The Great Disorder

The Great Disorder

Politics, Economics, and Society
in the German Inflation, 1914–1924

Gerald D. Feldman

New York   Oxford   OXFORD UNIVERSITY PRESS

Oxford University Press

Oxford   New York
Athens   Auckland   Bangkok   Bogota   Bombay
Buenos Aires   Calcutta   Cape Town   Dar es Salaam
Delhi   Florence   Hong Kong   Istanbul   Karachi
Kuala Lumpur   Madras   Madrid   Melbourne
Mexico City   Nairobi   Paris   Singapore
Taipei   Tokyo   Toronto

and associated companies in
Berlin   Ibadan

First published as an Oxford University Press paperback, 1996

Published by Oxford University Press, Inc.
198 Madison Avenue, New York, New York 10016

Oxford is a registered trademark of Oxford University Press

Library of Congress Cataloging-in-Publication Data
Feldman, Gerald D.
The great disorder : politics, economics, and society in the
German inflation, 1914–1924 / Gerald D. Feldman.
p.   cm   Includes bibliographical references and index.
ISBN 0-19-503791-X; ISBN 0-19-510114-6(pbk.)
1. Inflation (Finance)—Germany—History—20th century.
2. Monetary policy—Germany—History—20th century.
3. Economic stabilization—Germany.
4. Germany—Economic policy—1918–1933.
5. Germany—Economic conditions—1918–1945.
I. Title.   HG999.F45 1993
332.4'1'094309041—dc20   92-19725

9 8 7 6 5 4 3 2 1

Printed in the United States of America
on acid-free paper

For Norma

Preface

This book is intended to be a history of German society between 1914 and 1924 centering on the depreciation of the mark—from 4.2 marks to the dollar to 4.2 trillion marks to the dollar—and the creation of new currencies that were denominated once again at 4.2 to the dollar. Adding twelve zeros to the exchange rate and then lopping them off again constituted more than an arithmetic exercise. For the great majority of Germans, the Weimar inflation was a truly traumatic experience with incalculable consequences, and in the modern history of inflation it has attained paradigmatic status despite some extraordinary hyperinflations in places like Hungary, China, Germany once again after 1945, parts of the former Soviet Union, and eastern Europe. This is, in part, because the hyperinflation of 1922–1923 was the most spectacular of its kind ever to hit an advanced industrial society with a market economy and also because Weimar's inflation underwent such a protracted development. Though money may not be everything, virtually every significant aspect of life is influenced in some way or other by the quantity and quality of money. In this sense, the German example, extending over a ten-year period, provides the historian with the inestimable opportunity to study the full experience of a great inflation in "slow motion."

Inflation is a monetary, financial, and economic phenomenon arising from the decisions of persons who are acting in response to economic interests and theories, political considerations, social pressures, and cultural attitudes. Any one of these aspects and perspectives, or some combination of them, can serve as the basis of a study of the Weimar inflation. The interest here, however, is in their interaction and in identifying what was most significant, most central, at any given time in the unfolding story of the inflation.

To realize this aim, I had to deal with some highly complex and demanding technical and theoretical issues. Reparations—the constant preoccupation of Germany's rulers—is one of these, and the course of the inflation is unintelligible without some reasonably detailed comprehension of the management (or mismanagement) of the reparations problem. Similarly, one cannot understand the making or ending of the inflation without exploring the debates on monetary policy, both theoretical and practical, conducted by Germany's political and economic leaders. Thus, as I try to show in this book, the "technical" issues, whether of reparations or of monetary policy, whether of price regulation or foreign trade controls, require attention because of their important political and social consequences. Since we now live in a time in which international debt, monetary policy, and balance-of-payments issues are more and more the stuff of front-page reporting in the newspapers, I hope that many of the economic issues discussed here will ring familiar bells, even for the less economically versed of my readers.

It should be clear, however, that this is not an economic interpretation and that the larger arguments of this book do not support economic determinism. Similarly, it takes no ideological stand with respect to the "primacy" of foreign versus domestic policy or history "from above" versus history "from below." Rather, my work deals with the interaction of foreign and domestic policy, just as it deals with the relationship between those in authority, on the one hand, and those who were sometimes ruled and sometimes imposed their will on their leaders, on the other.

In the most basic sense, I intend this book to be a work of general history that contributes to an understanding of the problems of democratic governance and social stability in advanced capitalist societies. The Weimar Republic has become (and I hope will remain) the most dramatic and fateful historical case of the breakdown of democratic institutions and social order in such a society. Although it has become quite fashionable to make analogies with Weimar whenever a society has serious problems, I am skeptical about using the Weimar experience, or any other major historical episode, in anything but a heuristic manner. The real gain from the history of the Weimar Republic is some insight into the mechanisms by which great disorders are created and lead to even greater disorders; it also provides an opportunity to reflect on paths not taken and on the consequences of asymmetries in economic, social, and political development, that is, failed modernization.

Toward this end, I have tried to reconstruct the history of the German inflation as comprehensively and as accurately as possible. A current tendency of American historians is to question whether we can engage or even claim to be engaging in such enterprises and whether "objectivity" is possible. This is a book about what happens when money, the representation of value, loses its correspondence to reality, and this phenomenon may have some heuristic value for current debates about historiography. Insofar as the "objectivity problem" is concerned, I hold the view that the evidential rules and canons of historical scholarship exist as necessary and potent antidotes to human frailties. This is the reason why they should be treated as normative values and not simply as convenient instruments or rhetorical devices. In any case, I have tried to make this a work of continuing value for my fellow scholars and readers by providing material in the text and documentation that can be used to refute my arguments or open the way to alternative interpretations in our common search for the truth.

The research for this book began some fifteen years ago and the writing a decade ago, and I am deeply grateful for the material and personal support I have received along the way. As the bibliography will show, I have produced a variety of articles during these years, a number of which have been taken from the manuscript and some of which have found their way into the manuscript. I am thus also indebted to the institutions and persons mentioned here for their support in completing these studies and to the publishers for allowing incorporation of portions of them here.

A National Endowment for the Humanities fellowship assisted me at a very preliminary stage of my research, while Professor Knut Borchardt provided me with a base in his institute in Munich along with his invaluable advice and friendship. I also wish to thank Professor Gerhard A. Ritter and the late Professor Thomas Nipperdey for their encouragement, intellectual companionship, and friendship during my two stays in Munich. The bulk of my research was supported by a generous grant from the Volkswagen Foundation, which was given to me as part of the larger international project on Inflation and Reconstruction in Germany and Europe, 1914–1924. That project entailed the collaboration of some fifty scholars and led to the publication of a remarkable number of articles and books. I am extremely thankful to have had the opportunity to exchange ideas and to work closely with so many fine scholars and wonderful people in the course of our symposia and in our workshop, and my work and life has been very much enriched by the experience. The project had two homes, the Historische Kommission zu Berlin and the Institute of International Studies at the University of California, Berkeley. Professor Otto Büsch and the staff of the Historische Kommission were extraordinarily helpful to me at every stage of the way, as was Carl Rosberg, the former director of the Institute of International Studies. Mrs. Karen Beros and her staff have been especially attentive to my needs and requirements, and I thank them for their warm support and good cheer. I also wish to thank the Committee on Research of the University of California, Berkeley, for its assistance at various times.

When I began writing this book, I had the opportunity to try out my ideas at the Lehrman Institute, which gave me a fellowship in 1981–1982 and organized seminars to discuss my work. The criticisms and comments I received played a crucial role in the conceptualization of this book, and I wish to thank Nicholas Rizopoulos for organizing these events and the participants for making them so fruitful. This year of putting my work and ideas together would not have been possible without the support of a German Marshall Fund fellowship.

A substantial portion of the first eleven chapters of this work was written when I was a Fellow of the Historisches Kolleg in Munich in 1982–1983. The Historisches Kolleg is supported by the Deutsche Bank Endowment for the Support of Scholarship in Research and Teaching and the Stifterverband für die Deutsche Wissenschaft. This study recounts portions of the histories of the Deutsche Bank and of the Stifterverband, and I hope that both those parts and the entire eleven chapters are worthy of the opportunities afforded me as a Fellow of the Historisches Kolleg. I am especially grateful to Dr. Elisabeth Müller-Luckner for making my stay in Munich so pleasant and to Elsa Lang and Georg Kalmer for their many kindnesses.

In September of 1987, I was an invited guest at the Rockefeller Center at Bellagio, where I did some revision, and then in 1987–1988 a Fellow at the Institute for Advanced Study in Berlin, where I completed most of the second half of the book. These were wonderful experiences in marvelous places made all the more splendid by daily exchanges with interesting and interested colleagues and friends. I would like to thank Professor Wolf Lepenies, the director of the Wissenschaftskolleg, and his staff for making my year in Berlin so rewarding.

This study is based on work done in many public and private archives and libraries. It would take too many pages to thank each and every archivist who helped me to find necessary materials, and to single out any one of those working at the archives listed in the bibliography would be unfair to the others. I would, however, like to express my gratitude to them as a collectivity and give a special word of thanks to the archivists in Potsdam, Merseburg, and Dresden who helped me before the fall of the Wall and did their best to supply the resources I needed despite many bizarre obstacles and senseless regulations invented by the old re-gime. I would like to thank Mrs. Edith Hirsch for placing the papers of her husband, Julius Hirsch, at my disposal and Mr. Dieter Stinnes and Miss Else Stinnes for making the Hugo Stinnes Papers available to me.

I am quite confident that I would never have been able to complete this book without the help of able and devoted assistants, some of whom became my collaborators on related projects. The fact that many of them now bear academic titles and have produced fine historical works, some to be found in the bibliography of this book, is salve for my conscience, as is the fact that many of them have become and remain good friends. At very early stages of my work on the German inflation, Heidrun Homburg, Irmgard Steinisch, Andreas Kunz, and Kees Gispen worked for me on this project and then with me on various related projects. Martin Geyer and Paul Erker, two first-rate historians then in the making, assisted me during my stay at the Historisches Kolleg. Ulla Chapin and Anne MacLachlan contributed significantly to this book with their assistance, as did Jonathan Zatlin. A special word of thanks must go to Karin MacHardy, who put most of the materials for *The Great Disorder* in order and assisted me on this and related projects with unfailing energy, great competence, and her characteristic good humor.

I owe Sheldon Meyer of Oxford University Press a great debt of gratitude for encouraging this project over many years, showing endless patience, and accepting a good deal more than he bargained for with such good grace. Scott Lenz has been an understanding, encouraging, and truly diligent copy editor.

Parts of this book have been read by Richard Bessel, Thomas C. Childers, Peter Jelavich, and Larry Jones, and I am grateful for their comments and suggestions. Jan de Vries read a substantial portion and gave me very good advice. The manuscript was read from beginning to end by three great experts and dear friends, Carl-Ludwig Holtfrerich, Harold James, and Peter-Christian Witt. Their great expenditure of time and the care with which they read the manuscript saved me from making serious errors and helped to improve the argument. I alone, of course, am responsible for the content of this book.

There is another person who has assisted me on this project and read this manuscript through—indeed, more than once—and that is my wife, Norma von Ragenfeld-Feldman. She is responsible for reducing absurdly long sentences and successfully eliminating much muddle in my book—and in my life. She has been a loving and indispensable companion, dear friend, and wise counsellor during the years this book was being written, and it is to her that this book is dedicated.

Berkeley, California   G. D. F.
January 1993

Contents

Illustrations

Tables

Abbreviations

AA   Auswärtiges Amt
Abt.   Abteilung
ACDP   Archiv für Christlich-
Demokratische Politik
der Konrad-Adenauer-
Stiftung
ADGB   Allgemeiner deutscher
Gewerkschaftsbund
(General Federation of
German Trade Unions)
AdSt   Akten des deutschen
Städtetages
AEG   Allgemeine Elektrizitäts–
Gesellschaft (General
Electric Company)
Afa   Arbeitsgemeinschaft freier
Angestelltenverbände
AfS   *Archiv für Sozialgeschichte*
AfSS   *Archiv für
Sozialwissenschaft und
Sozialpolitik*
AHR   *American Historical
Review*
AN   Archives Nationales
Arbeno   Arbeitgeberverband
Nordwest

BAK   Bundesarchiv Koblenz
BAP   Bundesarchiv Potsdam
BayHStA   Bayerisches
Hauptstaatsarchiv,
München
BgA   Bergbau-Archiv

CEH   *Central European History*

DAZ   *Deutsche Allgemeine
Zeitung*

DBB   Deutscher Beamtenbund
(German Civil Servants
Federation)
DBFP   *Documents on British
Foreign Policy*
DDP   Deutsche Demokratische
Partei (German
Democratic Party)
DHSG   Deputation für Handel,
Schiffahrt und Gewerbe
DHV   Deutschnationaler
Handlungsgehilfenverband
(German National Retail
Clerks' Association)
DMA   Demobilmachungsamt
(Demobilization Office)
DMV   Deutscher
Metallarbeiterverband
(German Metal Workers'
Union)
DVP   Deutsche Volkspartei
(German People's Party)

EHR   *Economic History Review*
EWB   Eisenwirtschaftsbund (Iron
Trades Federation)

FWH   Friedrich-Wilhelms-Hütte
FZ   *Frankfurter Zeitung*

GLA   Generallandesarchiv
GStAPrK   Geheimes Staatsarchiv
Preußischer Kulturbesitz
GStAKM   Geheimes Staatsarchiv
Kulturbesitz Merseburg
GuG   *Geschichte und Gesellschaft*

HA	Historisches Archiv
HAAA	Handelspolitische Abteilung des Auswärtigen Amts
HADB	Historisches Archiv der Deutschen Bank
HA/GHH	Haniel Archiv/ Gutehoffnungshütte
HAPAG	Hamburg-Amerika Linie
Hiko	Historische Kommission zu Berlin
HK	Handelskammer
HStA	Hauptstaatsarchiv
HZ	*Historische Zeitschrift*
IG	Interessengemeinschaft
IWK	*Internationale wissenschaftliche Korrespondenz zur Geschichte der deutschen Arbeiterbewegung*
JMH	*Journal of Modern History*
JNS	*Jahrbücher für Nationalökonomie und Statistik*
Kl. Er.	Kleine Erwerbungen
KRA	Kriegsrohstoffabteilung (Raw Materials Section)
KWG	Kaiser-Wilhelm-Gesellschaft
LA	Landesarchiv
LHA	Landeshauptarchiv
LHStA	Landeshauptstaatsarchiv
LPP	Landespreisprüfungsstelle (State Price Examination Agency)
M.A.N.	Maschinenfabrik Augsburg-Nürnberg
MB	Zusammenstellungen der Monats-Berichte der stell-vertretenden Generalkommandos (compilation of the monthly reports of the Acting General Commanders)

MdI	Ministerium des Innern
MH	Handelsministerium
MPG	Max-Planck-Gesellschaft
NA	National Archives
NGW	Notgemeinschaft der deutschen Wissenschaft
NHStAH	Niedersächsiches Hauptstaatsarchiv in Hannover
NL	Nachlaß
NStAO	Niedersächsisches Staatsarchiv in Oldenburg
PRO	Public Record Office
PVS	*Politische Vierteljahrsschrift*
RABl	*Reichsarbeitsblatt*
RAM	Reichsarbeitsministerium
RB	Reichsbank
RM	Reichsmark
RdI	Reichsverband der deutschen Industrie (Reich Association of German Industry)
RFM	Reichsfinanzministerium
RGBl	Reichsgesetzblatt
RWA	Reichswirtschaftsamt
RWE	Rheinisch-Westfälische Elektrizitätswerke
RWM	Reichswirtschaftsministerium
RWR	Reichswirtschaftsrat (Reich Economic Council)
RWWK	Rheinisch-Westfälisches Wirtschaftsarchiv zu Köln
SAA	Siemens-Archiv Akten
SäHStA	Sächsisches Hauptstaatsarchiv
SPD	Sozialdemokratische Partei Deutschlands
SRSU	Siemens-Rheinelbe-Schuckert-Union
StA	Staatsarchiv
SVS	*Schriften des Vereins für Sozialpolitik*
SWW	Stiftung Westfälisches Wirtschaftsarchiv

VC	*Volkswirtschaftliche Chronik*	*VSWG*	*Vierteljahrsschrift für Sozial- und Wirtschaftsgeschichte*
VdA	Vereinigung deutscher Arbeitgeberverbände		
VDMA	Verein deutscher Maschinenbauanstalten	WA	Werksarchiv
VfZ	*Vierteljahrshefte für Zeitgeschichte*	WA/ATH	Werksarchiv der August Thyssen-Hütte
VN	*Verhandlungen der verfassunggebenden Nationalversammlung. Stenografische Berichte und Drucksachen* (Berlin, 1919–1920)	WA/M.A.N.-A.	Werksarchiv Maschinenfabrik Augsburg-Nürnberg, Augsburg
VPI	Verband der Pfälzischen Industrie	WA/M.A.N.-N	Werksarchiv Maschinenfabrik Augsburg-Nürnberg, Nürnberg
VR	*Verhandlungen des Reichstags. Stenografische Berichte und Drucksachen* (Berlin, 1920ff.)	ZAG	Zentralarbeitsgemeinschaft

The Great Disorder

Introduction

The German Inflation in Collective Memory and Economic History

It was, a novelist wrote only a few years after the German inflation had ended, "an extraordinary time. Disorder seemed to be trump, even in the heavens. The constellations were certainly in a wild state and demanded that things be so—for it was a time when one had to believe in all that again, in planets and the stars under which one was born."[1] Of course, if one knew how to penetrate the meaning of the stars, the disorder was only apparent. An astrologer, writing in the midst of the hyperinflation of 1923 and carefully correlating the movements of the currency exchange rates published in the economic section of the *Frankfurter Zeitung* with those of the planets provided by the undoubtedly less widely consulted *Astronomical Ephemeris* of Raphael, confidently provided his readers with an astrological explanation of the development of the exchange rate between 1914 and 1922 along with a prognosis for 1923–1926. He insisted on the existence of "lawful relationships between the variations in the rate of foreign exchange and the course of the planets."[2] Whether such claims are more or less abstruse than present-day efforts to explain inflation by the "entropy state of the environment,"[3] that is, the costs of the increasing amount of energy unavailable for work, is hard to say. In any event, there has been a strong tendency to characterize the German inflation as an uncontrollable and unanalyzable natural phenomenon. This found especially dramatic expression in "Merkur," a novella of the early 1930s by the Rhenish writer Elisabeth Langgässer: "A dark, volcanic landscape with gigantic golden fruits completely filled on the inside with ash emerged out of the briny torrent, and alongside the first and largest crater, smaller brothers and sisters shot up, which also belched forth paper money, [and] which divided and subdivided until finally almost every city sat in its own lava."[4] Elsewhere she likens the inflation to an avalanche and a flood. Yet, even so cool a present-day analyst of the political economy of inflation as historian Charles Maier finds the language of natural catastrophe most suitable for describing the hyperinflation and its end: "Hyperinflations are the supernovas of the monetary firmament, exploding furiously only to collapse into the dark neutron stars of economic contraction."[5]

As some of the above illustrations show, the inclination to treat the German inflation as a traumatic, apocalyptic phenomenon which overwhelmed its defenseless victims antedated the events of 1933–1945. Thus, in a story of 1928 about an old Jewish businessman whose assets had been destroyed by the inflation, Arnold Zweig identifies his protagonist with a "lost generation about whose throats a doggedly harsh age had placed its rope."[6] The triumph of National Socialism served to heighten the significance and monumentality of Germany's inflationary experience. Economist Lionel Robbins wrote with unabashed certainty about the consequences of the inflation in 1937, calling it "one of the outstanding episodes in the history of the twentieth century":

Not only by reason of its magnitude but also by reason of its effects, it looms large on our horizon. It was the most colossal thing of its kind in history: and, next probably to the Great War itself, it must bear responsibility for many of the political and economic difficulties of our generation. It destroyed the wealth of the more solid elements in German society: and it left behind a moral and economic disequilibrium, apt breeding ground for the disasters which have followed. Hitler is the foster-child of the inflation.[7]

Former Chancellor Heinrich Brüning, corresponding with fellow exile and political scientist Eric Voegelin in 1941, was no less certain about the dire social and political consequences of the inflation:

I consider your sociological analysis of the absence of a new ruling establishment [*Herrscherschicht*] after the last war very important. I wish that you would mention that the conservative *Bürgertum** with whom one could have formed a strong conservative block in normal times was completely ruined financially and socially by the inflation. It became proletarian in its entire ideology. This is one of the astonishing factors which enabled the Nazis to gather together impoverished princes, unemployed workers and bankrupt peasants in the S.A. and S.S. Whatever the social strata they belonged to before, they were all poor and could reach an understanding with one another about nothing other than going to war. . . .[8]

Elias Canetti, writing after 1945, went much further and discovered in the Holocaust a replication of the inflationary experience:

In its treatment of the Jews, National Socialism repeated the process of inflation with great precision. First they were attacked as wicked and dangerous, as enemies; then they were more and more depreciated; then, there not being enough in Germany itself, those in the conquered territories were gathered in; and finally they were treated literally as vermin, to be destroyed with impunity by the million. The world is still horrified and shaken by the fact that the Germans could go so far; that they either participated in a crime of such magnitude, or connived at it, or ignored it. It might not have been possible to get them to do so if, a few years before, they had not been through an inflation during which the Mark fell to a billionth of its former value. It was this inflation, as a crowd experience, which they shifted on to the Jews.[9]

It is hard for a historian as heavily invested in the history of the German inflation as is the author of this book to resist the temptation to seize upon such testimonials to the significance of the inflation and to try to convince his readers that such claims are true. If this book bears witness to anything, however, it is to the pen-

alties of propagating illusion. Just as banks should adhere to reasonable coverage requirements in providing the liquidity that makes enterprise possible, so historians should adhere to sensible methodological and evidential standards in presenting the implications and significance of their labors. Thus, historians cannot and should not follow the lead of even so admirable and sensitive a thinker as Canetti and engage in the establishment of causal linkages by metaphor, especially where, as Canetti himself shows, metaphors were used to legitimate and carry out unspeakable crimes; nor should the historian appropriate the embittered reflections and prejudices of important historical actors as fact. Much will be said in this book about the effects of the inflation on the German *Bürgertum* and their consequences for German politics. Yet, there is no viable methodology for effectively linking these effects with the deficiencies of Germany's post-1918 political establishment. If Brüning's intuitive statement is correct, then one can only wish he had taken such perceptions into greater account in his own disastrous attempt to bring the Weimar Republic through its great crisis. Finally, Hitler was the foster child of a hydra of historical circumstances rather than of the inflation alone. Nevertheless, the kinds of connections between the inflation and the condition that produced National Socialism suggested by Lionel Robbins are susceptible to historical demonstration and analysis and will be explored in this book. It is possible to show an important relationship between the inflation, intensified anti-Semitism, increased right-wing radicalism, and a high degree of sociopolitical demoralization and anxiety. Nine years separated the end of the inflation from Hitler's assumption of power, however, and while the inflation is important for an understanding of the weaknesses of the Weimar Republic and the early history of National Socialism, its connection to the events surrounding the Republic's demise and Nazism's triumph are complicated and indirect. They do exist, and that is surely significant enough.

The difficulties of moving from easy generalization to actual demonstration of the consequences of the inflation undoubtedly help to explain why the inflation received so little

---

*For reasons to be made clear later, the term *Bürgertum* will often be left in the original and not be translated as "middle class" or "bourgeoisie."

Table 1. Dollar Exchange Rate of the Paper Mark in Berlin, 1914–1923
(in monthly averages)

	1914	1915	1916	1917	1918	1919	1920	1921	1922	1923
January	4.21	4.61	5.35	5.79	5.21	8.20	64.80	64.91	191.81	17,972
February	4.20	4.71	5.38	5.87	5.27	9.13	99.11	61.31	207.82	27,918
March	4.20	4.82	5.55	5.82	5.21	10.39	83.89	62.45	284.19	21,190
April	4.20	4.86	5.45	6.48	5.11	12.61	59.64	63.53	291.00	24,475
May	4.20	4.84	5.22	6.55	5.14	12.85	46.48	62.30	290.11	47,670
June	4.19	4.88	5.31	7.11	5.36	14.01	39.13	69.36	317.14	109,966
July	4.20	4.91	5.49	7.14	5.79	15.08	39.48	76.67	493.22	353,412
August	4.19	4.92	5.57	7.14	6.10	18.83	47.74	84.31	1,134.56	4,620,455
September	4.17	4.85	5.74	7.21	6.59	24.05	57.98	104.91	1,465.87	98,860[a]
October	4.38	4.85	5.70	7.29	6.61	26.83	68.17	150.20	3,180.96	25,260[b]
November	4.61	4.95	5.78	6.64	7.43	38.31	77.24	262.96	7,183.10	2,193,600[b]
December	4.50	5.16	5.72	5.67	8.28	46.77	73.00	191.93	7,589.27	4,200,000[b]
Average	4.28	4.86	5.52	6.58	6.01	19.76	63.06	104.57	1,885.78	534,914[b]

Source: Statistisches Reichsamt, *Zahlen zur Geldentwertung in Deutschland 1914 bis 1923* [Sonderheft 1 zu *Wirtschaft und Statistik*, Bd. 5] (Berlin, 1925), p. 10.
[a]In thousands.
[b]In millions.

attention from historians until the late 1970s. At that time, the situation was changed by some combination of the intellectual curiosity of persons like myself, contemporary concern with the origins and control of inflation, and, most important, a kind of logic that inheres in the trajectory of meaningful and fruitful research that at some point in the evolution of their enterprise makes it likely that scholars will give closer attention to phenomena about which they had contentedly generalized in the past.[10]

Some explanations certainly are needed for the fact that, with respect to the inflation, the historiographical landscape so long resembled what I once described as a desert with very few oases.[11] The horrendous consequences attributed to the inflation by Lionel Robbins were being regularly repeated in classroom lectures, textbooks, and popular historical works. Yet, these accounts almost invariably replicated the collective memory of the inflation as it was conveyed in personal reminiscences, memoirs, and fictional literature. That collective memory has certain crucial characteristics which go a long way toward explaining the historiographical blockage in dealing with the inflation. One of these is the tendency to confuse the trauma of hyperinflation with the entire inflationary experience. Indeed, what had for many years served as the most useful introduction to the inflation and documentary collection for American students bears the title *The German Infla-*

tion of 1923.[12] In reality, the inflation was a decade-long affair of considerable variation and complexity (see Table 1). It began in the First World War, increased substantially in the fall and winter of 1919–1920, slowed during a period of relative stabilization between the spring of 1920 and the spring of 1921, and made a dramatic leap upward to qualitatively new levels beginning in the late summer of 1921 and continuing through the winter and spring of 1922 before the true hyperinflation began in the summer of 1922. It was this hyperinflation that culminated in the infamous satchels, sacks, and wheelbarrows full of money and in the collapse of the mark in the fall of 1923; but even the hyperinflation is not characterized by a neat and steadily accelerating curve of disaster, since there was a relative stabilization of the mark in the early months of 1923.

While this longevity and variability received some recognition in graphic and verbal references to the long-term depreciation of the mark, their implications were consistently overlooked, thanks to the preoccupation with the dramatic denouement of hyperinflation. Yet the cataclysmic and, as this study will seek to show, by no means necessary conclusion to the inflation only lasted from July 1922 to November 1923, long enough, to be sure, to produce the trauma that has burned itself into collective memory, but not long enough to produce all the consequences attributed to the inflation. The conflation of the final and extremely chaotic period of inflation with the total experience made it all too easy for historians to write general accounts of the inflation that paralleled its popular and literary treatment. There are thousands of actual and millions of potential inflation stories and anecdotes, and the historians who have relied upon collective memory, have found it easy, satisfying, and understandably entertaining to dwell on these anecdotal aspects of the inflation. Indeed, it is unlikely that anyone who lived through the experience does not have a colorful story to tell. Thus, the noted Frankfurt School sociologist Leo Lowenthal was clever enough to use foreign currency at his disposal to enjoy the last days of the hyperinflation at a splendid hotel in Baden-Baden. His apparently less flamboyant contemporary, historian Felix Gilbert, then a student at Heidelberg, invested the fifty dollars he had received from an uncle by buying and selling pots of jam, "an item that people liked and needed and that would never spoil."[13] The hyperinflation seems almost to have been made for history-of-daily-life enthusiasts, but its historical significance can no more be constructed from such stories than can the generic behavioral differences of sociologists and historians. Semipopular and textbook accounts have oscillated between tales drawn from fact or fiction illustrating the characteristic disorder of the inflation and generalizations about the social consequences of the inflation, usually summarized in the ruin of the middle class and exploitation of the working class to the benefit of industry and agriculture.[14]

More often than not, there are fuzzy references to the role played by reparations or the effort to evade reparations in promoting the currency collapse, but nearly all accounts suffer from the compulsion to assign responsibility for the inflation, either directly or indirectly, to groups or representative individuals. While Reichsbank President Rudolf Havenstein with his allegedly false monetary theories and fearsome pride in the ever increasing money-producing capacities of the Reich Printing Office has served as something of a figure of derision, other purported makers and beneficiaries of inflation are viewed less benignly. Here, too, historical accounts have mirrored the tendencies of fiction. Literary works on the inflation are filled with profiteers and shady characters who live off the misery of those less adept at dealing with the monetary chaos. Especially noteworthy are the great wire-pullers of the inflation, most prominently the scarcely veiled representations of the great industrialist Hugo Stinnes, who appears as Kobes in Heinrich Mann's novella of the same name, as the mysterious merchant in Langgässer's "Merkur," and as Ottokar Wirtz in Erich Reger's *Union der festen Hand*. While a glance at the index of this study will certainly suggest the importance of Stinnes, the tendency of popular and textbook authors dealing with the inflation is to transform the "Merchant from Mülheim" into the symbol of inflation profiteering by industry and agriculture and to use him as a substitute for exploring the deeper issues involved in the inflation.[15]

The examination of those questions, particularly those of the function and consequences of the inflation and of the responsibility for the inflation, is extremely complicated and inevitably frustrating. This is especially the case the moment the inflation is taken seriously as a decade-long phenomenon. As economist Franz Eulenburg argued in his pioneering essay of 1924 on the social consequences of the inflation,

The disintegration of the currency did not occur in isolation but in constant connection with all the other factors of societal existence. It is itself only the consequence of factors underlying it. But these factors, in independence of the currency, exercise definite influences on their own which somehow find economic and social expression. There is a plurality of causes and effects which makes it difficult or almost impossible from the outset to derive all other factors from one single factor, no matter how outstanding.[16]

Not the least of the problems involved in confusing the inflation with the hyperinflation is that most of the social consequences of the inflation were present and actively described and discussed by contemporaries before the hyperinflation ever began. Indeed, it is extraordinarily difficult to distinguish many of the consequences of the war from those normally attributed to the inflation, especially since the inflation itself owed its birth to the war economy and its financing. Similarly, how is one to weigh the roles of demobilization, political revolution, world economic conditions, reparations, and domestic politics in promoting or constraining those redistributive phenomena and political conflicts usually ascribed to inflation? Matters are not helped by the notorious gaps in the statistics for the years from 1914 through 1923 and the unreliability of some of the available data, and it is truly frustrating that the last census prior to 1925 was taken in 1907. It is also easy to overdo the deficiencies in the statistics, however, and plenty of reasonably replicable economic and social data can be ferreted out of published and unpublished sources. Recent general, sectoral, and regional studies demonstrate that one can find satisfactory data if one seeks in the proper places.[17]

In the last analysis, the biggest problem in studying so protracted and complex an inflationary experience as the one examined in this book is the phenomenon of inflation itself, which in its very essence seems to conspire against its own investigation. Inflation depends upon monetary and other illusions and thus involves a high degree of intransparency. Inflations are said to "creep" at price increases up to 10 percent per year, to "trot" with yearly price increases between 10 and 50 percent, to "gallop" at rates above 50 percent per year, and to be "hyper" at and beyond monthly price increases of 50 percent. Recently, Charles Maier has subsumed trotting and galloping inflations under the rubric of "Latin"-type inflations.[18] Be that as it may, the German inflation of 1914–1923 crept, trotted, and galloped to various "Latin" rhythms, and ended up "hyper"; what the causes and consequences were at any given stage are anything but obvious. Since milder and even some of the more serious forms of inflation have been known to be accompanied by high levels of economic activity and employment, the more negative aspects of the inflationary process may become especially unclear and have at times been of subordinate significance to economists and historians. Indeed, one of the consequences of the Great Depression of the 1930s and the subsequent predominance of Keynesian economics is that the inherent difficulties involved in unraveling the

inflationary process conveniently interacted with current economic and political priorities to promote indifference. As economic historian Knut Borchardt has pointed out,

it is because the manifold distributive effects are so diffuse and unclarified that inflation can be allowed to go on so long without becoming an acute scandal. The effects do not spring forth in a manner visible to every person, as is the case with unemployment, where no scientific investigation is needed to determine who is unemployed. The unemployed are known by name and address. The reason why full employment has until recently been the unquestioned higher aim of economic policy is probably explicable by the asymmetry of the social consequences of unemployment and inflation.[19]

In fact, a good argument can be made that the revival of interest in inflation by economists in the 1970s was closely linked to the phenomenon of stagflation, the coexistence of persistent inflation with high unemployment and reduced productivity.

Both before and after this rekindled interest in inflation, however, Weimar Germany has provided the great laboratory for those economists who chose to invest their efforts in the study of monetary disorder. Thus, Princeton economist Frank D. Graham, who published the first major economic study of the inflation in 1930, noted that "[I]n the study of social phenomena, disorder is . . . the sole substitute for the controlled experiments of the natural scientists." While recognizing that chaos could reach the point of being unanalyzable, Graham was convinced that "perseverance" was preferable to "surrender" and sought "to discover what actually happened in Germany and either to bring the observed phenomena within the fold of accepted theory or else so to modify that theory as to give it a more catholic character."[20] The same theme was struck in Lionel Robbins's introduction to what has long been regarded as the classic study of the German inflation, Costantino Bresciani-Turroni's *Economics of Inflation*, which appeared in Italian in 1931 and in English in 1937. Robbins argued that "[a]ccidents to the body politic, like accidents to the physical body, often permit observations of a kind which would not be possible under normal conditions," and that "it is sometimes possible to snatch good from evil and to obtain insight into the working of processes which are normally concealed." In the case of the German inflation, "there is hardly any branch of the theory of economic dynamics which is not illuminated by examination of its grim events."[21]

Economists have tended to investigate Germany's great monetary disorder, however, from very different perspectives that have mirrored trends in the profession and current concerns. This may help to explain why Graham's book was rapidly eclipsed by Bresciani-Turroni's, which for many years became the standard reference work for economists and non-economists alike. Certainly this owed much to Bresciani-Turroni's international eminence as an economist and statistician, his direct experience as a member of the Reparations Commission during the inflation period, and the relative accessibility of his book. The chief reasons, however, probably lie in the fact that Bresciani-Turroni's theoretical orientation and conclusions about the effects of the inflation were at once firmer and more palatable than those of Graham. Whereas Bresciani-Turroni blamed the fall of the mark almost exclusively on German financial and monetary policy, Graham placed some emphasis on the role of reparations and, therefore, on the balance of payments. Most significant, Graham came to the rather startling conclusion that the inflation was of general benefit to the German economy despite its many unhappy social and political consequences, while Bresciani-Turroni insisted the inflationary boom, such as it was, distorted German economic development and was a source of stabilization crises. If the inflation had been so good for the German economy, Bresciani-Turroni rhetorically asked, then "why was the eventuality of a new depreciation considered almost with terror in German official circles, which from 1931 onwards have made some desperate efforts to keep the mark exchange stable?"[22]

There are many historians and economists today who would argue that the answer to this question was anything but self-evident, that the terror was misplaced, and that the wrong lessons were learned from the German inflation. They would insist that, whether because of limited maneuverability imposed by internal and external constraints or because of ill-conceived self-imposed agendas connected with ending reparations and imposing fiscal discipline, it was a tragedy for Germany and the world that policies of reflation and possibly of devaluation were not pursued. When Bresciani-Turroni was writing, however, recessions and even depressions were viewed as "natural" events related to the business cycle and could be made intelligible and even palatable as responses to and corrections of distortions in economic and fiscal policy and capital shortages. The depth of the depression was ascribed to lack of confidence arising from bleak economic and political circumstances. For Bresciani-Turroni, however, "confidence" was epiphenomenal in explaining inflation, the occurrence and termination of which were, in his view, determined by the money supply. His important book, therefore, was intended as an argument for the quantity theory of money.[23]

Insisting that the level of prices and the internal and external value of any currency were determined by the money supply seemed all the more necessary in the case of the German inflation. Not only had the Germans sinned by producing the greatest inflation ever experienced by an industrial society but also some of their major economic thinkers and political leaders had defended their actions by arguing that the German inflation was the consequence of Germany's adverse balance of payments resulting from reparations transfers and insufficient capital to cover imports. They claimed that this led to the outflow of German currency, the depreciation of its value on foreign exchanges, rising prices at home, and the need to print money to satisfy increasing demand. From the perspective of most quantity-school proponents, the Germans had not only a cavalier attitude toward the printing of money but also a completely unacceptable attitude toward money itself. Thus, many of their economic thinkers and leaders were followers of George Friedrich Knapp, the proponent of the "state theory of money," that is, the extreme nominalist position that money was not a commodity but rather a purely functional instrument created by the state to facilitate exchange. While Knapp was never the inflationist quantity theorists claimed he was, the German inflation did little to enhance the reputation of Knapp and his followers and put the balance-of-payments school into considerable disrepute. It is a measure of the atmosphere that while many of Graham's arguments tended toward the balance-of-payments school, his theoretical message was sufficiently mixed or veiled so that a proponent of the quantitative school, Ludwig von Mises, could praise the book in a review, studiously avoid the complexities of Graham's argument, and take the opportunity to fulminate that "[T]he German inflation, above all, was the outcome of the monetary and banking theory which for many years had obsessed the men who occupied the chairs of economics at the Universities, the men who governed the financial policy of the Reich, and the editors of the most influential newspapers and periodicals."[24]

By 1945, these were spent passions for economists, but the basic conflict, which some economic historians have dated back to early modern times, continued in the contest between Keynesians and monetarists. The former placed their emphasis on the real economy—questions of demand, employment, and consumption. Their analyses invited attention to nonmonetary sources of inflation: to shortages in supply and to cost-push inflation, where costs—above all, wages—drive up prices. The monetarists, in keeping with their conviction that the only way to control inflation is through management of the money supply, emphasize the demand-pull character of inflation and have developed various models of adaptive and rational expectations, either models of decisions about how much money to hold based on past experience or models attempting to show that people respond on the basis of expectations that conform to economic models.[25]

Faced with these disputes in the field of economics, one might well expect the rational historian to seek some subject other than the German inflation. Actually, however, both the Keynesian and monetarist schools have been very helpful in sharpening the perspectives the historian should employ and the questions the historian should ask in dealing with the subject. Paradoxically, this has been less the case with the monetarists, despite the fact that they have been far more engaged with the German inflation than the Keynesians. Their engagement,

however, has been almost exclusively with the hyperinflation, which has proven to be a unique and welcome laboratory for the testing of their hypotheses concerning the development of expectations.[26] Unfortunately, it has not been very helpful in accounting for the influence of political and other "exogenous" events that change expectations—precisely those events that interest the historian most. Nevertheless, this literature has been helpful to the historical investigation of the German inflation in at least three ways. First, it has encouraged the quest for better and more reliable data. Second, while the older literature certainly placed considerable if varying emphasis on the question of "confidence" in the currency, the monetarist focus on expectations has become a touchstone of historical analysis even where monetarist doctrine has not been accepted. Finally, the monetarist literature has provided important new insights on how inflations end and how and why stabilization works.[27]

The contribution of Keynesianism to the historical investigation of the German inflation has nevertheless been greater despite the fact that Keynesian economists have been most preoccupied with contemporary rather than past cases of inflation. Because of its emphasis on macroeconomic management to promote employment, growth, and stability, which has been heavily buttressed by the explicit concern with economic growth and development that came to the fore after 1945, it has become possible to give more serious attention and respectability to Graham's insights concerning the beneficial effects of the inflation for the German economy. Thus, Scandinavian economists Karsten Laursen and Jørgen Pedersen, in a 1964 study, positively evaluated the inflation from the perspective of its contribution to economic growth and full employment and blamed its hyperinflationary conclusion on an absence of policy—above all, with respect to mounting wage costs. The theme of the inflation's promotion of economic growth and reconstruction after World War I was carried on in pioneering articles by German economic historian Peter Czada, and in a study of the iron and steel industry by the present author. In his monumental comparative study of 1975, *Recasting Bourgeois Europe*, Charles Maier emphasized the contribution of inflation to immediate postwar stabilization by maintaining social peace.[28] In the context of such work, it became possible to turn the argument that the inflation was instrumental in the destruction of the Weimar Republic completely upside down, as did Knut Borchardt when he wrote that "it was only the inflationary financing of the public deficits in the years after 1918 that made it possible to begin the Weimar experiment."[29]

Finally, insofar as it is possible to speak of a rehabilitation of the German inflation, Carl-Ludwig Holtfrerich attempted the task in the most important work of modern economic history on the German inflation, *The German Inflation 1914–1923: Causes and Effects in International Perspective*, which appeared in German in 1980 and in English in 1986. Sober, persistently analytical, and splendidly researched, it is nevertheless quite radical in its conclusions. While some earlier works recognized the contribution of the German inflation to economic reconstruction and social peace, Holtfrerich goes quite a bit farther. He has positive things to say about even the hyperinflation, pointing to its advantages in eliminating Germany's domestic debt as well as important portions of the foreign debt created by speculation in favor of the mark prior to the hyperinflation. The inflation, in Holtfrerich's view, helped to wipe the slate clean, so to speak, and had positive redistributive effects in the direction of greater equality as well. In contrast to Bresciani-Turroni, who concluded that "the stabilization of the value of the mark, thanks to the limitation of the quantity, must be considered not as the *end* but as the *starting point* of the process of economic reconstruction,"[30] Holtfrerich, in conformity with the findings of recent economic analyses of German economic growth in the twentieth century, insists that the "demand deficiency" of the post-inflation period prevented the German economy from benefiting to the extent it should have from the inflationary reconstruction. For Holtfrerich, therefore, the stabilization marked an interruption of Germany's postwar economic reconstruction. Indeed, he even goes so far as to consider the German inflation as something of an international blessing by arguing that German demand for goods helped to pull England and America out of the depression of 1920–1921![31]

All this suggests that Ludwig von Mises, were he alive, would still be rather unhappy about the way German academic economists view inflation. It would be false to think, however, that Holtfrerich's conclusions are a demonstration of how one can come to love a subject one studies no matter how awful it might be. Rather, he is insisting that the German inflation be understood in the context of the real historical circumstances confronting historical actors at the time. He proceeds from the proposition that theoretical positions concerning inflation have inevitably been linked with policy prescriptions, and the latter are inextricably bound up with values. Given the protracted nature of the German inflation and its variability, Holtfrerich argues, a good case can be made that all the major theories have considerable explanatory power for specific phases and aspects of the inflation, but a cost-benefit analysis of the policy choices they imply depends upon the subjective preferences of the economist or historian making the analysis. Like Borchardt, Holtfrerich considers the ultimate determinants of the inflation to be political choices that promoted rather than impeded the progress of inflation. While Holtfrerich takes the position that the inflation proved the least unsatisfactory solution to Germany's economic, social, international, and domestic dilemmas under the existing circumstances, he asserts that there is no satisfactory way to defend such a position on purely objective grounds. This is not to say, of course, that an objective understanding of the "actual phenomenon of the inflation, its causes and its consequences"[32] is not possible. On the contrary. Objectivity does not preclude engagement, but it does make possible mutually intelligible discussion and the effort to persuade and possibility of being persuaded on the basis of shared methods and standards. It prevents the degeneration of scholarship into a babble of self-serving discourses.

The necessity of bringing contradictory modes of analysis and interpretation into confrontation and objectively testing them against one another as far as possible is of special relevance to this study. How is one to reconcile the traumatic idea of the German inflation passed down in collective memory and the progressively positive appraisal that began with Graham, moved on through Laursen and Pedersen, and ended up with Holtfrerich? Has some of the new scholarship treated the German inflation, as Charles Kindleberger once suggested, as nothing more than a "bad cold,"[33] thus creating the impression that the sociopolitical pneumonia that developed subsequently had nothing to do with the lengthy walk taken in a monetary blizzard? Even if one assumes that the economic consequences of the German inflation were overwhelmingly positive, how is one to measure the significance of its social, political, and psychological consequences, and how is one to assess the calculations and motivations of those who made the decisions that produced these results? What has been missing in the investigations of the German inflation has been a detailed narration and analysis of the roles and interaction of political and economic leaders, on the one hand, and social organizations and structures, on the other, for the entire period of the inflation. The goal of this book, therefore, is to explore politics and society in Germany in their domestic and, very importantly, in their international context from the onset of the First World War to the stabilization.

It is important to note that such an effort does not stand in contradiction or opposition to much of the economic literature on the inflation. The increasing tendency of economists and economic historians of a nonmonetarist persuasion has been to emphasize the political and social determinants of inflation, that is, to understand the inflation in structural terms and avoid what Charles Kindleberger has called "tight priors"—rigid and absolute theories that constrain rather than liberate the analysis of Germany's inflationary experience:

Economists seem frequently to take up the German inflation to prove some point in monetary or foreign-exchange theory and study little more than statistical series with no flesh and blood, no political parties, interest groups, politics, revolutions, violence, assassinations, etc. When they bring out their conclusions that the German inflation supports the theory they brought to its study, I am led to react with the Duke of Wellington when someone approached him and said "Mr. Smith, I believe"; "If you believe that you can believe anything."[34]

The argument of Kindleberger, Mancur Olson, and other historically and sociologically sensitive economists that inflations be viewed as products of distributional conflicts, both national and international, is well suited to the task of the historian of the German inflation. Indeed, as this book will show, the German inflation is as fine a laboratory for structural explanations of the inflation as it is for monetarist ones. At the same time, the case study is important at a more general level, for the conditions that lead to inflation lie at the heart of the problems of governance in modern industrial societies. Unhappily for Germany, that nation has served as the most important laboratory for those disorders and their most extreme consequences in our century as well. In order to understand why this was so, however, one must understand what was at stake, what was changed by the German inflation, and how those changes took place.

The Germany of Dr. Cornelius

In what is certainly the most famous but also the most detached and even Olympian work of fiction dealing with the inflation, Thomas Mann's *Unordnung und frühes Leid (Disorder and Early Sorrow)*, the protagonist is a history professor named Cornelius, a member of the "villa proletariat" forced to scrimp and save under the changed conditions of his class and to manage his emotions in a volatile environment of painful cultural transformation. Cornelius embodies the world that was lost after 1914 and the alienation induced by what had replaced it. He

. . . knows that history professors do not love history because it is something that comes to pass, but only because it is something that *has* come to pass; that they hate a revolution like the present one because they feel it is lawless, incoherent, irrelevant—in a word, unhistoric; that their hearts belong to the coherent, disciplined, historic past.[35]

It is, in truth, easier for Cornelius to make sense of the very different consequences of the debts of England at the end of the seventeenth century and of Spain at the end of the sixteenth century and to contemplate the futile struggle of King Philip of Spain and of the aristocracy against the forces of progress than it is for him to derive meaning from current cataclysms. The inevitability of massive transformation in the past provides the past with a stability of meaning and significance in the present, while current transformation is resented as an undermining of an alleged stability that has been lost.

Walter Benjamin viewed such reactions to the inflation very critically, suggesting that much of the upset over the inflation and invidious contrast with the prewar period was little more than the dissatisfaction of those who had been the beneficiaries of past circumstances. For them, the past represented "stability," while the present, which had dispossessed them, represented "instability." This blinded them to the fact that the past "stability" was for many nothing more than a "stabilized misery."[36]

There is yet another perspective from which the trauma of the inflation may be relativized. Economic and social historians have shown that there are endogenous forces at work in the evolution of modern industrial societies which promote certain kinds of structural change, so that the decline of the agricultural sector, the eclipse of old and the triumph of new industries, the growth of the service sector relative to the blue-collar work force, the increasing employment of women, urbanization and suburbanization, and the development of the welfare state are all phenomena which, over the long run, produce a considerable amount of convergence in our contemporary societies. Many of these processes were promoted or accelerated by the inflation but were going to take place in any case. It is important to remember, therefore, that the inflation in Germany between 1914 and 1923 was not an epoch, and the "immediate socioeconomic consequences of the German inflation," whether conducive to or retarding long-term trends, "must be relativized when considering long-term trends."[37]

Certainly Benjamin's relativization of the destabilizing effects of inflation as well as the arguments of those who take the long-run perspective have validity and importance. But an argument can also be made that the manner in which change takes place and the conditions under which it takes place also have their special consequences and that our understanding of major historical episodes will be distorted by a failure to devote sufficient attention to the immediate causes and effects of historical transformation and experience. Indeed, one of the brutal lessons of modern history, especially

German history, is that even change for the better in a social sense, like "modernization," may not in and of itself be beneficent and that some attention has to be paid to how and under what conditions change, transformation, and "modernization" actually take place. It would also be a mistake to appropriate disgruntled *fin de siècle* sentiments toward pre-1914 Germany, or Europe, and forget that the contempt shown by some alienated bourgeois youth for the material security and prosperity of their elders assumed a very different character and quality as a result of the disappearance of what Stefan Zweig called "the world of yesterday" in the turmoil of the war and inflation.[38]

For reasons neither as perverse or strange as they may seem in the light of overwhelmingly critical historical literature on the Second German Empire, it was possible for people to celebrate Germany's material well-being before 1914, that is, before it was sacrificed to militarism and imperialist ambition. The issue is not simply one of "doing justice" to the Germany of that time and understanding the period in its historical immediacy but also, above all, one of making intelligible why its passage had been so traumatic. Indeed, the most impressive paean to German prewar wealth and prosperity was provided appropriately and ironically enough by Director Karl Helfferich of the Deutsche Bank. Helfferich not only played a major role in the history of the inflation from its very beginning to its bitter end, but also gave especially destructive expression to the traumas of the Empire's fall and the inflation in his postwar career as a Nationalist politician. To his great chagrin, his famous work of 1913, written to celebrate Kaiser William II's twenty-fifth year on the throne, *Germany's Economic Progress and National Wealth* (*Deutschlands Volkswohlstand 1888–1913*), was to be used regularly in the postwar period as evidence of Germany's past prosperity in the debate over Germany's capacity to pay reparations as well as a bitter reminder to Germans of their fallen fortunes.[39]

While certainly a contribution to the cause of national self-glorification, Helfferich's book was a serious work by a major economist of the time, and it constituted the best available estimates of Germany's indisputable material progress over the previous two and a half decades. In fact, his estimates of the growth of the German national income remain useful if somewhat exaggerated by his failure, which he recognized but underestimated, to account for possible reduction in the real value of money due to price rises since 1900, while the savings rates he presented were proven to be underestimates by later scholarship. Above all, the book attested to what we would today call Germany's record of economic growth and social modernization. It was a work that reflected the values of Germany's business elite, its *Großbürgertum*, celebrating Germany's growth as an industrial and trading nation, its overtaking of England in key areas of production, its superiority to France because of its stress on labor and industry rather than mere gain from investment, and the nation's increased productivity and its capacity to find gainful employment for its growing and increasingly healthy population and thereby reduce the high emigration of previous times. This is not to say that Germans did not invest. On the contrary, according to his estimates, they invested over 20 percent of their annual income of forty-two billion marks. If Helfferich felt impelled to make some vague and dutiful references to the shadowy sides of industrialization and urbanization, he was nevertheless certain that the continuing shifts in occupation shown in the censuses of 1895 and 1907 were essential to explaining the growing welfare of the German people. Thus, the relative percentage of those employed in agriculture had decreased from 35.6 to 28.5 percent, while the percentage of those engaged in industry and in commerce and transportation had increased, respectively, from 38.9 to 42.5 percent and from 11.5 to 13.3 percent. Helfferich waxed no less enthusiastic over Germany's immense technological progress and its indebtedness to a superior educational system, and he expressed particular pride in the organization of the nation's financial and industrial institutions that led to high savings rates and exceptional efficiency. Helfferich was especially proud of the manner in which Germany combined organization and individual enterprise, including cartels, syndicates, communities of interest (*Interessengemeinschaften* or IGs), and concerns, which at once prevented a "planless and disorderly working against one another,"

while avoiding that "swallowing up of individual enterprises" that characterized the American trust.[40] In short, Germany's great success was owing to her uniquely organized capitalism. Even though the nation's estimated national wealth of three hundred billion to three hundred fifty billion marks lagged behind its major industrial competitors, Helfferich implied, William II's Empire had nevertheless achieved more in a shorter period of time and had done so more effectively through the careful and purposeful employment of her capital at home and abroad.[41]

As a liberal imperialist capitalist modernizer who was also deeply committed to the conservative idea of progress and reform within the context of Germany's existing political and social order, Helfferich was well aware of the political and social divisions in German society. He had been no friend of the Junkers and Conservatives, whose hostility to the great banks and industrialization was evident, even when tempered by tactical alliances with portions of industry on tariffs or in common hostility to the Social Democrats. As the costs of Germany's naval building program and army strained the national budget, Helfferich came out in favor of direct taxation in the Reich and, along with other major elements of Germany's business establishment, was more than a little vexed by Conservative successes in blocking Chancellor Bülow's finance reform proposals of 1909.[42]

This did not mean, however, that Helfferich and most of his allies in the fight for financial reform were prepared to take up the substantive constitutional and political issues that underlay the battle over tax policy. The concentration of direct taxation in the federal states and the dependence of the Reich on indirect taxation and the so-called matricular payments of the states, by which they allocated an assessed portion of their revenues to cover the Reich's requirements, served a variety of system-preserving functions. They strengthened particularist interests in the German federal system by maintaining the fiscal dependence of the Reich on the states, and they buttressed the political domination of the largest, wealthiest, and most populous of the states—Prussia. The Prussian Landtag, composed of a mainly hereditary and partially appointed House of Lords and a

House of Deputies elected under the infamously plutocratic three-class voting system was a bastion of Junker, Conservative, and heavy-industrialist power and often functioned as a barrier to the liberalizing and modernizing elements in the Prussian State Ministry and bureaucracy. Thus, while the Reichstag, with its system of universal and equal male suffrage, more and more reflected the transformation of Germany into an industrial mass society, Prussia, with its de facto control of the federal diet (the Bundesrat), retained basic control of legislative initiatives and exercised a veto power over liberalizing efforts by the Reichstag. Above all, Prussia's domination helped to underpin Germany's peculiar system of constitutional government under which the parliamentary bodies had the power to pass the budget but were denied the right to overthrow the government or present a new government from their own ranks. While the Reichstag elections of 1912 made the Social Democrats the largest party in the Reichstag and created a potential left-wing or reformist majority, Germany's government remained the appointed instrument of the Kaiser, who was, above all, concerned with the retention of his power over the army and foreign policy and the prevention of parliamentarization.[43]

In reality, as Wilhelmine Germany's recurrent political conflicts and periodic crises demonstrated, its political life was far more dynamic than the theory of German constitutionalism with its assumption of benevolent bureaucratic rule from above in harmonious consultation and with the regular approval of the elected representatives of the nation would suggest. The future of the system has long been debated among historians, some arguing that it was inherently unreformable, others claiming that Germany was undergoing a slow and unsteady but unavoidable process of parliamentarization and that the regime was capable of weathering its crises. The pessimists take their stand on the failure of even the most modest efforts to reform the Prussian suffrage system before 1914 and the inability to reform it prior to the development of a revolutionary situation in 1918. Similarly, they note the failure of the Reichstag elections to produce a stable and coherent opposition coalition to the government

composed of Socialists and liberals; the rallying of agrarian, industrial, and lower-middle-class forces in favor of the existing order and even reaction in the so-called Cartel of Productive Estates (*Kartell der schaffenden Stände*) in 1913–1914; the inability of the trade unions to achieve recognition from most of the employers and the unwillingness of the government to recognize collective bargaining agreements in public law; and the stagnation of political and social reform on the eve of the war. Optimists would argue that the perspective of 1912 is more predictive of the future than that of 1913–1914, especially since there was a cyclical downturn in the economy in 1913 which provided the environment, presumably temporary, of the conservative turn. Thus, the elections demonstrated that one could not roll back the political implications of Germany's industrialization, while the collaboration of the major parties, including the Social Democrats, in passing a one-time capital levy for the defense budget (*Wehrbeitrag*) in the Reichstag in 1913 had important and positive implications for the future. It demonstrated that direct taxation in the Reich was inevitable and that the political implications of such would have to be faced sooner or later. It also showed that the Social Democrats were becoming integrated into the political system, a point proven by their support of the war effort in August 1914, and that their accommodation would have been a practical necessity even if Germany had not gone to war. Germany could, after all, boast the most advanced social insurance system in the world, portions of which were already administered by and through Socialist trade-union organizations, and the largest trade-union organizations as well. In the last analysis, therefore, the forces of industrialization, modernization, and liberalization were likely to triumph and peacefully transform the system.

A definitive answer to what the course of imperial Germany's future might have been in the unlikely event of a protracted period of peaceful development can never be given, and, depending on one's position, one can extrapolate either from the elections of 1912 or the conservative turn in 1913–1914 forever and a day. What is relevant here is the manner in which the economic conditions, social structure, and the political culture of the Empire influenced politics and society in the German inflation, and a good way of getting at this problem is to consider some of the issues debated prior to 1914 and the terms in which they were framed.

While the materialism and philistinism of Wilhelmine Germany may have provoked dissatisfaction and a sense of social crisis in some circles, Helfferich's work of 1913 and the self-presentation of Germany's leaders prior to 1914 certainly suggest that there is much to the argument that economic success was an important element in the self-legitimation of the nation-state forged by Bismarck.[44] This was all the more the case because of the deep sociopolitical divisions within Imperial Germany, and Helfferich, in the 1914 editions of his work, was especially concerned to respond to Socialist criticisms that the increase of national income about which he waxed so enthusiastic was unfairly and unevenly distributed to the benefit of the propertied classes. Helfferich, analyzing the Prussian income-tax statistics for the years from 1896 through 1912, argued that the distribution of Germany's increased wealth over this period was remarkably even. His answer to the question, "Cui bono?" therefore, was "everyone." The achievement was not simply economic but, especially if one took social expenditures into account, also social.[45]

In making these arguments, Helfferich was participating in a contemporary debate that has spilled over into scholarly efforts to evaluate the material welfare of the German working class before the First World War. Helfferich certainly was correct in arguing that the German economy had been quite successful in providing employment. By interwar and today's standards, unemployment certainly was low, the available statistics showing rare instances of 6 percent unemployment and a normal level below 3 percent. Few would argue that these figures are entirely reliable, and if one excludes trade-union support for their unemployed members, municipal and local provisions for the unemployed were abysmally inadequate. The unemployed turned to such traditional solutions as taking agricultural work, part-time work, or migrating to other parts of the country. There is also good evidence that employers sought to maintain employment levels among their own skilled

workers. Employers attached importance to retaining their stock of workers, and they were anxious about the social danger that high levels of unemployment might present. In any case, large-scale unemployment was not a familiar problem in prewar German society and the phenomenon was viewed as a social and political danger. Such attitudes obviously had important implications for the response to inflation.[46]

Raging as well was a public debate over whether the working class really was getting a fair share of the national income and, if not, over who was responsible. There could be no doubt that the nominal and real income of the German working class had risen dramatically since unification and especially since 1890 and that there had been a marked improvement in the quality of life measured in terms of nutrition and other forms of consumption. Important modifications must be made to this broad generalization about the material progress of the working class. First, housing conditions may actually have become worse for many workers, particularly in the great urban and industrial areas where rapid industrialization and urbanization had produced miserable housing for disproportionately high rents. Second, and most important, the distribution of the material progress that had taken place was very uneven within the working class. There were enormous differentials in wages among the various industries and between skilled and unskilled workers, between men and women, and between the young and the mature. Thus while the yearly earnings of workers in the mining industry, the iron and steel industry, and the machine-building industry were, respectively, 1,587, 1,357, and 1,423 marks per year in 1913, those employed in the textile, paper-products, and stone-quarry industries earned, respectively, 860, 666, and 471 marks per year. In contrast to England, social insurance was based on worker contributions, and both the contributions and the benefits were based on income; this heightened the significance of the differentials. At the same time, there is strong evidence that skill differentials were beginning to narrow in the two decades before the war, which may have reflected the deskilling that accompanied prewar mechanization and rationalization but which also may have in some part been a response to the increased cost of living after 1900.[47]

It was that increased cost of living which provoked so much discussion and angry reproach from the forces of organized labor in the years prior to the war. The increase of prices was indisputable, and even Helfferich recognized that the money values in which he calculated Germany's national income might have undergone a "modest" diminution in value because of this factor. The cost-of-living index, using 1895 as a base of 100, rose to 106.4 in 1900, 112.4 in 1905, 124.2 in 1910, and 131.3 in 1912 before dropping to 129.8 in 1913. Prices for food and clothing moved in very close conformity to these numbers, while rent actually exceeded the average index. The impact of these rising prices may have been all the greater because costs, especially for consumer goods, the supply of which was greatly increased by technological innovations and improved transport, had dropped substantially during the mid-1870s and had then remained quite stable until 1895. These conditions changed after 1895, when capital-goods industries assumed the innovative role and required very high levels of investment. Prewar workers, therefore, had the impression that their real wages were diminishing, and some economic historians have argued that real wages either stagnated or actually decreased. The best data suggest, however, that real wages continued to rise and that it was high employment and high investment in capital goods along with growing demand for consumer goods which drove prices upward and slackened the pace of real wage increases. In any event, the real wage issue intensified industry-labor conflicts which pitted large employers and employer organizations against the Free (Socialist), Christian, and liberal Hirsch-Duncker unions. While unions fought vainly for recognition and collective bargaining rights, employers used their organized strength to lock out the workers, promoted "yellow" nonstriking unions, sought state support against picketing and more vigorous defense of strike breakers, complained about high costs and shortage of investment funds and the mounting difficulties of facing international competition, and challenged the further extension of social reforms.[48]

The battle between employers and workers over wages was only one of the fronts in the debate over what to do about what was persistently called *die Teuerung* (rising prices). The concept of inflation, which has its origins in the United States, was not employed in prewar Germany, either by economists or in the public discussion of economic questions.[49] While the prewar German Empire exhibited a variety of inflationary tendencies thanks to its military expenditures and the deficiencies of its taxation system as well as from endogenous developments in the real economy, the problem was not viewed in any systemic way or seen as parts of a process except by the Socialists who, from their Marxist perspective, viewed all dysfunctions in the system as illustrations of the faults of capitalism. Such explanations were not so readily available to such nonworker social groups suffering from rising prices as craftsmen, retailers, white-collar workers, civil servants, and even peasants, although lower-middle-class anticapitalism was not insignificant, and ultimately both Socialists and non-Socialists responded to the phenomenon in the same manner; namely, by placing the blame for the situation on one or more other groups. Thus, in the great Reichstag debates in 1912–1913 on rising prices, Socialists blamed agrarian tariffs, while agrarian representatives blamed "middlemen." The wholesalers and retailers returned the compliment by blaming producers, and a variety of groups blamed industrial cartels. Industrial interests divided among themselves as to whether they supported agrarian tariffs and industrial cartels or not.[50] Such lines of conflict and modes of interaction were to persist during the inflation, which was initially perceived and treated as an especially bad and persistent case of *Teuerung*. It is important, however, to recognize both the lines of continuity and the lines of differentiation between the pre-1914 debates about rising prices and those that took place once the war had started.

The lines of continuity were determined by certain peculiarities of Germany's political culture. Despite all the qualifications that must be made, the German political party system in both the Empire and the Weimar Republic basically remained locked into what German sociologist M. Rainer Lepsius has characterized as social-moral milieus. Thus, the Social Democratic Party served as an explicit representative of worker interests and the embodiment of a Marxist proletarian subculture. Conservatives were dominated by agrarian interests and expressed the values of the East Elbian agrarian elite. The Center Party was much more broadly based, encompassing the entire socioeconomic spectrum—workers and businessmen, peasants, craftsmen and merchants, and professionals—but remained almost exclusively Catholic. The National Liberals, often dominated by industrial interests, especially in Prussia, nevertheless had a considerable professional, lower-middle-class and even peasant constituency in the cities, towns, and villages of Protestant Germany, while the left liberals in the Progressive Party represented banking and commercial but also professional and other middle-class elements in the larger cities.[51]

Because the parties found it difficult to transcend their social-moral milieus, a condition at once promoted and exacerbated by their lack of executive responsibility, they also failed to expand their constituencies and integrate economic and other interests through the formulation of broadly based social and economic programs. While often highly susceptible to special interest pressures in day-to-day politics, they were also open to strong and direct competition from interest groups in the political arena. The articulation of economic and social interests and conflicts in Germany had a peculiarly organized character and found direct and public expression, more often than not, by the interest group rather than at the level of the political party. Indeed, Bismarck and his successors had encouraged interest-group politics as a means of reducing the role played by parties and the parliament and of promoting the public's concentration on economic rather than high political issues. While liberal institutions and ideas in Germany had advanced too far to permit the virtual replacement of the Reichstag by a People's Economic Council (*Volkswirtschaftsrat*) composed of interest-group and professional representatives, as Bismarck had once

advocated, corporatist ideas had a much greater resonance in Germany than in other advanced societies, and the language of politics emphasized occupation, profession, and *Stand* (estate).[52]

It is important not to confuse the "premodern" character of German corporatist language and the political vocabulary employed in certain areas of German politics with the real world out of which German interest groups had sprung and the actual conditions to which they addressed themselves. The roots of Imperial Germany's interest groups, like those of its political parties, lay in the rich associational life of nineteenth-century Germany rather than in the premodern estate system. This is as true of the agrarian interest groups founded by Prussia's notorious agitating aristocracy and the multitude of peasant organizations as it is of the great industrial umbrella, branch, and employer organizations. The major agrarian interest groups were products of the post-emancipation period, attained particular importance in the struggle for protectionism in the 1870s, and reached their apogee with the formation in 1893 of the League of German Farmers, a populist organization that used "democratic" and very modern techniques of propaganda and mobilization.[53] Similarly, the leading industrial associations (the Central Association of German Industrialists, representing heavy industry and certain large business interests, and the League of German Industrialists, representing regional, export-oriented, manufacturing interests) were, like the branch and employer organizations, products of Germany's industrialization and represented particularly advanced and modern forms of organization. It is also worth noting that the leading organizations of craftsmen and retailers did not have their roots in the guilds but rather in the problems of the liberal industrial order as they first manifested themselves with threatening severity during the Great Depression of 1873–1896 and persisted during the rapid industrial development of the subsequent period. Thus, the demands for the restriction of entry into the crafts, the strengthening of guild prerogatives, and increased attention from the government and parties had nothing to do with restoring the world of the guild master Hans Sachs, immortalized in Richard Wagner's *Die Meistersinger von Nürnberg*, but rather with protection against the growing might of industry and labor. Similarly, the plaints of retailers over "unfair competition" from itinerant peddlars, department stores, and consumer cooperatives, whether organized by the Socialists or by civil servants, were responses to the rapid development of the tertiary sector and had nothing to do with the preindustrial world.

A more potent argument can be made that the management and manipulation of some of these interest-group claims and the style of politics employed in connection with them may indeed have played upon nostalgia for the preindustrial age and certainly exploited and promoted anti-modern social and political attitudes with the purpose of preventing parliamentarization and the full and equal integration of the organized working class into the political and social system. This was especially true in the East Elbian regions. Such tendencies reached their height in 1913–1914 with the creation of the so-called Cartel of the Producing Estates, an attempt inspired by the League of German Farmers, in alliance with the Central Association of German Industrialists, and the *Mittelstand* Association of the German Reich, which encompassed a variety of craft and retailer organizations, to form a coalition against democratization, social democracy, and liberal politics. The cartel was loosely aligned with a variety of extreme nationalist and anti-Semitic groups—above all, the Pan-German League—and it represented a backlash against the Socialist successes in the election of 1912 and the more liberal tendencies finding expression in the National Liberal Party as well as an opportunistic response to the downturn in business conditions in 1913. Thus, it was possible to form a block of the politically and economically anxious that called for harsher measures against strikes and strikers, a cessation of social reform, greater protection for agriculture, and increased social and economic protection for the eternally hard-pressed *Mittelstand* of craftsmen and retailers.[54]

This was not the first time an effort was made to form such a block (*Sammlung*), and it would not be the last. Thanks to the economic reces-sion as well as its own stalemated policies with respect to recognition of the trade unions and suffrage reform in Prussia, the government was prepared to argue that the Social Insurance Reform Law of 1911, which provided a separate insurance system for white-collar workers with the obvious intention of distancing them from the blue-collar workers, constituted a "certain closure in our social legislation"[55] and that more emphasis would be placed in the future on economic than on social policy so as to provide industry with the "elbow room" it needed. Certainly this implied no more of a rollback in the social reforms of the previous decades than did the government's assurances that the existing system of agrarian tariffs would be maintained but not expanded. Insofar as the calls for a more active *Mittelstandspolitik* were concerned, Interior Minister Clemens von Delbrück, as one Deputy sarcastically noted, made the promise heard the previous year; namely, that they would be "taken under consideration."[56]

Perhaps the major achievement of this kind of interest-group *Sammlungspolitik* was to produce a high degree of callousness, cynicism, and class hostility in German political culture. Alliances between industry and agriculture were notoriously unstable because industry had no real interest in having to pay the higher wages and face the retaliation produced by agrarian protectionism, while agricultural leaders continued to complain about Germany's "over-industrialization," the flight from the land, and the high cost of industrial goods. In the last analysis, they were nothing more than alliances against domestic consumers and in favor of political reaction whose formation had periodically been defended since Bismarck's time as the "protection of the national labor" (*Schutz der nationalen Arbeit*). When agrarian leaders had the bad taste to claim that "rising prices were a measure of compensatory equity," Social Democrats responded that "the increasing prices, the hunger, the distress, the misery—*that* is the protection of the national labor."[57] While it certainly may be argued that the Social Democrats had, for ideological reasons, never done enough to exploit the differing interests of large, medium-sized, and small agriculture, the chasm between organized labor and agriculture and between urban consumers and rural producers surely was widened by the rhetoric of agrarian protectionism practiced by the agrarian leaders and defended by the government.

In the case of agriculture, the words of the government were at least matched by deeds, whereas when it came to the *Mittelstand*, the appeal to fears and anxieties produced few concrete results. Thus, State Secretary Delbrück declared in 1914 that "the process of dissolution of the old independent *Mittelstand* is progressing and, thereby, the buffer between capital and the revolutionary workers is disappearing; one day, some extreme occasion must bring about the great social revolution as the hour of death of our national body politic."[58] The demagogic appeal to the *Mittelstand* by their proclaimed allies in industry and agriculture was no less apocalyptic: "Because the broad groups of the *Mittelstand* are a bulwark against the red flood of Social Democracy, the latter has no interest whatever in the preservation of the *Mittelstand*; on the contrary, Social Democracy does everything it can to destroy the *Mittelstand*."[59] The reality was that neither the government nor industry was prepared to sacrifice economic progress in any serious way to make the *Mittelstand* content and that the *Mittelstand* itself was hopelessly divided into groups that often had conflicting interests. Not only did the two leading groups in the old *Mittelstand* of craftsmen and merchants have different interests, but also the new and growing *Mittelstand* of white-collar workers and middle- and low-ranking civil servants were often more consumer than producer oriented. The government had to tread lightly, for example, in trying to limit civil-servant participation in consumer cooperatives, and white-collar sales clerks were often in conflict with their retailer bosses. While a portion of the new *Mittelstand* was susceptible to right-wing status appeals, anti-Semitism and antifeminism—to the kind of right-wing populism that periodically expressed itself in prewar Germany among members of the old *Mittelstand* and peasantry—the group's future political trajectory was not written in the stars.[60]

The growing complexity and differentiation within the *Mittelstand* was indeed but one expression of these characteristics as they were to be found in the more elevated segments in the *Bürgertum*, a designation once used for those possessing urban citizenship rights under the old estate system but which had become the term applied, first, to the *Bildungsbürgertum*—those who possessed education and property (*Bildung und Besitz*) and served the state as bureaucrats and professors—and then extended to the *Wirtschaftsbürgertum*—those engaged in industry and commerce as capitalism developed, and those in the free professions as professionalization developed in the late nineteenth and early twentieth centuries. The high status of the educated elite and its life style set the tone for what became known as *Bürgerlichkeit*. The households of the *Bürgertum*, which certainly varied in income and were managed with considerable parsimony, were nevertheless characterized by a comfortable standard of living, cherished possessions of refinement and quality, one or a few servants to assist the mistress of the house in her basic tasks, a particular level of nutrition and mode of dining, an emphasis on appropriate attire, and a certain refinement of taste exhibited in the reading of literature of quality and the appreciation of certain types of music and art. While the *Wirtschaftsbürgertum* by no means always participated in the cultivation of the *Bildungsbürgertum* and often pursued narrow educational goals of a technical nature while succumbing to the temptations of ostentatious living, the model of *Bürgerlichkeit* was set by the *Bildungsbürgertum* and served to separate those who participated in its ideals, if not in its material advantages, from the proletariat. A classical education at the *Gymnasium* and university, paid for by paternal savings, and the expectation of a sustained period of uncompensated apprenticeship supported in a similar manner were hallmarks of this life-style which had its roots in the creation of an educated class of state servants at the beginning of the nineteenth century. The costs of education and training could amount to as much as between 30 and 50 percent of a family's expenditures. The *Bürgertum* thus constituted a unique and somewhat variable status group which set the tone for prewar German society, defining the ideals of the petite bourgeois *Mittelstand*, which had once been a major constituent element of the *Bürgertum*, for an upwardly mobile and striving technical intelligentsia of engineers and modern professionals which at once strove for recognition of its less classical education requirements while yearning for the status of the classically educated *Bürgertum*, and for the new *Mittelstand* of white-collar workers and lower and middle-range civil servants. Fears of proletarianization only served to heighten the significance of the model provided by the *Bürgertum* for other middle-class groups. *Bürgerlichkeit* rested, above all, on certain cultural values and practices based on an ill-defined but very real measure of material security. Nevertheless, it was one thing to clip coupons and another thing to be involved in business, just as it was one thing to serve or support the state and another to engage in partisan politics. The ethos of German *Bürgerlichkeit* contained a strong antimaterialist and even anti-industrial element despite its important contribution to capitalist accumulation, and the adaptation to advanced industrial values of technological and commercial competence and achievement was slow and halting. In contrast to the French and English bourgeosie, the members of the German *Bürgertum* used occupation to create their social identification, and took pride in being apolitical or unpolitical but always "state-maintaining" (*staatserhaltend*).[61]

For a state to be maintained, however, its leadership must know how to maintain the state. With regards to the history of the German inflation, the legacy of the prewar period is especially important in understanding the special assets and vulnerabilities of Germany's polity and society in confronting the phenomenon of monetary depreciation. On the one hand, Imperial Germany was a highly industrialized and organized society and, for these very reasons, possessed a wide range of in-depth defenses and structures capable of coping with monetary crisis. Interest-group development and the tradition of group alliances (*Sammlungspolitik*) were powerful instruments in the confrontation with inflation. On the other hand, the political stability of Imperial Germany rested upon the satisfaction, real or psychological, of the economic and status requirements of social groups and classes especially susceptible to the crises that began in 1914. Prior to that fateful year, the German working class, insofar as it was organized by the Social Democrats, faced an unstable array of industrial, agrarian, and lower-middle-class opponents who excluded them from participation in the political power exercised by a bureaucratic elite. That elite embodied both traditions of economic and social reform from above that permitted the *Bürgertum* of education and property, with which its leadership was identified, to have a free ride on the wave of economic modernization of the previous decades. It had come to terms, often quite enthusiastically, with Prussian militaristic traditions and had embraced a post-Bismarckian imperialism that was especially dangerous in an age of social Darwinism and in a nation with hegemonic inclinations, an unresolved relationship with the exercise of power, and an ambivalent attitude toward the legitimating functions of representative institutions. As this book will show, the specific political and social character of the German inflation and the trauma it created must be understood in terms of the legacy of German prewar development.

BOOK ONE

THE INFLATION IN WAR AND RECONSTRUCTION

*The dual nature of money, as a concrete and valued
substance and, at the same time, as something that owes
its significance to the complete dissolution of substance
into motion and function, derives from the fact that money
is the reification of exchange among people, the
embodiment of a pure function.*

Georg Simmel, *The Philosophy of Money*

PART I

THE FIRST WORLD WAR
AND THE ORIGINS
OF THE GERMAN INFLATION

VERTRAUENSMANN: Sie werden mich kennen; ich bin der Bürgermeister. Ich komme auch zu Ihnen wegen der Kriegsanleihe.

DIE FRAU: Ich habe schon Kriegsanleihe.

VERTRAUENSMANN: Um so besser. Dann wissen Sie ja schon Bescheid.

DIE FRAU: Aber wir haben kein Geld mehr.

VERTRAUENSMANN: Auch der Soldat wird manchmal denken, er hat keine Kraft mehr. Und doch gehts' weiter.

WAR BONDS AGENT: You know me. I am the mayor, and I want to talk to you about the war bond drive.

THE HOUSEWIFE: I have already bought war bonds.

WAR BONDS AGENT: All the better. You are already informed.

THE HOUSEWIFE: But we have no more money.

WAR BONDS AGENT: The soldier will also often think that he has no more strength, and yet he goes on.

Zur VI. Kriegsanleihe. Leitfaden und Nachschlageblätter zur Werbearbeit.

Chapter 1

Financing the War

The German inflation had its origins in the First World War, a war which profoundly altered the course of German history. During the 1970s and 1980s, some historians stressed the important lines of continuity in German history, such as the weaknesses of German liberalism and of the German parliamentary tradition, the special characteristics of German imperialism that are seen by some to run in a continuous line from as far back as 1848 up to the Second World War, and the role played by Germany's uneven economic and social development in preventing the timely decline of her preindustrial elites and social groups and in delaying the emancipation of the German working class. Although many of these arguments for continuity have come under increasing attack for being excessively teleological, it would be nonsense to reject the existence of a potent and unique historical legacy which is essential to any explanation of why German history took its indisputably disastrous course between 1871 and 1945.[1]

Needless to say, all nations have their unique histories and political cultures, and the manner in which the various contestants of the First World War managed their respective war efforts militarily, politically, and economically and the consequences of the war for their subsequent development were in no small measure determined by their prewar development.[2] This is not to argue, however, that their histories would have been the same if the First World War had never transpired or if it had not taken the form and character it did. The war was a historical turning point precisely because the domestic politics and foreign relations of the nations involved were irreversibly changed. Little wonder that those who could remember the world before 1914 looked back to it so longingly, whereas no such similar mass emotion was evoked by the "Golden Twenties" after 1945.

While these points might seem obvious, they are often overlooked by those preoccupied with the continuity of German history. To be sure, it is of great importance for German historiography as well as for the German historical consciousness to come to terms with the long lines of continuity that made Nazism possible, but it is also essential for historians to identify the point at which fascist solutions in general and National Socialism in particular became truly possible. Notwithstanding prewar Prussian militarism, Pan-Germanism, varieties of anti-Semitism, disgruntled shopkeepers and craftsmen complaining about department stores and big industry, broadly based anti-socialism and anti-parliamentarism, it is extremely difficult, if not impossible, to project the Third Reich or anything resembling it from the perspective of 1913. This is increasingly less the case after 1918 because Germany had been changed by the war in a manner so fateful as to provide its historical legacy, and especially the aforementioned components of its political culture, with an entirely different context in which to find expression. The First World War was the great transformer through which the currents of German history emerged with newly determined strengths and in newly determined directions. The financing of the war, the subject of this chapter, and the war economy, the subject of the next, were crucial elements in this process.

The Reichsbank, the Financial Preparations for War, and the Banking and Currency Laws of August 4, 1914

The German inflation began, as it was to end nine years later, with legal changes in the nation's monetary regime. Just as the laws of August 4, 1914, defining Germany's wartime monetary order were to provide the legal basis for that continuous expansion of the money supply that was to culminate in the hyperinflation of 1922–1923, so the hyperinflation was to find its termination after November 15, 1923, when the German Rentenbank went into operation on the basis of a law enacted exactly one month earlier. The analogies do not stop here. The five War Finance Laws of August 1914 were passed in association with eleven other laws dealing with wartime economic and social matters and a comprehensive Enabling Act permitting the Bundesrat to decree economic and financial measures without consulting the Reichstag. The Rentenbank Law of October 15, 1923, was actually decreed under an Enabling Act passed by the Reichstag on October 13, 1923. For all intents and purposes, the monetary measures of 1914 and 1923 had an emergency character and were the products of executive power and authority rather than of parliamentary discussion and debate.[3] Finally, and most significant, these laws presupposed that the citizens of the German Reich would accept the implicit contention upon which these laws were based; namely, that the monetary emissions which they sanctioned had real value.

This is no small matter when one considers how rapidly the German people seemed to put their faith in a new currency after experiencing an almost decade-long destruction of their faith in the old one. The Rentenmark and stabilization of 1923–1924 do indeed appear "miraculous" from this perspective. How was it possible for a state and its financial institutions to effectively defraud its citizens through a protracted inflation and then manage to employ its executive authority to gain acceptance for a new currency based not on gold coins that could be stored under a mattress or in the dark recesses of a cupboard but rather on paper notes allegedly backed by all the landed and industrial

wealth of Germany? This is one of the questions this book attempts to answer.

In any case, one must begin at the beginning, and in the beginning the German Empire's central bank, the Reichsbank, created paper money and said it was good. Of course, the Reichsbank had been issuing notes ever since its creation in 1876, and these notes were given the status of legal tender in 1909. Yet, these paper-money emissions were to take on a new character after August 4, 1914. To understand why this was the case, it is necessary to survey briefly the key aspects of the monetary constitution of the Reich before that fateful date.[4]

It lay in the very nature of the Reichsbank that its leaders bore heavy responsibility for meeting the needs of both the state and the private economy. On the one hand, it was a central bank of issue created by law and formally placed under the direction of the Reich Chancellor. He chaired the Curatorium composed of four others beside himself, one named by the Kaiser and three appointed by the Bundesrat. The Reichsbank Board of Directors was required to provide quarterly reports to the Curatorium. In practice, the Chancellor delegated his responsibilities as head of the Reichsbank to the Board of Directors. The latter was composed of a President, Vice President, and eight other Directors. On the other hand, the Reichsbank was a clearing house engaged in providing credit to some forty-three thousand of the most solid private industrial and commercial enterprises in Germany, discounting bills of exchange, and providing other services. It had branches throughout the country. Shares in the Reichsbank were held by major banks and enterprises, and these were represented in the general shareholders meeting of the Reichsbank held every year as well as in the Central Committee elected by the shareholders to oversee the operations of the Reichsbank on a regular basis. Not surprisingly, the fourteen members of this Central Committee—the counterpart of the supervisory board representing the ownership of major German industrial enterprises— were by and large the leaders or representatives of the leading German banks.

In reality, the Curatorium and Central Committee did not play any significant role in determining the policies of the Reichsbank and are

Rudolf von Havenstein, President of the Reichsbank, 1907–1923. (*Die Deutsche Bundesbank, Frankfurt*)

Otto Georg von Glasenapp, Vice President of the Reichsbank, 1907–1924. (*Die Deutsche Bundesbank, Frankfurt*)

largely of interest as reflections of the dual character of the Reichsbank and as bodies to whose discussions historians may turn for information about the bank's policies and the views of its leaders. The Board of Directors, allegedly a collegial body operating on the principle of majority rule, was responsible for day-to-day operations. Since 1908, it was dominated by the President of the Reichsbank, Rudolf von Havenstein (1857–1923) and the Vice President, Otto Georg von Glasenapp (1853–1928). A jurist by training, Havenstein had served in the Prussian Finance Ministry between 1890 and 1900 before gaining great distinction as President of the Prussian State Bank (*Seehandlung*). With his appointment to the presidency of the Reichsbank in 1908, this extraordinarily conscientious, hard-working, and tenacious administrator reached the height of his career and was fated to bear the chief responsibility for the policies of the Reichsbank from the very beginning to the virtual end of the inflation. Havenstein's chief adviser and colleague, von Glasenapp, was also trained as a jurist, but he had made his reputation at the Reich Treasury Of-

fice desk concerned with government debts, money, and coinage, and had served there between 1882 and 1907 before becoming Vice President of the Reichsbank. A broadly educated and cultivated man, von Glasenapp was deeply interested in literature, had an impressive command of the works of Goethe, and was reputed to have transformed his son's translations of Indian poetry into fine German verse while walking to work in the morning. It is impossible to say what relationship these creative capacities had to his tasks once he settled down at his desk, but Glasenapp was known to have played the most important role in framing the legislation that went into effect on August 4, 1914.[5]

Inventiveness is, in any case, the prerequisite for the leadership of any central bank, whose fundamental difficulty is to reconcile its commitment to provide the state and economy with the currency necessary to carry on their operations and its charge to maintain a sound currency. The manner in which these conflicting obligations are resolved and the claims which are made in connection with the solutions chosen, however, have a profound significance for the economic and social developments to which they contribute as well as for the psychological and political responses they produce among the nation's citizenry. In normal times, as the years before the war were thought to be, the Reichsbank's policies stirred relatively little debate and discussion, but the foundations for the legislation of August 4 were laid during those years, as were the Reichsbank's policies during the great inflation.

In many respects, the Reichsbank was one of Germany's most modernizing institutions, and it strove assiduously to create a modern currency system. In our age of paper money with its accompanying kaleidoscope of paper, plastic, and electronic credit instruments, it is difficult to imagine an industrial society, like the German Empire before 1914, in which 52 to 65 percent of monetary circulation consisted of coinage. The daily transactions of most Germans were conducted with ten- and twenty-mark gold coins; one- to five-mark silver coins; five-, ten-, and twenty-five-pfennig nickel coins, and one- and two-pfennig copper coins.[6] The Reichsbank, which had been assigned the task of "regulating the circulation of money in the entire territory of the Reich, facilitating currency transactions, and caring for the utilization of available capital,"[7] viewed this dependence on coinage with increasing disapproval. The dependence on coins and even on cash transactions with paper money was proving to be an ungainly way of doing business. As international tensions mounted in the prewar years, the Reichsbank also considered the excessive circulation of coinage dangerous because it could act as an extreme brake on the Reichsbank's ability to satisfy government liquidity requirements in the event of war. Thus, economic and military considerations went hand in hand as motives for Reichsbank policy.[8]

To counter these inconveniences and threats more effectively, the Reichsbank put substantial effort into educational and propagandistic activities designed not only to promote the use of paper money but also to encourage noncash transactions through checks and interbank transactions. The quantity and variety of paper money in circulation grew considerably prior to 1914. This was most noticeably the case with twenty-, fifty-, hundred-, and thousand-mark Reichsbank notes, whose total value increased from 1,951,000,000 marks in 1908 to 2,574,000,000 in 1913. The increased circulation of Reich Treasury Office notes (*Reichskassenscheine*) in five- and ten-mark denominations from 62 million to 148 million marks during the same period reflected the effort to substitute paper money for coins. Least significant was the increase of hundred-mark notes issued by the few remaining private banks allowed to issue money from 139 million to 147 million marks. At the same time, the Reichsbank sought to take the lead in encouraging noncash transactions by expanding the number of its clearing (*Giro*) accounts from 15,847 in 1900 to 26,148 in 1913. The sums of money thus handled grew from 163,632 million to 379,157 million marks in the 1908–1913 period. Here, however, the Reichsbank served primarily large firms and concerns engaged in big transactions.[9]

The Reichsbank's double motivation in promoting paper money and noncash transactions exposes the tension between Germany's status as a major industrial nation integrated into an international capitalist economy based on the gold standard and its position as a major military and imperialist power at the center of worsening international conflict. Germany's adherence to the gold standard in 1871 was virtually coincident with the creation of a united Germany, and it was the first of the major nations to join England in accepting the "rules of the game" of that monetary order. Those rules mandated virtuous fiscal and monetary behavior domestically and internationally. Thus, all states were expected to back their currencies sufficiently to maintain the exchange rate between their currencies and those of their international trading partners in the system and, theoretically, to ship gold to cover trade imbalances. In short, the system required that governments balance their budgets and that their private sectors control their liquidity.[10]

In practice, it was England's preeminent position as the financial and trading center of the world which was fundamental to making the gold standard work. The Bank of England, which functioned as a lender of last resort for the international trading community, was able to exercise a decisive influence on world credit conditions by changing the discount rate. Because an essential feature of the pre-1914 gold standard was that the pound sterling was a universally accepted currency and was treated as if it were as "good as gold," a Bank of England decision to raise the discount rate inevitably led to an influx of sterling-denominated assets and gold into London. The functioning of the gold standard, therefore, was inextricably connected with the regulative activities of the Bank of England, and these were effective because of certain presumptions concerning the soundness of the pound sterling.

Although the classical gold standard of the pre-1914 era was idealized after 1918 and has been treated as a Paradise Lost from time to time ever since, there is considerable evidence that it was already undergoing significant transformation before the war. There were signs that England was no longer able to maintain her hegemonic role because of her relative decline as an economic power and balance-of-payments deficit. The international monetary order appears to have been becoming hierarchical. Paris, Berlin, and New York increased their importance as financial centers, and the franc and mark played the "key currency" role in certain parts of Europe once reserved for the pound sterling. Most important, neither the British nor anyone else operated the gold standard according to the "rules of the game." Central banks employed a good deal of discretion and varied their gold-reserve ratios. In fact, something akin to what was later called the gold exchange standard—that is, a system in which reserve currencies were held in place of gold— was developing. Indeed, the prewar gold-standard system may already have been in crisis, as reflected in an increasing tendency to hoard gold in anticipation of war and, most serious, in general dissatisfaction with the Bank of England's gold reserve, as well as a growing challenge to the Bank of England by the joint-stock banks.

All this is not to say that the gold standard was facing imminent collapse from its own structural weaknesses. The greatest immediate threat was the anticipation of war because it encouraged the hoarding of gold and discouraged central-bank cooperation to maintain the sta-

bility of the system. The Reichsbank and other central banks worked together to alleviate economic and financial crises, but such cooperation became more difficult as international relations worsened. Whatever their seriousness, the endogenous problems of the system do not seem to have attracted much attention, and this was to have important consequences after the war by promoting illusions about the actual way the prewar gold standard functioned and by nurturing a fatal nostalgia for prewar conditions and monetary parities. In reality, leading participants in the system were finding it more difficult to follow the rules for both domestic and international reasons.

The Reichsbank certainly was committed to solid monetary policies and clung to prescribed coverage requirements for its monetary emissions. At least one-third of the notes issued by the Reichsbank had to be covered by gold or Reich Treasury Office notes (whose emission was very strictly limited) or by other precious-metal German and foreign coins, while the rest had to be covered by commercial bills (*Handelswechsel*). The discounting of the latter constituted the chief and most profitable commercial activity of the Reichsbank and involved the granting of credits, guaranteed by orders already placed, to firms for no longer than three months. In other words, these were short-term operating credits based on concluded business transactions, and this made them secure enough to act as secondary coverage for Reichsbank notes. Most important, the prewar holders of money issued by the Reichsbank had no reason to worry because they had the legal right to demand German gold coins for those notes.

The real source of confidence in Germany was not, of course, the knowledge that its citizens could hoard their money in the form of gold but rather the extraordinary growth and prosperity of the German economy. The Reichsbank and such great universal banks as the Deutsche Bank, Disconto-Gesellschaft, and Dresdner Bank had contributed mightily to that growth. Thus, the Reichsbank used its chief instrument for the control of the money supply—the discount rate—very cautiously and tried to keep interest rates low. At the same time, it acted as the lender of last resort to the great banks, a practice which permitted them to

keep relatively low capital and cash ratios to deposits and investments. Indeed, the Reichsbank, great universal banks, major provincial
banks, and the more exclusive and specialized
but highly influential private banks all worked
to maintain high liquidity in the economy and
supply German industry with generous
amounts of long-term and operating capital.

After 1905, however, the Reichsbank found
it increasingly difficult to meet its own coverage
requirements and became more concerned
about the inadequate manner in which the
great banks were covering their deposits and investments. This was especially evident in the
cyclical crisis of 1906–1907, when the Reichsbank discount rate, which normally ran between 3.5 and 5 percent jumped to between 7
and 7.5 percent because of the sharp decrease in
the Reichsbank's gold reserve. The crisis led to
the dismissal of Richard Koch as Reichsbank
President and the appointment of Havenstein
and Glasenapp, but this scarcely ended the difficulties with which Koch had been wrestling.
The problem with relying on the discount rate
was that its manipulation was not immediate
enough to cope with so relatively sudden a development as the gold loss in 1907; nor could it
deal with the long-term problem of the growing
dependence of the great universal banks on the
Reichsbank as a "lender of last resort." The
credit operations of these banks, and especially
those of the Berlin banks, were so extensive and
generous that in June 1914, for example, only
5 percent of their outstanding credits were covered by actual specie holdings. This was a good
demonstration of how little the prewar gold
standard was actually played according to the
"rules of the game." The reality was that the
"total supply of money had emancipated itself
very considerably from the amount of the gold
reserve."[11]

The Reichsbank was constantly striving to
increase its specie holdings, and one of the most
important measures toward this end after the
run on the bank's gold supply in 1905 was the
issuance of twenty- and fifty-mark notes in an
effort to drive the gold coins in these denominations out of circulation and back into the
Reichsbank specie reserves. Nevertheless, it
proved inadequate in the next Moroccan Crisis
of 1911, when the Reichsbank, in collusion
with the government and leading parliamentar-

ians, felt compelled to stretch its own coverage
limits on twenty- and fifty-paper-mark-note
emissions and then to have such practice made
policy in 1912–1913 by eliminating the three-
hundred-million-mark limit on the emission of
small notes. Under the impress of the tense international situation, the Reichsbank not only
intensified its campaign for noncash transactions, but also increased its gold purchases and
the amount of gold it hoarded in its vaults.
Thus, the amount of gold held by the Reichsbank climbed from 596 million to 777 million
marks between 1905 and 1912; it then rose to
1.17 billion marks in 1913 and to 2.09 billion
marks in 1914.[12]

Reichsbank President Havenstein continued
to plead with the banks to increase their reserves so as not to compound the difficulties of
the Reichsbank in the event of a national emergency and thereby weaken its "action radius,"
which was defined in formulary terms as "the
supply of commercial bills plus specie holdings
minus notes in circulation."[13] His efforts, however, met with only limited success. In 1908, he
managed to impose the publication of interim
balances, thereby providing an incentive for the
banks to behave more responsibly through the
year. After the 1911 political crisis, during
which the Reichsbank was forced to expend
considerable resources to cover the requirements of the banks, Havenstein inspired the
creation of a condition cartel to establish uniform interest rates among the great Berlin
banks and reduce competition (the *Berliner
Stempelvereinigung*). The Berlin banks were
willing to cooperate in this measure and shared
Havenstein's hope that the provincial banks,
some of which had already been taken over by
the Berlin banks, would feel compelled to enter
into the cartel. Similarly, they supported Havenstein's efforts to encourage the municipal
savings banks, where most savers from the middle and working classes kept their money and
with whom the great banks were also in competition, to place more of their assets in government paper rather than mortgages. On the eve
of the war, however, Havenstein found all these
measures inadequate for what he perceived to
be an increasingly dangerous situation.[14]

Thus, only a few days before Sarajevo, on
June 18, 1914, he summoned the leading bankers to a meeting at which he informed them that

the time for action had come. While accepting that Germany's extraordinary economic development owed much to generous credit policies, he felt compelled to point out that "our economic life has been based far too much on credit,"[15] and that this not only reduced the Reichsbank's ability to cope with a military emergency but also undermined Germany's ability to play an active role on international financial markets, extend the nation's economic and political influence, and maintain peace through financial strength. Havenstein argued that the concentration of capital in the banks was soaking up cash reserves and that therefore only self-restraint and higher liquidity on their part could correct the condition for which they themselves were responsible. The time for such a change, of course, was propitious because they found themselves in a period of economic slowdown. After the immense investments in industry and increased productivity of the previous decade, he thought a renewed upswing of great dimensions unlikely in the near term. The opportunity should thus be used to double the liquidity of the banking system over the course of three years, and two paths stood open: "the path of voluntary agreement and collaboration of the Reichsbank and the banking community, which we have previously employed, or legislation." As Havenstein pointedly warned, presenting the Reichstag with bank control legislation was a risky business. He did not want to see the banks put into a "Spanish Boot."

This offer of choice between the voluntary and the compulsory cartelization of the banking industry had long-term significance because it was paradigmatic for the wartime and postwar relations between the state and the business community. It also demonstrated the importance attached by both sides to the elimination of parliamentary interference. After decades of prosperity and economic growth, however, it was difficult to act as if one were in an emergency, and it would remain difficult to shake the mentality nurtured by years of success. Arthur Salomonsohn of the Disconto-Gesellschaft thought that the Reichsbank was acting out of "too much pessimism," reminded the assembled that "no country has come through critical times so well as Germany," and urged that further discussion be put off for a year to see how well the banks could manage to deal

with the problem on their own. Henry Nathan of the Dresdner Bank suggested that foreign assets held by the banks be included in the calculation of their liquidity, a proposition which evaded the question of whether those assets could be realized in the event of war. A number of the bankers stressed the concessions they had already made, pointing to the labor and cost involved in preparing interim balances and the sacrifices imposed by the cartel. They blamed the provincial banks and savings banks for being the real culprits in the liquidity problem. The opportunity offered by the Reichsbank proposal to force the provincial banks into line met with approval, but there was anxiety over the implicit change in the relations between the Reichsbank and the banks being called for by Havenstein. On the one hand, as Salomonsohn noted, the requirement that the banks maintain a specific level of liquidity meant that "the Reichsbank will become an agency of control over the banks for the first time"; on the other, as another banker remarked, the goal of Havenstein seemed to be to "make the banks independent of the Reichsbank." While Havenstein corrected him by arguing that the goal was making the banks "more independent" of the Reichsbank, the real issue was how much the Reichsbank was going to reduce its very convenient role as a lender of last resort for the banks by imposing compulsory organization and higher liquidity requirements. The meeting of June 18 ended with an agreement that the bankers would discuss the matter further and make counterproposals at a meeting scheduled for the end of August. By that time, Germany was at war, and banking control was not to be taken up again for another two decades.

It surely would be a mistake to interpret Havenstein's drive to increase the liquidity of the banks as the expression of a conservative credit policy on the part of the institution he led. On the contrary, it was precisely the liberality of the Reichsbank's intentions in the event of war that drove him in the direction of trying to control the banking system and thus make it easier to mobilize for Reichsbank purposes. The basic legislation for the eventuality of war was well prepared by the summer of 1914. Indeed, it was a worthy counterpart of the Schlieffen Plan, the risky military strategy that sought to overcome the problems of a two-front war by a bold assault on France through Belgium in the expectation that speedy success against Germany's strongest enemy would nullify the significance of a British entry into the war and compel an isolated Russia to come to terms or face the full might of Germany. Just as the military plan sought to compensate for Germany's potential inferiority by a risky policy of capitalizing on short-term advantages, so the financial plan tried to redress Germany's economic and financial isolation by employing instruments which had proven so potent in Germany's rise to economic power. For Havenstein, apppropriately enough, the chief enemy was England, whose "jealousy and ill-will toward our economic flowering, our growing world trade and growing power at sea is in the final analysis the basic cause of the world war."[16] He was convinced that the enemy, especially the English, expected Germany to collapse economically, and it was thus essential that Germany falsify such expectations by showing that the sources of her peacetime success would be even more serviceable in war. As he reported in late September 1914:

In no nation in the world is credit so well developed as in Germany; in no land is the progress of economic life so dependent upon credit and its maintenance as is ours. . . . We must under all circumstances by and large maintain payment of obligations and the obligations themselves. All our preparations for the financial mobilization were based upon this, and they have proven themselves superbly, and we can be truly proud that we, as the most productive of all lands on earth, alone among all the combatants, have come through without a moratorium. . . . The precondition for this continuation of economic activity was the most extensive use of the old source of credit, the Reichsbank, through which the generous granting of credit on the basis of the gradual increase of our war treasure and of the expanded elasticity provided by the wartime legislation was initially required. . . .[17]

The Reichsbank and government were indeed able to resist pressures for a debt moratorium from various interest groups and chambers of commerce at the outbreak of the war, and this success, unique among the warring nations, certainly was made possible by the financial laws prepared by the Reichsbank. Whether "Generalgeldmarschall Havenstein," as he came to be affectionately known, had a more solid foundation for success than his military counterparts, however, was another question.[18]

The fundamental characteristic of the Reichsbank policy surrounding the laws of August 4, 1914, relating to the German currency and monetary system was to transform the system radically while pretending that it was basically unchanged by the measures taken. The most important of the laws, the law which relieved the Reichsbank as well as all other institutions issuing money of the obligation to redeem paper money for gold on demand actually gave retroactive sanction to a decision taken by the Reichsbank on July 31, 1914, in violation of §18 of its charter. Indeed, Havenstein had as much of an interest in a rapid termination of the political crisis and getting on with the war as did General von Moltke. Moltke worried about the timetables of the Schlieffen Plan; Havenstein feared for his gold. The panic created by the international crisis in the last week of July caused thousands of people to line up around the Reichsbank and exchange their paper money for gold and silver, and this cost the Reichsbank 163 million marks' worth of its gold and silver reserves, and another 32 million in Reich Treasury Office notes. In order to prevent further losses, the Reichsbank took the initiative and suspended redemption and payment in gold on July 31, an action for which it was subsequently indemnified by the Reichstag. Thus, in Havenstein's words, it was "especially fortunate that the height of the political crisis lasted only five days. If it had lasted weeks, so that the crisis and panic would have slowly and ever more forcefully crept through the country, it would have weakened the Reichsbank very seriously. . . ."[19]

Allegedly thus fortified, the Reichsbank could fulfill its task of supplying the Reich with the vast sums of cash it needed to carry on the war. The actual problem of money creation on so large a scale was solved by a law that permitted the Reichsbank to discount short-term Treasury bills (*Reichsschatzwechsel*) and gave these bills a status equal to that of commercial bills as secondary cover for the monetary emissions of the Reichsbank. It is to be noted that these Treasury bills were renewable every three months. In other words, while the government was forced to "remind" itself that it was in debt to the Reichsbank for the amount in question, it could prolong such portions of its debt as

Das Gold dem Vaterland!

Gold gab ich zur Wehr

Eisen nahm ich zur Ehr

**Vermehrt unsern Goldbestand!
Bringt Euern Goldschmuck
den Goldankaufstellen!**

Der volle Goldwert wird vergütet!

Typical Reichsbank propaganda urging Germany's women to surrender their gold for the war effort. The placard reads: "Gold for the Fatherland! I gave gold for our defense and received iron as honorable recompense. Increase our gold stock! Bring your gold jewelry to the gold purchasing bureaus. Full gold value will be given in return!" (*Mueller and Graeff Poster Collection, Hoover Institution Archives*)

could not be repaid either through consolidation into long-term debt, by sale of war bonds, through tax receipts, or from other sources of income. This privileged status granted to Reich Treasury bills was viewed as a kind of compensation by the Reichsbank for the government's transfer of control over its entire gold treasure, its "war chest"—lodged in Berlin's Julius Tower—of a hundred twenty million gold marks from the French indemnity of 1871 to the Reichsbank.

While these measures greatly increased the amount of money the Reichsbank could put into circulation, its leaders sought in every way to emphasize that its basic coverage policies remained inviolable. Thus, the Reichsbank claimed that the fundamental guarantee of the soundness of its monetary emissions—the fact that at least one-third of the money had to be backed by gold and certain equivalents—remained inviolate. Indeed, such a preoccupation

with gold as that demonstrated by the Reichsbank is to be found only in Richard Wagner's *Das Rheingold*. Havenstein warmly praised the initiative taken by prominent persons to round up gold, noting how Frau Geheimrat Borsig, the wife of the Berlin industrialist, had gotten the administrators of "her village" to collect forty-five hundred marks in gold from its "450 souls," and how a neighbor had followed her example and collected another three thousand marks in gold. He was also quite proud of his brother-in-law, apparently a Mecklenburg official, who had mobilized the village mayors (*Schulzen*) to exercise a "mild pressure" on the Russian harvest workers to exchange the gold coins in which they had been paid for paper money. It was harder, of course, to shake native Germans out of the "mindless anxiety" that was making them hold on to their gold.[20]

The long-standing attempts to increase the specie supply by encouraging the use of paper money and noncash transactions now took on a patriotic and fetishistic quality of previously unimaginable proportions as the Reichsbank launched a five-year campaign against the hoarding of gold and for its surrender in return for paper money. The argument was always the same. The more gold the Reichsbank had, the more money it could issue. For every one mark in gold in the vaults of the Reichsbank, three paper marks could be placed at the disposal of the war economy. Reichsbank employees were chastised for failing to work after hours when patriotic citizens came to turn in their coins, and pastors were urged to preach the surrender of gold to their flocks in the countryside since the peasantry was particularly notorious for gold hoarding. By the end of 1914, the Reichsbank gold holdings reached two billion marks, but Germany's citizens were reminded by a broadsheet that five billion in gold had been coined and that it was their "holy duty" to give their gold to the Reichsbank. The public was also reminded that "every pfennig that is cleared without the use of cash is a weapon against the economic war of annihilation conducted by our enemy."[21]

A particular effort was made to get schoolchildren to campaign among parents and their elders and thus assist in the national quest for gold. Instructive little brochures were produced with stories illustrating how bright children, properly instructed by their teachers, could extract the golden treasures hidden by shortsighted adults. Reading a brochure like "The Goldseekers at Work," one wonders if the famed authoritarian upbringing of German children was not being sacrificed to Mammon by the Reichsbank. It tells the story of three *Gymnasium* students who verbally harass a fictional elderly grain merchant, Bernhard Lehmann, into turning in his gold for paper money and perform this patriotic deed during school hours with the approval of their teacher. It had apparently become acceptable, even charming, to tell Herr Lehmann that he was a "betrayer of the Fatherland" and "unthinking" because of his reluctance to part with the precious metal.[22]

More significant, however, were the economic arguments put into the mouths of these energetic youngsters. Thus, when Lehmann naively asks, "why should I give gold to the Reichsbank? 20 marks is 20 marks, whether in gold or paper, and what is gained if they have to pay me for it in paper?," the young hero of this tale, Schönfeld responds, "Oh no, Herr Lehmann. 20 marks is not 20 marks, at least not for the Reichsbank. For them 20 marks in gold in reality equals 60 marks in paper because they have the legal right to give 60 marks in paper for 20 marks in gold." The plot thickens as Lehmann asks, "Actually, what prevents the Reichsbank from printing *more* money than three times its gold holdings?" but remains unconvinced when he is told that this would violate the law. He argues skeptically that, "If the law does not suffice anymore, then another will be made, as now occurs with fabulous speed. And then the Reichsbank will give out four or five times as much paper with all the advantages you mentioned also being there." Undaunted, Schönfeld rises to the challenge, asking Lehmann if he would lend his money to someone with insufficient resources, even at a high interest rate. When Lehmann responds in the negative, his mind is prepared for the crucial lesson in the higher realms of state finance:

You see, Herr Lehmann, that's the way it is. And it is just that way with paper money. Why does everyone take paper just as readily as gold, although, for example, even a thousand mark bill is nothing more than a scrap of paper? *Because he knows that the Reichsbank is in a position to give gold for it at any moment, because he knows that he can count on the Reich.* What would happen if the Reich began to print notes without paying attention to its gold stock? It would immediately suffer a loss of confidence. The notes would no longer be accepted, especially abroad, or if accepted, then it would be like those profiteers who supply 750 marks or less worth of goods for the 1000 marks you pay them. A mark would only be worth 75 pfennig abroad or, as one would say, the mark has a low value (exchange rate). Every trading operation with foreign nations for such a state, therefore, means a huge loss. So it is with Russia now, which has frequently made a law like the one you have proposed and has printed banknotes without restraint. . . .[23]

As one might expect, the story ends with Lehmann cheerfully and appreciatively surrendering his hard-earned gold and the youngsters getting the next day off from school (*goldfrei*) for their achievement.

Alas, Schönfeld and his compatriots were not being rewarded for telling the truth, and Herr Lehmann's questions were very much to the point. If the Reich did not need, *à la Russe*, to pass a series of laws raising the amount of money it could issue, it was because the problem had already been solved by the Loan Bureau Law (*Darlehenskassengesetz*) of August 4, 1914, which provided a mechanism for increasing the money supply that made a farce of the one-third cover requirement. Naturally, this was not the officially stated purpose of the law. Officially, it was meant to provide a source of Lombard credit for the federal states and communities as well as the private sector in lieu of the credits provided in the past by the Reichsbank. Since the Reichsbank had to discount Treasury bills to fund the war effort, it was allegedly no longer in a position to grant additional credits to the states and industry without endangering its coverage requirements. To meet the needs of other government entities, private industry, and commerce, therefore, a parallel system of loan bureaus was prepared, and these banks could be set up, as needed, wherever there was a branch or office of the Reichsbank. The loan bureaus would provide three-month credits against a guarantee of either goods or securities.[24]

The fetishistic and ultimately very dubious

manner in which the Reichsbank sought to live up to its coverage requirements is most fully revealed by the loan bureaus. Thus, on August 16, 1914, the Reichsbank informed all its branches that it was turning down every request that it had received from the federal states to discount their bills, a measure which did not preclude private non-Lombard lending by the Reichsbank. The federal states were referred to the loan bureaus since there was a "strong public interest" in maintaining the Reichsbank coverage requirements and "the Treasury bills of the federal states in this regard cannot be placed on an equal footing with the Reich Treasury bills and cannot be considered as monetary coverage. If the Reichsbank were to discount such notes, this would not increase the amount of assets suitable for monetary coverage and, should it involve large amounts, it could present the danger of a violation of the coverage requirements."[25] The loan bureaus, the Reichsbank argued, had been created to solve the dilemmas of the federal states in this situation, and while the loan bureaus did require security and did charge a higher interest rate than the Reichsbank, these requirements were "moderate and appropriate" under the existing circumstances. This last point was undeniable, since the loan bureaus charged 6 percent while the Reichsbank charged 5 percent.

The worm was to be found elsewhere. While the state Treasury bills or other securities used to borrow from the loan bureaus were deemed unworthy of serving even as secondary cover for the monetary emissions of the Reichsbank, the loan-bureau notes themselves, that is, the officially recognized legal currency issued by the loan bureau in connection with their operations, could, insofar as they fell into the possession of the Reichsbank, serve as *primary* coverage for the Reichsbank's monetary emissions. In short, the loan-bureau notes which came to the Reichsbank automatically had the status of specie! The inflationary potential of these loan-bureau notes may perhaps be grasped best when one realizes that it was perfectly possible to use government war bonds as security with the loan bureaus to secure loan-bureau notes and then to use the latter to buy more war bonds from the Reichsbank which, because they were paid for in loan-bureau notes, permitted the Reichsbank to issue more money. Thus, whereas the fundamental purpose of war bonds is to withdraw money from circulation, the capacity of loan-bureau notes to act as primary coverage made it possible for war bonds to serve the exact opposite purpose than that for which they were intended! The only limitation on the issue of loan-bureau notes was the ceiling set under the law of August 4, 1914, of one and a half billion marks, a ceiling which could be raised whenever necessary. It was already doubled in November 1914 to help the first war-bond drive, and its ineffectiveness can be measured by the fact that 15,626,000,000 marks' worth of loan-bureau notes were in circulation in December 1918. The Reichsbank held 33.7 percent of such notes or 5,263,000,000 marks. On this basis, it could legally emit 15,789,000,000 notes of its own.[26] Clearly, Herr Lehmann should have kept his gold and sent Schönfeld back to school with his boot!

Needless to say, those responsible for the banking and currency laws of August 4, 1914, never imagined what the state of German finances would be like in 1918, or even in 1916. They expected the war to be short, and much of the decision making grew out of the experience of 1870 when there had been great difficulties with the financial mobilization. This time, the authorities intended to make sure that there were no financial bottlenecks and that every legitimate credit demand, public and private, would be satisfied. The desire of the Reichsbank to achieve this goal without damaging the integrity of the currency is perfectly understandable. Indeed, one- and two-mark loan-bureau notes played an important role in relieving the shortage of small change and bills caused by hoarding, and they were shipped out to the eighty-eight municipalities and twenty-five private enterprises that had issued 6,287,740 marks in emergency money (*Notgeld*) in August and September 1914 to deal with the problem.[27] The emergency money could thus be speedily withdrawn from circulation, something that was not to prove so simple in later years.

The question, nevertheless, remains as to why the Reichsbank laid the foundation for unlimited monetary emission while claiming that it was doing nothing of the sort. There was no reason why the securities put up to guarantee state and municipal loans, which by 1918 had consumed 84.5 percent of the credits of the loan banks, should lead to the production of notes that could act as primary coverage for Reichsbank monetary emissions while the Reich Treasury bills should have a lower status. If the currency depreciated, then the loan-bureau monetary emissions would depreciate as well, and there was no way in the world that the holder of loan bank notes could make a special claim for security of assets pledged to the loan bureaus.[28]

The dubiousness of the arrangement must be borne in mind because it illustrates that the practices of the Reichsbank were not simply the consequence of monetary theories popular in Germany that denied the inflationary consequences of increasing the supply of money and that overemphasized the dependence of the value of money on the gold stock. Whatever the role of monetary theory, there was no school that could justify the Reichsbank's sleight of hand in connection with the loan-bureau emissions.

It is significant that the earliest and most trenchant criticism came from the Hamburg bank director and monetary theoretician Friedrich Bendixen, who was an ally of George Friedrich Knapp and supporter of the state theory of money. In an article intended for publication in January 1915, Bendixen characterized the loan-bureau arrangements as the "greatest invention of all times" and tore into the motives and morality of the Reichsbank's monetary planning for war:

In the financial press, there even was great rejoicing over this "ingenious" new note emission and coverage system. I cannot decide if it is even to be found worthy of the German name, and it has done us damage abroad. If the German feels himself entitled to give paper as gold coverage—it is argued—then the allegedly effective gold supply that is claimed to exist is to be treated with caution. The result is that one simply does not believe us anymore. Thus we discredit our integrity and the healthy position of the Reichsbank with a hateful trick that we could easily do without. The use of the loan bureaus in connection with the war loans is something that cuts both ways. To be sure, it makes possible a splendid sign-up and places the national will to sacrifice in the best light. But, on the other hand, the ad hoc loans thus granted falsify the sum of effectively available capital, because with the help of the loan bureaus even a totally exhausted people can produce any number of billions. This is to be regretted because the actually available capital savings for the war loan is imposing in any case, and its effect is lost through the illegitimate increase.[29]

In Bendixen's view, the Reichsbank could have surrendered "the fiction that paper is gold," and, insofar as coverage of note emissions became an actual problem, "it would have been simpler to ask for a legal provision that empowered the Bundesrat to suspend the coverage requirements by decree." Bendixen did not think much of the effort to leave the banking laws untouched so as to "awaken the impression of extraordinary stability" and impress people with the notion "that one can keep things going in war with the same rules one uses in peace." He attacked the "cult" of one-third coverage, the manner in which the translation of every piece of gold into three pieces of paper money had become some kind of "natural law" for the public, which was being indoctrinated to regard this transformation as some sort of "miracle." While such "nonsense" was producing the desirable result of driving gold into the Reichsbank, Bendixen demanded of the Reichsbank leaders that "they should themselves be free of this popular error and not sink to their knees before their self-created idol of one-third coverage."[30]

Actually, as Bendixen well knew, there was something of a precedent for the loan-bureau notes in the Reich Treasury Office notes, which also served as primary coverage for Reichsbank emissions. Bendixen had devoted some attention to this currency before the war, and Knapp had expressed his warm approval of Bendixen's essay on the subject in 1913: "One should continually remind everyone of the nonsense involved in partially covering bank notes through uncovered Treasury office notes."[31] The irritating criticisms that were permissible in 1913, however, were intolerable in 1915, and Bendixen's article on the wartime currency arrangements could not be published until 1919 since "the confidence of people in Havenstein had to be spared"[32] for the duration. What Bendixen understood, however, was that this was a dangerous business, for what the state theory of money meant in the last analysis was that the currency's stability was dependent upon the state's capacity to maintain it through its authority and success. The depreciation of the currency would necessarily impugn the authority of the state, and making artificial claims for the currency by a variety of dubious methods would only damage both the state and the currency further.

Bendixen was not the only economist to fall victim to the censor. The sensitivity of the Reichsbank to criticism was apparent as early as August 8, 1914, when Glasenapp and Karl von Lumm of the Board of Directors responded to criticisms by Kurt Singer of the *Hamburgische Correspondent* that the Reichsbank had not been swift enough in terminating its obligation to redeem notes in gold and had failed to print enough notes in small denominations by warning Singer that if commentaries did not cease, they would have "to seek the assistance of the military authorities."[33] At the completely other end of the theoretical spectrum from Bendixen, one supporter of the quantity theory, L. Albert Hahn, was refused permission to publish an article in the *Bank = Archiv* on the grounds that his desire to discuss the great increase in the money supply and its role in the financing of the war would disturb the public. As he later noted, this was the beginning of a posture that was to be assumed repeatedly and with devastating consequences: "Placed before the choice of publicly exposing abuses and thereby effectively fighting them or keeping dead silent because of the danger of arousing mistrust, one decided for the latter course."[34] It is interesting that Joseph Schumpeter, despite his own reservations about metalist and quantity theories of money, stressed their relevance in 1918, not only because they pointed up phenomena not otherwise explicable, "but above all because there is seriousness and integrity in them, which we desperately need."[35] In sum, the central problem of August 4, 1914, was not the monetary theory, such as it was, upon which monetary arrangements were based. Rather, it was that the Reichsbank chose a path that threatened to compromise the authority of the state and the confidence in the probity of its measures and thus displayed what Bendixen trenchantly described as a "character deficiency,"[36]

the depth and significance of which he himself scarcely realized at the time.

Lest there be any misunderstanding, it should be made clear that the anthropomorphization of states and institutions, which are composed of human beings but do not function as individual human beings do, is a tricky business. It is important for the historian not to debase the medium through which he or she seeks to describe reality by substituting metaphors for explanation. Furthermore, it is not the business of the historian to dispense simple moral lessons. The historical status and significance of the deceptions and self-deceptions of those in authority depend on their consequences, and it is the latter which determine whether they are trivial and perhaps amusing or significant and even terrifying. In the first case, they may simply be noted; in the second, they require investigation and analysis. The "character deficiency" involved in the treatment of loan-bureau notes as primary coverage for Reichsbank notes would simply be one of the peculiarities of banking history were it not for the great German inflation. In the context of the latter, however, the banking and currency laws of August 4, 1914, become part of a pattern in which the constitutional, political, and socioeconomic evolution of Imperial Germany compelled or encouraged the exhibition of one "character deficiency" after another, which in aggregation and in combination with one another produced the momentous developments which are the subject of this book. One of those developments was that the real Mr. Lehmanns emerged from the war and its aftermath feeling that they had been deceived.

War Loans, War Taxes, and Exchange Controls

That the monetary arrangements of the Reichsbank were no isolated example of structural deficiencies in the governance of the German Empire becomes evident when one turns to the actual problems of war finance. Certainly the Reichsbank had no intention of flooding the country with worthless paper, and it discounted Reich Treasury bills in the expectation that the Reich would make a successful effort to cover its costs. There were three possible ways to finance the war. The first was by war loans; that is, the periodic consolidation of the short-term debt into a long-term debt owed to domestic war-loan subscribers. The second was by taxation. The third was by borrowing abroad. As is well known, Germany placed her primary reliance on domestic war loans. The chief theoretical proponent of this method, the economist Heinrich Dietzel, defended war loans on the grounds that they maximized the speed with which money could be raised while minimizing the resistance that the government was likely to encounter in its efforts to extract money and reduce purchasing power. This view was shared by leading members of the banking community, such as the influential Hamburg private banker Max Warburg, and it also conformed to the attitudes of the Deutsche Bank director who was to assume the position of State Secretary of the Treasury from January 1915 to May 1916, Karl Helfferich. The latter pointed to Germany's war-bond drives with great pride and disparaged the English efforts to fund a substantial portion of the war effort with taxes.[37]

The degree of English dependence on taxation may have been exaggerated by Helfferich as well as by historians, while the extent of German taxation may often be understated in comparative terms by the failure to take German state and local taxation into account. At the same time, the evidence suggests that Germany was far less able to afford dependence on domestic war loans than England because the London money market was far larger and had a much greater capacity and willingness to absorb the state debt to substitute for the decline in its normal international business. The Berlin market was substantially smaller, unused to dealing in Treasury bills, compelled to take over the financing of international as well as domestic trade, and unwilling to sacrifice domestic customers in order to hold government bills in what was expected in any case to be a short war. Thus, until 1917, three-quarters of the floating debt of the Reich was held by the Reichsbank, the amount decreasing to somewhat over half in 1917–1918. This meant that a great deal more of the German debt was rapidly monetized than was the case in England, especially since German municipalities bor-

rowed heavily from the loan bureaus. This monetary expansion as well as the collapse of overseas trade help to explain why more of the German debt was held outside the Reichsbank after 1917. Nevertheless, the comparative data on monetary expansion clearly demonstrate how much advantage the British had over the Germans in the fight against inflation. While the British monetary base and money supply at the end of 1917 had increased over the end of 1913 by 12 and 17 percent respectively, Germany's had increased by 56 and 50 percent. The corresponding figures for the end of 1918 were 32 and 25 percent for England and 76 and 52 percent for Germany. If, as recent scholarship has suggested, the source of the British advantage was in its superior money market as well as in access to foreign money rather than in its level of taxation, then this only strengthens the case for those who have criticized Germany's failure to make greater use of taxation to finance the war. If Germany could not borrow abroad and was unable to place a sufficient amount of its debt at home, then what other alternative was there but much greater dependence on taxation?[38]

It is significant that those who advocated financing a German war effort by taxation, most notably the economists Adolph Wagner, Johann Plenge, and Julius Wolf, did so in the context of the debate over a reform of the entire financial system of the Reich which had taken place before 1914. The major goal of such a reform was the shifting of the preponderance of direct taxation from the federal states to the Reich, a change that would have reduced the power of the federal states, especially Prussia, and greatly increased the power of the Reichstag. It would have propelled Germany significantly further along the road to parliamentarization. Not surprisingly, therefore, the chief prewar efforts failed, and even the capital levy for military purposes passed by the Reichstag in 1913 was accepted by the federal states only on condition that it would be a nonrecurring levy. The failure of prewar taxation reform efforts virtually decided the question of Germany's ability to finance the war by taxation. Given the past limits on the Reich's direct taxation activity and the fact that the actual administration of direct taxation remained lodged in the states, the dependence on war loans became unavoidable. Furthermore, and perhaps most decisive, an attempt to produce a tax reform during the war would have led to a major political debate and thus undermined the political truce (*Burgfrieden*). Finally, insofar as foreign borrowing was concerned, the imperial regime showed very little interest in what was to become so important for the Allied, and especially the French, war effort. On the one hand, Germany was not rich in allies or friends from whom she could borrow. As Havenstein argued with considerable pathos, "it was very clear to us that we were thrown back upon our own resources and that we could expect support from no one in this world war. . . . "[39] On the other hand, there was little genuine interest in securing funds by this means during the early years of the war. It appears that some initial efforts to procure money from the United States were killed by government procrastination despite the enthusiasm of Max Warburg and his Hanseatic colleagues. Thus, with each passing year of war, the German war-bond drives, while certainly bearing witness to the loyalty of the nation's citizenry, also testified to the vulnerabilities of Germany's domestic fiscal and financial arrangements and to German international isolation.[40]

The fictions surrounding the German financial war effort, like all such fictions, derived their plausibility from the fact that they were not totally divorced from experience. The German budget, for example, had always been divided into an ordinary and extraordinary budget. Before 1914, the former covered about 90 percent of expenditure and included both current and capital expenditures that were met from income. The extraordinary budget covered special capital expenditures that were either self-amortizing or were to be covered by special loans. While it is possible to detect certain dangerous tendencies in the use of the extraordinary budget before the war, the latter only began truly to live up to its name after August 1914, when it became the repository of all expenses involved in running the war, including the normal military budget, which was removed from the ordinary budget. The relief thus provided to the ordinary budget, however, was short-lived because the entire service on the debt created by the extraordinary budget, funded through war loans, was lodged in the ordinary budget. At the same time, traditional sources of income used to cover the ordinary budget, such as receipts from customs, the post office, and the railroads, were either sharply reduced, as in the case of customs, or turned into deficits as a result of the reduction or elimination of paying customers and their replacement by military consumers. Appropriately enough, the only Reich enterprises to make a profit during the war were the Reich Printing Office, the Reichsbank, and the loan bureaus. The Reich made these "profits" at its own expense.[41]

The actual financial fate of the Reich in the First World War may be most clearly seen by placing together the expenses of the two budgets and the income from traditional sources and war loans (see Table 2). The only surplus for the entire period was that combined in the ordinary budget for 1914, and it is virtually meaningless from the perspective of war finance since the debt service amounted to "only" a quarter of expenditures, the income from the 1913 capital levy was still relatively high (637.4 million), and customs receipts—560 million in 1914 in contrast to 359.9 million in 1915 and 130 million in 1918—reflected the fact that Germany had been at peace through most of the year. The decisive turning point in the financial history of the war came in the second half of 1916 and is clearly reflected when, on the one hand, war costs escalated to a new order of magnitude in comparison with the earlier period and, on the other hand, war-loan subscriptions fell significantly behind expenditure.

It should be pointed out that a more cheerful construction can be put on the situation during the first two years of the war than that shown in Table 2. This was provided by Karl Helfferich who, as State Secretary of the Treasury during the period in question, was not exactly a disinterested observer. Helfferich's argument here and elsewhere is worth reproducing, however, because he was one of Germany's foremost economic thinkers and writers, and he was to play an important role throughout the history of the inflation. Furthermore, this argument is also useful in highlighting the disastrous impact of the Hindenburg weapons and munitions program inaugurated in the early fall of 1916 and

Table 2. Income and Expenditure of the Reich, 1914–1918
(in millions of marks)

		Ordinary Budget			Extraordinary Budget		
		Expenditures	Income	Balance	Expenditures	Income	Balance
1914	Total	1773.5	2471.1	697.6	7004.3	4805.3	−2198.8
	Debt Service	470.4				4435.3*	
	(% of total)	(26.5)					
1915	Total	1875.9	1825.2	−50.7	23927	20495.1	−3431.9
	Debt Service	1346.0				20382.0*	
	(% of total)	(71.7)					
1916	Total	3066.8	2122.2	−944.6	24771.7	19751.9	−5019.8
	Debt Service	2616.8				19658.9*	
	(% of total)	(85.3)					
1917	Total	7073.3	8010.1[b]	−936.8	45121.8	26138.5	−18983.3
	Debt Service	6518.8[a]				23851.2*	
	(% of total)	(92.2)					
1918	Total	7545.6	7395.2[c]	−150.4	36884.7	23111.1	−13773.6
	Debt Service	6770.5				22738.2*	
	(% of total)	(89.7)					

Source: K. Roeseler, *Die Finanzpolitik des Deutschen Reiches im Ersten Weltkrieg* (Berlin, 1967), pp. 197, 199.
[a]Includes 2178 million marks in war-loan redemption.
[b]Includes 1200.2 millions in consumer taxes (668.8 millions in 1916) and 4842.7 millions from the 1916 war taxes.
[c]Includes 2032.8 millions in consumer taxes and 2409 millions from 1916 and 1918 in war taxes.
*Portion of income from war bonds.

the transition to "total war" under the auspices of the new Supreme Command of Hindenburg and Ludendorff.

Helfferich argued that the proceeds from the first four war loans (floated between September 1914 and March 1916) managed to cover the outstanding Treasury bills during this period (see Table 3). Therefore, according to Helfferich the war loans did what they were supposed to do, and the financial policy of the Reich was justified. There are, however, two technical problems with this argument. First, Helfferich employs the nominal worth of the war bonds without taking into account the fact that the actual amount received was below face value at maturation. Second, since the fiscal year began in April and ended in March while the biannual war-bond drives were launched in March and September, Helfferich was operating under the assumption that the results of the March war-bond drives could be counted as covering and even exceeding the outstanding Treasury bills of the previous fiscal year, an assumption that does in fact hold through the fiscal year ending in March 1916. What is less rosy, of course, is the situation during the intervening months. The most dubious aspect of Helfferich's argument, however, was the actual point he was trying to make: the method chosen to finance the

war was completely successful, and the major debt to be covered was that of the ordinary budget where the growing debt service had to be met.[42]

This posture was highly significant, however, because it provided the vantage point from which the purposes of wartime taxation were perceived; namely, the covering of the deficit in the ordinary budget to the total neglect of the burgeoning deficit in the extraordinary budget and, ultimately, the huge outstanding war-loan debt. Obviously, Helfferich and his colleagues were too intelligent not to be aware that these potentially horrendous problems could not be covered up by a bookkeeping device, but they insisted that it was impossible to deal with them until the war ended and its consequences could be measured. Especially in 1915, when he had high hopes for a speedy end to the war, Helfferich took the view that Germany could manage without raising taxes and that it could count on war loans and the printing press. He was no less frank about whom he expected to pay the bill. As he told the Reichstag on August 20, 1915, "The instigators of this war have earned this lead weight of billions; may they drag it down through the years, not we."[43]

A decision was made first to avoid and then, as financial and public pressures increased, to

Table 3. War Loans and Treasury Bills
(in millions of marks)

War Loan		Nominal Value	Outstanding Treasury Bills	Balance
I.	Sept. 1914	4.5	2.6	1.9
II.	March 1915	9.1	7.2	1.9
III.	Sept. 1915	12.1	9.7	2.4
IV.	March 1916	10.7	10.4	0.3
V.	Sept. 1916	10.7	12.8	−2.1
VI.	March 1917	13.1	19.9	−6.8
VII.	Sept. 1917	12.6	27.2	−14.6
VIII.	March 1918	15.0	38.9	−23.9
IX.	Sept. 1918	10.4	49.4	−39.0

Source: Carl-Ludwig Holtfrerich, *The German Inflation 1914–1923. Causes and Effects in International Perspective* (Berlin and New York, 1986), p. 117.

limit wartime taxation, but this still left a host of problems about the kinds of taxes that might be raised. A major difficulty in analyzing and evaluating Helfferich's policies, as well as those of his successor, Count Siegfried von Roedern, is sorting out their actual intentions from the constraints under which they were compelled to operate. The political constraints were the most important. Every tax measure threatened to disrupt the *Burgfrieden*, or what little was left of it as the war went on. Direct taxation by the Reich immediately stirred up the federal states, while new indirect taxes inevitably brought sharp criticism from the Social Democrats. Even if they so wished, neither Helfferich nor von Roedern was capable of revolutionizing the Reich taxation system in the midst of the war. Within these constraints, however, there was the question of how far they were prepared to go in doing the possible—specifically, taxing war profits. Here, one can demonstrate a great difference between Helfferich and von Roedern. Helfferich was profoundly liberal in his attitude toward war profits and was also convinced that industry had to have every possible incentive to produce for the war effort as well as to recover its position and reconstruct after the war.[44] In May 1916, von Roedern replaced Helfferich, who was appointed State Secretary of the Interior. Shortly after taking over his new post, von Roedern began to press for the control of war profits, only to be resisted by Helfferich. Von Roedern was to prove more severe in his tax measures during the last two years of the war and, what was even more telling, began to plan for a comprehensive tax reform. What can be argued, therefore, is that Helfferich's eco-

nomic liberalism and conviction that generous incentives were the only way to promote production made him less resistant to conservative efforts to retain the existing archaic tax structure, while von Roedern was more genuinely a victim of the political and social constraints on higher taxation and basic reform.[45]

Whatever it was that should have been done, it is necessary to register the inadequacy of what actually was done. Insofar as direct taxes are concerned, the Reich government felt compelled to follow the model established in 1913 and use special nonrecurring taxes rather than move in the direction of a Reich income tax. Thus, in June 1916 the Reichstag passed an extraordinary war levy on corporations and physical persons aimed at taxing excess profits and increases in wealth. In April 1917, a 20 percent surcharge was placed on the 1916 tax, and a new war levy was imposed for 1918. Beginning in June 1916, there were also substantial increases in indirect taxes, especially on tobacco, all beverages, freight and personal travel, and postal and telegraph services. In June 1916 a turnover tax was introduced for the first time and was raised two years later. Finally, in April 1917 an important new 20 percent coal tax was initiated.[46]

As Table 2 shows, the new taxes reduced but did not eliminate the deficit in the ordinary budget. While left-wing pressure helped to sharpen and strengthen the direct taxes passed in 1918, the entire result bespoke the inertia created by the financial constitution of the Reich as well as by the initial unwillingness to tax effectively. The direct taxes, based by and large on self-assessment and the inadequate and varying assessment methods employed in the federal states, provided numerous opportunities for evasion. Furthermore, the taxes could be paid in war bonds. A particularly ironic aspect of the reliance on indirect taxes, especially on new taxes like the coal tax, was that the Reich, as the chief non-household direct or indirect consumer of coal because of its centrality to the war economy, was really taxing itself. The turnover tax was hard to implement effectively because of the inadequate personnel available, while the actual costs were largely passed on to the consumer. The most that can be said for the Reich's wartime taxation was that it came close to realizing its inadequate goal of covering the deficit in the ordinary budget.

Germany's war-bond drives, therefore, remained at the center of the nation's effort to finance the war, and they provide yet another revealing and long-lasting contribution to the history of the German inflation. The war loans were relatively successful in covering the Treasury bills placed by the government prior to the fall of 1916, but after that time, they failed of their purpose. The first of the war-bond drives proved to be a model for the rest. For the business community, the government offered a billion marks' worth of bonds yielding 5.63 percent with an average term of five years, while the general public was offered war bonds which could be turned in at any time but which, if held for ten years, were to yield 5.38 percent with a conversion right into normal government bonds at 4 percent. Subscribers in amounts over a thousand marks could pay in as much as four installments, but these had to be completed within two and a half months. The banks, especially the savings banks, gave the Reichsbank a helping hand in its efforts by permitting early withdrawals and extending the deadlines for their customers to pay the money owing for war-bond purchases. The success of the first war loan was somewhat alloyed by the fact that considerable assistance was given to customers without the cash to buy war bonds by the loan bureaus. The latter provided some 921.8 million in loan-bank war-bond loans at a favorable rate of interest. Twenty-one percent of the first war loan was financed in this manner, but the portion of war loans thus financed

continuously declined and became quite negligible in the last two years of the war as the liquidity of those wishing to invest in war bonds made such borrowing unnecessary.[47]

Of much greater interest from the political and social points of view, however, was the changing composition of the war-bond subscribers. From the very outset, the Reichsbank had decided not to place the war loans with a bank consortium since it was convinced that no consortium would be willing to guarantee such large loans or, if it did, would charge so much for its services as to make the bonds unattractive to the public. The only solution, therefore, was "an appeal to the entire people" that would base itself on "ethical values, not merely personal gain."[48] Here, as in so many other areas, time worked against Germany's planners. The percentage of money collected from those investing a hundred thousand marks or more ranged between 55 and 60 percent of the total receipts for the first four bond drives, while it ranged from 66 to 82 percent for the last five loans. Those subscribing between six hundred marks and two thousand marks accounted for 13 to 15 percent of the amount collected from the first four loans but only for 5 to 10 percent of the last five loans. Subscriptions of over a million marks accounted for 8 percent of the intake from the third loan drive, but for as much as 25 percent from the seventh, 23 percent of the eighth, and 34 percent of the ninth war-loan drive. While it certainly was an achievement to increase the number of persons subscribing up to two hundred marks from 231,112 in the first drive to 4,076,649 in the eighth drive, and to increase those contributing three hundred to five hundred marks from 241,804 to 944,491 during this same period, the number of those contributing between six hundred and two thousand marks remained fairly steady between the fourth and eighth loans at about 1,300,000 persons. What these figures suggest is that the war was producing a redistribution of financial resources to the disfavor of the middle-class investors and savers to the benefit of those producing for the war effort and thereby in possession of substantial liquidity. Whereas middle-class savers seem to have played a prominent role in the early war-bond drives, they no longer had the same capital at their disposal during the second half of the war, while those being fed by the government with profits from war contracts were in a position to increase their war-bond holdings.[49]

The situation was noted as early as December 1916 by the Reichsbank, which expressed concern over the decrease in the number of those signing up from 5.2 million in the fourth drive to 3.8 million in the fifth, and that most of the decrease could be accounted for by persons who had invested up to twenty thousand marks. The difference in the total intake was made up by big investors; that is, those purchasing a hundred thousand marks or more in bonds.[50] The Reichsbank was anxious to maintain the popular and national character of the war-bond drives, and it stepped up its efforts to secure a mass sign-up. The statistics show that the number of persons purchasing bonds remained in the millions to the very end, even though the size of the total intake depended increasingly on the large subscribers. What the statistics cannot tell, of course, is who the small subscribers were. Just as one may deduce from the structure of the subscriptions that the role played by the urban middle class became less important in the second half of the war, so, too, one can get some sense of whom the Reichsbank hoped to tap from its propaganda.

The major group, certainly, was the peasantry, which always seemed to be in the foreground of every discussion of war-bond-drive propaganda because of its obvious ability to profit from the food shortages as well as its notorious unwillingness to part with its money. There is some evidence, however, that the working class appeared as a promising object of war-loan propaganda efforts in the latter part of the war. Thus, in the eighth war-bond drive of March 1918, the chambers of commerce identified 1,767 firms in which a special effort might be made to win worker subscriptions.[51] Over 29 percent of the 334,000 workers in question, about 125,000 of whom were female, contributed a total of 33.3 million marks, a result aided by the willingness of firms to collect the subscriptions in installments.[52] Too much should not be made of such evidence, but the alienation of the workers was probably no greater than that of the peasants by the end of the war, and the evidence would be in conformity with the improvement of the condition of certain portions of the working class relative to that of other social groups.

In any case, Reichsbank propaganda sought to appeal to the nation as a whole, whether it was to procure gold, encourage the use of noncash transactions, or, above all, promote the biannual war-loan drives. This propaganda, especially that supporting the war-bond drives, deserves serious attention. Initially, the Reichsbank seemed to rely largely on the press to promote the war-bond drives. Thus, whereas it had employed about seven hundred newspapers to publicize government loans before the war, twenty-eight hundred large and small papers throughout the country were used to push the first war-bond drive. Nevertheless, a major propaganda effort for war bonds was not found necessary until the fifth drive in the second half of 1916, but then the Reichsbank followed advice it received and went systematically to work. It established a massive and well-funded effort centrally directed by a special office in the Reichsbank and became something of a gigantic national advertising enterprise that displayed a remarkable degree of inventive ability. It pioneered in the use of trick film for advertising purposes, for example. Helfferich, both in and out of high office, played a major role in these efforts, and he seems to have been important in encouraging the use of these "Americanlike" techniques while serving as Secretary of the Treasury. The propaganda itself was spread through a well-organized voluntary network of thirteen hundred head agents and a hundred thousand regular agents throughout the country who made use of provincial printers for the rapid production of pamphlets, leaflets, and other such materials. These were addressed to the various concerns and fears about Germany's financial situation and sought not only to allay anxieties but also to instill a set of beliefs and promote a mood of confidence and willingness to invest in the German war effort.[53] This propaganda provides a useful measure by which to compare what the Reichsbank and government told the people was happening over against what was really happening and what the Reich leadership itself thought.

Early Reichsbank propaganda, for example, had placed special emphasis on how the alleged one-third coverage of the Reichsbank emissions maintained the exchange rate of the mark abroad. This was an argument that became increasingly shaky as the war went on. The Reichsbank continued to emphasize its gold hoard as a guarantor of the external value of the currency, but foreign exchanges showed more interest in the amount of marks in circulation, Germany's balance of trade, and her military fortunes. The reality was that the mark was "floating," and that its ups and downs were very much determined by the latest economic, military, and political news. The Reichsbank and the Reich government could not totally neglect these realities in their policy decisions. By the end of 1915, the increased note circulation within Germany as well as the reduction of exports had already negatively affected the exchange value of the mark to the point where the first exchange control measures had to be considered.

A decree on dealings in foreign currencies issued on January 20, 1916, marks the formal beginning of a decade of exchange controls and exchange regulations. Under this decree, the purchase and sale of foreign currencies could only be undertaken through the Reichsbank or one of the twenty-eight designated banks located in Berlin (thirteen), Frankfurt (eleven), and Hamburg (four). The Reichsbank could demand information about all business transacted with the use of foreign currencies and the setting of exchange rates, and their publication within Germany could only be done with Reichsbank approval. The increasing demands on the war economy and the blockade made new regulations necessary a year later, and on February 8, 1917, a new decree was issued which dealt not only with the use of foreign currencies but also with mark payments abroad. This decree effectively placed all imports and all currency operations with foreign nations under Reichsbank surveillance, a power which the Reichsbank shared through delegation with its branches and the twenty-eight banks.[54]

Prior to the launching of the Hindenburg Program in the fall of 1916, both the Reichsbank and the government had been encouraging exports wherever these did not interfere with the war effort, and certain industries were more than willing to oblige, even to the point of disregarding the demands of the war effort. The policy proved most effective as well as most problematic in the iron and steel industry, where forced organization into export syndicates ensured that the firms could take maximum advantage of high demand in neutral countries instead of underselling one another. Furthermore, organized selling abroad could be done in such a way as to secure not only a high profit in relation to costs but also a high exchange profit on the difference between the German and foreign currency in question through the calculation of the price in the foreign currency. The profits thus made were so extraordinary that the Reichstag insisted on their taxation and, in June 1916, an export levy (Ausfuhrabgabe) taxing away 5 to 7 percent of the profit—not 75 percent as demanded by some deputies—was passed. In the fall of 1916, however, the government was forced to ban most iron and steel exports for military reasons. To be sure, exports of these and other products could not be totally eliminated since the neutrals made their food and raw-materials exports to Germany dependent upon German willingness to export some coal, iron, steel, and certain finished products, but the total volume of trade diminished after 1916. Most important, the unfavorable balance of trade became worse. Indeed, to the estimated 11.1 billion gold-mark* trade deficit must be added another 4 billion gold marks in assistance to Germany's allies.[55]

Needless to say, the Reichsbank was anxious to improve but especially to stabilize the exchange rate of the mark. One possible method was to intervene with the German gold stock at strategic junctures. When the economist Kurt Singer suggested this to Havenstein, however, the latter responded as defiantly as the Wagnerian giant Fafner protecting his gold horde against Siegfried: "As long as I am in the Reichsbank, no gold leaves the bank."[56] As usual, he insisted that public confidence could only be maintained through the one-third coverage and that was why the gold was there. In reality, the Reichsbank had surrendered some nine hundred million marks in gold prior to

---

*A gold mark is an artificial unit used to measure the relationship between the value of a paper mark to that of the gold mark in August 1914. In 1914 one gold mark equalled one paper mark.

June 1918, of which fifty-six million had gone to pay for vital imports and the rest to assist Germany's allies. Nevertheless, the Reichsbank gold holdings remained stable during the last years of the war and reached a level of 2.55 billion marks before it ended—thanks to the continuous collection of gold coins, gold jewelry, and other gold objects from the public as well as the collection of two hundred million marks' worth of gold from the Russians under the Brest-Litovsk Treaty.[57]

Since neither massive exports of goods nor use of gold was an admissible means of stabilizing the external value of the mark, the Reichsbank was compelled to search for other solutions. One of these was to intervene in favor of the mark on neutral markets through the sale or use of foreign securities, foreign exchange, and German monetary claims against foreign neutrals. By this means, it was possible to give the mark a push upward by purchasing marks or to get imports without doing further damage to the exchange rate. On March 3, 1917, a decree was issued, which was soon to be elaborated by a complex series of supplementary decrees, that virtually compelled German holders of such resources to sell them or lend them to the Reichsbank. Approximately three billion marks in foreign securities and one billion marks in German securities were sold by the Reichsbank to help stabilize the external value of the mark and cover vital import costs.[58]

There was yet another important use to which such resources could be put—as a guarantee for foreign loans. One of the great claims of the Reichsbank's propaganda was that Germany's strength was being demonstrated by her capacity to fund the war on her own, while "the greatest weakness in the war financing of the enemies is their growing indebtedness abroad."[59] Quite aside from the fact that one could argue that dependence on outside sources increased the stake of others, especially the United States, in the fate of the Allies, the reality was that by 1916 even Helfferich wished Germany could find more help abroad. Furthermore, Germany did in fact borrow a great deal during the last two years of the war, and this borrowing had an extremely dangerous character.

These dangers are well illustrated by the large loans taken by a number of German cities—Berlin, Bochum, Dortmund, Heidelberg, Karlsruhe, and Freiburg—in early 1917. These cities, much strained by their wartime social welfare obligations, were becoming more dependent on the loan bureaus to cover their short-term needs but were constantly in search of long-term credit. They were approached by agents representing Swiss and Dutch interests with offers that seemed to answer their needs. The agents in question usually represented firms and individuals who had large mark holdings on account in German banks from prewar business dealings with Germany. The problem was that they could not bring these marks out of the country because of German currency controls, and, furthermore, they did not want to exchange these marks into their own currencies because of the wartime depreciation of the mark's exchange rate. A secure investment of this money—and German cities were viewed as such an investment—seemed the most promising way of using the money during the war. On the one hand, they offered the cities in question substantial ten-year loans at relatively low interest rates, usually 5 percent; on the other hand, they reserved the right to request repayment in the currency of their choice at the prewar parity. What this meant, of course, was that all the risk lay with the borrower. At the very minimum, the creditor was guaranteed his principle and interest if the mark did return to its prewar parity with other currencies. Insofar as the old parities were not restored, the creditor could choose the most favorable currency and thus make an exchange profit in addition to his interest. The Reichsbank objected mightily but belatedly to these arrangements and branded them as usurious and harmful to Germany's credit. At the same time, the government warned the large banks, firms, and cities trying to get long-term credits in Switzerland during this period—often to cover anticipated needs in the conversion to a peacetime economy when the war ended—to cease their efforts and not to take any credits without the approval of the Reichsbank.[60]

If the Reichsbank opposed such activities, it was because it wished to prevent borrowing not required by the immediate war effort and to concentrate the use of Germany's credit abroad in its own hands or in hands of which it ap-

Table 4. Average Yearly Exchange Rate of the German Mark, 1914–1918

	U.S. Dollar* (1 RM)	Swedish Kronor (100 RM)	Dutch Gulden (100 RM)
1913	4.20	112.50	168.74
1914 (end of July–December)	4.41	115.88	180.00
1915	4.92	127.82	200.10
1916	5.39	158.25	249.12
1917	6.45	207.33	271.92
1918 (Jan.–June)	5.17	163.92	220.79
1918 (June–Dec.)	6.50	203.83	297.08
1918 (12 mos.)	5.84	183.88	258.94

Source: Valuta-Tabellen 1914–1922. Sonder-Veröffentlichung der "Wirtschaftskurve," 2nd edition (Frankfurt a.M., 1923), pp. 5, 12–13, 29–30, 33–34.

*Berlin official notations, except for U.S. dollar which is indirectly calculated for 1917/18.

proved. The Reichsbank itself borrowed over two and a half billion gold marks abroad (repayable in foreign currencies), and private firms had borrowed an equivalent amount. The latter were often actually instructed by the Reichsbank to undertake such debts denominated in foreign currencies, and the Reichsbank usually guaranteed them. The Reichsbank's goal was to prevent a further depreciation of the exchange rates by large-scale mark payments abroad. The most famous of the private debts were the Swedish ore debts contracted by leading German iron and steel concerns for some seventeen million tons of ore purchased between 1915 and 1918. These debts were repayable in kronor, just as the debts contracted in the Netherlands were repayable in gulden and those contracted in Switzerland were repayable in Swiss francs. Germany, in short, emerged from the war with a substantial burden of debts denominated in foreign currencies, (Valuta-schulden).[61]

The calculation of the Reichsbank, banks, and firms involved, of course, was that the value of the mark would rise again once Germany had won the war. The loss being taken was considered temporary, and borrowing on these terms was justified for its service in helping to stabilize the exchange rate. And, in truth, the combination of measures taken to improve the position of the mark was relatively successful during the last two years of the war, especially when combined with such apparent German military successes as the great offensives in the spring of 1918 (see Table 4). Indeed, in the summer of 1918 Havenstein actually declared a significant improvement of the exchange rate

undesirable since it would lead foreigners to attempt to make an immediate profit by disposing of their mark holdings and would thereby destabilize the market. During the last year and a half of the war, Havenstein and his colleagues could claim that the mark was even more stable than the Allied currencies while the German gold reserve remained intact. The risky operations underlying this seeming stability were by and large known and at least in part understood only by those engaged in them.[62]

Whatever worries the Reichsbank leadership might have had, they did not want the public to share them, and the Reichsbank conducted a well organized campaign against financial and currency anxiety. The quality of their argumentation may be gathered from an article by lawyer Georg Reimann entitled "The interest on and Amortization of our War Loans. An Open Letter to Herr Meier."[63] This rather odd exercise in the abuse of history, which purported to answer a gloomy article dealing with the German war debt, was recommended by the Reichsbank to its propagandists as "being suitable in its fresh style for the instruction of anxious dispositions." Referring to the history of England between 1688 and 1815, Reimann pointed out that England persistently increased her national debt in war and yet emerged not only as the victor but also as the head of a great empire. Why had not her increasing debt produced the dire consequences that some had predicted? Using Macaulay, Reimann argued that, on the one hand, it was irrelevant how large a national debt was so long as it was internal and the nation's citizenry was in a position to pay off those holding the loans and, on the other hand, that the creative and industrial energies of the people were such as to create the wealth necessary to increase the national income well beyond that required by the debt. Thus, England's great industrial development made it possible for her to deal with her internal debt and rendered trivial the costs of her wars. To these explanations, however, Reimann added a third of his own, overlooked by Macaulay, and yet the "most important of all"; namely, the "depreciation of money." Reimann detected a secular trend toward the diminution of the purchasing power of money in all "civilized" nations, which Reimann exemplified by the extraordinary increase in the cost of land in Berlin-Schöneberg and in the Prussian countryside. He concluded from this "that the value of the money employed in paying back a debt after fifty years is much less than the value of the loan at the time it was made, even if the repayment is in exactly the same coinage as that used in making the loan." To be sure, the individual life was too short to get much benefit from this alleged trend, and each individual had to pay his debts during his lifetime, but the matter was entirely different when viewed from the perspective of the historical development of the great nations of Europe: "Here the depreciation of money plays the role of a slow but certain seisachtheia [a "shaking off" of burdens, referring to Solon's purported effort to bring social peace to ancient Athens by canceling private mortgages and personal debts], a casting off of the state debts." Thus Reimann triumphantly concluded, "The increase in the value of the existing national wealth conditioned by the depreciation of money combined with the newly created goods will so favorably influence the proportion of national wealth to state debts within the foreseeable future that the fears becoming so loud today will seem even to our generation as laughable exaggerations."

It is hard to say exactly how audiences for whom this exercise in debt repudiation fantasy was intended responded. That the Reichsbank should grasp at such a straw—rather unconventional economic and historical theorizing—in its propaganda efforts, however, was symptomatic of increasing public anxiety about Germany's financial future. When Director von Grimm opened a meeting in January 1918 to

prepare the propaganda for the eighth war-loan drive, he had to admit that there was a broad concern as to "whether the Reich will be able to bear all the burdens which the war has laid upon us, a concern which cannot be denied a certain justification."[64] Neither in his speech nor in any of the other statements at the meeting, however, was this disconcerting thought taken up. Instead, the emphasis was on Germany's economic strength, her glorious economic future, the failures and weaknesses of her enemies, and the absolute security of the German war loan, a loan formally guaranteed by the Reichstag and materially guaranteed by the productive and revenue-generating capacities of the German people. The Reichsbank was particularly anxious to counter rumors that the war-loan investors would be deprived of their rewards through government bankruptcy, a lowering of the promised interest rate, premature cancellation, or special taxes. Grimm insisted that the German people had to be told that "the German Empire will not go upon the easy path of state bankruptcy, either an open one or a veiled one."[65] They had to be reminded that the war loan was a gilt-edged (*mündelsicher*) investment; in other words, an investment of the kind permissible to savings banks, trusts, legacies, and other institutions and funds whose investment rights were under strict legal restraint. The risk lay with the government, not the war-bond purchaser. The latter had the right to cash in his bonds if he needed money, but the government was required to maintain the bond for its lifetime.

Nevertheless, a sober note did creep into the Reichsbank propaganda efforts during the last year of the war. The Reichsbank warned against dealing with the question of Germany's ability to hold out with such vague statements as "we can make it" and "the powerful German people will not collapse under the burden."[66] The fact that the German people could not hold out forever had to be admitted, but they had to be convinced that they could hold out as long as was necessary to break the will of the enemy. It was a question, in other words, of who could hold out longer. Even more touchy was the issue of the relationship between war indemnities and annexations and Germany's ability to meet h⁓ financial obligations after the war. The Reicl

Where the propaganda for the sixth war-bond drive of March 1917 stressed the expectations of victory through the introduction of unrestricted submarine warfare, the appeals surrounding the ninth war-bond drive of September 1918 suggested the need for a final big effort to protect Germany from its enemies. Thus, Lucian Bernhard's poster (*left*) reads: "This is the way your money helps you to fight. Transformed into U-Boats, it keeps the enemy shells away from you. Therefore, sign up for the war loan!" The tone of the words accompanying E. Thöny's drawing of workers gazing at a war bond (*right*) are clearly more defensive: "Now really do it! Show the Anglo-Saxon blood suckers what German workers can do. The German people's spirit and strength, the nation's riches, its sons' courage—these provide a guarantee that is strong and lasting. Entrust the Reich with your wealth! It all depends on each one of you!" (*Mueller and Graeff Poster Collection, Hoover Institution Archives*)

bank was somewhat concerned about the extent to which the proponents of a harsh peace were arguing that "without a large indemnity we will be *kaputt*." Such arguments would only serve, in the Reichsbank's view, to alienate the supporters of a peace of understanding and those who were convinced that Germany could not get a large indemnity. Consequently, the Reichsbank propagandists were told that "from the standpoint of our enlightenment work, it is desirable that if one wants to support the demand for a large war indemnity and annexations, then one should do so with something other than the argument that *without* this economic help we will not be able to bear our burdens."[67]

The domestic political atmosphere had, of course, changed since the halcyon days of 1915 when Helfferich could blithely and openly talk about the enemy bearing the "leaden weight" of the war costs. Euphoric expectations of military

victory aside, there were some good practical reasons for the rulers of the Reich to wish for a large indemnity. The federal states were particularly interested in such a solution as a means of obviating the need for a tax reform of the Reich, although Helfferich himself was not convinced that even an indemnity would solve this problem over the long run.[68]

How difficult it was to think of solving the Reich's financial problems without a large indemnity was demonstrated by the eminent national economist Edgar Jaffé, who expected England to bear between a third and a half of Germany's war costs. It is instructive, however, that he admitted that a major financial reform was necessary and that one would have to prepare for the eventuality of Germany having to bear the entire burden of her own costs. He warned that the failure to do so would lead to the "monstrous catastrophe" of currency collapse.[69] If there was no indemnity, Jaffé warned, then the only alternative was either an income tax burden so enormous that it would reduce the living standards of the German people, especially the middle classes, for years to come or, as he preferred, a massive levy on personal wealth (*Vermögensabgabe*) in favor of the state in the form of mortgages and interest-bearing titles on personal property and productive assets. On top of this, Jaffé then proposed taxation on a whole range of Reich enterprises and monopolies as well as on production and savings along with taxes on war profits and inheritances designed to cover the remaining war costs. While Jaffé's program has a certain long-term interest because of his effort to find an alternative to a completely unitarian Reich finance reform—Jaffé was to serve as the Finance Minister of the Bavarian revolutionary government of Kurt Eisner—his sober discussion demonstrates the growing awareness in relatively moderate circles of the financial day of reckoning that was in the offing, even if the war had a positive outcome for Germany. One dared not think of what would happen if Germany lost the war and was suddenly confronted with the demand for an indemnity from a victorious enemy.

While the censorship succeeded in preventing public use and discussion of the word "inflation," and the Reichsbank leadership insisted that rising prices and shortages of money were largely due to hoarding, it was hard for persons who thought about such matters to deny the reality that Germany was experiencing something more than a rise of prices (a *Teuerung*) of the kind experienced in the decade before the war. While the Reichsbank studiously avoided using the word throughout the war in any of its pronouncements or publications, Count von Roedern finally took the plunge in April 1918 and dared to speak before the Reichstag of the "money and credit inflation from which we undoubtedly now suffer."[70] By the summer of 1918, however, even Havenstein, was very worried. As he confessed in the privacy of the Reichsbank Curatorium meeting on July 4, 1918, only eleven days before the last of Germany's 1918 offensives was to have its abortive start followed by a French counteroffensive that signaled the beginning of Germany's military end:

The total circulation of Treasury bills has only decreased from 39 billion to 36.4 billion marks after the last war loan. At present, it is already 37 billion marks again. The absolutely necessary coverage of these bills after the war will be extraordinarily difficult if we do not get a large war indemnity. Even then, it will only be possible if the Reich completely covers its expenditures with ongoing or one-time revenues so that the Reich can use its extraordinary income at least to eliminate its floating debt in a few years.[71]

In truth, the 51.2-billion-mark floating debt was a novel and terrifying experience. The government and Reichsbank were paying for the war by printing more and more money while finding it increasingly difficult to control or tap the liquidity thus created. Enthusiasm for war bonds was waning, and not only among peasants who were hiding their money under beds and in stockings. The government sought to fight the decline of war-bond investment preference by placing restraints on the founding of new joint stock companies or the floating of new private stock and bond issues. This seemed all the more necessary because the states and municipalities were also draining the capital market through their increasing use of the loan bureaus and could be expected to continue to do so when the war was over. States and municipalities accounted for 25 percent of the borrowing from the loan bureaus in 1916, 74.9 percent in 1917, and 84.5 percent in 1918.[72]

The problem was not only one of getting those with large cash holdings to buy war bonds, however. There was also the danger that people might sell their war bonds. In August 1918 the Reichsbank felt compelled to instruct its branches to discourage the sale of war bonds unless an economic need to do so could be demonstrated. The problem was so serious by late summer that the Reichsbank decided to sacrifice appearance for reality and to refuse to boost the number of subscriptions to the ninth war-bond drive by accepting old war bonds as payment for new ones.[73] Such measures notwithstanding, Havenstein could only feel increasingly helpless in the face of the seamier consequences of the manner in which the war had been financed. A veritable speculative fever seemed to take hold on the stock exchanges in the spring of 1918, which he frankly blamed on "the profit increases of a number of enterprises and the great personal gains of the war profiteers," but which he also attributed to "an army of bank employees which form consortia reaching down to the female secretaries." He came to the conclusion that "effective help can only come from a large war tax."[74] Ironically, however, the Reichsbank also had to play down its desire to increase taxes in its battle against the money hoarding and in its efforts to promote war-bond sales. Peasants had to be assured over and over again of the confidentiality of their bank accounts, reminded that banks were much less likely to burn down or be robbed than homes, and endlessly told that there would be no special tax on their war-bond interest and no reneging on the obligations to war-bond holders.[75]

What is truly remarkable is that, as the war came to its end, the lack of public confidence in the government and its promises did not extend to the government's money, which was retained and hoarded out of anxiety that the government would confiscate bank and savings bank accounts in order to cope with the manifest financial crisis. After four years of pleading with the public to turn in its gold for paper money and then to put its money into the banks, the Reichsbank confronted a situation in October and November 1918 in which the public literally regressed into its old habits and began a run on the banks. On October 3, the Reichsbank telegraphed its various branches to contact local municipalities, important firms, and chambers of commerce and instructed them to produce emergency money in five-, ten-, and twenty-mark denominations for use until November 30, when the Reichsbank presumably would be able to supply the necessary amounts. By October 10, the Reichsbank instructed that these emergency notes could also appear in fifty-mark denomination, and that they would be valid until February 1, 1919. The Reichsbank emphasized that the measure was temporary and was meant to deal with local money shortages. It gave assurances that it had the capacity to print the money necessary once the immediate emergency came to an end. The problem simply was one of production.[76]

And, indeed, the economic correspondent for the *Berliner Tageblatt*, Felix Pinner, an informed observer, had no doubt that the Reichsbank could solve the printing problem; nor was he worried that the run on the banks or the printing of money to meet the shortage would be particularly inflationary. The former simply involved bringing out into the open an inflation veiled by interbank transfers through checks and other noncash instruments, and he did not think it likely that those taking out their money would spend it since the expectation of peace was causing people to hold back on their ordering and purchases in anticipation of lower prices. It was even possible that they would return their money to the banks when things calmed down. For the same reasons, the extra money printed might also be withdrawn in due course. What disturbed Pinner most was the lack of preparation for the crisis, which he viewed as typical of the entire administration of the war finances. In Pinner's view, every measure taken to deal with the inflation had come too late and had been inadequate, especially the taxation of war profits. However impressive the war-bond-drive results, in Pinner's view, Germany would have been better off if the price paid for the war materials had been kept lower.[77]

One might also argue that Germany would have been better off if the propaganda behind Germany's financial war effort—indeed, the propaganda behind her entire war effort—had been more truthful. The Reichsbank propaganda continued in the old way to the bitter end, however. The ninth war-bond drive was conducted in the fall of 1918 in the midst of Germany's totally unexpected request for an armistice. As always, Karl Helfferich was pressed into service to support the cause. He could no longer claim, as the Reichsbank had in its earlier propaganda, that Germany's war debt constituted no loss to the nation since the war loans involved nothing more than a transfer within the German economy. Nevertheless, he managed to play down the actual loss of German wealth caused by the war and stressed the sacred obligation to the war-bond holders. The commitment was backed by the "entire working strength and taxable capacity" of the German people. The unreality was heightened by Helfferich's typical patriotic rhetoric, his argument that the war was not only a secure investment but also a demonstration to the enemy "that we would rather go down in honor than wither away in shame."[78] The battles of the postwar inflation debate were about to begin, but now the basic issue, of course, was how the "leaden weight" of the unanticipated defeat would be borne by a German economy, society, and body politic vastly transformed by the war and inflation. It is to these transformations that we must now turn our attention.

Chapter 2

War Economy and Inflation

What Price War?

The great underlying issue of German politics after 1918 concerned the distribution of the costs of the lost war and, insofar as the domestic, non-reparations costs of the war are concerned, the redistribution of the burdens of the war as they had been determined in preliminary form by the organization and operation of the German war economy. It is necessary, therefore, to penetrate what economist Franz Eulenburg called the "veil of money"[1] and get to the more fundamental determinants of the character and consequences of the wartime inflation. Inflation, of course, is a monetary phenomenon, "a decline in the purchasing power of the monetary unit of account,"[2] but that does not mean it is self-explanatory. Havenstein was not printing money for the sheer pleasure of it, and he was not free to simply stop the presses. The money supply was increased to make possible the deficit financing of the budget, and the fact that this was done, the manner in which it was done, and the extent to which it was done were all the result of political and socioeconomic decisions taken by the government or of constraints felt by the government as a consequence of real or feared actions and reactions on the part of the groups and classes of which German society was composed. From the very outset, the significant determinants of the German inflation were structural ones.

Furthermore, there are good reasons to argue that political decisions were more potent than economic considerations in determining the course of the German inflation. Manifestly, the war would have been brought to an end much earlier than it was if economic considerations had had priority over political ones. Those who

had argued before the war that a long war was unsustainable for financial and economic reasons had underestimated the price that nations could and would pay to hold out, but their gloomy perspective was not incorrect in the long term. There was plenty of consciousness well before 1918 that Germany's economic and financial future was being jeopardized. The war was started and prolonged for political reasons, and the financing of the war was strongly influenced by political concerns as well. The same holds true of the economic conduct of the war, which, especially after 1916, fatally exacerbated the difficulties of its financial management.

This is not to say that it is impossible to abstract certain characteristics of the war economy from their political context; it is just as possible as isolating the purely monetary aspects of any inflation from its immediate historical context for purposes of analysis. It is interesting and by no means accidental that Franz Eulenburg, who was to produce what was for decades the most important analysis of the social consequences of the inflation, should have tried his hand at a "theory of the war economy" during the last years of the war.[3] According to Eulenburg, the war economy, while leaving modes of production, property relations, and the profit motive intact, nevertheless produces major changes and distortions in the national economy. The first of these is the distortion in the consumption of goods, since the determination of demand by private consumption, insofar as purchasing power will allow, is replaced by the demand of a war machine, the characteristics of which are entirely different from those of the private consumer. In contrast to the private consumer, who is moved to produce in order to consume, the military consumer produces nothing. Also, private consumption uses up goods in a gradual and reasonably predictable manner and thus permits the appropriate and timely repair and renewal of the productive apparatus. The military consumer uses up goods practically as rapidly as they are received and shows little concern for the repair or renewal of the productive apparatus. Even without increasing his prices, the businessman who produces for military purposes has a higher profit and can justify more rapid amortization of his plant and equipment because of the rate of military consumption. While some effort is made to correct this situation through systematic attempts to save raw materials and labor, such efforts can never make up for the extent of wartime consumption and therefore do not have the benefits of similar strivings in a cyclical downturn in peacetime. Naturally, military consumption takes place at the expense of private consumption, which is reduced both quantitatively and qualitatively. An especially crucial point in Eulenburg's conception, however, is that the phenomena just described are dynamic, that the balance between supply and demand is not simply reduced from one level to another but is perpetually being disturbed by the continuation of the war, and this threatens to produce increasing national impoverishment.

The second major economic disturbance generated by the war economy, according to Eulenburg, is to the free market and prices. The breakdown of international trade and the isolation of national markets are of themselves factors which change supply-and-demand relationships, but the most important influence is that of what is today known as demand-pull inflation; namely, money chasing an inadequate supply of goods for the war economy. Not only does the price of daily necessities rise, but also those articles which are of rather poor quality increase in price relative to those of better quality. The result is a general rise in the level of prices and reduction in the purchasing power of money. Price controls may dampen such tendencies, but they cannot be carried too far without driving the available goods from the market. Even without errors on the part of the purchaser in choosing from whom to purchase and in deciding what price to pay, and even

without deliberate exploitation and profiteering on the part of the producer or seller, a situation is created in which "the buyer knows no upper price limit"[4] when it comes to military purchasing or to buying vital necessities, and "the holder of certain means of production has a dividend fall into his lap, which in no way has anything to do with improper actions or arises in some [deliberately] unfair way, but is rather the simple consequence of the altered structure of the market."[5] Profiteering becomes the essence rather than the excrescence of the war economy.

Third, the war economy interrupts what Eulenburg calls the circulation process; that is, the process of capital accumulation and economic growth. Production is reduced through the removal of large numbers of workers from industry and the low priority given to maintenance and new plant construction. Consequently, there is an increasing undercapitalization of the economy despite savings made by war industries or by individuals unable to find goods to purchase. In a very literal sense, the war economy turns the purposes of normal economic life upside down: "While the wealth of a country is composed of the sum of useful things which serve the promotion of human welfare, nothing of this kind is to be found in the expenses for war."[6] The only check on this process is a bitter one indeed; namely, that a war economy "is only possible for a certain amount of time and threatens to come to an end because of its own exhaustion."[7]

The monetary inflation is the final disturbance for which the war economy provides a "unique experiment." Eulenburg views it as "merely the external expression of the self-generated purchasing power and demand produced by the Reich through its credit. . . . It is the consequence of the entire economy of indebtedness with which the war is being fought."[8] Hence it veils the unproductive activity of the war economy which has all the symptoms of an economic crisis and yet gives the appearance of an economic boom. Full employment and rising prices accompany diminishing national productivity and depreciation of the currency. The visible evidence of currency depreciation—rising prices—may follow from the less apparent phenomenon of its over-

supply, but the two processes do not have to operate in tandem with respect either to tempo or
incidence. They depend on the pace of war contracting and the way in which its effects spread
through the interconnections among the various sectors of the economy. Thus, the willingness of the military to grant high prices to encourage conversion to war production and to
foster high levels of military production lead to
a similar generosity with respect to raw materials and wages. The merchants and businessmen involved are permitted to charge high
prices for their services as well as to increase the
salaries of their employees. The workers and
employees can then increase their demand for
food and such consumer goods as are available.

Eulenburg was already able to note at this
early period in the history of the inflation, however, that not everyone was equally involved in
these developments. Different groups were variously affected by the wartime inflation. Those
already in possession of factories and plants
producing for the war effort or those with efficient agricultural holdings were in a position to
make a super profit because pricing policies in
the war economy were almost invariably based
on the costs of the least efficient producer. Also,
those skilled workers producing for the war effort gain relative to those working in less favored industries. Much less happily situated
were those living on fixed incomes, officials,
white-collar workers, and pensioners. They,
like those living on fixed investments, were, as
Eulenburg argued, being "proletarianized":
"Just as a new host of propertied persons is
being formed, so on the other side there is one
that has remained behind and has been made
declassé. The war is completely unsocial in this
respect in that it creates new wealth and property and creates a new poverty among those
who remain behind. The relationship between
creditors and debtors also suffers a significant
change in the process, that is, the old creditors
are those who suffer while the debtors profit significantly through the monetary depreciation."[9]

While such redistributive effects of wartime inflation seemed clear enough, there was
much less transparency involved in other aspects of the inflation. The fact that all nominal
values were rising, no matter how differentially,
was creating monetary illusions for contemporaries and, one might add, creates problems for
the historian. Obviously, the value of property,
both landed and industrial, was increasing
greatly, but so had the costs of purchasing or reproducing them again. One thing was certain,
the real national wealth had diminished during
the war, thus demonstrating that "the national
economy can be impoverished in war and yet
become richer in nominal terms."[10] Similarly,
it was quite possible for the income of the state
to increase, especially when a progressive income tax pushed the wealthy into higher brackets, but the costs of operating the government
were escalating beyond any planned new revenue. Nevertheless, through what is today called
an "inflation tax" based on the unplanned redistributional processes just described, the government receives some temporary relief.

Ultimately, Eulenburg was suggesting that
the war economy was potentially a form of national economic suicide, and this makes the
evaluation of a nation's wartime economic mobilization a very complicated matter. On the
one hand, the survival of the nation depends on
the success of its economic mobilization; on the
other, the more extreme and "successful" the
economic mobilization, the greater the dangers
to the long-term health of the economy and society. While some of the problems can be mitigated by occupying enemy territory and looting
in more or less sophisticated ways, and while
one can entertain the hope of making a defeated
enemy bear the costs, war remains an economic
gamble. Even Germany's leadership lost faith
in the ability of an indemnity to repair the financial damage. One of the most important implications of Eulenburg's analysis, however, is
not only that the financial and economic status
of the nation is endangered by modern war, but
also that its social order is threatened through a
redistribution of wealth and resources. Eulenburg did not treat the political and psychological consequences of this development, although
there is little reason to believe he was unaware
of them. In any event, it is worth noting how
early Eulenburg was able to identify the chief
characteristics of the inflation and that his ob-

servations rested upon his analysis of the German war economy.

It is significant that Germany's policymakers feared such social dislocations even before they became reality and demonstrated a notorious reluctance to undertake a full-scale economic mobilization. For as long as they could, they sought to meet the demands of the war in a piecemeal fashion. From the perspective of Eulenburg's analysis, these policies reflected a healthy concern for social and economic self-preservation. The less one destroyed, the less one would have to reconstruct. The greater the interference in the free play of economic forces, the more serious would be the distortion of market operations. Furthermore, a policy of economic liberalism was dictated by political and social conservatism. The more extreme the conversion to the war effort, the greater the harm done to the civilian branches of the economy and the weaker sectors of the economy, those "state maintaining" (*staatserhaltende*) elements of the middle class which were considered so crucial to the stability of the existing order. Similarly, the more one interfered in the relationship between workers and employers (for example, through the restriction on the rights of workers to move freely from job to job), the more one would have to grant the workers protection against employer abuse of labor-market restrictions. Economic liberalism was a conservative defence against both radical militarist demands for total war and the socialist dangers total war threatened to actualize.[11]

During the first two years of the war, therefore, both the military and the civilian authorities sought to contain the cost of the war in every sense. Manpower policy was designed to maximize the number of troops available to the army while limiting the exemption of workers to highly skilled men needed for key branches of production. Forced mobilization of the civilian population was rejected in favor of permitting the market situation gradually to absorb women and young persons into the factories and of encouraging labor-saving devices. If bad organization and an unexpected munitions crisis in late 1914 created a high degree of chaos in procurement, the Prussian War Ministry pulled in the reins through most of 1915 and 1916 by encouraging maximum use of existing facilities, ordering only as much as was thought necessary, and irritating war producers by seeking to control costs and profits. Thus, during the first two years of the war, there was much tension between the military authorities and leading industrialists. The latter objected to the unpredictability of military procurement (which prevented full utilization of plant facilities), stubbornly resisted the surrender of "business secrets" to government auditors, and protested efforts to hold down prices.

There were major conflicts over social issues as well. While many employers wished to limit the free movement of labor by military fiat, the War Ministry recognized that such one-sided interference with a traditional worker right would lead to employer abuses and would create social tension. Consequently, they encouraged voluntary collaboration between industry and labor to control labor turnover while maintaining fair wage levels. In cases of flagrant employer abuse, the military often interfered on behalf of the workers and—much to the distress of the heavy industrialists in particular—showed an increasing disposition to heed the advice of academic social reformers from the Society for Social Reform and to show a positive attitude toward the Socialist Free Trade Unions.

These "social" attitudes did not prevent or do away with deplorable working conditions arising from the suspension of hours-of-work limits and safety and health regulations, especially for women and youths; nor did they force the more reactionary employers to recognize and negotiate with the trade unions. Nevertheless, they were an obvious and necessary response to the Social Democratic decision to vote for war credits and the trade-union support of the war as well as the desire to keep the workers loyal to the war effort and maintain the *Burgfrieden*. The general policy was to promote voluntary agreements while vaguely promising some "new orientation" after the war rather than to preempt postwar decisions in the field of industrial relations. Here, as elsewhere, the effort to avoid compulsory measures and total mobilization and to maintain liberal economic practices had a conservative intent. Enlightened conservatism under wartime conditions, however, also demanded intervention on behalf of the workers in the name of fairness and of the claim made by the army and the state to be above party and class.

This is not to say that the authorities could cleave successfully to voluntarism and liberalism in all things. In fact, the groundwork for a full-scale economic mobilization was being laid between 1914 and 1916, and the basic characteristics of the war economy were also assuming shape. This was especially true in the area of raw materials, where measures of profound importance were undertaken as early as August 1914. Noting the danger that Germany would have insufficient raw materials, Wichard von Moellendorff, a technocratically minded engineer highly placed in the German General Electric Company (AEG), inspired the head of this corporation, Walther Rathenau, to go to the War Ministry and urge them to do something about the control of vital raw materials. The result of this initiative was the creation of the Raw Materials Section (KRA) of the Prussian War Ministry, initially under Rathenau and then under Lieutenant Colonel Joseph Koeth. A series of war corporations (*Kriegsgesellschaften*) were set up under the aegis of the KRA to control, purchase, store, and sell the raw materials in accordance with KRA guidelines. The concept of these corporations was provided by Rathenau, and they became the model for the organization of the war economy through their unique combination of industrial self-government and government supervision. While placed under the supervision of KRA Commissars, the corporations themselves were composed of businessmen who sold or used the raw materials in question. They provided the initial capital in return for a fixed interest on their investment—no dividends were paid—and they were responsible for the operation of the corporations. These "state licensed oligopolies,"[12] two hundred of which came into existence before the war was over, were not allowed to make a profit, but their control over raw materials placed their members in an excellent position to serve their own interests.

Industrial self-administration (*Selbstverwaltung*) and self-organization had a long tradition in Germany, where syndicates and cartels were favored and accepted, and it was thus quite natural for the government to turn to existing organizations in its mobilization efforts as well as to create structures like the war corporations. Wherever syndicates already existed (for example, the Steel Works Association and the Coal Syndicate), the government sought to employ them for the war effort. At the same time, it encouraged and promoted industrial organization. The industrialists were not always happy about this pressure, especially when they wished to break away from the constraints of their own organizations. When the Coal Syndicate threatened to split apart in 1915, the government warned that it would syndicate the industry by law unless the participants voluntarily retained the organization. Industrialists came to the conclusion that it was better to organize voluntarily than have the government do the job for them, and by the end of 1916 war committees (*Kriegsausschüsse*) had been established for nearly every branch of industry as well as an alliance made between the two great peak associations, the Central Association of German Industrialists and the League of German Industrialists. They formed a War Committee for German Industry.

The pressures to organize the industrial sector notwithstanding, the government's emphasis during the first two years of the war continued to be on voluntary organization and self-administration. At the same time, it could not but recognize the advantages of labor organization as well, and while refraining from using compulsion to bring industrial and trade-union organizations together, it clearly took a favorable posture toward collaboration and was especially supportive of the "working communities" (*Arbeitsgemeinschaften*) established in a few industries at the beginning of the war to manage initial unemployment problems and cooperate in matters of social welfare. Such arrangements, which were set up in the woodworking and certain other industries dominated by small and medium-sized plants, appeared as the apogee of the *Burgfrieden*.

The attempt of the imperial government and army to live up to its ideological claims of being above party and class and to preserve the *Burgfrieden* was not the easiest of enterprises. The combination of voluntary organization, gentle but firm persuasion, and subtle favor toward the trade unions had prewar precedents and was as acceptable to moderate businessmen as it was promising to moderate Socialists and trade unionists. It alienated heavy industrialists and other diehards in various branches of industry who had a long tradition of grumbling about "concessions to the street." The conciliatory policies pointed to an evolutionary rather than a revolutionary change. When it came to agriculture and the distributive trades, however, the wartime change of government policy was truly revolutionary. The farmer and the merchant, especially the retailer, once viewed as indispensable supports of the existing order against the Socialist threat, were suddenly transformed into the objects of regulation, prescription, and penalty in the interests of the industrial sector of the economy producing for the war effort.

The prewar protection of German agriculture at the expense of the German consumer had been the source of endless Socialist and liberal criticism. The protectionist policy had been defended as a means of maintaining a balance in the German economy proclaimed vital by those involved in agrarian production and considered essential for economic and political reasons by the prewar regimes. Frequently, protectionism was also defended as a means of ensuring Germany's food supply in wartime, although this was always a subsidiary justification for the policy. As it turned out, the argument proved more valid than most of its proponents ever imagined. Protectionism did not make Germany self-sufficient in foodstuffs, but it did encourage a level of agricultural productivity much higher than that of its chief free-trading opponent, Great Britain, and made it possible for Germany to survive the blockade in 1917–1918.[13]

Nevertheless, the blockade created a situation in which imports were severely restricted, while labor and matériel shortages were bound to reduce the productivity of German agriculture as the war progressed. This would have been quite bearable had the war been short, and the initial measures to deal with the problem were based on that expectation. Although the Bundesrat had extensive powers to control prices and undertake other measures under the Enabling Act, its initial actions in the realm of price ceilings, regulation of production, and rationing were slow and unsystematic. Ironically, the first initiatives came from the agricultural organizations themselves. Their leaders, wishing to combat speculation and avoid unpleasant political accusations, urged the imposition of price ceilings on wheat and rye at the end of October 1914 and later extended this request with respect to all cereal grains. They continued to favor price ceilings until the spring of 1915 before the increasing differences between the prices they proposed and those actually imposed made them realize that public pressure was turning the ceilings into an instrument of "consumer" rather than "producer" interests.[14]

The situation was made all the more irritating because they had turned down the alternative approach recommended by coal-industry leaders Hugo Stinnes and Alfred Hugenberg in September 1914 that a corporation be established to buy up two million tons of wheat. By holding back this wheat, prices would increase and consumption would be reduced in 1914 while the available supply in 1915 would increase. The Stinnes–Hugenberg argument, one that Stinnes repeatedly used for almost a decade, was that the high prices would guarantee the supply and could be covered by increased wages if necessary. This argument was rejected by the agrarian leaders at the time with the claim that such prices could not be paid by the lower middle class, and that the price ceilings agriculture proposed would prove most adequate for the situation. Nevertheless, agriculture rapidly became the chief target of what was called the controlled economy (Zwangswirtschaft).

Strong regulation became necessary because the piecemeal approach to prices, production, and distribution of foodstuffs did not work. The peasantry has never been quite as "backward" as some historians have claimed. Especially when engaged in diversified farming (as in the Rhenish-Westphalian region), peasants were quick to react to market signals. Price ceilings on one crop led them to concentrate on another, and when price ceilings on food crops began to make production for human consumption less profitable, they used those crops as fodder for their animals. When the government sought to control this practice, the farmers engaged in a massive pig slaughter in the spring of 1915. The end result was that the entire production of German agriculture came under government control. The government controlled not only the prices but also the use to which agricultural products could be put and the customers to whom the crops could be sold. Wheat, for example, had to be sold to the War Wheat Corporation (*Kriegsgetreidegesellschaft*) which monopolized the sale of German domestic wheat production as well as such foreign imports as came into the country. Farms were subjected to searches and the confiscation of hidden or unreported production.[15]

Unfortunately, these measures in no way ensured that the urban population would receive the food supplies it needed. Nearly all the measures came too late. Thus, bread rationing was not introduced until January 1915 in Berlin and later than that in the rest of the country. The price ceilings were not imposed in any coordinated manner so that the later a price ceiling was issued, the higher the price relative to its predecessors and the more the farmers favored production of the crops last placed under control. Most important, it was clear by 1916 that Germany was suffering from an absolute shortage of foodstuffs as well as declining production due to labor shortages, insufficient fertilizer, and equipment problems. The farmers found their profit margins inadequate and were increasingly hostile to the controlled economy, while the urban population complained about the inadequate supplies and high prices. The result was a growing black market, especially in those areas where the urban population could easily get to the countryside and purchase at the source. At the end of May 1916, an effort was made to pacify the complaints about the chaos in the regulations as well as correct distribution inefficiencies through the creation of a War Food Office (*Kriegsernährungsamt*). The new organization was intended to centralize the management of the food supply as well as ensure that those doing heavy industrial labor for the war effort would get enough to eat. Unfortunately, actual food shortages combined with the effects of past policies set real limits on what the new agency could do either about the situation or about the increasing hostility between city and country. At the same time, the creation of special categories of "hard working" and "hardest working" (*Schwer- und Schwerstarbeiter*) laborers who were entitled to extra rations produced tensions among the workers as well as between the blue-collar workers and other consumers.[16]

The peasants were not the only subjects of the controls placed on prices and the distribution of food and other vital necessities. The war marked the beginning of a decade of hell for the German retailer. Panic buying on the part of consumers was already evident in July 1914, and some retailers unquestionably took advantage of the situation to raise prices as well as to hold back their goods in the expectation of ever higher prices. It did not take long for public outrage to express itself or for the administration to take measures. The authorities, however, often created more problems than they solved because of their typically decentralized character. Price ceilings and other regulations against holding back goods were issued by the twenty-odd Deputy Commanding Generals responsible for internal security under the 1851 Prussian Law of Siege or by local civilian agencies using authority granted under the Law on Price Ceilings issued on August 4, 1914. As usual, the isolated price ceilings proved to be a primitive approach to a complex problem that made things worse, especially when they seemed to be inspired by medieval notions of a just price. They drove goods to those districts where there were no controls or where they were least obnoxious. Gradually, therefore, important articles of daily use became subject to centralized price ceilings by the Bundesrat, and the number of such items swelled to 763 by the end of 1916. The results were not very satisfactory, however, because the controlled items either disappeared into the black market or reappeared in stores as "foreign goods" or were packaged and reworked in some manner so as to make them sellable at a higher price.[17]

The stuff of which much of the controversy with the retailers was made, however, was not the price-ceiling regulations but rather the Bundesrat decree of July 23, 1915, against profiteering (*Preistreibereiverordnung*). The concept of excess profit introduced by the decree was a more flexible standard than the price ceiling because it made profiteering a function not of charging more than an allowed price but rather of making an "excess profit" on "objects of daily use." The courts then defined this to mean that "no one shall earn more on his goods than he did in peacetime."[18] Not only violators of these provisions were threatened with fines and even imprisonment but also those who sought to manipulate the market situation by holding back goods for speculative purposes or engaging in other unfair practices. While these may have been conceptual steps forward in the battle against profiteering—or a return to the "moral economy" of a bygone age with bans on forestalling and engrossing—they created a whole new set of complications by requiring some form of expert judgment to determine what constituted a just price and profit for the host of items on the market.

This was one of the tasks of the price examination agencies (*Preisprüfungsstellen*) created under a decree of September 25, 1915. These new institutions were charged with determining the appropriateness of prices in the various districts in which they were set up, assisting the authorities in controlling prices, issuing regulations for retailers, and providing the public with information. All municipalities with over ten thousand inhabitants were required to set up such agencies. Half of the members were to be producers, wholesalers, and retailers; the other half, independent experts and consumers. Each agency was to have a nonpartisan chairman. The decree also provided for the establishment of a network of price examination agencies at the district, provincial, and state levels with a center in Berlin. Until the fall of 1916, this central headquarters was the Reich Examination Agency for Food Prices. Then, it was placed under the National Economy Section (*Volkswirtschaftliche Abteilung*) of the War Food Office. By this time, there were over a thousand price examination agencies in Germany, the most important and active of which were located in the industrial districts.

These two decrees were by no means the only important regulations dealing with the selling of food and other vital necessities issued during the first years of the war. There were regulations requiring the public display of all prices in retail stores as well as the placing of accurate information on packaging. Particularly important were the regulations issued restricting newcomers from entering into the retail trade in basic consumer goods. Those who violated the regulations could lose their licenses, and a special effort was made to bar persons engaged in the so-called "chain-trade" (*Kettenhandel*); that is, superfluous middlemen whose "services" had the intention or the effect of raising prices.

This flood of organization and regulation was a response to the rising tension between consumers and retailers that accompanied the tension between city and country. The peasantry enjoyed the advantage of some measure of distance from the consuming public as well as the possibility of covering up its delinquencies more effectively. Retailers, however, lived among their customers, and their place of business was where the consumer actually faced the realities of shortages and rising prices. The shopkeeper and merchant thus became the objects of hostility and suspicion.

Furthermore, the hostility was organized. At the end of 1914, a host of civil-service, labor, and white-collar organizations joined with various organizations of housewives to form the War Committee for Consumer Interests, which later teamed up with other consumer groups to form the Working Community of Consumer Organizations. Its Board of Directors included such prominent Social Democrats as Deputy Robert Schmidt, who had a trade-union background; August Müller, the executive director of the Central Association of German Consumer Cooperatives; and Siegfried Aufhäuser, the head of the Socialist Federation of Technical Employees. Other members were Christian trade unionist Adolph Giesberts, liberal feminist Dr. Gertrud Bäumer, and well-known academic social reformers Professors Waldemar Zimmermann and Ernst Francke. Francke and the Society for Social Reform (which group he represented) were prominent among those providing advice to the civilian and military authorities, and August Müller became a member of the Advisory Board of the War Food Office in May 1916. The War Committee for Consumer Interests, therefore, was well placed to influence the government and the price examination agencies as well as to provide information to the public and disseminate its own point of view very widely.[19]

This propagandistic function was performed by a newsletter, "Consumer Economics in War" (*Verbraucherwirtschaft im Kriege*), which was sent out twice weekly in 1916 and also provided material for the press. The content of a particular issue of this two-page publication is a good illustration of the goals and style of the organized consumer propaganda. The issue of November 24, 1916, provided eight items for its recipients.[20] The first contained information on a petition to the War Food Office calling for price ceilings on horse meat, which "because of the shortage of other kinds of meat is very much sought, especially by those doing heavy labor, but which, because of the absence of price ceilings, has become monstrously expensive, often five times its peacetime price...." There followed a critical commentary concerning the recent confiscation of foodstuffs at the Berlin railroad station and post offices, apparently of goods sent by farmers to their relatives in the city. While the effort to equalize consumption was laudable, the authors of the article wished to remind the public that the recipients of these packages "are in no way only rich families, but often those who are suffering severely from the needs of the time," and that since these surpluses normally would never be freely given by the farmers, "one should view their import into the cities sympathetically."

The articles which followed had a much harsher tone. One severely criticized the city of Nürnberg for abandoning its attempt to centralize sausage making. The meat dealers insisted that only the individual butcher could produce good sausage and were proving the point by providing the city with inferior meat. Another attacked the mild punishment of a canned-goods producer whose meat products contained only 10 percent meat and who had overstated his daily production costs by two hundred forty marks. This individual had been fined only two thousand marks, the equivalent of seventeen days' worth of his unjust profit. The compilers of the issue turned their fire

against arguments that higher prices were the best means of getting the farmers to follow the regulations. The authors hoped that Field Marshall von Hindenburg's recent appeal to the farmers to do their duty would put an end to such calls for agricultural price incentives.

There followed two articles which touched upon another major consumer interest theme; namely, the disappearance of certain goods from the market and the availability of others only at extremely high prices. The authors wanted to know why cooking oil had not been available for months and why it had suddenly reappeared at astronomical prices. They also wanted to know what happened to skimmed milk, upon which the people were counting after whole milk had disappeared from the market. Was it being turned into cheese in order to increase the profit, or was it being fed to the animals? The publication then concluded with a lengthy poem, "For the Album of the Profiteer," which concluded by declaring that "You are worse enemies of your country / than are the Russians, Britains, and Frenchmen."

Such poetic flights of fancy as well as articles of the character just described were common in the urban and trade-union newspapers throughout the war. Little wonder, therefore, that retailers felt constantly on the defensive. In the early months of the war, they argued that the price increases were largely the consequence of military purchasing and panic buying by the municipalities. First somewhat gingerly, and then with much more vehemence, they attacked the purchasing policies of the municipalities, which, they argued, often bought up stores of low-quality food at excessive prices and thus created a situation in which the retailers looked like profiteers because they charged even more for better quality products. They claimed, not entirely without evidence and reason, that municipal purchasing would have been more effective and efficient if the advice of experienced local merchants had been taken, but they were most insistent that they could ultimately do a better job of procuring and selling food than the municipalities. At the same time, they pointed out that it was the municipalities themselves which had promoted the rise of profiteering merchants by permitting new persons, who were unable to pursue their old occupations because of the war, to enter the retail trades. Finally, the retailers contested the capacity of their old enemies, the consumer cooperatives, to do a better job of food procurement and of keeping prices low. They protested what appeared to be a growing preference being shown toward the cooperatives by the authorities.[21]

The greatest concern of the retailers, however, was that they were being singled out, not only for public disapproval but also for actual sanction by the authorities. It was indeed something quite new for this once respected part of the *Mittelstand* to find itself increasingly on the wrong end of the law. Unhappily, there was much to justify a growing feeling of paranoia. In July 1915, for example, the Deputy Commanding General of the First Bavarian Army Corps issued a decree threatening a year in prison to anyone who offered to sell or to pay for food at prices which were "inappropriately high" or "unjustifiably high." The same penalty threatened anyone who withheld food "without sufficient cause." The Deputy Commanding General in Münster, von Gayl, enthusiastically proposed to copy the order with such additional touches of his own as compelling those convicted under the decree to pay the costs of publishing the judgment in three newspapers chosen by the court. Not surprisingly, the Münster Chamber of Commerce strongly protested the proposed decree. They pointed out that the language was fuzzy. At its worst, it was an invitation to denunciations; at its best, it compelled retailers to fear loss of freedom and reputation. Indeed, the flood of regulations piled troubles upon troubles for the retailers. While the requirement that they display their prices seemed reasonable enough, it encouraged consumer groups to go about comparing prices without regard to quality distinctions and to launch complaints against retailers. Retailers were hauled into court without prior investigation and, even if acquitted, "being charged in itself tends, not only to damage the honor of the retailer but also to leave him tarnished in the eyes of the consumers, which naturally makes itself felt in his business and unfavorably influences his economic existence."[22]

Efforts by retailer organizations to persuade the authorities that they compel those making accusations of profiteering in the press to identify the group they were actually accusing—producers, wholesalers, or retailers—and to ban such accusations until there was an independent investigation by the Münster Chamber of Commerce were coldly rejected by General von Gayl. He seemed to feel that newspaper reports of profiteering were in the public interest.[23] In the course of 1916, a new and particularly unwelcome development alarmed the retailers; namely, the decision of certain large industrial firms to buy food and then sell it below cost to their workers. Not only did this threaten the economic life of the retailers by taking away business, but it also fortified the impression that the retailers' prices were excessive. The lack of solidarity shown by the industrial employers especially irritated the retailers, who thought that employers had every reason to join with retailers "against the widely spreading state socialist efforts."[24]

Actually, a situation was developing by 1916 in which a variety of traditional or assumed forms of social solidarity were breaking down and in which social relationships and attitudes were taking on an ugliness nurtured by hunger and want. The mood was well characterized by the Police President of Berlin:

The reproaches concerning the present food situation are directed primarily against the producers and against the middlemen, who are without exception identified as speculators and war profiteers and who are assumed to be mainly Jews. The criticism levelled by a portion of the Berlin population against the measures of the communal, state, and Reich authorities, however, is also not very edifying. In any case, there is here at the present time a feeling of irritation that is not to be underestimated, which stems from the conditions described, from the long duration of the war, and finally also a general nervousness produced by undernourishment and great overwork.[25]

This was by no means the only report of increasing anti-Semitism. The presence of Jews in the Central Purchasing Corporation (ZEG), which managed the government food import monopoly, and the traditional role of Jews as cattle and food merchants made them obvious objects of suspicion in a society already habituated to anti-Semitic charges. Thus, the Deputy Commanding General in Kassel reported a "substantial increase"[26] in anti-Semitism in Marburg and Gotha because of alleged high profits in the cattle trade and in the ZEG, and his counterpart in Stettin, Freiherr von Vietinghoff, regularly supported such sentiments with obvious personal approval. Whether with approval or not, however, the same information was relayed from Karlsruhe and Breslau. The Deputy Commanding General in Breslau attributed the anti-Jewish feeling to "the high war profits remaining in Jewish hands as well as to their efforts to escape service at the front." [27] The charge that Jews capable of frontline duty were working at desk jobs and in garrison duty provoked the War Ministry to undertake the compilation of its notorious "Judenstatistik," the interpretation of which became a subject of considerable controversy. One certain result was to intensify anti-Semitic sentiment.[28]

Yet another significant source of increasing anti-Semitism was the influx of eastern Jews from Russian Poland and Galicia whose personal style of life and business attitudes and practices were frowned upon not only by Germans but also by many assimilated or native German Jews. The war had increased the number of such immigrants considerably, as many fled to join relatives in Germany or simply came to take advantage of better conditions and opportunities provided by the German war economy. The situation was viewed with alarm, especially because of the fairly obvious German plans to annex large portions of Russian Poland in the event of victory. The Leipzig Chamber of Commerce, for example, decided to do something about the situation and petitioned the government not to make another German state out of the areas annexed lest the extension of citizenship rights lead to a flooding of cities like Leipzig with such persons. At the same time, it also proposed creating stricter requirements before permitting anyone to settle down and enter the trades in Leipzig. To be sure, the Chamber of Commerce denied any anti-Semitic motives behind its actions and claimed, possibly with some accuracy, that it was "acting in agreement with respectable Jewish merchants of our city" in the belief "that an excessive influx of inferior eastern elements [*minderwertige östliche Elemente*] is a danger to trade and commerce."[29] The problems connected with the east European Jews coming into Germany were not so easily solved and are significant for the social history of the inflation. The other problem of what to do with Jews in annexed territories was to remain unanticipatedly academic for a quarter of a century, after which time it was "solved" in a manner quite different from that proposed in 1916 by the Leipzig Chamber of Commerce.

While it is important to note this increasingly virulent anti-Semitism, it is also necessary to recognize that its context was one in which Germans were not being particularly nice to one another. The Thuringian states, for example, complained bitterly about the refusal of Saxony and Bavaria to permit food to travel over their borders into Thuringia, while Prussia complained that Thuringia was treating bordering Prussian territories in a similar manner. Then there was the increasing hatred between city and country, which was given particularly strong expression by women left at home to run the farms while their men were at war. When the butter ration for farmers was cut in the late summer of 1916, the anger was intense. As one peasant woman bitterly complained:

I have been working the farm alone now for a year, and I have as help one prisoner of war. When I come home tired in the evening, I have to clean out the cattle stall, and I wake up early in the morning to milk the cows. If the butter is now taken from me, then I will sell my cows, for which I can get a good price. I will only keep one for myself, which cannot be taken from me, and I will have less work. Soon I will not be able to go on. I will not slave away for the Berliners; they will not come and clean out my stall.[30]

Even proletarian solidarity was not unaffected, and many workers complained bitterly that they were not included among the "hard" and "heavy" laborers entitled to higher rations. There was a strong tendency for each group or class to blame others, and the hard-pressed retailers were not above arguing that the real fault for the high prices lay with the producers, wholesalers, and hoarding customers.[31]

In the last analysis, however, the retailers remained in the most exposed position and bore the brunt of much of the public anger and distress. It is important to remember that the bonds between retailers and their working-class customers had often been very close since the former were dependent on the welfare of the latter.[32] Relations often marked by trust and concern were now being undermined by suspicion and irritation. Not only did the tone of daily contact in markets and shops become harsh and unfriendly, but also the underlying rage over shortages and high prices began to find more violent expression. Thus, in Zittau in September 1915 a veritable egg-and-butter battle broke out between the market women and their customers as a result of disagreement over prices.[33]

Not all events of this kind were equally slapstick, however. Leipzig experienced three days of street disturbances in May 1916. The triggering incident occurred at a butter shop, outside of which a group of women and children had lined up in the early evening. Noting that there were women in the store already, those outside began to hurl insults and complain that the customers inside had been let in unfairly through the back door. When the angry shoppers began to bang on the window pane, the uniformed son of the owner, apparently home on leave, pulled out his pistol. An excited crowd gathered and stones began flying through the store windows before the police came to the rescue. That evening, however, six other food stores received the same treatment, while the following two evenings were filled with similar events in which clothing stores also fell victim to the crowd. Finally, troops had to be used, although there was no bloodshed. The authorities attributed the unrest to excitement over the intended reduction of the potato ration and the high prices. These were by no means isolated instances, and such disturbances by housewives and children were quite common in 1916. It is significant that the Leipzig authorities strove to prevent having these housewives stand in line as much as possible, a virtually hopeless endeavor under the circumstances. The lines were a place where the consumers could share their complaints and work up the kind of anger that produced events like those described. The greater danger was that these lines would become centers for the mobilization of a "counter public opinion" demanding an end to the war and reform.[34]

This danger was becoming a reality in 1916. The split in the Social Democratic Party (SPD), which was to culminate in the creation of the Independent Social Democratic Party (USPD) in April 1917; the first political strikes in Berlin in June 1916 in protest against the internment of Karl Liebknecht; and the increasingly vitriolic debate over war aims were all making a shambles of the *Burgfrieden*. From the standpoint of the government, the most alarming signal of war weariness was the diminished sign-up for the fifth war-bond drive in September 1916, and this seemed to have, in part at least, an explicit political motivation. As the War Ministry reported:

Almost all the Deputy Commanding Generals agree with one another in reporting that the tendency to sign up for the war-bond drive has decreased considerably and that the refusal to participate is often seen as a means of bringing about the end of the war. In fact, there are instances of hope that the drive will fail. Regrettably, it seems that in many cases those on leave from the front have militated against the loan. . . . Even if the total subscription, which has in the meantime been tallied, gives little evidence of the direct effect of this negative attitude, the actual sums subscribed individually are much less than before according to the reports of the Deputy Commanding Generals, and this is an important reflection of the public mood.[35]

The most alarming development, however, was the increasing number of food demonstrations that were taking a political turn. The process by which the problems of the food supply became the mechanism of overt expressions of war weariness and of social and political mobilization is well revealed by the demonstration in Dresden in November 1916 by some six thousand to eight thousand persons, predominantly—once again—women and children. The demonstration was organized by the Majority Socialists, largely by word of mouth, at the food-store lines and another important trouble spot—the offices where the wives of men at the front came to collect their government support funds. The Majority Socialists had a twofold objective. First, they sought to provide the workers with a means of venting their growing discontent over the food situation and the war. Second, they wished to distract attention from a Minority Socialist opposition rally for the imprisoned Karl Liebknecht. The Majority Socialist leaders wanted an orderly protest and not only arranged for a delegation to meet with representatives of the Saxon government and report back to the demonstrators but also were careful to urge only those workers to come who would not disrupt work at their plants. And, in fact, the demonstrators were by and large female home-industry and tobacco workers as well as workers who had a free shift. Such concern for the demands of the war economy notwithstanding, the delegation considered it essential to speak about more than the food problem with the authorities: "The labor leaders are trying to keep the people from taking unconsidered steps and will continue to do so in the future, but they cannot guarantee peace and patience over the long run if conditions do not get better. They consider it their duty, therefore, to point out the seriousness of the situation to the government. They must also express the wish that the government finally make an effort to secure peace."[36] The authorities responded by promising to do their best in dealing with the food supply and, above all, in distributing food fairly. They assured the labor leaders that the government was doing everything possible to bring peace, but that these efforts were contemptuously rejected by Germany's enemies. At the same time, they warned that the enemy's great hope was that the Germans would not hold out, and such demonstrations, however understandable their motivation, were likely to strengthen that impression.

If the political price of "holding out" was already becoming evident, so was the social price which the war was exacting from the German people. Whatever the statistical and other problems connected with prewar—and later—efforts to determine developments in the German standard of living, especially that of the urban population, certain tendencies seem uncontestable. First, the prewar urban population was increasing its consumption of such animal products as meat, fat, butter, eggs, and milk, while reducing its relative consumption of bread and especially potatoes. Naturally, the better off the family, the more this was the case, but the tendency was common among all classes. Second, one of the major characteristics of class and social differentiation between working class and middle class was the relatively large expenditure of the latter for "cultural" requirements. While the working class may have been improving its physical standard of living and perhaps benefiting more from entertainment, there was a significant difference in the quality

of life between the workers and the middle class. The latter not only ate and lived better, but also spent more on education, theater, books, and other cultural activities. Lower levels of the civil service and white-collar workers, as might be expected, engaged in a mixture of proletarian and bourgeois consumption patterns.[37]

There was considerable evidence by the spring of 1916 that the war was altering these prewar consumption tendencies in very profound ways. This was provided by surveys taken by the War Committee for Consumer Interests in April and July. The first of these surveys was used in comparison with the Reich Statistical Office survey of 1907–1908. The comparison showed that the proportion of family expenditures for food had greatly increased for all income levels so that middle-class "cultural" expenditures were being sacrificed to pay for physiological needs. Furthermore, at all income levels, the proportion of expenditure for vegetable as opposed to animal products had increased in such a way as to reverse the prewar trend. The middle class, therefore, was not being spared the diminution in quality of life imposed by the war so that this, as a worried analyst of the data warned, was "a very troubling sign and serves as a warning to those governing to do everything possible from the standpoint of economic and taxation policy even during the war but also afterward to prevent a grinding down of the *Mittelstand* and the rise of a 'barbaric' economy in which there are only 'rich' and 'poor.'"[38]

The leveling process was further evidenced in the July survey, which was taken after rationing had been extended to potatoes, and the rations for meat, sausage, butter, fats, and margarine had been reduced. While those earning a hundred to two hundred marks a month actually increased the number of grams of meat they consumed from 1,211 to 1,319 grams, the amount consumed by those earning two hundred to three hundred marks a month actually decreased from 1,439 to 1,417 grams, and those earning over three hundred marks reduced their consumption from 1,794 to 1,405 grams. The last group apparently found a replacement in fish, since their consumption of that food increased from 635 to 1,012 grams while the fish consumption of the other two groups declined. The statistics demonstrated, however, that all groups in society were spending more on and consuming more of canned foods and food substitutes to replace the rationed food. As the compilers of the July survey concluded with apparent approval: "Rationing in combination with the setting of price ceilings has thus had an economically equalizing, that is, a social effect."[39]

The desirability of this "social effect," however, could be contested:

. . . Even in the *Mittelstand* and in the higher classes of the population one now finds real concern and a depressed mood, especially with respect to the future. The leading elements of these strata, in which the large part of the active officer corps and the retired officer corps are to be found, now lie in excessive numbers under the earth, and with them the best bearers of the spirit of the German people. As such, they are not to be replaced, neither through the millionaires rising like mushrooms day after day from more or less international commercial and Jewish circles, nor through the Social Democrats, whose importance is increasing more and more. Now and in the future, the major danger faced by the economically and politically independent *Mittelstand*, the chief bearer of the German spirit, is being ground down between these two poles. One constantly encounters such observations with the anxious question: "What will actually happen when peace 'breaks out'?" Such views gain more and more ground.[40]

The social realities underlying these obviously reactionary, militarist, and anti-Semitic observations cannot be dismissed because of the unpalatable attitudes in which they are embedded. Indeed, the danger was that those realities would give the views expressed greater plausibility and virulence. Anxiety over rising prices (*Teuerung*) had crossed class lines and was helping to redefine and exacerbate traditional class and social hostilities.

The fact that increasing misery and leveling were going hand in hand made it possible for all affected groups to attack the system being employed to bring it about. Those purporting to represent the interests of the peasantry and retailers openly attacked what they described as a "state socialism managed exclusively through large capitalist organizations"[41] and charged that artificially low prices and the machinations of the ZEG were responsible for the diminishing availability of food. Such charges were not limited to such irascible reactionaries as General von Vietinghoff, however. The reformist Socialist economist Richard Calwer was particularly critical about the unreality of some consumer demands:

When one follows the public discussions of food profiteering during the war, then one is struck by two things: on the one side, one tries to find who is guilty for the fact that there are excessively high prices, and to be sure, if possible, a whole economic group, like the farmers, the merchants, the retailers, the banks, the industrialists, even at times portions of the consuming public itself. That purely objective reasons could bring about a sharp increase in prices is something that one does not want to grant in his anger over rising prices. On the other side, one cries out, in the knowledge that one is powerless, for strong help, which in such cases always means the authorities and the state. Like the child who, when it cannot help itself, calls for mother and father, so the consumers call for Father State when there are high prices.[42]

If Calwer fought against unrealistic consumer expectations, Friedrich Bendixen, speaking for the hard-pressed merchants of his native Hamburg, took an extreme free-market position and argued that allowing prices to reach their natural levels would lead to greater production and bring demand into line with supply. He was extremely skeptical of the usefulness of what he labeled "fortress communism": "We decree that when we have a reduced supply which cannot satisfy the usual demand, the market is disturbed and the increased prices are artificial and harmful to the common good. We destroy the clock because the hour which it shows displeases us just when we most desperately need a measure of the time."[43]

Bendixen's optimism that Germany could manage to feed itself if free economic forces were allowed free rein was not shared by all economic liberals. His friend Kurt Singer was convinced that the food deficit was so great that uncontrolled prices would lead to the speculative holding back of food and prevent the supplying of the poorer classes.[44] There was one uncontestably true point made by Bendixen, however; namely, that the consumer-oriented war socialism did not extend to the entire economy: "It exists for the nation's food supply. For the second part of our war needs, for armaments, weapons and munitions, it does not exist."[45] Bendixen sought to use this argument to demonstrate that productivity depended on a free market. What he failed to recognize, however, was that the war had created two markets, and that their status was by no means the same. Richard Merton, a leader of Germany's metals business, who was serving as adjutant to the head of the German field railways, General Wilhelm Groener, spelled out the problem for his chief in an October 1916 memorandum. Merton confirmed that the food supply regulations had a "socialist" character and hurt farmer initiative. If the inadequacies of the system were unquestionable, however, Merton shared Singer's view that the food supply simply was inadequate in absolute terms and required market control. The free market had become an unacceptable alternative because it would alienate the urban masses upon whose labor and morale military production depended.[46]

The Merton argument went to the heart of the issue, which, as usual, was political or, to be more precise, politically determined economics. The fact was that meat, vegetables, and dairy products were incapable either of shooting or exploding. In war, the "productive" sectors of the economy were those which serviced direct military needs. Insofar as its workers were consumers of agricultural products, it appeared logical to give their consumption needs priority over the interests of the agrarian and commercial sectors in the name of higher military production and the social peace it required. The political leadership of the Empire thus found itself alienating important segments of its old "state-maintaining" constituency—the propertied urban and rural classes and the civil service—without capturing the loyalty and affection of a working class to whom it was compelled to make constant concessions.

The controlled economy in food, which was soon to be extended to other areas of the consumer economy, had important implications for the character of the wartime inflation. As England demonstrated through its very different policies, the promotion of agricultural productivity and more equitable distribution by means of price incentives was a conceivable alternative to the controlled economy. The decision to hold down prices meant that the enormous expansion of the money supply would not be reflected in official consumer prices. The consequence was a "suppressed inflation," which, to be sure, had its short-term temporary advantages. It helped to justify lower wages than would otherwise have been the case and assisted Germans in being able to use their own currency in neutral countries to purchase necessary goods. Shortages of consumer goods and controlled prices also encouraged savings, which increased from 21.4 billion to 31.8 billion marks during the war and were largely available to the government in the form of war bonds. Money that might have been used for consumer consumption could thus be shifted to military production. Needless to say, the suppressed inflation produced powerful negative consequences. The absence of satisfactory price incentives and investment in agriculture led to a marked reduction in productivity after 1915, while the system of price ceilings distorted production since farmers invariably produced more of those products for which they could get more money. At the same time, there was a significant reduction in the quality of food. Finally, the controlled economy necessarily promoted black marketeering with all its attendant economic distortions and consequences for morals and morale. Inflation had thus been "suppressed," but for how long and at what cost?[47]

The Price of War

Though Germany's leaders were not oblivious to the threat posed by the war to the nation's economic, social, and political stability, their tragic incapacity to prevent the worst arose nevertheless from their very conservatism and from the constraints imposed by the political system of the Empire and the socioeconomic forces which determined its functioning. Total victory could only be won through total war. While important segments of Germany's political leadership were convinced that only total victory could stabilize the existing order, they were paradoxically compelled to enter upon the destabilizing path of total war in order to attain that victory. That is why the history of Germany's economic mobilization became the prehistory of the Revolution which toppled the old order.

As in the financial history of the war, so in its economic history; the second half of the year 1916 marks a break between two relatively distinct periods. The appointment of Hindenburg and Ludendorff to the Supreme Command at the end of August 1916, the launching of the Hindenburg Program immediately afterwards, the creation of the War Office in the Prussian War Ministry to oversee the total mobilization required by the Hindenburg Program, and the passage of the Auxiliary Service Law to mobilize the male civilian population on December 5, 1916, marked the end of the cautious policies previously pursued by the civilian and military authorities.

There was thus more than a little irony in the fact that it was Chancellor Bethmann Hollweg who fought successfully to bring the new Supreme Command (OHL) of Hindenburg and Ludendorff into power in 1916. Bethmann, who genuinely feared the revolutionary implications of the war and worried about defeat, deluded himself into believing that he could use the fame of and national confidence in Hindenburg to achieve a peace based on compromises and concessions the German annexationists would otherwise be unprepared to make. The Chancellor's reward was the installation of a military team committed to total war and total victory that was to create havoc in the economy, force the declaration of unrestricted submarine warfare (leading to the entry of the United States in April 1917), and then force him out of office in July 1917.[48]

This is not to say that the calculations of Hindenburg and Ludendorff and their advisers were much better than those of Bethmann Hollweg. The brain behind the Hindenburg Program, Colonel Max Bauer, and his chief industrial allies—Carl Duisberg of the chemical industry and the Ruhr industrialist Hugo Stinnes—had intrigued against the cautious procurement policies of the War Ministry for some time with the argument that Germany could only win the war by substituting machines for men and launching a vast weapons and munitions program. According to Bauer and his allies, new plants had to be created, skilled workers reclaimed from the front, and questions of

cost put aside. The effects of this economic adventurism on Germany's finances and the consequences for the economy were devastating. The latent transportation and coal shortages erupted in exacerbated forms and plagued both the war economy and the postwar reconstruction.[49]

The calculations and expectations that led to the creation of the War Office and Auxiliary Service Law were even more elaborate and misconceived than those that had produced the Hindenburg Program. Ludendorff and his grey eminence, Bauer, were political primitives and radical militarists who lived for war and were convinced that the rest of German society was obligated to join them in this dubious commitment. They cared neither for tradition nor for the more civilized values of bourgeois society, and the actual long-term consequences of their measures were irrelevant to them because they were convinced that all problems would be solved by victory. It was no accident that Bauer later became involved with National Socialism. It was also no accident that they acted in tenuous alliance with technocrats like Wichard von Moellendorff and a group of young bureaucrats and industrial and economic specialists who viewed the war economy as an opportunity to reconstruct German economic life in a rational, organized, and planned manner. The perception implicit in Franz Eulenburg's discussion of the war economy—that war economics was by its very nature inimical to economic rationality—was evaded or perhaps repressed in the enthusiasm over the opportunity the war seemed to provide to realize visions that could never have been put into practice under normal circumstances.[50]

Thus, in September 1916 Moellendorff, filled with enthusiasm, seized upon the Hindenburg Program as an opportunity to realize his longrange goals. Through his colleague, the great German-Jewish chemist Fritz Haber, Moellendorff communicated to Max Bauer the initiating schemes that were to lead to the creation of the War Office and the passage of the Auxiliary Service Law. The purpose of the former was to centralize the entire planning and organization of the economic war effort into one unbureaucratic, well-coordinated planning agency. For the Supreme Command and especially for

Colonel Bauer, it was an instrument of revenge against a War Ministry that had long stood in their way. For Moellendorff, it was the institutional framework for a new economic order. When finally established on November 1, 1916, under the leadership of General Wilhelm Groener, it was an administrative mish-mash lodged within the framework of the old Prussian War Ministry; this avoided having to create a new Reich agency by law and thus open up a discussion of the military constitution of the Empire in the Reichstag. Whatever its contribution to the war effort, it in no way compensated for the year of bureaucratic confusion and infighting that finally led to the subordination of the War Office to the War Ministry. Just as economic realities had compelled the OHL to accept a reduction of the Hindenburg Program by late 1917, so bureaucratic rationality forced a reduction of the activities of the War Office. In the meantime, there had been an immense waste of resources and energy.

The consequences of the Auxiliary Service Law were to prove even less correctable. For Moellendorff, the mobilization of the civilian sector meant the installation of a form of "Prussian Socialism" that would lead to the shutting down of inefficient plants, the rationalization of German industry, and the control and manipulation of the labor market in accordance with economic priorities. For many industrialists, who had been pushing hard for the control over labor turnover, civilian mobilization was a means of controlling labor, especially the workers exempted from military service or reclaimed from front duty. The Supreme Command shared this goal, but intended more. In the original plan of Bauer and Ludendorff, civilian mobilization included youths and women and involved such measures as the shutting down of the German universities. The Supreme Command also wanted to secure a national plebiscite for total mobilization through the passage of an actual law by the Reichstag. These plebiscital intentions were treated with alarm and mistrust by Bethmann Hollweg, Helfferich, and the more traditionalist elements in the War Ministry. They knew that the nation was too war weary to provide a plebiscital response to the Supreme Command's program, and they feared that the representatives of or-

ganized labor in the Reichstag would demand increased protection for labor and a greater role for the unions in return for accepting the restraints to be placed on the workers.[51]

These were the only accurate predictions made by Germany's leaders in the fall of 1916, and while Helfferich and his allies persuaded the Supreme Command to drop its demand for the compulsory mobilization of women, they were unable to prevent the increasingly powerful left-wing coalition of Social Democrats, Centrists, and Progressives from transforming the government bill in such a way as virtually to revolutionize the foundations of industrial relations in Germany. Not only were the trade unions recognized as the representatives of the workers, but they were also guaranteed a voice on the various committees set up and charged with determining which plants and enterprises were to be shut down and who was to be called up for civilian service. Most important, they served on the mediation committees and arbitration boards established to determine whether a worker should be permitted to change his job. The most fateful provision of the law, set forth in paragraph 9, pertained to this question. It required that a worker be permitted to change his job if he could demonstrate that he thereby attained a "suitable improvement of his working conditions." Obviously, this was a grotesque provision under wartime labor-market conditions and could only have the effect of increasing rather than restricting turnover as well as encouraging wage increases. It was also the price which Helfferich and his colleagues had to pay for their refusal to accept the efforts of the Reichstag, supported behind the scenes by Count von Roedern and Wichard von Moellendorff, to impose controls on profits. Helfferich warned that such controls would offend the industrialists and undermine their incentive to meet the goals of the Hindenburg Program. Needless to say, the trade-union leaders in the Reichstag were able to insist that the workers also have their incentive. What was left of economic liberalism in Germany by 1917, therefore, lay chiefly in the realm of industrial prices and wages. With the existing shortages, this could only promote inflation. On the one hand, enormous governmental production demands pushed up prices; on the other, the shortage of labor and the need to keep the workers quiet and productive pushed up wages. The wage-price spiral was "paid for" by monetary inflation.

The decisions taken in the last months of 1916 fixed the economic and social fate of the German people by pushing to their ultimate conclusion those tendencies already evident during the first half of the war. While an attempt must be made to assess the consequences of the war in quantitative and qualitative terms, it is important first to register the increasing helplessness and passivity of Germany's rulers in dealing with the condition of crisis which they themselves had created. If inflation is one of the results of weak government, as it most certainly is, then the increasing inability of the imperial government to control the special interests in the war economy must be counted as one of the major sources of the German inflation's severity.

The price-wage spiral unleashed by the new programs reached full speed by the summer of 1917. On the one hand, questions of cost were simply pushed into the background as the military procurement agencies and the war industries sought to carry out the Hindenburg Program and seemed ready to pay any price for the matériel and labor needed; on the other hand, those laboring in the war industries made increasing use of their market power and their organizations to secure the higher wages virtually sanctioned by the Auxiliary Service Law and legitimized by the food shortages, increased cost of living, and the incessantly mentioned industrial profiteering. Wage movements and strikes became the order of the day, and the growing political cast of the latter, which culminated in the famous peace strikes of January 1918, drove the trade-union leaders to demand and the authorities and employers to concede higher wages in order to prevent more dangerous developments. Yet, anxiety was also growing about how Germany would be able to compete in the postwar world with such inflated price and wage levels.[52]

The most comprehensive proposal for dealing with the problem came from Groener's adjutant, the industrialist Richard Merton. Just as Merton had argued the necessity of retaining the compulsory economy for foodstuffs, so he came to the conclusion that the war required firm intervention in the military-production sector as well. His views were expressed in a July 1917 memorandum "On the Necessity of State Intervention to Regulate Employer Profits and Worker Wages."[53] Merton began by bluntly pointing out that the accomplishments of those producing for the war had very little to do with patriotism and love of country. They were largely motivated by the quest for profit, and the longer the war lasted, the more producers were taking advantage of the booming market for military production. Not only had the appetite of industry increased with the eating, but its huge profits and exploitation of the situation had spilled over into the labor market, where wages were being bid up constantly by competing employers, while differences in wage levels were being created between the industries producing for the war effort and those producing peacetime products. Many of these differences had nothing to do with productivity but were simply a function of the vagaries of the wartime economy: "The workers know that their power has grown without limit, and the employers, especially the short-sighted ones or those who are to be viewed only as war industrialists and have no concern with the future development of the peacetime economy—and both together constitute a majority—can in large measure protect themselves against the increasing wage demands by increasing the prices of their products as they will, while the state, which is the final customer, can do nothing else under the present circumstances than agree to every price demanded of it."

Merton was particularly alarmed by a phenomenon which was to become one of the hallmarks of business practice in the inflation and which he correctly recognized to be undermining business morals; namely, the abandonment of firmly contracted prices in favor of arrangements in which either the price was left open or additional charges were allowed once all the cost increases occurring between the time an order was placed and the date of delivery had been calculated. This practice not only destroyed every incentive to keep costs down but also, because profits were calculated on the basis of a fixed percentage of costs, actually encouraged the disregard of cost increases. Merton placed the chief blame for these practices upon the producers of coal, iron, and steel—the raw-materials producers in heavy industry. He noted that the heavy industrialists were particularly reluctant to make long-term delivery contracts at firm prices, thereby forcing the manufacturers to abandon the practice of charging stable prices themselves.

Merton proposed that these problems be attacked by a virtual ban on further price increases for heavy-industrial products on the grounds that heavy-industrial profits were high enough already. This would make it possible to insist on stable pricing policies by all producers for the war effort. Indeed, he went so far as to argue that existing contracts should be revised toward this end. Most radical, however, was his proposal that legal measures be taken to put an end to the exploitation of the war economy by employers and workers. He urged increasing the war-profits tax to the point where "no war profits actually can be made" and the passage of a law permitting the War Office to take over the management of any company when this appeared the only means of settling differences over prices and wages.

The Merton memorandum was sent on by General Groener to Chancellor Michaelis on July 25, 1917, with an expression of his approval of its goals and the conviction that "it would bring a new note into our economic attitudes which perhaps would have a beneficial effect on our general domestic political situation."[54] A few weeks later, Groener found himself out of office, while Merton almost landed on a particularly dangerous section of the front. Groener had long been disliked by the industrialists and Colonel Bauer for being too sympathetic to the trade unions and was also opposed by influential persons in the War Ministry who wanted to cut the War Office down to size. Rumors of the memorandum leaked out and alarmed industrialists with access to the Supreme Command, although the precise role they played in the final decision is difficult to determine.[55]

Of greater significance, however, was the fate of the memorandum, the reaction of the civilian government leaders to its contents, and the subsequent discussion of the problems to which it was addressed among the Reich's rulers. Ap-

propriately, the memorandum was passed on to the Reich Office of the Interior, where it was subjected to vigorous commentary by Helfferich and his aides. Initially, Helfferich seems to have thought that the author was Moellendorff, who had become the *bête noire* of all opponents of further state intervention. In any event, these officials in no way shared Groener's sanguine expectations concerning the potential impact of the program. They thought that it would produce "endless political battles"[56] and that the left would try to use the situation to participate in employer profits. Obviously, they dreaded the thought of entering the Reichstag with a new piece of legislation relating to the war economy. Repeatedly, they warned against taking away material incentives allegedly essential to war production, declaring that "it probably will be impossible to maintain production at the unconditionally high levels necessary with reduced wages and lowered profits." Finally, they were frankly critical of further state intervention, commenting that the proposed legislation was destructive of "every private initiative." It would be nothing more than "a social state pure and simple." The proposal meant that "the War Office take German industry under its compulsory authority, when and how to be determined by the War Office."[57] These marginalia finally became the basis of a lengthy memorandum, probably by Helfferich himself, in which the author insisted, on the one hand, that "with pure ethical attitudes and enthusiasms one can in no way bring a war economy to its height," and, on the other, that the most important and productive industrialists wanted to remain "masters in their own house" and would never cooperate in becoming "civil servants of the economic state."[58]

These arguments for monetary incentives and for unfettered entrepreneurial initiative had by now become traditional, and Helfferich certainly believed them. Of course, there was much to be said for his claim that neither the personnel nor the skills were available to master the technical problems involved in assessing prices and wages throughout the country and revising existing contracts. His most compelling arguments, however, were political; they were also the most revealing because they demonstrated how much the price-wage spiral was

Karl Helfferich (1872–1924) as State Secretary of the Treasury in 1915. He served as State Secretary of the Interior in 1916–1917, was a prominent member of the DNVP after the war, and played a leading role in the stabilization of the currency in 1923. (*Library of Congress*)

a function of the powerlessness of the state in the face of the social and economic forces unleashed by the war economy:

. . . In view of the previous experience one cannot expect that the factory owners will voluntarily change in any substantial way their views about taking advantage of the boom and the appropriateness of war profits. In the numerous and very detailed negotiations last year concerning the limitation of the prices for coal and iron, the two pillars of our economic life, the intransigence of the interested parties with re-

spect to price decreases made itself apparent. Despite the high dividends, royalties, write-offs, etc., they are convinced that the prices and profits stand in proper relationship to the risk and consider further price increases, not reductions, to be justified. Should the factory owners be prepared to restrain themselves voluntarily under the Damocles Sword of the law, however, then the workers would only yield on the question of substantial wage reductions under direct and strong compulsion.

Helfferich was convinced, however, that the labor leaders would use every opportunity to get the plants under War Office control and that the government would find itself in the impossible position of trying to determine what actually constituted proper prices and wages. Just as he had warned that a law intended to provide plebiscital acclamation for total mobilization would end up with a legislative product based on parliamentary logrolling and increased labor power, so now he warned that the Auxiliary Service Law debate had provided a "foretaste of the conflicts to be expected" if a law on profits and wages were presented to the Reichstag.

The extent of Helfferich's cynical skepticism was really quite extraordinary. The old utilitarian argument for the free market had been that the pursuit of self-interest would serve the common good. Helfferich's argument, however, was that the free market was necessary because the alternative would require "a degree of unselfishness, sense of obligation, subordination" that were not to be found in human beings. Above all, as he made clear in the conclusion, these qualities were not to be found in German industrialists. He warned with incredible frankness that a tax that wiped out war profits would not only damage Germany's war effort but would also constitute a heavy liability for Germany's military future:

The German Empire would, after the introduction of such a tax, not be able to conduct a new war in the foreseeable future unless it was completely on the basis of a nationalized economy. For one should not overlook the fact with respect to high war profits that the employers almost without exception have run extraordinarily great dangers. They have done so in the hope that they would be compensated with a reward for their risk, and they would not act the same way in a new war if they have to pay out their profit in full.[59]

Conservative economic liberals like Helfferich and the industrialists he defended would someday be taught the meaning of placing the "common good before one's own good" (*Gemeinnutz vor Eigennutz*), and perhaps the popularity of the Nazi slogan becomes more comprehensible when placed in the World War I context. Actually, one wonders if all the German industrialists were quite as greedy as Helfferich suggests and whether the alleged German habits of subordination to authority and willingness to sacrifice for the nation did not exist at least to some degree. Certainly many of Germany's industrialists were aware that millions of Germans were also running some risks at the front, and there is good evidence that such major figures as the general director of the Gutehoffnungshütte, Paul Reusch, and the general director of the Maschinenfabrik Augsburg-Nürnberg (M.A.N.), Anton von Rieppel, were highly critical of industrial profiteering. Indeed, after the war, when Stinnes threatened to sue Merton for libeling German heavy industry, Reusch privately warned Stinnes that he would testify on Merton's behalf![60] In general, however, the weight of the evidence would appear to have fallen in Helfferich's favor, which was not very flattering to German industry and which was a constant source of distress to Treasury Secretary Count von Roedern, who had to pay the bills.

If one could file away the Merton memorandum, one still could not escape the problems which it addressed. In January 1918, the Prussian Minister of Public Works, Breitenbach, appealed directly to the Supreme Command to support his efforts to resist the price demands of the railroad-car manufacturers, which had increased 35.7 percent within a half year on the claim that this was necessary to meet past and anticipated material and labor cost increases. As Breitenbach noted, the price quotation contained "a much too high net profit," and would encourage new wage demands.[61] The Supreme Command responded with moral support, pointing out that the high prices and wages "lead to an unhealthy enrichment, on the one hand, and impoverishment, on the other hand, as well as to a very unhealthy dislocation of the social classes."[62] Among the officials of the newly created Reich Office of Economics (RWA), which had taken over the economic duties of the Reich Office of the Interior, how-

ever, the spirit of Helfferich remained alive and well. Thus, Helfferich's old aide, Ministerial Director Müller, reported with relief to his new boss, von Stein, that the Supreme Command had proposed no legislation, and Stein hastened to produce a new memorandum against legislative measures which largely repeated Helfferich's old arguments. While Breitenbach concurred in Stein's opposition to legislation, he could not refrain from pointing out that the rapidly increasing prices were dangerous not only because they threatened to bring about the financial collapse of the Reich, states, and municipalities but also because they created the possibility of a "complete economic collapse."[63]

Breitenbach, like most of his colleagues, was fully aware that he would have to live with inflation for the duration and that little could be done to man the first line of defense, the fiscal one. What worried him was what was to become the major concern of policymakers throughout the inflation, namely, the maintenance of some measure of relative price stability. This was what might be termed the second line of defense, and it was crucial if the economy were to function in some orderly, predictable manner. Undoubtedly, his position as head of Germany's largest railroad system and his sensitivity to the problems of postwar economic management made him particularly alert to this issue. In contrast to Merton, who touched on some of these problems from the perspective of business morality, Breitenbach's major worry was the destruction of that essential calculability upon which economic enterprise and profit making depended:

. . . Slowly rising prices, even when they stem from a gradual depreciation of money, may even have an enlivening effect upon economic life, since they strengthen the hope of a future profit. But if there is such a stormy price increase as in the past year, then a reasonable calculation of prices no longer is possible. Doing business becomes a gamble so that a very high premium for risk has to be calculated into every pricing decision. . . . In this way, the goods are made more expensive, the purchasing power of money is further reduced, and the further increase of prices and wages made unavoidable so that in the end there is such a general uncertainty in business life that no one dares to commit himself. This is now the case for entire branches of industry, as in parts of the electrical and machine building industries, rolling stock construction, etc., where it has become necessary to avoid binding price agreements. . . . If this becomes universal, then even normal conduct of business will become impossible and economic collapse will be unavoidable.[64]

Such concerns notwithstanding, Breitenbach favored an individual and case-by-case effort to bring industry to reason. He was much more ruthless in his approach to labor and sought to counter railroad-worker demands for wage increases by trying to get the army to reduce wages in state-owned weapons and munitions factories. Here he functioned very much as an employer and in some consonance with employer circles concerned about Germany's ability to compete on world markets with her "excessively" high wages.[65]

In general, however, wage reduction was a program which neither the military nor the civilian leadership was willing to support, not only because it was politically dangerous but also because they correctly recognized its economic impossibility. While there certainly was a tendency in the Supreme Command to complain that the workers were profiting at the expense of their brothers at the front and that Germany's *Mittelstand* was being crushed between industry and labor, a one-sided effort to bring down wages was firmly rejected by the military authorities at home, even when propagated as a step toward bringing down prices. Groener's successor, General Heinrich Scheüch, while as concerned as anyone about the "endangered *Mittelstand*," in which he included "the majority of the civil servants, officers, and pensioners, as well as all others on a fixed income and small craftsmen insofar as they do not have private wealth worth mentioning," argued that "many in the working class were suffering great need as well" and that "wages have not kept up with prices" except in the case of a "thin upper level" of workers. The attribution of high prices to rising wages was, according to him, a "misreading of economic realities," since the rising prices were responsible for the wage demands. He called, therefore, for a "systematic reduction of prices for foodstuffs and other necessities of life" as well as for raw materials. In his view, this could be accomplished by taking measures against wholesalers and other intermediaries between the producer and consumer.[66]

Scheüch's refusal to give any credence to those who tried to blame everything on wages certainly was laced with a very traditional military suspicion of merchants and those engaged in trade, a sentiment now reinforced by the utter helplessness of the regime in controlling either producer prices or wages. In fact, the best argument against the Merton program probably was the utter failure of the government to control black marketeering and the price of food and other vital necessities. From this perspective, a comparable government effort to deal with the wage-price problem in the industrial sector hardly appeared very promising. The government was capable of acting against industrial profiteering only in the most egregious instances, as in the case of the Daimler firm, which it placed under military control in the spring of 1918. This, however, was an isolated albeit spectacular case.[67] In the last analysis, government incompetence was delegitimizing government intervention.

German Society Between War and Peace

By the end of 1917, not only was the battle against the black market about to be lost, but also some of those in charge of the struggle seriously wondered if it was in the national interest to be successful. The extent of the disaster was candidly presented at the sixth meeting of the price examination agencies in Dresden in December 1917. The proportion of the food supply going through the black market had reached the point where the entire system built up by the government was in danger of collapse. To begin with, the public attitude toward the whole matter had changed so that "in large parts of the population the violation of the regulations is not felt to be wrong."[68] The evolving mentality was later described by no less a figure than Thomas Mann:

What did the people do? Since the future seemed uncertain to them, since no one could know what would happen, since beyond this the sons and husbands and brothers stood in the field and would perhaps not return, so that one could not see for whom one should actually save, and all the less so as the war was "so expensive" anyway, they bought whatever it was they could buy at whatever price. In the black market the German citizen could get a pound of rancid butter for twenty marks. The black marketeer played a dominant role in almost every German household, and to break the law in that one lived beyond his rations and quite sensibly overpaid for what one had illegally procured was viewed as unobjectionable and honorable.[69]

There were, to be sure, exceptions like Reichsbank President von Havenstein, who not only refused to use the black market but actually gave his bread and meat ration stamps away to the poor. Apparently, neither his charity nor his emaciated look were much appreciated by his friends, who felt that "the Reichsbank would have done better with a well-nourished instead of a half-starved President."[70]

What the officials at the Dresden meeting of the price examination agencies particularly noted was a vast increase in the range and complexity of black-market operations over the course of the year then coming to an end. Whereas previously it was the urban dweller who went out to the country and enticed the farmer to sell his foodstuffs, now the farmer was smuggling food into the cities because the only way the farmer could get boots, cloth, sugar, and fuel was by offering butter, eggs, and bacon in return. No only did such bartering of the necessities of life assume major proportions alongside the stepped up activity of the professional black marketeers, but also the ranks of the latter were now being strengthened by an increasing number of small-scale black marketeers from the *Mittelstand*. The *Mittelstand* found petty black marketeering a means of adapting to the price inflation and loss of real income: "The impoverished *Mittelstand* cannot pay the high prices needed for its own food supply. In order to get the food it needs in spite of this, it buys in larger quantities, which it then resells with a big price markup. It then uses the profit to pay for what it needs itself."[71]

More important from the standpoint of the scale of black marketeering, however, was that huge new markets that were particularly difficult to control had opened up. First, large firms had intensified the practice of supplying their workers with black-market products. This was a way of securing workers and keeping them fed and, one hoped, quiet. But it also meant that any effort to stop the illegal flow of food to and from the factories would be dangerous. Second,

the municipalities not only were inclined to tolerate black marketeering in situations where it was the only way to supply the local population, but also were actually known to have bought food on the black market themselves as well as to have exceeded the price ceilings in their purchases. They often excused their behavior by claiming that the competition from the industrial works made it necessary for them to engage in these practices.

Consequently, the question had been raised as to whether it did not make sense to distinguish the "black market" (*Schleichhandel*) from "illegal food supplying" (*Schleichversorgung*). It was, after all, easier and more practical to go hunting after the estimated half million black marketeers in Germany than to try to control the black-market activities of those who were supplying the population for more disinterested reasons and run the risk of irritating everyone. As officials from the industrial districts pointed out, the "illegal food supplying" often led to an "economic balancing out of things and prevented local disturbances," while the industrial supplying of the workers was something the workers had "become used to" and should perhaps be legalized. The spirit of these remarks was well captured by the representative of Greater Berlin, whose view of the black-market situation was "almost hopeless, in any case without illusions," while a representative of the agrarian area of Lippe suggested that the trading of agricultural goods for manufactured consumer goods needed by the farmers simply ought to be legalized.[72]

The entire discussion in Dresden was contemporaneous with the publication in the SPD newspaper *Vorwärts* of a memorandum by the Neukölln Municipal Council of December 3, 1917, in which the entire system of industrial and municipal use of the black market was described in vivid detail and in which the council quite bluntly expressed its intention of continuing its purchases unless the War Food Office could provide convincing and effective remedies.[73]

If the officials ultimately came down on the side of enforcing the regulations, it was because supplies were too short to grant total freedom and because the public would not tolerate the granting of a blank check to war profiteers and organized black marketeers to indulge themselves free of all anxiety and possible retribution. Even more important, the authority of the state, or what was left of it, depended upon an effort to uphold and maintain the law. The battle against the black market, aside from a more systematic attempt to attack the professional black marketeers, to increase controls and inspections at railroad stations, and to engage in such dubious practices as the systematic opening of the mails—in which Bavaria had pioneered—ultimately depended on increasing the supply of legally provided food. Here, one could not be very sanguine. Thanks to the "statistical demoralization" during the war, the producers deliberately understated their harvests and the consumers deliberately overstated their needs, so that "where one party swindles, the other thinks he has to swindle more. A very special optimism is required to think that it is possible to improve control over the supply."[74]

Certainly no one could be sanguine about the effects of the methods employed against the farmers. It was impossible to "enlighten" them, especially in the context of the unavoidably more forceful techniques being used to bring them into line. The often successful nighttime "inspections" of small mills and farms to check for false production reports and hidden stores "produced much bitterness among the people on the countryside," while the use of informers, so helpful in getting information about illegal cattle and pig slaughters, was "so poisonous and demoralizing in its effect as to make authorities doubt whether the advantages were greater than the disadvantages."[75] The certain consequence of all government attempts to control the food supply, and to do so with inadequate personnel, was to stir the resentment of the peasantry against what one historian has properly called an "affirmative action program for consumers."[76]

Even the very traditional respect of the farmers for the army was undermined in the spring of 1918 when soldiers were sent out to the countryside to confiscate fodder for military purposes, thereby starving the work animals. The agricultural workers, already in short supply, were demoralized as well. If the farm workers were unable to follow the model of their urban counterparts, who went out on strike and dem-

onstrated for higher wages and lower working hours, they could simply go to bed and report themselves "sick," and they began to do so.[77] A whole harvest was threatened, a harvest which strangers were going to take anyway to feed other strangers at prices which farmers deemed unsatisfactory. From the perspective of the farmers, the attitude of the workers and the authorities was nothing but hypocrisy. The workers were being supplied by the large firms and municipalities from the black market with the collusion and even the approval of the authorities. As for the workers, "on the one side they demand the strictest suppression of black marketeering, even in the big industries, but on the other side they gladly benefit from the black market supplies of food through the plants, and they set the condition that the supplying of the workers ought not to be reduced under any circumstances in the fight against the black market."[78]

The fight against profiteering was more complicated than that against black marketeering, but it also contributed its share to the breaking down of respect for law and authority. When the head of the Saxon Price Examination Agency, Professor Obst, reviewed in December 1917 the previous two years of activity by the agencies, he came to the sad conclusion that "the results do *not* stand in relation to the effort expended."[79] He blamed this, on the one hand, on the unhappy wording of the existing legislation and, on the other, on the profit seeking of commerce and industry and their hostility to the price examination agencies. While changes in the wording of the legislation were subsequently undertaken so that the War Profiteering Decree of July 23, 1915, appeared in revised form in a Decree Against Price Gouging (*Preistreibereiverordnung*) of May 8, 1918, the basic sources of tension were in no way eliminated, and the new regulations were indeed to generate endless new problems in the postwar period.

The July 1915 decree sought to impose a profit standard that was "just" or "appropriate" (*angemessen*) and placed under penalty those who sought to gain an "inappropriate profit for items that were needed for the pursuit of the war effort or items of daily necessity after taking into consideration the total circumstances, especially market conditions."[80] The fundamental paradox of both the old and the new decree was that they maintained the principle of private profit for merchants while placing the determination of what a legitimate profit was in the hands of the authorities. The principles under which such determinations were to be made were anything but clear, and the result was extraordinary confusion and an increasing uncertainty as to what the law actually was. Obviously, the merchants had every interest in defining the range of products under control as narrowly as possible, but both the network of price examination agencies and the courts tended to expand the list of items under control in the most extraordinary way. In April 1918, for example, the German Association of Toy Makers contacted all the chambers of commerce to complain that not only toys but even Christmas tree decorations had fallen under the anti-profiteering regulations.[81]

As might be expected, the biggest headaches involved the question of what constituted an "appropriate profit." In general, this was defined as the costs, including some allowance for salary and sometimes even for risk. The net profit was defined as the difference between these costs and the selling price and, in the interpretation of the courts, was not to exceed the net profit earned in peacetime. The trouble was that the experts consulted by the courts found it impossible to compare adequately peacetime and wartime costs or peacetime and wartime net profits, especially for new products never sold before the war. The most grotesque aspect of the measurement of net profits, however, was the tendency of the courts to think in absolute rather than in relative terms, so that, as one of the countless *gravamina* from retail organizations pointed out: "It is also incomprehensible why the merchant, who in peacetime made a net profit of 20 pfennig on an item with a value of perhaps 2 marks should now, when the same item costs 8 marks, also make only the same 20 pfennig profit on this 8 mark item."[82]

What ultimately threw the entire effort to determine a just price into total disarray, however, was the erroneous belief of the merchants that the decree of July 1915 left them free to base their prices on the market price. The courts ruled, however, that the market price was only one factor in price formation and that,

under wartime conditions of shortage, "emergency market conditions" (*Notmarktlage*) often existed and that traditional price determination when applied to such markets constituted an abuse for which a merchant could be fined, have his goods confiscated, have his business closed, and even be put in jail. While the decree of May 8, 1918, sought to remedy this ambiguity by omitting all reference to market conditions in the determination of an appropriate profit, market conditions could be subsumed in the "consideration of the total circumstances," and this left matters as uncertain as ever.[83]

The problem, of course, was that the government and the courts systematically refused to recognize the consequences of inflation. Insofar as the retailers were concerned, suppressing inflation had become a policy, and the results were inevitably bizarre. The effort by a committee of price examination agencies and the retail price specialist in the War Food Office, Professor Julius Hirsch (who was to become a major figure in the history of the German inflation), to set up national price guidelines for such individual items as school supplies, wood, ground black pepper, and cocoa beans, and then to illustrate the problems of determining costs by the example of the "calculations for sauerkraut in a factory that also sells vegetables and pickles,"[84] suggests that by 1918 the price examination program was firmly committed to the achievement of the impossible and that the potential for conflict between the retailers and the authorities would find its limit only in the actual number of items sold on the market.

The regulations concerning excess profits did not exhaust the sanctions of the decrees of 1915 and 1918, which also contained injunctions against hoarding in order to raise prices, collusion to raise prices, incitement to raise prices, and middleman operations that unnecessarily raised prices. Whether or not sales among merchants were legitimate efforts to promote economical distribution or were speculative ventures was, of course, extremely difficult to determine and necessarily provided further challenges for the authorities and the courts.[85]

It should not be thought that the retailers and wholesalers were totally unsympathetic to all these regulations. They had always supported restrictions on those allowed to engage in merchandising and marketing and persistently argued that the real problems stemmed from the "illegitimate" rather than the "legitimate" merchants. Thus, in Oldenburg the retailers sought to use the black market as an excuse to petition for the banning of door-to-door peddlers, noting that many war disabled were seeking to make a living in this manner and fearing that "the public would buy from the war disabled out of sympathy for them."[86] This particularly ugly example was part of a general pattern of resentment to be found among Germany's retailers over their disadvantaged position in the war economy. They asked why the civil servants and workers were allowed to get regular cost-of-living increases, and why industry, craftsmen, and farmers had to be encouraged by profits, while retailers were denied the right to exceed their prewar profit rates despite the fact that they were unable to sell as much as in peacetime. They viewed the supplying of food to the workers by the factories and municipalities and the favor shown to consumer cooperatives as threats to their existence from large-scale capitalism, on the one hand, and creeping socialism, on the other.[87]

It should be clear by now that one of the most fateful legacies of the war was a feeling throughout German society that various groups and individuals were unfairly advantaged or disadvantaged by the war economy and that many of the social and economic consequences of the war were unjust and illegitimate. These sentiments were to accompany the entire decade of the inflation and were to deepen and find dangerous and destructive political expression. They are, therefore, of great historical importance, and they are also profoundly difficult to analyze and evaluate. Even if the statistical data on income were complete, accurate, and reliable, which they are not, the problem of determining gainers and losers is by no means solved once the objective economic position of each of the major groups and subgroups of German society has been established. Such data are not a very satisfactory basis for determining changes in the quality of life, feelings of happiness and unhappiness, power and powerlessness, and political behavior; nor are they entirely predictive of the capacity of various groups to deal with

the problems of monetary depreciation and of the manner in which they were to do so over time. The relative positions of the various social groups at any given stage in the inflationary process is their point of departure for the next. The modern social and economic history of industrial nations, even in times of protracted inflations, is not the story of major upheavals but rather of constant jockeying, sometimes conscious and sometimes unconscious, for relative advantage. Finally, such developments must be placed in the context of the political and legal conditions which may determine the seriousness and significance of social changes.

In undertaking to determine the socioeconomic effects of the war economy, therefore, it is essential to bear in mind that the war was a losing proposition for Germany economically. In addition to the financial costs and the diminution of international trade, Germany lost 4 percent of her population—2,400,000 dead at the front and 300,000 civilian deaths through war-related deprivation and disease.[88] The loss in agricultural and industrial production was also severe (see Table 5), but the full measure of the war's consequences in terms of the exploitation of Germany's agricultural and industrial plant without satisfactory repair or capital investment is not yet fully evident in the wartime index numbers. What is indicated, however, is not only a general reduction in the growth of the German economy, but also an unevenness in the distribution of this reduced growth. Clearly, it was the consumer sectors that suffered the most, so that Germans may have been relatively well armed, but increasingly poorly fed, clothed, and housed. The question of winners and losers, therefore, must be placed in this unhappy economic context because it reduced the significance and pleasure of "winning" and called forth virulent sentiments among the losers.

This is the view from hindsight, however. Until the early summer of 1918, most Germans assumed a favorable outcome of the war, and their perceptions were based on this expectation and were grounded in the belief that what was distasteful or unjust in current conditions would be corrected. There was a general consensus, for example, that agriculture was doing well in the war despite its unanimous rejection

Table 5. Agricultural and Industrial Production Before and During World War I

Agricultural Production
(average yield per hectare in 100 Kg.)

	1901/13	1914/18
Wheat	22.7	18.3
Rye	18.6	14.5
Summer Barley	21.3	16.3
Oats	19.8	15.6
Potatoes	157.1	124.6

Industrial Production
(1913 = 100)

	1914	1915	1916	1917	1918
Non-Ferrous Metals	89	72	113	155	234
Mining	84	78	86	90	83
Iron and Steel	78	68	61	83	53
Merchant Marine	73	65	75	61	42
Construction Materials	88	69	59	58	35
Textiles	87	65	27	22	17
All Industrial Production[1]	81	66	63	61	56

Sources: D. Petzina et al., *Sozialgeschichtliches Arbeitsbuch. III. Materialien zur Statistisk des Deutschen Reiches 1914–1945* (Munich, 1978), p. 60; Rolf Wagenführ, "Die Industriewirtschaft. Entwicklung der deutschen und internationalen Industrieproduktion 1860–1932," *Vierteljahrshefte zur Konjunkturforschung,* Sonderheft 31 (Berlin, 1933), p. 22f.

[1] 1928 = 100; 1913 = 98

of the compulsory economy and difficulties in procuring the industrial and consumer items needed in the countryside. Indeed, to a great extent, the united agrarian front against the compulsory economy and the tension between city and country helped to hold in check the very serious potential differences among the farmers as well as to obscure the more general problems the war was creating for German agriculture. The compulsory economy, in reality, affected smallholders more adversely than large landowners, and there were periodic outbursts of resentment by western farmers against the relative advantages enjoyed by the East Elbian Junkers as well as bad feeling on the part of poorer farmers over the advantages richer neighbors seemed to enjoy in dealing with the demands of the authorities. Nevertheless, not only did all farmers have reasonably certain access to food, but also the rising prices, even the controlled ones, increased their liquidity and helped them to reduce their indebtedness. The macroeconomic realities of reduced productivity and undercapitalization were repressed thanks to a monetary mirage, on the one hand,

and preoccupation with the battle against the controlled economy, on the other. German agriculture appeared a winner, but it was constantly on the defensive and considered itself to be a loser relative to the industrial sector.[89]

Insofar as farmers compared themselves to industrialists, which they periodically did, they had reason for resentment, and it was a resentment that they could share with much of German society. The report of the Württemberg War Ministry in August 1918 was typical: "The extraordinary profits of the large corporations, especially the machine, munitions, sugar, cigar, and cigarette firms, iron smelting plants and coal mines, food processing plants, and the like, which announce unbelievably high dividends and other bonuses for the stockholders, partially in veiled form, along with the fact that these plants are always increasing the price of their products with the excuse of the general price increases, has to create bad blood and have the effect that the workers are always demanding higher wages."[90]

The profits of German industry, at least on paper, appeared outrageously high. The net profit of some forty-seven hundred German corporations increased from 1,656 million to 2,213 million marks between 1912–1913 and 1917–1918, while the profit as a percent of total capital increased from 10.9 to 13.7 percent and the dividends as a percent of total capital from 8.7 to 10.1 percent during the same period. The profits of the war industries were yet more significant. If one examines the deflated dividends as a percentage of capital for 1917–1918 for all of industry, they amount to 5.41 percent. Yet, for the iron and steel industry and the chemical industry, they were 9.60 and 10.88 percent respectively. What most upset the public, however, were the undeflated figures, which showed that the Phoenix concern paid a 20 percent dividend in 1916–1917, where it had "only" paid 12 percent in 1915–1916. In 1914–1915 it had a net profit of 15.4 million with 12.6 million in write-offs. In 1916–1917, the net profit was 52.4 million, and the write-offs were 16.7 million. The controls placed on the prices of basic iron and steel products in early 1917 by the Raw Materials Section were recognized by the big industrialists for what they were; namely, a cosmetic attempt to prevent German industry from totally alienating public opinion. As they and their protector, Lieutenant Colonel Koeth well understood, the great concerns were "mixed" enterprises producing everything from coal to finished artillery, and the loss taken on steel merchant bars was more than compensated for by the profits made on coal and on finished products. Furthermore, nothing required the firms to reveal the special prices they demanded for quick delivery or—often allegedly—higher quality products or their silent reserves.[91]

This is not to say that those doing business in the nonessential and peacetime industries were necessarily without reward. To be sure, certain industrial branches were reduced by as much as half their prewar number of plants in order to save on labor and raw materials. The cotton, glass, shoe, and soap industries were particularly hard hit. Of the seventeen hundred cotton-spinning and -weaving plants operating before the war, only seventy "high productivity" plants were functioning in 1918. These, of course, were making handsome profits and paying dividends between 13 and 16 percent, but the fate of those shut down was not really tragic since the Reich paid half a billion marks in compensation to such firms in 1917–1918.[92]

The liquidity of German industry—especially of the large corporations—had increased enormously because of the war, and this combined with raw-materials shortages had a significant effect upon the power relationships within the business community. The high liquidity and the government practice of immediate payment explain not only the virtual disappearance of commercial bills because of the elimination of the need for short-term credit, but also industry's increasing independence of the banks. Furthermore, these factors pushed forward the process of industrial concentration. Heavy industry expanded into shipbuilding and finishing and also enlarged its marketing operations at the expense of the commercial sector, which was already hurt by the wartime reduction of international trade. Vertical concentration was complemented by horizontal in the chemical industry, where important new steps were taken in the direction of what was to become IG Farben. In general, there was a strong tendency for larger firms to buy up smaller ones. This economic consolidation was accompanied by an organizational tightening promoted at once by the government for reasons of organizing the war economy and by industry itself as the most effective means of protecting itself against the government. Vast strides were made in the formation of industrial branch organizations (*Fachverbände*), especially in textiles, machine building, and the electrotechnical industries.[93]

While the industrialists certainly were the darlings of the war economy, their joys were not unadulterated. Under the best of circumstances, producing for a war economy is filled with irritations and difficulties, and dealing with the civilian and military authorities in Germany presented some special problems. They chaffed under the controls and bureaucratic procedures and, above all, worried about the future when German industry would have to reconvert to peacetime production, reestablish its position on world markets, and reconstruct its own exploited and overworked industrial plant. Insofar as the high war profits were legitimized by the future problems of reconstruction, the justification was sincere, and two problems loomed particularly large as German industry faced the future. The first was to regain its freedom from bureaucratic interference and ward off the intentions of planning enthusiasts like Wichard von Moellendorff and Walther Rathenau, who wished to perpetuate "war socialism." The second concerned the increased power of organized labor and the steadily rising wages. The latter, in the view of most employers, had to be accepted so long as food prices continued to rise, although they feared the rising wages would ruin Germany's competitive position once peace was restored.[94]

This last issue raises what is unquestionably the thorniest and most controversial problem of analysis in dealing with the war economy and, indeed, the entire history of the German inflation; namely, the economic position of blue-collar workers during this period. Happily, the ideological difficulties have become less difficult than the statistical ones, thanks to the collapse of East German scholarship insisting that the Majority Socialists and the trade-union leaders betrayed the German working class by participating in the war effort and, in the process, brought the working class nothing but political defeat and material misery.[95] This was never a very interesting mode of historical argumentation since it took its point of departure from what allegedly should have happened instead of what did happen. It was also factually false. The weight of the evidence comes down on the side of those who have argued that the political position of the working class, as represented by the reformist parties and trade unions, improved absolutely, and that the economic position of the working class, even though it deteriorated in absolute terms, improved relative to that of the *Mittelstand*. The problematic side of these developments is that they cannot simply be placed in the context of the long-term political and economic emancipation of the working class under reformist auspices, but must also be seen in the context of inflationary conditions that constantly tested the viability and challenged the legitimacy of labor's increased power.

Thanks in large part to the Auxiliary Service

Law, the Free, Christian, and Hirsch-Duncker unions began to increase their memberships and influence. During the first two years of the war, the unions had suffered severe membership losses because of the military call-up and because many workers, especially those exempted or reclaimed from the front, were not convinced that the trade unions could protect their interests. This changed during the last two years of the war (see Tables 6A and 6B), since the recognition given to the unions under the law, their presence on the mediation and arbitration committees, and the compulsory introduction of worker committees into all plants of any significant size all served to demonstrate that the unions were in a position to protect the interests of the workers. This impression was strengthened by the lively activity of the trade unions in protesting the food situation and by the willingness of the authorities to listen to such petitions and at least promise remedy. Undoubtedly, the obvious and loudly expressed unhappiness of the employers with the favor shown to the trade unions and the disfavor

Table 6A. Trade Union Membership, 1914–1919

	Socialist	Christian	Hirsch-Duncker
1913	2,574,000	343,000	107,000
1914 (1st half)	2,511,000	283,000	78,000
1914 (2nd half)	1,664,000		
1915	1,159,000	176,000	61,000
1916	967,000	174,000	58,000
1917	1,107,000	244,000	79,000
1918	1,665,000	393,000	114,000
1919	5,479,000	858,000	190,000

Source: Correspondenzblatt der Generalkommission der Gewerkschaften Deutschlands, Statistische Beilage, Nr. 20 (1920), pp. 78, 103.

Table 6B. Membership in the Socialist Metal, Miners, and Factory Workers Unions, 1914–1918

	Metal Workers	Miners	Factory Workers
1914 (July 31)	531,991	101,956	207,330
1915 (Dec. 31)	234,360	46,371	86,119
1916 (Dec. 31)	247,674	53,404	80,666
1917 (Dec. 31)	393,734	110,454	110,862
1918 (Sept. 30)	447,197	138,470	119,829

Source: Correspondenzblatt der Generalkommission der Gewerkschaften Deutschlands. Statistische Beilage, Nr. 20 (1920), pp. 78, 103.

shown to the so-called yellow, or nonstriking, unions, served to reinforce the case for trade-union membership. Membership increased most strongly in the unions serving those industries most vital to the war effort—the metal, mining, and factory-workers unions. In this trend toward greater union membership, however, the role played by new members, especially women and young workers, was of particular significance. The percentage of women in the Free Trade Unions rose from the prewar level of 10 to 30 percent by the end of the war, or from 200,000 to 430,000. This influx, however welcome, was not without attendant problems since these new members lacked trade-union experience and discipline and were prone to demonstrate and strike spontaneously.[96]

Protests, in the form of demonstrations and strikes, increased substantially in 1917–1918, beginning almost invariably with complaints about the food situation but rapidly taking on a political character, especially where the USPD was in a position to agitate. While officially opposed to strikes, the SPD and its allied trade-union leaders felt compelled to take over the leadership of such movements and direct them away from protest against the war itself and toward securing promises of better provisioning, higher wages, and domestic political reforms. The trade unions often did take the initiative in launching wage movements, a useful way of increasing membership and deflecting attention from political issues. These movements were difficult to resist, the employers tending to give way since the costs could be passed on in higher prices, and the government favored anything that would keep the peace and maintain production. The employers did try to hold the line, however, with respect to base wages, preferring to give cost-of-living supplements (*Teuerungszulagen*) in the obvious hope of keeping their options open for the time when the war would end and prices presumably would decrease. It is to be noted that the trading of prices and wages was often quite explicit, especially in the crucial coal industry, in which the Deputy Commanding General in Westphalia made a regular practice of promoting wage increases for the miners while urging the Prussian government to grant the coal industry's requests for price increases.[97]

These wage movements undoubtedly had a significant effect on nominal wages, especially in the war industries, but they are inseparable from the market situation which simply made it essential for the war industries to maintain or increase their work force. Unionization and rising nominal and real wages worked in tandem precisely where the demands of war production and the labor market left the employers and state authorities with limited options. At the same time, the increasing dependence on female labor combined with the rising prices reduced the pay differential between men and women so that the gap in nominal wages narrowed while the real wages of women actually increased relative to those of men after 1916 (see Table 7). The narrowing of sex differentials was accompanied by a narrowing of age and skill differentials as industry employed increasing numbers of unskilled and semiskilled workers. At Krupp, for example, the wages of women and youths under sixteen and between sixteen and twenty-one increased 150 to 180 percent between 1914 and 1918, while those of unskilled and skilled males increased only 87 to 110 percent. A similar pattern is to be found at the Bayer Chemical Works in Leverkusen. Such leveling notwithstanding, one is also struck by the immense differences between workers in war and nonwar industries.[98]

Reliance on existing wage statistics, however, can be misleading. They do not always take into account special premiums given to workers with children. They also fail to account for special food rations, most common in the big war plants, as well as food supplied at reduced prices through the firms. Most important, they do not account for family earnings. A family in which husband, wife, and children were employed in armaments plants was obviously in a different position than a female worker whose husband was at the front and who was supporting her children from her earnings in a textile mill and such government support funds as she might receive. The former families were able to afford some luxuries and were even known to have invested in war bonds. Such exceptional situations aside, however, family income certainly was of crucial importance in explaining how many workers made it through the war. The complexities involved in evaluating the real sit-

Table 7. Average Daily Nominal and Real Earnings for Men and Women in 350 Establishments, September 1914–1918
(March 1914 = 100)

	1914	1915	1916	1917	1918
Nominal Wages					
War Industries[1]					
Men	98.1	123.0	147.5	212.0	250.0
Women	80.9	129.6	173.3	232.6	284.7
Intermediate[2]					
Men	98.4	112.4	129.6	169.5	208.6
Women	91.2	105.6	125.0	172.7	225.9
Civilian[3]					
Men	89.3	106.1	109.7	140.5	176.3
Women	84.3	98.7	111.7	155.7	201.7
Real Wages					
War Industries					
Men	90.8	89.8	78.4	78.8	77.4
Women	76.4	95.3	92.0	86.7	87.9
Intermediate					
Men	92.3	81.6	68.3	62.8	64.2
Women	86.3	77.7	67.1	64.8	71.1
Civilian					
Men	83.5	77.5	57.9	52.7	55.5
Women	79.2	71.9	59.3	57.8	61.9

Sources: Reichsarbeitsblatt 17 (1919): p. 622, for nominal earnings; and Gerhard Bry, *Wages in Germany, 1871–1945* (Princeton, 1960), p. 211.

[1]metal working, machine construction, chemicals, and electrotechnical

[2]stone and earth, wood, leather and rubber, and paper

[3]foods, textiles, clothes, and graphics

uation of workers do not end here, however. Workers in small cities and towns earned less than their counterparts in the great industrial and urban centers, but they had more direct access to the food on the countryside. From the standpoint of nutrition, it mattered considerably whether a worker had a small garden (*Schrebergarten*) or not. Access to foodstuffs, therefore, was often more important than the actual wage. While there was much talk about younger workers having more money than they could handle and workers who were "war profiteers" because they were skilled and could benefit from a high base wage and piece rates, this certainly was not the condition of most workers. Some workers were able to save money only because there was so little to buy.

Basically, however, there is no reason to question the generally accepted contention that the real wages of the German blue-collar workers and their quality of life decreased during the war, no matter which of the price indices one uses (see Table 8). The problem was most serious for the more poorly paid workers, since

they were most inclined to purchase lesser-quality goods in the first place, and it was precisely for such goods that the demand was most extreme and the related price increases most serious. Not only did the quality and quantity of the available food continue to deteriorate, but also the problems of securing the basic necessities were compounded by clothing and housing shortages and their increasing cost. The price of woolen material for female clothing increased 1,720 percent and that of cotton material 1,405 percent between October 1915 and October 1918, while the price of material for men's clothes rose between 795 and 861 percent during the same period. The cost of shoes jumped 200 percent. In Magdeburg, the Deputy Commanding General reported that a set of clothes for daily wear that cost between thirty-five and fifty marks in peacetime cost from three hundred to three hundred fifty marks in May 1915, and the price of a man's shirt had gone from between two and a half and three and a half marks to between twenty and twenty-five marks. The miseries of the unaffordable prices were com-

**Table 8. Indices of Changes
in the Cost of Living, 1914–1918**
(1913 = 100)

	Wholesale Prices	Calwer (Food)	Reich Statistical Office/Bry (General Cost of Living)
1914	105	101	103
1915	142	143	129
1916	152	198	170
1917	179	213	253
1918	217	229	313

Source: Jürgen Kocka, *Facing Total War. German Society 1914–1918* (Leamington Spa, 1984), p. 22.

pounded by the malfunctioning of the bureaucracy. The Frankfurt War Office Bureau reported at the beginning of 1918 not only that the quality of shoe leather had deteriorated to the point where it was unusable, but also that the procurement of shoes required going to three different agencies, while the procurement of thread, nails, leather scraps, and other items needed to repair shoes required turning to ten additional agencies.[99] Finally, the housing situation steadily deteriorated, especially in the industrial centers. In April 1918, General von Gayl reported "calamitous" housing conditions in the Rhenish-Westphalian district. Essen was short ten thousand living quarters and Dortmund was in need of an additional two thousand.[100] As might be expected, this led to rising rents, and, much in the style of the management of food prices at the beginning of the war, the local military authorities began imposing rent controls and restraints on the rights of house owners to evict tenants in a helter-skelter manner. The Bundesrat finally acted to introduce some consistency into the handling of this problem in September 1918, by which time the landlords were already well integrated into the ranks of those disaffected by the controlled economy.[101]

Miserable as it was, however, the situation of blue-collar workers in the war industries takes on a somewhat different character the moment it is compared with that of white-collar workers and civil servants. While statistical information on the salaries of white-collar workers is very poor and scattered, the decline of their situation relative to that of blue-collar workers during the war is indisputable. The tendency toward equalization of the economic situation of

white- and blue-collar workers was already in evidence before the war, but then this most important element of the "new middle class" could still boast salaries that ran on average 15 percent higher than the wages paid blue-collar workers. The social advantages and pretensions of white-collar workers thus had some material basis. The war dramatically changed this situation. Employers actually reduced white-collar salaries during the first months of the war, and, in contrast to the blue-collar situation, even nominal salaries did not begin to increase during the war's first two years. When they began to rise in the second half of the war, it was at a much slower pace than the nominal wages of blue-collar workers. While white-collar organizations complained to military authorities that their members were receiving either no cost-of-living supplements or totally inadequate ones, the authorities in question admitted the "justifiability of the complaints" but pointed out that "a general regulation cannot be made due to the many-sidedness of the white-collar worker group and the totally varying employment conditions connected with it."[102] The suggestion that complaints should be dealt with on a case-by-case basis suited the employers quite well since they wished to maintain the "special" relationship with white-collar workers and also feared that salary increases could not as easily be reversed for white-collar workers after the war.

The discriminatory treatment against white-collar workers continued despite the Auxiliary Service Law, which included provisions for the creation of white-collar worker committees and also gave them the right to make use of mediation and arbitration boards. The legal changes brought about by the law, however, undoubtedly made white-collar workers even more acutely aware of the dilemmas involved in trying to maintain status distinctions in the midst of eroding real income. A stunning illustration of the transformation of mood and loyalty among white-collar workers was a meeting held between the Bavarian organizational leaders and the authorities in February 1918. A representative of the retail clerks pointed out that the situation of his colleagues had not been good even before the war but that "now the issue is to prevent having the entire class dissolve into

**Table 9. Nominal and Real Monthly Salaries of Higher-,
Middle-, and Lower-level Civil Servants, 1914–1919**
(salaries in marks; index, 1913 = 100)

	Higher-level			Middle-level			Lower-level		
	Nominal	Real	Index	Nominal	Real	Index	Nominal	Real	Index
1914	608	591	97.2	342	332	97.2	157	153	97.2
1915	608	470	77.3	342	264	77.3	157	121	77.3
1916	608	358	58.9	342	202	58.9	157	93	58.9
1917	660	261	42.9	420	166	48.6	213	84	53.6
1918	891	284	46.8	589	188	55.0	342	109	69.6
1919	1,105	245	40.2	778	187	54.8	582	140	89.3

Source: Jürgen Kocka, *Facing Total War. German Society 1914–1918* (Leamington Spa, 1984), p. 88.

the proletariat."[103] Comparison of the wages of workers with their own demonstrated that "in the course of the war an extraordinary disrespect for mental labor has taken hold." While he believed it difficult to set up collective wage contracts, he was convinced that a minimum wage was necessary and pointed out that the needs of white-collar workers was so great that the idea of striking was being discussed increasingly and noted that three clerks had been among the leaders of the most recent Munich strikes. The representative of the technicians at the meeting chose to stress the "more ideal side" of the problem. He found it inappropriate that the salaried employee, "who was supposed to be superior to the worker," could not get his organizations recognized by the employers, while the latter were willing to negotiate with blue-collar worker unions. This was not the only "slap in the face" (*Faustschlag ins Gesicht*) they had experienced, since white-collar worker committee members were more frequently dismissed and called up for military service when they strongly represented salaried worker interests than their blue-collar worker counterparts, and it was a regular practice at the Prussian military technical institutes to reclaim blue-collar workers and give them full pay while simply placing technical personnel on leave and giving them military pay. The implication clearly was that the government and employers were frightened of blue-collar trade unions and worker strikes but felt they could mistreat the salaried workers with impunity. While white-collar worker representatives at this meeting assured the Bavarian authorities that they were opposed to strikes, it was clear

from their words that attitudes were changing and that the salaried employees were showing an increasing readiness to unionize and to strike. Thus, the only white-collar trade-union group to grow during the war was the Socialist organization.[104]

If fully satisfactory statistical evidence on wartime white-collar salaries is hard to come by, the statistics on the civil service are more readily available and provide a stunning demonstration of the leveling effects of the war and inflation. As in the case of white-collar workers, civil servants suffered from stagnating nominal wages and brutally deteriorating real wages until 1917, when the former began to rise. However, it was the lower levels of the civil service that benefited the most (see Table 9). Germany's upper-level civil servants clearly were making a monumental if involuntary financial sacrifice for their country during the war, but even middle- and lower-level civil servants were not much better off in the end than workers in civilian industries.

In the last years of the war, this became a matter of great concern, as the military authorities in the homeland reported repeatedly on the proletarianization of the civil service and the dangers which this presented to state and society. Thus, a Deputy Commanding General received the following letter: "We struggle through from one day to another; we actually go begging. We civil servants will be pushed down completely into the proletariat. The food situation is daily more serious because it is an open secret that those who are dependent on the rations and do not have friends to help them through starve. The civil servant has few such friends, but when he has them, then there is the horrible danger that demands will be made upon him that stand in conflict with his office and his professional honor."[105] Instances of corruption did, in fact, increase in the last years of the war, but more fundamental was the sense that the civil service was in crisis and that something had to be done. While upper-level civil servants seemed to have maintained an outwardly passive stance and probably lived off past savings, their subordinates became more militant and began to protest conditions openly as early as 1916. They proposed the indexation of salaries to meet the higher cost of living and showed increasing tendencies to organize in the so-called "Interest Association of the German Reich and State Civil Service Organizations" (*Interessengemeinschaft deutscher Reichs- und Staatsbeamtenverbände*), which was created through the collaboration of a variety of existing organizations in February 1916 and had half a million members by the beginning of 1918. These groups had greater reluctance to launch strikes than white-collar organizations, but the effectiveness and attractiveness of union organization obviously was increasing, while the logic of the situation and circumstances, if not of status and tradition, was pushing large groups of civil servants in a more militant direction. Inflation appeared to be leveling the differences between those who worked for wages and those who received salaries to the point where a united front of the old and the new proletariat was theoretically conceivable.[106]

The Revolutionary Crisis and Its Limits

Who would have imagined such a state of things in August 1914? When Ludendorff's unsuccessful 1918 offensives ground to a halt and the enemy took the offensive in the late summer, the fundamental prop maintaining morale on the home front, the hope for victory, began to crumble. Matters were not helped by postcards from the front calling the war a "swindle" and remarks to the same effect by troops home on leave. While the authorities worried about a revival of political strikes after the long period of quiet that followed the successful repression of the January 1918 peace

strikes and the great military offensives of the spring, the labor unrest which developed in the late summer and fall was of a different character and had its own ominous implications. The workers began to demand a reduction of the long wartime working hours and claimed exhaustion due to the hard work and poor nourishment. Weariness of the most literal kind and demoralization were in fact taking hold, and with them an increasing disrespect for law and order as well as an unwillingness to make sacrifices. As the War Office reported in August 1918: "One of the most regrettable accompanying circumstances of the war is a serious slackening of general respect for law. Break-ins, robberies—lately especially robbery from the fields—poaching and crimes of violence are the order of the day. Moral laxity, the quest for pleasure, especially among young people, are spreading more and more widely. The demand for countermeasures, therefore, becomes ever more pressing."[107] The capacity to take countermeasures, however, was becoming more limited. With virtually the entire nation involved with the black market and the war going badly after all the promises of victory, the authority of the state was becoming shaky. Even in less troubled periods of the war, intermittent efforts to force young people to save their earnings had to give way in the face of resistance and trade union protest. By the end of the war, excesses were nothing more than an integral part of the general demoralization.

That this situation should have intensified particularist sentiments and attitudes in the Reich is not surprising, especially since the war economy had increased south German resentment of Prussia and its control of so much of Germany's raw materials and industrial resources. Anti-Prussian sentiment became particularly loud and vehement in Bavaria, and the Bavarian government turned to the Reich in alarm and in the knowledge that its fate was inextricably bound up with that of the Reich. The Bavarian government's response to this crisis as well as to later crises are of particular interest because they transcend Bavaria's own particularism and illuminate the condition of Germany as a whole. This certainly was the case with a memorandum submitted to the Reich government on September 6, 1918, which bluntly and effectively described public feeling about the economic situation only a few weeks before Ludendorff's totally unanticipated armistice request gave the *coup de grâce* to Germany's war effort.[108]

The memorandum began by pointing out that the Bavarian government had been aware for some time that public confidence in Germany's economic situation was in a state of deterioration. Socialist labor leaders had repeatedly pointed out in serious discussions that "they could no longer share the confidence of the government that we can hold out through the war economically. The physical and psychological capacities of the population have been so weakened by the long duration of the war with its heavy sacrifices and privations, that one must expect them to collapse." The labor leaders, who had tried to maintain worker support of the war effort, were now in danger of losing the confidence of the workers because "they were reproached for going along with a government that cannot fulfill its promises to improve the situation but instead demands new sacrifices and privations and thereby has lost the confidence of the people." The labor leaders were threatening to end their collaboration unless either the food situation improved or the government drew the "unavoidable consequences for its war policy" arising from its inability to provide the necessities of life. The goodwill of the government was no longer enough.

The Bavarian population was not primarily industrial, however, and the Bavarian attitude is particularly interesting because it conveys the views of a broad spectrum of public opinion. Thus, the authors of the memorandum insisted that views they described were not restricted to the working class but were echoed "by the peasantry, the middle class, the white-collar workers, and especially those who are called upon to assume leadership. Even clerics and civil servants have by and large lost their inner confidence in our ability to hold out and, after many disappointments, have become uncertain about what they can actually say about the situation and its further development without soon being contradicted by events." In the view of the Bavarian government, the situation could only deteriorate the longer the war lasted.

Shortages of food, clothing, coal, and petroleum would get worse and prices would rise. Recent measures to collect the last metal scraps and textiles "appear to people as an official demonstration of the progressive depletion of our last stocks." The people were embittered over their steady impoverishment and high prices which they blamed in large measure on profiteering.

Despite these gloomy prognostications, the Bavarian memorandum did not have as its purpose a call for the speediest possible termination of the war. Its fundamental goal was much more modest; namely, the dissemination of accurate information, "clarity about the present situation and future developments" so that people could be properly informed and encouraged to hold out. This pathetic call for accurate information by officials who probably understood the truth far better than they cared to admit is indicative of the position in which the authorities ruling Germany had placed themselves by the end of the war. It helps to explain the complete collapse of support for the war effort on the home front once Ludendorff's insistence that Germany request an armistice became public knowledge at the beginning of October. It also helps to explain the collapse of the Reich and state governments in the face of the revolutionary wave that swept Germany in early November 1918.[109]

There are many who argued at the time and some who might argue now that it was the war which revolutionized German political, social, and economic life and that the Revolution of November 1918 was at worst superfluous and at best a noisy and confused confirmation of what had already been accomplished. It is true that beginning with the Auxiliary Service Law, but especially after the July 1917 crisis which led to the downfall of Bethmann Hollweg, the Reichstag was dominated by the future Weimar coalition of Majority Socialists, Centrists, and Progressives* with the support in domestic matters of the left wing of the National Liberals†, and this coalition's activities were formally institutionalized in the so-called Inter-Party

---

*The functional equivalent of the post-revolutionary German Democratic Party (DDP).
†The functional equivalent of the post-revolutionary German People's Party (DVP).

Committee (*Interfraktioneller Ausschuß*). Despite the absence of formal constitutional provisions mandating parliamentary confidence in the government, the last two Chancellors of the Empire, Count Hertling (November 1917–September 1918) and Prince Max von Baden (October 3, 1918–November 9, 1918) were appointed after consultation with the Reichstag "majority." It is also true, however, that the power of the Reichstag remained formally limited by the Constitution and practically limited by the domination of the Supreme Command in all matters of foreign and military policy. Furthermore, the reform of the Prussian suffrage system, which was an essential prerequisite for effective parliamentarization, continued to be obstructed by the Prussian House of Lords as late as September 1918. While the Supreme Command's decision to ask for an armistice put an end to its overwhelming political power and terminated the resistance to reform in Prussia, the constitutional reforms proposed by the Prince Max von Baden government did not aim at a full parliamentarization of the Empire. Pressure from the Reichstag finally produced this result in late October, at a time when the question of the Kaiser's abdication had taken the political forefront because it seemed the only way to get an armistice from President Wilson. By this time, the revolutionary situation was far advanced, and rumors of the Kaiser returning home at the head of his army, as well as of army plans for a final call-up and naval plans for a final sally against the British navy, were more than sufficient triggers as well as justifications for revolution, the forced abdication of the Kaiser, and the creation of the Republic on November 9, 1918. In the light of this course of development, it is difficult to see how the political revolution could be termed superfluous.[110]

Much of the confusion about the German Revolution undoubtedly stems from its comparison with the "great" revolutions in France in 1789 and in Russia in 1917, although the fact that historians speak quite comfortably about revolutions in 1830 and 1848 which produced minor changes or were unsuccessful makes one wonder why the German Revolution of 1918–1919 cannot be treated with the respect it deserves. The revolutions of 1989 provide even more compelling evidence that 1789 and 1917 are not the only models of true revolution. Certainly the spreading of the councils movement from Kiel clear across Germany in a matter of days is about as spontaneous a development as one could wish, even if it lacks the cinematic possibilities provided by the Bastille and the Winter Palace. The real difficulty, of course, is that the November Revolution did not lead to a social and economic revolution and that the Republic it established came to such a sorry end in 1933, allegedly in large measure because of the "incomplete" Revolution of 1918–1919.[111] This basic criticism of the Revolution, however, only adds importance to the investigation of the complex relationship between the economic and social changes wrought by the war, on the one hand, and the socioeconomic history of the Revolution of 1918–1919, on the other. That is why this account of the origins of the inflation in the First World War will conclude with a discussion of this problem; it forms the basic point of departure for the Weimar inflation.

Two analytical points may be made at the outset. First, it is misleading to think of continuity and revolution as mutually exclusive. The idea that an important function of revolution can be to maintain and legitimize changes that have already taken place is an old one, but it deserves reiteration in this context. Second, there is reason to doubt whether a full-scale revolution in the sense of the "great" revolutions is possible in as advanced an industrial society as the Germany of 1918. One of the reasons for this is the dependence of the population upon the services of highly organized and articulated state agencies that makes running the risk of a total breakdown of the state structure unacceptable to most of civil society. Another, however, is that civil society itself is highly organized and has available efficiently led, self-interested economic and social groups and parties which have the mass bases, skills, and power to assume responsibility and "manage" the revolutionary crisis. The revolutionary wave, therefore, breaks upon dikes which may not always be strong enough to prevent flooding but which put limits upon its impact.

In the view of Germany's propertied classes, the war was a revolutionary experience. This was not because it had brought fundamental changes in the ownership of the forces of industrial and agricultural production. Nothing of that sort happened, and while the war certainly had favored an increase in the holdings and power of certain industrialists and encouraged the entry into industry and commerce of a motley assortment of munitions manufacturers, war profiteers, speculators, and black marketeers, the propertied remained in control of their possessions, and, if anything, the gap increased between those who controlled the forces of production and those who did not. What disturbed those engaged in industry and commerce, no matter how high their profits, was the loss of sole disposition over their property and operation of their enterprises because of increasing state intervention and regulation. This was the common nightmare of farmers and landowners, shopkeepers and merchants, great industrialists and craftsmen. The concrete wartime situation had created a considerable division among the propertied classes, to be sure. Most industrialists producing for the war effort silently favored the controls on agriculture and retailing and rents because they were the only way to maintain social peace and prevent a total loss of control over wages. The moment these groups contemplated the postwar period, however, they demonstrated considerable solidarity. They wished to undo the wartime revolution represented by regulation and control and to return to the world before 1914 by resuming their free individual or collective decision making without state interference.[112]

The irony was that they needed the state to achieve their goal. By 1916, they became aware of two barriers to this simple and straightforward purpose. First, the problems of the demobilization and transition to a peacetime economy (*Übergangswirtschaft*) would be complicated because of the disruptions created by the war both at home and on international markets. Second, and most worrisome, there were influential persons who wanted to maintain state controls through the demobilization and transition and even to make Germany's peacetime economy a "national" planned economy. Germany's industrial and commercial leaders were far more exercised during the war about the planned-economy schemes of Walther Rathenau and Wichard von Moellendorff than

they were about the Marxist visions of the Social Democrats. The problem, therefore, was to find state agencies that would perform the tasks necessary to put the economy on a peacetime footing in a manner that was at once efficient and friendly to the restoration of prewar conditions.

Germany's commercial and industrial leaders had long been unhappy with the services provided—or not provided—by the Reich Office of the Interior. Ostensibly charged with the handling of national economic questions, it was in fact horrendously overburdened even before the war while lacking competence in such crucial sectors as foreign trade, the food supply, and transportation. The goal of the business community, therefore, was to create a Reich Economics Office that would act in consultation and harmony with the interest groups. The problems of demobilization and transition to a peacetime economy at once made this aim more pressing while raising hopes that it could be achieved. It had been strongly resisted by Helfferich, not because he disagreed with the substantive policies of the businessmen, but because he did not want to reduce the powers of his office. As a compromise solution, Helfferich accepted the creation of a Reich Commissariat for the Transitional Economy in August 1916, which was placed under the leadership of Hamburg Senator Friedrich Stahmer. It was to be advised by a group of no less than four hundred representatives of the various economic interests. During the seventeen months of the Commissariat's existence, the Advisory Council never met, which undoubtedly saved the money and time of very busy people, and the Commissariat itself accomplished virtually nothing except to convey a commitment, shared by Stahmer and Helfferich, to the speediest possible restoration of a free economy. They were particularly hostile to any further military interference in the economy. The only significant dissenting voice in the Commissariat was that of Wichard von Moellendorff, who was convinced that the "impoverishment of the people" and the indebtedness of the Reich required something more than an economic restoration.[113]

However gratifying the basic attitudes of Helfferich and Stahmer, the lack of progress in the plans for the transition combined with the con-

tinued dissatisfaction over the absence of a special Reich office to deal with economic affairs in
some coordinated manner led to a new offensive by various segments of the business community in early 1917. These pressures, combined with those from the Reichstag and from
within the government itself, finally produced a
victory for the proponents of the Reich Economic Office, which was formally established
on October 1, 1917, under the leadership of an
ex-Mayor of Strasbourg and student of George
Friedrich Knapp, Rudolf Schwander. The RWA
took over the Reich Commissariat as well as a
host of agencies from the Reich Office of the
Interior and even from the War Office, but food,
foreign trade, and transport remained outside
its jurisdiction. Schwander's efforts to create an
integrated organization and plan for the transition to a peacetime economy did nothing to
improve his already weakened health. He resigned on November 20 and was succeeded by
Hans Karl Freiherr von Stein, a former Undersecretary in the Office of the Interior. Stein took
as his Undersecretary Dr. Heinrich Göppert,
who had formerly served in the Prussian Ministry of Trade and Industry.

Although Stein had flirted with some of
Moellendorff's national economy ideas before
assuming his new post, he entered office a
strong proponent of the rapid restoration of a
free economy and was thus in complete harmony with the economic liberalism of Göppert.
Both men, however, were convinced that the
demobilization and economic transition could
not be conducted without state intervention
and controls, a view in no way shared by Germany's leading commercial circles or by German industry. They wished to make use of the
existing war corporations and other self-governing war committees precisely because they
were convinced that this would confirm the
temporary character of the controls exercised
during the transition. This did not, however, reassure the by then morbidly suspicious German
business community.

There were, to be sure, moments when a realistic appreciation of the situation forced itself
on some of the business leaders. At an RWA
meeting with bankers and exporters in February 1918 to discuss the problem of postwar exchange controls, Göppert found a strong ally in
Reichsbank President Havenstein, who showed

considerable impatience with the notion that
controls on currency, imports, and exports
could be eliminated immediately at the end of
the war. Havenstein gave a bleak report on Germany's financial situation, the external depreciation of the mark, and the extent to which
Germany would need to import capital. He was
unconvinced by the claims of some exporters
and bankers that they could secure the credits
they needed easily if only allowed to go their
own way, and he was even less convinced by
their sanguine expectations of a large loan from
the United States. In Havenstein's view, Germany would need her foreign exchange to import vital necessities and could not simply
abandon exchange controls. He glumly pointed
out that "most of the problems would solve
themselves" if Germany could count on a war
indemnity, but this was not the case. While he
appreciated the international connections of
the exporters and bankers, he reminded them
that no loan would be large enough to cover
Germany's billions in debts and necessary expenditures and that Germany's "capital-rich
enemies" were unlikely to help Germany use a
loan to develop its economy and competitive
strength. Havenstein did share the widely held
expectation that the exchange rate would improve after the war, but he warned that there
would continue to be serious problems because
of Germany's negative balance of payments
and import requirements. To prevent the situation from becoming worse, controls had to be
maintained. Havenstein warned that most Germans did not understand the full significance of
the exchange-rate situation yet because of Germany's wartime isolation from international
markets. They would have to learn to "save and
work doubly hard" after the war.[114]

This was a rather sober and even pessimistic
view for Havenstein to take slightly a month before Ludendorff's anticipated spring offensives.
In a very real sense, the discussion showed that
the future debate over whether and how much
mark depreciation should be accepted as the
price for rejuvenating Germany's international
trade position had already begun. While an in-
corrigible free trader like Alfred O'Swald of the
Association of Hamburg Importers continued
to wonder if it were not best simply to pile up
debts in order to get trade and industry going
again, the more sober private banker Max War-

burg felt that Germany could not destroy all the instruments of control at her disposal in the transition to a peacetime economy. Göppert was grateful for this attitude and emphasized that the RWA did not wish to reach a premature decision nor be open to the standard reproaches that the government had failed to prepare for all eventualities.

It rapidly become clear, however, that distrust of the government and hostility to controls were overriding emotions in the business community. When Stein and Göppert tried to implement their very middle-of-the-road program in 1918 by presenting legislation for the reorganization of the textile industry under state control, they met with ferocious resistance from the industry and had to accept a watered down version of their program in the Reichstag. Their proposal for an Enabling Law on the model of that of August 4, 1914, to permit the Bundesrat to legislate on economic matters during the transition met with so much opposition that it was still tied up in the Reichstag when the Revolution broke out.[115]

The only effective actions taken in connection with the plans for the transition were those taken by the opponents of the RWA efforts, by the various commercial and industrial groups who organized repeated protests and petitions against economic controls in a mounting crescendo that began in the last quarter of 1917. The high point probably was a large meeting at the headquarters of the Hamburg–America Line in Hamburg on June 15–16, 1918, to which a hundred sixty Reichstag Deputies came on the invitation of the Hamburg commercial interests who had organized the event. The tone of the assemblage was set by the Hamburg–America Line's president, Albert Ballin. Ballin attacked the "dangerous intention of driving the national economy and the world economy into the barrack square."[116] Not all businessmen were favorably impressed by the meeting. Carl Duisberg, the great chemical industrialist and certainly no friend of government controls, found the entire tone very unconstructive:

It is not as if I am not as honest a friend of economic freedom as those Hamburg groups. But I failed to find in the Hamburg negotiations clear, positive indications of the way in which the matter is to be handled positively if the plans of the RWA are rejected

wholesale. For that there can be no total freedom immediately after the war is something the Hamburg circles have conceded. But then how is it supposed to be done, at least with those articles which are almost gone or are in only short supply?[117]

Such displays of moderation aside, however, the resistance experienced by the RWA was so great that it found itself in the fall of 1918 with no concept at all for a transitional economy and without even the instruments it required for achieving such purposes as it might define.

While commerce and industry did battle against the RWA's efforts to uphold the powers of the state in the transitional economy, agriculture and the retail trades lived in justified fear of a continuation of the controlled economy. They had every reason to be anxious, for while Stein and Göppert shared a long-term commitment to the restoration of the free-market economy, the man appointed as Undersecretary of the War Food Office in August 1917, August Müller, the first Social Democrat ever to receive such a high government post, could hardly be suspected of great sympathy for either agriculture or the food merchants. As he bluntly stated his position in December 1917:

Many people in Germany believe that the end of the war will also be the end of the price examination and anti-profiteering agencies. A dissemination of this view, not to mention its implementation, would however be fateful for the German people. On the day when peace comes, a ruined national economy will lay before us. The conditions which could develop within the Reich cannot yet be foreseen.... Under all circumstances, everything must be done to bring the prices of articles of daily use into conformity with the purchasing power of the people. It will be the task of the government to undertake a reduction of the price level and an adjustment to the existing levels of income with all its energy. All special interests will have to be set aside. Only the general interest counts. If we do not succeed in this, then there will be internal conflicts with unpredictable consequences. Here ... lies the great important tasks for the price examination agencies in the future.[118]

After much delay, these tasks were finally elaborated upon in July 1918 by Dr. Zahn, an eminent statistician and president of the Bavarian Price Examination Agency and Dr. Thiess of the War Food Office, both of whom advocated the continuation and even strengthening of price controls and regulation during the transition to peacetime conditions with the argument that they were absolutely necessary to prevent excessive profiteering and difficulties for the consumer during the time when other wartime controls and restraints were being eliminated. The decontrol of production and distribution would, in their view, necessarily lead to rising prices which had to be controlled. Indeed, they thought that particular attention would have to be paid to cartel and syndicate prices since the organized power of such bodies placed them in a good position to raise prices unjustifiably as well as prevent their natural decline. The proposals of Zahn and Thiess addressed what was to be a repeated problem in the coming period; namely, how to prevent decontrol measures from leading to unbearable shocks to the consumer or outright exploitation. At the very best, the adjustment of demand and supply on the liberated market would lead to a preliminary period of price increases before the anticipated sufficiency of supply would drive prices down. The object of continued price controls, therefore, was to cushion this process.[119]

These considerations and arguments were rejected, however, by the representatives of the merchant interests in the German Chamber of Commerce and Industry. At a meeting in Berlin on November 6, 1918, one of the syndics, Dr. Diete, attacked the analysis of Thiess and Zahn on the grounds that they failed to recognize that peace would bring changed expectations in the economy. During the war, Diete contended, merchants and consumers constantly anticipated rising prices, but "psychological conditions" would change with the coming of peace and both parties would operate with the expectation of falling prices; for this reason, it was best not to interfere and hamper what would be a natural process. While friendly to the notion of controlling cartels and syndicates, he insisted that this could best be done by creating a cartel office rather than by using the locally based price examination agencies. Diete then presented a resolution, which was passed, stating that industry and commerce would view the elimination of the price examination agencies as a "liberating deed."[120]

There was, however, another aspect to this question of continued price controls which made the entire question of whether prices would rise or fall quite secondary to other considerations; above all, the need to encourage employment through maximum incentive to

business activity. The Berlin industrialist Waldschmidt spelled this out:

... one is thinking now about how unemployment can be avoided after the war and about how good wages can be given through the employment of the workers streaming back from the front. Here one must hope and count on the contracts of wholesalers to the factories for staple goods, for which we know there is a huge market at home and abroad. The wholesalers, however, can only risk giving such contracts in large amounts when they are sure that they will not be prevented by price examination agencies, price ceilings, and other such vexations from demanding those prices which they undoubtedly must have to cover expenses, handling charges, reasonable profit, and especially risk. . . .[121]

Just as the producer had been given price incentives to produce for the war effort, so now merchants and manufacturers had to be similarly encouraged to provide employment. The difference, of course, was that now the market rather than the state was to provide the necessary inducements.

The unfortunate reality, however, was that Germany was not going to enjoy the luxury of a leisurely demobilization and conversion to a peacetime economy under free-market conditions but rather a hasty demobilization that would have to be conducted under the worst imaginable circumstances and a forced transition and economic reconstruction that would be filled with uncertainty and peril. By mid-October 1918, it was quite obvious that the military demobilization plans, which had been carefully designed to gradually bring back the soldiers in an organized manner in accordance with the changing economic priorities of the home front and in such a way as to guarantee domestic security, could be turned over to the archives. They were as obsolete as the wait-and-see attitude the employers had assumed with respect to labor's demands for recognition of the trade unions, continuation of labor's other wartime gains along with the creation of public labor exchanges based on parity between industry and labor, and the full-scale reemployment of the soldiers returning from the front by their prewar employers.[122]

In its efforts to prepare for the transition to a peacetime economy, the RWA had sought to meet some of the worker demands by lifting the restrictions on freedom of coalition and by preparing a Chambers of Labor bill that would provide labor with a formal institution to represent its interests comparable to the Chambers of Industry and Commerce and the Chambers of Agriculture. They also hoped to create an institution in which labor and industry could resolve their differences. As usually the case, the RWA's efforts were attacked by industry, especially some heavy industrialists, which accused it of acting out of "fear of the masses and the gutter."[123] The RWA bill presented to the Reichstag in April 1918 was not very well received by the trade union leaders either, since it failed to provide for chambers on a territorial rather than an industrial branch basis. It also did not meet union demands for worker committees, for compulsory mediation of labor disputes, and for full rights for the state railroad and other public employees. Trade-union leaders not only demanded a bill which fully integrated the advantages of the Auxiliary Service Law into the peacetime economy, but also reiterated the demand, which was the counterpart to that raised by commerce and industry that had led to the creation of the RWA, for the establishment of a Reich Labor Office to deal with labor and social questions.[124]

The stalemate on the latter question was broken in October 1918 when the new Max von Baden government created a Reich Labor Office with the trade unionist Gustav Bauer at its head. This was not the only concession to the Social Democrats made in return for their entry into the Cabinet assigned the task of negotiating an armistice. August Müller was made Undersecretary of the RWA and Robert Schmidt was made Undersecretary in the Reich Food Office. The Social Democrats thus received key positions in the Offices charged with economic and social questions. Indeed, on October 11 it was August Müller who took over the RWA committee charged with the preparation of the economic demobilization.

The RWA had lost none of its unpopularity with the employers, however, and it was soon to find that it had little confidence among the trade unionists either. The unions had never considered Müller one of their own, even if he was a Social Democrat, and they had wanted Robert Schmidt in the RWA. Ironically, however, it was Müller who had been responsible for the initial steps which ultimately brought the direction of the demobilization into hands other than his own. Discussions in the spring of 1917 between Müller and economist Professor Hermann Schumacher, who had close contact with Hugo Stinnes, had brought about a series of secret meetings in August 1917 between the trade-union leaders Gustav Bauer, Theodor Leipart, Alexander Schlicke, and Robert Schmidt, on the one hand, and the heavy industrialists Hugo Stinnes, Alfred Hugenberg, Emil Kirdorf, and Fritz Winkhaus, on the other. The two sides discussed war aims, the economic transition, and future social policy, and, apparently, Stinnes suggested that the trade unionists support industrialist war aims in return for recognition and other possible concessions. While it is quite likely that some of the trade union leaders privately hoped for some annexations, they had no choice but to reject the trade-off Stinnes was suggesting. In December 1917, new meetings were held, this time at Ludendorff's instigation, attended by the head of the Free Trade Unions, Carl Legien; the influential union journalist, Wilhelm Jansson; and Gustav Bauer for the union side, and a more variegated group of industrialists that included Walther Rathenau and Carl Deutsch of the AEG; Carl Friedrich von Siemens; and the business manager of the newly created Central Association of the Electrotechnical Industry, Hans von Raumer, as well as the omnipresent Stinnes. Once again, the meeting had no practical result, but von Raumer, an ambitious, energetic, and skillful negotiator, decided to pick up the initiative in July 1918.[125]

Nevertheless, the first serious negotiations only took place on October 2 when, of course, Germany was in a true crisis. Not only the more pliable Berlin industrialists from the electrotechnical and machine-construction industries associated with von Raumer's initiative but also Stinnes and his colleagues in the Ruhr were beginning to feel that "fear of the masses and the gutter" for which they had once excoriated the RWA and were ready to negotiate with the trade unions as well. On October 9, at a meeting with his colleagues in Düsseldorf, Stinnes was empowered to negotiate with the unions. These businessmen, as the managing director of the Association of German Iron and Steel Industrialists, Jakob Reichert, later reported, were convinced that the Max von Baden government could not last more than four or five weeks—an absolutely correct prediction—and that the industrialists had to turn to the unions in the absence of a reliable government and a mass base they could count upon. While silently turning their back on their erstwhile political alliance with the Junkers, such as it was, they explicitly rejected an effort to rally the *Bürgertum* to their cause since they were convinced that "there was no counting upon the *Bürgertum*, as it is constituted in Germany, in economic matters."[126]

Why were the labor leaders willing to enter into an arrangement with the industrialists? The answer lies in the fact that their fear of chaos and unrest was no less than that of the industrialists. They also shared the anxiety that the demobilization, if left in the hands of the military and civilian authorities who had mismanaged the food supply and so many other aspects of the war economy, would produce unemployment, misery, and Bolshevik conditions in Germany. A working community (*Arbeitsgemeinschaft*) of industry and labor in the demobilization would constitute an alliance of practical men who would have something to offer each other. Industry would provide its alleged economic and technical knowledge and skill; organized labor would provide its alleged control over the masses. In return for freedom to set the economy going again, industry would offer the long-sought recognition of the trade unions, employment for the masses, and social concessions.[127]

Obviously, the government could not be ignored since the provision of jobs required government contracts and government money. As Colonel Wurzbacher, the head of the Weapons and Munitions Procurement Agency, appropriately put the matter on October 15, 1918: "The Task is the adjustment to a peacetime economy, *and we take the view that work must be created for those returning, even if it should cost the Reich millions or billions.*"[128] Continuity of expenditure, however, did not mean continuity of personnel or procedure, and the industrial and labor leaders were very skeptical about Undersecretary Müller's plans to have the demobilization carried out by the regionally based War Office bureaus on the information received from new questionnaires. At a meeting

on October 16, textile industrialist Abraham Frowein bluntly announced that "90 percent of the material gathered by War Office questionnaires is not worth the paper on which it is written."[129] This view was shared by the powerful and influential Ernst von Borsig, the Berlin machine builder. The harmony with labor was well illustrated by the insistence of Socialist trade-union leader Schlicke and his Christian trade-union colleague Johann Giesberts that Müller's Demobilization Commission was too large to accomplish anything. While Müller sought to maintain his leadership role and the RWA's control of the demobilization, his position was sharply criticized by the head of the Raw Materials Section, Lieutenant Colonel Koeth, who roundly declared that "an energetic man must manage the business as his sole area of responsibility and one has to give him a usable instrument with which he can work."[130] This could not be Müller, who had too many responsibilities, nor the RWA Commission; nor could the War Office bureaus be the "bearers" of the demobilization: "The responsible bearers of the demobilization can only be the employers and the unions. They will be in the best position to deal with the workers and lead them, for the workers can only be dealt with by people in whom the workers have confidence."[131]

These remarks were strikingly similar in content to formal proposals made by Rathenau on the previous day to General Scheüch in which the industrialist explicitly recommended Koeth to head the new Demobilization Office. While there was some sentiment in favor of making Stinnes the "dictator" of the demobilization, especially on the part of Director Otto Henrich of the Siemens concern, Stinnes seems to have preferred remaining in the background as the dominant spirit behind the negotiations with labor. He certainly was the person with the clearest vision of what the future would supposedly bring, and it was a remarkably optimistic one for a German in the fall of 1918. He virtually dismissed the economic significance of France's military victory by contending that France would become very dependent on German coal and would be burdened with an excessive amount of ore and excess capacity in iron and steel. She would thus have to come to terms with German industry. Most important from Stinnes's point of view was the elimination of economic controls so that Germany could take advantage of the postwar boom he anticipated. As he pointed out at a meeting on October 26: "I expect a gigantic labor shortage about twelve months after the demobilization which will then last a few years. These two or three years must be used by us in Germany. After that the whole world will start saving. By then we must sit in the saddle abroad once again."[132]

Stinnes was convinced that this expansive policy could only be conducted in collaboration with the unions and was prepared to trade high wages for high prices. Undoubtedly, Stinnes was also too busy with his own enterprises and interests to undertake an administrative position as well as too inexperienced in government affairs. In any case, given Stinnes's goals, Koeth was an ideal candidate. Koeth had opposed Moellendorff throughout the war, arguing that war had to be treated as a constant emergency in which the needs of the hour had to take precedence over all long-term considerations. He was respected for his efficient leadership of the Raw Materials Section, and he seems to have known how to ingratiate himself with industry and labor. As Borsig cynically put the matter: "In labor questions he is more in the Social Democratic camp, while in economic questions he stands completely on the side of the employers."[133] The inflationary trade-offs could now be continued with the blessing of the government and the formal collaboration of industry and labor. It had been an expensive war. It was going to be an expensive demobilization.

The negotiations between the industrialists and the trade-union leaders in Berlin and in the Ruhr, therefore, really dealt with two sets of problems. The first was the future regulation of the relationship between industry and labor, and here a number of outstanding issues remained prior to the outbreak of the Revolution, especially in the Ruhr. While the employers were prepared to recognize the unions, create labor exchanges and mediation and arbitration boards based on parity, and pledge the reemployment of the returning soldiers, they resisted trade-union demands for total renunciation of support for the yellow unions, compulsory collective-bargaining agreements in all industries,

and the uniform introduction of the eight-hour day. On November 5, the first of these issues was settled with a compromise under which the employers agreed to end their financial support for the yellow unions if the other unions agreed to recognize those nonstriking unions still surviving after six months of financial starvation. This was to prove a great trade-union victory since it was most unlikely that the yellow unions could survive on their own, while the militant unions could now penetrate the large heavy-industrial and other plants where they had been weak.[134]

The other points of contention remained unsettled. If negotiations did not break down, however, it was because the second set of problems, those pertaining to the demobilization, became more pressing during the last week of October with the dismissal of Ludendorff, the growing demands for the Kaiser's abdication, and the unexpected harshness of the Allied demands with respect to an armistice. Initially, some of the employers seemed to have felt that the war might be continued, but this no longer was a reality by the end of October. Anxiety about the demobilization, therefore, bridged the differences between the two sides and led to the formation of an *Arbeitsgemeinschaft*. It was to determine the basic policies of the demobilization, push the government to give contracts, and promote the creation of employment opportunities. They also agreed to cooperate more effectively in supplying the workers with black-market food and to secure better coordination among the firms engaged in this activity. They were intent, as Stinnes declared, to get "rid of Berlin's tutelage relentlessly and forcefully."[135]

Between October 30 and November 5, von Raumer, Henrich, and Legien drafted a management-labor demarché declaring their willingness to "work together in unity concerning all questions pertaining to the demobilization and transition from a wartime to a peacetime economy" and calling for the creation of a Demobilization Office with "extensive executive powers" to be headed by a State Secretary and to be advised by a body composed of an equal number of trade-union and employer representatives.[136] Its purpose would be to supply work and support to the returning troops and oversee the reorganization of the economy. This demand was presented to Vice Chancellor Payer in the name "of the only power that still exists in Germany, the united employers and workers of Germany."[137] This presentation, not exactly flattering to the government, was followed by unabashed blackmail the moment Max von Baden and his colleagues showed some resistance in discussions with Stinnes, Legien, Rathenau, and Christian union leader Adam Stegerwald. The industrial and trade-union leaders threatened to withdraw their cooperation in the demobilization unless their demands were met. On November 7, the Demobilization Office was established with Koeth as State Secretary; the Bundesrat approved the new agency and granted it all the powers demanded by the proponents of the measure.

The dominant forces in the war economy had thus joined together to organize the economic demobilization and the transition to peace at the expense of a state whose authority had been completely undermined by its efforts to manage the war economy. What remained an open question was the exact balance of these forces, the representative character of those who claimed to speak for them, and the political legitimation of their actions. For there could be no doubt about the fact that on the eve of the Revolution, key issues of the constitution of German industrial relations still remained undecided; specifically, the extent to which collective bargaining would become universal and the problem of the eight-hour day. Also, the *Arbeitsgemeinschaft* was being created by a relatively small group of industrialists and trade-union leaders acting in an emergency but without a real mandate from their constituencies. Finally, their actions had been made possible by a political power vacuum, the duration of which would be limited.

Nevertheless, the socioeconomic path into the future was already being cut in October–November 1918 by the unanticipated collapse of Germany's war effort and the fear of a total socio-economic disintegration. That it was a path already set in significant respects by the war economy itself is not surprising. This was not the time to think of Germany's floating debt or the value of Germany's currency when making decisions. Concerning the latter, there was actually a good deal of optimism in Octo-

ber 1918, for while the position of the Entente currencies improved because of the military situation, the external value of the mark also improved in October with the prospect of peace. The industrialists, therefore, asked for an easing of the regulations requiring them to take payment in foreign currency for their exports, and their request was granted by Havenstein. On November 8, the day before the Revolution broke out, Stinnes and the general director of his Deutsch-Luxemburg concern, Albert Vögler, were pleading for the elimination of export restrictions and price ceilings on raw materials and were only denied complete success by the resistance of some of the manufacturing interests, who were worried that the iron and steel they needed might be exported at their expense but who themselves accepted in principle the idea that the elimination of price ceilings and of export controls should go hand in hand. The business demand for economic decontrol was on the march.[138]

Whether these gentlemen anticipated falling prices is doubtful, but the Socialist leaders certainly did not, and they, too, were putting in their claims for the workers. Thus, Socialist Deputy Hermann Molkenbuhr in an article, "Money without Value," openly predicted that the monetary depreciation would not disappear after the war and declared that "wages must be raised at least to the level that will permit the same standard of living as before the war." If the purchasing power of the mark had depreciated four to five times, then wages must be increased by that amount "even if there is the danger that goods will further increase in price." While Molkenbuhr did not address himself to the logical question of the value of wage increases if prices immediately increased as well, he was insistent that "the adjustment of wages to the purchasing power of money" was necessary for two reasons. First, it was the only means of restoring the productivity of labor to its previous levels. Second, the economy would require the consuming power of the labor force if industry were to find a market for its products and unemployment were to be avoided. Molkenbuhr's willingness to run inflationary risks and his emphasis on this adjustment's relationship to the restoration of labor productivity and to solving the unemployment problem are indicative of the priorities with which the labor leaders contemplated the future reconstruction.[139]

It was, in any case, certainly more realistic than the widely held position among economists during the war that Germany should have as her priority the reduction of prices and wages and the restoration of the gold standard and prewar parities. A much more sophisticated and prophetic rejection of this classical position was provided by Friedrich Bendixen in an article of October 1918. With his usual relentless honesty, the same honesty that had led him to unveil the realities behind the wartime monetary arrangements, Bendixen questioned whether a real basis for the old parities continued to exist given the changed economic conditions and relationships arising from the war. His answer was negative. Just as he had criticized the fetish of the one-third coverage requirements of the Reichsbank, so now he warned that an arbitrary clinging to prewar parities that neglected the "natural relationship in the commercial relations" and economic condition of nations which formed the ultimate basis of exchange rates could only lead to distortions. New, natural parities would have to be found, and this could only be done gradually as reconstruction proceeded at home and abroad.

What worried him most, however, was the belief that the forcible reduction of wages and prices would benefit Germany's export industries and improve her balance of payments and thereby make possible a restoration of old parities. He pointed out that a low exchange rate for the mark would provide an export advantage despite high wages, while a high exchange rate would damage exports even if wages were modest. He went on:

It is completely mistaken to see in the absolute value of the exchange rate a significant benefit for the national welfare and honor that is worth any kind of economic sacrifice. And it would be truly fateful to convulse the domestic market through a depression of prices and wages for the sake of this phantom. No statesman would take responsibility for what is from the social perspective so hateful a measure as the exercise of pressure on wages. But also a forceful reduction of prices would be anything but good policy. In all the measures that he takes, the statesman should think first about the effect on national production. . . . Just as inflation, that is, the excessive creation of money, creates a consumption crisis through the raising of food prices, so the "contraction" causes a production crisis. Reduction in the value of goods, unemployment, and credit crises would be the significance of such a fateful policy. Nothing is more bitterly necessary for Germany after the war than the mobilization of all economic forces for maximum production.[140]

Whether this was a clarion call to a new age of monetary Machiavellianism or a dire warning against living in accordance with obsolete doctrines remained to be seen. Whatever the case, Bendixen was not to stand alone in arguing that the primacy of production and the prevention of crisis made a policy of deflation, of contraction, the epitome of "foolishness." The path from Germany's inflationary war economy to her inflationary reconstruction could not have been more accurately or persuasively charted.

PART II

MANAGING THE CRISES:
FROM THE NOVEMBER REVOLUTION
TO THE KAPP PUTSCH

*Das Paradox, daß eine republikanische-
sozialdemokratische Regierung sich und die
kapitalistischen Geldschränke durch bezahlte
Arbeitslose und royalistische Offiziere verteidigen
lasse, sei zu verrückt.*

*The paradox that a republican-Social-Democratic
government allows itself and the strong boxes of the
capitalists to be defended by paid unemployed and
royalist officers is just too crazy for words.*

Harry Graf Kessler, *Tagebücher, 1918
bis 1937*

Chapter 3

The Economics of Revolution and Revolutionary Economics

Revolution and Demobilization: November 1918–May 1919

At the beginning of February 1919, three British officers boarded the "Armistice Express" in Cologne and traveled to Berlin under instructions to report back on conditions in the German capital and on the German food supply. Originally from London and having just gone through war-ravaged Belgium, they were impressed by the absence of any sign of deforestation in Germany; the extent to which the land was cultivated; and the substantial number of trucks, rolling stock, and locomotives standing idle along with huge piles of timber at the major railroad stations. Upon arriving at the noisy and crowded Potsdamer Station, where no one came to meet them, they encountered armed "Red Guards" who shouted that all baggage had to be examined but to whom neither the officers nor any of the other passengers leaving the station paid the slightest attention. They checked in at Berlin's famous Adlon Hotel, where they found "no sign of want of anything." The hotel was well heated and the dinner in the restaurant—mock turtle soup, boiled turbot and potatoes, a large plate of veal with vegetables and salad, stewed apples and "mokka" coffee at a price of eighteen marks—they rated as "good." The only unpleasantness was the theft of cigars and cigarettes from the suitcase of one of the officers while he was out of his room. Thus began their stay in Berlin, which lasted from February 2 to February 11, 1919, and which provided an impressionistic—perhaps it would be more accurate to say expressionistic—but revealing picture of Berlin

three months after the Revolution and on the very eve of the meeting of the National Assembly in Weimar.[1]

Lunch at the Adlon was less satisfactory than dinner, the roast beef being "very poor" and the pastry of the fruit tart "very dark and tough," but it became apparent, as they sampled a variety of Berlin's restaurants, that one could get plenty to eat if one dined out regularly and that the restaurants were crowded despite the high prices. To be sure, ration cards for meat and bread were required, but restaurant owners openly admitted that their food was procured on the black market—evidence that the black market was "rampant"—and it was possible to get meat, at very high prices, even in lower-middle-class restaurants on supposedly meatless days. Café fare was less satisfactory, the *Ersatz* coffee having "the color of coffee but no smell or taste whatever," but tea time at the Adlon did provide the sight of a "stout woman feeding her fat dog with bits of fancy biscuits," while a dinner put on for the officers by the local charity organizations "would have done justice to the Ritz in London."

Nevertheless, that dog was a very fortunate animal indeed, at least for the moment, since it apparently was one of the few left in Berlin. When the officers remarked on the absence of dogs and cats in the city, they were informed by the host assigned to them by the German Foreign Office, Major von Schweinitz, that "they have all been eaten and their skins used for leather." Clearly, this information was not intended to assure the officers that the food situation had thereby been solved. Schweinitz; Dr. Reinhold Schairer, the head of the Berlin Charity Organization Committee; Dr. Mertz, the "apparently able little Jew" from the Reich Food Office; Dr. Karl Melchior of the Warburg Bank—also a Jew, but apparently not the kind British officers immediately stereotyped as such—and the other local and ministerial officials and health experts who were interviewed all sought to impress upon the officers that, as Schairer put the matter, "conditions among the poor and the lower-middle class are almost desperate, and the only way to stop the spread of Bolshevism is to send prompt relief in the form of food."

The officers were indeed impressed with evidence of underfeeding, especially at an orphanage and other institutions where the food rations were enforced. They also noted that there was virtually nothing on sale at the main Berlin market but cabbages and turnips and that the vegetable soup prepared in the adjacent central soup kitchen for Berlin (which itself serviced hundreds of persons and was only one of the various soup kitchens throughout the city) was "not unpleasant to taste . . . but contained practically no fat." The president of the Board of Health, Dr. Bumm, and his colleagues presented a particularly gloomy picture of the effects of the food shortage, emphasizing especially the loss of resistance to infection and the increasing number of deaths of women during childbirth. Melchior had also stressed the soap and clothing shortage, the former being responsible for an increase in disease and the latter making work in winter weather extremely difficult. Melchior was particularly concerned with the problems of importing food. He seemed to place his main hope in the procurement of loans from the United States, but pointed out that the difficulties were such that "Germany is probably willing to go to any lengths in order to prove her good faith to the Allies, if she can obtain supplies."

Of this, the British officers were not entirely certain. While impressed by the pedigree and bearing of Major von Schweinitz, whose home on the Wilhelmstraße they visited, they were not entirely convinced by Frau von Schweinitz's claims that her older children never received milk, that the household existed only on rations, and that they had fish only three times

in the past year because all the fish was bought up by hotels and restaurants. They treated this information as "hearsay," pointing out that "there was no evidence, whatsoever, of scarcity or want in the outward impressions we got." At the same time, they were absolutely irritated by the responses of the military representative of the Reich Food Office, Major Keim, a "typical Prussian of the unpleasant type," and the War Ministry officials who contemptuously dismissed questions about the food stores in the hands of the military and resisted inquiries about the number of men still on military rations with the argument that the army was in a state of dissolution anyway and that the food supplies in military hands were negligible.

The greatest puzzle, however, was the quantity of food on the black market and the inability of the authorities to bring that market under control. In a conversation with two persons at their table in a restaurant, they learned that "people with money can obtain as much food as they want, provided extravagant prices are paid, and one of them admitted to having plenty of butter at home." The issue was of no small importance since, as the officers pointed out in a meeting with a committee of the Berlin Charity Organization Society, Allied willingness to relax the blockade depended upon the ability of those favoring such a policy to convince public opinion in the Allied countries that the need in Germany was as great as was claimed. The matter was discussed at great length, "but the main point of the German reply was to the effect that supplies obtained by this means were only a drop in the bucket, and mainly represented supplies which would otherwise have been retained for the producers' own consumption and would, therefore, never have otherwise become available for general consumption. Also, to completely stamp out this illicit trade would require a police force equal in number to two army corps, an impossibility under existing conditions, where the police are in a state of flux owing to Eichhorn, the late chief of the police force, having declared himself a Spartacist."

In fact, the absence of police was noted by the British officers, who thought it a good thing under the circumstances that the street traffic in

Berlin was far lighter than in Paris and London. The forces of law and order, which were largely military in character, were devoting their attention to the danger of riots, and machine guns were being mounted at various points in anticipation of difficulties when the National Assembly would begin its meetings at Weimar. Such ominous preparations notwithstanding, there was also much evidence of sheer indifference and pleasure seeking, which was reflected not only by the "ladies of the easy virtue brigade" who seemed "particularly anxious to forget hostilities" and solicited the officers in English along the Friedrichstraße, but also by the signs of a "mania for dancing" and numerous advertisements for balls. Thus, while street fighting was going on in a worker quarter of Berlin in which five persons were killed and fifty wounded, the "general public seem . . . quite content to enjoy themselves on the edge of a precipice." This, at least, was the impression of the officers as they sat in a cabaret on the same day, watching a "huge crowd of middle class men and women, the majority between the ages of 35 and 50 . . . waltzing and fox-trotting and drinking extremely expensive wines." The officers' evening ended with them passing a large crowd on the Friedrichstraße listening to a speaker. When they heard the words, "we must have fats," the officers decided to hasten to their hotel since it was not "a healthy topic for us to stop and listen to."

The officers not only were presented with demonstrations of middle-class demoralization but also saw and heard much evidence of working-class demoralization. The snow on the streets, for example, had not been cleared away, although Berlin had over two hundred thousand unemployed and those assigned to clean the streets earned between nineteen and twenty-two marks a day. Major von Schweinitz blamed the situation on the food shortage and

. . . has a theory that the masses have actually been mentally affected through insufficient nourishment. No one will do any work, the railways are in complete disorder and in bad condition, and regular running is upset by the various Government parties commandeering trains on short notice. The munitions works are idle. The position of many employers is rendered almost impossible by the men demanding a whole month's pay at Christmas and a month's holiday *per*

annum on full pay, i.e., the employer has to pay 13 months' wages for eleven month's work. Wages are very high, and while the hands cannot be compelled to work, they many not be dismissed. . . .

All the blame for the production difficulties was not placed on the workers, however. Dr. Ramm of the Agricultural Ministry admitted that the shortage of fertilizers was due to the military absorption of Germany's nitrate production, while the coal shortage was responsible for the post-Armistice idleness of the plants. A businessman placed particular emphasis on the shortage of such raw materials as tin, copper, and lead and seemed particularly anxious about Britain's willingness to reopen trade relations with Germany, a willingness simply assumed with respect to the United States and evidenced by a large notice at the Hotel Adlon bar that the American Chamber of Commerce in Berlin was functioning again.

Despite such interest in resumption of trade, however, the German authorities, to the constant irritation of the British officers, persistently emphasized the deleterious effects of the Armistice terms imposed upon Germany. They pointed out that Allied refusal to accept many of the trucks and locomotives surrendered under the Armistice was keeping the repair shops busy working for the Allies instead of for Germany's own requirements, and they seemed particularly outraged that Germany was being compelled to restore machinery taken from Belgium and France. The British officers' attempt to explain that Allied public opinion was somewhat different triggered an interesting reaction: "This led to several Germans talking together and starting a political argument among themselves, which ended in them all declaring themselves Monarchists at heart. One of them remarked that, speaking for himself, he often found it extremely painful to have to wait upon Ebert and Scheidemann, to which there was a chorus of approving grunts." Indeed, in their report, the officers frequently noted the continued presence of pictures of the Kaiser and battle scenes in the various offices and institutions they visited, and their conversation with a former Guard Regiment officer, who had been wounded many times and who had just enrolled in a free-corps unit, must have been particularly chilling: "He did not appear to have the slightest hostility, but remarked that of course Germany would have to have another war as soon as possible, probably within 20 years, as the present situation was unbearable."

What exactly was unbearable? Peace? Defeat? Allied demands? The "tragic" fact that beer "which formerly could be bought whole-sale for less than ld. a bottle, now cost 6d?" Which of the impressions gained by the British officers was correct? The impression on February 3?:

All the shops seemed well-stocked and the prices for articles such as cameras and field glasses were consid-erably lower than in England. Wertheim's (a large store of the Selfridge type) windows made a very good show; prices, however, ran high for most articles. The people in the streets seemed well-clothed and looked well-nourished. . . .

Or the impression on February 9?:

In the afternoon we went for an hour's drive. . . . The old orderliness in the streets is noticeably absent. . . . The horses one sees appear to be either in very good or in very poor condition. Those in good condition are said to be ex-army horses, and the poor ones have been working in Germany. There seemed to have been a distinct increase in horsed vehicles on the streets during the week. We have not seen or heard a single cat, or seen more than a dozen dogs during the past week. The untidy effects of the streets is no doubt increased by the motley array of untidy uniforms and semi-military attire of a large percentage of the men. Civilian trousers and a military cap and tunic, or mufti, under a military greatcoat and a bowler hat, are common. Berlin's bedraggled appearance seemed to strike us more strongly after we had been there a few days than at first sight.

One thing was certain; namely, that the help at the Hotel Adlon was grateful to receive the re-maining rations of the British officers as tips, "and these were evidently much more accept-able than money would have been."

This, however, was only of limited signifi-cance, since the question of how much the monetary depreciation was already provoking a "flight into goods" could no more be deter-mined from the preferences of the help at the Adlon in February 1919 than the experience of dining in Berlin's hotels and restaurants could be taken as ample proof that Berlin's cats and dogs—and Germany's mothers—were being needlessly sacrificed. The pleas for food and the machine guns in the streets did not demon-

strate that the Bolshevik threat was real, while the combination of malaise and pleasure seek-ing did not rule out the potential for seething re-sentment and mass mobilization. The tired as-surances given by Major von Schweinitz and his friends that the monarchy, the General Staff, and the old order were finished, however much to their personal regret, were no more to be taken at face value than the vicious certainty of the nasty young free-corps officer who calmly foretold a future that appeared quite unbeliev-able for the Germany of February 1919. The fu-ture to most contemporaries could only have seemed very uncertain indeed, and the concen-tration upon immediate necessities easily went hand in hand with a variety of contradictory and confusing sentiments.

The Germans had not made it easy for those British officers to assess Germany's political and economic condition. The sheer oblivious-ness of Germany's new rulers to symbols, for example, not only made it possible for the Kai-ser's visage and military exploits to continue to grace Berlin's official walls, but also created an environment in which monarchist sentiments could be openly expressed rather than furtively whispered. The peculiar combination of whin-ing and patriotic pathos which the British offi-cers encountered during their visit was not atypical of the unskillful manner in which the Germans had been presenting their economic needs and potentialities to the Allies. In fact, it was precisely the Germans' puzzling and con-tradictory behavior that had led to the British officers' mission. In the armistice negotiations with the Allies, the Germans had blended an undignified and tactless playing up to Wilson and Wilsonianism, declarations that "[A] peo-ple of seventy million suffers, but does not die," and claims that Germany's wheat supply would last only four to six weeks. While the posturing was more or less irritating, the contentions con-cerning the wheat supply particularly tested Al-lied credulity given the recency of the harvest. Why the Germans could not simply have de-clared the truth—that the supplies were holding at the moment but that they feared a major cri-sis in the spring—is difficult to understand.[2]

The Germans were not simply being disin-genuous, however, and their efforts to explain the situation were a consequence of its complexity and intransparency. Had the Germans been visibly starving either during or at the end of the war, judgment would have been simple and arguments clear and to the point. Potentially fatal malnutrition was not visible. Almost half the patients in Germany's mental institutions had died from hunger and illness during the war, and the condition of those in prisons and of others institutionally compelled to survive on the official rations was horrendous. This *de facto* policy of *triage* and an efflorescence of anxiety over the size and quality of the German population during the war were to inspire postwar medical arguments for euthanasia and its practice a little over a decade later.[3] What was visible in 1919, however, was a population dependent upon the black market and a variety of other makeshift solutions for its basic necessities. It had long ceased to have any advantage from its initial adaptation through weight loss to reduced supplies and a leaner diet and was now sullen, discontented, and demoralized by a deprivation that had lost all rationale. In this context, Allied continuation of the blockade and procrastination in the fulfillment of the obligation to supply the Germans with food in return for the surrender of the merchant fleet under the Armistice conditions appeared barbarous indeed. The French initially refused to let the Germans use some of their gold as security in paying for American food imports, while the Americans, however anxious to get rid of their food surpluses, found it impossible for domestic political reasons to lend the Germans money. It was not until early March that the French yielded to the pressure of England and the United States and agreed to let the Germans pay some twenty million marks' worth of gold, primarily to the United States but also to England and Australia, for food. When the imports finally came, they were too little and too late to avoid appearing as a formidable posting on the ledger of German bitterness and resentment.[4]

The conundrum of Germany's food situation was only part of the giant puzzle of trying to determine the actual state of German agriculture, industry, and finance which was to plague the peace settlement from beginning to end. In the German defense, it must be said that striking a proper balance was anything but easy,

as Socialist Finance Minister Albert Südekum pointed out in January 1919: "[I]f we paint things too darkly, then we drive away our own public and lessen the chances for a consolidation of the floating debt; if we do not paint things darkly enough, then we excite the appetite of the Entente."[5] In the end, the dilemmas facing the British officers in assessing Germany's situation have become the problems of historians and the subjects of their debates. The answers to the questions of whether the German Revolution might have been more complete and successful than it was and what burdens should and could reasonably have been imposed upon Germany depend upon such assessments.

Yet, as always, the consideration of alternatives can only clarify the force and power of realities. The actuality was that the basic decisions had been taken and the fundamental lines of development had been determined by the management of the revolutionary crisis between early November 1918 and the end of January 1919. The path into the future would narrow rather than widen by the end of the year, which is not to say that men did not have reason to hope that a better fate was attainable. Exactly what constituted a "better fate" also was a matter of controversy. The essential characteristic of crisis management, however, is the prevention of the worst rather than the attainment of the best, and the Majority Socialists who assumed power in Germany in November 1918 were convinced that the former rather than the latter had to be their goal.[6]

They were thus driven into a series of alliances with the forces of the old order. It must be recognized, however, that there was nothing intrinsically sinister about tactical arrangements with the old order to deal with pressing emergencies facing the SPD–USPD Council of People's Commissars which governed Germany almost immediately after the proclamation of the Republic on November 9, 1918, under the *de facto* leadership of Friedrich Ebert. The demobilization of six million men within an unanticipatedly short period of three weeks required collaboration between the General Staff and the new government. The so-called Ebert–Groener pact of November 9–10, 1918, in which Ebert promised to support the maintenance of military discipline while Groener agreed to manage the military demobilization and maintain law and order, in no way committed the new regime to a permanent alliance with the old military establishment. Similarly, the utilization by the new regime of bureaucratic experts as state secretaries and the dependence upon the old civil service for the management of the technical functions of governance did not have to fix future lines of policy. Working arrangements with the agrarian leaders to maintain the food supply did not preclude a future land settlement program, and temporary cooperation with the industrialists was no permanent barrier to socialization measures.

It also cannot be argued that the SPD's freedom of action was inhibited by the radicalism of the soldiers and workers councils. There can be no question that the Majority Socialists controlled the vast majority of the soldiers and workers councils which had sprung up throughout the country, as well as the Congress of Soldiers and Workers Councils which met in Berlin on December 16–20, and the Central Council of the Soldiers and Workers Councils which represented the councils thereafter.[7] The councils movement, at this stage, formed a type of social mobilization in the emergency, and while examples of excessive expenditure and interference with food and transport by the councils certainly can be found, there is a great deal more evidence of responsible management of food and other problem areas and, given the circumstances, of political moderation on the local level.[8] Insofar as the movement was inspired by any program or idea, it was a vague expectation of more thoroughgoing democratization and of the socialization of key industries. It is conceivable, therefore, that the Majority Socialists might have continued their collaboration with the USPD through an effort to maintain contact with the councils for the purpose of internal reform of a more vigorous kind than that which was actually pursued. Instead, the Majority Socialists pressed forward the call for speedy elections to a National Assembly, urged the quickest possible abolition of the councils, pursued an extremely dilatory tactic with respect to the socialization of key industries, and permitted their arrangements with the forces of the old order to take on the

character of firm alliances aimed against the demands of the left.

From the political standpoint, the most fateful decisions probably fell in the realm of military policy where the dissolution of the old army gave way not to a systematic effort to create a republican army but rather to the creation of free corps composed of the worst elements of the old army as well as young men thirsting for action denied them by the end of the war. The justification for this policy was the alleged Spartacist danger, which unquestionably was greatly exaggerated since the Spartacist leaders, Rosa Luxemburg and Karl Liebknecht, were fresh out of jail and the Spartacists themselves had little support in the working class. They were easily if brutally suppressed in their foolishly conceived and executed Berlin uprising in mid-January 1919. The major accomplishment of the military policy of the Majority Socialists was to force the departure of the Independent Socialists from the Council of People's Commissars at the end of December, thus reviving the wartime split in the ranks of German socialism and paving the way for a renewal and exacerbation of the tension between the SPD leadership and a substantial portion of its mass base or potential mass base. The violent turn taken by the mass movement in March–April 1919 and the development of an ideology with claims to political and economic co-determination rights through the councils were the outcome of mass disappointment in the failures of the Majority Socialists to live up to the reformist expectations of the Socialist workers at the outset of the Revolution.[9]

The timidity of the Majority Socialists had two sources. The first was a commitment to democratic legitimacy, which in practical terms meant an unwillingness to preempt the decisions of a democratically elected National Assembly or even to rule for any length of time without summoning such a body. Where the Independent Socialists wished to delay elections until they could undertake a thoroughgoing democratization of German polity and economy in collaboration with the councils, the SPD leadership, very much in harmony with the bourgeois party leaders as well as the other forces of the old order with which they were allied, pushed for early elections, which were held on January 19, and for the rapid meeting of the National Assembly, which took place on February 7. It is difficult not to conclude, however, that what underlay this urgency was a fear and unwillingness to exercise power alone for any length of time as well as a deep suspicion if not actual hatred for the mass movement represented by the councils. These tendencies arose out of the party's long history of legal opposition as well as the ambivalence built into a party that had for years combined revolutionary pretensions with reformist practice only to have power thrust upon it under the most miserable of circumstances. Its firm belief in the ultimate triumph of socialism only served to reinforce the dogma that this triumph could only take place when conditions were "ripe" and to neglect the importance of exercising political power effectively.[10]

The undeniable rottenness of economic conditions was the second major check on the Socialist will to power and clearly the most justified one. Revolutions, of course, do not usually take place under ideal circumstances, but one can hardly dismiss the international historical context in which the German Revolution took place. The Majority Socialists and a large portion of the German population were convinced that the alternative to the policy being pursued was the one employed in Bolshevik Russia. This policy was unattractive then, and the results make it even less appealing with hindsight. The Majority Socialists can hardly be faulted for wanting to avoid internal chaos and misery, thus making it possible for the Allies to invade Germany and destroy her unity. It would have required leadership of extraordinary vision, tenacity, political skill, and charisma to have steered the German Revolution along more truly fruitful paths leading toward the effective smashing of the right, controlling the left, reeducating the bourgeoisie, feeding and employing the people, and holding the Allies at bay while achieving all this. Germany lacked such leadership, a failing that was regrettable but in no way unique. Unhappily, however, she lacked even the more modest political talents that might have given the future German democracy firmer foundations and greater security.

All such criticisms notwithstanding, it is important not to underestimate the risks and difficulties faced by the SPD leaders and their bourgeois allies and to neglect their genuine accomplishments. Ebert was no Kerensky, and while it was unfortunate that he did not compel the military to take responsibility for the Armistice of November 11, 1918, and extremely regrettable that he chose to greet the returning troops as "unconquered in the field," he and most of his colleagues recognized that Germany had to make peace at any price. The Armistice terms signed by the Centrist politician, Matthias Erzberger, who was to fall victim to assassins in August 1921 as a reward for this and other acts of political courage, were extremely harsh. Germany was forced not only to withdraw its army behind its own borders, but also to evacuate Alsace-Lorraine and the entire left bank of the Rhine and to pull back thirty kilometers behind the right bank. The Allied occupation of the left bank, the costs of which Germany was required to cover, placed Germany at the mercy of the Allied forces. Additionally, Germany was required to surrender huge amounts of military matériel, most of the high-seas fleet, all its submarines, five thousand trucks, five thousand locomotives, and a hundred fifty thousand railroad cars. The last three items had to be in a condition to meet Allied standards, and the failure of many of them to pass strict inspection did, in fact, overburden German repair facilities. While Germany was required to renounce the Treaties of Bucharest and Brest-Litovsk and thus all of their material advantages from the standpoint of food and raw materials, the Allied blockade was to continue with food being supplied only in return for gold or hard currency. Havenstein raised strong objections to the use of Reichsbank gold as security for the loans taken in neutral countries to pay for food imports. In contrast to the ill-fated Kerensky government in Russia, therefore, the governments led by Majority Socialists Ebert (November 9, 1918–February 12, 1919), Scheidemann (February 13–June 20, 1919), and Gustav Bauer (June 21, 1919–March 27, 1920) were willing to provide their people with peace and bread at almost any price.[11]

They were also willing to provide work at any price along with a host of other social and eco-

The Cabinet of Philipp Scheidemann, February 13–May 12, 1919, at its first meeting in the Castle of Weimar. The numbers identify: 1. Robert Schmidt (SPD), Food Minister and later Economics Minister in the Bauer and Wirth Cabinets; 2. Eugen Schiffer (DDP), Vice Chancellor and Finance Minister; 3. Philipp Scheidemann (SPD), Chancellor; 4. Otto Landsberg (SPD), Justice Minister; 5. Rudolf Wissell (SPD), Economics Minister; Gustav Bauer (SPD), Labor Minister and Scheidemann's successor as Chancellor; 7. Ulrich Graf von Brockdorff-Rantzau (no party), Foreign Minister; 8. Eduard David (SPD), Minister without Portfolio; 9. Hugo Preuss (DDP), Interior Minister; 10. Johann Giesberts (Center), Postal Minister; 11. Johannes Bell (Center), Colonial Minister; 12. Georg Gothein (DDP), Treasury Minister; 13. Gustav Noske (SPD), Defense Minister. (*By permission of the Ullstein Verlag*)

nomic concessions to the working masses, and this, to a very high degree, in collaboration with the employers. The Revolution not only brought about a very major change in Germany's political system but also led to a major transformation of social and economic relations that was to give the Weimar Republic the most advanced, albeit no longer the most generous, system of industrial relations and social welfare in the world. Whatever their prewar and especially their wartime origins, the highly articulated industrial and social systems of the Weimar Republic were the chief and most lasting product of the Revolution with which it began. Weimar's pioneering experiments were at once its glory—because they pointed the way to the modernization of industrial relations and social welfare—and its tragedy—because they were born of revolutionary crisis management and inflation and became fatal sources of political conflict. They foundered on what have become classic problems of advanced industrial societies everywhere. One of these problems is

the creation of an integrated financial, economic, and social policy. Another is the resolution of the conflict between representation and leadership, a conflict which affects both institutions of intermediation, such as parliaments and interest groups, and executive organs in advanced industrial societies; this conflict is fundamental to the socioeconomic as well as the political history of the German Revolution.[12]

The trade-union and industrialist leaders who had been working toward an agreement before the Revolution, for example, did so under the assumption that they had the right and duty to lead their respective constituencies and to make agreements in their name. They did not allow the events of November 9, 1918, to disrupt their labors, which is not to say that they were oblivious to the significance of the Revolution for their decisions. The employers felt compelled to abandon their resistance to the universal introduction of collective-bargaining agreements and the eight-hour day, since it was obvious that the unions could not defend their agreement with the employers unless these concessions were voluntarily made now that the revolutionary government was likely to introduce them anyway. Interestingly enough, however, the employer surrender was not completely unqualified. Thus, the collective-bargaining agreements were to be introduced "in accordance with the conditions of the affected industry," while a secret protocol was drawn up making the final acceptance of the eight-hour day contingent upon its introduction in other civilized nations," and upon the government asking to have the issue regulated in the peace treaty.[13]

By November 15, 1918, therefore, the various organizations of industry and labor were able to sign what was to become known as the Stinnes–Legien Agreement. Not only did this agreement provide for the recognition of the unions, mandatory collective bargaining and wage contracts, worker committees in every plant with over fifty employees, the termination of employer support for yellow unions, and the introduction of the eight-hour day without any reduction in pay, but it also provided important arrangements for collaboration in the demobilization and even beyond. Thus, the employers pledged themselves to reemploy every returning soldier in his place of prewar employment, while the two sides agreed to collaborate in securing raw materials and contracts to make this employment policy possible. Most important, §10 and §11 of the agreement provided for the creation of a "working community" (*Arbeitsgemeinschaft*) to implement the agreement during the demobilization and in the future: "To carry out this agreement as well as to regulate further measures needed for the demobilization, the maintenance of economic life and the securing of the possibilities of existence for the workers, especially the war-disabled, the participating employer and worker organizations will establish a central committee based on parity with a sub-structure organized by branches."[14] The Central Committee's decisions were to have binding force unless objections were raised within a week. This laid the foundation for the so-called Central Working Community (*Zentralarbeitsgemeinschaft*, or ZAG), and Legien and von Raumer were as-

signed the task of providing for a temporary constitution. The latter was completed by December 4 and provided not only for the thoroughgoing organization of industry into working communities along branch lines, but also, in its opening paragraph, for the ZAG and its subgroups to discuss all economic and social questions affecting German industry or their particular industries.[15]

The willingness of the trade unionists to continue their negotiations with the industrialists surprised at least one employer. Walther Rathenau asked Legien on November 11 whether it was still wise for the trade unions to make the agreement since "the reputation of the union representatives could eventually be discredited by their forming what is more or less a coalition with the employers in the midst of such a movement."[16] Legien's response was that he and his colleagues had no intention of abandoning the agreement, which they viewed as the best way of dealing with the dangers to the well-being of the workers presented by the immediate emergency as well as a step in the direction of socialism. The latter could not be created overnight by a political transformation but needed a long period of time to develop. Legien and the trade-union leaders were convinced that the collaboration with the employers was necessary for the trade unionists to learn the tasks of economic management. Also, they were frankly suspicious of how much security could really be provided by political arrangements and were much more trusting of voluntary private agreements between the two parties. As Stinnes reported: "The trade unions say quite correctly that what is now introduced in a compulsory manner by the trade unions and actually has no legal legitimation does not have the same significance as a free accord between the unions and the participating industry, since the latter will remain while the former is something that can be repealed again."[17] Apparently, neither Stinnes nor the trade-union leaders put much stock in the legal legitimacy of the revolutionary government. Legien and his colleague and later successor Theodor Leipart of the Woodworkers Union aggressively defended their decisions. The most vociferous opposition among the trade-union leaders came from the rather conservative head of the Construction Workers'

Union, H. Paeplow, who was hostile to the Revolution, the workers councils, and the ZAG. He opposed the first two because they had unleashed the masses in a manner threatening to the unions, while he opposed the ZAG on the ground that it would alienate the masses still further and was impolitic. Legien and Leipart insisted, however, that the agreement had to be viewed as a revolutionary achievement on the part of the workers because the unions had thereby attained some of their oldest and most important goals. Legien explicitly rejected a more tactical and temporary alliance for the transition to a peacetime economy and bluntly stated that he hoped that "the partnership could be a lasting one."[18]

Indeed, whatever the view of the opposition trade unionists and later historians, it is important to recognize that the interpretation of the Stinnes–Legien Agreement as a revolutionary triumph for the workers was widely held among the employers and the first opposition to the agreement came from that side. At least three types of objections were raised. First, there were strong reservations about its terms. Fervent supporters of the yellow unions, like the Saar trade-association official Max Schlenker and Ruhr industrialists Paul Reusch and Heinrich Vielhaber, found the abandonment of the yellow unions dishonorable, while there were also strong objections to the schematic eight-hour day and universal collective bargaining for both technical and economic reasons. Such industrialists felt that those who had made the agreement were too influenced by the situation in Berlin and were too inexperienced in labor relations. Hans von Raumer was singled out with respect to this last charge. This leads to a second set of criticisms of the agreement; namely, that those who had negotiated it did so without prior consultation with their colleagues throughout the country and in complete disregard of the existing industrial and employer organizations and their leaders. Neither the negotiators nor those whom they pressured into signing the November agreement really had a mandate to act on behalf of their organizations or of industry as a whole. In fact, this was a legitimate complaint, since the persons who negotiated the agreement, however powerful, had received little or no authorization to do what they did,

while the persons who signed for the various industrial organizations had been presented with a *fait accompli* under conditions where travel and consultation were constrained by unrest and demobilization. Finally, while the employers by and large understood that they had to recognize and negotiate with the trade unions under the changed circumstances, many were reluctant to enter into a permanent relationship in which they would be obligated to discuss not only social but also economic questions with the union people. The proposed constitution for the ZAG aroused particular hostility, for it seemed "as if there is nothing left between heaven and earth that does not fall into the competence of the working community."[19] Especially strong objections were raised by the representatives of small and medium-sized firms, many of whom were not unprogressive and had never been as hostile to the trade unions as some of the big businessmen who had made the agreement. They were, however, organized along territorial lines and were unused to operating in a national context. The Saxon industrialists, for example, were particularly critical of the Berlin arrangements. They felt that the concessions made in Berlin were much more affordable for big industry than for themselves and warned about the consequences of having to discuss their economic decisions with the trade unionists.

At a meeting of the Federation of German Employer Organizations on December 18, 1918, the executive director, Fritz Tänzler, sought to defend the agreement by pointing out that it had been necessary to save the country from Bolshevism and arguing, as did his colleague from the Association of German Iron and Steel Industrialists, Jakob Reichert, on another occasion, that the agreement was the only way to find a mass base for sound economic policies given the "unreliability" of the German *Bürgertum* "which crept into every mouse hole at the first shot or the first revolutionary wave." It could not be counted upon to support the views of industry, "and there remained and remains nothing left but to turn one's eyes to the mass of workers, and then again to the organized mass, that is, the trade unions. . . ." Tänzler and his colleagues did not view this strategy from a purely defensive perspective, however. Just as Legien and Leipart viewed the ZAG as a means of developing the economic know-how needed for the future triumph of socialism, so the employers hoped to make a virtue of necessity and inculcate the workers and their leaders with the employer economic perspective. As Tänzler argued:

The goal [of the ZAG] is much broader and deeper. . . . The purpose is to introduce the workers much more than before, and more than was possible before, into an understanding of economic matters . . . to give them the opportunity to have the insight into the economic situation, the economic perspectives, the economic interconnections, which are the foundation of all social and wage demands, not in order to beat them in conflict but rather to convince them that there is a limit to where social and economic policy are compatible.[20]

While this hope was perhaps as naive as the belief entertained by the trade unionists that the ZAG would pave the way to socialism, such expectations must be taken seriously if the realities to which they were addressed are to be comprehended. Just as the behavior of the Social Democrats and trade unionists cannot be understood except in terms of their conviction that their lack of economic training and experience made dependence on professional and industrial experts necessary, so the employers who created the ZAG were convinced that employers and workers had common interests as producers, and that the workers could be made to understand the need to harmonize social and economic policy.

However splendid such ideals, German industry was not so easily brought into line, despite the power of the group which had negotiated the ZAG. This group played a decisive role in the creation of the Reich Association of German Industry (RdI) at Jena on February 3–4, 1919, and was powerful enough to gain acceptance of its policies concerning the trade unions. It did not, however, have the strength to withstand demands that the ZAG constitution be revised to separate economic and social questions so that the former would be dealt with in—as yet, uncreated—industrial branch organizations, while the latter were to remain the province of the employer organizations. Whereas the ZAG originators had supposed that the formation of the RdI would be determined by the intended gathering of all of German in-

dustry into working communities along branch lines, it was clear after Jena that the fusion, while still projected, would never be complete and that heterogeneity would continue to characterize German industrial organization even if the branch principle had achieved a goodly measure of implementation. A major result was that the substructure of the ZAG was very slow in developing. Although the employers preached the unity of social and economic policy, they were unable to realize it even in their own organizations, and, indeed, the desire of many employers to reduce the potential interference of the trade unionists and the state in their affairs was a disincentive to the rationalization of the RdI. It was very much in the interest of Germany's "organized capitalism" not to be too organized for its own good.[21]

These difficulties had not been anticipated, either by those who had created the ZAG or by the new head of the Demobilization Office, Koeth, who expected the ZAG to develop its substructure rapidly and thus provide the self-governing industrial branch organizations he hoped to employ to carry out the demobilization. Being a reasonable man, he knew that this would take a certain amount of time, and he also was convinced that the chief tasks of the working communities would be those arising once the troops had crossed back over Germany's borders. He conceived of the demobilization as a two-stage process. During the first stage, the troops would be brought home, and "only when the army has by and large come home will we be able to undertake a further regrouping and organization as the second act of the demobilization."[22] At that point, he hoped that the branch organizations would be at his disposal to provide information and advice as well as practical assistance in completing the transition to a peacetime economy.

Whatever reservations one may have about Koeth and his general conceptions, it is difficult not to be impressed with some aspects of his performance as head of the Demobilization Office (DMA), especially during the first month and a half of its operation. Koeth was a crisis manager *par excellence*, and his entire administrative philosophy was based on the principle of meeting the immediate emergency as effectively as possible without trying to anticipate or plan for an uncertain future. Both as head of the KRA during the war and as head of the DMA, Koeth considered his chief opponent to be Moellendorff, whose efforts to use emergencies to create complicated organizations and to lay long-term plans Koeth viewed as irrelevant at best and dangerous at worst.[23] Despite his distaste for the visionary approach, however, Koeth was not only highly intelligent, able, and forceful, but he was also persuasive, diplomatic, and sensible. What role his early Jesuit training played is difficult to say, and the fact that he was deeply affected by the death of the philosopher and sociologist Georg Simmel in October 1918 suggests that his interests were broader and deeper than most professional military men. While it is doubtful that his daily work was informed by any unrevealed deep principles or convictions, he certainly could act with remarkable common sense and balance in very difficult situations. At the same time, his purely functional approach left him extremely vulnerable once more substantive types of decision making were required and his dependence on the instrumentalities of crisis management was tested. At that point, he reached the limits of both his patience and capacity, although these were limits of which he was apparently quite aware.[24]

The soldiers and workers councils, for example, did not give Koeth as many sleepless nights as they did the SPD leaders of the government. Indeed, one suspects that if the latter had handled the councils with the same authority and calmness as Koeth, there might have been much less tension. Koeth's task undoubtedly was made easier by the fact that the representative of the soldiers-and-workers-council movement assigned to the DMA was Dr. Adolf Löwe, a twenty-six-year-old economist who just happened to be present in the room where the soldiers-and-workers-council leaders in Berlin were trying to figure out whom they should assign to represent the councils and oversee the activities of the various government offices. When they expressed puzzlement over the nature and functions of the recently created DMA, Löwe had the temerity to explain to them what it was all about and was rewarded with the assignment. It was one, in fact, for which he was highly qualified, having produced

pamphlets on the principles of the economic demobilization with a colleague in 1916 and on the social aspects of the demobilization in 1918. Like many young economists and officials at the time, he was an admirer of Wichard von Moellendorff, and his 1916 pamphlet is an interesting early example of the effort to organize a demobilization that would ensure full employment. He also had good connections with the trade-union leadership.[25]

One of the first acts of the DMA, however, was to scrap the War Office demobilization plans, and Löwe was not to have any opportunity to propose his more ambitious projects while in Koeth's agency. He did, however, have considerable success in his chief activity, which was to get the soldiers and workers councils throughout the country to cease interfering with the food and coal supplies and with the transportation system and to get them to cooperate with the DMA. Löwe, whose studies had included work with Simmel, seems to have gained Koeth's confidence and to have served unofficially as Koeth's private secretary.

Koeth was surprisingly positive toward the soldiers and workers councils. He did not want them intruding upon his work, but then again he did not want interference from the other government agencies in Berlin either. He specifically instructed that the councils be asked to help and that they have representatives in each of the war corporations "in order to eliminate the unduly felt mistrust" toward the councils.[26] He apparently shared the view of Löwe that the actions of the councils were often the result of ignorance rather than malice, and he pointed out that "[I]n general one has to keep in mind that we are having a revolution, and that under such circumstances conditions are bearable. The chief thing is to maintain calm and presence of mind, even in the face of transgressions by those in power at the moment, which are partially done from pure motives. The calm and presence of mind of the older and more understanding people must be carried over to the younger, more restless ones."[27] While unavoidably conscious of the difficulties created by the councils, Koeth persistently sought to make positive use of them wherever possible, whether in a specific instance of calling on them to persuade the workers in an airplane factory to take up lower paid furniture making or, more generally, by trying to communicate to them that "the unwillingness to work, on the one hand, and the high wage demands, on the other, must unconditionally lead to collapse."[28]

Worries such as these, however, tended to play a secondary role for Koeth during the early period of the demobilization. In the first week of the Revolution, he found it "incomprehensible" that employers would refuse to pay their workers for the days they were on strike and warned against the repetition of such "crude mistakes."[29] In collaboration with the Reich Labor Office, Koeth issued an Unemployment Relief Decree on November 13 which required the municipal authorities to provide support for the unemployed in the amount of the local wage as determined by the Reich social insurance regulations. Half the cost was to be born by the Reich, one-third by the states, and one-sixth by the municipalities. The decree of November 13 created immense difficulties for which Koeth was blamed. In reality, however, it was almost identical to legislation prepared by the RWA prior to the end of the war.[30]

A decree had been issued because there no longer was sufficient time to go to the Reichstag. Koeth's major interest was to have the workers and returning troops either employed or supported by the state. He was much less concerned about costs and wages. During the first meetings with his staff in November, he spoke of the Reich Treasury Office allocating twelve billion marks for emergency public works projects and then insisted that the Treasury had to encourage employers financially in view of their reluctance to invest their money under existing conditions. When the Treasury representative argued that "industry has earned so much that it can put itself back on its own feet," Koeth replied that "the millions earned will be quickly forgotten or quickly taken away."[31] The Reich did not need to offer high profits, but it did have to offer to pay to keep industry working. In the face of objections that there was neither a Reichstag nor a Bundesrat available to approve credits, that the "Reich debt was hanging in the air," and that officials were unwilling to violate their oaths by illegally providing money while the Treasury was reluctant to transform itself into a "warehouse,"

Koeth bluntly asked "whether the financial administration existed for the Reich or the Reich existed for the financial administration."[32] The next day, he warned against "false economy for so short a period," and renewed the pressure at the next meeting by pointing out that 90 percent of German industry would soon be without work and that subsidies from the Reich to the tune of two billion or three billion marks a month would be necessary.[33] Koeth was much more satisfied with the attitude of the Reichsbank, of which it was reported in mid-November that "the presses are working well at present" so that wages could be paid. The Revolution seems to have interrupted money production for five days at both the Reichsbank and the five private presses it was employing, but the revival of production was expected to calm things down as well as reduce the troublesome hoarding of money.[34]

Koeth was convinced that it was important to keep the workers employed at any price, and he was as indifferent to the costs of the employers as he was to those of the Reich Treasury. As the Socialist trade unionist in charge of handling unemployment in Berlin, Johann Sassenbach, reported:

We have found the greatest possible responsiveness in every respect from the Chairman of the Demobilization Office, State Secretary Koeth. All work creation proposals are granted by him to the greatest extent possible. Often, his orders constitute a terrible injustice to industry and the employers. They are not placed on a bed of roses. Many have double the number of workers they really need. . . .[35]

This is not to say that Koeth thought the workers should be put on a "bed of roses" either. While he obviously had a preference for terminating war contracts as rapidly as possible, he rejected the argument, apparently popular in certain worker circles, that "the workers after four years of heavy labor with little food can be accommodated if for once they have to vacation for a few weeks and despite that still receive their wages."[36] Supporters of this position argued that continued production under war contracts was simply a waste of raw materials, and the Bavarian government did in fact issue a decree on November 30 ordering the termination of such work by December 6.[37] Koeth, however, was unwilling to go this far, and he did not want the workers milling about. Instead, he ordered on November 21 that war contracts were only to be continued where they were absolutely essential to maintain employment, but that they were to be renegotiated so as to provide no profit to industry.

At the same time, he insisted that the employers had to make concessions on wages and working conditions. In mid-November, he mediated a conflict in the Hamburg shipyards and in other port cities, where tension between workers and employers was particularly high, and temporarily abolished piece rates and raised wages while establishing a "study commission" to recommend a final settlement. With the exception of the food industries, where he viewed the eight-hour day as a misfortune, Koeth was sympathetic to work-stretching policies and even opposed the use of labor-saving machinery in canal-building projects so as to increase the number of workers employed.[38] He called on the employers, "especially those who have earned well during the war," to do their share since "the Reich will give subsidies, but this can only be a small part of what is needed." When Ernst von Borsig pointed out that the employers were frightened by all the talk of socialization and were holding back, Koeth retorted that changes were indeed likely but that "one should not take what is written and spoken on both sides all that seriously." He reminded Borsig of the moderate Socialist arguments that it was not the time to undertake economic experiments and urged that "right now one has to get the economy moving again in order to take care of the people. One has to make an exception and work on the short run and then build up a new foundation. The attempt to look too far into the future can only cloud one's view at the present time."[39]

The problem, however, was that looking into the immediate future was becoming distressing as well. As the unhappy month of November came to an end and December brought new problems, it became clear that the Armistice was not bringing as much relief as anticipated; the transportation situation was getting worse, and the system threatened to break down if and when Allied food deliveries began to arrive. This would, in turn, influence the coal supply,

already reduced by poor production. The first phase of the demobilization was now nearly completed and unemployment was growing. As Koeth informed his colleagues, "the really difficult time is only coming."[40]

A good illustration of these difficulties was provided at a meeting between Ebert, various leading Berlin employers and trade unionists, DMA officials, and Labor Secretary Bauer on December 6. In order to save coal, the Berlin plants had been instructed to reduce their working day to five hours, the normal working day having already been reduced to eight hours by a decree of November 23, 1918, which essentially made the Stinnes–Legien Agreement on hours a matter of law. While the legal reduction of the hours of work was to be implemented without loss of pay, the mandatory imposition of short time to save coal would have meant a loss to the workers. During the war, the problem had been handled by government subsidies to compensate employers operating plants vital to the war effort for continuing to pay normal wages. This arrangement terminated on November 25, when such a category of plants officially ceased to exist, but the Unemployment Relief Decree foresaw assistance for those on short time. The scale of such support, however, hardly matched the wages earned by the Berlin metal workers, and the employers tried to anticipate worker demands. A number of them decided to provide 20 percent of the lost wages, while a number of others, often after threats of violence, had agreed to pay 75 to 100 percent of the lost wages. As Borsig pointed out, however, many of the firms could not afford to pay for nonproduction without eating up their reserves. They needed government help, and Borsig proposed that the workers be given 50 percent compensation for the wages, 30 percent from the government and 20 percent from the employers. He considered it important not to provide anything more, since increasing the amount would only further discourage workers who had come to Berlin during the war from leaving at a time when a new influx of between sixty thousand and eighty thousand returning soldiers was expected. Also, there was the problem of compensating only the metal industry despite the fact that all basis for such preferential treatment had disappeared.[41]

Ebert was particularly concerned about redirecting workers away from Berlin to where they were needed in the coal industry and in agriculture, while Bauer was worried both about the costs and about the problems of wages and morale. Although a trade-union leader, Bauer was a crusty and somewhat crude administrator who was remarkably critical of worker attitudes. As he pointed out, "the workers simply say: now the war profits have to come out, now we want them. I recently told them in a meeting: if you take the whole war profit, what remains for the Reich? The Reich wants to pay its debts with it. But one gets nowhere with these people that way; they have gotten it into their heads to get at the war profits and that has also been preached very energetically to them from the other side [the radicals]." Nor was Bauer unduly impressed by worker performance even when they were supposed to be working: "They demand that the five hours that they spend in the factories should count as work. Nothing is done there. They say: to produce weapons now makes no sense; we would rather do nothing."[42]

Only the Independent Socialist Dittmann, who represented the "other side," sought to take a different approach to the problems of both money and postwar psychology, pointing out that "[T]he Reich has thrown out so many billions for military purposes in the last four years, that it can sacrifice a few billions for the transitional period in order to keep disaster away" and that "the workers feel that the Revolution has liberated them from external compulsion, and they now also want a purely personal easing of their lot from the Revolution."[43] Treasury Secretary Eugen Schiffer thought that the wartime expenditures called for a different conclusion, of course, and the entire matter was temporarily settled by an agreement to compensate the metal workers for half their loss, the Reich providing 60 percent, the employers 40 percent of that amount. At the same time, Ebert was counting on the DMA and the ZAG to deal with the broader problem of redirecting the workers and returning soldiers to where they were most needed.

The time was fast arriving, in fact, when positive measures to implement the transition from the wartime to the peacetime economy would have to be taken. As Koeth turned to these difficult problems, he also found himself faced with a reviving RWA and once again in combat with the ideas of Wichard von Moellendorff. Also, August Müller had not taken the exclusion of himself and the RWA from the direction of the demobilization lightly and was intent on recovering control of economic policy. He had come to know Moellendorff and his ideas through wartime contacts. Müller had become a convert. He not only was willing to abandon traditional Socialist nationalization programs to Moellendorff's national-economy ideas, but also advocated the creation of a Reich Economic Council and the replacement of corporatist for parliamentary decision making in economic matters.

Thus, Müller invited Moellendorff to abandon his professorship at the Technical University of Hanover and become Undersecretary of the RWA. Moellendorff saw this as the golden opportunity to realize his program. Koeth now faced a genuine rival, and the policy differences were genuine and long-standing. All this occurred at a time when Koeth was already very unhappy with the growing criticism of his office and of his style of management that was appearing in the press and emanating from the RWA.[44] Koeth was never apologetic, either at the time or later: "Critics very rapidly and with complete accuracy established the absence of every creative idea in the Demobilization Office. Given the manner in which the Office had defined its tasks, such ideas were dispensable. We were not interested in a big program. What was necessary was speedy action and a mistake was better than a failure to do anything."[45]

The conflict came out into the open in late November and early December as both Koeth and the RWA leadership turned to the problem of what should be done to revive the economy, encourage production, and prevent unemployment. As usual, Koeth advocated a direct, short-term approach. He wanted a billion marks for an Assistance Fund for Industrial Enterprises (*Hilfskasse für gewerbliche Unternehmungen*), especially for small and medium-sized firms which needed help to start up again and were fearful of doing so because of the uncertain situation. As Koeth pointed out, it was impossible to demand that firms rehire their returning employees without also giving some

Wichard von Moellendorff (1881–1937), Undersecretary of Economics under August Müller and Rudolf Wissell. (*By permission of the Ullstein Verlag*)

support for actual production. While Koeth did not rule out state contracts for the firms in question, he clearly meant to use some of the funds for priming the private economy and wished to dispense them with a minimum of organization and regulation. The proposed Assistance Fund, therefore, is not to be confused with the billions already allocated for public works projects— 1.6 billion by the Prussian railroad authorities for the production of locomotives and rolling stock, and 4 million for related equipment; 1.5 billion for building construction; 600 million for canals and waterways; and 80 million for the Reich Post Office.[46] Rather, it was meant to serve as a stimulant to the private sector through the reduction of risk. The only requirements would be the payment of interest on any profits made and the promise to maintain a certain number of workers as well as a certain level of wages.[47]

The proposals of the RWA, designed by Moellendorff, were much less modest in cost, scale, and intention. While not denying the ne-

cessity of some immediate subventioning of firms to encourage production, he viewed this as hopelessly inadequate because it would not really create the incentive for long-term production and would not encourage reasonable wage or price levels. Once the money was used up, the problems would simply return in worse form. Instead, the RWA proposed that the Treasury set up a Reich Fund of five billion marks for a longer-term solution. The economy would be organized into self-governing economic associations (*Zweckverbände*) for the various sectors and branches on the basis of joint industry-labor participation, and these associations would have the task of applying for and using the funds in accordance with government guidelines. The fundamental goal was to create mechanisms for macroeconomic management by the state: "In times of crisis, financial help by the state for the economic associations, in times of boom, taxation of the economic associations (tax associations) through the state; initially, the speedy distribution of a five-billion mark Reich fund for the granting of credits, capital participation or the ordering of goods by the economic associations; gradual transformation of the Reich Treasury into a chief banker."[48] The goal, in short, was to integrate economic, social, and financial policy. In more modern, "Keynesian" language, pump priming would be used to overcome slumps and unemployment, while taxes would be used once recovery had taken place to correct the deficit spending. The plan would cost money, but it was money one could recover: "The operation of a Reich Fund agency unquestionably requires financial losses by the Reich. If, however, one considers the role of the Reich with respect to the national economy in the moderate Socialist sense to be such that the Reich helps to bridge over bad economic periods in order to produce better economic periods and to benefit from them, then the temporary loss of money appears less frightening than a fatalistic acceptance of an economic catastrophe."[49] Furthermore, by assuming the role of chief national lender or banker, the state would also be in a position to influence through its regulations wages and prices as well as the market directly as a purchaser of industrial goods and a "giant warehouse" ready to place goods in the hands of the commercial sector for sale to the consuming public. From Moellendorff's point of view, such arrangements would eliminate bureaucratic mismanagement, since the impulses and ideas would come from the self-governing economic associations which would also have responsibility for carrying them into action. They would also eliminate the opportunistic individualism that typified the liberal free economy. The economy would be organized and forced to assume responsibility. The state would be there as a policymaker and arbitrator of the last resort.

Koeth thought the program a nightmare, particularly under the conditions existing in the winter of 1918–1919. He argued that it required too large-scale and extensive an organization and prevented the handling of the immediate emergency in the manner he proposed. This argument was undoubtedly more sincerely meant than his rather disingenuous claim that his own program did not stand in the way of the RWA plans which would require time to be realized. Moellendorff was fully aware that Koeth's way of doing things was one of the chief threats to his ideas and characterized them as "the opportunism which has ruined every truly complete economic reform for years, because it counts on a gradual automatic return to the prewar situation."[50] Unfortunately for the RWA, however, it confronted not only the animosity of Koeth but also the resistance of the liberal State Secretary of the Treasury, Eugen Schiffer. Schiffer's opposition to the RWA plans, which was not only financially but also ideologically based, was something of a mixed blessing for Koeth however. Schiffer was not at all inclined simply to hand over a billion marks to the DMA. Bureaucratically, therefore, it was a three-ring circus that performed before the Council of People's Commissars on December 12, 1918, when Ebert and his Cabinet were called upon to decide how to proceed with the next phase of the demobilization.

It was an important meeting in the broadest sense because it revealed the possibilities and constraints of the nascent Weimar Republic as its leaders faced the dilemmas of integrating their economic, social, and financial policies, and it thus provided important precedents for the future. The major result of the meeting, an allocation of five hundred million marks to Koeth to spend on subventions to enterprises needing help for the conversion to peacetime production or to start up production, bore witness to the dominant influences determining such policy discussions; namely, the immediate emergency, on the one hand, and financial anxieties, on the other. Koeth was eloquent and straight-forward, and it was impossible to send him away empty-handed: "I have always had a difficult situation in the war dealing with the other two offices. I do not have any greater ideas and far-reaching thoughts in my office. I only have to see how to get through the next weeks. . . . I cry out for help; I have only a small idea: how do I get from one day to the next."[51] He claimed he needed a sum of money at his disposal so that he did not have to beg for each individual case. He was grateful to Schiffer, but not that grateful, pointing out that the two hundred fifty million he had finally extracted for certain emergency projects was "easily spit into the air" after a war like the one just fought. Above all, he sought to distinguish clearly his proposal from that of the RWA, pointing out that his chief purpose was to get the existing economic system moving again and assuring his colleagues that reasonable discussion with the employers, such as those he had recently conducted in the shipyards, would bring both sides to reason and prevent an abuse of the subsidies he was requesting.

Schiffer was not convinced, pointing out that subventions were a dangerous business leading to corruption and the whetting of appetites that could not be satisfied. He forcefully argued that it was precisely the fact that the war had cost so much that made it important to put an end to the kind of financing that had gone on during the war. His greatest concern, however, was the plans proposed by the RWA. While having no quarrel with the "greatness of the idea . . . that we should combine the social, economic, and financial points of view," he found the plans presented by Müller "extraordinarily questionable" and feared that "with the huge sums that are supposed to be placed at [their] disposal for priming the economy one will, I believe, bring economic life into disorder."[52] Schiffer contested the availability of the information necessary to accomplish the tasks proposed by the

RWA, but his entire criticism was more fundamental. While very much a critic of Helfferich's management of the wartime state finances and taxation policies, Schiffer shared Helfferich's skepticism about man's ability to live up to the expectations of economic regulators and planners. Given the regime he was serving, Schiffer refrained from attacking socialism as such, but he did attack the notions of combining state intervention with an individualistic, capitalistic economy: "I contest the idea that the state, as we have it, and that people, such as those we have, are in a position to control things."[53]

One of the most interesting aspects of the discussion was the strong support Schiffer received from Eduard Bernstein, then a member of the USPD but clearly as much a reformist Socialist as ever. Quite typically, not only for reformists like himself but also for most of the Socialist leadership throughout the Weimar Republic, Bernstein took the view that capitalist economies had to be run according to the laws of capitalism, and he was profoundly conservative in his fiscal attitudes. On the one hand, he showed no interest whatever in the RWA program; on the other, he strongly urged limiting the help asked for by Koeth. He shared Schiffer's suspicion of subventions. Bernstein argued that the sum asked for by Koeth would only serve to increase inflation:

... What kind of effect will it have when the public knows that 1 billion is available to support industry in general. . . . I do not believe that the workers will then be inclined to hold back in their demands. We stand before a bottomless pit. I cannot hold it against the workers when they demand higher wages when the purchasing power of their wages sinks. . . . From whence will come the billions that are being demanded? They can only come from an increased use of the printing presses. Whatever one thinks about the influence of the [printing of] notes on the purchasing power of money, there is a point at which the printing press [must] affect the purchasing power of money in the form of inflation. Thus the purchasing power of money sinks more and more and the wage demands increase. Economic policy must be directed toward bringing about a cleansing of economic conditions [Sanierung] and to work against everything that makes the conditions and conflicts worse. . . . We still have a bourgeois economy. We know that Socialism is moving forward . . . but in the largest part of our economy we remain a bourgeois economy, the economy of free competition. Subventions

have the tendency to work against this and to drag out and make more difficult the restoration of sound economic conditions. We get an unhealthy development of the market, an unhealthy development of wages, and these are things that make the demands, as they are presented here, appear extraordinarily questionable to me. . . .[54]

These arguments made an obvious impression on Ebert. Without rejecting the RWA proposals, he simply pointed out that they required presentation in written form. Further discussion was tabled. At the same time, he explicitly supported Bernstein's argument that large-scale subventions would have a bad effect on the workers, while agreeing with Koeth that a flexible system of support in special instances was desirable. Thus, Koeth ended up with five hundred million to spend until April 1, 1919, and could set up his Assistance Fund for Industrial Enterprises.[55]

The first days of the new year found Koeth a very unhappy man, however, and it is doubtful that he would have been much cheered even if he had the full billion marks he requested. Germany's armies had returned across the borders and were in a state of dissolution. This did not disturb Koeth, who had argued all along that it was hopeless to try to control the return of the troops once they had reached German soil and that the urge to go home should not be challenged but rather encouraged. Koeth, however, apparently had some illusions of his own behind his very practical and understanding approach toward the Revolution. He seemed to think that it would be possible to direct and organize the labor force and gain control of the situation, but this was the reverse of what happened after mid-December. Reports streamed in stressing ill-discipline and unwillingness to work, while the railroad system was jammed, coal production sank, and shortages were reported everywhere. When Koeth's "study commission" set up to make proposals concerning labor conditions on the docks produced a report recommending wage reductions and the reintroduction of piece rates, the dock workers held a mass protest on January 5, marched to the trade-union headquarters, threw out the functionaries, and, after launching a general strike a few days later, occupied the building.[56]

The Upper Silesian situation was particularly serious because of Bolshevik-inspired unrest and Polish incursions, and things were made worse by the fact that there, as in the shipyards earlier, the workers took their revenge for the long tradition of harsh and brutal supervision by forcing dismissals and even attacking supervisors and other plant and mine officials.[57] Were it not for the relative mildness of the winter, the situation might have been "catastrophic." The developments in Berlin were particularly alarming. In early January, eighty thousand unemployed were officially reported, but it was clear that the actual number was far greater and would almost triple in the course of the next sixty days. The unruliness of the workers made it difficult for the civil servants to deal with them, and the employers were calling for protection.[58] At a meeting on January 6, Koeth appeared to be at his wits' end. He concluded the session by telling his staff that he did not think they could go on for many more weeks and declared that he did not know whether the inability to recognize the facts was due to "lack of intelligence or delusion." He could not understand "how every German is not red with shame when he sees how we have decayed." He despairingly concluded: "Things will have to come to the point where each person will have to reach for his rifle so that we can at first give ourselves some breathing space in the East. As things are going now, we are at the edge of the abyss and perhaps it would be better if this situation ends as quickly as possible. Then, those who remain can perhaps experience better times."[59]

If Koeth was losing his grip on the situation, then one of the chief sources of his difficulty was the Unemployment Relief Decree of November 13. The decree had left the setting of support levels to the municipal authorities on the basis of official local wages, and these were invariably higher in the big cities. Initially, the rates were fairly moderate, but the pressure of soldiers and workers councils and the unruliness of the unemployed themselves soon began to force them upward. The situation was particularly serious in Berlin, where the high local wages kept from leaving those who had come to do war work, attracted persons who did not want to work in the first place, and, of course, promised to make

things worse as the actual Berlin workers who had been at the front finally came home. The municipal authorities were profoundly discontented with the tasks thrown into their laps. As Mayor Wermuth personally wrote to Ebert in mid-December, the entire burden of unemployment relief management and distribution, work creation, and labor exchanges was placed on the municipalities. The Reich and state authorities "are very free in providing lectures on how the communities are supposed to carry out the tasks assigned to them," but were failing to take any positive measures to deflect the workers away from the big cities.[60]

Repeatedly, Wermuth and his colleagues suggested a minimum unemployment relief of three marks per day for the entire Reich so that the unemployed would have some incentive to leave the big cities, and they also called for a time limit on the support of those who were not permanent residents of the cities. This proposal received some support from the Prussian Minister of Commerce, Fischbeck, who in December advocated not only a minimum but also a maximum unemployment relief rate of four and a half marks per day so that a situation would not be created in which Dresden paid six marks while Berlin paid four marks. But the proposals for a minimum rate and for time limits on the payment of supports were rejected by the demobilization authorities and by Labor Minister Bauer. In their view, conditions in the Reich were too divergent to allow for a single rate, and it was impossible to impose a three-mark minimum because there were many areas of the country in which the actual daily pay for work was less, while a time limit on the receipt of support for nonresidents violated the free movement of labor.[61]

With the coming of the new year, however, pressure grew to increase the unemployment-relief payment scales, and the demands were not limited to Berlin. The Mayor of Altona made a desperate plea in mid-January that the Reich introduce maximum scales for unemployment relief. From an economic point of view, Hamburg and Altona were an economic unit, so that actions taken in one city easily affected the other. Initially, the unemployment support in both cities was set slightly higher than the official local wage: four marks for a single man, three marks for a single woman, six marks for a married couple, and one and a half marks for each of the first three children and one mark for each child thereafter. Altona had a ceiling of eight marks for an entire household. Since someone on public-works projects received nine and a half marks per day, there was some incentive to take such work rather than receive unemployment relief. However, the unemployed of Hamburg, with the help of the Hamburg Soldiers and Workers Council soon forced an increase in the payments by one mark, with a ceiling for a household of eleven and a half marks. Altona tried to deal with the situation by setting its ceiling for household unemployment relief at nine marks and raising the pay for public-works labor to ten and a half marks, but they were unsuccessful. Hamburg not only raised its rates again, but it made the increases retroactive to December 1; a meeting of the unemployed in Altona demanded the same rates as Hamburg. In the end, the ceilings were simply eliminated, and the new, increased scale was made retroactive to January 1. As the Mayor of Altona pointed out, this meant that the daily wage of the worker employed on public-works projects had to be raised once again, and this was now so high that the regular wages of privately employed workers also had to be raised. The increased labor costs, however, were causing prices to rise and reducing business activity, which, in turn, was increasing unemployment and thus leading to the further "dissipation of municipal resources under the pressure of the unemployed."[62]

The authorities in Berlin, of course, faced the worst situation because of the size of the city and its role as Germany's political center. The representatives of the unemployed in Berlin could turn directly to Koeth as well as to other Reich, Prussian, and municipal officials. At the beginning of January, they demanded a doubling of the unemployment supports—an increase from four to eight marks per day, including Sunday, for males over twenty, with proportionate increases for males and females in the same and lower age groups. The city administration did not contest the need for an increase given the higher cost of living, but Wermuth worried about the influence on the rest of the Reich as well as upon wage levels and, quite naturally, municipal finances. The city made a counterproposal which differed only slightly from that of the unemployed, and Koeth urged acceptance of the city's offer, pointing out that the arrangement could only be financially feasible for a few weeks anyway. Koeth feared, however, that it would last for months because of raw-material and coal shortages and that the number of unemployed would increase. To the arguments of the unemployed that money from the capitalists could be used to pay the costs, Koeth rejoined that "the peace will be dictated by the enemy in the most rigorous way, and the burdens arising from it will have to be born chiefly by the capitalists. Even with the socialization of all the plants, one still has to have the necessary operating capital." The representatives of the unemployed, however, were patently uninterested in such considerations. As one of them bluntly remarked: "I want to make it clear that the unemployed everywhere demand higher scales. The collapse will take place even without an increase in the scales. The unemployed, however, must in any case not suffer because of it. If we don't succeed with the demands of the unemployed masses, then they will try to use force to attain them over our heads."[63]

To attribute this attitude to selfish exploitation of the weakness of the government would be as simpleminded as to push aside the fact that these workers felt entitled to a greater share of the pie, however reduced its size, on the grounds that they had been through four years of war and deprivation. Those speaking for the unemployed were not simply threatening the government but were also intent on bringing to its attention the misery of the unemployed— their hunger, the ill-health that required a richer diet, and the lack of clothing that made it difficult for them to take emergency public work because they were simply too cold or too inadequately clothed to do the jobs. When the Berlin unemployed "settled" for a daily rate of seven marks for unmarried male workers and eight marks for those who were married and "compromised" by agreeing not to get paid for Sunday, they were hardly on the road to prosperity; nor was the willingness of only four hundred fifty unemployed to take on construction work in the outlying Grunewald district of Berlin, where the city was in a position to offer two thousand jobs, necessarily a sign of bad will or laziness on the part of the unemployed. The representatives of the unemployed were frank in stating that ten to twelve marks per day were too little to make it worthwhile for workers to take on the job, even when the city increased the value of the daily wage by two and a half marks by throwing in a meal. The costs of travel to work, additional food needed to gather the strength for heavy labor, and wear and tear on clothing which could not be replaced very easily or cheaply did not make the taking of such a job a very attractive or even rational proposition. There was thus a distinct relationship between the shabbiness of the clothes worn by the returning soldiers in Berlin and the fact that the snow was not being cleared away despite the high unemployment.[64]

The dilemma was that the unemployment relief was a necessary social measure arising from the war and, like most of the other measures taken in connection with the war, had nothing to do with sound economics and finance. At the same time, the war and Revolution had created expectations on the part of the unemployed workers and a realization that they were sufficiently numerous to impose their will on the government. The borderline between demands based on principles of elementary social justice and those based on conscious employment of brute force is not always clear, anymore than is the borderline between good social policy and sound economic policy. When one considers, for example, that in Munich the wife of an unskilled day worker with three young children received an average of six and a half marks' support per day in October 1918, and that the entire family received thirteen marks per day after he returned and found no employment, then it is difficult to see how, on the one hand, the relief could be called excessive given the increased cost of living and family food requirements as a result of his return, and why, on the other hand, he should take a public-works job for thirteen to fifteen marks a day. From an economic point of view, of course, paying this man to do nothing was difficult to justify, while his continued unemployment was undesirable from both a social and psychological point of view. Finally, there was both danger and injustice in the leveling effect produced when one paid thirteen marks to an unskilled Munich laborer whose average wage in April 1919 was fifteen marks and the same thirteen marks unemployment relief to a skilled worker who could earn twenty-two marks if he could find employment. Justice, however, required that the unskilled worker receive enough to keep body and soul together; the state simply could not afford to justly reward the unused talents of the skilled worker.[65] August Müller, ever anxious to criticize Koeth, might complain that a family of many persons gets the maximum pay of the government Councillor (*Regierungsrat*) as unemployment support,[66] but it was inflation, not the admittedly problematic decree Koeth had taken over from his predecessors, that was producing this result.

Furthermore, the decree was not responsible for the demoralization arising from the war. Welfare swindling was a natural addition to the black marketeering and other forms of illegality that had become endemic in German society. Trade unionist Sassenbach estimated that 25 percent of the unemployment payments in Berlin were illegitimate, and he had to establish a Criminal Division at the unemployment offices to deal with it. Members of the Berlin Republican Guard made a regular practice of claiming unemployment supports. Workers regularly made claims for nonexistent family members. A favorite trick was to register in two different districts of Berlin—for example, Schöneberg and Wilmersdorf–and then collect from both offices. It was impossible to catch all such cases, but they heightened the need to do something about the general situation.[67]

The government sought to do something about the deficiencies of the Unemployment Relief Decree of November 13 by issuing a new decree on January 15, 1919, whose provisions were designed to reduce the unemployed in the cities and increase the leverage at the disposal of the authorities in putting the unemployed to work where they were needed, for example, in agriculture and mining. Thus, municipalities were instructed to limit the support of the nonresident unemployed to four weeks, except in cases where they had established residence with their entire family or could not move because of illness or because their hometowns were under Allied occupation. Furthermore, §8 of the decree of November 13, which was designed to force the unemployed to take suitable employment if offered, was now strengthened so that unemployed persons could be forced to take work in another location and work with which they were not familiar but for which they were medically fit. Family men who took work in another location were guaranteed continued support for their families. Finally, the new decree established ceilings on the supports, which were to be no more than one and a half times the local wage defined by the insurance offices.[68]

Koeth's mood in mid-January was so desperate, however, that he wanted to go even further and to issue a decree making it possible to draft all able-bodied persons, especially young people, into agriculture and coal mining. Koeth likened his proposal to the Auxiliary Service Law, but he had not forgotten this law's problems and urged that a decree be issued before the National Assembly met, since the latter would at once politicize the proposed law and also pass it too late to be helpful in the spring planting. His scheme, which can only be called politically harebrained under the circumstances and another illustration of Koeth's surprising loss of control at this time, received very little support from his colleagues, who urged that they wait upon the efforts to "turn the screws" by means of the revised §8 of the new Unemployment Relief Decree of January 15.[69] Nevertheless, Koeth stubbornly pressed on with the drafting of his proposed decree despite warnings that the Council of People's Commissars would never risk issuing such legislation. Interestingly enough, only in the Central Council, increasingly influenced by Koeth's friendliness and his efforts to cultivate the councils movement, did someone have the temerity to ask, "[S]ince we had compulsory labor in the war, cannot the Socialists manage to have compulsory labor for their own Socialist Republic?"[70]

Within the actual government, however, the situation was being used against Koeth. August Müller, blessedly free of responsibility for the demobilization, could afford to paint the economic situation of the country in the darkest colors, warn against plans to expand the activities of the DMA, and go so far as to argue that "the Demobilization Office is a foreign body in

our organism. It must disappear as soon as possible. The working against one another of the various agencies, which is worse than ever before, must stop."[71] In a meeting called by Müller, propaganda aimed at persuading the unemployed to take work in the country was stepped up, but Koeth's compulsory labor service proposal never reached the Council of People's Commissars.

Indeed, by the end of January, Koeth was back to his old realistic self. This was demonstrated by the tone and content of a series of meetings concerning the unemployment situation and the need for workers in the mines and on the farms. The full complexities of the situation now received their due. The illusion that the authorities could simply move thousands of workers or young people to the mines and farms had been dispelled by the fact that the mines did not have adequate housing and that the necessary boots and clothes had to be supplied first. Koeth also recognized that the shortages of raw materials meant that employment could not be provided for masses of workers from Berlin and elsewhere at the moment. Furthermore, the sending of large numbers of workers to agriculture, while highly desirable, had its limitations. These were created, on the one hand, by the simple unsuitability of many unemployed for such work and, on the other, by the frequent unwillingness of farmers to employ workers from the cities because of their inexperience, expectations, and radicalism. The negative attitude of the farmers was particularly noticeable in Saxony, where it seems that many workers did want to do such work, undoubtedly in order to get more food. In any case, as Koeth openly admitted: "The city people do not want to go to the country and the farmers do not want to take the city workers."[72]

Koeth was extremely sensitive about the Unemployment Relief Decree of November 13, and the official line of the DMA was to blame the cities for surrendering to the terror of the unemployed and granting excessive support scales. Koeth certainly knew, however, that such terror was not easily resistible. It is hard to imagine him arguing that the Mayor of Mannheim, for example, was cowardly in coming to terms with the unemployed after they burst into his office and left him with head wounds.[73] Although Koeth now placed his hopes on the decree of January 15 rather than on any new compulsory legislation, he reduced his expectations here as well. The burden of persuading or forcing the unemployed to take available work lay with the labor exchanges, and it was clear that neither of these tasks was particularly easy. Propaganda by the labor exchanges ran into the "psychological condition of the mistrust of the worker for the academically trained and better-clothed person."[74] Actual enforcement of the regulations was unpleasant at best and precarious at worst. Leipzig officials who seized the unemployment support control cards of those who refused to take available jobs were "cursed in the crudest manner, insulted, and even threatened." At the end of January, an official holding control cards was actually assaulted by the unemployed: "They kicked him with their feet, tore his uniform, also tried to get hold of his stamp, and one of them grabbed the hand in which he held the control cards and bit his thumb until he bled."[75] The police were summoned but felt helpless in the face of the crowd, which was only quieted down after a local trade-union official from the Leipzig Soldiers and Workers Council pacified the men. He pointed out to them that the officials had to do their duty and were proletarians like themselves. It was "unworthy of a worker" to mistreat them.

Not all the efforts to implement §8 were equally dramatic, but the incident is a good indication of the mood of the returning veterans. Contrary to myths cultivated by the political right in the later Weimar Republic, the failure to bedeck the returning veterans with laurel wreaths was not the consequence of mistreatment but rather of the fact that most of the army had drifted rather than marched home. The returning soldiers were by and large given work when they wished work and often came back in a rather aggressive mood, either demanding their support and a measure of relief from their hardships or demanding and receiving their old jobs and making the most of regulations requiring their reinstatement.[76]

The attitude of male white-collar workers, especially commercial clerks, is particularly interesting because it demonstrates this aggressiveness as well as the dilemmas of social justice and social policy in the demobilization. While the manual workers often seemed to welcome the opportunity to go on unemployment relief after the strains of war work or military service, the returning white-collar workers appear to have been very anxious to get on with their careers and were frustrated by the poor business conditions in the commercial sector that made their employment difficult or impossible. In Mannheim, for example, the white-collar workers, clerks, and technicians were furious at being put on unemployment relief. The tone of their petitions was bitter: "As thanks for our four-and-a-half years of service we are out on the streets without jobs for the simple reason that we did our duty to the utmost and to the last. We looked forward to coming home and returned with the firm and holy intention of reconstructing our shattered existences and putting our best energies into the construction of the new state."[77] They particularly resented conditions at the labor offices, where they had to wait for unemployment relief, pointing out that "you cannot expect educated people who have served in the war and whose health has suffered . . . to subject themselves without reason to the inclement weather and to stand daily without enough food before the labor office for hours at a time." They were no less angry over claims that it was "financially impossible" to meet their demands for higher support. In an expression of their deep resentment against those who had stayed at home as well as against the blue-collar workers, they asked, "who gave us cost-of-living supplements and salaries during our . . . service?" and "how it was financially possible that the workers laid off between Christmas and New Year—who earned immense amounts during the war—received 70 percent unemployment relief?" The greatest hostility, however, was expressed toward those women who continued to be employed in the public and private offices and businesses. The male veterans demanded that, with the exception of widows, women be systematically replaced by veterans. They were quite prepared to see female workers receive the unemployment supports the veterans were now receiving if they were truly needy, but "we will not tolerate that women whose brothers and fathers are already employed in city plants and agencies should also be employed there while thousands of war veterans are without work."

The release of blue-collar and white-collar female workers had long been intended as part of the demobilization, and it was one program which appeared to meet with very little overt protest from the women affected. The demobilization agencies and the government were particularly anxious to shift women—above all, young ones—into domestic service or back into such industries as textiles. Undoubtedly, many women, especially those from the middle class who had entered war work for patriotic or temporary financial reasons, were happy to give up their occupations. Many employers, however, were reluctant to give up their female workers, in part because they could pay them less, but also because they were reliable and experienced.[78] Most important, while it was difficult in the face of the strong antifeminine stance of the blue- and white-collar workers to make the point, the reality was that many women needed to work and that they were being unjustly treated. Thus, at a meeting in Dortmund of the various demobilization agencies and white-collar union representatives in January 1919, there was a veritable storm of proposals for the elimination of female employees. The only voice of resistance came from a female union representative who gingerly suggested that women, too, had some problems:

In order that there not be any misunderstandings, I would like to stress that the Working Community of Female Unions takes the view that the veterans are to be employed first and that the women who are not dependent on employment are to be let go. What shall the unemployed women do? Not a word has been said about that today. . . . That all of us women should be occupied in households, as is demanded, is out of the question, for you must realize that an endless number of female workers will be set free who want to take up housekeeping again. . . .[79]

The truth was that female employment had been rising even before the war and that many women were dependent on an earned income and would need to have one in the future. As one female official shrewdly pointed out:

You are speaking for those male white-collar workers who must have their bread and not realizing that later you yourselves might be also in the position of having to care for your daughters, that your four or five daughters will come home, sit down at the table and

say, papa, we are not allowed to work in the offices. I believe that you will not exactly see the task of providing for your daughters as a happy state of affairs. I therefore ask you . . . to put aside all hostility.

The attachment to prewar social and cultural habits helps to explain why certain aspects of the demobilization, such as the release of female workers, were more successful than others, such as the effort to get the unemployed to help out on the land. The attitude of white-collar workers toward this effort is revealed by the interchange between a government official and a white-collar representative at the 1919 Dortmund meeting. The official pointed out:

. . . If the gentlemen turn down other suitable work, then their need cannot be so great. The shortage of workers on the land is very large. Many of the gentlemen who want to be employed in the large cities come from the countryside. But they cannot decide to return to the land (interjection: To do what, load dung?), even if they must load dung. Work is not shameful. The Americans have given us a good example here. . . .

The white-collar worker representative did not agree:

We must above all proceed from the view that we have to bring the people into positions suitable to their accomplishments and abilities. In general, I would like to comment with respect to the remarks of the government councilor that we do not have American conditions here in Germany.[80]

Clearly, therefore, the Unemployment Relief Decree of January 15 involved some serious problems of implementation, and Koeth had obviously become aware of them by the end of that month. Indeed, at a meeting of January 31 with the representatives of the state governments, he informed them in a matter-of-fact way that the unemployment situation in most of Germany was not really as bad as that in Berlin, but that there simply was not enough work for the unemployed for the time being. He was as conscious as anyone of the role played by threats of violence in making the implementation of the decree difficult and undoubtedly agreed with those state representatives who argued that it was a "power" question and expressed appreciation for the government's efforts to quiet things down with the free corps wherever necessary. Nevertheless, it was the old, illusion-free, commonsensical Koeth who now spoke once again. He showed little tolerance for the employers inundating him with complaints about high wages: "We must accustom ourselves to the idea that we will also have to count on a significantly higher wage scale in the future. The fear that the wages will develop in an unreasonable way seems unfounded. The world market will bring things into order." More generally, he stressed that "one ought not to demand too much from the workers; the revolution has played itself out in peaceful forms until now, and one needs time to sober up."[81]

Actually, the Revolution was now entering its most violent period, but as Ebert pointed out at this meeting of January 31, ". . . if one has sufficient means of force, then governing is easy; it has been very difficult to create a military force; finally, we have succeeded. The government will do everything necessary to bring our economy into operation again and to eliminate the transportation difficulties."[82] This was amply demonstrated between the middle of January and the end of April, when the free corps and regular army were used to smash, often with considerable brutality, strike movements and uprisings in the Ruhr, Central Germany, Berlin, Braunschweig, Bremen, Hamburg, and Munich. There can be no question about the fact that these were political movements, a second revolutionary wave. Politically, there was disenchantment with the performance of the Majority Socialists, dissatisfaction with the National Assembly elected on January 19, and disapproval of the SPD's entry into a coalition with the Catholic Centrists and the bourgeois Democrats in February. The trade union alliance with the employers and the delay of socialization in the mining industry gave rise to frustration and violent protest. At the same time, a new conception of the role of the councils emerged in which factory councils would have a voice in socio-economic management of enterprises with the objective of democratizing the economy. The councils would provide a training ground for the democratization of society and the triumph of socialism. Now, in contrast to the first phase of the Revolution when their purpose was unclear, the councils appeared as much more conscious alternatives to the establishment of a purely liberal parliamentary state ruled by the traditional combination of parties and interest groups.[83]

As is always the case in such movements, there was a peculiar blend of romanticism and intellectual idealism, on the one hand, and more dubious aims and forms of behavior, on the other. The movement must ultimately be placed in some broader historical perspective.[84] It was patent that some idea of democratization from the bottom up and direct democracy underlay the seizure of coal mines and factories and the attempt to run them through worker direction. Such goals found expression in the writings and actions of Karl Korsch in Germany and Antonio Gramsci in Italy. They transcended simple notions of nationalization, but it would be a mistake to dismiss the importance of socialization itself. As the district President in Merseburg reported in early February: "The masses are no longer in the hands of their leaders. The idea of socialization has completely turned the heads of the great mass."[85] At the same time, one cannot simply disregard the evidences of gangsterism among this "great mass." The martyred Rosa Luxemburg and Karl Liebknecht must not be confused with all their followers, and there is no reason to believe that the speaker at a meeting in Berlin on February 27 was atypical when he called for the rallying together of the unemployed to secure the mass necessary to fight the regime and told his listeners: "Comrades, again I say to you, we will only come to our goal through terror and radicalism. There will be a great massacre [*Mörder*], perhaps even worse than St. Bartholemew's night in France."[86]

Both the ideals and the brutalities of the mass movement, however, must be comprehended in terms of the complex socio-economic and psychological background out of which they arose. One great center of unrest was the large metal factories in Berlin and other major cities, in which highly skilled workers served as revolutionary shop stewards and assumed the leadership of a mass of skilled and unskilled workers. Other important centers were the mines in the Ruhr, the docks in Hamburg, and the huge chemical and lignite mines in central Germany. The war had intensified already existing trends in the direction of large-scale industrial enterprises in which masses of workers were mixed together and in which the work process was frequently diluted through the employment of unskilled and semiskilled labor. During the war there had been a vast expansion of these plants, especially in Berlin, central Germany, the Rhineland, and the Ruhr. Some giant new plants had been created literally in a matter of months, as was the case with the Leuna chemical works in the Merseburg-Halle region. The workers in these plants frequently came from outside the region and were often young persons. Furthermore, neither the housing nor the food situations were satisfactory. In the allocation of food, for example, Merseburg continued to be treated as an agrarian region despite the proximity of the Leuna works. The food situation in the Ruhr was always a problem, especially in the mining industry. Miners were entitled to a totally inadequate ration of nineteen hundred calories instead of the four thousand to five thousand they required. Much of the unwillingness to work and the demand for a six-hour day in the mining industry must be understood in terms of sheer physical exhaustion as well as the feeling that miners deserved special consideration because of the difficulties and dangers of their work and thus should have a shorter working day than the eight-hour day created by the Revolution.[87]

While many of the ideals and goals articulated by the radical leaders were shared by both young and old workers, the former obviously were more prone to violent measures. It is reasonable to suppose that the prewar demographic trends (which substantially increased the cohort of young people in the urban industrial areas of Germany) combined with the specific influences of the war (in which young people were employed in large numbers with substantially higher pay and—especially when their fathers were absent—with unusual independence) to create a situation in which youth could play an important and radical role.[88] These problems were anticipated well before the unsuccessful end of Germany's military effort. At a meeting of officials in January 1918, one expert pointed out:

Even in peacetime the young male workers were often viewed in administrative practice as a difficult element in the population, and especially insofar as one was dealing with "family-uprooted" youths, who prematurely, upon leaving school or shortly thereafter, are separated from the parental home and find employment on the labor market. I can assume that the accompanying problems then observed are generally known as well as the fact that during the war this naturally unstable and restless group of young workers has greatly increased. What before the war was a strange exception is now to be sure not the rule, but is still a truly frequent phenomenon.[89]

The tendency of such young workers to be spendthrift had led to efforts on the part of the authorities to curb their activities as well as to attempt to control their "unbearably increased self-consciousness" and to force them to save portions of their wages (*Sparzwang*). Those planning the demobilization had hoped to organize the integration of these young workers into the peace-time economy in a careful and disciplined way. Such intentions were scrapped along with the rest of the demobilization program in November 1918, and the young workers were now more uncontrolled than ever.

Finally, the role played by demoralization cannot be overlooked in understanding the wave of violence and upheaval that swept Germany in the spring of 1919. Dancing was not a pleasure limited to bourgeois Berliners. There were no less than 209 public dancing parties in Dortmund in January 1919, and the efforts to set an early curfew for such activities were abandoned because the workers threatened the police.[90] Of much greater moment, however, were the sentiments described in the report of a British military officer sent to examine conditions in Bavaria during the first week in April, the week when the extreme left established a dictatorship of the councils in Munich that led to the bloody seizure of power by Communists and to an even more brutal suppression by the free corps during the following week:

The greatest danger lies in the fact that the nerves of the German people appear to have broken down. A people of little political understanding, they imagined, when the Armistice was signed, that peace was immediately at hand and the privations of four-and-a-half years were over. Five months have passed, and their exaggerated hopes of a speedy peace, of quick supplies of food and clothing—hopes unduly encouraged by a somewhat reckless press—have been disappointed. Hope deferred has made the German heart sick. From the heights of hope of last November—and in spite of the disaster that had overtaken them the Armistice was hailed with genuine joy in Germany—they have plunged into the depths of despair. And it is this despair which has given Bolshevism its chance.[91]

While the revolutionary strikes and uprisings were too deficient in competent leadership and too uncoordinated with one another as well as too lacking in general support from the bulk of the population to succeed, they had important short-term and long-term consequences. First, they provided the Ministries, especially the Labor Ministry (RAM) and the Economics Ministry (RWM) with the opportunity to reestablish their authority and develop their own programs, and they also heightened the importance of the Reichstag and its legislative potential. Second, they compelled the trade unions to begin the process of reconsidering the extent of their commitment to the ZAG and to start paying more attention to their own constituency and to the reestablishment of contact with the shop floor. Third, they confirmed the impossibility of conducting a "second stage" of the demobilization in which the DMA could force the unemployed to work in agriculture or mining or, for that matter, to work under administrative pressure. The crisis management would have to continue, and the second wave of the Revolution raised fears of a third wave and reinforced governmental tendencies to buy social peace at any price through food subsidies, wage increases, and other costly measures. Thanks to the revolutionary situation, the legacy of the demobilization for Germany's finances was to be large and prolonged.

The recovery of the Ministries and the Reichstag and the beginning of the trade-union retreat from the ZAG went hand in hand. The ZAG vision was that of the most thoroughgoing societal corporatism, that is, the virtually untrammeled self-determination by interest groups and professional organizations in economic and social affairs.[92] Thus, the trade unions had themselves requested that the Stinnes–Legien Agreement be published in the Reich Register (*Reichsanzeiger*) of November 18, 1918, and this gave it a semiofficial character, while the actual accomplishments of the agreement—the eight-hour day, freedom of coalition, collective bargaining, worker committees, mediation boards, public labor exchanges based on parity, and the obligation to rehire returning troops—had been legislated by decree

along with a host of other social measures, such as the regulation of unemployment supports, limitations on the rights of employers to fire workers or shut down plants, and improvements in the social insurance system. These measures were decided upon with little or no consultation with the ZAG or even in the face of its opposition.

Gustav Bauer, who stayed on in the Scheidemann government as Labor Minister in February 1919, was an old trade unionist, but he had taken his post without consulting Legien and was intent on carrying through his own program.[93] The obvious loss of union control over a large portion of the workers, made evident by the situation in the winter and spring, convinced Bauer that the RAM had to undertake measures of its own. While the trade-union leaders were prepared to abandon their old demands for worker chambers and were absolutely hostile to the workers councils on the grounds that the need for them was obviated by the ZAG, Bauer came to the conclusion that something had to be done to satisfy worker demands for organs of direct representation. On February 22, he decreed the establishment of worker chambers for the mining industry as a concession to the mass movement in the Ruhr and shortly thereafter ordered his subordinates to begin drafting a Factory Councils bill. While the leading trade unionists remained committed to the ZAG, the events of the winter and spring had made them aware that they had alienated much of their membership by the pro-ZAG policy and had also failed to establish contact with the thousands of new members who had streamed into the unions in 1918–1919 (see Table 10). Every fourth new member,

Table 10. Development of Free Trade Union Membership, September 30, 1918–December 31, 1919

End of Quarter	Total Membership	Increase	% Increase
3rd 1918	1,468,132		
4th 1918	2,866,012	1,397,880	95.2
1st 1919	4,677,877	1,811,865	63.2
2nd 1919	5,779,291	1,101,414	23.5
3rd 1919	6,562,359	783,068	13.5
4th 1919	7,338,132	775,773	11.8

Source: Heinrich Potthoff, *Gewerkschaften und Politik zwischen Revolution und Inflation* (Düsseldorf, 1978), p. 41.

however, came out of the group that was under twenty years of age, workers who had the least experience with unions and union discipline.[94] By late spring, Legien and his colleagues were well aware that they faced opposition to their policies at the forthcoming Nürnberg Trade Union Congress scheduled to begin at the end of June, and they were quite irritated by the slowness with which the employers had moved in setting up branch working communities. While not yet prepared to see anything positive in the factory councils, the trade unionists were no longer willing to place all their hopes for realizing their goals in the ZAG and had begun to think they "could push through their aims by legislative means."[95]

No less important than this self-assertion of the RAM was the revival of the RWM, and this process, too, owed much to the political strikes and unrest in the first quarter of 1919. While the star of the RWM rose, that of the DMA set. August Müller had worked assiduously toward this end, but he was not to enjoy the final triumph. His own opposition to socialization had become so pronounced and open that his opponents in the trade unions and the party were able to argue that he was a liability. Müller yielded to pressure and resigned on February 13, to be replaced by the important trade-union leader Rudolf Wissell who, if anything, turned out to be a more impassioned and sincere supporter of Moellendorff's ideas than Müller. Koeth saw the handwriting on the wall when, on the same date, he was denied the full rights of a Minister on the grounds that the DMA was a temporary institution. Undoubtedly, the job itself had lost much of its charm for him. On February 20, he told a group of reporters that the DMA was going to be dissolved in the spring and informed Scheidemann on March 3 that he was hoping to complete the task of dismantling his agency by April 1. He frankly indicated that his disagreements with the RWM made the speedy end of his duties desirable, especially since the tasks of organizing the economy and transition in its final phases belonged to the regular ministries anyway. Actually, the DMA was not dissolved until May 1, Koeth stepping down on the following day, but it had essentially ceased to play an important role in the course of March.[96]

During this same period, the RWM under Wissell and Moellendorff demonstrated a new aggressiveness, taking advantage of the demands for socialization by the miners to present a Socialization Law, which passed the National Assembly on March 23, 1919. While ostensibly making state appropriation of an industry possible with suitable compensation, the law actually paved the way for the implementation of Moellendorff's national economy ideas in the coal sector. The existing cartels and syndicates were joined in the Reich Coal Council, in which labor was also represented and in which the state retained veto powers. At the same time, the RWM leaders turned to the task of propagating their ideas among the leaders of the ZAG, hoping to use the working communities as a foundation for setting up self-governing bodies in every branch of industry to serve the purposes of Moellendorff's national economy program. By the end of March 1919, therefore, the ZAG had to deal with increasingly formidable Labor and Economics Ministries and a newly constituted Reichstag as well. The days when industrial and trade-union leaders could dictate how the government was to organize the economic transition were over.[97]

The ZAG, in fact, decided not to raise any protest over the projected dissolution of the DMA. This decision not only reflected a recognition of its own failure to live up to its promises, the opposition that was finding expression among the employers and workers, and the vigor with which the RWM was pursuing its aims, but also mirrored the divided opinions within the ZAG over Koeth's performance. Despite some criticism of his Unemployment Relief Decree of January 15, Koeth's popularity with the trade-union leaders had, if anything, increased because of his positive attitude toward wage increases, the reduction of working hours, and other measures aimed at satisfying and pacifying the workers. Understandably, the employers were far less enthusiastic about these measures and, indeed, viewed many of them as unnecessary and dangerous. In fact, all sorts of rumors were going around about Koeth. At the Jena meeting of the nascent Reich Association of German Industry, Koeth was said to have threatened to establish and support worker chambers unless the industrialists got on with the creation of working communities and to have declared that "the unrest of the workers was well-founded because the government had not yet told the workers what the result of the Revolution was."[98]

It was even reported that Koeth had threatened to carry through socialization himself. The last contention is most unlikely, since Koeth was always careful to be neutral on the subject of socialization, arguing that one had to work with the existing system until the demobilization was over. Ernst von Borsig, who considered most of the charges against Koeth exaggerated, made a point of showing that some of the remarks attributed to him by the employer rumor mill were untrue. Still, Borsig had to confess that "I don't completely trust him."[99] He found it difficult to decide whether it was Koeth's obvious ambition and opportunism or his lack of knowledge and false calculations that were responsible for some of his actions that were offensive to employers. In economic questions, Koeth certainly had yielded to heavy-industrial demands and lifted price ceilings and export restrictions on iron and steel products. To be sure, he had also put an end to piecework in the shipyards, for which he was attacked with hateful and insulting correspondence from the major industrialists concerned, but Borsig simply attributed Koeth's action to inexperience. Whatever the case, the employers were not unhappy to see Koeth go and the DMA to disappear. The big supporters of the ZAG—Borsig, Vögler, and Jakob Reichert—now entertained high hopes that Bauer and Wissell, with whom they had been in contact, would support and make use of the ZAG in a manner desired by the employers. While the Ministers certainly encouraged the ZAG, albeit for their own purposes, they undoubtedly also found such promises useful in isolating Koeth as well as strengthening an organization important to the maintenance of social peace. There can be no question that industry had found Koeth too pro-labor for its tastes.[100]

The irritation in employer ranks probably was heightened by the simple fact that the demobilization was proving to be a very costly proposition conducted to a significant extent at their own expense as well as at the expense of the Treasury. From the perspective of the real situation, the unemployment statistics provided by the trade unions were altogether too rosy, and they are most useful in indicating certain trends rather than in providing absolutely reliable information on the state of the labor market (see Table 11). Many of the new trade-union members flooding into the organizations failed to report their unemployment, especially since new members had to wait a year before receiving union assistance. Nevertheless, given the enormity of the labor-market problem, the formal percentage of unemployed was remarkably low, even during the worst months of January and February 1919, an impression that is heightened when one considers the deliberate policy of dismissing female workers wherever possible.[101]

These aggregate statistics do not, of course, reveal sectoral and regional differences, both of which were of particular importance. The percentages of free trade-union unemployed textile workers were 10.6 percent for January and 14 percent for February 1919; those of construction workers were 17.3 percent and 14.2 percent for the same months, although this was seasonal since the percentages went down to the 5 percent range during the next two months. Metal-worker unemployment was 4.7 percent

Table 11. Unemployment in Germany, November 1918–March 1920
(percent of trade-union members)

	Men	Women	Combined
1918			
November	.3	2.8	1.8
December	.5	5.2	5.1
1919			
January	6.2	7.0	6.6
February	5.5	8.0	6.0
March	3.6	4.8	3.9
April	4.8	6.8	5.2
May	3.5	5.0	3.8
June	2.1	3.8	2.5
July	2.8	4.2	3.1
August	2.6	4.8	3.1
September	1.7	4.0	2.3
October	2.3	3.9	2.6
November	2.7	3.8	2.9
December	2.8	3.6	2.9
1920			
January	3.3	3.6	3.4
February	2.7	3.6	2.9
March	1.9	2.1	1.9

Source: BAP, RWM, Nr. 6033, Bl. 88.

and 4.8 percent for the first two months of 1919. Berlin, with its 275,000 unemployed, and Saxony, with its 234,000 unemployed, in mid-March 1919 were real trouble spots in comparison even to Düsseldorf with its 52,000 and Munich with its 38,500 unemployed at the same time. The actual work of the demobilization was accomplished at the local level, where the district Presidents served as Demobilization Commissars and worked hand in hand with local authorities, employers, and trade-union functionaries. Koeth was correct in pronouncing the effort to get the unemployed to take up agricultural work a "fiasco" and in noting with disgust that the farmers in the east were once again employing Polish workers as before the war, though his complaints took little account of what happened when local authorities did have some success in getting workers to go to the countryside. Thus, young people sent to East Prussia by the Düsseldorf Demobilization Committee certainly came back better fed, but their clothes, which were quite precious under existing conditions, were ruined, and the working conditions they had encountered made a repetition of the experiment impossible. A more systematic effort to send Düsseldorf workers to harvest the sugar-beet crop in the province of Saxony seems to have presented delousing problems of enormous magnitude, though it could boast of some success thanks to factory inspectors sent to ensure that conditions were not totally unsuitable for city workers.[102]

Unfortunately, the "success" of the demobilization and the reduction of unemployment was not accomplished with such measures but rather with a high degree of systematic and enforced waste and inefficiency. The DMA itself paved the way by maintaining work on some war contracts almost until the end of January. Thus, of the 10.3 billion in outstanding war contracts on November 10, 1918, 2.4 billions' worth were actually carried out by January 31, 1919. An almost equal amount was canceled, while 1.3 billions' worth were converted to peacetime production contracts and 2.7 billion terminated on the basis of a monetary settlement. The balance that remained at the beginning of February, which totaled 1.5 billion, was

either to be settled through a monetary payment or maintained as emergency public-works projects. In short, wasteful and expensive war production was continued in order to maintain employment.[103]

While utterly impossible to measure or aggregate, however, it is obvious that the real unemployment was being veiled by deliberate policies of overemployment and "stretching"— producing inventories for which there were no orders, operating machinery at low capacity, undertaking superfluous repairs, and the like. Decrees requiring the rehiring of returning troops, the maintenance of certain levels of employment, the hiring of at least one disabled veteran, or the banning of the shutting down of plants except under special conditions all virtually guaranteed inefficient production and waste.

Bavaria provides some interesting illustrations of how shortages of raw materials and uneconomic use of plant facilities worked themselves out. A cotton-spinning plant which had employed 471 persons in June 1914 had slightly more than half that number, 269 persons, in May 1919. Its production, however, was reduced from 215,480 kilograms before the war to 38,325 kilograms in April 1919. Relative to the number of spindles in actual use, however, the number of employed had doubled while the production had sunk by half. Likewise, a locomotive factory had increased the number of its employees from 2,030 to 2,810, but its production had decreased from 5,085 tons per month before the war to 3,200 tons afterward. A bicycle factory produced 3,600 wheels with the help of 388 workers in the last prewar month, but produced only 600 wheels with 409 employees in April 1919.[104]

In the Düsseldorf region, which was heavily industrialized, very few workers were let go because the firms were compelled to stretch work by the Düsseldorf Demobilization Committee, and every instance in which an employer sought to shut down or reduce the number of employed led to negotiations with the Committee and the factory inspectors with the objective of preventing such actions. The Elberfeld Demobilization Committee maintained employment in its textile plants by imposing a four-hour shift.[105] There is, therefore, no reason to question the generalization of the Bavarian report on the demobilization that

... the chief burden of the readjustment losses was borne by commerce and industry. The relatively good position of the labor market was only upheld by the fiction that industry could employ the larger portion of the workers. In actuality this was impossible given the halved coal supply, the raw-materials shortage, the continuation of the blockade, the uncertainty of the situation. The cost of the transition, therefore, had to be covered in large measure by the reserves of industry. These were probably not small in the case of a large number of plants because of the wartime boom.[106]

There are evidences of great strain on some industrial enterprises. A sugar-processing firm had to shut down two of its plants and feared it would have to close completely if worker wage demands persisted.[107] Upper Silesian industrialist Ewald Hilger was probably not exaggerating when he reported privately to his colleagues on March 1, 1919:

Now I'll tell you how things are doing financially. I can give you some details here, also about situations where I am informed. I know that a large work in Upper Silesia, which employed perhaps 25,000 workers, entered the Revolution with a bank account of 12 million marks. Today it has bank debts of approximately 10 million marks. Therefore, the Revolution cost an easy 22 million marks without anything added. Then there are the expenditures caused by the supplements to the officials and the workers, which amount to about 1,000 marks a head for the workers per year. That makes 25 million more alone for the workers, but that is not the total wage bill. The total wage bill is much higher than the 6–7,000 per man per year. There are worker families which earn 2–3,000 marks per month without any further effort. When sons and daughters work, then you have such circumstances. The collapse is absolutely unavoidable. I don't know how it can be prevented. The works here had to use their bank credit and to put up their holdings as security; and whether we can succeed in getting the wages we need to pay the workers in the coal mines and smelting plants on March 15 is very doubtful.[108]

Nevertheless, few such illustrations of astronomical worker wages are to be found in the sources despite continuous complaints about endless wage demands and the low productivity of workers. The dominant theme is the using up of reserves and the danger of economic collapse. Thus, a survey taken by the Duisburg Chamber of Commerce at the end of February 1919 on the effects of the Revolution did not bring forth comments that certain firms were going to shut down because of the costs but only some comments that they should shut down because of the uneconomic operation of their enterprises. Of far greater concern, however, were the low productivity and the unwillingness to work. There was fear that these would render Germany uncompetitive once international trade was restored.[109] The same concerns were expressed by the Bavarian demobilization report, which is all the more significant because it was not unsympathetic to the high wages themselves, pointing out that wages could not be called "senselessly high" since they were not worth much in real terms. The author saw the problem caused by the unquestionably large increases in wages since the outbreak of the Revolution from two perspectives. First, "the issue is not that the real wages of the workers have increased substantially but that their income has been better able to adjust to the depreciation than that of the *Mittelstand*." Second, and far more serious from a national economic point of view, "the wage increase per unit, or more simply put, the sinking productivity of the industrial worker" was the most serious consequence of the demobilization and threatened Germany's reentry into the world economy.[110]

These problems become all the more significant when placed in the context of the financial legacy of the demobilization, which was reported to the DMA at one of its last meetings, on April 10, 1919. These costs had amounted to 3.5 billion marks for January, 2.7 billion for February, and 2 billion for March. The total deficit stood at 160 billion marks. The Finance Ministry was not overly concerned about the high wages, since "the increase of the wages carries its own corrective because the purchasing power of money has sunk so much."[111] More harmful was the fact that the wage increases were being granted on a case-by-case basis, creating constant instability in the economy. Still, wages could double as far as the Finance Ministry was concerned without seriously affecting domestic production. The matter only became serious the moment Germany had to import food and raw materials. At that point, Germany could only offer increasingly worthless money which, despite its depreciation internationally, was still overvalued from the Finance Ministry's perspective. They feared that Germany would literally go hungry in the coming years and was trapped in a vicious circle. The domestic tranquility of the country and the restoration of its production depended on the workers receiving sufficient food, but in order for that food to be purchased, there had to be sufficient tranquility and productivity to pay for it.

By May, as Germany was about to face the new shock of Allied peace terms, the Revolution had been suppressed and the demobilization had run its course, but both the dangers of the former and the basic problems exposed by the latter persisted. The workers were continuing to demand the improvement of their lot, and the precedent for using strikes and violence to attain their ends was firmly established. The Revolution had been transformed into a wage movement, and the answer to the question of how the costs were to be paid was anything but obvious. The new leadership in Berlin was well aware of the situation's complexities, compounded by the fact that two groups of workers, the miners and the railroad workers, were positioned to strangle the economy in order to attain their goals. When the crisis with the miners abated somewhat, the railroad workers created a more serious situation in April as they became the vanguard of a general movement on the part of the civil servants for greater militancy. The discussion of these problems at a meeting of the Reich Food Ministry on May 5, 1919, is a fitting signature on the legacy of the Revolution and demobilization on the eve of the crisis that would arise with the peace treaty.[112]

The demands of the railroad workers, like all other worker groups, were justified by the price levels and the absence of sufficient food and clothing, and while much attention was paid to these problems, the discussions were anything but uncritical of worker contentions. In considering the situation, Undersecretary Hirsch of the Food Ministry gave a very balanced account of the sources of the nation's rising prices. The first source was the wartime and postwar monetary policies with their inadequate note coverage, heavy borrowing, and inadequate taxation. The second was the high wartime and

postwar demand for goods that could not be met, the unfortunate procurement policies pursued by the authorities, and the black market. The final source was labor, where the eight-hour day, the elimination of piecework, the "economically incomprehensible" controls on the dismissals of superfluous workers, and "above all the wage increases resulting from the special power position of the workers" all helped to drive up prices. While recognizing that it was often hard to define which was primary—prices or wages—Hirsch was convinced that wages had moved ahead of consumer prices, both official and those on the black market, since the Revolution. Nevertheless, in considering what to do, aside from the usual battle against black marketeering and efforts to tie wage increases to observable price increases, Hirsch could only come up with proposals to increase food imports from abroad in order to satisfy worker demands and, possibly, to give special food premiums to such key groups as the miners and the transport workers.

Many of Hirsch's colleagues shuddered at the thought of reviving the wartime system of special rations for certain categories of workers since this had produced considerable resentment and had led to the spreading of demands from one group of workers to another. Indeed, it had appeared as a reward to those who were in a position to blackmail the government with threats to shut down the economy. Furthermore, there was no loss of love among some of the groups, especially between the miners and transport workers; they each had a tendency to blame the other when the coal shortage was attributed to either one of them. Special food premiums, as one railroad official reported, could indeed have disastrous consequences: "The Westphalian workers told me that they will beat the railroad workers to death if they struck, but if Berlin gave in, then they would really let the mines be flooded." Hirsch's colleagues, therefore, were much more enthused about increasing food imports, whatever their cost. In somewhat desperate terms, Prussian Finance Minister Südekum spelled out the logic of this position:

The problem cannot be solved by theoretical considerations; only one way is possible, and that is to promote imports, in order to satisfy the workers in particular but then also the general public. It is a matter of state necessity for Prussia against which every consideration of the Reichsbank's attitude has to be set aside. Every price and every kind of concession is justified to prevent the shutdown of railroad traffic in Prussia. What is not feasible through the ending of the inflation is possible and can be carried out if work becomes possible as a result of improved provisioning with food. In this regard, there is no reason to consider the exchange rate, since every foreign merchant is really only influenced by his mistrust of the general conditions in Germany.

The policy of the demobilization had been to buy social peace at any price. Post-demobilization policy seemed to be headed in the direction of buying productivity at any price.

Planning Financial and Economic Reform in the Shadow of Peacemaking, January–July 1919

While it would be easy enough to take Südekum's remarks as a good illustration of the governmental passivity and helplessness that were to propel the inflation on its course, it would be a mistake to underestimate both the desire and the will to seek happier solutions. To be sure, Südekum in May 1919 was virtually repeating arguments he had used in January 1919. In reply to the reproaches of the then Baden Finance Minister Joseph Wirth, who protested that the liberal wage-supplement policies of Prussia and the Reich were setting loose demands in Baden which were unaffordable, Südekum insisted that a railroad worker strike could not be risked in the middle of the demobilization and that concessions had to be made (a point Wirth was to understand altogether too well one day when he faced Germany's greatest railway strike three years later as Chancellor). At the same time, Südekum was far from casual about the situation, which he blamed on the "frivolous wage and labor policy that was pursued in the last years of the old regime."[113] He also understood it as a legacy which Germany's new leadership had to master, among other things, by telling the truth: ". . . we move about in a world of appearance. To be sure, we are living well today. But there is no substance available to justify our living as we live. That way is just not truthful. And we have to have the cour-

age to say it. . . . We have a moral obligation to do so. We must tell the people how things really are."[114] Even the Bolsheviks, Südekum insisted, had begun to understand that labor discipline and incentives for managerial and labor productivity were essential. In rather apocalyptic terms, Südekum argued that "[I]n the seventeenth century this land was the stage for a monumental struggle of religious world views. The battles were fought out here. And now in the twentieth century, if things go further, this land will be the ground upon which the battle between western culture and Bolshevism will be fought out. The battle will be decided in Germany. . . ."[115]

While it is hard not to think of Germany's subsequent "defense" of "Western culture" without cynicism, the argument made in the context of 1919 did have a tragic legitimacy. Germany did stand between East and West and, of all the major industrial societies, faced the greatest problem of harmonizing the revolutionary socioeconomic and political tendencies set loose by the war with the task of reconstructing a stable economic and financial order in the context of a liberal parliamentary democracy and within the framework of a severely shaken international system whose economic organization was capitalist. Somehow, Germany's new leadership had to operate within domestic and international constraints which were often quite simply irreconcilable and to do so with inadequate instruments in a hostile environment. Whatever their weaknesses, faults, and errors, the persons who assumed leadership or found themselves in positions of responsibility in 1918–1919 and afterward were not only burdened by power but honestly sought to bail out the ship of state financially and economically. It is important to remember that the situation with which they had to deal was one they inherited. It was the political leadership and officialdom of the old regime which had failed to prevent the mutilation of the nation's finances and the disruption of its social system. Thus, the invidious comparison in favor of the old regime that was to gain increasing currency with Weimar's failures really arose from various mixtures of nostalgia, illusion, and outright malice.

Some of the failures of the new regime were

simply unavoidable under the circumstances. There was a conscious desire on the part of some of Germany's political leaders for an integrated social, economic, and financial policy. The barriers to this goal, however, were not simply a function of policy disputes but also of inadequate information and underdeveloped instruments for procuring it. Despite a large government apparatus for its time and a world-famous Reich Statistical Office, the basic data needed for economic and financial planning and management often were simply not available because of the chaotic conditions and inadequate personnel and facilities. Time was needed to create the essential informational base for the formulation of integrated policies.[116] Time, unhappily, was never on the side of the Weimar Republic. It would be a grave injustice to Weimar's new rulers, however, to suggest that they did not seek to confront the nation's problems directly or to overlook the extent to which their measures marked a significant change in Germany's governance. What is remarkable is both the extent to which the alternatives and possibilities were consciously realized and articulated and the interplay between conceived options and overwhelming constraints.

A case in point is the man who assumed the leadership of the Reich Treasury Office in November 1918 and then served as Finance Minister in the Scheidemann government between February and April 1919, Eugen Schiffer. Though he never emerged either as one of the heroes of the Revolution or as one of Weimar's more distinguished leaders, he deserves more recognition than he has received for his performance in 1918–1919. A former National Liberal who joined the new Democratic Party after the Revolution, Schiffer was a confirmed economic liberal. He strongly opposed the plans of Müller and Moellendorff in December 1918, and the continuation of these policies under Wissell probably played an important role in Schiffer's decision to resign in April 1919.[117] Nevertheless, Schiffer's administration must be given credit for building upon the plans and programs devised during the last year of the war

by the hapless Count von Roedern and by the talented Undersecretary who served them both, Stefan Moesle. The plans paved the way for the great finance reform that Matthias Erzberger was to push through between July 1919 and March 1920.

Schiffer had an unquestionable and admirable commitment to telling the truth about Germany's economic plight as well as to placing the responsibility where it belonged. From his first pronouncements on Germany's financial situation before the German Chamber of Commerce and Industry on December 9, 1918, through his major address to the new National Assembly on February 15, 1919, Schiffer lashed out at the economic consequences of the Hindenburg Program and at Germany's method of financing the war. While no friend of the soldiers and workers councils, he showed little patience with rightest efforts to deflect attention from the real issues by concentrating on alleged financial abuses by the councils. Quite properly, he was more concerned about the immense costs of the demobilization and the need to control government expenditures. Similarly, he was fully cognizant of the role played by the financial constitution of the old regime in preventing a more satisfactory handling of war costs.[118] In a very important meeting with the Finance Ministers of the various states on January 29–30, 1919, he bluntly told them that "[i]n the past the representatives of the states have always warmly declared their complete understanding for the needs of the Reich. But this understanding has not always been put into practice. For if this understanding had been acted upon, then we would not have carried on the false finance policy during the war which we did. It was only because of the resistance of the individual states that we were forced into a one-sided financial policy without reducing debts and without developing our taxes. I believe we must all learn from the past."[119]

Both the past and the present, however, stood in the way of the Ministry's ability to plan for the future. Directing the Reich's finances in the midst of the Revolution presented certain legal novelties which Schiffer, a jurist by training, felt very keenly. One of these was that the Reich had been spending money without any legal authorization. The old regime's last request for a credit of fifteen billion marks had been presented to the Reichstag without having been passed when the Revolution broke out. The Reich Debt Administration (*Reichsschuldver-waltung*), whose officials were bound by a special oath not to increase the government debt without legal authorization, refused to issue the appropriate documents. Rather than strain their consciences, Schiffer and his colleagues decided to make use of the Reich's status as a "legal person" which, like any legal or physical person, could issue bills and encumber itself (*Wechselfähigkeit*) if a bank would accept them. Schiffer issued such bills in the name of the Reich, and they were accepted by the Reichsbank which then issued the necessary bank notes. By the end of January, the government had received sixteen and a half billion marks in this manner, and while Schiffer could defend his actions on the grounds that the Reich "was an organism which had a right to exist," he was uncomfortable with its dependence on what were "to a certain extent private debt obligations" and wanted retroactive legitimation from the National Assembly.[120]

This, of course, he received, but his discomfort with the entire procedure is perhaps indicated by the fact that he mentioned taking only fifteen billion in credits in this manner to the National Assembly; that is, the amount of the last credit request, while the additional one and a half billion had been mentioned only in the confidential meeting he had with the state Finance Ministers. Ultimately, however, this was all of little moment, since he had to ask for a twenty-five-billion-mark credit anyway to cover the expenses of the demobilization already incurred or anticipated during the coming months. Here, too, Schiffer wished he could put an end to the employment of "fictive emergency budgets." He pointed out that "in setting up the budget during the war we have worked with numbers while conscious that they were false. I do not think it right to continue operating this way. We must go over to orderly conditions."[121] Nevertheless, the inability to predict either income or expenditure for the immediate future, not to mention the uncertainties connected with the peace treaty, made it necessary to continue operating in the old manner at least temporarily. Schiffer only could hope to indicate the general lines of a future normal budget before the National Assembly.

If the expenditures of the Reich were surrounded by problems of legality and uncertainty, so, too, were the efforts to reform the Reich taxation system and increase Reich income. On the one hand, Schiffer did not think action could wait until the creation of a new constitution, and he and Moesle considered it imperative that the basic lines of financial reform be laid out and that tax measures be prepared; on the other hand, the development of a comprehensive reform program and its implementation could not be accomplished immediately. The program Schiffer presented to the Council of People's Commissars on December 12, 1918—the same meeting at which he had battled so successfully against the demands of both Koeth and Moellendorff—mixed immediate with long-term intentions. The war-profits tax was to be increased from 60 to 80 percent of all excess profits for 1918, and the way was to be prepared for a tax on all capital gains between 1914 and 1918. Corporations, therefore, were required to set aside 80 percent of their increased earnings for the year in anticipation of them being taxed away, and persons were required to prepare an inventory of their assets so that rapid assessment could be made once the necessary legislation was passed. Schiffer and Moesle also announced their intention to prepare legislation for the taxation of higher incomes by the Reich and for an expansion of the inheritance tax. Additionally, indirect taxes were to be increased and new ones introduced.[122]

While Schiffer was anxious to announce the new program and lay the groundwork for its implementation, he was convinced that the taxes themselves had to be properly prepared and legislated. This is not quite as obvious and banal as it seems. Some of the People's Commissars, particularly USPD Commissars Emil Barth and Hugo Haase, were anxious to have immediate action in order to satisfy worker demands for the taxation of war profits and personal wealth, and they warned that the masses would not be satisfied by mere declarations of intent. While not insensitive to such arguments, Schiffer and Moesle emphasized the immense technical problems involved in preparing and implementing new tax legislation. They pointed out that the various direct taxes were intimately related to one another and could not simply be legislated without paying attention to the dangers of double taxation and inequities. As later developments were in fact to show, the Finance Ministry was greatly understaffed, while the most experienced personnel were employed by the various state Finance Ministries because it was there that most of the tax assessment and direct taxation were carried on under the old regime. Furthermore, the taxation of nonliquid wealth presented special problems not only of assessment but also of collection, since payments in kind were anticipated in certain instances, making possible the not entirely welcome prospect of the Reich being turned into a warehouse and market for second-hand goods (*Trödelmarkt*). The tax program announced by the government on December 30, 1918, therefore, concentrated on the immediate need to tap war profits and wartime capital gains, while leaving the other aspects of the program largely to statements of intention.[123]

Even this, however, alarmed the state governments. They were already worried about plans by Hugo Preuss and other framers of the nascent constitution to destroy their taxing powers and were resentful they had not been consulted by Schiffer and Moesle before the new program was issued. They also feared that they would not have the wherewithal to cover their own vastly increased wartime and postwar expenses. At the meeting of the various Finance Ministers in Weimar on January 29–30, 1919, these sentiments received particularly strong expression from the south German Finance Ministers, especially the Bavarian Finance Minister Jaffé, whose rather unique commitment to both socialism and particularism as well as his expertise in the taxation field made him the spokesman for those seeking to retain the income tax for the federal states.[124] Schiffer had himself created a degree of confusion and had played into their hands to some extent by using an income of a hundred thousand marks as the point at which the Reich would begin to participate in the collection of the income tax. Quite aside from the fact that because of the in-

flation this no longer constituted as high an income as once was the case, Schiffer had meant it only to illustrate his apparent intention to set a minimum level at which the Reich would directly tax incomes. Presumably, the taxation of lower incomes would stay in the hands of the states.[125]

Once Schiffer and Moesle realized the confusion they had sown, they retreated from specifying a figure and became more open about the fact that Reich priorities would have to come first. Schiffer not only made it clear that the old system of matricular payments could never meet Reich requirements, but also speculated as to whether a complete reversal of the old system was not in order so "that individual states as well as the municipalities would to a greater degree benefit from the Reich taxes."[126] Schiffer found a good deal of sympathy among the north German Finance Ministers who simply realized where the locus of future taxation would have to lie. Thus, an official of the Prussian Finance Ministry pointed out that if the projected tax on capital were to be paid in installments over a period of twenty to thirty years, then this was a form of income tax, and he thought it unwise to have a situation in which Reich, states, and municipalities were all going to tax incomes in an uncoordinated manner. He found it "surprising" that the Reich Treasury Office "does not want in a radical manner to pursue the way that would be logical from its point of view and draw exclusively upon capital and income for itself and [then] give the federal states and municipalities what they need for their tasks." He suspected that this was in fact the Treasury's real intention and that "it views the co-taxation of higher incomes as only a first step along this path."[127] This, however, was to be a program for the future, and while Schiffer was putting Germany on a road to financial reform, he neither seems to have worked out nor to have pressed for a full-scale change while in office.

The technical and manpower problems that plagued tax reform not only affected the drafting of legislation but also hampered effective action to prevent flight of capital and the hoarding of money. While legislation to prevent capital flight was issued immediately after the Revolution and strengthened in January, there were horrendous accounts of capital flight. The Hamburg authorities reported that a firm had transferred fifty-two and a half million marks to the Netherlands through various banks in only two weeks. Investments had been made in northern Schleswig in the expectation that the area would be given to Denmark.[128] While certainly distressed over such developments, Schiffer and Moesle warned against panic or the illusion that one could effectively close down the borders. Similarly, Schiffer rejected proposals that the Reich restamp all money and negotiable paper in an effort to combat hoarding. On the one hand, he lacked the personnel and facilities to conduct such an operation; on the other, what could he do about German money abroad? This did not rule out extraordinary measures, however, and Moesle informed the state Finance Ministers that the secrecy of bank accounts could no longer be maintained under conditions where it was essential to uncover hidden wealth. Obviously, this would further encourage private hoarding, but it would impose limits on some of the larger-scale efforts to transfer or hide wealth for purposes of tax evasion.[129] Here again, therefore, there were simply physical limits to what could be accomplished, and the Finance Ministry's hope was that a fair tax system and a repetition of promises to honor Germany's domestic obligations, especially with respect to war bonds, as well as a restoration of order would lead to a strengthening of taxpayer morality.

Holders of war loans were not only worried about repudiation or taxing away of their holdings but also about state bankruptcy arising from Allied demands, and this obviously was always very much on the minds of the Finance Ministry officialdom. The evidence suggests, however, that such concerns promoted rather than discouraged the move in the direction of tax reform. Thus, when the question of whether a financial reform would only whet the appetites of the Allies was brought up in the Council of People's Commissars, the notion was rejected on the grounds that the tax program would demonstrate how little Germany really had at her disposal.[130] Although the German leadership was alarmed by rumors that Allied demands were going to be enormous and by increasing evidence that this was to be the case,

the German position was that Wilson had promised a peace of understanding and that the Entente and its American ally would yield to economic reason and not ask for more than Germany could pay. Economic rationality and the needs of European reconstruction were expected to triumph over the quest for revenge.

Thus, when asked by Baden Finance Minister Wirth whether Germany was bankrupt, on the verge of bankruptcy, or heading toward it, Schiffer replied that the answer depended on what kind of peace Germany received. He saw little point, however, in discussing figures which Germany could or could not pay. Using imagery that was to become both popular and common in dealing with the reparations question, Schiffer compared Germany to a business: "We have to operate here like a merchant who has come into a difficult situation through the collapse of his business. He simply says, good, I pay this and this. But if you demand more, then I can undertake no obligations. So long as it cannot be determined what demands are going to be made upon us, for so long we cannot say how our future is going to look."[131] What seemed obvious to him, however, was that Germany's capacity to pay was very limited, that it depended upon the production of goods requiring foreign raw materials and foreign credits, and that Germany's credit depended upon paying off already heavy obligations to neutral countries. This left little for a war indemnity, although a partial solution might be found in the use of German labor to reconstruct the devastated areas of France and Belgium. In order to pay any reparations in cash, Germany would have to recover economically, and the neutrals did not have enough money to supply the necessary credit. Only America was in such a position, and this carried the danger of American economic penetration of Germany, "a danger which we must, however, look straight in the face, since without it we cannot go forward."[132] As the negotiations with the Americans over credits for food imports were demonstrating, however, they were demanding cash and refusing to give credits. Germany, therefore, was being forced to use the gold needed to import raw materials and to back her currency. The Reich thus faced complete loss of its credit, and this meant, as Schiffer realized, dependence ultimately upon the credit and connections of the German business community:

> It is a fact that the individual economic credit of persons and enterprises in Germany is greater than the economic credit of the Reich. And we must keep these economic entities strong. We have to use them in order to be able to get back into international economic life. All these connections must not be cut. We must be careful here. The negotiations are very difficult. We must have as our goal getting the biggest possible loan in foreign currency as soon as possible which we can use to get food and raw materials. We need to revive our economic life and create the wealth with which we can pay. And this wealth can only be the products of labor. We do not have any other assets.[133]

Again, however, Schiffer did not intend to rely solely on outside help and was firmly committed to using taxation to withdraw purchasing power from the economy and to bring down prices. When asked whether he really believed that Germany could pay her enormous domestic debt, he replied that

> . . . with the confiscation of a portion of the wealth at hand, be it directly or be it in the form of an interest-free compulsory loan, so that there is a sinking of prices and the purchasing power of money is correspondingly increased . . . [we] can bring order into our finances and . . . can get ourselves out of the *Schlamassel* without having a state bankruptcy. But if these conditions are not fulfilled, then . . . we are not to be saved. For with the present insane prices and wages our plants quite naturally cannot work rationally, above all when they must be so severely burdened [financially] by the state.[134]

Insofar as it was possible, therefore, Schiffer tried to achieve domestic financial stabilization independently of Germany's future external obligations. This appears to have been less true of his successor, Bernhard Dernburg, a banker and former Colonial Secretary, who replaced him in April 1919 and remained in office through June. Dernburg was notably unproductive, although a good measure of his undistinguished performance certainly arose from the general preoccupation of the government with the problems of the peace treaty.[135]

The full measure of the complex interconnections between the peace settlement and, especially, the reparations issue, on the one hand, and the management of Germany's domestic affairs, on the other, can only be fully comprehended in an examination of the entire history

of the Weimar Republic, but broad outlines were already coming into both consciousness and reality even before the treaty's terms were known. This was particularly the case with the dogma that Germany had to have an American loan, the notion that only a "businesslike" approach to the problem of reparations was appropriate, and the assumption that Germany's international credit was by and large a function of the credit of her leading entrepreneurs and firms. All this was clearly established even before any of the treaty terms leaked out and had profound implications for German domestic politics. The Weimar Republic could never be a state with true domestic political autonomy. Its entire existence operated under the shadow of a lost war and the burdens the war left behind as well as a Revolution viewed with hostility by a substantial portion of the population and with insecurity and dissatisfaction by those who were supposed to be its beneficiaries.

The Revolution had been made to ensure the peace, but the peace somehow had to be made compatible with the gains of the Revolution. It is extremely important to recognize that both before the presentation of the treaty and then for some time afterward, there was a basic assumption that the fulfillment of its terms would have to be consonant with the achievements of the Revolution and that social stability and domestic peace had primacy over all other concerns. Christian trade-union leader and sometime Minister Johann Giesberts, for example, argued in the Cabinet in March 1919 that "the standard of living of the German worker and his social achievements must remain secure. We must present this as a precondition by making reference to domestic political conflicts (Bolshevism), etc."[136] Two months later, when the Economics Ministry summoned a group of industrial leaders to discuss the possibility of offering the Allies capital-stock participation in major German enterprises in return for territorial concessions, especially with respect to the Saar and Upper Silesia, Free Trade Union leader Umbreit welcomed such ideas but pointed out that "[T]he workers will nevertheless have to protect their own interest. They have to place importance above all on maintaining what they have achieved in social policy. . . . All the workers who labor in the service of foreign capital must place the greatest value on maintaining our social legislation as well as our hours and wages."[137] Quite aside from the commitment to maintain social gains was a very simple practical consideration; namely, that the German worker was unlikely to be inspired by slaving away for the Allies. Dernburg was frankly fearful about the German people learning what the future had in store for them if the Allied demands were to be upheld since "the chief thing is that the German people maintains its courage, that it does not say: if we have to do all that in addition, then we won't work at all, then we would rather take unemployment relief. Then chaos will come."[138]

As Schiffer had indicated, however, Germany's leadership was dependent not only upon labor to fulfill the nation's international obligations but also upon the credit of Germany's economic leaders and enterprises, and one of the most profound consequences of both the peacemaking process and the peace treaty itself was the powerful position in which it placed the German industrial and banking community (*Die Wirtschaft*). This did not occur against the opposition of organized labor, but often with its approval and even at its insistence. An incredible illustration of this occurred after Erzberger had prevented Hugo Stinnes from serving on the Armistice Commission because the industrialist was an internationally known annexationist and thus a political liability. The ZAG sharply protested this decision on the grounds that Stinnes was an indispensable expert, and Legien went so far as to declare that he simply could not understand how political reservations stood in the way, since "when it comes to questions of existence for our industry, other considerations have to be decisive."[139]

The business community did, in fact, play a dominant role in preparing the German position on the peace treaty as well as in negotiating with representatives of the Allies, but the chief burden was carried by the bankers, especially by the Hamburg bankers Max Warburg and Carl Melchior. There were, of course, close connections between the German banks and German industry. Nevertheless, there were also important differences of style and attitude, the bankers being not only more cosmopolitan and commercially oriented but also more politically liberal and moderate. This was especially true of Warburg and Melchior, both having close American connections, opposing unrestricted submarine warfare, and extremely critical of the rampant annexationism and jingoism that had characterized right-wing industrial and agrarian circles during the war. Like the leaders of the German government beginning with Prince Max von Baden, they must be held responsible for failing to inform and prepare the German people for the fact that Wilson's Fourteen Points could form the basis of a harsh peace; yet the internationalist and free-trading aspects of the Wilson ideology were commitments which Warburg, Melchior, Schiffer, and Dernburg shared with the American President, and there is no reason whatever to doubt the sincerity of their desire to reconstruct the international economy through the restoration of prewar international monetary and commercial relationships on the basis of free trade and international cooperation. While recognizing that high monetary demands would be made upon Germany, they operated under the conviction that Wilson had promised a peace based on Germany's capacity to pay for her share of the damage and destruction wrought in the war-torn regions and that such payment could and would be made possible by a large-scale international loan to set Germany on her feet again.[140]

Whatever the virtues or defects of such a program, it is important to bear in mind that it stood in considerable contradiction to that of the RWM under Wissell and Moellendorff, so that there were irreconcilable differences between Germany's peace conference strategy and strategists, on the one hand, and the plans and planners charged with the reorganization of her domestic economy, on the other. Wissell and Moellendorff stood in an adversary relationship to Warburg, Schiffer, and Dernburg, and if the differences remained unresolved through nearly the entire period of the Scheidemann government, it was because two sets of circumstances made the positions of both groups momentarily impregnable. Warburg and his friends were needed for negotiations with the Allies, while Wissell and Moellendorff were able to ride the wave of worker unrest in the spring to promote their programs and even gain support from industrialists who were willing to play along with Moellendorff's national economy schemes in order to prevent socialization.[141]

It was not only fear of worker unrest and socialization that was making industrialists more tractable and willing to discuss the schemes of Wissell and Moellendorff in the spring of 1919, however. They themselves were becoming aware of the difficulties involved in ending economic controls and in the restoration of complete economic freedom. Decontrol, for example, had produced dangerous conflicts between iron and steel producers and machine builders and other manufacturers dependent on raw materials. The raw materials producers had persuaded Koeth to relax export restrictions, remove price ceilings, and relax controls requiring exporters to receive payment in foreign currencies. These measures, taken in November–December 1918, were backed up with promises that the availability of raw materials, especially iron and steel, would increase, that prices would moderate, and that the mark would increase in value. Instead, iron and steel producers held back their goods in anticipation of price increases, imposed onerous conditions, and raised prices massively in January and then again in February. The response of the manufacturers was one of loud protest. They accused the Ruhr magnates of being more willing to enter into a working community with the trade unions than with their fellow industrialists and of exploiting their power. In some cases, the manufacturers went so far as to threaten support of socialization as a means of ending their long-standing conflicts with their raw-materials suppliers. The more moderate and politically sensitive heavy industrialists became alarmed and persuaded their colleagues to pursue a conciliatory course. As a result, prices for most heavy-industrial products were held steady between February and April and then moderately increased after negotiations between the iron and steel producers and their customers. The experience, however, had been a bitter one and intensified the already existing mistrust between the industrial branches.[142]

The problem of exchange controls caused even more difficulty. Despite their basic commitment to a free economy, both Havenstein and Schiffer favored retention of the decree on exchange controls, albeit for somewhat different reasons. The Reichsbank wanted to get its hands on as much foreign exchange as possible in order to pay the interest on the debts to neutrals. The Reich Finance Ministry saw the exchange controls as a barrier against capital flight. Nevertheless, both wished to promote exports and, on November 1, 1918, the Reichsbank had been persuaded to leave the question of the currency in which export business was to be conducted up to the exporters. The fall of the exchange rate led the Reichsbank to retreat from this policy and to ask that billing be calculated in foreign exchange while leaving open the question of the currency in which payment was to be made. The result was confusion among the exporters. The fact that the food imports from America had to be paid for in foreign currency increased the demand for the latter and revived the inclination to reintroduce the requirement that exporters receive payment in foreign currency. At the same time, the value of the mark was still expected to improve sometime, and machine builders, for example, were prepared to demand foreign exchange for short-term orders but not to run the risk when making contracts that would not be completed in a year or more. It was possible, of course, to demand payment in the mark equivalent of a strong foreign currency based on the exchange rate being quoted on the day of payment.[143]

Ultimately, such decisions, like decisions about prices, depended on what one was selling. If there was no serious competition, it was an optimal situation; for example, an export syndicate so situated could ask the highest possible price and require payment in foreign currency or marks calculated in such a way as to eliminate the risk of exchange loss by insisting upon payment in accordance with the exchange rate in effect on the day of payment. Where German businessmen faced strong competition, then there was a strong tendency to underprice and dump goods and to accept payment in marks on unfavorable terms, a policy which was necessarily harmful to German national economic interests. Furthermore, there was the danger that foreign buyers would take measures against such dumping practices or that they would, as had the Swiss, insist on paying in marks for their iron-wares imports. The ability to create industry-wide unity against such measures and to enforce regulations was hampered not only by such "natural" causes as the existence of a large number of firms with highly diversified products typical of certain key export industries, but also by the situation in the occupied areas, where it was proving impossible to implement export and import regulations because of Allied policies. This "hole in the West" was a serious barrier to the enforcement of German customs regulations and was one of the most important arguments of those advocating an end to all foreign-trade controls. In spite of this problem, however, industry was confused because it was divided, and it was divided because conditions varied so greatly from industry to industry. Yet as Reichert (surely no enthusiast for excessive government regulation) pointed out, "the luxury of competition as in peacetime is one the German economy can no longer allow itself."[144] There was at least a minimum need for industrial self-regulation by export syndicates which would be in a position to create binding prices and payment terms designed to ensure maximum benefit to the industry and the national economy and prevent Germany from being bought out at bargain-basement prices because of her currency depreciation.

Just as the revolutionary uproar had given Wissell and Moellendorff an oppportunity to implement their program in the coal sector, so the obvious need for some kind of regulation in the area of exports provided the RWM leadership with an opening for the introduction of their organizational schemes into industry. It was one of the few instances in which the otherwise rather rigid and doctrinaire Moellendorff demonstrated flexibility and tact in the development and presentation of his schemes. He did not pursue his original plan of creating economic associations for each industry which would then, among other things, organize the regulation of exports, for the pressing nature of export regulation to prevent dumping caused him to concentrate his attentions there and to attempt to use export controls as the wedge for the attainment of his larger organizational goals. Thus, he proposed the creation of some

seventeen export control boards (*Außenhandelsstellen*) for the various industrial branches which would, in turn, establish sub-boards (*Außenhandelsnebenstellen*) where appropriate. The textile industry, for example, was to have nine sub-boards, while the paper industry was to be limited to two such sub-boards, one for paper production and the other for paper processing. Wherever possible, the export control boards were to act as successors of the wartime central bureaus. The entire system was to be placed under the direction, as was the case during the war, of a Reich Commissar for Exports and Imports, and each export control board was to have a Reich Commissar (*Bevollmächtigte*) and a committee of no more than sixteen persons representing producers, merchants, and consumers, each of these groups having an equal number of labor and management representatives. The fundamental idea, as with all the national economy schemes, was to produce self-regulation by the interested parties under government surveillance. By the end of July, export control boards and sub-boards existed in metals, construction materials, paper, synthetics, textiles, leather, chemical, and grocers' goods.[145]

This emphasis on export organizations did not mean a loss of interest in the creation of the broader industrial organizations of which they were meant to be a part, although only in the textile industry did such organizations exist before Wissell and Moellendorff left office in July. Here, again, they sought to sell and implement their program through existing organizations, turning to the ZAG, the Association of German Iron and Steel Industrialists, and the Reich Association of German Industry. They encountered very little enthusiasm or encouragement. The problems Wissell and Moellendorff faced in dealing with the ZAG were not very different from those experienced by Koeth. The effort to use the ZAG to realize their various goals and programs was frustrated by the incompleteness of the ZAG organization. Nevertheless, there were also important differences. Koeth had purely short-run constructions in mind and basically sympathized with the liberal and voluntaristic principles on which the ZAG was based. Wissell and Moellendorff, by contrast, intended to use the ZAG as part of a complicated and grandiose corporatist organization of the entire German economy that would include agriculture, the crafts, and the commercial sector as well as consumers. The working communities would be turned into executive organs of a planned economy. Although sympathetic to Wissell (who was a trade-union colleague), Legien was by no means certain he wished to have the odd combination of greater power and reduced freedom which the RWM was offering, and it is a measure of the retreat of the ZAG from its previous pretensions that Legien and his colleagues in the ZAG leadership emphasized the consultative as opposed to the executive functions of the ZAG, urging that the RWM consult with the ZAG about all legislation and insisting on the power to nominate the personnel for the various bodies the RWM meant to create.[146]

The industrialists themselves were divided about the RWM program, which at once appealed to their belief in industrial self-government and threatened to limit their freedom of action. Their dilemma arose from the fact that they were convinced that international trade and other aspects of economic life simply could not be left totally unregulated under the existing circumstances. They also needed government backing to make the implementation of industrial trade-association policies effective. Jakob Reichert, for example, supported the creation of compulsory export syndicates so as to maximize export profits and agreed to the necessity of export controls. As head of the wartime Central Agency for Exports and Imports for Iron and Steel, he had become convinced of the system's advantages and believed that it had to be maintained as long as there was a significant difference between the domestic and international value of the mark. Nevertheless, he was very hostile to Moellendorff's grand design because he saw behind it an end to true industrial self-government and its replacement by government tutelage through an instrumentalization of industrial organizations and the ZAG. He wished to maintain the ZAG as an autonomous alliance of "producers." As he cogently argued:

... The Working Community above all is constructed on a free foundation. The Reich Economics Ministry thinks of and needs compulsion. The Work-

ing Community very wisely limits itself to economic and social *policy*; The Reich Economics Ministry interferes in *business* activity. . . . A further difference between the two structures is that the organs of the Working Community are composed on the basis of parity of workers and employers from *industry*. In no case do industrial employers work together with merchants and consumers in the same organs. The solidarity, of whose importance the Working Community is convinced, is for us an entirely different one from that presented here by the Economics Ministry.[147]

The relationship between the RWM and the industrialists was made even more difficult by the fact that Moellendorff had a tendency to present his programs in a highly abstract and schematic manner which left his hearers at once puzzled and terrified, the former because they were never quite sure of what he wanted, the latter because they shuddered at the thought of establishing new organizations after years of governmental controls they had found obnoxious. There were, to be sure, a few notable instances of industrialist sympathy for the Moellendorff program—for example, paper products industrialist Hans Krämer and certain circles of the chemical industry—but the more general spectrum of opinion ranged from absolute hostility, especially in small and medium-sized industry, to opportunistic collaboration on the part of those who feared socialization. General Director Vögler, for example, thought the entire business would "waste much costly time with unproductive labor." Nevertheless, "we always have to bear in mind that the government, whether it wishes or not, is forced to interfere in the economy. It would be better in the general interest of industry to collaborate than only to conduct opposition and thereby not improve the situation in any way. The severe opposition of commerce to the Reich Economics Office is certainly understandable, but commerce has through its approach—of this there can be no question—only strengthened the position of Wissell."[148]

The reaction of commercial circles, above all in the Hansa cities of Hamburg, Bremen, and Lübeck, certainly was notable for its absence of tact and perhaps reflected the feeling that the German merchant had nothing to lose but the chains of the compulsory economy. The war had severely reduced international trade, and the blockade continued to delay the restoration of commercial contacts and connections. A hallmark of the management of the war economy had been the effort to exclude merchants and middlemen as much as possible, and it was no accident that the more syndicalized and concentrated industries which handled their own marketing were friendlier to the RWM plans and export controls than other industries as well as relatively indifferent to the plaints of the commercial sector. Commerce had an obvious and simple interest in increasing imports and exports as much as possible, and this put it in direct conflict with Wissell and Moellendorff who were intent on pursuing as autarkic a policy as possible, thus in effect exacerbating the conditions about which the merchants had been complaining throughout the war.

One may be certain, therefore, that Wissell would have preferred a trip to the dentist over one to Hamburg in April 1919, but he went nevertheless and tried to persuade the businessmen there to give up their opposition and accept the fact that Germany could afford neither to import without restraint nor to export whatever she wished at any price without destroying both the currency and the economy. The response was as icy as could be expected, the president of the Hamburg Chamber of Commerce, Franz Witthoefft, attacking the RWM program as deleterious to economic recovery and suggesting that the bureaucracy was neither intelligent nor honest enough to fulfill the tasks assigned to it. The reaction became unpleasantly hot, however, thanks to Bremen coffee merchant Ludwig Roselius, who launched a vituperative public campaign against Wissell and especially against Moellendorff, identifying the national economy program with Bolshevism and hysterically warning that it would lead to Germany's destruction. The meeting marked the beginning of a continuous protest campaign throughout the spring and early summer by the various commercial groups and organizations.[149]

Most typical of the campaign against the RWM as well as illustrative of the concrete issues to which it was addressed, however, was a petition of May 1919 by the Hamburg-based Association of German Exporters calling for the end of export controls except for such vital necessities as food, coal, nitrates, and iron. The argument was that the system of minimum prices, however profitable during the war, was proving hopelessly counterproductive as international trade was being restored and Germany was faced with severe competition from other nations. Many products could no longer be sold at the excessively high prices being dictated from Berlin. This was illustrated by letters from Scandinavia and Switzerland appended to the petition as well as by the universal complaints about the clumsy and slow workings of the export agencies. A firm wishing to export dyes had begun making requests for minimum price information on February 17 and still had not received a satisfactory reply by May 15, despite a dozen exchanges of correspondence. The system often functioned as an invitation to smuggling. The minimum export price for aspirin, for example, was such as to encourage Germans to smuggle it out at a lower price with the help of French officers in the occupied areas and still make a handsome profit. The exporters objected not only to the bureaucratic nature of the system, however, but also to the way it created conflict between industry and commerce and threatened to drive the merchant out of business. This was illustrated by an association of aluminum utensil producers in Lüdenscheid which used the export agency to enforce special provisions for the sale of goods. The association itself confessed that its purpose was to exclude the merchants from the sale of these products by making it profitable only for the manufacturers themselves to sell abroad. Ultimately, the merchants argued, this was not in the interest of Germany's reconstruction or German industry, because few firms or industries were large or concentrated enough to handle their own export business, but experienced export merchants were prepared to go to every corner of the world and sell even in small amounts at high prices. The petition concluded:

Industry and commerce have a great interest in working hand in hand and the central bureaus as well as the many manufacturers associations are committing the greatest injustice when they try to press the merchants to the wall. If the government agrees with that type of procedure, then let it ban commercial activity, so that the merchant at least knows where he stands. . . . If the government, however, is convinced of the utility of exporting for our economy, then let it

Max Warburg (1867–1946). (*By permission of the Ullstein Verlag*)

free the export trade from the chains of the central agencies. . . . Only a free export trade can . . . be in a position to procure the so desperately needed foreign exchange.[150]

The high point of the criticism of the new RWM program undoubtedly was a speech by Max Warburg on June 27, 1919, at the founding of the Oversees Club in Hamburg at which he called for "a new free trade."[151] Certainly the most articulate and measured spokesman for the commercial interests of his native city, Warburg's views were of particular importance because of his central role in the negotiations with the Allies as well as his weight within the German business community. In March he had warned Havenstein against retaining exchange controls once peace had been concluded, citing as the most practical reason that, "if retained, then there is the danger that they will be overrun by the force of circumstances, that is, that they will be ignored by exporting circles just as already thousands of war regulations are treated by the population as if they do not exist. . . ."[152]

Most revealing of his position and that of his colleagues in the commercial sector, however, was his commentary on the Wissell program,

probably composed in mid-May 1919.[153] The memorandum contained the usual criticisms and arguments against the bureaucratic restraints to which the commercial sector had been subjected, emphasizing the embitterment caused by frustrating trips to Berlin, where it was necessary to run from office to office to secure permission from the various agencies. Similarly, Warburg presented the usual arguments for the freeing of initiative and the importance of increasing trade. He strongly urged that such controls as were retained be decentralized so as to make possible the speedy settlement of problems.

Warburg's remarks were particularly interesting, however, in three respects. First, he was unusually explicit about the points of conflict between industry and commerce and the reasons for the latter's lack of enthusiasm for the branch organization that underlay both the recently created Reich Association of German Industry and the RWM plans. Whereas industry was organized according to its products, commerce was organized in terms of the regions with which it traded, so that the interests of the latter seemed irrelevant to the former:

The great Hamburg merchant who today for example exports bicycles or brewing machinery together with all the other German export products, to Venezuela will—with his small fraction of the bicycle export market—get just as little hearing in the discussions of the relevant branch organization as his other colleagues who take care of exports to the other parts of the world and who together account for 100 percent of the export business."

This profound structural difference and the tendencies toward industrial cartelization and syndicalization were creating the danger that commerce would be excluded or that its interests would be neglected despite its fundamental importance to the German economy. But it was no accident that the views of the iron and steel industrialists and the merchants were so different, since the former were highly organized and had a powerful central bureau for imports and exports that frustrated merchant demands for greater flexibility. While the wartime situation permitted the charging of exorbitantly high prices to neutrals, Warburg warned that the restoration of international competition would change this situation and make the merchant's flexibility in setting prices and responding to market opportunities more necessary.

Second, Warburg argued that the concern about Germany's exchange rate was not a good reason to maintain controls: "In the financial situation in which we find ourselves we have, at least in the next decade, no interest in having our currency come even near its previous worth again. We only have to work toward a stabilization of our exchange rate. This stabilization can only be attained in free monetary transactions." German ability to export thus depended upon a reduced value for the mark, while the conduct of business required that the value be relatively stable. Government measures promoted gambling instincts and encouraged speculation against the mark in Warburg's view, while freedom of transaction would enable German bankers to engage in exchange transactions of their own that would act as a counterweight to foreign speculation. In the absence of fixed exchange rates, Warburg was convinced that the best counter to speculation lay in the free play of the market where private enterprise had a natural interest in stable conditions.

Finally, Warburg welcomed the idea of foreign capital investment in Germany and viewed the relaxation of controls as the best means to encourage it. Investment by foreigners would mean an import of capital and would thus raise the value of the mark itself. In fact, he urged that Germany seek such foreign investment in German enterprises, especially by those with whom Germany was likely to enter into friendly economic relations. Here, as elsewhere, Warburg's views ran counter to those of the RWM, which were strongly nationalist and autarkic. This is not to say that Warburg was not a fervent nationalist himself. Indeed, he argued that the peace-treaty terms, with their territorial losses, made it particularly important not to have extreme foreign trade restrictions since they would only serve to increase the separation of annexed or occupied areas from Germany. Fundamentally, however, he viewed Germany's recovery as a function of its successful reintegration into the international capitalist world through the restoration of economic freedom.

The uncompromising demands for the restoration of free trade and the extreme nature of the attacks on Wissell and Moellendorff from the commercial sector undoubtedly would have been more counterproductive than they were except for the fact that they helped to fuel the much more potent opposition to Wissell from within the Scheidemann government while the Allied peace terms decisively undermined the RWM's position. The RWM's Cabinet opposition came from two sources. On the one hand, Finance Minister Dernburg and Treasury Minister Georg Gothein, both of the DDP, were economic liberals and opposed the RWM for ideological as well as practical reasons; on the other hand, Socialist Food Minister Robert Schmidt also opposed the RWM schemes because he was convinced that they would destroy the chances for the socialization of ripe industries and other traditional Socialist goals, and because they ran counter to the efforts of his ministry to import food for the workers and thus start up the economy once again by encouraging productivity. Given the incompatible economic programs advocated within the Cabinet, it is no wonder that the Scheidemann government never developed a clear economic policy, a task it could put off because of its immediate domestic and international problems. Since the issues dividing the Cabinet could not be fought out on the level of principle without tearing the government asunder, each of the relevant Ministries pursued its own policies with considerable autonomy, and conflicts found subterranean expression, so to speak, in heated debates over spheres of authority. The most serious of the latter were those between two Socialist-led Ministries, the Food Ministry and the RWM, and these provided Dernburg and Gothein with welcome opportunities to deepen the conflict between Wissell and Schmidt as well as promote their own liberal solutions.[154]

The disagreements finally came to a head at the beginning of May over the issue of food imports and their payment. While Schmidt and his liberal colleagues wanted to increase food imports and loosen export restrictions in order to procure the necessary foreign exchange, the RWM tended to favor raw materials imports over food imports and wished to maintain strict controls on foreign trade. On May 5, Dernburg informed the Cabinet that the future financing of food imports had become a major problem and suggested that exporters be encouraged by being allowed to retain 20 percent of their foreign-exchange proceeds instead of being forced to deliver all their foreign exchange to the Reichsbank. In addition, he proposed such other measures as the mortgaging of enterprises and merchant ships to procure foreign loans and the creation of a single authority to decide such matters "in order to avoid competency conflicts."[155] On the following day, a "Dictatorial Committee" was created with Wissell as chairman and Gothein and Schmidt as members along with Erzberger and Undersecretary Toepffer of the Foreign Office. Toepffer was to handle the management of committee operations. The purpose of the committee was to examine and decide upon the measures necessary to procure foreign currencies.[156] When the committee met on May 8, decisions were taken to let exporters keep 20 percent of their foreign exchange proceeds, to give coal exporters 20 percent of the value of their exports to purchase additional food for the miners, and to undertake other measures to help exporters purchase the foreign raw materials they needed. That the ultimate purpose of the entire action was to loosen up the foreign-trade restrictions was left in no doubt when Dernburg explained the purpose of the new committee to the National Assembly in precisely such terms.[157]

Wissell and Moellendorff were not prepared to stand by idly and have their entire program undermined in this manner. Instead of eliminating the Reich Food Ministry by taking over its functions, as he had hoped, Wissell now found himself presiding over a committee forced upon him by Ebert and Scheidemann at the behest of Dernburg. Its true purposes were to sacrifice the RWM program to Schmidt's insistence in promoting food imports and to back the Dernburg-Gothein effort to restore free trade. Wissell and Moellendorff, therefore, decided to use the Dernburg speech to force the Cabinet to make a decision as to what kind of economic policy it wanted. They accused Dernburg of using the food-import issue as a device for sabotaging the RWM foreign-trade policy. Having reluctantly relented in his opposition to the use of foreign exchange to buy food instead

of raw materials, Wissell now found that even raw materials were to be used to buy food. Wissell regarded such a policy as short-sighted and viewed his continuation in office under such conditions as impossible. In order to help the Cabinet come to a decision, he submitted a memorandum and a lengthy economic program. The latter had originally been given to Labor Minister Bauer in the hope that it could become the basis of a common Socialist program in the Cabinet. Significantly, Bauer had never responded, and so the memorandum, which was dated May 7, 1919, and was accompanied by a letter from Scheidemann, was sent under Wissell's name alone. In fact, the document, largely the product of Moellendorff's pen, had been composed in April and had been sent already to the Socialist Cabinet Ministers.[158]

The significance of the memorandum lay not in its novelty, since most of its ideas had been propagated by the RWM for months and by Moellendorff for longer, but rather in its comprehensive character and the challenge it presented not merely to the liberals but also to the Socialists. Fundamentally, it was a bid for power in the name of unifying economic, social, and financial policy. Wissell argued that the people were losing faith in the government because of its unsteady and unstable policies and the unclear division of responsibility for basic economic policy. He charged that Socialist principles were being sacrificed "to the democratic principle" and coalition politics.[159] As a result, Germany was not in a position to confront her changed economic circumstances with clarity and effectiveness. That economic situation was described in the blackest possible terms. Because of the war, "Germany has become poor and unemployed."[160] Burdened by war costs and Allied demands and excluded from world markets by blockade and discrimination, it was thrown back on its own resources. To meet the new situation, the economy had to be organized and regenerated from within. Once again, therefore, the RWM strongly advocated its comprehensive organization of the economy along branch lines and its proposal for a Reich Fund. At the same time, it accused the Socialist parties of holding on to obsolete notions of socialism and combining these with "petty bourgeois" notions of individual freedom instead of embracing the idea of socialism propagated by the RWM, the *Gemeinwirtschaft* concept, which the RWM defined as a "national economy that is systematically managed and socially controlled for the benefit of the national community."[161] In their view, the government had to go beyond blaming the old order and crying poverty. It also had to provide ideals, since "the frighteningly profit-oriented striving of the German working class of late, on the one side, and the drawing power of confused foreign ideas, on the other side, reveals that our socialism suffers from poverty of ideals."[162]

In its actual eight-point program, the RWM called for the reorganization of the economy, using the councils principle for regional organization and the branch principle for industry, and proposed the extension of the national economy organization used in the coal and potash industries to the electrical power industry and the grain-milling industry. At the same time, it urged that the new taxes on property and wealth be used by the Reich to buy into industrial enterprises and to create thereby a large number of enterprises that combined public and private ownership. The administration of the Reich enterprises and the Reich's share holdings in private enterprises would lie in the hands of a Reich Assets Bank (*Reichsvermögensbank*), which would also administer the Reich Fund. In order to discourage food imports and gain control over their unhappy effects on the economy, the RWM urged partial payment of worker wages in food and clothing and the raising of the bread price so that the Reich would have a fund at its disposal with which to give extra rations to the miners and other workers whose labor could be expected to promote the inflow of foreign exchange. The disciplining of labor demands was to be furthered by a law on labor peace which would severely restrict the right to strike in vital industries by requiring mediation and a nine-tenths majority vote of the workers before a strike could begin legally. Finally, the determination of economic policy was to be placed in the hands of an Economic Committee composed of the Economics Minister as the chairman, the Labor Minister, and the Finance Minister, all of whom were to be committed to the national economy program. The instructions of the Economic Committee were to be binding on the Food Ministry, Foreign Office, and all other government agencies dealing with economic affairs.

The RWM memorandum was obviously a severe challenge to the Scheidemann Cabinet, since it would have turned the RWM into the dominant Ministry, but it also was politically daring in its insistence that the German working class could be called upon to trade its material demands and right to strike for the implementation of a national economy program based on a high degree of autarky and self-discipline. It is difficult not to characterize the program, whatever the virtues of certain aspects and the high motives of its authors, as politically tactless and doctrinaire. Moellendorff certainly was both, and his expectation that Germans would choose "to be poor in order to be pure"[163] had a strong air of unreality. It also had strong intimations of authoritarianism. The tactics of the RWM may have been, to some extent, the product of the atmosphere of the Ministry, many of whose leading officials had become devotees of its author, as had Wissell, who behaved like a convert. In any case, the memorandum of May 7 was presented in such a way that it would mark either the beginning or the beginning of the end of the RWM program.

Both Gothein and Schmidt were intent on making sure it was the latter and presented sharply critical countermemoranda. Gothein's was the more prosaic of the two, engaging in traditional liberal attack on over-organization and economic controls, which he viewed as an invitation to further black marketeering and smuggling. He was especially disdainful of the RWM efforts to achieve maximum economic self-sufficiency, pointing out that "an autarkic economy is utopian for any more or less civilized people, most of all for the Germans"[164] and insisting that Germany had to restore her position in international trade. Whereas Gothein played the traditional economic liberal, Schmidt played the traditional Socialist. He pointed out, with considerable justification, that the Coal Socialization Law had not really quieted the workers down and that the national economy scheme had nothing to do with so-

cialization as defined by the Erfurt Program—
that is, "the transfer of possessions from private
to social property."[165] He dismissed the overblown emphasis on organization in the RWM
memorandum by pointing out that "it is not
the organization of the Reich Economic Council that will save our industry from enslavement
but rather the return to intensive work which
has priority today."[166] While not objecting to
greater coordination of policy, Schmidt argued,
not surprisingly, that the Reich Food Ministry
had to be included in the decision making because of its importance under existing conditions.

Of much greater interest was the manner in
which Schmidt dismissed the RWM claims that
Germany was hampered in both its production
and its ability to reenter the world market. In
Schmidt's view, this simply was not true. While
agreeing that reduced coal production and
labor difficulties were a problem, Schmidt
pointed out that there were plenty of important
industries with domestic raw materials at their
disposal which had orders from abroad: iron
and steel, small iron wares, machines, potash,
chemicals, wood, bricks and cement, glass and
porcelain, for example. If these industries had
enough coal and if they and agriculture could
get enough workers, then both a domestic and
an international market stood waiting. Thus,
"the problem is put in a completely wrong way
by the Reich Economics Ministry from a national economic point of view. At present the
problem is much less one of getting contracts
for industry and much more one, as in the war,
of shifting workers to those industries which
have possibilities of work without fully using
them."[167] Indeed, Germany was in a position to
offer "devastating" competition on the world
market:

This superiority over the competition finds expression in the pricing of goods on the world market. It
suffices alone to point to the fact that the value of our
currency has fallen to one-third of its value. Through
this unfavorable rate of exchange we are in the position where we can offer our goods at approximately
one-third of the domestic price to foreign customers.
But since wages have increased considerably abroad
in the countries with which we compete, we have an
advantage when offering our products which the
competition simply cannot match. The [RWM]
memorandum emphasizes difficulties in reestablish-

ing foreign connections. They exist, but at no time
will it be so easy for us to establish these connections
as at the present time when the unfavorable exchange
rate gives us the possibility of competitive superiority
on the world market.[168]

Schmidt's argument lacked the rigor, austerity, and virtuous tone of the RWM memorandum, but it had the virtue of accessibility to
mere mortals uninitiated in the mysteries of the
national economy doctrine, of being optimistic
at a time when there was very little cause for optimism, and of offering what appeared to be
feasible solutions to what were otherwise
intractable problems. Party affiliations notwithstanding, Schmidt really was closer to Warburg than to Wissell, and he had joined with important segments of the German business community in grasping the possibilities offered by
monetary depreciation for the restoration of
Germany's position on world markets.

On the day the Wissell and Schmidt memoranda were submitted, however, the difficulties
facing Germany attained new heights with the
announcement of the peace terms. This pushed
the Cabinet conflict over economic policy into
the background. An awareness that the terms
could be extremely harsh existed before their
presentation, but the fact that they were dictated rather than negotiated made dealing with
the problem in a concrete manner virtually impossible, so that the government oscillated between illusion and panic. The former was illustrated by the guidelines for the German peace
delegation of April 21, 1919, whose dream-like
interpretation of Wilson's Fourteen Points
went so far as to contemplate a referendum in
Alsace-Lorraine and the limitation of Germany's financial obligations to the damage
done in the occupied areas. The German government hoped that the bill could be paid
largely in goods rather than cash. While willing
to tax herself to "the utmost," Germany needed
to pay not only her external but also her internal debts and could only make payment after
receiving a loan permitting her economic recovery.[169]

The panic developed once the realities were
faced squarely, as was the case when Dernburg
discussed the financial capacity of Germany before the Cabinet on April 26, 1919. He had to
admit that "the French economic situation, if it

is at all possible, is even sadder than our own."[170] While its industrial areas had been destroyed, an impoverished world was in no position to purchase French luxury exports. Clearly, therefore, Germany would have to pay something, but Dernburg was convinced that this was impossible until there was an economic recovery and that Germany could only become a "good debtor" if the Allies would have the patience to wait a year or two. Exactly what the French were supposed to do about their own plight during this period was not discussed, but Dernburg warned that if the Entente turned the reparations debt owing to them into a first claim on German resources, then the result would be disaster. If Germany did not pay its debts to the neutrals, it would not have the credit needed to import and produce. At the same time, he warned that the domestic debt had to be paid as well. He claimed that Germany's war bonds did not lie in the hands of pensioners or coupon clippers but rather in the hands either of business people who had directly invested in the hope of renewing their plants and replenishing their empty inventories with the returns or of "countless little people" whose money had been put into war bonds by savings banks and public and private insurance funds and institutions. Dernburg warned that "if we shake an important part of our social structure, if we do not pay old age insurance, accident insurance, do not fulfill our obligations, do not pay life insurance, then German economic life will come to a standstill."[171]

In contrast to Schiffer, who had been relatively optimistic about what could be achieved through taxation, Dernburg seemed overwhelmed by the problems, pointing out that the reserves had been eaten up since the Revolution while expenditure had increased. He had been granting money for the war disabled, food subsidies and the like, but everyone knew from where this money came:

A decision of the National Assembly is made. On its basis, Reich Treasury bills are printed and on the basis of the Reich Treasury bills notes are printed. That is our money. The result is that we have a pure assignat economy. We have pure paper money. . . . What can we pay? We do not have foreign currency. We do not even have enough of the foreign currency that is needed in order to pay what is necessary to feed

our people under the Brussels Agreement. . . . Should we now, since we do not have it, offer some sum payable in German marks? As I said, we can send as much German marks as the people want to have, since it only has to be approved by the National Assembly; in general, it is a job for the German Reich Printing Office, and the other printing plants can be called upon. That is obvious. But the enemy cannot use the German mark; they can't do anything with it.[172]

Hence, Dernburg at once recognized that the French needed real money and felt that Germany was in no position to provide it in the immediate future. He could only hope that this was recognized. The upshot of the entire presentation, however, was a retreat into passivity, as illustrated by the decision not to do anything about the tax program for the time being "because of the general situation."[173]

The announcement of the peace terms thus constituted an immobilizing shock, even if the final reparations sum was not to be announced until May 1921 after a commission had the opportunity to determine Germany's capacity to pay. The failure to state the final sum meant a perpetuation of the uncertainty that had plagued Germany since the conclusion of the Armistice, while the actual losses and obligations imposed by the terms combined with the Allied decision to include such items as war pensions among the war costs for which Germany was liable could only increase the sense of hopelessness. It appeared that insofar as Germany could recover, that recovery would only serve the benefit of her enemies, and this material loss and deprivation was compounded by a profound sense of injustice. The "war guilt" clause introducing the reparations section of the Treaty became a fixation for the Germans, and the humiliation was compounded by the provisions calling for the surrender and trial of Germany's wartime leaders, its virtual disarmament, and the loss of all colonies.[174]

If in retrospect it is clear that the Treaty preserved German unity in the face of French designs on the Rhineland and certainly was no worse than what the Germans imposed on the Russians at Brest-Litovsk and would have imposed on a defeated Entente,[175] it is important to bear in mind that mankind does not live in a state of retrospective observation and eternal gratitude that things are not as bad as they might have been. It had been a great mistake for the Germans to underestimate the potential harshness of a treaty produced under the aegis of the Fourteen Points and an even greater mistake for Germany's leadership not to make this clear to the German people as well as subsequently to overstress the war guilt question in trying to modify the terms.[176] It would be ridiculous, however, to argue that the Treaty did not violate both the letter and the spirit of the Fourteen Points and that it was not extremely harsh. No amount of prior preparation would have made it appear just to the German people. Such preparation would have had an important domestic political function, especially if accompanied by a systematic effort to place the blame for Germany's plight on the old regime. This would have helped pave the way for dealing with the problems of reconstruction in the context of the Treaty. Instead, the Treaty became the most horrendous of the legacies of the old regime placed on the back of the Weimar Republic, and no matter what its justice or injustice and no matter how understandable in its historical context, it must be accounted as a disaster of the first rank.

The territorial terms of the Treaty involved the loss of Alsace-Lorraine, most of Posen and West Prussia, Memel, Danzig, and the German colonies. The Saar was placed under French control until 1935, when a referendum was to decide its fate, and referenda were to be held in Eupen-Malmedy, North Schleswig, portions of East and West Prussia, and Upper Silesia. The left bank of the Rhineland and the Bavarian Palatinate along with Koblenz, Cologne, Mainz, and Kehl were placed under Allied occupation for from five to fifteen years as security for the fulfillment of the Treaty. Thus, Germany lost 10 percent of its population, one-eighth of its territory, 43.5 percent of its pig iron capacity and 38.3 percent of its steel capacity. The occupation gave the Allies a potential stranglehold on Germany's chief areas of industrial production, and Germany was liable for the costs of the occupation. At the same time, it was liable for the payment of twenty billion gold marks to the Allies before May 1, 1921. Further, it was to issue a hundred billion gold marks in bonds as a guarantee of future payment of reparations, although these bonds were

to bear no interest until the final sum was set. To be credited against these amounts were proceeds from the sale of German property in enemy countries, Reich property in the annexed territories, the value of the merchant ships and railroad stock and other goods delivered to the enemy under the Armistice agreements as well as the value of the twenty-five million to forty million tons of coal Germany was required to deliver to France, Belgium, and Italy yearly, the 25 percent of German pharmaceutical and dye production to be delivered yearly until 1925, and reconstruction material delivered in kind and labor services agreed upon for the reconstruction of the devastated areas. It is to be noted that Germany was to receive no credit for German property confiscated by the Allies during the war or for the private losses of her citizens in the annexed areas, although the Reich was obligated to compensate its own citizens and enterprises for such losses. Germany was also obligated to pay foreign creditors for their claims against private German citizens for prewar debts on the basis of a "clearing" agreement designed to deal with such claims. Furthermore, the value and price of those items to be credited against reparations were to be determined by the Reparations Commission, a matter of no small importance since German and Allied estimates often turned out to be very different. However these estimates turned out, they would most likely fuel the bitterness felt over a Treaty whose terms can reasonably be described as harsh and humiliating.[177]

The presentation of the Allied demands pushed the entire debate and discussion concerning the RWM economic program into the background, even though Wissell and Moellendorff believed that the Treaty made their program more necessary than ever. Nevertheless, the conflict over the program continued to play a role because the German counterproposals to the Allies almost invariably collided with the intentions of the national economy program. These counterproposals were of two types. First, there were the suggestions, which seem to have been supported by Gothein, Erzberger, and Dernburg, for Allied participation in German enterprises as an alternative to territorial demands and monetary payment. These seem to have been encouraged by American industrial and banking circles and were discussed at a meeting of over sixty industrialists with government officials under the chairmanship of Wissell on May 24, 1919.[178] While Wissell emphasized that any such foreign participation in German enterprises would have to be done in a manner consonant with the national economy program, Gothein stressed the importance of foreign capital, especially American, to Germany's reconstruction and even secretly hoped that Germany might get back some of its merchant marine by this means. Gothein's positive stance was supported by Carl Duisberg, who suggested that foreign capital might participate in Germany's new nitrates works and who agreed with Gothein's suggestion that individual industrial groups make contact with their foreign counterparts to discuss capital participation in German enterprises. Duisberg also thought that a German initiative would make a virtue of necessity, since "the bad situation of our currency will make it particularly easy for foreign capital to enter our economy. It is therefore in our interest to prevent this by making proposals of our own and above all to avoid having the control of our economic life fall to the enemy." Duisberg suggested that the German corporation law might be employed to create preferential stock (*Vorzugsaktien*) with multiple voting rights that would be reserved for German stockholders so as to maintain German control. In his view, the coal, nitrates, and potash industries were particularly attractive to foreign investors.

This positive attitude was not shared by all Duisberg's colleagues, however. Some objected simply out of fear of foreign domination, while Carl Friedrich von Siemens questioned the efficacy of the project. He pointed out that the Allies had different interests, England and America viewing Germany as a dangerous competitor whose technology they wished to appropriate, while France was too poor to invest in Germany and wished to secure raw materials and money gratis. There was considerable confusion over the modalities of foreign participation in the German economy. While some, especially those friendly to the national economy program, argued that the best way to protect German interests would be to have in-

dustry organized into large groups under Reich leadership, Gothein and others stressed that the Americans did not want to deal with the government but rather with private industrial branches. Negotiations, therefore, would have to be conducted by the industries themselves. Exactly how such private arrangements were supposed to change the provisions of the Treaty was not made clear by Gothein, whose conviction that it would ultimately lead to pressure for a revision of the Treaty appeared to be a long-run rather than a short-run calculation. Notable for his absence from the meeting was Hugo Stinnes, a matter of no small importance, since Stinnes, like most of his colleagues in the Ruhr, was unwilling to allow French participation in German industry without corresponding German participation in French industry.[179] Ultimately, the end of May was too late to launch such an effort to change the Treaty. This served as yet another illustration not only of the desperation and confusion created by the Allied terms but also of the manner in which the terms increased the significance of Germany's industrial interests and helped undermine the organizational efforts of the RWM.

The second and most serious and important effort to offer a counterproposal to the peace terms also had such implications. It was the work of Max Warburg and represented a desperate effort to find a means of opening up a discussion with the Allies and securing some territorial concessions by means of an offer of a hundred billion gold marks, which Warburg himself and all those involved thought vastly beyond Germany's capacity. The figure had its origins in the amount of bonds that Germany was supposed to issue as a guarantee against the future final sum. The Warburg proposal differed from the Allied terms (in addition to the immediate establishment of a final sum), first, in having the initial twenty billion in payments fall due in May 1926 instead of May 1921 and, second, in making interest free the annuities in which the balance was to be paid. Under the Allied plan, the balance would bear interest once it was finally set. The major problem with the Warburg proposal, which was rejected by the Allies, was that it did not address the problem of providing some immediate relief to France and Belgium and, in effect, made German recovery the condition of payments.[180]

The program becomes more significant from the historian's perspective in light of the manner in which Warburg had to fight for the approval of his colleagues in the peace delegation, especially that of Finance Minister Dernburg. The latter was convinced that no fixed sum could be offered because of the uncertain state of Germany's economy and that an international commission of Allied, German, and neutral experts should determine what Germany really could pay. Warburg argued, however, that "there are moments in life when one ought not to calculate but must find courage, even if one cannot back it up with numbers, to save an asset, which the Reich still appears to be. It is the deadlock which we have to break, and I want to give you the courage to take on the great obligation even if this will perhaps not be understood in Germany and even if the pecuniary sacrifices which Germany must make will be inhumanly large."[181]

Even when finally persuaded to support the Warburg proposal, Dernburg almost undermined it by proposing that the final eighty billion be paid off in annuities of a billion per year for eighty years! No one, in fact, was able to state how the offer actually was to be made, and there was a general feeling among the delegates that it was "insane" even when it was thought necessary. The fact that it failed of its purpose and did not meet Allied needs or demands should not obscure this fact; nor that the "present value" of the offer, estimated between thirty billion and forty billion marks, was fairly close to what both the French expert Louis Loucheur and the British expert John Maynard Keynes thought Germany actually could pay.[182] Finally, the offer was not an easy one to propose in the German political context. Warburg had decided not to run for the Hamburg City Assembly in March 1919 because "already at that time in Hamburg as in all of Germany there was a strong anti-Semitic movement which would not have made it possible for me to act beneficially in the Assembly."[183] A leaflet was widely circulated singling out Warburg as the "father of the 100 billion offer," noting that the Jew Dernburg was Finance Minister and that the Jew Bernard Baruch was the financial ad-

viser to Woodrow Wilson and calling for an end to the "rule of this international power so alien in its nature to our race."[184]

The hundred-billion gold-mark offer is symptomatic of both the foreign and domestic political efforts of Germany's rulers during this period. It was inadequate to meet the demands of the situation, but this was only to be expected in a situation which made impossible demands and promoted intolerable choices. While the growing crisis over the Treaty terms in May and June made further work on a tax program and a final decision on the economic program virtually impossible, these issues continued to exercise those responsible for a solution and reached a remarkable level of articulation precisely at the height of the foreign-policy crisis. This was not so much the case in the cabinet, where skirmishes replaced the potentially major battles launched by the RWM memorandum at the beginning of the month. Thus, on May 28, Wissell had another set-to with Dernburg and Gothein over proposals to relax foreign-trade restrictions, a situation that repeated itself on June 7, when Wissell angrily accused the Dictatorial Committee of undermining the RWM policy before a decision on it had been made. The committee had recommended the elimination of all controls on foreign exchange as well as the elimination of export controls for entire groups of products. The argument was resolved by a resolution paralyzing both sides. The Dictatorial Committee was not to change existing regulations but only to make individual exceptions, and the RWM was to issue no decrees with legally binding power for the coming two weeks. Obviously, therefore, nothing very profound was happening at the Cabinet level.[185]

Yet, there was a serious discussion about future economic policy taking place in the publications of economic experts and, quite symptomatically for the course being taken by the continuing debate over the RWM economic program, in Schmidt's Reich Food Ministry. While the peace terms had demonstrated that the days of uncertainty were far from over, they also cleared the air with respect to what might be considered reasonable goals for Germany's economic future. One of these certainly was not the return of the mark to its prewar value. The economist Richard Hauser bade a formal farewell to this notion, for which he had argued in the *Bank = Archiv* in 1917, by publishing a new article with the contrary view in the same journal on July 1, 1919. Hauser pointed out that "the abnormal has become normal" and that the entire economy and society had adjusted itself to new levels of prices and wages, so that a return of the mark to its prewar worth would provide an incredible bonus for creditors and an unbearable burden for the economy. The most for which one could hope, in his view, was "to maintain the exchange rate first at a level not too distant from that existing at present . . . through the discount and exchange policies of the central bank. . . ." The restoration of money-market operations would make this even more difficult, so that it might only be possible to stabilize the exchange rate "for certain longer periods" until the gradual settling down of international financial relations would make possible the establishment of a new parity and a devalued German mark based on gold.[186]

This view was shared by Willi Prion, a professor at the Commercial University of Berlin, who was a close adviser to the Finance Ministry and who provided a lengthy expert report in the spring of 1919 which addressed itself to the problem of reducing prices and thus creating a greater measure of domestic economic stability.[187] In Prion's view, the inflation was a consequence of excessive purchasing power in the economy chasing after too few goods. Consequently, the problem had to be attacked, on the one hand, by increasing production and, on the other, by reducing liquidity through taxation of income and especially wealth. Ideally, the two processes should proceed in tandem so that increasing tax receipts would coincide with falling prices and thus be more effective than would be the case with rising prices. Recognizing the time required for tax reform, Prion argued that to accomplish this purpose price reduction could only begin from the side of production, of the supply of goods: "The increase of sellable goods, first food, must provide the initial thrust to the downward movement of prices. Cheaper food, generally reduced expenses for daily living, termination of wage increases, reduction of the especially high wages, increased production, greater supply of goods—that alone is the

way to a reduction of prices."[188] As a way out of the "vicious circle" created by the inability to lower wages or prices because of the disagreement between those who wished to begin with prices and those who wished to begin with wages, Prion proposed the subsidization of imported food so that the reduced food prices would eliminate the excuse for high wages.

The ultimate goal of Prion, like that of Hauser, was therefore the relative stabilization of the value of the mark. This did not mean Prion wished a return to prewar prices, which he felt could only be a matter of "memory." The fact was that the "depreciation of money would have to be accepted as a permanent phenomenon," and that the stress would have to be on "steady prices" rather than "the achievement of a low level of prices at some time or other."[189] Furthermore, like Hauser, Prion thought such a return to prewar prices and money values profoundly unjust and dangerous. It would magnify the profits of the war profiteers, give an unfair return to war-bond holders, and unjustly disadvantage debtors. Those who made debts in bad money would have to pay back in good money with the corresponding greater effort, and those, like many civil servants, who had to incur debts in order to survive during the wartime inflation, would now be doubly penalized. There was one class of debtor that would above all be severely affected, Prion emphasized, and that was "the Reich and to a lesser extent the states and municipalities, who have piled up debts upon debts during the war":

The Reich alone has up to April 1, 1919, taken 180 billion marks in debts. For at least two-thirds of this sum, the Reich received depreciated money, and this money was in fact all the more depreciated the later the indebtedness took place. The 180 billion marks ought not to be worth much more than 90 billion marks in peacetime currency. If the Reich were to repay these 180 billion marks in good money, then it would mean a splendid deal for the creditors. The interest and repayment would have to be procured through taxes, would thus have to be taken and then given by the Reich. But the collection of taxes will be more difficult if levies and taxes must be raised in the old nominal amount of 180 billion marks for the debts of the Reich from the reduced nominal income of the individual as a result of reduced prices and reduced sales. The taxes would be more oppressive, and even if on the other side the outlays of the Reich for interest and amortisation would flow back to the people, still those who pay the high taxes and levies and those who receive the high interest and capital returns are not always the same persons. The already existing hardships in the distribution of burdens and advantages would be increased, multiplied, even made unbearable in many cases.[190]

For this reason, price reduction through increased production had to be accompanied by a fair but effective tax policy that would permit the Reich to repay its debts in values that fairly reflected the depreciation of the currency since 1914. Economic recovery as well as what could be construed as equity under the existing circumstances required that debtors—above all, the state—be given some edge over creditors through economic policy.

There was however another solution being proposed of which Prion was well aware. Friedrich Bendixen, first in March 1919 and then in June, proposed that the problem be solved through inflation rather than price stabilization. Pointing to the continually decreasing value of the German war loans on the exchanges and the burgeoning debt of the Reich, Bendixen concluded that the Reich could never take in enough in taxes to repay what it owed— "every effort to collect the monstrous sums through taxes will weaken our productivity and thus reduce receipts and drive the Reich to economic collapse." The only solution, short of official bankruptcy, therefore, was to pay the war-loan debt in the manner in which the Reich had paid for everything else: "Only the transformation of the war loans into money can bring salvation."[191] At one stroke, the Reich would fulfill its obligations, either by printing the money necessary to pay off the debt or by providing Reich Treasury bills which could be turned into money. The Reich would eliminate its debts, provide the economy with all the stimulation inflation had to offer, avoid the deadening effects of brutal taxation, and, as Prion put the matter in commenting on Bendixen's proposal, "be able to begin a new life on the basis of a new money."[192] Inflation would be a means of salvation, a method of cleansing the finances of the Reich and constitute, to use modern parlance, the ultimate tax. Solon's *seisachteia* would be revived![193]

Bendixen's program was rejected with vari-

ous mixtures of horror and distress, and Prion himself expressed the hope that so drastic a solution would not be needed. The Treaty terms, however, had not only strengthened Bendixen in his convictions but also shaken Prion. Publicly, to be sure, the latter continued to advocate his relative stabilization program while emphasizing that more productivity and sacrifice than ever would be required. Privately, however, he took a somewhat different line. Thus, at a meeting of the Commission for Price Reduction of the Food Ministry on June 23, 1919, in which Reichsbank Vice President von Glasenapp sharply rejected the Bendixen scheme and pointed out that "the consequences of such an action would be a price revolution the likes of which we have never seen, and that the Reichsbank would be ruined," Prion admitted that he could not take Bendixen's view either, "but that one must still consider whether things will develop along these lines anyway in the short or long run."[194]

Thus, as early as the spring of 1919, the fundamental issues of equity in a stabilization had already found explicit expression. On the one hand, there was the conviction that the state had to fulfill its obligations to its creditor-citizens, albeit with due regard for the changed worth of the money involved; on the other, there was the contention that economic recovery, not equity and good faith, was of primary importance and that the slate might have to be wiped clean at a stroke.

Whatever the ruminations of the experts, however, Germany's leaders were not prepared to make the radical decisions of 1923 in the early summer of 1919 and, indeed, the other great radical decision that might have been made, the rejection of the peace treaty terms, was not made either. Most of German industry, large portions of the bourgeois party leadership, and leading Social Democrats, including Scheidemann, advocated rejection of the Treaty, and whether the Weimar Republic, Germany, and the future of the world might not have been better served by such a decision will never be known. The greatest dilemma was faced by the Social Democrats. It was neatly put by one of the agents used by the government to deal with the Americans, Walter Loeb:

You ought not to forget that Social Democrats sit in leading positions in our government today, whose obligation it is to see to it that social legislation can be made. But this is impossible if the peace treaty is signed. It certainly is a cynical thing to see imperialism triumphing over democracy on the one side and capitalism triumphing over Socialism on the other side, but the idealists unfortunately have not been proven correct. . . .[195]

While the employers and trade-union leaders in the ZAG were able to join in a protest against the Treaty, Legien was convinced that Germany had to sign. On the one hand, he argued that the workers would not agree to anything else; on the other, he proclaimed that it would be no more than a "scrap of paper" since "world revolution" would soon sweep over the Allied nations.[196] Although this certainly involved a good deal of wishful thinking, Legien's fear that nonsignature would lead to chaos and that the hungry workers would simply go out into the countryside and steal the food they needed was much better grounded. It was ultimately more persuasive than Carl Duisberg's disingenuous argument that the Treaty "would mean the death of Socialism not only in Germany, but in the world altogether, at least for the next generation."[197] In the last analysis, not only most of the Social Democrats—including that supreme realist Gustav Noske—but also Erzberger, Foreign Minister Bernstorff, and Dernburg came down on the side of signature "even if they hold the conditions now as before to be unfulfillable."[198]

Whether the acceptance of the Treaty on June 28, 1919, would mean the death of socialism—a prospect which really could not have upset Carl Duisberg all that much—remained to be seen, but it did signal the last battle over the RWM national economy program. The new government of Gustav Bauer, formed on June 21, 1919, and composed initially of Social Democrats, Centrists, and the Bavarian People's Party, was in no way a real improvement for Wissell, despite the departure of his DDP opponents Dernburg and Gothein because of their party's opposition to signature of the Treaty. The new Chancellor, a trade unionist who had shown little sympathy for Wissell's ideas and who Wissell felt had little feeling for the problems of production because of his

white-collar background, had treated the RWM proposals with critical indifference during his previous tenure as Labor Minister. Wissell placed more hope in the new Labor Minister, Alexander Schlicke, who as head of the great Socialist Metal Workers Union allegedly had more understanding for the productionist orientation of the RWM scheme. Wissell continued to face his old enemy, Robert Schmidt, however, who stayed on as Food Minister. Schmidt was constantly on the telephone with National Assembly Deputies and trade-union leaders seeking to undermine Wissell's position and stir up opposition to the RWM. On the Centrist side, Erzberger, the new Finance Minister, was known to be unfriendly to the RWM program, while the new Treasury Minister, Wilhelm Mayer of the BVP, could hardly be enthusiastic about Wissell's open opposition to the very existence of his Ministry and desire to absorb most of its functions into the RWM in connection with the projected Reich Assets Bank.[199]

While it is conceivable that Bauer and his colleagues would have preferred to drift along in the matter of economic policy without bringing the fundamental issues to a head, Wissell pursued the same tactic of forcing the issue that lay behind his memorandum of May 7 for the Scheidemann government. Thus, in a letter to Bauer of June 21, he emphasized that he had agreed to remain in office in the new government without a formal decision on his program only because of the peace treaty crisis, but that he would only continue on if his program were formally accepted, which, among other things, meant the elimination of the Treasury Ministry and the Dictatorial Committee. That the direction of the new government ran contrary to that of the RWM was amply demonstrated both practically and theoretically during its first days. In the face of a serious new railroad-worker strike threat, the Cabinet decided on June 26 to deal with the situation by offering to subsidize the price of food imports and thus negate the need for a wage increase. The decision was strongly influenced by the ideas of Willi Prion in the Commission for Price Reduction of the Reich Food Ministry and was strongly seconded by Undersecretary Julius Hirsch of the same Ministry. Whereas the ideas of the RWM had been energetically represented by Privy Councillor Ernst Trendelenburg at earlier meetings of this commission, this no longer was the case in late June and early July.[200]

A much more direct attack on the program was provided by Treasury Minister Mayer on July 5, however, who in a memorandum tellingly characterized the entire RWM program as "geometry . . . not economics." He warned that Americans, in particular, viewed it as a "product of the German bureaucratic spirit, to some extent of German militarism applied to economic conditions. . . ."[201] It would thus discourage foreign investment while continuing the compulsory economy and all the corruption associated with it. Mayer dismissed the plan for a Reich Assets Bank as bureaucratic and superfluous, pointing out that so far only fifty million of the two hundred million marks in the Assistance Fund for Industrial Enterprises created during the demobilization had actually been called upon. The problem in starting up the economy, in Mayer's view, was not a shortage of cash but rather raw-materials shortages and bad economic and social conditions. He was skeptical about the possibility of controlling strikes and warned that the effort to restrict strikes through wage and profit control would prove technically impossible and ultimately would discourage enterprise and productivity.

On July 7, Wissell set down the final plea for his program as Economics Minister. He defended the RWM organizational plans as the only way to depoliticize the economic issues dividing employers and workers, producers and consumers, and city and country: "We must unburden politics from economic problems and conflicts as much as possible, that is, we must make possible the expression of such questions and differences on an economic basis."[202] Insofar as the Reich Fund was concerned, he pointed out that the raising of both agricultural and coal production were the most pressing requirements for the economy and that these were, by and large, problems of settling workers on the land and in the coal producing areas. The Reich Fund could be used for land settlement and to build houses, as many as fifty thousand of these, in the Rhenish-West-

phalian coal producing areas. Once again, he reiterated his fundamental opposition to an approach based on cheapening the cost of food and clothing as a means of reducing prices and warned that "if one cheapens the consumption without raising production, then one only increases the demand and thereby provides an incentive to a renewed increase of prices."[203]

At the decisive Cabinet meeting of July 8, 1919, however, Wissell found himself totally and depressingly isolated. His Socialist colleagues, to a man, rejected the RWM program. Bauer not only reiterated the criticism of Socialist theoretician Rudolf Hilferding, who had charged that "Wissell's planned economy is a danger to the realization of socialization,"[204] but also contested the notion that the economic organization of workers, employers, and consumers would bridge existing conflicts and depoliticize them: "Employers and workers will very quickly unite at the cost of the consumers. Stinnes had already declared during the war that in case of victory the workers and employers would divide the booty. The most dangerous aspect of the program is the limitation of trade."[205] Undoubtedly these remarks only reinforced Wissell's impression that the new Chancellor was primarily interested in consumer problems and the consumer point of view. The strongly antitheoretical and hardnosed attitude of Wissell's Socialist colleagues came particularly to the fore in the remarks of Interior Minister Eduard David, who pointed out that theory had always followed rather than preceded real life, especially in the complicated realm of economics, and that the driving force for 90 percent of humanity was not the "social motives" stressed by the RWM but "private interest." Finally, SPD Party chairman Hermann Müller pointed out to the assembled that "just as only the black market helped us out of the war economy, so only smuggling will help us out of the planned economy. The most important solution to the problem of getting credit is personal credit abroad."[206] The role played by the bad experiences with the war economy in undermining the support for the national economy ideas as well as the overwhelming concern with getting foreign credit through the use of channels available to the German business community could not have been more plainly indicated. Nevertheless, as one considers these remarks by Germany's Majority Socialist leadership, it is difficult to imagine that they would not have received the complete approval of the Hamburg Chamber of Commerce. The non-Socialist Cabinet members had little need to add anything, and the consequence for Wissell and Moellendorff was very clear.

On July 12, they resigned in considerable bitterness, a sentiment undoubtedly increased by the appointment of Robert Schmidt as Economics Minister two days later, and the achievement of that unification of the RWM and the Reich Food Ministry which Schmidt had so successfully resisted for as long as Wissell remained in office.[207] If Wissell and Moellendorff had run aground because of their impolitic approach, moral rigidity, and utopian technocratism, they had nevertheless raised the central issues of coordinating economic, social, and financial policies. Whatever one may think of their answers, they had addressed the problems, and what they had wished to prevent was precisely what occurred during the next eight months.

Chapter 4

The Chaotic Path to Relative Stabilization
July 1919–March 1920

Searching for Solutions: The Erzberger Tax Program

Whether Wissell and Moellendorff could have prevented the developments in the months which followed their departure from office is an open question. In any case, they were able to stand on the sidelines and, with more than a touch of *Schadenfreude*, watch the economy virtually run amok as a great inflationary wave rolled over the country. If this inflationary surge cast a certain pall over the Bauer government during its first nine months (between July 1919 and March 1920), it is nevertheless important to recognize that it could also claim important accomplishments in the realms of financial, economic, and social policy. A balanced assessment of these complex and politically fateful months is in order, especially since they are justifiably tainted by the decisive shift to the right politically that found its most extreme expression in the Kapp Putsch of March 1920. This turn to the right was not simply a reaction to the Treaty, and it must be understood in terms of a complicated undercurrent of social protest and political conflict arising from the upsurge of inflation. The Bauer government sought both to respond to the social unrest and political pressures that pulled them in conflicting directions and to develop effective policies to deal with the unhappy situation they had inherited. The task of reconstructing the nation's economy and finances under such conditions was not an easy one, and German politics ensured that it would be thankless as well.

The new government was strongly inclined to follow the advice of Willi Prion to attack the reconstruction problem by increasing production at all costs and to subordinate financial and currency considerations to economic ones. His views were widely shared, and the emphasis on productivity inevitably fueled the clamor for decontrol, as an article by the shrewd and influential economic commentator Felix Pinner in the *Berliner Tageblatt* of June 21, 1919, amply demonstrated. Like Prion, Pinner opposed a state bankruptcy and the effective cancellation of Germany's domestic debt which would accompany it, possibilities that were producing lively discussion at this time. Pinner admitted that the dependence on war bonds had been a great and unsuccessful gamble, however, and he sharply attacked suggestions that the obligation to repay the bonds be written into the new constitution. He likened this to a provision that every German had a right to three pounds of butter per week at the official prices. Bondholders had no reason to expect full return on their value under existing circumstances. In Pinner's view, the low notation of the German war bonds on the exchanges was unavoidable until there was a financial reform. While the Reichsbank could take advantage of the situation and repurchase some of the bonds at a lower price, the bonds could only be paid for with money based on Treasury bills. The long-term debt was being reduced through the increase of the short-term debt, and financial reform was therefore essential.[1]

Moreover, Pinner argued that financial reform required a solid basis in economic recovery and this could only be achieved if the shortage of goods was relieved through increased domestic production and imports. For this reason, he criticized the Reichsbank and the Exchange Decree provisions requiring that all imports paid for in foreign exchange be subject to Reichsbank approval. He found this "narrowminded" and accused the "old gentlemen" in the Reichsbank of failing to adapt to the "spirit of a new order and a new orientation that has set in since November 9, 1918." It was they who had accepted the high war profits and been responsible for the "manufactured" bond-drive successes and, like the old regime, pursued a policy of "prestige" rather than actual results and continued to treat the worth of the currency purely in terms of its external value as mirrored by the balance of payments. He considered this obsolete:

No one today would doubt anymore that what is expressed in them [the exchange rates], aside from the political factors, is the internal value of the money which is in turn conditioned by the entire financial and economic situation domestically. If we want to improve the exchange rate, then we must raise the internal value of the money, and if this happens, then our credit abroad will improve. We will only be able to improve the domestic value of the money when we reduce our price levels, and this in turn is only possible through the setting aside of the shortage of goods, the raising of domestic production, and a real easing of imports and exports.

Pinner charged the Reichsbank with failing to understand this and lumped its policies together with those of Wissell's schemes for a planned economy based on allegedly self-governing bodies. In Pinner's view, it was a fantasy to think that the nation's dissatisfactions could be remedied in such ways:

The German people, for five long years undernourished and undersupplied through blockade and self-blockade, first of all needs a sufficient supply of goods to regenerate themselves again physically and morally and to once again be capable of and willing to work. If these goods are denied them by the authorities, then they will help themselves, and the black market, against which there is no resistance, will supply some of the goods at much higher prices and much to the detriment of the economy and the currency.

Pinner's editorial, like Prion's recommendations, signaled the policies that were going to be pursued by the RWM under its new leadership. While it would be tempting to treat Pinner's remarks as a triumph of common sense

over dogmatism, the matter is not quite so simple. On the one hand, Pinner underestimated the degree to which the Reichsbank was prepared to surrender monetary to productivist considerations; on the other, he overestimated the salutary effects of removing all restraints on commerce and the capacity of the economic policy he advocated to produce the stable conditions he thought necessary to make a financial reform feasible and effective. Pinner's article is significant as an illustration of how much sober and informed opinion was behind the underlying economic policy concepts of the Bauer government and helps to illuminate their difficulties.

Pinner's insights notwithstanding, the Reichsbank would not really be that much out of tune with the new policies, and the tensions between the Reichsbank and the government were to move along somewhat different lines than Pinner suggested. Clearly, the Reichsbank leadership was concerned to reduce imports, increase exports, and procure as much foreign exchange as possible, but it in no way presented itself as a barrier to the foreign trade policies inaugurated in the summer of 1919. Its major concerns lay with its domestic functions and, as before the war, it was torn between its role as a form of service station to which commerce, industry, and now primarily the government could turn for the liquidity required to keep operating and its role as the guardian of the soundness of the currency. The war had transformed the task into something of a nightmare. The liquidity of industry and commerce were such that they did not need to "tank up" at the Reichsbank with their commercial bills, while the government was forever discounting Treasury bills and thus perverting the real-bills doctrine which lay at the heart of German banking practice.

These activities had produced increasing discomfiture among the Reichsbank leaders, and if those worthies had found the Revolution little to their taste, it cannot be said they had in any way been negligent in trying to serve the leaders of the new Germany as well as they had served those of the old. True to the service-station principle, they were genuinely troubled by the shortage of money in the fall of 1918 and were resolved not to allow the economy to run

short in the future. This was not easy. The capacity of the Reich Printing Office was limited,
and while plans were laid for its rapid expansion, something had to be done in the meantime. The Reichsbank first tried to use some
private Berlin printing houses, but surveillance
and quality control proved extremely difficult,
and the forgery problem, which had already attained serious dimensions, was increased. Happily, a temporary answer was provided by the
Austrian State Printing Office in Vienna, which
had very modern equipment and apparently a
considerable unused capacity now that it no
longer had a vast empire to service. Despite
complaints from the unemployed Berlin printers, the Reichsbank, which had expanded the
number of its employees by the thousands, was
convinced that it had done its share to reduce
unemployment and had a higher duty to produce quality bank notes. It contracted with the
Viennese to print the fifty-mark notes that were
needed until such time as the Reich Printing Office was in a position "to satisfy all requirements."[2]

This by no means implied, however, that the
Reichsbank looked forward to using such increased capacity or intended to permit the requirements to become boundless. This was
made clear to Finance Minister Erzberger in an
important memorandum of July 1, 1919, a
memorandum which marks the beginning of a
two-year series of anxious appeals by the
Reichsbank for the government to reduce its
expenditure and consolidate the floating debt.
Havenstein and Glasenapp pointed out that the
number of short-term Treasury bills in circulation had increased 48 percent between October 1918 and mid-June 1919, that is, from 48.2
to 71.4 billion marks. The Reichsbank had
been able to rediscount 27.5 billion. Another
fifteen billion had been sold to the Prussian
State Bank (*Seehandlung*) in return for loan-
bureau notes which the Prussian State Bank
had procured with securities in its possession
for the express purpose of being able to exchange its loan-bureau notes for Reich Treasury notes. After this operation, however, there
were still 28.9 billion unplaced Reich Treasury
bills in the Reichsbank. Naturally, this increase
in the floating debt was accompanied by a for-

midable increase in the currency in circulation,
69 percent to be specific, which amounted to an
increase from 16.7 to 28.3 billion marks between the end of October and mid-June 1919.
During the same period, according to Havenstein's approximations, the number of loan-
bureau bills had increased from 12.6 to 19.8 billion, 11.2 billion of which were in free circulation while 8.4 billion—as over against three billion at the end of October—lay in the
Reichsbank as "cover" for monetary emissions.

Gone, however, were the days when the
Reichsbank enthusiastically defended this system of note coverage, whose dubious character
Bendixen had exposed so long ago. The gold
supply had been reduced from 2,550 to 1,150
million marks' worth of gold to pay for food imports, and the only way the new Treasury bills
and their corresponding monetary emissions
could be covered was through the loan-bureau
notes. That was why the Reichsbank had to ask
the Prussian State Bank to borrow from the
loan bureaus. In this way, the Reichsbank could
then get hold of loan-bureau notes with which
to purchase Reich Treasury notes and still have
the one-third coverage it required for its monetary emissions. Though a somewhat complex
operation, its significance was very nicely
summed up by the authors of a Reichsbank
memorandum who confessed that "[t]he legally prescribed one-third coverage, the so-
called specie coverage, at present consists of
only 12 percent in gold and 88 percent in loan-
bureau notes."[3] In contrast to the prewar period, the Reichsbank now held very few commercial or municipal bills, which had once provided part of its coverage, and thus "the note
issuance is as good as if it were exclusively based
on Reich Treasury bills; they are, to be sure,
short-term, but always have to be prolonged
when they fall due and their total amount continuously increases." The Reichsbank was fearful that the time would come when normal economic conditions would lead to a reduction in
the high liquidity of the economy and the Treasury bills in circulation would come streaming
back into the Reichsbank for further rediscounting. The Reichsbank would then find itself trapped. It would no longer be possible to
bring new Treasury bills into circulation be-

cause of the demand for cash holdings, and the Reichsbank would thus steadily increase its Treasury-bill holdings while continuing its increased monetary emissions. An incredible paper inflation would be the result. In the last analysis, therefore, the credit of the Reichsbank rested completely on the credit of the Reich, a reality veiled by the arrangements of August 4, 1914.

Having predicted, rather accurately, what the earthquake would be like, the Reichsbank leadership nevertheless refrained from actually criticizing the unsoundness of the paper structure which it had described. It did, however, demonstrate a good sense of the preconditions for creating a sounder one. It specifically attributed the monetary inflation to the increase of the floating debt and roundly declared that the only cure was to stop this debt expansion through "extreme austerity and the speediest possible implementation of a comprehensive tax program that permits the coverage of Reich expenditures with its own receipts."[4] Indeed, the Reichsbank now assumed a threatening tone and pointed out that it had already given signs that it meant business. While it had met all the demands placed upon it by the government during the war and until the acceptance of the peace treaty, it now questioned "whether the unlimited acceptance of Reich treasury bills continues to be compatible with our responsibilities."[5] While apparently chary of threatening to refuse to discount Treasury bills presented by the government, the Reichsbank did warn that it might refuse bills submitted by private persons and institutions for rediscount.

Whatever the actual beliefs of the Reichsbank leaders with respect to the origins, nature, and cures for inflation, no proponent of the quantity theory could have asked for more than the Reichsbank's insistence that the source of the inflation lay in the increased public expenditure and floating debt and its threat to cease discounting Treasury bills.[6] The Reichsbank called on the government to undertake a policy of austerity and demanded that measures also be taken to reduce the floating debt. Specifically, the Reichsbank urged that negotiations with the Belgians and the French be conducted to remove the eight billion marks in formerly

occupied Belgium from circulation. Above all, it called for major tax measures, especially a large tax on capital and a forced loan to be imposed on all persons having an income over ten thousand marks. While willing to have half the tax on capital paid in war bonds, the Reichsbank was, above all, anxious to reduce the enormous liquidity in the economy and, of course, the number of Reich Treasury bills in circulation. Curiously enough, however, the Reichsbank did not address the role played by the loan-bureau notes in promoting liquidity or the fact, for example, that war and government bonds could be used as security with the loan bureaus. It was almost as if the Reichsbank was intent on making sure that it could inflate the currency whenever necessary. In any case, it clung to the loan bureaus with considerable tenacity, and its major concern was to put an end to the perversion of their purpose by the Prussian State Bank, which was using them as a dumping ground for Reich Treasury notes and a funnel for the transmittal of loan-bureau notes to the Reichsbank. It hoped that the loan bureaus could once again serve the private economy and issue loan-bureau notes backed up with securities genuinely placed in the private sector. The loan-bureau emissions could then once again provide "a not unsuitable substitute for specie coverage" from the bankers point of view. Clearly, in the short run, the Reichsbank held on to the war-created fictions for dear life. In the long run, it hoped that the progressive reduction of Reich Treasury bills in its portfolio with concurrent reduction of the liquidity in the economy would increase the demand for short-term capital in a reviving economy and lead to the reintroduction of the commercial bill, and "thereby one would have regained a healthy basis for monetary emissions and the credit of the Reichsbank."[7]

The dreamlike quality of the conclusion of the Reichsbank's memorandum is as significant as the hard-headed demand that the Reich shape up its finances. There was a goodly measure of naiveté in the notion that the fictions connected with the loan-bureau notes could once again be made believable and that the real-bills doctrine could rapidly be made to function in its prewar manner. Nevertheless, if the

Matthias Erzberger (1875–1921), Reich Finance Minister 1919–1920. (*Courtesy of the U.S. National Archives*)

Reichsbank leaders were allowing wishful thinking to get the better of them in the summer of 1919, they had some reason to take heart given the new energy being shown on the part of the Reich financial authorities and especially its energetic, ebullient, resourceful, and optimistic new leader, Centrist Matthias Erzberger. Erzberger had indeed made speedy action the condition of his accepting the onerous Finance Minister position. What distinguished Erzberger's remarkable tenure as Finance Minister was not his specific contributions to the content of the major reforms over which he presided, but rather the manner in which he picked up on the plans and programs developed by his predecessors and the officials of his Ministry— above all, Stefan Moesle, Johannes Popitz, Friedrich Saemisch, and Friedrich Carl—and then forced them through with a vigor, skill, and insistence rarely found, not only in the Weimar Republic but also in governments anywhere throughout modern history. It rapidly became clear that a new tone of aggressiveness, greater clarity of intent, and an absolute determination to move speedily and at all costs characterized the new leadership of the Finance Ministry.[8]

Erzberger's enemies were many, especially those who resented his role in the Peace Reso-

lution of 1917 and the signature of the Armistice Agreement and the Treaty of Versailles. This mercurial and not always careful politician was an ideal target for Karl Helfferich and others with an interest in obfuscating the sources of Germany's plight. The campaign against Erzberger, therefore, was well under way, but Erzberger was adept at repaying discourtesies in kind. Thus, in his first address as Finance Minister to the National Assembly on July 8, 1919, he concurred fully with his predecessors in blaming the war and its financial mismanagement for the state of Germany's finances, but his denunciation of Helfferich as the "most frivolous of all Finance Ministers"[9] called forth a storm of hisses and catcalls from the right side of the house. These were to become the regular accompaniment to his addresses to that body.

Erzberger joined his predecessors in refusing to declare Germany bankrupt and argued that the repayment of the war-bond debt was a social responsibility. He differed from his predecessors, however, in openly stressing the redistributive and social purposes of his tax program, declaring that "income from capital must bear a much greater share of the burden than income from labor" and announcing, in a phrase that was to become famous, that "a good finance minister is the best socialization minister."[10] Of particular importance was that there was no further ambiguity about the reorganization of the national tax system. The burdens placed upon Germany by the peace treaty made it absolutely essential to centralize the administration of taxation in the hands of the Reich and to give the Reich a virtual monopoly of direct and indirect taxation. The extent to which the Reich would use these powers was made clear when Erzberger outlined his immediate tax package, beginning with the oft proclaimed extraordinary levy on war profits and capital gains and continuing with taxes on inheritance, transfers of landed property, and a variety of indirect taxes. He announced his plan for a one-time Emergency Capital Levy, the famous "sacrifice for the Reich in its hour of need" (*Reichsnotopfer*), as well as a national income tax and an increased turnover tax.

For Erzberger, these taxes were a matter not only of fiscal necessity but also of fairness and justice. The salvation of Germany could only come, in the last analysis, through "work, work, work," but Erzberger implied that labor's sacrifices had to receive compensation through a just tax program: "The State will try through radical laws and radical implementation of laws to make good the injustices of the war. The broad masses of the people have been waiting since the revolution for the great sacrifices on the part of the propertied classes."[11] In his view, there was no time to lose, and he called on the Reichstag to pass the legislation in question, above all the creation of a national tax administration, before it went on summer recess. He reminded them of the importance of fighting inflation: "Whether rich or poor, we all have too much paper money in our pockets. When the paying of taxes starts, our wallets will become thinner."[12]

The administrations of the various federal states already knew that Erzberger meant business because they had been the recipients of a lengthy memorandum sent out on July 6, 1919, which pointed out that "no thinking person" would continue to question the necessity of turning the administration of taxes over to the central government now that the lion's share of the national expenditures lay with the Reich. Whereas before the war the percentages of national expenditure among Reich, states, and municipalities were, respectively, 41.9, 21.8, and 36.21 percent, they were now 70, 10, and 20 percent.[13] On July 13, Erzberger faced the various state Finance Ministers in Weimar and assessed the needs of the Reich at 17.5 billion marks and those of the municipalities and states at 6.5 billion. The 24 billion marks that had to be raised required a vast administrative reform and the deficit of 6.5 billion that he calculated as remaining after his program had been passed required a Reich income tax which would have to be gathered at the source, that is, through withholding from wages and salaries as well as a tax on capital gains of perhaps 30 percent. Erzberger recognized that the "loss of a tax which is the backbone of the financial systems of the individual states naturally means the greatest possible sacrifice,"[14] but he insisted that the cleaning up of the deficit was impossible unless there were a Reich income tax and that this required that the Reich take over the entire administration of taxes so as to bring uniformity and efficiency into the system. His deadline for the formal transfer of all taxing authority to the Reich was October 1, 1919.

Not surprisingly, these claims were contested by the Bavarian Finance Minister, Speck, who pointed out, not incorrectly, that "the proposal of the Finance Minister takes away the last vestiges of independence from the states. The natural consequence of the sacrifice of their financial independence will be the loss of their political independence."[15] He warned, too, that it would destroy municipal government. While the majority of the state Finance Ministers recognized the necessity of the change, which one of them properly described as "revolutionary," they worried about becoming totally dependent on the Reich in cultural as well as all other matters and were resistant to the speed with which Erzberger aimed to take over their tax administrations. Erzberger met this resistance in part with threats to impose federal control agencies on the state tax authorities if they refused his plan, in part with concessions granting a certain amount of tax income to the states and promising a suitable formula for the distribution of funds among the Reich, states, and municipalities (*Lastenausgleich*) that would be commensurate with their burdens. Thanks to these techniques, Erzberger was able to push through his major work of administrative reform as well as the first parts of his tax program by August 19, 1919. Next to the actual creation of the Republic, it probably was the most revolutionary act in the history of the Weimar Republic.

This being the case, it is not surprising that the National Assembly debate over the Erzberger tax reform became the occasion for the expression of counterrevolutionary sentiment and resistance to the Treaty of Versailles. While Socialists may have objected to some of the proposed indirect taxation and Centrists to the inheritance tax, the virulence of the right-wing attack on Erzberger and his program forced the pro-republican parties to concentrate their efforts on the support of the Finance Minister. Right-wing opposition could not really focus on the institutional aspects of the Erzberger tax reform, for while they could wax sentimental about the special qualities of the state tax administrations, warn against employing unitarian principles in such a manner as to destroy the individuality and morality of the agencies to be integrated into the projected Reich Taxation Authority, and question the feasibility of making the change so quickly, they realized that centralization of the system was unavoidable. As for the criticisms of his timetable, they were dismissed by Erzberger with his usual optimism. He was convinced of the necessity and feasibility of nationalizing the taxation system by October 1 and stressed how important that would be in making possible the implementation of uniform assessment procedures throughout Germany for the projected capital levy and income tax. He hoped that these assessments would be ready by April 1920.[16]

The opposition could make itself more effectively felt, however, in a general attack on the Republic and on Erzberger personally, as well as in a specific opposition to some of this tax proposals, above all the Emergency Capital Levy. It was thought that the attack on the Emergency Capital Levy could, in turn, be used to begin the formulation of a right-wing strategy of resistance to the Treaty of Versailles in which opposition to effective taxation could be linked to opposition to the Treaty. While all of these tendencies were to become more explicit and articulated in the second series of debates on the tax program when the National Assembly convened in Berlin after the summer recess, they had their beginnings in the debates in Weimar in July and August. Thus, representatives of the DVP and DNVP sharply attacked the high expenditures of the republican regimes, accused the government of bloating the civil service, and complained about the alleged financial abuses of the soldiers and workers councils. Nostalgic appreciations of the old regime for its efficiency and probity were combined with a studied neglect of the role played by the war in Germany's financial misfortune. The extreme rightist Deputy Reinhard Mumm used the occasion to declare explicitly that Germany's armies had been stabbed in the back in November 1918. Naturally, the left responded by saying that Germany owed her miseries to the war and the maladministration of the old regime and that it was the Republic which was at last undertaking long-needed reforms evaded by the old regime. While the Reichstag President strove to keep the debate focused on the concrete issues of tax reform, it was impossible to exclude the campaign of defamation launched by Helfferich, which involved an attack on Erzberger's political and financial honesty and finally led the government to launch a libel suit against Helfferich at the beginning of September.[17]

Of greater material significance to Erzberger at the time, however, was the concentrated attack on the Emergency Capital Levy, which destroyed his hopes of having this tax passed before the summer recess. The proposed levy spared low incomes entirely but then taxed the wealthy with progressing harshness, charging 10 percent for the first fifty thousand marks and rising to 50 percent for those with capital of three million or more. Since the entire tax could not be paid immediately without disrupting the economy, Erzberger proposed that it be paid over thirty years in interest-bearing installments. Erzberger was convinced, however, that those affected would wish to pay off the tax rapidly within the first few years, and his optimistic expectation that he could get two and a half to three billion marks a year from the tax rested on this assumption.[18]

This was a miscalculation of historical importance, since inflation would work against Erzberger's expectations. Indeed, it cannot be emphasized enough that the entire Erzberger program was based on the assumption of increasing currency stabilization. He was convinced that people would have an incentive to surrender the excessive liquidity in the economy: "Although the one-time levy is distributed over decades, it is evident on the other side that a large portion of the income from it will come soon and can be used to set aside the paper economy, for the hoarded paper bears no interest while the tax debt must be paid off with interest."[19] Erzberger argued that if every German had sacrificed properly and signed up for war bonds to the extent of 30 to 40 percent of their capital, then the Emergency Capital Levy would not be necessary. That levy was nothing more or less than a means of annulling that portion of the debt that could have been prevented during the war were it not for the triumph of "mammonism." As always, he emphasized the social intent of the levy and its potential "anti-plutocratic effect."[20]

This is not to say that Erzberger was unaware of the importance of encouraging capital investment. This concern explains his willingness to stretch the Emergency Capital Levy over decades as well as his opposition to a forced loan (*Zwangsanleihe*), the pet scheme of the Reichsbank and the alternative pushed by some of his right-wing opponents. The obvious advantage of a forced loan would have been to provide speedy returns and a measure of relief for the Treasury. Erzberger had more extensive goals, however. He did not think that the forced loan of 10 to 20 percent proposed by the Reichsbank would be adequate. Even some of Erzberger's critics, the DVP Deputy Becker, for example, had reservations about the forced loan on grounds that it would create an impression of national bankruptcy and ruin Germany's credit.[21]

The truth was, however, that the extreme right had no interest in an effective tax program so long as the reparations bill was unsettled. Deputy Kraut of the DNVP suggested that the Emergency Capital Levy be put off until the reparations bill was presented in May 1921 and that the government make do with a forced loan. To this Erzberger bluntly responded, "[I]t is not possible for the Reich Government to wait until the date which Deputy Kraut has suggested before cleansing the Reich finances. . . . Any government . . . which does not turn decisively and quickly to the cleansing of the Reich finances is not worthy of having the fate of the German people in its hands."[22] With even greater irritation, Erzberger rejected claims by the right that the Entente would seize the receipts from an Emergency Capital Levy for reparations instead of permitting them to be used for purposes of domestic stabilization. Erzberger denied that any such Allied rights existed under the peace treaty, assured that the levy would be annulled the moment that such claims were made, and stressed that Germany's credit abroad depended upon measures of domestic stabilization. Clearly, however, the contention had been launched that the proceeds from a thoroughgoing system of taxation would, in the end, only fall into the pockets of the Allies. The Treaty of Versailles was becoming an effective weapon against the reforms needed to strengthen the new German Republic.

If Erzberger believed that his program would promote stabilization and that the taxes could be collected, he was not and could not have been oblivious to the dangers of tax evasion and flight of capital. The newspapers had been carrying articles reporting the names of firms being set up for the express purpose of transferring German capital abroad, and such transfers had been going on since the Revolution. At the same time, the tax program planned by Erzberger was so Draconian that the effective assessment of personal wealth would suffer if the privacy of bank accounts were maintained. Too much was at stake to permit continued secrecy. The amounts held by the great Berlin banks had increased by fourteen and a half billion marks between 1913 and the end of 1918, while the holdings of savings banks had increased by eleven billion marks. Erzberger firmly declared that the measures he intended to take were such that "a halt will be made before no safety-deposit box at home or abroad—we have ways and means of getting at those abroad—and even the straw sack of the peasant out there will not be safe from the tax officials . . . and the stocking also!"[23] The first means by which Erzberger intended to accomplish this purpose was the Law Against Capital Flight and Capital Flight Abroad, which went into effect on September 8, 1919, to replace the old and by this time defunct Foreign Exchange Decree of February 8, 1917. To make international trade easier, the old provisions requiring reporting all transactions involving monetary transfers abroad by the businessmen involved were replaced by a requirement that the banks do the reporting and provide explanations to the tax authorities. While the business and banking communities had grave reservations about such a violation of the privacy of banking transactions, the National Assembly passed the law with the provision that it remain in effect only until October 1, 1920. By that time, it was optimistically presumed, the tax assessment procedures would have been completed and the need for the law obviated.[24]

Erzberger had more extreme measures in mind, however. He hoped to get at the money that had already fled abroad as well as the money hidden in the peasant stockings by requiring the exchange of bank notes and the stamping of all securities. What was not stamped would become worthless. This method had already been employed by the Czechoslovak Republic, albeit more for nationalist than for monetary reasons. Erzberger believed that the exchange of hundred- and thousand-mark notes could be achieved by the end of the year and the rest by March 31, 1920. He also believed that it would be possible to get foreign banks to report the deposits of Germans and to persuade the Entente to confiscate unreported securities held by Germans in their countries for reparations. He hoped that the neutrals could be pressured into cooperating as well. Havenstein, however, resisted these plans in one panic-filled communication after another. He warned that the Reichsbank could not possibly print enough money in time, that the proposal would promote a severe drop in the exchange rate, and that the result would be monetary demands upon the Reichsbank that it simply could not meet. He constantly referred back to the situation at the end of 1918 and the panic produced by the shortage of money arising from the military collapse and revolution. However, "everything that we had experienced would be child's play compared to the conditions which would necessarily develop in the second half of December if Your Excellency's intention is realized. . . . Strikes, disturbances, tumult and uprisings would be unavoidable. Bolshevism would victoriously raise its head and complete anarchy would be the result."[25]

Erzberger's case was not helped by the fact that in July rumors concerning his intentions had been followed by a fall in the exchange rate of the mark and that subsequent declines in the rate were attributed in part to such reports. Erzberger blamed the exchange-rate situation on other factors, but the technical reservations raised by the Reichsbank put him into an impossible situation, even if the new Law Against Capital Flight provided him with powers to order an exchange of bank notes or the stamping of notes. However irrepressible his ardor and great his optimism, he simply could not

run the risk of undertaking a measure which the Reichsbank declared technically impossible and thus risk leaving the nation with an insufficient supply of money. At the same time, he remained unconvinced by the Reichsbank arguments for a forced loan as the best means to get at hidden capital but agreed with the Reichsbank that an effort to launch a large-scale voluntary bond drive was most unlikely to get much support and would only hurt the Reich's credit. As a compromise, Erzberger supported a floating premium loan repayable at 10 percent more than its principle and bearing 2 percent interest as well as exemption from the inheritance tax. The results were a good illustration of the depths to which the nation's credit had sunk in the eyes of its own people and how little could be expected from a voluntary approach. The loan drive brought in 3.8 billion marks, half of it in war bonds. The war bonds, which bore 5 percent interest, had sunk so low in the public estimation that they were valued on the open market below mortgage bonds bearing 4 percent interest.[26]

It was not, however, upon such stuff that Erzberger's optimism was based but rather upon his remarkable success in pushing through his great reform of the Reich financial system and the first parts of his tax package in the space of less than two months as well as his expectation that he would meet with continued success when the National Assembly reconvened in October. Along with this came certain other considerations which were reflected in a rather extraordinary confidential report which Erzberger gave to the Reichsrat on September 19, a report in which he bubbled with enthusiasm and hopefulness on a variety of fronts. He began by announcing that the wheat harvest had been particularly good, so that it might be possible to provide better quality bread and even raise the bread ration. At the same time, worker productivity was improving, especially among the miners, and there was an increasing willingness to do piecework again. He hoped that unemployment relief could be eliminated by the end of the year and be replaced by a system of unemployment insurance based on worker, employer, and government contributions and in which the self-government of the fund would act as a barrier to the abuses from which the unemployment relief system was suffering. He also had good news on the international front. The Allies were showing an interest in holding a conference on stabilizing the various currencies, and growing tension between England and France could only help Germany. The increased concern with Germany's problems and the desire to improve its finances were being strongly underpinned by the effects its depreciated currency was having on international trade. Erzberger was reported to have argued that

At present Germany, because of the situation of her currency, is by far the cheapest producer and the most competitive land on earth. America, Switzerland, and Denmark are completely filled up with goods which they have produced for Germany as their best customer and which they now must seek to sell. Where directly before the conclusion of peace, profiteers and swindlers came to the German Government with insecure offers, we are now being approached by official representatives with clearly defined offers and financial proposals, and it is clear that England is very afraid that America will get ahead of her and must do everything possible in order not to come too late.[27]

In addition to such competitive considerations, according to Erzberger, the Allies were also worried that Germany's succumbing to Bolshevism would destroy Germany as a customer, make the collection of reparations impossible, and make possible the infestation of their own countries with the Bolshevik disease. He predicted the conclusion of agreements with the United States, England, and the Netherlands for the purchase of food and raw materials on the basis of credit and expressed the expectation of receiving a thirty million dollar cash credit from the United States. This credit could then be used to buy marks abroad and raise the value of the currency. He warned that other government authorities, municipalities, and private companies should not try to get credits abroad, since this could only reduce the value of the mark and cross up the purposes of the Finance Ministry. Further, he suggested that it might be useful to have the German coal prices rise to world-market levels since this would increase the value of the coal deliveries under the Treaty and have a positive effect on

the currency even if it caused difficulties for German industry.

Given the continuing deterioration of the German currency and other difficulties faced by Germany domestically and internationally, Erzberger's ebullience left some of his listeners more than a little skeptical. As the Saxon delegate reported: "I must confess that the light touch with which the Reich Finance Minister paints the change for the better on the wall appears rather uncanny to me. Erzberger has been an optimist all his life and has on one day expected glorious things which he has completely set aside on the next."[28] Erzberger's optimism was indeed excessive and premature, and its most valuable function probably was to fuel his salutary activity without which things certainly would have been much worse. Nevertheless, his remarks did point up the rank order of the Bauer government's priorities and those realms in which it hoped progress would be made: the food supply, worker productivity, increasing exports, and gaining foreign credits. Erzberger could not expect the effects of his tax program to take hold until the coming year. Any improvement in Germany's circumstances before then would have to come in the economic rather than the financial sphere. How justified was his optimism of mid-September 1919?

The Policies of the Economics Ministry under Schmidt and Hirsch

Any assessment of Germany's economic prospects at this point must first of all be made in terms of the goals which the RWM had set for itself, goals very close to those of Pinner as described at the beginning of this chapter. Pinner had obviously been well-informed about the struggle between Wissell and Schmidt and understood the latter's priorities. Although Schmidt had assumed office on July 14, it was not until September 19, the day Erzberger was giving his cheerful report to the Reichsrat, that the new Economics Minister presented the guidelines of his economic policy to the Cabinet. The delay probably was due to the difficulties Schmidt faced in taking over the RWM and finding a suitable Undersecretary. The Ministry was filled with Moellendorff followers, and this meant that his replacement would inevitably face great hostility. After toying with the idea of appointing Carl Melchior of the Warburg firm, Schmidt finally chose a man with whom he had already been associated in the Reich Food Ministry, Professor Julius Hirsch, who came strongly recommended by both the well-known economist and pioneer of modern accounting methods, Professor Eugen Schmalenbach of the University of Cologne, and by the Berlin Chamber of Commerce. Hirsch was to remain in office until the fall of 1922 and, thus, to play the central role in economic policy formation during the coming three years. His expertise lay in the field of commerce, which he taught in his part-time position at the University of Cologne, and he had distinguished himself in the Berlin Price Examination Agency during the war. A brilliant and imaginative intellectual, Hirsch lacked some of the diplomatic qualities desirable in political and administrative affairs and does not appear to have been terribly popular among his colleagues. Undoubtedly, some of his problems were compounded by his Jewish background. In contrast to Moellendorff, Hirsch was a believer in the market economy, but he was also pragmatic and supported controls when he saw no alternative. If he had any goal, it was the rationalization and modernization of the economy through the encouragement of what he considered to be the more positive forces in the free market. At the same time, he was committed to the protection of consumer interests and to the fair distribution of the burdens that had been placed upon the German people.[29]

The "guidelines" of September 19 constituted the first major policy statement of the new RWM leadership, which deliberately chose not to present a formal program "with far-reaching goals" because of the "lack of clarity in the direction of our economic development."[30] By and large, therefore, the guidelines addressed immediate problems of economic management and are best viewed in the context of actions already taken by the RWM, the problems arising from them, and the actual situation when the guidelines were formulated.

From the standpoint of the RWM, the central internal problem facing the German economy was labor productivity, but the full significance of this problem can only be understood when its political dimension is taken into account. There were formidable barriers to increased productivity. One of these was persistent labor unrest. In their efforts to blame the condition of the German economy on the Revolution, the right wing was already playing upon the waves of strikes rolling over Germany since November 1918. When Erzberger had declared that Germany could only recover through "work, work, work," one of the his DNVP opponents maliciously picked up Erzberger's words to declare: "What is the picture in reality today? Not work, work, and again work, but strike, strike, and again strike!"[31] In a rhetorically moving response, Erzberger, to the repeated cheers of the Social Democrats, reminded the National Assembly of the great suffering of the working masses in the industrial centers:

For what have they had? Only that which was absolutely necessary in order to vegetate like animals! Did they have the bread to eat, as in peacetime? And the bread ration itself is so small that despite all medical claims, in which I do not believe, no person in Germany can live on the rations which the Reich has allowed. . . . For does not Deputy Mittelmann know that the broad masses of our people today have no shirts, no stockings, and no shoes anymore? A people that is so undernourished over the course of the years, when this goes on for four years, will become sick, and our people are sick. Our people must be made healthy again. You can never solve this problem if you don't give our people more and better nourishment. . . .[32]

Providing food was, in fact, the centerpiece of government policy. On June 28, the Cabinet had voted to subsidize the cost to consumers of food imports. These subsidies were expected to amount to one and a half billion marks. The price charged consumers for various items purchased by the Reich agencies from abroad would be lowered substantially; for example, a kilogram of flour from 4 to 1.30 marks, of bacon from 16 to 6.8 marks, and of meat from 15 to 7.80 marks. The costs of the subsidization program were to be divided among the Reich, states, and municipalities, each paying one-third. This arrangement led to some difficulties. On the one hand, many municipalities were importing food on their own and were success-

Julius Hirsch (1882–1961), State Secretary in the Economics Ministry, 1920–1922. (*Courtesy of Mrs. Edith Hirsch*)

ful in demanding that their purchases be counted in the contributions they were expected to make to the program. (Similarly, municipalities in the occupied areas also insisted that the increased ration they were being forced to provide with purchases from Entente military stores—the so-called La Morlaye ration—be included.) On the other hand, other states and municipalities objected on the grounds that they could not afford the costs and that they faced the ugly choice between turning down the much needed imported food or increasing taxes on precisely those who were meant to receive the subsidization.[33]

This subsidy policy, which also included a program to reduce the price of textiles and clothes controlled by various Reich agencies, was based on the recommendations of the Commission on Price Reduction set up in the spring to find ways and means of preventing a railroad-worker strike; it cannot be said that its recommendations were made with any great enthusiasm. Hirsch, a member of the commission, was very skeptical, pointing out that re-

duced food prices in the occupied areas had not led to reduced wage demands, while his colleague, Gert von Eynern noted that "it is rather a matter of indifference whether one increases the state deficit through higher wages to the railroad workers or through subsidies to reduce food costs." In the last analysis, it was "hard to decide what one should strive for, high wages or lower wages and lower food prices."[34] If the decision was taken in the end to subsidize food costs, it was not with any expectation of seriously influencing prices or wages or the financial situation directly, but rather of increasing the willingness to work and thus achieving real price and cost reductions through increased productivity. Little wonder, therefore, that Hirsch found the results of the commission something of a "fiasco."[35]

If so, however, they were not easy for the RWM to escape. Although the subsidization was supposed to be limited to three months, that is, until October 6, 1919, the RWM decided on September 18 that the increased costs of imported food resulting from the fall in the exchange rate could not be carried by the population without a new wave of wage demands. Another three and a half billion in subsidies, therefore, was proposed and then approved by the Cabinet for the period ending March 31, 1920. Nevertheless, the RWM was already anticipating another wage movement because of the need to raise the bread price in the winter. Under the impending change in the taxation system, however, the costs of the continued subsidy would have to be born entirely by the Reich. What the RWM thought of its own actions may be measured by its guidelines of September 19: "the policy of subsidies for food costs cannot lead to a real reduction of prices, since the subsidies must be covered by taxes. This policy, certainly unavoidable for the coming winter, can only be temporary, for a further increase of the tax burden is unbearable given the state of our indebtedness."[36]

The great hope, therefore, lay in the achievement of higher productivity, and here, of course, the government, especially the Majority Socialists who dominated it, was in the odd position of at once having to defend the workers from right-wing attacks on their low productivity by emphasizing the role played by food and clothing shortages while at the same time having to put increased pressure on the workers to settle down and work harder. What is particularly interesting is that the Socialists themselves do not seem to have been entirely convinced that the low productivity and reluctance to work were simply a function of hunger. Hirsch had argued repeatedly since May that the workers were taking advantage of their new power position without experiencing serious objections from the Socialist leaders for whom he worked. At no time did he question the seriousness of the food problem, and he placed special stress on what he considered the outrageous clothing prices. However, at the decisive meeting on the question of food price subsidies on July 11, the weight of his argumentation was not on the side of the "official standpoint" that the sources of reduced productivity and wage demands were to be found in the shortages and high prices. Those problems were already present during the war, Hirsch argued, "while the circumstances described here only developed since December 1918. Therefore, the alterna-

tive view is that the ultimate reason for the present situation lies in the changed power situation of the workers."[37] This could be demonstrated by the fact that wage increases had exceeded price increases during the first half of 1919 while productivity had decreased. This is not to say that Hirsch was unsupportive of the import subsidy policy, but he was insistent that it had to be paid for in higher productivity at a time "when the entire economy is functioning like the railroads; the operating costs are higher than the returns; one is working continually with an increasing negative balance." Hirsch went so far as to argue that "the added purchasing power of the workers today probably encompasses amounts which are just as high as the additional purchasing power of the war profiteers; in the case of the workers, however, it is not held back to be used as capital but rather streams back into the market and increases prices."

Hirsch was no conservative. Indeed, he was to become the darling of the Social Democrats and would earn the hatred of the right during his tenure as Undersecretary. His criticisms of the attitude of the workers were widely shared among the Socialist leaders, not because they had lost sympathy with the workers or their problems or lost sight of the role played by shortages and high prices, but because they were now, in large part, responsible for making sure that the economy functioned and because the life of the Republic depended upon increased production.

This was especially true in the coal-mining industry which, along with the transport sector, provided the major bottleneck in getting the economy moving again. No one contested the hardships and dangers faced by the miners or the inadequacy of their food supply, and it was obvious that the mines had been run down in the course of the war and that the loss of the Saar production was serious. It was also a fact, however, that Germany had only half the coal supply of 1913 available in 1919 and that the production of the Ruhr mines had sunk to 71 percent of the prewar level despite the availability of more miners. Since production per hour reached its prewar level in October 1919, the production loss could only be explained by reduced hours of labor and that, relatively speaking, more workers were doing fewer shifts than in 1913.[38]

Claiming the right to special treatment, the miners had successfully forced a reduction of the shift underground from eight and a half to seven hours in April 1919, and since the new hours included the full trip to and from the workplace, the effective working time could run as low as four and three-quarters hours. Despite this fact, there was a very strong movement among the miners for a six-hour shift, which the government had only managed to stall temporarily in August by setting up a special committee of experts to investigate the feasibility of a six-hour shift in the industry. While the hours-of-work question was also a source of conflict with employers, who saw no other path to increased productivity than the laying on of extra shifts, there was more harmony between employers and trade unions on the wage question. Just as the miners claimed that they deserved special consideration with respect to hours and that the introduction of the eight-hour day throughout German industry should mean the special reduction of their workday, so they claimed the right to receive the highest industrial wages.

Although the owners of mixed enterprises (that is, large vertical concerns stretching from raw coal to finished products) demonstrated some resistance to this concept, the "pure" mine owners were more tractable, asking only that the unions support coal price increases to cover the costs of wage increases. This practice, begun during the war, continued even though the trade unionists were fully aware that "one demand promotes another just as one price increase pushes another. We must also realize that the demanded coal price increase will set loose a new series of price increases and that the miners will in the last analysis also have to bear the costs in the form of still higher prices for food and other necessities."[39] The negotiations for the first industry-wide contract in coal mining, which opened on September 19, began with both sides making "traditional" claims—the miners for top wages and the employers for a price increase. This obviously was no contribution to government efforts to reduce prices, and the only hope was that any contract would pave the way to increasing productivity.

The problems of controlling labor, however, were not limited to the private sector. While miners claimed special privileges on the grounds of their importance and their dangerous work, civil servants of all types, who had become better organized after 1918, were demanding redress for the long years during which their interests had been neglected. The railroad workers were proving to be the most outspoken and dangerous of the public employees. Indeed, it was their strike threat that had forced the government to adopt a policy of subsidizing food imports. The postal workers and the multitude of other office workers and officials were also demanding an improvement of their conditions. Not only did the increasing restiveness of the civil servants threaten the economy with paralyzing strikes during the second half of 1919 but also the increasing evidence of corruption among the civil servants suggested that the famed German bureaucracy would degenerate entirely if something were not done.[40]

Furthermore, while the growing enrollment of civil servants in trade unions was something of a mixed blessing to the new political leadership of Germany, the latter could not be unaware of the fact that more conservative political forces were ready and able to woo the civil servants. This became very evident in the Reichstag debate of August 1, when the DVP Deputy from Duisberg, Otto Most, made a ringing speech in favor of assistance to the neglected civil servants, stressed the extent to which they had become indebted in order to maintain their living standards, and expressly played upon status feelings by pointing out that young miners in the Ruhr were making more than civil servants with years of experience and military service. For the government, however, such differences raised more complex problems. The treatment of civil servants had to be coordinated among its various agencies, and also it had to take into account the effect of such treatment on private industry. The Prussian mining authority, for example, had tried to deal with the increased cost of living by granting basic wage increases, while the railroad authority sought to maintain base wages by granting cost-of-living supplements instead. The consequence was that the employees of the state-owned mines started demanding cost-of-living supplements on top of their higher base wage. Manifestly, major concessions of whatever type would inevitably influence the private sector, especially since the miners constantly referred to the "easy" situation of civil servants when calling for shorter hours and higher pay for themselves.[41]

To remedy these problems, the Labor Ministry began to discuss the creation of a Wage Office (*Lohnamt*) in the spring and summer of 1919. Its purpose would be to coordinate policy. These efforts were interrupted, however, by the outbreak of a new crisis in July and August, when the public employees threatened to strike unless they received a special supplement to assist them in buying clothing and other necessities (*Beschaffungsbeihilfe*), the purchase of which they had been compelled to forego during the war. Initially, the government sought to parry this demand by offering an advance on a cost-of-living increase, but this was viewed as inadequate. As one Hamburg civil-servant representative put the matter:

The question is already acute. New debts are constantly being piled on the old, and if the civil servants continue to wait, then their demands will suddenly burst forth with an elementary force. The lower civil servants have not been able to make purchases during the last five years. . . . The financial considerations are of subordinate significance. The state can find ways of getting the money. Otherwise it would not have offered the advance payment. In addition to the raising of the cost-of-living supplements, we must demand a supplement to get out of debt [*Entschuldungszulage*].[42]

While the Prussian Finance Minister Südekum opposed this concession at the decisive discussion on August 15 on the grounds that the civil servants had no right to strike and the costs would be too great, the Reich leaders were fearful of strikes and a growing communist influence among the civil servants. Erzberger, who certainly was concerned about finances, unequivocally supported concessions for political as well as economic reasons since "no group [*Stand*] has been treated so badly during the war as the civil servants. One would simply open the gates wide to bribery if one does not help out."[43] Help out they did, and both the Cabinet and the National Assembly agreed to a thousand-mark assistance grant to married

civil servants, six hundred marks to single persons, and two hundred additional marks for each child. Half the grant was to be given in September, the rest in December. The difficulties of holding the line on pay increases by trying to substitute food subsidy programs could not have been more crassly demonstrated.

Little wonder, therefore, that increased productivity was seen as the only way out of this mess. If both Erzberger and Schmidt claimed they saw signs of improving labor productivity in mid-September 1919, the RWM guidelines did little to veil the fact that there was a long way to go and that the labor and productivity questions remained the central sources of concern for the RWM. The author of the document—by all internal evidence, Hirsch—continued to see the chief source of the problem as the "changed power position of the workers," to view the "increase of labor productivity as the chief goal of economic policy," and to see the solution in "the greatest possible identification of the worker with the results of his labor."[44] Piecework, premiums, and other incentives were strongly recommended, and the RWM stressed the need to prevent any reduction of working hours in mining and went so far as to express the timid hope that the influence of workers from districts needing coal would "to some extent" persuade the miners to work an extra shift.

This concentration on labor productivity, however, is not to be confused with an "antilabor" policy. The problem of restoring labor morale after the First World War was an international one, and that it should have been particularly serious in the defeated nations is hardly surprising. The particular danger in the German case was that the struggle to improve labor productivity took place in the context of increasing counterrevolutionary sentiment that caused many to play upon labor's restiveness and criticize the government for failing to contain it. Furthermore, the government remained committed to fulfilling some of the socio-political goals of the Revolution. Bauer and other Socialist leaders did not have the same objections to factory councils that they had to the now defunct soldiers and workers councils. The Bauer regime was preparing legislation during the fall of 1919 to create factory councils throughout German industry, and the RWM guidelines outlined the contribution a "real factory democracy" could make to productivity, just as they proposed the creation of a temporary Reich Economic Council to seek compromises among "competing productive interests" and of further cooperation with the ZAG. While wishing to promote labor–industry collaboration to the greatest possible extent, the RWM was aware that both sides were behaving in an inflationary manner: "The latest developments have led to a situation in which labor groups, in order to raise their wages, have promised the employers to help secure price increases which are often far beyond that which is required by the wage increases."[45] The RWM, therefore, spoke of the need for greater surveillance of industrial policy, especially the coordination of price and wage policy. There was also emphasis on the need to ration coal, fight the black market in coal, and ensure that the most productive plants were favored.

Similarly, the new RWM leadership was distinctly committed to consumer protection. The dysfunctionalities of the controlled economy in agriculture were undeniable, and the controls on oats, eggs, vegetables, fruit, and fish had been lifted in the spring, while controls on skins and leather had also been ended. The results, however, had not been gratifying. Prices for these products had soared rather than simply risen, and this now served as a warning for the future. The RWM had no intention of decontrolling grains, bread, meat, or potatoes. Schmidt got into a nasty public altercation with the Socialist Prussian Agriculture Minister, Otto Braun, who, based on his own judgment that the controlled economy was too bureaucratic and simply promoted black marketeering, responded to mounting agrarian complaints by arguing that either decontrol or higher price ceilings for basic food products were necessary.[46] Quite in keeping with this policy of maintaining restraints, the RWM, in its guidelines, called for the continuation of the anti-profiteering regulations and the price examination agencies, although it hoped that prices would be determined more by consultation than litigation. At the same time, a very positive attitude was taken toward the municipalization of the sale and distribution of vital necessities

and the expansion of consumer cooperatives. Retailers had very little to cheer about when it came to the new RWM leadership.[47]

Indeed, a careful reading of the RWM guidelines of September 19 suggests that not economic liberalism but rather pragmatic *dirigisme* was going to replace the planned-economy program of Wissell and Moellendorff. Agricultural policy was conspicuous by its absence in the guidelines, a clear indication of the intention to leave the compulsory system as it was and of the continued subordination of agricultural interests to the needs of industrial recovery. The savage attacks on Braun in the Socialist press provided good evidence that Schmidt and Hirsch were very politic in being silent. The retention of the anti-profiteering regulations showed that no change could be expected here either, while the document contained more than a few hints that industrial prices and wages would be monitored with greater energy. Also, the document was not totally without indications of long-range intentions. The RWM complained that existing conditions were producing an "economic step backwards" through an "unmistakable strengthening of the competitiveness of small and medium-sized plants and the retardation of the development of large-scale plants." Of even greater potential significance for the long-run was the specific mention of the need for the state to play a role in the formation and organization of capital for the "reorganization of the national economy"[48] if the private sector continued to prove unwilling to put its capital at the service of economic reconstruction. In short, there was a strong hint that the government might seek to direct investment for purposes of industrial rationalization and modernization.

If the *dirigiste* tendencies and undercurrents of the new RWM guidelines were unclear or subdued at this point, this was, on the one hand, because of the RWM's absorption with immediate problems and uncertainties and, on the other, because of its extremely liberal foreign-trade policy. It was this, more than anything else, that made the new leadership of the RWM appear so radically different from its predecessor. What better evidence of this could there be than the enthusiasm of Hamburg's Reichsrat representative, who found Hirsch's presentation of the new policy on September 4 "thoroughly sympathetic and in its basic points in complete agreement with the oft expressed views of Hamburg and the other Hanseatic cities."[49] In reality, neither Schmidt nor Hirsch ever believed in completely decontrolling imports but only justified their attitude by the utter hopelessness of controlling them effectively because of the "hole in the West." In its guide-lines, the RWM went so far as to assign the imports through the borders of the occupied areas with a major responsibility for the fall of the exchange rate of the mark then taking place.[50] It made little sense to ban the import of coffee, for example, if it were going to come into Germany through the occupied areas anyway. The only effect of import controls would be to make the price higher. Insofar as the free traders in Hamburg and elsewhere celebrated RWM liberality about imports, therefore, they mistook helplessness for policy and repressed the fact that this helplessness arose from Germany's inability to establish sovereignty over her own borders.

Under existing circumstances, Schmidt and Hirsch were quite willing to permit a foreign trade policy that was damaging to the exchange rate. The decontrol of exports, except for vital food and raw materials, unlike the involuntary decontrol of imports, rested on the premise that exporters would be advantaged and their gains would compensate for the inevitably increased price of imports as a result of the depreciation of the mark. Additionally, this liberal export policy would provide employment and help reestablish Germany's position on world markets. While certainly not opposed to the export control boards and their continued operation, Schmidt and Hirsch had no intention of imposing them on any industry in the manner advocated by their predecessors, and were in fact prepared to give way to south German demands that special delegates be appointed from their states to the export control boards since such decentralization would help to speed up the export of products that remained under the control of such boards. The object, in short, was to unleash an export offensive and to reduce the barriers to its success as much as possible.[51]

This policy brought the RWM into conflict with the ZAG and especially with the leaders of those industrial groups who counted on the export control system to maintain high price levels for German exports and thus maximize exchange profits while sparing Germany charges of dumping and the retaliation that might follow. Hans von Raumer of the electro-technical industry and Hans Kraemer of the paper-products industry were particularly incensed at the RWM, but Schmidt and Hirsch seemed oblivious to the dangers of their export policy. In their guidelines, they dismissed the threat of foreign reprisals, viewing liberal export policy as the appropriate pendant to the liberal import policy, pointing out that cheap German exports would always find a way out anyway, and opposing an exaggeration of Germany's "self-blockade," since "the permanent need for Germany to export in the future makes it necessary that German products find their way abroad in the greatest possible amounts. This is more important than the immediate securing of the greatest possible return on their worth."[52] Unofficially, Schmidt expressed to Kraemer the hope that "a further worsening of our exchange rate might have a good result insofar as the Entente will be inclined to initiate an international understanding on the exchange rate."[53]

There can be no question that this very risky sudden liberalization of foreign-trade policy, which had involved the lifting of the Foreign Exchange Decree, was being conducted in the expectation that it would help the Allies to see the necessity of altering their policies in the occupied areas and doing something to help Germany stabilize her finances and economy. Erzberger's optimism as well as his willingness to propose such radical measures as the exchange of all of Germany's bank notes, on the one hand, and the optimism expressed in the RWM guidelines with respect to the anticipated benefits of a liberalized export policy, on the other, rested on the anticipation that the Allies would understand the grim realities and come to reason about helping Germany out of her difficulties. In the absence of such Allied help, however, the policies of both Ministries were at once problematic and somewhat contradictory. Insofar as Germany could not get a stabilization and reconstruction loan, programs for exchanges of currency or stamping of paper assets could only serve to undermine confidence in the mark and discourage people from holding on to it. This was tantamount to discouraging the one potential form of large-scale credit Germany did have; namely, the speculative holding of German currency by foreigners. At the same time, the RWM's engagement in an inflation-conditioned export drive could be harmonized with Erzberger's plans if it were a temporary measure designed to secure agreements making stabilization possible. In the absence of such agreements, it would lead to a buying out of Germany and foreign complaints about German dumping and retaliation. If Erzberger and Schmidt worked together in harmony, as they apparently did, it was not because their policies were coordinated but because they both operated with optimistic assumptions about what the Americans and British were prepared to do, assumptions for which there was relatively little solid evidence.

This is not to say that they did not try to turn their hopes into realities. On September 18, the two Ministers personally requested an interview with Lieutenant Colonel Thelwall, the commercial expert in the British Military Mission in Berlin, a request which the latter explained as the consequence of "the extreme anxiety which the German Government feels with regard to the present financial and economic situation of Germany and the prospects of the coming winter."[54] He went on in his report: "Very great emphasis was laid on the importance of rapid assistance being forthcoming, if progressive disintegration and final collapse are to be avoided. Effective help in a month's time would be more appreciated than ten times the amount in twelve months." The Germans asked that they be allowed to levy customs in gold and that they be permitted to reestablish German customs controls and enforce their import and export regulations at the borders of the occupied areas. The Germans argued, accurately, that they had levied customs duties in gold before the war so that the continuation of this practice did not violate peace treaty restrictions on an increase of German tariffs, while the continued refusal of the occupation authorities to permit duties calculated in gold deprived Germany of much needed revenues. While Germany had once received 700 million gold

marks a year from such revenues, it was now collecting 132 million in paper, the equivalent of 26 million in gold. The refusal to honor German customs practices and laws was not only turning the occupied areas into a haven for smuggling to and from the West but also creating grotesque distortions in the flow of trade. Czech exporters, for example, found it cheaper to send goods to Dresden via Alsace than by the usual direct route.

The Germans also requested immediate financial assistance in the form of an international loan by England and the United States with the participation of their Allies and the neutrals nearest to Germany. Erzberger proposed that those participating send representatives of their trade and foreign ministries and central banks to such a meeting and pointed out that "by making the loan an international one in which practically all the European states had a share, it is considered that the odium attaching to the granting of financial support to Germany alone would be avoided." While Erzberger stressed the need for speed in the negotiation of what was obviously meant to be a large-scale international stabilization and reconstruction loan, he was also anxious to have England assist in a "temporary and speedy measure"; namely, a sterling loan of ten million pounds, half to be paid off in six weeks and the rest at the end of the year. The purpose, as Thelwall reported, was "to use the money thus obtained for the purchase of marks in neutral countries and, with characteristic optimism, he considers that by judicious manipulation of such purchases he could bring the mark down to 30 in a few days." Since the pound sterling stood at 109.90 in Berlin on the day of this conversation, Erzberger's expectations from such an operation were nothing short of fantastic. Once again, however, they explain the boldness and riskiness of his stated intention to call in and exchange all of Germany's money at home and abroad. Finally, on a less dramatic level, Erzberger urged that Allied merchants be encouraged to promote commerce with Germany by lending raw materials to be worked into manufactured products in return for a fair return on the sale of such goods as well as by bartering Allied goods sold in Germany for German products.

It is significant that Thelwall's report concerning these proposals was quite positive. He was in fundamental agreement with the Germans on questions pertaining to trade control in the occupied areas and the levying of customs in gold, pointing out that

... it is useless for them to endeavor to effect financial and industrial improvements so long as they are denied proper control over their most important frontier, a denial which also affects adversely their commercial relations with their other neighbors. Further, the conditions created by the present lack of control and supervision in the occupied territory, as far as imports and commercial transactions generally are concerned, only tend to promote a large amount of speculative and unsound business which is of no permanent value to either Germany or the Allies and is undoubtedly a contributory cause to dangerous fluctuations in the rate of the mark which not only make transactions with Germany almost impossible, but have brought this country to the verge of bankruptcy.

Given the scope of the German financial goals, he was necessarily more cautious in passing judgment on them, but he did stress the political aspects of the question because Germany "was now about to enter upon what will probably be the most difficult months since the Revolution." While political violence had died down, he warned that the economic difficulties would be serious and that "if by any chance it should bring matters to such a pitch that orderly government becomes impossible in Germany the possibility of a union with the Russian Soviet Republic must be contemplated." Thelwall thought the danger "remote, but sufficiently real to make some action, even if it be only the opening of financial negotiations, well worthwhile." The alternative would be to run the risk of "bankruptcy or political anarchy," which would not only deprive the Entente of the fruits of victory but create "so vast an area of disturbance that it would practically be impossible to restore it to a state of order again."

Apparently, however, these were risks the Allies and the United States found either nonexistent or acceptable. The British made some concessions in October and November 1919 by agreeing to controls of border trade in food products and then by conceding that customs be calculated in gold at the beginning of 1920, but it was not until late March that the Allies finally acceded to the enforcement of German customs regulations in the occupied zones. The "hole in the West," therefore, remained open throughout the fall and winter of 1919–1920. Large-scale international loans and credits were not to be had either. There certainly was long-term substance to Erzberger's belief that English fear of American competition and desire to restore London's position as the world's financial center predisposed Great Britain to assist Germany, but it was a bit too soon for such tendencies to have positive consequences. At the moment, Germany's efforts to play on the potential Anglo-American rift backfired since they took the form of unconfirmed rumors that got back to the Americans and were suspected of being "inspired by the standard German desire to sow distrust."[55] Actually, Erzberger was sincerely pro-English and had openly spoken of England as the clearing house for Germany's foreign trade, a remark which his domestic political enemies used when claiming that the Americans were refusing to give Germany a large loan because of Erzberger's "dilettantism." They argued that if Germany had a "respectable" Finance Minister such as Warburg, Dernburg, or even Helfferich, the American businessmen "who are appearing here in great swarms, partially in order to see if we are still capable of surviving, particularly in order to conclude large delivery contracts,"[56] might bring more favorable reports home. Increasingly, Erzberger was being portrayed as Germany's nemesis both at home and abroad.

Actually, the failure of Germany to receive an American loan at this time had nothing whatever to do with Erzberger's person or policies, and there was something truly pitiable about the way in which Germans grasped at every hint of American help and were preyed upon by the most dubious characters claiming to have American connections. Thus, in the very communication in which the Reichsbank was warning the Foreign Office that a person who claimed to represent a large syndicate capable of providing food and raw materials for credit was a "swindler," it noted that "under the existing circumstances Germany must place the greatest value on credits from America; we therefore consider it desirable that all offers, even if they perhaps promise little result from the outset, be considered and that the opportunity be taken to subject them to appropriate scrutiny."[57]

Fortunately, the German government also had reliable informants who told the simple truth, such as Wall Street broker F. A. Borgmeister who, in seeking to renew his connections with Germany in August, frankly reported:

As soon as communications were reestablished and trading with the Central Powers became possible, my office became right active. I suggested various credit arrangements, some of which have been accepted by the banks; others are in the course of negotiation. At the same time all kinds of possible and impossible credit proposals—the latter predominating—appeared in the market. They must have been prompted by the desire of certain exporters and some profiteers to make a killing. The idea prevails at this time in such circles that once the credit question is solved, almost any price can be settled on the German and Austrian consumer. The banks are holding back, and as far as proposals of the above category are concerned, their conservatism adds to the advantage of the Austrian and German consumers. . . . At present nobody knows what to do and what is being done. Banks like the Guarantee Trust Co., National Bank of Commerce, and others inform me that nothing will be done until peace is ratified and until they have a clearer view of the financial and industrial situation in Germany.[58]

An even more cautious attitude was expressed at the end of the year, when another reliable informant listed a series of uniformly pessimistic statements by leading American bankers. Without the assistance and guarantee of the government, the banks were unwilling to launch a major international loan effort, and the U.S. government was dead set against further international lending under its auspices. The American public was hardly ready to be mobilized to repeat the wartime Liberty Bond drives for foreigners and, worse yet, for Germans in peacetime. To be sure, there was much talk, especially at banquets and celebrations of various sorts, about helping the hungry and bankrupt Europeans: "After a good dinner, one often feels that one wants to help the whole world out of its misery; but before the hand manages to reach the wallet in one's pocket, the benevolence has largely been discounted. As the situation is today, Europe has little help to expect, unless it pays cash or gives first-class securities. The old principle 'everyone for himself

and the devil take the hindmost' is once again the everyday slogan."[59]

It was a slogan most appropriate for Germany in the fall and winter of 1919–1920, as an unprecedented wave of inflation shattered all calculations and expectations and forced the government to rethink many of its economic prognostications and programs (see Table 1). Whereas the RWM guidelines of September 15 had stressed the worker productivity problem and reflected the impact of worker unrest and demands of the revolutionary period while only hinting at the problem of controlling industrialist policies, the situation seemed quite different a month and a half later. To be sure, both domestic and foreign observers reported a settling down of the workers and increased willingness to work and even to do overtime. Insofar as this happy development was being frustrated, it was by the coal shortage, which became particularly serious during the winter and explains why the productivity question remained a major source of contention in the mining industry. Relatively speaking, however, the problem of labor discipline became secondary to an incredible breakdown of discipline taking hold elsewhere in the economy and even in the government.

The external depreciation of the currency was itself a symptom of this deterioration of discipline, a fact that became quite apparent when the authorities made inquiries among the banks and the various German consulates. There was universal agreement that the "hole in the West" (the smuggling engaged in by both the Germans and foreigners which was either tolerated or virtually encouraged by the Allies) was a major source of mark depreciation. Fundamentally, this was a steady problem, and it did not account for the sharp drops and fluctuations in the worth of the mark that took place in mid-August. These were almost invariably the result of large sales of marks abroad, in this case from two sources: "The first are those Germans who have sent marks abroad for purposes of capital flight. They apparently want to protect themselves against the stamping of their money by throwing their German notes on the market at any price in order to buy neutral or enemy currencies. The other purchasers are apparently those Reich agencies which buy foodstuffs abroad and pay for them through the sale of marks."[60] This is rather solid evidence that the Reichsbank was correct in arguing that Erzberger's tax program and his stated intention to exchange currency notes and stamp securities—there was no announced plan to stamp the currency—hung as a "Damocles sword" and encouraged flight from the mark, a situation that was made all the more disastrous by its coincidence with the abrogation of the Foreign Exchange Decree.[61] A flood of "best orders" (sales of marks for foreign exchange at the best possible price) rolled over the Netherlands and Switzerland in particular and created a measure of panic. Indeed, there were rumors of an incipient German devaluation or declaration of bankruptcy, of diminished chances for an American loan, of strikes and coal shortages. What one report described as "the relentless pessimism with which the majority of Germans judge the future of their country, and with which even the directors of the leading German banks have expressed themselves concerning the economic future of Germany" necessarily took its toll on the exchange value of the mark.[62]

This was particularly distressing because it was possible, after all, to speculate in favor of the mark as well as against it, and some persons, at least, were aware that many of the mark holdings abroad were in the hands of foreigners counting upon making a profit someday from a German recovery. As the well established Lübeck merchant house of L. Possehl & Co., which conducted its business with Scandinavia, pointed out in a revealing petition to the government:

Foreign speculation in mark notes is our only salvation today given stagnating exports. It was our good fortune that every peasant in Denmark bought mark notes and securities in the hope that the value of the mark would go up again after peace was restored. . . . The situation is similar in Sweden, where many large and small speculators took advantage of the low value of the mark to purchase it. All these people place their hopes in the arrival of normal conditions in Germany and then consider an increase in the exchange value of the mark to be self-understood. These many hands are today the reservoir for receiving the mark notes and securities which Germany is sending into the outside world. We believe that Germany must do everything possible to encourage these many hands—our helpers—and must avoid every-

thing that might make them anxious. The rumor reaching Sweden that the mark notes would be stamped called forth a real panic. . . . Even many northern banks had the idea that the bank notes in their possession could become worthless if they overlooked some formality. In any case, countless persons decided to free themselves from holdings which were threatened with confiscation and thereby enormous holdings of marks were thrown onto the market.[63]

The relative significance of such speculative engagement—and disengagement—in marks at this time is difficult to determine, and it is rarely mentioned in the sources dealing with the fall and winter of 1919. However, it was to become a factor of crucial importance throughout the history of the German inflation, so that this lonely hint by a well-informed firm is of great significance. For Erzberger, whose primary concern was to reduce the liquidity in the economy and promote a return to sound finance through heavy taxation at home and long-term credits abroad, such considerations were secondary. He was hoping to achieve stabilization, not survival through foreign speculation. In the absence of success in procuring foreign credits, however, the role that might be played by speculative support of the mark could not be discounted, and care had to be taken with respect to the psychological disposition of the speculators.

Care also had to be taken about the way in which the government went about using its money to buy food and raw materials abroad. The manner in which the Reich agencies had undertaken to sell marks—the second source of foreign mark sales at this time—was anything but conducive to the promotion of confidence. The money market had, so to speak, anticipated Germany's foreign food purchases and discounted for it, but it had not anticipated that "the purchases would be undertaken by the Reich authorities without consultation with one another and in the most unskillful manner imaginable in that the entire purchase in the amount of 20 to 30 million marks was thrown onto the market all at once."[64] Worse yet, the sins of August and September were repeated in November, when purchasing orders for foreign currency amounting to as much as twenty million marks were sent out in a single day, creating panic among foreign holders of marks and forcing the exchanges in the Netherlands and Norway to go so far as to refuse to purchase German marks on November 4.[65]

Although a Foreign Exchange Procurement Board (*Devisenbeschaffungstelle*) had been set up at the beginning of September 1919 to coordinate government purchasing activities, its inexpert performance remained a source of difficulty. That such expertise was desperately needed was demonstrated at the end of November, when the Reichsbank bitterly complained that government mark sales had set back the improvement of the mark between November 22 and 25. Confidence in the mark had probably increased because of rumors that the negotiations to plug the "hole in the West" had been successful, but the happy trend was not only halted but also significantly reversed by the sale of a hundred fifty million to three hundred million marks for foreign exchange on November 24 and 25. To compound the problem, the purchases had not been made from the great banks but rather from other firms which, however respectable, could not offer to sell foreign exchange they had on hand to the government without first buying foreign exchange abroad to maintain their holdings. This increased the massiveness of the foreign-exchange purchase and could necessarily undermine the recovery of the exchange rate. The Reichsbank insisted that "mark purchases abroad, if they cannot be avoided, should under all circumstances be undertaken only with the greatest caution and only through such firms and agencies where one is certain that they subordinate their own advantage out of consideration for the market situation."[66] Coordination with the Reichsbank and other agencies was essential, all the more so as the Reichsbank was itself paying off large wartime credits in foreign exchange and had benefited by a billion marks from the all-too-brief 12.5 percent improvement of the mark when paying off those debts. Since the Reichsbank, by the end of December, had paid back 1,848.7 million marks in debts fully and another 1,983.8 million in partial principal and interest, its concern with the improvement and stability of the exchange rate and desire to prevent untoward actions by the government which might undermine it were quite understandable.[67]

To correct all these problems and ensure greater coordination, Erzberger created in December an advisory council of government and Reichsbank officials as well as experts from the private sector for the purpose of guiding the Foreign Exchange Procurement Board. Such prominent bankers as Max Warburg and Paul von Schwabach; the head of the Metallgesellschaft, Richard Merton, whose experience on the international metals market presumably gave him special qualifications; and Independent Socialist economist Rudolf Hilferding were also invited to serve. The representatives of the private sector were far from enthusiastic about taking this responsibility. This was particularly true of Richard Merton, who fretted both about the composition of the group and about its purposefulness. He worried that the non-Berliners would find it hard to get to meetings, so that the decisions would be made by the unlikely pair of Schwabach and Hilferding: "Since I take the view that Miss Currency is the legitimate daughter of capitalism, I can well imagine a healthy currency issuing from Lord Rothschild and Miss Morgan, but not from Herr Schwabach and Herr Hilferding."[68]

Ultimately, however, he wondered if the currency really could be saved and if it really were in the interest of the private sector to remain tied to the finances of the state and the interest of the Reichsbank. Merton was more than a little skeptical of the influence of the directors of the great banks, who because of their "monumental Treasury note holdings" and seats on the Reichsbank curatorium were too caught up in the fate of the existing currency to face the possibility of a state bankruptcy.[69] While conceding that the currency might be saved if the Treaty of Versailles were rapidly revised and Germany thereby made worthy of international credit once again, and confessing that the "bad position of the exchange rate of the mark was the best glue holding the Reich together today," he wondered if the private sector should not at least be prepared to separate itself from "the state and the bad state currency" and thereby at once complicate the problems of Germany's external enemies and withdraw the private sector "from the influence of domestic politics."[70]

If Merton's industrialist colleagues had found him too radical in a statist direction during the war, they were now finding him too radical in precisely the opposite sense. Director Kurt Wiedfeldt of Krupp, to whom the above lines were penned, shared Merton's distrust of the great banks and regretted that the more autonomous private banks had lost influence before the war. He went on to note that "at first sight, there is much to be said for your idea that the Reich and the state be allowed to collapse financially and that the German private sector keep away from this collapse and establish itself on an independent basis with respect to its money and credit."[71] Nevertheless, Wiedfeldt thought it advisable to "weigh the consequences more carefully," a requirement Merton in no way questioned. What is significant about the exchange, however, is the seriousness of these two industrialists, who certainly must be counted among the more responsible, moderate, and cosmopolitan of Germany's industrial leaders, simply to "go it alone" if necessary in total disregard of the state and its currency. It helps to make more comprehensible the extent to which certain industrial groups were prepared to solve their problems, especially their foreign debt obligations, in total disregard of government policies and interests.

Like the Reichsbank, several major German firms and industries had wartime debts payable in foreign exchange. Some of these debts were guaranteed by the Reichsbank, others were not; but just as the Reichsbank was concerned to maintain Germany's credit abroad by paying off its debts to the neutrals so the businessmen in question were anxious to maintain their credit and ensure their supplies of foreign raw materials by paying off their foreign-exchange debts as quickly as possible. This was especially the case with the German iron and steel industrialists, who had purchased over seventeen million tons of Swedish ore between 1915 and 1918, much of it on credit and repayable in kronor. Most of the debts were to fall due by July 1, 1920. According to one calculation of March 1919, they amounted to a hundred twenty million marks. It was a debt that made the great industrialists nervous, particularly because it steadily increased as the mark depreciated.[72]

The restraints imposed by the Reichsbank and the government on the repayment of the debt had thus become an increasing source of worry and irritation. The Reichsbank was, to be sure, the guarantor of many of these debts, but the industrialists wondered if the Reichsbank could supply the necessary foreign exchange in an emergency. As early as January 1919, General Director Hasslacher of Rheinstahl declared that "I want to remain an honest fellow who pays his debts and does not need to claim that I would have paid gladly except that my government prevented me from doing so."[73] In March, August Thyssen, who apparently had larger foreign-exchange holdings abroad than some of his colleagues, suggested they pay 25 percent of the debts immediately and another 25 percent when the notes fell due so as to show good faith to the Swedes.

Until the summer, however, the great industrialists demonstrated considerable restraint, a posture which changed quite abruptly with the acceptance of the Treaty of Versailles and became more and more ruthless as the exchange rate deteriorated. Encouraged by the lifting of exchange controls and alarmed by the decline of the mark, which made it even more expensive to buy kronor, some of the firms displayed panic in their efforts to discharge their debts as rapidly as possible. Unhappily, the tendency of government agencies to purchase foreign exchange wildly on the market encouraged the industrialists to act similarly. Actually, this panic was not entirely convincing since the German industrialists had cleverly stored up their ore supplies before the end of the war, and the Swedes, desiring to increase rather than diminish German dependence on their ores over the long run, were prepared to make concessions regarding the rate at which the debts were paid off and the terms of payment. Max Warburg, for example, became thoroughly annoyed at the industrialists and thought that advantage should be taken of the Swedish willingness to wait: "We are driving ourselves to destruction if everyone now . . . secretly sells mark notes in order to be able to meet his obligations. If things keep on this way, then the mark notes will become unsalable."[74]

As things became worse, some of the firms turned to the government, demanding that it should assume some of the responsibility for the matter since it was at the government's request that the debts had been made in the first place. The iron and steel industrialists were not the only group to make this claim, and the government took the posture that increased indebtedness through exchange deterioration was an "indirect" war cost and therefore not its responsibility. Nevertheless, there was a strong inclination on the part of the government to make an exception in the case of the ore debts because of the importance of the iron and steel industry and the economically disruptive consequences of the industry's efforts to pay the debts on its own. In December, for example, Erzberger suggested that the government-owned Hibernia mines be leased to the Swedes under a complicated scheme that would have put off the debt payment for ten or fifteen years.[75] Nothing came of the proposal, but the RWM then took up the problem only to find the industrialists unwilling to supply it with the needed information about the size and distribution of the debts among the various firms. The industrialists were as anxious to avoid government interference in their affairs as they were to pay off their debts. They therefore proceeded to take matters into their own hands and managed to liquidate most of the debts by October 1920.

The methods employed by these industrialists not only had a negative effect on the exchange rate but also affected German domestic price levels in a very serious manner and, indeed, increased the growing chaos in the domestic economy. They were engaging in four practices which were viewed as particularly harmful. First, they exported iron and steel in order to secure foreign exchange and thereby increased shortages at home. Second, in July they abandoned the restraint they had shown on the home market and began to raise prices regularly. Thus, pig iron, which stood at 438 marks a ton in July, cost 516.60 in August, 651.50 in October, 1,323.50 in November, and 1,775 in April. Third, on October 9, they renounced the stable pricing policies they adopted in April, which they now characterized as an "act of stupidity." This meant that manufacturers no longer had any clear idea of what they would have to pay for their iron and steel

when it was finally delivered. Fourth, and most serious, in the late winter they began to demand partial payment in foreign exchange from their domestic customers, often at a rate below that of the official exchange rate.[76]

Quite understandably, this situation created enormous difficulties for the manufacturers of finished products using iron and steel and led to a breakdown of industrialist solidarity. From the standpoint of the national economy, the most profitable exports were those with the most labor added, that is, finished products. Exports of iron and steel, therefore, were uneconomic, except for their producers. At the same time, orders for finished products tended to be long-term, so that changes in costs resulting from sliding-scale raw materials prices and demands for special forms of payment made calculation of final price impossible. Manufacturers of machines and other products employing iron and steel had a decision to make. They could absorb the increased costs and possibly even sell at a loss, or they could introduce sliding-scale provisions into their own contracts, cancel their old contracts, or change prices retroactively. Naturally, such measures would not be treated with favor by customers and, indeed, the fall and winter of 1919–1920 was a period when the reputation of the German industrialist and merchant sank dramatically. As the Association of German Machine Builders noted on January 23, 1920, "[T]he cancellation of export contracts, especially those which had been concluded in the summer of 1919 at fixed prices, has evoked a bitter reaction abroad at times, and the machine builders have been accused of violating equity and good faith."[77] The Reich Association of German Industry warned its members that it was unethical to add supplemental charges to bills to cover increased costs when there was no provision for this in the contract and pointed out that the reputation of German industry was being ruined by such practices.[78] By February, the matter had become so serious that the RWM, the Foreign Office, and the Reich Commissar for Exports and Imports were all issuing similar warnings to German businessmen, especially against such shady practices as making fictitious claims that they could not get permission to export in fulfillment of their contracts. The government noted that "the bitterness of foreign customers . . . is causing them to purchase more in enemy or neutral countries."[79]

Obviously, heavy-industrial demands for partial payment in foreign exchange or for payment calculated in foreign exchange or for payment in scrap calculated at an artificially low price were not likely to promote goodwill on the domestic market either. The situation was particularly bad when such demands were coupled with an exploitation of shortages so that, as first in the case of coal and now in the case of iron and steel, the availability of raw materials often depended on the customer's willingness to make some special concessions or to bribe the producer in some form or other. Furthermore, the tactics of the iron and steel producers were copied by other suppliers whose products were in whole or in part based upon imported raw materials that had to be paid for in foreign exchange.

These practices promoted instability in various ways. They threatened to create a widespread demand for foreign exchange throughout the country, thereby producing a great array of persons and firms seeking small quantities of foreign exchange in an uneconomic manner while greatly increasing the overall demand for foreign currencies at the expense of the mark. At the same time, they served to promote an approximation of domestic and international price levels and thereby an unbearable and insupportable general increase of domestic prices. While this was the goal of some of the iron and steel producers, it was not a goal to which either the government or large portions of industry subscribed. Finally, they tended to create a situation in which the formation of domestic prices would become dependent upon the frequent variations of the exchange rate. It is important to recognize, however, that the Germans in 1919–1920 did not view this problem from the perspective of 1922–1923. The anxiety at this point was not hyperinflationary adaptation to exchange rates. There is no evidence of serious concern that the mark would cease to be a measure of value altogether. Rather, the problem was viewed as one of excessive instability in the conduct of business and excessive price fluctuations. The problem, as defined by contemporaries, therefore, was

how to restore a reasonable amount of stability to domestic and foreign trade.

Not surprisingly, some thought was given to the possibility of resurrecting the old exchange control system, and even Director Mankiewitz of the Deutsche Bank argued that the practices just described were proving so conducive to hoarding of foreign exchange and speculation that strong legislation was desirable. Most bankers present at a meeting of experts called to discuss the problem in early April 1920, however, advised against resurrecting the Foreign Exchange Decree. Warburg, for example, argued that it simply could not be implemented effectively when so many firms were involved in the use of foreign exchange. Dr. Hjalmar Schacht of the Nationalbank, who would one day preside over Germany's stabilization, took a somewhat different position, which is particularly interesting because it shows that calculation in terms of foreign exchange rates was not yet viewed as a genuine threat to the German currency and that stability of business conditions was the paramount concern:

The reason for the calculation in foreign currencies in domestic commerce is not simply the wish for price increases, and also not simply the demand of heavy industry to cover foreign exchange debts. To a large extent it is the effort to find a secure and uniform basis for calculation. To this extent, the demand for payment in a foreign currency is not without a certain justification. One should therefore issue a decree that every purchaser can free himself from payment in foreign currency by paying in marks at the day's exchange rate. In that way we would, on the one hand, show some consideration for industry and, on the other hand, eliminate the demand for foreign currencies.[80]

This had, in fact, become the practice of the porcelain industry. Nevertheless, most of the experts, including Professor Prion, shared Warburg's view that no decree would be truly effective and that the best approach would be to work on the trade associations and cartels and syndicates to make them realize the dangerousness of their actions and to get them to exercise moderation and self-restraint.

This, however, simply was not working in many cases. The RWM had been trying to use persuasion without any great success since July, and not only the Ministry but also important groups in industry became convinced that nothing could be accomplished without regulation. Indeed, by the turn of the year, rumors were circulating that Schmidt was going to be replaced, possibly even by Rathenau, and that, whoever his replacement, as Director Wiedfeldt of Krupp reported to his chief, "the RWM will push the Wissell–Moellendorff plans further in some manner. Undersecretary Hirsch is already on this route. He is particularly pushing the fusion of the iron industry. . . . I still do not clearly see what these people want."[81]

Neither, exactly, did Schmidt and Hirsch, but experience was helping them to define their goals and determine their methods more clearly. They learned, for example, that they would have to assert state authority more vigorously since it was virtually impossible to get industry to act in what they conceived to be the national interest. When Hirsch tried to persuade the iron and steel industrialists in September that the coal shortage was a good opportunity to work toward the trustification and rationalization of the industry, the great industrialist Peter Klöckner responded that "we do not need to play hide-and-seek here. Industry as well as the banking world has no confidence in the present government," while Wiedfeldt declared that "the general uncertainty and concern about the future causes every firm to keep its financial situation as liquid as possible above all so that, if it is necessary, it can at least have as respectable a bankruptcy as possible."[82] Were it not for government decrees mandating syndicalization, the great concerns would truly have gone each to its own way, and the RWM had to prolong the Steel Works Association by decree so as to ensure some uniformity of behavior and collective responsibility. At the same time, the behavior of the Steel Works Association and the growing storm of protest from its manufacturing customers convinced Hirsch that more forceful measures were necessary to bring the great concerns into line and protect the consumers of iron and steel products.

In a memorandum in December, Hirsch sharply attacked heavy industry for its exploitative practices and proposed the creation of a self-governing body that would bring together raw-materials producers, manufacturers using iron and steel products, and merchants and give all concerned, including the government, a voice in the export, pricing, and condition-of-payment policies of the producers. While Hirsch certainly intended that the iron and steel producers had enough foreign exchange to pay their ore debts, he was insistent that this could and would be done in a more satisfactory manner through a mixture of self-regulation by all parties concerned and government surveillance. While the raw-materials producers were horrified to find large portions of the machine-building and electro-technical industries teaming up with the government in this manner, the manufacturers, as one of them put it, had no intention of committing "hara-kiri" and turning down the proffered assistance in the name of a nonexistent solidarity with the iron and steel men. After numerous delays and complicated negotiations, Hirsch issued a decree in April creating the Iron Trades Association (*Eisenwirtschaftsbund* or EWB) and thereby earned the undying hatred of heavy industry.[83]

The most dramatic indication that the RWM of Schmidt and Hirsch was reversing its policies and picking up on at least some of the plans of Wissell and Moellendorff, however, was the issuance of a Decree on the Regulation of Imports and Exports on December 20, 1919, a decree which laid the groundwork for a network of export control boards composed of the representatives of industry and labor for nearly every branch of industry and which placed the activities of these self-regulating bodies under the surveillance of the Reich Commissar for Imports and Exports. This reversal of the RWM position on export controls was a classic illustration of the dilemmas of decontrol following the war. On the one hand, the retention of wartime controls of imports and exports would have been a somewhat fruitless "self-blockade" after July 1919. They were simply ineffective to a great extent because of the "hole in the West," but they were potent enough to hamper Germany's reentry on the world market. On the other hand, the RWM could not project the extent to which the sudden turning away from foreign trade controls and weakening of the existing controls would lead to totally insupportable circumstances because the government leaders could not anticipate the extent of the depreciation of the mark in the fall and winter. Characteristically, the RWM's chief

Table 12. Purchasing Power Pars of the British, French, Italian, and German Currencies as Percentages of the Exchange Rate of Each of Those Currencies Against the Dollar, July 1919–June 1920

	British Pound	French Franc	Italian Lira	German Mark
1919				
July	95.9	81.5	95.7	224.4
August	98.4	94.1	104.1	229.6
September	97.0	95.7	107.3	240.0
October	93.0	91.7	107.7	241.0
November	95.1	97.4	113.7	288.6
December	103.1	110.1	123.4	315.2
1920				
January	107.0	108.8	114.4	260.4
February	109.1	121.7	145.7	311.4
March	99.6	113.1	141.0	258.7
April	96.9	128.6	159.6	222.8
May	102.4	126.2	131.7	178.1
June	99.8	120.1	125.6	163.8

Source: Frank D. Graham, *Exchange, Prices, and Production in Hyper-Inflation: Germany, 1920–1923* (Princeton, 1930), p. 118.

concern during the summer had been excessive imports, but it consoled itself with the notion that these would be compensated by increased exports. It played down the dangers of dumping. By the fall, however, it had become evident that dumping was out of hand and that Germany was in danger of being "bought out" as well as becoming the subject of foreign reprisals against the short-sighted export policies of some of her manufacturers.[84]

This was something that many leading industrialists and trade-association officials had understood all along, and it was why they had objected to the Schmidt–Hirsch policy of decentralizing existing foreign-trade controls and refusing to expand the system. No one knew better than they how short-sighted businessmen could be, and they were also aware of the fact that many businessmen simply did not understand the extent to which the mark had depreciated abroad. Many businessmen were as prone to the monetary illusion, to the confusion of a nominal with a real increase of their cash receipts, as were workers. Such businessmen believed that they actually were making a profit simply because they were selling at a much higher price in marks than before the war. This was especially true of businessmen who did not have to buy raw materials abroad and were only beginning to enter the world market again. Iron and steel industrialists, for example, were friendlier to export controls at

this time because they had learned the great difference between domestic and foreign prices and to calculate in foreign currencies during the war thanks to the fact that they had to buy ore abroad and were permitted a certain amount of export business. Small machine builders, furniture manufacturers, and producers of other finished products, however, did not have the same awareness because they bought their raw materials domestically at prices which were either controlled, as in the case of coal, or held down "voluntarily" out of fear of control, as in the case of iron and steel. In all cases, these prices reflected relatively low real-labor costs which were, in turn, a product of rent controls and continued controls on or subsidies of food prices.

Naturally, everybody in Germany was complaining about rising domestic prices during this period, but prices and wages were still well below world market levels, as demonstrated by the comparative domestic purchasing power of the mark against other major currencies (see Table 12). Indeed, one of the more cynical claims of the iron and steel producers in the fall and winter of 1919–1920 was that their high prices and harsh payment conditions were teaching manufacturers the difference between German domestic and world-market prices and thus encouraging them to export at appropriately high prices. The Association of German Machine Builders, of course, was not taken by such pedagogy, but it was concerned enough about the problem to hire Professor Prion to provide its members with a lecture on why higher nominal prices were not higher real prices. The point was that Germany did have a substantial export advantage, but insofar as exporters and manufacturers failed to take the difference between domestic and world market prices into account, or were insufficiently aware of the difference, they were often simply throwing goods away and taking a real loss.[85]

By November 1919, the situation had reached serious proportions, and foreigners were beginning to complain about German dumping. Switzerland provides a particularly interesting illustration of what was happening. At an economic conference held in Bern on October 16, many of the Swiss industrialists present openly called for protectionist measures against Germany. These demands were rejected by the Swiss government because it recognized that Switzerland's industry was too heavily export oriented to abandon free trading policies lightly and because Swiss consumers would resist an increase in their domestic price levels and would raise wage demands. Furthermore, some of the loudest complaints came from the electro-technical firms newly established during the war that had to face foreign competition and from paper producers who were being compelled to give up a lucrative wartime monopoly. The illegitimacy of their protectionist demands were all the greater because the German electro-technical and paper-products industries were in fact maintaining export controls for their industries and were careful to export at reasonably high prices. Other Swiss industries, however, had more legitimate complaints. German furniture makers offered modest bedroom furniture for about 160 francs, a fancier bedroom set for 455 francs, and a desk for 69 to 80 francs, while the Swiss charged for the same items, respectively, 400, 1,932, and 270 francs. Small iron wares and bicycles were also being sold by the Germans at extremely low prices not justified by market conditions. These industries were dumping by any standard. Moreover, the matter was serious. Furniture demand, for example, was very great, and German consular officials in Switzerland concluded that "German exporters were bad businessmen and, with respect to the interests of the German economy, one can only regret that they throw away their products at such prices."[86]

Ultimately, of course, the Swiss had every interest in raising the value of the mark. Their tourist industry depended to a great extent upon German visitors, and Swiss banks had large amounts of marks in their possession whose value had so depreciated that the Swiss government passed a regulation permitting the amortization of exchange losses over a number of years so that the banks could pay current dividends. Even so, the Elektrobank, which financed electrical works and railroads, was so overloaded with depreciating currency that its president, Dr. Julius Frey, was compelled to announce that there would be no dividends for 1919. To correct such conditions, most Swiss businessmen and officials believed that Germany had to export, and they were prepared to accept a measure of German exchange dumping, be it intentional, be it unintentional, so long as it was temporary. As a German official warned, however:

The agitation for protective measures will undoubtedly continue and will also have a chance for success if the underpricing continues. For this reason, it is very much in German interests to have this underpricing limited to a reasonable degree. Delivery of goods at half the price or less than they cost abroad means wasting (*Verschleuderung*) Germany's national wealth and, above and beyond this, risks important export interests. Care should be taken that goods should not be delivered to Switzerland at prices which over the long run must bring the German export business to a halt.[87]

Within Germany itself, such concerns received public expression from Felix Deutsch, general director of the AEG who, in an article in the *Vossische Zeitung* of November 9, 1919, emphasized the extent to which German products were being sold at prices excessively below those of their competitors. That something had to be done about this "selling out" of Germany was by this time recognized by nearly all, with the usual important exception of the Hansa cities. This became clear at a meeting of the Reichsrat on November 18, at which there was expressed strong support for the introduction of self-governing export control boards to regulate exports for all the relevant industries. It was, in effect, the scheme proposed by Wissell and Moellendorff without their long-range and elaborate organizational purposes. Hirsch, to be sure, continued to argue that the recent fall of the mark was due to the "hole in the West" and capital flight, but he left no doubt about his agreement with the need for stricter foreign-trade controls. He emphasized that the use of export control boards would be based on the principle of self-government in industry and that he hoped to avoid all bureaucratization. That is, the boards were not intended to be part of some grand plan in the style of Moellendorff. At the same time, he announced that legal measures would have to be taken to compel the various industries to organize export control boards on the basis of parity between labor and industry and to accept a government role in their operation and in the enforcement of their decisions.[88]

While it is reasonable to suppose that Schmidt and Hirsch would have come to this conclusion themselves, the organized forces of industry and labor in the ZAG certainly played a major role in promoting and in defining the manner in which it was to be realized. Hans von Raumer and Hans Kraemer had opposed the liberalization policy all along, but they were also shrewd enough to press Socialist journalist Wilhelm Jansson into their service. A Swedish citizen who had risen high in the Free Trade Unions, Jansson was able to emphasize criticisms and complaints which the German unions had received from their Swiss, Dutch, and Swedish counterparts about the unemployment being caused by unfair German competition and also, in close collaboration with von Raumer, to enlist trade-union support for a system of export control boards to be organized with the assistance of the ZAG and to be based on parity between industry and labor. The task of such boards was to determine minimum export prices on the basis of wage rates raw-materials prices, and the exchange rate.[89]

The participation of the trade unions was particularly important because of the thorny issue of how to handle the export profits, especially the profit being made on the difference between the foreign and the domestic price and the exchange profit resulting from the calculation of the difference between the two. There was much sentiment in Socialist circles for an export tariff that would tax away this profit, a plan unanimously opposed in industrial circles as well as by most of the authorities on the grounds that an expert determination of the proper tariff for the various products simply was impossible from a technical point of view and that the government would have a strong tendency to abuse such a tariff for fiscal purposes and thereby undermine the will to export. As a solution to the problem, Jansson proposed an export levy (*Ausfuhrabgabe*) of up to 5 percent on the price charged abroad, a levy that would be used for the specific purpose of "improvement of the situation of pensioners, invalids, and other groups with relatively low incomes."[90] This appeared to be a happy solution from every point of view. It saved industry from the export tariff, pleased labor by promising to relieve the lot of inflation victims by a charge against the profits made from the inflation, and sought to provide Erzberger, who appears to have been skeptical about the measures, with a source of increased income to finance the social insurance system at a time when its benefits were not keeping up with prices. Thus, a second decree issued on December 20 laid the basis for a system of export levies to be imposed by the export control boards established under the Decree on the Regulation of Imports and Exports of the same date.[91]

All this brought little joy to Hamburg's merchants and bankers or to those industries and industrialists who felt that the problems would solve themselves in the end and that they were being locked into a new bureaucratic system. Nevertheless, it was the ZAG, or the organized forces of industry and labor, that had promoted and helped to create the system of foreign trade controls and export levies in their postwar form. Given the general distaste for the controlled economy in industrial circles, however, the situation was not without its ironies, and Economics Minister Schmidt, who had been subjected to many attacks by the ZAG leaders for opposing the system initially, could not resist noting them to the ZAG General Assembly in December 1919:

Gentlemen, what you in your circles and also in commercial circles have otherwise stressed so emphatically, freedom of commerce and trade, of these I have heard nothing today, and I am very happy that you have come to the view that at the present time and under the given circumstances, it is necessary to introduce regulation, to employ compulsion where you believed only a few months ago that complete freedom was necessary.[92]

Needless to say, Schmidt was himself conveniently underplaying his own contributions to the abandonment of controls and his lack of heed to the warnings of those who criticized his policy. Still, there is no evidence that those critics had anticipated the degree and extent of the external depreciation of the mark anymore than had Schmidt, and it was this unprecedented and unexpected collapse of the exchange rate that had changed the views of the RWM and also led to the successful counteroffensive of those favoring controls. Furthermore, the "buying out" of Germany was a matter not only of foreign trade in the usual sense but also of domestic commerce. Germany's borders were constantly being crossed by merchants and individuals seeking German goods at cheap prices. Thus, Danish retailers were entering North Schleswig and buying everything in sight, while Dutchmen were crossing over into the area around Osnabrück and driving whole herds of live cattle across the border. Even the Hamburg Chamber of Commerce thought it high time that something be done about the bribing of border officials and such illegal traffic.[93]

The buying out of Germany was not limited to the border regions. In December, various associations of department stores and shops and retailers in Berlin decided to charge all foreigners a surcharge of from 20 to 25 percent on all items bought in their businesses. Upset by such discriminatory practices, the British economic expert in Berlin, Thelwall, summoned a director of Wertheim's department store to discuss the matter and was told "that this rule had been introduced to prevent foreigners from depleting the stocks in shops, as all goods were so extraordinarily hard to replace, but, on being pressed by me, he had to admit that it is quite easy to circumvent the resolution by using a German as an intermediary for a small consideration."[94]

Thelwall found even more "unjustifiable" a decision by the Association of Hotel Proprietors and the Association of German Pension Keepers to charge foreigners 25 percent more than the regular price. In January 1920, such practice became official government policy, and the chambers of commerce were asked to levy surcharges of as much as 150 percent on certain of the scarcer items purchased by foreigners. Shortly afterward the government proposed the levying of a special tax on foreigners visiting German spas and vacation centers. Some of these measures were undertaken with more than a touch of xenophobia and resentment against foreigners, but there was also recognition that they could prove impossible to administer or would ultimately backfire. All foreigners could not be identified, and there was certainly no wish to ruin the tourist business. As a consequence, the discriminatory practices were applied rather unsystematically and with some reservations.[95]

Indeed, Germans had more to worry about than the buying out of German cuckoo clocks on the cheap. Of much greater concern was the danger that foreigners might use the weakness of the mark to buy up German landed property and to gain control of German enterprises. While there was considerable evidence that foreigners were buying up landed property, the extent of such purchases in 1919–1920 is difficult to determine. Baden introduced a provision that changes in landed property had to have government approval, while the RWM contemplated issuing residence requirements or provisions similar to those of Baden for the entire nation. A major difficulty with all such measures and proposals was that they probably were violations of Article 276 of the peace treaty provisions preventing economic discrimination against the Allies. The same held true of provisions against foreign capital penetration into Germany, but here German firms had found an effective means of protecting themselves in the issuance of special stock that gave preferential voting rights and in arrangements providing that the supervisory boards and boards of directors of German firms had to be German. While foreigners appeared reluctant to invest heavily in German firms during this period because of the uncertain conditions, these provisions, which were widely undertaken, must have discouraged notions of controlling German industry. The fear of foreign penetration, however, was extremely strong and was one of the major reasons for the RWM's direct involvement in the entire question of the Swedish ore debts. It feared that either some of the heavy-industrial firms themselves or the manufacturers being forced to pay for iron and steel would welcome foreign penetration as a means of solving their financial difficulties. This anxiety also explains why the government was prepared to act against the great iron and steel concerns by setting up the Iron Trades Federation and why many manufacturers agreed that compulsory measures were essential.[96]

It should come as no surprise that the parlous state of the German economy, the mounting deficit, the depreciation of the mark abroad, and the rising prices at home would all be laid at the door of the government. Throughout the fall and winter there were rumors of impending state bankruptcy, and they persisted no matter how often they were denied. At the end of January, the Reichsbank repeated with ever more urgency the warnings which it had issued when the Bauer government took power, declaring that "the exchange situation has reached such a point of seriousness that the coming of a financial and economic catastrophe with fateful consequences is immediately approaching."[97] It saw the only solution in "saving" and "working," and called for a ban on luxury imports and the restoration of the prewar hours of work.

Whether any government could have tried this recipe in early 1920 is very doubtful, but the boldness of the Reichsbank at this juncture reflected the low credit of a government whose zig-zag course in the realm of economic policy had not produced much public confidence. Whatever the reality, it appeared to have first pursued a policy of decontrol and then to shift back to the ideas of Wissell and Moellendorff. The apparent lack of direction even produced a certain nostalgia for the old RWM leadership. Thus, the Independent Socialist Reichstag Deputy Simon admitted that he and his party had found the Wissell program too bureaucratic and insufficiently Socialist,

. . . but just the same, Wissell had the conviction that we could not come through without a planned economy, and he had at least given some thought to it. . . . Wissell fell because of his planned economy, and thereby we have fallen into a chaos that has shaken our economic life much more than the strikes. Through this planlessness in our economy, a handful of people have learned how to soak up millions if not billions from the people. . . . The Reich Economics Minister Schmidt has performed a great service for the capitalists with his policies. . . .[98]

If this was so, however, then the capitalists were proving insufficiently appreciative. Schmidt and Hirsch were criticized by the business community for a variety of sins both of commission and of omission. What was conveniently overlooked by the critics, however, was how badly divided they were themselves and the extent to which they, like the government leadership, were responding to unanticipated changes in an unprecedented economic situation. An outstanding illustration of this was the stormy debate within the business community over a pamphlet of December 1919 by the business manager of the Association of German Iron and Steel Industrialists, Jakob Reichert, entitled "Salvation from the Foreign Exchange Crisis." In this passionately and skillfully argued propaganda piece, Reichert propounded the idea that Germany's great hope lay in allowing domestic prices to reach world market levels. He confessed that he himself had originally anticipated a stabilization of world price levels after an initial period of price increases following decontrol and had thus been agreeable to domestic price restraint. Recent developments had proven this wrong, and the only solution for Germany was to accept the realities and allow domestic prices to rise. He called for complete decontrol of domestic prices, but for strict export controls so that German exporters could receive full value in foreign exchange for their production. Reichert was convinced that the high postwar demand for German products would continue for some time so that handsome export profits could be made. The decontrol of the domestic market, however, would encourage production, put an end to shortages, and eliminate black marketeering. Reichert recognized and accepted the fact that this would lead to soaring prices, require the further use of the printing press, and lead to wage demands, but he saw nothing wrong with any of these developments under the circumstances and specifically declared that wages should not be lowered. This mixture of domestic decontrol and export regulation, not the "consumer socialism" of Hirsch with its price controls and other restrictions, was the best way to end corruption and black marketeering, free the goods that were being hoarded, and encourage production and capital formation.[99]

If Reichert's pamphlet was a good illustration of practice being transformed into self-serving theory—in this case one designed to interpret the ruthless practices of the iron and steel industry as a service to the nation—it should be noted that it was a policy which its advocates sincerely wished to extend to the entire economy, especially to agriculture. Thus, at the December meeting of the supervisory board of the Reich Grain Corporation, Alfred Hugenberg insisted that shortages could only be eliminated by the restoration of the free market, while Stinnes declared that "the compulsory economy leads us to complete ruination. The wheat is flowing abroad. The wheat prices must therefore reach world market levels as rapidly as possible. . . ."[100] He urged that this be done in collaboration with the ZAG and shared Reichert's view that wages should be increased as much as necessary to meet the costs. Ultimately, the increased productivity and availability of food would bring both prices and wages down.

The slogan "onward to world market prices," however, found limited acceptance, even in business circles. The government leadership rejected it on the grounds that it would lead to an uncontrollable price-wage spiral and unprecedented chaos and disorder. As Erzberger argued before the Reichstag:

To have this goal before our eyes at this moment and to base our measures upon it will lead to a complete collapse of our economic life and to revolution in another way. For you cannot raise food prices by two, three, four, and five times. That's impossible. You also cannot raise wages at one stroke by so many times. For at the moment when the exchange rate improves again, there will have to be a downturn in our economic life once again—an eternal rising and receding tide that never comes to rest—an economic life that never permits secure calculation.[101]

These fears were shared by leaders of the banking sector as well as leading manufacturers and some heavy industrialists themselves. There was a general consensus that it was ultimately desirable to bring German domestic prices into line with world market prices, but the process had to be a gradual one. Some industrialists pointed out that they did not even know what world-market prices were under the existing fluid conditions, while others feared that world prices might soon drop, and Germany would be left with a domestic-prices structure ruinous to its exports. Thus, even if Erzberger was anything but popular in business circles, his views on the world-market price question were fully in line with those of major segments of the business community. The latter, therefore, was divided and hesitant, and while it recognized that productive incentives had to be provided, foreign debts paid, and capital resources reconstructed, it wanted protection against exploitation by those in control of vital resources. The primary consumers in industry, like the final consumers of basic necessities, continued to look to the state for protection. The controlled economy appeared necessary to maintain order, even though it was a source of disorder as well.

This is not to say that Wissell and Moellendorff were correct or realistic. No less profound an observer than Joseph Schumpeter, who had served on the short-lived German Socialization Commission and then as Austrian Finance Minister from March to October 1919, questioned the efficacy of all attempts to organize the economy through Socialist or other compulsory methods under postwar circumstances. Schumpeter was convinced that a successful reconstruction could only be carried out on a capitalist basis and sharply criticized the "childish belief in the state" that illustrated the German bourgeoisie's lack of self-confidence and led to an unshaken acceptance of the controlled economy even in the face of its "most severe failures" and the knowledge "that the German people owes its survival during the war only to the illegitimate remnants of private economic activity." He was even more caustic in his treatment of that class of intellectuals who made a practice of turning "future possibilities" into "demands for the present." The result of their influence, according to Schumpeter, was the inability "to accept clear facts, to give life its right to live and to see that every merchant who smuggles a train car of coal into a factory through all the artificial barriers, does more for the people than all the learned writers who, in a completely pre-Marxist manner, act as if people had a free choice between possible forms of organization. But that changes nothing of the broad lines of our fate."[102]

A Winter of Discontents

That fate, however, was not only economic but also political and social, and the great tragedy was that just as the demands and needs of the governed constrained the range of choice and decision making of their leaders, so the inevitable compromises underlying those decisions produced the no less inevitable discontents among the nation's citizenry, discontents heightened by the intransparency surrounding the decision-making process, its purposes, and its consequences. Most people, after all, are not Schumpeters, and they find it difficult to treat the black market as an economic good. They are equally unenthusiastic about letting private interests run amok in times of scarcity and want, however beneficial the ultimate results of the "invisible hand." At the same time, they are not prepared to freeze or starve out of reverence for bureaucratic decrees. That their attitudes are somewhat contradictory is not immediately apparent, and only a government prepared and able to employ the most Draconian methods would have been in a position to impose economic controls without tolerating their violation. One day Germany was to have such a government, but happily this was not the case in 1919–1920, and this meant the acceptance of various mixtures of economic freedom and economic control. At the "grass roots," this could only produce an intensification of the distress and confusion which had taken hold during the war and which had discredited the old regime. This Shirt of Nessus was now worn by the Weimar Republic.

Weimar's disastrous inheritance from the previous regime was especially evident with respect to the food supply, by now an endless pre-

occupation of whoever had the misfortune to rule in Berlin. The decontrol of various food products as well as of certain commodities, especially leather, had led to price increases that were unanticipatedly high, and this dissuaded the RWM from pursuing the decontrol of basic necessities any further. The maintenance of controls, however, and the prices being paid to the farmers for controlled products, were leading to what was tantamount to an agrarian delivery strike. At the end of November, the RWM reported that the grain supply, taking all available sources into account, would only last until March 1, 1920, thus leaving a five-month gap before the harvest that could only be covered by such undesirable measures as further imports or cutting the ration. The Reich Wheat Corporation and the RWM, however, were convinced that the official harvest estimates which they had drawn up were about two million tons below the actual wheat harvest, a view strengthened by the fact that the farmers had delivered over a million more tons of wheat in 1918 than in 1919. Deliveries between September and November had been fairly satisfactory because of delivery bonuses paid to the farmers, and it was obvious that similar inspiration would be necessary to extract more wheat in the future. The unsatisfactory delivery totals, however, could not be blamed on the harvest itself, but rather upon the "transport and coal shortage, the black market, and especially the unwillingness of the farmers to deliver for the previous, in their view, excessively low prices."[103] On December 4, the Cabinet authorized the payment of delivery premiums for bread grains, barley, and potatoes, premiums which the Reich Wheat Corporation scheduled to run from two marks per centner (110.23 pounds) for delivery of up to 70 percent of the minimum requirement to fifteen marks per centner for delivery of 110 percent of the minimum requirement. The problem, of course, was how to pay the costs of these premiums, and the only answer seemed to be raising the bread prices and other controlled food prices.

The entire situation threw Mayor Wermuth of Berlin, a member of the Reich Wheat Corporation, into a fury. He protested in the name of Germany's cities, pointing out that the premiums should have been decided upon earlier and that "the situation of the cities is desperate, the potato and meat supply has collapsed." Wermuth found it outrageous that the Reich was raising prices just as it was bringing its food subsidy program to an end. He attacked this "burdening of the mass of consumers" and called for harsh measures to bring the farmers into line. Joining with other representatives of the urban interests, Wermuth engaged in a sharp altercation with Hugenberg and Stinnes concerning their advocacy of world-market prices and pointed out that "agriculture is in a much better pecuniary position than the urban population" and called for "protection of the consuming public against the policy of force propounded by big industry."[104]

By mid-January, Wermuth was writing to every member of the Cabinet and warning that there was a catastrophic shortage of wheat and potatoes in the offing and a real danger of hunger if something were not done. This pessimism was not shared by Schmidt, who believed that the supply would prove satisfactory in the end, a posture which earned him strong criticisms from the Democrats in the Cabinet, Schiffer, Koch, and Gessler, all of whom urged him not to follow the model of the wartime governments and fail to tell the people the truth. The Democrats feared that large imports would be needed and pointed out that the required foreign exchange to pay for them was not available. Germany would be "Austrianized," that is, she would have to follow the Austrian example and put up her public enterprises as security for loans to pay for food and raw-materials imports. The only way to generate the foreign exchange was to export, but this required transportation and coal. Here, however, the government was facing new crises in January. On the one hand, there were transport strikes; on the other, radicals were trying to persuade the miners to impose the six-hour shift on February 1. It appeared as if the very conditions which had plagued the Bauer government when it first took office were not only repeating themselves but were actually doing so in exacerbated form at the beginning of the new year.[105]

The relationship between city and country and agriculture and government certainly were worse. Delivery premiums were helpful, but they did not smooth the resentment felt by farmers against the controlled economy. Controls were maintained for basic products despite an endless succession of complaints and petitions from agrarian organizations because, as Schmidt made clear, only the well-off would be able to eat if there were total decontrol. As evidence, he cited impressive studies by Professor Silbergleit concerning the cost of living in Berlin. Working from the medical assumption that a person needed 3,000 calories a day, Silbergleit found that in November 1919, 1,819 calories were provided from rationed and price-controlled food at a cost of 10.58 marks a week, 628 calories from decontrolled foods at a cost of 24.80 marks a week, and the remaining 553 calories from the black market at a cost of 16.87 marks a week. The weekly cost of a minimum diet, therefore, was 52.25 marks a week. Were all foods to be decontrolled in February, then the cost per person per week would jump an additional 41.75 marks to 94 marks. A family of five would need 208.75 marks more per week to meet its minimum food requirements. Manifestly, this would require extremely large wage increases, and this would make it impossible either to export cheaply or to import sufficient amounts of food.[106]

The other side of the argument, however, was that continuation of the system would lead to the disappearance of the food supply. As one informed critic noted, it was impossible to pay ten thousand marks a ton for rye in Holland while offering only seven hundred marks per ton to German farmers, and the situation was not improved by offering nine hundred marks a ton. Little wonder that large amounts of food were being exported abroad illegally, hoarded, or sold on the black market: "[T]he morals of our people simply cannot stand up against the temptations." Furthermore, it was not only the farmers who were at fault, since "every train is full of people who have begged potatoes from the peasants with great complaints and effort."[107] Hoarding was not a vice practiced exclusively by private persons, since many municipalities, including those run by Socialists, were buying up excess supplies of food and storing them in anticipation of shortages.[108]

All this was true, but the greatest suffering still was among the urban consumers, and the hoarding and profiteering were producing un-

One of the consequences of the food shortage in Berlin in 1920. Men, Women, and children waiting outside the slaughter house to purchase meat. (*By permission of the Ullstein Verlag*)

rest and dangers to civic peace. Real conditions were movingly described by a Mormon missionary:

Prices are very high. The wages are high, but it requires two weeks of labor to earn a sufficient amount to buy a pair of shoes; it takes the pay of one day's labor to pay for a pound of lard; butter is 15 marks a pound. The bread is course, sour and indigestible. There is little coal for the winter, and much suffering will result from the lack of warm clothing. At a large store in Zwickau, Saxony, all the girls were examined with the view of recovering 50 cases of missing underwear, the girls being suspected of having stolen them. They were found upon examination to be going entirely without underclothing.[109]

To be sure, many workers, especially in the Ruhr, had little gardens from which they supplemented their diets, and others had relatives in the country. The great mass of wage earners and those living on fixed incomes—the latter often being worse off than the workers—were compelled to suffer all the miseries of insufficient food and clothing at constantly rising prices while knowing full well that many shops,

especially in the big cities, were full, that those with money could get whatever they wished, and that the farmers certainly had enough to eat and were violating the regulations.

Fearful of open disturbances and riots, both the Reich government and the various state governments attempted to take more effective and organized measures to enforce the controls. In Saxony, where serious riots had taken place in the summer, special watch patrols were set up to intercept illegal operations between farmers and Saxon mine officials, the former supplying flour and meat for the miners in return for coal. Things there had gone so far that the mine officials were putting advertisements in the papers offering two carloads of briquets in return for the right to hunt deer or in return for wheat, while farmers were taking the coal they had received in exchange for food and selling it by the wagonload in the big cities.[110] The idea of bridging the gap between city and country by establishing surveillance committees in which farmers as well as urban consumers would work together was particularly popular in government circles. In Saxony, a State Price Office was set up in November, but when Saxon Economics Minister Schwarz remarked to the advisory council of this body that agriculture was making monstrous profits, the agricultural representatives protested his remarks vigorously, and one of them simply resigned.[111] This was more than a matter of touchiness. The conflict between city and country reached new heights at the turn of 1919–1920, often to the point of violence, and it is essential to recognize that the problem cannot be understood simply in terms of the suffering of urban consumers at the hands of rapacious peasants. Unfairness and injustice were built into the system and lay on both sides.

This was painfully illustrated by the reports of the control commissions of the State Distribution Agency for Greater Berlin. This agency had been created in May 1917 by the then Prussian State Commissar for the Food Supply, Dr. Michaelis, to coordinate the food supply of Greater Berlin. Control commissions placed under its jurisdiction were set up throughout Prussia in May 1919 for each district where the farmers were under legal obligation to deliver food to the urban areas. The commissions were assigned the tasks of conducting inspections and audits to ensure that the farmers were reporting and delivering their production in accordance with the regulations rather than selling on the black market or exceeding the quotas they could retain for personal consumption. The farmers were supposed to be represented on the commissions by persons from outside their own district, and one of the purposes of the commissions was to "enlighten" the agrarian population about the dire distress in the cities and thus smooth relations between city and country. In reality, however, the commissions were dominated by consumer representatives and, as "auxiliary organs of the police authorities," their conciliatory functions obviously were secondary. Understandably, therefore, farmers were reluctant to participate, not only for the simple reason that they found the obligation too time-consuming, but also for the very human reason that they did not wish to be in conflict with their fellow farmers. They demonstrated their hostility to the commissions

through passive resistance and various forms of obstructionism.[112]

The flavor of relations between the control commissions and the farmers can be gathered from a somewhat extreme but far from anomalous incident in the village of Ratzdorf in November 1919. Acting on the basis of an anonymous report that the family Schostag had slaughtered one of its pigs without the requisite prior reporting of its intentions, four members of the Ratzdorf Control Commission suddenly appeared at the family home in the evening and confiscated the meat from the slaughtered animal along with two and a half pounds of butter which had apparently been retained illegally. The commission was fortunate neither in its choice of victims or in its tactics. The family was one of the poorest in the village and was composed of a sixty-nine-year-old wife, her crippled seventy-year-old husband, and a shell-shocked son, the only survivor of the three who had gone to war. The pig was very underweight and had to be killed before it died of natural causes. According to the *Landrat*, one of the commission members saw fit to pull out a revolver, hold it to the chest of the old woman and warn her that resistance was useless. According to the gun-toting commission member, his threats were made in response to the son's unleashing the vicious family dog. Whatever the truth, the affair at the Schostags did unleash the village on the commission when it returned to Ratzdorf two days later, and the commission required police protection to avoid being treated roughly and chased away.[113]

Indeed, commissions often needed protection, even when they did not engage in provocative actions of the type described. They met with persistent resistance, both active and passive, just as they were frustrated by the manner in which the *Landräte* and village authorities defended and protected the peasantry. Thus, the lengthy reports of a commission sent to Ostprignitz in January 1920 were a continuous tale of woe, for while the police could protect them from violence, they were not terribly useful in getting the farmers out of the village pub, restoring their memories when questioned, or putting their records in order. The farmers were much more mobilizable for meetings against the controlled economy, where it was argued that "a cessation of the investigations by non-experts can only increase the will to produce, while their continuation provides reason to fear the greatest dangers to the food supply."[114]

It is important to recognize that the worst conflicts and the greatest resistance did not come from the big landowners or wealthiest farmers. As one of the Berlin agencies reported, "[W]e have found that the estates generally fulfill their obligations, while the small and medium-sized owners leave much to be desired with respect to their deliveries."[115] Of course, the estate owners detested the controlled economy every bit as much as the others, but they undoubtedly were better able to handle the demands made upon them and too politically vulnerable to resist. What this meant, however, was that the battle in the countryside was often between the needy, and that the heart of the conflict lay in access to food rather than property ownership alone. This is demonstrated by the inability of the control commissions to rely on the support of agricultural workers. At a meeting of the various control commissions in February 1920, it was reported that "there could be no talk of solidarity between the agricultural and industrial workers. . . . The farm workers were primarily interested in extracting as high a food allowance in kind (*Deputat*) for themselves through the collective bargaining contracts as is possible without concerning themselves about the distress of the industrial workers."[116]

The rage and cynicism that marked relations between city and country in the wake of the controlled economy, therefore, were not the fruits of propagandistic manipulation or pre-industrial sentiment—which is not to deny all role to these factors—but rather of direct experience and conflict in which the poorer farmers and peasants were often put upon the most. As the Ratzdorf Control Commission noted in an attempt to justify its actions: "We cannot make a distinction between poor and rich in our investigations and will not even do so in the future. The big farmer says that the small ones profiteers, and the small farmer says that the big do so. It follows that we cannot distinguish between them."[117]

Such attitudes and circumstances could only deprive law enforcement of its legitimacy, a fact not lost upon one of the more thoughtful of Berlin's consumer leaders, who pointed out in a memorandum of January 1920 that

during the war the realm of criminal justice was expanded into an area which did not arise from the people's sense of justice but rather was born of the emergency of the moment—the controlled economy, with its regulations which penetrate so deeply into the life of the farmer. It is not only that the farmer (as well as other large parts of the population) completely lack the sense of violating the law when transgressing these regulations, he almost generally denies the purposefulness of the decrees, which he only sees as oppressive and burdensome for his production.

As a consequence,

The penal provisions of the controlled economy lack a foundation in popular sentiment—namely among those who are primarily affected by them. How much harder and more unjust must the effect be upon them that every infraction, even the smallest, of these regulations which receives its penalty through the courts stigmatizes the "delinquent" publicly for the rest of his life, or at least for years. . . . The woman, who perhaps without sufficient understanding of the weight of her action, sells a few eggs in an illegal manner or delivers too few liters of milk, is considered to have just as much a criminal record as a burglar who has taken someone's property. . . .[118]

From this perspective, the writer argued, it was hardly surprising that the *Landräte* would be disinclined to impose the law in their districts. Hence, he proposed the decriminalization of minor violations of the regulations and the implementation of a scale of fines that would act as an economic disincentive to such violations as well as the removal of jurisdiction to an independent authority and the speeding up of legal procedures. Yet, there was little that could make better a system which, whatever its necessity under the circumstances, was fundamentally unworkable and demoralizing.

Furthermore, it is worth remembering that the peasants and farmers had a good deal more to resent in the realm of discrimination against them than these controls. If they were suddenly on the wrong side of the law, it was because they were on the wrong side of what they perceived as a social revolution. While delivery strikes by farmers were sharply condemned, disturbances and strikes by industrial workers were rewarded with wage increases. While price controls were imposed on agricultural products, the production costs of farmers as well as the prices of the goods they had to buy often seemed totally un-restrained. The farmer could not claim the eight-hour day, that boasted revolutionary achievement of the industrial workers, and while the Socialists demanded high food pro-duction, they agitated among the agricultural workers, unionized them, and undermined the traditional patriarchal relationships that ex-isted on the land. Last, the high unemployment supports paid in the cities appeared to act as a disincentive to agricultural labor. Thus, in Ba-varia, one official reported in September 1919 that "there is much bitterness among the agrar-ian population concerning the unemployment supports, the continuing strikes, the short hours of work enjoyed by the industrial workers and the efforts to spread dissatisfaction among the farm workers and hands," while another re-marked that "in the farming circles there is now the view that the performance of the peasants, who have fed a nation of 67 million for five years is undervalued. The peasant asks, how has agriculture been thanked for this? They take the view that the municipalities and Jewish mer-chants take the high profit while the peasant gets nothing."[119] If the government lived in fear of the workers, why should it not live in fear of the peasants? The successful blackmailing of the government was being turned into a na-tional sport and was also further undermining the new regime's chances of gaining some loy-alty from the rural population.

This resentment, however, was not limited to peasants. Those who had taken power after No-vember 1918 had, if anything, intensified the conflicts which the old regime had with the re-tailers during the war. At least the monarchy had paid lip service to the maintenance of the commercial and industrial *Mittelstand*, but the new rulers of Germany were in many cases be-lievers in the inevitable decline of the *Mittel-stand* and supported consumer cooperatives and the communalization of the procurement, storage, and sale of basic consumer items. It was not unwarranted for a retailer to declare that "we have previously considered ourselves to be part of the *Mittelstand*. The Social Democrats do not want a *Mittelstand*. No one should be better placed than the worker. . . ."[120] When they attacked the special provisioning of the miners as a "profiteering view that the entire ex-

istence of the state must be adapted to the sole wishes not only of the workers but of single groups of workers . . . ,"[121] they were expressing a sentiment that was even shared among many workers. At the same time, the retailers often found themselves in conflict with industry, not because of some generalized preindustrial an-ticapitalist sentiments, but because many plants were purchasing directly from wholesal-ers to provision their workers and even selling their products directly to farmers in return for food. Despite a common rhetoric about the need to restore the free market, industry also seemed to disregard the retailers.[122]

This feeling of being exploited and singled out for discrimination was especially strong when retailers confronted the delivery and pay-ment conditions imposed on them. These had already become harsher in wartime, but the re-tailers were truly outraged by those of 1919–1920. Thus, textile producers demanded pre-payments ranging from one-third to the full price, immediate payment in cash upon deliv-ery, and imposed all kinds of special charges to cover packing, insurance, and the like. It mat-tered little whether it was the wholesaler or the retailer upon whom the terms were imposed; both complained about the policies of the pro-ducers. But while the wholesaler could then im-pose similar terms upon the retailer, the entire situation "necessarily hits the retailer with spe-cial force since he, as the last purchaser of goods, does not have the same possibility of passing on the harsh delivery conditions."[123] The government did not permit the retailers to include the increased and arbitrary charges in their prices.

The republican regime not only maintained the wartime anti-profiteering legislation the re-tailers had found so offensive but actually began to expand it as prices rose dramatically at the turn of 1919–1920. On November 27, a de-cree establishing special antiprofiteering courts was issued. It was designed to provide more ex-peditious handling of profiteering charges as well as to expand the range of items falling under the black marketeering decrees and to in-crease the penalties for violations. There was no appeal from the judgments of these new courts.[124] A further source of discontent was provided by the turnover tax that was passed by the Reichstag on December 24, 1919. One of the provisions of the new law was that the tax could not be passed on as a supplement to the price but could only be taken into account in the calculation of costs. For those selling food, this was exceptionally onerous. Insofar as there were price ceilings, there was no way to pass on any of the tax at all without violating the ceilings. Where there were no ceilings, there still were very narrow margins allowed between costs and prices by most municipalities. Worse yet, these varied extraordinarily, so that while Berlin allowed 10.2 percent, Barmen permitted a 13 percent margin for most foods, but then there were cities which allowed as little a profit on margarine, for example, as 1.95 to 6 percent. Understandably, the Federation of Food Merchant Associations called for a revision of these margins and greater uniformity, a request to which the RWM did not respond for a full month before indicating that it was planning such a revision.[125]

Especially obnoxious and humiliating from the standpoint of the retailers was the growing tendency on the part of the authorities to inspect or even "make a raid" on retail stores and shops. These became more frequent as the public became more alarmed at rising prices and suspected the storekeepers of selling goods they had bought cheaply at newer and higher prices and thus making an allegedly exceptional profit. In Offenbach am Main, for example, this led to a series of systematic but discreet visits by police and Offenbach Price Examination Agency officials to various shops to check up on costs and prices. It was determined that about one-quarter of the clothing and shoe stores thus visited should receive citations for price violations and profiteering. This initiative was recommended to other price examination agencies since, "under the present threatening circumstances, which easily could lead to unrest and plundering, it is necessary to take the initiative and make use of the legal right to inspect salesrooms . . . and get a precise idea of actual circumstances."[126]

Naturally, the retailers detested such initiatives, but not all customers supported them either. When officials discreetly entered through the back door of a Saxon butcher shop suspected of illegally selling rolls with its sausages

and found no less than 241 rolls, the butcher's wife rallied the customers, and a number of the latter, "by external appearance belonging to the better classes," angrily accosted the officials with such remarks as "why should it matter to you if we pay for it" and sent the officials packing.[127] Needless to say, the authorities were more than a little annoyed to encounter such responses despite the constant demands for action against black marketeers and profiteers. The problem, however, was that there were different publics—the public that noted angrily how those with money could buy their rolls and sausages, and the public that felt entitled to use its money to buy what would only be made available in any case if someone were prepared to pay the high price.

As in the past, the retailers blamed much of the difficulty on hoarding, price gouging, and unnecessary middleman operations, as well as the entry of newcomers into the field. The situation had, if anything, become worse since the Revolution. In Berlin, the number of retailers had increased by twenty-five thousand since 1914. In Königsberg, the number of food stores had quadrupled since that time, while the number of cigar stores had quadrupled since 1918. The government, in its effort to promote the employment of returning veterans, had been loathe to discourage this development despite the available legal mechanisms. Some of the states were more lax than others, and the established retailer organizations were by no means always prepared to oppose new entries either. The stable population and the shortage of goods in comparison to 1914 meant that more persons were in the business of selling fewer goods, not to mention the traveling salesmen and office personnel needed to service these retail operations.[128]

The problems involved in acting against the proliferation of street stalls in Berlin illustrate the kinds of difficulties involved. A case could be made for the increase of those selling fruits and vegetables since this promoted the accessibility of those products and prevented spoilage, but the same could not be said for those selling such smuggled luxury items as cigarettes, soap, and chocolate. In the final analysis, however, "a general ban on street vendors in Berlin simply cannot be carried out because of the social and political situation. One has to consider the fact that certain elements are brought into a relatively orderly type of existence through street vending who might otherwise be engaged in dangerous activity."[129] This was not only a big city phenomenon, since itinerant peddlers played a role in the countryside comparable to that of urban vendors. For practical purposes, therefore, only the established merchants were the actual subjects of the host of regulations governing prices, requiring their posting, and permitting the examination of books and accounts, just as it was they who were at the mercy of producers, large-scale merchants, and consumer cooperatives. It was something more than paranoia that made them declare that "the retail trades are strongly endangered by the consumers, and by the wholesalers as well as industry. The retailers must join together and seek to influence the entire economic policy of the government. It must be the task of the retail trades to oppose every form of communalization. It must also turn against the anti-profiteering courts and many other new institutions of the Socialist state. For this purpose, collective action is necessary."[130] Thus, like other economic groups in this period, the retailers gathered sums of money to support and even elect to the Reichstag political representatives who might champion their interests. The loudest and most numerous voices in the Reichstag, however, were those of the representatives of industry and organized labor. The limited effectiveness of retailer power (or of the craftsmen, who had their own special complaints against the new state which provided them with insufficient credit and coal and which promoted cooperatives) was quite obvious. The increasing tendency toward fragmentation and narrow interest-group politics, however, could only have a negative effect upon the political integration which the Republic required for its success.

Clearly, the breakdown of social solidarity, already evident during the war, was being compounded by the inflationary wave that marked the nine months following the acceptance of the peace treaty. A condition was being created in which nearly all classes of society felt disadvantaged and exploited to the benefit of others and in which loss of confidence in the state was combined with deep and not easily specifiable resentments throughout the society. Much of this resentment was aimed against the working class, which appeared advantaged by the Revolution because of its organized power, stranglehold on an economy dependent on increased productivity, unpredictable oscillation between strikes and collusion with industry, and successful wage demands. The fact that there were other groups in society worse off than the workers—pensioners, invalids, and others living on fixed incomes—could no longer be denied. Trade union support for an export levy that would aid such persons constituted a revealing effort to compensate such groups by those advantaged by the inflation. Labor, however, had the power to bring the economy to a halt, especially certain groups of workers, and however unsuccessful the Revolution may have appeared to disgruntled Socialist workers, it seemed genuinely effective and real to other groups who had lost power and government support. The controlled economy had become identified with the triumph of socialism for peasants, retailers, craftsmen, and businessmen.

The power of labor was also a problem from the perspective of the Reich government, and the controlled economy and various other concessions to labor were essential if labor were to be controlled and productivity increased. The attitudes and policies of those in power, including the trade-union leaders, seemed almost to confirm the widespread notion that the workers were the illegitimate gainers from an increasingly unpopular revolution. The gap between the old trade-union leadership and its vastly increased trade-union membership had widened substantially, as was pointedly illustrated by remarks made by Legien to a trade-union leadership meeting in the fall. To the amazement of his colleagues, Legien said that there were far too few strikes going on, and when asked if he had gone crazy, he responded "that the workers will only come to reason again through a series of unplanned and unsuccessful strikes, since only such failures can shake the authority of the wild leaders. . . ."[131] His view that the recent collapse of a wild metal-workers strike "was a step on the way to recovery" certainly could have been expressed by the employers as well. Such angry cynicism, however, could not hide the fact that the old trade-union leadership was in trouble, as evidenced by the triumph of the Independent Socialist Robert Dißmann over the old chairman of the German Metal Workers Union (DMV), Alexander Schlicke, at the DMV's October congress. The DMV, the largest of the Socialist trade unions, also decided to leave the ZAG and thereby return to the old principle of class struggle.[132]

Even without such powerful warning signs, however, Legien, Chancellor Bauer, and other leading Social Democrats understood that compromise had its limits. While anxious to settle the workers down and increase production, they were not prepared to sacrifice what they considered to be the legitimate claims of the workers or surrender what remained of their hold on the workers. They could hardly dismiss the significance of rising prices for the real wages of the working class, and while willing to see the farmers get premiums and higher prices in return for larger deliveries and to work at persuading the workers that the farmers should get more for their products,[133] they insisted that something be done to raise wages to meet the bread and potato price increases that had been scheduled for January 1920. Thus, on December 18, Labor Minister Schlicke wrote to the ZAG urging that the employers grant a six- to seven-mark-per-week cost-of-living supplement to cover the increased food costs. Since most industries now had collective contracts that were difficult to change, and since both industry and the authorities were anxious at least to hold the line on basic wage rates, the cost-of-living supplement was considered the best way to deal with the emergency. Schlicke hoped that the employers would realize the importance of a speedy and a voluntary response to the situation. While the employers on the directing board of the ZAG could not help but recognize the problem, they resisted Legien's proposal that they recommend a two-mark-per-day supplement for workers throughout the country. The employer representatives insisted that the supplement be adjusted to the number of family members being supported by individual workers, an obvious effort not only to take its special character into account but also to favor older, married workers over young, single workers. While the unions and many employ-

ers as well opposed such "social wages" and believed in equal pay for equal work as a matter of principle, the trade-union leaders were not disinclined to accept the employer suggestion. Undoubtedly, they felt a certain reluctance to give more than necessary to the young, single workers who were causing them so much trouble. Nevertheless, agreement was hard to reach because the employers were reluctant to urge a uniform handling of the problem throughout the country and thus revive resistance to "dictation" from Berlin and employer hostility to the ZAG. Legien had to warn that if the employers did not act voluntarily, "then the trade unions will be forced in this instance to come down on the side of the workers since the claims of the workers are completely justified."[134] In the end, the employers yielded and passed a resolution urging regional arrangements on the basis of recommendations from a ZAG committee, while the trade unions agreed to a concluding paragraph to the resolution pointing out the high cost and sacrifice being imposed on the employers and the need for higher productivity. The resolution was widely, albeit often reluctantly, followed by employers throughout the country.[135]

Such achievements, insofar as they could be so designated, did not pacify the far left, and while trade-union leaders, much to the irritation of employer colleagues, had come around to supporting a moderate Factory Councils Law that was passed by the Reichstag on January 13, 1920, the law was viewed with great hostility as a blow to the ZAG by employers, while the far left responded with a bloody riot in front of the Reichstag.[136] This, however, was not the central labor issue at the turn of 1919–1920, either for the government or for the leaders of labor and industry. That issue was the need to increase production to meet the higher costs of imported and domestic food. Here, as in so many other realms, policy had changed since the summer of 1919. The policy then had been to hold the line on wages by reducing or maintaining existing price levels and then link wage increases to productivity. The unanticipated inflationary wave had ruined this policy, and the government had gradually come to the conclusion that it had to ride the wave rather than resist it. It thus now sought to secure increased production and export advantages by adapting to the inflationary situation in the short run, while hoping that prices and wages would stabilize in the long run. The posture of the government toward the inflation and wage questions was frankly expressed by Christian trade-union leader and Postal Minister Johannes Giesberts in a revealing letter of December 20:

... not the wage question, but rather the labor question stands in the center of our national economic problems. Confidentially, I want to tell you that here in government circles no one counts on the mark returning to its full value. If we can bring it to half its peacetime level, that will be the maximum. At present it is only worth a tenth of that. We will, therefore, still have large price increases during the next half year, which we will have to follow with our wages if our workers are not to hunger. Otherwise, let me alert you to a very noteworthy phenomenon. Despite the increased coal prices and steel prices and despite the very much increased wages, Germany's export industry is blossoming. For example, I get equipment, machines, and materials in my postal ministry only with difficulty, while on the other side, the same industry has huge export contracts and exports at prices 100 percent higher than our own.[137]

It made sense, therefore, to give the workers more, particularly the miners, whose production was the key to economic revival. Giesberts pointed out that if the coal miners would work an extra shift or two, the extra production could be used for export and the foreign exchange thereby gained could be used to purchase food and raw materials necessary to keep Germany's workers fed and industry in operation.

Furthermore, as Giesberts and his Ministerial colleagues were shortly to discover, it would be dangerous and short-sighted to hold the line on wages. The government had tried this in mid-December, when it disregarded civil-service-organization demands for a 150 percent cost-of-living supplement and voted for a 50 percent supplement instead. The response was a surprising and unexpected wave of demonstrations followed by strikes of railroad workers and officials at the beginning of the year. The fact that railroad officials had joined up with the railroad workers was especially alarming. The government response was twofold. On the one hand, it declared a state of emergency in the affected areas and gave the State Commissar in the Rhenish-Westphalian area, the Socialist Carl Severing, special powers as well as the right to employ the assistance of General von Watter and his troops. The unauthorized strikes were broken and disciplinary action taken against the civil servants. On the other hand, negotiations were conducted with the civil-servant organizations in which Erzberger and the Cabinet rescinded the decision of December 15 and agreed to a 150 percent cost-of-living allowance in return for a public condemnation of laziness and corruption in the civil service. While the exact victor in the situation is difficult to identify, a pattern had been established. The government would use force to keep the economy functioning in the face of the more determined forms of blackmail by key groups of workers, but it was willing to pay cash to prevent the contest from being carried to its ultimate conclusion. This technique was next to be employed with the miners.[138]

At the turn of the year, as in the summer, coal production was the key economic problem, and the government once again faced the demand for a six-hour shift and a threat to introduce it by strikes if necessary. The radicals in the Ruhr set February 1 as their deadline. The commission set up to study the question in the summer had come up with a report recommending against a reduction to six hours for economic reasons, a report with which the Majority Socialist trade-union leaders agreed. The latter, however, including their respected leader, Otto Hué, played a particularly undistinguished role in the affair, opposing the reduction of hours but trimming when they faced their people in the Ruhr. On this issue, however, the government could not compromise, and most trade-union leaders throughout the country, who had their fill of coal shortages, opposed the miners. In the persons of Severing and von Watter, the government had the necessary instruments to enforce their position. Thus, on January 24, Severing declared bluntly that he would use "*all* means at his disposal, even against the trade unions themselves" to prevent the unilateral introduction of the six-hour shift by the miners. He warned that strikers and persons who left the pits early would be subject to dismissal, denial of unemployment support, and even imprisonment. As usual, however, the carrot accompanied the stick, and the miners received a new wage contract increasing wages and vacation time, while the employers were granted their usual price increase.[139]

The next step was to repeat the process to get the miners to work an extra shift a week. On the one hand, the government threatened to allow overtime work at 25 percent pay per hour, a procedure that would have led to a "mad" rush to get overtime hours by miners seeking to increase their incomes. From the standpoint of the unions, this was the worst possible solution. On the other hand, the government suggested that a happier solution was possible in the form of an agreement with the unions under which the miners would receive a 100 percent premium for each extra shift they worked as well as extra food rations at a reduced price. The extra rations would be financed from the price increase allowed the employers, two marks of which would be devoted to the cause. Additionally, they would have access to extra rations at the regular prices as well as clothing. On February 18, 1920, an agreement to lay on an extra shift in accordance with these terms was signed. It was a major triumph for the government. Though it had begun the year in dread of a struggle to prevent the six-hour shift, it had managed not only to preserve the seven-hour shift but also to get the miners to work an extra shift. The extent to which the miners were responding to pleas from the ZAG, the government, and the general public that the economy could not function without these concessions is difficult to determine. One may be certain, however, that the threat of force, which had credibility, as well as the promise of extra food, clothing, and financial reward, especially among the miners with families, proved decisive.

Were these, then, to be the "achievements" (*Errungenschaften*) of the Revolution? Even a Christian trade unionist found his treatment by Severing, Bauer, and other Socialist and trade-union leaders unpleasantly reminiscent of the style and tone of the old regime. The Democratic Minister of the Interior, Erich Koch, did not quite agree, but the praise he lavished on the Socialist labor leaders in his diary could make one wonder:

What a sensible person Severing is. What do those heavy-handed, vacillating bureaucrats of the old regime imagine when they claim that they would have the better cure for our masses, who have gone insane, than such sensible and experienced persons in this area as Bauer, Winnig, Severing, Hué. If only we had come to an understanding with these people earlier.[140]

This praise might have been less problematic if the socio-political context in which it was made had been more satisfactory. The terrifying fact, however, was that these successes, such as they were, were taking place as the forces of German democracy were losing both public support and power to a resurgent right. Almost as if by a natural process, the necessary and inevitable taming of the left required by the economic situation was unleashing the right. As Ernst Troeltsch noted in December:

The sinking of the exchange rate and the insane price increases denote the coming of a catastrophe against which all government is powerless. The means of dealing with the situation planned and proposed by the government only serves today to make the coming misery of the masses clear and, without oneself seriously knowing other ways to deal with the problems, one blames the government for both the situation and the remedies. Therewith begins the period of general disappointment, the yearning for the good or, in any case, the better past. The old patriotic circles and the old social order, which was surprised, stunned and for a time completely helpless are taking heart again and using the order created by the democracy along with the only now completely apparent indications of the economic consequences of the war and the Revolution for a passionate struggle against the bearers of the present government and against the Revolution in general.[141]

The infamous political manifestations of this were to be found in the hearings of the Reichstag Committee to Investigate the Collapse in the late fall of 1919—in which Hindenburg and Ludendorff publicly expounded the stab-in-the-back legend—and the Helfferich campaign against Erzberger, which the latter won in the courts at the further expense of his reputation. This was followed by an assassination attempt in which the Finance Minister was slightly wounded and for which the "idealistic" young culprit was sentenced to a year and a half in prison, a sentence which could be interpreted as an encouragement to better shots.[142]

Though Erzberger had managed to steer important elements of his tax reform through in December, the task he faced in the new year was much more difficult. Now there was a vocal and mobilized opposition arguing that the Emergency Capital Levy would destroy the credit and investment capabilities of Germany's economy while serving the goals of the Entente. It goes without saying that personal enemies like Hugenberg and Helfferich used the debate to further vilify and excoriate Erzberger who, for the extreme right, had come to symbolize the Republic. For the Bauer government, he was an indispensable liability, for as one observer remarked, "[W]ho shall take over his legacy? His successor can only complete his work; a change of course in the tax reform is no longer thinkable for financial reasons."[143]

Whatever the inadequacies and deficiencies of the Erzberger tax program—the reform of the system itself was a lasting and monumental achievement—it is important to recognize that it was nothing short of revolutionary in its comprehensiveness and was viewed by many as a veritable rape of the propertied classes. Thus, a specialist invited to explain the tax laws to the liberal Hansa-Bund in mid-December 1919 described them as "the worst sort of violation of the bourgeoisie for the benefit of the propertyless manual workers."[144] It was not so much a matter of the individual taxes, each of which was worthy of consideration, but the "accumulation of these taxes is complete insanity since they each burden the same shoulders." It appeared as if the intention was to "eliminate capitalism" and carry out the egalitarian aims of the French Revolution for the benefit of the proletariat. He feared that it would destroy all incentive for the outside world to help Germany. The credit of the Reich had already sunk to the level of Guatemala, and the credit of Germany's private entrepreneurs would now be ruined also. Ultimately, he warned, the workers would suffer most, but in the meantime Germany would not be able to reconstruct.

The businessmen in attendance did not need to be convinced that Erzberger was sentencing them to financial death, and they were in accord that the burdens had to be distributed differently. Department store owner Oscar Tietz was quite explicit on this score:

It is unquestionable that the state needs money and plenty of it. But to get it, one has to approach the problem with reason and not unreason. . . . If I want to pay my debts, then I must work more and save more. Instead, the Revolution began its "improvements" by reducing the hours of work. But things could work out with the eight-hour day if employers were obligated to require overtime. One could pay 125 percent for this overtime, of which the workers would receive 40 percent and the rest could go to the state or the municipality. Then the workers would have their advantage and the state would get its money from labor and not from capital.

Indeed, for old opponents of democracy, the Erzberger tax program was a nightmare come true. It is, after all, infinitely more agreeable to predict disaster than to experience it. Thus, Berlin industrialist Ludwig Waldschmidt lamented that the tax program was a natural consequence of equal suffrage, "for when someone, who does not possess anything gets the power to dispose of the wealth of others, then the wallets of the propertied will be emptied in a very short time." He "had always predicted that this levelling would have to have these consequences, and is only surprised at the speed with which the prediction is now being fulfilled." For the majority of Germany's propertied classes, liberals as well as conservatives, Erzberger had carried out the alleged aims of the Revolution under the worst possible conditions and in the worst conceivable manner.

By the time Erzberger had finished pushing through his program, it was tainted both by the attacks upon his person and by this almost universal disapproval of Germany's economic leadership. Worse yet, the future did not bode well for the implementation of the program. As influential banker Franz Urbig noted: "The moral strain imposed by the inheritance tax, the capital gains tax, the Emergency Capital Levy, etc., are such that even the normal taxpayer is not up to it. People take the view that it is too much all at once."[145] It is fair to say that most of the critics of the Erzberger program strongly disapproved of the tactics of Hugenberg, Helfferich, and the DNVP, which they viewed as nothing more than the waving of a "red flag" that incited the Social Democrats and made a reasoned discussion of their arguments impossible. Max Warburg, for example, was an opponent of the Emergency Capital Levy, but personally urged Hugenberg to change his tactics. Warburg argued for a *Burgfrieden*, since "we will get no credits abroad so long as we continue to work against one another and slander one another as is the case now."[146]

Hans von Raumer was also a strong critic of the tax levels imposed by Erzberger and even proposed that an effort be made to persuade the labor leaders in the ZAG that the taxes would take away industry's operating capital.[147] He rejected an invitation to join the DNVP, joining the DVP instead, because he considered the DNVP's policy a "calamity":

Those people hang on to the 9th of November, which without a doubt did bring great misfortune, but do not understand that the Revolution as such began on August 1, 1914. They view everything that changed since the prewar period as a consequence of the 9th of November, instead of drawing the necessary consequences from the fact that it was the war that was the revolution and that one must secure and organize the great amount that is new and worthwhile. . . . They are so horribly unclever. If they were calm, reasonable, and behaved only as participants in the reconstruction, then political leadership would fall into their laps like a ripe fruit. Instead of this, they excite the chauvinistic movements and manage to weld the shaky government majority together more. To this is added the stupid anti-Semitism.[148]

These divisions in the ranks of the political opposition on the right certainly served the survival of the Republic, while the absence of a sufficiently powerful party on the right and the lack of clarity in the entire domestic and international situation made a mass mobilization comparable to that which had taken place and could still take place on the left extremely difficult. The existence of "republicans of reason" and of persons who tried to think in terms of economic reconstruction on rational terms surely was positive, but Raumer missed the potential and the importance of extreme rightist irrationality and the fact that anti-Semitism was something more than just "stupid" at this point in German history. Political irrationality and anti-Semitism were nurtured by the growing intractability of Germany's problems.

It was incredibly difficult to focus the attention of the masses on the great long-term issues facing the political leaders in Berlin. Many of these issues simply fueled public discontent and impatience. The actual consequences of both the Treaty of Versailles and the tax reform were still future in very great measure, and the recriminations over the lost war were very much an activity for resentful higher civil servants, politicians, academics, students, and ex-officers. For the great mass of the population, however, high politics had taken a very minor place beside daily cares. As one official noted: "[T]he

concern with immediate material advantage dominates the entire life of the people. Such other important developments and questions as the new constitution, the *Anschluß* of German Austria, the question of whether to have simultaneous or confessional schools are almost entirely ignored."[149] Not "policies" but rather the failure to control the black market and rising prices was the chief source of popular disenchantment with the government, and social protest mounted as shortages and inflation cut across traditional class lines and created a general impoverishment and anger. It is in this context that the frequently noted spread of virulent anti-Semitism needs to be considered.

Playing upon anti-Semitic sentiment was an old tradition in reactionary and conservative circles, and the prominent role played by Jews in leftist and liberal political and journalistic circles helped to strengthen the links between anti-Semitism, on the one hand, and anti-liberalism and anti-Socialism, on the other. What distinguished the post-revolutionary anti-Semitism, however, was its summons to violence as well as its overt violence and its concrete relationship to day-to-day experiences with shortage and inflation.

Beginning in the spring of 1919, pamphlets began to appear all over Germany, circulated by such organizations as the Committee for National Enlightenment and the Defence and Defiance League (*Schutz- und Trutzbund*), propounding acts of violence against the "Jewish plague," suggesting that Jews be placed under preventive arrest, promising Jews that "we will spit you on pitchforks," charging that Jews "have created the present conditions" and that this "was nothing less than high treason . . . and deserves death," and calling for the killing of Jews, "for they incite you against each other and stir up strife." While the propaganda frequently emphasized the role of Jews in leftist parties, it also repeatedly addressed itself to "Socialist-minded workers" and was spread about in factories and industrial towns.[150] That such efforts were not entirely fruitless was demonstrated in Chemnitz in August 1919, where systematic anti-Semitic propaganda had been promoted by the far right in that already radicalized city. As an observer reported: "[T]he seduced masses were to be made ripe for pogroms. The politically less schooled citizens found themselves misled from each and every side and believed that they could only express their bitterness through radicalism."[151] Although the food riots and plundering which took place in the city were attributed to leftist agitators, one of the most distinctive characteristics of the disturbances was the hunting after Jewish "profiteers" and "smugglers" by groups of housewives and, especially, youths. A Communist noted with great distress the effects of the anti-Semitic propaganda on the demonstrators: " 'The Jews, yes, the Jews. They eat all the fresh meat and we must eat the completely spoiled and canned meat!' Such and similar views were expressed, and it is difficult to free such people from their false views."[152]

The growing connection between social protest over economic conditions and anti-Semitism was not limited to the street, however, and while leftist Deputies of all stripes officially and usually sincerely deplored it, they were not always resistant themselves. This was sadly illustrated by a National Assembly speech of the SPD Deputy from Oppeln, Roman Becker, attacking the decontrol of leather and the resulting high prices and export to places like Poland, where there was a desperate need for leather and extremely high prices were paid. To the enthusiastic applause of his Socialist colleagues, Becker played on anti-Polish sentiments:

Warschwosky, Auerbach, and Sickmann from Lodz and Stchowsky and Alexandrowitsch from Warsaw ply their trade in huge numbers in Breslau and Berlin. They came over the border with false and expired passports. Today they have completely valid documents. Proudly they sprawl in their typical manner in the first-class compartments of the express trains; they have business to do. One can earn money from the distress of the people.

Lest the names did not suggest that more than just Poles were involved, Becker went on to wonder aloud how it was that the Reich Commissar permitted such persons to export, and then to make a more explicit insinuation for which he earned approval from an unexpected quarter:

One must almost come to the conclusion that there are persons in his surroundings who stand in disturbing direct contact with Polish-Jewish smuggling circles. (Hear! Hear! Right!)

Indeed, that it was possible for a Social Democrat to at last touch the hearts of the German Nationalists was demonstrated at the conclusion of his lengthy speech, when Becker was greeted not only with a "Bravo!" from his own party but also with "prolonged, lively agreement on the right."[153]

Anti-Semitism had assumed particularly ominous proportions in Bavaria after the suppression of the Communists in April 1919, and rising prices and shortages inspired anti-Semitic and anti-foreign demonstrations in Munich in March 1920. The mood of the Landtag under such pressure was typified by a Democratic Deputy who called for life imprisonment and even the death penalty for large-scale profiteers and smugglers. The Social Democratic regime of Johannes Hoffmann found itself bombarded by claims that Jews were being favored by receiving the right to have white flour included in their ration for making Passover matzohs, a contention denied by the government and the Rabinnate. The sensitivity to this issue, however, is demonstrated by the fact that Socialist Interior Minister Fritz Endres, who personally felt that the Jews were being favored, decided to complain to the Reich agencies since "things cannot go on this way."[154]

There was, however, a more pressing and serious area of official preoccupation with the Jewish population; namely, the considerable influx of Galician and east European Jews that had begun during the war and stepped up in the chaos which followed. There can be no question that some of these persons were involved in black marketeering and especially in illicit monetary and foreign-exchange trading. They were apparently particularly active in Berlin on the Grenadier- and Dragonerstraßen in the so-called *Scheunenviertel*, which became notorious for such activities. In February 1919, the Reichsbank saw fit to make them the subject of a particular memorandum to the Interior Minister claiming that

Because of their shrewdness, their connections with one another and with third parties, and their skill in using loopholes in the regulations . . . to get around the legal requirements, a complete success against their mischief is unlikely to be achieved . . . unless it proves possible to keep these unwanted foreign guests, whose presence from a political as well as from a food and housing perspective is not exactly advantageous, out of Germany.[155]

A year later, the situation had become even more troublesome because of the large numbers of Polish and Galician Jews who fled Russia to escape violence, war, and bad conditions. Over seventy thousand such persons were in Berlin, most of them illegally. Saxony was also seriously affected because of its location. The Chemnitz Chamber of Commerce, for example, complained that foreigners were compounding the food, housing, and employment problems of the town as well as promoting black marketeering. The eastern Jews were viewed as "drones" in the economic process who made everything else more expensive. The authorities did recognize that these people were virtually forced into illegal activity since they did not have proper papers and could only procure food by illegal means. Unhappily, the attitude of the indigenous German Jews toward the newcomers remained mixed. While aid societies sprang up in an effort to protect and assist the eastern Jews and protect them from arrest and deportation on the grounds that they were legitimate refugees, the resident Jews of Leipzig actually opposed "allowing these elements to stay in the country."[156] Among the general population and the authorities, there was a general desire to deport these Jews, but this was easier said than done. The Poles either refused to take them back or threatened them with arrest and punishment, and the affected Jews themselves often fled from the trains in which they were being deported. Serious consideration was given to putting them into internment camps, but there was concern that "putting them in internment camps will offend the circles supporting Jews in America and will thus exercise unfavorable influence on the future relations between Germany and the United States."[157] Obviously, these eastern Jews constituted a social problem of considerable difficulty, but their most important sociopolitical effect was to help inflame and focus a more generalized rabid anti-Semitism being fed by social and economic conditions.

The sinister quality of this anti-Semitism became particularly evident in the promotion of concrete measures against all Jews and the sowing of the seeds of such distrust between Jews and non-Jews that even measures of Jewish self-protection took on a self-defeating quality. The German Defence and Defiance League, ever imaginative, circulated a list of "recommended non-Jewish firms" in a large number of cities. When the Frankfurt Jewish Womens' Organizations threatened a boycott of those businesses that did not publicly come out in opposition to the anti-Jewish boycott effort, the Frankfurt Retailers Association expressed great irritation. It pointed out that the Jewish and Christian merchants had worked together in its ranks for over twenty-five years and that this good relationship would be destroyed by a Jewish counterboycott. At the same time, the association threatened to sue the Defence and Defiance League, and, sometime later, the German Chamber of Commerce and Industry formally condemned the league's efforts to "damage merchants simply because of their origin."[158]

Clearly, many Jews, along with large segments of German society, were involved in black marketeering, smuggling, capital flight, and such activities. Insofar as they were disproportionately involved in commercial activities for historically conditioned social and cultural reasons, Jews could be singled out for their contributions to the general demoralization of German society taking place because of conditions that had nothing whatever to do with the Jews but a great deal to do with the political groups that were manipulating the Jewish "question." In a society that had been known for its lawfulness and orderliness, the national descent into varieties of illegality certainly was traumatic, and it was undoubtedly a relief for many to project onto the Jews behavior that they did not wish to think of as "German." Reason certainly could not win out in the context of a quantitatively and qualitatively transformed anti-Semitism that sought expression in radical action as well as in discriminatory legislation. Though wealthy Jews or persons of Jewish origin, like the bankers Max Warburg and Franz von Mendelssohn, sought desperately to use their foreign connections to get credit for a nation without credit, and though the Jewish "copper kings," Aaron Hirsch & Sohn, used the familial relationships with the firm of J. P. Vogelstein in New York to secure copper imports on credit and thereby help to keep German industry going, many Germans saw themselves and their nation as being mysteriously expropriated by a Jewish "international" and concentrated their attention on the paranoid question of how Galician Jews always managed to find relations in German and other European cities. By 1920, the term *Volksschädling* had become a widely accepted code word for the Jew, a term used to identify those who injured the people but which also suggested a noxious insect whose elimination could only serve the public good.[159]

The horrors of the future, however, may have been presaged, but they were not preordained by these grim developments, and the significance of such phenomena in 1919–1920 lay in their function as a reflection of the growing self-disgust within German society and its relationship to social protest arising out of the postwar hardships as well as the enormous uncertainty with which Germans faced the future. The condition of the country in the late winter was brilliantly described by the British Ambassador, Lord Kilmarnock:

Looking at the situation as a whole, it would seem that, while there are indications that the German workman has realized the seriousness of the crisis, and is ready to do his best in the interests of his country, little permanent improvement can be expected without substantial help from the Allied Powers. Disorders may, and probably will for the present, be suppressed by the Government, production may increase by the help of small loans from the neutrals, and the coming of spring bring some alleviation of the conditions of life, but without raw materials, better food, and clothing, no real stability can be attained. As the price of defeat and in expiation for their past crimes the German people may be forced to make bricks without straw—they cannot make them without clay. If my judgment is correct, we have the spectacle of a people beaten in war, torn by revolution, physically exhausted, suffering from privation and nervous strain, despondent, sometimes almost despairing, but still capable of an effort if it sees the slightest chance of success; a Government believing itself to be democratic, and having the support of the saner elements of the nation, threatened by the ever-present threat of anarchic violence, maintaining itself, as of necessity by methods indistinguishable from those of the autocracy, inclining therefore more and more to the right, faced by innumerable difficulties within and without, but on the whole managing, in spite of faults due to inexperience and the inefficiency of many of its organs, to keep the nation from falling into chaos; in addition a large class of war profiteers and people who are living recklessly on their capital on the principle that it is better to get what enjoyment they can before the money is taken from them by overwhelming taxation, filling the restaurants and the dancing halls, crowding the theatres where new plays of abysmal decadence compete in obscenity with revivals of the medieval dramas; and in the background, temporarily quiescent, helpless indeed for the moment, but not altogether hopeless of the future, sinister, resentful—the devotees of reaction watchful of their opportunity, ready even if it is said to help the extremists to plunge their country into chaos if thereby their own eventual aims may be served[160]

A gloomy picture, to be sure, but a balanced one that provides realistic bases for measuring the "successes" of the Bauer government. Bauer's regime was gradually beginning to dig Germany out of the mud, however problematic its methods and limited the possibilities. And what the government could not do, others were doing for themselves. A great tax reform had been passed. By the end of February, the labor situation looked the brightest since the Revolution. The miners had agreed to work an extra shift. The Reichsbank and the iron and steel industrialists had paid off large portions of their wartime debts, a notable feat in the context of the extraordinary depreciation of the mark abroad and one that could not but have a positive influence on foreign observers even if one may express great reservations about the way in which the industrialists had gone about the task. Also, it was impossible to overlook the fact that German industry was very busy and making its presence felt on the export market. As one businessman somewhat painfully noted, "[T]he most depressing thing about the present situation is a certain prosperity among individual enterprises and the absence of any credit on the part of the Reich and the states."[161] While this comment had more than a little significance for how the inflationary situation was being used and who was being strengthened by it, it must be noted that things were improving even for the government.

The single most important illustration of this was the negotiation for a Dutch credit which began under Erzberger's aegis in December 1919 and reached the stage of a final draft on January 20, 1920. Under the proposed agreement, Germany received a ten-year credit of two hundred million gulden, sixty million for food purchases and a hundred forty million as a revolving credit for raw-materials purchases. The credit carried a 6 percent interest charge and a German obligation to sell ninety thousand tons of coal a year to the Netherlands and to permit the Dutch half ownership of certain German mines on the border. Erzberger hoped that this credit would become part of an international economic and monetary understanding in which Germany would be included, a view shared in some Dutch circles. Actually, the proponents of the credit had to overcome not only the opposition of Dutch business circles angry at losses suffered in doing business with Germany and refusals by German firms to deliver at agreed upon prices, but also the unwillingness of the French to agree to coal shipments to the Netherlands when they were entitled to first call on German coal sent abroad. The German government, however, hoped to disarm such French objections by arguing that production would increase under the new extra-shift agreement with the Ruhr miners. They went on to ratify the agreement secretly in March in the hope that the French would prove reasonable. Erzberger had already announced his negotiations with the Dutch to the National Assembly in December, as a demonstration that Germany's credit was not as bad as his opponents claimed, and the rumors concerning the agreement certainly were conducive to improving Germany's status among the world's investors.[162]

The Reich government was not alone in being able to secure foreign credits. The City of Berlin seems to have been able to borrow 70,800,000 marks abroad, mainly from America, in the course of 1919, and it is reasonable to assume that a respectable portion of the 220,000,000 borrowed by that city in 1920 as well as the millions borrowed by other cities in the course of 1920 were taken in the earlier part of that year.[163] Thus, on April 1, 1920, one of the most active representatives of German financial interests in the United States, Martin Nordegg of the Deutsche Bank, reported from New York that "many millions in German city bonds and also industrial obligations have been placed here." The business was not being done by big banks or brokers, but rather by "about fifty small firms . . . not one of which enjoys the kind of reputation that would make it worthy of large-scale sales."[164] Nordegg hoped this would change, and he urged that the Erzberger premium loan be marketed in the United States.

It is important to note, however, that promoters of such speculative investments had no conscious intention whatever of cheating their customers or persuading them to purchase obligations that would later be paid in depreciated currency. Quite to the contrary, Nordegg even imagined there to be some risk on the German side: "The most important thing is that sympathy for Germany be created with each purchase of such paper. Even if Germany will have to repurchase these obligations at a much higher price, then it will at that point be in a position to do so anytime, and in the meantime it will have created an atmosphere here which can only be of great advantage to us."[165] Germany could be expected to have to pay something for the goodwill that would promote her recovery.

During the second half of 1919, and especially during the last quarter of that year, German bonds did appear on the New York market and were bought with dollars in the hope of making an exchange profit when the mark improved. Furthermore, the speculative tendencies did not end here. On the one hand, there was a growing tendency for foreigners to open up German bank accounts, so that in 1919 approximately 35 percent of the holdings of a group of leading banks were from foreign sources. On the other hand, there was an increasing tendency on the part of American exporters to hold on to marks received in payment from Germany in the hope of making a speculative profit. It would appear, therefore, that German import surpluses in 1919 were being in goodly measure paid for with the help of what amounted to a growing short-term capital export to Germany for speculative purposes.[166]

Germany had a great interest in the promotion of such tendencies for obvious reasons, and there is some evidence that there was a need to promote them actively. Ludwig Bendix, a former banker with Hallgarten & Co. in New York, who had lectured at New York University on banking, was particularly prominent in encouraging both the German government to set up a financial archive and agencies to provide the American investing public with information about opportunities to invest in German securities and enterprises. He also urged that the American government be informed about Germany's credit needs and the importance of Germany as an importer of American products. The shrewd manner in which he operated is well illustrated by his telling the American Treasury Department that British importers were selling foodstuffs, often American, and raw materials to Germany on three-month credit guaranteed by German purchasing syndicates and banks. His objective, of course, was to inspire the Americans to follow suit and compete with the British for the German market. While Bendix strongly supported the efforts of his government and of people friendly to Germany, like American banker Paul Warburg, to promote long-term reconstruction credits, he was no less concerned about encouraging short-term credits and the placement of municipal bonds and other such assets through a systematic effort to propagandize the German-American community and other potentially friendly groups through films, written propaganda, and especially the churches.[167] Even in the absence of such a systematic effort, however, Germany was profitting from a growing tendency on the part of Americans not only to give short-term credits to cover the price of their exports but also to follow in the footsteps of the many Danes, Swedes, Dutch, and others who had been speculating since the war on an improvement of the mark.

The international financial maneuverability of the Reich was being increased not only by such credits and speculation, however, but also by the very active policy of the Reichsbank to procure foreign exchange and thus be in a position to intervene on international money markets and put an end to its total helplessness in dealing with the exchange rate. Since mid-1919, the Reichsbank had been gradually but systematically increasing its holdings in foreign bills and checks. Its major source of such foreign exchange was German exporters who needed money before they could collect the bills due them and to whom the Reichsbank provided marks at a guaranteed rate. At the same time, the Reichsbank proceeded to gather as much of the foreign-exchange holdings in the hands of its branches as it could and also made a practice of selling the foreign securities that it could lay its hands on for foreign exchange. Between June and December 1919, it secured over

a billion marks in foreign exchange by this means, 870 million of it through its hyperactive representative in the Netherlands, Dr. Fritz Mannheimer, whose energetic services were praised to the skies by the Reichsbank leaders and who was to serve as their chief agent for a host of transactions for years to come. Even before the turn of the year, the Reichsbank had already used some of this newly acquired foreign exchange to support the exchange rate of the mark, although it was not yet in much of a position to do anything about the dismal condition of the German currency. Nevertheless, it continued to increase its holdings during January and February of 1920 even as the mark declined more precipitously than ever, a process which then accelerated through the spring. In January, its holding in foreign exchange amounted to 1.1 billion; in February, 2.1 billion; in March, 4.3 billion; in April 8.1 billion; and in May 11.9 billion. Measured in dollars, this was an increase from $17 million to $256 million. Thus, the financial potential of the Reichsbank had increased substantially by the end of May.[168]

Yet another important weapon in the German arsenal was the measures taken by the government to control the foreign trade situation, specifically, the Decree on the Regulation of Imports and Exports of December 20, 1919. By the turn of the year, the export control boards were being rapidly constructed, the government was showing an increasing determination to ban unwanted imports, and, while there was little inclination to revive exchange controls, the Reichsbank was working hard at persuading exporters to take payment in foreign exchange. The export control boards, once formed, could impose such a regulation on their members. Most important from the standpoint of the effectiveness of foreign-trade regulations, real progress was being made toward plugging the "hole in the West." In the second half of February, State Secretary Hirsch traveled to Paris to negotiate with the influential economic expert in the French Foreign Office Jacques Seydoux. Hirsch bluntly pointed out that "anarchy" was reigning in the occupied areas, and that the French might just as well forget about collecting reparations if the conditions there persisted. While the French took offense at some of Hirsch's remarks, Seydoux, at least, seems to have been friendly enough to invite Hirsch to a tea party at which all sorts of luxury foods of the type being smuggled into Germany were served, and to participate in two meetings at which Hirsch outlined the details of closing the border. Undoubtedly, these negotiations were smoothed by Hirsch's perfect French. The Germans were still compelled to wait a few weeks for success, but the French formally imposed German customs sovereignty on March 22; the actual implementation took place a few days earlier. Hirsch, overjoyed at this success, began receiving reports about how long lines of merchants were waiting outside the borders with illegal imports and made sure that "not a gram" was let in.[169]

This was not the only German foreign policy success in the first months of 1920. The Germans also enjoyed a political triumph when the Allies decided to withdraw their demand for the delivery of German "war criminals" for trial. Thus, a particularly disturbing and somewhat gratuitous source of international and domestic friction was eliminated. While there remained troublesome signs on the international front, especially the appointment of Raymond Poincaré to chair the Reparations Commission on February 23 and French complaints about insufficient German coal deliveries on February 8, the German reading of the international situation at the beginning of March was such that they could begin contemplating a revisionist effort. This seemed all the more desirable in the light of the Allied invitation to the Germans to submit their own reparations proposals and thus speed up the determination of the final reparations bill within four months of the coming into force of the Treaty of Versailles on January 10, 1920. On March 1, Privy Councillor Kempner of the Reich Chancellery and Undersecretary Hans Albert presented the Cabinet with a memorandum aimed at encouraging a German initiative.[170]

In this document, they placed particular emphasis upon the changing attitudes toward the treaty terms outside France. The growing influence of Keynes's *The Economic Consequences of the Peace* was their key piece of evidence, but they also could cite numerous criticisms of the treaty by English and American leaders and by

international financial leaders and experts meeting unofficially in Amsterdam in October and November 1919 who had called for an international conference to consider the world's currency and economic problems. While such developments might seem to provide grounds for a major effort at revision of the entire Treaty, the authors of the memorandum viewed this as premature and felt that the initiative for a comprehensive solution had to come from abroad. Instead, they urged a more restricted German proposal on reparations "which would automatically become broader"; that is, to use the invitation to present a reparations proposal as a wedge for the ultimate reconsideration of the entire Treaty. This approach would also be justified by the fact that "the circumstance that Germany is not to know the extent of her obligations for a longer period, makes it impossible to balance the receipts and outlays of the Reich. An orderly budget, the basis of every health economy, cannot be set up for this reason."[171] While Keynes had argued that Germany could pay thirty billion gold marks, Kempner urged that Germany offer only twenty billion in cash beyond the already performed payments in kind and services, a just sum on the basis of Germany's incapacity to pay as demonstrated by her economic situation—above all, the food, clothing, and serious coal shortages. They argued that if Germany delivered the forty million tons of coal in 1920 required by the Treaty, then it would only have 19.1 million tons left for home heating, agriculture, and industry instead of the 59.1 million that might be available and that was already below requirements.

The tactics proposed in this memorandum were approved by a meeting of the government leadership on March 3, in which there was a consensus that the old hundred billion goldmark offer was invalidated by circumstances and that the Keynes book had created a new situation as well. A decision was made to set up a commission of bankers—Warburg, Melchior, and Urbig were explicitly named—and experts, especially noted economist Moritz Bonn, to formulate a memorandum. At the same time, Reconstruction Minister Otto Gessler was instructed to pursue further his efforts to organize the reconstruction of the devastated areas in

France and Belgium through payments in kind and labor services.[172]

It is important not to overdo the positive character of developments in February and early March 1920 and neglect the economic miseries, continued high inflation, and political disorder of this period, but the determination to take major steps in the direction of getting Germany out of her economic mess was unquestionably there. Hirsch, for example, was formulating proposals for the organization of German capital imports and credit so as to ensure flow in the most positive direction—proposals that bore interesting resemblances to Moellendorff's projected Reich Fund. Especially noteworthy was the discussion of ways of terminating Reichsbank note production and undertaking currency reform at a meeting of experts on March 11, 1920. Hirsch suggested that the printing of money might be limited to what could actually be covered by available foreign exchange and bills on hand. Socialist theoretician Hilferding was notably traditionalist and conservative in his monetary views. While advocating high taxes and denying that high wages were responsible for increased inflation, he seemed perfectly willing to allow domestic prices to rise to world market levels, viewed calculation in foreign exchange on the domestic market as a stabilizing factor, and argued the "necessity of gold coverage of the note circulation. We need a new Reichsbank without state involvement, but above all the granting of credit by the bank only against produced goods and thereby perhaps a transition to a gold currency. Perhaps later the establishment of a clearing office."[173] It is a long way from such a discussion to monetary stabilization, but the meeting is indicative of a continued belief that the currency could be stabilized and would be stabilized under the right conditions.

The difficulty of achieving such conditions, however, was demonstrated only two days after this discussion when, on March 13, Wolfgang Kapp launched his famous Putsch with the help of General Lüttwitz and bands of free-corps troops. As Hirsch later noted, the swastika appeared on German military helmets for the first time. The Putsch was a miserable failure, which at once reminded the world that the German right was not dead and, through its defeat by a general strike, that the remobilization of the left was possible, at least when the Republic was in danger.[174] Quite aside from the political threat, however, what worried the business community most was the Putsch's possibly adverse effect on the universally observable progress that had been made in bringing the workers to a higher level of productivity and the visible signs that the exchange rate was improving. Thus, while some businessmen were sympathetic with the "ideals" of some of the putschists and all were for calling for a new election as soon as possible in the expectation that the right would make great gains at the polls, businessmen deplored the Putsch for its timing and consequences as well as for the political stupidity it reflected. As Carl Duisberg angrily and not untypically commented:

Just at the moment when we begin again to work more than before, at least in the mines—and coal is the chief thing at the moment—when in London the recognition is mounting that through the imposition of the Versailles Treaty one has committed a fearful political stupidity and accordingly that the exchange rate begins to improve, the military party, and then under the leadership of a man who is a notorious reactionary, again throws everything overboard and forces our workers into a general strike and demonstrations that are unnecessary because nothing will be achieved that way.[175]

In reality, the general strike was more necessary than Duisberg claimed, and if there were anything questionable, it would be the manner in which many of his colleagues refused to take a clear position against the Kappists as well as the subsequent use of right-wing rebel troops to put down the left wing uprising in the Ruhr. Nevertheless, the upshot of these happenings and ambivalent republican successes was to confirm and strengthen the indicators pointing to some measure of political and economic stabilization.

For those who watched the exchange rate, the positive trend was undeniable, both before the Putsch and then afterward. In Amsterdam on March 8, 100 gulden bought 3,340 marks. On March 12, 100 gulden bought 2,602 marks. Happily, the Putsch interrupted telegraphic communications with the outside world so that the mark could only be quoted unofficially, but even then, its setback was brief. On March 16, during the Putsch, it was back down to 4,000 marks for 100 gulden, but three days later the recovery resumed, and one could buy 100 gulden for 2,000 marks.[176]

The great burst of inflation that had gripped Germany since the summer of 1919 appeared to be over. What exactly had been learned from it and whether its resumption could or would be prevented remained to be seen. While by April 1920 most Germans had become aware of the devastation wrought to their economy since 1914 and had come to experience inflation as a veritable way of life, the path to reconstruction was anything but obvious and the question of whether or not they could live without inflation had yet to be asked or answered.

PART III

RELATIVE STABILIZATION AND INFLATIONARY RECONSTRUCTION, APRIL 1920–MAY 1921

. . . it is worse, in an improverished world to provoke unemployment than to disappoint the rentier.
—John Maynard Keynes, *Essays in Persuasion*

Chapter 5

The Trials and Tribulations of Relative Stabilization

The Relative Stabilization as a Historical Problem

The control of inflation is a political question, but this is not to argue that the successful control of inflation is always a demonstration of political virtue. It is, in truth, nothing more or less than a manifestation of political power by a government that feels secure enough to pursue a stabilization policy despite what seems to be its unavoidable economic and social consequences; namely, an economic crisis with its attendant high unemployment and weakening of labor's ability to secure improved wages and working conditions. This power may be the product of the repressive force at a government's disposal, the support of a substantial body of public opinion, or some combination of the two. The price may be necessary and even desirable when compared to that paid for galloping inflation or hyperinflation, but this presupposes that the political price is tolerable as well.

This obviously was the case in Great Britain and the United States, where firmly established political democracies could withstand the shocks of a deflationary economic policy without suffering serious political consequences. Also, in contrast to Germany, the power of finance capital remained extremely strong in England. The determination to subordinate economic to financial policy had been asserted very early in England by the Cunliffe Reports of August 1918 and December 1919, the acceptance of which pledged the nation to take the steps necessary to restore the gold standard as soon as possible. Once the demobilization and its accompanying difficulties were over and the initial surge of postwar demand for goods had been somewhat satisfied, the Bank of England abruptly terminated the postwar boom by raising its discount rate significantly in April 1920. In the United States, this process had already been started by the Federal Reserve in November 1919, but the decisive blow was dealt in the first two months of 1920 with a l.25 percent increase in the discount rate. The determination to conduct a fiscal and economic "regime change"—that is, to reduce public spending, balance budgets, and restrict demand through tight money policies—was incontrovertible, and the response of the economy was a tribute to the credibility of the governmental and financial authorities. By summer, both nations and, indeed, most of the industrial world were plunged into what was known as the Great Depression until a new standard for "greatness" was established a decade later.[1]

In both Great Britain and the United States, the deflationary policy was preceded and then accompanied by a significant increase in political repression and a turning away from the pro-labor policies that had characterized the wartime and demobilization periods. In England, the government played upon "supposed abuses of unemployment insurance, the fears of small investors, and the great mass of residual middle-class hostility to working-class aspirations"[2] to create a consensus for its policies and pave the way for repeated blows against labor, while in the United States the Red Scare, Palmer Raids, and brutal suppression of strikes ushered in a period of political conservatism. In these societies, however, the fundamental political stability remained unshaken, and the political system remained unthreatened. Fear of the left assisted in the creation of a new consensus while the right, however one judges some of its actions, remained committed to democratic institutions and practices. That this did not have to be the case was demonstrated by Italy, where government success in reducing the budget deficit in 1920 left the country especially vulnerable to the world economic crisis of 1920–1921, promoted a sharp reduction of industrial production, and exacerbated social conflicts to the point where they not only destabilized but ultimately led to the destruction of the political system by the fascists after 1922.[3]

This international context is important if one is to understand the very different path taken by Germany during the world-wide depression of 1920–1921. It should be obvious from the preceding chapters that stabilization was viewed as a desired goal by most of the German political and economic leadership, who lived in anticipation, not of continuing inflation, but rather of an improvement of the exchange rate and a return to "normal" economic practices. Havenstein and Hilferding may have had very little in common, but they shared the conventional belief in a return to "sound money" through the limitation of government expenditure and restriction of monetary emissions. While the business community had little enthusiasm for the comprehensiveness of the Erzberger tax program, the need for heavy taxation and tax reform itself was accepted by most reasonable persons. The idea that the rates were too high was not a monopoly of Erzberger's right-wing opponents. Julius Hirsch thought them too high, and so did the Italian member of the Reparations Commission and later most famous of all students of the German inflation, Costantino Bresciani-Turroni, who criticized the "unduly high rates" as a "stimulus to evasion" and capital flight.[4]

Just as most German economic leaders knew that higher taxation and tax reforms were necessary, so they knew that manipulation of the exchange rate was no way to solve the problems of inflation. They would have agreed with banker Paul von Schwabach when he argued that Reichsbank and Foreign Exchange Procurement Board interventions to influence the exchange rate were palliatives: "In the last analysis the exchange rate is nothing other than a thermometer measuring economic conditions. If one artificially drives the temperature up, then first of all, it does not last long, and secondly, it does not make it warmer outside."[5]

Finally, Germany's leaders also shared the international conviction that inflation had to be fought with higher productivity and efficiency. As has been shown, the willingness to "get tough" with labor extended to the Social Democratic leadership, and its tactics in dealing with the railroad workers and miners undoubtedly emboldened industrialists and bankers to voice open criticisms of the eight-hour day in early 1920 and even to work actively for its suspension until the economic situation changed for the better. While this certainly was a point of difference with someone like Hilferding—who argued that the eight-hour day was by no means as deleterious as was contended and that the ultimate solution to the productivity problem was rationalization—the consensus on the need for higher productivity was well-nigh universal.[6]

The Kapp Putsch and the subsequent worker uprisings in the Ruhr and central Germany served as a reminder that what was at stake in German social and economic policy was the political system itself, while it also made clear that the alternatives to that political system threatened to destroy the German economy. Kapp and his fellow conspirators were unacceptable both at home and abroad. Ebert was on firm ground in arguing in his proclamation against Kapp that Germany would never get the foreign loan it needed under such leadership. Stinnes pointed out in a not exactly ringing but undoubtedly sincere and certainly realistic statement that "in economic life one has to come to terms with the present constitutional conditions, for Germany's economic life can only be rebuilt with the democratic states of the West. Germany could never come to a bearable relationship with England and America if prerevolutionary conditions are perceived to be an option here."[7]

The responsible right knew that it could not rule against the workers—at least not in 1920. The defeat of the Kapp Putsch, however, also gave the trade unions and the left an opportunity to make clear to whoever ruled in Berlin that the workers had no intention of abandoning their power and surrendering the gains of the November Revolution. The Nine-Point Program imposed by Legien and the trade unions at the end of the general strike demanded, among other things, decisive trade union influence on the economic and social policies of the government, economic and social equality for the blue- and white-collar workers and civil servants, socialization of the coal and potash industries, and confiscation of the property of farmers who had violated the food regulations. These, along with a variety of political demands, which included the purging of the bureaucracy and the army, became the basis of the so-called Bielefeld Agreement of March 24 aimed at ending the uprising in the Ruhr that had followed the Kapp Putsch. If the long-run danger to the Weimar Republic came from the right, the short-run problem was once again pacifying the left.[8]

It would be erroneous, therefore, to think that the governments ruling Germany after the Kapp Putsch had a free hand in financial, economic, and social policy and could pursue an Anglo-American course, even if they wished to do so. Furthermore, this was true of any viable government. To be sure, the Reichstag elections of June 6, 1920, were a dramatic turning point in the history of the Weimar Republic, reducing the Weimar Coalition vote from 76.2 to 43.6 percent while increasing the DVP and DNVP vote from 14.7 to 29.1 percent and that of the USPD from 7.6 to 18 percent.[9] Despite this shift toward the right and tendency toward extremism, there was considerable continuity between the caretaker Weimar Coalition government of the Social Democrat Hermann Müller, who held power from March 27 to June 21, 1920, and the bourgeois Coalition Cabinet of Centrist, DDP, and DVP Ministers under the Centrist Konstantin Fehrenbach, which ruled from June 25, 1920, to May 4, 1921. Müller's replacement for Erzberger as Finance Minister was Baden Centrist Joseph Wirth, who stayed on under Fehrenbach, as did DDP Interior Minister Erich Koch-Weser and Centrist Postal Minister Giesberts, both of whom had already assumed these positions under Bauer. Otto Gessler, the former Reconstruction Minister,

became Defence Minister under Müller and was to remain in this position until 1926. To encourage agricultural production, Müller revived the old Reich Food Ministry as a Ministry for Food and Agriculture and placed it under the until then little-known Centrist agricultural expert Andreas Hermes, who continued on under Fehrenbach. Finally, the changes in the Economics and Labor Ministries were less dramatic than might appear at first sight. Ernst Scholz of the DVP, who had made his reputation in municipal administration, replaced Schmidt as Economics Minister, but Hirsch was retained as State Secretary. A much more lasting change was the appointment of the cleric Heinrich Brauns as Labor Minister by Fehrenbach to replace Alexander Schlicke. Long associated with the Christian trade-union movement and the labor wing of the Center Party, Brauns was to remain in this office until 1928. His appointment could in no way be considered unfriendly toward labor. Indeed, he was to prove one of Germany's foremost proponents of social legislation, and, insofar as he sought to promote productivity and tie wage increases to productivity increases, he certainly was not at odds with his Socialist predecessors.[10] The reality, therefore, was that the mix of financial, economic, and social policies pursued before June 1920 could not be easily changed by the election results, except with the greatest caution. This was evident from the composition of the new government and was demonstrated by the policies it pursued.

A very important illustration of this, especially from the perspective of the history of the inflation, was the treatment of the civil service. In its efforts to quiet the unrest among the civil servants and government employees, the Bauer government had promised to produce a much-needed and long-awaited Salary Reform bill. Work was begun in late 1919, and a draft was finally produced in February 1920. The chief features of the bill were the reduction of the over one hundred eighty previous classifications of civil servants to thirteen and the reduction of the pay differentials between higher, middle, and lower levels of the civil service. The bill produced a goodly measure of protest, especially from the railroad workers, who demanded a higher classification than that provided. While there could be no question that civil-servant salaries were in desperate need of reform and improvement, there was also no denying that it was an extraordinarily expensive reform. When finally drawn up in March, the bill was expected to cost 3.9 billion marks for the year, of which only 1.3 billion were budgeted, leaving 2.6 billion to be covered either by taxes or, as was most likely, by the printing press. Obviously, therefore, the government had every interest in resisting the demand of the railroad workers for reclassification since it would start an avalanche of such demands.[11]

The Kapp Putsch strengthened the hand of the railroad workers as well as of the civil-servant unions, whose role in the general strike enabled them to claim greater consideration. The railroad workers turned the screws tighter in mid-April by threatening refusal to enter the service of the Reich when the impending nationalization of the railroads, which had been run by the federal states, took place. Their demands would have increased the cost of the civil-service reform bill by two billion marks, however, and Finance Minister Wirth chose to oppose the expenditure. Thus began what were to become a series of periodic battles with the civil-servant and public-employee unions. While the majority of the Cabinet supported Wirth, new Centrist Transport Minister Bell proved so weak in his attitude that Koch-Weser sincerely regretted the absence of the tough Socialist trade unionist Bauer, who knew how to put his foot down with the workers. Thanks to Wirth's tenacity, the classification change was defeated in the National Assembly, and the new Salary Reform Act was passed on April 28, while Bauer did, in fact, become Transportation Minister for the last two months of the Müller chancellorship.[12]

This hardly ended the problem, however, since the National Assembly left a reconsideration of the matter to the new Reichstag along with the touchy question of deciding on the civil-servant salary scales for the different areas of the Reich. In the meantime, the government was compelled to provide a cost-of-living increase of 50 percent for the civil servants on May 8, so that a substantial sum was added to the recently revised and significantly higher base rates under the new Salary Reform Act. As always, however, the public employees and civil servants remained dissatisfied, and they gave vent to their feelings in the June 6 elections, where some civil servants may have turned to the USPD. A great many more civil servants apparently turned to the DVP and DNVP which had made improvement of the lot of the civil servants a major theme of both National Assembly debates and the Reichstag election campaign. While the leadership of the German Civil Servants Federation (*Deutscher Beamtenbund* or DBB) worried about a decline in their parliamentary influence, the truth was that Finance Minister Wirth's problems with the civil servants and their parliamentary supporters had only begun. He was saddled with the unavoidable but expensive Salary Reform Act as well as with the need to complete the unfinished business which the National Assembly had left behind. He could look forward to periodic choices between undermining his financial policy by yielding to civil-servant demands and risking an economic standstill by resisting them.[13]

In the last analysis, however, the choice in this realm as in others would be to maintain peace and production at the expense of sound financial policy. There was a basic consensus in Germany on the need to subordinate financial to economic policy for the purposes of promoting reconstruction through the systematic effort to encourage agricultural and industrial production and maintain high employment, on the one hand, and a no less concentrated effort to maintain social peace and ameliorate hardships, on the other. To a considerable extent, these were policies dictated by the external and internal constraints upon any regime ruling Germany at this time; namely, the uncertainty as to what the reparations bill would be, the continued unavailability of a foreign reconstruction loan, and, of greatest importance, the need to contain the forces of upheaval. At the same time, however, a good argument can also be made that these policies were preferred options to less promising alternatives. The advantages of a deflationary policy of the type being pursued in England and the United States as well as certain other industrialized nations at this time were anything but obvious under German conditions, while *relative* stabilization seemed to make sense and to offer a host of benefits.

Indeed, when knowledgeable Germans contemplated the problem of inflation from a historical perspective, as did economists Kurt Singer and Alfred Schmidt in a special supplement to the *Bank=Archiv* in October 1920, they demonstrated how totally inconceivable the introduction of a rapid "regime change" of the Anglo-American type was to most reputable German economic experts at this time.[14] The authors pointed out how little information was available in the literature about the curing of inflation, in part because of the limited experience with inflation in modern advanced societies but "perhaps also because the recovery is an occurrence that is slowly carried out and is difficult to notice [and is a development] which is not founded upon the reestablishment of a stable currency but is rather crowned by it." That is, the actual currency stabilization and creation of exchange parities were viewed as a "technical matter" which could be handled once the economic problem—above all, the unsatisfactory relationship between goods produced and money in circulation—was corrected. From the vantage point of Germany's problems in 1920, the experience of past inflations—France after the Great Revolution, Prussia and England in the Napoleonic period, Russia in the nineteenth century, the United States during the Civil War, Austria in the 1860s, Italy in the 1880s, Chile in the two decades before the war, and Argentina before the reform of 1899—appeared of little relevance. Nearly all of the states in question were agrarian in character, comparatively uncomplicated in their industrial and banking organization, not yet integrated into a complex international monetary system, and, thus, "more robust and less sensitive to disturbances." All that was needed were "some good harvests and some reason" to correct the situation, while the inflation problem itself could be solved by a return to metallic currencies, a task made all the easier by the availability of sufficient supplies of precious metals.

From the perspective of postwar Germany, Singer and Schmidt argued that the most rele-

vant experience was probably that of Argentina, since that country's 1899 reform appeared to have been strongly influenced by agrarian, especially sugar-exporting, interests which were affected by and therefore sensitive to world-market conditions and currency relationships. The sugar interests were unhappy with trends toward an excessive increase in the value of the Argentine peso but wished to use the improvement of the exchange rate then taking place to create greater stability and thus at once prevent new surges of depreciation and defend Argentinian export capability. The reform, associated with Ernesto Thornquist, sought precisely such a stabilization through the establishment of a clearing bank to exchange the notes in circulation into gold and the latter back into new notes again while controlling the number of new notes sent into circulation. In choosing a rate of conversion, however, the reformers deliberately avoided a return to the old parity since "a conversion at parity would impose huge sacrifices upon the country without anybody deriving any benefit from it. . . . " A nation which has lived so long with a paper money economy, Singer and Schmidt argued, would suffer extraordinarily under a conversion to the old parity. Only during and after the war, when Argentina had a huge export surplus, did its leaders decide to go over to a gold-backed currency at a fixed parity, a decision which the German economists questioned in the light of Argentina's success with a policy of avoiding fixed parities for the peso and pursuing a policy of relatively stable exchange rates instead.

The Argentine model was extremely influential among German banking and currency experts. Hilferding seems to have had it in mind in his own reflections on the stabilization problem in 1920. In any case, two aspects of the Singer–Schmidt discussion are particularly important in revealing basic German attitudes toward their own inflation at this time. First, there was the assumption that an improvement in economic conditions, especially higher productivity and substantial exports as well as fiscal reform and reduced expenditure, had to precede monetary stabilization. Second, insofar as the immediate future was concerned, there was a strong inclination to think in terms of a relative stabilization that was tantamount to a devaluation within the context of continuing flexible exchange rates. Over the long run, a return to fixed exchange rates and the gold standard, the "European" model, remained the goal. The feasibility and even desirability of a full scale "regime change" along Anglo-American lines, however, was pushed very much into the background during this period. The relative stabilization from the spring of 1920 to the spring of 1921, therefore, must be viewed in this context.

What was the relative stabilization? To begin with, as the exchange rates on Table 1 (see page 5) show, it had nothing whatever to do with stabilizing the mark at anything remotely resembling prewar levels. The prewar exchange rate had been 4.2 marks to the dollar. By February 1920, the mark had depreciated to 99.11 to the dollar. Its improvement thereafter must be viewed relative to this low point. Thus, it was most impressive in June, when it stood at 39.13 marks to the dollar, while during most of the period, it averaged between 60 and 70 marks to the dollar. The conditions which had produced this improvement of the exchange rate have been discussed at the end of the last chapter, the advantages and limitations of the relative stabilization are best understood in terms of the larger economic picture during this period.

As Tables 1, 13, and 14 show, there were significant differences between the previous period, stretching from the signing of the Treaty of Versailles to the end of the Kapp Putsch, and the period of relative stabilization. The most significant ones, aside from the improvement of the exchange rate and its relative stabilization, were the sharp drop in the price of imported goods and the relative stability of domestic wholesale prices. The cost of living, however, for which an index was first established in February 1920, showed a marked tendency to remain high in 1920–1921, exhibiting slight declines in June–September 1920 and February–May 1921. Two previously observable trends continued throughout the relative stabilization, however. The first was the increase of the paper money in circulation, albeit at a reduced pace, from 59,607 million marks in March 1920 to 84,556 million marks in June 1921. The second, and most significant, was the dramatic increase in the floating debt during the same period from 91.6 billion to 185.1 billion marks.

From the standpoint of the containment of the major source of inflation, therefore, the period of relative stabilization must be viewed as a failure. While the reduction of the increase in monetary circulation was not unimpressive, falling from 9.4 billion in the first quarter of 1920 to 5.8 billion in the final quarter and continuing to decline in the first months of 1921, the causes scarcely reflected a fundamental shift in the direction of long-lasting stabilization. The development certainly was a happy one insofar as it was a consequence of the introduction of tax withholding in the second half of 1920 or, as in early 1921, reduced prices or the

Table 13. The Index of Wholesale Prices for Imported and Domestic Goods, and the Cost-of-Living Index*, July 1919–June 1921
(in paper marks; 1913 = 1)

	Imported Goods	Domestic Goods	Cost-of-Living Index**
1919			
July	3.55	3.41	—
August	4.29	4.24	—
September	6.18	4.65	—
October	8.21	5.03	—
November	11.62	5.63	—
December	15.08	6.33	—
1920			
January	27.31	9.61	—
February	40.63	12.10	8.47
March	40.14	12.48	9.56
April	34.41	11.92	10.42
May	25.84	12.93	11.02
June	21.17	12.35	10.83
July	18.98	12.60	10.65
August	20.40	13.32	10.23
September	22.28	13.53	10.15
October	23.28	12.94	10.71
November	23.62	13.39	11.18
December	20.23	13.23	11.58
1921			
January	18.23	13.62	11.79
February	16.60	13.20	11.47
March	16.15	12.82	11.38
April	15.60	12.80	11.27
May	15.23	12.66	11.20
June	15.95	13.20	11.67

Source: Statistisches Reichsamt, *Zahlen zur Geldentwertung in Deutschland 1914 bis 1923* [Sonderheft 1 zu *Wirtschaft und Statistik*, Bd. 5] (Berlin, 1925), pp. 16–17, 33.

*Unavailable before February 1920.

**includes food, clothing, housing, heat, and light.

Table 14. Paper Money and Treasury Bills in Circulation, July 1919–June 1921

	Paper Money (in millions)	Treasury Bills (in billions)
1919		
July	41,807	76.1
August	40,781	78.2
September	42,196	80.6
October	43,300	83.3
November	45,311	85.2
December	50,065	86.4
1920		
January	50,960	88.3
February	54,330	89.0
March	59,475	91.6
April	62,286	95.1
May	64,150	101.6
June	68,154	113.2
July	69,655	122.7
August	72,223	129.4
September	75,635	138.3
October	77,168	140.6
November	77,202	147.6
December	81,387	152.8
1921		
January	78,506	155.6
February	79,720	161.8
March	80,118	166.4
April	80,912	172.7
May	81,410	176.7
June	84,556	185.1

Source: Statistisches Reichsamt, *Zahlen zur Geldentwertung in Deutschland 1914 bis 1923* [Sonderheft 1 zu *Wirtschaft und Statistik,* Bd. 5] (Berlin, 1925), p. 46; and Carl-Ludwig Holtfrerich, *The German Inflation 1914–1923. Causes and Effects in International Perspective* (Berlin & New York, 1986), pp. 67–68.

anticipation of reduced prices. Less clear as a positive factor was the reentry of hoarded money into the market in the fall and winter of 1920 because of the dip in the value of the mark and the usual flight into goods whenever that occurred. Increased use of postal checking accounts and other forms of noncash instruments of payment also seems to have played a role, as did the disgorging of hoarded notes either because the assessments for the Emergency Capital Levy had come to an end or in order to escape higher assessment. Most important, the declining increase in the amount of money in circulation reflected the willingness of private persons and institutions to hold Treasury notes in response to changing business conditions, prices, and exchange rates. This reduced the Reichsbank Treasury note holdings and

the amount of money that needed to be printed.[15]

While true stabilization is not incompatible with some increase in the amount of money in circulation, however, it is incompatible with significant increases in the floating debt. The most important demonstration of the fragile and tenuous character of the relative stabilization, therefore, was the enormous increase of the floating debt. Two actions taken by the Reichsbank and the government in the late spring of 1921 put a fitting and sad signature on the relative stabilization as it drew to a close. First, on May 9, 1921, the Reichsbank Law was amended to suspend the one-third coverage requirement until December 31, 1923. The fictions of August 1914 under which Germany sought to "cover one paper currency with another" were finally abandoned.[16] Second, on June 1, 1921, the Reichsbank began to offer a premium for gold coins bought from the public, which was tantamount to a first official recognition of monetary inflation even if the fiction that the prewar paper mark was the equivalent of the postwar mark ("mark for mark" was officially maintained).[17]

This sorry end to the relative stabilization demonstrates its limitations and the continuity of constraints on German policymakers, but it does not totally obviate the question as to whether the relative stabilization was not a lost opportunity to save the mark. Some of the most distinguished students of the German inflation have so argued. Thus, in his classic study, Bresciani-Turroni claimed that "it would still have been possible to save the mark if the German Government had taken energetic measures to reestablish a balanced budget instead of allowing treasury bills to be discounted continually at the Reichsbank."[18] Ragner Nurske took a similar position: "The general level of German wholesale prices actually declined between March 1920 and June 1921, i.e., the period of the postwar slump abroad, and the inflation could perhaps still have been brought under control if appropriate measures had been taken at that time."[19] Was the relative stabilization a lost opportunity, and if so, why? Was there a "third way" around the Anglo-American deflationary policy and the inflationary path being taken by the Germans? These questions can best be answered by turning to the interaction between the real conditions within Germany and governmental practices at that time.

The Crisis of the Summer of 1920 and Its Consequences

Shortly after the Kapp Putsch, State Secretary Hirsch stepped out of the Cologne railroad station and was greeted by a placard declaring: "See what this 'comrade' Hirsch has given you. First, he promised to make the mark strong again. Now it is stronger, but we cannot export anymore. Instead of inflation, he has brought us unemployment and hunger."[20] The Communists responsible for the placard were not alone in their critical attitude toward the improvement of the mark. The *Frankfurter Zeitung* reported in late April that there was "widespread fear" of too rapid an improvement of the exchange rate, and the paper went on to warn that even the most effective of medicines, if taken in a single dose, could produce undesirable results.[21] The negative aspects of a more highly valued mark were increasingly apparent as spring turned into summer. Foreign customers began to find the cost of German goods too high, and domestic customers held back—indeed, engaged in a veritable "buyers' strike" (*Käuferstreik*)—either in the hope of lower prices or because price levels had risen so steeply during the inflationary winter that they could not afford to buy. Unemployment, especially in the manufacturing industries, rose substantially (see Table 15). Short time (*Kurzarbeit*) increased, although the precise amount of this important form of unemployment was not registered until 1921. No less disturbing were the numerous reports of firms closing down, some temporarily, others selling their machinery and simply going out of business. Not only was the inflationary boom of the fall and winter over, but it seemed to be replaced by a recession of no mean proportions caused not by deflationary measures on the part of the Reichsbank or the government but rather by the improvement of the exchange rate.[22]

Some people found the improvement too much of a good thing. Thus, the Leipzig Cham-

ber of Commerce supported stabilization of the exchange rate, but not "in the sense of a sudden but rather of a gradual improvement."[23] The Roofers Union, in early June, also welcomed the improvement of the mark in anticipation of a better and cheaper food supply but warned that it would lead to unemployment and called on the government to give "billions in contracts to all industries in an effort to overcome the downturn."[24]

The government and the Reichsbank certainly had considerable responsibility for the exceptional improvement of the mark thanks to the stock of foreign exchange they had purchased since the fall of 1919 and their use of it to improve and stabilize the German exchange rate. As Hirsch reported on June 3–4, over 25.4 billion marks in foreign exchange had been purchased, 14 billion between September and January and another 11.4 billion during the first half of 1920. While large amounts were required for the purchase of food and raw materials, it had become possible to maintain a reserve "which could be used for purchase and sales of foreign exchange in order to affect the

Table 15. Percentage of Unemployed and Short-time Union Workers, April 1920–December 1921

	Unemployed	Short Time
1920		
April	1.9	—
May	2.7	—
June	4.0	—
July	6.0	—
August	5.9	—
September	4.5	—
October	4.2	—
November	3.9	—
December	4.1	—
1921		
January	4.5	7.0
February	4.7	7.9
March	3.7	9.5
April	3.9	8.9
May	3.7	8.1
June	3.0	7.2
July	2.6	5.2
August	2.2	3.2
September	1.4	2.9
October	1.2	2.5
November	1.4	1.1
December	1.6	1.5

Source: Friedrich Hesse, *Die Deutsche Wirtschaftslage von 1914 bis 1923. Krieg, Geldblähe und Wechsellagen* (Jena, 1938), p. 480f.

exchange rate in a stabilizing manner. At least in this way one can hope to avoid strong shifts in the exchange rate." Hirsch went on to indicate that perhaps government funds could be used directly to influence the exchange rate to a still greater extent. As Hirsch himself recognized and as others pointed out, however, one could "affect the exchange rate in this manner to a limited extent, but the carrying through of a real stabilization in this way is out of the question."[25]

But "real stabilization" was not the agenda, and the problem, as Hirsch and his colleagues chose to define it, was how to prevent the improvement of the mark from turning into a total disaster for German exports. Their solution was the massive sale of marks for foreign exchange by the Reichsbank in coordination with the Foreign Exchange Procurement Board. As Havenstein later boasted, the exchange rate of the dollar "would have sunk even more if the Reichsbank had not jumped in with billions."[26] Hirsch also claimed credit for the achievement of bringing about a reduction in the value of the mark to a level at once favorable to exports and relatively stable for about a year: "I believe that I can claim that, if the initial stormy rise of the value of the mark gave way to a calmer development, then this was due to the very appropriate intervention of the Foreign Exchange Procurement Board, which at least managed to guide the unavoidable fall of the foreign currencies in a systematic manner, insofar as such things can be managed."[27] Hirsch boasted that they had been able to keep the mark at fifty to sixty marks to the dollar for almost five quarters and thus enable Germany to export profitably. Before these relative stabilization measures proved demonstrably beneficial in early September, however, Germany experienced a crisis during the summer and spring. This crisis was a very complicated one. It did not simply involve unemployment and unsatisfactory business conditions, although they were not comparable to what was being experienced in those countries that had chosen a deflationary path. The most dangerous aspects of the crisis centered about high consumer prices, and the full gravity of the situation in the summer of 1920 can only be comprehended if this wave of *Teuerung* is taken into account. It is the best point of entry into the domestic dilemmas of the relative stabilization.

The increased value of the mark and the decline in world prices accompanying the depression did, of course, have very substantial advantages for Germany from the standpoint of import prices. By early March, the price of foreign wheat had dropped from between 10,000 and 11,000 to 7,000 or 7,500 marks per ton. The Reich Wheat Corporation substantially increased its purchases abroad with the purpose of building a reserve as well as covering anticipated needs, a policy made possible by the reduced prices of imports. In June, its leadership stated that it intended "to remain continuously on the world market and purchase further in response to market opportunities and to exploit favorable conditions."[28]

This policy seemed to ensure that the supply would be sufficient, but it did not solve the problems of diminishing the dependence on foreign wheat, the need to subsidize imports, and the continued difficulty of increasing domestic production and deliveries. The situation on the domestic market was, in fact, worse than ever at the beginning of the relative stabilization. The President of the Reich Wheat Corporation, Dr. Kleiner, cheerlessly reported "that the Reich Wheat Corporation is in as critical a situation this year as never before." The daily domestic deliveries in June amounted to three thousand to four thousand tons as over against a six-thousand-ton requirement.[29] The political pressure to go after agricultural districts that were suspected of holding back their production was extreme, and "commando units" (*Stoßtruppen*) of twenty to thirty officials each were being sent on raids to such districts with some "positive psychological effects." Kleiner did not believe for a minute, however, that this would solve the problem:

The trade unions, the actual victors of the Kapp Putsch, have among other things demanded the relentless collection of all agrarian products under public control. In my view, however, it is utopian to think that a fundamental success in the realm of grain collection can be achieved through the *general* employment of force, especially military force.[30]

As usual, Stinnes pleaded for world market prices, but if this proposal remained politically unacceptable, his basic argument could scarcely be faulted: "Just as one cannot compel the miners to work, so one cannot compel the farmers to deliver. Our entire economy depends upon the increase of basic production, that is, the increase of coal production and agricultural production."[31]

The basic decisions to provide extra monetary incentives to the farmers and miners antedated the Kapp Putsch. In the case of the farmers, these took form on March 13, 1920, with the establishment of delivery premiums and guaranteed minimum prices. These were to be determined by an Index Commission for grains and other government controlled products. In the case of the miners, incentives took the form of special benefits provided by the overtime agreement signed at the end of February. Both policies were not simply continued but actually expanded after the March disturbances. The reestablishment of the Ministry for Food and Agriculture under Hermes, who was committed to the gradual decontrol of agriculture, encouraged incentives for agriculture. After the June elections, the policy of concentration on the encouragement of production became more open and pronounced. In a speech to the Reichstag in June, Hermes publicly supported food price increases in order to improve the supply. The Cabinet decided to decontrol potatoes on August 7.[32] Hermes viewed this policy as one of the "middle way," that is, "planned dismantling of the controlled economy as far as possible." While decontrol was "undesirable" for bread and wheat, Hermes emphasized that it was important "not to impose any regulations on agriculture that could not be carried out." He was convinced that "the price increases for wheat will have their good effects"[33] and blamed the insufficient meat supplies on the unsatisfactory prices offered producers. Consequently, he urged an increase in meat prices and further measures of decontrol in this sector. While this policy was pursued to the growing disapproval of the SPD and especially the USPD, it cannot be said that the Socialist parties offered any alternative other than the continuance of the old, unworkable system. Now out of power, they were in a position to take the "consumer point of view" and oppose policies which, in the case of the SPD, had actually been launched under their aegis.

Production incentives for the miners were made all the more necessary by the Allied demands for German coal deliveries at the Spa Conference in July, where Stinnes took the position that Germany should simply refuse Allied demands and run the risk of a Ruhr occupation. The trade-union leaders, fearful of what the workers would suffer in such an eventuality, sought to trade German concessions on coal deliveries for Allied financial assistance to feed the miners. Under the agreement reached on July 16, the Germans were to supply two million tons of high-quality coal per month for six months but were to receive a premium of five gold marks per ton to purchase extra food for the miners. This agreement was then used to maintain the extra-shift agreement to which the miners had pledged themselves in February, and this concession was further sweetened by the exclusion of the additional pay received from the detested withholding tax that had recently been introduced. Indeed, the government promised to push forward socialization and further irritated the employers by forcing them to take over the costs of a pay increase in May and then refusing to allow a price increase in August which even State Secretary Hirsch thought justified. This policy of granting wage increases while refusing price increases was repeated in October. The Labor Ministry, which had arbitrated the arrangement admitted that the mining industry "has reached the limits of its financial capacity."[34] Although the Spa Agreement was to have a negative effect on the domestic coal supply in the fall and winter, the government decided to concentrate its efforts on encouraging the miners without demonstrating similar consideration to the mine owners. The goal was to maintain industrial production and competitiveness through high coal production and low coal prices. Mine owners, after all, did not strike, had never been known to riot, and were terribly unpopular.

Preventing the Ruhr miners from getting out of control was very difficult even if the government was successful during this period, and it is important to bear in mind that, if the miners were "blackmailing" the nation at this time, the situation of these allegedly "elite" workers gave them every justification for dissatisfaction. An American investigator sent to explore the chances for the fulfillment of the Spa Agreement, found horrendous conditions, and his report is all the more impressive because of its conservative tone and its reliance upon both his direct observations and the information received from the Quaker mission in the Ruhr. In his view,

... the pith of the whole situation lies in the question of proper housing, clothing and feeding. When one sees miners working hundreds of meters under ground wedged in small shafts where the air is foul and full of dust and where the heat is such that men go stark naked, even without shoes, and still are dripping with perspiration, one can understand the importance of proper nourishment. All that the miner can take with him to eat during his seven hours of labor is a bread sandwich—formerly a slice of bacon, which is now not to be had. Miner after miner complained to me of the quality of the bread which some stated had been so bad at one time that they were laid up for several days with stomach trouble.[35]

Indeed, the quality of bread was a problem throughout Germany and was no small matter. When whole rye and wheat were not available, which was often for weeks at a time, bean flour was used as a substitute, and the bread used in the Ruhr in July 1920 was pronounced dangerous to health by an investigatory commission. The situation in Hamburg, the port of entry for much foreign wheat, was not much better, however. Complaints there were so loud that a meeting was held on the subject. It was determined that the foreign grain was "musty" by the time it arrived and the "potato flour available was absolutely unfit for use." The American Consul there seems to have ventured to taste the stuff and reported that "it would be a very difficult matter for anyone to state just what composed the ordinary bread sold on ration cards. Apart from the sour and mouldy taste, it contains some gritty substances that lead one to surmise it might be made of ground linoleum or saw dust."[36] Back in 1916, a major Hamburg baker had been prosecuted for making his bread out of ground straw, obviously an extreme case, but by 1920, the common folk in Hamburg and the miners in the Ruhr and Germans everywhere had been eating bread of low or abominable quality for at least five years.

For the miner with a family, however, the problems were compounded by the prices, which seemed to be unbearable despite all his special advantages:

While food of most kinds is to be had in stores and restaurants, prices are such that the miners cannot afford them, particularly those with families. Their daily meals consist principally of bread, potatoes and fresh vegetables with small rations of bacon and margarine. . . . Potatoes form the principal diet, as fresh vegetables are relatively expensive, but even the potatoes supply has been so short the past weeks that a miner with a family of wife and three children could obtain but ten pounds for the week.[37]

The housing shortage in the Ruhr district was estimated at a hundred sixty thousand while only four thousand new constructions were planned for the coming year. Insofar as clothing was concerned, the Quaker mission reported that "most children examined had no underclothes, and that many of the outer garments were made from piano covers, curtains, etc. From other sources was added that many families were without bed linen, and that many adults were going without underclothing as well as the children."[38] Both the Quakers and the American official observer were convinced that the "lack of energy" and interest shown by the undernourished children was also present in the undernourished miners and provided the main cause of the poor productivity, on the one hand, and the radical outbursts, on the other.

Whereas 1919 was the year in which the Revolution was transformed into a wage movement and in which the government and employers paid practically anything to keep the workers quiet, while the workers took advantage of the situation to "catch up" with the war profits of the employers, 1920 was the year in which the German workers confronted the tenuous character of their gains and were made conscious of their true impoverishment since 1914. This was now measured less in the unavailability of goods than in their unmanageable prices. This, argued Socialist trade unionists, and not ideology explained the susceptibility of urban workers to Communist propaganda:

Daily their standard of living goes down. And while they are not in a position to provide for their needs sufficiently, let alone to provide clothing or linens, a portion of the population wallows in the most extravagant luxury. When the worker goes through the streets with an empty stomach, in torn clothing, with shoes filled with holes, yes, often without underwear, then he sees on display in the shop windows the finest delicacies, articles of clothing, and linens in abundance. That has a much stronger effect than agitation. . . .[39]

Whatever the hardships and difficulties of employed skilled workers, these could not be compared with the problems faced by unskilled workers, the unemployed, the disabled, and widows. The impoverishment of such persons had now become frighteningly visible. For years they had put off replenishing their clothes, linens, and bedding. The shortage of bedding was a major source of deteriorating standards of cleanliness and of spreading disease, especially the flu, and a source of growing social problems as well. Many children simply were not going to school because they did not have suitable clothes or shoes. The furniture situation was not much better, a good deal of it having been progressively used over the years for fuel in winter so that a "pitiful emptiness takes the last vestige of livability from the accommodation."[40] When studies of household income and expenditure were undertaken for such persons in 1920, they revealed an intolerable gap between income and the most necessary expenditure, while never even troubling to explore how such "unnecessary" expenditures as transportation, clothes, shoes, and social insurance were being covered (see Table 16).[41]

If the unemployment relief payments in 1919 had been too high and a disincentive to work, this was no longer the case by 1920. The inadequacy of the relief was especially notable in the centers of high unemployment, Berlin, Hamburg, and Saxony. Thus, the American Consul in Saxony pointed out that "the individual receives insufficient to live as he formerly did but too much with which to die. Work must be found for them or the amount of money increased to do away with the discontent."[42] The level of desperation was particularly extreme in the Saxon Vogtland, whose embroidery industry blossomed before the war only to be virtually eliminated as a luxury industry and then to remain practically shut down afterward because of raw-materials shortages and poor market conditions. Not only the manual workers, but also the designers and white-collar workers found themselves destitute, while the employers were forced to sell their machines. In a pe-

tition for assistance at the beginning of September 1920, which was notable for its absence of class hatred and radicalism, the trade union secretary in Plauen pointed out that "the workers have sold their last piece of furniture and in their misery have even taken to selling their most necessary items, their beds."[43] He made special mention of the reports of the school doctors and midwives on the poor health of the population and noted that the unemployment relief was insufficient to "satisfy the most bare necessities." He then went on to warn that "this horrible misery finds its ultimate expression in madness and makes a social group ripe for anarchism." Only this could explain the recent disturbances and how as "faithful, industrious a people as the Vogtländer" could riot and turn to crime. His reference was to the rampage organized by Max Hoelz, the utopian head of the Communist unemployed in Falkenstein. The fear of another *Hoelziade* by this modern-day Robin Hood inspired trade unionists, employers, and the authorities to take preventive measures, but their appeal was not made until the damage had been done.[44]

Not all the petitions and protests of the unemployed were presented in so respectful a manner, and demonstrations of the unemployed in Hamburg and Saxony in the early summer often had a very alarming character reminiscent of the days of the Revolution. Thus, in Dresden at the end of July, the Saxon Labor Minister Heldt was forced to receive one delegation after another demanding that the Saxon government force Berlin to prolong unemployment relief beyond the twenty-six weeks allowed and also to increase the amounts granted. These demands found considerable support from the employed workers, who feared that the unemployed would seek work at any price and thus undermine the existing wage contracts. Demands were thus raised that the government force the employers to provide work. When Heldt objected and said that work was not created for forcing employers to hire people they did not need, he was told that "you Saxon ministers are nothing but an agency of Berlin. If you do not agree, then you will have the people at your throat; then you will see. The people will take care of things when they are angry enough. . . . We will not rot from hunger.

Table 16. Three Household Budgets for Disadvantaged Worker Families in Berlin, April-June 1920

The five-person family of a war disabled man who is fully employed in a gas works. His wife is only partially capable of working, and two of his three daughters are sick.

Income		Expenditures	
Wages	480	Rationed Food	475
War-Disabled Pension	35	Unrationed Food	225
		Rationed Fuel	40
		Soap	46
		Rent	30
Totals	515		816

The family of an unemployed worker whose wife is only partially capable of working and who has eight children.

Income		Expenditures	
Unemployment Support	442	Rationed Food	949
Pay for Cleaning of Rent-Free Living Quarters	5	Unrationed Food	500
Earnings of Daughter as an Apprentice	100	Soap	92
Totals	547		1,621

The family of an unemployed worker no longer entitled to unemployment support who has a wife and son.

Income		Expenditures	
Poor Relief	43	Rationed Food	380
Invalidity Pension	46	Unrationed Food	180
Earnings of Son as an Apprentice	130	Fuel	34
Earnings of Wife for Needlework	50	Soap	37
		Rent	29
Totals	269		660

Source: Merith Niehuss, "Lebensweise und Familie in der Inflationszeit," in Gerald D. Feldman et al., *The Adaptation to Inflation* (Berlin & New York, 1986), p. 249.

Before we die, we will first take along with us those who are responsible for these circumstances."[45]

The demonstrations and disturbances caused by the unemployed were by no means the most serious threats to public order in the summer of 1920. The most alarming development was the riots and plundering that spread throughout the country with the objective of forcing down prices, a movement whose spontaneity and scope, if not its character and consequences, were sufficiently impressive to rank it as a successor movement to the preceding wave of mass activism that had found expression in the creation of the councils in the fall of 1918 and the great strikes in the spring of 1919. That such mass behavior now took the form of "self-help" to bring down prices was highly significant as an illustration of the exhaustion of the political revolution and the intensified pre-

occupation with daily problems and cares. Obviously, Communist and other radical agitators had an interest in stirring things up and did their share to aggravate the outburst, but it would be useless to seek the source of the phenomenon in this quarter. Rather, it was to be found in an almost universal sense of impoverishment which cut across social classes and which expressed itself in the demand for an end to the *Teuerung*, the increased cost of living, and a *Preisabbau*, a reduction of prices. It demonstrated that, for the masses, inflation was not understood as an increase in the currency supply as a consequence of budget deficits but instead as soaring prices for insufficient goods.[46]

The intensity of this cry for price reduction was closely related to the specific situation of workers and employees in the spring and summer of 1920. The inflationary wave of the first part of the year had wiped out many of the real

Table 17. Indices of Retail Prices for Major Items of Household Expenditure, February 1920–June 1921

(in paper marks; 1913–1914 = 1)

	Food	Heat and Light	Clothing	Housing
1920				
February	9.48	5.01	17.99	1.67
March	11.01	7.08	18.56	1.71
April	12.29	8.79	18.58	1.75
May	13.22	8.83	19.25	1.76
June	12.80	9.20	19.25	1.78
July	12.52	9.38	19.07	1.79
August	11.70	9.68	19.04	1.83
September	11.66	9.46	18.83	1.84
October	12.60	9.71	18.87	1.87
November	13.43	9.74	18.89	1.88
December	14.27	8.86	18.77	1.91
1921				
January	14.23	11.75	18.85	1.95
February	13.62	11.96	18.85	1.98
March	13.52	12.15	18.51	1.98
April	13.34	12.67	18.07	2.03
May	13.20	12.81	18.07	2.03
June	13.70	12.81	19.38	2.09

Source: Statistisches Reichsamt, *Zahlen zur Geldentwertung in Deutschland 1914 bis 1923* [Sonderheft 1 zu *Wirtschaft und Statistik,* Bd. 5] (Berlin, 1925), p. 33.

wage gains of the 1919 wage movement, so that the real wages in the first months of 1920 had dropped to the levels of 1917.[47] The improvement of the mark in the early spring had led to a deterioration of business conditions and rising unemployment through the summer, a situation that was not favorable to wage movements. Prices, however, had risen sharply in the first months of 1920 and remained sticky. When the government began publishing its cost-of-living indices in February 1920, which were meant to serve as a guide for wage negotiations, they demonstrated the extent to which the cost of living had increased since 1913–1914 and the high levels of retail prices (see Tables 13, on p. 216, and 17). From the standpoint of the social situation, domestic retail prices certainly overshadowed such more positive signs as the improvement of the exchange rate, the decreasing cost of food imports, and the tendency for wholesale prices to stabilize. The extent to which Germans at this stage were paying attention to the new cost-of-living index or to the variety of unofficial indices being published by experts in professional journals and by others in newspapers is difficult to determine, but there certainly must have been a general awareness of how much prices had increased since

1914 as well as of the deterioration of the quality of life. It had now been six years since the war had begun, and people were sick and tired of what appeared to be endless price increases. Since the process of decontrolling administered prices or of increasing the prices of administered products was also under way, the inevitable price increases accompanying these measures also influenced the situation.

The most immediate and obvious source of aggravation seems to have been the high prices being asked for fruits and vegetables at stores and markets. Meat prices were so high, however, that cases were known in which butchers simply gave the meat away to municipal authorities for distribution among the needy since normal persons could not afford to buy meat.[48] As bad luck would have it, the withholding tax from wages and salaries was introduced in the summer of 1920, thus reducing the take-home pay of the workers and leading to worker protests and resistance. At the Bismarckhütte in Upper Silesia, for example, twenty thousand workers protested on June 25 and sent an appeal to President Ebert calling for an end to the 10 percent withholding tax along with a reduction of the prices for food, clothing, and other necessities, "so that we can have orderly economic conditions."[49] In Württemberg, especially in the Stuttgart area, the tension over tax withholding was particularly intense. The Württemberg government, after attempting to conciliate the workers, decided to close down the Bosch works and surround it with barbed wire, machine guns, and police. The workers, who were to be locked out until they agreed to accept the withholding system, sought to spread the movement and succeeded in instigating a general strike in Stuttgart and other localities. The workers were finally brought to heel, but they were particularly embittered by the fact that "the far-reaching taxes on capital and property passed by the National Assembly have not yet been brought into practice" so that "the 10 percent wage tax was . . . the first of the new regular taxes to be levied, producing the impression among the working classes that they were being unfairly treated."[50] In the Rhineland, the Bayer Chemical works in Leverkusen were forced to shut down, and there were strikes and demonstrations throughout the Ruhr. The employers, fearful that they would ultimately be forced to pay the tax in the form of higher wages—which did turn out to be the involuntary solution in some cases—and resentful that they were compelled to bear the brunt of protests over a law imposed as much upon them as the workers, called on the government for protection and for an easing of the regulations. The government provided both, and while insisting that the withholding system had to be maintained, it made some concessions with respect to very low incomes, limited the withholding on higher incomes to 10 percent, and exempted overtime pay in the mines. The government's task was made easier by the fact that the strikes were wild and that the trade unions refused to support the workers on this question.

The situation was much more difficult, however, when it came to the more primitive and spontaneous reactions of the masses to high prices and inadequate purchasing power. This is well illustrated by Hamburg, where serious disturbances broke out at the end of June. The problems of high unemployment and high prices combined to produce a particularly volatile situation. Disturbances had already taken place elsewhere in Germany, and the vendors of fruits and vegetables hoped to ward off difficul-

ties by "voluntarily" reducing their prices as much as 50 percent. Although the initial violence was triggered by a demonstration of the Hamburg and Altona unemployed, the more riotous activities truly got under way when a crowd gathered at the market where pushcart vendors sold their produce. The latter sought to calm things down by reducing their prices, but they soon found their carts overturned and their wares trampled. The crowd then turned to plundering shoe and clothing stores, and the violence rapidly spread to every section of the city. The police were not able to deal with the situation, and troops had to be called in. Indeed, before things had quieted down, lives had been lost.

The centrality of the price question was particularly evident in the deliberate effort on the part of some of the plunderers to give their actions a semilegal character:

In many instances the plunderers endeavored to cover their actions with a peculiar sort of legality by taking what they wanted and paying whatever price therefore that came to their minds. Bread was taken, for example, that was marked 5 or 6 marks per loaf and 2 marks left in its place; shoes marked 200 to 300 marks per pair were taken for 15 to 30 marks; fruits and vegetables that had been selling at 4 to 5 marks per pound were taken straight through at 1 mark per pound. . . .[51]

Much of the behavior, however, was nothing more than wanton plundering and destruction, many of the goods simply being stolen and nearly every store window in sight being broken. The introduction of martial law and the use of rifles and hand grenades finally put an end to the violence in Hamburg, but the troubles rapidly spread to Bremen, where storekeepers were forced to sell their goods for one-third to one-quarter of their price and where some plunderers also left only as much money as they thought proper.

The feeling that prices were not only too high but also unjustifiably high was widely shared and by no means without foundation, as was demonstrated by the complaints of the Saxon Economics Minister to Hermes at the end of July. He pointed out that the disturbances in Dresden, which had shut down the city food office and had finally compelled very expensive and undesirable concessions on the part of the city government to restore order, and similar events in other cities were the result not only of the sheer inability of the local population, often hard hit by unemployment, to buy at the stores. These consumers knew that the farmers were often selling meat and other products in the countryside for much lower prices and were themselves admitting that the meat and potato prices granted by the government were too high. In short, the farmers were taking these official prices into account when selling to wholesalers and retailers, but were quite prepared to sell more cheaply when given the opportunity to sell directly to consumers.[52]

This, in fact, was also one of the complaints of the chief victims of the wave of plundering that spread across Germany in the summer of 1920, the retailers, who angrily criticized not only the farmers but also wholesalers and producers of manufactured goods. Not atypical was the protest to the government of Oldenburg by the merchants of Rodenkirchen, who had decided to lower their prices rather than have a riot: "Our so-called 'voluntary action' was forced; it is an assault on those doing business here, the majority of whom gave in because the Social Democrats declared that the Communists in Nordenham were just waiting to come to Rodenkirchen to put things in order. It is an absurdity to blame the retailers for increasing prices. The root of the evil lies with the producers. . . ."[53]

The retailers of Delmenhorst were much less fortunate than their brethren in Rodenkirchen, however, since they apparently were not given the opportunity to take the initiative and lower prices. Instead, a mob of hundreds plundered and destroyed their shops in a riot that left one person dead and many wounded. Naturally, the retailers called for more police protection and pressed for an improvement in the government compensation they received under the Riot Damage Decree (*Tumultschadenverordnung*). They were especially incensed over the rather rubbery provision that compensation be given only to the extent that the continued economic existence of the victim actually was threatened by the damage after taking his entire economic situation into account.[54] Most aggravating to retailers here and elsewhere, however, was that the plunderings, as apparently was the case in

Bremen, were tolerated by the police and that some authorities, as in the Bavarian city of Aschaffenburg, organized and directed forcible price reductions. The Socialist Mayor of Aschaffenburg, who was also head of the Aschaffenburg Price Examination Agency, set up a price reduction commission in which retailers were a minority and which proceeded to impose 10 to 30 percent reductions.[55] Manifestly, some of the traditional labor leadership was seeking to prevent the worst by taking control of the movement and accomplishing its purposes in an "orderly" manner, just as they had assumed the leadership of spontaneous wartime and postwar strikes, but the retailers could hardly be expected to find this acceptable. As the Berlin department store owner Oscar Tietz pointed out on behalf of himself and his fellow merchants, they objected strongly to "a kind of shadow government being set up by the workers and the government while the government provides the defenseless retailers with no protection."[56]

As always, and not without justification, the retailers complained that they were the last link in the chain between producer and consumer and that it was they who paid the penalty for prices determined by others. Typical arguments were used by the speakers at a meeting of the local retailers in the Düsseldorf Chamber of Commerce in May, pointing out that producer associations were always raising prices, often to cover the costs of wage increases they had conceded to the workers, while the retailers were compelled either to foot the bill or to pass it on to the consumer with all the legal and physical risks this entailed: "We have often pointed out here, how the legislation in the Reich, the states, and the municipalities only knows how to prescribe a thousand regulations for the retailer, while leaving the manufacturer untouched. The outrageous conditions on the leather market, where huge dividends are being paid out while the little man on the street cannot afford shoes, are only too clear for all to see."[57]

A more statesmanlike posture was taken by the Duisberg retailers, who pointed out in a memorandum on food prices between July and October 1920 that the prices were a reflection of Germany's miserable economic condition, that the retail prices were necessarily limited by the competition among retailers, and that the exposed position of the retailers should not be used to turn them into scapegoats for more general conditions of shortage and impoverishment. Not without reason and not without insight, the authors deplored what was being done to German society as a consequence of the situation:

Since the German people have been severely affected in their material and moral strength through war and revolution, and since insufficient production has led to chronic shortage of food and consumer goods for a nation of 60 millions, one observes how entire portions of the nation grind against one another in mutual suspicion and insult, how especially the so-called consumers—to whom everyone belongs as soon as he acts as a consumer—make responsible now this and now the other economic group for all the damage and includes them in the charges of price gouging and profiteering.[58]

The only solution, in the view of the authors, was a restoration of the sense that all factors of production and distribution were interdependent and a concentrated effort to deal with the situation cooperatively rather than in mutual hostility and recrimination.

The bitter truth was that it was too late for *Gemeinschaft*. The dilemma for those in authority was how to deal effectively with the various elements of the crisis of the summer of 1920 while pursuing such broader goals as raising productivity, promoting reconstruction, and reducing government expenditure instead of simply surrendering to the demands of crisis management in the style of 1918–1919. The accounts that reached Berlin showed how difficult a task this was. Not atypical was a report by an official from Hanau, an industrial city near Frankfurt am Main, where some effort was being made to achieve the goals of common action espoused by the Duisberg retailers. The official in question had summoned a meeting of the various social groups and classes to discuss the situation. It was promptly branded a "theatre comedy" by the Communist-controlled local trade-union leadership. A commission representing agriculture, retailers, and craftsmen was set up which at once pledged to do its share to lower prices but strongly urged that the government lower potato prices and insisted that "the reduction of prices must begin with the prices of the industrial syndicates and the large wholesale organizations whose egotistic

price policy has made a reduction of prices by the merchants impossible despite a significantly more favorable market situation." They complained particularly about the high potash prices, which hurt agriculture, but also about the iron, wool, and textile prices. The Hanau official strongly supported the resolution of the commission, stressing how "extremely serious" the situation was:

Specifically, there is strong unrest in the metal industry, which has already led to scenes similar to those which have played themselves out in the Höchst Dye Works and the Kleyer firm in Frankfurt. Violence has only been avoided because the directors gave way to force and agreed unconditionally to a 10 percent wage increase to cover the tax withholding, a contribution of 30 to 50 percent of wages lost through short time and other demands. There is increasing unrest in other branches . . . , especially among the unemployed, whose number is continually growing.[59]

Policymaking in the Relative Stabilization

From the vantage point of Berlin, conditions such as those described in Hanau and the entire situation of the summer of 1920 were a severe setback, at once undermining government efforts to concentrate on longer-range problems and increasing those pressures which so often forced it to exacerbate its more fundamental difficulties in order to deal with its momentary dangers. The unrest created by price increases simply could not be brushed aside, although it was hard to tell whether, as in all aspects of the controlled economy, the laws themselves were making things worse or whether the correction of extremely difficult conditions through gradual decontrol and price incentives simply had to extract its ugly social and political price. Manifestly, the RWM could not and would not defend price reductions by violence and threats of violence, but it was committed to a policy of price stabilization by legal measures when justified and necessary. Its goal, however, was to promote stable prices by sound economic policy that would obviate the need for police methods.

Fundamentally, the RWM's policies were a counterpart of the gradual decontrol policies of the Food and Agricultural Ministry. The policy of partial decontrol and gradual dismantling of the remaining controls had its parallels in the realm of price-examination and antiprofiteering efforts. The economic free-for-all accompanying the rapid inflation in the fall and winter of 1919–1920 had reached the point where attempts to implement price regulations had proven at best absurd and at worst downright unjust. This was openly confessed by one of the leading officials of the RWM, Dr. Stern:

The most serious fault of the entire system seems to me to be that the difficulties involved in the examination of prices make control practically impossible and that this is already clearly understood by those engaged in business, and they take advantage of it accordingly. At this moment [April 1920], the entire price policy threatens to become an empty phrase, and we risk making ourselves laughable and accustoming those engaged in economic life to treat the laws as if they did not exist. In short, we are in the process of sawing off the branch upon which an economic policy must rest.[60]

One solution to the problem, cheerfully and ceaselessly advocated in commercial circles and by many important industrialists and experts, was to make a full return to a free economy, thereby eliminating the unenforceable regulations, the lengthy and expensive meetings of the price-examination-agency officials Dr. Stern was addressing, and the huge apparatus of officials and mass of paperwork involved in the controlled economy. Dr. Stern admitted that this was an option and that there was much to be said for it. It would not only simplify both the government and its tasks but also do away with the black market and the activities of all the parasites who were making a living by violating the various regulations. Goods would "come out of hiding," thus reducing the shortages, and open competition would terminate the host of unhealthy and inefficient economic enterprises whose lack of viability was veiled by the existing circumstances. Exports, although reduced, would no longer take place at the expense of the nation's substance through dumping practices. The attainment of world-market prices within Germany would compel the reduction of production costs, while the adjustment of wages and salaries and pensions to world-market prices could be mediated through a sliding-scale system permitting adjustment during the initial phases. Stern thus

had no trouble enumerating all the advantages of a return to the free market.

Nevertheless, it was not an option that the government or the Economics Ministry chose to take because they believed the disadvantages outweighed the advantages. A sudden conversion to the free market, in the RWM's view, would lead to a period of extreme volatility of supplies and prices and, instead of rationalizing the economy, would produce instability and create adjustment requirements for which some of the more technically advanced sectors of the economy were not ready but to which some of the less advanced and ultimately unviable enterprises might, in the short run, adjust more easily. The stability desirable for the strengthening of individual enterprises and the rationalization of industries in preparation for a future and more timely adjustment to world-market conditions would be undermined. At the moment, in the RWM view, German industry was not ready to enter into long-term, full-scale competition on world markets on even terms. Finally, the process of adjusting wages in the course of converting to a free economy would lead to labor struggles, since there would always be a lag between wages and prices, and while such conflicts might be welcome under conditions where productivity might be improved, this would not be the case where the health of German industry and German society was too poor to weather such conflicts. From all of this, Stern concluded that complete economic decontrol of prices was an unwise policy and that the fundamental goal of the government had to be the promotion of a reasonable measure of domestic price stability and a controlled and disciplined response to market conditions. For this reason, the Ministry welcomed the formation of trade associations and other forms of "crystallization."[61]

Manifestly, this was a policy which addressed itself to the symptoms rather than the causes of inflation and ran parallel to the interventions on the international money markets to induce exchange rate stabilization. This was because the malfunctioning of the economy was considered the primary disease and the inflation only a symptom. The relative stabilization was seen to provide an opportunity to promote economic recuperation under controlled conditions. This meant allowing the patient, the economy, to recover his strength, but not to leave him alone to exert himself unwisely or unnecessarily. As in agriculture, a very important change was taking place in government price policy that more or less recognized the futility of much of the previous effort to control domestic prices and that now gave primacy to economic and productive rather than social and moral considerations. As Stern explicitly declared:

The first goal of price policy accordingly is to so influence the formation of prices that it causes as little disturbance to the circulation of goods as possible. . . . Only secondarily is price policy a means to enact economic justice, a means of evening the distribution of the burdens and losses arising from the distress of the German people; and only thirdly is it a means of increasing personal ability to work and incentive to work by making life easier.[62]

At a series of meetings of the national and state authorities charged with price examination held in Würzburg and Giessen in April–May 1920, an attempt was made to draw up new guidelines in accordance with the new policy of giving primacy to economic considerations and of trying to induce price stability. The authorities now sought to identify three types of prices: prices determined by organizations of producers (*Verbandspreise*), wholesale prices determined by the market, and retail prices determined by the producer-association prices or the market prices to which would be added the percentage allowed the retailer to cover costs, risk, and profit. The trade-association or cartel prices were to be based on average member costs plus the traditional allowances for risk and profit and were to be communicated to the authorities who would then use them as a basis for defining the prices for those products. Where a normal market situation was determined to exist—that is, where supply and demand were functioning—the going prices were to be elicited through the commodity exchanges or other acceptable sources and viewed as the prices to be charged. Finally, the price examination agencies were to determine the additional charges allowed to retailers on the basis of the same principles used in determining the

suitability of trade-association prices; that is, some sort of average of cost, risk, and profit calculations.[63]

All this appeared very sensible, but there was a real question as to whether the so-called Giessen guidelines had any relation to the laws as written, their purposes, or the capabilities of the authorities. To begin with, the decrees really dealt with profits—a highly variable concept that ultimately could be judged only in individual cases—rather than prices. The objective of the RWM, however, was to stabilize prices and evaluate the suitability of prices rather than to preserve this or that businessman from bankruptcy.[64] On one level, therefore, the RWM was ceasing to question individual price and profit calculations insofar as they were not egregiously self-serving, while on another level, at least by implication, declaring that prices, however justifiable from the perspective of those making them, could be declared inappropriate if they were felt to be damaging to national economic interests. When it came to the determination of what was in the general economic interest, however, the only criteria seemed to be orderliness and stability as guaranteed either by organized economic groups or the operation of supply and demand on the market. While the government could and did, by law, interfere in the pricing operations of certain industrial associations—for example, coal, iron and steel, and potash—it had no such powers with respect to the host of other cartels and trade associations whose proliferation it was encouraging in the name of economic rationality and stability. Under existing legislation, accepting trade-association and cartel prices as the measures of acceptable and stable prices meant quite literally accepting the price dictation of organized industrial groups. Thus, immense discretionary power was being given to the cartels and trade associations, except insofar as the government had special regulatory powers.

Insofar as market prices were concerned, there were many precedents for declaring an emergency market condition, which is precisely what the courts had been doing for years so that retailers were at once told that they could charge a market price and then denied the right to do so because virtually every market situation could be defined as an emergency market situation under the miserable circumstances pertaining in wartime and postwar Germany. The RWM officials were convinced that the failure of the courts to accept market conditions as a basis for settling cases was often illegitimate from an economic point of view and helped to undermine efforts to maintain stable prices on a realistic foundation. In this context, they agreed with the retailers' complaints and did not think it reasonable for the courts, unschooled in economic matters, to impose social sacrifices on individuals for no sound economic reason. At the same time, however, some court decisions in early 1920 showed that the jurists were beginning to realize that normal market conditions were being restored and could thus be educated to accept market conditions as a basis for prices. This pleased the RWM officials immensely because, despite much discussion of the desirability of codifying existing antiprofiteering legislation and getting a new and more suitable law passed by the Reichstag, the RWM was extremely reluctant to make a legislative effort since the issue could not be discussed without an ugly battle between right and left. Furthermore, the feasibility of such an effort would be influenced by changes in the political constellation of the government. In short, political considerations meant that antiprofiteering legislation could neither be abrogated nor suitably reformed.[65]

The objective of the Ministry, after all, was to mediate as peaceful and untroubled a transition to free-market conditions as possible and in such a way as to encourage production. Insofar as high prices were a natural result of the gap between supply and demand, the best way to keep them steady was through collaboration with the organized sectors of the economy. The problem in the summer of 1920, however, was that these prices were often the product of the chaotic economic conditions of the previous winter and the bad habits that had developed over a considerable number of years. As an official from Württemberg pointed out:

About three quarters of a year ago the industrial groups, that is the associations, gave in to all wage demands in the expectation that they could self-understandably charge these increased costs in their prices. That produced a general increase in prices which was

perhaps even greater than the increase of agricultural prices. . . . The problem of profiteering is no longer the chief question, but rather how we are to come out of the distressing situation of overpriced goods. Our trade association prices are by and large the prices of 500 or more syndicates. They have determined the prices, but before the war they did not determine them according to an anti-profiteering system but rather on one based on the so-called optimum allowed by the relationship between supply and demand. . . . We are now in the situation not of a buyers' strike but rather of purchaser powerlessness because the population is not in a position anymore to bear the planless price increases that have taken place.[66]

No one believed that it was possible to oversee all these prices, but there was an increasing demand that they be monitored in some way. If one could not command producer price reductions in most industries, however, then one could at least let the "natural forces" of the market do their work, and, in this context, Hirsch viewed the summer crisis of 1920 as a "cleansing process" whose salutary consequences were not to be interrupted by misguided relief. Minister Scholz agreed:

I believe that the crisis is to a large degree caused by the fact that the German manufacturer has forgotten how to calculate, that he, incited by the possibilities of high profit through export abroad, has permitted himself to pay any price asked for raw materials and intermediate products, and that he could also afford to do this until the change in the exchange rate. Now, we have to reconstruct from the back to the front. On the one side, one has the merchants, and on the other side, one has the purchasers. Every interference in this cleansing process is a disturbance, a taking of sides in the conflict between merchant and purchaser.[67]

In the last analysis, therefore, antiprofiteering activity and price examination were to remain largely concerned with the prices of food and basic consumer items, and while vigorous efforts were made to prevent retailer profiteering, especially in Saxony and Bavaria, the official policy was, in fact, to pay more heed to legitimate retailer complaints and to allow them to take risk and monetary depreciation into account. Retailers themselves recognized that "the price examination agencies cannot be denied a certain right to exist under present conditions simply for political reasons,"[68] and they welcomed the Giessen guidelines insofar as these sought to reduce the legal uncertainty to which retailers had been subjected, to expressly recognize the market situation as a factor in the formation of prices, to permit daily price changes to be taken into account, to allow expert testimony before charging someone under the regulations, and to show great caution in the imposition of penalties, especially prison sentences. How much consolation the friendlier posture of the RWM toward the retailers provided while they were repairing their windows and assessing the damages of the summer of 1920 is, of course, difficult to say.

Obviously, the unrest throughout the country made the formulation and implementation of policy difficult. The same was true of policy coordination, inevitably a problem under the best of circumstances and even when there is basic agreement about aims and goals. In the face of the socioeconomic and political pressures of this period, however, the tendency to see things less broadly and to view everything from the standpoint of the individual Ministry—the notorious *Ressortstandpunkt*—was necessarily intensified. This created a measure of tension between the Labor Ministry and the Economics Ministry and a good deal more tension between both those Ministries and the Finance Ministry.

From the very beginning, Labor Minister Brauns took the position that the sources of the crisis were economic and that the chief responsibility for the ultimate improvement of the situation rested with the Economics Ministry. He considered it essential, however, that the public—above all, the workers—be given the sense that the two Ministries were working together to improve the employment situation, ameliorate hardships, prevent employers from using the crisis to fire workers or needlessly shut down their plants, and, above all, keep the lid on prices. This effort, at once to pay full respect to the prerogatives of the RWM and to commit the RWM to the social perspective of the Labor Ministry, took the form of a memorandum to the RWM on June 25 proposing close cooperating in dealing with labor-market, wage, and price problems and suggesting that this intention be communicated to the various Ministries and state governments as rapidly as possible.[69] Hirsch, however, saw no real necessity for setting things down in a general circular, and it was

not until August 15 that he so informed the RAM. While concurring with the view that coordination and cooperation were essential, he took the opportunity to put a different emphasis on the questions raised by the RAM. This was especially the case with reference to the closing of plants because of insufficient business or inadequate coal supplies. Whereas the RAM had stressed the importance of preventing plant shut downs, Hirsch pointed out that "it is essential for the carrying out of my economic policy that only economically important industrial branches be supported." Similarly, in matters of wage policy, he argued that "economic principles must be placed more in the foreground."[70]

The RAM was by no means unmoved by this last argument. At a meeting of officials from the various Ministries on July 7, the RAM representative agreed completely with his RWM colleague on the need to prevent the unrest over prices from being transformed into another large wage movement that would drive prices up even more and went so far as to declare "that the Reich Labor Ministry, in the conviction that the intrinsic value of the labor being performed is not the equivalent of the wages being paid today, is also striving for a reduction of wages."[71] Unhappily, in his view, these efforts were being undermined. The reasons he gave suggested that the policies of his colleagues in other Ministries were responsible. Thus, he attacked high food prices in an implicit criticism of the Food Ministry price incentives to agriculture. Labor Minister Brauns was, in fact, a strong opponent of the minimum-price policy that had been introduced earlier in the year and viewed it as a source of the price increases that were irritating the workers. The RAM, however, was also unhappy with the Economics Ministry and the Finance Ministry for their support of coal price increases. While the RWM was willing to permit coal price increases to promote greater employer investment in the mines and worker housing, and the Finance Ministry wished to reduce the subsidies it had been paying for the feeding of the miners by making the consumers pay the costs, Brauns took the view that coal price increases inevitably raised all prices and should therefore be avoided. If Brauns was in conflict with the RFM over this issue, however, he allied himself with Wirth in criticism of the Transport Ministry for what he viewed as the excessively high wages paid to the railroad workers, which were used by the workers in private industry to justify their wage demands. Under these circumstances, the RAM, like the trade-union leaders, found itself in the hapless situation of trying to contain wage demands:

The trade union leaders are completely clear about the serious dangers which the continuous wage increases signify for our economy, but they also cannot go against their followers and run the risk of having them go into the radical camp. The Reich Labor Ministry, therefore, shares the concerns of the Reich Economics Ministry fully, but must point out that every increase in the price of coal and bread as well as every coal wage increase in the state plants brings its efforts to nought.[72]

A particularly important illustration of the manner in which the crisis of 1920 at once undermined efforts to solve basic problems while promoting inadequate solutions to immediate difficulties is unemployment relief. Since the winter of 1919, the governments ruling Germany had worked assiduously to reduce the amount of unemployment relief, prevent its abuse, provide productive unemployment relief on public-works projects and in the private sector, and replace the entire unemployment relief system with an unemployment insurance system. When it came to tightening the screws on unemployment relief, the government could boast considerable success. Maximum scales established in April 1919 were not raised until May 1920 despite a doubling of wages and a great increase in the cost of living during this period, although a winter supplement had been granted in October 1919 and certain modifications were made in January 1920. The maximum benefit for a single male over twenty-one rose from three and a half to six marks in February 1920, to five to eight marks in May, and to seven to ten marks in November, at which level it remained until August 1921. The maximum unemployment benefit a Berlin family of four could receive in June 1920 was ninety marks, although the minimum cost of subsistence was three hundred four marks.[73]

The Reich government had also worked to prevent local authorities from exceeding the maximum rates. A decree of October 10, 1919, ordered the withdrawal of all Reich unemployment relief funds from municipal authorities exceeding the maximum scales. It was less rigorous in preventing municipalities from raising the official local wage scales used for purposes of determining social insurance rates in various parts of the country, but since these were well below the wage scales actually paid and could not be used to justify exceeding the inadequate minima for unemployment relief established by the government, there was no genuine "laxity" here either.[74]

The rigor with which the Finance Ministry watched over unemployment support expenditures is well demonstrated by its protest against a Labor Ministry telegram to the various state governments of May 29, 1920, inquiring about the desirability of special grants to assist the long-term unemployed. The Finance Ministry effectively blocked such proposals. The only concession the government would make in recognition of the consequences of rising prices for the unemployment relief system occurred in August 1920, when the percentage of lost pay required to qualify for relief by short-time workers was reduced from 70 to 60 percent.[75]

The Finance Ministry not only battled with considerable success against tendencies to raise the relief scales but also stoutly resisted efforts on the part of the states hardest hit by unemployment to promote a redistribution of the burdens imposed by the unemployment problem. Under the various decrees issued to deal with unemployment in 1919, the Reich paid half the costs of unemployment relief while the states and municipalities paid one-third and one-sixth respectively. Especially poor municipalities could petition for additional grants from the Reich, but no provision was made for giving special assistance to those states such as Saxony and Hamburg which had extraordinarily heavy unemployment. Indeed, Saxony, Hamburg, and Berlin had three-quarters of the unemployed. Not surprisingly, Saxony took the lead in seeking to correct the distribution of federal unemployment relief. Initially, Saxony, with the support of most of the other major states, argued that the Reich should take over the full burden of unemployment relief once it had also appropriated the chief source of state revenue, the income tax, when the Erzberger reform went into effect on April 1, 1920. The Finance Ministry, however, unequivocally rejected any increase of the Reich contributions to unemployment relief, let alone the assumption of complete financial responsibility. While the Saxon Reichsrat Delegate used the occasion to point out what a "capital mistake" it was to render the states so powerless through the tax reform, he confidentially confessed to Dresden that he had no idea how the Reich was supposed to provide the huge sums needed "except through the printing press."[76] At the same time that the Reich Finance Ministry was refusing to consider any increase of its contributions, particularly when it was nationalizing the railroads and thus assuming state financial obligations in this area, the Reich Labor Ministry turned down all proposals for a reduction of benefits or changing of regulations that came from the states on the grounds that it was hoping to have a new unemployment insurance law passed within a year and, therefore, that it was pointless and impolitic to tinker with the existing arrangements.[77]

Temporary or not, however, these arrangements became ever more unacceptable to the hardest-hit states as the unemployment crisis of the summer developed and then continued in milder form in the fall as a result of coal shortages. Since the Reich refused to grant any relief, the high-unemployment states now sought a solution at the expense of those states suffering from less unemployment, Baden and Mecklenburg for example, and argued, not without justification, that unemployment was a national problem and that some form of equalization of burdens among the states was necessary. It did, after all, seem unfair that, in May 1920, Saxony, with 7.78 percent of Germany's population, should bear 25.83 percent of the unemployment relief expenses paid by the states or that Hamburg, with 1.79 percent of the population, should pay 45.09 percent of the state contributions, while the Mecklenburgs, with 1.28 percent of the population, should provide only .43 percent of the total state unemployment relief contributions. The Saxon government argued that Prussia and the Mecklenburgs, with their profitable agrarian areas,

which were unaffected by the unemployment, were far richer than Saxony and should have a higher share of the burden. It considered it inequitable "that the Saxon state should take over the costs of the political relief of the entire Reich by more than a quarter and thereby fall prey to financial disorder for the benefit of the other states and the Reich."[78]

In July, Hamburg proposed that the costs of unemployment relief be distributed according to population, a plan which Saxony also supported because, among other things, it would not increase the burdens of neighboring Bavaria, whose population and unemployment percentages were just about in line. Apparently, they also had some hope that the Prussians would accept the plan for political reasons, especially since the Reich Labor and Finance Ministries agreed that the existing system was unfair and were prepared to support any arrangement that did not increase the burdens of the Reich itself. The Prussians, however, while "platonically recognizing" that Saxony was bearing an unfair share of the costs, cried poverty and argued that every state must bear the burdens "which fate had placed upon it."[79] By this time, it was late October, and the negotiations had been dragging on since May without any progress whatever having been made in the redistribution of the unemployment relief burdens of the states.

In fact, it was to take seven more months of haggling to produce a modest agreement in May 1921 which was not implemented until November 1921. Efforts by Braunschweig to increase the Reich share of the costs met with the usual rejection, and a proposal by Hamburg in December 1920 that one-twelfth of the total Reich contribution to the unemployment relief be put into a fund to be distributed to the most burdened states while the Reich provided an additional one-twelfth received the support of the RAM and Saxony but was opposed by the majority of the states and, of course, the Finance Ministry. Bavaria, which had supported this proposal, finally came up with a proposal of its own that found acceptance. The Reich was to cease its special assistance to needy municipalities and give the money to the overburdened state governments instead. The latter would, in turn, determine which municipalities were most needy. While this arrangement had the advantage of simplifying the process of determining which municipalities were most desperate by placing the decision with the allegedly more knowledgeable state governments, it alarmed the municipalities because they feared being short changed by the states, which were calling for more help themselves. Also, it did not entirely please the Saxons, who saw little advantage to the plan unless the actual sums available for such purposes were substantially increased. Nevertheless, the solution was finally implemented in a decree of November 1, 1921, the delay possibly the consequence of the abatement of unemployment as well as the political crisis over reparations in the spring of that year and the governmental changes which followed.[80]

Action was finally taken, probably because no one could foresee any longer when the long-planned unemployment insurance system would be introduced. A Labor Ministry bill had actually gone through the Cabinet in mid-1920, only subsequently to be subjected to fatal criticism by the Finance Ministry. The RFM thought the bill inadequate from the standpoint of easing the financial costs of the existing relief system, and the RAM, after some initial resistance, decided to withdraw its bill in November 1920 and deal with the entire problem in a new memorandum which was circulated in February 1921 and was based on the proposition that economic conditions were too uncertain to establish a new unemployment system immediately. Instead, it proposed a temporary unemployment insurance scheme which would use the existing system of unemployment relief as a mechanism of transition by having the employers and workers contribute to the unemployment relief along with the public authorities and by having the system administered through the sickness insurance funds. The public authorities were to pay one-third, one-sixth of which would come from the Reich, one-ninth from the states, and one-eighteenth from the municipalities. Even this, however, was too much for the RFM, which approved the basic tendencies expressed in the memorandum but argued that the public authorities should provide no contribution whatever and that the entire burden should be carried by the employers and workers. The road to an unemployment insurance system thus remained very unclearly charted, and such a system was not to be created until 1927![81]

A fundamental purpose of unemployment insurance, of course, is to reduce the stigma of the dole from unemployment relief by basing support on regular contributions from those directly involved. Yet another path to this end, and indeed a much more satisfactory one, is the provision of work to the unemployed through public works, be they directly contracted by the public authorities or subsidized. As has been shown, various efforts were made to provide and even force work on the unemployed through emergency public-works projects during the demobilization, while ideas were also developed, especially by Moellendorff, for the regular control of unemployment by pump priming through a Reich Fund during business downswings.

With the steady reduction of unemployment relief scales, the problem of forcing the unemployed to work became a secondary issue, although there was some discussion in 1919–1920 of compulsory labor service for young people as a means of promoting reconstruction and reducing unemployment. The interest in finding an economically and psychologically sound substitute for unemployment relief remained, however, and led to provisions for "productive unemployment relief" in decrees of October 1919 and January 1920. In contrast to the support of public works projects, which took the form of financial assistance to cover additional expenses involved in providing work to the unemployed, the new program empowered the RAM, with the approval of the Finance Ministry, to provide subsidies to municipalities to support measures that would be likely to promote the reduction of unemployment relief. The extent of the subsidies was to be determined by the number of unemployed who could be removed from the rolls by such means. A fundamental goal was not only to spend less money on unemployment relief, but also to spend less public money altogether, so that the subsidy was not supposed to amount to more than the saving on unemployment. While this appears as a somewhat utopian expectation at first sight, it must be understood in terms of the conception of the productive unemployment relief as part of a system that was to include unemployment insurance and careful coordination with labor exchanges. Productive unemployment support was also intended to provide a pump-priming mechanism in times of economic downturns. A major consideration, as the RAM pointed out in a note to the RWM on August 26, 1920, was to "revive industrial life through measures taken by the public authorities."[82]

As always, those involved were rapidly confronted with the inescapable question of whether they could or should afford such measures. In mid-May 1920, for example, the Reich had requests for grants from productive unemployment relief amounting to 1,929,314 marks that would have provided employment for 3,633 persons. The projects involved included canalization in Coburg, building renovation in Bremen, street construction in Meiningen, and the building of sports fields in the Prussian city of Lüneberg and the Thuringian town of Schwetzingen. This was trivial, however, compared to the seventy-eight million marks allocated by the Reich to employ sixteen thousand workers on public works in Berlin. The total costs of the employment program in Berlin set up in August 1920 amounted to 295 million marks. While the City of Berlin was thus to pay the lion's share, it found itself forced to request a forty-million-mark prepayment by the Reich in October 1920 because it did not have the means to pay the workers involved.[83]

Indeed, the original notion that productive unemployment relief would prove less expensive than simple unemployment relief had turned into fantasy. By August 1920, a project was considered worthy of support if it cost only twice or, in special cases, two and a half times the sum needed to maintain the employed workers on relief. Brauns had, in fact, proposed to Wirth that they go as high as three times the amount of unemployment relief saved, arguing that the measure, even if regrettable from the perspective of Reich finances, was necessary "under the present circumstances—if only to avoid political difficulties."[84] In October, the German Municipal League (*Deutsche Städtetag*) petitioned to raise the limit to four times the cost of the unemployment relief saved. As RAM's Dr. Weigert, who was in charge of the program, had pointed out back in July when predicting precisely such a development, the local authorities viewed the program to be nothing more than a continuation of the old emergency public works programs. This was not the only way in which the purpose of the two programs became confused in practice. Originally, the costs of productive unemployment relief were to be divided in such a way that the Reich paid one-half; the state involved, one-third; and the municipality, one-sixth. A decree of May 6, 1920, however, allowed financially troubled municipalities to be relieved of all financial obligation for the subsidization with the approval of the Finance Minister. On July 31, some limit was set on the entire system by an RAM directive instructing that the limit to which the productive unemployment relief funds could be used for a project was one-half its cost.[85]

Nevertheless, the municipalities were by no means certain the Reich was doing them a favor with these various concessions since the costs for many municipalities appeared disproportionate to the benefits and the further deterioration of municipal finances they entailed. As the Mayor of Altona pointed out in November 1920, the full cost of public construction work in his city amounted to fifty-eight and a half marks per day, of which the Reich was paying thirty marks. Unemployment relief, by contrast, cost eighteen marks per day, of which the municipality paid three marks or only one and a half marks "if it had the good fortune to be recognized as being especially poor." From this perspective, it really paid to let the unemployed worker remain unemployed, while the productive unemployment relief was "such an unprofitable form of help from the Reich that one cannot really work with it."[86] If cities, nevertheless, sought subsidies for productive unemployment relief, it was for sociopolitical reasons; that is, because workers and trade unions believed that some form of employment was better—and safer—than relying on the dole and because some cities undoubtedly were prepared to spend money on city improvements even if these were, as the RAM called them, "economic luxuries."[87]

The Labor Ministry was indeed concerned that the municipalities would ruin their finances through the undertaking of one public works project after another, that some of the projects simply were economically unproductive, and that a more general effort had to be made to get urban workers to depart from the cities and do work in the countryside or be retrained for other occupations. The Ministry thought this all the more necessary because it anticipated "chronic" unemployment once the summer crisis was over and felt that long-term solutions had to be found. No one had very great illusions given the limited success of past efforts to move workers to the countryside and to persuade female workers to undertake domestic work. As one official put it, "[T]he agrarian employers look with horror upon urban workers, and the same holds true when it comes to the employment of female factory workers in domestic service."[88] The expectations of such workers simply were too high, and then there were certain types of work, such as sugar beet growing, that were apparently so onerous that only those who had traditionally done such work—Poles, for example—could be so employed. Furthermore, while one could point to some successes in retraining workers (for example, a case in which a number of unemployed workers had completed courses in furniture making), such efforts could also prove abortive in the immediate crisis (in this case because the furniture industry was one of the worst victims of the recession).

Fundamentally, the perspectives of the RAM and RWM on the long-term problems of the German economy were not dissimilar. Both Ministries spoke of the need for a "regrouping" of the labor force along more economically rational lines. As Hirsch argued: "We will not be able to avoid a regrouping of the means of production and the labor force of the German economy, independently of the question of 'crisis' and 'non-crisis.'"[89] He saw little point in placing exaggerated hopes in the transfers of industrial workers to agriculture, but he was convinced that there was much more room for employment in canal building and especially in home construction and similar activities.

An argument could be made, after all, that "more expensive constructions are still cheaper than unproductive unemployment relief."[90] That this argument was made by Minister of the Treasury, Hans von Raumer, who had close connections with the electrotechnical industry, in favor of the subsidization of water-power works is not surprising but hardly the full story. Hirsch had made similar arguments for completion of the Midland Canal between Hanover and Magdeburg, and a case could also be made for other large-scale projects, such as the expansion of the Berlin subway system. In general, there was a growing tendency for the Reich to promote employment in various industries directly, to give out large public sector contracts of its own, and to undertake projects in which the states rather than the municipalities were involved. This was particularly the case with respect to contracts for the reconstruction of the devastated areas of northern France and Belgium, the rebuilding of the German merchant marine, the construction of trains and locomotives and repair of the worn railroad system, and the supply of clothing and shoes to miners, agricultural workers, and other needy groups in connection with the Reich subsidies for such programs. Federal government contracts for such purposes dated back to the demobilization, but they intensified and became increasingly organized in late 1919, largely because of the interest in shifting as much as possible of the reparations burden into actual reconstruction with German materials and labor, and also because the states actively pursued such federal contracts and strove to avoid conflicts with one another through the so-called Contract Equalization Agency they set up for this purpose. That agency rapidly assumed the role of an information center on reconstruction and other contracts and regularly distributed confidential material about available opportunities.[91]

For obvious reasons, the Reich government itself was reluctant to get into the business of subsidizing individual industries and private firms directly from the productive unemployment relief funds. It therefore urged firms to turn to the Assistance Fund for Industrial Enterprises to help and encouraged the creation of an economic bank to provide credits. This unwillingness to provide subsidies was strengthened by the strong sense that it would be "misplaced to interfere in the cleansing process which economic life is now undergoing by granting loans or subsidies to individual firms. The result would be no other than that the workers in the plants will be kept busy for yet another few weeks thereby increasing inventories and making things even worse."[92] A more positive view was taken of assisting companies which were retooling to increase exports and of helping indirectly industries whose activity seemed to serve important social or economic purposes.

Thus, in the early summer of 1920, the government took a hand in the revival of the Pirmassens shoe industry, whose economic difficulties arose from the fact that it was prohibited from exporting shoes because of the domestic scarcity but was unable to find domestic customers at a price that would cover its production costs. The authorities recognized that there was something absurd about a situation in which "shoes in the value of many millions were lying in storage while the lack of shoes and other articles of clothing was compelling agricultural workers to make constant wage demands."[93] The shoe industry made an arrangement to supply a pair of shoes to the domestic market, especially to agricultural workers, at a low price in return for every pair it was allowed to export. In a similar action, the Emergency Textile Provision Corporation, a government company that had previously been charged with supplying inexpensive clothes from the military supplies, was empowered in May 1920 to purchase from private firms as well and proceeded to give contracts to the south German clothing industry. Of greatest importance, however, from the standpoint of both decreasing unemloyment and government expenditure, were the public-works contracts provided by the Reich Post Ministry, which provided large sums for the repair of post wagons, repair of post offices, procurement of equipment, and, most important, replacement of overhead by underground cables. Similarly, the Reich Transport Ministry reported itself to be in a po-

sition to provide sixteen billion in contracts for 1921. The impending transfer of the waterways to the Reich in April 1921, like the already undertaken nationalization of the railroad system, placed the Reich in a position of responsibility for the reconstruction of these enterprises but also in a position to allocate contracts. As Reich Transport Minister Groener put it, one could "concentrate contracts in those places or at those times where unemployment is especially high."[94] In addition to such outright expenditures, the Reich also provided low-interest loans and grants to states, including Prussia, for soil improvement and land redemption.

From the standpoint of increasing employment and economic activity, however, there was no area comparable in importance to that of housing construction, and there was complete agreement between the RAM and RWM that this was the industry most worthy of promotion in fighting the unemployment problem. Public pressure to increase housing construction and to fight unemployment by this means was also very great, as demonstrated by the emphasis placed on this sector in Reichstag discussions and in trade union petitions to the government. Before the war, 16 percent of all those working in industry and the crafts were in the construction sector, and an average of 30 percent of all investment between 1851 and 1913 was in nonagricultural housing construction. It was the industry which traditionally promoted and also helped to stabilize levels of economic activity, but the conscious application of its countercyclical potentialities—that is, the deliberate promotion of housing construction as a means of encouraging economic activity during downswings in the business cycle—was unknown before the war. This was because home builders usually had no more than 10 to 25 percent of the capital needed, so that construction costs normally had to be covered by first and second mortgages. First mortgages came from banks and covered 60 to 70 percent of the costs, while second mortgages were provided by private persons at a higher rate. The regulation of business activity by the discount rate made construction cheaper in times of recession and more expensive in times of boom, but the time lag between the decision to invest and actual construction meant that private investors were slow to respond to changing circumstances and usually ended up investing in a pro-cyclical manner, withholding their investments in times of recession and increasing them in times of high business activity. All this made home and building construction more expensive than necessary and had a particularly negative effect upon lower-class housing construction despite the increasing population during the prewar period.[95]

The war had a devastating effect on home construction, reducing the number of new homes made available from a yearly average of about a hundred seventy thousand between 1900 and 1913 to a hundred eighty thousand for the entire period 1914–1918. Because of the war economy, housing problems were greatly increased in industrial areas. The war did decrease immediate demand through deaths and a reduction in the number of marriages, but the war economy exacerbated the problems of already crowded areas and created shortages in previously uncrowded areas. It was easy enough to predict that this situation would worsen drastically when the war was over. The incentives to private enterprise in the housing field, however, were greatly reduced by the controlled economy in housing, which had been introduced in September 1918 and then stepped up. The regulation and control of rents and the right of the authorities to force persons with empty houses and other facilities to take in renters meant that private builders and owners could only expect reduced profits and generally reduced disposition over their property. Obviously, if the seven hundred thousand needed units that were already anticipated by the old regime in February 1918 or the one and a half million estimated by the more socially minded governments of 1919–1920 were going to be built, there would have to be substantial government assistance.[96]

During the demobilization, three billion marks in subsidies were allocated to cover all building costs. This amounted to more than 130 percent of what would have been spent in peacetime. Because of the enormous increase in the costs of all building materials, however, this proved to be an impossible and unjustifiable subvention of the home builders and a change

was made in 1920 under which the Reich was to lend one-third of the extra cost per square meter, calculated according to an established norm, at a very low rate of interest, while the states and municipalities were to provide another third each. Such additional costs over the prewar period as were not covered by the described formulas were to be covered by rent increases. Furthermore, the actual costs of the entire subsidy program were to be raised by taxes on rents and homes. Although this bill was brought before the National Assembly at the end of 1919, it was so strongly opposed by renters, who did not want to see their rents raised, and by house owners, who feared that they would end up getting even less in rents than they were already, that no party in the Reichstag wished to defend the measure before the June 1920 elections. Also, there was a lengthy struggle over the Reich's plan to collect the tax itself and thus centralize the control of housing subsidization. Consequently, special tax funds were not available in 1920–1921, although the Reich was involved in the financing of 90 percent of the 108,307 units built or reconstructed in 1920 and 70.5 percent of the 141,498 units built or reconstructed in 1921.[97]

This inability to spur on home construction to a greater extent was a source of endless frustration to both the RWM and the RAM, especially since they were convinced that virtually the entire unemployment problem could have been solved by this means. Instead of employing 1,750,000 persons, as was the case before the war, the construction industry was giving work to only a few hundred thousand. Were Germany able to produce the number of homes produced before the war, then it was estimated that one and a half million more persons could be employed, assuming one took employment in construction materials, furniture, and other related branches into account.[98]

The construction-materials industries themselves (the producers of cement, bricks, tiles, gypsum, wood, etc.), had proven to be a major bottleneck. On the one hand, these industries were often very dependent on coal deliveries and suffered particularly from coal shortages as well as from the transport, labor, and other problems besetting the economy. Naturally, this affected their prices in a very significant way and helps to explain why the original subsidy program proved unworkable. On the other hand, these industries were beset with inventory problems insofar as they did produce because the domestic market was too weak to sustain them while government restrictions on their exports made it impossible for them to compensate for their domestic losses and continue operation. In the course of 1920, the RWM had some success in relieving these problems. By dismantling controls on exports and encouraging cooperation among producers, the profitability of the industry had increased and actual domestic price reductions began to take place. As in the case of the shoe industry, a more liberal export policy certainly reduced what was available to the domestic market but had the positive effect of increasing profitability and making possible delivery to the domestic market at somewhat reduced prices. Despite such progress, however, the RWM gloomily noted in September 1920 that "a loosening up of the construction market is not noticeable since the question of cost subsidies is not yet clarified."[99]

Ultimately, it was the financial problem that stood in the way, and in November 1920, the RWM and RAM decided to coordinate their efforts since "through such common action one may expect a strengthening of our position over against the Finance Ministry."[100] Not only did they agree to fight for the allocation of one and a half billion in subsidies for 1921, but they also intended, here in accord with the RFM, to push for the passage of the long-delayed rent tax. Yet, they could have few illusions about the extent to which such revenues would solve the problem. Between 1918 and 1920, the Reich alone had spent 1.63 billion marks on housing construction and another 300 million on coal-miner housing. Additionally, a special coal price increase in December 1919 provided a levy of six marks per ton for miner housing. If one added the state and municipal housing-construction subsidies, then a total of four and a quarter billion marks in public monies had been made available. The results were not impressive, and the monies for miner housing proved so inadequate that the RWM began to look for ways and means of finding a source of credit so that the special funds could be used to

pay interest and amortize the loan rather than pay building costs directly. Thus, if government-subsidized housing construction was inflationary, then inflation was also undermining the capacity of such subsidization to achieve its purpose.[101]

Nevertheless, the relative stabilization and notable reduction in the cost of building materials gave reason for hope. The RWM–RAM fight to get a Cabinet allocation for housing in 1921 was successful, 1.5 billion marks being allocated, to which 700 million from the coal levy and the state and municipal subsidies can be added for a total of 3.7 billion marks. Furthermore, a rent tax passed in June 1921, under which the Reich and states could jointly levy a 5 percent tax on rents and the municipalities could levy another 5 percent and, with special permission, yet another 5 percent. Yet the rent tax was expected to bring in no more than 3.2 billion marks during the twenty-year period of its anticipated existence and to provide funds for only some fifty thousand units. The Socialists voted for the law with grave reservations and ultimately only to prevent the control of the housing program from being taken over completely by the states.[102]

The entire realm of housing construction provided a classic illustration of the vicious circles into which social and economic policy in the early Weimar Republic were driven. The SPD opposed rent increases for obvious social reasons, but it is important to recognize that Germany's low wage levels and export advantages depended upon the maintenance of low rents, so that even construction industry advocates of substantial rent hikes conceded that complete decontrol of rents was impossible.[103] Although the Socialists claimed that the major problems could be solved by socialization of the construction industry, one wonders how sincerely they believed their own rhetoric on this subject. In Germany, the construction industry did not build houses for sale but rather on order from investors. The real dilemma was finding the wherewithal to build, and the Majority Socialists parted company with the USPD and joined the other parties in opposing the use of the printing press to carry out various schemes, some of which can only be called harebrained, to finance housing construction through the issuance of "emergency construction money." The proponents of such ideas, among them the bourgeois land-reform and homestead enthusiast Adolph Damaschke, argued that the new emergency construction money (*Baunotgeld*) would be secured by the constructions themselves, while other like-minded souls called for the issuance of special money or bonds based on a compulsory mortgage of all existing property in Germany. Left-wing trade unionists picked up these ideas and developed plans in which loan-bureau notes with utterly fictional "coverage" would be employed. Thanks to the presence of supporters of these various projects on the Labor Ministry's Standing Advisory Commission for Homesteads, the ideas were brought to public attention and, when rejected by the Labor Minister, were "appealed to the higher body" of a rally at the Circus Busch by a group of extreme left-wing trade unionists who claimed to be speaking for the trade unions.[104]

These proposals so alarmed the Reichsbank that it sent a lengthy memorandum in January 1921 to the Labor Minister expressing its hostility toward such schemes. The Reichsbank had no taste left for the creation of new forms of money. Once one started, where would one stop? Were not shipbuilding and waterpower and waterway construction also important? It would also be possible to create special currencies for these activities. Not only would this increase the inflation, but it would also add to the chaos by producing forms of money of unequal worth and value because this form of currency would be discounted by those receiving it on the basis of their estimate of its true worth and security. In the view of the Reichsbank, some of the arguments employed by proponents of the previously discussed schemes were downright frivolous. Thus, the Reichsbank felt compelled to point out that the argument that the twelve billion marks spent on food imports in 1920 could have been saved if only the money had been put into homesteads and that Germany could actually export food if six million Germans would cultivate gardens was utterly ridiculous because wheat and cattle were not garden products.[105]

Far more distressing than such manifest nonsense and economic quackery, however, was

the tendency, especially on the part of the far left, to promote and encourage a fatalistic attitude toward the inflation which was reflected in the notions that "our currency is already so fundamentally destroyed that there is nothing left to destroy" and that "just as one fights prairie fires with counter-fires, so one should fight inflation with counter-inflation" and that "concern for the people and the Reich must come first and only thereafter concern for the currency." The Reichsbank feared that such overly simple agitatorial phrases and sloganeering would ruin all sense of the relationship between the currency and the nation's economic condition and destroy the relative stabilization which both the Reichsbank and government were trying to maintain as a means of promoting the ultimate recovery of both:

It is difficult at any specific point in time, almost impossible, to determine where there is more cause and where there is more effect in the causal relationship. If the economy collapses, then the currency goes with it. If the currency as measured by the exchange rate, drops, as it has periodically, then it drags the entire internal situation unredeemably along with it. We have every reason to avoid repetitions of such catastrophic developments with their attendant price, wage, and even political movements.

From this perspective, argued the Reichsbank, it was very important to recognize that much remained to be destroyed in the mark and that every diminution of its worth had profound effects on prices and wages and could ultimately create conditions comparable to those existing in Austria and Russia, whose currencies were being ruined. It was "just for this reason that the Reichsbank had stood up so decisively for the balancing of the Reich budget, for a speedy collection of the Emergency Capital Levy and for forced loans."

This attack on fiscal and monetary irresponsibility and sloganeering certainly would have been more edifying if the Reichsbank had a better wartime record of its own. Furthermore, the Reichsbank memorandum against the proposed financing of home construction by ever new and more imaginative uses of the printing press had a broader purpose. It provided the Reichsbank with an opportunity to attack "the all too widespread tendency to burden the public purse excessively with purely economic functions and to expect from it salvation from all difficulties." It had been found all too agreeable to give out paper money so that the individual lived off the Treasury, personal responsibility was lost, and "our people to the greatest extent are condemned to an uneconomic condition." The time had come, in the view of the Reichsbank, that "the individual must be turned back again to his own resources, to his own strength, to his inventiveness and responsibility." While not denying that the public authorities had a role to play, the Reichsbank insisted that a change in attitude was necessary so that this role would be viewed in terms of how much it might be minimized rather than maximized.

This was not the only occasion during this period when Havenstein warned that Germany might be heading toward "Austrian and perhaps even Russian conditions" because of the increased amounts of currency in circulation as a result of the increasing debt of the Reich. He was not at all shy about using the term "inflation" to describe the situation in an appearance before a Reichstag committee in December 1920:

This growing flood of paper today truly is inflation and the beginning of an assignat economy. It is inflation with all the fateful consequences that are clearly evident today, even if one rejects the quantity theory as I do. The floating debt and the amount of paper money in circulation have for some time been the barometer of the outside world in judging our currency situation, and our economic and financial conditions, which are viewed with a very critical eye. The growth of both strengthens the mistrust which is there in any case and acts as a heavy burden and increasing pressure on the currency. . . . The danger is just as great at home. The destruction of our financial conditions and our money also grows here as the flood of paper grows with each passing week and month and depreciates the currency from the monetary side.[106]

If the floating debt continued to grow, therefore, it was not because either the government or the Reichsbank were seeking to promote inflation or encouraging uneconomic expenditure at the turn of 1920–1921. Quite the contrary, they were seeking ways and means of maintaining stability and encouraging efficiency. The problem was that the circumstances were not conducive to sound economic practices. The unemployment problems and price disturbances of the summer had followed upon the burst of inflation and virtual civil war of the previous winter, while the fall of 1920 and the winter of 1920–1921 brought coal shortages, a tendency of the exchange rate of the mark to move downward, and new tensions over layoffs and high prices as well as continued impoverishment of large numbers of people. The government may have viewed the "cleansing process" brought on by the downturn in the economy positively, but the Berlin authorities could not permit plants to shut down and sell out at will in the face of mounting trade union complaints and potential high unemployment. The RWM, while certainly more partial to letting economic forces cleanse the economy than the RAM, also worried that firms would not only close down temporarily or out of necessity but also simply sell their equipment and machines for immediate monetary advantage and thus do great harm. The government was particularly anxious to prevent foreigners from buying out competing German companies and then closing the newly acquired plants to eliminate the German competition. Consequently, on November 8, 1920, the government issued a decree on plant shut downs and dismantling (*Stillegungsverordnung*) that required all such actions be reported to the Demobilization Commissar—usually the district President— and enjoined such firms from in any way taking action until its legitimacy could be determined. This would be done by the authorities in consultation with the factory council, whose task it was to investigate ways and means of keeping such plants in operation. Needless to say, this was a profound interference with the rights of the factory owner and ran against traditional principles of capitalist economics. It made the shutting down of uneconomic enterprises extraordinarily difficult. The trade unions explicitly instructed the factory councils to recognize that all shut downs were not illegitimate and that many would be necessary. Factory councils were told to take the entire economy and not only local conditions and interests into account. Nevertheless, the trade unions viewed the decree not only as an important means of expanding the role and responsibility of the factory councils, but also as "a first step on the way to a legal public control over the means of production."[107] That the decree was especially hated by the employers is obvious, and it constituted one of an increasing number of points of conflict between industry, on the one hand, and the government and trade unions, on the other.

This decree was thus a perfect illustration of the constant tension between the RWM policy of releasing the forces of the private economy and the socioeconomic constraints that limited this policy. Furthermore, the constraints in question were not only felt or intuited by the responsible officials involved but also were constantly given expression by highly organized groups. The contradictions in government policy were not simply the product of a compromise between its conviction that the compulsory economy had to be dismantled and its desire to prevent unrest and upheaval, but also a function of complex patterns of conflict and cooperation between organized industry and labor. One of the major consequences of the crisis of the summer of 1920 had been to increase the conflictual aspects of that relationship as well as to threaten those instruments of economic monitoring and control which the RWM had built up in the course of the fall and winter of 1919–1920.

These tendencies were particularly evident in the debate over export controls and the export levy, issues which also serve to demonstrate the manner in which the mercurial character of the entire inflationary period undermined governmental efforts to maintain and effectively utilize the instruments it had painfully forged to gain a measure of control on the economy. The export control boards and export levy had been legislated at the end of 1919 in response to the problems created by the underpricing of German exports, on the one hand, and the need to tax export exchange profits for the benefit of the worst victims of the inflation and to hold down domestic prices, on the other. The formation of the export control boards was pushed ahead in the early months of 1920, while the RWM set to work on calculating the levies and finally issued a schedule on April 22 which was to go into effect on May 10, 1920. In short, the entire system went into operation at precisely the time when the exchange rate of the mark improved dramatically, the prices of many German ex-

port goods on world markets became less competitive, and the exchange profit from exports either decreased significantly or disappeared altogether. Also, the adjustment of prices downward to deal with the changed market condition was particularly difficult when the manufacturer had paid high prices for the raw materials he used during the winter of 1919–1920. Given these conditions, it was not surprising that many industries and businessmen turned sharply against the entire system with considerable irritation and frustration. As one businessman remarked with exasperation: "We are encircled by a system that hampers every activity. . . . What is correct today is false tomorrow."[108]

The special delicacy of the situation lay in the fact that the export-control-board system and the export levies had been organized with the active participation of the ZAG, and the trade unions had developed a stake in the system. They viewed the boards as a means of gaining a voice in foreign-trade questions, while they considered the levies an important social concession wrung from the employers. The problem, as was usually the case with the ZAG, was that decisions made in Berlin were disavowed or undermined by the businessmen or trade-union members elsewhere. That is, the peak associations were not always supported by their constituencies. In this instance, the pressure of businessmen on their trade-association or peak-association leaders left the ZAG employer representatives in Berlin either paralyzed or forced to disavow the arrangements made with their trade-union colleagues. Since the employer representatives were loathe to go back on their agreements, they tried desperately to persuade the union leaders to reconsider their positions.[109]

The pressure was all the stronger because important employer groups were quite prepared to act unilaterally. In mid-May, the Association of German Machine Builders met and attacked the export levy, to the very great embarrassment of its president, Dr. Kurt Sorge, who was also president of the RdI and a member of the ZAG Board of Directors. His situation became even more difficult at the beginning of August, when the RdI itself called for the elimination of the export levy, and by September the employers were asking the trade unionists to join them in opposing the levy on the grounds that the previous profits were no longer being made, prices had to be calculated very precisely, and the levy was only serving to increase unemployment by ruining business. This the trade unions would not accept. They did not deny that conditions had changed and were prepared to agree to a lowering of the rates where appropriate, but they thought the levy essential to tax such exchange profits on exports as were being made and also viewed the levy as a means of forcing producers and manufacturers to reduce domestic prices.

Here they stood in alliance with Secretary Hirsch and the RWM. Hirsch argued forcefully, often in harmony with his erstwhile critic Rudolf Wissell, for the retention of the entire system in the periodic debates over the question before the temporary Reich Economic Council (vorläufiger Reichswirtschaftsrat or RWR). The latter, a large and cumbersome implementation of the corporatist elements in the "council" idea in which representatives of the various economic groups met to discuss the economic and social policies of the government, took up its work on June 30, 1920, and became the chief locus of debate and discussion on these and other major social, economic, and financial issues during the coming years.[110] The first of the many debates on the export levies and export controls took place during the first week of the RWR's existence, on July 6, 1920, and the RWM used the occasion to warn against allowing short-term economic developments to lead to decisions that would be regretted later. Rudolf Dalberg of the Reich Commissariat for Exports and Imports noted that only a few months before some people had been arguing for an equalization of domestic and world-market prices and pointed out that, if that had happened, "we would have double the prices at home today and could not export; we would be forced to reduce to reduce wages and prices. The political consequences of such an action are obvious."[111]

Hirsch made a lengthy and particularly forceful argument for the system of export controls and levies. Many German goods could still easily be dumped due to the low wages and other domestic costs and foreign retaliation

would be the outcome. There had to be some guarantee that products needed for domestic purposes were not exported to the point at which there were domestic shortages. It was necessary to make certain that the returns on exports were the equivalent of their value and did not constitute a veiled shifting of capital abroad. The system also was a means of restoring German business morality on international markets by compelling exporters to sell at fixed prices and keep to their contracts. Hirsch also maintained that an appropriate export levy should be collected for social, economic, and political reasons. The most basic ground for maintaining the system, even under changed conditions was that

... we are still in an absolutely insecure situation with respect to our exchange rate. No person can guarantee that the whole game of last year ... will not repeat itself from one day to the next through external interference or some domestic happening, and if we have dismantled everything, then we will be in the same desperate situation as during the past year and will have to do the same work all over again. ... We are uncertain with regard to possible exports, uncertain with respect to the demands that will come from the Entente, uncertain whether or not a depreciation of the mark can occur again because of our general monetary policy. Already for these reasons alone the controls cannot be set aside and their basic retention is necessary.[112]

Such arguments, to be sure, did not convince the general director of the Hamburg-America Line, Wilhelm Cuno, who found the whole system too bureaucratic and was convinced that the German economy would recover only if the "export, price examination, and other official agencies disappeared as soon as possible."[113] Wissell, also a member of the RWR, attacked as a delusion the notion that Germany could return to the happy times before 1914 because Germany had become "as poor as a church mouse,"[114] and if Cuno was complaining about the bureaucracy of the export control boards, then he was complaining about the bureaucracy of German industry itself since the boards were organized and managed by the German trade associations. In fact, many of the industrialists and businessmen were quite irritated at the functioning of their own organizations, and it was no accident that many of the "association men" (Verbandsmänner) from the trade associations were more favorable to the export control system than the businessmen for whom they worked.[115] Most important, however, the problems of the spring and summer had reopened the export decontrol issue, strengthened the arguments for a dismantling of controls, and created new grounds for conflict between industry and labor.

Indeed, the employers were demonstrating an increasing disposition to run the risk of open conflict with labor. Recession and periods of unemployment, after all, are traditionally a time when employers have the upper hand in dealing with the unions, and while conditions in Germany were in no way as favorable to the employers as in the United States and Great Britain, the tide seemed to be turning, and there was a marked tendency toward employer resistance and aggressiveness in the spring of 1920 which further shook the already insecure foundations of the ZAG. An important instance of the employers getting their backs up occurred when when the RAM and ADGB joined together to ask the employers to provide one-third of the cost of unemployment relief for workers on short time. This was intended, among other things, to discourage employers from increasing the number of short-time workers while counting on the public purse to compensate the workers for the lost wages. The employer representatives in the ZAG turned down the proposal with the argument that "the high point of the boom is past. We stand before a crisis and the number of short-time workers is so great that it is impossible for industry to make the sacrifice demanded." Even more serious, however, was that this was coupled with a warning that "the driving up of prices cannot go on this way. An end has to be made to this, but a stop must also be made to the climbing wages."[116] On May 20, 1920, the Association of German Employer Organizations secretly advised its members to refrain from granting further wage increases so that German competitiveness could be maintained. As with most such secrets, it leaked rapidly, and the trade unions protested mightily, insisting that "the reduction of prices is the precondition for the adjustment of wages, which must base themselves on the real cost of living,"[117] that is, on retail prices at the local level.

It would be misleading to suggest that important aspects of the previous cooperation and agreement, such as they were, did not remain, however. In the hard-hit textile industry, for example, cases were known in which an employer showed his books to the factory council and informed it that he would have to shut down if he could not lower wages. In one such instance, the employer managed to secure an agreement under which his workers received twenty-four hours of pay for forty-six hours work with a promise that the lost wages would be repaid when the firm could solve its credit difficulties.[118] Furthermore, employers and workers often worked hand in hand in trying to reduce export levies, although it was not always easy to tell who was taking whom by the hand. Trade-union leaders anxious to maintain the levy claimed that the employers were inciting the workers councils to support them against the levies and were being "misused" out of ignorance.[119] Many businessmen—above all, those with small businesses—could also be ignorant about the dangers of dumping, and factory councils were not beyond putting their interests in maintaining employment before national economic interests either. There is every reason to believe that the Commissar for Imports and Exports, Trendelenburg, was being honest when he responded to complaints from a Swedish official over German dumping by not only blaming the ignorance of small, inexperienced firms new to the export market but also admitting that some larger firms were at fault. Many of the latter had "internal difficulties" and were "actually forced by their factory councils to push sales abroad at too low prices so that they do not have to let any workers go."[120]

The anti-employer polemics of the trade-union leadership cannot always be taken at face value. While the trade unions protested employer efforts to hold down wages collectively in May 1920, they themselves placed their chief emphasis on price reductions and were suspected not to have been entirely unhappy about the employer move to hold wages to existing levels. Labor Minister Brauns certainly interpreted the official trade-union posture as one dictated by politics rather than wage hunger: "The trade union leaders are completely clear about the dangers which the constant wage increases present to our economy; but they cannot contain their followers without running the danger of having them wander into the radical camp."[121] Nevertheless, there is some evidence that the workers as well as the trade unions were disposed to exercise wage restraint. Throughout the late summer and fall of 1920 there was a considerable reduction of strikes and wage movements, which reflected the general interest in stabilization and price reduction. There was also an important change in the locus of conflict. Small and medium-sized industry, hard hit by the downturn and by credit problems, proved particularly hostile to wage increases, and strike activity tended to shift from large to small and medium-sized industry.[122]

Indeed, by the end of the year, the government could boast some real successes in its price reduction efforts. Coal price increases were steadily refused by the Cabinet throughout 1920, while iron and steel prices were reduced voluntarily a number of times during the course of the year. Price reductions could also be noted for construction materials and other basic products. Of course, no one could argue that the condition of the economy was satisfactory just because exports had increased and unemployment had been somewhat reduced. Coal shortages continued to cause slowdowns and production difficulties, and the economy could in no sense be said to be working at capacity. Furthermore, for the individual consumers, prices continued to be exorbitant and a source of severe social tension. It was not only a question of the sufferings of the working class; also severely affected were all those living on fixed incomes, pensioners, retired persons living on small capital investments (*Kleinrentner* or petite rentiers), students, widows, and disabled persons. The desire, therefore, to go after profiteers and reduce prices on consumer goods was not simply a "proletarian" issue. Better said, these were the issues of a society that had become increasingly proletarianized, at least in reality if not in mentality. The RWM, like the rest of the government, was sympathetic, but it felt compelled to view these problems as secondary.

As in the spring of 1920, the RWM continued its efforts in the later part of the year to orchestrate a peaceful and untroubled transition to free-market conditions as rapidly as possible and in an manner that would encourage production. The high prices were viewed as the natural result of the gap between supply and demand, and the best way to keep them steady, the RWM was convinced, was through collaboration with the organized sectors of the economy. At Coburg in October 1920, Dr. Stern warned price-examination-agency representatives against overestimating the importance of the price question and, in effect, failing to recognize that their purpose now was to come to terms with the consequences of the inflation in the name of increasing production:

The significance of the inflation is to be found largely in the fact that it continually shifts the relationship between those with fixed sources of income and those with variable sources of income in favor of those who have control over goods and property [*Sachbesitz*]. This redistribution [*Umschichtung*] is without doubt very harsh, but it is not the decisive thing for the price question. A stabilization of the currency or a move back to more favorable currency relationships will certainly prevent the profits made in the German economy from being further distributed according to the momentary accident of access to goods. Leaving aside the significance of variations in the exchange rate for the security and order of markets in which goods circulate, however, they will neither increase the amount of goods available nor lower the amount of goods available in an appreciable sense. Yet, it is the improvement of this relationship between supply and demand for goods that is the heart of the matter, because it means little if I earn 10,000 marks and then need 10,000 marks to live or whether I have to spend 5,000 marks and only receive 5,000 marks. But it makes a real difference if I can get twice as many goods for my day's labor.[123]

It was precisely this sort of thing that made the regimes in Berlin so hated and detested by Weimar's enemies on both the right and the left as well as so unsatisfactory even to those they may have been trying to encourage. The right-wing government in Munich under Gustav von Kahr, ever concerned about the impoverishment of the old middle-class constituency which had been the backbone of that state's political and social stability before the war, wanted the Reich to act against the cartels and industrial trade associations it held responsible for the high prices as well as the host of profiteers and middlemen who it accused of exploiting the shortages and high prices since the war. While certainly supportive of the productionist policies of the Economics Ministry, it expected the Reich not simply to inquire of the cartels what their prices should be but actually to make sure that the north German capitalists and monopolists were not making an excess profit. It accused the Berlin government of not doing enough to fight profiteers, supported Draconian punishments, and actually tried to implement harsher regulations and legislation of its own in the fall of 1920 that further inflamed the quarrels between the Reich and Bavaria over foreign and domestic policy. The left-wing government in Dresden, which came under the leadership of the Socialist Wilhelm Buck in November 1920, also found the RWM's attitude toward the price question wanting. While also anxious to have big business placed under stricter controls, the Saxon government was much more worried about the food prices its large and frequently unemployed urban working class had to pay and expected the price examination agencies to devote their attention to the reduction of basic commodity prices. While the Bavarian and Saxon governments sang the same song of complaint in different keys, the more commercially and industrially oriented states of Hamburg, Bremen, and, to some extent, Prussia read the language of the Economics Ministry to mean that the entire effort to control profiteering and prices was becoming increasingly superfluous and hoped, on the one hand, to see the enterprise dismantled and, on the other hand, to stalemate Bavarian, Saxon, and other efforts to strengthen the price examination agencies and the antiprofiteering laws. For them, especially the Hansa cities, the RWM was moving too slowly and cautiously.[124]

Thus, by the turn of 1920–1921, the tone of the meetings of price-examination agency officials had become both bitter and cynical. When placards with drawings by the great left-wing artist Käthe Kollwitz were used in the antiprofiteering propaganda of the Prussian police, people thought they promoted class hatred. Prussian police representative Dr. Falck responded by suggesting that it was not the drawings that provoked such hatred against the propertied classes but rather reality:

On the one side, unheard of luxury which individuals enjoy at the expense of the broad masses, the expenditures at delicacy shops with attractive and beautiful wares, with tasty and the most delicious things of every kind to eat, which only a fraction of the population, the war and revolution profiteers, have for themselves, and on the other side the hundreds of thousands and even millions of undernourished elderly persons, women, and children who are broken in strength and spirit.[125]

The passion of Dr. Falck should not be taken lightly since his use of the Kollwitz drawings had earned him numerous obscene and threatening letters which included murder threats.

It was not only Dr. Falck who felt that he was living on the razor's edge as 1920 came to a close. It was a sentiment shared by major industrialists, trade-union leaders, and government officials. As Rathenau pointed out in an interview with Bresciani-Turroni of the Reparations Commission in early October, "the workers are much quieter at present than during the past year and are working well, but the social crisis is not past. Any incident can let loose new serious difficulties."[126] The trade unions were also very uncertain about the situation and were singularly unaggressive. At the end of September, they published another recently discovered "confidential" circular of an employer association to its members. This circular opposed all wage increases, urged employers to respond to selective strikes with district-wide lockouts, asked that they refuse to accept arbitration decisions raising wages, and called on them to reintroduce piece work when renegotiating wage contracts and to attempt to extend the workday wherever the authorities would permit it. Also, they were to propagandize among union leaders, factory councils, mediators and arbitrators to make them understand the necessity of reducing wages, especially the wages of young unmarried workers. The Socialist General Federation of German Trade Unions (ADGB) responded to this document with remarkable caution: "We certainly do not want wages to continue at their present height forever. The condition for a reduction of wages, however, as has been pointed out repeatedly, is a prior reduction of the prices of the most necessary foodstuffs. So long as this does not happen, a reduction of wages is unthinkable."[127]

In the general movement for cost-of-living increases at the end of the year, in which the railroad workers and coal miners were particularly active, the ADGB again assumed a very

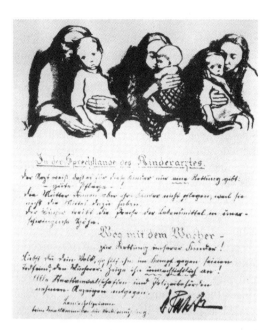

The Sick Woman and Her Children: "This woman was brought to the sickbed by an insufficient diet. She could become well again with good nourishment. What she needs is available, but she cannot pay for it because of the unheard of prices. WHAT WILL BECOME OF HER CHILDREN? Profiteering daily undermines the strength of countless human beings and leads them—to an early grave. THEREFORE, DO AWAY WITH PROFITEERING! If you love your people and Fatherland, then file a *written complaint with us* against every profiteer!"

Waiting Room at the Pediatrician's: "The doctor knows that there is only *one* way of saving these children—good nourishment! But these mothers cannot feed their children because they do not have the means. The profiteers drive the price of food to unmanagable levels. AWAY WITH PROFITEERING—to save our sick! If you love your people, then help them in their struggle against their deadly enemy, the profiteers! File a *written complaint with us* against them!"

Käthe Kollwitz, Three Leaflets Against Profiteers of 1920, commissioned by the Police Agency attached to the State Commissar for the Food Supply and signed by its head, Dr Falck. They each conclude by calling on the population to file a written complaint against profiteers with the authorities. (*Copyright © 1993 ARS, NewYork/VG Bild-kunst, Bonn*)

At the Doctor's: "DOCTOR: 'The child is severely undernourished. He needs *milk*, *eggs*, *meat*, and *lard* daily.'
MOTHER: 'Herr doctor, I do not have the money; *I cannot even manage to buy those things available with ration cards!*'
DOCTOR: 'That's how *profiteering* takes things to the point where *our youth* go to ruin! Can you quietly stand by and let that happen? *Everyone* must help in the struggle against this worst enemy of the people. File a *written complaint with us* against every profiteer.'"

cautious role, deciding that "the directors of the federation cannot undertake a general direction of wage policy. In movements on a large scale, such as those of the miners and the railroad workers, in view of the fatal effect such strikes can have on our economic life, there is to be a prior understanding between those unions and the federation. . . ."[128] It would appear, therefore, that the Socialist trade union leadership was very uncertain about its appropriate posture in 1920, that it accepted the desirability of wage reduction in principle, that it opposed any major action that might have a serious effect on the economy, and that its one and only precondition for cooperation with the government and employers was a reduction of food prices. Since the government's decontrol policies tended to result, at least initially, in price increases, this meant that trade union policies of self-restraint were certainly not guaranteed.

The ADGB sought a way out of this difficulty at the beginning of 1921 that also reflected its desire to restore collaboration. In the ZAG, the trade unionists tried to persuade the employers to join in alliance against high agricultural prices and in opposition to the relaxation of controls on agriculture. Put in somewhat schematic terms, an alliance of industrial against agrarian producers would save the trade-union leaders from having to surrender either to a rigid "producer" or to a rigid "consumer" point of view. The employers, however, refused to join in such an out-and-out alliance against agriculture, not because they were friendly to high food prices or had much sympathy for agriculture, but because they supported decontrol and considered agricultural controls as self-defeating as industrial controls. From their perspective, it was better to have expensive bread than no bread at all. Thus, in April 1921, they flatly rejected a proposal that the ZAG come out in favor of maintaining controls on wheat, promising to cover the cost of a bread price increase with a cost-of-living increase "after taking into account the reduced prices of other necessities."[129]

The drawing of lines between labor and industry and the increased resistance and aggressiveness of the latter were even more evident in early 1921 than they had been in the last half of 1920. Poor business conditions and the world economic crisis absorbed employer attention,

and employers repeatedly pointed to the massive wage reductions and high unemployment in Great Britain and the United States and suggested that Germany had better get in step with these developments to remain competitive. Wage reductions appeared all the more justifiable in the light of the real cost-of-living reductions at this time, and the employers were pleasantly surprised when they received sudden assistance from the government in the form of a decision by the Socialist State Commissar in the Ruhr, Ernst Mehlich, that the cost-of-living increase granted before January 1921 to the Dortmund workers no longer was justified and that wages should return to those stipulated in the original contract. The employers were as overjoyed as the unions were dismayed. The industrialists hoped that the labor leaders would now learn that just as they had always demanded wage increases when there were price increases, so would they have "to draw the consequences of a reduction of the cost of living."[130]

At the same time, the employers were not always willing to let the government do their work for them and demonstrated a readiness to go it alone in their battle with the trade unions. The Labor Ministry shared not only the employers' desire to adjust wages to the actual cost of living, but also their goal of bringing wages into line with productivity, a much more serious matter since it switched the emphasis from the social to the economic aspects of wages. In March 1921, Labor Minister Brauns made a desperate effort to implement this principle by trying to tie a wage increase to an overtime agreement in a coal industry arbitration. Privy Councillor Friedrich Sitzler of the RAM pleaded with the employers on Brauns's behalf to accept the decision and thus enable him to declare it binding so that

he could show that he is also prepared to use a decision against the workers, something that the employers had always doubted! For the Labor Ministry, the matter is of fundamental importance since here for the first time in an arbitration decision the connection between wages and productivity is stated. We want to extend this procedure to other mining areas . . . and to other branches of industry. The Labor Minister has taken a very personal interest in the success of this first effort.[131]

Hugo Stinnes and his fellow mine owners, however, were uncooperative. Stinnes argued quite simply that the workers would come to terms and accept overtime once they had a few weeks of work without a wage increase and without overtime pay.

While this mining dispute finally was settled on the basis of a very complicated compromise which left the basic issues undetermined, the implications of the episode were far-reaching. First, the conflict clearly hearalded the transition from the quest for higher production at any price to higher production at a price that was profitable. Second, it anticipated the two means by which this last goal could be reached; namely, governmental arbitration in favor of the employers, and employer use of the market to bring the workers to terms. The inclination to rely on the market was a reflection not only of employer distaste for government interference but also of an increasing sense that the market was turning in their favor and that the workers had to be stopped from depriving industry of the capital and flexibility it needed to deal with economic realities. That is, industry was coming increasingly to resent the power being exercised by labor and its economic effects. The emotional component is hard to measure, but it is well suggested by a diary notation of Julius Hirsch of March 1921: "A very serious hatred of the workers is manifesting itself, even among the liberal employers."[132]

Nowhere was the burgeoning conflict between "social" and "economic" priorities more pronounced than with respect to the unemployment and short-time work questions. Although the employers had flatly rejected Labor Ministry and trade-union proposals of May 1920 that the employers contribute to the payment of short-time workers, the ADGB revived this idea in late February 1921 in the context of a full-blown unemployment program. Concern with the problem was not only conjunctural. On the one hand, the sanctions being threatened by the Allies at this time in connection with the reparations issue appeared likely to increase unemployment; on the other, the trade unions were under great pressure to take some action because independent unions of the unemployed had been formed and the unemployed were also the favorite target of Communist agitation. The ADGB, therefore, called on the government to grant contracts to relieve the situation that would require the employers to give the unem-ployed jobs through the reduction of hours and the limitation of profits. The trade unions also demanded that union representatives be called upon to oversee the carrying out of these proposals and that the employers assume a portion of the costs of short-time unemployment support. Insofar as the financial side of the proposal was concerned, the ADGB declared that "In order to insure that the carrying out of the proposed measure does not lead to a further increase of inflation, we demand most emphatically the immediate collection of all taxes on property."[133]

Thus, by February 1921, the trade unions had decided on a full-scale program of their own and an assault on the employer position involving work stretching, hours-of-work reduction, government pump priming, participation in economic decision making, and effective taxation of those with wealth and property. Whereas only a few months earlier they had sought to come to terms with the employers, talk about wage reductions in return for lower prices, and stress the need for economic efficiency, they now were far more responsive to the pressure from their own ranks, especially since employers had proven so intransigent. When a young economist, Alfred Striemer, who had been placed in the higher echelons of the ADGB as part of a general effort to strengthen the command of economics and quality of argumentation of the unions attacked the work-stretching proposals on the grounds that they would increase production costs and prices and thus reduce worker purchasing power and suggested that it was a mistake to ignore "economic necessities because of social policy reservations," he was sharply countered by the leading ADGB editor, Paul Umbreit. Umbreit did little to contest Striemer's arguments. His main interest was to defend the primacy of social policy, and he bluntly stated that "if economic and social effects are set in opposition to one another, then the social interests have to be given precedence as the more important of the two and any economic disadvantages simply have to be swallowed on that basis."[134]

This posture was understandable, but it was not terribly rational, and it boded ill for the future of industrial relations in Germany. It suggested an abandonment of economic thinking

on the part of the trade-union leaders in response to the masses at their back and the increasingly dogmatic assertation of the primacy
of economic considerations by some of the
leading employers. It was a formula for confrontation that offered very little by way of constructive solution to the desperate problems
Germany was facing and even less by way of
hope of success for labor since the relative stabilization was revealing long-range prospects
that were anything but promising for the consolidation and perpetuation of labor's revolutionary gains. Labor advocated social programs
for which there was no sound money, demanded that industry behave in a manner that
was neither natural in terms of industry's interests nor rational in terms of the changing economic and political situation, and found itself
incapable of formulating a program to protect
its interests realistically in the face of the crisis
whose coming seemed to constitute the only
point of consensus in German society. The
basic compromise on which the Weimar Republic had been founded, cooperation between
industry and labor, had proven shaky every
time inflationary trade-offs appeared untenable
or in need of modification. It was hard not to
conclude that the compromise depended on inflation and had been bought at the expense of
inflation's victims.

The Gloomy Balance of Relative
Stabilization

If the contest between industry and labor and
between economic and social considerations
was sharpened as a consequence of the relative
stabilization and had been intensified by the
deliberate government policy of increased decontrol and acceptance of short-term price increases as the precondition for their stabilization under freer market conditions, it must be
recognized that the days when social considerations could be significantly subordinated to
economic ones still seemed very far off. This is
particularly obvious when one considers the
position of the government vis-à-vis its own
employees at the turn of 1920–1921. Its problems in this area were all the worse because of
Wirth's desperate commitment to reduce expenditures on the bloated and uneconomically

functioning civil service. The Salary Reform
Act of April 1920 had left the civil servants and
government workers with quite a few dissatisfactions and grievances, and these were intensified in July when an advance that had been
granted to the civil servants in March began to
be deducted from their salaries so that, despite
the raises granted in April, the salaries paid were
actually lower during precisely those months
when the retail food prices were increasing so
seriously. The Finance Ministry stubbornly refused any attempt to turn the advance into a
special supplement and thus restore normal
pay, although the Reich Statistical Office confirmed trade-union statistics on the inadequacy
of railroad-worker pay and the RWM repeatedly assured trade-union and other petitioners
that there was no hope for a decrease of prices
on the basic necessities of life until substantial
productivity gains took place. By September,
the unrest among the civil servants was so bad
that the German Civil Servants Federation
(DBB) asked that the already agreed-upon 50
percent cost-of-living allowance be doubled. At
the September 22 meeting of the Cabinet,
Wirth not only threatened resignation if the demands were not rejected but also tried to secure
an agreement that the Finance Minister's positions on budgetary matters could no longer
simply be overridden by a simple majority as
well as a commitment to a reduction in the size
of the civil service.[135]

It is hard to believe that Wirth had many illusions, however. While he was trying to find
ways to reduce the eighteen billion-mark railroad and postal deficit for 1920, the very workers involved were pressing for concessions that
would only increase it. On November 10, the
DBB launched a new movement for wage and
salary increases and other increases adding up
to 2.3 billion marks. Wirth sought to strengthen
his hand by turning to the state governments,
from which he did find strong support. The
Prussians admitted the justice of the civil-servant demands but thought them financially impossible and warned that the Reich would end
up footing the bill for the costs to the states if it
surrendered. The Bavarians were much more
negative, arguing that "in many Bavarian circles the last increase of civil servant salaries produced a certain hostility toward the civil servants."[136] Even the Saxons were prepared to

risk a strike, warning that surrender would unleash similar movements among the workers in private industry. There was particular irritation over the way the DVP had been playing politics with the civil-servant problems and thereby encouraging the movement. Thus, the DVP had presented an interpellation in the Reichstag on November 6, pointing out that "civil servants, pensioners, and retired persons are helpless in the face of the cost of living and need a thoroughgoing improvement of their cost-of-living supplements."[137] Wirth would have none of this. Fortified by the support of the state representatives, he persuaded the Cabinet to grant civil servants nothing more than a small increase of the supplement for children and then only in the more expensive areas of the Reich.[138]

While many of the Cabinet members believed that the high demands of the civil servants arose from the competition among the various unions, their decision to pursue Wirth's policy was tantamount to a declaration of war on all the involved unions. It was followed by growing tension, passive resistance, work slowdowns, and increasing talk of a strike. A railroad-worker strike presented international as well as domestic dangers, since it would have terminated deliveries of coal to the French and given them an excuse to impose sanctions. Once again, therefore, the Cabinet and the beleaguered Wirth found themselves under pressure from the political parties, especially the DVP, with its strong inclination to capitalize upon the civil-servant support it had received in the June 1920 elections. Even Wirth's own Center Party was prepared to bend. Indeed, nearly every political party was prepared to make a case for the civil service, albeit for different branches of it. Thus, while the SPD supported increases for the lower civil service, the DNVP emphasized the plight of the higher civil service. By the turn of the year, the entire issue was becoming the center of a political crisis. While the Cabinet continued to hold firm and issued an antistrike decree on December 2, Transport Minister Groener was warned that the unions were losing control of their workers and that the railroad workers in the occupied areas were showing an inclination to play upon French desires to take over the railroads.[139]

Ultimately, it was probably this fear of loss of control over the railroads in the occupied areas that broke government resistance to civil-servant demands by mid-January 1921. The government simply could not hold out, despite a Reichstag victory in early December achieved largely by Wirth's impassioned pleas. Political criticism continued to mount along with the threat of a strike, and the government faced its classic foreign-policy dilemma. In order to demonstrate its will to fulfill the Treaty of Versailles, the government needed to show fiscal restraint. Insofar as it demonstrated such restraint at the expense of powerful social groups, however, it ran the risk of the kind of social unrest that would leave it open to foreign imprecations. The immediate threat of social unrest appeared greater than the long-term dangers of fiscal improvidence, and so it surrendered. After long and complicated negotiations, the Cabinet found itself deciding between two proposals, one granting a cost of living increase ranging from 55 to 70 percent at a cost of 368 million marks, the other granting supplements ranging from 60 to 70 percent at a cost of 585 million marks. Ultimately, the negotiators managed to get the cheaper proposal through, but Wirth really did not seem to care much anymore:

The Reich Minister of Finances believes, insofar as he can judge the views of the Cabinet, that they are not prepared to have a peaceful outcome fail for a few hundred million. Still the difference is not inconsiderable. Also, one has eventually to draw the consequences for the war disabled. Finally, we have to think of building an emergency fund of perhaps 500 million for the small rentiers in order to protect a large number of our fellow German citizens who are not social pensioners and who are not working from dying of hunger.[140]

Such reflections cast a certain pall over the relative stabilization and turn Germany's socioeconomic survival in 1920 into something of a puzzle. As Lord Kilmarnock commented on January 18, 1921:

What we are witnessing in Germany is the capacity of a highly gifted people to make good to some extent commercially and economically despite a radically unsound financial situation. There is no financial bottom at all to the present modest commercial revival, nor any prospect of one. Whether it is possible under modern conditions for a bankrupt nation permanently to improve its health while remaining bankrupt, there is no way of knowing.

Economically, again, the improvement is really very superficial. The standard of life to which the great mass of the urban population seems to be adapting itself is considerably lower than what would be thought tolerable in this country. Whether the adaptation is more than apparent, and whether, if real, it is permanent, these are questions which every one will answer according to his taste.[141]

The remarks of the harassed Wirth about the small rentiers and other inflation victims or those of Lord Kilmarnock are of great importance because they point up the truth behind an increasing German effort to play on its poverty in ways that were sometimes less convincing. Take, for example, the remarks of retired Deutsche Bank director Carl von Gwinner, reported by the British Ambassador D'Abernon in November 1920:

Nothing could be more gloomy than his analysis of the present position, unless it be his forecast of the future. Germany was absolutely ruined; every month she was going deeper into the mire; taxation was already at an extravagant rate; the whole of the middle classes were ruined, while the former rich were now semi-paupers. To take his own case, he had more than a million sterling before the war, but 60 percent of this would be taken for an emergency levy, and he would pay another 60 or 70 percent income-tax on the revenue derived from what was left of his capital. Under these circumstances, he could not keep up his house or estate, while he found it extremely difficult to sell them.[142]

Somehow one suspects that Gwinner and his fellow bankers were not quite yet "semi-paupers," and it was not at all clear who was actually being beggared. Gwinner's friend, Swiss banker Dr. Julius Frey of the Schweizerische Kreditanstalt and the Elektrobank, for example, thought he was being victimized. The Elektrobank apparently was in as much trouble in 1921 as it had been in 1919, and he was disgusted with German business attitudes. As he frankly told Gwinner:

. . . almost daily we have to hear how in German heavy industrial circles one not only feels comfortable with the present exchange rate conditions, but declares in all seriousness that even an increase of the rate of the mark to 15 will end all German competitiveness on international markets. That we foreign creditors are simply being ruined by the present exchange rate, that we once gave our German debtors a good 123.45 gold francs for 100 marks and now shall be rewarded with 8 or 9 francs for it and that our participation in German enterprises even with 10 percent dividends is not even bringing a one percent return on our investments, for that no one in Germany

appears to have any feeling anymore. There is no lack of pretty words about labor and saving, but they are not translated into deeds. The state budget is ever more expensive, the inflation ever greater, and the end cannot be anything other than the great debacle unless one seriously and as quickly as possible tries to bring about a change. Does one still have the strength to do so?[143]

The German industrialist attitude described so angrily by Frey certainly was no secret. The December 11, 1920, issue of the *Frankfurter Zeitung* quoted remarks by the powerful Ruhr industrialist Peter Klöckner to the effect that the further depreciation of the mark offered the only opportunity "to protect our land from starvation by promoting large-scale exports."[144] Nevertheless, there was also considerable discomfort in Germany about what was going on. Back in September, the same influential newspaper expressed envy of those countries managing to cut their budgets, an envy which Wirth certainly shared, and in February 1921 the Association of German Metal Industrialists wondered how long Germany could remain an "oasis" in the world economic crisis.[145]

Still, the outside world did not always share this view. In January 1921, one of Richard Merton's English business colleagues wrote to ask about conditions in Germany:

Over here our alarmists or rather pessimists say that, whereas our workmen are idling for excessive wages, your working classes are slaving like niggers—the result being that we buy everything from motor cars to children's rattles from Germany at half the price which our English goods cost.[146]

Merton's response to this tasteless prose provided a remarkably well-balanced picture of Germany during the relative stabilization as well as a reasonably good example of opinion among influential and knowledgeable Germans.[147] He agreed that the Germans had a great export advantage but denied that it was because of the reason given. To be sure, worker productivity had improved substantially since the Revolution, but undernourishment, political agitation, and raw-materials problems continued to affect productivity adversely. In Merton's view, the "only significant reason" for German competitiveness was the exchange rate, which made German real wages much lower than those paid elsewhere, and it was this "difference in the international measure of the volume of a unit of labor" which "naturally comes in large measure to the benefit of the German producer, that is, the employer, and even to those who continuously import raw materials at international prices." Needless to say, the more labor contained in the product, the greater the advantage for the German producer, so that in some industries the profit margins were extraordinarily high—for example, in those producing electrotechnical products.

Merton did not think this situation would last. If the exchange rate remained stable, then wages would rise and thereby reduce if not destroy the German advantage. The balance would be much more rapidly restored if, as he hoped, the Allies would pursue a "reasonable policy" toward Germany and thereby promote so rapid a recovery of the mark that the export advantage arising from the difference between the internal and the external value of the mark would evaporate. Manifestly, the improvement of the exchange rate would not be without its price: "Here in Germany people are fully conscious of the fact that an improvement of the exchange rate would mean a heavy blow for German exports, for it would naturally not be possible to reduce wages at the same tempo as the exchange rate improves." Profits would deteriorate. Furthermore, sales at home as well as abroad would be negatively affected since customers would hold back in a repetition of that "buyers' strike" that had taken place when the relative stabilization first began. Merton reminded his English friend that purchasing power had deteriorated badly:

The impoverishment of the *Mittelstand* becomes ever greater. You do not realize how many people, not only from the *Mittelstand* but also the better placed circles and on down to the workers, have covered part of their expenses by selling something from their possessions, jewelry or some other such thing. Despite the apparent prosperity of the last years, the great mass in Germany could make no savings and this holds for the large part of the so-called rich as well, including my own person. Savings or an increase of wealth have been managed only by the so-called profiteers, who cannot be caught by taxes, but this group as a whole is not very meaningful among the totality of consumers.

Furthermore, Merton went on to point out that "a very large portion of German consumption among the middle income groups, for example, white-collar workers, is paid for by speculation on the bourse." This was especially true among bank employees, but it was a more general phenomenon when the mark was down and stock and bond prices were rising. It was possible to speculate on the bull market and thereby pay for the replacement of worn out shoes and clothes. Once the mark increased in value, speculation in a bear market would be less attractive and more limited, and this would have a significantly negative influence on German domestic consumption.

Indeed, while the existing situation was unhealthy, Merton recognized that a stabilization would lead to a serious economic crisis in Germany and to heavy unemployment, "which naturally in our situation could have extremely dangerous political consequences [in comparison] for example to England where the government enjoys more power and authority." Nevertheless, Merton wished that the risks could be run so as to "get out of the existing situation." First, a way had to be found to restore the finances of the state and cease the printing of money. The precondition for this, Merton insisted, was that "the Treaty of Versailles be more or less thrown out." In Merton's view, its only effect was to destroy both the consumptive and productive power of one hundred million central Europeans to the detriment of worldwide recovery. He concluded:

Thus, in my view, this is the way the situation looks from a general point of view and thereby also, in the long-run, from the private perspective as well. From the private perspective, naturally, one can also pursue a short-sighted policy and can do well under the present circumstances. But one must be clear about the fact that it is a short-sighted policy and should not be surprised when the entire story ends one fine day with a colossal crash in which even the greatest are laid low. For this reason, I prefer it privately, even though the Metallbank and the Metallgesellschaft are among those who have understood how not only not to become weaker but actually stronger despite all the difficulties, if even we are properly subjected to the crash which can lead to a recovery, because over the long run I have the conviction that it will be better for us than the present, highly unsympathetic situation which in the end no one enjoys.

Merton's preferences aside, the dilemmas of the relative stabilization and the contradictory sentiments and ideas it evoked could hardly have been more sharply presented. In the face of the socioeconomic and political conditions existing in Germany in 1920, it is difficult to see how a genuine effort toward stabilization was possible. A decade later, hindsight may have made Bresciani-Turroni more confident about treating the relative stabilization as a lost opportunity for the permanent stabilization of the mark, but when he reported for the Reparations Commission on the situation in Germany in late February 1921, he was more hesitant in his conclusions:

Under actually existing conditions, measures concerning the stabilization of the mark would be premature. However, that does not justify at all the fatalism which has taken hold in certain circles or the idea that nothing is capable of stopping the fall of the mark because it depends on general economic conditions. Experiences which we have had with monetary reform in the past demonstrate that one can obtain good results through wise measures. It is necessary however to recognize that a monetary reform depends upon certain economic conditions.[148]

Economic conditions, as this great Italian student of the inflation was suggesting, however, were a product of will and not only of fate. The battle between short-run and long-run considerations in Germany's economic reconstruction was a crucial aspect of the relative stabilization that must now receive attention, especially since it would determine the future of German development once the great debacle which so many Germans expected finally came.

Chapter 6

What Kind of Reconstruction? The German Business Community Faces the Future

A Credit Organization for German Industry?

Mankind's ability to survive sustained periods of chaos and even disaster seems to rest upon remarkable capacities of adaptation and an uncanny ability to make use of desperate conditions to serve not only short-run but sometimes even long-run purposes. Obviously, these capacities are not possessed by or made available to all, and periods like those through which Germany was passing between 1918 and 1923 are Darwinian episodes in which not only survival but also the redistribution of economic and social rewards were determined by access to goods and especially to credit as well as a substantial measure of speculative luck. Such periods are neither morally edifying nor economically and political healthy, and one of the major impulses behind the cries for organization and planning at such times is the wish to reduce the role of the fortuitous and give both control and direction to forces that would otherwise run amok in the service of special and immediate interests to the detriment of the "general good." The problem with these organizational and planning efforts is that they tend to be outrun by events and are resented as inhibitions and barriers to the next set of seemingly appropriate adaptations. As Jakob Goldschmidt of the Nationalbank argued:

I consider it impossible, at the present time, when we are going through complete revolutions politically and when everything is in flux economically, to lay down guidelines for the future. I believe that no expert will have the courage to engage in the business of prophecy in that manner, especially after the experiences of the last years, in which we have seen that all prediction and attempts to create fixed structures have had unfortunate results. I believe that very many discussions and considerations concerning the practical development of the economy would not have been necessary if one had not, through altogether too much organization and bureaucratization, treated the situation of yesterday as the truth of today. . . .[1]

But how was one to act upon anticipations of the truth of tomorrow? Reasonably informed persons were fully aware as to how profoundly unstable and vulnerable the entire financial structure of the economy was and the extent to which Germany faced a credit crisis threatening not only the long-term capital requirements of industry but even short-term needs for operating capital. Lord D'Abernon, who began a six-year stint as British Ambassador to Berlin in October 1920 and who brought considerable economic and financial expertise and experience to his post, was easily convinced of the seriousness of Germany's problems even if he was to become very critical of the German way of dealing with them.[2] When he asked why the Germans were presenting their financial situation in so gloomy a light when the government had not yet even begun collecting the large revenues anticipated from its tax program, Reichsbank Director von Glasenapp tried to show that German pessimism arose not only from the problems of collecting the taxes but even more from what would happen if and when normal financial conditions were restored. Glasenapp explained the delay in collecting the taxes by the problems involved in the reorganization of the nation's tax administration, a response Lord D'Abernon apparently found illuminating since it had English parallels. Germany, therefore, had to continue financing its expenses through increases in the floating debt. When D'Abernon inquired whether the floating debt was being placed successfully, Glasenapp explained that the Reichsbank was having little trouble placing the Treasury bills it was discounting for the government because of the abundance of cash on the German market, an abundance, however, that "could only be described as apparent since it rests exclusively on the creation of fictional capital by means of inflation."[3] Both the savings banks and the other banks had vastly increased their outside deposits, and in order to keep this money in the most liquid form possible, it was placed in Treasury bills which could be rediscounted at any time, even before they fell due. The consequence was that because of the inflation "an apparent abundance was being created which did not conform to the true economic conditions of the country and which makes it impossible to work effectively against the actual dearth of capital used in normal circumstances by means of the discount rate."[4] Thus, nations rich in capital, like the United States and England, actually had higher discount rates than Germany. The danger was that as soon as the government was collecting large amounts of revenue, the quest for the necessary funds would lead to a disgorging of the Treasury bills, and in the process, there would be a dramatic revelation of the chimerical character of the present surfeit of liquidity.

Havenstein provided an even more explicit scenario before the Reichsbank Curatorium in September 1920. He explained that there was no point under existing conditions for the Reichsbank to use the traditional method of raising the discount rate to attract foreign capital and ration domestic borrowing. It was impossible to attract foreign capital by such means because no one abroad had that kind of confidence in the German economy. The Reichsbank could not raise its discount rate above 6 to 7 percent and was thus in no position to compete with the 8 to 9 percent offered by the Anglo-Americans. A larger increase of the German discount rate would make domestic pro-

duction and exports more difficult without significantly affecting the most important source of credit within the German private economy, which was not the Reichsbank but rather the private banks and savings banks. Only when the huge liquidity was reduced through the collection of taxes would the Reichsbank regain its old influence over the money market and be in a position to employ the discount rate effectively. This prospect, however, did not give Havenstein much joy either. The projected soaking up of the money in the banks through industrial and municipal bond issues and especially through taxes would compel them to turn in their Treasury bills to the Reichsbank for cash so that the Reichsbank, instead of holding forty billion in Treasury bills (as was the case in September 1920), could anticipate holding eighty to ninety billion, and "its credit would thereby be endangered to the highest degree and perhaps ruined."[5]

When Havenstein was talking about the lack of confidence in Germany abroad as a barrier to foreign investment, he was talking about solid investors willing to take long-term risks. As every informed person knew, however, the economy was actually being sustained by an enormous flow of foreign speculative capital inspired by the weakness rather than the strength of the mark. This was speculation that sought to gain either from short-term fluctuations in the German currency or from a long-term bet on Germany recovery. It had begun in 1919 and assumed such massive proportions in the course of 1919–1920 that at least 36 percent of the deposits in the seven major Berlin banks was said to come from such sources.[6] While estimates varied greatly, the significance of the amounts of marks and mark-denominated assets held by foreigners inside and outside Germany was indisputable. Thus, American packers selling to Germany accepted marks in payment in 1919 and during the first half of 1920, and there is evidence that they were still holding millions of these marks in 1922. The sale of German industrial and municipal securities had stepped up dramatically in 1920, and it was estimated in October 1920 that as much as a hundred million dollars in German industrial securities had been sold on the American market, while thirty million dollars in municipal bonds had been placed as well. Furthermore, many persons were speculating in German money pure and simple. Thus, in late 1920, the American firm of George H. Perkins & Co. in Washington, D.C., offered six-month options on marks ranging from forty dollars to control ten thousand marks to three hundred dollars to control a hundred thousand marks and suggested a possible profit in the first case of a hundred dollars and in the second of a thousand dollars. While the U.S. Commerce Department was well aware of what was going on, it opposed intervention:

We believe that practically all Americans who buy these German securities and notes are very well aware of the risk they are taking and that they do not consider these purchases an investment but essentially a gamble. Also, there is no effective way of protecting certain classes of so-called investors who habitually prefer to play long chances. If they do not put their money into blue-sky oil stocks, they will put it into German mark notes or other European notes of uncertain value. These people know that they are gambling and we know of no effective way that this government can save them from themselves.[7]

The German authorities and business community did not lose much sleep about the risks being taken by American speculators either, and were well aware that "every waiter, errand boy, and cowboy, even in the most out-of-the-way places speculates in marks, since he always has left over the *one* dollar for which he can buy 100 marks."[8] The eminent statistician and economist Ernst Wagemann went so far as to argue that Reichsbank note emissions were to be encouraged because they promoted a "welcome form of foreign granting of credits" by stirring further speculation in favor of the mark.[9] Manifestly, this speculation in the future recovery of the mark was helping to maintain its worth, but it was not without its dangers to the German economy itself. The speculation created an instability which made doing business difficult and often ran counter to German government efforts to stabilize the exchange rate at a level it found satisfactory. Furthermore, it opened the exchange rate to deliberate manipulation. Thus, for example, between November 12 and 18, 1920, the mark suddenly improved in New York from eighty-eight to sixty-three marks to the dollar. The change was attributed to the election of President Harding

and rumors that the Americans were going to return the German property that had been sequestered during the war. There were strong suspicions, however, that the mark was being deliberately manipulated to improve American export opportunities to Germany and to encourage the Germans to buy food and raw materials. Whatever the case, one could assume that speculation, whether in response to major events, such as the decline in the mark's value that could be anticipated when the reparations terms were made known, or whether deliberately undertaken to influence economic conditions, would continue.[10]

The great fear, however, was that some major untoward development or combination of circumstances would lead foreigners to cease their speculation in favor of the mark. The massive deposits held in Germany would then be liquidated along with the money and assets held abroad. Not only would Germany thus be deprived of this source of foreign exchange, but it would also be drained of foreign exchange by the sale of marks. At the same time, the mark would sink into worthlessness, especially if the foreign flight from the mark were accompanied by the resale of Treasury bills to the Reichsbank by the banks in order to satisfy the cash demands of their customers. The ultimate nightmare was described in very concrete terms by industrialist Hans Kraemer at the Reich Economic Council in October 1920:

The banks are "swimming in money." What will happen, however, at the moment when one really goes about collecting taxes in Germany? Until now that has not been the case. What will be at the moment when the Reich Emergency Capital Levy is collected? This time will perhaps also come some day, even if I do see some smiles of doubt on many faces. Above all, how will things be when the wishes of the Reich Economic Council are carried out and the boundless increase of the currency is finally dammed and when the outside world one day, for foreign or domestic reasons, takes its deposits, which have reached 30 billions and, in my view, constitute a very substantial part of the deposits of the German banks out of Germany for speculative reasons, or with the further sinking of the mark, when the outside world uses this money to buy up German goods again.[11]

Hans Kraemer was one of those who was convinced that German industry could not afford to surrender to the monetary illusion if it were to have a successful economic reconstruc-

Georg Bernhard (1875–1944). (*By permission of the Ullstein Verlag*)

tion and that ways and means had to be found to master the credit crisis that would inevitably strike the economy once the excess liquidity had been removed by taxation and stabilization. This view was promoted above all by Julius Hirsch and by a number of leading industrialists, especially Dr. Hans Jordan of the cellulose industry, a member of the Presidium of the RdI. It was also vigorously supported by the influential editor of the *Vossischen Zeitung* and of the economic journal *Plutus*, Georg Bernhard, who was a left Democrat and a member of the Reich Economic Council. There was thus nothing surprising about the fact that the March 1920 issue of *Plutus* provided Hirsch and Jordan with an opportunity to present their schemes for the cooperative organization of industrial credit in Germany.[12]

Hirsch's concern with this question went back at least to the September 1919 economic policy guidelines presented to the Bauer Cabinet in which the then new RWM leadership stressed the importance of reconstructing Germany's industrial capital base and pointed out that if those in possession of capital continued to withhold it because of the political and economic uncertainty and to flee taxes, then "a taking over of capital formation by the state will have to be considered in the form that the state

itself undertakes the building of new plants for important industries, finances them and then runs them in the form of mixed economic enterprises."[13]

The seriousness of this intention became evident in early 1920, when Hirsch sent Chancellor Bauer what the latter's Undersecretary described as a "memorandum with a radical new proposal in view" on "Capital Formation and Capital Creation."[14] The fundamental assumption of the Hirsch memorandum was that the supplying of capital from private sources was not keeping pace either with the need for operating capital or, more important, with the need for long-term capital to renew and rebuild Germany's industrial plant. Presented at the height of the inflationary wave during the first months of 1920, Hirsch was able to point to complaints throughout industry about the rising prices of raw materials, especially imported ones, and the difficulties being created for those with debts payable abroad in foreign currencies. He was particularly concerned about the dangers of "foreignization" (*Überfremdung*); that is, that Germans would sell their firms to foreigners or be bought out because of these problems. Hirsch's major concentration, however, was on long-term capital formation to renovate and rationalize Germany's industries at a time when, for example, new machines cost at least fifteen times their prewar price. Unhappily, those with capital were showing an extreme reluctance to invest because of fears of taxation, threats of socialization, labor unrest, and general uncertainty. As a consequence, capital was not being employed for national economic productive purposes: "It creeps away from oppressive taxation into expenditures of the most unproductive sort, on the most expensive furs, hand-cut chairs of dubious origin, and cubist pictures of the most unclear color. It even creeps into raw materials of all kinds, along with the hoarding of money, there is the hoarding of blocks of iron, wood, and even suits of clothes."[15]

The problem, in Hirsch's view, was how to put this capital to use in the service of the national economy before foreigners would gain enough faith in Germany's long-term productive capacity to buy up German industry on the cheap. One of his particular concerns was mobilizing the large amounts of German money abroad for capital investment at home, and he was convinced that it might be possible to bring together Germany's industries and banks in a cooperative effort to turn those mark holdings as well as a portion of export profits into a credit based on the issuance of bonds backed, on the one hand, by a Trusteeship Bank (*Treuhandbank*) organized with industrial and banking participation and, on the other, by the Reich itself.

While Hirsch placed major emphasis on self-organization by the business community to secure credit, he considered state investment essential to further guarantee the credit and also emphasized the need for a measure of control and direction of investment. As he pointed out, there were precedents for this. During the war, the nitrates industry had created an equalization fund to use part of its profits to help the less developed plants in the industry, and a portion of the coal-industry profits were being used to support the construction of miner housing. A similar notion of controlling the use of industrial profits lay behind the idea of employing the rent tax for home construction and the social export levy. Hirsch might also have added his own efforts to persuade the iron and steel industrialists to create an equalization fund from their profits to help pay the Swedish ore debts and thus put an end to the harsh pricing policies and payment conditions they were forcing on their domestic customers. Finally, the proposed bank could be employed at once to attract foreign capital and prevent foreign control. Its assets could not be expropriated to pay for reparations as they would not belong to the Reich. At the same time, the bank could refuse to assist any firm seeking foreign credit unless that firm made provision against foreign control.

The entire scheme was typical of Hirsch's thinking and of his commitment to maintaining the primacy of private economic initiative and organization with just that measure of state control and influence necessary to place national above private economic interests. Although the affinity to the Reich Fund and Reich Assets Bank projects of Moellendorff was obvious, Hirsch's plan was likely to be more appealing to industrial interests because it was less statist and complicated. Hirsch did, in fact, find the RdI leadership "very sympathetic" to the

industrial bank idea when he discussed the matter with them on January 24, 1920.[16]

Nevertheless, there was anxiety about the role Hirsch assigned to the Reich, and this undoubtedly was one important motive driving Hans Jordan to make a proposal of his own for a "credit cooperative of German industry." In his memorandum of February 1920,[17] Jordan agreed with Hirsch's diagnosis of the problem, but he placed much more emphasis on Germany's long-term ability to secure foreign, especially American, capital if it balanced its budget and offered enough security. The speculative American engagement in Germany was taken as evidence of confidence in "our basically industrious population, our valuable highly developed industrial plant, the personality of our entrepreneurs, and our technical intelligence,"[18] and Jordan was convinced that a more solid American engagement was possible. To secure it, however, German industry had to take the path of self-help. This could not be accomplished in sufficient measure either through equalization funds and mechanisms of the type emphasized by Hirsch or by the banks. What was needed was an organization of German industry to produce credit through cooperation and solidarity within the industrial community, while the banks and the Reichsbank would lend their technical assistance to this effort. Jordan argued against the state assuming any significant role in securing foreign credit since, on the one hand, it was already burdened by reparations and other external and internal demands and, on the other, industry would be distrustful of the state out of fear that its intervention would be used for purposes of further taxation and socialization. What was needed, therefore, was a voluntary gathering together of industry in a "general credit cooperative" which would place its combined resources and credit behind the cooperative as a guarantee both for the credit provided to its members and for the credits received from foreign sources.

Manifestly, the organization would have to be careful to provide credit fairly and equitably and would have to take the needs of commerce and agriculture into account. Most important, however, was that it remain a purely private affair and be left free of all responsibility to collect taxes or to provide economic services to the state. Otherwise, Jordan warned, it would be "dead" from the start because of internal opposition and lack of confidence. Insofar as foreign exchange was necessary to cover import payments, it was to be secured through free agreement between the cooperative and the Reichsbank and Foreign Exchange Procurement Board. While the private character of the cooperative would keep it free of Allied efforts to seize its resources, as might not have been the case if the state were involved, the legal status of the cooperative and its membership would enable it to offer foreigners the opportunity to participate financially in German enterprises but prevent them from exercising any control.

The resources and credit behind the cooperative would put it in a position to issue what was tantamount to its own money for foreign trade. Jordan proposed that the organization be permitted to issue a commercial paper of its own which could not be used in domestic commerce. This short-term paper was to bear 2 percent interest and attain its face value in the course of the year, at which time it would have to be turned in for payment in the currency of a foreign state based on gold. Basically, the cooperative was to control all imports of raw materials and to mediate all foreign credits for such purposes. Furthermore, it was to do more than secure short-term credits and issue short-term paper. It was also to issue long-term bonds bearing 6 to 8 percent interest based once again on the security provided by the combined resources and credit of its membership. Jordan felt that such bonds

would probably be taken by American banks, because the costs could be recovered by selling them again to the public. Such long-term loans in dollars based on a broad guarantee of the cooperative membership would be suitable to replace the missing operating capital needed for foreign trade, to relieve the passivity of the balance of payments and, together with the short-term bills and foreign exchange from abroad, to ensure orderly private economic intercourse with the outside world.[19]

Jordan shared Hirsch's view that it was important to employ the existing industrial groups—that is, the branch organizations of industry—for the credit institution and to have labor represented, as was the case with the export control boards. He proposed that the cooperative be managed by a nine-person curatorium, which would appoint its officers, and that a thirty-person executive committee be created to represent the various industrial groups involved.

On February 18, Jordan presented his plan to some of his colleagues on the RdI, representatives of agriculture, and officials of the relevant Ministries. It was intended to be purely informational and, like the memoranda under discussion, was inspired by the difficulties various industries were having at the time in purchasing raw materials and paying off their foreign-exchange debts. There was, therefore, a positive disposition toward the idea of doing something about the credit problem through a cooperative effort on the part of the various economic groups. The recent development of the export control boards seemed to offer a suitable instrument for realizing some of Jordan's ideas. Nevertheless, there was much criticism and even alarm. There was some concern that the organization proposed by Jordan was too complicated, a view shared by Hirsch, who also argued that Jordan's exclusive concentration on credit for the purchase of raw materials from abroad overlooked what appeared to him the more important problem of gathering in Germany's floating mark circulation for purposes of long-term modernization.

The most serious and penetrating criticism, however, came from Privy Councillor David Fischer of the Finance Ministry, who strenuously opposed the plan. His greatest fears, which were shared by the Reichsbank, were that the economic groups in the credit cooperative would control virtually all the foreign exchange coming into the country and literally replace the German currency with a currency of its own. The proposal, therefore, had extraordinary political and economic implications. As Fischer reported:

The question was raised from my side whether in fact, as the remarks of Dr. Jordan suggested, the entire influx of foreign exchange into Germany was to be concentrated in the projected new organization. This would mean a separation of industry from the Reich economy, which has already occurred in the case of the known and very regrettable hoarding of foreign exchange abroad, and it also means the ruin of the banks, the Reichsbank, and the finances of the Reich. If one intends to establish a state on a largely private economic basis, to set up a new organization of the productive groups through the use of foreign currencies that have been procured, then one must also take over the foreign debt of the previous economic and state organizations.[20]

Fischer's worry was dismissed by Jordan and his colleagues from the RdI, who pointed out that the memorandum specifically stated that the foreign exchange needed for food imports and Reich expenses would be left to the Reich and the Reichsbank. The industrialists claimed that they were only interested in participation in the foreign-exchange supply insofar as it involved foreign trade. The misunderstanding, however, had greater significance than they pretended, for it raised profound questions of the relationship between Germany's economic reconstruction and the political control of the economy. Insofar as an effort was to be made to organize the reconstruction, the issue was who was to do the organizing, and the control of credit necessarily involved the control of investment and the potential control of the reconstruction. The Hirsch plan sought to reserve this ultimate control for the state and to maintain a measure of state involvement in the control of credit and the direction of investment. The Jordan plan sought to remove the state from such involvement, but if carried through under postwar German conditions, it was tantamount to a program for the virtual domination of the economy by organized industrial interests.

This problem of the control and direction of the German economy, which was one of the fundamental issues of Weimar politics, surfaced but briefly in these discussions, only to be submerged in the consensus that existed between the Reich Association and the Economics Ministry that some kind of organization was needed to provide the guarantees necessary to secure credit. Hirsch had intended to present his program to the Cabinet, but the Kapp Putsch pushed such matters into the background. Nevertheless, the two memoranda became public property thanks to their publication in *Plutus* in early March, and the interest in industrial circles remained quite strong. At the first membership meeting of the RdI on April 14, 1920, the business manager, Walter Simons, who was to become Foreign Minister

under Fehrenbach, made a strong plea for action to solve the credit problem. He pointed out that some industries had sufficient foreign exchange and exports to solve their capital problems but that the majority did not, and these industries were in danger of going under. He praised the Jordan plan, arguing that foreigners would not give Germans credit simply because of their "beautiful eyes" but would demand securities. Therefore, "we can do nothing more wrong than to sit down and wait until the outside world becomes so friendly as to help us recover with a large-scale credit action."[21] He strongly urged that industry help itself and do something about its own situation so as to attract foreign financial assistance.

Nevertheless, virtually nothing was done until the late summer of 1920, when the "discussion" of the problem was suddenly revived in the form of virulent attacks by its opponents in response to rumors that the plan for what was now being called a Reich Economic Bank (*Reichswirtschaftsbank*) was going to be implemented. The chief opposition came from the chambers of commerce, the banks, the Reichsbank, and the Finance Ministry. They were reacting to what they viewed as a new offensive on behalf of the idea by State Secretary Hirsch and Ministerial Director Pritschow of the RWM, who allegedly began their initiative by proposing that the Foreign Exchange Procurement Board employ part of its foreign-exchange holdings in connection with the project and who instigated an abortive meeting on the proposal in the board in late July. When Glasenapp announced that the Reichsbank would give no support to the idea, Economics Minister Scholz was reported to have left the meeting remarking that "he no longer had any interest in the matter."[22] It was then claimed that Scholz's interest was revived shortly afterward by Hirsch and Pritschow, who now argued that the fundamental reason for creating a Reich Economic Bank was social; namely, the giving of credits as a means of fighting unemployment. Rumor had it that Hirsch and Pritschow wanted to become the directors of the new bank and that they planned to give trade-union representatives a position of parity in the organization.

The exact reliability of all this confidential information supplied to and by the chambers of commerce is very difficult to determine. It certainly was true that the Reich Economic Bank idea (as was the case with Moellendorff's Reich Fund program of 1918–1919) was now linked with the unemployment question and that Scholz, in the context of the unemployment problems and other difficulties of the summer of 1920, had come to the conclusion, as he informed the Cabinet on September 7, that there was a need for "a great credit institution, which under the most accommodating conditions would place the needed means at the disposal of the cash-starved factories and help them to overcome the difficulties caused by fluctuations in the exchange rate."[23] Scholz wondered if a solution might not be found in a tapping of the resources of the savings banks and the clearing center (*Girozentrale*) of the municipal banks, which he himself had helped to establish in 1907–1908.[24] Apparently, there was also some further talk of employing the resources of the Foreign Exchange Procurement Board and some discussion of giving tax breaks to firms that would place their credit at the disposal of the proposed Reich Economic Bank as well as of using the profits of the various war corporations now under Reich control.[25]

Whether it was true that Hirsch and Pritschow had personal ambitions to direct the bank is unclear. Hirsch certainly was an ambitious man. Since his original memorandum had spoken of giving labor a role in the supervision of the bank, that part of the story appeared plausible, although this did not necessarily mean that Hirsch wanted to give the unions parity. What was not true was the alarmist rumor that the plan was going to be implemented by the Cabinet on September 4 following discussions with the Reichsbank Directors. All Scholz did on September 7 was to bring up the idea and secure approval for conducting further discussions despite the fact that heavy opposition from the banks was to be expected.[26] The rumor that the government was going to act quickly, however, created some panic among the plan's opponents and helped stir up sharp anticipatory reactions.

The most important of these was a fairly scurrilous protest by the Hamburg Chamber of Commerce. The authors frankly admitted that they were responding to rumors and newspaper reports and suggested that the project was not one supported by the government but rather was the result of "private wishes on the part of certain gentlemen in the Reich Economics Ministry."[27] The imputation that personal ambitions were at play helped to sharpen the broader and more familiar thrust of their lengthy attack. Their chief charges were that the plan would lead to a revival of the controlled economy in new guise, that the "centralization and monopolization of foreign exchange" would lead to the further burdening of commercial activity and the hated tendency of excluding the commercial sector from economic life, that it would produce unnecessary and undesirable competition for the banks, and that it would lead to a redistribution of capital from the deserving to the undeserving because there was no real mechanism by which the new agency could determine who was worthy of credit and who was not.

This missive was followed by an open and behind-the-scenes struggle against the economic bank scheme. The Hamburg Chamber of Commerce made certain to distribute its letter to other chambers of commerce, some of which promptly joined forces with Hamburg. The United Chambers of Commerce of Frankfurt and Hanau did so on October 1, adding to the Hamburg arguments the charge that the new institution would bring partisan political interests into Germany's credit organization.[28] The Cologne Chamber of Commerce added its opposition at the end of October by emphasizing the inflationary potential of the new bank.[29] Most impressive from a public relations point of view was a declaration by the leading Berlin banks of September 28, 1920, which appeared in the advertisement section of leading newspapers, stating that the banks were "in a position to meet every justified credit requirement of industry and commerce, that they have always done so readily in the past and will also do so in the future." The banks pointed out that numerous chambers of commerce, the Reichsbank President, and leading experts supported this position and warned against "an enterprise that will not bring the hoped for advantages but will lead to a waste of Reich resources." The "newly planned clothing of the project in the form of unemployment support" in no way altered this negative judgment in the eyes of the leading banks.[30]

The behind-the-scenes battle against the Reich Economic Bank was no less energetic. The Reichsbank leadership apparently was cautious about coming out openly against the plan and only decided to do so under pressure from the leading Berlin banks. The Reichsbank was especially opposed to plans to employ the four to five billion marks in profits from the war corporations to supply the capital for the new institution. The Reichsbank feared that this would only increase the need for printing further bank notes and also expressed anxiety that the organization would be much too complicated and too costly.[31] The Finance Ministry was much less measured and reserved about expressing its opposition. Even before the concrete plans of the plan could be formulated and presented, State Secretary Moesle informed Scholz of his misgivings. Moesle objected to the idea of a new agency that could act independently of the RFM in granting and distributing credits that came in part or in whole from Reich funds. What disturbed him most, however, was the idea of fighting the existing economic difficulties by countercyclical methods:

Most important, but also most questionable, is the purpose which the projected institute is intended to serve in combatting slumps on the market and in general production. Here one must vigorously act against the attempt to bring about an improvement in our economic situation through further inflation. Such an effort can only fail while doing the worst damage to our Reich finances and the general welfare. Where slumps in production have taken place because of market problems, the giving of credits can only bring temporary relief, which will lead to an increase of expensive inventory holdings and encourage industry not to undertake the necessary liquidation of those inventories. Making credit easier will not only hinder price reduction. The institution also will lead to the giving of credit to undeserving persons and enterprises.[32]

This was precisely the view taken by many of the bankers, especially the outspoken Jakob Goldschmidt. At a meeting in the RWM on October l to discuss the matter, Goldschmidt echoed Moesle in stressing the uselessness of giving credits to relieve a business crisis:

The placing of fresh means at the disposal of industry and commerce can only produce a temporary improvement, which will then lead to an even more severe collapse. The German economy is already in the middle of a crisis. He [Goldschmidt] wishes, in the interest of the German economy, that an elemental crisis will occur as soon as possible. . . .[33]

Such remarks, however, could only confirm the arguments of proponents of the plan that something had to be done to break the monopoly of the banks over credit, which placed many businesses at the mercy of the banks and gave the banks a "horrendous power position in economic life." These critics charged that "the great banks have decided to undertake a cleansing of German economic life by limiting the granting of credits in order to force the death of those plants less capable of survival, and this to be sure in the hope of bringing about a rehabilitation of those plants that remain."[34] The Deutsche Bank, for example, had denied its branches the right to grant credits in excess of a hundred thousand marks without permission, and its Berlin office, almost without exception, refused the granting of larger credits. If this continued, proponents of the economic bank argued, then there would be increasing shutdowns and massive unemployment, so that the Reich would end up having to pay huge sums in unemployment relief. The economic bank, therefore, lay very much in the interests of industry, and the plan's proponents could not understand the opposition of the chambers of commerce or industrial groups in certain regions, such as Saxony, where unemployment was such a problem.

One reason for the opposition was fear of reviving government controls, and another might have been the commitment to traditionalist capitalist principles as expounded by Goldschmidt. To an industrialist of the stamp of Hans Kraemer, who was willing to trade a certain amount of government economic involvement in return for the positive results it could bring and who did not feel bound by the rigid rules of classical doctrine, the position of Goldschmidt was nothing more or less than a "capitalist catastrophe policy," and he felt that "everything had to be done to avoid the catastrophe." To be sure, Kraemer was not prepared to absolve industry of all responsibility. In fact,

. . . industry bears responsibility in part itself for the fact that it is not at full capacity because it has got into the habit of selling at profiteering prices. The balances of the enterprises which have come out now show the unheard-of profits that have been made. Industry must itself reduce its prices, but the consequences of that will be that the reserves will be used up and there will be a further demand for credit.[35]

Over and over again, Kraemer warned that the collection of taxes would also lead to a huge demand for credit, that the German industrial plant needed renewal, and that the entire monetary foundation of the banks was built on a dangerous combination of Treasury bills and speculative foreign deposits. Goldschmidt, however, was relentless and blunt in his reply:

The German economy is in the middle of a catastrophe that has to run its course with the elimination of small enterprises. A support of enterprises that are not capable of survival must not occur. . . . He has long given up prophesying how the future will be. . . . It is impossible to bring about a general remedy for the collapse which stands before us. If a guarantee of the Reich is necessary for the various credits that are given, then a further monetary inflation is unavoidable. The credit question can only be solved in each case on an individual basis. One cannot operate according to a bureaucratic scheme.[36]

Even critics of the proposals and those with reservations, however, were not prepared, in most cases, to go quite as far as Goldschmidt and share his enthusiasm for an enlivening and refreshing economic *Götterdämmerung*. Reichsbank Director Friedrich admitted that there might be a need for assistance of some kind, while others pointed out that the banks had denied certain industries and plants credit in a manner that seemed unjustified and that had even necessitated Reich intervention. Such persons conceded that a distinction had to be made between the purely private economic perspective and the broader perspective of what was best for the economy. A means had to be found, therefore, to funnel and channel credit for the latter purpose. As everyone recognized, however, the use of the central clearing agency of the savings banks, which largely handled savings-bank funds, would require a Reich guarantee because of the legal requirements that savings bank funds be placed only in absolutely secure (*mündelsicher*) investments. This was not the most welcome of solutions, and there

continued to be division over whether there was a true credit shortage and what should be done if there were. Consequently, at the conclusion of the October 1 meeting, Scholz asked that a working committee be set up to review the question.

Even this met with opposition from Wirth, who protested that he had not been present at the September 7 Cabinet meeting at which Scholz was empowered to take further steps and that he was not present at the October 1 RWM meeting on the subject either. He insisted, in the name of the "unity of the government," on being consulted and involved in all future discussions.[37] It was largely due to Hans Kraemer, one of the most active industrialists on the Reich Economic Council, who joined forces with Jordan and Georg Bernhard as well as with Hirsch, that the issue was kept alive in the face of such powerful opposition. Their cause was strengthened by the fact that they could argue, as they did repeatedly, that the proposal dated back to discussions within the RdI and that Foreign Minister Simons had supported the Jordan plan at the April RdI meeting. Thus, when Kraemer used his position as Chairman of the Economic Policy Committee of the RWR to bring the question of credit help for industry before his committee on October 11 and to propose a special subcommittee to investigate the question, he, Jordan, and Bernhard were able to reject the claims of the banker Salomonsohn that the committee was being presented with an "omelette surprise" by arguing that the "omelette" was a good many months old and that it was high time that it was served up. Hirsch used the occasion to hit particularly hard at the suggestions that motives of personal ambition were behind his pushing the issue, pointing out that the RdI was repeatedly inquiring about what was happening and expressing fears that economic difficulties, be they exports or a new burst of mark depreciation, would lead to credit problems for industry. A major difficulty by this time, however, was that a variety of projects had been under discussion and no one was sure which project, if any, was being proposed and exactly what the Economics Minister himself had in mind.[38]

In order to define the problems and their possible solutions, therefore, the RWR's Economic

Policy Committee decided to establish a special subcommittee to "consider measures to deal with the financial needs of the productive estates." The subcommittee began its meetings on October 19, 1920, and held a total of eleven meetings between that date and July 14, 1922. The first ten of these were held between October 20, 1920, and February 1921 and were largely devoted to hearings in which experts from the world of banking and industry were interrogated as to whether there was in fact a capital shortage and what means could or should be used to relieve the credit problems of industry. The last two meetings, in November 1921 and July 1922, took place during an entirely different phase of the inflation, are mainly interesting for the light they shed on the changes that had taken place, and will be considered in a later chapter. These lengthy meetings, like most meetings of the RWR and its committees, produced no practical results whatever, but they provide a remarkably revealing picture of both credit and banking conditions and the economic thinking of many of Germany's most important and influential economic leaders.[39]

No one contested the fact that the banks were "swimming in money" or claimed that there was a credit shortage because of insufficient liquidity. What emerged from the testimony and discussion, however, was that the credit conditions being offered by the banks since January 1920 had become considerably more severe, amounting to an increase of 15 to 20 percent and that there was a extreme disproportion between the interest that the banks were giving on deposits and what they were charging for credit. While offering only 1.5 percent interest on deposits—and in some cases actually charging customers for holding their money—they were charging between 9 and 12 percent interest for credit and often even more. The actual interest charge was usually 7 percent, the rest being accounted for by a variety of commissions (*Provisionen*). Customers with a credit line, for example, were charged each quarter for that portion of the credit they did not use in order to compensate the bank for keeping the money available. Other imaginative provisions had also been introduced. As a representative of the Berlin clothing industry, which was apparently particularly hard hit by these credit conditions,

complained, the banks had a cartel with a monopoly of credit through which they were able to enjoy a "monopolistic" position in economic life:

The banks today form a cartel. We have to deal with a condition cartel in banking. I am a convinced supporter of cartels, but this support means in my case also that the limits of cartels must be drawn, and these are determined by the general economy because otherwise cartels cannot perform the functions which are expected of them. This monopoly by the banks lacks any control by competition or the public. This makes it possible for the banks to exploit—I mean this in the best sense without any other implications—the need for credit and leads to a situation in which production is hampered to such an extent that its justification needs to be considered.... If one thinks of credit as a means of production, and if that means of production stands today at 10 percent and is 2 percent too expensive, then there is a burden placed on production which, at a time when price reduction is more necessary than ever, can and should be born only if its inner justification and necessity can really be indisputably demonstrated.[40]

Thus, while credit was allegedly available, businessmen of this type found it more satisfactory to reduce their production than to expand it because the credit they needed simply was too expensive. Finally, there were loud complaints that in many instances the banks were offering particular customers credit only on condition that they paid interest as high as 20 percent with the obvious objective of cutting them off altogether.

The answer to these complaints by the illustrious bankers called to testify before the committee was that it was as nonsensical to compare prewar and postwar interest rates as it was to compare the prewar and postwar price of butter. Like everything else, banking had become more expensive, and they also found it somewhat odd that the textile cartel was complaining about the banking cartel. The inflation itself had vastly increased the need for more personnel in the banks, as well as for expansion of facilities, so that wage and material costs in the banking industry were higher than ever. To the great irritation of the banks, they were particularly burdened by having to perform new services for the tax authorities because of the requirement that all paper assets be placed on deposit and the termination of the privacy of bank accounts. The bankers claimed that it was impossible to give higher interest on deposits or demand less for credit under such conditions. They added that credit in Germany was cheaper than in other industrial countries while the risks were greater. One banker reminded the committee that there had been relatively few bankruptcies in Germany during the spring when the mark suddenly rose in value, and this was because the banks had stepped in and helped, as apparently was the case in the textile and shoe industries. "Just think what kind of risks have resulted from these credits given by the banks," he told the committee.[41]

Hilferding, another expert witness, viewed the bank charges somewhat differently. While agreeing that increased costs and risks played a role, the banks also could take advantage of certain circumstances that operated very much in their favor. They were able to offer such low interest on deposits because people were unwilling to put their money into government bonds and other long-term fixed interest-bearing assets. The banks could thus offer a repository for money upon which one could draw at any time and which had nowhere else to go. Similarly, the commissions and interest charged by the banks were possible not only because there was a condition cartel in banking but also because the Reichsbank had not been providing industrial operating credit in the form of commercial bills so that businesses were being compelled to turn to private banks when they were short of operating capital. In Hilferding's view, the distinction between commissions and interest was purely verbal and arbitrary. The banks decided what they could charge, 10 percent for example, and then divided up the amount in categories they thought most palatable psychologically.[42]

While most of the bankers repeatedly emphasized their risks and costs, Warburg conceded that the gap between interest on deposits and interest on loans possibly was excessive and suggested that the banks had been overly inventive in concocting novel commissions. He preferred that interest honestly be called by its name but pointed out that "if you see the costs and burdens which the banks have today and how through a strike of bank employees they shoot up by millions, then one cannot think ill of the banks and bankers if they create a certain

reserve through the invention of commissions."[43]

The hearings labored particularly under the difficulty of confusion between the problem of credit for long-term capital investment and the difficulties of finding operating capital. The proponents of the economic bank were constantly trying to focus on the danger that the credit structure was too vulnerable, that the future could bring a severe credit crisis, and that something had to be done to prepare for the emergency. They foresaw a time when there would be neither enough operating capital nor enough long-term capital to renew and rebuild the German economic plant. They felt it was erroneous for the representatives of the banks to continue to deny that there was a problem and simply to claim that they were in a position to provide all the credit that was needed.

Warburg sought to allay such fears. He pointed out that the banks actually wanted to give industry credit since their investment in Treasury bills and other forms of government paper could only be viewed as "second class." He knew of no deserving firm that had been denied money and suggested that the banks had found a solution to the great sums needed as a result of the inflation by forming credit consortia to help out firms when necessary. As he colorfully explained:

When today a great industrial enterprise, which earlier needed 3 million now needs 30 million and the individual bank is unwilling to give this credit . . . , then a credit consortium is formed. . . . With the help of this credit consortium and with the help of our greatest helper, the Reichsbank, which ceaselessly prints notes, we will always be in a position to give every credit that is demanded. (*Laughter*) The credit shortage will only start at that moment when the Reich and the currency become solid and we no longer, as before, have inflation. There can be no talk of a credit shortage until now.[44]

Warburg seems to have maintained a measured optimism that Germany could pull through her credit difficulties if she were smart and lucky. He warned against a complicated scheme like that proposed by Jordan, pointing out that foreigners did not take kindly to the German penchant for complexity and would not go along if "we demand complicated brainwork." They wanted clear security and not so insecurable a security as the "solidarity" of some collectivity of industries and firms. Warburg shared the view of others that no one would be impressed by the guarantee contained in a credit cooperative because there would be no way of monetizing it if the credit could not be repaid. Foreigners would give credit, Warburg argued, for the purchase of raw materials that would be turned into finished goods in Germany and resold abroad (*Veredlungskredit*), and he pointed out that they were flooded with credit offers of this nature on excellent terms from the United States, England, and the Netherlands which they were turning down because of domestic and world-market conditions. These offers were being given because the mark "enjoys an unbelievable confidence in the outside world which we ourselves do not share." Germany was living on "the credit of earlier decades" and the belief that it would recover. At the same time, the excess production abroad was so great, that the outside world had to offer credit, and it was because of Germany's inability to take advantage of all of it that "England, etc. are choking on their raw materials, and that is why there is the terrible crisis which we will, I hope, be partially spared in our misfortune, even if we unquestionably will experience it to some extent."[45]

It certainly was more agreeable to listen to Warburg than to Goldschmidt, who relentlessly stressed that Germany's failure to undergo a major economic crisis was a sign of its misery rather than its health, who pointed out that England and America by not trying to prevent this crisis with "brute force and bureaucratic organization" were ensuring that it would be shorter, who prayed that the crisis would finally come so that "we can slowly return to a healthy state," and who boldly asserted that the high interest rates for credit were beneficial and could go even higher.[46]

Goldschmidt denied that there was a capital shortage or a credit shortage and pointed out that twelve times more capital had gone into industry through the founding of corporations and the increase of capital stock in 1920 than in 1913. Capital stock increases of 7.5 billion and incorporations worth 909 million in 1920 stood over against 440 million in capital stock increases and 212 million in incorporations in 1913. Additionally, 1.5 billion in industrial

bonds had been sold. The capital market, therefore, could hardly be said not to be functioning, and Goldschmidt, like his colleague Salomonsohn, argued that the banks were not and should not be in the business of providing credit for long-term plant expansion and renewal; this had to come through the traditional means of incorporation and capital stock issues. While many private firms were reluctant to surrender their independence or family character by becoming corporations, there were important tax inducements for doing so. It was, in any case, unfair to ask either the banks or the taxpayers to bear risks that could be properly distributed by such readily available and traditional means. The bankers insisted that the banks only had a responsibility to provide operating capital to firms which were good credit risks, and even then not to those which produced goods for which there was no market and that would only make things worse. Throughout the hearings, they were strongly supported in this posture by the availability of a lengthy Reichsbank memorandum of November 8, 1920, which unconditionally opposed the artificial easing of credit through an economic bank or through any other plan.[47]

Georg Bernhard and his allies were well aware that it was not customary for banks to grant credit for long-term capital improvement or to grant operating credit on anything other than traditional banking principles; he was also aware that the larger and richer industries themselves were often playing the banker for their customers by granting credits. He questioned, however, whether the existing state of affairs was either equitable or economically sound. It was, after all, not entirely an act of fate that certain firms were in a position to raise their capital, grant credits, and receive credits from bank consortia or simply do without banking help:

We find ourselves in a type of upheaval, so that those who prepared their tax payments on time and placed them into liquid reserves, who properly declared their holdings during the war and who did not do a variety of things which they viewed as unpatriotic, are in the remarkable situation that their capital has not increased to the same extent—perhaps because they did not belong to a branch where large war profits were made—and the new purchases cost them much more than they have readily available.[48]

Bernhard rejected the simple equation between good banking practice and the general welfare of the economy. He argued for an economic bank because "such a bank would be in a position to supply the difference between the credit that is privately possible economically and that which is necessary from a [national] point of view."[49]

In the last analysis, this was an argument which addressed itself to the problems of medium-sized and small industry, and especially to the industries which manufactured finished products. Director Mann of the textile industry splendidly illustrated these problems for the committee. Those producing finished products from yarn were forced to pay in advance for the yarn but could at best hope to receive payment from their own customers thirty days after delivery. In other words, they received no credit from their suppliers but were compelled to give credit to their customers. Furthermore, their suppliers were often so tardy in delivering the yarn that the customers for the manufactured goods had disappeared by the time the yarn had arrived. Under these circumstances, it was perfectly understandable that the banks had to be cautious, but Mann wondered "whether some very special consideration must not be given to the special character of an industry in one of the most important industrial branches in Germany, and if the granting of credit does not have to be evaluated in an entirely different way than is apparently now the case."[50] There were also important sociopolitical reasons for giving credits since the industry was a large employer and, under the new law on the shutting down of plants, was not in a position to respond to slack demand by discontinuance of operations. In short, some account had to be taken of a situation in which traditional economic laws and practices were not operative and, indeed, had not been operative for some time.

The bankers and other critics of the economic bank program, however, were unswerving in their opposition to deviations from traditional banking practices. They opposed especially every suggestion that the reserves of the savings banks be tapped for capital invest-

ment in industry. Under the Prussian Regulation of 1838, savings banks were permitted to invest only in first-class paper, usually various types of government bonds and mortgages. These investment limitations along with the desire to promote savings served as the justification for their tax-free status. In reality, the savings banks were already undergoing a major transformation. Under legislation passed in 1908, they were allowed to engage in checking and clearing (*giro*) services. The pace of such change increased during the war, when the savings banks were used by the Reichsbank to place war loans and when these savings banks, either individually or in consortia, took over all municipal loans. The task of placing war loans among depositors was a first breakthrough in the old restrictions on the administration of securities by savings banks. The postwar tax legislation of the fall of 1919, which required that all securities be deposited in banks for tax purposes, could not be implemented without the use of the savings banks. The government was thus forced to concede to the savings banks the right to hold and administer all types of securities and by decrees of October 9, 1920, and April 15, 1921, to enter into the business of buying and selling on the securities market. In many frontier and occupied areas, as well as in important business centers, the savings banks were allowed to deal in commercial securities for their customers, and they also were called upon to administer the multiplying financial activities of municipalities arising from the purchase and distribution of food and clothing.[51]

Nevertheless, the basic restrictions remained on the books, and while the savings banks held approximately forty-six billion in deposits at the turn of 1920–1921, their investment possibilities remained limited despite the obvious deterioration in the quality of their allegedly secure investments. The real value of mortgages, insofar as they were not rapidly paid off, had already declined significantly and were in danger of further depreciation, while the drop in home construction since 1914 reduced the importance of this form of investment. Most serious, however, was that the value of the war bonds and other government paper held by the savings banks appeared increasingly fictional, and there was growing concern about the fact that savings bank assets were being invested primarily in municipal loans. In Kraemer's view, the social and political changes wrought by the war and inflation and the impending consequences of the tax reform required a new approach to the use of savings-bank deposits:

If the tax legislation will be carried out in the sense desired by the Socialist portion of the German people, it will lead to a levelling of capital to the greatest extent and then the money will no longer flow through the great channels of the banks but will flow through a countless number of small channels into the repositories of the savings banks. . . . I would consider it economically short-sighted if we would not today give timely thought that these billions—which today come from the *Mittelstand*, the chief depositors of the savings banks—which are flowing into this great gathering point of the Reich Clearing Center, be directed back into the great pot from which German industry can be nourished.[52]

Not only the *Mittelstand* but also the workers were known to be using the savings banks to build up some savings whenever possible, and here, too, good political and social as well as economic arguments could be made for tapping these resources. As another committee member noted:

The entire social development which gives the broad masses enormously increased rights also without a doubt places upon them the responsibility to help the credit needs of the economy and to make the means which they have made available serve this purpose. It will be impossible to have the savings of the large mass of our people continuously go into the savings banks and then go the not-very-productive route of municipal loans, as is now largely the case. Also, the concept of first class security has become so fluid, that in many cases it can no longer seriously play a role. It must in my view be possible to fill the saving impulse of the broad masses with confidence in the productivity of our industry.[53]

All such arguments were rejected by representatives of the great banks, underlying all of whose arguments about the laws governing savings bank investments was a profound irritation over the expansionist tendencies of the savings banks evidenced in their creation of city, district, and communal banks which were guaranteed by the savings banks but which were free to invest as they wished. The Siegen Savings Bank, for example, attained considerable notoriety for its plan to open a municipal bank. It justified its intention in a memorandum of January 1921 by bluntly stating that it was in competition with the great banks. The Siegen Savings Bank argued that the growing concentration of Germany's banking system; the decreasing autonomy of the old provincial banks; the great banks' lack of interest in lending to craftsmen, merchants, and workers, as well as their reluctance to lend to municipalities, required countermeasures if the great banks were not to dictate terms on the local level. The Siegen Savings Bank claimed that savings banks and municipal banks would strengthen one another, the former placing its resources at the service of the latter, while the municipal banks, with their resources guaranteed by both the savings banks and the municipalities, would be placed in a position to service the needs of their communities. Displaying a measure of aggressiveness, the Siegen Savings Bank, the municipality, and their supporters, sabotaged efforts of the Deutsche Bank to take over the provincial Siegen Bank for Industry and Commerce. Indeed, the Deutsche Bank's opponents thought that it would be better if the Siegen Savings Bank would do the taking over and thereby get the office space it needed without having to erect a new building. It was useless for the allies of the Deutsche Bank to protest against this "confusing of the boundary between savings bank and bank" and "mixing of public and private activities."[54] By April 1921, government decrees permitted savings banks to deal in all forms of security transactions except those involving foreign exchange.

It is likely, therefore, that more than coincidence was involved when one of the expert witnesses for the big banks at the RWR subcommittee hearings singled out a letter sent by the Securities Section of the Siegen Savings Bank to its customers in January 1921 to illustrate the manner in which the savings banks, at least in his view, were violating their legal charge. The latter pointed out that there was a strong tendency for the public to invest in industrial securities even when stock quotations had dropped because "the worth of good industrial stocks appears greater to our customers than the illusory value of the German paper mark," went on to advise people "to buy good industrial paper on cheap days," and listed a host of promising companies as suggested investments. In this banker's view, if the savings banks were going "to enter into competition with the banks in this area" and also to use savings bank money to buy industrial mortgages and bonds, then they deserved to lose their tax privileges because they could no longer claim to provide the traditional security to depositors. He was totally unmoved by the argument that the losses on war bonds had been horrendous and that they were probably less secure than industrial securities.[55]

The leading bankers were more moderate in their opposition to proposals that workers be encouraged to invest in industry by being offered small shares (Kleinaktien) at favorable terms with the objective both of getting capital and of giving them a sense that they were participants with a stake in productive enterprise. Yet, the bankers were not enthusiastic either. Warburg and Goldschmidt feared that this would encourage speculation without being particularly effective, an argument that was criticized as pointless "moralizing" since a veritable speculative fever was gripping large portions of the population both at home and abroad. Within Germany, people were trying to make up for the reduced value of their pensions by finding a new source of income in playing the stock market. Just as marks were being bought up by speculating foreigners, so billions in pounds, francs, and Polish notes were floating about Germany which were "largely in the hands of small players."[56]

Throughout the subcommittee discussions, probably the greatest degree of consensus was over the need to mobilize the billions of marks privately hoarded by Germans trying to escape taxation and refusing to keep their money in the banks because of the abrogation of their rights of privacy. The expert witnesses were convinced that "millions and billions" would flow in, especially from the farmers. As one expert declared:

Gentlemen, I have contact with all Germany. It is the same in Baden, East Prussia, the Rhineland. Wherever we have information, it is the same thing. The people do not want the tax collector in their pockets and the money, which can be weighed in pounds and centner, goes not into the stockings but into the cupboards.[57]

The Reichsbank itself took up the cause of restoring the privacy of bank accounts, pointing out that "the state, even against its own wish and desire, is binding the capital market through its legislation and is now faced with the consequence of its own actions if industry now comes and asks it for the credit help which it had previously been able to procure itself." The legislation had to be changed so that "capital can move freely again without being followed every step of the way for tax purposes."[58]

Here the bankers and the Reichsbank were at one, and they were especially enthused about the one major proposal of the Reichsbank for relieving such operating capital needs as existed; namely, the reintroduction of commercial bills. Because of the wartime government payments in cash, high liquidity, and the demand by industrial trade associations for immediate payment in cash in the postwar inflation, commercial bills had virtually disappeared from use. The Reichsbank viewed the reintroduction of "solid commercial bills" in the amount of about twenty billion marks an excellent means of relieving operating credit difficulties in a safe manner. In the Reichsbank's view, commercial bills had a host of advantages. They permitted a three-month delay in cash payment; a portfolio of such bills, if solid, could be used to procure further credit. They also reduced cash requirements in the economy and thereby would make it possible for the Reich to reduce liquidity through taxation and long-term loans from the domestic economy without bringing the economy to a standstill because of a credit shortage. The Reich would then be in a position to purchase back its Treasury bills, while the Reichsbank and other banks would once again have reliable portfolios of commercial bills instead of dubious Treasury bills. That this vision of the prewar order of things, where credit for operating capital was given with solid bills based on real production and sales, proved so palatable to everyone was not very surprising. Only Kraemer expressed concern that the reintroduction of commercial bills would produce a fantastic credit demand by industry, but this arose from his worry that the banks might not be able to meet the demand, an anxiety which the banks declared unfounded.[59]

Thus, the one point on which the subcommittee on industrial credit could reach a measure of harmony was with respect to doing something old rather than to creating something new. By the time it finished hearing testimony in February 1921, all the various projects proposed since early 1920 had been successfully buried by their opponents inside and outside the government. The chambers of commerce and bankers fired salvo after salvo against the plans, especially at the bankers convention in Berlin on October 25–27, 1920.[60] Reference was made to the Brussels International Financial Conference of the previous month, at which the European financial leaders and experts had attacked all forms of unproductive spending and deficit spending and had called for a return to traditional fiscal and financial practices. While the Jordan plan could be rejected on the grounds that it would be impossible to organize industry for the purposes intended and that a credit cooperative would not have the experience, knowledge, or personnel to review credit applications effectively, the economic bank scheme and all notions of the Reich serving as a guarantor of industrial credit could be attacked on the grounds of violating economic orthodoxy and as potentially inflationary. As Frankfurt banker and economist Ludwig Hahn argued in the *Frankfurter Zeitung*:

We have until now, and that is bad enough, a financial inflation, that is, an artificial excessive creation of purchasing power to satisfy the financial demand. One must guard against adding to this financial inflation an industrial and commercial inflation, which perhaps already exists latently in many places. Whether the interest rates in giving credit to industry and commerce are to be raised or lowered—in Brussels as is known the overwhelming inclination was the view that the interest rates are in general too low—over this one can argue, but there can be no doubt that the firm boundary of every credit expansion is the possibility of its being repaid. . . . Our financial inflation had its beginning at the moment when the Reichsbank, hardly noticed by the broad public, began to discount Reich Treasury bills instead of commercial bills, whereby the fate of the currency became tied to the fate of the state finances. The creation of an economic bank with the goal of giving credits when repayment is insecure would be a step of no less major significance. It would place a new burden on the currency at a time when the old is threatening its collapse.[61]

Both the Reichsbank and Finance Minister Wirth conjured up the spirit of Brussels in their opposition. In a harsh memorandum to Scholz on October 27, Wirth absolutely refused to support any Reich guarantee for industrial credits. Noting that the traditional method of dealing with excess demand for credit had always been for central banks to raise the discount rate, he went on to point out that

In countries with orderly economic and financial policies this practice is pursued now also, and the financial experts at the Brussels Conference have unanimously associated themselves with these tried and true principles. Now it is not to be denied that in the present period of transition, the low value of the mark, the reconversion and reconstruction of industry, and the high wages have, among other things, created extraordinary credit conditions. But whether the consequence of this should be that one reverses these recognized principles previously followed generally among financially strong states, in other words, that instead of limitation of credit, it should be increased and made easier to obtain, seems very dubious to me.[62]

There is some evidence that Scholz did not even need this letter from Wirth or the Reichsbank memorandum, since he began his address to the bankers convention by informing his listeners that the project no longer existed for him and that at no time had he sought to present a proposal to the RWR subcommittee, despite repeated requests for one.[63] The Reichstag also did its best to bury the proposal by passing a resolution on March 19, 1921, reserving for the Reichstag the right to grant government credits to industry and even banning the granting of such credits under the emergency economic powers.[64] With these decisions, both industry and the Reich effectively turned their backs on the last of the efforts, which had begun with Moellendorff, to involve the Reich in long-term investment activities aimed at industrial reconstruction and countercyclical pump priming. Insofar as anything had emerged from the entire discussion, aside from a great deal of information on credit conditions and attitudes in the German business community, it was a commitment to permit private industry to conduct its own reconstruction and to a return to traditional prewar credit practices. And all this was done in the name of financial orthodoxy and resistance to inflation.

The participants in these discussions, however, were well aware that the processes of economic reorganization and reconstruction were taking place in certain sectors without much concern with the debate over the credit problems of medium-sized and small industry. The most significant developments, in fact, were in the realms of banking and big industry, where the very conditions that were producing so much concern for the proponents of the economic bank and direction of investment had served to call forth a remarkable process of concentration and reorganization. The years 1920–1921 constituted the most crucial phase of this development, for the relative stabilization made it possible to act upon the conditions which inflation had helped to create.

Restructuring the Private Sector: The Gospel According to Stinnes?

The German inflation has traditionally and correctly been identified with a hectic process of concentration accompanied by unprecedented speculation and the building of huge economic empires. The same ambiguity attaches to these developments as it does to all other aspects of the inflationary reconstruction. Much of what occurred conformed to long-term structural tendencies in German economic development; for example, the absorption of provincial banks by the large Berlin credit banks; the vertical concentration of heavy industry backward into coal mining and forward into various forms of finishing as well as marketing; and the cartelization, syndicalization, and organization of various industrial branches into trade associations for economic and sociopolitical purposes. From this viewpoint, the inflation "accelerated" the "natural" evolution of the German economy, although it may have done so in a distorted and distorting manner in important instances. The dilemma for the historian of the inflation is to define in what ways the inflation specifically influenced the rationale of decision making and the manner in which these processes took place. As always, it must be remembered that inflationary influences are difficult to separate from those of the international and domestic conseqences of the war. Finally, it is necessary to distinguish between contemporary perspectives, goals, and motives, on the one hand, and later consequences, on the other.

Only in this way, for example, is the behavior of many of Germany's eminent bankers intelligible. The arguments made by them that Germany was not suffering from a capital shortage, which was to turn into demonstrable rubbish in a short period of time, reflected the fact that the banks were enjoying an unprecedented boom in 1920–1921 fueled by a government-induced inflation. The war marked a downturn in the fortunes of the banks, especially when compared to industry. The most important branches of industry "prospered" during the war itself, and since the government made a practice of paying for its orders promptly and was industry's chief customer, industry had little cause to borrow or use commercial bills. The banks, deprived of their usual business in commercial bills and in regular stock market transactions, were reduced to the function of "deposit banks lending chiefly to public authorities."[65] While making modest commissions on the sale of war bonds, expenses of the seven leading Berlin banks increased by almost 20 percent between 1913 and 1918 because of the mounting number of noncash transactions, inexperienced personnel, and rising salaries. Generally, wartime bank dividends were lower than those of 1913. The banks, to be sure, were very much in tune with wartime centralization tendencies, the great Berlin banks pushing forward their prewar drive to absorb provincial banks as well as increase their share of total deposits from 53.4 percent of all banks with over a million marks capital in 1913 to 65.6 percent in 1918, and to do so despite the expansion of the public banking sector. Perhaps most striking was the dramatic shift in the share of capital and reserves as opposed to deposits and current account balances as percentages of total liabilities among the eight great Berlin banks. While there was a long-term tendency for share capital to diminish in importance relative to deposits, the war qualitatively accelerated this trend, which then continued during the postwar inflation. Such a shift in the bases of liquidity naturally favored short-term over long-term engagements, especially as increases of capital never seemed to accomplish their purpose for very long.[66]

The most important line of continuity between the wartime and postwar inflationary periods was the extraordinary involvement of the banks with the finances of the Reich. Naturally, this created a rather delicate and often ambivalent relationship between the great banks, on the one hand, and the Reichsbank, on the other. During the war, for example, the head of the Rheinische Kreditbank, Richard Brosien, had sought to impress Havenstein by holding as much as fifty million marks in war bonds and Treasury bills on the bank's own account, but his bank chose to cut its losses very rapidly in the first half of 1919 by dumping these holdings onto the market or participating in certain consortia to buy up war surplus materials which could be paid for with such paper.[67] In general, however, the banks felt obliged to undertake a less radical disengagement from their war-bond holdings, and they joined forces with the Reichsbank in August 1919 to create a Reich Loan Corporation (Reichsanleihe AG) based on the participation of all the banks with the objective of consolidating their war-bond holdings and stabilizing their market value.[68]

In practical terms, however, getting rid of war bonds meant increasing bank holdings in Treasury bills, and the troublesome engagement with the government's finances was thereby only intensified. Needless to say, the Revolution had not heightened banker confidence in or promoted friendly feelings toward the government. Thus, Deutsche Bank director Paul Mankiewitz complained that "the government pays absolutely no heed to the banks, which it believes it can annoy and use in every way."[69] Despite his irritation at the "Socialist" governments in Berlin, however, Mankiewitz seems to have maintained an ultimate faith in the state's solvency. When Director Klaproth of the Hannoversche Bank inquired what Mankiewitz thought of investment in long-term Treasury bills that would reach maturity in 1924, one of the latter's colleagues, Director Wassermann, replied with cautious optimism on his behalf:

While Herr Mankiewitz sees extraordinarily hard times coming for the private economy, he inclines to the view that the credit of the state cannot be shaken in its foundations and that the possibility of a state bankruptcy is barred for internal reasons. At the same time, Herr Mankiewitz limits himself to saying that this view of future developments, which is so favorable for the credit of the state . . . is so personal that he would not want to be bound by it as the giving of actual advice.[70]

Bankers, at least respectable ones, do after all have a reputation for caution and conservatism, and one of the grave difficulties that Mankiewitz and his colleagues faced in the post-war inflation was making intelligent judgments and decisions in what had become veritable madhouses by the turn of 1919–1920. Thanks to the spiraling public debt with its accompanying monetary and Treasury note emissions, the restarting of international trade along with the reopening of the stock market and the accompanying feverish speculation in currencies and industrial shares, the beginning of a spectacular—at least in numerical terms—process of capital increases and industrial consolidations, and the government use of the banks to impose its requirements for the deposit of securities and the providing of information relevant to tax assessments, the banks were not only "swimming in money," but drowning in work. It was a measure of this condition that Mankiewitz abruptly put off ongoing negotiations aimed at a fusion between the Deutsche Bank and the Hannoversche Bank as well as the preparations for the takeover of other major provincial banks at the end of January 1920:

You cannot imagine how burdened our offices are: the correspondence sections, the securities office, and the secretariat hardly find time to work properly through their agendas. There exist conditions in our offices which I never would have imagined possible in so orderly a concern as the Deutsche Bank. The day before yesterday we had the tiny task of handling over 13,000 individual orders. Our stock brokers are dropping from exhaustion. . . . Just as little as you, my dear Herr Klaproth, can get onto a trapeze, as little can we carry out tasks today which are beyond our powers. Germany went to defeat because it overestimated its strength and believed it could carry on war and do its work from the Caspian to the Baltic and from the Channel to the Duna. That was our misfortune, and we here at the Deutsche Bank want absolutely no disorganization. A bank which does not do its work with the customary care, circumspection and caution, does not have the right to make transactions at this moment.[71]

While political uncertainties and cost considerations undoubtedly also played a role in Mankiewitz's hesitation, the shutting down of the bourse for three days a week at this time so as to catch up with business—a practice that was to be followed periodically during the inflation—and the fact that the Berlin banking offices became notorious for having lights burning through the nights and enormous overtime expenses certainly were strong evidence that the inflation had created unprecedented conditions to which the bankers had to get accustomed.

Once spring and relative stabilization arrived, however, the great banks were in a position to return to their expansionary process in which massive capital stock increases were combined with the takeover of provincial banks. The way began to be paved for the greatest bank merger of the inflation, that of the Nationalbank and the Darmstädter Bank, which finally took place in July 1922 after the Nationalbank had taken over the Deutsche Nationalbank Bremen in 1920 and had then formed a fifty-year community of interest with the Darmstädter in 1921.[72] In June 1920, the Commerz- and Discontobank fused with a major provincial bank, the Mitteldeutsche Privatbank, to become the Commerz- und Privatbank, increasing its capital and reserves between 1919 and 1920 from 104.5 to 270.7 million marks. Although the Mitteldeutsche Privatbank had once been reputed to have a loose connection with the Deutsche Bank, Director Wassermann unconcernedly welcomed reports of the merger: "If the Commerz-Bank has now really become a great bank, then I would be extremely happy. We have a national interest in strong banks, but the meal was quite large and will produce digestive complaints."[73]

The Deutsche Bank, having been compelled to disgorge many of its important holdings abroad because of the loss of the war, had a particularly hearty appetite and took over the Hannoversche Bank, the Braunschweiger Privatbank, and the Privatbank zu Gotha—all of which had a combined share capital of seventy-nine million marks and fifteen million in reserves—in November 1920. These fusions with major provincial banks required the Deutsche Bank to raise its share capital from 275 to 408 million marks, 74.8 million of which were underwritten by a consortium led by one of the Deutsche Bank's affiliates, the Essener Credit-Anstalt. The new shares were kept in friendly hands by being offered either as an attractive option for old shareholders of the Deutsche Bank or used in exchange for the stocks of the banks involved in the merger. Furthermore, by its takeover of the Hannoversche Bank, the Deutsche Bank was able to increase its interest in two other major provincial banks, the Württembergische Vereinsbank and the Hildesheimer Bank (which it eventually was to take over) in 1924 and 1928 respectively. By their policy of fusion, the great Berlin banks thus became truly national banks with vastly increased responsibility and large networks of branches under their control. In 1913, the Deutsche Bank had 15 branches; by 1924, it had 142. The Commerz- und Privatbank increased the number of its branches from 8 to 246 during the same period.[74]

This imperialism was not always welcome in the provinces. When the Deutsche Bank attempted to take over the Elberfeld Bankverein in 1919, it ran into such opposition that it was compelled to beat a retreat, and its effort to take over the Siegen Bank for Industry and Commerce in 1921, as noted earlier, was also temporarily frustrated.[75] In fact, there was much public hostility to the Hannoversche Bank takeover:

It is simply not understood for what reasons so intrinsically well-constructed and distingushed an institution could give up its independence. The economic soundness of the move is contested, and above all much is made of the point that a new attachment to Berlin in the midst of the general cry "away from Berlin" [*Los von Berlin*] is a first class tactical mistake.[76]

Just as the savings banks and municipal banks sought to prevent this envelopment of local interests by the big Berlin banks, so some of the larger provincial banks sought to protect themselves as well. Thus, the Allgemeine Deutsche Credit-Anstalt, Leipzig (ADCA), which had been conducting a very successful expansionist policy of its own in Saxony and Thuringia, joined in a "close friendly alliance" with the Bayerische Hypotheken- und Wechselbank and the Barmer Bankverein as well as with the private banking house of Hardy & Co. in 1921, while a similar relationship was established between the private Berlin bank Mendelssohn & Co. and the Bayerische Vereinsbank. Although the Leipzig and Bavarian banks were allied with the Disconto-Gesellschaft, these other friendly relationships had the specific purpose of providing a counterweight to the great "D" banks by establishing agreements on a regional division of their markets, facilitating expansion into Austria (as in the case of the Bavarian banks), and conducting business in the Netherlands—all without involving the Disconto-Gesellschaft.[77]

There was nothing very mysterious about the motives of the great banks. They wished to expand, eliminate competition, and control and centralize the banking business throughout the country by gaining access to the capital and silent reserves of the prestigious provincial banks. This was necessary if they were to meet the challenge created by the development of large-scale industrial enterprises with increasingly large capital reserves as well as capital requirements. The role of the inflation in this concentration process was important. The high liquidity at once made possible and encouraged banking concentration, and certainly one of the best inflation hedges available to the banks at this time was the acquisition of the buildings, facilities, personnel, and shares of other banks. That this could be done on the cheap only added to its attractiveness. The great discrepancy between the value of the shares of the great banks and that of the provincial banks meant that provincial bank shares could be bought up at low cost even when rumors of an impending fusion suddenly increased their market value. Furthermore, the difference between the internal and external value of the mark enhanced the advantages of the great banks. Although share prices tended to rise whenever the exchange rate declined, the real value of the rise of shares was in no way equal to the depreciation of the mark. The tendency of fusions to occur when the mark fell may have been related to this phenomenon.[78]

While the power and advantages enjoyed by the large enterprises certainly played their role in the inflationary concentration process, especially in the industrial sphere where ruthless takeovers with scant regard for the wishes of

smaller enterprises often occurred, the use of persuasion remained good form when dealing with established and respected businesses and seems to have been particularly important in the courtship of fusion-shy provincial banks. Concentration was not only a policy of expansion by the strong against the weak but also a strategy of consolidation and defense in a very uncertain economic situation, and this line of argumentation figured prominently in the persuasive efforts of the great bankers. As Oscar Schlitter of the Deutsche Bank pointed out to a recalcitrant Supervisory Board member of the Siegen Bank, the concentration movement had the "explicit purpose of gathering together the forces that lie scattered about at those junctures where they can find the best support in the competitive economic struggle." Germany's dangerous political situation and her dependence on raw materials along with the depreciation of the mark could create demands which "the financial strength of the individual enterprise is incapable of meeting." For this reason, "economically weak enterprises must seek support more than before from the stronger." This was as true for banking as it was for industry in Schlitter's view:

At the present time many industries are still living on a certain excess of cash, so that the banks have increasing means which they can place to some measure at the disposal of other enterprises in need of money. How long this will last, however, cannot be foreseen, and perhaps the Siegerland industry will one day, instead of having the money which it is keeping in the banks at the present time, once again be in need of money. The existing provincial banks are not today any longer in a position to meet such demands on their own. The monetary depreciation today requires sums on short notice that previously were viewed as gigantic. . . .[79]

When industries were suddenly compelled to pay the costs of raw materials or wages without having immediate buyers or found it necessary to grant customers longer periods to meet their bills, Schlitter argued, their demands would prove more than the provincial banks could handle, and "only the inner strength of a great bank can do for the nation's industry what is necessary in order to hold out in the great economic struggle."

These arguments not only revealed why the great banks promoted and many provincial banks sought fusion at this time, but also exposed some of the peculiarities of the banking "boom" of 1920–1921. As the most direct beneficiary of the state's inflationary policies, the banking sector had "partially emancipated itself from the conditions of the German business world."[80] It did not suffer from the slowdown experienced by industry, and it was raking in huge paper profits from its interest and provision charges on loans, stock exchange, and money-market transactions. Dividends to the great-bank shareholders ranged between 7 and 12 percent in 1919, between 10 and 18 percent in 1920, and between 12.52 and 24 percent in 1921. The greatly expanded Deutsche Bank took the lead in every case. Large silent reserves were being set aside as well.[81]

What all this meant for the structure of the economy, however, was less certain. In the past, the banks had played a leading role in stabilizing the economy and pointing the way toward concentration and rationalization, but now critics charged that the banks were catering to the speculative fever gripping masses of Germans, accepting and indeed participating in the tendencies to water stocks by granting generous options on new capital emissions, and doing nothing to prevent the practice of creating majority blocks of stock to take over companies behind the backs of their directors for no apparently sound economic reason. The banks, however generous with their credits, were enjoying a boom "ensured by the increasing impoverishment of the Reich."[82]

It could also be argued, however, that if the inflation had "emancipated" the banks from the condition of industry, it had also emancipated important segments of industry from the influence of the banks. As one banker tersely put the matter, "the great industrial corporations in general rule the banks and not the reverse."[83] In truth, the inflation exaggerated what was a longer-range trend toward the self-financing of great industrial firms in Germany as well as the loosening of the very close ties that had once existed between certain firms and banks. The specific conditions of the postwar period undermined the traditional capacity of the bankers to influence the direction of industrial policy and even their will to do so.

If, for example, Arthur Salomonsohn of the Disconto-Gesellschaft got on well with Hugo Stinnes, one of whose great goals in life was to emancipate himself fully from the control of the banks, it was because Salomonsohn was supportive of everything Stinnes did, even to the point of nodding approval when Stinnes declared that it would be the task of the industrialists to restore the health of the currency while the men of finance handled the details.[84] Who would have imagined such passivity from Salomonsohn, whose competence and skill as a banker were undeniable and who stood at the head of the German bank which historically was most famous for its influence on industrial development? Stinnes's relationship with the aging but intractable head of the Berliner Handelsgesellschaft, Carl Fürstenberg, was less satisfactory. Fürstenberg resigned in protest from the supervisory board of one of the enterprises controlled by Stinnes because of opposition to the latter's policies. The relationship went from bad to worse when Stinnes tried to get an interest, albeit nothing resembling a controlling interest, in the BHG by purchasing forty thousand shares of its stock in March 1922 from a notorious Hungarian-Rumanian speculator, Emil Cyprut. Stinnes was also reported to have expressed the intention of buying a controlling interest the Deutsche Bank, which certainly intensified that bank's watchfulness over what was happening to its shares, and he did get control over the Barmer Bankverein in 1923.[85]

In the last analysis, however, it was less Stinnes's interest in taking over banks—Rathenau's AEG viewed the Berliner Handelsgesellschaft as its "house bank"—than the use of them made by himself and his fellow industrialists as well as by speculators like Cyprut and the relative voicelessness of bankers during this period that were significant. A good illustration of the role acquired by speculators was the famous purchase of majority control in the venerable heavy industrial Bochumer Verein in the fall of 1920 by Hugo J. Herzfeld. The latter, a former employee of Mendelssohn & Co. who had struck out on his own during the war as a broker for various municipalities seeking foreign and domestic loans, had already begun to deal in shares during the war. Then, the heirs of

Silesian magnate Prince Henkel-Donners-marck asked Herzfeld to dispose of the latter's more speculative ventures. The most important of these was the "Kraft" Iron Works, which Herzfeld sold to Dutch interests after the war. They in turn, sold the shares to the Stumm concern in 1921 at 1,000 percent of their face value. Herzfeld achieved real public notoriety in 1920 as the mysterious, slow, steady, and triumphant purchaser of Bochumer Verein stock. Herzfeld had no intention of being an industrialist, however, and after threatening to sell the stock to Dutch interests, he ended up doing business with Stinnes through the mediation of Jakob Goldschmidt of the Nationalbank who, like Salomonsohn, seemed to have worked well with Stinnes. Given Herzfeld's record, there was something to Stinnes's claim that he had "saved" the Bochumer Verein for Germany. Within a year of the Bochumer Verein sale, Herzfeld pulled off another coup, selling the Mansfeld Copper Works, also an old conservative enterprise, to the Metallbank and the AEG. Old established bankers like Goldschmidt and Salomonsohn competed for the business of Stinnes and Herzfeld but they did not determine their policies.[86]

A classic illustration of the incapacity of the great banks to guide or effectively influence the processes of concentration and fusion then underway was provided by the struggle between the Stinnes and Haniel interests for the control of the greatest South German machine builder, the Maschinenfabrik Augsburg-Nürnberg (M.A.N.) in the fall of 1920, a struggle which Paul Reusch of the GHH, representing the Haniel group, won by playing upon the fears and eccentricities of the M.A.N.'s chief stockholder, the Baron von Cramer-Klett. Although two eminent bankers on the M.A.N. Supervisory Board, Oscar Schlitter of the Deutsche Bank and Franz Urbig of the Disconto-Gesellschaft, favored Stinnes and were scandalized by Reusch's victory, all they could do was protest and adjust to the results.[87]

Nevertheless, Reusch was a great general director, an aggressive manager–entrepreneur with the money of a great old industrial family behind him and fully worthy of competing with Stinnes for the jewel of south German industry.

For the scion of an old banking family like Baron S. Alfred von Oppenheim of the famous private Cologne banking house, who sat on many industrial supervisory boards, some of the people who were gaining control of old industrial enterprises were a real irritation. He expressed satisfaction that the iron merchant firm of Ottenheimer, which had bought stock in the Witten Cast Steel Company in the hope of forcing it to give Ottenheimer its marketing operations, was being rejected by Witten. The latter dealt in specialty products and did not need the services of Ottenheimer, "which has become big during the war." Oppenheim drew a parallel between Ottenheimer and Cologne iron merchant Otto Wolff (who had also become a major industrial figure during the war) and angrily pointed out to General Director von Schaewen of the Phoenix concern that "one sees everywhere the bad consequences of the war and revolution profiteers, which are insatiable and seek to extend their interests further everywhere."[88] As both men well knew, however, Wolff's growing interest in Phoenix and his enormous marketing operation in nearly all the major west European and some east European countries could not be so easily resisted. In the course of 1920, Wolff became not only a major stockholder in Phoenix but also its chief marketing agent, a role which the two other producers, Rheinstahl and van der Zypen, had accorded Wolff more willingly. While the Phoenix management, with the warm encouragement of its Supervisory Board chairman Oppenheim, held out for a full year against Wolff's desire to monopolize its marketing, even in instances where Phoenix could do better on its own, it soon became evident that this would not work and that Phoenix could not at once cooperate and compete with the Wolff operation. In October 1921 Phoenix relented in return for participation in the Wolff enterprises, and further contracts were signed in May 1922.[89]

To a considerable degree, therefore, the great bankers were being reduced to intermediaries in the industrial concentration process, buying and selling at the behest of speculators, merchants grown rich through wartime business, and industrialists and employing their skills to get the best possible advantages for their cus-

tomers in a market whose ups and downs signaled both the speculation of a vastly increased
army of "players" and the machinations of
great industrial and merchant firms engaged in
concern building. Much of the activity was
caused by the increasing number of firms which
sought to get cash through incorporation. Some
of it was created by outright swindlers who
floated the stock of bogus companies and
played upon the urge of little people and even
workers to invest in "Schulze & Co." or some
Hamburg merchant house selling herrings as
well as other more or less plausible-sounding
enterprises with the objective of doing something with their cash, maintaining their standard of living, or trying to get rich quickly.[90]

These, however, were not the most significant developments. All they demonstrated was
that the less wealthy and well-informed were
following or at least responding to the same signals as the wealthy and knowledgeable. The
quest for paper investments that would at once
be safe and profitable and the flight from depreciating assets had begun during the war. The
flight from war bonds into industrial shares was
started by the great industrial firms. The Krupp
firm bought no less than 310 million marks'
worth of war bonds during the war but discreetly sold off the lion's share of them so that
it only held thirty-one million in war bonds
prior to the war's end and only eight million
marks' worth in December 1918. While the
shortage of operating capital appears to have
been the primary motive for Krupp's unwillingness to tie up its money in patriotic investments
for any length of time, its financial officers
hardly could have been oblivious to the shaky
character of this type of asset in 1918.[91]

Some took longer to come to this conclusion.
The decision of the Retailers Committee of the
Bochum Chamber of Commerce in September
1920 "to get rid of its entire holding in German
war bonds and to place as much of the receipts
as possible in good industrial bonds"[92] reflected
a further step along the path of preference for
industrial over government-backed paper assets. This was revolutionary enough, since it
was the former rather than the latter that was
always regarded as the blue-chip investment.
Increasingly, however, people recognized that
while fixed-interest industrial bonds may have

been a better investment than government
bonds, they were no hedge against monetary
depreciation and that industrial shares, even
though more speculative, were a better way to
beat inflation. Richard Merton's advice to a
Dutch friend who wanted to buy mark-denominated assets illustrates the point:

> If you want to do something, then I would not advise
> you in any case to buy fixed-interest assets, for then
> you are speculating on an improvement in the rate of
> the mark, but have no security in case the mark does
> not improve or gets worse. In my view, an investment
> in first-class industrial shares is to be preferred. To be
> sure, they have a low rate of return today. But an in-
> dustrial share, even if denominated in marks, repre-
> sents the part ownership of an enterprise which more
> or less retains its intrinsic worth no matter what the
> condition of the mark.[93]

He went on to advise the Dutchman to buy
shares of Felten & Guilleaume, a large cable
producer in Cologne, or of neighboring smelting plant and rolling-stock producers van der
Zypen & Charlier or perhaps of the AEG or
chemical firms like the Elberfelder dye works or
the Frankfurt firm of Höchst. Here, indeed,
were Germany's "real values" and hope for its
future.

How much of this hope, however, did Germany want to sell to strangers? One of the great
anxieties of the immediate postwar years was
that foreigners would take advantage of the low
value of the German currency to buy up majority control of German enterprises. The danger
of "foreignization" appeared very real, especially at the turn of 1919–1920. In retrospect, it
appears remarkable that foreigners by and large
limited themselves to currency and fixed-interest bond speculations, engaged only in sporadic
share investment, bought some real estate, but
did not make a more concerted effort not only
to "buy out" but also to "buy up" Germany.
The best explanation was probably that given
by Oscar Schlitter a decade later:

> . . . there were not enough people abroad who could
> judge German conditions sufficiently, and also not
> enough people who had the necessary confidence.
> You have to imagine that someone today would go
> and buy shares in Russia. Foreigners found German
> conditions just as alien as we today find many things
> in Russia alien from a commercial point of view.[94]

Perhaps there were some advantages to the socialization threats and sociopolitical unrest in

Germany after all! Nevertheless, the fears of "foreignization" were very real at the time, and many corporations took advantage of the laws permitting the issuance of stock with multiple voting rights (*Vorzugsaktien*). These were sold to the company's controlling interests at a particularly low price.

Such practices were open to serious criticism as an artificial means of protecting vested German interests and as violations of the basic principles of the joint stock company. Nevertheless, such stocks were issued by, among others, the great chemical firms which had been organized by Carl Duisberg into the "little" IG Farben trust since 1916, the family-controlled Siemens electrotechnical concern, the shipping companies, and the lignite-producing Rheinische Braunkohlengesellschaft led by Paul Silverberg. When August Thyssen asked Silverberg why he was issuing such stocks, Silverberg bluntly replied that "without them we would have lost control either to Petschek or to Stinnes or to you."[95] The answer is revealing as a demonstration of the fear not only of external "foreignization" by Czech coal magnate Petschek but also of internal "foreignization" at the hands of Silverberg's colleagues. Thus, even such a sharp critic of stocks with special voting rights as Baron von Oppenheim was prepared to surrender principle in order to keep Wolff from gaining control of one of Phoenix's shipbuilding works. As he told General Director Beukenberg, "As you know, I am no friend of preferential shares, but on the other side I don't want to be open to the reproach of having prevented measures that might have hindered a Wolff foreignization."[96]

Indeed, in 1919–1920 it seemed to many as if Phoenix was being both externally and internally "foreignized." Wolff was not only seeking to increase his own control and influence over Phoenix but was also involved in bringing Dutch interests into the firm. He sought to avoid appearing as the seller of Phoenix stock by having one of the Dutch enterprises he controlled act as an intermediary and was more than a little chagrined when the *Frankfurter Zeitung* revealed that Wolff was behind the operation. In reality, Wolff was being anything but unpatriotic since at least part of his arrangements had been worked out with Erzberger and the government, which had leased Wolff's stock to use as security for vital imports from the Netherlands. Furthermore, the arrangements for collaboration between a Dutch government-owned smelting works and Phoenix provided Phoenix with a source of raw materials and semifinished products as well as a market for its own finished products. While there was some difference of opinion with the Dutch over the number of supervisory board seats each side would get, the agreement was based on the principle of mutuality, and the Dutch were anxious to have German involvement in their own works. The German Phoenix leadership was not entirely certain that the agreement would be a paying proposition, but they were very happy to get the gulden the Dutch capitalists had to offer. As for the public, it was much relieved to learn that the foreign involvement with Phoenix was Dutch, since it had been rumored that the United States Steel Corporation had been buying up Phoenix stock. The entire affair, however, was viewed as a "warning signal" of what could happen.[97]

There had been other such signals, and German bankers and industrialists had become very wary. While American dollar deposits and stock purchases were welcome, American banks and control were not. The Mercantile Bank of the Americas was anxious to establish a branch in Hamburg in 1919–1920 and talked about making a loan of as much as five hundred million dollars to German firms. Max Warburg politely referred them to the Deutsche Bank for further discussion. The idea was to set up a corporation to administer the loan, but when the Americans suggested that the corporation get collateral for the loan by assuming ownership of the borrowing factories, the Deutsche Bank representatives became very discouraging, and the idea was dropped. Politeness toward Americans, of course, was the order of the day, but the German bankers at a meeting in Berlin to discuss allowing foreign banks to set up shop in Germany took the view that "operating in Germany should be made as difficult as possible for foreigners."[98]

While Dutch incursions had their benefits and American money without strings attached was always welcome, every French effort to gain control of German enterprises was viewed with antipathy and concern. Expanding from the base in the Saar given them by the peace treaty (where the French had paid the Mannesmann concern, the Stumm group, and other German companies a very high price for the majority control of important works), the French were reported to be buying into the south German finishing industry.[99] In early 1921, some German industrialists feared that the French would next try to pull off some great coup in the Rhineland, such as taking over the Rheinmetall firm. Rheinmetall, in association with Krupp (which held a large share of its stock), had been a major armaments manufacturer, and the coming of peace presented enormous reconversion problems which the firm sought to solve by trying its hand at everything from locomotives to typewriters. Instead of paying dividends of 26 to 28 percent, as had been the case during the war, the company had large bank debts and a great need of capital. It could get little help from Krupp, which had its own reconversion problems. Carl Friedrich von Siemens was particularly alarmed, fearing "that the policy of France is perhaps to cut off the Rhenish economic area from the rest of Germany and gradually make it a second Saar territory."[100] France would then control a region rich in raw materials and manufacturing plants and be able to dump raw materials and iron on the rest of Germany while being relieved of the need to import machinery and other manufactured products. Siemens suggested to three of his business colleagues in the west, Emil Kirdorf, Albert Vögler, and Hugo Stinnes, that they create a consortium with some banks and secure Krupp's cooperation in gaining control of Rheinmetall, a proposal Stinnes looked upon with favor provided that "we are at the helm, if only to make sure that the petty experimentation comes to an end and only production that is of long-term value is continued and expanded."[101] Rheinmetall, however, would have liked a connection with Siemens, which it found much more attractive than Stinnes's proposal that it produce motors for his shipyards or other proposals that the Gutehoffnungshütte and Phoenix join in a rescue operation. Rheinmetall wanted to produce for a concern making electrical products, and when the Siemens leadership concluded that it really would not pay to set up production in the Rhineland, the AEG and the Breslau train and railroad-equipment manufacturer, the Linke-Hofmann Works joined together to solve the problem.[102]

If Krupp had proven helpless in the matter, it was because its own difficulties were such that its chief director, Otto Wiedfeldt, had proposed in July 1921 that Krupp use its Mendelssohn bank connection to approach Rockefeller and U.S. Steel and offer a hundred million marks in Krupp stock in return for granting an American seat on the Krupp Supervisory Board. While this would have caused bad feeling against Krupp in the Ruhr, the firm would have had greater independence of the other Ruhr works in its policies as well as foreign trade advantages and money. Wiedfeldt was particularly fearful of the empire Stinnes was creating, warning that the latter "will try to group as many works as possible about himself and then put to us the question: Do you want to go along under the conditions which I set forth or do you want to stand up to us in isolation?"[103] Nevertheless, Gustav Krupp von Bohlen und Halbach rejected the Wiedfeldt proposal, which he found incompatible with the special "national" character and reputation of his firm.

The AEG, which emerged as the most highly capitalized of all the great concerns during this period, demonstrated that it was possible to prevent external "foreignization" successfully while securing foreign capital and expanding its own interests. Thus, it increased its share holdings in the cable producing Felten & Guilleaume firm in 1920, one purpose being to insure that Felton & Guilleaume would remain under German control since it had been forced to sell shares to a Luxemburg consortium in order to receive the raw materials and semifinished products once provided by works lost under the peace treaty. The AEG itself had serious raw-materials supply problems—above all, in copper—and sold twenty-five million marks' worth of its shares to the American Smelting and Refining Company through the banking house of Kuhn, Loeb & Co., whose owner, Otto Kahn, was related to the AEG's general director, Felix Deutsch. The shares were sold at a price which gave the AEG the equivalent of fifty million marks in dollars, while the danger of "foreignization" was prevented by treating the shares as a block and placing both their disposition and their voting rights under the control of a committee composed of two Germans and one American. The arrangement, in effect, avoided the crudities involved in creating special shares with multiple voting rights while actually strengthening the power of the AEG's management against any opposition. Rathenau praised his company's stock sale to the Americans as a "pioneering arrangement," and even proponents of the idea of an industrial credit cooperative who deplored the absence of an "organized economy" in which there would be general liability for foreign credits rather than a "tributary obligation to foreigners" appreciated the skillfulness of the AEG's capital raising techniques.[104]

The expansion and aggressiveness of the AEG was relatively unique for a finished-product manufacturer at this time, since the direction taken by the concentration movement was usually vertical in character and came from the initiatives of the great heavy-industrial producers of raw materials and semifinished products. While the AEG did engage in some vertical expansion (especially through the control it gained of the Lauchhamer AG in Riesa, which produced lignite, iron, and rolled steel, and the alliance with the Linke-Hofmann Works of March 1921 and the joint penetration of Rheinmetall which followed), it stressed horizontal concentration and had actually proposed a community of interest with its great competitor, Siemens. It was a proposition which Siemens rejected because it did not seem to offer a solution to Siemens's capital requirements and raw-materials needs and because of the very different views and policies of the two leaders of the concerns, Walther Rathenau and Carl Friedrich von Siemens.[105]

In general, horizontal concentration proved especially suitable for such fungible products as potash, which had been syndicalized and highly concentrated at this time under government auspices. The most important model for the use of horizontal concentration to organize and rationalize a more complex industry was provided by the "little" IG Farben which Carl Duisberg promoted between 1904 and 1916. This was true even though the chemical firms did some backward vertical concentration

through the acquisition of coal mines after 1918. Logically, rationalization through horizontal integration should also have been the path for the two leading automobile producers Daimler and Benz. The industry had overexpanded during the war and found itself after 1918 facing a diminished market and severe foreign competition. The French made a point of promoting sales of their own cars in the occupied areas. Unhappily, the German government did little to encourage the industry and even taxed cars and gasoline very heavily as luxury items. Although discussions between the two firms began in 1919 and were strongly encouraged by the Deutsche Bank, the entire effort made no progress during the course of the inflation. Post-1918 conditions proved very unfavorable for the development of the German automobile industry, which tended to move more toward fragmentation than rationalization.[106]

Ultimately, the inflation and postwar conditions were most conducive to the vertical concentration led by heavy industry, where there had been a long-term historical development of "mixed" concerns integrated backward into coal and forward into finishing and machine building. While the increasing fragility of the heavy industrial cartels before the war seemed to be pointing in the direction of trustification and rationalization along the lines being pioneered by the chemical industry, the outcome of the war confused the issues in a very serious way. It was significant that Albert Vögler, the general director of the Stinnes-controlled Deutsch-Luxemburg Mining and Smelting Co., strongly advocated horizontal trustification and rationalization both during and after the war. His proposals culminated in a memorandum of July 1919 suggesting that six or seven of the great Rhenish-Westphalian concerns join in a community of interest that would restructure and rationalize German heavy industry.[107]

This was not a program that appealed to most of heavy industry's leaders, including Vögler's boss, Hugo Stinnes, who favored going it alone and vertical expansion for reasons of both fear and opportunity. On the one hand, they wanted to be as strong as possible in the face of the domestic and international uncertainties and so that they could demand good terms in the event of having to enter a trust. Nearly all the concerns had suffered losses in Lorraine and Luxemburg, had heavy ore debts payable in kroner, and were simply too mutilated to accept Vögler's proposals. Indeed, the feeling that everything had been turned topsy-turvy and that they had to look to their own best interests resulted in the collapse of the already badly shaken giant cartel the Steel Works Association, and it was this that led the government to impose the Iron Trades Association on the industry. On the other hand, the situation was also one of opportunity. Not only had many of the great Ruhr firms built up large reserves thanks to their wartime profits, but they had also sold their holdings in Lorraine, Luxemburg, and other lost areas for lucrative sums paid in francs and were, in addition, offered compensation by the Reich on condition that they use the money to restore their productive capacities. Since the situation was not very conducive to undertaking significant new plant construction, it was both natural and necessary for these concerns to seek to recoup their losses by buying up or consolidating with other works. Basically, they faced three tasks. First, they needed to acquire secure sources of vital raw materials, especially ore and coal. Second, they sought to restore their capacity in iron and steel production, but they were also particularly anxious to expand into finishing and machine building which, because of Germany's low real wages and the expanded iron and steel capacity of Germany's competitors and former customers, had become the most promising source of profitability. As a corollary to this, they also hoped to modernize and rationalize both their old holdings and their new acquisitions. Finally, they needed to recover their lost markets, either by reestablishing or creating marketing organizations of their own or by allying themselves with other marketing organizations with appropriate facilities both at home and abroad.[108]

This is not the place to catalogue or detail the various efforts that went into achieving these goals of vertical concentration, but it is important to stress and analyze the role played by problems of inflation and reconstruction. Manifestly, the policies pursued by the great con-cerns were determined by immediate considerations, and the priority was given to the rebuilding of heavy-industrial capacities rather than to the rationalization of the heavy-industrial sector, even though it was obvious that France had vastly increased her productive capacity, the United States loomed larger than ever before as a competitor, and other nations had entered the field. The control over raw materials, especially coal, and the large profits made on the war production and high raw materials prices gave heavy industry an unusually increased leverage over manufacturers who might otherwise have resisted giving up their autonomy. The M.A.N. was largely moved to seek alliance with a major Ruhr concern by its raw materials and cash flow difficulties, and the takeover of the firm by the Gutehoffnungshütte and its leader Paul Reusch was bitterly resented in south Germany. Even so mighty a concern as Siemens was moved to make an alliance with Stinnes because of raw-materials and capital problems. Indeed, Siemens had hoped that the M.A.N. would join in the connection with Stinnes so that they could provide an industrial and geographical counterweight to the power of heavy industry and the Ruhr. It is interesting to note that the distaste for Prussia was shared abroad, and Reusch had cause to remark that "it is very noticeable how much South Germany is preferred over Prussia. At the M.A.N. the incoming orders are continuously in excess of production."[109]

If such were the fears of great manufacturers like the M.A.N. and Siemens, one can well imagine the nervousness of small manufacturers who faced the same raw materials and capital shortages without the same powers to negotiate and even resist. The Nationalist Party Deputy Quaatz worriedly wrote Vögler at the end of 1920 concerning the reaction of Ruhr businessmen to the Rheinelbe concern Stinnes and Vögler had forged by the union of the Deutsch-Luxemburg and Gelsenkirchener Bergwerke concerns: "In Altona there was great distress concerning the relations between heavy industry and manufacturing. Someone asked: Is it your intention as well as part of the Stinnes policy to compel the manufacturing industry to join the concerns by keeping up the prices of semi-finished products while depressing the price of manufactured goods?"[110] Quaatz emphatically rejected such notions, pointing out that Vögler had always argued that "the future of Germany on the world market depends on the finished product industries" and that the Rheinelbe concern and other heavy-industrial concerns "were neither in the position nor did they wish to swallow up the manufacturing industries." It is hard to imagine that those listening to Quaatz were very reassured and did not think that it was precisely because Germany's future lay in manufacturing that heavy industry had every reason to take over finishing and that Stinnes and his compatriots would digest the manufacturing firms whenever there was an opportunity to do so.

The evidence certainly supports such an interpretation. Each of the great industrial concerns expanded its holdings in manufacturing during this period, while at the same time expanding or reconstituting its raw-materials and basic-product foundation. This was, of course, made possible by the special conditions existing at the time, and the fact that some of the takeovers of this period were highly successful and have withstood the test of time is no demonstration that they would have taken place under other, more "normal" circumstances. They must be understood historically as the consequence of developments which particularly favored the heavy-industrial sector, and, insofar as they were mirrored to a less extent in other industries—for example, in textiles—they must also be recognized as triumphs of big business over medium-sized and small business. Needless to say, this had immensely important political and social as well as economic implications.

The expansion of the great concerns was not limited to Germany. The great concerns involved in imports and exports were not only able but virtually forced to conduct many of their financial and trading transactions outside of Germany and even under foreign names and flags. Of course, many of Germany's large enterprises, especially in the electrotechnical, chemical, and metals fields had always had foreign subsidiaries and marketing operations. Branches in neutral countries survived the war, while efforts were undertaken to rebuild the others. However, the depreciation of the mark,

on the one hand, and the war-generated hatred of Germany, on the other hand, required special measures and made the Netherlands an especially important site for the economic reconstruction being conducted by Germany's economic leadership. Between 1918 and 1921, at least 128 new companies were founded in the Netherlands with German capital. Eleven of these were banks, usually branches of major banks, while 106 were merchant firms dealing in exports and imports. Another 82 companies were set up in 1922–1923, most of them in 1922. Again, merchant firms and, to a lesser extent, banks accounted for the majority, followed by a few transport and holding companies.[111]

The Netherlands served as a major repository for German capital flight, but it became most important after 1919 as a source of capital and a place where foreign exchange could be procured, held, and paid out to cover imports. Thyssen set up a bank in the Netherlands as early as 1918 to service his needs, while the large German banks found it necessary to establish themselves there to handle the foreign-exchange requirements of their industrial clients at home. It was through Mendelssohn & Co.'s branch in the Netherlands, for example, that Krupp secured important loans, and Dutch investments also flowed into the heavy-industrial enterprises linked with Otto Wolff, Haniel, and Mannesmann. The Netherland's significance for foreign-exchange transactions is demonstrated by the fact that a market for forward-exchange transactions was set up at the beginning of December 1920. No such markets could be found in London or Paris at this time, and the Dutch operation was intended only for large dealers and high-class customers. In January 1921, for example, it would only handle orders for a minimum of a thousand pounds, twenty-five hundred dollars, twenty-five thousand francs, or a hundred thousand marks.

Most important, however, were the trading companies. The Netherlands provided a stable economic environment in which calculation was less problematic and international transactions and arrangements could be handled more easily than back at home. In some cases, the German character of these companies was easily recognizable—for example, the N.V.F.

Krupp Rederie en Transportmaatschappij; N.V. Lahmeyer & Co. Electriciteitsmaatschappij; Mercedes Daimler Autmotilmaatschappij. Apparently, a large enough number of them were recognizable because the Dutch government actually banned German firms from membership on the Amsterdam stock market, a measure which even the Hamburg Chamber of Commerce found understandable in the light of the "flooding of Holland with German firms" and which the Hamburg businessmen sought to correct through negotiation rather than countermeasures.[112]

A great many of the German firms, however, were not recognizably German, and this by intention. One of the reasons why so many of the great concerns were anxious to cease selling through the syndicates was that, in the words of Hasslacher of Rheinstahl, "every work will do better business abroad individually than through an association. We will do better business under a neutral or enemy commercial trading flag than we would if we came forward with syndicates."[113] The Gutehoffnungshütte did much of its international trading through N.V. Algemeene Ijzer- en Staal-Maatschappij "Ferrostahl," of which a third of the shares were owned, respectively, by the GHH, a consortium of the Metallgesellschaft and the Dutch trading firm of Wilhelm H. Müller, and a consortium of banks. Ferrostahl already had a worldwide organization with forty branches in 1921 and was planning to expand to between a hundred and a hundred fifty branches. Stinnes controlled an import and transport firm called Plattenberg, and this was only one of at least three trading companies he controlled in the Netherlands. As noted previously, Otto Wolff was especially at home in the Netherlands. While Wolff did his business with England through his Cologne offices and also had a Comptoir Industriel in Brussels for trade with Belgium, an Eisenag in Zürich for trade with Switzerland, and an Estag in Vienna for trade with Austria-Hungary and the Balkans, his Dutch operation was most elaborate, involving a holding company for all his Dutch enterprises with the unrevealing title of Delfstoffen-Maatschappij Hollandia in Amsterdam. The heart of his operations in the Netherlands, however, was the Nedeximpo, which handled trade with the Netherlands and

the Dutch colonies from an imposing well-located Amsterdam building with a cellar and first floor capable of holding large amounts of machinery and other items marketed by Wolff from the production of his own and associated enterprises. The top two floors contained offices, the efficiency of whose personnel was amply demonstrated by the firm's profitable balance sheet. Furthermore, in early 1921, Wolff was expanding this already formidable operation by negotiating control of the old Dutch firm of Dikema and Chabot.[114]

While most of the companies discussed were under German control, there was also a great deal of collaboration between German and Dutch interests in which the German role was deliberately hidden by mutual agreement. In April 1920, for example, Richard Merton of the Metallgesellschaft negotiated with van Deventer of one of the greatest Dutch trading companies, Wilhelm H. Müller, to set up a Wilhelm H. Müller Iron and Steel Corporation to sell at home and abroad. In addition to the two companies mentioned, the Rotterdam'sche Bankvereeniging and M.M. Warburg & Co. were also involved. It was agreed, however, in order to maintain the Dutch character of the company, "that all shares with multiple voting rights shall be in the name of the Dutch founders . . . , while it is internally agreed that all rights accruing to these shares shall be granted in practice in accordance with their actual ownership."[115] This was a cheap way of overcoming what Rathenau called the "discount for hatred"[116] German goods were sold and shipped under Dutch names throughout Europe, North and South America, and the British colonies thanks to these kinds of arrangements. This was a singularly important element of Germany's economic reconstruction during this period, for if Germany needed to do anything, it was to sell her products on world markets once again.

From this perspective, it was fitting that Hugo Stinnes, whose calling card read, "Merchant from Mülheim," became the living embodiment of Germany's inflationary reconstruction. In truth, Stinnes was a remarkable merchant, not only of goods but also of economic projects and social and economic programs. If Stinnes was not as representative of the German business community as many have thought and as he sometimes pretended, he nevertheless appeared as the chief representative of German industry and, to many persons, of Germany itself both at home and abroad. This has not always served his reputation well. Stinnes has gone down in history as the classic example of inflationary empire builder as well as one of Germany's "destroyers."[117] The collapse of his economic interests after his death in April 1924 has been used to illustrate the fragility of the inflationary reconstruction and to exemplify the unsound principles on which it was based. The sociopolitical activities of Stinnes have served to demonstrate the worst consequences of that narrow business approach which asserted the primacy of the economic over the social and political and which confused the private with the public good. Stinnes has been vilified as having the worst characteristics ascribed to Germany's industrialists—self-serving opportunism, arrogance, reactionary authoritarianism, and social indifference.[118]

Such totally negative portrayals of Stinnes are about as useless in making Stinnes's activities, power, and influence intelligible as one-sided laudatory biographies written by hack apologists.[119] His appearance was undistinguished and his dress was sober, and he could be unassuming to the point of insisting on carrying his own valise in the train station. He treated his own firm very much as a family enterprise, discussing matters of importance with his wife and placing heavy, excessive responsibility on his sons, Hugo Jr. and Edmund, particularly the former and younger of them.[120] Hugo Stinnes was not a particularly impressive speaker, giving the impression in his public performances of being "an aesthetic monk with a high, suppressed voice." Yet, contemporaries were fascinated by his person and captivated by the presentation of his ideas. Apparently, he was able to convey a sense of personal vision and prophetic certainty, and he seemed to offer practical solutions along with imaginative ideas in an environment not particularly rich in either. Unlike Rathenau, who spoke in the tone of an "enthusiastic holy man"[121] and whose ideas were difficult to follow and who did not always practice what he preached, Stinnes was constantly acting on what he thought and gave the sense that even the simplest business decision had a place in some promising program and some general scheme of things. The tactical and the strategic became so intertwined as to legitimize inconsistency and make failures and mistakes appear irrelevant. Stinnes seemed and still seems unanalyzable because he was a truly Promethean character whose business interests ranged far and wide, drew him into the center of domestic and foreign affairs, and kept him constantly on the move. While generally identified as Germany's greatest industrialist and passionately engaged with problems of production, he was ever attentive to the market. It was no accident that he called himself a merchant. His approach to problems, both economic and political, was determined by an almost obsessive concentration on what he deemed to be the economic logic of the situation to the studied exclusion of other considerations which he deemed irrelevant. He was uniquely optimistic and self-confident, traits seldom found in so great a measure among his rather sour and dour colleagues in the Ruhr. As his son Edmund pointed out: "At the bottom of his heart, he was an eternal optimist and he managed to inspire even his most skeptical partners with confidence and the firm conviction that problems could be solved and mastered. In critical situations he would say: 'I never give up hope. If they want to hang me and the noose is already round my neck, I simply think how often ropes have broken.'"[122] Needless to say, such an attitude put his opponents and critics at a very great disadvantage. It also made him quintessentially fit for a period of inflation and ideally suited to present a countervision to the national economy schemes of the technocrats and the socialization schemes of the left.

It was a vision that arose out of his personal career as a businessman. He was born in 1870 to a Mülheim-Ruhr family that had made its fortune in coal production as well as in shipping along the Rhine and in marketing coal. His formal technical training was relatively brief, but he demonstrated his uncanny sense for profitable technical and commercial combinations very early, first expanding his mining, river transport, and marketing organizations and then founding the Deutsch-Luxemburg Mining and Smelting Company in 1901. Within a decade, he had expanded it into one of the most important, vertically organized, heavy-industrial concerns. The Hugo Stinnes Firm (which controlled the Stinnes family coal-mining, shipping, and marketing interests), although formally separated from Deutsch-Lux, handled many of Deutsch-Lux's export and marketing operations and joined with Deutsch-Lux in 1911 to gain control of important shipbuilding and shipping firms in north Germany. They thus became involved in the shipbuilding and machine construction industries.[123]

This was by no means the only type of vertical expansion that interested Stinnes, however, and some of his most imaginative ventures were in the realm of electric power. In 1905, he joined with August Thyssen in gaining a majority control of the Rheinisch-Westfälische-Elektrizitätswerke (RWE), but then assumed the dominant influence as chairman of its Supervisory Board. The RWE expanded into the greatest power company in the country under Stinnes's prodding. This was done initially through the RWE's close links with the Stinnes mines, but the RWE went on at Stinnes's instigation to acquire Rheinish lignite mines. The opening of the Goldenberg Power Plant near Cologne in 1914, named after the RWE's leading engineer, in whom Stinnes had enormous faith, was the high point of this development. A ground-breaking achievement, it was the largest plant of its kind in Europe, and it was based on the close connections between the Rhenish lignite mines and the power works. The Stinnes-RWE ambitions found their only, albeit significant, limits in the resistance of various outlying municipal authorities and industrial interests to integration into the RWE network. At the same time, much of the expansion took place through collaboration with municipal authorities, who were to gain majority control of the RWE at Stinnes's instigation, thereby creating a model of what Stinnes meant by a "mixed enterprise" combining public and private participation. Basically, it was a regional enterprise heavily dependent upon and integrated with the local coal industry while serving the rest of the regional industry along with domestic consumers.[124]

Stinnes continued these processes of vertical expansion during the war. Deutsch-Lux moved further into manufacturing and was embarking on motor-vehicle and airplane construction at the war's end, while the RWE began to service Stinnes's attempts to break into the field of aluminum production. Had Germany won the war and realized the gigantic war aims which Stinnes supported, his empire certainly would have been breathtaking since he was deeply involved in the private economic efforts to penetrate the areas that were either to be annexed or to become part of the German spheres of economic and political influence. In preparation for such a state of affairs, Stinnes reorganized his firm in 1917, and the purposes he assigned to the newly created Hugo Stinnes Corporation for Shipping and Overseas Trade (*Aktiengesellschaft Hugo Stinnes für Seeschiffahrt und Überseehandel*) give some measure of his intentions and expectations:

Ocean shipping of every kind, including the production of all the necessary supplies and equipment both at home and abroad; trade in all products of the mining, smelting, chemical, and electrical industries, of agriculture as well as trade in goods, finished products, semi-finished products, and raw materials of every kind, especially food and fodder; mineral, animal, and vegetable oils; cotton and other textile raw materials, skins, jute, wood, cellulose, paper, and all products of the manufacturing industries; further the transshipping and storing of such products, especially insofar as they come from abroad or are going abroad. The corporation is also entitled to itself undertake the production, extraction, and manufacture of goods, finished products, and semi-finished products, and raw materials of every kind on its own.[125]

Faith in Ludendorff's ability to lead Germany to victory was one of the greater miscalculations of Stinnes's career, but there is no evidence that the loss of the war significantly affected his entrepreneurial ardor. To be sure, some belt tightening was in order, and in January 1919 he had instructed the heads of his own firm to release superfluous personnel and reduce expenses since "we can only still make very modest profits in the best of circumstances" and "it is inconceivable that we can operate further on the present basis."[126] Social and political attitudes also had to be changed, and Stinnes rapidly and unsentimentally made his peace with the new order. He had never been a fanatical opponent of dealing with the trade unions in any case, and the ZAG represented a bold and necessary accommodation. Similarly, during the war he had always argued that defeat would mean the end of the monarchy, and he came to terms with the political reality as well, joining the DVP in 1918, permitting the general director of Deutsch-Lux, Albert Vögler, to become a Reichstag Deputy in 1919, and successfully running for the Reichstag himself in the June 1920 elections. He refused Kapp his support for both foreign and domestic policy reasons. From Stinnes's perspective, all such matters were "superstructural" rather than "substructural," and he moved forward like a man possessed in dealing with his business affairs and in fighting for the principles he deemed correct.

The postwar situation encouraged Stinnes to transform his personal economic ambitions and his economic vision into a program for the defense of capitalism and a formula for economic reconstruction. He had always opposed economic controls, state planning, and, of course, socialization ideas propagated on the left and in certain academic and intellectual circles. He was committed to economic individualism and to the benefits of the entrepreneur's unfettered "reading" of market forces. The postwar development of his enterprises was meant to serve as a model for what he felt to be the appropriate economic organization required for the reconstruction.

Stinnes's expansion created something of a legend, and while admirers marveled at his performance, critics attacked him as a profiteer. Stinnes always professed a great distaste, disdain, and indifference concerning the negative publicity accompanying some of his activities, especially for the ignorance he felt it displayed, although he was very sensitive to reports affecting his reputation as a businessman and to public misreading of his real goals and actions. A major source of difficulty in dealing with Stinnes lies in the fact that neither contemporaries nor historians have been able to sort out his affairs easily. While it was obvious that he was a very well-to-do man who disposed of immense resources, exactly how much of the latter actually belonged to him was hard to determine. One of his closest collaborators, Karl Fehrmann, pointed out in a confidential memorandum for Stinnes's widow in 1952 that:

In the view of the man on the street and also a portion of the educated, Stinnes controlled the numerous enterprises—for example, Deutsch-Lux, the RWE and many others—exclusively as a capitalist, that is, as

the majority stockholder, while in actuality he held only a minority of the shares in almost all of the enterprises including the Stinnes family mines and controlled the enterprises completely only on the basis of his over-whelming personality.[127]

The power of Stinnes's personality crops up often enough in the sources and literature to give credibility to Fehrmann's emphasis on its significance, but its full importance only becomes clear when one demystifies the point and realizes that Stinnes's personality was a monetizable asset. It was a source of credit. The tenuousness of his hold on the enterprises allegedly under his control is demonstrated by his revised testament of March 1920, a revision he undertook as a consequence of changes in the tax laws. He stressed that the actual Stinnes trading and transportation firms could only be "economically secured" if the power of the house of Stinnes was maintained in the Stinnes family mines and at Deutsch-Lux. That the control of the latter, in which he placed the greatest stake, was no certain matter was emphasized by a warning not to permit Deutsch-Lux to issue multiple voting-right shares unless they were placed in the hands of Stinnes's own firms. His fear was that the other interests in Deutsch-Lux, probably the banks, and its management might use such stock issues to undermine the Stinnes family control. As he bluntly stated in a remark that revealed the gap that continued to exist between the owner-entrepreneurs and the management of great enterprises: "Despite my great esteem and fondness for Herr Vögler, I do not wish to have the foundation of my life's work become dependent on a company manager."[128]

A major reason for the dependence of Stinnes's trading houses on the control of Deutsch-Lux was that the actual Stinnes family firms were overextended, and Stinnes knew that their operations were very much a function of his personal credit at this time:

Those carrying out this will are to see to it that the termination of the great personal credit which will occur under any circumstances with my decease is taken into consideration in any limiting of business operations that is found necessary. After my decease care must in general be taken to conduct business without bank credits as soon as possible even if on a smaller scale.[129]

While it certainly is true that the Stinnes family enterprises had very solid foundations, it also

Hugo Stinnes (1870–1924), from a portrait made in 1921. (*Library of Congress*)

of the collapse of most of his trading operations abroad, and that "only fools and ignoramuses" could imagine that war and postwar profits could replace such losses and that "an overseas export business of 6 million tons today counts for nothing more than an inestimable 'good will'." Stinnes, however, was not asking for sympathy or mercy. He was aggressively demanding opportunity. If the value of his name was inestimable, this was more than could be said of the credit of the government trying to tax him. In his tax assessment report, Stinnes absolutely refused to consider the Reich's promise to compensate him for prewar foreign debt claims he had lost and insisted on subtracting the amount to be paid from his taxable assets, pointing out:

The Reich, which today has 236 billion in debts and whose burden of debt grows from month to month, whose credit worthiness is well shown by the value of its currency, that prints notes upon notes without any coverage and that has long been bankrupt. . . . This poor Reich cannot give any guarantees or present a prospect of their realization upon which a businessman can base his balances. The basis for my business is my personal credit at home and abroad. This credit is until now unshaken; I can get any credit I need today at home and abroad. But that will cease the moment I begin to enter on the path of economic collapse in my business.[131]

This attitude had profound political and economic implications. Clearly a Reich government so described was unfit and unable to reconstruct the economy and could serve the nation best by nurturing and supporting those with real credit and a true capacity to reconstruct the economy—Germany's business leaders. And who among these had more ingenuity and more credit than Hugo Stinnes?

must be recognized that he had a strong tendency to place more of a burden upon them than others might have felt justified through the exploitation of the credit opportunities opened up by his "personality."

This was not a point he was shy about making, even if its significance was not fully understood by others, but it also helps to explain his irritation when reports of his profits and wealth were used to attack him. When the tax authorities wrote to him in the spring of 1920 asking him to be sure to respond to the charges and claims in certain newspaper reports concerning his war profits and investments when making up his income-tax assessment declaration, Stinnes replied with a mixture of contempt and pride, pointing out that there were volumes of stories circulating about himself, but that "not a single one of the many hundreds of newspaper reports concerning my person has correctly brought out the *economic* facts and interconnections."[130] Stinnes claimed that few firms had lost as much as his had during the war because

His most immediate major task at the end of the war was rebuilding the heavy-industrial foundations of his empire, and this meant replacing Deutsch-Lux's losses under the postwar settlement and meeting the demands of the energy crisis by expanding his coal base. Here, the most promising possibilities were presented by the Gelsenkirchener Bergwerke (GBAG), headed by the venerable Emil Kirdorf. The GBAG had lost most of its iron and steel capacity in the defeat, and this meant that the GBAG and Deutsch-Lux could complement one another admirably. In August 1920, the two concerns entered into an IG called the Rheinelbe Union, and Stinnes found himself in control of the mightiest coal base in Germany thanks to his own mining interests as well as those joined together in the IG. Stinnes's attitude toward the coal-mining sector's reconstruction, however, was a very cautious one. While arguing ceaselessly that there was nothing more important than improving coal production, he insisted that this could only be done through high prices. On the one hand, such prices would permit the payment of the high wages needed to persuade the miners to work overtime; on the other hand, he wanted prices that would cover nothing short of an 85 percent amortization of new investment on the grounds that a rise in the value of the mark would make the paying back of such investments an intolerable burden. The RWM was willing to encourage new investment through coal price increases, but it opposed the spectacular amortization rates demanded by Stinnes. The Ministry also insisted on the right to oversee the use of additional funds to make sure that the coal-mine owners really were investing in their own industry and to ensure that the mine owners were not also borrowing from the banks and thereby doubly burdening their consumers by a combination of high prices and reduction of the available private funds for credit. Stinnes rejected such government oversight and restrictions as nothing more than the back door socialization of the industry, a view shared by his allies in the coal industry, especially the lignite industrialist Paul Silverberg, and by the banks, which considered the suggested control of the objects of their credit the "most monstrous" example of the controlled economy yet conceived. The result of all this was a stalemate between the coal interests and the RWM. The Ministry, not surprisingly, enjoyed the support of industrial and private consumer interests on these questions.[132]

Stinnes, however, meant business, and his public posture on prices was translated into private policy on investment. Thus, at the very first meeting of the Rheinelbe Union's leadership on August 18, 1920, a decision was taken to emphasize the "short-term" in bringing about an integration of Deutsch-Lux's Dortmunder Union with the GBAG mines, and thereby "avoid major new investments as much

possible because new plant is extraordinarily expensive under the existing circumstances and the present high demand might possibly recede very sharply in 2–3 years because of the strongly limited capabilities of an impoverished Europe." Similarly, despite the desperate need to attract workers to the mines, investment in worker housing was to be undertaken only "in the most limited degree" and "means provided by the Reich are to be used as much as possible in constructing worker housing."[133]

Stinnes's extraordinary effort thus to socialize the costs of rehabilitating the mines and increasing coal production while preventing socialization required more than a little audacity in the context of the socialization demands that followed the Kapp Putsch and the civil war in the Ruhr that had led to the creation of a second Socialization Commission and renewed debate over the issue in the summer and fall of 1920. Even this, however, was as nothing compared to his boldness in presenting "socialization" proposals of his own that urged the legal sanction and encouragement of vertical concentration.

In order to comprehend Stinnes's remarkable handling of the socialization question, it is necessary to understand his views concerning the coal industry and its future. The Ruhr mining industry was divided between two types of mining companies—the "pure" mining companies and the mines belonging to iron and steel, chemical, and electrical power companies. Typically, Stinnes were firmly ensconced in both camps, being the major shareholder of the family-owned Stinnes mines as well as connected with those under control of the Rhineelbe Union. While never underestimating the importance of coal to Germany's domestic economy and international power, he was convinced that the prospects for economic growth and expansion were to be found elsewhere, and he did not think the "pure mines" had much of a future. As he told his cousin August Küchen, the general director of the Matthias Stinnes Mining Company in August 1920, "the class of companies which pursue coal mining in order to make money on coal will more or less die out." Over the years, Stinnes had repeatedly urged the Stinnes mines to link up with a large iron and steel company like Deutsch-Lux, but apparently he had run into family opposition, and this opportunity had been lost through the Deutsch-Lux alliance with the GBAG. The bleak future Stinnes anticipated for the pure mines, however, was being brought much nearer by the socialization movement. At the same time, Stinnes viewed the transformation of the ownership of the mining industry as inevitable and necessary:

The mining industry will go over into the hands of every kind of consumer and public as well as worker control. The development in this direction conforms to the national and public economic interest and is therefore unstoppable.[134]

The process, however, could be preempted if other private interests gained control of the mines, and Stinnes urged that the three Stinnes mines in Essen be tied to the RWE while the Matthias Stinnes mines become associated with one of the cellulose-producing firms with which he was associated. The Stinnes mines, in other words, had to "socialize" themselves in order not to be socialized by less desirable agents.

There was true harmony, therefore, between the public policy Stinnes was advocating and his private practice, a point not lost on his critics but one to which he pointed with an almost sublime pride. At the very moment when he was gaining control of the Bochumer Verein and promoting the RWE's formation of IG's with the Roddergrube lignite mines and his three Essen mines in the fall of 1920, he was publicly and formally advocating his concept of "socialization" to the Socialization Commission. Because of the energy crisis, control of coal had become more than ever the key to the RWE's ability to expand its hold on the regional power industry as well as to maintain its control or influence over the gas works, tram lines, and industrial facilities in the region. Similarly, coal was the essential basis for the expansion of the iron and steel works. In bigness there was power and an ability to resist government and public pressures. Just as the big banks welcomed one another's expansion as a means of strengthening their hold on the nation's banking system, so was it possible for the great Ruhr enterprises to find something positive in one another's expansion. Thus, Stinnes and Vögler urged the Phoenix concern to enter into an IG with the great Harpener Mining Company and even went so far as to suggest that "this ring would then enter into relations with the Rheinelbe Union."[135] No fears of "indigestion" here! It all fit in with Stinnes's concept of "socialization." By advocating vertically organized "coal committees" in which the coal consumers would be granted a voice in pricing, production, and allocation of coal, and making provision for the "appropriation" of the mines when necessary, Stinnes was simply identifying socialization with vertical trustification of the type practiced by Deutsch-Lux and the RWE. Critics understandably argued that nontrustified small and medium-sized coal and energy consumers would be at the mercy of these giants, while Walther Rathenau presented a proposal of his own aimed at making the production and pricing policies of the coal producers "transparent" and subject to public control for the thirty-year period in which a compensated socialization of the industry was to take place. Rathenau warned that the Stinnes vertical concentration program would create a group of uncontrollable "industrial duchies."[136]

It is necessary to emphasize, however, that Stinnes truly believed in vertical integration and that his arguments before the Socialization Commission, in which he pointed directly to the RWE as an illustration of the regionally organized community of consumers and producers which he was advocating, were not simply self-serving. While such arrangements would obviously minister to the interests of the mixed industrial works and would diminish the power of Berlin with its centralizing, interfering, and socializing tendencies, Stinnes himself was no longer very fearful that socialization would take place by this time. It was possible, after all, as in the case of Director Kleine of the Harpener firm, to argue that the socialization threat was not really as great as feared but to resist vertical integration anyway. As Kleine told Stinnes's ally, Paul Silverberg: "I am not so convinced of the superiority of vertically concentrated trusts as Herr Stinnes and Herr Vögler and as you seem to have become in the meantime. I think that these great enterprises must first present practical evidence for their economic superiority."[137] Kleine particularly objected to forcing vertical concentration to take place by legislative means. Vögler, unlike Stinnes and Kleine, felt that the socialization danger was very great in the summer of 1920 and that vertical integration was a practical means of undermining socialization attempts by tying coal mines to other enterprises and thus effectively removing them from the coal industry. Still, Vögler feared that they would "face great surprises in this area" and, like Wiedfeldt of Krupp, wondered if Stinnes, when propagating the "vertical idea" as *the* solution to the socialization question, was not failing to recognize that "socialization today is above all that which it should not be, a political matter."[138]

Wiedfeldt was not convinced, however, that Stinnes's "suggestive power of presentation" was adequate to deal with the political forces behind the socialization movement: the industries without coal who were by and large unintegrated into large electrical power systems (for example, textiles and woodworking) and private consumers suffering from coal shortages, for whom "it was a matter of indifference to whom the coal mines belong" and who "would accept every change of regime which promised them more coal"; the Socialists and planned-economy theoreticians, who had been making socialization the final goal for themselves and the masses over the years; and the bourgeois government which needed some kind of political success with the left. Wiedfeldt was concerned that the miners would cease to work overtime if their socialization demands were not met and was convinced that the only way to undercut the socialization drive was by offering the unions a measure of direct financial participation in the industry through the issuance of small shares to the miners as well as granting unions representation on the supervisory boards of the mining companies. The Stinnes plan, in Wiedfeldt's view, would backfire unless one could win over the workers by offering a measure of co-determination. As Wiedfeldt shrewdly pleaded with Stinnes:

You know that I see in you one of the few men in whom we can place any hopes for Germany's future. Please do not take it ill, but you should not allow yourself to be intellectually captured by *one* great idea. To be sure, one-sidedness is the force that makes every idea fly. But here the issue is the speedy translation into reality, and therefore the political effect is important. And if I am not mistaken, Vögler, who is much more involved in politics than either you or I, has the same reservations as I do.

Characteristically, however, Stinnes remained unmoved when he was convinced that nothing was to be gained by compromising a basic economic goal. This was all the more the case because concessions to the demands of the socialization proponents might be premature and unnecessary: "In this time of political and economic emergency no one can know what the next weeks will bring. Possibly, a civil war and/or other war will make the socialization question become highly inconsequential."[139] He was prepared to have a number of small shares made available to "interested workers and employees" of the mines and viewed the matter of offering the trade unions a percentage of mining company shares as a "question of tactics" which was "not of great significance." What remained essential, from Stinnes's perspective, was the union of coal production and consumption, and a "period of two or four years were to be given in which the action on the side of the consumers and consumer organizations . . . must be brought to an end. Naturally, the precondition for success is that the consumer groups are brought together in forms that make it possible for them to act."[140]

Stinnes's bold effort, on the one hand, to create privately the kind of economic organization he wished to impose on the nation and, on the other hand, to have the organization given a legal status was not limited to the coal industry. He urged Wiedfeldt, whose previous government service had given him "so much practice in the framing of agreeable and disagreeable laws," to try his hand at framing suitable legislation for the "socialization" of the electric power industry and also for the "subdivision of our railroad system." This last suggestion was quite remarkable since the railroad system had just been taken over by the Reich in one of the very few implementations of a Socialist program in the history of the Republic. The notion that the railroad system was to be integrated into the regional systems of vertical organization Stinnes was trying to promote certainly conformed to Stinnes' search for the "most efficient" means of distributing coal. His interest in the recently nationalized railroads, however, had more far-reaching implications that were to have great importance a year later in connection with the reparations issue.

If in the summer of 1920 Stinnes was showing a tendency to take a hard line and risk a political fight for his economic position, by late October 1920 he and his fellow industrialists had succeeded in getting the government to eliminate socialization from its formal program, and they were even arguing that the effectiveness of their own socialization proposals depended upon the miners being willing to work overtime shifts. Furthermore, they pointed out that the miners would be more agreeable to longer hours if the transport and construction workers would agree to a ten-hour day—an obvious back-door attempt to break the eight-hour day. The aggressiveness can be measured in the tone of the Industrial Committee of the DVP, in one of the meetings of which it was concluded:

The severest criticism must be exercised by the party, and political terrorism must be energetically opposed. In the Socialization Committee, in any case, the employers left no doubt about the fact that one must even calculate on the eventuality of a civil war. The party must even let it come to an electoral battle over the sabotage of the economy through socialization. The prospects for an electoral campaign that was conducted with the slogan of raising the purchasing power of the mark would be favorable for the German People's Party.[141]

No such dramatic actions were necessary, however, since by the beginning of 1921 the coal socialization issue had been drowned in anxieties that the allies might be able to tap the proceeds of a nationalized coal system to get reparations. In the last analysis, therefore, Stinnes had been correct in playing down the actual danger of socialization while treating the entire debate as an opportunity to procure a public sanction for his private economic program.

In reality, Stinnes had no intention whatever of waiting upon any external authority to continue his national and international expansion or pursue a program of vertical concentration far more extensive than anything imagined by the more modest giants of the Ruhr—August Thyssen, Peter Klöckner, Otto Wolff, and Paul Reusch, all of whose concern building in this period stopped more or less with the acquisition of firms building bridges, machines, or motors and turbines and the development of international marketing organizations for their own production. When Stinnes began discussing a community of interest between his heavy-industrial interests and the Siemens concern, at the turn of 1919–1920, however, negotiations that were to culminate in the creation of the Siemens–Rheinelbe–Schuckert-Union (SRSU) in December 1920, he held forth the prospect of "a community of interest that would begin with wood and end with the completed machine."[142] Stinnes meant this literally. He had already invested in the purchase of forests in East Prussia as well as Russia, where he seemed to believe that a regime change would take place, and he had also become involved in cellulose plants, printing companies, and publishing. He anticipated a replacement of cotton by synthetic fibers. At the same time, his trading companies were expanding into the hotel business, taking over the Esplanade in Berlin among others, and spas. The practical importance to the Siemens concern of these forms of vertical concentration, which crossed over into the realm of conglomeration, could not have been very clear. However, Stinnes's control of the giant, central German lignite producer, the Riebeck Mining Company (which was also a major producer of industrial oil products, paraffin, and wax), was undoubtedly of greater attractiveness, as was Stinnes's growing involvement with Austria's largest iron-and-steel-producing enterprise, the Alpine Montangesellschaft, which seemed to offer valuable support for Siemens's involvement with the Fiat automobile works in Turin.

Given these perspectives, it is hard to imagine that the negotiations leading to the SRSU began with a prosaic effort by Siemens and his leading director, Otto Henrich, both of whom had worked closely with Stinnes to create the ZAG at the end of the war, to find a secure supply of steel dynamo plate and other vital materials. Deutsch-Lux's Philipp Weber plant in Brandenburg was a major producer of dynamo plate, and it was this that ignited the discussions. Siemens and Henrich were drawn into deliberations concerning a more general alliance by their great need for operating capital, and Carl Friedrich von Siemens seems to have been particularly hard-pressed by worried family members who feared for the liquidity of the firm under postwar conditions. Henrich, who was peculiarly susceptible to Stinnes's arguments, seems to have pushed the IG idea very strongly. In any case, he could argue that a community of interest with the Rheinelbe would provide a secure supply of raw materials and an enormous pool of operating capital, while Stinnes and Siemens would benefit from one another's worldwide trading organizations and affiliates. The coordination of production, technical collaboration, and rationalization were much fuzzier areas, since there was no way to organize the kind of continuous operations between the Rheinelbe Union and those of the Siemens enterprises that existed within large portions of the Rheinelbe Union. Both sides hoped to establish closer productive connections through the effort to bring the M.A.N. into the IG, a measure which Siemens also saw as a form of protection against heavy industry and north German dominance.

Essentially, the SRSU was not an "organic" concern based on integration of production but a true economic "dukedom" put together in almost dynastic style and founded upon Stinnes's visionary programs and Siemens's raw-materials and capital problems. It was no accident that the SRSU was in the most basic sense a holding company with the purpose of pooling profits and the disposition of monetary resources. It strove to solve the problem of procuring operating capital by permitting those involved to "employ the liquidity of other enterprises" and by acting as a bank that would "without interfering in the settlement of industrial transactions and without disturbing industrial enterprises in the disposition of their internal affairs, will take over the role of the financier, the clearing house." The founders of the SRSU specifically saw it as a means of self-protection against a "sick," incompetent, and interfering state, a form of "self-help" that would at once promote reconstruction and soften the blows of economic setbacks. As one of the Siemens executives argued:

. . . the first thing to do is to set up an economic program for the new economic body, to regulate imports and exports and the foreign exchange question; to reduce the costs of new acquisitions; to consolidate foreign enterprises and representatives; to deal appropriately with business cycles, preparing ahead for future better periods in times of slack, limiting sharp recessions through the production of stockpiles of appropriate goods. We need to take advantage of technical improvements . . . ; and to create an economic body that ought not to go unnoted and unasked for in any project that comes up in this world.[143]

This was nothing more or less than a privatization of the schemes of Moellendorff, Hirsch, Jordan, the RWM, and the RAM, and it reflected a contempt for the efficacy of state intervention and action along with a boundless optimism about what the large-scale self-organization of industry could do. The possibilities for intelligent and coordinated action did appear to be increased by vertical concentration. When the Rheinelbe Union was founded, for example, a decision was made to develop "carefully worked-out statistics," not only for the Deutsch-Lux and GBAG, but also "with respect to the neighboring firms and the entire German economy" and even for England and the United States. Stinnes pointed out that much could be learned from statistics on electrical power usage and changes in the volume of railroad freight and suggested that Rheinelbe make use of the information available at the RWE and his Hamburg shipping offices. Kilowatt-hour figures were, in his view, "one of the most sensitive measures of productivity," while freight statistics provided a good means of predicting future cycles of business activity.[144]

Naturally, the potential for generating statistics was vastly expanded with the creation of the SRSU, but it was also possible to have too much of a good thing. By January 1922, Vögler was telling one of his colleagues, Siemens finance director Köttgen, that 90 percent of the statistics they were generating were never read or used and that he had cut down his statistical staff to five men at Deutsch-Lux in order to save money.[145] This, of course, was no argument against the collection of statistics or the value of some of the information that was being exchanged, but the attractiveness of the SRSU was more than a matter of its informational services.

To understand its appeal, it is useful to comprehend it from the perspective not only of its founding concerns and executives but also of the firms who willingly entered its fold under the inflationary conditions of the postwar period. A good illustration is the metal-finishing firm of Karl Berg in Eveking, which specialized in aluminum but also was an important finisher of iron, steel, and other metals. The firm, a family enterprise led by Theodor Berg, was one of the three Vögler recommended to Stinnes as potential participants in an IG with Deutsch-Lux in the winter of 1920. The other two were firms in Werdohl, the Stahlwerke Brüninghaus and a wire producer, Fr. Thomé. Vögler was very enthused about the prospects of these enterprises and suggested that one year of their production alone would pay for a decade of dividends. The Berg firm was particularly attractive because its finances were in good order, it had no bank debts, and it could be expected to be an important finisher of Deutsch-Lux production as well as supplier of metals needed by the concern. Since the firm specialized in producing metal used by electrotechnical works, its potential usefulness increased as negotiations began toward the formation of the SRSU.[146]

The advantages for Berg, which entered into the IG with Deutsch-Lux in mid-1920, were many—beginning with money. Deutsch-Lux purchased two million marks in Berg shares at their face value and provided another two-million-mark interest-free credit, so the firm had four million additional marks in operating capital at its disposal. Then, Berg had an inside track on sales to enterprises associated with the Stinnes Firm, Deutsch-Lux, the RWE, and Siemens-Schuckert. Thanks also to Deutsch-Lux and Stinnes's connections and his considerable involvement with the major raw-materials producers, the Erftwerke and the government controlled Vereinigte Aluminium AG, Stinnes was able to help Berg out of its tangled relations with these and other firms, which sometimes competed and sometimes collaborated with Berg.[147]

Most of Berg's production, however, was exported, and it was here that the close Deutsch-Lux connections with the Stinnes export houses proved so important. Actually, Berg dealt with the Stinnes Hamburg headquarters of its overseas trading company directly. As Stinnes explained to Berg in October 1920, there was a big market for aluminum in England and the colonies, but "the aluminum consumers cannot or do not want to buy directly from Germany for political reasons." Happily, the Stinnes concern had "friends" in London, who were prepared to buy and stock aluminum on their own account and then sell it. To be sure, the Stinnes organization warned Berg that the market in England and the United States was tight, that Berg would have to make its prices more competitive and be more reliable in its deliveries, and that it would have to deal exclusively through Stinnes. If Berg agreed, however, then he "would see that success will not be wanting and your works will have sufficient orders."[148]

Stinnes's "friends" in London were the well-known trading house J. Russell Ferguson & Co. Ltd., with one of whose officers Hugo Stinnes, Jr., had negotiated the setting up of a company for the reexport of German aluminum, potash, and chemical products. Naturally, the firm's name, which had not yet been determined in 1920, was to be totally innocuous, and Stinnes, Sr., wished even to have the word "trading" kept out of it, suggesting that the name "Produx Corporation Limited" be used, possibly because this was the name of the company set up to handle Stinnes's exports in the United States. In any case, Stinnes's conditions for Berg sales through England and the United States were the same. Berg received 50 percent of the profit, while Stinnes and his foreign "friends" divided the remainder, two-thirds for the "friends" and one-third for Hamburg. Furthermore, Berg was persuaded to provide some material on consignment to facilitate the meeting of unexpected demands, but it was to be understood that the risk was to be born by Berg and that it was the task of the "friends" to get the best possible prices, thereby persuading Berg to increase consignment shipments. Selling German goods abroad obviously was a tough business, and Theodor Berg was particularly incensed when the Americans withheld thousands of dollars in payment for his aluminum until its quality had been demonstrated.[149]

Nevertheless, Berg seems to have been very grateful to Hugo Stinnes, Jr., for providing him with foreign offers that kept his plants busy and to Hugo Stinnes, Sr., and Vögler for their attentiveness to Berg interests and their solicitude. He had every reason to be. By 1922, the Berg firm was heavily indebted to Deutsch-Lux, and while Stinnes and Vögler had considerable confidence in Theodor Berg, they worried about complaints from the RWE and Siemens concerning the technical and commercial ability of the rest of Berg's management. Vertical concentration obviously had its advantages for the great concerns, but it also had its risks and could sometimes raise the interesting question of exactly who was capturing whom.[150]

This was a problem of which the SRSU leaders became increasingly aware. In March 1921, for example, Köttgen wrote to Vögler that a major rolling-stock producer wished to join the IG, but that he was uncertain "whether purely objective, let us say, vertical considerations call forth such desires or rather the question of liquidity. The last consideration probably plays the chief role today with the strong monetary depreciation that has set in."[151] Köttgen worried that Siemens might be badly weakened by such investments, especially if demand suddenly improved and forced a huge outlay of capital—which took a substantial time to recover in the electrotechnical business. Vögler agreed that they should be "very careful with further acquisitions."[152] Rheinelbe, he noted, had very little operating capital relative to its production, and Vögler was most interested in acquiring plants and firms with low capital requirements that offered a good market for SRSU production. He confessed that he had been warning against expensive alliances and takeovers for over a year, "but unfortunately I have not been able to succeed in getting my views accepted."[153]

The truth was that Vögler did not always have an easy time with Stinnes and was not always in accord with his employer's policies or methods. Strictly speaking, the Stinnes concern, with its major offices in Hamburg and Berlin and the worldwide network Stinnes was rebuilding, was an entity separate from Deutsch-Lux and the SRSU. For Stinnes, the trading and shipping operations, built up, as he stated in his testament, with "success and love," were nevertheless only a "means to an end"; namely, the "building up of our domestic economy and its productivity."[154] Vögler and Sie-

mens thought in rather less grandiose terms, and they were worried that their respective components of the SRSU would become entangled with the Stinnes firm and interests in costly ways that were not in keeping with any clearly defined agreements existing among them. Siemens was particularly sensitive to any suggestion that Siemens had somehow become part of the "Stinnes concern." Vögler had more tangible worries. In early 1920, for example, Vögler complained bitterly to Stinnes that the general director of the Stinnes concern in Berlin, Friedrich Minoux, was expanding the Stinnes interests by committing Deutsch-Lux funds without prior consultation with Vögler and went on to point out that he would "like to see the face of Herr Minoux" were he, Vögler, to act similarly in matters involving the resources of the Stinnes concern.[155]

More serious and revealing was an altercation between the two men in late 1920. Fundamentally, Vögler was a technically inclined, rationalizing, but conservative businessman who stood guard over the interests of Deutsch-Lux while promoting the expansionist goals of his dynamic employer. He did not enjoy currency speculation. When the mark began to appreciate in the spring of 1920, Vögler thought it was a temporary phenomenon, a view shared by other mistrustful businessmen.[156] He had established a policy of exporting for payment half in foreign exchange and half in marks, a policy which he justified by Stinnes's continual emphasis on the importance of Deutsch-Lux correctly judging market conditions but which he used in fact to avoid excessive risks. Vögler did not believe that either market conditions or the exchange rate could be judged for any sustained period. At the end of 1920, he seemed satisfied that his policy with respect to import payments was sound since it had produced no losses, although he confessed that it had led to "large missed profits, which certainly are quite painful."[157] Still, the firm had lost very little by the appreciation of the mark in 1920 while making up for it in the paying off of their Swedish ore debts.

While relying on Stinnes's trading organization when exporting and on Stinnes's advice in matters of exchange-rate fluctuations, Vögler fretted when Stinnes seemed to be jeopardizing the cash flow of Deutsch-Lux. Thus, when the mark began a sudden increase in value in mid-November 1920, just at the time when Stinnes was pushing forward his efforts to acquire the Braunschweig Mining Company (a lignite work of particular interest to the Siemens concern because of its proximity to Berlin), Vögler pointed out that the deal could only be made with the help of their foreign exchange holdings. He worriedly inquired of Stinnes if they should purchase marks at so unpropitious a moment, and then went on to point out that business had not been good and that huge sums might be needed for a transfer in a very short period, something which "he had pointed out repeatedly."[158] Stinnes was unmoved by Vögler's plaints, insistent upon the acquisition of the Braunschweig mines, and obviously unimpressed with Vögler's reading of the currency market. Stinnes's Swiss sources had informed him that the mark had risen because of American and Belgian mark purchases as well as the temporary cessation of Reich purchases of wheat and fodder. The government would soon be buying food again, and the mark would begin to depreciate once more and, indeed, had already begun to do so by the time Stinnes responded to Vögler. Stinnes the worldwide merchant obviously knew a bit more about the currency market than Vögler the industrial manager![159]

Stinnes, in fact, became rather annoyed with what he perceived as Vögler's excessive solicitude for the interests of Deutsch-Lux and Rheinelbe at the expense of Stinnes's trading interests. During the war, Stinnes let his domestic iron marketing operations suffer because he did not think it right to promote his sales organization while serving as chairman of the Deutsch-Lux Supervisory Board. After the war, he had agreed to Deutsch-Lux's acquiring a controlling interest in the well-established H. A. Schulte iron merchandising company, apparently because Vögler had argued that this company was uniquely positioned to market Deutsch-Lux products domestically. With the founding of the Rheinelbe Union, Stinnes found that the GBAG had coal merchant houses which were also being favored by the concern. Then, as if to add insult to injury, Vögler began urging Stinnes not to enter into marketing agreements with the French works. Trade, however, was Stinnes's life blood, and he lashed out angrily in late December 1920 at Vögler's presumption:

I *must* remain in the business of trading on a running daily basis, be it in coal, oil, or iron, etc., or I will lose touch with the market and not be able to evaluate business conditions. Every failure in the evaluation of the conjuncture will hit the Rheinelbe concern in the most terrible way, and in the end the public responsibility will be placed on me. *My world credit* is at stake, because unfortunately I am too much identified with the individual events and sales of the works. I cannot allow the instruments needed to form a sure judgement to be taken away.... How, for example, can anyone pursue a policy with respect to iron without being at home in the iron business of Europe's biggest iron producing country, that is, France?[160]

While the crisis between Stinnes and Vögler was rapidly straightened out, and a comprehensive agreement was made between Deutsch-Lux and Stinnes's overseas trading organization in February 1921,[161] it was significant for what it revealed about Stinnes and the empire associated with his name. Ultimately, he sought to give coherence and integration through his personal capacity to understand world economic conditions and act as a source of pure intelligence and business intuition. He was convinced that these conditions were objective and had a rationality that had to be obeyed but which, once comprehended, opened up endless possibilities so long as one did not stray outside their compass. From this perspective, pure political considerations were irrational and irritating. Vögler, a much more prosaic soul, found it hard to dismiss the realities which did not fit. He fully agreed with Stinnes about the desirability of making French business connections but had urged caution because "one also has to consider the fact that you are judged today first of all as a politician."[162] Similarly, it might have made good sense in early 1921 for the German iron and steel industry to shore up the international price of iron, and indirectly of steel, by buying up French and Luxemburg iron. Whether it was "politically correct to do so" and whether "German industry had any reason to help its French competitor out of its difficulties"[163] was quite another matter. For Stinnes, however, national considerations, international considerations, and business considerations were all so mixed up that it was impossible to tell where one set of interests let off and another began.

The politics of the SRSU, however, were no less thorny, and in June 1921 the conflict with Vögler ignited again, albeit in more agreeable form since the culprit now appeared to be Siemens's overseas trading organizations, which Stinnes found in potential or actual competition with him in Brazil, Mexico, Chile, the United States, and China. Stinnes angrily pointed out that it was he who had been identified with the founding of the SRSU and it was his name which was giving it entrance into the world markets:

You will comprehend more than anyone that it is impossible for me to invest just for dividends large amounts of money and a great deal of my energy in enterprises which are pursuing what in my view are false impulses—seeking to free themselves from my influence in every way so that I, who . . . is made responsible for every external action of the [SRSU] lose influence internally, that is, on the running operation of the business from month to month because of insufficient orientation.[164]

He feared that the SRSU would become "an obstacle" in his path and would damage his credit through a false policy. Once again, Vögler had to pacify his employer. While forthrightly pointing out that many of Stinnes's suspicions were unfounded and bluntly stating that the Stinnes overseas organization was not always as effective in providing customers as might have been wished, he assured Stinnes of Siemens's goodwill. In July, a meeting between the leaders of the two trading organizations appears to have smoothed out the difficulties. The entire episode suggested that Stinnes was having considerable difficulty keeping properly informed about his multitude of interests.[165]

As the messy affairs of the Alpine Montangesellschaft demonstrated, however, creative visions, good information, and speculative skills were not always sufficient to prevent untoward situations from developing in the unstable economic and financial environment of postwar central Europe. The Alpine was an enterprise having both promise and difficulties. The Italians had taken advantage of the low value of the Austrian krone to gain majority control of the Alpine right after the war, but Fiat's dream of having an independent heavy-industrial base rapidly turned sour when it was discovered that the Alpine had been cut off from its old sources of coal and coke in Czechoslovakia and that it was just not possible for Italy to solve this crucial problem. Only the Germans could replace the Czechs, and the Italians engaged Hugo Stinnes's Austrian counterpart, financier and industrialist Camilio Castiglioni, to sell a large portion of its shares to a German who might supply the needed coal and coke. In March 1921, these two kindred spirits met, and Stinnes bought two hundred thousand shares. In the summer of 1921, the SRSU became the Alpine's chief stockholder.[166]

Stinnes dreamt of using the Alpine to penetrate the Balkan market and hoped that German control of the Alpine would strengthen the bonds between Germany and Austria, but in the meantime he confronted the nightmare of the Alpine's finances and management. The concern was loaded with bank debts and was in desperate need of renovation and modernization, no easy task in the context of the terrible Austrian inflation. The Reparations Commission did not think it proper for Stinnes to supply coking coal to an Austrian concern when Germany was supposed to be making deliveries to the French. Initially, therefore, Stinnes had to arrange the purchase of expensive Czech coal to satisfy the Alpine's needs. Although Vögler appears to have supported the Alpine venture, it did not take him long to start worrying about it. Thus, while Stinnes was telling Vögler in August 1921 that the Alpine's difficulties were temporary and that the Alpine "must have very good returns if it knows how to produce and sell those products for which there will be market aplenty in the next few months," Vögler could only respond by stressing how critical it was to straighten out the Alpine's finances and that "it would perhaps interest you to know that on the Berlin stock exchange the generally low quotation of our concern's shares over against Phoenix, Rheinstahl, etc. is explained by our high Austrian obligations, which are viewed very critically on the exchange—this only for your information!"[167]

It is doubtful that Stinnes lost much sleep over this information, or indeed that there was much general questioning of the viability of the SRSU, the Stinnes enterprises, or the general process of vertical concentration at this point. And in truth, it is false to think of the SRSU as some kind of great inflationary speculative enterprise. The SRSU leadership and especially Stinnes may have been overextending themselves in some of their immediate operations, but it is important to recognize that their proclivity to employ short-term capital to finance long-term projects at this time had very conservative underpinnings. They studiously avoided risking their capital stock and their control over it. In December 1920 and again in May 1921, Salomonsohn proposed that the SRSU raise capital by selling on the open market one-quarter of the preferred multiple voting stock which had been created as a reserve when the SRSU was founded and which was held in its own portfolio for the specific purpose of speedily raising capital. On both occasions, this suggestion, which would obviously have increased the power of the banks, was turned down, with Stinnes warning against "foreignization" and the Siemens-Schuckert interests claiming that they had a commitment not to sell stock shares to the public.[168] Stinnes reacted with extreme sensitivity even to the suggestion of alienating the capital stock in any manner and, in September 1921, severely reprimanded Director Haller of Siemens for using eight million marks' worth of Bochumer Verein stock as security for a 1.3-million-gulden loan from the Dutch.[169] He also strongly opposed any watering of stock, rejecting a proposal by the Riebeck Mining Company in February 1921 to issue new stock at 250 percent of par in order to acquire the Braunschweig Mining Company and blocking a plan to raise the capital stock of the SRSU in April 1922.[170] Although Stinnes showed some interest in issuing short-term bonds in 1921, even this was not carried through. These conservative policies reduced the sums needed to service the obligations on long-term capital and, when accompanied by a policy of high amortization rates, permitted the building up of substantial silent reserves. Thus, while the SRSU gave the impression of swallowing everything in its path, strong defensive motives underlay both its founding and its policies. While giving the impression of being multiple forts along the routes

of the SRSU's colonization of German industry, these were in fact viewed as outlying fortifications for a great central fortress to be managed by the best generals equipped with the most modern technical equipment.

The AEG, despite its comparatively stronger capitalization, felt much more exposed. Its constant dependence on investors and banks willing to buy its shares and obligations was a source of worry to some of its officials, one of whom frankly told Henrich of the Siemens concern that he had "great concern about the continued existence of the AEG" and pointed to the high capital of the AEG, "on which it is extremely hard to pay interest and dividends, and which constitutes a very serious source of danger to the AEG." In his view, the AEG was poorly managed, had not done enough to keep up with technology during the war, and found itself competing even with some of the smaller electrotechnical firms in this respect. There was insufficient coordination of effort in the concern, especially in the realm of price policy. If serious competition and a downturn of business conditions took place, the AEG's weak reserves "would melt like butter in the sun." Henrich had the impression that the AEG continued to be very interested in some sort of horizontal IG with the Siemens concern and suggested that discussions in mid-1921 between Vögler, Rathenau, and Deutsch also had the objective of "reducing the capital of the AEG and at the same time gaining our superior technology."[171] This was not a program which the SRSU or Siemens were prepared to buy, either at this time or throughout the Weimar period, but the situation further underlines the anxiety and defensiveness accompanying much of the concern building in the inflation.

To the world at large and to most Germans at home, however, these concerns represented an unprecedented accumulation of economic power in the hands of relatively few enterprises and persons. They were political factors of great importance, but they also seemed to hold forth the promise of a reordering of the economy, serving as the basis for its reconstruction. Their coming into existence, whether for good or for ill, did mark a devastating defeat for advocates of socialization and of a government-directed or -supervised economic planning as well as for those who entertained ideas of a more egalitarian reconstruction of the German economy through a credit cooperative. Insofar as some persons were demanding "transparency"—and one wonders if Rathenau really would have wished it with respect to the affairs of the AEG—they would have to wait for another day. Inflation-conditioned concern building, by its very nature, defied the demands for transparency raised by its critics. Indeed, the economic actors themselves found it difficult and sometimes impossible to get a clear idea of their resources and real worth. One of the oddest things about the SRSU was that it was founded as a profit-sharing pool based on setting up a balance for the entire IG. Yet, at the first meeting of the IG Council on January 12, 1921, a decision was made to put off setting up this balance "because of the enormous and time-consuming work involved, since a precise determination of the values in question cannot be established under the present unstable conditions."[172] If Germany's greatest concerns could not figure out what their assets and reserves really were, how could lesser entities or indeed anyone get a clear notion of their real circumstances in postwar Germany?

In truth, it was necessary to learn to think in new terms, and one of the least appreciated contributions of the German inflation to the history of modern business lay in the pioneering work it inspired in the field of cost accounting. Just as inexperienced businessmen had to be taught in 1919 to calculate in foreign currencies when exporting, so they had to be taught to take monetary depreciation into account when drawing up their balances. Eugen Schmalenbach's classic work, *The Dynamic Balance Sheet*, was a product of this period as was Walter Mahlberg's *The Technique of Balance Sheet Valuation under Depreciated Currency*, to which must be added the studies of Fritz Schmidt and Willi Prion.[173] Schmalenbach and Prion were particularly active in trying to get their message across to businessmen and apparently made a considerable impression on the Association of German Machine Builders (VDMA) in 1920.[174] One of their basic points was that many of the supposed profits being made in industry were fictional (*Scheingewinne*), which made a bad and misleading im-

pression on the public, gave "high" paper dividends to stockholders, and permitted tax collectors to make large assessments that were not really justified by the condition of many of the firms. These authors pointed to the absurdity of depreciating prewar investments made in gold marks in their nominal paper mark equivalents and insisted on the necessity of accounting in such a way as to permit the replacement of the item in question under the altered monetary circumstances. This justified shorter depreciation periods at higher paper rates which would conform to the replacement costs or to the setting up of renewal fund accounts. Schmalenbach and Prion were anxious to have businessmen go over to such techniques and were no less concerned to remove a major barrier to this conversion by having the tax authorities recognize this necessity. By implication, this was a break with the principle of "mark for mark," to which the government officially held, and the difficulty was compounded by the fact that the tax authorities could point to the improvement of the mark in 1920–1921 as a reason to reject such accounting methods.

Of greater relevance here than the accounting problems, however, were the general economic issues which Prion and Schmalenbach were trying to get the business community to confront. While obviously sympathetic to the needs of business, they were in no way supporting Stinnes's notion of an 85 percent yearly amortization rate to cover coal-industry investments. Prion, in particular, argued for the necessity of bringing sound principles of private economic management into line with public economic interests.[175] In his view, the industrialists were responding to amortization problems in unhealthy ways. Some were simply putting off needed investments "until prices went down" while raising capital to cover operating costs and then paying high dividends or interest. Others were paying for their investments in new plant and equipment out of the year's profits, or from silent reserves, a practice known before the war and employed by such solid firms as the Bochumer Verein. They did so then, however, with the objective of keeping down the cost of dividends and interest-bearing capital. While trying to get the highest price for their production, the tough competition and close calculation required during the prewar period never would have allowed them to attempt to add the full cost of new plant and equipment paid out from one year's profits or from silent reserves into the current prices. This, however, was precisely what some businessmen were doing or trying to do during the inflation. They were attempting to deal with the vastly increased paper-mark cost of new plant and equipment by paying for them out of profits or silent reserves, amortizing them in terms of their nominal prewar cost, charging the lion's share against current operating costs, and then charging those costs against current prices. This was a supremely sound form of finance, but it was unfair to both stockholders and consumers. The former, who had paid prewar gold marks for their shares, were being forced to live in a monetary illusion by receiving high paper dividends on high paper profits. The latter were paying prices into which were calculated the full cost of plant and equipment that could be expected to produce goods and profits for years to come. As Prion pointed out, the already "tortured present" was being burdened with investment costs "which actually should be placed on the returns of a series of years," a good illustration of "how private economic and national economic interests can go in different directions." While accounting techniques could be developed to avoid this result, many businessmen were understandably loathe to deal with the "difficulties, uncertainties, absurdities [and] capital stock changes" and opted for safer solutions, so that the businessman "prefers to place the security of his works before general economic considerations."

How, then, were the interests of the national economy to be preserved? More was involved than dealing simply with ambitious, energetic, and skillful industrialists of the stripe of Stinnes, who understood how to exploit raw-materials shortages, inflation, and access to credit to build up empires and to charge as much as the traffic would bear against current costs in their prices. In such cases, there was at least a vision and economic promise that might, under favorable circumstances, compensate the national economy with long-term benefits for its

temporary exploitation. A no less basic dilemma was that there was an entire business community whose members were becoming hell-bent on maximizing their own security in what they correctly perceived as an inscrutable and perilous economic situation. A government with authority and reasonable freedom of action at home and abroad might have been up to the task of dealing with these problems, but this was not the case with those who undertook the leadership of the Weimar Republic. Furthermore, in the course of 1920–1921, they had the misfortune to face a business community which had bridged its differences sufficiently to present a reasonably united front against further government interference.

The government's efforts to protect the public interest were failing, and it was increasingly giving up the effort. The socialization of the coal industry had been drowned in a rash of incompatible proposals and purposes, while the effort to organize the iron trades became superfluous because relative stabilization and market conditions had driven prices down. By the spring of 1921, the Iron Trades Association itself abolished the price ceilings that it had been set up to administer and effectively committed suicide.[176] While the demand for socialization and control of the basic industries may have come from the left, the process owed much of its success to the deep divisions within the business community, in which finishers and manufacturers were pitted against raw-materials producers. Momentarily, the common bond of hostility against government interference nurtured by war and revolution was snapped, but as the relative stabilization developed, the common desire to throw off government controls and reassert industrial self-government reknit the business community. Vertical concentration played an important role by tying some of the more important finishing and manufacturing enterprises to heavy industry. On the one hand, the latter now found itself with new support in the trade associations and syndicates, where major allies of heavy industry like the M.A.N. and Siemens used their power and influence to contain and check tendencies to seek governmental assistance and support against heavy industry. On the other hand, heavy industry had learned a lesson from the experiences of 1919–1920 and now also desired a high degree of stability in pricing and payment conditions. Not only did the heavy industrialists pursue a policy of stable pricing through most of 1921, but C.F. von Siemens actually induced the Central Association of German Electrotechnical Industrialists to give up sliding-scale prices and adopt stable ones at the behest of his heavy-industrial allies.[177]

The German business community, however, was not simply a complex of great vertical and horizontal concerns which could afford to break ranks when it suited them in order to expand and then to consolidate their hold by dominating other large firms with great influence and power in various trade associations, syndicates, and cartels. The inflationary wave at the turn of 1919–1920 had reminded small and medium-sized industry throughout the country of the importance of organization. The government had forced the various industries to organize during the war so as to control the allocation of raw materials and contracts, and it had also compelled organization into export syndicates to prevent dumping. Now small and medium-sized industry had become aware of the importance of organization to the protection of their economic interests in dealing with the state and with consumers as well as to the maintenance of their independence against the absorptive tendencies of big business. In 1914 the VDMA had 246 member firms. By the end of 1918, the number had swelled to 814 and reached 949 by July 1921. The number of its branch associations had risen from 40 in 1919 to 139 in 1921. The Central Association of the Electrotechnical Industry had 286 member firms in 1918 and 400 by 1920.[178] These organizations and other trade associations in other industries were in a position to educate their membership about such matters as inflationary cost accounting, international market conditions, and exchange rates, as well as to discipline their export operations through the export control boards and to develop general policies on payment and delivery conditions designed to protect the liquidity of their members against the ravages of currency and price fluctuations both at home and abroad. This mass membership also provided a counterweight against the influence of the larger firms and was a constituency to which the "organization men" running the trade associations had to pay attention.

Whereas vertical and sometimes horizontal concentration provided large enterprises with the strength to weather economic storms, horizontal organization through cartels and syndicates joined together those unable to stand alone and unwilling or unable to become part of larger concerns. Cartels provided such firms with organizations of their own capable of dictating prices and delivery conditions to their customers. Favored both by practice and by law as a means of stabilizing prices and preventing ruinous and cutthroat competition, cartels and syndicates had a long history in Germany, and their acceptability was only increased during the war when the government forced cartelization and syndicalization for its own purposes. While anxious to recover their autonomy, the members of these organizations became increasingly aware of their advantages, especially under changed conditions. Whereas before the cartels and syndicates were used to maintain price levels in the face of cyclical changes, they now had the added problems of dealing with raw materials and currency difficulties. In the context of the postwar hunger for goods, the problem of controlling cutthroat competition had become much more complicated, but so had the possibilities increased of passing the burdens and risks of doing business on to the consumer if businessmen were properly organized.

The textile industry became a particularly notorious example of how a war-spawned cartelization and syndicalization were used in this period of growing decontrol to organize and protect the interests of an industry that was extremely heterogeneous and complicated. The new-found willingness to organize and remain organized was exemplified by the textile finishing industry, which had organized for the first time during the war. Its members rapidly created their own peacetime trade association in July 1919 composed of 741 members and organized in thirty-six cartels.[179] A more spontaneous creation was the German Cloth Convention, a condition cartel composed of a variety of small associations which banded together in resistance to the pressures of their customers and set up unified terms of sale which they then imposed on the consumers. While a convention of this sort could not create uniform prices, it could introduce its members to the mysteries of inflationary calculation and pricing. As one of the organizers explained concerning the calculation scheme he had developed:

But it was only a scheme in order once and for all to present the members, namely the small ones, everything that had to be taken into account in calculating today. There are in the German cloth industry still plants which operate just as they did in the days of our grandfathers. You should not forget that in the German Cloth Convention we have producers which have only a few looms and operate in rented rooms, but also large firms which have, aside from their own weaving mill, their own spinning plant, their own artificial wool factory and their own dying and finishing operation. . . . That is the reason for the impossibility of introducing uniform price regulations in the German Cloth Convention.[180]

Nevertheless, the membership was grateful for the knowledge it received and became conscious of the fact that one could not calculate as in the old days of gold marks. Other cartels and syndicates did not have these difficulties and were able to set up uniform calculation methods and even prices, and this was true not only in textiles but also in shoes, utensils, tableware, wood, and numerous other products. In 1920–1921 Germany had somewhere between two thousand and three thousand such organizations.

Their existence was one of the reasons why prices failed to come down as much or as quickly as they might have and as much as the government and consumers wished during the period of relative stabilization. Many of the textile organizations actually obligated their members not to reduce prices in the spring and summer of 1920. During the boom of 1919–1920, many of the same organizations had starved the domestic market in order to export and had insisted on the right to charge more than originally contracted if costs went up. When business conditions slowed down, however, they pointed to the dangers of rising wages and also claimed that the risks of changing business conditions had to be included in their prices. Some critics thought this a most peculiar conception of capitalism:

The risk of the entrepreneur also belongs . . . to the essence of capitalist enterprise. It is very odd that it is by and large precisely those business circles which resist every form of planned economy and come out for an unconditionally free economy who attempt to assure themselves the advantages of a controlled economy which lie in risk reduction. . . . That is a complete misunderstanding of the basic nature of the capitalist economy. In the old-style capitalist economy, the entrepreneur is a producer of goods. He does not produce goods on order . . . but he produces wares for the market. . . . At the time of production, he has no idea whether and how he will dispose of them. . . . If it is false to say that the consumer has a right to purchase as cheaply as possible at the expense of the producer in all circumstances, it is also improper to give the producers the right to put the risk of changing business conditions around the necks of the consumers.[181]

Furthermore, the disease was one that was catching, since wholesalers, who were often themselves organized, and retailers, insofar as they could get away with it, imposed unjustifiably large markups—25 to 30 percent on shoes and as much as 50 percent and more on furniture and clothes—and were thus obviously taking their cues from the producers.[182]

As a result, there was a revival of traditional attacks on cartels and syndicates for basing their prices on the least efficient producers and thus giving a "differential profit" to the others, as well as charges that they blocked efforts to reduce prices. Critics laid many of the unhappy social and political events of the spring and summer of 1920 on their doorstep. By the end of that year, demands were raised by the DDP Reichstag Deputy, Erkelenz, who represented the Hirsch-Duncker unions, and by the Bavarian representative to the Reichsrat, whose state government was distinguishing itself as a champion of lower-middle-class interests, that the RWM do something about the cartels and perhaps even present legislation for their control. The RWM did, indeed, feel obligated to look into the matter, setting up a cartel desk and initiating a series of meetings with representatives of industry, the wholesalers, and the retailers which began in November 1920 and continued through the fall of 1921. Of all the RWM's efforts to deal with the control of industry during the inflation, these unquestionably were the most pathetic. Nevertheless, they are revealing of the general problem of governmental action against organized private interests as well as of the concrete economic circumstances and competing policy goals which reinforced government paralysis.[183]

One of the major difficulties facing the RWM was getting reliable information on which to base policy. When it sought to survey the concentration movement in industry, for example, it depended largely on newspaper reports.[184] While it was in a position to demand the cost calculations of the coal, iron, and steel industries because of the special laws and regulations governing them, the same was not true with respect to the enormous number of other products and wide range of organizations in the rest of the German economy. Furthermore, there does not appear to have been any legal basis for such an investigation, and when the RWM sent out a request to various trade associations and cartels in the spring of 1920 asking them to provide information on price agreements, sales conditions, and the like, the matter was reported to the RdI, which in turn informed its members "that the demand of the Reich Economics Minister appears unjustified and that we do not regard a supplying of such overviews to Reich agencies to be desirable."[185] Actually, however, supplying the RWM with all the information it asked for might have been just as subversive since the Ministry did not have the personnel to evaluate it. Even if the RWM chose to investigate and maintain surveillance over three hundred of the more important cartels, it was estimated that this would require at least twenty experts, not to mention the necessary secretarial and office help—and this at a time when its budget was being cut and it was losing some of its best people to higher paying jobs in industry! Thus, while a majority of the Reichsrat may have shared Bavaria's view that the RWM should do something, there was no majority to increase the RWM budget sufficiently to make the vote meaningful. Whatever they felt about the substance of the issue, therefore, the RWM officials were virtually forced to choose the path of trying to elicit voluntary co-operation from the involved parties, above all the RdI.[186]

The RdI was not, in fact, totally unresponsive, at least to the problem. Lessons had been learned from the 1919–1920 primary consumer revolt here too, and there was alarm over the buyers strike as well as the rioting and plundering of shops in the spring and summer of 1920. Industry had learned that it had to settle its own internal quarrels and present something of a united front against government interference. It could not simply disregard the fact that the decrease in prices had lagged very far behind the improvement of the exchange rate during the relative stabilization. For this reason, the RdI itself launched a campaign to lower prices in the spring of 1920 while attacking the violence used against retailers and the arbitrary lowering of retail store prices by municipal authorities. In short, it sought to mollify the retailers as well as to short-circuit their criticisms of industry. In answer to retailer demands for public scrutiny of cost calculations and profits, the RdI activated its own Cartel Bureau (*Kartellstelle*) and called for meetings between producers, wholesalers, and retailers to organize and carry through the private mediation of disputes. This effort culminated in an agreement in July 1921 among the three peak associations—the RdI, the Central Association of German Wholesalers, and the Association of German Retailers—to negotiate all conflicts concerning cartels and conventions among themselves, to encourage their member associations to do the same, and to strive "not to bring differences to any government agencies or before the public."[187]

Exactly how effective these shrewd actions were is difficult to measure, but certainly the representatives of the retailers had also had their fill of government regulation. While the Hamburg Chamber of Commerce could always be counted upon to point out that the government did not have the necessary expertise to deal with cartels, that there was a danger that it would once again "go way over the mark" with controlled-economy measures and operate with "inappropriate methods," it truly was echoing the views of the organized retailers of Hamburg, who also felt that government action was not necessary.[188] From the very outset of the RWM's investigations, the chief aim of the representatives of the retailers was to gain recognition of their organizations from the producers and to be consulted by the RWM. Oscar Tietz argued that "one-sided dictates from the cartels can be eliminated by the creation of an agency which is designed to bring the parties to the negotiating table."[189]

In its meetings with the RWM, the RdI representatives and other experts argued, quite simply, that conditions were too fluid and complicated for anyone to have a clear overview or to formulate clear policies. The generally recognized fiasco of the Iron Trades Federation was pointed to as an example of the government's inability to regulate business relations. The high prices were blamed on the costs of raw materials and currency fluctuations. It was this, in their view, which had produced excessive speculation. The industrialist representatives argued that one of the major purposes of cartels and syndicates was to eliminate the speculative element, which necessarily produced tension with the merchants, the essence of whose activity involved speculation.

Insofar as the arguments against cartels on the grounds that they promoted inefficiency were concerned, the concrete situation also served to reinforce the arguments for doing nothing. A traditional support for cartels in Germany had always been that they prevented American-style "trustification" and protected individual economic existences. This was a social argument that emphasized the value of protecting medium-sized and small industry and that stressed quality production over rationalization through ruthless and "unfair" competition. As a leading textile industrialist, Abraham Frowein, argued in defense of cartels that sought to provide a common basis for price calculation:

The quality of the goods produced has improved; the consumer has the benefit. All members are compelled to produce well. The possibility of competition is not eliminated. Everyone can produce what he will, but he has prescribed how he is to assess each cost factor in production. . . . Had we not come to an understanding about uniform bases for calculation and the setting of prices—and here we are dealing with a wage industry—then it would have led to a sit-

uation where goods would have been dumped at prices way under costs by the strongest firms. The effect would have been that only very few firms would have been left and we would finally have come to a trustification. I am of the view that the method of maintaining as many independent existences as possible is to be preferred to the free play of forces that finally leads to the maintenance of only few enterprises ruling the market.[190]

Exactly how such a view was compatible with the oft-discussed need to rationalize the German economy is not clear, but then neither was it clear exactly what constituted rationalization under the existing circumstances. Quite aside from the fact that the government itself was committed to a policy of preventing the shutting down of factories in its efforts to maintain employment levels, government-induced or -forced shutting down and syndicalization of industries could only be accomplished with compensation to those negatively affected. If the government had to pay compensation, however, then perhaps it was cheaper to allow the cartelized cement industry, for example, to produce at 30 percent of capacity and still make a profit.[191] Was it proper, however, that the Saxon textile firms were making a 30 percent net profit working at 40 to 50 percent of capacity when they had only been making 3 percent on full production during the war?[192] Both of these bizarre situations, however, could be presented as the consequence of the odd circumstances in which the definition of an optimal policy was not possible. Government intervention, it was claimed, could only make things worse.

Apparently, the RWM was coming to this conclusion itself. In November 1921, it decided against coming forward with a cartel law because "the form that economic policy concerning the cartels should take, [the creation] of normative regulations for the behavior of cartels, cannot be set for the long run today" and because "a cartel law, in view of its basic significance, would lead to difficult parliamentary battles and would be useless in its final form."[193] Even the compromise solution created by the RWM, a thirteen-member Cartel Council (*Kartellbeirat*), composed of representatives of the Reichstag, Reichsrat, and Reich Economic Council, was created in a self-admitted "do nothing" spirit; namely, to "give in somewhat to parliament and public opinion" while preventing "accidental decisions" in the three bodies represented, to prevent Reichsrat interference in economic administration, and finally to force the transformation of "criticism into positive proposals."[194] The RWM piously hoped that the pressures of public opinion and the self-control and self-administration as well as collaboration of producers and merchants would prevent abuse. A clearer revelation of the retreat of the government from economic regulation and of the decision to favor the self-reconstruction of the German economy and to favor producers over consumers would be hard to find.

Perhaps this was the correct or only practical policy under the circumstances, but it seems to reconfirm the limited potential of the relative stabilization period as an opportunity for the government either to control or to guide the path being taken by the German economy. If anything, the 1920–1921 period was one of governmental surrender to the forces at work in the economy, a permitting of the free market to reassert itself within the context of the self-consolidation of the major economic groups. Whether this development can be properly characterized as counterrevolutionary is questionable since the Revolution was not very rich in economic programs or solutions, and, in the last analysis, it was those economic institutions and practices created during the war that were being overthrown or undermined. As has been shown, the social achievements and social constraints of the Revolution remained in place, at least for the time being. Whether they were ultimately compatible with the economic path being chosen was another matter. And whether this economic path was likely to produce optimal patterns of investment and economic growth was also unclear. That is best measured later in the context of a broader evaluation of the consequences of the inflation. If the German economic reconstruction and the inflation had a very Darwinian character, one must also bear in mind that this in no way meant that it was totally disorderly or random. One can detect a system with a certain ecology of its own in which great whales swam in the same waters with very big fish and in which a great many medium-sized and small fish could also survive in relative safety if they swam in schools. Like most such systems, however, it was subject to severe external disturbances. It was not "natural" in the first place, but rather the product of adaptation to major prior disturbances made at heavy cost to other forms of life in its environment. It was a system that by its very circumstances was at once exposed to even more massive external disturbance and conditioned to respond by extracting ever more massive sacrifices from the weaker and more vulnerable species within its waters.

PART IV

REPARATIONS AND THE DOMESTIC MANAGEMENT OF THE GERMAN INFLATION

Inwiefern ist Ihrer Meinung nach D'Abernons These, daß das deutsche Geld hauptsächlich unter einer zu großen Notenemission litt, richtig?

D'Abernons These ist ganz unrichtig. D'Abernon sprach wiederholt auch mir gegenüber von einer Stabilisierung der Mark. Als ich ihn frug, ob seine Regierung für die Übergangszeit an unsere Seite treten würde, um uns materiell und politisch zu unterstützen, lehnte D'Abernon ganz entschieden ab. . . . Die Notenpresse war einfach nicht stillzulegen, und damals lebten wir noch, um das noch hervorzuheben, in einem quasi liberalen Staat. Was der totale Staat kann, das durften wir nicht einmal andeuten, sonst hätte man das Haupt verschiedener hoher Führer der Industrie aufs Schafott legen müssen.

To what extent in your view is D'Abernon's thesis that Germany's currency suffered chiefly from an excessive emission of notes correct?

D'Abernon's thesis is completely incorrect. D'Abernon repeatedly also talked to me about a stabilization of the mark. When I asked him whether his government would come over to our side during the transition in order to support us materially and politically, D'Abernon refused very decidedly. . . . The note printing presses were simply not to be shut down, and one must emphasize that at that time we still lived in a quasi-liberal state. We could not then even hint at what the total state can do, for otherwise one would have had to put the heads of various top leaders of industry on the block.

Wirth responding to a reporter's questions in exile during the Nazi regime, BAM, NL Wirth, Kr. 4

Chapter 7

The Presentation of the Bill

Spa, Brussels, and Paris

Reparations is the Pandora's box that must be opened if the breakdown of the relative stabilization of 1920–1921 and the subsequent galloping inflation and hyperinflation are to be understood. The London Ultimatum of May 1921, which set the reparations bill at 132 billion gold marks and set up a payments plan under which the Germans were to pay two billion gold marks in annuities and approximately another billion yearly in the form of 26 percent of the value of their exports, reached Berlin on May 6 and brought down the Fehrenbach government. It was accepted on May 10, 1921, by a new government under Joseph Wirth. This marked a real turning point. The fulfillment of the London Ultimatum became the central issue of German domestic and foreign policy, was intimately linked to the issue of stabilization, and dominated public discussion of taxation, social policy, and economic policy. The origins of the London Ultimatum and German efforts to cope with it, therefore, are central to the history of the German inflation.

Even today, this is not easy terrain for the historian. The Germans blamed the Allied reparations demands and the efforts to fulfill them for causing the galloping inflation and hyperinflation, while the French blamed the Germans for ruining their currency deliberately in order to evade reparations, a view widely held outside France as well. Historians have found it difficult to transcend the partisan struggle, and the battle, which found its most extreme expression in John Maynard Keynes's attack on the Treaty and Etienne Mantoux's bitter attack on Keynes,[1] is frequently refought with new evidence, recycled old evidence, and theoretical speculation. The older historiography tended to take the side of the Germans by blaming the French for indulging in a shortsighted intransigence that frustrated British attempts to find a rational, businesslike solution to the reparations question and permit the peaceful reconstruction of the European economy. In the 1970s, a new historiography, making use of freshly opened French archives, economic theory, and the cheerful post-1945 solutions to the Franco-German rivalry, has sought to demonstrate that the British were often more unreasonable than the French, that the French were much more sensible than previously supposed, and that it was the Germans, aided and abetted by the duplicitous British, who undermined and aborted French efforts to secure a peaceful and satisfactory solution.[2] It would be unfortunate, however, if the welcome discoveries concerning the complexities of French reparations policy were to be used to create the illusion that the German story was a simple tale of treaty evasion and bad faith.[3] The following discussion should dispel any such notions.

To begin with, the very capacity of the governments of the Weimar Republic to conduct a coherent and effective foreign policy was hampered by the disorderly state of its foreign policy establishment, on the one hand, and by its uncontrollable domestic distractions, on the other. The fact that the German Foreign Office was undergoing major reorganization and did not have the benefit of strong leadership and direction during most of the 1919–1923 period meant that foreign policy decisions were particularly susceptible to a multiplicity of influences—often incompatible ones—from both inside and outside the government.[4] The early Republic's domestic instability, however, was an even more serious barrier to the effective handling of its pressing foreign-affairs problems. This was not simply a matter of the frequent changes of government, but also of repeated putschist efforts, political violence, and assassinations. A powerful demonstration was provided by the difficulties the German government had in developing the reparations proposals it was supposed to submit to the allies within four months of the ratification of the Treaty of Versailles on January 20, 1920. The Bauer government's efforts to undertake this task, begun in early March 1920, were interrupted by the Kapp Putsch. The Müller government was clearly a caretaker government, and the Allies themselves waited upon the installation of a new government that would follow the June 1920 elections before getting down to serious negotiations. As a consequence, the first government to have to deal with the reparations issue in direct confrontation with the Allies was the Fehrenbach government, which assumed office on June 25 and thus had very little time to develop its policies before facing the Allies at the Spa Conference scheduled for July 5. Fundamentally, it was forced to pick up where its predecessors had left off.

The time pressure, however, was unwelcome for more fundamental reasons. German hopes had been raised substantially by the publication of Keynes's *Economic Consequences of the Peace* at the end of 1919, a masterful polemic against the Treaty which discredited the performance of its makers in a manner that would take historians years to modify and bring into more balanced perspective and which, through its dogged insistence that the salvation of European civilization and capitalism depended on giving primacy to economics over politics, branded the Treaty as a barrier to reconstruction and a source of inflation. Keynes shared Lenin's view that inflation, with its arbitrary redistribution of wealth and promotion of profiteering, was a menace to the existing economic and social order. Keynes further warned that there was no viable way of transferring the payments demanded of Germany without permitting it a level of exports that would become unbearable to the recipients. He thus called for a scaling down of the demands to be made on

Germany, a cancellation of inter-Allied debts, the elimination of trade barriers, and the stabilization of exchange rates through a large-scale international loan.[5]

Keynes was as effective a promoter of his work as he was a writer, and his book rapidly enjoyed large sales in England and the United States. Furthermore, it was translated into a great many languages. In the case of the German edition, Keynes paid five thousand marks to cover the translation costs by the noted national economist Professor Moritz Bonn, although it might be mentioned that Keynes more than made up for this expenditure in royalties and compelled the publishing house of Duncker & Humblot to increase the rate of his royalty in order to compensate for mark depreciation.[6] It was to be expected that the Germans would love the book, that the French would hate it, and that the English and Americans would learn from it and correct past mistakes.

If the book fell on fertile ground, this did not mean the seeds had sprouted or that the sprouts would blossom in quite the way desired by the Germans. It was one thing to be disenchanted by the Treaty, another to be captivated by the German case. While Paul Warburg of the Federal Reserve Bank could approvingly report to Moritz Bonn that "Keynes's book has made a great hit here," he had to admit that some of the anti-German papers "have gone out of their way to knock it." Furthermore, while public sentiment was "moving in a satisfactory way,"[7] financial conditions were not too good and opposition to the Treaty was also inhibiting an American settlement with Germany. Some Americans found Keynes's treatment of Wilson unfair and were totally unsympathetic to Keynes's proposal that America renounce its financial claims on the Europeans.[8] When a prominent member of the American Relief Administration declared the Keynes book a "Godsend," he also pointed out that the European mess had left Americans "without pride in American participation" in the war and "largely tending to draw back into our shells again and remain there." While he was of another mind, he felt compelled to say that the United States had expanded its currency "far beyond the normal," had "never been a lending nation until now," and had to look to its own problems.[9] As Americans were becoming suspicious of all Europeans, they were hardly likely to become less suspicious of Germans. Thus, a businessman interested in ending his industry's anti-German boycott called upon German industry to

help to remove the very bitter feeling which now exists in this country against everything German. It is felt very strongly that if we help Germany to her feet she will again fly at our throats. No evidence has yet been offered that the heart of Germany has changed. She is sorry she has lost the war, but she does not yet appear to regret the policy which relies upon force for the attainment of her national ambitions.[10]

English attitudes were also ambivalent. While one of Keynes's correspondents agreed that the "plight of civilisation" was too desperate to permit impossible demands on Germany, he found Keynes's presentation of Germany's plight very forgetful of the wrongs Germany had and would have committed: "When you speak of Germany as ringed round with enemies for at least a generation it recalls a phrase of, I think Helfferich, who looked forward to her being ringed round by tributary states paying her vast sums for a similar time."[11] Although public opinion in England, as in America, certainly was becoming highly critical of the Treaty and of French "militarism," suspicions of German militarism certainly persisted and were fed by German procrastination in carrying out the disarmament clauses of the Treaty. Similarly, the economic difficulties that intensified in the course of the year strengthened the case of those who thought the Treaty economically dysfunctional, but the enthusiasm for an economically reconstructed Germany capable of serving as a respectable trading partner for England was tempered by Germany's distressing postwar commercial practices.

England had sympathized with Germany's desire to plug the "hole in the West" and thus control imports and exports at her borders in the occupied territories, but the system introduced by the Germans in March 1920 rapidly became a source of repeated British protests and nasty altercations in Berlin. It was a system, of course, which irritated German businessmen

as well, but it realized its worst qualities when applied to foreigners:

In its construction the German apparatus for foreign trade shows on the one hand an absolute ignorance of, or disregard for, the first principles of commerce and, on the other, an ingenuity for those details which will require the employment of the largest possible number of officials, will waste endless time, will enable preferential treatment to be given to friends or compatriots, will favour corruption and will facilitate the evasion of the terms of the Treaty of Peace. . . .[12]

It should be noted that the French, who certainly had been less concerned about the "hole in the West," were even louder in their complaints. In May 1920, the Association of French Merchants and Industrialists of the Rhineland openly protested the German regulations and their implementation. This provoked a public reply from the German chambers of commerce of the occupied territories defending the necessity of the German measures, whose purpose, as they pointedly remarked, was "the maintenance and reconstruction of the German national economy, which is supposed to fulfill the hard conditions of the Treaty of Versailles." It is also amusing to note that these same German businessmen, having done their patriotic duty, privately wrote to the RWM pointing out that "there are great abuses in the handling of the import and export regulations which make the upset of the French merchants in the occupied area appear at least in part understandable."[13]

No less serious, however, were the growing criticisms of German dumping in England. The depressed business conditions there were forcing British producers to sell ever more cheaply in order to meet their debts, but many of them were not able to sell cheaply enough to undersell the German competition. The "great German rival" appeared to be "reawakening," and anxious British businessmen began calling for protection against countries which used their depreciated currencies to gain trade advantages.[14]

Lloyd George pursued a policy that mirrored conflicting British attitudes. Growing differences with the French did not blind him to the necessity of preventing the French from going it alone. He was intent on forcing the Germans to live up to feasible obligations and to show good faith in trying to live up to those that were more dubious. Thus, at the San Remo Conference in April 1920, Lloyd George pressed his French counterpart, Millerand, to invite the Germans to a conference to discuss a global reparations sum and other Treaty issues. The British Prime Minister promised to support coercive measures in the event of German failure to fulfill its obligations. The agreement to negotiate directly with the Germans meant bypassing the Reparations Commission, which had formal responsibility for setting the reparations sum, and Millerand insisted that the Allies establish their own standard for a final sum and annuities before meeting the Germans. In the negotiations among Allied leaders and experts at Hythe in mid-May and Boulogne on June 21–22, the so-called Boulogne Plan became the basis of Allied policy. Under this scheme, Germany would be liable to pay a total of 269 billion gold marks over the course of forty-two years: three billion per year until 1926–1927, six billion per year until 1930–1931, and seven billion per year thereafter until 1963. While a minimum three billion annuity was to be required throughout the entire period, the Reparations Commission could reduce annuities after 1926 if German economic conditions so required. This was in line with the proposal of Joseph Avenol, the French financial officer at the London embassy, that the annuities be linked to changing economic conditions in Germany. Odd as it may sound, these formidable numbers represented a substantial concession on the part of Millerand, who was already under severe attack from the French hard-liners. The fact was that few Frenchmen were overly interested in what they might be collecting in 1963 and were most concerned about what was known as the "present value" of the reparations settlement; that is, the immediate worth discounted at 5 percent. Both publicly and at Hythe, Millerand had pushed for a reparations bill with a present value of a hundred twenty billion gold marks, for which he had been heavily criticized at home. By the time of the Boulogne meeting, however, he was convinced that this could not be imposed and had settled for a scheme with a present value of approximately a hundred billion gold marks.[15]

For the Germans, as for the French, disputation over the global sum was very much a function of the current payments that would be demanded of Germany. Not without justification, the French argued that their reconstruction and financial stabilization took priority over Germany's, while the Germans insisted that they could not pay significant reparations in cash until they had the time and financial assistance necessary to stabilize their finances and achieve reasonable levels of production and export capacity that could be sustained without the aid of inflation. Nevertheless, this clash did not totally preclude the possibility of at least partially transcending the concentration on the financial aspects of the reparations issue by shifting the emphasis to reparations in labor and in kind and by trying to find solutions through the medium of economic cooperation. Such arrangements not only promised relief from the "transfer" problem but also opened the prospect of a *modus vivendi* with Germany's most powerful and dangerous neighbor.

The high point of German efforts to organize the reconstruction of the devastated areas of France through the use of German labor came in the fall of 1919, and they failed far more because of French resistance than because of difficulties from the German side. The German trade-union leaders, who played an important role in the negotiations, were enthused about this form of reparations since it involved fulfillment of what they considered a reasonable obligation, which would at the same time help to relieve German unemployment and possibly reestablish the alleged proletarian solidarity with their French counterparts supposedly shattered by the war. It was precisely on the absence of such solidarity, however, that the entire effort foundered, since rank-and-file hostility in the French unions was very substantial and French union leaders feared that the German presence would only increase their unemployment problems.[16]

It was no less difficult to establish cooperation between French and German capitalists, although here the resistance came from the German side and the key players were in heavy industry. The French dreamt of using their newly acquired heavy-industrial capacity in Lorraine to become a great heavy-industrial power. They hoped to use their ore supply and the coal deliveries required under the Treaty to force German industry into an alliance involving mutual stock participation in which the French would be the senior partner. The German industrialists recognized, however, that the long-term advantage was theirs if they could just hold out. They knew that they were not dependent upon French minette because of the availability of Swedish ores and other production techniques. While their spokesman, Hugo Stinnes, looked forward to cooperation with French heavy industry in the shape of a customs union, the arrangements of which would reflect the real relative strength of the two industries, he and his colleagues were careful to avoid responding too energetically to the direct overtures from the French industrial side which were encouraged by the chief advocate of Franco-German industrial cooperation in the French Foreign Ministry, the economic expert Jacques Seydoux.

This dilatory tactic became particularly evident in connection with the most onerous of the reparations in kind imposed upon Germany—coal deliveries to be credited against the reparations account at the low German domestic price. While the German obligation to make such deliveries under the Treaty did not begin until April 1920, the Germans had agreed in August 1919 to deliver 650,000 tons per month for the remainder of the year in return for a reduction in the amounts of coal the Germans were to supply once the Treaty clauses went into effect. They only delivered 350,000 tons, however, and remained in arrears during the next quarter year as their delivery obligation under the Treaty actually increased to two and a half million tons. The amount was regularly reduced at Germany's request and still only half met. While strikes, transportation difficulties, and production problems certainly were factors in the German shortfall, it was clear that Germany was giving precedence to its own needs and was far more willing to dispense coal at the world market price. Stinnes was prepared to talk with the French industrialists, but only on his own terms. Thus, he turned down an invitation to Paris in late May 1920 with the arguments that there was no point in discussing the situation until the German elections had been held, that agreements over coal deliveries would require the participation of the German trade unions and agreements on overtime, and that the overtime question could only be dealt with under calmer political circumstances.[17]

All this made the French industrialists quite frantic, and while they appealed to their government to force the Germans to come to terms, they also were prepared to pay higher prices, albeit not the English price, and were willing to talk privately with German industry. In early June, Stinnes met secretly in Paris with a small group of French businessmen, where he developed a plan for coal deliveries to be handled on a purely private basis with double payment for additional coal deliveries and special arrangements to provide German miners with extra food and clothing. State Secretary Hirsch was apparently informed of the meeting and plan, but the French government does not seem to have been at all involved. Stinnes obviously intended to turn the entire reparations question into a private business affair and revise the Treaty through the back door.[18] In the process, he also hoped to make changes in the hours-of-work question in Germany's coal mines and railroads. Stinnes seems to have been convinced that the French government would surrender to what he defined as economic reality, and that it was the task of the German government to force the issue by holding the line on cash reparations as well as reparations in kind. Thus, in April 1920, Stinnes, whose views were echoed by then executive secretary of the RdI Walter Simons and Krupp director Wiedfeldt, sharply criticized the government's intention to present a reparations proposal, as called for by the Treaty, and refused to associate himself with a memorandum written at the behest of Warburg and Melchior by two officials of the HAPAG firm dealing with the reparations issue. Stinnes did not think it possible even to discuss reparations under the existing economic circumstances and thought it tactically unwise as well since it would worsen the German situation "while with the continuation of the present situation the unstoppable depreciation of the franc will serve us well." Insofar as reparations were to be paid at all, it could only be when "certain basic changes of the Peace Treaty are attained"; namely, the introduction of universal military service based on a militia system, the termination of the occupation of German territory or the relief of Germany from the burden of further occupation costs and transport interference, the reintegration of the Saar into German economic life, the restoration of Germany's capacity to have a sufficient merchant fleet, and the creation of "economically bearable circumstances in the East."[19] Stinnes had no illusions about the possibility of such revisions under the existing circumstances, but he did not think any reparations could or should be offered until the changes were enacted.

This was not a policy any responsible German government could pursue, and the French government had very different ideas in mind. At the end of June, the Reparations Commission found the Germans in default on coal deliveries, which ensured that the coal question along with the disarmament issue would dominate the upcoming Spa Conference. This did not bode well for Lloyd George's plan to use the Spa meeting to begin a face-to-face discussion of reparations. In a personal meeting with Millerand on July 4, Stinnes told the French leader that an effort to impose impossible deliveries on Germany would lead to "war" since "a people driven to despair will and must attempt to free itself from the impossible conditions which have been forced upon it."[20] Thus, it was perhaps just as well that the issue of cash reparations did not assume the center of the stage at Spa.

Indeed, Stinnes managed to put on a remarkably offensive performance in his capacity as a delegate in Spa, for which he earned considerable applause at home and which gave Lloyd George the sense that "for the first time he had met a real Hun."[21] Nevertheless, the British Prime Minister was not prepared to have his "Anglo-Saxons" forget their interests so that the "Franks" could get all the coal they wanted at the "Huns" domestic price and occupy the Ruhr if their wishes were not met. The British had their own coal to sell, and they compelled

the French to accept a compromise under which the Germans would supply 2 instead of 2.4 million tons of coal per month for six months, for which the Germans would receive the difference between the German domestic and the British price as well as freight costs and a five mark per ton premium to assist the miners as a loan to be deducted from the German credits toward reparations. The Germans received this compromise in the form of an ultimatum, however, and its acceptance was anything but certain. Stinnes seemed convinced that resistance was worth an occupation of the Ruhr, in which he expected the French to bloody their nose and be forced to come to terms. He was supported by banker Franz Urbig. Walter Simons, now Foreign Minister, also seemed prepared to accept Stinnes's arguments. It was only thanks to other experts in the delegation—Walther Rathenau, Carl Melchior, Moritz Bonn, and Bernhard Dernburg—that relations with Lloyd George were smoothed out and that Simons and Fehrenbach were persuaded to accept the ultimatum. Rathenau bluntly asked Stinnes if the French could collect two million tons a month or even more if they occupied the Ruhr. They would then be in a position to sell the surplus coal at the world market price to the Germans themselves and thereby collect cash reparations by selling the Germans their own coal! Stinnes admitted this was possible and thereby lost the support of Simons and Fehrenbach, but he did not take his defeat lightly and gave vent to an anti-Semitic outburst, charging that Germany's resistance to humiliating demands had been broken by persons with an "alien psyche."[22]

Stinnes was not an anti-Semite, but anti-Semitism was so much in the air as to make this mode of lashing out both natural and convenient. Stinnes's egocentricity, however, had become a matter of national and international import. By publicly standing up to the Allies, he had become the darling of the political right and, through his untoward remark, helped to make more respectable their anti-Semitism. At the same time, his open disagreement, not only with his fellow experts but also with the responsible political leaders, reflected industrialist pretensions in the realm of foreign policy damaging to the authority of the state. The Allies were increasingly to ask who really ruled in Berlin and would come up with the answer that it was German industry. As Moritz Bonn, who was to be especially singled out for Stinnes's opprobrium, noted:

As much as I am impressed by Hugo Stinnes as a businessman and organizer, so lamentable does he appear to me as a politician. The attempt to shift the entire question onto the track of anti-Semitism that is now being pursued by the entire rightist press is only the response to the password spoken by Stinnes before his departure from Spa. He will yet manage to make people who have the greatest reservations about the socialization of the coal industry for economic and financial reasons give up their resistance in order to prevent the attempt to set up a state within the state.[23]

The internal battle at Spa foreshadowed the coming battle over reparations between those who were prepared to risk an Allied occupation and pursue a policy of passive resistance and those who advocated a "policy of fulfillment" in the hope that time, economic realities, and a changing political constellation would serve the cause of revisionism. Although reparations were supposed to be discussed at Spa, the issue was evaded on all sides. The Germans decided not to mention a final sum and studiously avoided indicating the yearly annuity they thought they could pay because they were convinced, quite correctly, that the amount they were prepared to offer would prove totally unacceptable to the Allies. Instead, they chose to present memoranda on Germany's economic condition, its tax burden, and the capacity to pay, the last document placing great stress on reparations in kind because of Germany's present inability to pay cash. They submitted these materials only two days before the Spa meeting; that is, for the record rather than for serious discussion.[24]

Even though undiscussed, the German documents presented at Spa did not go unnoticed, and they cast an important light on the entire relationship between reparations and inflation. The British Ambassador to Berlin, Lord D'Abernon, was impressed by the contradictory nature of Germany's financial situation. On the one hand, taxation had increased enormously since the Armistice, to the point of constituting "almost unbearable charges on capital and commerce." On the other hand, there had

been an "incredible" increase in the floating debt and in the currency in circulation. D'Abernon recognized that German solvency would ultimately depend on whether the tax receipts would come in and on the control of the debt, but he credited the Germans, at least in early July 1920, with "an enormous effort to avoid bankruptcy." This drove him, however, to an important conclusion that was to form a point of contention during the coming three years; namely, that the "vigorous endeavour to increase revenue made during 1919 and 1920 goes to disprove [the] contention that uncertainty as to amount of indemnity must paralyse efforts towards financial recuperation."[25] This was an argument that can easily be extended to the proposition that German stabilization policy was largely a function of domestic policy and that the credibility of German complaints about reparations could be measured in terms of the good faith shown by the Germans in straightening out their own affairs. Would the Germans be able to maintain their commitment to financial housecleaning in the face of the economic and social difficulties so evident at the very time of the Spa meeting, when government measures of decontrol and tax withholding were being met with a wave of rioting, plundering, and strikes, and in the face of a final reparations bill, the presentation of which was less than a year away?

Many of Europe's economic and financial experts, Keynes being the foremost among them, had been arguing for some time that the solution to these problems, which (with the exclusion of the reparations burden) Germany shared with the other nations of eastern and central Europe and even with France and Italy, had to be an international one because the problems were international. In October 1919, a group of leading bankers and economists had met in Amsterdam at the behest of the Governor of the Netherlands Bank, Gerard Vissering, to discuss the world financial situation and had subsequently drafted a memorial to the League of Nations calling for an international financial conference (to which the defeated powers would also be invited) to discuss a "deflation of the world's balance sheet"[26] and international cooperation toward the end of granting of long-term international stabilization and reconstruction loans. While declaring it "evident that Germany and Austria will have to bear a heavier load than their conquerors," the authors warned that "the load of the burden and the period during which it is to be borne must not . . . bring about so drastic a lowering of the standard of living that a willingness to pay a just debt is converted into a spirit of despair and revolt." They were equally insistent, however, that

no country . . . is deserving of credit, nor can it be considered a solvent debtor . . . that will not or cannot bring its current expenditure within the compass of its receipts from taxation and other regular income. This principle must be clearly brought home to the peoples of all countries; for it will be impossible otherwise to arouse them from a dream of false hopes and illusions to the recognition of hard facts.

Furthermore, the borrowing nations would have "to provide the best obtainable security," and this would mean that the international loans would have to be a first charge against their budgets and all other "indebtedness whatsoever whether internal debt, reparation payments or interallied governmental debt." In the case of Germany, it would also mean special security including specifically the "assignment of import and export duties payable on a gold basis."

Manifestly, the Germans had a great stake in the internationalization of the debt problem. An invitation to participate in such proceedings was in itself of value given their pariah status. An international loan that was a first charge against their receipts, even with onerous guarantees to the lenders, held forth the promise of an international effort to reduce reparations to bearable levels as well as to change the status of reparations as a first charge against German obligations. Needless to say, the French were much less enthusiastic, and they would only agree to a Brussels International Finance Conference (scheduled for September 24 to October 8, 1920) if it were to have a purely advisory function and to avoid all discussion of the reparations issue. The Germans, therefore, could once again present the perilous state of their finances to a public forum, but were prevented from overcoming the French taboo on the reparations issue.

The conference itself roundly condemned inflation as an "unscientific and ill-adjusted method of taxation"; called for a return to the gold standard; and affirmed the international financial community's commitment to the deflationist prewar economic verities of balanced budgets, high interest rates, central banks that were free of political influence, and privatized international lending based on sound banking principles. Trade barriers were strongly criticized, as were exchange controls, which were declared "futile and mischievous." The report singled out food and coal subsidies and high unemployment supports as well as freight and postal rates that did not cover costs as practices which all governments should abandon "at the earliest practicable date." The conference urged the League of Nations to establish an International Credits Organization to oversee the lending of money to nations in need in return for clear guarantees of repayment in the form of tangible assets or revenues.[27]

This fell far short of the kind of comprehensive international approach that was needed, and was, indeed, nothing more than an internationalization of the "Old-Time Economic Religion." The need for something more was comprehended by at least some contemporaries. Alexandre de Celier, the highest permanent official in the French Ministry of Finance, who was surprisingly sympathetic with many of Keynes's basic ideas, pointed out that "a minimum of solidarity" was indispensable in financial matters, and that the countries which had suffered most in the war could hardly reduce their inflationary policies if the more prosperous countries pursued extremely deflationary policies. He suggested to Keynes that this issue be taken up at Brussels.[28] Keynes could not have agreed more that "one of the greatest obstacles to the financial rehabilitation by external loans of all of the continental countries is to be found in the deflationist policy which is being pursued both here and in the United States." He did not think, however, that "reasons of foreign finance" would bring about a change in this policy because "the internal grounds upon which it is based" were "of too fundamental a character to allow concessions of this kind." The United States presented the most formidable barrier because of its Federal Reserve system, and a change of the law was not "practical politics at present." Consequently, a discussion at Brussels would not have "practical consequences," which "alas! is true of most of the discussions, whether at Spa, Brussels, or elsewhere."[29] Thus, the Brussels International Finance Conference was a monument to the domestic constraints on international understanding. The French would not permit a discussion of reparations, and the Anglo-Americans would not discuss a relaxation of their deflationary policies. Only the German delegates were free, because the German public was solidly behind a presentation of Germany's financial troubles on any and every occasion.

The Brussels International Finance Conference, however, also called for a speedy determination of reparations, so that both those who were to pay them and those who were to be paid could be relieved of the uncertainty that was impeding their budgetary decisions. The time was rapidly approaching when the Germans would be required to do a bit more than describe the holes in their pockets, and here the catalogue of economic and financial sins established at Brussels, which were a veritable description of the way Germany had managed her affairs since the war, and the fiscal standards sanctified by the Finance Conference were to combine with the reparations issue in a most unpleasant manner. At Spa, plans had been laid for a conference of experts to convene within a few weeks at Geneva to discuss Germany's finances and reparations proposals. For a variety of reasons, not the least of which were inter-Allied differences, the Allies rescheduled the conference for December 15–22, 1920, and relocated it to Brussels. Furthermore, the recommendations of the Brussels meeting were to be submitted to a high-level conference of the Allies to be held in Geneva, to which the Germans were to be invited in an advisory role. Thus, the Germans had almost five months to prepare their case and their proposals for Brussels with the prospect of further negotiations at Geneva.[30]

This period of grace, however, did not lead to any significant revisions of the general line of thinking that had been developed before Spa but rather to an increased commitment to certain positions that was made in a very charged and nervous atmosphere. The first of these was that Germany required the determination of a global reparations sum by May 1921, as called

for by the Treaty, but that it was necessary for the Germans to delay proposing a figure of their own because of their uncertain and unsatisfactory economic situation. This was no easy posture to take. The uncertainty surely was demoralizing. As general director Deutsch of the AEG pointed out:

At that moment when we know our situation and can come to terms with the Entente about payments, when we know what we will have to pay, we will also be able to get ahead in our economic life. I do not know if you have a real understanding of how much indifference and lack of interest has taken hold among workers and staff, because no one knows any longer what will happen to us, because everyone says that everything is useless because we are racing ever farther into the abyss. If we only would once and for all know what we have to pay and that the payments are possible even with the greatest efforts, then interest in working will return.[31]

For Foreign Secretary Simons, however, there was more at stake than relieving such tensions. Under the Treaty, there were ten categories of costs and damages for which the Germans were liable and a Reparations Commission with vague and broadly defined powers that could hound Germany for years to come. From this perspective, as he noted when speaking confidentially, the setting of a global sum would be a "monumental revision of the Peace Treaty. An entire set of terms of the Peace Treaty will be set aside *ipso jure* the moment a global sum is determined."[32]

The German tactic, therefore, was to arrive at a final reparations bill through the back door of determining a flat sum (*Pauschalsumme*) based upon Germany's ability to pay, reduced by payments in kind already made to be credited against reparations, and conditional upon Allied willingness to remedy certain disadvantages to Germany arising from the Treaty. Upper Silesia would have to remain German; Germany would have to receive most-favored nation treatment and a guarantee against economic reprisal; customs sovereignty at Germany's borders would have to be restored and maintained; occupation costs would have to be limited; and German property in Allied hands would have to be returned.[33]

Needless to say, the Germans recognized that they would have to make some proposals for immediate reparations payments and for some kind of payment schedule, and this presented them with the greatest difficulties. As always, they favored payments in kind because they wished to hold on to the gold they had left and needed their foreign exchange to pay for imports and maintain what remained of the mark's value and stability. The Economics and Labor Ministries were particularly anxious to have annuities paid in kind or in labor, since the employment problems in the second half of 1920 appeared to demonstrate that full employment could not be expected in the foreseeable future.[34] Ideally, the Germans hoped to avoid all cash annuities until their budget was in balance and their currency stabilized, but they recognized that something would have to be offered and concluded that a billion-mark annuity was all that could be managed provided the aforementioned conditions were met. At the same time, Moritz Bonn developed schemes to tie increases in the annuities to improvements in Germany's economic situation. There was some talk of increasing German annuities as the exchange rate of the mark improved, an arrangement that potentially could have involved the Allies accepting marks, but it was clear that the Allies could only accept such a scheme if the base exchange rate was set at a fairly high level. The most popular idea, developed by Bonn, took the form of a complex index designed to measure increases in Germany's prosperity as the basis for annuity adjustments. The resemblance to the Avenol idea of linking higher payments to increased prosperity is obvious, but the German concept, quite appropriately, arose from a concept in German bankruptcy law under which a debtor increases payments to his creditors as his position improves (*Besserungsschein*).[35]

Nevertheless, the Germans had no intention of being *that* bankrupt. The Austrians were providing a splendid example of the depths to which such *amor fati* could lead. Austria, with its huge deficits, inability to collect sufficient revenues, and galloping inflation, was distinguishing itself as Europe's economic "basket case" in the fall of 1920. With their imperial days behind them and no pretensions to great power status, however, the Austrians could accept humiliating, albeit not excessively humili-

ating, rescue operations. They positively welcomed the "foreignization" of their enterprises, since Austrian industry required direct foreign investment if it was to survive. The arrival in Vienna of the branch of the Reparations Commission assigned to deal with Austria in the spring of 1920 was greeted positively by the Viennese. Since the Austrians were in no position to pay anything, and the Allies were anxious to prevent an *Anschluß* with Germany, the only function that the commission could perform was to urge the financial support of Austria, which is precisely what it ended up doing. It rapidly became clear, however, that the price of such a rescue operation would be restriction on Austria's financial and economic autonomy.[36]

Leading German officials and politicians were obsessed with the Austrian "model"; Havenstein was making analogies with Austria's "Assignat" economy throughout the fall; and developments in Austria were repeatedly brought up at a series of meetings between government officials and the Reich Economic Council in October–November 1920. Ministerial Director Fischer of the Finance Ministry emphasized the price Austria was paying for an international loan: "As is well known, the Austrian section of the Reparations Commission has set up a complete financial control. The Austrians are bound hand and foot and must accept every kind of influence on their domestic legislation, on their taxation, on their trade policy, etc."[37] The Germans were desperate to avoid such control. Thus, an early proposal that a portion of Germany's budget or revenues be set aside for reparations was dropped because it would give the Allies a means of exerting control on Germany's internal affairs.[38] The Austrian analogy made clear that not only Germany's economic autonomy but also its great-power status was at stake. German government officials were very alarmed over reports that the French intended to ask for five billion gold marks in first-class German industrial shares as security for reparations until Melchior assured them that this was technically and politically impossible since the Treaty contained no provision permitting this and an effort by the German government to purchase such shares for this purpose would destroy the currency once and for all.[39] What was happening to the Austrians, however, was something the Germans could not accept for themselves. Fischer insisted that "we must struggle with all our strength against such financial control, because it will lead to the enemy's mixing into all our vital interests."[40]

It would take more than such words, however, to dispel the gloom. Rudolf Wissell was filled with resignation: "It won't be much better with us than with the Austrians. To have to say that is hard, but I cannot do otherwise."[41] The Cologne banker Louis Hagen, for whom Allied interference was a daily reality because of the occupation, was even more pessimistic: "If we have today presented Austria as a frightening example and it is said that the price of foreign help is to surrender all independent control over our economy, then gentlemen, I must say that we are running the same danger. In my considered opinion we are surely in not too long a time in the same Assignat economy that Austria has already." He thought the currency situation so "hopeless" that Germany should "seriously consider whether to present a progressively increasing annuity to our enemies."[42] He was not even sure it was proper to offer a billion-mark annuity for the year 1930! Foreign Minister Simons sought to counter some of the pessimism. While not denying that Germany was "always only a few steps behind Austria in this race toward the abyss," he insisted that it could and should make a "Telemachean leap" over the abyss by making a manageable offer and persuading the Allies that it could only pay its debts if given an opportunity to bring order to its finances.[43]

The strategy chosen by the Germans was a dangerous one, and they knew it. While there was reason to hope that the British had what the Germans considered to be realistic expectations, the French and Belgians obviously expected more. Louis Hagen, for example, recognized that the French economic situation was not good "and even more unfavorable than our own"[44] because the French were having a hard time selling their products. While he thought that some of the French leadership was beginning to moderate its demands, the kind of offer the Germans had in mind was bound to be "disappointing." After a visit to the Nether-

lands and discussions with neutral colleagues in mid-October, however, he returned home with the impression that a billion-mark annuity offer would be greeted with "a storm of outrage."[45] The DNVP Deputy Hermann Dietrich had come away with similar impressions in discussions with foreigners and wondered if it made sense to make proposals which they knew would be met with angry rejection.[46]

While Simons suggested that some of the outrage would be "feigned"[47] to satisfy public opinion, Bonn was becoming increasingly concerned that the German proposals were going to be contradictory and inadequate. The contradiction lay in the fact that the Germans were claiming that they wanted to establish a fixed reparation sum while really offering a variable thirty-year annuity scheme, the actual value of which was contingent upon improvements in the German economy. The present value of their offer, therefore, could vary from thirty to ninety billions. As he colorfully put it, they were offering the Allies a "bone" to start with, while the "meat" on the "cutlet" was being offered in the form of higher annuities that would accompany increased solvency and prosperity. Since Boulogne, the Allied notion had been that a prosperity index would be "decoration" on a scheme of high fixed annuities; given the German desire for a fixed reparations bill, it was only logical for the German scheme also to treat the prosperity index as "dressing" on the "bone." If Germany wished to establish a fixed sum, did it not make sense to offer a higher initial annuity that would be more acceptable to the Allies? Concerned that the German position was illogical and contradictory, Bonn also pointed out that offering an initial annuity of one billion gold marks while demanding in return that the Allies guarantee the return of Upper Silesia, limit the occupation costs, and accept the other conditions being stipulated was "giving less than the enemy already has, and I do not believe that we will get through that way."[48] He reminded his colleagues that the "sum of a billion marks is arbitrary, as everything here is arbitrary" and that it was determined by the fact that they had to offer something. Considering the German goals both of attaining a fixed sum and of standing a chance in negotiation with the Allies, however, Bonn came to the conclusion that Germany should offer a sum that would have some weight. He thought it worth the risk for Germany to offer more than it thought it could pay, especially if a scheme were then developed to test its feasibility along the way.

Bonn's idea, however, was rejected by Havenstein in almost hysterical terms. Havenstein saw nothing problematic in offering the Allies less than they were getting already because it was necessary to reduce what Germany was paying if recovery was to be possible.[49] He preferred to play the "honorable merchant" and run the risk of a *Diktat*:

... I fear a *Diktat* much less than I fear a voluntary increase of our payments over the possibly still bearable one billion mark offer. For such a voluntary offer ... will make us into a dishonorable bankrupt. We will not escape an offer made voluntarily, even over time. Over time, however, we will get out from under a *Diktat* if we present our honest convictions as to the maximum that we can pay. It must be presented so forcefully that the mood and convictions of the neutrals and in the enemy countries will be strongly influenced. ... This change of opinion must gradually lead to a recognition of the madness of a *Diktat* that is excessive.[50]

Louis Hagen went even further in supporting Havenstein:

We must explain and show what our situation is. If forceful measures are then taken, then I think ... frivolous as this may sound, that the earlier the catastrophe which the enemy is bringing upon us comes, the earlier will the healing process begin.[51]

Who was bringing catastrophe upon whom was a complicated question, but Keynes was probably correct in arguing that every major continental nation was doing its share. The French seemed more intransigent than ever and appeared disposed "to use the Reparations Commission as an instrument for the purposes of the political, military, and commercial Hegemony of Europe." As for Germany, that nation "from lack of nourishment I suppose, continues half-witted, and most of what emanates from them is impracticable and crazy."[52] There was indeed a tone of desperation among Germany's bankers, industrialists, and politicians as they finally confronted the reparations question in late 1920. This belligerent mood was no monopoly of the right. Carl Legien responded to charges that the Germans were unsupportive

of the international labor movement by accusing the English and French workers of showing only weak solidarity with their German brethren. He charged the Treaty of Versailles with "destroying Germany," robbing it of its "industrial freedom," and compelling it to "bleed" for the "senseless maneuvers" of the Entente. He protested as bitterly as Havenstein and Hagen about the occupation costs and about the fact that Germany was being forced by the Disarmament Commission to destroy plants and machines that had been converted to peacetime use. Legien was outraged that Germany was forced to deliver 10 percent of her milking cows, which he viewed as a deliberate attempt to kill German infants and children. As for the repeated French threats to occupy the Ruhr and the danger that it would be occupied in the winter, Legien warned that "not a ton more coal would be produced" and that the German miners would flood the mines, which would destroy Europe both economically and politically and clear a path for Bolshevism.[53]

In such an environment, the Krupp director Wiedfeldt found it plausible to regret that they had not risked a confrontation in July at Spa. Instead of accepting the "two million ton *Diktat*," they should have let the French invade the Ruhr. The French had no coal at the time, while the Germans had much more of it and little need for heating fuel. Under such conditions,

... the Germans in the non-affected areas would have unanimously turned against the occupation, which would have permitted national feeling to express itself. Just at that time even the workers would have responded, if not with a strike, then with passive resistance. Then coal production would have been so reduced that not only the other Entente powers but also various industrial circles in France would have declared: "now let's stop these military stupidities and get out of the Ruhr." Then we would have put to an end this constant threat of a dagger blow against our economic heart forever. But the gentlemen in Berlin, namely the government, did not have the courage to take a great risk, although in our desperate situation only playing with high stakes could bring relief.[54]

The government was not in a mood to play for "high stakes" in November either. It grimly anticipated a Ruhr invasion and was supportive of apparent trade-union plans for a general strike but opposed to acts of sabotage. Cabinet members also feared that the cutting off of Berlin's coal supply would lead to a Bolshevik takeover of Berlin. The French, however, would not be the only ones to blame. The unwillingness of the Kahr government in Bavaria to disarm its population and insufficient coal deliveries because of miner unrest in the Ruhr threatened to provide the French with the excuses they needed. As Fehrenbach put the matter: "What France and Lenin–Trotsky have not managed to accomplish, is reserved for the Bavarian People's Party—the destruction of German unity and the surrender of the Ruhr."[55]

Not to be outdone by Kahr, Stinnes was also putting on a rather extraordinary performance of his own. In a conversation with Lord D'Abernon on November 12, 1920, Stinnes provided a very bleak view of Germany's future. He feared unrest in the Ruhr and Silesia and claimed stabilization was impossible so long as Germany's civil service was so swollen. He expected a crisis in February because of the exchange rate and difficulties in buying food, and he feared both Communist uprisings and a French invasion of the Ruhr. The discussion took a very bizarre turn when Stinnes described the scenario of a red uprising:

The Russian plan was to detail two prostitutes to take care of each policeman and by this means the police would be rendered powerless. The women were paid heavily with Russian money. Herr Stinnes appeared to think that against such insidious methods for anaesthetizing the forces of order, civilization was almost powerless.[56]

While D'Abernon undoubtedly did not take Stinnes's overheated imagination very much to heart, he did take Stinnes, who "is universally recognised here as the most powerful private individual in the country," quite seriously. He hoped to persuade Stinnes that the opposition to the Spa agreements had proven unwise and, in effect, to take a more constructive attitude. In this, D'Abernon could have little hope of success. When C. F. von Siemens asked Stinnes whether or not to accept the government's invitation to serve as an expert at Brussels and Geneva, Stinnes urged him not to go. He did not think that anything could be accomplished so long as "elements" like Professor Bonn had a dominant influence and feared that Siemens

would find himself in the same situation as he and Wiedfeldt had found themselves in Spa:

Whoever does not have the courage to say No in the desperate situation in which Germany exists right now—and I do not believe that the present government has such courage—will take on new obligations that cannot be carried out and thus pull the noose somewhat closer around our throats simply in order to put off the necessary decisions for another few months.[57]

Bonn did go to Brussels as one of the experts attached to the delegation composed of Carl Bergmann (a former Deutsche Bank official who had become the Foreign Office's chief reparations negotiator), Havenstein, and Schröder of the Finance Ministry, but the government did not follow Bonn's advice on negotiating tactics and the character of a German offer. The Havenstein position had won out. Germany's delegates were instructed to give a straightforward account of Germany's financial and economic situation, describe the measures being taken to improve it, avoid offering a final sum, emphasize reparations in kind, and forcefully present the conditions, especially regarding Upper Silesia, under which they could begin to pay bearable reparations.[58]

The Germans knew that the conditions of their finances and their trade policies as well as the disarmament issue had cost them much of the credibility that had been gained at the time of the Erzberger tax reform. Germany's inadequate tax receipts and her deficit had already received severe criticism at the Brussels International Finance Conference, and the French press had taken up these issues as well as the high dividends paid by German corporations. The government made a systematic effort both before and during the Brussels Conference of Experts of December 16–22, 1920, to deal with these criticisms. It argued, not without cogency, that the dividends were paper dividends and that it could no more be claimed that they were high when measured in real terms than it could be said that five chairs were 500 percent of a piano. Similarly, they argued that real production costs were veiled by food subsidies, rent controls, and the failure of the railroad system to cover its true costs. In short, industrial production was being subsidized for social and economic reasons, and the impression of great profitability was false.[59] This very argument, however, shifted attention to Germany's budgetary practices, floating debt, and taxation. At Brussels, the Allied representatives demonstrated an uncommon interest in that rationale behind Germany's continued maintenance of ordinary and extraordinary budgets, since the latter now included not only the war costs but also the costs arising from the war, which included food subsidies of seven billion marks for the 1919 demobilization period and three billions in compensation to German citizens for losses under the Treaty, and the eighteen billion marks in railroad and postal deficits. That is, the floating debt of the Reich, everything covered by Treasury bills, was in the extraordinary budget, while the interest payments were placed in the ordinary budget. Schröder tried to assure the Allies that Germany was making every effort to put an increasing number of expenses in the ordinary budget, as had been the case with the three billion spent on food subsidies in 1920.[60]

When the Allies tried to find out what the budget for 1921–1922 would be like, however, Schröder was unable to say and, indeed, pointed out that the budget for 1920 was not fully completed. Schröder and his colleagues were not very convincing. Only eight days before giving this testimony, Schröder had tried to persuade the Cabinet not to put the full 5.8 billion requested by the Food Ministry for food subsidies into the "temporary emergency budget" for 1920 in view of the Brussels Finance Conference's criticisms of such unproductive expenditures and because "it would not be advantageous for the forthcoming reparations conference in Brussels, if yet more funds for the cheapening of bread grain prices are taken into the budget." He urged that only part of the money be appropriated right away because he feared that the German government would be accused of "letting the reins on its finances slip." The majority of his colleagues disagreed, however. They saw no point in alarming the German consumers or in hiding the truth from the Entente.[61]

How could they hide or disavow their social expenditures when, at the very time the German delegation was holding forth in Brussels, Wirth was being attacked as a "Dictator" by the civil servants for trying to hold the line on cost-of-living increases and the railroad workers were threatening to strike in January? Wirth had instigated the appointment of a Reich Commissar to Simplify and Unify the Reich Administration back in October, but he joined with the rest of the Cabinet in late December in finding unacceptable the report of Reich Commissar Friedrich Carl for failing to take into account the increased needs of the Reich government. Carl justified his austerity proposals in terms of saving money and preventing Entente financial control, and his response to Cabinet members' rejection was to threaten resignation. His promise not to state his views to the press "aggressively" was something less than reassuring.[62]

It was impossible for the Germans at Brussels to deny that the bureaucracy was bloated or that the railroad and postal deficit was being increased by excess personnel. One could only claim that the railroad and post had been running heavy deficits in part because of needed repair and reconstruction work as well as because of the costs of railroad nationalization. The German delegation had to admit that the immediate future would bring higher deficits. Erzberger had privately confessed to representatives of the Reparations Commission in Berlin that "nothing has been done to remedy this disastrous state of affairs" and that "it will be necessary at all costs to dismiss 100,000 employees and workmen engaged after the war to reduce the number of unemployed."[63] At the Brussels assemblage, Lord D'Abernon pointed out that the railroads had a hundred thousand more employees than before the war, and the Reich government had twenty-five thousand more.[64] The German delegation was in no position to contest such criticisms and could only give assurances of Germany's intention to reduce expenditures.

Allied efforts to determine what the Reich's revenue would be were met with comparable vagueness, and this probably came as no surprise. Erzberger, the man most responsible for the tax reforms, told the Reparations Commission agents in late November 1920 that a precise estimate of income from taxation would not be available until May 1921 because the bills had only gone out in August. He was more optimistic about his Emergency Capital Levy, since the administrative preparation and organization for this tax was in good order and since one-third of the amounts was to be paid in two installments (on February 1 and August 1, 1921) and the remaining two-thirds was to be paid over thirty years and he thought the government could take in seventeen billions.[65] At Brussels, Schröder made much of the increased tax revenue resulting from withholding and the fact that the ordinary budget probably would be balanced. He emphasized the extremely high charges on the rich and sought to demonstrate how a businessman with a million marks who retired to a hundred-thousand-mark house in a Berlin suburb would be left with nine thousand marks at the end of the year after he had paid his taxes and fuel bills. Schröder had to admit, of course, that a businessman who remained active and productive would not be so hard hit, and Schröder's interlocutors were far more interested in what was going to be done to reduce expenditure and decrease note circulation than they were in such extreme cases as the one described.[66]

The simple fact was that Germany's heavy direct-taxation program had been far more impressive when the deficit had been lower. The British Treasury's financial expert, R.G. Hawtrey, had already analyzed the situation from the perspective of the German documents presented at Spa and had come to the conclusion that the time factor and deficits were threatening to undermine the German direct taxation efforts even if they were very impressive on paper. The delays attendant upon the development of the necessary administrative machinery and the problems of assessment were compounded by the fact that the taxes on capital were to be paid in installments. As Hawtrey shrewdly argued:

[T]he interval during which this deficit will accrue, that is to say, before the new direct taxes come into full operation, is full of danger. . . . A valuable stabilizing influence is to be found in the preparation by the taxpayers for the payment of the direct taxes. They will tend to restrict expenditure and put funds temporarily into Treasury Bills. But should they be led to expect great increases in the paper prices of commodities, the opportunities of speculation will more than counteract that tendency, and traders will prefer to realize bills and lay out the proceeds in purchases of additional stock-in-trade. The currency position being thus weakened, the consequent discredit of the mark might destroy the whole fabric of direct taxation.[67]

German leaders were by no means indifferent to such dangers. The Emergency Capital Levy had failed to produce sufficient revenues because it allowed taxpayers to delay payment or pay in war bonds. Since the economic situation had improved sufficiently to justify faster and higher payments, and since payment by war bonds only served to decrease the fixed debt of the Reich but not its floating debt, Wirth concluded that a bill requiring an accelerated collection of the Emergency Capital Levy and the War Profits Tax was essential. He pushed it through against heavy opposition from the DVP and the DDP by threatening to resign.[68] Havenstein was very alarmed and, along with Mankiewitz of the Deutsche Bank and others, pushed for his program of a compulsory loan, which had been rejected by Erzberger in favor of a totally ineffective voluntary premium loan in 1919. Havenstein was convinced that a compulsory loan, combined with a restoration of the secrecy of bank accounts, would ferret out hoarded marks, encourage the rapid payment of the Emergency Capital Levy, and solve some of the cash-flow problems of the Reich. It should be noted that this idea enjoyed some left-wing support, since Fritz Naphtali of the ADGB looked with favor upon such a measure provided the loan could not be cashed in for loan-bureau notes and thus become another indirect means of increasing rather than decreasing the floating debt.[69] In any case, what had become apparent by the turn of 1920–1921 was that the postwar tax reforms were proving inadequate to meet the increasing floating debt and that further taxation would be necessary in combination with reduced government expenditure. What was not apparent was how this was to be done in the context of severe domestic pressures to spend more money and growing insistence on the part of the DVP and the political right after their victory in the June 1920 elections that the tax program be implemented in a "liberal" manner.[70]

In the meantime, what was to be done about reparations? The Brussels Conference of Experts left the answer very uncertain. That was one reason why it was the most pleasant of the postwar international conferences dealing with reparations and was probably more harmonious than most of the meetings among the Allies. The Allied experts appear to have been very objective in their questioning and investigations, and the Germans were forthright and open. The fact that Seydoux, who was not a member of the Reparations Commission, served as the head of the French delegation also promoted a good environment, and the Belgian chairman Delacroix seems to have been very effective and evenhanded. When the conference was adjourned on December 22, it was with the intention of meeting again on January 10.[71]

From the German perspective, however, what made Brussels particularly hopeful was that both Seydoux and D'Abernon, in private meetings with Bergmann and other German delegation members, seemed anxious to solve the reparations issue in ways that would take German problems into account. Unhappily, the ways being proposed were very different. Seydoux, reflecting views held in important circles of the French government, recognized the immense difficulty faced by Germany in making cash payments in the near future. He was also altogether too well aware of the problem of arriving at a fixed reparations sum that would satisfy public opinion in both countries. He therefore developed proposals, which he first presented at Brussels and then in modified form to the German negotiators in Paris in early January 1921, for a period during which both the setting of a final sum and cash payments would be set aside in favor of payments in kind based upon Franco-German economic cooperation. While he had refrained from mentioning annuities for the provisional period at Brussels, the revised version of his proposal in Paris resembled the Boulogne scheme, at least to the extent of calling for a German obligation of three billion gold marks per year for five years. The emphasis, however, was to be on payment in kind and payment of a portion of Germany's export profits. Seydoux's basic purpose was to relieve the transfer problem created by Germany's adverse balance of payments and give the Germans every incentive to produce and balance their budget. Thus, German industry would supply not only unfinished but also fin-

ished goods and even labor which the German government would compensate. A revolving mark fund would be created for this purpose, but there would also be some compensation to German industry in francs. Part of all such payments in kind would be credited against reparation at German export rather than internal prices, a major incentive to German industry. Thus, German industry and the German economy would be allowed to keep some portion of their gains from their deliveries to France, while a comprehensive program of agreements between French and German industry to facilitate trade and the employment of the mark fund to permit French businessmen to buy into German industry would provide the foundation for comprehensive economic cooperation.[72]

The German Economics Ministry had long been interested in such plans which, among other things, would help to maintain employment in Germany. Furthermore, German policy continually sought to encourage reparations in kind over cash. Bergmann was especially friendly and encouraging to Seydoux at Brussels in their discussions, and there can be no question about the fact that the French proposals were taken seriously and as a sign that moderation was on the march in Paris. Nevertheless, Bergmann, to the irritation of some of his advisers—above all, Director Le Suire of the Economics Ministry—ended up taking a somewhat dilatory attitude toward the Seydoux proposals at the conclusion of the Brussels meetings because Lord D'Abernon, arguing that they should take advantage of France's reasonable mood and reflecting Lloyd George's mania for setting a final reparations sum rather than his own preference for a provisional solution, was urging the Germans to offer eighty-five billions in present value; that is, some fifteen to twenty billions below the Boulogne scheme. When D'Abernon and Delacroix, who joined in this effort, responded affirmatively to Bergmann's idea that the eighty-five billions would be declared the total war costs for which Germany would be responsible but that the actual amount to be paid would be considerably less, Bergmann was even more enthusiastic. He thus encouraged an interruption of the Brussels discussions to consult with Berlin on the theory that, as he told his delegation, "time is working for us."[73]

This was not the perception of either Le Suire or Moritz Bonn. The former wanted to keep the matter away from the Reparations Commission, the home of which was Paris, and to take advantage of what he felt to be Seydoux's genuine desire to increase Germany's capacity to pay by giving her some relief. In Le Suire's view, there were too many financial people involved in the discussion, including D'Abernon and most of the German delegation, and he welcomed the influence of Seydoux, whose main interest was commerce, as well as the idea of moving the reparations issue into a series of conferences like the one held at Brussels where experts could make sensible arrangements.[74]

As for Bonn, he thought that D'Abernon had a tendency to underestimate the difficulties with the French and continued to feel that Germany had to make a substantial offer that would be taken seriously. This was the issue from Bonn's perspective rather than the question of reparations in money or in kind. Both constituted transfers of real wealth which would have to be paid for by the German taxpayer. In either case, Germany needed time to recover and credit to help pay both her imports and her deliveries or payments to the Allies. In this sense, the Spa accord, under which Germany received a premium to feed her workers in return for deliveries, was a model. Germany's need for such a "double credit" became clear once one remembered that Germany was surviving largely because of speculation with the mark and the buying out of Germany. An acceptance of reparations in kind meant a reduction of Germany's export capacity, and Bonn warned that

we thereby give up the temporary advantage we enjoy from our depreciating currency. But insofar as we deny ourselves dumping because we do not have excess goods anymore, we renounce the most effective argument for the international attempt to improve our currency. The danger of dumping because of our bad currency is, along with our inadequate purchasing power, the chief reason why the states with large amounts of capital are interested in our situation.[75]

Germany's own requirement to stabilize her currency, however, would remain whether payments were made in kind or in gold "since if we give goods at world market prices and compensate the producers in world market prices, then it costs us just as much financially as if we bought goods denominated in gold."[76] The fact that payments in kind relieved the transfer problem did not mean that they relieved the stabilization problem. If anything, they only highlighted the latter since one could not pay German industrialists endless amounts of newly printed marks for their deliveries to the French without making the inflation worse.

Another interesting problem, however, was whether Germany's industrialists were prepared to collaborate in any way with the proposals being considered to solve the reparations question. Much to Foreign Minister Simons irritation, the various industrialists approached by the Foreign Office had refused to participate in the Brussels negotiations, largely because of the opposition from the Ruhr, and the only nonbanking businessman who served as an expert, Wilhelm Cuno, the general director of HAPAG, was closer to banking circles than he was to heavy industry. The industrialist attitude is all the more remarkable when one remembers that Simons had been executive secretary of the RdI. The Seydoux plan, however, obviously required the cooperation of industry, and Simons therefore decided to approach the RdI president Kurt Sorge to see if he could persuade industry to participate in the talks with the French. When various industrialists agreed to do so, however, it was under two conditions. The first was that the Reich not accept any fixed obligations in the negotiations. The second was that the proposal of the Deutsche Bank director Oscar Wassermann that German industry surrender 10 percent of its production for purposes of reparations, a proposal that might have been tied to the Seydoux plan, be dropped.[77]

This did not make dealing with the industrialists any easier. At a meeting in Essen on January 8, 1921, in which Simons and various members of the RWM tried to impress upon the industrialists the urgency of responding to the Seydoux proposals, they met with a steady stream of objections. Klöckner, for example, opposed letting French iron products into Germany without reciprocation and rejected buying minette unless the price was lowered. The iron industrialists claimed that they could not afford to surrender any of their foreign exchange for reparations purposes. Von Buttlar of the RWM responded by pointing out the good results of recent negotiations between the German and French dye industries under which an agreement had been reached on sales territories as well as an arrangement under which France would own shares in the dyes syndicate while the Germans would put capital into three French works. He also remarked, apparently with approval, that the French viewed the interpenetration of French and German industry as a foundation for a later political understanding. What was to be accomplished thirty years later in the wake of a second world war, however, could not be achieved in 1920. The iron and steel industrialists insisted that their situation was different from that of their dye industry counterparts and that they did not have the capital needed to invest in the Lorraine works. Furthermore, however desirable were agreements with the French, they felt it was premature to enter into them under existing circumstances. Stinnes stated the calculations of German heavy industry as bluntly as possible:

The French are under the pressure of a much too expanded iron industry which does not have a sufficient market. We have the greatest interest in letting this disproportion work itself out fully and to win time. It is impossible at present to offer the French any foreign exchange. We need the foreign exchange ourselves, especially for the payment of our food supplies. If we come to an economic understanding with the French, there is the danger that England will deny us help. We should not ruin things with England, which will be more useful to us than America.[78]

Stinnes nevertheless agreed that three representatives of industry should negotiate to "find a *modus vivendi*" with the French, although it is difficult to tell from these remarks exactly what those named—Vögler, Klöckner and himself—were to negotiate about.

Simons was none too happy about the naming of Stinnes, whom he viewed as a liability in negotiations after the outburst at Spa, but the RdI insisted, and Simons quickly backed down. Insofar as actual policy was concerned, Simons and Stinnes were in fundamental harmony in January, and this was important because the negotiations in Paris had taken a difficult turn. The agreement between Simons and the indus-

trialists to refuse a temporary arrangement under which Germany would pay fixed annuities for five years was becoming increasingly incompatible with the desire not to "ruin things with England." Lord D'Abernon had now reverted to openly supporting what had always been his personal position and joined with Seydoux in urging the Germans to accept a provisional solution under which Germany would accept five years of substantial fixed annuities. While the formal resumption of the Brussels meeting scheduled for January 10 was postponed, negotiations among the experts continued in Paris during most of January and were not interrupted even by the government crisis in mid-January which brought down Premier Georges Leygues, who was suspected of being too soft on the Germans. He was replaced by Aristide Briand, but President Millerand continued to exert strong influence in foreign-policy matters and kept the discussions going. D'Abernon was continually emphasizing the importance of keeping the French reasonable by accepting the Seydoux proposals. If Simons were to take a completely negative stance, he would run the danger of alienating the British and strengthening the French hard-liners. He was counting heavily on the United States exerting a strong influence in Germany's favor in order to relieve its own economic difficulties by procuring Germany as a good customer and finding a source of capital investment, but American action could not be expected before Harding took office in March.

Stinnes agreed. At a meeting in the Foreign Office on January 14, Stinnes argued that

. . . one should not avoid negotiations on a provisional arrangement in principle because he [Stinnes] believes that the later the final reparations are set, the better for us. In his view the world economic situation is developing in a way that is making things harder for the masses everywhere. One will have to create consumers. We have to hold out through the period of "things being more and more unbearable." In a few years, people will be calculating in pennies again. In any case, we must wait until America sits at the table with us.[79]

This is not to say that Stinnes or Simons were prepared to accept a provisional settlement. The question was one of talking until the Americans could enter the scene. As Simons defined the strategy, it was "no rejection of the plan of Seydoux, but a statement that the plan needs careful study because the demands made on Germany require examination from an economic point of view; effort to be made at direct contact between the industrialists on both sides; the basic goal is to put off the final setting of the German reparations payments until the United States can join in the negotiations."[80] On the following day, January 15, Simons asked the Cabinet to empower him to discuss the Seydoux plan so that "its impossibility could become obvious during the negotiations and the Americans can come to help us in the meantime. By discussing it we will also help to prevent a Poincaré government."[81] Once again, the Germans were convincing themselves that time was on their side.

In the short run, this most certainly was not the case, as the Germans were horrified to discover at the end of January 1921 when the Allies themselves completed the task of burying the Seydoux plan and the provisional five-year annuity scheme upon which Seydoux and D'Abernon had united. The chief responsibility for this lay with Lloyd George, who was unalterably convinced that neither Germany nor the world could achieve stability so long as a final reparations sum was not set. As one historian has argued, "[W]hat he does not seem to have understood was that the only thing more unsettling to German finance and the German economy than an unspecified total was one which exceeded the German's own rather modest estimates of their capacity to pay."[82] Lloyd George had other concerns, however. He was deeply worried about Britain's high unemployment and economic difficulties, and he wanted to end German dumping. At the same time, he felt that something had to be done to prevent reparations from becoming ruinous to British and European economic recovery. He also was anxious to produce settled circumstances so that the United States would play a more constructive role on questions of debts and European economic reconstruction. Finally, Lloyd George was anxious to keep the French under control by forestalling Franco-German agreements at Britain's expense and also preventing the French from using reparations in kind to take more than the 52 percent of reparations to which they were entitled. If Lloyd George was prepared to get tough with the Germans, it was, of course, first and foremost for Great Britain's good, but it was also meant to set limits on the French as well by forcing them to settle for what they could realistically get and to pressure the Germans to put their own house in order.

Taking advantage of a scheduled meeting of the Supreme Council in Paris on January 24–29, 1921, to discuss German fulfillment, the Prime Minister stunned the French by disregarding the work done by the experts at Brussels and in Paris and calling for the immediate setting of a final sum and annuities to present not to "experts" but rather to the German political leadership itself. The first victim of this bombshell was Briand. He and his predecessors had not dared to bring the Boulogne scheme before the Chamber of Deputies because any government that did so would be sent packing. If forced to come out into the open, they could only do so with huge sums, and the new Finance Minister Doumer, pointing to French "bankruptcy," called for a final sum with a present value of two hundred billions and annuities of twelve billion per year. He recommended that the Germans pay for this by reducing their imports. Lloyd George would have none of this:

If Germany had to pay these 12 milliards of marks within her own territory, she could do it easily, but when you ask her to pay it, not in paper marks, but in gold marks, that is, in marks which have full face value outside Germany, then comes the difficulty. It is no use referring to the forests of Germany, and the railways of Germany, and the mines of Germany, and the land of Germany; you cannot transport the land of Germany or the forests of Germany over the frontier. . . . supposing you seize the railways of Germany; you will have to collect your revenue in paper marks. . . . M. Doumer said Germany can increase her exports and diminish her imports. Well, there is a limit to her diminution of imports. The vast majority of what she imports is either food or raw materials or essential machinery for her industries. If she does not get these her people will starve, or her industries will starve. Then she certainly could not pay an indemnity. If she increases her exports, where to? Her best customers before the war, were Central Europe and Russia. It will take years before they can buy. Is Germany to increase her exports to England, or to France, or to Italy, or to Belgium? If she does she can only do so by displacing the labour of our own work-men. Is she to increase her exports to neutral mar-kets? If she does she will do it at the expense of our own trade there.[83]

Lloyd George was convinced that if they went on procrastinating, the Germans would go on printing, and soon "not all the *camions* in France will be able to carry the indemnity across the frontier because the mark will be so depreciated that it will require at least one *cam-ion* for a gold franc!"[84]

As at San Remo and Spa, so at Paris. Lloyd George was prepared to commit himself to the use of force in return for reasonableness from the French. He thought it necessary to "use all the authority given by the treaty to compel her to put herself in a position to pay." He did not venture an opinion as to whether Germany was "letting herself go" for political or tactical rea-sons or because the government was too weak to impose the necessary taxation, but he consid-ered German taxation insufficient compared to England and France and thought that railway and utility rates had to be raised and indirect taxes imposed on liquor and tobacco. In his view, Germany was "not telling her people to contribute; and the result is that the mark is be-coming more and more worthless."[85]

Briand sought in vain to persuade Lloyd George that the expert discussions on a tem-porary annuity scheme should continue, that the Reparations Commission establish the amount to which Germany was liable on May 1, and that the actual full amount that Germany could pay be established later when the situa-tion was clearer. Lloyd George had no interest in making domestic politics easier for his French colleague and threatened to go home leaving everything unsettled unless the French returned to the Boulogne scheme and then summoned the German leadership to Paris to reach an agreement. He was, to be sure, pre-pared to accept "improvements," such as a tax on German exports as part of the reparations payments in line with their general interest in adopting measures "to prevent unfair compe-tition by Germany with the industries of Allied countries."[86]

Briand was forced to yield, and the upshot of the Paris discussions was a series of resolutions communicated to the German government on January 29, 1921. In addition to making vari-ous demands concerning disarmament and threatening sanctions, the Allies made major reparations proposals. Germany was to pay a rising scale of annuities biannually in gold marks beginning on May 1: two annuities of two billion in 1921–1923; three annuities of three billion in 1923–1926; three annuities of four billion in 1926–1929; three annuities of five billion in 1929–1932; and thirty-one an-nuities of six billion in 1932–1963. In addition, it was to pay forty-two annuities amounting to 12 percent *ad valorem* of its exports payable two months after the close of each half year. Further, it was to provide the Reparations Commission with the facilities necessary to cer-tify the value of its exports, to pledge that nei-ther the German government nor any govern-mental entity under its control would embark upon a credit operation without the approval of the Reparations Commission, and to pledge its customs receipts as security for the fulfillment of its reparations obligations. German liability for occupation costs would continue. The Ger-mans were invited to come to London at the end of February to discuss these proposals.[87]

The German reaction was one of predictable outrage, but it is useful to bear certain facts in mind before considering it. The Paris proposals were unquestionably a departure from the terms that had been discussed at Brussels and in Paris by the experts, but it must be remembered that the Germans themselves were pursuing a dilatory tactic and were committed to an un-acceptably low global figure and annuity. If the Seydoux proposals had offered the most hope-ful way out in the entire early history of the rep-arations issue, it was not a way out the Germans were prepared to accept, although it was also doomed because of Lloyd George's hostility to a provisional settlement. Given these facts, it is necessary to recognize that the Paris proposals were no great departure from the Boulogne scheme and thus consistent with Allied policy as it had developed since San Remo. The nom-inal value of the Paris proposals was some forty-three billion below that of the Bolougne scheme, the difference being made up in the levy on exports. The value of the levy could be assessed optimistically or pessimistically, but the English did not think the present value of the Paris proposals was more than a hundred ten billion gold marks; that is, about eight billion more than the Boulogne scheme.[88]

Thunder from London: From Sanctions to *Diktat*

From the German perspective, of course, the entire proposal was impossible and Germany was being placed under a financial control reminiscent of that imposed on Egypt. Simons felt that the rug had been pulled out from under his feet and contemplated resignation. Reich President Ebert, however, warned against his resignation or that of the Cabinet. A basic decision was made to mobilize German and world opinion against the Paris proposals and to try to avoid an Allied *Diktat* before a decision had been reached on Upper Silesia and America's new President had a chance to intervene. Simons played an active role in the mobilization of public opinion and the creation of a united front with an angry address to the Reichstag on February 1 in which he attacked the Paris resolutions as the "economic enslavement of the German people."[89] He then traveled to south Germany and made a major speech in Stuttgart defending his decision to go to London but assuring the nation that Germany would stand fast. He expressed regret that the Brussels negotiations could no longer be carried forward but rather disingenuously pointed out that while a provisional payments arrangement might have been possible before the Paris proposals, now "the German people will see rising like an apparition behind every provisional arrangement some monstrous figure of gold billions."[90] Individual protests were made by the German state parliaments. The government directly sought to mobilize the trade unions, warning that the Allies intended to make "permanent helots" of the German people, and the ADGB sent forth an appeal to the workers of the world to stand behind their German brethren.[91]

There is no reason to doubt the sincerity of the German claim that they could not fulfill the obligations proposed in Paris. In a confidential meeting on February 7 in the RWM, State Secretary Hirsch declared that the carrying out of the Paris demands "will unquestionably mean the economic end of Germany," since at existing export levels it would leave virtually no foreign exchange for imports of food and raw materials. Because of the restrictions on German tariff policy imposed by the Treaty, he found it difficult to figure out how Germany could even effectively control nonessential imports. There was wide agreement with Simons that any German counteroffer had to be based on Germany's productive capacity and that every German offer would thus inevitably outrage the Allied public as much as the Entente demands had enraged the Germans. Whether Simons was doing much to improve the Allied mood by holding a speech in Karlsruhe in which he explicitly denied German war guilt, however, was very doubtful.[92]

As had been the case prior to the Brussels conference, the German Foreign Office held a series of meetings with experts from banking, industry, and labor in February to seek advice on the counteroffer to be made in London. The group divided in a now familiar pattern. The leading Ruhr industrialists—Stinnes, Vögler, Klöckner, Wiedfeldt—and the chemical industrialist Carl Duisberg and Havenstein took a pessimistic view and urged against presenting any global sum or offering provisional sums beyond what they considered to be the absolute maximum. Their posture did not have the aggressiveness that had characterized Stinnes's performance at Spa, however. Stinnes himself seemed anxious to gain time and emphasized that it was important at some point to come to terms with Germany's most dangerous neighbor, France. Duisberg was particularly concerned about Germany's labor force and the dangers that acceptance of impossible terms would bring. He was distressed over the lack of opportunity for young chemists, but he was also fearful that the workers would emigrate if conditions were made too harsh: "We should not take beer away from the workers and make cigars and tobacco so expensive that they can no longer smoke. I warn you very emphatically: do not touch the eight-hour day . . . do not neglect the psyche of the workers! We want to keep the eight-hour day."[93] He seems to have been very much influenced by a severe strike at his plants in Leverkusen, but the fact that there was talk of the Paris proposals requiring an increase of the working day from eight to fourteen hours gave his fears a broader basis. While the Socialist trade unionist Silberschmidt worried that mention of increasing the hours of work might suggest that they had already come to accept the necessity of an increased workday, Stinnes insisted that it had to be mentioned, and the Christian trade unionist Baltrusch thought it essential to inform the workers about the danger which the Entente demands ultimately presented to their working conditions and well-being.[94]

Another group of experts, led by Rathenau and including Melchior and Bonn, took a more optimistic stance and argued that Germany should run the risk of a larger offer than she thought possible to fulfill. Rathenau feared for German credibility. He pointed out that the Allies knew that Germany was exporting a billion marks' worth of coal already, that she had large-scale imports of unessential goods, that substantial portions of the German population were living as well as their counterparts elsewhere, and that "above all one knows about Germany in these two very troubled years that, to be sure in part through selling ourselves out, but in part also through the realization of profits, we have acquired assets abroad which I do not want to calculate here but which go well beyond estimates. That is known abroad and it will therefore be very hard for them to understand and it would even be very difficult to make intelligible that we cannot pay a pfennig more than what we are now providing in coal."[95] He thought Germany's productive capacity was much greater than had been estimated and that one had to "leap over the ditch" and make an offer that would show Germany's good faith and win over public opinion whether the Allies accepted it or not. He stressed the importance of the "imponderables," reminded the group assembled of the influence of Keynes's book, and looked forward to creating a situation in which Germany's economic problems and obligations would become part of a discussion of worldwide reconstruction.

Neither the Ruhr industrialists nor the officials of the government shared this optimism. Vögler was certain that the "billions could only be paid at the cost of our exchange rate," and

Schröder of the Finance Ministry pointed out that "not even the biggest tax increase" would pay for reparations and that whatever future economic improvements there might be, the initial reparations payments would "have to be covered by the printing press."[96] In such an environment, it was very difficult indeed to decide on a counteroffer. The numerous experts upon whom Simons had counted and who had met off and on between February 9 and 25 found themselves incapable of producing a usable proposal, and finally Simons turned to a small group composed of Melchior, Wiedfeldt, Cuno, and Bergmann.

They turned up with a proposal that had as basic assumptions that the Upper Silesian plebiscite would be in Germany's favor and that Germany would be granted full economic freedom and equality. While the Paris resolutions were declared "economically and financially unfulfillable," Germany should make a counteroffer with a present value of fifty billion marks, a figure which they arrived at by employing the Allied offer to permit the Germans to pay off the entire indebtedness stated in the Paris resolutions before 1923 at 8 percent. In reality, however, the proposal was to offer what was claimed to be thirty billion marks, since the drafters worked on the assumption that Germany would be credited with at least twenty billion marks for payments in kind and services prior to May 1921. An expert commission was to be set up to determine what should be credited against reparations. In order to pay these thirty billions, Germany was to be allowed to float an international eight billion gold-mark loan bearing 5 percent interest that would be declared nontaxable for foreign lenders. The amortization of this loan would begin five years after issuance at 1 to 1.5 percent. Additionally, Germany would pay one billion marks a year, primarily in kind, for the coming five years, as well as contribute with its labor to the reconstruction of the devastated areas. Insofar as Germany's reparations bill was not covered by the international loan and these payments, the balance would bear 5 percent interest beginning in 1926. The proposal explicitly stated an intention to raise the balance of the debt through additional international loans if at all possible. In place of the 12 percent export levy proposed by the Allies, the Germans suggested an index scheme that would measure improved German capacity to pay and be used to increase such annuities as were necessary. This system would only go into effect, however, after May 1, 1926.[97]

This proposal was approved by the Cabinet on February 25, although both the DVP Treasury Minister von Raumer and the Centrist Postal Minister Giesberts found it excessive. Both Simons and Bergmann realized that the proposal might not be accepted, but they thought it would impress the English and Americans and would produce a "moral success in the entire world."[98] That they could entertain such nonsense was a reflection of the German domestic political environment and of the mood of fatalism that had begun to grip Germany's political leadership. The Bavarian delegate chosen to accompany Simons on his fateful trip to London, State Councillor von Meinel, noted that the Foreign Office's preparation of materials for the meetings, especially its foreign-trade statistics, was nothing short of "sloppy." The dilemma was that Simons could not pursue a "catastrophe policy." He had to make proposals, but these were bound to be unacceptable, and one had "to be prepared for the worst." Meinel saw only two possible bases for the Allies to grant concessions. The first was that their excessive demands would make it impossible for Germany to maintain its social legislation and that this would produce a reaction from their own working classes, and the second was that the Germans would be compelled to flood their countries with German goods to such an extent as to be against the interest of the Allies themselves. Meinel thought it would be a great success if the Germans could just manage to draw things out until Harding became the U.S. President, although he had to confess that he did not really place much hope in Harding either. In fact, Meinel seemed to share the fatalistic mood he had encountered in Berlin; namely, that

. . . in certain circumstances one will accept even the most extreme Entente demands with the idea in the back of one's mind that the general world situation will improve for us in a few years. This is naturally a most dangerous experiment and would lead to the further impoverishment of the German people,

under which condition the termination of the eight-hour working day would be self-understood.[99]

The German counterproposal, however, was also a "dangerous experiment." Predictably, Lloyd George was enraged by the German counteroffer, which was presented by Simons in London on March 1 in a manner so clumsy as to make the bad situation worse. The experts at Brussels had only been willing to credit German payments until then at eight billion, not the twenty billions claimed, and even if the Allied appraisal was somewhat too low, the German estimates of the Saar mines and the German maritime fleet were patent exaggerations, while the inclusion of the value of the fleet scuttled at Scapa Flow bordered on the grotesque.[100] The present value of the thirty-billion goldmark German offer, when discounted at 5 percent after 1926, was really twenty-two billions, about a quarter of what had been proposed at Paris. The Prime Minister could not understand why the British government should force its citizens to pay taxes on bonds used to pay for public housing but not on bonds used to help the Germans take out an international loan to pay for reparations. He had also been more than a little chagrined by Simons's speech in Karlsruhe, since German war guilt was not a subject on which the Allies were prepared to negotiate. Briand, of course, found the offer no less unacceptable, although he expressed some sympathy for Simons, "who possessed a great deal of civic courage in that he was able to make such proposals, about the nature of which he could not be ignorant, since he was a clever man."[101] Both Briand and Lloyd George recognized that the proposals reflected the weakness of the German government and its inability to deal with domestic opposition, and they viewed the proposals as the creation of Stinnes and the industrialists and a defeat for the German moderates. In reality, of course, the German counterproposals exceeded Stinnes's wishes, and had even been opposed by Wiedfeldt, one of the narrow circle of "experts" Simons had worked with before departing for London.[102] The proposals, however, did produce precisely the reaction predicted by Bonn and Rathenau.

If the Allied leaders blamed the German

counterproposal on Stinnes, it was nonetheless Simons who had to receive the incredible dressing down administered by Lloyd George on March 3 in London. The Prime Minister angrily declared that "the counterproposals mock the treaty,"[103] sharply criticized the manner in which public opinion in Germany had been whipped up during the preceding weeks, and accused the Germans of acting in bad faith. If the Germans had come in with objections to forty-two years of payments or had proposed a reasonable alternative to the 12 percent export levy, there would have been something to discuss. He devoted particular attention to Germany's failure to levy taxes comparable to those of the victor nations, reminding Simons of how Great Britain had taxed its citizens during and after the war, while pointing out that "Germany has made no such effort. Today her apparently gigantic debt has been reduced almost to the amount of her prewar liabilities by a process of depreciating her currency. She has nominally imposed very heavy taxes on wealth, but everyone knows that they are not fully collected."[104] Lloyd George laid particular stress on Germany's indirect taxation, which he termed "ridiculously low," especially on alcoholic beverages, tobacco, coffee, and tea. While Great Britain had abolished food and utility subsidies, Germany was spending thirty billion a year on them. In short, Lloyd George found the German counterproposals "provocative" and considered it a "sheer waste of time" to discuss them.

When it came to Stinnes and his friends, however, Lloyd George intended to employ deeds, not words. Unless the Germans either accepted the Paris proposals or came up with discussable propositions of their own by March 7, sanctions would be imposed—specifically, the occupation of Düsseldorf, Duisberg, and Ruhrort; the retention of a portion of receipts on German exports to Allied countries; confiscation of the customs at the borders of the occupied area for the same purpose; and the establishment of an Allied customs line between the occupied and unoccupied areas. Briand had urged more military measures and extensive occupation, but Lloyd George argued for an emphasis on economic measures. The occupation of the chief ports for the shipment of coal

was meant to bring the sanctions home to Stinnes's doorstep, so to speak, while the seizure of German export profits and customs duties as well as the potential reopening of the "hole in the West" had a similar aim of hurting Germany economically but also of preventing the kind of public anxiety in England and France that would attend severe military measures.[105]

As was always the case, there was more than a touch of British self-interest in their sanction proposals. While they were cold to reparations in kind because they saw this as a means for France to collect more rapidly and perhaps in fuller measure than England, the idea of collecting reparations through a levy on German exports was most appealing at a time when bad economic conditions at home were fueling resentment in some circles against increasing German exports and exchange dumping. The Germans were not helping their cause very much, however, by a certain amount of obnoxious economic chest thumping. Thus, in mid-February, Ambassador Stahmer warned against "continuous references to the powerful development of Germany's economic life, as well as statements concerning great dividends and profits, the founding of new companies and the formation of syndicates" which were avidly followed by British protectionists.[106] Nevertheless, it was not at all clear as to exactly what British self-interest was in dealing with Germany. Thus, Stahmer also reported that many persons in British economic life had taken note of the manner in which the Spa Agreement and the forced surrender of the German merchant marine had hurt two of the most important British industries, coal mining and shipbuilding. They were fearful that the demands made upon Germany by the Paris proposals would lead to a further "strengthening of German industry, which will be necessitated by the burdens placed upon it" and worried about what this "would mean for English industry on the English and world market."[107] The solution to the conundrum presented by German reparations was not very clear, but there is good evidence that Lloyd George thought he could help solve the problem by proposing the passage of laws that would permit the British to abscond with 50 percent of the German export receipts. By this means, the

British Treasury would benefit by collecting reparations without having to deal with the transfer problem because the Germans would compensate their businessmen for their losses; or if the German government refused to provide compensation, then at least the German exchange dumping would be coming to a halt and English industry given a boost.[108]

Although the levy on German imports had become something of a pet project for Lloyd George, he could not but have been aware of strong opposition to such a scheme within the government itself as well as from important sections of business and labor. More generally, the Prime Minister seems to have continued to entertain hopes that all sanctions could be avoided by the Germans coming to terms. Simons and his colleagues were indeed anxious to keep the talks going, and this produced some rather bizarre proposals. One of these was an idea concocted by Rathenau involving a German offer to take over the forty-five billion gold-mark debt owed by the Allies to the United States, as well as the floating of an eight-billion-mark loan for the reconstruction of the devastated areas. In this way, Germany could bring in the United States, without whose help Rathenau was convinced the reparations problem could not be solved and have the advantage of repayment in modest installments at a low interest rate.[109] As Moritz Bonn was to note in a scathing criticism of the plan, the Allies would consider it nothing more than the "usual German swindle . . . and rightly so."[110] The Rathenau plan amounted to an annuity of 1.4 to 1.8 billion per year. At the time, the Allies still had not paid any interest or amortization on their debts to the United States, and this, when combined with the projected 4 percent interest rate, made the debts rather more agreeable than that which the Allies had in mind for the Germans. Since the English owed more to the Americans than the Germans, it would transform the Allied formula under which France was to receive 52 percent of reparations into one in which she received 31.5 percent while England received almost 50 percent. By implication, the plan was also extraordinarily insulting to the Allies since it suggested that the United States would prefer a country in the miserable financial shape of Germany as its debtor to the Allies, and it would also rob the Americans of the potential use of the inter-Allied debts as a means of forcing moderation on France and England. There was also the not insignificant problem that Germany and the United States were still technically at war and that the proposal would have put Harding in an "impossible position."[111]

Once the impossibility of this proposal was realized by the German negotiators themselves, their only hope, ironically, was to return to the line of negotiation they had previously rejected and suggest a temporary arrangement for five years on the basis of the hated Paris proposals. While declaring it impossible to come to agreement on a final sum, they offered a provisional settlement under which Germany would pay two billion marks a year for two years and three billion for the following three years as well as 12 percent of the value of its exports for each of the five years. Since fifteen billion was beyond its capacity to pay, Germany returned to the idea of gaining permission to float an eight-billion-mark tax-free international loan whose servicing would have priority over other obligations. The preconditions with respect to Silesia and German trading rights remained. From the German perspective, this was no small change of policy, since it involved doing precisely what they had declared to be impossible. Indeed, Havenstein had composed a very lengthy protest against Simons's original offer at London, and Simons was in fact exceeding his instructions and would have been disavowed had it not been for Reich President Ebert's support. Simons's efforts, however, came too late. The environment was too poisoned for a provisional settlement, especially one conditional on the vote in Upper Silesia. As Lloyd George argued in a final meeting with the Germans on March 7, the German proposal "is not a proposal for five years; it is a proposal for five weeks."[112] On March 8, the sanctions were imposed.

Simons manifestly did not return to Berlin in glory. He had departed from the Berlin station to the shouts of "remain firm, do not give in!,"[113] only to come back without having remained "firm" and without anything to show for his concessions. Stinnes sharply attacked Simons and the government for showing a lack of leadership, ideas, and foresight and was especially critical of the helter-skelter manner in which the experts had been employed. The industrialists were particularly upset at the notion that they might be identified with Simons's decisions. Wiedfeldt wanted Hans Kraemer to call a meeting of the experts to disavow the Foreign Minister's actions, and Simons, anticipating such actions, publicly absolved the experts of any responsibility for his decisions in London. But what really annoyed the industrialists was the idea of being used by the government as experts while the real decisions were being made by a small group of advisers unknown to the public. Stinnes was not alone in entertaining the view that the government had some special obligation to businessmen when they agreed to serve as experts. As Hans Kraemer told Wiedfeldt, "It would seem to be out of the question that German businessmen should place themselves at the disposal of the government in the future if the Cabinet or individual ministers at the same time work with a second group of experts which proves itself to be more pliable than the one known to the public."[114] Simons, his skin perhaps toughened by his meetings with Lloyd George, defended himself worthily against Stinnes, assuring the latter that he cherished his advice but pointing out that he was not Stinnes's "young man." While Stinnes argued that the people in the government responsible for the London debacle had to step down, neither his own party nor most of the Reichstag were prepared to withdraw their confidence. Stinnes himself was hardly bursting with new ideas, and, temporarily at least, the sanctions seemed to be having precisely the effect Lloyd George had intended. Stinnes thought that the sanctions were "unbearable" and that "it therefore was unthinkable that we should evade any negotiations which the enemy might eventually offer."[115]

Whether the sanctions were quite as "unbearable" as Stinnes claimed, however, was as yet uncertain. Even before they were imposed, officials of the RWM viewed them as a "double-edged sword."[116] Commerce in the occupied area would obviously be affected, but the imposition of customs barriers and controls between the occupied and unoccupied areas was an expensive and complicated business, and the

volume of trade was such that the contribution to reparations would be very small. Even the collection of a 50 percent levy on exports to England, France, and Belgium, which constituted one-sixth of Germany's trade (or eleven billion paper marks), would only bring a return of five billion paper marks. Indeed, the major barrier to the Reich compensating exporters for such losses was that it would constitute an indirect recognition of the legality of the sanctions, which the Germans contested. Thus, exports to these countries were likely to suffer, although it should be noted that one of the more bizarre logical implications of the Lloyd George 50-percent reparations recovery program from exports was that it gave the Allies a patriotic reason to buy German products and thereby help their Treasuries.[117]

The major German concern was domestic unemployment, already a significant problem. Little compensation for the trade losses in the west could be found in the east, especially since Germany had imposed restrictions on trade with Poland and Romania for political reasons. Stinnes and officials of the RWM emphasized the need for government subsidization of domestic construction with tax breaks and low mortgage rates, and the great Ruhr industrialist also urged that the time had now come to get rid of the export control system, since Germany needed to export whatever she could and the system itself threatened to become a weapon in the hands of the Allies. Even Stinnes's DVP colleague, Treasury Minister von Raumer, however, warned against "letting the workers believe that one wants to use the opportunity provided by the sanctions to terminate export controls."[118]

The leading German industrialists did seem anxious to take a principled stand in resisting the sanctions. Thus, while a few called for the compensation of eventual losses, either by the state or through an equalization fund set up by the business associations themselves, the leaders of the RdI firmly opposed the principle of compensation. As Kraemer put the matter: "We consider this position to be the logical consequence of our effort to get the government to turn down the Paris demands. It is completely impossible to take the position that the Reich government should turn down the Paris demands, that is, to permit a break to take place with our enemies and then to take the position that the Reich should compensate all the amounts taken away because of it."[119]

The German business community truly was in a fighting mood. The Hamburg Chamber of Commerce called for a boycott of British goods and continued the boycotting of Antwerp in favor of Rotterdam which it had already begun in January as a means of pressuring the Belgians on reparations issues. Wiedfeldt wrote directly to the government urging the boycotting not only of Antwerp but also of all Entente goods. He viewed the situation as one of "economic war" and urged that Germany use such power as it had left as producer and purchaser not only to strike at the Entente but also to conclude trade treaties then being negotiated with Sweden and Switzerland and to enter into arrangements with other neighboring states and clarify German relations with Russia. Like Stinnes, he wanted to step up economic activity and reduce unemployment within Germany through "a great construction program with the expenditure of large amounts by the Reich."[120]

Naturally, the industrialists were not indifferent to losing money, but there was a general consensus among them "that the present political position was merely a passing phase and that the Allies and Germany would in the near future be obliged by the force of economic laws to resume negotiations in order to arrive at a firm agreement."[121] They rightly felt that Allied, especially British, businessmen would not take well to Lloyd George's 50 percent tax on imports from Germany. There was a storm of business and labor protest against the German Reparations Recovery bill presented to the House of Commons on March 10. Critics argued that the Germans would send their goods through neutral countries and that the effort to identify those imports which were German would revive all the bureaucracy and interference with trade that had characterized the hated war economy. The Prime Minister was accused of trying to bring in protectionism through the back door. As for labor, it was already strongly in opposition to the coal deliveries imposed on Germany which made the German miners work overtime in order to provide coal to the French that could have been imported from England. The British owners were thus in a position to use the depressed coal market to fire miners and depress wages, an effort that culminated in a great labor conflict in April. The new sanctions were seen as the continuation of the war by other means and were rejected for the harm they did to British exports and the fight against unemployment. Passed on government insistence, the Reparations Recovery Act went into effect on April 1 and was a demonstrated failure by the end of the month. German imports dropped spectacularly, while neutrals complained bitterly about British interference with their trade and British prestige suffered severe damage. For all intents and purposes, the Reparations Recovery Act ceased to be implemented, while its Franco-Belgian counterparts were never put into effect in the first place.[122]

The Germans were more worried about the occupation of the Ruhr ports and the proposed new customs arrangements in the Rhineland, although here, too, a wait-and-see attitude was adopted. There was some feeling, not limited to the Germans, that the projected customs line between the occupied and unoccupied areas would not prove technically feasible, although German businessmen in the Rhineland were convinced that the successful imposition of the customs control would be "catastrophic." Since the new customs arrangements were not to be introduced until April 20, however, the basic sentiments were those of impatience and uncertainty. No one knew what would happen and the conditions under which they would have to work, and the result was a substantial diminution of business activity.[123]

The remarkable thing was how little the exchange value of the mark was affected by all these untoward events. The rate in New York fluctuated between a low of 64.50 on March 9 and a high for the first nineteen days of the month of 62.10 on March 19. In part, the low level of business activity was itself a cause of the currency stability. The Germans were well supplied with food for the time being and the slowdown in business activity had reduced their raw-materials import requirements. The reduction of money-market activity was furthered when German banks ceased to buy on the Paris and London exchanges because of uncertainty about the security of their bank balances in those cities and about the manner in which the export levy was going to be collected. The signals in March and April for the future of the mark were not good, but they were not very clear either, and there was great international interest in reading the future in a favorable rather than gloomy light. As the Reparations Commission observers in Berlin noted:

Emphasis too has been given to a statement that, inasmuch as foreign countries in the period since the Armistice have become possessed of such a quantity of Mark-notes, which have been estimated at 30 milliards of paper-marks, and of such a quantity of mark-script, estimated at another 30 milliards of Marks, that alone must provide a certain stability to the German valuta as against unfavorable tendencies. It is surmised that a fresh fall in the Mark would do as much damage to foreigners as it would be bound to do to Germans.[124]

This imperviousness of the exchange rate of the mark to bad news continued through March and April despite a variety of untoward occurrences. The Communists staged a violent but abortive putsch in central Germany during the last ten days of March. At the same time, the reparations question become more and more of a nightmare. While the Germans claimed that they had paid the full twenty billions in reparations before May 1, 1921, required under the Treaty, the Reparations Commission would credit them with no more than eight billion. On March 15, the commission informed the Germans that they were owing twelve billion by May 1 and demanded that one billion in gold or foreign exchange at the dollar exchange rate be paid by March 23, a task the German government declared completely impossible. On April 16, the Reparations Commission, responding to the failure of the Germans to meet its demands, called upon the Germans to place all the gold and silver in the Reichsbank in its Cologne and Koblenz branches, a demand which the Reich rejected on April 22. The Allies, therefore, were well prepared to declare the Germans in default on May 1 and, if they wished, occupy more German territory.[125]

The relative stability of the mark was even more remarkable in the face of grim fiscal news and some significant evidence that German resistance to inflation was weakening significantly. The budget for 1921–1922 estimated a

deficit of forty-five billion marks, which included 6.7 billion for the railways. From the perspective of the 1920–1921 deficit of almost eighty-three billion marks, this was not unpromising, provided that one did not remind oneself that the deficit for 1920–1921 had once been estimated at 51.3 billions! The call of Stinnes and Wiedfeldt for a government-subsidized, large-scale building program to counter the negative effects of sanctions on domestic employment and activity, a summons echoed by strong trade-union complaints about unemployment, was being answered with substantial appropriations.[126] It was anything but easy to estimate the effects of changes in the income tax laws on March 24, 1921, aimed at increasing revenue by reducing the number of tax brackets from fifty-one to ten. The most perplexing problem was estimating what the government could really collect by way of direct taxes not subject to withholding. The government did give some indication that it was taking Allied complaints about its insufficient indirect taxation to heart when it decided to reduce its subsidization of the tobacco industry by imposing a 10 percent tax increase despite objections from the Saxon government that this would reduce German competitiveness with the English manufacturers and lead to unemployment.[127]

In the balance, however, the tone of German monetary management was being perceptively changed by the mounting conflict over reparations. This was most evident with respect to the Reichsbank, where Havenstein was combining a very sharp line about what was and what was not a feasible reparations policy with a decision to lay bare the short-term irreparability of the Reich's finances and to make the inflationary financing of the German economy as transparent as possible. As noted earlier, Havenstein had sent a formal protest to the Cabinet against Simons's original offer in London and had warned urgently against going beyond it. His language was nothing short of apocalyptic: "I . . . consider the London offer and the obligations that arise from it to be impossible and unbearable for our economy and our finances and fateful, if not fatal, for our exchange and our monetary system. A further increase of the offer will make this effect even more unquestionable."[128] For understandable reasons, Havenstein had never shown any great enthusiasm or optimism about Germany's economic situation since the end of the war, but his presentation to the Reichsbank Curatorium on March 21 was unprecedentedly dismal and reflected a considerable change of accent. Whereas in September 1920 he at least took a positive view of Germany's export situation, presented tax and other proposals for the improvement of the situation, and stressed the importance of balancing the budget, he now gave priority to the improvement of Germany's balance of payments, placed domestic measures of stabilization in second place, and emphasized that "the precondition for the recovery of the German economy, especially the German monetary system is the limitation of the war indemnity to a level compatible with the greatest strain we can take."[129]

Whereas only a few months before Havenstein had fretted about "Austrian" conditions, he now almost took the "Assignat" economy in stride, pointing out that the situation under which the budget could only be covered by the printing press "will as far as one can tell have to continue for another few years." The amount of paper money in circulation in 1920 had increased from 37.5 to 75 billion, but the money given out by the Reichsbank in return for Treasury notes tended to disappear because of hoarders, capital flight, and the negative balance of trade. Havenstein was not even impressed with the decrease of money in circulation in the last quarter of 1920 and in January 1921, although he did admit that improved tax receipts and moderate price reductions had helped. He attributed it chiefly to panic sales of marks for foreign currencies, however, and to the fact that hoarders, responding to the Reichsbank's call-up of old fifty-mark notes for replacement, had decided to trade in their old notes, often damp and wet because of the manner in which they had been stored, for new ones. Basically, the Reichsbank President saw no end in sight to this situation either. Havenstein concluded his presentation to the Curatorium rather dramatically by announcing his intention of requesting suspension until December 31, 1923, of §17 of the Reichsbank Act requiring one-third coverage of Reichsbank note issues. He emphasized that this would not lead to a deterioration of the coverage requirements, since it only amounted to "an honorable admission that we have a paper money economy."[130]

Havenstein of course was absolutely correct that the formal termination of the one-third coverage requirement had little practical significance since the fictional coverage had only been maintained since 1919 by the Prussian Seehandlung's taking out loans in loan-bureau notes that it did not need. The Seehandlung could no longer afford the debt, and there was no point to a reduction of the coverage requirement since that would hurt the credit of the Reichsbank even more. It was best, therefore, that the true coverage of Reichsbank emissions—that is, gold, silver, foreign exchange and assets abroad—be stated and that the loan-bureau notes stored in the Reichsbank for coverage purposes be allowed to circulate.[131]

Although Havenstein's decision had gone unchallenged in the Reichsbank Curatorium and by the government and was to go uncontested in the Reichstag, which passed it into law on May 4, some questions were raised in the Reichsrat. Concern was expressed about the impression the change might make on world opinion, and there was also fear that the Entente might think itself entitled to demand the Reichsbank's gold for reparations on the grounds that it no longer was legally required as coverage. Havenstein, however, insisted that the one-third coverage could only be maintained by "swindling manipulation" and that this would harm the prestige of the Reichsbank even more. If the Entente wished to use force to take the Reichsbank's gold, it certainly would not be stopped by §17 of the Reichsbank Act, and he believed that such an action would so destroy the German currency and capacity to pay that it was not in the interest of the Allies. Furthermore, it was not gold coverage but rather the one-third coverage requirement that was being suspended. Indeed, Havenstein pointed out in remarks that may help to explain the timing of his decision to bring in the suspension of §17, that its effect in hostile countries would be to force them to "recognize the great danger which hangs over the entire financial situation of Germany and perhaps to ask themselves whether common sense and their own interests do not make it necessary to depart from the incomprehensible path they are now pursuing."[132] Havenstein's fatalism was shared by the Reichsrat members. As the delegate from Saxony put the matter:

There is no other way and means to create money except that now being used. The connection between the credit of the Reich and that of the Reichsbank is too close. If the Reichsbank, in order to put its own affairs in order, refused to discount the Treasury notes of the Reich and thereby force the Reich Treasury to try to get its notes discounted on its own, then the Reichsbank could not rediscount its Treasury notes. Then very soon no bank would take a Treasury bill of the Reich any more.[133]

It was possible to argue, of course, that precisely the connection between Reichsbank and Reich finances made the retention of some kind of coverage requirement desirable. The Saxon Finance Minister had privately expressed the view that the coverage requirements were the "last dam" against a "boundless inflation," and wondered if the assets of the great banks and some other forms of coverage might not be found.[134] A similar anxiety was expressed publicly by Georg Bernhard's *Plutus*, which complained that the matter had never been taken to the Reich Economic Council, warned that there was "no more agreeable form of governance for demagogues and dumbheads than the printing of notes," and wondered if the Reichsbank's efforts to educate the government and the public to the realities of Germany's financial situation by maximizing the transparency of the Reichsbank reports would really have much effect. It grimly concluded that "even the present condition of our money and our financial condition would be bearable if somewhere in the Reich government there was the will or the ability to undertake a comprehensive restructuring (*Sanierung*). But where is this will, where is this ability, where is the man who would allow us to hope that both could be effectively joined together?"[135]

"He" certainly was not in the Fehrenbach government, which was truly at the end of its tether in March–April 1921, and all it could fall back upon was what *Plutus* described as a "childish belief in American help in its distress."[136] German efforts to get the United States to intervene were at once odd and clumsy to boot. An attempt to use Vatican good offices to get American mediation collapsed in mid-April when it was leaked in the press. The next effort was suggested by a group of U.S. businessmen trying to open up business contacts with Germany. In their conversations with Labor Minister Brauns, they urged that the Germans make a direct appeal to Harding in the form of an invitation to arbitrate. This was a rather unusual and, given the relatively recent German experience with the placing of their fate in the hands of an American President, risky form of appeal. The Reichstag and the parties were in no way properly prepared. Sent on April 20, the invitation to arbitrate was promptly rejected two days later. Harding and Secretary of State Hughes were willing to offer their good offices to convey a German offer to the Allies as a basis for further negotiation between the two sides, but they were not willing to arbitrate. This was followed, on April 24, by the presentation of a German offer of a sum of fifty billion gold marks to be paid as much as possible in kind and services as well as from an international loan floated for this purpose. Insofar as this did not suffice, Germany might take over some of the Allied debts to the United States and offer security in the form of a mortgage on the Reich railroad system and customs receipts. The U.S. government passed the note on, but it made clear in a note of April 29 that it did not believe that the German offer would be acceptable to the Allies. This marked the defeat of the foreign policy of the Fehrenbach government, which decided unanimously to resign on May 4.[137]

While the German offer was notably vague in various details, it did, in fact, contain some changes in German position. In offering fifty billion gold marks present value and two hundred billion marks in annuities, the Germans were making their largest offer yet. The program for a large international loan was reiterated, although the Germans offered to pay a billion within three months. Furthermore, while not explicitly saying so, they were no longer claiming that they had paid the twenty billion gold marks required before May 1. Privately, they had recognized that the experts who had calculated twenty billion gold marks at London had "erred in the most reproachable manner," and that the Allied claim that only eight billion had been paid "was right or at least more correct."[138] As usual, the offer was contingent on certain conditions, although the reference to Upper Silesia was veiled in terms of a condition that there be no further reductions of German productive capacity.

All this had indeed been too little too late, and the Allied leaders had begun meeting at Hythe on April 23–24, 1921, and then in London on April 30–May 5, 1921, to map out their future course. Briand blamed the incapacity of the Germans to present a satisfactory solution on German public opinion, but he also agreed with Lloyd George "that every nation has to struggle against public opinion."[139] In truth, both men were looking for a way to escape their domestic pressures, Briand from the cry for an occupation of the Ruhr, Lloyd George from the complaints at home that the Treaty was responsible in part for the one and a half million unemployed and for preventing England from doing what it really wanted to do, which was to "get on with business."[140] The British Prime Minister continued to think that the best route was to force the Germans to accept reality under the threat of a Ruhr occupation, while forcing the French to accept reality with the promise of British support in a Ruhr occupation if that proved necessary. Whatever the agreed upon proposal was, it would be presented in the form of an ultimatum, and this was indicated to the German Ambassador Stahmer and through Lord D'Abernon on April 28–29.[141]

On April 27, the Reparations Commission announced that it had determined Germany's liabililty to be 132 billion gold marks. It should be noted that this did not take into account German capacity to pay, as was required under the Treaty in determining what Germany would actually pay, nor did it state a schedule of payments. The crucial questions were whether the French would refrain from demanding action on the grounds that the Germans would have been twice declared in default by the Reparations Commission for failure to deliver one billion marks by March 23 and the twenty billion marks required by May 1, 1921, and whether they would agree to an actual schedule of payments that Great Britain could accept as the basis for an ultimatum to the Germans. In both cases, the answer was yes. Briand had no intention of going it alone.[142]

The London Ultimatum was largely an English creation, and there can be no question that it was meant to veil a significant reduction of Allied demands. The debt of 132 billion gold marks was purely formal in any immediate sense because the debt was divided into A, B, and C bonds—the first amounting to twelve billion (that is, the amount not credited against the twenty billion to be paid by May 1), the second amounting to thirty-eight billion, and the third amounting to eighty-two billion. However, the Reparations Commission was to issue only the A and B bonds between July 1 and November 1, 1921, while the C bonds could not be issued or bear interest until the Germans had covered the interest and sinking funds under the A and B bonds. For all intents and purposes, therefore, the Germans had a fifty billion gold-mark obligation for the foreseeable future (the amount they had offered on April 24), and there can be no question that the entire London schedule could be viewed as a way of reducing the reparations bill without the Allied publics being fully informed of what was going on. This was recognized by at least some German politicians, one of whom optimistically argued that "the Entente will only demand the 50 billion marks, not the rest. They have only called for the rest for domestic political reasons."[143]

Nevertheless, the burden being imposed could hardly be viewed lightly by the Germans. The Germans were required to pay two billion gold-mark annuities plus a variable annuity of 26 percent of their exports. It was an improvement over the Paris annuity scheme, which increased at a fairly rapid pace to six billion a year, but in contrast to the German proposal of a billion, the annuities demanded in London were much more substantial and reflected a higher interest rate. Although no provision was made for an international loan along the lines proposed by the Germans, they would now be permitted to seek such a loan, and this was a useful modification of the terms of the Treaty of Versailles. While the annuities would obviously be the major German concern, it is important not to dismiss the potential significance of the C bonds from the standpoint of the continuing German uncertainty about the nation's long-term economic future. The Germans, therefore, had nothing to celebrate when they received the London Ultimatum on May 5, which not only contained the aforementioned reparations program but also further disarmament demands. They were given until midnight of May 11 to accept it or suffer an invasion of the Ruhr valley.[144]

As had been the case for some time, some of the leading industrialists as well as right-wing politicians in the bourgeois parties were prepared to run the risk of a Ruhr invasion. Not only did the London Ultimatum appear as a "second Versailles," but it arrived at a time when nationalist sentiment was being further stirred up by events in Upper Silesia. The referendum there had produced a 60 percent majority for Germany, to which the Poles responded at the beginning of May with an uprising. The French were showing favor to the Poles, while the British supported the maintenance of law and order and gave tacit support to the resistance exercised by German free-corps units. While a powerful argument could be made for acceptance of the London Ultimatum in order to strengthen British support of the German cause, the right found it hard to resist succumbing to its rage over both events and using the nationalist reaction for domestic political purposes.

Thus, Ernst von Borsig complained bitterly over the failure of the government to insist that the Allies fulfill their obligations under the Treaty and protect the Germans in Silesia as well as resist the impossible demands being made by the Entente instead of

continually crawling into a mouse hole out of fear that something might happen this time and thus further putting off again and again the catastrophe that will finally come. It is indisputable that these demands that are being made here cannot not be fulfilled during the next few years, and that this horror without end will go on until we finally succumb to the uncertainty. It is therefore much better to take the worst now than to let things go on because finally the time will come where it is no longer a matter of our giving promises but of realities which we cannot handle, and then it will be too late. Then we will say: had we only then been serious and not taken upon ourselves that which we could not do.[145]

Borsig recognized that an occupation of the Ruhr would only indirectly affect his interests, which lay in Berlin and Silesia, and he was heartened by the Ruhr industrialist Paul Reusch, who frankly expressed the hope that the Ruhr would be occupied and that the enemy would even march as far as Königsberg and thereby wake the German people up:

I mean, when the enemy has occupied all of Germany, then the national consciousness will express itself in a completely different way in the German people than before, and when the enemy occupies the Ruhr area, then a portion of our workers will fall away from the Social Democrats and left-liberal parties and join the national current. That is probably also a reason why left-wing circles are for accepting the Ultimatum, because they fear that otherwise their following will swim away from them.[146]

Similar sentiments were voiced by the Bavarian Minister-President von Kahr, who not only was convinced that the Reich had every reason to be thankful to the Bavarian "thick-headedness" that had kept them from disbanding their civil guards, but also argued that the Social Democrats were digging their own grave with their policy of surrender. As the Saxon Ambassador reported concerning an interview with von Kahr:

. . . the experience, especially in Bavaria, is that the national idea is winning more and more ground among the workers. He pointed to the National Socialist Workers Party in Bavaria, in which the workers are strongly represented. This last view was expressed to me yesterday by another source. Before I was of the view that the National Socialist Workers Party was not a factor to be taken seriously in the political life of Bavaria. Through the policy of the Entente and domestic developments, the page actually seems to have turned. In this respect I must also think of a remark made to me some time ago by one of the best known Social Democratic leaders: "In the not too distant future a great national wave will go through the entire German people. It will be the hour of truth for my party, and if we do not grasp it correctly, then we will suffer severe losses!"[147]

For the moment, however, world history was not to be determined either by the thundering of Reusch or by the goings-on in Bavaria. While the London Ultimatum could draw so odd a couple as general director and DVP Deputy Vögler and USPD Deputy Ledebour into agreement that "Entente-capitalism" had to be fought, their motives and programs were really quite different. Vögler and his colleagues wanted to turn down the London Ultimatum and run the risk of a Ruhr occupation, and they were especially anxious to use the crisis to get rid of the export levy and export controls with the argument that they were German inventions which the Allies would be able to employ as weapons against the Germans themselves. Ledebour's concern was that the Allies, through their demands, were threatening "to throw into the dust heap Germany's entire social legislation and bring about a horrible exploitation of the German worker."[148] This did not mean, however, that Ledebour supported resistance to the Ultimatum. The consequences for the workers were rather clearly spelled out by Undersecretary Hirsch in a secret meeting with the Reichstag Deputies. While the worst immediate effects could be avoided by the fact that the railroads had twenty-two days supply of coal and that the coal supply, aside from the gas works, was satisfactory, the Allies would be in a position to charge the Germans the world-market price for their own coal, and, most important, within four to six weeks, unemployment would increase between one and one and a quarter million. There would thus be two million unemployed in Germany, and an estimated half million and quarter million, respectively, on the dole in such trouble spots as Berlin and Saxony.[149]

Under such circumstances, it was difficult for those with responsibility to indulge in reveries, nationalistic or otherwise. The mighty Stinnes was moved from dreams of worldwide economic reconstruction to hard politics by Simons's appeal to the Americans in late April and the Allied ultimatum of May. After the failure of the London conference in March, he seems to have retreated into a fantasy in which an "Economic League of Nations" would be created for the reconstruction of Europe, whose member states would give credits to cover the financial costs of the war. This would be made possible by the levying of a special tax on coal and certain other raw materials, the proceeds of which would be surrendered to the League. The League would then give out tax free loans to those nations needing them. The events of late April and early May now reminded him that the Allies thought the money should be pro-

vided by Germany alone. His answer was to return with renewed energy to the project of getting rid of the Fehrenbach government, and especially Simons, whom he viewed as incompetent, and Wirth, whom he viewed as "left" and an executor of Erzberger's tax programs. He wanted a Cabinet of personalities with "discountable signatures." His candidates for the Chancellorship were either Wiedfeldt or Stresemann.[150]

As so often was to be the case, both domestic politics and international realties stood in the way of Stinnes's goals. Wiedfeldt thought the matter over and came to the conclusion that it was the wrong time for a businessman to take the helm. If a "new flag" was to be hung out, it had to be a "labor flag," since a labor person could win sympathy abroad and get away with a certain disregard for Treaty obligations and diplomatic niceties. He thought the Centrist labor leader Stegerwald, well known for his nationalism, ideal for such purposes, provided he would take his economic advice from the side of industry. The world was not yet ripe for Stinnes's economic reconstruction ideas, and, in the meantime, Germany would have to raise taxes in order to make some payments. These taxes would have to be unpopular indirect taxes, and their passage "would be easier with a labor secretary."[151]

Stresemann was willing, indeed anxious, to take power, and since he intended to take a firmer line in foreign policy, he had sought a coalition with the DNVP. With the arrival of the London Ultimatum, however, he realized that the new government would have to begin with a basic surrender to Allied demands and that some form of cooperation with the SPD would be required. His views were shared by von Raumer, but not by Stinnes, Vögler, and the majority of the DVP deputies, who voted against accepting the Ultimatum. The basic dilemmas of the moderates in the party were now revealed. A policy of international conciliation and fulfillment could not be carried out except in conflict with the heavy-industrial wing of the party, and no coalition could be formed with the DNVP on such a basis. This meant that the DVP needed some alliance with labor, if not with the Social Democrats then at least with the left Centrists who were prepared to make concessions on taxes and social issues to fulfill Germany's international obligations. Although the DVP had played the major role in undermining the Fehrenbach government for the purpose of taking the reins itself, it ended up with nothing to offer because of its refusal to accept the Ultimatum.[152]

Strictly speaking, the caretaker Fehrenbach government could have accepted the Ultimatum itself, but Ebert was insistent that the new government would have to take the responsibility. By May 9, it became evident that the Center, SPD, and USPD were prepared to accept the Ultimatum, while the DDP decided to let its members vote according to their conscience, and the BVP, DVP, and DNVP were pledged to vote against it. Since the USPD would not enter into a coalition with the Center, the new Chancellor would have to come from the SPD or Center. The SPD, while anxious to restore its voice in government, and initially calling for a Bauer chancellorship, could take little pleasure in the prospect of having chief responsibility and thus repeating the unhappy circumstances of November 1918 and June 1919 and ultimately accepted the notion of entering a Cabinet under a Centrist leader.

The new Chancellor, therefore, would come from the ranks of the Center. The latter's problem once the Ultimatum was accepted would be precisely the opposite of the DVP. It would need an opening to the right as well as the support of the left, and the party had indeed been willing to accept a Stresemann chancellorship until the DVP declared itself against acceptance of the Ultimatum. One possibility was the former BVP Deputy and then Ambassador to France, Mayer-Kaufbeuren, who, however, refused. They then turned to Prussian Minister-President Stegerwald, who was noted for his anti-Marxism and who had just completed the painful process of forming a minority bourgeois government in Prussia following the February elections there. He also turned down the post; however, along with Labor Minister Brauns, he strongly urged another candidate, the Lord Mayor of Cologne, Konrad Adenauer, who had already developed a reputation as something of a "strong man."

If there was a candidate who could make an opening to the right, it was Adenauer, and this was well demonstrated by the four conditions he set forth for taking the job: acceptance of his tax program, which involved substantially greater emphasis on indirect taxes and cancellation of the recently passed revisions of the income tax law; termination of socialization efforts for the immediate future; introduction of a nine-hour work day; and the right to appoint and change his own Ministers independently of the parties. Adenauer's candidacy was treated with great seriousness by his party because it offered a real alternative to the only other truly plausible candidate remaining, Wirth. The latter was identified with the Erzberger tax program, which Wirth had used as the foundation for his own legislation as Finance Minister, and was friendly to the left. The DVP had wanted him removed from any future coalition government with the Center, and this meant that it would be very hard to reestablish the connection with the DVP if Wirth were Chancellor. Adenauer, by contrast, had strong support from such industrialist leaders in the party as Florian Klöckner and ten Hompel, but also such labor-oriented leaders as Brauns and Stegerwald. His tax policies and his willingness to discard the sacredness of the eight-hour day, however, gave him no small entreé to the DDP and DVP and, once known, were to bring him no small criticism from the Socialist trade unions and left-wing parties. When the Adenauer chancellorship was being considered on May 9–10, there was too little time to conduct new negotiations with the SPD and other parties to see if Adenauer's conditions were acceptable, and the party therefore fell back on Wirth, who only accepted the onerous office under strong pressure from his colleagues and President Ebert.[153]

On May 10, 1921, Wirth assumed the chancellorship of a minority Weimar Coalition Cabinet composed of himself as Chancellor, Foreign Minister, and Finance Minister, along with his fellow Centrists Brauns (Labor), Giesberts (Post), and Hermes (Food and Agriculture); the Social Democrats Bauer (Vice Chancellor and Treasury), Gradenauer (Interior), and Schmidt (Economics); and the Democrats Schiffer (Justice), and Gessler (Defense). Groener remained on as a nonparty Transport Minister, and he was soon joined later in the month by Friedrich Rosen as Foreign Minister and

Walther Rathenau as Reconstruction Minister. On the same day, the Reichstag accepted the London Ultimatum by a vote of 220 to 172, with some DVP Deputies breaking ranks with their party to vote for acceptance. It marked the end of a particularly undistinguished chapter in the history of European international relations. The most imaginative solution to the problems, that proposed by Seydoux, was buried thanks to Lloyd George's opposition to a provisional solution and British suspicions of Franco-German economic cooperation, on the one hand, and the German tactic of playing Britain and France off against one another and stalling in the groundless expectation of an American intervention on Germany's behalf, on the other hand. The result was a *Diktat* which veiled very substantial potential long-term concessions to Germany without confronting the immediate problems of Germany's failure to put her economic house in order. As for the Germans, they could now expand their domestic conflict over fulfillment of what many regarded as a new Versailles. All the young Republic's newest Cabinet of political "old timers" had to do now was figure out how to pay the bill. The great domestic struggle over the distribution of the costs of the lost war could begin in earnest, and so could the penultimate and ultimate phases of the Great Inflation.

Chapter 8

The Domestic Politics of Fulfillment, May 1921–January 1922

Fulfillment and Its Fiscal Limitations

A rather misleading case can be made that the Germans had not acted in good faith in the negotiations and discussions that took place between July 1920 and May 1921. In its extreme version, this charge neglects both the very real efforts that the German government had made to reform its taxation system, increase production, and reduce expenditure as well as the powerful domestic constraints preventing post-Revolutionary German governments from being as forthcoming in their negotiations with the Allies and as effective in their fiscal policies as the situation demanded. Nevertheless, the criticisms of German behavior are not without basis and cannot be dismissed. One need turn neither to critical historians nor to Allied polemics for such an argument. The Germans provided enough testimony of their own. Bonn, Melchior, and Rathenau had questioned the credibility of the German negotiating tactics and had pointed out that German proposals and counterproposals were constantly based on an underestimation of Germany's economic potential. This irritated the Allies and made a *Diktat* almost inevitable.

Such self-criticism had a domestic political counterpart with respect to the government's handling of its fiscal and financial problems; namely, the argument that the government was permitting paralysis to take hold whenever it needed to confront the issues of setting its own economic house in order. The negotiating tactics in Brussels, Paris, and London and the failure to take action back at home fed upon one another. As one Socialist critic pointed out, "in-

sofar as reparations are concerned, the Reich Finance Ministry unfortunately has seen its task in the past year as always to try to demonstrate that we *could not* pay, instead of working out plans of how we should bear the burdens which were in the offing in any case."[1] There were bourgeois critics as well. Georg Bernhard, as chairman of the Finance Committee of the Reich Economic Council, had to struggle in April against both colleagues and government officials who thought it useless or untimely to discuss funding the government debt or the problem of private German foreign exchange holdings abroad. With some exaggeration, he complained that for two and a half years German financial policy had avoided taking thoroughgoing measures because of relations with the Entente or some other difficulty. More tellingly, however, he argued that it would have been a disaster if Lloyd George had actually accepted the German proposals made in London in March but had insisted that the Germans describe how they were to live up to the obligations they themselves had proposed. In his view, Germany was unprepared to pay even half a billion gold marks a year or, indeed, promise to pay any sum immediately in good conscience.[2]

The Wirth government gave an appalling demonstration of Bernhard's point in its efforts to pay the first billion gold marks due to the Allies by August 31, 1921, and it is worth contemplating the gory details of what this payment involved.[3] Under the Ultimatum, the Germans had to supply by May 31 a billion gold marks in the form of gold, approved foreign currencies, or three-month Treasury bills endorsed by ap-

Joseph Wirth (1879–1956). (*By permission of the Ullstein Verlag*)

account of the Bank of France and the other half to the Bank of England. This demand that dollars be used exclusively to make payment was essentially maintained for the remaining eight hundred fifty million, since the three-month Reich Treasury bills deposited with the Deutsche Bank, Dresdner Bank, Darmstädter Bank, and Disconto-Gesellschaft were denominated in dollars. This caused not only technical difficulties, not the least of which was the great reluctance of these banks to become involved and the extreme measures they took to protect themselves by storing up large amounts of foreign currency, but also raised the cost of payment by promoting speculation and increasing the demand for dollars as over against other currencies.[4]

The balance of eight hundred fifty million was paid by a variety of complicated and troublesome methods. The government was able to purchase another four hundred thirty-nine million in foreign exchange and convert it into dollars. In part this was accomplished by the Foreign Exchange Procurement Board and in part through the Reichsbank and its branches. Industry was persuaded to turn in some of its foreign exchange for marks after a direct appeal by Wirth, Havenstein, and the big banks. Thus, the export control boards delivered an average of eighty million gold marks a month between May and July from their average receipts of three hundred million gold marks a month at that time. Wirth made a special appeal to some of the big concerns for a three-month loan from their foreign-exchange holdings on which he promised to pay lost interest and other costs. He tried to raise a hundred fifty million gold marks in this manner, and there is a record of his receiving three million gold marks from Krupp, two million from Deutsch-Luxemburg, and one and a half million from the large chemical concerns.[5] Another fifty-eight million was raised by putting up nine hundred thousand kilograms of silver as security in Switzerland, Sweden, Denmark, and the Netherlands. Most of the silver was moved by some ninety railroad boxcars, although some was shipped by sea and river transport. The Reich also parted with some seventy-three million in gold—sixty-eight million coming from its remaining gold stock and fifteen million acquired through sil-

proved German banks. In keeping with their earlier proposal sent through the United States, the Germans were able to offer a hundred forty million gold marks immediately in ten different sorts of foreign currency and another ten million in gold, but the Reparations Commission insisted that the nine non-American foreign notes offered be converted into dollars—which, unlike the franc and pound, were convertible into gold at this time—and then be paid at the Federal Reserve Bank of New York, half to the ver sales and gold purchases within Germany for this purpose. The gold was packed in five hundred sixty cases and sent to the United States on four steamers just before the deadline. Finally, the remaining two hundred seventy million gold marks needed to pay the first reparations installment were raised through a loan negotiated by Fritz Mannheimer, the energetic Mendelssohn Bank representative in the Netherlands. After a nearly successful effort to mobilize French banking houses for this purpose, Mannheimer pulled together a consortium of Dutch and English banks to lend the money to the Reichsbank. This achievement astonished even the Netherlands' leading banker Vissering, who wondered how anyone besides himself could raise fifty million gulden in his country.[6]

Such accomplishments aside, however, it was inconceivable that such financial gymnastics could be regularly repeated. At least some of the industrialists who had turned in their foreign exchange for the cause were resentful and skeptical. Vögler, for example, had received a personal letter from Havenstein inviting him to come by and negotiate Deutsch-Luxemburg's contribution and felt that his arm had been twisted to no purpose: "It is nothing but throwing sand in people's eyes when one puts the touch on business circles now and then proudly announces after some time that we have punctually delivered the first billion. In reality, it is becoming more and more obvious that we are not even capable of mobilizing the first relatively modest sums."[7] This was true. Valuable reserves had been mortgaged or surrendered, two hundred seventy million gold marks remained owing to new creditors, and the throwing of marks on the market to raise four hundred forty-six million in June, July, and August had contributed mightily to the deterioration of the exchange rate, which had gone from 62.30 marks to the dollar at the end of May to an average of 84.31 marks to the dollar in August. The Reichsbank had been shorn of its supply of foreign exchange and had the obligation to pay back the two hundred seventy million borrowed gold marks. This meant that it was in no position to intervene on behalf of the mark as it had done throughout the relative stabilization, which had now come to an inglorious end. Havenstein not only fretted about not being

able to act in the present but also feared for the future and was digging in against any further alienation of the gold remaining in the Reichsbank since they would need it "at a later new ordering of the currency on the basis of a lower devalued level."[8] At the moment, however, one could only dream about a stabilization based on a devalued mark. For Havenstein and his colleagues at the Reichsbank, the prospect created by the payment of the first billion in gold was more currency depreciation. On the one hand, the entire effort only confirmed their view that "Germany with the best of will is completely incapable of fulfilling the demands made upon it by the Ultimatum."[9] On the other hand, they could see no way of not cooperating with government efforts to pay reparations. While intent on retaining what was left of the Reichsbank gold reserve, Havenstein was willing to repeat the wartime efforts to get the public to surrender gold in its possession even where this produced rather indifferent results.

There was, of course, another policy option offered by the hard-line opponents of fulfilling payment obligations. Helfferich, for example, had lost his old wartime enthusiasm for increasing the gold stock of the Reichsbank and now not only argued that it was not worth the trouble but actually had the temerity to claim that it was politically disadvantageous because of the "justified disgruntlement of those who gave their gold at full value for paper marks out of a sense of patriotic duty."[10] Havenstein found it easy enough to counter this irritating argument by pointing out that he could see no difference between urging people to turn in their foreign exchange or foreign denominated assets and their gold. The gold, in any case, was not being bought for the Reichsbank, but for the Reich, and it was absolutely necessary to pay reparations. A representative of the Bavarian government, however, reminded Havenstein that he himself had once remarked that the gold in private hands was a useful reserve for the time when Germany would put her currency on a new basis. From the Bavarian perspective, a successful effort to procure the gold was tantamount to eating up the reserve and "spilling it down the bottomless barrel of reparations." Havenstein's response to this argument was much less determined. He suggested that the reserve would be lost anyway, for "if the gold is not bought by the Reich, private buyers would get hold of it for the high profit and bring it over the border."

It is useful to remember that the political dimensions of this discussion transcended the practical question of whether it made sense to get Germans to sell more gold to the Reichsbank. When two young right-wing fanatics pumped twelve bullets into the body of the vacationing Matthias Erzberger while he was taking a walk in the mountains on August 26, 1921, they were also participating in the domestic German reparations "debate." Helfferich had stood at the forefront of the campaign of character assassination in which the former Finance Minister was castigated as the embodiment of what had ruined Germany from the July 1917 Peace Resolution through the Armistice, the Treaty of Versailles, and the Emergency Capital Levy. If Helfferich's famous polemic, "Away with Erzberger" (*Fort mit Erzberger!*) was not meant as a literal invitation to murder, it served, nevertheless, as a legitimation for all those who actively or passively welcomed such a consequence. Thus, the official organ of the Bavarian government, while condemning this "way of making harmless" (*Art der Unschädlichmachung*) an allegedly unsavory politician, could not resist making Erzberger "co-responsible for the unfortunate outcome of the war, as well as the so devastating effects of the Treaty of Versailles and its acceptance which came about because of it."[11]

As if it were not enough to murder the man, it seemed as if some of the same conditions and persons that destroyed Erzberger were bent upon undermining his work as well and making a mockery of that unwarranted optimism that had propelled him when he risked reputation and life in the service of the Republic. In the month of Erzberger's assassination, August 1921, taxes accounted for 29.64 percent of German expenditure. It was, to be sure, a very bad month, although not as bad as December, when the figure was to drop to 28 percent. However, the average amount raised by taxation in the fiscal year 1920–1921 (April 1, 1920–March 31, 1921) was 36.31 percent, and it was to be 44.52 percent for the fiscal year 1921–1922. Erzberger had anticipated that taxes on income would ac-

count for about a third of tax receipts, but in August 1921, they only accounted for 15.56 percent; in the fiscal year 1920–1921, for 18.81 percent; and in the fiscal year 1921–1922, for 24.33 percent. Not only had the dead ex-Finance Minister's calculations gone awry, but so had his social intentions. The income tax schedule had been organized with the object of having those in the lower-income brackets, most of whose taxes were paid through withholding, provide 30 percent of the receipts, while those with higher incomes, whose wealth was subject to assessment, were to provide 70 percent of the receipts. In August 1921, the ratio was 54 percent to 45 percent, an improvement over the average for fiscal year 1920–1921, to be sure, when it was 100 percent to 0 percent, but quite in conformity with the ratio for fiscal year 1921–1922, which was 53 percent to 47 percent. Furthermore, when one considers that the last four months of fiscal year 1920–1921 were the high point of receipts from the Emergency Capital Levy and that the returns from this tax were fading into insignificance (that is, from 13.38 percent of all tax receipts in April 1921 to 1.06 percent of receipts in March 1922), then it could be argued that the real tax burden on the better-off classes was actually decreasing.[12]

This was not the consequence of some dark and evil plot on the part of the authorities or the propertied classes. Rather, it was the result of an effort to combine a major administrative reorganization of the nation's financial administration with the implementation of a massive tax reform under conditions that became increasingly detrimental to the morale of the authorities as well as to the morality of the taxpayers and that more often than not brought out the worst in both. In his necessarily hurried efforts to push through his taxes and organizational reforms, Erzberger had made compromises with the state governments which were now revenging themselves mightily. Prussia and some of the south German states had been permitted to block the nationalization of the revenue collection offices. The result was a cumbersome network of twenty-six state finance offices, a thousand finance offices, and two hundred forty customs offices, some of which had overwhelming workloads and insufficient and inexperienced personnel. The mere administration of the new taxes would have been difficult enough, but the technical problems of assessment, Berlin's genuine efforts to make the system more effective, and the lobbying of special interests with the government and the Reichstag produced a veritable flood of administrative orders and decrees, amendments to existing legislation, and new legislation that drowned the officials in paper and problems. By October 1921, the Wirth administration itself had produced fifteen new pieces of tax legislation to add to the twenty legislative acts passed since 1918. Not surprisingly, the officialdom from top to bottom found it difficult to master the problems presented by all these new laws and the implementing regulations that came pouring down in their wake. All too often, it became preoccupied with picayune questions and lost sight of the larger goals of the original Erzberger program.[13]

The worst consequence of this situation was the horrendous delay in tax assessment. The assessments for 1920 still were uncompleted in the fall of 1921, and while the first bills were then going out and it was becoming possible to demand prepayments for 1921, there was increasing public anger over the manner in which wage and salary earners had been forced to pay their taxes immediately while the wealthier were benefiting both from being able to hold on to their money as well as from the effects of depreciation. This was not the only inequity. Many civil servants not only had to pay withholding but also were subject to additional payments for 1920 because the withholding did not cover their income bracket. How were these persons supposed to save money to pay in 1922 on their 1920 income if they were living solely from their salaries? It was also becoming clear that many persons with lower incomes, be they casual laborers who would not work for employers who withheld taxes or persons in the free professions who did not report their fees and income, were falling through the tax net. Of far greater concern, of course, were the inequities in dealing with higher incomes. Successful lobbying, for example, had enabled farmers to avoid paying taxes on the increased value of their assets, while stockholders received no such benefit. An "undue hardship" clause opened

the way to appeals from the accelerated collection of the Emergency Capital Levy. A modification of the law burdened one finance office with ten thousand requests for repayment of overpayments, requests to which a Finance Ministry decree had given priority over all other finance-office tasks.

In short, the evidence was multiplied throughout 1921 that the tax system had failed of its purpose and, furthermore, that a sense of inequity was undermining tax morality among those subject to assessment. As in the case of price controls and the antiprofiteering laws, those who faithfully fulfilled their obligations and reported accurately increasingly felt like fools. Furthermore, there was some evidence that the officials were not encouraging tax morality in every instance. This was especially true in the east, where an investigation showed that large landowners who accurately reported were urged by officials not to make life difficult for the landowners who underestimated their wealth and income. Inflation was the most prominent factor undermining the effectiveness of the system, not only because delays in assessment were permitting taxpayers to pay less in real terms than would have been the case earlier, but also because it was becoming easier to pass the costs of higher taxes on to the public in the form of higher prices. As in 1919, when the "war profiteers, who were supposed to become poor people, actually became richer"[14] by passing costs on to customers in the thirst for goods that had marked the inflationary wave, so this process seemed to be repeating itself in the summer and fall of 1921. The happy circumstances at the beginning of the year, when the relative stabilization had brought a slight reduction in prices and wages and had made it difficult to pass tax costs on to the public, had evaporated.

Most dangerous, however, was a growing tendency to view tax evasion positively for political reasons. As one official reported with evident discomfiture to the Finance Committee of the Reich Economic Council:

I have found increasing evidence from my discussions with the Tax Office Chairmen and the Presidents of the State Finance Offices, that in these rather important positions the view is widely held that it is not our duty to carry out the tax laws to the maximum. It is in the interest of our people that we retain certain reserves, that we do not yet extract all that we can to throw into the mills of the Entente. This view is actually there and it has its influence.[15]

There were powerful arguments against it to be sure; namely, that there was no way to save the "reserves" given the long-term needs of the Reich and, especially, that it was unfair to those living on fixed incomes because the laxness could only take place in the realm of assessment and could thus only benefit landowners, industrialists, and persons with wealth and property. Nevertheless, the signs were growing that the reluctance to pay taxes was becoming something more than a natural human inclination. It was being justified by economic rationality and even patriotism.

This resistance to assisting the government's fulfillment policy also found expression with respect to the problems of what to do about the holding of and widespread speculation in foreign bank notes and foreign exchange. The problem was highlighted by the government's wild hunt for foreign exchange to pay the first reparations annuity, but it was also related to the general problems of tax evasion and especially to the problem of preventing the further depreciation of the mark. A major difficulty was that there was no accurate way to measure the problem. It was a given, for example, that the official figures on imports and exports were fairly worthless. In April 1921, Anton Feiler, the economics editor of the *Frankfurter Zeitung*, reported at a Reich Economic Council meeting that State Secretary Hirsch had remarked that there might actually have been a balance between imports and exports at the time because "imports and exports were being falsified for the purposes of capital flight. Imports are exaggerated with the purpose of more easily permitting the actually unused portion to be kept abroad, and at the same time the exports are set at a lower level for the same purpose, to leave the surplus profit abroad."[16] All this meant that Germany might have had a better balance of payments if the firms holding and using foreign exchange had brought more of their foreign exchange home. But how much of it? No one could question that German industry and commerce needed to keep some of its foreign exchange abroad to conduct business.

When the Reich Economic Council heard experts on the question of whether or not to urge the reintroduction of exchange controls, the general response was negative. As might be expected, representatives of the Hamburg commercial community were particularly opposed, arguing that merchants and businessmen were chronically short of capital and could not behave like rentiers and let their foreign exchange abroad remain idle. It was in the German interest to encourage the speedy and effective conduct of business operations by permitting businessmen the unhampered disposition of their foreign exchange. But was it in the interest of the German economy, Socialist critics asked, for a German industrialist to use his foreign exchange to buy up shares of the Austrian Alpine Montangesellschaft, especially at a time when the Food Minister was complaining that he could not find the foreign exchange for food imports? The banker Louis Hagen responded in the affirmative, pointing out that there would soon be a surplus of coal and that it was useful for Germany to be able to sell her coal to concerns in which Germans had a major voice. From Hagen's standpoint, Stinnes and his colleagues could only be praised for pursuing so farsighted an economic policy that opened up important future prospects for German industry.[17]

A less flattering picture was presented by Director Wassermann of the Deutsche Bank, who agreed that much of the foreign exchange held by firms abroad was maintained for the purpose of making speedy responses to business opportunities, but who also admitted that both private persons and businessmen had substantial foreign exchange and currency holdings because of their lack of confidence in the solvency of the German state. Thus, the government would be unable to tap these resources because "there is an absence at the present time of the civic sense" required to make exchange controls work.[18] The great banks had, in truth, never been very happy with the government's decision in 1919 to terminate the wartime centralization of control over foreign exchange and to let exchange controls lapse. Yet, as one expert with close contacts to bankers noted, "the same circles are also of the view that the power of the state over conditions, as they have in the meantime developed, is no longer sufficient to bring about such centralization."[19] He questioned whether it was feasible for the state to reemploy the badly compromised instruments it had surrendered. Fatalism had become the order of the day.

The "Appropriation of Real Values" and the Tactics of Fulfillment

The acceptance of the London Ultimatum, therefore, did not lead to the kind of domestic financial reordering that might have made a sustained policy of fulfillment, let alone the actual carrying out of the London schedule, even remotely possible. Furthermore, the second half of 1921 witnessed a deterioration of the mark from which it was never really to recover. These are well-known historical facts, but the problem confronting the historian is to determine as well as possible the particular mix of internal and external causes of this great failure of governance as well as its relationship to the depreciation of the currency. It should be obvious that internal and external factors cannot be neatly separated except for analytical purposes and, further, that the debate about whether foreign or domestic policy had "primacy" in the determination of events is not very helpful in this context. What must be understood is the fateful interaction of international political and economic relations, on the one hand, and domestic politics, on the other. The paradox of reparations was that they imposed demeaning obligations on the German state while undermining the legitimacy and stability required by the state to fulfill them. This parlous condition was reflected in the virtual impossibility of deciding upon and implementing a long-term solution as well as by the manner in which all short-term measures not only failed to work but even compounded the problems. Growing fatalism in the face of inflation was the inevitable outcome of these conditions.

Manifestly, the acceptance of the London Ultimatum required a long-term response to Germany's financial miasma, and the Wirth government confronted precisely such a proposal at the very outset of its tenure in office. It was a proposal that had strong Socialist and

trade-union support. As was so often the case with Socialist programs, its origins and formulation came from elsewhere, this time from State Secretary Hirsch, who was once again working under Robert Schmidt. It was a program for the "appropriation of real values" (*Erfassung der Sachwerte*) and was formally presented to the Cabinet on May 19, 1921, and then developed in an expanded and somewhat revised form in another memorandum of June 27.[20] The basic assumption of the program was that no amount of taxation could meet Germany's reparations, and that it would be a fundamental error to resort to a repetition of the Emergency Capital Levy. Not only would the latter fail to raise the necessary sums, but it would lead to renewed flight of capital abroad and discourage the saving needed for investment at home. Furthermore, it would perpetuate the social inequities of which everyone was becoming more conscious; namely, that "the owners of paper values have been the chief bearers of the burdens placed on wealth, while the owners of the means of production have largely been able to free themselves of these burdens through their prices."[21] If the RWM had itself promoted this tendency through its productivist policy, it was now obviously becoming more concerned about employing the resources transferred by the inflationary process to the public good. Hence, it would be socially more just, politically more feasible, and financially more satisfactory to tap the substance of the nation's productive wealth in order at once to deal with the reparations emergency and to stabilize the currency.

Hirsch proposed, therefore, that the German state hold a 20 percent mortgage on agricultural property and on urban housing as well as a 20 percent share in all industrial and commercial enterprises. These state-held mortgages, shares, and bonds were to be valorized; that is, denominated in gold and thereby made invulnerable to paper-money depreciation. The real values thus placed at the disposal of the Reich would have a twofold function. First, they would provide a form of valorized income, since the Reich would collect yearly the standard 4 percent and 4.5 percent interest paid to the holders of mortgages on agricultural and housing mortgages and would also get a 6 percent return on industrial and commercial profits. Second, these Reich holdings would constitute security for large-scale borrowing abroad by the Reich to stabilize the currency and fulfill the Treaty.

Not surprisingly, critics of the plan were to charge its proponents with trying to introduce socialism through the back door, but Hirsch seemed to have no such intentions. His calculations, in fact, presupposed the termination of the various forms of "consumer socialism" that had been so sharply attacked during and after the war; namely, the controlled economy in agriculture and rent controls on urban housing. In short, higher food prices and rents were the precondition for the success of the scheme. Furthermore, government participation in the equity of industrial and commercial enterprises, while requiring the incorporation of unincorporated enterprises, was not meant to carry any voting rights or right to "hinder the free economic activity of the enterprise." As for agriculture and housing, so with regards to industry and commerce did Hirsch argue for an end to price controls. Prices were to be allowed to rise to their natural levels, and the need to cover real costs was to force economic rationalization. The Reich, through its participation in the ownership of the productive portions of the economy was expected by Hirsch to tap some 20 percent of the real returns arising from decontrol and from freeing liquid capital from the threat of expropriation and thereby encouraging its investment in the nation's productive resources.

From this perspective, the "appropriation of real values" was always meant to be a great deal more than a tax program. As Moellendorff had once sought to use the transitional economy for purposes of converting the war economy into a peacetime planned economy, so Hirsch was seeking to use the reparations payments crisis to realize his particular vision of a controlled liberalization of the economy designed to force rationalization in such a manner as to ensure that the Reich would be able to fulfill its financial obligations in the context of increasing monetary stabilization. In contrast to Moellendorff, Hirsch had no intention of letting the state oversee the rationalization process or interfere directly in its course in order to impose some grand plan. He would only support state mea-

sures designed to encourage rationalization. These could be negative, as in the case of decontrol of prices; they could be positive, as in the case of import and export policy. Hirsch wished to impose rigid controls on imports, especially of luxury items, and to maintain export controls and minimum export prices as well as export levies so long as they were justified. Here there was a similarity with Moellendorff, as there was in Hirsch's recognition that a social policy was an essential component of any total program, but Hirsch eschewed Moellendorff's inclination to commandeer labor according to some master plan. It was manifest that rationalization would create employment problems, while decontrol would raise prices. The transition, therefore, would require an organized effort to deal with these potentially dangerous developments. He urged that the labor surplus be employed on projects aimed at strengthening the economic infrastructure; that is, in the building up of Germany's transportation, electrical, and water-power networks as well as in construction, pointing out that these sectors had employed more workers in peacetime than were presently unemployed. He also envisioned the government's playing a role in the raising of wages and salaries to meet the price pressures created by decontrol, presumably through its arbitration and mediation agencies. Hirsch's chief goals, however, were to stabilize the currency by giving the state a real foundation for covering its domestic deficit and securing foreign credits and to promote the kind of rationalization that would ultimately bring down costs and prices and enable Germany to compete and generate the export surplus it needed.

This program did not have a ghost of a chance politically, and it is doubtful that even its Socialist supporters thought of it in terms of an integrated total program, however much they may have been in favor of its various component parts. Unlike Wissell and Moellendorff, Schmidt and Hirsch presented no ultimatums to the Cabinet and remained on the job until November 1922. In the last analysis, the "appropriation of real values" had a political function as a threat rather than as a promise. It was presented at a time when the redistributive effects of the inflation and government policies in favor of holders of real assets were becoming

blatantly obvious, when both Allied and domestic pressures were making increased indirect taxes on consumption inevitable, and
when the no-less-inevitable reduction of subsidies and controls on basic necessities of life was
bound to bring domestic prices closer to world-
market levels and thus increase the advantages
of those with control of productive resources
and real values. Politicians who purported to
represent the working masses simply had to demand that the sacrifices being imposed by the
London Ultimatum be more equitably shared.[22]
Otherwise, the bulk of the burdens would fall
on wage and salary workers through withholding, on consumers through indirect taxes, and
on holders of liquid assets through depreciation.

The real issue, however, was the way in
which the holders of real values could be called
upon to do their share. Wirth, in his dual role
as Chancellor and Finance Minister, as he later
confessed, had "rejected the plans of the Reich
Economics Ministry from the outset because of
the impossibility of carrying them out politically."[23] But he did not do so openly, and, indeed, in his presentation of the then new government's program to the Reichstag on June 1,
1921, he declared that

aside from the unavoidable burdening of consumers,
other sources of income must be sought. In this respect, the government is considering primarily those
in possession of tangible assets less affected so far by
the monetary depreciation, namely the so called gold
values. . . . What is primarily involved are those values which bring profits, be it because of favorable
business conditions or be it because of the attainment
of world market prices. Under all circumstances, we
must prevent the war profiteers and the revolution
profiteers from being joined by reparations profiteers.[24]

This had been preceded by a statement revealing that he planned to introduce taxes on assets
"which could be carried out without damage to
the economic process" and in which he concretely mentioned an expanded corporation tax
and an expanded tax on bourse operations to
tap the speculators.

Nevertheless, his veiled reference to a possible assault on "gold" assets did not go unnoticed, especially after a press indiscretion revealed some of the details of the RWM
proposal, and a DNVP Deputy charged that

within the Wirth Cabinet plans were being
hatched to tax urban and rural property and all
of industry in a way that was tantamount to an
"expropriation."[25] While the DNVP motion of
no confidence in the new government was defeated, the debate following Wirth's speech revealed the profound weakness of his minority
government, which depended for its survival on
the support of either the Independent Socialists
or the People's Party. Neither the right Centrists
nor the Democrats could be expected to support the RWM tax proposals, and both were
anxious to bring the DVP into the government
as soon as possible. The big problem was how
to get the DVP to join the Cabinet and get the
SPD to agree to a "great" coalition with the
DVP. For the time being, the DVP was willing
to support a lukewarm motion of confidence
because it wished to avoid prejudicing the impending League decision on Silesia, while the
SPD pondered whether it should pay the price
of entry into the Prussian Cabinet held out by
the Centrists by acceding to DVP membership
in the Reich Cabinet. From the perspective of
domestic politics, the Wirth government
seemed unlikely to survive very long, while the
expectations attached to its existence in the
realm of foreign policy—the termination of
sanctions and a favorable decision in Upper Silesia as the reward for acceptance of the London
Ultimatum—were no less shaky. It was symptomatic, therefore, that Socialist Vice Chancellor Bauer fretted in late June that the entire discussion of a tax program involving the
appropriation of real values "could lead to an
endangering of the present coalition," and that
Hirsch constantly complained in his diary that
"Bobbie" Schmidt was not supporting him and
wondered if he should not take his leave.[26]

The fate of the RWM proposal, therefore,
was decided in the Ministries and Cabinet, not
in the Reichstag. The chief arguments against
the plan itself were provided by the officials of
the Finance Ministry, especially by State Secretary Heinrich Zapf, who had replaced Stefan
Moesle at the beginning of the year.[27] Zapf
viewed the participation of the Reich in the
ownership of Germany's private resources as
unnecessary and unwise. Insofar as the Reich
was to receive a regular return on its ownership,
he could not understand why the same effect

was not attainable by means of taxation. If the issue was rapidly to raise certain sums in the manner of the Emergency Capital Levy, then this could just as easily be accomplished through a compulsory loan or even a "voluntary" loan backed by the threat of an appropriation of real assets. Zapf also warned that the states were coming to depend upon property taxes and the industrial tax (*Gewerbesteuer*) now that they no longer were able to levy income taxes and that even the Socialists were supporting the proposals of the states and municipalities to solve their fiscal problems in this manner. The RWM program would undercut these efforts.

Zapf was sharply critical of the expectations of Schmidt and Hirsch. He contested the theory that the Reich would get the 4.8 billion yearly in interest from its mortgage on agricultural property. Extrapolating from recent studies made by the Prussian Finance Ministry of potential returns from a property tax, he calculated that no more than 1.2 billion could be collected. As for the return on the proposed mortgage on urban housing, this could only be achieved by a staggering increase of rents that would cause great social disruption. At the same time, he feared that the new mortgages held by the Reich would lead to a depreciation of existing mortgages, a phenomenon already demonstrated in the depreciation of existing mortgages because of new mortgages taken out to pay the Reich Emergency Capital Levy. Insofar as Reich participation in corporations was concerned, Zapf warned that the worth of industrial enterprises was extraordinarily difficult to calculate under existing conditions and reminded the Cabinet that it had already given up the effort to create a special office to undertake such valuations for the Emergency Capital Levy and that the personnel and resources needed to realize the RWM program simply were not there. He did not see how the Reich could fail to become involved in matters pertaining to the administration of enterprises, since the participation in profits had as its logical corollary the participation in losses. He feared that the end result would be constraints on the efficient functioning of management and reduction of the gains that could be made from existing and expanded capital gains and cor-

poration taxes. Indeed, in Zapf's view, the only way of dealing with the Entente demands and the nation's domestic requirements was to expand existing taxation possibilities to the maximum and try to increase the efficiency of administration and collection.

Underlying the conflict between the Economics Ministry and the Finance Ministry, however, was a profound difference over the limits of fulfillment. Both sides agreed that the London Ultimatum could not be fulfilled through normal taxation, but while Hirsch and Schmidt were prepared to take dramatic steps to move toward stabilization and create what they believed to be a basis for fulfillment, Zapf and his colleagues were unwilling to adopt what they considered a risky and untenable program that would only slow down or prevent the Entente from facing the inevitable. Zapf feared that the Hirsch–Schmidt plan would provide the Committee of Guarantees set up to oversee the fulfillment of the London Ultimatum with a convenient mechanism for taking over the administration of the Reich holdings, and he deplored the possibility that the Reich would create legal forms that would permit this. It was more appropriate, in his view, "to exhaust the existing sources of taxation to the utmost, to present the entire situation to the Committee of Guarantees clearly and openly, and to leave it to this commission to suggest what else can be done." He was convinced that it would "then rapidly come to the conclusion that the demands of the Ultimatum cannot be fulfilled through taxation," although less certain that it would "draw the necessary consequences."[28] If this did not happen, however, then Zapf and his colleagues had no difficulty drawing their own conclusion. Even with the utmost exertion in the realm of taxation, they would "have to make extensive use of the printing press for a protracted period" to meet their monetary requirements.[29]

While there is no reason to doubt the sincere conviction of these Finance Ministry officials concerning the impossibility of meeting Allied demands and the untenability of the RWM program, they at once represented and reflected the political stalemate inside and outside the Cabinet. Zapf was close to the DVP, and his collaborator, State Secretary Franz Schroeder, sympathized with the DNVP.[30] Thus, although neither party was in the Cabinet and these officials could be counted upon to fulfill their responsibilities loyally, their conception of those obligations was not free of political significance. In warning against "experiments" and the dangers of giving the Allies a mechanism through which they might gain control over the economy, however, the Finance Ministry officials could expect strong support in the Cabinet.[31] Reconstruction Minister Rathenau sounded like a typical industrialist when commenting on the RWM plan:

> ... it was not desirable that the state have large amounts of [economic] substance in its hands. The Entente will then have the possibility of getting hold of it, and the State on the other side will have the temptation of employing the capital resources placed at its disposal in ways that are not purposeful. The carrying out of the plans of the Reich Economics Ministry means the beginning of socialization, but the present economic situation does not permit experiments.[32]

In such a context, the Finance Ministry and Cabinet could do little more than operate along familiar lines. No less than fifteen tax bills were sent to the Reichsrat in the course of the summer, most of them proposing indirect taxes. The most important of the the indirect taxes was a greatly increased turnover tax, a tax which of necessity would encourage industrial concentration by the tax advantage it gave to the transfer of goods within as opposed to between corporate economic units. As compensation to the consumers, the Cabinet followed the recommendations of the Finance Ministry and presented bills to increase the corporation tax and proposed a series of measures to improve and expand upon the purposes of the Emergency Capital Levy. Collection was to be speeded up and new assessments were to be made every three years so as to take inflation into account. Additionally, a tax was to be imposed on capital gains made since the end of 1919. The proponents of these measures never believed they would suffice. Hirsch presented strong arguments warning that those with liquid assets would again be the hardest hit insofar as they did not send their capital abroad or flee into real values, the incentive to save would be further weakened, those with real values would

simply pass the costs on to the consumers, and any effort to put teeth into the proposed measures would be as politically controversial as his own program. Whatever the outcome, the battle over the tax proposals remained to be fought in the Reichstag, while the question of the appropriation of real values was relegated to discussion in the Reich Economic Council and the Socialization Commission, two uniquely ineffectual bodies with an increasing reputation for talking all proposals to death. As fall approached, therefore, the entire tax program was more or less up in the air and so was the question of how Germany was to pay the next installments on reparations as well as its other obligations.[33]

The question of how and on what basis Germany was to pay its variable annuity, defined as a 26 percent charge against its exports by the Ultimatum, was also unanswered. This mode of tapping alleged improvements in Germany's economic situation for the purpose of reparations was filled with complications. From the Allied perspective, it was essential that the variable annuity add at least one billion gold marks per annum to the fixed annuity so as to provide the minimum of three billion needed to cover interest and amortization on the Series A and B bonds. Insofar as the variable annuity might bring in more money, the Reparations Commission could begin considering the activation of the C bonds. The implication of this effort to tap German export gains, of course, was the promotion of German exports.[34]

This, however, had some peculiar consequences of which the British especially were becoming keenly aware. While the 50 percent levy on German exports to Britain under the Reparations Recovery Act was reduced to 26 percent in May 1921, ceased to be a "sanction," and henceforward was to be credited against the variable annuity, experience had already demonstrated that Britain derived little benefit and much potential harm from the arrangement. On the one hand, the levy could easily be circumvented by indirect exports to England via the Netherlands or some other neutral country; on the other, it could only intensify the already observed tendency of the Germans to shift their exports from Great Britain, France, Belgium, and Italy to the neutrals, eastern Europe and the non-European world. Thus, whereas exports to the former had been 31.4 percent in 1913, they had dropped to 15.5 percent in early 1920. Exports to the neutrals had increased spectacularly from 21.9 percent in 1913 to 55.9 percent in 1920, while the share of German trade with non-European countries other than the United States and especially to eastern Europe had drawn much closer to the share of exports to western Europe. German exports had, to be sure, been halved since 1913, but the strong competition in such markets worried British observers.[35]

The 26 percent variable annuity levied on exports was most obnoxious to the Germans and presented a variety of dilemmas, the most major of which was the attitude to be taken toward exports themselves in the light of the particular index of economic improvement chosen by the Allies. In a revealing memorandum of May 1921, Paul Beusch, the head of the Intelligence and Information Section of the Reich Finance Ministry, a Centrist who had been a close adviser of Erzberger and held a similar position with Wirth, seriously questioned the desirability of orienting the German economy "in a strongly one-sided manner toward export capitalism" rather than concentrating more on the domestic economy until it "was ripe for new world economic successes."[36] He argued that Germany had fought the war for a world economic position and lost it and that now the nation "pushed back to a continental line of development," especially since it did not have a fleet and had lost its merchant marine and colonies. The dangers of external dependence had been amply demonstrated by the war; Germany faced the danger of tariff barriers if too successful; it was undesirable to expose the domestic economy to the instabilities of the world economy. All this suggested to Beusch that Germany should not force exports but rather reenter the world market from a position of strength through reconstructing its domestic economy.

Beusch believed that the reparations problem reinforced his position. He feared that vastly increased exports could present a completely false picture of the German economy, while exposing Germany to increased Allied exploitation. If Germany maintained a low level of exports, then the variable annuity would be kept at a level that would make the "ominous 82 billion" (that is, the C bonds) virtually worthless. This would provide a powerful incentive to revision. Allied enthusiasm for the *Londoner Diktat* would also be diminished if Germany became more self-sufficient and imported less, thereby damaging the trade of the western powers.

The Foreign Office was more enthusiastic about exports than Beusch because its economic experts viewed the creation of a more favorable balance of trade essential to Germany's recovery and prosperity, but they shared Beusch's concern that the Allies be kept from receiving more than a total of a billion from the variable annuity each year. They urged a variety of measures to deal with this problem. Insofar as it was not possible to find some other index of "prosperity," it was necessary to promote industries like shipping and such mechanisms as the establishment of branches abroad that would hold on to export profits and thereby veil improvements in Germany's trade balance. Similarly, it was necessary to stress finished-product industries, since exporters in such industries had a greater margin when declaring the relationship between cost and profit. More generally, the Foreign Office advocated a more planned export drive that would concentrate on areas and countries that would not retaliate against Germany and in which Germany could successfully compete. In their view, the problem of the statistics used in determining the variable annuity had to be separated from the issue of export policy: "The striving to attain a low export figure should not be allowed to become a means of hindering exports, for then it will never be possible to get an active balance of trade again."[37]

Rathenau thus had a point when he told the French Minister of the Liberated Regions, Louis Loucheur, who had devised the index, that it was a bad one that could lead to very unstable and contradictory export policies by successive German governments.[38] Loucheur himself recognized its problematic character, but it proved extraordinarily difficult to find an alternative because the Germans were not interested in an alternative that would "work" but rather in making the variable annuity as harmless as possible. The Germans came up with a very good argument against using exports as an index of increasing prosperity by pointing out how difficult it was to measure exports in the case of a nation that engaged in so much finishing of imported goods and in transit trade, but the various alternatives they proposed all proved unacceptable to the Committee of Guarantees. At the same time, the index proposed by the Committee of Guarantees— namely, one that would combine exports with the exchange rate—made economic sense but was rejected by the Germans because it carried with it the danger that the Allies might then seek to interfere with German foreign-exchange policies. By September, the stalemate had reached the point where the Germans had, at least temporarily, given up trying to find a solution while recognizing that they had to assure the Allies of at least a billion from the variable annuity. For political reasons, they had to make new proposals, but the German Index Commission was in agreement that "the index must be so constructed that acceptance by the Entente is not to be expected."[39]

The desire to prevent the Allies from direct interference in German economic life also led the Germans to avoid any proposals to collect the 26 percent through the export control boards. Here again, they had a perfectly cogent argument; namely, that this would be extraordinarily cumbersome and inadequate. What this meant was that the 26 percent levy would have to be calculated from trade statistics and paid by the government from the same sources as the fixed annuities.[40] This was not without its advantages in 1921, because the effect of the payment of the first billion of the fixed annuity at the end of August along with other developments had produced so horrendous an effect upon the exchange rate and had led to so much speculation against the mark that the Committee of Guarantees was persuaded in September to credit German reparations in kind against the first two and a half billion variable annuity payment due on November 15.[41]

As had been the case from the very beginning, payments in kind remained a favored form of reparations on the part of the Germans; in the summer of 1921, it appeared as an especially useful means to show that Germany was sincere in its policy of fulfillment and thereby produce a more favorable impression abroad. This was an important short- as well as long-term goal, since the Germans were anxious to end sanctions as rapidly as possible and to secure a favorable League decision on Upper Silesia. The chief responsibility for this aspect of the fulfillment policy lay with Walther Rathenau, who felt himself to be a representative not only of the Democratic Party in the government but also of German industry. Before entering the government, which he had done with great hesitation under strong pressure from President Ebert,[42] he had consulted with leading industrialists, including members of the DVP, as to whether they regarded his entry into the government to be useful. His position on the appropriation of real values was what one would have expected of an industrialist, and it was fully in keeping with his conception of his role as a representative of industry that he made a practice of consulting quite frequently with the leadership of the RdI concerning what were to become his very controversial negotiations on reparations in kind with Loucheur that began on June 12–14 at Wiesbaden and resulted in a preliminary agreement on August 25–26 and a final agreement on October 6–7.[43]

Intended as an important step in the direction of Franco-German conciliation, the Wiesbaden Agreement provided for the payment of seven billion gold marks in reparations to France between October 1921 and May 1926, any part or all of which could be in kind. French orders for German goods and their execution were to be handled by private organizations on both sides with prices to be set more or less by mutual agreement. There were provisions for arbitration of differences, and Germany was not to be required to provide goods for which it lacked the necessary raw materials or which exceeded its productive capacities or were needed at home. These were all advantages over the existing situation for Germany since they permitted Germany to switch a substantial portion of its gold payments into deliveries in kind and thus transform the financing of these reparations from a matter of financing through foreign exchange to one of domestic financing. The agreement placed restrictions on what France could demand by way of material for reconstruction and thus limited its rights under the Treaty of Versailles. They also enabled the German suppliers to deal on a basis of parity with their French counterparts.[44]

From an economic point of view, however, there can be no question that the Wiesbaden Agreement had severe disadvantages for Germany. The most serious of these was the great concession made to what Loucheur frankly described as the "popular notion of a stream of gold" from Germany in the French public and press.[45] France was only entitled to 52 percent of the reparations paid yearly, and the payments in kind could eat up the French share of Germany's cash payments. To solve this problem, Rathenau agreed that Germany should only be credited up to 35 percent and no more than one billion marks of her payments in kind for any of the four years under which the agreement was to run. The remainder was to be credited against payments for the period 1926–1937 at 5 percent interest instead of the 8 percent interest granted prepayments under the Treaty. Germany would, Rathenau disingenuously declared, become France's "banker."[46]

Of course, neither Rathenau nor anyone else really believed this, and the true purpose of the agreement, as of the entire policy of fulfillment, was to move toward revision through active compromise and demonstrations of goodwill wherever possible. From this perspective, the Wiesbaden Agreement was an experiment in trying to reach an accord with France rather than an exercise in rational economic arrangement. Rathenau, having discussed the arrangement with various industrialists (one of the leading German industrialists and a member of the RdI, Emil Guggenheimer of the M.A.N., had even participated in much of the negotiation), believed he was acting in accord with industry. He was quite shocked, therefore, when Hugo Stinnes, who had neither attended any of the meetings he had held with the industrialists nor breathed a word of opposition, pronounced the agreement "extremely bad" (*überaus schlecht*) in a short, imperious letter to him on October 19, Stinnes went on to express bewilderment as to how "Dr. Walther Rathenau can make a contract with options in favor of the other party, which in no way express his intelligence and business acumen." Stinnes thought it a great mistake for Germany to deny itself the

opportunity to capitalize on the next boom by placing the French in control of German goods that the French could then sell on the world market. He also questioned the political wisdom of the arrangement, suggesting that the British would take offense and that this would negatively influence their position on Silesia. His conclusion was ominous, informing Rathenau that "in my view, the agreement and those who produced it will and must be criticized and fought."[47]

Rathenau felt compelled to respond in considerable detail, arguing that the agreement provided that the materials were only to be used in the devastated areas and that the agreement made provision for abrogation in 1923 if the Germans so desired. Stinnes, however, was certain that the French could find ways and means of diverting the German goods and did not think that a nation as weak as Germany was in a position to abrogate anything. Rathenau had been authorized to quote Lord D'Abernon to the effect that the British had no objections to the agreement. This was not very convincing either, since Lord Bradbury on the Reparations Commission held up the agreement for months on the grounds that Germany was in no position to offer more than she was proving unable to pay already. Stinnes was thus to be proven correct about British suspicions of Franco-German cooperation.[48]

Rathenau was on firmer ground in complaining that neither Stinnes nor later vociferous critics of the agreement, like Jakob Reichert, had ever commented on the agreement or made any constructive criticisms before it became public. Stinnes maintained that Rathenau had asked back in June that "industry and its representatives in the People's Party should not prevent you [that is, Rathenau] from being actively successful abroad," and Stinnes had "kept his promise insofar as it was within his power until the results were out."[49] This, however, was more than a little misleading. Stinnes and Rathenau had differed profoundly in their approaches to the reparations problem for some time. Most important, Stinnes's assault on the Wiesbaden Agreement was part of a pattern of behavior toward the Wirth government by Stinnes and his allies that had been developing since Wirth assumed office and that was to have important political consequences in the fall of 1921.

This pattern, quite simply, was to let the Wirth government struggle with its immense problems and come up with proposals which, however problematic and short-term, appeared to have the support of various industrial leaders. Only then did Stinnes and his allies come forward with a sharp attack on decisions already taken and with proposals designed to undermine the programs of an already shaken government. This tactic had a dual consequence. On the one hand, it encouraged the government to seek the help of industry and to increase its dependence upon it, a proclivity arising directly from the impossibility of pursuing the policy of fulfillment without its cooperation and support. On the other hand, the sabotaging of the government's plans by its critics within the industrialist camp could in no way eliminate the dependence on industry. Indeed, the effect was to further increase the need for industrial support on terms that strengthened the hand of its more extreme leaders. The drift to the right became self-sustaining thanks to the momentum provided by the London Ultimatum, and the character of this movement was to be most forcefully demonstrated by the events surrounding the so-called "credit action of German industry" in the fall of 1921.

The Credit Action of German Industry

Wirth was fully aware that neither his nor any other tax program would be passed and operational in time to mobilize the resources necessary to pay the five hundred million gold marks due in January and the two hundred fifty million due in February 1922. In the summer of 1921, however, he was convinced that these payments had to be made so that further time could be bought for the Allies to realize that fulfillment ultimately was impossible. He concluded that the most promising solution was to seek assistance from industry. In the course of his negotiations with industrialists to secure foreign exchange to make the first reparations payment, he had met with sufficient cooperation to be optimistic. Only Hugenberg, who represented the extreme wing of the DNVP, refused

to cooperate, while the leadership of the RdI and even Stinnes seemed prepared to help out.

They had a number of good reasons for doing so. Although the position of his government was becoming weaker by the failure of the Allies to lift sanctions and settle the Silesian question in Germany's favor, both Wirth and the industrialists could continue to entertain the hope that they would receive at least these rewards for signing the London Ultimatum. So long as these matters were not decided, it appeared destructive for responsible persons to compound the problems the Entente was already making for the Wirth government. At the same time, the plans for the "appropriation of real values" were anything but dead and buried, and both worker and middle-class displeasure with what was viewed as industrialist profiteering and the lively discussions of these issues in the Reich Economic Council, the Socialization Commission, and the press provided Wirth with useful "background music" for his approaches to industry. Wirth, to be sure, wanted to prevent the Socialists from adopting the RWM program at the forthcoming SPD Party convention in Görlitz scheduled to begin on September 18, and he hoped that the party would there take a more positive view of bringing the DVP into the government, but the upcoming Görlitz meeting was also a very useful means of pressure in his dealings with the industrialists. Finally, while Wirth had rejected the RWM program for actual participation in the ownership of Germany's industrial resources, he appeared more favorable to a scheme proposed by Rathenau under which the government would receive interest-bearing bonds covering long-term payments of the corporation tax which it could use to borrow money abroad.[50]

Rathenau thought this a "harmless" form of government participation in industry, a view that seemed to be shared initially by such leaders of the RdI as its president, Kurt Sorge; its managing director, Hermann Bücher; Hans Kraemer; Felix Deutsch; Otto Wiedfeldt; and Ernst von Borsig when he met with them at the "Automobile Club" on August 9.[51] It alarmed others however, among them the moderate Hans von Raumer but also Albert Vögler and Hugo Stinnes, and it is likely that Rathenau was given the latter's views in person while visiting him late in August in Heimburg, where Stinnes was recovering from an automobile accident.[52] These reactions, however, reflected the variety of opinions within industry as well as the importance attached to the views of Hugo Stinnes.

For political and possibly also for personal reasons having to do with his accident, Stinnes seems to have avoided making public statements of his views during the summer of 1921. He had disapproved of the acceptance of the London Ultimatum but had refrained from exacerbating the division within the DVP because he recognized that some of those who supported acceptance did so because of the Upper Silesian issue. Nothing could persuade him, however, that DVP leaders, like von Raumer, were correct in agreeing to an unfulfillable arrangement. He was glad that the right-wing parties had refused to support acceptance of the Ultimatum, since "whoever signed no longer has a signature which can be discounted (diskontfähig) and therefore can hardly be considered when it comes to the conclusion of a real peace."[53] He was particularly appreciative of an article by Keynes recently published in his own *Deutsche Allgemeine Zeitung*, which demonstrated that an economic program based on the London Ultimatum was bound to be an "absurdity." He continued to hold to his plan for a general worldwide reconstruction through a collaborative bearing of the costs among the various nations. Stinnes, therefore, had developed very firm views and fixed positions before his colleagues in the Reich Association of German Industry turned very actively to the problem of answering the Wirth government's call for help in meeting the next reparations payments.

Although Stinnes was allied with Alfred Hugenberg on some issues, he did not share the latter's deep antagonism and hatred for the democratic Republic. Stinnes seems to have had no interest in political forms whatever and tended to view the political problems, be they international or domestic, from his own particular economic perspective. By the summer of 1921, he had convinced himself that the key to domestic fiscal reconstruction was the privatization of the railroads and other government and municipal enterprises and blamed the domestic deficit on the waste and mismanagement in these areas. The target was an easy one since there was universal agreement that the railroads had been overstaffed to fight unemployment and that the rates were too low. Also, in taking over the railroads, the Reich had saddled itself with the debts of the old systems and the enormous problems of repair and replacement arising from the war and deliveries to the Allies. For Stinnes, however, privatization became an *idée fixe*, undoubtedly because he imagined it could be fit in with his larger economic schemes but also because he could treat it as a *deus ex machina* to solve the domestic fiscal crisis and to provide security for foreign loans once reparations had been sensibly regulated. Thus he argued that "only when one has placed the elimination of economic parasitism (*Luderwirtschaft*) in the state and municipal enterprises at the forefront of every tax program can we then see what truly is needed by way of taxes."[54]

Stinnes's disgust with the mismanagement of the railroad and postal systems and other public enterprises was universally shared in industrial circles along with an extremely critical attitude toward the size of the civil service and its inefficiency as well as the undue complexity of the tax system. Nevertheless, most of the leading industrialists who met in preparation for discussions with Wirth scheduled for September 7 did not think it politically wise to state conditions to the government. This was as true of those who had opposed acceptance of the Ultimatum, like Carl Duisberg and Otto Wiedfeldt, as it was for those who, like Wilhelm Cuno of the Hamburg–America Line, had supported acceptance. The two greatest concerns of these businessmen were to ward off the RWM program and the Rathenau alternative, and to get off with as little compulsion and expense as possible.[55]

A solution to their dilemmas was offered by Hans Kraemer, who came up with the idea of using industry's credit abroad to procure one and a half billion in gold marks to be charged against future taxes. As Kraemer and Bücher argued in their meeting with Wirth on September 9, this was the surest and best way of procuring the gold values the government was seeking. Otherwise, whether it collected stocks or bonds, it would be dealing in paper values.

They took a very hard line with respect to the program for the appropriation of real values, pointing out that they had no intention of voluntarily placing such resources at the disposal of the government to be wasted on paying for a domestic deficit produced by inefficiency and waste. Duisberg pointed out that "the trade unions are uncomprehending when it comes to economic questions, while they have a much better understanding of social problems. . . . the threats of the Social Democrats make no impression. If they want to destroy the German economy, then industry will stand by as the gravediggers."[56] They would only help with the payment of reparations to tide things over until the Allies were brought to reason by the further deterioration of the world economy.

Despite Duisberg's bravado, these industrialists were quite worried and made no bones about their fears when later trying to persuade Stinnes to go along with their scheme. Wirth's demand that industry make some kind of offer before the SPD convention in Görlitz had not been without effect, and both Bücher and Kraemer stressed the threat from the left. Kraemer feared a "united left" from Wirth to the Independent Socialist Crispien and argued that his scheme "at least produces *gold*, protects us from brazen assaults and brings a sacrifice to the Fatherland that demands respect."[57]

Stinnes, however, remained quite unmoved by the arguments of Bücher and Kraemer and expressed his views in a remarkably blunt and bold response to both of them.[58] He shared their desire to avoid bringing down the government, not because he feared a leftist government, but because the pending Upper Silesian decision made a crisis undesirable. He did not agree, however, that special measures were necessary to organize the supply of foreign exchange since he felt certain that receipts from exports would be sufficient to squeak through with reparations payments in the spring, albeit at the cost of a further deterioration of the exchange rate. In short, as far as Stinnes was concerned, the government could continue to live from hand to mouth in paying reparations, and he was in no way perturbed at the prospect of further currency depreciation. He had no intention of making the slightest concession by way of encumbering real values "for this government

and I might say for any government that we have had since the Revolution . . . since we would thereby irredeemably destroy the last pillars of the German national economy for nothing." He was certain that the government would take any money that it was given and "grind it to dust in its wasteful economy" and that the end effect of buying time in this manner would be the "undermining of industry's credit abroad and thereby an extraordinary speeding up of the downfall of the private economy."

Stinnes thought that Kraemer was fooling himself by believing that government guarantees to industry were worth anything. The only guarantee that would count, in his view, was industrial control over the real values owned by the state:

In the present situation there is only one possibility, namely that the state and municipal enterprises be given up or taken over by the private economy. The domestic budget could thus immediately be brought into balance without any significant new taxes, while the private exploitation of the railroads, the post office, the forests, etc. would probably produce surpluses for Germany so that the German industrial group that had taken them over would be in a position to take over certain moderate obligations in gold. . . .

In addition to this "guarantee" to German industry, the state would also have to promise to eliminate superfluous personnel from all levels of government so that the productive economy would cease to be saddled with the costs of these "drones."

Once again, Stinnes reiterated his firm belief that Germany's former enemies would soon take an interest in promoting its monetary stabilization for their own self-preservation and that the costs of the war would be shared "at the cost of an economic league of nations." There was, therefore, only one tactic that made sense:

What Germany must do is to wangle through this period [*sich über diese Zeit wegzulavieren*], without endangering the German economy and making it uncompetitive, and at the same time to use this time to liberate the democratic state from tasks which only the old authoritarian state could solve and relatively badly at that.

Stinnes's logic was really quite simple. If the state could not manage its problems without the help of industry, then it was the task of in-

Hermann Bücher (1882–1951). (*By permission of the Ullstein Verlag*)

dustry to insist that the state manage its problems in the manner defined by industry:

In my view, we face an extraordinarily critical situation during the coming weeks. Industry must show if it is capable of helping the state in this difficult but partially self-imposed situation, but the help is only possible if industry has the courage to set uncompromisingly those conditions which alone can make the assistance effective. If the preconditions are established and if we can count on the money not being uselessly wasted once again, then in my view we should not be small-minded in our efforts to reach the point where all the possibilities for another international settlement will be reached.

Bücher, who had the unenviable task of trying to define a program for the RdI that would have strong general backing and would keep Wirth and the Social Democrats from coming out in favor of an appropriation of real values, simply did not think Stinnes's approach the appropriate one, either domestically or internationally. At a meeting with two of Stinnes's chief agents, Thomas and Osius, Bücher presented an entirely different conception of the situation. What is striking about Bücher's po-

sition, however, is that while it certainly was more alarmist and hence more compromising than that of Stinnes, it was probably even more calculating and was by no means lacking in its own peculiar arrogance. As Osius reported back to Stinnes:

In the view of Bücher, it is necessary to delay the financial collapse of the Reich at least until, as anticipated by Keynes, the summer of next year. By then, the economic crisis of the Entente powers with an interest in us, especially the British, will have intensified to the point where in order not to be dragged down into the general debacle there will automatically be a change in the burdens placed on Germany. On the other side, a too early German bankruptcy brought about by the occupation of the Ruhr and other measures will have unbearable consequences for us. Therefore, if one now agrees that industry will collaborate in the procurement of 270 million gold marks in foreign exchange, then this is not to be viewed as an inconsistency after wishing to turn down the Ultimatum, but rather a tactical measure designed to ensure that the collapse of the government and the Reich comes only at the moment in which it can be exploited by the right-wing parties for reconstruction.[59]

What divided Bücher and Stinnes, therefore, was not the goal of using the economic and fiscal crisis to enable industry to dictate a new set of policies to the government but rather the timing of this development. He and his colleagues had not been shy about criticizing government wastefulness and arguing that the railroads and post office should be put on a self-paying basis, but they were unwilling to make privatization a firm condition of industrial assistance because they knew this would place Wirth in an impossible political situation.[60] Like Stinnes, Bücher wanted to take advantage of the improved export possibilities created by the recent depreciation of the mark, an advantage heightened by the fact that industry had been able to stock up on raw materials relatively cheaply during the past period of relative stabilization. The more unemployment this produced in England, the better. In the meantime, however, he wished to avoid forcing the various issues and to prevent a crisis that would bring a left-wing government to power. Osius, however, seemed to share his chief's reluctance to have the DVP assume direct responsibility for the policy of fulfillment, and he questioned Bücher's fears of a left-wing victory. He regarded Wirth as too "unreliable" to trust and saw no reason to "pull Wirth's cart out of the mud."[61]

The initiative, however, clearly lay with Bücher. As so often occurred in the history of the RdI, the compromises, whether with labor or with the government, tended to be worked out by the organization men and prominent industrialists residing in Berlin. They were most directly exposed to the political situation and were under greatest pressure to act. This also meant that they constantly faced the danger of disavowal by their colleagues in the provinces, whose hostility to Berlin and its political environment was very strong. Bücher, who had just come to the RdI from the Foreign Office, certainly was aware of the dangers, just as he was sensitive to the government's domestic and international difficulties, and wanted to find a solution that would at once satisfy the government and be based on a consensus, however unenthusiastic, in the ranks of the RdI.[62]

In this he was strongly supported by Kraemer and Wiedfeldt, and on September 13 they received near-unanimous support from the Presidium of the RdI to go ahead with the Kraemer plan and negotiate with Wirth. At the same time, the industrialists were insistent that industry not go it alone and that the banks, agriculture, and urban property owners also participate in the risks involved in the credit operation. The banks were especially important because of their international connections and holdings in German industrial assets, and the RdI leaders arranged for Wirth to invite five of the leading bankers to join in a discussion at the Reich Chancellery on September 14. Apparently, the bankers came under the assumption that they were going to discuss tax questions and were more than a little surprised and chagrined to find that they had really been invited to discuss their participation with industry in using their assets as a guarantee for foreign loans to cover reparations payments until the summer of 1922. They were most unenthusiastic, protesting that the banks had no "real" assets worth speaking about, questioning whether it would even be possible to get credits sufficient to make the reparations payments, and doubting that it even made sense to take the large-scale and long-term international credits they

felt essential without a scaling down of reparations. Salomonsohn, who was closely connected with the Stinnes interests, created considerable tension by questioning whether the industrialists present had the right to speak for all of industry, a challenge to which the textile industrialist Frowein responded by declaring that he and his colleagues in the RdI leadership considered themselves to be the representatives of industry and would resign if disavowed. The pressure on the bankers was made all the stronger by the government's pressure on industry. Rathenau warned that a token effort to raise money—in which industry would ask the banks to procure credits abroad and then report back some inadequate results—simply would not do. Industry had to pledge to raise a certain amount against future taxes (going so far in a private meeting that evening as to name an amount of three billion gold marks), and the banks would have to do their job of negotiating the credits against industrial assets. While the bankers insisted that they would first have to consult with the rest of the banking community, they not very surprisingly agreed to join in the effort and to set up a committee to work with industry in a meeting with the Chancellor on September 17. They also agreed with the industrialists who had initiated the credit action that the entire effort needed the political foundation of a broadened Cabinet—one that would include the DVP.[63]

Any other decision would have produced a major crisis dangerous to all segments of the business community because news of the September 14 meeting leaked out on the very day it took place and was then confirmed by the government.[64] The leak was very much in the interests of Wirth's political program, since it gave him a weapon with which to promote his goals for the Görlitz SPD meetings. He had thrown the "political ball" to the RdI; they had caught it and now could throw it to the left with considerable success. On the one hand, the SPD Congress refrained from giving formal support to the appropriation of real values, a decision which owed much to the influence of President Ebert and for which Wirth was especially grateful. On the other hand, the delegates had sanctioned a coalition with the DVP, thus opening up the possibility of a widening of the government along the lines desired by both Wirth and the moderates in the RdI.[65] Even the leaders of agriculture seemed to be cooperating. When Wirth met with them on September 26, they appeared willing to do their share, whether by direct participation in the credit action or by accelerating their payments of the Emergency Capital Levy. They reserved their decision for the outcome of the Munich meeting of the RdI on September 27.[66]

The concretization of the proposed credit action was no easy task. How voluntary was industry's "voluntary" offer going to be? Among the RdI directors only Hugenberg, who was anxious to sabotage the entire plan, argued that those willing to assist should simply step forward and offer their credit and that legal compulsion was to be avoided at all costs. The others understood that they had gone too far to follow his stricture and "remain standing and not go beyond the point that one happily has not overstepped until now."[67] Kraemer, Sorge, Siemens, Jordan, Mann, and Frowein, among others, all recognized that some form of compulsion would be necessary if the burdens were to be fairly shared and if industry were not to be blamed, as Siemens put it, for leaving the country in the lurch. Both because they had no solution to the problem and because they wished to avoid a battle at the membership meeting, they decided to have Kraemer present their intentions and secure support for a vaguely worded resolution while turning the modalities of the credit operation over to a small committee.

The tactic worked, but the well-attended membership meeting that left at least one observer with the sense that the RdI had attained a "major position among the political power factors" in Germany was not without its difficulties for the leadership.[68] Kraemer was skillful enough in presenting his case, assuring all and sundry that DVP entry into the government was not a condition for the credit offer, having no illusions about Germany's actual capacity to fulfill the Ultimatum, and insistent that the government do something about its financial mismanagement. When the RdI leadership was pressed on how the credit offer was actually supposed to function, Jordan replied quite vaguely, making it clear that purely personal credit and

not the substance of German industry was to be offered as a guarantee, emphasizing that the paying of the loan would be credited against taxes, and terminating the discussion with a declaration that the details would have to be worked out. While it was difficult to criticize a plan that was so vague, some members, like the German Nationalist iron wares industrialist van der Kerkhoff, were very unhappy that there was going to be any plan at all; others sharply attacked the RdI leadership for having undertaken promises to the government without wider consultation and for its inability to present concrete proposals. The vast majority were unwilling to disavow the leadership, and even so hostile a member of the RdI Board of Directors as Hugenberg appeared to go along with his colleagues' plan. Thus, only five of the few hundred businessmen in attendance voted against the resolution that had been presented. Much more symptomatic of the potential division in industry's ranks on the policy of fulfillment was the manner in which both Rathenau and Reichert were warmly applauded at the public sessions during the next two days for their contradictory presentations on foreign-policy issues. Clearly, there was a potential opposition that could be mobilized if given the time and excuse to do so.

Time there certainly would be, for the resolution Bücher formally transmitted to Wirth on October 17 did nothing more than state the intentions of the RdI to enter into negotiations with the government after developing a plan and establishing as the preconditions for the action the participation of the other sectors of the economy and "the carrying out without delay of effective measures to eliminate the present financial mismanagement, which undermines the credit of the Reich and private industry."[69] Ominously, however, Bücher informed Wirth that, although the special committee established at the Munich meeting had met, no concrete proposals would be made public until there had been consultation with and approval of a membership meeting. Even more ominously, he noted that the earlier discussions had been based on the premise that the German economy would remain intact. The effect of the League decision to partition Upper Silesia and to give the major industrial regions to Poland, a decision which became known on October 12, would also have to be considered by the RdI membership.

Nevertheless, Bücher and Kraemer had no intention of leaving the government in the lurch and using the unhappy situation in Upper Silesia to bury the credit offer. Indeed, not only were they prepared to face down industrialist opposition that might take such a position, but they were also quite accepting of the new difficulties that were bound to arise from decisions that had been taken in the Reparations Committee of the Reich Economic Council with respect to the credit offer. There, the members of a subcommittee under the chairmanship of Rudolf Wissell, who had been organized to debate the various proposals for the taxation of real values, came to the conclusion that the industrial credit offer would require some legal foundation obligating the members of the various economic sectors involved to do their share. The task was assigned to Max Hachenburg, a distinguished expert on commercial law from Mannheim, who developed the draft of a law establishing a Credit Community, of which all persons engaged in industry, commerce, and agriculture holding assets above a certain level would be compulsory members. The Credit Community would be divided into various self-governing organizations representing the various economic sectors whose task it would be to distribute the obligation of paying the interest and amortization on the proposed loan among their members as well as the credits against future taxes they would receive. The proposal had the strong support of Wirth, as well as the labor representatives on the subcommittee, Wissell and Hilferding. Kraemer, speaking for industry, initially opposed the proposed *Lex Hachenburg*, warning that "if I present this to the Reich Association, it will box my ears."[70] In the end, however, Kraemer recognized that some form of legal obligation would be necessary and supported the measure, a draft of which was sent to the Finance Ministry for further consideration on October 4. He undoubtedly also realized that it had provided a means of defeating Socialist proposals that the RWM program for the appropriation of real values be implemented if industry had not raised the credits by April 1, 1922. Hachenburg argued that industry

could never get credit abroad if its substance was threatened in such a manner. Stinnes, of course, was unmoved by such tactics. He strongly opposed the measure in the Reich Economic Council and smilingly assured Hachenburg in private conversation that foreign lenders would not give industry the money anyway.[71]

The presence of such strong opponents of the credit action as Stinnes and Hugenberg on the RdI credit committee could not have been very helpful to Bücher and Kraemer in their efforts to push the credit action forward, and the leakage of the Hachenburg proposal to the press added fuel to the opposition in industrial ranks. The action of the Reich Economic Council suggested that the RdI credit committee was not going to be as autonomous in its decision making as was intended. Georg Bernhard's support of the plan and of the credit action certainly was bound to arouse suspicion. Bernhard had been advocating a corporatist organization for industrial taxation under which the major industrial and branch organizations of industry would be responsible for the assessment and levying of taxes, a scheme critics from the business community and elsewhere viewed with great alarm. It was attacked as a new variation on the hateful controlled economy of the wartime period, a means of endlessly interfering in the internal affairs of industry and an impractical idea that would foster hostility and conflict within the business community. The Hachenburg proposal smacked strongly of such ideas even if it was addressed to a proposal that stemmed from industry itself.[72]

A further complication was that the supporters of the credit action on the credit committee appear to have taken steps without much consultation with their colleagues. Thus, when Kraemer reported to the Chancellor on October 18 that "industry" had negotiated with the younger Lord Rothschild during his visit on the previous day and had also begun discussions with the Swiss for a two hundred fifty million gold-franc loan, he was really talking about unauthorized negotiations between certain industrialists and the potential lenders. Both the British and the Swiss were only willing to make twenty-five- or thirty-year long-term loans backed by German industry, and Rothschild intended to clear the matter with the British government and then turn to the City and even go to America to promote the effort. Bücher and Kraemer strongly approved of using the credit action for long-term loans only. The sharp depreciation of the currency then taking place meant that German industry would probably be exporting more than it was importing during the coming months and would need to reserve some of its credit for later purchases of depleted stocks of raw materials. Nevertheless, both Bücher and Kraemer clearly felt that the credit offer should be made. While reiterating the standard position that the London Ultimatum was "unfulfillable" and that the question of how much longer one should pay was nothing more than a "matter of expediency," Bücher also asserted that "it is the view of industry that payments must continue temporarily" until economic conditions abroad promoted a revisionist view. The credit action and approach to foreign lenders was an integral part of this policy. Kraemer argued that if the offer succeeded, then something would have been achieved, while if it failed, "then our inability to pay will have been demonstrated." It was one thing to make such statements to the government and its party leaders, however, and quite another to act as if these views and actions actually represented the will of the RdI credit committee. There was good reason to believe that Hugenberg and other German Nationalists had only given their assent to the credit action at Munich because they, like Stinnes, believed that foreign lenders would never give the credit anyway. From this perspective, the talks with Rothschild could only be alarming.[73]

RdI president Sorge was also concerned that Bücher and Kraemer were creating a false impression. Quite justifiably, Sorge was never regarded as one of the most inspiring or inspired leaders of German industry, but he was an honest representative of his very divided constituency in every sense of the term. A DVP Deputy as well as an industrial leader, he felt it essential to warn his party leader Stresemann in mid-October against a misreading of the situation. He thought it important that his DVP colleagues be aware that the credit offer had been a very shaky affair from the outset and that he opposed public and press discussions that gave the impression that it had taken definitive form. Sorge was particularly disturbed by remarks of Director Kraemer that the Upper Silesian situation was of no relevance to the credit offer and argued with considerable justification that there was strong feeling in the RdI that the credit offer *would* necessarily be influenced by the Upper Silesian decision; Kraemer, as a party to the discussions, could not but have been aware of that fact. He also warned Stresemann against misconstruing the credit offer, as Wirth apparently was doing, as a vote of confidence for the government. He was certain that the credit offer never would have gone so far if it had been so regarded. Rather, the RdI was prepared to aid "any government which can convince us with specific guarantees, that this last economic asset of Germany will not be used uselessly and in vain, but rather with the greatest possible prospect of saving the German economy. In this sense, industry as such has no intention of having a direct effect on the retention or departure of the Chancellor and the entire government."[74] Sorge himself warned against entering the Wirth government at so unpropitious a moment since industrialist participation might make government efforts to revise the Treaty more difficult. In short, Wirth was to be left with the responsibilities and the defeats.

The entire political situation in October 1921, therefore, was almost tailor-made to delegitimize the policies of Bücher, Kraemer, and their allies. If they needed anything, it was a government in Berlin based on a broad coalition running from the SPD to the DVP that at once stood behind them by containing the demands for an appropriation of real values while threatening to implement the RWM program if the industrial opponents of the credit action carried the day. Instead, they had a government that was more inclined to fall apart than to become more inclusive. The Socialists continued to insist on the taxation of substance and even went so far in late October as to threaten nonsupport of the indirect taxation program if they did not have their way. They demanded that a stabilization of the mark through effective taxation was essential in the face of currency depreciation and rising prices and called for a stabilization of the mark through effective taxation. The DDP, however, argued that such

a program, which the SPD regarded as a precondition for persuading the Allies to revise the
Ultimatum, had to have Treaty revision as its
precondition and had to be accompanied by
measures designed to increase productivity, a
veiled term for modification of the eight-hour
day. The same view, only more strongly stated,
was taken by the DVP, which also rejected any
linkage between the success of industry's credit
action and the taxation of real values. As the
DVP Party leader, Hugo, put it:

The credit action of industry must remain a matter
for industry; it is unsuitable for domestic political debate. He can assure that industry wants to carry
through the plan seriously. The seizure of real values
. . . could only be a last resort in the case that one
came to a foreign policy accord about the entire reparations issue.[75]

It was an absurdity, of course, to treat the
credit offer, which had been a response to the
threat of the seizure of real values, as if it had
nothing to do with domestic political issues,
just as it was hopeless to treat what the Allies
would necessarily consider as the essential evidence for the credibility of German claims that
they could not pay (namely, effective taxation
to stabilize Germany's currency and finances)
as a consequence rather than the precondition
of a revision of reparations. A compromise such
as that proposed by Hirsch—who argued that
industry should be given its chance to pursue
the credit action but that if it did not produce a
specific sum by a specific time, then the amount
needed should be raised by the seizure of real
values—got nowhere. The political parties were
too fixed in their positions to unite on a program that would have asserted their political
will. Industry's peak association, whose key political role was a reflection of the weakness of
the political system, lacked the internal cohe-
sion needed to fill the breach. Kraemer and
Bücher had to struggle in a political vacuum,
and their opponents were permitted to take the
initiative.

The Upper Silesian decision, while certainly
and justifiably resented by all, also came to
serve as an excuse or weapon to achieve the political purposes of the moment. Unable to get
the parties of a potential Great Coalition to
agree on a program, Wirth gave way to pressures from his own party and the Democrats,

and his Cabinet resigned on October 22 over
the humiliation of the decision at Geneva about
which they had learned a full ten days earlier,
thus highlighting to the benefit of the right an
Allied decision that had not been entirely unanticipated and for which once again the public
had not been properly prepared. The failure to
form a coalition based on a common program
was then repeated during the next few days,
whereupon a new Wirth "Cabinet of personalities" was formed on October 26 at the behest
of a personal plea by Ebert that Wirth remain
in office. Although Stresemann would have
liked to have done otherwise and had indeed
hoped to replace Wirth, the DVP was too fearful of losing voters to the DNVP and too divided to enter the government in the context of
the Upper Silesian situation. The DDP also formally withdrew but permitted Gessler to remain in the Defense Ministry and left Rathenau free to decide for himself on remaining
in office. The Reconstruction Ministry was in
fact left unfilled. Wirth turned the Finance
Ministry over to Hermes and assumed the Foreign Ministry himself. Otherwise, the new Cabinet closely resembled the old, both in its composition and its divisions. Most significant, the
parties most closely connected with industry
were not represented in the Cabinet. This ensured that industry, whose control of Germany's most important economic and financial resources gave it the decisive role in the solution of Germany's reparations and domestic
problems, could once again make profoundly
political decisions without having political responsibility.[76]

The increasing political influence of industry, and especially of its right wing, is well revealed by Rathenau's decision to resign. Although Rathenau claimed that the Upper
Silesian debacle and party loyalty made this
step necessary, the attacks on his Wiesbaden
policy by Stinnes and Reichert and the sense
that he did not have the confidence of industry
played a decisive role. On October 26, he had
confidentially asked RdI president Sorge
"whether industry wished his remaining in the
cabinet or whether it no longer considered him
to be the suitable person, as he will make his decisions dependent upon this."[77] Significantly,
Sorge, who probably would have preferred

Rathenau to remain, felt impelled to ask Stinnes's opinion. Stinnes, speaking for Vögler as well as himself, admitted that he could not foresee that Rathenau's departure would necessarily improve things, but "in any case did not want to take even the slightest responsibility for the conduct of [the government's] affairs by giving a positive answer on his remaining [in office]."[78]

The way was, in any case, free for a full-scale attack on the credit offer within the RdI. It is important to recognize, however, that this opposition was uniform neither in its composition nor in its motives. While heavy industry, as represented by Paul Silverberg of the lignite industry, Stinnes, Jakob Hasslacher of Rheinstahl, and Reichert, played a very major role in mobilizing and representing the opposition, Wiedfeldt of Krupp was a major spokesman for the other side. Furthermore, while very special economic motives defined the position of Silverberg and Stinnes, who were both identified with the DVP, Hugenberg, Hasslacher, and Reichert were leading DNVP figures and were far more concerned to undermine the policy of fulfillment on political grounds. Similar motives can be adduced for the very active opposition expressed by leading representatives of the small iron-wares industrialists from the Rhineland, especially van den Kerckhoff and the Hamburg shipbuilder Rudolf Blohm, but these political motives were also often combined with a fanatical opposition to all forms of government interference and a distrust of the syndics and "organization men" who ran the industrial associations in Berlin. Finally, there were undoubtedly a great many businessmen and industrialists whose views were far from clear and who might find both Rathenau and Reichert very clever and applaud them both. Most businessmen were not privy to the wheeling and dealing of the big industrialists and their more active colleagues and were prepared to temper their tendency to support one side or the other for reasons of interest or political inclination by their equally strong desire to prevent disarray in industrial ranks and compromise differences. These businessmen were the people the opposition wished to win over at the special membership meeting of the RdI that the leadership felt compelled to summon for November 5 in

Berlin to consider the credit action in the light of recent political and economic developments—the Upper Silesian debacle, the unprecedented deterioration of the mark then taking place, the Hachenburg proposal for a Credit Community, and the final version of the Wiesbaden Agreement.[79]

Taking the right tone in trying to use these developments to destroy the credit action was a tricky business because pure German Nationalist attacks pleased the converted but tended to backfire elsewhere. The fulminations of the DNVP Deputy Paul Bang in the press, for example, may have gratified the reactionary shipbuilder Rudolf Blohm and his ilk, but their appeal was limited. Bang characterized the RdI decisions at its Munich meeting as a "national misfortune" in which industry had "voluntarily allowed a rope to be placed about its neck" because of its support of the policy of fulfillment. He attributed that policy's support to an "alien journalism" he identified with the liberal *Frankfurter Zeitung* and *Vossische Zeitung* and with persons like Georg Bernhard (that is, Jews and the Jewish press). "What," he asked, "do these people know about *German* needs, *German* politics, and *German* economics?" The results, Bang argued, were to be found in the Upper Silesian decision and in the fall of the mark. Hence, it was essential that industry "protect itself against its own representatives" and rescind the credit offer.[80] While persons like Bang certainly were more upbeat in November when all their disastrous predictions seemed to be coming true, even so tireless a critic of constructive politics as Hugenberg had become sensitive to accusations of representing an "unfruitful German National opposition" and were aware that they faced an uphill battle in the ranks of industry.[81]

It was important, therefore, that they find powerful allies who might appeal to those unlikely to be won over by Nationalist political appeals, and here the chief assistance was provided by Hugo Stinnes. Stinnes continued to have his eye on the German railroad system, forests, post, and municipal enterprises, and while certainly a critic of the fulfillment policy, he was far more interested in using the credit offer for his own purposes than in ruining it. From the very outset, therefore, he tended to brush aside Hugenberg's principled argument against the credit action with quintessential Stinnes logic: "If something is to come out of the [credit] help, then one will have to make difficult concessions to industry which lie in the interest of the state."[82] Hugenberg wanted to ruin the state; Stinnes wanted to appropriate it. The privatization of the state enterprises had thus been transformed into a state interest, while the exact content of industry's sacrifices had become fuzzy indeed.

It would be false to think, however, that Stinnes's willingness to use the privatized state railways as security for an alleged industrial credit offer was tantamount to a readiness to sacrifice German control over those railways. Foreign businessmen had gotten wind of the privatization movement, and in mid-October both Transportation Minister Groener and Stinnes were approached by persons representing English and American railroad interests and the banks allied to them with the question of how the Germans might respond to a takeover of 30 to 40 percent of the privatized German system in return for paying some 60 percent of the German reparations bill. Stinnes would have none of this, declaring that "such a participation of a foreign group, should the railroads be privatized, is out of the question. So strong an influence can just as little be conceded to foreign capital in our railroads as it can be conceded in our industry."[83] He felt somewhat differently, of course, about foreign—and German—participation in the railroad systems of other countries:

Things would be different if one developed an East European railroad community, to which could be joined, besides Germany, the railroad systems of Austria, the border states, Poland, and the Danubian lands. Then it would be possible to have a participation of Anglo-American capital in relation to the foreign rail systems brought into that railroad community.[84]

A remarkable mixture of nationalism and cosmopolitanism indeed!

When it came to the government in Berlin, however, Stinnes could only play the tough businessman because he could not identify its policies with the national interest. Indeed, he had no compunctions about ordering Carl Friedrich von Siemens not to compromise the interests of the SRSU by approving of the industrial credit action. He thought it had even been a mistake to have supplied foreign exchange in the summer, and it was not to be repeated. In effect, industry had to demand that any credit action be based not on its own present substance but rather on substance added by the state itself:

If one gives us the opportunity to make gold values out of the state enterprises, then we can consider how far industry can help out on the basis of gold values *that are to be newly created.* If the way is not opened for this, then not the slightest thing ought to be done, since we will thereby pointlessly drag industry into the bankruptcy of the state.[85]

Stinnes had the strong support of lignite industrialist Paul Silverberg in this program, although it was by no means obvious that the rest of industry was equally enthusiastic about taking over the railroads. In any case, the actual organization of the opposition for the November 5 Berlin meeting was less the work of Stinnes than of Silverberg, Reichert, and a variety of like-minded industrialists and associations. Silverberg, acting in the name of the lignite industry, saw fit to inform the RdI leadership that the conditions on which the Munich meeting had come to its decisions had changed, while Reichert urged his fellow DNVP businessmen to attend the meeting and called a special session of the DNVP industrialists on the night before the RdI was to meet. The coal-mining-industry branch organization urged that the credit offer be withdrawn and that a compulsory mark loan, the interest and amortization of which would be backed by the proceeds of certain taxes, be used to make the next reparations payments. At the same time, some of those who could not attend made sure to inform the RdI membership of their views, as was the case with the Employer Organization of Hamburg-Altona. It wired that its members "condemn most strongly the credit project . . . [and] demand unconditional withdrawal of the Munich . . . decision."[86]

The special membership meeting of the RdI on November 5 to reconsider the credit offer was attended by some twelve hundred persons who filled the Marble Room of Berlin's posh Hotel Esplanade. The credit offer had been the subject of repeated indiscretions, and the RdI put up a great barrier at the entrance to the hall, had the credentials of all who entered checked, and barred the press. The effectiveness of these precautions may be measured by the fact that detailed reports of the meeting, some of them quite inaccurate, appeared in the afternoon—the meeting did not end until six p.m.!—and evening papers, and it is doubtful that even the closing of the side doors to the hall, which had inadvertantly been left open, would have made a great difference. It was bound to be a dramatic event, a meeting that was supposed to determine whether the credit of industry would be available for the credit of the Republic or whether *die Wirtschaft* would refuse its help. A positive decision could be expected to strengthen the policy of fulfillment and the domestic position of the Wirth government. A negative decision might create circumstances that would lead to an occupation of the Ruhr and would certainly stir up renewed demands by the Socialists and others for the taxation of real values and other harsh measures against industry. Finally, it was a critical day for the young Reich Association of German Industry, the leadership of which faced the prospect of disavowal. German industry was threatened with division and its peak association with disintegration. And all of this was taking place in the context of an unprecedented collapse of the mark.[87]

The RdI leadership had prepared as well as possible for a meeting in which they knew they would be on the defensive. Sorge opened the proceedings with a sharp attack on the Upper Silesian decision but warned against permitting the detestable behavior of Germany's enemies to influence the decision on the credit offer. It had to be discussed along "sober and purely objective" lines, and it was in the context of this plea that Sorge announced the presence of Reichsbank President Havenstein to repeat remarks he had made to the RdI directors on the previous day. It was thus made clear to all that the authority and influence of the Reichsbank and its president were to be placed behind the credit offer in the course of the meeting.

Bücher then took the floor to present two resolutions. The first declared that the RdI maintained its resolution of September 27 to place its credit at the disposal of the Reich despite its reduced capacity because of Upper Silesia, and it empowered its credit committee to continue its work. It was doing so on condition that the government and Reichstag would correct the mismanagement of the economy and would "not disregard the well-founded and objective suggestions of industry as [they had] in the past." The second resolution instructed the credit committee to determine speedily the legal forms and obligations involved in the credit offer as well as the manner in which the latter would be credited against taxes in such a way as to take into account variations in the exchange rate so that those who had contributed would receive full value on the duty thus discharged. Manifestly, while the government might collect taxes in paper, industry had no intention of being reimbursed in paper!

Nevertheless, this second resolution openly accepted the principle of legal obligation, and Bücher addressed that issue very directly in his skillful speech in support of the resolutions. He admitted that the Munich resolution had been based on the idea of voluntarism but stressed that the members of the credit committee had in their very first meeting come to the conclusion that a legal obligation defining what individual businessmen would have to contribute was unavoidable. He accurately argued that this conclusion had been reached independently of the Hachenburg proposal.

No less directly, Bücher attacked the mining industry's proposal for a compulsory loan in marks, pointing out that the Reich needed foreign exchange, not marks, and that a renewed massive purchase of marks on the open market to make reparations payments would lead to yet a further reduction in the value of the currency. As if in a warning to those who calculated that the already evident export spurt produced by the depreciation might be pushed even further at the expense of Germany's competitors, Bücher in effect reminded them of the dangers of too much of a "good" thing and of the value of striving for relative stabilization. If Germany were to allow herself to be bought out and to exhaust her raw-materials supply, it would mean much higher import prices for essential goods and a huge increase in domestic prices, wages, and salaries. Were there then to be even the slightest improvement of the exchange rate of the mark, the result would be a "catastrophe" for Germany on world markets, not to mention the damage that would in the meantime have been done to the credit of the Reich and of industry.

Bücher sought to impress on his listeners how essential it was for Germany to buy time so that economic conditions could drive the Entente to reason. He was as optimistic that this was to occur as he was certain that a retraction of the credit offer would lead to a left-wing backlash at home and to sanctions, including a Ruhr occupation, from abroad. Bücher concluded by making a personal plea to the members that they not cut the lines of communication they had established with the Reich government in connection with the credit action.

The attack against the credit action began with speeches by Silverberg and Hugenberg, both denying that they had any partisan political motivation—a claim more plausible in the case of the former than the latter—and both arguing that the conditions under which the credit action had been accepted had changed. Silverberg contended that the entire effort was pointless since Germany had not even been able to make the first payment without employing the Reichsbank's gold. Risking German industry's substance had no justification, in his view, and he openly stated that he did not take Socialist threats to seize real values seriously. He offered the compulsory paper-mark loan as an alternative way of tiding the government over. He also made a special point of attacking the Wiesbaden Agreement, claiming along the lines being argued by Stinnes that it would deprive Germany of the goods it needed to take advantage of its export advantages. As for Hugenberg, he made a great show of confessing that he had erred in supporting the plan at Munich and leveled his fire against the introduction of compulsion into the plan. He warned that industry would lose all control over its resources through the plan while having no guarantee that its conditions would be met by the government. In the end, all the profit would go to foreign banks, which would collect "colossal interest," and the action would be repeated until all of Germany's substance was eaten up.

Silverberg and Hugenberg were followed by von Raumer and Havenstein, the latter certainly being the most important card in the deck of those who supported the credit action. Both men stressed the importance of choosing the right moment to declare Germany's incapacity to pay and warned that such a declaration before the completion of the impending Washington Disarmament Conference would hurt Germany's chances of benefiting from the financial discussions and decisions expected to take place at that meeting. The foreign bankers with whom the RdI representatives had been dealing had made it clear that the progress of the loan negotiations would have to wait upon the end of the conference. Von Raumer went so far as to argue that a premature declaration of German incapacity to pay would lead "to the confiscation of the deposits of the German banks and the entire fleet of Herr Stinnes," and he placed particular emphasis on the domestic political dimension, pointing out that the political parties were dependent upon the help of industry and that the "economic parties" (by which he presumably meant the parties associated with industry) would lose all their influence.[88]

While the response to von Raumer simply mirrored the divisions among those in attendance, Havenstein's remarks were received with attention and respect by all. He was admired both for his integrity and for the manner in which he bore his numerous burdens. It was the greatest of these, the currency, that was uppermost in his mind. If industry turned its back on the credit offer, the result would be "acts of force and the absolute collapse of our currency." Like von Raumer, he thought that reason would triumph with time and a deepening economic crisis but that if industry

leaves the path it has taken, then it will have a catastrophic effect on the currency and exchange rate. The outside world will view such an act as the reflection of bad will and a catastrophe policy. Domestically, the masses will not understand the decision. All will be against industry.[89]

Havenstein insisted that the withdrawal of the credit offer would be nothing more or less than gambling with the welfare of the nation.

As if to demonstrate this daredevil spirit, General Director Hasslacher of Rheinstahl changed the entire tone of the discussion with a defiant attack both on the Munich decision and on the RdI leadership:

The politicians have only dragged us in the mud until now. He [Hasslacher] speaks for the occupied area. All his colleagues think the Munich decision is a mistake. . . . Reparations are only to be paid by raising production and lowering costs. He asks, with what right do the workers make demands on industry when they themselves hold on to the eight-hour day. . . . No one in the West fears an occupation of the Ruhr, which is already occupied. We will deal with the slogan of appropriating real values just as we dealt with the slogan of socialization. Many works have voluntarily given their foreign exchange to the Reichsbank, but if compulsion is used, that will stop. He would like to know who actually called the credit offer into existence. Only one representative of West German heavy industry actually was heard.[90]

Hasslacher went on to question the prognoses of the opposition. In his view, economic conditions abroad were improving, while the Wiesbaden Agreement would make it impossible for Germany even to take advantage of her falling mark. He repeatedly pointed out that the catastrophe was coming anyway, that an "honorable merchant" could not subscribe to the credit offer, and that one had to have "the courage to tell the truth."[91]

It is likely that Hasslacher's indelicacies were not especially welcome to some of his leading allies, however much they had warmed the hearts of lesser-known followers in the audience. The RdI leadership was in an aggressive mood and felt strengthened by Havenstein's support. Hugenberg had tried to attack the motives and tactics of the leadership in the meeting of the credit committee on the previous day and had been sharply rebuffed. He and Silverberg, therefore, opted for a more sober tactic at the membership meeting. Hasslacher appears not to have been aware of the change, and his remarks were strongly and sharply challenged by two of the more eminent supporters of the credit action, Carl Duisberg and Otto Wiedfeldt.

In the context of the meeting as well as of his wartime record with respect to profits, labor relations, and annexations, Duisberg's remarks, apparently delivered with considerable passion, were truly remarkable. Although a member of no political party, he declared that he had a "democratic world view." He had opposed accepting Allied demands from Versailles to the London Ultimatum, but once they had been accepted, he felt obligated to accept them as well. He regarded the expression "real values"

as nothing more than a slogan, and he thought the RWM program "insane." These were, in any case, not the issues for Duisberg, who had very little use for the moralizing of the opposition. He juxtaposed the "clever merchant" to Hasslacher's alleged "honorable merchant," who was self-righteously prepared to withdraw the credit offer. Duisberg, however, proved himself to be honest as well as clever, and he bluntly sought to demonstrate that the moral position of Germany—especially of German industry—was not as strong as was being pretended:

Up to now, nothing has been done for the fulfillment of reparations. He asks each person what he has paid so far. Of the 132 billion, only one billion has been paid. He must state that actually nothing has happened until now. The tax bills will open up the eyes of many. If industry does not take a voluntary initiative, then it will be forced, and it is not the elephant-like steps of Herr Bernhard in the Reich Economic Council that he is talking about. A departure from the Munich decisions is a violation of equity and good faith, it destroys domestic harmony and takes away the faith in industry. . . . We must avoid the basic mistake that our financial administration made during the war, namely, having no foreign creditors abroad. If we now had such a creditor, then it would prevent socialization and this laying of new burdens upon us. . . . Industry can certainly bear a billion marks. The taxes being called for impose completely different burdens. . . . This is the first time that industry does something for the welfare of the nation; unfortunately, it has always failed to do so before.[92]

Wiedfeldt disapproved of these last remarks, but he pointed out that the idea that German industry had done nothing was the "dominant view in England."[93] He also conceded that while some had sacrificed foreign exchange to help the government in the summer, others had not. He showed complete impatience with the pretentious negativism of the German Nationalists, who, he believed, were behind the entire Fronde against the RdI leadership even if he did not say so openly. He pointedly remarked that the German people were not like the Irish and did not have two and a half centuries of resistance to England behind them. The German people were "spiritually exhausted and do not dream for a moment of resistance."[94] There was one trait which he identified with the Germans for which he did not care at all, and he found it reflected in Hasslacher's remarks, which he deeply resented: "To designate one's own position as the honorable one, is to make that of the other dishonorable. Such a view can only be held in Germany."[95]

In the last analysis, however, Wiedfeldt and his allies knew that the great danger came not from the Nationalists, who had, to be sure, rallied their troops to the meeting but whose numbers—not to mention whose authority—were less than what was needed to pose a decisive threat to the leadership, but rather from their alliance with their "big cannon," Hugo Stinnes. The latter had acted honorably throughout, in Wiedfeldt's view, since he had stated his opposition to the credit offer from the beginning, and the fact that he was untouched by the political fanaticism of Hugenberg, Hasslacher, and van den Kerckhoff was also understood. Given Stinnes's immense authority, as well as his uncanny powers of persuasion, much depended upon how he would act. Wiedfeldt had fought hard with Stinnes on the previous day over the latter's proposed mortgaging of the railways and other government enterprises, and Stinnes had impetuously declared that he would break up the RdI and resign from it. The Krupp director assured Stinnes that industry would not support a mortgaging of the railroads, and this appeared to have silenced Stinnes. At the membership meeting itself, Wiedfeldt, in anticipation of Stinnes, who was the next speaker, directly assaulted the Stinnes proposal. He pointed out that the Entente already had the right to use the Reich's enterprises as a guarantee and that he would consider it politically and economically undesirable for the Allies to exercise those rights. However, "to offer such a mortgage voluntarily goes far beyond and is much worse than the credit proposal under discussion."[96]

Stinnes's appearance, the great dramatic event of the day, would demonstrate the extent to which he could counter the influence of Havenstein as well as how far he was prepared to go in aligning himself with the German Nationalists. It was a skillful performance. On the one hand, Stinnes presented his entire program by reading his correspondence with Bücher and Kraemer of early September. Everyone, therefore, was informed of the actual program. On the other hand, he presented a resolution of his own which empowered the RdI credit committee, which was to be expanded to include the banks, to continue its negotiations with the government for financial support under certain conditions:

Security must be given that the Reich government and Reichstag will introduce an austere financial policy and that the economy will be freed from its constraining shackles; that the many superfluous employees in the enterprises and bureaus will be let go, whereby these unproductive existences can be made productive. Industry must have suitable guarantees to cover the interest and amortization of the proposed gold loan.[97]

As Stinnes explained, he did not wish to cut off discussions with the government, however much he wished that they had never been started. Nevertheless, while not specifically mentioning the railroads, he had produced a resolution vastly different from that proposed by Bücher at the beginning of the meeting. Industry would now be in a position to dictate conditions, and the principle of legal obligation went unmentioned.

Director Mann, an RdI director, had intended to come forward with a motion to support the position of the leadership, but it became obvious that Stinnes had profoundly altered the situation. As he later told colleagues, "here we experienced the remarkable fact that what alone mattered to this fascinating personality Stinnes was to conceal what he was up to and thereby to kill the entire thing."[98] A stream of speakers, among them the influential Ernst von Borsig, followed Stinnes to the podium to support his resolution, and it appeared as if the tide was turning decisively in favor of the opposition. At this point, Mann came to the conclusion that a simple resolution of support would no longer do and disingenuously argued that Stinnes's motion differed very little from that proposed by Bücher and suggested that a committee be appointed to come up with an acceptable draft combining the two. Mann's obvious goal was to get the matter off the floor and back under control, but both Bücher and Sorge felt that the substantive issues should not be evaded. Bücher pointed out that the Stinnes draft had omitted all mention of compulsory participation, and Sorge bluntly stated that unless the final resolution was based on the Munich decision, he and his colleagues in the RdI leadership would feel disavowed and would have to resign. The meeting was then recessed for almost an hour while a committee of Stinnes, Silverberg, Hasslacher, Duisberg, Borsig, and Wiedfeldt sought to hammer out a draft acceptable to all.

The end result was a compromise resolution which left many of the most important ends loose. In a formal sense, the Munich resolution was maintained since a credit committee, expanded to include the banks, was authorized to negotiate "initially" with the Reich to give "the most far-reaching support to the Reich for reparations payments." What this meant was that Stinnes agreed that negotiations might also be conducted with foreign lenders after negotiations with the government had begun and, as Stinnes specifically conceded, that not only industrial credit but also foreign exchange could be made available to the government. Insofar as the conditions for industry's help were concerned, these were more sharply formulated than in the original Bücher resolution, although the question of privatization of the railroads was left open. Thus, the resolution demanded austerity in government finances and decontrol of the private economy, while it called for the management of government-owned enterprises to be carried out in such a way as to relieve rather than burden the public purse. The final sentence hinted at privatization and was meant to pacify the demands of Hugenberg and his supporters for an emphasis on voluntarism: "Industry must have the security that through its collaboration unproductive enterprises will be made into productive ones that will realize profits sufficient to cover the interest and amortization on the projected monetary loan and will relieve industry which is voluntarily engaging itself." In negotiating this line, however, Stinnes explicitly assured his colleagues that he realized that no guarantee was possible without some form of legal obligation on the part of the individual businessmen. Most important was the general acceptance by both sides that any final arrangement worked out between the credit committee and the government would have to be submitted to yet another membership meeting.[99]

Needless to say, the vast majority of those who had waited to hear the results of the committee's work and vote on the resolution had little idea of exactly what had gone on behind the scenes and what the rather rubbery resolution actually meant. There was general relief that the leadership did not have to be disavowed, and only seven persons voted against the resolution while five abstained. Sorge openly stated his own bewilderment and failed to understand why a new resolution was needed. Wiedfeldt tried to reassure him that the final resolution was bearable but also confessed that he was fed up with the RdI, urged Sorge to resign, and argued that the Stinnes interests, which represented the largest German concern, should replace Sorge and the Krupp interests in the chairmanship of the RdI.[100]

This did not occur, and it was indeed easier for Stinnes to influence the policies of the RdI by not taking a direct role in the management of its affairs than by doing so. The issue of the privatization of the railroads and the firing of thousands of its workers became central, and fatal, to the entire credit action, as it moved toward its torturous demise in November and December. Thus, when the industrial leaders met first with trade-union leaders and then with Wirth and other government officials on November 10, it became clear that the privatization of the railroads had become a precondition for the credit action.

Peculiar as it might appear, Stinnes and some of the RdI leaders hoped to have the trade unions as allies in the privatization scheme. With his usual indifference to politics, Stinnes actually viewed the privatization program as one of the chief tasks of the Central Working Community he had forged with Legien three years before.[101] He noted and probably did whatever he could to promote the antagonism felt by many workers toward the railroad workers, and there certainly was some sympathy with the idea of privatization among the leaders of the Christian unions as well as irritation at the mismanagement of the system among the Socialists. In presenting their plan to the trade unionists, Stinnes and his colleagues were very open about their intentions and calculations.[102] They proposed that the privatization be implemented on the basis of an Enabling Act that would be passed simultaneously with the initiation of the credit action. Stinnes insisted, quite plausibly, that this could not be done against the will of the workers, while Silverberg admitted that industry's plan was "revolutionizing" but necessary. The intention was not to throw thousands of workers onto the street, but rather to find new employment for them through a massive government land-settlement policy that Stinnes announced would cost some twenty billion marks. Exactly how the government was to produce this not-inconsequential sum was not revealed, but Stinnes's real point was that the outside world would only help Germany if her economy was made healthy. This could not be done through taxes, but only through following the model by which German industry had recovered. If the railroads followed the model of industry, then "they would not even be recognizable in 12 to 18 months." Industry "was intact and was the only part of the economy capable of getting credit," but this was personal credit, and it could not be risked for a "five-month stay of execution." Stinnes warned that "by May things will be even worse than now. The Reich will fall apart and all that will be left will be a formation like Austria in central Germany." He rejected the idea that the German export offensive would bring the outside world to reason. He certainly was for continuing it "but not talking about it," and he cogently pointed out that it was based on an exploitation of German labor through low wages that might be defensible if used for short-term gains but that certainly could not be continued for forty-two years of annuities. None of this, however, did much to win the hearts and minds of the trade unionists. While the Christian leader Baltrusch was willing to "go part of the way with industry," he warned that complete privatization was out of the question. The Socialist trade-union leader, Adolf Cohen, however, issued a total rejection, pointing out that they would rather forget the entire credit action than accept such conditions and that they would fight the industrial plan "with all the means at our disposal." Bücher could only respond by begging that the Socialists not came to any overhasty decisions before hearing industry out.

In meetings with Wirth and other government leaders, Sorge initially trod rather gingerly and tried to cover up industry's changed approach by saying that the "basis for the credit action had shifted somewhat," but Wirth wanted a clear answer, since it appeared to him that "the idea that industry would provide credit on the basis of its own substance seems to have been given up." Bücher sought to soften this change by arguing that industry's credit could not amount to more than fifty million pounds, which was clearly insufficient, and that a solid base could only be created if the railroad system operated at a profit. Since the Reich was incapable of bringing this about, the railroads had to be placed in private hands. Siemens also sought to put a better face on the matter by pointing out that industry had always insisted on guarantees in connection with the credit offer, but Stinnes, as always, was much more aggressive, virtually arguing that industry was doing the government a great favor with its privatization program since he viewed it as an "enormous risk."[103]

Stinnes's enthusiasm for the privatization of the railroads was genuine, but it was not shared by all of his allies, let alone by his opponents on the credit issue in the RdI. Thus, Rudolf Blohm may have welcomed the privatization issue as a means of sabotaging the credit offer but was most unenthusiastic about privatization since, as he told Hugenberg, "I fear that it will give Herr Stinnes the means by which at the very least he can gain an overwhelming influence over the railroads and the post office."[104] The Stinnes scheme was also opposed by the leadership of the electrotechnical, textile, and foodstuffs industries. Krupp executives Wiedfeldt and Sorge, as well as Gustav Krupp von Bohlen und Halbach opposed it, and Duisberg had nothing but contempt for the entire idea. In Duisberg's view, it was an illustration of how Stinnes "seldom thinks deeply, but usually only acts, while leaving it to others to do the work." One piece of work Duisberg apparently did not intend to do for Stinnes was sinking his good money into the railroads.[105]

The Socialist trade unions, of course, had no intention of giving Duisberg any such opportunity or of allowing the "appropriation of real values" to be transformed into what the Socialist trade-union leader Tarnow called the "appropriation of Reich values," and their direct response was to issue Ten Demands with Respect to Taxation and Financial Policy on November 21, which called for the implementation of the RWM program for government participation in real assets, socialization of the coal industry, a host of tax measures aimed at the propertied, foreign exchange controls, higher export levies, control of private monopolies, and reform in the management of the railroad system.[106]

This was precisely the reaction which Duisberg and like-minded supporters of the credit action had feared, and he could only hope that the projected discussions between the RdI credit committee and the banks would get the credit action launched again before things became worse.[107] An important concern, of course, was what the government would do. There was no question in Wirth's mind that industry's demands could not be met, and he deplored the RdI's November 5 resolution because "it gave no consideration to domestic political conditions." Wirth could hardly ignore SPD charges that the Stinnes plan would turn Germany into a "money republic par excellence" and would meet with the "united resistance of labor." Not surprisingly, Transport Minister Groener, whose battles with Stinnes went back to the war, fought tooth and nail against the idea of privatization and roundly declared that it was "Stinnes's intention to rule Germany economically and thereby politically." Groener contested that the deficit simply was the product of mismanagement, pointing to the effects of the war on the system and assured one and all of his intention to bring about reforms. The attack on the railroads had in fact backfired miserably thanks to Stinnes. When his fellow industrialist Paul Reusch complained bitterly to Bücher that Groener had set up a propaganda agency to cover up the mismanagement and constant concessions to "the factory councils and the other lazy good-for-nothings" in the railroad and postal system and called on the RdI to counter such self-justificatory efforts, Bücher assured him that the RdI had every intention of doing so. He blamed Groener's success on the precipitous behavior on November 5 of the RdI, which sought to turn the Stinnes resolution into immediate policy without preparing the public: "I already warned in the discussions at that time that it

was self-defeating to go before the public with such a far-reaching demand which ran against the feelings of the great mass of the people without the necessary preparatory work having been done."[108]

Even with better preparation and without Groener's opposition, however, privatization was politically untenable. But this also made the credit offer virtually impossible, and the problem for Wirth remained how to raise the money he needed to pay the next reparations payments, the due dates of which were rapidly approaching. In Wirth's view, a domestic political crisis over the situation was pointless because it would not lead to a widening of the government in the existing situation.[109] The deterioration of the mark was undermining Germany's credit further and driving Wirth to the conclusion that only a reparations moratorium could save the situation, but the Allies were insisting that the next payments, intended for Belgium, be made before a moratorium could be considered. The long-term credits supposedly to be gained from the shaky RdI credit action could not even be negotiated until the Washington Disarmament Conference (then in progress) came to an end. The only solution, therefore, was short-term credits, a device already tried in the case of the Mendelssohn credit for the first reparations payment and the repayment of which had proven extraordinarily difficult.[110]

Even if Wirth had wished to strike back at industry for its performance on November 5, this was no time to do so, for the grotesque consequence of the reparations situation was that he needed help from wherever he could get it, either to procure short-term credits or to be able to demonstrate that they were not to be gotten. In close collaboration with Havenstein and Bücher, therefore, he launched a two-pronged approach deliberately designed to lead nowhere. On the one hand, he asked Havenstein to appeal directly to Montagu Norman, Governor of the Bank of England, for short-term credits. On the other hand, he addressed a letter to Bücher on November 12 asking industry to provide five hundred million in foreign exchange as a short-term credit to the government independently of the long-term industrial credit action still under discussion. Both the

sending of this letter and the response were pre-
arranged between the two men. Bücher was to
respond negatively, pointing out that industry
could not take the credit needed without destroying its capacity to buy raw materials and
provide the government with foreign exchange
to import food in the coming year. The Reparations Commission was to be informed of this
reply once the reply from London, also expected to be negative, was received.[111]

Here was an arrangement between industry
and the government that could work; that is, a
prearranged request and refusal fashioned to
demonstrate Germany's incapacity to pay! It
should not be thought, however, that Wirth had
entirely given up on a real credit action by industry. Indeed, to promote the cause, he decided to create his own committee composed of
the industrialists Hugenberg, Kraemer, and
Bücher and a number of eminent bankers, including Havenstein, Mendelssohn, Melchior,
Urbig, and von Stauss.[112] The fact that a majority of bankers served on this committee was not
lost on hostile industrialists, like Rudolf
Blohm, who suspected that Wirth was intend-
ing to play off the two groups against each other
and that the bankers viewed the credit action as
a means by which they could recover their lost
position *vis à vis* industry:

The banks have naturally suffered from always having to work only in paper. For them, the financing of
this huge gold action is naturally made to order. I also
attribute to the banks enough perspicacity to know
that it will not just be one action. If the Reich now
gets the help of industry, then it will take this extraordinarily agreeable way for each of the 132 or more
billion and the resistance will become more difficult
each time. The banks would like to take the entire
leadership in their hands right now and negotiate the
credit independently with the foreign lenders. Before
the war industry was to a large extent in the power of
the banks, while in the war and afterward industry
had rewon its independence. That is a thorn in their
flesh, and they grabbed hold with both hands once industry came forth with its unfortunate credit idea.[113]

The paranoia of persons like Blohm undoubtedly was intensified when the Hachenburg proposal formally passed the Reich Economic
Council on December 10 and was sent to the
government to be framed into legislation. Yet,
even Hirsch had ceased to take the matter seriously. He thought it useful to push the plan for-

ward for domestic political reasons, but he did
not think it had any further significance for the
reparations question. By this time, the government had decided to seek its salvation in a moratorium and return to its tax program. The
credit action was dead and with it the most genuine phase in the life of the policy of fulfillment.[114]

As might be expected, the arrogance and self-
serving defiance of German industry was
sharply attacked in the left-wing and liberal
press, and the posture of industry also made a
very bad impression abroad. From a historical
perspective, however, these criticisms skirted
the fundamental problem raised by the credit
offer, which would have existed whether it succeeded or failed. Some contemporaries understood this problem from the outset. The question was why this kind of solution had to be
considered in the first place. As Anton Feiler
had pointed out in a meeting of the Socialization Commission on October 7, the state allegedly had the power to enforce the general obligation to pay taxes just as it had the power to
demand universal military service. In this context, the industrial credit offer reflected a breakdown of state power:

What we do not have today is the power of the state,
and this as much with respect to its organization—
the apparatus does not function—as above all with
respect to the political power which must be exercised for these purposes. It is just this plan of industry
that is for me a sign of the weakness of the state which
we presently experience. The state would in and of
itself be legally completely in the position to force by
order that which is being voluntarily being offered. It
is certainly legally in the position to do so, but it does
not feel politically strong enough. Rather we stand
before the fact that once again confirms the line of
Lassalle: "The true constitution is the existing power
relationships." That means in other words: independently of the state, alongside the state there exist
social forces and powers which are stronger than the
democratic parliament. This is the fact before which
we stand.[115]

This danger existed for Feiler even though industry at the time appeared to be tying its fate
to that of the democratic state. After November
5, even this positive consideration had proven
untenable, and yet where was the state to turn,
a state without credit, a state with inadequate
authority and power, a state succumbing to inflation?

Salvation from London?

The government's inability to procure support from the most important social group in German society with access to credit only served to strengthen the tendency to seek salvation abroad. This inclination was particularly reinforced by Moritz Bonn, who had a very strong influence on Wirth and reparations policy during this period. Bonn had visited England, where he held discussions with Sir Basil Blackett, who served as a reparations expert, and he seems to have had access to Ambassador D'Abernon in Berlin. Bonn does not appear to have thought much of the industrial credit offer as a solution to the reparations problem. As he told Wirth in a letter of November 18, he doubted that the international credit market could provide the long-term credits required on the basis of the securities industry had to offer, and he believed that industry needed what credits it could get for itself and to assist the government with food imports. That is, the industrial credit proposal was a dead end even without the "unfulfillable conditions" the RdI had presented. Bonn saw only two possibilities to deal with the immediate crisis that would be created by the demand of the Reparations Commission for the payment of the January and February installments. The first, which appeared to be favored by Blackett in his conversations with Bonn, was a short-term credit to serve as a bridge while a moratorium was negotiated; the second, which he considered undesirable for psychological reasons, was either the sale of the gold in the Reichsbank or mortgaging the gold to the Bank of England. Most important, in his view, however, was to maneuver the Reparations Commission out of the decision-making process through a direct appeal to Lloyd George since a Bank of England loan would only be possible with the support of the English government. If the Bank of England would not grant a credit, then one could begin considering a cessation of payments and had to weigh the consequences both of a Ruhr occupation and of the kind of control of German finances which some Englishmen considered the essential precondition for a loan.[116]

While Wirth, Havenstein, and the Reich government had little disposition either to mort-

gage the gold in the Reichsbank or to submit to financial control, the basic program of approaching the English for a moratorium and loan and circumventing the Reparations Commission was very much on the agenda at the end of 1921. Whereas the Reich government had placed its hopes in American intervention prior to the London Ultimatum, so now it sought to be rescued with a moratorium on payments through English intervention. In contrast to the situation at the turn of the previous year, however, reports from England indicated good reason to expect some positive support from the English. Continued high unemployment and economic crisis at home and conflicts with the French over disarmament and Near Eastern issues were driving Lloyd George and other prominent Englishmen inside and outside the government to question the feasibility of the schedule of the London Ultimatum and to seek a program of international economic reconstruction that would include Germany. Movement toward a settlement in Ireland and a positive turn in relations with the United States as well as signals that some French leaders were interested in a more sensible management of the reparations question also encouraged the British government to turn its attention to problems of European economic reconstruction.[117] In Wirth's view, the French thought in political terms, while the British thought in economic terms, and only the latter way of thinking could bring Germany relief and prevent the occupation of the Ruhr once Germany announced that it could not make its January and February payments. The Germans, to be sure, had every reason not to take British support for granted. The leaders of English finance and government continued to suspect the Germans of promoting inflation and state bankruptcy to escape reparations and to entertain a fairly rosy picture of the state of German industry. In early November, Wirth was very fearful that the British had accepted the "fairy tale so zealously propagated by the French that we are faithless debtors who are capable of paying but are trying to set in motion a deceptive bankruptcy by artificially increasing our inflation."[118] What the French press was saying was well summarized by the German embassy in Paris:

The German bankruptcy is being systematically prepared in order to evade the fulfillment of the treaty obligations. The whole thing is a big swindle. The government is also guilty because it continuously prints new paper but is not at all serious about its plans to appropriate the available wealth and income. Everybody is speculating and buying foreign money in order to bring down the mark. Industry, especially the great companies are fully employed and are making plenty, but place their money abroad. Everywhere outside of Germany, large firms are being acquired with German capital. Taxes are not being paid, but huge salaries are granted in order to make the purchasing power of the mark worse. In one and the same breath, there are complaints that every demand of the workers for increased compensation are given in to and that the employers are abusing their power over the workers by depressing wages and thereby keeping costs as low as possible for the purpose of dumping. In general, the view is that Germany is working systematically toward bankruptcy because it knows that "weakness is the equivalent of victory."[119]

The French naturally had a very special interest in making Germany's weakness the price of defeat rather than the path to victory. They viewed the stabilization of the mark as a means of encasing the Germans in an Iron Maiden of reparations.

The German government was well aware that there was widespread feeling in Europe that the Germans were deliberately promoting inflation to escape reparations. In Naples, for example, where "not only merchants and bankers, but also shopkeepers, white-collar workers, small artisans, lawyers, and students" were losing four-fifths of the lire they had invested in marks thanks to the depreciation the German currency was undergoing in the second half of 1921, a leading newspaper was warning "that things will soon come to the point where the Reichsmark, which has been bought with the 'savings' of the entire world, will only be useful as wallpaper."[120] As the local German representatives reported, however, businessmen in the area continued to entertain an "incomprehensible optimism with respect to the financial situation of Germany, which has its chief source in the false belief that the German government has artificially brought about the fall of the mark with the clever calculation that it could thereby demonstrate its inability to make reparation."

The sunny disposition of Neapolitan holders of marks was not shared by their counterparts in Amsterdam and London. Thus, when Ludwig Bendix of the Foreign Exchange Procurement Board went on a tour of the financial centers of the Netherlands and England at the end of 1921 before returning to his post in New York, he found the Dutch much less friendly to Germany than before and reported that "this change of attitude is partially to be explained by the extraordinary losses which the Dutch commercial world and especially the Dutch public has suffered from holding marks."[121] Similarly, the editor of an influential British journal gave some very Calvinistic warnings to Moritz Bonn:

The point is tens of thousands of people have invested in German currency. Now the German financial policy is clearly to expedite technical bankruptcy as a demonstration of Germany's incapacity to meet the gold mark reparations, and this is the point we have reached. But there is a psychological and human corollary which I submit is of vital German importance. It is this: Everybody who bought German marks paid tribute to the industry and efficiency, the power and the financial honesty of Germany. In plain words, they put their money on German recovery; they banked on you. If you repudiate, or the currency gets depreciated beyond all chance of recovery, tens of thousands of people, who would be good friends of Germany, will become *bitter enemies.* . . . The danger today is that you are abusing the confidence of tens of thousands of foreigners in peace, thereby alienating the immensely strong lien which you hold through marks on the world's sympathy.[122]

Private creditors and mark speculators, however, were to discover repeatedly that they were not the ones to determine the economic and political relations among great powers. Also, the financial interests involved could be said to have had their own stake in giving the Germans a breathing space, since German bankruptcy would hardly serve the London banks who had invested five million to six million pounds in credit to German importers.[123] This was a substantial speculation on the future of the German mark. Bendix found the British bankers in a listening mood, therefore, despite their distress over German financial and monetary mismanagement. His discussions with Goodenough, head of Barclay's Bank, and McKenna, head of the London Joint City and Midland

Bank, were especially notable since "both gentlemen emphasized to me that a moratorium on Germany's reparations obligations had to be striven for in England's interests," and McKenna went so far as to suggest that his French banking colleagues were beginning to take a similar view and that the American banking community and even the Morgan firm were beginning to contemplate doing something to alleviate the situation. To be sure, the two English bankers were adamant that the Germans had to pay for a moratorium by ceasing to print new money and balancing their budget, and Bendix tried to reassure them by pointing out that the Reichsbank had only accelerated its printing in order to meet reparations demands so that the diminution of Germany's reparations obligations would necessarily lead to an improvement of its budget and a slowing down of the printing press.[124]

Thus, there was a mood in England that German leaders could and did cultivate. Professor Moritz Bonn and the general director of the AEG, Felix Deutsch, had also visited London in an effort to influence opinion there. Havenstein's appeal to Norman for credits, for example, was directly inspired by British banker Lord Kindersley of the Lazard Brothers firm (he was also a Bank of England director), who had been involved with the Mendelssohn loan made in connection with the August reparations payment and who had told Wirth that the British were ready to make a loan if the payment schedule were changed. The fact that Kindersley had lost a son in the war and was viewed as anti-German and that he worked closely with Bradbury, the English representative on the Reparations Commission, only added significance to his intervention.[125] The foundation for Havenstein's request to Montagu Norman was all the more propitious because Norman had invited Havenstein to London earlier in the fall in connection with the opening up of an account at the Bank of England designed to facilitate Reichsbank international transactions and reduce speculation. Havenstein had found his reception in London "surprisingly friendly and personally warm" and thought Norman and his colleagues showed great understanding of German conditions.[126]

Indeed, if Germany was having a difficult time being received back into the community of nations, Havenstein, at least, was well on the road to being received back into the community of central bankers. In an extraordinarily friendly personal letter of December 10, writing as "one Central Banker to another," Norman declared Havenstein's visit a "turning point" and expressed hope that the reparations negotiations in progress would lead to a strengthening of the Reichsbank *vis à vis* the German government. He considered this essential, since

... a Central Bank which is so much dominated by its own Government as to have no independence or initiation and even no right of protest is not in a fair position and therefore cannot play its part either within its own country or, still more, alongside other Central Banks. That is for instance the present position of the Bank of France, and we all lose by it. In varying ways the position of the Netherlands Bank and the Bank of England and even of the Federal Reserve Bank is different and more independent; and, now that we have more or less emerged from the domination of our respective Governments which during the War was unavoidable, all Europe will gain from it.[127]

Norman urged Havenstein to strengthen his ties with Vissering in the Netherlands and Benjamin Strong in the United States and to feel free to call on him for further assistance.

One of the peculiarities of the situation was that this letter followed Norman's formal refusal of December 5 to give Havenstein the loan he had requested. Odd as it may sound, the manner in which Norman refused Havenstein's loan request was also encouraging. On November 25, Havenstein had asked for a long- or short-term loan of five hundred million gold marks, offering German customs revenues or currency receipts from exports as security but explicitly refusing to pledge the Reichsbank gold. Norman, in his reply of December 5, 1921, pointed out that the securities offered by the Germans required the approval of the Reparations Commission and went on to deny the loan request with wording that was intended to be helpful to the Germans. In fact, Norman had shown the document to Rathenau before sending it and did "not think he was displeased with it."[128] The wording also had the tacit consent of

Sir Robert Horne, the Chancellor of the Exchequer. The most crucial sentence read, "I have consulted with those best competent to form an opinion and I have to say, in reply to your request, that under the conditions which at the present time govern the payments due during the next years by the German Government to the Reparation Commission, such advances cannot be obtained in this country."[129] The English were thus providing the Germans with an excellent basis to call not only for a moratorium but also for a revision of the schedule of the London Ultimatum. The policy of fulfillment, the fundamental goal of which was the demonstration of Germany's incapacity to pay, seemed to be working.

Stinnes was hardly one to take this view, but even he was creating the impression of a breakthrough in London. He was in London from November 19 to November 23, allegedly on private business, but actually to propagate his railroad privatization scheme as part of a general plan for a central European railroad consortium as well as the creation of an international consortium for the reconstruction of Russia. Stinnes, of course, was representing Stinnes, even if he sounded as if he were representing Germany, but he did manage to meet privately with Lloyd George and British reparations expert Sir Basil Blackett. While his railroad schemes do not seem to have produced much of an impression, and his program for using the privatized German railroads as a security for a loan to make the upcoming reparations payment aroused the suspicion that he was only serving his own interests, his Russian plans certainly must have been more attractive to Lloyd George, for whom the international reconstruction of Russia was an important element in his own plans for an international conference to organize world economic reconstruction. Stinnes also struck a responsive cord with Lloyd George when he pointed out that "Germany has a million too many employed in national enterprises including the railways. They had to be dismissed."[130]

Such remarks were not terribly helpful to Rathenau, whom the British had invited to London to discuss the proposed loan. (The talks were really understood to be a discussion of a projected reparations moratorium.) During his stay, from November 28 to December 9, followed by another visit from December 18 to December 23, Rathenau, in effect, served as Wirth's unofficial envoy. One of his chief tasks was to attack the view that Germany was deliberately courting bankruptcy through inflation and to strengthen Lloyd George's disinclination to follow French demands that any relaxation of the schedule of the London Ultimatum be accompanied by strict controls on German finances.

It appears to have been a very successful venture. Rathenau played upon Germany's role as a defender of the West against Bolshevism as well as upon the Prime Minister's guilt feelings over the Upper Silesian decision. He cogently suggested that the Allies had failed to strengthen German parliamentary democracy and that a Ludendorff government could not have been treated worse than the Wirth government. Apparently, Rathenau made a powerful impression and undermined some of the arguments that the Germans were deliberately promoting the inflation. The British leaders dropped their interest in having the Reichsbank gold and industrial assets as security for a new reparations arrangement, although they continued to insist that the Germans eliminate their food and railroad subsidies.[131]

For some of the British leaders, however, the Germans continued to make an impression of passivity and seemed to lack a program. The influential newspaper publisher Lord Beaverbrook thought Rathenau "one of those pedagogic Jew philosophers with no clear view of the position and no particular plan to solve the difficulty."[132] Industrialist James H. Dunn, who admired Stinnes and appears to have "managed" the Ruhr industrialist's English visit, took a broader view of the problems posed by the German pilgrimages to London in his conversation with Rathenau:

You have come here and continued the work begun by H[ugo] St[innes]. He has set the ball rolling and you are pushing it a little further. We are all glad to have this opportunity of discussing the position with you but we cannot help feeling that the good work done by one of you is undone again by the statements of another of you. That the good work stated by H. St. is somewhat paralyzed by your endeavors and so it goes on. First came Prof. Bonn, then Deutsch, then Havenstein, now you. In between we saw H.St. and we were certainly impressed with his views. But the views of all of you somewhat differ and there is not enough agreement. And that makes it difficult for us to act. Why don't you go back and get the German Government to have 3 to 4 men appointed, who come here with proper authority and full power to negotiate. . . . What is your plan now? I do not know whether you have one. But if I may make a suggestion, it strikes me that the only means of making headway is that a committee be appointed of which you form part and certainly H.St., as his views have impressed us and that further you be fully authorized by your Government not only to ask for time but also to take up the whole question right from the beginning of the Treaty of Versailles but with power to act on behalf of the Government and with authority to ask us to approach our former Allies. Has it occurred to you that if you had succeeded to raise the money to make the Jan[uary] and Feb[rua]ry payments, you would only defer the evil, but not gone to the root of it![133]

Rathenau, who had been pumping Dunn for information about what Stinnes had been up to in London and getting little for his efforts, assured Dunn that he was not opposed to returning to London with Stinnes in the future. From other sources, however, Rathenau was hearing that Stinnes had been going about saying that there was not much point to helping Germany until it balanced its budget and ceased printing money, and Rathenau complained that Stinnes was undermining his own efforts to get the English to provide help first.[134]

The rivalry between the two industrial leaders certainly did not contribute positively to German efforts in London at this time, and Montagu Norman may have been correct in emphasizing the Havenstein visit as the "turning point." Norman certainly was correct in his overall estimation he gave to Havenstein of the relative impressions made by Stinnes and Rathenau:

Many people here will attribute the present negotiations to the visit of Stinnes. I did not see him but I heard about him. I do not know why he came: his standpoint is *not* the same as yours and I doubt if he achieved any good—financially or politically—unless perhaps for his own business. Or they will attribute them to Rathenau. But that also is not true though his views are wide, and not unlike yours, and he has made a good impression and helped towards a European understanding.[135]

Be that as it may, what was competition in London was a great political battle in Berlin, as

was demonstrated by the debate in the Reichstag Foreign Affairs Committee on December 22.[136] As was to be expected, Helfferich launched a brutal attack on the Wirth government and its policy of fulfillment, accusing it of accepting impossible obligations, misleading the public into thinking it could fulfill them, and then suffering one defeat after another while ruining the currency at the same time. The Wiesbaden Agreement had, according to Helfferich, produced no relief, and the moratorium request had come too late. He lashed out at the Hachenburg proposal, which would have made it possible for the Allies to use the industrial credit offer to seize German private property and thus control the German economy. He was no less critical of English demands for an end to food subsidies and the raising of postal and railroad rates as well as the bringing of coal prices to world market levels. Germany would then no longer be able to compete on the world market. Helfferich concluded his tirade by calling for Wirth's resignation.

Stinnes was at once more moderate and more deeply insulting to Wirth and Rathenau in his own indomitable way. He alleged that he was only reporting on his impressions from London, which he admitted were favorable, since economic conditions were forcing the British to face up to the fact that when a German worker earned one and a half shillings a shift because of the German currency while a British worker earned eight to nine shillings for the same work, high unemployment in England was bound to be the result. The problem was to start producing goods and gaining purchasing power again after years of destroying both, and the reparations problem had to be seen as an economic rather than a money problem. Wirth's approach, which Stinnes identified with the latter perspective, was shipwrecked. As Stinnes explained:

The Reich Chancellor enjoys a not insubstantial personal sympathy because of his goodwill in trying to fulfill the obligations that have been taken on. But he does not have authority. His signature is not discountable. But we need for the forthcoming negotiations, in which our reparations obligations have to be reduced to a bearable level, men who can give the other side an absolute guarantee that they can and will actually carry out what they have signed.[137]

Stinnes argued that the Wirth government had compromised itself by giving in to blackmail and by failing to find a way out of the dilemmas which it had itself created. Rathenau was accused of being little more than a philosopher who had presented ideas in England which the English viewed as utopian. He insisted that the nation had to be represented in future negotiations by persons who had the confidence of the people and of the other side.

The trouble was that Stinnes, in admitting that Germany's prospects were the best they had been in the past three years and in pointing to the change in British attitudes, was undercutting his own argument, and this point was made by Wirth and his defenders, all of whom recognized that the fall of Wirth would undo the very real successes of fulfillment. Stinnes himself had no answer to this and, indeed, disclaimed that he was trying to bring down the government and alleged that he was only trying to report on his impressions from England to the confidential committee meeting, a disclaimer very much inspired by Wirth's warning that he would now fight for the political life of his government in parliament and in public.

In the ensuing weeks, Stinnes's attack on Rathenau as an "ethical philosopher" and "theoretician" proved even more abortive. It became more than evident that Rathenau had gained the confidence of the English political leadership and stood in the forefront of the struggle to gain the reparations moratorium Wirth had formally requested on December 14, 1921. Lloyd George not only actively pressured Briand at their December meetings in London to accept the moratorium proposal and eschew demands for the financial control of Germany in return for his support of the Wiesbaden Agreement, but also negotiated with Rathenau concerning these questions. He planned to have the moratorium agreement into which he had pressured Briand ratified at the Allied meetings in Cannes scheduled for the week of January 6, 1922, intended to invite a German delegation, and also planned to set the path there for Germany's full-scale participation in the Conference on International Economic Reconstruction to be held in Genoa in March. Wirth was not behindhand in cultivating the British and encouraging broader perspectives on Anglo-

German relations either. At a large dinner at his residence on January 5, the first such event since 1918, Wirth made a point of talking confidentially with Ambassador D'Abernon, during which discussion the Chancellor praised "the broadening of [the] reparation discussion into [the] wider problem of European restoration" as a "master-stroke" and suggested that England thereby had assured Germany's friendship for years to come and, indeed, perhaps the century. Wirth expressed alarm at the manner in which France had forged a chain of military allies in central and eastern Europe and suggested that England and Germany had to work together, taking the view "that Germany is England's advance post on the Continent or I shall say an advance post of Anglo-Saxon civilization. Like you, like America, we must have exports, only by trade can we live. That must be the policy of all three countries." Wirth also was confident about the domestic situation, assuring D'Abernon that the tax program would get through and that both the extreme left and the extreme right were under control. D'Abernon was impressed by Wirth's confidence and reported that there was "little doubt . . . that [the] policy of following England, which suffered temporary eclipse after Geneva, is now again dominant and probably stronger than before."[138]

The French had not disappeared from the scene, of course, and there was no ironclad guarantee as to what would happen at Cannes. Formally, the scheme worked out between Lloyd George and Briand in December did not provide for a moratorium but rather a reduction of 1922 reparations to seven hundred twenty million gold marks in cash—five hundred million in reparations and two hundred twenty million in occupation costs—and one and a quarter billion gold marks in deliveries in kind. Obviously, this was a vast improvement over the London Untimatum schedule, especially since the full reparations in kind were most unlikely to be collected as France hardly would be willing to be flooded with German goods in so large an amount. This agreement was ratified at Cannes, thereby eliminating the January, February, and April payments, as well as the 26 percent export levy for the period in question. All was not perfect, to be sure.

Briand's government fell during the meeting, and he was replaced by Poincaré. This made a final action on the moratorium request impossible, and the decision was passed back to the Reparations Commission, which proceeded to pass a provisional postponement requiring the Germans to pay thirty-one million gold marks every ten days beginning January 18 and to submit its plans for reforming the budget and monetary policy as well as its reparations proposal for 1922 within two weeks. Rathenau's efforts at Cannes to persuade the Allies that Germany could not afford even the seven hundred twenty million marks and to convince them that the German economy was really in a parlous state did not prove entirely convincing. Yet, he had achieved more than met the eye. A real danger of Allied control of the German economy had also been thwarted. Some of the British reparations experts had wished to impose a "technical adviser" on the Reichsbank with the power to veto the creation of new money, but Rathenau's persuasive powers and the reluctance of Lloyd George, Bradbury, and Horne to interfere so massively in German internal affairs won out at Cannes. While there continued to be interest in pressuring the Germans into taking steps to get their house in order and to make the Reichsbank autonomous of the government, measures of effective control had been killed for the time being despite the replacement of Briand by Poincaré on January 12.[139]

When Rathenau and Wirth appeared before the Reichstag Foreign Affairs Committee on January 19, therefore, their position was stronger than ever. The danger of Ruhr occupation had been averted, and the British had given up the "superstitious belief nurtured by the French . . . that Germany is an ill-willed bankrupt." Germany could expect to play a role in Genoa and in the reconstruction of Russia, and if the coming to power of Poincaré meant that there would be some unwanted frosts, "we will not sink back into the complete darkness of the year 1921 in the year 1922."[140] As they had in December, Helfferich and Stinnes attacked Rathenau, but they did not do very well. The claims that Germany's remaining obligations for 1922 were excessive and unfulfillable simply did not ring true, and the Wiesba-

den Agreement could now be presented by Rathenau as an "icebreaker." Helfferich asserted that the economic conditions imposed on Germany in connection with the partial moratorium were designed by the English to ruin German competitiveness and the German economy because "the cessation of note issuance is completely impossible; it would mean the cessation of salary payments to the civil service and interest payment on debts, and the complete bankruptcy of the state will be the consequence." Rathenau, however, was fully prepared to show that Helfferich was wrong:

There can be no talk about a sudden and complete cessation of the issuance of uncovered money. He even told Lloyd George that. We have been put into a morphine intoxication by the inflation because we have not noticed our sliding down into the abyss; we must get to a deflation. But one cannot undergo a morphium withdrawal cure suddenly, but can only do it gradually, and thus we can also only deflate gradually.[141]

Rathenau also sought to dispel fears that Germany would undergo high unemployment by a move in the direction of deflation:

Our present competitiveness has its basis in our continuously sinking exchange because of the inflation. We are thus performing penal labor; our middle class is being ruined; the workers and civil servants are subjected to deprivations. It is unworthy of human beings to be competitive on this basis. Even with a gradual ending of inflation there will still be a certain difference between the external and internal value of the mark which will enable us to work further even if the motor will have to work harder than it is now.[142]

Stinnes was neither the only speculator in Germany nor the only person whose private and public interests were mixed. Back in November, when he had entered into his semiofficial missions to London, Rathenau had told Julius Hirsch that "actually we must now make an end to the inflation. I have in any case set things up so that I have a full billion marks at my disposal at the AEG."[143] Hirsch clearly was correct in not viewing this as the most "brilliant of speculations," but this was from hindsight, and Rathenau had little reason to change his monetary arrangements at the turn of the year. Rathenau's optimism after his triumphs in London and at Cannes is understandable, but was he right? At Cannes he had impressed the political world with his comparison of Allied treatment of Germany with that of the owner of a donkey who had sought to increase his return on the donkey's labor by conditioning it to eat less and less. Finally, the owner achieved complete success when the donkey learned not to eat anything and died.[144] It was easier to find a successful parable to persuade the English about Germany's limited capacity to pay, however, than it was to find one to persuade the Germans to move toward stabilization. Could Germany do so without external compulsion? Was it possible to produce a gradual stabilization? These were to be the great questions of the year 1922.

Chapter 9

The Transition to Galloping Inflation

Theory and Policy

The turn of 1921 to 1922 is a good vantage point from which to analyze the process by which Germany was succumbing to inflation. At this time, the situation by no means appeared hopeless, as demonstrated by the improvement of the mark and a measure of stabilization from December through February and by the optimism with which Rathenau had spoken of a gradual transition to a deflationary policy. Events since May 1921, of course, had fed arguments on both sides of the contemporary debate over the responsibility of reparations for ruining the German currency. Germans could claim that the severe distress of the mark was the product of Allied mistreatment of Germany and the reparations payments and that the improvement was a consequence of the relief being granted and the prospects of further Allied concessions and even of financial help in the future. Allied critics of Germany could claim that the Germans had been successful in using their inflation to blackmail the Allies into concessions and would do so again unless stringent controls were imposed on German monetary and fiscal policy. These differing views were to fuel an increasingly tense theoretical debate between the proponents of the balance-of-payments theory of the inflation, who tended to stress the role of reparations in causing the increased inflation, and the proponents of the quantity theory, largely but by no means exclusively in the Allied camp, who were often highly critical of the reparations demands but nonetheless argued that the source of the inflation was the budget deficit and the use of the printing press and that an endogenous stabilization was possible and essential. These theoretical debates were more than intellectual exercises. They at once reflected and influenced policy options, and the theoretical positions accepted at the highest levels of government and among Germany's economic leadership were choices between or among competing priorities.[1]

The historian, of course, cannot understand and evaluate the interaction of contemporary debates among economists and the decisions of political leaders by making the analysis dependent upon judgments with respect to the correctness of one theory or the other. Historical actors may have very compelling reasons to opt for a less over a more intellectually satisfactory theory. The essence of historical explanation is neither the accumulation of facts nor the verification of theory, but rather the understanding and interpretation of events through the discovery and elucidation of their relevant context. That context may or may not contain genuine alternatives for the historical actors, but it is important to distinguish between those alternative scenarios which have historicity (could have taken place in the real world) and those which do not have such historicity.

The period following the acceptance of the London Ultimatum is crucial to any analysis of the precise role played by reparations in causing or promoting the depreciation of the currency as well as in understanding the role of reparations in affecting the domestic management of the inflation. This is especially the case because the tendency for the Germans to blame the inflation on reparations and for the Allies to accuse the Germans of promoting inflation to escape reparations increased in 1922, when galloping inflation accelerated and then gave way to hyperinflation. As this happened, these charges began to be self-fulfilling prophecies, and it becomes very difficult to sort out how the Gordian Knot of hyperinflation had been tied. The problem, therefore, is to recapture the process by which its configuration became so intransparent and its tightness so irreversible that the employment of a sword whose hilt was a new currency and whose blade was a new monetary, fiscal, and economic regime remained the only available solution.

There can be no question that a pronounced turn for the worse took place in the summer and fall of 1921. To be sure, the critical mass of long-running problems that ultimately caused the collapse of the currency were in place by then—the budget deficit, increased floating debt, the bundle of internal and external commitments that could not be met because of inadequate tax receipts and an inability to get a sufficiently large foreign loan, and the domestic political stalemate that limited the ability of any government to take effective action. These conditions existed, however, during the first wave of postwar inflation in the fall and winter of 1919–1920 and during the relative stabilization from the spring of 1920 to the spring of 1921 without triggering anything like the dramatic depreciation of the currency of the summer and fall of 1921. At the worst point of the previous period of currency depreciation, in February 1920, one dollar was worth 99.11 marks, whereas at the height of the inflationary wave of 1921, in November, the dollar was worth 262.96 marks before "stabilizing" in December and January at close to 192 marks. While the necessity of financing the first reparations payment due in August 1921 under the London Ultimatum schedule was bound to have a negative effect on the mark, the extent of the deterioration was a shock to both domestic and foreign observers and raised the specter of complete currency collapse through a foreign and domestic flight from the currency. That is, there was some perception of an ominous qualitative change in the character of the inflation.

Both the surprise over the degree of depreciation and the anxiety over the conditions surrounding it are well illustrated by a lengthy speech by Julius Hirsch to the Finance Policy Committee of the Reich Economic Council made on November 11, 1921. Hirsch was asking for the support of new legislation designed to place foreign currency operations under greater surveillance, but he took the occasion to deal more generally with recent developments. The value of this source is high for two reasons. First, the deliberations were confidential, and Hirsch went to great lengths to stress the importance of maintaining the confidentiality of certain of his remarks. Second, and most important, Hirsch was anything but a fatalist with respect to the inflation, and his controversial programs to promote stabilization and a policy of fulfillment were earning him considerable hostility from the right. He was no apologist for those who might seek to use inflation to sabotage reparations, and he was a strong supporter of domestic initiatives to fight inflation.

Hirsch began by reiterating remarks already made by Chancellor Wirth to the Reparations Committee of the Reich Economic Council which characterized the claim that Germany had deliberately promoted the depreciation of the mark as "complete nonsense" and roundly declared that "no people consciously brings about such a national disaster, least of all the Germans."[2] He emphasized that they were caught completely by surprise, "that for us the exchange catastrophe came completely unexpectedly, that it was never anticipated to this extent by anyone, that it also could not be expected by anyone." Looking back to June and July, Hirsch argued that one of the first sources of the sharp drop in the value of the mark, initially unrecognized in its full import by the German authorities themselves, was the reopening of the "hole in the West" through the Allied sanctions undertaken in March. This was a problem with which Hirsch had more than a little familiarity, since it had proven a major source of the importation of unwanted goods into Germany and uncontrolled exports at very cheap prices at the turn of 1919–1920. Its closure, which Hirsch had helped to negotiate, had certainly contributed to the relative stabilization. Hirsch estimated that about a billion paper marks' worth of goods per month had flowed into Germany between April and August 1921 as a result of the sanctions, thereby exacerbating an already serious balance-of-trade deficit. He felt this reflected a real contradiction between Allied financial and commercial demands: "[O]nly two things are possible:

either we give our money for champagne . . . or we make reparations payments."[3] While these imports drained Germany of needed foreign exchange, receipts from exports also dropped significantly in the spring because of the sanctions and the Upper Silesian uprising. The importance of these factors in bringing down the exchange rate was unclear at the time, but even the Allies were being made aware of the situation by the fact that they were not getting as much money as anticipated from the 26 percent levy on German export profits.

Hirsch was hardly seeking to blame the mark depreciation on champagne imports, and his greatest worries were not about the "exogenous" sources of the depreciation but rather about the interplay between these and certain "natural" reactions they called forth. Thus, the drop in the exchange rate in August was "strongly accentuated" by a phenomenon which "from hindsight one can call nothing other than a natural development"; namely, that the merchant or producer who saw that the payment of reparations through the purchase of foreign exchange and the taking out of foreign loans was affecting the value of the mark came rapidly to the conclusion that things could only get worse and therefore increased his import of raw materials before they would become more expensive through increased mark depreciation. Thus, the import surplus in August was approximately three billion in marks as against one billion during the previous months.

This speculative tendency was only intensified by the Upper Silesian decision, the impact of which was very serious. Hirsch did not discuss the internal ramifications of the decision— namely, the fact that the chief argument used to justify acceptance of the London Ultimatum and the policy of fulfillment was that Germany would retain Upper Silesia[4]—but he did argue that it had a profound effect on foreign financial circles, especially in neutral countries, which came to the conclusion that "Germany will not be fairly treated." Hirsch was convinced that this negatively influenced their willingness to lend money to Germany or to continue to speculate in favor of the German mark:

In August every conceivable prospect was still held out to us, but in September and October there was the reverse, and thus key circles abroad developed the sense that Germany was not in good hands; Germany will not be well treated. Thus, the circle of those who had bought marks throughout the entire year, who had shown themselves willing to take marks, become smaller and smaller.[5]

Hirsch was not prepared to place excessive stock in fears being expressed by "the most expert of experts" that "the famous forest of Macbeth" was actually moving against Germany in the form of a massive unloading of German currency. While it was true that some Swiss banks were ruthlessly alienating their mark holdings, the reactions of money market notations to the latest news about reparations and other events affecting Germany seemed to suggest that the speculative interest of those holding marks was quite alive. What was dying was the inclination to acquire more marks. Half with relief and half with fear, Hirsch noted that the renewed "buying out of Germany" was taking different forms in 1921 than it had at the turn of 1919–1920. There seemed to be little interest in the purchase either of property or of stocks, apparently because government rent controls and other regulations were found unattractive, there seemed to be serious doubts about the long-term profitability of many German firms. Instead, foreigners were buying goods and often keeping them in Germany for future use or sale.

What disturbed Hirsch most, however, was the extent to which Germans were beginning to flee from the mark themselves, their inclination to sell marks abroad and to stock up on raw materials and other goods in anticipation of further mark depreciation. One of the most distressing results of all this was the undoing of the considerable successes in holding down prices and wages during the later phase of the relative stabilization. The miners were demanding and getting an increase, and this was bound to trigger other wage demands and to affect prices. Experience had shown that it was virtually impossible to bring down paper-mark wages and prices, which meant that one would have to operate on a new level of depreciation and that those living off fixed incomes would lose yet another third of the value of their holdings and earnings unless relief was provided.

As Hirsch pointed out, however, there was no reason to suppose that the deterioration of the mark would have to stop at its present, previously unimaginable level. The true seriousness of the situation, from his point of view, only fully came into focus when one turned from the fairly familiar modes of domestic flight from the mark to a phenomenon which was quite new and which Hirsch chose to present and illustrate in rather dramatic and personal terms:

Another consequence has set in which must once and for all be spoken about in all frankness here, but where I again must ask that not a syllable escapes outside concerning what I am going to say now. Something has taken hold which one can call the domestic sabotage of the mark, and it is a completely natural occurrence, one which no one can consider a crime in and of itself. I would like to use examples in which I myself encountered it. It is the following: about four weeks ago, when the dollar rate sprang on one day from 150 to 190, a relative dropped by and said: "I simply do not know what to do anymore; my goods are being torn from my hands, but I simply cannot sell them. Before we had a turnover of 6 to 7 million marks a year—it is a very respectable business—but now we have the same turnover in one month. But I would rather not have it because no matter what price I charge, the whole business is worth a quarter less the next day. What should I do? For the moment I have stopped selling, but I cannot do this over the long run. What remains? I will not be able to do anything but somehow or other to sell in gulden."[6]

The practice obviously was not limited to Hirsch's relatives, and he pointed out that it was to be found in the Krefeld silk industry, in the Rhine shipping industry, among persons advancing mortgages in East Prussia, and even among certain employees. Perhaps most fateful was that accountants were beginning to recommend it to their clients. The danger was obvious: "The mark will no longer be treated as a subject of calculation but will only serve as a means of payment while the basis of calculation will be the dollar." The next step was not hard to imagine. The mark would cease to be either a basis of calculation or a mode of payment. The threat, therefore, was that even a *relative* stabilization would no longer be possible:

Gentlemen, we do not stand before the question: an exchange rate with the dollar of 300 or 500? We stand before the question of whether we want to have a national currency at all; we stand before the question of whether we can remain independent at all with our existing monetary conditions, whether we want to remain independent at all, and I believe the very fact

that we all want to be is the most important reason for us to use every conceivable means to come out of this dreadful situation.[7]

How credible was Hirsch's account of the events surrounding the alarming deterioration in the value of the mark during the last half of 1921? No one would quarrel with the importance of the massive mark sales and other operations needed to make the first reparations payments as an immediate source of currency depreciation, but the interesting aspect of Hirsch's account was his stress upon the role played by events prior to the reparations payments as well as upon the way in which certain tendencies in domestic behavior were intensifying the monetary problems in a qualitatively new way. The evidence suggests that he did indeed pinpoint the major sources of difficulty as well as properly describe the increasing domestic flight from the mark as a phenomenon that had more to do with circumstances than intentions.

The sanctions, whose consequences are no more precisely quantifiable than the undergrowth of a jungle, certainly appear to have worked against German government efforts to conduct a responsible trade policy. Although the Allies promised to lift the sanctions by September 15 if the first billion in reparations was promptly paid, the promise was not kept until October 1, a belated concession which did very little for the domestic credibility of Wirth's fulfillment policy.[8] Between early March and the end of September, therefore, the occupied region was subjected to a policy designed to undermine the German economy in a systematic fashion. German firms in the occupied areas complained that they could neither take on new short-term contracts to deliver to their customers in the unoccupied regions nor count on receiving the raw materials they needed because of Allied customs barriers and regulations. As a consequence, many firms were compelled to shut down or put their workers on short time while Allied firms took over their business with the unoccupied areas.[9] These charges were confirmed by the American Legal Adviser to the Inter-Allied High Commission, Manton Davis, in a very critical report of August 4 which frankly questioned the good faith of the Allies:

Every effort is being made to divert trade channels from Germany to the Allied nations. The licensing system, as operated, is admirably adapted to injure Germany: to make the whole Rhineland dependent upon the Allied nations and independent of Germany; to divert into Allied hands profits from Rhineland trade, which profits, in the hands of Germans, might be collected through taxation and applied to reparations. This procedure tends toward leaving reparations unpaid, thus justifying both the retention of the present sanctions and the application of others.[10]

Davis was even more dismayed by the manner in which the Allies had undermined German efforts to control unnecessary imports: "Perfumes, cosmetics, wines, liquors, leather goods, expensive wearing apparel, cigarettes, fruit, etc. are being admitted across the western frontier into the Occupied Territory without regard to the needs or present demands of the country." Although the average alcohol consumption in the Rhineland was three million liters a month, licenses for twenty-three million liters were issued for the month of May. Davis could only conclude that the Allies themselves were contributing to a future German default on its reparations obligations and that "Germany would be in a strong moral position to assert that she was being punished for acts brought about by those who were punishing her."[11] This, indeed, was precisely what the Germans argued in their efforts to end the sanctions.[12]

Both Germans and Allied observers testified to the renewed "buying out of Germany" but also to the hoarding by German consumers. The situation in the occupied areas was particularly distressing. Thus, the retailers of Duisburg complained of the "plundering of the retailers by foreigners with highly valued currencies" but were even more distressed by "dark and uncontrollable elements" who went from shop to shop buying up goods for resale at higher prices.[13] The British observed similar tendencies in Cologne, but also in Berlin:

Though Berlin is not so near the frontier as Cologne, and has therefore suffered less from the incursion of foreigners anxious to benefit by the exchange in making purchases, very much the same phenomenon has been witnessed here in regard to dealings in retail shops. Many shops declare themselves to be sold out; others close from 1 to 4 in the afternoon, and most of them refuse to sell more than one article of the same

kind to each customer. . . . In almost every camera shop . . . the sight of a Japanese eagerly purchasing is still a common feature. But on the whole, as far as Berlin is concerned, it is the Germans themselves who are doing most of the retail buying and laying in stores for fear of a further rise in prices or total depletion of stocks.[14]

While retailers in the occupied areas were encouraged to sell to foreigners at higher prices, it was much more difficult to control domestic tendencies to hoard or to buy luxury items or to engage in a host of other undesirable practices associated with a flight from the mark and a general demoralization. As a Bavarian official reported in early November:

The fall of the mark to less than two pfennig in worth has brought a real anxiety among the propertied classes. Everyone seeks to do something with their money. Everything is bought that can be bought, not only for present need, not only for future use, but in order to get rid of the paper and have objects to exchange when the time comes that it is worth absolutely nothing. In Augsburg, the throng at various businesses was so large that the owners had to close their doors and let the buyers waiting outside in by groups. In Memmingen, the farming population during the last weeks, namely during the yearly market, totally bought out the manufactured product, textile, and shoe stores. . . . There has been speculation to an extent never seen before. The bank employees have been especially active in this respect. Recently, the Café Königsbau in Augsburg opened up a luxury restaurant with such sumptuous decoration as not to be found even in Munich. There one can see how the foreign-exchange profiteers use their money.[15]

The prohibition of unwanted imports and the discouragement of expenditures on luxury items were very real concerns of the German authorities at this time, although no one was under the illusion that these measures would provide the margin that would make the payment of reparations possible, and, more often than not, the concern over excess consumption of luxury goods was the product of moral and social considerations. In Bavaria, for example, reactionary Minister-President Gustav von Kahr took upon himself the unpromising task of legislating Protestant abstemiousness for Bavarians. His effort was in no way connected with Treaty fulfillment, which Kahr strongly opposed, but rather to allay the social discontent produced by conspicuous excess. Bavarian efforts to have the Reich pass a law against gluttony (*Schlemmerei*) were likened by the British Consul to "the decrees of old-time Puritans or the freak laws of certain of the modern States of North America, making gluttony a penal offence." As Consul Sneed sneered:

The preamble of the bill states that popular indignation at the excesses of profiteers constitutes a social danger. . . . They draw a nice distinction between habitual gluttony and occasional overindulgence on festive occasions: apparently the underfed man in the street will be less shocked at the sight of fifty gross eaters issuing in a body from a banquet than at that of the closed shutters of a mansion where a profiteer nightly consumes his portion of champagne and paté de foie gras. The argument adduced is that feasts are desirable to light up occasionally the dark hours of Germany's need.[16]

Far more serious were the discussions of closing down luxury industries or taxing them very heavily, but here, too, there were limits imposed by common sense and economic rationality. Steel industrialist Beukenberg might complain bitterly that the reduction of wage differentials was making it possible for young workers to indulge themselves in the latest fashions and might fume over the latest rage for hats—"now it is a green hat, then it is a bright hat, another one every three months"—but he warned that the shutting down of such industries would put many workers on the dole. His colleague Abraham Frowein of the textile industry pointed out that either one revived medieval sumptuary laws defining who was allowed to wear what or one frankly recognized that "even the worst economic circumstances never suppresses the need of the people for adornment."[17] It was also difficult, if not impossible, to distinguish between luxury goods and quality goods. It was not even clear what constituted luxury goods for purposes of taxation. Producers of pianos and other musical instruments insisted their products were educational rather than luxury items; the leather industry joined with similar groups in fighting against the luxury tax on the grounds that much of what they produced was not luxurious; film theatres warned that they would be ruined by a 50 to 60 percent tax on tickets.[18]

Far more problematic and significant than the attendance at the movies, however, was the attendance at the stock market and the mass speculation in stocks and currencies. Informed ob-

servers felt that there was a direct relationship between the orgy of stock market speculation that had set in with the currency depreciation in the late summer and the luxurious ostentation of those who were "playing" the market:

Stock market speculation today is the organized flight from the mark. What externally appears as wild speculation on the stock market has a deeper significance which is rooted in the problem of investment. The boundary between investment [*Anlagegeschäft*] and speculation no longer can be precisely separated at a time when the return on an investment diminishes in the same ratio as the value of the paper mark and when therefore even the solid capitalist, if he does not want to impoverish himself from day to day, must acquire real values. This alone has led to an extraordinary increase in stock market business. It has been strengthened through the continuous depreciation of money, which explains the permanent bull market for securities, and the fact that profits from speculation appear not only as a lucrative but also as a permanent and risk-free source of income. A by-no-means insignificant portion of the population today gets the largest portion of its income from such speculative profits. And the otherwise often completely inexplicable purchasing power of the German population for luxury articles is primarily attributable to the fact that relatively many persons still profit easily and quickly from such business and strive to place this money in those tangible goods which increase the pleasantness of life.[19]

The decline in the mark that set in during the late summer of 1921 had indeed produced an orgy of stock market speculation that went beyond the excesses of the previous period of mark depreciation in 1919–1920. The index of share prices, which had remained relatively stable during the first half of the year, shot up from 100 in May 1921—the same level as January—to 337 in November before declining to 263 in December.[20] In August, the Berlin exchange was so overloaded with business that it shut down three days a week. By November, it was open only one day a week. Banks were taking orders for shares only until ten in the morning and were increasingly refusing smaller orders. The speculating public was dealing not only in the shares of established firms, often encouraged by their quest for capital, but also in the shares of previously unknown companies, the origins of which were obscure and balance sheets unavailable.[21] The officers of the exchange finally decided to ban all "guests" from the floor, as conditions had become dangerously crowded, and even after the ban the exchanges were filled with hoarse, screaming traders and brokers who tended physically to crowd one another out in the tumult. When a physician appeared on the floor of the exchange one day, it turned out that his purpose was not to "relieve the sore throats of the stock exchange brokers or tend to the hands crushed in the crowd"[22] but rather to join directly in the speculative fray. There was a price to be paid for such small time speculation, however. The market notation of shares was closely linked to the value of the mark, and when the latter suddenly began to rise against foreign currencies in December 1921, share prices fell rapidly and millions were lost, to the unrepressed glee of Georg Bernhard's *Plutus*:

The fall of share prices on the exchange . . . [has] led to millions in losses, namely of the small speculators, who considered it a natural right to live nobly from daily stock exchange profits. Many of these small speculators were not in a position to pay off their credit engagements because the bank bureaus were very rigorous in demanding payment. . . . A mass of persons who had become, if not rich persons, then people who were rich in profit taking, have returned again very quickly to the shadows, and it is said in Berlin that at the end of last week almost as many automobiles were offered for sale as were sold during the entirety of last year. Even the Berlin taxis are complaining about the decline in their use and their earnings.[23]

There were more serious and dangerous losses at this time, however, in the more elite speculative game of the currency market. Before 1914, it had been the preserve of a select few whose mathematical skills, instincts, and experience enabled them to fathom the minuscule variations to which prewar currencies were subject and to engage in the business of currency trading and arbitrage. Their inflation period successors were a new breed, the "prima donnas of the banking business,"[24] the much sought-after currency speculators who had demonstrated a knack for playing the market at a time when every bank was desperate to hire those possessed of this suddenly indispensable yet rather rare talent. Such persons, not to be confused with the small-time operators on Berlin's Grenadierstraße, often held the fate of banking enterprises in their hands, and it was understandable that those who showed promise

were rapidly raised to the level of branch directors of major banks or partners of private banks. Their role appreciated as the mark depreciated, but sometimes they were poorly chosen or inadequately controlled, and the blind trust placed in them sometimes led to major disappointment and even disaster. Thus, Director Römer of the Munich branch of the Pfälzische Bank, a respected enterprise founded in 1886, managed to ruin the bank at the end of 1921 by speculating in favor of the mark and losing three hundred fifty million from one day to the next. Römer was viewed as a person of scholarly talent and mathematical ability, and he did, in fact, calculate correctly in acting on the "international secret tip" that the mark would rise on November 11 because of the opening of negotiations with the Reparations Commission in Berlin. It was just that he seems to have speculated in favor of the mark slightly too early and with far more money than responsible bank management at the bank's central headquarters in Ludwigshafen ever should have allowed. As a result, the Deutsche Bank had to come to the rescue, which it did by swallowing up the Pfälzische Bank.[25]

The entire affair, which was by no means an isolated one, illustrated the loss of control that had overtaken some responsible members of the business community at this time. As the extreme example demonstrates, however, those involved were not thinking in terms of supporting or fleeing from the mark for political reasons. Römer was speculating in favor of the mark, and his interest was not, in any case, in the problem of fulfillment—it was in making a "killing." To do so, however, one had to try to anticipate political developments and their economic consequences. The decision to speculate for or against the mark was not a decision to influence policy but rather to predict the influences of policy. At the height of the mark depreciation and during the greatest excesses of the stock-market and currency speculation in early November, for example, *Plutus* warned that the calculations of the speculators were quite dangerous:

They argue something like the following: the fall of the mark brings an export boom, and a German export boom exacerbates Anglo-American unemployment (which is now the worst it has been in a century). This world crisis finally makes it necessary to change Germany's payment obligations and also forces action to deal with Germany's financial misery. A mixture of *dette publique* and payment reprieve will be the consequence. Will this come and when? It might come very soon; it might come very late. The probability is that it will be neither too long nor too short a time. No one knows whether the dollar will reach 300, 400 or 500 by that time. But that then the dollar could fall to 70 and 50 marks is by no means out of the question.[26]

In a manner now familiar and, of course, informed by the first episode of accelerating inflation suddenly giving way to relative stabilization in the spring of 1920, the author of these lines worried that while "the fall of the mark is bad, a sudden recuperation would almost be worse" because it would lead to "domestic purchaser strikes, decline of exports on the world market, unemployment, a gigantic stock market crash, no dividends, bankruptcies of banks and industrial enterprises, etc., etc." The sudden improvement of the mark in December, with its attendant disasters for some speculators and financial institutions, only seemed to confirm these points and teach "the lesson of these stormy days that the way to a final cleansing [*Sanierung*], when we finally once and for all take this path, will lead us through a severe economic crisis. This crisis will be all the more difficult, severe, and long, the more extreme the fall of foreign currencies and the improvement of the mark until the point is reached where stabilization is possible."[27]

However critical *Plutus* and its editor Georg Bernhard were of many industrialist practices and policies, their commentaries appear to be a reasonable reflection of the attitudes of the more responsible elements of the German business community at this time. When they fled from the mark, they did so reluctantly, and they struggled constantly to read current economic and political trends directly and make the correct disposition of their liquid resources. They really had little choice in the matter.

A good illustration is provided by the Deutsche Bank director and supervisory board chairman of the Mannesmann concern, Max Steinthal, who regularly provided General Director Bierwes with information and advice on the currency situation. Thus, in early November ber Steinthal advised closing a deal in marks despite the depreciation, disgustedly remarking that "I do not believe that the entire productive capacity of our nation of sixty million, despite all the production difficulties with which Germany has to struggle, can change from one month to the next and be valued at one-fourth its worth in line with the movements of the foreign currencies, for this would bespeak the rise in the value of the dollar from 75 to about 300 [marks]."[28] A month later, he commented on how the drop in Mannesmann stock prices from a high of 1800 to 1305 was being viewed almost casually and how the latter price, which would once have been regarded as "exaggerated," was now considered relatively cheap. As he frankly admitted, however, the price of shares had very little to do with what was going on in the company but rather was a function of the exchange rate of the mark, which he now assumed would improve, "even if with large variations," a fact confirmed by the astonishing upward movement of the mark on the New York exchanges because of rumors concerning a possible moratorium and loan for Germany.[29] When Poincaré replaced Briand in mid-January, Steinthal felt that "an entirely new situation" had been created and suggested to Bierwes that "it is not impossible that in a little time there will again be an opportunity to sell foreign exchange at favorable prices."[30] Because of Mannesmann's important Czech interests, Steinthal observed the movement of the Czech koruna very closely and in late January was very uncertain whether Bierwes should carry out a plan to sell large amounts of korunas or not. On the one hand, the koruna had been doing particularly well against other currencies and might increase; on the other hand, he had confidential information that the Czech government was trying to bring down its market value for economic reasons. Initially, he took a neutral stand on the sale, pointing out that "an industrial enterprise like ours is not there to speculate constantly in every currency." When it became evident four days later that "even a government is not in a position to determine the rate of a currency in accordance with its will," he concluded that perhaps it was advisable to hold on to the korunas for a while after all.[31] Indeed, Steinthal was at this point becoming more cautious about the sale of foreign exchange altogether. Thus, he urged holding on to the proceeds from sales to South Africa, something he had not done back in November, pointing out that "even if as whole foreign currencies are subject to heavy variations and are therefore not steady, the possibility that Germany's deadly enemy Poincaré might bring about a change through some measure is not to be dismissed lightly. Presently, one will have to limit oneself to observe such measures and their consequences for the foreign exchange markets."[32]

This was a joyless activity for most of Germany's businessmen. The prominent M.A.N. director Guggenheimer did not think much of speculation or of speculators, and he saw the "ruining of hundreds of existences" in the December 1921 mark recovery as a positive development for the economy and a means of returning them to honest and real labor. In his view, truly productive enterprises and businessmen, especially those engaged in international trade, had a natural and necessary interest in stable conditions. Germany was "never suited to autarky," he argued, and "speculation is the worst enemy of world economic relations, which require stability and security more than anything else." Nevertheless, he had to admit that, thanks to the insecurity of the circumstances in which they operated, the statement of an industrialist that "we are all actually no longer manufacturers but have become speculators" was absolutely correct, involuntary speculators to be sure, but speculators nonetheless. In domestic commerce, no one could tell what the marks he was receiving one day would be worth the next because of rising labor and material costs, but the worst problems were in foreign trade. Everywhere there was a tendency to return to the practice of sliding-scale prices, so cheerfully abandoned during the relative stabilization, in order to ensure that costs and raw-materials costs would be covered. The old debate about whether exporters should ask for payment in foreign or German currency had been revived, some, like Guggenheimer himself, arguing that only the collection of foreign currency made sense, while others insisted that this was tantamount to eliminating the mark as a currency for calculation purposes. Many were

evading the issue and trying to reduce risk by charging half in foreign currencies and half in marks. Whatever the case, doing international business had become a currency guessing game. When something went awry, businessmen no longer asked themselves the old question of why they had failed in their economic understanding and had calculated wrongly but rather the speculator's question of why black had turned up instead of red.[33]

Nevertheless, this did not mean that businessmen had ceased trying to calculate according to the familiar rules, that they were deliberately seeking to sabotage the currency, or that they were not resisting the temptation to succumb to inflationary expectations. The best evidence is provided by the iron and steel industrialists, who were, by and large, stalwart opponents of fulfillment and who by past experience were peculiarly well versed in all the high and low arts of inflationary pricing. They had been so well behaved during the relative stabilization that the Iron Trades Federation had dropped its price ceilings and become virtually defunct, and it was a measure of their faith in the mark at that time that even Vögler, the leading manager of the Stinnes iron and steel operations, was billing in marks when he could have billed in foreign currencies. The depreciation of the mark in late summer brought vastly increased demand and much higher prices for iron and steel products within Germany, but the industrialists warded off worker demands for new price ceilings in the Iron Trades Federation by agreeing to a more informal arrangement establishing price guidelines (*Richtpreise*). At the same time, however, they agreed to deliver at fixed prices, a very risky decision given the fact that they were flooded with orders and had signed contracts for delivery much in advance. Apparently, they were convinced that they were dealing with an illusionary boom (*Scheinkonjunktur*) and that they should support stabilizing policies.[34] Ironically, it appears the manufacturing industries took the lead in abandoning fixed-price contracts toward the end of 1921 by reintroducing clauses allowing for additional charges for increased labor and materials costs. Given the fact that the time span between order and delivery tended to be longer for manufacturers of finished products than for producers of primary products, this change of policy was by no means radical, especially as it did not link price changes directly to exchange-rate changes. In retrospect, businessmen in late 1921 failed to anticipate the effects of inflation adequately, and this only reinforces the impression that they were genuinely surprised by the end of the relative stabilization and that they did not realize the inflation's full implications for their own business operations, let alone for the conduct of Germany's foreign relations.[35]

While they certainly thought it splendid that the renewed German export boom was promoting unemployment elsewhere, thereby encouraging sentiment for a Treaty revision, this was a by-product of policy rather than policy itself. Although it clearly was in the interest of exporters to bill and receive payment in high-valued foreign currencies once the value of the mark began to decline, it was not until the last two months of 1921 that one export control board after another, often at the urging of both the Reichsbank and the government, required this of their members.[36] The practice was not always welcomed by Germany's customers, especially when they were anxious to unload their accumulated mark reserves or use them to make cheap purchases in Germany and thereby recoup some of their losses on the exchange. In Naples and southern Italy, for example, the change of policy ruined many new small firms, the founding and continued existence of which depended on cheap purchases from Germany in marks, since they could afford neither to pay in lire nor (as was often the case with the larger and more-established firms) to put their mark holdings into German banks and use marks to buy stocks or goods. The more marginal firms needed to use their marks to buy stocks and goods in order to operate. Worse yet, the national pride of these Italian businessmen was often hurt by the demands of some German firms for payment in pound sterling rather than lire.[37]

In a world of floating exchange rates, not all good currencies were equally good or were even comparably good at different times, as the comparison of the relative worth of the mark to those of the various currencies at its first low point at the beginning of 1920 and on October 15, 1921, demonstrates (see Table 18). It is un-

derstandable, therefore, why German exporters who were insisting on payment in foreign currencies would prefer pound sterling to lire. The currency payment requirements of the Germans, however, produced bad feelings even among those nations with very highly valued currencies for somewhat different reasons. Swedes, like Italians, still thought they might make a speculative exchange profit on the side if they continued to pay in marks, but the Swedes were particularly dependent on various German products and were especially resentful when they were forced to pay high prices. They could understand why Germans wanted payment in Swedish kronor, but they thought it unfair that German goods were specially priced in Swedish kronor or Danish and Norwegian kroner and that these prices were all different because they were geared to the relative purchasing power and markets of the countries in question. In rather contradictory fashion, Swedes complained not only that the prices they had to pay for some German products were unfairly high but also that what they had to pay for others were often artificially low because of exchange dumping. While greater discipline was being exhibited by German producers in late 1921 than had been shown in the inflationary wave of 1919–1920, exchange dumping continued in a roundabout way because German wholesalers often exported goods allegedly bought for the German market illegally or with doctored licenses and then undersold Swedish sellers of the same products.

Table 18. Exchange Rate of the Mark Relative to Other Major Currencies at Its Low Point at the Beginning of 1920 and on October 15, 1921

	Beginning of 1920	October 15, 1921
U.S. Dollar	103.65	149.60
English Pound Sterling	349.65	576.40
100 Swiss Franc	1,798.00	2,877.10
100 Danish Kroner	1,698.50	2,727.20
100 Dutch Gulden	4,196.00	4,945.05
100 French Franc	713.60	1,083.90
100 Belgian Franc	729.25	1,071.40
100 Italian Lire	584.40	594.45
100 Swedish Kronor	1,998.00	3,411.55
100 Norwegian Kroner	1,949.00	1,813.15

Source: Report of the Economics Minister to the Reich President on the Economic Situation in September 1921, BAK, R 43I/1947, Bl. 622.

The thirty thousand Swedish summer travelers in Germany also took advantage of the mark prices whenever possible, so that a German camera that sold in Sweden for 384 kronor could be bought for the mark equivalent of 135 kronor in Germany. Thus, the entire currency situation promoted conditions under which not only Germans undercut Germans but also Swedes undercut Swedes. As producers, Swedes, like their counterparts at this time in other countries with highly valued currencies, faced unemployment, wage cuts, and depressed conditions and complained about German dumping and sometimes even called for tariffs and other trade barriers. As consumers, they welcomed the lowest German—and also Austrian and Polish—prices they could get. All this made the danger of countermeasures of a protectionist kind from Sweden much less serious than they were from Switzerland, Great Britain, and the United States. Nevertheless, German Foreign Office officials in Sweden stressed the importance of stricter export controls and higher export levies as well as strong pressure on German exporters to insist on payment in Swedish currency.[38]

In the last analysis, however, what forced the government to reassert its controls over exports and imports and introduce some new measures to control foreign exchange in the fall of 1921 and the winter of 1921–1922 was both foreign and domestic political pressure. On the one hand, the Allies were persistently threatening to levy the 26 percent reparations export tax on individual exports rather than seek to collect its equivalent by lump-sum payments from the German government. Even if businessmen were convinced that the export boom was nothing more than a temporary phase and a *Schein-konjunktur*, it was impossible to deny that large export profits were being made and that the German government's good faith depended upon some effort to tap this potential source of revenue. It was also in its own economic interest to prevent the waste of national resources produced by dumping, and the export levy was viewed not only as a source of revenue but also as a disincentive to dumping. On the other hand, the Socialists and other left-wing critics of the government, already angered by the failure of tax collection and demanding the appropriation of real values, were no less insistent that

the export-control and exchange-control system and the export levies be vigorously revived and implemented.[39] The government's measures, both those taken and those planned, led to angry debates in the Reich Economic Council and constant complaints from affected businessmen. The Hamburg merchants were in the forefront and argued that German exports would diminish because of the requirement that payment be made in foreign currency and, further, that it would appear as a renunciation of the mark by Germans themselves and thus bring the currency into further disrepute. As always, they warned that the delays and bureaucratic problems would lead to the loss of millions in business.[40]

The desire of the Reichsbank and Reich Economics Ministry officials to get the foreign trade situation in hand is indisputable, but their growing pessimism and fatalism must also be recognized. In private conversation, the Reich Commissar for Imports and Exports, Ernst Trendelenburg, and Director Friedrichs of the Reichsbank confessed that many of the control measures would hurt business without being terribly effective. They admitted that the "most important reason" for the measures was "to convince the Entente that official Germany was doing everything in order to procure the gold payments needed for the reparations obligations." As the Hamburg Representative in Berlin, Justus Strandes, reported:

In the course of the lengthy extended conversation the questions of the fulfillment of the reparations obligations and the prospects for the development of the worth of the mark were taken up. Privy Councillors Trendelenburg and Friedrichs diligently emphasized that they had to be cautious and reserved in stating their opinions. Nevertheless that could only poorly disguise the fact that they had no confidence in the future. It was completely clear that they themselves defended the measures without truly believing that they would be of much use and only so that nothing be left undone. Along with the already noted remark that what has been planned must be carried out in order to prevent an intervention of the Entente and even more damaging measures, there were a variety of intimations about putting off the catastrophe. I came away again, as so often of late, with the impression that for those circles in the know there is fear that our financial strength, especially with regard to reparations, will come to an end soon and that all efforts are being made to hold it back in the hope that one might still succeed in getting an easing of our obligations.[41]

This was simply the counterpart of the fatalism that was also gripping the tax authorities at this time. When some weeks later Strandes suggested to State Secretary Zapf of the Finance Ministry that more money would be gained from effective implementation of the tax laws than from export regulations, Zapf "complained about the failure of the state tax offices. What is lacking is the energetic initiative of these intermediate agencies, so that the Reich Finance Ministry actually finds it necessary to maintain a special control apparatus to monitor the tax offices on a constant basis. The most severe regulations for the speedy assessment of taxes have been issued, but in the end the implementation depends once again on the people involved."[42]

If there was any official involved in these matters who was firmly committed to taking action, it was Julius Hirsch, who, as noted earlier, alarmingly described the events surrounding the deterioration of the mark at the Finance Policy Committee meeting of the Reich Economic Council on November 11, 1921. As the author of the program for appropriation of real values and of many of the measures taken to control exports, his credentials as an opponent of the inflation were impeccable. Yet, in that very speech, Hirsch betrayed the fatalistic tones and the sense that Germany could not help itself until the Allies helped it existing among his colleagues. Thus, he argued that "the entire situation lies at the moment in the hands of the Entente and lies at the moment in the hands of the Reparations Commission. The decisive word would then be spoken if one would say to us that the purchase of foreign exchange in the immediate future is not required to such and such a degree."[43] He believed that this would lead to some measure of recovery for the mark. The opportunity thus provided could then be used to undertake measures against the flight of capital, the domestic use of foreign currencies, luxury imports, and excessive consumption, and, above all, inadequate tax collection. In short, Germany needed a breathing space to take proper action on the home front.

Unhappily for Hirsch, however, his grasp of what was necessary and desirable exceeded what was politically possible, and one has a sense from the entire context of his speech that he was aware of the disparity between the drama of the circumstances he had described and the means available to cope with them. The speech was written to support a measure whose fundamental provision was to require that all domestic exchanges of marks and foreign currency be reported to the tax authorities. As Hirsch pointed out, such transactions were not being made illegal, and since the tax offices were so overburdened already, that one would have to wait and see if they could do anything with the information. At the very best, the measure would discourage such transactions and identify some of the more significant instances; at its worst, it would encompass those foolish enough to report their actions and miss the large speculators against the mark who knew how to cover their tracks. Hirsch was even more pessimistic when it came to controlling the sale of marks abroad. For this, he ruefully told his listeners, one would need the authority of the Kaiser, trenches, and something much larger than the hundred-thousand-man army allowed under the Treaty. In a more serious vein, Hirsch did think that more could be done to gain control of foreign-exchange profits from exports as well as to secure neutral and Allied assistance in identifying and bringing back German foreign-exchange holdings abroad. Finally, Hirsch argued that the chief area in which something had to be done was taxation, which presented "extraordinary difficulties" from a political point of view: "This is a regrettable situation, but I do not believe that we can evade regrettable situations very much longer. We must find the courage to deal with difficult tasks."[44]

As one wit interjected, "the regrettable thing is that we have so many regrettable situations." The projected law was not meant to interfere with the activities of businessmen dependent upon foreign raw materials and regularly engaged in international trade, and it was not meant to punish Berlin cab drivers asking for payment in foreign currency either. One of its purposes was to discourage businessmen from demanding payment in foreign currency from their domestic customers, a practice for which those in the jute business and engaged in silk weaving seemed to have gained notoriety. The proposed legislation was also intended to dampen unnecessary dealing in foreign exchange. No one could believe the legislation was going to be very effective. Critics frankly charged that the law was composed mainly of "loopholes" because it failed to deal with those who did the most business in foreign exchange. The actual delivery of foreign exchange gained in exports, like the question of billing and receiving payment in foreign exchange, was regulated through the self-administrative activities of the exchange control boards in cooperation with the government. Thus, in January 1922, most of the major industrial groups producing for export were committed to deliver all their foreign currency proceeds to the Reichsbank "minus what was necessary for their own needs," while others required themselves to deliver a fixed percentage (usually 60 percent) of their foreign-exchange receipts.[45] These were, to say the least, very elastic arrangements since those involved basically determined what their foreign-exchange needs were. The projected law did not impinge on this system of self-regulation.

Georg Bernhard was particularly acerbic about the legislation's inadequacies. In Bernhard's view, the use of foreign currencies in domestic German commerce threatened Germany's monetary sovereignty and had to be banned before "Austrian conditions" were produced and every small merchant began not only to calculate in foreign currencies but also to insist on payment in them. At the same time, he and others were concerned with the problem of how to limit the number of those entitled to engage in foreign-currency trading and foreign currency transactions.[46]

But how was one to distinguish between legitimate trade in foreign currencies and speculation? Furthermore, as Socialist Max Cohen pointed out, it was not speculation in foreign currencies but the lost war that was responsible for the depreciation of the mark. Another Reich Economic Council member suggested that the effort to control speculation was comparable to the effort to control prostitution and would ultimately cause more problems than it was worth. As was so frequently the case, the issue ultimately boiled down to the impression on the Allies. The head of the Berlin stock exchange, Privy Councillor Lippert, agreed com-

pletely with Max Cohen that the lost war and not speculation was the source of Germany's difficulties, but in his appearances before the Guarantees Commission, he had the impression that the Allies thought that Germany was deliberately supporting speculation to force Treaty revision and that therefore "at least formally something should be done in order to avoid the impression that speculation really plays a role here."[47]

There can be no question about the fact that Germans did have a goal of proving that reparations were the source of the difficulties confronted by Germany's trading partners as a consequence of the fall of the mark. Thus, while they tried to show good faith, often without much real belief in their measures, on the one hand, they also sought to prove the harmfulness of the London Ultimatum to the outside world, on the other. They did not promote exports to force a revision of the Treaty of Versailles, but they were quite conscious of the political uses of the export weapon and could be very explicit about them. As one businessman put the matter in arguing against excessively strong export controls and high export levies, "I must underscore that it is a necessity, not only economically but also politically, that the German export business can be as active as possible, naturally always under the precondition of charging respectable prices, so that we can increase the economic difficulties of other countries and in that way come nearer to a revision of the treaty."[48] When the Danish Foreign Minister complained that 121,000 persons had crossed the Schleswig border into Germany on the so-called "*Valuta*" trains" and that Danish industry and trade were suffering from lack of business because of the cheap German competition, his German interlocutor responded that "he had come to the wrong address and that he should first turn to the Entente and bring about a change of the Treaty of Versailles." As the German Ambassador noted, however, this response was positively received since "the minister himself is one of those persons who from the very beginning recognized the unfulfillability of the Versailles Treaty and its destructive effects on all of Europe, and he made no bones about this fact, at least to me. He completely understood that we are not in a position to undertake thoroughgoing measures."[49] Switzerland, whose reward for having a currency as highly valued as the dollar and the yen was to find itself in the throes of a terrible depression, also viewed the reduced purchasing power of Germany and her exchange dumping as a major source of her difficulties. Here, too, the German Chamber of Commerce in Zurich and the German Foreign Office representatives worked assiduously to cultivate the opposition to the Treaty. As one German official reported, "we have here in government, banking, and industrial circles zealous and sworn helpers against those interests maintaining the Versailles Treaty. Not the least of our tasks is to support them further in their work."[50]

Manifestly, the Germans were not inventing the growing international hostility to Versailles out of thin air. They were cultivating a widely felt perception. If they had no compunctions about using their inflationary export advantages to promote unemployment abroad and the cause of Treaty revision, they were by no means sanguine about how long such techniques would work. Thus, in drawing up the guidelines for a meeting of the Reich and state Economic Ministers at the end of 1921, the RWM's major emphasis was on stabilizing domestic prices, as much as possible, and international trade relations as well. Most significant, the Ministry refused to operate under the assumption that the condition of high employment created by the inflationary boom would persist, and it actually drew up plans for "work creation in the impending recession." While calling for a moratorium on public contracts and productive unemployment support under existing circumstances, the Ministry urged that preparations be made for a downturn, "since a sudden turn in the present economic boom can be expected anytime."[51] Furthermore, such a downturn was by no means viewed negatively since it conformed to prevailing economic doctrine. As things stood, the advantages of high unemployment and recession abroad were bound to turn into disadvantages within the foreseeable future. In Sweden, for example, major wage cuts were being undertaken, often with the agreement of the workers themselves. As the German Ambassador reported, "it is not to be ruled out, therefore, that a consequence of

the systematically conducted wage reductions will be that the moment is not far off for many Swedish industries previously unable to meet the German competition when they can enter into competition with German products once again."[52]

At the same time, the high hopes entertained by Germany for both financial support from and increased trade with the United States appeared substantially diminished in the fall of 1921. Ironically enough, this was a result of both the tumbling mark and the very successes which low exchange rate of the mark had permitted Germany on European markets. Thus, not only did American bankers appear very cold to the idea of handling a German reparations loan that might be floated in the United States (a fact confirmed by agents of German banks in the United States), but also German-Americans were in some cases disposing of marks they had bought out of loyalty to the "Old Country," arguing that the Upper Silesian decision only reinforced the developing feeling that help given to Germany would end up in the pockets of the French and therefore was pointless.[53] There were even rumors, false in all but one case, that New York banks were refusing to trade in German currency because of its violent fluctuations. Importers, customs agents, and transport firms handling German goods were all complaining of heavy losses on their mark holdings used to transact business and were beginning to feel that the mark was going the way of the Austrian Crown. American producers and politicians were spreading horror stories about the manner in which the Germans had already flooded European markets with their products and were now doing the same in America. Since the ruling Republicans were committed to protectionist measures, doing business in the United States could only be expected to become more difficult. And this was taking place at a time when the German export effort in the United States was anything but distinguished. Thus, the leading American customs broker for German products reported:

The importers of German wares generally complain about bad and delayed deliveries. They are told by manufacturers that goods ordered in December can only be delivered between March and April, and this no longer in mark but rather in dollar prices that are 50 percent higher than the price originally agreed upon. . . . These conditions are a result of the sharp fall in the mark, and an increase in the value of the mark would produce an improvement. A further consideration in getting German goods on the market here is that the German Government has to grant a permit before something can be exported, and that the manufacturers there find it hard to buy raw materials. If the mark were higher, then they would be in a position to supply themselves with foreign raw materials. In the meantime, the importers here do not know what they can buy and at what prices. If the price question were regulated, then American orders for German goods would be much larger.[54]

These problems could be found in the entire range of German export products, from textile machines and inexpensive leather gloves to artificial flowers, porcelain, and standing clocks.

Once again, the Germans were being reminded that, paradoxically, the inflationary export advantage required a goodly measure of stability if it were to be maintained. Little wonder, therefore, that Germany's leadership held on so desperately to the policy for which they had opted back in 1919; namely, for a program of relative stabilization based on the maintenance of a limited export advantage through a regulated difference between German domestic and world prices and through a policy of gradual dismantling of controls and subsidies at home.

While these purposes were obviously incompatible with the kind of reckless inflationary policy of which the French accused the Germans, German opinion was almost unanimously negative with respect to a genuine stabilization until certain basic preconditions were satisfied. While the most important of these was a lower long-term reparations settlement (a revision of the London Ultimatum), German attention was no less riveted on the difficulties of making payments in the near term under any schedule. From this perspective, the entire process had to begin with a moratorium, the terms of which would take the delicate nature of Germany's domestic recovery into account and would involve the reintegration of Germany into the world economy and the granting of credits that would make it possible for Germany to reconstruct its economy as well as meet its financial obligations.

Before criticizing such expectations as irrational, it is useful to remember that they had a good deal of plausibility from the German viewpoint and a great deal of confirmatory evidence in recent experience. The relative stabilization had produced some very promising developments before it came to an end. There had been a marked tendency for domestic prices and the cost of living to stabilize and thus to complement the diminution in the cost of imported goods evident throughout most of the period.[55] Once the London Ultimatum went into effect and reparations payments had to be made, the already unfavorable balance of payments shifted significantly to Germany's disfavor, the exchange rate took a disastrous turn for the worse, and the costs of imports as well as domestic prices and the cost of living began to shoot upward. This was experience, or at least one way of reading experience, but it was also reinforced by the balance-of-payments theory of inflation, which was the dominant, virtually "official" theory in German academic and political circles. Leaving variations among various proponents of the theory aside, the theory held that a passive balance of payments led to an outflow of paper money and a rise in the price of foreign exchange. The rising cost of foreign exchange necessarily increased the size of the budget deficit as well as of commodity prices, which also increased the deficit. This was the process that allegedly produced inflation, and the increase in the quantity of money was a consequence of exchange depreciation of the mark rather than its cause.[56] Naturally, this was grist for the mills of the critics of fulfillment and the Treaty of Versailles, and it was no accident that Karl Helfferich became the most important publicist for the theory as well as serving as one of the leading intellectual exponents of the position.

It would be totally erroneous, however, to view the balance-of-payments theory as nothing more than an instrument of right-wing politics. It was a theory which took its point of departure from real economic factors and which argued, sometimes to excess but never without some cogency, that a modern state and economy had demands which were inelastic. Germany had to import certain quantities of food and raw materials, the argument went, and there was no way to obviate the basic demand for imports through an endogenous solution of restricting the currency supply and balancing the budget.[57] One of the foremost proponents of this argument was Moritz Bonn, who would hardly be numbered among the intransigents on the reparations issue. He was identified with the proponents of fulfillment, had considerable access to and influence on Wirth and Rathenau, and regularly provided material and arguments for the German reparations negotiations. It is worth noting that his views at this time were similar to those of the American economist John M. Williams and the Italian expert on the Reparations Commission Bresciani-Turroni.[58]

Bonn felt quite justified in placing a substantial portion of the blame for the situation that developed after May 1921 on reparations:

... I personally have the impression, and I believe that experience confirms it, that if we did not have to perform any obligations for the Allies, if we did not have to make any reparations payments, then the German balance of payments would not become worse. the experiences which we made with the Spa Agreement, that is from the summer of 1920 until 1921, where the dollar by and large remained steady and where the payments which we made served to pay for credits granted us, point in the direction of there being a certain balance without reparations. At the moment when we bring in reparations, the picture naturally shifts. ... The reparations burden comprehends 33 percent to 40 percent of our foreign obligations every year. That is a rigid sum, so long as certain requirements exist. In this way the balance of payments cannot be put in order.[59]

He recognized, of course, that reparations were not Germany's only economic problem; it was also a heavily indebted land, and its economic survival had been made possible by "wild credits"[60] from abroad. He suggested, however, that those giving the credits were not totally misguided in their speculations since Germans held substantial assets abroad and also hoarded assets at home in order to protect themselves from the inflation. In pure economic terms, Germany was a creditor as well as a debtor nation, even if the foreign denominated assets in German hands, the full extent of which could not be statistically determined, were not presently bringing much benefit to the nation.

Bonn took heart from the fact that foreigners were continuing to speculate in favor of the mark even as Germans were increasingly inclined to abandon it after May 1921.[61] This only heightened the significance he attached to the balance-of-payments problem in explaining the inflation and was another illustration of how much better things would have been without reparations. As matters stood, the outside world was in a very real sense paying for the impossible situation in which Germany had been placed:

... the grant of credits we have from abroad is in many respects a very agreeable form of credit. For the moment at least, it largely bears no interest. Insofar as mark notes are involved, it costs absolutely no interest, but even where German securities are involved, it does not cost any interest against our balance of payments so long as the people believe that the mark will be worth more later and the interest is left in Germany.[62]

Bonn was not suggesting that this situation could go on forever, but he did forcefully argue that it was one important reason why a real stabilization (the establishment of a fixed relationship between the mark and the dollar) was "hopeless" under existing circumstances. All that was possible, in his view, was a measure of "regulation" that might involve the setting of a price ceiling on gold-denominated exchanges but certainly not a minimum price. The attempt to do both would be disastrous:

On that day when the German government . . . announces its intention that . . . let us say, the dollar shall neither rise above 200 marks nor fall below 198 marks, the whole business is at an end. For, at that moment when everybody knows the mark can rise no further, the many billions (people speak of 70 billions; nobody has counted them) invested by foreigners in mark balances in the hopes that the price of the dollar would fall and that of the mark rise substantially, will be thrown on the market and cause such a *deroute* as no organization on earth could contain.[63]

The strength of Bonn's analysis lay in his effort to find solutions that took into account what he conceived to be the full range of unpleasant realities with which Germany had to cope: Germany's import needs, the reactions of those who had speculated on the mark, the necessity of a moratorium and foreign loans, the political necessity of paying France something right away, and the probability of never having the total German obligation set by the Allies reduced very much. Bonn did not think it possible to have a moratorium so complete that France received nothing, because it was obvious that the French had created a budget deficit for themselves which they expected German reparations to fill. He felt that Germany could not escape paying less than a billion a year from its present balance of payments. This, however, constituted the interest needed to pay the private short-term debts Germany had contracted. Like any debtor, Germany could, of course, try to declare bankruptcy or arbitrarily reduce the interest, but these would constitute political rather than financial decisions and would bring the entire "political machinery" into play against Germany.

The only solution, therefore, was to consolidate the short-term private obligations into long-term foreign bonds—that is, a funded debt. Thus, for the next five to seven years, the servicing of the short-term obligations would not be in interest but rather in the form of five billion to seven billion in bonds issued in connection with this debt consolidation. Money would still have to be borrowed to pay the French, but the amount would be more modest—Bonn estimated one and a half billion dollars. When Germany turned to the Americans, however, it would not be with a declaration that "the money which you have given us is lost, but please be so kind as to lend us more."[64] Bonn believed that Germany could be in a position to begin paying the interest on such a modest loan by 1923–1924, when the clearing payments on prewar obligations were to come to an end. By that time, Germany would have had the breathing space needed to get its domestic finances in order and the value of the mark would have risen to the point at which forced loans would no longer be necessary at home because of the restored confidence and because foreign banks could be called upon to support a stabilization loan on terms far more honorable than those which Austria was being compelled to offer at that time.

Bonn's proposal demonstrated that the balance of payments theory was not incompatible with a realistic and responsible approach to the financial and international obligations of Germany. While the entire set of calculations and expectations presented by Bonn turned out to

be too good to be true, it is not inconceivable that the kind of policy he advocated and the spirit behind it might have produced real results if the German government had had the strength and conviction to carry it out consistently and in the face of its domestic opposition. Such a program, however, would also require the acceptance of the Allies, and here Bonn was totally in tune with the Wirth government in placing all his hopes on the British to keep the French in tow and to lead the Americans toward responsibility. Bonn had lived in America and maintained close contacts with prominent American scholars and businessmen, but he was convinced that the Americans would not take the lead in the financial reconstruction of Europe. Like Germany's political leadership, therefore, he welcomed the weakening of the American economic position in Europe during 1921. American trade with Europe in 1921 was 50 percent below 1920, and the dollar, much to German relief, had lost some of its exceptional edge over other currencies. The pound was gaining relative to the dollar and so was the significance of England to Germany. Close relations had been struck up between the Reichsbank and the Bank of England, and the latter had begun to conduct business for the former in a most profitable manner. The United States had an interest in European reconstruction and, to be sure, was suffering from unemployment, but the influence of unemployment on the British was much more serious and was compelling the British to think in terms of reintegrating Germany into the world economy and doing something about the reparations muddle. Bonn could thus speculate that once the pound reached parity with the dollar, "London would take the financial leadership once again" and get the Americans to join in a program of loans to Germany.[65]

This was not to say that it was simple to deal with the British. British economic ideology was considered a very special problem by Germany's leaders. As Bonn put it:

The Allies, chiefly the experts of the British government, who are very much influenced by classical national economic theory, above all the quantity theory, have become addicted to the idea that one can stabilize a currency when the finances have been put in order and when no new notes are printed. They think that then the matter will be in order, and they operate from the line of argument that, if one does not print any notes, then one brings about a shortage of money, and that through this shortage of money one attains lower prices domestically and thereby reduces imports and increases exports.[66]

Bonn rejected this conception by positing the high inelasticity of imports in an economy like Germany's. When Chancellor Wirth solicited a memorandum from Bonn in late January for use in negotiating with the Allies, the economist stated in no uncertain terms that "never in the history of the world of finance has a community indebted abroad been put right simply by setting its domestic house in order."[67] Rathenau, whose own speeches at international conferences and other occasions during this period were heavily influenced by the balance of payments theory of the inflation, sharply attacked the idea that Germany had only to stop printing notes and balance her budget as an "alien way of looking at things."[68]

Actually, it was not quite that "alien." Germany did have prominent and respected economists who held to the quantity theory of money: Walter Eucken, Ludwig Mises, Karl Schlesinger, Alfred Lansburgh, Ludwig Pohle, and L. Albert Hahn. The German quantity-theory proponents were also strongly influenced by the writings of the Swedish economist Gustav Cassel.[69] Their writings on the German inflation and their influence were to increase substantially in 1923–1924, but their theories enjoyed little favor within Germany in 1921–1922 and ran counter to the position taken by Wirth, Rathenau, and other German political leaders that currency reform would have to follow the attainment of a favorable trade balance and fiscal reform. Thus, the thoughts of the editor of the journal *Die Bank*, Alfred Lansburgh, when he argued in two articles that appeared at the turn of 1921–1922 for an immediate currency reform, were very much out of season:

Experience teaches that in a country with a constantly fluctuating currency a normal budget cannot be adhered to. This is rendered still more difficult with a budget so heavily encumbered by war reparations as the German budget. To place the sanitation of the finances after the currency reform is to postpone it *sine die*, i.e., up to the time when the German budget has been stabilized by means of foreign cred-

its. These foreign credits would force Germany to make unnecessarily heavy sacrifices, as such credits are only granted to a country with a depreciated currency on very hard conditions, whilst for countries with a normal currency they are not only cheap but also, to some extent, superfluous. But it is of still greater importance that the reform of currency should not be placed temporarily behind the balancing of imports with exports. As has been pointed out repeatedly in this periodical, the low exchange value of the currency is not the result of the constant excess of imports but the excess of imports has been the inevitable result of the depreciation of the money by the issue of notes. It is unimportant to how large an extent a country is indebted to foreign countries, so long as its currency is equivalent to gold. The indebtedness has no unfavorable influence upon the daily balance and the exchange value of the currency.[70]

Lansburgh advised the cessation of note printing and the covering of the state's needs by loans and taxes and the creation of a new currency that would be exchanged for the old marks at a fixed ratio. The reform would also involve the establishment of regulations for the liquidation of debts that would take into account the value of the mark at the time when they were contracted. Lansburgh was aware of the dangers posed by the huge amount of marks in foreign hands, and he argued that the government would have to be cautious in announcing the reform so as to foil speculators. At the same time, he urged that the German banks form a consortium, eventually to be enlarged into an international syndicate, to secure the credit needed to turn the notes in foreign hands into a loan. Finally, Lansburgh insisted on the necessity of separating the note-issuing functions of the Reichsbank from the giving of credits to the government and proposed that a separate and independent section of the Reichsbank be established for the former purpose. Since this note-issuing section would have both the power and the obligation to restrict the money supply, it would need only a small gold reserve to cover its emissions.

Lansburgh was especially critical of the Reichsbank for its low discount rates and its increasing inability to market Treasury bills.[71] Between 1918 and 1920, the Reichsbank had been able to market between 52 and 75 percent of its discounted Treasury bills, but in November 1921 in excess of one half of the discounted Treasury bills were on reserve in the Reichsbank, and it was forced to issue increasing numbers of notes as these Treasury bills began to accumulate. The situation was such as to lead the American economic observer Maurice Parmelee to wonder if the "vicious circle between the Government deficit and currency inflation" could be broken and whether it would be possible to stop before "the exchange value of the depreciated currency has fallen to zero."[72] The French assignats and the policy pursued by Bolshevik Russia, which were deliberate policies of debt repudiation, were two illustrations of this process. Parmelee did not think the German government so revolutionary or "so irresponsible as to wish to repudiate its debts by underhanded methods," but he was convinced that an immense tax reform was necessary if there were not to be a complete currency breakdown. He did not see how anything like the Lansburgh proposal could work unless fiscal reform came first.

Reichsbank President Havenstein certainly was no revolutionary and was a model of responsibility. He fretted about the way in which the Reich Treasury bills were increasingly backing up into his vaults. He told his Curatorium in December 1921, "[D]espite the continuing high monetary liquidity, the German money market is not able to take this huge mass of treasury bills to the same extent as previously had been the case. Ever larger amounts remain hanging in the Reichsbank and thus increase the circulation of paper money."[73] Nevertheless, Havenstein could see no virtue whatever in the kinds of solutions proposed by Lansburgh and other quantity theorists under existing conditions, and, indeed, the pressure coming from the Allies had the effect of driving him further and further into the balance-of-payments-theory camp.

This is a point worth emphasizing, for while Havenstein and his colleagues at the Reichsbank hardly had much to offer the world by way of monetary theory, their posture toward the inflation problem had been dictated more by practical than theoretical considerations. Until the May 1921 Ultimatum, their Reichsbank reports had continuously stressed the importance of controlling inflation by bringing down the budget deficit, and only with the events of the second half of 1921 did their priorities change

so as to make them appear as undeviating adherents of the balance-of-payments school. Havenstein bristled at the charges that the Reichsbank was a party to the alleged creation of an artificial inflation, and while he was prepared to swallow Allied demands that the Reichsbank be made autonomous of the government, a condition he in fact felt to exist already, he was outraged at the idea of a technical adviser to control the printing of money. This he held to be a violation of the integrity not only of his bank but also of all central banks, a view apparently shared by Montagu Norman, and he was more than willing to provide a memorandum for German negotiators putting forth his views at the end of December 1921, a memorandum which well reflected the increasing calcification of the Reichsbank's position with respect to the causes and cures for the German inflation.[74]

Havenstein hotly contested the notion that Germany had anything to gain from an artificial inflation and state bankruptcy. It would be "insanity," lead to "Austrian conditions," create a measure of unrest that would endanger the political order, make the balancing of the budget impossible, and destroy Germany's ability to produce and trade. In his view, the inflation was the necessary consequence of the adverse balance of payments that, as the events of the previous half year demonstrated, was decisively determined by the reparations obligations and by the domestic deficit. Havenstein emphasized, however, that the balance of payments and reparations problems were decisive for the domestic deficit, so that even if the latter were corrected "through further increase and rapid collection of taxes, which can hardly be increased any more, and through the collection of fees and duties that have been decided upon, the note presses will still be compelled to remain in motion as well as the passivity of the balance of trade."[75]

The reparations undermined confidence at home and abroad, according to Havenstein, and it therefore was impossible to raise loans under existing conditions. The Reichsbank *had* to discount Reich Treasury bills, and Havenstein took full responsibility for this policy by flatly stating that "neither the Reich Chancellor nor any Reich authority has ever put pressure on the Reichsbank Direction to grant credits to the Reich. Rather, we have always voluntarily decided to accept the Treasury bills offered by the Reich for discount."[76] It was an autonomous decision, and, by implication, granting the Reichsbank "autonomy" would not change behavior which Havenstein viewed as natural for any other central bank of issue, except perhaps in the United States, operating under similar circumstances. If the Reichsbank did not discount the Treasury bills, then disastrous consequences would necessarily follow. The Reich could not market the bills on its own without the Reichsbank behind them, and a possible alternative, the issuance of Treasury notes (*Kassenscheine*) by the government, could not be accepted in exchange for Reichsbank notes and would thus also depreciate rapidly. A technical adviser could not alter the realities of the situation:

Would such a person seek to prevent the discounting of the Treasury bills necessary for the coverage of the Reich expenditures or to issuance of notes or the transfer of payments from accounts, this would have the effect of immediately stopping all payments of the Reich and make impossible as well the payments of wages, salaries, and other disbursements to the population, that is, would lead to the bringing of the entire economic life of Germany to a halt and to serious domestic unrest.[77]

The primary responsibility of the Reichsbank, in short, was to keep the economic life of the nation going, and stabilization could only be attained when the balance of payments was improved to the point where balancing of the budget would become possible. Only then would the speculation and hoarding of German bank notes, either for speculative reasons or out of anxiety or to evade taxes, "which have risen to an unbearable measure," come to an end.

Most important about Havenstein's position are his priorities, not his monetary conceptions. He was not indifferent to the amount of money in circulation, and he argued privately that the twentyfold increase of money in circulation over peacetime—from five and a half billion to a hundred billion—could not be justified because the standard of living of the broad masses of Germans had been reduced by 60 percent. Thus, by simple subtraction he concluded that

there was a "real inflation" of some forty billion marks in circulation, which he largely attributed to the amounts being hoarded at home and abroad. He also recognized, quite correctly, that reparations in kind were inflationary because they were exports that produced no foreign exchange and that had to be paid for by the government. He was thus grateful that the Allies at Cannes had reduced the payments in kind foreseen under Rathenau's Wiesbaden Agreement by limiting them to two years. In Havenstein's view, the payments in kind could only be done with the printing press, for if those engaged in this business were forced to accept Treasury bills, then they would soon lack the liquidity to cover their costs. The Reichsbank President thought the widely held view that industry had billions abroad a "fairy tale" and did not think that such conclusions could properly be drawn from heavy industry's rapid paying off of its ore imports a few years before. The amounts involved were too small relative to the kind of money being talked about, and the fact that only about five hundred million of the three billion in exports during the previous year had been paid for in foreign currency suggested that the reserve of foreign exchange available to industry was inadequate. This is not to say that Havenstein wished to leave increased foreign currency reserves from exports in the hands of industry, but he felt strongly that the Reichsbank could not do its job of intervening to stabilize the exchange rate and meet the other needs and interests of industry if it did not have the appropriate resources at its disposal. He argued that selling abroad for foreign exchange rather than marks was "of great significance . . . since thereby large amounts of foreign exchange can be concentrated at one place and one can operate with them just as one can operate with large masses of troops."[78] The major priority in collecting foreign exchange for Havenstein, therefore, was not to pay reparations or to engage in an immediate stabilization but rather to keep the economy going while preventing wild exchange fluctuations.

The priorities of the German balance-of-payment theorists and the political and economic leaders who joined in their position were rational and plausible, just as were those of Poincaré and the other French leaders who said very little about economic theory but who wished to solve France's financial difficulties and reparations at one and the same time by turning the entire reparations problem into a credit operation under which reparations bonds would be internationally marketed. Holders of such bonds would demand security, and the French demand for controls on German fiscal and monetary policy appeared necessary to attain their goal.[79] The Germans were constantly tossing export, import, budgetary, tax, and other figures about at one another and at the Allies, but neither they nor the foreign recipients of this material were overly impressed with the accuracy of what they were producing. The American Economic Consul in Berlin, Maurice Parmelee, dutifully reported whatever the Finance Ministry produced by way of budget and tax information on a regular basis but no less regularly concluded with confidential comments on the "obscurity" of the material and the "contradictions" between one set of data and the next, a condition vastly exacerbated by the manner in which items were shifted about between the "ordinary" and "extraordinary" budget, all of which indicated the "confused state of the German public finances and the more or less chaotic financial conditions in Germany at large."[80]

The German leaders had every reason to try to preserve their fiscal autonomy and conduct a reconstruction consonant with Germany's great-power pretensions. They also had every right to attempt a way out of their dilemma compatible with their need to maintain order, a problem of which Wirth was brutally reminded in late January by a dangerous railroad strike. Yet, there was a very real danger that their employment of the balance-of-payments theory in their negotiations with the Allies for a moratorium would blind them to the serious gaps in their credibility and would drive them into a position of intransigence that was a good deal less pragmatic than the theory they espoused. It might become both possible and "logical" to slip into a position of principled opposition to the ordering of German finances unless demands for a moratorium were met.

This danger did not go unnoticed on the German side. In the discussion of the reparations problem in the Socialization Commission between July 1921 and March 1922, the interest

had shifted very markedly from a stress on balancing the budget and stabilization through effective taxation and other domestic measures to the balance of payments issue. Bonn's influence had proven quite strong during the last sessions held in March, and the eminent statistical economist Robert Kuczynski became increasingly alarmed over the tone and political implications of both the discussion within the Socialization Commission and the statements of Germany's political leaders, especially Rathenau's treatment of the quantity-theory advocates abroad:

I must say that I find it extraordinarily regrettable when that [theory] is presented here as an alien way of looking at things. During the war we have so often regarded that which was thought, not only by the political world, but also by the scholarly world, as an alien way of thinking. Our honored member, Dr. Rathenau had also done that often enough. I believe that we here should distance ourselves from this attitude and should rather work through and take a position toward that which is generally recognized by the scholarly world even if we do not agree with it.[81]

Kuczynski thought it neither intellectually sound nor politically wise simply to reject the opposing point of view, a fault of which he accused Bonn, and simply toss about trade statistics that were not entirely reliable and that really did not settle the issue:

I mean, the least the supporters of Professor Bonn could do would be to refute seriously the so-called alien way of thinking, which happens to be general outside of Germany, and they ought to consider among themselves whether they should not take the position upon which I and perhaps other members of the Commission stand, which is that, on the one hand, one can view as the ideal solution for Germany that Germany be granted a moratorium for five to seven years, but that on the other hand, if we do not receive this moratorium, which we also regard as self-understood, then we must take measures to achieve a stabilization of our currency through the cleansing of our finances and the reestablishment of the balance of the Reich budget, which you all unconditionally called for five months ago in your first report after the discussion of the reparations question.[82]

The policy prior to May 1921 of waiting upon a fixed reparations sum and failing to undertake serious measures of domestic stabilization, whatever its positive advantages from the perspective of German domestic peace and economic reconstruction, had led to the post-London Ultimatum conditions that gave such plausibility to the balance-of-payments theory. The threat now was that the notorious tendency of German scholarship to treat a scholarly argument as a set of theological tenets reflecting both Truth and national superiority would combine with the kind of self-righteous whining and self-encircling diplomacy characteristic of the Wilhelmine era to produce new disasters.

The Great Wage Push

Whatever the deficiencies of the balance of payments theory and the manner in which Germany's leaders conducted foreign affairs, it is essential to record that these were also responses to the exigencies of democratic politics and to the anxieties about popular unrest to which any government had to pay heed after the war and Revolution. The tragedy of the Weimar Republic unavoidably produces a goodly measure of wishful thinking in the form of counterfactual propositions about the postwar settlement imposed upon Germany. One can reasonably argue that the cause of German democracy and domestic stability would have been served best if reparations had never been imposed and inter-Allied war debts had been rapidly cancelled after the war. Alternatively, the future of the world might have been a happier one if the French had been allowed to separate the Rhineland from Germany and open the way to new territorial arrangements in central Europe. In the first instance, German domestic development could have enjoyed an autonomy that it simply could not have as long as its governments were confronted by a reparations charge against their national income estimated by sober economists today to range between 10 and 12 percent.[83] Nearly all Germans viewed this charge as unjust, and it heightened and legitimized antidemocratic and conservative political and social positions that would certainly have been difficult to maintain under other circumstances. In the second instance, it would seem obvious that a strategic solution to the German question eliminating Germany as a great power would have reduced substantially the significance of its domestic political traditions and development and obviated the rather overdone debate among German histo-

rians concerning the primacy of domestic as opposed to the primacy of foreign policy in determining Germany's development. Neither of these scenarios occurred, and they are not very useful counterfactual propositions. The reality was that a domestically troubled and economically disabled Germany confronted a reparations bill which was certainly beyond its domestic political capacities whatever the bill's theoretical feasibility. What this meant was that while no German government could manage the domestic situation without taking the foreign policy constraints imposed by reparations into account, the response of any German government, especially of one with democratic pretensions, to the conditions created by Germany's reparations creditors depended significantly on domestic conditions. The domestic political stalemate was such that the self-confidence of the government in domestic political management constantly required external support. That was why Wirth's mood was so buoyant in early January in his conversations with D'Abernon; the prospect of a moratorium and a role for Germany in European reconstruction enabled him to speak confidently about dealing with his domestic problems.[84]

Only a month before, however, he had spoken in very different tones to British diplomat and economic expert Joseph Addison, to whom he commented in the gloomiest manner of the dangers created by rising prices, labor discontent, and the possibility of serious unrest. The effect of Wirth's remarks was heightened by the semidarkness in which the two men spoke because of the utility-worker strike in Berlin and because Addison regarded Wirth to be "a man of quiet determination, with a leaning towards optimism, and who does not suffer from the almost universal German defect of viewing all difficulties through a magnifying glass."[85] The Chancellor appeared quite distressed because of reports that women appeared to be in a particularly belligerent mood and were likely to "inflame their male relatives." Addison was convinced that the situation was threatening to German democracy:

It cannot be expected that the working classes should be expert economists and should understand the close relation which exists between the price of a pair of boots in Berlin and the mark value of a dollar in New York. They not unnaturally attribute excessive prices and their distress to everything except their natural cause, and above all, to the maneuvers of a gang of speculators and oppressors of the people, who are supposed to be in close league with the Government. The present situation, therefore, has a distinct political bearing in that it increases the lack of esteem for the present form of Government, which, so far as I have been able to ascertain, exists to a greater or lesser degree even amongst those classes which *prima facie* would be supposed to support it.[86]

The sudden improvement of the exchange rate in December, as Addison recognized, did not really make the situation better, for "whatever advantage may accrue to public finance, such a change cannot fail, if maintained or accentuated, to entail the usual consequences of too rapid deflation, and to add unemployment to the many disadvantages with which the population of Germany is at present contending."

These problems were not new, and it is difficult not to have a sense of *déjà vu* as yet another Weimar regime, for the third year in a row, confronted year-end or post–New Year problems of public-service-worker unrest (especially in the railroads), a new round of coal-price and wage increases, and the puzzles of how to manage inflationary interest-group and social pressures, ward off the consequences of deflation, and avoid offending the Allies at the same time. History never quite repeats itself however, and these problems had taken on new qualities after the acceptance of the London Ultimatum.

The strains in the relations between organized industry and labor had increased markedly in the course of the relative stabilization. Industry attempted to hold down wages and salaries, restore differentials, increase hours, eliminate or reduce export controls and levies, and take advantage of unemployment and short-time to roll back some of the advantages gained by labor since the war and shift the emphasis from social to economic considerations in the determination of public and private policy toward labor. For all its protests and emphasis on the priority of price reduction, organized labor exercised a goodly measure of wage restraint—in part because economic conditions and Germany's international problems had placed it on the defensive, and in part because it did not have economically convincing counterarguments at its disposal—and sought to find means of continuing its collaboration with industry. By early 1921, however, pressure from the rank

and file and anxiety over unemployment were shifting the balance in favor of a more uncompromising stance, tempered only by the desire to maintain cooperation with industry in dealing with the foreign policy crisis surrounding the London Ultimatum and the Upper Silesian question. If nothing else, the leaders of both industry and labor could continue to protest Allied demands and measures in common.[87]

The tide against wage restraint was turned in the summer of 1921, and the ostensible cause was a 50 percent bread price increase on August 15, 1921. The background of this event is to be found in the evolution of the government's food supply and agricultural policy. The Centrist Food Minister Andreas Hermes, who had taken office in March 1920 and continued to serve in that capacity until he assumed the post of Finance Minister in March 1922, devoted most of his efforts to dismantling the system of food controls, with the objective of increasing the supply and ending black marketeering and ultimately reducing the need for foreign food imports and government subsidies. His efforts, strongly supported by Wirth, had been significantly assisted by the relative stabilization, which reduced food import costs. Nevertheless, Hermes was fully aware of the need to practice decontrol in a manner that ensured the supply of food, especially bread, in sufficient quantity and at a controlled price. For this reason, he planned to introduce a transitional system of grain levies for the new agricultural year beginning August 15, under which the farmers would be required to deliver a quota of their production at a price determined by the Reich but would be free to market the remainder. This projected dual-market system met with antagonism from the farmers, who wanted a return to the free market in wheat, while it was considered by the leading consumer interests an inadequate way to protect the food supply and maintain prices. Hermes, however, remained convinced that it was the only socially acceptable way of moving toward a free market and resisted the pressures coming from both sides. While sticking to his plan, he strongly opposed price increases until an adequate supply of wheat was available. The acceptance of the London Ultimatum undermined this goal because Chancellor Wirth felt that significant bread price increases were essential to reduce subsidies. Wirth hoped the increase would at once assist the cause of making the first reparations payments and show the Allies that Germany was on the road to abandoning the much criticized food-subsidy system. Hermes, supported by Labor Minister Brauns, was prepared to accept a 33 to 50 percent bread price increase for the economic year beginning in August, but Wirth wanted increases in both July and August. Hermes, warning that these increases were bound to cause unrest and major wage demands, finally found sufficient Cabinet support to force Wirth to settle for a projected four-billion-mark savings in subsidies through a single 50 percent bread price increase on August 15.[88]

The trade-union leaders had expected the Hermes program to bring a bread price increase from the day they learned of the plan and had tried in April to mobilize the employer leaders in the ZAG against any relaxation of controls on the wheat producers. The employers refused to oppose the government program, just as they had earlier refused to join in an alliance with the trade unions against the farmers and in favor of the controlled economy, but General Directors Krämer and Sorge assured Theodor Leipart, who had assumed leadership of the ADGB after Legien's death, and the other trade union leaders that a wage increase would be the logical result of a bread price increase. Still operating in the glow of the waning relative stabilization, they hastened to point out, apparently without objection from Leipart, that the wage increase would naturally have to be one which did not raise the prices of all other products and, further, that any subsequent reduction of bread prices would also have implications for wage levels.[89]

Such speculations could easily be dispensed with when the issue was taken up in the ZAG again on July 7. The bread price increase was a foregone conclusion, and the trade-union leaders saw fit to remind the employers of what had been said in April and asked that the ZAG call for negotiations to arrange a general supplementing of wages and salaries outside of existing wage contracts. The employer representatives claimed they could not commit themselves without instructions, and Leipart decided to increase the pressure when they next met on August 11 by pointing out that the price

of everything was going to go up and that "the trade unions are thus forced to make demands that could perhaps make the employers want to hide their heads in their hands."[90] At this meeting as well as on August 19, the employers took the position that the actual consequences of the bread price increase were not yet evident, that a few employer representatives in Berlin could not dictate to the rest, and that specific conditions obtaining in the various industries would have to be taken into account in determining what wage supplements, if any, would be granted. For the trade-union leaders, however, the situation was too serious to make such a response acceptable now that the anticipated and, in their view, preventable price increases had come:

The workers agree with the employers that the workers are not helped when the printing press is set in motion and a few more paper marks are received. In order to have relatively healthy conditions, the workers had proposed to begin with the reduction of prices at that point where the price increases started, namely in agriculture; the other economic areas would then follow. This proposal was not met with any reception. On the contrary, agriculture is now trying to attain world market prices. But the consequence of this effort will be that one will have to pay world market wages. One should also think about the fact that the *Arbeitsgemeinschaft* has been much attacked lately and that the opposition to this institution of ours has increased. If the ZAG remains passive in this matter, then it will be grist for the mills of the opposition.[91]

Sorge and his colleagues pointed out that opposition to the ZAG also existed among the employers and that a centralized regulation would not be acceptable. The trade unionists seemed to understand this and settled for a resolution urging that the bread price increase be taken into account in those wage negotiations having not already occurred.

The employer representatives in the ZAG were well-advised not to go beyond such recommendations, for on the day before the resolution was passed, the powerful Association of German Metal Industrialists instructed its members to reject wage increases based on the bread price increase and to refuse negotiations on this subject in any central organization, including the ZAG. The association argued that wage increases should not be granted to anticipate an increased cost of living that had not yet set in, especially since this would only serve to justify new demands if and when prices did go up. Additionally, employers were urged to point out to trade-union negotiators that "only now would the effects of the Versailles Treaty and the acceptance of the Ultimatum show themselves in all their severity and that the resultant impoverishment of all classes of the German people, also the workers, would have to be suffered in common."[92]

The trade-union leaders were not in any mood to listen to such stuff, however, and when less than a week later an employer representative in Stuttgart tried to argue against a demanded wage increase on the grounds that prices had not yet gone up, Germany was not competitive, and the international situation made belt tightening essential, the metal-workers' representative replied that

Baurat Fischer's lesson in national economy is appropriate for a professor, but not for hungry workers. The workers do not have any responsibility for the depreciation of the money anymore than they have for most of the price increases. Other circles are to be held responsible for that. . . . The cost of living has increased by ten to twenty times since 1914, but wages only by six times. It is thus impossible to buy clothes, linens, boots, etc. On the other side, there has been a steady increase of dividends which does not stand in any relation to the depreciation of the money, and it does not appear that the employers are prepared to renounce higher profits for economic reasons.[93]

The altercations on this and other occasions involved a good deal of bandying about of cost-of-living and wage index statistics, both sides at once claiming validity for those which were most useful and questioning the value of the statistics and charging political motives when they were unfavorable.

The wage movement of August 1921, while supported by the trade unions in a general way, was anything but a disciplined and coherent trade union effort. Leipart had tried in vain to coordinate the wage demands of the various unions, and efforts by union negotiators to settle on what they considered appropriate cost-of-living supplements were often rejected in close votes by the workers.[94] The demands made were often in substantial excess even of what could be anticipated as the consequence of the bread price increase as well as of the actual cost

of living in August. To the informed observer, it rapidly became clear, on the one hand, that the workers were responding to an unusual combination of real and environmental indications that the trend toward price stabilization was at an end and, on the other hand, that the workers were determined not to let inflation undermine the recovery, such as it was, that they had made since the war. They intended to anticipate the inflation.

There were a host of signals to which they were responding. In August 1921 the workers were not only confronted by the bread price increase, but also by higher prices for other food products because of a drought which reduced the supply of potatoes, vegetables, and milk. At the same time, the implications of the first reparations payment were brought home to them by the announcement of Wirth's unprecedented tax program, which included a host of indirect taxes that were bound to raise the price of consumer goods. Then, there were some less tangible but all too visible influences that incited worker demands: the host of foreign summer visitors who were enjoying German resorts and goods on the cheap, the speculators on the stock exchange and in the money market and the reports of sensational share price increases, and the manifest increase in the flight from marks to goods on the part of businessmen and consumers wealthy enough to anticipate price increases. As early as June 1921, a Berlin official noted that "the buying out of Berlin shops by foreigners from countries with strong currencies increases. They arrive at the Stettiner railway station in rumpled suits and leave it newly clothed with stately leather suitcases."[95]

Finally, a good deal of inspiration was being provided by two very powerful groups within the ranks of labor itself, the civil servants and the coal miners. The former, led by the German Federation of Civil Servants (DBB), were raising demands which not only the government but even the ADGB found totally unacceptable. Even more serious than the fact that they would cost the government an additional thirty billion marks a year was that they called for the elimination of differentials and the establishment of an automatic sliding-scale wage that would be adjusted to price increases (indexation). While the government managed to evade

In the West, the accursed hole is wide open behind Goch.

The shy smuggler goes under cover since he does not like the green color.

"Bang!" goes the border guard's rifle; smuggling is not so easy anymore.

The Dutch come in swarms; their money weighs heavily.

"Warehouse Germany." Here the miracle of making oneself beautiful and plump is quickly accomplished.

By means of this picture, any child can see what "barbarians" the Germans are.

Emergency money issued by the town of Goch near the Dutch border in January 1922. Many towns and cities issued emergency money prior to the hyperinflation to satisfy the need for small "change." Considerable imagination and effort were often put into the design of such money to advertise the town for tourist purposes or tell its history, but some of the money was used to convey a political message, usually attacking the Treaty of Versailles and its consequences. In this case, the "Accursed Hole in the West," the buying out of Germany, and the war against illegal smuggling by the "green police" at the border provided the subject matter of these very colorful fifty- and seventy-five-pfennig notes.

serious discussion of this issue and to outflank the civil-servants' unions by offering substantial increases in the cost-of-living supplement provided for in the Civil Service Reform Act of 1920, the achievement of a compromise that would cost the government "only" seventeen billion to eighteen billion obviously did not help Wirth's efforts to control government expenditure. The fact that a major social group had come out in support of the automatic adjustment of its wages and salaries to inflation did not bode well for the future and undoubtedly did its share to stir other groups of workers.[96]

As for the coal miners, they too were making fateful strides in the adaptation to inflation. Until this time, wage negotiations in the mining industry had been decentralized and conducted in the various mining districts, and this meant that the wage levels took some account of the different price structures and conditions in the various districts. On July 20, 1921, however, the unions came forth with wage demands that were addressed to the coal *Arbeitsgemeinschaft* in Berlin and pushed for centralized wage negotiations on the grounds that the increased cost of living existed throughout the Reich. Centralized negotiations were particularly advantageous from the union point of view because they permitted the negotiators to focus their energies and consolidate their demands in one place rather than repeat their efforts district by district. They also were of advantage to the employers, however, since they would promote the united front often sorely absent in wage negotiations despite repeated agreements among the employers of the different districts to cooperate with one another. Furthermore, the extreme nature of the trade-union demands—an increase of twelve marks per man per shift for the entire industry—and the fact that they could not easily be justified by the increased cost of living, placed the employers in an excellent position to concede both centralized negotiations and a pay increase in return for a price increase. Thus, on August 19, August Schmidt of the Socialist mining union declared that "wherever the mining industry is not in a position to bear the costs of the wage increase demanded alone, there must eventually be a price increase of mining products," a view seconded by his colleague Steger from the Christian mine union.[97]

Nevertheless, the employers offered an increase of only eight marks per shift, and it took the mediatory efforts of Labor Minister Brauns to produce a compromise of ten marks per shift on September 1, which was followed by a decision of the mine owners to raise prices by twenty-one marks per ton a few days later. In order to appreciate the significance of this trade-off, it is necessary to note that the average price of anthracite coal had been forcibly held

by the government at 198.40 marks per ton between May 1920 and March 1921, despite moderate wage increases for the miners throughout that period, and that the increase to 227.40 marks per ton allowed in April 1921 reflected Cabinet consensus that an increase was fully justified. The new increase to 253.90 was also accepted by the government, but this second increase within less than half a year suggested that the tide was turning and that the practice of trading off wage for price increases was resuming.[98]

When all the above developments are taken into account, it seems clear that August 1921 brought about a significant transformation of labor's attitude in the direction of adapting to inflation no matter what the economic consequences. As one expert, who was by no means antilabor, put it in a sharp criticism of those determining and defending trade-union wage policy:

The reservation that every further increase of the nominal income of large portions of the people that is not absolutely justifiable economically and that takes place without a comparable increase in the goods produced, is not only pointless but also leads to a reduction in the domestic purchasing power of the mark while at the same time increasing the money in circulation and reducing the exchange rate against foreign currencies—the reservation concerning the *circulus vitiosus* of all watering of wages played no role among the literary champions of the great wage movement in the worker and white-collar worker press. Since the German paper mark was being subjected to new tumbles because of the gathering of the gold payments needed to cover the first billion in reparations and the accompanying speculation in any case, these wage policymakers did not feel that they had to give special heed to the new watering of income produced by the domestic depreciation of the mark. On the contrary, the newly begun weakening of the exchange value of the mark has fortified the determination behind the wage policy of the workers and civil servants to go the whole way this time and anticipate all these mark depreciating tendencies through higher wage increases before they occurred.[99]

The most extreme illustration of this attitude in the labor camp was provided, appropriately enough, by the head of the Socialist Agricultural Workers Union, Georg Schmidt, who openly argued that the policy of agrarian controls should be abandoned and that world-market prices should be matched by world-market wages.[100] Even without such inspiration, how-ever, the trend was clear by September 1921: in-dustry was gradually giving up its relative sta-bilization policy of resistance to wage demands and simply surrendering and then increasing its prices.[101]

Such developments were not what most trade union leaders had in mind, despite their support of the August wage movement. Georg Schmidt's attack on the controlled economy and call for world-market prices and wages were openly disavowed.[102] While Independent Socialist trade-union leaders, like Robert Diß-mann of the metal workers, continued to de-fend the controlled economy, even those who questioned its efficacy felt that it was impolitic for trade union leaders to agree to its abolition. They viewed the idea of attaining world market wages as absurd and rejected it as the fantasy that one "could pull oneself out of the mire by one's own pig tails."[103] Put in less colorful terms, the problem was that the high wages of American workers, for example, did not nec-essarily buy as much in America as did paper marks in Germany, and American wages were not as well supplemented with social benefits as were those paid in Germany. America also had much higher unemployment.[104]

Similarly, the ADGB leaders were sharply critical of the civil-servant associations' de-mands, which they attributed to lack of orga-nizational and negotiating experience. Leipart and others also felt that the wage–price trade-offs were a path to disaster, and another trade-union leader criticized the factory coun-cils for being nothing more than "employer representatives" because of their willing ness to accept price increases in return for wage increases. These trade unionists argued that

the representatives of the workers must sharpen their consciences. They cannot collaborate in the pricing policies of the employers and ought not to be exces-sively influenced by occupational or industrial branch considerations, but must rather be aware that they are not only representatives of the producers but also the consumers.[105]

For this reason, the trade-union leaders fought against a response to the situation that

was based solely on wage increases. Their con-cern with the tax program and support of the appropriation of real values were efforts to tran-scend a purely reactive policy toward inflation that concentrated on wage increases. They sought to provide the government with the means both to maintain its social policies and to carry out the policy of fulfillment while fight-ing against a taxation system under which the chief burdens would fall on the mass of con-sumers.

Despite these good intentions, the pattern set in the summer continued through the fall and winter. The civil servants were especially restive and in October 1921 forced the government to grant new cost-of-living increases costing be-tween twelve billion and thirteen billion marks. These new costs, which could only be covered by the printing press, scarcely give the full pic-ture of the fiscal damage being done, however, because the Civil Service Reform Act of 1920 mandated that increases in Reich civil-service pay scales had to be complemented by state, municipal, and other governmental agencies as well. The decision of the Reich government thus produced panic among the municipal au-thorities throughout Germany, who held an ex-traordinary meeting of the Congress of German Muncipalities on November 11 to insist that the Reich cover the new costs immediately, since many of them did not have the necessary cash on hand, and also that the Reich make pro-vision for coverage of future raises by more eq-uitable distribution of income-tax proceeds.[106]

The October increase produced profound dissatisfaction among the lower-level civil ser-vants. Although their salaries had in real terms reached 97 percent of prewar levels, they had for the first time since April 1920 received pro-portionately less of an increase, albeit by ex-tremely small percentages, than the middle- and higher-level civil servants. The fact that the former were only up to 65 percent and the latter only up to 54 percent of their prewar salaries did nothing to still the passion for equalization of differentials which the inflation was used to justify. As added spice to this unhealthy brew, the civil servants in the countryside were mo-bilizing on their own in protest against the higher salaries being paid to the urban civil servants who benefited from the regional classifications on which salary levels were partially based.[107]

As a final complication, municipal authorities in Prussia and elsewhere were required to adjust their civil service pay scales to those of the state government, which was nothing short of "Sisyphean labor" in Prussia's ninety-four municipalities and agrarian districts. In Berlin, this undermined efforts to get more work for less pay out of its officials and thereby control municipal payroll expenses. The result was an orgy of expensive trade-offs and special-interest politicking. First, there were three days of ceaseless negotiation between the municipal authorities and the civil-servant union representatives. As one of the former recorded:

A macabre final scene: in the smoke-filled magistrate's meeting room there sit numerous exhausted organization representatives slumped in the comfortable chairs. A box of Brazilian cigars and a number of Grenadines with enough rasberry liqueur help me to fight off every bout of tiredness. Smokers are always at an advantage in tiresome negotiations.[108]

The arrangements made under these unedifying conditions were only the prelude to a new round of wheeling and dealing between civil-servant interests and the parties in the city parliament, which threatened to undermine the agreed-upon plan. The parties vied with one another in their solicitation of the civil servants they thought politically friendly to their side. While the left concentrated on the lower officials, the bourgeois parties sought to woo the higher civic officials and academics. The debates were not a credit to municipal parliamentary government:

Characteristic for the handling of such huge bills was that there were special battles over the pay of individual persons. Thus we could not prevent the placing of the Schöneberg city hall restaurant *Meister* in the pay group of the city executive secretaries. The Schöneberg wine cellar guests had the majority.[109]

The private sector was no less troubled. A major new wage movement began in October, which the Association of German Employer Organizations (VdA) immediately declared in now familiar tones to be unjustified by prices and nothing more than a deliberate attempt to achieve world-market wages by taking advantage of the boom accompanying the depreciation of the mark. They confessed, however, that the employers themselves were responding no less slavishly to the boom and were inclined to behave as they had in August and September by refusing to follow VdA wage guidelines and simply giving in to union demands in order to keep production going. This was producing especially unhappy results in some branches of industry, since the tendency to emphasize the cost-of-living component in wage increases meant that the increases easily granted by industries enjoying the boom were being forced upon those industries not doing as well. The cost of living, after all, was increasing for all workers, no matter what the condition of their branch. Furthermore, the big increases granted in some industries and not others were causing workers to migrate to the higher-paying industries, and the result was recriminations between groups of employers, especially in the metals and textile industries. What disturbed the VdA leadership most, however, was that the combination of preoccupation with the boom and concern with such major economic and political issues as taxes, the Wiesbaden Agreement, and the industrial credit offer were distracting attention from the issues of wage policy.[110]

Wage policy was, in truth, a problem for the employers, the trade unions, and the Labor Ministry. It was impossible not to be critical of the degree to which differentials had been reduced by the need to keep up with the cost of living as well as by the renewed tendency to decouple wages from productivity. One employer approach to the problem of squaring social with productivity concerns was the so-called social wage, which involved giving additional compensation to workers with families. Some firms had actually set up equalization funds among themselves, with the aim of increasing the money available to firms with large numbers of married workers with children. The trade unions opposed the social wage for the obvious reason that it was discriminatory against younger workers and tended to favor workers who were most dependent on steady work and least likely to strike. At the same time, the manifest injustice being done under inflationary conditions to workers with families and the obvious advantages enjoyed by the unmarried could hardly be dismissed, and there was much talk in union circles of having the government provide the social component. This was not exactly an inflation-fighting proposal, and one of the chief goals of Labor Minister Brauns was to use his mediation and arbitration powers to balance social and productivity considerations, a goal which the employer organization leaders branded as "mercantilistic." They, however, were not able to boast much success in their own efforts to accomplish the same end. Ultimately, all the employers could argue was that the wage component of production was becoming increasingly excessive, that insufficient capital was available, and that Germany was fast becoming uncompetitive.[111]

The trade-union leaders were not blind to these problems, and they faced the double task of arming the workers against the depredations of inflation and the anticipated depression. They were very aware that even if their primary task was to defend the immediate interests of the workers, the long-term interests of labor required German productivity and competitiveness. The angry set of Ten Demands proclaimed on November 21, 1921, in response to the collapse of the credit offer strenuously rejected the privatization of the railroads but strongly stressed the importance of straightening out the finances of the railroad system and other public enterprises, a position which sat ill with the unions' traditional call for the socialization of the coal-mining industry.[112] And while union leaders loudly renewed the demand for the appropriation of real values, at least the Majority Socialists among the trade-union leadership entertained no illusions that this constituted much of a solution to the immediate international and domestic crisis.[113] Thus, Otto Schweitzer of the white-collar trade unions frankly admitted that the Ten Demands had primarily a tactical purpose and had been presented with the objective of supporting Wirth's fulfillment policy and forcefully responding to the industrialists. In his view, the London Ultimatum was unfulfillable, and Germany could do nothing until Allied demands became bearable. The Majority Socialist trade-union leaders were particularly irritated with the manner in which such Independent Social-

ists in their ranks as Robert Dißmann of the DMV and Josef Simon of the Shoemakers Union became victims of their own rhetoric, talked about a general strike to force through their tax program, and actually appeared to believe that the appropriation of real values was some kind of panacea for labor's problems. Quite aside from the fact that Fritz Tarnow, Wissell, and other SPD trade unionists felt that the tax program was a matter for the political parties first and foremost, they pointed out that a tax program based solely on direct taxation would be found unacceptable by the Allies, who had been insisting on increased indirect taxes all along, that many of the direct taxes would hit consumers indirectly in any case, and that the appropriation of real values would take at least two years to get under way and, when effectuated, would also harm the workers because it involved directly tapping the means of production for reparations. Given this attitude, it is hard to take seriously Leipart's veiled threat in a meeting with Wirth on January 12 of a general strike if the appropriation of real values did not become part of a tax reform. The trade-union leaders put up very little resistance to Wirth's arguments that there was no majority in the Reichstag for such a reform as well as his warning against imposing yet another assessment program on the tax authorities. What really made the trade-union leaders nervous was the potential effects of Allied demands for tax reform and for the termination of food subsidies on their constituencies. One trade-union leader pointed out to Wirth that "the trade unions are not dogmatists on the question of the appropriation of real values. But they must insist that the existing taxes actually be collected with the greatest possible speed. Further, it is unthinkable for domestic political reasons to terminate the subsidies for food now while raising taxes on consumer items without there being some visible sacrifice by the propertied."[114]

Indeed, it was impossible for the trade-union leaders not to view any program for the fulfillment of reparations and the balancing of the budget with mixed feelings. On the one hand, there was some inclination to see the end of food and other subsidies very positively and even a willingness to discuss, as had the Christian trade unionists, some new arrangement for the railroad system. On the other hand, there was a genuine fear that the Allies would impose financial controls that would, for example, leave a total vacuum in the support of the unemployed by compelling the dismantling of the existing unemployment support system without making an employment insurance system possible. In 1918–1919, industry had filled the breach with its reserves and work-stretching policies, but industry no longer felt obliged so to act in 1921–1922. When both the Labor Ministry and the trade unions proposed at the end of 1921 that the employers agree to put away some of their profits from the existing boom to meet the costs of supporting the unemployed if and when business conditions turned for the worse, Bücher of the RdI coolly replied on behalf of industry that "in view of the present large-scale variations in the exchange rate and in consideration of the fact that there are eighteen new tax laws being presented which in part not only tax profits but also capital, there is already great uncertainty in business calculations, and it is completely impossible to accept the proposals of the representatives of the workers."[115]

The trade-union leaders responded by threatening to call upon the government to implement its proposed measures by emergency decree, but there is no evidence that the employers lost much sleep over this threat. In fact, despite deep differences concerning an equitable distribution of the costs of the lost war and the Treaty, industry and labor continued to be drawn together at the leadership level because both sides had their attention riveted upon the diplomatic situation at the turn of 1921–1922. In the context of the external threat and wage–price trade-offs, they could converse with one another in an atmosphere of limited confrontation. Their agreement on the impossibility of fulfilling the London Ultimatum was the bedrock of what remained of their relationship.

Thus, the *post mortem* on the industrial credit offer in the ZAG in late January 1922 was a very genteel affair, a condition undoubtedly helped by the fact that the discussion had been put off for weeks. Bücher tried to rationalize away the defeat of the moderate industrial forces he represented by arguing that Germany could not have received the long-term credit

she needed by means of the credit offer in any case. Evading the role played by domestic conflicts in causing the failure of the credit action, he gave classic expression to the primacy of foreign policy: "It is a great mistake that in Germany domestic and foreign policy are continually mixed up with one another, instead of our getting together in external matters. So long as we do not recognize our common interest and find the way to positive collaboration, the government will remain an executive committee of the Entente, which is what it is now. The policy of fulfillment to the limits of our capacity to perform is a purely negative matter and no positive deed."[116] Exactly what constituted a "positive deed" remained undefined, aside from participation in the forthcoming Conference on International Economic Reconstruction in Genoa. Bücher seemed to view Germany's greatest advantage to be the fact that "we have an infectious effect because of our attack on the employment levels in other countries,"[117] although he admitted that this German export advantage was beginning to deteriorate.

Bücher's emphasis on the primacy of foreign policy and the need to push the Allies by exporting unemployment was shared by some Socialist trade-union leaders and strongly supported by the Christian trade-union leadership. Thus, in another such meeting, the Socialist textile-union leader Kreil saw "the greatest weapon of the Germans is, on the one side, that they fight unemployment in their own country through payments in kind and, on the other side, cause unemployment abroad or even increase it."[118] However, other trade-union leaders, Wissell for example, doubted that one could separate foreign and domestic policy, felt that Germany's export advantage had very little depth because of the development of competitive industries abroad during the war, and wondered why Germany was having such a hard time collecting more taxes when the workers were paying a great deal more than before. The general Socialist answer to the long-term problem of competitiveness was to push technological development, a solution with which every industrialist could agree and which provided Stinnes with a marvelous opportunity to complain about the aging of the coal-mining industry, the shortage of capital, and the need to prevent unemployment by getting rid of the controlled economy (including rent controls) and thereby help industry to get the operating capital it needed. Both he and Borsig took a very conciliatory position on the length of the working day, blaming the productivity problem on the failure to make use of the actual hours worked. Stinnes roundly declared that "an elimination of the eight-hour day is not necessary if there is intensive work during these eight hours. But today in Germany there are two million people unproductively employed. The railroads alone use at least 400,000 persons who could be productively employed elsewhere."[119]

While there is no evidence that the Socialists were prepared to take this bait, Schweitzer did go so far as to urge the cessation of state subsidies and a reform of the railroads that would make them profitable. The Christian leader Baltrusch was in many respects even more challenging than his Socialist colleagues by arguing that a free economy also meant the elimination of cartels, trusts, and monopolies, and that true cooperation between industry and labor required that the latter be given a much more important role in industrial matters, "since political rights alone are not sufficient for the workers." Industry, in short, would have to give labor a role in economic decision making if there were to be cooperation in solving these problems. Furthermore, industry would have to take some responsibility on its own, and Baltrusch reproached the industrialists for "lacking the good will to take responsible positions in the government."[120]

How well taken this point was may be gathered from a letter Hans von Raumer sent to Stresemann on December 14, 1921, asking that he not be considered as a replacement for the Social Democrat Schmidt as Economics Minister should a Great Coalition government be formed. As a general proposition, he was opposed to DVP participation in the government under existing circumstances because of the divisions in the party. Those divisions meant that every foreign policy crisis during the coming months—and he anticipated many—would lead to a coalition crisis and the absence of an effective government precisely when it was needed. Most important, however, he could see little point in assuming a Cabinet position that

would involve domestic political decisions that could only be taken by a DVP Minister against severe opposition from the left. This was a responsibility best left to the Social Democrats:

Insofar as the taking over the Economics Ministry is concerned, I cannot repress my purely objective reservations about taking over this ministry from the Social Democrats just at the time when the Social Democrats are seeing the endless difficulties which precisely this ministry will have to overcome in the coming years. These difficulties will arise because our exports will stagnate and a large, perhaps unsurpassed unemployment will force the economy to confront the most difficult questions. A way out of these difficulties will be opened up only by a complete turning away from the previous socialist economy policy. Above all, an increase of the working day and of labor productivity will be the fundamental preconditions. For the realization of the English demands—increasing the coal prices and the railroad rates to world market levels, the dropping of every subsidization of the bread price—will place the people before the necessity of covering through labor the needs which were covered by the printing press before.[121]

Unfortunately, Raumer's point was very well taken. Why should industry take responsibility for a fulfillment policy which many of its leaders opposed when labor and its bourgeois political allies could do so instead and at the same time be forced in the process to clear the path toward the unpopular domestic programs favored by industry? Raumer accurately reflected the unhappy contradiction between the policy of fulfillment supported by the trade unions and SPD, on the one hand, and the mechanisms by which social peace and the relatively increased advantages of labor as a consequence of war and revolution were being maintained, on the other. Just as organized labor had dealt with the unrest of 1918–1919 by encouraging the degeneration of the Revolution into a wage movement, so it reluctantly surrendered wage restraint during the summer of 1921 because it saw no alternative to the anticipation of inflation. The workers were not going to wait around until they found such an alternative in any case. Similarly, one consequence of the acceptance of the constraints of parliamentary coalition politics in 1918–1919 was the necessity of accepting a tax compromise such as that to be hammered out under Wirth's leadership in the winter of 1921–1922. Thus, bourgeois profit seeking and compromises served to spur labor's wage push, and that push could easily serve as a justification for the abandonment of self-restraint in the pricing considerations and practices of the business community. As for reparations, they were the convenient but by no means ill-chosen scapegoat for everyone. The government could not respond to the pressures from the Allies to fulfill the London Ultimatum schedule in blissful disregard of the tensions at home, and it was not being given enough time to cope with them. In October 1921, Berliners were engaged in the panic buying of clothes and shoes, but in late November the plundering of clothing and food stores required a ban on public meetings and demonstrations.[122] The domestic situation was becoming dangerous again. Under the circumstances, therefore, it is not surprising that the theory, the practices, and the conditions that would drive Germany into hyperinflation were reaching maturation by the beginning of 1922.

Chapter 10

The Vicious Circles: From Galloping Inflation to Hyperinflation, January–July 1922

The Paradoxes of Compliance

While the chief sources of the German inflation were endogenous, the catalyst of inflationary development between the spring of 1921 and the summer of 1922 was reparations. Expectations with respect to the currency both at home and abroad were profoundly affected by the status of the reparations issue. When demands were made upon Germany which the Germans and substantial portions of the outside world felt were unfulfillable, the consequence was a loss of confidence in the mark abroad and a surrender to inflationary tendencies at home. When reparations obligations were reduced, or even when the prospect of relief and external assistance appeared on the horizon, the exchange rate improved and the will to combat inflationary tendencies on the German domestic front increased. Thus, although the inadequacies of the German domestic efforts to fight inflation are incontestable, their extent certainly is more open to debate than some critics of German theory and practice have suggested. The role of the reparations issue during this period cannot be downplayed. It became the preoccupation of the Wirth government and of its opponents, both sides advocating policy options that were very risky. The opponents of fulfillment were willing to hazard policies that certainly would have destroyed and ultimately did destroy the currency and bring Germany to the border of domestic collapse. Nevertheless, it is essential to recognize that the policy of fulfillment by no means lacked certain adventurous aspects.

Since Wirth and Rathenau basically calculated that they could only restore what they perceived to be sanity in the reparations issue by demonstrating the limits of German capacity, their efforts required a repeated tempting of Germany's economic and political fate. The domestic contest over fulfillment thus increasingly became a battle over the manner and extent to which Germany should run the risk of ruin, and it was inevitable that the gulf between the two positions narrowed rather than widened as the reparations crisis deepened.[1]

At the Cannes meeting of the Reparations Commission on January 13, 1922, the Allies had given the Germans two weeks to come forth with proposals for dealing with their financial and monetary affairs and for the future payment of reparations. Allied experts, however, also presented certain broad areas of reform which were considered necessary, and the Germans responded to these proposals on January 27. On the surface, the Germans responded quite positively, promising to raise taxes, levy both involuntary and voluntary internal loans, collect customs duties on a gold basis, significantly raise the domestic price of coal as well as postal and rail rates, abolish subsidies, prevent the export of capital, and grant autonomy to the Reichsbank. They studiously disregarded the Allied call for a limitation in note issue, however, and they were evasive in responding to the Allied request for a reparations payment plan. The experts at Cannes had proposed that, for 1922, the Germans pay 720 million gold marks in cash and a maximum of

1,450 million gold marks in kind and that the recoverable occupation costs for 1922 come out of the payments in kind and then be fixed for future years. In reply, the Germans simply applied the balance-of-payments theory to the situation and argued that Germany was facing a two billion mark import surplus and that cash payments could only be covered by foreign-exchange purchases while payments in kind would require imports of raw materials needed for manufacture. The result, therefore, could only be a further deterioration of the exchange rate, a new reparations crisis, and the possibility that no reparations could be paid in 1923. Hence, Berlin asked for a reduction of payments in 1922 without specifying an amount and argued that future payments would depend upon Germany's ability to get an international loan.[2]

It is a measure of the ambiguous and mysterious quality of German responses to Allied demands, especially when they involved German fiscal and monetary intentions, that they could produce diametrically contrary reactions in the same person within only a few days. Thus, the British Reparations Commission representative Bradbury initially found the German proposal "thoroughly disappointing" and thought it "obvious that the Germans do not believe the Cannes figures feasible and do not intend to make any serious effort to reach them."[3] He was unable to tell whether the projected forced loan discussed in the German proposal was to be levied in paper or gold marks and unable to discern the relationship between the tax proposals and the budget. After some reflection, however, Bradbury thought that the Germans were showing goodwill and actually wondered whether their plans for reducing the bread subsidy and raising railroad and postal rates were not "so drastic" as to "go beyond what will prove to be practicable."[4] On both occasions Bradbury was certain that the French would not be satisfied. Even when questioning German good faith, however, he argued that trying to force guarantees on the Germans was pointless because the Allies would find themselves "either without a German Government or with a large number of kettles of inedible fish on our hands." The Germans, in his view, had to have a chance to settle their domestic finances before

paying reparations since "the only other alternative is Reparation crises every six months."[5]

This was precisely the kind of impression the Germans wished to create, but the point being made was also well taken because conditions were such that, in the absence of the kind of currency reform and rigorous deflationary policy which no responsible German politician was prepared to implement at this time, even measures fully in keeping with Allied proposals were bound to have very mixed if not negative results. Germany required relief from the international pressure and an opportunity for a new relative stabilization of the mark to take hold so that the Wirth government could gain some control over the domestic situation. Unhappily, the reparations crisis proved to be continuous between February and June 1922, and so was the deterioration of the exchange rate. In order to understand the interaction between German domestic policies and the reparations problem, however, it is useful to focus on the measures taken by the Wirth government to satisfy the Allied demands and the manner in which they were affected by both internal circumstances and mark depreciation.

The Allies were particularly adamant that the Germans eliminate their subsidies, although the French and British interpreted the meaning and significance of Germany's cheap food, coal, and transport prices differently. As Chancellor of the Exchequer Horne explained to Melchior in a conversation in February 1922, "while the French view the subsidy policy as a conscious effort to prevent reparations payments, British public opinion is very agitated about these subsidies for *the* reason that English industry, which already suffers so much from the sinking of the exchange rate of the mark, is further weakened in its competitiveness through them."[6] From the "psychological standpoint" of France and England, therefore, it was essential to eliminate the subsidies. While Melchior defended the need for these subsidies to maintain order after the Revolution, he confessed that an earlier start might have been made in eliminating them. At the same time, however, he pointed out that the mark depreciation arising from the response to the reparations demands of the Allies made an effective raising of railroad rates virtually impossible because one could not raise them every two weeks. The problem, however, was by no means limited to this particular subsidy but involved all of them, as an examination of German efforts to deal with the question of food and coal prices, low freight rates, and other forms of subsidization demonstrates.

There is no better place to begin than with the food subsidy question, a classic illustration of the problems of managing the inflation under the combined internal and external pressures to which the German government was subjected. Quite independently of the Allied demands, Wirth and Hermes hoped to eliminate bread subsidies and intended to introduce a 75 percent increase in bread prices in February on top of the 50 percent increase of the previous August. In fact, the Cannes conditions were extremely helpful in justifying a measure they were going to take anyway. The trouble was that Hermes still had to ask the Cabinet for a retroactive increase of 6,372,000,000 marks in the 1921–1922 budget to cover the subsidy since August. The subsidy had been budgeted at an exchange rate of sixty-five marks to the dollar, and this had obviously become fictional. Furthermore, foreign grain purchases between May and September were made on credit in order to spare foreign exchange for the first reparations payments and were thus more expensive. Wirth and Hermes hoped for better times in 1922 and had allocated only 954 million marks to subsidize cereals in the 1922–1923 budget. This was a substantial reduction, to be sure, but as Wirth pointed out to the Reparations Commission, both the 6.37 billion and the 954 million were based on an average exchange rate of a hundred eighty marks to the dollar. Should the exchange rate rise to an average of three hundred marks to the dollar, the amounts entailed would increase, respectively, to 8.6 billion marks and 5.2 billion marks.[7]

Thus, the scheme for the abolition of food subsidies could end up with the costs of food subsidies increasing anyway, and this is precisely what happened by June when the exchange rate was over three hundred marks to the dollar. This by no means exhausted the difficulties. Hermes's plan called for the purchase of a million tons of foreign wheat as a reserve, and this had to be paid for in foreign exchange.

The Reich Wheat Board, therefore, had to turn to the Foreign Exchange Procurement Board, which had the onerous task of deciding how available foreign exchange was to be spent as well as on foreign-exchange purchases for the needs of the Reich. Since the Reich was eliminating its subsidies, the Reich Wheat Board did not feel that it could buy on credit without a guarantee from the Reich Finance Ministry against losses on the exchange rate. The question of whether to use available foreign exchange or to buy on credit also presented some interesting tactical problems with respect to the Allies. On the one hand, a good argument could be made for taking credit, since foreign credit was available for wheat purchases but not for reparations. Foreign exchange could then be spared for reparations purposes while "the fact that Germany is becoming a debtor with private obligations to a further extent could under circumstances also be useful some day."[8] On the other hand, to the Foreign Office, the potential pressure that private lenders might impose on the Allies in the future was less important than the making of an immediate impression by burdening the money market with foreign-exchange purchases to pay for the wheat and thus assuring that "in the further discussion of the reparations payments, the difficulties in procuring foreign exchange will not go unrecognized."[9] Possibly for this reason, and possibly also because the Finance Ministry was uncertain it had a post in the budget to guarantee against foreign-exchange losses for wheat purchases, a decision was made to use existing foreign exchange to pay for the imports. In April, this was creating such difficulties that the Foreign Exchange Procurement Board was recommending that foreign exchange reserved to pay for reparations be used for wheat purchases, a decision the Cabinet was unwilling to take for fear that the Allies and others convening at the Conference on International Economic Reconstruction in Genoa at this time would show little sympathy in the light of the famine in Russia and the miserable food conditions in other parts of central Europe.[10] These were not conditions, however, which the German government had any intention of imposing on its own people. Over the protests of the farmers, Anton Fehr, Hermes's successor as

Food Minister, decided in the spring that the wheat levy would be continued into the next agricultural year, and while Hermes complained that "a new subsidy policy" was being introduced, the inflation made a full transition to a free economy in agriculture too dangerous to try.[11]

Social pressures were no less important in determining the fate of the Wirth government's plans and promises with respect to eliminating the deficit in the railroad and postal systems. Here, too, there was a commitment to undertake reforms that antedated the discussions at Cannes. In addition, there was the pressure that came from the industrialists wishing to privatize the railroad system. Railroad Minister Groener fought tenaciously against these plans, arguing that the railroad system's deficits were correctable as demonstrated by the fact that the deficit had been reduced from 87 percent in 1920 to 32 percent in 1921. He expected to balance income and expenses in 1922. The personnel in the system had doubled since 1914, but he had already eliminated about fifty thousand persons and planned to eliminate another twenty thousand, or 3 percent of those employed in the system, by March 31, 1922. More important, he was trying to work out an hours-of-work law that would break with the schematic eight-hour day, which was unsuited to the railroads, as well as to develop a Railroad Finance Law that would separate the railroad system from the general financial administration and put it in the position of having to pay its own way. The postal system was less sanguine about its ability to balance its budget, which Minister Giesberts thought would take two or three years, but here, too, there was the expectation of greater flexibility in working hours through a new law governing the civil servants.[12]

Unfortunately for these Ministers and Chancellor Wirth, just at the time that Wirth was announcing all these good intentions along with massive rate hikes to the Allies at the end of January 1922, the railroad workers and other groups of civil servants were about to launch the only major civil-service strike in German history.[13] The strike, which broke out at the beginning of February, was the culmination of months of agitation and disatisfaction not only

over the increased cost of living and the unwillingness of the government to meet the various financial demands of the civil servants but also with the increase of pay differentials in October and the program for a change in working hours. The last issue won the sympathy of many of the trade-union leaders despite outright Socialist opposition to a railroad strike and serious reservations about the programs of the civil-servant unions. Initially, Wirth, with the strong encouragement of industry, which worried about civil-servant demands spilling over into the private sector, took a tough line and supported the intransigent stance of Groener. The strike was declared illegal, the emergency powers of Article 48 of the Weimar Constition were invoked, and many striking workers and officials were subjected to disciplinary action that involved dismissal and even arrest. As the strike threatened to spread to the postal workers and other civil servants and beyond its north and central German centers, however, Wirth came to the conclusion that it was better to sacrifice economic to political considerations. Wirth's fears of chaos were reinforced not only by reports he received from the strike centers but also by the pleas of Carl Severing, the Prussian Interior Minister. Severing was not one to give in to unreasonable worker demands, as demonstrated by his severity in dealing with striking coal miners two years earlier, and this undoubtedly gave his anxieties credibility. Severing argued that

If 50,000 postal employees in Berlin alone are added to the striking railroad workers, then the situation will become insupportable, and the large factories especially will be shut down. The consequence will be food shortages and plundering. The Reichswehr will then have to be employed as a last resort, and then civil war will be at hand. It is established that the Soviet Government is supporting the KPD with money.[14]

Over the strenuous objections of Groener and Hermes, and despite severe criticism from the DVP and DNVP for backing down in the face of a "revolt of the civil servants," Wirth decided to negotiate with the striking unions on February 7. He agreed to revise the pay scales so as to reduce differentials, to withdraw the hours-of-work bill under consideration, and to discuss the issue of automatic indexation of wages and salaries to the cost of living. This strike was to mark the high tide of civil-servant militancy, and Groener took full advantage of the Railroad Workers Union acceptance of the government's right to undertake disciplinary measures. Nevertheless, the concessions made by Wirth certainly compromised Groener's plans for making the railroad system pay for itself in 1922. In fact, there were indications of a change in Groener's attitude toward the privatization question in late February, and he was reported to have said in private conversation that balancing the railroad budget was no longer possible and that "one would sooner or later have to consider the possibility of denationalizing the railroads."[15]

In any event, Groener apparently readjusted to deficit spending even if he did brave the wrath of the unions in his post-strike purge of the railroad system. New pay demands in March led the Railroad Ministry to project an additional twenty-four billion in its deficit for the year.[16] In May, the civil servants were demanding increases that would increase the deficit by another ninety-six billion. Postal Minister Giesberts bluntly declared that there was no way in which he could cover the pay increases in the postal system through rate increases, since recent rate increases had led to a drop in the use of the mails. He wondered how Germany was going to justify a ninety-six billion mark increase when it was telling the Allies that it could not meet their recent demands for a sixty billion mark tax increase. He also felt it important that the increases be tied to a serious discussion of increased productivity with the unions, since "so long as there is so little productivity in the state enterprises, profitability cannot be expected."[17] In contrast to their positions at the beginning of the year, however, Hermes and Groener were in no mood to do battle with reality. Thus, Hermes argued:

It is a mistake to link this question to the pay question. It is an obligation of the government to create internal peace and satisfaction first, and only then can the reparations payments be dealt with. There is a great difference between collecting 60 billion in new taxes and making available the means to pay the civil servants in distress. These increased expenses are a consequence of the fall in the mark which, in its turn, is again conditioned by foreign-policy circumstances.[18]

Groener was in complete agreement with Hermes and, while anxious to deal with the hours-of-work question, argued that the pay increase was a consequence of the "general economic situation" and that orderly circumstances in salaries could only be created when the exchange rate was stabilized.

There were, to be sure, very substantial freight and passenger rate increases between February and June 1922, and substantial postal rate increases as well. Freight rates, which were subjected to monthly increases of 20 to 50 percent, managed to climb from an average of 47.9 percent of their 1913 gold-mark value to 98.4 percent in June before dropping precipitously to 48 percent in July. The real cost of a third-class passenger fare though nominally increasing during this time actually declined from 18.5 to 11.1 percent of its 1913 gold-mark value, while the cost of sending a domestic letter increased from 21.3 to 31.8 percent of its 1913 mark value. In short, rates continued to be too low while inflation ate into the real value of rate hikes.[19]

The failure to valorize these rates appears less astonishing than one might otherwise think when one considers them in terms of the sum of economic and social policies pursued by the Reich governments. In some instances, as in the case of third-class railroad fares, social considerations certainly played a role since those who rode third class were less well-off, although the rates for the higher classes were also disproportionately low.[20] More generally, however, it is necessary to recognize that the low rates for public services offered by the Reich undoubtedly reflected the basic effort to keep the economy going and competitive while maintaining employment and public order. Since these prices were controlled by the government, they constituted one area in which the proposition "mark for mark" could be applied, especially when maintaining such rates was in the interest of relative stabilization. Finally, the failure to make timely increases also undoubtedly had something to do with government expectations about inflation. Quite aside from the fact that anticipatory behavior on the part of government agencies would have been the most powerful of signals to the rest of society to follow suit, the extent of the deterioration of the mark's exchange rate was not anticipated, and the hope for relative stabilization continued even as conditions became worse.

This is especially well demonstrated by the one area in which the German government had broken with the "mark for mark" doctrine and had established the principle of valorization—namely, customs. Under the Treaty of Versailles, Germany could not raise her tariffs for five years and was compelled to give the twenty-seven nations with whom it had been at war most-favored-nation treatment. In 1919, however, Germany managed to persuade the Allies that such tariff protection as was left it was worthless because of the currency depreciation and that its customs receipts, an important part of prewar income and one of the sources of German revenue that was specified as a guarantee for reparations, were doomed to worthlessness if they could not be valorized. As a result, Germany received the right to collect customs either in foreign currency or in an amount of marks determined by a multiplier that was supposed to be based on current exchange rates and prices.[21]

One of the things that "astonished" the Allies was that the multiplier used seldom reflected the actual exchange rate and, further, that even the amounts that should have been collected on the basis of the existing multipliers were not collected.[22] Two factors seemed to be at work. First, the government effort to promote and maintain stable trade conditions as well as expectations appear to account for the slow reaction to circumstances. Thus, a multiplier of 8.0 was used from June 1920 through September of 1921. It was consistently below the exchange rate and domestic wholesale price indices and thus had no protectionist consequences of any significance. Then it was increased during the last months of 1921 to 13.3, 24.5, and 40.0, where it remained through February. During the period December 1921–February 1922, the multiplier exceeded the wholesale price index for domestic products and would continue to do so until it fell behind in June. Second, the income from customs was affected by the right of Germany to cancel import duties on items it considered important to the economy, and this right was exercised very extensively as part of the government's efforts to keep prices down

and German competitive capacity high. At Cannes, the Allies called upon the Germans to take measures to increase their receipts from customs. The Germans responded to this demand by undertaking to increase the multiplier regularly and by shortening the time in which such changes were announced in order to foil those who rushed their imports in order to beat the increases. The multiplier did make it possible for customs to keep up with inflation better than railroad rates. However, since between half and three-quarters of the imports into Germany in 1922 liable to customs were exempted from duty, the returns remained below what they should have been. In short, while government expectations about inflation began to show some signs of change, its economic policy of subsidizing the German export effort did not, and it was mark depreciation rather than the gold tariff that provided German producers with such protection as they enjoyed during this period.[23]

One of the key areas in which the government had imposed both its expectations of exchange stability and its social policies of internal pacification as well as its economic policy of export expansion was coal taxation and pricing policy. The coal price question was the linchpin of both government and industrial efforts to maintain price stability and the competitiveness of Germany's finished-product industries. Any coal price increase was bound to make itself felt throughout the economy. During the relative stabilization, the Cabinet, over the objections of the Economics Ministry, had placed a lid on coal price increases and had sought to promote increased productivity by granting wage increases rather than by giving the coal-mine owners much financial incentive to invest and rationalize. Although coal production had improved significantly since the war and lignite production had increased dramatically, anthracite production lagged behind 1914 levels. Coal shortages continued to plague the economy thanks to inadequate production, the loss of coal-producing areas in the Saar and Upper Silesia, and coal delivered for reparations. Quality had deteriorated. The overtime agreement had lapsed in the spring of 1921, and it had proven impossible to reach a new agreement during the rest of 1921 and for most of 1922.[24]

The coal-price and coal-tax question was a source of particular irritation for the Allies, and the British especially were insistent on a change. While the British claimed that the pressure they were applying for an increase in the coal tax and in German coal prices had nothing to do with their commercial interests, the fact that they were major producers and that the French were getting their reparations coal booked at the very cheap German domestic-market price could hardly be overlooked. Whereas in May 1921 the Germans were credited twenty-four gold marks per ton for reparations coal, in November they were credited only six gold marks, and the depreciation of the German mark was estimated to have brought the Germans 78.7 million gold marks less credit for their coal deliveries between June and November than would have been the case had the exchange rate remained at its May 1921 levels.[25]

More generally, while the price for a ton of Ruhr coal had risen from 193.40 marks in March 1921 (when the first increase in almost a year had been allowed) to 405.10 in December and January, the price in dollars had declined from $3.18 to $2.11, while the price measured according to a dollar index based on 1913–1914 prices had declined from 111.2 to 73.8—that is, 57 percent of its real price in 1914. Finally, mention should be made of the fact that an important portion of the price, slightly more than fifty marks per ton during this period, was composed of the coal tax and social levies to support worker housing and other social costs, so that the actual price received by the industry was substantially lower when measured against prewar real prices.[26]

To pacify the Allies and for fiscal reasons, the government began contemplating an increase of the coal tax in July 1921 and actually increased it by 40 percent in November, albeit with few illusions that this would impress the Allies any more. The legislation, however, provided for future increases or decreases dependent on the world market situation.[27] The major question that began to develop at the end of the year was what to do about Allied demands for an adjustment of German domestic to world-market prices. While the government clearly was committed to only a gradual movement in this direction, primarily by increasing the coal tax to reduce the gap between the domestic and world-market prices, a conflict was developing within the coal industry and within industry more generally over a proposal boldly announced by Stinnes in mid-December 1921 for a dramatic increase of prices to world-market levels as soon as possible.

In Stinnes's view, the mining industry had made no progress whatever during the previous eight years in improving its productive capacity. Because of territorial losses and insufficient productivity, Germany was no longer self-sufficient in coal production and could not become self-sufficient again unless new shafts were opened that would make up for the wearing out of those that had been opened in 1913. The effort to keep coal prices low and to take limited write-offs could not continue, according to Stinnes, because the Allied demand that Germany raise its coal prices to world-market levels meant that time was running out. Within the foreseeable future, Germany would lose its competitive advantages and the money needed to improve the mining industry's productive base would no longer be available. He argued, therefore, that the coal prices had to be increased immediately for the specific purpose of providing the wherewithal to open at least eight new shafts and to mechanize the industry. Stinnes was strongly seconded by Silverberg of the lignite industry, who bluntly argued before the Reich Coal Council in January that it would be nothing less than a "national misfortune" if the gap between domestic and world prices "would be completely filled by taxes." Opposition to fulfillment played no small role in animating Stinnes and Silverberg, as became obvious when the latter declared that the big question was, "are we going to bring about the coal price increase by increasing the coal tax as now budgeted in order then to have the monies taken for reparations, or are we going to use it for the internal improvements Germany needs?"[28]

This rather dangerous line did not go unchallenged. One of the trade-union representatives on the Reich Coal Council pointed out:

The mining industry must have the necessary means of maintaining itself. But there is something I do not understand. You say: it is better that we hold on to the money that the higher prices give to mining in order to get our mines in operating condition than that we deliver the surplus to Paris via Berlin. But we do also have reparations obligations. In my view, we cannot get around these reparations obligations. We cannot simply declare: we do not have anything and we cannot pay anything. One day we will be shown that we have to pay. . . . The mining industry must also provide whatever is in its power to meet our obligations.[29]

Silverberg responded by claiming that he knew this but that Germany had to be placed in a position where she could pay. Stinnes, however, was in no mood to beat about the bush. Wherever one went abroad, he argued, people were aware that Germany could not pay, and he opposed making believe that Germany could:

Above all we do not want to go under and to be torn apart, and that is what we will do if we act as if we can pay and cannot pay in reality. The two billion spoken about in Cannes can in no case be paid. The economy cannot be managed as it has been so far; the other powers are not willing to put up with it anymore. You see it in the fact that their first condition is that the printing should not go on any more. Then naturally the opportunity to swindle others with worthless paper will also cease. . . . We can neither barter away our real values nor our labor abroad. First we want to bring our Fatherland back into condition again, and then we can pay without bleeding ourselves white beforehand.[30]

For tactical reasons, Stinnes wanted a massive and sudden price increase before the projected Conference on International Economic Reconstruction met in Genoa, and he recognized that it was important to deal with the wage question as well. Obviously, price levels would rise and the miners would have to get their due, and he urged that the industry be generous in its negotiations with labor.

It would be false to think that fulfillment was the only issue involved in the coal price increase, however, since many industrialists as hostile to fulfillment as Stinnes were nonetheless very opposed to his coal price program. Indeed, his chief manager Albert Vögler did not hide his unease. At the end of January, he wrote to Stinnes pointing out that his iron and steel firms had lost fifty-two million marks and would have shown losses of even more were it not for the use of exchange profits to reduce them. He warned that the costs in December demonstrated that "the iron industry cannot bear any more major coal and wage increases. . . . If the miner wages are again raised,

then wages in all the other industries will automatically follow. I fear that business will stagnate all along the line."[31]

But for Stinnes this was all the more reason to press forward with his coal-price-increase program. This becomes clear from his performance at a meeting of the directors of the RdI on February 22, 1922, in which he and Silverberg had to defend themselves against sharp criticisms from colleagues in the iron, steel, and manufacturing industries who had insisted on putting the coal price increases Stinnes advocated on the agenda. The meeting was a last-ditch effort to overturn Stinnes's successful efforts to win over the Economic Committee of the Coal Mine Owners Association in mid-February, at which only General Director Hasslacher and Vögler, with understandably less vigor, had opposed him. The critics of Stinnes then appealed to Gustav Krupp von Bohlen und Halbach, who was extremely hostile to Stinnes's program, and it was he who urged a final appeal through the RdI.[32]

At the meeting itself, Paul Reusch was particularly vociferous in arguing against an immediate adjustment of domestic and world-market prices: "The consequence will be a further increase in wages and the making of competition more difficult on the world market. The mining industry, despite all the difficulties raised by Dr. Silverberg, ought to have acted in a timely manner to increase its production, and if this did not happen, then the consequences should not be imposed on everyone else."[33] Stinnes could speak more freely in this company since labor representatives were not present, and he pointed out that the danger was that the difference between domestic and world-market prices would be made up for in wage demands insofar as it was not made up for in the coal tax and other tax increases. Thus, nothing would be left to take care of preparing for Germany's future coal needs: "This is the last moment available to build the new coking ovens and mining shafts we need from the necessary price increases. Once the stability of the currency has set in, we will have the same struggles the other countries are now facing. If we are to survive these struggles, we must take the necessary steps now." All this did not persuade manufacturers like Oscar Funcke of the iron wares industry, who felt only a small increase in coal prices would be possible if his industry were not to become uncompetitive, and he could see no reason why the new shafts should not be paid for by raising capital in the usual manner rather than using higher prices that would ruin everyone else. Silverberg skillfully sought to undermine the arguments of both Reusch and Funcke by playing them off against each other. He implied that Reusch could well afford to be sanctimonious about what the mining industry should have done since he headed a mixed concern in which the profits of the non-coal producing sectors could pay for the development of the coal mines. If all the coal mines were integrated into mixed concerns, then this would be a disadvantage for the rest of industry, and he thus suggested that people like Funcke had an interest in the development of the independent mines. Furthermore, if their competitiveness was being harmed by the coal price increases, then they should seek relief through a reduction in the coal tax. From this it followed for Silverberg that "if one is going to take a stand against the coal price increase, then the point of attack should above all be directed at the coal tax."

Vögler also was prepared to attack the coal tax as a means of compensating industry for the burdens of a coal price increase, but he, nevertheless, had the courage to criticize the notion of his employer Stinnes that things would be improved with a coal price increase. It would simply raise material and wage costs once again, and this would get the industry nowhere:

If higher productivity is not demanded for the wage increase, then it is a vicious circle which will never bring us to stable circumstances. . . . On the other side, one has to bear in mind that an approaching of world market prices will not take place because the coal price increase will lead to a worsening of the mark. There are no world market prices.

Stinnes agreed with Vögler on the need for greater stability but disagreed with him on the idea that one could get more productivity from the workers and thought that the plant deficiencies that were causing poor-quality coal production were more central than higher wages in creating the existing difficulties. He warned that Germany would have to import more and more coal if new shafts were not created and that this would lead to much higher prices for the unin-

tegrated manufacturers and great tension in industry. Silverberg, too, showed a reluctance to challenge the workers head on, arguing that "it is best not to speak of increased labor productivity. It certainly will come, but only if it is not demanded by us."

What emerged from this obviously difficult meeting was that industry was badly divided and that many of its members were uncertain and even frightened by Stinnes's program. Bücher, good organization man that he was, did the best he could by declaring that all present recognized the justification for the mining industry's demands but that the consequences could be formidable, and he therefore hoped that the objections raised would be taken into account by the mining industry. In reality, not even the business managers of the coal organizations were convinced by Stinnes's contentions. Any coal price increase would bring labor and material-cost increases, and by the time these worked themselves out along with further drops in the exchange rate, very little would be left over for investment or even increased write-offs. As Coal Commissar Brecht wearily and fatalistically concluded, "The plans of Herr Stinnes are thus incapable of being carried out. Nevertheless it is necessary to try to get as much as possible as write-offs for the capital that needs to be found. One should also consider that if new plant is created in sufficient amount and production is thereby increased, then perhaps the controlled economy will be eliminated."[34]

On March 1, coal prices were raised from 468.10 marks per ton to 601.70, then to 713.20 on April 1, and to 907.50 on April 20. Needless to say, wage hikes accompanied these price increases, but the April 20 increase constituted something of a breakthrough since it involved a price increase in response to a wage increase in the middle of a month. By May, German coal prices had reached world-market levels, which led to a hiatus in wage demands that abruptly ended in June when further mark depreciation led to new wage increase and an increase of coal prices to 1,208 marks per ton on July 1.[35]

The predicted effect on the rest of industry became rapidly evident, and the March 1 coal price increase marked the end of the iron and steel industry's efforts to stabilize its prices as well as the surrender of the effort made even in late 1921 to avoid open-ended contract conditions. If the workers had abandoned wage restraint in the late summer of 1921, the most important employer groups followed suit in the winter of 1922. On March 2, Vögler reported to Stinnes that they had still managed to avoid the formal introduction of sliding-scale prices in the iron industry, although they were anticipating monthly price increases based on impending coal and turnover tax increases as well as railroad rate increases. He expected that they would soon have wage indexation as in Austria and noted that in Hagen the employers had agreed to an arrangement whereby the final wage for any given month would be determined on the 15th of the following month so as to take inflation into account. If the industrialists were gradually surrendering their previous policy of maintaining price stability, they were doing so angrily and reluctantly in many cases. The Krupp director Bruhn actually attacked Stinnes in the presence of worker representatives at a Pig Iron Association meeting, but the feeling that Stinnes had shifted the balance in pricing policy and the resentment over it was more widespread.[36]

Disapproval, however, was not a spur to virtue but rather an incentive to further abandonment of the commitment to the stabilizing behavior that had characterized the iron and steel industrialists during the previous months despite the sacrifices this may have entailed. Price stability was a public good, the support of which depended upon a consensus that the benefits it brought exceeded the personal sacrifices involved. Stinnes had called this proposition into question and, in the process, had made it attractive to jump on the "running board" of the vehicle he had set in motion and become a "prisoner" on its journey. Increasingly, businessmen had to ask themselves whether their continued individual adherence to principles of price stability mattered in the context of its increasing abandonment by others and whether they were not doing themselves more harm by continuing along the path of virtue. Such behavior certainly was encouraged by divisions within cartels, where the case for a collective change of behavior in the direction of abandoning stability could be made on the basis of the behavior of other such groups, and it was also encouraged by the balance-of-payments theory

to which most employers held and which encouraged the feeling that all stabilizing measures were pointless without a new approach to reparations by the Allies.[37]

Thus, in the Steel Federation meetings between February 28 and March 1, the chairman, Ernst Poensgen, certainly deplored the 28 percent coal price increase but then pointed out that the inability of the iron industry to hold prices had led many firms to argue for freedom to price as was required by the situation and for the introduction of sliding-scale prices. They could no longer bear the kind of losses they had taken as a result of holding on to fixed prices at the end of 1921. This proposal was voted down by a very close vote (in one case, the representatives of a firm divided over the issue), but significant price increases were voted on this occasion and in the coming months which were tantamount to sliding-scale prices. Most interesting was the situation at the end of May 1922, a month when the coal industry had refrained from new price increases. While some iron and steel industrialists argued that they should also exercise restraint in order to improve Germany's competitive position, another group strongly disagreed, arguing against "public good" considerations by pointing to the behavior of others and the futility of holding back. Thus, they claimed that "in the price question one must primarily be guided by the cost structure and tactical considerations about appropriateness must take second place. The market at present is still giving orders. It has swallowed significantly higher prices in the months just past and can still take a moderate increase. Other branches of industry have known how to use their advantage in a very different way and are in no way embarrassed to demand what is to be had."[38] Only the fear that the workers and primary consumers in the Iron Trades Federation would vote to reintroduce price ceilings and bring a revival of the kind of government intervention that had taken place before the relative stabilization led to the defeat of those supporting a price increase on this occasion, but they decided to increase prices in June if there was a coal price increase, and that is precisely what happened.[39]

What should be manifest from this discussion of the German compliance with certain of the Allied economic demands raised at Cannes or earlier was that they tended to be counter-productive with respect to halting inflation. It is easy enough to attribute this to the unwillingness of the German government to clamp down on labor and industry and force a radical deflationary cure, but could the German government have been expected to countenance starvation and undernourishment because of insufficient food supplies or impossible prices along with the paralysis of the railroads and other vital services in order to attain total victory over the civil-service unions, possible shortages of raw materials and unemployment through rigorous application of gold import duties, and labor unrest by trying to stop wage increases while the Allies were insisting on the unfreezing of coal prices? How, exactly, was Germany's weak democracy, still fearful of violent unrest, to negotiate the transition to deflation in the context of a reparations obligation whose necessary implication was the lowering of the standard of living of the German people? Could German leaders mediate a distributional conflict whose major function, no matter who won, appeared to be serving the well-being of Germany's enemies? Whatever the justice or injustice of reparations and whatever the theoretical arguments for German capacity to pay, the effect of Allied reparations at this time was to place the German government before impossible alternatives and to unleash and legitimize the self-serving policies of the country's industrial leadership.

Fulfillment Policy in Crisis

These dilemmas of the Wirth government were most apparent with respect to taxes, the substantial increase and rapid collection of which were at the center of the Allied requirements as well as of Wirth's efforts to maintain the reduction of reparations payments, enable Germany to qualify for an international loan, and keep his government in power. It was also the focal point of the conflicts between Germany and the Allied powers from the Cannes conference in mid-January to the assassination on June 24, 1922, of the man Wirth appointed Foreign Minister on January 31, Walther Rathenau.

What Wirth had presented to the Reparations Commission on January 28 by way of a revenue program was the so-called one hundred billion mark "tax compromise" he had been hammering out in painful negotiations with the parties in his coalition—the SPD, the Center, and the DDP. He also consulted regularly with the DVP. The compromise consisted less of an arrangement of differences between the government and the parliament, as is usually the case in tax legislation, than a tediously negotiated trade-off of competing taxation principles among the parties. The tax package which Wirth presented to the Reichstag in the summer was one in which the conservative elements in the Center Party and the parties to the right of the Center agreed to high levels of direct taxation on income and property in return for left-wing acceptance of high levels of indirect taxation.[40]

Socialist and trade-union acceptance of the compromise was simply a surrender to realities. The Allies and the bourgeois parties insisted on higher indirect taxation. There was no majority to be had for the appropriation of real values, and Wirth's warnings against placing new assessment burdens on the tax authorities undoubtedly had some effect. Finally, nothing was to be gained from bringing down the government. The February 1921 elections in Prussia had only confirmed the trend toward the right already shown in the June 1920 Reichstag elections. The workers were bound to suffer from the fall of Wirth. As the ADGB leader Tarnow put the matter in late January, "if the government falls before the Genoa Conference, then the mark will fall immediately. The burden of taxes is not nearly as great as the burden of a collapse of the mark. . . . If a halfway acceptable tax program is possible, then that is the way we should go."[41]

What helped to make the tax compromise "halfway acceptable," at least in part, was a 200 percent increase in the property tax and the decision to impose a graduated compulsory loan to be subscribed to by all persons with over a hundred thousand marks in property during the period July–December 1922. The loan would not bear interest until October 31, 1925, after which it would bear interest of 4 percent, and then 5 percent a year later. This measure was expected to raise a billion gold marks. It was intended for the sole purpose of covering reparations costs and could be increased if it proved insufficient. The bourgeois parties had great reservations about the loan, but they, too, were under strong pressure to impose sacrifices on the wealthy. Thus, Hans von Raumer of the DVP confessed to Stresemann that he had to think of the compulsory loan "not as an industrialist but rather as a politician" and support it because it was "very popular among the broad strata of our voters [and] also the entire *Mittelstand*, which belongs to us and for whom things are going badly" and who were insisting "on a visible sacrifice from the propertied."[42]

The dilemma, of course, was that inflation had a way of making such sacrifices invisible by making them nonexistent. Thanks to depreciation, Erzberger's Emergency Capital Levy had brought in less than a billion marks by 1921, and while the Wirth program provided for a speeding up of collection in 1922, the assessments on which it was based turned the entire tax into such a farce that there was nothing left to do but absorb its remnants into the tax program passed in the course of 1922. Similarly, the tax on postwar profits was proving such a cumbersome matter for the tax authorities and was so unproductive that it was also to be replaced by a surcharge on the tax on capital gains. What then was to be the fate of the compulsory loan? When first proposed, its papermark value was placed at forty billion. In April, when it was still being considered, the sum had gone up to sixty billion, which was then raised to seventy billion at the time of its final passage in July. Collection, however, was to be based on assessments of wealth as of December 31, 1922![43]

The history of the compulsory loan testified to the immense difficulty faced by the Wirth government in passing and putting into effect its tax program. Time was of the essence, and so, clearly, was valorization. Wirth certainly appeared to have the best of intentions. When presenting his program to the Reichstag in January, he declared that "in connection with this great legislative program one will have to examine with respect to the other taxes whether and to what extent they will have to be adjusted to the development of the the currency,"[44] but he stressed also that this would have to be done in a manner consonant with the rapid collection of taxes and the effective functioning of the tax authorities. While this suggested that val-

orization was a long way off, Wirth was much more serious about increasing the speed with which taxes were collected and, above all, getting his tax compromise through the Reichstag as rapidly as possible. He needed to pacify the Allies and strengthen his case abroad. Unhappily, the railroad strike in February and DVP anger at his handling of the strike as well as his naming of Rathenau as Foreign Minister delayed matters further.[45]

This was a dangerous delay. The French had never found the German proposals of January 28 very convincing, and the British were having second thoughts about the seriousness of German intentions, even though they continued to resist Poincaré's demands for controls. The fact that things were not going well became clear from reports from Paris sent by State Secretary Fischer, the Chairman of the German War Burdens Commission, who Wirth and Hermes had sent to promote a "reasonable decision" by the Reparations Commission with respect to the German note of January 28. Understandably, Fischer devoted his major efforts to cultivating Bradbury and trying to undermine his monetarism. Bradbury continued to press for a monthly limitation on short-term Treasury bills and note issue based on the December 1921 level, to which Fischer responded with the argument that such a limitation was pointless since Germany hoped to issue fewer bills and notes if the mark improved but that there was no way it could guarantee holding to such a limit if the currency were to collapse. Similarly, Bradbury expressed particular interest in the autonomy of the Reichsbank. He placed less emphasis on the legal side of the problem than on the need to place a stronger personality in the leadership of the bank who would dispel the widely held view that the Reichsbank was too acquiescent to government demands. Here, Fischer sought to convince the Englishman that such demands reflected a failure to understand German conditions, since a struggle between the Reichsbank and the government hardly would be beneficial to anyone. Fischer claimed that "circumstances" would prove stronger than any personality, and that if it was the leadership of the bank that was at issue, then new legislation would hardly solve the problem. Bradbury was most critical about the compulsory loan, which he viewed as inadequate in the light of the anticipated one hundred eighty billion mark deficit and wanted assurance that the receipts would be used to pay for reparations and not to fill up holes created by the failure of other taxation measures. Here, Fischer sought to be as reassuring as possible, pointing out that the maintenance of Allied reparations reductions for the year and positive decisions from the Reparations Commission that would raise the exchange rate would make it possible for the entire return on the forced loan to be devoted to reparations. Fischer became most concerned, however, about Bradbury's proclivity to propose an insistence on currency reform as a guarantee for reparations:

I urgently pleaded with Bradbury to refrain from demanding such a reform proposal now because no one can presently say what will become of the mark. So long as there is any hope whatever for the maintenance of the purchasing power of the mark, one ought not to talk about the introduction of a new currency. That is a crime against the German economy, which today is completely based on the mark. With such demands, one puts the cart before the horse. A currency reform and the reduction of the circulation must be the natural consequence of the economic reconstruction; it cannot be artificially forced to bring about a possible financial recovery by another route. It is difficult to say how much I was able to convince Bradbury with my arguments since he is still rather rigidly committed to the Anglo-American monetary ideas.[46]

Fischer went on to stress the importance of avoiding sharp demands and difficult or unacceptable guarantees that would only serve to promote pessimism within Germany and destroy all hopes for an international economic recovery. Under such circumstances, Fischer warned, it would not even be possible to pay the seven hundred twenty million gold marks currently demanded by the Allies.

Insofar as the Germans being able to count on the forthcoming Conference on International Economic Reconstruction in Genoa to provide a basis for relief in the context of world wide reconstruction, the signs were also rather gloomy. The French were most unenthusiastic about the conference and insisted that the reparations issue be excluded from the discussions, while the Americans, who it was felt held the key to international recovery if they would only participate and show a willingness to annul Allied war debts, refused to become formally involved. For the Germans, American cancellation of the war debts would clear the path for the elimination of the London Ultimatum's C bonds, which hung over the Germans like a "Damocles Sword." As things stood, the French expected that the bonds would begin bearing interest in 1926, while the Germans hoped to delay this unhappy event until 1929. The Genoa conference itself, therefore, could not be counted upon for salvation, a point concerning which there could be few illusions and which was viewed with increasing fatalism in the course of February 1922. Thus, when Sir Robert Horne told Melchior that nothing decisive could be expected to occur with respect to reparations either at Genoa or during 1922 and that the Germans would simply have to make the best of the situation, Melchior replied that "then nothing will remain except, as in the past at Versailles, Spa, and London, to accept conditions and figures where we know very well that we cannot meet them."[47] By late February Rathenau was urging that the Genoa conference be thought of as a "first link in the chain" of a series of conferences rather than as a solution to immediate problems.[48]

The repeated delays in the forging of even this link, however, were distressing, as was also the absence of a response from the Allies to the German note of January 28. At Cannes, the Germans had been required to pay thirty million marks every ten days until a decision was made about reparations relief for 1922, and this was proving more and more difficult because of the renewed decline of the mark. Rathenau bluntly told the Reichstag Foreign Affairs Committee on February 28 that "in his view a part of the obligations could be covered by the compulsory loan. For the rest, we will probably have to turn to the printing press. Our own dire interest and the demand of the enemy that we give up printing money cannot be fulfilled in this year. There thus arises the most dangerous conditions for the domestic situation in Germany as well."[49] He informed the Deputies, with a well-advised request for the strictest confidentiality, that the Reichsbank was giving consideration to following the French model for "guarding against the inflation" by creating a new form of interest-bearing scrip valid for two years that would be something between bonds issued on a government loan and paper money. What Rathenau presumably had in mind was the seven billion franc loan which the French government had given itself to cover "recoverable" reconstruction expenses.[50] That the Germans should have been contemplating the issuance of a new monetizable paper in anticipation of future income or loans to cover the reparations payments with which the French expected to cover their own monetizable paper on "recoverable" expenses is a commentary in itself on where European domestic and international politics were heading. For the time being, it was the French, not the Germans, who had the margin to engage in such droll speculations, and the Germans refrained from issuing yet another negotiable paper for the time being.

In truth, the Germans were running out of room for financial maneuver. The March 18 reparations payment drained the Reichsbank of most of its reserves of foreign exchange derived from the surrender of export profits. What remained was needed to cover private obligations, and the purchase of more foreign exchange on the market would make the exchange rate even worse. On March 21, therefore, the Finance Ministry urged that the Reparations Commission be informed that Germany was unable to meet its March 28 payment.[51]

On the same day, however, the Reparations Commission finally sent its response to the German government which relieved the Germans of the payment due on March 28 but maintained the seven hundred twenty million goldmark requirement for 1922. The balance owed was to be paid on the fifteenth of each month for the rest of the year. Eighteen million was to be paid on April 15 and fifty million each month thereafter. The German difficulties in paying thirty million gold marks every ten days and the effect of these payments on the exchange rate hardly could be overlooked by the Reparations Commission, especially when compounded by the thirty-five million gold marks per month in clearing payments the Germans owed until March 1923 and the ninety million francs owed France for 1922 on liquidations in Alsace-Lorraine. Under such circumstances, even the French felt it necessary to come around and accept the Cannes schedule as the arrangement for the year. The immediate relief given Germany notwithstanding, this was bound to be a disappointment to the Germans, and it appeared doubtful to the well-informed American observer on the Reparations Commission, Colonel James Logan, that the Germans would be able to meet the new schedule past August.[52]

Most devastating from the German point of view, however, was a second note of March 21 which coldly laid down a series of conditions for the maintenance of the reduced level of reparations payments. Most of these set deadlines of April 30 or May 31 for the fulfillment of German pledges made in their January 28 note, but some set forth new requirements. The most significant of these was a demand that sixty billion paper marks in additional taxes be voted before May 31 and that forty billion of these actually be collected by December 31. The German government was strongly urged to avoid complicated taxation measures and to develop schemes for the automatic increase of taxation pegged either to increased government expenditure or to changes in the exchange rate. Finally, Germany was to agree to Committee of Guarantees supervision of the progress being made in reducing the debt and expenditures through the creation of regular mechanisms for the provision of information and for consultation with the Committee of Guarantees. This could be interpreted as a demand that Germany accept financial control over its budget. If these conditions were not fulfilled by May 31, the Reparations Commission reserved the right to restore the London Ultimatum schedule and declare Germany in default.[53]

The Reparations Commission notes were an extraordinarily severe blow to the German government because of their tone as well as their content, and there was complete unanimity within the Cabinet that the demands for sixty billion more in taxes and financial control had to be refused. They would never pass the Reichstag in any case. Wirth viewed the tone of the Allied response, which paid no tribute whatever to German efforts, as "likely to damage and to weaken the core of German democracy."[54] There was particular disappointment at Bradbury's failure to protect the Germans from such demands, and this was blamed on his "mistaken" conceptions about inflation, but the attention of the government was now riveted on handling the domestic problem created by the Allied response. There was a real danger that the policy of fulfillment would be totally discredited, that the right-wing elements in the DVP would win out, and that support for the tax compromise, especially the forced loan, would disintegrate. It could now be argued that the fulfillment was a disaster internally and externally. On the one hand, the fulfillment policy could be held responsible for the collapse of the mark and the increased cost of living; on the other hand, the evidence suggested that Poincaré, not Lloyd George, was in control of Entente policy.[55] President Ebert was both incensed and concerned:

The present situation is similar to the situations which we have often experienced since the Armistice. Every time it has been said in such cases that some country or other has failed us. We must now deal with things from a domestic political point of view. A large portion of our people had hopes for a substantial improvement since Cannes, and that is just the reason why the position gained ground that our policy was correct. The significance of Poincaré's coming to power has been underestimated on many sides. He [Ebert] has not been surprised by what has happened. In the last few days, there has been a strong drop in morale. For the Chancellor's speech, a firm posture with a patriotic undertone must be found.[56]

Ebert also warned against placing too much hope in the Genoa conference, which he thought Lloyd George had so overloaded with participants and issues as to make unmanageable. At the same time, he and the Cabinet were anxious to maintain and strengthen the policy of fulfillment and the tax compromise against the right by demonstrating, as Rathenau emphasized repeatedly, that the policy was not an end in itself, that it had served to keep the French out of the Ruhr, and that it had contributed much to undermine support for the London Ultimatum schedule. It was necessary, therefore, to say no while leaving the door open to negotiation. The Allies had to be persuaded that they were undermining the currency through their demands, as demonstrated by the money-market reaction, and endangering the reparations program in the process. Indeed, as

the Reich Economics Ministry noted in a memorandum, a continued decline in the exchange rate because of such events would enable the government to collect much of the additional sixty billion being demanded because of the currency depreciation and thus fulfill the Allied demand for new taxes without doing a thing![57]

There was no reason to believe that the Allies would find such a proposition as humorous as it was, however, and vigorous nationalist speeches could backfire. Rathenau remembered well how Stinnes's speech at Spa had offended the British,[58] and this could be neither the desired effect of Wirth's address to the Reichstag nor the German response to the Allies. Nevertheless, Ebert, Wirth, and Rathenau were disappointed and agitated, and their anger put them in a risk-taking mood. It was impossible to pin their hopes on Genoa, and since Great Britain had the greatest stake in Genoa, they thought it best to take a firm stand before the conference in the hope that the Reparations Commission would be kept on the leash by Lloyd George's desire to avoid further ruining the atmosphere surrounding the conference in which he had invested so much of his political capital.[59]

On March 28, Wirth gave an angry speech to the Reichstag denouncing the Allied demands, stressing their impossibility, and pointing out that the government could hardly pass an additional sixty billion in taxes by May 31 when it was preoccupied with the Genoa conference scheduled to begin on April 10 and to last for weeks. He defended the policy of fulfillment by stressing that it was a step-by-step policy that was not being pursued for its own sake but rather to bring about a reasonable long-term solution to the reparations problem, a policy that was bound to produce some crises such as the one presently being faced.[60] Wirth's performance was well received and gave the government strong Reichstag backing which Rathenau intended to exploit.

Thus, when Rathenau appeared to address the Reichstag on the next day, he followed a surprisingly friendly speech by Stresemann for the DVP. It rapidly became clear that Rathenau was especially obsessed at this time with the fall of the mark and the ruin it was bringing to the German middle class and German cultural life, a theme Stresemann had also emphasized. He forcefully blamed the reparations payments Germany had been making for ruining the currency and causing all the misery Germany was experiencing and, to the evident approval of most of the Reichstag, showed no little irritation at Allied monetary theory:

Over and over again we encounter the notion that if the value of our money has been ruined this can only be because we have printed money. The recipe which we are given against this is: stop your printing press, bring your budget in order, and the misfortune is ended! A grave economic error! For a country with an active balance of payments, the recovery of its currency is possible by pursuing a deflationary policy, establishing a balanced budget, and stopping the printing of notes. But things are different for a country with a passive balance of payments. I challenge anybody with a knowledge of economic life to show me a way in which a country with a passive balance of payments can find it possible to make continuous gold payments without the help of foreign loans and at the same time keep its exchange rate intact. (Very true!) The attempt has never been made to give such a prescription, and it cannot be given. (Interjection by the Social Democrats: Helfferich! *Laughter*.) For a country that does not produce gold cannot pay in gold unless it buys this gold with export surpluses or unless it is borrowed.[61]

This was the kind of speech that could drive an otherwise very sympathetic Englishmen like Ambassador D'Abernon to despair. He fretted over the manner in which Rathenau "went out of his way to declare himself an advocate of further inflation."[62] It was a measure of Rathenau's rather uncompromising mood at this point that he turned down an invitation from Poincaré to come to Paris to negotiate and that he overrode the objections of State Secretary Fischer and Finance Minister Hermes and decided to send a strongly worded response to the Reparations Commission before Genoa. Fischer and Hermes argued that no response was required by the note since they were planning to make the April 15 payment anyway, fruitful negotiations were being conducted with the French about payments in kind, and the situation was best handled by negotiations. Rathenau, however, insisted that risks now had to be taken and that they could not return to the "old forms." It was better to respond while the Reparations Commission was "handicapped" by the Genoa meetings.[63]

The determination of Wirth and Rathenau to take a new tack became even clearer on April 4, when an initial draft of the projected reply to the Reparations Commission was branded as too weak, especially in the context of the speeches they had given in the Reichstag. They were especially preoccupied with the deterioration of the domestic economic situation and the need to stress these domestic dangers to the Allies. Wirth argued that they would "shortly be in a situation where they would not be in a position to pay one gold mark in reparations because of the need to import food," while Rathenau warned that "the dollar could be 450 the day after tomorrow and soon stand at 600. Also, a dangerous shortage of money in industry is becoming evident. The note of reply must therefore state that we cannot provide the 720 and 1,450 gold millions at the present time." Rathenau was convinced that the upcoming Genoa conference made the moment favorable for a "change in policy." Rathenau's impetuous tone further disturbed an already nervous Hermes, who opposed an outright refusal to pay what was demanded for 1922. Hermes agreed that they had to refuse the demands for the additional taxes and financial control, although he had originally proposed fudging the former question by arguing that the compulsory loan was tantamount to fulfillment of this Allied demand, but he urged that the 1922 payments problem be put in the context of the need for a foreign loan to cover these payments as well as those of the next few years. Hermes was prepared to accept a "change of tactics," but not a "change of policy," a distinction to which Rathenau agreed but then made rather semantic by once again insisting that the currency had collapsed to the point where one could no longer operate as one had in January and that therefore "it is better to use the present dollar rate to declare our inability to pay."[64]

Rathenau's conviction that the currency and financial situations had reached an intolerable state and his willingness to push matters to a head were further demonstrated by his reaction to the news on April 4 that the Reparations Commission had decided to appoint a special committee to evaluate Germany's qualifications for a foreign loan. The Belgian Reparations Commission member Bemelmens had even assured Rathenau that this was a means of getting an opinion from a committee of bankers that reparations would have to be reduced and would thus spare the Reparations Commission the responsibility for such a decision. Nevertheless, Rathenau's response upset Bemelmans, who was anxious to have the various payments-in-kind agreements that had been worked out rapidly passed by the Reichstag. According to Rathenau, the situation had changed entirely because of the fall of the mark, and he even blamed the Reparations Commission for the dire straits in which Germany found herself. He was apparently more impressed by a telegram from Bergmann in Paris indicating that the demand for sixty billion in taxes was made necessary by "French circumstances" and that the German reaction had failed to recognize this and made the problem worse. In truth, the Allied note contained "loopholes" designed to make further negotiations possible and had substantially watered down French demands for the kinds of controls that had been placed on the Ottoman Empire and China before the war. Bergmann, therefore, had good cause to warn against a German overreaction that would provoke the other side. But this caution was only to be of limited value. Rathenau now drew the conclusion that the German "no" had to be expressed in "more conciliatory form."[65]

The upshot of these discussions was a German note to the Reparations Commission of April 7, 1922, detailing the miseries of the German currency and circumstances, disingenuously suggesting that the compulsory loan took care of the demand for higher taxes, and turning down Allied supervisory proposals as incompatible with German sovereignty while stating a desire to negotiate further. While welcoming the projected bankers' investigation of Germany's loan qualifications, the German government formally requested implementation of Article 234 of the Treaty of Versailles calling for an examination of Germany's capacity to pay and asked that this be conducted by experts from nations that were not a party to the Treaty. Even Logan, who felt that reparations would have to be scaled down and doubted that the Wirth government could meet the other Allied demands, thought the German note "stupid" in view of the projected Bankers' Com-

mittee review of the loan question and considered it a clumsy effort to force the reparations question on the Genoa conference. The French attitude naturally stiffened, and while they agreed not to declare Germany in default before the May 31 deadline, they refused to accept the notion that there were any "loopholes." On April 13, the Reparations Commission responded by sticking to its position while denying that it had any intention of violating German sovereign rights. This left open the way to further discussions of Germany's difficulties, but the German response had done nothing to improve the atmosphere either for Genoa or for what was to follow.[66]

Domestically, the new Wirth–Rathenau line was a great success. Right-wing Deputies, Helfferich and Stinnes included, were "agreeably disappointed" by the government's position, which refuted rumors that Germany's industrial assets would be mortgaged to pay for a reparations loan. Stresemann, supported by Stinnes, praised the handling of the international-loan question and emphasized that what was needed was a loan that would be used to pay the total reparations bill and not something that would simply cover a few years of difficulty. This, however, was not Rathenau's view, and the limits of the change of policy quickly became apparent when Rathenau pointed out that "we could find it absolutely necessary to seriously discuss a small loan which would give us a breathing space for the next few years. The cover for this loan should not be a mortgaging of our industrial assets, but we must unfortunately reckon with a mortgaging of our customs for such a loan."[67]

It is important to recognize that Rathenau's turn to a harder line did not mean that the fulfillment policy was dead or that he was now marching in lock step with his rival Stinnes. The latter had leaped well ahead of Rathenau. Stinnes's business contacts with the leading representative of the French coal industry, Baron de Lubersac, had been increasing, and he had been the recipient of overtures from French industry to enter into economic collaboration. Most significant, Poincaré had invited him to come to Paris in March for discussions, one of apparently many such invitations he had been receiving to come there to discuss Franco-Ger-

Foreign Minister Walther Rathenau (1867–1922) in the automobile in which he was assassinated. (*By permission of the Ullstein Verlag*)

man relations. Stinnes, his sense of self-importance obviously confirmed by the apparent French conviction that negotiating with him would be useful, had refused with infinitely more bravado than Foreign Minister Rathenau. Not only did he insist on an official invitation, a remarkable demand for a private individual, but he also set as "conditions" the evacuation of the Rhineland and Saar, the return of smelting plants he had claimed were taken illegally, and a customs union with France. Stinnes also appears to have felt that he could take such a position because of his rather peculiar interpretation of Poincaré's motives with respect to the Reparations Commission note of March 21: "Poincaré deliberately is demanding the impossible because the French do not want to enter with us into economic relations with the English but rather because they want to enter into an economic agreement with us against England."[68] Stinnes did not think that Genoa would bring any positive results for Germany since it was a place where "only talks would be given."

In addition to Stinnes, Bücher of the RdI took a much gloomier view of Genoa than Wirth and Rathenau while by no means entertaining Stinnes's fantasies about French goals.

Bücher, in some contradiction to his repeated emphasis on the role that exported unemployment would play in bringing England to terms, questioned the belief of those who supported the policy of fulfillment that the Allies could be made to see reason because "the economic thinking of those on the other side is so little schooled in matters of international economics that a turnabout will only take place when Germany is completely ruined."[69] If the RdI agreed to participate in the preparations for Genoa, provide memoranda, and send Bücher and possibly other experts, it did so with rather bad grace and with the reservations that the "working conditions" for the experts had to be "bearable" and that "the total situation be judged favorable for their collaboration."[70]

While the ostensible goal of the Germans at Genoa was to secure a foreign loan to assist them in their reparations payments, the discussions among the experts who gathered in Berlin prior to the conference revealed considerable division not only over the possibility but also over the desirability of success. Witthoefft, of the Hamburg Chamber of Commerce, reported to his colleagues, "many people in Berlin were of the view that we should not take any international loan now since such a loan would only serve the Entente while making Germany weaker. Above all one must bear in mind that the satisfaction of France will lessen the conflicts between France and England, which is not in Germany's interest."[71] Warburg, usually a moderate, took an extraordinarily harsh line, arguing that it was "utopian" to think, as Havenstein apparently did, that the central banks could organize international currency stabilization once there was a foreign loan. In his view, stabilization would be impossible so long as the reparations obligations continued. He was particularly alarmed at English demands for the payments of taxes according to their dollar value so that the real value of tax receipts did not automatically sink with the fall of the mark:

Such a procedure is completely unthinkable, because it would throw overboard every individual's estimate of his yearly expenditures and every overview of tax payments. Our financial weakness makes a cessation of the inflation completely out of the question. For the inflation is a consequence of the financial weakness, just as fever is a consequence of illness. One therefore has first to get rid of the financial weakness if one wants to get rid of the inflation.[72]

While the fact that the government was unable to calculate its receipts or deal with its obligations apparently disturbed Warburg not a whit at this point, his tone must be interpreted as yet another illustration of the same kind of total frustration Rathenau and Wirth had experienced as a result of the Reparations Commission note of March 21. Warburg was, in fact, in a rare mood of desperation: "Herr Warburg went on to say that he personally takes the position that if we do not get a loan, then we should simply stop payments altogether. The financial situation would then be hopeless, and the Entente could then themselves see how they get the money."[73]

Warburg admitted that this extreme position was not taken by the delegates to Genoa and that opinions varied. What certainly was demonstrated by Warburg's remarks and report, however, is that a shift had occurred across an important portion of the political spectrum. For those who still shared it, the commitment to fulfillment had been severely shaken and had taken on a much less conciliatory character. The Germans were now prepared to take risks and pursue an "active" policy.[74]

This became particularly evident at the Conference on International Economic Reconstruction at Genoa, which began on April 10 and lasted until May 19, with the signing of the famous Rapallo Treaty between Germany and Russia on April 16, an arrangement which preempted a perceived but unreal danger of an Allied arrangement with Russia at Germany's expense and ended Germany's isolation while it guaranteed Russia against its nightmare of a West united in its economic and political dealings with the Soviet state. While the agreement strengthened the ongoing military and economic ties which had developed between the two states and promised to serve German industrial ambitions for a preeminent role in Russia's reconstruction, it was a severe blow to Lloyd George's plans for European cooperation and reconstruction and gave much credibility to French warnings about the Germans.[75] That is, it was not the high road to reparations relief and an international loan or a solution to the May 31 deadline imposed by the Reparations Commission. In point of fact, the chief proponents of fulfillment, Wirth and Rathenau, had made a major contribution to the cause of their domestic political opponents.

This was all the more the case because the German performance at Genoa was as undistinguished and unsuccessful as the conference itself. In keeping with their practice since Versailles, the German delegation came loaded with learned and intelligent, sometimes ponderous, and always self-serving studies dealing with the major economic issues under discussion. Of more importance was the fact that the delegation was badly and visibly divided. Hermes, Moritz Bonn, Hirsch, Bergmann, Melchior (the financial and economic officials and experts of moderate disposition) were chiefly concerned with securing an international loan and getting reparations relief and opposed the Rapallo decision. Hirsch and the RWM had long been calling for an agreement with Russia, but they took the view that it could just as well have been done earlier in Berlin.[76]

While these people were concerned with the reparations problem and getting a loan, others in the delegation, most notably Hermann Bücher and Hans von Raumer, were showing considerable enthusiasm for the Rapallo arrangement, in which industry had a great interest, and indifference or even hostility to using the conference to secure an international loan and stabilize the German and international economic situation. Quite early in the conference, for example, Bücher became alarmed at proposals by Fentener van Vlissingen, the Dutch financier and prominent shareholder in the German Phoenix Company, that an international loan be funded with the guarantee of the difference between the paper and gold value of German industry's stocks and bonds. Vlissingen claimed that this difference contained enough gold value to guarantee a loan and that it would raise German production costs to international levels, an idea very appealing to businessmen in the neutral countries upon whom Vlissingen had considerable influence and with whom (especially the Swiss) he was working closely. Vlissingen thought the time had come for Germany's inflationary reconstruction to give way to a sounder form of development. His argumentation, as reported by Bücher to Stinnes, showed genuine sensitivity to the redistributional consequences and dangers of the inflation, which was all the more remarkable for coming from so capitalist a source:

Van Vlissingen starts from the presumption that the previous tendency of German industry—to employ the large paper mark profits to expand its plants or to create reserves abroad—has been correct, but that it becomes a severe mistake at the moment when the internal enrichment of industry becomes overstretched. He defines this as follows: In Germany we have two types of persons, the one being the great mass that constantly loses and becomes impoverished, the other being a small number that constantly gains. Both will go to ruin the moment in which the system of the enrichment of the one and the impoverishment of the other collapses, whether because it has become unbearable for the masses or because of the power of foreign policy developments. For in the last analysis, the fate of German industry is also dependent upon the fate of the entire people. For industry, therefore, the important thing is to recognize and not to miss the moment in which it is called upon to save the situation through the employment of its productive gold values as the only credit-worthy asset in the German economy. He considers this moment to have come.[77]

While German industrialists certainly wished to bring German production costs into line with those of their major competitors, they had no desire to do so by mortgaging their own assets under the existing circumstances. In the view of the leading German industrialists, the time for an end to the inflationary reconstruction, the international economic consequences of which van Vlissingen and his neutral colleagues were so anxious to end and in whose interests he obviously was speaking, had not come. Bücher asked Stinnes to explain to Vlissingen that the Dutch banker was acting against his own interests as a major shareholder in German enterprises, a task which Stinnes seems to have conducted with success even if it did not spare Vlissingen serious attacks in German industrial newspapers and threats against which Stinnes subsequently had to defend him.[78]

The Vlissingen proposal, however, seems to have been Bücher's only alarming moment at Genoa, and he was later able to send a relieved report to Stinnes that the "Russian intermezzo" seemed to have put an end to all efforts to arrange an international loan at Genoa. While he certainly was pleased that Germany's need for a loan was recognized by the Financial Committee at the conference, he shared von Raumer's view that the financiers were making a mistake in treating the projected loan as a purpose in itself instead of realizing that Germany needed four or five years free of Allied harassment to catch its breath.[79]

If anything, however, Genoa helped to ensure greater exposure to French pressure than ever before and was a disaster for both the Germans and Lloyd George despite such technical accomplishments as laying the groundwork for the establishment of a gold exchange standard, the actual implementation of which must have seemed as far away as ever. In their final interview on May 18, Lloyd George made it more or less clear that Wirth and Rathenau, whose attention was now riveted on the May 31 Reparations Commission deadline, could no longer really count on him to stand between them and Poincaré. He warned against giving Poincaré an excuse to act, since the latter was obligated to consult with his Allies but not to follow their advice. He urged continuation of the fulfillment policy since "Wirth had saved his country," and when Wirth pointed out that "he must have some chance of extending some hope to the German people within the next fortnight," Lloyd George responded "that Germany must go right down before she could rise again, but that was merely a policy of despair. The next few years were the difficult ones for Germany. The civilized world would gradually say that Germany was doing her best and must be given a chance. Then things would get easier."[80] Perhaps Rathenau, who had thirty-eight days left to live and was deeply distraught over what the inflation was doing to German society, should have asked whether a civilized Germany could emerge from this process.

Whatever the case, at least one member of the German Cabinet had not waited upon Genoa and had been troubled by the Rapallo policy from the outset, Finance Minister Hermes. Convinced that something had to be done to ward off a declaration that Germany was in default on May 31 and an occupation of the Ruhr, he followed the request of the Belgian Reparations Commission representative Delacroix, with whom he had unofficial meetings at Genoa and who was anxious to break the impasse, and went off to Paris with the approval of the Cabinet to see what could be done. Hermes, Bergmann, and Fischer negotiated with Bradbury and Seydoux an arrangement between May 13 and 24 that was formally announced by the Reparations Commission on May 31 after its acceptance by Germany three days earlier. Although Bradbury and the English government were as fed up as ever with the manner in which the Germans were managing their finances, they continued to argue for moderation, and Hermes appears to have been able to persuade Bradbury that Germany could not balance its budget without a loan. Both men agreed that it was important to switch the discussion of Germany's liabilities from the Reparations Commission to the Bankers' Committee appointed by the Reparations Commission in early April. Since a final resolution of the reparations question was impossible at the moment because of Franco-German differences, an interim solution based on a loan was necessary. The result of this meeting of minds was a new agreement aimed at maintaining the partial moratorium for the remainder of 1922 while compelling the Germans to get their house in order. The Allies withdrew their de-

mand that Germany raise another sixty billion in taxes in return for an agreement that Germany would cap its floating debt at the level of March 31 and would meet any further increase by new taxes that would not be payable in discountable Treasury bills. The objective, of course, was to prevent revenue collection from becoming a veiled mechanism for the increase of the floating debt. Germany's acceptance of this arrangement was made conditional on the approval of the foreign loan being discussed by the Bankers' Committee. Assuming that Germany received this loan, the German government was to refrain from asking the Reichsbank to issue more marks unless the proceeds of the loan were insufficient to meet reparations payments due after April 1. Finally, the Germans agreed to the Committee of Guarantees' right to supervise the collection of revenue and expenditure insofar as this was within the bounds of what was provided by the Treaty of Versailles and the London Ultimatum but made the additional concession of supervision of direct taxation collection at the federal and state levels. As Poincaré correctly noted, the agreement was filled with "loopholes" favorable to Germany. On the one hand, it depended on Germany's receiving a foreign loan; on the other, the German obligations to discuss their budgetary affairs with the Committee of Guarantees were placed in the context of full respect for German sovereignty, and there was thus no effective control over how the Germans were spending their money.[81]

Poincaré may have been disapproving, but Wirth was furious. In his view, Hermes had exceeded his authority and made excessive concessions, the most onerous of which was the agreement to raise taxes if the floating debt increased over the March 31 level. Wirth did not think it possible to raise new taxes and wanted to stick by the earlier German refusal to do so. The majority of the Cabinet, including Rathenau, supported Hermes, who repeatedly pointed out that the so-called Bradbury Plan was the only way of safely passing the May 31 deadline and yet continue to be considered for the loan on which the entire plan was contingent anyway. If Wirth finally relented very reluctantly and under strong pressure from Rathenau and Ebert, it was because of news that Bradbury was threatening to resign and leave the Germans to the tender mercies of the French.[82]

The Bradbury Plan was contingent on loan negotiations which were expected to be coupled with banker demands for a revision of the London Ultimatum schedule for four or five years, but it also had very revolutionary implications for the German approach to the inflation. Hermes was fully aware that it meant a reversal of the German insistence that stabilization had to precede rather than follow the satisfactory adjustment of German finances. As he rather daringly told a small group of Reichsrat delegates on May 30:

We had to enter into the obligations of the Bradbury draft in order to allay the suspicion . . . that we did not have the goodwill to stem our inflation. The carrying out of the obligations certainly does mean a change in our previous financial and economic policy. But in his [Hermes] view it is absolutely necessary to stem energetically the constantly increasing inflation which, with its ever new price and salary increases, threatens to develop finally into the complete depreciation of the mark and lead to Austrian and Russian conditions. So long as we cannot attack the illness of the mark and bring about its stabilization, all attempts to bring our budget into order are in vain. Of course, we could never do this out of our own power, but we probably can with the granting of a foreign loan. Through the stabilization of the mark we can have a recovery of our finances, naturally also with difficulty for our economy, and crisis conditions for our industry as well as for agriculture. But he sees no other way to prevent state bankruptcy.[83]

Even if Hermes continued to hold the view that Germany could not stabilize on its own without a foreign loan, he had obviously been infected with what Rathenau had once described as an "alien conception." While it is uncertain whether Hermes was equally open about his lapse of faith in the balance-of-payments theory before the Reichstag Foreign Affairs Committee, Helfferich knew what might be called "Bradbury's Disease" when he saw it. Helfferich laced into the agreement, insisting once again that the depreciation of the currency was not a result of inflation but of the reparations obligations and that a reduction of the inflation would not produce an improvement of the exchange rate but rather "an economic ca-

tastrophe as a consequence of the financial bankruptcy of the Reich which must unfailingly occur if the emission of uncovered notes has to be stopped."[84]

True or not, the Gospel According to Helfferich was no defence against French bayonets, and the Centrists, Socialists, and Democrats in the Cabinet, with the exception of Wirth, had supported acceptance of the Bradbury Plan on the simple grounds that it was a means of avoiding the worse alternative, buying time, and possibly getting a loan. As Dernburg of the DDP put the matter: "We had to accept the agreement in order to get past the 31st of May. It is absolutely clear that the money printing presses cannot be stopped. But we must first of all think polititically here, not economically and should not take a completely negative standpoint. Moreover, we always have a free hand to turn down the loan if it appears to offer us excessively unfavorable conditions."[85]

If this appears somewhat cynical and lacking in good faith, however, Dernburg's remarks take on a milder appearance when placed in the context of the open and straight-forward calculations and program offered by Hugo Stinnes. Stinnes showed little interest in the theory of inflation and stabilization and concentrated his attention on the politics and economics of stabilization. He first surveyed the world economic situation, arguing that the United States and Great Britain were showing signs of recovery while France remained in deep financial trouble and had an excess production of heavy industrial products. From this he drew bold conclusions for German policy:

Insofar as the presently demanded shutting down of our note printing presses is concerned, we must not overlook the fact that in our printing of notes lies a kind of emergency weapon against the exaggerated demands of the Versailles Treaty. The French have the threat of further occupation as their sole means of pressure to push through these demands. But such an occupation will hardly bring them any advantage.

After providing statistics on the overproduction of coal in the Entente countries, Stinnes went on to point out

that until now anxiety has driven our policy, namely the anxiety over French threats to occupy further territories of the Reich. This threat will suffer the fate common to weapons which are blunted by continuous use. An occupation of the Ruhr would naturally be a severe test for the area, for one can see in the Rhineland what occupation means. On the other side, however, one must soberly consider the interests of all of Germany and whether through such an occupation of the Ruhr area the French would actually accomplish something. After what he has said, he must absolutely deny this and he therefore urgently warns against letting our policy be determined by the occupation of the Ruhr area. In his view, the French will themselves have the greatest disadvantage from such a step over the long run.

Stinnes then went on to reject the plan to seek a loan that would give Germany a few years of "breathing space" and, in contrast to his somewhat benign view of a French Ruhr occupation, to present the effects of the loan policy in very alarmist terms:

England above all is striving for an improvement of the mark so as to reduce the pressure of our exports by means of the breathing space and the projected loan. The result will be immense unemployment in Germany, for we will not find enough markets for our production. In addition, German products will be boycotted by most of the nations of the world through differential duties and other measures. One has to imagine for oneself what the domestic consequences will be, namely factory shut downs and unemployment, in other words, very large labor struggles that will so convulse our economy that one can only warn in the most urgent manner against promoting this development through our own actions. One should only think of a stabilization of the mark when there is a favorable world economic situation [*Weltkonjunktur*], which we then would have to be in the position to be able to exploit fully. If one were to try today to stabilize the mark in the projected manner, then conditions in England and America would be completely in order in any case, while we, France, and Russia would be completely *kaputt*. Only a definitive regulation of the reparations problem can save us from ruin economically.[86]

In Stinnes's view, the final sum would have to be very low. Thus, he advised against taking a loan to help out for the next few years and suggested "to help ourselves out with small loans if necessary from month to month until a definitive regulation of the whole reparations question through the entry of the United States would be possible." Stinnes saw such American involvement as part of a regulation of Allied war debts as well. He concluded by expressing his concern that the arrangements made by Hermes and Bergmann in Paris had prejudiced

the stand he wished Germany to take, strongly urging against a long-term "breathing space" policy, and pleading that the government not bind the Reichstag to such a policy so that the Reichstag would be in a position to disavow it.

Stinnes's application of his speculative talents to politics was truly remarkable. Fundamentally, he was advocating a conscious and deliberate policy of nonstabilization and confrontation, even if it meant occupation of the Ruhr. It all was a bit too much for Robert Schmidt, the Socialist Economics Minister, who became increasingly apoplectic as he responded to Stinnes. In his view, the "stabilization of the currency is the heart of our entire economic policy," and he insisted that the inflation was responsible for the wage conflicts and unrest then plaguing the country. He suggested that matters had to be viewed from the standpoint of the workers as well as the employers, and the former were being devastated by the inflation. It was when it came to Stinnes's attitude toward a Ruhr occupation, however, that Schmidt went completely out of control, his face turning red and his anger becoming unrestrained. He insisted that a Ruhr occupation would lead to the falling apart of the Reich, something the policy of the government had managed to avoid so far, and that "while it is possible that the occupation of the Ruhr might bring no harm to individual businessmen and perhaps even some advantage," he had to represent the public interest energetically and oppose such a policy. He then bluntly declared that "in any case, it seems to me that Herr Stinnes has only represented his personal interests in his remarks."[87] The USPD Deputy Dittmann joined in the personal attack on Stinnes, which was soon extended to an attack on the industrialists generally; special mention was made of the manner in which the Upper Silesian industrialists were accommodating themselves to the Poles.

Chancellor Wirth was not happy with Schmidt's attack on Stinnes, especially since his own doubts about the Bradbury Plan were far from allayed. Indeed, at this point he was more anxious to work with the People's Party than ever and felt frustrated that every time he made a step in this direction, he was put down in one way or another.[88] He made little effort to hide the reluctance with which he supported the decision to seek a loan, stressing that it was the lesser evil. He admitted that it was preferable "to leading the people once again into catastrophe," but he was frank enough to admit that while the government was striving for a financial and economic breathing space for a few years, he thought the real breathing space would only last a few months, after which it would face profound political questions with respect to accepting the terms of an international loan if it came through. For this reason, he seconded Stinnes on the question of the Reichstag taking a position with respect to the Bradbury Plan, warning that those "who go along as accomplices are liable to be taken prisoner" as well and insisting that the Cabinet alone should and would take responsibility for the agreements made by Hermes.[89]

Depending on one's perspective, the situation at the beginning of June 1922 may be described as fluid or as totally mixed-up and confused. The first, more benign description could be justified by the indirect involvement of the United States through the entry onto the scene of an important new factor in the person of the American banker J. P. Morgan. While the United States had continued to hold itself aloof from direct involvement in European affairs and the Genoa conference, the Harding–Hughes administration was anxious to promote European recovery as part of American recovery. This view, and the position that German recovery and stabilization were the key to the entire European situation, had become widely held in American banking, industrial, and agricultural circles. The State Department strongly supported the idea of the Bankers' Committee to consider an international loan to Germany and, while vetoing the appointment of Benjamin Strong of the Federal Reserve, secretly nominated Morgan for the task. The sending of a private banker meant to relieve Washington of official involvement and prevent linkage with the problem of Allied debts to the United States.[90]

Morgan, however, was the last man on whom the Germans might be expected to pin their hopes. Until this time, Morgan had enjoyed a reputation for being notoriously anti-German and had gone so far as to declare that his firm would never do business with Germany and had even refused to purchase first-class paintings coming from Germany. His willingness to travel to Europe and participate on the Reparations Commission Bankers' Committee was justifiably interpreted as a turning point not only in American willingness to get involved but also, much less justifiably, in American attitudes. Morgan was known to share the growing feeling in American financial circles that the reparations bill had to be cut to manageable size. This was bad enough from the French point of view, but when he began taking the position on the Bankers' Committee that much of any loan given to Germany would have to be used to pay for food and raw materials imports and that the amount available for reparations would have to be limited, rumors began to fly that he had turned pro-German. Actually, the rumors were nonsense and reflected nothing more than the sober business approach being taken by Americans acquainted with the German situation.[91]

Exactly how much American money was available was unclear since the business revival in the United States could be expected to draw off some of the immense liquidity that was being heavily invested in foreign bonds in early 1922. German economic expert Ludwig Bendix strongly urged that the German government prevent a disorganized effort by private and government agencies to get capital in the United States, but he placed strong emphasis on the renewed interest in doing something for Germany.[92] Thus, the Germans, who had sought salvation alternately from the Americans before the London Ultimatum and from the British prior to Genoa, were now once again pinning their hopes on the Americans.

The question of how the Americans were to be used, however, was where the confusion became evident because the Germans were officially pursuing a policy in which none of their leaders were to prove absolutely confident and in the success of which some of them did not have any interest. The tendency to leap at every opportunity of American aid and support which had characterized the period prior to the London Ultimatum was much diminished by 1922, and this was especially apparent in the ambivalent attitude toward the Bradbury Plan in the German Cabinet and the outright hostility toward a "breathing space" loan in important sectors of industry. This hostility was shared by the former chief executive of Krupp, Otto Wiedfeldt, who went to Washington as German Ambassador in May 1922. He had left Germany in a state of some bitterness, angry at the industrialists who had suggested he was not an "honest merchant" in connection with the industrial credit offer he had supported and critical of the Wirth–Rathenau performance at Genoa and Rapallo for undermining the clear coalition of Germany with the Anglo-American powers for which he hoped.[93]

Despite such differences, Rathenau thought Wiedfeldt uniquely suitable for the American post. The Americans had asked the Germans not to send a "big name" but rather someone who understood economic questions. This ruled out most of the career diplomats. Most of the available businessmen did not have the necessary diplomatic skills, while those who did, like Cuno, did not have enough of a private fortune to go into diplomatic service. Furthermore, Cuno was "no genius."[94] Stinnes, with whom Wiedfeldt spoke before his departure, shared Rathenau's view of Wiedfeldt's suitability. If Wiedfeldt had opposed Stinnes on the industrial credit offer, however, he now stood on his side in the matter of a loan, despite Rathenau's instructions that he was to do everything possible to get the "breathing space" loan. While assuring the Foreign Office that he was carrying out instructions and urging American bankers to support the loan, he reported with no little satisfaction that opinion was turning against the loan because it was held that it would only serve France and French armaments. Bankers were allegedly urging that Germany not ask for an international loan because "it is too early; you have to wait; do not lose your nerves, or you will end up in complete misery." Wiedfeldt did not hide his own agreement: "I hold to be acceptable only an international loan based on the coverage of total obligations that are reduced to a bearable level, whereas I hold interim and partial loans to be nothing more than damaging obligations. They lead to special mortgaging of assets and to interference in our political and economic auton-

omy and can only be anticipated to make our situation worse."[95]

Undoubtedly, therefore, he was well satisfied when the Bankers' Committee reported to the Reparations Commission on June 9 that it did not consider it possible for Germany to receive an international loan under existing circumstances. The report, left unsigned by the French representative on the committee, was a blow to the French position, and it was meant to be. Poincaré had objected to any consideration of the actual reparations bill by the committee and then publicly attacked tendencies to "amputate" the reparations settlement in a speech of June 2. As a result, the report not only declared that Germany could not expect a large-scale international loan so long as the reparations bill established under the London Ultimatum remained unchanged (a position shared by both Morgan and the British banker Kindersley from the outset), but also did not consider Germany qualified for a large provisional loan to cover its needs for the coming five or six years or even for a very small loan of one billion or one and a half billion to cover reparations for the coming year. Kindersley had initially been inclined to support the large provisional loan, but Poincaré had so annoyed him that this project was rejected on the grounds that subscribers would remain uncertain as to what France would do after the provisional period ended. Insofar as the small short-term loan was concerned, Morgan argued that it was too small to be floated on the American market under existing political conditions, especially the lack of Allied agreement. While the French were furious (especially at Belgian chairman Delacroix) about what had happened, Bergmann, who had pleaded with great passion and effect for at least the small loan to help Germany in its misery, returned home feeling very positive about the manner in which his applications had been rejected.[96]

The initial draft of the committee report was so anti-French that it had been toned down. Bergmann had actually been consulted by Morgan about the conclusion, and he considered the manner in which the report ended the most important achievement of the negotiations—an appreciation shared by Rathenau, who regarded it as "the greatest progress which the government's policy has enjoyed since the London Ultimatum."[97] This conclusion called for the gradual transformation of reparations from intergovernmental debts to debts among private capitalists that would depend upon relationships of credit rather than force and be based on normal trade and currency relations. Bergmann was particularly pleased by the friendliness shown toward him and the sympathy expressed concerning Germany's plight, although he admitted that his task had not been made easier by a Stinnes speech attacking the notion of a "breathing space" loan that would stabilize the mark at an "artificially high" level. Matters were not helped by newspaper commentaries declaring that the danger of a provisional loan was greater than that of a further depreciation of the mark and expressing relief over the adjournment of the Bankers' Committee meetings and, with that, the avoidance of the "greatest of dangers," namely, the stabilization of the mark. Bergmann had to admit, however, that he had come to entertain his own grave reservations about the utility of the small interim loan for which he had fought so hard and concluded "that I can actually no longer regret that the small loan has not come about now."[98]

The joys of receiving nothing were, of course, limited, especially since Kindersley, to make a gesture toward both the French and economic virtue, had insisted on the inclusion of a statement that Germany had to make itself worthy of credit by placing its finances on a stable basis. While it was theoretically possible to assume the position of simply letting the mark collapse—a policy Hirsch attributed to speculators and to those he colorfully described as the "reparations sadists," who were prepared to let the German people suffer every misery in order to prevent the enemy from collecting anything—this was not a policy the government was prepared to pursue.[99] Bergmann warned that the happy political developments he reported would come to nought if Germany did not keep to its pledge to get the floating debt under control through the tax program and other measures promised. The "impossible," he emphasized, however, could not be done in the event

of an Act of God. In the case of Germany in 1922, God acted through exchange rates, and the news of the Bankers' Committee decision had brought the dollar rate from 278 on June 8 to 313 on June 13.[100] Bergmann had been impressed by a Helfferich article advocating that Germany refuse to purchase foreign exchange if the dollar rate went above a certain level and was happy to learn that this proposal came from Rathenau and Wirth. Bergmann pointed out that Bradbury had already indicated that the Reparations Commission would recognize the necessity of preventing a total collapse of the currency arising from the need to buy foreign exchange to satisfy reparations obligations. To the regret of Hirsch, the press had reported that Germany had enough foreign exchange to meet the June and July reparations payments, but Rathenau suggested that they try to use some of this foreign exchange to push up the value of the dollar in order to control "fantasies" about the future value of the dollar and thereby bring the American currency back to the "bearable" level of 270.[101]

Bergmann supported Rathenau in the idea of throwing some fifty million to a hundred million gold marks' worth of gold or foreign exchange into the "whirlpool" for the purpose of reducing the value of the dollar. In truth, the dilemma faced by the Cabinet at the meeting of June 13 at which these problems were discussed was extraordinary, and it became worse as the month progressed. Prior to this time, the support of the mark at certain levels had served to encourage foreign speculation while preserving employment at home because of export advantages that came with the differential between the internal and external value of the currency. If Germans ceased to believe in the value of their money, however, and based their decisions on the dollar, then the domestic foundations of the inflationary export and employment policy would collapse in the near future. Could one still achieve relative stabilization and prevent the collapse of the domestic economy at the same time? The game depended upon fantasies on both sides of the Atlantic. Americans had to continue believing that the mark would rise, and Germans had to continue believing that the mark was worth something at home. Bergmann, whose travels had taken him to America and Germany in the past year, joined Rathenau in believing that these illusions could be perpetuated even though he saw the signs that they were beginning to dissolve. Thus, he thought the proposal to reduce the value of the dollar would achieve support in New York because of the overspeculation on the mark:

I believe that if one got into contact with suitable circles in New York, one could bring forth a very nice movement [in favor of the mark], even of long duration under the present favorable foreign policy situation. The purchasers of marks have naturally become somewhat timid and cautious, but they are there. They show up on the day after we have a favorable exchange rate. The people want to see something for their money. They buy, perhaps foolishly— that is what I experienced in New York last fall.[102]

Bergmann expected New York speculators to appreciate the "favorable" manner in which the Bankers' Committee had turned down a loan to Germany, but New Yorkers lived far away, and how was one to persuade Germans that affairs had taken another turn for the better? Rathenau might talk about how it was "progress from the long-term perspective" and was not receiving the public appreciation it deserved, but fighting the domestic pessimism was becoming more and more difficult. As Bergmann noted in true bewilderment:

I cannot at the moment say how we are supposed to present the whole business to the public in order to suppress the pessimism that exists among us. I can give no good advice right now. But I must confess, that I do not find myself able to deal with things in Germany any more. For as long as the loan negotiations went on we said: now we face the terrible danger of the depreciation of the dollar; now come the bad times. If the loan—thank God!—is eliminated, then the line is that now we face dreadful times because no loan has been granted. I believe that the pessimism has thus become deeply rooted.[103]

A condition was developing in which no policy could help restore confidence in the mark within Germany, and its economic parallel was visible in conditions which Hirsch described and which Wirth recognized to be "exactly like Austria"; namely, that "where before the external depreciation was in the habit of running ahead of the internal depreciation, now it is the reverse."[104] The fact that agrarian and industrial

leaders thought that the falling exchange rate was still good for exports only made things worse. Hirsch felt that Germany could hold out another two months with the foreign exchange at its disposal before there would be a crisis over reparations payments under the partial moratorium. The difficulties, however, would be accompanied by immense domestic problems because German prices would reach world-market levels and there would be serious unemployment. He thus anticipated a dangerous domestic crisis in the fall and winter.[105]

For the moment, the German government sought to tread water and give some support to the mark until the fruits of the "victory" provided by the Bankers' Committee could be realized. Reichsbank President Havenstein was even more optimistic about the Bankers' Committee decision than Rathenau, while he did not share Rathenau's anxiety about the fall of the mark or think that the dollar was overvalued. He rejected the idea of a massive intervention in early June, arguing that Germany's foreign-exchange resources should be husbanded, and he persisted in a policy of small doses, which added up to some 159 million gold marks fruitlessly expended to bring down the dollar between June 9 and July 15. It is doubtful that the larger doses desired by Rathenau would have turned the tide in any case. A possibly more promising proposal was that this use of foreign exchange earmarked for reparations be supplemented by taking a loan in Switzerland and the Netherlands to cover the remaining five hundred million gold marks owed in 1923 under the Clearing Agreement on prewar debts. The idea was to influence the exchange rate by improving the balance of payments, but this notion was also squelched by Havenstein.[106]

The policy of fulfillment continued in a similarly desultory fashion. While the failure of the loan effort relieved Germany of the requirement to raise new taxes to meet reparations, an effort was made to carry through on previous promises and avoid a political crisis. The compulsory loan was pushed forward and finally passed in mid-July, although in early May Hirsch had already concluded, presumably because of the depreciation and its late passage, that it would not bring in much in 1922 and would be unlikely to bring in the anticipated returns in the future either. The entire tax compromise had, in fact, been passed, although what was probably more important was that tax collection had definitely become more effective in the first half of 1922, and, when combined with government cutbacks on expenditure, revenues actually managed to cover ordinary expenditures. They did not, of course, cover reparations. This and such positive developments as the increases in the coal tax, the reduction of subsidies, and the increase of the duties calculated in gold values undertaken at the behest of the Allies were now all threatened by the renewed deterioration of the currency in response to the decision of the Bankers' Committee.[107]

Germany had also met Allied demands for a reform of the Reichsbank, although the significance of this was largely a product of British imagination. Indeed, the real significance of the measure was to Havenstein, who, during his visit to London in October 1921, had asked for and received Montagu Norman's support for the legislative strengthening of the Reichsbank's position against the government. The Autonomy Law passed on May 26 and formally went into effect on July 24, 1922. It provided for the continued "supervision" (*Aufsicht*) of the Reichsbank by the Reich government but removed the Chancellor from his role (purely formal though it had been) in the direction (*Leitung*) of the bank. The object of the reform was to provide the Reichsbank with the ability to resist government demands that it discount Reich Treasury bills. Havenstein, of course, always denied that he had ever involuntarily discounted Treasury bills, and the reasons he gave for welcoming the measure hardly could have been reassuring. He did think it helpful for the Reichsbank to be able to resist government pressures to undertake measures harmful to the bank, and he cited as examples Erzberger's idea of bank-note stamping and pressures to mortgage the gold in the Reichsbank. That is, he used illustrations of behavior that might be related to currency stabilization! The best measure of the law's futility with respect to Allied goals was Helfferich's support of the bill. Although he deplored any action taken under Allied pressure, he welcomed freeing the Reichsbank from control of the republican and parliamentary government and rejected as pure

"quackery" the notion that the printing press could be stopped by anything but a revision of the Treaty of Versailles! Havenstein could not have agreed more. Like Helfferich, he was most anxious to keep the Entente from having any influence on the Reichsbank and fought successfully against proposals by Georg Bernhard in the Reich Economic Council to provide for the exploration of further measures to sever the link between the issuance of notes and the coverage of the Reich's budget. This, Havenstein warned, would play into the hands of the Entente, for "so long as the reparations burden remains, there is no other means to procure the necessary means for the Reich than the discounting of Reich treasury notes at the Reichsbank."[108]

This was not a position Poincaré was ready to accept, and while the German government bided time and awaited the arrival of the Committee of Guarantees in Berlin to discuss measures of supervision and control, the inflation and social situation were becoming worse. Fundamentally, as a British observer put it, "the German Government would appear to be 'waiting for something to turn up.'"[109] Poincaré was increasingly moving in the direction of turning up with his troops, the only logical conclusion given his unwillingness to consider revision.[110] At a meeting with the British leaders and Morgan in London on June 19, he argued for the control of Germany's budget, currency, and exports and thought it had been a mistake to have the Bankers' Committee meet before such controls had been established. The dilemma was well expressed by Treasury Secretary Horne:

The difficulty was that they were in a vicious circle. Germany said she could not stop the emission of paper money and repay her obligations unless she was able to raise a foreign loan, and she could not raise a foreign loan unless she could pay her obligations. This was the vicious circle they were in. His view was that Germany should meet her expenditure by the normal means of raising revenue to meet expenditure. Germany had undertaken to restrict her paper if she could obtain a loan. But as she could not obtain a loan, he feared that the promise to restrict the paper circulation was only a pious aspiration.[111]

Morgan presented the "vicious circle" in even broader terms and implied that it was a reflection of the inability of the Allies to face economic realities and decide on what it was they wanted. He emphasized the known fact that he was not pro-German and did not want German obligations cut down but stressed that the Germans had to be put in a position to pay if one wished them to pay and that the implications of their prosperity had to be accepted:

The only chance was that Germany know the total amount of what she had to pay. So long as that was an uncertain quantity, liable to be increased if Germany was prosperous and to be diminished when she was not, a state of depression would be produced in Germany which would, in Mr. Morgan's view, prevent her from putting herself in a position to pay.... If she was prosperous she could pay a great deal of money; otherwise she could not. Broadly speaking, Mr. Morgan appeared to think that the Allies must make up their minds as to whether they wanted a weak Germany who could not pay, or a strong Germany who could pay. If they wanted a weak Germany they must keep her economically weak; but if they wanted her to be able to pay they must allow Germany to exist in a condition of cheerfulness, which would lead to successful business. This meant, however, that you would get a strong Germany, and a Germany that was strong economically would, in a sense, be strong from a military point of view also.[112]

The upshot of the entire discussion was that the Allies were in a stalemate; Poincaré was convinced that the Germans were manipulating the inflation to build up their railroads and merchant fleet and gain markets at the expense of England and France, and the British were arguing that some of the German reconstruction was legitimate and necessary if the Germans were to pay reparations and were warning against excessive controls. In the end, all involved agreed that they were in a "provisional period," without defining what the final result was going to be.

One thing was certain, Germany was not in a state of "cheerfulness," but quite the reverse, and the evidence of impending crisis was to be seen everywhere. Germans were now living in fear of both the depreciation and the appreciation of the mark. The former was causing prices to skyrocket so that, as a British observer reported, the workers themselves did not know what kind of wage increases to ask for, and the employers, who were fleeing from the marks into goods and engaging in hectic activity, had no choice but to give in. The public appeared totally surprised by the suddenness and rapidity

of the latest depreciation. At the same time, everyone was fearful that domestic prices were beginning to reach world-market levels and that the entire inflation boom would collapse. Many were afraid that a recovery of the mark would turn Germany's high tax levels into personal financial agony. A great change had taken place in any case. In contrast to the previous year, there was a growing fatalistic attitude about both the fall of the mark and the occupation of the Ruhr.[113]

The Coming of Hyperinflation

Fatalism about the future, however, is not the same as fatalism about everyday life, and Germany's leaders were, above all, concerned to keep the economic activity and employment produced by the inflationary boom going for as long as they could. Without sufficient coal this was not possible, and it was this problem, so often the subject of debate between them, that brought Stinnes and Rathenau together on the evening before Rathenau's murder and, appropriately enough, on the eve of Germany's descent into hyperinflation.

It is important to recognize that the character of the coal problem in 1922 had changed substantially since 1919–1920. The full potential quantity and the quality of production were held back by run-down collieries and coking plants and by the inability of the government and the owners to persuade the miners to enter into any long-term overtime agreement because of their suspicion that the eight-hour day would be thus ended through the back door. Nevertheless, the amount of coal available within Germany's changed borders were 94 percent of what it would have had at its disposal *after* reparations coal deliveries within the same territorial area. In the first five months of 1922, Germany had actually been a net exporter of coal in the amount of two and a half million tons. Nevertheless, she was on the verge of becoming an importer of coal to the tune of ten and a half million tons between June and December of 1922. The source of the shortfall was the inflation boom, above all in iron and steel, which required large amounts of high-quality coking coal. This was the kind of coal Germany was required to deliver as reparations to France and Belgium.[114]

Germany thus began to import coal from England both for immediate needs and to create some stock for the coming winter. This coal was bought at the world-market price, although it was exempted from the 40 percent coal tax in order to make it purchasable in Germany. Even with such measures, however, the situation seemed so potentially dangerous in June that the Reich Coal Commissar ordered reductions of coal available for industrial purposes. If the orders were carried out, there was a real danger that the gas and electrical supplies in the Ruhr would be disturbed and that not only cokeries and smelting plants but also Siemens–Martin steel plants would be shut down. The industrialists, among them Stinnes, had no intention of taking responsibility for this and went off to Berlin to have the orders changed. In a meeting on June 23, Economics Minister Schmidt found himself in agreement with the industrialists but insisted that Foreign Minister Rathenau be consulted because of the possible effect on reparations deliveries. Rathenau was also in full accord with the industrialists, suggested they offer British coal in place of the coking coal needed by the Germans, and was willing to arrange a meeting with the Committee of Guarantees.[115]

Back at his hotel, Stinnes encountered Bemelmens, the Belgian representative on the Reparations Commission, and informed him of the coal situation, pointing out that while the Allies had a right to be informed of German production problems in a timely manner, they also had to understand that emergency "situations could suddenly arise, given the unrest which has affected all classes of the German population because of the continuous increase of the cost of living and the catastrophic fall of the mark. It is impossible for us in these times to risk bringing large numbers of the German working people out on the street and letting them demonstrate because of heavy losses of production and wages, and that insofar as we prevented this, we are the same time serving the interests of the Entente."[116] Bemelmens was quite sympathetic but pointed out that one should avoid any conflicts and suggested that the French would soon come around to agree-

ing with the views of the Americans, English, and Belgians and accept a final arrangement of the reparations and loan questions.

While Stinnes was using his persuasive powers with Bemelmens, Rathenau was dining at the home of the American Ambassador Houghton. He decided to have Stinnes called over to join Houghton and his other guest, Colonel Logan, to explain the coal situation. Stinnes arrived at 10:30 in the evening, and the conversation lasted until 1:30, when Rathenau accompanied Stinnes back to the Hotel Esplanade, where the two men continued talking until 4:00 in the morning. Already at Ambassador Houghton's, the conversation had rapidly drifted away from the coal situation to the general problems of the inflation and reparations and had revealed a rare harmony between Stinnes and Rathenau, two normally competing figures, about the origins and character of the German inflation as well as the condition of Germany.[117] Both industrialists pointed out that the inflation arose out of the need to find employment for the returning soldiers, maintain internal order, and prevent Bolshevism. Rathenau compared Germany with an army that was completely surrounded and which "in order to save its existence is forced even with the greatest losses to break through in order to secure air and the chance of survival for the majority."[118] Stinnes spoke of the inflation as a "political necessity." "It was," he said grimly, "a question of your money or your life, and when compelled to choose between the two, he always gave up his money."[119] While the Americans present agreed that inflation was preferable to death, they qestioned whether its continuation was acceptable and raised the accusations that had been made that Stinnes wished to promote the inflation further. Stinnes hotly denied this, declaring that "anyone who suggested that he [Stinnes] wanted to see the Austrianization of Germany was a fool."[120] He was prepared to take his deflationary "medicine" once there was a reasonable reparations settlement, but he opposed a small loan that would leave things worse than before. The Americans agreed, Logan pointing out that this was also the position of Morgan, but they were very skeptical about Stinnes's tactics and suggested that he was playing into French hands by not supporting the stabilization of German finances necessary to qualify for a loan. Stinnes, possibly encouraged by his conversation with Bemelmans, countered with a rather optimistic scenario in which Germany would receive in only a few months' time a modest loan that would be accompanied by the end of the occupation, sanctions, and the existing reparations arrangements and would be given equality on world markets.

It is unclear from the accounts whether Rathenau poured any water into this rather heady wine. It is most likely that he chose simply to yield to Stinnes's proclivity to spin forth his visions. It is clear, however, that the two men and the Americans did agree on certain very important matters. Rathenau and Logan shared the view that the payments to the Entente would have to stop under existing circumstances and that probably only one more of the installments under the moratorium could be paid, an attitude that filled Stinnes with enthusiasm and led him later to claim that the differences between himself and Rathenau no longer existed. Before Stinnes had arrived, Rathenau appears to have indicated to the Americans that reparations might reasonably be set at fifty billion gold marks. They agreed that all subsidies and economic controls would have to be ended and that greater worker productivity would have to be required. In this last regard, the two Germans found themselves well behind their hosts in vigor and rigor. Whereas Stinnes and Rathenau thought that it would be possible to persuade the German workers to labor longer to pay modest reparations and create a positive balance of trade, Houghton was skeptical, pointing out that "in his experience in America as well as in England only through the bitter Must of hunger could the masses be brought so far that they realized that only higher labor productivity and a productive economy could bring salvation." Houghton did admit that the German workers were very advanced and industrious, apparently in contrast to the laborers at home, and that this perhaps justified the optimism of Rathenau and Stinnes.[121]

In truth, however, Rathenau was not in an optimistic mood at all, which may help to explain why he did not take as much exception to Stinnes's comments as he could have, despite his own increasingly hard line on the reparations question. He actually asked Stinnes to explain his personal attacks on himself to the Americans, which Stinnes did with his usual line that Rathenau's signature "could not be discounted" because he had approved the Cannes and March 21 payment schemes even though Germany could not meet them. Rathenau went so far as to say that he agreed with Stinnes but that a member of the government could not simply operate on "business principles" and had to take "political exigencies" into account.[122] Stinnes's answer to this all along had been that an industrialist of Rathenau's calibre should never have entered the government in the first place, and he expressed the hope that Rathenau would resign as soon as possible, a request which Rathenau laughingly refused, pointing out that someone had to do the work and that he had entered the government in the hope of serving the country.[123]

In truth, however, serving the nation had been hard, and Rathenau was showing the strain. In the course of the day, he had been the victim of a brutal verbal assault by Helfferich in the Reichstag on the inadequacy of the German response to French policies in the Saar. Helfferich used the occasion to attack the entire policy of fulfillment, pointing out that it "has brought about the frightful depreciation of Germany's money, has crushed our *Mittelstand*, has brought countless persons into distress and misery, has driven countless persons into despair and suicide, has delivered up substantial valuable portions of our national capital to foreigners, has shaken the foundations of our economic and social order."[124] After arriving at Ambassador Houghton's, Rathenau had concentrated his agitation on the Helfferich speech and its potential consequences. As the evening wore on, however, possibly under the influence of Stinnes's rhetoric and certainly moved by his own doubts about fulfillment, Rathenau focused his bitterness elsewhere. He complained about how onerous it was to be constantly hounded by Germany's former enemies with notes and demands and pointed out that if the German people knew what passed over his desk, it would strengthen the reactionaries even more. While he explained the necessity of the inflation along lines similar to those of Stinnes, he also said that it had gone too far. He viewed the inflation as a "necessary transfer of capital from one class to another" required by Germany's wartime impoverishment.[125] He pointed out very gloomily that "a people that had become as poor as the German people could no longer sustain broad classes of the population living off wealth and pensions [and investments],"[126] a position which the Americans questioned given the fact that Germany was sustaining a host of inflation profiteers. These were not the people of whom Rathenau was speaking, however, but rather the educated middle class, the improverishment of which obviously touched him deeply. Rathenau lamented the decline of German morale, which he attributed, among other things, to the assassinations and attempted assassinations of major political figures, and he appeared depressed throughout the evening. As Logan reported, Rathenau likened Germany's situation to that "of a sane man taken and confined against his will in an insane asylum during a long period with the result that he gradually assimilates the mental traits of his associates."[127]

While the two Americans tended to discount many of Rathenau's remarks as the "old stuff," Logan admitted that he was at least "50 percent impressed," and he certainly was moved by the events of the late morning, when two right-wing murderers using a submachine gun and a hand grenade assassinated Rathenau. It was a fate of which Rathenau had been continuously warned both officially and unofficialy since he took over the Foreign Office.[128]

The effect was to rally supporters of the Republic in ways unseen since the Kapp Putsch, but it was also to deepen the economic crisis and social conditions creating the bitterness that was producing the environment of violence and political murder. As Hirsch noted a few days after the assassination:

The adjustment of our domestic prices to the dollar rate is taking place with uncommon rapidity, and with it grows the bitterness of the broad masses. This embitterment is the true soil on which Organization C and its associates flourish, and even the counter-demonstrations have their deepest economic basis in the growing immiseration of the masses. The atmosphere of murder and putschism thickens itself progressively with the rising dollar.[129]

The workers who demonstrated in support of the Republic and of the Law for the Protection of the Republic that was passed as a result of the assassination were struggling to keep body and soul together in the face of constantly rising prices, but they continued to have the organized power to raise their wages; and as the remarks of Stinnes and Rathenau at Ambassador Houghton's suggested, important elements in industry continued to think of courting them. Von Raumer, for example, saw the failure of the loan effort and the rapid attainment of world-market prices in Germany as an opportunity as well as a threat. He did not underestimate the latter, warning that unemployment would bring catastrophe and the possible tearing apart of the Reich through invasion and separatism. In contrast to his attitude at the end of 1921, however, he now could foresee a real basis for collaboration with labor by trading off increased wages and salaries for the only thing that could justify them—increased productivity. Since labor was insisting that industry had not done enough to modernize technically, von Raumer contemplated satisfying this demand through a legal requirement that firms plow a part of their returns into a tax-exempt works-renewal fund. Most important, however, was a common front on reparations, which Raumer thought the Bankers' Committee report now made possible. One could then go about the tasks of solving both the socioeconomic and the reparations problems in unity with the Socialist and Christian labor organizations in a working community as had been done when the ZAG was established during the Revolution.[130]

Where did the nonindustrial middle classes, the misery of which Helfferich had invoked in his Reichstag speech and the fate of which had so distressed Rathenau on the night before his death, fit into this arrangement, however? Who was making an *Arbeitsgemeinschaft* with them, and where were the organizations through which they could be meeting the endlessly rising cost of living? As the British Consul in Frankfurt reported:

It is a situation which cannot but give cause for grave anxiety, for the educated classes, deprived, in a great majority of cases, of the right to live and bring up their families in decency, are becoming more and more hostile to the Republic and open in their adhesion to the forces of reaction. Coupled with this movement, a strong and virulent growth of antisemitism [*sic*] is manifest. It is, indeed, no exaggeration, but merely a statement of fact, to say that cultured Germans, men and women of high social standing, openly advocate the political murder of Jews as a legitimate weapon of defence. They admit, it is true, that the murder of Rathenau was of doubtful advantage, for, as is well known, the late Minister had strong Monarchist sympathies and, as his writings showed, was himself, to a not inconsiderable extent, an anti-Semitist. But, they say, there are others who must go in order that Germany shall be saved.[131]

The murder of Rathenau also dealt a mortal blow to the mark. Between June 24 and July 1, the exchange rate of the mark moved from 345 to 402 marks to the dollar. On July 31, it stood at 670 marks to the dollar. More than Germany's newest political catastrophe was at work of course, but the combination of the Bankers' Committee report and the assassination did much to complete the destruction of confidence in the mark abroad that had begun in the fall of 1921. As Ludwig Bendix reported from New York on July 3: "While the standing German offer of marks, relatively speaking, found willing acceptance until the middle of last month, there has been a complete absence of any demand for German currency since that time. With this has been lost an important support which the mark has previously enjoyed."[132]

At the same time, the loss of confidence in the mark at home intensified the flight from the mark and led to unprecedented rises in prices and wages. Industry, heavily organized in cartels and associations, had begun imposing severe payment conditions. At the same time, the practice of sliding-scale prices spread throughout the business world. The result was the severe credit crisis about which industrialist Hans Kraemer and the economic writer Georg Bernhard had warned a year and a half earlier. The question as to what would happen if the outside world ceased speculating on the mark was now being answered. At its final meeting on July 14, 1922, the Reich Economics Council's Sub-Committee on Production Credit, no banker stood up, as had been done eighteen months earlier, and proudly announced that the banks were "swimming in money." Germany may have been swimming in money, but the banks were unable to supply all that was needed to keep up with price and wage demands. As a result, they were being increasingly forced to hold cash rather than Reich Treasury notes, which were flowing back to the Reichsbank in

alarming numbers. Unless the liquidity crisis paradoxically caused by the inflation was overcome, German industry would grind to a halt for lack of the operating credit needed to keep going, and massive unemployment and turmoil would be the result. There was only the one solution, widely agreed upon in industrial circles, of massive reintroduction of bills of exchange which could be discounted at the Reichsbank. Havenstein, in full consonance with the principle that his fundamental task was to keep the economy going, agreed on the necessity of this measure. As Kraemer reported, Havenstein had declared that "the Reichsbank viewed the development during the next weeks with horror, with the greatest alarm, since it is at the moment no longer in a position to market treasury bills, that on the contrary treasury bills in extraordinary amounts are flowing back to the Reichsbank. He declared to us that it is necessary for industry to take energetic measures to reintroduce commercial bills as rapidly as possible."[133]

This was advice which industry was happy to accept, and the various cartels and trade associations hastened to accept bills of exchange in their transactions. It was dangerous advice, and its more responsible supporters, such as Georg Bernhard, knew it. The discounting of commercial bills could easily be abused and become a new source of inflation if it were not controlled, but even Bernhard considered it a necessary transitional measure to the inevitable deflation. Thus, on the one hand, he argued that "we face a situation in which there is only one source of money in Germany left, and that is the Reichsbank, and it cannot give out any more notes because we only have four billion in commercial bills outstanding, while everything else are state issued bills. It is thus absolutely correct that we create commercial bills; then the Reichsbank can issue money." On the other hand, he warned that "when one has as inflationary a situation as we have, then one runs the danger of eternalizing the situation by bringing out new masses of notes. Just as much as I think it self-understood that we return to bills of exchange in the present situation, just so dangerous do I consider the dangers that can be connected with it if we do not watch the credit situation closely."[134] Bernhard's anxieties, however, were not shared by some prominent businessmen. For the banker Salomonsohn, inflation was nothing more or less than money in excess of what was needed for business, and since so much money had been hoarded and still was abroad, he did not consider the inflation as large as was being pretended. He, and others in industry, had high hopes that the "the deterioration of the mark will once again open up the possibility of being competitive abroad," and thus lead to a new inflow of foreign exchange, thereby relieving the credit situation.[135] Whether this would happen remained to be seen, but Havenstein could be counted upon to do his share. As the Reichsbank President cheerfully reported to the Central Committee of the Reichsbank on July 28, the amount of domestic bills of exchange and checks in the portfolio of the Reichsbank had increased from 922 million at the end of December 1921 to 6,581 million on July 23. The big breakthrough had come in June, since the amount had increased gradually though most of the year, and had then leaped from 2,681.6 million on May 31 to 4,571.4 million on June 30. The demand was now so great that Havenstein felt justified in calling for an increase of the discount rate from 5 to 6 percent, a proposal that was accepted after some debate about raising it to 7 percent. The Reichsbank was now adding a private inflation to the public one created by the discounting of Reich Treasury bills.[136]

The hyperinflation had thus begun, and the jump in the discounting of Treasury bills in June and July combined with the shutting off of the foreign speculative spigot gave quantitative reinforcement to the impact of the Bankers' Committee decision and the murder of Rathenau. The domestic and international problems of Germany could not be separated, and at the beginning of July Labor Minister Brauns felt that an appeal to the Allies was necessary to hold back the slide into disaster. The anxiety was heightened by a printers' strike which prevented the printing of money and government documents.[137] Since Allies knew that Germany had money at hand to make her July reparations payment, Wirth and the Cabinet felt they had to make yet one more fifty million goldmark reparations payment under the reduced 1922 schedule before asking for relief once

again. Yet, it was simply impossible to argue, as had been the case in the past, that the reparations payments were responsible for the most recent collapse of the mark. Germany had not been buying but rather selling foreign exchange to shore up the mark. Not only could no direct link be established, but as Julius Hirsch noted, the news that Germany might not make further payments and thus would not be buying foreign exchange was nevertheless increasing the price of the latter. Furthermore, there was substantial evidence that the balance of payments was not excessively passive as evidenced by the foreign exchange collected from exports and the amount of foreign money being brought in by tourists. Hirsch attributed the decisive role to "pessimism" and came to the conclusion, especially after reports from New York showing very little speculative activity against the mark there, that the depreciation's "single truly permanent source" lay in Germany itself. The huge demand for foreign currency in Germany was no longer a result of what it needed to pay abroad but rather of the demand for foreign currency in internal transactions.[138] Like the increasingly unmarketable Reich Treasury notes which were backing up on the Reichsbank, so the entire inflation was backing up on the German people themselves.

Thus, the endogenous sources of the inflation—Germany's fiscal, monetary, and socioeconomic condition—had finally overtaken the exogenous ones that had dominated and veiled them since the summer of 1921. Reparations did not cause the German hyperinflation, and the Germans did not make the hyperinflation in order to escape reparations, but reparations had proven a disincentive to stabilization. Furthermore, the ceaseless preoccupation with reparations had necessarily interacted with political and social currents in Germany so as to become a decisive factor in shifting the political balance from the left to the right. That was the meaning of the failure of the credit offer and the increasing intransigence of Wirth and Rathenau after March 1922 as well as the efforts of Rathenau to find some common ground with Stinnes during those few hours that remained to his life. While Wirth and Rathenau had made notable achievements in discrediting the London Ultimatum schedule in Britain and America, they had not convinced the French or anyone else that Germany had been managing her domestic finances properly. Fulfillment was a tactic, a short-term policy; it certainly was not a conviction. Since the war, the domestic advantages of inflation for the maintenance of social peace, reconstructing the German industrial plant, and reestablishing Germany on world markets had served to reinforce the "inflation consensus," which had also been heavily boosted by the reparations issue. With the coming of the hyperinflation, the domestic price of these policies and of the tacit consensus on which they were based was to become as brutally apparent as its fragility and untenability. The great question now was whether it would still be possible to stabilize before the currency collapsed and the Ruhr was occupied.

Chapter 11

Stabilization Debates and Political Crises, August 1922–January 1923

Reparations and the Stabilization Issue, August–November 1922

The galloping inflation and the hyperinflation were having disastrous effects upon Germany's society and polity. Both Rathenau and Wirth had predicted such a result if Germany were not granted some respite from Allied demands. It is impossible, therefore, not to take very literally the desperate appeal made by Wirth for Papal intervention on Germany's behalf at the beginning of August 1922. He warned that Allied demands were creating conditions which were reducing the "*Mittelstand* to beggars" and could only lead to more political murder, desperation, and the kind of circumstances that had already devastated Russia. Wirth, "as the responsible director of German policy and as a faithful son of the Catholic Church," pleaded that the Holy See intervene in what he called the "final hour" to prevent Allied measures of force from totally destroying the German economy and to call for a reduction of the demands made upon Germany to a "bearable measure" as well as for a "sufficient breathing space" within which Germany could restore its currency and finances.[1] Both the new pope, Pius XI, and his Secretary of State, Cardinal Gasparri, were indeed concerned about the economic plight of both Germany and Europe. Gasparri had hoped that the Conference on International Economic Reconstruction in Genoa would pave the way to a more reasonable solution by linking war debts and reparations and by bringing about a constructive American role, but the divine blessings asked for the conference had obviously not been granted. The German Am-bassador Bergen had cultivated Gasparri's quest for a satisfactory solution to the reparations problem in a variety of ways, not the least important of which was by supplying Gasparri with the Italian edition of Keynes's *Economic Consequences of the Peace* in July. Bergen thus followed up Wirth's letter to the Pope by urging Gasparri to represent the view that "after the collapse of the German currency, gold payments during the next few years were totally out of the question, and later only possible to a limited extent."[2]

Just as Wirth sent an ardent appeal to the Pope on August 4, so he sent an even more impassioned entreaty to Lloyd George on the same day stressing the political dangers of the deteriorating situation in Germany. The public, Wirth argued, was blaming the fulfillment policy of his government for its miseries, a policy Wirth claimed he had pursued faithfully for a year "with patience and hope for improvement." What he now confronted was the sheer exhaustion of his people, and he reminded the Prime Minister of the service Germany had performed for European democracy: "The German democratic government saved bourgeois society in central Europe from Bolshevism after the great catastrophe of the war and thereby has in my view performed a great historical service for the bourgeois social order in the world. The total immiseration of the German people makes the continuation of this policy, which serves Europe as a whole, impossible." Not only could Germany no longer make monetary payments, but it would soon be unable even to finance payments in kind. Wirth asserted his intention of pursuing the policy of fulfillment as long as possible but warned that it would inevitably be "shipwrecked on the naked reality of the depreciation of the mark" if "outside help" did not come, he twice emphasized, "at the right time." Payments in gold and "exaggerated" coal deliveries could no longer be made, for "if we do not put a limit on the further immiseration of the German people, then German democracy is lost." The "cry of agony" of those in the middle classes, who were being turned into "beggars," was indescribable, and it was therefore essential that no measures of force be taken against Germany and that Germany be given the breathing space needed to meet demands of a bearable nature.[3]

The immediate purpose of these diplomatic efforts was to gain British support at the forthcoming London Conference of August 7–14, at which the Allies were to consider the German request for a moratorium as well as general policy with respect to Germany's obligations. Their language and significance, however, was more than tactical. There is no reason whatever to question the sincerity of Wirth's conviction that his domestic situation was desperate. He was horrified to read an article in a Bavarian newspaper associated with the Bavarian People's Party accusing him and other supporters of fulfillment of giving Germany's wealth away to "foreign money magnates," further declaring that "the fulfillment politicians have the increased cost of living on their conscience. They throw the small rentiers, workers, and civil servants into bitter distress. Living on their salaries as ministers and deputies, they do not starve and they will not freeze in winter; they and their wives can afford expensive furs. And you . . . ? How can you stand German government people who sell you out day after day?" Wirth complained angrily to the German Episcopal authorities that such an article should appear in a paper calling itself Christian and indicated that, after its publication, he was in no way surprised at receiving a letter from a Bavarian priest who predicted that he would in all probability shortly meet a violent end and stand before his Judge.[4]

More prosaically, Wirth could hardly treat the stability of his minority government lightly. His domestic political problems were compounded by seemingly endless conflicts and distracting negotiations with Bavaria over the Law for the Protection of the Republic and other issues involving Bavaria's "sovereign rights." Quite aside from the thorny constitutional issues, the constant challenges from Bavaria were harmful to the domestic prestige of the Reich government and dangerous to its international security because they constantly raised the issue of separatism.[5] More generally, however, and most important, Wirth had little confidence that he could undertake the necessary measures to deal with the economic and social situation at home because "the decomposition of civic spirit [staatlichen Geistes] is far advanced, and it will be very difficult to take or carry out the measures needed to relieve the distress of the German people."[6] It is in this context of deeply felt pessimism concerning Germany's capacity to recover entirely on its own that Wirth's desperate search for outside assistance is to be understood.

Wirth's humiliating and frustrating efforts to procure a moratorium provide ample evidence of the problems encountered by his policy, although this is not to argue that the policy was not justified under the circumstances. On July 12, 1922, the German government had formally requested a two-and-a-half-year moratorium on cash payments. That is, following a last fifty million gold-mark payment of July 15 under the reduced schedule set up in March 1922, no further cash payments were to be made until 1925. Thus, the Germans asked for the suspension not only of the reduced schedule but also of the May 1921 London Ultimatum plan, which was scheduled to go back into effect at the beginning of 1923. Furthermore, their request included a reduction of the monthly clearing payments agreed to in June 1921 from two million to half a million pounds sterling.[7]

Even before the German request for a moratorium could be considered for approval at the highest levels, the Germans had to make concessions to the Allied Committee of Guarantees involving further surveillance over German measures against capital flight and provision of statistical information. While Finance Minister Hermes felt that these concessions, however obnoxious, at least preserved German sovereignty, barred administrative interference, and preserved the secrecy of tax records, Wirth feared "that with each request for a moratorium we go further in the direction of Ottomanization."[8] Nevertheless, Wirth preferred to concede freely what might otherwise be imposed by an ultimatum and was undoubtedly relieved that the Reichstag was not in session and that he could present its Foreign Affairs Committee with a *fait accompli*. Nevertheless, the increased supervision of German affairs was resented by the public, while the American observer Logan wondered if such measures really were very helpful in securing Germany the loan which everyone on the Committee of Guarantees recognized to be necessary since "it might be difficult to get a lender to advance money if told that it was necessary to keep three or four policemen with the borrower so as to prevent his running away."[9]

Poincaré, however, was in a policing mood and was very cold to the idea of a long-term moratorium. Indeed, State Secretary Bergmann reported from Paris on July 29 that Poincaré viewed the collapse of the mark as a deliberate German swindle and, even more ominously, cautioned against a renewal of "false hopes" in British ability or willingness to resist Poincaré.[10] These points were rapidly demonstrated both before and during the London Conference of August 7–14. Thus, Poincaré not only refused the German request for a reduction of clearing payments even before the London meeting, but he responded to the German default on the August payment by ordering measures of surveillance and control over German assets connected with the clearing arrangements and threw out some five hundred German citizens from Alsace-Lorraine for good measure. As far as the moratorium issue was concerned, he came to London insisting that any such concessions to Germany be coupled with the granting of "productive guarantees" to the Allies. The "guarantees" not only included that the Bad Ems Bureau set up in 1921 to grant export and import licenses for the occupied area be maintained but also called for the restoration of a customs boundary between the occupied and unoccupied areas, the surrender of the Prussian state forests and mines in the Rhineland and Ruhr to the Allies, the surrender of 60 percent of the shares of the great chemical works on the left bank, the confiscation of tax

receipts in the occupied areas in the event of delayed reparations payments, and increased control on German exports by the Committee of Guarantees.[11]

Not surprisingly, Lloyd George refused to go along with such a program, and the conference broke up without agreement and with France appearing extremely isolated. The danger was that Poincaré might decide to act in isolation, a possibility made much more real by his decision of July 12, the same day the Germans requested a moratorium, to set up an interministerial committee to examine the question of an occupation of the Ruhr. Naturally, this was not known to Wirth, who was receiving positive reports that Poincaré would fall in October and be replaced by Loucheur, but it made more sense to base German policy on fear than on optimistic speculations. Poincaré only had to thunder to make the mark fall, as it did when the London Conference broke up over his recalcitrance on August 14 and as it did again after Poincaré held a speech at Bar-le-Duc on August 22 in which he threatened unilateral action if French views on a moratorium were not heeded.[12] In contrast to early June, when a certain amount of "bad" news for the mark, such as the refusal of the Bankers' Committee to approve a loan for Germany, could be secretly welcomed as a long-term piece of "good" news, the German government was unable to find any solace in news that negatively influenced the exchange rate in the late summer and fall of 1922. France's isolation could become more dangerous than advantageous. Thus, when urging the Bavarians to do nothing that might imply a threat to the unity of the Reich, Wirth pointed out that "we stand before such difficult weeks and months, that we need to stick together unconditionally at home. The isolation of France and the collapse of the mark are circumstances such as have never been encountered in German history."[13]

The uncertainties involved in getting help from the English and the need for extreme German caution were well reflected by the situation of Austria and Wirth's handling of a visit by the Austrian Chancellor Seipel and his Finance Minister, Count Segur, in August. The Austrians had hoped to stabilize their currency with the help of Austrian and foreign-owned banks in Austria, but the latter had set a condition that Austria get a fifteen million pounds' credit in London. Contrary to expectation, the English rejected the Austrian request and told them to turn to the League of Nations for a solution. This convinced Seipel that he indeed had to secure international assistance. In late August, he made a round of the relevant European capitals to secure support, starting with Prague, then visiting Berlin, and finally ending up in Verona. Seipel was fully aware that he could get little help from Berlin but was apparently somewhat taken aback by the harshness of his reception. Wirth, in some contrast to Ebert, took a sharply negative stance on giving the slightest hint of interest in an *Anschluß*, rejected the idea of helping Austria by mobilizing German financial assets in Austria for a loan, and showed no interest in making it easier for Austria to export to Germany despite the marked growth in German exports to Austria. Wirth was manifestly unwilling to get involved at a time when he had enough troubles of his own, and his hostility may also have reflected some recognition that the path chosen by Seipel could easily become his own. Like Seipel, Wirth was seeking international help for Germany, but unlike Seipel, who was to make a successful plea for a loan before the League of Nations in early September, Wirth was not prepared to accept financial control. In contrast to Austria, where the Socialists feared financial control as a mechanism to roll back social reforms and felt that stabilization could be attained by efforts from within the country itself, both the left and the right in Germany resisted external controls; Wirth could count on a consensus with respect to this question. Germany, after all, was a great power, even if it could only exercise the traditional brusqueness with which great powers treated smaller ones in a curt rejection of Austria's pleas for sympathy.[14]

Whether Berlin would fare any better in London than Vienna had, however, was very much an open question. Indeed, developments during and subsequent to the London Conference only proved that Bergmann had been correct in his doubts about the British. Not the least of the reasons for Poincaré's hard line had been the Balfour note of August 1, 1922, which declared that Britain was prepared to give up reparations

claims as well as claims on the Allies to the extent that the United States would act similarly with respect to Britain's debts. Offensive to both the United States, which was made to appear as a barrier to international reconstruction, and France, which had wished to take its own initiative and resented the prospect of having to pay its allies in full while being asked to accept less from Germany, the note made it even more difficult for Britain to go overboard in her concessions to Germany. Furthermore, the British leadership had no desire to do so. Feeling overburdened by taxes, the British public viewed German reparations as necessary and justified, while the British government was fully prepared to support harsh measures if the Germans did not clean up their financial act. At the same time, the British leaders, who thought in very economic terms, recognized that a German stabilization would necessarily produce a depression, and British support for a moratorium was meant to assist the transition from the unavoidable travails of stabilization to more normal economic circumstances.[15]

The British counterproposals at the London meeting and their subsequent policy reflected these motives and goals. Although prepared to have the Reparations Commission accord Germany a moratorium until the end of 1924, the British argued this should only be granted if the Germans had proven their readiness to stabilize their finances. In the meantime, a moratorium for the remainder of 1922 was to be attached to certain old and new conditions. The former involved implementation of the autonomy of the Reichsbank, upon which the British, as usual, placed a special and exaggerated significance; fulfillment of the pledges and measures already agreed upon with the Committee of Guarantees; and maintenance of the 26 percent export levy. To ensure collection of the levy, German customs receipts were to go into a special account available to the Germans only so long as they were following the instructions of the Reparations Commission. Similarly, Germany's state-owned mines and forests were to be placed under supervision if there were any default on coal and lumber deliveries. These conditions were meant to satisfy the French demands for "productive guarantees" but were only to become operative in the eventuality of default rather than as preconditions for reparations relief.[16]

Nevertheless, the British proposals filled the Germans with alarm. Wirth thought that he had gone the limit on concessions involving Allied control, and now he found himself faced with new demands. Since the Germans were already behind in their coal and timber delivery obligations and the situation was likely to get worse, the supervision of the state mines and forests was virtually inevitable. Not only was there reason to fear the depletion of German forestry resources and further drastic increases in the already excessively high wood and paper prices, but the Reich also would face an immense battle with the state governments, especially an intensification of the ongoing struggle with Bavaria, which had large forest resources. Furthermore, the Germans were expected to accept this proposal for a five-month moratorium without any guarantee that the long-term moratorium would be granted. If Germany were to encumber these valuable resources on a long-term basis, what would it be able to offer as security for the international loan it was hoping to get if a reparations settlement could be reached? The entire proposal was all the more disturbing because it had been concocted by the British reparations expert Bradbury, who was known to be sympathetic to Germany's problems and who was in considerable difficulty with the British Foreign Office and government for his initiatives. When Bergmann told him that the German government could under no circumstances use the state-owned coal mines and forests as a guarantee, Bradbury warned him, as Bergmann reported to the German Cabinet, that "we should not fool ourselves about England's position. It is in a disagreement with France, but Lloyd George is in a tight corner and could eventually find a scapegoat for his policy. . . . Bradbury also said that it would be false to speculate that the situation would remain as it is. The break between England and France will *not* continue. The Belgians will have to go along with what the French do. England would not prevent French stupidities."[17]

The upshot of all this was that some kind of basis had to be found for a moratorium, an issue left totally up in the air after the London Conference. Since the Germans were unwilling to use the state mines and forests as guarantees, their negotiators at the Reparations Commission could only put up precisely that which they were trying to stop giving in the first place, gold payment or, more specifically in this instance, part of the gold still remaining in the Reichsbank. This, however, was a proposition as damaging to Wirth's prestige and domestically difficult as the use of the state mines and forests for the same purpose. In this instance, it would run against the loudly pronounced slogan Wirth adopted at this time, "first bread, then reparations,"[18] and would bring him into headlong conflict with the Reichsbank just as the use of the mines and forests would have brought him into conflict with the states.

This was, in fact, precisely the conflict which did erupt as the question of finding a suitable basis for a short-term moratorium gave way at the end of August to an effort simply to evade the issue for the rest of the year. Since the remaining payments for 1922 were to go to Belgium, that country's position became crucial to subsequent developments. Although inclined to compromise with the Germans, the liberal Belgian government faced domestic political pressures that forced it to abandon its moderate position and lean more heavily toward France. Since Poincaré was dead set against a moratorium and the Belgians could not simply surrender their claims, a scheme was developed under which the two hundred million gold marks owing Belgium would be paid in the form of German Treasury bills guaranteed by the equivalent amount of Reichsbank gold to be deposited in some neutral place agreed upon by the Germans and Belgians. The American James Logan seemed to have played a major role in bringing about this arrangement. It was warmly and, to the irritation of the British Foreign Office, publicly supported with considerable fanfare by Bradbury and voted for by the somewhat overwhelmed and confused French representative Dubois, who was subsequently compelled to resign by Poincaré for his pains.[19]

Both the plan to use Reichsbank gold as security for a moratorium and the idea of using it as security for six-month Treasury bills to be given to the Belgians in lieu of reparations payment helped place Havenstein and what remained of his gold hoard in the center of discussion at this point. He had agreed to assume a guarantee of as much as eighty million gold marks to support a moratorium, provided that the Reich abandoned the plan to use this amount in gold to cover wheat imports and supplied the necessary foreign exchange instead. While Food Minister Fehr argued that "bread is just as important as a moratorium," Havenstein took the position that "a moratorium of five months is of the greatest significance, also for the mark."[20] He had not the slightest intention, however, of mortgaging two hundred million in gold to pay reparations to the Belgians, a point he made in very blunt terms to the Cabinet on August 30:

We stand at a turning point in the fate of Germany. The question is, has the time come to close down the policy of fulfillment? He affirms this. That policy had been necessary since the London Ultimatum, but it is now no longer feasible. The mortgaging of the gold in the Reichsbank is impossible, for without it a later reconstruction cannot be carried out. . . . The gold is indispensable for a later devaluation. He is happy that the autonomy of the Reichsbank now demonstrates itself to be a blessing, for in this way the Reich Chancellor can evade a severe crisis of conscience.[21]

The Reichsbank was, in fact, digging in against any alienation of its gold for reparations purposes at this time. On August 29, Havenstein had made a passionate speech before the Economic Policy and Reparations Committees of the RWR in which he stressed the utter pointlessness of risking the billion marks in gold left in the bank without a new reparations settlement that would make stabilization possible. If there were such a settlement, however, then the sacrifice of the gold for reparations would not be necessary because stabilization would be possible.[22]

The Reichsbank strategy was spelled out quite precisely by its influential Statistical Section in a memorandum of September 2, which urged that Germany play upon the Allied, and especially the English, vision of a return to prewar currency relationships and the gold standard. Thus, the Reparations Commission's demand for a gold guarantee was viewed as a contradiction of the demand that Germany stabilize, since the gold was the last available backing for the currency. If the gold went, then the credit of the Reichsbank would disappear, economic life would collapse, and the Entente

would never get any reparations while Germany would descend into Bolshevik conditions. The Allies were also to be reminded of their own citizens who had counted on the viability of the German currency:

Since the gold is the only backbone of our currency, with its loss the approximately 200 billion paper marks in foreign possession in the form of German mark notes, securities, mark denominated assets will necessarily be totally depreciated. Through a taking away of the gold, the Entente will cut into their own flesh and betray their own countrymen, who in confidence in the credit of the Reichsbank conditioned by its gold have remained in possession of "marks."[23]

If there was a touch of blackmail in these lines, there was also a sincere commitment to the prewar European economic order based on gold, an order from which Germany could not be excluded without damaging all nations at a certain level of "economic culture." The mission of the Reichsbank, therefore, was a European one, and it was employing its autonomy for purposes also in the interests of Germany's enemies: "A farsighted and well-considered policy of the Reparations Commission should therefore be directed first and foremost toward the unconditional retaining of the gold in the Reichsbank."[24]

Wirth was fully prepared to use the autonomy of the Reichsbank to prevent losing the Reichsbank gold, but he refused to abandon the policy of fulfillment. As he had told the state government representatives a few days earlier, while it was necessary to refuse to give guarantees for any short-term arrangements, the basic policy had to be continued:

The goal of our political work during the last two years can be summarized as striving to get away from senseless gold payments and attain a sensible solution to the reparations problem. We can tally as successes the isolation of the French system of revenge and the changed position of England. One only needs to compare the position of England now with the time of the London Ultimatum. In short, the issue has always been how to go from impossible to possible obligations.[25]

This policy certainly seemed to work, albeit painfully and precariously, in early September. Wirth, with the support of his Cabinet, absolutely refused to pledge the Reichsbank gold in support of the six-month Treasury bills provided to the Belgians. He was particularly sympathetic to Havenstein's refusal to deposit his gold as security in the Bank of Belgium, arguing that he would rather risk a Ruhr invasion than risk starving his people by giving way to this Belgian demand. He also refused the Belgian proposal that German industry be asked to guarantee the bills, since he knew full well that Stinnes and his colleagues would use the situation to make politically dangerous demands. Here Wirth was absolutely correct. When Hermes touched on the issue in discussions with Stinnes, the latter immediately said that the question could only be discussed in the context of a privatization of the railroads and concessions to industry with respect to export controls, the right to procure foreign exchange, and reduction of interest rates.[26]

Happily, the short-term problem of giving a guarantee to the Belgians could be solved through the good offices of Bradbury and the British Treasury's support. Havenstein was able to travel to London and secure a Bank of England guarantee of two-thirds of the Treasury bills given to the Belgians on the basis of the fifty million in Reichsbank gold already on deposit in the Bank of England. While the Reichsbank was not obligated to prolong the bills after six months, the Bank of England was pledged to prolong its guarantee for a year. The Wirth–Havenstein policy of holding firm had paid off. Only the fretful Hermes had wanted to instruct Havenstein to offer more than the fifty million already in London, arguing that "the situation is such that, if we do not have an understanding in the Belgian matter, then Germany will move toward chaos. But if we have chaos—and he considers the situation extraordinarily dangerous—then the gold treasure in the Reichsbank will not be of much use; it will melt like butter in the sun." Wirth, in a heated exchange with Hermes, warned against a "policy of anxiety," and not only won the day but also proved correct.[27] Insofar as the clearing payments were concerned, the British and French managed to collaborate on a compromise with the Germans for a change. Under the new arrangement, concluded after lengthy negotiations on October 21, 1922, Germany was to pay 24.2 million over a six-year period, commencing in July 1923. For this purpose, Germany was to issue Treasury bonds which, if unpaid by the due date, could be exchanged by their holders for bonds that might serve as legal tender for the payment of German taxes and customs. Thus, stop-gap measures had been found to spare the Germans further cash payments in 1922, but the deadlock over a moratorium continued. It was a dangerous situation because Lloyd George's position at home was getting weaker and the possibility was growing that Britain and France might settle their Near East conflicts and start working together again to Germany's detriment.[28]

It was of no small significance that the one development on the reparations front that appeared promising to the Germans and even mollified the French somewhat was the progress of German efforts to promote deliveries in kind and the increasing privatization of these activities. The dilemma was that these arrangements also threatened to have increasingly inflationary effects and constituted a further reparation-induced emasculation of the state by industrial interests. What, however, was Wirth to do? When Bradbury proposed in late August that the Reparations Commission appoint "controllers" (*Überwacher*) to determine if Germany were fulfilling her coal and wood delivery obligations and that forests or mines which were reported in default be placed under Allied control, Wirth not only resisted in order to prevent Allied seizure of German resources and the foreign control of one of the most important income-producing assets available to the states but also welcomed an alternative in which the Allies could only impose the kind of sanctions inflicted for breaches of private contracts. That is, if deliveries in kind continued to be funded by the Reich but were arranged on the basis of private contractual obligations between German and Allied businessmen, then they would only be subject to the conventional penalties provided under the private law of contract. State-owned mines and forests thereby would be once removed from the tentacles of the Reparations Commission.[29]

This privatization of payments in kind had significant precedents prior to the summer of 1922. The Belgians had begun the practice in an effort to escape the complicated procedure provided under the Treaty of Versailles, whereby lists of desired materials had to be sent to the

Reparations Commission, which then evaluated their appropriateness in terms of the reparations schedule and transmitted its requests to the German authorities who, in their turn, went about procuring what was necessary. In this way, those Belgians with claims could seek out their own German suppliers, and the Reparations Commission and German authorities could then be brought in to approve the arrangements. Not only was the procedure thereby made less bureaucratic, but the Belgian government was also relieved of potential charges that it was giving business to Belgian industry's German competitors. A major difficulty from the German perspective was that the Reconstruction Ministry officials, for all intents and purposes, lost all influence over the choice of German supplier and the terms of payment. Rathenau's Wiesbaden Agreement sought to establish some basis for control of the process of ordering and supplying materials by requiring organization on both sides, but the Cuntze–Bemelmens Agreement of June 2, 1922, with Belgium and the Gillet–Ruppel Agreement of June 3 with France gave considerable latitude for individual contracting between those in the devastated areas and German suppliers.[30]

In the face of the proposals to treat the state mines and forests as "productive guarantees," the German government seized upon these precedents and negotiated with the German coal industrialists on the question of delivery contracts for the supply of reparations coal until the end of 1923. Stinnes, who took the lead in the negotiations with the government, was prepared to enter upon such contracts provided that the miners were willing to enter into a new overtime agreement and maintain it for the entire period in question.[31] Such an effort to step up coal production in order at once to satisfy Allied demands in a safe manner and reduce the costs involved in importing English coal was bound to be very costly. The acquiescence of the miners to a new overtime agreement could only be bought with very substantial wage increases as well as a 50 percent premium for the six overtime hours. If the trade unions finally agreed to an overtime agreement to go into effect on September 1 despite strong radical and Communist as well as rank-and-file opposition, it was largely out of fear of a French invasion of the Ruhr.[32]

Similarly, the coal mine owners were also insistent upon full compensation for their efforts and asked for payment a month in advance in the decisive negotiations on August 29. Most revealing, however, were the political implications of the arrangement, which Stinnes was reported to have spelled out in no uncertain terms:

He [Stinnes] must further emphasize that, if industry and with it the private sector now ties itself closely with the Reich and the national economy, then industry also has to be brought into active participation in the negotiations concerning economic reform measures. The economic reforms must extend to a more productive arrangement of general work performance. Those measures which industry considers to be generally necessary will be stated at the appropriate time. We must break with the system of low productivity and the unfree economy.[33]

Stinnes then went on to inform the Cabinet that he had been engaging in very confidential negotiations with French industrialists and a French Senator. He wished to know if the government was agreeable to having these discussions continue and, once again, whether it was prepared to "carry out general economic reform measures in collaboration with industry." While the record of this meeting contains no direct response from Wirth to these questions, the evidence of Wirth's position is reasonably clear. On the one hand, he approved the continuation of Stinnes's negotiations as a means of placing reparations in kind on a private contract basis and preventing the seizure of government-owned mines and forests. On the other hand, only a few days after the meeting in question, he responded to similar domestic political demands from Stinnes by calling them "completely pointless" and insisting that "such demands can only be discussed with his *party*."[34] That is, such programmatic issues would have to be discussed in connection with a widening of the government to include the DVP. Nevertheless, it was manifest that the development of the reparations issue and the problem of "productive guarantees" had promoted yet another major step in the constantly increasing dependence of the German government on industry.

This was all the more the case because of the extraordinary energy and initiative of Hugo Stinnes, who set the tone for industry's expanding involvement in both foreign and domestic affairs during this crucial period. It was Stinnes, rather than his colleagues on the Rhine and Ruhr, for example, who had grasped at the opportunity for the direct negotiations with French industry concerning which he had finally informed the Chancellor on August 29. The initiative came from the French, who feared that the visible liberation of German heavy industry from dependence on French minette ore and the restoration of German freedom to set new customs duties in 1925 would set the seal on the already evident competitive disadvantages of French heavy industry. Some of these French industrialists doubted that France's political leadership could protect them over the long run and thought it was best to come to terms with their German counterparts while France still enjoyed important advantages. It was a measure of German industry's growing self-confidence that Paul Reusch and other Ruhr heavy industrialists responded to initial French overtures in the spring by saying that they were willing to talk, but only if France was willing to discuss evacuation of the Saar and other occupied areas. This line was pursued with even more harshness in early August, when August Thyssen responded to a request from French industrialist Senator Japy to negotiate by declaring that it was "premature" for such discussions and that "so long as there is no real peace with conditions for Germany that are bearable, such a getting together in the contemplated manner seems to me impossible."[35]

Stinnes had no intention of taking a line different from that of his colleagues, but he was prepared to pursue different tactics. He accepted a request for a personal conversation with Japy, which complemented talks he was holding with the Marquis Guy Jean de Lubersac, another French industrialist who was also the President of the General Confederation of Cooperatives of the Devastated Areas. These discussions were conducted in mid-August at Stinnes's Heimburg, a property he owned near Wiesbaden, and they strengthened Stinnes's conviction that a direct interindustrial agreement over payments in kind would not only relieve the immediate reparations crisis but also pave the way for a more general settlement of the outstanding issues between Germany and France. Like Stinnes, the French industrialists with whom he spoke also seemed to feel that it was time for businessmen to take the initiative.

Japy argued that "the French industrialists have come to the conviction that professors and lawyers cannot govern at the present time. The past policy of France has led to a dead end. One has to seek new paths and must come to an understanding with Germany."[36] He complained that French industry had become totally dependent on Italian and Spanish workers who took their earnings home and that the best solution would be to bring the army home and create a native stock of workers. Japy pointed out that the French budget would never be balanced if Poincaré's policies continued to be pursued, and he strongly suggested that the Prime Minister was on his way out.

All of this could only strengthen Stinnes's interest in concluding an agreement with de Lubersac involving direct arrangements for the shipment of wood and other construction materials to the devastated areas. This agreement, which was worked out between August 14 and September 4, provided that Germany would deliver materials to be credited to reparations at a price not exceeding that of the domestic price in France. To promote German productivity for this purpose, the French would agree to have certain portions of its reparations coal given to the firms involved, which would be distributed by the Stinnes firm in collaboration with the coal syndicate. Stinnes's construction firm, the Aktiengesellschaft Hoch- und Tiefbau, in collaboration with a bank consortium headed by the Dresdner Bank, would act as the intermediary in the distribution of orders and contracts, while de Lubersac's firm would perform the same function on the other side, and both would receive a 6 percent commission for their efforts.[37]

Stinnes, Director Fehrmann (his chief aide in these arrangements), and Bücher of the RdI were all aware that Stinnes's action was very much open to criticism. Ostensibly an enemy of the fulfillment policy who had criticized Rathenau for making an agreement based on similar principles, Stinnes could easily be charged, in the words of Fehrmann, with trying to "enrich himself on the national misfortune." The rumors of Stinnes's negotiations were flying fast and furious, and there was talk at the Reich chancellery that "Herr Stinnes is selling the German coal and iron industry to France." As always, Stinnes did an excellent job of persuading himself in preparation for the task of persuading others:

H[err] St[innes] pointed out that a practical realization of the fulfillment policy—which all of us wanted to be within the bounds of the bearable—is not *de facto* possible for the Reich. This is demonstrated, for example, by the wood deliveries: the states give no wood to the Reich and the Reich no longer has the power to have its way with the states. Only private businessmen can accomplish that because they are in a completely different situation when it comes to reaching understandings with one another. He [Stinnes] makes pledges, for example, and by holding various discussions in Bavaria, he manages to get those difficult people to deliver wood. He is fully aware that the plans made at Heimburg create political difficulties for Reich Chancellor Wirth and, in the last analysis, also put the unions in a difficult situation. They all wanted to conduct fulfillment policy and have thus made many political and economic sacrifices without accomplishing anything. But now this shall be achieved by precisely the man who has been reproached not only for his position at Spa but, beyond that, for always wanting to sabotage the policy of fulfillment. State Secretary Hirsch has already argued in the cabinet that H[err] St[innes] has come around. This is not correct. H[e] has always been for the policy of fulfillment, albeit for one within the bounds of reason and within the bounds of what is bearable for our national economy.[38]

Stinnes claimed that his agreement contained no promises that could not be fulfilled; it provided more coal for Germany and, unlike the Wiesbaden Agreement, for full and immediate credit for German deliveries. He also saw it as a stepping stone to more general political agreements with the French. Stinnes was operating from these perspectives and was obviously unconcerned by the fact that the Reich, thanks to the higher price of materials in France, would be burdened with fairly large costs and that his own company would gain considerable control over the construction materials market.

Stinnes's high opinion of himself and sense that he had something genuinely visionary and comprehensive to offer was strongly reinforced by those with whom he dealt. De Lubersac made it a condition of the arrangement that Stinnes take the central place for Germany in the negotiations since "only his name calls forth that measure of trust and confidence in France which is necessary."[39] De Lubersac was fully aware that the same could not be said of himself in either country and that everything

depended on the manner in which the French government would respond to the proposals. In order to avoid "unnecessary dust," therefore, the content of the talks was to be kept secret, although the existence of the conversations was made known to the two Foreign Offices, primarily because correspondence was conducted through their diplomatic couriers.

The entire situation was most revealing of the asymmetrical relationship between industry and the state in the two countries. De Lubersac informed his government in full, waited upon its reaction, and was in no position whatever to determine the tone taken by the government toward Germany. Stinnes told Bücher of the RdI to urge the Chancellor "in a cautious manner" to avoid taking a sharp tone in the negotiations with the French "but under no circumstances to provide the personally so unreliable Dr. Wirth with any facts" concerning the negotiations with de Lubersac.[40] Stinnes further suggested that Bücher inform President Ebert about the situation, since Ebert was "the decisive person ... also for the policy of Dr. Wirth."[41] When the French government finally gave de Lubersac the green light to go ahead with the agreement, it did so with the provision that reparations coal would only be granted to the German companies involved in reconstruction work if Germany fulfilled the entire program of the Reparations Commission and satisfied French demands.[42] Stinnes, in contrast, chose to inform Wirth of the negotiations on August 29 in the context of demands that the government work with industry on a yet to be announced economic program.

The excitement created by the Stinnes–Lubersac Agreement must be placed in the context of the deadlocked international situation in the late summer and early fall of 1922 and the apparent inability of the Wirth government to find a way out of its dilemma. Any movement was bound to bring attention and even admiration, and Stinnes always did things in a grand style. This is not to say that the limitations of his achievement were not recognized even within his own circle. Thus, the London reporter of the Stinnes-owned *Deutsche Allgemeine Zeitung*, Dr. Adler, reported that the English were filled with a sporting admiration for Stinnes's latest maneuvers, especially in the light of their own keenly felt lack of economic leadership and stagnation, and Stinnes was spoken of as "the only man in Europe today who knows what he wants."[43] This did not mean that the English necessarily were optimistic about the agreement or convinced that it would have happy results. Poincaré's acceptance of the arrangement was seen as a purely tactical maneuver aimed at satisfying the population of the occupied areas, and there were strong doubts that the French would buy an economic solution at the expense of their political interests. While the agreement was also seen as a shrewd move on the part of Stinnes to guarantee a market for himself and jobs for German workers in the event of a slump, its problematic financial basis was quite obvious. Industry might make high profits, but the costs to the government were likely to increase the inflation even more.

There were more than sufficient grounds for such concern. Since Stinnes saw the entire agreement as a stepping stone to a political agreement with the French and a comprehensive internal economic reform program, however, the more problematic specific aspects of the agreement could only appear as secondary to him. Furthermore, he succeeded in nurturing a similar attitude by appealing to those whose interests might also be positively influenced. Thus, at the end of September, he made a special trip to Bavaria, a state especially important because of its timber resources, to persuade both government and business circles of the advantages of his program. He seems to have succeeded. Not only did he impress Count Lerchenfeld with the optimistic view that France was beginning to realize that an agreement with Germany was in the best interests of both, but he also managed to convince the initially sceptical Bavarian industrialists of the benefits of his agreement with de Lubersac, so that "apparently one expects here that all the construction companies will have contracts."[44] Neither Stinnes's political optimism nor the positive expectations of the agreement with de Lubersac were shared by every major businessman, however. Hjalmar Schacht of the Darmstädter and Nationalbank, for example, was very critical of the plan. In his view, a moratorium on all payments in gold and in kind was essential, and he considered Stinnes's program

futile from an international perspective and dangerous internally. In a trenchant criticism, he pointed out that

A German moratorium is hard for France to accept in her present psychic and economic condition without securities or some other form of compensation that eases her own finances. Germany has now offered wood and coal deliveries *under private guarantee*, which is the equivalent of a political failure of the present system of government and a further squandering of the little trust which the new state form has won until now. It seems very doubtful to me that France will be satisfied with the German offer under the pressure of world opinion because France herself has been financially irresponsible and because payments in kind cannot relieve her financial distress. Under no circumstances will we achieve a longer moratorium with our proposals but only continue to drag from one short-term payment delay to another, always having to make new concessions, squandering our tangible capital even more, and above all accomplishing nothing for our currency. France does not want and cannot seriously make use of payments in kind; France wants *money*. It is only for money that France will give us the needed moratorium.[45]

As an alternative, Schacht proposed that Germany and France jointly secure an international loan, the interest and amortization of which Germany would pay from the profits collected on some of its leading exports. In this way, the French would get money right away in return for giving Germany a five-year moratorium. These exports were to be placed under the control of a state-supervised export monopoly run by persons from the industries involved. In this way, the German government would regain control of the reparations question while state involvement would be kept to a minimum, and Germany would have the ability to bring its house back into order. While such a state export monopoly might be obnoxious to the industrialists involved, it was no more insufferable than the existing system of grain levies and rent controls which Schacht expected to disappear once Germany could function normally again. It was impossible, after all, to bring about a general improvement without doing someone harm, "and no legal measure can be more unjust than the manner in which the depreciation of the mark itself hits large groups."[46]

Schacht had discussed his ideas with business associates in the United States, among them John Foster Dulles and James Morgan, as well as bankers and officials in France, and he claimed that his ideas had been met with considerable interest. There is no evidence that they were met with equal interest in Germany, however, and Schacht's hour was yet to strike. For the moment, despite its worrisome aspects and dangers to the autonomy of the state, Stinnes's initiatives seemed most important and hopeful.[47]

The double-edged character of Stinnes's achievement was even more worrisome to the Independent Socialist Deputy Rudolf Breitscheid, who at once praised and condemned Stinnes in a meeting of the Reichstag Foreign Affairs Committee:

... here we see the connection between politics and business. From the standpoint of reparations, the agreement is not unfavorable, but it is suspicious that Herr Stinnes has conquered a monopoly for himself. It is regrettable that the government did not bring about such an agreement itself and that it is without influence on the agreement before us. Herr Stinnes's party fought against the Wiesbaden Agreement and subsequent agreements, and now Herr Stinnes makes a business out of it. Stinnes gets the profit, but one must also objectively recognize that he gets the credit for having contributed to the relaxation of an extremely dangerous situation in the reparations question. ... He, Breitscheid, protests however when Herr Stinnes and his party wishes to gain political influence through this achievement. The German workers will not allow that such agreements are concluded on their backs.[48]

Helfferich vigorously came to Stinnes's defense, pointing out that the "agreement shows what the German entrepreneur can accomplish" and that "the time had come to put an end to class conflicts." The test of this proposition, however, was not the Stinnes–Lubersac Agreement but rather the economic and social program of which it was a part, and here Breitscheid knew very well whereof he spoke. In reality, the crucial issue facing Germany was ceasing to be reparations, which were no longer being paid anyway, and achieving stabilization.

The seemingly uncontrollable fall of the mark and the reparations problem were making serious consideration of stabilization unavoidable. Good news about reparations, such as the agreement with Belgium, not only brought little improvement in the mark but also failed to stop its decline. The fall of Lloyd George on October 19 and his replacement by Bonar Law, who was committed to a better relationship with France, was only one of what by now had become a host of factors that promoted the mark's depreciation.[49] The British pressure on the German government to introduce stabilization measures on its own was bound to grow. This was especially evident in the case of Bradbury, who was very friendly to the idea of a moratorium and whose independent role was bound to diminish under a new regime. When Bradbury came forth with a plan in the Reparations Commission, however, it was almost as displeasing to the Germans as to the French.

Bradbury's chief goal was to provide the Germans with an opportunity to make themselves capable of paying reparations. While proposing a moratorium for at least two and possibly five years, the payments in gold and in kind owing were to be covered by German bonds in the amounts provided by the May 1921 London Ultimatum schedule of payments. The bonds for delivery in kind were to be credited to the Germans to the extent that they did not increase the deficit. To ensure that the Germans would not increase their deficit through excess expenditure, a commission appointed by the Reparations Commission was to fix the price at which the Reichsbank gold would have to be sold to cover any deficit. Such sale would become necessary because a new Reichsbank law would prohibit it from covering such a deficit except through gold sales. In Bradbury's view, this would obviate the need for actual controls, although he did propose that the Reparations Commission be moved to Berlin, thereby placing the kind of watchdogs in the capital which would make Germany attractive to foreign lenders. At the same time, these provisions would enable the governments holding the reparations bonds to guarantee them and satisfy their own cash requirements. While Bradbury foresaw a readjustment of the entire reparations question in the course of the moratorium period, the Germans viewed the whole plan as a *de facto* restoration of the London Ultimatum schedule compounded by the credit crisis and depression which Bradbury explicitly and unconcernedly stated were bound to hit Germany under his plan. As for the French, they were especially upset by the absence of any genuine financial control whatever and no guarantee that the entire plan would not collapse. Their response was to have their new representative to the Reparations Commission, the tough and able Louis Barthou, present a program for direct control of German budgetary and taxation planning.[50]

Both Bradbury and Barthou, however, held the common assumption that Germany could undertake effective measures of stabilization before there was any definitive new reparations settlement that might reduce German obligations and before receiving a stabilization loan. This was different from the view taken by the Bankers' Committee back in March and very different from the view taken by Wirth, Havenstein, and other leading German policymakers, especially in the Finance Ministry. Wirth needed to find a way of persuading the world that he and most German leaders were correct in their claim that Germany could not stabilize without outside help in the form of a loan and a better reparations settlement. Thus, he hit upon the idea, so to speak, of getting outside help that would make the case for getting outside help. He sought at once to "depoliticize" the question and reinforce the German position in dealing with the Reparations Commission by asking an international group of financial experts to evaluate Germany's economic situation and make recommendations concerning the stabilization question. For this purpose, on October 18, he invited Keynes; British banker Robert Brand; Swedish economist Gustav Cassel; the President of the Swiss Banking Association, Louis Dubois; Dutch banker Gerard Vissering; a Russian banker residing in Paris, Kamenka; and American economist Jeremiah Jenks to come to Berlin and convene a conference. Wirth was optimistic about what they would produce. Keynes and Cassel had already publicly stated that the existing reparations demands could not be fulfilled, while Vissering had signed the Bankers' Committee report in June. Dubois, known to be pro-French, was also reported to have said that Germany could not stabilize on its own. His presence, along with that of Kamenka and Jenks, gave the entire arrangement an aura of fairness.[51]

Quite another question was, however, whether the Reparations Commission or the Allied and German publics would be genuinely receptive to a "depoliticized," "expert" solution. The various efforts to deal with the reparations and stabilization problems at this time must always been seen against the background of the increasing fatalism among some highly placed persons about a French invasion of the Ruhr. Just as Poincaré was moving closer to action in the Ruhr, so some leading German industrialists were willing to accept the worst. There was, for example, at least one influential German industrialist whose despair was so great that he seemed interested neither in Stinnes's payment-in-kind arrangements and efforts to negotiate with the French nor in Wirth's attempts to find a peaceful way out of the crisis. At the end of October, Peter Klöckner refused to come to Berlin or go to Paris to negotiate on future coal and wood deliveries, arguing that the rising wages and prices were such that a further burdening of the economy could not be accepted and that Wirth should refuse to make any further coal deliveries after November 1 unless they were compensated in francs. The consequences were very clear to Klöckner: "I am fully aware that such a declaration can lead to an invasion of the Ruhr and a confiscation of the coal. But I am also completely clear as to the fact that one has to face the attendant misery and that it is today a hundred times more correct to accept these consequences than to bring about the complete collapse of the German Reich through a continuation of the fulfillment policy."[52] Poincaré and Klöckner thus demonstrated how much was at stake in the great stabilization debate of the fall of 1922.

The German Stabilization Debate and the Fall of Wirth

The reparations crisis in the late summer and fall of 1922 served as a catalyst for the growing political polarization over the stabilization problem. But in order to understand the impact of the expert reports in early November and the political crisis that brought down the Wirth government on November 14, 1922, it is necessary to explore the conflict over stabilization within Germany itself. Customarily, the division over stabilization is seen from the perspective of the conflict between the proponents and opponents of fulfillment, the conflict between left and right, or the conflict between industry and labor. This mode of analysis, while certainly having some validity and utility, is not entirely adequate to the complexity of the situation.[53]

The problem with these categorizations is that they understate the extent to which the consensus had grown that fulfillment was impossible and that the stabilization problem had to be confronted. That was why Wirth could claim that he was continuing the policy of fulfillment while refusing to make any further payments and Stinnes could claim that he had always been a supporter of fulfillment in the context of his agreement with de Lubersac. Similarly, although it was possible to debate the feasibility of stabilization under existing conditions, even those who were most optimistic about Germany's ability to pull the mark out of its nosedive through a new surge of export profits recognized that the stabilization problem had to be faced seriously. The real debate was over the preconditions for stabilization and the manner in which it was to be accomplished. A more fruitful, albeit more complicated, way of structuring the conflicts over these issues than the traditional ones would be to distinguish between those who felt that the only way Germany could get on the road to stabilization was by receiving outside assistance (a reduction of reparations and a foreign loan) and those who argued that the bases for stabilization had to be created by action on the domestic front. This division cut across the camps that had argued for and against fulfillment and had profound implications for the domestic politics of stabilization. It often created strange bedfellows. Thus, those who gave primacy to an external solution included Chancellor Wirth himself, Rudolf Havenstein, and such industrial leaders as Hermann Bücher, Hans von Raumer, and Wilhelm Cuno. Those who stood in the other camp, who were convinced that Germany could and should undertake internal stabilization measures on the grounds that these were both possible and necessary for receiving outside assistance were a more heterogenous and even incompatible lot, including Julius Hirsch; Rudolf Hilferding; the liberal economics editor

of the *Frankfurter Zeitung*, Anton Feiler; Moritz Bonn; Georg Bernhard; Hugo Stinnes; and the lignite industrialist Paul Silverberg.

Those who gave priority to an external solution were largely moved by the sense that Germany's economic, financial, and, above all, sociopolitical situation was too fragile to sustain the necessary domestic measures without the legitimation and support that would be provided by a new reparations arrangement and a foreign loan. This was certainly true in the case of Wirth and Havenstein, although it must be said of the latter that his primary concern at this time was his gold. Bücher was equally passionate on this subject, however, and he had responded to rumors that the government might have to mortgage and ship out some of the Reichsbank gold in order to get an agreement with Belgium by asking the RdI to take an unequivocal stand in opposition to such measures, for "our economic situation is such that not even a single little bit of Reichsbank gold ought to be given out. The gold must be there to fight against possible hunger in the winter. *The gold in the Reichsbank is the last reserve we have to be able to meet a sharpened economic crisis.*"[54] Bücher, whose background was in the Foreign Office, tended, in any case, to see international economic reconstruction as the key issue and always put the question of economic cooperation among the world's businessmen and an international loan as the first order of business, a view that the internationally oriented HAPAG director Cuno tended to share. For Raumer, who was more sensitive to domestic political problems, it was essential to square one question away at a time, and the international one assumed priority because there was more consensus on the need to change the reparations schedule and procure a loan. As he had pointed out to Wirth in May, "foreign policy difficulties can be more easily handled by us at a time when there is no unemployment. Once we are in the midst of an unemployment crisis, then the conflicts between employers and workers and between their respective political parties can be so severe that a unified stance in foreign policy questions would no longer be possible."[55]

The price of waiting passively for external help, however, was permitting the inflation to increase and running the risk that the Allies and Americans would make the entire effort to secure reparations relief dependent upon domestic stabilization measures accompanied by humiliating controls. Within the government itself, the most active and energetic supporter of domestic stabilization initiatives was Julius Hirsch. Frantically urged by his father and relatives to quit his post and not expose himself to the fate of Rathenau,[56] Hirsch chose instead not only to remain in Berlin but also to respond to the hyperinflationary development with a comprehensive economic and financial program to promote stabilization that could only increase the ranks of his enemies. Hirsch first gave expression to his views in a confidential memorandum on "The Currency Catastrophe" of July 4–5, 1922, ideas for which he then fought within the government during the next quarter of a year. He also presented his program in surprisingly attenuated form to a joint meeting of the Economic Policy and Export Levy Committees of the Reich Economic Council on August 17, 1922.[57]

As in November 1921, so in August 1922, he had the unenviable task of reporting on the latest inflationary developments to the Reich Economic Council in the context of proposing specific and manifestly partial measures for dealing with inflationary developments—the reporting of domestic foreign-exchange purchases, in the first instance; the increase of export levies in proportion to the currency depreciation, in the second. Now, however, Hirsch was taking a radically new line.[58] Whereas in 1921, he tended to blame reparations and be rather fatalistic about effective action domestically in the absence of a diplomatic success, he was now convinced that fatalism was impossible and action was necessary in the form of a "total system."[59] Thus, Hirsch took the reparations situation as a deplorable fact. What could be done about it was being done, but this in no way justified standing by and permitting disaster to befall Germany in the winter. The inflationary employment boom then going on was, in his view, nothing more than a sign of disintegration and impending economic collapse (*Verfallskonjunktur*), and the bad harvest threatened to impose unbearable food import costs on the government. Hirsch emphasized that the deficits in the balance of trade and of payments could not explain the continuing mark deterioration since the summer. The balance-of-trade deficit during the first six months of 1922 was twelve billion paper marks, which Hirsch did not find frightening under the circumstances and which could not explain the hyperinflation. The balance of payments also could not have been a significant source of the extreme depreciation because the last reparations and clearing payments made had come from foreign-exchange reserves already at hand and thus had not involved money purchases abroad. More serious was the "strike of the mark purchasers" abroad, but Hirsch noted that at least the foreigners had not been selling their marks to any substantial degree. The real problem, in Hirsch's view, was the domestic flight from the mark, which had taken on such proportions that Germany was rapidly heading in the direction of having two domestic currencies, the paper mark and foreign exchange. People were no longer simply fleeing into goods, a major source of the employment boom, but also buying and selling foreign currencies within Germany. That is, the tendency to calculate in foreign currencies but give and receive payment in marks was giving way to the exclusive use of foreign currencies as a means of escaping the rapid mark depreciation. Foreign exchange was thus taking on an entirely new function, and this with devastating consequences for the mark and for the economy because now foreign exchange was being purchased for purely domestic transactions. A truly ironical situation had developed. Whereas in the past Americans had sold their raw materials to Germans for marks which they held (thus giving Germans a free loan based on positive speculations about the future of the German currency), now Germans were selling their goods to Americans for dollars which they retained, thus, in effect, "giving the Americans a dollar loan."[60] The process was proceeding like an avalanche, and Hirsch warned that it would not only bring those still functioning with marks into utter misery but also bring about a collapse of the economy itself.

What is striking about Hirsch's performance before the Reich Economic Council, however, is that his proposals were presented in a very gingerly manner that was in marked contrast to the firmness of his July memorandum and the energy with which he pursued his stabilization project within the government. He couched his plans before the Reich Economic Council in the form of suggestions to which he hoped the RWR would respond with expert opinions advising the government. He stressed the need for a "moral transformation" that would restore a measure of unity to the nation, not only in the sense that one part of society would not live in wasteful luxury at the expense of another but also that policy decisions would transcend interest group egoism.

Hirsch argued that measures had to be taken in the areas of economic, financial, and currency policy, all of which were to be conceived as an integrated program. The economic policy measures involved efforts to restrain consumption and increase production. In Hirsch's view, the import of luxury goods, especially tobacco and alcohol, had either to be made prohibitively expensive through import duties or actually banned, and he also raised the question as to whether German agriculture should not be prohibited from producing grain alcohols. With respect to increasing production, Hirsch placed his chief emphasis on overtime in the mining industry in order to reduce the foreign-exchange expenditure required to import coal. On the financial side, Hirsch argued for substantially increased government taxation of profits made in foreign exchange (that is, of the export levy) and urged the possibility of a small foreign loan to cover the remaining costs of the Clearing Agreement to ease the government's foreign-exchange requirements. Significantly, he said nothing about the security to be given for such a loan. Hirsch was even more coy with respect to the currency measures that might be taken. He pointed out that some people were calling for very strong exchange controls, employing either the recently introduced Austrian measures requiring that all those purchasing foreign exchange be required to state their reasons for doing so, or the selective auditing of the use of foreign exchange. Hirsch expressed reservations about both methods, suggesting that the German economy was too complicated to sustain the first approach and that the second

would produce an even worse black market in foreign exchange than already existed. The present situation, he pointed out, was one which not only encouraged but even required the hoarding of foreign exchange for domestic transactions, for "who will prevent someone from buying goods which had been purchased with foreign exchange and whose price rises with the value of the foreign exchange?"[61] In order to prevent the speculation in foreign exchange, Hirsch suggested, one had to create an incentive to invest marks in some other form of valorized medium of exchange; he had in mind some form of gold-backed security that could take the place of foreign exchange. He urged that a committee be formed to consider such a proposal.

When one considers what Hirsch really wanted to do, then it becomes obvious that his performance before the RWR was a desperately diplomatic effort to create a positive atmosphere for a program which could only be carried out if the government had the ability and will to assert its authority in the face of a hailstorm of objections emanating from both private interests and governmental agencies. He was trying to defuse the contentious issue before the Reich Economic Council, the raising of export levies, by placing it in the context of a broader appeal to its members. He wanted them to think about the export-levy problem in the context of a general domestic program to fight the hyperinflation. Hirsch had a very good idea of what that program should be. He wished to raise the gold premium on German customs duties between 8,000 and 8,500 percent and to impose substantial import-duty increases on coffee, tobacco, and other luxury items. At the same time, he wished to increase the export levy in proportion to the currency depreciation so that the much increased export profit made from the substantially increased difference between German domestic costs and export receipts arising from the hyperinflation would be tapped. Hirsch believed that an additional levy averaging 4 percent might even serve as partial security for a loan to cover German expenses under the Clearing Agreement, although the chief security he wished to provide was a portion of the gold in the Reichsbank. Hirsch in no way shared Havenstein's view of the gold in the Reichsbank:

Such a loan is to be gotten immediately insofar as the gold treasury and the silver deposits in the Reichsbank now available are put up as security. It is impossible to see what value this Nibelungen hoard can have for the national economy if not to prevent that national disaster, namely civil war, which most immediately threatens as a result of the currency collapse. Thanks to large-scale imports, the largest portion of the wheat supply for the coming fiscal years has been secured. This hoard lying there immovably has long ceased to have a function in our currency policy. Austria, which does not possess such a hoard, has seized upon the foreign exchange holdings of the private banks. The German people did not surrender gold to the Reichsbank so that it should lie there immobile at the time of their greatest distress and not relieve the immiseration of the most important classes of the people! Perhaps a third of the gold and silver treasure would be more than sufficient to secure the clearing loan.[62]

Nor was he as cautious about increased exchange controls as he claimed before the RWR. In his July memorandum, he pointed out that controls similar to those imposed on Austria would be necessary if only because the Allies would force them upon the Germans if they did not initiate them voluntarily. He thought such exchange controls could be effective if rapidly installed, but it was true that he did not think that exchange controls could work in and of themselves if there were not some alternative available to those persons requiring some kind of valorized medium of exchange to cover their legitimate business operations. His solution to this problem was a domestic gold loan of four hundred million marks which would form the basis for the issuance of gold Treasury certificates of five hundred gold marks or more bearing 4 percent interest and guaranteed by a fund composed of the income received from the export levy and from the increased income received from the coal tax as a result of the September 2, 1922, price increase. The certificates could be bought with foreign exchange or paper marks at their gold-mark value on the day of purchase and turned in for paper marks at their gold equivalent on the day of sale.[63]

It was a measure of the antagonism with which any program of stabilization through internal measures would be confronted that not a single part of the Hirsch program escaped severe criticism and opposition, whether from within the government or from economic interest groups. Thus, when Schmidt and Hirsch presented their proposals for reduction of imports through heavy duties at a Cabinet meeting on August 14, they ran into opposition both from State Secretary Zapf of the Finance Ministry and State Secretary von Simson of the Foreign office. The first argued that the employers and workers had first to be consulted before the duties on coffee and tobacco could be raised and felt that it was necessary to wait until the Reichstag and Reichsrat convened again in October. The second stressed that a prohibitive duty on coffee imports would hurt Germany's foreign relations. Hirsch, who considered the situation an emergency that could not wait until October and who knew full well that it was pointless to ask the employers and workers in the cigarette and cigar industries how they felt about raising tobacco duties, found himself frustrated by the Chancellor himself. Wirth felt not only that expert opinion had to be sought on whether or not these import control measures should be undertaken but also that the entire RWM program should await the results of the then concluding London Conference. A few days later, Wirth and the Cabinet did approve some significant import restrictions despite Foreign Office worries about Brazil's attitude. The results, however, do not appear to have been very impressive, since Economics Minister Schmidt was complaining in early October that the effort to reduce tobacco imports had failed and that corn imports for purposes of making *Schnaps* were actually increasing, in total contradiction to the government's policy.[64]

Raising export levies was no simple matter either. When Hirsch appeared before the RWR on August 17, primarily to push an increase in export levies, he knew that he faced powerful opposition. While he had the support of the Foreign Office, which feared anti-dumping measures from Germany's trading partners, and of the trade unions, he faced a veritable mobilization of industrial and commercial interests against export-levy increases. On August 11, the German Chamber of Commerce and Industry had called a meeting of representatives of the leading interest groups to discuss the subject and, in collaboration with the various state governments, met with Hirsch the next day to protest his plans for a doubling of the export levy. They were especially irritated by the trade-union support for the measure in the RWR since there was general agreement that "the worker representatives on the export control boards, who have learned to calculate and stand in close connection with actual practice, would go along with us. However, it was feared that the worker representatives in the Reich Economic Council cannot be persuaded to change their mind, and this especially because the term 'exchange profit' has become a slogan against which it is difficult to fight."[65] The arguments of industry were clearly expressed by Paul Reusch in a personal letter to Hirsch. He pointed out that "in view of the general shortage of money and the severe price increases because of the fall of the exchange, industrial activity is declining noticeably and the cancellation of already given contracts are the order of the day. A doubling of the export levy is unbearable at a time when the specter of unemployment stands before the door."[66] The state governments, led by Prussia, played a particularly important role in warning against a schematic increase of export duties, especially for those industries heavily dependent on raw-materials imports and for those whose business had been declining. The Bavarian representative reported that the industrialists in his state were enraged, while his colleague from Anhalt asked for a special dispensation for the airplane industry and the representative from Thuringia insisted on special consideration for the textile industry. The individualization of the increases, of course, was a guaranteed formula for delay. Hirsch reminded the interest groups that the RWM was usually accused of acting too late, and he asked how it was supposed to be effective if it had to review some fourteen hundred items and consider seventy-five protests from various interest groups.[67] Thanks to the support of the labor representatives in the RWR, Hirsch was able to gain a slim majority for an average 60 percent increase of the export levies. He promised to give special consideration to industries in difficulty, however, and both the RWR and RWM were

flooded with petitions from both individually interested parties and state governments, especially Hamburg, asking for relief.[68]

If Hirsch's policy of raising export levies did nothing to increase his popularity in the business community, his plans and actions in the field of exchange controls were a genuine failure from every perspective. The extent to which he was personally responsible for the fiasco in which his efforts ended is hard to determine because it is somewhat difficult to disentangle the actions of a government whose functioning left a great deal to be desired and which was on its last legs. There can be no question about the fact that Hirsch had told the RWR committee the truth on August 17 when he had expressed skepticism about the efficacy of exchange-control measures in and of themselves. He always planned to combine new regulations on access to foreign currencies and their employment with the provision of an alternative form of security for businessmen seeking safe monetary backing for their domestic operations; that is, his proposed domestic loan and gold-denominated Treasury notes.

He was less than truthful, however, in downplaying the fact that he intended to undertake measures to control foreign currency speculation in Germany. He had already presented a draft of a law to a meeting of Reichsbank and government officials in the Economics Ministry on August 11. It was intended to build upon the restoration of exchange controls begun in February 1922 when foreign-exchange transactions were restricted to a limited number of banks and reporting of such transactions was required. The projected new legislation aimed at making permission of the finance offices a condition of foreign-exchange transactions. Only banks and enterprises certified by the chambers of commerce could purchase foreign exchange without first securing permission, but they were required to state the purpose for which they were doing so. Were they found to be "speculating" rather than securing foreign exchange for legitimate business requirements, then their right to purchase foreign exchange without permission would be withdrawn. The proposed law also sought to ban both the use of foreign exchange in domestic retail transactions and the calculation in foreign exchange, although an exception was made for sales to foreigners and in the occupied and border areas.[69]

"Speculation" under existing conditions, of course, was very hard to define and even harder to control. The representatives of the Reichsbank, Director Kaufmann, and of the Reich Commissariat for Exports and Imports piously declared that they did not necessarily oppose the projected law, since something had to be done about the situation, but they were most concerned about providing business with the liquidity it needed and were quite frank in stating that they did not think that the proposal would be very effective because of the complexity of the economy and the loopholes in the legislation. The representative of the Prussian Ministry of Commerce went so far as to object to the ban on the purchase of foreign exchange as a capital investment since it was the only "economically sound form of saving." Everyone wondered how the law could really be carried out. Hirsch did not dismiss these objections and pointed out that he had no intention of bringing in a "façade law." The bill's necessary "corollary" was the proposed domestic gold loan and gold-denominated Treasury bills.[70]

Here, however, he also ran into powerful opposition from the Reichsbank, the Reich Finance Ministry, and the Reich Labor Ministry, all of which argued that the Reich would be running an enormous risk by undertaking a valorized obligation which would have to be paid back in three months. There was some fear that the new gold-denominated Treasury bills would lead to a further depreciation of the mark and become a new object for speculators. A social objection was also raised. If the new gold Treasury bills were issued in the high denominations intended, then "the capitalists would, to be sure, have a valorized form of liquid capital, but this path would be closed to the less well-off."[71]

The Reichsbank took the lead in the battle against Hirsch's proposal. On August 29, Havenstein made a powerful plea before the Economic Policy and Reparations Committees of the RWR against using the Reichsbank gold to guarantee a clearing loan and also used the opportunity to attack the gold Treasury-note proposal:

And now to the question of the flight from the mark! Here also I have no doubt that there will hardly be a person who would give up the foreign exchange and currencies with which he today protects himself against the monetary depreciation to buy these gold treasury bills (Very true!), for these gold Treasury bills are a very uncertain factor. They will fall due in three months at the earliest. The Reich will not be in a position to discount them. They can only be sold on the free money market if takers are available. The market notation will vary because one does not know whether the mark will rise or fall on the day they come due and because the confidence in the credit of the German Reich is more or less lacking. They are thus no substitute for foreign exchange, and therefore no one will buy them.[72]

Hirsch sought to counter this opposition in a full-blown presentation of his plan to the Cabinet on September 15, before which he reiterated that foreign-exchange controls were futile in the absence of an alternative secure form of liquidity, especially since the Reichstag was not to go into session until the second half of October and would certainly take some time to pass such legislation. He did not think that the new gold Treasury certificates would cause a further decline of the paper mark. It was the public's loss of confidence that was promoting the depreciation, especially the workers, who were now anticipating currency depreciation with their wage demands. Hirsch felt the interest-bearing gold Treasury certificates he was advocating would diminish the existing overconsumption and provide an incentive to save. He also denied that the Reich really was running a risk by issuing such certificates. The domestic loan was short-term enough not to overstrain confidence, and it was to be backed by a guarantee fund whose real value would increase if the paper mark depreciated further and thus cover the risk or, if the value of the mark improved as expected, would decrease along with the diminishing risk.[73]

Typically, events overtook the debate in early October. Apparently, Hirsch did not have a very easy time explaining to his increasingly panicky superior, Economics Minister Schmidt, the vital link between the gold loan and legislation against speculation in foreign currency. Even when Schmidt finally caught on, his focus continued to be on taking every conceivable and inconceivable measure to fight the effects of the hyperinflation on the workers.

It was a measure of this desperation that Schmidt, to the horror of the official of his Ministry, took very seriously a Bavarian memorandum of September 28 filled with bizarre statist proposals for control of the economy. The Bavarian Minister-President Lerchenfeld had presented the document to appease consumer opinion in his state but rapidly sought to distance himself from the document after it was subjected to severe attacks from Bavarian economic interests and the studied neglect of the Reichsrat. Lerchenfeld was thus quite discomforted by Schmidt's continued interest.[74] Schmidt, however, was in a very anticapitalist mood, pointing out that "large portions of industry and commerce do not wish a strong improvement in the mark."[75] The Economics Minister was not alone in his anxiety and feeling that something had to be done immediately to fight speculation in foreign exchange. There was strong sentiment that action was necessary. The Commander of the Berlin Schutzpolizei, for example, welcomed news of measures against speculators, noting that he knew of one case in which a person was making millions by using a grain purchasing firm run by a friend as a cover for his speculations.[76] The government also felt it should do something before the Reichstag met. Stresemann, certainly no enemy of business, was pressing for action against speculators. Last, and anything but least, Schmidt and other Cabinet members feared that the Allies, who were supposed to resume their reparations negotiations in Brussels in the near future, would force the Germans to take action if they did not do so themselves.[77]

In all this the Cabinet had been bestirred by Wirth, who was out of Berlin but wired a request that something be done about foreign-exchange control for domestic and international reasons. Since he was trying to move in the direction of a Great Coalition government, the fact that both Stresemann and Hilferding supported exchange controls made action very desirable. At the same time, the "small breathing space" being provided by the negotiations with Belgium had to be used: "Activity must be demonstrated under all circumstances so that the outside world sees that we have not surrendered in despair to our fate."[78] The upshot of all this pressure was a decision by the Cabinet on

October 7 to have the President use his emergency powers and issue a decree against foreign currency speculation under Article 48. Hirsch was instructed to make the necessary arrangements with the Reichsbank and Finance Ministry to implement the decree. At the same time, a decision on the internal loan and gold certificates was put off.[79] Neither the Reichsbank nor the Finance Ministry showed much enthusiasm for these proposals—the former agreeing to them only on condition that the Reichsbank not be required to use its resources to back them, the latter grudgingly agreeing to take responsibility while openly doubting their efficacy. Thus, the Foreign Exchange Control Decree was approved on October 11 and promulgated the next day without any decision having been taken on the gold loan plan.[80]

What the Foreign Exchange Control Decree meant for Hirsch can be gathered from his diary:

7.10. *Cabinet decides on Foreign Exchange Control Decree . . . beginning of the end . . .* [On] 11. and 12.10. the Foreign Exchange Control Decree had to be overhastily brought out. Upon announcement the dollar drops from 3,100 to 2,400 and then immediately after appearance climbs back to 2,700. 13.10. Bobbie [Schmidt] places my office at disposal because of Foreign Exchange Control Decree. . . . And with the climbing dollar there begins an unheard of agitation against me. The Reich Chancellor is hardly back, then one turns him against me. The banking "experts" naturally stand to a man on the enemy side and prepare defeats for me in the Reich Economic Council; the Reichsbank agitates; the right-wing press foams. 19.10. Storm in the Reich Economic Council. The Reich Chancellor does not stand behind the Foreign Exchange Control Decree. Storm of petitions. . . . 24.10 Bobbie writes his letter of resignation, but crisis is declined. Public opinion turns against me as the source of the economic misery, *Berliner Zeitung am Mittag, Der Deutsche, Deutsche Allgemeine Zeitung*, the Reich Association of German Industry move in unheard of sharpness against Bobbie. . . . I am repeatedly declared finished in the Reichstag. . . . And all this at the turn of my 40th year.[81]

The Foreign Exchange Control Decree in fact was highly vulnerable to criticism. It had been issued without any consultation with the interest groups, and its provisions were both vague and alarming. Most immediately, businessmen were concerned about its effect on already concluded contracts, but they also argued that they could no longer function effectively if they were in any way involved with the domestic sale of products involving foreign raw materials or acted as intermediaries for foreign imports. The Hanseatic cities were particularly outraged, pointing out that the decree would force all importers to move out of Germany since only then could they sell to their German customers for foreign exchange. Most worrisome, however, both to merchants and businessmen was how to protect their operating capital and maintain business activity if they could only deal in marks in their domestic transactions and if they were forced to calculate in marks. In sum, the Foreign Exchange Control Decree unleashed a flood of complaints from every branch of industry and commerce. This bore testimony to the enormous extent to which the economy was already functioning on the basis of foreign exchange in both international and domestic business. As a consequence, the government had to issue a host of modifications on October 27, but these necessarily increased the loopholes in the decree. Indeed, if the decree was meant to impress the Allies, it failed of its purpose. The British Commercial Attaché Thelwall pointed out that speculation could go on anywhere and that the banning of speculation in Berlin would simply drive it elsewhere. He thought that the Germans were overemphasizing the significance of speculation, which was a symptom rather than cause of their problems, and, along with the German business community, was convinced that the decree would make even more complicated their already cumbersome foreign trade regulations. Ambassador D'Abernon agreed and acidly commented that the new regulations "belong to a class of legislation which it would be flattery to call childish. The spirit which has inspired them appears a combination of the Prussian passion for regulating and restricting everything, with the impulse of a Kaffir medicine man to smell out somebody if anything goes wrong. Nothing could be more false than the diagnosis: nothing more futile than the treatment."[82]

All this, of course, was anything but fair to Hirsch. He never viewed antispeculation measures alone as effective means of dealing with the currency problem, while the specific faults

of the decree were to some extent attributable to the speed with which he was forced to act. However, it is anything but self-evident that the results would have been happier if he had consulted endlessly with all the interested parties. Furthermore, Hirsch was now more than ever a victim of the Reichsbank autonomy upon which the British had been so insistent. The debacle of the Foreign Exchange Control Decree only strengthened the hand of the Reichsbank and Finance Ministry in their opposition to what Hirsch had always considered the essential pendant to the decree; namely, the domestic loan and gold Treasury certificates. On October 20, the Reichsbank struck hard at this aspect of the Hirsch plan in a memorandum that not only presented the old arguments but also roundly threatened to cease discounting Reich Treasury bills if the government carried out the gold Treasury certificate plan as intended. In short, the Reichsbank threatened to withdraw the support it had given the government since 1914 through the discounting and rediscounting of Treasury bills. Its preconditions for continuing to do so were, first, that there would be no rediscounting of the projected gold Treasury certificates either by the government or by the Reichsbank and, second, that the amount of such certificates be narrowly circumscribed to one hundred million gold marks and, third, that the foreign exchange and paper marks paid for the certificates (the proceeds of the loan) be deposited in the Reichsbank to be used in a manner to be determined in agreement with the government. Thus, the Reichsbank was prepared to accept a severely truncated version of the Hirsch gold certificate plan, but only if it had control over the funds collected. If the RWM persisted in its program, the Reichsbank was prepared to employ its "ultimate means" of coercion.[83]

Hirsch was not the only enemy Havenstein had to fight in trying to protect his gold hoard, however. During the first three weeks of October the Reparations Committee of the RWR had been meeting at the instigation of Rudolf Hilferding to discuss the possibilities of domestic stabilization measures, and a formidable array of prominent persons had come forward to argue that Germany had to do something on its own to stabilize the currency and that the

Reichsbank's gold should be brought in to assist in this effort. It was Hilferding who initiated the series of meetings and hearings on this problem and who had opened them up with a major speech on October 2 in which he left no doubt about where he stood.[84] Reviewing the history of the inflation, Hilferding pointed out that it had gone through three stages. First, there was the war and failure to finance it through taxation. Second, there was the period after the Armistice when Germany financed its imports by selling marks abroad or by letting foreigners speculate until the saturation point was reached. Finally, there was the present period, in which the mark was depreciating because of internal causes; namely, because it was ceasing to be a measure of value in which anyone had confidence. Hilferding rejected the notion that inflation had certain self-curative powers at this final stage so that by encouraging exports and discouraging imports one could create a new relative stabilization. In an advanced industrial society, economic and social conditions set limits on the restriction of imports, and he suggested that now Germany was paying for the failure to make good use of the relative stabilization in 1920–1921. The hyperinflation, by discouraging all saving and by increasing demand, was creating a credit crisis compounded by what Hilferding denounced as the false policy pursued earlier by industry and the banks of granting excessively large dividends and not doing enough to build up capital and reserves. The credit shortage was leading to a vast increase in currency circulation thanks to the Reichsbank's credit policies, and this, in turn, acted upon the floating debt and the government deficit. How was Germany to break out of this situation?

Hilferding pointed out that even if it appeared that some countries facing major inflations could only achieve stabilization on the basis of outside loans, the German situation made internal stabilization measures practicable. Germany had a billion marks in gold in the Reichsbank, and, in Hilferding's view, this gold could be mobilized if it were mortgaged instead of being allowed to lie dead in the vaults of the Reichsbank. If one thereby satisfied Germany's real needs for foreign exchange while introducing strict measures of exchange control, then it would be possible to stabilize the mark. At the same time, the opportunity could be used to control state expenditure and move toward a balanced budget. Hilferding made it absolutely clear that he viewed his proposal as an alternative to the increasingly discussed notion that the gold could only be used to back up an entirely new currency. He recognized that this might be possible but argued that it would only be possible "through the collapse of the entire economy of the state."[85] He preferred to stabilize the mark at some level between its domestic price level and its external value so as to mitigate a possible deflationary crisis and keep the production process going. It was a policy, in his view, that would not only carry Germany through the winter but that would also make an "active reparations policy" possible, "while today we must count on being dictated to once again because we do not voluntarily do that which economic reason and our own interests require."[86]

Georg Bernhard shared Hilferding's view that the breathing space in reparations had to be used and pointed out that great progress had been made in balancing the regular budget. What was needed was capital, a point that he had been making for years, and the only way to counter the flight of capital was to produce a measure of stabilization that would encourage the return of capital from abroad or from hiding at home. Like Hilferding, he felt that the Reichsbank had an obligation to use its gold to support even a temporary stabilization so that the opportunity could be used to deal with Germany's foreign and domestic difficulties. Arthur Feiler of the *Frankfurter Zeitung* seconded these arguments by attacking the fatalism that had been created by the "eternal mixing up of domestic and foreign questions" and insisted that "many things which could have been done to cleanse our domestic economy have been hindered by the feeling that the reparations burden stood before us and this finally has become a block against doing anything that is good for our economy." Feiler joined in the attack on the Reichsbank by arguing that, instead of serving as the "conscience of industry," it had stood by passively and "believed that it could do nothing other than give in to the fate that was rolling over it."[87]

Needless to say, these sentiments did not go without challenge. On the one hand, there were strong differences of opinion over Germany's economic situation. Hirsch, Hilferding, and Bernhard all took the view that the German balance of payments was relatively favorable at the moment and was being made worse by the credit policies of the Reichsbank. On the other hand, there were disagreements as to the best tactic for Germany under existing international and domestic political conditions. Havenstein left no doubt about where he stood on both sets of issues. In his judgment, the German balance of payments was passive by at least two billion marks a year, and not enough foreign exchange was coming in. Only half of Germany's exports were being paid in foreign exchange because so much trade was going to the east, to countries with poor currencies. Thus, Germany was only bringing in between one and a quarter billion and one and a half billion in gold values, and the Reich was taking away half. What remained for the private German economy was insufficient to cover the required four and a half billion in imports, and the missing balance could only be covered by selling marks. This, in Havenstein's view, was why the mark had to fall and why Hilferding's arguments for the use of Reichsbank gold were to be rejected:

It is a mistake for Hilferding to assume that one can effectively support the mark with the help of 300 million gold marks from the Reichsbank gold. It is a further error of Hilferding to think that the Reichsbank would only sacrifice its gold *temporarily* in this way. Things in reality are such that the exchange rate of the mark will only very temporarily be improved with this 300 million, and that 300 million will be *permanently* lost to the Reichsbank. The Reichsbank gold is *not* dead, as Herr Hilferding and Herr Bernhard maintain, it is rather the *fundamental support* of the bank. The strength of the bank rests only in its gold reserve, and if one takes its gold, it is as if one cuts off the locks of Samson's hair. The policy recommended by Hilferding and Bernhard therefore is a Delilah policy, the act of a Herostratus. Only with its gold can the Reichsbank remain worthy of credit and work for the German economy. If a portion of her gold is taken for the purpose mentioned, then the direct consequence of this action will be a further rapid fall of the mark. Precisely the opposite of what Hilferding wants will happen.[88]

On a rather less emotional plane, textile industrialist Abraham Frowein, a powerful figure

in the RdI, concentrated less on the problem of the Reichsbank gold than on the danger that Germany would stabilize, possibly at too high a rate to export successfully, and then find herself faced with new Allied demands. He felt it essential to at least wait and see what was going to happen in Brussels. This view was sharply challenged by Christian trade-union leader Baltrusch, who reflected the sentiment in both Socialist and Christian trade-union circles and who pointed out that there was no longer time for the old recipes—first, because the domestic situation was getting extremely tense and the workers were beginning to listen to the Communists and, second, because the Allies were losing all patience:

It is not true that we can go to Brussels with the old program, that we can say, you must first help us, then we will help ourselves, because the will to help Germany is, so to speak, divided. There is certainly a conviction in the world today that yearly payment of two and a half billion gold marks is something impossible, that the conditions of the London Ultimatum are senseless. But on the other side there is a very deep mistrust abroad also as to whether Germany will operate correctly with the means which eventually might be placed at her disposal. And the way in which we have handled our currency in the past has promoted the conviction abroad, also among neutrals, that this would not be the case. . . . We can only go to Brussels if we can show that we have done with our own power what has been asked of us. Only then will we get that loan, will the moratorium be prolonged which will extend our breathing space. On the other hand, if we don't do it, then that development will set in which will lead to an absolute catastrophe for our state finances with all of its domestic political consequences.[89]

On November 1, the majority of the Economic and Finance Policy Committees of the RWR supported the position of Baltrusch, Hilferding, and Bernhard and urged the introduction of measures to stabilize the mark, but the report was kept secret in order to avoid embarrassing the government or prejudicing the international experts who were meeting in Berlin.[90]

Much to the dismay of the embattled Wirth and those who had counted upon a report that would confirm the necessity of outside help to Germany prior to its taking stabilization measures, Baltrusch's view that Germany was going to be expected to take the first initiatives received very strong confirmation from the committee of international experts Wirth had invited to Berlin to consider Germany's financial situation. The experts met in Berlin during the last days of October and the first week of November concurrently with the Reparations Commission, which had come to receive concrete German proposals. The Social Democrats had feared that Wirth and the other opponents of self-initiated stabilization measures would preempt the autonomous decision of the foreign experts by bringing them into contact solely with officials, financial experts, and businessmen who shared the views of Wirth and Havenstein and that "the foreign experts might be frightened away from making positive proposals for the support of the mark." The Socialists therefore urged that Hilferding, Feiler, and Professors Moritz Bonn and Alfred Weber—"experts from those circles who place the greatest value upon an immediate action to support the mark"—be brought into contact with the foreign experts.[91] It certainly was true that the government pinned some hope on the influence of Melchior, Cuno, the banker Urbig, and Professor Hermann Schumacher, who stood on the side of Wirth and Havenstein. Nevertheless, Hilferding was asked to appear before the experts, albeit as a representative of the SPD rather than as an economic expert.[92] It is doubtful, however, that this jockeying mattered much. Keynes was quite friendly with Melchior and Cuno, whose expert advice the government had also sought and who held the view that nothing could be done to stabilize before a definite reparations settlement was reached. He also had personal contacts with Bonn, who had translated his famous reparations book. Insofar as the matter at hand was concerned, Keynes and Bonn had become convinced that Germany could and should undertake some immediate stabilization measures on its own and simply had to do so to get a foreign loan. They continued to feel that reparations had to be lowered to ensure permanent stability.

As is so often the case when experts are called together, the committee of foreign experts disagreed and produced two reports. The majority report—signed by Keynes, Cassel, Brand, and Jenks—took the position that a permanent stabilization was impossible under existing circumstances because of German financial policies and the terms of the Treaty of Versailles. Unhappily for Wirth and Havenstein, however, the majority report went on to argue that a provisional stabilization was possible under existing circumstances since the trade deficit was not excessively large. It called for a two-year moratorium on reparations payments and a concentrated German effort to balance the budget and keep it in balance. Under such conditions, the report argued,

. . . an immediate stabilization is possible by means of Germany's own efforts. Indeed we go further. Certain technical conditions are now present—the large gold reserve, the scarcity of currency, the margin between external depreciation on the one hand, the degree of internal inflation and internal depreciation on the other, which render the position unusually susceptible to control. At the rate of 3,500 marks to the dollar the gold in the Reichsbank now amounts to about twice the value of the note issue. This is an unprecedented situation. No other currency has fallen into decay with so great a potential support still unused.[93]

The majority report concluded with a stabilization plan involving the creation of a Board of Foreign Exchange Control within the Reichsbank which would fix the rate of the mark and have the Reichsbank gold at its disposal to maintain the rate so fixed. The floating debt of the government was to be held at a specified figure and all further credits to the government covered by funded loans. Along with these measures, the German government might, with the permission of the Reparations Commission, seek the support of a foreign banking consortium and secure a loan backed by the Reichsbank gold. Exchange controls were to be abolished, and the interest rates raised to a sufficiently high level to ensure the stabilization.

The minority report, possibly influenced by the fact that Dubois was trying to put together a consortium to lend money to Germany that included French banks, was even more unsatisfactory from the standpoint of the German government. It placed more emphasis on the role played by Germany's negative balance of payments in explaining the inflation than did the majority report. Unlike the majority report, however, it made no mention of reducing reparations demands. The minority report called for a new gold mark to be created by a "Money Bank" that would back up the gold currency with the gold from the Reichsbank for which the latter would receive an equivalence in shares. The currency was to be pegged at a level substantially above the present purchasing power of the paper mark. In the view of the minority report, therefore, the stabilization would require a five hundred million gold-mark loan from an international consortium which would have to be backed by the gold deposited in the "Money Bank." The Money Bank would undertake to purchase paper marks with the object of raising their value, and a transitional period was foreseen in which the two currencies would coexist until a gold standard could be restored and the paper marks exchanged for gold marks, at which point the Money Bank could be dissolved. In contrast to the majority report, the minority report called not only for the balancing of the budget but also for specific measures against the flight of capital, the reduction of the civil service, and the increase of working hours.[94]

In addition to the majority and minority reports, the three bankers—Brand, Dubois, and Vissering—presented a special report on the possibility of forming an international syndicate to assist Germany with a five hundred million gold-mark credit. They urged what was tantamount to the reconstitution of the international Bankers' Committee under the auspices of the Reparations Commission to consider the granting of such a credit for two years with the understanding that it would be guaranteed by the proceeds from the Reich customs. The Reichsbank would be expected to match the international loan with a five hundred million gold-mark credit of its own guaranteed by its gold. Germany was to be relieved of reparations payments during the period of the loan, and the repayment of the international consortium was to have precedence over all other Reich obligations. Brand, very much in keeping with the majority report, indicated German credit was too low for the City to support a loan unless it was guaranteed by the Reichsbank and unless there was certainty about the extent of German obligations.[95]

These reports manifestly challenged the Wirth government's official position that a moratorium and final reparations settlement had to precede any domestic steps necessary for stabilization. They also contested Havenstein's policy of unwillingness to put up his gold as security for an interim stabilization. The most powerful case for an interim solution within the circles advising the government was made by Moritz Bonn, who was a supporter of the balance-of-payments theory but who nevertheless now felt that the risk of putting off a final solution to the reparations had to be taken if Germany were to get out of the domestic and international crisis in which it found itself.

Playing the devil's advocate, Bonn suggested two arguments against an interim solution. The first was that it would not restore economic health or eliminate the causes of Germany's distress. He considered this argument valid only if the moratorium were to be for a few months. If Germany were to have a three-year moratorium with an opportunity to stabilize in freedom from international reparations crises, then it was hard to imagine that conditions would be worse for the German economy than they were at present. The second and much more serious argument against an interim solution, in Bonn's view, was that Germany might be so well recovered after three years that far more would be demanded of it than in an immediate final reparations settlement. Bonn felt, however, that Germany would be unable to make a satisfactory offer under existing circumstances. Either it would be too low to be acceptable to the French or it would be a high sum based on some uneducated guess concerning what Germany's capacity would be three years later. Bonn argued that it was economically illogical and short-sighted to oppose an interim arrangement in fear that more reparations would have to be paid in the end:

Should the moratorium bring about such a recovery of Germany that after it was over we could pay substantially larger sums than presently appears possible without damaging our further development, then this would be no misfortune from the German point of view. The goal of German policy must not be the prevention of a financial gain for France but rather the avoidance of an economic catastrophe for Germany.[96]

Bonn went on to point out that he himself had always taken the view that the international banking community would provide no money to Germany before the reparations bill was reduced and settled but that this argument was no longer valid because, on the one hand, Germany's chaotic economic situation made a calculation of its capacity to pay nothing but wild guesswork and, on the other, the setting of an acceptable sum in the context of continuing Allied fantasies about German capacity would lead to demands for securities and economic controls of precisely the kind Germany was trying to avoid. Bonn's own guess was that Germany's capacity to pay reparations would be shown to be far less than anyone presently thought once decent statistical work were possible and the results of a quiet period of recovery could be examined. He thought that large portions of German industry would fall into foreign hands because of the capital shortage and that this in itself would limit Allied interests in too high a final reparations sum. Another possibility suggested by Bonn was that Germany provisionally accept a target reparations sum of forty billion gold marks—the Allies were thinking in terms of forty to fifty billion— and that this amount be treated as provisional depending upon the extent to which Germany recovered by 1926 in comparison to 1913. The amount could then either be increased or decreased depending on the results of this test. Bonn himself guessed that the final reparations obligation would then be twenty billion. The advantage of such a procedure, however, would be that so presently unacceptable a sum would not have to be stated.

Bonn's fundamental point in this exercise, of course, was to stress the importance of a tactful political solution that would save Germany from disaster. In this respect, as he frankly admitted, his stabilization plan was very close to that of the Social Democrats', both in its intention and in its point of departure: As he emphasized to Hermes on November 6, Germany could not stand on principles that no one else found reasonable. The experts were going to say that Germany could stabilize, and Germany wanted a loan. If so, the implications had to be accepted: "It is naive to expect that international finance will risk 500 million of its own money in the form of loans when we fear that 500 million in German gold could be lost. I

think it possible to get a loan if we risk the gold, otherwise not." In Bonn's view, a turning point had come that would have to be dealt with courageously and sensibly if the situation were to be saved. The time for "overly clever half measures" was past, and failure to face the situation would lead to a "catastrophe."[97]

Hugo Stinnes also had been making this argument, albeit with a very different program of internal stabilization in mind. He was making it ever more loudly and sensationally as well as in his private international diplomacy precisely during these crucial days in early November when the Reparations Commission was sojourning in Berlin along with the committee of international financial experts and when the Wirth government was at once seeking to satisfy the Allied demand for a program and to broaden its base so as to include the DVP. The financial and monetary crisis along with the reparations crisis were thus hopelessly entangled with a government crisis, and the Stinnes stabilization program is the final ingredient necessary to bring all three into focus.

Stinnes was a passionate advocate of the proposition that Germany had to seek a path to stabilization on its own before it could ask for relief from abroad. This put him at odds with many of his industrialist colleagues, who were as convinced as Wirth and Havenstein that nothing could be done until reparations were scaled down and Germany received both a moratorium and a loan. Where Stinnes differed from the nonindustrialist advocates of a domestic stabilization initiative and found strong support among his fellow industrialists, however, was in switching the focus of domestic stabilization measures from financial to economic ones. While a year earlier he had almost singlehandedly swung the pendulum in the RdI from willingness to make a credit offer to the government for reparations purposes to a refusal to do so unless the railroad system were privatized and used as security, now in the hyperinflationary crisis, with no less single-mindedness, Stinnes focused on the elimination of the eight-hour day as the one and only path to stabilization.

When Hermann Bücher, in the spring of 1922, proposed that the RdI develop a comprehensive program on all pertinent economic, financial, fiscal, and social policy which it could use in presenting a united and clear front before the public and government, Stinnes and his chief ally at this time, Paul Silverberg, seized upon the opportunity to push the RdI in the direction they felt essential. Bücher's emphasis was gaining a comprehensive settlement of reparations and international economic relations through international business cooperation. He argued that industry and the German government should seek a reduction of reparations and the elimination of trade barriers to German exports and promise, in return for such concessions, to undertake the domestic reforms required for stabilization. Silverberg and Stinnes sharply criticized this approach. They did not disagree with Bücher's foreign policy goals, but they were very pessimistic about Bücher's contention that the French, British, or Americans would be moved to support the German position by arguments about the restoration of the world economy. Instead, Silverberg proposed that primacy be given to domestic affairs and that industry and government join in a battle with the left over the eight-hour day, the demobilization decrees that prevented the firing of redundant workers, and the entire system of economic controls that had hampered industry since the war. The restoration of the ten-hour day—twelve-hour shifts in the continuously running plants of heavy industry—would, according to Silverberg and Stinnes, increase production and lower costs to such an extent that Germany would become attractive to foreign creditors.[98]

Few industrial leaders needed persuasion about the evils of the eight-hour day and the various controls on the economy, but some found it difficult to understand the passion with which Stinnes and Silverberg gave priority to domestic "reforms." Cuno, for example, argued against a rigid program:

I want to take up the idea in the economic program that, as you believe, one should move in two phases, first create order in our own house and then take up the foreign policy questions. I would like to ask that these questions not be taken up so separately in time and in action. Recovery internally depends on recovery externally. We would then achieve a contemporaneous perspective on the internal and external problems. We should in general demand a *separation of economics from politics.*[99]

Stinnes, however, was insistent on the order in which German goals were to be achieved:

I believe that we must hold to a definite sequence. A basis must be established for an international negotiation, so that we cannot be reproached at every negotiation that the German economy is managed in such a way that it always has a passive balance, that is, at least two billion marks too little is produced. . . . We have to have the courage to tell the workers and the government: what you are running is an economy of deceit. You have to work!! Things cannot go on any longer this way. If we are not capable of surviving ourselves, then the outside world will have absolutely no interest in helping us. I believe in any case that even if we achieve a higher level of work productivity, we will only just succeed in getting an active balance of payments. We must become active. *First we have to come to increased work, then the stabilization of the currency on the day when one is certain that the reparations problem has been solved.*[100]

All this in no way meant that Stinnes had given up his idea of trying to conduct the economic reconstruction in cooperation with organized labor. Cuno was by no means less belligerent than Stinnes and Silverberg, and he argued that tactics were secondary and that industry should challenge labor if it did not cooperate. Silverberg, while sharing the view that industry should speak its mind and fight labor if necessary, nevertheless thought that public opinion had to be taken into account and that it was essential to maintain contact with the leaders of the labor movement. In his draft program of early August, he went so far as to include the statement that "the necessary struggle against unwillingness to work, which must be fought in the interest of the entire people, can only be carried out in common collaboration of employees and workers." This view, too, was not shared by all industrialists. Paul Reusch, always a critic of the ZAG, commented that "the unwillingness to work is not to be fought by the common collaboration of employers and workers, but by a strong government that has the courage to act energetically and ruthlessly. We do not have a government in Berlin, but only various bureaus at whose head there are more or less capable bureau chiefs. We have a factory for laws, which are disregarded by a large portion of the population because the government has no authority and is not strong enough to impose its will."[101]

Nevertheless, Stinnes was by no means prepared to abandon the policy of crisis management in collaboration with the trade unions
and moderate elements of the SPD, a policy
that was all the more to be recommended politically in the wake of the uproar over the murder
of Rathenau and the increasing tendency of the
SPD and USPD to join forces. The great question was whether he could persuade them to
support his program, a proposition not quite as
bizarre as might initially appear. It was the Majority Social Democrats, after all, who had
pushed for greater productivity in 1918–1920
and who had been prepared to use force even
against trade-union leaders to get an overtime
agreement in the mining industry in early 1920.
It was not entirely amiss, therefore, when Stinnes wrote personally to the man most responsible for that policy, Prussian Interior Minister
Carl Severing, in early July 1922. Stinnes
warned Severing that there were signs that exports would soon decrease if steps were not
taken to maintain German competitiveness
and "to use the inflationary wave in order once
again to thrust forward on overseas markets."
This was all the more necessary because matters
were coming to a head with the Entente. It was
very important, in Stinnes's view, that Germany "not lose her breath." He compared the
situation with that faced by Severing in early
1920 and argued that the means of defense remained the same: "We must in the shortest possible time produce more coal and also produce
more in manufacturing through overtime, and
we must no longer strike. If you can see a way,
at first of using key persons to influence the
miners and workers in other industries, then I
will gladly make my best efforts to help as
well."[102] Whatever the role played by Severing
in 1922, the fact that a new overtime agreement
was concluded demonstrated that such efforts,
as well as the generous wage policy at which
Stinnes was hinting, were of some avail.

Stinnes took a surprisingly positive attitude
toward the unification of the SPD and USPD
finally consummated in September 1922 and
felt it important that the government be broadened to include the DVP in a Great Coalition
government. Stinnes agreed with Stresemann
in opposing the entry of the USPD into the
Wirth government, as had been proposed by

the SPD in the wake of the Rathenau murder,
but raised no objections when Stresemann
pointed out that people like Hilferding and Rudolf Breitscheid could prove acceptable in a re-
united SPD. He went on to state that "in view
of the future of the trade unions and in general
I am of your opinion that a *fusion* between the
Majority Socialists and the reasonable part of
the Independents should be promoted wherever possible."[103] Stinnes's perception that the
unification of the two Socialist parties would increase trade-union influence was fully justified.

Such influence was all the more desirable because many of the trade-union leaders appeared
to be in a very pessimistic mood thanks to the
hyperinflation. At the Free Trade Union Congress in June, the radicals launched a major attack on the ZAG, to which Wissell responded
less with praise for the ZAG's accomplishments
than an argument that it was necessary to maintain the influence of the trade unions during the
inevitable stabilization crisis that would follow
the inflation. If the opposition wished to claim
that the ZAG had done nothing to improve the
lot of the workers, then one also had to ask what
the trade unions had accomplished. Wissell answered his own question: "Then I must tell you
honorably and openly, our powers were insufficient to bring about this improvement in their
lot."[104]

In mid-August, Bücher was able to report an
even more potentially receptive atmosphere
among the trade union leaders. At a meeting of
the ZAG directors, Grassmann of the ADGB
suggested that the ZAG meet to discuss the general situation and the means of preventing a
"total collapse."[105] He spoke openly about the
unhappy situation in the unions and the flood
of anxious inquiries from members and made
no effort to hide the fact that "the trade union
leadership does not at all feel secure." Bücher
also had the feeling that their financial situation
was not good and that they were having a hard
time supporting their large number of functionaries by trying to raise dues which the workers
seemed unwilling to pay. While Grassmann
made the usual complaints about the farmers
and food prices, neither he nor the other trade-
union leaders objected when Bücher suggested
that the unions were bound to decay if they did
not develop new ideas. Bücher blamed the

unions for always putting the wage question in the forefront at a time when everyone had to make sacrifices and criticized them for failing to rally the masses behind a sound economic policy:

Until now they have only rallied the masses behind them with radical slogans and phrases. With these one cannot move forward. We must make the demand that the industrialists are recognized as the leaders in economic policy. As an example, I brought up your [Stinnes] person. I said that it makes a truly childish impression to an objectively minded person when I continuously read in the Social Democratic press about "Stinnesization," "Stinnes lackey," "exploitation," etc., although they must know themselves that Hugo Stinnes creates more bread for the workers than all the trade unions taken together.

Once again, Bücher noted not only an absence of opposition but also a tone of agreement. He found their respect for Stinnes very "interesting," as he did the fact that they blamed the politicians for the newspaper articles. Bücher concluded that "they also wanted cheerfully to place themselves behind an economic program of the industrialists; one only has to find a form that is acceptable for them."

All this certainly must have reinforced Stinnes in his feeling that he could win the trade unionists and reasonable Socialists over, especially since he felt that wages had to be raised under existing conditions. If he recognized this, however, then he expected the workers to recognize that the eight-hour day, the very existence of which foreigners were taking as a sign either of Germany's well-being or bad faith and which, he claimed, was making it possible for foreigners to buy up German works for a song, could not be maintained in its present form.[106] Curiously enough, however, very little was done to pick up on the signals sent by the trade-union leaders. One reason appears to have been the increasing lack of interest in the ZAG on the part of the leaders of the Association of German Employer Organizations, whose activities were not well coordinated with the RdI and whose representatives did not always attend ZAG meetings. Another probably was that all employers were not as willing as Stinnes to increase wages and resisted calling for a general wage increase to match bread price increases. Last, Stinnes was preoccupied during this period, not only with his own business affairs and

agreement with de Lubersac but also with a variety of other personal initiatives in both foreign and domestic policy. He did not appear prepared to come forth with his full program, either in his dealings with Chancellor Wirth or in discussions with the trade union leaders.[107]

In fact, he preferred to pour out his ideas in private conversations with or memoranda to foreign leaders and to undertake such activities sometimes in consultation with President Ebert but never with the full knowledge of Wirth since, as he told the American Ambassador Houghton, he "did not trust the Chancellor's discretion."[108] In this instance, he was referring to what the Ambassador considered a "remarkable document," which Stinnes had presented to de Lubersac for consideration by the French government. In addition to de Lubersac and Houghton, it had also been made available to President Ebert and Ambassador Wiedfeldt.[109]

The document in question demonstrated that Stinnes planned to solve not only the German stabilization problems but also the world's problems. He began with Germany, pointing out that its "untenable position" was the consequence of insufficient productivity, government controls, "foolish tax legislation," along with the Treaty of Versailles, which, "through its economically unfulfillable terms and through its grave psychological blunders, has ruined Germany financially and morally." As a solution, he proposed that the Allies evacuate the occupied areas of Germany by April 1, 1923, and abandon all sanctions and interference in German internal affairs. In return, Germany would hold a plebiscite in which the German people would be asked to agree to work overtime for as long as was necessary to gain a favorable balance of trade and to cover the costs of interest and amortization of a gold loan. The loan would pay the costs of reconstructing Belgium and France and serve to stabilize the German currency. Stinnes calculated that these tasks would require two hours overtime work for ten to fifteen years. Germany would also abandon all domestic economic controls and subsidies. In return for these actions, Germany would expect most-favored-nation treatment in international trade. The German mark would be stabilized at the level "at which it will find itself after the stabilization and reparations loan had been insured," and this stabilization would be guaranteed by a ban on strikes in all industries of "vital importance" and the placing of all public enterprises on a profitable basis so that they "become fit to serve as a foundation for the international gold loan." The tax laws would be revised so as to stimulate thrift and promote capital formation, and crimes against property would be subject to "extremely severe punishment." The civil service would be reduced to a minimum, and all laws passed or issued since 1914 would be reexamined for their influence on production. Middle-class persons ruined by the inflation would be provided with state assistance "so that they may support themselves decently and not, in their despair, become a danger to Germany and the world." Finally, "after all this preliminary work has been done, Germany and France, in conjunction with England, Italy, and Belgium, will have to approach the United States of America in order to try to arrange the indebtedness between the nations and thus make possible a final liquidation of the consequences of the war of 1914–18."

Stinnes seemed to feel that he could head a German negotiation team in Paris with these proposals, which he had given to de Lubersac to discuss with Poincaré. In fact, without telling Wirth exactly what the program was, he had brought de Lubersac into contact with Wirth for the purpose of having the Frenchman assured that such a negotiation could take place with the full approval of the German government. His personal diplomacy by no means ended here, however. While he strove for negotiations with the French and cultivated Houghton, he recognized the importance of not neglecting the British, who, he recognized, had contained the French on crucial occasions.[110] Thus, he found six hours' time on October 29 to enlighten in apparently fluent English two British steel industrialists, John Craig and Sir William Larke, as well as J. I. Piggott, the British Commissioner at Cologne. Stinnes hoped to win their support for one of his pet projects, an international conference of businessmen to recommend solutions to the world issues. He hoped the Americans would take the intiative in calling such a meeting, and he felt the French

were beginning to pursue a more economically minded and industrially oriented policy because of their own currency and reconstruction difficulties. He outlined his position on Versailles and overtime work very much along the lines of his memorandum for Houghton but was quite blunt about expressing his concern over unemployment and his willingness to see Germany print as much money as necessary to help the workers keep up with the depreciation and to promote German business activity until the mark ran out of domestic purchasing power. This insistence that Germany hold out at all costs until she received favorable terms also conditioned his somewhat excited response to the question of what Germany would do if the French used measures of force. He warned that "no power on earth will then prevent a German alliance with the reconstituted Russia and the resulting war of extermination against France, beside the horrors of which the last war would pale. We are fully alive to the fact that the price of this war will be the destruction of Germany between the Rhine and the Elbe, but we should be willing to pay even that price."[111] This, however, was a lapse from his otherwise optimistic mood, which also extended to internal affairs, where Stinnes boasted that he was a "personal friend" of "the saddler," President Ebert, who was "in full agreement with his ideas." It is a measure of the effect of a prolonged exposure to Stinnes that Piggot concluded his report by declaring that "the leaders of the Socialist Party have certainly a tremendous respect for him, and when his hour comes, as I fully believe it will come, to lift Germany out of the morass in which she now finds herself, the workmen and the bulk of the people will turn to him as the saviour of their country."[112] Lord Kilmarnock of the Berlin embassy was less entranced, finding Stinnes's willingness to keep the printing presses rolling the most interesting part of the interview. He pointed out that Stinnes neglected "French popular feeling" and thought him "unduly optimistic" about the willingness of the German workman to go back to prewar working hours in order to pay reparations. He also noted that production under the latest overtime agreement in the mining industry had so far produced enormously high wage costs but not much increased production.

In the meantime, however, Wirth was trying to save the country, and Stinnes, despite his similar goal of bringing the DVP into the government, was making life very difficult for the Chancellor with his criticisms and private negotiations. The situation was particularly tense at the end of August, when Stinnes was telling his staff that "the government is letting the reins slip to the ground. Actually others must rule today; the ministers cannot do so."[113] Stinnes was particularly annoyed that Wirth had taken over the Foreign Ministry after Rathenau's death, but he also felt that the Economics Ministry and Finance Ministry needed to be placed in "expert hands." He viewed Hirsch as someone who was "hostile and intriguing," however friendly on the surface—to which adjectives were added "incompetent" and "insensitive" to the needs of industry after the October 12 Foreign Exchange Control Decree. Stinnes responded to contentions that the Socialists would insist on Economics Minister Schmidt's retention with the comment that "they will have to come to terms with it; otherwise the country will bear the consequences."[114] If Stinnes also wanted Finance Minister Hermes replaced, he nevertheless discussed his discontents with him, a matter bound to irritate Wirth, who suspected Hermes of wanting his job.

Most annoying, however, was Stinnes's constant access to President Ebert. The situation at the end of August provides an excellent illustration of how this connection functioned. On August 31, Stinnes visited Ebert to discuss the reconstruction of the government, pointing out that it was the right time for such an action since industry had been coming to the aid of the government with the de Lubersac negotiations. He suggested that Wiedfeldt be invited to take over the Foreign Office and that Raumer or the Rheinstahl director, Becker, be given the Economics Ministry, while the SPD retain the Interior Ministry. Ebert appears to have been in complete agreement with Stinnes but had "some anxiety about his own party" and expressed the desire to delay the decision until after the party congress in mid-September, a

delay Stinnes considered "impossible" but which, nevertheless, lasted even longer.[115]

Wirth himself seemed to be of a divided mind about giving up the Foreign Office. Close advisers argued that it strengthened his position, put him in the tradition of Bismarck and Bülow, and ensured unity of policy. Others pointed out that the burden was too heavy and that there would be some advantage to having a conservative Foreign Minister carry out the government policies. Wirth seemed willing to take the latter tack and initially asked Max Warburg, who refused, among other reasons, because "with the mood in Germany such as it is, I think it a great mistake for the regime to name a minister of Jewish origins to the Foreign Ministry."[116] Cuno was then raised as a possibility because of his excellent English connections, but when Wirth later pursued it, he ran into the usual problem Weimar governments faced when they tried to bring businessmen into the government; namely, that the conditions set were likely to undermine rather than strengthen their Cabinets. Cuno declared that he could not take office so long as a "rational economic policy was not possible" because of the "overwhelming influence of trade unions of Socialist and Catholic observance" and that he could not do so until there was "homogeneity in the views of the most important ministries, among which is also the Reich Economics Ministry."[117]

By late October, Wirth's struggle to keep his Cabinet and policies afloat was taking its toll of his energy and patience. Matters were not helped by repeated bouts of illness and rumors that rightist assassins planned to launch an assault upon his house. The Chancellor remarked to one official that "each day that I am still alive is granted to me by God."[118] He was irritated by what he referred to as the "shadow government" of President Ebert. Ebert was consulting with Stinnes, although he had also approved the Foreign Exchange Control Decree so sharply criticized in industrial circles. There probably was much less substance to Wirth's suspicions of Hermes. While the two Centrists had disagreed on how to respond to Allied pressures, Wirth's willingness to believe rumors that Hermes was plotting with the Social Democrats to become Chancellor was grounded more in his state of agitation than in reality.[119]

Wirth's conviction that the time had come to broaden and unify his government in connection with the forthcoming visit of the Reparations Commission and the foreign financial experts was a far more rational perception. During his brief vacation in the middle of October, the pressure from the left had led to the issuance of the ill-fated Foreign Exchange Control Decree. While the left was demanding financial and currency stabilization measures, the right was fighting them and demanding the end of economic controls and the abandonment of the eight-hour day. Wirth was intent on broadening his government to the right, which meant concessions on hours of work, but he also knew he could not go over to the free economy demanded by industry and that the hours-of-work question would have to be handled with delicacy. The rapid depreciation, as well as the political situation in England and France, demanded action. On October 23, he summoned the Cabinet and declared that the time had come for a "concentration of forces," for a broadening of the government with the object of creating a unified policy. Claiming for himself a right to determine the general guidelines of the government without a vote of the Cabinet and of restructuring the personnel of the Cabinet in collaboration with the President, Wirth was indicating his intention of abandoning the policy of fulfillment and of realizing his wish to create a Great Coalition government. This would also mean the "concentration of economic forces," for "unless [increased] labor productivity is freely undertaken, the German people are no longer to be saved."[120]

Thus, Wirth was not only trying to broaden his government to the right, he was also moving personally to the right. This necessarily increased the already existing tension between himself and the SPD, a tension which had been growing for months as Wirth took an increasingly hard-line course on the reparations issues. There were also powerful pressures from within the Center Party to create a Great Coalition, especially from Christian trade-union chief Adam Stegerwald, who had supported the formation of a "working community of bourgeois parties faithful to the constitution" in July that

included the DVP and that was meant as a political counterforce to the developing block of Socialist parties.[121]

Just as the Social Democrats were becoming more sensitive to left-wing pressures through their union with the USPD, so Wirth was becoming more responsive to right-wing criticisms as he strove for a Great Coalition. He was turning very distrustful of Social Democratic leadership in economic affairs and became infuriated over the problems created by the Foreign Exchange Control Decree of October 12, remarking that its defects would have to be corrected even if this meant cutting off Hirsch's "antlers."[122] While Hirsch and Hilferding were basing their argument, among other things, on claims that the German balance of trade was relatively favorable at this time, Wirth was hearing that the German government agencies preparing the forthcoming Reparations Commission and foreign expert visits, especially the Foreign Office, were complaining bitterly about the inadequacies of the German trade statistics. They thought the unfavorable balance estimates were too low because the Reich Statistical Office was calculating export receipts in paper-mark values, had an inadequate means of determining the real value of imports, and was using the prewar techniques applicable to stable monetary conditions. Thus, on October 24, Wirth wrote a very personal letter to Economics Minister Schmidt, pointing out the important implications of this finding for German foreign and economic policy:

If our foreign trade statistics are false to that degree and if our balance of trade is passive to the extent that must be assumed after the results of these discussions, then the situation in a series of domestic and foreign questions must be seen completely differently. The question of the stabilization of the mark— even under the precondition of being freed of all cash reparations payments for a number of years—must be judged completely differently where there is such a passive balance of trade than when one uses the previous numbers as a basis. The question of the export levy and the import bans have to be evaluated upon another basis than before. I am seizing upon these questions only as examples; the foreign trade balance is of the greatest significance for our entire economic policy, and we have robbed ourselves of one of the most effective propaganda tools in the struggle to relieve our reparations burdens and against the Treaty of Versailles in that the horrifying situation of German foreign trade has remained unknown at home and abroad.[123]

This is a document of exceptional importance for both the long-run and the immediate evaluation of Wirth's policies. On the one hand, it is decisive evidence against the contention often made by the Allies that Germany was *deliberately* overstating its trade deficit since, if this were true, it would be impossible to explain why Wirth and others were becoming convinced that the trade deficit was being underestimated and calling on the Economics Minister to use his powers to improve the methods being employed by the Reich Statistical Office.[124] On the other hand, it helps to explain Wirth's great reluctance to accept the proposition that Germany could undertake effective stabilization measures autonomously as well as his willingness to openly turn his back on the fulfillment policy. It is important to recognize that Wirth's conclusion was a logical but not a necessary conclusion. An alternative was that provided by Moritz Bonn, who was willing to turn the statistical uncertainty into an argument for an interim solution. But if one drew the opposite conclusion, as did Wirth, then the logic of the position was to emphasize the importance of external assistance in the reparations negotiations and increased productivity in the domestic negotiations. The ultimate domestic political goal was to rally a Great Coalition for this purpose and thereby carry out this program on the basis of the political "concentration" for which Wirth was striving.

During the first week of November, Wirth sought to hold his government together and win the support of the DVP by pursuing a tactic of waiting upon the reports of the foreign experts. Thus, on November 4, a note was handed to the Reparations Commission taking the standard position that stabilization without a final reparations solution was impossible but that measures had to be taken to bring about a control of the depreciation through an international loan. The note also contained the promise of Reichsbank collaboration in such an effort, with the unstated assumption that the bankers would not provide the requested credit of five hundred million gold marks without a moratorium. In short, Wirth avoided asking for a moratorium, thereby annoying the French still

further because he assumed that the bankers would insist upon it. At the same time, he defended his dilatory tactic against Socialist criticism with the argument that he could hardly present a program to the Reparations Commission without having the report of the foreign experts.[125]

When Wirth learned the unexpected content of the no less unexpectedly divided findings of the experts, he chose to take what was most agreeable in the reports as the basis of German policy while at the same time deciding to put more stress on the need to pursue stabilization. Thus, he emphasized the criticism of Versailles in the Keynes–Cassel report and the call for a large foreign loan in the minority report while downplaying the argument that Germany could stabilize on its own. At the same time, he tried to get his potential allies on the right, especially in the DVP, to take a much more positive stance toward stabilization for practical political reasons. In Saxony, where state elections were held on November 5, the Communists had doubled their vote and, together with the United SPD, had the basis for a potential Marxist majority. Wirth brought the lesson home to the Reichsrat Foreign Affairs Committee on November 8:

The goal of German policy must be the stabilization of the mark. It is therefore very regrettable that many industrialists have lost their belief in the mark. In the Saxon electoral battle, this slogan played a great role. It was shown that a portion of the *Mittelstand*, which is expropriated by the depreciation of the mark, went with the left. At the same time he [Wirth] has fought strongly against the premature surrender of the Reichsbank gold wanted by many politicians on the left.[126]

The exacting question of how to deal with the Allies was thus complemented by the arduous task of forming a Great Coalition. The Social Democrats were arguing that they were willing to take "personalities" into the government who were economic experts connected with the DVP but were opposed to bringing the DVP officially into the government at the moment. Their fundamental concern was the known hostility of leading persons in the DVP, especially the industrialist wing, to the eight-hour day. On October 30, the party publicly declared that it could not accept a "laying hands on the eight-hour day" and declared the precondition for increasing production to be stabilization of the currency.[127] While taking the position that the DVP had to be brought into the government as a party, the government continued to suffer from the usual divisions between its more compromising and more militant elements, and much depended on the extent to which it could stress its moderate face and disarm the suspicions of the Socialists.

It was just at this point, however, that Stinnes chose to demonstrate that the misgivings of the Socialists were very well-founded. At the end of October, he was not only talking about his program of increasing productivity through longer hours and the dismantling of economic controls, but he was also beginning to pursue it actively in consultation with leading persons in the DNVP. Thus, he made contact with Helfferich and asked him to work together with another leading industrial representative, Quaatz, and the DNVP Deputy and iron and steel trade association official, Reichert, to "draft a complete change of the Versailles Treaty and at the same time to draw up the legislative changes which are necessary to bring about healthier conditions."[128] What was unknown could not hurt, but on November 9, 1922, the fourth anniversary of the German Revolution that had produced that achievement so precious to the Socialists—the eight-hour day—Stinnes chose to talk more openly about his program at a widely reported meeting of the Reich Economic Council. It was a speech which had the sanction of the RdI, and it must be understood as an integral part of a decision by individual industrialists and also their organizations to come out openly with that domestic economic "reform" program to which Stinnes had referred in his August meeting with Wirth on the de Lubersac accord.[129] Thus, it was sandwiched between two other events to which the worker parties and organizations were bound to respond with alarm. The first was a personal letter from August Thyssen to Wirth on October 14, 1922, which had been leaked to the public. Thyssen called upon Wirth to take the lead in the fight against the "undifferentiated eight-hour day," and branded it as "the greatest misfortune which the Revolution could bring to Germany."[130] The other was a lengthy two-day

meeting of the directors of the ZAG to discuss the crisis and the possibilities of cooperation. The idea of such a meeting had been raised by the trade unions in August but only achieved realization in the late fall. It had originally been scheduled for November 3–4 but was then put off to November 10–11 and was held at the Siemenshaus in Berlin. What all this meant was that the Stinnes speech was part of a steady diet of exposure to the economic program being developed by the RdI to deal with the crisis.

The speech itself was not only dramatic in its content, but also in its circumstances. Georg Bernhard began the meeting by reporting on the findings of the international experts, pointing out that they conformed to the recommendations made by RWR committees dealing with the stabilization problem and urging that a resolution be passed reporting the recommendations of the RWR to the press and urging the government to follow them and the corresponding advice of the international experts. Bernhard took the occasion to launch a scarcely veiled attack on Stinnes, arguing that while most industrialists were opposed to further depreciation (because it threatened to eliminate their capital), there were a few with an opposite interest whose activities attracted international attention. These persons,

who play a great role in industry and whose strongly creative industrial character I otherwise do not call into question, construct their great combinations and financial transactions by contracting extraordinary debts and that these debts, with which they buy real values to carry through their combinations, decrease in value as the inflation increases.[131]

Bernhard insisted that such individuals wished to stabilize the mark at as low a basis as possible in order to get rid of their own debts and increase their holdings, even if this involved the further immiseration of large numbers of German people.

Stinnes was absent at the time these remarks were made, but his cause was taken up by Frowein and Salomonsohn, the former insisting that Stinnes wanted stabilization as much as anyone else but that everyone had an interest in the mark not being stabilized at so high a level that there would be an economic crisis, while the latter charged Bernhard with vilifying Stinnes and praised Stinnes's patriotism.[132] Demands were made that the debate be broken off until Stinnes could arrive to defend himself. Bernhard sought to clarify his point by arguing that the real issue was the level at which stabilization would take place. Stinnes, in Bernhard's view, wished to lower that level by eliminating all subventions for food and rent controls, thereby reducing the real purchasing power of the mark within Germany and only then permitting stabilization to take place. It was in the midst of this debate over whether Stinnes had or had not been vilified by Bernhard and the latter's efforts to explain the real meaning of his attack that Stinnes himself arrived and began his address.

Stinnes was not the sort of person who said one thing in private and another in public if he could help it, and his remarks were made with his typical frankness and certainty as to the correctness of his diagnosis and solutions. After reminding everyone of how badly affected his enterprises had been by the outcome of the war, he went on to point out that the reconstruction was a practical question and that he was no dogmatist with respect to horizontal and vertical organization. Both had their purposes. He did not deny that some businesses were suffering more than others in the inflation or that those with larger means at their disposal and better connections at home and abroad were in a more favorable position to deal with the situation. They could hardly be expected to stand with "their arms folded" and wait upon events.[133]

In Stinnes's view, nothing could be more dangerous than to take measures which would prove useless in a few months and thereby to expose Germany to the Austrian danger of being taken over by foreign capital. As it was, foreigners were planning to buy up German property and industry according to his information. The best defense was to do something about Germany's production, which was twenty-two hundred million gold marks short of what was required to supply its needs domestically, let alone pay reparations. Stinnes argued this could only be done, on the one hand, through Germany terminating subventions and controls on its economy and, on the other, through the Allies recalling occupation troops from Germany and granting it equal trading rights

with other nations. Transcending these measures, however, was increased work through overtime, specifically, additional hours without overtime pay for the foreseeable future until Germany's balance of payments was such that it could take care of its own needs and also cover the interest and amortization on the international loan needed to stabilize the mark and cover a reduced reparations bill.

Stinnes was more than willing to discuss the calculations behind his opposition to stabilizing the mark at too high a level:

Now as to the level of the stabilization! Because of the monstrous sums of paper marks in circulation, it would mean, if we stabilized at too high a level, that we would be making a monumental contribution to foreigners since these foreigners have these marks in their pockets, and the higher one stabilizes, the higher the contributions to those who have purchased the marks relatively cheaply. We would above all, if we chose to bless the workers and civil servants, and all those who are on fixed wages with too high a stabilization at a time when the alleged advantages of the controlled economy are being lost, have to do something about those nominally high pay levels for which they had won in the form of weak paper marks. And since one cannot expect the kind of insight that would be needed for these levels not to be stubbornly defended, we will be involved in new wage struggles. The precondition for any successful stabilization in my opinion, is that strikes and wage struggles will be ruled out for a long time. If you want to launch a stabilization with strikes, then in my view the stabilization will be at an end in two months.[134]

From this perspective, Stinnes made no bones about his opposition to a "stabilization at any price." The eight-hour day could be kept, but the German workers had to suspend it as well as their right to strike until the economy was in order. The time had come to tell the German people they could not lose a war and work two hours less, and the time had come to stop the "palaver" and permit people like himself and Salomonsohn to do something more productive than hold speeches in the RWR. Similarly, one had to speak clearly and honestly to the Reparations Commission. Reparations and payments in kind to reconstruct the devastated areas could be made, but only if they were reduced to acceptable levels and if the other burdens of the Treaty were eliminated. If these things were done, and Germany were treated as an "enterprise," then it would be worthy of credit and its support could become part of that settlement of the outstanding economic issues left over by the war—a resolution of which Stinnes dreamed.

It was to Bernhard's great credit that he was able to challenge Stinnes after his remarkable performance and point out that they were dealing with a political and not simply an economic issue, that the world was composed of more than businessmen, that there were disagreements even among the latter as to the level at which stabilization should take place, that it was unclear from Stinnes's description if there really was any point at which stabilization could take place, and that the speculation had to end. Most relevant from the standpoint of the existing domestic political debate, Bernhard questioned the assumption that an international loan could simply be paid off by more work and pointedly asked if they could accept this proposition "as if the entire reparations loan had to be paid by the workers and as if the war had only been lost for the workers."[135]

The labor leaders present at this meeting and during the next two days of discussion in the ZAG in truth found it difficult to accept Stinnes's proposition that, on the one hand, it was not "prudent" to debate the eight-hour-day question but, on the other, that they had to realize that extending the hours of work was the only way in which the German workers could have a decent existence under existing circumstances.[136] Bücher and Fritz Tänzler of the VdA took Stinnes's line on both foreign and domestic political matters, and Stinnes repeated his arguments once again. The trade-union representatives were clearly on the defensive, the Christian leader Baltrusch showing more inclination to make concessions on the hours-of-work question by recognizing the need to move away from the "schematic" eight-hour day than his Socialist colleagues. His view that all modifications had to be done in collaboration with the trade unions was shared by the Socialists, who wished to maintain and strengthen labor's rights of co-determination. The Socialist trade-union leaders, however, were most insistent on the need for labor to protect itself through the controlled economy, whatever its faults, and through a rapid stabilization. They sharply criticized the manner in which certain classes had been able to protect themselves

against inflation and that those very groups were now demanding that labor sacrifice its own interests.[137]

While the lines were hardening, some important representatives on both sides at the level of the political parties were searching for a means of achieving collaboration in the ongoing domestic and international crisis. A small program committee had been set up on October 26 in which Hans von Raumer and Rudolf Hilferding played the chief roles, and it was able to come up with guidelines for the management of government expenditures and the budget. Most important, a compromise was worked out so that the eight-hour day was to be maintained in principle under Reichstag regulation while limited exceptions were to be allowed through contractual agreements between labor and industry or by sanction of the authorities.[138]

The recommendations of this committee formed the basis of the Reparations Note to the Allies of November 14, 1922, which was sent at the urging of Hermes and sought finally to provide the concrete proposals the Reparations Commission had long been demanding. The reports of the international experts were appended to the note. While continuing to argue that a genuine stabilization would not be possible unless there was a definitive reparations settlement, the German government for the first time accepted the proposition that a temporary action supporting the mark would be possible. Though the government persisted in its contention that foreign help was essential (thus adopting the position of the minority foreign) experts report on this issue, it did express a willingness to use the Reichsbank gold to back up the five hundred million gold-mark loan being sought. There was to be a three-year moratorium, although deliveries in kind were to continue, and the Reichsbank was to place its gold at the disposal of the loan provided that the Reparations Commission approved the repayment of the international loan as a primary obligation of the Reich. The exchange rate of the mark was then to be raised and regulated and an internal gold loan secured—half to be used to repay the international loan, the other half to pay reparations. The government was to balance the budget, cease presenting the Reichsbank with unfunded Treasury notes, introduce an austerity program, and increase productivity. Germany was to be granted commercial sovereignty on her western borders.[139]

Although the Reparations Note of November 14, which was to become the basis of German policy until the Ruhr occupation, contained significant concessions by Wirth and Havenstein to those who were arguing for stabilization measures based on the security of the Reichsbank's gold, it was not to serve as the policy foundation for the Great Coalition government which, in the persons of Raumer and Hilferding, had basically agreed on its principles. The decision and the direct responsibility for the failure to establish a Great Coalition government lay with the Social Democrats, whose Reichstag Deputies met on November 14 and decided they could not remain in a government in which the DVP was officially represented. Stinnes's speech of November 9 played no small role in this decision, and those opposed to the Great Coalition questioned whether people like Raumer and Stresemann would be capable of resisting the influence of Stinnes and the hard-liners in the DVP. While some Socialists, especially Prussian Minister President Otto Braun, warned that this would lead to a shift of the DVP to the right, the Socialists, despite Hilferding's cooperation with von Raumer, had their eyes on their critics to the left. The dilemma faced by the Socialists was most clearly stated by Rudolf Breitscheid in a private conversation shortly after the crisis. As the Hamburg lawyer Klügmann reported,

Dr. Breitscheid said that the time for a Great Coalition is not yet ripe. As much as he personally views collaboration with Dr. Stresemann and his wing to be possible, that party is unfortunately burdened by its right wing. On the other side too, the workers at this time do not yet have the necessary insight to understand a coalition with the German People's Party. Nevertheless, it is possible that the working masses themselves could press for such a collaboration in the foreseeable future. To my objection that the leaders have to lead the masses and not be led by them, he countered by noting the danger of these masses being radicalized as a result of the increased cost of living and the distress accompanying it. He repeatedly emphasized how extremely difficult it was for him and his party to calm down somewhat the agitation of the masses over [the party's] stance.[140]

Just as the ability of the SPD to overcome this resistance from within its ranks and enter a Great Coalition (especially after Stinnes's November 9 speech) must remain an open question, so, too, is it difficult to determine whether the moderates in the DVP could have overcome the growing intransigence of Stinnes and the fixing of the RdI on the Silverberg–Stinnes program. The reality was that the test would not be made.[141]

The SPD decision of November 14, coming hot on the heels of the promising situation of the previous day, left Wirth with the feeling he had no choice but to resign. It could be argued that his government had the majority necessary to stay on, and Wirth himself later blamed Stegerwald for having successfully put on so much pressure for a Great Coalition government that the option of continuing the existing government had been closed.[142] This tends to overlook Wirth's own suspicions of Hermes at the time, the difficulties he was having with Ebert, and his own bouts of exhaustion. It also neglected the rather brusque manner in which Wirth had presented the SPD with what was tantamount to an ultimatum to either join a Great Coalition or accept the consequences.[143] In the last analysis, however, the fall of Wirth reflected the deep division the hyperinflation had opened up in the relations between industry and labor and the increasing rigidification of their positions on the central problems of inflation and reparations. It can be argued that unless Wirth could achieve his ultimate goal of securing an external solution to the stabilization problem, the battle between the two sides supporting diametrically opposed internal stabilization measures would have to be fought out with all the dangers that would entail. Domestic political considerations dictated the need for an external solution. It can also be argued that Keynes, Bonn, Hirsch, Hilferding, and Bernhard were all fighting for a viable alternative that might have worked and that was very much worth risking in the light of what was happening and what was to follow. Its failure may have been overdetermined since it is difficult to see how such a program could have been carried through in the face of Wirth's deep belief that Germany had to have outside help for any stabilization, Havenstein's attachment to his gold, Stinnes's passionate conviction that only his program for domestic stabilization was acceptable, and a political, economic, and social environment that militated against rational decision making in the national interest. Nevertheless, the stabilization of 1923–1924 was to take place under even less propitious circumstances, and November 1922 may be viewed as the lost opportunity for stabilization that has genuine historicity.

Business at the Helm? The Policies of the Cuno Government

The man asked by Ebert to form a new government, Dr. Wilhelm Cuno, was no less anxious than his predecessor to avoid a deep domestic political conflict and to form a Great Coalition government. Like Wirth, he hoped that relief from abroad would provide a foundation for a final stabilization at home. Cuno had not begun his career as a businessman but rather as a civil servant, serving first in the Reich Treasury Office before taking over the leadership of the Reich Grain Bureau during the war. It was there that he was discovered by the then head of the Hamburg–America Line, Albert Ballin, who brought him into the company as a director at the end of 1917. When Ballin committed suicide in November 1918, Cuno became his successor. Although a Catholic from Thuringia, Cuno adapted to the Hamburg business community with great rapidity and was widely respected for his negotiating skills and valued for his Anglo-American contacts. Because of these qualities and experience, his name had often been raised for important government posts, first as Finance Minister to replace Erzberger in 1920 and then as Foreign Minister in the last months of the Wirth Cabinet. Ebert undoubtedly was particularly well disposed toward him. Cuno had been a strong supporter of Ebert's presidency and had openly and unequivocally accepted the Republic. This was a quality not often to be found in a businessman whose political sympathies were on the right. Although variously reported to have political views lying between the DVP and DNVP and between the Center and DVP, Cuno, who belonged to no party, was probably closest to the DVP in his positions and viewed politics from the perspective of a businessman. What that meant, as he told his colleagues in the RdI in early September 1922, was that they had to demand "*separation of the economy from politics. We should represent to the government with great vigor*

that our economic freedom of movement should not be constrained by politics. So long as we are dependent on a government in which there is no one who knows the economy, we cannot expect a recuperation to take place."[144]

If there was no small irony in Germany's next Chancellor arguing for the separation of the economy from politics, a task apparently only achievable by a businessman assuming the political leadership of the nation, it certainly would have been lost on Cuno and most of his fellow businessmen. Cuno's actual understanding of the manner in which a parliamentary democracy was supposed to function was minimal at best, and his basic conception was that of a government of "experts" supported by a broad coalition of parties. Where Wirth, who had an infinitely better sense of the political realities, failed, Cuno was hardly likely to succeed. The Center balked at his proposal to make Hermes Foreign Minister because of the dispute between Hermes and Wirth, while the SPD continued its resistance to a coalition with the DVP and was particularly insistent on the retention of Schmidt and Hirsch. If Cuno was anxious to do anything, it was to get the Economics Ministry into pro-business hands, however, and the effort to establish a Great Coalition thus failed.

All this left Cuno more disgusted with the parties than ever, but Ebert, who was angry with the SPD for not heeding his call to enter the Cabinet and who had been impressed with Cuno for some time despite political differences, would not let the putative Chancellor give up. Neither Ebert nor most of the parliamentary leaders were willing to run a new Reichstag election under existing conditions, and Cuno was encouraged to form a nonpartisan government of "experts," a "government of deeds" (*Regierung der Arbeit*), as he chose to call it, which was finally formed on November 22, 1922. Even this had not been easy. He had no luck in getting practicing businessmen to join his government, and his initial appointment of Karl Müller as Minister for Food and Agriculture produced a crisis only a few days after the Cabinet was formed when Müller was sharply attacked by the Social Democrats because of his opposition to the grain levy, and they threatened to expose his separatist connections in the occupied area. Müller was a right-wing Centrist closely associated with Catholic conservative agrarian leaders in the Rhineland. He had apparently suggested that the peasants could turn to the French authorities in their efforts to resist making their required grain deliveries.[145] His replacement was Hans Luther, the Mayor of Essen, who was to became a central figure in the history of Weimar politics and economics. The other "experts" in the new Cabinet were Frederic von Rosenberg, a career diplomat, as Foreign Minister; Groener, who was retained as Transport Minister; and Heinrich Albert, a career civil servant who had previously served in the Reich Chancellery, as Treasury Minister. The other members of the government were all party people ranging from the Center to the DVP—Brauns and Hermes, staying on in their posts; Rudolf Oeser of the DDP, taking over the Interior Ministry; Eduard Hamm, the Bavarian Democrat and former Bavarian Minister of Commerce, assuming the influential position of State Secretary in the Reich Chancellery; and two DVP Deputies, Rudolf Heinze as Justice Minister and Johannes Becker as Economics Minister. Of all these appointments, the most noteworthy and thus the most sharply criticized from the left was that of Becker, who had been a director of the Rheinstahl corporation, was considered a representative of heavy industry, and had been an outspoken advocate of ending economic controls.

It would be too simple to deduce from these appointments, however, that some major change in foreign and domestic policy was about to take place under the new government, that, as the far left claimed, Stinnes was in the saddle. Cuno's personal relationship with Stinnes had been strained over sharp differences concerning the reorganization of the shipping business, and Stinnes had quit the HAPAG Supervisory Board in 1921 because of these disagreements. Cuno was also closer to Bücher's view that the impulse for Germany's recovery had to come from foreign assistance than to Stinnes's narrow concentration on domestic economic reform and the hours-of-work question. Also, while Cuno and Becker could indeed be counted upon to support tendencies toward untrammeled economic liberalism in the RWM previously held in check by Schmidt and

Hirsch, Cuno's programmatic advice came from more moderate and politically astute sources, his colleague from the HAPAG Dr. Hasselmann, who was a member of the DVP, and Hamm, who had been a strong critic of business profiteering as Bavarian Commerce Minister.[146]

Both the political situation and the personnel surrounding Cuno, therefore, dictated a program that stressed continuity rather than policy change. This was especially evident in his foreign policy posture, which was based squarely on the German Reparations Note of November 14, although Cuno coupled this with a much more explicit appeal to Great Britain and the United States to support a reasonable final reparations settlement so as to make Germany truly worthy of credit. He adopted Wirth's "first bread, then reparations" slogan. Similarly, while Cuno emphasized the need for reduction of expenditures and other budget-balancing measures along with more effective tax collection and the increase of industrial and agricultural productivity, he also promised to assist the needy, protect the small craftsman and businessman against cartels and trusts, and keep wages in line with prices. In sum, Cuno presented a program which the bourgeois parties could support and the SPD could tolerate despite reservations about Becker and concerns about the right wing of the DVP.[147]

Beneath the surface of this massive effort at accommodation, however, lay a continuity in the tactical paralysis that had so hampered the Wirth government in dealing adequately with the reparations problem as well as differences of opinion that made the new regime a most unpromising vessel in which to negotiate the increasingly stormy international and domestic waters. Few thought Cuno would remain in power very long. It was not simply a matter of trying to deal with the different views of the parties; the parties themselves were divided. In the DDP, for example, Moritz Bonn openly associated himself with a position very close to that of the Social Democrats, whom he credited with "getting things rolling." The problem, he insisted, was a "political," not a "technical," one, and it was necessary for the Germans to "turn the tables" by presenting their own reparations plan along with a moratorium effort so that they could get the loan they needed. From this perspective, he was sorry that the former government had not developed a plan even before the foreign experts came. It was not that Bonn thought that Germany could solve its problems alone, but rather that he believed that outside help needed the inspiration of German initiatives:

A temporary stabilization of the mark can only take place if we gain a breathing space and hold the mark at its previous level. Then we can turn all the forces and views around, which have previously worked against us. With respect to our currency, we find ourselves in a ring, which can only be broken from the outside, and that to be sure only by getting the outside world to believe in Germany's future. Then the balance of payments and also the balance of trade will be turned around. This process of transformation will not be easy. It will lead to interruptions in economic operations. This problem is not to be approached from the side of the eight-hour day, but rather from the currency side. If we get the moratorium, then we should set all our forces working for a stabilization of the mark. If we do not get that, then everything is finished. We should only view the moratorium as a means to an end, and we should work out not only one but many detailed plans for the stabilization action. The decision does not lie with us, but with the others. We should prepare things in such a way that a negative decision will become impossible.[148]

This point of view was contested by Deputy Gothein, who was close to industrial interests and who argued that the entire problem was as "statistical" as it was "psychological." The balance of payments, Gothein insisted, had to be straightened out, and this could only be done by increasing productivity, reintroducing large wage differentials, reducing the number of civil servants, and liberating the economy from controls.[149]

It would be too simple, however, to treat this difference of opinion purely in terms of the conflict between industry and labor. Bonn was no Social Democrat, and the disagreement between himself and Gothein was not over the desirability of higher productivity and the reintroduction of wage differentials but rather over the point of departure to be taken in dealing with the problems of stabilization and reparations. Fundamentally, it was an argument between those who emphasized finances and those who emphasized economic production in dealing with these issues. Thus, when the Stin-

nes concern director Osius was asked by the new Foreign Minister Rosenberg what Stinnes thought about the participation of bankers as official experts in projected negotiations with the Allies, Osius reported to Stinnes that "in my answer I clearly emphasized the primary [significance] of the productive economy [*Produktionswirtschaft*] against the secondary significance of the financial side [*Finanzwirtschaft*], and showed on the basis of previous developments (the neutral experts, etc.) what kinds of dangers arise when finance is granted a dominant influence on questions which in the first instance involve production."[150] This should not be construed as a demonstration of some clear division of opinion between industry and banking or of unanimity within the ranks of the one or the other.[151] The actual condition was one of disarray, a situation that was to make Cuno's efforts to deal with the reparations and stabilization by the method of calling upon the support of the leading members of the business community well-nigh impossible.

It is, to be sure, important to recognize that the international situation was anything but stable and that the Germans did not face a world of objectivity and rationality. Poincaré certainly did nothing to make an international settlement based on financial principles any easier. Thus, when the Dutch banker Vissering and his Swiss colleague Dubois went off to Paris in mid-November to persuade Poincaré to accept the German Reparations Note of November 14 and to reconvene the Reparations Commission's Bankers' Committee and to do so quickly so as to include J. P. Morgan, who was then in Europe, Poincaré used an interpellation in the French parliament to state (subsequently naming Morgan explicitly) that there was no hurry since the bankers could be brought in to meet any time they were wanted. The obvious implication was that Morgan and the bankers would always be there if there was money to be made and that this was the extent of their interest in helping out with the reparations problem. This certainly was unfair to Vissering and Dubois, the first of whom was not only worried about the Netherlands' large holdings in increasingly worthless marks but was also concerned about the number of Germans flooding over the border seeking food or a more peaceful political atmosphere. Dubois also feared a domestic collapse in Germany. He felt that the German Revolution of 1918 had a bad influence on Switzerland, and he did not want it repeated. Most of all, Poincaré infuriated Morgan, who was very sensitive about the motives attributed to him. When Vissering and Dubois managed to engineer the scheduling of a meeting between Poincaré and Morgan for November 22, Morgan indicated that he did not feel there was any point in coming to Paris unless the French Premier accepted the basic principles of the Bankers' Committee laid down in June, whereupon Poincaré claimed he could not see Morgan because of a Cabinet meeting. Manifestly, the advice of international bankers was not as eagerly sought in Paris as in Berlin. A doubly piqued Morgan sailed home on November 24, while Vissering and Dubois left Paris hoping that Poincaré's fall would not be far off.

It is difficult, however, to see exactly what wonders Poincaré's departure would have wrought. President Millerand was, if anything, more belligerent than the Premier himself, and the opposition to Poincaré was directed against his domestic rather than his foreign policies. Furthermore, the international constellation was relatively favorable. Mussolini was likely to support energetic action, and the Belgians were unlikely to resist them. The new British Conservative government and its Foreign Minister Bonar Law were more sympathetic to France than its predecessor and keenly annoyed by incidents involving the harassment of Allied disarmament inspectors in Stettin, Passau, and Ingolstadt. While hardly likely to be supportive of a Ruhr occupation, the critics of German policy in the Foreign Office could be expected to gain in influence. Two developments at the end of November were indicative of the direction in which events were moving. On the one hand, the British agreed in the Reparations Commission not to press for an immediate consideration of the German stabilization plan in return for a French agreement not to ask that Germany be declared in default on her timber and coal deliveries. On the other hand, the French Cabinet decided on November 27 to occupy the Ruhr rather than negotiate should the Germans be declared in default and instructed the French

Ambassador in London to request that the projected Brussels meeting be held no later than December 15 and that the Allied Prime Ministers meet before that date to coordinate policy.[152]

Bergmann, who was being sent around Allied capitals at this time to keep the government informed and to test new proposals, could thus only report bad news from Paris. The members of the Reparations Commission were at a loss as to how to advise Germany, insofar as they had any interest in giving Germany any advice at all. The Belgian delegate Delacroix wondered if Cuno could not use his influence with industry to get the help needed for a temporary stabilization of the mark, a possibility Bergmann rejected so long as it was not coupled with a moratorium that would last a few years. The American observer Boyden went so far as to argue that any plan presented by the Germans would be rejected because of the mere fact that it was German and fatalistically suggested that Germany simply declare that it was the task of the victors in the war to come up with an acceptable plan. While Bergmann thought Boyden's perceptions had considerable validity, he did not think Germany could run the risk of being presented with plans involving varieties of sanctions. Bergmann's gloomy report was supplemented by another from Max Warburg, who transmitted a personal letter he had received from Keynes indicating that "the German Government is psychologically mistaken in putting foreign assistance in the forefront of their plan," as had been done in the German Reparations Note of November 14, and that the bankers could only be expected to help if the Germans first helped themselves. Keynes also warned against trying to support the mark simply by interventions. A genuine maintenance of the exchange rate decided upon was necessary.[153]

As rumors and reports of the French preparing to act in the Ruhr increased during the last week in November and the first week in December, it became obvious to Cuno that Germany had to present something to the London meeting of the Allied leaders. He seized upon what appeared to be a very promising plan by the Deutsche Bank director Wassermann, which had been submitted to Hermes and concerning which Delacroix had responded with interest in his conversations with Bergmann.

Wassermann considered a stabilization of prices and thus of the currency necessary in order to maintain order and secure the food supply in Germany, a stabilization that was to take place "at a level corresponding to the internal depreciation of the mark."[154] Wassermann considered a stabilization impossible without the suspension of cash payments and deliveries in kind, especially of coal, the importation of which had cost 29.8 billion paper marks during the previous nine months, and also a "suspension of the unbearable occupation of the Rhineland." At the same time, the Allies had to be offered an "equivalent." Something also had to be done to show that Germany was willing to take seriously Allied "slogans" concerning German capital flight and demands for the use of the Reichsbank's gold resources to stabilize. This was all the more necessary because the Allies were likely to raise impossible demands in Brussels, while Germany could expect little by way of foreign loans and then only at unacceptable conditions. He was trying to provide "a proposal from our side to the Entente at a suitable moment which will at least demonstrate our goodwill to bring about a settlement."

The Wassermann proposal was for the Reich to issue gold bonds bearing 4 percent interest plus .5 percent of the original value each year, the entire issue to be amortized over a period of fifty-one years. They were to be guaranteed by the customs receipts of the Reich. A portion of the bonds were to be given to the Allies in place of the reparations to be paid during a projected two-year moratorium. While recognizing the desirability of keeping this amount as low as possible in the expectation of a reduced final reparations settlement, Wassermann argued that something had to be done to satisfy French needs for cash to deal with their difficult financial situation. Therefore, he suggested a maximum of one and a half billion per year in bonds for the coming two years. While the amount of bonds available to the Allies in place of reparations was to be limited, the second portion of the bonds, which were to be unlimited in quantity and amount, were to be placed on the domestic German market and could be bought for foreign currency or assets denominated in foreign currency. The proceeds from the sale of the gold bonds marketed in Germany were to be retained to a maximum of one and a half billion marks and used to balance the budget and stabilize the currency. Receipts in excess of this amount were to be given to the Allies as reparations with the understanding that for each billion gold marks so paid, Germany would receive a one-year extension of her moratorium. Wassermann felt this a fair return for the advantages of receiving cold cash instead of bonds.

A major purpose of the Wassermann plan, of course, was to lure back such German capital as had flown abroad or was being hoarded in Germany for purposes of capital flight or tax evasion. Real incentives, therefore, had to be provided. One of these was that the bonds given the Allies be indistinguisable from the bonds sold at home, thus making it possible for both non-Germans and Germans to market the bonds on an equal basis. A second even more important incentive was to make the entire bond issue free of taxation, especially the capital gains, income, and inheritance taxes, for all time. This was tantamount to an amnesty for past tax evasion as well as a nullification of taxes that might have been owing, and it was to be guaranteed by a restoration of the secrecy of bank accounts and cancellation of the requirement that all securities and liquid assets be placed on deposit in a bank.

Whatever the morality of ensuring that the rich remained rich and that those who had protected themselves against both inflation and taxation would be guaranteed their gains, the Wassermann plan unquestionably had advantages for Germany in that these gains would be put in the service of the nation in a very advantageous manner. In contrast to earlier proposals for seeking a loan abroad, Wassermann's proposal relieved Germany of the need to beg for such a loan. In fact, Wassermann suggested that Germany could ride piggyback on Allied efforts to market the bonds in order to pay cash, and, since the reparations bonds and the domestic bonds would be indistinguishable, Allied guarantees of the bonds would have to cover bonds held by German nationals as well. They would thus be acting indirectly in the interest of Germany. Under such circumstances, in Wassermann's judgment, even the use of the

Reichsbank gold for purposes of assisting the stabilization effort would no longer be dangerous.

Both the Wassermann plan and the upcoming conference of Prime Ministers in London provided the first test of whether the presence of a businessman at the helm of German affairs would create the cooperation between government and industry so lacking under Cuno's predecessors. The results were anything but encouraging. Originally, Cuno seems to have contemplated meeting with representatives of the various interest groups but then decided to refrain from holding such a meeting before presenting a new reparations offer to the London gathering. Instead, he asked Hermes to inform some bankers, Becker to speak to industrialists, and Rosenberg to confer with some leading Socialists. This approach was productive of both rumors and misunderstandings, especially with Stinnes, who along with Silverberg and Peter Klöckner, had been empowered to negotiate in Paris concerning the coal problem and other economic issues. When Cuno and Becker held a meeting with Stinnes and Reusch on December 6, neither of the government leaders had said a word about the Bergmann mission, although Becker had hinted at a possible German offer to the Entente. The Bergmann mission also had not been mentioned in a meeting which followed on the same evening between Foreign Minister Rosenberg and Stinnes, in which "reparations, a more active German foreign policy, a German–Austrian customs union and . . . the denationalization of the railroads" were discussed.[155]

When on the next day, stories were circulating in the press that Bergmann had been sent on a special mission to make a government offer and that Stinnes stood behind such an action, Stinnes composed a furious letter to Cuno stating that while the management of the government was the business of the Chancellor and Cabinet, he had a right to demand honesty as "a man who had placed himself and his connections at the service of the fatherland in its distress" and that "what happened last evening, or better said what failed to be said was dishonest and misleading."[156] Similar letters were addressed to Rosenberg and Becker. If these remarkable documents were not sent officially,

but only handed to Becker privately for his information, it was because Becker had gotten wind of the problem, assured Stinnes that he had been instructed to inform Stinnes and had already informed Vögler, and made clear that he had been waiting for a suitable moment to discuss the question with Stinnes himself. Nevertheless, Stinnes was only somewhat mollified. He told Becker

with all clarity that he can only go along with a policy of which he is precisely aware and which provides for a final solution. If the government, which has the right to determine policy, wants to go in other directions, as for example, to propagate the Wassermann ideas, then it must provide timely and full information [to the industrialists being asked to negotiate for the government] so that it does not put those people in a situation where they either have to act against their convictions or to refuse to collaborate in a critical moment, possibly even with a public statement of the fact that their own government has deceived them.

Stinnes made it clear that he "had more to lose than a portfolio" and that he could not tolerate being kept in the dark after he had placed his person at the disposal of the government.[157]

If this was an extraordinarily arrogant way to treat one's government, especially on the part of the leading representative of a group that was constantly complaining about the government's "lack of authority," the basic point made by Stinnes was, nevertheless, well-taken thanks to the by now internationally recognized dependence of the German government on industry which Stinnes had done so much to create. When Bergmann confidentially presented the Wassermann proposal to Bradbury and Bemelmans prior to its formal presentation to the Allied Prime Ministers meeting in London on December 9–11, the Reparations Commission members immediately pointed out that the plan, in addition to offering too low an interest rate on the bonds in their view, had the major weakness of nowhere giving assurance that German industry stood behind it. Cuno's response demonstrated that he was coming to think a bit more about the complexities of the relationship between business and politics. Bergmann was instructed to say that "under existing conditions, the solution of the reparations question is only thinkable under the strong leadership of the government. The prior asking of all the economic factors has previously always ended up with no results because of the conflicting views. We must therefore renounce consulting all circles without distinction before taking each step."[158] Since the Wassermann plan involved an interim solution of a largely financial and banking nature, he had consulted the bankers and could count on their support. When the time came for a discussion of a final reparations solution, he would consult with industry. In Cuno's view, it was understandable that industry would be reluctant to participate or show much enthusiasm for interim solutions, and there was not enough time to persuade them under existing circumstances.

Cuno was learning, however, that this was shaky logic. On December 11, after the Allied Prime Ministers had turned down the German proposal, Stinnes's *Deutsche Allgemeine Zeitung* (*DAZ*) made a point of declaring that industry had never been consulted and was opposed to the plan and that industry could only support a plan involving a final reparations settlement. The article provoked a storm of protest against Stinnes and German industry, which was accused of betraying rather than helping the government out of its great difficulties. On the following day, Cuno used the occasion of a speech before the Reich Economic Council to declare that "the relation of economic circles to the government should be that the government leads and business supports the government. There is here no power factor, no center of power in the economy which is strong enough to take the leadership out of our hand."[159] The manner in which the incident ended suggested otherwise. Thus, concern over domestic attacks on the reliability of the DVP members of the Cabinet and, above all, about the international impression led to a "clarification," agreed upon between Foreign Minister Rosenberg and Stinnes's press man Humann, stating that industry had been willing to cooperate despite the fact that it had not been informed. Stinnes made a point of informing his most important colleagues that this was an "agreed upon game."[160] Similarly, the president of the RdI, Sorge, hastened to declare that the *DAZ* was not speaking for the RdI, which stood behind the Chancellor. The reality was, however, that Cuno himself had felt forced to assure all and sundry in his RWR speech that every

relevant interest would be consulted about German reparations proposals and expressed his own support for a final solution even if interim measures might be necessary. In the last analysis, Cuno did not seem to be able to count much more on industry's support than his predecessor.

Fundamentally, the Germans were right back where they had started after the meeting of Prime Ministers in London, except that the situation had become more dangerous. The Germans had proposed the Wassermann plan as an alternative to securing a foreign loan and as a four- to five-year interim solution and had coupled it with a call for an end to all trade discrimination against Germany. While the Allies, as usual, were unable to agree on a program of their own in London, they at least had no trouble rejecting the German proposal. The English and Belgians found it more promising than the French, but they all agreed that it did not provide sufficient security and guarantees. The German plan *was* more of a step forward in the sense that Cuno had gone even further than Wirth in offering to undertake stabilization measures autonomously, but the political constellation was increasingly unfavorable for the Germans. The British were anxious to bring about a Near Eastern settlement at the forthcoming Lausanne conference and thus toned down their differences with the French, although those differences certainly were there. Poincaré was refusing to accept any reduction of German obligations unless they were complemented by a reduction of French obligations to England and the United States or the acceptance of the C bonds provided for under the London Ultimatum in place of regular French debt payments. He would not hear of a domestic German loan that involved tax benefits for the German capitalists, to whose machinations and resistance he attributed Germany's failure to pay reparations, and declared that any moratorium would have to be coupled with control over the German budget and productive guarantees made readily available by the occupation of Essen and Bochum.[161]

As always, the British opposed measures of compulsion and, to show goodwill, indicated a willingness to forgo the German and Italian debts in return for a sensible settlement. Insofar as the latter was concerned, they adopted a new plan by the ever-inventive Bradbury. The plan called for the cancellation of the bonds provided for under the London Ultimatum and a setting of the German debt at fifty billion marks, including occupation costs. The German government was to issue immediately bonds in this amount bearing an interest of 5 percent. Germany was to receive a four year moratorium, after which it was to begin paying two billion a year for the next four years, and then two and a half billion for the next two years, after which it was to pay either three and a third billion or two and a half billion depending on whether an arbitration commission composed of representatives of Germany, England, and one neutral state decided it would be in a position to pay the estimated seventeen billion in back interest on the debt in its annuities. In return for the moratorium and this arrangement, Germany would be required to stabilize the mark within six months and balance its budget within two years, while an Allied and neutral control council would be given extensive supervisory powers over Germany's fiscal policies. At the same time, Germany would be freed of all fear of sanctions so long as it was not found in violation of these obligations.[162]

This plan, which was soon to be renamed the Bonar Law plan, was conveyed by Bergmann to Cuno on December 11 with Bradbury's urging that the Germans adopt and present it to the Allies themselves, a procedure which Bergmann questioned on the grounds that the French would turn down anything that the Germans suggested. At the same time, Bergmann urged Cuno to give the plan a "careful examination" and, should it prove at all acceptable, to give it precedence over any German proposal since "Sir John, with his egotism, will strongly fight against every independent German plan because he considers his plan to be much better than any other under all circumstances."[163] While the Allied intention of meeting in Brussels on December 15 was abandoned, a decision was made in London to meet in Paris on January 2, and the French were indicating a willingness to compromise on certain issues, such as their demand for an occupation of German cities in order to achieve an agreement. The Germans, therefore, faced a new deadline to come up with proposals of their own, and once again Cuno had to find a suitable solution as rumors of impending French action in the Ruhr grew.

The situation at the end of 1922 was a telescoped version of that which had existed in the months prior to the London Ultimatum. The German government then, as at this time, had found itself wrestling with the question of choosing between temporary and permanent solutions, trying to come up with an acceptable reparations figure, calculating that one or the other of the Anglo-American great powers would come to their rescue, trying to make policy in the face of severe domestic differences and tensions, and encouraging private negotiations between German and French industrialists as a basis for settling the outstanding differences between the two countries. The situation in late 1922, however, was much more threatening. The 1922 crisis was taking place in the context of hyperinflation, not relative stabilization or even galloping inflation, and it seemed as if the country were on the verge of severe internal unrest and possible dissolution. Reports were streaming in concerning French machinations in the occupied areas, separatist activity, and mounting social unrest. Anxiety over a French invasion was thus coupled with a growing feeling in some quarters that the existing occupation was becoming totally intolerable and calls for a more active government policy to eliminate it.[164] Oddly enough, the disunity among the Allies had taken a turn which also made the situation more threatening to Germany at the turn of 1922–1923 than it had been during the previous two years. For political and financial reasons, the French were more inclined than ever before to act on their own, while Britain could no longer be counted upon to constrain France by operating in concert with it, as had been the case with the sanctions of March 1921 and the London Ultimatum, or by employing the sort of pressure used by Lloyd George at the end of 1921 and during the first months of 1922. Belgium could not be expected to resist France, while all that could be anticipated from Mussolini was noisy inactivity on the side of France.

Beginning in mid-December, Cuno undertook a two-pronged effort to meet the challenge of this unhappy situation. On the one hand, he sought to involve the United States financially and politically in an effort to solve the reparations problem and ward off French action; on the other, he tried to develop a reparations program for presentation to the Paris meeting of the Allies scheduled for the first days of the new year. In both cases, he worked in close consultation with Germany's business leadership.

Thus, on December 12, Stinnes met with Cuno, Rosenberg, and Becker to discuss instructing Ambassador Wiedfeldt to approach J. Pierpont Morgan about assuming the leadership of an international bank consortium that would give Germany a large enough loan over the course of the coming four years to cover the costs of stabilizing the mark as well as all reparations and other obligations under the Treaty of Versailles "so that Germany will become a free state again."[165] No definite sum was to be asked for, but Wiedfeldt was instructed to indicate an amount of ten billion gold marks. Wiedfeldt also was to inquire as to what kind of security Morgan would think appropriate and, without making any offers, to let drop that "it is not impossible to provide properly managed railroads as a basis, perhaps even to come up with a guarantee of a surplus for these railroads on the part of industry insofar as it has the dominant influence on their operation."[166] The negotiations for this loan were to be conducted with Paris because of the connection with the Treaty of Versailles. Stinnes also seems to have persuaded the government to couple this inquiry with a further question for Morgan concerning Stinnes's pet scheme for European economic reconstruction; namely, whether Morgan would be

willing simultaneously with or immediately after these negotiations ... to negotiate in the United States concerning a second loan which would have to be guaranteed by certain international industries (e.g. coal, iron, steel) and the proceeds of which would be designated to serve the purpose of the great work of reconstruction, so necessary and useful from an economic point of view, in Central Europe and South East Europe and to abate for a number of years the difficulties of unemployment, which otherwise would become unbearable?[167]

It is most unlikely that Cuno thought that these proposals would be taken up immediately by Morgan or that they would have much practical meaning for the upcoming meeting in Paris, although it is very probable that Stinnes pinned much greater hopes on their short-term

promise. Rather, Cuno was probably fishing for the naming of a sum by the world's leading banker that he could then use in the formulation of the German plan. Whatever the case, Morgan refused to be drawn into such schemes or intentions and responded with the position he had been stating since June; namely, that the question of a loan could only be discussed when the politicians had settled on a fixed reparations sum. At the same time, he expressed distaste for the idea of a world reconstruction syndicate, which he characterized as the "dreams of a distant future."[168]

There were dreams entertained by American leaders at this time to which Cuno could appeal, however—for example, a settlement of European differences under American guidance. Cuno was well aware that one of the chief barriers to a settlement with France and to relief from the occupation of German territory was the French desire for security. Cuno, therefore, asked Wiedfeldt to inform Secretary of State Hughes that Germany was prepared to sign a thirty-year nonaggression pact with the powers interested in Germany's western borders under American guarantee along with an agreement that no war would be fought except on the basis of a referendum by the people. If the effort to pander to Ambassador Houghton's frequently reiterated call for a "people's referendum to end war" was transparent, the proposal fell on fruitful ground because the American government was becoming more and more concerned both about unilateral French action and, like the British, about the alternative danger of a Franco-German economic accommodation at the expense of the Anglo-American powers. The Cuno proposal, therefore, was transmitted to the French, who promptly rejected it and thereby drove Hughes to be even more forward in suggesting America's willingness to assume a leadership role. In a speech to the American Historical Association in New Haven on December 29, 1922, Hughes offered to help solve Europe's economic and reparations problems by providing expert opinion on German capacity to pay and a new reparations settlement if the Europeans would agree in advance to accept the recommendations given.[169]

It was, however, much too early for the ideas that were to develop into the Dawes Plan and

Locarno Treaty, just as it was too late for the kind of thinking that went on among the experts summoned by Cuno to assist in formulating a proposal for the Allied conference in Paris. The bankers who met on December 13 and were then joined by leading industrialists on December 16 and at subsequent meetings on December 21 and 28,[170] for example, consumed a remarkable amount of time discussing whether or not Germany should make the end of the Rhineland occupation a condition of any offer. In general, the bankers, especially Cologne banker Louis Hagen, recognized that this was a political rather than an economic issue and that Germany was likely to get nowhere with the Allies in asking for anything more than an improvement of the conditions of the occupation, a view shared by two of the industrialists from the occupied area, Carl Duisberg and Julius Flechtheim of the Köln-Rottweil AG, as well as Hermann Bücher of the RdI. Nevertheless, Franz Urbig of the Disconto-Gesellschaft did break ranks with his fellow bankers on this as on other issues and joined Reusch, Klöckner, and Silverberg in arguing that economic recovery was impossible without ending the occupation provisions of the Treaty. Reusch was perhaps most insistent, claiming that the continuation of the occupation would wear down the population of the Rhineland to the point where they would accept separatism and that south Germany, with which he had close contact, would then follow. In some contradiction to the negotiations Stinnes was conducting with French industrialists, Reusch, who also favored economic negotiations with French industry, and Klöckner reminded Hermes and Becker, who represented the government in the discussions, that the industrialists had made the end of the Rhineland occupation a condition of economic negotiations. In the end, Hermes, with Becker's support, pointed out that while an end of the occupation might be the condition of some economic agreement, the financial offer under discussion involved the "life of the nation" and could not be prejudiced by such a precondition.[171]

This was not the only point at which the political analyses of the participants contrasted oddly with the realities of the situation. Although the "Bonar Law plan" devised by Brad-bury was condemned by almost everyone, including Bergmann, who cautiously urged that some effort might be made to include aspects of it to please the British, Urbig used the occasion of the discussion of the plan to launch into an anti-British tirade in which he claimed that the plan reflected England's goal of at once preventing Germany from ever becoming a serious competitor again while ensuring that Germany could manage to buy British products. Silverberg was also suspicious of the British, arguing that they only resisted a French occupation of the Ruhr because they feared French competition and that England was the actual driving force in the reparations issue because it wanted to keep Germany dependent on English coal. He echoed the argument that Stinnes had been making since 1918 that the French would be driven to an economic understanding because of their dependence on German coal and excess capacities in Lorraine. While this last point had an important element of truth, even if it was of secondary importance to those who were making the decisions in Paris, the most bizarre political intimation was made by the otherwise sober and constructive Melchior, who noted that Hamburg colonial circles were suggesting that Germany might be able to pay more if it were given back the administration of some of its colonies since it was "certain that Germany could get more out of these than their present owners."[172]

A more serious subject of discussion, even if not of immediate relevance to the matter at hand, was the question of increasing worker productivity. Urbig, Reusch, and Klöckner all justified their positions on both trying to end the Rhineland occupation and securing a reparations settlement that was low and definitive with the argument that the workers would never increase their productivity so long as they thought they were working for the Allies and not Germany itself. Thus, Reusch argued that "a definitive solution is the only possible way, since we must know when we would stop having to pay. To a great extent, the laziness into which the German people have fallen after this war is to blame for the collapse of the mark that has created such difficult conditions for us. But this laziness cannot be eliminated if the people do not have a goal before themselves."[173] The idea that the workers would accept longer hours if they were convinced about the goal was one that Stinnes had also propagated as late as the previous month, and it was thus of no small significance that his ally Silverberg did not share this optimism at the meeting. Silverberg saw the situation "darkly" because of the negative attitude of the workers and did not "believe that higher productivity is to be expected when one provides a goal for the increased productivity." The latest negotiations in the Reich Economic Council seemed to show this in Silverberg's view, and he reiterated his program of giving paramount importance to "the solution of domestic problems" by urging that it was necessary to negotiate at the same time on financial, economic, and occupation questions. But "hand in hand" with such efforts had to be a change in the hours of work "so that the German economy will be freed of all the chains in which it has been placed during the last four years."[174]

Silverberg admitted that these problems could not be solved by January 2, which prompted the undoubtedly irritated Hermes to argue that time was being lost by such ruminations and that it was necessary to concentrate on what could be done in preparation for the Paris meeting. Duisberg, who agreed with Silverberg that the workers and unions did not yet realize the need for longer hours but who shared Reusch's view that they had to be given a goal, also argued that the question facing them was primarily political and that the primary target of negotiation had to be France. When it came to a concrete offer containing financial terms, however, Duisberg was no more able than any of his colleagues to suggest a plan likely to satisfy the Allies. There was much confused discussion as to whether Germany should offer a "definitive" or a "provisional" reparations plan, which ran parallel to an argument over whether it should pay annuities or raise a fixed sum in a loan and which were periodically punctuated by suggestions from Melchior and Bücher that a provisional solution could show the way toward a definitive solution. Coherence was not served by the fact that Wassermann first argued that an international loan was unattainable and then, a few days later, when he apparently began to realize that the danger of a

Ruhr occupation was real, enthusiastically supported a Duisberg–Flechtheim proposal for periodic international reparations loans guaranteed by the mines, forests, and railroads of the Reich. A fifteen billion mark loan would be raised immediately, thus satisfying France's need for cash. The subsequent payment of reparations would then be pegged to Germany's ability to get international credit. There was some recognition of the fact that both England and France would only accept a figure of at least fifty billion rather than the twenty billion dominating the discussions, while it was pointed out that the present value of Bradbury's plan was really twenty billion if one took his projected discount rate of 8.33 percent into account. Still, there was also strong feeling that Germany should only offer what it could really pay, and everyone agreed on how ill-advised was the previous practice of making concessions once negotiations had started. The high point of compromise with political reality was provided by Melchior, who suggested that they start with fifty billion but then subtract what Germany had already paid and issue a loan at 2.5 percent. It was to be paid off in annuities varying between a billion and 2.4 billion over a fifty-year period.[175]

As so often was the case when there was confusion in the ranks of the businessmen, Stinnes was able to gain the advantage by coming up with a coherent program and train of thought. On December 20, Cuno met with the leaders of the RdI, after which a committee composed of Bücher, Hagen, Melchior, Silverberg, Stinnes, and Urbig was formed to write up a proposal. It met the next day and came up with a majority report that was in substantial part a verbatim rendition of ten points produced earlier by Stinnes. It contrasted markedly in content and tone with the results of the expert discussions formulated by Hermes after their meeting on December 16. At the earlier date, the majority of the experts took the position that Germany had to pursue an active reparations policy that would seek a three- to four-year moratorium and a temporary solution as the path to a final one. The government was urged to develop a plan that would also offer political, financial, and economic guarantees to France and that would actively promote economic negotiations. It was then to consult with the experts about this plan. The most disputed point of Hermes's summary on December 16 had been the question of whether or not to make the termination of the Rhineland occupation as a condition of any plan, and here, Hermes and Becker had held firm against Reusch and Klöckner.[176]

The Stinnes-inspired majority report of December 21 took an entirely different tack and seemed intended to spare the government the need to develop a plan. It began with the proposition that the German economy was in a state of steady deterioration, which made Germany incapable of making any payments until the deterioration was ended and the economy was made productive and could produce a surplus. For "economic and psychological reasons," such a state of affairs could only come about if Germany had "economic and political freedom," and this required the "wiping out (Abgeltung) of all the economic and financial burdens arising from the Treaty of Versailles." This could only be achieved by the payment of the final sum of fifteen billion marks, which was to bear no more that 5 percent interest and 1 percent amortization, and Germany was not to pay more than nine hundred million marks a year. To satisfy the needs of the Allies and fulfill its function, this sum had to be found as soon as possible, and this could only be done by means of an international loan guaranteed primarily by a first mortgage on the German railroad system. Further guarantees and the guarantee of the productivity of the railroad system "on the part of German business" were to be negotiated with those granting the loan. Finally, there were to be negotiations for a restructuring of international commercial and economic relations as well as consideration of the ways and means necessary to pay off the international loan and stabilize the mark. These, obviously, were veiled references to the granting of most-favored-nation status to Germany and to the implementation of the Silverberg program for the elimination of the eight-hour day and economic controls.[177]

All this, of course, was the Stinnes program at the time of the industrial credit offer in the fall of 1921 redivivus. On only one point did Stinnes's colleagues on the majority drafting committee deviate from his proposals, and that was to leave out his call for direct economic negotiations between French and German heavy industry for a long-term compromise in their mutual interests. It is likely that this was for the tactical reason of not wishing to alarm the Anglo-Americans who were expected to provide the loan.

The more interesting question, however, is whether those involved, with the exception of Stinnes, truly believed that this program had any realistic chance of success. Melchior certainly must have had his doubts, for on December 23 he wrote to Stinnes reporting on Brand's position. Brand, who came from Lazard Frères, one of the "best informed and most influential financial houses," had served on the international commission of experts, during their visit to Berlin in November, was a partner of the leading banker called upon by the British government in its reparations discussions, Sir Robert Kindersley, and was stating strong opposition to big international loans. He did not think them "feasible" or "desirable" and did not think that they would bring stability. Melchior regarded this communication of no small importance, since the question of whether Germany should propose a large final sum or develop a scheme based on annuities depended on the size and kind of international loan it could get.[178]

For Stinnes, however, the road to an international loan lay through a Franco-German understanding. He responded to Melchior that he saw things differently because he was informed that nationalist circles in France were thinking in terms of getting twenty-five billion gold marks. He was convinced that if Germany offered fifteen billion with 5 percent interest and 1 percent amortization, the French would settle on a compromise of twenty billion with 4 percent interest and 1 percent amortization. A loan based on such a settlement would sell very well, especially "if the states taking it over granted it freedom from taxation of every kind." Stinnes optimistically pointed out that "I do not have the slightest doubt that, for the purpose of covering the consequences of the world war, this loan, distributed in segments over three or four years, will be accepted if France and Germany negotiate with the Americans in alliance with England and Italy." Apparently unperturbed by the fact that he was treating speculations as a matter of certainty, Stinnes then went on to argue that France would accept the proposal if the inter-Allied debts were wiped out. It could then comfortably shift the blame for the failure of the Treaty on the other powers. What was essential, therefore, was that Germany gain France's trust by not offering what it could not perform, and Stinnes thought Melchior would agree that "that which I want and which very large influential circles in France also want, can only be reached through clear, unreserved solutions and not through offers which the other side, with its existing extraordinary mistrust, would perceive as a renewed German effort to defraud."[179]

In reality, the evidence for Stinnes's speculations was very weak indeed. The sporadic industrialist negotiations with their French counterparts had been so unproductive as to drive Reusch to argue, most unusually for a German industrialist at this time, that the government had to take the lead in promoting them. Cuno, who had also hoped to make direct contact with influential Frenchmen anxious for a settlement with Germany, had encouraged contacts between Schacht and Senator Bergeron, the head of the French Senate's Foreign Affairs Committee, and had himself received the Senator in late December. The discussions were very friendly, but hardly reassuring since Bergeron emphasized that the reparations bill could not be expected to be reduced under the existing political constellation. And even the most promising efforts at Franco-German cooperation, the arrangements with de Lubersac, were turning a bit sour, a matter of which Stinnes certainly was aware because of de Lubersac's complaints about the unsatisfactory results of the deliveries program. Favorable rumors from Paris, therefore, had to be treated cautiously. Melchior had also heard that the French might settle for twenty-five billion, but he remained convinced that an "elastic" rather than a "fixed" offer was the better tactic since the latter was more likely to be rejected by the French Cabinet.[180]

In the end, a compromise proposal was worked out which while heavily influenced by Stinnes also bore traces of some of the earlier proposals, especially that of Wassermann, and owed its final form to Melchior. The first point of the proposal skirted the issue of a final sum simply by leaving it unmentioned. Instead, operating on the basis of Germany's present situation, the proposal called for the floating of a twenty billion mark loan through an international consortium bearing 5 percent interest and 1 percent amortization. That portion of the proceeds of the loan which covered interest for the first four years was to be held back, and the amortization was to begin after that time. Insofar as the loan was subscribed to in Germany, half the proceeds were to be retained for purposes of stabilization and other German requirements. The second and third points of the proposal provided for the participation of Germany's creditors in later improvements in Germany's situation. Thus, in 1927 and again in 1931, Germany would float a five billion gold mark loan on each occasion if the financial consortium that had given the first loan determined that Germany had the credit to offer such a loan under normal credit conditions. Point four dealt with the question of guarantees and securities for the loan, which were to be negotiated with the consortium. No mention was made of German public enterprises, while specific reference was made to the fact that German industry and banking "despite their concern as to whether the offer has not already exceeded Germany's capacity, are resolved to support the government in its implementation."[181] It promised that the Reich would issue the necessary legislation to mobilize all groups in the economy toward this end. The final point promised to undertake necessary measures to stabilize and improve productivity, while calling on the Allies to provide Germany with a position of economic equality in world trade and specifically making the evacuation of Düsseldorf, Duisburg, and Ruhrort a condition of the German offer as well as the "soonest possible dismantling" of the occupation of the Rhineland.

Despite the low sum of the projected loans, the decision to base the offer on an international loan, and the very dangerous concession to the Ruhr industrialists involved in making the evacuation of the three cities a precondition of the offer, the final discussions with the industrialists on December 29 were not without serious tension. In the morning discussions, Stinnes had warned that he would fight the government if it pursued policies with which he disagreed. Later in the day, Silverberg took up where Stinnes had left off by expressing special hostility to point four, which declared that industry stood behind the offer, a proposition he contested in the name of the Ruhr industrialists who had participated in the discussions. The precondition for accepting a twenty billion gold-mark offer, he emphasized, was the government's carrying out of the "domestic reforms" in his program. By this time, Cuno seemed to feel that he had put up with enough from his erstwhile industrialist colleagues. As Bücher reported, Cuno responded, "externally calm but inwardly upset," that he had just learned from Bonar Law that there was no purpose to Germany making any offer that did not have the support of the business community and went on:

The government is honorably striving to work together with business and must rely upon it. It is impossible to get complete agreement among experts on such portentous questions. The responsibility for what is done lies with the government, which carries out its charge with the best of will and which strives to take into account all objectively presented reservations. But if the government is told from some side of economic life or from individual persons in economic life that if the government does not do something in the direction of the opinion held by that person, then it will be fought with all the means available, then he [Cuno] is resolved to lay down his office. . . . The reforms which Herr Silverberg considers necessary have also been supported by himself in the Reich Association and one cannot ask of himself that he make up by January 2 for what had failed to be done earlier or was impossible to carry out earlier. The important thing is that one begins to negotiate as quickly as possible.[182]

Bücher felt called upon to answer these remarks by stating that the experts had given their views as individuals and not as members of any group, although they all had to try to rally the support of the group with which they associated. As far as he could tell, there was little difference among the experts as to what could actually be paid and that those who had pleaded for a higher figure for political reasons had tried "with more or less skill to find a formula that looked like much but really brought little." The ultimate policy and the question of tactics had

to be decided by the government, and he personally would oppose any opposition from individuals or industrial groups against the government "*so long as the effects of the negotiations pursued by the government do not lead to financial obligations which go beyond that which the experts hold to be truly bearable.*"[183] Bücher also suggested to Cuno that he consider whether "a certain opposition would not be agreeable to the government, although this opposition must certainly be influenced by the government itself and carried on with its agreement." Nevertheless, Bücher and possibly Silverberg recognized that Cuno was not getting an opposition he found either agreeable or useful. In private conversation, the Chancellor intimated to Bücher that he was prepared to resign at the first sign of overt opposition and that he had already discussed the matter with Ebert, and Bücher felt impelled to urge Stinnes to make sure that the *DAZ* avoided criticism of the government before the Paris negotiations and in discussing a German offer.

Stinnes remained unmoved, however. In a New Year's Day note to Bücher, he expressed dissatisfaction with the Melchior draft, which he viewed as the kind of compromise he had anticipated, and went on to make it clear that he had little use for the government and every expectation of new struggles, especially at home:

We will have monumental battles in Germany from the side of industry, for Cuno and Hermes are not reliable and do not have any insight into production. Every foreign-policy success will make them arrogant, and they will forget that the path of suffering of internal reparations [*Leidensweg der inneren Reparationen*] will only begin once the paths in foreign policy are cleared.[184]

Stinnes left no doubt about the fact that he was in a fighting mood as the new year began and that he shared Silverberg's insistence that economic reforms were necessary. He called for the full implementation of that program for extending the hours of work and removing economic controls, for otherwise Germany would be "*kaputt* domestically." He was manifestly fed up with the effort to bring the trade union leaders to terms and was ready to abandon the alliance of 1918 by making full use of the secret concessions given by the trade unions during the Revolution. He asked Bücher to search out the secret protocol which made the eight-hour day contingent on its international acceptance as well as the protocol permitting recognition of the yellow trade unions if they survived despite the absence of employer support. The yellow unions would support overtime work, and "we will have to break the tyranny of the present inferior [*minderwertigen*] trade-union leadership." If they chose to face reality that would be "all the better," but it was clear that Stinnes was prepared to reverse his policy and no longer believed that an agreement could be achieved voluntarily. Similarly, he was not prepared to promise Bücher that the *DAZ* would not attack the government. While he had, in fact, given instructions that nothing oppositional should be written without his personal approval, what he would do depended on the "honesty of the government." As he reflected on events since the end of the war, he believed more than ever that his personal influence abroad depended upon his "courage to say the truth" and to "draw the economic consequences" and that he should continue to do his "duty." One could only trust the political leadership when there finally would "some day come a cabinet of really first-class men."

This was a quality of which Cuno and his colleagues could not be accused, and it is manifest that they entered the year 1923 with a program guaranteed to deepen its inevitable crises. Whether it would have been possible to have come up with an offer that might have prevented the occupation of the Ruhr that began on January 11 may be questioned, but the offer developed by the Cuno government was so inadequate to the situation that Bergmann himself was reluctant to present it to the Allies in Paris at the beginning of January. He did not have to do so, since the Allies compounded Germany's difficulties by their own quarrels. Bonar Law presented the Bradbury Plan and at the same time proposed the cancellation of French, Belgian, and Italian debts minus the gold deposits already in German hands and the end of Belgian priority in the receipt of reparations. This infuriated an already angry Poincaré, guaranteed the failure of the conference, and obviated the need to even hear the German proposal. Enough of it was already known to guarantee its rejection in any case. Britain now

stood isolated in the Reparations Commission, which had already found Germany in voluntary default on its timber deliveries on December 26 and then followed up the Paris conference by finding Germany in voluntary default on coal deliveries. The way was thus paved for the Ruhr occupation of a few days later.[185]

The history of the final German offer before the occupation demonstrates that there was considerable validity to Poincaré's notion that German policy was being dictated by its industrialists and that the only way to bring Germany to heel was by invading the Ruhr. This is not to say that the French reparations policy was wise or that the German businessmen who advised Cuno—himself one of them—were not sincere in their beliefs and conviction that Germany could not pay more than was being offered. Yet, it is one thing to argue that important elements of the German business community were a barrier to a sensible settlement of the reparations problem and quite another to suggest, as did some Frenchmen, that the hyperinflation and the reparations stalemate were some kind of interconnected plot to destroy the Treaty of Versailles. Furthermore, the British and Americans did not believe that the reparations program set up by the London Ultimatum could be realized, and there seems to have been quite a few doubting Frenchmen, not to mention Belgians and Italians as well.

This makes all the more plausible the argument that the driving force of the inflation throughout 1922 was the political situation—above all at the international level but also domestically. While economists have struggled with determining whether inflationary expectations were adaptive (in the sense that the demand for money was determined by the experience of past price changes) or rational (in the sense that people responded to fiscal news at the proper time and in some anticipatory measure that is predictable), the essential point for the historian is that "fiscal news was political news, diplomatic news, and especially military news."[186] In short, political news of various kinds determined expectations, which seems to fit well with the rational expectations model. Contemporaries seemed to have been well aware of this process. Thus, in a report on the exchange rate of the mark and the dollar in

Table 19. The Correlation Between the Dollar Exchange Rate of the Mark and Political News in 1922

Date	Exchange Rate	Political News
Jan. 5–9	201–163	Opening of Cannes Conference Conference and news of constructive plans
Jan. 13–21	178–200	Briand resignation; new Poincaré policy; Reichstag taxation debate
Feb. 1	204	German railroad-workers' strike
Feb. 8	199	End of railroad strike
Feb. 18–27	209–228	Postponement of Genoa conference (Feb. 20) and Boulogne agreement not to discuss reparations at Genoa (Feb. 27)
March 4–7	238–261	English coalition government crisis
March 7–9	261–250	English crisis over and Allied Finance Minister recommendation for a moratorium
March 11–April 4	257–326	Negative reports and expectations concerning Genoa conference
April 4–12	326–296	Hopeful feelings about Genoa
April 17–25	300–252	Positive reaction to Rappalo
April 25–May 22	252–314	Reaction to disappointments connected with end of Genoa
May 22–June 2	314–272	Hopeful feelings about bankers' conference in Paris
June 4–11	272–318	Failure of bankers' conference
June 23–24	331–345	Murder of Rathenau
June 28–July 31	374–670	Conflicts with Bavaria over Law to Protect Republic and with France over reparations
Aug. 5–19	764–1254	Tensions with Bavaria and France and between France and England
Aug. 21	1171	Agreement with Bavaria on Aug. 21
Aug. 22	1301	Poincaré Bar le Duc speech
Sept. 2–6	1351–1251	Positive reports from Reparations Commission on moratorium and agreement with Belgium
Sept. 6–13	1251–1602	Bad news on negotiations with Belgium
Sept. 21	1396	Agreement with Belgium
Sept. 23–Oct. 10	1409–2973	Crisis in Asia Minor
Oct. 10–12	2973–2473	Allied agreement with Turks
Oct. 18–20	2903–3568	Fall of Lloyd George
Nov. 8	9172	Low point of deterioration since late October
Nov. 15–21	7533–6190	Response to Cuno appointment
Nov. 28	8795	Rumors that French plan to enter Ruhr
Dec. 18	6115	Reports that United States favored new reparations arrangements
Dec. 28–31	7588–7368	Renewed rumors of French intransigence

Source: Orsen N. Nielsen and Rudolf E. Schoenfeld, "German Exchange During 1922," February 13, 1923, NA, 162.5151/1048.

1922, two American consular officials, Orsen N. Nielsen and Rudolf E. Schoenfeld, demonstrated a connection between international and domestic political developments and the exchange rate during the entire year (see Table 19). The importance of this contemporary analysis does not lie in whether or not it fits perfectly in each and every instance with the sum total of responses to the various signals in political, economic, and social affairs that determined expectations. The banker Max Steinthal, who handled the foreign-exchange account of the Mannesmann firm, for example, paid very little attention to the Near Eastern situation in mid-October and felt that the signals sent by the inadequacies of the projected internal gold-loan scheme and efforts to stop foreign-exchange speculation, the reports of the latest Bradbury plan, and the poor harvest explained the con-

tinuing drop of the mark and decided to hold on to thirty thousand English pounds since "when I take all these factors into consideration, I cannot believe in a subsequent improvement of the mark."[187] The most important point is that, in the aggregate, people were increasingly responding to the mix of signals in the same way, by and large negatively, and that they were responding, above all, to the outcome of political events that might affect the future situation. Thus, whereas reparations payments exercised a strong influence on the mark in the second half of 1921, they were of secondary significance in the first five months of 1922 and were overshadowed by such political events as the Conference on International Economic Reconstruction in Genoa. This was fully in keeping with the tendency for expectations to eclipse past events. Thus, the agreement with Belgium on September 21 went virtually unreflected in the exchange rate as attention focussed on the Near Eastern situation, where Germans feared that English preoccupations would leave France with a free hand. No sooner was the Near Eastern situation settled, however, then attention centered on the English Cabinet crisis, once again to the detriment of the mark. The American observers thus felt justified in arguing that "the rate of exchange seems to depend on the future outlook almost to the exclusion of the past. The past affects the exchange only as it affects the future."[188]

This is not to say that Nielsen and Schoenfeld were prepared to accept the notion that the collapse of the mark was purely determined by political circumstances. It was, in their view, the culmination of a process in which the government had permitted an excess circulation of currency and in which industry, exhilarated by repeated inflationary waves and the appearance of prosperity and then thrown into anxiety by the stagnation accompanying every readjustment from the last inflationary wave, seemed incapable of doing anything other than calling for the issuance of more money by the government.

Could one then argue that just as industry blocked all political agreements that might have put an end to the inflation, so it stood in the way of a cessation of inflation for economic reasons as well? How was the behavior of the German business community to be explained? An interesting perspective on German behavior that takes political and economic behavior into account was provided by Ambassador Houghton, who had discussed the inflation and reparations problems with numerous leading German economic leaders. He had come to accept the arguments of Rathenau and Stinnes on that fateful night in late June that the inflation was a necessary means of dealing with the postwar sociopolitical problems of Germany which had gotten out of hand. Houghton shared the view of Melchior, however, that the industrialists and German government had not deliberately promoted the inflation to escape reparations. The problem lay elsewhere:

I do not believe that to escape paying reparations any national suicide was planned. . . . The truth, I believe, is that the German bankers and industrialists are

mighty poor economists. They have had plenty of experience in a constantly growing and expanding volume of industry and trade, they have had no experience whatever, until the present, in a decreasing volume of industry and trade, such as, for instance, both the United States and England have experienced several times. The net result is that they do not understand the present situation. They are, I believe, not competent to meet it. They need English and American help in particular to work themselves out of the hole into which they have fallen. They have made many efforts to dig themselves out, but no two of them agree. None of them seems to be able to separate the various factors and to analyze the exceedingly complicated situation which has developed. The first effective analysis made was the so-called Majority Report of the Committee of Experts. That is sound. That should have been adopted by Wirth, and I am hopeful that before the reparations question takes final form it will be adopted by Cuno and his government. Otherwise the wreckage will, if possible, be made even more complete.[189]

The "wreckage" in fact was to become greater than ever, but Houghton did put his finger on a central problem that helps to explain how it came about and why it was that so many sober, rational German industrialists and bankers could have behaved with such political irrationality in 1922 and provides some insight into the fantasies of Stinnes as well. The incapacity to find a sensible solution, however, was not limited to German businessmen. Germany's leading politicians and diplomats also seemed more willing to gamble in terms of their rigid preconceptions than to accept the risks required by facing reality. There were some exceptions. Hermes, even if not the strongest and most appealing of political leaders, seems to have taken the arguments made by Moritz Bonn to heart. Both inside Center Party circles and in the Cabinets in which he served, he argued that Germany should show a willingness to accept obligations beyond its capacity, not quibble over "a few billion more or less," and recognize that there was no way of predicting what conditions would be like in ten or twenty years. This was no way either to convince or to get the assistance of the outside world. As he pointed out in reviewing the mistakes of 1922 from the perspective of the even greater disasters of 1923,

Instead of holding fast to a fixed formula with a stubbornness which is incomprehensible to the world and which is not even founded on economic facts, Germany would have been much better off to have tried to demonstrate stronger empathy for the mentality of the rest of the world by coming to terms with the general opinion and thereby tried to secure a more favorable judgement of Germany. Then it would have been easier to argue for an appropriately long moratorium for Germany as a precondition for such a larger [reparations] program.[190]

Germany had bought time through inflation, but the time had run out. The hyperinflation was exposing the limits of Germany's inflationary reconstruction, revealing the real social and economic damage being wrought and raising the question of how these problems were to be dealt with in a political culture so inadequate to the problems of Weimar's shaky democracy.

BOOK TWO
THE HYPERINFLATION

An inflation can be called a witches' sabbath of devaluation where men and the units of their money have the strangest effects on each other. The one stands for the other, men feeling themselves as "bad" as their money; and this becomes worse and worse. Together they are all at its mercy and all feel equally worthless.

Elias Canetti, *Crowds and Power*

PART V

SOCIETY, STATE, AND ECONOMY
IN THE HYPERINFLATION OF 1922

Ich hab' Dich gern, mein Freund,
weil Du Devisen hast
und weil Du's dann und wann
mir schon bewiesen hast.
Ich hab' Dich gern, weil du gut spekulierst
und an der Börse auch niemals verlierst.
Ob Du nun Franken hast, ob Du nun Gulden hast;
wenn Du Verständnis nur für meine Schulden hast;
alles and're ist nur Schein,
bloß Devisen müssen's sein. . . .

I go for you, my friend,
because you have foreign exchange,
and because now and then
you have proven it to me.
I go for you, because you speculate well
and never lose on the stock exchange.
Whether it is francs you have, whether it is gulden
if only you have understanding for my debts;
everything else is just so much show,
it just has to be foreign exchange. . . .

Harry Hauptmann, *Die Dame mit dem Monokel*

Chapter 12

The Year of Dr. Mabuse:
The Hyperinflation and German Society in 1922

1922 was a banner year for the German film. In London, the long-planned first postwar presentation of a German movie finally took place with the showing of Ernst Lubitsch's *Madame du Barry*. Appearing under the title of *Passion* and starring Pola-Negri, the film sold out nightly to audiences entranced by its star, admiring of its technical achievements, and undoubtedly greatly entertained by Lubitsch's skill in presenting great historical events as the outcome of the all-too-human behavior of the well known historical characters populating his film.[1] Two of the most famous productions of the silent film era, F. W. Murnau's vampire thriller *Nosferatu* and Fritz Lang's *Dr. Mabuse: The Gambler*, appeared in Germany at this time. Following in the steps of the pioneering expressionist work of Robert Wiene, *The Cabinet of Dr. Caligari* (1920), these films reflected a fascination, often ambivalent and certainly politically and socially significant, with the tyrannical powers exerted by inhuman and superhuman creatures. While the blood-sucking protagonist of Murnau's film was not an unsuitable figure for this unhappy year of exploitation, profiteering, and impoverishment, the character of Mabuse, taken from a best-selling novel by Norbert Jacques, was a genuine and conscious product of the inflation. It told the tale of an evil genius possessed of hypnotic powers whose chief satisfaction was "playing with human beings and human fates" and whose sinister "exercise of the power of willing" enabled him to prey upon a world that had surrendered to speculative fever and a gambling mania. Mabuse's victims invite their victimization, be it in the hectic madness of the stock exchange, where the exercise of Mabuse's unidentifiable power drives values up and down without any apparent rhyme or reason, or be it through their restless search for pleasure and sensation in the secret club run by inflation profiteers. The habitués of these establishments were greeted with a choice between cocaine and cards, and the hapless rich young American who was foolish enough to choose the latter ended up losing his money and then his life to the machinations of Dr. Mabuse. The environment in which these people moved was not uncultivated, but Lang made it clear that their "higher" and their "lower" interests were not as far apart as one might think. Thus, when Dr. Mabuse is asked, "What do you think of expressionism, Doctor," he replies, "Expressionism is nothing but a gamble. Everything is a gamble."[2]

These films reproduced the psychological and moral currents of their time, thus helping us to explain why they "spoke" to contemporaries. They do not, of course, explain why everything had become a "gamble" or even explain what the "game" actually was. They do tell us much about popular perceptions—the appeal of the notion that the truth could be revealed by looking through the keyholes or listening at the doors of the mighty and the tendency to attribute the growing inflationary chaos either to human folly and incompetence or to superhuman and demonic machinations.

"Looking through the keyhole" can, even if very incompletely, reveal something about the game and its stakes. When a discussion in February 1922 in London between Carl Melchior and Chancellor of the Exchequer Sir Robert Horne turned to the long-term effects of the German monetary depreciation, it did expose the consciousness of informed contemporaries about the national and international stakes of the inflation. Melchior spoke of the "enormous redistribution of wealth which has taken place in Germany . . . especially the extraordinarily strong position which the owners of industrial and agrarian property have gained because their debts, mortgages, and bonds only have slightly over two percent of the value they had when the debts were first contracted. Urban property owners will also have this advantage once rents are decontrolled." Horne was no less blunt, however, reminding Melchior that the German state was also slated to become a beneficiary of the inflation. From this perspective, Germany's present financial miseries and economic problems were deceptive. Horne called attention to

the splendid position of Germany's finances in the next generation, when the reparations payments will be completed. The domestic German debt will be minimal thanks to the depreciation of the mark. This future position of Germany is well understood in England and we are completely alert to the fact that we are nurturing a fearful competitor for later on. If the English government for general reasons tries to support Germany despite this, then Germany must in any case convince the world that she is doing her utmost in the reparations question.[3]

The trouble was that Wirth was not in a position to wait for the next generation when Germany's finances might be "splendid." His problem was to ensure that Germany survived financially through the year. The Weimar governments had also been gambling that the processes of domestic redistribution and economic reconstruction could take place without civil war at home and invasion from abroad, and the game was turning against them in both arenas. In the last analysis, the fundamental thrust of the policies advocated by Stinnes and by Wirth was quite similar. Both wished to buy time for Germany's economic reconstruction and financial stabilization under advantageous conditions. The difference lay in the tactics proposed, but it is important to recognize that in politics, tactical differences are often differences of substance because they can profoundly alter both the chances of attaining desired goals and

even the goals themselves. It was Stinnes's outrageous approach to the achievement of his aims—his insistence that the reparations be scaled down to what *he* considered an acceptable level, that the Allies surrender their political interests to what *he* considered a sound international economic arrangement, and that the mark be stabilized at that level which *he* viewed most advantageous to Germany—that transformed his calculations into a formula for political adventure.

The policy of fulfillment, however, was also a dangerous game because it consciously undertook the risk of domestic political conflict and severe financial and economic hardship in order to prove that fulfillment was impossible and thus gain the breathing space necessary for a gradual stabilization that would be socially, economically, and politically tolerable and that would permit Germany to reenter a reconstituted international economic order with an advantageously devalued currency. That was why, for example, Havenstein insisted on hoarding rather than gambling with his gold. Germany's leaders were well aware that they were presiding over a massive redistribution of assets in German society and that the state was taxing away the claims of its citizens against the state through inflation. This policy was dangerous enough, but it was at least tolerable so long as there was the hope that a sound basis for financial and economic reconstruction could be created that might smooth over and ameliorate the damage and resentment created by these policies. Since the fall of 1921, however, this hope was dealt one brutal blow after the other and was being replaced by a consciousness of injury, loss, and genuine crisis. The foreign and domestic policies of Wirth during his last months in office (between August and November 1922) and of his successor, Wilhelm Cuno, prior to January 1923 can only be understood in the context of the escalating domestic crisis and disorder in German society and politics just as these conditions were themselves the product of foreign and domestic policies which no longer were working. Indeed, nothing seemed to be working, including the efforts of Nobel Prize–winning chemist Fritz Haber (a man intensely concerned about the consequences of the inflation for German science and culture) to pay off reparations by finding a means of extracting gold from the seas![4]

The history of the hyperinflation, like that of the entire inflation, is comprehensible only in terms of the interaction of domestic and international developments as well as the interaction of the "rulers" and the "ruled." The dilemma of the historian is not to decide which of these is more "important" but rather how to deal with the fact that a work of history can never be three dimensional. The coming of the hyperinflation created a qualitatively different situation for Germany's rulers and ruled, and the realities of this new predicament must be brought into focus. Whereas both the reparations demands of the Allies and the efforts to cope with them had by and large provided the context for the domestic history of the inflation since May 1921, the situation after July 1922 was one in which the inflationary process was significantly liberated from its external determinants and appeared increasingly autonomous. This domestic inflationary crisis imposed major new imperatives on the political leadership both within and without Germany and thus changed the character of the policy discussions. There was not only a debate about whether Germany should and could stabilize under existing conditions, but also a mounting discussion of what kind of stabilization there should be. Hyperinflation compelled Germans to confront the most extreme consequences of the inflationary reconstruction and redistribution of assets, raised the question of whether or not to take immediate measures against them, and opened the issue of whether the inevitable future stabilization should confirm the consequences of the inflation and hyperinflation or seek to reverse or correct them. The films and literature of the period expressed the dilemmas of a society victimized by intransparent forces and uncertain as to whether it could best recover its way by going forward or trying to find its way back to the path it had left.

Mark for Mark?

An important measure of the growing crisis within Germany was the increasingly open recognition of the falsity of the most basic of all the monetary propositions of the German government since 1914; namely, that the prewar mark was interchangeable with the postwar mark. The principle of "mark for mark" was the legal basis of all economic transactions in Germany, and it was the necessary fiction upon which the inflationary reconstruction had taken place. Now, however, the suspension of disbelief was becoming insupportable. This was so not simply for those who engaged in business involving imports and exports, who had already made various adjustments and thus had a firm foundation for further adaptation to the worsening situation, but also for those having purely domestic economic and financial interests.

The discomfiture was particularly evident in legal circles. While the courts of the Weimar Republic have gone down in history not for their support of the Republic but rather for the reverse, their treatment of the proposition "mark for mark" demonstrated a considerable reluctance to depart from the tradition of judicial positivism and an unwillingness to override the will of the lawgiver. In retrospect, the Reich Supreme Court (*Reichsgericht*) had taken an important step in the direction of judicial review and thus on the path to challenging the authority of the legislature with a decision of April 1921 asserting its right to review the constitutionality of legislation, but the anti-democratic and anti-Republican implications of this step in the Weimar context do not seem to have been at all clear at the time. Furthermore, while it has been argued that the assertion of the doctrine of judicial review by the Weimar courts was primarily aimed at protecting property rights against incursions from the democratic state, the evolution of court challenges to the legislature (being intimately linked with the problems created by the inflation) suggests that such an overly simple Marxist interpretation from hindsight does not adequately explain this important development. Quite aside from the fact that any decision on either side of the question of "mark for mark" could only have the effect of favoring one class of propertied persons over another, the criticisms of the court for its reticence on the "mark for mark" doctrine by no means came from one clearly defined point on the political spectrum.[5]

It is more than a little ironic, for example,

that "Morus" (Richard Lewinsohn), the leading economic writer for the critical left-wing
journal *Die Weltbühne* (which regularly compared the disparities between the sentences
given to left-wing and right-wing political criminals), should have been one of the most outspoken critics of the courts for their lack of initiative. In an article of December 1921 on the
well-publicized trial of Max Klante—who was
accused of swindling some sixty thousand persons into investing in his projects—Morus suggested that Klante's activities were as nothing
compared to what was going on quite legally on
a national scale and accused the Reich Supreme
Court of demonstrating an "unsurpassable ignorance of the world" by its insistence that the
measure of value existing in 1900 had not
changed and by its failure to realize that a
twenty mark gold piece now bought thirty
thousand paper marks. He invidiously compared the English and German judiciaries and
praised the former for its inventive use of the
common law in dealing with such problems. In
a remarkable plea for judicial activism, Morus
declared that

where the legislative machinery fails, it is the task of
the free judiciary to correct the failures and fill in the
holes in the laws. . . . The German judge, who never
is allowed to dare to say something that is not in the
books even now, where it is necessary, does not have
the courage to free himself from the paragraphs and
to hand down judgments in accordance with what is
just, not according to the letter of the law but in free
assessment of the real circumstances. Whoever before the war gave gold has today to take back one-
twelve-hundredth as the full value, and no gold
clause protects the creditor from state sanctioned expropriation by the debtor. But perhaps there lies the
rub. The state as the greatest gold mark debtor dares
not admit that the principle and interest on the loans
which it took for good money before the war and during the war can today only be paid back with scraps
of paper (*Papierfetzen*) and only in this way. In common terminology: The Reich dares not admit the
bankruptcy of the state, which it actually has long entered, and the German judge, state-maintaining as he
is, glosses over and covers up this situation and endlessly enlarges the economic insecurity with the fiction of a legal security that has long ceased to exist.
When will the statesman come, when will the legislator come, when will the "High Senate" come to free
us from this "Klante System?"[6]

Actually, the German judiciary did not need
such provocation. The sense of unease, the feel-

ing that it was an accomplice in a swindle, and
the argument that the courts had an obligation
to protect citizens who were creditors or wards
of the state from expropriation through monetary depreciation had become widespread
among prominent jurists after the onset of galloping inflation in the late summer of 1921 and
intensified as the situation became worse. The
discussion that began at this time was to become one of the most bitter political issues of
the Weimar Republic, but its initial phase reflected the concrete dilemmas faced by the jurists arising from conditions which they had not
anticipated. Furthermore, the discussion itself
is significant as a reflection of the transformation of inflationary expectations following the
summer of 1921 and the increasing crisis that
accompanied it. This is well illustrated by the
burst of concern over the "robbery" of the
wards of the court.

The responsibility of Germany's jurists and
judges for overseeing the assets of trusts subject
to court supervision and ensuring that monies
were placed in secure "gilt-edged" investments
became an especially neuralgic point as the inflation progressed. The courts had always exhibited a preference for Reich, state, or municipal bonds and, during the war, war bonds. The
real value of these assets by 1922 had deteriorated substantially, but insult was added to injury by their reduced market price in paper
marks. Thus, if and when court-appointed
trustees were granted permission to cash in
some portion of such assets on behalf of their
charges, the return was below even the nominal
value. The entire situation was exposed in late
1921 when the Duisburg jurist Stiel published
an article in a major legal publication bearing
the somewhat sensational title "The Robbery of
the Wards of the Court." Stiel made two proposals to remedy the situation. The first was
that the state provide compensation to victims
by making up the difference between the nominal and market values of the bonds. The second, and far more important, proposal was that
the courts allow trustees to invest the money of
their charges in industrial stocks or bonds or
property where there might be some chance
that the values of the assets would keep up with
inflation.[7]

Stiel's article spoke to the "souls" of some

judges. One, who had permitted a trustee to sell five hundred marks in war bonds to relieve the distress of his charge for only three hundred eighty marks on the market, thought it a "duty of honor" for the state to make up the difference and thus not appear as a "faithless guardian of orphans."[8] The Finance Ministry refused all requests for compensation, no matter how dire the need, because of the financial plight of the Reich and the fear of setting a dangerous precedent. In a few instances, municipalities had stepped into the breach despite their own financial difficulties.[9]

Stiel's article attracted the attention and concern of the the Prussian Ministry of Justice, which in early December 1921 called upon the Presidents of the provincial Superior Courts (*Oberlandesgerichtspräsidenten*) to comment on the Stiel proposals. Their reactions, most of which were sent in between February and April 1922 and thus coincided with a round of further currency depreciation, were generally negative. At the very most, there was some sympathy for the proposition that the Reich should provide some compensation for the deterioration of the market value of war bonds. The Superior Court President in Königsberg argued that modest compensation should be given to truly needy cases as a means of allying "irritation" and "resentment" but would go no further. As he pointed out,

... the fate of the wards is the same as that of all the others who, in confidence in our previous financial situation, had bought so-called gilt-edged paper before the war, mainly above its market rate, and who now find it at 70 percent or 60 percent of its face value. The people tell themselves that these losses are an unavoidable consequence of the lost war. . . . The only thing that causes bitterness is that the state had then used all its resources to pressure the trustees to put all available money in war bonds and that now not a word is heard to the effect that the small and smallest war-loan subscribers should receive state compensation for their losses on the market when they are forced to sell.[10]

The judges continued to think it improper for the courts to permit trustees to invest in industrial shares and other assets previously considered risky. The Superior Court President in Düsseldorf had gone to the trouble of consulting the Düsseldorf Chamber of Commerce, and its response showed the dim prospects faced by small investors. While the Chamber of Commerce agreed that a change of court investment regulations was probably the only means of preventing the total depreciation of gilt-edged–backed trusts, it questioned whether it was not already too late because the depreciation had progressed to the point where, whatever the ups and downs of the currency, "the return of the paper value to its gold value is completely out of the question."[11] The crucial question, however, was whether there was any kind of industrial paper whose paper-mark value would keep up with depreciation and thus act as a hedge against inflation. There were, to be sure, a number of enterprises whose shares represented real values, but these were in the hands of certain families or shareholders and could not be bought on the market. The majority of industrial shares, however, while certainly issued by solid enterprises, could in no way be guaranteed to keep pace with inflation. Their fluctuations did not necessarily reflect the conditions of the enterprises themselves but rather speculative activities at home and international developments. At the very most, therefore, the Düsseldorf Chamber of Commerce could recommend that a portion of trusts be placed in first-class industrial bonds, the value of which was likely to be at least as good and probably better than that of the so-called gilt-edged assets previously accepted by the courts.

A number of the judges pointed out that the court normally chose as trustees persons who were unlikely to speculate. Such persons had neither the inclination nor the ability to enter the market, especially a market that could bring down even experienced players as had occurred in early December 1921. While more of a case could be made for investment in land or in goods, the price of land had risen beyond what most trusts could cover, while goods involved problems of storage and maintenance and, in turn, could put the courts and their trustees in the unpleasant position of becoming involved in hoarding and shifting around goods in a manner that would drive up prices. In at least two instances, the judges objected to the inquiry of the Justice Ministry itself on the grounds that it promoted speculation on a total state repudiation of the assets it had created. As the Superior Court President in Cologne pointed out,

Every position taken by the lawmaker in this area will lead to mistrust. Many will draw the conclusion that the lawmakers *themselves* doubt the security of those assets previously seen as gilt-edged. The Reich and the states must maintain confidence in their own future and strengthen such feelings in the population. They should not agree to legal measures that could lead to the questioning of this self-confidence. The result will be a further depreciation of Reich and state obligations, from whose effects not only the wards would suffer.[12]

Not all the judges, however, were willing to engage in such whistling in the dark. In Celle, the Supreme Court President pointed out that no trustee was willing to put the money in his charge into government paper any longer and that, in effect, everyone recognized the "veiled bankruptcy" of the state that could not be declared for obvious political reasons. It was no less clear that "the present situation cannot be a lasting one."[13] What would take its place, however, was a matter of speculation. Possibly, the Allies would simply force Germany to stop printing money, in which case this judge doubted that the government could afford to make good its domestic debts while fulfilling its obligations to the Allies. Yet another option was the creation of a new currency for which, as under Napoleon, the old paper currency would be exchanged at a fixed ratio. Under such circumstances, a revaluation might take place in which mortgages would probably be treated more favorably than government bonds. This judge, like his colleague from Marienwerder, however, was convinced that nothing was to be accomplished by switching the investment of trustee assets so late in the game.[14] They both appear to have been impressed with proposals that provision be made for a legal revaluation of monetary obligations that would remove the speculative character of future creditor/debtor relations and modify or correct the injustices committed by the past depreciation of the currency.

The chief proponent of such legislation was State Secretary Oskar Mügel of the Prussian Ministry of Justice, who published his views in the leading legal journals in October 1921 and February 1922 and also presented them for debate at the Berlin Lawyers' Association in November 1921.[15] He very appropriately disassociated the Ministry from his views, but proposals of this kind from so highly placed an official were bound to attract attention. Although similar analyses and arguments can be found in the writings of other jurists, most notably in those of the Leipzig jurist Alois Zeiler, whose interest in the problem dated back to December 1918 and who followed Mügel with a speech of his own at the November 3 meeting in Berlin,[16] the publication of Mügel's recommendations, coming as they did in the midst of the galloping inflation, marks the actual beginning of serious public discussion of what, if anything, should be done about creditor/debtor relations during and after the inflation.

Mügel operated under the assumption that a stabilization could not be expected for the foreseeable future. On the contrary, the mark could be expected to deteriorate further. Thus, the "restoration of a gold currency which would put an end to the monetary depreciation all at once is out of the question for a long time."[17] The problem, therefore, was how to make the depreciation "more bearable," especially since it was threatening to break down economic relations by making it impossible for anyone to grant private credit or for the government to issue domestic bonds. Mügel's answer was the passage of legislation to valorize all future creditor/debtor relations on the basis of the gold mark. Just as the German government had been calculating import duties in gold—at least in theory—so now everyone would calculate credit and mortgages in gold marks as of the date of the projected law's promulgation. The gold mark value of paper marks would be set less arbitrarily than the gold import duties, however, and Mügel was inclined to use the quarterly average value of the paper mark abroad. Thus, if a person borrowed a thousand paper marks when the gold mark was worth ten paper marks, then he would be required to pay the equivalent of a hundred gold marks; if he repaid at a time when a gold mark was the equivalent of fifteen paper marks, then he would have to repay fifteen hundred marks; if the gold mark was the equivalent of five paper marks, then he would have to repay five hundred marks. In this way, neither debtor nor creditor would have an unfair advantage because of changes in the value of the currency.

Mügel was fully aware that no such easy solution could be found for debts contracted earlier, since it was impossible to account for all the complicated and different situations involved. For example, if those with old unpaid debts were suddenly required to pay back the full amount in gold marks, they would be treated unfairly in comparison with those who had been fortunate enough to have paid their debts earlier. All debtors had calculated on paying their debt in paper marks, and many now found themselves victims of the depreciation and price increases themselves. They could not afford to pay off their debt in gold marks calculated on the basis of value at the time the debt was contracted. Among these, Mügel included the state and argued against robbing "the Reich of the advantage arising from its loan debts having become less oppressive with the progress of the depreciation."[18] As a general rule, therefore, Mügel proposed calculating all such debts in gold marks only as of the date when the projected law would come into effect. Creditors, in short, would be protected against further depreciation but be forced to accept what had taken place in the past, although Mügel was prepared to grant additional compensation to creditors in case the mark increased in value to the point where the creditor could receive full value. Mortgages were to be increased to reflect the increased value of the land or property involved. Finally, wages, utility, and transportation rates, taxes, and fines were to be calculated in terms of their gold value. If the paper mark would remain the basic currency, therefore, calculation would nevertheless take place on a gold basis, thereby eliminating the need for premiums for risk and a good deal of the unhealthy speculation required by the existing situation of uncertainty.

Mügel's ideas came in for considerable criticism. Georg Bernhard viewed them as typical of the kind of legalistic thinking that failed to take national economic interests into account. More specifically, the Mügel proposal entailed nothing less than the abandonment of German monetary sovereignty because a gold-mark currency of the type proposed would not be a new currency but rather the old currency as determined by the rate of the American dollar. Germany, Bernhard predicted, would thus become completely dependent upon foreign manipula-

tion of the mark rate and would actually be encouraging speculation against the mark.[19] Mügel did not deny the legalistic nature of his thinking, which he had based explicitly on the doctrines of the early nineteenth-century German jurist Savigny and on the basic concept of "equity and good faith" (*Treu und Glauben*); nor did he disagree with the charge of his most vociferous critic, Dr. Springer, another Finance Ministry official, that the use of the gold mark as the basis for calculation addressed the symptoms rather than the causes of the monetary depreciation. Mügel simply argued that it was neither just nor economic to continue giving bad money for good and that it was the duty of a good "doctor" to relieve symptoms and promote the healing process when he could not bring about an immediate cure.

For Springer, however, Mügel's proposal would only make the disease worse. Springer's most fundamental objection was that it was impossible to regulate such matters so long as there was no stabilization since "there are few things more dangerous in economic life than the artificial alteration of the factors which influence it, because here things are so intermeshed with one another that one can never forecast with any measure of probability the consequences that will result in any individual instance."[20] He was very critical of the use of the external value of the mark as a basis for calculating its gold value since the purchasing power of the mark was higher in Germany than abroad and, like Bernhard, warned against encouraging speculation against the mark as well as the promotion of world-market prices in Germany. Springer also felt it wrong to tilt the balance of advantage so strongly in favor of the debtor and seriously questioned the possibility of achieving equity *post facto*. How was one to determine a suitable solution for recalculating mortgages when they had been taken out by different persons at different times and under different circumstances and where some had been paid off and others not? Furthermore, where was the equity in treating holders of war bonds less favorably than holders of mortgages:

That the Reich can pay back its debts in nothing but the present currency, that is in paper marks, is clear given the situation of its finances and is presumed by the speaker [that is, Mügel]. But I could really not understand it if I had given the Reich in its need large sums of money in return for war bonds and would then remain stuck with the resulting loss in value while a less patriotic neighbor, who instead of signing up for war bonds had put his money in mortgages, would now be given an adjustment. Perhaps I had actually mortgaged my house to him in order to get the money to buy war bonds![21]

Mügel maintained his conviction that his solution was both economically rational and legally necessary, and he expanded his arguments with complicated illustrations of how his proposals would work. As he confessed, however, economic, not legal considerations would determine the fate of his program, a view shared by the officials of his Ministry, who felt that the decision on such matters had to be left to the Ministries charged with economic affairs.[22] Others, most notably Zeiler, were more persistent, and they were heartened by a decision of a Polish Superior Court of February 25, 1922, in favor of a mortgage holder who had refused to accept nominal payment of an old mortgage in the depreciated Polish currency. While this decision was later reversed by the Polish Supreme Court, Zeiler and others strongly approved of the manner in which the Polish court had argued in terms of general "equity and good faith" to assert creditor rights, sought to promote legislation banning the repayment of mortgages until the currency was stabilized, and tried to persuade the government to support the revaluation of mortgages. The German government, however, took the position advocated by Springer; namely, that it was unfair to single out mortgage holders for special compensation and that the government could not afford to provide similar benefits for government bondholders.[23]

Indeed, while Mügel may have felt certain of the proposition that "that which is just is in the end also that which is economically useful,"[24] the evidence was anything but as conclusive as he claimed. In fact, it was nothing short of ambiguous and confusing. The deterioration of the mark in 1922 was not only damaging to Germans with liquid capital invested in German marks but also to the foreigners who had speculated on the mark. Just as German trustee courts were contemplating the possibility of granting the right to invest the money of court

wards in stocks and real estate, so some enterprising North Americans were trying to save what could be saved of mark holdings in a similar manner. In September 1922, a group of American and Canadian investment dealers, in collaboration with some German investment houses and banks, established a holding company with the title of the United European Investors, Limited. Chartered in Canada and placed under the presidency of the former Secretary of the Navy and future Governor of New York and President of the United States, Franklin D. Roosevelt, the company was established with a capital of six hundred million marks and sixty thousand U.S. dollars. It offered common stock with a par value of ten thousand marks or one dollar. The company proposed to take the marks provided by its investors and place the money in hotels, apartment houses, industrial shares, mortgages, and other assets presumably invulnerable to inflation. Since the mark had a higher value in Germany than abroad, it appeared possible to upgrade the purchasing power of the depreciated marks and put the increasingly worthless money to some profitable use.[25]

It has not been possible to determine how much interest was shown in this venture, which, in any case, was undertaken too late to have been of much use. The new company certainly could not have been of much promise to a German-American like Mr. Carl Fincke of Chicago, Illinois, who had paid $197.50 to the Chicago firm of Wollenberger & Co. at the beginning of 1916 for a thousand-mark German war bond on deposit in the vaults of the Dresdener Bank in Berlin. When Fincke read newspaper reports that Ambassador Wiedfeldt had given assurances that the German government had "laid aside" funds to pay back "every cent" of the $6,682,000 invested in such bonds by German-Americans, he promptly wrote to the Dresdner Bank asking when he might be receiving his check for $197.50.[26] Ambassador Wiedfeldt found the reports very embarrassing. What he had actually said was that dollar-denominated debts would be paid back in dollars when the German government was in a position to do so, and he found it painful to have to issue a clarification when he was pounced upon by reporters as he stepped off the boat after a trip to Germany in November 1922. As he sadly reported:

We receive frequent requests from veterans associations, burial societies, and similar German-American organizations, which had once put their assets into war loans out of pro-German feelings and which now ask the Embassy to help them get back in dollars the equivalent of what they had paid for the war loans. Naturally, we have to turn them down. It is unavoidable that these groups, which are by and large without much means, should be bitter about this since the financial status of their organizations is thereby severely damaged. It is understandable that a certain resentment has thus taken hold in German-American circles, but nothing can be done about it.[27]

In the balance, official German representatives in the United States actually welcomed what appeared to them exaggerated and what certainly were sensational stories of American losses from mark speculation and deliberately decided not to issue official denials or explanations. The *New York World* estimated American losses at 904 million dollars, an amount which German banking experts questioned because it treated as losses monies invested in German shares and other assets whose real value had not necessarily been affected by the monetary depreciation. In reality, the newspaper estimate was not far off the later official estimate of 770 million dollars, but the really important matter was that the newspaper reports could be interpreted as pro- rather than anti-German. Thus, they were accompanied by comments by German bankers and noted Anglo-American financial experts and economists who frankly stated that Germany had been the recipient of an interest-free loan that had held it above water for two years but which then blamed the losses of foreign mark investors on Entente policies and reparations. How could Germans take out normal loans when there was a first mortgage on their credit in the form of reparations? Furthermore, these commentators pointed out that the losses were not as great as they appeared from a broader economic perspective because the capital exports to Germany had provided the means by which Germany could import food and raw materials and thus provide American agriculture and business with orders during the depression. American speculators, from the lift boy to the millionaire, had financed an important portion

of these American exports, Dutch economist G. W. Bruins was quoted as arguing, and the cessation of such speculation under the impress of the mark depreciation would hurt American business. Without such speculation, the Germans never would have been able to import anything approximating what they had, and, by implication, recovery from the depression would have been more difficult. Little wonder, therefore, that German officials viewed such articles as helpful to the German side of the reparations question and conducive to American intervention on Germany's behalf.[28]

As in Germany, therefore, so internationally did the German inflation involve a redistributive process which produced some macroeconomic benefits at the expense of individuals and specific classes. The process had nothing whatever to do with "equity and good faith" and was, if anything, antithetical to international economic ethics. What, however, would have been the price of maintaining such standards? Could they be maintained? There were a few instances in which creditors did have protection against German debtors, and these cases serve as illustrations of the dilemmas involved in trying to apply the principle of "equity and good faith."

Foremost among these were the municipalities which had taken out loans payable in foreign currency during the war, often despite warnings from the Reichsbank and government, but sometimes prior to receiving such warnings. As the depreciation of the mark progressed in 1922, they not only began to fear but sometimes experience the price of their folly.[29] Prior to this time, the Congress of German Municipalities had taken the position that equity and good faith and the international credit rating of Germany's municipalities required that debts with a gold clause had to be paid in full. Thus, when the Mayor of Wittenberge, which in 1917–1918 had taken out loans repayable in gold marks, called upon the Congress of German Municipalities in early 1921 to promote a law under which such loans could be repayable in marks, his colleagues opposed any such action and pointed out that the speculative character of Wittenberge's action no matter what the outcome of the war should have been quite evident.[30] A similarly negative response was given to the city of Flensburg, which was trying to renegotiate a ten-year loan that it had taken out in Switzerland in August 1916 and that was hurting the city's credit. The Swiss were not co-operating, and Flensburg argued that the Reich should come to its aid since it had agreed to repay the loan in foreign currency in view of

repeated declarations of the Reich government and the repeatedly strengthened confidence that a defeat of Germany in the world war need not be considered within the range of human calculation. Already at that time, as is now known, the Reich government had good reason to doubt a favorable outcome to the war and it is generally recognized that it would have been more correct if the German people had been informed about the full seriousness of the situation at that time. If that had occurred, then the responsible authorities of the City of Flensburg certainly would have been more cautious in the matter of the loan.[31]

Whether the Mayor of Flensburg was being disingenuous or not is difficult to say. His loan was not due until 1926, and his major concern appears to have been the capacity to raise new monies rather than repay old debts. Mayor Charbonnier of Liegnitz, for example, appeared immune to the experiences of a lost war and dangerous speculations. In his view, the only way new housing could be constructed in the cities was through the taking of long-term loans repayable in foreign currency. The profit on the exchange rate difference between the mark and the foreign currency would allegedly permit housing construction at the prewar price. When Charbonnier heard rumors that the Mayor of Berlin had been able to raise a new loan repayable in gulden in the Netherlands, he sent off a letter asking for more information. The reply should have been sobering. Berlin was one of a number of cities that found itself "in a big fix" because it had taken out loans payable in foreign currencies and only wished that it had "gotten out of the trap of payment in foreign exchange on time." Some were fortunate enough to be able at least to pay the interest in German currency, but others were stuck with short-term debts payable in foreign currency. Berlin was one of these. It had borrowed one and a half million gulden due in February 1922. As a result, it had to purchase gulden at the unfavorable exchange rate in order to be able to pay at least part of the debt; for the rest, it had to take out a new forty-year Dutch loan.

It was the reports of this loan that had so enticed Charbonnier! The interest and principle of this consolidation loan was repayable in gulden. Whether Charbonnier decided to forget about his housing projects or to grasp at new opportunities offered municipal authorities in other cities by Danish and other foreign lenders is unclear. Most municipal officials seemed to understand that short-term loans repayable in foreign currency were too great a risk in the hyperinflation, while long-term loans might be worth considering. After all, a long-term loan repayable in marks could also be a tricky business. It was conceivable that a loan received in bad marks might have to be repaid in good ones someday! Many cities simply gave up on borrowing for the time being, especially since the market, even the United States bond market, had become so poor. Thus, if Charbonnier wanted to take out a foreign loan, then Mayor Böss of Berlin could only wish him "better experiences than those who now sit on their foreign loans and cry for help."[32]

By the second half of 1922, their cries for help were taking on very concrete form and were no longer being rejected by the Congress of German Municipalities. In part, this was because of the growing panic over the currency collapse; it was also because the problems of the affected municipalities were similar to those of other individuals and groups of so-called *Valuta* debtors (*Valutaschuldner*). Not all private debtors who had during the war contracted debts repayable in foreign currency had been in a position to deal with their obligations as easily and ruthlessly as the German iron and steel industrialists in 1919–1920. The most important class of debtors were those who had taken out mortgages and/or made debts payable primarily to Swiss but also to Dutch creditors. The most prevalent numerically were, by and large, South Germans, but also, apparently, some Ruhr businessmen had taken out mortgages on their properties from Swiss insurance companies or other Swiss lenders and had to repay in "hard cash"—"*klingende Münzen*," to use the picturesque German term—in "gold currency" or, in a few instances, Swiss francs. The total in mortgages held by Swiss lenders was estimated at a hundred fifty million gold marks. A comparable group was the owners of ships and barges used on Germany's domestic waterways who had continued the prewar practice of taking out mortgages in the Netherlands. Yet another class of debtors consisted of public and semipublic corporations established in south Germany to purchase milk and cattle in Switzerland during the war. Private firms and individuals who had purchased raw materials payable in foreign currency also constituted a debtor group. These last two categories of debtors mentioned owed their money in foreign currency and were in a situation analogous to that of the Swedish-ore debtors, except for the fact that they had not paid off their debts. Another group of private individuals with similar difficulties were the interned German soldiers and civilians who had received medical treatment in Swiss hospitals and spas. Lastly, there was a group of major German insurance companies which had insured Swiss citizens and were obligated to pay their benefits in Swiss currency. The companies might easily have fulfilled this obligation had they not been compelled under German law to place the premiums they had collected in marks or allegedly "gilt-edged" mark denominated assets and then forced to continue to put the premiums into such assets after the war by the Reich Supervisory Office for Insurance. The amount owed Swiss customers was estimated at a hundred twenty-five million gold marks in July 1922, while the amounts owing to persons of other nationalities for similar reasons had not even been calculated. If these firms went bankrupt trying to pay off their Swiss customers, thousands of Germans insured by the same firms would also suffer.[33]

In purely formal legal terms, many of these debts could simply have been paid off in German paper marks. This was especially the case with mortgages, since an agreement to pay in gold or "hard cash," as opposed to an agreement to pay in a specific foreign currency, had ceased to be binding in Germany under a still operative Bundesrat decree of September 28, 1914. Thus, in 1920, some German courts had rejected the demands of Swiss creditors for mortgage interest payments five times higher than the nominal mark value. Such decisions were manifestly harmful to German–Swiss relations and to German credit, and a compromise was worked out in the German–Swiss Agreement of December 6, 1920, aimed at protecting Swiss creditors from excessive losses and German debtors from bankruptcy. The agreement (which is also interesting indirect evidence of the expectations of the German government during the relative stabilization) gave the Swiss creditors a choice between prolonging mortgages for from ten to fifteen years in return for higher interest payments or settling for a compromise payment of the mortgages in paper marks that would be substantially lower in real value than the original mortgage and interest. If the first choice were taken, then the Swiss creditors would be paid interest, the nominal sum of which was to be multiplied to take depreciation into account.[34]

The agreement was a disaster. The German debtors, many of whom had been transformed overnight into big debtors by the agreement, were unwilling to have their interest payments valorized, sabotaged the agreement either by refusing to pay the additional interest or any interest at all, and created a noisy Protective Association of Swiss Gold Mortgage Debtors to lobby for relief. The Swiss were furious, accusing the Germans of bad faith, and began to take the debtors to court again. The collapse of the mark in late 1921 and throughout 1922 compounded the problems because the German–Swiss Agreement of December 6, 1920, did not even provide multipliers to cover the depth to which the German mark had sunk relative to the Swiss franc. For most of the debtors, the interest was now truly unpayable. The situation of the Swiss creditors appeared more hopeless than ever when the Reich Supreme Court ruled in May 1922 that the debts covered by the 1920 agreement attached to the person of the debtor but not to the property. If the owner of the property happened to have sold the property and the present owner had taken over the mortgage, the latter had every right to discharge the mortgage on the property in paper marks, while the actual debtor, if one could identify and extract anything from the luckless individual, was responsible for the debt as valorized by the German–Swiss Agreement. At the same time, the court decision was tantamount to an open invitation for those debtors who had previously been unable to sell their properties because they were presumably encumbered to now sell what in many cases was the only tangible security for their debts.[35]

The Reich government found itself in a most unenviable position as a result of these developments. Initially, the Swiss refused to consider a renegotiation of the agreement, while Finance Minister Hermes stoutly resisted the pressures from the Protective Association of Swiss Gold Mortgage Debtors. The latter's abusive pamphlets against the Reich government and demand for help, however, rapidly attracted the attention of both the Reich Economic Council and the Reichstag as well as the affected state governments. The municipalities with debts payable in foreign currencies also joined in with demands for legal and financial assistance and protection from the Reich and in the arguments of the Swiss mortgage debtors. In part, some of the panic, even with respect to long-term debts, arose from the feeling that the inflation was never going to end. Thus, the idea of seeking a moratorium, a proposal seriously considered by some of the debtors, was treated with skepticism by others. As one pessimist declared, "it is most unlikely that the exchange rate situation will improve significantly in the next decade."[36]

While a good moral case for government assistance existed all along for the cattle dealers and other merchants who had incurred their debts in order to procure food at the government's behest during the war or for the soldiers interned in Switzerland, many of the mortgage debtors now argued that they, too, had a moral right to government assistance as a result of the German–Swiss Agreement of December 6, 1920. If the German government had not made the agreement, they could have paid off their debts in paper marks. Instead, they were being forced to pay more and more because of the inflation. And who was responsible for the inflation? The answer would have been music to the ears of Poincaré! As one irate member of the Reich Economic Council, who also represented the interests of pensioners, put the matter:

... the Reich is legally obligated to help the *Valuta* debtors. The Reich is unconditionally responsible for the financial policy of its highest officials. By preventing the timely payment of the debts because of the existent legal regulations, the *Valuta* debts were made in the first place, and the mark depreciation has

been brought about chiefly through the inflationary financial policy of the Reich. The German League of Pensioners, therefore, intends to take the Reich to the highest court on behalf of its members in order to make the Reich liable for the debts incurred by its members through the monetary depreciation. [I] propose that the Reich Committee also take the position that the Reich government is liable for all the damages arising for the *Valuta* debtors out of the conditions described. Then all the discussions about how the *Valuta* debtors are to be helped will become superfluous. One should not argue that the Reich does not have the means. By taxing real values, the possessors of which have previously had all the advantages of the inflation, there will not only be sufficient means to pay for these costs but also to pay a good portion of the reparations debts.[37]

It is most likely that these remarks bespoke more the tone of those who felt cheated by the government than their realistic expectations. A more serious argument was made by those— and here the indebted municipalities and the Congress of German Municipalities were prominent—who claimed that there were a growing number of good examples and precedents for forcing foreign creditors to accept increasingly worthless currencies in payment for debts. Italy, Yugoslavia, Portugal, and Greece had all issued regulations making debts owed abroad payable in their currencies, sometimes with a modest percentual premium and often on condition that a moratorium be granted on the principle. The French had refused to recognize any special obligations arising out of contracts between Alsace-Lorrainers and the Swiss. Swiss insurance companies were paying off their obligations in German marks, which German law ironically enough required, while the Swiss government was providing considerable relief and protection to its citizens seeking to collect from the Germans. The Poles, much to the outrage of the German public, had insisted that debtors in the former German portions of Poland be permitted to pay mortgages and other debts owed to German banks and creditors in Polish marks. The Austrians, less because they were more delicate than because they were in a more delicate situation, had passed a law permitting the city of Vienna to settle its debts payable in foreign currencies with Austrian kronen, a law which the city then used to negotiate repayment on favorable terms with its creditors. From this unedifying perspective on international behavior, therefore, a decision by the German government to pursue similar policies was by no means inconceivable.[38]

Nevertheless, it was not one to be chosen lightly by a state with pretensions to great-power status, on the one hand, and with a high degree of dependence on foreign credit and international trade, on the other. While the Swiss, Dutch, and other creditors certainly must also have been aware of the options available to Germany, the authorities in Berlin sought to maintain their respectability within reasonable limits. An assumption of the debts, whether of individuals, corporations, or municipalities, was clearly impossible because of the Reich's own financial difficulties, and no category of debtor could be encouraged to follow the proposal that they speculate by buying the foreign exchange they needed and paying off their creditors before things became worse. Yet, various modes of indirect assistance in the form of relief from rent controls, tax benefits, and exclusion from export controls and levies could be provided as means of assisting the debtors. In addition to such demonstrations that the Reich government was willing to make some sacrifices to help the debtors out, it also sought to come to terms with the Swiss through an agreement, finally concluded in June 1923, limiting the multiplier to four times the amount of the interest owed, terminating litigation against the German debtors for two years, and promising Swiss intervention with the Allies to allow a Reich guarantee of the later payment of the debts. In return for having the interest payments rendered worthless, the Reich agreed to make the present mortgagees responsible for payment of the debts on their properties.[39]

The government had a good deal more trouble in trying to solve the problems of the insurance companies. Because these insurance companies were under government supervision, the government had a direct responsibility for the inability of the companies to cover their obligations payable in foreign currency. This was tacitly recognized by a belated decision in December 1921 to permit the investment of premium reserves from foreign policyholders in assets denominated in the currency in which payments would have to be made. Under pressure from the affected insurance companies, the Reich began to negotiate an arrangement with the Swiss and Dutch under which insurance payments in their respective currencies would be partially paid up in the proper currency, while the rest would be given in 3.5 percent interest-bearing certificates to be paid off in twenty or twenty-five years. A special fund was to be set up for this purpose, two-thirds of which would be provided by the Reich and one-third by the Swiss to guarantee interest and amortization. The projected agreement, however, ran into ferocious opposition from those insurance companies which had not written policies payable in foreign currencies, for the government proposed paying the interest on the certificates through a levy of 9 percent on the premiums of newly contracted policies. The companies with foreign-denominated obligations argued that the other insurance companies had been giving rebates on the premiums of new policies and that this allegedly unbusinesslike behavior justified asking them to sacrifice on behalf of their colleagues with debts in francs and gulden. The result was a veritable civil war in the insurance industry, with the "*Valuta*-free" companies forming a protective association in Dresden to fight what they viewed as an outrageous plot aimed at making them pay for the mistakes of the government at a time when rising personnel and other costs were making the industry less profitable. They saw no reason why twenty-five companies still holding themselves above water should risk going under for eight companies which had failed even to report their foreign currency obligations in their yearly business reports and had continued to pay dividends to their domestic customers as if everything were normal. These charges appear to have been justified, since insurance companies were only required to report their obligations in foreign currency in early 1923. Since the Reichstag appeared to side with the "*Valuta*-free" companies, the government decided to conclude a temporary arrangement with the Swiss in October 1922, which was then prolonged during the following year. The problem was further complicated by the fact that the Reparations Commission denied the German government permission to use its own funds to assist the insurance companies.

Ultimately, the dilemma was "solved" after the stabilization, when some of the companies involved did go bankrupt, and the Swiss government ended up coming to the rescue of its citizens.[40]

While the German government sought to do the best it could to maintain Germany's standing as a creditor, for whatever it was still worth, it had to contend with an intensification of tendencies, already quite apparent in 1919–1920, for Germans to stretch court decisions in order to escape their financial and economic obligations to foreigners. Even when refusing to assist municipalities in their efforts to overturn contracts requiring the repayment of debts in foreign exchange, the Congress of German Municipalities had noted the possibility of finding relief through court decisions based on the so-called *clausula rebus sic stantibus.*[41]

This principle held that all contractual arrangements assumed prior conditions without which the contract never would have been made and the disappearance of which might render a contract null and void. Beginning in 1920, some German courts ruled that a contract might be cancelled or its terms subject to renegotiation if conditions were such as to make fulfillment impossible or "ruinous" to one of the parties. In the prewar period, this principle had been rejected in German legal circles as threatening to legal predictability and security (*Rechtssicherheit*), but under the impress of the first inflationary wave at the turn of 1919–1920, some courts showed an increasing inclination to make rulings that gave greater scope to §157 and §242 of the Civil Code—the former providing that transactions had to be carried out in "good faith," and the latter maintaining that contractual obligations were to be fulfilled in accordance with "equity and good faith." While most courts took a fairly conservative posture with respect to the obligations of parties to a contract, conditions at the end of 1921 and in 1922 necessarily multiplied the number of contract cases before the courts and led to increased judicial activity. Important ammunition for a more flexible approach to the nonfulfillment of contracts and alteration of contracts was provided by noted legal scholar Paul Oertmann, who argued that every contract presumed a certain "equivalence" in the performance of both parties. This was the assumption of the equity and good faith clauses in §242 of the Civil Code; if the "equivalence" ceased to exist, then the contract might be nullified.[42]

While German jurists were groping their way as pioneers in the development of a modern law governing the nonfulfillment of contracts, German businessmen were anxiously following court decisions in their desperate effort to escape the ill effects of contracts concluded before or during the early stages of the collapse of the mark. During the relative stabilization, they had made considerable strides in improving their international reputations by ceasing to make spurious claims that they could not fulfill contracts because of barriers placed in the way by the export control boards and by negotiating contracts based on fixed terms. While it would have been madness to have concluded contracts in anything but foreign currency or with provisions taking mark depreciation into account in 1922, the problem of getting out of previously negotiated contracts or insisting on changes had become more delicate.

Here, the evolving decisions of the German courts seemed to offer a very happy way out of the mess, and it was not long before German businessmen were sending their domestic and foreign customers learned summations of cases and opinions by company lawyers or printed compilations of German court decisions allegedly sanctifying the cancellation or revision of contracts.[43] These documents and the practices that accompanied them did little for the reputation of either the German legal establishment or the German business community. Dutch business associations called on their government and members to launch protests in Berlin, to refuse to accept contracts with open-price clauses, and even to take legal action to have German goods confiscated in response to nonfulfillment of contracts.[44] The British Board of Trade sent out a circular warning British businessmen against the shady practices of the Germans and the difficulty of securing relief in German courts. One irate Englishman wrote to the "Chancellor of the Reichstag [*sic*]," pointing out that

. . . Germany should export today 3 times as much as she does but for the fact that nearly everyone who does business with Germans gets cheated. If they do not get cheated then they do not get deliveries. For instance my friends and I have just lost about £2000 through buying marks to pay for blankets when the exchange was about 2000 to the £1. The blankets were never delivered so we now have lost nearly all our money because the exchange [is] 30000 to the 1£.[45]

German business organizations and Foreign Office officials were very worried about this behavior. They pointed out that foreigners understood that some German businessmen were in serious trouble and were prepared to negotiate but that the sending out of court decisions and persistent breaking of contracts was, "first of all, a great mistake by the German firms and, second, a piece of stupidity that might possibly not be repaired later."[46] The court decisions could by no means be interpreted as a blank check permitting businessmen to break their contracts because of any change of circumstances. The German Consul General in Amsterdam was particularly distressed because he was quite well-informed of the court decisions, which were anything but consistent. Some, for example, only permitted the cancellation or change of contract if fulfillment would prove "ruinous" to one of the parties, and all the decisions required that the changed economic conditions could not have been foreseen by the contracting parties. This German official, at least, was most skeptical about the pretension of all the German businessmen that the mark collapse was totally unexpected:

It is generally known that heavy reparations burdens have been placed on the economic life of Germany and that, quite aside from these burdens, it has not proven possible to bring the ordinary budget into balance. The result of this condition is that a few billion uncovered mark bills are issued every week. For an objectively thinking merchant, the logical consequence of this situation must be a progressive deterioration of the mark. To be astonished over this economic development and its consequences is improper in my view. The German judiciary, however, is almost to a man of the view that this logical consequence is not to have been overlooked by the German manufacturer.[47]

These were well-taken points indeed. Even the most cursory examination of the flood of litigation and dealing with contracts since the war shows that there was much confusion, contradiction, and revision of lower-court decisions by higher-court ones.[48] A balance was to be drawn at the end of the year by the jurist Hans-Carl Nipperdey. German courts would con-

done breach of contract only in cases in which there was simultaneous fulfillment of a number of difficult conditions: a total change of circumstances that could not be anticipated, demonstrable goodwill on the part of the party seeking to overturn the contract, manifest economic ruin of the plaintiff if the contract remained in effect, the nonspeculative character of the arrangement, and a balance of expected performance by both parties. In the face of such conditions, Nipperdey could only advise settlement through mediation out of court.[49] This view was shared by the German Consul General in Amsterdam, who pointed out such cases could lead to decisions against German defendants. At the same time, the legal costs—involving high retainers, hourly fees, and percentages of the winnings that were calculated in gulden—were likely to alienate Dutch businessmen seeking redress in German courts.

It must also be said, however, that most German lawyers needed the money, and one of the ironies of Nipperdey's discussion of contracts and monetary depreciation is that it was addressed to the problem of "Monetary Depreciation as a Legislative Problem in Private Law," the projected central item on the agenda of the Twenty-third German Congress of Lawyers scheduled for September 12–13, 1922. Unfortunately, the "beautiful, hospitable" city of Hamburg, "where the extraordinary increase of prices was particularly strongly felt,"[50] had been chosen as the site, and the Association of German Lawyers decided to cancel the event because too few of its members could afford to attend. Nipperdey remarked, "It seems as if the monetary depreciation itself resists scholarly consideration. It has become so monstrous, that it prohibits discussion of itself by the jurists."[51] As the lawyers and other members of the free professions, learned professions, and middle class in general had discovered, the inflation was destroying not only legal certainty and security but their own financial and economic security as well.

"The Distress of the Intellectual Workers"

The experience of inflation as an economic disorder bringing privation and hardship and as a social disorder damaging to traditional styles of life and values was evident before the hyperinflation. The reduced standard of living of middle-class persons who had lived in reasonable comfort and security before the war, the redistribution of assets and income within German society, and the often unwelcome changes in power, influence, and cultural values evident in postwar Germany were hardly novelties in 1922. But hyperinflation did change the context and character of these phenomena, just as it qualitatively changed the nature of creditor/debtor relations in such a way as to provoke the debate over the continued validity of the mark-for-mark principle. There are, after all, differences between relative and absolute change; hard times and disaster; precarious survival and extinction. The coming of hyperinflation appeared to undermine all chances for a breathing space that might lead to stabilized conditions and recovery. Prior to the hyperinflation, those left stranded by the monetary flood could entertain the hope that the waters would recede, various forms of relief would come, and rescue would prove possible. Now the hyperinflation appeared as an endless torrent which would drown all who had not already been brought to safe shores and high ground. Those groups excluded from the labor market by age or disability aside, none seemed more affected by this turn of events than the so-called *geistige Arbeiter*—the intellectual workers in the free professions, the arts and sciences, and all those who professed to be "bearers" of Germany's cultural and intellectual traditions.[52]

Such persons probably were quicker and more willing to draw analogies between what had happened in Austria and what was going on in Germany since they were undoubtedly more impressed by the cultural similarities between the two countries than by differences in size and economy. The collapse of the Austrian krone and the parlous state of Austria's "intellectual workers" could not but help produce analogies in the minds of Germans. The apocalyptic mood was reported by the British Consul in Frankfurt am Main, who recounted the remarks of a well-known professor with whom he had spoken:

The position of Germany, he said, is in some respects more serious than that of Austria, for the latter country has certain advantages and attributes which we do not possess. One of these advantages is that, unlike the Germanic Empire she is not a new state but an ancient one strongly imbued with historical and traditional associations. She has, moreover, what this country possesses only in an inferior degree, namely considerable potential wealth in her museums and galleries. If the dry rot really sets in, Germany's ruin will be more rapid and more complete than that of her neighbor, for Germany's strength lies in her science and in her learning and with them, the capacity for acquiring knowledge, and for accurate and detailed research work, go hand in hand with industrialism. As things are today, Professors, Teachers and Men of Science are not given the right to live; many of them indeed, will probably die in the coming winter for lack of food, clothing and warmth. Their sons, instead of following their fathers' careers, as they have done for generations past, will, by the force of circumstances, turn to manual labour as a means to earn their bread. Labour . . . has already begun to rule in Germany and there is no demand for brains; that is to say, brains have no longer a marketable value. The result can only be a catastrophe for Germany and the downfall of civilisation in Central Europe, if not, indeed, in the whole world.[53]

The influence of Spengler's *Decline and Fall of the West*, the second volume of which appeared in 1922, undoubtedly did much to feed such sentiments, but most of those who did mental work were probably most concerned about their own decline and fall as mirrored by conditions in Austria. As one lawyer argued to his colleagues:

We finally have to learn to think beyond tomorrow and to ask where we will be in a year. The answer is as dismal as can be and can be stated in a word: Austria. . . . We are always one year behind Austria. The calculation is exact, as everyone who knows Austria is aware. Insofar as one can prophesy, we will be exactly where Austria is in October 1923, in other words with a depreciation of the mark ten times its present level. We have to come to terms with this fact and learn to face up to it. Some will say, that the value of cases will increase with the depreciation, but experience teaches that the value of cases does not increase in proportion to depreciation. (Very true!) In Austria, the legal profession has, so to speak, been sentenced to ruination [*zugrunde gerichtet*].[54]

The chief victims of the situation were not the judiciary, who were civil servants and thus entitled to salaries, cost-of-living increases, and pensions, as well as freedom from overhead costs, but rather the independent lawyers who enjoyed none of these benefits. This independence, however, did not mean that they were completely free agents or that they did not have a fixed place in the legal system. The civil and criminal courts were required to use their services (*Anwaltszwang*), and they were attached to specific courts (*Lokalisierung*). Most important, they were subject to a specific fee schedule (*Gebührenordnung*) based on the monetary value of what was being contested and the fees defined for the various stages of a legal action. While a lawyer had the right to negotiate a fee that deviated from the schedule with his client, this was a risky matter since the defeated party was required to pay the scheduled fee but not the negotiated legal costs of the victor. Fees for criminal cases were fixed at a lower level, as were those in which a lawyer was called upon to act on behalf of clients too poor to pay. Costs of travel to distant courts and per diem expenses were also regulated by government schedule. Prior to 1914, this system at once provided Germany's independent lawyers (the number of which rose from 7,262 in 1903 to 12,324 in 1913) with a reasonably good living as well as a special status between the commercial occupations—which were preoccupied with pecuniary gain—and the civil service—which was beholden to the state.[55]

What had once been a source of special pride as well as an often higher standard of living than their colleagues in the civil service, rapidly became a formula for penury during the inflation. The increase of fee schedules was a cumbersome process, accomplished through Reichstag legislation in 1918–1919 and, following the passage of a law in July 1921 permitting adjustments by decree, through the issuance of decrees. The lawyers had to pay a high price for this concession, which was granted with great reluctance by the Justice Ministry; namely, a ban on the right of the Association of German Lawyers to issue guidelines or standards for its members in negotiating additional payment from their clients. While practically every other occupational and professional group in German society was being allowed to organize and collectively determine or advise uniform standards of remuneration to deal with the inflation, the lawyers were deprived of their rights to use their organizations for such a purpose. Some went so far as to question the constitutionality of the situation since it appeared to prejudice the freedom of coalition of lawyers.

The anger over this restriction was fueled by the manifest inability of the government to issue decrees often enough and fast enough to keep up with inflation. The first decree increasing the schedule appeared in August 1921; four decrees were issued in 1922; eight were to be issued in 1923. The increases in allowances for travel were also persistently inadequate. It was not uncommon for the client to travel second class while the lawyer traveled third class to save on expenses. The sums involved in litigation did not increase in proportion to the depreciation even before 1922, and the disparity grew thereafter. At the same time, the interest in litigation decreased—a mixed blessing, since the reduction of litigiousness often undoubtedly was a consequence of financial inability to defend one's legitimate rights in court. The number of cases tried before courts dropped from a yearly average of 2,632,160 between 1911 and 1915 to 1,559,851 in 1921. At the same time, overhead costs increased. Secretarial and other office help demanded the same cost-of-living increases enjoyed by their compatriots in private industry and government offices. While older lawyers with small practices could put their wives and daughters to work for them, larger urban practices required the help of regular employees. Furthermore, no office could be run without such basic requirements as paper, light, and heat. In short, a substantial number of lawyers found themselves in desperate straits by late 1922, and some were actually giving up their practices to take jobs in commerce or industry. Under such circumstances, it was little wonder that the Association of German Lawyers thought it more important to have its representatives discuss "the distress of the lawyers," than to attend an unaffordable meeting in Hamburg on monetary depreciation and the law.

The proposal of the association was a radical one, although not as radical as some would have liked. It did not call for the total elimination of the fee schedule, as some wished, but it did ask that the schedule be treated as nothing more than the minimum required to cover overhead costs and that legislation be passed permitting lawyers to ask for an "appropriate compensation" (*angemessene Vergütung*) without requiring prior agreement as to the exact fee assessed the client. Supporters of this proposal as well as those who wished to eliminate the fee schedule argued that it was nothing but blind social prejudice and status pretension to argue the holy writ that lawyers could only charge a fixed amount in accordance with the monetary worth of the case. Were doctors indifferent to the number of visits they made to a patient? How could lawyers, who were daily called upon to deal with the problems of economic life, pursue such a policy while knowing full well that the businessmen they represented would go bankrupt if they did not take all costs into account when selling their products? Nevertheless, there remained those lawyers who were reluctant to see their profession as just another business: "What I treasure in the legal profession is that I do not have to bargain and negotiate with every client about what I can and cannot demand. . . . I esteem the businessman, but I do not want to be a businessman. . . . I want to have the fee schedule because I want to be bound by fee schedules and law as a person with a legal public status and then be free to secure what is appropriate through agreement."[56] Furthermore, as this lawyer argued, the principle of appropriate compensation and the fee schedule were incompatible; who was to determine what was "appropriate"? The end result, he feared, would be endless complaints by clients over the interpretation of what was fair and what was not.

This, however, was an argument that cut both ways. It was also possible to argue that if the lawyer was a person with special status in public law whom the courts had to employ, then the time had come for lawyers to be taken into the civil service. Since it was now the jurists in the civil service rather than the private lawyers who were doing better financially (thus completely reversing the prewar situation), one should make the best of the situation. One lawyer suggested that the government should pay the overhead costs of lawyers just as they paid the costs of the secretaries and clerks of judges. In this way, at least some measure of independence could be maintained. The truth was that the lawyers and their spokesmen were confused and torn by unattractive options. On the one hand, they wished to have the advantages of businessmen, who were able to take changing

costs and currency depreciation into account, without becoming completely commercialized. The corollary of this stance was the call for a limitation on the number of persons allowed to study and practice law, the so-called *numerus clausus*. Such demands were intensifed by the increasing number of former officers or persons who might have become officers entering law as well as the increasing interest shown in the profession by women. Furthermore, there was a growing interest in expanding the activities of lawyers beyond the courtroom into the realms of business and government consultation but also into the courts in which they had not previously been allowed to practice; that is, the commercial, industrial, and labor courts. On the other hand, the lawyers wished to maintain their status as a free profession and not become civil servants while insisting that the government honor their public functions and their special status. Underlying the entire discussion was often a deep resentment against both the social classes who were overtaking them and a political regime that appeared to be actively presiding over this process. One lawyer expressed this particularly well:

If we want to go back to the origins of our distressed situation, then it is the domestic policy of our government that is to blame. We belonged to the good *Mittelstand*. That has changed. The previous fourth estate now takes our place. Every party strives to win over the fourth estate, and we can see where this leaves us. In the face of this, we have to give up the principle of preaching self-help without actually practicing it. Insofar as we can help ourselves, we should do so. But we also want to exercise our right to demand protection by the state in view of the monetary depreciation promoted by the pay scales of the civil servants along with the reparations payments and which, through no fault of our own, has created the situation that the compensation for our labors steadily sinks despite our great efforts.[57]

Such feelings were often aggravated in direct confrontations between representatives of the profession's interests and the Socialists. Thus, in the discussions held in late 1922 in the special subcommittee of the Reich Economic Council set up to study ways of improving the situation of the intellectual workers, one of the Socialist labor representatives, Hugo Cohn, responded critically both to claims that the lawyers were overly burdened by employee costs and to their desire to try cases before the labor courts. He pointed out that

the salaries of white-collar workers in law offices were very bad even in peacetime, when things were going well for the lawyers, because the lawyers always thought of themselves first. The workers do not wish to allow the advantages they have gained for themselves through the labor courts to be endangered by the dragging out of disputes that would result from letting the lawyers into these courts. Moreover, if the lawyers are allowed to practice in them, then the number of those going into law and the distressed situation of the lawyers will become even greater.[58]

These harsh and almost insulting remarks were somewhat softened by another labor representative, who pointed out that those involved in the labor courts, like those dealing with industrial and commercial courts, wanted them run according to economic and social rather than narrow and often irrelevant legal principles. According to this trade unionist, most lawyers were poorly trained to deal with such problems. The spokesman for the lawyers, Dr. Hachenburg, a liberal jurist with considerable economic expertise, found the attitude provocative and thought it a "social obligation to care as much for the free professions as for the other social groups." It is significant that he was seconded by Ludwig Heyde, the editor of *Soziale Praxis*, who had long fought for the improvement of the social condition of the workers but who felt that "the general lack of understanding in worker circles for the distressed situation of the intellectual workers is very regrettable." He attributed this misery to the generally bad economic situation which had diminished the demand for "relative luxury goods." It reminded him of the time of the guilds, when one had also sought to preserve cherished institutions in a collapsing market and a changing world. This combination of sympathy and fatalism did little to improve the condition of the lawyers. In February 1923, the Reich Economic Council subcommittee unanimously voted to support the lawyers in their call for the removal of restrictions on their freedom of coalition and for a change in the fee schedule and, by a majority, to support the use of lawyers in the labor courts. Yet, this did very little to improve their worsening condition under the circumstances.[59]

If legal services could be considered a "relative luxury good," could the same be said of medical services? While some lawyers pointed to doctors as a model of a free profession that charged what it thought necessary, others reminded them that people were no longer going to private doctors because they could no longer afford the fees. At the same time, the majority of doctors, who were dependent on the health insurance funds, faced increasing impoverishment and became discontented and bitter. Neither commercialization nor "socialization" seemed to offer them protection, and the conflicts between the leading organization of the medical profession and the representatives of labor were markedly more severe than those involving the lawyers.

To a great extent, the conflicts were a massive intensification of the prewar problems of the medical profession. While the professionalization of medical practice prior to 1914 had helped doctors in Germany to attain both prestige and higher incomes, medical practitioners also confronted a vast expansion of the compulsory medical insurance system. By 1914, approximately 50 percent of all Germans were enrolled in health insurance programs (*Krankenkassen*), and it was estimated in 1908 that as much as 90 percent of all practicing doctors were devoting as much as 75 percent of their time in work for the health insurance funds.[60] What this meant was that doctors, despite their membership in a free profession, found themselves to an increasing extent in the position of employees of the health insurance funds as well as in a state of growing dependence on health-insurance-fund schedules of payments and honoraria. The payments were based on a fixed amount per member of the insurance program, while the honoraria were calculated according to the services rendered by the physician in individual cases. There were thus manifold possibilities for conflict between the doctors and the health insurance system, especially with respect to the payments, honoraria, and types of services that could and should be given to patients. Prior to 1914, doctors fought and, by and large, won bitter battles with the health insurance programs over these issues. Their success was largely due to the organization of a majority of doctors in the Association of German Doctors, more popularly known as the Hartmannbund, after its founder, Leipzig doctor

Hermann Hartmann, who not only promoted the organization of the medical profession but also, with increasing and visible success after 1900, encouraged the use of the strike weapon as a means of bringing the health insurance funds to terms. Whereas the funds were required by law to supply medical services, the doctors, as members of a free profession, were under no such obligation. Thanks to collective action and a ruthless policy against outsiders, the Hartmannbund was able to develop what was tantamount to a system of collectively negotiated agreements with the health insurance funds that strengthened both the economic position and professional autonomy of doctors.[61]

The anomalous situation in which trade-union methods were used to protect the special interests of a free profession was well reflected in one of the few prewar demands of the Hartmannbund which had only limited success; namely, the insistence that the health insurance funds hire all doctors who wished to work for them and thus permit patients a "free choice of doctor." Most health insurance funds, especially the increasing number under Socialist influence, stoutly resisted this demand on the grounds that it would substantially increase costs and undermine the control of health insurance programs over their medical employees. Many doctors also opposed it for being too costly as well as threatening the more lucrative contracts possible under a system in which the number of doctors hired by a health insurance fund could be limited. Concern about an "overproduction" of doctors increased prior to the outbreak of the war and did not abate after 1918, despite the fact that 10 percent of the twenty-five thousand doctors at the front did not return.[62]

In 1921, there were 36,186 doctors in Germany (or one doctor for every 1,700 inhabitants), whereas in 1909 there had been 30,558 doctors (or one doctor for every 2,400 inhabitants). In large cities, however, the 1921 ratio of doctors to population was 1:950, while it was 1:2,250 in small towns and in the countryside. Socialist commentators suggested that the "overproduction" of doctors and some of their misery could be alleviated if they were willing to leave the cities. The misery was nevertheless

scarcely deniable, and the medical association and its publications and allies pinned the blame on the "exaggeration of the insurance concept"[63] through the rapid expansion of compulsory and voluntary health insurance under the Weimar Republic to include agricultural and domestic workers, home workers, and workers and employees in the public sector. Advocates for the medical profession claimed that the insurance had been extended to persons who could well afford to pay for private care, while critics suggested that much private care was being given and never recorded and that doctors were taking additional money "on the side" from patients. Yet, the stories of health insurance fund doctors who were forced to take jobs as waiters or sell sausages and *Schnaps* at places like the Anhalter Station in Berlin were too widespread not to be credible, as were reports of those who played fast and loose with professional ethics and engaged in quackery to make ends meet.[64]

Not surprisingly, therefore, the struggle between the Hartmannbund and the health insurance funds became more extreme than ever before, especially since legislation passed following the establishment of the Republic increased the power of worker representatives in the health insurance funds, while both the expansion of those entitled to insurance and the economic situation made the doctors extremely dependent on the health insurance system. What the official historian of the Hartmannbund sarcastically referred to as the "blessings of parliamentarism"[65] led to increasing radicalization of the doctors in their struggle with the health insurance funds over honoraria. In 1920, the Labor Ministry had to mediate medical strikes in Berlin and elsewhere triggered by the raising of the entitlement to insurance from those with incomes of twelve thousand to twenty thousand marks. The Ministry made significant concessions to the demand for the "free choice of doctor," but the coming of the hyperinflation increased the environment of hostility and conflict, particularly because of the failure of the health insurance funds to grant satisfactory honoraria as a consequence of their own financial difficulties and rising costs.[66] The doctors now demanded the passage of a law granting "free choice of doctor" (so that no health insurance fund could exclude a doctor), fees that kept up with inflation, and relief from the tax on alcohol as well as reduced telephone rates. There were calls for the introduction of the *numerus clausus* to restrict the number of persons who could enter the profession and, at the same time, for permission to advertise for patients. The basic question, however, and one not only raised by Socialists, was whether the acceptance of every doctor who applied to the health insurance funds would do anything about the actual plight of the doctors. The representatives of the profession did not gain much sympathy by their strike threats, and the publication of statements to the effect that "for we doctors to put ourselves on a brotherly basis with the workers means to lose the last remainder of our self-respect"[67] hardly helped the situation. While recommending the "free choice of doctor," the Reich Economic Council subcommittee dealing with the intellectual workers refused to recommend a law mandating such a system. Others noted that there was a contradiction between trying to restrict competition through the *numerus clausus* and promoting it through allowing advertising. Even more than lawyers, doctors wanted to be protected from both commercialization and socialization, from the brutal struggle for existence which they were facing, and from being transformed from members of a free profession into civil servants subject to planning. To some, it seemed that the assumption of civil-servant status was either inevitable or welcome or both, and this threat of socialization made the non-Socialist doctors more radical than ever and more willing to intensify their prewar practice of combining trade-union tactics with anti-Socialist politics. When doctors' strikes broke out in Berlin in 1923, it was the Socialist doctors who played the role of strikebreakers.[68]

A doctors' strike, of course, was a serious matter, but could the same be said of the long-threatened Berlin actors' strike that finally broke out in December 1922? The actors, a substantial portion of whom had been unionized, certainly took themselves very seriously. They were particularly outspoken during the relative stabilization in 1920–1921, their more aggressive leaders demanding yearly contracts, a month's paid vacation, two free evenings a week, and all the rights of self-protection against being laid off or fired granted normal white-collar workers through their factory councils and the decrees limiting the right of employers to shut down plants. These demands arose quite naturally out of the socioeconomic situation of the acting profession after the war. Most actors found themselves in a two-front war against the theatre directors, on the one hand, and the "stars," on the other. The vast majority of actors were hired on the basis of short-term contracts, were overworked during the season, and were then compelled to make do with whatever work they could find during the summer. The jobs they had to take were often humiliating and always ill-paid so that they were, in effect, "proletarianized." This was more or less the condition of the next, middling group of actors, who were fortunate enough to be able to make ends meet by taking work on the side in the film industry. Only a small group of "stars" were in a position to get high fees for individual performances and to make large sums doing films in addition, often to the detriment of their theatre work since these "big earners" (*Schwerverdiener*) were notorious for refusing to attend rehearsals regularly because of their film commitments. The actors' union, therefore, demanded that the theatre directors hire a full ensemble, guarantee that it could make a living for the full year from its work in the theatre, and only conclude special contracts involving honoraria with the agreement of the theatre actors' council.[69]

The managers and owners of the theatres rejected such demands, arguing that they could not take the risks involved and that such claims were inappropriate for an artistic profession. The actors, despite the miserable economic situation of many of their number, were divided over the more extreme position taken by the leadership of their organization.[70] What is extraordinary, however, is that actors, and the opera singers who joined with them in their strike of December 1922, should have had anything to strike against given Germany's condition after the First World War. Both the opera and, to a very significant extent, the theatre in prewar Germany had prospered thanks to the support of the royal and princely courts, and these institutions were held on to tenaciously after 1918 because of their peculiar place in Germany's cultural life. Thus, when the American reporter for the *New York American* and other Hearst newspapers, Karl H. von Wiegand, in 1919 asked the new intendant of the Berlin State Opera, Max von Schilling, whether Germany, in the light of its financial situation and international obligations, really needed some thirty-odd opera houses, Schilling unhesitatingly replied in the affirmative: "To Germany and the German people opera is a cultural necessity. Music is a part of the Soul of Germany. The opera is educative and inspiring. It has become a part of our education—a part of our intellectual life. We cannot, must not let it be lowered in quality, we must not alone keep it up but endeavor to maintain the highest standard."[71] Schilling warned that the opera could never become a "paying business proposition" and was quite insistent that the new Socialist regimes had to take over where the Kaiser and princes had left off and pay the deficits so that people could continue to afford tickets. He brushed aside suggestions that the Socialists might not wish to subsidize an institution of so little interest to the workers with the argument that the real problem was that the Berlin opera was housed in too small a building and that larger facilities would at once make it possible for more persons to attend and to increase receipts. By 1922, Berlin, in fact, had three opera houses, the state-run Deutsche Oper in Charlottenburg, the Kroll Opera House, which was supported by the *Volksbühne* (the Socialist organization which strove to make culture available to the workers), and the Volksoper in the Theater des Westens. The last of these and the newest was the product of a dedicated group of founders who set up a nonprofit corporation to fund an affordable opera. Whether or not Berlin could afford to have three high-quality opera houses under hyperinflationary conditions, however, was a genuine question. Even progressive, socially minded critics wondered if it made sense to perform a work like Beethoven's *Fidelio* in the Volksoper and argued that the producers had underestimated "the effort, the mental concentration, the level of humanity that are necessary in order to be appropriately receptive to the full worth of a great musical work of art."[72]

Manifestly, there was more room for theatres, not only because many more new works were available that could be produced more cheaply, but also because theatres could put on entertainment requiring minimal effort to understand. There was, of course, much difference of opinion as to what fell into the category of "tasteless honky-tonk [*Tingeltangel*]"[73] passing for theatre. Karl von Wiegand waxed indignant over the manner in which it was "as if the revolution had stirred up the very dregs of the German mind and soul." By this he did not simply mean the sex films and nudity on stage, but also the so-called legitimate theatre itself: "On the legitimate stage Wedekind's 'Pandora's Box' is the limit to which the vileness of eroticism, sensuality, and brutality, has gone. It is the 'limit'—the very mental and psychic gutters. It is the sequence to Wedekind's 'Erdgeist' (Earth-spirit). It surpasses the latter in all that is vile in human nature. Two lust murders take place on the stage. It has played to crowded houses for weeks at the Koeniggraetzer theatre, which makes a speciality of Ibsen and Strindberg."[74] The first uncut presentation of Arthur Schnitzler's satire on social hypocrisy and sexual morality, *Der Reigen,* opened in January 1921 in Berlin-Charlottenburg's Kleines Schauspielhaus to right-wing stink bombs and charges of "Jewish pornography,"[75] and the state attorney later in the year sought to prosecute the director, producer, and performers for "creating a public nuisance through immoral actions."[76] If the number of theatres in Berlin did not decline during the inflation, however, it was not because of the thrills provided by Wedekind and Schnitzler, but rather because the majority of theatres were maintained through a variety of means which included public subvention and private trustification as well as exploitation of their actors and actresses and pandering to public demand for triviality and sensationalism.

There can be no question about the fact that the old legitimate theatre in Berlin and throughout Germany was highly dependent on government subsidization. In Berlin and Munich, the government provided nine million marks each in 1920 to support two major theatres each, while ten other major cities spent a total of 29,388,000 marks to support a total of fourteen theatres. Substantial subventions were also given to provincial theatres. When the state could not help, trustification seemed to be the only answer, especially in Berlin, where the Rotter Brothers Concern controlled six of the largest Berlin private theatres, while Felix Hollaender struggled to keep together the theatres previously run by Max Reinhardt.[77]

If the German theatre blossomed during the relative stabilization, albeit not to everyone's taste, it was because of this combination of public subvention and private support for either cultural or purely commercial reasons. Nevertheless, the change in audience was noticeable, since the old middle class that had previously gone regularly to the theatre found it increasingly difficult to pay for tickets; a new clientele of *nouveaux riches* and foreigners played a major role in supplying the audience for opera and stage productions. This is not to say that the entertainment industry survived because of these two classes, and it is difficult to determine how much and what portions of the middle class were spending their money in this way. Author and critic Alfred Döblin perhaps offers more than a clue concerning this question. He noted the filled movie houses, theatres, and restaurants in August 1922 with amazement and was struck by the willingness to buy even the most expensive tickets. People seemed to be willing to live for the day and to spend their money as quickly as they got it. When he looked about at the audience during an intermission between acts of Strindberg's *Dance of Death* at the Kleines Theater Unter den Linden, he saw a "not very select, very rich public, but good and simple *Mittelstand*, a great deal that had the look of white-collar workers."[78]

With the progress of the hyperinflation, however, the theatres, both public and private, genuinely feared for their very existence. How long, after all, could or would white collar workers sacrifice what Döblin described as "between four and twenty-two breads" for seats at a new Strindberg production? In April 1922, a good ticket at the Berlin theatre cost 227 marks; in October, the price was 1,000 marks. Deficits in the publicly supported theatres grew larger, while subventions could no longer keep pace. The same held true for Germany's great orchestras. The Berlin Philharmonic had been re-

ceiving a subsidy from the city of sixty thousand marks in return for putting on a series of popular concerts for low ticket prices, but the hyperinflation had so negatively affected the orchestra's finances that the magistracy felt compelled to provide a seven-hundred-thousand-mark subsidy in November 1922.[79] As in every other realm of cultural life, so in the theatre, opera, and concert stage; the wages and salaries of nonprofessional help rose more rapidly than the pay of actors and soloists who were not top stars. The situation of the actors became more desperate than ever, and it was this, above all, that triggered the December 1922 strike.

It was a strike that worried even leftist friends of the theatre, like Siegfried Jacobsohn, a major critic and editor of the *Die Weltbühne*. In September, he predicted that the hyperinflation would bring about the economic collapse of the theatres by Christmas, and the strike seemed to confirm his predictions.[80] He sharply criticized both sides. The actors had failed to face the reality that they were in the same miserable boat as other intellectual workers: "What will become of the countless journalists, painters, *Dozenten*, doctors? If 682 of the 2,300 Berlin lawyers do not have an income of more than 18,000 marks, then they have the choice of starving or changing their hopeless profession; and when they are forced to, they make the choice one by one. They and whatever no longer has a function cannot expect to be kept going by a pathetically impoverished people for their own sake, for the sake of their beautiful eyes, beautiful voices, beautiful legs."[81] As for the directors, he accused them of being mercenary and forgetting that the situation required sacrifices from them as well. He urged both to realize that many theatres would have to close and that it was the chief responsibility of both actors and managers to ensure that artistic values were protected in the process.

Such nonpartisan Olympian posturing was not appreciated, however. Producer Berthold Viertel reminded Jacobsohn in a bitter reply that actors and producers like himself were not dealing with a majority of managers and owners who cared about art or were experts, but rather with speculators and trusts of theatre owners who, with their "George-Grosz faces," played the role of "vampires," sucking the blood of both the theatre as an institution and those who worked for it by trying to service a public thirsting for sensations and stars and to profiteer at the same time. Thus, there was "a disorder, growing from above and from below, that destroys everything."[82] In Viertel's view, the actors' strike, by the sheer shock effect of intellectual workers employing proletarian methods in the struggle to maintain the dignity of their craft against commercialization, was serving the art. Was this not also posturing, however? By what right, after all, did actors in the Germany of 1922 claim a year's pay for eight month's work and put on a proletarian pose while refusing to do the proletarian labor that many other intellectual workers were forced to do under existing conditions? The argument could also be made that the actors stop pretending that they were defending ideals and fight for the economic conditions they could realistically attain under conditions requiring the rationalization of the theatre business.[83]

It was one of the peculiarities of the inflation, and especially the hyperinflation, to lay bare the economic relationships of patronage, dependency, and intermediation upon which intellectual work rested and to do so in a manner that promoted hostility between the intellectual workers and those upon whom they were economically dependent. Theatre managers and owners were in conflict not only with actors but also with the authors of the plays and pieces they commissioned over honoraria and the question of royalties. The struggle between the authors of scholarly and literary works and publishers, however, was especially intense, achieving public notoriety shortly after the inflation through a lengthy and often bitter debate between authors and publishers in *Die Weltbühne*.[84]

Actually, however, the battle had been going on for some time. In 1900, the General Association of Writers had been founded, primarily for the purpose of protecting the interests of authors in matters of copyrights and honoraria, while the Leipzig Academic Protective Association, founded in 1903, was set up for the purposes of keeping the price of scholarly publications under control and promoting their dissemination as well as "protecting scholarly authors against the superior economic power of

the publishers when concluding contracts."[85] Conflicts between authors and publishers over the transfer of copyrights from one publisher to another, pricing policies, and honoraria increased dramatically during and after the war because of increased printing and paper costs and publishers' price increases of books. An investigation of these problems by the Association for Social Policy (*Verein für Sozialpolitik*), which was completed in 1922, bore testimony to a sorry state of affairs in which authors were either left defenseless against publishers or failed to exercise such rights as they had. The situation in scholarly publishing was particularly bad, since publishers were demanding subventions from organizations devoted to the support of scholarship and state or city governments to completely cover their costs. They would never take full responsibility or pay honoraria for works by other than well-established scholars, and then only for texts and reference works. As one critic pointed out, "that the German private publisher 'makes sacrifices for scholarship' is a phrase that is not made true by frequent repetition."[86] He wondered if the Anglo-American system of university presses was not the proper solution for Germany, while some critics went so far as to advocate the creation of cooperative presses by authors or the socialization of the book publication industry. Most people viewed such plans to be impracticable under existing conditions. The problem of properly rewarding creative work increased as inflation diminished the value of honoraria and advances while publishers were able more or less to adapt to conditions. The response of publishers to writer complaints often only served to fuel writer resentment. While it might be reasonable for publishers to argue that scholars had to depend on their salaries and not on honoraria for their income and that the state had a responsibility to raise academics to a higher level of the civil-service scale, it was more than a little provocative under the conditions of the inflation for a publisher to draw upon Adam Smith's argument that the "liberal and honorable professions" were by nature "underrecompensed." Smith had drawn an analogy between the free professions and an "unfair lottery." In a fair lottery, the winner gains what the losers had lost, but those who gambled on making a living from a free profession could by no means count on making a living from their work even if they were successful.[87] Was it not also possible to argue, however, that the living creative artists and their heirs were entitled to a guaranteed minimum income from their labors and that this constituted nothing more than an extension of German social policy?[88]

This is precisely what leading organizations of writers and artists were claiming. In November 1920, representatives of various organizations of playwrights, film scriptwriters, composers and orchestrators, and artists met in the Berlin Weinhaus Rheingold to discuss measures to relieve the plight of those in their professions and came up with a scheme for a 5 percent cultural levy (*Kulturabgabe*) to be placed on all books, sheet music, and concert performances—including works whose copyright had expired. The levy was to be used for the purpose of assisting contemporary intellectual workers in these fields. The proposal subsequently was revised in a memorandum for the Reich Economic Council which increased the proposed levy to 10 percent of the sale price. While the levy was to be paid by the consumers, the publishers were required to provide a strict accounting of their costs, and the levy was not to be included in any discount given to retailers.[89]

The proposal infuriated publishers, especially since it appeared to be instigated by old enemies of the industry and also because it had been made without any serious consultation with publishers. It is hard not to agree with the publishers in their criticism of the projected cultural levy as a pretentious absurdity:

The so-called "cultural levy" is nothing but a fine sounding name for a new special tax on intellectual cultivation at the cost of all who buy a book, piece of music, or picture, who go to a concert or movie or who hear an orchestra play. It is a special tax for the benefit of a single group, the intellectual workers. . . . One must raise the question as to what are the implications when one group declares itself in distress and especially important culturally and demands of the state that it tax the entire nation on its behalf? By the same right, needy chemists, technicians, machine builders could ask for a special tax upon everything that is covered or had once been covered by the patent laws. Just as one could tax the Bible or the works of Homer, Beethoven, and Rubens, so one could tax hammers, pincers, or saws for the benefit of needy inventors . . . since these tools also were once invented. . . . The entire nation is in distress. We find ourselves in "a shrinking economic basis for a highly cultured people." No one has enough anymore. Certainly one cannot disregard the fact that the material compensation for intellectual work has remained behind that of manual labor during and after the Revolution. . . . But whoever places himself and his fate upon so uncertain a foundation cannot complain if the ground gives way when his creative powers fail or because he lives in a time of crisis.[90]

This is not to say that the publishers did not indulge in a goodly measure of dubious self-righteousness of their own. The hostility of the publishers was exacerbated when they were summoned by the Reich Economic Council to testify and were told that they would be handed a detailed questionnaire to fill out that would seek to penetrate into the mysteries of the business. The fact that the publishers were being widely criticized for profiteering at the expense of their authors and that the publishing industry was not represented on the Reich Economic Council made the entire situation appear even more ominous. Happily for the publishers, the hearing was meant to be informational, and they were not required to testify under oath. The representatives of the industry came dead set against answering the questionnaire, which they treated in a most insulting fashion, and the result was a very stormy session of the subcommittee on May 30, 1921. The Berlin publisher de Gruyter roundly declared that he could not and did not want to answer the questionnaire and that the only way he could explain calculations was on a book-by-book basis. This was met with disbelief on the grounds that publishers certainly must have had some general basis for making their calculations; the Commercial University of Berlin taught a course in publishing in which the question of pricing surely was discussed. De Gruyter and his colleagues irritatedly suggested that those on the committee had no understanding of the field whatever and were prejudiced against the publishers. Although committee members (one of whom was editor Georg Bernhard) pointed out that they were not a group of authors either but did have a responsibility to investigate charges that publishers were making enormous profits while authors were receiving as little as one and a half marks on books that were selling for fifty marks, they received no enlightenment from the publishers whatever. De Gruyter and his friends ended up more or less walking out of the hearing.[91]

The publishers, not unlike the theatre managers and owners, viewed themselves as patrons, friends, and promoters of the arts, and it certainly is true that such publishers as Kurt Wolff, Ernst Rowohlt, Paul Cassirer, and Reinhard Piper promoted Dadaism, Expressionism, and other forms of experimental literature and art. They did take risks and could well present themselves as "conscious intermediaries between the Spirit, Art, the Idea, and a Public."[92] These were not mere phrases, and there is no neat way to separate Kurt Wolff's genuine interest in promoting the work of poet, novelist, and dramatist René Schickele from his extraordinarily close attention to questions of honoraria and marketing strategy. Thus, he waxed enthusiastic over Schickele's comedy, *Die neuen Kerle*, which he praised as a splendid portrayal of "the boundless corruption and spiritual rottenness of the German *Bürgertum* . . . the counterfeit and scheming intimacy of bourgeois life, the political opportunism, the corrupting effect of the war profiteers."[93] However anxious to win Schickele away from Cassirer, however, Wolff would offer him no more than a 15 percent instead of the usual 20 percent royalty, although he was willing to give him a five thousand mark advance. He claimed he could print more copies and thus sell more if he paid a lower royalty and told Schickele with typical straightforwardness:

Think the matter over quietly. I do not doubt that you will realize we are right. Let me remind you that I immediately said yes to your financial requirements, which were objectively high despite the inflation. There is nothing I can do about the fact that intellectual workers cannot earn anything anymore these days. You see that we are not at all petty. Now make it possible for us to work for you the way one in the end must work for Schickele.[94]

Schickele accepted the offer and apparently continued to work well with Wolff despite reservations about the way Wolff was compensating him during the hyperinflation. Until 1923 Wolff seemed quite content with the "keenness to buy and purchasing power" of the reading public despite the monetary depreciation.[95] Radical poet Erich Mühsam, who spent much of the early Weimar Republic in jail, took a very different view of Wolff, however. Wolff had acquired his work from Cassirer just before the war, and Mühsam felt that he had learned what it meant to be "thrown to the Wolff." He accused Wolff of opportunism, of neglecting his works when pacifism was unpopular and then promoting them after the Revolution, and of exploiting him at all times, and he called on his fellow authors to escape the "vampire fangs" of the publishers.[96]

A similar bitterness is to be found in the reactions of the poet Klabund (Alfred Henschke), who actually wrote a satirical poem entitled "The Intellectual Worker in the Inflation." It described an author of a monograph who had received a three mark honorarium. He worked nights selling sausages at the Anhalter Station in Berlin so that he could save enough for his coffin and prayed that he might die and reawaken in a new life as a "foreign exchange dealer, diamond cutter, or sewer cleaner."[97] Klabund himself was quite prepared to remain a poet, but he insisted on being treated no worse than the others who labored on books: "We demand our right, our right to be measured by the same yardstick as all the others who are professionally involved in the production of books. We do not want to be treated better, but also no worse than the typesetters, printers, and bindery workers."[98]

The discrepancy between the treatment of writers and those involved in book production had been a source of complaint since 1920,[99] but the sense of unfairness was compounded by the strong feeling that publishers were not only failing to reward their authors properly on domestic sales but were also making an extraordinary profit on foreign sales under the export control system reintroduced in 1920. As in other industries, the system had been instituted to guarantee that German books would not be dumped on world markets for ridiculously low prices and that the German economy would profit from the foreign exchange received from exports. It was passionately supported by most publishers and by their organizations as a means of keeping domestic German book prices lower at a time when the old German reading public was increasingly unable to afford books and scholarly journals. By imposing a 100 percent surcharge on books sold in countries with highly valued currencies and a 60 percent surcharge in countries with currencies medially valued, such as the lira, publishers claimed they were able to stay in business and continue production while at the same time remaining competitive abroad. Thus, for example, R. Tagore's *Home and the World,* published in the German edition by Kurt Wolff, cost three pounds, whereas the London Macmillan edition cost six pounds in 1920. The publishers of the *Annalen der Physik,* a world renowned physics journal, insisted that the only way they could stay in business was by charging foreign subscribers eight times the peacetime price, while the publishers of a major text on venereal diseases pointed out that by charging foreigners three hundred sixty marks, they were able to keep the domestic price at one hundred eighty marks.[100]

As was the case in so many industries, however, there was considerable disagreement about the export control system. A minority of publishers, including Kurt Wolff, thought it harmful for the very same reasons producers found it harmful in other industries. It complicated business, alienated and discouraged foreign customers, and was ineffective against smuggling through Germany's often very leaky borders.[101] Some writers, like the Rhenish author Herbert Eulenburg, shared this view, arguing that it was destroying the interest in German cultural achievements abroad. While he agreed with his publisher Kurt Wolff on this question, however, he sharply criticized Wolff for profiteering from the export control system at his expense. Thus, at the beginning of 1923, Eulenburg received more money from one American interested in a personally autographed copy of his book than he was to receive during the entire year for his life's work. The American had sent him a dollar! He, like so many other authors, blamed the publishers for failing to share any of their export gains with the authors and for tenaciously holding on to the principle of mark for mark in fulfilling their contracts.[102] Yet, Wolff was not prepared to ac-

cept all this as an injustice. He agreed that the authors had been paid in paper marks but reminded Eulenburg that they had also enjoyed advances against royalties which had higher real value than the honoraria would have had if they had been paid over time. He made no pretence of denying the advantages publishers enjoyed in comparison to their authors:

It is far from my intention to disregard the fact that in the end the author in general stands at the coffin of the mark more weakened than an economic enterprise such as a publishing house, for the publisher has had the possibility of using certain business techniques to create equivalents which, if they did not fully compensate for the mark depreciation, at least prevented the complete ruin of his operation. I am thinking of the inflation profits made through the possibility of being able to pay with bills of acceptance for new stocks of paper and printing and binding bills and then paying off the commercial bills of acceptance with currency that was worth less than on the day the bills were issued. Without such crutches the German publishing business would have had to shut down long ago.[103]

Wolff's argument, in effect, was that the relationship between publisher and author was a microcosm of the inflationary economy, an economy in which those in control of productive resources or engaged in actual production that could immediately be realized in salable goods survived at the expense of those who lacked these advantages.

This is not to say that all intellectual workers suffered equally. René Schickele was able with some painter friends to purchase a home during the inflation, and Eulenburg seems to have survived the inflation very nicely.[104] Similarly, many painters did very well in the inflation, at least if one is to judge by contemporary commentaries. Thus, in February 1920, a leading art journal reported:

The art market is feverish. Things are being bought without even being seen, and there is a shortage of goods everywhere. What should one do with the paper money? Then one remembers that pictures, prints, books, and antiques are objects of value, of variable exchange rate, to be sure, but of rising artistic worth. In exhibits, every third item has a slip of paper marked "sold." And since a reactionary art does not exist anymore, and since everyone paints and draws in the modern style, the expressionist laughed at yesterday becomes a publicly renowned artist and capitalist over night. Now he begins to grumble about the paper money himself, fears the capital levy, seeks to buy houses or farms and begins to hold back his works.[105]

An exhibition catalogue of early 1923 commented on the problematic character of the modern art rage in not dissimilar terms:

On the Sociology of the New Art

1912: Hearts were aflame; the artists starved, struggled, and displayed. The Blue Rider galloped exultantly through the howling philistines. Three art dealers who served it fought against bankruptcy. A small, slowly growing clientele of awakening buyers and followers were in the closest personal contact with the artists and dealers. How wonderful was this year!

1922: The artists ward off the intruding herd of buyers through private secretaries, others sell only abroad, and those who have fully arrived do not sell at all. The travelling and resident art dealers who sit in salons filled with easy chairs and who all love and understand Paul Klee are legion, and mouths are aflame.[106]

Art and artists had indeed been sucked into the whirlpool of the inflation at an early stage. Foreign buyers had acquired many old masters and valuable works of German and non-German art in Germany before the creation of an "Art Guardian" (*Kunstwart*) and export controls in early 1920 sought, with what effect it is difficult to say, to put an end to the buying up of Germany's art treasures.[107] More important for living artists, however, was the veritable craze for art purchasing in 1919–1920 (prior to the relative stabilization) which had been induced not only by the flight from the mark but also by the desire to avoid taxation and in the belief that the new taxation would not be effective. The mania was to be found high and low, so that the sellers of kitsch, who had previously achieved a certain notoriety at beaches and spas, were to be found populating the city streets at this time. The relative stabilization and the increasing reality of the tax threat put an end to this phase of the art boom. The coming of the galloping and hyperinflation renewed the art fever—albeit to a lesser extent because the tax laws no longer were favorable to evasion by this means and because postwar conditions were not conducive to the building up of fortunes that could be used to invest in expensive art. Many of the new purchasers who streamed into the art exhibitions and auctions between 1919 and 1922 were persons who had made their profits from the war, the black market, or dealers in scarce goods, the so-called *Schieber*, or those who worked for them.[108]

The portrait of the artist as successful merchant of his wares and winner over inflation, however, certainly was overdone. Some artists did indeed possess a remarkable ability to market their work to rich buyers for very high prices and to persuade them to donate their works to museums. Max Liebermann appears to have fallen into this category, although even he was not always successful in getting the high prices he wanted. Others, like Ernst Barlach, could count not only on the skills but also on the financial generosity of an experienced and skilled art dealer. Thanks to Paul Cassirer, Barlach remained free of immediate financial worry at the end of 1922 and expected his good fortune to continue for as long "as the rich people are really rich" but also feared that the conditions of his life could become comparable to those living in Russia, where it was reported that a teacher made two hundred fifty million rubles but was unable to buy clothes.[109]

Few artists, however, had the patronage of a Cassirer, and most had extreme financial difficulties well before the hyperinflation came to plague them. This was evident in the organization of some seven thousand artists out of an estimated ten thousand artists working in Germany into the Economic Reich Association of Fine Artists (*Wirtschaftlicher Reichsverband bildender Künstler*) and the monthly publication throughout the remaining years of the inflation of an official journal with the very unaesthetic and rather jarring title of *Art and Economics* (*Kunst und Wirtschaft*). The journal was filled with complaints about inadequate copyright protection, illicit copying of works, plagiarism, and other violations of intellectual property rights. The new organization and its journal also sought to protect artists from exploitation by materials manufacturers and houseowners. They complained bitterly about the low quality and high price of paints, warned against exploitative merchants of equipment, encouraged the formation of cooperatives for the sale and purchase of artistic supplies, and demanded special protection and controls on ateliers. They also fought for free admission to museums on uncrowded days.[110]

While strongly supporting a cultural levy, artists and writers staunchly opposed the imposition of the luxury tax on their works. The battle against the luxury tax—referred to by one representative of the artists as the "creation of a bureaucratic soul unaware of art"[111]—entertainment taxes, and turnover taxes on artistic works and performances assumed a very special place in the economic program of the artists, a battle in which they were joined by theatres, book publishers, art dealers, and other interested parties. The argument against such taxes was that they made the sale of artistic work too costly and that the producers of cultural goods and values needed special protection. As usual in such discussions, those engaged in them ran up against the thorniest of all questions; namely, what constituted art and whose economic activity should be relieved of taxation. Famed theatre producer Max Reinhardt claimed that he had left Berlin because of the entertainment tax and the competition of the movies. Was only the theatre to be protected? The circuses were also claiming that they were providing the people with "edification," a point unlikely to receive extensive elaboration in the Reichstag but splendidly made by the owner of a circus in Carl Zuckmayer's inflation play *Katharina Knie*:

This is the end of world history! The entertainment tax! Has anyone heard of such a thing! When they can't think of any other way of doing us in, then they think of the entertainment tax!! I really would like to know where they find the entertainment!! Climb up on the high-wire sometime and take a look at the world while handling the balancing-pole. It is, I tell you, a damned serious business, not entertainment. And for the people who have to watch, with their behinds on a hard wooden bench and their heads straining on their necks to look upward until they get a stiff neck—that is no entertainment, you know, it's unhealthy, and they get nothing for it, not a bloody cent.[112]

Needless to say, not everyone thought that this was the sort of stress that should be tax exempt. Those with more selective cultural preferences pointed out that if the tax were abolished altogether, then "the *St. Matthew Passion* and *Parsifal* would be put in the same pot with horse races, boxing matches, fan dancing,

etc."[113] Similarly, it was one thing to make it possible for the suffering *Mittelstand* or young people to go to see the theatre, hear music, or buy books, another to support the ostentatious pretensions to culture by the *nouveaux riches*. It could be argued that it was precisely because such persons were not taxed that sheet music for orchestral and chamber music was disappearing while publishers serviced upstart demands for fox-trots and two-steps.[114] Did it make sense, as was finally decided, to tax art works sold by art dealers but not those sold by artists themselves in their ateliers? The public prejudice against the middleman and distributor of vegetables, meat, and underwear was being extended to the art market. Paul Cassirer pointed out that the tax was perfectly justified when dealers sold old masters or when they sold the works of Max Liebermann but that it threatened young artists who depended on the dealers to present their work to the public. "How is an artist who lives four flights upstairs in the north of Berlin to sell his pictures," Cassirer asked and went on to point out that "the prices are also depressed there, for the artist often sells so as to keep the buyer from going away. Thus the artist who is young and poor is penalized."[115]

These protests against the taxation of the arts could boast some very minor successes. Thus, in March 1922 the Reichstag, in an unusual state of mirth and to outcries of "the Great Coalition," unanimously voted to exempt the works of living artists and those who had died within fifteen years from the property tax.[116] For obvious fiscal reasons, however, the Reich and municipal governments found it impossible to do away with the other taxes on artistic work and entertainment entirely, and while a variety of complicated and not insignificant concessions were made, the tax problem remained a source of constant dissatisfaction and bickering with the authorities and of tedious debates within the Reich Economic Council.[117]

Art, after all, could not be immune from the consequences of the lost war or the Treaty of Versailles. If the railroads were to be taken out of their bankruptcy then freight rates had to be increased and special rates could no longer be granted for shipments to exhibits. The representatives of the artists now feared that work done in Düsseldorf, for example, would no longer be seen in Munich and complained about the laughably low sums of insurance offered by the railroad system for artistic works. As one of the leading representatives of the artists somewhat melodramatically grumbled, "the artists can no longer see the 'state' as its friend anymore. At the same time they are surrounded by enemies on all sides."[118]

While many artists supported the Weimar Republic and were grateful for the support given to artists and architects by commissions and by the establishment of such institutions as the Bauhaus and municipal deputations to deal with artistic questions, others felt that the new Republic was not as supportive of artists as its predecessor and that it was insensitive to their problems. Weimar's most famous artists tended to be identified with the Republic, but the majority of artists were not famous, and many were alienated from the Republic for political and economic reasons. Thus, there was an "Association of Artists and Intellectual Creative Workers" allied to the German Nationalist Party and a "German-Völkish Anti-Semitic Artists Group" that stood in opposition to the "Socialist Artists Cooperative" and that severely criticized the state-supported Bauhaus and other such institutions. The hyperinflation promoted such anti-Weimar radicalization.[119]

In the last analysis, however, the majority of artists found themselves facing economic problems quite similar to those of other intellectual workers in the hyperinflation and, indeed, not so different from those involved in any business. If a sculptor offered a bronze for twenty thousand marks in May 1922 and was called upon to keep to his price in September, then he took a hundred-thousand-mark loss on materials alone. The obligation of dealers and exhibition halls handling such matters was hard to determine, but many an artist felt cheated. In August 1922, the Economic Reich Association of Fine Artists drew up a price schedule for all types of artistic productions to guide its members and subsequently published regular price lists and multipliers to be used in helping its members to keep up with inflation. Such help notwithstanding, most artists were finding it virtually impossible to make ends meet. This

was especially the case for the majority, who had never benefited much from the "false boom" prior to the hyperinflation, but it was becoming true even for those who had done well. This explains the intensification of artists' struggle for a cultural levy and their growing interest in promoting the creation of an Emergency Society for German Art (Notgemeinschaft der deutschen Kunst).[120]

In doing so, they were consciously copying the model of the Emergency Society for German Science and Scholarship (Notgemeinschaft der deutschen Wissenschaft or NGW) and were deeply impressed by the apparent success of scholars and scientists in winning public and private support for science and scholarship after the war. Scientists and scholars, of course, had the advantage of powerful organizational bases from which to press their case; namely, the universities and academies, as well as the Kaiser-Wilhelm-Society for the Promotion of Science created in 1911. The latter, founded under the inspiration of Friedrich Althoff of the Prussian Ministry of Culture, theologian Adolf von Harnack, and Nobel Prize–winning chemist Emil Fischer, sought to mobilize private as well as public funds for the support of special institutes for advanced research and thereby at once relieve the overburdened universities and retain Germany's competitiveness in the face of the kinds of private resources being mobilized for the promotion of science elsewhere (for example, the Rockefeller Institute in the United States). After the war, those concerned with the maintenance and reconstruction of Germany's scientific position in the world could boast an experienced and talented group of academic managers and bureaucratic policymakers with the experience and connections needed to mobilize the necessary resources. Harnack, Fischer (until his death in 1919), the chemist Fritz Haber, and the physicist Max Planck, to name a few of the most important persons in the first category, worked hand in hand with Friedrich Schmidt-Ott (who had made his career under Althoff) and two other experienced bureaucrats—Friedrich Glum and Ernst Trendelenburg. These persons had very close contact with industrialists and bankers who had long shown an interest in and support for science and scholarship, most notably Carl Duisberg, but also Albert Vögler, Gustav Krupp von Bohlen und Halbach, and the bankers Eduard Arnhold and Franz von Mendelssohn. They also rapidly learned the art of cultivating the Reichstag, where they could count on the active support of what was a virtual science and scholarship political constituency, for which the Center Party Deputy Georg Schreiber served as the chief spokesman.[121]

All of these contacts and experiences, however, would have meant very little had not the purpose of the fund-raising and lobbying been as economically and culturally compelling as it was. The contributions of German science to the growth of the German economy were obvious, and it was no accident that the chemists and chemical industrialists had taken the lead in these matters. At the same time, the situation after 1918 was one in which it was more than natural and easy to pull at the German historical heart strings, to remember the days after Jena when the university reforms of Wilhelm von Humboldt paved the way for Prussia's recovery, and to argue that at a time when Germany's military power was no more, it still had the economic potential and spiritual resources needed for its reconstruction if they were properly sustained.

In reality, the great interest after the war, unfortunately one might argue, was not reform but money, and it was this that led to the founding of the NGW on October 30, 1920. The first steps toward its founding were taken by leading academics who empowered Harnack to appeal on their behalf to the National Assembly for funds to restore subscriptions to scholarly journals, to support the publication of scholarly work, and to finance some major projects. This initial and unsuccessful effort was superseded by a more systematic approach by Fritz Haber and Friedrich Schmidt-Ott. They developed the idea of creating a "self-governing" emergency society encompassing all scientific and scholarly institutions to serve as "the center of coordination and interest representation for *Wissenschaft* in organizing and propagating the support of research through the state and business community."[122] Alongside the NGW, the forerunner of the present day Deutsche Forschungsgemeinschaft, there was established an-

other organization that is the predecessor of its modern German counterpart—the Association of Foundations of German Scholarship and Science Stifterverband für die deutsche Wissenschaft, a kind of holding company for business financial support to science and scholarship created under the inspiration of Carl Duisberg, Albert Vögler, and Arthur Solomonsohn. Haber and Schmidt-Ott were also involved in promoting this centralization of business giving, and the original idea was that the Association of Foundations and the NGW would work closely together and coordinate policies.[123]

Actually, things did not work out quite as planned. The Association of Foundations ended up in competition for money with the Helmholtz Society for the Support of Physics, which had been set up slightly earlier, and it took some time to work out a satisfactory formula for distributing business funds. The scholarly and bureaucratic leadership of the NGW was worried about both the Helmholtz Society and the Association of Foundations, Haber especially fearing that "the establishment of an industrial autocracy in the plants of science, which decides things with its money, is a cheerless prospect for the future."[124] They did not want funds to be drained away from the NGW or to be directed toward purely utilitarian goals, a possibility which Harnack saw as the "American conditions" he had always tried to avoid despite his interest in industrial money.[125]

In the last analysis, however, the problem of getting substantial amounts of business money proved even more difficult than getting such money with no strings attached. The monies provided to the NGW by the Association of Foundations were given in the form of a capital fund, and the NGW was expected to make use only of interest. More generosity was shown to the Kaiser-Wilhelm-Society, but its business money was largely directed to institutes whose establishment and support was in industry's interest—for example, the institutes for coal and ferrous-metals research. Both organizations, therefore, were primarily dependent on public funds, especially from the Prussian and Reich governments and felt compelled to present very utilitarian arguments not dissimilar to those made with the businessmen in order to justify government expenditures. Thus, while the nascent NGW was successful in getting a large initial appropriation in 1920, Haber reported that the Minister of Finance's "willingness to provide 20 million in the budget to be passed in September is exclusively thanks to his faith in the future success of chemistry. I avoided mentioning philology and everything connected with it."[126] The Kaiser-Wilhelm-Society (KWG), being older and more established, could take a more aggressive approach and, indeed, one that was filled with remarkable arrogance toward the new, Republican government. In asking the Prussian government for money to cover the KWG deficit in 1920, for example, Harnack spoke of its "moral obligation" to provide money and saw fit to remind the Minister of Culture that the citizens who had supported the KWG in the past were "no longer in a position to secure its survival through a new large-scale rescue operation in the state of today which is based on such different foundations."[127] He took a particularly critical attitude toward the civil-service pay increases, which had added to the difficulties of the KWG. By implication, the government was therefore obligated to compensate the KWG for the lack of confidence felt by Germany's business community and for giving pay raises to Germany's civil servants.

The period of inflation was, on paper at least, a period of expansion for the KWG, so that the number of institutes increased from nine to sixteen between 1918 and 1923. Needless to say, such expansion as there was took place prior to the coming of hyperinflation and in the context of cutbacks within a number of important institutes in 1920. The policy of "expansion" reflected a policy of starting up institutes already planned and accepting money in the expectation that the funding, both private and public, would persist. This was as speculative as the basic financial policy of the KWG itself, which seems to have presumed that the inflation was a passing phenomenon and that the liquid capital it was building up prior to 1922 was secure. Instead of building up debts which might have been repaid in depreciated currency, the leadership of the KWG sought to cover its rapidly increasing expenses with its no less rapidly de-

preciating capital. Its fixed-interest bond investments were only converted into industrial stocks in March 1922. The NGW followed a similar policy, so that it only began receiving interest on the capital provided by the Association of Foundations in 1922. The interest amounted to 2.4 million marks. By 1923, its 162,139,116 paper-mark capital was worth some 3,543 gold marks.[128] By late 1922, the entire effort to reconstruct German science and scholarship seemed endangered because of the hyperinflation, and dependence on public monies, especially on the part of the NGW, was extreme.

The status of science and scholarship, however, was such that it could demand and became the subject of a lengthy debate in the Reichstag in mid-November 1922, where Georg Schreiber painted a grim picture of the condition of Germany's scientific and scholarly institutions, pointing to the inability to purchase or feed experimental animals and guinea pigs, to maintain equipment, and to buy glass test tubes. He spoke at length about the decay of libraries and museums, the inability to buy books and journals, the foreign purchases of German books and libraries, and the prohibitive cost of scholarly works. Schreiber's pleas on behalf of the NGW and the support of science found a general echo among his colleagues in the Reichstag, although it is interesting to note that Julius Moses, the SPD spokesman on cultural matters, took advantage of the occasion to criticize Germany's industrialists in a not entirely Socialist manner for their failure to do enough for science. He compared them unfavorably with the "Japanese Stinnes," Hoshi, who had made substantial grants to the NGW, as well as with the American industrialists who had set up the Carnegie and Rockefeller Foundations and asked, "where is our big industry, where are our great banks, which are swimming in money?"[129]

The fears expressed by Schreiber, Moses, and other Reichstag Deputies were well taken, and there was significant evidence that Germany's scientific and scholarly plant was breaking down and that Germany's international standing, damaged in some fields by foreign boycotts and hostility in the immediate postwar years as well as by penury, had deteriorated. In May 1921, for example, the British Consul in Zurich reported on the impressions of leading Swiss surgeons who had just returned from the German National Medical Congress in Berlin: "They told me that they were much disappointed at the results. It appeared to them as if German surgery had learned nothing from the war, and no new theories had apparently been scientifically tested. The German surgeons and doctors give the impression of men, who were mentally and physically exhausted and unable, for the present at all events, to hold that high standard in the scientific world which was theirs before the war."[130] This was, of course, a theme on which one could capitalize in appealing to those (like Abraham Flexner of the Rockefeller Foundation) who continued to believe that German science was essential to world progress. Thus, Schmidt-Ott and physiologist Emil Abderhalden appealed directly to Flexner, the latter warning that "if the scientific activity of Germany collapses, if it fails in the matter of succession, then a perceptible regression over the whole world is bound to take place."[131] To prevent such "regression," the Rockefeller Foundation set up a special committee to promote medical research, not by grants to universities, which it regarded as too nationalistic and reactionary, but rather by the support of talented workers in "neglected" fields—like genetics, where, unfortunately, the political consequences turned out to be even worse.

The outside world was not always so helpful, however, and the attitude toward foreign presence in German *Wissenschaft* was very ambivalent. Directors of KWG institutes complained that many talented scientists and young persons were going into industry or going abroad because of poor working conditions and inadequate compensation. At the same time, to their very great discomfort, the KWG institutes felt compelled to take on a substantial percentage of their scientific personnel from abroad, often from former enemy countries. Such persons were required to cover their own costs as well as the costs of their research animals or equipment and to pay a fee for the privilege of working in the institutes. It is a measure of the anxiety felt about this situation that the KWG

adopted a policy of denying regular assistant status to foreigners.[132]

What all this demonstrated, and what the debate in the Reichstag confirmed, however, was that it was not really possible any longer successfully to separate a discussion of the maintenance of German science, scholarship, and artistic life from a discussion of the social condition of their practitioners. Natural scientists were better supported than humanists, scholarship was better treated than the arts, and some artists, writers, and performers were better off than others, but the artists who were so terribly impressed with the NGW and wanted to create something comparable for their own field were missing the point. Neither the NGW nor the KWG had any social functions. They were in the business of supporting research, not researchers,[133] and the condition of Germany's scholars, teachers, and university students by 1922 amply demonstrated that these groups, so central to Germany's educated elite, were at the end of their economic tether. As in the economic, so in the cultural sphere was the government trying to maintain and reconstruct institutions and structures, but the hyperinflation was making it increasingly impossible to neglect the personal impoverishment and accompanying bitterness and resentment which, to some extent, was the product of its policy.

Germany's university professors were very conscious and explicit about the change in their economic and social status in the postwar order, and the Association of German Higher Educational Instructors spelled out their complaints in a comprehensive memorandum of October 1922 which followed upon over two years of petitions and meetings with the officials of the various state governments. Prior to the war, the German professor could boast a moderately good income which permitted him to live decently, purchase books, go on research trips, carefully educate his children, and "grant himself the longer yearly vacation trip (*Erholungsreise*) which is especially necessary for every intellectual worker."[134] The association argued that it was on the basis of this relative freedom from financial care of those who had successfully climbed the arduous path to the full professorship that Germany's great fame in science and scholarship rested. The professorial salary was relatively modest, a price paid for his independence as teacher and scholar and tenure at a specific university. What accounted for the financial well-being of the professor, therefore, were two other sources of income. The first was fees paid by students to attend lectures and seminars, most of which went to the professor himself—the rest being used by the state to equalize conditions for professors teaching the less popular subjects with fewer students. The second was the fees for state and academic examinations. The importance of these income sources is demonstrated by a breakdown of the average incomes of professors before the war. A professor in Berlin received a basic salary of 7,200 marks, teaching fees of 7,700 marks, and 1,000 marks in examination fees, bringing his total income to 15,900 marks. His colleague in the provinces made less—6,400 marks basic salary, 4,000 marks in teaching fees, 1,000 marks in examination fees; that is, 11,400 marks a year. Additionally, professors frequently made as much as two thousand marks a year from scholarly publication, consultations, and other such professional activities. Clearly, therefore, the economic status of the professoriat was highly dependent on fees, especially for professors without permanent tenure (*außerordentliche Professur*), whose basic salaries were lower, and for the *Privatdozenten*, who had qualified to teach by achieving their *Habilitation* but who had not yet received a regular appointment.

What the organization of Germany's professors referred to as the "one-sided disadvantaging" of the professoriat arising from its peculiar status between the civil servants, on the one hand, and the free professions, on the other, began during the war when lecture and examination fees decreased while the cost-of-living supplements for higher civil servants failed to keep pace with inflation. But the hardest blows were struck after the war. The number of students swelled because of the returning veterans, so that professors often taught additional courses, and special inter-semester programs were set up to help the veterans make up for lost time. What all this meant for the professoriat, however, was a great deal more work for a great deal less real pay.

The implementation of the Civil Service Pay Reform Act of April 1920 in the academic sphere was extremely damaging to them, especially in Prussia. The basic salary was kept relatively low, as before the war, although the Ministry could grant special supplements to particularly exceptional scholars. Most important, the portion of lecture and examination fees left to a professor was calculated in such a way that his income from such fees could actually be reduced by as much as 1,750 marks, even when the number of students he taught doubled. At the same time, the fees for lectures, seminars, and examinations were kept relatively constant in order to avoid imposing further burdens on the already impoverished students. Whereas the average income from teaching fees in Berlin had been 7,699 marks a year in 1913, it had only increased to 8,945 marks in 1921, while the average for eight Prussian provincial universities increased from 4,077 marks to 6,822 marks. The increases in base pay and guaranteed instruction fees granted in 1921–1922 did not solve the basic problem; namely, that professors had suffered a severe loss of real income and a harsh decline in their relative status within the civil service. Doubling the guaranteed lecture fee from two thousand to four thousand marks could not be viewed as very satisfactory when civil-servant salaries had multiplied twentyfold. While the professor stood at the same level in 1920 as a higher civil servant, by 1922 the income of the former was some thirty-two thousand marks less. Each across-the-board cost-of-living increase in the civil service increased the differential, a situation rendered all the more disheartening by the notorious fact that the higher-civil-servant salaries had increased least satisfactorily relative to inflation so that their organization was complaining that, as things stood, the lifetime income of a higher civil servant was only 1.35 percent higher than that of an unskilled worker.[135]

Not surprisingly, therefore, the professors called on the state governments to increase basic salaries to at least that of the higher civil servants, to increase instructional and examination fees, and to permit all but those with the very largest numbers of students to keep most of their instructional fees. Their organization was highly critical of the state governments, especially the Prussian government, for making promises to remedy the situation without fulfilling them and warned of both the short- and long-term consequences of the situation:

The natural consequences of the bad income of the professoriat must initially be the deterioration of its health as a result of aggravation, undernourishment, care, and indebtedness, and then the reduction of its ability and willingness to work. Further it will look for profitable work on the side. Whoever can do so because of his talents and specialty will place himself as a "working professor" alongside the "working student." In the course of the years the poor pay will necessarily effect the composition of the instructional staff. Whoever is still young enough to learn a new line of work, will leave; whoever is old enough, will retire in order to find a side profession or be able to live more cheaply. Experience has shown that the most capable persons can only be won through special bonuses, and the insupportable situation already has developed in which newly appointed younger professors are substantially better paid than the older ones.[136]

Needless to say, the number of such young professors were few and far between, and the condition of the *Privatdozenten*, who had traditionally never received salaries while they awaited their summons to a chair unless they had some special teaching appointment, had become parlous in the extreme. Before the war, they had usually made a living from occasional teaching assignments, scholarly writing, and invested family income. The postwar situation had undermined all these means of livelihood, and the organization of those *Privatdozenten* without civil-servant positions, the work of which was supported by the Association of German Higher Educational Instructors, was constantly striving to persuade the state governments to provide the *Privatdozenten* with more teaching opportunities and to give them salaries. After a meeting in August 1922 with the Prussian Minister of Culture, the organization was able to report that the Ministry "recognizes that the *Privatdozent* of the old type, who devoted the major portion of his time to scientific labors without having fixed regular income, is no longer possible under present circumstances in Germany." Nevertheless, the government neither could nor wished to support everyone in this position, and while it was prepared "in the interest of the progress of science . . . to in-

crease the teaching appointments of a small number of *Privatdozenten* to the point that they reach the existence minimum," the rest would have to find some other means of support while pursuing their scholarly work in their "free time."[137] Sometimes, of course, they could pick up some scholarly work on the side, as happened when a totally unknown American offered six dollars (eighteen thousand marks on October 12, 1922) to have explained certain points of both the general and special theories of relativity. The individual in question, a Dr. Max Talmey of New York City, reserved for himself the right to decide if the explanation offered was satisfactory or not, having had an unsatisfactory experience on a previous occasion. If it did not reach him by January 12, 1923, he would be obligated to pay only postage and paper costs. So far had the status of the German academic fallen![138]

This was an offer which many of Germany's students probably would have been happy to take, since large numbers of them were doing less agreeable work under often less agreeable conditions. After 1918, many of Germany's students were compelled to earn their way doing nonacademic work, and this marked a radical change in their life-style when compared with the prewar period. The condition of Germany's students had indeed become the subject of international concern and a reason for assistance. This was yet another source of invidious comparison between the indifference of German industrialists and the concern of foreigners.[139] Aid from the United States, Great Britain, the Netherlands, Switzerland, and Scandinavia as well as from various church organizations sought to ameliorate the miserable lot of Germany's university and technical university students. Their numbers had swelled since the end of the war, rising from 71,676 in 1914 to 108,694 in 1922.[140] Their situation, however, reflected the declining fortunes of the lower-middle and middle class from which they largely came and which, prior to the war, had sufficient savings or investments to make uninterrupted study as well as probationary periods of unrecompensed preparation for the judiciary, academic life, and the higher civil service possible. The situation of both this class and its young student members was sympathetically described in early 1922 by a female British social worker engaged in student relief work:

It has certainly been a shock to me to see how the middle class lives, what terrible poverty there is to be found behind closed doors. In well-furnished houses there are chairs devoid of leather which has been used for shoes, curtains without linings which have been turned into garments for the children, and a woman student lucky enough to possess a nightdress or two has cut them up to wear as chemises, using the odd bits from the sleeves and hem to make pocket handkerchiefs. This sort of thing is not the exception but the rule. I know many families where before the war two servants were kept, now they do their own housework; and instead of dinner in the evening they have plain brown bread and weak tea without milk or sugar, and only one meat meal a week. Many a man and woman student earns his or her own money to pay for their studies at the university, and often support their families as well. Educated men work in mines or at the docks during the vacation, while women go into factories or shops.[141]

Many of these students undertook this unfamiliar labor on farms and in factories in a very idealistic spirit, often viewing it as an opportunity to bridge the old barriers between the educated and less educated classes and often frustrated by the rejection they found from suspicious and even resentful workers.[142] If more than half of Germany's students found work fairly easily during this period, it was because of the inflationary boom; this hardly portended well for the future. Indeed, there was no guarantee that working in order to study would achieve its goal. As one student from Breslau reported:

The boundless inflation totally destroyed my budgetary arrangements. I was in danger of using up my entire resources in a very short time if I did not find some extraordinary source of income. I took advantage of the opportunity to work during the school holiday. With the money I first saved, I put my clothes in order. The persistent inflation forced me to increase my expenditures from day to day. I earned 250 marks per day in August, 500 in September, and 630 in October. Living in that area was so expensive that I only had a surplus of 6,000 marks for the semester. My present costs are 2,000 a month, an amount beyond my past calculations. How long will it be possible for me to make do with the money saved? I need 2,000 marks alone for the payment of the fees. I can make it with the greatest possible parsimony until Christmas, and then my further study will be in question.[143]

At the same time, the entire phenomenon of student work worried the older generation of scholars, who felt that outside physical labor robbed the students of their energy and was too distracting to permit quality work or contemplation. One suspects that lethargy and preoccupation with nonacademic matters was more a product of undernourishment, miserable housing, and illness, then of work *per se*. The leadership of the Association of Hanoverian Agricultural Housewives Associations, which was constantly urging its members to supply food and other assistance to the Göttingen student dormitory, pointed out that some students were simply too ill to work and were not making enough in any case. They urged their member associations to take on a few "*Petstudenten*" from among the poorest students to receive special packets.[144] Critics of the situation, therefore, certainly had reason to fear that the economic situation was a massive discouragement to scientific and scholarly study for its own sake. Students in the postwar period showed a distinct preference for practical fields of a technical or economic nature and an increasing disinclination to go into scholarly pursuits or pursuits requiring long apprenticeships and offering little monetary reward. The future of German science and scholarship was in danger and with it the economic survival and social status of the bearers of German *Kultur*, of those responsible for its reproduction. Indeed, for racially minded scientists, like geneticist Otmar von Verschuer, who joined with his Tübingen colleagues in conducting racial surveys and organizing health services for the students, the stock of Germany's future leadership, its *Führerschicht*, was endangered.[145]

The regular appearance of statistical analyses dealing with the household expenditures of middle-class households and of higher civil servants during the hyperinflation, therefore, were charged with social and political meaning. All such statistical studies carried a message; namely, that the amount of household income spent on food and household requirements had risen substantially while the amounts spent on education, culture, and other previously normal components of an intellectual worker's life had decreased significantly (see Table 20). As

Table 20. The Structure of Expenditure of a Higher Civil Servant's Household 1913/14–1923
(in percent)

	1913/14	1920	1921	1st	2nd	3rd	4th
				1922 (by quarter)			
Food	27	49	44	40	33	45	52
Household	10	14	16	16	15	11	13
Other	63	37	40	44	52	44	35

Source: Carl-Ludwig Holtfrerich, *The German Inflation 1914–1923. Causes and Effects in International Perspective* (Berlin & New York, 1986), p. 257, derived from *Die Wirtschaftskurve*, I (1922).

one study after another pointed out, however, the full impact of these changes had to be understood in qualitative terms. The increased proportion of expenditure for food had been accompanied by reduced quality and quantity of the food consumed, while the increased household expenditure took place in the context of reduced expenditure for rent and household help and higher expenditure for poorer quality clothing and for utilities.[146]

It could, of course, be argued that it was high time that income was more equitably distributed in Germany, especially in times of distress, and that a comparison of the relative minimum existence requirements for a higher official and an unskilled Berlin worker and their real incomes was not to be taken as tragically as the advocates of the intellectual workers pretended (see Tables 21A and 21B). To this, the latter replied emphatically that it was "in no way" unfair that the higher official had a minimum existence that was 33.8 percent higher than an unskilled worker before the war, since "this small additional income was, viewed from a private economic point of view, the repayment of capital expended in the public interest but, when viewed from the perspective of the national economy, the funds from which the studies of a new generation would again be covered."[147] Even for those prepared to recognize fatalistically that "our young academics will hardly be recruited in the future from the circles of parents who had studied," the statistics led to a deeply pessimistic conclusion; namely, "the destruction of those circles who had previously represented German culture. Whether the placement of the others at a higher level will occur with sufficient speed so that this culture will not have already disappeared is doubtful."[148]

For others, to raise this question was to answer it automatically in the negative. While it might be possible to lower the requirements for entrance to advanced studies and to make examinations easier, the price would be a lowering of quality and the undermining of German intellectual work. If the German people were not to slide into the "condition of fellahin" within a generation through the "absence of scientific and scholarly leaders," then it was essential "to reestablish the earlier healthy relationship in the assessment of intellectual and mechanical labor, and this in the foreseeable future."[149]

When the Association for Social Policy met

Table 21A. The Comparative Minimal Existence Compensation for a Higher Official and Unskilled Worker, 1913/14–October 1922

	Salary of Higher Official	Wage of Unskilled Worker
1913/14	1.338	0.650
April 1922	0.785	0.714
July 1922	0.950	0.823
October 1922	0.891	0.701

Source: Hans Guradze and Karl Freudenberg, "Das Existenzminimum des geistigen Arbeiters," *Jahrbücher für Nationalökonomie und Statistik* 65 (1923), p. 333.

Table 21B. The Comparative Real Compensation of a Higher Official and Unskilled Worker, 1913/14–October 1922

	(a) Higher Official	(b) Unskilled Worker	Ratio (a) to (b)
1913–1914	1.000	1.000	1.000
April 1922	0.587	1.235	0.475
July 1922	0.710	1.424	0.499
October 1922	0.666	1.213	0.549

Source: Hans Guradze and Karl Freudenberg, "Das Existenzminimum des geistigen Arbeiters," *Jahrbücher für Nationalökonomie und Statistik* 65 (1923), p. 333.

in Eisenach on September 20–21, 1922, to "celebrate" its fiftieth anniversary, there was no small irony in the fact that it chose as the subject for its meeting the "distress of the intellectual workers." The Association had been founded in large measure out of concern for the condition and well being of the working class in an industrializing, capitalist society, and yet now it was devoting its jubilee to the economic distress of its own class in unavoidable comparison with that of the workers! One speaker went so far as to call the trade unions a "state within the state," while another spoke of an "intentional or unintentional dishonorableness" when trade unions spoke of "hunger wages" in their wage demands under existing conditions; however, there was also a strong undercurrent of resentment against the power of organized capital.[150]

This was especially evident in the widely reported speech of sociologist Professor Alfred Weber, whose chief concern was whether intellectual workers had any future at all. While all civilizations had known something akin to intellectual workers (for example, the Chinese mandarins), the development of modern industrial capitalism, in Weber's view, was successively undermining and eliminating the social classes which had once supplied them. First, it had eliminated the patriciate and landed aristocracy, which had earlier supplied a class with sufficient wealth and leisure time to pursue intellectual work, and now it was dispossessing the class of *Rentenintellektuellen*, of persons capable of pursuing their intellectual interests or of supporting children who would pursue such interests by dint of the returns they received on invested capital. It was this financial underpinning that had made it possible for intellectual workers to undergo long, unpaid apprenticeships and to accept relatively low compensation when established in their professions as well as to have the freedom and independence to engage in the kind of public-spirited intellectual activity that characterized the Association for Social Policy. The crisis was compounded by the impoverishment of the state, which could no longer afford to support either the institutions serving the intellectual workers or the intellectual workers themselves. The great danger now was that everything intellectual and spiri-

tual would become a "dependency of economic forces" (*Anhängsel der Wirtschaft*): "Just as the state today is exposed to mediatization through the organized economic forces, so are also the intellectual and spiritual spheres in danger of decaying into dependence upon economic forces."[151] Weber had little hope that either the *nouveax riches* or the capitalist classes would provide the wherewithal to maintain intellectual labor in the near future. The parvenus were too preoccupied with making money and speculating, while the capitalists also were unable and unwilling to devote their resources and time to provide the foundation for intellectual labor. In the last analysis, Weber pinned his hopes for the reproduction of intellectual workers on what he called the working intellectuals (*Arbeitsintellektuellentum*)—managers, engineers and technicians, lawyers, and doctors who, under better economic circumstances, might provide the bases for the intellectual workers of the future. At the same time, he urged his fellow intellectual workers to cease their aloofness from politics and to become engaged in party politics and to mobilize young persons to do so in order to impress upon the parties and state the necessity of preserving and promoting intellectual labor.

Weber was a supporter of the Republic, and the audience to which he spoke was not hostile to the Republic, but there was an inconsequentiality to his analysis that left very unclear the substance of the political participation he advocated. Not surprisingly, he criticized the Marxist contention that the intellectual workers were part of the superstructure instead of the substructure. As far as he was concerned, this was an unwarranted contention that was being transformed into a self-fulfilling prophecy. He concluded that both the state and the leading economic forces had been acting in error, the former by failing to attend to its need for a spiritual and intellectual foundation, the latter for believing they "could continue to exist in a stateless structuring of society" and thus ignoring that "this stateless society will come to ruin through class conflicts."[152] As one of the more Marxist-oriented participants in the meeting, Carl Grünberg pointed out, however, Weber's entire analysis of the economic collapse of intellectual workers seemed to do nothing more than document the dependence of intellectual work on the evolution of the forces of production under capitalism.[153] He was seconded by left-wing economist Emil Lederer, who pointed out that intellectual workers were in no position to match the economic power of the organized economic interests in industry and commerce and insisted that the problem could not be solved except by addressing the "crisis of capitalism" itself:

The crisis of capitalism, which has principally become a psychological crisis through the destruction of broad middle strata, has severely shaken the bases of existence of the intellectual classes. We cannot re-establish them by curing the symptoms; we cannot solve the crisis of intellectual work without at the same time opening up the question of how social labor is at all possible at higher levels. We have to deal with the crisis of capitalism if we want to do away with the crisis of intellectual labor. And, therefore, the entire discussion, even if many participants do not wish it to be so, points to the question: labor in society is manual *and* intellectual labor, and under what conditions of compensation are they possible under the present form of highly organized monopoly capitalism?[154]

The tendentious terminology may be dismissed, but the relevance of Lederer's implicit concern that manual and intellectual labor be treated as constituent parts of an entire socioeconomic system rather than as totally separable and possibly antagonistic elements was constantly being demonstrated. Georg Bernhard, for example, complained bitterly about the high price of paper, which was having a ruinous effect on the publishing and newspaper industries and was particularly damaging to intellectual workers, and strongly suggested that it was not timber deliveries to the Allies but rather deliberate private and state policies of holding back on timber cutting in order to achieve higher prices that was responsible for the situation.[155] Yet, in his review of the meeting at Eisenach in his journal, *Plutus*, he opened with a comparison of manual and intellectual labor that could only produce resentment. He pointed out that there was a sure way of determining how much intellectual labor went into any kind of occupation under existing conditions: "The more the intellect involved, the less the pay. The more the brutal muscular force involved, the higher the pay." He went on to

argue that this was the basic meaning of the German Revolution:

The meaning of this revolution is documented more in the wage revolution than in the political revolution. While one can debate the extent to which it has been a political revolution, no one can ever debate that it was a social revolution. The meaning of this revolution was the ascent of the fourth estate. It was not the victory of a party, but it was the victory of the masses. And the first economic consequence of this revolution is an improvement of those lowest classes as compensation for the relatively worse pay they received before.[156]

The discussion at Eisenach was seen by Bernhard as the price the Association was paying for the success of the goals for which it began fighting fifty years before! For Bernhard, this was a piece of irony, not a legitimation for the resentment of the "uprooted," who blamed the Revolution for what the war had wrought.[157] Similarly, the left-wing *Weltbühne*, in its commentary on Alfred Weber's talk, also had no intention of feeding right-wing resentments when it agreed that the "public spirit" had been "mediatized" by the economic forces of capitalism. Yet, it went even further than Bernhard in its elitist specification of the transvaluation of values that had taken place:

Everyone knows today the examples of the magistrate's assistant who until recently earned absolutely less and who today earns relatively less . . . than a doorman; the school director who earns less than his janitor; of engineers and architects who are more miserably paid than their locksmiths and masons. It is just these last examples which clearly demonstrate the immoral perversion of conditions—immoral because they involve a reversal of means and ends. For the mental labor of the master builder is the precondition of the manual labor of the stone bearer and not the reverse. He who draws a plan, creates a new spiritual value (*Geistwert*); he who brings together bricks and cement in a wall, creates a new physical value (*Sachwert*). And this is the key point: the creation of physical values today is exclusively—and this exclusivity is the difference from past times—more highly valued than the creation of spiritual values. . . . And what does this reversal otherwise mean than the mediatization of the spirit by the economy?[158]

Whereas this writer blamed the war, which he considered unnessary and against German interests, for the situation of Germany and the intellectual workers, others chose to focus on German powerlessness abroad and the new political order. As one German Nationalist Dep-

In *Simplicissimus,* a cartoon by E. Thöny on the changed social conditions of the educated and the working class in 1922. The new proletariat—a poor intellectual worker asks for a warm spoonful of soup.

uty put it, "the economic development together with a lack of understanding for the significance of intellectual work has since the Revolution lead to an undermining, even to a dismantling of intellectual culture . . . which must revenge itself in the bitterest manner in the foreseeable future."[159] The Republican regimes and their Socialist Ministers thus became the literalization of the prewar fears and anxieties of the *Gebildete* about the fate of German *Kultur* if the old regime were ever overthrown. The anti-Republican spirit was particularly evident in a substantial portion of Germany's university students, but also in large numbers of teachers and university professors, and it manifested itself in insults to the Republican flag and such gestures as the ostentatious refusal of most students to attend the celebration of Gerhard Hauptmann's sixtieth birthday at the University of Berlin.[160]

Thus, while members of virtually all parties could express dismay at the economic distress of intellectual workers, worry about the future of Germany's cultural life, and deplore the preoccupation with material concerns in almost identical language, the political consequences

of this unanimity were most unlikely to serve the cause of the Republic. The reasons for this were well understood by pacifist and pro-Republican DDP Deputy Walther Schücking, who recited in the Reichstag the miseries of intellectual workers in the usual appalling terms but also saw fit to mention that the universities and *Gymnasien* had done little to adapt themselves to the needs of a more modern Germany—as for example, by promoting the study of modern languages—and that the conservative spirit among teachers and in the universities reflected the fact that the bourgeoisie and, in certain key fields, the upper bourgeoisie continued to dominate the faculties and student bodies. For him, the failure of the Berlin students to honor one of Germany's great creative artists reflected an absence of "political culture," the kind of political culture of which Swedish Socialist Branting boasted by noting that the University of Uppsala saw fit to honor him despite the fact that the students there, in large part, belonged to another party. As Schücking sadly noted, "we do not have this political culture today. What does it mean to have political culture? It means to also respect the political opinions of those who think otherwise and to be willing to work with them for the best of the Fatherland."[161] This was a penetrating comment indeed, and the hyperinflation virtually guaranteed that the German political culture in the sense of the highly fragmented bundle of antagonistic political traditions, positions, and attitudes which constituted Weimar's inheritance from the German past would persist and flourish to the detriment of the "political culture" of which Schücking spoke.[162]

The challenge of the hyperinflation, in short, was as moral and cultural as it was social and economic, and the hard truths of socioeconomic reality were detested and rejected because they challenged the assumptions upon which German society had long functioned. When "Morus" made reference to the "long proletarianized German worker, who had until now known best how to secure his minimum of existence, [but] can no longer eat his fill after the latest price increase," he received an infuriated letter from a "mental worker," who insisted that the workers had been "deproletarianized," that the wives of urban workers were to be seen in the markets buying legs of veal and saddle of venison which the wives of even the best-off doctors and lawyers could no longer afford. "Where," he asked, "is the non-mechanical, the intellectual work even approximately so well paid as the mechanical labor whose wage, as is well known, is depressed by female labor? How would it be if you would for once concern yourself with our fate, instead of with that of the less than ever proletarianized worker?"[163] Morus's response was to point out that the relative increase in the pay of unskilled workers was a universal, not simply a German, phenomenon, that most of the workers' pay was being consumed in the cost of food, and that intellectual workers had to face the fact that the social and psychic consequences of the war were, among other things, that people were more concerned about getting their *Schnaps* and tobacco than about contemplating works of art or seeing their doctor. Intellectual workers not only had to organize like everyone else, including the allegedly individualist entrepreneurs who were cartelizing and syndicalizing at an unprecedented rate, but also had to face the reality that they could no longer remain the chief consumers of their own products and had to widen their clientele.[164]

From the perspective of both intellectual workers and large portions of German society, however, the consumers of art and culture had been widened to include elements for whom they could only have the most extreme distaste; namely, the war and inflation profiteers, the nouveaux riches, and especially the *Schieber* (those persons who dealt in scarce goods and articles in violation of the antiprofiteering laws and other regulations). Much newspaper and magazine space was taken up in poking fun at the *Schieber*, especially in Berlin, where the figure of Raffke (named after the verb *zu raffen*, "to snatch up"), the boorish newly rich businessman whose money had been made by dubious means as a war profiteer and inflationary wheeler and dealer in scarce goods, appeared regularly in print, illustration, and in cabaret pieces. Raffke was the sort of person whose wife regularly referred to their recently bought home as "ancestral" and confused an *Oratorium* with a *Moratorium*, while he himself refused to pay the demanded price for a Rubens because it was a "used" picture, drank his beer out of a bottle even at the opera, and periodically took time off from the vulgarities of Berlin night life to taste what was passing for high culture. He bought Expressionist art for tax evasion or investment purposes and filled his house with unread books.[165]

Famed Weimar critic and writer Kurt Tucholsky, an "intellectual worker" who was briefly and despairingly forced to take a bank job to make ends meet during the 1923 hyperinflation and often wrote songs and other works under the pseudonym of Theobald Tiger, immortalized Raffke for Berliners in a cabaret song for the 1922 revue of Carl Rössler, "Things Are Topsy-Turvy" (*Wir stehen verkehrt*). The song portrays Raffke as the "latest thing" to be found everywhere. As the famed Raffke, he can whistle at public opinion, and as the "finest of fine numbers" who appears regularly in the *Berliner Illustrierte Zeitung*, he can afford champagne, lobster, and women, just as he can commission paintings for his bathroom, even though he does not know whether a Botticelli is a cognac or a cheese. Thanks to his dividends and thirty supervisory board seats, his thick fingers are bedecked with a "salad" of pearls and diamonds, while he shifts the proceeds of his various dealings to the Bank of England and "always makes dollars." In short, whether as money-maker or as consumer, Raffke, as the refrain of the song went, "always digs in, really digs in" (*Ich knie mir rin, ich knie mir richtig rin!*).[166]

There was another vision of the *Schieber*, however, one more formidable and more culturally threatening. It is to be found in the portrait of the *Schieber* (1920) by Heinrich Maria Davringhausen, an early example of the so-called "new objectivity." Here, the *Schieber* appears in an environment of urban modernity, cold, aloof, working in an empty office with the tools of his trade—pencil, paper, and telephone—amply supplied with cigars and modestly with wine, intense, confident, and businesslike. The complexity of this figure was well captured by a satiric and socially penetrating article by Roland Schacht of December 1922 with the title, "Defence of the *Schieber*." In it, the *Schieber* defends himself against the various charges made against him by society. To the ac-

The Raffke family doing its Christmas shopping, December 1922. The scene was a display in one of the windows of the Wertheim department store in Berlin. (*By permission of the Ullstein Verlag*)

cusation that he breaks the law, he responds that he had sold meat illegally throughout the war and that no one objected to buying it from him: "On the contrary. I was a sought after personality. 'My *Schieber*,' people said fondly of me. Without me many more would have starved. I was the salvation of children, the refuge of the weak, the sun of the convalescents, the consolation of the worn out. . . . But do not think that I earned my money without work and care. Nothing was wasted through me. Entire storehouses did not spoil through me, and entire deliveries of goods were not unusable, as was the case with the authorities who presumed to take the food supply in their hands instead of us. . . . I worked, and God blessed my work."
To the charge that he enriched himself at the cost of others, the *Schieber* responded that everyone did so, and who was to judge what "suitable" compensation was? The incompetent, he argued, were in the majority, and the state and its officials hardly deserved more. Most devastating, however, were the words Schacht put into the mouth of those who criticized the *Schieber* for being uneducated and boorish:

Now you say, the *Schieber* is uneducated. Yes, I only went through grammar school. Why did not the educated, who had the say before, make the grammar schools better? When I see what kinds of fatheads most of the educated are, how they allow themselves to be led around by the nose by their newspapers, their politicians, their bureaucrats, do you think I envy them? No one can take me in. I understand my business, and thoroughly at that, and when I am asked, I say my piece. The rest is of no concern to me. The scholarly experts? They do not even agree with one another. Just think of the nonsense which the economists, those big shots, talked during the war. Intellectual activity? We cannot all be intellectually active. And are you not doing business with your intellectual activity? And for that matter, who is buying your special luxury editions, your folios of paintings, who is going to your concerts and theatre? Exclusively we *Schieber*. Do we not have intellectual and artistic interests? From whom would you cultivated people, who tolerated the war and its miserable management, live today, if we were not buying up your stuff. We are an economic blessing. We are the new men who are replacing the dried up *routiniers*, the people with the worn out traditions. We know what we want and we stand by what we do. We do not go into raptures of William Tell and then stand at attention before William the Second. We are not anti-Semites and we do our shopping at Wertheim. We are the children of the people, who are making it. We

Heinrich Maria Davringhausen, *Der Schieber* (1920). (*Photo by Walter Klein,* Foto-meister, *courtesy of the Kunstmuseum Düsseldorf im Ehrenhof*)

are the true revolutionaries. *Schieber*? We are Germany's future.[167]

"The Most Characterless Land on Earth"

All this was very clever, but it did nothing to remedy the miseries into which the hyperinflation was driving entire groups of Germans and the anxiety, physical misery, and distress arising from the conditions that permitted the *Schieber* to ply their trade. The hyperinflation was an economic as well as an emotional disaster for the small rentier (*Kleinrentner*) and other pensioners as well as for all those living on social security and social welfare of various kinds. The sale of personal valuables and household possessions by such persons from the *Mittelstand* in order to meet day-to-day living costs had been going on since the end of the war, but it became so ubiquitous in 1922 that house-

wives' associations in Berlin and other major cities undertook the painful task of disposing of such people's cherished possessions. This lower-middle-class "self-help" took the form of establishing sales bureaus, in the Berlin case within the secure confines of a savings bank, to which both sellers and buyers could come, and where experts were brought in by the housewives' associations to ensure that the sales prices would be as fair as possible under the circumstances. The situation was genuinely pathetic:

A walk through the small salesroom with its tables and glass cases is heart-rending. There lie spread out so many lovely things so pleasing to the eye . . . wonderful Turkish and embroidered silk shawls, finely carved figurines, old porcelain, clocks, inlaid pearl, embroidered linens, silver utensils—everything in short that once decorated a house is assembled here. . . . There is some old piece, a picture, a porcelain dish, a vase, which appears to the loving but unskilled eye of the owner as a true rarity and who, if

The *Mittelstand* sells its cherished possessions. (*Bundesarchiv Koblenz*)

she must part with it, wants to receive as much as possible. One now has to tell her that it has neither material nor artistic value, and the sick, embittered souls are always inclined to take this as a personal affront and bad will.... A look out the window—there slides by the restless life of the metropolis, the fine silk stockings and expensive furs, there sit autos with the fat figures of *Schieber* inside, and here inside, in the quiet room, an impoverished Germany quietly and painfully weeps in its silent misery.[168]

Actually many of the inflation victims in this situation were not quite entirely as passive as these lines would suggest. Some 90,000 to 170,000 of Germany's 250,000 to 330,000 small rentiers were organized in the German Rentiers' League (*Deutscher Rentnerbund*) and its various affiliated associations in 1921–1922. Some two-thirds of these were women, usually widows and spinsters. The majority of the males, who were usually over sixty years of age, had been independently employed members of the *Mittelstand* or former officers and white-collar employees, while a substantial number of the women had no occupation. In a great number of cases and in contradiction to the social

pretensions of their propaganda, their economic status bordered on that of the proletariat even before the inflation, but they could have anticipated surviving on interest from small savings and investments. They were thus especially vulnerable to the inflation, and the propaganda of the Rentiers' League was filled with hostility to the government and social resentment. In August 1921, the Rentiers' League demanded that the government exempt all rentiers with incomes of less than six thousand marks from the bread price increase and protested having to pay the capital gains tax.[169] A month later, its Bavarian branch took a threatening tone, pointing out that the civil servants would stand up to a man if their pensions were cut and asking if "it does seem a mockery of us small rentiers when our assets are continuously being decimated thanks to the previous mistakes of the state while that same state, on the one hand, fights profiteering and, on the other hand, publicly offers 340 marks for a 20-mark gold piece once again in the newspapers? Is the state not thereby giving itself the greatest imaginable reward for its common profiteering? If the money is there for these *Schieber*, then the money is there for us."[170] One of the Rentiers' League's favorite themes was reminding the government that it was responsible for departure from the gold standard and for failing to put Germany back on it. In the hyperinflation, it took an extreme creditor position, arguing that the government's monetary policies lacked all political justification in the light of its failure to accomplish any of its political goals, the controlled economy and the helter-skelter decisions of the courts on contracts were demoralizing, and the only way out of the situation was for the courts to be genuinely free of politics and parties by insisting that all monetary obligations be calculated in gold marks even if they had to be paid in paper marks. In this way, the letter of the law requiring acceptance of paper marks would be maintained, but the courts would restore "justice."[171]

The Reich government was relatively slow to accept a special obligation to the small rentiers; the states and municipalities had taken the lead in supporting those who were impoverished by the inflation. By late 1921, however, the municipalities and state governments were calling on the Reich to assist them, and the Reich did begin to give assistance for the first time at the end of the year.[172] What made the problem particularly difficult was the general feeling that the small rentier should not be treated in the same manner as those on social security because "the small rentier stands at a completely different social level and to them it means something very different when they are required to live on the same sum as a social pensioner."[173] At the same time, they were for all intents and purposes receiving welfare or poor relief, and the growing budget deficits made it necessary to individualize relief by using such criteria as sole dependence on capital investments, genuine need, and the reaching of retirement age. While accepting no formal obligation to aid the small rentiers, the Reich Labor Ministry did recognize that insofar as they had financial need arising out of general economic conditions and did not have an entitlement to social security, they needed help from the Reich as well as states and municipalities. Thus, the Reich agreed to provide some fifty million marks to cover a third of

the costs of assisting needy small rentiers through the granting of annuities in return for a posthumous claim on their assets, a method in which Mecklenburg-Strelitz had pioneered. It was anything but popular since the self-worth of many of the small rentiers appears to have been tied to their roles as aunts and uncles from whom something could be inherited. The Reich also allowed for other appropriate forms of help for those who met the necessary tests of need and age, such as placement in old age homes or the subsidization of food, clothing, and other necessities. These Reich funds were only available, however, if the states and municipalities first provided their share of two-thirds of the costs and supported only those who met Reich conditions for assistance.[174]

By February 1922, the Reich was contemplating an increase of its subsidy to two hundred million, and some Reichstag Deputies were proposing an increase to five hundred million to cover the costs of assisting not only the small rentiers but also a host of miscellaneous groups who were not covered by social insurance programs and who were in dire straits— for example, women hired to do domestic work in homes, white- and blue-collar workers with serious family problems, persons dependent on recently received inheritances, and the like. Funds were necessary to subsidize the rising costs of bread, milk, and potatoes for such persons, and there seemed no point in pushing through separate bills for each category of the growing number of needy. The dilemma, which was to become typical of all aspects of social welfare involving the sharing of responsibility by the Reich and the states and municipalities, however, was that the Reich was trying to reduce and control its financial obligations while the states were seeking to shift all the costs to the Reich because of their own parlous economic situations as well as the increasingly desperate financial condition of the municipalities. Though the Reich refused to widen the categories of those entitled to the help given to needy small rentiers, the accelerating currency collapse did force the Labor Minister to provide an initial five hundred million marks and then a billion marks in the course of the budget year. No less symptomatic, however, was the observation of the Labor Ministry that its funds were

not as rapidly used as might have been anticipated, and then only for a limited number of
those involved. The chief beneficiaries of the assistance were the weakest of the weak; namely,
women who were too old or too inexperienced
to enter or go back into the job market or to follow the lead of some of the male rentiers and
engage in speculation. At the same time, the
Reich guidelines for receiving assistance required that the state and municipal governments go through the tedious process of passing
new appropriations of their own, while many of
the municipalities were simply unwilling to
take on further social obligations and also
found that the Reich guidelines, which had to
be relaxed, placed them in the position of continuously having to deny the poor in order to
aid the poorer.[175]

They were placed in a similar position with
respect to those receiving social insurance and
security benefits, and this meant nothing more
or less than that Germany's famed social insurance system, which dated back to Bismarckian
times, was threatened to its very core by the hyperinflation. The essence of that system, the intention of which was to promote a measure of
social stability as well as social security, was the
substitution of the insurance principle for welfare or poor relief. The worker or employee and
employer contributions were intended as investments in the present and future security of
the individual and his or her family. The difference between the social pensioner and the small
rentier was that the latter could engage in speculative investments if he or she wished, while
the monies paid by the former had by law to be
placed in nonspeculative investments. This was
especially the case with respect to invalid and
old age insurance. In contrast to the funding of
sickness and accident insurance, which employed a cost-averaging method (*Umlagever-
fahren*) that was based on relatively short-run
determination of requirements and sought to
cover most costs by contributions rather than
by return on investments, invalid and old age
insurance were based on the so-called capital
coverage method (*Kapitaldeckungsverfahren*);
that is, contributions served as a forced investment in the system which would be repaid
through the income-generating capacities of the
system itself. Since these forms of insurance de-

pended upon the interest from long-term investments, eligibility was determined by a procedure under which a person qualified only
after a certain period of investment in the system (*Anwartschaftsverfahren*).[176]

From hindsight, it is obvious that the German social insurance system, especially that
portion of it that depended upon long-term returns from invested assets, was in jeopardy by
1918, but the principle of mark for mark promoted a tendency to concentrate on immediate
problems under the assumption that an eventual stabilization of the existing currency would
restore a reasonable value to the investments.
The number of persons covered by social insurance was increased, benefits for accidents were
made more generous, and waiting requirements for veterans were relaxed. While the
measures taken by the post-1918 governments
were accompanied by considerable talk about a
thoroughgoing reform and coordination of the
entire system, the patchwork approach taken
with respect to immediate problems added to
its complexity. The upshot was a host of complaints about confused regulations, increased
discretion on the part of individual insurance
bodies, the loss of uniformity, and intensification of such old problems as the battle between
doctors and sickness insurance funds.

The result was two concurrent dilemmas. On
the one hand, the real value of the investments
of the system were constantly deteriorating
and, with the coming of the hyperinflation,
were dwindling into worthlessness. Nevertheless, the social insurance organizations not only
remained passive in the face of the evaporation
of their assets, but they in fact encouraged the
Reichstag to make a substantial increase in benefits in July 1922 by claiming that they were
"swimming in money."[177] The government
called for yet another increase in October, arguing that the needed funds would come from
the existing contributions and an increase of
contributions in 1924. Obviously, the ever
higher paper-mark wages were the source of the
liquidity of the social insurance system and its
borrowing against the fictional returns on its increasingly fictional capital. Matters were made
worse for the operating capital of the system by
the continued practice of having the higher
classes of workers pay a lower proportion of the

contributions, particularly since practically no one was working at the old lower wage scales anymore. The dangerous nature of the system's investment practices did not go entirely unnoticed. In December 1922, one of the leading white-collar unions, the German National Retail Clerks Association (Deutschnationaler Handlungsgehilfenverband, or DHV) asked that the Reich Insurance Board for Salaried Employees should change its regulations so that only one-twelfth instead of one-quarter of its money had to be invested in government bonds and thereby avoid becoming "an institution for the compulsory confiscation of employee salaries."[178]

On the other hand, while wages were being tapped for worthless investments, the pension and other social insurance payments already being paid out represented a confiscation of past savings. The second dilemma, therefore, was that the inflation was undermining the very principle of insurance itself. To correct this injustice while maintaining the integrity of the insurance principle, the Reich would have had to adjust pensions to the depreciation, a question actually raised by the Socialist Justice Minister Radbruch in September 1922 and rejected on the grounds that it would "start an avalanche" in which mortgage holders, creditors, and indeed everyone victimized by the destruction of paper assets would descend on the government for assistance.[179]

The only alternative to valorization of insurance benefit payments, however, was a growing dependence on welfare—precisely the kind of poor relief for which the social insurance was intended as an antidote. The Reich sought to avoid this consequence for as long as possible; first, by granting supplements to social insurance that had to be repaid by the social insurance organizations. Since these repayments could be in war bonds at their face value, this was a veiled Reich subvention of social insurance. Another approach, pursued especially in 1920, was to require additional payments from the insured to cover the supplements, a policy made all the more dubious by the insistence that the money thus collected be added to the "investments" of the social insurance system. Then, the Reich sought to evade the inadequacy of the social insurance payments by try-

ing to have them supplemented with welfare payments by the municipalities, a policy sharply criticized by the latter, some of whom warned that this was not in the interest of the pensioners since "it will lead to passive resistance in many of the municipalities, at times even to efforts to drive the pensioners out of their localities."[180] By December 1921, however, it had become utterly impossible for the Reich to escape passing a law implementing emergency assistance to needy social pensioners under which the Reich provided 80 percent of the assistance. Proposals that all social pensioners receive supplements to their totally inadequate payments were rejected in an effort to maintain the fiction that welfare could still be separated from insurance and that it could be individualized. The call for sparing the states and municipalities the additional financial and administrative burden was also turned down for the related reason that the local authorities were responsible for welfare.

These basic policies were maintained throughout 1922 as the amounts granted by the Reich increased in their usual inadequate manner. Municipality after municipality reported that it could not manage to provide the additional support necessary and that the law of December 1921 imposed a burden greatly in excess of what was already being spent on poor relief. Especially objectionable from the perspective of the municipalities was that the Reich relief for social pensioners required the establishment of yet another bureaucratic agency to deal with welfare problems, the costs of which had to be carried by the municipalities without any Reich support. In many cases, the needy pensioners or members of their families would have to be dealt with by the old municipal welfare agencies as well as by new agencies set up to implement the new law. As the City Council of Halle complained:

On the one hand, the Reich and state use every appropriate and inappropriate opportunity to point out that the municipalities allegedly are much too wasteful and are not careful enough with their money, but on the other hand, they compel the communities against their will to set up new and very costly administrative agencies which have no practical value and which could be spared without any disadvantages at all. . . . The entire effort is also to be severely criticized because the social pensioners are only *al-*

legedly being offered a "special" care, while they, because of the inadequate support provided by the Reich, are actually remaining as before in the poor relief, which has been designated as a second-class form of care in a completely superfluous manner in order to make things look better than they are. The difficulties this creates for our practical work do not seem to have become clear to the ministerial experts.[181]

An important calculation of the authorities in Berlin, however, was that (as with the support given for small rentiers, so with the support for the social pensioners) only the most desperately needy would apply. This was Labor Minister Braun's actual calculation in pushing through the December 1921 legislation, and it is very likely that many social pensioners failed to take advantage of the new "opportunity" either out of pride or sheer exhaustion and that many municipalities simply failed to take the necessary measures because of the costs involved. One may be certain that the municipalities did not make it easy for the pensioners to qualify for their maximum entitlements under the emergency measures, and it was understandable that pensioners demanded the transformation of the emergency supplements into regular pension entitlements "so that the hardships of the needy are eliminated, for the city authorities judge need to their advantage for financial reasons in order to save on their supplement costs."[182] In a very real sense, these expropriated pensioners were being exposed to a double injury. As with other groups who had anticipated getting real value for their investment, they found it, in the words of one worker, "an outrageous injustice that, we earlier paid yearly contributions amounting to approximately 48 gold marks, which is the equivalent of 28,800 marks today, and receive a pension entitlement after 25 years of service of 220 marks monthly or 2,640 marks a year."[183] Additionally, however, in order to get some extra, desperately needed though still very inadequate support in the hyperinflation, they were expected to meet the qualification requirements of some ungainly new agency considered superfluous and demeaning by the very municipalities responsible for its establishment as well as costly and absurd by the state governments.[184]

In fact, Germany's municipalities and a substantial number of German citizens had already had their fill of such agencies. Quite pertinently, the Magistracy of Halle, in opposing the new regulations for social pensioners, made specific reference to the widespread discontent with the special agencies that had been set up to determine the support of some 1.5 million disabled veterans, 525,000 war widows, 1.3 million orphans, and 164,000 parents entitled to consideration for benefits under the National Pension Law of 1920.[185] The workings of this law provided Georg Grosz with an extraordinary source of material. While all war disabled were entitled to a fixed pension whatever their class or rank, they had to apply for this, and the amount of the pension ranged from 25 to 100 percent depending on the degree of disability. The system aimed at returning as many disabled veterans and widows to the job market as possible, a goal encouraged by the legal requirement that every employer hire one disabled veteran for every twenty-five to fifty employees and hampered by the failure to have similar legislation for widows. In the case of the latter, the fact that such persons were often best suited to lower-level civil-service jobs had ambivalent consequences. While the Labor Ministry made a substantial effort to have as many widows hired in the postal system as possible, for example, the efforts made to reduce personnel and expenses in the system stood in some contradiction to the employment policy.[186] Decisions concerning the entitlement to pensions were handled by some three hundred offices throughout the country, and all pensions granted prior to the law had to undergo review. Some three million applications were reviewed between July 1921 and February 1923, the largest number being handled in early 1922. Doctors had to determine degrees of disability, while the offices had to determine eligibility under a system where a maximum income level, regularly but insufficiently changing under inflation, was an important element in the question of entitlement. The unholy combination of bureaucratic backlog, frequent arbitrariness, complex and constantly changing regulations, and inadequate levels of support to keep up with prices produced deep resentment and sullen disgust. The civil service was a special object of hatred, since its procedures were seen as a self-serving technique designed to

keep the bureaucracy overstaffed and to provide its members with salaries that were a far
cry from the benefits provided its "victims." In
January 1922, for example, when the minimum income index stood at 1,600 marks, a
fully disabled veteran received 1,034 marks, a
widow 716 marks, and a civil servant 1,965
marks. The key point, however, was that the
disabled and the survivors of Germany's lost
war were increasingly being viewed as just one
more group of charges against Germany's taxpayers and one more excessive financial burden
under circumstances where everyone was struggling with hyperinflation.[187]

To be sure, all sense of civic spirit and voluntarism had not been lost, as shown by the
housewives who helped those compelled to sell
their household possessions, or the Aid to the
German Aged (Altershilfe des deutschen
Volkes) created in 1922. The Central Association of German Invalids and Widows met with
leading trade-union, party, and employer organization representatives in August 1922 to
try to persuade them to collect some portion of
earnings and profits for the purpose of helping
the two million Germans incapable of working
to avoid hunger and to prevent a further increase in the notable number of beggars on Germany's streets. While Germany's pensioners
were forced to live on six hundred marks a
month, others were living in luxury, millions
were being spent on alcohol and tobacco, and
Germany's plants and factories were running
full blast. Could not this booming economy be
tapped by voluntary means? The trade-union
representatives did suggest that the workers
might be willing to contribute some pay from
overtime work to assist but insisted that industry and the banks also indicate a willingness to
contribute from their resources. In the end, the
Central Working Community agreed to lend its
support to a proposal by the Labor Minister
that a German Emergency Aid Community
(Deutsche Notgemeinschaft) be established to
call on the German people to collect monies
and goods for the needy voluntarily. In so
doing, however, the ZAG urged that the number of those to be served by this charity be limited to those on poor relief, since it did not believe that meaningful sums could be collected
for all those in distress.[188]

The condition of Germany in the hyperinflation was indeed a strange one. On the one side,
there was a booming economy with scarcely
any unemployment; on the other side, there
was increasing economic and social misery.
The situation which had led the organization
representing invalids and widows to appeal to
the ZAG was exactly the same that led the
famed Berlin zoo to ask if the ZAG would not
support the performance of a free hour of overtime work to keep the zoo open, a request
turned down on the grounds that the ZAG was
a central organization not responsible for rem-
edying local problems. This was a wise decision
since Hamburg's popular Hagenbeck Animal
Park was also on the skids.[189] The great problem
in 1922, however, was not feeding animals but
feeding people who could not afford the price of
food, and the mounting insolvency of Germany's municipalities was what made the problem appear insoluble.

This insolvency was most clearly demonstrated in September 1922, when the central
clearing banks (Girozentralen) through which
the savings banks served the credit needs of the
municipalities announced that they were no
longer in a position to supply them with credit.
At the same time, the loan bureaus began to refuse to discount municipal bills of exchange. A
further source of liquidity, the issuance of
emergency money, had already been sharply restricted by law in July. Foreign loans were
scarcely to be had anymore. This condition of
approaching bankruptcy marked the culmination of tendencies that had begun during the
war and had intensified because of the Erzberger tax reform and postwar conditions. On the
one hand, the social responsibilities and expenses of the municipalities had increased substantially; on the other hand, their powers of
taxation had been significantly reduced. In addition to the extraordinary rise in social expenditures, personnel costs had increased thirty-
one times over between 1918 and 1922, so that
the Reich was forced to take over 60 percent of
all municipal and wage salary supplements
made after September 1921. As was the case
with its assistance for social purposes, however,
the Reich aided the municipalities with great
hesitation, while the municipalities argued that
the Reich should assume full costs because of

their loss of taxing powers. The Reich complained that the municipalities were not sufficiently economical, even as the municipalities protested that the Reich was both ruining and confusing their finances with late payments of the portions the income tax owed them. As the Westphalian cities pointed out in November 1922:

1923 is already approaching, and the transfer of the final portion of the amounts [owed the cities] from the Reich income tax for 1919–1922 remains outstanding. Paying the municipalities a portion of what is owed in the form of 135 percent of what is owed on the 1919 tax receipts some three years late has put the municipal finances in disorder. Very costly expenses of 1919 are supposed to be covered with the depreciated marks of 1922. That is impossible. The currency depreciation has forced the municipalities to cover running expenses temporarily with millions in expensive discounted bills. The interest burden for these is thoroughly uneconomic and must be paid at the cost of the Reich. Covering them has not been possible since the payments in the depreciated marks of 1922 do not suffice. Even worse is the moral effect. The sense of financial responsibility is being undermined by the inability to have a clear idea of what municipal budgets will be like.[190]

Fundamentally, the cities were struggling along by borrowing in anticipation of funds to be received, sometimes from further borrowing. Efforts to improve their tax base by adding a municipal surcharge to the Reich turnover tax were frustrated by the Reich Economic Council and the Reich itself, while the taxes on trades (*Gewerbesteuer*) and on property were paid quarterly in depreciated currency and were bitterly resented by small tradesmen and businessmen. The most successful taxes were the hotel, entertainment, and drinks taxes. The entire situation was driving the municipalities in the direction of running public utilities and municipal enterprises along more commercial lines. While the bourgeois parties in the municipal councils protested increasing municipal "socialism" and competition with private enterprise, the left-wing parties objected to the increasing priority being given to economic as opposed to social considerations in the management of municipal enterprises.

As 1922 drew to a close, however, such measures were more of long-term than of short-term interest. The Reich supplements for personnel costs covered only officials, not workers and employees in the municipal works. While the supplements, unlike the back taxes owed the municipalities, were paid in advance every quarter, the money was often spent before the rising salaries for which the supplements had been given could be paid. Thanks to the refusal of the clearing banks and savings banks to give further credit after September 1922 and of the loan bureaus to continue to give credit for unsold municipal bond issues, many cities were unable to pay their employees or their bills on October 1, 1922. The Reich came to the rescue with an "extraordinary prepayment" of monies owed to the cities but claimed it could not repeat this without undermining the financial equalization scheme worked out among the Reich, states, and cities. The task of determining which municipalities were needy and giving them help would have to be done by the states.[191] In effect, the Reich was treating the municipalities in the same manner as the municipalities were being compelled to treat its citizens on poor relief; namely, require them to undergo a means test and humiliating and ungainly procedures in order to get assistance.

The Congress of German Municipalities blamed the Reich for creating the difficulties in the first place, and also blamed the Reichsbank for refusing to discount municipal bills. The Reichsbank was not amused by what it chose to call a "slip of the pen" on the part of the Congress. While the cities chose to make a comparison between themselves and merchants or industrialists who were being given credit on the basis of securities presented, the Reichsbank took the view that securities could not be given for municipal assets which offered no real guarantee of payment. The Reichsbank was only prepared to make an exception in the case of the purchase of food for the needy for the coming winter. In cases where the municipalities were selling the food directly to the poor at subsidized prices, the Reichsbank was prepared to accept municipal bills of exchange with the condescending but by no means unwarranted condition that "in all cases the practice is to be followed that the receipts from the sale of goods to the population should be used exclusively for redeeming the bills issued for their purchase."[192] It was a measure of the low esteem in which municipal credit was held that the merchants had great reservations about taking credit from the Reichsbank on the basis of the bills issued by the municipalities.[193]

The upshot of this situation could only be grudging support dishonestly given. The Reich, supported by the Reichstag, refused to provide municipalities with an interest-free loan to overcome their difficulties or to simplify procedures by distributing the money to all the cities. Instead, it offered prepayments on money due to the municipalities in the form of block grants to the states with instructions that the prepayments only be given to needy cities. The fact that the Reich was always behind in its payments and that the municipalities had been forced to borrow in order to cover their bills seems to have been a matter of indifference in Berlin. At the same time, it was manifestly impossible for municipalities to deal with their problems unless they were provided with liquidity. To deal with this problem, Prussia, to take the most important example, rigidly followed the guidelines in distributing Reich prepayments for needy municipalities and charged them a higher interest than the Reichsbank. In December 1922, however, the Prussian government permitted the Prussian State Bank to give the municipalities over four billion marks in prepayments on municipal bond issues which had not yet been placed on the market. These credits, like an additional two billion in credits from the loan bureaus to cover the operating expenses of municipal enterprises, were to have the guarantee of the Prussian state. Special Municipal Credit Certificates (*Kommunalkreditscheine*) were issued for this purpose. The Prussian State Bank agreed to accept them and, with the approval of the Reichsbank, use them as security with the loan bureaus. Thanks to this imaginative approach, the collateral in the form of securities held by the loan bureaus grew from 14,122,000,000 to 210,407,000,000 marks between the end of 1921 and the end of 1922. For January 1923, therefore, the liquidity problem of the municipalities appeared to be "solved," since the clearing banks reported that the "money situation is still very fluid."[194]

What must always be kept in mind, however, is that these bizarre arrangements were still being made in the context of an economy operating at a very hectic pace and suffering from very minimal unemployment. While an underclass of pensioners, widows, orphans, and disabled persons was being kept more or less alive through inadequate welfare and varieties of poor relief, these people did not share the company of any substantial number of unemployed. Emergency measures for the poor, therefore, could be accompanied by reduction of expenditures on the unemployed, as was the case in November 1921 when Labor Minister Brauns cut back unemployment support entitlements and promoted a cutback in productive unemployment support. Needed increases in support payments were deliberately withheld for foreign policy reasons until inflationary developments in the fall made increases unavoidable, thus placing those who were unemployed in a position of dependence on poor relief analogous to that of the indigent unemployable.[195] Implicit in this situation, however, was what might be called the ultimate nightmare; namely, a situation in which hyperinflation was accompanied by high unemployment.

It was more than natural that such fears should find early and explicit expression by the Saxon authorities, since Saxony was especially prone to high unemployment. At the same time, as the most densely populated and industrialized area in Germany, its population suffered especially from food supply problems and was very reactive to price increases. Even during the last phase of the galloping inflation, therefore, the Socialist government of Saxony was particularly outspoken in calling for strong measures to deal with the rapidly increasing costs of the basic necessities of life. In a memorandum on the increasing cost of living sent to the Reich government and Reichsrat in May 1922, it argued that the situation was dangerous to public safety and order and that no one should be lulled by the relative absence of public disturbance until that point. If things had been quiet in Saxony, "it is only thanks to the fact that there has been an economic boom for a year and a day in which there is only a very small number of fully unemployed persons. There would, however, be immediate reason to have worse fears if suddenly the boom slowed down and the number of unemployed would rise. Even with higher unemployment support rates, unemployment and, at the same time, so sinful an increased cost of living as at present would be unbearable."[196]

In the view of the Saxon government, the astronomical prices were by no means justified because the price increases were outstripping the rate of currency increase. The prices could only be explained by profiteering on the part of persons with access to goods, by cartel pricing, and by corporations using their profits in order to satisfy the hunger of stockholders for higher dividends. The Saxon authorities cited the sharp rise in sugar prices and the shortage of sugar since the removal of controls as a typical example and accused the refineries of creating an artificial shortage and high prices by selling most of their production to the producers of chocolates and luxury baked products servicing rich Germans and foreigners at any price that was asked. Rising meat prices were blamed on the illicit sale of cattle over the borders and to high-priced areas by dealers and analogous charges were made with respect to potatoes and other decontrolled agricultural products. The high price of clothes and shoes was blamed on machinations by wholesalers, swindling, and cartel pricing. The Saxon government felt that the time for half measures and dependence on the price examination agencies was past. The Reich was urged to impose a much higher export levy so as to ensure that export profits would benefit the economy as a whole; to assume control over prices, wages, and tax payment in important plants; to establish surveillance committees of producers, merchants, and consumers to aid the price examination agencies in checking prices and in restricting entry and practice in retail and wholesale trade; to increase the grain levy from 2.5 million to 4.5 million tons; and to reintroduce economic controls on potatoes and sugar.

This was an extreme position indeed, and it ran against the policy of decontrol pursued by the Wirth government, a fact which may explain why no answer to the memorandum was sent to Saxony.[197] Nevertheless, the Saxons were not alone in worrying about the rising cost of living and the need to step up the war against profiteering. The Prussian Ministry of the Interior was concerned enough in March 1922 to order tours of inspection in major provinces, undertaken primarily in May and June, and

these reports revealed, on the one hand, the immense difficulties faced by the antiprofiteering effort and, on the other, the growing public frustration and bitterness over the situation.[198] The organized effort to combat profiteering varied in effectiveness geographically. It appeared better organized in the east than in the west and in cities than in the countryside. The cities with large quantities of readily available food were understandably less sensitive to the need to fight profiteering than those dependent on supply from the outside. Breslau and Düsseldorf had notably competent organizations, but the Rhineland province in general suffered badly from the Allied occupation, the loose border controls, the large number of foreigners and amount of foreign currency with their price-increasing effects, and the hostility of farmers and tradesmen to the regulations. Separatist sentiments were, in fact, attributed to efforts to enforce the laws. Quite often, the antiprofiteering agencies were badly understaffed and lacked expertise, the latter compounding the most universal and serious problem encountered in the struggle against profiteering; namely, the inability of the authorities to provide satisfactory counterarguments to the experts sent to the courts by the chambers of commerce to testify on pricing questions. Almost invariably, these experts took the side of the defendants, and the courts were severely criticized for dismissing too many cases and for inadequately penalizing violations of the law. As might be expected, the antiprofiteering laws met with nothing but hostility from industry and commerce, which argued that the only real profiteers were the so-called "wild traders" who traveled around, often in the company of ladies of dubious reputation and in an ostentatious style, and were very difficult to catch. The frustration of the population generally found expression in a feeling that there was no point in participating in the effort and undergoing all the disagreeable consequences of personally making charges when one could just as well respond by demanding wage and salary increases. The cynicism was heightened by the growing realization that attacking high prices and profiteering could no longer begin and end with the retailer but had to extend to the wholesalers and the cartelized producers. Here, control of books, expert testimony, and oversight were particularly difficult, and there had been very little success.

Nevertheless, the Prussian inspectors warned against any letting up on the effort, which would meet with resentment and resistance from the population and a total loss of self-control by merchants and producers. Of this there was already sufficient evidence, as certain staples were no longer to be had. Marmelade producers had bought up most of the fruit; the candy and liquor industries, most of the sugar. Citizens of Stettin, for example, were unable to buy fish except from inland dealers at high prices. Above all, something had to be done to fight the deep sense of inequity that surrounded the steadily climbing prices. Thus, wherever the inspectors traveled in the western and central provinces of Prussia, they found workers, employees, and civil servants expressing over and over again their resentment that wage and salary increases never led to a genuine improvement of their situation and that they were taxed at the source, while businessmen were able to use price increases to better their situation, to calculate tax payments in their pricing, to hide their full wealth, to delay payment, and thus to leave those receiving wages and salaries as "the lone bearers of the burdens of the state." An even harsher version of the same views was to be found in the eastern provinces:

One demands that the producers and the merchants like the workers and civil servants participate to their fully appropriate extent in the general distress, and that this finds visible expression in their style of life. Thus, no merchant, who in the prewar period ever could have thought of buying a house or an automobile through his business activities should be able, as is observed a hundred times over, to do so in this time of great distress. These persons could only have found the money for these purchases through profiteering prices, and one asks if the revenue offices have done their duty in assessing their taxes. . . . The population itself finds no greater satisfaction then when false tax declarations are discovered, for it does not trust the tax declarations of the big earners in any way. Because of the excessively slow working of the courts in profiteering cases, a demand has arisen for the creation of people's courts [*Volksgerichte*] for the speedy judgment of indicted profiteers.[199]

The sense that profiteering and profits had gotten out of hand did not simply come from below. At the end of March 1922, the Bavarian

Minister of Commerce and Industry, Eduard Hamm, a leading figure in the DDP and certainly no enemy of industry, sent a confidential memorandum to the leading trade associations and business organizations of Bavaria sharply critical of what he considered to be excessive industrial profits. While certainly agreeing with the view that the chief cause of the increased prices and cost of living lay in the international situation and reparations problem, he nevertheless felt that more and more persons were becoming disturbed over the excess dividends being passed out to stockholders, especially in the form of the right of old stockholders to buy new stock at severely reduced prices and thus increase the real worth of their holdings very substantially. While admitting that much of industrial profit making was purely illusory and granting that reserves needed to be assembled for the hard times that would undoubtedly come, he nevertheless missed sensitivity and tact in a great deal of the behavior of businessmen with respect to both prices and profits, and he appealed to their social conscience:

There is also the question of whether such plants, before they give such high profits to their stockholders, have done everything that one might at this time consider the task especially of successful economic ownership, namely, a multiplication of the contributions to the housing and education of the workers in their own plant and locality, care for those classes of our people who are suffering most from the present price movement, namely, the *Mittelstand* and the small rentiers, care for the maintenance of the scientific and technical capacity of the German people, care also especially for the scientific goals of state and other public service institutions and for the students.[200]

The reaction to Hamm's remarks in Bavarian industrial circles was very sharp. Both businessmen and their organizations stressed that wages had risen far more than dividends, that the future was anything but rosy, and that if, as Hamm admitted, many of the supposed profits were purely paper profits, then it was the task of the responsible authorities to enlighten the public instead of add to the misinformation, jealousy, and anticapitalist sentiment fostered by the left-wing press. One company claimed that the price increases were due to the high commissions taken by the merchants. Insofar as the question of supporting worthy causes was concerned, the argument was made that it was not the workers, the middle class, or the new rich that did most of the private giving but rather industry. In one case, however, a firm responded bluntly and negatively to the effect that "the heads of private enterprises have to take care of their stockholders first," that the tax burden was very heavy, and that "in more profitable years one first has to think of building reserves for worse times."[201]

Most significant, the officials of the Reich Economics Ministry, to whom Hamm had also sent his memorandum, responded not very differently from the Bavarian businessmen, also arguing that the paper profits were more apparent than real. They, too, rejected a proposal by Hamm for the surveillance of profits on the grounds that the effort would be in disproportion to the results and that, as long as profits tended to be in paper marks, it was virtually impossible to determine what excess profits were.[202] The furthest they would go was examining the cost calculations of leading firms suspected of profiteering. The truth was, however, that the officials in the Ministry charged with the controlling of profiteering were not prepared to follow calls in either Saxony or Bavaria for a control of profits or of cartel pricing.

This became very obvious at the meeting in Dresden of the Price Examination Agency representatives on May 23–24, 1922.[203] The reaction of the Bavarians was always a matter of concern to the RWM, since there had actually been demands for the death penalty for profiteering emanating from that state. As it turned out, however, the head of the Munich Agency, Bretzfeld, took a very moderate tone, pointing out that "we have to have the courage to destroy the illusion of the masses that we can influence the economy with police measures. We destroy the authority of the state by decrees against profiteering which underpin this illusion, for sooner or later it will be shown that these are only words and that deeds will not follow because they cannot follow."[204] Ministerial Director Hüttenheim was surprised and pleased to hear such common sense from this quarter but went on to point out that not only the authority of the state but also the functioning of the economy was at issue and that "we should not destroy the entire economy by pursuing a price policy which makes it impossible for the busi-

ness community to do business."[205] What this meant was that the RWM was trying to hold fast during the last phase of the galloping inflation to the principles it had laid down during the relative stabilization; namely, to sacrifice considerations of social policy and equity to the inflationary economic reconstruction process. As the economy moved in the direction of hyperinflation, the Ministry was prepared to accept pricing policies that ensured the continuation of economic activity, even if this meant sacrificing the goal of price stability that had been so important in the relative stabilization. The only question was how far they were prepared to go in this regard.

The ultimate limit would have been the acceptance of prices based upon calculations of reproduction cost, as opposed to the policy traditional since the war, at least in theory, of basing the calculation of cost on what had been expended at the time the item was made or sold. Under stable monetary conditions, of course, prime costs (*Gestehungskosten*) and reproduction costs (*Wiederbeschaffungskosten*) are seldom so far apart that they cannot be covered by provision for risk. When they are not, then the bankruptcies that ensue are considered normal sacrifices in the cyclical ups and downs of capitalist economies. Under unstable monetary conditions, however, the reproduction price reflects the effort to find a price that will cover cost increases that result from inflation alone, and in extreme inflationary conditions, its determination involves an anticipation or speculation of what the inflation will do to future costs. Had this problem of covering the costs of mark depreciation been discovered only in 1922, when it became the subject of constant discussion, it would have been very strange indeed. What made the discussion so very important in 1922 was that the rate of inflation was such as to make the acceptance of pricing in accordance with reproduction costs a decision to promote and accept an unheard of level of inflation.

This was a consequence toward which men naturally preferred to walk rather than to run, as well demonstrated by the most extraordinary address at Dresden of the RWM's specialist in these matters, Privy Councilor Wodtke. As usual, the RWM was faced with demands for a change in the wording of the antiprofiteering decrees, the faithful still hoping that the problems of the laws would be solved by a change of wording that would ban an "excessive price" instead of an "excessive profit." Wodtke did not think such word games, which had originated in Austria and had much support in Bavaria, worthwhile. The faithless, who were to be taken much more seriously because they constituted the major peak associations of commerce and industry, were proposing that the law be changed to read that "a price is not to be considered to contain an excessive profit and is not to be viewed as an unallowable increase of prices if it is in conformity with the market situation or if the reproduction costs of the goods sold are its basis. The market situation is not to be considered if it is temporarily impossible to bring goods on the market or if, through unfair machinations, an emergency market situation is created."[206] This was too much for the RWM since it was nothing short of an acceptance of the reproduction price at a time when monetary depreciation was the major source of price increases and when the very fact of monetary depreciation was encouraging a flight into goods. A great many prices were being determined by cartels, and merchants tended to take every potential price increase into account in making up their own prices. This could only serve to promote inflationary expectations, and Wodtke was convinced that "satisfying this demand will mean an increase in the tempo of monetary depreciation."[207]

If depreciation were to be contained at all, Wodtke argued, then some discretion would have to be left to the authorities in turning down price increases, even at the risk of some legal insecurity. For this reason, he objected to a recent Reichstag committee resolution asking that "the standards of evidence for price profiteering be clearly defined so as to make possible an incontestable objective determination of violation of the decree."[208]

Under the existing unprecedented and unanticipated inflationary conditions, such definitions would only hamstring the authorities, who needed to ensure the satisfaction of legitimate business and consumer interests. He thought it especially important to influence the courts to interpret the decrees along lines that recognized economic realities rather than registered social and moral prejudices. Progress had been made in getting the courts to accept prices based on market situations that would take both business and consumer interests into account. If goods were in short supply in a market, for example, it made sense for the courts to encourage their reappearance by allowing the seller to anticipate a real profit but not to gouge the consumer. In the view of the RWM, this was a reasonable way of preventing profiteering while keeping businessmen in business.

Most worrisome from this perspective was a Reich Supreme Court decision of July 7, 1921, which barred sellers from taking monetary depreciation into full account in their pricing. The court ruled that the full cost of currency depreciation could not be passed on to the consumer, and the RWM considered this decision economically untenable. While the RWM opposed the acceptance of reproduction costs as the basis of price determination, it insisted that a businessman at least had to recover the full costs of the item he was selling and that those full costs had to take into account the full previous monetary depreciation. The fact was that the antiprofiteering laws had not been framed with the inflation in mind but rather to prevent the abuse of shortages and emergencies. To tell people that they could not recover their full costs and take the monetary depreciation into account was to encourage them to hold on to their goods and to discourage all commerce and trade. In a trenchant criticism of the Supreme Court's motives, Hüttenheim argued:

It is a mistake at this late date to equate a mark with a mark, as the Supreme Court does, when it makes the price plus some extra charges the equivalent of the sales price and merely seeks to take the monetary depreciation somewhat into account. . . . The situation in which monetary instruments whose values are continuously subject to great variations are treated as things of equal value cannot be sustained. If our general measure of value, called the mark, has become false because of changes that have taken place, then it must be corrected and must be given precisely that value that it had when the goods were purchased. But we can only do this if at times of falling mark value and increasing depreciation we allow the seller to add charges to cover this development. Then the seller has at least the security that he will recover the full monetary value of his goods. The incentive to the economic activity of capital is restored once again. Transfer of wealth within our society [*Volksgemeinschaft*] which the Supreme Court wishes to prevent because it violates its social feeling, namely that the holder of paper marks will bear the full depreciation of the currency and therefore be more unfavorably placed than the holder of goods, cannot and should not be fought through the price decree, which is not there for that purpose, but by another means, primarily that of taxation. . . .[209]

This was a rather remarkable statement made all the more remarkable by the fact that Hüttenheim cited with approval the views of State Secretary Mügel of the Prussian Ministry of Justice and his arguments for a valorization of business transactions on the grounds that "a condition in which monetary units whose worth is constantly subject to great variations are treated as objects of equivalent worth should not be allowed to become a permanent state of affairs."[210] The fact that Hüttenheim's wording appeared to exclude the notion that *past* obligations should be subject to revaluation only heightened the extent to which the RWM was sanctioning the redistributive workings of the inflation. It was the Reich government, after all, that had made the mark-for-mark principle the law of the land and that banned the acceptance of any other currency or even calculation in other currencies for purposes of domestic business. While Hüttenheim stressed that taking depreciation into account was nowhere excluded by the wording of the antiprofiteering decrees, this hardly did away with the inconsistency involved in suddenly claiming that the Supreme Court was mistaken in treating the mark as a mark in present and future transactions without calling into question the status of past transactions. True consistency lay in the policy of promoting and maintaining industrial production at all costs, a policy which also permitted the loose attitude toward credit that led to the discounting of commercial bills in increasingly enormous amounts during the summer and fall of 1922. What this meant was that those who had access to goods and access to credit were to be favored, and, as Hüttenheim's statement demonstrated, the social consequences were anything but mysterious to those making policy. It was not implausible for Hüttenheim to argue that tax policy was the instrument by which the injustices of the inflation might be corrected, but this required the speedy collection of taxes and their valorization. Instead, the government was becoming more and more dependent on wage and salary withholding for such revenues as it received, and since

the employers were required to turn in their payroll tax receipts on a quarterly basis, employers were receiving an interest-free loan from their employees which they were able to pay back in depreciated currency![211]

Obviously, producers had to adapt to hyperinflation by calculating in terms of real values and real costs if they were to survive. The unavoidable fate of those who failed to make such an adjustment was well illustrated by a popular anecdote about a rope manufacturer who had become convinced that he could do splendid business by selling his rope for ever increasing amounts of paper marks. He rapidly became a millionaire and then a billionaire, but each time he used his capital to buy hemp, he noted that he progressively received less hemp for more money and that his production steadily decreased. Finally, the day came when he could produce only one piece of rope, and he used it to hang himself at the gate of his desolated factory.

As the economic correspondent for the *Berliner Tageblatt*, Felix Pinner, pointed out, however, such factory owners seldom drove themselves to such a sorry end and that the normal scenario by September 1922 was a very different one. The factory owner had used his paper marks to expand his plant and construct new buildings. He had not forgotten his comforts, perhaps having bought a villa and an automobile or two which he could charge off as business expenses on his tax return. Furthermore, he was not blind to the danger that his capital investments could turn out to be dead capital, and this had led him to purchase foreign currencies—not only to buy raw materials but also as a reserve for the future. Insofar as he did not have enough operating capital at any time, he borrowed from the bank monies which he then repaid in depreciated currency, further enabling him to increase his substance at the cost of others. In order to protect himself against depreciation, he assiduously worked in the meetings of his trade association to have prices calculated not only on the basis of reproduction costs but also in foreign currencies, just as his balances were also increasingly calculated in gold or foreign currencies.[212]

This ideal-typical model of business behavior in the inflation was not anything the RWM wished to encourage, and it helps to explain the resistance to accepting the so-called reproduction price. So long as the domestic purchasing power of the mark continued to be higher than its worth abroad, the RWM wished to avoid calculations in foreign currencies that permitted an excess profit totally unjustified by domestic costs and prices. The reality, however, was that the cartels and trade associations, and not the authorities, were issuing the guidelines. The number of cartels in industry had increased from six hundred to seven hundred in 1905 to fifteen hundred in 1922, while wholesalers had forty organized cartels, and retailers ten, or at least these were the number of cartels whose existence was admitted.[213] With the coming of hyperinflation in the late summer and fall of 1922, the iron and steel industry, for example, haggled over new prices, first every ten days, then every week, while at the same time introducing automatic increases to cover changes in the price of coal and other raw materials. They stretched their imaginations to devise delivery conditions and contract terms to protect themselves from losses and to maximize their gains. The spirit in which these decisions were made was well described by one of their own number: "Nothing resembling a higher point of view is given consideration in the negotiations anymore; it seems as if everyone sees the collapse coming closer and closer and wants to still grab for himself beforehand whatever can be snatched up."[214] Whereas previously the manufacturers acted as a brake on the raw-materials producers, situations now developed in which the former took the lead in developing harsh-delivery conditions and calling for price increases.

This is not to say that the relationships among the various elements of the business community were always so friendly. Quite to the contrary, they often took on a remarkable degree of hostility since the fundamental goal of each party in the chain of production and distribution was to protect itself to the maximum while letting someone else hold the paper marks. It was a game of economic Old Maid or, as one would say in the German context, a test of who would be left holding the *schwarzen Peter*.[215] In the textile industry, for example, the relations between the producers and wholesalers could not have been worse, the latter complaining bitterly about the open-ended prices of the former that compelled wholesalers to pay for each wage increase or other cost increase between the date an order was placed and the date the goods were actually received. They took particular umbrage at the policy introduced by the large weaving mills in the spring of 1922 requiring even the oldest of customers with the best credit to pay 25 percent in advance the moment they placed an order. Wholesalers, however, were hardly models of innocence, and one critic argued that consumer cooperatives were being cut out of business under their pressure and that "the wholesalers dictate conditions to industry today, while industry follows their command. In this way the prices for the consumers, whose income has not kept up, are increased by ten percent."[216] The craftsmen also got into the act, and their prices led to demands that "profiteering from services" (*Leistungswucher*) be included in the regulations.[217]

As always, retailers were the most vulnerable, and insofar as the price examination agencies and police did much of anything in the realm of fighting profiteering and preventing pricing on the basis of reproduction and replacement costs, they turned out to be the chosen targets of such efforts. They felt surrounded by enemies. As one retailer pointed out to his Reichstag Deputy, the Socialists were preventing the retailer from receiving just recompense because "Mr. Majority Socialist [Economics Minister] Schmidt wants to destroy the retail trade in order to promote his consumer cooperatives. He does not consider that he thus deals the death blow to a major group of taxpayers." At the same time, consumers and the prosecuting attorney's office were constantly "looking behind the wrong bush" in their search for the origins of the high prices, since "no prosecutor troubles himself about the boundlessly increased price demands of manufacturers or industry." He went on,

I would like to see the face of Herr Stinnes when an envoy of the police comes to his residence and demands the presentation of his invoices and records, as has lately become the sport of the local price examination agencies in dealing with the retailers. The legitimate merchant, who is simply fighting for his existence, but also has to worry about paying the terrible tax burdens placed upon him, is treated under the penal provisions as the equivalent of a cutthroat, a swindler, a burglar.[218]

Even after one discounts for hyperbole, it is difficult not to conclude that the hyperinflation had completed the process of turning the antiprofiteering laws into a worthy successor of the controlled economy in agriculture insofar as absurdity and unenforcibility are concerned. The situation by late 1922 was simply chaotic. Neither the authorities nor the retailers were clear about the extent to which the inflation could be taken into account in setting prices, and complaints about the legal uncertainty (*Rechtsunsicherheit*) were universal. In the Dresden district, for example, the authorities had pursued 225 cases of alleged violations of the regulations between May 1 and October 31, 1922. One hundred thirty cases were dropped; sixty-seven were sent to the prosecutor's office, and twenty-eight were still pending. Of the sixty-seven cases under consideration, fifteen had ended in some penalty, ten had been discontinued, and forty-two remained pending. In short, the majority of the cases was dropped, and it should be noted that, aside from the stigma of being found guilty, those penalties exacted through fines were paltry because they were paid in paper marks according to obsolete schedules.[129]

The authorities confessed that they had neither the personnel to enforce the regulations nor a clear sense of what the regulations meant. There was a growing disinclination to obey or enforce the price-posting regulations, which threatened to result in store windows being turned into an unsightly mass of lengthy and constantly changing numbers. Such fines as were levied were extremely light "since the compulsion to maintain the posted prices in a period of rapid monetary depreciation while the rest of the commercial world is allowed to take reproduction costs into account is viewed as an undue hardship."[220] There seemed to be a consensus among the Saxon authorities "that the retailer is much less to blame for the price increases than the producer or wholesaler."[221] At the same time, the authorities noted that the reluctance of consumers to bring profiteering retailers to court was increasing, although it was hard to tell whether this was "because a seller is seldom found guilty, or because they fear that the seller will not give him any food."[222]

While such motives must unquestionably have played a role, consumer behavior and perceptions certainly also must be considered since they probably led to a certain degree of collaboration between some consumers and retailers. Consumers were hardly faultless with regard to pushing up prices, since they were getting rid of their money as rapidly as possible and hoarding whatever they could as their purchasing power steadily diminished. At the same time, retailers, in their struggle with wholesalers and producers could at times take on the appearance of advocates of consumer interests, particularly in the context of such outrages as wholesalers buying out retailers' stocks in order to resell them to other retailers at higher prices. Some of the more hard-pressed retailers simply gave up. A few engaged in a sellers' strike in late 1922, while some struck back at their wholesalers in a most peculiar manner by simply selling off their goods at prices below what they would need to replace them, thereby placing themselves in a position of not being able to afford to buy from the "profiteering" wholesalers and having to sell to consumers. Apparently, it was this development that persuaded the Reichsgericht in Leipzig to revise its previous posture and, in a decision on December 19, 1922, to recognize the right of retailers to take domestic monetary depreciation fully into account in their pricing. It followed by only a few days upon a new set of RWM instructions along precisely the same lines. To be sure, these changes did not constitute an acceptance of the reproduction price, and no *carte blanche* was being given with respect to the calculation of prices. But the court, undoubtedly influenced by the Economics Ministry, in suggesting that the cost-of-living index might serve as a foundation for pricing calculations, had moved radically away from its old position. As a leading wholesaler organ noted with no little satisfaction, "[T]he principle of mark for mark has thus been given up insofar as the antiprofiteering laws are concerned."[223]

The collapse of restraint and self-restraint in the first months of the hyperinflation was viewed with horror and opprobrium in many quarters. Thus, when the representatives of the price examination agencies met anew in Hannover in November 1922, the mood was grim. The manifest inability and unwillingness of the RWM to control the cartels and their exploitation of consumers, which one official described as a victory of the "economic policymakers" over the "politicians," was deplored for its political and moral consequences. Dr. Bretzfeld, the same Munich official who only half a year earlier had argued that efforts to control the situation by decrees and laws could only ruin the authority of the state, now felt Germany was facing anarchy:

Until now, the extreme left and extreme right have been separated by a dam, the *Mittelstand*. This dam is disappearing day by day. A great portion of this barrier has already collapsed, and we will soon see the *Mittelstand* simply ceasing to exist. In particular the entire bureaucratic apparatus in Germany will no longer be in a position to hold out economically. Then, in place of the professional civil service, we will have the party functionaries. With this, however, the barrier to the extremes will be completely eliminated. The final struggle will come, and one will only have to ask who will finally emerge as the ruler from Germany's ruins, the Bolshevik or the great capitalist. The path which we are on and which has the disappearance of the *Mittelstand* as an element, leads to a war of all against all.[224]

What is important about this apocalyptic vision is not whether either the social analysis or the prognosis conformed to reality but rather the manner in which the hyperinflation had transformed this previously relatively sober official into a prophet of doom. That it was a Bavarian who spoke these words is by no means insignificant. The condition of Bavaria during the hyperinflation, the proposals emanating from it, and the behavior of its population bespoke the rising tide of anxiety, the morally ambivalent behavior, and the shame and outrage which existed throughout Germany but which expressed itself with peculiar virulence in that state.

All this was not entirely new, of course. Bavaria had distinguished itself with periodic fits of moral pretension as the Reich's *Ordnungszelle* while it remained a haven for right-wing extremism and resistance to the Republican governments in Berlin. The antics of the former District President of Upper Bavaria and Min-

ister-President from March 1920 to September 1921, Gustav von Kahr, had included demands for stringent prosecution of profiteers, antigluttony legislation, and other morally "cleansing" measures. Even when out of office, Kahr continued to enjoy wide popularity among Bavarians, probably because this sober, stern, narrow-minded, anti-Semitic, anti-industrial, anti-Socialist, Protestant administrator conjured up a vision of Bavaria that Bavarians wished to continue to entertain despite its remoteness from reality. Kahr's fulminations against Berlin satisfied Bavarian prejudices. As the British Consul in Munich noted, "[T]o the Bavarian, Berlin is a cesspool of atheism and vice, a sordid market where culture is at a discount and only the money-grubber flourishes, a town without a soul, a city in Germany, but not a German city."[225]

In reality, Bavaria was anything but a center of virtue and innocence, and the posturing of its politicians was not unrelated to fear of a breakdown of political order, which, under Bavarian conditions, meant an increased danger from the political right. Thanks to its strong agriculture and possibly to more stringent controls, Bavarian prices had remained below north and central German levels until the spring and summer of 1922 when galloping and then hyperinflation hit with particular ferocity by bringing Bavarian prices into line with the rest of the country and creating no end of anxiety for the Bavarian political leadership. As the Saxon Ambassador to Munich reported, "when one considers the psychological attitude [here], especially of southern Bavaria, which is completely unwilling to suffer and bear in the manner of the rest of their German fellow citizens, then one can completely understand the concern of the responsible circles here."[226] Their confusion about how to respond was well reflected in Commerce Minister Hamm's attacks on industrial profiteering, on the one hand, and the liberal line taken on profiteering controls by Bretzfeld in Dresden, on the other.

By September 29, both confusion and political unrest had increased to the point where Minister-President Count Lerchenfeld felt compelled to send a memorandum, which was more radical in many respects than that of his Saxon counterpart some months earlier, to the government on the increased cost of living.[227] Lerchenfeld stressed the impoverishment of the "mass of the *Mittelstand* . . . , which had always counted as the most reliable support for the state," and he devoted considerable attention to the need to resist Allied demands as well as to maintain domestic order, balance the budget, and increase productivity. Like his Saxon counterpart, Lerchenfeld blamed much of the situation on the cartels and called for "prophylactic measures" against them, and he urged Draconian measures against profiteering, including "penitentiary, expulsion, the work house, confiscation of property, ban on continued business activity, and closing of the business." Lerchenfeld did not think it fair that only farmers should be forced to make sacrifices in the form of the grain levy and urged that commerce and industry also be compelled to surrender a portion of their goods at reduced prices. At the same time, he called on the Reich to take positive steps to aid the needy through bread price reductions, increased support for small rentiers, reduction of freight rates for food transports, cheap provision of coal and fuel, and reduction of the coal tax. He also urged wage and salary increases, especially for civil servants, where justified.

These proposals were accompanied by repeated challenges to economic liberalism and an insistence on the primacy of state interests. Thus, "where the state and the economy have come into conflict with one another, economic considerations must retreat wherever the existence of the state is placed in question." No reverence whatever was given the laws of economics, which "are only an expression of the fact that certain conditions bring about certain results. But they do not say that these conditions themselves are always necessary and that every attempt to influence them by state measures must be inadequate." In fact, Lerchenfeld concluded his memorandum with an argument for autarchy until Germany had recovered sufficiently to return to the world market, and he even suggested that all prices and wages should be stabilized at their prewar levels and that insofar as food imports were necessary and had an effect on the currency, the costs should be born by the state. He concluded with a dramatic defense of his proposed return to the controlled

economy: "The major reservation that this would mean a step backward into the hated controlled economy should not be decisive if the means in general appear suited to prevent a catastrophe for our economy and our state. No government should give its people the freedom to throw themselves into destruction and the compulsion not to step before falling into the abyss is no compulsion at all."

Only the Bavarian Socialists showed much sympathy for the memorandum, and Lerchenfeld confronted a storm of protest both from within his government and from business interests, which forced him to retreat and contributed to his fall shortly afterward. The document did contain a mass of contradictions. One simply could not increase exports and prevent unemployment while forcing producers to limit production to vital necessities, and one could not simplify the administration while undertaking a full scale surveillance of cartels and syndicates and reviving the controlled economy. It was impossible to reduce railroad and postal deficits while reducing railroad and postal rates, and one could not reduce the Reich deficit while raising civil servant salaries and subsidizing coal and food for the poor. These inconsistencies were compounded by the difficulties of reconciling the memorandum with previous Bavarian policies. Whereas in the past Bavaria had opposed the grain levy, called for the reduction of the export levy, attacked Reich efforts to provide cheap clothing and shoes to the poor, and opposed price ceilings, it now came out for diametrically opposed policies. Whereas previously the Bavarian Forest Administration had held back wood for fuel and paper production and promoted high prices, Lerchenfeld was now calling for generosity in the supplying of wood and low prices. Normally, Bavaria approved of expensive food and luxury imports to support its tourist hotel business, but now these were opposed as part of a mysterious autarchy program. In short, behind the radical anticapitalism of the Lerchenfeld memorandum, there was a maze of confusion and contradictions not to be found in its more straightforward, Socialist Saxon counterpart. What characterized both, however, was a fear of increased radicalism and the breakdown of public order.

While the Lerchenfeld proposals were buried under a pile of criticism and contempt, conditions in Bavaria, as elsewhere in Germany, steadily deteriorated. The Bavarian peasantry was a particularly undisciplined lot and showed no inclination to make sacrifices for anyone, other Bavarians included. Indeed, the peasants' behavior ranged from the most fine-tuned response to monetary and monetary-exchange conditions to orgies of self-indulgence of every kind. A major source of the increased cost of living in Bavaria was that the countryside was being flooded with merchants from north and central Germany who came with the purpose of buying up food at higher prices. Although these transactions involved a host of irregularities, as one official pointed out, "the peasant would have to be an angel if he wanted to resist the continuous temptations."[228] Of this there was no danger whatever, and when combined with the other forms of collective peasant behavior—first the hoarding of money and then its rapid expenditure on consumer goods, home improvements, and new farm construction; the endless complaining about the grain levy and repeated threats of a delivery strike; and a rapidly growing interest in consuming as much *Starkbier* and having as many peasant feasts as possible—the result could only be resentment and hatred toward the peasants on the part of the rest of the population. By late 1922, in Bavaria, as in the rest of Germany, there was a marked increase in plundering on the land and generalized anxiety that there would not be enough food.

This anxiety had been increasing over months, creating an enormous amount of difficulty, for example, at the time of the first postwar showing of the Oberammergau Passion Play in May 1922. Fears that hundreds of thousands of Americans and other foreigners would come to Bavaria and gobble up the food supply led to threats of violence by the Penzberg miners and considerable disturbance until the government successfully assured the population that the foreign exchange brought in would permit the hotels to feed the tourists exclusively with imported food. As things turned out, far fewer tourists came than expected, and they left far more speedily than desired, primarily because Munich was considered the most conspicuous illustration of a phenomenon for which Germany was becoming notorious; namely, the cheating and mistreatment of foreigners by officials, hotels, merchants, and anyone else a tourist was likely to encounter in his or her travels.[229]

Germans could not be expected to treat foreigners better than they were treating one another, however, and the conditions that drove Saxony and Bavaria to send their memoranda were worse than ever by the end of the year as the political extremes began to mobilize. In Saxony, control committees of the type advocated by Buck were being set up against the will of the government by Communists and radicals to hound and plague a helpless and resentful peasantry and to try to force their will on the merchants as well. An effort was made to mobilize not only workers but also disaffected lower-middle-class persons—civil servants, policemen, doctors—"to take the distribution of food, housing, and clothing into their own hands, with force if necessary."[230]

In November 1922, a Communist agitator from Erfurt visited Straubing and Passau to urge workers to follow the lead of their brethren in Saxony and Thuringia, declaring that the "leaders of the revolution have remained standing half way to the goal."[231] While provincial President von Pracher was anything but happy to have such missionaries in his district, his major problem was how to deal with the conditions that had led to the control committees, and those conditions were as Bavarian as they were Saxon. He reported that the peasants were holding back their grain or selling only the cheaper varieties while keeping the rest until the price increased further. Penalties for profiteering were too low to serve as a disincentive to the various illegal activities being conducted. At the same time, the peasants were getting a taste of their own medicine and were outraged when "doctors, veterinarians, druggists, lawyers, notaries, and other representatives of the free professions" were forcing the peasants to pay for professional services in food calculated at the prewar prices. In summing up the political and social situation in lower Bavaria, von Pracher demonstrated that the Munich Price Examination Agency official Bretzfeld had good reason to think in apocalyptic terms:

The political situation is tense. The concern about one's daily bread is increasing not only among the workers, employees, and civil servants, but also among a large number of those who are self-employed, not to speak of the military and social pensioners and the small rentiers. In the cities and in the better-off agricultural districts, the antagonisms are particularly pronounced. On the one side there are the various wholesale and other merchants and the better-off farmers, on the other side there are the consumers who are struggling with necessity. It is obvious that under such circumstances the political antagonisms should also become ever more severe. The discontent of the laboring people is directed chiefly against the Jews and the peasants, as one can hear daily in the conversations which are conducted in the railroad trains. The National Socialists appear to find increasing membership. If they do not always show the necessary self-restraint, on the other side they form a not to be underestimated check for the left radicals for whom the creation of a dictatorship of the proletariat appears as the ideal.[232]

To whom, after all, were a "sick" people supposed to turn? The message of shame and self-disgust was preached in a variety of venues from the beginning of 1922 to its even more miserable end. Thus, on New Year's eve, Cardinal Faulhaber delivered his customary sermon in the Frauenkirche in Munich, where he urged that his listeners carry something of the seriousness of the Sermon on the Mount into the coming carnival (*Fasching*) season: "Gluttony and amusement can only embitter the famished at home and awaken abroad the impression that the economic distress and incapacity of our people to pay are not to be taken seriously. . . . The moral nadir of our people is marked by many sad symptoms, most crassly through the glorification of the work of the flesh, through the contamination of the blood in the bodies of our people, through the poisoning of public behavior. More shameful than the black shame in the occupied areas are the negro dances in the unoccupied areas."[233]

It was also possible, however, to fantasize about employing shame for self-curative purposes and about the means through which such self-help could come about. The hero of Norbert Jacques's novel *Dr. Mabuse: The Player*, super-detective Wenk, offered opportunities for recovery. Wenk unequivocally rejected his minister's claim that the German people were healthy by stating that "it is sick through and through. From what can it be healthy—after

such years and such a life." His bitter words persuaded the minister to "leave nothing untried" and to create a new post for Wenk. The latter surrounded himself with a group of young people whose money was not new and who had been driven into political and personal opposition by the fallen social order with which they identified themselves. He knew he could count on them because their sense of guilt was exceptionally strong thanks to their awareness that they had failed to resist what had come to pass when they should have.[234]

From this perspective, the Reich's observer in Munich missed the point somewhat when he wrote on November 9, 1922, that the rallies and demonstrations of Hitler and his National Socialists were largely "empty slogans, mostly with 'völkisch' and anti-Semitic content and, as social wrapping, the struggle against Mammonism."[235] While he correctly captured the social character of the movement as a catch-all party composed of workers, students, members of the *Mittelstand*, and many officers and other bourgeois persons who had moved out to the countryside and as a party disliked by the peasants and living off the "despair of the ever more miserable *Mittelstand*," he probably underestimated the psychological power of Hitler's message and its role in the steadily increasing enthusiasm for the movement in Bavaria, especially later in the month following Mussolini's triumph in Italy.[236] Unlike Cardinal Faulhaber, Hitler offered a secular solution, and, unlike Wenk, he was real. Yet he played on all the themes of shame and outrage which had become so acute in the hyperinflation. This is well illustrated by a speech he made on August 19, 1922:

This Germany stands in remarkable contrast to the Germany there once was. The earlier honesty, freedom of opinion, system of justice, etc. have been turned into their opposite. An unexampled characterlessness is taking hold of our people, and its government nurtures this characterlessness in that debauchery and place-hunting has become so widespread that in this three past years Germany has become stamped as the most characterless land on earth. The Revolution preached the struggle against capitalism, but actually it has destroyed the small saver and small tradesman while cultivating big capital and big commerce. It has promised to make the worker free. Today the worker toils so that Germany can pay reparations and earns only one-third of his wages while the rest is slave labor. On the one side the distress of the small rentier, pensioner, and war cripple, on the other side shameless gluttony with the state doing its part in that it marches at the head with its unsurpassable mismanagement. Where the earlier state used its means stingily, although it was rich and powerful, this weak republic throws its pieces of worthless paper about wildly in order to enable its party functionaries and like-minded good-for-nothings to feed at the trough.[237]

Needless to say, Hitler blamed Germany's condition over and over again on the Jews, on the "Jewification of the economy," and, in effect, on the "Jewification" of German life. It was this that was destroying the *Mittelstand* and undermining its well recognized functions in German life:

A Jewification of the economy as in Russia is unavoidably taking place here also. The only opponent in this process is the *Mittelstand*, which represents individual existence and is therefore also the political opponent of the type of state which permits this type of Jewification. Thus the *Mittelstand* is the genuine national *Stand*, for those on the right are depraved and those on the left are victims of agitation. And its most valuable task is to make the bridge over that division of the classes which must ruin a people. It is the class that ties together poor and rich. Its most significant characteristic is its relative purity of race.[238]

The implication was obvious. All that was obnoxious and corrupt in German life, what the Germans were doing day after day in the course of the hyperinflation, reflected a "characterlessness" that was not really in character but consisted of the machinations of the Jews and their helpers in a "characterless government" that pursued a policy of fulfillment until it was too late. Its "worst crime" was the "printing of paper money."[239]

Chapter 13

Facing Disaster:
The State and the "Productive Estates" on the Eve of the Ruhr Occupation

The French occupation of the Ruhr on January 11, 1923, was to create, however briefly and confusedly, a new context for the issues of stabilization and inflation that was nevertheless not entirely unfamiliar. Actions conducive to the worsening of the inflationary situation and attempts at relative stabilization were to become instruments in the struggle against the French and were to take on the "decisionist" quality of financial and economic practice during the war as well as of the crisis management aimed at pacifying the unrest of the first postwar years. It would be false to think that history could repeat itself, however, since years of inflation (and, above all, the year of galloping inflation between the summers of 1921 and 1922) and the hyperinflation since July 1922 had changed the consciousness of the participants in the inflationary process.

Fundamentally, the broadening recognition of the consequences of the inflation, together with the adaptation to them, meant that inflation would lose much of its rationale as well as its rationality. The inflation had depended on a certain consensus about the primacy of economic reconstruction in an environment of relative social peace. This had promoted a redistribution of assets enabling the state to eliminate a large portion of its domestic debt and assisting producers of goods to rebuild their plants and recapture some of their markets under conditions of relatively high employment and low wages supplemented by imperfectly operating price and rent controls and

food subsidies. The consensus was based to a high degree on illusion and differential learning both within Germany and internationally. The holders of real assets, the organized, and the knowledgeable depended upon the willingness of others to hold paper assets and/or their inability to reject and get rid of them, the inadequate organization on the part of the inflation victims, and a persistence of monetary illusion arising either from ignorance or slow learning. The hyperinflation marked the breakdown of the confidence in the currency both at home and abroad and the increasing dissemination of knowledge about the consequences of living in a monetary illusion. The past willingness to play the inflationary game was fading, insofar as it had not disappeared altogether, and this was why a consensus was developing that stabilization was necessary. No one could doubt, however, that the stabilization would bring a crisis since it necessarily involved surrendering the capacity to combine export advantages with that assortment of voluntary and involuntary arrangements in the realms of taxes, wages, social welfare, and working conditions by which the various "productive estates" had been pacified. Thus, while the consensus on the need for stabilization was growing, the differences over the distribution of its burdens were perforce increasing as well.

The Ruhr occupation, therefore, could only defer but not prevent the stabilization crisis widely anticipated before the invasion. As Georg Bernhard wrote at the end of 1922,

One must therefore accept the fact that the year 1923 will under all circumstances be a crisis year. Under all circumstances, for if the stabilization does not take place, then the dollar rate will increase into the immeasurable, and then the further inflation will certainly produce a crisis because of the capital shortage arising from it. If on the other side there is a stabilization, then there will be a crisis because of the reasons mentioned. But one must go through such a crisis. Disturbances of the economic mechanism in a capitalist economic order cannot be eliminated without crises. And it is under all circumstances better that we have a stabilization crisis as a transitional crisis with hope for a rapid final recovery than an inflationary crisis, which has to end in complete stagnation and the dying out of the German economy or with a social revolution.[1]

The occupation of the Ruhr ensured that Germany would experience both crises and would come very close not only to political upheaval but to political dissolution as well. Whether the inflationary crisis of 1923 could have been avoided without the Ruhr occupation is difficult to say, but it is important to recognize that Germany was heading toward that inflationary crisis well before January 11. In order to understand the place of the Ruhr occupation in the history of the German inflation, therefore, it is essential to comprehend the situation of the "productive forces" of the economy—business, labor, and agriculture—in the hyperinflation of 1922 and consider the condition of the German economy and its prospects on the eve of the political events that culminated in the total destruction of the mark and which made inevitable a stabilization based on a new currency and new domestic and international arrangements.

The Financial and Currency Crises

One of the most important characteristics of the hyperinflation was that the private sector joined the state in seeking to keep afloat by means of fiat instruments of exchange. This meant that industry and agriculture began to share with governmental authorities the tension between doing everything possible to keep operating by inflationary measures and seeking to escape the monetary illusion by attempting to valorize revenues and find some real means of accounting for assets and liabilities. Once industry and

agriculture began to face the same dilemmas as the state, however, concentration on the question of how to maintain the remaining productive resources of the nation meant that the private fiscal crisis would assume priority over the public fiscal crisis. In order to understand how this happened, it is necessary to begin with a consideration of the condition of public authorities themselves.

The hyperinflation undermined an increasingly successful effort by the Wirth government to reduce expenditure, balance the budget, and make tax assessment and collection effective. The high point of success had been in the spring of 1922, when the combination of increased revenues from taxes and reduced expenditure had made it possible to cover ordinary and extraordinary expenditure out of revenue and even to have something left over for reparations (see Table 22).[2] This promising state of affairs was made all the more agreeable by the distribution of tax receipts, especially the income tax, which produced for a short period a relative distribution of receipts between taxes based on withholding (PAYE or "pay as you earn") and taxes based on assessment akin to what Erzberger had in mind in his tax reform (Table 23). Thus, in February 1922, the high point of what can only very loosely be called a trend, the percentage of collected income taxes based on assessments not only exceeded the percentage collected by withholding, but did so in the proportions Erzberger had intended. The tendency of receipts from assessed taxes to exceed or nearly equal the wage tax lasted through May, after which the situation became as bad as it had been in May 1921. The devastation wrought by hyperinflation on the government's efforts to secure its income through taxation rather than Treasury bills is most evident, however, when one takes note of the decreasing percentages of government income acquired from taxes of all types as compared to the percentage of issued Treasury bills in the course of the budget year 1922–1923 (see Table 24). The "successes" between February and August 1922 were largely a consequence of the sending out of tax bills for 1920 at the end of 1921 along with prepayment bills for 1921 and the sending of bills to those with very large incomes between May and July 1922. Hyperinflation nullified much of these

Table 22. Real Government Deficits, Revenues, and Spending, 1919–1924
(million marks per quarter deflated with the wholesale price index; 1913 = 1)

Quarter	Deficit[1]	Revenue[2]	Spending[3]	Cash Reparations
1919				
1st	1,501	—	—	0
2nd	3,394	987	4,381	0
3rd	1,977	854	2,831	0
4th	780	653	1,432	0
1920				
1st	348	397	745	0
2nd	1,188	542	1,730	0
3rd	1,648	843	2,490	0
4th	743	1,389	2,132	0
1921				
1st	196	1,904	2,100	0
2nd	1,816	1,819	3,635	319
3rd	1,230	1,410	2,640	451
4th	916	1,103	2,019	460
1922				
1st	499	1,205	1,703	347
2nd	297	1,293	1,590	177
3rd	585	888	1,473	92
4th	826	646	1,472	149
1923				
1st	1,054	628	1,682	99
2nd	1,091	743	1,798	30
3rd	2,654	415	3,062	6
4th	1,928	803	2,730	0
1924				
1st	177	1,947	2,124	0

Source: Steven B. Webb, "Fiscal News and Inflationary Expectations in Germany after World War I," *Journal of Economic History* 46 (September 1986), p. 779.

[1] Deficit: the change in the government debt (bonds and outstanding Treasury bills, except for Treasury bills at the Reichsbank backing government deposits).

[2] Revenue: taxes plus receipts from railroad and post.

[3] Spending: revenue plus deficit

achievements and placed a premium on going to court to contest assessments and thereby reduce the real worth of payments still further by the simple process of delay. Indeed, since both the wage withholding and the turnover taxes were paid on a quarterly basis, the effect was to give the employers and sellers of goods what was tantamount to an interest-free loan which they could repay in depreciated marks.[3]

The sociopolitical consequences of this situation were anything but pleasant, and they were felt most keenly by the SPD, which had voted for the tax compromise under Wirth with the expectation that the billion gold marks allegedly to be raised under the forced loan finally passed in July 1922 would provide some compensation for their assent to higher indirect

taxes. The loan was subscribed to in paper marks according to the dollar rate in April 1922; that is, at a ratio of seventy paper marks to one gold mark. The hyperinflation made a mockery of the entire effort, which brought in half the projected amount during the subscription period of July 1922–March 1923. Naturally, the Communists made the most of Socialist embarrassment and the universal complaint of salary and wage earners that they, and they alone, were paying taxes at full value. The Socialists objected that they could not conceivably have known what was going to happen to the mark when they agreed to the compromise and that the tax program would have even been more unjust without their agreement. At the same time, they called on the government

Table 23. Yield of PAYE and Assessed Income Tax in Percent, April 1921–March 1923

	PAYE	Assessed Income Tax
1921		
April	93	7
May	87	13
June	83	17
July	64	36
August	54	46
September	51	49
October	55	45
November	50	50
December	57	43
1922		
January	65	35
February	30	70
March	43	57
April	51	49
May	50	50
June	58	42
July	62	38
August	57	43
September	58	42
October	72	28
November	75	25
December	82	18
1923		
January–March	87	13

Source: Peter-Christian Witt, "Tax Policies, Tax Assessment and Inflation: Towards a Sociology of Public Finances in the German Inflation, 1914–1923," *Wealth and Taxation in Central Europe. The History and Sociology of Public Finance* (Leamington Spa, 1987), pp. 154–55.

to change the assessment system so as to take depreciation fully into account.[4]

This was not something the government was prepared to do. The Finance Ministry's response to the manifest inadequacy of the forced loan was to propose changes to the Reich Economic Council and Reichstag in December which were anything but convincing. Lifting the seventy billion paper-mark ceiling on the loan and proposing a doubling of the valuation on physical assets hardly constituted solutions to the effects of inflation on the expectations associated with the forced loan. In truth, the Reich Economic Council had never entertained any such expectations in the first place, the majority of its members having opposed the forced loan on the grounds that its failure was predictable when it was first proposed in March. They could see no point in further tinkering in December. Hilferding bluntly de-

clared that "what is being presented to us has very little significance; it basically seeks to secure a doubling of the tax revenue in the face of an inflation rate of 50 to 100 percent. According to the estimates of the Reich Finance Ministry, the law should bring 140 billion instead of 70 billion. Whether it will bring so much remains to be seen and above all whether the 140 billion will actually be what we now understand it to be in March or May of next year also remains to be seen."[5] Unpredictability, however, was precisely the argument the Finance Ministry was using against calls from the left for taxation in gold or some other fixed value. While legislation was being prepared to take depreciation into greater account in all of the Reich's taxation, full valorization was explicitly rejected on the grounds that it only made sense in the context of a general stabilization. Once one began to valorize one part of the economy, the

Table 24. Percentage of Reich Income from Treasury Bills and from Taxes, Budgetary Years 1921–1922 and 1922–1923

	Treasury Bills	Taxes
1921–1922		
April	53.76	45.43
May	39.26	59.82
June	58.78	40.53
July	49.88	49.19
August	69.72	29.64
September	60.31	38.78
October	54.04	45.04
November	54.59	44.46
December	71.43	28.00
January	49.38	49.65
February	42.08	56.71
March	38.92	60.04
1922–1923		
April	40.28	59.06
May	31.83	67.54
June	24.48	74.77
July	36.92	62.41
August	42.55	56.88
September	78.75	20.87
October	74.92	24.61
November	69.03	30.41
December	82.87	16.75
January	67.18	32.27
February	81.19	18.20
March	85.32	14.34

Source: Peter-Christian Witt, "Tax Policies, Tax Assessment and Inflation: Towards a Sociology of Public Finances in the German Inflation, 1914–1923," *Wealth and Taxation in Central Europe. The History and Sociology of Public Finance* (Leamington Spa, 1987), pp. 156–57.

Finance Ministry argued, it would be necessary to take similar steps with respect to others—for example, wages and contracts—and the result would be a further abandonment of the mark, this time under government auspices. Lastly, the Ministry rejected the notion that stable tax rates could be established when prices were so unstable.[6]

If this debate over valorization and the inequities of the tax system was in many respects a repetition of the arguments made when Erzberger's tax package and the Emergency Capital Levy drowned in the earlier waves of inflation and delayed assessment, the hyperinflation had, nonetheless, brought about a very real change in the character of the tax debate. On the one hand, the old slogan of seizing "real values" now gave way to an explicit call for valorization in terms of some stable monetary unit; on the other, the effort to use taxation as a means of absorbing excess liquidity was made very problematic because hyperinflation created a profound liquidity crisis. The perennial complaint of farmers and businessmen that taxes deprived them of the capital they needed for investment and operating costs suddenly took on a truly dramatic quality under hyperinflation and tended to relativize concern over the insufficient revenues produced by the tax system by shifting attention to the problem of providing enough liquidity to keep the economy going. Just as the beginning of a genuine stabilization debate as a consequence of the hyperinflation changed the balance in favor of the political right on the question of hours of work and economic controls, so the hyperinflation and attendant credit crisis undermined efforts, at least in the short-run, to rectify the tax system.

The entire situation and, indeed, history of the inflation as well as prediction of its future course was admirably summed up by Dr. Bücher of the RdI in a spirited assault on the idea that reforms of the forced loan or other taxes made any sense at all under the conditions existing at the end of 1922:

If you attempt to bring the total depreciation which we have in Germany—and we are heading toward a total depreciation, of this there is no doubt—into one formula, then it is that, first, there was the depreciation of pensions and liquid capital wealth while one at the same time had very good conditions in industry and a relatively favorable living standard for the producing groups in comparison to the others; the second stage was a complete depreciation of the *Mittelstand* alongside only relatively good conditions in industry and in the productive sectors; the third stage is a depreciation of operating capital; the fourth is unemployment and the complete collapse of our economy. That is a rough formula. . . . We are today in the third stage, namely, the depreciation of operating capital.[7]

Bücher pointed to the growing stock of commercial bills at the Reichsbank as evidence of his contention and went on to argue that while the nominal value of government revenues was rising, the actual value of this income, once deflated by the wholesale price index, was approaching zero. Over the previous half year, the income-tax receipts had lost two-thirds of their value, and this made it irrelevant whether the forced loan amounted to seventy, a hundred forty, or even two hundred ten billion. Germany, therefore, was "being driven in giant steps toward the absolute bankruptcy of the state." Under such circumstances, it was pointless to burden the business world with taxes which were not worth the cost of collection.

Bücher was not suggesting that this condition should be continued or that an effort should not be made to find some stable basis for taxation. He and his colleagues did have a program, although the valorization of taxes certainly did not stand at the top of the priority list. The crucial point, however, was that the credit crisis deflected attention from the problems of tax reform to those of finding operating capital and strengthened the hand of those who argued that the Erzberger reform was harmful to capital formation. In the context of the hyperinflation, however, it was less the long-run goals of tax policy than the short-term effects of the existing system that irritated businessmen. Profit, for example, was defined as an increase in the inventory value of property. Under conditions of hyperinflation, it was quite possible for a piece of property or for inventory to increase in value from two hundred thousand to two million marks between 1921 and 1922, for the "profit" to be taxed at 60 percent, and yet for the actual value not to have increased one iota in real terms. A situation thus arose in which the distinction between capital and income was being confused, and while it was possible for the government to decide to tax both, it was dangerous to tax the former as if it were the latter under conditions of capital shortage. Finding a way out of this situation, however, was not easy, even for its critics. As interested as businessmen were in making it clear to the German public and the Allies that many of their alleged profits were illusory (*Scheingewinne*) and that a proper accounting would reveal their true status, they rejected proposals by Professor Schmalenbach and others that the government require them to present their accounts in accordance with an index geared to inflation and be made to go over to gold balance sheets by 1926. Their argument was that many businesses were operating with two balance sheets already. The creation of a third for purposes of coping with the inflation problem would overburden their staffs. Most important, such balance sheets would ruin their credit while exposing them to unjustly harsh payments under existing taxation regulations which, it was claimed, were more informed by legalistic and bureaucratic than economic considerations. An especially important consideration was that gold-mark balances would inevitably lead to worker demands that wages also be calculated in gold or index marks and that domestic prices would also have to be so calculated. Thus, while calling for long-term reform and simplification, they demanded immediate relief that would take monetary depreciation into account and permit them to hold on to the reserves necessary to retain operating capital. Commercial circles—above all, wholesalers—were even more energetic in raising such demands than industry since commerce, in contrast to industry, had almost all its capital tied up in goods for market rather than in fixed plant. The government, therefore, was under extremely strong pressure to relax assessment regulations for enterprises because of the hyperinflationary conditions.[8]

The pressure for a relaxation of taxation regulations as a means of relieving the capital shortage is well exemplified by the debate at this time concerning the restoration of the secrecy of bank accounts and the requirement that domestic securities be placed on deposit in banks. Prior to the decree of October 24, 1919, German banks were required to provide the authorities with information about their customers' accounts only in cases where someone had been indicted for a criminal offense. The decree, ostensibly directed against the flight of capital but actually concerned with the prevention of tax evasion, unquestionably placed a major burden on the banks by requiring them not only to hold all domestic securities on deposit but also to provide up-to-date lists of their customers and all information required by the revenue authorities involved in the normal levying of taxes. Conceived as a temporary measure to ensure the effectiveness of the Erzberger Emergency Capital Levy, the regulations had been maintained despite strong opposition from the banks and the Reichsbank. Indeed, the great banks, savings banks, and credit banks showed rare unanimity in their opposition to the regulations, in part because of the amount of time and staff needed to carry them out, but primarily because they were convinced that the regulations destroyed the traditional relations of trust and confidentiality between banks and clients to the point where people used the banks as little as possible. The bankers and their organizations argued that the relationship between bankers and their customers was analogous to that between doctors and their patients or lawyers and their clients. Most important, the reluctance to use banks was leading to an uneconomic use of capital, depriving the economy of liquidity, and encouraging rather than discouraging tax evasion and flight of capital.[9]

Although the regulations were already the subject of growing criticism and opposition in 1920–1921, the Finance Ministry, reinforced by reports from the revenue offices throughout the country, had refused to abandon the system. The tax authorities claimed that they received extraordinarily important information through the banks and that the system's main defect lay in the announcement of its temporary character since this encouraged holders of securities to refrain from collecting interest in the hope that the lifting of the regulations would protect the securities they were hoarding at home. If they were deprived of this expectation, then they finally would be compelled to deposit their securities in order to collect on their interest and could then be properly taxed.

Thus, at the beginning of 1922, Hermes refused to listen to the cries of the bankers for a change.[10]

The hyperinflation and attendant credit and liquidity crisis, however, opened the way for a full-scale assault on the system later in the year. The Reichsbank was particularly active in the campaign, taking a leaf from the Finance Ministry's book and presenting a thick collection of reports from its branches all over the country in emulation of the RFM's practice of buttressing its arguments with reports from the revenue offices. In a lengthy report to the RFM of October 9, 1922, the Reichsbank argued that the regulations were undermining its effort of many years to encourage noncash transactions by driving people to hoard money, conduct business on a cash basis, and thereby undermine the financial condition of the banks as well as the healthy functioning of the economy. The Reichsbank openly recognized that the chief motive for this behavior was tax evasion, but it insisted that "the tax legislation through its incentive to hoard money and its incitement to irrational economic management has increased and accelerated the effects of the monetary depreciation and the increased cost of goods."[11]

The evidence that huge sums of paper money had been hoarded was indeed quite compelling. Thus, when the Reichsbank called in the fifty-mark auxiliary notes it had issued in 1918 for exchange, large amounts turned up in their original packing and in numerical order. Further evidence that they had been hoarded was that they smelled of earth or cement, were often mouldy and mouse eaten, and were sometimes burnt at or beyond the edges because they had been hidden away in ovens or near ovens. There was indeed reason to believe that substantial sums had been burnt up in barns and other fires in the countryside and that substantial sums had also disappeared in the growing number of robberies. Bank authorities also reported that people were asking for large sums in hundred-, thousand-, and, most recently, ten-thousand-mark notes and that they explicitly stated that they wanted bills in such large denominations for purposes of convenient storage. Although eighty billion marks in ten-thousand-mark notes had recently been issued,

scarcely any of these notes were showing up in circulation.[12]

The reports from the Reichsbank offices were replete with colorful illustrations of the length to which people were going to spurn the banks and evade the tax authorities. Typical were the reports from Krefeld, where a businessman kept a million marks in a safe at home; a female pensioner reported the theft of twenty-thousand marks, although she had only admitted to possessing eight thousand marks at the time of her tax assessment; a farmer hoarded forty thousand marks in a milk can which was so stuffed that he had to shove recently received money into the can with his foot; and a tax official found a hundred thousand marks hidden around the house of a bicycle manufacturer. In Stettin a firm reported that the Pommeranian estate owners with which it did business often carried anywhere from five hundred thousand to seven hundred thousand marks in their suitcases to pay for purchases and frankly admitted that they preferred to forego interest than have to answer "burdensome" questions from the tax authorities. Peasants were particularly prominent as hoarders, of course, and the tales of their experiences were not lacking in humor. For example, one peasant found nearly all of the fifteen thousand marks he had stashed away eaten by pigs, while another nearly fainted when he came home to find that his wife had lit the oven to make the room warm for a visiting neighbor and thus burned up the one hundred eighty thousand marks hidden there.[13]

While such stories could be multiplied many times over, they did little to change the behavior of those involved, to make them more willing to put their money into banks or to invest in even the "safest" of securities. On the contrary, farmers, millers, slaughtering houses, small businessmen, doctors, and dentists were all increasingly insisting on payment in cash and were refusing even to accept checks placed into their bank accounts. The problems created by hoarding were compounded, on the one hand, by unjustified borrowing and, on the other, by unnecessary purchasing. It was noted that especially at times when heavy payments were necessary—for example, the end of the year or the dates on which tax payments were due—people who most certainly had cash on hand chose to borrow instead, despite the high costs. At the same time, there was a good deal of hoarding of goods as well as money, especially by peasants. In Augsburg, for example, individual peasants were reported to have purchased "6 bicycles, 7–8 sewing machines, 2 motorcycles, automobiles, 6–8 pairs of boots, supplies of linens, clothes, materials for as much as 25 to 30 years, etc."[14] It should be noted that the Reichsbank was not alone in reporting such stocking up by peasant consumers at this time. The Bavarian authorities were constantly mentioning such purchases and especially the buying of pianos and similar luxury items by peasants.[15] Whether borrowing or purchasing without real economic justification, however, the consequences were always the same; namely, increasing the demand for capital and undermining the position of the banks.

This was especially evident, argued the Reichsbank, in the unsatisfactory character of the increase in deposits of all kinds (*Fremdgelder*) relative to the capital stock (*Eigenkapital*) of the great banks, savings banks, and credit cooperatives. The capital stock of the banks had been depleted substantially since the beginning of the war, and this made deposits all the more important if the banks were to be in a position to supply credit. According to Reichsbank calculations, however, deposits had increased very inadequately relative to inflation, while the volume of deposits open to withdrawal within a week had shifted dramatically against deposits with longer periods of withdrawal. These calculations were well-founded. While the nominal value of deposits and current account balances in the Berlin banks had increased from 11,568.9 million marks in 1921 to 1,618,230 million marks in 1922, the gold value based on the dollar exchange had decreased from 2,626 million to 925 million gold marks during the same period. The percentage of very short-term deposits and current account balances in the Berlin banks had increased from 60.6 percent in 1918 to above 75 percent in 1919–1921 to 93 percent in 1922.[16] At the same time, the Reichsbank authorities noted that savings banks were feeling compelled to alienate their holdings of war bonds at a great loss, and there was sub-

stantial danger that some of them would have to close down their credit activities. A major consequence of these conditions was that Treasury bills were streaming back into the Reichsbank because of the demands for cash in the banking system, and the entire credit system was in danger. From this perspective, argued the Reichsbank, the advantages of tax collection under existing regulations were far overshadowed by the dangers to the economy, and it called on the government to eliminate the regulations of the decree of October 1919 in their entirety.[17]

This view was by no means universally shared. While there was general agreement on the need to eliminate deposit requirements for fixed-interest securities on the simple grounds that the cost of their deposit no longer stood in relation to what might be gained from the regulation, there was much less enthusiasm in both left-wing and liberal circles and in the Finance Ministry for a return to prewar regulations. The compromise proposed by the government was to eliminate the requirement that the banks provide a list of their customers to the revenue authorities but not to relieve them of the obligation to respond to inquiries relevant to the assets of their customers. While the banks argued that this was insufficient, critics like Georg Bernhard pointed out that the regulations in question hardly explained the reluctance to deposit money in banks,

for much stronger than the fear of taxation is the fact that a bank or savings account is exposed in full measure to the monetary depreciation. But the bearing of this depreciation, as for example by the hoarding of bank notes, was during the past year a much stronger form of taxation than any of the schedules which exist in any German tax law. The banks will certainly not be flooded with depositors even after the restoration of the confidentiality of bank accounts, and this because the interest and commissions which they grant and calculate are not likely to entice a mass increase of new depositors and because the banks in truth do not really want a flow of small accounts. On the other side, the repeal of the control measures, even if their direct effect is not very great, will be very harmful indirectly because it will eliminate a psychological barrier which still influences countless taxpayers to make truer declarations.[18]

Bernhard was correct, and the fuss made by the Reichsbank and its allies in banking and other sectors of business over the regulations governing bank secrecy and the depositing of securities was in growing disproportion to their importance. Insofar as the hoarding of money was not being punished by hungry pigs and chilly wives, it was proving a genuine victim of the "inflation tax." It was no accident that the major victims of this increasingly self-destructive hoarding—peasants, small merchants and businessmen, and professionals—were precisely those who were least able to manipulate liquid assets and currencies with speed and efficiency, although as the reports demonstrated, these groups also were learning to borrow and to flee into goods even if they could not entirely surrender their irrational need to hold on to large bundles of increasingly worthless cash for dear life. All this did not prevent DNVP Deputies Helfferich and Reichert from claiming at the end of November that if the secrecy of bank accounts were only restored then "the money and credit shortages could in large part be steered." Hermes frankly rejected this proposal on "political grounds," and it is hard not to conclude that Helfferich and Reichert knew better themselves and had other reasons for pressing the issue.[19] Whatever the case, so long as the hyperinflation continued on its trajectory, it mattered not a whit if the hoarded money remained in circulation to fuel price rises or rotted in milk cans and was replaced by new production from the printing presses. Most important, the inflationary process could scarcely be halted so long as the Reichsbank continued to meet the combined needs of the public and private economy by creating more and more money on the basis of the constant discounting of Treasury notes and bills of exchange.

Havenstein and his colleagues were fully aware that they were responsible for the rapid increase of very dangerous processes which would, if continued, inevitably spell disaster in the foreseeable future. Nevertheless, they accepted and even promoted them in the firm conviction that there was nothing else that could be done if the economy was going to continue functioning. One such process was the familiar discounting of Reich Treasury notes, but now under conditions where they became in-

creasingly unmarketable. Thus, the amount of Reich Treasury bills issued increased dramatically in the second half of 1922, while the percentage held outside the Reichsbank sank no less spectacularly—from 50.7 percent in January to 20.8 percent in December (see Table 25).

The inability of the Reichsbank to market four-fifths of the outstanding Treasury bills was intimately related to two other processes; namely, the sporadic but extremely significant stepping up of Lombard credits and loan-bureau activities and the Reichsbank policy of discounting short-term commercial bills on a large scale that really took off in July 1922 (see Table 26). The mounting credit crisis, on the one hand, caused the banks to alienate their Treasury bill holdings in order to procure the cash needed to meet the credit demands of their customers and, on the other, induced the Reichsbank to offer credit itself either through the discounting of commercial bills or by giving credits through the increasingly active loan bureaus. The granting of Lombard credits directly through the Reichsbank was, to be sure, relatively insignificant with the exception of November 1922, when the direct Lombard credit was used to finance the domestic purchases of grains and the grain imports by the Reich Grain Corporation. The procedure was necessary for technical reasons; namely, to provide security for the credit until the legal limit

Table 25. The Floating Debt of the Reich and the Proportion Held Outside the Reichsbank in 1922

	Total Value of T-Bills (in billions)	Percentage Held Outside the Reichsbank
January	255.9	50.7
February	263.0	48.9
March	272.1	46.2
April	281.1	44.7
May	289.4	42.1
June	295.3	37.0
July	308.0	32.5
August	331.5	24.7
September	451.1	22.5
October	603.8	21.0
November	839.1	19.9
December	1,495.2	20.8

Source: Deutschlands Wirtschaft, Währung und Finanzen (Berlin, 1924), p. 62.

Table 26. **Outstanding Credits Granted by the Reichsbank and Loan Bureaus in 1922***
(in millions of paper marks)

	Commerical Bills	Lombard	Loan Bureau
January	1,592	20.5	13,867
February	1,857	62.3	12,617
March	2,152	20.7	15,064
April	2,403	134.3	13,182
May	3,377	54.4	14,441
June	4,752	59.0	25,083
July	8,122	141.3	25,423
August	21,704	173.0	36,729
September	50,234	61.5	35,935
October	101,155	624.4	51,146
November	246,949	51,425.0	91,706
December	422,235	774.0	252,043

Source: Statistisches Reichsamt, Zahlen zur Geldentwertung in Deutschland 1914 bis 1923 [Sonderheft 1 zu *Wirtschaft und Statistik*, Bd. 5] (Berlin, 1925), p. 52.
*Excluding discounted Treasury bills.

on the issue of loan-bureau notes could be raised. Once this had occurred, the credit was transferred to the loan bureau where, for "technical reasons" once again, it was backed by Reich Treasury notes rather than the grain itself. At the same time, the Reichsbank estimated that the credits granted by the loan bureaus for this purpose would amount to as much as two hundred fifty billion marks by the end of March. Even without this specific credit, however, it is manifest that the loan bureaus were playing the kind of major role in the credit market they had not played since the war. In July, the Reichsbank had expanded the amount in industrial shares that could be put up as security by the loan bureaus, although it warned against conducting such operations for speculative purposes, and by the end of the year the loans granted were backed by such shares as well as large quantities of grains, sugar, metals, and other commodities as well as the Treasury notes serving as proxy for grain. Since the certificates issued on the basis of loan-bureau credits could serve as coverage for monetary emissions, the loan bureaus resumed their wartime function of serving as a mechanism for increasing the money supply. Similarly, just as war bonds had served as collateral in the portfolios of the loan bureaus and thus as a means of increasing rather than decreasing the inflation, so now certificates issued in connection with the

forced loan could also be used the same way. Once again, the liquidity removed from the economy by one means served as the basis for its restoration by another.[20]

Credits provided by the loan bureaus, however, were of limited use for the growing demands of the private economy since these credits could only be given against specific forms of security and were tied to specific valuation criteria.[21] In the case of the discounting of commercial bills, however, the Reichsbank actually took the initiative in promoting this type of credit. The desirability of reintroducing sound commercial bills had, of course, been discussed for some time as a means of relieving short-term capital requirements and providing the Reichsbank and the banking system with more solid forms of coverage. In the second half of June 1922, however, as Germany teetered on the brink of hyperinflation, the Reichsbank seized the initiative to promote the reintroduction of commercial bills as a means of alleviating the mounting private credit crisis. This decision was taken at a time when the Reichsbank itself was experiencing a crisis as a result of its inability to market Treasury bills and in anticipation that the banking system would unload its stock of Treasury bills back onto the Reichsbank.

Thus, on June 22, Reichsbank officials met with the representatives of the leading banks and peak associations of commerce and industry to persuade them to promote the reintroduction of commercial bills.[22] It was a Reichsbank effort that had two very remarkable aspects in the light of subsequent developments. The first of these was the assumption that the reintroduction of commercial bills would either have no influence on the inflation or might even slow it down. Havenstein argued that "the expansion of business in commercial bills will be without significance for the inflation insofar as the bills are only an instrument of credit and not a means of payment."[23] On the face of it, this was a reasonable assumption if the bills were backed by real orders and were not repeatedly rediscounted. Indeed, Havenstein hoped that a substantial portion of the bills would be discounted by the Reichsbank and would provide some solid paper coverage for a change. Such anticipations stood in some contradiction, however, to the problematic arguments for the reintroduction of commercial bills produced only two days before within the Reichsbank itself:

Nothing will be changed with respect to the increase in the circulation of money by the reintroduction of commercial bills, if the bills only serve to secure and permit the prior liquidity of short-term credits in commercial dealings. For by being discounted at the bank, it takes on the character of monetary capital in the form of an acceptance credit that is scheduled to fall due later but that is immediately available as means of payment, a credit in one's account, or bank notes and therefore in the last analysis appears as additional purchasing power on the market. The inflation thus remains as it is in its full measure. But it is to be hoped that a portion of the newly created acceptance material will retain the quality of a direct means of payment and will be used in its original form in commercial activity as a means of payment in that the original issuer as well as every subsequent owner of the bill will endorse it over to a third party as was done to a large extent before the war. If this means of payment becomes common, then the acceptances thus used in commercial commerce will actually function as a means of payment and contribute to slowing down the creation of bank notes.[24]

Obviously, such lines would have provoked sharp criticism from quantity theorists—were such persons allowed within the portals of the Reichsbank—although it should be recognized that the argument was perfectly consistent with the traditional real-bills doctrine under which the Reichsbank had operated before the war. What made its traditional functioning implausible under existing conditions is well demonstrated by the other peculiarity of the meeting called by the Reichsbank on June 22; namely that the Reichsbank, banks, and businessmen who did support the reintroduction of commercial bills were by no means having an easy time persuading some of the leading businessmen and their organizations to accept the credit opportunity they offered. Given the feeding frenzy on commercial bills about to begin, this reluctance is surprising and very revealing of the business community's general preference for caution and security over inflationary adventure. As Director Wassermann of the Deutsche Bank, himself a proponent of commercial bills, pointed out, businessmen and especially their trade associations and cartels were averse to giving credit and preferred cash payments within strict time limits for very good reasons. On the one hand, it was best to get cash while it was still worth something; on the other, giving credit was tricky because

the seller no longer knows the business condition of his customer in the same way as before. Each businessman today tries to make himself look poorer than he really is. That is because he does not have any confidence in his holdings because of the political and economic situation and therefore undervalues it. He is just as little able to judge the situation of his neighbor. He cannot tell if his customer has covered his foreign exchange requirements abroad. So long as he does not have any reliable material on this, he cannot give any credit.[25]

Given the speculative environment—above all, in foreign exchange—the granting of three-month credits seemed particularly risky. Many wholesalers, for example, were counting on receiving dollars but feared that the dollar, and thus the value of such payments, would drop sharply if there was a sudden agreement on reparations. At the same time, some also had customers with heavy debts payable in foreign exchange, and they feared giving credits to such customers since the dollar might continue to rise. Anything could happen, and they had to protect themselves. Similarly, cartels and trade associations were reluctant to change payment conditions when prices were changing so rapidly. If industry led the way and relaxed its terms to wholesalers, then wholesalers could relax their terms to retailers. The problem, so to speak, was to get everyone to speculate on commercial bills together. Havenstein, of course, did not present it this way but rather argued with words that he could later have been forced to eat that "a skilled merchant certainly must find it possible to clarify and then distinguish among the situations of his customers even if they are at first intransparent and then decide to whom he should give credit and to whom not."[26] In the last analysis, however, those present at the meeting were confident that commercial bills could be successfully reintroduced for the simple reason that more and more businessmen were finding it impossible to meet the payment conditions they themselves had established because of the accelerating inflation:

Where the conditions functioned perfectly two months ago, a large part of our clientele today are no longer in a position to fulfill the conditions. Things have changed completely in the recent past. A large part of the clientele drags out their payments four to six weeks; If we do not want to lose out, then we must agree. Large industrial firms that previously insisted on cash payment now accept bills. An acceptance is always better than an open debt. Insofar as the small and medium-sized firms are concerned, they no longer fulfill the condition of paying in cash since they only get their money in three to four months and cannot otherwise pay for their new raw materials. Thus, things are moving toward the acceptance of commercial bills as if a law of nature were in operation. If a businessman does not mobilize his means through bills, then he will not be able to get wares abroad.[27]

What this implied, of course, was that bills of exchange would be needed because the entire business community was running out of money, and if this were true, then it certainly made a mockery of the arguments that it was possible to issue only "solid" commercial bills to "solid" businessmen or that it was possible to do much distinguishing among customers. Indeed, the entire cry for the reintroduction of commercial bills was nothing but a reflection of the growing desperation in the Reichsbank and in the business community created by the credit crisis. Despite the danger of increasing the hyperinflation, there was a general agreement to promote the reintroduction of commercial bills.

The Reichsbank was especially prominent in this effort, its most significant promotion of the cause taking the form of a widely noted and influential article by Privy Finance Councillor Friedrich of the Reichsbank Board of Directors in the *Bank=Archiv* of July 15, 1922, dealing with the problem of fighting the credit shortage.[28] Later called by one critic a "literary summons to a credit-needy business world,"[29] Friedrich virtually invited the business community to discount commercial bills at the Reichsbank. It would be unfair to say that he was totally oblivious to the danger of what was being proposed. He admitted that the credit crisis was inflation-induced and that an argument could be made for a "radical cure" in the form of cessation of production and unemployment. His response was fully in keeping with the long-

standing practice of rejecting such solutions for social and political reasons. He argued that "the accompanying developments and transitional phenomena would in all probability be such that every serious person, no matter what his political orientation, must do everything to act against such a crisis." While insisting that the use of such credits for the building or expansion of new plants would have to be viewed very critically, he stressed that "in general everything must be done to procure the short-term capital through credit."[30] Similarly, Friedrich rejected the notion that everyone who asked for credit could or should receive it and asserted that commercial bills would only be discounted for goods that could be marketed and that everything possible had to be done to avoid providing speculators with money. Nevertheless, the basic message was very positive:

Developments during the last months have already led to a clearly discernible large flow of bills to the banks. At the same time, a further, significantly larger, consciously promoted development along these lines is very much to be desired.... A bank portfolio with good commercial bills ought *ceteris paribus* to be many times larger than the holdings of regular and current account holdings. Even from the perspective of the relationship between assets to deposits of the banks, there are no insurmountable reservations to be had, because they are in a position to rediscount the bills, which must be viewed as a liquid means of the first order, in appropriately increased amounts at the Reichsbank, provided that the latter is ready and willing to take on correspondingly higher amounts. Now, the Reichsbank itself has an interest in having its assets which, as in general has also previously been the case with the private banks, have been completely composed of Reich Treasury notes, improved once again by the entry of good, normal commercial bills.[31]

If a liberal credit policy was risky, Friedrich declared, the times demanded "more courage, decisiveness, and readiness to take responsibility." He did not deny the danger of further inflation through such a policy, but this would increase in any case if the Reich Treasury notes continued to flow back to the Reichsbank. From this perspective, the commercial bills were much less dangerous than the Treasury bills since "the bills bear the source of their repayment in themselves; they must be paid back when they fall due; prolongation seldom takes place, whereas the Reich treasury bills are always prolonged."[32] While some of this was whistling in the dark since the Reichsbank was continuing to discount Treasury bills and the commercial bills would inevitably be repaid in paper marks and the Reichsbank would thus be repaid in depreciated marks unless the discount rate was extraordinarily high, it could certainly be argued that the inflation would be even worse if industry's liquidity crisis were to lead to decreased production while the Reichsbank continued to fund the government deficit. The stoppage of production while the printing presses continued to roll would only force up prices and accelerate the flight from the mark.[33] Whether the Reichsbank could at once discount the commercial bills and prevent their abuse was, of course, another question.

Furthermore, it would be an error to think that the massive reintroduction of commercial bills during the months following the publication of Friedrich's article was simply the result of Reichsbank encouragement and thereby to overstress the responsibility of the much-maligned Havenstein and his bank. The business community's inhibitions of the late spring, such as they were, gave way by the end of summer to disbelief that it had taken the Reichsbank so long to resurrect the commercial bill. From the perspective of German industry, Bücher declared in a meeting of early September, "the Reichsbank is to be blamed for not making use of the time available" to prepare for the credit and liquidity crisis, although he cautioned against personally blaming Havenstein "in view of the great services of this man."[34] The RdI directors at the meeting were certain that more "services" were going to be required because of the disastrous credit situation. Saxon textile industrialist Otto Moras went so far as to suggest sending a delegation to the Chancellor to demand not only that bills of exchange be rediscounted on a larger scale but also that a greatly increased amount of money be put into circulation. He personally did not think "that the worth of the German mark will be very much influenced if we print more money," and he emphasized the seriousness of the situation for individual enterprises of the type that existed in Saxony as compared with the large concerns of Rhineland-Westphalia, which were in

a much better position to get money. Moras warned that his industry was beginning to have to cut back on production and that unemployment was looming ahead unless something was done:

There is no longer enough operating capital. It is impossible to adjust to the constant leaps in raw materials prices, wages, etc. Until now we have tried to deal with the situation by limiting purchases, reducing inventories, cutting the time given customers for payment, increasing exports and demanding prepayments from our customers. The shortage of capital is keeping us from maintaining operations. Also, the exports of the textile industry are made much more difficult because we have come increasingly closer to world market prices, have even in part exceeded them. Added to this we still have the two percent turnover tax here in Germany, the huge transportation and insurance costs, while the countries with good currencies are increasingly approaching prewar conditions with respect to these costs.[35]

The discussion triggered by Moras's remarks showed that he was anything but alone in his complaints and demonstrated the complexity of the problem and the difficulty of sorting out its various components. At the most primitive level, the production of money simply was not keeping up with demand, so that firms had to send messengers daily to the banks, where they waited in line to get huge sacks of bills to carry back to the plants in order to pay wages. Bücher and RdI leaders had already been in contact with Havenstein about the "production" problem, which had been much worsened by printing strikes, unwillingness to work extra shifts, and the refusal of the Reichstag to permit the Reichsbank to give contracts to private firms. The shortage of small bills was particularly serious, although their production was also becoming a bit ridiculous because it cost some eighty pfennig to produce a one-mark piece. Havenstein had suggested that the firms provide their workers with short-term chits (Gutscheine) which might be used to buy necessities, although Reichsbank officials warned that these should be kept in low denominations since a recently produced five-hundred-mark bill with a good watermark had, nevertheless, been fairly well counterfeited within three days of its appearance! Havenstein had given assurances, however, that he was developing a production plan that would meet industry's needs.

Of course, this would not solve the credit problem, which had deeper causes, as Wilhelm Jordan sadly reminded his colleagues now that the credit crisis he and Hirsch had predicted during the relative stabilization was upon them. No one was "swimming in money" anymore despite the vast increase in the amounts of money in circulation. Industry had withdrawn its cash holdings at the banks in order to cover costs, and the banks had turned in their Treasury bills to the Reichsbank, which was now "choking" on them, in order to get cash to provide insufficient credit at very high interest rates. At the same time, the banks were reluctant to discount commercial bills in sufficient quantity because the Reichsbank was not doing so. Jordan pointed out that the Reichsbank had, by and large, failed to revise its prewar credit listings and asked: "When, for example, a middle sized firm is listed by the Reichsbank at an earlier time with a credit of 300,000 marks, what can it do with this credit, which has not been increased by a pfennig today?"[36]

Yet another matter of great concern to the industrialists was the collapse of the forward market in foreign exchange, which had been reopened during the relative stabilization and which was being closed down by the banks as a result of the hyperinflation. Prior to July 1922, there had been a premium on the mark expressed in the negative annualized percentage difference between the spot rate of the mark and the forward exchange rate—the so-called swap rate—added to the interest rate on the domestic money market. On the one hand, this had encouraged foreigners to hold funds in German banks where they were guaranteed more of their currencies than earlier expended when they reconverted their marks at the guaranteed forward exchange rate. On the other hand, the same forward exchange premium on the mark enabled German businesses holding foreign exchange, but in need of marks, to cover running expenses by selling the amount of foreign currency they needed to a German bank for marks while at the same time purchasing the equivalent amount of foreign currency on the forward exchange market for future delivery. So long as there was a reasonable premium on the mark on the forward exchange market, the risk for the German banks was bearable as was the in-

terest rate for the German businessman.[37] However, the premium on the mark disappeared in July 1922, while the daily money rate also began to rise (see Table 27). At the same time, the increasing illiquidity was further indicated by the sharp rise in the interest on current account credits, levied in large part, as had become the custom since 1918, in the form of commissions, and even the Reichsbank began to raise its discount rate in August, along with its growing acceptance of commercial bills. Some people, of course, were prepared to pay any interest rate. Cologne banker Seligman reported that "he had been offered interest at a hundred percent per month on German marks, Dutch currency having been offered as collateral. The only explanation of such an unheard-of interest rate is the fact that the money was wanted for speculative purposes and that the speculator expected the mark to drop to less than half within the month. Of course, only sums of not less than 50,000,000 marks would be dealt in at this rate."[38] The average businessman in Cologne and elsewhere was not a speculator, however, and neither was the respectable banker. In Cologne, bankers were lending only to industry and the government and refused to sell foreign exchange except against cash delivered within twenty-four hours.

Even at the cost of higher discount rates, therefore, it was to the Reichsbank that industry felt compelled to turn as liquidity decreased. Stinnes, to be sure, might fume at the banks for closing down their forward exchange transactions so suddenly, declare the 67 percent interest they were demanding "such a misfortune, that it cannot be borne," and argue that "a serious word" with the bankers was necessary, but even he must have realized what one of his colleagues made explicit; namely, that the banks were understandably unwilling to speculate on the foreign exchange market under the existing circumstances. Thus, Stinnes argued that "the only salvation" was a "proper discount policy by the Reichsbank" and that "the credit and money shortage can only be set aside if the Reichsbank can be brought to perform the great deed it had performed at the outbreak of the war, when it accepted every form of bill presented to it. . . . The other banks can do as good as nothing. If the Reichsbank does not print

Table 27. Short-term Interest Rates in Percent Per Annum, 1922–1923

	Reichsbank Discount Rate	Daily Money Rate	Forward Margin Against Sterling*	Effective Rate of Interest on Current Account Credit
1922				
January	5	4.50	−4.3	
February	5	4.28	−3.0	10
March	5	4.54	−0.8	
April	5	4.38	−0.2	
May	5	4.34	−0.6	
June	5	4.91	−0.3	
July	5	5.40	3.3	12
August	6	6.50	12.5	
September	7	7.40	43.3	
October	8	7.75	92.3	50
November	10	8.22	163.6	
December	10	9.21	92.9	
1923				
January	12	11.05	104.1	
February	12	25.67	285.2	
March	12	11.00	77.6	
April	18	12.70	89.4	
May	18	20.15	143.6	
June	18	19.35	141.3	
July	18	92	452.8	
August	30	283	658.5	
September	90	1606		
October	90	1825		

Source: Carl-Ludwig Holtfrerich, *The German Inflation 1914–1923. Causes and Effects in International Perspective* (Berlin and New York, 1986), p. 73.

*Expressed as percent per annum of spot rate. Negative sign implies premium on the mark.

more notes, they [the other banks] also can be of no use."[39] Stinnes urged that they send a small delegation to Havenstein to promote a more liberal policy and a low discount rate, a proposal strongly supported by Bücher, who persuaded the industrialists not to bother going to the Chancellor since "we would thereby put ourselves on the same level as the trade unions and one will handle us with phrases."[40]

There can be no question that Havenstein did his best to increase the production of money. At the end of December, he reported a substantial improvement in the situation thanks to the establishment of a third shift at the Reich Printing Office, the simplification of printing procedures for smaller notes, the giving of contracts to private printing houses for the production of auxiliary notes, and the granting—against the original intention if not the letter of a law of July 1922—of permission to municipalities and industrial firms to issue emergency money. All such monetary emissions had to be backed by full-value security placed on deposit with the Reich Credit Corporation or the Reichsbank; that is, to be fully covered so as to prevent the giving out of emergency money to be used as a source of self-financing by those issuing it. From this perspective, the emergency money issued, which was the equivalent of some 7.6 billion gold marks at the beginning of 1923, was not inflationary. Nevertheless, the increasing use of emergency money was not without tensions. Industrialists objected to the .5 to 1 percent commissions demanded by the agencies issuing the money in the Rhineland and Ruhr, and considerable effort had to be made to create emergency money that was as uniform as possible and that had the confidence of the public. There could be no question about the fact that the emergency money was very helpful. When Cologne, which had previously issued only fifty-pfennig notes began issuing twenty-, hundred-, and five-hundred-mark notes, it provided immediate relief. The relief, however, could only be temporary, and the most significant next development in this area was that both municipalities and industrial firms strove to secure permission to issue emergency money in advance of actual need under the assumption that wage and price increases would exceed the Reichsbank's printing capacity and objected to Reichsbank demands that security be put up for the amount requested rather than the amount really issued.[41]

When it came to satisfying business demands for great liberality in the granting of commercial bills, Havenstein's attitude was probably less passive than his actual behavior. Though Havenstein was a hearty supporter of the reintroduction of the discounting of commercial bills, he nevertheless had to be urged and pressured by industry to discount bills to the extent that he did. Thus, at the Curatorium meeting of September 26, Havenstein announced that "the Reichsbank is extending the concept of commercial bills as far as possible," but then went on to warn that it could not carry the entire burden of government and private credit and could "therefore only give credit on short-term bills, has to control the purpose for which they are used, and must not create fictive capital by giving long-term investment capital."[42] That there was cause for concern was demonstrated a month later, when Havenstein told the Reichsbank Central Committee that "he could not escape the impression that the obliging attitude of the Reichsbank is not now and then misused to request credit that is not economically justified, that for example, serves to hold on to stores of goods, or to buy excessive stocks of goods in order to profiteer from further price increases."[43] While not thinking that the Reichsbank could accomplish much by raising the discount rate under existing circumstances, Havenstein argued in November that the increases he had imposed were a necessary "warning signal" to all classes about the growing "economic impoverishment" as well as a signal that the Reichsbank would not support use of the credits to procure unnecessary raw materials and foreign exchange. All this was repeated once more in December at the meeting of the Reichsbank Central Committee, but now with an explicit recognition that the policy did indeed carry inflationary dangers with it. Thus, while only a few days before Havenstein had told the Reichsbank Curatorium that the use of commercial bills "still had a wide field for expansion before it attained its previous importance in economic intercourse,"[44] he now called

for a stricter policy by both the Reichsbank and the loan bureaus and pointed out that "it will not do and will ruin our monetary system completely if commerce and industry, states and municipalities, mortgage banks, and cooperatives try to run their administration and business to a large extent with the credit of the Reichsbank and the loan bureaus, that is, through the creation of fictive money." Though the total amount given in real terms was much less than in the prewar period, the percentage of Treasury bills combined with the commercial bills discounted by the Reichsbank—half of all the commercial bills in circulation—and the loan-bureau credits demonstrated that the bank was approaching the limits of what a central bank of issue could or should do to support the private economy. The impoverishment of Germany "cannot and ought not to be prevented by the boundless increase of the inflation," Havenstein argued, and then even more frankly declared that "it cannot be belied that under the present circumstances even the credits which are to be recognized as economically desirable have the tendency to increase the inflation in Germany, so that the fight against the taking of credit is at the same time a fight against the inflation."[45]

But how was Havenstein to do battle with the giants of German industry, to whom he felt compelled to give direct access to the Reichsbank for the discounting of commercial bills? For Stinnes, the opportunities thus provided were something of a dream come true. In late October, he reported to Vögler that Havenstein had agreed to grant the Siemens–Rheinelbe–Schuckert–Union (SRSU) a four-billion-mark credit permitting the various works in the IG to draw bills of exchange amounting to half of their deliveries to one another. The amount of the credit, which was raised to six billion in early November, was based on the projected sales of the concern during the coming three months. The bills could be drawn on the Reichsbank branches in Essen, Bochum, Dortmund, and Berlin but had to be reported to the central offices of the Reichsbank, which could order a halt of credit if the limit were exceeded and to which the internal deliveries within the SRSU had to be reported. The Reichsbank did not even pick up on the hint dropped by Stinnes that he was willing to provide some security. The heavy-industrial group in the SRSU had been desperately seeking a "new way" of getting further credits while reducing its bank debt, and the way had been found. Stinnes could not help but be mightily pleased, for thereby "we have made ourselves independent of the banks here and . . . can still make timely purchases of large amounts of foreign exchange."[46] At the same time, he cautioned Vögler not to make the same mistake as had been made the previous year when large amounts of foreign currency had been purchased just as the mark began to rise. Vögler, in his hunger for cash because of the constant wage and materials cost increases, was very content to have so large a credit at his disposal and, while assuring Stinnes that he would be careful, also suggested that there was little danger of a rising mark: "A currency which is so dragged down cannot in my opinion ever again have a significant improvement. Even foreign speculators will be careful about trying with the mark after its steady decline."[47] The trick for both Vögler and Stinnes as well as for others in a position to turn it, was to get rid of mark holdings as quickly as possible and to pay running expenses and other obligations by credits as much as possible. As Vögler had pointed out to an official of the concern handling its affairs in Zürich, "the only secure way of doing things is the procurement of money through outside credit, so that someone else gets the depreciated marks back."[48] For a gigantic concern like that presided over by Stinnes, the ideal "someone" was the Reichsbank because of its low discount rate. By February 1923, the SRSU had overdrawn the credit by 2 billion marks, the GBAG having received 3.6 billion, Deutsch-Lux 2 billion, the Bochumer Verein 1.2 billion, and the Siemens group 1 billion. Whereas at the end of August Stinnes had been putting tremendous pressure on a projected consortium of bankers—headed by representatives of the Dresdner Bank—to back the arrangements made between his Hoch- und Tief construction firm and the French in connection with the Stinnes-Lubersac Agreement, at the end of December he absolutely rejected this idea, pointing out that "the matter cannot be handled in this way; we would then be com-

pletely under the control of the [Dresdner] bank and could on longer work directly with the Reichsbank at all."[49]

Stinnes, Vögler, and Siemens could hardly be faulted for taking advantage of credit opportunities previously available only to the Reich, and neither could the others favored by the Reichsbank's largess. Furthermore, circumstances rather than sinister intentions drove them to these policies and impelled them to hold as much of their resources in foreign exchange as possible. This is well demonstrated by the convergence of the foreign-exchange policies of the heavy-industrial and electrotechnical groups in the SRSU. In July 1921, the SRSU had decided to keep a third of all its liquid capital in foreign exchange, but the electrotechnical group, heavily dependent on the Reich for contracts, wished to avoid the impression of hoarding foreign exchange and kept its foreign-exchange holdings below the amount decided, only keeping enough to cover needs. While the heavy-industrial group had all of its liquid resources in foreign exchange in the spring of 1922, Siemens & Halske held only 26 percent and Siemens-Schuckert only 68 percent of its cash on hand in foreign exchange on May 1, 1922. By July 15, the policy had become insupportable, "need" had to be defined in long-run terms, and the percentages of liquid capital held in foreign exchange for the Siemens group were 97 and 100 percent respectively. The Siemens group had thus caught up with the heavy-industrial group in its foreign-exchange policy, if not yet in its share of discounted bills credited at the Reichsbank.[50]

The form of credit offered by the Reichsbank, however, was not easily accessible to all firms for certain purely technical reasons and was by no means always sufficient to meet the needs of many applicants. On the one hand, firms in the manufacturing industries—the machine construction industry, for example— were often unable to provide requisite security because they could not guarantee completion of orders within the time allowed by normal commercial bills. This helps to explain why many important firms apparently did not take advantage of the Reichsbank credit that might have been available to them as well as the peculiar advantage enjoyed by the SRSU thanks to the imaginative manner in which Stinnes had tied the Reichsbank credit to deliveries within the giant concern and to prospective rather than actual sales.[51] On the other hand, the taking of credit via commercial bills necessarily influenced the credit status of borrowers. A way out of this dilemma was found by firms and concerns which were members of the trade associations dealing largely in such products as coal, pig iron, and steel. In the late fall, agreements between the Reichsbank and the Coal Syndicate and the Pig Iron Association were made permitting them to discount bills of acceptance on behalf of their members. Stinnes played a major role in negotiating the agreement between the Coal Syndicate and the Reichsbank, with the result that the GBAG further exceeded the credit limit allowed the SRSU. In the case of the Pig Iron Association, up to five billion could be drawn on behalf of firms using foreign ores. At the end of November, representatives of the Steel Federation, a loose association of steel producers which did not market the products of its members in the manner of the other two syndicates, negotiated with Director Kaufmann of the Reichsbank for a similar arrangement whereby a Steel Finance Corporation would be formed to act on behalf of the individual producers. In this way, their credit would not be directly impaired, and they would not be compelled to damage their business and the economy further by asking for payment immediately on the day of delivery. They claimed that the existing system led to a loss of two-thirds of the profit between the day of delivery and the day of payment. Thus, both the distress of the producers and that of their customers would be relieved by such an arrangement. Kaufmann proved friendly to the idea, although not to the proposal that the Reichsbank make between forty billion and fifty billion marks available, a reaction anticipated by steel industrialists. The entire scheme apparently was thought up originally by August Thyssen, who was worried about tendencies among the steel industrialists to abandon the paper mark entirely in domestic transactions, a step he thought impossible until "a new strong government has found a way out." While the

plan was pursued, there was some feeling that the end result would be that a flood of commercial paper would replace the flood of currency without any positive result in the end.[52]

The steel industrialists were not alone in their concern. How much did German businessmen want to promote the loss of confidence in the mark by openly abandoning it, even in internal transactions? Ambassador Stahmer reported from London that English trust in the mark was being undermined not only by the German calculation of export prices in foreign currency but also "by the procedures at the Leipzig Fair, that is, the fixing of prices in foreign currency even for trade in domestic goods," which was "taken as the clearest possible demonstration of the lost confidence in our own currency."[53] The use of commercial bills might ease the pressures to go over to foreign currencies and dampen slightly the proclivity to tighten payment conditions, but for how long? If Saxon textile industrialist Moras had argued in one breath for harsher payment terms and a liberal commercial-bill policy, his colleague from Westphalia, Müller-Oerlinghausen, pointed out that "the introduction of commercial bills has great dangers. Herr Moras has very rightly pointed out that the textile industry is especially helped out by demanding prepayments. By means of commercial bills, the credit problem is put off somewhat. Afterward, we face precisely the same catastrophe. One should warn against acting too harshly. The collapse of the domestic market will only be speeded up that way."[54] It was typical of business behavior at this point, however, that the tendency toward world-market prices was pushed forward at the very time when the dangers were being recognized. Thus, at the RdI directors meeting on September 6, machine-construction industrialist Reuter informed his colleagues of a recent decision by the Berlin Price Examination Agency favoring pricing on the basis of reproduction costs and asked if the RdI should come out in favor of a radical reform of the antiprofiteering laws. The answer was almost uniformly positive, even if industry, with its mass of cartels and syndicates, was not directly affected. The porcelain manufacturer Rosenthal reported that members of commerce and industry had met at the Leipzig Fair and had agreed to oppose the antiprofiteering regulations altogether because retailers were being ruined. That Stinnes strongly supported such pricing was only to be expected, and it was very clear that industry had come to the conclusion that the one way in which it, and wholesalers, could escape the charges of being solely responsible for the high prices was by making common cause with retailers. As one industrialist put it, "[W]e have every reason to fight the antiprofiteering laws. The retailers are being ruined by them. . . . We ought not to take the consumer point of view but we must represent the producers."[55] Even extreme conservative Rudolf Blohm was apparently a bit taken aback by the enthusiasm for letting go the reins, and he pointed out that "everything has a limit" and reminded his colleagues that numerous associations were insisting on full payment at the price on the day of delivery while at the same time demanding 80 percent prepayment. He thought the RdI ought to say that the remaining 20 percent in such instances should be fixed at the delivery-day price.[56]

But how does one create order in disorder and set limits on a process that was becoming inexorable? The hopelessness of the situation was well demonstrated by Hirsch's ill-fated Foreign Exchange Control Decree of October 12, 1922. The decree backfired and had to be modified because importers, manufacturers, and wholesalers would not accept the sacrifices which had been imposed upon the retailers since the war. The decree in its original form suddenly imposed upon all the risk previously limited only to the retailers; namely, the obligation to deal only in marks. Thus, whereas before the importers, manufacturers, and wholesalers had responded to the galloping inflation and hyperinflation by doing their business in dollars and pounds—thus assuring that they could calculate on replenishing their stocks— the decree suddenly obligated them to do their business in marks. Only those purchasing foreign goods or raw materials could employ foreign currencies, and then only to pay foreigners. In order to deal with the risk involved in allowing any time at all to pass between their receipt of marks and conversion into foreign currency, the firms involved felt that they had to add as much as 10 percent to their prices. The effect

was to raise German prices above those abroad, despite Germany's lower labor costs. A further consequence was to force manufacturers to buy from foreign importers and use foreign shippers, thereby avoiding the problem of converting foreign exchange on hand into marks. The Hamburg–South American Steamship Company appeared fully justified in complaining that the decree was undermining the effort to rebuild the German shipping industry by forcing it to speculate on the stability of the mark. While German manufacturers and exporters were allowed to collect their bills in foreign exchange and expected the shipper to offer fixed charges for goods sent for export, the shipper was now expected to bill and receive payment in marks for goods sent on a three and a half month voyage during which crews and expenses would have to be covered in foreign currencies.[57] Little wonder that Hamburg and Bremen raised a storm of protest and that they were successful in getting importers and shippers exempted from the requirement that they sell only in marks. Manifestly, manufacturers were better able to deal with the currency conversion risk (*Valutarisiko*), especially if they were also exporters, although this did not stop them from complaining about the decree.

Major complaints, however, came next from wholesalers, who argued that manufacturers were transferring the risk to them and that they, in turn, were forced to transfer the risk to retailers. Particularly alarming and threatening were the reports from wholesalers and their organizations dealing in vital consumer necessities. The coal dealers complained bitterly about the limitation of their profit to 3 percent by the Reich Coal Council, pointing out that such an arrangement only made sense if bank credit were readily available or if customers could be billed promptly and collection made speedily. Under conditions where coal prices were continually responding to changing wage, transport, and material costs, no prediction was possible, and a higher allowable profit appeared the only way of helping wholesalers to protect themselves from the increasing number of payment delays by normally reliable customers and to maintain their own status as customers who could be counted upon to pay their bills to producers on time. Here, at least, the merchants could count on the sympathy of Stinnes, a coal merchant himself, who described the existing system as "suicidal."[58] Whereas the coal dealers wanted help from the coal producers, the dealers in foodstuffs, especially in grains and potatoes, felt they could turn to the government since their continued functioning could be viewed, especially in the industrial West, as an issue of public security. They were not, to be sure, prepared to accept just any kind of help. They rejected a proposal made in the summer of 1922 by the Socialist district President in Düsseldorf, Grützner, that the cities in the region set up a credit association for the consumer cooperatives and the wholesalers. Quite aside from not wishing to be associated with the hated consumer cooperatives, wholesalers feared the proposal was a move back to the controlled economy and toward the communalization of the food supply. In these views, they were supported by the then Mayor of Essen Hans Luther as well as the Mayor of Duisburg Carl Jarres. Luther insisted that the cities were in no position to get credits and that the cooperatives and wholesalers had to get credit on their own. The wholesalers agreed and proceeded to impose very harsh credit conditions on retailers and to turn to the banks. They were soon complaining, however, that the provincial banks, many of which had been taken over by the large Berlin banks, were not as forthcoming as they had once been and were very "schematic" in their treatment of wholesalers. Consequently, they asked the Reich to supply a guarantee for the credits they needed in lieu of the security which they were unable to supply themselves.[59]

Under the conditions described, the interest of industrialists and wholesalers in calling for the elimination of the antiprofiteering regulations and the implementation of pricing according to reproduction costs by retailers became increasingly logical. The case was well put by the large Westphalian textile firm Gebrüder Rath in repeated pleas for the cancellation of the decree in even its revised versions. Under a revision of October 27, those paying bills in a foreign currency after December 15 were required to procure the needed exchange as of the date on which the bill fell due and not, as had been the practice, at the time the order was ac-

cepted. In practical terms, this meant that a firm owing three hundred gulden could be forced to order its gulden at a moment when they could be bought for two thousand marks only to find that, by the time the gulden arrived, they cost three thousand marks. If such a situation were multiplied by all the other costs, then it was clear that the government was ordering manufacturers to work at a loss by prohibiting them from stabilizing their costs. The same held true for retailers, and "we are of the firm conviction that no law can force someone to knowingly work for his own ruin." Gebrüder Rath was fully aware that what it was supporting was tantamount to a vast increase in prices, but "if our substance is not to be wasted, then we must go through this price rise, cost what it will. In the last analysis, it lies in the interest of the entire national community . . . , for just as that portion of the people composed of pensioners and those no longer productive have fallen victim to the depreciation of the mark, so, as certain as is death, will all the other classes follow." From this perspective, they concluded, the producers, wholesalers, and retailers all had the same interest, "for all are equally disadvantaged by the monetary depreciation."[60]

This last statement certainly was somewhat premature, but it was very significant, for it demonstrated that the incentive to maintain differential advantages arising from the inflationary process were breaking down in the wake of the increasing disadvantages. Those who had come to conclusions similar to those of Gebrüder Rath were increasingly accepting the implications of this de facto march in the direction of valorizing their pricing in terms of foreign currencies. This was especially the case with those businessmen who were not in a position to function by steadily discounting commercial bills at the Reichsbank. Thus, in mid-November, the Koblenz Chamber of Commerce, after hearing a lecture by a leather manufacturer, unanimously accepted a resolution calling for a change of the commercial code that would favor the setting up of gold-mark balances. Similarly, at the beginning of the new year, the Association of Wool Carders and Wool Yarn Spinners was sending around a brochure showing its members how to set up gold-mark balances for 1921 and 1922. It was also offering the material to other businessmen and chambers of commerce at cost (four hundred marks). In contrast to the situation in the first three quarters of 1922, at least these businessmen were now convinced that such a procedure was necessary and pointed out that "the way in which the productive power of our industry and work opportunity for our people can be saved in the course of the coming year of the most difficult economic circumstances can only be found through the unreservedly clear understanding of our own situation."[61] Businessmen were beginning to want to know what their real balances were.

This yearning for some solid foundation for calculation and for an escape from the risks of paper money were by no means limited to industrialists. As Alfred Lansburgh put the matter, "that portion of the German people capable of judgment wants nothing more to do with the mark."[62] When they used the mark, they immediately converted it into something else, and the search was on for stable alternatives. Industrialists and merchants who were engaged in domestic business and farmers, who also did not have access to foreign exchange, were especially anxious to find some solid base from which to conduct business and to secure their assets. Farmers found it especially attractive to use their own products for such purposes. Oldenburg and Mecklenburg began to offer valorized bonds based on rye and grain, while some private organizations established mortgage bonds or other forms of securities based on rye or coal. In certain instances, potatoes and kilowatt hours were also used. The states floating such securities were themselves in the business of selling rye and other grains and could back their interest-bearing paper with their receipts from the sale of these products. The receipts from the sale of these securities were used to lend money to farmers, who were then obligated to repay the loans according to the price of rye. A good illustration of the issuance of securities based on coal was the Mannheim Power Works Co., which issued securities worth between five hundred and ten thousand kilograms of coal. Since the price of electricity tended to move in consonance with the price of coal, the company, which supplied a very large area, believed that it could always cover its ob-

ligations with its receipts for supplying electricity. These were, of course, tricky forms of valorization in that they depended on the price of single products. Furthermore, they were anything but interchangeable, since people had enough trouble converting paper marks into one other form of currency without now having the additional task of converting various commodity-based currencies into others. At the same time, they also had a dubious side in that they gave those investing in such securities a stake in the high price of the commodities in question and shifted the risk from actual producers to the public.

In a similar effort to find an alternative valorized currency and to escape the risks of dealing in paper marks, an important movement developed at the turn of 1922–1923 for the creation of gold accounts or banco marks. The term dated back to a currency employed by seventeenth- and eighteenth-century Hamburg merchants who, appropriately enough, wanted a currency that would have fixed value and be free of state manipulation. In contrast to this banco mark, the one discussed in the German hyperinflation, which had been strongly propagated by Dr. Dalberg of the Reich Economics Ministry, was not to be backed by silver or any other precious metal but was rather meant to serve purely as a unit of account in bank-mediated transactions. If cash payments were actually required, they were to be paid in paper marks at the rate designated when the account was opened. A number of banks had already opened such accounts for their customers in 1922, whether for savings or business purposes, and the idea seems to have been strongly supported by the savings banks and their clearing center as a means of encouraging savings and of making business easier.

In early December, the Central Association of German Wholesalers was calling upon the government to permit recognized firms to open gold-mark accounts with the Reichsbank that would be guaranteed by calculation in dollars or some other high-value currency. In its view, this would end the use of foreign exchange in domestic transactions and the imposition of conversion risk charges on retailers and consumers. The Reich Association of German Industry took up the cause in mid-January 1923, arguing that the creation of a banco mark, denominated in gold or at the rate of one gold mark to the English shilling, would enable both producers and retailers to calculate properly. As things stood, retailers were hampered by both the decree against speculation in foreign currencies and the antiprofiteering laws, but a valorized mode of calculation would enable them and everyone else to function in an economically sound manner. This was an obvious effort to create a united front in pricing between producers and merchants. The idea owed much to the advocacy of Dr. Dalberg of the RWM and was viewed sympathetically by highly placed officials on both the national and state levels. For understandable reasons, these plans and proposals worried the Reichsbank, which feared that the risk of dealing in paper marks would be shifted entirely to itself and was undoubtedly even more concerned by suggestions that a special new bank be set up to handle the banco accounts. As far as the Central Association of German Banks and the Banking Industry was concerned, the proposal appeared very alarming because it either imposed an unbearable obligation or invited participation in an incredible absurdity. On the one hand, the banco accounts could be covered by foreign exchange. In this case, the banco-mark plan would not be dissimilar from a privatized version of Hirsch's proposal for a domestic gold loan aimed at reducing the incentive to deal in foreign exchange in domestic transactions. On the other hand, the banco accounts would have no real backing at all, and the banco mark would be a "monstrosity," a "*Valuta* currency of calculation with paper mark coverage."[63] Whatever the case, these ideas reflected the increasing tendency toward the privatization of currency, mounting impatience with trying to do business in a hyperinflationary environment, and a yearning to pass the "*schwarzen Peter*" of the paper mark to anyone who could be induced or forced to take it.

The Economic Crisis

Manifestly, the aspects of the political economy of the hyperinflation demonstrate that it was an economy in crisis. Those involved in it on a day-to-day basis were obviously living from hand to mouth, even when they were doing very well or thought they were doing very well. It is thus important to contextualize their behavior in terms of some broader appreciation of the condition of the German economy and its relationship with the outside world during the pre-Ruhr–occupation phase of the hyperinflation.

The determination of the real condition of the German economy in the hyperinflation has exercised the skills of economists and economic historians since the hyperinflation itself. Both at the time and subsequently, the German balance of payments has been a matter of debate and controversy. How much money did foreign speculators lose on the mark, and how much did Germany gain? Was the German balance of trade negative or positive in 1922, and how big was the trade deficit between 1919 and 1922? How great was the flight of capital from Germany during this period? To what extent were German holdings abroad necessary to pay for imports, and to what extent were they illegitimate? A major difficulty with the investigations of these questions is that they all arose in the context of the reparations issue and the problem of Germany's capacity to pay, a context highly conducive to the production of underestimates on the German side and overestimates by Germany's enemies and critics. Even more problematic from the perspective of the historian writing long after the event, however, is that while the aggregated effect of German financial and economic decision making in both the public and private sectors may have been to keep German payments below what they might have been if the Germans had devoted all or at least more of their efforts to paying their international bills, the primary concern of most Germans involved in economic life was to do as well as they could under existing circumstances rather than to create some creditor's utopia. From the viewpoint of German businessmen in 1922, the extent to which foreigners had speculated away millions on the mark, the amounts of German capital stashed away or invested abroad, and the degree to which receipts from inflationary export advantages were higher than ever paled in significance in the face of the stoppage of foreign speculation in favor of the mark and the shortage of capital and credit, the danger that capital kept abroad would have to be repatriated if one wished to continue operations in Germany, and the increasing evidence of German noncompetitiveness on world markets.

This was precisely the point John Maynard Keynes sought to make in one of his own contributions to the "Reconstruction in Europe" series in the *Manchester Guardian* on "Speculation in the Mark and Germany's Balances Abroad" of September 28, 1922.[64] Keynes readily admitted that the "bankers and servant girls" who had together speculated on the mark and German recovery had provided Germany with "her much-discussed international loan, and on the easiest terms imaginable—as for interest, most of it bears none; and as for capital, only such proportion is repayable as Germany may herself decide when she comes to fix the value of the paper mark."[65] He estimated that, as things stood, they had lost 96 percent of their capital. He calculated the amount involved at between eight billion and ten billion gold marks, while the McKenna Committee, which had access to German bank reports in its efforts to prepare material for what was to become the Dawes Report in 1924, put the figure at between 7.6 billion and 8.7 billion gold marks. This estimate, which was a compromise and was politically influenced, does not stand up well against the most recent research findings of Carl-Ludwig Holtfrerich, which put the speculative capital transfer to Germany at fifteen billion gold marks.[66]

Whatever the sum, however, and whatever the aggregate net gain to the German economy from the perspective of hindsight, there was much to Keynes's argument that the "loan" was a disorderly and ultimately improvident solution to the problem of Germany's reconstruction:

Yet it must not be supposed that Germany, too, has not paid a penalty. In the modern world, organization is worth more in the long run than material resources. By the sale of paper marks Germany has somewhat replenished the stocks of materials of which the war and the blockade had denuded her; but she has done it at the cost of a ruinous disorganization, present and still to come. She has confiscated most of the means of livelihood of her educated middle class, the source of her intellectual strength; and

the industrial chaos and unemployment, which the end of the present inflationary boom seems likely to bring, may disorder the minds of her working class, the source of her political stability. The money of the bankers and the servant girls, which would have been nearly enough to restore Europe if applied with prudence and wisdom, has been wasted and thrown away.[67]

Most important, the interest-free loan was no longer being given because of the complete collapse of confidence in the German situation. The function of speculation, as the Belgian economist Maurice Frère pointed out in an intelligence report for the Reparations Commission in October 1922, was to "anticipate events," and speculators had simply ceased to believe in German recovery.[68]

A similarly sober view was taken by Frère toward another much-discussed subject at this time and subsequently; namely, the flight of capital from Germany. In his view, there was no way to prevent capital flight under existing conditions, and he went so far as to argue that "to prevent persons resident in Germany from changing their savings into foreign currency is tantamount to opposing by force, not only the opinion but also the interests of the majority of the public." Here, too, the issue was confidence, and one could not "impose this confidence by force."[69] If there was anything that fired the imaginations of Germany's critics, however, it was this capital flight, and rather extraordinary estimates were circulating about. This was one of the major charges of the Allies against German industry, and it was echoed by anticapitalist critics within Germany itself. Both Germans and non-Germans made considerable effort in 1922 to try to determine the amount and character of the flight of German capital. Keynes, after consulting with leading bankers in Germany and elsewhere, concluded that "the total of Germany's foreign resources probably falls short of two milliard gold marks and certainly cannot exceed three milliards."[70] He actually thought it was closer to a billion.

There were other estimates floating about. Erzberger gave the figure of three billion in November 1920; Sir Robert Horne suggested not more than two billion in August 1922; while McKenna estimated four billion in the fall of 1922 and later, in the famous report of January 1924, provided a figure of five billion to six billion gold marks. Not surprisingly, Havenstein and Warburg as well as other Germans sided with Keynes, and the full truth will never be known.[71] Vissering and van Meulen, the two Dutch bankers Keynes consulted, came up with widely divergent estimates for German holdings in their country, the former suggesting about four hundred fifty million gold marks (250–300 million gulden), the latter arguing for about a billion gold marks (750–800 million gulden). In his response to Keynes, Vissering did not feel he could answer the question as to how much of these German holdings was necessary for business and how much was hoarded, while van Meulen stated his belief that "by far the greater part of the sum mentioned is to be regarded as hoarded capital" since only between twenty-five million and fifty million would be necessary for actual trading purposes. In his article, Keynes chose to treat Vissering as the more "authoritative" of his sources, and perhaps he knew best, but van Meulen chose to remind Keynes that the Netherlands was filled with "branches of German banks, branches of German banking firms, Dutch banks founded with German capital, Dutch commercial concerns founded with German capital and various other institutions, whose principal object consists in helping their German founders to do business with foreign countries." The profits were often kept in the Netherlands, and the dividends were kept low, so that the enterprises involved were growing richer and were "in a position to conceal a great deal of their wealth, which remains hoarded on behalf of their German shareholders until the time will come, when no further danger exists in Germany of excessive taxation or even confiscation." Similarly, Swedish banker Marcus Wallenberg estimated that most of the German kronor-denominated assets were hoarded capital and thought that there were some three billion goldmarks' worth of German capital held in the United States, England, and Argentina, which when added to the 2.3 billion he thought held on the continent came to a total of 5.3 billion. What is interesting is that Wallenberg did not treat this, at the time, extremely high estimate as an argument that the money could somehow be mobilized for reparations but rather declared that "it seems impossible to dispose of a

very great part of those for payments of indemnities" and in no way changed his belief that a five-year moratorium was necessary.[72] At the rate things were going in Germany in 1922, after all, it could be argued that the German capital flight was an asset best left untouched until conditions could be stabilized and the capital could be repatriated for useful purposes.

Just as Germany's balance of payments was being negatively influenced by the loss of foreign speculative capital and the incentive for Germans to flee the mark, so the brightest point on the balance-of-payments horizon, the German export drive, was darkening as well. Even the Wirth government was distrustful of its own trade statistics, which had produced excessively positive results for the first eight months of 1922 and led to an effort to reform the way in which foreign trade was calculated.[73] The statistics subsequently generated did not eliminate contention. The export statistics were particularly unreliable because of smuggling through the "hole in the West" and elsewhere, because domestic prices were often given for goods rather than their much lower export prices, and because the price quotations in marks often failed to do justice to what was finally received from foreigners. These defects, it is to be noted, could lead to overestimates as well as underestimates of export receipts. Prices quoted for German exports in 1922, for example, appear to have been about 30 percent less than world-market prices and about 15 percent higher than 1913 prices. The Reich Statistical Office, however, presented the value of German exports at two-thirds of their 1913 price. Thus, the Statistical Office appears to have gone overboard in responding to the call for a change of its methods by assessing the value of German exports for the entire year 1922 below their actual worth. The real issue, of course, is not the size of the surplus, insofar as any may have existed for a brief period in 1922, but of the trade deficit. The Reich Statistical Office later calculated a trade deficit of eleven billion gold marks for the period 1919–1922 and a deficit of 2.2 billion gold marks in 1922. Calculations by the Committee of Guarantees of the Reparations Commission in 1924 put the 1918–1922 deficit at between 4.5 billion and 6.5 billion gold marks, with the 1922 deficit at between .5 and

Table 28. The Value of German Imports and Exports in Gold Marks, 1913, 1919–1922

(at 1913 average prices)

	1913	1919*	1920	1921**	1922
Imports	11,206	2,587.9	3,947.2	5,750.1	6,311.5
Exports	10,199	1,986.0	3,724.0	4,503.9	6,199.4
Deficit	1,007	601.9	223.2	1,246.8	112.1

Sources: R. Pilotti, "The Value of German Imports and Exports from 1919 to 1923," Reparations Commission. Delegation of the Committee of Guarantees, Feb. 16, 1924, Library of Congress, Ayres Papers; and *Statistik des deutschen Reichs* 310 (1924), I.2.

*Approximately calculated by the Exports Section of the RWM on the average prices of the subcategories of the customs schedule of 1913. Values for 1920–1922 calculated by Reich Statistical Office on the average prices of the various numbers of the customs schedule of 1913.

**Export figure obtained by multiplying by 1.5 the figure of 3,003 million gold marks given by the Reich Statistical Office for the period May–December 1921.

1.0 billion gold marks. Whatever the correct figures might actually have been, there was a deficit, especially since 2.6 billion in reparations payments for 1918–1922 must be added in. Nevertheless, if one wished to be optimistic, then it could be argued that, in the absence of reparations payments, imports and exports seemed to be approaching some measure of equilibrium, and that this would be a major plus in the event of stabilization measures and a restoration of confidence (see Table 28).[74]

None of this would have provided very much consolation to German businessmen and economic leaders as the year 1922 drew to an end, and with good reason. While the inflationary export "boom" was at its height in 1922, the achievement in the second half of 1922, as was also true during the last months of 1921, was based on dumping; that is, by selling well below world-market prices (see Table 29). The value of German exports decreased substantially between the first and second half of 1922, while the proportion of exports paid in foreign currency increased dramatically because of the accelerating exclusion of the mark from international commerce.[75] Another interesting measure of what the German economy was paying in real terms for conducting its international trade under hyperinflationary conditions was provided by the economist Frank D. Graham, who compared potential with actual expenditures for imports and receipts from exports using 1913 values and assuming the operation of the gold standard. Thus, Germany spent 1,759,839,000 less on imports in 1922 than would have been the case under 1913 condi-

tions, but received 4,290,186,000 gold marks less from her exports. In calculating the ratio of potential to actual return from exports for the last three months of 1922, he found that the return in percent was, respectively, 50.1, 47.7, and 48.6 of what it would have been under 1913 conditions.[76]

While real losses clearly correlated with higher rates of inflation in late 1921 and late 1922, there was a major difference. Germany still appeared reasonably competitive in late 1921 and even early 1922, while evidence abounded in the second half of 1922 that German competitive capacity was being lost—its leading western competitors had recovered from the world depression of 1920–1921, had

Table 29. Indices of Average Export Prices, 1921–1922

(1913 = 100)

	1921	1922
January	—	72
February	—	79
March	—	72
April	—	74
May	131	90
June	109	99
July	101	78
August	98	59
September	86	61
October	66	59
November	45	55
December	63	65
Average	80	64

Source: R. Pilotti, "The Value of German Imports and Exports from 1919 to 1923," Reparations Commission. Delegation of the Committee of Guarantees, Feb. 16, 1924, p. 13, Library of Congress, Ayres Papers.

taken measures against German dumping, and had begun underselling the Germans and also serving their customers more speedily and reliably.

The alarming news was coming in from everywhere. In May, the German consulate in the Netherlands, Germany's most important customer in 1922, reported that German bids for various types of rolled steel and pipes were being rejected in favor of Belgian and English competitors. Whereas German competition in the printing trades had once been "catastrophic," now German offers were underbid by Dutch competition. The Germans were also disadvantaged by "freight costs, longer delivery times, export permissions, retroactive price increases."[77] In the furniture industry, German prices were being rejected even though they were at the very minimum allowed by export control boards, and the German General Consul thought the export control boards were showing insufficient awareness of Dutch market conditions. Where the Germans were competitive, as in cigars and shoes, enormous pressures were placed on the Dutch government to simply ban German imports, although the Dutch government inclined to raising tariffs instead.[78] In the United States, where strong antidumping measures were to be included in the Tariff Act of 1922, the German General Consul in New York, nevertheless, showed less concern with German dumping than with German inability to compete with the English, French, and Japanese, as well with the American producers of porcelain. Either the German prices were too high and were irritating to Americans because less was charged in other countries or they were insufficiently competitive for importers to make an acceptable profit.[79] Similarly, while German producers were complaining about Swiss import restrictions, the German Consul General in Zurich reported in December that German producers were losing out for a variety of reasons. In the case of electrical machines, where the German export control board was very flexible, the problem was that German producers were selling at world-market prices while the Swiss were simply underbidding the competition in order to maintain employment. The Consul General wondered if the 8 percent export levy made any sense under such conditions. When it came to boilers and similar products, the German export price simply was too high, especially because of the Swiss tariff. As for eye glasses, the German syndicate seemed unaware of the lower Swiss price. The problems involved in selling German ready made clothes in Switzerland were variously blamed on the German export levy and the fact that German suppliers of material charged German manufacturers a higher price than Belgian suppliers charged Swiss manufacturers.[80]

Such reports were bound to heat up the already more than lively battle over export controls and export levies. The government responded to the hyperinflation in the summer of 1922 by seeking a substantial increase in export levies across the board. Every conceivable argument was used against the "schematic" increase of one hundred percent proposed by Hirsch. The government of Hamburg, for example, forwarded complaints from Hamburg–South American Steamship Company, which pointed out that it was under pressure to keep its freight rates much lower than the English and American competition because otherwise exporters of cement, paper, and other products sent to Brazil and Argentina would no longer be able to compete, and then there would be nothing to ship. The claim was that the export levy was so high that the shipping companies had to subsidize these exports through artificially low freight rates. Frustrated in their efforts to prevent export levy increases, the opponents of the levies turned, as in the past, to trying to get the levies reduced on a product-by-product basis—especially for those items using imported materials, paints, weapons and munitions, textiles, and soap, for example. This was a wearisome process, and efforts to eliminate the levies in their entirety were constantly met by RWM claims that the prices of industrial securities were very high, that there remained sufficient margin for export profits, and that reductions would encourage anti-dumping measures by importing nations. These arguments were answered by counterclaims that the German securities market was filled with watered stock and that anti-dumping measures were a reflection of hostility toward German competition and would in no way be influenced by export levies. Furthermore, dumping appeared unavoidable if some German industries were to retain anything of the markets in which they had finally reestablished themselves. The small iron-wares industry, for example, was not only faced with tariff barriers in Belgium, France, and the English colonies, and growing American competition, but it also found it impossible to stock up on raw materials, as could be done before the war, because of the constantly changing prices and the shortage of operating capital. The conflicts over the levies were compounded by debates over the question of which countries were to be billed in foreign currencies and which were to be treated as countries with depreciated currencies and billed in marks. Portugal was a particularly contested case.[81]

The bottom line in all these discussions was the question of unemployment and the argument that it was better to eliminate levies than jobs, and reductions were made whenever it could be shown that unemployment was serious or a danger. In such cases, one could count on the support of the worker representatives in the RWR, although the Economics Ministry often refused to cooperate when Schmidt and Hirsch were in power. In mid-November, the employers made a new effort and were more aggressive in their discussions with worker representatives. Now it was the turn of the industrialists to make the "schematic" proposal that export levies be reduced to 1 percent. The trade-union representatives claimed that conditions in industry varied too much to allow for such a solution. They went on to argue that the best route to the improvement of exports was "through rationalization of production methods, especially through the consolidation of plants." The response of the employers was to refuse all responsibility for unemployment arising from the export levy, one businessman pointing out that

if it would be possible through the elimination of the export levy to employ even a small number of workers in every plant, then the reduction of the export levy would have fulfilled its purpose. A rationalization of the productive process and a consolidation of plants is not as easy to effectuate as the worker representatives assume. The employers are in any case striving to maintain their plants at a high level of productivity in their own interest. At present, the extraordinary lack of operating capital and the housing situation, which hinders the resettling of workers, stand in the way of the restructuring of plants along the lines demanded by the workers.[82]

In raising the rationalization issue, however, trade-union representatives were on very dangerous ground. Thus, at a meeting in the Reich Economic Council on November 25, General Director Krämer readily admitted that a variety of industries were engaged in dumping pure and simple. The head of the export control board of the paper industry, to which Krämer belonged, then showed this to be the case for his own industry, a fact confirmed by the paper-industry worker representative. While the paper industry, which imported 80 percent of its raw materials, had been able to maintain high employment levels earlier in the year, the situation deteriorated in the summer and became especially difficult after the raising of the export levy in September. Contracts from abroad had severely diminished, and export prices were below the German domestic price in many cases. Thirteen percent of the workers in book printing were unemployed, and 17 percent were on short time. The only relief from the situation was being provided by the Reichsbank and various municipalities needing printers for the production of money, clearly not a promising long-term solution. Krämer, like representatives of other industries, did not blame wages for the situation and readily admitted that German real wages were well below those of workers abroad. When a worker representative asked why an industry whose wages were one-tenth of those paid abroad could not compete, the answer was "that foreign industry often has more modern machines, longer working hours, and fewer constraining conditions in their labor contracts, thus making it possible, in contrast to Germany, for the worker to tend more machines."[83] A few days later, the employers renewed the charge. This time, the initiative came from the textile industry, which claimed that the ban on workers tending more than one loom put the German industry at a competitive disadvantage. Krämer followed up with exact figures showing that "the use of the labor force abroad ... is much more intensive. This is why it is possible in many branches of textiles for foreigners to compete so well with German wares despite the high wage costs."[84]

Such information was based on very concrete reports from firms in the industry to their chambers of commerce. Thus, the important Westphalian firm of M. van Delden & Co. in Gronau provided specific information on the reasons for its declining export advantages in late October:

Now one would think that the German textile industry would again be offered great export opportunities with the sinking of the mark. But this is not so. Holland as well as England are cheaper in many articles today. . . . This is because Holland as well as England are experiencing an economic crisis in their textile industries and therefore sell in part under cost while at the same time making the greatest conceivable efforts to force down their costs. It is interesting for example that in the neighboring Dutch textile industry at this time, a struggle is going on to increase the weekly work week from 48 to 52 hours while maintaining the present weekly wage. Furthermore, it is possible in Holland for a worker, as in Germany before the war, to tend four or more looms, while the effort to implement this generally in Germany has been in vain. . . . Added to this is that German industry, in contrast to the Dutch and English, is not supported by its government agencies but rather actually hindered in its competition on the world market through bureaucratic interventions.[85]

The reference, of course, was to the recent measures dealing with foreign exchange and the increases in the export levy. If the government wished to tax away 60 percent of a firm's profits, that was one thing, but to impose a 6 percent levy on its anticipated gains beforehand was, in the view of this firm, to make the firm noncompetitive, to take away such profits as it might make, and to threaten to tear asunder overnight international connections it had laboriously reestablished since the war.

How much credence is to be given to such arguments? The evidence from less interested sources suggests that the arguments and complaints of some of these businessmen were well-founded and also provides some basis for understanding both the extent and the limits of the inflationary reconstruction grinding to a halt at this time. As an American Consular report of early January 1923 on conditions in the textile industry on the Dutch border shows, half the spindles of the van Delden firm, one of the largest on the Continent, were idle, and the problems of the firm were typical of the double bind in which the firms in the region found themselves. On the one hand, they were being squeezed by the growing cost of raw materials and shortage of credit; on the other, they suffered, strange as it may sound, from a shortage of labor. The first problem is familiar enough. The industry was dependent on foreign raw materials, the real cost of which was steadily increasing with the result that the firms were forced to diminish their stocks since bank credit was either unavailable or too expensive for them to maintain stores of cotton and other such materials in sufficient quantities. The labor problem arose from the shutting down of much of the industry during the war and the tendency of many of the workers in the region to seek work in heavy industry. It was compounded by the difficulty of procuring the skilled Dutch workers upon whom the industry depended both before and after the war. In order to maintain the remaining stock of workers, the firms often took on "work for wages"— that is, contract work for foreign firms, which severely limited their initiative and independence—and provided food at cheaper prices to their Dutch workers. At the same time, they had invested in housing construction with the objective of enticing a new stock of workers, especially refugees from the east, to come to the region. By the turn of 1922–1923, however, their efforts were breaking down. It was becoming too expensive to hold on to the Dutch workers, and for every skilled Dutch worker lost, six Germans had to be let go. Coal prices were not only astronomical, but the production needed for the textile mills was totally inadequate because German miners in the region were seeking employment in the Netherlands. At the same time, it had become clear that the gains from exports in no way covered the costs of replacing raw materials. Lastly, no stimulation could be expected from the local domestic market because the purchasing power of the population was insufficient to meet its dire need for clothing. Little wonder, therefore, that firms found it impossible to take on long-term contracts since they were uncertain they could cover the raw-materials costs and were putting their workers on short-time of one or two days a week.[86]

Not all industrialists were in quite such dire straits, however, and credence must also be given to reports that their holding back in the purchase of raw materials was less the result of the immediate situation than the anticipation of the future. As another American official in Rhineland-Westphalia reported:

It is quite certain . . . that the industrials purchased foreign exchange heavily throughout the year and that they have sufficient credit abroad in the form of foreign currency to purchase raw materials. It appears, therefore, that the real reason why industrials do not purchase raw materials is the general uncertainty regarding industry and trade, or rather speculation as to the future turn of affairs. It appears that they are in doubt as to whether they can gain more by retaining the foreign exchange which they purchased or by purchasing therewith raw materials. Bankers here do not deny that the industrials are heavy holders of foreign exchange purchased when the mark was considerably higher than it is at the present time.[87]

The trouble was that there was good reason to be pessimistic. When yet another American diplomat investigated Saxony in August and tried to figure out why the Saxon industrialists had been so terribly gloomy at their annual May meeting when business was booming, he came to the conclusion that the melancholy was justified. Another report in December simply confirmed the deterioration. In August, unemployment was low in comparison to prewar times, but so was productivity thanks to the abolition of piece work, reduced working hours, and the shortage of skilled workers. Many of the latter had been killed in the war; others had aged; young workers disliked serving as apprentices; and the small pay differential between skilled and unskilled workers served as a disincentive to the development of skills. Much of the industrial activity in 1922 was concentrated on the completion of orders given in 1921, and there was a marked decline in new orders. While substantial amounts of money were being invested in industry, this was not money earned from production but rather some foreign investment and a great deal of money that came from paid-up mortgages by people who were trying to save what could be saved from depreciated investments. At the same time, the previous cost advantages were disappearing as the workers began to press for real wage increases. Wages increased 270 percent between November 1921 and July 1922, while the dollar rate only increased 87.6 percent. The credit crisis reduced the ability of the industrialists to replenish their stocks and to step up dumping practices. By December, the situation was much worse. The most prosperous part of the population appeared to be the farmers, who were paying off their mortgages in depreciated marks and using the money to buy consumer items. The stabilization of the Czech koruna had greatly increased the price of Bohemian coal and had also led to a flood of Czech buyers—not only of goods but also of real estate, which could be had very cheaply because of the rent controls. Those Germans with money to invest feared a collapse of the industrial stock market and were also following the general inclination to buy whatever goods they could lay their hands on. As for the rest of the population, its purchasing power had deteriorated to the point where those who wished to get rid of their money did so by acquiring secondhand goods.[88]

The reality was that the hyperinflation, in contrast to the preceding periods of relative stabilization and galloping inflation, was characterized by a strong tendency toward retrenchment, a pulling back from new construction and plant expansion. Study of the investment decisions of major firms in the machine-construction industry—the M.A.N., Krupp, the Maschinenfabrik Esslingen, Schenck, and Klöckner-Humboldt-Deutz—demonstrates conclusively that the high points of investment decisions for leading firms in this industry were months when the mark and prices were at least relatively stable, when the firms in question had substantial bank deposits. There was a great unwillingness to increase debts for such purposes, and the floating of capital stock issues for plant expansion was substantially below that of the prewar period in real terms. In short, the plant construction and expansion boom in early 1922 and, insofar as it was continued, in the second half of the year was primarily the product of decisions made before the hyperinflation began.[89]

Further powerful evidence for this analysis is provided by other major concerns. The Mannesmann concern, for example, had allocated

185 million marks for new construction in July 1921 and another 125 million in March 1922. In October, another 1.5 billion was appropriated, two-thirds of which was to cover increased costs on this building program, and the rest of which was to cover "urgently necessary" construction. A decision was made, however, "to carry on the expansion only to the extent that the corporation has the necessary financial means available."[90] In December 1922, the Phoenix concern decided to appropriate more money for the completion of its old program as well as approve some modest expansion, especially of housing for miners, but it had access to Dutch capital, calculated in gulden, and instructed that the necessary materials be purchased immediately so as to reduce cost overruns. In doing so, it carried on a policy decision taken back in April to draw on its foreign exchange reserves to cover loans for its new construction program. Krupp took another tack, however, deciding to seek credits only for the maintenance of existing plant and to refrain from taking any credits for new construction.[91]

Whatever the variations, it was clear that the construction boom between the fall of 1921 and the spring of 1922, which was largely concentrated on the construction of new plant, office buildings, and company housing for workers, was slowing down substantially. A good illustration of the mood among industrialists was provided by Catholic industrialist Peter Klöckner, who sadly informed the pastor of the area in which his concern's mines were located that he could no longer authorize the provision of funds for the building of a church and urged him to cease construction if he could not find funds elsewhere. As he glumly noted:

Conditions have so changed in the last months that the industrial enterprises have the greatest concern as to how they are going to provide the wages and salaries for their workers and employees. The resources of the works have shrunk or disappeared. Our substance has already been strongly employed, and all enterprises without exception have to make an effort to protect themselves from collapse. Under these circumstances, there remained nothing more that our administrative offices could do than to order no more new constructions and to restrict what is already under construction as much as possible. The same fate has been experienced not only by industrial en-

terprises but, as must certainly not be unknown to you, all the cities. Even in the cities, construction work has been interrupted. One leaves the houses standing, irrespective of whether they are at the foundation stage or are at the first or second story. Necessity at present compels everyone to the greatest retrenchment. Despite this distress we receive almost daily requests for support, not only from the Cardinal in Cologne, but from all the bishops, cloisters, and not the least from the great Center Party. Everyone's treasury is empty and everyone believes that they can still quickly consume something from the riches of industry. No one can get used to the idea that industry was rich once upon a time and that this wealth has long been a thing of the past.[92]

Such decisions by firms and concerns in the summer and fall of 1922 to pull back from the feverish construction activity of the earlier part of the year caused no little anxiety. The labor representative on the Supervisory Board of the M.A.N., while accepting the financial considerations that made a limitation of the construction program necessary, nevertheless pleaded that the board consider "whether various productive constructions could not perhaps be taken up again in the interest of the employees and workers."[93] Most dramatic had been the public announcement of the Siemens–Rhein-Elbe–Schuckert–Union in the summer of 1922 that it was ceasing work on all its construction sites with the exception of the nearly completed plants at the Bochumer Verein. Trade-union economist Fritz Naphtali was somewhat less convinced than the worker representative at the M.A.N. that such radical decisions were justified by the shortage of operating capital, at least not in the case of the SRSU with its huge resources and completely unwatered stock. Yet, Naphtali had to admit that the phenomenon was too widespread to suggest that all the firms involved had the option of raising capital stock in order to complete projects. Whatever the case, he described the results as dramatically as Klöckner:

In fact according to available reports, constructions expanding industrial plants as well as constructions of worker housing that had been begun are being shut down incomplete, and that which the Stinnes trust has made known to the broad public is not limited to it alone. There are similar shut downs of construction sites, stoppages of plant renewal, cancellation of contracts for replacement materials among other industrial groups in substantial amounts. Cases are known in which the work on constructions is left at a stage where protection against deterioration does not appear to be present so that the observer has the impression as if, as in the outbreak of a strike, the work had suddenly been stopped without preparation and in haste.[94]

For Naphtali, this demonstrated the importance of the abortive efforts to organize the capital market in 1920 and the mistake that had been made by the bankers and others in failing to realize the necessity of organizing a nation's labor and capital resources.

Stinnes obviously thought differently, and his decision, while rapid, was by no means purely reactive and unreflecting, although it did involve some miscalculation. The high point of liquidity in the SRSU had been reached in December 1921, and Stinnes had hoped to maintain the huge construction program at the beginning of the year without having to borrow through coal price increases. By late May, he had come to the conclusion that a period of holding back with orders and new construction was necessary: "I have the impression, that in a few months the overemployment of German industry will let up, that material would become more available and also cheaper, so that we should wait patiently with contracts. I also wish that we do not overextend ourselves, but come to a resting point from which we can undertake new engagements."[95] He instructed the various directors of the SRSU and the Rhenish-Westphalian Electrical Works (RWE) to make a survey of construction work in progress and then ordered the cessation of all construction that was not near completion. Similarly, he urged the RWE to get rid of "dispensable technical and commercial personnel . . . since we cannot under any circumstances tolerate an excess of personnel in the coming extraordinarily difficult period."[96]

The motive for the building stop at the SRSU and RWE was not only Stinnes's expectations about future business conditions, however. He was, along with many other industrialists, extremely upset about the rising wages in the construction industry and the number of miners and other workers who were taking advantage of the situation. The construction boom was hurting coal production as well as construction

costs, and Stinnes's cutback in June was undertaken in collaboration with other firms and concerns in the Ruhr facing the same problems.[97] No less important a motive, however, was the unwillingness of Stinnes to issue new stocks or to float bonds. He insisted that the enterprises with which he was associated make due with returns from sales and, after his arrangements with the Reichsbank, with commercial-bill credits. A major reason for this conservative policy was fear of "foreignization." At the same time, however, Stinnes also pursued a very conservative dividend policy in comparison to that of concerns like Phoenix and Rheinstahl, which were paying out two and a half to three times as much on their shares. Stinnes felt that there were not only economic grounds for controlling dividends but political reasons as well, although Vögler thought the low dividends kept the quotations of SRSU stock unnecessarily low. This in no way impressed Stinnes, however, who did not believe that people were buying stock systematically at this time with the level of dividends in mind.[98]

Stinnes undoubtedly was correct, since the evidence was that both foreigners and Germans, insofar as they were willing to invest in any German liquid asset, were investing in industrial shares as a form of long-term investment. Until mid-October 1922, the share market had been quite depressed, since the belief that industrial stocks were a good inflation hedge had dissipated at the end of 1921, but then prices picked up thanks, in part, to the increased liquidity that came with the discounting of commercial bills. Foreigners were showing some interest in German stocks. Generally, this was not because they were trying to take advantage of their absurdly low value to take over German enterprises. While it was true that, for example, the market value of Daimler's stock was the equivalent of 327 cars and that of the Tietz department stores of 16,000 suits, the German business world had fairly well protected itself with preferred multiple voting shares sold only to a limited circle of holders. Foreigners bought the shares because it was virtually the only thing they could do with the increasingly worthless marks they held. The other alternative was buying real estate, which occurred in significant quantities, but which was problematic so long as rent controls continued. As for the German purchasers of stock, many found the Foreign Exchange Control Decree was a particularly important incentive to invest in stocks if they were not among those who could safely speculate in foreign exchange. This helps to explain why prices went up dramatically during the last two and a half months of 1922. While there was some concern of another crash on the market, as on the "Black Thursday" of December 1, 1921, the prices of shares reflected the fact that the market was already discounting in anticipation of bad business conditions. There was thus a feeling that industrial shares would keep pace with inflation and not fall much in a stabilization. The real value of German shares, of course, was seriously depressed, and they could only be held as a long-term investment. While the dividend rates were very high, the real value of the dividends was quite low, and firms and concerns were clearly holding on to most of their profits rather than distributing them.[99]

It would be a mistake to think, however, that this dividend policy did not "get on the nerves" of major shareholders. The publisher Walther de Gruyter, who had substantial shares in the Gutehoffnungshütte (GHH) and who felt pressed by tax problems—a good deal more pressed than he felt about the complaints of authors about his honoraria—thought it was time to tell General Director Reusch "a thing or two" at the beginning of 1923. He insisted that the dividend policy had to be changed. The problem was not simply the GHH, but rather the dividend policy pursued throughout the business world since 1918, which in de Gruyter's view was being dictated by the "overheated but work-shy . . . soul of the people." De Gruyter, in a comparison by no means unique, demonstrated the "absurdities" of the practice of paying dividends in watered-down form on past profits by comparing the earnings of GHH stockholders and workers. The former had received a dividend of 57.6 million marks for the business year 1921–1922 in January 1923. Using January as a base, the GHH was paying its forty thousand blue- and white-collar workers 28.8 billion marks a year. The stockholders were thus getting 0.2 percent of the wages and salaries paid to GHH employees. In de Gruy-

ter's view, this was "an expropriation policy with the most serious social and general consequences." As a solution, de Gruyter proposed that the stockholders be paid a dividend for 1922–1923 that was many times that of the previous year and that they be granted an interest-free loan against it of a few hundred percent of their nominal share holdings. This would provide stockholders with the kind of relief that would make them ready to sacrifice higher dividends for the GHH again in better times.[100]

What appeared on the horizon was not better times. Not only were export markets deteriorating while the opportunities on the domestic market were also diminishing, but hopeful possibilities for developing new markets abroad also seemed to be collapsing. The great plans for German development projects in Russia and trade with the Russians are a good illustration of the brutal manner in which the hyperinflation cut off the progress of the German industrial and commercial reconstruction effort. Such projects could only be operated on the basis of credits to the Soviet Union, an increasingly dubious proposition by the summer of 1922 because of the illness of Lenin and the increasing influence of radical elements. Nevertheless, in agreeing with his fellow industrialists that the project had to be given up for the moment, Stinnes felt compelled to comment that "it is a shame that the worsening of the economic situation and of the purchasing power of the mark in Germany is bringing all foreign projects to a standstill."[101]

But then what projects would remain? Was Germany to return to the condition of 1918–1919, when industry depended upon state contracts to maintain employment and keep the economy going? Something like this was already happening in certain areas, and the Stinnes–Lubersac Agreement and growing interest of certain branches of industry on reconstruction contracts were simply new variations on the familiar theme of a privatized "productive unemployment insurance" based on state subsidization. This was especially evident in the railroad-car industry, which was largely occupied with government contracts and reconstruction contracts in the fall of 1922, but a substantial portion of the contracts of the Siemens concern at this time also came from the state.

Just as Stinnes rallied businessmen to participate in the reparations-in-kind program in Bavaria in September, so in the following month he sought to mobilize industry in the Rhineland and the Ruhr to take up his offer to broker the reconstruction contracts. He himself viewed the reconstruction contracts as a means to take up some of the slack created by the cessation or reduction of construction work in Germany. The Stinnes–Lubersac Agreement, however, was not only important itself but also served as a clarion call, so that by November 1922, twelve similar agreements had been concluded, and firms were competing with one another in France, Belgium, Italy, and Yugoslavia to get contracts. The costs of this increasingly uncontrollable enthusiasm for reparations in kind, however, could only be paid by the state and thus constituted an inflationary form of productive activity. As one of Reusch's directors bluntly put the matter, "Stinnes probably hardly thought that his agreement with Lubersac, which is exclusively concerned with the destroyed territories of Northern France, would have such an effect. If it continues to go on, our economy will drown in a flood of paper."[102]

This was not to be the only or the last time that one of Stinnes's grandiose ideas was to grow over his head, as was being amply demonstrated at the end of 1922 by the Alpine Montangesellschaft which, thanks to mistakes in the handling of its foreign-exchange holdings and bad management, was unusually hard hit by the economic crisis that struck Austria as the krone began to stabilize in anticipation of the action by the League of Nations to save Austria. Neither Stinnes nor his Italian counterpart in the control of the Alpine, Camillo Castiglioni, were prepared to let their investment sink, however, and new funds were poured in despite the nervousness of Vögler and Siemens, who feared that the entire enterprise was a bottomless pit. Stinnes, however, saw a bottom to the pit, and here, as in so many things, Austria served as Germany's future writ small.[103]

Stinnes certainly held management responsible for the various mishaps that had befallen the firm, and his chief complaint was that it had permitted productivity and profitability to drop. A "cleansing operation" (*Säuberungsarbeit*) was necessary, and this required that "the workers and the officials must be cleaned out,

costs must be reduced at least 20 percent."[104] The organized workers at the Alpine, apparently working under the illusion that Stinnes would prove more sympathetic than Castiglioni and the Austrian management, frequently sought to appeal to Stinnes over their heads. In early December, they composed a memorandum pointing to the high unemployment and low wages at the company and asking that, instead of the working day being lengthened to twelve hours in the continuously operating factories, the workers be put on four-hour shifts so as to provide employment. A response was composed to be issued in Stinnes's name which was designed to destroy further illusions about Stinnes's position and which certainly was in the spirit of Stinnes's intentions at this time. It began by pointing out that Austria was going through its present crisis because the Austrian people and state had been consuming more than they had been producing since the war. The eight-hour day and social laws as well as low productivity made Austria uncompetitive:

Against this there is only *one* cure, reducing the cost of production through increased work, better utilization of the work force, and efficient organization of the plants. Reduction of wages must be numbered among the austerity measures. Under the present circumstances, wages must be as low as possible for the unit of time worked, and [the wage] can be increased through more work time and greater labor intensity.[105]

There was no room, therefore, for programs which called for the employment of more workers than necessary while reducing the hours of work. This could only lead to collapse, not to economic reconstruction.

The message was clear. The burden of reconstruction rested upon the workers now, and this was precisely the point being made increasingly in Germany while it was beginning to be implemented in Austria. Stinnes was hardly the only person making it; he was just arguing for it more loudly, clearly, and consequentially than most others. His views were easily echoed by less strident voices. Thus, an American observer analyzing the industrial outlook in Germany in December 1922 concluded with the question, "shall labor solve the problem?" and replied:

Naturally organized labor as a unit is not yet ready to forego the eight-hour day. This was an achievement of the revolution of 1918 and it will not be easily surrendered, but there can be little doubt that a reversal to longer working hours will yet be reached. . . . The greatest of the trades unions, the Allgemeiner Deutscher Gewerkschaftsbund . . . will not readily yield unless or until the industrial situation becomes so acute from lack of orders and prohibitive prices of raw materials that closing down of works becomes obligatory. As that course is unfortunately no vague hypothesis of a remote future the necessary incentive to labor to concede the point of length of working hours may not improbably be forthcoming in time to avert a catastrophe. At all events, without labor's willing cooperation and sacrifice, it may be, of some of its cherished ideals, no action by the national government can bring about the industrial recovery which must come to Germany before it will regain the confidence of foreign peoples.[106]

The Social Crisis

How is one to interpret this concentration on the problem of working-class productivity at this stage of the inflation? In the space of only four years, the most basic achievements of the working class in the German Revolution were being challenged, and a powerful consensus was emerging outside working-class circles that labor would have to make massive sacrifices if the nation were to survive economically. The atmosphere surrounding the discussion of the hours-of-work question, the other social gains of labor, and its wage levels makes it impossible to overlook the strong element of social resentment that was involved. The "intellectual workers" and the *Mittelstand* deeply resented the relative deterioration of their economic position. Affection for the proletariat did not grow with proletarianization, but rather the contrary feeling developed. These groups, however, had little love for the capitalists either, and the interpretation of employer militancy has to be seen in somewhat different terms. The simplest explanation is that capitalists—and capitalism—are necessarily exploitative and that the employers were out to bleed the workers dry. This idea received its most extreme expression in a short story of Heinrich Mann, "Kobes" (1925), a veritable caricature of Hugo Stinnes, in which the propaganda chief of a concern roundly declares: "The *Mittelstand* has delivered what it was worth. Honored be its memory. But now more work has to be done. The workers' time has come. They have more than only money to lose to us. Twenty hours daily

work!"[107] While there certainly is no evidence that Stinnes or any other major industrialists were so deliberately and consciously manipulative and cynical, reliable testimony suggesting a determination to instrumentalize the plight of labor to achieve employer goals of longer hours for less pay does exist. In October 1922, the British Commercial Secretary in Berlin, Thelwall, after noting the growing inability of the workers to keep up with prices and the danger of riots and strikes, went on to remark that "it must not be forgotten that the German employer, aided by certain political elements, still wishes to obtain greater ascendancy over the working classes and to strike a further blow at social democracy. In his opinion one of the best means of achieving this end is to so reduce the working classes by starvation misery that they will agree to almost any terms. A deliberate provocation of conflict from the employer's side may, therefore, also be looked for, should the opportunity seem favorable to him."[108]

The evidence for such interpretations, however, is very mixed, and while employers sensitive to currents of public opinion certainly were aware of the growing weakness of labor's position in the course of the galloping inflation and hyperinflation and were increasingly inclined to take advantage of the situation, both Mann and Thelwall were overstating the rapacity of the employers. In so doing, they underestimated the role of worker militancy as an incentive to employer mobilization but also as a deterrence to employer overestimation of what was possible.

This was amply demonstrated in south Germany in the winter and spring of 1922, when workers and employers in the metal industry fought a bitter and protracted battle over the employer demand that workers surrender the forty-six-hour work week they had enjoyed since the Revolution and accept the forty-eight-hour work week commonplace throughout most of the country. The peculiarity of the situation in this region was that workers had enjoyed a free Saturday afternoon before the war on a forty-eight-hour week and were able to impose a reduced work week during the Revolution on the grounds that they also were entitled to achieve some reduction of working time. The arrangement had always been a source of irritation to employers, but the conflict really began to heat up in the fall of 1921 when the industry found itself with many export orders and an insufficient number of skilled workers. Under the existing labor contracts, employers could ask for two hours overtime if they could demonstrate pressing reasons and secure the approval of the factory council. When seeking to exercise this right, however, they found workers either unwilling to do the overtime or only willing to do it if wage concessions were made. Not without justification, therefore, they sought to escape dependence on the goodwill of workers for overtime work by making concessions on wages, overtime pay, and vacation pay dependent on the installation of a forty-eight-hour work week. If workers wished to retain the free Saturday afternoon, then they would have to work longer than eight hours on some week-days.[109]

Employers rapidly discovered, however, that the rank-and-file workers were even more adamant about working time than the trade-union leaders. The workers not only voted overwhelmingly against proposed contracts increasing working hours but also readily participated in selective strikes when the employers held their ground. The employers, with the strong support of their national organizations and encouraged both by misinformation suggesting that it was the trade unions which had stirred up the workers and by a more accurate sense that public sentiment was turning against the workers, then proceeded to lock out some 250,000 metal workers in the spring of 1922. Both sides demonstrated extraordinary tenacity, and the deadlock was only broken in May 1922 thanks to the arbitration of the Reich Labor Ministry and the Bavarian Social Ministry in a scarcely veiled victory for the employers on the hours-of-work question. The trade-union effort had suffered from the divisions between the Socialist DMV, the effectiveness of which was undermined by Communist propaganda and activity, and the Christian and Hirsch-Duncker unions. The latter unions were more compromising from the outset and recognized that public opinion was against the workers.[110]

From the Socialist perspective, however, more was at stake. They correctly recognized that the struggle would spread to other areas and industries in which forty-six hours were being worked and that the cause of the workers involved had been badly compromised by the outcome of the metal-industry conflict. Thus, in the summer of 1922, the dispute over this issue in the bookbinding industry was concluded with an industry-wide arbitration decision under the chairmanship of no less prestigious a personage than Wichard von Moellendorff. The board decided unequivocally in favor of the employers. The paper manufacturing industry took advantage of this decision to abolish Saturday work and add forty-eight minutes on to weekday work, arguing with considerable cogency that it made more sense to operate efficiently five days a week then to operate uneconomically for four hours on Saturday when time was lost in starting and heating the machines for only half a day. If the textile workers were treated more favorably by another arbitration board, it was probably because of the large numbers of women and youth employed in the industry. The employers refused to accept the decision, characterizing it as a surrender to the workers in contradiction to the real views of the neutral government officials appointed to the board. The language of the decision in truth did not carry much conviction, and the primary object of the decision appears to have been to buy a year of tranquility in the industry. If so, it was unlikely to be very successful since the employer organization urged its members to take up the struggle on the district level.[111]

What worried Socialist union leaders most about these conflicts was that the lengthening of weekday work beyond eight hours in order to preserve the free Saturday afternoon seemed to drive a wedge into the maximal eight-hour workday established under the Stinnes–Legien Agreement. These anxieties had been heightened by government proposals for an hours-of-work law submitted back in November 1920, which stressed the forty-eight-hour week rather than the eight-hour day and was very generous in its setting of the conditions under which overtime might be enforced by the Labor Minister and by employers. Since that time, the trade unions had restructured the projected legislation in lengthy meetings in the Reich Economic Council between November 1921 and December 1922. They opposed the separate legislation for blue- and white-collar workers in the government proposals and insisted on a more rigorous enforcement of the eight-hour-day principle. While accepting the necessity of some overtime and greater flexibility, they demanded that exceptions require factory-council approval or that they be written into labor contracts. It was a measure of the tension and deadlock between trade-union and employer views that the trade-union proposal emerged triumphant from the Social Policy Committee of the RWR by a very thin majority in December 1922, while the employer version was voted for by a similarly thin majority of the RWR plenum.[112]

Most troubling about the entire discussion in 1922, however, was that while workers were desperately trying to hold on to the eight-hour day, the support for the eight-hour day was collapsing, not simply under the weight of the attacks of employers but also because of a lack of public support. As Leipart admitted three years later: "You know that the attacks did not simply come from the employers. Much more important was that, it was almost a religious belief that went through the entire people into the ranks of the workers themselves that the German people could only be saved in its distress by more work."[113] It was bad enough that so influential an expert on labor problems and social policy as the chairman of the Society for Social Reform, Heinrich Herkner, should choose Stinnes's *DAZ* to come out sharply against the harmful effects of the eight-hour day and the trade-union tactics in December 1922, but it was even more depressing for trade unionists to hear similar words from an old Socialist trade unionist like Max Cohen in the RWR. Cohen pointed out that just as Robert Schmidt had declared both his continued belief in socialization and his conviction that the experiment was impossible under existing conditions at the most recent SPD Party Congress, so he, despite his belief in not only the eight- but even the seven-hour day, had to say quite openly that

despite this conviction, I will always take the position that the eight-hour day be broken through as frequently as possible. (Interjection: Out of high regard for the *Schieber!*)—Not out of high regard for the *Schieber*, but out of high regard for the German people, who in its immense distress cannot make due

with the eight-hour day. (Very true!) . . . And I must say that I wonder about the courage of my compatriots, who now, where the dollar is climbing to such heights, where each person feels that, if we do not bring about a change, we are steering toward a collapse into which we will all be drawn in—I wonder about the courage of those who believe that things can be saved with a reduction of productive performance.[114]

Cohen's Socialist colleagues were also filled with wonder at what they took to be his suggestion that the workers were responsible for the situation, and while Cohen denied that he had said any such thing, the implication at the minimum was that the workers would be responsible if they did not come to terms on the hours-of-work question. Under the conditions of 1922, it mattered very little if both trade unionists and even a few employers, like Robert Bosch, could argue that hours of work were not as important as increasing productivity through rationalization and better use of the eight-hour day, at least in the more advanced industries.[115]

The important point was that people believed that more work was either *the* key or an important key to saving the situation, and it followed from this that workers were being stubborn, self-serving, and exploitative in rejecting this solution. The heavy industrialists and leading industrial leaders from other branches who supported them received a positive reception for their position on the eight-hour day because there was a general consensus that productivity was the crucial problem and there was not enough time to solve the problem by rationalization. Their position was made all the stronger by the sense that trade-union leaders who rigidly stuck to the eight-hour day really did not care about rationalization or efficiency. It was difficult to understand, for example, why a Socialist trade unionist from the paper industry, Stühler, would not accept a forty-eight-hour work week divided over five days that would provide workers with a full two-day weekend. Making reference to the Socialists associated with the *Sozialistische Monatshefte*, who were more economically oriented in their thinking, an employer organization official pointed out that "thus party dogma stands above everything even for Herr Stühler, even if the economy is ruined by it. Economically minded Socialists like Julius Kaliski, Cohen-

Reuss, Lindemann, Dr. Striemer, with their proposals concerning the eight-hour day based on economic reflections are not listened to; they are described as traitors to the workers, and it would not be surprising if they were soon thrown out of the party."[116]

The Social Democrats and trade unionists were too internally divided and too much off balance and on the defensive to throw such persons out of the party for arguing, in effect, that the schematic eight-hour day was a poor first line of defense against the mounting assault on the eight-hour day. They themselves, for example, had supported overtime work in the coal-mining industry for the sake of increased production and they were fully aware that their control over the rank and file was diminishing in more ways than one. If many workers opposed the slightest concession on the hours-of-work question, others, especially older married workers, were often willing to do overtime work. Indeed, the "wild" overtime shifts performed by such miners prior to the overtime agreement in the mining industry of August 1922 had proven more productive than the overtime performed by formal agreement. The overtime thus led "to the increased earnings of a number of workers, but . . . also to a not insignificant increase in the costs of the mines without bringing any advantage to the general public worth mentioning."[117] Even if the overtime agreement showed better results toward the end of the year, the inadequate productivity and the high cost of English coal imports needed to compensate for the shortfall provided the industrialists with strong arguing points against not only the current hours-of-work policy but also against the wage policy of the trade unions and the government. Indeed, the crucial

question during the last weeks before the Ruhr occupation was whether the coal mine owners could succeed in holding the line on wages in the coal-mining industry and thereby propel other industries to follow their example in an effort to maintain German competitiveness.

This effort, aborted by the Ruhr occupation, must first be comprehended in the context of the preceding months of debate and uncertainty about what to do about the level of wages and salaries in the ranks of industry, labor, and government. Employer attacks on the level of worker wages were hardly a novelty, but they had been repeatedly parried, so to speak, by political conditions as well as the circumstances of the inflation, and they were even more frustrated by the first months of the hyperinflation. The spontaneous wage movement at the beginning of the galloping inflation in August 1921 was a major setback to employer efforts to stabilize or reduce wages during the relative stabilization. Sporadic efforts to keep wages under control by no means ceased, however. At the end of the lockout in the south German metal industry in late May, for example, employers in Württemberg, to the surprise of both workers and authorities, showed great reluctance to make a generous financial settlement on the grounds that "the high point of the boom had actually passed during the strike."[118] The fate of such attempts to hold back wage increases once the hyperinflation had struck, however, is well demonstrated by the huge and increasingly more frequent nominal wage increases in the major industries of Württemberg (see Table 30). For industries filled with export orders, as was the case in Württemberg, or heavily engaged in construction during the summer building season, there was a premium on pro-

Table 30. Hourly Wages in the Major Industries of Württemberg, January 1914, January–October 1922

(in paper marks)

	1914	1922			
	Jan. 1	Jan. 31	July 1	Oct. 1	Oct. 4–24
Construction	0.64	12.20	32.00	100.00	120.00
Metals	0.60	10.33	22.85	78.00	98.50
Timber & Wood	0.62	11.80	24.50	80.00	98.00
Textiles	0.60	9.50	20.60	73.00	93.00

Source: "Economic Conditions During the Quarter Ended September 30, 1922," of Oct. 25, 1922, NA, 862.50/470.

duction and a great reluctance to quibble over wage levels. On the one hand, wage increases were simply passed off in higher prices, so that, for example, tires ordered in early September for eleven thousand marks each were sold three weeks later for twenty-five thousand marks each. On the other hand, most employers seemed to recognize the need to provide their workers with the minimum salaries needed to keep up with the rising cost of living. The average cost of living for a family of five in Stuttgart had risen 9.4 times between January and the end of September 1922, while the hourly wage of workers had increased by between 6.7 and 8.6 times. If more than one member of the family were working and if overtime were available, then weekly earnings probably enabled such a family to manage. The greatest threat to the standard of living undoubtedly came from the increased short time at the end of September caused by raw-materials shortages, which involved the loss of as much as two or three workdays.[119]

Certainly one could find instances, such as the chauffeur of the British General Consul in Munich who was married and had one child, where wages more or less kept up with prices in 1922 and the family was able to buy some butter and meat. The workings of the hyperinflation, however, are well reflected in the differing appreciations of this chauffeur's situation in August and November 1922. In the former month, Consul Seeds commented that

the working classes do not suffer to the extent which certain foreign observers are inclined to believe. Were it not so, they would not be in a position to devote to comparatively expensive amusements the portion of their wages which they do at present. The consumption of food has certainly decreased, but some German physicians admit that a reduction in the quantities consumed in prewar days is rather salutary than otherwise.[120]

In November, he was much less casual about the diet of the working classes:

It is of course a truism that the prewar standard of living has long been beyond the reach of the great mass of the population and such comparisons are in my opinion of no practical use. What is of importance at the present moment is the fact that the wages now generally paid here . . . could not meet even the modest food requirements of my chauffeur's small family, let alone such items as rent, clothes, heating and

taxes. To arrive at some sort of balance it would be necessary to deduct . . . not only butter, which must be taken as an unjustifiable luxury in present conditions, but also all expenditure . . . on meat and sausages while considerably reducing some of the remaining necessaries.[121]

The situation of workers in the last months of 1922, while certainly relatively better than that of persons in the *Mittelstand*, constituted a serious setback in the recovery of the economic position of the working class, such as it was, since the war. The sources are unanimous on this point, whether for chemical-industry workers and printers in Berlin (see Table 31), railway workers and Ruhr miners (see Table 32), or textile workers (see Table 33).[122] Berlin workers, both skilled and unskilled, were being pushed back to or below the subsistence level, as were most of their counterparts throughout the country. This includes the miners, whose need for overtime and strong tendency to seek work in the construction industry during the building boom earlier in the year and then to seek work in the Netherlands to the great detriment of production in the last months of 1922 becomes quite explicable once the real wages of this allegedly most-favored group of workers is shown up for what it was.[123]

The situation was not without its frustrations for employers, however, since the hyperinfla-

Table 31. The Weekly Wage of an Unskilled and Skilled Chemical-Industry Worker and a Printer in Berlin in 1922 in Relation to the Minimum Existence Requirement for a Married Couple with One Child
(requirement = 100)

| | Chemical Worker | | |
	Unskilled	Skilled	Printer
January	114.24	119.77	115.69
February	115.29	121.21	111.96
March	103.45	108.88	94.09
April	105.35	110.65	97.17
May	118.68	124.78	107.80
June	110.20	115.97	105.00
July	90.17	98.71	85.74
August	78.16	85.68	63.48
September	79.60	87.29	63.45
October	69.84	76.44	65.82
November	58.72	64.41	51.49
December	69.39	76.11	58.20

Source: Rudolf Meerwarth, "Zur neuesten Entwicklung der Löhne," *Zeitschrift des Preußischen Statistischen Landesamts 1922/23* 67 (Berlin, 1923), p. 339.

Table 32. Average Real Weekly Wages
of Railway Workers and Ruhr Miners as
Per Collective Agreements in 1922
(1913 = 100)

| | Railway Workers | | Ruhr Hewers and Haulers |
	Skilled	Unskilled	
January	69.3	93.5	83.1
February	58.6	79.0	76.8
March	49.4	66.7	76.3
April	61.8	84.6	73.8
May	75.3	102.0	80.7
June	78.4	106.8	75.7
July	70.9	96.5	69.5
August	66.3	91.0	59.1
September	83.4	114.4	75.6
October	53.3	73.5	51.6
November	48.5	66.9	52.6
December	55.0	76.2	62.2

Source: Carl-Ludwig Holtfrerich, *The German Inflation 1914–
1923. Causes and Effects in International Perspective* (Berlin &
New York, 1986), p. 234.

tion encouraged *Gleichmacherei*, the leveling
of differentials against which they had been protesting since the war. This was a view shared by
the Labor Ministry, and even trade unionists
often were concerned to maintain skill differentials as well as sex and age differentials. The
situation of unskilled workers in the railroads
certainly fueled the criticisms of the government management of that industry, but the situation in the textile industry also showed how
the problem of providing workers with minimum wages needed to live undermined all efforts to reestablish strong differentials. In the
case of the textile industry, this does not, to be
sure, entirely explain the relative advantage enjoyed by female workers, a phenomenon re-

Table 33. The Real Weekly Wages of Skilled
and Unskilled Male and Female Textile
Workers in 1922
(1913 = 100)

| | Skilled Workers | | Unskilled Workers | |
	Male	Female	Male	Female
April	85.5	94.7	88.9	95.5
July	84.9	96.1	93.2	99.2
October	70.3	81.5	76.1	83.2
November	61.5	71.0	65.9	71.6
December	74.6	86.5	81.0	91.2

Source: Statistisches Reichsamt, Zahlen zur Geldentwertung in
Deutschland 1914 bis 1923 [Sonderheft 1 zu *Wirtschaft und Statistik*, Bd. 5] (Berlin, 1925), p. 42.

sulting from the fact that two-thirds of the
workers employed in the industry were women.
Thus, women in this industry received an average of 70 to 85 percent of the male wage,
whereas the percentages of the male wage were
60 to 65 percent in the chemical industry, 60 to
68 percent in the wood and metal industries,
and 55 to 72 percent in the paper-products industries. The pressure to raise the relative wage
levels of female workers was increasing, however, and this, too, worried employers.[124]

Under these conditions, it was difficult to
conduct a very reflective wage policy in daily
practice. The longstanding debate over the "social wage" became even more complicated and
confused than it had been during the previous
years. Opinions on the "social wage" were as
sharply divided as ever within the ranks of industry and labor. Officially, both sides favored
wages based on performance rather than family
situation. As the employer organization for the
paper and wood-products industries pointed
out, however,

The abnormal conditions under which we are compelled to live also require extraordinary measures.
Undoubtedly, it is significantly more difficult for a
married worker to hold out with himself and his family under the present cost of living than the unmarried worker. So long as the wages are so strongly influenced by the increased prices, it seems appropriate
in any case to give special consideration to family fathers in the wage system. In actuality they are taken
into account in almost all the group collective wage
agreements today. Even in the ranks of the free trade
unions, the position on the social wage is not uniform; one finds in the trade-union press many voices
which are for a social compensation under the existing circumstances. Despite this, the official position
of the free trade unions against the social wage has
been retained.[125]

This was true, and the official reason for this opposition—namely, that the social wage would
encourage employers to let go or refuse to hire
older workers—also remained the paramount
official basis of the trade-union position. In
some contradiction to this argument, however,
was the fact that many employers showed a
preference for older, married workers because
they were more stable and reliable. It was not
uninteresting that in one wage negotiation, the
ADGB union representative argued against a
proposed doubling of the family supplements
on the grounds that the employers were thereby

creating a "Praetorian Guard," and that an ar- bitration proposal thought too modest by the unions was accepted by the Berlin metal work- ers largely thanks to the vote of the married workers who had been won over by the high family supplements.[126]

While it is difficult to determine the extent to which such "egotistical" motives influenced the trade unionists who opposed the social wage, ADGB leaders, including Leipart, were fully aware that the unions were being criticized for an "unsocial wage policy."[127] Nevertheless, he and the majority of the leadership of the ADGB confirmed their opposition to the social wage in late November 1922, insisting that it was one thing to differentiate between skilled and un- skilled workers and between older experienced and younger inexperienced workers and quite another to provide a wage based on family cir- cumstances. An adequate minimum wage would deal with the social component of the wage problem, but a social wage would endan- ger productivity, expose older workers to firing in an economic crisis, and alienate the single workers. Leipart argued that many single work- ers did in fact support family members, that their household costs were no less than those of workers with a family and often more, and that many worker families enjoyed the benefit of having more than one person employed. In re- sponse to arguments, especially but not exclu- sively from representatives of the white-collar- worker unions, to the effect that the social wage was too widespread to eliminate and that im- mense misery would be created if it were dis- mantled, Leipart responded that the very fact that the system was so widespread and could later be used to reduce wages for all workers provided an incentive to get rid of the social wage. Insofar as fathers of families faced a social problem because of the size of their support ob- ligations, Leipart argued, it was the responsibil- ity of the state to assist through tax relief and so- cial welfare.

By the end of 1922, however, the social wage was a very difficult system to eliminate, since it was to be found in many of the major industries despite the strong reservations of employers. In the Berlin metal industry, the wage of a married skilled, semi-skilled, and unskilled worker with one child exceeded that of the unmarried

worker by, respectively, 6.48, 7.06, and 8.02 percent. Furthermore, in order to neutralize ar- guments that the system would later be used to eliminate married workers, the Berlin metal in- dustrialists and some in other industries intro- duced equalization funds under which all member firms contributed an equal amount for the additional support of married family men without regard to the actual number of single and married men they employed. The logic of employers who accepted such a system was not very different from that of the influential trade- union leader Alexander Knoll, who rejected Leipart's argumentation by pointing out that "wages today make it impossible for a family fa- ther to eat his fill. Adequate pay is not to be had today. For this reason the social wage provides worthwhile help. Equalization with respect to taxation and a favored social treatment of the family father through public means is unthink- able in the present situation."[128]

Here, as in so many other areas, however, hy- perinflation was changing the terms of the dis- cussion. The debate over the social wage was becoming secondary to the battle over adapting wages to hyperinflation through sliding-scale wages and the "gold wage." Although govern- ment cost-of-living statistics had been regularly used in wage negotiations since February 1920, both employer and worker organizations op- posed the automatic adjustment of wages to a cost-of-living index. Here, as in the case of the social wage, opinions were divided, and prac- tice deviated from the official position in both camps. The argument for indexation was that it saved the time and energy required by the ne- gotiations conducted every two to four weeks in most industries, through which wages were more or less adjusted to the changed cost of liv- ing anyway. There was a whole list of argu- ments against indexation, however, many of which were shared by both sides. The most im- portant was that it would destroy all interest in keeping prices under control. Furthermore, there were immense difficulties in creating a proper index. If done schematically, it would fail to take the special problems of individual industries and local circumstances into ac- count. If done on a more individual or local basis, it would lead to difficult negotiations and conflicts over the index which would end up being no less unpleasant and time consuming than what was taking place anyway. Employers questioned whether it really would be possible to lower wages if the cost of living receded and saw the entire system as a means of setting wages in favor of the workers. Trade unionists opposed to the system insisted that it was nothing more or less than an installation of subsistence wages.[129]

The evidence for and against the sliding-scale system was indeed very mixed. Labor Minister Brauns had come out in support of sliding-scale wages in February 1922, and much attention was paid to the experience with the system on a national scale in Austria, where it had been introduced in late 1921 to compensate workers for the elimination of food subsidies, and in the German cities of Flensburg, Breslau, and Brandenburg, which had chosen to experiment with it. In Austria, the wage supplements were determined by an employer–labor Index Commission created under government auspices. Originally meant as a guide for wages where collective labor agreements did not exist, the method was rapidly taken over not only by the government but also by various private industries. The Austrian trade unions had considerable experience in working out indices for the increased cost of living, and under their influence, the indices established by such commissions tended to be higher than those set forth by the Austrian Federal Statistical Office. As the Austrian hyperinflationary crisis rapidly developed in 1922 and was accompanied by signs of economic crisis and growing unemployment, the indices were criticized by employers for being too high, and, most important, employers claimed they could not stay in operation if the wages continued to be so schematically adjusted. They pointed out that, unlike the state, they could not print money. The entire system was in crisis by September 1922, when worker dissatisfaction led to a strike threat on the part of two hundred thousand Austrian metal-industry workers and employees. This was finally settled in a compromise under which the workers accepted a supplement less than that called for by the index. The trade-union decision was purely pragmatic. The workers would have lost more in a strike than they would have gained,

and there was a general fear that a massive strike by the metal workers would spread to the rest of industry and trade and would jeopardize the Austrian negotiations for a League of Nations loan in Geneva. A decision to strike also had tactical dangers. The promising negotiations in Geneva had stabilized the inflation somewhat, and the union leaders feared that a successful struggle to rigidify the application of the index could soon become the foundation for a reduction of wages. In short, the Austrian experience provided arguments for all sides of the indexation question, as did the Flensburg experiment, where employers in the transport industry claimed they could no longer afford full indexation and workers felt unable to accept a pay cut in March 1922 when prices dropped slightly. Generally speaking, employers were more critical than trade unionists, but both sides viewed the system with great skepticism, while the Society for Social Reform first supported and then opposed sliding-scale wages.[130]

The new and touchiest issue that developed as a consequence of the hyperinflation, however, was the idea of the gold wage and the sometimes related notion of world-market wages. The context and logic of the call for a valorized "gold" wage was well described by one of its advocates:

The battle for a sliding-scale wage is bogging down. A struggle for a gold wage begins. Here and there it is already demanded by the workers. The goal of wage stabilization has remained the same, only the technical means of the stabilization is different. With the sliding-scale wage there is the adjustment of prices to necessary goods; with the gold wage, there is the fixing of wages in peacetime marks which will be paid out in paper marks according to the price of the golden twenty mark piece! The model is Stinnes, who sets twenty gold pfennig per line for advertisements in his *Deutsche Allgemeine Zeitung*. The labor market only wants to follow the market for goods. The industrialist calculates in dollars; the wholesaler demands his price with a supplement based on the worth of the mark on the payment due date; the retailer strives for reproduction cost prices. In the Reich Economic Council, a memorandum of the Cologne Professor Schmalenbach is discussed, which proposes replacing the paper-mark balance required by the commercial law with a gold mark balance. All these strivings will only be helpful to the national economy if each group does not have only its own interest in mind, but rather when the entire means of measuring value, be it for prices, or wages, or taxes, will be uniform.[131]

Here, as in the case of the sliding-scale wage, it was a measure of the novelty of the hyperinflation and the general uncertainty it produced that the Society for Social Reform's organ, *Soziale Praxis*, while stating its opposition to the gold wage, felt compelled to provide considerable space to its advocates as well as to its critics.

In September, *Soziale Praxis* published a proposal by Bührer, the Mayor of Offenburg, urging that wages be pegged to the notation of the dollar. Bührer made it clear that he was no advocate of world-market wages or of the reinstallation of prewar wage levels. In his view, the impoverishment of the country made a return to prewar wages and salaries impossible, but both productivity and social peace did require a "simple but sufficient" income for workers and civil servants based on some generally accepted measure of value.[132] As in the *Soziale Praxis*, so in the official organ of the ADGB, the *Correspondenzblatt*, space was given to the cause of valorized wages. In this case, the advocate was the influential head of the Woodworkers' Union, Fritz Tarnow, who also denied that he was supporting world-market wages or even that he wished a return to prewar wages. He argued that the existing real wages of workers had to be guaranteed and they needed protection against getting more and more worthless paper while all other groups in society valorized their prices.[133]

The arguments against this position both within and outside the trade unions, however, were still overwhelming. There was, of course, the standard argument that using the dollar value of the mark in domestic transactions would effectively eliminate the mark as a unit of value and promote a vast increase in the number of paper marks needed. More important, the purchasing power of the mark was still higher in Germany than it was abroad, and the effect of wage payments in dollars or gold would be to drive the entire economy up to world-market levels. Employers were in no position to pay such wages, and the result would be an economic collapse in which Germany would lose its remaining export advantages and be unable

to sell at home as well. As might be expected, the peak employer organization, the VdA, was strongly opposed to the valorization of wages. While appropriating many of the arguments used by trade union and other critics of the gold wage, Dr. Meissinger, who managed the VdA Wage Policy Committee (*Tarifausschuß*), was especially hostile to those who made a comparison between "reproduction prices" and "reproduction cost wages":

The businessman who thinks in national economic and moral terms has on his own begun to determine the practical effects of the reproduction price that crosses the border into profiteering and has thus committed himself to the maintenance of the purchasing power of the mark. The reproduction price should keep plants in operation and keep the economy functioning for the general good without increasing the income available for the personal use of the employer beyond that which is claimed by the workers in each wage increase. A reproduction wage . . . would raise the portion of the wage costs that is still acceptable to keep the plants operating beyond the present real wages and one-sidedly favor the workers over the remaining portion of the population. The reproduction wage would not only guarantee the present but also the future wage. Every such guarantee, which is tantamount to an automatic adjustment of wages, is impossible for us. The public must finally realize that in a politically and economically prostrate state, neither real wages nor the blossoming economy required can be guaranteed without at the same time sealing the doom of the economy.[134]

Meissinger's reference to businessmen who thought in "national economic and moral terms" in their setting of prices carried with it the implication that not all businessmen were so self-restrained, and he and like-minded businessmen and officials in the VdA were fully aware that disciplining the labor force required a considerable amount of self-discipline in industry and that this could not be taken quite so much for granted as his remarks implied. The VdA paid close attention to efforts to reduce costs and wages among Germany's competitors and was convinced that such efforts had to be matched in Germany. Each move in the direction of relative stabilization presented a potential crisis in Germany because of the way in which wages and other costs were approaching world-market levels, and it was a fundamental tenet of VdA policy to maintain the higher domestic purchasing power of the mark relative to its value abroad. Special attention was necessarily directed toward the most basic costs of food and transport, and each rise in prices or in freight rates was noted with alarm and concern. At the same time, the VdA worried about rising prices for agricultural products and the growing insistence of the farmers on a higher price for their deliveries under the grain levy. In short, the VdA had been anticipating a crisis of wage policy because of Germany's inability to contain domestic costs.[135]

What had been expected since the spring became a reality in September when, the VdA argued, wage increases, especially in coal mining, seemed to exceed the increased cost of living. The VdA claimed that the workers were the one group whose wages had reached prewar levels while productivity remained well below that of 1913. More overtime and piecework were proclaimed necessary, as well as greater differentiation in the wages of skilled and unskilled and especially younger and older workers, and the employer organizations were urged to coordinate their granting of wage increases with one another on both branch and district levels. An appeal for "greater discipline among the employers" was made. They were urged to avoid secret agreements with their workers exceeding official wage contracts as well as provisions for retroactive payments in new wage contracts, and they were warned especially against agreeing to the prepayment of wages or salaries.[136]

Underlying this call for discipline was a considerable conflict within employer ranks that paralleled the struggle among the trade-union leaders between those who called for restraint and those who felt that there was no longer any point in trying to control prices and wages. A simple political analysis of these positions is not possible for either camp. Tarnow was not a radical trade unionist anymore than his opponents on the question of the gold wage, while metalworker leader Dißmann opposed both the sliding-scale wage and the social wage and argued, very much against the more economically oriented position of the leading trade unionists, that the principle of class struggle had to guide the wage demands of the unions. Similarly, Stinnes supported pricing on the basis of repro-

duction costs and was basically willing to see paper-mark wages rise with prices, but this hardly suggested that he was "soft" on labor anymore than his strong stand on working hours made him "harder" on labor than some of his less outspoken and noisy colleagues. In fact, many of those who disagreed with Stinnes on matters of prices and wages were downright conservative and even reactionary and, in contrast to Stinnes, were opposed to the eight-hour day as a matter of principle rather than as an economic necessity. The Wage Policy Committee of the VdA, which had sent out policy instructions to its members in late September, issued at the same time a statement drawn up by Meissinger which was highly critical of the manner in which industry, commerce, and agriculture were driving up prices, calculating in foreign currencies, and, more generally, undermining the internal purchasing power of the mark. Meissinger argued that a continuation of these policies made the development of a wage policy by the VdA impossible and was largely responsible for the call for gold-mark wages. The statement blamed employers for showing "indifference" to the wage question and to the guidelines of the VdA, thus making it possible for both the government and the people to think that they could return to the prewar standard of living without greatly increasing productivity, and it summoned the leading organizations of industry to pursue a more coordinated policy toward this end.[137]

For those who could "read between the lines," this sharp criticism from within the employer camp reflected the tension between those who emphasized "economic policy" and those who emphasized "social policy." Translated into organizational terms, this was a tension between the RdI and the VdA. For a genuinely reactionary industrialist like Director Gok of the shipyard firm of Blohm & Voss, who was a member of the VdA Wage Policy Committee, the great danger was that the VdA would be mediatized by the Reich Association. As he pointed out to his boss, Rudolf Blohm,

I personally would hold such a development to be very regrettable and unfortunate because thereby, on the one hand, the boundless interest politics of a Stinnes and, on the other hand, the muddy pacifist policy of compromise as embodied in Bücher would gain decisive weight. I am of the view that the tendency to let the gold mark or world price take hold even in wage questions is devastating for our economic existence, and the maintenance of the domestic purchasing power of the mark, upon which the wage policy of the VdA is correctly based, in contrast to the gold-mark tending policy of the Reich Association under Stinnes's influence, is to be promoted and must be promoted.[138]

From this perspective, the struggle of certain business organizations and groups to hold the line on wages and to roll back not only wages but also prices must be seen as a struggle not only against the demands of the workers and the interventions of the Labor Ministry but also within the ranks of industry itself. For obvious reasons, this struggle took place, above all, in the ranks of heavy industry, where the cost of coal and related labor costs were of prime importance to the general structure of prices within the economy and where, in the case of iron and steel, the growing noncompetitiveness of German industry was particularly evident.

The dramatic developments in heavy industry began in the fall when the Ruhr Coal Mine Owners' Association launched an offensive to protest the extent of the wage increase given the miners for September by an arbitration decision of the RAM. The mine owners claimed that the wage increase exceeded the rise in the cost of living by 10 percent and that it set the dangerous precedent of anticipating a higher cost of living in October and declared that "our economic life desperately requires a holding back in the granting of wage increases—at least so long as there is no recognizable increase in productivity—and that the workers, who by and large have so far understood how to maintain the purchasing power of their wage, must also at least temporarily bear for once a relatively modest 'factor of self-denial' (*Entbehrungsfaktor*) in their style of life, which has been silently accepted to an unprecedented extent by the broadest circles of the German people."[139] The coal mine owners threatened to boycott future mediation proceedings if the Labor Minister continued to view wage questions from a "political" rather than an "economic" perspective. They were especially angry that the head of the mediation committee, Prussian Minister of the Interior Severing, had decided on a new

raise for October 15, and then, under worker pressure, proceeded to set it back to October 7 and then to October 1 under pressure of the unions and apparently out of fear of the Communists. The coal mine owners argued that the price increases required by this wage hike were beyond what the economy could sustain.[140]

The truth, however, was that the declining value of real wages of miners and nearly every other group of workers made further increases necessary and also required more frequent payment of workers in order to deal with the rapidity of price increases. The major employer effort in November was less to resist wage increases than to make their acceptance contingent on the lengthening of the working day. Thus, when Wirth summoned the representatives of the ZAG to the Chancellery on October 5 to urge private industry to follow the lead of the government and increase wages to meet the projected doubling of the bread price in November, an action made necessary by the need to increase the payments for the grain levy and above all by the higher cost of imported wheat, Tänzler, the managing director of the VdA, and his counterpart in the Wholesalers' Association, Keinath, both expressed reservations about a centralized response. They pointed out that wage negotiations were now so frequent that the matter could be dealt with locally and went on to insist that little could be achieved by such "small means" and that only increased productivity could solve the problem. While the government, in truth, wished it could avoid raising the pay of the civil service and thereby unleashing new wage increases in industry, subsidization of the bread price to the full extent necessary was impossible because of the offence it would give to the Allies. As for the trade unions, they were ready to negotiate about overtime on a case by case basis but not to violate the eight-hour day, and they asked their usual question as to why employers should be able to raise prices in an organized manner while workers should not respond in a similarly unified style to get higher wages.[141]

The attitude of employers in these negotiations was, of course, part of a general campaign against the eight-hour day, of which Stinnes's famous November 9 speech in the Reich Economic Council was simply the high point. The entire approach of employers, however, distressed the government and especially Labor Minister Brauns. This was not because he did not sympathize with the employer position. Brauns, as had long been the case, was friendly to employer demands that wage increases be linked to productivity, just as he wished to restore differentials and, indeed, return to the kind of wage structure that had existed before the war. He could hardly disregard the political dimension, however, or make believe that the loss of real purchasing power by the workers did not require an immediate response. Thus, in early November, he tried get the mine owners to behave more agreeably by pointing out that he had persuaded the trade unions to agree in principle to longer hours in connection with the reparations program of the government and the international loan negotiations and pointed out that "one has to pay attention to the psychological moment in all these questions. The eight-hour day is a dogma for these people, which cannot be set aside just like that. One has to proceed very diplomatically." Similarly, in answer to complaints that the government had failed to press for the lengthening of the working day on the streetcars in Berlin, Socialist Reich Commissar for the Ruhr Mehlich assured mine owners that he had succeeded in increasing the working day on public transportation in the Ruhr in many instances.[142]

As the year drew to a close, however, it was the employers who decided to press their initiative rather than wait upon the RAM. On December 19, the Steel Federation decided to reduce the price of steel bars by twenty-three thousand marks a ton, a measure which was intended at once to make the industry competitive again and to signal a general effort to hold prices. The decision was a victory for those employers like Paul Reusch and the Wage Policy Committee of the VdA who wished to prevent domestic prices from reaching world-market levels. Reusch detested the eight-hour day, but he was not terribly interested in the grandiose plans of Stinnes and Silverberg either. He simply wanted to keep business operating and saw no end in sight unless industry moderated its prices and imposed similar moderation on labor by getting the government to stop supporting wage increases. The crucial issue, therefore, was whether the steel industry decision could be used by the coal industrialists to refuse a pay increase in January and thereby hold down coal prices. For if coal prices were raised, then steel would have to follow and the entire price reduction effort would get nowhere.[143]

Following their pricing decision, the Steel Federation and the Northwest Group of the Iron and Steel Association sent a joint appeal to the RWM and RAM to support a wage stop in January for the coal mining industry. Reusch wrote directly to Cuno, with whom he was personally friendly, to point out that the steel industry had set a "good example" with its price decrease and that Cuno "would perform a great service for the entire economy if he would succeed in influencing the Reich Labor Minister to present a blunt 'no' to the demands of the miners. The drop in the rate of foreign exchange will only have a corresponding effect domestically if an end is made to the wage and salary increases clear across the board."[144]

Brauns was inclined to take this position even without Cuno's pressure, however, for when the mine owners personally went to Brauns on December 20 to ask that the negotiations with the mining unions scheduled for December 28 be put off until later in the month, they found the Labor Minister sympathetic. The overtime agreement had been suspended for the Christmas holidays, and he thought it psychologically useful that no wage increases be negotiated for the period after January 15 until overtime had been resumed. At the same time, there was some hope that the price reduction in steel and price stability in coal might have a positive effect on prices in general and thus obviate the need for a response to the bread price increase scheduled for January 15. The effort to promote stability was also seen as a good move in the context of the impending Allied reparations negotiations scheduled for the beginning of the year.[145]

It was only a matter of days, however, before the entire effort was brought to a dead halt by all the parties involved. The trade unions insisted that negotiations be held for a raise on January 1, and Brauns installed an arbitration commission which, on January 8, awarded the miners a seven-hundred-mark increase retroactive to January 1 and another twelve hundred marks effective on January 12. While the mine owners refused to accept the decision, which left open for the moment the question of whether Brauns would declare it binding, the Pig Iron Association had broken ranks with the Steel Federation and decided to raise its prices on January 4, thus forcing the Steel Federation to raise its prices five days later. This totally undermined the moral foundations of the federation's previous plea that the government hold the line on coal-miner wages. The hyperinflation had made the pursuit of "high policy" among the industrialists virtually impossible.[146]

At the same time, however, there was more than a little evidence that all of this had created a demoralization which boded ill for the future powers of resistance of the miners and the working class in general. Some sense of the mood of the miners on the eve of the Ruhr occupation can be gathered from the reports of an official of the Prussian Mine Office from the Ruhr at the turn of 1922–1923. He pointed out that the mood of the workers was depressed and that their hopes for some gradual relief from the rising prices had been in vain: "The desire to return to the old circumstances where the housewife could buy for 10 marks or less substantially more than she can now buy for 10,000 marks, and the wish for a return to the old wage relationships have become almost general."[147] Although overtime work had been suspended for the holidays, many workers wished they had continued and were, in effect, surrendering to trade-union and radical pressure. While the wage demands raised by the miners had been rejected, everyone was convinced that they would be granted because the cost of living had become more expensive. Additionally, the miners were fearful of a French invasion and believed that they would be forced to bear the brunt of the burdens this would impose. Finally, they were depressed by the signs of an economic crisis in the finishing industries and yet felt compelled to raise new wage demands because of the high cost of living and their anger that workers in some other industries were violating the industrial pay hierarchy by earning more than the miners. The ultimate mood, however, was one of "strong resignation. . . . The inclination to do something active, to strikes or practical actions as in the years 1919

and 1920 has for the moment completely vanished. Apparently, large sections of the workers now understand that economic development is a stronger force than they had previously supposed so that it cannot be mastered by organizations and unions."[148]

The power of economic circumstances weighed no less heavily in the agricultural sector, but here the danger to internal peace and stability was even greater than that arising from the increasing but still uncertain militance of employers. It was difficult enough to force workers to increase their work time, quite another matter to make them confront—along with large portions of the rest of German society—the renewed menace of hunger, especially a hunger that would be largely attributable to prices rather than supply. Even under the more favorable circumstances of late 1921, the authorities felt convinced that "the population will not put up with another turnip winter."[149] The fear of a repetition of the conditions of 1916–1917 was much greater, however, as Germany faced the winter of 1922–1923.

In addition to the many other headaches created by the onset of hyperinflation, the government also had to cope with a poor grain harvest in 1922. This was a harsh blow to government efforts to dismantle the controlled economy and end the food subsidy policies which were so severely criticized by the Allies. Although the world price of agrarian products had been halved since 1921, the deterioration of the currency made the purchase of foreign wheat extraordinarily difficult. By spring, it was clear that the grain levy, against which the farmers were fighting tooth and nail, would have to be continued, and the Reichstag so voted on June 21. Two and a half million tons of wheat were to be delivered to government agencies at a fixed price, one-third by October 31, and one-sixth, respectively, on December 31, January 31, February 28, and April 15. This was a risky decision. Many peasants and farmers were in open rebellion against the system and were even running the risk of judicial action and heavy fines in their resistance.[150]

At the same time, those who chose not to violate the law constantly worked to change and weaken it. Having lost the basic battle over the levy on the 1922 harvest, the agrarian interest groups next called for the reduction of the amounts to be supplied on the grounds that the reduced supply made it essential for them to have more left to sell on the free market and for the exemption of small and medium-sized farms from the levy. This, too, was unsuccessful, but hyperinflation gave them a further basis for attacking the levy, since the price offered by the government became increasingly inadequate. The prices stated by the Reich Food Ministry for the first third of the levy due for delivery by October 31 could well be termed totally inadequate by early September. Even those who criticized the notorious hoards of money held by the farmers would have found it difficult to argue that such savings were sufficient to cover production costs, especially the mounting costs of agricultural machines and fertilizer. Like industry and commerce, agriculture faced a credit crisis, and the president of the Prussian Central Cooperative Fund, which brokered credit to farmers provided by other credit cooperatives in Prussia, warned both the Prussian and Reich governments that he could only discount bills on behalf of the farmers at the Reichsbank if farmers could guarantee sufficient receipts to cover the credits granted. The payments specified in the law were inadequate, and farmers would be unable to purchase fertilizer for the next harvest.[151]

Against this situation, of course, had to be set the problems of the urban populations, for whom the price increases of food in 1922 and especially in the second half of the year could only have been traumatic. The importance of the lower price of the rationed amounts of bread that could be bought against stamps is evident from the fact that, in Berlin, the price of such bread was less than half that sold on the free market (see Table 34). While the cost of food for a married couple with a child between seven and twelve years had increased by "only" 46.1 percent over the course of 1921, the increase was 3,655.6 percent between January and December 1922. In December 1922, the yearly minimum expenditure for a family of four in Berlin broke the million-mark barrier, assuming such barriers even meant anything anymore.[152] What made the situation at once worse and more complicated, however, is that the relative expenditure on food and rents actually declined over the year because the costs of heat and light, clothes, and such other items as taxes, newspapers, schooling, insurance, medical care, eating out, and miscellaneous expenditures had increased disproportionately (see Table 35). Indeed, disturbances in the Ruhr cities of Oberhausen, Hamborn, and Mühlheim in early September seem to have been especially focussed on the prices of textile articles, shoes, soap and washing products, and fish.[153] Agricultural interests could and did point to the fact that the price rises for nonagricultural products, from which farmers also suffered, well exceeded the prices for agricultural products and that they were involuntarily subsidizing the rest of the economy. Furthermore, they were even supported at a meeting of the ADGB leadership in late September by the head of the Socialist Agricultural Workers Union, Faaß, who protested the unsatisfactory prices offered the farmers for the grain levy, pointed out that production could only be increased if the farmers received a reasonable price and stressed that agricultural workers were bitter about being asked to subsidize the food of the urban population while other workers made no such sacrifices. An article dealing with the subject had

Table 34. The Price of 1,000 Grams of Rye Bread and Wheat Bread in Berlin, January–December 1922

(WS = with stamps, NS = without stamps)

	Rye		Wheat	
	WS	NS	WS	NS
January	3.91	7.48	5.00	14.00
February	4.62	8.27	6.00	16.00
March	6.74	10.79	9.00	19.00
April	7.39	12.25	9.75	25.00
May	7.68	12.35	10.00	23.00
June	7.93	13.02	10.50	24.00
July	8.60	18.69	11.75	33.00
August	12.70	27.97	17.00	49.00
September	18.42	53.49	25.75	100.00
October	22.37	110.46	32.75	124.00
November	55.83	280.00	75.00	362.00
December	153.69	363.70	200.00	546.00
Average (1922)	25.82	76.85	34.38	111.25
Average (1921)	2.96	5.35	3.52	10.80*

Source: Hans Guradze, "Die Brotpreise und Kosten des Lebensbedarfes in Berlin im Jahre 1922," *Jahrbücher für Nationalökonomie und Statistik* 65 (1923), p. 255.

*August–December 1921.

Table 35. Weekly Expenditure for a Berlin Family with Two Children in January and December 1922 and Expenditure for 1992

(in marks and in % of weekly expenditure)

	January 1922		December 1922	
	Marks	%	Marks	%
Food	257	46.90	8,154	32.62
Housing	11	2.01	193	.77
Heat & Light	43	7.85	2,084	8.34
Clothing	128	23.34	8,361	33.45
Other	109	19.90	6,202	24.82
Week	548	100.00	24,994	100.00
Entire Year 1922 Based on Weekly Expenditure	28,600		1,303,900	

Source: Hans Guradze, "Die Brotpreise und Kosten des Lebensbedarfes in Berlin im Jahre 1922," *Jahrbücher für Nationalökonomie und Statistik* 65 (1923), p. 256.

been rejected by the ADGB newspaper as a danger to the effort to reduce prices. What about other prices, however? As Faaß angrily commented: "One certainly cannot speak of bread profiteering if one does not at the same time talk about coal, textile, and paper profiteering. The agrarians are only viewed from a partisan standpoint. This is false from the standpoint of the national economy. We must follow a policy of raising production, and this means that we must also give the farmers that which they deserve, otherwise we will drive a wedge between those working the land and other strata."[154]

Faaß was not alone among trade-union leaders in taking such an attitude. Josef Diermeier, the head of the Bakers' Union, once a great enthusiast for the controlled economy and an opponent of Faaß, had suddenly been transformed into a supporter of the free market in food and even opposed the strong demand of the ADGB for reintroduction of controls on sugar. His reasoning was anything but intransparent:

The food question is the most important problem. But our representatives have put forward demands that are not in the interest of our food industry. If the grain grown in Germany could be supplied for food, then a better bread than the bread provided for stamps could be made available. Agriculture now wants to reduce the grain levy in order to have higher prices. . . . Sugar is certainly an important food, but chocolate and bonbons are a better form of nutrition than a bad piece of bread. We can expect a rich supply of sugar in Germany this year. . . . If we forbid its utilization for production, then we open up new paths for the black market. Even now we are suffering

under the demands being raised, for while the Christmas season normally begins at this time, we now have 10,000 members of our profession unemployed.[155]

For ADGB leader Peter Grassmann, who was seeking to promote a unified policy, the newfound harmony between Faaß and Diermeier was anything but reassuring. In fact, it bespoke the increasing weakness of the ADGB under the impact of the hyperinflation:

A noteworthy aspect of today's debate is that those representatives who have been most contrary to one another have found themselves closest together. Faaß identifies the raising of wheat prices as the precondition of being able to push through the necessary wage increase for the agricultural workers. From his perspective, he is right. But it goes against our interests and shows how deeply the conflict between city and country has cut. We now face the danger of losing at this time the last bastion of republican sentiment on the countryside, the agricultural workers. I know of no bridge over this chasm. . . . Despite the extensive debate, my conviction that we have gone the only and correct way with our demands remains unshaken. No less unshaken is my realization that we in Germany do not have the power of setting aside the source of our misery effectively. It is shattering for the German spirit to come to such realizations. The belief of the masses in the power of the ADGB extends far beyond our real power situation. We have to change that; the members must be made to understand the limits of our power, our capacity.[156]

Clearly, the ADGB could not come out for the full-scale decontrol of the agrarian sector. How could it when the authorities of a city like Mainz came to the conclusion in the fall that they were facing a winter as bad as any experienced during the war? Mayor Külb not only desperately pleaded for financial help but also called for the restoration of controls on sugar so that the supply would not be used for inappropriate purposes.[157] The Socialist parties and free unions had, of course, gone much further and had called for the reintroduction of the controlled economy, demanding that the entire grain supply along with the potato crop and other vital necessities be delivered up at a controlled price. Angry speeches in the Reichstag in which Communists sought to outdo Socialists in making such demands had a hollow ring.[158] Neither Wirth's Agricultural Minister, Fehr, nor his successor, Luther, could support a return to the controlled economy, a system for which there was very little sentiment among the various state agricultural Ministers. Thus, in September, Baden Minister Remmele pointed out that the "general morale and the necessary state authority" were lacking, while his Bavarian colleague Wutzlhofer, who had more than a little experience with rebellious peasants, insisted that "with compulsion or a dictatorship, nothing can be done with the peasants, as the Russian example demonstrates."[159] Even the Socialist Economics Minister in Württemberg, Keil, strongly supported an increase in the price offered for the levy, as did the influential Oldenburg Minister-President Tantzen, who had otherwise made himself extraordinarily unpopular in agrarian circles by recommending the valorized taxation of agriculture through taxation of the real value of production.[160]

As a result, prices for the levy were substantially raised in late October by the Wirth government, which employed an index scheme to determine the increase and thus provided another illustration for the workers of how a producer group was able to more or less index prices while wages fell behind. The point was further brought home when the government raised the bread price in November while employers resisted an across-the-board wage increase.[161] The same scenario was repeated at the end of the year under the new Cuno regime and its Food Minister, the former Mayor of Essen, Luther. The Prussian government sought to create a much closer link between compensation for the levy and increasing production by proposing that farmers receive a mandated amount of fertilizer instead of a price increase, but this was rejected by both Luther and Hermes as unfeasible and involving expensive imports. Both felt that a substantial increase in the price paid for the levy was essential in order to ensure that the deliveries would be made and, most important, that farmers would be encouraged to produce for the next harvest. As the former Mayor of an industrial city, Luther was most concerned not to reduce the bread ration if at all possible and was genuinely uncomfortable with the price rise that would have to take place in January. This meant that production came first:

The Reich government has to make sure that as much domestic wheat comes in as possible, and this by every means, such as a ban on use of wheat for fodder, etc. But the job is not done this way alone. The farmer must also have the feeling that the demands made of him do not go beyond his capacities. The difficulties for agriculture involved in preparing for next year's harvest are very great. On the one side, agriculture has had very good earnings this year also, but on the other side, the profits have been placed in goods which the farmer cannot sell again.[162]

As usual, the Socialists raised objections to the increase, albeit this time to the amount rather than the increase *per se*, even though it was less than proposed by the majority of the Reichstag. The tension was heightened by the projected price increase scheduled for January 15, especially since employers were trying to resist raising wages while the government was seeking to calm public opinion by guaranteeing adequate compensation to cover the increase. Even the one bright spot on the agrarian scene, the good potato harvest, was given a distinctly negative side by the decision to "stretch" the bread supplied the population by mixing in potato. While the authorities hoped that the amount of "stretching" required would not cut into the quality of the bread significantly, there were already complaints about the quality of such bread as had been so treated. Of course, no one expected the farmers to reduce the quality of their bread in any way, and a further intensification of the conflict between city and country was to be expected. So, too, was further bitterness over the shortage of milk because of its use for cheese and other more lucrative purposes, and even Luther's suggestion that milk for urban infants be subsidized was rejected by Hermes in the latter's desperate struggle to avoid anything that smacked of food subsidization. Some funds finally were allocated for this purpose, but at the end of 1922 it seemed as if the worst conditions of the war might be replicated during the coming year.[163]

But there had been no hyperinflation during the war and no threat of coming depression either. The various governmental authorities had paid farmers and civil servants in money whose value was unquestioned and had done so on time. The use of the printing press went unquestioned, as did government expenditures. None of this was true in late 1922. Complaints abounded that farmers were not being paid on time for their deliveries and that cities and municipalities were falling behind in their social services because of late payments from the Reich. Dependence on the Reich under the Erzberger reform had revolutionized the finances of the states and municipalities, and the latter, in their bankruptcy, were complaining that the Reich, in its bankruptcy, was threatening to bring down the entire edifice of the state. The linking of civil servant salaries and salary increases throughout the nation to those of the Reich provided states and municipalities with repeated fiscal traumas. First in October 1921 and then in September 1922, many municipalities faced the prospect of being unable to pay their civil servants because they confronted such pay increases without the cash they needed. In certain instances, this was because the Reich had failed to transfer funds owing from the Reich income tax, and in all cases the Reich had to come to the rescue with prepayments made against transfers owing or to be made in the future. Just as the social insurance system had disintegrated into a welfare system by late 1922, so the attempts at an orderly arrangement of finances between the Reich and the states and municipalities had degenerated into a system of ceaseless negotiations over *ad hoc* grants for various emergencies. As one critic remarked, this had turned the self-government at the local level into "a concept without content because the feeling of self-responsibility of the states and the municipalities for their finances, which is the best teacher and means of

training for thriftiness, is gradually being killed by the grants from the Reich."[164]

Early in 1922, high hopes had been entertained for a law that would determine the portions of Reich taxes upon which the states and municipalities could count as well as define further their taxing powers. By October 1922, when the matter was discussed in the RWR, the entire effort had taken on a quality of hopelessness. The head of the German Congress of Municipalities, Mitzlaff, pleaded that "we want to get out of the disorderly system of advances, where with each item, unemployment support, war disabled support, etc., a great negotiation starts up again as to whether $\frac{7}{10}$ or $\frac{6}{10}$ is to be carried by the Reich, and we want to have an orderly system under which the Reich provides us with larger portions [of taxes]."[165] The representative of the Reich Finance Ministry, however, pointed out that trying to correct legislation prepared when the dollar stood at three hundred marks at a time when the dollar was eight thousand marks was like "trying to square the circle" and claimed that

... the Reich has given the states and municipalities much more than it had. If that is not enough—the Reich also does not have enough! We find ourselves in a desperate situation, which shows us that the collapse is not before the door but already there. And in this situation to throw percents back and forth at one another really has very little purpose. Whether we say today 60 percent to the civil service pay supplements or 70, 80, or 85 percent is all the same; even if you received 85 percent it would not be enough. One should tell us what the Reich should otherwise do but give these supplements. Should the Reich cover your deficits with taxes? Then it will have to use the entire income tax, the entire turnover tax, and probably the entire coal tax.[166]

Precisely this situation, however, fueled the increasing attacks on the expenditures of the governments at all levels and upon the social system which was associated with the growth of an increasingly disliked civil service. Ironically, as Mayor Lohmeyer of Königsberg pointed out, his city even needed an increased staff to collect municipal taxes despite the fact that the bulk of taxation now lay in the hands of the Reich, and this was not all. There was "the Labor Exchange Office, the Unemployment Support Office, the War Disabled Office, the Widows and

Orphans Office, the Small Rentiers Office, the Social Pensioners Office, the Rent Mediation Office." Most unproductive of all, however, was the Housing Office, which, in one large city, employed one hundred persons—the equivalent of the number of housing units given out during a month. Lohmeyer admitted that it was "the most senseless thing imaginable," but he also insisted that "it is not to be avoided; so long as there is a shortage of housing, we must have a Housing Office. And it is obvious that we cannot now get away from the control of housing. These are things which we unfortunately have to bear as a matter of necessity and which besides have the unpleasant aspect that everyone who deals with them curses them because the problem of dividing two dwellings among ten people is insoluble."[167]

This was a situation which virtually invited strong attacks on the government for wastefulness as well as an intensification of the attacks on the civil service which had been going on for some time. The repeated civil-service increases and demands were the subject of sharp and severe criticism in both the industrial and agrarian press, which not only challenged the amount of the increases but also noted the peculiar advantage which civil servants enjoyed of receiving payment on a quarterly basis in advance. Such public sentiment undoubtedly strengthened the hand of government in its resistance to the civil-servant organizations in October and November and prompted its decision to act unilaterally in providing the civil servants what it thought it could afford. It mattered little that in November 1922 the real salaries of civil servants had dropped to one of their lowest points in the history of the inflation. The negative public image of civil servants and the growing hostility to the government's mismanagement of the inflation was what really counted.[168]

The bizarre situation is nicely illustrated by the salary arrangements for Eduard Hamm, the newly appointed State Secretary in the Chancellery under Cuno. He took over his job on November 22 at a salary of 285,000 marks a month to be paid in advance quarterly. During the month of November 22–December 31, however, his salary had risen to 371,280 marks. Its construction reflected the importance of the

"social salary" paid civil servants as well as the importance of cost of living supplements (see Table 36). Unfortunately, the real value of these impressive sums was about one-third of what Hamm would have earned before the war, and, as he showed in his own calculations in preparation for a meeting between the Chancellor and trade-union officials on December 28, 1922, civil-servant increases lagged far behind the increased cost of living.[169]

The trade-union officials who met with Cuno, like the civil-servant unions, had all come to the conclusion that constant wage and salary increases were getting the working class nowhere, that something had to be done about prices, and that stabilization should not be achieved on the backs of the civil servants and workers. Just as industry, agriculture, and commerce seemed to be mobilized against labor and its demands at the end of 1922 and were collectively arguing that stabilization required increased productivity, so white- and blue-collar labor and the civil servants appeared, for the moment at least, united in their demand that profiteering be ended, that prices be lowered, and that the rich bear their fair share of taxes. In short, the hyperinflation was producing sharp class divisions that were beginning to override some of the differences within and among the different social groups of those with and without property.[170]

Similar tendencies toward class polarization had existed during the last months of the war and prior to the Revolution of November 1918, and it is important to note the differences between the two situations. In 1918, the revolu-

Table 36. The Monthly Salary of State Secretary Eduard Hamm, November 22, 1922, and November 22–December 31, 1922

	Nov. 22	Nov. 22– Dec. 31
Basic Salary	108,500	141,050
Local Supplement	6,000	7,800
Supplement for 3 Children	7,500	9,750
Special Local Supplement	12,200	15,860
Cost of Living Supplement	146,000	190,320
Spousal Supplement	2,000	2,600
Ministerial Supplement	3,000	3,900
Total	285,600	371,280

Source: NL Hamm, private possession.

tionary situation benefited from the bankruptcy of a discredited Imperial regime and the promise of a Wilsonian peace as well as the prospects of internal reform. In 1922, the forces of the left stood on the defensive in shaky support of a Republic racked by hyperinflation, ruled by a conservative government, under assault by propertied classes who now felt strong enough to question the legitimacy of the social achievements of the Revolution, and threatened with imminent foreign invasion in the west. The brightest prospect for the future was a stabilization, as had taken place in Austria in November with the cessation of the printing presses, that would bring massive unemployment in its wake. In the meantime, there were numerous reports that the *Schieber* who had profited from the Austrian inflation were moving northward to Berlin to satisfy the cravings of the gluttons and others who were noticeably living luxuriously from speculation and inflation profiteering.[171]

Most alarming were reports from trade-union leaders in the occupied areas. The important ADGB leader in Düsseldorf, Heinrich Meyer, was deeply disturbed by the mood of the workers in early December. After talking with Meyer, State Secretary for the Occupied Areas Brügge reported,

. . . there is more and more feeling among the workers as a result of the difficult economic emergency that "there is no purpose to clench one's teeth and stay with the German Reich when things can be better another way." In a word, the workers are beginning to waver. The workers are not only being worked on by syndicalists and Communist agents, but also by the emissaries of the Separatists and French agents. The argument is being used that the introduction of payment in francs will produce better circumstances. The argument in favor of payment in francs is promoted with the greatest energy by Smeets [a Rhenish separatist].[172]

The trade-union leaders no longer seemed to have the workers under control. Radical elements were claiming that the inflation was artificially produced by the government and industry and that the latter was preventing a reparations settlement. The workers were especially discontented about the withholding tax and the fact that the propertied were escaping real taxation.[173]

Against reports of wild strikes in Ruhr cities, Communist disturbances in Cologne and Düsseldorf, and other such events must be set the organized patriotic rallies against the Separatists and the anti-French feeling that was strongly felt in the working class. A British official in Cologne reported in early December that he anticipated passive resistance if the French chose to invade and quoted Mayor Adenauer, "a person of wide influence and considerable power," as saying that "we would try to fill France's mouth so full that she would be compelled to spit out the mouthful."[174] Perhaps, the *Schieber* would then continue on their way to Paris. For the moment, however, the hyperinflation had created immense social and political tension in German society and an economic impoverishment and sense of social injustice comparable to that which had existed at the end of the war. Whether Germany could survive the widely anticipated French occupation of the Ruhr under these circumstances remained to be seen.

PART VI

THE RUHR CRISIS, END OF THE MARK, CURRENCY REFORM, AND STABILIZATION

Die Hausfrau endlich wieder lacht.
Was hat Erlösung ihr gebracht
Aus Not und Geldentwertungsnacht?
Die Rentenmark von unserem Schacht.

The houswife finally laughs again.
What has brought her salvation
From distress and the dark night of
  monetary depreciation?
The rentenmark of our Herr Schacht.

Abelshauser et al., eds.,
Deutsche Sozialgeschichte

A Disordered Fortress:
Passive Resistance, the Cuno Government,
and the Destruction of the German Mark

The Insupportable Mark:
Financing Passive Resistance

The fate of the German mark in 1923 rapidly overshadowed the prolonged deterioration which it had undergone since 1914 and even its parlous condition in 1922. How, after all, can a deterioration of 1:1,500 against the dollar between 1919 and the end of 1922 compare to the 1:4,200,000,000,000 ratio of the mark to the dollar at the end of November 1923? From this perspective, it was perfectly correct for even so knowledgeable a person as Willy Prion to contrast the "small inflation" until the end of 1922 with the "big inflation" of 1923.[1] And yet, the events of 1923 in major respects completed processes well under way in 1922 or before. Indeed, one can even argue that the crisis year of 1923 recapitulated in exaggerated and often grotesque form the entire range of decisions and conditions that had propelled the inflation since 1914, but did so in such a way that the ultimate delegitimation of the inflation could only be achieved by carrying the inflation to a literalized conclusion; namely, the liquidating of the mark. The "bigness" of the 1923 inflation helps to explain not only why the more positive aspects of the postwar inflation for Germany's reconstruction were lost to collective memory but also why the preexisting condition of hyperinflation in the last half of 1922 has often been enveloped in historical consciousness by the much greater catastrophe of 1923.

The German government was remarkably ill-prepared for the entry of French troops into the Ruhr on January 11, especially if the experience with sanctions in 1921, the continuous public discussion in France, the rumors throughout the second half of 1922, the various signals of impending French action, and the manner in which some German industrialists had virtually courted a French move are all taken into account. A military response, of course, was out of the question, but amazingly little was done deliberately to store up coal and raw materials for such an eventuality or to prepare appropriate fiscal and financial measures or to create organizational structures and devise an appropriate strategy for what was to become the policy of passive resistance. If 1914 offered any lessons with respect to the necessity of economic and financial preparation for an international crisis, there was no evidence that those charged with the leadership of Germany in 1923 had learned them. While the Reich Printing Office and the private printing houses that were used to print money had a capacity of one hundred billion marks a day (as much as had been spent on four years of war), this formidable productive capability was no foundation for a financial program to deal with a Ruhr occupation. In fact, in early January the Reich was running out of its last Reichstag credit approval and needed to be very careful with its spending until the ninth supplementary appropriation to the 1922 budget became law on January 16. A tenth supplementary appropriation bill was in preparation which, like its predecessor, was primarily concerned with covering the increases needed for the civil servants. An appropriation

Wilhelm Cuno (1876–1933). (*Library of Congress*)

containing specific provisions for Ruhr occupation costs was only ready for presentation on January 29 and was not passed until February 16.[2]

One reason for this delay apparently was that Cuno believed to the bitter end and despite much evidence to the contrary that an international conference would be held. Another, less simply demonstrable, explanation is that the same mood of passivity and drift that had allowed the reparations crisis and the inflation to reach the point they had also inhibited the government from confronting the impending occupation of the Ruhr in any systematic manner. Indeed, insofar as any actions were being planned with respect to the inflationary situation, they moved precisely in directions least responsive to the domestic requirements of a Ruhr occupation. Not only were price increases for the railroad, the post, coal, and bread planned for January, but the coal mine owners refused to accept a government mediation-

board decision raising wages, and the metal workers in Berlin and elsewhere were planning to go out on strike in protest against a similar employer response to a government mediation award. That is, both major price increases approved by the government and an employer offensive to hold the line on wages were in progress just at the time when a Ruhr occupation was likely to begin. While government mediators were authorizing wage increases to compensate for price increases, employers were seeking to keep wages down in order to carry through some projected price decreases. Thus, insofar as the government had not been inactive, it was a participant in contradictory policies which compounded the dangers for the formation of a united front against the French.[3]

Once the Paris reparations conference ended in failure on January 4, the French formally requested the Reparations Commission to find the Germans in default and thus to provide an excuse for action. The Reparations Commission did so on January 9, but French military preparations were already quite evident on January 6. Germany's leaders could no longer behave as if negotiations were likely and as if they could risk major industrial and social conflicts within the country. While the idea of "passive resistance" had been vaguely bruited about as a possible response to a French invasion, it was in no way a government policy prior to the event itself. In fact, what the government, the trade unions, and employers would do beyond launching loud international protests was far from clear. For employers, defying the French involved serious financial risks—specifically, the seizure of their production or plants. For the trade unions, especially the Socialist unions and the SPD, recent history weighed heavily on any policy of resistance that might be chosen. They in no way wished to encourage nationalist, right-wing adventurism, be it of the old conservative DNVP variety or of the new and growing fascist species. Making common cause with employers could easily evoke the discredited *Burgfrieden* policy of August 1914, and this at a time when support for the *Arbeitsgemeinschaftspolitik* was strongly opposed by a powerful and growing minority in the trade-union movement and when employer–worker tension was extremely severe. At the same time, trade-union leaders had little taste for an alliance with the Communists, who were intent on using such a crisis for revolutionary purposes. Similar concerns militated against calling a general strike, especially in view of the manner in which the general strike in March 1920 had concluded with an armed uprising in the Ruhr. In short, 1923 was neither 1914 nor 1918. There would be no united front on the basis of a *Burgfrieden* because the left could no longer accept either a foreign policy or a domestic policy dictated by a right-wing government and its allies; nor would there be the kind of crisis management based on *Arbeitsgemeinschaft* that had helped contain the Revolution because the relationship between the two sides had soured and the great task of the trade unions was to save what could be saved of the achievements of the Revolution. Insofar as there was going to be a common front, it would be against the French rather than for some set of joint policies and goals.[4]

In the setting of policy toward the French occupation in early January, two personages stand out in particular, President Ebert and Hugo Stinnes. Ebert not only took the initiative in summoning Socialist and trade-union leaders to discuss their intentions with him on January 8 but also presided over the first serious Ministerial meeting on the policies to be pursued in the event of a French invasion on January 9. The Reich Chancellery had, to be sure, not been totally inactive; Hamm had also independently asked that ADGB representatives come by the Chancellery on January 8 and had drawn up an agenda of issues to be dealt with and basic policies to be pursued by the Cabinet. Nevertheless, Ebert seems to have been very resolved to have the Cuno government decide on a united course of action and to make sure that it was backed up by the Social Democrats and their trade union allies. While wishing to avoid offending the other powers and to keep the door open to negotiations with the French, he was determined to encourage a tone of resistance, pointing out that "appeals to the world are a worn out method and have brought us little success in the past." Stressing the importance of standing on the grounds of the Treaty and thus denying the French any excuse for violating Germany's rights, he thought that the world

would understand a suspension of German payments and deliveries in view of the French effort "to tear out our economic strength and our economic soul from our body."[5]

Ebert knew, however, that workers would take their cue from the behavior of employers and that much depended on the willingness of industry to make sacrifices. In this respect, he was very heartened by the decision of the Rhenish-Westphalian Coal Syndicate on January 9 to move its offices to Hamburg and thereby deprive the French of the personnel and material necessary to procure the coal for which their entry into the Ruhr would ostensibly be intended. Ebert thought that it was "clever that the mine owners take the first step and make the first sacrifice. This must so be accomplished that the workers are filled with respect and courage."[6]

The decision to move the Coal Syndicate from Essen to Hamburg owed much to the pressure exerted by Stinnes in collaboration with the venerable Kirdorf. They seemed to have had difficulty persuading some of their colleagues of the wisdom of this step, as evidenced when Stinnes wrote to Kirdorf a few days later that "without you and me, the coal syndicate would not have been moved, and without this transfer, the resistance against the external enemy would not have gotten going as has now happened."[7] They also met with opposition from some of the Socialist trade-union representatives on the Reich Coal Council, who feared that the French would respond with harsh measures taken largely at the expense of the workers and also suspected that the move might provide a step toward dissolving the Coal Council and eliminating the trade-union role in pricing and other decisions. The trade-union representatives on the Coal Council were divided on the issue, however, and had no vote on the location of the syndicate.

In any case, Stinnes certainly had no such difficulties in his talks with ADGB leaders on the afternoon of January 9, when he informed them of the impending decision. As was his wont, he was quite frank about his feelings as well as the options running through his mind. He pointed out that the French, especially French industrialists, had been courting him for some time but that he had constantly rejected proposals for a 60 percent French participation in German heavy industry and refused to consider any arrangements for capital participation at so high a level and without provision also being made for German participation in French industry. Furthermore, neither he nor his colleagues would enter into such discussions unless the Saar and Rhineland were first evacuated. Stinnes was certain that the French would someday accept such conditions, just as they would accept less reparations than the German government was now offering. In the meantime, however, he had no illusions about France's ability to undertake measures that would make life very difficult for both employers and workers. He doubted the French would go so far as to cut off the supply of wood to the mines, since this could terminate coal production for as much as a year and hurt them severely, even if it hurt the Germans more. Stinnes pointed out, as he had since 1918, that the French iron industry was totally dependent on German coke, and he confidentially informed the trade unionists that, under the most extreme circumstances, one could blow up the cokeries and that he would not hold back from personally placing the dynamite necessary for such an operation. It would take three months to rebuild the cokeries, enough time to ruin the French iron industry, and this would be the "surest means of forcing France to enter into negotiations with Germany on a reasonable basis." Stinnes made it immediately clear, however, that his purpose was not to pursue a "catastrophe policy" and that he hoped for and expected negotiations to take place. He pointed out that "it is self-understood, however things may go now, that heavy industry would one day come to negotiations with France because such an understanding must take place one way or another." Stinnes hoped that, when the time came, "there would not again be attacks on himself and against heavy industry in general because of their negotiations with France." He assured the trade unionists that such negotiations would only be carried on in a "national sense."[8]

Stinnes's concern was well-founded, since he aroused as much suspicion among the workers when he was silent as when he was in the limelight. When he disappeared from the Ruhr for a few days in mid-January—he had been privately warned by the British that the French might take him hostage and his doctor had ordered a rest—a trade-union leader at the Gutehoffnungshütte anxiously remarked to Director Woltmann that "one hears so little lately from Herr Stinnes. In worker circles there is the fear that Stinnes at present wants to keep a free hand in order to come forth at the right time with a special agreement with the other side."[9] Woltmann was able to provide reassurance by pointing out that the move of the Coal Syndicate to Hamburg was largely on the initiative of Stinnes, but the episode is revealing of the distrust entertained by the workers. Stinnes himself thought it important that he stay in the background at this time. He was very conscious of how much controversy surrounded his person and was convinced of the need for national unity "in common suffering and common hatred." Indeed, he was even reluctant to play an overly prominent role in the passive resistance policy implied by the transfer of the Coal Syndicate, a policy he recognized would require substantial sacrifices from his colleagues in coal and iron. He thought that while their "suffering is necessary . . . it is also much better if people like Thyssen stand at the front rank and commit themselves than if the action takes place under my name."[10]

This is not to say that Stinnes refrained from exerting a major influence behind the scenes when he thought it essential to his general purpose of promoting a clear national commitment to passive resistance. Furthermore, he was encouraged to play such a role. Cuno summoned Stinnes to a January 11 meeting with himself, Foreign Minister Rosenberg, Economics Minister Becker, and Stresemann to discuss the Reichstag session scheduled on January 13 to deal with the government policy toward the occupation. Stinnes, with the support of those present, urged Cuno to insist on a clear vote of confidence in his policy and to come to the meeting with an order in his pocket to dissolve the Reichstag if he were not granted the kind of support and authority necessary. Stinnes intended, and was encouraged, to see Ebert also and to urge him that such an order be prepared; he did so later in the day. Ebert knew his Social Democrats better than Stinnes, however, and felt reasonably certain that they would stand behind the government, especially since he himself was doing so. Nevertheless, he assured Stinnes that "if necessary, he would not shy away from the most extreme means."[11]

As anticipated, most Social Democrats had little difficulty standing behind Cuno in protesting the French employment of force in the Ruhr and in supporting defensive measures, especially since Cuno stressed the illegality of the French action and emphasized his continued support of the Reparations Note to the Allies of November 14, 1922, as well as his commitment to the proposals made by his own government. He made it clear that the response would be peaceful and called for prudence on the part of the German people. While forty-nine SPD Deputies, mainly former USPD members, stayed away from the meeting and six abstained, the rest of the SPD Deputies joined with the bourgeois parties to support the government by a vote of 283 against 12 KPD votes.[12] The problems were that no one, including the leaders of the government, was certain as to exactly how and to what extent to resist the French and that the industrial and labor organizations and their members were also divided and uncertain in their attitudes.

This became clearer during the coming days and weeks as the passive resistance policy and its organizational foundations evolved. Since the proclaimed purpose of the French military presence in the Ruhr was to protect the Belgian and French engineers sent in to secure the "productive guarantees" for German reparations payments, the so-called MICUM (*Mission Interalliée des Mines et des Usines*), the first act of passive resistance was for Coal Commissar Stutz to order a cessation of coal deliveries to the occupying powers on January 11. This was followed two days later by the suspension of all reparations payments and deliveries in kind under agreements of March 15 and June 3, 1922. A key question, however, was whether the Reich railroad system would continue to function as usual or become involved in the passive resistance. At a meeting on January 10, the Reich Transport Ministry resisted such involvement, arguing that the French would then either force the railroad workers to move trains for the occupation authorities or take over large portions of the system and thus make life harder for the population. It soon became obvious that the conveying of occupation troops and of reparations coal to France and Belgium would make a mockery of the entire resistance effort, and the nonparticipation of the railroads in the resistance rapidly called forth complaints, particularly from the industrialists. Vögler reported that "the coal industrialists do not understand why they should risk their necks while the railroad system follows the orders of the occupation authorities to the letter."[13] Reusch, who was in Berlin and in daily contact with Cuno, was incensed over the behavior of the railroad authorities and seems to have been particularly active in urging Cuno to take action and to step up the passive resistance program. In any case, the upshot of these complaints and pressures was an order on January 19 barring the railroads from transporting coal to Belgium and France and instructing the railroad workers and officials to carry out only the orders of the German authorities. Cuno was very insistent that they so act in both the old and the newly occupied areas.[14]

As German passive resistance took shape, the French responded with a variety of repressive measures and sanctions. Among them were the seizure of German customs and tax receipts in the occupied areas, the declaration of martial law, the arrest and fining of German coal mine owners for refusing to follow French orders, and the expulsion, usually on short notice and with considerable brutality, of German civil servants who refused to carry out occupation-authority orders. While these measures fueled the mood of resistance among employers and workers and even some sporadic acts of violence which led to loss of life, the evolving conflict also raised questions as to how the German government was going to handle the financial and economic problems arising from its policy of passive resistance.

The problem of providing industry with the necessary credit to conduct the passive resistance policy appeared at the very moment when the policy began; namely, with the decision of the Coal Syndicate to move to Hamburg. The sudden move meant that the syndicate would be delayed in paying the mines for coal delivered, and Stinnes coupled his announcement of the decision to move to Hamburg with a request that the Reich, the Reichsbank, or both provide means to cover the shortfall. The response of the government was to guarantee a Reichsbank credit of up to one hundred fifty billion marks in three-month bills for the mines. These, at least, were credits and would be repaid, albeit in money of uncertain value. The decision to ban coal reparations deliveries, however, opened up an even more serious problem. What would happen if the French decided to confiscate the coal? The Reich would have to import even more English coal, and this would be very damaging to the currency. As Melchior reported after a discussion with Hermes on January 12, however, the government viewed the struggle as one that could determine the fate of Germany for generations and that, in this context, "the question of an eventual further strong depreciation of the German currency is only of secondary significance historically."[15] Presumably, the government anticipated taking a similar attitude toward another group of high costs that would arise from French confiscation of the coal; namely, the fact that the Reich could be required to compensate the coal mine owners under existing law. In effect, this would be as costly to the Reich as when normal reparations deliveries were being made. Yet, without such compensation the mines could only pay their workers for about four days, which meant that someone would have to compensate the miners either for producing the coal seized by the French or for being idle. The bottom line was that the workers in the occupied areas could only hold out if they either were provided with work for which they could be paid or were compensated, at best, for doing unproductive work, at worst, for enforced idleness.

Similar dilemmas arose with respect to the decision of the Rhenish-Westphalian industrialists to boycott French imports and to cancel orders from French and Belgian firms at the end of January and demonstrated that the solidarity and iron will within industrial ranks was not all such hard-line industrialists as Stinnes and Reusch wished they were. A leading industrialist in the machine-construction industry, General Director Reuter, complained that he did not know where he could get the kind of cast

steel he needed if not from the enemy works from which he had ordered deliveries, and he apparently fought hard against denying the French the statistical information they would demand when permitting such imports. One industrialist at a meeting to discuss the problem emphasized that all business contacts could not be cut off, while another expressed fears that the firms in the unoccupied areas would use the situation to steal away customers as they had done during the 1921 sanctions. While it was not good form to doubt the success of passive resistance publicly, Director Vielhaber of Krupp told a colleague that "the strength of the French is much greater than ours and that they will be able to hold out longer than we can; despite all, we will come to a bad end."[16] What all this made manifest was that one could not assume that businessmen in the occupied areas would or could hold out at all costs or that the business community could be counted upon to maintain its solidarity.

Ultimately, however, the success of passive resistance would depend upon retaining the support of the workers, and the industrialist leaders supporting the policy knew that they had to terminate their attempts at a wage stop immediately. The nascent test of strength with the miners over the wage increase for January was simply aborted in favor of a new price increase to compensate for the wage increase. The employer attitude was nicely summed up by an official of the Essen Chamber of Commerce: "A few million more or less should play no role now when the final fate of Germany is at stake."[17]

As during and after the Revolution, so in the Ruhr crisis was the maintenance of employment considered the single most important weapon against both the internal enemy on the extreme left and the external foe seeking to take advantage of Germany's domestic tensions. Quite early in the conflict, therefore, the Reich undertook a strong commitment to devote whatever resources were necessary to prevent unemployment. Its most important measure was a system of wage guarantees (*Lohnsicherung*) designed to ensure the payment of two-thirds or, in exceptional circumstances, the entire wage of workers employed on "unproductive" work. A similar arrangement was

Table 37. The Dollar Exchange Rate of the Mark and the Wholesale Price Index in January and February 1923

		Exchange Rate	Wholesale Price Index*
January	2	7,260	—
	5	8,700	1,670
	15	11,875	2,131
	25	21,600	3,286
	31	49,000	—
February	5	42,250	5,967
	15	19,500	5,388
	24	22,775	5,257

Source: Statistisches Reichsamt, *Zahlen zur Geldentwertung in Deutschland 1914 bis 1923* [Sonderheft 1 zu *Wirtschaft und Statistik*, Bd. 5] (Berlin, 1925), pp. 10, 18.
*1913 = 1.

made for short-time workers. Employers were expected to use their own resources to pay the workers first, and Reich funds were only to be used thereafter in accordance with agreements made in Cologne and Düren on February 10 providing for joint determination of such circumstances by trade unions and employers. Manifestly, it was a system which had to be bolstered by government credits to the industries in question. In the event that workers did have to be laid off, they were then to benefit from the more familiar forms of assistance; namely, productive unemployment support and regular support, except that those laid off "directly" because of measures taken by the occupying powers were to get higher levels of support, possibly their full wage, instead of support according to the usual schedule. Needless to say, the arrangements were a fiscal time bomb predestined to explode if the Ruhr conflict went on for any length of time.[18]

Even without the immediate appearance of unemployment, however, those supporting passive resistance and paying its price could not but be aware that further inflation was not without its dangers and feel compelled to warn of the very active Communist propaganda effort in the Ruhr and the desire of the Communists to turn the resistance against the French into resistance against the Cuno government and the capitalists as well. One of the chief goals of the Communists was to play upon the inflation question and to make a special appeal to women, who were felt to be particularly sensitive to the inflation and most directly hit by its

impact because of their daily encounters with food and other consumer prices. The problem was not, of course, limited to the occupied areas. On January 19, Socialist Thuringian Minister-President Frölich sent an anxious plea to Cuno for action against the enormous price increases of the previous days. ADGB Secretary Knoll had called for the reintroduction of the controlled economy two days earlier, arguing that the "*Valuta* blockade" was as bad as the wartime blockade and justified extreme action.[19]

The anticipation of the Ruhr occupation and the actual event itself triggered a devastating deterioration of the mark along with a sharp increase in prices (see Table 37). It thus raised difficult questions of policy for a regime committed to reducing and eliminating the controlled economy in food and increasing production incentives through higher prices as well as making major concessions to industry and commerce with respect to the antiprofiteering laws. While refusing to rewrite the laws or accept the principle of reproduction pricing, the Justice and Economics Ministries had sanctioned a loosening of the regulations through the concept of the "market price" in a major memorandum of December 17, 1922. This "middle ground position" meant that mark depreciation could be taken into account in pricing, although it left open the way for decisions that might keep prices below levels normally justified when a market was determined to be "in an emergency."[20] Needless to say, this provided neither legal security for sellers nor much protection for consumers, especially since many prices were determined by cartels and trade associations. The question of how to deal with these problems in the context of the Ruhr occupation only magnified the dangers of the conflict between producers and consumers and the government's difficulties in dealing with it.

The most comprehensive statement of the Cuno government's response to the various economic and social requirements of the situation immediately after the Ruhr occupation was provided by State Secretary Hamm in a memorandum of January 17.[21] It was significant that Hamm began with measures to be taken in connection with the control of immigrants, travelers, and tourists in Germany. The major concern, as always, was "*Ostwanderer*," largely a code name for Jews, and others suspected of being money dealers, profiteers, and *Schieber*, but Hamm's lengthy discussion of measures to be taken to charge higher prices in hotels, theatres, and restaurants for all foreign tourists, students, and his interest in proposed special fees and taxes on foreigners demonstrated the extent to which the government had appropriated the widespread and growing xenophobia. Hamm not only enthusiastically supported strict passport controls at the borders and in trains but also showed great enthusiasm for police control—better said, harassment—of foreigners seeking to do business or find housing in Germany. He was in no less a policing mood with respect to certain other objects of public resentment and governmental concern; namely, gluttony, consumption of alcohol, and the mania for dancing and inappropriate celebrations and entertainment. As always, the definition of gluttony remained as difficult as when the Bavarians first proposed measures against it in December 1921, and Prussian efforts to tax *Schlemmerei* also ran into definitional difficulties. More success could be expected in the war against the misuse of alcohol by banning public advertisement, restricting the sale of intoxicating liquor and arresting drunks, and limiting the production of spirits. Similarly, the holding of public entertainments could be limited and sharp curfews imposed. These were not the only police measures Hamm proposed. He urged strong action against the growing plague of trade in stolen metals, not only from factories but also from private persons.

The major cause of the increased thievery clearly was a result of the demoralization produced by the inflation and the difficulties many workers had in securing vital necessities. When it came to measures that might be taken to deal with the rising prices, however, Hamm's proposals were much more liberal, combining a peculiar measure of *laissez faire* in economics and generosity in social policy. What this reflected was that Germany's rulers no longer had much faith in the viability of the old answers to the crises they had experienced since 1914 and that they lacked genuinely new solutions to a crisis like the Ruhr occupation.

Since the food supply was more or less secure until early summer, Hamm recognized that price rather than supply was the main problem. To deal with the supply problem, he proposed that the grain levy be collected by March rather than April 15, and he thought a voluntary agreement by the farmers to renounce the price increase planned by the Food Ministry would have great political effect as well as avoid a battle with the Socialists. Whatever Hamm's hopes were, however, he certainly was not very sanguine about controlling grain prices on the free market. He did not think price ceilings could be made effective without requiring delivery of the entire crop, a totally unrealistic enterprise at this point, and could only piously hope that the farmers would exercise restraint. While thinking that price guidelines could be established for potatoes, he had no expectation whatever that meat prices could be regulated. Hamm supported restrictions on the use of grain flour to make pastry and of barley to make beer, as well as on the use of milk for butter, cheese, and chocolate, but he felt that the milk-price question could only be dealt with by voluntary agreements with the farmers. The Reich, nevertheless, would have to subsidize the cost of supplying milk to the needy. With respect to the much discussed efforts to restrict entrance into the food trades, Hamm remained unconvinced by the optimistic arguments of the authorities in his native Bavaria, although he was prepared to explore such action.

Hamm's actual proposals for dealing with economic, financial, and social issues were more likely to increase the inflation than the reverse. While a decision had been taken on January 16 to maintain the coal tax, Hamm emphasized the importance of suspending the tax, a major source of government income, if the French made any effort to seize the revenues collected or if the continuation of the Ruhr struggle made this desirable. In order to maintain the coal supply, the Reichsbank would have to make foreign exchange available to buy English coal. Coal might be saved by reducing unnecessary use of energy, but Hamm also suggested running factories only five days a week toward this end. When it came to the much disputed order controlling speculation in foreign exchange, Hamm argued for a consolidation of the existing legislation on the basis of recent experiences, which was tantamount to a codification of the various relaxations of the regulations. In a similar tone, he urged stronger surveillance of cartels and trade associations with respect to pricing, but he totally rejected the kind of direct measures to ban price increases or control prices proposed by the Bavarian and Saxon governments in their 1922 memoranda. Instead, he proposed greater collaboration between government, industry, and consumers in trying to maintain or lower prices on a voluntary basis. Hamm pointed out, not incorrectly, that the controlled economy had to a great extent been responsible for the exfoliation of trade associations and cartels by requiring their creation. In his view, much of the bitterness against the cartels, some of which he felt legitimate, could best be corrected by free and voluntary agreements and collaboration in the manner of the ZAG. Furthermore, he was convinced that much good would be done by providing trade-union leaders and left-wing economists with information about how pricing decisions were being made and with access to company records, especially in the construction and wood industries, about which the trade unions had complained quite strongly. In this way, such critics would realize that many seemingly unjustified price increases were absolutely necessary from an economic point of view and could be trusted when they sought to enlighten the population.

At this point, Hamm apparently did not think it possible to remedy the depreciation of the mark by technical means, but he strongly urged a reduction of unnecessary imports, not only for economic reasons but also to demonstrate that a nation so mistreated was in no position to import. At the same time, he considered an expansion of the social role and intervention of the state essential. While calling for the greatest possible promotion of wages based on productivity in state-owned enterprises, he argued, in somewhat contradictory fashion, for a much stronger emphasis on the social wage. In fact, he urged not only that young single workers be paid less but also that they be taxed more and be required to contrib-

ute higher social insurance payments. Exactly how such schemes were to be implemented while maintaining social peace is difficult to say, and it certainly is not surprising that this oft-repeated position of the Cuno government was never seriously discussed. It was more likely that Hamm's proposals for increased state efforts to maintain employment through emergency public works and for mediation to prevent major labor disputes would be implemented and that measures he proposed to adjust state support of pension and welfare recipients to the monetary depreciation would succeed.

On the very day that Hamm had composed his program, Hilferding had been urging him to take more drastic measures—above all, with respect to currency policy, which Hilferding insisted was the only way to combat the uncontrolled movement of prices. He had argued that the Finance Ministry should take control of the entire foreign-exchange resources of the country in collaboration with the Reichsbank and banks and secure the foreign exchange necessary for the purchase of wheat and coal, using the gold resources of the Reichsbank if necessary. He suggested that the dependence of industry on the Reichsbank and excessive granting of credit be reduced by compelling the various industrial groups to assist one another with credit and especially by forcing the nonexporting industries to assist the export industries. He urged the control of the prices of selective key cartels—the iron industry, for example. Finally, Hilferding believed that sliding-scale wages would work better in the German political context than they had in the Austrian and supported their introduction to prevent wage conflicts.[22] All this was undoubtedly too much for Hamm. His own program, of which substantial portions became or were to become government policy, demonstrated how averse he was to drastic action to influence the exchange rate through currency measures.

The problems created by the Ruhr occupation could not really be managed by this odd mixture of Calvinist moralism and economic liberalism. It certainly must have been gratifying to see the Berlin hotel owners voluntarily restrict the meat, butter, and egg consumption of their guests and refuse either to serve French and Belgian visitors or to sell French and Belgian products. An eleven o'clock curfew for theatres, movies, cabarets, and restaurants, and bans on public dancing and the sale of alcohol to minors as well as restriction of electrical advertising promised to make Berlin appropriately gloomy and ensure that the nation's plight could be contemplated with sobriety. Such measures could not, however, cure the dizzying collapse of the mark.[23]

It became obvious to Hamm and Cuno within only a couple of weeks that something "technical" had to be done to prevent the total collapse of the mark. What had originally been thought to be the great danger to the success of resistance to the French—namely, the coal supply—had proven not to be so serious after all. Many of the major mines lay outside the area of occupation, increased coal supplies could be secured from Upper Silesia and other German mining regions, reparations coal had been diverted, and, apparently to the surprise of the government, substantial stocks of coal were stored up in the unoccupied areas. But there were some problematic reasons for the adequate supply. On the one hand, large amounts had been and were being imported from England; on the other, use of coal had been reduced because of the high prices. Both factors pointed to the devastating potentialities of the extreme depreciation rates of January. The more coal the Reich had to import to run the railroads, the more scarce foreign exchange would have to be used. Increasing the railroad rates to deal with this problem would simply compound the difficulties of an industrial system already heading toward a slump before the invasion began. Few industrialists could be as buoyantly optimistic about their situation as Carl Duisberg in early February. IG Farben had plenty of coal, and while it might not be able to export the material it was producing if the French refused to grant export licenses, it had sufficient stocks in the unoccupied areas and in its warehouses abroad "to supply dyes and pharmaceutical products to the world for another three months."[24] The chemical industry could thus continue to provide foreign exchange to the Reich.

Much less comprehensible, however, was the enthusiasm of textile industrialist Frowein. One of his colleagues indeed accused him of sticking his head in the sand in arguing that the crisis in his industry antedated the occupation and that all would be well so long as wages kept up with prices. All that seemed to matter for Frowein was to keep on producing money to support the great struggle: "What do billions mean; what does it mean that we need so and so many billions per week in our factories; it does not mean anything. . . . It does not mean anything for the outcome of this struggle. The issue is not what is printed on the pieces of paper which are circulating in the country, and so long as we can do that, we can hold out."[25] Other textile industrialists were more worried, especially when they were operating with Dutch credits which were running out. Potash producers and others were also alarmed that it was beginning to pay for them to carry their production by horse and buggy in the manner of their forebears rather than to pay the increased railroad rates. Most disturbed were the worker representatives, especially from industries like the shoe industry in which 75 percent of the workers were on short time in December and no one could keep up with prices. From the perspective of these businessmen and trade-union leaders, the export market was collapsing and the domestic market was being ruined by the exorbitant prices. They needed credits and price stability, and the two were ever more contradictory.

In the third week of January, the Reich and private concerns and firms asked the Reichsbank for credits amounting to two hundred seventy billion marks, or 15 percent of its capital, while in the fourth week the amount requested was four hundred billion, or 20 percent of its capital. On January 18, the Reichsbank had raised its discount rate from 10 to 12 percent per annum, a most unimpressive discouragement to borrowers under the circumstances. As Havenstein made clear, however, the purpose of the increase was less to discourage unnecessary borrowing than to encourage people to purchase or hold on to Treasury bills and thus slow down the process by which they were flowing back to the Reichsbank. The discount rate of the Reichsbank was to be raised to 18 percent

Table 38. The Floating Debt of the Reich and the Proportion Held Outside the Reichsbank in 1923

	Total Value of T-Bills (in billions)	Percentage Held Outside the Reichsbank
January	2,081.8	22.7
February	3,588.0	17.9
March	6,601.3	31.0
April	8,442.3	26.3
May	10,275.0	21.9
June	22,019.8	16.7
July	57,848.9	7.1
August	1,196,294.7	17.5
September	46,716,616.4	3.2
October	6,907,511,102.8	0.5
November 15	191,580,465,422.1	0.9

Source: Deutschlands Wirtschaft, Währung und Finanzen (Berlin, 1924), p. 62.

in April, 30 percent in August, and 90 percent in September. The influence these increases exerted on the holding of Treasury bills, such as it was, was inadequate to staunch so profusely bleeding a wound (see Table 38).[26]

Critics of the Reichsbank, whose number was growing, were especially disparaging of this key element in the Reichsbank's "passivity" in the face of the hyperinflation throughout January. More generally, they were convinced that the Reichsbank had the means to intervene to prevent the further collapse of the mark. Hamm's discussions with Hilferding, as supplemented by meetings with Hermes, Becker, and Stresemann took on new significance for Hamm when the dollar shot up to forty-four thousand marks on January 30. This not only brought a huge price increase in its wake but also undermined morale since it seemed to reflect the pessimism of the business community.[27] The fact that the mark appeared to have a higher value in New York than in Berlin was especially disturbing. This suggested both that the mark was being torn down by domestic demand for foreign exchange and that it was being undervalued at home. At this point, therefore, Hamm was willing to contemplate Reichsbank intervention and greater control of foreign exchange. Cuno was of a similar mind, especially after a dramatic visit to the occupied areas at the beginning of February. As he told the Cab-

inet: "There is now a situation in which politics has to lead the economy."[28]

Indeed, the Reich Chancellery at this time was providing its own grotesque illustration of how important it was to arrest or at least dampen the flight from the mark in its handling of an "emergency help" fund placed at the special disposition of the Chancellor and deposited with the banking house of Delbrück, Schickler & Co. The bank was instructed to put the money in some secure, valorized asset but not in foreign exchange which had to be purchased for other purposes. Its advice, which may be taken as a good illustration of what bankers were suggesting to their clients at this time, was that the Chancellery avoid putting the money in German industrial shares because the Ruhr occupation had depressed the market. While preferring investment in either privately or publicly issued German securities denominated in rye or coal, it revealed that demand was so great that the existing issues had already been bought up. Consequently, it could only recommend investment in certain solid foreign shares available on the German market, such as the Hispanic-American Electricity Company (the shares of which were denominated in pesetas but which could be purchased with marks), or to buy silver. Even then, the bank warned that the demand for these shares by Germans seeking to invest without violating the Foreign Exchange Control Decree was very high and the price was constantly rising. The Chancellery would find it hard to escape the paper mark![29]

Workers, of course, could not normally contemplate such alternatives, but one of the most potentially dangerous possibilities if the rapid depreciation of the mark continued was that the French might begin to offer an alternative currency by introducing the French franc in the occupied areas. They had introduced the franc in the Saar, and it was alarming that the French mining engineer who had been put in charge of the MICUM, Paul Frantzen, had been responsible for the economic policy there. German industrialists who had dealt with Frantzen did not think his techniques would work under the very different conditions existing in the Ruhr, and a very strong point in favor of this view was provided by the trade-union leaders who warned against being seduced by the alleged stability of the French franc. Prices in the Saar had sky-rocketed since the introduction of the franc, but neither wages nor social benefits compared with those of Germany. Nevertheless, some government officials thought that the French would make their move once they had successfully cut off the occupied area and that the situation might be favorable because of lack of worker confidence in the mark and yearning for a stable currency. In short, the wage problem would provide the wedge for the French. There is no evidence that the government viewed this as an immediate danger at the end of January or that it was prepared to do much by way of prevention. Suggestions for propaganda among the workers or the issuance of special regulations against the use of the franc in daily transactions were deemed unwise since they would draw French attention to anxieties about the problem. The best solution was seen in providing the occupied areas with enough marks to pay wages, avoiding emergency money wherever possible, and studying what measures to take were the danger to become actual.[30]

If the government was moving toward a more active policy to control the depreciation of the mark at the end of January, it was not because of the danger of the French introducing their currency but rather because the passive resistance policy was being threatened by the constant increase in prices. At the same time, the Reichsbank also found itself under immense pressure in the Reich Economic Council, where Hilferding and Bernhard sharply attacked the Reichsbank for failing to use its gold reserve to stop the fall of the mark. They demanded the centralized control of foreign exchange and complained that the discount rate was too low and the amount of credit being given by the Reichsbank too high. As had so frequently been the case since the report of the foreign economic experts in November 1922, Hilferding and Bernhard cited the expert view that no currency had ever collapsed to such an extent with as much gold available as then in the Reichsbank and claimed that it would take very little to turn the tide in the current depreciation.[31]

Turn the tide, but toward what end and with what means? The Reichsbank position during the first weeks of the mark collapse was that its limited resources of foreign exchange were insufficient to take effective action against the wave of doubt about Germany's future reflected in the plummeting exchange rate of the mark following the Ruhr occupation. Only late in the month did the Reichsbank leadership purportedly have a change of heart, which led to a massive intervention in early February. Subsequently, Havenstein sought to explain the development between mid-January and early February by arguing that the Reichsbank "could only use moderate means and moderate interventions to restrict the catastrophe . . . but it could not think of breaking the development and forcing it to recede by making heavy sacrifices from our indispensable last reserves." Havenstein insisted that such an effort would have been doomed to failure from the start. Intervention only made sense when the dollar increased "by leaps and bounds" at the end of January because of unscrupulous speculation and when it became clear that the dollar was "undervalued." Having determined at this time that intervention was necessary "for political reasons," the Finance Ministry made a decision, Havenstein claimed, that "came at the right moment and was willingly taken up by the Reichsbank."[32]

Havenstein's rather unconvincing account suggests that the Reichsbank would have remained more or less passive even after the situation became more conducive to an active policy. Furthermore, it was the decision of the Chancellery and especially the insistence of Finance Minister Hermes to place political considerations first and to demand energetic action from the Reichsbank that decided the matter. In fact, there had been a very serious battle between the government and the Reichsbank over a major effort to support the mark. Hermes and Cuno, strongly influenced by State Secretaries Bergmann and Schroeder, realized that the only effective way of bringing prices down or at least controlling them was to stop the mark depreciation. Since the gold in the Reichsbank was 500 percent of the value of the marks in circulation, the technical situation was favorable. What was not favorable was the attitude of Havenstein and Glasenapp. They repeatedly recalled the lack of success they had in trying to support the mark with mild interventions in the summers of 1921 and 1922 and were only moved to relent in their opposition when Hermes threatened to resign and Cuno indicated he might do the same unless the Reichsbank gave way. Even then, the Reichsbank leaders raised opposition on an almost daily basis at the onset of the mark support effort.[33]

Havenstein and Glasenapp were not, of course, being perverse in their reluctance to place their most precious resources at the disposal of the passive resistance effort, which hardly could be considered a sound business investment in any immediate sense. It was a politically motivated and very risky policy whose payoff, if there was any, could only be reaped in the future. Thus, Havenstein explained:

The motives for the intervention of the Reichsbank with stronger means were chiefly of a political nature. In agreement with the Reich government, which had launched a passive resistance policy against the enemy occupation, an attempt was made to subject the leaping price increases which accompanied the fall of the mark to a halt or, wherever possible, to downward correction in the interest of our holding out economically.... The intervention did not therefore have as its purpose the permanent and final stabilization of the mark. Such an undertaking will only become possible when the reparations problem is seriously brought to a solution. What it [i.e., the mark-support action] had as its purpose was, chiefly for political reasons, to recover for the German economy and productive plant for as long as possible a time a somewhat calm and even course which would offer the opportunity for steady work and greater calculability. The further purpose was to free the market from wild and unscrupulous speculation and to protect the German people from a further rapid price increase which would have exhausted it. This all seemed doubly necessary at a time when the action of the French and Belgians had finally created once again a determined and complete unity of the German people and everything had to be set aside which might be likely to endanger it once more.[34]

Neither the government nor the Reichsbank was overly sanguine about the longevity of their effort and did not think that the support of the mark would last more than four weeks when first implemented. In mid-February, however, there was a bit more optimism. Hermes thought that the effort could continue another six weeks, a view also held by some of the leading bankers.[35] In fact, it lasted eleven weeks, until mid-April, before breaking down, and the

Table 39. The Dollar Exchange Rate of the Mark and the Wholesale Price Index, March 1–August 14, 1923

		Exchange Rate	Wholesale Price Index*
March	1	22,800	—
	5	22,768	5,120
	15	20,875	4,750
	24	20,915	4,827
	29	20,975	—
April	5	21,133	4,844
	14	21,110	4,923
	18	25,000	—
	25	29,900	5,738
May	5	34,275	6,239
	15	42,300	7,105
	25	54,300	9,034
June	5	62,500	12,393
	15	107,700	17,496
	25	114,250	24,618
July	3	160,000	33,828
	17	218,000	57,478
	24	414,000	79,462
	31	1,100,000	183,510
August	7	3,300,000	483,461
	14	3,000,000	663,880

Source: Statistisches Reichsamt, *Zahlen zur Geldentwertung in Deutschland 1914 bis 1923* [Sonderheft 1 zu *Wirtschaft und Statistik,* Bd. 5] (Berlin, 1925), pp. 10, 18.
*1913 = 1.

intervention on behalf of the mark begun in February continued through mid-June. The results between February and mid-April were not unimpressive (see Table 39). Both the exchange rate and the level of prices held reasonably steady—indeed, remarkably so under the circumstances—and this raises questions about how the mark support action was organized, why it was successful, and what caused its breakdown.

The intervention of the Reichsbank took the form of large sales of foreign currencies for German marks both abroad and in Germany. The full record of currencies sold and paper marks received only hints at the complexity of the operation and certainly does not betray how the means to cover these foreign-exchange sales were found or were expected to be found (see Table 40). Between February 1 and March 15, to take the most crucial and successful period of the mark support action, the Reichsbank sold foreign exchange both abroad and at home for paper marks amounting to a total of 178 million gold marks (see Table 41). An important

Table 40. The Reichsbank Intervention to Stabilize the Mark, January 23–June 19, 1923

	Swiss Fr.	Dutch Fl.	US $	UK £	Paper Marks *(in Millions)*
Currencies Sold to Support the Mark and Paper Marks Received					
Jan./Feb.	4,754,200	15,605,022	5,194,901	3,019,474	= 714,161
March	12,000	10,937,053	1,432,482	2,640,395	= 394,970
April	1,909,200	25,223,625	3,565,200	5,774,430	= 897,953
May	2,660,000	10,748,979	3,654,500	1,924,000	= 700,630
June	2,400,000	4,140,000	2,186,500	1,021,500	= 803,144
Totals	11,735,400	66,654,679	16,033,583	14,379,799	= 3,513,858[1]
Repurchases					
March		9,099,591		436,750	= 118,949
April		4,264,604			= 35,364
Balance					
	11,735,400	53,290,484	16,033,583	13,943,049	= 3,359,545[2]

Source: BAP, RB, Nr. 6406, Bl. 301

[1] = 459,904,000 gold marks
[2] = 429,404,000 gold marks

element was the sale and repurchase of foreign exchange in the Netherlands, where Mannheimer directed the action for the Mendelssohn bank.[36] So, specific foreign currencies were sold for the mark with the objective not only of raising the price of the mark but also of reducing the value of the currencies in question so that the German stock of foreign exchange needed for coal, grain, and other raw-material import purposes was maintained or increased. Slightly less than half of the actual expense of the intervention was covered by foreign exchange surrendered from export profits and other such sources. The Reichsbank additionally provided a large portion of its own foreign-exchange reserves for the operation, while the reserve of foreign exchange in the form of guaranteed Treasury bills to cover the bonds issued on the reparation payment to Belgium were also utilized. Lastly, the Reichsbank sold Reich gold holdings and put up its silver as security from its deposits abroad.

The hardest decision of the Reichsbank, of course, was the use of portions of its precious-metals reserve. One of the most interesting revelations made by Havenstein in connection with this decision was that these reserves were far greater than the public accounts of the Reichsbank indicated. As he informed the Reichsbank Curatorium in "strictest confi-

dence" on March 21, the Reichsbank silver supply, most of which was deposited abroad in case it needed to be used in an emergency, was worth not the four billion paper marks stated in the official Reichsbank statements on March 7 but rather 387 billion paper marks. The worth of silver was, to be sure, quite variable, but it nevertheless constituted a "truly valuable silent reserve."[37] Most of it was abroad and served as a Lombard security. Until mid-April the Reichsbank neither had to sell nor take Lombard credits for the 1,004.8 million gold marks in gold in its own vaults or on deposit abroad. Such gold as had been sold came from the Reichsbank purchases for the account of the Reich. Nevertheless, Havenstein believed it necessary to anticipate the sale or mortgaging of Reichsbank gold by commencing with the packing and shipment of gold to supplement the sixty-five million gold marks already held in foreign central banks, and he was able to report that both the Swiss National Bank and the Bank of England were willing to take gold on deposit and provide a Lombard credit if and when it were necessary. They were, in other words, willing to give what was tantamount to material and moral support to the passive resistance effort for which the mark support action was intended.[38]

The mark support action of the Reichsbank

Table 41. The Mark Support Action of the Reichsbank,
February 1–March 15, 1923*

Direct Mark Purchases	Amounts in Millions of Gold Marks
In America	10.5
In Holland	36.4
In England	30.2
In Berlin	
foreign-exchange sales = 170.4	
less foreign-exchange purchases = 15.9	
Berlin Balance	154.5
Forward Exchange Mark Purchases	27.9
Total	259.5
Less Foreign-Exchange Purchases	
In Holland = 80.6	
In England = 1.0	−81.6
Total Expense in Gold Marks	177.9

Means Used to Cover the Intervention as of March 15	
Treasury Bill Reserve	16
Advance Against Reichsbank Silver	15
Sale of Reich Gold	25
Reichsbank-owned Foreign Exchange	36
Subtotal	92
Foreign Exchange for Exports and Other Sources	86
Total	178

Source: BAP, RB, Nr. 6406, Bl. 227.

*As estimated by the head of the Statistical Section of the Reichsbank, Kauffmann, for the Curatorium meeting of March 21, 1923.

by no means stilled those who had been critical of Havenstein and his policies. On the contrary, Havenstein's measures seemed to confirm those who argued that the Reichsbank could have done more all along and who felt and continued to feel that the Reichsbank did not have a sufficiently comprehensive policy. Such patriotic Germans as Georg Bernhard or Anton Feiler were unwilling to give full vent to their reservations in public because of the Ruhr crisis, but they left little unsaid about the past and present policies of the Reichsbank in a meeting of the Reich Economic Council of February 8, 1923. The very success of the Reichsbank action raised the question as to why it had not been taken under more propitious circumstances. As Feiler asked, "Why has the interventionist activity of the Reichsbank succeeded in bringing the exchange rate of the dollar down from 50,000 to 38,000; why did not this activity take place when the dollar was at 8,000; why has the demonstration now been made that an intervention is possible without the measure

having been taken earlier?"[39] Bernhard went even further. Even if one granted the worst motives attributed to the French in undertaking the Ruhr action, he argued, then it was still necessary to recognize that the French had only been able to act because Germany did not get a foreign loan, for "had we gotten a loan earlier, then it would have been possible to make payments, and the French, even if they had the same intention, would have at the very least found it extraordinarily difficult to carry through."[40] When one asked why Germany did not receive a loan, Bernhard's answer was that "the non-granting of a foreign loan as well as the entire dragging out of the regulation of reparations is in the last analysis to be attributed to the fact that absolutely nothing has been done on the German side to even somewhat awaken the confidence of foreign creditors." After Bücher, in a tone of some outrage, asked Bernhard how he could say such a thing, Bernhard told him in no uncertain terms that it was because Germany refused to break out of the vicious circle under which it would not receive a loan until there was a reparations settlement, while a reparations settlement was the precondition for a loan. In Bernhard's view, the precondition for a reparations settlement was to undertake internal stabilization measures, and Austria, by undertaking such measures prior to getting a loan, had demonstrated that this was possible. When Bücher objected that Austria could only secure a loan by accepting humiliating conditions involving financial control and that Austria was not saddled with reparations, Bernhard pointed out that Germany was not Austria and that Germans had the duty to prevent being dictated to by doing what was necessary. As to the role of reparations, Bernhard thought "that the collapse of the currency is not a consequence of the reparations payment. I want to make that very clear, and if I have not publicly expressed this in this form before and do not have the intention of doing so for the time being, it is because I do not want to open myself up to the reproach that I am the person who has weakened the front."

Thus perceived, the intervention of the Reichsbank appeared in its existing form to be nothing more than a perpetuation of the policy that had brought on disaster in the first place. Bernhard was not blaming the Reichsbank for making the inflation by yielding to government demands for money, and he recognized that the Reichsbank was in no position simply to say it would not print money anymore. But he objected to the Reichsbank suddenly placing its foreign exchange and gold at the disposal of an intervention. This could not protect the currency in and of itself because it was not "part of a chain of measures" of the kind that he, Hilferding, and Hirsch had been demanding all along; that is, the combination of foreign exchange controls with a domestic gold loan. He noted sarcastically that the Foreign Exchange Control Decree had been retained despite all the criticisms and Hirsch's departure from office, and this suggested that it was unavoidable. The big question, however, was whether the package of measures desired by Hirsch, including credit restrictions and valorized taxation, would not now be implemented in the crisis. As Christian trade unionist Baltrusch, another of the advocates of internal stabilization measures in the fall of 1922, argued once again:

The general adaptation of the people to the rapid mark depreciation, the insufficient collection of taxes, the possibility of making extraordinary profits through the late payment of taxes, further, the possibility of undertaking large foreign exchange and goods speculations by taking Reichsbank credits, and finally, the fact that even foreign exchange that is supposed to be surrendered, is borrowed against, and that the loan then received, which will be paid back in depreciated money, is used to make new foreign-exchange purchases when the foreign exchange is at a lower price—all these facts must necessarily lead to a monetary depreciation that is larger than is justified by the condition of our balance of payments and our finances.[41]

Not all members of the Reich Economic Council committees were equally convinced that the package of measures (which was voted for by varying majorities) proposed by the Reichsbank critics really solved the basic problems. Bücher thought that the members of the RWR committees would one day read the protocols of their meetings and think they had been a "house of fools" in believing that financial remedies could correct the insufficient exports and low productivity which he held responsible for the situation. ADGB official Tarnow thought differently, however, and remarked with pathos that "when later in quieter times, the monetary development of our period will be told, then no person will any longer truly understand why no one took action here, why these things could develop completely unhindered and unregulated."[42]

The fundamental problem with Havenstein was that he always seemed well aware of the risks he was taking but seldom felt he could reduce them significantly. He understood how great a gamble the mark support action was, and he was especially anxious to secure the support of the German business world. Whereas before the Reich Finance Ministry had an account to its credit with the Reichsbank, the account now transformed by the mark support action into a debit account since the cost was being charged to the Reich. If this account, along with the amounts to be expended on further interventions, were to be covered and if the Reichsbank were to keep its gold, then something would have to be done to reduce the other obligations of the Reichsbank as well as to save and add to the stock of foreign exchange available for future interventions on behalf of the mark. Nevertheless, Havenstein continuously had to be pushed to make the mark support action part of a "package" involving heavy demands on the business community.

It must be recognized that even without such demands, the support action had painful implications for the private sector which were evident from its very beginning. Those who had bought goods or assets for foreign currency during the time of extreme depreciation found themselves caught up short. Some of this was quite beneficial, especially in the case of grain merchants who had hoarded large amounts of grain and were now compelled to sell their stores. Similarly, exchange speculators who had anticipated that the mark support action would be short also lost heavily, although it is important to recognize that the "speculators" were not only new enterprises spawned by the inflation but also old established firms which had guessed wrongly in their desperate attempts to cope with the inflationary situation. Against their losses, however, could be set the general good of the economy through the ability to purchase coal, wheat, and other raw materials for less foreign exchange. Another difficulty lay in the level at which the mark was stabilized. While most businessmen did not seem to take the view of Stinnes or Rhenish banker Louis Hagen that the entire support of the mark was a mistake and that industry was unable to export because of the drop in the value of the dollar, the traditional worry about keeping the mark low enough to sustain the German export advantage was no less important now than it had been in the past. Apparently heavy industry had urged Havenstein to maintain a rate of between twenty-three thousand and twenty-five thousand paper marks to the dollar and found a rate of twenty-one thousand or less harmful to exports. Havenstein himself admitted that the mark had risen higher than he wanted, although he was happy that this had reduced the cost of English coal imports in Hamburg. Domestic price levels, to be sure, did not go down because of the improved condition of the mark but rather stabilized somewhat. Clearly, domestic producers and sellers did not trust the situation sufficiently to lower prices, but this also had its advantages since it forced buyers to make greater use of their monetary reserves.[43]

Despite these problems, Havenstein believed that industry and commerce had an obligation to assist the government and the Reichsbank in their effort, that their resources were substantial enough to make a significant contribution, and that they could be counted upon to give support. He thought, however, that this support could take a form that would at once be free of risk and promise a profit. Typically enough, the answer given to the problem of building a fund of foreign exchange that could be used to cover the mark support action was provided not by the Reichsbank but by Finance Minister Hermes. Apparently strongly influenced by Carl Melchior and State Secretary Bergmann, Hermes proposed the launching of a fifty-million-dollar Treasury loan that could only be subscribed to in foreign exchange and that would be repaid on April 15, 1926, at 120 percent. Havenstein immediately took up the idea and made a careful distinction between this dollar Treasury loan and the gold loan proposed by Hirsch and Schmidt a few months earlier. He "thanked God" that the Hirsch plan had never been implemented since it involved the Reich guaranteeing the value of a loan in six-month bonds that could even be subscribed in paper marks. Havenstein was obviously correct in noting that the Hirsch plan would have proven disastrous in the vastly increased hyperinflation following the Ruhr occupation, but he conveniently forgot Bernhard's point that the plan had been suggested as part of a general stabilization program which, among other things, was to pave the way for a reparations arrangement that might have prevented a Ruhr occupation. He also tended to dismiss the possibility that those investing in the loan might hold on to their foreign exchange and purchase the needed foreign exchange on the market, thus working against one of the purposes of the mark support action.[44] Be that as it may, Havenstein undoubtedly believed there was no inconsistency in his accepting the Hermes plan after having so forcefully attacked the Hirsch plan a few months before:

This time the situation is different. The matter is not one of shifting the depreciation of money from the business community to the Reich, but here the matter is one of taking foreign exchange from industry and commerce against gold Treasury certificates with the obligation of paying them back after three years, and that with an interest premium. That was an honest way of doing business, and it was an idea that was developed in the Finance Ministry and that was immediately very much welcomed by the Reichsbank for the purposes for which the gold Treasury certificates were meant to serve as well as from a general perspective.[45]

The reasons Havenstein gave for his enthusiasm, however, betray why his enthusiasm was so misplaced and why it was most unlikely that the plan could ever succeed. The first of these was that the Reichsbank faced "a monstrous storm of requests for credit . . . to which no end is in sight." A balance had to be created to prevent a "weakening of confidence in the steadfastness of the Reichsbank," especially since its foreign-exchange reserves were being entirely used up by the intervention. The dollar Treasury bills would, in Havenstein's view, create precisely such a balance. Second, the intervention and dollar Treasury-bill scheme demonstrated to the world that "the Reich and the Reichsbank intend to hold the dollar on a steady level and to fight new, wild, unscrupulous speculation under all circumstances." Finally, the dollar Treasury bills would provide the foreign exchange needed for imports at a time when Germany's chief industrial region was in no position to secure foreign exchange by exports.

But if those who were storming the Reich and the Reichsbank for credit were also expected to supply their credit givers (the Reich and Reichsbank) with credit, and to do so under conditions that were likely to become worse rather than better, then some kind of breakdown was inevitable. Georg Bernhard was to make the argument that, under the circumstances of the national mobilization for the Ruhr conflict, a compulsory domestic loan whose repayment in gold was guaranteed would have had a resounding success. It would have been welcomed by a much larger portion of the population anxious to have a secure form of investment. Whether the application of the Hirsch plan for a domestic gold loan would have made sense under the seemingly unstabilizable conditions of 1923 Germany is difficult to say. Whatever the case, the dollar gold loan floated by the Reichsbank and a consortium of large banks under a law of March 2, 1923, was meant to support a situation that could only become progressively worse. Furthermore, the loan was highly dependent for its success on the existence of a large

enough body of subscribers with sufficient foreign exchange at their disposal and the will to invest it in the dollar-denominated Treasury bills. That such subscribers had the right to put up the dollar loan certificates as security for loan-bureau credit may have provided some incentive for investment, but it also demonstrated a fateful line of continuity from the financing of the war to the financing of passive resistance.[46]

Havenstein's commitment to support the mark certainly made him more alert than ever to the problems created by the Reichsbank's liberal credit policies. Seconded by Economics Minister Becker, Havenstein was completely unwilling to consider Hermes's argument at the end of January that the Reichsbank provide its commercial credit on a gold- rather than paper-mark basis, but the Reichsbank did agree to become more restrictive in its credit granting. Havenstein undoubtedly had a point in arguing that the chief problem continued to be the government deficit and the discounting of Treasury bills and that it would be impossible to keep the economy going with valorized credit. Also, Havenstein was convinced that there were large resources of foreign exchange that needed to be tapped and that credit restriction was an important way of flushing out some of the foreign exchange held by businessmen by forcing them to use their own resources rather than ask for unnecessary credit. It was also a way of working against abuse of the credit to speculate in foreign exchange or stockpile goods without sound economic reason. Thus, in early February, a telegram was sent to the various Reichsbank branches instructing them to avoid increasing the discount credit lines of old customers whenever possible and to reject new applicants. Also, they were to show the greatest reserve in granting credit by insisting on information on the use to which the credit was to be put, by increasing the discount rate, and by refusing to provide credit for the purchase of foreign exchange.[47]

The results of these efforts do not appear very impressive when one considers the amounts of private lending by the Reichsbank even at the high point of the mark support action between February and mid-April 1923 (see Table 42), and they are not. Indeed, they seem almost a

Table 42. Outstanding Credits Granted by the Reichsbank and the Loan Bureaus in December 1922 and January–November 15, 1923*

	Commerical Bills	Lombard	Loan Bureau
In Millions of Paper Marks			
December 1922	422,235	774.0	252,043
In Billions of Paper Marks			
January 1923	697	95.3	381
February	1,829	27.4	708
March	2,372	2.1	1,147
April	2,986	20.5	1,464
May	4,015	61.0	1,892
June	6,914	188.5	2,867
July	18,314	2,553.0	3,987
August	164,644	25,261.0	14,176
In Trillions of Paper Marks			
September	3,660	99	941
In Hundreds of Trillions of Paper Marks			
October	1,058	42	115
November 15	39,530	536	1,996

Source: Statistisches Reichsamt, *Zahlen zur Geldentwertung in Deutschland 1914 bis 1923* [Sonderheft 1 zu *Wirtschaft und Statistik,* Bd. 5] (Berlin, 1925), p. 52.

*Excluding discounted Treasury bills.

mockery of a Reich Economic Council resolution of February 8 calling on the Reichsbank to undertake "energetic restriction" of credit to business and, in particular, to refuse to discount bills that were purely financial rather than commercial in purpose. Nevertheless, when the Reich Economic Council debated the problem of Reichsbank credits to private industry on February 21, there were powerful complaints against the Reichsbank on both sides of the issue. As usual, Georg Bernhard, Hilferding, and their allies sharply attacked the inadequacies of the Reichsbank credit-restriction policies and demanded that the Reichsbank set its interest rate at the going rate being charged by the regular banks so as to discourage lending effectively. Bernhard cited the Berlin clothing industry as an illustration of how liberal credit policies encouraged businessmen to hoard raw materials, finished materials, and foreign exchange. He claimed that credit banks were springing up like "mushrooms" to service those who had goods to put up as security. Feiler picked up on this theme to show how the Reichsbank was encouraging various portions of the business world to profiteer at the expense

of others to the point of virtual expropriation. Those with direct access to Reichsbank credit were particularly fortunate because their bills were discounted at 12 percent, and they were thus always making a profit on the depreciation. Then, there were those who had what was tantamount to indirect access to Reichsbank credit because their banks were willing to discount their bills at 30 to 50 percent, by no means an unbearable rate under hyperinflationary conditions. But the greatest profiteers here, as Feiler noted, were the banks, for they then discounted the commercial bills they had accepted at the Reichsbank for 12 percent and were able to pocket the difference between the Reichsbank discount rate and the interest rate they charged and, of course, pay off the bills in depreciated marks three months later. Thus, all those with access to these credits were in a position to maintain their substance while the rest were stuck with paper marks, and it was this result that Feiler and the Reichsbank critics laid at the door of the Reichsbank.[48]

In his defence of Reichsbank policies, Reichsbank Director Dreyse did not contest that "smart businessmen" were trying to avoid putting their own money into their businesses and to live off credits instead. But he fatalistically pointed out that "this was not to be prevented and one has to accept it at the present moment."[49] He insisted, however, that the Reichsbank was clamping down on credit requests and would continue to do so. At the same time, he strongly defended the interest-rate policy of the bank on the grounds that it had a special function in keeping the economy going and in trying to make milder the inevitable crisis. He also took the occasion to express regret for unintended hardships caused by the Reichsbank credit restrictions.

It was, in fact, very difficult to determine what constituted legitimate credit requests and what did not. Bernhard himself admitted that the Reichsbank had an obligation to help businessmen seeking to maintain supplies of materials needed for production. A representative of the small and medium-sized municipalities pleaded that the Reichsbank control its discount rate since any increase would lead to even greater increases by the banks upon whom the municipalities depended. He also argued that an increase of the Reichsbank discount rate would increase the already enormous debt of the Reich. While everyone at the meeting could agree that money should not be provided for speculation in foreign currencies, the question remained whether it was really illegitimate for a manufacturer of furs to use credits to purchase foreign exchange to buy furs? A fur manufacturer thought so, especially since he claimed that the finished furs were to be exported. Hilferding, however, did not think that the exports were sufficient to justify wasting foreign exchange on them in the existing emergency. To him, it was further proof that a central agency to control foreign exchange was necessary.

The matter was seen very differently by textile industrialist Frowein. He had traveled from the Rhineland through the night to the meeting in Berlin "under not entirely simple circumstances" to warn against the existing Reichsbank policy as well as to reject the one advocated by Hilferding:

The practical situation is that the Reichsbank restriction . . . has led to a circumstance today in which a large number of plants actually face the question of closing down. (Interjection: Or selling their foreign exchange!)—Herr Hilferding, I will return to that shortly.—They face closing because it is no longer possible for them to get the paper marks to pay wages. It is a terrible mistake . . . to throw the entire mass of employers in Germany into one pot when such a large number of plants is closing. . . . Do you seriously believe, that the great mass of those textile industrialists employing workers have any foreign exchange reserves at all after having produced primarily for inventory for six months and who have only actually worked for inventory during the last months because they did not want to sharpen the serious crisis which has come upon our land by releasing even more workers and cutting back production even more than has taken place already? That's the way things are! The raw materials at the disposal of these industries did not help me at all. I can assure you . . . that it was the Dutch credit that was employed in order to be able to import these raw materials. Thus a large portion of industry has no foreign exchange which it can sell but rather obligations in foreign exchange which it will sooner or later have to cover with the goods it has produced or wants to produce. . . . From whence should come the paper money, if not through the bills which then are given directly or indirectly to the Reichsbank for discount. Things have gone so far that absolutely solid commercial bills . . . have been turned away. In one case, these commercial bills were accepted by a major bank. But the head of the branch of the bank in Wuppertal, whom I met at the station yesterday, said to me: "I am travelling to Berlin because we are also completely at the end. The Reichsbank makes such difficulties when accepting our bills that we cannot make further credit available to industry." That is the real situation.[50]

Frowein was reflecting the basic views of the Reich Association of German Industry, which was complaining to the Reichsbank that the credit restriction effort was causing great hardship and was insisting that individual instances of abuse were no justification for a generalization of the credit restriction. While the Reichsbank hastened to assure the RdI that no full termination of credits was intended, it made clear in no uncertain terms that it expected industry to use its own resources. The condition described by Frowein was certainly accurate for important parts of industry. To some extent, this seems even to have been true of German heavy industry. Apparently, some industrialists did take advantage of the mark support action to purchase foreign exchange in the expectation that "they would never get it so cheaply again,"[51] but there is little to suggest that industrialists could afford to do much gratuitous speculating under 1923 conditions. Reusch, for example, reported in late February to the head of his supervisory board, Karl Haniel, that he had bought a hundred thousand gulden and then sold them at a profit, but then gloomily remarked that "the shortage of money forbids a further speculation" and that "we will have to eat up our foreign exchange during the coming months." Nor was he alone, since Vögler had told him ten days earlier that Deutsch-Lux had been compelled to sell two hundred thousand English pounds.[52]

This was not the sort of news Havenstein wanted to hear. At the end of February, he set out on a series of trips to leading industrial and financial centers of Germany to market the gold loan. He seemed personally convinced that there were at least one and a half billion gold-marks' worth of foreign exchange in Germany and another billion in foreign notes. If 10 percent of this amount were subscribed to the gold loan, all would be well. As might be expected, he counted strongly on heavy industry in the Ruhr, both because he thought it had substantial foreign-exchange holdings and because of its stake in the Ruhr conflict. Thus, he made a dramatic secret visit to Essen in the last week of February and summoned a small group of industrialists to discuss the matter with him. He was not at all pleased to be told that, in view of the situation in the Ruhr, he "had not turned to the right address."[53] Klöckner was particularly outspoken, pointing out that his concern did not have a sufficient supply of foreign exchange for more than half a month and that it was again selling marks for foreign exchange in order to pay for foreign scrap. To prove his point, Klöckner, who was joined by the directors of Deutsch-Lux, Rheinstahl, and Phoenix in claiming insufficient supplies of foreign exchange, offered to show his books to Havenstein. Klöckner later noted that Havenstein "was very unpleasantly affected since he had personally assumed that industry had much larger supplies of foreign exchange."

This was by no means all that the great Ruhr industrialists had to offer Havenstein by way of problems. Klöckner took advantage of Havenstein's visit to inform him that

the manner in which the Reichsbank is now handling the credit question must very soon bring about a complete standstill in industry. . . . If the Reichsbank

or the Reich does not help out in the most generous way, then we would prefer to close down the works and let ourselves be compensated by the Reich for the shutdown wages. I expressly emphasized that there exists an absolutely insane risk for our concern in operating on the credits. Assuming that we hold out for six months and are compelled to accept 50 billion, and assuming that the mark would then improve, then we would have to pay better money for the bad marks. Besides this, our stocks would very seriously drop in price in such a case and we could then have losses in our concern which would not be overly estimated at 30–40 billion. Herr v. H[avenstein] could not belie this danger and he also did not take it ill when I told him that our concern would have to very seriously consider the credit in this regard, for I did not want to finally find myself a bankrupt in the second half of my life.[54]

Vögler pointed out that his concern was in the same position and proposed that the Reichsbank provide 100 to 150 billion in credits for the nine major concerns in the Ruhr—Thyssen, Rheinstahl, Phoenix, Hoesch, Haniel (GHH), Krupp, Deutsch-Luxemburg, Klöckner, and Mannesmann—to be transferred via the various branches of the Reichsbank. They intended to set up a finance corporation which, like the Pig Iron Association, would distribute Reichsbank credits. Havenstein encouraged the firms to get together in this manner and also assured them that he would attach no demands for foreign exchange in giving these credits. He accepted the principle that it was the task of the firms in the unoccupied areas to supply foreign exchange and intended to tighten credit there toward that end.[55]

It should be obvious that these credit arrangements were, by and large, an extension of the pattern that had been established in 1922 before the Ruhr occupation. The major difference, of course, was that now credits were increasingly granted to produce for inventory or even unproductively. The important point with respect to the negotiations conducted in late February and early March, however, is that the contributions of the Ruhr industrialists to the dollar loan were closely linked to the credit arrangements they were making with the Reichsbank and the government. Thus, after Havenstein had taken his leave from Essen, the industrialists worriedly discussed what they should do about Havenstein's appeal. They came to the conclusion "that the Rhenish-

Westphalian industry cannot avoid signing up for the gold loan," and the very fact that they had to come to such a decision is a good indication of how uneasily they viewed the investment. Nevertheless, they realized that "if the Rhenish-Westphalian industry wants to be able to maintain itself before the German public, then it ought not to sign up for less than 10 to 12 million gold marks," or two and a half million to three million dollars' worth of the fifty-million-dollar loan.[56] Apparently, a proposal by Vögler that they contribute 5 percent (the lower figure) finally was accepted, the assumption being that the great banks would take over 50 percent of the loan and the commercial and industrial firms with foreign exchange at their disposal would supply the remaining 45 percent. Individual contributions by the Ruhr concerns were to be based on steel production during the previous year. At the same time, Havenstein agreed to a hundred billion paper-mark credit to the Ruhr industrialists and also agreed to permit them to borrow up to 90 percent (instead of the normally allowed 60 percent) of their investment in the dollar loan. In effect, they were underwriting the gold loan with discounted bills that they would repay in depreciated marks, which they expected to be repaid in gold value for their investment in the gold loan. Even this was not sufficient for Reusch who, while willing to accept Vögler's proposal, strongly felt that the trade-off had to be carried much further:

If the Reichsbank strongly supports us with credits . . . then we must . . . also support the government in bringing in its gold loan. It would be advisable if, in connection with the signing of the gold loan, we would negotiate with Havenstein over a further credit beyond the 100 billion already placed at our disposal with the object of giving the individual works further credits in proportion to their participation in the gold loan. We should not therefore remain satisfied in being able to borrow on 90 percent of the gold loan we signed up for, but must demand further credits beyond this.[57]

Reusch was loudly patriotic and committed to the Ruhr struggle, and he certainly would have denied that he was placing profit before resistance to the French. At the same time, he and his colleagues felt entitled to consider how much risk they were going to take and for how long. They accepted the government demand

that they employ their own resources and the credits granted them to cover the costs of unproductive labor and the prevention of layoffs, and they did not take advantage of the government wage guarantee funds until the end of June. Nevertheless, they were more than a little anxious to avoid dangerous risks to their financial future that could have turned out very badly once the crisis was over. As a consequence, they haggled with the Reich Finance Ministry between the end of February and the middle of April before setting up a Steel Finance Corporation to purchase the unsold production of the eleven leading Ruhr concerns with bills discountable at the Reichsbank and guaranteed by the Finance Ministry. The major issue was the terms on which they would buy back their production, and the fundamental goal of the industrialists was, at a minimum, to get a guarantee against any loss whatever because of changed market or currency conditions and, at a maximum, to take all of the gain that might arise from changed conditions. Understandably, Hermes and his Ministry found such terms unacceptable and finally proposed a sharing of the risk whereby the concerns would take their credits half in marks and half calculated in pounds sterling. While this did not please the industrialists at all, they were in desperate need of credits and were faced with huge stocks of steel which could only be monetized by this means. Vögler seems to have been particularly instrumental in arguing that the crucial thing was to get an agreement of some kind and then get better terms from Hermes later. The agreement was thus signed on April 14.[58]

Throughout all these negotiations, the industrialists seemed to assume that the passive resistance would only last a relatively short time and apparently also counted on the exchange rate to hold. More generally, they, like the government in Berlin, were living from hand to mouth. At the same time, however, they were beginning to wonder how far they could afford to go in resisting French imprecations. A particularly significant illustration was putting a halt to the successful French confiscations of coke by severely reducing production and by making the existing stores unusable with the help of tar and sulfuric acid. The first measure had been requested by the Reich Coal Commissar, while the sabotage proposal came from mine directors. When the Coal Mine Owners' Association met on April 17 to discuss these issues, Director Winkhaus raised the question of whether they really wanted to destroy a hundred billion marks' worth of coke, and Klöckner created something of a sensation by making the point even more sharply:

We as administrators of the property of stockholders do not have the right to simply destroy such highly valued assets. One has at least to ask the true mine owners, if they are agreed. He [Klöckner] then referred to the experience which we had with the authorities in Berlin at the founding of the Iron [sic] Finance Corporation. The contract for the said corporation only came into existence after lengthy efforts and in an insufficient arrangement between the government and the companies. Instead of the requested 800 billion, one only received 300. The experience was that the Berlin agencies are not inclined to make great sacrifices for industry, and he referred especially to the resistance of Reich Finance Minister Hermes.[59]

In Klöckner's view, the coal industrialists needed to demand the creation of a Coal Finance Corporation similar to the one established for the iron and steel industry, and he was especially worried about the huge amount of bills the Coal Syndicate had discounted. He thought they should be taken over by the Reich and warned that energetic steps were the only way to avoid being "left in the lurch." Furthermore, Klöckner did not wish to destroy the coke but rather actually to increase, not restrict, production. He argued that French President Millerand would drive Poincaré from office soon, negotiations would take place sometime in June, and they had to have coke supplies in order to employ the workers and deliver reparations. Klöckner was not alone in taking this position, but most of the mine directors felt that it would give an undesirable signal to the French. They therefore decided to restrict production, but not to destroy the coke in storage and, above all, to make a strong appeal for more aid from Berlin.

That these negotiations, discussions, and reflections took place in mid-April was of no small significance, for they betrayed the critical phase into which the Ruhr struggle was now entering. Fundamental to the increasing difficulties of the passive resistance policy was that the French were progressively tightening the screws in the Ruhr. The French occupation was hardly a model of efficiency and competence and was often characterized by an odd mixture of bumbling and brutality. But its fundamental conception, the pénétration progressive devised by Marshall Foch prior to the invasion, was admirably suited to induce gradual exhaustion both in the occupied and unoccupied areas while avoiding immediate chaos and starvation in the areas under Franco-Belgian military control. Thus, the expansion of the occupation itself took place over six weeks and was only completed with the entry of French troops into the ports of Mannheim and Karlsruhe at the beginning of March. At the end of January, the French began to ban systematically the export of products from the occupied to the unoccupied areas, starting with coal and coke, and concluded with the establishment of a customs line between the two parts of Germany in early March. At the same time, the occupying forces gained increasing control over the railroad system, expelling German railroad officials who refused to follow orders, establishing their own Regie to administer the system, and, on March 1, introducing visa and pass requirements for those traveling between the occupied and unoccupied areas. By mid-March, the occupation was in a position actually to occupy some state-owned mines and to begin to transport coal and coke. This, when combined first with restrictions on the use of coke and coal by Germans in the occupied areas and then the actual ban on the use of coke at the end of March, increasingly enabled the French and Belgians to supply their own needs while progressively shutting down industry in the occupied areas. By May, one-third of the normal coal and coke transport had been resumed, a clear indication that time was working for the French. During this entire period, the passive resistance was further undermined by French seizure of money sent by the Reichsbank to support the resistance as well as arrests; the fining, imprisonment, or deportation of those refusing to follow orders; and a barrage of propaganda aimed at sowing divisions within the population. Time and power clearly were on the side of the French.[60]

By early spring, therefore, the "heroic" period of passive resistance was coming to an end.

This was demonstrated not only by the growing demand that the government take steps to enter into negotiations with the French but also above all, by the evident failure of the dollar loan in early April, on the one hand, and by the failure of the mark support effort with the resumption of the depreciation of the mark on April 18 (see Table 40, on p. 644).

The fact that the dollar mark loan was only one-quarter subscribed must be understood not simply as a blow to the effort to support the mark and the passive resistance but also as a profound humiliation for the Cuno government and for Havenstein. The latter had expected at least half the loan to be subscribed and angrily declared that the loan had proven a "miserable failure" which he attributed to the fact that "all parts of the business community have failed us." He was least disappointed with heavy industry, which contributed substantially despite the opposition of Stinnes, who told Hermes that he had no intention of supporting the effort but promised not to oppose it on patriotic grounds. For Cuno, the attitude of the Hamburg merchants and bankers was a hard blow. Their apparent unwillingness to do their share was particularly galling. Cuno resented the pessimism of his closest business associates, especially since he was confident that his Ruhr policy would succeed, and he felt "left in the lurch" by industry and the banks and warned that this would have bad consequences someday. Cuno made no effort to hide his resentment in a talk with Max Warburg at the end of March and threatened to publicly identify those responsible for the failure in a discussion with leading bankers in mid-April.[61]

Warburg, who had personally put much effort into the loan drive, had to admit that "I have never received so many refusals and have never walked about so much with the whip; only a French officer can outdo me." In response to Cuno's charge that there were Hamburg businessmen who were "enthusiastic about speculation against the mark," Warburg conceded that "it is definitely the case that some firms here cannot entirely distinguish between speculation and arbitrage." It was also true that "the general political situation has naturally held back many from putting up their small savings which they still have in foreign exchange."[62] Warburg urged that a special Commissar be appointed to put pressure on firms and municipalities that had not done their share. At the same time, he also argued, both to Cuno and publicly, that the results of the loan demonstrated that the German people did not have the resources that had been assumed either by those abroad or by critics at home. This point was taken up by the Hamburg Chamber of Commerce, which felt called upon to defend its businessmen against criticisms from Reichsbank officials by pointing out that Hamburg had made a very substantial contribution to the loan when measured against other areas and that Hamburg businessmen had much greater need of their foreign exchange.[63]

None of this was terribly edifying. One could indeed find many good reasons for the failure of the dollar loan aside from the dangerous political situation. Business conditions were bad; the requirement that only foreign exchange be used limited the number of potential subscribers; and the loan faced competition from the growing number of loans based on rye and coal. The supply of such valorized investment opportunities was rising to meet the demand. In addition to the rye loans of Oldenburg and Mecklenburg, the Prussian State Bank and the province of Hanover had also issued rye loans, while Saxony and Cassel had issued lignite loans. The Baden Electric Power Company had issued a loan based on anthracite coal, and those bonds, providentially, could be converted into a legally established new German currency! In addition to such internal factors harmful to the gold-loan effort, there were also external ones. Damage had certainly been done by the noisily made French claim that the Reich had no right to guarantee such a loan without permission under the Treaty of Versailles, a position subsequently rejected by a majority of the members of the Reparations Commission. The Reichsbank had also failed to show the same verve, skill, and imagination it had demonstrated during the days when it was promoting war loans. The amount of the loan against which subscribers could borrow was left unclear until after the loan had been floated. The Reichsbank had only engaged the great banks in the effort and had failed to use small and medium-sized provincial banks, where there were substantial amounts of foreign exchange. Reichsbank propaganda tended to treat the loan as a charitable enterprise rather than a business arrangement.[64]

Whatever the causes, the results of the loan could only lead to melancholy conclusions. Warburg might seek to assure Cuno—or himself—that world opinion was moving in the right direction and that "the French would collapse in the Ruhr action,"[65] but a critical observer only had to make comparisons between the results of the dollar loan with the highly successful loans floated in Swiss cantons and small Swiss cities or with the one hundred billion francs in loans subscribed to by French citizens despite the French budget deficit and the uncertainty about how much would be received from Germany in reparations. How was Germany to get a foreign loan when it could not raise an internal one of relatively modest proportions for so great a nation? As Ludwig Lewinsohn concluded, "credit is a matter of faith, and a state which has lost the faith of its own citizens, is unworthy of credit."[66]

In the second half of April, however, the sins of omission that had led to the failure of the gold loan seemed compounded by sins of commission in connection with the fall of the exchange rate of the mark that began on April 18–19. Manifestly, it would only have been a matter of time before the mark support action would collapse under the weight of the note production to finance passive resistance, the failure of the gold loan, and the worsening economic circumstances. Nevertheless, the abnormal demand for foreign exchange in the days prior to April 18 and the onslaught of foreign-exchange purchasers on that "black day" made it impossible for the Reichsbank to continue to buy marks without exhausting its resources in a matter of ten days. Havenstein, already sorely disappointed and angry over the failure of the dollar loan, was nothing short of infuriated by what he considered to be much worse behavior; namely, "special interests . . . whose demands on the foreign exchange market and on the Reichsbank rose from week to week and finally reached a level such as went far beyond the normal need of our economy." This was accompanied by the revived activity of the daily speculators, who equally "undisturbed by the

well-being of the nation" made the Reichsbank's task more difficult. Most aggravating, however, was that "in this time of most difficult struggle for Germany, serious circles in our economy also believed they had the right to cover themselves in large amounts, not only for the necessary requirements of the near term but also beyond this to maintain a supply or to replenish foreign exchange they had used." Havenstein bluntly declared that such behavior, even if not so intended, was nevertheless an "attack from behind on the great common battle front and the action which the Reich and the Reichsbank have led in the interest of our policy and our economy."[67]

Harsh words indeed, especially when combined with reported remarks by Cuno to the bankers about being stabbed in the back by business. The press immediately took up the matter and pointed a finger at the person to whom numerous influential persons and journals were attributing the debacle, Hugo Stinnes, whose concern was reported to have made large purchases of British pounds in the days prior to the collapse of the exchange rate. Reports were also circulating that Siemens had made such purchases. The suggestion was that these massive, unauthorized purchases had, on the one hand, made a barely controllable situation impossible and, on the other, had set a model for others to follow in the days after April 18. These charges were taken very seriously in the Reich Chancellery, where Hamm called for a close examination of Stinnes's foreign-exchange operations, and they became the subject of a lengthy investigation by a special committee of the Reichstag in the spring and summer of 1923.[68]

Both Siemens and Stinnes immediately wrote to Havenstein protesting their innocence. Siemens pointed out that his concern had bought no foreign exchange in March, while they had sold $907,500 and had also subscribed $150,000 to the gold loan. In the first days of April, he had bought $125,000 on the forward exchange, and between April 1–25, he had sold $423,000 in foreign exchange. Thus, his firm had not been buying foreign exchange to any great degree but, on the contrary, was selling large amounts. He also pointed out that the heavy-industrial side of the SRSU had bought only very small amounts of foreign exchange during this period. Stinnes confirmed this in his letter to Havenstein, in which he also announced the publication of the information in the *DAZ* to demonstrate that the attacks in the Socialist and liberal Ullstein press "lacked the slightest foundation." Since Havenstein's charges had fed these false reports, he called on Havenstein to clarify the situation, "all the more so as you know that, despite my rejection of the foreign exchange policy of the Reichsbank and the Reich Finance Ministry, I do not belong to those who at the time of Germany's economic struggle against France would, in the pursuit of special interests, attack the government from the rear."[69]

It was a measure of the tension developing between the Reichsbank and industry at this time that a conflict even developed over Havenstein's efforts to correct the impression that he was in any way confirming the newspaper charges against Stinnes. Havenstein's clarification was presented by the *DAZ* in much stronger language than he himself intended, whereupon he demanded a further clarification. This the *DAZ* refused and issued a threat that it would oppose the Reichsbank and Havenstein on all fronts. The "declaration of war" apparently emanated from Stinnes's press chief, Hans Humann, who frequently had to be kept on the leash by his boss. The episode ended with Stinnes assuring Havenstein that he had no intention of warring with the Reichsbank; he also promised a further clarification in the *DAZ,* which, however, he never seems to have authorized.[70]

Siemens and Stinnes were telling the truth when they stated that they had not been buying large amounts of foreign exchange for the SRSU and had, in fact, been selling such currencies. What the government soon discovered to its great irritation and what the Reichstag investigation found, however, was that Stinnes had sought to purchase ninety-three thousand pounds on April 13 and had actually purchased sixty thousand pounds on that date. The purchase was not intended for either the SRSU or the Stinnes concern, whose officials were responsible for the effort, but rather for the Reich Railroad Central Office to cover purchases of English coal. The Stinnes concern handled these coal purchases for the railroads and had

undertaken the currency purchase to cover a coal bill of ninety-three thousand pounds which was due on April 14.

It is no easy task to sort out the variety of improprieties involved in these transactions, and it is not surprising that the Reichstag investigation committee finally tended to exonerate the Stinnes firm of intentional wrongdoing while placing chief responsibility on the Railroad Central Office and the government. The initiative clearly did come from the Railroad Central Office, which had a long record of struggle with the Reich Coal Commissar and the Economics Ministry concerning both its supply of coal and its mode of financing foreign purchases. While the railroad management sought to assure itself of a fixed amount of coal, the Commissar tried to maintain a measure of flexibility in the distribution of coal and promote import reduction. Whereas the railroad authorities found it most efficient to get their foreign exchange directly through the banks, the RWM and Finance Ministry, under strong pressure from the Reichsbank, wished to have the foreign exchange purchased from the Foreign Exchange Procurement Board. In this way, they would have a clear view of, as well as control over, how much foreign currency was being purchased on behalf of government agencies and could make sure that such purchases were carried out in a manner consistent with the effort to support the mark. In late January, Groener agreed to get his foreign exchange through the Foreign Exchange Procurement Board, provided that it was available on time and in sufficient quantities at especially satisfactory terms.[71]

In the second half of March, the Transportation Ministry became concerned over what it perceived to be a diminution of supply from the Foreign Exchange Procurement Board and began to fear that it would not meet its obligations, especially the ninety-three thousand pounds it needed to pay on April 14. This engagement had not been reported to the Foreign Exchange Procurement Board until April 10. Then, the Transportation Ministry faced extremely severe criticism in the Foreign Exchange Procurement Board's Advisory Council for failing to give prior notice of this obligation and was accused of trying to hoard coal rather than simply to cover operating needs. It was strongly urged to stretch out the deliveries it was receiving so as to reduce the amount of foreign exchange needed at any one time and to reduce its reserve from thirty-two to fifteen days. At the same time, there was no reason for the Transport Ministry to worry about covering its bill on April 14 with foreign exchange it already had on account with the board.

Nevertheless, on the same day, the Ministry sought to find some other solution to its foreign-exchange difficulties by inquiring if various import firms with whom it did business, the most prominent of which was the Stinnes firm, could not supply the foreign exchange needed from stocks of foreign exchange which might be in their possession. On April 12, the Stinnes firm wrote to the Ministry declaring its readiness to procure the needed exchange and, on the same day, without any authorization whatever, approached five banks seeking to purchase the foreign exchange needed. On the following day, it managed to purchase sixty thousand pounds. During negotiations over the next three days, the Transport Ministry decided to accept the sixty thousand pounds to cover its coal bill and drew on its account with the Foreign Exchange Procurement Board to cover the remaining thirty-three thousand pounds. The sixty thousand pounds, the purchase of which was never formally authorized, certainly eased the Ministry's problems. Manifestly, then, the Transport Ministry acted irresponsibly in failing to report its bill due on April 14 and in accepting the unauthorized foreign exchange purchased from the Stinnes firm rather than covering the entire ninety-three thousand pounds from its account with the Procurement Board. It also was at fault for failing to find out if the Stinnes firm had sufficient stocks of foreign exchange, and there is no evidence that the Stinnes representatives ever suggested that they had stores of exchange and would not have to go out onto the market. Indeed, it is difficult not to conclude that the Ministry was more concerned about finding a way around the restrictions being imposed by the Reichsbank and other government agencies than it was in preventing the massive purchase of foreign exchange on the open market. Undoubtedly, there must have been something about the tone

of the Ministerial officials that suggested to the Stinnes-firm officials that fast help was needed. But it is no less obvious that the firm was quite ready and willing to overlook its lack of authorization and to take an action which could not go unnoticed on the market. Approximately four hundred thousand to five hundred thousand pounds were transacted daily on the Berlin money exchange, and a private effort to purchase ninety-three thousand pounds by so prominent a firm as Stinnes's could hardly escape the attention of those in the business. In this sense, the affair probably played some role in the breakdown of the mark support action a few days later.[72]

What makes the affair significant, however, is not the issue of "guilt." There is no evidence that any of those involved had any intention of sabotaging the government effort, whatever some of them may have thought of it, and the heavier burden of responsibility certainly lies with the Ministry rather than the private firm. The real problem was that the Ruhr occupation simply replicated the dilemmas arising from the interaction between the public and private sectors that had already been evident in the war. The German economy could not function without the railroads, and the latter could not function without coal, and coal had to be purchased through private import firms. All involved had a short-term stake in the others' improvidence, and each action had its own rationality and legitimacy. It was, however, no way to deal with a crisis that was at once domestic and international, and the events described were a symptom of the problems of governance which had plagued one Weimar regime after the other.

Of all those who had ruled Germany since 1918, however, Cuno was the least suitable person to guide his nation out of the morass. He profoundly misread the political situation and the way in which he could use his powers most effectively. This was well demonstrated in a report by his business associate, Arndt von Holtzendorff, on a conversation with Cuno in early April:

Cuno very much regrets that he has been given so little power as Chancellor to do things internally as he would like. In foreign policy, he will attain his goal, but in domestic politics the Reich government has damned little influence. In Prussia, there is a Socialist government; in Bavaria one that is completely to the right; in Saxony a Communist one and in Thuringia another Socialist one. This naturally makes it enormously difficult for the Reich government to impose its will. Here only a dictatorship can really bring about a change, but that is naturally impossible now.[73]

In reality, there was little reason for Cuno to think he could attain his foreign policy goals at this time. Furthermore, it was precisely the devastation wrought by the Ruhr occupation and passive resistance that continued to make the domestic situation more and more dangerous. Passive resistance was turning the claim of the right that the path to domestic stabilization lay in solving the reparations problem into a self-fulfilling prophecy. The irony was that it really made little difference anymore whether one argued for the primacy of internal stabilization measures or of an international settlement. In either case, the initiative had to come from Germany. The chief obstacle to a reparations settlement, however serious the problems posed by Bavaria, did not come from the internal problems Cuno mentioned, but rather from his own erstwhile colleagues in industry. They did not give him the support he needed to pursue a passive resistance policy for as long as might have been necessary for a successful diplomatic action to put the reparations question on a new basis, assuming one believes that passive resistance could have produced such results. This was amply demonstrated by the failure of the dollar loan and the collapse of the mark support action. At the same time, the industrialists were anything but helpful in promoting a diplomatic program that stood a reasonable chance of success. There was no evidence, as some well-placed persons believed, that the "new intentions of making the mark worse" attributed to Stinnes had the purpose of demonstrating that Germany could not pay reparations and thereby excluding sensible solutions in government discussions with industrial leaders on the reparations problem.[74] The very fact that this could be believed, however, demonstrated that the internal barriers to a solution of the Ruhr problem were much more in his own camp than Cuno was willing to recognize. By late April, however, the realities were imposing themselves in such a way that an increasing number of persons realized that the major question was whether Germany could find a way out of the Ruhr crisis before it was too late.

Crisis Mismanagement: Cuno's Foreign Policy in the Ruhr Crisis

In early March 1923, the then young and always very nationalistic historian Gerhard Ritter sent a letter to his mother that is something of a monument to the analytical failings of the Prussian school of historiography he would later so brilliantly represent. Filled with enthusiasm, pride, and patriotism, he wrote:

We once again have a state that acts and not only "fulfills." And wondrous enough is the effect; the misused state which was yesterday so despised, which was treated by industry practically as a powerless marionette . . . is today again the leading force in public life. The *state* determines the exchange rate of the dollar; the *state* has the railroads in the occupied area firmly in its hands; the allegedly so international big capital suffers martyrdom in order not to be alienated from the German state. . . . And with this respect for its own state, the German people recovers its own self-respect.[75]

For Ritter, the most important immediate consequence of this imagined state of affairs was in domestic rather than foreign policy. He thought the "unity of all classes" in the occupied areas more impressive than that achieved during the war because "now for the first time those who are 'propertied' and those who are 'governing' stand farther forward at the front than the little man from the masses." He was thrilled at the spirit of self-sacrifice that supposedly filled the land, although he admitted somewhat disingenuously that "as a civil servant . . . the state solicitously eases these sacrifices *very much*. If the prices are fabulous, so are the salaries."

Developments during the weeks following Ritter's remarks amply demonstrated that a more pathetic misreading of the real situation of the Cuno government is hard to imagine. The "State's" ability to control the value of the mark was only one of many illusions disproved by events in the spring of 1923. Insofar as the railroads were concerned, a "State" did indeed gain ever firmer control over the system in the occupied areas, but it was the French state. If there were any true "martyrs" of the passive resistance policy, it was the transportation workers and officials, who bore the brunt of the French policy of reprisals and expulsions and who found themselves increasingly bewildered by and resentful of the policy of so-called "elastic resistance" which the government had begun pursuing in mid-March. In contrast to "strict" resistance, "elastic" resistance involved the acceptance of certain regulations of the occupation authority, such as requesting export and import licenses or automobile permits as a means of either maintaining a modicum of economic activity in the occupied zone or of sanctifying existing practice. The most extreme illustration of the elasticity of this form of "resistance" was provided by the coal-mining industry. Employers and miners contended that they could continue production so long as they did not have to do so at the point of French bayonets and in total obliviousness to the fact that the French were confiscating the coal at the pitheads and transporting it to France! Furthermore, at the beginning of the passive resistance it was the mine owners and miners who had complained bitterly about the failure of the railroad personnel to join the movement; now the railroad workers and officials were complaining that they were making all the sacrifices while the mining industry continued business as usual.[76]

Ritter's notion that the French occupation had called forth a unity of classes was largely fantasy. There was not even much unity within the classes, especially if the tension between Socialists and Communists is taken into account. As for the collaboration between industry and labor, it never really got off the ground. The organizations represented in the ZAG did, to be sure, declare their intention to collaborate in matters of wages and prices and engaged in the well-practiced art of wage-price trade-offs, both before and after the mark support action, as well as in a measure of wage and price restraint during the mark stabilization. A truer measure of the constraints placed on collaboration by the growing tensions of the previous years, however, was the fiasco of the so-called "Ruhr Assistance" (Ruhrhilfe). Set up by the ZAG under government inspiration in late January, the organization was to gather contributions to assist Ruhr workers who were unemployed or on short time. The basic idea was for each worker in the unoccupied areas to contribute one hour's wage a week to the cause, while the employers would provide four times as much. Commerce and agriculture were called upon to contribute as well. Although the leadership of the ADGB argued passionately that the chief burden was being carried by employers and that the Ruhr Assistance was a way of making sure that employer monies did not go into the hands of rightist fanatics, important trade unions (most notably the AfA and DMV) refused to give any funds to an organization in which employers were involved, and numerous local trade-union organizations took the same hostile position. At the end of April, the Ruhr Assistance had collected five billion marks, not the twenty-five billion anticipated, and it was soon merged with the German People's Fund (Deutsches Volksopfer) set up by the government to help widows and pensioners.[77]

Underlying the failure of the of the Ruhr Assistance was the feeling that employers and propertied classes were not really at the forefront of the struggle against the French, as Ritter imagined, but rather potentially or actually at the forefront of those seeking to make an arrangement with the French at the expense of the German working class. Certainly, at some moments workers had good cause to be impressed by the stand taken by some employers, Fritz Thyssen, for example, who faced a French court-martial and was sent to prison. Furthermore, some employers had an almost fanatical will to resist, as in the case of Paul Reusch. This did not mean, however, that Reusch and other tough-minded supporters of passive resistance did not wish or work for a settlement, and they invariably felt that big concessions by labor would have to be a major, if not the major, foundation for terminating the conflict in the Ruhr.

Industrialists could hardly be faulted for facing reality, of course. Stinnes thought it important that the French be shown that they could not do whatever they wished with the Germans, but he recognized, as he told Stresemann in mid-March, that time was on the side of the enemy and felt that Cuno was making a mistake in treating the passive resistance as an end in itself. Similarly, he wrote Ambassador Wied-feldt that things were going well in the Ruhr but that it was important to negotiate with the French before Germany's breath ran out. It was perfectly proper for Stinnes to confide in fellow Germans, and the views cited were at one with many trade-union and Socialist leaders, who were making the same criticisms of the govern-ment. Far more problematic was the willing-ness of leading shareholders in the Phoenix concern, Otto Wolff and Werner Carp, to hold a meeting with the French Consul in Düsseldorf in late April at which they criticized Cuno's slowness in coming to the negotiating table; they also suggested discussions with leading French industrialists close to the authorities in Paris as a possible means of leading to talks at the governmental level. Most serious, however, was the action by some businessmen, like banker Rinkel of the Solomon Oppenheim firm of Cologne, who had previously served as a go-between in Franco-German heavy-industrial relations. He stated quite openly to an Ameri-can businessman that Germany could well af-ford to pay large reparations but that no Ger-man offer would be accepted because the French wanted to create a separate Rhenish state, and he intimated that he saw no way of preventing the French from achieving their goals.[78]

As anxious as Stinnes was for an understand-ing with France, he showed no readiness to ac-cept a settlement at any price and was particu-larly hostile to the idea of French participation in German industry, let alone French control of the Rhineland. As he put it to Wiedfeldt, "When I am facing a blackmailer, I would rather give him my wallet with its contents than the key to the house."[79] In reality, however, Stinnes continued to hope that France could be bought off with the mortgaging of state enter-prises and the increased labor of the working class. Thus, in a visit to Rome at the end of March, Stinnes met with the American steel in-dustrialist Judge Gary to discuss the situation. When Gary asked whether Stinnes thought the Germans had done everything possible to fulfill their reparations obligations, Stinnes re-sponded in a way that would have confirmed the worst trade-union suspicions. As Stinnes later recorded:

I told Judge Gary that I could in no way say that; on the contrary, I have often told my German country-men in the labor force and especially the Social Dem-ocrats that they were acting very unfairly and even criminally because, through the Socialist economy, they were impairing production to such an extent that even without the reparations sums the economy would be passive by two billion gold marks. Despite this, as a German I must refuse to accuse my coun-trymen in the labor force and the civil service before the assembled public of other nations, since I must find new ways to an orderly economy in common ef-fort with my fellow countrymen and that this is pre-cluded if one reproaches them beforehand before third parties.[80]

What was essential, Stinnes argued, was that the "Socialist economy" be eliminated and that all state- and municipally-owned enterprises be privatized and made productive. Germany did require outside help, and it was essential that the leaders of the German economy get to-gether with foreign creditors and determine the circumstances under which Germany might become a reliable debtor. Stinnes was certain that under such conditions, the German people "would be absolutely good for a certain not too high amount of reparation." Indeed, "if the German people could purchase freedom through productive labor, then they would cer-tainly do it and not prefer laziness to no free-dom. But, one must present the alternative to the population in order to bring about a sure change of present conditions."

It is doubtful that this was what Ritter meant when he spoke of the propertied as standing far-ther forward at the front than the masses, al-though it is manifest that Stinnes had a good many of his own illusions. But then again a sub-stantial amount of illusion permeated the thinking of Germany's leaders even as they haltingly faced some of the realities of the situ-ation. Stinnes, however dubious his solutions, certainly had a point in suspecting that Cuno and Foreign Minister Rosenberg were pursuing the passive resistance policy for its own sake. The same criticism was being made not only by the political left but also within the Cuno Cab-inet and in most political circles outside the DNVP and right wing of the DVP. Most wor-risome in the first months of the passive resist-ance was that Cuno and Rosenberg seemed to be taking the position that negotiations and a settlement would be impossible so long as the

French remained in the Ruhr. When pressed on the issue by the constantly worried Thüringian Minister-President Fröhlich in mid-February, Brauns told the Reichsrat Delegates that discussion of the problem of negotiations in public would weaken Germany's position and was to be avoided. He went on to point out that the position actually was that Germany would not negotiate "under the force of bayonets," a formula which he viewed as "rather flexible."[81] This was not, however, very reassuring, especially since the pronouncements of Cuno and Rosenberg not only sounded like the statements coming from the extreme right—especially from its major spokesman in the DNVP, Helfferich—but also seemed to confirm suspicions that government policy was, in fact, being influenced by Helfferich. Cuno had served in the wartime Treasury Office and had ties to and been an admirer of Helfferich ever since. Rosenberg had worked closely with Helfferich in the prewar Foreign Office, and Becker had economic views identical to Helfferich's and had been notably supportive of Helfferich's positions in the Reichstag.[82] Little wonder, therefore, that government pretensions to moderation were often suspect and that many were concerned that Cuno and Rosenberg were digging themselves into a pit from which they would be unable to emerge.

It had, of course, become traditional for postwar German governments and industrial leaders to expect that one of the great powers would toss a rope for them to climb out. As usual, opinions differed as to which of the great powers would play the savior. Stinnes seemed to believe that the French could be brought to terms by some combination of economic reason, passive resistance, and an international business arrangement, but they had to understand that a relationship with Germany meant partnership and excluded control of German industrial assets. He placed little store in an Anglo-American intervention and felt that a "continental block without Anglo-Saxon leadership the best for us Germans," since it logically would give "us the upper hand or at least equality." As he once allied with Thyssen in the prewar period, even though he found Krupp and Haniel more sympathetic personally, so he now preferred to come to an arrangement with the French and

Russians. At the same time, he was certainly seeking to engage in business with prominent American and British business leaders, presumably like Judge Gary, on a worldwide scale. The major problem, of course, was that nations were not businesses and their leaders could not function as businessmen. The more immediate difficulty was that the French government and even opposition leaders treated overtures by Stinnes's representatives with a cold shoulder. They had little reason to do otherwise since Stinnes was certain that the twenty billion goldmark offer which the German government had refrained from making public in December made for a suitable basis for negotiation provided "the entire controlled economy, the entire Socialist economy in Germany, is laid aside." Here, the help of those lending money to Germany would be essential, since Germany seemed incapable of accomplishing these internal reforms on its own. In short, Stinnes offered an unacceptable amount, the payment of which depended upon the capacity of international bankers, cheerfully "assisted with the advice of Germany's economic leaders," to pressure Germany into a reform of its internal policies. The French not only refused to consider such terms but also darkly indicated that much higher reparations, the continued occupation of Essen, and the creation of a Rhenish state with internationalized railroads would provide the only suitable bases for an agreement.[83]

Reports of these demands only strengthened the inclination of the Cuno government and business leaders allied with it to look to the United States and England. Not the least important of the reasons for Cuno's appointment had been his close American business connections, but these were proving of little avail in the early months of the Ruhr crisis. Ambassador Houghton was most sympathetic and constantly urged a more active American policy in Washington while advising the Germans against presenting a fixed offer in the belief that a bankers' committee would not advise a sum greater than Germany could pay. On the point of a fixed sum, he differed with Fred I. Kent of the Bankers Trust Company. Kent, however, also wished the United States to intervene and used his trip to the International Chamber of Commerce in Rome to hold discussions with political and economic leaders in Paris and Berlin. His discussions with Poincaré led him to urge that Germany offer a fixed amount. Feeling strong isolationist pressure, however, U.S. Secretary of State Hughes was unwilling to budge from his stand of December 1922. This had included a readiness to participate in an expert investigation and report on the reparations situation and to encourage a comprehensive political and economic settlement provided that France first requested American good offices. The State Department's response to Houghton's interventionism and close relations with Cuno was to keep the Ambassador in Washington for two months after he returned home for a visit in May and thus out of contact with Cuno while his regime went through its worst agonies.[84]

The British had proven only somewhat less frustrating to German intentions. Here, too, informal business contacts were used, such as those of Arndt von Holtzendorff with his cousin Sir Eyre Crowe, and Paul Reusch with Sir Eric Geddes, a former Transport Minister through whom the Germans hoped to contact Bonar Law. The Reusch mission, carried out on April 24, was especially important, not because it accomplished anything but rather because the instructions given to Reusch were a good illustration of Cuno's inconsequentiality and that odd mixture of whining and blackmailing that had been the hallmark of Germany's prewar diplomacy. On the one hand, Reusch was told confidentially to inform the British that Germany could hold out for weeks at best, not months. On the other hand, he was instructed to warn that Germany was prepared to use her last economic resources in the struggle and that the longer it lasted, the less there would be to cover reparations. The present German government was prepared to accept a "reasonable" reparations settlement and carry it out. In contrast to some other German government which might accept more but be able to perform less, Cuno claimed that his was regarded as Germany's last government capable of giving its signature in good faith. It was essential, therefore, that England and the United States summon a conference of experts. Germany would then immediately raise a loan of sixteen billion gold marks while the experts decided on a final sum. Ger-

many would also offer guarantees, which were not specified, and would resume deliveries of reparations in kind.[85]

The Reusch mission was predictive of the inadequacies of any response Germany might make at this point, even if the English had responded to German urging. On April 20, Lord Curzon, yielding to his own domestic pressures that Britain do something, made a speech in the House of Lords urging Germany to take the first step and make an offer and specify guarantees. Curzon claimed that this would lead to some progress. In reality, Curzon had no reason whatever to be so sanguine since the French resented any British intervention at this point and were unwilling to entertain any offer to which preconditions might be attached. Insofar as the Germans were concerned, the forces driving the Cuno government to do something were largely internal, namely, widespread criticism of the government for its diplomatic inactivity. It did not take Cuno and Rosenberg long to find out that the Curzon speech involved no change in British policy. There is some evidence that they might have limited their response to a speech in the Reichstag were it not for the fact that the press simply assumed and expected that the German response would take the form of a note. Furthermore, there were immense pressures from within the Cabinet, especially from Hermes and Brauns, as well as from state governments and trade unions for Germany to make a formal response.[86]

The uninspiring consequence of this situation was the German Note to the Allied Powers of May 2, 1923. The note reaffirmed the German intention of continuing passive resistance until the areas occupied since January were evacuated. It then picked up on the German reparations plan devised prior to the occupation under which Germany offered a total of thirty billion gold marks. Twenty billion of these were to be paid through loans by July 1927, and the remainder was to be paid in five-billion-mark installments in 1929 and 1931 from additional loans raised for this purpose, unless an international committee determined that Germany could not manage the payments or needed more time. During the four-year moratorium on the first twenty billion, Germany was to pay no interest, and the interest on the payment of the loans was to be taken out of the loans themselves thereby setting the real value of the offer at fifteen billion gold marks. Since the most favorable British proposal yet made, that devised by Bradbury and presented by Bonar Law at Paris in January, had set a global sum of fifty billion gold marks with terms giving it a real worth of twenty-five billion, the German offer of May 2 was bound to make a terrible impression on the British. This fact, obvious to the critics of Cuno and Rosenberg both within and without the regime, did not prevent the German note from declaring that the offer was the absolute limit of Germany's capacity. The possibility of a rejection of the German offer was dealt with by a proposal that, in such an eventuality, an international commission be set up to review the entire reparations question as had been proposed by Secretary of State Hughes. Although Germany would in no way formally obligate itself to accept such a commission's findings, the moral effect of such a report would be as good as binding. Finally, no concrete guarantees were offered. The May 2 note left this question to future negotiations while pointing out that the Reich was prepared to undertake legal measures requiring the private sector of the economy to place its resources behind the service of the reparations loans.[87]

The logic of Cuno and Rosenberg was that they could not offer more for Germany than had been offered in January, for otherwise they would be indirectly justifying the French occupation. It was not an argument likely to satisfy the politically sensible either at home or abroad. Hermes seriously thought of resigning, and others found the substance and the tactics employed inadequate to the situation. The criticism, implicit and explicit, began even before the note was sent. Stresemann, for example, greatly irritated Cuno and Rosenberg by writing that "life and death do not depend upon whether Germany has to pay a billion more or less, but whether the Rhineland and the Ruhr remain German may very well depend on it."[88] There had, in fact, been a severe struggle within the government over the note, Bergmann advising a more generous offer with the support of Brauns, Reconstruction Minister Albert, and Schröder of the Finance Ministry. As one member of this group noted, Cuno was even more

pedantic than the "otherwise very mentally rigid and short-sighted Rosenberg." The Chancellor compounded the damage by his overdependence on special interests for advice:

Cuno has a peculiar idea of numerical offers. He feels himself responsible for every decimal point. I often have the impression that he believes he must make an offer that measures the ability of Germany to pay to the last dot on the "i." He must therefore more or less say: I have calculated the German ability to pay at 35,555,555,555 marks and 55 pfennig and therefore propose to pay this sum. Once again the Reich Chancellery is getting testimony from every conceivable expert from industry and banking. . . . Once again it makes the old mistake of consulting interested parties as experts and lets them have a say in the amount that Germany can pay. This method will revenge itself this time as it has with past governments. . . . But it is noteworthy that those who rule in Germany always underestimate their own power and strengthen their enemies.[89]

The same point was made very candidly by Carl Melchior on May 10 after a very anxious Cuno had summoned him to discuss what all were now anticipating to be a very negative response to the German note. Cuno realized he would be called upon to raise the German offer and to be concrete about guarantees. But while he recognized that it might be politically correct to offer more and then hope that a more reasonable sum would be accepted in quieter times, he did not feel he could now lead a government that would do so. Melchior agreed that Cuno could not now offer a higher sum, but he was convinced that the German government could gracefully retreat from the thirty billion by suggesting that a commission of experts raise the amount if it came to other conclusions about Germany's capacity. Melchior thought it essential, however, that there be a clear and precise specification of the guarantees put forward. Otherwise, Germany would be accused of perpetrating a "dishonorable bluff." When Cuno pointed out that Bücher of the RdI was supposedly working on the guarantees question but had not turned up anything for months, Melchior bluntly replied that Cuno could expect no results if he relied on the RdI or some conference of German experts:

As things stand with us, each group will try to shift the burdens on to the other. If he [i.e., Cuno] wants to have a historic success for Germany and a change in our present plight, then he must have the courage to accept the enmity of industry and other economic circles and of the press dependent upon them. I can only think of negotiations with the Reich Association such that he summons Privy Councilor Bücher to tell him that . . . industry has a choice between taking on an obligation in gold or accepting participation [in its enterprises], and they must make proposals as to which of the two evils they view as the lesser. One of the two is necessary.[90]

At the same time, Melchior urged Cuno to stay in office, since his departure could either lead to a Socialist Cabinet and the danger of a civil war, in which Bavaria, Pommerania, and East Prussia would leave the Reich, or a new bourgeois Cabinet with insufficient authority to rule. For Melchior, therefore, the only solution was for the Cuno government to act decisively and independently and strengthen its hand against both the interest groups and the centrifugal political forces with which it was confronted. So long as Cuno could get a majority in the Reichstag, Melchior thought it a "complete misconception of democracy" for Cuno and Rosenberg to consult widely about each diplomatic note they sent rather than decide for themselves on such matters.

Melchior was impressed that Cuno did not appear offended by the rather open criticism of his leadership, which implied that Cuno might be the problem rather than the solution. Perhaps Cuno did not comprehend Melchior's message. Whatever the case, the course he pursued during the next few weeks demonstrated little ability or inclination to follow Melchior's advice. His situation, of course, was no easy one with either the parties upon whom he relied for support or within his own Cabinet. A widely noted article by Stresemann calling for a great sacrifice on the part of industry to maintain the integrity of the Reich sharpened the conflicts with the DVP, while the DNVP leader Hergt made a speech warning that his party would strongly oppose any concessions beyond those already made. The mere placing of the question of a mortgage on private property on the agenda of a commission established to investigate various aspects of the reparations question provoked opposition from industrialists in the Center and DVP. At the same time, Foreign Minister Rosenberg threatened to resign if Germany responded to sharp British and French criticism of the German Note to the Allied

Powers of May 2 by raising the total amount of the German offer. Hermes strongly urged such a step, while Cuno, strongly protective of Rosenberg but also ailing and torn by conflicting advice, seemed prepared to accept a higher amount if proposed by an international commission of experts. Confidence in Cuno was waning on all sides, and comparisons were being made with the end of the war along with sarcastic remarks that Germany had not even been spared a "second Michaelis." Any new German note, therefore, would have to find a way around the deep division in the government itself.[91]

With respect to the question of guarantees, the handling of the "productive estates" proved especially thorny. Cuno's approach to industry showed little of that firmness and clarity of purpose called for by Melchior. In fact, these qualities were shown by industry, which expected to play a major role in the negotiations of any settlement and was not very shy about stating its position in responding to Cuno and other government leaders. In all of this, industry was encouraged by Helfferich, who urgently advised that "the employers (finally!) take the leadership on the reparations question into their hands."[92] Stinnes, of course, was always ready to take the initiative. He advised Cuno in mid-May to concentrate on reparations rather than political questions in his next note to the allies, to offer annuities and evade the issue of a final sum, and to consult with the foreign powers about the note before sending it so that he could be assured of a positive response. These were all actions Cuno was to take, probably even without the advice of Stinnes.

Far more significant were Stinnes's views on the guarantee question, both in his conversation with Cuno and at the RdI meetings held in mid-May to discuss this issue. He noted that the Treaty of Versailles had made the assets of the Reich, not the private property of its citizens, liable for the payment of reparations, and it followed from this that the enterprises of the Reich had first to be put up as security in any reparations arrangement so "that the private individual would be burdened only to the lowest conceivable extent." Stinnes had a very concrete and by now very familiar program for accomplishing this goal. The state-owned enterprises—above all, the railroads—were to be separated from state management and placed under the control of "management corporations" (*Betriebsgesellschaften*) which would be obligated to pay the state a yearly lease denominated in gold values with which the state could then pay off its international obligations. This payment would be guaranteed by the members of the management corporations, who would come from the private sector, and the private sector would thus be responsible for operating the enterprises at a profit sufficient to pay the lease. Stinnes did not rule out the possibility of having the trade unions participate in the management corporations, probably in the expectation that their involvement would make them understand and take responsibility—or, in a perfectly plausible alternative interpretation, implicate themselves—in the economic and social measures required to pay the lease.

The demands upon the state, however, by no means ended here. Stinnes felt that the time had come for the various governmental authorities at all levels to eliminate their ownership of enterprises. Some of them were producing such products as sausage and margarine and were competing with private enterprises by using taxpayer money, thus serving the interests of parliamentary members who sat on their supervisory boards. The time had come for the state to reduce its activity, concentrate on its "governmental functions," and increase the quality of its administration, as well as the authority of the state, by reducing its size and activity. As usual, Stinnes called for the elimination of the controlled economy, although he made a significant exception in the matter of housing. While this might be taken to demonstrate that the housing situation was so bad that even the strongest advocate of a free economy could not support the termination of controls in this area, it is important not to overlook that rent controls constituted an indirect subsidization of wages at the expense of the middle-class house owners which was by no means disadvantageous to the employers.

In fact, Stinnes was even more unabashedly self-serving than usual in his discussion with Cuno. There was nothing particularly noteworthy about his insistence that the tax system had to be reformed in a way that would encourage capital accumulation and thereby ultimately increase rather than lower tax receipts. Far more interesting was his argument that "extraordinary measures" had to be taken to make the annuity payments that would be part of any reparations settlement and that the bases had to be found in the "two pillars" of "property and labor." With respect to the former, he called for a "compulsory gold mortgage" on all immovable property. There was no point in trying to encumber liquid capital because it could so easily be made to disappear, and it was dangerous to encumber operating capital. As a ferocious enemy of the "foreignization" that had taken place during the inflation, Stinnes thought it particularly important to tax real assets. Thus (to use his most revealing example) by imposing a forced mortgage on the real assets of the Pheonix concern, its Dutch stockholders would become "liable to pay a tribute on the German reparations," and the same would hold true of the many foreigners who had bought up German real estate. Foreigners, in short, would be compelled to cover an important portion of the forced loan and would be encouraged to pay it off rapidly!

Stinnes argued, not surprisingly, that labor's share of the burden would have to take the form of increased hours of work. But he gave this requirement an imaginative twist by suggesting that it had to be viewed as a kind of "mortgage" on the eight-hour day, which could be "paid off," and thus the eight-hour day could be restored when the means of production could be improved enough to make that possible. This would at once appeal to the "psyche" of the workers and would establish a parallel between the burden on property and the burden on labor. This was not the only way in which Stinnes intended to appeal to the workers. He also argued that every effort had to be made to restore the real wages of the workers to their prewar levels and went so far as to declare that "those portions of the employer group which cannot manage this—and these will probably not be a few because of the outcome of the war—are unsuitable for their task and it is logical in terms of the recuperation of our economic circumstances that they be eliminated as employers in the course of events." This was nothing less than an open declaration that the rationalization and economic recovery would have to take place at the expense of small and medium-sized business. If Stinnes was to some extent returning to his 1918 idea of finding some basis for restoring the collaboration of big business and labor at the potential expense of small and medium-sized business, he had not cast aside the concern about those who had been expropriated through the inflation. Indeed, he argued that a "modest gold pension" had to be paid such persons—by the state, of course—and this not as "a social pension, but explicitly as a compensation for the fraud committed against them through the inflation. Actually, all persons who trusted their money to the state and thereby helped it through investment in fixed interest obligations and similar securities have been defrauded of their property through the manipulation of the state."

It is difficult not to wonder at this point how Stinnes felt about the holders of 1908 bonds issued by the Deutsch-Luxemburg concern, who had been informed in early February 1923 that the bonds would be paid off on April 1. When one incredulous bondholder who was obviously not given to such celebrations of April Fool's Day asked if the concern really intended to pay him twelve thousand worthless marks in return for his investment, he was assured by the Legal Division that this indeed was the intention. He was also informed that "in taking this position, we find ourselves in the same position as the Reich, the states, the municipalities, the savings banks, the mortgage banks and the other debtors, whose debt exists in a simple sum of money and who can similarly pay off their debt through the submission of its nominal amount."[93] An intelligent guess as to Stinnes's feelings about this problem would be that the state should be responsible here as well. Who, after all, had made the inflation?

What is important to recognize, however, is that while Stinnes was quite original, especially in the way he framed his arguments, he was not *that* original, either in paying off his bonds or in his views on the guarantee question. They were shared to a very great extent by his colleagues in the RdI. When Cuno and Becker appeared as supplicants—and that is the only term one can use—before the Presidium of the RdI on May 15, the Chancellor was roundly criticized for

failing to consult with industry before sending his Note to the Allied Powers of May 2. He was told that industry could not put up guarantees if it were not made a party to the relevant negotiations and effectively compelled to reassure the industrialists that he would not promise more than Germany could pay as well as consult them in the future. Total opposition was expressed to foreign participation in German enterprises as a method of guarantee and strong opposition to any mortgage of German customs receipts. The business leaders also insisted that the Reich and states mortgage their enterprises first. Peter Klöckner was especially outspoken in his demand that no mortgage be placed on industrial assets which could not be paid off in a generation and that industry receive the assurance from labor that it would work more intensively. Finally, he bluntly asked Cuno if the government was ready "to proceed with the transformation of the revolutionary economy into a rational economy."[94]

While Cuno and Becker raised no objection to the substance of the RdI demands, they did raise some practical concerns and also warned about tactics. The enterprises of the states could not be mortgaged as easily as those of the Reich for political reasons, and Cuno was particularly concerned that the hours-of-work question not be made a formal condition of a guarantee by industry. He was convinced that the guarantee question had to be solved first, after which the government could be "helpful" in the matter of internal reforms, especially since the outside pressure for a settlement would aid the cause. Similarly, Becker cautioned that stress on the hours-of-work question would lead to an "immediate collapse of the defensive front on the Ruhr."[95] Many of the industrialists were in a radical mood, literally expecting the Cuno government to be a "cabinet of German business."[96] They were infuriated when it did not thus behave and were inclined to present an ultimatum in return for their assistance. Nevertheless, the cooler heads of Bücher, Sorge, and Lammers were able to prevail somewhat. Sorge was particularly worried that industry would be accused of trying to evade its obligations and warned that "the mood in the political parties from the left to far into the People's Party is in no way friendly to industry."[97]

While the formal response of the RdI to the Chancellor on the guarantee question of May 25, 1923, reflected the moderating influence of Lammers rather than the sharp line desired by Silverberg, it was not the sort of offer likely to gain industry warm public appreciation. Insofar as the state enterprises could not provide the entire amount needed once they had been put on a profitable footing, the private sectors of the economy could provide up to five hundred million gold marks a year. Industry, however, could only provide 40 percent of this amount, and then only if the reparations issue were settled in a satisfactory manner, if Germany were given a moratorium and granted most-favored-nation status, and if the controls on business were eliminated and labor productivity increased.[98]

The content of the RdI offer, which leaked out in somewhat distorted form before it was released in full by the government on May 29, made a justifiably bad impression. Even some businessmen found it embarrassing. Banker Arthur Solmssen objected both to the form of the offer and to the manner in which it had been made public. Heinrich von Thyssen-Bornemisza, one of the co-owners of the Thyssen enterprises, was not only concerned about the bad impression made by the note but also attacked the manifest inadequacy of the offer, pointing out that "the outside world will never understand that the economically weaker element, namely the Reich with its railroads, etc., should do more than industry, agriculture, shipping, and commerce, etc. If one wants to commit oneself to figures, then I would reverse the relationship to one-third by the Reich and two-thirds by industry, agriculture, etc."[99] There was also some nervousness about the RdI's assault on the eight-hour day. As the banker Robert Bürgers contemptuously remarked, "[T]he eight-hour day is regarded by the workers as the most important remainder of the achievements of the glorious revolution. For the largest number of workers, it is an untouchable relic, and a systematic encroachment upon this allegedly so beneficial institution will call forth immense domestic resistance."[100] Bürgers himself thought it more important and politic to do something about restoring wage differentials, and he undoubtedly had a point.

The Socialist trade unions responded to the RdI in precisely the way one could have anticipated, expressing outrage at the inadequacy of the RdI offer, accusing the industrialists of an unwillingness to pay their fair share of taxes, and denouncing them for abusing their economic power and seeking to take advantage of the distress of the state. Indeed, they saw in the posture of the RdI a "complete reversal of the relationship between business and the state. Industry seeks here to negotiate with the state as an independent power and presents demands where the matter is one of fulfilling the duties of citizens toward the state. The attitude of industry leads one to the conclusion that it wishes to solve the entire problem of reparations on an industry-to-industry basis to the exclusion of the state. The authority of the state must be unbearably weakened if the Reich government agrees to the conditions of the Reich Association."[101] Such sentiments were by no means limited to the left-wing workers in the Marxist parties. The Christian-trade-union leaders were equally incensed. They saw the existing taxation system and the industrialist stress on indirect taxes as meaning that "the great mass of consumers, thus in essence the workers, will have to bear the costs of the four-year international slaughter. Such a solution is unacceptable to us Christian national workers." The industrialists' reparations offer would mean that "the majority of the German workers would be reduced to *Lumpenproletarier*, who would have to toil through their lives to the point where their tongues hang out. But we workers do not have the intention of permitting ourselves alone to be thus worn out."[102]

The Reich Chancellery, therefore, had good reason to be concerned by the consequences of industry's attitude, especially since that attitude seemed to be getting more extreme. Reports that Bücher had been telling foreign industrialists that the negotiations would be conducted on an industry-to-industry basis without direct government participation were noted with some alarm, and there was downright irritation over the fact that Bücher had been invited to participate in Ministerial discussions devoted to framing a legal basis for the projected guarantee. It was one thing for the government to receive and consider expert advice in written form, another for it to have interested parties participate in the framing of legislation. Things had come so far, however, that the RdI saw itself as an equal or even superior to the state. In a personal letter of clarification, Bücher informed Cuno that, although previously insistent that the only reparations arrangement that could be made was one based on a global sum, he had now come to the conclusion that the best approach was to offer annuities. In short, industry now sanctioned this approach. While prepared to accept a one-time levy on wealth to get payments rolling, he specifically warned against any regular special tax on wealth to pay for reparations. Finally, while recognizing that other interest groups that were asked to put up security for the new offer might have suggestions modifying the ones proposed by the RdI, Bücher made it clear that these would have to be presented to the RdI Presidium for examination. As he explained, "Without such an opportunity for examination on our side . . . we must view our expert report as a self-contained whole from which in our view it is improper to take out individual parts if one intends to count upon the readiness [to give assistance] expressed in our letter of May 25 in the course of any form of further action."[103] The government, in short, would have to accept the terms of the RdI as they stood unless the RdI agreed to modify them.

The tone of the leading agricultural organizations with whom Cuno negotiated was not very much different from that of the industrialists. Here, too, the government was criticized for acting without prior consultation in sending its Note to the Allied Powers of May 2, and assistance was made conditional on the creation of a final reparations settlement, the restoration of economic freedom, acceptable levels of taxation, and the reestablishment of law and order in the country.[104]

It was, therefore, with very contingent and restraining preconditions that the Cuno government proceeded to frame a new Note to the Allies of June 7, 1923. Nevertheless, the note did represent considerable progress in Germany's approach to the reparations question. It set no preconditions with respect to the French occupation, left the determination of a final sum to an expert commission, and offered an-

nuities insofar as a loan could not be arranged. Most important, for the first time it offered concrete guarantees in the form of a mortgage on the Reichsbahn, which was to be made independent of the regular government administration. Proceeds from duties and excise taxes on tobacco and alcoholic products were also to be mobilized. In addition to the five hundred million gold marks per year to be guaranteed from Reich sources, a further five hundred million was promised through a guarantee by the major economic sectors to be raised in the form of a mortgage or tax.[105]

Even before sending the note, the German government was aware that it would be received favorably by Great Britain, the United States, and Italy and would also find Belgium basically well-disposed to the proposal. Poincaré, unfortunately, was not equally impressed and refused to consider any offer that did not involve the termination of passive resistance and the statement of a satisfactory concrete reparations sum. Furthermore, he opposed the replacement of the Reparations Commission by a committee of experts and did not find the guarantees offered sufficiently concrete. Insofar as the goal of the Cuno–Rosenberg effort was to win over the British and weaken the Franco-Belgian front, it scored considerable success, and marked the beginning of increasing tension between Britain and France over French recalcitrance. Unfortunately for Cuno, all this was taking place too late to do him much good. As Stresemann noted toward the end of June, "the state of political matters is that England is showing a great deal of activity and appears to be filled with goodwill to do everything possible in order to liquidate the Ruhr action, but in the last analysis everything still depends on France and there is no visible inclination there to come to an agreement with Germany. I see the future very darkly in this respect."[106] Especially dangerous was the fact that this British "activity" resurrected a pattern that had plagued the diplomacy of reparations at earlier dates when Britain seemed to be on Germany's side. That is, the British, in their increasingly righteous irritation at the French, encouraged the Germans to hold out—in this case with their passive resistance policy—without ever taking or being able to take sufficiently rapid or significant actions to help the Germans benefit from their policy. While Rosenberg waited for his policy of winning over England to produce results, Germany was falling apart, and the Cuno government was becoming the victim of the domestic crisis it had done so much to spawn.[107] The real significance of the German Note to the Allies of June 7, therefore, insofar as it did not move Germany along toward the kind of long-run settlement of reparations that was to take place months later, was what it revealed about the disintegration of public authority in Germany.

Crisis Mismanagement: The Domestic Crisis of the Spring and Summer of 1923

The incompetence of the Cuno government was one of the chief sources of the crisis of governance that struck Germany during this period. This was a subject on which Germans of nearly all political persuasions had reached a rare measure of consensus by the summer of 1923. As Hans von Raumer told Stresemann in late July, "[I]n my view, one cannot say that the Socialists are wrong in arguing that the Cuno cabinet pursues a very unskillful domestic policy and that they are above all completely lacking in plans and ideas in their economic policy. It is regrettable to note that the disappointment in this regard unites capitalists and Socialists in the same criticism."[108] Since the Cuno government based its power on the pretension that it was a nonpartisan administration of "experts," with special competency in the economic area, and had come into office because of the failure to establish a Great Coalition government, the formation of a Great Coalition of opposition to its economic policies constitutes just about the most telling testimony to its deficiencies one can imagine. The single most important measure of Cuno's failure was the horrendous hyperinflation (see Table 40, p. 644) and its accompanying social and political disorder. The question naturally arises as to what Cuno and his government did to deal with this disaster as it progressed after the collapse of the mark support action in mid-April 1923. The importance of such decisions lay in the fact that the time was needed for Germany's diplomatic efforts to succeed, and this meant that the economic and financial credibility of the passive resistance effort had to be maintained. A proper appreciation of the inadequacy of the Cuno government, therefore, can only proceed from an appreciation of the forces at work that made effective action so imperative following the collapse of the mark support action.

Passive resistance was a phenomenally expensive enterprise. By the end of June, the Reich had guaranteed about two and a half trillion paper marks in credits granted by the Reichsbank, the Reich Credit Corporation, and the Prussian Central Cooperative Bank. Some 1.6 trillion of this amount given to heavy industry was partially to be paid back in valorized form based either on the pound sterling or the price of pig iron. In addition to heavy industry government-guaranteed credits had been granted to banks in the occupied areas, to wine growers to maintain operations, and to various cooperatives for the purchase of food and clothing for the population of the occupied areas. Furthermore, between January and the end of June, the Treasury had actually provided 5.2 trillion marks in funds for the Ruhr conflict— an average of a trillion marks a month. Most of this went to the Labor Ministry to cover social costs and to the railroads and post to cover the deficits arising from the occupation. The effects on the railroad budget were particularly significant. Prior to the occupation, the railroads had accounted for 31 percent of the income of the Reich budget while accounting for only 18 percent of its expenditures. This surplus was now lost, as had been the surplus from the Saar and Upper Silesia. The hard-pressed railroad system was thus deprived of its most profitable territories while being forced to pour huge amounts of money into the purchase of English coal to keep the system running. Because of the continuing decline of the mark and increased wage costs, an average expenditure of one and a half to two trillion marks on credits per month was anticipated for July–October 1923; that is, a minimum of six trillion marks for the coming four months.[109]

In reality, of course, these astronomical numbers are not very enlightening about the real expense of the operation. The costs for the months of July and August, however fantastic the paper-mark sums, were not substantially higher when calculated in gold marks than the costs for June. A steady state of disastrous expenditure had been achieved by early summer. The Reich Statistical Office put a great deal of effort into calculating expenditures for a projected later attempt by the government to demonstrate Germany's diminished capacity to pay reparations because of the Ruhr conflict in another one of those lengthy and futile "expert" reports with which Germany had been responding to Allied demands since 1919. By these calculations, the fiscal damage to the Reich and the states by the first six months of the Ruhr struggle was an estimated 827.6 million gold marks, using the wholesale price index as a measure, or 703.8 million gold marks, using the dollar exchange rate as a measure. The capital loss to the Reich through the credits it granted was estimated at 444.8 million gold marks calculated at the wholesale price index and 404.4 million gold marks calculated according to the exchange rate of the dollar.[110]

Perhaps the most interesting calculation was the estimate made of the extent to which the Ruhr crisis had added to the "normal inflationary requirement"—a most revealing terminological indication of government adaptation to inflation in the last months of 1922. The "additional inflationary requirement" created by the Ruhr crisis for the public and private sectors amounted to 426 million gold marks over and above the "normal" requirements for the six-month period (see Table 43). These various costs did not take into account the costs to the economy involved in reduced production and exports as a consequence of the Ruhr occupation, a situation which was driving the German economy back to the disastrous levels of 1919 and truly terminating the economic reconstruction.

It was in no way surprising that the private sector wished to minimize the damage of the Ruhr occupation to itself as much as possible and to employ the credit arrangements made with the government and Reichsbank toward this end. The tactics by which such goals could be achieved were clearly demonstrated in the case of the Steel Finance Corporation. If the steel industrialists had most reluctantly agreed to terms under which half their credits would be valorized, the resumption of mark depreciation

Table 43. Inflation Requirements of the Reich and the Private Sector, September–December 1922 and January–June 1923
(in millions of gold marks)

	Reich	Private Sector[1]
Average Monthly Requirement for:		
September–December 1922	266	53
January–June 1923	314	86
Additional Average Monthly Requirement	48	22
Total Additional Requirement for Six Months	288	138

Source: "Schädigungen Deutschlands durch den Ruhreinbruch," a confidential memorandum of the Statistisches Reichsamt, undated, summer of 1923, GstAPrK, Rep. 84a, Nr. 1410, p. 18.

[1]Use of the Reichsbank through the submission of bills of exchange and the rediscounting of Treasury notes, and use of the loan bureaus less the amount of Treasury notes in free circulation.

after the collapse of the mark support action gave them a perfect opportunity to complain about the terms to which they had just agreed. With a good deal of self-righteousness and even more disingenuousness, they pointed out that the manner in which the credits were being given violated the government's own claims that a mark equaled a mark:

It is incomprehensible that the ministry has fought against giving paper mark credit until now when one considers that only the paper mark is valid everywhere in Germany, that the Reichsbank only discounts paper mark bills of exchange, that it deducts the exact amount of paper marks stated on the bills when they fall due, and that furthermore all the banks have one type of account, that they give paper marks and later demand back the same number of paper marks along with interest and charges, and that finally, in our entire economic life no distinction is made between paper marks which are given and then received back, and that even in the case of the Reichsbank notes only the number of paper marks are given which appear on their face regardless of the note's date of issue.[111]

The author of these lines certainly was as aware as his colleagues in heavy industry of the advantages of paper-mark debts in improving the real position of concerns under existing circumstances. Krupp, for example, calculated on June 4, 1923, that the real value of its paper-mark debt had diminished by 1,601,000 gold marks during the previous week because of the depreciation of its paper-mark debt while its supply of foreign exchange had remained stable.[112]

Since the paper mark was now serving the interests of both the government and heavy industry, it is not surprising that they finally decided on a policy of mutual accommodation with respect to the credit arrangements of the Steel Finance Corporation. The government wanted to encourage production as much as possible to prevent further unemployment and needed to finance the steel firms for this purpose. The heavy-industrial firms intended to claim compensation for their losses in the Ruhr crisis and therefore found their debt to the government a means of ensuring that they would be in a position to deduct their claims against the government from the monies owed to it. Thus, industry agreed to some portion of its credits being valorized, while the Finance Ministry increasingly reduced the amounts of the credit subject to valorization—first from 50 to 33.33 percent in the case of the first credits taken, then in June and July on a sliding scale from 25 to 5 percent as the amount of credit taken increased. Also, steel industrialists were able to get these credits at 6 percent interest, or at a third of the absurdly low rate charged by the Reichsbank.

In considering these policies, it is necessary to bear in mind that the alternative to thus supporting the productivity of industry, even when it was nothing more than productivity for the purpose of piling up production, was to pay for the unemployment of labor with all its attendant economic and political dangers. The costs of the decisions taken to pay guarantee wages for unproductive employment, and to supply productive unemployment support as well as higher levels of unemployment support in the occupied areas wherever necessary, began to be seriously felt in March and increased steadily in significance in the spring and summer. For the same financial reasons that had undermined the productive unemployment support program prior to the Ruhr conflict, this form of work creation played a relatively small role in dealing with the unemployment problem. The Reich found it too expensive, and the municipalities did not receive enough help from the Reich to make it work. Actual unemployment support was becoming increasingly important

and increasingly dangerous for two reasons: first, because the higher levels provided in the occupied areas encouraged unemployed from outside those areas to come to seek benefits and, second, because the benefits were inadequate even when they were the equivalent of the basic wage since they did not cover the lost overtime needed to meet rising prices. Sometimes, moreover, the benefits were an incentive to unemployment. Hotel workers who were unable to make tips because of the reduced number of travelers were known to have urged their employers to fire them since they could do better on unemployment relief. It was difficult not to note that the railroad workers and officials who had been expelled or were unable to work under the French received their full wages and salaries and were doing much better in many cases than those who were able to work. Little wonder that Hermes viewed the wage guarantee system as "unfortunately leading increasingly to conditions of the greatest corruption and demoralization."[113]

The major question, therefore, was whether the wage guarantee system could be made to function without totally destroying the finances of the Reich. Control over the validity of claims for the compensation of unproductive wage costs was an especially serious problem. The Düren Agreement of February 10, 1923, providing for joint employer–trade-union collaboration had broken down, in part because of French harassment. Their efforts to seize government funds provided for such purposes made it necessary to locate control in the so-called external economic bureaus (WASTs) set up on the borders of the occupied areas. Mutual suspicion also contributed to the breakdown. Whether with dishonest intent or not, there had been many cases in which the monies intended to cover wage guarantees were confused with monies provided as credits to employers, and the businessmen were often suspected of using the wage guarantees to enrich themselves.[114] Whatever the case, by June the payment of unproductive labor costs took on major importance because of the tightening French controls and seizures of raw materials. The most significant development in this regard was an agreement reached in June between the Northwest Group of the Association of Iron and Steel Industrialists and the Reich under which the latter was to pay two-thirds of unproductive labor costs and employers were to cover the remainder. What constituted "unproductive labor" was to be determined by five district commissions composed of management and labor. Disputes were to be settled by an Arbitration Board headed by Dr. Syrup of the Reich Labor Administration. The entire arrangement, which was similar to one created for the coal industry, disturbed not only the Finance Ministry but even the usually friendly Economics Ministry, which apparently found the control mechanisms insufficient. However, the plan was pushed through by the Labor Ministry, which wished to maintain employment at all costs. These costs were substantially increased in July by an arrangement which obligated the Reich to increase its contribution as production decreased below half of what it had been in the last months of 1922. If production fell below 10 percent, then the Reich would have to cover all the unproductive labor costs. This new settlement was, in part, a compensation to the industrialists for the government's refusal to extend the logic of paying for unproductive labor costs, as the industrialists began to demand, by also paying for unproductive operating costs.[115]

In considering these agreements and provisions, one must, of course, also bear in mind that prices and wages were rising in an increasingly uncontrolled manner following the collapse of the mark support action. Prior to this time, there had been some slight reduction of wholesale price levels (see Table 40, p. 644), although it really would be more appropriate to speak of their relative stabilization, especially since in March, for example, the cost-of-living index was actually 8 percent above that of February. In mid-February, the RWM sent an entreaty to the various industrial and commercial peak organizations to put their patriotism before their inclination to disregard the stabilization of the mark in their pricing.[116]

As might be expected, the RWM received protestations claiming good behavior and demonstrations of an assortment of price reductions, but most interesting were those responses which threw the burden of reducing prices right back at the government. The German Chamber of Commerce and Industry pointed out that the Reich had raised freight rates, postal rates, coal prices, and rents precisely when the mark had improved and thereby had done much to negate any beneficial effect. Food prices had been similarly raised. While recognizing that these increases had been scheduled before the mark support action had taken effect, the organization called on the government to undertake its own price reduction program in these areas. Even more ironic was a similar demand by agricultural interests, which presented a resolution to the RWR in early March calling on the government to bring the prices of necessities into line with incomes. While Socialists Wissell and Hilferding were always ready to welcome such proposals, chemical industrialist Carl Duisberg expressed astonishment that agriculture, which had always demanded a free market, should suddenly come forth with a resolution that smacked of further economic controls. As the proponents of the resolution explained, however, neither labor nor industry understood or chose to understand what the farmer representatives were driving at; namely, a reduction of coal and potash prices so that farmers could afford to buy the fertilizer they needed at prices within their income limits. Industry had managed to raise its prices to world-market levels, and if the farmers could not do so because of the Ruhr situation, then it was the task of government to find some means of lowering the prices of raw materials needed by farmers! The argument, of course, was not without cogency, and there was much complaining about cartel resistance to price reduction, although the RWM insisted it did not have the personnel or money to conduct thorough investigations. It is important to note, however, that potash and coal prices were reduced under government influence in the price stabilization effort. Similarly, the government held back on its plan to eliminate its subsidy on the price of grain delivered under the levy. The argument in late February and throughout March had been to use whatever financial reserves were necessary to prevent an immediate series of price increases. As State Secretary Trendelenburg bluntly stated the policy in late February, "we must awaken the belief that this is the last wave of price increases even if we ourselves do not entirely share it."[117]

Once the mark support action collapsed, however, prices increased quite literally by leaps and bounds. Coal prices rose from an average of 114,117 marks per ton in April to 129,288 in May, 320,893 in June, and 1,126,742 in July; pig-iron prices soared from 623,613 marks per ton in April to 1,253,968 in May, 2,634,700 in June, and 8,924,806 in July. The Reich cost-of-living index (1914 equals 1) mounted from 2,954 marks in April to 3,816 in May, 7,650 in June, and 37,651 in July.[118] A more concrete illustration of the rise of the cost of living is to be found in the account of the cost of basic necessities for a four-week period for a working man, his wife, and two children (aged six and ten) by the American Consul in Cologne. On April 11, it was 433,509 marks; on April 25, it was 463,366 marks; on June 6, it was 981,233 marks; on August 14, it was 83,706,541 marks.[119]

Such circumstances made it utterly impossible to maintain the wage stabilization effort that had accompanied the mark support action. The Socialist trade unions had mixed feelings about this attempt to maintain wage levels and found themselves divided and rather disadvantaged in their efforts to confront what appeared to be a concerted front of government and industry aimed at the prevention of wage increases. The mine-workers' union was most cautious in making wage demands, recognizing the necessity of keeping down coal prices, and agreed in February to put off a wage increase until May. But other unions felt that there had to be more immediate adjustments to prevent further encroachments on the real living standard of the workers. Basically, the ADGB pursued a policy of leaving the wage issue to individual unions while it supported wage stabilization whenever possible. It did so on the basis of an agreement with the government, which had, in turn, promised not to make public pronouncements in favor of keeping the lid on wages since "the unions did not want to appear as acting under the pressure of the government."[120] An apparent violation of this agreement in early March led to protests by Leipart, and the difficulties of the ADGB position were more than amply demonstrated when members called the entire policy into question at the very time when the mark support action was collapsing.

On the one hand, there was a good deal of evidence that the Employers Association (VdA) was making a concerted effort to hold the line on wages, and this was, in fact, the case. Thus, the Wage Policy Committee of the VdA called upon its members to resist wage increases in March and April. It took the position that wage increases during February had been so high that they had enabled labor to recover from its losses at the end of 1922 as well as to compensate for the minor increases in the cost of living that had taken place since then. The VdA argued in a tone much friendlier to the government's economic policies than that taken by some of the RdI leaders. While accepting in principle the position that wages had to be adjusted to rising prices, the VdA strongly urged its members to stand behind the mark support action of the Reichsbank. It argued that if employers were going to support the government's efforts to hold down wages, then they also had to support the government's restrictive credit policies, despite all the hardships entailed. This enabled the VdA to criticize wage concessions very strongly and declare that it was the "economic and patriotic duty" of employer organizations to reject arbitration awards raising wages in April.[121] While admitting that prices had gone up 8 percent in March, the VdA insisted that the price increases at the beginning of the month had been corrected in the second half.

On the other hand, in making this statement, the VdA was, in fact, following the line of the RAM and the Chancellor, although both denied any intention of opposing wage increases when price levels justified them and contested that they had broken trust with the unions by seeking to show that statements on the issue had been misconstrued.[122] The denials and corrections left the ADGB with the impression that the RAM was in a very confused state and that it had subordinated itself to the RWM. The normally conciliatory Paul Umbreit bluntly declared that "the Labor Ministry deserves our distrust since it has apparently fallen into dependence on the Economics Ministry." One of his colleagues expressed anxiety over the instructions being given to the mediation and arbitration boards, warning that "the declaration of arbitration decisions as binding is very dangerous. I fear that this method will be used to reduce wages one day."[123] Thus, even before prices began to rise again, trade-union leaders were mobilizing to demand that the government either significantly lower prices or accept suitable wage increases and were assuming a hostile attitude toward what they viewed as systematic collusion between employers and the government.

At the same time, they sought to remind the employers of the pledge made in January to do their utmost to meet worker needs in wage negotiations and to at least keep real wages at their January levels. In the trade-union view, the tacit pact made between the two sides at the onset of the passive resistance was being broken by employers. Leipart had already protested against the VdA policy at the ZAG directors' meeting of April 16. He returned to the charge at a tense ZAG meeting on April 23 in which, strongly seconded by the Christian mine-union leader Otte, he protested the manner in which employers were turning down arbitration decisions raising wages. The significance of this meeting as well as of debates in the Reich Economic Council at this time, however, is that they marked the onset of what was to become a continuing two-track discussion between employers and workers that was to last until the end of the inflation. On the one hand, the two sides debated and deepened their differences on the relationship between wages and basic economic and social policy; on the other, they wrestled with the dilemmas of trying to find a way to determine wages under conditions of extreme hyperinflation. Of course, there had been concurrent debates about basic policy and the nitty-gritty issues of setting wages since 1918. What made these discussions different was that employers were moving more actively to realize their agenda while the normally manageable issues of day-to-day wage determination, usually handled by adjusting wages to the monthly cost-of-living index, appeared increasingly insoluble.[124]

Reacting to trade-union complaints about employer wage policies, employers now consistently blamed the situation on the various economic controls. These, they claimed, made it economically impossible to maintain real-wage levels as German prices attained world-market levels and the insufficient productivity of the economy came home to roost. Moreover, with considerable support from the RWM, industrialists had taken a very bold step toward the economic freedom they craved when they made a desperate but unsuccessful effort to eliminate the export control boards in late March and early April. To their usual and by no means unjustified complaints about the morass of bureaucratic regulation, high cost, excess officialdom, and inability to make a sufficient profit, employers now also insisted that the days when businessmen would sell abroad for marks and dump at unprofitable prices were over. The lessons of inflation had been learned, and the government could ensure sale for foreign currencies and the turning over of foreign exchange by much simpler procedures. The trade unions, certainly motivated by fear of losing their voice in foreign trade matters, responded that it could not be known if the conditions leading to the creation of the boards in the first place might not return and that it would be insane to dismantle the system only to have to re-create it. They also spoke rather vaguely about using the boards to control domestic prices, that is, as a mechanism to control cartels. While the unions succeeded in blocking the total dismantling of the system, they were compelled to agree to a substantial extension of the list of goods freed from export controls and levies.[125]

Employers intensified the pressure to move further in this direction after the collapse of the mark support action and sought to connect their demands with the wage issue. Bücher was especially formidable in presenting their case. Since the collapse of the mark support action made it impossible for German producers to hold back in their foreign-exchange requirements any longer, everything had to be done to promote exports. He noted that "we have gradually become clear about the fact that we have only lasted through the last four years because of the depreciation of our currency. Our entire economy has survived through the stupidity of others. . . . for otherwise we could not have outlasted the extraordinary deficit in our trade balance and even more in our balance of payments."[126] Bücher insisted that most of the trade advantage had come through access to cheaper raw materials, not low wages, an argument which produced some bitter mirth on the part of trade unionists. It was not an argument, however, which Bücher was prepared to drop.

He certainly agreed that wages were low if one simply argued that wages had only increased by 1,800 to 2,400 times over, while the mark had depreciated by 5,500 times, the cost of iron had increased by 12,000 times, and that of copper by 8,000 times. The important point for Bücher, however, was that wages could only be considered too low if the labor productivity that went into the manufacture of an item were the same as it had been before the war. This was not the case. At Siemens, for example, the effectiveness of workers measured by labor input into items of manufacture before the war was 9.5 hours of productivity in a 8.45-hour working day, whereas in the last few years it had been 6.48 hours of effective production for an 8-hour day. From this Bücher concluded that "the individual wage is too low, but the input into the manufactured article is much too low to allow the same wage as in the prewar period."[127]

Tarnow, Leipart, and other trade-union leaders found more than a little sleight of hand in Bücher's argumentation. While agreeing that wages were an economic and not simply a social problem and conceding that there was a great deal of unproductive labor in the economy, they found it difficult to believe that the prices being charged in Germany's highly cartelized economy were natural and justifiable. In Tarnow's view, Germany was still competitive because of its low wages, and he found the posture of the industrialists very contradictory:

We see that when it comes to wage determination, the fiction of prices below world-market levels is tenaciously retained, and that one studiously seeks to stabilize wages at the level at which they are found. That is, you want, on the one hand, to keep production costs low, under world-market parity and want, on the other side, to fully realize the possibility of getting world-market prices. One cannot do both of these things at the same time. You must then join with us in a common wage policy that will justify your demand for world-market prices. But you cannot do the one and seek to neglect the other.[128]

Otte was even more pointed about the contradictions in the employer position at the ZAG meeting on April 23:

The employers wish the support of the workers in eliminating the coal tax, the demobilization decrees, etc.; they want freedom for the economy. On the other side, there are the cartels, which one-sidedly set prices. It will not do to turn down wage increases by

pointing to the government's mark-support action while the cartels continue in their activities without paying any attention to the intentions of the government.[129]

What was becoming clear at this point, therefore, was that the leading employer groups were seeking to maintain German competitiveness almost entirely at the expense of labor's wages and justified their position by the alleged low productivity of labor and the low productivity of the economy. Employers in no way answered the trade-union charges concerning cartel pricing by telling workers to investigate retailers who failed to bring down their prices and by supporting the continuation of rent controls. Insofar as competitiveness was not to be maintained at the expense of the workers, it was apparently to be maintained at the expense of retailers and house owners![130] This is not to say that the trade unions were fully candid either. The amount of unproductive labor in the economy was a very sticky issue for the trade unions. Were higher wages to be bought at the cost of unemployment? Otte, calling for "more precise calculations" by employers, really failed to address this issue, and at least one trade-union official pointed out that England had solved the problem of unproductive labor by creating massive unemployment.[131] Of course, it was easier for employers to suggest sacrifices on the part of the *Mittelstand* than it was for the trade unions to disregard the unemployed. Nevertheless, the problems and possibilities of some renewed accommodation between industry and labor at the expense of important portions of the middle and working class remained in the background as an important possibility in the long-term rearrangement of the economy and management of the wage problem.

The immediate handling of the wage problem, however, also posed some thorny problems of mutual accommodation, and these, however much jockeying there might be for long-term advantage, had to be solved immediately. At their meeting on April 23, the employers more or less recognized that they could not continue their effort to maintain February wage levels if the already evident collapse of the mark support action led to significant increases in the costs of living. At the same time, the trade unions were demanding the adjustment of wages to prices, but the employers were unclear as to how this was to be understood. Construction workers were asking for wages that were higher than those of miners, while woodworkers were demanding adjustment to the wages of metal workers, and workers in government enterprises were demanding the same wages received by metal workers. From the employer standpoint, this could only lead to "going around in circles." One answer, which Wissell had been giving for some time, was a sliding-scale wage adjusted to the inflation rate. Employers, however, continued to resist this, one of them pointing out that "whether the living standard of a person can be maintained at a specific level depends not upon the will of the employer but rather upon the laws of the economy."[132]

At the same time, it was manifest that the pressure on employers to change their policy was increasing mightily. Before deciding on their policy for May, they turned to the government, warning that a general increase of wages would not only undermine the effort to hold the line on prices but also force a major increase of inflation because of the quantities of money that would be required. As things stood, the monthly wage for workers alone amounted to half the money in circulation. While Cuno was unable to meet with the VdA representatives, Brauns did so and subsequently claimed that he had urged them to make sure that wages kept pace with prices.[133] The VdA Wage Policy Committee paid little attention to this plea in its May circular, declaring that "the trade union demand in the *Zentralarbeitsgemeinschaft* for a guarantee of the real wage of January of this year is unfulfillable, just as unfulfillable as the striving of the workers for a gold wage [that is, a valorized wage] at the present time."[134] Once again, the VdA warned against accepting arbitration awards favorable to worker demands. Wage increases were not justified by the economic situation, and a recently granted wage increase to the miners for May had been pre-arranged in February and was intended to restore the miners to the head of the wage hierarchy. While not necessarily convinced that the miners should be accorded this special position, the VdA thought it important that the structure remain untouched and that the line be held against a new wage–price spiral.

The events of May, especially in the Ruhr, demonstrated the dangers of continuing such a policy of resistance to worker wage demands, but they also showed that the fears of anarchy in the wage structure were well justified. The warnings came early. On May 3, the head of the Metal Workers Union, Dißmann, wrote personally to Brauns to complain that the decision of the mediator in Dortmund to refuse worker demands was simply insupportable in view of the price index during the previous weeks and that strikes, once begun, would spread rapidly. On May 12, the Socialist provincial President in Düsseldorf sent his own warnings about some new decisions by the Dortmund mediator, who had just issued an award giving the skilled metal worker a wage of 1,875 marks while giving unskilled textile workers 1,910 marks in another ruling. The unskilled textile workers were thus getting more than the coal miners, who were engaged in their own negotiations and obviously would take notice of the decision; the metal workers could be counted upon to make new demands so that they could once again pull ahead of the textile workers. On May 16, wild strikes broke out at the Kaiserstuhl mine in Dortmund, and on May 20 the wild-strike movement began to spread throughout the western Ruhr involving some three hundred thousand workers.[135]

Communist agitation and the actions of the so-called Communist Centuries (*Hundertschaften*) clearly played an important role in promoting the strikes and, above all, in the actions of political violence that led to the occupation of town halls and to clashes with police. The alarmed trade-union leaders, however, were unanimous in attributing the situation to the inflationary problem. This is evident from the description of the circumstances by the mine-union leader Husemann:

Because of the monstrous sudden increase in the cost of living brought about by the collapse of the mark and the completely unsatisfactory results of the wage negotiations, the bases for a strike movement in the Ruhr were created which were carried out by Communist, syndicalist, and unorganized elements with an indescribable terror. The members of the Free and all the other unions were brutally and ruthlessly driven from their work places by the so-called Communist Centuries, who were greatly augmented by all kinds of riff-raff. Armed mobs went from factory to factory and in this manner brought economic life to a halt.[136]

Similarly, his colleague Schmidt argued that "the Communists are perhaps the source and bearer of the movement, but the ground was laid by the insufficient concessions by the employers and the attitude of the government."[137] The trade-union leader in Mainz, Schreiber, took exactly the same line, while spelling out more clearly the dangers of the situation:

The last wave of increased living costs, which affected us more severely than elsewhere, has brought the masses to a pitch of excitement that allows for no further escalation. The employers declare that they cannot raise the money needed to make up for the higher prices to even some extent because of their inability to sell. Just as the wages are low, so are the support payments for the unemployed. For some time now unknown agitators, who come from outside, have been plying their trade here and captured reports show that they plan things in this district similar to what has taken place in the Ruhr during the last few days. These irresponsible elements want to bring in Centuries, disarm the police, and occupy public buildings. Whether they will succeed is another matter. Unfortunately we have to state that even our most reasonable people, including leading persons, have completely lost their nerves and treat the situation not only with indifference but actually with approval. This development would not be possible here if the distress and misery were not so great. . . . That the masses are driven to despair under such circumstances is only too comprehensible.[138]

While outrage at the French was strong enough to maintain passive resistance, "the attitude of the employers with respect to raising wages and the striving of the KPD are creating circumstances which can hardly be handled" and were bound to nurture feelings that "the sacrifices which the workers are making in this economic struggle are useless and becoming senseless" and that "the *Diktat* will come. The railroads will fall under French control and the separation of the Rhineland as a buffer state will result."[139]

Neither Brauns nor the trade-union leaders could evade these messages any longer. In response to union complaints, Brauns insisted that he had done nothing to hold back wage increases since the collapse of the mark support action and had even exceeded the cost-of-living index in raising miner wages in late May. As the strongest piece of evidence for his goodwill, he pointed to a letter he had sent to the VdA on May 25 in connection with the price increase for bread in June in which he called upon them to show "understanding" and "fully compensate for both the direct and indirect burdens resulting from the bread price increase."[140] The letter, which was released to the press, infuriated employers. They claimed, in an apparent lapse of memory, that they had always compensated the workers for bread price increases and complained that Brauns's action seemed to confirm charges that the employer wage policy was responsible for the recent Communist successes. Furthermore, they insisted that they had been making policy in consultation with the government all along and rejected the suggestion that being "understanding" involved surrendering totally to the demands of the other side. Finally, they suggested that the Labor Ministry, in calling for compensation for both the direct and indirect costs of the bread price increase, reversed its own previous policies.[141]

The underlying problem of these and subsequent altercations was that previous experience and policies were no longer very helpful in dealing with wages at the existing levels of inflation. The difficulties of measuring real wages by the cost-of-living indices used at the time is well illustrated by considering the results of using three different methods of calculating the cost of living in relation to wages. The first two of these define a monthly real wage, based on the weekly wage, for unskilled and skilled workers in the Berlin chemical industry (see Table 44). Method A is based on the official cost-of-living index used since 1920, which took an average of the cost of living on the sixth and twentieth days of every month. Method B takes the calculation of the *Berliner Industrie- und Handelszeitung*, which takes the average of a day chosen from each week of the month. While both methods show the leveling of wage differentials, the second demonstrates that the greater the frequency with which the cost of living is calculated, the lower the real wage of the workers in question. The trouble is that even the second method cannot give an accurate picture of real wages once the mark support action collapsed and hyperinflation began to accelerate. This is clearly demonstrated by another calculation used by the *Berliner Industrie- und*

Table 44. The Real Monthly Wages of Berlin Chemical-Industry Workers, January–June 1923

(married with one child; 1914 = 100)

	Method A		Method B	
	Unskilled	Skilled	Unskilled	Skilled
January	85.60	64.60	66.39	50.35
February	81.38	61.60	78.44	59.38
March	94.51	72.59	86.33	65.95
April	102.50	78.70	85.94	65.65
May	103.51	79.09	83.83	64.05
June	136.08	103.33	108.77	82.59

Source: Rudolf Meerwarth, "Zur neuesten Entwicklung der Löhne," *Zeitschrift des Preußischen Statistischen Landesamts 1922/23* 62 (Berlin, 1923), p. 340.

Handelszeitung, which started to calculate daily changes in the cost of living on April 14, 1923. This method makes far clearer not only the loss of real income for both kinds of workers when compared to 1914, but also the exhausting instability of their situations in hyperinflation as their real wages began to fluctuate unsteadily from week to week (see Table 45).

If salaries and wages were following too slowly upon the inflation, then a way had to be found to make them more adequate through more rapid and frequent calculation of the cost of living along with more frequent salary and wage adjustments. This, at least, was the conclusion to which Brauns came in late June, when he proposed that they continue to be negotiated every month, but that they rise in between in accordance with an index agreed to by both sides.[142] The trade-union leaders had come to the same conclusion and sought to convince the employers at the ZAG by pointing out that the cost-of-living information came out too late to be of use and that some index method had to be found. As usual, they met resistance from employers, who emphasized that their balances were also subject to depreciation and that the Austrian experience with indexation had not been satisfactory. They even went so far as to suggest that retail prices had not risen as much as wholesale prices so that one could not speak of a "catastrophic sliding of wages."[143] An index, it was claimed, would push prices up, and the technical difficulties would lead to even worse conflicts between industry and labor than already existed. Furthermore, valorized wages would in no way solve the currency problem. As always, the trade unions countered with an

insistence that prices could not be calculated in gold while wages continued to be calculated in paper. They took a more positive view of the Austrian experience than the employers and, above all, stressed that workers were extremely bitter, a fact certainly confirmed by the increasing amount of labor unrest. In the last analysis, they were quite desperate for an agreement, as evidenced by the plea of the white-collar leader, Aufhäuser, for employer cooperation:

If the trade-union leaders wished to take the mood of the workers into account, then they would have to demand peacetime wages. If this demand is not presented, then it is done out of consideration for the general economic situation. He [Aufhäuser] agrees . . . that the currency problem cannot be solved with the demand for valorized wages, but we find ourselves in a corner at the present time and must find a way out. The solution to the currency question has to await further negotiations. What we now have to do is to find a way to get through the transitional stage in the least contentious a manner possible. . . . In the establishment of a formula, he sees a technical aid to make wage negotiations easier. If one decides on short-term contracts of about four weeks, then one can negotiate about a reduction of the wages if the cost of living retreats, for the workers do not care so much about paper wages, but rather want a compensation that enables them to make it through and takes away the insecurity they feel that comes from their pay constantly slipping behind the depreciation of the mark.[144]

Aufhäuser had been especially prominent in this discussion, having authored an interpellation in the Reichstag in early June concerning this question and having proposed there the development of some automatic adjustment mechanism for wages. Brauns had treated this proposal with some skepticism and had placed greater emphasis on a better cost-of-living index. Within the ADGB, however, there was a good deal of skepticism about every solution. A discussion of the question among the ADGB leaders on July 4–5, 1923, makes depressing reading. Paul Umbreit pointed out that all the proposals discussed since the beginning of the hyperinflation seemed unsatisfactory. The return to the peacetime wage, or the wage calculated in gold, and the sliding-scale wage all had their disadvantages. The first would have "catastrophic" consequences by creating unemployment, while sliding-scale wages would deprive the unions of their function in negotiating wages. His colleague Brey, from the Factory Workers Union, added gloom to the gloom:

Although I have tried very hard, I have found no formula for that which should be achieved. We have neither the economic nor the legal power to achieve this goal. I do not believe that we can work against the monetary depreciation through any regulation. All artificial interventions in the regulation of the economy have failed until now, and the attempt to protect the consumers through the state has been a farce. If the power at the disposal of the state has failed, we will not be able to achieve the desired goal as worker organizations. We must strengthen the authority of the state as an instrument and put it into a position to counter the employer organizations and their measures. Through no wage policy can we get around the economic power of the employers. This consideration has not been taken enough into account in the public debates. But we must avoid awakening hopes that lead to disappointments; that is something we cannot handle.[145]

Tarnow, who had raised the entire issue of gold wages in 1922, was somewhat less pessimistic. On the one hand, he warned against confusing valorized wages with peacetime wages, arguing that the latter were impossible under existing conditions. On the other hand, he pointed out that valorized wages had become possible because the businessmen were valorizing their prices. Once the odd situation of the index of real prices being below the index of wholesale prices was remedied by the retailers going over to gold pricing themselves, the way would be paved for valorized wages. While the unions called for a valorization of wages and proposed the use of some kind of centralized measure to provide a basis for wage increases between negotiations, the exact means of valorization remained undetermined, and, given the differ-

Table 45. The Real Weekly Wages of Unskilled and Skilled Workers in the Berlin Chemical Industry, April 14–July 20, 1923
(married with one child; 1914 = 100)

	Unskilled	Skilled
April 14–20	93.46	70.88
April 21–27	87.93	66.46
April 28–May 4	82.96	62.91
May 5–11	89.29	67.82
May 12–18	82.72	62.83
May 19–25	73.23	55.62
May 26–June 1	75.14	57.01
June 2–8	63.46	48.15
June 9–15	92.62	70.08
June 16–22	77.58	58.74
June 23–29	75.69	57.38
June 30–July 6	75.72	57.22
July 7–13	63.22	48.05
July 14–20	75.88	57.68

Source: Rudolf Meerwarth, "Zur neuesten Entwicklung der Löhne," *Zeitschrift des Preußischen Statistischen Landesamts 1922/23* 62 (Berlin, 1923), p. 340.

ences between the workers and employers, the establishment of a joint employer-worker committee to come up with a formula could not be viewed with much hope. In the meantime, the government urged both sides to agree on using government cost-of-living indices, now issued twice a month, or other suitable local or regional indices in setting wages.[146]

The crisis of wage valorization, of course, was part of the larger and fundamentally insoluble problem of providing adequate support for the unemployed, small rentiers, social pensioners, widows, and war disabled, for all of whom the travails of hyperinflation were being multiplied by the collapse of the currency. Now more than ever, misery promoted an angry sensitivity to inequity, and the civil servants, who represented and carried out the misguided and ineffective policies of the state, became a special target of general protest at this time. The civil-servant organizations had managed to procure a significant improvement in their pay in March 1923 despite the government's stabilization effort, and after the collapse of the mark support effort, they fought a successful battle for the indexation of their salaries. The great achievement of the agreement concluded with the government on July 19, however, was to compound the advantages of prepayment of salaries on a monthly or quarterly basis by having partial future projections of the increased

A small firm transports wages from the bank on August 15, 1923, when a gold mark was worth a million paper marks. (*Bundesarchiv Koblenz*)

cost of living prepaid in their salaries. Furthermore, these prepayments were made on the basis of biweekly and then weekly calculations. The agreement thus contained built-in corrections to the real-wage instability from which wage and salary earners normally suffered. Clearly, when the German Federation of Civil Servants spoke of this system as being "the best and only well-functioning one of the inflation,"[147] it knew whereof it spoke.

Understandably, no other group showed equal enthusiasm. The private sector was particularly outraged, not only because a dangerous model was being supported by the government but also because the shortage of cash needed to make wage payments was substantially worsened by the large outlays to the civil servants under the prepayment system. Even more bad blood was caused by the obvious collusion between the government and the civil-servant unions, the intransparent manner in which they had reached their agreement, and the obvious political favor shown to them. The tone of the most important bourgeois reformist organ, *Soziale Praxis,* well conveyed both the social tensions and the dangers arising from this situation:

It seems significant to us that public opinion is now gradually turning against the civil service to an extent that gives great concern. How much hostility is daily directed against that portion of the employed German people with civil service status is shown by the press and also even by those parties which previously supported the civil service through thick and thin and now press for a reduction of the civil service. . . . The civil service can be sure that this attitude will not halt before its "well-earned rights," but will demand sacrifices. The chasm which has developed among academically trained persons during the last years is now taking on the sharpness of a class conflict between the civil servants on the one hand and the doctors, lawyers, writers, etc. on the other. . . . At a time when the non-civil service stratum of cultured Germans can hardly enjoy meat once a week and is literally fading and wasting away—leaving aside its renunciation of the most vital spiritual goods—it is time that the civil servants themselves develop some self-restraint in further pursuing a policy which has arisen out of the competition of the parties for their favor and the shameful weakness of the government. It has turned the broadest circles of the people against the civil service even though a relationship of firm confidence between the civil servants of the Republic and the people is now more desperately needed than ever.[148]

Conditions had, in fact, reached the state in which both the previously relatively quiescent cultured and some of the less cultured were taking matters into their own hands. In Saxony, doctors went out on strike in July to protest the inadequate pay they were receiving from the health insurance funds. Beer drinkers in Thuringia put on a consumers' strike at the same time, while in a rare show of cooperation, Saxon cigar makers, wholesalers, and retailers shut down for three days in protest against having to pay both the cigar and the turnover tax.[149] Strikes by professionals, consumers, and businessmen in a marginal industry, however, were most unimpressive compared to the pressure put on the government by organized labor, the increasingly organized unemployed, and, needless to say, big business. It was more than a weak government could handle, and the Cuno regime pursued economic control policies which were veritable caricatures of those pursued by its predecessors.

This was especially well exemplified in the ongoing war against profiteering. The government was utterly helpless in dealing with the heart of the problem—namely, cartel pricing. The inability to do anything significant about cartel pricing was made abundantly clear in late June when the price examination agency officials met in Stuttgart. The Bavarian representative attacked the failures of the government, characterized the Cartel Advisory Council set up in the Reichstag as a "piece of decoration" and pointed out in frustration that control of the cartels was the only way to prevent the economy from being "raped" and that it would determine "who will rule in the future, business or the state."[150] Insofar as the government showed any boldness, it was in seeking to control "service profiteering" by doctors, lawyers, and other such service providers, to enforce the rules against profiteering and dealing on the cattle and food markets more strictly, and to tighten the controls on those entering into the retail trades. Quite naturally, retailers sought to do what others were doing—namely, to valorize their pricing—but the government went to considerable pains to prevent this. While recognizing that retailers were caught between the "wholesalers who dictate conditions and the consumers who have little purchasing power," the government feared that the retailers, once set loose, would try to use prewar prices as their standard and would fail to take into account low rents and wages. This could only fuel the demand for wages denominated in gold values. Thus, while the reality was that much of the economy and many retailers were calculating according to the index and the exchange rate of the dollar, a decision was made to fight price valorization on the part of retailers and maintain controls on them.[151]

Whatever the justification for focusing on the small merchants at an earlier date, if there ever was one, it had certainly become increasingly cynical and hypocritical since most of the rest of the economy and, above all, the larger businesses calculated and operated in valorized terms. As Georg Bernhard argued:

Large business is absolutely valorized. However small business is not valorized. The small man is now on a treadmill. He cannot have a valorized investment if he does not want to violate the exchange regulations, which to be sure the majority of people, even the smallest, do now as before. . . . But in what kind of situation is the small person who is honest? Take the small merchant, the small craftsman. The state, which in no way thinks of in any way moving against the big fellows, is constantly preoccupied with the profiteering decrees and every possible regulation which ties the knot tighter around the small fellow. . . . For what is the real issue in the reproduction price? If a person has placed his money in valorized form, he does not need to calculate according to the reproduction price . . . . You punish a man for profiteering if he calculates according to reproduction costs. But you do not give him the possibility of putting his money in valorized form. . . . It is in my view immoral for the state to use a double standard and to do so demagogically. Thank God one can no longer throw sand in the eyes of the masses. The great mass of people has for quite a while now seen through the situation because they experience in practice in their own lives that which they could not fathom theoretically.[152]

Retailers, however, were not the only middle-class group deprived of the power to valorize. By 1923, the real value of rents had been reduced to a pittance, and small house owners dependent upon rental income for their livelihood were in no position either to make ends meet or to repair their properties. If they were retailers as well as house owners, they had a double complaint against the controlled economy. More typical was the condition in which members of the *Mittelstand* were at once beneficiaries and victims of the workings of controls in the hyperinflationary setting. Many retailers were victims of price controls and beneficiaries of rent controls, just as many

Berlin retailers protest the government's antiprofiteering measures, August 1923. The sign reads: "Because of the impossibility of securing sufficient supplies due to the various government measures against retailers, the retailers of Greater Berlin will be closed on Thursday, August 9. From August 10 on, business hours will first be *reduced to six hours." (By permission of the Ullstein Verlag)*

house owners were victims of rent control but beneficiaries of the depreciation of their mortgages. Matters were further complicated by the fact that some house owners were compelled to sell off their properties, often to foreigners, to make ends meet and thus ended up with paper marks for their chief real assets. Many were able and clever enough to pay off their mortgages in 1922 and the early months of 1923, but others would not or could not do so. All of this undermined solidarity in the *Mittelstand* and promoted bitterness and confusion.[153]

The movement to provide creditors protection against debtors, already the subject of so much discussion and writing in 1922, was turned into a live political issue on March 1, 1923, when the DVP Deputy Adalbert Düringer introduced a bill calling for a five-year moratorium on mortgage repayments to which lenders denied assent. It was a shrewd proposal. On the one hand, it would put a stop to the flood of repayments against which mortgage holders and mortgage bondholders were totally defenseless. Düringer purportedly had been inspired to act by a Bavarian mortgage banker, perhaps the same banker who reported that

day by day we hear the bitterest reproaches at our counters. I only wish that the opponents of the Düringer bill would go through our files . . . so that they would have a conception of the flood of redemption notices streaming in. I would prefer even more if they would spend a few hours at our mortgage bond windows and observe the heated arguments with the mortgage bondholders concerning the redeemed or to-be-redeemed bonds. Then they would know the disappointment and bitterness that reigns among the hundreds of thousands of . . . mortgage bondholders. . . . We cannot comprehend how those charged with responsibility for Germany's fate and fortune could really allow it to come to pass that our real estate credit, to which Germany owes so much for its past prosperity and which is also so indispensable for a solid reconstruction, must be buried in the grave.[154]

On the other hand, the moratorium left open both the possibility of friendly agreements between creditors and debtors prior to 1927 and the possibility of revaluation of debts if the mark failed to recover a reasonable measure of its value.

Düringer faced almost total opposition within his own party, from the Reichstag, and especially from the government. The moratorium could only have one purpose; namely, preparing the way for revaluation if the mark did not recover. What was to prevent similar claims from being made against holders of industrial bonds or war bonds? The effect of such uncertainty and claims would be to destabilize any stabilization, and it is not surprising that government, industry, and the banks united against the proposal, and the Reichstag killed the measure in committee and then in plenary session. The issue remained very much alive, nevertheless, because of the anger of the creditors—most Germans were angry in 1923—and because of significant evidence that the judicial system was moving in the direction of supporting revaluation. The signals being given by the courts were, to be sure, contradictory. The Cologne *Landgericht* ruled in one case that there was no means under law to prevent the paying off of a prewar mortgage in paper marks since the court had no right to anticipate the legislature, which it viewed as the ultimate source of law. The higher Darmstadt Appeals Court, however, in two decisions of March 29 and May 18 argued that repayment in paper marks violated the provisions for fairness and justice and equity and good faith in the Civil Code. The decision was strongly influenced by the court's President, Dr. Georg Best, who was one of the leading proponents of revaluation.[155]

All of this was very worrisome to the government, especially the DVP Justice Minister Heinze. He was convinced that the mark would never recover its worth and feared that Düringer's proposal would lead not only to fiscal disaster but also to endless litigation and an army of officials to handle the problem. Consequently, an effort was made to mobilize the opposition to a moratorium and revaluation by submitting the matter to the Reich Economic Council for an "expert" recommendation in early May. The RWR could, indeed, be counted upon to support the government's position, although the eminent jurist Hachenburg, who had been converted to support the Düringer proposal after initially opposing it, made an eloquent argument on its behalf. He stressed the strong public feeling against the

"enrichment of the debtor at the expense of the creditor" and urged that the RWR transcend formal legalisms in coping with the problem.[156] The most powerful and forthright argument for burying the entire matter came from Rudolf Hilferding, who found himself in a "Great Coalition" with the employer and business representatives in opposition to the Düringer proposal:

It is certainly very regrettable that because of the monetary depreciation those classes have suffered who are of extraordinary importance for our entire culture, that the *Mittelstand* has been decimated in a manner that is extremely destructive to our entire spiritual life. But one must also say, that it is completely impossible to want to help those affected in this manner. . . . It is completely impossible to intervene here except through social and charitable measures in individual cases. But . . . we cannot today turn back a movement upon which in the end our entire economy has had to base itself. And if we want to judge the matter from a purely economic standpoint, then we must say that . . . it is the one plus in this development that our agriculture and our industry have strengthened themselves extraordinarily through this elimination of their debts and, as a consequence, are potentially capable of bearing the great burdens which they will have to carry in the future.[157]

Hilferding felt that one had every right to expect that the increased ability of industry and agriculture to pay taxes as a result of the elimination of their debts would be employed for the public good, but he rejected the idea that the mortgage holders had some special claim or, indeed, any more of a claim than government and industrial bondholders. The interests of either all these debtors had to be sacrificed to the reconstruction of the finances and economy of the nation or none, and Hilferding's answer was quite clear.

Needless to say, neither industry nor agriculture shared Hilferding's vision of their taxability, but it was obvious from his stand and from the thirteen to three vote against the Düringer proposal in the RWR that the SPD's chief economic thinker and the forces of industry and agriculture could travel a goodly stretch together while trading blows over hours, wages, and other issues of direct interest to the workers. They certainly had a common interest at this point in promoting the valorization of new credits and transactions in terms of some reasonably stable values. The old mortgages might have been disappearing, but new ones were needed. The irony and cynicism involved were not the products of deliberate intention on the part of the actors but rather of the situation itself. Thus, slightly over a month after voting down the Düringer proposal, the RWR Economic Policy Committee met once again to consider a bill, this time one prepared by the government, for the creation of valorized mortgages. The RWR endorsed the measure, which was subsequently passed by the Reichstag and became law on June 23. The legislation provided by the denomination of mortgages in rye, wheat, fine gold, or the price of other goods or services—for example, the value of an hour's labor. As a representative of the Justice Ministry put it, "reverence for traditional forms has to give way to life's necessities." Farmers had to buy fertilizer. To do so, they needed credit, and they had to offer their property as security. No one would give real credit any more against unvalorized paper marks; hence, the need for the legislation. Formally, the government was in no way abandoning the principle of mark for mark since the mortgage was not being denominated in marks at all.[158]

If one believed this, of course, one could believe anything. Hilferding characterized the bill as being "for the first time a principal change in the previous legal fiction that a mark is a mark."[159] The government representative did, in fact, recognize that the bill was just one more act of recognition that the paper mark was ceasing to be an object of value in daily economic practice. An especially good illustration of this process was provided by the insurance business. Major companies began writing insurance in Festmarks during the spring of 1923; that is, insurance valorized in terms of the government-set gold customs rate, a rate which was advantageous because it corresponded much more to local prices than the dollar rate. Thus, a property insured for a thousand Festmarks which burned down on January 31, 1923, would have been worth 3,235,000 marks if paid on that date—the gold customs rate then being 3,235 marks. If the insurance were paid on March 30, when the customs rate was 5,095, the company would have to pay 5,094,938 marks.[160] Clearly, the quest for stable values on the basis of which one might valorize transactions and assets (*Wertbeständigkeit*) was exercising many a fertile German imagination.

One could also argue, however, that the minds most important to the management of Germany's economy and finances were being insufficiently exercised, while an excess of imagination was being demonstrated by others. The importance of the government bill for the creation of valorized mortgages was that it triggered a serious discussion of both these problems in the RWR and helped to focus criticism of the Cuno government's policies as well as to propel the formulation of a genuine program of fiscal reform and pave the way for the subsequent monetary reform. The number of different modes of valorization being employed certainly was problematic, and while of subsidiary importance during the Cuno period, the form valorization should take was to gain in significance in subsequent discussions. As so often was the case, Hilferding understood the long-term implications best, pointing out that this variety of valorized instruments of exchange available was likely to be very harmful in a stabilization since it seemed mistaken to him to denominate mortgages in rye, wheat, coal, and other items which had always been regarded as especially variable in price. Hilferding thought it important to return to the traditional measure of gold. Bernhard shared this view and also suggested that mortgages denominated in gold would increase the pressure on agriculture to rationalize and at the same time prevent the development of a large body of mortgage bondholders with an interest in high rye or wheat prices. Hilferding and Bernhard were unable to carry their point in the bill, primarily because the agrarian interests claimed that the farmers could measure their actual encumbrance far better in rye than gold and the government chose to support their position. The battle over this issue remained to be fought.[161]

The more immediate problem was the totally odd behavior of the Cuno government. Hilferding could not understand the contradictory attitudes of both the private sector and the government, which admitted that valorization was spreading and even encouraged it but then did not draw the full consequences:

I find it to be incongruous and contradictory that, on the one side, business accepts valorization in private contractual and private economic relations and that, on the other side, it refuses to adapt to valorization in the other direction, just as the state, on the one side, represented by the Reich Justice Ministry, recognizes valorization as a self-understood factor while, on the other, the Reich Finance Ministry and the Reich Economics Ministry do not take the same position.[162]

If the private economy could secure the value of its revenues and assets, then certainly the state and the Reichsbank could do the same. Trade-union leader Schweitzer could not agree more. As might be expected, he called for the valorization of wages, but far more important in this context was his opposition to "dealing with the shift from a paper to a gold currency piece by piece instead of dealing with the problem as a whole and at least making the effort to handle the question as a totality."[163]

This was not the style of the Cuno government or the Reichsbank, and the currency and fiscal policies they had pursued since the collapse of the mark support action in mid-April were singularly inadequate to the situation they confronted. The effort to control speculation in foreign currency provided a particularly splendid illustration of these failures. The demand for foreign exchange had been a source of the collapse of the mark support effort, and the problem was bound to be intensified once the mark began depreciating again. Cuno, in his irritation over the business community's lack of support of the gold loan and reports that the mark support action had itself been sabotaged by industry, seemed ready to take some action to tighten up on speculation in foreign exchange. Though he did not want to go as far as a centralized agency for the control of foreign exchange constantly advocated by Hilferding, he at least wanted a decree that required the reporting of all foreign-exchange holdings. In this way, the government would have an inventory (Bestandsaufnahme) of the available foreign exchange in the country, would have greater capacity to determine how much of it was being held illegitimately, and would also be able to exercise some psychological pressure against speculators as well as to encourage further support of the mark. No one could entertain the illusion that the implementation of the proposal would

move mountains, but it nevertheless provoked sharp protests from commerce and industry. Their most cogent argument against the proposal was that it would do little good since those seeking to evade discovery could easily do so, while the evaluation of those who did and did not legitimately hold foreign exchange would take more time than it was worth. More significant was the Hansa city importers' fear that the government was moving toward a centralized control agency and that foreign-exchange holdings which exceeded their immediate obligations would be confiscated. They did not expect such behavior from the Cuno government but felt that a future "evil" government would do so and noted recent statements by former heads of the RWM Schmidt and Hirsch. Rather amazingly, Hirsch's successor, State Secretary Trendelenburg, "did not totally reject the correctness of such fears,"[164] and he considered quite plausible the Hansa merchants' claim that they had not contributed much to the government's gold loan because they had sharply reduced their foreign-exchange holdings during the mark support action. Clearly, the product of such governmental sympathy and business pressure could only be a weak solution, and this found expression in two new decrees of May 8. They subjected the employment of foreign exchange in international trade to the scrutiny of the Foreign Exchange Procurement Board in Berlin and subjected exchange offices (Wechselstuben) to licensing and required them to surrender all foreign currencies received to the Reichsbank within three days.

But the hesitations of May then gave way to the panic of June. The private demand for foreign exchange mounted enormously for both business and speculative purposes, and it was now more difficult than ever to tell them apart. Those in the import–export business with dollar or other foreign-currency accounts found the temptation both to abuse the trust of their clients and to speculate against the mark irresistible.[165] More visible, but no less damaging, to the interests of the government was the endless trading with currency by illegal "corner banks" (Winkelbanken) in Berlin and elsewhere. The basic problem was that those dealing in foreign exchange that was not under the control of the Reichsbank were dealing at higher rates than those being quoted on any given day and were thus adding to the instability of the money market. Hamm warned the Chancellor in a memorandum of June 16 that public opinion was turning against the government for its inactivity. He feared that farmers would refuse to accept paper marks for their products in the fall and urged that something energetic be done to absorb foreign exchange to support the mark as well as to move in the direction of creating accounts and forms of investment in fixed values. On the same day, Hermes fired off a memorandum to Cuno pointing out that the state was at the end of its financial tether and that the currency was in danger of total collapse under existing conditions. He demanded greater control over the expenses of the Ruhr conflict.[166]

The crisis, and an effort to stabilize the mark while waiting upon reaction to the German Note to the Allies of June 7, did produce new and surprisingly drastic government action with respect to speculation in foreign exchange. Its primary expression was the new Foreign Exchange Control Decree issued under the Emergency Powers provided by Article 48 of the Weimar Constitution on June 22, 1923. This provided that foreign exchange could only be bought and sold at the official rate quoted in Berlin on the day on which the business in question was concluded. It established, in short, a unitary exchange rate (*Einheitskurs*). Since the Berlin currency exchange was only open two days of the week, this meant that someone closing a deal on a day when the exchange was closed had to wait until 4:00 P.M. of the following day in order to determine the allowable exchange rate. Further decrees during the next two weeks sought to tighten both the access to foreign exchange and the potential for circumventing the unitary exchange rate. Thus, a decree of June 29 imposed more stringent qualification requirements for each and every request for foreign exchange but also permitted the Reichsbank and government to specify the types of imports for which foreign exchange would be provided. Most rigorous, however, was a decree of July 3, which banned all forward exchange transactions for the mark in an effort to fight the bear market, which meant that importers had to cover their risks immediately. At the same time, futures trading in commodities was banned to put a stop to the practice of acquiring foreign exchange to cover bogus purchases that were never seriously intended but that would provide an opportunity to speculate. Finally, the unitary exchange rate was also extended to the government's dollar Treasury bills, which were being quoted higher than the dollar itself and being purchased to circumvent the Foreign Exchange Control Decree of June 22.[167]

Cuno and his colleagues were well aware that the creation of a unitary exchange rate would be devastating to the import business and frankly told the Cabinet that "the Hamburg import trade will scream; consideration for individual occupational groups, however, is no longer possible; it is self-understood that every compulsory measure is unhealthy."[168] Nevertheless, Cuno acted with the strong support, and possibly at the instigation, of the German Bankers Association and after consultation with the RdI. A member of the Finance Ministry explained to a British embassy official why the bankers had behaved so remarkably:

The big banks are patently afraid of the political situation; they fear that, if social disturbance breaks out, they will be the first object of attack. In the circumstances they desire to place themselves in a favorable light by showing that, for their part, they do not agree with this frantic speculation in foreign currencies which has brought with it the depreciation of the mark and a phenomenal rise in prices.[169]

These bankers and the Finance Ministry apparently saw the unitary exchange rate as being directed against the estimated million speculators in foreign exchange in the country and especially the "corner bankers" in Berlin and other large cities who offered a higher price for foreign exchange after the bourse closed. Such transactions were now illegal, and since such businesses "are generally run by people of doubtful character (Galician Jews and the like)," the expectation was that they would be blackmailed by their employees and driven out of business. The British observer found all this somewhat naive, since a similar measure in Austria had only driven the speculators into the cafés and other undercover locations where they soon constituted a "black bourse" that ended up influencing the exchange rate on the legal bourse!

The government itself recognized that the fixed exchange rate could not work for very long since it was impossible to control the mark quotation on the international market arbitrarily. It had only acted after the RdI assured the government that industry had enough foreign exchange to hold out for a month. At the same time, one could not paralyze the import business for longer than that either. Furthermore, these antispeculation measures were intended to be limited not only in time but also in scope. Suggestions that the banks undertake measures to restrict and control the supply of foreign exchange to business were rejected. Wassermann of the Deutsche Bank pointed out that there were some four thousand banks dealing in foreign exchange in the country and the banks were in the business of carrying out the instructions of their customers, not policing them. They preferred to leave the determination of the purposes for which foreign exchange would be granted to the Reichsbank. At the same time, the bankers firmly rejected Hilferding's renewed plea for a central agency to control the use and distribution of all foreign exchange. Director Ritscher of the Dresdner Bank pointed to the bad experience of the Austrians, where the effect of this type of institution was "a strong drop in the Austrian crown, a strong drop in imports and great increases in prices. The unfavorable effects were only eliminated when Austria, after surrendering her independence, received large foreign credits after some time."[170]

These dangers were also potential consequences of the new German measures, however, and everyone involved was aware of them. The success of the unitary exchange rate really depended on a renewed effort to stabilize the mark, which the Reichsbank sought through interventions and gold sales, and by securing business cooperation in purchasing dollar loan certificates and surrendering foreign-exchange holdings. To some extent, industry was undoubtedly moved to assist by the same anxiety that had led bankers and industrialists to accept the unitary exchange rate. Thus, the banking consortium handling the dollar loan floated the rest of the fifty million it had guaranteed, and industry showed a disposition to do its share as well. Siemens and the AEG seemed most conscientious, as did a small number of other

major concerns, although the satisfaction of the Reichsbank with industrial promises rapidly gave way to new warnings of credit restrictions if the results continued to remain unsatisfactory.[171] The pressure seems to have been to good effect. Carl Duisberg, whose own chemical industry was setting an excellent example, seems to have been particularly outspoken in mobilizing the RdI to promote the effort. As in the first mark support action, however, it was not a model Cuno's associates in Hamburg were prepared to follow. They responded to Reichsbank calls for help from commerce by pointing out that "the situation of commerce is different from that of industry. As is well known, the latter had profited colossally during and after the war and had good earnings. Just the reverse has happened to commerce, which has been so weakened through the results of the war that not much could be expected from it."[172]

Underlying all this, however, were grave doubts about the unitary-exchange-rate policy as well as serious opposition to it. Economics Minister Becker was skeptical from the start, while Reconstruction Minister Albert thought it "the falsest measure that we could take."[173] Hermes's support of the measure was singularly uninspiring, since he openly admitted that the results would be small and felt that everything depended upon a foreign policy success. While everyone appeared willing to sacrifice the interests of the Hamburg exporters to buy a spell of stability, there was great fear that opposition from another quarter—the banking and industrial interests of the Rhineland—would lead to the creation of a "black bourse," two currency quotations, and the collapse of the passive resistance effort. These interests, led by Louis Hagen, who proved particularly obstreperous, wasted no time in announcing on June 23 to the Reich and Prussian governments their refusal "to recognize the decree under any circumstances."[174] It took a joint effort by the leading banks and the government as well as the support of the RdI to bring the Rhenish businessmen to heel by threatening to cut off all credits, close down their accounts, and prosecute them if they violated the law. Cuno personally warned the Rhenish business leaders summoned to Berlin on June 27 that he intended to stick by the decree and succeeded in isolating Hagen. At the same time, he promised that Berlin would supply foreign exchange at the fixed rate if the major cities would aggregate and report their requirements daily to Berlin.[175]

The trouble was that anyone with a special claim upon the government for foreign exchange could learn to do what Cuno had urged the Rhinelanders to do and to do it to excess. This was true even of some Hamburg merchants, who were, after all, importing food and other vital necessities. The new decree might slow business down in Hamburg, where 75 percent of all transactions involved foreign currencies, but it could not be allowed to stop it entirely. The combination of not knowing the exchange rate except at certain times of the day—and thus having to rely on bankers to complete transactions—and not knowing what percentage of one's foreign-exchange needs would be allocated on any given date threatened to have devastating consequences in the case of food imports. Thus, American food importers in Hamburg threatened to ship their food elsewhere unless the government allowed the German importers enough foreign exchange to cover their bills. As a consequence, Hamburg food importers were granted 20 to 30 percent of their daily foreign-exchange requests. This was an open invitation to increase the size of such requests so as to get a larger supply of foreign currency while complaints continued that the Reichsbank was not supplying enough. In mid-July, the Reichsbank furiously rejected such complaints, pointing out that business was getting as much foreign exchange as had been the case before the latest effort to support the mark and that all the demands being made were so excessive that actual requirements could be met by supplying only 4 percent of the foreign exchange being daily demanded. The problems of the new system were compounded by the unwillingness of those holding foreign exchange to give it up at a Berlin rate for the mark substantially below—varying from 20 to 50 percent—the exchange rate for the mark outside Germany and their fear that they would never be able to replace what they had surrendered. Thus, on July 10 even Director Ritscher of the Dresdner Bank was rediscovering the virtues of a centralized control of foreign exchange; he informed State Sec-

retary Hamm that the banks might actually welcome such a system since it would take them out of the foreign-exchange business and relieve them of the "odium" now connected with it.[176]

As for the Reichsbank, there was no "odium" which it was not spared. Most reluctantly, the bank had once again given in to Cuno's call for an effort to support the mark, which it viewed as a futile effort to "swim against the stream" from the outset.[177] Since the first mark support effort seemed to have failed partially because of insufficient consultation and collaboration with the banks and industry, a major effort was made to work with both and to gain support for that other measure of despair—the unitary exchange rate. If the big-time speculators were neutralized and made to cooperate, then one could launch an attack on the mass of speculators. Unhappily, the Reichsbank's and government's mark support strategy here reached the limits of their imagination. The mark support interventions by the Reichsbank, which began on June 19, were very much in the style of the pre-February 1923 interventions of too little too late while they added some new deficiencies to the old. Whether what one British observer termed "another . . . convulsive and desperate attempt to bolster up the mark by throwing foreign currency on the market" and another called a policy that was "completely insane" could have accomplished anything at all is doubtful. But Havenstein's method of backing up the unitary exchange rate made little sense because he concentrated the interventions in Berlin rather than abroad, where the gap between the Berlin and the international quotations might have been closed somewhat. Instead of "gaily" satisfying "the demands of the public by the sale of foreign currencies," as the economic expert at the British embassy cynically suggested to Bergmann, Havenstein should have satisfied public demand for the dollar loan certificates: "My point is, give the Germans here the Dollar Loan; it is after all only paper manufactured in Germany; it costs nothing and is repayable in three years, but do not give them sound money; keep the *Devisen* for more useful ends."[178] Actually, this was something the Reichsbank was trying to do by getting businessmen to accept dollar loan certificates for their foreign exchange gained from exports and, likewise, for the credits they received from the Reichsbank. Nevertheless, insofar as the Reichsbank was finding itself forced to pursue the more cynical approach suggested by the Englishman, it was most uncomfortable with its actions and wished to dampen rather than encourage the increasing speculation in the dollar loan certificates. As Glasenapp reported in mid-July:

It is also to be noted that we not only have to buy marks abroad and give up foreign exchange on the domestic market, but we have also not been able to avoid the giving of dollar loan certificates for marks. Astonishingly, a strong demand for such certificates against payment in paper marks has developed, and the certificates have attained a higher notation than the dollar itself. The speculators therefore first buy dollars and then use the dollars to buy dollar loan certificates which they then sell again for a profit. Under these circumstances, we have to try to reduce the market value of the dollar loan certificates by selling them for marks. This is undesirable because our gold is mortgaged to the later redemption of these certificates without our having received the appropriate foreign exchange for them.[179]

The Havenstein policy was not only costing foreign exchange and compromising the gold-loan certificates, however, but was also eating into his precious gold supply. Between May 15 and July 31, 223.6 million gold-marks' worth of gold were sold, 113 million of which went to cover the Reichsbank guarantee of the Treasury notes issued in connection with the 1922 reparations for Belgium. The purpose of the new Reichsbank mark support action was to bring the mark below a hundred thousand paper marks to the dollar, and it failed miserably. The value of the mark improved somewhat between June 19 and 27 and then deteriorated rapidly again thereafter. On July 14, Glasenapp was still justifying the support action by arguing that without it "no one knows where the dollar would stand today," but on July 28, Havenstein announced the end of the support effort to the Chancellor and further concurred with Becker that the unitary exchange rate had to be lifted since it was destroying Germany's business life and its international credit. That action was taken on August 4.[180]

Nothing, however, fed the growing public dissatisfaction with the Reichsbank more than its credit and discount policies, which appeared increasingly bizarre as the hyperinflation progressed. On July 11, Havenstein appeared before the Reichsbank Central Committee to ask for an increase of the discount rate from 18 to 25 percent. He justified his request by pointing to the immense increase in the Treasury bill, exchange bill, and Lombard credits of the Reichsbank (see Table 43, p. 670) and wondered if it were not time to "bring our discount rate somewhat into line with conditions on the open market,"[181] where average interest rates for daily money were 72 percent at the end of June. As in April, when the rate had been increased from 12 to 18 percent, Havenstein did not expect much from the measure. It would be another "warning signal" and might lead to a greater absorption of Treasury bills by the public. Whether Havenstein's wishy-washy presentation emboldened the bankers on the committee to oppose the measure more strongly than might otherwise have been the case is difficult to say, but with the exception of Carl Fürstenberg of the Berliner Handelsgesellschaft, committee members were unanimous in their opposition and managed to defeat the proposal on this occasion. They insisted that it would compel the private banks to raise their discount rates and that the effect would be to raise price levels and hurt consumers. Industry would find it more difficult to function, and the result would be high unemployment. Salomonsohn, who had fought even against the April increase and who felt vindicated by events, could only see political reasons to take the step; namely, the impression that would be made on the workers and the Entente. While he thought that there might be some benefit from sending the British and Americans a signal that Germany was near collapse, he could see no other advantage. Havenstein's idea that the public might hold more Treasury bills, he pointedly remarked, "rested on an error, for today even those circles which had previously held Treasury bills have the desire to put their money in valorized assets and have a distaste for Treasury bills."

Remarkably, it was not Havenstein but rather Glasenapp who made the strongest case for a discount rate increase and demonstrated that a new consciousness was dawning on at least one high Reichsbank official. Whereas the bankers argued that the increasing inflation made a 25 or 30 percent discount rate too high,

Glasenapp countered that it was precisely the high inflation that made such an interest rate too low:

It is basically, as one expresses it in the newer literature, a kind of "negative rate." If I give someone money for three months today at 25 percent, then the debtor can in general expect that the money, when he repays it, will be worth much less than at the time when he received it. It is therefore an extraordinary advantage for the debtor. Basically, he did not pay any interest, but actually received something additional. But that is also the charge that is raised against us from all sides, namely, that we charge too low a rate to the credit taker, that the debtor gets an extraordinary advantage.[182]

That something so incredibly obvious should have been told to a group of bankers, and this by an experienced Reichsbank official who spoke as if he had just learned something new, is extraordinary, although perhaps less extraordinary than the failure to raise the discount rate in July. Even more remarkable was the continued resistance of the committee when it met again on August 2. This time, Havenstein asked for an increase to 30 percent, pointing out that the situation was much worse and that the private banks were charging 1 percent a day or 360 percent a year since the second half of July. Nevertheless, Havenstein and the directors suffered another defeat, this time by an eighteen to five vote. They insisted on renewed discussion of the matter, however, and finally had their way.[183]

Havenstein's struggle to raise modestly the discount rate, while certainly not comparable to the tenacity and conviction characterizing his struggle against a stabilization effort that could have reduced his precious gold supply back in 1922, does demonstrate that his policies had considerable backing not only from his directors but also from the bankers on the Central Committee. Havenstein surely was correct in arguing that the discounting of Treasury bills— that is, the increasing floating debt—was a more important source of inflation and a greater danger to the credit of the Reichsbank than the commercial bills being discounted for the private sector. Increases of the discount rate, in and of themselves, would not have the desired consequences and would increase the costs of production. And Salomonsohn was correct in pointing out that the public was searching for valorized assets and was reluctant to take Treasury bills anymore, so that raising the discount rate could not significantly decrease the Reichsbank Treasury-bill holdings. Also, the Reichsbank leaders had good reason to be irritated by demands from both the left and the right that they refuse the Reich any more credit and cease printing money. Glasenapp called such outcries "nonsense" and pointed out that "just the people who give us this friendly advice would themselves be immediately outraged and would criticize most energetically the unavoidable collapse of our economy as well as our financial organization that would follow."[184]

All of this did not exonerate Havenstein, however, but rather pointed to the real fault of his policies and, one must hastily add, of the policies of the Cuno government—namely, their inconsistency and inconsequentiality. If important sectors of the economy were not only calculating in real values but also valorizing their assets and trying to operate with valorized means of exchange, then why not promote this tendency so that the need for papermark credits would be reduced, and one could begin to function with valorized credits and effective discount rates? It was precisely here, however, that the Reichsbank and the bankers stoutly resisted all notions of setting up gold accounts, as was being called for by important sectors of industry and commerce with the support of Economics Minister Becker. The latter had been arguing since late April that no mark support action could succeed unless those holding foreign exchange could be offered a safe alternative investment. Typically for the Cuno government, however, what was supported by one Minister was opposed by another. In this case, Finance Minister Hermes apparently shared the view of Havenstein that establishment of gold accounts was too risky an experiment to try.[185]

The discussion of the so-called banco mark and gold accounts had been going on since the end of 1922 and had picked up considerably during the late winter and early spring thanks to the publicity provided by Dr. Dalberg of the RWM.[186] The pressures for action increased greatly after the first mark support action collapsed, and the issue was on the agenda for discussion in connection with the renewed effort to support the mark and the creation of a unitary exchange rate in June. Significantly, the matter was put off for further exploration by a committee under the chairmanship of Becker.[187] Nevertheless, there was little doubt where the Reichsbank and the bankers stood. The argument remained that such accounts were very risky because there seemed to be no way the banks could protect themselves against devastating losses if they opened accounts denominated in real values and then the mark began to recover to a rate higher in value than that of the special accounts. Similarly, it was pointless to give valorized loans since there was no guarantee that the debtors would be good for their debts in a few months. In fact, there did not seem to be much point in doing anything, or at least this was the impression left by a lengthy attack on Dalberg and the supporters of valorized accounts and valorized credits by Director Friedrich of the Reichsbank in the influential *Bank=Archiv* on June 15, 1923. He insisted that, so long as stabilized conditions did not exist, gold-mark accounts and credits were filled with "difficulties, dangers, and impossibilities" that would lead to a "shifting of risks to the banks and the Reichsbank."[188]

Such powerful opposition along with the negative attitude of Hermes could provide little inspiration to those who wanted to pursue the gold-account question. The committee created on June 20 did not meet until July 19, months after the Dalberg proposals and the public discussion had begun and weeks after a decision had been taken to set up the committee. Indeed, the action seems to have been inspired by instructions from Cuno of July 10. Cuno had apparently been very impressed by a discussion with a Hamburg businessman and DVP member, Walther Dauch. Dauch had argued that since the business world was accounting in gold, the time had come to pay wages in gold and thus restore a measure of order among the workers. In Dauch's view, what was needed was not the further financing of the government by the printing press but rather stable assets and an export offensive. Whatever Dauch or Cuno or Becker thought, their views were shared neither by the majority of members of the expert committee nor by Hermes. The committee was

badly divided but did think that in certain cases involving the use of foreign exchange as security, such accounts as well as valorized bills of exchange might be possible. As for Hermes, he responded with lines that had by this time become liturgical for German leaders and bankers: "So long as the reparations question is not finally settled in a way that German payment obligations are brought into line with Germany's real capacity, it is not possible to make Germany's balance of trade and payments active. So long as this is not accomplished, however, every new currency created as a substitute for the paper mark will fall prey to a new depreciation."[189]

Perhaps so, but this formula for passivity, which Hermes also used in defending his tax policies by arguing that "the healing of our circumstances can only have its point of departure from the foreign political side,"[190] could no longer work. German society was moving massively to disown the paper mark, and each step in the direction of valorization made the failure to take another intolerable. The inability of the government to provide a clear and comprehensive program under such circumstances was an act of self-destruction and provided critics of the regime with a field day. The meeting of the Economic and Finance Committees of the Reich Economic Council on July 11, 1923, was a veritable *auto-da-fé* with Hilferding acting as Grand Inquisitor in the condemnation of the government.

The subject of the meeting was the consideration of the report of the Subcommittee on Currency Questions for measures in the area of currency, finance, and wage policy. The report had grown out of the earlier meeting dealing with the creation of valorized mortgages and reflected the rising sentiment for a comprehensive program to deal with the hyperinflation. It directed its primary attention to the problem of attacking the Reich deficit, the floating debt, and the excessive monetary emission and declared that the stabilization of the currency could only take place with the balancing of the budget. The work had to begin with the finances of the Reich and its tax system, and the report called for the greatest possible adjustment of prepayments on income and corporation taxes to the monetary depreciation as well as the frequent and rapid adjustment of railroad, postal, and other government rates. Concerning the Ruhr conflict, the report demanded that it be financed by valorized surcharges on existing taxes and the issuance of a long-term gold loan to which one could subscribe in paper marks. For the Reichsbank, the report prescribed gold-denominated credits, interest, bills, and accounts; the acceptance of foreign-exchange deposits; the creation of a foreign-exchange fund from industry against gold certificates for the purpose of backing a new currency support action; and assumption of a guarantee of the interest on a long-term valorized loan. The authors of the report recognized that calculation in gold or other fixed values was unavoidable but insisted that it could not be limited to the private economy but had also to extend to municipalities, states, and the Reich. Similarly, if prices were calculated in gold, the same had to be true for wages, and while gold prices could not be introduced until gold prices were generally and openly stated, the adjustment of wages and private and civil-service salaries to a finely tuned index, agreed upon and regulated by industry and labor, was essential. The report also called for "appropriate reproduction cost" pricing for wholesaling and retailing. Lastly, the authors recognized that these measures in and of themselves would not eliminate the deficit, which required a program of governmental austerity, a unified economic policy, and the elimination of inflationary hindrances to industry as well as an increase in the productivity of the economy.[191]

The passage of the report, which proceeded with relatively little of the usual recriminations between the industrial and labor representatives was in and of itself a reproach to the government and reflected a kind of Great Coalition in the making. Hilferding, in his presentation of the report, however, drove the point home. He began by pointing out that, for the French, the moment when the victory of their policy would be decided was fast approaching. The French were most interested in the "consequences" of a termination of passive resistance on their terms; namely, "that such a capitulation in certain circumstances could mean the unleashing of a civil war and the disintegration of Germany. That is what is at stake; that is what we

are confronting."[192] Hilferding blamed this condition on the failure to act effectively in dealing with the existing situation. He noted that the private sector of the economy was increasingly seeking to "free itself from the state economy and the currency and to put itself on its own feet and its own currency." This was happening because nothing was being done about the "real source of the inflation, the budget." He sharply attacked the policy of waiting upon outside help for salvation and the notion that one could not make "an honest, upright and honorable tax policy but must wait until somehow by some mysterious means the balance of trade will first become active and then somehow the balance of payments will improve." Instead, the government had persistently created artificial purchasing power and was thus running the danger that, at some point now not too distant, it would no longer be accepted, and catastrophe would result. Hilferding likened the policy of the Cuno government to that pursued during the war, when there also was the illusion that the war would be short and that no firm internal measures had to be taken and that negotiations did not have to be initiated. The Reichsbank, instead of pursuing a credit policy, had pursued a subvention policy with its propagation of commercial bills. Hilferding was particularly acerbic in dealing with the foreign-exchange policy of the government, which at once rejected the centralization of exchange control and then lodged it in the Reichsbank—where it would have no effect—while undertaking to create a unitary exchange rate that was unworkable and that made importing impossible. The government had "undertaken the technical measures and forgotten the economic ones."[193] At the same time, the Reichsbank, which Hilferding treated with utter contempt, had demonstrated boundless incompetence in its efforts to intervene in support of the mark by concentrating on domestic rather than foreign markets. Hilferding, however, refused to accept the government's excuses for its inaction by pointing to Reichsbank autonomy, for he was convinced that "an energetic government that disposes of some authority would be able to do what is necessary without changing the law." This, however, was only a prelude to a devastating and more general attack on the way in which the government itself had been managed. He assailed not only the lack of integrated policy at the highest levels but also the inability of the Ministers to control the government enterprises and to enforce policy down the line. He noted with interest the poor representation of the government at the Reich Economic Council sessions on the currency problem:

We must demand of the government that it finally become clear about its own economic policy. It behaves most peculiarly. I believe that in the Currency Committee there was no government representative at the first meetings. Today, I believe that the government is very weakly represented. . . . It is not even a matter of bad will. I am convinced that actually each ministry says: it has nothing to do with me; it has to do with the other ministry. Financial policy and currency policy have to do with the Finance Ministry. Foreign exchange policy has to do with the Economics Ministry. A whole group of important things, such as the entire question of wage negotiations belong to the Labor Minister. But there is more! The Finance Ministry has no control over the financial administration—it sounds paradoxical but it is true—for more important than the entire Reich financial administration is the administration of the government enterprises, und the Finance Ministry has nothing to say about the financial administration of the government enterprises. The Railroad Minister, the Postal Minister forbid it. While the Reichsbank was doing its mark support action, Herr Groener was conducting his coal policy that was made in terms of months and years into the future. It was a misfortune that this coal policy happened to ruin the currency policy, but since these are two separate ministries, it is not something that has anything to do with the Cabinet. We do not have any economic policy in this government, because it is no economic policy if three or four different principles of economic policy are meshed with one another in the Cabinet. We do not have a Cabinet, gentlemen! We have a political association which debates. (Very true!) We do not have any real leadership. We do not have unity. We do not have distribution of responsibility. Beside that we have no relationship between this Cabinet and the Reichsbank, and that is the basis of all the evils. This is something that has finally got to be said out loud so that it will change.[194]

The charges were true, and those in and close to the Cuno government knew it. The Foreign Exchange Procurement Board periodically complained about the Railroad Authority's violation of directives, which demonstrated that the situation had not changed much since April.[195] The DVP leader, Dr. Leidig, complained bitterly to Stresemann in July about Economics Minister Becker's unsteady policy and expressed grave disappointment about the failure of Becker to lead people like Hermes and Brauns, which is precisely what industry had expected from an industrialist in that position. He had to admit that the jokes about the "expert" Ministry in the Socialist press were well-taken, and he expressed admiration for the way the Socialist Severing managed his Ministry in Prussia.[196]

Even more pathetic was Hermes. By early August, under pressure from Cuno, he had accepted the necessity of gold accounts and was holding meetings with the leading experts on the question of putting taxes on a gold basis rather than continuing to attempt to deal with the situation on the basis of unsatisfactory indices. At this point, Hilferding could say quite bluntly that the hour had come because the farmers were already refusing to accept the currency and Germany faced the imminent danger of hunger revolts, while Moritz Bonn was pointing out that a new gold-note bank would have to be set up besides the Reichsbank since experience had shown that inflation was always leaping ahead of valorization. Hermes's heart was not really in the matter. He blamed the Reichstag for its failure to support adequate tax measures in the past, a charge that certainly was true but that reflected on his leadership. The character of that leadership was expressed by him in a veritable swan song:

One seeks today the great decision. We are not so lacking in decisiveness as you believe. We feel decisive about doing that which is necessary, but above all decisiveness about not doing something stupid. That seems to me to be the first principle in these nervous days: not to do something false. One looks for the great, liberating deed. I have no qualms about saying to you: There is nothing for Germany to do in the present situation than to muddle through with certain half measures. That is my personal view, and there will be no liberating deed. . . . If there is not a change in the foreign policy situation, then our deeds can only help to prolong our stay of execution.[197]

Insofar as the Cuno government was energized in the last weeks of its existence, it was by certain impending signs of disaster which had to be dealt with immediately and by a few supporters who sought to save it from collapse. The chief source of specific crisis at this time concerned the food supply. Not only were the farmers threatening not to take paper currency, but the Reichsbank was finding itself unable to supply the foreign-exchange necessary to import vitally needed foodstuffs. At a Ministerial council meeting on July 27, Ebert complained bitterly that he had to struggle with Havenstein to get him to surrender his dollar loan certificates against paper marks so that food could be bought, and Havenstein had only relented after an agreement that he could keep some ten million gold-marks' worth of certificates on hand. A decision was made to give top priority to those needing foreign exchange to buy foodstuffs, and Hermes presented a program for valorizing taxes, advancing the payment dates, and instituting a new Rhine-Ruhr tax to finance the passive resistance effort. Sensing a measure of panic in the Reichstag over the mark collapse of July, Hermes and Cuno were now able to get Reichstag support for taxation measures and valorization which would have been denied them or seriously compromised by logrolling earlier. Indeed, Hermes was even prepared to contemplate a new currency based on rye as proposed in discussions with Helfferich at the beginning of August.[198]

The situation was also serious enough for Cuno to appeal to industry in a meeting on August 3 for a large-scale subscription of fifty million gold marks to cover the remainder of the dollar loan and thereby provide the foreign exchange needed to buy food. He promised a host of economic actions viewed as necessary by industry, including the introduction of gold accounts, termination of economic controls, and the like. But he insisted that the precondition for success was that the business community support the government and warned against making all kinds of reservations and conditions which "politically would be neither bearable for the government, nor for the people."[199] This, however, did not stop the industrialists, in their meeting on August 3, from demanding the termination of the unitary exchange rate, the continued discounting of bills of exchange at the Reichsbank with no obligatory introduction of gold credits before November 1, the elimination or reduction of export controls, and the ability to discount dollar loan certificates at the loan bureaus. Cuno escaped this graceless situation by choosing to treat these conditions as "wishes, which are also wishes of the Reich government."[200]

Cuno did seem to have sent the leaders of the RdI into something of a panic with his warning that, if the government did not have more foreign exchange, the food supply could only be maintained two or three weeks and that the Reichstag was likely to take that which was not voluntarily given. The Presidium and directors of the RdI met on August 2 and 7 and agreed to assess all the major groups of industry one or more quotas of a hundred thousand pounds to be used to purchase dollar loan certificates from the Reichsbank within less than a week. In a truly remarkable, italicized passage, the RdI leader declared that they were of the opinion that "*the capitalist economic system would be carried* ad absurdum *if it cannot succeed in immediately supplying from business the means now needed.*"[201] Apparently well atuned to the capacity for carrying matters *ad absurdum* in certain industrial circles, the RdI appended a Reichsbank letter pointing out that the objective was to procure foreign exchange already in the hands of industry and that no purpose would be served by industrialists going out on the market and buying foreign exchange! To further emphasize the seriousness of the situation, Carl Friedrich von Siemens wrote personally to his fellow industrial leaders indicating that what was involved was not exaggerated pessimism but rather the true state of affairs and bluntly stating the alternatives: "If the entire amount is not secured within 8 days, the government will only have the possibility either of resigning or undertaking rigorous measures of compulsion through the confiscation of foreign exchange, etc. Both would mean an end of the Ruhr action and the end of the Reich."[202]

Apparently, most of industry was sufficiently moved by this appeal to turn up with the cash, although the shipbuilding industry claimed incapacity to supply its full quota. Furthermore, not all industrialists willingly fell into line. The shipbuilder F. Schichau paid his five thousand pounds but also took the opportunity to tell the leaders of the RdI that he had little if any confidence in them and that they had permitted the management of the Ruhr conflict to "strengthen the unions at the cost of industry."[203] Nevertheless, Schichau had apparently not missed an important point made in Siemens's letter; namely, that the industrialists could borrow between 60 and 80 percent of the dollar loan certificates in marks from the loan bureaus! Another shipbuilder noted with irritation that while his industry was supposed to turn up with two hundred thousand pounds, entire branches of the Bremen wholesale and merchant business were being asked to give only between one thousand and three thousand pounds, although it was well known that some of them, especially those engaged in the cotton and textile trade, had plenty of capital.[204] Given the attitude of the commercial sector, however, it was probably fortunate if the Reichsbank collected even that much. In fact, the entire operation was one that manifestly would be hard to repeat.

Yet, Cuno and his advisers were convinced it would have to be repeated since ninety million gold marks a month were necessary to cover food and raw-materials purchases, and new negotiations were begun with the business leaders for another hundred-fifty-million-mark gold-loan subscription. Under this renewed pressure, the banks came up with a radical proposal for the outright confiscation of foreign exchange, a proposal which the government tabled for the time being in favor of preparing legislation which would empower the peak associations of industry, banking, and commerce to impose a levy upon their members to cover the new requirement. While the peak associations resisted the idea of being transformed into semipublic agencies for such purposes, they finally did declare themselves ready to impose new levies on their members. At the same time, Cuno hoped that a big propaganda campaign with publication of the lists of major subscribers would have a powerful moral effect and inspire savings banks and cooperatives to join in the effort and set up special valorized accounts. He also expected the Reichsbank to support the dollar loan certificates from sinking below the exchange rate of the dollar. In this way, immediate needs would be covered and the "foreign exchange blockade" against Germany would be broken.[205] Cuno, of course, had been trying to drag full support for the dollar loan out of the business community since

March, and it is hard to escape the conclusion that only the distressing state of the country and cries of panic, along with threats from himself and his erstwhile friends in the business community, had finally done the trick.

Indeed, not only was Cuno prepared to apply more vigorous pressure on the business community during his final weeks in office, but he also showed a disposition to act against the Reichsbank and its leadership. The radical abandonment of Reichsbank support of the mark in connection with the termination of the compulsory exchange rate was opposed by the government, which felt that some countermeasures had to be taken to the unavoidable increase in depreciation that would follow upon the end of the controlled exchange rate. Havenstein refused to heed government wishes and provide fifty billion gold marks—to be taken from foreign exchange provided for food purchases rather than the gold supply—in further support of the mark. This led Cuno to push forward plans to change the banking law to limit the Reichsbank's sovereignty and to force the resignation of Havenstein or Glasenapp and possibly both. In short, Cuno was prepared to abrogate the Reichsbank Autonomy Law imposed by the Allies, a law which had, of course, never functioned as the Allies intended. Faced with these threats, Havenstein relented on August 9. He agreed to a new, limited intervention which was to be conducted in close cooperation with State Secretary Bergmann and the former Siemens director and present general director of the Deutsche Werke, Otto Henrich, who would serve as representatives of the Chancellor. Clearly, government patience with the Reichsbank and its leadership had grown as thin as it had among its critics outside the government.[206]

Indeed, the last weeks of Cuno's regime were marked by the programmatic effort that was lacking since he had taken office. This was thanks to Hamm, who presented a financial and economic program on July 25. It incorporated much of what the Reich Economic Council committees had recommended earlier in the month, but also provided for an anti-unemployment program of housing construction and emergency public works. Even more important, because of Cuno's total acceptance of the program, was a memorandum by Minister Albert and Otto Henrich of July 27. This addressed the tax problem in a surprisingly sharp manner and called not only for the rigorous valorization of taxation but also for an assessment system that made corporations and individuals pay according to their true wealth. At the same time, the memorandum insisted that a much larger domestic stabilization loan was needed than what had been tried before and proposed a five hundred million gold-mark loan repayable at 6 percent interest after thirty years to stabilize the currency. Half the loan would be subscribed to in foreign exchange, the other half in paper marks. While demanding severe sacrifices from business, however, these proposals were coupled with a program for the dismantling of all constraints on the economy. The two men recognized that the program would inevitably run into the opposition of all parties but argued that a decisive program would be welcomed by the broad masses, who were more interested in ending their misery than in party programs.[207]

This may have been the kind of program Cuno had fantasized about when he created his Cabinet of "experts," and he made the program his own. Both the program and the actions of the Cuno government demonstrate that some of the elements of a fiscal and economic "regime change" were being put in place and that there was a growing consensus about the need for action.[208] Nevertheless, it was too late for Cuno to preside over such a change, even if the Reichstag, the business community, and other interests were sufficiently panicked to accept measures they had previously refused to consider. The government in Berlin was worn out. While visiting Berlin in August, Warburg had the impression that Hermes was totally "used up" and that Cuno was "tired of office." The Chancellor was drained physically as well as emotionally from the attacks on his person in the press and hoped to leave office once the loan from business had been worked out.[209] More important, however, was that Cuno's regime had drained the nation and that he was losing the confidence of leaders of the right and center as well as the SPD. Within the DVP, moderate industrialists, particularly Leidig and von Raumer, were pressing for a Great Coalition and a

Stresemann Chancellorship, while important elements in the Center were abandoning Cuno and calling for a new broad government as well. The issues, both economic and political, were perhaps most clearly put in the DDP by the banker Hjalmar Schacht:

The financing of the Ruhr struggle has a distressing similarity to our financial posture during the war. It is even worse, since we are operating not with loans but only with the printing press. The judgment has fallen as a consequence of what the government has not done since the collapse of the mark support action. The situation today has a great similarity with that of October 1918. The government does not understand what is at stake. Parlamentarism in Germany will lose all credit today if it does not now show decisiveness in expressing its power. If this government is allowed to muddle on, parliament will bear the responsibility. The present government is not capable of finding a way out. Is there any way out at all?[210]

In Schacht's view, there was a way to create "the great democratic front needed to maintain the resistance on the Ruhr"; namely, the introduction of a tax measure that would soak up huge amounts of paper marks immediately and "under all circumstances, the cutting off of paper mark credits." Schacht was strongly seconded by his fellow banker Melchior in calling for a currency reform on a gold basis and the collection of taxes in stable values.

The stabilization consensus had thus reached a stage of development where antagonistic forces could find their way to one another in a manner that had not proven possible at the end of Wirth's tenure of office. The crisis was sufficiently great to make compromise both necessary and possible and to bring enough anxiety into the more recalcitrant elements in the business community to promote a passive reaction to Cuno's impending fall. Furthermore, Cuno may have been moving toward a stabilization program of his own, but it was too late because his entire effort had been subject to Rosenberg's expectation that England would save Germany from France. On August 12, Lord Curzon did write to Poincaré declaring the Ruhr occupation illegal and calling for an expert determination of the reparations bill, but Poincaré was in no way moved to abandon his policy. This left Germany facing more of the chaos created by passive resistance. Cuno could only present the Reichstag with a success that brought no real hope, especially since the Cuno regime remained committed to continuing the passive resistance policy. While it was prepared to consider "certain changes" if it dragged on into September in order to secure the food supply, it continued to be insistent on depriving the French of coal and coke and assistance in running the railroads.[211] How any stabilization program could succeed under such conditions is difficult to see. In any event, an impending Socialist vote of no confidence led to Cuno's resignation on August 12. The new government on the "broadest basis" being called for by the Social Democrats was already in the making.

Stresemann, who had been widely recognized as the "coming man" since Rathenau's murder, knew that the crisis in which Germany found itself could only be mastered in alliance with the left. What one could expect from the right was well demonstrated by Alfred Hugen-berg who, in a letter to Stinnes, urged that Albert Vögler be put up for the Chancellorship since Stresemann, in Hugenberg's view, "has neither nerves nor is he of firm character, nor does he have political instincts and thus he never does the right thing at the decisive moment, as is shown by his wavering with respect to the Peace Resolution, the Ultimatum, etc. He simply embodies Germany's weak, politically unfruitful *Bürgertum*. I therefore think it highly probable, if not certain that, if he becomes Chancellor, it will be fateful for the German *Bürgertum*."[212] The preference for Vögler over Stresemann provides some measure of the quality of Hugenberg's own "political instincts." Nevertheless, whether Stresemann and his Finance Minister, Hilferding, the most formidable critic of the government's financial policies since the onset of the hyperinflation, could "do the right thing at the decisive moment" remained to be seen.

Chapter 15

The Politics of Currency Reform, August–October 1923

A Republic in Crisis

The Germans, at least until the very recent past, have not been notable for their political achievements, and the mismanagement of the nation's affairs that produced the situation faced by the Stresemann Great Coalition government when it assumed office on August 14, 1923, is yet another troubled chapter in an unhappy history. Credit, however, should also be given where it is due, and the emergence of the Weimar Republic and of Germany intact from the crisis of the summer and fall of 1923 was a remarkable political acccomplishment. The weathering of a crisis of such proportions inevitably depends upon having a goodly measure of fortune in misfortune, and, in contrast to the fatal crisis of a decade later, a concatenation of assets in the form of persons and circumstances was at hand to make survival possible. Major credit certainly must be given to Gustav Stresemann, one of the great political figures of the twentieth century, but it is also necessary to recognize that England and the United States had developed a vital interest in Germany's stabilization. Neither political skill nor foreign support, however, made the outcome any more inevitable than the deficient political leadership and international indifference at the turn of 1932–1933 made Hitler's triumph inescapable. Furthermore, there is no cause to romanticize the management of the 1923 crisis since it involved a heavy social, economic, and political mortgage on the Weimar Republic's future and played no small role in laying the groundwork for the disaster of 1933. What is important for the historian is to attempt to recapture the depth of the crisis, the options facing decision makers, the reasons for their choices, and the tenuousness of the solutions at almost every step of the way. There are no "miracles" in history.

The Weimar Republic provides marvelous opportunities for the comparative study of crises, and 1923 invites comparison not only with 1933 but also with 1918. As is so often the case, however, such comparisons often do more to expose differences than to reveal similarities. Just as the launching of passive resistance at the beginning of 1923 tempts natural if somewhat misleading comparisons with August 1914, so the manifest breakdown of the German effort in the summer of 1923 suggests comparison with the collapse of the German military effort in 1918 and the Revolution that followed in its wake. Here, too, the parallels are deceptive, even though some of the major personalities involved in dealing with the 1918 crisis were to show up to manage some of the problems in 1923 and some of the techniques employed were to be similar. The spontaneous movement from below in 1918 turned out to be a force for order—first, because the soldiers and workers councils met with so little resistance and, second, because they were dominated by Majority Socialists whose fundamental interest was the restoration of order. Indeed, the forces of counterrevolution, insofar as they were mobilized at all, acted under the aegis of the SPD once the actual revolutionary danger was past. Similarly, foreign occupation and the threat of invasion were, oddly enough, forces for order in 1918–1919. French ambitions in the Rhineland were a threat rather than a reality, and the English

Gustav Stresemann (1878–1929) after assuming the office of Chancellor in August 1923. (*By permission of the Ullstein Verlag*)

and Americans could be counted upon to act as a check on French aspirations as well as a stabilizing influence in their zones of occupation.

How different was the situation in the summer and fall of 1923! The forces of right-wing and left-wing radicalism were now mobilizing in various parts of the country, separatist movements were gaining strength, the French appeared to be achieving their ambitions, and the English and Americans, whatever their criticisms of the French, had so far done little or nothing to help the Germans out of their misery. Whatever the incidence of lawlessness and disorder in Germany in 1918, it could be tempered and controlled by the hope of peace and the anticipation of normalization and recon-

struction. The crisis of 1918–1919 had been managed by inflationary trade-offs; the veiling of unemployment through work stretching and reduced hours; and the collaboration of industry, labor, and the state to force farmers to supply the urban population at cheap prices. The crisis of 1923 was, among other things, the consequence of inflation and veiled unemployment, of the breakdown of worker–employer relations, and of the rebellion of farmers reflected in their growing refusal to accept the existing currency for their products. For what could one hope in 1923? The crisis of 1923, therefore, was a far deeper crisis than that which brought forth the controlled Revolution of 1918–1919 because it was characterized by a despair and rage provoked by monetary disorder and social disruption which threatened the very existence of civil society itself as well as the political order and the integrity of the German state. Whereas the crisis of 1918–1919 led to a successive narrowing of dangers and alternatives, the situation in the late summer and fall of 1923 seemed to be one in which everything was becoming possible.

This was the situation which the Stresemann government had inherited from the Cuno regime. It was not inappropriate, therefore, that part of that legacy was a decree of August 10 issued by Ebert and countersigned by all the members of the Cuno government that greatly extended the powers of the Reich government to prevent the forcible overthrow of the government. It provided for the direct suppression of political literature calling for or inciting the violent overthrow of the regime. State governments were required to follow such Reich Interior Ministry instructions and could be subjected to Reich execution for failure to comply. The new Stresemann government entered upon its duties with a keen sense that it had assumed office in a fateful moment for the Republic. Socialist Deputy Otto Wels explicitly stated that his party was supporting the new government "because it is the last possible constitutional government" and was prepared "under certain circumstances even to defend the Republic against Bolshevik labor disturbances with armed force."[1] Stresemann, too, perceived the new government as "the last constitutional Cabinet," while his Socialist Vice

Chancellor, Robert Schmidt, frankly stated that "a measure of dictatorship would have to be exercised by the government in order to gain control of the situation."[2] Schmidt, like Wels, saw a great danger in the increased Communist agitation and mobilization, but he thought the right-wing *völkisch* movement much stronger than its three Reichstag seats would suggest. This view was shared by the Reich Commissariat for the Surveillance of Public Order, which took worried notice that the "bloodthirsty language" employed by both the left and the right "is always used to press for action and assumes the inevitability of an impending civil war."[3]

The fundamental task of the Great Coalition government of Stresemann was to liquidate the bankrupt policies of the right—above all, in foreign affairs—while imposing discipline and hardship on the workers and other social groups whose increased productivity was viewed as the key to recovery by the right. The final days of Cuno and Hermes in office had not been without accomplishment, especially in the area of taxation; a panicked Reichstag had accepted new tax measures it had previously been able to resist all too easily in the face of Hermes's half-hearted approach and agreed to a higher degree of valorization through accelerated indexation. Implementation, however, was left to the new regime. Stresemann was compelled to run the political gauntlet which Cuno escaped by departing from office. Things could only get worse before they became better, and Stresemann inevitably had to extend and deepen the general crisis in which Germany already found itself when the new government took power. During its seven-week tenure (between August 14 and October 3), the first Stresemann government set in motion the new tax program passed by the Reichstag, prepared the way for a currency reform, and came to the conclusion that it had to terminate passive resistance, which it did on September 26. The implementation of the tax legislation of August 11, for example, meant that large groups previously spared from paying real taxes because of inflation would suddenly find themselves facing genuine tax burdens under unaccustomed if not yet fully effective pressure. The new legislation had imposed a Rhine-Ruhr Levy doubling the prepayment on income taxes for Au-

gust, October, and January and then using a multiplier of 400 instead of the multiplier of 25 as provided by the March 1923 legislation. Furthermore, the multiplier for October and January could be raised if there was further depreciation. The already heavy automobile tax was increased by fifty times the amount in effect on September 1. At the same time, the beer tax was raised, and the period allowed for the payment of all consumer taxes to the Treasury was shortened. Especially onerous from the standpoint of business and agriculture were the new Enterprise Tax (*Betriebssteuer*) and Land Levy (*Landabgabe*) under which all industrial and business enterprises were to pay twice the amount of wage and salary withholding to which they were obligated for the coming six months, and every farmer was to pay one and a half gold marks for each two-thousand-marks' assessment on his land as calculated under the 1913 Defense Levy. Finally, a law governing the interest on unpaid taxes permitted the revenue authorities to impose supplementary interest charges on late taxes so as to compensate for depreciation.[4] The new taxes were to be enforced immediately, and thus the Stresemann government would have to face the political right as the collector of real taxes as well as the liquidator of the passive resistance policy. At the same time, it was obvious that the stabilization measures, especially the new currency reform, would require further sacrifices from all the major social groups and new battles over the distribution of burdens. Before discussing the plans and actions of the government, therefore, it is essential to explore the context of the sociopolitical crisis in which they took place and which they exacerbated, at least in the short run.

At the time of Cuno's departure from office, most of the danger seemed to be coming from the extreme left, where the Communists had been planning a general strike to bring down Cuno. Cuno's fall and effective police action in Prussia took the wind out of the movement's sails, at least momentarily, but Communist leaders were frank in speaking of the aborted strike as nothing more than a "delay" in their plans and in characterizing the new Stresemann–Hilferding regime as nothing more than a "helpmate of capital." One of their more imaginative modes of agitation, especially under the hyperinflationary conditions of the summer of 1923, was to circulate thousand-mark notes of 1921–1922, apparently printed in Russia, with the statement on the reverse side that "we take the liberty of informing you herewith that we have taken over the business of the bankrupt firm of Cuno, Hermes & Co.," followed by the names of Stresemann, Hilferding, and others.[5]

More immediately worrisome than the danger of a Communist-inspired general strike was the situation in Saxony, where a left Socialist government beholden to the Communists had taken over in April under the leadership of Erich Zeigner. Certainly out of conviction but also in an effort to fulfill promises to the KPD, the Zeigner government in July had forced through the Landtag an amnesty for those found guilty of crimes against property committed to relieve the distress of the culprits or their families and for those who had performed abortions. The measure was bitterly opposed by the bourgeois parties. They questioned its constitutionality, since it appeared to be a violation of Reich law, but undoubtedly they were even more concerned about giving a license to thieves and abortionists. Indeed, the propertied classes in Saxony and Thuringia felt that their state governments virtually condoned their persecution by promoting worker control commissions to fight profiteering and ensure adherence to the food regulations and by tolerating the so-called Communist "Centuries" (*Hundertschaften*) ostensibly set up to fight the fascist danger from Bavaria. The Centuries, armed with truncheons and even more dangerous weapons, were viewed, not without considerable justification, as Communist terrorist organizations by peasants and businessmen. Even the Saxon government could not warm up to a Communist proposal made in July that two such Centuries be attached to each unit of the State Security Police so as to provide the force necessary to meet the fascist menace.[6]

These debates and discussions, however, were the tip of a truly dangerous iceberg of genuine want and social tension and resentment being reported in grim detail daily to the authorities in Dresden. Not untypical was the account of events in the district of Kamenz, where

the "progressive depreciation has brought the prices of all foodstuffs to a level which is unbearable for the consuming public. There are complaints about the shortage of milk, butter, and meat as well as all other foodstuffs. The working population of the cities and the larger industrial municipalities have thus been placed in a condition of great excitement and the result has been various outbursts and demonstrations in the district."[7] On August 16, five hundred workers from the Hutschenreuter porcelain factory in Radeberg organized a march to the nearby farming village of Kleindittmannsdorf, where they discovered and confiscated large amounts of dairy products. Receipts were left with farmers for the food taken, and the latter were forced to promise to supply Radeberg. The municipal authorities in Radeberg were implicated in the affair with demands to declare the actions of the workers legal. A few days later, butchers were sent to the village to slaughter livestock for Radeberg. Demonstrations over higher prices and house searches and confiscations by control commissions elected by workers were conducted in other villages in the vicinity as well. These were "tolerated by the anxious farmers without resistance." Workers found some, although not much, food being held back by farmers, and consumers were, above all, angry at outside merchants who had already bought up large amounts of food. Nevertheless, renewed demonstrations took place at the end of the month.[8]

The farmers were not always so passive, however. Not only did they insist upon and receive police protection against poor folk who stole from the fields, but they also ventured to show a measure of defiance themselves. Unhappily, such resistance usually took anything but edifying forms. In an act of downright meanness, some farmers in Niederoderwitz, near Zittau, so thoroughly harvested their grain that nothing remained for the poor who customarily collected scraps from the fields, and one even went so far as to beat a child who tried to make use of a scarecrow made of grain. These farmers got off relatively easy, however, when a crowd of some three hundred workers descended upon their property and drove them around for a while in a cart.[9] Being thus "taken for a ride," a form of "degradation ritual" regularly repeated in dealing with recalcitrant farmers and businessmen, certainly was terrifying but not terminal. The treatment suffered by a farmer and his wife at the hands of striking miners in the Stollberg region was much less benign. When one of the couple was reported to have sarcastically played upon the term "*Hundertschaft*" and the situation of the workers by remarking, "here comes the *Hungerschaft*," thirty or forty men entered the couple's home, assaulted them, and tore off their clothes.[10] Understandably, therefore, most farmers were quite passive when dealing with the Centuries or with spontaneously formed groups of consumers who posed as "Centuries" and plundered their fields when not prevented from doing so by older workers anxious to maintain order. Those farmers who responded to worker complaints that they had no food or milk for their children with statements such as "let them eat stones" and "let them drink water" apparently had never heard of Marie Antoinette and ran considerable risk in thus giving vent to their bitter feelings toward consumers.[11]

Some of the most serious actions against farmers and retailers occurred in the context of employer–worker conflicts over wages. Wage disputes increased steadily after May, and the trade-union leaders steadily lost control over the situation. As the Chemnitz police reported: "[T]he more left a speaker in the presentation of demands, the more adherents he found, a situation of hopelessness called forth by very real distress."[12] Employers who resisted such demands were intimidated, harassed, compelled to bedeck themselves with red flags or wear self-deprecating signs and then march in a parade, and exposed to other humiliations and even violence. The mistreatment of factory owners and managers in Saxony became increasingly notorious. It is important to note that the victims in Saxony, by and large, were those who managed medium-sized and small plants and were especially hard-pressed in their efforts to cope with the hyperinflation. Not untypical was a report on the events in Penig in mid-August:

In Penig, as in other places, special negotiations between employers and workers took place as a consequence of the economic emergency, whereby the payment of a special economic assistance benefit . . . was agreed upon. As of today, the payment has only partially been made, the reasons given being the shortage of means of payment or, in the case of small factories, the lack of cash or credits. In this connection as well as in the course of implementing the general strike slogans of the Communists, there were assaults on employers. The employers or directors of the plants were forcibly, or at least under the pressure of the demonstrators, compelled to march along in the demonstration parades, where they sometimes had red flags pressed into their hands. At the market place, the employers were exhibited before the crowd, which amused itself at their expense and treated them disrespectfully. In one case, where the employer was not at home, they took his wife instead, who then suffered a nervous breakdown in the market place.[13]

Economic and political motives were sometimes explicitly intermingled on such occasions. On August 17, a variety of marches were held calling for the deposing of the newly established Stresemann government in which employers were forced to close up and march to the music of the parades.[14] It would be a mistake, however, to overstress the role of political agitation to the point of forgetting the extent to which a generalized anger and barbarization had taken hold, especially among young people and women, whose violent behavior is repeatedly mentioned in reports. This phenomenon was especially evident in a wage and strike movement among the construction and metal workers in the Erzgebirge in July, where a sixty-year-old metal industrialist was nearly beaten to death by demonstrators "under the influence of women standing near" the scene until he was rescued by "sensible workers."[15] Indeed, the members of the Centuries were often far more moderate than the working-class persons they claimed to serve. The industrialist who reported this incident also admitted that the Centuries had "previously maintained peace and order" and criticized merchants for holding back food and thereby creating uncontrollable unrest among the masses. Indeed, some middle-class persons seem to have been as verbally uncontrolled as certain farmers. An innkeeper in Freiberg had the temerity to throw unemployed workers out of his establishment after telling them that he did not tolerate persons "without collars or pressed shirts" in his establishment.[16] As this innkeeper discovered when his inn was reduced to a shambles and he was roughed up, the unemployed were particularly inclined to violence and were a problem even for the Communists who sought to recruit them. When Communist leaders tried to calm down a violent three-day demonstration of the unemployed in Leipzig at the beginning of June, the response of the mob, along with the hurling of stones at the speakers, was "we are not KPD and we are not SPD. We are making our own action, and we do not need you."[17] While the Communists were quite prepared to terrorize employers and other members of the propertied classes in an "orderly" manner by compelling them to march at the head of parades draped in red flags and wearing self-abusive signs, they also sought to maintain control of the permanent-wage movement and strike situation created by the hyperinflation, and this proved to be no easy task. When the Communists peacefully settled a strike in Leipzig in mid-August, for example, they confronted an angry membership that ostentatiously tore up their party cards.[18]

Saxony, of course, was in the hands of the "reds," a condition which ensured that most of the seething resentment in bourgeois and agrarian circles would find limited and usually cautious expression. Fascists (*Hakenkreuzler*, as they were called after the swastika symbol) had to tread warily in Saxony and Thuringia, while more daring members of the movement risked being beaten up. As conditions deteriorated in the late summer, however, and especially after the new Stresemann regime came to power, the extreme right become more emboldened. This was particularly evident in mid-September, when the National Socialists and the various nationalist associations organized "German Days" in the border towns of Coburg and Hof. These giant assemblages of tens of thousands combined the elements of a popular nationalist festival with the consecration of flags and political speechmaking. Most of the participants seem to have come from Bavaria and the Tyrol, but a substantial number of Saxons appear to have participated, especially from the Vogtland, where the movement seems to have had some appeal to workers despite the government ban on the *Hakenkreuzler*. Less surprising was its appeal to some Saxon businessmen. A report that the industrialists of Plauen were going to supply the Nazis with trucks to go to Hof led to

worker patrols being set up to inspect trucks going to and fro on the road. Despite altercations between workers and noisy participants traveling through Saxon railroad stations, violence seems to have been kept to a minimum, although there were some Nazi assaults on Jews and Communists.[19]

If Saxon Socialists and Communists saw Bavaria as a breeding ground of fascism and a jumping-off point for violent action against themselves, the perception on the other side of the border was that the latent civil war would erupt with an invasion by the Saxon Centuries. In Bavaria, as in Saxony, the root cause of the anticipated political violence was seen in the dismal economic situation. Thus, the *Regierungspräsident* reported from Würzburg:

Almost everywhere the view reigns that the situation of economic distress must speed up the allegedly unavoidable bloody confrontation between right and left. For this reason, right and left are busily propagandizing and arming themselves, whereby by all counts the Social Democrats are being pushed more and more into a defensive position. This is probably also the explanation for their increasingly public blind hatred against the right in word and deed. One anticipates that the confrontation will open with the penetration of portions of the red army from Thuringia into Lower Franconia. I do not think that fears of this kind are well-founded, for on the left one knows that the government is strong enough to suppress any uprising.[20]

Even if one accepted this prognosis, however, the same writer had to recognize that disaffection had become universal:

The mood of the entire population is extremely agitated and dissatisfied. Big business, wholesalers, and especially agriculture, which find themselves in an economically more favorable situation, feel themselves oppressed beyond what they deserve by the new taxes, while the mass of the consuming public suffers heavily under the pressure of the measureless price increases and, far into the civil service, are embittered by the boundless profiteering of the peasants, from whose "tax-shyness" they expect the destruction of the people and the state. It is worth noting that the recently reported actions of Communist workers against landowners and peasants in central and north Germany have been viewed as justified self-help even in the ranks of the middle class and that similar actions in Bavaria would not be considered unwelcome.[21]

Thus, peasant leaders chose to call Stresemann and Hilferding "Jewish international wretches

[*Lumpen*] not only because they approved the new tax bills but also because they immediately implemented them without allowing for any reprieve,"[22] while other Bavarian peasant leaders suggested that a skillful leader could easily bring peasants and bourgeoisie together "against the new Socialist tax policy."[23] Nevertheless, many of the projected allies of the peasants were reported to be joining with hungry workers and stealing from the fields of the peasantry. If there was a measure of unanimity about anything in Bavaria, it was hostility to foreigners and tourists and the desire to hang *Schieber* and other "parasites." For some observers, the situation was reminiscent of the fall of 1918 in creating a mood at once fatalistic and revolutionary.

Authorities in Würzburg reported in early July that

the mass of the population is in a similar mood with respect to the decisive battle on the Rhine and Ruhr as it was regarding the war in the fall months of 1918. Under the pressure of price increases and in view of the fact that a portion of the people live in superfluity while another portion is immiserated and even slowly starves. They often no longer believe in success. The word "swindle," which played such a fateful role at the end of the war, is frequently heard again.[24]

There was, however, an important difference. The revolutionary mood was much more widespread and "this time is also the product of national concerns. Large industry, commerce, and agriculture are all subject to the most serious reproaches, along with the government naturally, that allegedly does nothing."[25] A most revealing portrayal of the temper in Bavaria was provided by the police authorities in Bayreuth:

The mood of the people is phenomenally agitated. The workers are enraged by the rising prices and unemployment. The patriotic associations are above all extremely upset over the leadership of the Reich government in foreign policy, the giving up of passive resistance, and the negotiations with the Entente. The peasants work with all their means against the new tax laws. The well-known Baron von Gagern even called openly for tax sabotage and resistance to compulsory collections in a peasant assembly. The resolution of the peasants was sent to the other peasant chambers as a model. Each circle expresses dissatisfaction with the government in line with its own particular interest and demands a change of conditions.[26]

While conditions in Saxony and Bavaria gave Berlin growing cause for concern, the greatest source of anxiety certainly was the increasingly desperate situation in the old and new occupied areas on the Rhine and Ruhr, where profound demoralization and increasing unrest and violence were gripping all classes of society. Sentiment among the organized workers, who were the backbone of the passive resistance, was graphically and poignantly described in a report of early August from a trade-union leader. The deterioration of the situation was the product not of any single event or series of events but rather of "an unending sum of relatively small but still extraordinarily torturous measures of pressure which make life here more and more unbearable. Each person has the feeling that the noose around his neck is getting increasingly tight, and that the point will come where breathing is completely impossible; there is a foreboding in the air that very great and perhaps frightful things will happen to the population of the occupied territories."[27] Though this union leader greeted the recent increase of workers into his union, he recognized that the new entrants were not acting so much out of conviction as out of an "instinctive feeling that one should have a girder on which to cling" in the anticipated explosion. A major source of all this pessimism, of course, was the increasing deprivation. The cities of the occupied areas resembled "beleaguered fortresses." They were cut off from all but the most basic foodstuffs, from normal wares, and from tobacco for months; not a single store stayed open for normal hours any longer, and most stores were open only two hours a day.

This union leader further emphasized that workers in the occupied areas had a strong sense of having been left in the lurch by Berlin and were extremely cynical about the policy pursued by the Social Democrats, who, it was generally held, were so desperately seeking to escape the charge of stabbing the passive resistance effort in the back that they had fallen prey to the illusions of the Cuno government about England's will or capacity to save the day. Indeed, this failed policy was viewed as part of an "endless chain" of recurrent "terrible disappointments" in foreign policy. The workers thought little of "heroes" of the stamp of the recently executed National Socialist Schlageter and felt victimized by "unknowing and incompetent government officials and corrupted press people," and it was little wonder that they were becoming indifferent to separatism or even supportive of it. This was especially the case because of the widespread conviction that bankers like Louis Hagen in Cologne and leading industrialists, who were issuing—and allegedly profiteering from the issuance of—enormous amounts of emergency money, were supportive of a Rhenish Republic.

While some leading businessmen were wrongly suspected of separatist leanings, the suspicion that members of the Rhenish business community, especially in the Düsseldorf region, were something less than firm in their commitment to the struggle with the French was quite well-founded. At a confidential meeting of the Düsseldorf Chamber of Commerce on August 29, the mood was anything but heroic. There were loud complaints about the excessively high wages paid to labor, which were also driving up the salaries of white-collar workers, while the prepayment of civil servants was encouraging speculation. German industry was no longer able to compete; the government was taking too long in compensating the firms for expenses arising from the occupation; the new taxes were extremely burdensome; and "there is a feeling of great bitterness against the government on the part of the firms."[28] The majority of those present were convinced that passive resistance was becoming increasingly more difficult, that they could hold out for a few weeks longer at the most, and that an understanding with the French was necessary before the time came "when no airplane would be fast enough to bring us to Paris to sign everything that is demanded." The demoralization was well illustrated by the fact that new firms were opening up in Düsseldorf to sell material confiscated by the French. Most worrisome, however, was the short supply of food, the danger that any further blockage in the supply would lead to hunger, and the growing evidence of Communist influence.

There was good reason for such fears. As one official reported, "the shortage of money, on the one hand, and the insufficient wages, on the other hand, have produced such feeling among the workers, that Communist elements have found it easy to incite the greatest unrest in the factories."[29] Legally elected factory councils were being replaced by revolutionary councils in many plants, and employers were unable to resist the wage demands being made. The fault in this official's view, however, often lay with the unwillingness of employers to grant the wages needed as well as the failure of the government to use its mediation and arbitration powers to impose sensible and uniform wage scales. In the Cologne woodworking industry, workers with comparable skills were getting fifty-one thousand marks, a hundred twenty thousand marks, or a hundred eighty thousand marks an hour thanks to the *ad hoc* manner in which the wage question was being handled. The loss of any sense of order or direction in wage scales was even better illustrated by complaints of the Socialist miners' union in Essen in early September that the miners were extremely agitated not only by the increased cost of food but, above all, by the fact that they, as the "chief support of the economy," were receiving 50 percent less in wages than the metal workers. Whereas the latter were receiving 31,269,000 marks a day, taking family supplements and piecework premiums into account, the top miners' wages were only 16,816,000 marks a day.[30] Under such circumstances, strikes and violence were likely, and it would be impossible for the trade unions to retain their authority.

There were, in fact, a whole series of Communist incited strikes throughout August in the mines and other industries, but even more alarming was the breakdown of law and order because of the increasing shortage of food and other goods. A report of August 9 noted that strikers in Gelsenkirchen attacked police, who then used their weapons, killing one striker and wounding ten others. Police were also attacked in Dortmund by demonstrators angry over the food situation, while Communists fought with fascists in the same city. In Vohwinkel, the supervisor of the consumer cooperative was beaten up; stores were plundered in Recklinghausen; food riots in Krefeld led to deaths and injuries. At the same time, the fields in the vicinity of Krefeld were being plundered by bands of city-dwellers. In Aachen and its surrounding villages, riots quickly turned into "plundering expeditions in which shops and farms were raided for provisions." When a mob of twenty thousand to thirty thousand persons tried to force the police to release arrested rioters, a police charge led to the death of ten persons and the wounding of many others. A less dramatic but by no means insignificant sign of the collapse of order was that railroad lines were being systematically plundered of copper wire. As part of their campaign to intensify the pressure on the population, the French claimed that such thievery from the railroads under their control was sabotage and imposed a severe fine on the city of Essen. At the same time, they intensified their own confiscations and sequestrations from the Ruhr plants and regularly seized money sent by the Reichsbank to cover wage costs, going so far as to blow up the safe of the Reichsbank branch in Gelsenkirchen and to occupy the printing plants involved in the production of emergency money for some of the Ruhr municipalities.[31]

French behavior guaranteed their continuing unpopularity and made it unlikely that much of the population would discover any redeeming qualities in the separatists.[32] The entire situation, however, inevitably produced increasing pessimism and a feeling that the French would in the end be able to work their will. This made the government decision in early September to seek a means to end the passive resistance and negotiate with the French a particularly delicate matter. Rumors began to circulate immediately and called forth the inevitable comparisons with 1918:

A comparison is being drawn, not without justification, with the premature announcement of the armistice offer to the troops in 1918 that had led to the feeling at the front of "why make sacrifices now when the capitulation is about to take place." Similarly one fears in the Ruhr that the entire resistance will collapse prematurely if there is even the slightest weakening demonstrated from above.[33]

Needless to say, the danger did not only come from the left but also from the fanatical nationalist right, whose response to Stresemann's efforts to bring an end to the passive resistance was well described by another observer:

There is the wildest outrage among these circles over the "treason" of the Chancellor. One says quite openly that Stresemann will have to follow Rathenau and Erzberger as soon as possible. Nationalist in-

stincts are being whipped up to a fever pitch. The situation is pictured as if the defensive struggle could be carried on much longer and that the victory would be ours if only a Jewish government, as in 1918, was not now selling us out and betraying us. Hilferding, the Austrian Jew, and Stresemann, the half-Jew [sic!], naturally have no understanding for our national worth and for the honor of the German name. These and similar remarks are to be heard again and again these days. Any type of rational perspective is impossible for these circles. Everything is based on emotion and upon a naive and dangerous overestimation of German strength both in terms of material and morale.[34]

The greatest incentive to the new government taking the measures it did, however, was the food situation, the seriousness of which was recognized by anyone with a sense of reality on the right and the left. At the end of July, for example, Stinnes and Thyssen had appealed to Ambassador Houghton for American assistance because they believed there would be famine in the Ruhr within two or three months without outside help. Houghton reported that the situation was indeed grave. Bad weather and transportation conditions had led to a real shortage in Berlin, but there was also the problem that the "tremendous fall in the mark has tended to make farmers and wholesalers loath to part with such provisions as are on hand."[35] Most dangerous, however, was that the impending potato harvest would not reach the Ruhr because the transportation system, always strained by the need to bring in the potatoes between August and the October frost, would simply be unable to do the job under occupation conditions and that the nine million people of the area, also suffering from shortages of milk and fats, would simply starve.

The dangers, indeed, were not to be exaggerated. A foretaste of what might come was being provided by reports of firefights between farmers and unemployed coal miners who had descended in bands to plunder the fields. Not only would the passive resistance collapse under such conditions, but anarchy would replace it.[36] It is in no way surprising, therefore, that much of the initiative and pressure for currency and fiscal reform came from Cuno's Minister for Agriculture and Food and former Mayor of Essen, Hans Luther, who had been retained in the Stresemann government and who was well acquainted with the food-supply problems of the Ruhr.

In Luther's view, in fact, "the chief ill which also affects the food situation lies in the monetary area, specifically the shortage of foreign exchange and the destruction of the domestic currency."[37] The harvest was satisfactory; there was sufficient oil in the country to make margarine; adequate supplies of other fats were on their way to Germany. The problem was prying the food from the farmers and getting the foreign foodstuffs out of consignment by procuring the necessary foreign exchange. Although there was pressure from Thuringia, Saxony, and other quarters to reintroduce controlled economy measures, Luther remained firm in the decision to abandon the last vestiges of the controlled economy in agriculture that had passed into law on June 23, 1923, and had been accepted even by the SPD in final recognition of the system's almost decade-long demonstration of bankruptcy. It was, indeed, a decision taken against the system rather than for the benefit of agriculture. Luther insisted that the price benefits of the grain levy had been lost in the costs of administering and enforcing the system and the lower bread price was largely due to either veiled or open government subsidization. His solution had been to impose a two-hundred-twenty-million gold-mark tax, half of which was payable on August 1 and the remaining two quarters on January 1 and April 1, to enable the government to cover reducing food costs for the poor. Little wonder, therefore, that the agricultural interest groups showed little gratitude for the substitution of a system of controls that forced them to deliver their products at reduced prices by a system of taxation that forced them to sell their products to satisfy the revenue officer. They lashed out by demanding "a complete about face from past methods of governance and the pernicious parliamentarism, especially the policy of socialization and expropriation by means of taxation."[38]

Luther, however, was relentless about forcing farmers to deliver through the increased tax burden, just as he was resolved to use this food emergency to extract as much foreign exchange from industry as possible while pushing the Reichsbank to give priority to food imports in its supplying of foreign exchange and to do so at 100 percent of the level required. Nevertheless, the linchpin of Luther's program, a pro-

gram he had already begun supporting and advocating in the Cuno government, was the creation of a valorized currency. As he argued in a memorandum for the Chancellor of August 22, 1923, the other measures he had taken could only bring partial success, and the agrarian sector of the economy could not be made to function normally and effectively over the long run by means of the pressure of taxes but only by means of normal market forces. These could only operate properly if the grain business ceased to be a "wild speculation" because of currency oscillations. He warned against toying with the idea of a government grain monopoly or other compulsory measures, which would require a huge staff and for which there was insufficient time even if they were desirable. A valorized currency would obviate the need for any kind of compulsion. Indeed, he envisioned eliminating the Reich Grain Board, the activities of which would be unnecessary once an acceptable currency could be created:

Hans Luther (1879–1962), Food Minister and then Finance Minister in the Stresemann Cabinets. (*By permission of the Ullstein Verlag*)

As soon as our economy is based on a valorized currency, the procurement of foreign exchange will no longer create difficulties. Above all, this will be the case if gold accounts are set up at the same time. These gold accounts will attract foreign exchange, because continuing to hold back foreign exchange by private enterprises and private persons will appear uneconomic since it will lead to a loss of interest and also constitute a gratuitous enrichment of the outside world.[39]

Once the new Stresemann government was in office, Luther vigorously pursued his goals by calling Stresemann's attention to a plan of Karl Helfferich, a plan Helfferich had already presented during the last days of the Cuno regime and one Luther was prepared to support. It was to prove the point of departure for the currency reform of 1923.

The Struggle over a Currency Reform Plan

At first glance, there would appear to be no small irony in the fact that it was Karl Helfferich who came forth with the plan that would trigger Germany's currency reform and eventuate in the "miracle" of the Rentenmark. After all, his wartime policies had done so much to promote the German inflation, and his intention of placing the "leaden weight" of war costs upon Germany's enemies had significantly contributed to the prolongation of the war and to the burdens under which Germans had labored since 1918. Helfferich's performance in 1923 appears less ironical, however, if his plan is put in its proper context. On the one hand, it should be seen as the culmination of the nominalist monetary theory and neo-liberal economic policy that had informed his thought and actions since the beginning of his career. On the other hand, it was a direct response to the loud demand for a new and reliable instrument of exchange by those engaged in agriculture and industry. These points are important because the Helfferich program and the alternatives proposed to it had profound implications for Germany's subsequent political and socioeconomic development. While it certainly is true that Germany was heading toward the monetary and fiscal "regime change," as it is called by economists today, the "regime change" was by no means as tidy as it might appear in the retrospective analyses of economists, and it certainly was not prepackaged. The essential task for the historian seeking to reconstruct something approximating what really happened is to explain why a specific kind of "regime change" took place, why the alternatives failed, and what historical significance is to be attached to the results.

The Helfferich proposals for currency reform were formulated in the final weeks of the Cuno regime. They were a product of a general willingness of the DNVP leadership to maintain the political truce during the Ruhr crisis as well as Helfferich's access to the Cuno government and high standing as a monetary theorist. Helfferich had drawn up a plan for an "emergency currency, a transitional currency,"[40] during a July Swiss Alpine vacation, "up there in the mountains where the good ideas come to one,"[41] and descended with an actual draft of a law for discussion with Cuno, Hermes, and Luther at the beginning of August. The fundamental assumption of the project was that the Reich was in no position to create a currency that would win confidence either at home or abroad, and this made it essential that the task be undertaken by the "free forces of the economy," the so-called "economic occupational estates [*wirtschaftliche Berufsstände*]." Industry, agriculture, and commerce, including the banking and transport sectors, were to establish a currency bank for the purpose of issuing a Roggenmark ("rye mark"). The new bank was to begin its activities with a capital of one billion Roggenmarks—an amount increased to one and a quarter billion Roggenmarks in the subsequent version—to be raised by agriculture, industry, and commerce. The statutes of the bank were to be determined by the peak associations representing these economic sectors but were to be subject to the approval of the Chancellor, who was also to have a maximum of two vetoes over proposed presidents of the otherwise independent bank. The bank was to be tax-exempt. The capital of the bank was to be backed by real values (*Sachwerte*) in the form of first-charge encumbrances denominated in rye on all farms in the amount of 5 percent of the valuation for the prewar Defense Levy (*Wehrbeitrag*). Half the capital of the bank was to be raised by agriculture, the other half by commerce and industry.

Mortgages would be imposed on these three sectors. The rye-mortgages bonds, calculated in a later draft at a rate of eight marks Defense Levy valuation serving as the equivalent of one centner rye, were to bear 5 percent interest per annum. These mortgage bonds would form the basis for the issuance of rye bills (*Roggenrentenbriefe*), bearing 4 percent interest per annum. Roggenmarks, fully backed by and convertible into rye bills—two hundred Roggenmarks were to be the equivalent of the value of one ton of rye—would be issued and be considered legal tender as of the date specified in the projected law. Strict limits were to be imposed on the government's credit with the new bank. While the new bank was to provide the government with the equivalent of three hundred million, later three hundred seventy-five million, goldmarks' worth of Roggenmarks to assist it to redeem its short-term debt, this was to be given in lieu of the Enterprise Tax passed by the Reichstag on August 11. Any additional credit given to the Reich in return for Roggenmark-denominated Treasury bills was to be limited, the amount of 2.1 billion marks being specified as the maximum in the later Helfferich draft. Helfferich conceived of the new currency bank as a profit-making institution designed to serve primarily the private sector. The bank was conceived as a transitional institution, with an anticipated two-year life span, the money-issuing powers of which could be taken away once the Reich was in a position to buy back its Treasury notes and return to a gold currency. At that time, the bank could convert its own assets into gold-currency equivalents. In the event of liquidation, its subscribers would be repaid. Half of any profit would be given to the groups running the bank "for the promotion of the economy," while the other half would be disposed of in accordance with a law passed by the Reich.[42]

It is likely that Cuno, who had assented to the plan prior to his resignation, intended to make Helfferich head of a small commission to work out the currency reform, and Helfferich certainly expected to exercise considerable influence on the government. Helfferich amply demonstrated the kind of leverage his plan might afford the interests he represented at the meetings of the Reichstag Revenue Committee to discuss the projected taxes on industrial and agrarian enterprises prior to the fall of the Cuno government. Helfferich and DNVP Deputy Schiele, who was closely tied to agrarian interests, objected to the taxes on the grounds that it was intolerable to impose a double burden on agriculture and industry. If these sectors were to place their assets behind a new currency, then, they argued, it was unfair to impose a new tax in addition; Hermes apparently agreed that such a tax would have to be credited to industry and agriculture under such circumstances.[43] The Helfferich plan proposed to credit the projected bank's initial loans to the government against the tax.

The fall of the Cuno government and the replacement of Hermes, who was far from popular in right-wing circles at this time, by the even more threatening figure of Hilferding was a severe setback for Helfferich and his conservative friends. Cuno had, in fact, warned Stresemann against appointing a Socialist Finance Minister, since the successful implementation of a currency reform required the confidence of the business community; in his view, no Socialist could command such confidence.[44] This unhappy prognosis seemed to find confirmation in the Reichstag on August 15, when the Revenue Committee successfully moved a resolution calling upon the government to draft legislation that would reform the finances of the Reich and restore its credit "through the burdening of the assets of the economy and through the transition to a valorized currency."[45] Helfferich sharply attacked the resolution, pointing out that much "nonsense" was being spread about through the use of the term "valorized" and that the real question was finding a "means of payment that was genuinely based [*realfundiertes Zahlungsmittel*]." He warned that such a currency could not be founded by the state and that a currency based on the "appropriation of real values" would be comparable to the "*mandats territoriaux*" that had replaced the *assignats* in the French Revolution. If Helfferich conveniently overlooked the fact that both French currencies had failed not because of their backing and inadequate convertibility but rather because of their overissue, his main point, in any case, was that the new currency had to be based on the active participation of the "occupational estates" (*Be-

Finance Minister Rudolf Hilferding (1877–1941).
(*By permission of the Ullstein Verlag*)

rußstände) and that "it would be fateful in the situation in which we are in to proclaim to the world that one wants to reform the currency through an appropriation of real values."[46] He was in no way pacified by Hilferding's assurances that the "occupational estates" would be consulted and asked to collaborate, since the issue was no longer simply "collaboration [*Mitwirkung*]" but rather active involvement: "The matter must rest upon the credit of the *Wirtschaft*. As a consequence, the *Wirtschaft* must be given a much greater freedom of action than what the Social Democrats today imagine. Otherwise, that which you are considering will be nothing but an illusion and a betrayal of the people."[47]

Though Helfferich's alternate resolution failed in the Reichstag by a heavy margin, he, nevertheless, continued to have good reason to feel that his cause was not lost where it might count the most, despite the unwelcome presence of Hilferding—namely, in the new government. Luther was anxious to promote Helfferich's program, and Economics Minister Hans von Raumer also wished to gain Helfferich's collaboration and expertise for a projected currency reform. It was a measure of Helfferich's crucial role at this point that he felt he could set conditions before agreeing to present his ideas to the Cabinet, and he informed

von Raumer that he would only collaborate if the project were based on the voluntary participation of the economic groups involved and not turned to their disadvantage and if the promise of Hermes with respect to the tax on enterprises were kept by the new government; namely, that the tax would be covered in the credits granted by the new bank to the government. On August 16, von Raumer officially assured Helfferich that the latter's conditions would be met, and Helfferich agreed to present his ideas to the Chancellor and other Cabinet members on August 18.[48]

Despite their distaste for the new government, Helfferich and his colleagues in the DNVP were anxious to take advantage of von Raumer's promise of "autonomy for the *Wirtschaft*" and the chance to "buy agriculture free" from the Reichstag's "enterprise-tax Marxism." Not only might this tax now be negated, but the projected currency bank could be a means of keeping Germany's finances out of Allied control while putting the government on "pension" through the projected "rationing" of credits.[49]

It was thus quite fitting that Helfferich was flanked by the leading spokesmen for industry and agriculture in his party, Reichert and Schiele, when he presented his plans to the Cabinet on August 18.[50] If Reichert's recollections of a few months later are to be believed, and they appear plausible enough, then the meeting began with an altercation between Helfferich and Hilferding that exposed the basic differences characterizing the debate during the coming weeks. Helfferich responded to Hilferding's invitation to present his plan by asking the new Finance Minister if he did not have ideas of his own. Hilferding took up the challenge by confirming his metallist position and indicating that he wished to divide the Reichsbank—a part of which would continue to deal in paper marks and be left to its fate, while another part would operate with a new gold currency backed by the gold in the Reichsbank. When Helfferich countered that there was not enough gold left after so much had been sold or mortgaged, Hilferding responded, in a manner Reichert thought typical of a "Finance Minister of the revolutionary period," that one could use the gold a second time and also suggested that one might follow the Austrian example of a currency not fully covered by gold. Helfferich professed to be shocked by Hilferding's attitude, warning the new Finance Minister not to begin his tenure with a "fraudulent bankruptcy" and pointing out that Germany did not enjoy the stable economy of the Austrians. In his own presentation, he argued for exploitation of the "imagination of the people" and pointed out that the recent law on valorized mortgages had already legalized the use of mortgages based on rye, coal, potash, and other fungible commodities. In the end, however, the meeting was inconclusive. On the one hand, Hilferding agreed to the establishment of a commission of political leaders, bankers, and economic experts to review the Helfferich project. On the other hand, the new Finance Minister seemed preoccupied with the question of how he was going to cover his expenses during the coming weeks, tax collection, and ways and means of getting his hands on foreign exchange. It was, in truth, somewhat distressing to be confronted with an anticipated revenue during the coming four weeks of 169 trillion marks as over against an anticipated expenditure of 405 trillion, 240 trillion of which were to be poured into the Ruhr struggle; nor did it help Hilferding to face the future with confidence when Reichert responded to even the intimation that some effort might be made to cut down on Ruhr expenses with the admonition that Hilferding should not "expect to make any savings on the Ruhr battle!"

Where then? The emerging debate on currency reform took place in the context of the government's efforts to deal with the Ruhr crisis and determine what to do first in a situation where it was no longer possible to differentiate between long-term and short-term solutions because it was virtually impossible to think of anything but the short term. The dilemma of the new government was already set when Stresemann first addressed the Reichstag on August 14, warned against allowing expectations of English support to induce "political lethargy," and declared that "the best activity in foreign policy which we can develop is creating order in Germany's situation at home."[51] When Hilferding turned to this task in support of Stresemann's efforts to strengthen the domestic front

until the French would agree to negotiations, he confronted an utterly demoralizing situation. As he told the Reichsrat on August 22, he had thought he had a good sense of the financial situation of the Reich when he took office but had to confess that "what he has discovered in the meantime exceeds his worst expectations, and that the financial situation of the Reich is to be described as very dangerous, practically desperate."[52] Indeed, it was so bad that he refrained from presenting any figures to the Budget Committee of the Reichstag in his first meeting with that body on the same day.[53] Taxes had become "incidental" as a means of covering Reich expenses, and the German economy had become so burdened with unproductive costs that it was in no position to "come even near to paying prewar wages." Yet, this was precisely what was being demanded by the workers, who were insisting that their wages be denominated in gold and were asking for increases that Hilferding considered unaffordable. The shortage of paper money was leading to the illegal issuance of uncovered emergency money. Hilferding estimated the amount of emergency money in circulation as running between sixty trillion and seventy trillion paper marks and suspected that the illegal issues were being privately encouraged by industrial firms needing the paper to pay wages. The most serious problem was the shortage of foreign exchange to cover imports, a situation that all agreed had to be met with compulsory measures along with incentives to surrender foreign exchange. Even Economics Minister von Raumer, a representative of industry, thought harsh measures had to be taken, angrily remarking in a Cabinet meeting that "it has always been an abuse that industry, whenever one came too close to its supply of foreign exchange, took to a flight into goods. It procured and stored huge stocks of foreign raw materials in place of foreign exchange. One must also act here and take measures that prevent industry from covering its raw materials needs for a longer period of time than perhaps two months."[54]

Hilferding recognized that it was somewhat contradictory to turn on the tax screws and seek voluntary subscriptions to the gold loan at the same time, but he could see no way out. One could hope for some results, however, under two conditions. On the one hand, he wanted to compel those with foreign exchange to pay their taxes in foreign exchange unless they were prepared to declare under penalty of perjury that they were in no position to do so. On the other hand, he was willing to offer a virtual amnesty for past violations of foreign-exchange regulations and tax violations by inviting those with foreign exchange to use it in subscribing to the gold loan with a guarantee that no questions would be asked about where the money came from. In the last analysis, however, Hilferding had to "admit that the Reich government is in no position to develop an actual financial program today, that it has to see its true task far more in getting through the next difficult weeks, and above all preventing a further fall in the exchange rate, which would have a very dangerous effect because of the attendant increased prices and the great agitation of the population."[55] But if this was the case, then how could Hilferding realize Stresemann's slogan that the best foreign policy under the circumstances was a sound financial policy? At the Reichstag Budget Committee meeting on August 23, Hilferding first identified himself with Stresemann's position, only, as one alert observer reported, to contradict himself a few minutes later:

The Reich Finance Minister held firmly to this position today and declared that a real foreign policy could only be made possible though a control of the exchange rate allowed by the possession of a sufficient fund of foreign exchange. But in another connection, the Reich Finance Minister had yet to let the reverse of the statement hold true. After mentioning the monumental expenditures of the defence of the Ruhr, he conceded that, from a broader perspective, even a harsh tax policy and the planned control of foreign exchange could not lead to a cure without the plugging up of this hole. He therefore concluded: "A good foreign policy is the best financial policy!" Here the circle in which we are caught is revealed. The program of the Reich government will be: to win time through the projected measures and to use this time to come to agreement in the Ruhr struggle.[56]

When the Cabinet met a week later, on August 30, however, time seemed to be running out at too fast a pace. The dollar stood at eleven billion marks; the floating debt between August 21 and 31 increased 832.8 trillion marks, and the floating debt in discounted Treasury bills on August 31 was 1,196,294,527,397 marks. Hilferding bluntly told the Cabinet that he "could

see no way out from the financial side," despite increasing revenues from taxes, and that, in the last analysis, what they faced was "a foreign policy problem."[57] Government councilor Stockhausen cruelly noted in his diary that "Hilferding, the Socialist-Jewish Finance Minister, makes a helpless and desperate impression. The waves of paper trillions burst over him. I believe he yearns for those blessed times when a certain portion of his body did not press upon a ministerial chair!"[58] If Stockhausen prayed that "God protect us from the white flag of November 1918," however, he also recognized that Hilferding had no monopoly on depression in the Cabinet, which was convened to give "morphine injections," possibly in the form of a valorized currency, to prolong the life of a dying cause. Nevertheless, Hilferding had the most difficult position in Stresemann's Cabinet, both in terms of his area of competence and in terms of his party affiliation. Listening to his colleagues and reviewing his experiences of his first two weeks in office reinforced his conviction that a "foreign policy solution" was the only way out, but this did not mean that he was advocating the abandonment of passive resistance:

In his [Hilferding's] view, the situation is the following: Germany stands before collapse. We can only be saved by measures which are effective in a very short time. All the measures previously discussed last too long. Valorized currency does not solve the problem. Nothing can be done by technical means alone. If he is reproached for not making proposals, then this is because he is convinced that only an operation in the area of foreign policy can help in the present situation. . . . Also, loosening up passive resistance is extremely dangerous, since it will be treated as a worker betrayal. The French must be told that we are ready to take definite measures if they give us the possibility of restoring government in the Ruhr.[59]

It could, of course, be argued that Hilferding was now being hoisted on his own petard, that he was now making an argument for which he had criticized his predecessor; namely, that effective financial measures at home could not be undertaken without creating suitable conditions through foreign-policy successes. It is important to remember, however, that conditions in the summer and fall of 1923 were very different from the situation the year before and that it was not Hilferding's fault that the claim that Germany needed outside assistance to undertake an initial stabilization had been transformed into a self-fulfilling prophecy by the protracted Ruhr conflict. The deeper source of Hilferding's paralysis, however, was his fiscal and financial conservatism. He found it difficult to support or willingly undertake bold strokes of an unorthodox nature based on what he perceived as inadequate preconditions. At the same time, he was obviously afraid that the most important precondition for an effective financial policy—the termination of the passive resistance in the Ruhr—would burden the left with yet another stab-in-the-back legend.

If these somewhat contradictory convictions, perceptions, and tensions undermined Hilferding's administrative effectiveness, however, it is also important to realize that the internal opposition and obstacles which had paralyzed his predecessors were as much on the scene as ever. Personally, Hilferding was committed to the "most severe and brutal" exercise of his office to cure the currency and fiscal situation. He firmly believed that "economic policy considerations, however important they might be, must today retreat before considerations of currency policy." And, in a most un-Marxist manner, he expected that "as never before, every German today must maintain the unconditional primacy of the state over personal interests."[60]

What Hilferding encountered, especially from those on the right, was anything but edifying. The government was flooded with petitions requesting delays in tax payments and warnings that people could not be expected to pay such high taxes on so short a notice and subscribe to the gold loan as well. More serious, Hilferding's appointment was used as an excuse, especially by agrarian interests and the DNVP, to engage in open or veiled tax evasion and incitement to tax sabotage, and this certainly must have tempered the government's initial successes in collecting valorized taxes. The appointment provided an important focus of right-wing mobilization against Berlin, and government-inspired criticism of DNVP propaganda led Helfferich to warn that his collaboration in the creation of a new currency was being jeopardized.[61]

In reality, bad will was not even necessary to undermine much of the potential initial success of the new taxes because, as so often in the past, the administrative timing of the measures served the cause of tax evasion. The increased revenues were anticipated from the stepped-up prepayments on corporation taxes due on August 15 and 25, the Rhine-Ruhr Levy due on August 25, and a prepayment of the turnover tax for July on August 15. The decree governing the turnover tax was only promulgated on August 8, while the announcement of the other taxes appeared on August 11. Taxpayers had to be individually informed of their obligations, especially since there was a general consensus that the tax system had become an incomprehensible jungle for all concerned. Finally, the law required that taxpayers whose payments were overdue had to be warned before the revenue offices could take action against them. While the effectiveness of the German postal system might have made a speeding up of the process possible, the revenue offices lost about a week in their collection procedures, and, since the taxes were subjected to higher indices than used previously but were still not denominated in gold values, taxpayers were once again paying in depreciated currency. Accelerated indexation of the kind now being used might have worked in 1922, but it was doomed to failure in the hyperinflation of late 1923![62]

Hilferding's efforts to round up foreign exchange were also filled with frustration. He had never placed much faith in the voluntary surrender of foreign exchange, and even the leaders of banking and industry with whom he consulted felt that compulsory measures were essential if the food supply were to be secure. On August 25, the emergency powers of the President were employed to issue a new foreign exchange decree under which all persons and corporations holding foreign assets between August 10 and 20 were required to pay, respectively, one or two gold marks in foreign exchange or its equivalent for every ten thousand paper marks in such assets to support the levy for the purchase of foreign grains. The payments on this levy were to be credited toward the new gold loan of the Reich or against valorized tax accounts. To improve the implementation of this measure, which yielded a hundred seventy million gold marks, yet another decree was passed on September 7 establishing a Commissariat for Foreign Exchange, which was placed under Ministerial Councillor Fellinger of the Prussian Ministry of Commerce, who was given extraordinary powers to require the surrender of foreign exchange in subscription to the Reich gold loan and who assumed control of the four-hundred-person Foreign Exchange Procurement Board. Two further decrees of September 17 placed strict controls on exchange brokers and required exporters to sell only against highly valued foreign currencies, to use their foreign exchange for measures approved by the Reich, and to surrender at least 30 percent of their foreign exchange at the Reichsbank against marks, the gold loan, or credit on a gold account.[63]

While the leaders of the peak associations of banking and industry felt that they had to come to the aid of the government in the emergency, their constituencies were not in an equally giving mood. On the very day that the decree of August 25 was issued, observers noted heavy purchases of foreign exchange and suspected that all those effected by the new decree were rushing to buy up the foreign exchange they would shortly have to deliver.[64] Such behavior was truly subtle when compared to the views expressed at a meeting of major Cologne industrialists on August 22, who not only ranted and raved that the "intention to increase taxation and to collect the taxes more strictly is obviously a forerunner of proletarian socialisation," but who also insisted that "they must have solid money" and were thus "dependent on foreign money." They therefore intended "to make use of our foreign branches and entrust the foreign currency to them." This would make them "free of the German exchanges" and permit them to be their "own masters." The industrialists unanimously concluded that "on the whole we must be in violent opposition to the new Government. We must hold together and show a united front. We must consider the government's appeal for large amounts of foreign money from this perspective. The government appeals for our help, on the one hand, while on the other hand, it seeks to pick our pockets without any compensation."[65]

Little wonder, then, that the various new exchange control decrees and the appointment of a Foreign Exchange Commissar were greeted with considerable skepticism. As one newspaper pointed out, "if the decree is to have any real success, then it can only be by bringing certain portions of the *Mittelstand*, who have sought to escape the monetary depreciation by [placing into foreign exchange] the small portion of what remains of their assets or their even smaller new savings, into a trying conflict of conscience. At long last, by now one should have learned from the experiences of the last years that a decree which appeals only to the integrity of the little man through a combination of compulsion and amnesty while evading the real issues, can have no practical effect."[66] Indeed, the new Foreign Exchange Commissar, Fellinger, an apparently pleasant and reasonably competent young man, had few ideas himself how to go about finding illegitimately held foreign exchange. He told a British official on taking office that he had no intention of going after little people with small amounts of foreign exchange since, "if no general settlement is come to and if social disorder does break out, it is realised that such small sums will be invaluable to small people in procuring the necessaries of life." When considering great firms like AEG, he did not have the faintest idea how much of their holdings were really superfluous. Furthermore, decreasing exports meant that this important source of foreign exchange was drying up. He apparently planned to devote much of his energy to going after speculators who had large amounts of foreign exchange held in small banking operations that had "grown mushroomlike in Berlin." Fellinger's appointment did indeed mark a stepping up of the number of razzias undertaken against cafés and similar sidewalk establishments in Berlin and elsewhere, but there was considerable doubt as to whether these operations were worth the effort. In the last analysis, therefore, Fellinger did not think force and other measures would produce much, and success would ultimately depend upon his "being in a position to offer a stable counter value."[67]

The new gold loan launched by Hermes at the end of his term in office was, if anything, bound to heighten demands for such stable values. The gold loan, in contrast to the dollar Treasury loan issued during the first mark support action, did not yet have the recognition of

Great Britain and the United States, and the Reparations Commission had protested its issuance, albeit with British abstention. Thus, when August Haniel of the major stockholder family in the GHH asked General Director Reusch about surrendering foreign negotiable assets he had inherited in the gold loan, Reusch advised against such an action because the gold loan was unprotected and it was better to pay the inheritance taxes than to "put good money in the gold loan."[68] For political reasons, big industry and the banks had indeed followed the government summons to subscribe and put their necks "in the sling." Bücher of the RdI and even some of his sharpest opponents in the Reich Economic Council left little doubt about what they really thought, however:

We put ourselves behind the gold loan, but we left no doubt that the gold loan, in the form in which it has been issued, is no gold loan, for it is not secured. Claiming that this loan is secured by the nation's assets is an empty phrase (Interjection: It's a bluff!). Also it's not covered; in its present form there is no security that the Reich is really in a position to keep it valorized. That is what counts. (Bernhard: Very true!) Such a means of payment must be created.[69]

Whatever his reservations about the schemes of Helfferich and others, Hilferding had at least sought to satisfy the cries of business and agriculture for valorized accounts and to provide as much encouragement as possible for them to feel they were getting a good return on the foreign exchange they surrendered. In these efforts, he took up where his predecessor had left off in battling with the Reichsbank and its leadership. By the time of Cuno's demission, the desire to see Havenstein depart from office ran across political and social lines. While the Social Democratic *Vorwärts* called for Havenstein's resignation on August 17, ex-Chancellor Cuno was recommending Jakob Goldschmidt of the Darmstädter und Nationalbank, who purportedly had the support of Stinnes. Senator Böhmers of Bremen mentioned Hjalmar Schacht as a possible candidate, as did the *Frankfurter Zeitung* (which also proposed State Secretary Bergmann). Manifestly, each party had its own reasons for wanting a change, the left assaulting the Reichsbank's credit policies and discount rates, the right deploring Haven-

stein's resistance to gold accounts and currency reform. More generally, there was a feeling that Havenstein and some of his colleagues were simply too old and inflexible for the tasks they faced.[70] Forcing Havenstein out of office could require special legislation amending the Reichsbank Autonomy Law. Lord D'Abernon, whose comment on Havenstein's rapturous reports on the Reichsbank's printing capacity was that "such insanity has never before been spoken outside a lunatic asylum,"[71] assured Stresemann, who seemed worried that the financiers in London would refuse Germany any credit if Havenstein was fired, that everyone believed that the inflation was the chief cause of Germany's financial situation and that "it would be difficult to reconcile this view with a demand that the chief inflationist be left in undisturbed control."[72]

Nevertheless, members of the new government had serious reservations about creating special legislation just to remove Havenstein and hoped that persuasion might work. On August 20, Hilferding proposed holding off with the creation of gold accounts until Havenstein could be induced to resign. Unfortunately for all concerned, Havenstein had no intention of resigning under pressure. Sharp attacks and demands for his resignation in the press and the Budget Committee of the Reichstag only made him more stubborn than ever. Stresemann and von Raumer discussed resignation with him on August 21 and found themselves confronting a strong defense of Reichsbank policies along with a promise to introduce gold accounts. Attempts to mobilize the persuasive powers of President Ebert were also of little help. All Stresemann could report on August 30 was that Havenstein intended to resign on March 30, 1924, and might leave office earlier but that "his honor" required that he not leave under pressure and that he be allowed to defend his policies before the Cabinet.[73]

In reality, Havenstein was digging in with a mixture of concession and defiance, and there was quite a bit of defiance in the concessions. On August 18, the Reichsbank opened up its counteroffensive with a note to the Finance Minister indicating its intention to reduce its paper-mark credits as much as possible and to go over to valorized credits. Nevertheless, it insisted that the problem of unjustified credits to industry was a very small one and that the great difficulty for the Reichsbank lay not in credits to business but rather in the discounting of Treasury bills for the government, especially in the exploding government quest for credits to pay civil-service salaries and the costs of worker efforts to attain prewar wage and salary levels. The Reichsbank could no longer participate in a process that would send the mark down the path of the Soviet ruble and destroy both the private economy, by making it noncompetitive, and the Reichsbank itself. Havenstein and Glasenapp welcomed the intention of the Reichstag and government to move in the direction of valorizing taxes and balancing the budget but insisted that these intentions would now have to be taken literally. Consequently, they informed the government of their decision to cease granting uncovered credits to the Reich on December 31, 1923, if the Reich did not by that time at least balance the ordinary budget. They also called on the Reich to undertake certain emergency measures, the most important of which was the use of the gold loan to pay salaries. The effect of this measure would have been to discredit the loan and pervert its purposes, and it is hard to escape the conclusion that the memorandum was a scarcely veiled effort to shift attention from the Reichsbank and put the government under immense pressure.[74]

Four days later, and certainly under the impress of the uncomfortable interviews between Havenstein and the leaders of the government, the Reichsbank finally agreed to the establishment of gold credits and accounts on a limited basis in a memorandum filled with hesitation, reservation, and skepticism. Conveniently overlooking the fact that the proposals for using gold accounts and credits as a means of reducing dependence on foreign exchange had their provenance in proposals by Hirsch, Dalberg, and Schmidt back in August 1922, the Reichsbank claimed that all the proposals that had been made failed to protect the bank from the risks of exchange depreciation. Thus, the Reichsbank had to seek "new ways," and these could not be found "from today to tommorrow."[75] At the same time, it was uncertain that the economy could bear an indebtedness in gold

marks without large numbers of bankruptcies. Whatever the case, the Reichsbank was not prepared to give normal discount credits denominated in gold values without a change in existing legislation. It was willling to offer valorized Lombard credits through the loan banks, an obviously more clumsy and conservative way of meeting this demand.

The strongest and sharpest response of Havenstein and his supporters to their critics, however, came at the Central Committee meeting of the Reichsbank on August 25, when Havenstein made a point-by-point defense of himself with his usual odd mixture of plausible and absurd argumentation. He correctly pointed out that the chief source of the inflation was the discounting of Treasury bills and that much of the credit granted to the goverment and to municipalities had been given in the interest of the Reich for the purpose of purchasing food and and raw materials. But he then went on to insist, obviously employing the real-bills doctrine, that while the granting of credits certainly increased the amount of money in circulation, this did not have an inflationary effect insofar as these credits were "economically necessary." "Unjustified bills of exchange," in contrast, were inflationary, and it was against these that the Reichsbank had to be on its guard, and he welcomed the introduction of valorized credit as a means of reducing such credit requests.[76]

What made this statement nonsense, of course, was that it was virtually impossible to distinguish between justified and unjustified demands. As an internal Reichsbank memorandum written only a few days later noted:

With the rapid progress of the depreciation, the entire private economy necessarily ever more speedily adjusts itself to being financed exclusively by the Reichsbank, for it is generally . . . considered a crime today to maintain credit balances at the banks and making debts is viewed as the height of business wisdom. A typical example of this is the Berlin discounting business of the A.E.G. For months now it has only paid in acceptances, initially running for three months, but now, because of their rejection by the local discount business, running for 30 to 60 days. If one wishes to stop this boundless exploitation of the Reichsbank and to effectively force business to use its own means and reserves, then I see only the stoppage of paper mark discount business as an absolutely certain means of doing this.[77]

Furthermore, if Havenstein was "welcoming" the introduction of valorized credits, he was doing so rather slowly when time was of the essence. While he was perfectly correct in arguing that the proportion of Treasury bills discounted at the Reichsbank had increased disproportionately, the amount of private bills and other forms of unvalorized credit had doubled and was likely to grow, while Lombard credits had been reduced. What this suggested was that private business was anticipating a conversion to valorized credit by the Reichsbank and was trying to take advantage of unvalorized credit before it was too late.[78]

The rest of Havenstein's self-defense ran along traditional lines. He played up the Reichsbank's role as the credit source of last resort in keeping the economy going, emphasized that it was politically impossible not to assist the Reich in its travails, defended his low interest rates as justifiable under inflationary conditions, and praised the expansion of the Reichsbank's printing capacities. At the same time, he indicated a willingness to provide valorized credits and gold accounts based on so-called "stable marks" (Festmark) pegged to the pound sterling. Havenstein chose the pound sterling because it continued to be the dominant currency in world trade, but he subsequently began to reconsider the question because of the dollar's popularity in Germany and the fact that the valorized tax accounts being opened by the financial authorities were denominated in dollars. Havenstein warned that the Reichsbank, in dealing in both paper and valorized means of payment, was being put in a very difficult position and that it needed absolute security for the latter. Thus, the stable-mark accounts would have to be based in large part on foreign exchange. The plan being developed called for a minimum 80 percent payment in foreign exchange. The right to pay up to 20 percent in paper was to be an incentive to open the stable-mark accounts. The Reichsbank would deal primarily in large accounts and leave the opening of smaller ones to private banks. Havenstein insisted that the Reichsbank could not simply go over to valorized credits so long as it was not sure of the economic consequences and that it was best that "it follow the general development."[79]

At long last, therefore, Havenstein had a program to answer to demands for stable-mark accounts, although timing remained a problem since he did not anticipate being able to introduce the new measures until the second half of September. His pronouncements at the August 25 meeting, however, had a more fundamental purpose. The Central Committee meeting was used by Havenstein and his allies to demonstrate loyal support for the bank and its leadership. Thus, Director Grimm made it clear that Havenstein's policies were those of the entire Board of Directors, and Director Kaufmann lauded the Reichsbank as the "heart of the economy" and warned that a change of leadership would deprive the bank of unique experience and technical knowledge. The most fulsome and extraordinary defense of Havenstein came from banker Salomonsohn, who cited Tallyrand in suggesting that the removal of Havenstein would be a true blunder and even worse than a crime; he spoke disparagingly of the "agitation" against the Reichsbank and intimated that the Reichsbank may have gone too far in its concessions to demands for gold accounts and credits. Long a defender of Havenstein in the Reich Economic Council, Salomonsohn's importance stemmed from his position not only in the Disconto-Gesellschaft but also in the leading banking associations in Berlin and the country. Actually, in calling for a vote of confidence in Havenstein at the meeting, Salomonsohn was representing no one but himself, since his banker colleagues had refused to support a similar vote of confidence in their associations. Furthermore, his effusive support of Havenstein's self-defense and program, which was well reported in the press along with Havenstein's remarks, was tantamount to an attack upon the government. This was made all the more evident because Salomonsohn saw fit to remark that "we are all of the view that those truly to blame for the present situation are not the Reichsbank, the Reichsbank Directorate, and the esteemed Herr President; those really to blame are our political leaders, especially of our financial policy, who can in their turn exculpate themselves by pointing to the unhealthy party system and the attitude of the Reichstag."[80]

Havenstein's counteroffensive may not have convinced any of his critics, but it worked to keep him in office for the time being. Hilfer-ding's frustration with the Reichsbank contin-ued unabated. Von Raumer was exasperated over slowness with which the Reichsbank en-couraged the surrender of foreign exchange be-cause of its apparent illusion that further inter-ventions on behalf of the mark might work and its odd preoccupation with the danger that it might suffer a financial loss if the value of the mark were to rise. Neither Minister, however, seemed prepared to press the point as August came to an end. On August 30, Stresemann even contemplated building a "golden bridge" to Havenstein by acceding to his wish to appear before the Cabinet to defend his policies, an ex-ercise which the Cabinet in the end appears to have been spared. The Chancellor warned against trying to force the Reichsbank President out without being certain about who his succes-sor would be, and this put an end to the battle against Havenstein for the time being.[81]

The stalemate with the Reichsbank only served to intensify the uncertainty and panicky atmosphere. Hilferding appeared paralyzed and looked to Stresemann to find a foreign-pol-icy solution while Stresemann warned that "no solution can be found in foreign affairs in a short time"[82] and that it was essential to keep the economy intact and give the people the sense that the government was getting the situ-ation in hand. If Hilferding was not offering much assistance on this score, neither was the Chancellor's DVP colleague Hans von Rau-mer, who appeared no less fretful and uncertain than Hilferding and presented a very grim view of the economic situation to the Reich Eco-nomic Council and Cabinet at the end of Au-gust. What distinguished Hilferding from von Raumer, however, was that the former persis-tently transcended class interests in his quest for a solution to the nation's problems, a charac-teristic he shared with Stresemann, while von Raumer almost invariably took the perspective of industry, which, in a manner typical of its leadership, identified its well-being with that of the nation.

In von Raumer's view, industry was heading toward a great crisis with uncommon rapidity. There was an extreme shortage of capital thanks to the sudden leap of wages and salaries and rising prices. Germany no longer was com-petitive, as was proven by the unsatisfactory re-sults of the recently held Leipzig Fair and the sharp drop in exports. In short, the game was up:

We in business can no longer live from the depreci-ation of the currency. That has exhausted itself. At the beginning we lived from the outside world falling for our mark. One can easily put it that way. We re-ceived a bonus of billions in gold à fond perdu. Then we lived from the capital of our pensioners. That has also been used up. Then we lived from the reserves of our enterprises. You only have to look at the liquidity of the plants to realize that this is also gone.[83]

Von Raumer insisted that the German price level was being ruined by the anticipation of de-preciation and the use of indices in setting wages and prices, to which he added the low productivity of non-piecework labor. His most immediate solution was to eliminate export controls and levies and the tax on coal, thereby removing administrative and financial burdens on trade and lowering the costs of basic raw ma-terials. At the same time, he manifestly antici-pated increased unemployment, longer hours, and lower real wages as the only means to eco-nomic recovery over the longer run. Compar-ing the economy to a sick organism, von Rau-mer argued that it could only be kept alive if its most vital parts were saved while others were al-lowed to decay and wither, and he foresaw many years of difficulty. The actual process of healing could only begin with a cessation of the printing of unbacked money and a balancing of the budget. Until this was possible, industry had to be helped in every way possible, and the printing press remained the only alternative to anarchy.

The Socialists and left liberals who listened to von Raumer were not especially impressed with his therapy. They seriously questioned whether the only solution to Germany's competitive problems was reducing the cost of labor and doubted the advisability of eliminating the coal tax and all export controls and levies at a time when Germany's fiscal condition was so par-lous and when economic conditions were so uncertain. The essential point for von Raumer, however, was that "industry must uncondition-ally be sustained in the immediate future. The solution of financial questions is secondary."[84]

This was not a very convincing argument at the end of August 1923, and it was even less im-pressive if one takes into account von Raumer's helplessness in the face of precisely those developments in the coal industry that were leading him to insist on the elimination of the coal tax. When coal prices came to exceed world-market prices in August, it was because the introduction of automatic adjustment of prices to all cost factors and the indexation of coal mine wages at the beginning of the month had created a situation in which miner wages rose faster than the dollar during the first half of August. Von Raumer came into office in the middle of that month committed to keeping coal prices at or below world-market prices. But neither he nor the primary consumers of coal represented in the Reich Coal Council were able to make any headway against the insistence of both the coal mine owners and the unions that they did not have the strength to fight it out with the miners. Indeed, the coal interests not only demanded an end to the coal tax as the only means of keeping their prices under control but even went so far as to call for a levy on the price of imported coal in order to bring it up to the German price! Even Stinnes opposed this last proposal, but Stinnes and his colleagues did keep up the pressure on von Raumer to accede to their other demands. While representatives of the finishing industries told von Raumer that he should have permitted the price increases at the end of August only "over his dead ministerial body," Raumer not only accepted the increases but even permitted the setting of the coal price on a gold basis. This "linking together of the most important domestic product, that is coal, with the dollar, which in large measure depended on foreign policy developments, without the counterweight of a valorized means of payment within Germany" was viewed by industrialists dependent on coal as a key source of the increasing collapse of the economy.[85]

Even if von Raumer was prepared to argue that the financial situation of the state was secondary, he also had to face the fact that both the economic and financial requirements of industry had reached the point where currency reform was necessary. Here, too, his leadership was less than inspiring. While he apparently did not think that the introduction of the new currency being called for by industry and agriculture was possible until the Ruhr conflict was ended, he thought the Helfferich plan a suitable basis and urged that work on the project be

begun immediately. Von Raumer's performance was indeed most revealing of the highly complex economic and political context of the currency-reform discussion. The initiative for the reform came from agriculture and industry, and it was conceived in terms of serving their interests. At the same time, the entire discussion was deeply embedded in the call for increased labor productivity and liberation of the private economy from restraints. Currency reform, as it was taking shape as a concrete program, therefore, was part of a right-wing agenda and reflected the strong tendencies of those economic groups whose power the inflation had strengthened to break loose from the control of the state and to strive to dictate social and economic policy.

For those in the government with a broader vision—above all, Stresemann and Hilferding—the question was whether they could ride with this right-wing agenda while containing it. The circumstances made Great Coalition politics and even a certain tacit collaboration with the more rational elements of the DNVP possible. Hilferding was a fiscal conservative and knew that prewar wages were not possible and that some modification of the eight-hour day and reduction of the costs of government were essential. Von Raumer wanted a stabilization with Socialist collaboration. Most important, if the Cabinet could begin moving toward a loosening and eventual termination of passive resistance at the end of August, it could do so with some encouragement from industry. There were, to be sure, choleric hard-liners, such as Paul Reusch, who wrote in early September that "Stresemann is the Chancellor of capitulation. The Chancellor speaks and his Social Democratic ministers act and will force him to negotiate directly with France in a short time." While recognizing that the costs of the passive resistance were enormous, he nonetheless cynically commented that he "fears that the Reich one day will be compelled to stop its payments and that then the one productive activity of the government, namely, the printing of notes, will come to an end."[86]

The reality was that the Social Democrats were quite cautious in promoting the dismantling of passive resistance, but for understandable reasons Hilferding did not view the printing of money as a productive activity. His desire

to impose greater accountability on the big industrialists with respect to their demands for
wage supports and credits compelled them to
confront their own dilemma. On the one hand,
they threatened to shut down and throw their
workers out onto the streets; on the other, they
pleaded that the government help them because
the unemployment would be dangerous for reasons of domestic and foreign policy. Underlying all this was an anxiety, as Reichert put it,
that the the accusation would be made that "the
iron industry stabbed the Ruhr struggle in the
back."[87] Insofar as industrialists were not
blindly nationalistic or totally defeatist, therefore, they were now being forced to recognize
that the Ruhr conflict was becoming an alba-
tross for them as well as the workers. The effort
of Stresemann to find a way out, therefore, was
very much eased by the fact that he could report
and von Raumer could affirm that Stinnes and
Vögler had told them "that no day should be
lost in entering into negotiations with the
French."[88] Indeed, one major industrialist,
Otto Wolff, was already holding discussions
with the French with Stresemann's knowledge.[89]

Despite the desperate situation and the ago-
nized condition of his chief Ministers, therefore, Stresemann was able to guide his Cabinet
forward along three basic lines at the end of August. First, a committee of the relevant Ministers was set up to pursue both the currency-reform question and ways and means of
extracting additional foreign exchange from the
economy. Second, steps were to be taken to re-
organize the passive resistance along more satisfactory lines while efforts were made to
achieve a negotiated settlement. Third, von
Raumer was permitted to reduce the coal tax so
as to lower coal prices and to eliminate the export levy on the condition that he agreed to the
raising of revenues from other sources. It was,
of course, easy enough to compromise so long
as too many hard and fast decisions did not
have to be made, and this held true not only
within the Cabinet but also in the unofficial collaboration between the Stresemann government and the DNVP leaders.

For the DNVP, involvement in the currency
reform project cut both ways. On the one hand,
it opened up the promise of greater influence
and popularity; on the other, it held the danger

of becoming implicated in the Republic and its
politics. For someone as stubbornly uncompromising as Alfred Hugenberg, this was no easy
matter, and the complicated considerations underlying the participation of Helfferich and others in the currency reform plans easily came to
the surface in Hugenberg's ruminations on his
unaccustomed cooperativeness. Thus, upon
finding that his schedule would not permit attending a meeting of experts finally summoned
for August 29 to discuss the Helfferich plan,
Hugenberg confided to Jakob Reichert:

> In a certain sense I was happy that, because of the late
> invitations, I had a reason each time to avoid sitting
> down to deal with these problems with Herr Hilfer-
> ding. On the other side, I concede to you, as I have to
> Herr Stinnes, who also was of your opinion, that it is
> desirable today to show the masses that the positive
> ideas for solutions come from the right, even if the
> seeds spread about are largely overwhelmed by the
> weeds. . . . The only question is whether a sustained
> period of participation in the daily political struggles
> leaves enough strength of nerve in the end so that one
> remains effective at the final hour.[90]

The question of currency reform, in the last
analysis, was a matter of high politics as well as
a conflict of special economic interests and a
contest among those who held different theoretical positions on currency and economic policy. That is why it was very complex in nature
and therefore one of those potentially enerva-
ting exercises Hugenberg dreaded. On the one
hand, the Helfferich plan soon found itself in
competition with other plans whose essential
basis was the creation of a new currency denominated in gold. On the other hand, there
was a conflict between those plans which envisioned a new currency bank designed to liberate
the private economy from the state finances
and those plans or ideas which placed their
chief emphasis upon solutions designed to uphold the autonomy of the state, its power to
control the issuance of currency, and its ability
to exert greater influence on the private economy. The debates over these issues began with
a meeting of experts under Hilferding's chairmanship on August 29 and then continued on
in hearings and debates in the Reich Economic
Council and in the Reich Cabinet itself during
most of September.

The basic positions, however, were staked
out during the first ten days of the discussions

which began on August 29. It was quite understandable that Helfferich's plan should be the focus of attention since it had been worked out earliest, was very well thought through, and addressed the perceived needs of the most important interest groups. This also gave him an advantage in responding to criticisms and alternative proposals. He did not contest Hilferding's charge that the plan offered nothing more than a "technical means" which would not suffice by itself but warned that "without such a technical means we could go to ruination."[91] He reminded that Germany was not Russia and could not go over to a barter economy. The consequences would be like those of the Thirty Years War and would be crowned by a civil war. Typically, he argued that the primary source of the inflation had been the Treaty of Versailles, to which now was being added an "internal cause," the decline in productivity. He did not expect the reparations problem to go away, but a means had to be found to eliminate the government deficit, provide a temporary medium of exchange, and pave the way for the establishment of a gold currency on the basis of an international loan. Helfferich readily admitted that, from a theoretical standpoint, there was no difference between basing his projected currency on rye or gold. His chief argument was psychological; that is, the need to create a medium of exchange that invited confidence in a society that had become "psychopathic" in its distrust of gold-denominated assets. The German people could, so to speak, "relate" to rye. The same would not be true with the "stable marks" Havenstein and some of the Reichsbank officials were suggesting as a potential transitional currency with the obvious purpose of avoiding the establishment of a competing currency bank. The gold loan certainly did not invite much trust. As for Hilferding's idea (first developed at the meeting of August 18 but not set down in writing until September 10) to create a transitional currency based on the gold in the Reichsbank and to divide the Reichsbank into paper-based and gold-based portions, Helfferich continued to argue that there simply was not enough gold available.[92] In essence, he was arguing that it was better to create a fiction that inspired confidence— that is, in the restricted emissions of an inde-

pendent bank based on rye and backed by first-charge mortgages on the land and assets of the participants—than a reality that would prove unworkable.

Needless to say, agrarian interests were most favorable to the plan, especially since this envisioned a tariff on rye that would protect its domestic value. Also, since the prewar Defense Levy had imposed an artificially low contribution on agriculture, it was highly unlikely that agriculture would ever be able to contribute half the capital of the projected currency bank. Industrialist and banker enthusiasm, even when it was strongest, was tempered by serious reservations about the use of rye. The DNVP shipbuilder Rudolf Blohm greeted the plan, even if it brought only temporary relief, because he agreed with Helfferich that it was the only way to prevent a continued sellers' strike by farmers. What most enthused him, however, was that it provided a way to circumvent the tax on enterprises. Yet, Blohm worried about basing the new currency on a commodity whose price on the world market was unstable and feared that the coupling of the rye mark with the paper mark might also create difficulties.[93] The banker Urbig, also willing to accept the plan, expressed similar concerns, but Wassermann of the Deutsche Bank wondered how the money was to be used to buy foreign exchange abroad. The problem, of course, was that the domestic acceptance of a currency that was not denominated in gold did very little for industrialists engaged in foreign trade. The "most normal thing," according to von Raumer, was to follow the Austrian model and set up a gold-note bank in which the Reichsbank participated but which was completely independent of the Reich finances. He even envisioned some foreign capital participation, "for the chief thing in my view is to get off dead center and get a means of payment that is accepted. I must say that I can only welcome every foreign investment in our economy, even politically."[94] In his desperation to find some immediate solution to the crisis and his recognition that gold was a "swindle" in the eyes of the farmers, however, he seemed ready to accept the Helfferich plan more or less unchanged. Bücher, however, took a different view, pointing out that "industry can only work with gold," and Luther, the chief advocate of the Helfferich program in the government, also began moving toward gold on August 29 by arguing that "psychology" spoke for rye, thus making rye backing desirable, but that the new money had to be denominated in gold.[95]

Helfferich's plan had always been tied up with the task of providing farmers with an incentive to deliver their produce, and this necessarily led those in industrial circles concerned with a currency reform to wonder if it was the most satisfactory alternative from their perspective. As early as August 12, economic journalist and editor of the *Berliner Börsenzeitung* Walter Funk had begun publishing a series of articles urging the creation of an autonomous gold-credit bank with foreign participation to serve the needs of industry and commerce. The projected bank would give the Reich a gold credit to assist it in getting its finances in order. Funk later claimed that his articles had exerted a strong influence on industrialist thinking, and his proposal certainly resembles both the ruminations of von Raumer about what he thought to be an ideal solution and the actual proposal developed by a special committee of the RdI under Hans Kraemer's leadership in the last days of August.[96] The Kramer proposal envisioned the establishment of the gold-note bank as an autonomous corporation with a capital stock of five hundred million gold marks, two hundred million of which were to be provided by the founding consortium. Kraemer and his colleagues assumed that industry had more foreign exchange at its disposal than was believed and that the restoration of bank secrecy and a reasonable interest on the investment would provide adequate incentives for subscribers. Foreign investors were to be invited to subscribe up to one-third of the capital, and the Reichsbank was invited to participate to an appropriate extent with an option to increase its holdings in the future. While the seat of the bank would be in Germany, its basic assets would be kept in a neutral country. The bank would have the right to issue gold thalers equivalent in worth to the American dollar. In return for this right to issue money, the Reich was to receive an interest-free loan for the life of the bank as well as a portion of its profits for the support of the paper mark until the old currency was eliminated.[97]

The Kraemer or RdI plan was apparently in the hands of the government as early as September 1, since in Cabinet discussions on that date, Hilferding seemed to favor it over the Helfferich plan because it was "closer to gold" in its backing, while Luther favored the Helfferich plan because it could be implemented more quickly and with greater certainty. Unlike the RdI plan, which depended upon voluntary subscriptions, the Helfferich plan would have a legal basis. At the same time, Luther made clear in a personal memorandum for Stresemann of September 3 that he was now firmly on the side of using gold rather than rye as the basis of the new currency. He had come to the conclusion that Helfferich had exaggerated the psychological issue. Although he himself had been the person who had urged the acceptance of rye mortgages on the Reich Justice Ministry at the beginning of the year, he now saw evidence in recent public behavior that a rye currency was no longer necessary psychologically:

By this I mean not only the conversion of all wholesale transactions in gold. The conversion has also taken place in retailing. Buyers in large retail stores see the prices on tables which are calculated in gold marks and are pegged to the shortest term changes in the index numbers. One already sees prices in gold marks on many shop windows these days. This development has transpired quite a while ago in the book trade. Even in the Reich Revenue Service gold accounts as tax accounts have already been established. I conclude from this that the public is in the process of accustoming itself to the idea of gold again and has in part already done so. All our propaganda for the gold loan would be pointless if one could not count upon this fact.[98]

Correctly noting that the rye basis was in no way essential to the Helfferich plan, Luther went on to warn that a gold-denominated currency based on rye would easily invite speculation on the price difference between rye and gold and that "rye profiteers" would be added to the "war, revolution, inflation, and occupation profiteers" with which Germany had already been blessed. It was not possible to corner the market in gold, but it would be possible to do so in rye.

Helfferich, to be sure, did not easily surrender his position on rye. He seems to have maintained it in the discussions in the RdI on September 3, when a special committee was set up to pursue the currency reform question, and in a meeting of September 5 among the experts appointed to discuss the question by the Finance Ministry. The Ministry had gone so far as to draw up two versions of potential legislation based on the Helfferich plan, one basing the projected bank on rye, the other on gold. Helfferich continued to make "psychological" arguments and to insist that the new currency should be based on a product that Germany had and could reproduce, and this clearly was rye and not gold. At the meetings on both September 3 and 5, however, Helfferich and industrialists Lammers and Frowein appeared inclined to try to pursue both plans simultaneously; that is, to implement the Helfferich plan for domestic purposes and the gold bank for German foreign trade.[99]

Thus far, the initiative clearly lay with Helfferich and Kraemer. Hilferding, whatever his objections, assumed a rather passive role. He had every reason to find the RdI plan even more objectionable than that of Helfferich, and his "favoring" of the former because of its gold basis must be viewed as a maneuver. It is not inconceivable that he anticipated an easier time in taking an initiative of his own once the Reich Economic Council's Currency Committee began its hearings on September 6, since this would constitute the first more public and wider consideration of the plans. Organized labor was represented on the committee, and Hilferding might have pinned some hopes on other old allies from previous RWR debates— Georg Bernhard, who was to chair the meetings; Anton Feiler; and Julius Hirsch, who was one of the experts called upon to testify.

When the committee met on September 6, it was confronted with yet another plan, which was important not only for its source but also for the manner in which it helped to focus some of the key issues at stake in the entire discussion. The author of the plan was Friedrich Minoux, the general director of the Berlin division of the Stinnes concern who, writing under the pseudonym of Friedrich Pilot, had set forth his ideas in Stinnes's *Deutsche Allgemeine Zeitung* on August 23 and, thus, manifestly with Stinnes's approval. Although Minoux was a member of the Currency Committee of the RdI, his plan does not seem to have received any serious attention in the deliberations of the RdI or the government. That it suddenly

showed up as a third plan in the discussions of the Currency Committee on September 6 seems to have been the result of a special request by a member of the committee made during a preliminary presentation of the Helfferich and Kraemer plans on September 4.[100]

Of all the currency reform plans, Minoux's was without question the most total and radical. It was intended to create a new currency on a firm gold basis and thus bypass the kind of interim solution projected by the other proposals. Also, in contrast to the other plans, the Minoux plan envisioned a solidly funded Reichsbank with greatly expanded resources as the chief institutional instrument of the reform and called for the funding to come from taxation by the state. Minoux estimated that the total national wealth of Germany before the war was three hundred fifty billion gold marks and that this had been diminished by a hundred fifty billion. He proposed an effective taxation of the remaining two hundred billion through a one-time levy of 5 percent. Rejecting Helfferich's notion of using the Defense Levy, Minoux proposed an entirely new assessment that was to begin with all persons and corporations estimating their own worth immediately—under penalty of prison sentences, loss of civil rights, and confiscation of property for those who deliberately understated their wealth or assisted in such action and lesser penalties for negligent reporting. Debentures were then to be issued for the ten billion gold marks thus collected, three billion of which were to serve as the basis of a new currency issue of eight billion marks. The bonds, which entitled the Reich to a share in the ownership of the Reichsbank, would bear 10 percent interest but be unredeemable for seventeen years and be marketed by the Reichsbank only against foreign exchange, precious metals, and jewels. The remaining seven billion marks collected by the Reich from the levy on assets were to be used by the Reich to get its affairs in order. The seven billion were also to be turned over to the Reichsbank, which was to issue debentures, in this case bearing 5 percent and redeemable at any time. The Reich could then secure funds from the Reichsbank up to the worth of these assets. The new currency would thus be fully covered. Minoux estimated that it would take about two months to prepare the new currency and coins needed for the reform. The new currency was to be fixed at the old parity of 1 dollar equaling 4.20 marks. The plan called for a rapid elimination of the old currency, which was to be supported as much as possible—Minoux calculated at a millionth of its gold worth in late August—and then exchanged within two days, the deadline being somewhat extended for money held abroad.

The Minoux plan certainly had some of that combination of grand thinking and forthrightness which seems to have characterized the operations of the Stinnes concern itself. Not only was the plan intended as a final reform, but it also offered substantially more liquidity to the economy and to the government than either of the other two plans. Tacked on to the plan were also certain expectations about the government's use of the money and future behavior which bore the unmistakable imprint of Stinnes's stabilization program. The money placed at the disposal of the government was meant to provide the government the means to get itself straightened out within a year. The funds would allow simplifying the tax program, eliminating excess personnel, putting government enterprises on a profitable basis. Lifting economic controls of all kinds—above all, the demobilization decrees—restoring prewar working hours, and eliminating cartels and syndicates. Minoux anticipated high unemployment as a result of the release of redundant workers and officials, but he expected that the money available to the government under his proposal would enable it to undertake productive unemployment relief and thus permit the unemployed to contribute to the productivity of the economy. While the proponents of the Helfferich and Kraemer plans certainly entertained similar expectations for a final stabilization—with the probable exception of the elimination of cartels and syndicates and the work-creation strategy to deal with unemployment—and while Funk had spelled out a host of similar demands for decontrol and fiscal belt tightening in his articles, Helfferich and Kraemer knew they were presenting interim plans and were careful not to link these with potentially controversial political demands.

This was all the more appropriate given that the Helfferich and Kraemer plans necessarily weakened rather than strengthened the govern-

ment. While the Minoux plan called for effective taxation of real values to secure the capital of the Reichsbank, the Helfferich and Kraemer plans were based on private guarantees or investments, and the Helfferich plan even involved tax relief. Neither of the two plans could be said to be particularly generous to the government with assistance in its financial plight, the Helfferich plan offering some three hundred million gold marks in return for a tax break, the Kraemer plan offering a possible hundred million marks as compensation for the right to issue notes. More important, both plans presumed that the successes of their projected new banks would rest upon their being private and independent of the discredited state and its finances. The attitude was most extreme in the case of the Kraemer plan, in which the bank's resources would be placed in a neutral country because, as he bluntly told the RWR committee, "we want them to be secure not only from the clutches of foreign powers but also secure from the clutches of circles who find themselves temporarily in power at home."[101]

While Minoux offended worker representatives by openly calling for the end of the eight-hour day, he won considerable approval at the RWR committee hearings for his defense of the integrity and authority of the state and the Reichsbank against the pretensions of Helfferich and, above all, the RdI. As the observer from Hamburg noted, Minoux, "to the astonishment of the worker [members], who took notably little part in the proceedings," argued that "it was impossible for the state to place its monetary monopoly, which is a basic sovereign right of the state, in the hands of private professional organizations. In his view, bringing the capital abroad would not serve to increase the credit of the currency bank, since this would be taken as an expression of the fact that the German circles involved themselves view the domestic political situation as desperate."[102]

This was not the only "astonishing" idea Minoux entertained, and he was by no means operating as a spokesman for Stinnes. What is striking here is the resistance he put up to the attempt to use the currency-reform issue to undermine the authority of the government. Significantly, Minoux's opposition to a rye currency and currency banks established by interest groups in independence of the government was strongly seconded by another expert at the hearings, Hjalmar Schacht:

It has been stated that the German Reich nowhere abroad—one can even say at home—still has sufficient confidence to entitle it to produce a currency that can have international acceptance. It is always said that there is still such confidence in the *Wirtschaft*, but that the state has lost it. I do not want to investigate whether the state or the *Wirtschaft* is more to blame for this, but want to place this factor calmly in the foreground of the discussion. I think it is completely wrong to propagate this view further, for that which Herr Minoux has said is completely correct in my view: If we do not succeed in restoring confidence in the state finances, then all these projects will not help. For we will never be able to handle the great questions of state policy through a mere confidence in the *Wirtschaft* . . . and I therefore consider it under all circumstances proper with respect to all the projects presented that the state, no matter how the organization is set up in detail, should receive a completely authoritative influence on this institution, not upon its technical and commercial leadership, but certainly upon those tasks of the institution where it must be put under state control in its capacity as a note-issuing bank for the state.[103]

Whatever the virtues of the Minoux plan as an alternative to its competitors, its primary function at the meetings of the Currency Committee of the RWR was to focus attention on the deficiences of the two other plans. Bücher admitted that the Minoux plan could be carried out most quickly but tellingly remarked that it required an "absolute dictatorship" as a precondition.[104] Bernhard and Feiler, whose views were very close to those of Hirsch and Hilferding, found the Minoux plan a convenient way of supporting a solution approximating the goals of Hilferding without actually accepting the Minoux plan. Thus, on September 7, with most of the members of the committee gone elsewhere, Bernhard and Feiler pushed a resolution rejecting the Helfferich plan because it was based on rye and the RdI plan because it would lead to a further repudiation of the mark. The vote was seven to four, with the employers constituting the minority. The resolution called on the government to move toward a balancing of the budget by reduction of the Ruhr expenses through a small dictatorial committee and urged a levy on assets along the lines proposed by Minoux for the transition period along with a severe discount policy to eliminate the private

inflation. The Helfferich and Kraemer plans were further rejected for violating the sovereign right of the state to issue money, a power that had to remain in the hands of the Reichsbank. In their stead, the Bernhard–Feiler project proposed that a maximum be determined to the inflation, after which the gold of the Reichsbank along with collected foreign exchange be combined into a currency fund. Gold notes were to be issued on the basis of the currency fund, which was to be supplemented by precious metals, bills of exchange, and the other methods proposed by Minoux. The paper money in circulation was to be exchanged for the new notes at the going rate of exchange. The Reichsbank was to retain its autonomous character, but the influence of the government was to be increased, and the capital of the Reichsbank was to be augmented by shares based on gold, foreign exchange or gold credits, and mortgages. This was not, of course, the Minoux plan, but what was manifest from this resolution was that the only plan that had made any impression on its authors was the Minoux plan, primarily because it placed state interests above private ones and held open the promise of a genuine taxation of real values. It is thus no accident that Minoux was mentioned positively twice in the resolution.[105]

Needless to say, the Bernhard–Feiler resolution decided nothing, even in the Reich Economic Council, whose combined Economic and Finance Policy Committees were scheduled to discuss the Currency Committee findings on September 11 and anticipated hearing the views of the government—above all, the Finance Minister. In fact, the vote had been pushed through early in the day on the 7th so that the Cabinet, which was scheduled to meet in the late afternoon, would have a chance to consider its recommendation. At the same time, some of the Currency Committee members who were absent at the time of the vote were busy working through yet a new draft of the Helfferich proposal with Finance Ministry officials for presentation to the Cabinet, and this apparently still was going on while the Cabinet was meeting. As a result, the Cabinet went through another inconclusive meeting, with Hilferding treating the entire subject in a very tentative manner by stressing the need to clarify the relationship between the projected new bank and the Reich and emphasizing that all that was being talked about was an auxiliary currency, that any currency was endangered so long as the budget was not balanced, and that the existing currency had to be supported against full repudiation and have some value if exchanged against the new currency. But how was one supposed to support the existing currency through increased demands for the surrender of foreign exchange when one was also counting on the foreign exchange in the economy to support the new bank? Hilferding could only resolve this conundrum by declaring that the new Foreign Exchange Commissar would begin by taking unproductive foreign exchange from hotels and sanatoria and see how that worked, a proposition supported by von Raumer and denounced by the Social Democratic Vice Chancellor Schmidt and Interior Minister Sollmann. Schmidt insisted that one had to go after the banks and industrialists, whom he accused of speculating, while Sollmann suggested that von Raumer did not understand the mood of the country and that time was of the essence. While the Socialists vented their displeasure on von Raumer, Luther expressed his exasperation with Hilferding. While leaving little doubt that he did not think a new bank would succeed if the Reich had too much direct influence upon it and that he inclined to a gold rather than a rye basis for the new currency, Luther insisted impatiently that the Cabinet had to demonstrate that it had a "firm goal" and demanded almost in the form of an ultimatum that Hilferding present a "definite project" by Monday, September 10.[106]

Hilferding did indeed show up with a plan at the Cabinet meeting on September 10. Both the plan and his remarks concerning its competitors seemed to parallel the attitudes taken in the Bernhard–Feiler resolution as well as reflect the influence of Moritz Bonn, who had provided Hilferding with a series of critical comments on the Helfferich plan and proposals of his own at the beginning of the month. Needless to say, Hilferding had independent thoughts and positions on these matters, and it is hard to trace the personal contact and interaction that certainly took place.[107] In any event, the Hilferding plan—which never took the form of more than

seven "guidelines," and thus in no way reflected the kind of drafting process that the Helfferich plan had gone through in Hilferding's own Ministry—began with the proposition that the transition to a valorized currency would only be possible once the deficit was covered, but that it would be possible to create an interim currency for a limited period. Since the Reich would have to continue printing money to pay for the uncovered portion of the budget, it would not be possible to fix a rate of exchange between the new money and the old without dragging the new currency into the inflation. However, since the new currency was meant to pave the way toward a final gold currency, it had to be both backed by gold and denominated in gold. This was also essential for purposes of international trade. Since the Reich was not to surrender its sovereign rights of note issue and since the creation of a new interim currency required a gold basis which had to be secured quickly, Hilferding proposed that the problem be solved by lodging the new bank within the Reichsbank. This seemed all the more logical in view of the Reichsbank's intention of opening gold credits and accounts on September 20. Hilferding thus projected the creation of a new bank in the form of a private corporation in which the Reichsbank would participate through a substantial portion of its remaining gold as well as its gold accounts, and this gold-note bank would take over the entire valorized operations of the Reichsbank. In order to strengthen the bank and assist the Reich, a 5 percent mortgage would be imposed on the capital value of the private economy which would not be used to cover note issues but rather to cover the issuance of gold bonds by the bank. A portion of these bonds were to be given to the Reich as compensation for the note-issuing rights of the bank, while the remainder were to serve as an interest-bearing investment for subscribers.

Hilferding assured the Cabinet that his plan could be implemented within ten to twelve days of Reichsbank agreement. He argued that it had the advantages of maintaining the note-issuing powers of the state. In contrast to the RdI plan, which simply neglected the finances of the Reich, it offered the Reich genuine assistance; in contrast to the Helfferich plan, which required no real sacrifice by those whose assets were being mortgaged, the possessors of capital would be required to put up real assets. Whatever its virtues, the belated presentation of a new plan by the responsible Minister certainly threw the rest of the Cabinet off balance and created a delicate and rather confused situation. Stresemann was most concerned about having money available to pay off the French if he could get them to end the occupation, and he worried that the private economy might be doubly burdened. Von Raumer seemed inclined to support the introduction of both the Hilferding and Helfferich plans since he viewed the former as insufficient to cover the needs of agriculture and the retail trades. This argument was made much more strongly by Luther, who correctly recognized that the Hilferding plan was extremely deflationary and insisted that the three hundred sixty million gold marks it would make available for the private economy would be totally inadequate in an economy with a prewar circulation of five billion. This was especially the case since people were likely to hoard a valorized currency. While Hilferding appeared to feel that he could get foreign investment in the bank and had contacted Vissering and Dubois toward this end, the basic issue of providing sufficient liquidity appears not to have been discussed. Nevertheless, because of the emergency and Stresemann's desire for speed, the Chancellor pronounced Hilferding's plan accepted by the Cabinet, although this apparently was not meant to involve a total exclusion of the Helfferich plan. The press was to be informed of the government's intention to establish a gold bank, and nothing was to be said about further consideration of the Helfferich plan.[108]

Georg Bernhard's *Vossische Zeitung* carried the first reports of the Cabinet's decision and intimated that the Helfferich and RdI plans had been turned down and the Bernhard–Feiler program unanimously adopted by the government. Nevertheless, Bernhard himself was extremely irritated by the way the matter was being handled when he appeared to report the Currency Committee's findings before the joint meeting of the RWR Economic and Finance Policy Committees on September 11. The interpretation of the government's decision had been deduced from a rather cryptic press release. Bernhard had assumed that this was because Hilferding intended to reveal his views at the meeting. Hilferding had not shown up, however, and Bernhard felt compelled to complain that "through the notice which all we citizens have read in the newspapers, the sphinxlike position of the Finance Minister on this question is actually only increased rather than the mystery in any way being cleared up."[109] Bernhard was fearful that the notice would lead to a further repudiation of the paper mark by the public, a fact confirmed by a representative of the consumer cooperatives on the committee, who warned that "if the government does not immediately declare that the paper mark is maintaining some value, then you will have no more food next Saturday."[110]

Bücher, who had been one of those involved in working with Finance Ministry officials on the revision of the Helfferich plan while the Currency Committee had been voting to support the Bernhard–Feiler proposal, was especially irritated by the news in the papers and commented that "if I do not want to behave like a fool myself, how can I now occupy myself with these matters without knowing the status of all the preparatory work and what the position of the government is." He called for an adjournment of the meeting until the government was ready to say where it stood since "everything else is meaningless chatter and can only increase the division of the German people still more. I do not want to be responsible for that in these days, when we are right on the brink of collapse."[111] Bücher's sentiments were widely shared in the committee, and August Müller, thinking back to 1918, could not help expressing a certain *déjà vu*: "Whoever has been in a responsible position during a collapse will not be surprised by such happenings; it is the return of things he has already experienced once before."[112]

Hilferding's absence actually had a rather prosaic cause, as he explained to the joint committee on September 12, namely, a previously scheduled Reichsrat meeting. At the same time, in explaining his plan, he also gave an important hint as to why his position had been so unclear and unenergetic with regard to the various new currency programs. The creation of a valorized currency would necessarily endanger the paper mark, and "I state quite openly that, so long as the deficit is not covered, I must recognize this danger, and it was for just this reason that I exhibited a certain hesitation in the carrying out of this idea."[113] In truth, Hilferding's speech repeatedly exhibited the deep conservatism of his thinking. The new currency had to be based on real values, and the only ones he recognized were gold, precious metals, foreign exchange, and first-class bills of exchange. He rejected "fictive capital" as a basis for the currency, and while willing to accept Helfferich's mortgage scheme on the assets of the economy as a supplementary means of supporting the projected measures, he would not go further. His refusal to turn the new bank over to the "occupational estates" reflected a comparable conservatism with respect to the state and its role in the economy. The state could not surrender its note-issuing power to the so-called occupational estates since "what occupational estates are is not at all very clear. We do not have a social order based on estates, but we have equality under the law. The law knows no estates. It is not a comprehensible juridical concept."[114] If what was really meant, however, were the various peak associations, then Hilferding viewed this as no less problematic. The peak associations were by no means equal. Some were more powerful and better organized than others, and these would inevitably have the upper hand over other groups and over the Reich itself: "The idea, therefore, of giving the control of the bank to the peak associations, while on the other side the Reich would give these peak associations the right to impose burdens on the private economy in specific ways, that is, to control the distribution of tax burdens to such an extent—this idea did not seem fully compatible with the task of the government to watch over the general interest and to maintain the authority of the state."[115]

These were true and important points, but was this the kind of statement to make before the RWR under the existing circumstances? The most devastating comment on Hilferding's speech came not from the side of business or agriculture, but from his own camp. Rudolf Wissell pointed out that the time for programmatic

statements was past and that reality had to be faced. He poignantly remarked:

The inflation in which we find ourselves at this time is murdering the Republic; it will be the gravedigger of our Republic. That mixture of despair and bitterness which is the mood of the people will not abate if these explanations of the Reich Finance Minister become known to the public through the daily press.[116]

It remained for yet another Social Democrat, August Müller, to give vent to his frustration over the crisis of governance which he saw reflected in the remarks made by Hilferding and von Raumer at the meeting:

In general, I must say that when I consider the impression left by the remarks of the Finance Minister and the Reich Economics Minister, then I ask myself: How is it possible that any people in the world tolerates such a failure of political leadership (Very true!) as is to be found here in Germany? I assure you, that there is no people in the world that would have permitted the things that have occurred to us in the last decade with such lamb-like patience as the German people. I believe that there is no people more upright, industrious, moral, healthy, and easily manageable people in the entire world than the German people, and if despite this it has been brought into such misfortune, then it is not the fault of the people but due to the fact that it has never found leadership (Very true!) with the ability to make of this people what one could make of it. That is the fateful thing! With all the good nature which I attribute to the German people, I still believe that it is actually very doubtful whether it can still bear the things which are descending upon it.[117]

Whatever the good nature of the German people, that of the members of the joint committee was more limited, and the meeting was not without the usual exchanges about worker productivity and about who was hoarding foreign exchange. Nevertheless, the tone of Wissel's and Müller's remarks was truer to the general tenor of the discussion, which was one of worry, even panic. Certainly the industrialists had been taken aback by the Cabinet decision of September 10, and Frowein reported that at an RdI meeting prior to the joint committee meeting an overwhelming majority of those present came out in support of the Helfferich proposal as an interim solution. That is, they were no longer willing to press their own plan. The important thing was to persuade farmers to sell their harvest, and Frowein urged that they cease blaming one another for the loss of authority of the state and accept the fact that any interim bank created needed to be independent of the discredited state and Reichsbank. He was seconded by representatives of agriculture and the merchants. The former pointed out that for months farmers had been subjected to bands of thieves and robbers, that no one could protect them anymore, and that, at the same time, they could no longer pay for machinery and basic needs. The latter reminded his colleagues that for years retailers had been subjected to what was tantamount to expropriatory regulations and that they had now run out of paper money and dollars. Unlike the situation in the occupied areas, which he pictured as "swimming in money," wholesalers and retailers in the unoccupied areas had run out of goods. They had to have money that was guaranteed and could no longer tolerate "this counterfeiting."[118]

It cannot be said that Hilferding's friends on the committee and the supporters of the Bernhard–Feiler resolution responded very impressively to such remarks. Feiler claimed that the panic was the result of the "phantom" of a valorized currency that had been spreading through Germany during the previous two weeks and pointed out that the examples of Austria and Argentina demonstrated that it would take years to bring a currency into order once it collapsed. He pontificated about the inflation tax as "the heaviest, the most fearful, the most fateful and the most objectionable tax there ever was"[119] but argued that it had to be replaced by taxes that enabled the state to function again rather than by schemes that deprived the state of the wherewithal it needed to exist. When he turned to the concrete issue of how one was to persuade farmers to sell their harvests under existing conditions, his response was to suggest that they be paid in certificates from the gold loan or in exchange for fertilizer and agricultural machinery or in return for chits entitling them to a certain amount of nitrate fertilizer. Such arguments made it easy for Bücher to score a point by ridiculing the idea of "nitrate money" as yet another new form of currency, while an agrarian representative pointed out that farmer cooperatives were already mediating barter arrangements. Even So-

cialist Max Cohen felt that Feiler's concentration on the need to restore state finances and balance the budget was pointless under existing conditions and expressed a willingness to accept any interim solution, even Helfferich's.

All this horrified Bernhard. Not only had the Helfferich plan "reappeared," but it had done so in its most dangerous form—namely, the Roggenmark, which was suddenly supported by Frowein and Max Cohen.[120] He tried to weaken the arguments for the Helfferich plan by suggesting that it would take two or three months to implement and that it would destroy the credit of the Reichsbank, although Bücher responded by raising the question of what made Bernhard think that the Reichsbank would accept Hilferding's plan. Bernhard was, nevertheless, resolved to bring the resolution of the Currency Committee to a vote. His twenty-three to twenty victory, if it could be called that, was something less than glorious, and because of the closeness of the vote, it was further tarnished by the decision to send forward the alternative resolution presented by industrial and agrarian members of the committee which explicitly supported the Helfferich plan as an interim arrangement.[121]

Thus, for all the virtues of Hilferding's arguments against the Helfferich plan and any other plan based on the "occupational estates," his hesitations had proven impolitic, and his own plan stood on very shaky ground. In fact, the decision of the Cabinet on September 10 to support his plan was a Pyrrhic victory for the Finance Minister. The industrialist leaders in the RdI were enraged over the manner in which the Cabinet had suddenly turned its back on the Helfferich plan. Rumors were about that the SPD Reichstag delegation leadership—above all, Deputies Müller and Wels, who feared placing any new bank of note issue in the hands of the economic interest groups—had persuaded Hilferding to oppose the Helfferich plan and that partisan politics had thus once again triumphed over what the RdI leadership perceived as the national good. While it is doubtful that Hilferding really needed to be persuaded by his party colleagues, the situation served to mobilize the industrialist Centrist Reichstag Deputy Rudolf ten Hompel, who was in contact with another Centrist industrialist on the RdI Currency Committee, Clemens Lammers. Fortuitously, the Center Party Reichstag delegation was scheduled to meet about other matters on the morning of September 13, and ten Hompel took advantage of the meeting to gain a hearing for Lammers, who was also furious about the government's about-face. Among those present were the Centrist Postal Minister, Höfle; and Minister for the Occupied Areas, Fuchs. Both confessed that they had been so burdened by the affairs of their own Ministries that they had paid little attention to the various currency schemes presented to the Cabinet. Höfle promised to get the issue put on the agenda of the Cabinet meeting scheduled for later in the day and to present the RdI position at the meeting.[122]

If Höfle carried out this mission successfully, it was because the way had already been well prepared by other events. Stinnes and Vögler had paid Stresemann a visit shortly before the meeting, and the Chancellor had assured them that the Helfferich project was not dead but was only considered an inadequate final solution to the currency question. At the same time, Hilferding was forced to report that the Reichsbank was making difficulties, having expressed a wish to separate itself completely from the finances of the Reich, and that it was working on a response to his own plan. While he maintained his position and seemed most preoccupied with the support of the paper mark to the greatest extent possible, only Schmidt spoke against the Helfferich plan. Even before Höfle presented his views, von Raumer called for a return to the Helfferich plan, and Luther reported that the food market was chaotic and the situation desperate. Höfle noted that while the public was satisfied with the government's performance in foreign affairs, the general impression was that the government's inactivity in domestic matters could only be explained by deep divisions. He urged the Helfferich plan as an interim solution. Stresemann had apparently come to the same conclusion. His chief reservation about the Helfferich plan seemed to be that it might stand in the way of his efforts to come to terms with the French. He considered it essential, therefore, that the encumbrance placed on the economy as a basis for the pro-

jected bank not be considered a first charge in view of Germany's reparations obligations. He seemed even more concerned, however, about the food supply and agrarian resistance, especially in view of the danger of an Italian–Yugoslav war, which might encourage German farmers to hold back their food for export. Pursuit of the Helfferich plan thus seemed essential to the majority of the Cabinet for purposes of domestic pacification, and the decision of September 10 was essentially reversed. The plans for a gold-note bank and an interim arrangement to ensure sale of the harvest were to be pursued simultaneously. A special Cabinet committee chaired by Hilferding was established composed of Luther, von Raumer, and Sollmann.[123]

These decisions undoubtedly defused what could have been a major political conflict over the currency-reform question. Helfferich was understandably embittered by the Cabinet decision of September 10, which seemed to make a mockery of his labors. His response was to release the full text of his original proposal to the right-wing *Kreuzzeitung*, in which it was published on September 14 as the prelude to a campaign against the government. While the publication could not be prevented, Lammers and von Raumer were able to persuade Helfferich to refrain from attacking the government.[124]

Matters were further simplified on September 14 when the Reichsbank formally stated its absolute refusal to collaborate in the Hilferding plan. The Reichsbank insisted that the public would totally reject the paper mark if the Reichsbank were divided and one portion issued paper marks that had no backing whatever. It adamantly condemned any effort to take the Reichsbank's gold for another institution as nothing short of a "rape," a "forcible confiscation" of private property that would bring the German government and the Reichsbank into disrepute throughout the world.[125] The true goal, in the view of the Reichsbank, had to be separation of the finances of the Reich from the Reichsbank, and here the Helfferich proposal was viewed as most promising under the condition that it be modified in such a way that it would provide credit only to the Reich and thereby not threaten the functions of the Reichsbank. Drawing upon the commentary it had already presented on the Helfferich plan on September 11, the Reichsbank argued it was fully capable of supplying the credit needed by the private economy and proposed that the capital of the new bank be reduced as well as the encumbrance on the private economy from 5 percent to 3 percent of the Defense Levy. In the Reichsbank's view, the Helfferich plan offered an excessive amount of credit to the private economy and the Reichsbank warned that the co-existence of two national credit banks would lead to a private credit inflation which, it was claimed, did not presently exist since the real value of the Reichsbank's paper-mark credits was far below real requirements. Manifestly, the Reichsbank was only willing to accept the Helfferich plan if it relieved the Reichsbank of the government debt while permitting the retention of the Reichsbank's position as the private economy's lender of last resort. Under such circumstances, it could anticipate an improvement in the value of its own note issue, and it was for this reason that the Reichsbank rejected any fixed rate of exchange between the currency issued by the Helfferich credit and its own paper marks.[126]

Havenstein was in a position to complicate but not to block the Helfferich plan. The same was not true of the Hilferding plan, which was effectively buried by the Reichsbank memorandum of September 14, thus leaving the Helfferich plan as the only viable alternative in the existing emergency. Emergency or not, it would take another two weeks before the necessary legislation was passed and constitution of the new bank was ready and still another two weeks before the bank would be called into existence.

One reason for this was continued dissatisfaction within the government with the Helfferich plan. Since Hilferding seems to have recognized that his own plan was doomed on September 14, he approached Helfferich personally on that day in an effort to win Helfferich over to the idea that the new currency bank would best be constructed within the framework of the existing Reichsbank. Hilferding seems to have argued that this would reduce the personnel needed by a new bank, speed things up, and answer to the Reichsbank's objections to a competing bank of note issue providing credit to the private economy. Undoubtedly, he

also hoped that this would expedite the transition to a final currency reform and genuine gold-note bank. After thinking the matter over, Helfferich responded negatively four days later. He did not deny that Hilferding's proposal would make things easier but insisted that the important thing was confidence, and he doubted that "in view of the severe shaking of confidence in the Reichsbank notes and the Reichsbank itself, even the best foundation for Reichsbank notes can be of any help anymore."[127] At the same time, he recognized the importance of close collaboration between the two institutions and suggested that the Reichsbank could act as an intermediary in the granting of credit to private industry and commerce, but not agriculture, from the capital of the new currency bank.

While Hilferding moved forward with his usual hesitation, Luther once again seized the initiative and held a meeting with Director Friedrich of the Reichsbank on September 15 to hammer out a mutually acceptable draft that would be based on the Helfferich plan but take into account the various objections that had been raised. During the following two days, Luther discussed his plan with von Raumer and his currency specialist, Dr. Dalberg, and a final draft was then hammered out under State Secretary Schroeder of the Finance Ministry. While the basic principles of the Helfferich plan were retained, there were also important changes.[128] First, the new bank was to be based on gold, not rye, and the new currency was to be given the name Bodenmark (literally, "earth mark"). Thus, two "psychological" needs would presumably be satisfied at once. On the one hand, the transition to a final gold currency would be eased; on the other, and here one can only suspect the linguistic motivation, those who doubted the solidity of gold and trusted rye would, in a land unused to earthquakes, find a mark identified with the earth calming. It was most unlikely, however, that the economic interest groups would find the second major change made by Luther very much to their satisfaction. Whereas Helfferich had conceived of the interest on the encumbrance on agriculture, industry, and banking as constituting a replacement for the Enterprise Tax and thus involving no real surrender of resources, Luther intended the private economy to make a real sacrifice. Not only would the Enterprise Tax remain in place, but the encumbrance would bear 6 percent, of which no more than 3 percent could be deducted as a share of the profit of the bank. Interest on the mortgage would, therefore, have to be paid. Finally, the new currency bank was not to provide direct credit to the private economy. Instead, it was to accept bills of exchange on a gold-value basis from the private economy and then rediscount these bills at the Reichsbank in order to provide the needed cash to industry. The Reichsbank's functions as a source of private credit would thus be preserved.

When Hilferding presented this new draft to representatives of the business world at a meeting on September 19, they objected strongly to the retention of the Enterprise Tax and the fact that they would now have to make genuine interest payments on the encumbrance on their assets as well. Agriculture was even more alarmed at the gold base of the new bank and the requirement to pay in gold rather than rye and objected strenuously to having to pay the counterpart of the Enterprise Tax, the Land Levy. On September 25–26 these issues also produced sharp altercations between von Raumer and Hilferding in the Cabinet. Von Raumer claimed that he had promised Helfferich in writing that the three hundred million to be received by the Reich would serve in place of these taxes and that the government was breaking its word by failing to honor the preconditions it had accepted for Helfferich's assistance. Von Raumer feared that agriculture might refuse to cooperate as a result of the new arrangement. Hilferding insisted that the taxes in question were the only gold taxes at his disposal and that he could not surrender them, especially since the mortgage encumbrance for the new bank would only become effective on April 1, 1924. He saw no point in setting up the new bank if he would not be in a position to balance the budget with taxes. He was strongly backed by Schmidt, who did not consider personal promises made to Helfferich binding on the Cabinet, thought agriculture could well afford the tax now that the controlled economy had been abolished, and warned that the Socialists could not go along with tax relief. While Luther seemed inclined to a compromise through a

partial coverage of the taxes by the mortgage interest payment, Stresemann, obviously concerned about Socialist defection and clearly worried about the bank project becoming bogged down once again, came down firmly on the side of Hilferding.[129]

The pressure to do something by the end of September had, in fact, increased immeasurably, and Stresemann had good reason to believe that the currency bank plan in its existing form would be accepted. The alternative appeared to be that the inflation would tear the country apart, especially with the termination of passive resistance on September 26. Urgent warnings were coming especially from Prussia, where the DVP Finance Minister, Ernst von Richter, sent a lengthy plea for speedy action to Hilferding:"The transition to index calculation, the Reichsmark's loss of function as a measure of value, and the month-long not always objective and endless preoccupation of the public with the currency negotiations in the Reich agencies destroy the mark day by day in increasing measure even as a means of payment. The failure of the Reich to provide a substitute threatens to bring anarchy, splitting off from the Reich, and disintegration."[130] Von Richter pointed to growing tendencies toward self-help in the form of arbitrary creations of valorized money on a local basis and in complete disregard of the Reich's interests. Agricultural banks were requesting permission to issue rye notes to pay agricultural workers, and in the province of Saxony, such workers were refusing to accept cash for that portion of their wages not given in kind. The danger thus arose that it would be impossible not only to get farmers to deliver to the cities but to get the harvest into the barns!

The chaos being created by the various forms of emergency money in circulation was bad enough, but an especially threatening situation was arising in the border areas. There were reports from the portions of Upper Silesia retained by Germany that people there were expressing regret that they had not voted to become Polish in view of Poland's stronger currency. Germans in the Huldschin area were talking about wanting to join Czechoslovakia, and the Danish krone was undermining pro-German elements in Schleswig. Thus, while fully sympathetic with all the objections to the various currency solutions and the desire not to undertake a reform before the costs of supporting the Ruhr were reduced or terminated, immediate action nevertheless was necessary in von Richter's view because "we have reached a point where the currency misery threatens to bring the disintegration of the Reich and economic and political disintegration. The loss of currency unity will mean the loss of the unity of the Reich."

Hamburg was providing an especially telling illustration of these dangers. The government there was increasingly concerned that it would be unable to pay for food and coal, and while plans were made to use a valorized loan recently issued by the city to assist in getting food and retailers were being permitted to sell on the basis of the exchange rate of the dollar, the sense was growing that more drastic action was necessary. At the Hamburg Chamber of Commerce meeting on September 14, the DVP Deputy Walther Dauch proposed the creation of a valorized money for Hamburg backed up by foreign exchange which "would be issued the moment the Reichsmark is no longer accepted as payment." He went on to argue that "this is not far off" and called for the creation of "a private institution independent of the state" to issue the new money. The proposal was referred to the banking section of the Chamber of Commerce for immediate action.[131]

Since Germany's salvation would also depend upon help from abroad, the outside world's view of Germany's situation was of no small importance, and here, too, there was ample evidence of a disintegration of Germany's position. The Foreign Office reported in late September that the mark was viewed as worthless in New York and no longer was noted on the exchanges. Even more dangerous was the discussion in the London papers, where the argument was being made that sooner or later Germany's finances would have to be put under Allied control. In Amsterdam, Zurich, and Stockholm great skepticism was being expressed about Germany's capacity to bring its currency in order without a restructuring of its finances and economy, one of the Swedish papers going so far as to say that "all the talk in Germany about a gold currency is empty blabber."[132]

Such reports were forcing the rest of the Cabinet to adopt the line Luther had adopted weeks before—namely, that the Helfferich plan, as modified, was the only way out—and were also compelling Hilferding and von Raumer to come to terms with the plan and with one another. In the same way, the situation was also compelling the leaders of industry and agriculture to give strong support to the plan despite their serious reservations. This became very apparent when the Finance Committee of the RWR met to consider the final government proposal on September 28.[133] Bücher, taking a view similar to that of the aforementioned Swedish newspaper, argued that they had managed to talk the paper mark to death and that the interim solution proposed was the only solution. This in no way prevented the committee from discussing the subject for slightly over nine hours before voting to support the government proposal by a fifteen to three vote with two abstentions. The chief opposition came from Georg Bernhard who, in collaboration with Hermann Fischer (a Cologne Democrat), presented an alternative resolution. The resolution also seems to have been influenced by the ideas of Julius Hirsch. Bernhard and Fischer proposed that the Reichsbank cease discounting government Treasury bills, discount normal bills of exchange only in gold marks at the prewar dollar parity, and otherwise give only gold-denominated Lombard credits. All exchange controls were to be lifted, and the Reichsbank was to open gold accounts against both paper marks and foreign currency. In order to straighten out its finances, an operation Bernhard thought could be completed in a quarter of a year, the Reich was to increase the gold loan. At the same time, to satisfy demands for a valorized trustworthy interim currency, coupons from the gold loan could be used as currency for a restricted period of time and had to be accepted by government agencies at full value.

This extremely conservative and restrictive resolution reflected the strong opposition to the government's modified Helfferich plan among important DDP leaders. Bernhard opposed any interim solution that, in his view, opened up the danger of a new inflation by permitting two banks and two currencies to coexist. He took the position that a new bank tied to the state finances and based upon a fictitious capital would offer no guarantees against the repetition of previous abuses. What the government now termed the Neumark (or "new mark") would be doomed to depreciation because it would be a "money machine" for the state and a new means by which certain industrial circles could enrich themselves. England and America, with their "puritan" monetary views, certainly would not recognize it. Thus, Bernhard condemned the entire proposal as a "massive fraud"[134] and regretted that Hilferding had abandoned the sound monetary principles he had previously represented to put his name to it.

It was a measure of Bernhard's weakened position at this juncture that the only significant support he received came in the form of a rambling and disjointed attack on the idea of returning to a gold standard by the non-Socialist white-collar trade union leader Wilhelm Beckmann. The monetary views he presented were, if anything, the reverse of Bernhard's, and he castigated gold currencies and the deflations they required as a source of crisis in the service of international finance capital. Thanks to this lower-middle-class anticapitalism, however, he was able to grasp what he termed to be the "social dynamite" implicit in the government proposal; namely, the destruction of "the last rays of hope" of all those with fixed incomes and investments who had been hurt by the inflation for a revaluation of their entitlements and assets.[135]

Under the circumstances, however, such arguments could only provide ammunition to Bernhard's critics. The time for theory, good or bad, was long past. As one supporter of the plan noted: "Everyone acquainted with monetary theory knows that he must put all his theoretical convictions in the file cabinet if he wants to support this plan. Especially Dr. Hilferding had to do this, for everything that he has always fought against is actually being put into practice by this currency bank law bearing his signature. Of this there can be no doubt. One thus sees that people in politically responsible positions must in certain circumstances act in opposition to their conviction."[136]

Hans Kraemer was most effective in making

this point about his own person. He gave an impassioned argument for the government plan while reminding everyone that he had supported and continued to support the RdI plan. He likened Germany's situation to that of a flood in which the only way to save oneself was to climb on the roof. The projected bank was the only way he could see to mobilize the harvest. When Bernhard interjected that there was another way, Kraemer shot back, in an obvious reference to Hirsch, "but then show me another means than—please excuse me—these bloody theories that one can create a gold bank by sitting down a former very clever state secretary and having him make a draft bill."[137] If there was going to be a gold bank, then he preferred his own to Hirsch's since the backing would be safely kept on neutral soil. Furthermore, Kraemer expressed astonishment that those who had been crying for the appropriation of real values for years should now oppose a plan that involved precisely such an encumbrance of real values as called for in the government draft. If industry now agreed to these burdens, however, Kraemer frankly admitted that it was only because there no longer was a choice. In contrast to Bernhard, Kraemer considered the paper mark doomed: "The paper mark is not to be saved, never as a paper mark, and if you confiscate the very last drop of Germany's assets, you cannot save this paper mark which has lost its notation, its value, its reputation, and all confidence. You must introduce a new currency." He did not deny Bernhard's charge that the new interim currency would begin to depreciate, but the problem was to buy time and not to follow theory—one had to get through the winter. "I [Kraemer] can empathize with the farmers when they take the position that: my corn has real value; my wheat is gold; what you put in my hands is nothing; it runs through my fingers."[138]

It was precisely with such arguments that Luther was able to win the approval of the Reichsrat for the draft bill on October 1, from whence it was sent to the Reichstag.[139] The debate in the Reich Economic Council on September 28, however, also made clear the limited character of the harmony which had been achieved. Indeed, the consensus on the new bank and currency, such as it was, only intensified the deep divisions over the more basic financial and economic reforms upon which the successful transition from an interim currency to a new stable currency would depend. The willingness of the RdI leadership and the representatives of the agrarian interest groups to go along with the government's currency program was not without conditions, some explicit, some implicit. Furthermore, the "sacrifices" required of their constituencies only served to intensify their insistence that the reforms they demanded—severe reduction of the civil service and social programs, dismantling of economic controls, and suspension or elimination of the eight-hour day—be implemented. Bücher was quite solemn on this point: "The representatives of industry present feel themselves obligated to say that their agreement would be made impossible if the government, under renunciation of a simultaneous solution of the complex of questions of which it is aware, tries to carry out the currency plan without consideration of the other problems." He knew full well that there was an uncomfortably large number of politically charged issues to be handled, but their accumulation arose from the fact that "one did not listen at the time and no authority could be found to carry out what many recognized to be necessary. The authority was lacking. But now the questions are so pressing that it is a matter of life or death." If Bernhard wished to talk about a defrauding of the people, then he should look elsewhere than the economic groups supporting the currency reform; namely, "to the views of those who out of cowardice preach theories against their own inner convictions without having to translate their consequences into practice."[140] The agrarian leader Crone-Münzenbrock was no less adamant that the currency reform depended upon a new, better said, an old way of doing things economically:

If we do not get back to productive work, if we don't get to the point where our taxes bring real returns and further if all this chatter about socialization [and] factory councils does not cease, then these measures will have no success. In a short time, the disaster will be dragged out further. The army of civil servants must be reduced appropriately. There must be productive work. The thousands upon thousands, who are today in housing offices and rent control offices must be

channeled into productive work. There must be pay according to performance. There must be overtime. In short, we wish that the peasants be taken as the model of what it means to work. Then you will very soon have the basis for a sound currency, also the basis for the gold currency desired by Herr Bernhard.[141]

The undercurrent of hostility toward the workers among the industrial and agricultural leaders was so extreme that even the banker Hans Fürstenberg took umbrage at the implication that "the entire misfortune of the past few years in Germany is to be placed on the account of the workers" and reminded his colleagues that their constant discussions of the mistakes made by the Reichstag and government in the past years suggested that "a very large measure of the blame for our present disaster lies in the insufficient and deficient decision-making capacity of the so-called leadership with which we have been blessed during the past few years."[142] Such remarks, however, had their own political implications, and one of the more notable characteristics of the discussion in the RWR Finance Policy Committee was the manner in which not only the representatives of propertied interests but even more the labor representatives at the meeting decried the political partisanship which stood in the way of the necessary stabilization measures. The Christian labor leader Baltrusch was particularly insistent that decent persons of goodwill had to join in making decisions that were not bound by partisan considerations. The Socialist Max Cohen, who did, to be sure, stand on the right wing of his party, was even more obdurate: "One cannot give this state, above all these political parties, a money covered by gold into their hands. After all the experiences which we have made with the political parties, we must assume that, if we were to get a really valorized currency—and this holds true for all the parties, from left to right—they would also grind it into dust. One can only give the political parties a valorized currency when they have contributed something to bringing the economy into order. If you give it to them beforehand, then they will in all probability waste everything and leave the economy in its old state."[143] If the new currency bank was intended as an interim measure to bridge an immediate socioeconomic emergency, it also posed a challenge to the political system because of the general consensus that a more basic financial and economic regime change was necessary and, thus, raised the question as to whether the existing political regime was capable of carrying through such a transformation. The subsequent history of the currency reform, therefore, must be considered in the context of this questions.

Dictatorship or Enabling Act?
Retaining Democratic Legitimacy

The decision to terminate passive resistance unconditionally on September 26, 1923, was a triumph of political reason and economic necessity but a setback for Stresemann's foreign *and* domestic policies. If Stresemann had begun his tenure as Chancellor by calling for a solution to Germany's domestic problems, this was not because he entertained the illusion that Germany's internal problems really could be solved autonomously but rather because he had reason to hope that a running start on the resolution of domestic problems would buy the time needed to negotiate an end to the Ruhr struggle. Foreign policy success would then reinforce the process of domestic reconstruction by holding out the hope of external assistance. Unhappily, the hopes he pinned on the British and then on French willingness to negotiate failed to materialize while the runaway inflation and costs of the continued passive resistance made continuation of the Ruhr effort impossible. He came to the grim conclusion that "passive resistance has become a weapon more directed against the Reich than against the enemy."[144] This was a realization to which Hilferding had come soon after taking office and the reason why he began speaking about the necessity of a foreign policy solution to the problems of government expenditure and currency collapse. The relationship was expressed very aptly by August Müller:

Those who consider the state to be unsuitable to act as the bearer of a currency reform action because it enjoys neither assets nor confidence are correct for only so long as it does not succeed in getting rid of the Ruhr question in some way. On the day when this question is solved, the state will again have a greater

mass of confidence and of potential to act economically and politically, and can again collect revenues. That is a foreign policy matter, and for this reason the whole situation is a foreign policy problem. I do not see how it is at all possible to create the preconditions for a solution if the Ruhr situation and its consequences shall continue.[145]

As Stresemann also recognized, however, terminating passive resistance unilaterally was a dangerous business, especially since there were those like the Mayor of Duisburg, Karl Jarres, who wished to do this in an aggressive and potentially suicidal manner. Jarres became the chief advocate of the so-called "ditching" policy (*Versackungspolitik*); that is, combining the abandonment of resistance with a declaration that the Treaty of Versailles was null and void so long as the the illegal occupation of the Ruhr continued. Jarres, whose views were shared by a number of leading right-wing industrialists and politicians, including Albert Vögler and other members of the DVP, was convinced that the Ruhr could only be saved by an international conflict brought about by the intervention of other powers against France. Stresemann sharply opposed this approach. While having no intention of signing away German territory, he continued to hope for negotiations and warned that "breaking off relations with the invading powers now and rejecting the Versailles Treaty means leaving the population of the occupied areas to their fate and removing every legal foundation on the basis of which other powers could use their influence to the benefit of Germany."[146]

In taking this stand, Stresemann was strongly supported by the Socialist State Commissar for Westphalia and the Unoccupied Area, Mehlich, and the Socialist trade unionists, while his chief opposition came from within his own party. The conflict within the DVP had, in fact, been brewing for at least two weeks and reflected the increasing dissatisfaction with Stresemann's handling of domestic questions, especially the situation in Saxony but also wages and economic controls, as well as the stalemate in his negotiations on the Ruhr. Stinnes and Vögler had encouraged the negotiations but began to lose faith in Stresemann's ability to resolve the conflict with the French. At the same time, Stinnes appears to have become genuinely fearful of civil war in Germany. At a meeting of the DVP Reichstag delegation on September 12, he accused Stresemann of failing to accomplish enough during the previous five weeks, warned that there would be a "civil war in Germany in two weeks," insisted that a new money had to be created and that more work had to be done, called for action against Saxony and Thuringia, and remonstrated that "not a day must be lost, for otherwise the street will bring down the Stresemann Cabinet."[147]

Stresemann sought to defend himself by noting that the business community was itself divided over the kind of currency reform it wanted and that the Socialists were seeking to promote productive support of the unemployed. He did not see how one could eliminate the demobilization decrees in the unoccupied areas at a time when unemployment was increasing so massively. On the wage–price question, he actually took the offensive against Stinnes, recalling that "when our colleague Stinnes strove for world market prices in his industry, I pointed out to him that world market prices will lead to gold wages and gold wages would make us unable to export." This, however, was too much for Vögler who decided to speak his mind to the Chancellor:

One cannot conduct foreign policy when one is not master of domestic policy. . . . In times of crisis political leaders must keep their nerve. I told the Chancellor: let the Rhine and Ruhr stew (*schmoren*), but do not capitulate. The Chancellor should not reproach us about our price and wage policy. For the past year and a half there have been no wage increases in mining except through the power of the arbitrators. Certainly we strove for world market prices two years ago. Was that wrong? We would then have had unemployment two years ago. Better then than now.[148]

Vögler was even more hostile when the party leaders met on September 25 after Stresemann had informed the political leaders of his intention to end passive resistance: "A false domestic policy is the cause of the capitulation. Everything that Stresemann said yesterday to justify his surrender of passive resistance was absolutely false. . . . If the Reich Chancellor cannot decide to conduct a powerful economic policy, then we ought not to give him any vote of confidence, for otherwise we are co-responsible for ruining our economy along with our people."[149]

While both Vögler's remarks and the subsequent vote of the delegation to oppose negotiations with the French reflected a good deal of grass-roots sentiment within the party and great concern over how the Bavarians might behave, it also exposed a growing insistence on a more aggressive posture toward labor and a conviction that the government could never settle matters in the Ruhr satisfactorily. Stinnes in fact showed his hand when he opposed a proposal that the government be forced to withdraw its instructions for the ending of passive resistance by declaring that "you can place your confidence in the fact that we from the occupied area will conclude a modus vivendi with the French that will preserve Germany's dignity."[150] Clearly, since the government was to abandon passive resistance and the French were refusing to negotiate with the government, then the French could only negotiate with the leadership of the occupied areas, that is, with Stinnes and his colleagues.

Yet another example of how Germany's business leadership was taking a more radical line in domestic affairs with the ending of passive resistance and were turning against Stresemann is provided by Cologne Banker Louis Hagen, whose views at this time were noted by Max Warburg,

If and when the Rhineland will make itself independent, he could not himself say; he fears that if Bavaria jumps out of line, the Rhineland is not to be held. The only solution he sees is a cabinet restructuring after the Social Democrats are shipped out and the Centrist deputy [*sic*!] Adenauer is the successor of Stresemann. So long as we do not operate more reasonably than before economically—longer worker hours, fewer civil servants, fewer pensions, lifting of all control regulations—he sees no salvation.[151]

A movement to "ship out" the Social Democrats and remove Stresemann constituted not only a rejection of the political concept of accommodation between the parties of labor and industry but also a turning away from the social compromise upon which the Republic had been based with the creation of the Zentralarbeitsgemeinschaft in November 1918. As badly tarnished as that organization was, it continued to function and even enjoyed a certain tension-filled resurrection as a locus for the discussion of economic and social policy in August–September 1923.

The initiative came from the employer organizations, which on August 9 decided to open up a new round of negotiations with the trade unions in the ZAG concerning the question of finding an acceptable and uniform means of establishing valorized wages so as to reduce the role of government arbitration and endless wage talks. Underlying this purpose, however, was the longer-term goal "to use the question of a valorized wage to discuss the real wage problem in general and thereby to open up the entire question of increasing production and to attempt an agreement with the trade unions on this question."[152] A Wage Commission with ten representatives from each side was established on August 14, and guidelines were hammered out between August 20 and September 1. The major concern of the trade unionists was to prevent the further deterioration of real wages by guaranteeing valorization through the reduction of pay periods, thus ensuring that the workers could use their money rapidly. The trade-union leaders assured the employers that a gold wage was a distant rather than an immediate goal so long as the entire economy was not operating on a gold basis, and they also agreed to take regional differences into account rather than rely solely on the Reich cost-of-living index. As for the employers, they persistently emphasized that increased unemployment would be the only result of extreme demands and that the condition of industry was so parlous that the trade unions had to decide whether they wanted to work with employers or go it alone and "suffer shipwreck."[153]

The guidelines finally approved on September 1 were devised by the lending director of Siemens, Köttgen. The object of the scheme was to provide a degree of stability in future negotiations by fixing a basic wage for a period of at least four weeks and then introducing a multiplier based on the anticipated increase in the cost of living during the coming week to determine the weekly wage. Multiplier errors in one direction or the other would be corrected in calculating the wage for the following week. What was thought to be the thorniest aspect of the arrangement was the question of the basic wage once the economy stabilized. Employers conceived of the basic wage as one calculated in

gold pfennig and based on the prewar wage with downward calculations for lower rents, lower productivity, and current market conditions. The trade-union leaders were fearful that this would have bad results for important groups of workers and preferred to leave the issue for quieter times. Finally, a compromise was worked out which recommended the gold-pfennig wage but did not rule out using the paper-mark wage of more recent vintage as a basis of calculation.[153]

What the negotiation exposed was the tragic situation of the trade-union leaders and their weakness. On the one hand, they saw few alternatives to the proposals of the employers and were desperate for some immediate calculability; on the other, they could not appear weak to their constituency. As Köttgen told Siemens, "Naturally, we also touched upon the level of real wages in the discussion. The trade unions also agreed on the impossibility of going as high as the peacetime wage. They are not prepared to concede this openly however. A great deal of enlightenment in this area will be necessary."[155] "Enlightenment" was not the real issue, however, but rather trust and self-restraint. The Socialist trade-union leader Franz Spliedt, put the issue quite directly:

He does not think it proper when the workers are told, produce more, and then we will come out of the dilemma. It can be shown that it is precisely in the industries in which work is more intensive than before the war that the difficulties are the greatest. Nevertheless, it can be conceded that there are many plants in which productivity is not commensurate with wages, and the unions are quite ready to seek ways of dealing with these difficulties. The employers see the solution in eliminating the veiled unemployment. But one must ask: how do we get through the period in which the unemployed are on the streets? To support them in the way that, for example, England has is hardly to be thought of in Germany, and it will not do to give them only unemployment support. The economy is sick because the employers and workers have no confidence in one another. The employers complain that the workers do not produce enough and make the plants incapable of survival. The workers say that the employers fail to fulfill their obligations. Perhaps both are not entirely incorrect.[156]

Ernst von Borsig, who was the chief employer representative at these meetings, however, insisted on "enlightenment" and the argument, repeated over and over again by employers, that "unemployment had to be fought with unemployment":

He suggests the following for consideration: If temporarily only a limited number of workers were employed in a factory, wherever possible with increased hours of work, then this portion of the work force could be sufficiently paid and would become capable of consuming. The ability to consume would increase turnover of goods and this would increase work opportunity. In this way we would slowly return to normal levels of employment after a certain period of transition in which unemployment support would have to be paid.[157]

At the same time, however, Borsig could not refrain from making the reproach repeated over and over again by employers and by Economics Minister von Raumer during this period; namely, that the coal miners in the unoccupied areas, instead of working doubly as hard as before, were producing less. If this were otherwise, "the Ruhr struggle could have been kept up longer. It is irresponsible that coal has to be brought in from England instead of an effort being made to cover the gap in production."[158]

The impression made by such strictures was limited, however, in the face of the immediate problems faced by both employers and workers in implementing the guidelines negotiated in late August and signed on September 1. As was later confessed, they turned out to be appropriate for the "more or less steady monetary depreciation" of late August but not for the "colossal fall of the mark" of the first week of September, and many firms, faced with inadequate resources, were refusing to follow the guidelines and were firing their workers. They did not feel that they could afford the base pay or that they could make commitments on a four-week basis, and Borsig felt compelled to ask the trade-union leaders at a stormy meeting of the Wage Commission on September 10, that they "not overlook the fact that industry had to be ready to meet every situation."[159] Exactly what workers were supposed to do was left unanswered. Union leaders were outraged that all their discussions appeared to have been purposeless, especially since their assumption was that the guidelines were meant to deal with catastrophic inflation. Employers were themselves more than a little embarrassed by the situation, and Köttgen, in particular, urged that they not

cease to negotiate because circumstances made the guidelines obsolete. The truth was that neither side had anticipated that the inflation would become so bad that the multiplier simply would not function. While the VdA membership was rebelling against the guidelines, trade-union leaders feared that they would lose credibility if the guidelines were not followed. They pleaded that the VdA publish the guidelines and instructions for their implementation and promised, in turn, to discuss the productivity problem. As a result, the guidelines were published, as the VdA explained, "for the psychological and domestic political tranquilization of the workers."[160] This was done, however, with no expectation that the guidelines could be implemented, and the VdA in its circular of September 19 made no secret of the fact that it considered the effort to deal with the situation as "Sisyphus labor." It claimed that "with the best of will, we cannot see how it will be in any way possible to maintain the present real wage at its level with the continuing destruction of the currency and the continuing crisis of production."[161]

This characterization of the guidelines as "Sisyphus labor" infuriated the otherwise very compromising Spliedt who, at the September 19 meeting of the Wage Commission, attacked the "gold hunger" of industry and agriculture. He accused them of saving their substance while telling workers either to work nine hours or be unemployed three days a week. He pointed out that millions were going to be unemployed and would go hungry because there was no money to support them, and the time had come for employers to decide whether they wanted to work together with trade unions or let things take their course. While Borsig, Bücher, and other employer representatives defended themselves against charges of duplicity, they also recognized that their goal of negotiating a basic settlement was being jeopardized by their inability to deal with the immediate crisis and decided to affirm their support for the guidelines and their recommendation that its terms be carried out "where conditions anywhere at all permit it."[162]

The reality was that "multipliers" were no longer working, either with respect to taxes or wages, and interim arrangements were necessarily problematic without a basic reform program. When it came to considering reforms, however, employers continued to stress low productivity because of reduced hours, vacations, sick leave, state interference, and diminished labor intensity, while labor leaders blamed poor nourishment and profiteering. Whereas trade unionists insisted that the "private controlled economy" of the cartels had to be regulated, employers argued that it was inconsequential to attack the cartels for protecting economic incompetence and high prices while defending demobilization decrees that prevented the closing of unprofitable plants. They accused the trade unions of functioning as "wage cartels" which imposed their demands through binding arbitration by the government. Looming over the entire discussion was the spectre of growing unemployment and the anticipation of greater unemployment in the future at a time when the government was indicating that it could not maintain existing levels of unemployment support. Employers persistently reiterated the argument that "open unemployment was more rational than veiled unemployment" through work stretching and the maintenance of unprofitable enterprises. Trade unionists insisted that the restrictions on plant closings be maintained until the unemployment support system was properly regulated. They feared that otherwise the employers would close down plants on a large scale the moment they were no longer constrained by the demobilization decrees. The future seemed very dark indeed if employers were to have their way. While employers regularly pointed to the English model, Spliedt tried to hammer home the fact that Germany faced a very different situation: ". . . England pays unemployment support to an extent that is unknown in Germany. Things here are such that the Finance Ministry is saying that it can no longer maintain the existing benefits as they have been. If financial control were to be imposed on us in the course of our negotiations with France and Belgium, then he does not see how we should deal with the unemployment problem."[163]

Underlying these discussions and debates was the question of whether the ZAG could collaborate in dismantling many of the arrangements that had formed the basis of its creation in November 1918 without dismantling itself.

It had been easy enough to take the corporatist path to inflation, but could the same path be taken to deflation? The motive driving forward the negotiations in 1923 was the same as it had been five years earlier; namely, in the words of trade unionist Tarnow, "that free agreements are to be preferred to legislative ones."[164] A decision was taken on October 1 to draw up a position paper stating the points of concurrence and dissension between the two sides with the objective of working toward a common program.

It cannot be said that this was a very hopeful venture given the fate of the ZAG's 1918 pretensions and the chasm between the position of at least the Socialist trade unionists and employers. More fundamentally, however, the deficiencies of corporatist solutions were even more likely to exhibit themselves in 1923 than they had after 1918. On the one hand, the economic and social issues were more the stuff of high politics than ever, and it was difficult to imagine how even the weakened Weimar state was going to turn these issues over to private determination under existing circumstances anymore than it was going to turn its powers to issue money over to "occupational estates" or peak associations. In the last analysis, the legitimation of all private understandings between industry and labor would have to come from the executive and legislative authority of the state. On the other hand, experience had shown that the peak associations were of varying strengths and divided among themselves and within themselves. There was no real guarantee that their private undertakings would be accepted by or be binding upon their constituencies.

If there was to be an understanding on the "regime change" Germany would be forced to undergo, therefore, it would have to be on the political level. At the same time, there would have to be a government united enough and strong enough to make decisions and impose its will. While the corporatist temptation arose in 1923, as in 1918, from the feeling that the basic issues could never be solved by the partisan politics that seemed to dominate the Reichstag, the real issue was whether it would be possible to run the country in 1923 without resorting to authoritarian government. Even the Social Democrats were prepared to accept a measure of "dictatorship" to deal with the situation. Through most of Stresemann's first month and a half in office, however, the precise character of the powers to be given to the government did not have to be determined because the Reichstag had been adjourned. It did not convene between August 15 and September 27, and then met for two days to debate the abandonment of passive resistance before adjourning again until October 6. The prospect of having to bring all the necessary measures of financial reform before the Reichstag was not one that any member of the Cabinet, and certainly not Hilferding, could look forward to with any confidence. At the Cabinet meeting of September 30, Hilferding frankly questioned whether the government could survive such discussions and whether the entire situation would not lead to a spreading of the idea of a right-wing dictatorship, already much discussed in the press. For these reasons, he proposed getting parliamentary agreement to an enabling act that would give the government the necessary powers to deal with the financial and political crises and then to have the Reichstag adjourn. This was a program which the entire Cabinet presumably could support. Nevertheless, it provoked a severe crisis in the government and a reshuffling of the Cabinet prior to the reconvening of the Reichstag on October 6.[165]

This reconstitution of the government meant that, for the moment at least, the crisis created by the termination of passive resistance had been resolved in favor of a constitutional solution. It is important to recognize, however, that extra-constitutional solutions had been taking very real shape during the preceding weeks and appeared as very real alternatives during the government crisis at the beginning of October. Such alternatives inevitably centered about the head of the Reichswehr, General Hans von Seeckt, who would necessarily play a leading role if the situations in Saxony and Bavaria got dangerously out of hand. It was understandable, therefore, that Stresemann and Ebert should have held discussions with Seeckt on September 22 about declaring a state of emergency and having the Chancellor then pass on his powers to Seeckt, who would thus become a kind of "emergency Chancellor." In the last week of September, therefore, Seeckt understood that he might become the head of the government, possibly at the summit of some form of Directory.[166]

Ebert and Stresemann were not the only persons looking to Seeckt, however, and this made the entire situation potentially threatening to the future of the political system established in 1918. Seeckt was by no means averse to serving as the instrument for a massive change of the political regime as well as the socioeconomic order. On September 19–20, Seeckt had been approached by prominent agrarian leaders who, wishing the "elimination of Social Democratic influences on the government," assured Seeckt that he had their confidence and that they would place large amounts of food at his disposal if a dictatorship were established. Next, the DNVP leaders Hergt and Count von Westarp visited Seeckt on September 23 to inform him that they had no confidence in Stresemann and favored a "military chancellorship." Seeckt was not inattentive to such suggestions, but he was urged by his chief advisers to be cautious and to avoid becoming a "dictatorial chancellor with *one* party." They thought it important that he be allied with the more "reasonable portion of the workers," and Seeckt did, in fact, receive representatives of nationalist trade-union organizations on September 24.[167]

Even more dangerous were the appeals that Seeckt come to terms with the patriotic defense associations, whose major center of activity was Bavaria. Not only did the Pan-German Heinrich Class urge Seeckt to take action at this time, but the philosopher Oswald Spengler also came to prod Seeckt to collaborate with the patriotic defense associations. To Seeckt's credit, he seemed to have little patience with either of these gentlemen, telling the former that he would move against any violent action, be it from the right or the left, and privately describing Spengler as a "political fool," whom he wished would "go under with western civilization."[168] The less humorous side of the encounter was that Spengler had been sent to Seeckt at the instigation of Paul Reusch, whose industrial and newspaper interests in Bavaria and general political posture had brought him into close contact with the patriotic associations. Nor was

Reusch the only industrialist who had shown an interest in reconciling Seeckt with those organizations. Stinnes, through his leading directors in Berlin, Osius and Minoux, had been involved in such efforts as early as February 1923, and he himself had brought Seeckt and Ludendorff together at Minoux's Wannsee villa. The goal at that time had been to secure collaboration in the event of a need to resist the French by force, and a temporary agreement to collaborate may have been worked out.[169]

In mid-September, however, Stinnes seems to have had action on the domestic front rather than the Rhine and Ruhr in mind, as evidenced by a rather dramatic conversation he held with Ambassador Houghton on September 15. Stinnes announced that the resistance on the Ruhr was reaching its end, that Germany's economic situation was desperate, and that the only salvation was a return to prewar hours. He was quite prepared to see wages doubled or tripled toward this end, but he was convinced that German workers would not accept the reality voluntarily. A "dictator" had to be found, therefore, who would be given full powers but who would also be *bürgerlich* and speak the language of the people. Stinnes assured Houghton that such a man had been found in the great movement emanating from Bavaria which was determined to reestablish the monarchies. All the right-wing parties would join the cause, as would the industrialists and a substantial number of moderate people as well. The movement was prepared to wait until the harvest had been brought in before it took action, and Stinnes was especially concerned that it not act prematurely but rather in response to Communist provocation. Since millions would be unemployed by the middle of October, it was likely that a Communist uprising would take place, and the Bavarian movement would then be forced to respond. He also anticipated that Ebert would call a person or a committee of three to replace the allegedly incompetent Stresemann and his government and have disposal of the nation's military forces. Parliamentary government would be ended and all the barriers to productivity would be swept away in a matter of three weeks.[170]

Houghton was genuinely puzzled, and with good reason. At one moment Stinnes was talking about an initiative from Bavaria led by a popular leader; at the next, he was suggesting that the matter would be settled from Berlin through an initiative by Ebert. The Bavarian initiative certainly reflected the mood on the far right in that state if not the confusion and divisions among those putative rescuers of the nation. The most popular leader was Crown Prince Rupprecht, who was monarchist enough but certainly not *bürgerlich*. Ludendorff fell into this category and was the most likely candidate since Stinnes apparently and incomprehensibly continued to have confidence in him. The other candidates were Hitler, whose popularity was growing but who Stinnes thought quite mad after a meeting arranged by Ludendorff, and Gustav von Kahr, viewed increasingly as the "coming man" and certainly an admirer of Stinnes. As for the "Berlin solution," it inevitably meant Seeckt and possibly Wiedfeldt, who had been summoned back from the United States by Stresemann, and the increasingly politically active Minoux.[171]

In any event, Stinnes seemed obsessed with danger of civil war in the very near term, as was evident from his remarks at the DVP Deputies' meeting on September 12, and was filled with the conviction that his increasingly Draconian socioeconomic program had to be implemented by whatever means necessary. Thus, he responded on September 29 to a request from his DVP colleague from Hamburg, Walther Dauch, for such a program by going beyond his usual demands for complete economic freedom, the selling off of all government enterprises, the elimination of the eight-hour day, the reduction of the civil service, and tax reform. He also proposed what was tantamount to forced labor in the form of emergency public works for the unemployed at wages reduced by 20 percent, insisted on the "at least temporary elimination or banning" of all collective bargaining agreements and syndicates "insofar as they have the effect of making production more expensive or hampering exports," called for a ban on strikes in vital enterprises and the protection of strikebreakers, and urged heavy customs duties on all unnecessary imports but also for the protection of agriculture and new industries. While prepared to accept a yearly percentage encumbrance on capital, Stinnes advocated an end to the taxation of wages and withholding and supported only a very low, unprogressive income tax. In this way, taxation would not stand in the way of production. He grimly concluded that "whoever, even when given dictatorial power, wishes to make good all that has been made bad in the last nine years and, aside from this, wants to make serious progress over the prewar period, will have to devote two to three years of ceaseless labor for this purpose."[172]

Ultimately, however, it was not the DNVP and agrarians, the Pan-Germans and patriotic associations, or Stinnes who were to exercise the greatest direct influence on Seeckt as he contemplated the possibility of being granted dictatorial powers at the end of September, but rather Stinnes's general director, Minoux. On September 25, Minoux visited Seeckt and expounded a program that, as an aide of Seeckt's reported, "is enormous in all areas and would change Germany in its entire structure. It means a life and death struggle, but would lead to the recovery of Germany if it succeeds. 'Seeckt is completely taken with the powerful effect of this personality.' "[173]

Exactly how influenced Seeckt was can be demonstrated by the drafts of a government program and government declaration Seeckt produced at the end of September, which reflected not only Minoux's influence on Seeckt but also the extent to which Minoux had liberated himself from Stinnes in important ways. Minoux, for example, was prepared to accept substantial French participation in German enterprises without insisting, as did Stinnes, that Germany be granted participation in French enterprises. His calculation, apparently, was that the French would be attracted to an arrangement whereby, in combination with Germany, they would be in a position to destroy English and American competition. Minoux also opposed the complete privatization of publicly owned enterprises and allowed for foreign participation in their stock. He was prepared to maintain the eight-hour day in principle, while allowing for legitimate exceptions. Although he wished to replace the trade unions by occupational chambers, he accepted the right to strike. His tax program and currency stabilization program, in contrast to Stinnes's, was based on a genuine encumbrance of real values. Thus, Minoux and Seeckt, while agreeing with Stinnes on the need to favor private enterprise and roll back many of the gains of labor in 1918, especially collective bargaining agreements, differed with Stinnes in that Minoux, true to his currency reform program, favored state interests over private interests. At the same time, both Minoux and Seeckt were more explicitly in favor of constitutional reforms raising the voting age and introducing a second chamber based on the "productive estates" as well as increasing the autonomy of the federal states in matters of taxation and finance.[174]

Minoux was, in fact, thinking increasingly in political terms, and while his politics may be viewed as very dubious, it was quite different from the narrow concentration on economic measures that preoccupied Stinnes. The difference became especially apparent when Minoux objected to the publication of Stinnes's September 29 letter to Dauch on political grounds. Stinnes momentarily yielded to Minoux, but, in a letter of October 7, he suggested that he should no longer stand in the way of Minoux's political goals, which Stinnes privately thought excessively "Messianic," and that the time had come for an end to their twelve years of business collaboration.[175]

By the time this letter was written, Stinnes's politics of confrontation and that of his allies in the DVP and heavy industry had proven quite destabilizing and dangerous in their own right. The abandonment of passive resistance and the opposition to the Stresemann approach within the DVP was being used by the right wing to force the Socialists out, create a new government that would include the DNVP, and openly call for the elimination of the eight-hour day. This was the fundamental thrust of the party delegation's rejection of Stresemann's Ruhr policy on September 25. Similarly, it was also the purpose of a unilateral decision by the Ruhr coal mine owners at Unna on September 30 to reintroduce the prewar eight-and-a-half-hour workday, including time spent going to and from the workplace, effective October 8. This would have been a clear violation both of the Stinnes–Legien Agreement and of the law passed in July 1922 governing labor in the mines. The action was temporarily kept secret and implementation delayed for a week in the expectation that the decision could be used to force a change to a government that would support the industry's action. At the same time, public pressure was applied by a telegram to Stresemann informing him that the recent arbitration decision raising coal miner wages could not be accepted by the industry unless the coal tax were reduced by the amount necessary.[176]

This was not the only threat from the right directed against the Stresemann government at the end of September 1923. The Bavarian government responded to the termination of passive resistance by declaring a state of emergency and appointing Gustav von Kahr as General State Commissar. On the one hand, drastic action appeared necessary in Bavaria because of Hitler's assumption of the leadership of all the right-wing patriotic associations and combat leagues in the state and the danger that fighting would break out between left and right in Bavaria itself. On the other hand, von Kahr's known opposition to the policies of Berlin made his appointment a challenge to the central government. Ebert and Stresemann responded immediately by declaring a state of emergency in the Reich and granting powers to General von Seeckt parallel to those given to von Kahr in Bavaria. Manifestly, the co-existence of two parallel states of emergency threatened the sovereignty of the Reich, and the danger was made quite palpable in the first two days of Kahr's rule. Seeckt's ban of the Nazi *Völkischer Beobachter*, which had defamed Seeckt and Stresemann for having Jewish wives, was defied by the Munich authorities. Additionally, von Kahr suspended the regulations for the carrying out of the Law for the Defense of the Republic. Finally, the Bavarian police stopped the shipment of gold from the Reichsbank branch in Nürnberg to Berlin. The Bavarian authorities claimed they feared for the security of gold traveling through Thuringia and Saxony, while the Reichsbank insisted it needed the space in the Nürnberg vaults for the huge amounts of paper money they anticipated Bavaria would require in the coming weeks. Underlying the conflict, of course, was the disposition of the Reichsbank's gold and the authority of the Reich.[177]

The Socialists in Stresemann's Cabinet—Hilferding, Schmidt, and Sollmann—were at one in seeing the developments in Bavaria as a move against the Social Democrats and in the direction of the increasingly discussed right-wing dictatorship. At the same time, they feared bringing the matter before the Reichstag, lest the Coalition be brought down by the issue, and they knew that Seeckt and his generals were far more inclined to use force against Saxony and Thuringia (with whom conflict had raged for weeks over Zeigner's disclosures concerning the "Black Reichswehr" and the activities of the Communist Centuries) than to run the risk of Reichswehr shooting on Reichswehr in Bavaria. Seeckt ruled out immediate military action in Bavaria at the Cabinet meeting on September 30, while ominously pointing out that "we are approaching the time for a Directory under which a clear economic program will have to be made." His comment, however, must be seen in the context of Hilferding's call for an enabling act at this very meeting, as well as remarks by Interior Minister Sollmann made along similar lines as Seeckt's, though for very different political purposes:

Force alone will not do. The economic and social policy questions have to be solved in a nonpartisan way. The storm warnings from left and right are constantly increasing, and it is to be feared, if it came to violent actions, that the consequences would be such as to throw the German people back for decades. It is thus the task of the Great Coalition to keep the Reich and people together, which can only occur if broad circles of the people are behind it. It is generally felt that dictatorial measures are necessary, but we must find a form for them that does not lead to new upheavals.[178]

Sollmann was convinced that the necessary powers could be received from the Reichstag and that they could demonstrate that the members of the Cabinet were no mere "tools of their party delegations."

Indeed, the Socialists in the Cabinet appeared to be demonstrating real independence at a Ministerial conference on October 1 summoned to formulate the government's position in requesting an enabling act from the Reichstag. When Labor Minister Brauns announced that he supported an eight-hour day in mining, including time spent going to and from the workplace, and that he favored an extension of hours for all non-dangerous occupations, Schmidt's only response was to urge that, when it came to the hours-of-work issue, "one should act and not talk too much."[179] He also expressed his dismay that miners in Silesia were working seven hours at a time when Germany had to import coal from England. Clearly, therefore, the Socialists in the government were prepared to accept Braun's conception of a "sanitary working day" in place of the existing arrangement, and they were prepared to see social as well as economic and political questions regulated by the projected enabling act.

Unfortunately, the same did not hold true for the Socialists in the party delegation and, above all, the trade union leaders, who balked at the idea of surrendering the great achievement of November 1918 and objected to including social questions in the enabling act. Needless to say, this suited the *fronde* against Stresemann within his own party quite well, since they insisted not only on the inclusion of social questions but also on the exclusion of the Socialists from the government and their replacement by the DNVP. Had the Social Democrats agreed to the inclusion of the hours-of-work issue in an enabling act, Stresemann could undoubtedly have held his government together despite the problems in his own party, but even his trenchant argument that heavy industry opposed Brauns's hours-of-work program and was convinced that it could get even longer hours failed to move the SPD's trade-union contingent. Initially, Stresemann himself seemed to have thought of creating a minority bourgeois Cabinet composed of "experts" like Wiedfeldt, Luther, Minoux, and Schacht, but neither the Center nor the DDP would accept such a solution. That a new Great Coalition government reemerged on October 6 after the collapse of the first Stresemann government three days earlier was thanks to a variety of complex circumstances: the obduracy of the DNVP, which refused to serve with Stresemann; the support which Stresemann continued to receive from Ebert, who asked him to form a new government; the backing of his own party delegation, the majority of which refused to drop him; and the realization of the Great Coalition parties that the considerations which had brought them together in the first place were, if any-

thing, more operative in October than they had been in August. Thus, a compromise formula on hours of work was reached that was basically no different from that of November 22, 1922, under which the eight-hour day would be maintained in principle, while exceptions would be allowed either by contractual agreement or by law in cases where needs of production and lower costs made it necessary. As part of the compromise involved in reviving the Great Coalition Cabinet, an agreement was reached to exclude the questions of hours of work and pensions from the projected enabling act. Furthermore the enabling act would remain in force only so long as the new government was maintained in its existing composition and would, in any case, lapse on March 31, 1924.[180]

Were it not for the *fronde* in the DVP and the short-sighted interest politics in the SPD, the entire crisis might have been avoided, and it also must be said that the outcome reflected a weakening of the Great Coalition itself. Both Hilferding and von Raumer were no longer in the government—the former, by DVP demand; the latter, because he found his situation impossible in the light of the tensions within his own party. While one could argue that neither had put on a particularly impressive performance, they did represent two of the most solid backers of industry–labor collaboration. To be sure, the new Economics Minister, Josef Koeth, had worked well with the SPD in the past and could boast past successes in crisis management. He was a fitting person to preside over the liquidation of many of the measures that had been taken during the demobilization. Also, Hans Luther, who now took up the position of Finance Minister, had proven to be one of the most competent people in the last two Cabinets. Nevertheless, with only Schmidt, Radbruch, and Sollmann in the government, the SPD influence certainly was weakened. This is not to say that the role of industry had been strengthened. On the contrary, and much to the annoyance of Stresemann, industry had remained at once aloof and threatening, and Stresemann reproached the industrialists for "failing" to take responsibility. Bücher rejected such charges with that typical mixture of disingenuousness and sanctimoniousness that characterized RdI relations with the government:

He [Bücher] would view it as a misfortune if the fate of the Reich were directed by men from industry, since regardless of all their other qualities, they lack the special skills and knowledge of the professional civil servants, who have learned administration from the start. Service to the Fatherland is a life work and not some incidental occupation. But the failure of the leading men of the *Wirtschaft* of which the Reich Chancellor complains, is also justified by the fact that, in the last four years under the dictatorship of Marxism, no personality has managed to implement an objective view serving the general interest in dealing with the parliament and the unions. Until this situation is changed, one cannot count on an entry of economic leaders into the government.[181]

Bücher and the RdI president Sorge were, nevertheless, sharply criticized for failing to exert sufficient influence on the government, especially by Saxon and other medium-sized industrial interests, and Bücher was so incensed by such criticisms that he offered their chief spokesman, Rudolf Schneider, his position if he thought he could do better. Thus, while industry evaded all involvement in the government, it was under strong pressure to take a hard line in dealing with Stresemann and his Cabinet.

The Socialists and trade-union leaders, therefore, now had every reason to be anxious, and their support of the Enabling Act passed on October 13, like their participation in the government, was an effort to prevent the worst. There was most certainly a "worst" to prevent, as demonstrated by the opposition to the Enabling Act on the part of the racists, Bavarian and Hanoverian particularists, Nationalists, and Communists. The Nationalists and Communists hoped to prevent passage by absenting themselves from the house and, in the anticipation that some of the Great Coalition Deputies would also absent themselves in opposition, thus deprive the bill of the two-thirds majority it needed. In that eventuality, Ebert and Stresemann were prepared to dissolve the Reichstag and rule by decree under Article 48. This was a luxury they could have enjoyed for ninety days, since the Constitution allowed sixty days for the holding of an election and thirty more before a new Reichstag had to convene. Stresemann made his intentions public in the well-founded expectation that Great Coalition party members opposed to the law would be inspired to show up for the vote rather than face a protracted rule by decree and an election campaign. The Communists, as might be expected, played upon Socialist concessions for all they were worth, the KPD Deputy Frölich arguing that while the Italian fascists at least had to march on Rome and do something to create their dictatorship, in Germany the Reichstag installed the dictatorship itself. In a revelation which certainly suggests that great German employers did not always have reliable office security, Frölich read Stinnes's programmatic letter to a "DVP deputy," which corresponded exactly to the letter of September 29 to Dauch, as an illustration of what was in store for workers under the new legislation and the dictatorial proclivities of employers. For the Social Democrats, however, this only proved the wisdom of their decision, for as Hermann Müller pointed out, even if the letter were authentic, it only reflected the views of Stinnes, who had "outgrown" any party. For Müller, the way chosen by the SPD was the way to prevent a "Mussolini policy," and the Enabling Act was "the only way to save democracy in Germany."[182] Indeed, Müller's perception of the advantages of the Enabling Act seemed to be shared by Hermann Bücher, who bitterly remarked at an RdI meeting on October 12 that the measure did not reflect the wishes of their organization and that, "if it is accepted, the *Wirtschaft* will be delivered up to a cabinet in which the Social Democrats have the dominant influence."[183]

It surely was a commentary on the state of German democracy that it could only be saved by an act permitting the government to rule by decree and, where necessary, to set aside the basic rights of the Constitution. Yet, it is impossible to see how the government's stabilization program could have been implemented without the adjournment of the Reichstag, which lasted from October 13 to November 20. At the same time, Socialist participation and the Enabling Act also gave the government a much strengthened position in dealing with the high-handed tactics of some of the leading industrialists. Indeed, these tactics were already being discussed at the Reichstag debate on the Enabling Act in connection with reports of industrialist negotiations with the French following the termination of passive resistance.[184]

The industrialists *were* negotiating with the French, and there was nothing necessarily treasonous or devious about this. The end of passive resistance meant that productive work would have to be resumed as quickly as possible for both economic and social reasons. The government had announced its intention of systematically reducing the wage guarantees, payment for unproductive labor, and credits through the Coal and Steel Finance Credit Corporations before terminating them fully by October 20.[185] Manifestly, therefore, either production would have to resume or the plants be shut down and the workers sent out onto the street, and the resumption of production could only be done in collaboration with the French, who were in occupation of many of the mines and who were confiscating stocks of coal, iron, and steel. Furthermore, the French had come into the Ruhr to collect reparations, and it was inconceivable that they would simply allow German heavy industry to resume production without demanding a resumption of payments in kind as well as possible cash payments through the tax on coal and export levies. Would the Reich credit such payments against the reparations account and compensate the industrialists? In short, the ending of passive resistance and the refusal of the French to negotiate with the German government meant that the Ruhr industrialists would have to do so. Considerations of both patriotism and self-interest required that the industrialists undertake such negotiations in concert with the government in Berlin. For Stresemann, these negotiations held open both a promise and a threat. On the one hand, they could serve as a bridge to later government-to-government negotiations; on the other, they could be used by the French to promote separatism in the Rhineland, especially if industrialist self-interest overwhelmed patriotic considerations. Since the industrialists tended to confuse the two under the best of circumstances, the situation was very dangerous indeed.

Exactly how dangerous was demonstrated by the Otto Wolff concern, which included the large enterprises of Phoenix and Rheinstahl and which decided to act independently of its fellow concerns and the Reich and approach the French on October 1. The concern had been particularly hard hit by French confiscation of its iron and steel production and was under strong pressure from the Dutch shareholders who dominated the concern to get back to business. Wolff himself, along with Werner Carp and the banker van Vlissingen, represented these interests. Thus, they used the end of passive resistance to inform the French High Commissioner Tirard that they were ready to accept French terms involving payment of the tax on coal and other forms of regulation but complained that "the social legislation of the Reich had let power slide into the hands of the trade unions, and the inflation as well as the tying up of the goods produced had taken away their capital."[186] Tirard showed no particular interest in discussing the social legislation of the Reich, the changing of which he considered to be their problem, but he did show an interest in talking about the autonomy of the Rhineland and the introduction of a new currency in the area. Wolff and his colleagues refused to discuss such political questions and proceeded to negotiate with the Interallied Engineers Committee (MICUM) on the actual terms under which production might be resumed. These were harsh. The Wolff group was required to supply reparations coal gratis, repay back coal taxes and pay future coal taxes to the French, as well as pay an export levy on its iron production. In return, it would be paid for its deliveries to the railroads in the occupied areas, allowed to charge whatever price it wished to customers, and to export with the MICUM's permission. At the same time, the French negotiators intimated that they would expect to keep German iron production at the existing French level, a rather grim prospect since the French were operating at 40 percent of capacity.[187]

Wolff did inform the government about his negotiations, but Stresemann was profoundly displeased on both procedural and substantive grounds with the unilateral action of the Wolff group. He blamed Wolff for undermining his own efforts to get Paris to negotiate by demonstrating that the industrial leadership in the Ruhr could be brought to terms one by one. While recognizing that Wolff's arrangement imposed no financial burdens on the Reich, he felt that Wolff had undermined the authority of the government by coming to a fixed agreement and had prejudiced the efforts of other industrialists and the government to come to terms with the French. The French desire to keep German production at low levels was particularly distressing and only strengthened Stresemann's resolve to emphasize Germany's willingness to pay reparations and to seek a reparations settlement at the governmental level so as to justify and require a return to the highest possible levels of production in the Ruhr. Wolff's only response to Stresemann's reproaches was to argue that he had to get his works in order because he employed a hundred thousand workers, although it was clear that the special problems of his firms, Dutch interests, and Wolff's hostility toward the Coal Syndicate were key motives.[188]

Wolff's actions were also deeply resented by his colleagues in the Ruhr, who were preparing a more concerted negotiation effort with greater government involvement and who were not quite prepared to resume production at any price, at least not at any price they alone would have to pay. The most problematic aspects of the Franco-German industrialist negotiations were revealed at the very outset when the coal industrialists began planning future sessions at their meetings in Unna and Bochum on September 30–October 1. They resolved to resume work, but to do so on the basis of a unilateral decision to restore the prewar hours of work on October 8. Their expectation, however, was that they would have a friendly government in Berlin that would also abolish the tax on coal so that they could raise miner wages. At the same time, they formed a Committee of Six to negotiate with the French—Stinnes, Vögler, Peter Klöckner, von Velsen of the state-owned Hibernia Mining Co., and directors Herbig and Janus of the Coal Syndicate. Before beginning their negotiations with the French general Degoutte on October 5, they were careful to secure permission from the Reich government to enter into such discussions. This, however, was no barrier against improprieties, at least on the part of Peter Klöckner who, under the impression that Degoutte was a sympathetic fellow and highly critical of the Ruhr workers, decided to bare his soul to the Frenchman by holding forth on the plight of German industry and the mistake it had made in reducing hours in 1918. Klöckner pointed out that he and his colleagues were planning to rectify the situation on October 8 and were informing Degoutte that their intention required French support. It was a bad mistake. Degoutte was no more willing to become a vehicle of the social dismantling pro-

grams of German industrialists than Tirard, and he reminded the industrialists that the eight-hour day was German law and that the French had no intention of violating German social legislation. Though Stinnes skillfully shifted the discussion to questions of other ways in which the French could promote the resumption of production and the terms on which this might be accomplished, the damage was nevertheless done. News of Klöckner's *faux pas* leaked to the press, and the French spread leaflets about on October 7 assuring workers that they had no intention of violating the eight-hour day. On top of it all, industry faced an unanticipated and unwanted new Great Coalition government in Berlin. Although some of the mines had already posted notices of their intention to increase the work day, the government mines backed down immediately. Stinnes wanted to put off the implementation of the Unna decision by one day in the totally unfounded expectation that the new government could be persuaded to approve the decision, but the majority of his colleagues voted on October 10 to call off the entire attempt to impose a *Diktat* on the already infuriated workers.[189]

This was not the only matter on which Stinnes and his colleagues on the Committee of Six were frustrated when they met with the government on October 9. Unlike Wolff, who wanted government compensation for the coal tax payments to the French but felt compelled to agree to pay the tax for a month without knowing if and when he would be repaid, the Committee of Six wanted the government to compensate them for coal tax payments, losses on confiscated coal and other materials, and payments in kind. These were only a few of the "questions" sent to the government on October 7 with a request that they be responded to on October 9. The Committee of Six also wished to know if the government was prepared to have them continue negotiations with the French on terms that involved priority in deliveries to the occupied areas and in full independence of the Reich Coal Commissar and Coal Syndicate. The coal industrialists further asked if the government was prepared to abrogate the tax on coal so that they could negotiate on acceptable terms with the French and if the government was prepared

Labor Minister Heinrich Brauns (1868–1939). (*By permission of the Ullstein Verlag*)

to support them in increasing working hours in mining to eight and a half hours a day in the occupied and unoccupied areas as well as to annul the demobilization decrees along with a decree of July 17, 1923, issued in connection with the wage guarantee payments, which prohibited the firing of workers in the occupied areas. In conclusion, Stinnes emphasized that the financial situation of the concerns was very critical.[190]

When Cabinet members met with the Committee of Six to answer these "questions" on October 9, there was considerable irritation on both sides. Stinnes was furious at the stories in the newspaper accusing the industrialists of treason and demanded that the government even go so far as to censor such stories. Brauns, while deploring the news reports, did not veil his annoyance at the indiscretions over the working-hours question in the negotiations with Degoutte and expressed regret that worker representatives were not taken along for the negotiations. While he assured employers that an increase in hours of work was on the agenda, he made it clear that there would be no return to prewar working hours and that he intended to modify but not totally eliminate the demobilization decrees bearing on the release of workers. The government was even less forthcoming on money matters. Stinnes's concluding comment about the financial straits of the concerns was not meant simply for effect, but rather to pave the way for a "start-up credit" of between a hundred fifty million and two hundred million gold marks on top of the additional financial sacrifices and compensations asked of the government. The industrialists warned that without such credit there would be chaos in the area and the French would achieve their goal of controlling the most important heavy-industrial area of Europe. Neither Brauns nor Luther were overly impressed. The former pointed out that if this were indeed the French goal, then there would be no point in pouring more money into the Ruhr; the latter, echoing a question raised by Degoutte in his negotiations with the same gentlemen, asked if they could not get the needed credit through their works and connections in the unoccupied areas. What was manifest in both discussions, however, was that the industrialists, insofar as they had reserves, were unwilling to commit them and wished to generate credit through the assets and political support of the Reich.

While the finances of the great concerns are anything but transparent, there is some evidence that some had such assets. Reusch, in reporting on the situation of the GHH in early September to August Haniel, for example, made mention of "liquid resources" that he did not want to put down in writing and pointed out that the concern "was not yet in bad shape," even if it had "used up portions of silent reserves which we undoubtedly will find necessary when the currency stabilizes." Similarly, in writing of the concern works in the unoccupied areas, he pointed out that while a few had been compelled to go into debt to pay the "insanely rising wages and material costs," they were all in solid shape. To prevent financial difficulty, he had, "despite a large number of orders, instructed that there be a substantial reduction of working time in order to have the necessary means to pay for wages and material." Thus, "[T]here are reserves available everywhere from which we draw, and which will help us through the coming difficult period."[191]

These were not resources the industrialists were going to sacrifice in making arrangements with the French. Dutch financier van Vlissingen seemed to feel that the agreements the Wolff group had made with the French would not lead to any practical results since the greatest buyer of Ruhr products was the rest of Germany. The consequence would be high unemployment and chaos in the Ruhr unless the German government provided the credits needed to tide the Ruhr industrialists over. Van Vlissingen was certain that "the Ruhr magnates are not going to use their available capital for this purpose so long as they have no guarantees as regards the political future of the Ruhr, and for the same reason the international money markets would equally refuse to finance the Ruhr industries at the present time. The result will be wholesale unemployment and destitution for which the French Administration will have no possible remedy."[192] At the same time, Vlissingen and the German directors of Phoenix believed that the French terms reflected a gross exaggeration of the kinds of profits the Ruhr concerns had been making. As Ernst Poensgen of Phoenix told one of his colleagues, "Phoenix, although it was convinced of the impossibility of fulfilling the demands, signed the agreement in order to keep in closer touch with the MICUM and thereby to gradually bring it around to realizing the unfulfillability of the conditions."[193] This, of course, sounds suspiciously like the old policy of fulfillment which "honest merchants" had rejected when practiced by Wirth and Rathenau, but Poensgen and Vlissingen seemed to think it was the only way to bring the French to their senses, even if it involved risking an increased measure of chaos in the Ruhr.

Stinnes and his committee seemed to feel differently, not in that they were prepared to fulfill less, but rather in that they were prepared to fulfill more under the right circumstances. To be sure, Stinnes was not going to sacrifice his resources either. One of his officials responded to a renewed French suggestion that the industrialists use their foreign resources by bluntly stating that the assets abroad were worth more than the holdings in Germany and they would rather

sacrifice the latter than the former.[194] Nevertheless, Stinnes preferred not to risk chaos in the Ruhr if he could get Reich help, and he tried to convince the government that such an investment would be worth making:

. . . the creation of order in the unoccupied area, especially the energetic implementation of extended work time, will immediately increase the confidence of foreign capital to such an extent that industry will be in a position to receive substantial credits. At the same time, the credit of the Reich will also be so increased that the currency can be reconstructed. In the face of this perspective it is not so questionable to increase the inflation temporarily, especially since the [real] amount of money in circulation in the Reich is extraordinarily low.[195]

The Cabinet, however, was in no mood for Stinnes's latest invitation to speculation. Stresemann did not see how the government could give a "start-up" credit to industry while claiming that it was in no position to pay any reparations in the near term. Koeth, with the evident approval of the Chancellor, stated his negative reaction with his usual decisiveness:

The chief question is, should one today put another pfennig into the Ruhr or not? There has to be absolute clarity about this. He personally is of the view that not another pfennig should be put in, come what may. One should then give the following instructions to the industrial groups: we advise you to get into contact with the occupation authorities; we permit you to negotiate about economic, but not about political questions. The reproaches made against industry in the press must stop. My proposal will perhaps have the result that we will initially lose the Ruhr territory. If we do not act this way, however, then we could also lose the unoccupied area under certain circumstances as well.[196]

With such backing, Stresemann was in a position to reply negatively by letter to Stinnes on October 12. Citing the struggle "for the naked existence of the German people," Stresemann reported the Cabinet's decision to refuse any credits beyond those already scheduled to terminate on October 20 and to reject any guarantee of compensation for reparations coal deliveries, confiscated coal, or coal tax payments. The Cabinet agreed to abrogate the tax on coal on condition that there was a reduction of the price of coal in the amount demanded by the Finance Minister. Stresemann authorized continued negotiations with the occupation powers on economic matters that did not touch upon

German sovereign rights. Those rights included the ownership and control of the railroad system. Lastly, Stinnes was reminded that existing law governed the hours of work. Stresemann assumed he was aware that a new regulation of this question was being worked out. As Stresemann had pointed out to the Cabinet the day before sending the letter, "especially in the matter of hours of work it is important that the measures to be taken should not be allowed to appear as responses to the demands of the representatives of industry."[197]

These were hard but necessary decisions that liberated the government to do precisely what Stinnes's proposal would have set at risk; namely, to focus on currency and fiscal reform in the hope that a strengthened German heartland might be in a position to save what could be saved of its precious periphery and secure outside support to shore up its tenuous existence. Nevertheless, the final phase of legislating currency reform was to prove as conflict ridden and protracted as previous phases.

Koeth, ever impatient, was particularly anxious to move the creation of a new currency forward, and he rapidly ran into conflict with Luther, whom he considered too dilatory and overburdened. He privately urged Stresemann to find a Finance Minister with "expertise and energy" and regretted that Schacht (with whom he had worked closely as one of the Darmstädter Bank's delegates to various supervisory boards and who had been considered as a replacement for Hilferding by Stresemann) had been passed over because of charges by Undersecretary Schröder of the Finance Ministry that Schacht had used his position as a currency expert in the Belgian occupation to favor the Dresdner Bank with which he was then associated. Schröder was close to the DNVP, and there was strong right-wing hostility to Schacht, whose currency reform ideas were anti-agrarian and who took the pro-parliamentary line of the DDP. The charges were launched with such suddenness, however, that Stresemann did not have enough time to check them out and thus opted for Luther.[198]

Koeth's criticisms of Luther, however, overlooked the powerful last-minute objections to the currency reform plan that Luther intended to institute by decree under the new Enabling Act. Indeed, Schacht was one of those who criticized the Helfferich plan as modified by Luther and Hilferding and which bore the latter's signature. Both in a newspaper article and in a private letter to Stresemann of early October, Schacht warned against a currency backed by anything other than gold. What was required was a "healthy currency," and while such a currency would necessarily bring out into the open the veiled crisis already existing, such a crisis was "not only unavoidable, but desperately to be desired."[199] His chief charge against the currency bank was not simply its unsound foundation in an unredeemable form of coverage but, above all, its linkage to the financing of government expenditure. Both of these deficiencies would virtually guarantee that the new currency would enter the scene already discounted against other currencies. Fundamentally, Schacht viewed the projected new mark as another form of "inflation money" because it was being created to cover state finances. A gold-currency bank, in contrast, could legitimately help the state by paying for the concessionary right to issue money while concurrently providing a means of enforcing both fiscal restraint and productivity. At the same time, a special arrangement could be made with agriculture to bring in the current harvest. He thought there was both enough gold and enough foreign exchange about to create a bank that would satisfy the needs of the economy, especially since the support of the outside world could be counted upon. In Schacht's view—a perspective that was to play a most important role in the later stages of the currency reform—the outside world had a great interest in German recovery from the inflation, and "even a mere moral support of foreign interests, which is certainly to be attained in a suitable form, would be a great help and, by inner necessity, the new gold bank would form the center from which a recovery of our entire economic life could take its start."[200]

Schacht was not the only prominent source of criticism of the government's currency bank plan. The DDP, of which Schacht was a prominent member, stated its formal opposition, thought the plan would take too long to implement, and called for a rapid return to a gold currency. Julius Hirsch also publicized and submitted a plan of his own for a restoration of a gold currency and the redemption of the paper marks at some fixed rate.[201] The most serious attack on the government plan, however, came from the powerful Central Association of German Banks and Bankers, members of which presented their views in a meeting with Luther on October 8 and then in writing on October 10.[202] Bankers took the position that a new currency stood no chance of success as long as the French were occupying parts of Germany and conditions were not normal internally. They also feared that the issuance of a new currency would encourage the French to introduce their own currency in the occupied areas. If they decided to speak out with a "serious warning in the last hour," it was because of their special responsibility in monetary matters. Though bankers disagreed with Schacht on the possibility of creating a new currency of any kind immediately, they agreed with him that the basis of the new currency was unacceptable and that the new currency would be discredited from birth. The full conservatism of their position was expressed in their objections to the devaluation of the paper mark implicit in the plan through its linking of the old and new currencies by means of some forthcoming redemption of the former through the latter. In their view, this would be especially damaging to Germany's credit since "foreign holders of mark notes would justifiably view such an act as a one-sided and arbitrary abrogation of their rights to the legal coverage of their notes." Bankers alleged that it would be extremely difficult to receive foreign credit in the future if this were done. They were especially critical of the idea of making the new currency a legal currency of the German Reich and pointed out that if, as they obviously anticipated, the new currency were to go the way of the old, then not only would those who had sacrificed for the new currency be fatally disappointed, but it would become virtually impossible for the government to receive the public confidence necessary to issue a new currency again. Finally, they objected to the legal and accounting confusion that would be created by an interim arrangement under which the medium of monetary obligations would be changed twice over.

The banking association did recognize that some interim solution to assist the Reich and the economy was necessary and that no solution would be without its negative features. Still, bankers argued that the existing plan was so bad that their alternative was worth proposing. They advocated the passage of a law that would permit the Reich to issue a limited amount of the gold loan in the form of certificates no smaller than half a dollar and no larger than ten dollars which would not be legal currency but would have to be accepted in lieu of legal currency by all offices receiving and disbursing monies in the Reich. The interim currency thus created would be backed by the occupational groups called upon to back the money of the government's bank, except that the investment would be in the gold loan rather than a hypothetical mortgage.

Luther was not insensitive to the various objections to his own plan any more than he was to complaints of Helfferich and the industrialists that they would be doubly burdened because of the continuation of the Enterprise Tax and Land Levy along with the interest on the annuity payments on the mortgage for the new currency. Nevertheless, he considered action necessary, especially since he had the approval of the other economic interest groups and the agreement in principle of the Reichsrat. The Enabling Act now gave him the mechanisms by which to modify the plan to meet such objections as appeared valid. The most important of these was the argument against the co-existence of two legal currencies, especially since the new currency was being potentially tied to a paper currency that might be impossible to stabilize. His solution was not to treat the new currency (now called the Rentenmark) as a legal currency but rather as a medium of exchange that would be accepted by law in all offices handling money in the Reich. The new appellations, "Rentenbank" and "Rentenmark," also had a happy psychological advantage, since they not only reflected the fact that the new money was based on the annuities paid on the mortgage of the assets of the productive classes but also conjured up memories of the highly successful nineteenth-century *Rentenbriefe*, which were the state-guaranteed bonds issued after the emancipation of the peasants on which the redemption of peasant holdings was paid to the landlords.[203]

At the same time, something had to be done to deal with the fact that the new money could not be issued for at least another four weeks because the initial expectation that the Ruhr expenditures could be immediately liquidated could no longer be met. Some of the social expenditures could only be more gradually liquidated. Thus, yet another interim measure was deemed advisable, and this was to follow the bankers' proposal in part and employ a limited amount of the gold loan, two hundred million gold-marks' worth, as a form of interim currency that could subsequently be turned in for Rentenmarks once they were issued. Insofar as the complaints about the Enterprise Tax and Land Levy were concerned, Luther was not prepared to relinquish either, especially since a decree had been issued placing all taxes on a gold basis on October 11. He hoped that both industry and agriculture would find compensation in the abrogation of the tax on coal—which was decreed on October 15. He also promised a thoroughgoing reform of taxation as part of the general task of reforming the finances of the Reich then being undertaken.

Having made such concessions and promises, Luther went forward with the issuance of the decree establishing the Rentenbank, which was dated October 15 even if actually promulgated on October 17. On this last date, the Cabinet also agreed to the appointment of the DNVP Deputy and former Prussian Finance Minister August Lentze as head of the Administrative Council of the new Rentenbank. Three days later, Luther presided over a meeting in his Ministry at which the Rentenbank was formally established and in which further appointments to the Administrative Council were made. Undoubtedly, every effort was being made, as demonstrated by the appointment of Lentze, to name persons reassuring to right-wing, agrarian, and industrial circles. As one member of the Finance Ministry sarcastically put it, "they belong to that class of people

whom the policy of inflation has enriched and whom the ineptitude of Division III of the Treasury (Tax Revenue) has allowed to escape the payment of their just dues to the State."[204] Certainly, such stalwart and notably reactionary agrarian leaders as the Chairman of the Agrarian League, Gustav Roesicke, and the Chairman of the Confederation of German Peasant Associations, August Crone-Münzebrock, as well as the Bavarian populist peasant leader Georg Heim and the DDP agrarian leader Hermann Dietrich bespoke the goal of creating a currency that would satisfy farmers. The appointments of Bücher, Hilger, Sorge, Siemens, and Urbig obviously was intended to reflect the commitment of industry and banking to the project. Nevertheless, industry demonstrated its limited confidence when its representatives at the first reading of the implementing regulations of the Rentenmark law on October 27 rejected a provision making the incitement to refuse acceptance of the Rentenmark punishable, although they were to agree to this provision after the Rentenmark was introduced because some of their compatriots demonstrated its necessity.[205]

It should come as no surprise that the new measures were treated with considerable skepticism by outside observers; not untypical was the attitude of a British economic expert in Berlin, Finlayson:

The sum total of all these wonderful measures is that Germany will be faced with four different currencies:

    I. The old paper mark
    II. The New Rentenmark
    III. The Reichsbank Gold Notes
    IV. The small denominations of the gold loan

My general conclusion in regard to all these new-fangled schemes remains the same—the whole business is a scheme, and not too ingenious at that, of camouflage. The basis is not solid—that alone can be created by a sound financial policy on the part of the Reich.[206]

Only credibility would bring confidence, and credit. The great tests of Germany's ability to end the Great Disorder were yet to come.

Chapter 16

The Politics of Stabilization, October–November 1923

"Regime Change" or Change of Regime? The Stresemann Government between Communist Insurgence and Fascist Putschism

Stresemann and his Cabinet realized that the effective functioning of the new Rentenbank as an interim arrangement prior to a permanent stabilization depended upon a genuine transformation of German fiscal and economic practice. The central question was whether this change could be achieved without disaster or some combination of disasters: the total disintegration of the political system, the dissolution of national unity, or a loss of national independence. Could the Weimar political system survive if its government reneged on its social commitments? How could a social *démontage* be achieved without unleashing the latent civil war between the extreme left and the extreme right? How was a fiscal and socioeconomic regime change to be legitimized in such a way as to preserve the parliamentary government created in 1918? The real achievement of the stabilization was less the so-called "miracle" of the Rentenmark than the political successes of the Stresemann governments, which were then consolidated under his successor Wilhelm Marx. They saved both parliamentary democracy—albeit by the dangerous method of circumventing some of its major assumptions and requirements—and German unity and sovereignty while they liquidated the old currency and took the measures that were needed to get the economy going again and receive external support.

The future of German democracy and German unity hung in the balance in the fall of

1923, and it was very likely that the political system established in 1918 would remain highly vulnerable in the years to come. The stabilization, however much welcome to all by the time of its arrival, was not to rest on consensus or on the clear triumph of any set of interests but rather on universal dissatisfaction. Agriculture and business were already registering their displeasure with the growing tax burden in August and September. Stresemann's unwillingness to create a completely right-wing government, make way for some kind of authoritarian regime, and countenance the high-handed effort to abrogate the eight-hour day unilaterally in the Ruhr had shattered the hopes for such measures entertained by Germany's industrial leaders. Industrialists did not consider the Enabling Act of October 15, 1923, to be favorable to their interests. The squabbling in his own party notwithstanding, it was much easier for Stresemann to keep a leash on the industrialists at this point than it was to impose the government's will on labor and the civil service. The industrialists, after all, were anything but popular, and they had no mass movement behind them. Their links to the German fascists, such as they were, were weak, and the Nazis were, at any rate, incalculable. The organized masses who counted stood on the left, and if these masses were mobilized, it would be against industry.

While industrialists had become bolder in making their demands upon labor, some of them and some of the industrial and employer organization leaders persisted in the view that the trade unions had not lost their value either as an instrument for the containment of the workers or as a valuable buffer against the bureaucratic regulation of industrial relations. Thus, despite the fiasco of the ZAG's efforts to establish guidelines for the valorization of wages in August and September and the gloomy prospects for a successful agreement on a common set of principles to guide industrial relations in the stabilization, the two sides continued to use the Wage Commission of the ZAG as a venue for their efforts to explore whether there were any bases for mutual understanding. At their meeting of October 1, they were apparently optimistic enough about their ability to deal rationally with one another, despite a somewhat heated discussion of their differences, to establish a small drafting committee to draw up a list of areas of agreement and disagreement for further discussion. They also managed to agree on a set of revisions one week later which were to be discussed on October 15.[1]

The results of this discussion were not very impressive. As always, the two sides could agree on blaming the war and reparations for Germany's plight, asserting that worker wages should not be allowed to fall, and confirming that increased productivity was the best means of maintaining worker living standards. The real differences, of course, were in the distribution of sacrifices and in determining the conditions and tempo of the demands to be made on workers. The unions insisted that legal action be taken to control the cartels, while employers, undoubtedly aware that cartel legislation was on the government's agenda, failed to come up with an explicit position on this question. After much negotiation, the two sides were able to agree on a common language concerning the housing market and rent controls and were calling for the gradual raising of rents to prewar levels and the gradual elimination of rent controls as increased wages might make this possible. Originally, employers had sought a rapid decontrol of rents, but they retreated from this posture, a concession undoubtedly made all the easier by the fact that the sacrifice would be borne by house owners. Employers were in a less giving mood on the so-called demobilization decrees limiting employer rights to fire redundant workers and requiring "work stretching." Though both sides agreed that open unemployment was preferable to veiled unemployment, union leaders felt that the restrictions were essential so long as the existing crisis lasted. What was noteworthy was that union leaders were willing to see the restrictions lifted under more stable conditions, and this may have induced employers to agree to the proposition that unemployment support could only be ended when it was transformed into unemployment insurance and that the two sides had to work together to relocate redundant workers. As always, the thorniest point of contention was the eight-hour day. The trade unions wished to make exceptions contingent on employer demonstrations of need and formal inclusion in wage contracts, while the employer organizations insisted that such tiresome procedures deprived them of both flexibility and productivity. In the employers' view, Germany not only had to restore prewar production levels but also had to increase productivity by 25 percent without additional compensation in order to pay reparations.

The fact that trade unions were willing to concede the dismantling of the demobilization decrees and the abridgement of the eight-hour day by mutual consent demonstrated their interest in a negotiated settlement with the employer organizations. It was all the more noteworthy in the context of the unilateral attempt of the Ruhr coal industrialists to abrogate the hours-of-work regulations in early October, an effort which cast a pall over the discussions of October 15. Tarnow had begun the meeting by asking Borsig and his associates if they were still authorized to negotiate on behalf of industry. Borsig replied positively, but with the caveat that decisions would have to be approved by the peak associations. Yet, even in this highly charged atmosphere, both Borsig and Tarnow agreed, as had Legien and Stinnes in 1918, that the matters being discussed "were better regulated between the parties by negotiating than through laws."[2]

The trouble was that now the tables were turned against the workers, and trade-union leaders had much more reason in 1923 than in 1918 to wonder if the government and Reichstag could protect their interests. Their willingness to talk to the employer organizations, even in the face of the high-handed tactics of the

Ruhr coal mine owners, can only be explained in terms of their financial weakness, the exhaustion of the workers, and their fear that the government might also exploit these circumstances to act against worker interests. As Leipart explained to his fellow ADGB leaders at a meeting on October 16: "It appears that the government now feels strong enough to master the situation without the help of the trade unions. One may conclude from this that not only the employers but also the government has realized the weakness of the unions."[3] There was some inclination on the part of a few of the trade-union leaders to try the *Arbeitsgemeinschaftpolitik* once again, but its loss of credibility in Socialist trade-union circles over the previous four years combined with the most recent performance of the Ruhr industrialists did not make it a very promising option. In the last analysis, trade-union leaders were doing little more than keeping the lines of communication to employers open in the crisis.

Yet, what could one expect from a government which seemed more or less prepared to implement the policies advocated by employers and was planning an hours-of-work bill that would undermine the eight-hour day? An especially pessimistic appraisal was offered by Robert Dißmann of the Metal Workers Union:

The basic issue is: Who will bear the costs of the war, of the Ruhr conflict, of reparations? Without a doubt, it is the workers who will pay. What we are now experiencing shows us that this is the way everything is going. We can thank the employers for the present situation, and now they are also trying to rape us economically and politically. The Enabling Act is directed solely against the left. The draft of the hours of work law requires nothing less than that the workers place themselves at the feet of the government. Bavaria, the state of siege, the Enabling Act, the hours of work law—they all belong logically together. The enemy is moving systematically against us. Do we have a chance to avoid the conflict? We have already avoided it for too long. I fear that a further retreat this winter will lead not only to the loss of more rights but also to the loss of the confidence of workers.[4]

The growing discontent among the organized workers was undeniable, and the ADGB had been flooded with petitions from all over Germany and deputations from the large Berlin plants calling on the unions to take a tougher stance in order to retain the confidence of the

workers. Nevertheless, Leipart and most of the other union leaders rejected proposals for large demonstrations, protest strikes, or a general strike as utterly useless under existing circumstances. The Construction Union leader Paeplow warned that a general strike would lead to a civil war because the masses would descend upon the countryside in search of food, and he ruefully concluded that "it is our ill fate that today, where we have to employ the most extreme means, we are too weak to do so."[5]

Now, more than ever, the majority of the trade-union leaders worried that the masses, once set in motion, would be beyond all control. Furthermore, they could not but be aware that they were not only dealing with male workers, an increasing number of whom were unemployed, but also with female workers and housewives whose desperation was becoming increasingly visible. As the women's trade-union leader Gertrud Hanna warned:

The distress of the women exceeds all bounds. Women have to wait for hours for food, while at the same time knowing for sure that the prices of other necessary foodstuffs are increasing significantly. It is no wonder that women often take the lead in disturbances and plundering. Unfortunately, the workers often do not show understanding for the cares of the women and often show very little concern for the rightful interests of women in competing for jobs. The difference in pay is taken by and large as self-understood. In many branches of the economy, but above all in the political area, women are the decisive element. We must therefore pay more attention to the interests of women than before.[6]

Tarnow and his fellow trade-union leaders agreed that the condition of the German worker had been reduced below that of "coolies," and they were convinced that only the government could provide the necessary relief. Their chief priority was a currency reform, so as to put an end to the bizarre circumstances under which not only the housewives and workers but also their own organizations were forced to function. It was impossible to deny, for example, that labor was being used unproductively when the trade-union printing house was compelled to attach a tax stamp–filled sheet measuring ten feet long to one of its bills of exchange and on which each tax stamp had to be carefully canceled by hand![7]

Indeed, the head of the Factory Workers Union, Brey, was prepared to put quite a bit of faith in the government. He attacked those of his colleagues who claimed that the government was ignoring the trade unions and pointed out that the Socialists in the government were doing the best they could under circumstances beyond their control: "That which has taken place in the Ruhr and in economic life has been uncontrollable, and it is questionable whether things would have turned out better if the critics had been there in place of the government. We are very dependent in our economic life, and we will not be able to master the situation even with a gold currency if we do not succeed in getting an international agreement."[8] He dismissed calls for the sequestration of the harvest, pointing out that past experience and peasant resistance in the present demonstrated the futility of such efforts. He also defended the necessity of the Enabling Act as the only means of overcoming the obstinacy of the various special interests. He even went so far as to suggest that the hours-of-work bill being contemplated would have to be accepted.

Brey was not alone in his views, and some of his colleagues noted that Labor Minister Brauns had made concessions on unemployment supports in the occupied areas. The real question for the majority of the Socialist trade-union leaders was whether they could maintain a measure of influence on the government under existing circumstances and whether the government would keep trade-union interests in mind and strengthen the unions. Thus, when the leadership of the ADGB, AfA and Socialist Civil Servant Union (ADB) held their first joint meeting on October 17 with the objective of making their views known to the government and the public, the tone was more restrained than militant. Tarnow asked the government to recognize that the trade unions were the best supporters of the Republic and unity of the Reich and were trying to prevent rather than cause a social explosion. Labor Minister Brauns also sought to be reassuring, insisting that the government had no intention of dismantling social supports, declaring that new arrangements on hours of work would be accompanied by action against the cartels, and affirming that the government was set against returning the workers to their prewar circumstances.[9]

Clearly, the government had the upper hand, but this hardly meant it could rest easy in the chaos of the final weeks of the inflation. Furthermore, there was no certainty that the measures that were undertaken and displeasing to labor could be enforced and made to stick. Both the Socialists and the trade unions confronted volatile constituencies which were not as sensitive as Brey to the constraints, both domestic and international, that would be entailed in any long-term stabilization.

It is a measure of Stresemann's desperate situation in the fall of 1923 that he seriously contemplated sacrificing important elements of German sovereignty as a means of legitimizing the "regime change" being pursued by his government. He thought the situation might be eased if the responsibility for unpleasant measures could be shifted from the German government to some external authority. Just as the Germans had once seen their inflationary future mirrored in Austrian conditions, so now they looked to Austria as an exemplar of a major financial and economic reform and balancing of the budget (a *Sanierung*) they needed to undertake. It was, to be sure, a very uncomfortable model. The acceptance of the Geneva Protocol in November 1922, under which Austria had received an international loan through the League of Nations, carried with it acquiescence to humiliating international controls of Austrian finances. The League appointed a High Commissioner, the Dutchman Alfred Zimmermann, to oversee state finances as well as control the funds collected for customs and tobacco.[10]

However unpalatable the Austrian model, Stresemann nevertheless was extremely anxious to get together with the Austrian Chancellor Seipel to exchange views on the management of state crises. Unfortunately, Stresemann found himself going from one crisis to another, so that the efforts to meet at the Bodensee at the end of September and beginning of October and then again at the end of October were aborted. Extensive informational meetings were held between the Austrian Austerity Commissar (*Sparkommissar*), Hornick, and representatives of his German counterpart,

Friedrich Saemisch, as well as various German state Finance Ministries in Bad Reichenhall on September 14–15, when Hornick provided detailed information on the techniques used in the drastic reduction of the Austrian civil service. Even more indicative of Stresemann's desperate search for a solution, however, was that he sent a special emissary to Seipel at the end of October to discuss Seipel's experiences with High Commissioner Zimmermann and "whether the government was able to rely on him as a support against the Left."[11] Seipel expressed considerable satisfaction with the role played by Zimmermann, not in the sense that the latter had forced him to take any actions directly but rather that the parliament understood that measures he had undertaken in connection with reducing the civil service and reducing wages were the kinds of policies wished by Geneva and Austria's creditors. At the same time, Seipel stressed that Zimmermann's effectiveness depended upon his being independent of the Austrian government and a representative of a "foreign body."

Indeed, Zimmermann, the highly conservative and domineering former Mayor of Rotterdam, seems to have had the ambition of making Berlin his next stop after straightening out Vienna and was also being mentioned for such a job. According to the British Ambassador, the High Commissioner found Stresemann's interest in visiting Seipel very promising:

Dr. Zimmermann said he was firmly convinced that with a new currency, a small loan to start it, a new Bank of Issue, and a foreign control, stronger perhaps than here, Germany was capable of reviving even more rapidly than Austria had done, and, in a very short time, of paying reparations. Countries whose currency had gone to pieces had a great advantage over others; they started with a completely clean sheet; their National Debts had vanished into thin air, and in this sense it might be said that the war had cost them nothing, whereas the victorious nations were burdened by huge liabilities. The same applied to Municipal debts, debts incurred by the State Railways, and other Public enterprises. . . . he quite realised that the German problem was infinitely more complex than that of Austria . . . but he was firm in his conviction that once the currency was stabilized on a sound basis Germany could be put on her feet in an astonishingly short time.[12]

Whether Germany would want or be compelled to accept the services of a Dr. Zimmer-mann was a question for the future, however, and, as in Austria, the planning and first steps in the direction of stabilization had to be taken without either foreign loans or foreign overseers. The work had begun in Stresemann's first Cabinet with the genuine activation of the man Cuno had appointed as Austerity Commissar, the head of the Reich Audit Office (Rechnungshof), Saemisch, who had the task of developing plans for the reduction of expenditure at all levels of government. This was no easy task. Saemisch was successful in securing approval to attend all Cabinet meetings, and he worked closely with Hilferding and then Luther in attempting to implement mechanisms whereby the Finance Minister would be able to make effective the priority of fiscal over all other considerations in Ministerial planning granted him by the Cabinet in 1920 and by regulations issued on December 31, 1922. An effort to establish a rigid system of Treasury control under which the Finance Minister would have absolute veto power over proposals to which he objected was already partially in place. The Finance Minister's powers had been greatly increased, and a Cabinet override of his veto had been made complicated and difficult. Similarly, a plan to install permanent Finance Ministry delegates in all the ministries with the power to veto all unbudgeted expenditures and cost overruns was softened in such a way as to place the chief responsibility on the budgetary officers within the Ministries, while the Finance Ministry reserved the right to send delegates for informational purposes. These measures, which included severe penalties for unauthorized and uncontrolled expenditures, were in force by November 7.[13]

The major obstacle to budgetary control lay not only in the efforts of the various Ministers to keep their authority intact within their Ministries, but also in their understandable desire to resist reductions in programs and personnel they considered essential. Prior to Stresemann's taking office, Saemisch had refrained from creating an overall program and sought instead to work with individual Ministries and agencies to reduce personnel and costs. Stresemann and Hilferding wanted a genuine austerity program, however, and Saemisch supplied a lengthy and detailed document of over two hundred pages on August 31. He urged, however, that it be kept secret so that they would not be drowned in objections even before they began.[14]

The most serious barrier to fiscal reform, however, was the civil service, which would obviously be the chief victim of any program for the reduction of government expenditure. Stresemann and Hilferding had been at one in their intention to eliminate quarterly salary prepayment for civil servants and reduce the size of the bureaucracy, a policy that was very popular in all but civil-servant circles and the political parties or portions of political parties supporting them. As long as the passive resistance continued, the government had to be careful about offending the civil servants and their organizations, especially since the civil servants often bore the brunt of the resistance in the Ruhr. A most dramatic illustration of the Stresemann government's willingness at least to begin defying the civil-servant organizations, however, was the speed with which quarterly prepayment of salaries was temporarily suspended. The Finance Ministry received approval from the states on August 30, after which the Cabinet sent the measure to the Reichsrat on September 4 and secured passage in the Reichstag on September 27.[15]

The civil servants viewed the introduction of weekly pay as an effort by the Finance Ministry "to dismantle the professional civil service and put it on the same level as the workers."[16] In one instance, a civil-servant group went so far as to suggest that the safety of the state depended upon the well-being of the civil servants now threatened by the new pay arrangement since, in the event of a Putsch, "they would have to obey a new government all the more quickly, the greater their distress."[17] Far more worrisome to the civil-servant organizations than this measure, however, which was supposed to be temporary, were the rumors about government plans to permanently reduce the size of the civil service. Hilferding did not deny the reports but tried to assure the organizations that these plans constituted neither an attack on the "well-earned rights" of the civil servants nor an effort to dilute the quality of the civil servant by hiring non–civil-service clerks and other personnel in their place. Nevertheless, the civil-servant organizations were very dissatisfied with

the explanations being given to them and wished to be consulted about the measures under consideration.[18]

There were good reasons for such concern. Hilferding's initial approach, which took the form of a draft law presented on August 23 and discussed in Cabinet on September 10, seemed relatively mild. It called for forced retirements and early retirements with pensions and moving costs and even providing similar benefits along with one-time compensatory settlements for civil servants on probation or without tenure. These measures were to be followed by the state governments as well. The Hilferding draft was not well received either in the Reich Chancellery or by the Socialist Interior Minister Sollmann. The Chancellery officials thought the proposal went too far in trying to avoid hardships and was too narrow in scope because of its failure to deal with reductions of contractual personnel. These higher civil servants were inclined to take a much harsher attitude toward non-tenured civil servants and government employees and workers but, at the same time, warned against creating a situation in which a thousand civil servants would be put on pension but ten thousand white-collar workers would replace them. In their view, every category of government employee had to be encompassed by the legislation. This was a central point both substantively and tactically. The inflation and bloating of government payrolls had created a certain unity of interest among the various categories of government workers. If the government was now going to begin to disgorge a large proportion of its labor force, then the issue of which categories were to bear the brunt of the process was of no small importance. One civil-servant organization, for example, was already demanding in September that contractual employees had to go first before any civil servants were released. As for Sollmann, he was most concerned about further damaging the morale of the civil servants as well as relations with the states, and it was this difference between Hilferding and Sollmann that delayed a settlement of the issue during the first Stresemann Cabinet.[19]

The standoff ended in October, when the new Finance Minister Luther had an Enabling Act at his disposal with which to decree a solution. The inspiration by no means came from him alone. The Democrats and especially Transportation Minister Oeser had given strong support to the Enabling Act, since "only by this means could he have a way of reducing the excessive personnel and other personnel costs of the Reich Railroad System."[20] Reich President Ebert also spurred Luther on. On October 10, he sent Luther a personal letter pointing out that the Enabling Act now eliminated any legal need to pay heed to the "well-earned rights" of the civil servants and reminding him that public opinion "viewed the existing civil service policy as one of the chief causes of the financial nadir in which we find ourselves."[21] Ebert called for a strict hiring freeze, even if this would destroy the expectations of those completing their training, and the establishment of fixed quotas for reductions in government employees with a higher percentage being fixed for contractual than for civil-service employees. He also asked for a reduction of pensions for civil servants who had other sources of income. While Luther demonstrated some inclination to negotiate about these plans with the civil-servant organizations, which would have kept a promise made by Stresemann on September 11, Labor Minister Brauns opposed any negotiations at the Cabinet discussion of the projected law on October 17. In Brauns's view, the Enabling Act had changed the situation, and there was no reason to negotiate with interest groups at a time when one did not even have to consult the Reichstag. The matter was resolved by a decision to present the draft law to the civil-service trade unions and receive their suggestions but to refrain from negotiation or commitment to modifications. The Cabinet approved the legislation despite Sollmann's continued reservations, thereby accepting a 25 percent reduction of the personnel employed by the Reich, beginning with three 5-percent reductions by the first day of each of the first three months of 1924 and concluding with a 10 percent reduction to be completed before July 1. On October 27, the Civil Service Reduction (*Beamtenabbau*) Decree, now renamed the Personnel Reduction (*Personalabbau*) Decree became law.[22]

The change of name was much more than a diplomatic gesture toward the career civil ser-

vice. It seems to have been inspired by Mayor Carl Goerdeler of Königsberg, who was one of the representatives of the Congress of German Municipalities at the discussions of the measures held with state and municipal government officials in the Finance Ministry on October 19–20. Goerdeler was a member of the DNVP, and his views certainly reflected those of the career officialdom. The change of appellation was part of a more general proposal he presented under which civil-service personnel would be released beginning with, respectively, temporary employees, married women, regular employees, and only then moving on to untenured civil servants and tenured civil servants. While not challenging the government's intention of forcing the retirement of those over sixty-five and, with the concurrence of their superiors, of career civil servants between sixty and sixty-five, civil servants with seniority were to be favored. Not only did the Finance Ministry assure the municipal and state representatives that the personnel reduction would be carried out in such a manner, but the breakdown of the categories of Reich employees dismissed or retired by March 1924 shows that the promise was kept. Of the 396,838 out of 1,592,214 Reich employees retired or dismissed (a 24.9 percent reduction), 32.9 percent were workers, 49.7 percent were contractual employees, and only 16.3 percent were civil servants. Of the 134,507 career civil servants dismissed, 127,354 came from the railroads, post, and Reich Printing Office. Of the 576,083 railroad workers employed on October 1, 1923, only 186,658 were left on March 31, 1924, while the number of workers in the post and Reich Printing Office had been more than halved.[23]

It is important to recognize, however, that existing circumstances played altogether too well into the hands of conservatives like Goerdeler. There were powerful arguments for a rapid and drastic reduction of the personnel working for the Reich of the type which took place, not only because of the financial situation but also because of the general consensus that the civil service was bloated in precisely those areas where state workers and contractual labor were most numerous. As the head of the Congress of German Municipalities, Mitzlaff, pointed out:

There is unquestionably a great inflation of civil servants in the Reich administration at the present time. It is well known that in the postal service and railroads, where the largest portion of the civil servants in the Reich administration are lodged, there is a civil service apparatus that far exceeds its performance and actual need. If the Reich wants to cut back in a wholesale way, then this is justified without further ado by conditions in its large enterprises.[24]

This posed a horrible dilemma for the more militant and especially the Social Democratic civil-servant trade unions, which were committed both to the democratization of the civil service and to providing job security to employees and workers on the government payrolls. On the one hand, they knew that personnel reduction was necessary; on the other, they were aware of how tenuous their solidarity was with the workers in private industry. The leader of the ADB, Falkenberg, was a strong supporter of a united front, but his remarks at a joint meeting of the ADGB, AfA, and ADB leaders on October 17 were anything but confident and can only be understood against the background of long-standing worker hostility to the size and priveleges of the civil service, the relative indifference of the labor leaders to such civil servant demands as civil-service worker councils similar to those granted the blue- and white-collar workers, and the fact that solidarity was anything but promoted by an increasingly proletarianized society:

We are not against a reduction of the civil service, but we decidedly reject the plan now before us. The only purpose of the plan is to eliminate the republican civil servants. We are of the view that the reduction should begin at the upper and not at the lower levels. We have only common interests with the workers, and we want to join in to support their previous rights. But the workers must also support our efforts to have a civil service councils law. Common understanding is the precondition for collaboration in all questions. We have the power, if we only want to use it. We want to be united in our will to see a new time begin.[25]

As Falkenberg and the union leaders allied with him discovered when they met with Finance Ministry officials on October 22–23, however, the power lay elsewhere and the "new time" that was beginning had precious little to do with what Falkenberg had in mind. No attention was paid to their proposals for the reduction of the retirement age and, above all,

that the "organizational and legal reforms" precede the taking of action and that the organizations be consulted regularly in order to avoid a planless personnel reduction and hardships.[26] As the regular trade unions were insisting that modifications of the eight-hour day be conducted in consultation with the unions, so the civil-servant unions were calling for consultation in personnel reduction. In both cases, the response was that the emergency was too great to allow for clumsy procedures and consultation, and these arguments were very plausible under the circumstances.

Yet another illustration of how the crisis was undermining the legitimacy of the movement toward democracy and equality with which the Republic had begun and the possibilities of greater solidarity among wage earners is the way in which women were affected by and treated under the Personnel Reduction Decree. Women were particularly vulnerable because, as a petition of the Federation of German Women's Associations (Bund deutscher Frauenvereine) of November 6, 1923, pointed out, they had only been allowed to enter the school, post, and railroad services as full-fledged civil servants after the Revolution and thus had not had time to go through the necessary probationary period in many cases. Even worse, however, was that their rights as permanent civil servants as well as their constitutional rights to equality of treatment were no longer secure since the decree mandated the release of married female civil servants if they were financially secure. While they were able to get a government promise to review the implementation of the decree to avert great hardships, the evidence is that they suffered disproportionately from the firings in the postal service.[27]

They were, of course, able to make stronger claims for their role in the field of social welfare and teaching, where their work appeared especially important and necessary. Most of this activity, however, was performed on the state and especially the municipal level, where the reduction of the civil service could not be conducted as radically and schematically as in the Reich. Indeed, the municipal leaders pointed out to the Reich Finance Ministry that their situation was particularly serious because of the manner in which the Reich had been and was continuing to shift social and other responsibilities on to the municipalities. Nevertheless, the state and municipal authorities welcomed the Personnel Reduction Decree (under which the Reich intended to empower the states to order personnel reductions on the municipal level through enabling acts of their own) not only because it gave them greater flexibility in reducing their civil services but also because it gave them a lever for encouraging the reduction of the responsibilities imposed upon them by the Reich in the field of social welfare. Whatever the necessity of employing women in social welfare, therefore, there was a general understanding that the reduction of social welfare itself would inevitably attend upon personnel reduction.[28]

This point was demonstrated on the very day that the Personnel Reduction Decree went into effect, when Luther also issued regulations for the carrying out of the austerity program of the Reich government agreed upon by the Cabinet on October 10. Thus, every government agency was required to submit its plans and budget for review, and to do so with the instructions to refrain from all but the most necessary legislation and measures in mind. Luther also provided a detailed list of no less than forty measures involving either the suspension or delaying of social and other types of reform legislation as well as new measures aimed at reducing costs and improving the Reich's financial situation. In his meetings with the state and municipal authorities, the basic principles of future welfare practice were laid out very clearly:

Public welfare should only be practiced to the extent absolutely necessary: a) turning away from all experiments, b) suspension of all unessential tasks, c) turning away from exaggerated institutional care, d) transfer of all not absolutely essential publicly supported tasks to private welfare; reawakening and further promotion of self-help and neighborly assistance, e) reduction of staff to what is absolutely necessary and extensive use of persons willing to take honorary offices.[29]

What this was to mean in practice was reduction of the number of those entitled to assistance after prior use of all their available resources, the direct and indirect compulsion of those on welfare to work, severe limitation of support for "asocial persons," and consolidation of the various categories of relief and the

authorities dealing with them. A host of educational measures for teacher training, vocational training, and training of midwives was to be eliminated, suspended, or receive reduced funding. The important Youth Welfare Law of 1922 was to receive similar treatment, as were the agencies established for the benefit of various forms of welfare cases (including war disabled), and monies for the Red Cross and refugees. A similar posture was taken toward legislation for plant protection, caring for those with tuberculosis, and fighting of venereal diseases, and the list ominously concluded with "the limitation of all expenditure for cultural and welfare purposes even if they rest upon constitutional provisions."[30]

The paradox was that the government was trying to dismantle or reduce its social expenditures at the very moment when the need for expanded welfare was becoming more desperate than ever before. This was not simply because the numbers of those in distress was increasing but also because the social insurance system (the system of health, accident, and old age insurance) was entering the final stages of disintegration under the impact of hyperinflation. The Labor Ministry subsequently compared its condition to that of a great bankrupt enterprise that had ground to a halt, and voices were being raised against its ever being allowed to resume production again. The hyperinflation was thus threatening one of the few remnants of Bismarck's Empire upon which the Republic's founders had hoped to expand by appearing to force a return to poor relief in place of social insurance.[31]

This was true even of the health insurance system, which experienced a third less demand for its services in 1923 than in 1922. This was not because Germans were healthier but rather because sick-leave pay had become worthless, and it made more sense to work while one was sick or return to work prematurely than starve. Labor Minister Brauns was well aware that the insurance funds were facing almost insurmountable odds in their efforts to stay afloat and provide services effectively:

The price of medications is calculated by the chemical industry in gold; the merchants add 30 percent to the price and the pharmacists 75 percent. The chemical industry charges according to the going dollar value in selling medications. Such a pricing policy, against which my ministry is helpless, must have a devastating effect upon the health insurance system. The expenditures of the health insurance funds are largely calculated in gold currency, while its receipts are in paper or indexed currency. It is as impossible to collect insurance premiums in gold as it is to pay gold wages. The same tense relationship exists between the contributions to the health insurance and the costs of health and hospital care; here the price of coal plays a decisive role. The health insurance offices made heroic efforts to master their difficulties. The health insurance system is now newly faced with destruction by the extended and continuing unemployment. The number of members will decrease rapidly and the number of those reporting sick will rise sharply, a natural phenomenon whenever there is a sharp increase in unemployment.[32]

At the same time, however, a Reich government bent on budget balancing was increasingly reluctant to bail the health insurance funds out. The extreme hyperinflation only served to heighten the recriminations between doctors and health insurance boards. The former accused the latter of wasting money through overorganization and bureaucracy. The boards charged that there were too many doctors providing excessive and overly costly treatments and that they, along with pharmacists, were pandering to irrational patient demands for medications made excessively expensive by the collusion of pharmacists and the greed of drug companies. The government in Berlin found merit in the arguments of both sides. It responded by applying the Personnel Reduction Decree of October 27 to the health insurance boards and, most important, by issuing a decree of October 30 permitting health insurance boards to increase their supervision of medical treatments and dismiss doctors who provided needless services, to force patients to pay a tenth of the cost of perscriptions, and to favor pharmacists who lowered their prices.[33]

The decree of October 30 unleashed a storm of protest and defiance on the part of the doctors and pharmacists. The Medical Faculty of the University of Göttingen protested that the new powers given to the health insurance boards turned the unprofessional officials into "legislators, prosecuters and judges" in their dealings with the doctors and not only endangered public health but also "demeaned" the medical profession.[34] If the practice of the

Württemberg health insurance organization was any measure of the new situation, then the doctors had something to complain about. Bills presented by pharmacists were subject to review by a staff of one doctor, two pharmacists, and several inspectors, while doctors' bills were reviewed by a number of doctors and the statistical section of the fund. The review of each lower official was checked by a higher official, with the result that the expense and effort involved was in total disproportion to the money saved. Furthermore, the fund was accused of competing with private agencies by running a host of luxury services and speculating in real estate. In early November, the doctors and pharmacists began to demand direct payment from their patients and thus participated in a growing wave of medical strikes. And if that were not enough, employers joined with the doctors and pharmacists in criticizing the health insurance system by suggesting that it had grown too large and needed decentralization and debureaucratization. The critics claimed that the larger firms could manage their own funds with fewer personnel and "the relations with doctors and pharmacists would be placed on a business-like basis and would be far more cordial and beneficial for the insured."[35] Whether such solutions would or could work remained to be seen, but it was clear that the government's efforts to cope with the hyperinflation had increased the hypertension in the health insurance system.

The chaos in the health insurance and accident insurance systems at this time was part and parcel of the immediate hyperinflationary disorder. Since these insurance systems more or less operated on a pay-as-you-go basis, one could anticipate a stabilization of contributions and services with the creation of a valorized currency. The cries for the reform carried on the old conflict between doctors and funds over the question of the right of patients to choose their own physicians as well as the concern of employers over the costs of the system. No one was seriously proposing its abolition. The old-age and invalid insurance system, however, was far more vulnerable to extreme proposals.

The reason, of course, is that it was, by and large, bankrupt. The government had relaxed its regulations governing the security of insurance fund investments in the course of 1923, but not all the funds had acted with sufficient alacrity. When the Association of German Occupational Organizations reproached the Labor Ministry in October 1923 for allowing many of its members to go bankrupt, the Ministry responded with great irritation, pointing out that the regulations had been relaxed all through the year and that it could not understand why some insurance bodies had taken advantage of this fact while others were still holding large quantities of worthless government and municipal bonds. The Ministry's irritation was all the greater because it had paid most of the accident insurance benefits for the year while the insurance funds only had to pay their (in the Ministry's view) bloated staffs.[36]

In reality, the relaxation of the investment regulations had come too late for most of the insurance funds. One notable exception was the White-Collar Workers Insurance Fund. Its success is to be explained by its recent vintage, having been created in 1911, and by the fact that it was not obligated to begin paying pensions until 1923 as well as by its apparent speedy response to the possibilities for valorizing its assets. The Reich, states, and municipalities, however, were hardly innocent bystanders in the bankruptcy of the insurance funds, since the depreciation of the bonds held by the funds was the depreciation of their debt. Similarly, it was the funds which now bore the burden of the mortgages in which they had been compelled by the Reich to invest in 1920–1921 in support of the government's housing construction program. Yet another benefit gained by the Reich from the hyperinflation at the expense of the social insurance system was that the 110 million mark contribution it was obligated to pay under the original system to cover a fifty-mark supplement for invalids and widows and widowers and a twenty-five-mark supplement for orphans was no longer being paid because the supplement was worthless.[37]

To be sure, the Reich was paying 80 percent of the support being provided by the municipalities to social pensioners who passed the means test, payments which were effectively completing the regression of the social security system into a humiliating system of poor relief. To save on these sums, it was pushing the in-surance funds to collect contributions that were indexed, and this enabled them to give two million pensioners a supplement of a hundred million marks each on October 1, an amount that was to be multiplied tenfold on November 1. Although inadequate, these payments could be deducted from the municipal supports, and this saved the Reich money. The difficulty, of course, was that the social insurance contributions were made in the form of insurance stamp purchases negotiated through the post office, and by the time the money thus collected reached the insurance funds, the stamps had lost most of their value.[38]

Did it make sense to continue the old age and invalid insurance system at all under these circumstances? By October, the government had already decided to leave the care of the socially insured to the insurance bodies, even if this meant higher contributions, severely reduced services, and release from the restrictions on the use of what remained of their capital resources. As one expert commentator pointed out, "the provisions made in the past are pointless; provisions made for the future are at present just as pointless; our age is left completely to itself and can in the present only care for the present."[39] The question, therefore, was not simply one of collecting valorized contributions and of organizational rationalization. Payment of benefits was supposed to come from accumulated invested funds, and these investments were now worthless, except in the most unlikely eventuality that the Reich would permit a revaluation of such assets. In the view of Mayor Luppe of Nürnberg, whose analysis appeared not only in the socially conservative *Deutsche Allgemeine Zeitung* but also in the social reformist *Soziale Praxis*, the entire system should have been liquidated on November 1, thereby eliminating the entire costly administrative apparatus and saving the Reich and employers the need to make further contributions. The savings thus made would make up for the additional cost of welfare support for pensioners in need. In Luppe's view, the suffering thus created was unavoidable:

Certainly there will be hardships for civil servants and employees and for a portion of the pensioners; certainly it is painful to take leave for a protracted period of the social security insurance system of which

Germany was rightfully proud . . . , but there is no other solution, since *an impoverished land cannot support a pension system.* My proposal will at least maintain health system services for as long as possible without the monstrous apparatus of the insurance system.[40]

However dire the fiscal straits of the Reich government and the demands of the impending currency reform, the Reich government appears at no time to have entertained the total abandonment of the social security system. Loyalty to the Bismarckian heritage undoubtedly played a role here, but so did practical considerations. Defenders of the system certainly made reverent references to the work of the "great Chancellor," but they also warned against the demoralizing consequences of returning to the antiquated system of poor relief. On the one hand, they expressed the conviction that administrative reform and consolidation of the entire system were necessary. On the other hand, they remained loyal to the principle of insurance. The dilemma of what to do about the evaporation of the investment of the social security system was answered by the Finance and Labor Ministries with a call for a change of the system; namely, the reconstruction of the old-age insurance system on a cost-coverage rather than capital-coverage requirement. The *de facto* transition to the cost-coverage system already employed in the sickness and accident insurance funds was being allowed to take place by the government in the old-age and invalid insurance system as well. This was seen as the way out of the dilemma created by the bankruptcy of the system and the perceived inability of revaluating assets after stabilization. In the short run, the insured were being forced on poor relief, but in the long run, the reconstitution of the system on a cost-coverage foundation through employer and worker contributions and a measure of government support seemed the best way of cutting back Reich responsibility while making sure that workers and employers had no excuse to drop out of the system. No one thought the future rosy, and the Labor Ministry intended to impose "a ruthless cost-cutting in administration, a reduction of services and a lowering of contributions." Nevertheless, it remained "unshaken in the conviction that the social insurance system can and

must be maintained. The demands for the abrogation of the social insurance system are highly regrettable, especially at a time when the workers are being called upon to assume new burdens."[41] Politics and principle, therefore, militated in favor of the system and, indeed, even its extension. As one defender of the system put it, "how can one recommend the transformation of insurance into poor relief while one is right now and with complete justification at work transferring the unemployment support system into unemployment insurance. The principle of contribution and corresponding service, which is the foundation of our worker insurance, is a very healthy one and should not be transgressed."[42]

The paradox that the government was planning to expand the social insurance principle to the unemployed at the very moment when the existing social security system seemed to be in its death throes must also be understood in terms of fiscal calculations with respect to both the hyperinflation and the anticipated stabilization. The degeneration of the existing social insurance system into poor relief and welfare was presumed to be a temporary condition. Contributions by employers and workers were seen less as a foundation for entitlements than as a means of taxation for reduced welfare services based on demonstrated need and as an incentive to administrative rationalization.[43]

This was patently evident in the decree of October 15 issued under the Enabling Act which governed the future financing of the unemployment relief system. Under the new dispensation, four-fifths of the costs of unemployment relief were to be covered by worker and employer contributions, but such contributions were not to exceed one-fifth of their respective contributions to the health insurance system. The remaining fifth was to be supplied by the municipalities, although this contribution was not to amount to more than one-quarter of the combined employer–worker contributions, a regulation changed in February 1924 to make the system even more dependent upon employer–worker contributions. Strictly speaking, therefore, the Reich and states were no longer to be involved in unemployment relief, although the new decree did provide for federal and state grants in high unemployment districts

**Table 46. The Number of Supported
Unemployed and Dependents Per Thousand
in the Major German States in 1923**
(by quarter)

	January	April	July	October
Prussia	2.7	9.2*	6.6	24.1
Bavaria	2.1	5.9	3.9	17.6
Saxony	8.4	20.5	11.8	61.0
Württemberg	0.7	2.9	1.9	8.0
Baden	1.0	4.4	5.3	9.2
Thuringia	4.0	10.5	7.4	42.6
Hessen	0.7	2.0	7.7	37.4
Hamburg	11.0	23.5	15.3	64.8
Bremen	8.0	21.1	11.8	31.3
Reich	3.1	9.5	6.6	27.0

Source: Reichsarbeitsblatt, 1923, Nr. 3, p. 47; Nr. 9, p. 173; Nr. 15, p. 317; Nr. 21, p. 441.

*Excluding the Rhineland.

where the combined funds did not provide sufficient support. What must be emphasized is that, whatever the long-run significance of this decree as a step in the direction of the Unemployment Insurance Law of 1927, it was anything but unemployment insurance under the circumstances pertaining in 1924. No one had a right to unemployment relief unless they could demonstrate need and that their unemployment was somehow "war related." The tightening of the regulations governing such support as well as the increasing tendency to reduce support for short-time workers and to eliminate the cost-intensive productive unemployment support were necessitated by the limited funds available from workers, employers, and municipalities. At this same time, they also could be mandated by the state and federal governments insofar as they were called upon to come to the rescue. There was, in short, nothing about the motivation for the new measures and their context that could in any way be called reassuring about the future of Germany's unemployed.[44]

The projected bleakness of the future, however, was as nothing compared to the hopelessness and misery of the present. In October and November 1923, unemployment seemed to be getting totally out of control (see Table 46). This was especially the case in the occupied areas, where all estimates spoke of at least two million unemployed, not including family members. In the major cities of the Ruhr, if one

takes other persons on welfare into account, at least half the population was in need of public support. There were fifty thousand unemployed in Bochum, a hundred thousand in Düsseldorf, and ninety thousand in Dortmund. In the unoccupied areas, the number of supported unemployed reached 1.5 million at the end of November, while the number of those on short time numbered 1.8 million, bringing the total number of those unemployed or on short time in Germany to between four million and five million persons, exclusive of dependents. Thus, between twelve million and fifteen million persons were in need of support in the final weeks of the hyperinflation.[45]

If the unemployed seemed to stand at the center of the social disaster of late 1923, this was not because they were the most disadvantaged. Widows, the disabled, social pensioners, and aged rentiers were now deliberately given lower levels of welfare support as part of a kind of social triage favoring the potentially productive over the unemployable or the less employed.[46] The mounting unemployment was the critical test of the ability to master the fiscal crisis and conduct the social *démontage* in progress at this time because the unemployed had been considered the nation's most serious social danger. Weimar governments had hesitated and continued to hesitate about running the risks of mass unemployment. Since the end of the war, the control of unemployment had been an important domestic legitimation for inflationary policies. The price of stabilization would inevitably be high unemployment, and the question of whether the government could survive high unemployment and fiscal constraints on the support of the unemployed without producing the kind of chaos and revolutionary danger that had been feared since 1918 remained to be answered. On the one hand, unemployment was a means of disciplining labor; on the other, the disciplining of labor could only be achieved if the revolutionary danger from the left could be contained at an acceptable price.

The price worried responsible politicians and officials. It was hard to neglect the anxious voice of Mayor Böss of Berlin, who warned in mid-September that widespread unrest and plundering were inevitable if unemployment and short-time work continued to increase, that the damage caused by such unrest in Berlin would cost ten times more than the recent upsurge of violence in Breslau arising from similar causes, and that the events in that city had proven that it was cheaper to finance public-works programs than to pay the costs of disorder and its suppression. At the very moment when Böss was writing, the maximum weekly unemployment benefit in Berlin for a family of four was 88,500,000 marks, while the minimum needed for substinence was 683,300,000,000 marks. Böss felt confident that radical elements seeking to take advantage of the situation could be contained, but he pleaded for timely prevention instead of costly cures.[47]

Similar warnings over like conditions were coming from that other great center of unemployment, Saxony, where pleas for assistance were backed up with reports of plundering and intimidation of merchants by hungry unemployed, women, and youths. Brauns, however, was no longer willing to give the Saxons or other hard-hit areas special consideration, pointing out "that at the moment when the Reich is declaring its inability to continue payments to the Ruhr, he cannot take responsibility for making special financial concessions to other parts of the country."[48]

Furthermore, events in the traditional high-unemployment areas of Saxony, Thuringia, and Hamburg during the last weeks of October made it abundantly clear that Communist ability to stir up and mobilize the unemployed was not translatable into successful revolutionary action. The insurrectionary tactic decided upon by the Comintern in September now culminated in the fiasco of the "German October." The entry of Communists into the Zeigner government in Saxony on October 10 and the Frölich government in Thuringia on October 16 (ostensibly for the purpose of providing a united front and barrier against a Bavarian fascist march on Berlin but actually for the purpose of preparing the way for a Communist march on Berlin and Munich) gave the Reichswehr commander and holder of executive powers in Saxony, General Alfred Müller, a welcome opportunity to ban the proletarian Centuries and send troops into major Saxon cities on October 21. Even before the Reichswehr employed force against the Communists,

however, the KPD suffered a major defeat from the ranks of labor when the left Socialists in the Conference of Factory Councils, which the Communists had initiated in Chemnitz on October 21, turned down a Communist summons for a general strike and thus rejected the effort to trigger a general revolutionary movement in Germany. The harebrained character of the Communist effort and their lack of support among the workers was made evident in Hamburg, where the KPD leadership, whether because of misperception or poor communications, unleashed a totally unsuccessful uprising on October 23. The KPD leadership seemed to have felt that the "special economic and political situation in Hamburg" had been highly propitious for such an action:

The unemployed and short-term workers in the week of October 13–20, at a time when bread already cost 4.2 billion marks, by and large did not receive even 10 million marks. There was plundering of food stores in various parts of the cities. The distress and dissatisfaction of the *Mittelstand* was also very great. On Saturday, the 20th, there were demonstrations and bloody encounters between the police and the unemployed. 40,000 shipyard and dock workers were involved in a union-approved wage movement.

They rapidly discovered that the situation was not so revolutionary after all in the course of their attacks on the Hamburg police and other strategic points on October 23. The poorly prepared and organized but bloody effort was supported neither by the organized workers nor the lower middle class and was harshly suppressed by the well-armed police. From this, the Hamburg KPD leaders drew the rather uninspiring lesson that "the entire Hamburg uprising shows that we were not yet strong enough to carry out the final struggle."[49]

Though the unemployed in the traditional areas of high unemployment—Berlin, Saxony–Thuringia, and Hamburg—were not a revolutionary threat, the growing number of unemployed in the occupied areas of the Rhine and Ruhr, nevertheless, presented its own very special dangers to the unity of the Reich. The cessation of wage guarantees that accompanied the end of passive resistance meant that the unemployed workers would now be genuinely unemployed and would be dependent on unemployment supports. Initially, these were twice those paid in the unoccupied areas, but they were reduced to one and a half times that of the unoccupied areas on October 20 and were to be on a par with the unoccupied areas after November 1. As the British High Commissioner in Koblenz reported on October 19, the supports given on that date were just above starvation levels, especially because the cost of living was much higher in the occupied than the unoccupied areas. Since the mark was deteriorating more rapidly than the weekly support level was being set, a situation of genuine desperation was being created. Most reluctantly, the government decided on October 25 to pay 15 percent more unemployment support in the occupied areas than in the unoccupied areas after October 31, but this could hardly do much to alleviate the situation. On October 29, the British Consul in Cologne reported serious disturbances in Düsseldorf, where "looting of shops and vehicles containing foodstuffs is of daily occurrence. . . . Both in the neighborhood of Düsseldorf and other cities the townsfolk in increasing numbers are making excursions into the country in search of food and those who have no money form themselves into marauding bands."[50]

A depressing but revealing analysis of the situation in the Ruhr was provided by Mayor Geyer of Bochum at a meeting of the representatives of the occupied areas with Stresemann in Hagen on October 25:

We are not prophets of doom and gloom. I have been in the occupied area for a long time, and I have experienced all kinds of happenings there. But I have never witnessed the kinds of things I have seen on today's trip from Bochum to Hagen. I have never encountered such hordes of people starving and wandering about.[51]

He was happy to learn of government plans to ensure that food would reach the area, but he pointed out that the food also had to be paid for and that

Nothing has yet been said about how the population is supposed to get money into its hands during the next few hours in order to buy the always and ever increasingly expensive food needed just to survive; whether it be valorized or unvalorized money is irrelevant. The only source of income for most of the people now is unemployment relief. . . . How long unemployment relief can be paid depends upon the financial strength of the Reich. . . . In our view, un-

employment relief today is no longer a social support but rather, after the largest portion of the population are recipients, an economic and financial expenditure . . . thrown away capital which one day can no longer be paid.

The only logical conclusion that could be drawn from these facts was that the economy had to be started up again as soon as possible. In Geyer's view, this was what the people cared about most at this point:

The population is fully resigned and is thankful for the prospect of every piece of bread that is held out to it. I am convinced that if we can offer up even some well-founded prospect of providing the population with work and thus with earnings, that we will then overcome the difficulties and that we can maintain the territory in one or another form for the Reich. If this does not happen then, in the view of those of us in public life, it's all over.

These remarks are especially interesting because they reveal the extent to which, from the standpoint of the government, the situation was filled not only with threat but also with a glimmer of promise. The privations of the Ruhr occupation and years of inflation and shortages had beaten the Ruhr population, and not only them, into a state of potential docility in which they might welcome the opportunity to earn their bread under previously unacceptable conditions. The key questions were whether one could bridge the period to the reactivation of the economy and deal with the existing chaos and whether the area could be held for Germany in the process.

Both the Communists and the French in the occupied areas were taking advantage of the situation, the former by stirring up the unemployed, the latter by urging the introduction of the French currency as a solution to the miseries of the population and encouraging the separatists, who made use of disgruntled unemployed, farmers, and merchants as well as jailbirds and other dubious elements. Operating from the center in Düren, the separatists launched a spate of putsches on October 21 in Aachen, Trier, Koblenz, and Bonn. While these were more or less effectively handled by the local authorities, they were a source of continuing concern both to local authorities and to Berlin. This was especially the case in the Bavarian Palatinate, where leading Social Democrats, although disavowed by the national party, used the rightist control of Munich as an excuse to identify themselves with proposals for a separate state and even separation from Germany.[52]

Needless to say, a major source of distress and unrest for all elements of the population was the currency situation. It was especially serious in the occupied areas because of French sequestrations of money sent by the Reich and the uncertainty about whether the new currency scheduled to be issued on November 15 would be allowed in the region and, no less important, whether conditions in the region would not ruin the new currency just as it had helped to bring down the old. The delay of the German currency reform was caused, in large measure, by the continued unemployment supports in the occupied areas, and this now played into French hands. There was a contradiction between the effort to reduce the amount of unemployment support being given in a gradual and humane manner and the need for a rapid currency reform so that the economy could function again. German businessmen in the occupied areas were at the end of their tether because of the currency situation. At a meeting of leading Rhenish businessmen in the Cologne Chamber of Commerce on October 16, one "very prominent personality" argued for the creation of a new Rhenish currency. This idea was rejected by his colleagues and the Chamber's president, Louis Hagen, who urged great caution and coordination with Berlin. As a government observer reported, however, "there could be no question that an immediate solution to the currency question was felt to be the first and most pressing necessity. The currency depreciation in the occupied area is so far advanced that one must expect a cessation of the possibility of making payments in paper marks in the next eight days. Prices are climbing in such a way that the production of money cannot meet the need."[53]

The separatist outbursts only brought the point home more clearly, and when the so-called "Economic Committee" for the occupied areas—which was composed of leading interest-group representatives and officials—met in Cologne on October 22, it followed Louis Hagen's proposal to create a new committee charged not only with the task of restoring the

Rhineland economy but also with the responsibility of negotiating with the French on behalf of the various interested parties. These Rhenish leaders—some the most prominent and active of whom were Adenauer, Hagen, Jarres, the DVP Deputy Paul Moldenhauer, Vögler, and the ADGB leader Heinrich Meyer—were by no means prepared to embrace separatism or even act in independence of Berlin. Yet, they could hardly be unaffected by the realities that the clock was ticking away the life of the existing currency, that the Reich might be compelled to set the Rhineland adrift, and that there were strong forces, especially within the Rhenish Center Party, that were toying with alternatives to the existing relationship between the Rhineland and the Reich and Prussia. While prepared to wait upon the direct information and instructions Stresemann and other members of the Berlin government intended to provide in a meeting in Hagen on October 25, they found it hard to contain either their pessimism or the alternatives with which they were toying.[54]

Both the pessimism and the alternatives found expression at a preliminary discussion among the Rhenish leaders in Barmen on October 24 in preparation for the next day's conclave in Hagen. For Louis Hagen, the currency question continued to hold a central place in his concerns because he saw neither how the food supply could be guaranteed without an acceptable currency nor how the unemployment situation could be dealt with once all the large mining companies closed down. The impending currency reform offered no solution:

The Rentenbank planned by the Reich is also worthless for the Rhineland, because, for example, the required encumbering of landed property with a mortgage ... will not be permitted here. On the other side, a currency on a French basis is also impossible because it will lead to an unbearable influence by the enemy on our administration and economy. The currency question is not simply an economic, but to a high degree, a political question.[55]

In the ensuing discussion, two political alternatives were presented in addition to Jarres' old "ditching" program with its banking on a major international crisis to come to Germany's rescue. The first, made by Moldenhauer, opposed any *de jure* separation of the Rhineland from either the Reich or Prussia but insisted that the *de facto* loss of Reich and Prussian sovereignty over the region had to be accepted as a reality. Moldenhauer thought the only acceptable solution to be one in which the Reich empowered the newly established committee to satisfy the most important economic requirements of the region by having its own currency, budget, and taxation rights. For Adenauer, who presented an alternative plan, the Moldenhauer proposal simply perpetuated the "lawless" state of affairs already existing and made the region a "French Colony" without in any way protecting the interests of the Reich. Instead, Adenauer suggested separating the Rhineland from Prussia and at least facing the possibility of separating the region from the Reich in the form of a new state structure, but doing so through negotiations that would relieve the Reich of the burdens of Versailles and the region of the occupation and Rhineland Commission.[56]

However one interprets Adenauer's motives—whether as an expression of his anticipation of impending disaster and desire for a "western" solution to the German security problem, which seems most plausible, or as wishful thinking by an ambitious politician seeking to rally the Rhenish Center Party behind him and offer the French a "decent" alternative to the separatists he despised[57]—both the Moldenhauer and the Adenauer proposals had as their common denominator the assumption that the currency reform would require the Reich to effectively abandon the Rhineland to its economic fate. The threat that the Reich would cease all support of the region as part of its stabilization program certainly was central to the entire discussion of alternative solutions to the Rhenish question, and there was a genuine consciousness that the fate of the Rhineland became ever more problematic as the opening of the Rentenbank on November 15 came nearer.

This was especially evident in the gloomy Cabinet and Ministerial discussions on October 20 and 24 prior to Stresemann's appearance at the Hagen assemblage. Luther was quite explicit about the negative implications of his program for holding on to the Rhineland:

The credits must be stopped under all circumstances. For the moment, the schedules valid in the unoccupied areas shall be applied with respect to the unemployment support. The social pensions must also be limited or terminated. If we do not succeed in cutting loose from the inflationary economy through ruthless choking off of Reich expenditures, then the only prospect we have is general chaos. Even the Rentenmark has no point if we do not manage to create clear financial conditions by that time. He intends to set up a gold-based budget concurrently with the introduction of the Rentenmark. It will balance receipts and expenditures. It will assume a rump Germany and exclude reparations payments.[58]

If there was any hope at all, it seemed to lay with the recent reports from Stinnes on the negotiations between the Committee of Six and the MICUM. The industrialists seemed willing to cover the costs of reparations deliveries and past coal tax payments through loans from abroad if the Reich would promise compensation once its finances were in order and would agree to credit present tax payments. This last concession was viewed as trivial since the tax payments were worthless under existing conditions. A much more problematic point was that the French were insisting on continued payment of the tax on coal. The tax had been abrogated by the government on October 15. The industrialists were unwilling to pay the tax, and the Reich was unwilling to compensate them if they did. The French also were making other demands with respect to German financial support of the French-controlled railroad system and occupation costs. The promise of the industrialist–MICUM negotiations, therefore, were shaky at best. Nevertheless, Stresemann, strongly backed by Interior Minister Sollmann, who continued to argue for special levels of unemployment support for the occupied areas, was willing to do whatever he could to hold on to the occupied areas: "Even if one must count upon a break between the occupied and unoccupied area, then this must take place with a handshake: 'We will come again.'"[59] He made the same point with even more pathos on October 24: "We cannot finance the struggle any longer. The goal must be to separate in love, not in hate."[60]

This continued pessimism, however, was accompanied by a marked softening of Luther's position—possibly under the influence of Sollmann; Brauns; the Minister for the Occupied Areas, Fuchs; and his own roots in the region—as Stresemann prepared for his journey to Hagen. While Luther continued to declare that "a clear decision is unavoidable," he also admitted that "a period of transition must be given so that the people do not suddenly stand before nothing."[61] In a memorandum of October 24, intended to help Stresemann buy time and which Luther later rationalized away with the argument that promises could be made because they were still in a period of paper currency, Luther agreed to the continued payment of unemployment supports and civil-servant salaries in the occupied areas at a level 15 percent higher than in the unoccupied areas. He thus enabled Stresemann to put off decisions that might have further compromised the Reich's control over the occupied areas in the Hagen discussions.[62]

Stresemann's performance at Hagen on October 25 was extraordinary, an achievement made all the more stunning by the fact that he was ill and physically exhausted and was coping with the crisis in Saxony-Thuringia and the even more uncontrollable situation in Bavaria at the same time. Everywhere Stresemann was seeking to restrain and constrain, to limit the actions of others while maximizing his own room to maneuver and seize opportunities. This was especially the case in the Hagen meeting, in which he strove to close the door on the proposals advocated by Jarres and Adenauer, while permitting something akin to the Moldenhauer solution since it was impossible to deny the Rhenish leaders all authority to negotiate with the French on local conditions and essential to provide a formal alternative to the separatists. He blasted away at Jarres' call for a formal break with France by likening that more to Germany's disastrous race to issue a declaration of war in 1914 and insisted that it was essential to exhaust all possibilities that would let the blame fall on the French. At the same time, he treated Adenauer's quest for a formalization of the situation as illusionary, warning that France would milk a new Rhenish state while continuing to make demands on the Reich because no French government would see such a new state structure as anything but German at heart. The crucial thing, therefore, was to maintain existing structures and the rights of the Reich. Stresemann thus salvaged that critical measure of openness in the situation required to ensure that the Reich would be in a position to maintain and reassert its rights in the occupied areas. By refusing to accept any of the alternatives proposed, all of which would have compromised the Reich's powers in the region, and by offering hope, he foreclosed decisions by others.[63]

In this effort, Stresemann was strengthened by Luther's concessions of the previous day on continued special support for the occupied areas, by the backing of the Ministers of the state governments in a meeting on the Bavarian question, and by the willingness of the mine owners to shoulder temporarily some of the costs of an agreement with the MICUM. He was also heartened by reports that British Prime Minister Baldwin intended to state publicly his opposition to any effort to divide Germany, by similarly positive news from the United States, and by General Smuts's speech in London on October 23 calling for a moratorium. He had reason to hope, therefore, that a German note of October 24 to the Reparations Commission expressing Germany's willingness to pay reparations but asking that the commission review Germany's ability to pay under existing conditions might receive a positive reception. Poincaré continued to appear intransigent, but his domestic political and financial difficulties were hardly a secret, and, indeed, on the very day of the Hagen meeting, October 25, France finally agreed to the British proposal for the establishment of an expert committee under American leadership to review Germany's financial capacity.[64]

In dealing with the Rhenish leaders, Stresemann's most delicate problems were in making a convincing presentation of his financial plans, on the one hand, and in dealing with the currency reform issue, on the other. While insisting that the new currency had to be sound and that austerity was necessary, he created an atmosphere of vagueness about whether special support for the occupied areas would cease and when this would happen. Stresemann openly stated that he did not share Luther's optimism that a balanced gold budget could be created on January 1: "I cannot share this optimism. I consider it impossible because there are certain expenditures which the Reich cannot avoid."[65] The dilemma, of course, was that these expenditures could not be met with more worthless paper, and here Louis Hagen, Adenauer, and others joined forces in trying to extract from

Stresemann whether the coming currency reform could really be enforced in the occupied areas. The Chancellor was something less than reassuring. He admitted that the new currency could only be introduced if there was a guarantee that the French would not confiscate it or turn it into an object of speculation with the objective of destroying its worth. He pointed out that, in contrast to traditional government money, the new money did not, strictly speaking, belong to the Reich but was rather given to it under guarantee of the economic sectors and had, therefore, to be handled more carefully than regular currency. While Adenauer emphasized that the French would take the money the minute the Reich ceased to pay the occupation costs in the old occupied areas (as was intended if the Reparations Commission did not provide some relief) Louis Hagen thought sequestration secondary because of his conviction that the French would never permit the mortgage on private assets in the occupied areas. Stresemann found it impossible to hide his own doubts on this score, and his unconvincing assurances only provoked Hagen, Adenauer, and others to raise the possibility of creating a separate currency for the occupied areas.

Hagen openly recognized the political dangers of such a step, warning that it would create "a new source of discord among our people,"[66] but he did not feel that they could go on without a valorized currency for more than a few days. Adenauer was even more dramatic, addressing himself directly to the Chancellor with the remark, "that you will have to concede to me, Herr Reich Chancellor: if there is no means of payment there anymore, then the people will beat one another to death." Adenauer was not, in any case, waiting upon events and announced that he had already summoned representatives of the various Rhenish cities to Cologne to issue a valorized emergency money. He also pointedly remarked to Stresemann that there might not be enough time to follow all the requirements recently laid down in a Finance Ministry decree governing the coverage of such money but that the requirements could be met retroactively since "conditions are such that things can explode any hour."[67] Under the circumstances, however, such proposals were welcome to Stresemann since he was seeking to encourage rather than discourage provisional

arrangements. Without wishing to prejudice the will of his Finance Minister, he assured Adenauer that this was no time to "dot i's" in carrying out decrees and that he and Ministers Fuchs and Sollmann, who were also present at the meeting, would defend such actions in the Cabinet, and he urged the cities to issue their emergency money as rapidly as possible. This interim solution was, in fact, widely welcomed by those attending the meeting. Stresemann, who fainted after the meeting, was able to leave Hagen knowing that unwelcome actions had been warded off and time and room for maneuver had been gained as he confronted the mess awaiting him in Berlin.

This maneuverability was increased further when Stresemann, with Luther's support, agreed on November 1 to compensate the Ruhr industrialists for their losses under the MICUM Agreements once the Reich finances were put in order. This problematic decision was justified by Stresemann and Luther on the grounds that unemployment support would have been more costly and that everything had to be done to hold on to the occupied territories. Nevertheless, it was opposed by Brauns, while the Social Democratic members of the Cabinet, who had never been consulted, abstained.[68]

Despite such "successes," there was good reason to wonder whether Germany could survive the remarkable combination of external and internal crises to which the country had fallen prey, and it could be argued that many Germans were doing everything conceivable to prevent the nation's pulling through. However friendly to Germany, General Smuts in a private conversation with Melchior expressed astonishment over the strong centrifugal tendencies in Germany, which he had always thought to be far more internally strong and united. Melchior used the occasion to suggest that this was not a natural condition but rather a product of the war and inflation:

I pointed out that Germany has lived in a pitiless state of war for the past nine years and that, as a result of this condition of privations, social dislocation through the economic submersion of our best circles, namely the educated middle classes, and finally through the feeling of hopelessness and national despair, a condition of general nervous excitement has set in which has to be taken into account if one wants to understand German conditions. In the last analysis, every state is composed of human beings, and among us eight or nine of every ten men is suffering from nervous illness. The exception naturally is the rural population which as everywhere is least affected by political changes.[69]

Certainly there was much to this interpretation, but the American correspondent Karl von Wiegand thought the problem more deeply rooted and privately reported:

The good old Reich is like a ship that has hit the rocks and is slowly going to pieces. The French ought to be happy at the prospect of attaining their goal, namely the dismemberment of the country. As to that, the Germans are in no small way to blame. They are at one another's throats like a lot of wolves instead of standing man to man by the ship and forgetting their petty quarrels. Germany is still a group of "tribes," not a nation or a people. The political horizon of most of them, and that includes the so-called leaders, doesn't extend much beyond their physical eyesight. They would rather be right and go to Hell than to be somewhat wrong occasionally and win out. It's in their blood and it runs back to the days of the Thirty Years War. As I wrote in one of my despatches the other day from Munich, Bavaria of today reminds me of the time of the feudal barons. Every "Big Chief" has his own army and is going to save the country in his own way, or the country can go to the . . . Bowwows.[70]

Conditions in Bavaria certainly spoke as much for Wiegand's interpretation as for Melchior's. The biggest "chief" in Bavaria after September 26 was General State Commissar von Kahr, who had been appointed by Minister-President von Knilling and whose high-handed tactics and protection of the host of right-wing paramilitary organizations in Bavaria ensured that the coexistence of two states of exception, one in the Reich and one in Bavaria, would maximize the already severe tensions between Munich and Berlin. The conflict between the two governments focused on the status of the Reichswehr commander in Bavaria, General von Lossow, who had referred Berlin's ban of the *Völkischer Beobachter* to von Kahr—thereby effectively negating it—and who had given primacy to the orders and authority of von Kahr over Defense Minister Gessler and the Reich government. When von Lossow finally was relieved of his command on October 20, Bavaria responded by assuming authority over the Seventh Reichswehr Division and retaining von Lossow in command.[71]

The fact that the Reich position was supported by the other state governments at a meeting on October 24 does not seem to have made much impression on the leaders in Munich, and the continuing standoff with Bavaria was one of the worst of Stresemann's tribulations. The more publicized aspects of the problem obscured yet a further issue of no small importance to the impending stabilization; namely, the fact that one-quarter of the Reichsbank's precious metal reserves were stored in Bavaria, that General State Commissar von Kahr insisted on being consulted about their transport to Berlin, and that there were vague intimations that some Bavarians were inclined to use the metal to back a currency of their own and reassert some of their prewar financial privileges. Indeed, Stresemann's sentiments about German and Bavarian political behavior were not much different from those of von Wiegand:

I really have the feeling that we will in the end not fall to the enemy but to ourselves. . . . Ajax fell through Ajax's strength. That is what one will someday place on the gravestone of the German people, if it does not free itself from partisan antagonism and the conflicts of the tribes, all of which mean nothing in comparison with the suffering of the entire people, and finally learn to separate the important from the trivial. All the things that have gone on between Munich and Berlin are trivial when one realizes that they ought not to come to a head right now [and] to one's having the feeling that the Reichswehr is not even a unified instrument in the hands of the German Reich.[72]

"Trivial" though they may have been, however, Stresemann's fear of the right-wing militants in Bavaria and lack of confidence in the loyalty of the army made it impossible for him to act decisively against Munich. Not only did the government refrain from a serious consideration of the use of military force against the Bavarians, but also the Reichsbank representative sent to Bavaria to deal with the transport of the precious metals stored there, Director Vocke, acted more like a petitioner than a representative of the legal owners of the metals. When Defense Minister Gessler sought to cut off payment to the Reichswehr in Bavaria, he was supported only by the Socialists and strongly opposed by Luther. It was precisely the differential treatment of Bavaria and Saxony that led to the resignation of the Social Democrats and the collapse of Stresemann's second Great Coalition government.

To be sure, the disposition to intervene in Saxony and Thuringia had been prepared by months of legitimate and well-grounded com-

The "German Day" of the Völkisch-Nationalist right and the Nazi S.A. in Nürnberg, September 9, 1923. (*By permission of the Ullstein Verlag*)

plaints of terror and mistreatment by Saxony's industrialists, farmers, and shopkeepers, and Stresemann's Saxon origins and political affiliation certainly predisposed him to their cause. His and Gessler's decisions to permit Reichswehr intervention in Saxony and Thuringia and then to use violent encounters between the troops and the workers as an excuse to appoint a Civil Commissar for Saxony on October 27 and to conduct a Reich Execution in Saxony on October 29 to eliminate the Communists from the government, however, were grounded in more immediate political considerations. With the Zeigner government out of the way and the Thuringian situation under control, the Reich had eliminated the "danger" to Bavaria and, with it, Bavaria's excuse for mobilization against the Communist threat on its borders. At the same time, Stresemann's tough action would also take some of the wind out of the sails of right-wing critics of his domestic policies. This is not to say that Stresemann wished to see the SPD leave his government. In contrast to the other bourgeois members of the Cabinet, who felt that the Bavarian situation could not be dealt with so long as the Socialists were in the government and who seemed anxious to move

to the right, he considered their presence highly desirable because of the economic and social decisions that would have to be taken in connection with the stabilization. Nevertheless, the political realities justified the risk, and this also explains why his action against Saxony had President Ebert's support. Whether one can similarly justify the risk taken by the Social Democrats, who were as much moved by the desire to maintain party solidarity as by righteous indignation, in abdicating power at so perilous a time both domestically and internationally is another question.[73]

The entry of the Reichswehr into Saxony with marching bands playing did have a certain tasteless quality, and even someone as happy to see the Communists kicked out as General Smuts felt that the "warlike-military" form of the operation was untoward and had created a bad impression in England. Yet, it is important to note that military control was welcomed by those who had felt victimized by the extreme-left regimes of the past:

The Saxon Bourgeois population greeted this development. The entire life in the towns suddenly took on another aspect. The shops which had previously closed their show-windows throughout the day, opening, if at all, merely the entrance door in order to be able to shut down at once in case of a repetition of the daily riots of the unemployed, again displayed their goods. The cafés and restaurants in the cities whose guests had repeatedly been forced to leave were again opened. In Dresden . . . the public spirit seemed entirely changed. Instead of the dead impression, which the closed shops had given to the city, the streets again became full of life, more cheerful and crowded, quite in contrast with the situation when everyone hurried away from the center of the town in order not to be molested by occasional riots. The reintroduction of the change of guard of the Reichswehr was cheered by thousands, throwing flowers on the soldiers, who seemed a protection to them and a guarantee for the discontinuance of the frequent riots which had occurred. The police force felt relieved at the support of the military authorities and at being no longer exposed to reproaches from their chief for energetic repression of the tumults and for not having been lenient enough toward the rioters, who usually bombarded them with stones and bottles.[74]

While the American observer making this report pointed out that "reasonable workmen" were also glad to see an end to the disorder, he admitted that they viewed the martial law as having the aim "of suppressing the laborers, of depriving them of the franchises won by the revolution and of making them again entirely dependent upon their employers," and he also felt compelled to point out that the high unemployment, high prices, and employer demand for the ten-hour day without increased wages "provided a good argument for influencing even reasonable workmen to believe in the above suggestions."

The danger that the socioeconomic measures of stabilization and the class conflict would be settled by bayonets surely was one reason for the Social Democrats to have thought twice about leaving office. The Communists had helped to bestir the right without gaining the allegiance of the left, and the latter was terribly weakened. As Sollmann himself had noted, the Reichswehr in Saxony had seen fit to recruit volunteers among extremely dubious elements, especially from the Stahlhelm, whose Halle branch had circulated a summons to its members in mid-October reading: "We wish the internal and external liberation of our Fatherland. Domestically, the overcoming of the Marxist, Jewish, pacifist world view, elimination of the red terror, gathering of all Germans on a national, volkish foundation."[75] Fascist and authoritarian forces had been strength-

ened. If they did not strike, it was only because the easy victories over the Communists had taken some of the wind out of their sails and because they were geographically and politically disunited. Though the reinforcement of the Bavarian border police and mobilization of various patriotic bands under the notorious Captain Ehrhardt on the Thuringian border were quite sensational and produced a good deal of sporadic violence, Reichswehr general Reinhardt's troops prevented the civil war that might have broken out had the Centuries and Bavarian fascists been left to their own devices. In northern Germany, where the right had been relatively quiet following an abortive putsch by the "Black Reichswehr" under Major Buchrucker on October 1, extreme right-wing organizations, especially in Pomerania and Brandenburg, now apparently looked primarily to Bavaria for action against Berlin, although both the northern leaders in the Agrarian League and some of the Bavarian leaders hoped that the Reichswehr would act in the person of General von Seeckt. At the end of October, Seeckt himself was once again contemplating the idea of a Directory of Seeckt, Minoux, and Wiedfeldt.[76]

The confusion and stalemate on the extreme right was strikingly revealed during a trip by the head of the Bavarian State Police, Colonel Hans von Seisser, to Berlin on November 3, when he visited with Seeckt, Minoux, and various agrarian and right-wing paramilitary leaders to test the waters; von Kahr and the Bavarian leaders hoped that the right-wing leaders in Berlin were prepared to act and that Bavaria could then support them. What Seisser discovered, however, was that the Reich Agrarian League and the leaders of the paramilitary leagues in the north, Colonel Friedrichs and Otto von Below, were looking to Bavaria. Director Kriegsheim of the Agrarian League was action-oriented enough, to be sure, declaring that the Agrarian League intended to continue fighting Stresemann and Ebert despite the departure of the Socialists from the Cabinet and that, as part of the struggle, they would hold back food. Nevertheless, both he and the paramilitary leaders pointed out that the patriotic associations and combat associations in the north were too weak to act alone and were waiting upon Bavaria.[77]

Although Seeckt was suspect to these groups and the Bavarian leaders, the support of a Directory by Seeckt and Minoux was known to Seisser and his superiors and constituted an alternative form of action that might be taken in Berlin. Seisser found much sympathy from Seeckt for Kahr's goal of a "national dictatorship" and "thoroughgoing measures against the Socialist garbage"[78] but a frustrating insistence on legality and caution. He found this as much the case with Minoux as with Seeckt. On the one hand, Seisser tried to reassure Minoux that Ludendorff and Hitler had given "binding assurances" to Lossow and himself that they would not undertake a Putsch, that both the troops and police were absolutely loyal to their leaders, and that the forces on the Thuringian border were under control. On the other hand, Kahr needed to know what was going on in Berlin because the situation had become very unclear as a result of the departure of the Socialists from the government and the situation had become "very difficult to bear. Bavaria is daily being pressed by the leagues, but also from North Germany to translate its plans to cleanse the Reich from the South into deeds." Minoux insisted, however, that the Bavarians simply had to live with the tension and avoid premature actions, a position he had been urged to take in dealing with the Bavarians by his former boss, Hugo Stinnes:

One has to have the nerves to wait, even if one runs the danger that the hunger and distress would become even greater. Only when things are hopelessly bad for the people, will they call for salvation or go over to self-help, which will then justify action from the other side, that is, the right. He must under all circumstances refuse under the present domestic situation and very especially in view of the international situation to participate in an undertaking which, like the Kapp Putsch, is directed against the constitution. For the same reasons, a pure military dictatorship is completely impossible. The power to be sure would lie with the soldiers, but this power must be covered on the outside by a civilian authority.[79]

Minoux shared the view, attributed to the Reich Agrarian League leaders, that the SPD withdrawal from the government was a "skillful chessboard move" behind which stood Ebert, whose refusal to sanction a non-parliamentary regime had been expressly stated in a private conversation with Minoux. Consequently,

Minoux believed that a break with both the President and Chancellor would be needed.

Whereas Minoux was counting on a break with Ebert, Seeckt was preparing the way for the replacement of Stresemann with the help of Ebert. Convinced that the extreme right could only be contained by a Cabinet that included the DNVP and knowing that the Nationalists would not enter a Cabinet under Stresemann, Seeckt now sought Ebert's support for a new "small cabinet with the character of a directory having exceptional powers" and received Ebert's permission to ask Ambassador Wiedfeldt in Washington to head such a regime.[80] Although Seeckt fired off a letter to Wiedfeldt on November 4 and, during the following days, responded to inquiries from Stresemann by making absolutely clear his view that it would be difficult if not impossible to restrain the right if Stresemann remained in office, Seeckt was careful not to declare that the Chancellor no longer had the confidence of the Reichswehr. Ebert responded to Stresemann's offer to resign by asking him to remain in charge of his rump Cabinet.[81] Indeed, Stresemann was able not only to contain Seeckt's pressure for a right-wing government and his resignation, but also to roll back the plans of the members in his own DVP who wished a sharper course to the right, arguing that this was the only way to persuade farmers to deliver food to the cities. They were bitterly critical of the failure to solve the currency and price questions, to change the course of social policy, and to come to terms with the Bavarians. In a dramatic encounter with the DVP Reichstag delegation on November 5, Stresemann, while certainly not stilling the criticism which continued during the next few days, dispelled any illusions that he was about to step down either under pressure or under force; he would not flee Berlin as had the government in the days of the Kapp Putsch:

This week will decide whether the patriotic associations will risk a battle. Civil war will mean loss of the Rhine and Ruhr and a Franco-Rhenish embrace. For this reason, the first requirement is order at home. The government has enough Reichswehr near Coburg, and the Reichswehr has declared that it would respond to any effort to coopt them by shooting. If the Reichswehr fails, then these groups will triumph. Then there possibly will be a German Nationalist dictatorship. I am sick and tired of leading a dog's life—

intrigues in the DVP, the attitude of the Pomeranian Agrarian League, treason to the Fatherland. How can one only deliver food if one likes the government? If the bands penetrate into Berlin, then I will not go to Stuttgart; then let them shoot me down on the spot where I have a right to be. Stop the conflict over the composition of the cabinet now, help me with economic and financial advice. An understanding with the Bavarian government is possible, but not with Kahr and the patriotic associations.[82]

At this moment, only Stinnes ventured to attack Stresemann to his face, arguing that the currency collapse was the result of his failure to follow a "production policy" and that "whoever cannot come to terms with Bavaria cannot rule in Germany." Stinnes was certain that England and the United States would be happiest to deal with a "legitimate right-wing government,"[83] a view Stresemann contested, arguing that "England, America, and even France would regard his fall as calamitous and that under these conditions he could not surrender his post."[84] While Stresemann and Stinnes agreed that a military dictatorship was undesirable, Stinnes privately believed that Wiedfeldt would be called back to serve as Chancellor and Foreign Minister, while Minoux would take over the Finance Ministry. The program of the new government would be

the reduction of the powers of the national state and local governments to the one naked function of preserving order and the alienation for a definite number of years of all other functions . . . to private ownership and control to the end that unproductive labor may be reduced to a minimum, that these functions may be efficiently and profitably managed and that a share of these profits may thereby be obtained for reparations purposes.[85]

Nevertheless, whatever the differences among most DVP politicians and businessmen, they were virtually at one in rejecting the extremists in Bavaria, and Stresemann's point about Kahr was very well taken. This was amply borne out on November 6, when the extremely influential HAPAG lobbyist Arndt von Holtzendorff visited Knilling and Kahr at the behest of Hamburg's most influential businessmen—Cuno, Warburg, and Melchior. The Bavarian leaders were most unlikely to be impressed with the views of Jewish bankers. They were also unlikely to be very impressed by Smuts's view, conveyed to Melchior, that the

Bavarians should suspend their quarrel with the Reich until the international situation was settled. Cuno, however, retained considerable popularity among the Bavarian rightists, and a message from him might make some impact. Cuno had just returned from the United States, where he had been trying to win financial support for Germany from various banking circles and to get more political backing for the German position from President Coolidge and Secretary of State Hughes. He then went to London on a similar mission. Cuno was especially anxious to keep the Bavarians from doing something stupid and sent Holtzendorff to emphasize the importance of civil order in Germany for the securing of English and American support against the French.[86]

Both Knilling and Kahr took the usual Bavarian line by assuring Holtzendorff that they had no aggressive intentions, that there was more danger from Pomerania and Mecklenburg than from Bavaria, and that the forces on the Thuringian border were necessary for Bavarian security. At the same time, they made no bones about their lack of support for Stresemann, and Knilling bluntly called for a right-wing government with dictatorial powers. He was not the least impressed when Holtzendorff warned that this would cause a general strike, replying that such a strike would be broken in two days since "the trade-union treasuries are empty and the hunger is hurting." Von Kahr was even more emphatic, banging his fist on the table and declaring:

"In Bavaria one obeys me and marches and shoots on order against whomever it might be, but no rifle will fire without my order!" He [von Kahr] went on that Germany has to group itself around Bavaria, and he regrets that he was not allowed to march into Saxony, for he would have brought order there in the shortest time. Now, once the Reichswehr turns its back, the old *Schweinerei* will start over again in Saxony.

Holtzendorff found the conversation most unsettling. While Knilling seemed relatively reasonable and hinted that he did not sympathize with everything that von Kahr said, the latter "gave the impression of being an absolute fanatic; even his eyes, I would almost say, are not those of a normal person."

Normal or not, however, von Kahr's strength and popularity derived from the appeal of his radicalism to those who felt victimized by the horrendous social and economic conditions he had been summoned to master. As one official reported,

> The dictatorship can only be popular through the employment of the penitentiary and death sentence against social parasites [*Volksschädlinge*]. There appears no higher ideal to the downtrodden people than the reduction of prices. Since the previous methods moved too much along the old tracks and were either ineffective or too slow, nothing remained but the economic isolation of Bavaria, the closing of the borders despite all threats of being deprived of coal and potatoes.[87]

In his role as special protector of Bavaria, von Kahr did gain short-term popularity by forcing farmers to deliver food to the cities, reducing rents and beer prices, and prosecuting profiteering cases with increased vigor. His bans on strikes and political demonstrations and his restrictive policies toward the left were undoubtedly also welcome in some circles. He seems to have enjoyed special popularity for his high-handed and brutal expulsion of Polish Jews, some of whom turned out to be old, well-established Bavarian Jewish families. This "pioneering" effort in what was to be one of the most fateful anti-Semitic acts of the later Nazi regime was often accompanied by gratuitous physical violence against Jews. Although they were reported to have made a "good impression" among Kahr's followers, the expulsions were protested by Bavarian industrialists. They certainly caused deep concern in Berlin, where fear of Polish reprisals and anxiety about a backlash in the United States, just at the moment when the Americans were being courted for both charity and diplomatic support, added to Berlin's displeasure with the goings-on in Bavaria.[88] All this did not prevent Kahr from fantasizing about his German mission, however, and he "celebrated" the November 9 Revolution with a "Manifesto on the Fifth Anniversary of the Red International over Germany" by announcing the victory over Marxism and declaring "the task of the age to be the creation of a new German person" by providing a "binding life idea" to the disunited masses inherited from the Revolution.[89]

There were, of course, even wilder and more rabid saviors of Germany in Munich in 1923,

and if some native Bavarian Jews were voluntarily fleeing Munich at this time, it was in fear that violent pogroms would be launched if Hitler and his National Socialists assumed power. Kahr, in fact, was beginning to lose popularity. As the British Consul General reported:

> Much as Herr von Kahr is liked and respected as an honest downright man, the suspicion has now dawned upon the Bavarians that he is not a very clever one. He has not, in fact, got the brains to be a dictator in a delicate and complex political situation. He never appears to consider in advance the possible or even probable consequences of his acts. Allusion has already been made . . . to his foolish orders regulating the price of beer, which no sooner had they been issued than they were found unworkable. He has been equally unsuccessful with an order attempting to regulate the prices charged in shops whereby the price should at least remain stable for the day and not fluctuate with every telegraphic report from Berlin as to the fluctuation of the dollar. He has issued orders to the police respecting the expulsion from Bavaria of certain categories of Jews . . . and when it was found that they must inevitably lead to international complications . . . they have not been enforced. His prestige has consequently suffered. He is abused by Hitler for his weakness, he falls foul of Knilling and the Bavarian Government for his obstinacy and lack of finesse in dealing with Berlin and he is chided by the public for not fulfilling their expectations.[90]

The Hitler–Ludendorff Putsch of November 9, 1923, demonstrated that the danger of the Nazi alternative was real enough, although it also showed the limits of the Nazi threat in 1923. Von Kahr was caught by surprise and cut a miserable figure in the entire affair. He and Seisser felt compelled to turn against the Nazis and, in the process, significantly to reduce the Bavarian threat to the Reich as well. As in the case of the Communists in Saxony, Thuringia, and Hamburg, so in the case of the fascists in Bavaria did geographical localization of the movements also isolate the latent civil war which they represented and kept the putschist danger on the periphery. The situation was very different from what it was to be a decade later.

Nevertheless, Hitler and his followers never could have developed that measure of strength which they did have or risked a putsch had they not enjoyed a considerable amount of sympathy as a result of the desperate conditions of the hyperinflation. Since the Nazis, like von Kahr, tended to treat the peasants as inflation profiteers, they appear to have been quite content to see the Putsch put down. The Nazis also seem to have received little worker support despite claiming to be a workers' party, although it is noteworthy that the workers in lower Bavaria appear to have been passive and even positive. As the local authorities reported, "workers are more moved by the development of price and currency conditions than political matters," and "in worker circles, even in a large portion of those that lean to the left, there is sympathy for Hitler, from whose enterprise one had hoped for an improvement of the economic situation."[91] If this was the case among some workers, it was even more so among students, who were probably most enthusiastic about conquering Germany—and getting something to eat at the same time:

As a rule one has no conception of the unbelievable distress ... which exists among the students. Many do not know how to still their hunger, and even less whether they can continue to study next month. Naturally, it would be a form of salvation for them to be enrolled in an army where they had regular meals and could eat their fill. The local authority believes that this is a not to be underestimated factor in the entire Hitler movement. A host of young people now living from hand to mouth hope thereby to rise again economically.[92]

Of all the analyses of the socioeconomic and political aspects of the Hitler Putsch, perhaps the most penetrating was supplied by the district President of Schwaben and Neuburg, Count von Spreti, who pointed out that the entire Nazi effort was hopelessly contradictory. As a unitarian movement emanating from Bavaria, it ran counter to Bavarian interests while at the same time being unacceptable in the north precisely because of its Bavarian origins. Its success could only be explained by the toleration of the Bavarian government, which was unwilling even to react against the *Völkischer Beobachter*'s open call for civil war. The National Socialists had simply capitalized on the nationalist and patriotic movement in Bavaria, but they were no more responsible for it than they were the labor party they claimed to be. In reality they were revolutionary:

The National Socialists have not created this [nationalist, patriotic] current, but they have exploited and misused it. Alongside the patriotic current there is namely yet a second, revolutionary current in the *Mittelstand.* All those who have had especially to suffer under the consequences of the war economically and socially, have become dissatisfied. The officer, the civil servant, the intellectual worker, the pensioner, the businessman, who have sunk down to the level of the distressed portions of the population, are embittered and jealous. They are in part a dangerous revolutionary element. Hitler and his people understand how to effectively exploit this fact. Slogans like "down with the November criminals, to the gallows with the profiteers and *Schieber,* with the black and white Jews" had magical power. Often they were treated as lapses. One should not take them ill, for one was dealing with patriotically minded people. In order to gather this protective cover firmly about themselves, one approached the youth, gave them uniforms, divided them in regiments and bataillons and kept them busy playing military games to satisfy their youthful ambition. Thus the heart of the matter was veiled. The heart of the matter was not mainly the patriotic idea but the revolutionary idea. Hitler can thank his success primarily to that. Quite justifiably, the National Socialist *Schwäbische Volksstimme* which appeared in Neuburg a.D. claimed the name *"National Revolutionaries"* for the National Socialists.[93]

What the events of November 9, 1923, had made clear, however, was that the "national revolutionary" would have to wait for another day and that it would have to capture Germany "legally" from Berlin. The "German Mussolini" had failed, and with the successful suppression of both the extreme right and the extreme left, Stresemann was in a position to compel the social forces which had supported them to settle into their discontents. Finally, although this was by no means totally clear at the moment because the government crisis was anything but over, the events in Saxony, Hamburg, and Bavaria had more or less set the seal on the schemes for creating a Directory. Seeckt, to be sure, continued to exercise emergency powers and remained a major political factor, but he had no inclination to act alone while his potential collaborators had no disposition to act. Minoux was insistent upon waiting for a condition of disorder that was much less likely to arise or take threatening form after the defeat of the Communists, and it was hard to pin hopes on a militant right that had been discredited by the Bavarian fiasco. As for Wiedfeldt, he was genuinely unwilling to play the role Seeckt wished to assign him. At the very time that Seeckt was asking him to assume a role in a Directory, Wiedfeldt was warning Berlin that any military government or effort at monarchical restoration in Germany would do damage to Germany's efforts to secure American support. He responded to the coded telegrams he had received through the Hamburg–America Line asking him to assume a role in what he termed a "dictatorship" by assuring Stresemann that he had nothing to do with them. Stresemann, therefore, had good reason to jest with Ambassador Houghton about reports of a Wiedfeldt Cabinet, and he made a point of releasing Wiedfeldt's disavowals to the press. The reality was that Wiedfeldt was not a political amateur like Seeckt and Minoux. When Wiedfeldt finally responded to Seeckt's letter of November 5 asking him to participate in the Directory on November 24, he pointed out that the creation of what he, out of consideration for English and American political values, termed a "protectorate" could not rest on the bayonets of the Reichswehr but rather required broad public support if it were to be able to deal effectively with the outside world. He did not feel that he himself enjoyed such backing since no party stood behind him, and he had the confidence neither of agriculture nor of most of organized labor. Indeed, he reminded Seeckt that he even represented a minority position in industry, as had been demonstrated by his having been on the losing side in the industrial credit offer of November 1921. While Wiedfeldt modestly excused himself on the grounds that he had been out of touch with internal German politics for too long and could do more good in the United States, it was quite clear that he never had any inclination to become a party to the Directory schemes and that he, like Stresemann, was convinced that one could not stabilize the economy with a regime that had the complete hostility of any of the major social groups, including organized labor.[94] Despite the Cabinet crisis, therefore, Stresemann's fundamental political approach to stabilization was strengthened by the events of November 9.

Introducing the Rentenmark

Whatever the historian's perception of the march of events from hindsight, however, it is necessary constantly to bear in mind that the Great Disorder was at its height at the end of October and the first weeks of November. The understandable concentration of historians on the more dramatic and decisive political upheavals in Saxony, Hamburg, Bavaria, and the Ruhr necessarily distracts attention from the extent to which the entire country was descending into chaos because of the hyperinflation. Kahr's organized anti-Semitic actions against the eastern Jews attracted the ire of Berlin for political and diplomatic reasons, but extreme measures against the Jews took place in the capital itself.

On November 5 and 6, angry mobs attacked the Jews in the Scheunenviertel around Alexanderplatz, plundering and wrecking shops and going from house to house and along the streets attacking anyone who looked Jewish, especially the easily identifiable Galician Jews, who were severely beaten and whose clothes were torn off. The pogrom-like actions of the mobs certainly must be seen in the context of the general plundering triggered by the raising of the bread price to a hundred forty billion marks on November 5, the reaction to which led to a reduction of the bread price to eighty billion the next day and the reintroduction of bread cards. The actual events in the Scheunenviertel were sparked by the violent reactions of unemployed workers, to whom Galician Jews apparently offered gold loan certificates in exchange for the emergency money with which unemployment support was paid. Oddly enough, the certificates were offered on good terms, beneficial to the purchasers if not to the government, but the atmosphere was poisoned not only by the distress of the workers but also by constant anti-Semitic agitation from the extreme right-wing press, the long-festering hostility to the Galician Jews, and reports that the Jews had bought up all the emergency money. This environment and the repeated cry, "beat the Jews to death," certainly is more relevant to understanding what happened than the scholastic question of whether the event was an actual pogrom or only what the critic Alfred Döblin described as the unloading of tension on the Jews and a present-day historian views as a part of the "every-day life [*Alltag*] of the inflation."[95] Far more relevant and illuminating than such catchwords in assessing the breadth and depth of anti-Semi-

Security Police with fixed bayonets clear a Berlin street where plundering has taken place. (*By permission of the Ullstein Verlag*)

tism in Germany at this time is the fact that such outbursts also took place in Erfurt, Nürnberg, Coburg, Bremen, and Oldenburg, and one wonders what would have happened if Hitler's Putsch had lasted longer and been more successful. Max Warburg certainly had no doubt. After hearing reports that anti-Semitic outbursts were in the offing and that agitators had been singling out his name in the streets, he fled Hamburg for the second time in slightly over a year—this time, to be sure, only for the twenty-four hours it took until the Munich Putsch was put down.[96]

In order to explore the hyperinflation as a final stage of a longer process of monetary disintegration and to explain the transition to stabilization, however, one must turn away from these spectacular events as well as from the well-known phenomena of people carting sacks full of money to meet payrolls and housewives waiting outside factories to collect and spend their husbands' pay as rapidly as possible. The chaos of this final phase can only be made intelligible and analyzed when one contemplates what the leaps of the exchange rate of the mark to the dollar during the final month of the hyperinflation (see Table 47) meant for the daily lives of those who were exposed to them as well as for the economy as a whole.

The task is made more difficult by the fact that the leaps in the official dollar exchange rate of the mark do not leap enough, because on October 21, the government issued a new foreign-exchange decree prohibiting the publication and use of any exchange rate except that officially established in Berlin. This final effort to control the exchange rate of the mark prior to the initiation of the Rentenmark hearkened back to the last abortive effort to create a unitary exchange rate in June 1923 and provoked the same skeptical responses as well as the usual hostility from commercial circles. As Lord D'Abernon wryly commented, the depreciation between October 19, when the measure

Table 47. Official Berlin Exchange Rate of the Paper Mark to the Dollar, October 15–November 20, 1923*

October	Exchange Rate	November	Exchange Rate
15	3,760,000,000	1	130,000,000,000
16	4,100,000,000	2	320,000,000,000
17	5,500,000,000	3	420,000,000,000
18	8,160,000,000	5	420,000,000,000
19	12,000,000,000	6	420,000,000,000
22	40,000,000,000	7	630,000,000,000
23	56,000,000,000	8	630,000,000,000
24	63,000,000,000	9	630,000,000,000
25	65,000,000,000	10	630,000,000,000
26	65,000,000,000	12	630,000,000,000
27	65,000,000,000	13	840,000,000,000
29	65,000,000,000	14	1,260,000,000,000
30	65,000,000,000	15	2,520,000,000,000
31	72,000,000,000	16	2,520,000,000,000
		17	2,520,000,000,000
		19	2,520,000,000,000
		20	4,200,000,000,000

Source: Statistisches Reichsamt, *Zahlen zur Geldentwertung in Deutschland 1914 bis 1923* [Sonderheft 1 zu *Wirtschaft und Statistik,* Bd. 5] (Berlin 1925), p. 10.
*Excluding Sundays and days when no official notation was made.

was announced, and its implementation three days later was "equal approximately to one mark for every second which has elapsed since the birth of Christ."[97] The banker Carl Melchior was more concerned with the longer term consequences of the measure and privately warned the government that the deliberate overvaluation of the paper mark at a time when businesspeople were forced to accept the paper mark but were calculating in gold values would lead to excessive increases in domestic prices.[98] The new decree was not greeted with the same hue and cry from Hamburg as its June counterpart but rather with a tone of *déjà vu* and a decision to make the standard complaints through the Hamburg representative in Berlin. This undoubtedly was because there was no foreign demand whatever for marks and thus little effect on international commerce. Furthermore, the June experience had demonstrated the futility of the measure in the occupied areas, and it was likely that the "hole in the West" would function again. It was also fairly clear that the motives of the government were primarily domestic. On the one hand, the unitary exchange rate was aimed to quiet consumer anxieties about the food situation by forcing shopkeepers to accept the paper mark at a controlled rate of exchange, and a regulation requiring food stores to stay open during normal business hours shortly followed. On the other hand, the gold

loan was exempted from the unitary exchange rate in the hope that this would increase demand for it while demand for foreign exchange would be reduced. Despite its unpopularity in business circles and Koeth's hostility, it can be argued that Luther had made the correct decision in seeking to slow down the domestic depreciation of the mark during this crucial period. Much would depend on the avoidance of too great a gap between the external value of the mark and the controlled exchange rate and the manner in which the gold loan was marketed.[99]

Whatever the case, the unitary exchange rate was reestablished for political reasons, and its futility in the occupied areas was demonstrated immediately. The reason, quite simply, was that the official rate was one-third to one-fifth below what one could get exchanging dollars for marks privately in unoccupied Germany and even more worthless in occupied Germany. In the Cologne area, the average rate of exchange of the mark to the dollar was 14,871,875,000 for the week October 15–22, rising to 92,288,000,000, for the week October 23–29, and to 1,190,714,000,000 for the week October 30–November 5.[100] The official exchange rate, therefore, was of little importance in the Rhenish-Westphalian region.

Conditions in the occupied areas were symptomatic of the urgent need for rapid currency reform. The cost of living in Cologne on October 22 for a family of four for four weeks for the barest necessities was 504,695,395,848 marks. It had increased by 602.31 percent to 1,563,104,700,000 marks on October 29 and then rose another 608.71 percent by November 2 to 15,554,575,000,000 marks. A "multiplicator" (multiplier) was used to calculate wages and was based on the exchange rate, which varied according to the highly volatile political circumstances of this period. Furthermore, while the multiplier used in the unoccupied areas was based on the official exchange rate of the mark in Berlin, that employed in the occupied areas tended to follow the quotations of the branches of foreign banks in the area and were thus often more than 50 percent higher. Even so, the officials charged with setting the multiplier did not always follow the exchange rate. For example, during the first days of the week of October 15–22, the multiplier was only one-half or one-third of the gold parity, while it was more or less at gold parity at the end of the week. What such varying calculations and the use of the multiplier meant for workers was described by the American Consul in Cologne:

Wages are usually paid weekly, that is, on Fridays, after working hours. Last Friday, the Multiplicator . . . was 27 billions. After receiving their pay there was hardly any opportunity to make purchases as it was the end of the working day, and the next day, Saturday, the Multiplicator was 65 billions, and was raised successively to 250 billions before the next payday.[101]

Some firms, like Krupp, sought to reduce such difficulties by paying their workers every three or four days, and white-collar workers in the Ruhr seem to have been paid every three to five days. Special payments in kind and cash prepayments aside, however, weekly pay seems to have remained the rule for most blue-collar workers.[102] The multiplier was used by everyone, but as the U.S. Consul in Koblenz reported, some merchants, unable to deal with its fluctuations and tiring of consumer complaints about the manner in which merchants sought to survive by allowing themselves safe margins, had simply gone over to calculating in francs. Such merchants would still accept payment in marks at the daily bank rate, but some farmers in the region simply insisted on payment in francs for their potatoes, even if they were half rotten. Another illustration of the manner in which people were "adapting themselves to cir-

cumstances,"[103] albeit in a somewhat less radical fashion, was the use of so-called "merchandise certificates." The Cologne Association of Importers of Meats and Fats used certificates good for a certain number of pounds of American lard which they sold to the cities and employer organizations. The lard for the workers was then purchased from the retailers with these certificates after a percentage was added for taxes and profit, thereby enabling the retailer to replenish his stock.

As this illustration shows, rather complex techniques could be developed to deal with the loss of real purchasing power in the hyperinflation. Certainly, the certificate solution was more sophisticated than that used by the Berlin metal industrialists at the end of October. They finally responded to the astronomical increases in bread prices and the growing worthlessness of the wages they were paying simply by giving their workers a daily compensation of "three breads."[104]

Berlin, of course, was particularly tense, but the situation in the Stuttgart area and Württemberg may be taken as a good illustration of conditions in a less historically prominent unoccupied area of Germany. As elsewhere in the country, the long-established practice of denominating export sales in foreign currencies was now being extended to the retail trades and domestic transactions, albeit in an indirect manner. The American Consul explained:

The retail stores in Stuttgart have now adopted the Gold Mark as a price basis or ground price. As there are no gold marks in circulation, in order to convert the price into paper marks with which the purchaser pays for the goods, a multiplier is used. This multiplier varies from day to day according to the Berlin rate of exchange on New York of the day previous. To give a concrete example: On October 21, 1923, half a metric ton of egg shaped coal briquettes were purchased at a price of Gold Marks 44.30. The bill was presented on October 22nd and paid for the same day. The multiplier on that day was 2,858,000,000 equals 126,610,000,000 paper marks which was the amount actually paid. Had the purchaser delayed one day in making payment, a multiplier of 9,523,000,000 would have been used and the coal would then have cost him 421,868,900,000 paper marks; had he delayed another day he would have had to use a multiplier of 13,366,000,000 so that the cost would have been 592,113,800,000 paper marks, or nearly six times as great as he actually paid. Under these circumstances the purchaser pays his bills on the date of receipt of the goods so as to avoid loss through depreciation in the value of the paper currency. The seller on the other hand gets rid of the paper marks just as soon as possible for the same reason.[105]

These practices are familiar enough from the past history of the inflation, but their acceleration produced some variations and consequences that were qualitatively different from the past. Transactions had been made utterly frenetic, even when compared to 1922. The advantages to the buyer of delaying payment had been significantly diminished by the use of the multiplier, while the seller quite literally could not wait to get rid of his money. In the last analysis, however, both were being driven out of business because hyperinflation was driving prices out of reach:

As the mark declined in value, prices and wages rise. But at times when there is an extraordinary drop in the value of the mark, prices do not rise as rapidly as the mark falls. Therefore, conversions made at such times show prices and wages in dollars to be very low. After a few days of rapid decline, the mark usually becomes stabilized for a short time and prices generally continue to rise to such an extent as to be very high when expressed in American currency. It is only by taking statistics over a considerable period of time that it is possible to obtain a true picture of the rise of prices expressed in American currency. In October 1922, one meter of woolen suiting cost $2.00 while in October 1923 the price was $7.50; shoes last year cost from $2.50 to $3.00 per pair as compared with $7.50 at present. In other words, the purchasing power of the dollar is today about 400 percent less than a year ago.[106]

The largest retail store in Stuttgart reported not only that it had experienced a big decrease of sales but also that what it had sold had not covered expenses and that it would be unable to restock. Needless to say, the chief industries of the region—paper, leather, textiles, automobiles, and machines (especially the first three)—were finding it hard to sell both at home and abroad. As everywhere else in Germany, these circumstances had a devastating effect on worker wages and consumption. In the Stuttgart area, in real terms, textile and wood workers received less than one-tenth, metal workers less than one-eighth, and construction workers less than two-thirds of their prewar hourly wages on October 15, 1923. The actual value of the wages could vary 100 percent from one week to the next, and the differentials necessarily caused bad blood.

Indeed, what is most difficult to recapture or replicate is the immense nervous strain which the conditions imposed on all forms of economic activity and socioeconomic relationships:

We see in economic life how a grating struggle is carried on between suppliers and customers by means of an endless and fruitless correspondence, which is again and again concerned with payment conditions, that is, in other words about the question of who should bear the loss which today is entailed by owning marks for one day, even for a few hours. The same struggle over the distribution of the risk of depreciation dominates and poisons the relations among banks, industry, and commerce. Above all, however, this shatters the relations between employers and workers in the factories. The wage and salary earner is in constant unrest over the moment of his payment, because the time of payment decisively determines whether the paper mark wage is capable of securing the real goods needed for the support of himself and his family. The question of payment in the morning or the afternoon often plays practically the same role as negotiations about a wage rate difference of 100 percent. Under the pressure of this constant agitation about time of payment, the employers for their part are forced to use every means to get cash payments from their customers with the greatest possible speed. This then again causes every consumer to be burdened with a multitude of worries about getting rid of his money quickly at the right moment and at the right place. Today he had best pay his gas bill, tomorrow his electricity, the day after next, meeting the deadline for paying his newspaper subscription at the old price. And thus it goes on, each person, especially each housewife is under pressure to spend the money received quickly and correctly. In many cases it is not made easy to get rid of the money. A wearing, hour-long standing on line, today at the tax offices, tomorrow at the post office, and the next day at the gas company is necessary. To this is added the worst worry about the periodic complete absence of certain foodstuffs. At one moment potatoes are not to be had, the next time the milk supply ceases even in the modest confines allowed by the ration cards, the third time payment for potatoes is demanded not in marks but in dollar certificates, the procurement of which, leaving aside the going exchange rate, involves effort and cost.[107]

Little wonder that Ernst Barlach exclaimed in a letter that he found "every hour and every minute spent not thinking about money or money worries an immeasurable blessing."[108]

Unhappily, there was more and more money and kinds of money to think about as amounts required for purchases became astronomical. During the final months of the hyperinflation, monetary production reached its apogee, especially the manufacture of emergency money (*Notgeld*). If the Reichsbank failed to meet the demands of the economy for paper money, it was not for lack of effort. There were 2,504,956 trillion paper marks (equal to 353.1 million gold marks) in circulation at the end of October, 400,338,326 trillion (equal to 551.7 million gold marks) at the end of November and 496,585,346 trillion (equal to 393.6 million gold marks) at the end of December. While the physical difficulties of managing such large amounts in daily transactions were unavoidable, the Reichsbank did its best to produce larger and larger bills to remedy the situation. In addition to the Reich Printing Office, eighty-four printing establishments were directly involved in monetary production, and another forty-eight were assisting as well. In 1923, over thirty paper factories were producing for no other purpose, while twenty-nine galvanized-plate manufacturers delivered four hundred thousand plates for the printing of the money. On September 27, a fifty-million-mark note was issued; one-, five- and ten-billion-mark notes followed early in October; on November 2, matters had progressed to the point where the Reichsbank issued a hundred-trillion-mark note. The announcement of these new notes was made with all due formality and specifications given as to design, color, and other characteristics. It is noteworthy, nevertheless, that the reverse sides of these notes were left blank and that the Reichsbank reserved the right to recall the notes and exchange these against another currency in January and February 1924.[109]

All this was quite insufficient, however, and though the Reichsbank's new bills had taken on some of the qualities of emergency money in appearance and in the suggestion that the time of their circulation would be limited, there were still over fifty-eight hundred sources supplying emergency money in the last months of the Great Inflation. On the one hand, this emergency money was essential to keep portions of the economy going; on the other, it exacerbated the hyperinflation. In considering this emergency money, it is important to distinguish between authorized emergency money backed by

real values and fiat money without any backing at all. The first category included the money issued by the Reich Railroad System and the money issued on the basis of the gold loan and dollar Treasury certificates. The amount of such money, about three hundred and fifty million gold marks, was more or less the equivalent of all the Reichsbank money in circulation. To the second category belonged yet another four hundred trillion to five hundred trillion in paper without backing. In short, the total amount of emergency money was twice the amount of Reichsbank money in circulation, and nearly half the emergency money was fiat.[110]

All sorts of money was being issued by firms, municipalities, the states, and other public and private agencies. The Reich Finance Ministry strove to regulate and control the issuance of such money and to make sure that it was backed by real security, but control was lost in the last two months of the inflation. The unbacked emergency money issued by private firms and municipalities at this time was a quintessential illustration of the inflation as something of a "racket" in the public good. The Krupp firm, for example, according to the firm's own records, received through the issue of emergency money an interest-free loan during the hyperinflation of twenty-three million gold marks, which was about four million more than the average earnings of the firm during the business year 1923–1924. Much of the money was unbacked, although the firm claimed that it was backed by the securities it held in other firms, such as Mannesmann. What was really thought of the obligation involved in this "backing" was demonstrated at an internal discussion, in which it was pointed out that "given the present paper mark depreciation, these emergency money obligations play no role any more, so that the securities actually stand freely at our disposal."[111] Krupp's name, of course, counted for a great deal, and even the Reichsbank seems to have given out some Krupp money, but it was used chiefly by Krupp workers and the citizens of Essen to buy food. Typically, the emergency money of firms like Krupp were used in company stores and local retail stores and eventually flowed back into the firm. The public service aspect of the "racket," therefore, was very real, for as an internal report noted with regard to the last months of the inflation:

The company store on the one hand and the emergency money printing plant . . . on the other were the most important operations of the firm; they both made possible the ultimate continuation of the firm and of the population and thereby saved their existence. That the production of emergency money as a consequence of the inflation brought the firm a not inconsequential profit should not be ignored.[112]

Similar operations were conducted by municipalities, and, indeed, Krupp's performance was a model of probity compared to that of the Rhenish town of Ödenkirchen and its savings bank, which conspired together to issue trillions more in emergency money than was actually required by the population, lent its newly created money to various banks and private persons at 200 percent interest a month, and then later refused even to redeem some of the emergency money that had landed in the vaults of the branch of the Reichsbank in Mönchen-Gladbach.[113] The issuance of emergency money undoubtedly was more controlled in Württemberg than in the Rhineland, and yet it was later determined that more than thirty cities, ten banks and savings banks, and ten firms had given out emergency money in an illegal or irregular manner. Since the permission to grant such money was usually granted on the basis of frantic telegraphic interchanges between those claiming the need to do so, the government in Stuttgart, and the Finance Ministry in Berlin, the borderline between regularity and irregularity was increasingly blurred, and it is no wonder that the Württemberg government later dropped all charges against violaters of the regulations on the ground that the emergency had been too great. Its sympathies clearly lay with those who felt the need to issue the money, especially since it fully identified with complaints about the failure of the Reich government to fulfill its obligations to muncipalities on time and felt that the Reichsbank was failing to send enough money to the state and was favoring the north over the south.[114]

Even emergency money with backing, however, was not always accepted, and if one depended upon it, then it was best to stay home. A trip from Stuttgart to Berlin with such money was an "incalculable adventure," in which perfectly respectable businessmen could easily end up at the railroad station's traveler's aid office (*Bahnhofsmission*). As the Württemberg representative in Berlin reported, a day did not pass

where business people do not turn to the embassy to complain that the Württemberg money is not accepted anywhere here. . . . In large part they are Württembergers who have travelled here with only Württemberg money and found themselves in the most embarrassing situation because they cannot survive with it and cannot even buy a ticket to go home. . . . Naturally, it is completely impossible for me to help out in these cases, and I have to send them away.[115]

The enormous varieties of money, even valorized money, in circulation, however, were also a danger in another sense because they created immense confusion and increased insecurity. This played no small role in the violence in Berlin in early November. As a major newspaper reported:

Naturally, the nervousness of the public is fed by the fact that they cannot distinguish among the various forms of money in circulation with respect to their value. The gold loan is confused with the dollar certificates, and the new municipal money denominated in portions of the dollar is not familiar at all.[116]

What money could be familiar when new monies were constantly being created and others were being planned? Button marks? Someone proposed to the editor of the *Frankfurter Zeitung*, apparently in all seriousness, a currency reform based on buttons, whose various denominations would be determined by quality and type. Since buttons were readily available, and quite familiar to all housewives, the new currency could be introduced rapidly![117]

The button mark would at least have had the virtue of being a national currency, which could not be said of most of the currencies circulating, and one of the worst dangers to the unity and monetary sovereignty of the Reich and to the forthcoming currency reform were some of the valorized currencies issued or under discussion at the state level. The most famous and obvious of these, the projected special bank of issue for the occupied areas that might become necessary if the Rentenmark could not be introduced there, was not the only danger in this respect. The businessmen of Hamburg, critical of the

Rentenmark project from the start and most favorable toward Schacht's idea of a gold-backed currency, were already contemplating the creation of a special bank of issue in September.[118] If they held back, it was primarily because the creation of a "German dollar" would finish the destruction of the paper mark. Thus, when Mayor Diestel was under severe pressure from the dockworkers to pay valorized wages, the leading firms of the city chose to lend him fifty thousand pounds and bide their time. The Communist uprising of October 23 convinced them that they could no longer wait upon Berlin to create a valorized currency, and the Hamburg Bank of 1923 was founded two days later by 103 Hamburg firms, 64 of which were banks and the remainder commercial and industrial firms and shipping companies. These firms were permitted to open gold-denominated accounts in return for the deposit of U.S. dollars or other solid currencies. The bank then deposited all the dollars it received in American banks, and the monetary issue of the Hamburg Bank of 1923, initially twelve million gold marks and ultimately to rise to forty-six million gold marks, was fully backed by dollar deposits.[119]

The new currency, made in the city mint, was issued in two- and five-gold-mark notes and subsequently in gold pfennig as well. They were popularly known as "giro marks" and officially stamped as "clearing certificates" (*Verrechnungsanweisungen*). They enjoyed rapid acceptance because of their full dollar backing. On November 4, the shipyard workers and shipping company personnel were the first to receive payment in the new money. Since the new bank could hardly satisfy the demands of all the workers in Hamburg, and it was impossible to have one set of workers receiving gold marks and the other paper, the Senate of Hamburg also purchased large amounts of the Reich gold loan and was thus in a position to issue gold-loan emergency money to satisfy demand. Officially, the Hamburg giro marks were meant to serve only until the time when the new Rentenmark would be available in sufficient amounts, and the money-issuing operations of the bank were expected to terminate at the end of November. As early as October 31, however, the shipbuilder Rudolf Blohm was urging the issuance of longer-term certificates, on the one

hand, so that workers would save them and thus be in a position, as he concretely put it, to buy new boots and a new suit in a few months and, on the other hand, so that farmers would have the kind of solid money needed to ensure that they would supply Hamburg with food at the next harvest.[120]

The assumption, of course, was that retailers, who were calculating their prices on the basis of the exchange rate, would start to calculate in the new currency and the real values it represented. This was a very big assumption, and the impulse to save Hamburg giro marks as a longer-term investment became all the greater because of the regulation that paper marks had to be accepted in domestic commerce and its exploitation by retailers. Such abuse was possible because the value of the paper mark relative to the dollar was kept artificially high by the unitary exchange rate set in Berlin. Retailers were taking advantage of this exchange rate to calculate their prices at the official rate and then charge their customers accordingly, irrespective of whether they were paying in paper marks or giro marks. Hamburg employers complained bitterly, as did workers, that it was outrageous to charge a worker paying in giro marks 1.38 gold marks for bread, or the exorbitant price of thirty-three cents, because the official rate for the gold mark was one billion paper marks at the moment and for the dollar was 4.2 gold marks. The bakers claimed that the cost of the American flour they purchased was well over the official exchange rate, and that they were thus entitled to calculate a price of 138 billion paper marks or 1.38 giro marks for a loaf of bread. This was a good illustration of why the unitary course did not work, but the practice was totally unfair to the giro-mark customer. This battle between retailers, who were now stating their prices in foreign-exchange values, on the one hand, and industrialists and workers, on the other hand, would presumably end once the paper mark ceased to be printed and the Rentenmark came into force. As the American Consul in Hamburg cynically noted, however:

Whether the [Rentenmark] will meet with a much happier fate than the paper mark is more than doubtful. Personally I see no reason why it should. A note covered by a mortgage on a part of the assets of a country's population is merely an invitation to take part in a lawsuit in which you are both plaintiff and defendant, and the chances of gaining which are nil. It is to be added that people are already commencing to hoard Hamburg goldmarks which they have bought at prevailing low rates, on the practical certainty of being able to cash them for paper marks or dollars at a much higher rate later.[121]

All this demonstrated the extent to which the Reich was in danger of losing control of price levels in Germany not only prior to the issuance of the Rentenmark but even after the reform took place. The pricing policies of Hamburg retailers illustrated the manner in which the unified exchange rate was serving to drive up real prices within Germany and making the downward adjustment of real wages to meet the requirements of stabilization even more difficult than it would be in any case. It was no more possible to dictate the exchange rate successfully at this time than it was to compel retailers to ask for paper marks for their goods. The fixed exchange rate was, in essence, "a new form of setting price ceilings,"[122] and German merchants now had almost a decade of practice in their circumvention. Within the Cabinet, Economics Minister Koeth led the fight to permit retailers to denominate their prices in gold values, and he won his point on November 2 despite the reservations of some of his colleagues. There really was little choice, however, because this is what retailers were doing anyway, and if Berlin did not act, then decisions would be made on the state or local level. Württemberg and Baden had already formally permitted shops to state prices in gold values. The Prussian Justice Ministry and police were about to tolerate such practices themselves, and it was difficult to reject their pleas that the Reich make uniformity possible by taking the initiative.

Concurrently, the Cabinet decided to extend the unitary exchange rate to the gold loan. The attempt to use an uncontrolled exchange rate for the gold loan as a means of soaking up paper marks and increasing demand for the gold loan had failed because the Reichsbank had delayed its delivery of the gold-loan emergency money purchased through the banks with large amounts of paper marks by big customers. The delay permitted a depreciation of the real value of the paper marks used to purchase the gold loan, increased the paper-mark liquidity of the

banks, reduced interest rates, and promoted speculation in foreign exchange and securities with the paper money. Once the Reichsbank realized its mistake, it began to demand payment and thereby produced a shortage of both paper marks and the gold-loan marks because the banks now hoarded the latter. The Finance Ministry decision to allow the gold-loan marks to float having thus failed of its purpose, there remained no choice but to include the gold-loan marks in the unitary exchange rate and treat them like the dollar. The experience provided further proof that the Reichsbank leadership was inadequate to the tasks of the stabilization and did not bode well for the ability of the government and Reichsbank to meet the demand for the forthcoming Rentenmark in a timely fashion.[123]

More immediately, the creation of the Hamburg Bank of 1923 demonstrated what could happen if the Reich delayed much longer with the currency reform. Hamburg was the only state to found a genuine bank of issue, although a Holsteinische Goldgirobank was also being created in Kiel. The idea, however, was widespread and the tendency to act on it increasing. This was, of course, especially the case in the Rhineland because of its special problems, and a committee composed of Mayor Adenauer; the bankers Louis Hagen, Robert Pferdemenges, and Wilhelm von Waldthausen; and the industrialists Vögler and Silverberg had drawn up a plan by early November for a bank of issue with capital of a hundred million to a hundred fifty million gold marks. They were working closely with other Rhenish leaders, such as Rhenish banker Georg Solmssen of the Disconto-Gesellschaft, Mayor Jarres of Duisburg, and Moldenhauer. For the moment at least, they refrained from action because Berlin was holding them back with promises of more valorized money and the prospect that its negotiations with the Allies for the acceptance of the Rentenmark in the occupied areas might be successful. The signals from Berlin were mixed, however, and Solmssen noted that some Finance Ministry officials seemed to be suggesting that they might welcome "being released from the financing of the Rhine and Ruhr areas."[124]

This made the maintenance of the monetary sovereignty in the rest of Germany all the more important, however, and heightened the significance of the Hamburg example. A special problem was being presented by the four states with private note-issuing banks—Bavaria, Baden, Württemberg, and Saxony—which had been arbitrarily exceeding the contingents approved by the Reichsrat. While it was true that the contingents had totally failed to keep pace with the depreciation, the unilateral increases of these contingents were a challenge to the authority of the government and the Reichsbank.[125] The issuance of new valorized currencies, therefore, could be viewed as the logical next step in a progression of such challenges. In Baden, a bank of issue was created for the limited purpose of purchasing the harvest, and the government there had assisted by placing its forests as security for its "Baden-Dollar." Württemberg was holding back because it wished to use its forests as a guarantee for a foreign loan. Saxony was less inhibited; it had pledged some of its resources for a loan it had already taken out and yet was, nevertheless, using what it had mortgaged to back the gold-denominated money it was issuing! The Bavarians made vague threats of issuing their own currency and intimated that they might use the Reichsbank precious metals stored in Bavaria to back it, but warnings by industrialist Robert Röchling that Bavaria's economy was too integrated into that of the Reich to go it alone seemed to have a sobering effect. Nevertheless, the situation did cause industrialists and the Bayerische Vereinsbank to consider following the Hamburg example, but Bavarian Finance Minister Wilhelm Krausneck seems to have been rather cool to the project. He feared that the new money would be rapidly hoarded and refused under all circumstances to open the valuable Bavarian forests to exploitation for such purposes. Still, plans were afoot to have the Bavarian power works issue a gold-backed scrip. Bremen, Hessen, and Oldenburg were also working on money-issuing projects.[126]

Most serious potentially was the pressure from the Prussian Agriculture Minister for a Prussian bank of issue to satisfy farmers, and the undesirability of such a step was spelled out very clearly by the Centrist Prussian Minister of Welfare, Heinrich Hirtseifer, on November 10. While agreeing that the issuance of a valorized

currency was of the utmost urgency, he pointed out that the real questions were when and by whom such a currency should be issued. The timing, in his view, depended upon a reduction of expenditure—"above all, the cessation of the monstrously increased expenditures for unemployment support in the occupied areas during the last two weeks," as well as such more long-term measures as the proper collection of taxes, increased exports, and especially increased hours of work. Once the preconditions had been met, however, then the issuance of the new currency was the task of the Reich, not Prussia:

If the Reich does not retain monetary sovereignty, then one will have such a monumental step backward into particularism, that the domestic political consequences cannot be taken seriously enough. The creation of a Prussian valorized currency is only to be considered in my view if the preconditions for the establishment of a valorized currency in the Reich are present but the Reich does not move toward a currency reform despite the fact.[127]

Luther did not really think the preconditions were present, but he was moving toward the reform anyway, as he confessed to the Finance Ministers of the states on the very day Hirtseifer was penning the above-quoted lines. Luther and his leading officials conveyed an "impression of hopelessness." They appeared "overworked" and "at sea" and "lacked the slightest inclination to hold the meeting."[128] Luther repeatedly emphasized that he had only agreed to the issuance of the new currency on November 15 under the "pressure of the street" and that he considered the timetable "too hasty." Two situations troubled him particularly. First, not enough of the new money was being produced to satisfy demand. This had been a concern from the outset, but the November 15 currency-reform date was now being put into doubt by the outbreak of a printers' strike on November 10. The strike was motivated in Luther's view by the "fear that numerous printers could be let go if the money presses are shut down." Furthermore, the Reichsbank and the Post Office were claiming that they could not institute clearing operations for the new currency before December 1. He also did not think it possible to set a fixed rate of exchange between the Rentenmark and the paper mark by

November 15, since it was unclear whether the three hundred million Rentenmark to be set aside for this purpose would be available.

The second distressing circumstance of which Luther complained was that his intention to use the Rentenmarks available on November 15 primarily to pay the government employees at all levels of government had been undermined by the Administrative Council of the Rentenbank, which had decided that half of the available money had to be used to satisfy the needs of industry and commerce. This meant that only the civil servants and clerical help could receive partial payment in Rentenmark initially and that this would amount to 30 and not the originally intended 50 percent of their pay. If the states and municipalities were going to get any of the new money for their workers, it could only be through negotiating for a share of that made available to their local industries. Since the printing of paper marks would cease on November 15, all government entities were going to have to reduce their expenditures and cut their payrolls if they were to have enough money available to pay their employees.

Needless to say, the state Finance Ministers found this report of the Reich Finance Ministry detailing what the situation would be like in five days time anything but reassuring. The Prussian Finance Minister, von Richter, was especially upset that Rentenmarks would not be made available for purchasing food and warned that the cities would starve if they could not offer a valorized currency to the farmers. Furthermore, he and his colleagues reminded the Reich Finance Ministry that the basic taxing power lay with the Reich, that the Reich was appropriating much of the taxes that were supposed to go to the states, and that they remained dependent on the Reich for subsidies. These points were made even more sharply by the Hamburg State Finance Councillor, Lippmann, who blamed the disastrous increases in prices in Hamburg on the unitary exchange rate, shortage of valorized money, and continued use of the paper mark. He pointed out to Luther that "If the Reich credits are now closed off, the states and municipalities, in order to prevent chaos, must eventually issue money themselves." So long as they could not collect valorized revenues themselves, they were dependent upon Reich credits and could not pay

these back in valorized form. This was indeed a touchy issue, since the Finance Ministry had recently sent around a note to the states informing them that repayment of all future paper-mark credits would be valorized. It was a measure of the Finance Ministry's anxieties about the availability of sufficient sums of the Rentenmark that Ministerial Director von Schlieben now clearly hinted that the note was not to be taken seriously. He urged the states to call up any credits from the Reich already allocated but not yet taken and explained that "the states will in this way gain possession of larger amounts of paper marks for the transitional period. For the Reich, the calling up of these sums will be advantageous in that the money will still be at its disposition until November 15, while after the 15th such paper amounts based on treasury notes that have already been discounted can no longer be granted." When the Hamburg Finance Minister explicitly pressed von Schlieben on the question of whether or not these loans would be valorized, Schlieben responded that "he could only advise the states to call up the money and what happens later will work itself out."

If this was a most uninspiring performance, it must also be said that the position of Luther and his staff was an impossible one. They could not issue money unless it was printed, and the printers were on strike. It was hard at once to be responsible for maintaining liquidity and reducing it; that is, for organizing the issuance of the new currency and determining its relationship to the other available media of exchange, on the one hand, and for presiding over retrenchment and revenue collection, on the other. Matters had been allowed to "work themselves out" for years, and the results were visible to all. The technical questions involved in converting the entire economy to valorized media of exchange had to be managed with more technical precision than the strains on the Finance Ministry would allow and ingrained habits of the Reichsbank would permit.

The most solvable of these problems proved to be the printers' strike. On November 11, General von Seeckt exercised his emergency powers to ban strikes in all plants producing bank notes and to take the strike leaders into protective custody. Most effective in breaking the strike and forcing a rapid negotiated settlement was the manner in which the printers' tasks were energetically taken over by some of the workers and officials at the Reich Printing Office and especially by the strike-breaking organization set up to deal with stoppages in vital public works, the Technical Emergency Service (Technische Nothilfe). Thus, while certainly reducing the quantity of Rentenmark available on November 15, the strike did not delay the currency reform.[129]

Seeckt's actions, however, were not always equally welcome. Seeckt was construing his responsibilities for maintaining public welfare and order rather broadly, and while the government does not seem to have objected to an order of November 13 encouraging the closing of luxury restaurants, bars, and dance halls and their conversion into shelters and soup kitchens for the poor, Luther protested strongly against an order issued by Seeckt permitting the states, provinces, and municipalities to issue emergency money to secure food and fuel. While such money was not to be issued except insofar as its backing was accepted by the Finance Minister, Luther was not appreciative of Seeckt's interference in financial and economic matters and of what could be construed as a green light to new currencies on the eve of the currency reform. His protest to Stresemann may have been all the more impassioned because of an apparent lack of support from President Ebert, to whom he had complained in Seeckt's presence.[130]

Most serious were Luther's problems with the Reichsbank. On November 13, he formally protested the way it had marketed the gold loan. He accused the Reichsbank of poor management in its inadequate production of the gold-loan certificates and of harming the finances of the Reich while enriching the banks through its selling of the gold loan without demanding immediate payment of the paper marks to which it was entitled. The Reichsbank hotly rejected these charges, claiming that careful and not poor management was responsible for the delay and, in a later response, pointing out that "the Reich, which has brought about the inflation and has derived the greatest advantage from it for its finances cannot complain if, in one instance, the effects of the inflation for once are to its disadvantage."[131]

The most important issue, however, was the competence and not the arrogance of the Reichsbank, and the capacity of the Reichsbank leaders and their organization to deal with the tasks for which they would be responsible in the currency reform caused concern within as well as without the Reichsbank. On October 16, the organization of Reichsbank officials wrote to Stresemann, pointing out that the confused organization and working relationships within the Reichsbank made it technically incapable of working effectively with the new Rentenbank and arguing that the leadership had to undergo a fundamental change in their organizational attitudes and technical practices if "they were to fulfill the economic tasks of the Reichsbank in its collaboration with the new currency bank."[132] Within the Cabinet, there was a complete consensus that the best way to change attitudes in the Reichsbank was to change the leadership, and on November 5 it came to the formal conclusion that Havenstein and Glasenapp were no longer able to fulfill their tasks and that they should not be allowed to benefit from the provisions of the Civil Service Reduction Act permitting exceptions to mandatory retirement. This judgment was duly conveyed to Ebert, who then reported it to Havenstein with the request that the Reichsbank begin thinking about a successor, especially since Havenstein had already indicated his intention to retire at the end of 1923. Havenstein, however, chose to take his stand on the Bank Autonomy Law, under which he was appointed for life, and claimed that the Reichsbank did not fall under the Civil Service Reduction Act. He also was quite unresponsive to Ebert's rejoinder that the press attacks on him as the Reichsbank President had stopped and he could thus leave without creating the impression that he had been driven out by his critics.[133]

The stalemate with respect to the leadership of the Reichsbank presented serious problems not only because of the lack of coordination between the Reichsbank and the Rentenbank but also because of the difficult question of when and how a fixed relationship should be established between the paper mark and the Rentenmark and the manner in which the paper marks were to be redeemed. The Cabinet in a meeting of November 3 had decided to move in this direction and try to guarantee some fixed redemption value for the paper mark. This seemed to be the only means of stopping the free fall of the paper mark then effectively under way despite the fixed exchange rate and ensuring that the paper marks would have some value until there was a sufficient number of Rentenmarks to go around. There was considerable disagreement, however, as to how this redemption of the paper mark was to be carried out. The banker Rudolf Loeb and the Currency Committee of the Central Association of German Bankers argued for the creation of an autonomous Conversion Bureau (Konversionskasse) which would raise three hundred million gold marks through a special tax on assets. The Conversion Bureau would issue certificates redeemable in gold value for up to three years which would be exchanged for paper marks at a fixed rate, while those obligated to pay the tax could at once purchase and surrender the certificates for this purpose. The scheme, which Luther favored because it would allow a considerable amount of money to circulate in the transition, had the advantage of leaving both the Rentenmark and the gold loan unburdened by the paper mark, a matter of no small interest to the private banks which held large quantities of the gold loan. It also called for the creation of an expert bankers' committee to advise the government on currency matters and ensure unity, a scheme which certainly would have vastly increased the power and influence of the Central Association of German Bankers within the government as well as over and against the Reichsbank. Two other schemes were proposed as alternatives. One, recommended by Professor Warmbold, an agricultural expert and director of the Badische Soda- und Analin-Fabriken, and strongly supported by Economics Minister Koeth, called for the creation of a special gold loan to redeem the paper marks and thus make available a valorized alternative to the paper marks. A second, the original plan under the Rentenbank Law, which set aside three hundred million Rentenmark for the redemption of the paper money, was favored by the Reichsbank.[134]

Assuming the acceptance of any of these plans, there still remained the question of the rate at which the paper mark was to be exchanged. On November 5, the DVP had passed a resolution, which Stresemann communicated to the Cabinet, that the paper marks be exchanged for the gold marks by January 1, 1924, at a rate of one hundred billion paper marks for one gold mark. The resolution was never implemented, but it is most convenient for demonstrating what could have happened if the government had acted prematurely in setting the conversion rate of the paper mark. The problem was that the amount of paper marks issued by the Reichsbank increased from 19,153,087,468,907 marks on November 7 to 92,844,720,743,031 marks on November 15, while the floating debt increased from 21.5 to 191.6 quintillion marks during the same period. Indeed, between November 13 and November 15, the floating debt had increased by seventy quintillion so that, had the exchange rate proposed by the DVP been maintained not the projected three hundred million gold or Rentenmark earmarked for the redemption of the paper marks, but rather 1.9 billion gold marks or Rentenmark would have been required. Clearly, a fixing of the relationship between the paper mark and the Rentenmark would be an important aspect of the stabilization, especially since the Rentenmark was purely for domestic use and the external stabilization required a pegging of the paper mark. Determining the moment at which this pegging would take place and the appropriate level, however, was no simple matter.[135]

While both Luther and Stresemann recognized that these various tasks and decisions were beyond the capacities of Luther and his staff alone and that someone was needed to devote full attention to currency matters, they also realized that the logical person to oversee the currency reform, the Reichsbank President, could not be so employed because Havenstein simply was not up to the job. As a result, they seem to have settled on the idea of appointing a Currency Commissioner (*Währungskommissar*) with virtual Cabinet rank. Stresemann's choice for this position, which he probably viewed as the stepping stone to the presidency of the Reichsbank when that office became vacant, seems to have been made as early as October 23. On that date, he asked Reich Supreme Court President Simons to judge the merit of charges made by State Secretary Schröder of the Finance Ministry concerning alleged improprieties committed by Hjalmar Schacht during his service in the German occupation administration of Belgium. By November 2, Stresemann was able to inform Schacht, with whom he had been negotiating, that Simons adjudged him fully eligible for public office. There is reason to doubt that Luther initially shared Stresemann's enthusiasm, especially since Schacht had been one of the most open opponents of the Rentenbank and Luther appears to have favored letting Schröder devote himself exclusively to currency matters rather than create a new office. When Rentenbank president Lentze asked for a voice in the appointment of the new Currency Commissioner on November 6, Luther put him off on these grounds. Also, Luther seems to have asked and been turned down by two other persons, probably bankers, before asking Schacht. Stresemann's personal commitment to Schacht seems to have been increased by the Cabinet crisis and the pressure from the Democratic Party. He promised the DDP that he would consider Schacht for the post of Currency Commissioner on November 6. In any case, Schacht knew of his selection on November 11, was formally asked by Luther the next day, and accepted with an enthusiasm suitable to the as yet to be revealed dimensions of his ambition. Schacht had distinguished himself at the Nationalbank, and Jakob Goldschmidt strongly supported his appointment to a government post since both men well understood that Schacht was not the kind of man who could play second fiddle to Goldschmidt over the long haul. The new position of Currency Commissioner did, indeed, carry exceptional prerogatives. Formally placed within the Finance Ministry, the Currency Commissioner was permitted to attend all Cabinet meetings, at which he would exercise an advisory voice. He was directly responsible to the Cabinet in all currency matters, and no Ministry was to undertake any measure relating to the currency without his countersignature. In the case of a difference between the Commissioner and any of the Ministers, the matter in contest was to be decided by the full Cabinet. To Hjalmar Schacht, therefore, was given the task of overseeing the currency reform inspired by Helfferich and set in motion by Luther.[136]

First, however, the Rentenbank had to start operation and the new currency had to be issued. The Rentenbank was conveniently and appropriately located in offices belonging to the Reich Debt Administration which were across the street from the Reich Printing Office and near the Reichsbank. In keeping with the austerity drive, the staff of the new bank was kept as small as possible, and the task of assessing the mortgage to be placed on agriculture and industry and collecting the necessary taxes was left to the Finance Ministry. The printing of the new currency had actually begun before the Rentenbank was formally founded, but the government was anxious to produce a currency with more character and distinction than that which was rolling off its presses in such obscene quantities. Germans were going to experience dealing with coins and portions of the mark again, one- and two-pfennig coins of copper with a small admixture of tin and five-, ten-, and fifty-pfennig pieces of bronzed aluminum, all of which were to be printed in the Prussian mint. Special care was taken in the production of the Rentenmark notes, which took place in the Reich Printing Office and a select group of private printing houses, and not only for the obvious purpose of preventing forgery. The notes were issued in eight denominations running from one to a thousand Rentenmark, printed on both sides, and bearing on the front the formidable names of the Administrative Council members of the Rentenbank. This format was meant to promote confidence in the new currency, and a design suggestive of grain products produced on paper of quality may have further served the cause, at least among those whose products the new currency was meant to extract. Despite the early start, however, production of the new money was slow, and the printing strike made matters worse. On November 10, only 78,275,000 gold-marks' worth of the new currency was available, an amount which increased to over two hundred million by November 15 but was still a far cry from the 3.2 billion maximum emission provided under the law. After all, though the success of the new currency depended upon quantitative constraints, it also depended upon its being available.[137]

It was this anticipated shortage of the new currency which had made Luther hesitate about carrying out the reform as quickly as others wished. The very thirst for a valorized currency that made keeping to the deadline virtually imperative also threatened its satisfaction. Given the limited amount of Rentenmarks available, it was inconceivable that clearing operations for the Rentenmark and its use for postal checks could begin until December. The Rentenbank had itself contemplated asking Luther for a delay but then opted for the "lesser evil," considering it wiser to satisfy public demand that a valorized currency finally be issued in however momentarily inadequate a quantity and, no less important, "to have the moment of the shutting down of the printing press for new Reich debts come as soon as possible."[138] The conservative Administrative Council of the Rentenbank had every incentive to bring on this day since §16 of the Rentenbank Law gave it a potentially powerful voice in government expenditure. Once the Rentenbank had given the government the three-hundred-million-Rentenmark interest-free loan earmarked for the buying up of the Reich Treasury notes, the remaining nine hundred million interest-bearing credits which had to be given to the Reich within two years were subject to Rentenbank approval.

Indeed, the potential exercise of this power almost delayed the issuance of the Rentenmark, for in a final decisive meeting attended by Luther, Schacht, and the Rentenbank and Reichsbank officials on November 14, Luther insisted that he needed a hundred million Rentenmark for the continuation of the Ruhr struggle and, noting that the Rentenbank appeared disinclined to give the credit, threatened to withhold his signature for the launching of the Rentenmark the next day. Unfortunately for Luther, his position had been undermined by his own staff, since Ministerial Director von Schlieben had already issued instructions that 30 percent of the next salary payment for government officials be paid in valorized currency, and these orders could not be rescinded. On November 15, 1923, the Rentenmark went into circulation, and the Reichsbank ceased to discount Reich Treasury bills and issue paper money. Luther was to get his hundred million, but the episode certainly must have brought home the truth of the remark made to him by a financial leader after he had signed the decree creating the bank that "the Rentenbank would

pull the shirt from off his back within a month." Similarly, Kastl of the Finance Ministry remarked that "the Treasury has sold itself body and soul to the new Institution; no foreign Committee of Guarantees, he added, could possibly have such a stranglehold on Germany's finances."[139]

The extent of the stranglehold remained to be seen, but the initial relief to the Reich's finances were palpable, especially because of the manner in which the rate of exchange between the Rentenmark and the paper mark was set in the first days of the currency reform and then maintained thereafter. Until the issuance of the new currency, the government sought to maintain as high a unitary exchange rate for the mark as it dared to control domestic speculation against the mark. With the appearance of the new currency, the Reich had every interest in reducing the value of the paper mark as much as possible in order to diminish the real value of the debt it would have to repurchase with Rentenmark while stabilizing what was left of the currency at a level that would gain acceptance nationally and internationally. At the same time, there was some difference of interest between the Reich and Reichsbank, on the one hand, and the Rentenbank, on the other, since the Rentenbank was anxious to increase its profits by selling the Rentenmark for as many paper marks as possible. Everyone concerned certainly was very dissatisfied with the mere doubling of the fixed exchange rate on November 15 to 2.2520 trillion paper marks to the dollar or 600 billion paper marks to the gold mark. One possible way of dealing with the situation was to follow a Reichsbank proposal and close down the exchanges for a few days and then reopen them with a new exchange rate. The other was to heed to objections of the banks and the position taken by Schacht and leave them open in the hope that the events of November 15 would improve the value of the paper mark on foreign exchanges and create a better basis for setting a new value for the paper mark in Berlin.

Schacht and the bankers won the debate, and the exchanges were kept open. Nevertheless, the pressures for a rapid decision and stabilization of the paper mark were very strong, especially from Koeth, and on November 20, the fixed exchange rate (especially advocated by the head of the Statistical Section of the Reichsbank, Dr. Kaufmann, but most popular among those outside the Rentenbank involved in making the decision) was chosen. From the outset, the Reichsbank and Rentenbank had hoped to make the Rentenmark equal to the gold mark, and since the gold mark was always considered equal to $\frac{10}{42}$ of the dollar, the exchange rate could be set at 4.2 trillion marks to the dollar. One would return to the prewar parity simply by lopping off twelve zeros. The decision of November 20 was opposed by some members of the Rentenbank, and even Schacht seemed to have some doubts in December, although he always claimed that he defended it tooth and nail. It certainly was not binding on foreign exchanges, where the paper mark rose to as much as 6.7 trillion on December 1 before it settled at 4.2 trillion on December 3. This decision initially to let the currency depreciate substantially and then to fix the exchange rate and maintain the level at which it was fixed was one of the outstanding features of the stabilization. Although Schacht told Allied financial experts in January that he did not know why the mark had held at this level, he seems to have understood well enough the source of his effectiveness when he told the Cabinet on December 3 that in his efforts to influence the value of the new currency, "he did not place himself on the foundation of the policy of intervention previously employed by the Reichsbank, but rather sought to exert influence through the supply (*Geldseite*). A sharp restriction of the money market has actually had a salutary effect."[140] Indeed, it made it possible to redeem the debt of the Reich at the Reichsbank for two hundred million instead of three hundred million Rentenmark!

Ironically, on November 20, the day all those paper marks Havenstein had produced were stabilized at 4.2 trillion to the dollar, Havenstein suddenly died, thereby ending the battle over his retirement and undoubtedly adding a tincture to the confidence required for the stabilization. In a very real sense, the appointment of Schacht had already reduced him to irrelevance, and there is something utterly pathetic about the lengthy letter sent to Ebert on the day before his death in which he protested the notion that the Personnel Reduction Decree could be applied to the Reichsbank or used to retire members of its Board of Directors and warned that this would do immense damage to the

"Magna Carta" of the Reichsbank—that is, the Reichsbank Autonomy Law. Havenstein's character and role were shrewdly appraised by Max Warburg:

He was an extraordinarily sympathetic personality, with an unbending sense of duty and honorable character, but not up to the present situation. Since the beginning of the war, obedience and subordination to the presumed superior authority, be it the General Staff, be it the Reich Finance Ministry, be it the Reich Economics Ministry, had become so much a part of his flesh and blood that, even where it would have been possible, he did not know how to maintain the independence of the Reichsbank. Even after the independence of the Reichsbank was confirmed by special Statute, he could not bring himself to strong independent action. The difficulties should not be underestimated since it was always a matter of whether one wanted to stop the inflation and thereby extinguish it. International and domestic political developments tumbled one upon the other. Despite this, I have the impression that a stronger hand could at many points have changed the course.[141]

That course was now being changed by hands that were stronger or at least more desperate and more open to pressure in a new direction. Reichsbank Vice President von Glasenapp formally assumed control of the Reichsbank until the selection of a successor could be completed, and he stood squarely behind the currency reform. While reiterating all the wearisome verities of the balance of payments theory of the inflation and insisting that Germany could not stabilize and move to a true gold currency without reparations relief and outside assistance, he was no less adamant in demanding that the interim period of Rentenbank credits be used to reduce spending, balance the budget, and increase productivity. The Reichsbank itself pledged to do its share, and not merely by ceasing to discount government Treasury bills. In a noted speech to the Reichsbank Central Committee on November 29, Glasenapp proclaimed his intention to put an end to the private credit inflation launched in the summer of 1922 by pointing out that "we must continue in our effort, through the limitation of the granting of credit, to force business to actually use the valorized means of payment given to it. No possibility must exist for the recipient of valorized means of payment to hoard money because he is in the position to get hold of paper mark money through credit."[142] On December 1, the Reichsbank issued an order requiring all future credits to be valorized and requiring all borrowers to recognize as legally binding their obligation to repay credits at full value, although Schacht was still complaining on December 3 that the full conversion to valorized credit could only be expected a few days hence and was sharply critical of the continued existence of the loan bureaus and their practice of lending dollar Treasury certificates. This practice was finally ended on March 2, and the loan bureaus closed down on April 30, 1924.[143]

Similarly, the Reichsbank, strongly driven on by Schacht's insistence that "emergency money is not to be confused with monetary emergency,"[144] moved against the fiat currencies that had played such an important role in making the hyperinflation so extreme. On November 17, the Reichsbank announced that it would not accept any more uncovered emergency money after November 24, a concession designed to wipe the slate clean. The only exception was the occupied areas, to which Schacht traveled on November 25 and where, despite intense hostility, he insisted on a speedy deadline for the conversion of uncovered emergency money. The original deadline of November 24 was extended to December 1 by the Reichsbank, a modification which Schacht considered excessively generous, and then implemented despite Degoutte's threat to force the Reichsbank branches to accept the money. If necessary, the Reichsbank was prepared to close its branches to defy the French general's order. In any event, such action was unnecessary, and the threat to the Reichsbank's decision came not from the occupation authorities but rather from some angry Mayors who wished to employ the occupation authorities to force the Reichsbank to accept their uncovered emergency money. The Reichsbank also took an extremely hard line against accepting the 114.7 quintillion marks in emergency money issued by the railroads after the Finance Ministry agreed to provide the Reichsbank ninety million Rentenmark to cover the paper. As Glasenapp insisted in his speech of November 29, the nation had to be taught that the "impoverishment and shortage of capital cannot be eliminated through artificial capital, the granting of credits and inflation."[145]

The Reichsbank was undoubtedly coming to believe in these measures under the crack of Schacht's whip, but it is also important to remember that it was now somewhat fettered in its decisions by the Rentenbank. While the Reichsbank was free to set the interest on the 1.2 billion Rentenmark in credit it would have at its disposal for the private economy, the Rentenbank nevertheless exercised its right to insist that the credits had to be granted and repaid in valorized form and that any depreciation charges had to be paid to the Rentenbank. Although these conditions do not seem to have caused conflict between the two banks, a nasty quarrel did break out over how much of the interest on Reichsbank loans made in Rentenmark was to go to the Rentenbank. The Reichsbank claimed, not without justification, that it had to bear the costs and risks of holding, distributing, and lending the Rentenmark and thus deserved the lion's share of whatever interest it collected. Finally, on December 1, an agreement was reached on the first six hundred million Rentenmark to be made available to the Reichsbank for the private sector under which the Reichsbank was to provide the credits in equal measure to agriculture and industry at interest rates determined in consultation with the Rentenbank. The Rentenbank was to receive 30 percent of the interest thus collected, and the agreement could be terminated on April 1 with one month's notice. Lentze and his colleagues could not deny that most of the costs were those of the Reichsbank, but they also wished to gather "experience" and keep their hands free in case they could collect more interest, which the owners of the Rentenbank were, in effect, paying to themselves.[146]

In addition to driving hard bargains with the Reichsbank, the Rentenbank leaders also took a dictatorial tone in their dealings with the government. They not only immediately demanded a prospective budget drawn up in gold values from Luther but also secured his agreement that any portion of the interest-free three-hundred-million Rentenmark credit not used to buy up the government debt would be subject to Rentenbank approval in the manner of the interest-bearing nine hundred million available to the government. Since Schacht ended up using only two hundred million, the remaining hundred million was subject to Rentenbank approval. Perhaps this made the Rentenbank leader feel they were getting some compensation for the decision to grant Luther his hundred million for the Ruhr on November 15. Whatever the case, the money was not granted graciously. In fact, the Rentenbank leaders saw fit to visit Stresemann on the inauguration of the Rentenmark to reproach him for this demand and lecture him concerning their views on foreign and domestic politics, demanding the end of the eight-hour day, termination of compulsory collective bargaining, reform of the unemployment support system, and all manner of other social, economic, and financial reforms. While Stresemann may have found this outrageous performance useful in his dealings with the representatives of the occupied areas, since it enabled him to remind them that "one should not forget that the Reich government now finds itself to a certain degree under the trusteeship (*Vormundschaft*) of the Administrative Council of the Rentenbank,"[147] it is hard to believe that he did not find the experience humiliating. Nevertheless, he did not protest, and this brought forth sharp criticism. The *Frankfurter Zeitung* found it "at once regrettable and indicative" and went on to remark that "there are today in Germany astonishing notions of dictatorship: the exclusion of the parliament and the introjection of the chief powers of the private economy appears to be the ideal for many people today." Deputy Wels, in an angry speech in the Reichstag on November 20, charged that the budgetary power of the Reichstag had apparently gone over to the Agrarian League and the Reich Association of German Industry.[148]

These criticisms were not far off the mark, and while the Reich was granted some six hundred forty million marks' worth of its interest-bearing credit by the beginning of December, Lentze proudly noted that most of its requests had been turned down. As he explained:

The Administrative Council has taken the firm position that it is not there, perhaps like the Reichstag, to criticize and approve, or to make suggestions of all kinds and thereby to take upon itself a responsibility it does not have—for then it would always be the scapegoat of the government—but it views its task as preventing under all circumstances a diminution of

the inner worth of the Rentenmark. . . . It views all questions from the monetary perspective. . . . The guarantors of the Rentenbank and the purchasers of Rentenmark notes and Rentenmark bonds shall be protected from losses insofar as this is within the power of the Administrative Board. . . . All requests which deal with individual agencies, as for example, the railroads, have been turned down. . . . One must stubbornly hold to the principle that only the Reich Financial Administration shall receive grants. If it chooses to make the demands of others its own, then it does so on its own responsibility. It has never been left in doubt that it can receive no more from the Rentenbank than a total of 900 million Rentenmark of interest-bearing credit, and that this can be increased by that portion of the interest-free credit insofar as it has not been used, but otherwise cannot be increased.[149]

Certainly, the limitation of credit to the government and the protection of the new currency *were* genuine responsibilities of the Rentenbank, but the reference to the Reichstag and the interview with Stresemann demonstrated that something more was involved; namely, that, as Kastl put it, "their conservatism will be opposed to any democratic handling of the finance problems on the part of the Treasury."[150]

The specific danger of the Rentenbank solution had all along been that the agrarian and industrial interest groups would undermine the authority of the democratic state toward which they felt either hatred or indifference, and though Hilferding, Stresemann, and Luther had eliminated the most overt dangers of the Helfferich plan, they had not exorcised its spirit. This was amply demonstrated by the major industrial representative on the Administrative Council of the Rentenbank and the man who, ironically enough, Kastl was to succeed as executive manager of the RdI in 1925, Hermann Bücher. In an unusually sharp and even rude series of remarks and altercations in the Reich Economic Council on November 13, Bücher sharply criticized Luther, with regard to the budget he had presented to the Rentenbank, for excessive expenditure, conducting social policy for its own sake, and, above all, for failing to recognize that no budget could be balanced without a favorable balance of trade. The primacy which Bücher attached to the balance of trade and the need to increase productivity was challenged, as it had always been, by Georg Bernhard and Anton Feiler, both of whom insisted that a nation could ruin its finances even while having a favorable trade balance and that primacy had to be given to state finances and balancing the budget through effective tax collection. They both shared Bücher's view that productivity had to be increased, but as Bernhard noted, "it has been the misfortune of our discussions for years now that whenever the question of the cleaning up of our finances and the currency question are being debated, the discussion is shifted to the productivity question."[151]

While this remark gave the labor representatives in the RWR the opportunity to yell out that it was "always the same old gramaphone record" and for Bücher to shout back that his need to constantly repeat his arguments "is Germany's misfortune," the heart of the difference, as Feiler made clear, was whether one would ask, "what do we need and what do we impose on the economy?" or, "what can the economy bear?" In Feiler's view, it was the first and not the second question that had to be given priority. He in no way questioned that state expenses had to be kept to a minimum under existing conditions,

But this minimum must be given, for one finally has to also recognize that the state must also survive, and I permit myself to say that I miss this point in all that is said. . . . Paying taxes has never been something that has been loved, and it has truly never been so unloved as in this year of grace 1923.[152]

In a rather pointed illustration of how starving the state of the money it needed served special rather than national interests, Feiler noted that the Reich Economics Ministry had been trying to set up a cartel bureau for some time so that it could gather information on cartels, a matter made all the more urgent by the Decree Against the Economic Abuses of Cartels issued by the government on November 2. Yet it did not have sufficient personnel to do more than produce

a pile of unfiled newspaper clippings. The Reich Association of German Industry in contrast has set up a very complete Cartel Bureau, which has taken over these tasks in a very complete manner. Here you have the situation that the state cannot create its necessary aids, but the Reich Association of German Industry is in the position of giving the state the possibility of addressing this problem. That's the situation.[153]

Bücher's response to all this was to announce proudly that his Cartel Bureau employed only two academics and a female secretary, was based on voluntary reporting by industry rather than state compulsion, and yet was able to do a better job. That, of course, was not the point, but rather that the poverty of the state was compelling it to turn to the wolf to watch the chicken coop, and Feiler was incensed at Bücher's intimation that the Rentenbank would not give the state money, that it could stretch the credit out over two years if it wished, and that its primary responsibility was to the bank and to those whose assets had been mortgaged to create it. He accused Bücher of trying to turn the Rentenbank into a nonstatutory "power factor," while Bücher rejoined that "this is what separates us: you pursue power politics and we want to help the *Wirtschaft*." The final and most telling thrust, however, remained to Feiler: "I want to give the state power, and I consider it a fateful misfortune for Germany that the *Wirtschaft* makes the state powerless. That is what separates us."

This point is all the more relevant when one considers that the implementation of the currency reform took place in the midst of a Cabinet crisis and that the pressures from the right were not limited to the gentlemen in the Rentenbank. Employers in the Ruhr were both frustrated and furious about their inability to reintroduce the prewar hours of work and eliminate the other demobilization decrees restricting their freedom of action. Paul Reusch's attitude was typical: "I don't think much of the new money. So long as we do not change our economic and social legislation from the bottom up and make sure that we work more than in the prewar period, every new currency that we create will depreciate."[154] On the one hand, the government had forced employers to retreat from their unilateral effort to impose longer hours in early October; on the other, it had extended the demobilization decrees on October 27 until November 17 in the hope that it could get labor and management agreement to an hours-of-work law to which both sides so far had raised strong objections. Employers, on the brink of signing agreements with the MICUM that would lead to a resumption of work and which they did not feel they could fulfill without the longer work day, thrashed about from one possible solution to another. Direct negotiations with the trade unions failed to produce agreement because workers were furious over the attempted employer coup in the hours-of-work question and unconvinced that the extra hours were necessary at a time of unemployment and transportation difficulties. General Degoutte deliberately played upon the conflict by suggesting that the agreements could be carried out without additional work time. Though some employers toyed with threatening not to sign the MICUM Agreements unless the workers agreed to longer hours, the fact that a quarter of the firms had already come to terms with the French made this tactic inadvisable. In early November, they felt forced to turn to governmental authorities, both local and national. An especially promising avenue seemed to be opened by the hated Hours-of-Work Decree of November 23, 1918, which permitted the Demobilization Commissars to extend the hours of work whenever the public interest and especially the prevention of unemployment so required, and the Ruhr industrialists prepared to make such an appeal to the Demobilization Commissar in Düsseldorf. At the same time, they increased the pressure on Berlin.

On November 10, Peter Klöckner sent a truly impassioned plea to Brauns pointing out that no plant could stay open without an extension of the hours of work, angrily protesting that Germany was being forced to buy English coal because the government had failed to find a way to reintroduce the eight-and-a-half hour day in the mines, and claiming that the workers were anxious and willing to return to work "for ten hours and even twelve hours if they could only earn money again and provide their families with better conditions of life."[155] Klöckner called upon Brauns to bring out an order permitting the extension of the working day, a plea echoed by Stinnes in a letter to Luther of November 14 asking that Article 48 or the Enabling Act be employed to permit individual works to negotiate a return to prewar hours with their workers.

More was involved in this demand than the hours question, of course, since plant-by-plant determination of working hours would have undermined the entire system of collective bar-

gaining, a point certainly not lost on Stinnes and the other industrialists seeking to roll back the entire collective bargaining system at this time. The paramount concern, however, certainly was the hours of work. Stinnes brushed aside all claims that there was a contradiction in asking for longer hours when there was high unemployment. The essential thing was to lower costs and make Germany competitive. Once new contracts began to flow in, employment would increase. The alternative would be that the entire currency reform effort would come to nought and that France would succeed in its goal of "denationalizing" the population and industry of the Rhine and Ruhr. Stinnes was even more forthright than Bücher in asserting the primacy of productive over financial considerations, calling for the maximum reduction of government functions and the direction of large amounts of Rentenmark and gold-loan notes to industry so that workers could be compensated for their additional labor. The six months bought in this manner would be worth "a certain inflation" since this would create the foundation for a true stabilization.[156]

For Stinnes, as he confided to his son Edmund on November 16, the restoration of prewar hours would permit Germany "to capture the world market anew," while the reduction of prices arising from the reduction of costs would revive demand. The foot-dragging in Berlin thus irritated him to no end.

Stresemann is a weak man, who to be sure has moved more to the right in the last few days, but who does not dare to take the decisive step in the labor question and without this step there can be no currency reform, and no recovery of the economy and naturally also no reparations to France. The most depressing thing in all the negotiations with the enemy is that one cannot deny our guilt on one point. If Germany, instead of lazing about, had worked after the war as it had before the war, then everything would look differently, for then Poincaré would have had no excuse to do that which brings Germany ever closer to disintegration. Luther and Koeth both see the situation correctly, but cannot prevail.[157]

Despite his dim view of Stresemann and much of his Cabinet, Stinnes did expect the speedy reintroduction of a longer working day, and he had good grounds for optimism. Labor Minister Brauns had already been preparing the way for an effective change in hours of work.

On October 30, he issued an Arbitration Decree (*Schlichtungsverordnung*), scarcely noted in the context of the other dramatic events taking place at the time, which vastly increased the powers of the Labor Ministry to intervene in labor disputes and to issue binding arbitration decisions if the parties could not agree. Both through its powers to appoint Labor Ministry arbitrators and to issue guidelines for their decisions, the new decree placed the Labor Ministry in a position to exercise a powerful influence on wages and working conditions. While the decree later was to become a source of bitter conflict between the Ministry and industry, its fundamental function in 1923 was to pave the way for the forcible introduction of longer hours and lower wages. Indeed, the decree must be understood in the context of Brauns's intention to let the demobilization decrees lapse on November 17 whether or not the trade unions and employers were willing to accept the hours-of-work bill he was proposing. Once the decrees lapsed, only the Hours-of-Work Law for the Mining Industry of 1922, the old Industrial Code, and existing collective bargaining agreements would govern working conditions. Employers would then be in a position to give notice on the existing collective bargaining agreements in all industries, including mining, and the Labor Ministry would be in a position to use its binding arbitration powers in favor of longer hours should new agreements prove unattainable. The major heavy-industrial organizations were aware of Brauns's plan to let the demobilization decrees lapse by November 17 at the latest, which undoubtedly explains Stinnes's confidence, and the real question when the Cabinet discussed the issue on November 15 was whether the longer working day would be legislated by law or decree or simply left to the collective bargaining-binding arbitration processes.[158]

Although Brauns told the industrialists that he was unwilling to use Article 48 to decree the hours-of-work bill before the Reichstag because of the opposition from both industry and labor, this is precisely what he did call for at the Cabinet meeting. Revealing his own preference for ensuring that employers were not given a completely free hand and for maintaining the influence of the trade unions, he also suggested that he might add some further restrictions on hours of work, presumably in line with his concept of the "sanitary work-day." Interior Minister Jarres, in contrast, favored letting matters ride for a year before trying to regulate the question and proposed government subsidies to the trade unions to help them retain their influence despite the damage that this would cause to their position among the workers. He was seconded by Luther, who warned that "if the economy is now not brought into operation, then we are lost. With the exception of our labor power, all our reserves are used up." He supported the Transportation and Postal Ministers on the need to increase the hours of work in government agencies and plants and also thought that higher officials had to be forced to work ten hours. Transportation Minister Oeser wished to have the new hours legislated under Article 48, a position supported by Koeth, who insisted that "one has to show one's colors." Ultimately, Stresemann came to the same view, although he was initially reluctant to use Article 48 on the grounds that it would be disloyal to issue decrees on the hours-of-work question after it had been explicitly excluded from the Enabling Act.[159]

The decision, in any case, was not one that was to be his. Stresemann's sincerely intended goal of keeping the Social Democrats in the government and doing the best he could to recognize their legitimate interests under conditions in which they were the underdog did not receive any reward. Instead, it was the SPD which brought a no-confidence motion before the Reichstag on November 20 over the government's differential treatment of the Saxon-Thuringian and Bavarian uprisings, and the Social Democrats voted with the Nationalists and Communists to bring down the government on November 23.

It was a measure of the short-sightedness of the SPD vote that whereas they rejected Stresemann, it was Stresemann who rejected the schemes of the Nationalist leader Hergt for a Directory of Seeckt, Wiedfeldt, and Minoux and some kind of fuzzy alliance with right-wing patriotic associations like the Stahlhelm and the Young German Order. The putative "Directory" amply demonstrated the lack of viability that made its creation impossible. Seeckt was fulminating against the "failure" of the currency reform only five days after it had been implemented with complaints that prices were rising and speculation increasing. He demanded in contradictory fashion that "the unitary exchange rate be abolished and a fixed exchange rate between the paper mark and Rentenmark be established" and insisted that "all reservations of expert financial circles be set aside."[160] Privately, he confessed to his sister that he was a "novice" in economic and financial matters and although convinced that a "measure of dictatorship" was necessary, would "welcome it if a man could be found."[161]

Manifestly, he did not feel himself to be the man, and while quarreling with Luther over the currency reform and with Ebert over the retention of his exceptional powers, he was not prepared to challenge the civilian authorities himself. Wiedfeldt, however, was not willing to play a leading political role either. As far as Minoux was concerned, even Stinnes had become doubtful, privately confessing that he "does not have the impression that he [Minoux] will be called to play the role which might have been given to him with proper leadership. In his Messianic belief in himself he has apparently often expressed himself without restraint at the false moment. On the dangerous and slippery terrain of politics one must be able to keep one's mouth shut and not blabber, or at least only rarely and in good company."[162] Indeed, Stresemann was able not only to contest Hergt's contention that "the rule of big business and big agriculture would be popular" but also to challenge the notion that such a government would be acceptable abroad by pointing out that Stinnes himself had stated that the German Nationalists were "no political export article."[163]

If a right-wing government and Directory was unacceptable, however, so was a dissolution of the Reichstag and new elections under the chaotic and dangerous circumstances still existing in Germany. Efforts to form a government of "experts" under former Treasury Minister Hans Albert and coalition governments under Centrist leader Stegerwald or the former DNVP and now DVP Deputy Siegfried von Kardorff in the week following the no-confidence vote all failed because they were either unacceptable to the right without changes in the composition of the Prussian government or unacceptable to the left because they would require such changes. Ebert had only turned to Kardorff and Stegerwald after the moderate, experienced parliamentarian and widely respected Centrist leader Wilhelm Marx had turned him down on November 24 and persisted in his resistance during the next few days.[164]

The stalemate was particularly unbearable to Luther. He did not need Seeckt to tell him that the currency reform was hanging in the balance, that prices were shooting up, and that the situation was dangerous. Seeckt's high-handed interference, obviously inspired in part by critics of the Luther–Schacht policy in the private economy, only compounded the uncertainties of the situation. Luther firmly rejected Seeckt's call for an end to the fixed exchange rate, warning that this would lead to a complete collapse of the paper mark and would thus endanger the food supply even more. A degree of continuity in the exchange rate was essential, and both he and Schacht were counting on their firm policy of holding out while the number of Rentenmarks in circulation increased and confidence in the new currency grew.[165]

But Luther was a good deal less upbeat when appearing in his capacity as caretaker Finance Minister before the Reichsrat on November 28 to present his First Emergency Tax Decree. He did insist that all rumors to the effect that the Reich was continuing to print money were false and attributed them to the misleading impression created by the fact that the hundred million Rentenmarks for the Ruhr were being paid out in paper marks and that twenty-day private bills were still being temporarily discounted by the Reichsbank. At the same time, he reiterated his position that the currency reform had been introduced too quickly and against his vote, and he warned that the Rentenmarks available to the government were fast running out. Luther expressed despair over the resistance he was getting with respect to the reduction of the civil service and warned "that if the severest measures are not taken overnight, then every effort to save the situation is hopeless." His greatest concern was to increase government revenue, and he declared that "the Rentenmark is lost if very substantial revenue is not already collected in December." He remonstrated that "under such circumstances, all legal reservations must be silenced. The people want to survive, and a responsible government must therefore consider itself obligated to make use of Article 48." At the conclusion of his remarks, Luther apologized for his aggressive tone but pointed out that "he and all his co-workers labor under the sense of fearful danger that the currency reform that has been introduced will be destroyed."[166] This certainly would be the case if a real government were not formed soon, and Luther decided to force the issue by writing to Ebert on November 30 that a caretaker government could not deal with the situation and threatening to resign if a new government were not formed immediately.[167]

This demand was satisfied on that very day, however, when a minority coalition government of the Center, DDP, and DVP was formed under Wilhelm Marx, with Stresemann as Foreign Minister; Luther, Brauns, and Jarres continuing on in their previous posts; and the Bavarian Democrat Eduard Hamm as Economics Minister and Bavarian People's Party Deputy Erich Emminger as Justice Minister. Even this did not end the political crisis, however, for while the SPD was willing to tolerate the new government, especially because of its support of Stresemann's foreign policy, it resisted the call for a new Enabling Act to implement the various measures required for the stabilization. All this put Luther more into a panic than ever. As he confidentially told the Reichsrat on December 5, the Rentenbank credits would not even last until Christmas because of the continued credits for the occupied areas and the need to back up the emergency money of the railroads with Rentenmark. He had "already lost eight precious days, without moving forward on the passage of the tax laws. If he does not succeed in getting substantial revenues in December, then the catastrophe is unavoidable. . . . If the German people is to still have a chance to save

itself from the abyss, then the present government must be able to take the necessary measures without any hindrance and delay. If the extraordinary powers are not granted, then he sees no hope for salvation."[168]

Indeed, Stresemann thought the new government might fall in a week, after which new elections would be the only possibility and would, he predicted, lead to the election of an extremist Reichstag including a hundred Communists and twenty or thirty rightist Deutsch-Völkisch Party members. However dangerous such a Reichstag, in Stresemann's view it would at least have the virtue of forcing the various responsible parties to pull together and behave more sensibly. Happily, the joyless election predicted by Stresemann was put off to a safer time because the Socialists came to their senses, albeit only after Ebert threatened to govern by means of Article 48 and it became clear that only the DNVP had an interest in seeing elections conducted under the state of emergency and that Germany would receive no financial support from abroad if the law failed. The new Enabling Act, which was passed on December 8 and was to remain in effect until February 15, 1924, encompassed all measures necessary to meet the existing emergency. Social insurance and hours of work were no longer exempted. As Marx noted, "the cabinet wants to have a calm period in which to finish all the responsible and necessary work which is necessary in view of the miserable condition of our economy and finances. Decrees must be issued to which the Reichstag would never give its approval, but which it will perhaps accept if the responsibility can be shifted to the government."[169] The only concession made by the government was a promise to consult with a special Reichstag committee and the Reichsrat on important measures. The Marx Cabinet now had the powers it needed to confront the very real threats to the currency reform as well as to take the measures required for its success.

Chapter 17

Saving the Stabilization, December 1923–April 1924

Establishing Credibility

Needless to say, the believability of the currency reform had not automatically been established by its implementation. Such credibility would depend on repeated confirmation, especially through direct and usually unpleasant experience demonstrating that the government meant business. Neither the Munich lawyer Karl Lowenstein nor his friends, for example, believed that the Rentenmark would end the inflation. Returning from a trip to Italy and having arrived at the German border after November 20, however, he confronted valorized train fare that had to be paid with much more money than he had. When he asked the agent at the ticket counter how he was supposed to get to Munich, that worthy pointed to the dozens of hanging watches in his booth and invited Herr Lowenstein to join the crowd of those who had pawned their watches as security for a train trip. The experience undoubtedly contributed to the revision of Lowenstein's attitude toward the currency reform.[1]

Efforts were also made to enforce respect for and faith in the new currency. To be sure, some businessmen were outraged at the idea of accepting the Rentenmark as a full-valued currency. It is not surprising that some Hamburg businessmen should feel this way. They had always been critical of Berlin's currency policies, and Hamburg had its own valorized currency. As one angry business group protested to the Hamburg Chamber of Commerce:

The fraudulent monetary policy of the Reich during the last five years has buried all business morals, but this latest confidence-man operation is the crowning moment. The government of a German state threatens those who do not consider the Rentenmark which it has just brought into circulation to be of equal worth to the Hamburg Goldmark with humiliating penalties! This makes it seem as if those who counterfeit money can successfully employ the power of the laws against forging coins and notes against those who operate and *must* operate with the circumspection of a decent merchant![2]

While the Hamburg merchants do not seem to have challenged the government at this point, others did, and the government did indeed use compulsion. Two days after the Rentenmark was issued and the fixed exchange rate of the paper mark was being rapidly increased, the military commander in Saxony ordered the speedy arrest of "parasites on the body of the nation" who tried to persuade workers to sell their valorized currency for amounts of paper marks somewhat higher than the day's quotation.[3] When officials in upper Bavaria relayed rumors that the Rentenmark was being valued at twenty gold pfennig in Switzerland and seventy to eighty gold pfennig in Munich, the authorities in Munich replied that orders had been issued to arrest businessmen who refused to accept the new currency at full value. It was less easy, of course, to silence the Bavarian People's Party leader, Baron von Soden, who gave a particularist speech on November 25 deprecating the new currency and calling upon Bavaria to issue its own valorized currency. While the audience unanimously approved the creation of a Bavarian currency, it was a good deal less than unanimous in its approval of von Soden's attack on the Rentenmark. What this revealed was that the thirst for valorized currencies had become unquenchable. Indeed, prob-

Inflation money on the pyre. (*By permission of the Ullstein Verlag*)

ably most persuasive in turning public opinion in favor of the Rentenmark was the combination of yearning for the new currency and its scarcity. In lower Bavaria, for example, civil servants were extremely resentful that Jewish hops dealers and other commercial circles, thanks to their supposed "good connections," had allegedly gained access to the new money earlier than civil servants, although the latter were supposed to be paid in the new currency first. Could there be a better recommendation for the Rentenmark than that of the detested Jewish merchants?[4]

Nevertheless, it would take more than valorized train fares, police methods, and the significance lower Bavarians attributed to the monetary preferences of Jewish merchants to guarantee confidence. Despite the Rentenmark's stability, its acceptance by those who would count most in the end remained tentative during the first months of its existence. As the American Vice Consul in Hamburg, Maurice Walk, reported:

... there are defects it is said, inherent in the new plan, which will make the depreciation of the Rentenmark inevitable. In the opinion of these people the State in the near future will be forced by the pressure of ever-increasing deficits into some manner of inflation to maintain the functions of government. The arrangements announced by the financial bodies

to accommodate the Rentenmark transactions have been made with this possibility in view. The banks will not accept Rentenmark deposits in gold accounts but have separate Rentenmark accounts. Since a gold account obligates the bank to repay the same gold value which was deposited, the refusal to accept the Rentenmark in gold accounts shows a lack of faith in the stability of the new currency on the part of precisely those elements in the community which are looked to for leadership in financial affairs. It is difficult to blame the banks for being cautious, but caution in such matters is very difficult to differentiate from suspicion. Other bodies, such as manufacturers' syndicates, and—to mention a conspicuous case—the management of the Frankfort Affair [*sic*], state openly in the published selling conditions that the Rentenmark will not be accepted in payment on the same basis as stable foreign monies, but only after a discount. If the Rentenmark is discredited the fault will be due in no small measure to such public manifestations of distrust by those very groups which should exert themselves to generate a confidence in its stability.

On balance, however, Walk was optimistic because the

possibilities of inflation are patently exhausted. It had its.advantages and at one time was probably a necessary policy. But if it had a historical function that function was certainly outlived after the summer of 1922. From that time until the adoption of the Rentenmark the country was castigated with the evils of an outworn program that the Government was unable or unwilling, perhaps for political reasons, to alter. There seems to be no doubt that such internal opposition has ceased at last, and that the business world is now supporting the government sincerely in the new project of currency reform.[5]

Whether the possibilities of inflation can ever be exhausted, however, is an open question, although they are obviously more exhausted after a hyperinflation than a more moderate inflationary experience. Germany had, after all, experienced relative stabilization between the springs of 1920 and 1921, an easing of inflationary indicators between December 1921 and February 1922, and a relative stabilization between February and April 1923. The last-mentioned stabilization effort had come in the wake of hyperinflation, and while one may plead that its failure was caused by the continued Ruhr crisis, there was no guarantee that Germany's international problems would be solved satisfactorily when the stabilization effort of the fall of 1923 was undertaken. Clearly, there was more recent and substantial precedent for the government succumbing to inflationary practices in order to keep operating than the reverse.[6] Things were different this time because of a critical combination of measures and also because the stabilization consensus was broad enough to make the bitter medicine temporarily palatable and the government was prepared to exert its authority despite the political risks.

A powerful example of the changed environment was provided by the railroad system, which had been refused a loan by the Rentenbank in keeping with its practice of lending money only to the Finance Ministry and which was no longer qualified to receive government subsidization. In fact, the railroad system was not only ceasing to serve as a prime illustration of Germany's mismanagement and woes but was well on its way to becoming a paradigm for their solution. The railroad system had already been close to balancing its budget at the end of 1922, but the process was interrupted by the Ruhr occupation. When confronted by the inability of the Reich to provide the foreign exchange needed to buy coal for its winter needs in the fall of 1923, it had managed to procure a loan of four million pounds sterling from an English banking consortium headed by the banking house of Schroeder with the approval and participation of the Bank of England. In return for the loan, it had to put up its lignite mines as security and procure a guarantee in hard currency from German banks and shipping firms. Thanks to the aid of the houses of Bleichröder, Mendelssohn, and Warburg, as well as the Hapag and other firms, the guarantee was secured. The conditions, as Warburg noted, were "onerous," but the arrangement had political as well as economic benefit because "by this means the English government would develop an interest in the profit of the German railroads, and would if necessary oppose French plans with respect to the railroads on the Rhine and Ruhr."[7] Oeser's true goal, however, was to balance his budget and make his railroad system self-financing by separating it entirely from the Treasury. He pursued this aim by a rate policy which, as he frankly admitted, made him many enemies and by a brutal personnel policy. Finally, on February 12, 1924, the Deutsche Reichsbahn was established as an independent enterprise under the Enabling Act, although its rate and personnel policies remained subject to approval.[8]

Needless to say, normal Germans could not take pound sterling loans to make it through the cold winter, and while previous stabilization attempts had been marked by decontrol efforts and price increases, one of the hallmarks of the stabilization of 1923–1924 was the government's willingness to tolerate a far broader level of misery than it had in the past. As one observer reported in early January, ". . . there is complaint of suffering among people who are not able to buy enough fuel at prevailing high prices to keep warm. There is considerable unemployment and but little to distribute as unemployment doles, while wages are not sufficient to enable people to cope successfully with the high cost of living."[9] While the Reich did provide some funds for states and municipalities to purchase coal for the needy, the fundamental problem was that one-quarter of all Germans were in need of some support at the turn of 1923–1924. At the end of November there were between four million and five million unemployed or short-time workers in Germany, including those who were not receiving any support, and if one includes their families, then the total amounted to between twelve million and fifteen million persons. Furthermore, the high point of unemployment was not to be reached until January 1924. To their numbers, of course, must be added pensioners and rentiers, many of whom were now more in need of assistance.[10]

There was not much Christmas spirit emanating from Berlin in late 1923. Transportation Minister Oeser had given instructions that railroad employees in the occupied areas should not be fired before Christmas and urged that firings under the Personnel Reduction Decree not take place at holiday time, although this hardly gave anyone much to look forward to in the new year. The Labor Ministry certainly was not in a very giving mood at a meeting on December 18 to discuss the support of pensioners and rentiers. The state government representatives were informed that only half the amount granted during the previous three months would be available during the coming quarter. The number of those receiving support would, therefore, have to be even more severely limited, and he urged "strict testing of need, rigid application of legal support requirements [by the families of those being supported], and greater attention to possible employment possibilities."[11] Greater use was to be made of private charity, especially through collections of money and clothes, soup kitchens, and shelters. A special point was made of the fact that support of the unemployed, which was itself being restricted and reduced, would have to be higher than that of the pensioners and rentiers and that the number of unemployed was increasing. Not surprisingly, therefore, the Saxon Labor Minister Georg Elsner, when subjected to one of the usual fruitless Communist resolutions in the Saxon Landtag calling for higher support of the unemployed, gloomily responded that "I know that the justified hopes of the unemployed are kindled by this resolution, and there is nothing I would like to do more than be able to say that we are in a position, if not in this form, then in a more modest one, to give something to the unemployed. I am convinced that thousands of unemployed will be sitting home during the holidays with hardly dry bread at their disposal. There can be no doubt . . . about the distress of the unemployed, but the goodwill of the Labor Ministry and of the Finance Ministry founders on the impossible situation we face."[12]

There was a striking emphasis on charity, both foreign and domestic, to meet the situation, and there was some criticism by foreigners of the failure of German institutions to take care of their poor and starving. The official German response and attitude was effectively presented by Agricultural Minister von Kanitz at a meeting of the Food Ministers on December 18:

Welfare efforts have assumed large proportions, for example, soup kitchens. Berlin especially has been a model during the last four weeks, but there is still much to do. The reproach from abroad that the Germans are doing nothing for their starving fellow citizens is absolutely unjustified. . . . Much has been given, but there is more to do. I fear that the charity donations on the part of agriculture and industry will be diminished by the increasing tax burdens. The German people are certainly the best in the world; the good naturedness, the quiet sufferance with which the German people bear hunger, will and must be an incentive to do everything to eliminate the food market problems.[13]

Germans certainly needed and were grateful for help from abroad, especially when it was well and fairly administered and was not tainted by the favoritism and corruption which sometimes marred German charity operations. There was considerable satisfaction with the manner in which the Swiss administered (in Württemberg and Baden) the free meals provided by a substantial number of their cities. When the Mayor of Bendorf on the Rhine learned of American collections for Germany, he felt impelled to write and ask for help for his town, 65 percent of the citizens of which were unemployed and many of whom were starving old rentiers. The American Consul in Koblenz had little difficulty recommending the cause since he reported that the distress was visible to even the casual observer. As always, however, one also noted extravagance by those who were more fortunate. While expressing his sympathy for "the countless thousands" of Germany's "starving inhabitants" and the "old moneyed middle class . . . eking out a miserable existence supported by Government, by municipalities and by charitable organizations, and bearing their lot with admirable fortitude," the U.S. Consul in Hamburg noted that "their places had been taken by a new set of people, comfortably well-off and making money even in these hard times by anything but praiseworthy methods."[14] Similarly, an American on the expert commission that visited Berlin was rather perturbed when invited to visit a soup kitchen in Berlin on a Sunday to discover that they were all closed: "They do not feed anybody on Sunday."[15] The banker Arthur Young had a similar mixed impression when he visited Saxony. He found shops frequented by inflation profiteers in a position to buy pineapples, grapefruit, and caviar for prices higher than in Washington, D.C.; he also found that wages were so low that "it is hard to see what the poor people do."[16]

Certainly such disparities, which had been striking foreign visitors trying to figure out what was going on in Germany since the end of the war, were not the intention of Brauns or Luther, for whom financial and economic recovery were paramount. Brauns, in contrast to some members of the Cabinet, for example, showed no patience whatever to the pleas of Seeckt that the reduction of pensions and miserable salaries paid to civil servants in December 1923 would hurt the morale of the army and police. Brauns insisted that the "entire social dismantling which the Reich Labor Ministry is now undertaking and the great hardships for those affected, will be endangered if the law for the reduction of pensions is not carried out."[17] It was grim enough that the salaries of civil servants, which were placed on a gold basis in December, ranged from 39 to 75 percent below those of 1913, but it was even more painful when Luther announced that full salaries could not be paid as scheduled on December 17 and expressed the hope that revenue would permit full payment four days later. This necessarily hurt the morale of the civil servants, and the situation was no better in the new year: "The civil service is depressed, disturbed and angry over the reduction of their salaries, the loss of their savings and interest, to which on the other side has been added the lengthening of their working hours and rumors about the reduction of their vacations and the danger of personnel reductions."[18]

The condition of the working class was certainly no better and often worse, and it is important to recognize that government intervention proved virtually as central to the increasing of hours and reduction of real wages of the workers in private industry as it was for the civil service. It was the government that had permitted the demobilization decrees to lapse on November 17 after issuing the decree extending the practice of binding arbitration on October 30. The final and most crucial step in the process of extending the working day in the private sector was the Hours-of-Work Decree Brauns issued on December 21, 1923, which maintained the eight-hour day in principle while permitting the ten-hour day in normal plants and the twelve-hour day in continuously operating plants through administrative exception or collective bargaining agreement. For the situation in the winter of 1923–1924, it was most important that §13 of the decree permitted employers to give three-day notice on existing collective bargaining contracts and thus open up negotiations for new contracts involving an extension of working hours. Under the existing conditions, there could be no doubt that the Labor Ministry would then use its binding arbitration powers to extend the working day.[19]

While workers were understandably unhappy with the manner in which the Labor Ministry presided over the dismantling of the eight-hour day and the reduction of real wages in the stream of collective bargaining negotiations unleashed by the RAM deccrees, it is essential to recognize that industry, too, was far from pleased with these arrangements, even when gratified by the results. The more ferocious employers—above all, in the Ruhr—were against any enthronment of the eight-hour day, even if purely in principle, and hoped to eliminate collective bargaining. More moderate employers, while certainly willing to take advantage of their upper hand, preferred to maintain collective bargaining but detested binding arbitration because it meant potential state control of labor relations. They preferred risking future tests of power with the workers in negotiation and even strikes and lockouts to accepting bureaucratic regulation that might shift in favor of the workers once conditions changed. Officially, the Socialist trade union leaders also opposed state interference in collective bargaining, but their loss of membership and weak position in 1923 made them highly vulnerable, and they were unprepared to accept an offer from Bücher in January 1924 to maintain the ZAG and join forces against binding arbitration. They had to recognize that Brauns was seeking to maintain and strengthen the unions, if nothing else than as a bulwark against the growing influence of the Communists, and also that Brauns absolutely refused to accede to employer calls for freedom from the requirement to enter into collective bargaining agreements. The mutual trust between industry and labor, such as it was, and the alliance against the state of 1918 were no longer possible, and it was preferable to protect collective bargaining through binding arbitration than to let the economic forces operative in the stabilization place all at risk. Thus, the ZAG collapsed in the first weeks of 1924 when the Socialist unions withdrew from membership.[20]

What such a description of the formal arrangements among state organizations, industry, and labor cannot convey is the hostility, the frustration and depression, and the bitterness that characterized much of the relations between workers and employers in the stabilization. Certainly, the morale of the Ruhr workers had been undermined by the Ruhr conflict and by payments for doing little or nothing, but the statement of a director to his workers that "the behavior of the workers in the factories since the beginning of the Ruhr struggle has been a much less satisfactory one than before" and that "the *Schlamperei* must cease" surely was poor recompense to the workers for their patriotism and was at once vengeful and condescending.[21] It is a good deal less surprising, of course, to find a Saxon employer like the DVP Deputy Noack explaining the disciplinary and economic advantages of unemployment and low unemployment supports to a stormy session of the Saxon Landtag. He insisted that the cost of living would be brought down by

. . . you will not like to hear it—increasing labor productivity, more intensive work, and lengthening of the work day. (Commotion on the floor of the house). You do not fancy it, but it is so. Naturally the number of the unemployed will thereby increase, but the costs of production will be less, foreign and domestic orders will increase, and the number of unemployed will decrease again. (Very true! on the right). The way to an improvement in our economic circumstances is through an increased unemployment and higher labor productivity. (Very true! on the right.) Whether you want to hear it or not, it is so.[22]

Some workers unquestionably "got" the message even without Herr Noack's gratuitous assistance. One official noted that "the chief

thought among the workers is to get work at any price and not to be thrown out onto the street. The amount of the wages and length of the working day is considered only secondarily. The economic distress has pushed the affairs of the trade unions and organizations as well as political activity into the background."[23] It would be a mistake, however, to overestimate the passivity of the workers. The year 1924 was to be filled with lockouts and with strikes, militance and radicalization.[24]

The low real wages which accompanied the systematic increase of working hours did much to confirm opinions that the costs of the war and inflation were being disproportionately imposed on the working class. Whereas in the relative stabilization of 1920–1921 the unions had fought with some success for the principle that the reduction of prices had to precede or at least accompany the reduction of wages, they were left with little or no opportunity to debate or discuss the issue in the stabilization of 1923–1924. Employers not only had been very slow about valorizing wages despite their own calculation in fixed currencies but also had insisted that worker demands for payment on a gold basis could not take place until there was sufficient valorized currency circulating in the economy. Most important, they were united in a policy of stabilizing wages at 30 percent below prewar levels—even at 40 to 50 percent below 1913 rates in the case of some employer organizations—in order to take into account the impoverishment of the economy and high production costs. At the same time, they intended to restore the differentials between skilled and unskilled, older and younger, and male and female workers.[25]

This policy was implemented with the stabilization of wages at the end of November and beginning of December, and it was maintained during the next few months in the face of strong opposition from unions and workers and considerable labor conflict. The unions argued, with much justification, that the diminished purchasing power of money since 1913 and the stickiness of prices meant that real wages had been reduced by 70 percent rather than 30 percent, while employers claimed that the period was a "transitional" one and that prices would fall significantly once there were enough Rentenmark in circulation and merchants had a chance to respond to lower production prices. They were especially anxious to hold the line because they knew that rent controls were bound to be relaxed and that wages would have to be increased to take housing costs into account.

The dispute over wages was further complicated by a sharp disagreement within the government itself. The Labor Ministry, like the Economics Ministry, was anxious to establish long-term collective bargaining agreements with wages set somewhere between two-thirds and four-fifths of prewar earnings, and the signals given by Brauns to the arbitrators appointed by his Ministry exerted a strong influence on their decisions. Apparently, this was not enough for the Finance Ministry, which had set what it admitted to be extremely low wage and salary levels for state employees and, in mid-January, urged Brauns to use the Enabling Act to force the arbitration boards to make public-service pay scales the standard for private industry. What this would have meant in practice can be exemplified by comparing the highest paid train conductor and a skilled Berlin metal worker in 1914 and 1924. The former was earning 1,500 marks a year in 1914; the latter, 1,458 marks. In December 1924, the comparable yearly wage was 980 marks for the train conductor and 1,248 for the metal worker. That is, the *nominal* gold wage of the train conductor was 65.3 percent of his 1914 salary, while that of the metal worker was 85.6 percent of his 1914 income. The real wage, of course, was much lower since the cost of living had increased substantially since 1914. Both Brauns and Hamm sharply attacked the Finance Ministry proposal, which sought to impose the consequences of the fiscal crisis of the state on those working in the private sector and spare the government the unavoidable pressure from the state employees for an improvement of their miserable wages and salaries. They objected to the idea that the state should dictate wages and rejected as spurious the argument that so great a depression of wages and salaries would bring down prices in a healthy manner. They responded to this claim by pointing out that there were limits below which purchasing power could not sink without damaging the economy

itself and undermining German industry's effort to be internationally competitive without destroying the domestic market. In their judgment, the wage reduction effort required greater emphasis on the reduction of prices.[26]

It is important to recognize that this view was widely shared by employers. In fact, some were incensed by the absurd prices being demanded for consumer goods by farmers and merchants. A Rhenish metal firm complained in mid-November that meat prices ranging from half a pfennig to a mark before the war were now ranging from 3.20 to 6.50 marks. As had been the case in Hamburg when it had issued its giro mark, so now throughout Germany were merchants using the coexistence of valorized currencies with an artificial unitary exchange rate for the paper mark to jack up their gold prices. Often they claimed that their prices were taking "world increases in prices" into account, but even allowing for fertilizer costs, it was very hard to see what relevance world price increases had for the price of German meat, fruit, and potatoes. The situation was no better a month later in Berlin, where a skilled chemical worker was receiving 21.60 marks for a forty-eight-hour workweek as compared to 25.50 in 1913 for a fifty-one-hour workweek, while the cost of food for himself and a family of three had risen from 9.34 marks in 1913 to 15.51 marks. Nevertheless, the employer organizations took the position that wages should not be increased and sought to influence the retailer organizations to lower their prices. Prices did, in fact, decrease in Berlin by 8 to 10 percent in January. While workers in the Berlin metal industry asked for an increase of wages from fifty to sixty pfennig an hour, employers called for a reduction of wages to forty-three pfennig an hour before both sides settled on an hourly wage of forty-eight pfennig. Before the war, they had earned fifty-five pfennig, but the purchasing power of their wage then had been 40 to 80 percent greater.[27]

By mid-December, the Reich Economics Ministry was devoting a good deal of its energy to this problem by promoting the reduction of prices, and this necessarily meant continued pressure on retailers and merchants who directly or indirectly served the consumer. One of the more important new instruments in the hands of the RWM was the so-called Decree Against the Misuse of Economic Power, or Cartel Decree of November 2, 1923, which had been issued by the Stresemann government. Legislation against the pricing abuses of cartels had been demanded for years, of course, and action was finally taken because the measure was viewed as a "political precondition" for extending the hours of work. The law could in no way be construed as anti-cartel legislation, since the maintenance of cartels was considered "essential" and a deliberate effort was made to avoid using "heavy artillery." Rather, the decree sought to strike a "middle road," emphasizing supervision of cartels through the gathering of information and intervention through cartel courts in cases of egregious abuse that could not be rectified by government pressure and mediation.[28]

A more immediate and potent inspiration to retailers was provided by General von Seeckt, who employed his emergency powers on December 7 to order that stores display their prices in gold marks. For retailers, this had the advantage of reducing the number of zeros that had to be attached to every item they sold, while for the Economics Ministry it was a welcome opportunity to recondition merchants to think in gold values. On December 17, the RWM distributed a Memorandum on Appropriate Gold Mark Prices which purported to establish the prices of the most important items purchased by consumers in 1913 and then an appropriate market price under existing conditions. The memorandum postulated a "genuine price increase" of 60 to 70 percent and then sharply differentiated between consumer goods whose prices were influenced by foreign imports and those primarily of German origin. At the same time, the memorandum sought to change the manner in which wholesalers and retailers thought about prices. On the one hand, it sought to delegitimize such inflation practices as calculating currency depreciation and depreciation risk in pricing; on the other, it challenged inherited notions of levels of operation and profit and argued that an impoverished economy could be operated on pre-1914 assumptions. In the process, it was also very critical of the gap between producer and wholesaler prices and the interest rates charged to mer-

chants by banks. In the last analysis, the memorandum was a highly diplomatic document, asserting that "1913 prices were a thing of the past"; though the reduced income of labor meant that German prices would have to remain behind world-market price increases, at the same time consumers would have to understand that supply and demand set necessary limits on all government intervention in pricing matters.[29]

In any event, controls against profiteering not only continued but were even intensified at the turn of 1923–1924. Bavaria, where von Kahr continued to rule despite being discredited by his involvement with Hitler prior to the Putsch, seems to have been particularly diligent. The mere presence of criminal inspectors in various towns led to "voluntary" price reductions by bakers and butchers, while the arrest of a couple for selling geese for 1.60 to 1.80 marks per pound (when the going price was 1.10 to 1.20 per pound) and the confiscation of thirteen geese demonstrated a vigilance typical of the Bavarian authorities.[30] Such actions were not a peculiarity of the South, however, for numerous retailers and wholesalers were cited in November and December for excessive prices and profiteering in the Duisburg area. While many of those charged were subsequently acquitted, the pressure certainly was significant, and the claims of those charged that they were reacting to exorbitant interest rates from the banks and profiteering led to citations of the banks as well. In any event, Hamm was able to report to the Cabinet on January 11 that prices were being reduced by the coal industry and other cartels and that the banks were also moderating some of their terms.[31]

Fundamentally, however, there was a continuation of that constellation of social forces that had prevailed during the inflation with the difference that deflation was replacing inflation and thus increased the foundations for resentment by making the situation more severe. Previously, farmers had complained about the controlled economy, even when it had actually disappeared and despite the fact that they had paid no real taxes and had been well fed and supplied for all their difficulties. Now, they had the feeling "that the golden times of the last nine years are coming to an end."[32] No longer able to take advantage of the *Schieber*, who were out of business, they suddenly found themselves surrendering their produce for low prices and paying heavy taxes. Craftsmen and retailers also remained discontented, complaining loudly about the harsh credit conditions of the banks and angry at big industry for continuing to supply its workers with food at cheap prices and for the neglect of the interests of the *Mittelstand*. In a lengthy gravamen, the retailer organizations warned that "independent existences are almost only to be found in retailing and small business. Very little is left of the once blossoming, strongly rooted German *Mittelstand*." Consequently, they demanded support and protection against big industry and labor.[33] Under the strong economic pressures of a deflationary economy, they became particularly hostile to social costs. In a small Bavarian town, local officials reported that "the view is quite widely expressed in employer circles and even among the insured that the entire social insurance system has been transformed from a 'good deed' to a 'plague.' The district peasant chamber, which has little truck with social considerations in general, is engaging in a systematic resistance to the sickness insurance, which has never enjoyed any popularity among the farmers from the beginning."[34]

This did not mean, however, that the *Mittelstand* was now allied with industry. As had been the case since the war, the basic debate remained that between industry and labor, while what had changed, or had been changing as a result of reparations pressures and the hyperinflation, was the relative advantage between the two sides. The Labor Ministry had ensured that there would be no total victories, or at least no victories that would preclude a labor comeback, and there was plenty of evidence that both sides preferred to jockey rather than fight a total war. This was demonstrated, for example, in a debate in the Social Policy Committee of the Reich Economic Council on the future of German social policy in mid-January 1924. It was a remarkably statesmanlike affair in which employers, while insisting that social policy had to be reduced to the bounds of the economically possible, nevertheless argued that

We do not need to follow the "like it or lump it" policy of the Americans in the area of social policy, which is simply "work or you die." In America, there is no social welfare policy at all. We certainly don't want that. But insofar as questions of how far we want to go in our social legislation and welfare are concerned, the outside world has a voice today. We need foreign credit, and the outside world asks: what are you going to do with the credit? We cannot afford things they cannot afford.[35]

Needless to say, the worker representatives objected to the notion that social policy should depend solely on what employers claimed they could afford, for this would be the end of all social policy, even if they did agree on the need for the rationalization of the social insurance system. For Bücher, however, the lesson of the existing situation was a different one:

It seems as if we have learned nothing in the last four years. What is the situation. You on the worker side have had control of things. (Objection on the left.) Yes, only now that the time is past do you deny it. You have had the decisive influence on the government for four years, for a Republic—and you must know this as Republicans—can only be led by a majority, and you have had it. You have had an absolute majority (Interjection from the left: not since 1920!)—or at least a qualified majority, in that you were able to have the decisive influence because of the divisions in bourgeois society.... After things went so far that in August we stood before an abyss and no person knew the way out, then things turned about somewhat and now the scales fall on our side, which we embody as employer representatives. This is the time to draw the consequences.... I would very much regret it if the employers now made the same mistakes that you have made in the last four years (Interjection from the left: You have gone very far along that road already!), and I promise you, that insofar as I have influence, I will always strive for the employers to find a way to industrial peace.[36]

If it was up to the right-wing Socialist Max Cohen, this goal would not have been difficult to achieve since he felt that workers and their organizations had abused their power and that many of the economic considerations raised by employers were valid. Furthermore, he reminded his colleagues on the left that "much more has been taken from the *Mittelstand*. I believe that a host of such people are being ruined today, which is not the case with the workers."[37] Perhaps so, but it was not something that seemed to perturb the great industrialists very much. One of their leading spokesman compared the inflation to a flood:

What happens in a . . . deluge? Each person tries to bring his life and property to dry land; the water climbs higher and higher and one grasps for the high ground; many naturally run out of strength and there is no room for all on land. Thus many go under and others lose only their property but they have at least saved their naked existences. (Interjection from the left: Many were not allowed to save themselves!)— Yes, but they were the stupid ones who let themselves be prohibited from acting when their survival was at stake; they naturally were wiped out. (Interjection from the left: think about the foreign exchange decree!)[38]

Director Dahl remained unmoved, pointing out that the flight of capital had saved resources for Germany, and he was seconded in his paean to what was frankly labeled as the basic principle of "self-interest" (*Eigennutz*) by another of his colleagues.[39]

Germany, however, was more than its industrialists and workers. There were others for whom the stabilization meant obvious loss, whose only card in hand was the Old Maid, and who felt cheated. They had little incentive to accept the discipline implied by the Rentenmark–paper mark ratio established on November 20, 1923. Furthermore, those expropriated by the currency reform finally found a potentially effective foundation for their claims within days of the issuance of the Rentenmark. Indeed, perhaps the most dangerous of all the threats to the stabilization made its appearance on November 28, 1923, and then hung like the Sword of Damocles over the new government and especially over its sorely tried Finance Minister. On that date, the Fifth Civil Senate of the Supreme Court in Leipzig ruled in favor of the defendant, a Berlin lawyer who had given a mortgage to the plaintiff and was being sued by the latter for refusing to accept paper mark payment in the amount due. It was a rather odd case involving a thirteen-thousand-mark mortgage on a property in the former German colony of Southwest Africa, and there was some uncertainty as to whether the situation was governed by German law, since the two parties lived in Berlin, or by the British law obtaining in the former colony. The mortgage had been given during the war and was repaid on schedule with full interest in April 1920, since which time the case had been heard by two courts which had both decided in favor of the plaintiff. What made the

Supreme Court's reversal of these decisions especially ironic was that it was most unlikely that it would have done so had the paper mark retained some genuine nominal value in 1923. Alois Zeiler, a Supreme Court judge in close contact with some of his colleagues involved in the decision and a revaluation enthusiast, for example, did not think that the decision of November 28 would have been taken had the mark been stabilized at a level comparable to the Austrian krone (14,400 to 1). In fact, the Austrian courts had rejected revaluation and thus accepted a virtual expropriation of creditors. The Supreme Court only acted on behalf of the creditors after the paper mark had been reduced to worthlessness and a new valorized currency had been issued.[40]

Nevertheless, it was a momentous and even revolutionary decision. It marked the culmination of a period of growing legal uncertainty created by a mounting number of contradictory court decisions on the revaluation question. For the first time, the Supreme Court came down clearly on the side of those jurists and courts (above all, Dr. Georg Best, the President of the Darmstadt Superior Court) who insisted that the courts had a responsibility to act on behalf of the principle of equity and good faith enshrined in §242 of the Civil Code if and when the state refused to do so. Abandoning the tradition of legal positivism that insisted that it was the task of the courts to apply legislation in accordance with its specifications rather than review it in terms of intentions or general norms, the court now saw fit to evaluate the validity of the prewar legal-tender legislation in the light of totally changed and unanticipated circumstances:

The legislator . . . did not contemplate an essential depreciation of paper money, especially one so great as developed steadily after the World War and the Revolution. With the collapse of the paper mark there ensued a conflict between these currency provisions on the one side and, on the other, all those various legal provisions which aimed to prevent a debtor from being in a position to rid himself of his obligations in a manner which cannot be reconciled with the requirements of good faith and with commercial usages, that is to say, with the overriding mandate of Art. 242, Civil Code. In this conflict, the last-mentioned rule must take precedence and the currency legislation must give way, because . . . at the time of its enactment it was not foreseen that such a collapse of the currency might occur that the results could not be reconciled with the basic rules of good faith and with fairness; so that a strict application of its provisions in this situation was not contemplated.[41]

The decision was a major step toward the introduction of judicial review in Germany and, hence, "revolutionary" in its implications, and the step was taken in the context of a claim that existing law could be overturned in the name of such general legal clauses as "equity" and "good faith." It is important to note, however, that the decision in no way specified any form or level of revaluation. In fact, the principle of equity and good faith implied that each case would have to be considered on its own merits and take into account such factors as the changed value of the debtor's property, the time of purchase and mortgage repayment, and the economic circumstances of the parties. A new "Age of Litigation" seemed to be dawning for the sorely tried Weimar Republic.

Certainly it may be argued that the judges did not much care about the Republic and that their decision was self-interested to boot. Leftist critics of the Weimar judiciary had every reason to ask if the judges would have dared to make such claims under the monarchy, and it is noteworthy that the court chose to base its decision not on §151 of the Weimar Constitution which enjoined that the economic life of the nation must be based on "justice" and §153 which barred expropriation of property without "suitable compensation" but on so flimsy and "shapeless" a foundation as §242 of the Civil Code.[42] At the same time, the judges came from precisely that social stratum most negatively affected by the hyperinflation. Georg Best, who held 97,600 prewar marks in mortgages, had an obvious interest in revaluation.[43]

Yet, these are hardly satisfactory explanations for the judicial reaction; it must really be placed in the context of a festering grievance to which the government had simply failed to respond. The rejection of the Düringer proposal to place a moratorium on mortgage repayments except by mutual agreement in the spring of 1923 had only served to accelerate mortgage and bond repayment. In late October 1923, for example, Bavarian mortgage banks were repaying their prewar bonds, offering to pay 1,000,000 percent more than the par value. The bondholders were thus being offered one twenty-five thousandth of what they had loaned and were being threatened with payment at nominal value if they refused the offer. The banks claimed, with some justice, that they had no choice since the farm loans they had made were being repaid in completely depreciated currency thanks to the failure of the Düringer proposal and the manner in which both the Bavarian and the Reich governments were catering to farmers. The banks felt all the more impelled to act because they were afraid that the debtor organizations might force through legal measures revaluating mortgages. In fact, the Bavarian government itself had urged a moratorium on mortgage repayments in the Reichsrat in September 1923 which had been turned down by the then Justice Minister Radbruch with the argument that a moratorium was superfluous since any decision on revaluation could only be made after stabilization and would then certainly be retroactive.[44]

Radbruch, like most of his Socialist colleagues, was an opponent of revaluation at this time, however, and his answer was not convincing. Furthermore, it did not reflect the distress within the judiciary over a perceived loss of faith in the courts and the law as a result of the expropriation of mortgage holders through payment in depreciated money. When the Prussian Justice Minister, the Centrist revaluation supporter Hugo am Zenhoff, asked the Prussian Superior Courts' Presidents to give their views on the revaluation question, many responded by pointing to the increasing breakdown of confidence in the legal system. Zenhoff himself composed a memorandum urging support for the Bavarian moratorium proposal on November 15, condemning the "immoral" manner in which mortgages had been paid off, and warning that

It is obvious that such a failure of the legal order must lead to a serious shattering of legal sensibility and confidence in the state. That this has already transpired is plainly evident from the numerous newspaper articles, decisions by protective associations and private petitions which continuously reach me. It is especially regrettable that the losses of this kind more often hit those who have modest savings upon which they depend for their support and who thus fall into the bitterest misery.[45]

Am Zenhoff warned that if the legislators failed to take action, the courts would feel impelled to do so. His comments demonstrated that the forthcoming Reich Supreme Court decision, at which Zenhoff hinted, was very much in the air. At the same time, he rejected the idea that there was any reason to fear that the revaluation of private debts would carry over into public or foreign paper-mark-denominated debts:

I have the impression from numerous petititions that the population finds it much easier to come to terms with the depreciation of war bonds and other bonds than with the nominal repayment of private debts. They take the view that the individual has made a sacrifice for the community which cannot be repaid because of the unfortunate result of the war. But it is different if the debtor is a private person. Here it is justifiably found to be unbearable that the disadvantage of the depreciation should hit the creditor alone, while the economic position of the debtor has improved during and after the war and the debtor very frequently finds himself in much better circumstances than the creditor. I do not believe, therefore, that there will be resistance if public loans are exempted from the general revaluation. This also serves to weaken the reservations which the Commerce Minister has raised concerning foreign holders of public loans. They, or at least the most influential foreign circles, have understood for some time now that the Reich and the states are incapable of paying for the foreseeable future, namely for as long as they are overburdened with completely unbearable reparations burdens.[46]

Even here, Zenhoff wondered about the advisability of paying off public debts in purely nominal terms, but his concentration and that of the Supreme Court was on private credit relations.

It is worth noting that these views were not shared by every jurist. In early January, after the Supreme Court decision of November 28 had unleashed considerable debate within the government and the press, President Wernek of the Superior Court in Naumburg in Prussian Saxony sharply and bluntly criticized the view that a "mistake" had been made by the government in upholding the principle of mark for mark and made no bones about the advantages of the hyperinflation:

The depreciation of mortgages is only a partial reflection of the depreciation of monetary capital, and that is only a partial reflection of the catastrophe which has befallen our people and economy. One of the few true things which the leaders of the French state have

said about Germany is that Germany, however much the consequences of the war may have fallen harder upon her than the other participants, at least has the advantage of having been liberated from all the debts piled up before and during the war. I have never encountered any doubt that the depreciation of liquid capital has been fortunate for the nation as a whole, however fearfully hard and unfair it has often been for individuals. One has only to imagine what the situation would be if one had not done what the decision characterizes as a "mistake" and had not sought to maintain the principle mark for mark to the very last, but rather had allowed a revaluation of all monetary claims in conformity to the depreciation. The public debt would have been incapable of numerical expression, the collapse of the currency would have occurred at an even more extreme and destructive pace, and it is impossible to imagine that we could have come out of our financial misery by any means other than a Depreciation Law that without doubt would have spared no liquid capital whether backed by security or not. Domestic pacification would not have been attainable by any other means. If that is now taking place slowly and with hesitation, then we owe this happy circumstance chiefly to the depreciation of our liquid capital.[47]

Indeed, Wernek was brutally concrete about the situation. He noted that most of the farmers had paid off their mortgages and that it was precisely this that made it a paying proposition for them to produce despite low prices. He saw no way to legitimize the separation of private from public debts, especially if one took into account that much of the postwar public debt was contracted by cities and provinces for construction projects and other capital investments. Similarly, the province of Saxony had been able to peddle its emergency money because it was able to state openly that the propertied classes in the province were free of debt and thus in a position to pay taxes. In fact, the government's entire stabilization depended upon the debtlessness of agrarian and industrial producers and house owners, who could now be compelled to pay taxes. Wernek warned against any attempt to undo the past and subject the currency reform and the state itself to new shocks. On the contrary, "equity and private legal relations must make way for the welfare of the state."[48]

Luther could not have agreed more. He was counting on the taxation of debtor inflation profits to balance his budget and understandably likened the Supreme Court decision of November 28 to the explosion of a bomb. The sin-

**Table 48. Revenues of the Reich from Customs and Taxes,
December 1923 and January 1924**

(in millions of gold marks)

	December	January
Total	312,321.9	503,463.9
Of Which Was Received from:		
(a) wage and salary withholding	37,351.8	74,716.9
(b) assessed income tax	3,129.3	90,079.7
(a) + (b)	40,481.1	164,796.6
(a) + (b) in Percent of Total Revenue	12.9%	32.7%
(b) in Percent of Total Revenue	1.0%	17.9%
Corporation Tax	529.7	34,903.0
Percent of Total Revenue from Corporation Tax	0.17%	6.9%

Source: Karl-Bernhard Netzband and Hans Peter Widmaier, *Währungs- und Finanzpolitik der Ära Luther,
1923–1925* (Tübingen, 1964), p. 149.

cerity of his taxation efforts was unquestionable, driven on, as they were, in an atmosphere of panic resulting from the rapidity with which the government entitlement to Rentenmark credits was being used up. The role played by panic was particularly evident in the First Emergency Tax Decree of December 7, 1923. It had to be issued under Article 48 because of the Cabinet crisis and the delay of the passage of the new Enabling Act of December 8. The object of the decree was to increase government revenues very substantially in December and January by requiring prepayment of half the January installment of the Rhine-Ruhr Levy by December 18 in gold marks and by placing the prepayment of the turnover tax for December and January, which was itself increased, on a gold basis with retroactivity for November. In pushing this highly successful measure through the Cabinet, Luther showed no sympathy whatever for warnings by Agricultural Minister Kanitz that agricultural production would be harmed and by the claims of Economics Minister Hamm that craftsmen would be ruined. Luther warned that only farmers would suffer from reduced production, one of the obvious purposes of the heavy taxation being to force them to produce and deliver, and flatly declared that no exceptions could be made for craftsmen or anyone else.[49]

On December 19, after weeks of work by the officials of his Ministry, Luther took a next and more comprehensive step by issuing the Second Emergency Tax Decree, this time under the powers granted by the Enabling Act, which

completed the work of placing all taxes on a gold basis. The greatest difficulties lay in finding some basis for collecting income, corporation, and other direct taxes for the years 1923 and 1924. The hyperinflation made sensible assessment of incomes for 1923 an impossibility, and the balances of most corporations, except for the few that had gone over to accounting in gold values, were as nonsensical as they were useless. Nevertheless, Luther was intent on collecting as much as he could, and the result was a series of complex if crude regulations designed to achieve this purpose. No assessments were to be made for 1923. However, a "fifth quarter" was attached to 1923, and 1922 assessments and payments of non-wage earners and corporations were used to charge income and corporation taxes for 1923 taxes calculated in gold values. At the same time, prepayments for 1924 were to be estimated and collected on the basis of such measures as turnover, production, and assets. However unsatisfactory from a "scientific" point of view, this enabled Luther to collect substantial sums immediately until the formidable and unexpectedly time-consuming difficulties involved in establishing gold balances could be overcome. In January 1924, income and corporation taxes, especially assessed income taxes, constituted a truly significant portion of the greatly increased real revenues of the Reich (see Table 48). As in the case of the first decree, Luther received loud complaints from those affected, especially the farmers, who even threatened to rally before the Finance Ministry offices on the Wilhelmplatz with their threshing machines, tractors, and other farm implements. Despite their grumbling, however, the farmers refrained from such dramatic gestures, and Luther later attributed their relative passivity to their identification with the Rentenmark and realization of their stake in it.[50]

There were other cows that Luther wished to milk, and his greatest challenge came not from farmers but rather from the revaluation enthusiasts he confronted while struggling to appropriate inflation profits through his projected Third Emergency Tax Decree. Specifically, he wished to impose significant but nonrecurring taxes on the inflation profits made by enterprises that had issued bonds and paid them off in depreciated currency, on those who had repaid credits in depreciated money, and on those who had profiteered from the issuance of emergency money. He attached particular importance to a projected recurring tax on rents (*Mietzinssteuer* or *Hauszinssteuer*) under which house owners would be allowed to raise rents gradually from 40 to 80 percent of prewar levels between April and December 1924, while the public purse would take a percentage of the higher rents, beginning with 10 percent in April and rising to a 30 percent level by the end of the year. Thus, while the house owners would once again get rents that would allow for improvements and encourage construction, the state would tax away the inflation profit they had made through the depreciation of mortgage values. At the same time, Luther made the rent tax the centerpiece of the tax equalization among the Reich, the states, and the municipalities which was also to be regulated by the decree. The inflation had overthrown previous arrangements and forced the financing of the states and municipalities upon the Reich. The Finance Ministry wished to restore the responsibility of the states and municipalities for their own basic expenditures by allocating certain tax proceeds to the states, and the rent tax was to be the most important of these.[51]

Luther's hostility toward revaluation, which was exceeded in high government circles only by that of Schacht, can thus be well understood. There can be no doubt that if Luther had his choice, he would have responded to the Supreme Court decision of November 28 by generally banning revaluation, and the first draft of

his Third Emergency Tax Decree did precisely that. While his position on some modest revaluation for private mortgages may, in fact, have softened by mid-December, when the matter came up in the Cabinet and in the Reichsrat, his stance remained decidedly negative. His greatest concern was that the revaluation mania would spread to all forms of indebtedness and especially to war bonds and other government obligations. He found it difficult to determine on what basis private and public creditors should be distinguished, and it was hard to see why public obligations which were treated as absolutely secure by prewar courts should be treated less favorably than mortgage bonds which were not so recognized. Even a 10 percent revaluation of the sixty billion war bonds still in circulation would cost the government six billion gold marks and would thus constitute an unbearable burden. Luther was no less perturbed about the international side of the question, noting that since the Supreme Court decision a strong market for German bonds had been developing in London while the protective association informed by German mark-denominated asset holders in the United States were calling for a revaluation of such assets through an international clearing agency. Indeed, the court decision had opened up the possibility of great rewards for foreign and domestic speculators. In Luther's view, most persons had unloaded their paper-mark-denominated assets well before the hyperinflation, and those who had acquired them during the hyperinflation and were acquiring them under the influence of a possible revaluation were doing so for speculative purposes. Thus, just at the moment when Germany was striving to unburden itself of some of its reparations obligations, "a new kind of reparations in the form of the payment of the old mark obligations will take hold through which future generations of Germans will still be afflicted."[52]

This was not the only comparison Luther drew between the two kinds of "reparations." The Supreme Court's notion that each case should be treated in terms of the debtor's ability to pay was precisely like the formula in the Treaty of Versailles that had produced so much "continuous and unbearable lack of clarity."[53] Not only would there be endless legal squabbling about obligations to creditors with all the attendant uncertainty about the credit worthiness and, most important for Luther, the tax liability of those involved, but the entire venture would require an army of officials to gather information and adjudicate cases at a time when every effort had to be made to reduce government costs. Luther, therefore, insisted that the individualization of revaluation was a genuine impossibility for it "would mean a retroactive replaying of the inflation at the moment when the German people are beginning to breathe again, after they have only just come into the possession of a valorized currency and have painfully once again gotten used to operating on a gold basis.[54]

These were powerful arguments, and they were strongly supported in major sections of the business community. The Bremen Chamber of Commerce, for example, warned against the chaos and uncertainty which individual revaluation of all postwar obligation settlements would create, especially that of properties which had changed hands repeatedly during the inflation.[55] As Luther came to realize, however, such arguments were only sufficient to prevent individual revaluation and the revaluation of government obligations, not to overthrow the principle of revaluation in its entirety. A complete ban on revaluation threatened to arouse already embittered segments of the population upon whom moderate bourgeois politicians counted for votes and support. As an official from upper Franconia reported: "The half-official declaration according to which the Reich will act against the revaluation of mortgage bonds and war bonds has been very severely condemned. It means nothing more than that, in accordance with the program of Social Democracy, the plundering and impoverishment of the *Mittelstand* under the guise of law will continue."[56] It was not only Social Democracy, however, but also capitalism that was resented. A few weeks later, the same official commented that "one was surprised that it was at all possible to consider a ban on revaluation and sees in this once again the overwhelming influence of big industry, the big merchants, the banks, and the people from the bourse, who have long ago placed their old wealth in safety at home and abroad."[57] Certainly, Marx and his colleagues

had no desire to be tarred with the Socialist brush. Although Stresemann could join with Luther in turning down revaluation of war bonds on the grounds that the state had the right "to impose its will ruthlessly on its citizens in its distress," he could not condone such ruthlessness by citizens toward one another and saw both international and domestic advantages in legislating some measure of revaluation of private debts. Turning some of Luther's arguments against their author, the Foreign Minister claimed that

Foreigners have repeatedly justified their claims of Germany's ability to pay reparations by saying that it is the only state which carried on the war for nothing and is not burdened with state debts. From this perspective, he [Stresemann] views a limited revaluation as a foreign policy advantage. But he also feels that he must come down basically on the side of revaluation for domestic political reasons. The idea of fully proletarianizing by law just those classes which had earlier been state supporting is unbearable. One must also bear in mind that the credit worthiness of Germany will suffer extraordinarily through a dismissal of the debts. One can activate taxable potentiality by demanding sacrifices from those who were the real exploiters of the inflation.[58]

In presenting these arguments, Stresemann was supporting the position of Justice Minister Emminger and his State Secretary, Kurt Joël, who all along had argued that responding to the Supreme Court with a blanket ban on revaluation would be nothing short of a confiscation of property that would undermine the status of the judiciary and the rule of law in Germany. Their solution was to legislate a 10 to 15 percent revaluation of mortgages, thereby limiting court discretion and making possible simple and speedy settlement of claims. Although sympathetic to the creditors and anxious to maintain respect for the judiciary, Emminger and his Ministry were not prepared to accept the more pretentious claims of the judiciary reflected in a public letter from the Judges Association of the Supreme Court of January 8, 1924, that was apparently engineered by Alois Zeiler. It expressed concern that the government might ban revaluation and claimed that the Supreme Court had a right to declare a law invalid on the basis of equity and good faith. This went well beyond the claim, not yet asserted at this time, that the Court could review laws for their constitutionality, and neither the Court nor the Justice Minister were willing to have the judiciary legislate the mode and terms of revaluation.[59]

It must also be recognized that Emminger's projected 10 or 15 percent revaluation was not designed to satisfy creditor fantasies, which often ranged between 40 and 100 percent. The quest for a sensible solution was not helped much by the fact that some could claim that God and morality, speaking through the Catholic prelates, were also against a revaluation ban. The Church, which had been forced to invest in blue-chip government securities, was neither a disinterested party nor pretended to be one. Nevertheless, Marx and Brauns, the latter a priest himself, found it very distressing to read the widely publicized sermon by Cardinal Faulhaber of Munich on the Seventh Commandment against stealing and an open letter from Cardinal Bertram of Breslau accusing the government of expropriating the Church. Brauns's position was especially difficult because he stood on the side of Luther in supporting a ban on revaluation. As he later confessed, in responding to the reproaches of a theologian, no issue had caused him more inner conflict in his four years in office, and yet "what is decisive for us, who have the obligation before God and our conscience, is to protect the interests of the State and not to drive the German Reich and the German people into even greater misery and thereby in the end endanger the State and the Church anew." He could see no reason why the broad masses should pay the costs of satisfying the claims of relatively few and thought it destructive to create a situation in which mortgage holders and house owners would be at each other's throats while both claimed Christian justice for their cause. In the last analysis, "a real and true solution for these difficult questions does not exist," and it was necessary to "cut through the Gordian Knot."[60]

Brauns's posture also reflected the special tasks of his office, his personal consciousness of the trials he was imposing on the labor force, and his feeling that it was more important to promote home construction than recompense old mortgage holders. Understandably, the members of the Cabinet most concerned with the future of those classes which had profited most from the inflation, agriculture and industry, were most supportive of Luther and a revaluation ban. Agricultural Minister Count von Kanitz, Economics Minister Hamm, and Interior Minister Jarres, who was closely associated with the industrialists in the Ruhr, thus joined Luther in trying to stop revaluation. By early January, however, it became clear to all of them, including Luther, that a very modest revaluation would have to be written into the Third Emergency Tax Decree if the Reichstag was not subsequently to overturn it. The Cabinet continued to battle over whether it should be 5, 10, or 15 percent, inclining toward 10 percent before Emminger, claiming pressure from the political parties, pushed the figure up to 15 percent on February 13 against the wishes of the Agriculture and Economics Ministries. Since the Enabling Act was to expire the next day, there was considerable incentive to compromise so as to be able to issue the decree on February 14.[61]

The revaluation provided by the Third Emergency Tax Decree could hardly be called a serious victory for creditors, and it was not surprising that the Central Federation of Associations of Building and Property Owners had expressed willingness to accept a 10 percent revaluation on February 4 and that the leading business associations urged that no further changes be made in the decree on February 26. While critical of the measure, they preferred the certainty of 15 percent revaluation to more "upheaval."[62] Under the provisions, all direct mortgage and debenture claims had to be made before December 31, 1924, and were to be interest free until January 1, 1925, when they would bear 2 percent for the first year and increase by 1 percent until January 1, 1928, when a constant rate of 5 percent would come into effect. The debt could then be paid in installments, or in a lump sum after January 1, 1932, if both parties agreed. Since no interest was collected retroactively and repayment was to be made at a relatively low interest rate, the 15 percent revaluation was tantamount to a 90 percent real loss on the original asset. Debts made after January 1, 1919, were to be calculated at the gold-mark rate on the day they were contracted. It was fully in the spirit of these regulations that the debtor could appeal against full application of the revaluation if able to demonstrate that serious economic injury might result! Furthermore, certain classes of debts were to be treated differently from direct private debts. Much of the mortgage debt in Germany had been held in the form of mortgage bonds issued by mortgage banks, and these were only subject to revaluation insofar as they had not been cashed in or held after January 1, 1919, pursuant to the kind of legal requirements imposed on churches, foundations, and similar institutions. The unextinguished claims against savings banks and insurance companies were to be revaluated to the extent that their assets had been revaluated and could then be assigned either to claimants or, if they were too small, to a foundation. Finally, while the decree recognized the possibility of a revaluation of government debt, no revaluation was to take place until Germany's reparations obligations had been paid.[63]

Subsequent developments were to demonstrate that the Third Emergency Tax Decree marked the beginning rather than the end of a protracted new debate over revaluation, but the issue in the winter of 1923–1924 was making the stabilization stick, and the Third Emergency Tax Decree succeeded in this purpose. To be sure, there was another joust with the judiciary when the Berlin Superior Court ruled on February 23 that the decree's revaluation provisions were invalid because they were confiscatory and thus in conflict with §153 of the Weimar Constitution, but the decision was overturned by the Reich Supreme Court's Civil Senate on March 1, which accepted the legal validity of the decree and thus retreated from the extreme position that it, or at least some of its members, had taken earlier. The Court had succeeded in forcing the government to accept revaluation, but the government had produced a decree basically favorable to the debtors and to the most important debtor of them all, the state.[64]

For Luther, in fact, the entire revaluation discussion was an unfortunate distraction from the real purposes of the Third Emergency Tax Decree, which were taxation and the balancing of the new budget he had established. The atmosphere was influenced by the presence of international experts in Berlin in early February

for the purposes of determining the condition of the German economy and paving the way for a reparations plan and the possible granting of loans to Germany. It was an atmosphere very different from one that had prevailed the last time experts had come to Berlin in November 1922. The days when Germany's leadership tried to argue that it could not stabilize without a foreign loan were over. As Luther impatiently told the Reichsrat on February 2: "I have been told repeatedly that it is hopeless to pursue the earlier policy of claiming that an ordering of our domestic circumstances can only begin when we have a foreign loan. I have always been told: you first must show that you can at least survive on your own."[65]

The revaluation issue had cut into but not altered his plans. Clearly, he would have preferred to be spared revaluation calculations in his tax on industrial bonds. Nevertheless, the revised decree imposed a 15 percent tax on all bonds paid off before February 14, 1924, whereas the tax on those paid afterward was to be 2 percent of the face value after deduction of the 15 percent revaluation. This was to be the most significant of the nonrecurring taxes on inflation profits since the taxes on inflation gains of those who took credits and issued emergency money, though provided for in the decree to satisfy public opinion, were not really technically calculable and never actually implemented. From Luther's perspective, the most important achievement of the Third Emergency Tax Decree was the equalization agreement arrived at with the states and the passage of the rent tax so closely associated with it. In the hard bargaining on the equalization agreement, Luther had to contend not only with an effort by Bavaria to restore the prewar taxation privileges of the states but also with the inevitable monetary demands of the states themselves. In effect, he was compelled to buy them away from seeking to roll back the system created by Erzberger by offering them not only the proceeds of the rent tax but also a higher portion of the income and corporation taxes as well as certain other taxes. What the Reich gained in return was not only the complete elimination of the salary subsidies it had been paying to the state and local civil service by April 1, 1924, but also liberation from responsibility for the implementation of the entire welfare system, education, and police functions. The greatest losers in the entire arrangement were the municipalities, which now found themselves dependent on their state governments for their share of these tax proceeds despite their disproportionate share of social burdens and responsibilities.[66]

In achieving his hard-fought victory, Luther also faced complications in the Cabinet and could count on strong opposition when the Reichstag reconvened. Brauns, while backing Luther on the revaluation question, strongly objected to leaving the rent tax entirely to the states without making any strict provision that a certain portion of it would be used for house construction. He thought it important that the tax also be used as a means of supporting his Ministry's labor market and social policies. Luther, however, was unable to secure an agreement of the states to such a requirement and took the position that the states had to be given every possible encouragement to deal with the new financial burdens imposed on them. Other members of the Cabinet, especially Emminger and Jarres, questioned whether the rent tax would really bring in enough for the states to fulfill their tasks. Throughout these discussions, Luther remained persistent. He designated the rent tax as "the financial core" of his proposal and insisted that "without it there is no possibility of putting the budgets of the Reich, states, and municipalities in order. Whoever turns down this tax has to want a new inflation."[67] Luther never denied that the entire tax program could fail, but only if the foreign pressure prevented Germany from recovering. In that event, nothing could help, while if the stabilization program were allowed to go forward, then he was convinced that the program would exceed expectations.

Although Germany was to enjoy the novel experience of a budget surplus in 1924, the tax program was sharply criticized on both the right and the left. The DNVP demagogically called for a 100 percent revaluation and complained about the burdens placed on agriculture; the SPD attacked the rent tax as unsocial and proposed its replacement by a 200 percent increase in the tax on assets and urged a speedier and more broadly based revaluation that would show greatest favor to the poorer farmers and elements of the *Mittelstand*. It is difficult not to characterize the SPD demands as political grandstanding, even if the Socialists had good reason to claim that the bourgeois government was showing special favor to industry—they would have even better reason to think so as time went on. The conversion to revaluation was patently political and a belated effort to make inroads among groups the SPD had been neglecting and alienating for years. It seems to have been hastily conceived, and the Socialist trade unions continued to argue against any revaluation until the reparations issue was settled. The argument for taxing capital more heavily certainly had much to recommend it during the inflation and perhaps in the tax reform discussion of 1925 but did not constitute a very convincing program for the provisional tax arrangements of the winter of 1924. That was not the time to solve "structural" problems through sophisticated taxation techniques, assuming the Social Democrats or any other party were capable of such an operation in this period of their history. Whatever the defects of Luther's Second Emergency Tax Decree, he finally forced industry and agriculture to pay some real taxes. Luther's argument that time did not permit the assessments necessary for a special tax on wealth in his Third Decree and that such a tax would not produce the kind of revenues that the rent tax would bring in rings true.[68]

In the context of present and future reparations obligations and a universally recognized shortage of capital that would necessitate the taking of foreign loans at high interest rates, there was little incentive to punish industry for its past sins. Indeed, as Moritz Bonn, who certainly was no uncritical advocate for industry pointed out, the repatriation of capital that had fled Germany since 1918 would only be possible if it were not threatened with confiscation. Such repatriated capital would, in any case, serve not to lighten the tax load on the masses but rather to pay for reparations and imports. He thus concluded that

The political situation in Germany makes a revival of new confiscation efforts not probable at present, provided that the economic distress does not take on too extreme forms. There is also little inclination today to misuse taxation for the purpose of shifting the distribution of wealth and income. Experience has shown that, under the given distribution of power, radical tax measures do not hit the big interests but rather are shifted by and large to those of medium and small means.[69]

Obviously, this was unjust and could be very dangerous politically in the long run, but the issue in 1924 was not to achieve justice but rather to save the currency reform and prevent a return to chaos, and this could only be accomplished by strengthening the authority of a badly battered state in the context of the existing political situation. The parliamentary system was not functioning as it was meant to function, and much of this had to do not only with the destructive politics of the DNVP and KPD but also with the unwillingness of the SPD to take political responsibility in the situation. It is hard to fault Luther for fearing that the Third Emergency Tax Decree would be overthrown once he permitted the Reichstag to make any changes, and it is noteworthy that the more moderate elements in both the DNVP and the SPD cooperated in passing certain necessary measures connected with the currency and banking reform before the dissolution of the Reichstag on March 13. The hiatus between this event and the Reichstag elections of May 4 gave the government further chance to consolidate its achievements and further stabilize the stabilization.[70]

A New Order:
Credit Stops and Credit Starts

If this was a stabilization without much democratic legitimation, it was also one that set severe limits on forces inimical to Weimar democracy and threatening to the unity and autonomy of the nation and the state. The stabilization obviously was favoring the views and interests of the more powerful elements in the German business community as well as large agrarian and right-wing forces. Nevertheless, as the transformation of Helfferich's original currency proposal and the restructuring of working conditions, wages, and social policy had demonstrated, these groups were being denied a free hand. The point is further reinforced when one turns to the final aspects of the stabilization that

need to be considered: the appointment of Hjalmar Schacht as President of the Reichsbank on December 22, 1923, the suppression of currency separatism reflected in the Rhenish Gold Note Bank scheme that was being pursued with French support by leading businessmen and officials in the winter of 1923–1924, the laying of the foundations by Schacht and Stresemann against the opposition of Stinnes and Helfferich for a new banking and currency system and for the reparations and foreign-loan arrangements that were to culminate in the Dawes Plan, and, finally, the choking off of revived inflationary tendencies emanating from the private sector of the economy by the severe policy of credit restriction introduced by Schacht in April 1924.

The mere enumeration of these aspects of the stabilization indicates the central role which Schacht played, but his appointment, which was recommended by the Cabinet and Reichsrat on December 12, was anything but uncontested. The chief opposition came from the directors and Central Committee of the Reichsbank itself, which had enthusiastically supported Karl Helfferich from the outset and now responded by launching a slanderous and demeaning campaign against Schacht. Helfferich was portrayed as "the only person known to us who has in full measure the qualifications for the Reichsbank presidency." The Reichsbank directors lauded him for this renown as a theoretician and for his "creative power," pointing to his Rentenbank plan as the prime illustration. They insisted that he enjoyed wide confidence at home and abroad and assured the Cabinet and Reichsrat that he would withdraw from politics upon assuming the post. Schacht, in contrast, was described as someone who lacked the experience and distinction required for the job, a person who was wanting in creative ability, and someone who had opposed the Rentenbank scheme only to take credit in a recent speech in Hamburg for having stabilized the mark. Schacht's alleged misconduct during the occupation of Belgium was dredged up with loving attention to detail, and the government was reminded that the Reichsbank President had to have an "immaculate past." The Reichsbank Directors strongly suggested that Schacht's presidency would hurt the reputation of the Reichsbank and that his past would un-

Reich Currency Commissar and Havenstein's successor as President of the Reichsbank, Hjalmar Horace Greeley Schacht (1877–1970). (*Die Bundesbank*)

dermine his authority with the Reichsbank staff and pleaded that a leader with whom they did not feel comfortable working not be forced upon them.[71]

The Central Committee of the Reichsbank chimed in with a vote in favor of Helfferich and a declaration of the "unsuitability of Schacht." Schacht did have supporters on the committee, one of whom was Franz von Mendelssohn. Warburg, who was unable to attend the December 17 meeting and who viewed the nomination of Helfferich "with horror," probably would have voted for Schacht or abstained. While uncertain of Schacht's qualifications, Warburg felt that "he has the advantage . . . of being Aryan; he speaks good English and French and likes to take responsibility; he has always had good luck."[72] A good deal more certainty was expressed by Cologne banker Baron von Oppenheim, who saw fit, in the name not only of the banks of the occupied areas but of industry and commerce, "to declare quite openly that Dr. Schacht does not enjoy the respect (*Ansehen*)

which a Reichsbank President should in their view have."[73]

In the last analysis, however, Helfferich's liabilities were greater than those of Schacht. In the Reichsrat, as might be expected, Bavaria warmly supported Helfferich, while Saxony reminded the Delegates of Helfferich's mismanagement of the nation's finances in the war, his opposition to tax reform in the Republic, and his political role. The most decisive opposition was Stresemann's, who pointed out in a letter that Helfferich's appointment would ruin his negotiations for Allied loans, and, indeed, the head of the Bank of England, Montagu Norman, had made known his opposition to Helfferich's appointment. At the same time, what the Prussian Delegate characterized as the "rare hatefulness" of the attack on Schacht probably was counterproductive, and the reason for the hostility of the Rhenish business community was obvious. Schacht had earned its hatred by refusing to continue to accept its uncovered emergency money. Nevertheless, it was difficult to appoint a candidate the Reichsbank directors found distasteful. In the balance, however, most of the Reichsrat Delegates thought Schacht would bring a desperately needed change of course to the Reichsbank, and they saw the opposition of the Reichsbank directors as a "test of strength between the Reichsbank and the Reich government."[74]

What was truly at stake was perhaps most clearly articulated by Moritz Bonn, who had apparently been asked by his fellow DDP member Economics Minister Hamm to express his views on Schacht as well as on two other candidates apparently suggested by the Reichsbank as alternatives in the event Helfferich was turned down—Franz Urbig of the Disconto-Gesellschaft and former Economics Ministry official Heinrich Göppert. Bonn was in no way surprised by the support given Helfferich:

The Reichsbank, if it is properly led, is the one economic power position from which the state is in a position to successfully fight the assault of the special interests. It is well known that this has not happened until now because the special interests have overwhelmed the [Reichsbank] leadership. It is equally clear that the special interests make desperate efforts to bring a person into this position who has their confidence. The efforts of the Central Committee to bring in Dr. Helfferich can only thus be understood.[75]

In Bonn's view, Helfferich's appointment would be a "scandal" because his excessive "political passionateness" disqualified him and because "his Rentenbank project created a monument to the most monstrous favoritism for profiteering interest politics." Bonn argued that Göppert did not have any special qualifications for the job; but the same could not be said about Urbig, who had both technical skills and a strong personality. Urbig, however, had been too much a part of the problem to be the solution:

Until now he has always been an interested party and has never raised his warning voice against the destruction of the German currency from which the most influential circles in Germany cheerfully and consciously profited. He is, as he himself has always emphasized, a catastrophe-policy person, who has the view that we must go through it and that only the destruction of the German currency and the German economy will make the solution of the reparations question possible.

Schacht, in contrast, was being opposed precisely because

he has shown how one must do the job and has not spared the special interests even if they come from his own professional circles. . . . The fact that there is resistance is not an argument against but rather an argument for his appointment. The German business community must learn to obey, not to command, and when they see that they cannot enforce their will, they will fall into line right away, and they will give their confidence to the Reichsbank President since they need his confidence even if they have declared beforehand that they were not to be had for him.

Finally, while objecting to party affiliation as a test for such a post, Bonn felt that political considerations were a plus in Schacht's appointment:

Herr Dr. Schacht has been a faithful supporter of the Republic and our party from the beginning. He has already demonstrated his ability. It would show a lack of self-respect if the party and the Republic would let fall one of its supporters who has demonstrated the talent necessary for one of its most important posts because his capacities are found disagreeable by the opponents of the Republic and especially the opponents of a strong and well-ordered state authority.

The Cabinet came to its decision on December 22, 1923. However bitter the irony, Schacht's appointment must be viewed in its historical context as something of a victory for the Republic.[76]

In any event, Schacht, in alliance with Stresemann, contributed much to maintaining the monetary and physical unity of the Reich in December and January. They did a spectacular job of undermining the autonomous policies being pursued by leading Rhenish bankers and industrialists—the most prominent of whom were Louis Hagen and Hugo Stinnes—and the leading politician with whom they were allied, Konrad Adenauer. All three were convinced that the salvation of the occupied areas and the settlement of the international crisis required, first, an orientation toward France in which the founding of a Rhenish gold-note bank would be based on German and international participation; second, the reconstruction of industrial relations by agreements between German and French heavy industries with mutual minority participation in certain of each other's enterprises and trade agreements; and, third, the separation of the Rhineland from Prussia as a new state within the Reich. By November 1923, the bank issue was at center stage since industry was in desperate need of credit and the entire region lacked valorized currency. The Rentenmark, assuming it was allowed to circulate in the occupied areas, was a purely domestic currency and could thus be of only limited assistance to industry. If the French should refuse to allow the Rentenmark to circulate or threaten to confiscate it under certain circumstances, then the situation would be even worse. Furthermore, there was reason to doubt that the Allies would permit industry and agriculture in the area to participate in the mortgage on which the Rentenmark was based. In any case, there was every reason for Hagen and his friends to develop concrete plans for a bank of issue with the chief French negotiator, Tirard, with whom they had been discussing these matters for some time. For Tirard, the projected bank was the last hope for prying the Rhineland loose from Germany, since it had become quite clear that the separatists were seriously supported by no one in the Rhineland but the French.[77]

In the last analysis, this was not a very promising project for the French, however. Just as the delay in the issuance of the Rentenmark had been creating an intolerably dangerous situation for the German government in October and early November, so the founding of the Rhenish bank and its going into operation had to take place quickly—indeed, very rapidly because the situation in the occupied areas was so dangerous. For Hagen and Stinnes, the solution was very simple in that they hoped that the French would allow the Rentenmark into the occupied areas in return for the German government's permission to create the Rhenish bank. The workers could thus get paid in Rentenmark and order could be maintained while business would have access to gold credits. Tirard's perspective, needless to say, was quite different. He was not in the Rhineland to set up banks based on majority German participation and on French and international capital to provide German industry with credit, and certainly not to assist the Germans in reestablishing their sovereignty with the Rentenmark! The interests of the German and French negotiators in the Rhineland, therefore, were very different and even contradictory, and this opened substantial opportunities for Berlin. Prussian Welfare Minister Hirtseifer, for example, recommended taking advantage of the time needed to create the Rhenish bank to teach Hagen and the French a permanent lesson. On the one hand, Berlin would refuse to issue the Rentenmark in the occupied areas; on the other, it would terminate all supports for the occupied areas, thus leaving the French to cope with the problems of the region at a time when their own finances were becoming increasingly shaky.[78]

While this rather risky policy was not pursued, the fact that it could be seriously entertained at this time reflects the profound weaknesses of the French position, even without taking into account the fact that their allies were unwilling to support them. The Marx government chose a rather different tactic from that suggested by Hirtseifer. Rather than abandoning the support of the occupied areas, the Cabinet chose on December 2 to continue unemployment and other forms of welfare support at rates equal to those of the unoccupied areas. The costs were to be covered by the elimination of support for short-time workers throughout the country and by reducing the number of those entitled to support. The calculation, cor-

rect as it turned out, was that the resumption of production would begin to reduce the number of unemployed. Indeed, both for the sake of his negotiations with the Allies and to provide the French with no excuse for confiscations, Stresemann fought and won a tug-of-war with Luther for the continued payment of occupation costs in the old occupied areas. Finally, the Cabinet decided not to introduce the Rentenmark officially into the occupied areas after Tirard vetoed a British effort in the Rhineland Commission to allow its introduction and protect it from confiscation. While Berlin did permit Rentenmark to be sent via postal clearing and other means, it was unable to use the Rentenmark to pay wages and salaries in the occupied areas and also refrained from issuing the Rentenmark that were to be covered by mortgages on assets in the region.[79]

Under these circumstances, officials in Berlin could not reject the Rhenish bank proposals out of hand, as Schacht, Stresemann, and their allies in the Cabinet would have preferred, but they did make their acceptance of the idea as difficult and as complicated as possible. It was hard to deny that the Reich government had legitimate concerns—such as whether the notes of the new bank, which were to be backed by at least 75 percent in gold or foreign exchange, were to function as real currency. The government was also perturbed by the fact that foreign participation in the bank was going to vary between 45 and 50 percent, since it feared that such heavy foreign participation might preclude later dissolution of the bank or its absorption by a German institution. The last point was particularly important to Schacht, who hoped to establish a gold discount bank that would provide credit to German industry on a national basis and was hostile to regional enterprise with a similar purpose that could not be absorbed when the time came. Hagen sought to brush off Schacht's objections at a meeting on December 6 by saying that the bank would not be a bank of issue since its notes would be nothing more than a "transformed foreign exchange note" like the Hamburg giro mark. He did concede that the foreign participation in the bank would make its absorption into a national entity difficult but pointed out that the entire

Rhenish business community wanted and would stand behind the new bank and that the alternative was a Franco-Belgian creation with the participation of "less reliable" German firms. Schacht was as unconvinced as he was unmoved. He was anything but happy about the Hamburg giro mark and intended to stop the Hamburg Bank of 1923's emissions as soon as possible. In any case, that bank's currency was meant to serve Hamburg, not an area of fifteen million persons, and it was a fully backed note and thus a genuine "transformed foreign exchange note." There was no foreign participation in the bank, and it could easily be taken over by a German discount bank. In the face of these objections, Adenauer suddenly argued that negotiations with the French and Belgians had gone so far that they could not pull back without being accused of engaging in "camouflage." If anything, this could only have increased Schacht's hostility to the plan.[80]

A week after this meeting, Stinnes turned up in Berlin for a conference with members of the Cabinet to urge support of the Rhenish bank scheme. He sought to disarm objections by suggesting that the French had not absolutely rejected a proposal that the 50 percent German participation might eventually be transferred to a national gold discount bank. As usual, however, Stinnes also had on this occasion at once narrower personal and broader international matters on his mind. He specifically requested that he be allowed to fuse the plants in the occupied areas of the three great Ruhr enterprises of the Siemens–Rheinelbe–Schuckert–Union, the Gelsenkirchener Bergwerke, the Deutsch-Luxemburg AG, and the Bochumer-Verein without paying the large tax involved. In the negotiations and arrangements with French industry he anticipated, it was essential that the German firms be as strong as possible, and such a fusion would serve that purpose. As he assured the Ministers: "If this happens, then German capital can maintain itself. This is the key to the entire reparations question. In general, the occupied area will without a doubt develop into a new state structure, which will have the independence of a federal state without the boundaries of the German Reich. This state will have the mediating role between France and

Germany. It must be free of the burdens of the peace treaty to do this."[81]

Not surprisingly, Luther refused to finance Stinnes's personal foreign policy with tax relief, noting that such a step would have meant approval of an overarching Franco-German industrial agreement which required Stresemann's approval. As far as the Rhenish bank was concerned, Rhenish negotiators now found themselves shuttling between Berlin and their French interlocutors. While they tried to wrest some further concessions from the French—above all, that the Rentenmark would be safely admitted into the occupied areas if the bank scheme was accepted—Schacht and his colleagues were busy making the negotiations between the Rhenish leaders and the French as difficult as possible. The fundamental goal of the Berlin leadership was to ensure that the unity of the Reich and its sovereignty would be maintained. Thus, Hamm dreamed up the clever idea of asking that the bank be called the Rhenish-Westphalian Note Bank, thereby belying its separatist character. Further conditions involved the secure entry of the Rentenmark into the occupied areas, the subordination of the bank to the Reichsbank in matters of discount and monetary policy, the severe restriction of its minting rights, its taxability, and its complete integration into a future Reich gold-note bank. Were the French to accept such terms, they would find themselves participating in and helping to organize the financing of not merely Rhenish but of German industry! Not surprisingly, therefore, Hagen reported on the last day of 1923 that the French would not agree to the immunity of the Rentenmark from confiscation and that none of the parties involved could really accept subordination to the Reichsbank or the absorption of the bank into a future Reich institution.[82]

What really divided the two sides of the German dispute was that they were looking to different quarters for salvation. Stinnes, Hagen, and Adenauer were after an agreement with the French, while Schacht, Stresemann, and the Cabinet were looking to the United States and England. Stinnes "urgently warned against paying attention to English promises," while Hagen urged the government "not to listen to

English enticements; the English are dishonest and speak out of both sides of their mouths."[83] Adenauer was most explicitly pro-French and open in expressing the position of the Rhenish leaders:

In our view, significant help is not to be expected either from America or England. We face France alone. The domestic situation of Germany is such that if it does not succeed in straightening out its relationship to France in a reasonable period of time, it will probably break apart and the occupied area will in any case not remain in the German Reich. That is why Germany, even at a high price, must seek an understanding with France. . . . In France, one wants reparations and security. The French demand for security is to be taken seriously and is at least for the future objectively justified.[84]

It was precisely upon the United States and England, however, that the government was counting to escape the alleged French stranglehold described by Adenauer. To be sure, the Berlin authorities had finally learned that the American and British cards had to be played at the same time but somewhat differently if one were to beat the French. As had been the case since 1918, the Germans had found it very difficult to know where to turn for help in the United States and had often followed false leads and consorted with dubious or marginal characters in their search for American assistance. The latest victim of the mysteries of New World politics and economics had been former Chancellor Cuno, who had gone off to the United States in the fall of 1923, when he had become involved with a professor of economics from Cornell University, Jeremiah Jenks. Jenks, who had served as one of the international experts who visited Germany in November 1922, claimed to have close connections with New York banking circles and offered to organize an American consortium to finance a German currency reform and travel to Germany to arrange things. Much to the irritation of Wiedfeldt, the plan seems to have been taken seriously not only by Cuno but also by some people in the Foreign Office, and Wiedfeldt felt impelled to disabuse those who had been swayed by Jenks of their fantasies as to who really counted on Wall Street:

The fact that the President of his university happily gave him leave is taken by Wall Street as a sign that he is no loss to the university. I can only repeat that

it is an illusion to assume that great American banks would allow a professor, and not a first-class one at that, to negotiate so important and interesting a project as a currency bank. If they are considering such a venture or want to take part in such plans, then they send their own people. The German banks would do the same.[85]

Wiedfeldt reported that Cuno had made an international fool of himself and had become the butt of wry and sarcastic reports in the business press. He went on to advise:

We have lost a war and are in misery. Only the top people are good enough for us, and in dealing with them, we should go proudly to the front door. But if we creep in through the servant's entrance and allow ourselves to be seen going arm-in-arm with porters and hawkers, we will be treated like them and accordingly shown little respect.[86]

The task of winning over the Americans was not helped by the fact that the Germans oscillated between servility and arrogance. The death of President Wilson occurred just when the Expert Committee on Reparations was visiting Berlin in early February 1923, and editorials suggesting that the late President was "either a maniac or a liar" were not exactly opportune in dealing with Republicans like General Charles Dawes or Democrats like Owen D. Young and the other prominent members of the committee. Chemical industrialist Carl Duisberg also did not strike a welcome chord and left the impression of "real Prussianism" when he told one of the experts that Wilson had "betrayed Germany," compared the United States to Fafner in Wagner's *Rheingold* for sitting on its hoards of gold, and suggested that the United States was "too rich." The man who deliberately stamped on Ambassador Houghton's foot as a party of Americans was leaving a concert in Potsdam also produced a certain distress. It was hard not to conclude that "the Germans are always clumsy, especially at critical times."[87]

Happily, most of the Germans the American experts encountered, especially the bankers, made a very favorable impression both intellectually and socially, and Stinnes kept his options open by telling Ambassador Houghton that "the industrialists would not sign up with the French pending the outcome of the Com[mittee]'s work."[88] Stinnes, of course, had a very solid relationship with Houghton, and some Americans continued to be impressed by "the ruthless power of Stinnes" and to think "that it is almost essential that any settlement have his approval." Not all the Americans were taken in by the aura of the great industrialist, however. The expert Leonard P. Ayres did not think that Stinnes was likely to approve of the experts' proposals but was not certain it really mattered much because "Stinnes is said to have overwhelming debts due to the sudden stabilization of the mark, and it may appear to his advantage to bring about the devaluation of the Rentenmark."[89]

Furthermore, however difficult the Germans were and however contradictory an impression they left, both Washington and Wall Street were anxious to encourage a settlement with them. Duisberg's reference to Fafner was, in fact, well-taken. The Americans were sitting on a huge gold horde and had the alternative either of obeying the rules of the gold standard by expanding money circulation and credit in the United States, thereby reducing the value of the dollar and making it easier for the Europeans to pay off their debts and compete with the United States, or they could use the treasure to finance the recovery of its European creditors and customers. The second option was impossible, however, so long as Europe was in political, economic, and monetary chaos. Helping the Germans, therefore, appeared to be in the American national interest, especially if one could push Europe to rejoin America on the gold standard at the old parities as rapidly as possible, thereby tipping the balance in the rivalry between New York and the dollar, on the one hand, and London and the sterling standard, on the other, in favor of the New World. For the Germans, both the American search for European stability and the rivalry between New York and London opened up splendid possibilities for playing the English and Americans off against one another. This had already been demonstrated by the Hamburg Bank of 1923, whose giro mark had been denominated in dollars. As a result, a regular competition developed between London and New York which was very helpful to the discounting of the Hamburg Bank bills since, as Max Warburg noted, "England sought to rewin its dominance over the international money market, while the rich,

but inexperienced Americans tried to gain this dominance for themselves."[90]

This was a game which Schacht now played in reverse, as he developed and carried through his plan for a gold discount bank designed to finance imports for the German economy and pave the way for a reconstruction of the German currency on a gold basis. The rug would then be pulled out from under the feet of the Rhenish-Westphalian Gold Discount Bank, and the Rentenmark could then be replaced by the gold-backed currency Schacht had wanted in the first place. While Schacht had already been developing the ideas even before his appointment as Reichsbank President, that office gave him the power to implement the amendment to the Bank Law issued in connection with the Rentenbank Law which permitted the Reichsbank to issue gold notes. The Reichsbank had not done so because of its shortage of gold and foreign exchange, but Schacht could now seek assistance from abroad to remedy this situation, and he turned immediately to England and Montagu Norman.[91]

Norman invited Schacht to London immediately upon the appointment of the new Reichsbank President and personally welcomed Schacht at Liverpool Station on New Year's eve. A prouder entry into the front door of what Wiedfeldt had characterized as the "top people" is difficult to imagine, and Schacht only consorted with leading bankers and politicians during the visit which Norman had orchestrated for their mutual purposes. What made the new year truly joyous, however, was not simply the first-class company but also Norman's obvious willingness to support Schacht in word *and* deed. Norman had made no secret of his dislike of the Rhenish-Westphalian Gold Discount Bank scheme, and while Schacht was in London, Norman formally responded to the inquiry of an involved Belgian banker about English participation by stating that the Bank of England would not participate because it did not view the Rhenish bank as compatible with the interests of the Reichsbank. After showing Schacht the letter, Norman confidently told him that "I killed the Rhenish Bank." The visit was also used by Norman and Schacht to mobilize the English banking house of Schroeder and its head, Baron Bruno Schroeder, to influence his nephew in Cologne, Kurt von Schröder of the J.H. Stein Bank, against the Rhenish bank scheme in which he had been an important participant. Indeed, Bruno Schroeder cynically suggested that the English agreed to participate in the bank if it were based on the conditions laid down by the German government, conditions which, of course, were totally unacceptable to the French. Similarly, the British were incensed that the MICUM Agreements had been concluded without the participation of the German and British governments and were in no way going to finance private arrangements between German industrialists and the French government at the expense of British interests. Stinnes and his colleagues had sought to get financial help from London to cover the costs of the agreements and were turned down, which undoubtedly helps to explain Stinnes's sharp hostility to the British at this time. As Schacht cheerfully reported, however, "the attempt by Stinnes and his allies to find money in London has apparently not only been turned down for financial but also in strong measure for political reasons. People say here that if France wants to exploit the Ruhr by the present methods, then let it also take care of financing the MICUM Agreements."[92]

If Norman and Schacht "hit it off" very well, it was because the two central bank leaders were thinking along parallel lines, and their ideas were held among leaders of the City as well as by the head of the Dutch central bank, Vissering, with whom Norman worked closely. Schacht's gold-discount-bank plan was intended, among other things, to repatriate German capital that had fled Germany during the inflation and thus provide an amnesty for those who had violated the foreign-exchange laws. Schacht was not interested in the morality of such an effort, and neither were the English bankers with whom he spoke. It was indicative of the atmosphere that Reginald McKenna, the chairman of the Joint City and Midland Bank, who was to head the expert committee assigned the task of determining the amount of German capital abroad, welcomed Schacht's proposal. Schacht was "agreeably surprised":

He [McKenna] also considers it possible that the German foreign holdings, be it that they are held abroad, be it that they are held as foreign notes in

Germany, are mobilized by a new gold bank and that these foreign assets, in part through the issue of stock, in part through the issue of bonds, in part through the issue of notes be captured and made mobile and useful for German economic life. He considered the precondition for this the depositing of the fonds of such a bank abroad in order to keep them from the grasp of the French. This possible assault by the French upon a projected gold bank played a great role in all the conversations here. There is apparently great hostility here in the City toward the French use of force in dealing with private economic affairs.[93]

The repatriation of German capital abroad, however, could never be sufficient for the funding of the gold discount bank, and Schacht emphasized the importance of getting foreign capital to participate and noted the success of the Hamburg Bank of 1923 in getting rediscount rights. The idea was welcomed by the British, who, however, complained that the Germans had developed the unfortunate habit of constantly thinking in terms of the dollar, which led to an "artificial driving up of the dollar," and suggested that "one would find more sympathy in London if one would depend on the pound sterling."[94] "Sympathy," of course, was precisely what Schacht was looking for, and Norman had already been developing a plan for mobilizing British and international support for a new German gold discount bank based on the pound sterling. In fact, Norman looked on Germany as a major ally in his effort to reestablish the pound sterling as the major international currency with London as its center. Thus, when Norman asked Schacht if the Germans would mind having their finances straightened out by the same person who had performed this task for Danzig and Austria— that is, himself—Schacht assured Norman that "we would rather fuse later on with two healthy than with two sick bodies." Norman then pursued this remarkably revisionist conversation by inquiring whether he thought Germany, in the event of a reacquisition of Danzig and an *Anschluß* with Austria, would recognize its debts to the Bank of England! Even more extraordinary was Norman's suggestion, seconded by Niemeyer of the Treasury, that the Reichsbank participate with the Bank of England in the reconstruction of the finances of Czechoslovakia and Poland, a proposition which Schacht found far more palatable in the former than the latter case. In any event, all this signaled to Schacht that some important English financial circles viewed Germany not simply as a promising debtor that might help to restore and shore up the pound sterling's position but also as an ally in the reorganization of Europe under British monetary and financial tutelage. Of greatest immediate moment, however, was that Schacht returned home with an offer by Norman to mobilize a three-year five-million-pound credit for a German central gold-note bank at 5 percent interest—half the German rate—in collaboration with the central banks of England, Sweden, the Netherlands, and Switzerland, under the assumption that the new bank would operate on a pound sterling basis, as well as a rediscount credit for another five million pounds sterling. While the Bank of England would be represented on the Supervisory Board of the bank, the Germans would maintain majority control despite the fact that they would provide a minority of the capital.[95]

When the overjoyed Schacht returned home, therefore, he was in a much stronger position to face the challenges presented by the advocates of the Rhenish gold-note bank and potential objections from the expert committees dealing with the reparations issue and the restructuring of Germany's monetary and financial system. The Cabinet was able to stick hard and fast to the terms it had laid down to Hagen, which the French had found quite unacceptable. At the same time, Schacht pushed his project forward by going off to Paris, where he presented his scheme to the experts on January 19. He reported on his impressions and tactics in a personal and revealing letter to Stresemann:

The whole world is astonished here over the momentary ideal situation in Germany. The mark is stable; foreign trade is active; the tax revenues are splendid. I strive in every conversation to make clear to these people that how these conditions are, as is often the case in very long and severe illnesses, the final respite before death. I try to make it clear to them that the trade balance is a result of the fact that we do not have any more means of buying raw materials and goods from abroad which we need for our industry. I tell them that the present tax revenues are the final drops of juice being squeezed out, and that we will stand before the final end in a few weeks, that the taxes will not come in for very much longer. I tell them that, to be sure, the poor people today can buy because of the stability of the exchange but that the rich people can-

not produce anymore and that there soon will be no products there anymore for the people to buy. I summarize the entire exchange situation thus: the currency has been stabilized by our bringing commerce and industry to a standstill.[96]

Schacht had, in fact, presented his plan with admirable clarity and in a very blunt but appealing manner as something that "might be done without the interference of the politicians, in other words . . . a business solution to the problem."[97] The assets of the bank would be held abroad for this reason, since this would provide both Germans and foreigners with assurance that the assets would not be touched for political reasons. At the same time, the presence of foreigners on its Supervisory Board would give them insight into Germany's finances, which, he hoped, "will lead to cooperation in the settlement of reparations on a business basis." The Reichsbank, however, would manage the issue of the new bank just as it managed the issue of the Rentenbank to ensure a uniform discount policy and a movement in the direction of one currency once the reparations problem was regulated.

Schacht reported that he could tell by the "positive interjections, nodding of heads and the like," that the Americans and British were favorably impressed, even if the French in their "usual sadistic and formal legalistic manner" continued to suggest that "things are going splendidly in Germany, that Germany can pay much more and that everything that we Germans have done so far is only hypocrisy and camouflage."[98] Fortunately for Schacht, things were not going very splendidly for France. As one American expert noted, Paris "is full of the profiteers and speculators of all Europe. Our commercial attachés say that they see everywhere in the restaurants and public places the men and women whom they saw a year or two ago in Warsaw, in Vienna, and in Berlin."[99] And, as another reported, this was having happy political consequences: "The franc has fallen very opportunely and the result has been a great increase of reasonableness in this country."[100]

The real danger to Schacht's plans, as Norman, who had traveled incognito to Paris to lend those plans his support, worriedly informed Schacht, was that the Expert Committee might hold up the creation of the bank by insisting that its establishment be conditional on the concurrent implementation of the committee's other recommendations. The information called forth those stubborn and reckless characteristics of Schacht that were to play an important role at later, even more fateful junctures in German history. He told Norman that he did not wish to be put in the situation of "experiencing another collapse of our currency" and that "I, since I have a precise view of the situation, want to take the necessary measures in a timely manner beforehand and . . . will place the entire responsibility on the Committee" if it held things up. While Schacht hoped to "rescue the gold bank from the claws of the committee," he was worried enough that hard-line politicians might undermine the basic English and American desire to come to a sensible reparations settlement to urge Stresemann to spare no effort in showing the Allies and Americans

how serious our situation is. Doing this, in my view, involves not trying anymore to squeeze out further performance from the German people. In this respect, we are facing not a judge but an executioner, who will turn the screws for as long as a drop of blood exudes from our members.[101]

Schacht went so far as to urge Stresemann to cease paying occupation and English Recovery Act costs and to refuse to finance any more MICUM Agreements. Above all, he thought it important "to come to the Committee's aid with facts" by shifting the emphasis in reports on Germany's condition from improved trade balance and revenue collecting to "what these figures really mean, namely the last drops of blood of a body in its final convulsions." It was important, therefore, that the experts be provided with a steady stream of "alarming reports" and "striking figures" while in Berlin and also be given the opportunity to hear the gloomy views of leading businessmen and economic experts.

Even as Schacht was penning these lines and repeating his stark metaphors, positive news was coming through—for example, that Poincaré was unwilling to see Stinnes or his people unless it was as official German representatives. Furthermore, the Expert Committee commented positively on the gold-discount-bank

plan in an official communiqué of January 22, and while it persisted in placing the bank's establishment as part of the general reordering of German financial affairs, its statement was vague enough to allow for earlier action on the bank and promising enough to bury the Rhenish-Westphalian Gold Note Bank scheme. At the Cabinet meeting of January 26, Schacht urged that Hagen be told that there was no further need for discussions of a Rhenish bank after the Expert Committee's communiqué. Hagen and his allies seemed to realize this themselves, for they informed Marx on January 29 that the negotiations had been terminated and would only be resumed if the gold discount bank did not come into being. Schacht also seems to have become more reassured and calm once back in Berlin, since he raised no objections to the continued payment of occupation costs for the time being.[102]

Undoubtedly, Schacht's confidence was increased by Norman's labors on his behalf. Norman not only used his contacts with the experts to secure an agreement in principle to consider the rapid founding of the bank, albeit originally only after the Committee had returned from its impending trip to Berlin, but also secured the support of Prime Minister Ramsay MacDonald and the formal cooperation of Vissering. Thus, when Schacht chose to make a speech in Königsberg on February 7, discussing the gold-note plan and warning against wasting further time in its implementation, what appeared as a unilateral action to force the hand of the experts meeting in Berlin was in fact a tactical maneuver that had the backing of the Bank of England and the British government. On February 10, the Expert Committee gave way and accepted the plan with the provision that the new bank would be merged with the gold bank of issue that was planned for Germany by the committee. If anything, Schacht welcomed this condition since he intended to have Germany go over to a gold currency either through the projected new bank of issue or, if the proposals of the experts were rejected by Germany, through use of the right of the gold discount bank to issue up to five million pounds in currency.[103]

Even if Germany were to go over to the gold standard, however, the gold-discount-bank plan of Schacht and Norman was intended to

have a pound-sterling basis and obviously involved giving the Bank of England, which
would supply the initial credits, a very special
position in the handling of German credit and
trade operations. This understandably alarmed
the Americans, who correctly saw it as an effort
to regain the pound sterling's and London's position, and it also ran afoul of the plans being
developed by the American expert Professor
Edwin Kemmerer of Princeton University for a
new Reichsbank based on convertibility into
gold rather than into the most solid but still
fluctuating European currency. In one of the
more bizarre episodes of the entire story, Kemmerer, the ever-active Jenks (who was in Paris
for the wedding of Dawes's daughter), and
Leonard Ayres of the Expert Committee traveled incognito to Amsterdam on March 11 to
try to persuade Helfferich to accept the Kemmerer plan and to oppose the pound-sterling
basis for the gold discount bank devised by his
old rival Schacht. This clumsy effort, which
caused considerable consternation among the
leaders of the Expert Committee, did not work,
any more than did attempts to mobilize Bücher
of the RdI. Helfferich was appalled by the Kemmerer plan, which called for substantial foreign
control over the new bank of issue, and while
anti-English and critical of the pound-sterling
basis for the discount bank, he could not but be
impressed by the low interest rate the English
were offering. Ever the devious politician, Helfferich sought to attack Schacht for agreeing to
the Kemmerer plan and to create a certain confusion in the minds of Reichstag Deputies between the gold-discount and the bank-of-issue
proposals. Schacht was easily able to win the
day, however, by arguing that he had not yet
agreed to any bank-of-issue plan and had only
won great advantages for German industry
through the gold-discount proposal.[104]

One of the final acts of the Reichstag before
its dissolution was the approval of the Gold Discount Bank scheme on March 19, 1924. The
bank was formally created on April 7 and demonstrated that Germany was able to get the best
of both the old and the new worlds. On the one
hand, Norman mobilized guarantees for the
British credit to the Reichsbank from the central banks of the Netherlands, Ireland, Sweden,
Austria, Japan, and Italy and thus demon-

strated the continued potency of his network.
On the other hand, the Americans responded to
what they considered a challenge to Wall Street
and the dollar as well as an opportunity to make
money by joining the movement to give credits
to Germany. Paul Warburg, the head of the International Acceptance Bank, which had been
created to mobilize credits for American exports, formed a consortium of American bankers who offered the new Gold Discount Bank a
twenty million dollar credit at 6.5 percent interest, a very attractive offer at a time when the
Federal Reserve discount was 4 percent. The
venture had the unofficial support of the Federal Reserve Bank of New York. Schacht was
wary of binding himself at this point and only
took five million on April 26. These bills, of
course, would have to be denominated in dollars and be payable in New York, just as the
British credits had to be denominated in pound
sterling and payable in London. For Schacht,
however, having a dollar credit was of great importance since it was a means of avoiding the
exchange-rate risk involved in granting credits
in dollars and then having only pounds to back
them up. Schacht was also moved to caution by
reports that other American banks were interested in joining the Warburg consortium but
were first making inquiries in Paris about the attitude of the French government, which was
positive. This suggested to Schacht that the Allied and Associated powers were continuing to
consult one another on such matters and that
German policy had to take such collusion
among its erstwhile opponents into account. As
he told the Reichsbank Curatorium, "the people do not do anything, whether it is out of anxiety or friendship, that is not somehow arranged
with one another."[105]

It was a shrewd observation. The Americans
may have been powerful competitors and creditors of the Allies, but they felt uncomfortable
giving credits in Europe without signals from
the British, whose networks and understanding
of the European economic situation were un-
rivaled. Similarly, France, while severely weakened and more "reasonable," had demonstrated its ability to affect the political
environment. Germany's wartime enemies,
therefore, could pull together even as they
pulled apart. By June, however, Schacht was

ready to take more American money, and the Gold Discount Bank accepted another twenty million dollars' credit from the Americans. Thanks to the English and American rivalry, the credit of the new bank had risen from three hundred million to five hundred million gold marks within two months of its creation! There was no way Norman could object to the German acceptance of these American credits, and Schacht was in a taking mood.

Norman's battle for the primacy of the pound sterling and London also served to modify the plans developed by the Dawes Commission for the projected new German bank of issue. Norman was anxious to have the German Reichsbank as a partner of the Bank of England in the reconstruction of Europe, and for this reason he proved an invaluable ally of Schacht's in modifying major aspects of the Kemmerer plan detrimental to English and German interests. He was able to do this quite simply by threatening to withhold Bank of England support from the new bank of issue and from the anticipated American loans that were to be given in connection with the plan. It was well understood that American investors would not touch the loans without English support. Most important for Norman, of course, was making it possible for the new bank to operate on a pound-sterling basis, and he and his allies forced the Americans to agree to leave open the question of the gold convertibility of the bank's money. As for Schacht, the decision to make the new bank a reformed Reichsbank rather than an entirely new institution fit in quite well with his plans, both institutional and personal. Both he and Norman wished that he remain in his present position! Most troubling, however, was the question of the control over the operations of the bank and the finances of the Reich. The Kemmerer plan would have placed the bank outside of Germany and under foreign control, and the loan to Germany would have involved controls over German finances similar to those of Austria. Given the past record of the German Reichsbank and government, an argument for such controls could be made and even Stresemann had toyed with the idea of accepting such controls back in the fall. Indeed, the French were so suspicious of the Germans that they actually suggested, to the considerable

amusement of the Americans, that the comptroller of the bank individually sign each of the bank notes; one of the experts "calculated it would take one man 400 years to sign the notes providing he worked seven hours a day, providing he had a short name, and providing that none of the notes meanwhile wore out."[106]

Norman was not concerned with such antics but rather with what were, to him, the undesirable features of the Kemmerer scheme restricting the bank's autonomy. He viewed them as a barrier to the integration of the German central bank into his program for international central bank cooperation under British leadership, characterizing the control measures as "unnecessary, or costly, or vindictive."[107] Thus, Germany was to be spared the oversight of Dr. Zimmermann, and the final plan presented in April imposed a 40 percent coverage requirement as the chief control on the new bank and projected a stabilization loan of eight hundred million gold marks for the new Reichsbank to increase its gold holdings, to help in the transfer of initial reparations payments, and to demonstrate international confidence in Germany's stabilization. In contrast to the loans provided Austria and Hungary, the new loan was not intended to help balance the budget.

Needless to say, Germany was not Austria or Hungary but rather a fallen giant which had created considerable difficulties for all the great powers and the international economy even when laid low. This alone makes dubious the possibility that the kinds of controls imposed on smaller nations could be imposed on an unoccupied Germany with any success. Of more immediate significance, however, was that the Germans were doing a fine job of balancing their own budget, as demonstrated by the reduced expenditures and increased revenues of the Marx government while the experts were doing their work. Most important, as they were completing their report in early April, Schacht was demonstrating precisely that independence of special interests Moritz Bonn had anticipated and that leadership of the economy and enforcement of the rules that Norman expected to find in Schacht as a central-bank leader.

A public-sector inflation had triggered the German inflation, and the termination of the regime of public deficits marked the beginning of the end of the inflation. The final phase of the hyperinflation, however, had also been characterized by a private-sector inflation resulting from the Reichsbank's discounting and rediscounting of commercial bills, and it was quite appropriate that the stabilization should culminate with fierce measures by the Reichsbank to nip a potential new private-sector inflation in the bud. On April 5, 1924, Schacht ordered a credit stop under which the credits granted by the Reichsbank were not to exceed the amount outstanding on April 7. As new credit became available, it was to be redistributed in accordance with anticipated economic and commercial benefits to the economy. It was an extraordinary decision presented by Schacht to the Association of Saxon Industrialists on April 9 in an appropriately dramatic manner:

I believe that the Reichsbank is in the position of Odysseus, when he had to sail between the monster Scylla and the whirlpool Charybdis. Charybdis is the whirlpool of a new currency inflation, and Scylla is the monster of economic paralysis which snatches the crew from the ship of the national economy and swallows them in her maw. I believe that the Reichsbank can make no other choice than that which Odysseus made; that is to say, it must seek to avoid the Charybdis of inflation and steer close to Scylla, who may indeed snatch and swallow a certain number of the crew, but will allow the rest to pass unscathed.[108]

Actually, Odysseus had been sailing rather close to Charybdis during the previous three months, and the whirlpool had not gone unnoticed by anxious observers. An essential feature of the stabilization was that stoppage of the printing presses was accompanied by an infusion of capital into the economy in the form of Rentenmark and that the Reichsbank continue to discount commercial bills, albeit at a high interest rate of 10 percent in fully valorized repayment. As production and business activity resumed, unemployment decreased significantly by March. The trouble was that increased credits played a major role in this process. Thus, Reichsbank credits in millions of gold marks grew from 470.5 on January 31 to 1,169.3 on February 29, to 1,558.2 on March 31, and to 1,742.7 on April 30 before decreasing to 1,661.1 on May 7.[109]

What lay behind much of the business activity during this first phase of the stabilization, however, was a perpetuation of habits developed during the inflation. As the economic commentator Felix Pinner argued in an editorial in late February, the danger to the Rentenmark came not from the state but from the private economy,

... in short, the *Wirtschaft*, spoiled in a business sense through an almost uninterrupted ten-year boom and degenerate from a national-economic point of view, does not wish to face a stabilization crisis as unreservedly as is in the interest of achieving a final monetary and economic stabilization. Without a doubt—if one excludes adventurers who will never come to rest but will only calculate in terms of shifting values—there is hardly a businessman in Germany who consciously wishes to return to inflation, who does not basically realize that healthy currency conditions will in the long run benefit the private economy. Nevertheless, broad circles of the German business community have not brought themselves to burn the ship of inflation or to surrender the inflationary mentality once and for all.[110]

Instead of using their resources, especially their foreign exchange, to create markets at home and to compete abroad, these businessmen were hoarding their resources and charging excessive prices while engaged in constant "credit making." At the same time, agriculture was also demanding more and more credit, while the banks, legitimating their demands by their high costs and loss of resources, were charging interest rates of 18 or 24 percent or more. Pinner warned against a "watering of the Rentenmark," and pointed out that the Rentenmark was "a substitute for the gold mark" and had to be protected.

Such warnings, followed closely and collected by the Reichsbank, had been appearing regularly in the press since the end of December and were especially frequent in the second half of February. The authorities were urged to "free themselves from the idea that credit operations which are carried out in a solid business manner cannot be inflationary."[111] Informed observers suspected that the increasing amounts of Rentenmark credits were being used by industry to stock up on foreign exchange. Another paper warned that "just as before the Reich ruthlessly presented its demands to the Reichsbank, so today the private economy imposes itself by claiming the threat of ruin. There is the danger in this private inflation that the increase of the amount of money in circulation will undermine anew the confidence which the world is again placing in the mark." The Rentenmark credits were blamed for maintaining high price levels and encouraging the banks to charge excessive interest rates. Leading newspapers insisted that the existing system of credit rationing was insufficient, that more severe restrictions were necessary, and that the Reichsbank had to use the raising of the discount rate—its traditional and now once again viable first line of defense against excessive granting of credit.

In March, the Rentenmark, despite the fact that it was a purely domestic currency, was beginning to turn up as an object of speculation abroad and was selling at a discount. In Hamburg, always a source of problems in such matters, food merchants were discounting Rentenmark payments for foreign imports at a range of 15 to 66 percent. Another source of irritation for Schacht was that he had to provide agriculture with more credit than the original Rentenmark Law provided in order to cover nitrates costs. At the same time, he was infuriated to find that currency speculation was increasing within Germany again, this time in the French franc. Despite high discount and interest rates, inflation rates had increased by 7 percent between February and March and by 18 percent between March and April. In Schacht's view, there was only one answer to the growing speculation on a new inflation. It was not to be found in increasing the discount rate, despite the enthusiasm for this in the press, and certainly not in his predecessor's practice of intervening on behalf of the currency. Rather, Schacht chose the unanticipated path of a rigid and unparalleled credit stop on top of the rationing system already in effect. He was convinced that it would terminate inflationary expectations; force producers to use their hoarded foreign exchange; and compel consumers to reduce their expenditure and learn to think in terms of real values, save again, and drive prices down. The creation of the Gold Discount Bank gave him the capacity to conduct this credit-restriction operation without hurting the most credit-worthy exporters while at the same time letting drown speculators and enterprises that could not stay above water. From this perspec-

tive, the increase in the number of bankruptcies from 47 in the first quarter of 1924 to 346, 948, and 564 during the next three quarters was a welcome development. As Schacht told the Reichsbank Curatorium at the end of April:

The basic principle of the Reichsbank is above all not to let the currency fall. Whatever happens, I believe that it is much easier to bear unemployment again through industrial inactivity and great losses through the sacrifice of industrial substance, than that we drive the entire nation through the horrible insanity of inflation once again. And I must say that I have so far found understanding among credit seekers in need of money for this situation. That is the principle which will serve as the guiding star for the Reichsbank and myself in the coming period.[112]

Schacht certainly exaggerated the amount of "understanding" he received, but his action and the harsh consequences he anticipated did establish a high measure of credibility for his claim that the Reichsbank was going in new directions. It also helped to reinforce support for the foreign-policy approach advocated by Stresemann and a more positive reception for the Dawes Report, which appeared on April 9, 1924, two days after the credit stop went into effect. The report, although not the definitive settlement of the reparations question which the Germans had once so adamantly demanded, did provide Germany with a genuine breathing space in the form of a moratorium and a program for escalating payments with a prosperity index to assist in their determination. A portion of the income of Germany's railroads and receipts from various import and excise taxes were to be employed for reparations payments, and the railroads were to be mortgaged to Germany's creditors as a guarantee. The precondition for the plan, however, was the maintenance of that unity and basic German autonomy from foreign control for which Stresemann had fought so hard, and the plan was predicated upon substantial American assistance to Germany. While the battle over the acceptance of the plan was yet to be fought in the elections and in domestic debates for the coming months, it was more than mildly significant that the Reich Association of German Industry saw fit to announce that it saw the plan as a "significant step forward over all proposals that have previously been made" and was prepared to accept the plan.[113]

The foreign and currency policies pursued by Stresemann and Schacht had been a great defeat for Stinnes, who, weary and sick, told one of his collaborators in mid-March that he had kept on his feet in the hope "that there would be negotiations which would really carry us forward and for which he had to be fresh, but that vain Stresemann knows how to do everything better." He then went on, in apparent utter despair:

... I have had much time to think things over and have come to the realization that only a war can bring us out of our situation. Our beautiful Ruhr district will be completely destroyed in the process, and for that reason I have in my inner self written off my entire possessions there. ... Yes, there is no point in deceiving oneself, and I am just as certain that we will win this war against the French and that we will get back everything again, the Ruhr territory, Alsace-Lorraine, and more, if we only have people at the top who know what they are doing, fellows who are free of feelings, with strong nerves and a clear understanding.[114]

Stinnes obviously did not understand or appreciate the defeat which was being meted out to France, and his private interests undoubtedly here as on so many other occasions stood in the way of his understanding. The performance of Karl Helfferich with respect to the Dawes Report is rather less comprehensible and probably can only be explained by those traits of his personality that always limited the constructive use of his remarkable intelligence in the service of his country. He attacked the plan as a "Second Versailles" even though it met many of the demands he had been making for years, and he ranted against "the curse of signing unfulfillable obligations and the curse of transgressing against the spirit of national self-assertion."[115]

The Reich Cabinet interrupted its consideration of the Dawes Report and its other tasks for two memorial services in April. On April 10, Hugo Stinnes succumbed to his illness, and on April 24 Karl Helfferich was killed in an Italian train crash. Havenstein had departed only a few months earlier. It was as if Charon had worked overtime to bring the great figures and symbols of the German inflation, the great credit givers and credit takers, to the Other Shore. The Great Disorder had come to an end.

Epilogue: A Mortgaged Democracy

The German inflation should not be viewed as an isolated phase in the history of the Weimar Republic or Germany. This is not only because its legacy is to be found in every aspect of the life of the Republic and because the inflationary experience was constantly conjured up to influence contemporary politics; it is also because many of the conditions that had given rise to the inflation and had driven it to its disastrous hyperinflationary conclusion persisted through the stabilization and depression and played an important role in the destruction of the Republic. It remains then to consider the consequences of the inflation and to place them in longer-term historical perspective.

From Deflation to Deflation

The German inflation—above all, the hyperinflation—presents profoundly difficult problems of moral and political as well as economic and financial accounting. In their more tactless moments, Germans could mix these categories up in a very self-serving manner. Thus, when the Prussian State Bank wrote to Miss Liesbeth Eichstaedt of Beloit, Wisconsin, informing her that her account of 3,621,886,000 marks had to be closed without repayment because all accounts below ten billion marks (one gold pfennig) had been terminated, the bank could not resist the temptation to score some moral and political points:

You have been met by the same fate as numerous German investors, who, during the last year, have utterly lost their prewar mark deposits as a result of the disastrous and progressive depreciation of the German mark. In contrast to many of these small savers

of prewar times, you were perfectly aware, when opening the account in German marks, of the speculative character of this investment. When opening your account in January, last year [1923], you received for the $5 check on New York M. 88,764.-, i.e., about 4,000 times the prewar equivalent. We also regret the sad conditions in Germany, but they are the consequences of the late war which ended disastrously for Germany through the entrance of America.[1]

A similar charge could not, of course, be made against the neutral Swedes, who found themselves the victim of a "*Valuta* swindle" of three hundred million kronor. While here, too, one might argue that people speculated at their own risk, the loss to the Swedish national economy was the equivalent of half a year's state budget. Furthermore, when one took into account that the "entire world had given money to the Germans," then it was hard not to conclude that the Germans had turned the inflation into a "splendid business operation."[2] The Germans could, of course, try to counter such claims by pointing out that Swedes and others had chosen to speculate on the currency of a militarily defeated and economically wounded Germany rather than on the currency of victorious France and that they had participated in the "buying out of Germany" as tourists and businessmen. The Swedes, in their turn, could respond that the Germans had charged them special prices for accommodations and goods and, most important, that German exporters had exploited their inflationary advantages and had been paid for their goods in highly valued currencies. In the last analysis, however, irrespective of the fate of individual holders of marks and mark-denominated assets both within Germany and abroad, it was impossible not to conclude that the German national economy had profited from the inflation and hyper-inflation by liquidating most of its internal and non-reparation foreign debt.

This fact raised the uncomfortable question: "Was this monstrous swindle carried out inten-tionally or was it an avalanche which no one could stop?"[3] The Swedish commentator who posed this query in early 1924 admitted that it could not be answered with a simple yes or no. He at once acknowledged the sincerity of the Wirth governments in seeking to control the sit-uation and recognized the culpability of the Reichsbank and Germany's industrialists in the granting and taking of paper-mark credits. Ger-many's leaders certainly did not plan either the inflation or the hyperinflation. In the face of ex-treme domestic and international constraints, however, they either found it necessary or chose to exploit inflationary opportunities at crucial points, especially in the fall of 1922, and failed to take appropriate measures to contain the av-alanche. The inflationary gains made by Ger-many were the product of sometimes willful and sometimes unwillful negligence, but not of systematic planning and intention.

Given the domestic and international situa-tions, it is hard to disagree with those economic historians who have claimed that Germany's economic reconstruction was accelerated by the inflation and even the first months of the hyperinflation and that the inflation, therefore, was the least undesirable means of dealing with Germany's problems in the first postwar years. From this perspective, the collective memory of the inflation, so often promoted by literati, some historians, and even some economists, that tends to conflate the hyperinflation with the entire inflationary experience and portray it as an unmitigated disaster is historically inac-curate and misleading. At the same time, how-ever, the collective memory of the inflation cap-tures aspects of the hyperinflation obscured by the rosy glow of the inflationary reconstruction. Even in purely economic terms, the inflation-ary reconstruction was clearly coming to an end in the fall of 1922, and 1923 *was* disastrous, the index of industrial production falling from 70 in 1922 to 46 in 1923 (1913 = 98; 1928 = 100). That is, there was an inflationary reconstruc-tion but very little if any hyperinflationary re-construction. Most of the plant construction

and plant renewal and other types of private and public investment were budgeted prior to the spring of 1922, and the second half of that year was a time of retrenchment. The collapse of the inflation "boom" was well in progress be-fore the costs of passive resistance made it total, and certainly one could argue, as did Julius Hirsch in October 1923, that "the Ruhr occu-pation has caused much greater damage to the national economy than would have resulted from the paying of reparations."[4]

Whether one could successfully argue that the events of 1923 were more damaging finan-cially than if the Germans had been compelled to pay off their domestic and foreign creditors in money that had some value is less easy to as-sess. Certainly, by November 1922, at the time of the visit of the international experts, many foreigners had already disengaged themselves from the mark, since the percentage of foreign bank accounts in the seven leading German banks had decreased from 36 percent at the end of 1920 and 1921 to 11 percent at the end of 1922 and was only 2 percent at the end of 1923. It is reasonable to assume that Germany had al-ready received the most valuable portion of her interest-free loan from foreign speculators by the fall of 1922, and, as Keynes had noted in September of that year, Germany was in a po-sition to set the level at which those speculative engagements were to be stabilized. While the total ruination of the currency in late 1923 un-doubtedly proved quite persuasive in securing reparations relief and foreign loans once Ger-many had stabilized, it could be argued that a less traumatic and dramatic stabilization in the fall of 1922 would have given foreign lenders an interest in reducing reparations in any case and that the price of German bonds might have been higher and the interest rates charged Ger-mans under such circumstances might have been lower than the abnormally high interest rates Germans had to offer and pay between 1924 and 1929.[5]

These, of course, are counterfactual rumi-nations, and they are as speculative as the con-templation of what Weimar's fate might have been if it had been spared the political and so-cial disasters of 1923—the putsches from left and right, the weakening of German democ-racy, the revaluation controversy, and the collective memory of the death of the mark. The events of 1923—indeed, the inflation and hyperinflation more generally along with their sociopolitical causes and consequences—may have been overdetermined, but this only strengthens the point that it would be a grave mistake to make a simple conversion from the perception of the inflation as a political and social disaster of the first magnitude that has been handed down to us by collective memory to a view of the inflation as the best available means of reconstruction under the existing circumstances. The hyperinflation did have catastrophic consequences, and though there is no methodologically satisfactory way to do a cost-benefit analysis comparing the inflationary reconstruction with the sociopolitical and economic price of the inflation's denouement, it is, nevertheless, essential to recognize that they are forever linked by the hyperinflation.

This does not mean that the historian should replicate the connections made in the popular imagination, fulminate against the social and moral iniquities of the inflation, and evaluate the consequences of the inflation from the perspective of utopian economic systems or abstract ethical ideals. Ironically, the inflation effectuated "a massive redistribution of income and wealth . . . in an egalitarian direction."[6] Between 1913 and 1925, earned income as a percentage of all income grew from 50 to 65 percent, while the percentage of unearned income decreased from 50 percent to less than 35 percent. The number of those earning fifty thousand marks or more decreased from 8.4 to 2.8 percent.[7] Unfortunately, this did not necessarily make Weimar Germany a better, happier, or more stable society. This means that one must consider and evaluate not only the social and economic consequences of the inflation but also the consequences of achieving certain results by inflationary means and then explore how these results played themselves out under post-inflationary conditions.

However "egalitarian" the redistribution of income, certain economic groups and sectors clearly were more advantaged by the inflation than others. This in no way guaranteed that they would emerge strengthened by the inflation. The classic example of how winners could emerge as losers in the inflation, to borrow the apt description of Robert Moeller, was provided by the agrarian sector.[8] As long as German domestic production costs remained below world-market levels—that is, until the second half of 1922—the inflation provided a constraint on German imports that substituted for tariffs. Against such protection, of course, must be set the controlled economy, the slow and painful dismantling of which reflected the secular diminution of agriculture's economic and political power as well as the acceleration of this process by war and revolution. It is important to remember that the last step in the elimination of the controlled economy, the removal of controls on bread, was undertaken by Luther on October 15, 1923, in the context of an effort to extract wheat from farmers through high valorized taxes as well as a currency they could trust. The taxes accomplished their purpose, compelling farmers not only to sell their very good harvest but also to do so at excessively low prices while having to borrow to get fertilizer and other necessities for the coming season. While there can be no question about the fact that the liquidity of the agricultural sector was increased by food shortages and, above all, that the evaporation of about 13.3 billion marks in debts and mortgages—largely at the expense of urban creditors—was a genuine inflation gain, it is important to consider the distribution of these gains and the manner in which they were employed.[9]

The chief debtors both before and after the war were the large landowners in the east and large and medium-sized farmers more generally, and it was they, above all, who had been best positioned to buy machinery and make improvements during the relative stabilization of 1920–1921. There is abundant evidence that the peasants in particular did not employ their high liquidity during the inflation to modernize their farms or engage in more rational management. First, they hoarded their money and then, as they learned to distrust it, they speculated despite their lack of experience or invested in their households. Whatever the benefits of new linens and pianos, they were not of much use in reconstructing the agrarian sector. The hyperinflationary practice of using grains meant for human consumption as fodder in order to escape selling the grains for worthless marks helped bring the livestock supply up to near prewar levels, but this was not an investment that was of much immediate advantage in the stabilization. Indeed, there is no significant evidence for an inflationary reconstruction in agriculture, which in 1925 employed 30.5 percent of the economically active population while contributing only 16.2 percent of the net domestic product. As Germany's "major low-productivity occupation,"[10] it enjoyed disproportionate political importance, and while this did not save it from a taxation rate that between 1924 and 1930 was 3.7 times the prewar period, it also earned it a goodly measure of favored status in credit—especially in 1924–1925 when credit conditions were quite tight for other sectors—government subventions, and, most important, tariff protection after 1925. The results were disastrous. The credits were often used to pay taxes and cover current expenditure and, especially on the large estates in the east, were used to cover irresponsible luxury expenses. Many farmers also borrowed in the expectation that a new inflation would once again wipe out their debts while increasing prices; instead they were confronted with declining prices and increasing indebtedness, the percentage of interest paid on returns rising from 5.6 percent in 1925 to 7.5 percent a year later and to 13.82 percent by 1932.[11] The old panacea—tariffs—proved insufficient to protect German agriculture from the agrarian crisis that began in 1927–1928, while agrarian protectionist demands caused increasing tension between agriculture and industry as well as consumers. The agrarian radicalism already evident in the response to the controlled economy during the inflation and to high taxes at its end was revived in the late 1920s in the face of tightening credit, low prices, and increasing numbers of bankruptcies.

While not much can be said in favor of agriculture's gains as a consequence of inflation and hyperinflation, there is much greater reason to speak of industry's emergence from the inflation in a strengthened position. Using 1913 as a base (1913 = 100), the ratio of nominal capital in 1925 in Reichsmarks (RM) to nominal capital in marks in 1913 was 130 in machine construction, 134 in iron and steel, 136 in mining, 178 in utilities, and 227 in chemicals.

These ratios, to be sure, are not that impressive when one considers that the purchasing power of the Reichsmark in 1925 was 30 percent less than that of the mark in 1913.[12] Furthermore, some of the moral freight loaded on to these figures by some historians shoves aside the consideration that industrial societies depend upon the prosperity of industry; from the perspective of national prosperity, it is not entirely perverse also to ask if German industry emerged sufficiently strengthened by the inflation to perform its economic tasks. After all, there was no economic virtue in not taking advantage of inflationary opportunities, and businessmen who were unable to liberate themselves from the control of conservative bankers or were unable to follow their expansionary inclinations certainly understood this. A paper manufacturer testifying after the stabilization was most grateful for the support his firm had received from the banks during the war, when it had huge debts and inadequate markets, but was not at all happy with its subsequent influence: "We have an old factory that should be expanded. The management takes the position that it should be expanded during the inflation. The bank says: that can bring us into hot water and lead to a bankruptcy. The expansion is thus delayed due to the influence of the banks. But now it is being carried out and naturally costs gold marks; it will be very expensive. The bank takes the view today that it is unquestionably correct that it is done today because one did not know earlier how things would be. The management takes the view that it should have been done earlier, for then it would have cost nothing."[13]

Since a certain stigma is attached to getting something for nothing in capitalist economies, such observations are rare, and it is hard to draw conclusions as to whether German industry took sufficient advantage of its inflationary opportunities. Indeed, the concerns of contemporaries and later analysts have usually been preoccupied with the less positive sides of the inflationary industrial reconstruction and especially its quality. Julius Hirsch told the American expert Arthur N. Young in January 1924 that "the fall of the mark led to the conversion of German liquid capital into fixed capital investments, which to a great extent are not really economically needed. This, he thinks, means much waste."[14] Young also thought that many of the investments "may prove uneconomic" but also confessed that "the situation is so complicated that one hesitates to make any prediction."[15] In one area at least, American critics did not find judgment complicated at all; the Dawes Commission characterized the allegedly vastly increased numbers of locomotives and rolling stock in the German railroad system, the excess supply of which could stretch on a line from Berlin to Cologne, as "megalomania."[16] After the stabilization crisis in 1925 and the Great Depression, the charge that the inflationary investments of German industry and the flight into goods more generally had been wasteful and created useless overcapacities attained greater plausibility. The collapse of the Stinnes empire in 1925 served at once as a symbol and a symptom of the inflationary hangover. The negative estimation of the inflation's effect on subsequent industrial development was asserted by Bresciani-Turroni in his pioneering work on the German inflation and has remained one of the chief criticisms of the inflationary reconstruction ever since.[17]

If this interpretation is correct, then what does it mean to speak of German industry as a "winner" in the inflation, and does it even make sense to talk about an inflationary reconstruction? One can speak in these terms only if one is quite precise about what it meant to "win" in the inflationary context. In a memorandum of 1924, the Reichsbank Statistical Section produced a reasonably balanced description of how Germany's industrial concerns had made it through the inflation:

. . . they were in a position to protect themselves against depreciation by using their available paper marks to expand their plants and buy up raw materials. . . . At the same time, their extended relations abroad enabled them to procure foreign exchange and to gather assets denominated in foreign currencies. In the final analysis, their size and solid foundation made it possible for them to profiteer from the depreciation by being creditors to a greater or lesser degree. The utilization of these possibilities was all the more beneficial, the sooner it began, that is, the earlier the tendency toward prolonged mark depreciation was recognized. . . . But one must guard against generalization; for the employment of the business methods described was not always compatible with the old, solid business principles of the firms. The great majority of the industrial firms suffered severely under the consequences of the depreciation. This is shown first of all in the watering down of capital undertaken even by first-class enterprises, along with the increased tendency toward fusion and finally, if only in certain cases, in foreign penetration.[18]

There is strong evidence for this mixed estimation of industrialist behavior during the inflation. Carl Friedrich von Siemens, for example, frankly confessed in 1925 that the profit-pooling arrangements underlying the SRSU made little sense: "Because of the inflation we have, in part through force of circumstances, in part through our own fault, allowed ourselves to be driven into unclear circumstances, into engaging in obscure manipulations. . . . If these conditions were to come out into the open, then it would be a disgrace of the first order for all who bear responsibility for them."[19] One of the reasons why some of the more peculiar arrangements of the inflationary period did not become public knowledge was that many businessmen themselves could not evaluate their own situations, let alone make them transparent in the new gold-mark opening balances required for 1924 by a decree of December 28, 1923. The Reichsbank anticipated that the creation of gold balances would give an "objective picture" of the situation of the various firms and concerns, and the authors of the decree seem to have believed that requiring the enterprises to place their gold and paper-mark balances side-by-side would expose the relationship between the two; the reality was that in many cases the new gold balances had precious little to do with the paper-mark balances and were really the product of expectations and calculations concerning the future.[20]

The first of these points was demonstrated by responses to a proposal that the requirement for the simultaneous presentation of the two balances simply be dropped. The Kronen Brewery in Dortmund argued that

. . . the old paper-mark balance is nothing more than a playing with numbers which has no purpose at all because each point in time during the inflation had a different measure of value, and an addition at the end can provide no picture of the condition and value of an enterprise. The profit and loss account of the last paper-mark balance is composed of numbers which have no economic meaning. There is no connection between the paper-mark and gold-mark balances. One can only draw a line and begin anew with the gold-mark balance. The sins of mark-for-mark law cannot be rectified. It is completely irrelevant whether the new gold-mark balance shows other figures than the old paper-mark balance because they have nothing to do with one another.[21]

This viewpoint was shared by the Deutsch-Luxemburg concern and by numerous other firms, one of which cynically argued that changing the regulation was unecessary since the "paper mark balances are completely meaningless; they can be dressed up with the greatest of ease and made to serve any purpose."[22] There were some exceptions to this general attitude of either opposition or indifference, such as the August-Thyssen Hütte and the Harkort Company, both of which argued that the publication of paper-mark balances was in the interest of the stockholders of those corporations obligated to publish their balances and did have some worth.[23]

These attitudes undoubtedly were influenced by the manner in which different firms had conducted their internal accounting during the inflation. The more important determinant of the new balances, however, were expectations about market conditions, credit possibilities, and taxes. Little wonder, therefore, that many firms held back to see what others were doing before coming forth with their own balances and that the gold-mark balances—which were, above all, important for the future financial disposition of the enterprises involved—are so problematic. A good illustration of the kinds of conjectures involved was provided by Max Steinthal of the Deutsche Bank in his efforts to advise the Mannesmann concern. While admitting that it was seductive to support the prestige of the concern by claiming that the substance of the concern had remained intact and thus undertaking little or no consolidation of the share capital, he was convinced that such a consolidation and reduction of capital value had very important advantages. Not only would the consolidated shares have a higher value on the market but also, most important, the concern would not be obligated to pay a 10 percent dividend in order to maintain the shares at par. Since it was the firm's long-stand-

ing practice to put half of any such dividend in silent reserve, maintaining the existing share capital of 192 million marks would require an unrealistic effective profit of 28 million marks. Steinthal urged that the existing share capital be reduced by one-third, pointing out that the firm would thereby be compensated for the loss it had suffered in accepting four million in gold marks in return for floating 70.5 million in shares during the inflation. Finally, Steinthal warned that maintaining the existing share capital would necessarily increase the concern's tax burden substantially.[24]

The great temptation in placing a high estimation on existing fixed assets and inventories and in avoiding too severe a consolidation of capital shares was less prestige than the ability to attract capital. This need for capital apparently influenced the iron and steel industry to overstate its worth. By pursuing this policy, Krupp, for example, had to squander its silent reserves to produce favorable balances and ended up in serious trouble in 1925.[25] Indeed, it is misleading to draw favorable conclusions from the comparison of the nominal capital of enterprises between 1913 and 1925, not only because of the 30 percent disparity in purchasing power of the currency but also because enterprises in 1913 enjoyed the benefit of large amounts of silent reserves that had been built up during the previous years of prosperity. This was not the case with their post-inflationary counterparts. It is also important not to treat shareholders as inevitable "winners" in the inflation. By and large, they had fared better than bondholders and mortgage bondholders, who had lost 85 percent of their gold values under the 1924 revaluation, but much depended on whether they had purchased prewar shares or invested in the capital issues of the inflation. Even when the opening mark balance was close to the prewar capital value of the firm, the consolidation of shares meant that old shares were treated on an equal par with new shares. Ironically, in this one instance where the principle of mark for mark continued to be upheld, the benefit accrued to inflation rather than prewar investors! Finally, the joys of shareholding after the stabilization were not comparable to the prewar period, the average market value of industrial shares being 20 percent and the average dividend being 28 percent lower in Weimar's "good" years of 1926–1929 than in 1905–1913.[26]

The condition of German industry certainly would have been worse without the inflationary reconstruction, but it would be a mistake to overestimate the depth of that reconstruction and an even greater mistake to think that its longer-term consequences were as positive as they could have been or should have been. While the chemical industry is a prime example of a "winner" in the inflation, its leaders were not overly enthusiastic about the conditions of German industry or their industry in 1924–1925. An internal memorandum exploring the situation of the IG Farben group in April 1925 admitted its relative good fortune by noting that the stabilization was showing that "a great number of enterprises did not make any progress in the period of inflation but rather that there has been a goodly measure of loss of substance."[27] Furthermore, as the memorandum acknowledged, the stock of IG members had been heavily watered during the inflation, and the members had decided to consolidate shares at a ratio of five to one. Their liquidity, to be sure, had been used for substantial plant expansion, improvements, and the building up of inventories, a process completed by a limited amount of borrowing abroad at the beginning of 1924. While the need for capital was worrisome, however, the chief concern after the inflation proved to be excessive inventories. The group expected very high demand at home and abroad following the inflation and the ending of the Ruhr crisis, only to discover that demand was relatively low and competition keen. Though the concern was making somewhat more money and though production had increased in certain areas in comparison to 1913, the situation was, nevertheless, disappointing. Indeed, the export market had been reduced relative to the domestic market, inventories remained excessive, and, as the report gloomily concluded, "a *large* increase of business is not to be anticipated in the foreseeable future."

Such data suggest that German industry suffered from something much deeper than inflationary excesses and that it is a mistake to judge the inflationary reconstruction from the perspective of the so-called stabilization crisis that

lasted from the summer of 1925 to the summer of 1926. The inflation, certainly, had encouraged the launching of a host of fly-by-night firms and dubious investments which experienced a well-earned collapse in the stabilization. Such cases were not unimportant politically since they helped to form the public image of the inflationary economy and did much damage to the Republic. The most spectacular illustration of this was provided by the case of Julius Barmat, a Russian Jew who had worked closely with some leading Social Democrats in the importation of foodstuffs from the Netherlands after the war and had then begun speculating with credits from the Prussian State Bank and the Postal Service during the inflation until his operations collapsed in late 1924 under the burden of a ten-million-mark debt. The case was used by the far right to launch accusations and charges of bribery and treason against politicians associated with Barmat, among whom were the Centrist Postal Minister, Anton Höfle, and former Chancellor Gustav Bauer. Bauer and Höfle were compromised, but other targets, Socialists Ernst Heilmann and President Ebert, were victims of a smear effort. The importance of the entire affair was that it provided fodder for right-wing propaganda against Jewish *Schieber*, Socialists, supporters of the Republic, and "municipal Socialism" and was an ideal way of whipping up the resentment of middle-class victims of the inflation and all those who felt that milk and other food supplies had been shifted about to the detriment of themselves and their children.[28]

The record number of 31,183 bankruptcies and 19,586 more firm liquidations than openings between the third quarter of 1925 and the end of the second quarter of 1927 reflected difficulties that were less sensational but much deeper and more economically significant than the misadventures of Barmat. The most notable financial aspect of the crisis itself became the troubles of certain large enterprises and the need of the banks, the Reichsbank, and the government to undertake "cleansing" and rescue operations for major enterprises—above all, the Stinnes and Stumm concerns. At the same time, the crisis assumed important economic and social dimensions because of the inability of big industry to dispose of its inventories, thereby demonstrating its "excess capacity," and unemployment of one million by the end of 1925 and three million by March 1926.[29]

A so-called "cleansing crisis" (*Reinigungskrise*)—that is, a deflation crisis—had been anticipated as a necessary consequence of the inflation. Its beginnings after the Reichsbank credit stop of April 1924 had been mitigated and its full impact delayed by the sudden influx of the Dawes loans in 1924 and, in the Ruhr especially, by government compensation to heavy industry for the costs of the MICUM Agreements and damages of the Ruhr occupation. Indeed, while never attaining the notoriety of the Barmat affair, the discovery in January 1925 that eleven of the largest concerns in the Ruhr had received compensation in the amount of seven hundred million marks provoked a considerable amount of outrage in worker and middle-class circles. The sum, amounting to 10 percent of the Reich budget for the year, was given without parliamentary approval, erroneously booked in a most suspicious manner, and granted on the basis of extremely inadequate accounting by the recipients. Even if one granted the shaky claim, defended by Stresemann before a special Reichstag investigatory committee that convened between 1925 and 1927, that the monies had been given in accordance with Stresemann's promises to the Committee of Six on November 1, 1923, the procedure employed was indefensible and the committee's conclusion that overpayments had been made was inescapable. The scandal, such as it was, was buried by the protracted investigation, and its most positive consequence, aside from temporarily improving the liquidity of the concerns involved by dubious means, was to provoke the leading trade unions and representatives of middle-class and municipal interests in the Ruhr to press their claims and receive thirty million Reichsmark "social" compensation for their losses in 1927.[30]

Some great concerns were in too much trouble, however, to benefit much from such assistance and save themselves from bankruptcy by measures of self-help. The financial difficulties of the Stinnes concern—not to be confused with the Siemens–Rheinelbe–Schuckert–Union, which simply drifted apart with the re-

alization that it no longer served anyone's interests—was the most dramatic case. Not only had Stinnes become the symbol of the inflation, but also Stinnes's heirs had quarreled among themselves, and conflicts arose between members of the family and the huge bank consortium called upon to handle the concern's financial woes. It became the most extraordinary example of the allegedly distorted investments and industrial organizations created by the inflation. But was inflation the real malaise, and, if so, in what way? An informed contemporary like Carl Duisberg, who in tense collaboration with Carl Bosch was responding to the 1925 crisis and excess inventories and productive capacities for dyes by creating the expanded IG Farben, saw the Stinnes case in more complicated terms:

The difficulties in the house of Stinnes throw sufficient light on the previous development of our sick economic circumstances and show only too well the unhealthy basis on which it all rests. The primary blame lies in the illiquidity of the German money market, which forces enterprises in demand of credit to cover their needs quite often with short-term credits and are then unable to meet their obligations when they fall due. But to me the Stinnes case demonstrates very clearly that strict rules govern the efforts of enterprises to concentrate and join together and that it is a dangerous game to weld together unselectively all possible areas of business, which are intrinsically alien to one another, in one concern.[31]

In addition, that Stinnes's heirs lacked the talents needed to run a conglomerate in an age before conglomerates is not surprising, and familial conflicts certainly added to their problems. At the same time, the extent and significance of the Stinnes collapse can easily be exaggerated. While the bank consortium forced the family to sell off many enterprises, Hugo Stinnes, Jr., managed to rescue the core of his father's coal-mining business by an arrangement with American investors. The Deutsch-Luxemburg concern, which joined the other leading heavy-industrial concerns in the miseries of excess inventory and overcapacities, also took IG Farben's route of trustification and horizontal concentration and joined in the formation of the Vereinigte Stahlwerke in 1926. In the last analysis, the solution to the Stinnes problem was rather paradigmatic of the solutions to the problems of German industry in general between the end of the inflation and the Great Depression. Excessive holdings were reduced and remaining enterprises consolidated; bank consortia were called in to help with refinancing; rescue operations were conducted and fusions were undertaken, sometimes with the help of government subsidies (as in the case of Krupp) and tax relief (as in the case of the Vereinigte Stahlwerke); and, most important, American loans, whether made directly or through the intermediation of German banks, greased the wheels of these endeavors and the expensive and rather dubious "rationalization" of German industry which followed. Significantly, however, many of these investments proved no more successful than the allegedly unsound inflation investments, and industry blamed its profitless prosperity not on high fixed costs thereby created but on high wages, high taxes, and high social costs. The latter were also blamed for the insufficient funds available for investment.[32]

Indeed, the new round of concentration and, it should be noted, cartelization and German industry's dependence on foreign capital, government subsidies, and tax breaks sounds suspiciously like the way industry functioned during the inflation, as does the blaming of labor and government for its failures. Furthermore, "overcapacity" appears to have remained a problem to the bitter end. If so, how much responsibility can be placed on inflation-induced overcapacities for the problems of the subsequent period, and do those problems not have to be placed in a broader context? As Carl-Ludwig Holtfrerich has argued:

The reason why the productive capacities constructed during the inflation proved unprofitable and in need of rationalization after 1924 was not simply that the basis for investment appraisal had been unsound when they had been embarked on, causing them to extend the economy's productive potential in the "wrong" direction. It was also a consequence of general demand deficiency in the post-stabilization economy, flowing from an investment ratio *at that time* which was low by comparison with the periods of normal growth before 1914 and after 1948. Thus demand deficiency not only caused much of the fixed capital stock to seem unproductive; it also left a large part of the labor supply unemployed. It cannot be blamed on the preceding inflation. . . . "Structural weakness" is much more to be discerned in the low investment activity of the later 1920s, whatever its

domestic or international causes, than in the high investment activity of the early 1920s.[33]

From this perspective, the post-inflationary "readjustment" and stabilization crises of 1924–1925 are not the transition to a period of relative stagnation structurally immanent in the inter-war German economy but rather an interruption and delaying of the reconstruction that was taking place during the inflation and that was to resume after 1933 under a regime willing to overcome the previous impediments to growth and take advantage of immense capacities that had been allowed to lie fallow. Post-devaluation Britain and New Deal America demonstrate that it was not Nazi ruthlessness that provided the key to the recovery but rather the willingness to change policy. The essential point, however, is that the investment activity of the inflationary period should be placed in the context of the prewar growth and the periods of reconstruction in the 1930s and 1950s. From the viewpoint of economic growth, excluding the two world wars, 1924–1936 is the aberrant period.[34]

Needless to say, one must avoid carrying such arguments to the point of perversity and making the inflation "normal," but these considerations help to focus attention on how and why the evils wrought by the inflation enjoyed so rich an afterlife while the good had to be disinterred by economists. Two of those evils were inflationary price expectations and their maintenance by the vastly increased number of cartels and trade associations that had developed during the war and inflation. Both played no small role in intensifying the so-called stabilization crisis of 1925. Thus, critics viewed price levels as an "aftereffect of the inflationary way of thinking."[35] Reichsbank President Schacht and the Luther government openly attacked the pricing policies of the trade associations and cartels, and there was a new debate over the application of the decrees against price gouging and profiteering, the reactivation of the antiprofiteering police, and a more rigorous application of the Cartel Decree of 1923.[36]

The stickiness of German prices and the rigidification of industrial organization in counterproductive ways, which persisted right through the Great Depression, were symptoms of more basic limitations on German industry's capacity to make full and effective use of its in-flationary reconstruction. The most important of these limitations was the credit crisis and the role played by the banks after the inflation. In fact, one of the paradoxes of the inflation is that the banking industry emerged as a loser in the inflationary redistribution but, nevertheless, at least in the case of the great Berlin credit banks, was in a position to regain a great deal of the power and influence lost after the war. The fact that the nominal capital in banking and com-merce in the opening gold balances of 1924 was 30 percent of what it was in 1913 is the most superficial and unreliable indicator of the in-dustry's problems. War and inflation cost the banks a third of their capital and reserves, and the losses were born unequally in this sector, private banks suffering more than savings and cooperative banks. The most significant devel-opments from the perspective of the credit structure were that the capital stock and re-serves of the banks had dropped from 7.1 bil-lion marks in 1913 to 1.9 billion RM in 1924 and 2.3 billion RM in 1925 and that the ratio of stock and reserves relative to deposits had been reduced significantly, from as much as from prewar levels of 1 to 3.5 to post-inflation levels of 1 to 15. The heavy reliance on short-term de-posits meant that the term structure of credit operations was very much shortened following the inflation. Needless to say, deposits had dropped dramatically in all banks except pri-vate banks from a total of 33.6 billion marks in 1913 to 9.8 billion RM in 1924, while deposits in savings banks during the same period had been reduced from 19.7 billion marks to 600 million RM. Within the banking industry itself, the great Berlin banks had emerged as the ben-eficiaries of a systematic process of concentra-tion, which, however, meant that the 1924 bal-ances, while much reduced from 1913, were only as high as they were because they included the assets of the provincial banks they had ab-sorbed. Yet, the inflation had also called forth significant countercurrents to this concentra-tion in the form not only of savings banks and municipal banks, which had expanded their ac-tivities into realms previously reserved for the credit banks, but also of special industrial banks, agricultural banks, and trade-union and civil-servant banks. As the Statistical Section of

the Reichsbank gloomily noted in 1924, "this strongly overblown proliferation of bank orga-nizations stands in juxtaposition to the truly frightening German capital shortage and the anticipated heavy impositions under the peace treaty, which will probably make it almost im-possible for the German people to build up large amounts of savings and fructify the Ger-man credit institutes with them."[37]

Here, as in so many other areas, the inflation had promoted modernizing tendencies under very unpromising conditions. The "overcapac-ity" of the banking system certainly reflected some of the more bizarre features of the infla-tion, and with the reduction of the number of zeros that had to be dealt with, there also came up to 60 percent reduction in the number of bank employees. The expansion of banking ac-tivities and in the number of types of banks is a different matter, however, and may be viewed as steps in the direction of the more flexible, multipurpose banking systems of today. Such secular trends, like the long-term reduction of the ratio of capital and reserves to deposits in the banking system, may have had benificent consequences over the long run, but they were burdens in Weimar. They only highlighted the vulnerability of the Weimar economy in the face of the growth requirements of a modern in-dustrial society. On the one hand, the expanded system required greater liquidity, and time was needed to refill the balance sheets of the banks. On the other hand, the only way the banks could achieve this goal was by reducing and re-stricting the credits they gave until their bases were sound enough to give credit without se-vere risk.[38]

Strictly speaking, such severe credit restric-tion is precisely what should have happened under the stabilization regime, the very ideolog-ical essence of which was the primacy of finan-cial and fiscal restraint over economic and so-cial considerations. Germany's stabilization, it must be remembered, was part of a more gen-eral attempt to restore what was presumed to be the prewar financial and fiscal order by return-ing to the old parities and resurrecting the gold standard. In reality, of course, the old parities meant that currencies like the mark and the pound, after the British return to gold in 1925, ended up overvalued, while the "return to gold" was really the installation of a gold exchange standard propounded at the Conference on International Reconstruction in Genoa in 1922. In the case of Germany, special measures were taken to put into practice the "lessons" learned from the inflation by breaking with important prewar practices that had maintained liquidity and promoted economic growth before 1914. Not only was Reichsbank lending to the government restricted to the small sum of a hundred million RM and the discounting of four hundred million RM in Treasury bills, but the Reichsbank also broke with the old "real bills" doctrine under which it discounted commercial bills for all customers while seeking to control the amounts discounted through the discount rate. The credit stop of April 1924, which was much praised by Montagu Norman introduced a policy of credit rationing that sought not only to restrict the amount of credit given but also to discriminate between favored and unfavored industries and firms and make clear to the credit banks that the Reichsbank would no longer function as a lender of last resort upon whom they could count in a crisis. In sum, the response to the practices of the inflation was to create structural tensions between the Reichsbank, on the one hand, and the Finance Ministry, on the other. It was also to give the Reichsbank substantial capacity to inhibit the credit banks in the exercise of their functions and to place a premium on safe, secure, and unimaginative investment policies by the banks. A pro-cyclical, deflationary bias was built into the system in which the government could literally find itself unable to pay its bills because of a current accounts deficit and in which the banks could find themselves without liquidity as the result of insufficient backing from the Reichsbank.[39]

The purposes of the post-inflationary order could be defeated or modified if there was enough money—of necessity, foreign money—around and if the sociopolitical pressures to operate countercyclically were sufficiently potent. This was, in fact, the case in 1926, when the Finance Minister in the second Luther government, Peter Reinhold, launched public-works programs and gave industry major tax breaks to fight the depression. These decisions, however, followed continuous efforts on the part of the

government to persuade Schacht to lower the discount rate and relax credit rationing, actions he only took when they would no longer have much effectiveness in fighting the depression. Schacht justified his posture by arguing that excessive taxes on industry, unjustifiable municipal expenditures for social and cultural purposes, and insufficient economic rationalization were the real sources of the economic malaise. Similarly, the government was also frustrated in its efforts to bring about a reduction in the interest rates charged by the banks as part of its general effort to lower price levels. The banks, with Schacht's encouragement, had played a major role in the rescue operations for Stinnes, Stumm, and other large concerns in difficulty during the credit crisis of 1925, but the support of the bankrupt, even with Reichsbank or government guarantees, at once required and justified high interest rates and restrictive credits toward other credit seekers. Thus, not only were loans called in, but also creditworthy firms were denied credit, thereby worsening the depression and increasing the hostility toward the banks. This, of course, did not stop banks from taking credit for their role in liquidating Stinnes and other great concerns "in a form bearable for the general public." In its report for 1925, Jakob Goldschmidt's Danat Bank expressed considerable satisfaction not only at the success in cleaning house in industry but also at the bank's own success in firing large numbers of employees hired during the inflation and in cutting down on superfluous branches. To its distress, banks still had to suffer constant complaints about their interest rates and conditions that lacked "objectivity." One could not expect that "in a capital-starved land like Germany, in which the rebuilding of capital can only proceed very slowly, normal interest rates will obtain.... The earning capacity of the banks must be such that, aside from an appropriate return on their capital, it will also allow a gathering of resources that will make it possible for them to solve the great tasks of a national and general nature which press upon the attention of the banks."[40]

In reality, this "gathering of resources" never took place, not only because there was insufficient time and opportunity prior to the onset of the world economic crisis but also because the banks were dependent on American short-term money while the Reichsbank did everything possible to discourage long-term loans on the grounds that they were inflationary. It was a situation which made banks extremely cautious, and the practice developed to lend primarily either to older industries that were allegedly safe or to enterprises guaranteed by the government for political or economic reasons. At the same time, the proportion of industrial investment monies coming from the great banks during the stabilization had increased enormously over the inflation, ranging from about 57 percent in 1926 and 1928 to over 70 percent in 1925 and 1927 and to as high as 95.1 percent in 1929.[41] While many industries felt neglected by the banks and, in the case of enterprises large and powerful enough, circumvented the German banks and borrowed directly from American lenders, it should be noted that the policies of the banks were not without risk, since they often of necessity made long-term investments with short-term money. After the bank crashes of the summer of 1931, this practice was viewed as one of the cardinal sins committed by banks, but as the very knowledgeable State Secretary Hans Schäffer argued in a revealing memorandum, it was, in fact, common practice before the war: "The financing of the German economy and a portion of the financing of the public sector was conducted . . . in such a manner that first short-term credits were taken from the banks for the projected investments as was required by their progress and, afterward, when the investments had progressed sufficiently and when the market offered special opportunity, these short-term credits were transformed into long-term loans." The bank credits based on foreign loans in the period from 1924 to 1929 were nothing more or less than a continuation of traditional practice: "The idea which lay behind these short-term loans was the same as the financing of the prewar period." What had changed, of course, was the capital base on which the banks rested after the war and inflation, the absence of that class of savers and investors ruined by the inflation, and the international economy and world-market situation. Yet, while the vulnerabilities had increased, the mechanism that had previously existed to mitigate their consequences and tide the banks over—namely, the Reichsbank's willingness to function as the lender of last resort and accept their bills—had fallen prey to the post-inflationary stabilization regime. At the same time, the risks taken by the banks must also be considered in the context of the alternative risks of holding back on credits, which explains why the government encouraged such lending prior to the depression. As Schäffer confessed, "[T]he Reich government . . . which had already begun to suffer in its budgetary disposition from the deteriorating business conditions, also had to fear that a policy of holding back credit would create further difficulties. For reasons of economic and social policy, they wished to delay the recession to a time when a burdening of the labor market would be less fateful in its effect because of the reduced flow of employable workers."[42]

The problems of organizing credit, directing investment, and countercyclical measures to fight unemployment were all issues addressed by Wichard von Moellendorff, Julius Hirsch, Georg Bernhard and others in the Reich Economics Ministry and the Reich Economic Council during the inflation. They remained unanswered then and subsequently, with fatal consequences. It is thus manifest that the stabilization did not stabilize, and war and inflation left a legacy of vulnerability in the form of a stabilization regime unable to succeed in dealing with the continuing domestic and international pressures that had driven the early Weimar regimes to succumb to inflationary temptations. There was a substantial discrepancy between the traditionalist fiscal and economic ideology under which the "regime change" of 1923–1924 had taken place and the real behavior of the Weimar governments between 1925 and 1929. The Reich ran a budget deficit every year from 1925–1926 to 1931–1932, deficits often veiled in their full extent by the device of treating loans being planned or negotiated as if they had been received. By December 1929, the Socialist Hermann Müller government and its Finance Minister, Hilferding, were in the grotesque position of not knowing how to cover a current accounts deficit of one and a half billion marks, which was quite modest compared to Great Britain's sixteen-billion-mark shortfall but extremely difficult to manage because of the harsh German money market and the uncooperative posture of the Reichsbank and its President, Schacht, who urged that the Reich declare its inability to meet its obligations to the states and delay paying the civil service for ten days. For Schacht, the situation was an opportunity to at once impose greater austerity on the economy and to show that the latest proposed reparations settlement, the Young Plan, was impossible. Hilferding and Müller were also convinced that a financial reform was necessary but were insistent that wages and social services had to be maintained at existing levels to achieve this goal since the public, remembering 1923–1924, would only tolerate reductions if the currency were threatened. They, at least, were not prepared to push the panic button of inflationary danger.[43]

What underlay this condition was not only the violation of the dogma of the balanced budget, allegedly enshrined by the stabilization, but also the rapid breakdown of the stabilization ideology that consumption should be sacrificed to production and that social benefits, wages, salaries, and employment policies should reflect this disposition. Thus, the German social insurance system was not abandoned or maintained at its very low level of 1923–1924, but was actually rapidly reconstructed and expanded in 1927 to include unemployment insurance. Whereas social expenditure had amounted to 19.3 percent of all public expenditures in 1913, it amounted to 37.4 percent in 1925–1926 and 40.3 percent in 1929–1930. Even if one argues that these percentages include welfare costs arising from the war, they still placed Germany well ahead of any industrialized nation in social-benefits expenditure.[44]

If this seems virtually miraculous in view of the damage wrought by the inflation to the assets of the social insurance system, the wonder ceases in the face of the changed mode of financing the old-age and survivor insurance funds. The funding of this insurance was converted from the old method based on long-term capital coverage and lengthy qualifying procedures to payment on the basis of short-term assets—that is, contributions. Needless to say, this made the system highly susceptible to economic shocks, a vulnerability made all the worse by the inclination of the late Weimar governments to borrow against social insurance reserves to cover current account deficits.[45] By then, the Reich was running deficits, and the actual legislation reconstructing the social insurance system was the product of 1924–1925, when the Reich was running its only surplus. Why the abandonment of such restraint when fiscal restraint seemed to be working? The answer was clearly provided by the Economic Service of the Transfer Committee set up under the Dawes Plan in a report of October 1925:

It must . . . be admitted that the provisions recently voted by the Reichstag involve an increase in public and private expenditure which might well have been postponed. In view of the enormous surpluses from 1924, the rapid (and, in the opinion of many, overgenerous) settlement of the Ruhr compensation payments, the relatively undemocratic nature of the tax reform, and the imminence of the new customs tariff established more especially for the benefit of the industrialists and landed proprietors, it will easily be understood that the Reichstag was obliged on one point to yield to pressure from the working classes and that the Government resistance was weak: the voting of the new Social Insurance laws was the forced ransom for other legislative measures passed at the same time, in July and August 1925.[46]

As the report also noted, German workers did not regard the deductions as a charge but rather as a favored form of saving, while many employers considered their contributions as "an insurance premium for social peace" and as preferable to paying the higher wages that would be demanded otherwise. The Luther government also defended the new social legislation against the complaints of Ruhr coal industrialists as essential in view of the destruction of savings in the inflation and the need to protect those dependent upon wages and salaries.[47] At the same time, however, it also found itself having to defend the Labor Ministry and arbitrators against charges that they were permitting wages to reach excessively high levels, and such attacks were to increase steadily until reaching a crescendo in the Great Ruhr Lockout of 1928 when the heavy industrialists sought to destroy the system of binding arbitration that had been created at the end of the inflation. Industry, more generally, charged the Labor Ministry and trade unions with creating a system of "political wages" that exceeded what productivity would justify and that, along with high social costs and taxes, were responsible for the insufficient rate of investment in Germany.[48]

While the defects of binding arbitration (the most important of which was to permit industry and labor to evade responsibility for wage levels) are unquestionable, it is highly doubtful that the arbitrators did much more than determine wages in accordance with market conditions. As the events of 1923 demonstrated, it was a system required to preserve collective bargaining in the face of the desire of some employers to return to prewar labor–management relations. While employers complained about the way the system worked, it was the attitude of the more reactionary of the employers that had made the system necessary in the first place. Much more of a case can be made for the argument that real wages rose in excess of productivity between 1925 and 1931 while investment levels remained deficient (see Table 49). The net investment quota had decreased from 16 percent between 1910 and 1913 to 10.5 percent between 1925 and 1929, while 75 percent of the investment money was provided by foreigners or the state. These facts are generally admitted even by those participants in the scholarly debate on the roots of the economic crisis who do not place the chief emphasis on the role of wages and social costs in explaining the illness of the German economy.[49]

Table 49. Real Wages and Per Capita Production for German Industry and Percentual Change over the Previous Year, 1924–1932

(1913–1914 = 100)

	Hourly Wage Rate		Hourly Earning		Per Capita Production	
1924	82	−18%	86	−14%	74	−26%
1925	95	13%	103	17%	88	14%
1926	102	7%	109	6%	82	−6%
1927	104	2%	114	5%	104	22%
1928	110	6%	125	11%	106	2%
1929	115	5%	130	5%	106	0%
1930	122	7%	131	1%	92	−14%
1931	125	3%	132	1%	76	−16%
1932	120	−5%	125	−7%	61	−15%

Source: Gerhard Bry, *Wages in Germany, 1871–1945* (Princeton, 1960), p. 362; and Charles Maier, "Die Nicht-Determiniertheit ökonomischer Modelle," *Geschichte und Gesellschaft* 11 (1985), p. 281 (percentages corrected for arithmetic errors).

The recovery of labor's position in the stabilization period, which also included a return to the eight-hour day and forty-eight-hour week, is unquestionable, but it should not be overdramatized. The initial recovery in 1925 was started from an extremely low level, and the rate of increase slowed down dramatically because of the depression in 1925 and 1926. This initial recovery effort was very hard won, 1924 having been a year filled with strikes and lockouts. Furthermore, it was bought at the cost of relatively high unemployment. At the same time, it is important to recognize that the pressure for higher wages reflected not only an effort to achieve some compensation for political defeats akin to the demand for restoration of the social insurance system, but also a combination of reaction to years of deprivation and continuing inflationary expectations. Indeed, inflationary memories and expectations served as a natural disincentive to saving, and this made it highly unlikely that the inflationary transfer of resources from middle-class savings to wages and salaries would be channeled to investment rather than consumption. The time was not ripe for the kind of "growth pact" between industry and labor that existed after the Second World War.[50]

This combination of compensatory consumerism and inflationary expectations emerges repeatedly from investigations of the retail trades undertaken in the late 1920s. When asked if the preference for butter over margarine reflected better economic conditions, a store owner replied, "No, I personally explain the change from margarine to butter by the fact that our people had bad margarine during the war. The poor people would rather buy butter. They say: 'I spread butter on my bread and forget about the sausage. Then at least I know what I am eating; I don't want to see margarine anymore.'"[51] A witness from a consumer cooperative reported, "I have found that before the war people actually were not as demanding in the choice of food as they are today. These increased demands have probably been created by the food problems which developed after the war and in the inflation. In addition to this, people today probably place more value on quality."[52] In explaining the desire for better quality meat, a butcher noted that

... there are various factors responsible for this change of taste. First, the wartime food supply—the public had a real revulsion after the war against the meat products it ate during the war. It thus sought to find the best of what was once again to be had. The inflation strengthened this tendency. People bought the best because they did not know whether the money would be worth anything the next day. But then the social attitude has changed as well. The worker today wants to have the better things, just like those who are better off.[53]

Workers, but not only workers, were more prepared to borrow to pay for clothes and furniture, while at the same time remaining suspicious of the currency. As the manager of a small department store testified:

... Business for credit in the postwar period is a different kind of business than it was before the war. Before only the very poorest people bought on credit. The better-off workers could already buy a suit for 30 or 25 marks over the counter with two weeks' wages if they were somewhat frugal. In today's credit business one deals not only with the better working-class customers but also with tradesmen and middle and even higher civil servants, insofar as furniture is being purchased, where before the war these people had enough cash and kept away from this kind of business. The better-off workers feel themselves today to be more or less lower middle class, and they have taken on the requirements of the earlier lower-middle-class person without having the latter's firm foundation of assets. On the other side, sales have increased sharply. In general, the sense of thrift has relaxed. People are fearful that the German mark will not remain firm and want to enjoy something from life, and they spend their money today on clothes and externals of every kind.[54]

While patterns of thrift and more traditional modes of expenditure for cultural and educational purchases probably persisted among higher civil servants, the white-collar workers, lower- and middle-level civil servants, and workers, especially in urban areas, seem to have adopted new and more modern habits of consumption and entertainment.[55] All this took place in an uneasy environment in which inflationary anxieties, class tensions, and status and occupational prejudices colored opinion. They all came bubbling to the surface in 1927 when the civil service made its bid to recover its economic position and receive compensation for the blows it had received during the stabilization. Thanks to the support of the Centrist Finance Minister, Heinrich Köhler, who was joined by the DVP and DNVP, which sought to

court the civil service, what began as a modest pay increase escalated into an average pay increase of 25 percent. It was a proposal which enraged both Centrist and Socialist labor, which not only viewed the expenditure as a threat to unemployment benefits and other social expenditures they deemed more worthy, but also saw it as an incitement to further criticism of government expenditure and as an inflationary measure. Status hostility played no small role in the bitter debate, the Christian unionists charging that "... the educated can despise those who come from the *Volksschule*; and the government official, secure in his tenure, can treat his fellow citizens like dirt ...," while proponents of the Köhler bill warned that the "'bourgeois' and peasants have no desire to let themselves be shoved aside by the 'workers,' that is to say, the trade union secretaries."[56] In a pattern reminiscent of the inflation, workers responded to the huge civil-service salary increase by seeking "compensation" through a major wage movement in 1927 and 1928, which, of course, produced intensified conflict between labor and industry. At the same time, they and others also remembered to where such spiraling of demands could lead. Thus, in 1927, there were reports of hoarding of foreign currencies and of workers in western Germany suddenly beginning to ask that their wages be paid in foreign currencies. While such outbursts of inflation anxiety may have swiftly abated, it is worth noting that long-term contracts and life insurance policies throughout the stabilization contained gold clauses.[57]

Reparations, that unwanted but fatal distraction of Weimar politics, did not go away while these developments were occurring, and the Reparations Agent observed them with concern. As a Transfer Committee expert reported with respect to the civil-service salary issue, "... it would seem that the Reich can no longer resist the pressure brought to bear by the interested parties, who draw their arguments ... both from the inferiority of their salaries in real value in relation to what they received in 1913, and from comparison with the wages paid by private undertakings. Other States, tried like Germany by the war and currency depreciation, are, it is true, still obliged to keep the salaries of their officials, or at least of those in the highest positions, at rates much below those of before the war. . . . In Germany the progress of general recovery and the degree of prosperity make such conditions of existence seem intolerable."[58]

What had proven intolerable, however, were not the conditions demanded by prosperity but rather the conditions demanded by depression. This had been amply demonstrated during the one year when income and imports were reduced to a point where Germany actually ran a trade surplus and could autonomously transfer reparations—the depression of 1925–1926. The price of this "achievement" was unemployment that peaked at 22.6 percent in January 1926. It was not a situation that the government felt capable of sustaining, and it responded with the countercyclical measures and pattern of spending that produced the subsequent deficits. Cries for the correction of these deficits and for reforms came from the Reichsbank, the Reparations Agent Parker Gilbert, and German industry, all of which wished to control foreign borrowing by municipalities for allegedly "nonproductive purposes" and for a rationalization of the governmental structure. Especially after the civil-service pay hikes of 1927, it seemed imperative to compensate for the increased costs by reducing the number of civil servants, a task on which there had been no progress since the reductions of 1924, and to do so by eliminating the duplication of activities by the bureaucracies of the states and municipalities. Reform was indeed in order, and a good argument could be made that both fiscal responsibility and democratization would have been better served if the Reich had allowed the states and municipalities to secure assets commensurate with the responsibilities that had been imposed on them. The loudest cries for *Reichsreform*, however, came from precisely those groups which were hostile to what they considered Weimar's excessive parliamentarization and which wanted a more authoritarian management of the nation's finances.[59]

Reform of the governmental structure thus became linked to demands for a new round of social dismantling and authoritarian reform of the constitution, and the insistence on such measures was legitimized, as had been the case during the last years of the inflation, by the rep-

arations question and by the onset of a mounting fiscal crisis of the state and increasingly bad business conditions. Negotiations for a final settlement of the reparations issue in the form of the Young Plan were thus accompanied by a new industrialist offensive, signalized by new demands for the "freedom of *die Wirtschaft*" and by a famous assault on the social and economic policies of the Republic in an RdI pamphlet with the ominous title of *Recovery or Decline*. Just as in 1922 and 1923, the industrialists insisted that stabilization and the Dawes Plan required a rollback of government expenditure, social costs, taxes, and wages, and the privatization of public enterprises was necessary, so now they argued that an "internal Young Plan" was required to effectuate these measures for a new recovery.[60]

There was indeed a deep continuity between the ends of the inflation and stabilization periods, and it was openly stated by Hans Luther— Food Minister and Finance Minister at the end of the inflation, Chancellor during the depression of 1925–1926, and Schacht's replacement as President of the Reichsbank in March 1930. After leaving the Chancellorship in early 1927, he became head of the League for the Renewal of the Reich, an organization funded and supported by industry for the purposes of promoting reform of the Reich in a more centralized and presidential direction. It was in that capacity that he took advantage of the invitation to contribute a lead article to the January 1, 1930, issue of the *Bank=Archiv* by reflecting on "1923 and 1930."[61] While immediately dismissing the notion that a comparison of those years could be made with respect to the dangers to the currency as nothing but "irresponsible chatter," he strongly argued that the key similarity was the need to balance the budget by thoroughgoing reform. The Enabling Acts had permitted the government to accomplish this end in 1923 and 1924, but Luther readily admitted that the stabilization regime of that time could not be maintained, that a measure of relaxation and opportunity had to be created, and that a period of recovery based on foreign assistance was necessary. The loosening up, however, had been carried too far, and the basic crisis had not been resolved. It could not be solved through the economic forces in German society alone, for in a poor and politically weak country like Germany, the action of the state was necessary to ensure high productivity and the proper direction of resources. The reform of the economy thus depended on the reform of the Reich itself so as to restore confidence, produce a reduction of interest rates, and make investment possible again. If 1930 was like 1923, therefore, the new crisis should not be handled like the old through emergency measures that temporarily quieted political mismanagement of the economy through excessive parliamentary interference. The opportunity had come to undertake the sorts of more fundamental changes that could not be brought about in 1923. As the historian Harold James has pointed out, Luther "reinterpreted the economic and fiscal issues as political and constitutional ones."[62]

Luther was not alone in this tendency, and the new Chancellor in March 1930, Heinrich Brüning, was at one with the new Reichsbank President in this respect, as were the clique of higher officials, politicians, and military men around President Hindenburg who brought Brüning to power. In contrast to Stresemann in 1923 and 1924, they opened up the Pandora's Box of alternatives to liberal parliamentary democracy and thus permitted, indeed encouraged, the new economic crisis to become a crisis of the Republic itself. This time, deflation not only would be made to stick but would be an instrument for "restructuring the state" as well as for eliminating rather than reducing reparations.[63] Just as reparations had been used to justify the inflation, so now they were used to justify deflation. Historians may debate whether or not Brüning had more freedom of action to pursue a reflationary policy than he claimed, but the passion with which the deflationary policies were pursued and the unwillingness to seek a parliamentary basis for his policies cannot be explained in terms of economic policy alone. Instead of suppressing the civil war between Nazis and Communists, which had moved from Saxony, Hamburg, and Bavaria to the national level, it was allowed to expand as a means of bullying the Social Democrats into a policy of toleration.

The Social Democrats and other non-radical groups were terrorized into accepting the deflationary policies of the depression by fear not only of Nazis and Communists but also of inflation and the manner in which this fear was manipulated by Brüning and the bureaucracy to serve their ends. There can be no question about the fact that the fear was real—not limited to the endless number of petitions from lower-middle-class groups urging the government to refrain from all inflationary measures, but also in the strong support given to deflationary measures by Hilferding and other Socialist and trade-union leaders throughout most of the crisis. Quite aside from the restrictions imposed upon Germany by treaty commitments, going off gold or devaluation in Germany carried entirely different implications than it did in Great Britain because of Germany's inflationary experience. Obviously, inflation anxiety could be used, and ironically enough, British politicians made regular reference to the horrors of Germany's inflation in defending their own conservative fiscal and monetary policies right through the elections of 1931.[64] At the same time, sober economists who were by no means fraught with anxiety over inflation themselves nevertheless feared that the inflation trauma of the German people would cause panic in the face of reflationary measures. Thus, Professor Gerhard Colm argued in November 1931: "Every inflation today would in a certain respect spring over the curative stages as we came to know them in around 1921 and 1922 and very quickly lead to the catastrophic situation of 1923. We understand by inflation all measures which by intention or perhaps through unintended success lead to a situation in Germany in which regular income is drawn not from profits, taxes, etc., but rather from the printing of notes."[65] While it can certainly be argued that the governmental authorities, many of whom were well aware of the difference, had a responsibility to educate the public concerning the difference between inflationary and reflationary policies, it is also important to recognize that the "anti-inflationary consensus" frequently found expression in accusations against big industry and agriculture as well as the Nazis and Communists for being supporters of inflation. This made it all the harder to conduct reflationary policies under democratic auspices in Germany, and it is not

surprising that industry, as it moved more and
more toward the conclusion that reflationary
policies were necessary, latched on to Franz
von Papen and his "new state," which held out
the possibility of introducing work-creation
measures without resurrecting either trade-
union power or the social welfare system,
though doing so in an authoritarian, anti-par-
liamentary manner. The possibility of conducting reflationary policies without running headlong into accusations of promoting inflation
was only realized by Hitler, who overcame the
inclination to express inflation anxiety with
more potent reasons for anxiety in the form of
the S.A. and Gestapo.[66]

From *Geldmenschen* to *Hitlermenschen*

If there was a continuity of problems between
1923 and 1930, there was also a disparity of out-
comes. Germany's leaders between 1930 and
1933 obviously miscalculated what massive unemployment, a rollback of the social welfare
system, and measures creating even more extreme misery than 1923 and 1924 would bring.
They also failed to realize that the undermining
of parliamentary democracy would create an
unprecedented social and political crisis and
unleash forces and tendencies in the political
culture quite beyond their control. To what extent and in what ways, if any, did the inflation
contribute to this outcome beyond the impulses
provided by anxiety over inflation itself? There
is no contesting the fact that it was the Great
Depression and not the inflation that was the
driving force in making it possible for National
Socialism to come to power in January 1933.
The horrendous unemployment, wage cuts, and
general impoverishment of the Great Depression proved a far greater danger to German democracy than inflation ever had, and the case
for the inflation having saved German democracy during its early turbulent years by preventing precisely such conditions can be and has
been made here and elsewhere. As has also been
argued here, however, it is erroneous to think of
the inflation in splendid isolation from the rest
of Weimar's history, and it is certainly hard to
accept a comparison between the hyperinflation and the Old Testament's "Year of Jubilee"
in which all debts are cancelled and subordinate

Election poster used by the Völkisch-Social Block in
the 1924 elections showing the "achievements of the
Revolution," where the "paper-money economy,"
already added to the burdens of Versailles, is now
being supplemented by the high taxes of the stabilization. The working masses, therefore, should vote
for the extreme right. (*Mueller and Graeff Poster Collection, Hoover Institution Archives*)

relationships dissolved every fifty years with the
cards "dealt out afresh" so that the "capitalist
contest for power, profit, and property could be
recommenced."[67]

Quite aside from the fact that real property
had not been redistributed, it is of no small significance that those who had lost or felt they
had lost in the "Jubilee" remained around and
were anything but jubilant and often quite dangerous. The direct contribution of the inflation
to National Socialism and its success is difficult
to measure, but the existence of such direct
linkages is undeniable. Not only were inflationary conditions an important element in Nazi
propaganda and successes in 1923, but also resentments connected with the inflation and its
outcome have been shown to be of prime importance in the so-called inflation election to

the Reichstag of May 1924 when the Nazis received 6.5 percent of the vote. Their campaign deliberately targeted pensioners, small investors, and other inflation victims by characterizing the inflation as "finance Bolshevism" and history's "most shamelessly and ruthlessly executed expropriation" and by attacking the government for sanctioning its consequences in the Third Emergency Tax Decree.[68]

Though Nazi electoral successes came to an abrupt halt until 1929–1930 and inflation took a back seat in their propaganda during the Great Depression, the experience of inflation certainly was of some importance in the motivation of many followers of the movement. This is well illustrated in the autobiographies of Nazis collected by Theodore Abel. Not surprisingly, the inability to undertake or continue studies because of the depreciation of familial income is a repeated theme, as is the complaint of officers or their wives about the fate of their pensions. Some of these persons fled very early into the Nazi movement, but a more typical and illuminating illustration of the role played by the inflation is provided by a Berlin organ builder whose business collapsed in the inflation:

All hopes were in vain. The inflation put a miserable end to all my efforts. I couldn't pay my people. My assets had melted away. Once again we experienced hunger and deprivation. I fled from a government that permitted such misery, for I already at that time felt that it was not necessary to have an inflation in the unfortunate measure that it was carried through. But the purpose was achieved; the still somewhat prosperous *Mittelstand* was destroyed, that *Mittelstand* which was still an opponent of Marxism even if it did not have the slightest ability to fight against it successfully.

Although urged by friends to join one of the *völkisch* movements, he resisted in the conviction that "we could only overcome the misery if *one* man succeeded in uniting all German men who still knew what it was to be honorable." In the meantime, he went his unhappy way: "Used to deprivation, I greeted the smallest opportunities to earn some money, for thanks to the credit-taking economy (*Pumpwirtschaft*) of the government some small contracts came even my way from the church authorities."[69] He finally joined the NSDAP and SA in 1931 and seemed to have found considerable satisfaction in a life of adventurous street fighting. Clearly, therefore, it was not the inflation that brought this worthy into the movement, but the inflation was crucial in turning him against the "system." The inflation and the subsequent *Pumpwirtschaft* were, as far as he was concerned, of a piece. The difference between what the wife of a Nazi officer designated as *"Geldmenschen"* and *"Hitlermenschen"*[70] was that the latter viewed the problems of economics and therefore of inflation as a matter of will. Hitler made the point most clearly:

Inflation is lack of discipline. . . . I'll see to it that prices remain stable. That's what my storm troopers are for. Woe to those who raise prices. We don't need legislation to deal with them. We'll do that with the party alone. You'll see: once our storm troopers visit a shop to set things right—nothing similar will happen a second time.[71]

Nevertheless, the number of those willing to accept storm troopers in place of antiprofiteering legislation was not very widespread in the 1920s, and the deeper and ultimately more destructive sociopolitical consequences of the inflation took different forms. An important reason for this was that nearly every group in German society, with the exception of big business and big agriculture and the motley assortment of inflation profiteers who did not organize themselves for obvious reasons, could lay claim to being a "loser" in the inflation. Many of these claims, as in the case of organized labor and the broad mass of lower- and middle-range civil servants, could only be made if one abolished not only the distinction between inflation and hyperinflation but also the distinction between inflation and stabilization in one's political rhetoric. The trade unions, for example, could accuse employers of exploiting the inflation to make huge profits, to export at dumping prices, and ceaselessly to gather tangible goods at the expense of the entire population and then, in the end, to conduct a stabilization on the backs of the working class. Similarly, a civil servant, if conveniently forgetting the special advantages enjoyed by civil servants after the 1920 reform, could declare that "The inflation robbed us *Mittelständler* of the money saved from years of honest work," while at the same time he and his colleagues could claim to have been singled out for prejudicial treatment in

1923 and 1924.[72] Undoubtedly, all these charges and claims were true, but what was supposed to be done about them and about the no less legitimate claims and charges of those who had unquestionably been damaged or ruined by inflation and the stabilization regime of 1923 and 1924?

The answer was a dramatic descent into the most grotesque forms of interest-group politics. While interest-group politics had long played an exceptional role in German society and politics, one of the chief consequences of the inflation was to promote its exfoliation to the point of caricature while undermining the major bourgeois parties of the middle. The great breakthrough, not surprisingly, came in the Reichstag elections of May 1924, when the various middle-class and peasant regional and special-interest parties increased their vote from 3.7 percent in June 1920 to 8.3 percent, while the DDP received only 5.7 percent and the DVP 9.2 percent. More important, while the extremist parties (the Nazis and Communists) lost votes in the December 1924 elections—which reflected improved economic conditions and more genuine stabilization—the vote for the special regional-interest parties was 7.8 percent, the DDP receiving 6.3 percent and the DVP 10.1 percent of the vote. The special-interest-party vote, then, increased to 14 percent in 1928 in the allegedly most pro-Republican election since 1919, while now both the DDP and the DVP received lower percentages, 4.9 and 8.7 percent respectively. As recent research has shown, however, it is a mistake to give a purely economic interpretation to this proliferation of regional and special-interest parties. They were, in fact, anti-system parties and reflected disgust with the older liberal and bourgeois parties and with the Republic itself. The most successful of these parties, the Economic Party (Wirtschaftspartei), which represented house-owner and small-business interests, claimed that it was protecting the *Mittelstand*, which had been victimized by both the Revolution and the inflation, against capitalism and Marxism.[73]

The revaluation parties took up a similar stance against the two great ideologies of modern industrial society while attacking all the other parties for betraying not simply their interests but justice itself through their failure to support revaluation demands. These parties were, in fact, a good illustration of the manner in which single-issue interest groups had given way to single-issue parties with national pretensions. Originally, debtors sought to use an interest group founded in 1922, the Protective Association of Mortgages and Savers for the German Reich, to influence the bourgeois parties. Frustrated in their efforts to win support for revision of the Third Emergency Tax Decree, regional groups in the revaluation movement broke ranks with the interest-group approach prior to the December 1924 election to form the German Revaluation and Recovery Party in Saxony and the Revaluation and Reconstruction Party in Hamburg and Berlin to replace the Militant League of Beggars that had garnered some sixty thousand votes in the May 1924 elections. The two new parties received a hundred twenty thousand votes in the December 1924 elections, while the Protective Association (after breaking with the DVP and DDP) gave support to the DNVP, the German Racist Freedom Party (as the Nazis called themselves at this point), and the Center, all of which had courted the revaluation vote. The cumulative effect of all these efforts, especially in view of the relative recovery of industry and labor at the end of 1924, was to make a revision of the Third Emergency Tax Decree unavoidable. This took the form of a complicated compromise between the DNVP and the Luther government under which mortgages and other private debts were subject to 25 percent revaluation, while industrial bonds were to be revaluated at 15 percent and government bondholders were to receive between 2.5 and 5 percent compensation for the original gold value depending upon when they had purchased the bonds. Because of the parlous state of the recovery, the private and industrial debts, which would bear interest, did not have to be paid off until 1932, while the public debts would be settled by annuities over thirty years, although some public bonds could be redeemed immediately as determined by lottery and older needy bondholders were given a special preference.[74]

This was not what the revaluation groups had in mind, and they had more than a little cause to feel betrayed by the DNVP and the government. On paper, to be sure, the revaluation in Germany was fairly close to the 20 to 25 percent of value received by their counterparts in Italy and France after those countries had stabilized their currencies and exchange rates. In reality, the market value of the revalued assets was lower than their face value because of the delayed payment and low interest rates, and the practical value was decreased by the mortality of their holders. The situation was to be made worse during the Great Depression by moratoria. The important point, as Michael Hughes has argued, however, is that

psychologically . . . German creditors were not comparing their situation in 1925 to that of the French or Italians. Creditors believed the revaluation laws robbed them of justly acquired and vested rights. They hence compared their 1925 situation to their December 1923 situation, when the courts had granted them an individual revaluation that they believed would provide them with nearly full recompense.[75]

The issue, therefore, continued to fester and play a divisive role in politics. In 1926, a new National Party for People's Justice and Revaluation (Reichspartei für Volksrecht und Aufwertung) was founded which, along with the Economic Party, scored major gains in the Saxon state elections of that year and thus further destabilized bourgeois politics in that troubled state. The fundamental function of the People's Justice Party (as it was popularly called) was to play upon feelings of injustice and fears of proletarianization in the middle class while branding the other bourgeois parties as minions of plutocratic interests. Although stalwart defenders of the principle of private property, the revaluation parties were not above compromising this precept in order to expose the hypocrisy of the DNVP and to call attention to the prejudicial treatment of the *Mittelstand* by supporting a left-wing effort to hold a referendum with the goal of nationalizing the princely properties. Once again, the revaluation issue promoted that peculiar mixture of special pleading, interest politics, and organized *ressentiment* that robbed Weimar politics of the coherence and meaningfulness it so desperately needed.[76]

The bizarre combination of single-issue interest politics and pretentious claims to represent the *Mittelstand* and its alleged ideals of justice reflected the profound disorientation of a highly heterogeneous and much divided social group as it had emerged from the Second Empire through the traumas of war and inflation into the troubled modernity of the Weimar Republic. Habituated to thinking in corporatist and occupational language, nurtured on hostility to Socialism and suspicion of capitalism, and already well exercised in the interest-group politics of prewar Germany, its peculiar response to its loss of assets and status, increased dependency, and threatened values was virtually predetermined. War and inflation had dramatically and painfully accelerated what might be called the economization of life by creating a much closer relationship between class position and social mobility, on the one hand, and economic circumstances, on the other. The crisis of the intellectual workers, which persisted right on through the stabilization and took on forms completely reminiscent of those of the inflation during the Great Depression, was the most extreme illustration of this change.[77] In one way or another, this crisis affected every group in the so-called middle class as well as in all other social groups. If the inflationary experience promoted modernization and social change in Germany, it did so under the worst possible circumstances; namely, in the context of a massive loss of national resources and capital as well as defeat and humiliation and with a rapidity that made the change of circumstances brutally obvious. While the various middle-class protest groups spoke the language of corporatism and demanded social protection, they were really demanding compensation, opportunity, and increased income rather than a return to some ideal past. They were not as premodern as they sounded, and they were making a charge against the modernity of the present that addressed itself to very real conditions.[78]

There is also nothing premodern about the desire for social and political integration and the notion that the public good should take precedence over private gain. The inflationary redistribution of assets and opportunities dealt a powerful blow to these values, and the continuation of crass interest-group politics by the winners and the losers in the inflation was less than edifying. Little wonder, therefore, that bourgeois spirits (but, certainly, not only those) were uplifted by visions of a *Volksgemeinschaft*, a people's community, and by the slogan

Das Buch

Die Bücher

Cartoon (1925) from *Simplicissimus* showing the loss of traditional values. In the old Germany, one read "the book" around a table; in the new postwar and post-inflation Germany, the profiteer fox-trots, surrounded by books that serve only decorative purposes.

of *Gemeinnutz vor Eigennutz*, of the common interest before self-interest. It was not only Hitler who appealed to these sentiments, and it is noteworthy that, alongside the interest-group politics, there was a strong inclination for nationalist German burghers to seek at once sociability and community in the paramilitary exercises and other activities of organizations like the Stahlhelm. This, too, was a charge against a modern reality—namely, the consequences of Germany's failed political modernization.[79]

It was, of course, the war that had imposed the great mortgage on German democracy, but it was a mortgage with a variable interest rate that increased with each successive blow to the body politic. One of the greatest of these was the inflation, which caused the Republic to be identified with the trauma of all those who had lost out and with the shameful practices and violations of law, equity, and good faith that characterized the period. No less offensive than the misappropriation of money and goods, however, was the sense that there had been a misappropriation of spiritual values and a soiling of what the *Bürgertum*—above all, the *Bildungsbürgertum*—held to be holy. The so-called *Sittengeschichten*, the histories of manners and morals, of the inflation were simply an extension of this belief, so that the inflation added a powerful pornographic element to the political culture of Weimar with all the elements of shame and self-disgust and the projections onto others that came with it. In his *World of Yesterday*, Stefan Zweig claimed that

Nothing ever embittered the German people so much—it is important to remember this—nothing made them so furious with hate and so ripe for Hitler as the inflation. For the war, murderous as it was, had yet yielded hours of jubilation, with ringing of bells and fanfares of victory. And, being an incurably militaristic nation, Germany felt lifted in her pride by her temporary victories; while the inflation served only to make it feel soiled, cheated, and humiliated; a whole generation never forgot or forgave the German Republic for those years and preferred to reinstate its butchers.[80]

To say Germans were "ripe" is not to say they were ripe enough, and one must caution against drawing a direct line from the inflation to the victory of National Socialism. Nevertheless, if one considers the Hobbesian condition of German social and economic life during the hyperinflation, the ferocious outbursts of anti-Semitic and anti-foreign sentiment, the deepening of class hatreds and hostilities, then one finds evidence enough for a widespread introduction of elements of barbarism into the political culture of Germany that helps to explain the relative acceptance of political violence by the German *Bürgertum* during the later years of the Weimar Republic and that peculiarly hideous combination of indifference and careerism that characterized the behavior of so many intellectual workers in the Third Reich. Surely, the German inflation is one important reason why so many Germans defaulted not only on democracy but also on civilization itself.

Notes

Introduction

1. W.E. Süskind, "Raymund," *Neue Rundschau* I (1927), pp. 369–88, quote on p. 374.

2. Eduard Koppenstätter, *Die Markentwertung. Astrologische Begründung der Kursentwicklung in den Jahren 1914–1922 mit prognostizierter Währungskurve für die Jahre 1923–1926* (Ried, 1923). I am grateful to Dr. Martin Geyer for bringing this work to my attention.

3. Jeremy Rifkin, *Entropy. A New World View* (New York, 1980), p. 126.

4. Elisabeth Langgässer, "Merkur," *Erzählungen* (Düsseldorf, 1964), pp. 173–94, quote on pp. 187f. The novella was first published in 1932. For a fine analysis, see Eva Maria Welskop-Deffaa, "Die 'Inflationsnovelle' aus dem 'Tryptychon des Teufels.' Ein wirtschaftsgeschichtlicher Essay zur Nachwirkung der Inflation im Frühwerk Elisabeth Langgässers," in Gerald D. Feldman et al., eds., *The Consequences of Inflation* [*Einzelveröffentlichungen der Historischen Kommission zu Berlin*, Bd. 67. *Beiträge zu Inflation und Wiederaufbau in Deutschland und Europa 1914–1924*] (Berlin, 1989), pp. 287–330.

5. Charles S. Maier, "The Politics of Inflation in the Twentieth Century," in Charles S. Maier, ed., *In Search of Stability. Explorations in Historical Political Economy* (Cambridge, 1987), pp. 187–224, quote on p. 194.

6. Arnold Zweig, "Alter Mann am Stock," *Novellen* II (Frankfurt a.M., 1987), pp. 174–82, quote on p. 182. More generally on literary treatments of the inflation, see Gerald D. Feldman, "Weimar Writers and the German Inflation," in Gisela Brude-Firnau & Karin J. MacHardy, eds., *Fact and Fiction. German History and Literature 1848–1924* (Tübingen, 1990), pp. 173–83.

7. In the foreword to the English translation of Costantino Bresciani-Turroni's classic *The Economics of Inflation. A Study of Currency Depreciation in Post-War Germany, 1914–1923* (London, 1937), p. 5.

8. Letter of April 10, 1941, in Claire Nix, ed., *Heinrich Brüning. Briefe und Gespräche 1934–1945* (Stuttgart, 1974), p. 353.

9. Elias Canetti, *Crowds and Power*, translated by Carol Stewart (New York, 1963), p. 188.

10. For three illustrations of the confluence of contemporary concern and interest in historical experiences with inflation, see Fred Hirsch and John Goldthorpe, eds., *The Political Economy of Inflation* (London & Cambridge, Mass., 1978), the National Bureau of Economic Research–sponsored collection, Robert E. Hall, ed., *Inflation. Causes and Effects* (Chicago & London, 1982), and the Brookings Institution–sponsored volume by Leon N. Lindberg and Charles S. Maier, eds., *The Politics of Inflation and Economic Stagnation* (Washington, 1985).

11. Gerald D. Feldman, "Gegenwärtiger Forschungsstand und künftige Forschungsprobleme zur deutschen Inflation," in Otto Büsch and Gerald D. Feldman, eds., *Historische Prozesse der deutschen Inflation 1914 bis 1924. Ein Tagungsbericht* [*Einzelveröffentlichungen der Historischen Kommission zu Berlin*, Bd. 21] (Berlin, 1978), pp. 3–21. See also Gerald D. Feldman, "The Historian and the German Inflation," in Nathan Schmukler & Edward Marcus, eds., *Inflation through the Ages: Economic, Social, Psychological and Historical Aspects* (New York, 1983), pp. 386–99. Two very useful accounts of the inflation research that has been conducted by historians are Michael Schneider, "Deutsche Gesellschaft im Krieg und Währungskrise 1914–1924," *AfS* 16 (1986), pp. 301–20, and William H. Hubbard, "The New Inflation History," *JMH* 62 (1990), pp. 552–69.

12. Fritz Ringer, *The German Inflation of 1923* (New York, 1969). For all their interesting detail and factual information, the more recent accounts of Adam Fergusson, *When Money Dies: The Nightmare of the Weimar Collapse* (London, 1975), and William Guttmann & Patricia Meehan, *The Great Inflation. Germany 1919–1923* (Westmead, 1975), are less sophisticated and useful. The treatment of Otto Friedrich, *Before the Deluge. A Portrait of Berlin in the 1920's* (New York & London, 1972), pp. 131–44, is not lacking in insight but is submerged in his primary goal of being entertaining.

13. Felix Gilbert, *A European Past. Memoirs 1905–1945* (New York, 1988), p. 48. Lowenthal's adventure was personally related to the author.

14. A good illustration is Heinrich Böll, "The Specter that still Haunts Germany. Inflation," *New York Times Magazine* (May 2, 1976).

15. See the books by Fergusson and Guttmann &

859

Meehan referred to in note 12 for illustrations of these tendencies. See also Heinrich Mann, "Kobes," *Neue Rundschau* (1925), I, pp. 235–66; Erich Reger, *Union der festen Hand. Roman einer Entwicklung* (Berlin, 1946), and Langgässer, "Merkur," in *Erzählungen*, pp. 173–94. For typical textbook and general historical accounts, see Golo Mann, *Deutsche Geschichte des 19. und 20. Jahrhunderts* (Frankfurt a.M., 1958), pp. 695–99, and Gordon Craig, *Germany 1866–1945* (New York, 1978), pp. 448–56. Craig's discussion is certainly the best of this genre.

16. Franz Eulenburg, "Die sozialen Wirkungen der Währungsverhältnisse," *JNS* 67 (1924), pp. 748–94, quote on p. 748.

17. For the gaps in the time series, see the standard work of Walther G. Hoffmann, *Das Wachstum der deutschen Wirtschaft seit der Mitte des 19. Jahrhunderts* (Berlin, Heidelberg, New York, 1965). Wolfram Fischer & Peter Czada show that the figures which Hoffmann does provide are not without problems in their "Wandlungen in der deutschen Industriestruktur im 20. Jahrhundert," in Gerhard A. Ritter, ed., *Entstehung und Wandel der modernen Gesellschaft. Festschrift für Hans Rosenberg zum 65. Geburtstag* (Berlin, 1970), pp. 116–65. Exemplary pre-1945 sources of data are *Zahlen zur Geldentwertung in Deutschland 1914 bis 1923. Sonderheft 1 zu Wirtschaft und Statistik* (Berlin, 1925); Friedrich Hesse, *Die Deutsche Wirtschaftslage von 1914 bis 1923, Geldblähe und Wechsellagen* (Jena, 1938); Bayerisches Statistisches Landesamt, *Die Verelendung des Mittelstandes. Heft 106 der Beiträge zur Statistik Bayerns* (Munich, 1925), and *Sozialer Auf- und Abstieg im deutschen Volk. Statistische Methoden und Ergebnisse. Heft 117 der Beiträge zur Statistik Bayerns* (Munich, 1930); Robert Kuczynski, *Postwar Labor Conditions in Germany* (Washington, 1925); and despite its oddities, Ernst Schultze, *Not und Verschwendung. Untersuchungen über das deutsche Wirtschaftsschicksal* (Leipzig, 1923). Important recent works providing new statistical data are Carl-Ludwig Holtfrerich, *The German Inflation 1914–1923* (Berlin & New York, 1986); Steven B. Webb, *Hyperinflation and Stabilization in Weimar Germany* (New York & Oxford, 1989); Peter-Christian Witt, "Tax Policies, Tax Assessment and Inflation: Towards a Sociology of Public Finances in the German Inflation, 1914–1923," in Peter-Christian Witt, ed., *Wealth and Taxation in Central Europe. The History and Sociology of Public Finance* (Leamington Spa, 1987), pp. 137–60. What can be done on the regional level has been demonstrated by Merith Niehuss, *Arbeiterschaft in Krieg und Inflation* [*Beiträge zu Inflation und Wiederaufbau in Deutschland und Europa 1914–1924*, Bd. 3] (Berlin and New York, 1985); and Peter J. Lyth, *Inflation and the Merchant Economy. The Hamburg Mittelstand 1914–1924* (New York, 1990), while a good illustration of important new data generated by a sectoral study is Dieter Lindenlaub, *Maschinenbauunterneh-*

men in der deutschen Inflation 1919–1923 [*Beiträge zu Inflation und Wiederaufbau in Deutschland und Europa 1914–1924*, Bd. 4] (Berlin & New York, 1985).

18. For the different types of inflation, see Holtfrerich, *German Inflation*, pp. 11–14; Harald Scherf, "Inflation," *Handwörterbuch der Wirtschaftswissenschaften*, Vol. 4 (1978), pp. 159–84; Charles Maier, *In Search of Stability*, pp. 194–99; M. Bronfenbrenner, "Inflation and Deflation," *International Encyclopedia of the Social Sciences*, Vol. 7 (New York, 1968), pp. 289–301.

19. Knut Borchardt, "*Strukturwirkungen des Inflationsprozesses* [*Schriftenreihe des Ifo-Instituts für Wirtschaftsforschung*, 50] (Berlin & Munich, 1970), pp. 15f.

20. Frank D. Graham, *Exchange, Prices, and Production in Hyper-Inflation: Germany, 1920–1923* (Princeton, 1930), p. vii.

21. Bresciani-Turroni, *Economics of Inflation*, p. 5.

22. Ibid., p. 401n. Interestingly enough, Graham's views on the beneficial effects of the inflation were autonomously seconded in a much more theoretical and explicit manner by an Italian, the fascist economist Corrado Gini in his "Wirkungen der extremen Formen der Inflation auf den Wirtschaftsorganismus," *Weltwirtschaftliches Archiv*, N.F., 40 (1934), Bd. 2, pp. 399–436.

23. The points made here are especially clear when one reads his conclusion and appendix dealing with economic conditions in Germany until 1931, ibid., pp. 398–436.

24. Ludwig von Mises, "The Great German Inflation," in Richard M. Ebeling, *Money, Method, and the Market Process. Essays by Ludwig von Mises* (Norwell, Mass., 1990), pp. 96–103, quote on p. 96. Howard S. Ellis, *German Monetary Theory 1905–1933* (Cambridge, Mass., 1937), remains the best guide to the subject. See especially his analysis of Knapp on pp. 13–41 and his astute observations on Graham, pp. 279ff. Holtfrerich, *German Inflation*, pp. 156–72, provides a lucid account of the two theories. A more open contemporary defender of the balance-of-payments position was the American economist John M. Williams.

25. For the continuity of the debate over time, see Marcello de Cecco, "The Vicious/Virtuous Circle Debate in the Twenties and the Seventies," European University Institute Working Paper, No. 24 (Badia Fiesolana, San Domenico, January 1983). For an attempt to draw lessons from the post-1918 experience from balance-of-payments and quantitative perspectives, see Ragnar Nurske, *The Course and Control of Inflation. A Review of Monetary Experiences after World War I* (Geneva, 1946). On Keynesian and other models, see J.A. Trevithick, *Inflation. A Guide to the Crisis in Economics* (New York, 1980); Maier, *In Search of Stability*, pp. 189ff.; Holtfrerich, *German Inflation*, pp. 184ff.; Steven B. Webb, "Money

Demand and Expectations in the German Hyperinflation: A Survey of the Models," in Schmuckler & Marcus, *Inflation Through the Ages*, pp. 435–49.

26. Important examples are Phillip Cagan, "The Monetary Dynamics of Hyperinflation," in Milton Friedman, ed., *Studies in the Quantity Theory of Money* (Chicago, 1956), pp. 25–117; Jacob A. Frenkel, "The Forward Exchange Rate, Expectations and the Demand for Money: The German Hyperinflation," *American Economic Review* 67 (1977), pp. 653–70, and "Further Evidence on Expectations and the Demand for Money during the German Hyperinflation," *Journal of Monetary Economics* 5 (1979), pp. 97–104; Michael K. Salemi, "Adaptive Expectations, Rational Expectations and Money Demand in Hyperinflation Germany," *Journal of Monetary Economics* 5 (1979), pp. 593–604; Thomas J. Sargent, *Rational Expectations and Inflation* (New York, 1986).

27. Webb, *Hyperinflation and Stabilization in Weimar Germany,* provides a good illustration of how the monetarist literature has been put to valuable use for the historian. On the stabilization question, see especially Thomas J. Sargent, "The Ends of Four Big Inflations," in Robert Hall, ed., *Inflation: Causes and Effects* (Chicago, 1982), pp. 41–98, and Rudiger Dornbusch, "Lessons from the German Inflation Experience of the 1920s," in Rudiger Dornbusch et al., eds., *Macroeconomics and Finance: Essays in Honor of Franco Modigliani* (Cambridge, Mass., 1987), pp. 337–66.

28. Karsten Laursen and Jørgen Pedersen, *The German Inflation 1918–1923* (Amsterdam, 1964); Peter Czada, "Große Inflation und Wirtschaftswachstum," in Hans Mommsen et al., eds., *Industrielles System und politische Entwicklung in der Weimarer Republik* (Düsseldorf, 1974, reprinted in 1977), pp. 386–95, and "Ursachen und Folgen der großen Inflation," in Harald Winkel, ed., *"Finanz und wirtschaftspolitische Fragen der Zwischenkriegszeit* [*Schriften des Vereins für Sozialpolitik,* N.F., 73] (Berlin, 1973), pp. 11–43; Gerald D. Feldman, *Iron and Steel in the German Inflation, 1916–1923* (Princeton, 1977), and Gerald D. Feldman and Heidrun Homburg, *Industrie und Inflation. Studien und Dokumente zur Politik der deutschen-Unternehmer 1916–1923* (Hamburg, 1977); Charles S. Maier, *Recasting Bourgeois Europe: Stabilization in France, Germany, and Italy in the Decade after World War I* (Princeton, 1975, reprinted 1988).

29. Knut Borchardt, "Die Erfahrung mit Inflationen in Deutschland," in Knut Borchardt, ed., *Wachstum, Krisen Handlungsspielräume der Wirtschaftspolitik* [*Kritische Studien zur Geschichtswissenschaft,* 50] (Göttingen, 1982), pp. 151–61, quote on p. 154.

30. Bresciani-Turroni, *Economics of Inflation*, p. 401.

31. Holtfrerich, *German Inflation*, pp. 197–220, and the convenient summary of his conclusions on pp. 331–34. On the question of Germany's interrupted reconstruction, see Werner Abelshauser and Dietmar Petzina, "Krise und Rekonstruktion. Zur Interpretation der gesamtwirtschaftlichen Entwicklung Deutschlands im 20. Jahrhundert," in W. Abelshauser and Dietmar Petzina, eds., *Deutsche Wirtschaftsgeschichte im Industriezeitalter. Konjunktur, Krise, Wachstum* (Königstein/Ts., 1981), pp. 47–93. As the very title of his important work demonstrates, Harold James's, *The German Slump: Politics and Economics, 1924–1936* (Oxford, 1986), this periodization of German economic growth has gained general acceptance.

32. Holtfrerich, *German Inflation*, pp. 4–8, 97–101, 299–300, quote on p. 4.

33. The remark was made with reference to Gerald Feldman and Charles Maier in a comment on the latter's "The Two Postwar Eras and the Conditions for Stability in Twentieth-Century Western Europe," *AHR* 86 (April 1981), pp. 326–67, quote on p. 360.

34. Charles Kindleberger, "A Structural View of the German Inflation," in Gerald D. Feldman et al., *The Experience of Inflation. International and Comparative Studies* [*Beiträge zu Inflation und Wiederaufbau in Deutschland und Europa 1914–1924*] (Berlin & New York, 1984), pp. 10–33, quote on p. 32, and "Collective Memory vs. Rational Expectations: Some Historical Puzzles in Macro-Economic Behavior," in Charles P. Kindleberger, *Keynesianism vs. Monetarism and other Essays in Financial History* (London, 1985), pp. 129–38.

35. Thomas Mann, "Disorder and Early Sorrow," in Thomas Mann, *Death in Venice and Seven Other Stories* (New York, 1954), pp. 182–216, quote on p. 189.

36. Walter Benjamin, *Einbahnstraße* (Frankfurt a.M., 1969), p. 25.

37. See the remarks of Hans Mommsen in Büsch & Feldman, *Historische Prozesse*, p. 199. Some of the secular changes in question are discussed in Wolfram Fischer and Peter Czada, "Wandlungen in der deutschen Industriestruktur im 20. Jahrhundert. Ein statistisch-deskriptiver Ansatz," in Gerhard A. Ritter, ed., *Entstehung und Wandel der modernen Gesellschaft. Festschrift für Hans Rosenberg zum 65. Geburtstag* (Berlin, 1970), pp. 116–65. See also, Gerold Ambrosius and William H. Hubbard, *A Social and Economic History of Twentieth-Century Europe* (Cambridge, Mass., 1989), and Hartmut Kaelble, *A Social History of Western Europe, 1880–1980* (Dublin, 1989).

38. Stefan Zweig, *Die Welt von Gestern. Erinnerungen eines Europäers* (Frankfurt a.M., 1969). On the role of war and inflation in the disintegration of the *Bürgertum*, see Hans Mommsen, "Die Auflösung des Bürgertums seit dem späten 19. Jahrhundert," in Jürgen Kocka, ed., *Bürger und Bürgerlichkeit im 19. Jahrhundert* (Göttingen, 1987), pp. 288–315. The discussion of modernization here should not be construed as animosity toward the concept. See Gerald

D. Feldman, "The Weimar Republic: A Problem of Modernization?" *AfS* 26 (1986), pp. 1–26. On the need to relativize prewar anti-modernist cultural criticisms, see Thomas Nipperdey, *Deutsche Geschichte 1866–1918. Bd. I Arbeitswelt und Bürgergeist* (Munich, 1990), esp. pp. 824–34.

39. Karl Helfferich, *Deutschlands Volkswohlstand 1888–1913*, 3rd ed. (Berlin, 1914). The best study of Helfferich is John G. Williamson, *Karl Helfferich 1872–1924. Economist, Financier, Politician* (Princeton, 1971).

40. Helfferich, *Deutschlands Volkswohlstand*, pp. 46f.

41. Ibid., pp. 34ff., 83–85, 122f. For an interesting statement by Helfferich of the close relationship between German foreign investment and German industrial interests, see Peter-Christian Witt, *Die Finanzpolitik des deutschen Reiches von 1903 bis 1913. Eine Studie zur Innenpolitik des Wilhelminischen Deutschland [Historische Studien, Heft 415]* (Lübeck & Hamburg, 1970), pp. 197f. See also Williamson, *Helfferich*, pp. 111–13.

42. Williamson, *Helfferich*, pp. 113f.

43. For a positive view of German Constitutionalism, see Ernst Rudolf Huber, *Deutsche Verfassungsgeschichte seit 1789*, 7 vols. (Stuttgart, 1957ff.), esp. III, pp. 3–26, 766–85. For more jaundiced views, see Hans Boldt, "Deutscher Konstitutionalismus und Bismarckreich," Michael Stürmer, *Das kaiserliche Deutschland. Politik und Gesellschaft 1870–1918* (Düsseldorf, 1970), pp. 119–42, and, above all, Hans-Ulrich Wehler, *The German Empire 1871–1918* (Leamington Spa, 1985). An important criticism of Wehler's view is to be found in Thomas Nipperdey, "Wehlers 'Kaiserreich.' Eine kritische Auseinandersetzung," in Thomas Nipperdey, *Gesellschaft, Kultur, Theorie* (Göttingen, 1976), pp. 360–89.

44. For this argument, see Harold James, *A German Identity 1770–1990* (New York, 1989), Chaps. 3–4.

45. Helfferich, *Deutschlands Volkswohlstand*, pp. vi, 128–43.

46. See Linda Heilman, "Industrial Unemployment in Germany: 1873–1913," *AfS* 27 (1987), pp. 25–50 and Karl Christian Führer, *Arbeitslosigkeit und die Entstehung der Arbeitslosenversicherung in Deutschland 1902–1927 [Einzelveröffentlichungen der Historischen Kommission zu Berlin, 73. Beiträge zu Inflation und Wiederaufbau in Deutschland und Europa 1914–1924]* (Berlin, 1990), Chaps. 1 and 2.

47. On the wage question, see Ashok V. Desai, *Real Wages in Germany 1871–1913* (Oxford, 1968), p. 110, and Gerhard Bry, *Wages in Germany, 1871–1945* (Princeton, 1960), pp. 81ff. On the comparison between the German and English social security systems, see Gerhard A. Ritter, *Sozialversicherung in Deutschland und England. Entstehung und Grundzüge im Vergleich* (Munich, 1983), and Peter Hennock, "Public Provision for Old Age. Britain and Germany, 1880–1914," *AfS* 30 (1990), pp. 81–104.

For the improvement in nourishment in Germany, see Hans J. Teuteberg, "Der Verzehr von Nahrungsmitteln in Deutschland pro Kopf und Jahr seit Beginn der Industrialisierung (1850–1975)," *AfS* 19 (1979), pp. 331–88, esp. pp. 34ff.

48. For the data on cost of living and in the interpretation of the real-wage question, I follow Desai, *Real Wages*, pp. 97–105, 117, 125–26. For a more pessimistic appraisal, see Bry, *Wages in Germany*, pp. 71–74. Some of the difficulties in drawing conclusions from the available data are discussed by Jens Flemming and Peter-Christian Witt in "Probleme der Sozialstatistik im deutschen Kaiserreich," in their introduction to the reprint of the 1909 Reich Statistisches Amt, *Erhebungen von Wirtschaftsrechnungen minderbemittelter Familien im deutschen Reich,* and the Deutsche Metallarbeiter-Verband, *320 Haushaltsrechnungen von Metallarbeitern,* (Berlin & Bonn, 1981). On industrial conflict in prewar Germany, see the articles by Klaus Schönhoven, Hans-Peter Ullmann, and Klaus Saul in Klaus Tenfelde and Heinrich Volkmann, eds., *Streik. Zur Geschichte des Arbeitskampfes in Deutschland während der Industrialisierung* (Munich, 1981), pp. 177–236.

49. Borchardt, *Wachstum*, p. 152.

50. See especially the Reichstag debates in *VR,* Feb. 21–22, 1912, Bd. 283, pp. 180–236, and Jan. 20, 1914, ibid., pp. 6601–58.

51. M. Rainer Lepsius, "Parteiensystem und Sozialstruktur. Zum Problem der Demokratisierung der deutschen Gesellschaft," in Wilhelm Abel, et al., eds., *Wirtschaft, Geschichte und Wirtschaftsgeschichte. Festschrift zum 65. Geburtstag von Friedrich Lütge* (Stuttgart, 1966), pp. 371–93; Gerhard A. Ritter, *Die deutschen Parteien 1830–1914* (Göttingen, 1985), Chap. 3; Thomas Nipperdey, *Die Organisation der deutschen Parteien vor 1914* (Düsseldorf, 1961)

52. For a good survey of the development and role of interest groups, and the relevant literature, see Hans-Peter Ullmann, *Interessenverbände in Deutschland* (Göttingen, 1988), esp. Pts. I–II, which forms the basis of much of the discussion of interest groups which follows. On the language of German politics, see the suggestive article by Thomas C. Childers, "The Social Language of Politics in Germany: The Sociology of Political Discourse in the Weimar Republic," *AHR* 95 (April 1990), pp. 331–58.

53. See the classic article by Hans Rosenberg, "Die Pseudodemokratisierung der Rittergutsbesitzerklasse," Hans Rosenberg, ed., *Machteliten und Wirtschaftskonjunkturen* (Göttingen 1978), pp. 83–101.

54. On the Cartel, see Dirk Stegmann, *Die Erben Bismarcks. Parteien und Verbände in der Spätphase des Wilhelminischen Deutschlands. Sammlungspolitik 1897–1918* (Cologne, 1970), pp. 352–448. For an important and convincing warning against overlooking the archaic and premodern appeals to the old *Mittelstand* east of the Elbe, see Heinrich August Winkler, *Zwischen Marx und Monopolen. Der*

deutsche Mittelstand vom Kaiserreich zur Bundesrepublik Deutschland (Frankfurt a.M., 1991), pp. 1–17.

55. *VR*, Jan. 20, 1914, Bd. 292, p. 6637.

56. Ibid., p. 6647.

57. *Protokoll über die Verhandlungen des Parteitages der sozialdemokratischen Partei Deutschlands. Abgehalten in Chemnitz vom 15. bis 21. September 1912* (Berlin, 1912), p. 371.

58. Quoted in Robert Gellately, *The Politics of Economic Despair. Shopkeepers and German Politics 1890–1914* (London & Beverly Hills, 1974), p. 194.

59. Ibid., p. 184.

60. See especially David Blackbourn, "The *Mittelstand* in German Society and Politics 1871–1914," *Social History* 2 (1977), pp. 409–33.

61. See especially the essays by Jürgen Kocka, M. Rainer Lepsius, Dietrich Rüschemeyer, Thomas Nipperdey, Hans-Ulrich Wehler, and David Blackbourn in Kocka, ed., *Bürger und Bürgerlichkeit.* More generally, see Jürgen Kocka, ed., *Bürgertum im 19. Jahrhundert. Deutschland im europäischen Vergleich*, 3 vols. (München, 1988). See also Konrad Jarausch, *The Unfree Professions. German Lawyers, Teachers and Engineers 1900–1950* (New York & Oxford, 1990), pp. 1–26. There are some splendid illustrations of the complexities of German lower-middle-class and middle-class life and the life-style of the *Bürgertum* in Gerhard A. Ritter and Jürgen Kocka, eds., *Deutsche Sozialgeschichte. Dokumente und Skizzen. Band II 1870–1914* (Munich, 1974), pp. 322–54.

1. Financing the War

1. The classic statement of the German *Sonderweg* thesis and application of modernization theory to German history is provided by Wehler, *German Empire.* For the criticism of his position, see David Blackbourn & Geoff Eley, *The Peculiarities of German History. Bourgeois Society and Politics in Nineteenth-Century Germany* (Oxford and New York, 1984).

2. Gerald D. Feldman, *Army, Industry and Labor in Germany, 1914–1918* (Princeton, 1966) seeks to demonstrate this.

3. See Ernst Rudolf Huber, *Deutsche Verfassungsgeschichte seit 1789*, 7 vols. (Stuttgart, 1957ff.), 5, pp. 33f.; 7, p. 387.

4. For the constitutional status of the Reichsbank, see ibid., III, pp. 846f. See also, Carl-Ludwig Holtfrerich, "Relations between Monetary Authorities and Governmental Institutions: The Case of Germany from the 19th Century to the Present," in Gianni Toniolo, ed., *Central Banks' Independence in Historical Perspective* (Berlin & New York, 1988), pp. 105–59. The discussion which follows is based largely on Knut Borchardt, "Währung und Wirtschaft," in Deutsche Bundesbank, *Währung und*

Wirtschaft in Deutschland 1876–1975 (Frankfurt a.M., 1976), pp. 3–57. See also Reinhold Zilch, *Die Reichsbank und die finanzielle Kriegsvorbereitung 1907–1914* (Berlin, 1987), Chap. 1, and Heinz Habedank, *Die Reichsbank in der Weimarer Republik. Zur Rolle der Zentralbank in der Politik des deutschen Imperialismus* (East Berlin, 1981), pp. 13ff. There is an excellent brief summary of the German banking system in Karl Erich Born, *International Banking in the 19th and 20th Centuries* (New York, 1983), pp. 168–75.

5. See the short biographies of Havenstein and Glasenapp in the *Neue Deutsche Biographie* (Munich, 1953ff.), Vol. 8, p. 137, and Vol. 6, p. 428. On Havenstein, see also the insightful Felix Pinner, *Deutsche Wirtschaftsführer* (Charlottenburg, 1924), pp. 153–64.

6. H. Aubin and W. Zorn, *Handbuch der deutschen Wirtschafts- und Sozialgeschichte*, 2 vols. (Stuttgart, 1971, 1976), 2, p. 946.

7. Quoted in Habedank, *Reichsbank*, p. 13.

8. This is a central thesis of Zilch, *Reichsbank*, and it is very convincingly argued.

9. Ibid., pp. 14f. See also Deutsche Bundesbank, *Deutsches Geld- und Bankwesen in Zahlen 1876–1975* (Frankfurt a.M., 1976), pp. 2f., 14f.

10. For a brief discussion and references to the major literature, see Gerald D. Feldman, "Politik, Banken und der Goldstandard in der Zwischenkriegszeit," *Vom Goldstandard zum Multireservewährungsstandard. Neuntes nationales Symposium zur Bankgeschichte am 18. Oktober 1985 im Hause der Deutsche Bank AG, Frankfurt am Main. Bankhistorisches Archiv. Zeitschrift zur Bankgeschichte*, Beiheft 11 (Frankfurt a.M., 1987), pp. 11–20. See also the introductory chapters of Barry Eichengreen, *Golden Fetters: The Gold Standard and the Great Depression, 1919–1939* (Oxford, 1991).

11. Borchardt in *Währung und Wirtschaft*, p. 44.

12. Zilch, *Reichsbank*, pp. 92–101, 124–27. Bundesbank, *Deutsches Geld und Bankwesen in Zahlen*, p. 2.

13. Habedank, *Reichsbank*, p. 22. See also, Borchardt in *Währung und Wirtschaft*, p. 51f.

14. Havenstein's reliance on the voluntary cooperation of the bank, was much criticized by Johann Plenge, *Von der Diskontpolitik zur Herrschaft über den Geldmarkt* (Berlin, 1913). Here I follow closely the account if not the ideologically laden interpretation of Reinhold Zilch, "Zum Plan einer Zwangsregulierung im deutschen Bankwesen vor dem Ersten Weltkrieg und zu seinen Ursachen. Dokumentation," in B.A. Aisin and W. Gutsche, eds., *Forschungsergebnisse zur Geschichte des deutschen Imperialismus vor 1917* (Berlin, 1980), pp. 228–56, esp. pp. 228–33.

15. For the discussion and quotations which follow, see ibid., pp. 236–50.

16. From a speech, probably to the Reichsbank Curatorium, of Sept. 25, 1914, BAP, NL Havenstein, Nr. 2, Bl. 62.

17. Ibid., Bl. 64.

18. For the material on the moratorium issue at the outbreak of the war, see BAP, RB, Nr. 6342, Bl. 7–23, and the report, "Die Reichsbank in den ersten drei Kriegsmonaten," ibid., Nr. 6339, Bl. 21–43.

19. This discussion is based on Konrad Roesler, *Die Finanzpolitik des deutschen Reiches in Ersten Weltkrieg* (Berlin, 1967), pp. 18–40, and Heinz Haller, "Die Rolle der Staatsfinanzen für den Inflationsprozess," in *Währung und Wirtschaft*, pp. 115–55. For the quotation, see Havenstein's report of Sept. 25, 1914, BAP, NL Havenstein, Nr. 2, Bl. 89.

20. Havenstein speech of Sept. 25, 1914, ibid., Bl. 91.

21. BAK, R 28, Nr. 5, Bl. 5. For the other examples cited, see Nr. 3, Bl. 3; Nr. 4, Bl. 198–99, 405–6.

22. Gerhard Berghorst, "Die Goldsucher bei der Arbeit" (August 1915), BAK, R 28, Nr. 9, Bl. 128–33.

23. Ibid.

24. Carl-Ludwig Holtfrerich, *German Inflation*, pp. 115–17.

25. RB circular, Aug. 16, 1914, BAK, R 28, Nr. 3, Bl. 119.

26. Holtfrerich, *German Inflation*, pp. 64f., 115f.; Roeseler, *Finanzpolitik*, pp. 41–45, 141–45, 212–15.

27. Havenstein provided the details in his speech to the Curatorium of Sept. 25, 1914, BAP, NL Havenstein, Nr. 2, Bl. 96f.

28. Karl Elster, *Von der Mark zur Reichsmark. Die Geschichte der deutschen Währung in den Jahren 1914 bis 1924* (Jena, 1928), pp. 55–57.

29. Friedrich Bendixen, *Währungspolitik und Geldtheorie im Lichte des Weltkrieges* (Munich, 1919), pp. 27–28.

30. Ibid., pp. 28–29.

31. Kurt Singer, ed., *G. F. Knapp/F. Bendixen, Zur Staatlichen Theorie des Geldes. Ein Briefwechsel (1905–1920)* (Tübingen, 1958), p. 156.

32. Bendixen to Knapp, Feb. 9, 1915, ibid., p. 162.

33. Ibid., p. 165n2.

34. Albert Hahn, *Fünfzig Jahre zwischen Inflation und Deflation* (Tübingen, 1963), p. 10.

35. Joseph A. Schumpeter, "Das Sozialprodukt und die Rechenpfennige," *AfSS* 44 (1917/1918), pp. 627–715, quote on p. 714.

36. Bendixen, *Währungspolitik*, p. 26.

37. Roeseler, *Finanzpolitik*, p. 30; Habedank, *Reichsbank*, pp. 24f. On Helfferich, see Williamson, *Helfferich*. Chap. 4.

38. For this discussion of the comparative role of the money markets, see T. Balderston, "War Finance and Inflation in Britain and Germany, 1914–1918," *EHR* (1989) 42, pp. 222–44. Balderston seems to suggest in this important article that the old emphasis on differing taxation levels in Germany and England was misplaced. If one accepts his argument, however, then the only conclusion I can draw is that the significance of Germany's failure to adequately fund the war by taxation is far greater than has previously been thought.

39. Havenstein speech to the Reichsbank Curatorium, Sept. 25, 1914, BAP, NL Havenstein, Nr. 2, Bl. 95.

40. Holtfrerich, *Inflation*, p. 104ff. On the prewar financial system, see Witt, *Finanzpolitik des deutschen Reiches*. On the comparative financing of the war, see R. Knauss, *Die deutsche, englische und französische Kriegsfinanzierung. Sozialwissenschaftliche Forschungen, hrsg. von der sozialwissenschaftlichen Arbeitsgemeinschaft. Abteilung V, Heft 1* (Berlin & Leipzig, 1923).

41. Roeseler, *Finanzpolitik*, pp. 67ff.

42. Ibid., pp. 78ff.

43. Quoted in Williams, *Helfferich*, p. 131.

44. Helfferich's attitudes will be discussed more fully in the next chapter.

45. See Peter-Christian Witt, "Finanzpolitik und sozialer Wandel in Krieg und Inflation 1918–1924," in Mommsen et al., eds., *Industrielles System*, pp. 395–426, esp. pp. 404ff.

46. For this and the discussion which follows, see ibid., and Roeseler, *Finanzpolitik*, pp. 103–27, 163–66, and R. Kuczynski, "German Taxation Policy in the World War," *Journal of Political Economy* 31 (Dec. 1923), pp. 763–89. See also Carl-Ludwig Holtfrerich, "The Modernisation of the Tax System in the First World War and the Great Inflation, 1914–1923" in Witt, ed., *Wealth and Taxation in Central Europe*, pp. 125–35.

47. Roeseler, *Finanzpolitik*, pp. 56–57.

48. Havenstein speech to the Curatorium, Sept. 25, 1914, BAP, NL Havenstein, Nr. 2, Bl. 95.

49. Roeseler, *Finanzpolitik*, pp. 166–68, 175–77, 207.

50. Reichsbank circular, BAK, R 28, Nr. 6, Bl. 49.

51. Report of Jan. 19, 1918, BAK, R 28, Nr. 7, Bl. 85.

52. Reichsbank to chambers of commerce, Sept. 6, 1918, SWW, K1, Nr. 91.

53. On Helfferich's techniques, see Williamson, *Helfferich*, pp. 124f. See also Havenstein's description of the 1914 effort in his speech to the Curatorium of Sept. 25, 1914, BAP, NL Havenstein, Nr. 2, Bl. 95, and his postwar description of the system of June 22, 1920, BAK, R 43I/2391, Bl. 147f.

54. See Rudolf Kühne, *Die Devisenzwangswirtschaft im deutschen Reich während der Jahre 1916 bis 1926. Eine währungspolitische Reminiszenz* (Frankfurt a.M., 1970).

55. See Feldman, *Iron and Steel*, pp. 60ff. See also, Hesse, *deutsche Wirtschaftslage*, pp. 26–29, 61–63, 103f, 301–6, 336–39.

56. Singer, *Briefwechsel*, p. 176n1.

57. Haller, "Staatsfinanzen," in *Währung und Wirtschaft*, pp. 121ff. See also the report of the Saxon Ambassador to Berlin, June 25, 1918, SäHStA, Gesandtschaft Berlin, Nr. 1630, Bl. 11ff.

58. Elster, *Von der Mark zur Reichsmark*, p. 80, and Kühne, *Devisenzwangswirtschaft*.

59. BAK, R 28, Nr. 7, Bl. 82.

60. Reichsbank to Mayor Hans Luther, July 13, 1917, LA Berlin, AdSt, Nr. 2527, which also has other materials on the loans.

61. On the Swedish ore debts, see Feldman, *Iron and Steel*, pp. 14f., 55f.

62. Roeseler, *Finanzpolitik*, pp. 187ff.; Hesse, *Wirtschaftslage*, pp. 339f.

63. For the discussion and quotations which follow, see BAK, R 28, Nr. 7, Bl. 361.

64. Ibid., Bl. 83.

65. Ibid.

66. Ibid., Bl. 89.

67. Ibid., Bl. 87. For the consistency in Reichsbank leadership argumentation for the eighth War Bond drive, compare to Havenstein's speech at the University of Munich on March 11, 1918, BAP, NL Havenstein, Nr. 3, Bl. 171–82.

68. Williamson, *Helfferich*, p. 129.

69. Edgar Jaffé, "Kriegskostendeckung und Steuerreform," *SVS* 156 (Munich, 1917), Pt. 2, pp. 83–118, quote on p. 92. For a good discussion of the views of national economists on this question, see Dieter Krüger, *Nationalökonomen im wilhelminischen Deutschland (Kritische Studien zur Geschichtswissenschaft, 58)* (Göttingen, 1983), pp. 152ff. See also Roeseler, *Finanzpolitik*, pp. 180–86.

70. *VR*, April 23, 1918, Bd. 312, p. 4734. See also Roeseler, *Finanzwirtschaft*, pp. 130f., 137–40.

71. Report of July 5, 1918, SäHStA, Gesandtschaft Berlin, Nr. 1630, Bl. 23.

72. Confidential Reichsbank memorandum of Jan. 24, 1918, BAK, R 28, Nr. 9, Bl. 28f., and Roeseler, *Finanzpolitik*, p. 215.

73. Reichsbank to Reichsbankhauptstelle Breslau, Aug. 30, 1918, ibid., Nr. 8, Bl. 448.

74. Report of July 5, 1918, SäHStA, Gesandtschaft Berlin, Nr. 1630, Bl. 17–18.

75. Ibid.

76. Reichsbank to Reichsbankstellen and to the Prussian Minister of Commerce, Oct. 3, 1918, and Reich Treasury to the Federal States, Oct. 10, 1918, GStAKM, Rep. 120, AX, Nr. 27d, Bd. 1, Bl. 165–66, 172–73.

77. Felix Pinner, "Geldkrise," *Berliner Tageblatt*, Oct. 26, 1918, in ibid.

78. Berlin speech by Helfferich on Oct. 11, 1918, NStAO, Bestand 265, Nr. 421.

2. War Economy and Inflation

1. Franz Eulenburg, "Zur Theorie der Kriegswirtschaft. Ein Versuch," *AfSS* 43 (1916), pp. 349–96, quote on p. 396.

2. James Tobin, "Inflation: Monetary and Structural Causes and Cures," in Nathan Schmukler and Edward Marcus, eds., *Inflation Through the Ages: Economic, Social, Psychological and Historical Aspects* (New York, 1983), pp. 3–16, quote on p. 3.

3. For Eulenburg's analysis of the inflation, see *JNS* 122 (1924), pp. 748–94. The discussion which follows is based on Eulenburg, *AfSS* 43 (1916), pp. 349–96.

4. Ibid., p. 369.

5. Ibid., p. 376.

6. Ibid., p. 392.

7. Ibid., p. 393.

8. Franz Eulenburg, "Inflation. Zur Theorie der Kriegswirtschaft," ibid. 45 (1919), pp. 477–526, quote on p. 504. This important article was finished at the end of 1918.

9. Ibid., p. 512.

10. Ibid.

11. For this and the discussion which follows, see Feldman, *Army*, Chaps. I–II, and "The Political and Social Foundations of Germany's Economic Mobilization," *Armed Forces and Society* (1976), pp. 121–45. See also, Jürgen Kocka, *Facing Total War. German Society 1914–1918* (Leamington Spa, 1984).

12. Hans Gotthard Ehlert, *Die wirtschaftliche Zentralbehörde des deutschen Reiches 1914–1918. Das Problem der "Gemeinwirtschaft" in Krieg und Frieden* (Wiesbaden, 1982), p. 45. See also, Gerhard Hecker, *Walter Rathenau und sein Verhältnis zu Militär und Krieg* (Boppard am Rhein, 1983), pp. 201ff., and Friedrich Zunkel, *Industrie und Staatssozialismus. Der Kampf um die Wirtschaftsordnung in Deutschland 1914–18* (Düsseldorf, 1974), pp. 17–30.

13. Avner Offer, *The First World War: An Agrarian Interpretation* (Oxford, 1989), pp. 331–34.

14. For the organization and development of the wartime system of agrarian controls, see Martin Schumacher, *Land und Politik. Eine Untersuchung über politische Parteien und agrarische Interessen* (Düsseldorf, 1978), Chap. 1, and Jens Flemming, *Landwirtschaftliche Interessen und Demokratie. Ländliche Gesellschaft, Agrarverbände und Staat 1890–1925* (Bonn, 1978), Chap. 2. See also the older study by August Skalweit, *Die deutsche Kriegsernährungswirtschaft* (Stuttgart, 1927).

15. On the Rhenish–Westphalian peasantry and the controlled economy, see the important studies by Robert G. Moeller, *German Peasants and Agrarian Politics, 1914–1924. The Rhineland and Westphalia* (Chapel Hill, 1986), Chaps. 1–3, and his "Dimensions of Social Conflict in the Great War: The View from the German Countryside," *CEH* 14 (1981), pp. 142–68. More generally, see his insightful, "Peasants and Tariffs in the *Kaiserreich*: How Backward were the *Bauern*?" *Agricultural History* 55 (1981), pp. 370–84.

16. For a brief summary, see Feldman, *Army*, pp. 97ff.

17. Hans Geithe, *Wirkungen der Lebensmittelzwangswirtschaft der Kriegs- und Nachkriegszeit auf den Lebensmitteleinzelhandel*, (Halle, 1925), pp. 11ff.; and Lyth, *Inflation*, pp. 60–64.

18. Geithe, *Lebensmittelzwangswirtschaft*, pp. 17ff.; and Holtfrerich, *German Inflation*, pp. 76ff. For a good account of how the system of price ex-

amination worked in the states of Württemberg and Baden, see respectively, Gunther Mai, *Kriegswirtschaft und Arbeiterbewegung in Württemberg 1914–1918* (Stuttgart, 1983), pp. 374–416; and Klaus-Peter Müller, *Politik und Gesellschaft im Krieg. Der Legitimitätsverlust des badischen Staates 1914–1918* (Stuttgart, 1988), pp. 283–315.

19. Geithe, *Lebensmittelzwangswirtschaft*, p. 33; R. Meerwarth, A. Günther, and W. Zimmermann, *Die Einwirkung des Krieges auf Bevölkerungsbewegung, Einkommen u. Lebenshaltung in Deutschland* (Stuttgart, 1932), pp. 431–56. On the Society for Social Reform, see Ursula Ratz, "Sozialdemokratische Arbeiterbewegung, bürgerliche Sozialreformer und Militärbehörden im Ersten Weltkrieg," *Militärgeschichtliche Mitteilungen* (1985/1), pp. 9–33.

20. *Verbraucherwirtschaft im Kriege*, 1, Nr. 67/68, Nov. 24, 1916, Archiv des Bundes Deutscher Frauenvereine, Abt. 6, Mappe 6.

21. See the protests by various retailer organizations from different parts of the country in RWWK, 5/28/1, and 5/28/10.

22. Reichsdeutscher Mittelstandsverband to Handelskammer Münster, Aug. 9, 1915, RWWK, 5/28/1.

23. Correspondence of the summer of 1915 in ibid.

24. Reichsdeutscher Mittelstandsverband, Landesausschuß Rheinland und Westfalen to the Handelskammer Koblenz, Sept. 19, 1916, RWWK, 3/10/16.

25. Report of the Police President of Berlin, Aug. 19, 1916, MB of Sept. 8, 1916, BayHStA, Abt. IV, MKr., Nr. 12851.

26. MB of Nov. 17, 1916, ibid.

27. MB of Dec. 16, 1916, ibid.

28. See Werner T. Angress, "Das deutsche Militär und die Juden im Ersten Weltkrieg," *Militärgeschichtliche Mitteilungen* 19 (1976), pp. 77–146; and Werner Mosse and Arnold Paucker, eds., *Deutsches Judentum in Krieg und Revolution 1916–1923* [*Schriftenreihe wissenschaftliche Abhandlungen des Leo Baeck Instituts*, 25] (Tübingen, 1971).

29. Handelskammer Leipzig to the Saxon Ministry of the Interior, Aug. 10, 1916, SäHStA, Wirtschaftsministerium, Nr. 1546, Bl. 1–3. More generally, see Trude Maurer, *Ostjuden in Deutschland 1918–1933* (Hamburg, 1986), pp. 26ff.

30. MB of Sept. 8, 1916, BayHStA, Abt. IV, MKr., Nr. 12851.

31. Evidence is scattered throughout the MB in ibid. See also, Mai, *Kriegswirtschaft*, pp. 374ff., and Kocka, *Facing Total War*, pp. 121ff.

32. For an important correction to traditional notions of antagonism between the two groups, see Heinz-Gerhard Haupt, "Kleinhändler und Arbeiter in Bremen zwischen 1890 und 1914," *AfS* 22 (1982), pp. 95–132.

33. Geithe, *Lebensmittelzwangswirtschaft*, p. 41n1.

34. Reports of the Saxon Ambassador to Berlin,

May–June 1916, SäHStA, Gesandtschaft Berlin, Nr. 375, Bl. 18–19. On the role of the food lines and the creation of a "*Gegenöffentlichkeit*," see Friedhelm Boll, "Spontaneität der Basis und politische Funktion des Streiks 1914 bis 1918. Das Beispiel Braunschweig," *AfS* 17 (1977), pp. 337–66.

35. MB of Oct. 14, 1916, BayHStA, Abt. IV, Mkr., Nr. 12851.

36. Report of Nov. 2, 1916, SäHStA, Gesandtschaft Berlin, Nr. 375, Bl. 30–45, quote on Bl. 30.

37. Karl von Tyszka, "Die Veränderungen in der Lebenshaltung städtischer Familien im Kriege," *AfSS* 43 (1917), pp. 841–76. See also, Armin Triebel, "Variations in Patterns of Consumption in Germany in the Period of the First World War," in Richard Wall and Jay Winter, eds., *The Upheaval of War. Family, Work and Welfare in Europe 1914–1918* (Cambridge, 1988), pp. 159–96.

38. Tyska, *AfSS* 43, p. 876.

39. *RABl* 15 (1917), pp. 243–44.

40. Report by Freiherr von Vietinghoff, MB of Sept. 8, 1916, BayHStA, Abt. IV, MKr., Nr. 12851.

41. Vietinghoff in the MB of July 15, 1916, ibid.

42. Quoted in a speech of Nov. 8, 1915, RWWK, 5/28/1.

43. Singer, *Briefwechsel*, p. 23.

44. Ibid., p. 174n1.

45. Ibid., p. 17.

46. For the text, see Richard Merton, *Erinnernswertes aus meinem Leben, das über das Persönliche hinausgeht* (Frankfurt a.M., 1955), pp. 12–22. It is discussed in Feldman, *Army*, pp. 114ff.

47. On the controlled economy and inflation, I follow the arguments of Holtfrerich, *German Inflation*, pp. 85–91, and Offer, *Agrarian Interpretation*, pp. 64–66.

48. For a discussion of these matters, see Feldman, *Army*, pp. 135ff.

49. Feldman, *Army*, Chaps. III & V.

50. It might be noted that this marriage between military adventurism and technocratic opportunism was to be repeated in the Second World War. By then, Moellendorff's hopes had been so shattered that he committed suicide, and it was those much less troubled souls Fritz Todt and Albert Speer who carried his efforts to their logical conclusion.

51. Ibid., Chaps. III and IV, for this and the discussion which follows.

52. Ibid., Chaps. VII–VIII.

53. The Merton Memorandum is printed in Wilhelm Groener, *Lebenserinnerungen. Jugend, Generalstab, Weltkrieg*, edited by Friedrich Freiherr Hiller von Gaetringen (Göttingen, 1957), pp. 520–25, from which the quotes and discussion below are taken.

54. Ibid. For the original, see Merton to Michaelis, July 25, 1917, BAP, RWM, Nr. 3410, Bl. 3–8.

55. See Feldman, *Army*, pp. 373ff., and the more up-to-date discussion in the German translation, *Armee, Industrie und Arbeiterschaft in Deutschland 1914–1918* (Bonn, 1985), pp. 297ff.

56. Marginal comment on Groener's covering let-

ter by Geheimer Regierungsrat Mathies, BAP, RWM, Nr. 3410, Bl. 3.

57. Marginalia to the Merton memorandum, ibid., Bl. 6–8.

58. This quotation and those which follow are from an unsigned and undated memorandum, ibid., Bl. 15–21.

59. It is more than a little ironical that Merton, using rather strange but not unrevealing language for so nationalist and assimilated a Jew, wrote to Alfred von Batocki, the former head of the War Food Office in 1938, that his program had been rejected because it was too "National Socialist." See Merton to von Batocki, June 15, 1938, HA der Metallgesellschaft, Korrespondenz Richard Merton.

60. Merton to Dorothea Groener-Geyer, Feb. 26, 1955, HA der Metallgesellschaft, Korrespondenz Richard Merton.

61. Breitenbach to OHL, Jan. 14, 1918, BAP, RWM, Nr. 3410, Bl. 29f.

62. OHL to Breitenbach, Feb. 10, 1918, ibid., Bl. 33.

63. Ibid., Bl. 33–36, 43–45.

64. Note of March 12, 1918, ibid., Bl. 80–81.

65. See Feldman, *Army*, pp. 484ff.

66. Letter by Scheüch of Nov. 23, 1917, BAP, RWM, Nr. 3410, Bl. 65.

67. For a good discussion, see Bernard P. Bellon, *Mercedes in Peace and War. German Automobile Workers, 1903–1945* (New York, 1990), pp. 102–11.

68. For the protocol of this meeting of December 15, 1917, see GStAKM, Rep. 151, HB, Nr. 1032, Bl. 369.

69. Thomas Mann, *Gesammelte Werke in 13 Bänden. Bd. 13 Nachträge* (Frankfurt a.M., 1974), p. 182.

70. Hans Fürstenberg, *Erinnerungen. Mein Weg als Bankier und Carl Fürstenbergs Altersjahre* (Wiesbaden, 1965), p. 166.

71. Dresden meeting of Dec. 15, 1917, GStAK, Rep. 150, HB, Nr. 1032, Bl. 369.

72. Ibid., pp. 26–30, for these quotations.

73. See Ralph Haswell Lutz, *The Fall of the German Empire*, 2 vols. (Stanford, 1932), II, pp. 177–86.

74. Dresden meeting, Dec. 15, 1917, GStAKM, Rep. 151, HB, Nr. 1032, Bl. 375.

75. Meeting of the price examination agencies, Dec. 15, 1917, ibid., Bl. 370.

76. Moeller, *Peasants, Politics and Pressure Groups*, p. 44.

77. MB of June 15, 1918, BayHStA, Abt. IV, MKr., Nr. 12852.

78. Report of Oct. 15, 1918, ibid., Nr. 12853.

79. Meeting in Dresden of Dec. 15, 1917, GStAKM, Rep. 151, HB, Nr. 1032, Bl. 370.

80. Max Alsberg, "Wirtschaftsstrafrecht. Besonders die strafrechtliche Bekämpfung des Sozialwuchers," in Gerhard Anschütz et al., eds., *Handbuch der Politik* (Berlin and Leipzig, 1921), vol. IV, pp. 143–59, quotation on p. 150.

81. Deutscher Spielwarenverband an die deutschen Handelskammern, April 8, 1918, RWWK, 5/28/10.

82. Verein der Kaufmannschaft zu Münster an die Handelskammer für den Regierungsbezirk Münster, Sept. 10, 1917, ibid.

83. Alsberg, "Wirtschaftsstrafrecht," in *Handbuch der Politik*, IV, p. 150.

84. Meeting of July 9, 1918, GStAKM, Rep. 151, HB, Nr. 1032, Bl. 422–55, for the discussion of these problems.

85. Alsberg in *Handbuch der Politik*, IV, pp. 150ff.

86. Kleinhandelsausschuß Sitzung, March 12, 1918, NStAO, 265/147.

87. See the host of documents from the chambers of commerce in ibid.; and RWWK, 5/28/1, 5/28/10, 3/10/14, and 3/10/18.

88. Dietmar Petzina et al., eds., *Sozialgeschichtliches Arbeitsbuch III. Materialien zur Statistik des deutschen Reiches 1914–1915* (Munich, 1978), p. 27.

89. See especially Moeller, *German Peasants*, Chap. 3; and *CEH* 14, pp. 142–68.

90. MB of Aug. 15, 1918, BayHStA, Abt. IV, MKr., Nr. 12853.

91. Jürgen Kocka, *Facing Total War*, pp. 31ff.; Alfred Schröter, *Krieg-Staat-Monopol. 1914 bis 1918. Die Zusammenhänge von imperialistischer Kriegswirtschaft, Militarisierung der Volkswirtschaft und staatsmonopolistischen Kapitalismus in Deutschland während des Ersten Weltkrieges* (Berlin, 1965), pp. 93ff.; Feldman, *Iron and Steel*, pp. 57ff.

92. Kocka, *Facing Total War*, pp. 193n107, 194n116.

93. Feldman, *Army*, p. 469ff., and *Iron and Steel*, pp. 71ff.; Kocka, *Facing Total War*, pp. 29ff.

94. Zunkel, *Industrie und Staatssozialismus*, Chaps. 1–3.

95. A good example of this scholarship at its most sophisticated is Werner Richter, *Gewerkschaften, Monopolkapital und Staat im Ersten Weltkrieg und in der Novemberrevolution* (Berlin, 1959), esp. pp. 96ff.

96. Hans-Joachim Bieber, *Gewerkschaften in Krieg und Revolution. Arbeiterbewegung, Industrie, Staat und Militär in Deutschland 1914–1920*, 2 vols. (Hamburg, 1981), pp. 309, 922.

97. Feldman, *Army*, pp. 333ff., 388f. For a study of these conditions in Württemberg, see Mai, *Kriegswirtschaft*, Pt. III. Much also can be learned from the case studies in Gunther Mai, ed., *Arbeiterschaft 1914–1918 in Deutschland* (Düsseldorf, 1985).

98. On wages and differentials, see Feldman, *Army*, pp. 471f.; Kocka, *Facing Total War*, pp. 16ff. On the Krupp wages, see Waldemar Zimmermann, *Die Veränderungen der Einkommens- und Lebensverhältnisse der deutschen Arbeiter durch den Krieg* (Stuttgart, Berlin, and Leipzig, 1932), p. 382. On Bayer, see Gottfried Plumpe, "Chemische Industrie und Hilfsdienstgesetz am Beispiel der Farbenfabriken vorm. Bayer & Co.," in Gunther Mai, ed., *Ar-

beiterschaft 1914–1918 in Deutschland, pp. 179–210, esp. p. 189. See also Gunther Mai, "'Wenn der Mensch Hunger hat, hört Alles auf.' Wirtschaftliche und soziale Ausgangsbedingungen der Weimarer Republik (1914–1924)," Werner Abelshauser, ed., *Die Weimarer Republik als Wohlfahrtsstaat. Zum Verhältnis von Wirtschafts- und Sozialpolitik in der Industriegesellschaft* [*VSWG*, Beiheft 81] (Stuttgart, 1987), pp. 33–62, which parallels this discussion in many respects.

99. Zimmermann, *Einkommensverhältnisse*, p. 422ff.; Report of Commander in Magdeburg and of Frankfurt War Office MB of Jan. 15, 1918, BayHStA, Abt. IV, MKr., Nr. 12852.

100. Reports of July 15 and Aug. 15, 1918, BayHStA, Abt. IV, MKr., Nr. 12853.

101. Feldman, *Army*, pp. 459f.

102. MB of July 30, 1917, BayHStA, Abt. IV, MKr., Nr. 12851. More generally, see Kocka, *Facing Total War*, pp. 71ff., and Feldman, *Army*, pp. 465ff.

103. For this quotation and the discussion and quotations which follow, see BayHStA, Abt. IV, Mkr., K Mob 7d, Bd. IV, Bl. zu 67.

104. Kocka, *Facing Total War*, p. 96.

105. MB of Aug. 15, 1918, BayHStA, Abt. IV, Mkr., Nr. 12852.

106. Kocka, *Facing Total War*, pp. 98–102 and Andreas Kunz, "Verteilungskampf oder Interessenkonsensus? Einkommensentwicklung und Sozialverhalten von Arbeitnehmergruppen in der Inflationszeit 1914 bis 1924," in Gerald D. Feldman et al., eds., *The German Inflation. A Preliminary Balance* [*Beiträge zu Inflation und Wiederaufbau in Deutschland und Europa 1914–1924*, Bd. 2] (Berlin & New York, 1984), pp. 347–84.

107. MB of Aug. 15, 1918, BayHStA, Abt. IV, MKr., Nr. 12853.

108. BAP, RWM, Nr. 3420, Bl. 4–7, for the discussion and quotations which follow.

109. On Ludendorff's armistice request and the government crisis of authority, see Feldman, *Army*, pp. 503ff., and Kocka, *Facing Total War*, pp. 155ff.

110. For an excellent survey of the major controversies of Weimar history and the relevant literature on the revolutionary period, see Eberhard Kolb, *The Weimar Republic* (Winchester, Mass., 1988), pp. 3–22, 138–47. On the November 1918 Revolution, see Reinhard Rürup, *Probleme der Revolution in Deutschland 1918/19* (Wiesbaden, 1968), and Reinhard Rürup, "Demokratische Revolution und 'dritter Weg.' Die deutsche Revolution von 1918/19 in der neueren wissenschaftlichen Diskussion," *GuG* 9 (1983), pp. 278–301. See also, Wolfgang J. Mommsen, "The German Revolution 1918–1920: Political Revolution and Social Protest Movement," in Richard Bessel and E.J. Feuchtwanger, *Social Change and Political Development in Weimar Germany* (London, 1981), pp. 21–54; Gerald D. Feldman, Eberhard Kolb, and Reinhard Rürup, "Die Massenbewegungen der Arbeiterschaft in Deutschland am Ende des Ersten Weltkrieges (1917–1920)," *PVS* 13 (1972), pp. 84–105.

111. This is a central thesis of Heinrich A. Winkler, *Von der Revolution zur Stabilisierung. Arbeiter und Arbeiterbewegung in der Weimarer Republik 1918 bis 1924* (Berlin & Bonn, 1984).

112. The basic study of this problem is Zunkel, *Industrie und Staatssozialismus*. See also, Feldman, *Iron and Steel*, pp. 71ff.; Ehlert, *Wirtschaftliche Zentralbehörde*, pp. 53ff.

113. Ehlert, *Wirtschaftliche Zentralbehörde*, p. 60, for the quote and pp. 53ff. of this excellent study for the discussion which follows.

114. Meeting of Feb. 9, 1918, in the RWA on exchange controls, GStAKM, Rep. 120, C XIII, 1, Nr. 91, Bd. 3, Bl. 1–14.

115. Ehlert, *Wirtschaftliche Zentralbehörde*, pp. 70ff.

116. Ekkehard Böhm, *Anwalt der Handels- und Gewerbefreiheit. Beiträge zur Geschichte der Handelskammer Hamburg* (Hamburg, 1981), p. 179, and Zunkel, *Industrie und Staatssozialismus*, pp. 151ff.

117. Quoted in ibid., p. 153n73.

118. Meeting of the price examination agencies, Dec. 15, 1917, GStAKM, Rep. 151, HB, Nr. 1032, Bl. 324–62.

119. Meeting of July 9, 1918, ibid., Bl. 422–55.

120. Meeting of the Main Committee of the German Chamber of Industry and Commerce, Nov. 6, 1918, RWWK, 20/422/8.

121. Ibid.

122. On the irrelevance of the demobilization preparations, see Gerald D. Feldman, "Economic and Social Problems of the German Demobilization, 1918–1919," *JMH* 47 (1975), pp. 1–47.

123. Feldman, *Army*, p. 474.

124. Ibid., p. 473ff. See also the good discussion in Mai, *Kriegswirtschaft*, pp. 319ff., 426ff.

125. The account here is based on Gerald D. Feldman, "German Business between War and Revolution: The Origins of the Stinnes–Legien Agreement," in Gerhard A. Ritter, ed., *Entstehung und Wandel der modernen Gesellschaft. Festschrift für Hans Rosenberg* (Berlin, 1970), pp. 312–41. See also, Gerald D. Feldman and Irmgard Steinisch, "The Origins of the Stinnes–Legien Agreement. A Documentation," *IWK* 19/20 (1973), pp. 45–104.

126. Speech by Jakob Reichert to the Essen Chamber of Commerce, Dec. 30, 1918, reproduced in Gerald D. Feldman and Irmgard Steinisch, *Industrie und Gewerkschaften 1918–1924. Die überforderte Zentralarbeitsgemeinschaft* (Stuttgart, 1985), pp. 150–58, quote on p. 152.

127. See the revealing comments by the trade-union leaders at their meeting of Dec. 3, 1918, reprinted in Feldman and Steinisch, *Industrie und Gewerkschaften*, pp. 141ff. See also Gerald D. Feldman, "Die Freien Gewerkschaften und die Zentralarbeitsgemeinschaft," in Heinz Oskar Vetter, ed., *Vom Sozialistengesetz zur Mitbestimmung. Zum 100. Geburtstag von Hans Böckler* (Cologne, 1975), pp. 229–52.

128. Meeting of Oct. 15, 1918, BayHStA, Abt. IV, MKr., Nr. 14411a.

129. Ibid., Nr. 14412.

130. Ibid.

131. Ibid.

132. The meeting is reprinted in Feldman and Steinisch, *IWK* 19/20, pp. 69–76, quote on p. 72.

133. At the directors meeting of the Association of German Iron and Steel Industrialists, March 1, 1919, BAK, R 13I/156.

134. See Klaus Schönhoven, "Die Gründung der Zentralarbeitsgemeinschaft und die 'Gelben Gewerkschaften,' " *IWK* 26 (Sept. 1990), pp. 355–64.

135. Meeting between industrialists and trade-union leaders in the Ruhr, Oct. 26, 1918, HA/GHH, Nr. 3001242/7.

136. Erich Matthias and Rudolf Morsey, *Die Regierung des Prinzen Max von Baden* (Düsseldorf, 1962), p. 569.

137. See Legien's description in the *Niederschrift der konstituierenden Sitzung des Zentralausschusses der Zentralarbeitsgemeinschaft der industriellen und gewerblichen Arbeitgeber und Arbeitnehmer Deutschlands am 12. Dezember 1919* (Berlin, 1920).

138. Feldman, in *JMH* (1975). See also "Die Valutaverbesserung und das Exportgeschäft," *Berliner Tageblatt*, Oct. 15, 1918, and report from the Consulate in Bern of Oct. 17, 1918, GStAKM, Rep. 120, C XIII, 1, Nr. 91, Bl. 3, 85–88.

139. *Magdeburger Volksstimme*, Aug. 8, 1918.

140. Friedrich Bendixen, "Die Parität und ihre Wiederherstellung," *Bank = Archiv* 18 (1918/19), pp. 9–13.

3. The Economics of Revolution and Revolutionary Economics

1. The quotations and discussion which follow are based on a "Report on a Visit to Berlin, 2nd February 1919, to 11th February 1919," by Captains W.S. Roddie, Claude W. Bell, and E.W.D. Tennant, PRO, FO 371/3776/163/320–24.

2. Leo Haupts, *Deutsche Friedenspolitik 1918–19. Eine Alternative zur Machtpolitik des Ersten Weltkrieges* (Düsseldorf, 1976), pp. 239f.

3. See Robert N. Proctor, *Racial Hygiene. Medicine under the Nazis* (Cambridge, Mass., 1988), pp. 178f.; Paul Weindling, *Health, Race and German Politics between National Unification and Nazism 1870–1945* (Cambridge, 1989), pp. 284ff. The most notorious work advocating such policies appeared in 1920, Alfred Hoche and Rudolf Binding, *Die Freigabe der Vernichtung lebensunwerten Lebens* (Leipzig, 1920).

4. See Offer, *First World War*, Chap. 26, which parallels this discussion in many respects, although I think his discussion of Germany understates the degree of malnutrition. See also, Bruce Kent, *The Spoils of War. The Politics, Economics, and Diplomacy of Reparations 1918–1932* (Oxford, 1989), pp. 57–59.

5. Meeting of the Finance Ministers in Weimar, Jan. 29–30, 1919, GStAKM, Rep. 151, HB, Nr. 1444, Bl. 457–529, quote on Bl. 476.

6. Even the most optimistic assessment of the chances for greater democratization and even social revolution argue that the decisive period for action was prior to mid-January 1919. See Rürup, *Probleme der Revolution* (1968). For a discussion of the various phases of the Revolution, see Feldman, Kolb, and Rürup, in *PVS,* 13, pp. 84–105. The best accounts of the role of German Social Democracy in the Revolution are Susanne Miller, *Die Bürde der Macht. Die deutsche Sozialdemokratie 1918–1920* (Düsseldorf, 1979), and Heinrich A. Winkler, *Von der Revolution zur Stabilisierung*, Chaps. I and II.

7. The best studies of the councils are Eberhard Kolb, *Die Arbeiterräte in der deutschen Innenpolitik 1918–1919* (Düsseldorf, 1978), and Ulrich Kluge, *Soldatenräte und Revolution. Studien zur Militärpolitik in Deutschland 1918/19* (Göttingen, 1975).

8. In addition to the Kolb study mentioned in note 5, see Reinhard Rürup, ed., *Arbeiter und Soldatenräte im rheinisch-westfälischen Industriegebiet. Studien zur Geschichte der Revolution 1918/19* (Wuppertal, 1975).

9. This is a major theme of the works of Rürup and Kolb cited in notes 4 and 5. See also Peter von Oertzen, *Betriebsräte in der Novemberrevolution* (Düsseldorf, 1976).

10. See the excellent critique by Winkler, *Revolution zur Stabilisierung*, pp. 144ff.

11. For the Armistice conditions and their costs, see Statistisches Reichsamt, *Deutschlands Wirtschaftslage unter den Nachwirkungen des Weltkrieges* (Berlin, 1923), p. 10; on the overloading of the repair facilities, see Kurt Königsberger, "Die wirtschaftliche Demobilmachung in Bayern während der Zeit vom November 1918 bis Mai 1919," *Zeitschrift des Bayerischen Statistischen Landesamtes* 52 (1920), pp. 193–226, esp. p. 207. Also, see Susanne Miller and Heinrich Potthoff, eds., *Die Regierung der Volksbeauftragten, 1918/19*, 2 vols. (Düsseldorf, 1969), 2, pp. 279f., and Philipp Scheidemann, *Memoiren eines Sozialdemokraten*, 2 vols. (Dresden, 1928), 1, pp. 10f.

12. There is no precise English pendant to the German term *Sozialstaat*, which encompasses both the welfare state and the system of industrial relations. For an invaluable discussion in comparative perspective, see Gerhard A. Ritter, *Der Sozialstaat. Entstehung und Entwicklung im internationalen Vergleich* (Munich, 1989), esp. Chap. 5. The classic study on Weimar is Ludwig Preller, *Sozialpolitik in der Weimarer Republik* (Stuttgart, 1949).

13. Feldman & Steinisch, *Industrie und Gewerkschaften*, pp. 135–37 and *IWK* 19/20, pp. 102–3.

14. Feldman & Steinisch, *Industrie und Gewerkschaften*, p. 136.

15. For the development of the concept, see the Feldman & Steinisch, *IWK* 19/20, pp. 82–84.

16. Reported by Legien at a meeting of the chairmen of the various unions on Dec. 3, 1918, in Klaus Schönhoven, ed., *Die Gewerkschaften im Weltkrieg*

und Revolution 1914–1919 [*Quellen zur Geschichte der deutschen Gewerkschaftsbewegung im 20. Jahrhundert,* Bd. 1], (Cologne, 1985), pp. 542f.

17. Stinnes reporting to the iron and steel industrialists at a meeting of Nov. 14, 1918, Feldman & Steinisch, *IWK* 19/20, p. 88.

18. Dec. 3 meeting of the trade-union leaders in Schönhoven, *Gewerkschaften,* p. 590.

19. Feldman & Steinisch, *Industrie und Gewerkschaften,* p. 37.

120. Ibid., p. 34.

121. Feldman & Steinisch, *Industrie und Gewerkschaften,* pp. 37ff.

22. Meeting of Nov. 20, 1918, BayHStA, Abt. IV, Mkr., Nr. 14413.

23. Feldman, *Army,* pp. 279ff.

24. I have learned much about Koeth and other leading personalities of this period from a lengthy interview with Professor Löwe in June 1982. In exile, Prof. Löwe went under the name Adolph Lowe, but I shall use the German spelling here.

25. The pamphlet by Labor (a pseudonym) and Löwe, was published by the Kriegswirtschaftliche Vereinigung and bore the title *Wirtschaftlishe Demobilisation* (Berlin, 1916). He subsequently authored another pamphlet for the same organization, which the War Ministry banned and which only appeared after the war, *Soziale forderungen für die Übergangswirtschaft* (Berlin, 1918). On his relations with the councils, see Eberhard Kolb and Reinhard Rürup, eds., *Der Zentralrat der Deutschen Sozialistischen Republik* (Lieden, 1968), pp. 61f., 109, 112. Löwe later became a prominent and important member of the famous Institut für Konjunkturforschung and professor of economics at the University of Kiel. He went into exile when the Nazis came to power, he took a position as a professor of economics at a New School for Social Research in New York City. Important information on Löwe is scattered through Claus-Dieter Krohn, *Wirtschaftstheorien als politische Interessen. Die akademische Nationalökonomie in Deutschland 1918–1933* (Frankfurt & New York, 1981), esp. pp. 123ff.

26. Meeting of Nov. 12, 1918, BayHStA, Abt. IV, Mkr., Nr. 14412.

27. Meeting of Nov. 20, 1918, ibid., Nr. 14413.

28. Meeting of Nov. 23, 1918, ibid.

29. Meeting of Nov. 14, 1918, ibid., Nr. 14412.

30. *RGBl* (1918), p. 1305. See also Friedrich Syrup and Otto Neuloh, *Hundert Jahre staatliche Sozialpolitik 1839–1939* (Stuttgart, 1957), p. 326. The prehistory is discussed in Führer, *Arbeitslosigkeit,* pp. 131–43.

31. Meetings of Nov. 11–12, 1918, BayHStA, Abt. IV, MKr., Nr. 14412.

32. Meeting of Nov. 13, 1918, ibid.

33. Meetings of Nov. 14–15, 1918, ibid.

34. Meetings of Nov. 16 and 18, 1918, ibid.

135. At a meeting of Feb. 1–2, 1919, quoted in Schönhoven, *Gewerkschaften,* pp. 631f.

36. Statement by the People's Commissar in Braunschweig, Eckhardt, reported at the Reich Conference of Nov. 25, 1918, in Miller and Potthoff, *Volksbeauftragten,* 1, p. 214.

37. Königsberger in *Zeitschrift des Bayerischen Statistischen Landesamtes* 52, p. 196.

38. Meeting of Dec. 5, 1918, BayHStA, Abt. IV, MKr., Nr. 14413.

39. Meeting of Nov. 21, 1918, ibid.

40. Ibid.

41. Meeting in the Reich Chancellery of Dec. 6, 1918, in Miller & Potthoff, *Volksbeauftragten,* 1, pp. 262–76.

42. Ibid., p. 267.

43. Ibid., p. 274.

44. Ehlert, *Wirtschaftliche Zentralbehörde,* pp. 104f.

45. Joseph Koeth, "Die wirtschaftliche Demobilmachung. Ihre Aufgabe und ihre Organe," in Gerhard Anschütz, ed., *Handbuch der Politik,* 4 vols. (Berlin/Leipzig, 1921), 4, p. 165.

46. Meeting of Dec. 7, 1918, BayHStA, Abt. IV, MKr., Nr. 14413.

47. Koeth's ideas and much of the discussion which follows is based on the very important meeting of the Cabinet on Dec. 12, 1918, to discuss economic policy reprinted in Miller & Potthoff, *Volksbeauftragten,* 1, pp. 319–67.

48. "Denkschrift betreffend den Reichsfonds," in NL Emil Barth, SPD Archiv Bonn; and meeting of Dec. 12, 1918, Miller and Potthoff, *Volksbeauftragten,* 1, pp. 325f.

49. Memorandum of Dec. 20, 1918, NL Emil Barth, SPD Archiv.

50. Letter of Dec. 3, 1918, NL Barth, SPD Archiv.

51. Meeting of Dec. 12, 1918, in Miller & Potthoff, *Volksbeauftragten,* 1, pp. 325f.

52. Ibid., pp. 326–30.

53. Ibid., p. 328.

54. Ibid., p. 334f.

55. Ibid., p. 339f.

56. Hans-Joachim Bieber, "Die Entwicklung der Arbeitsbeziehungen auf den Hamburger Großwerften zwischen Hilfsdienstgesetz und Betriebsrätegesetz (1916–1920)," in Mai, ed., *Arbeiterschaft 1914–1918,* pp. 77–153, esp. pp. 143ff.

57. On Upper Silesia, see the useful if tendentious Wolfgang Schumann, *Oberschlesien 1918/19. Vom gemeinsamen Kampf deutscher und polnischer Arbeiter* (Berlin, 1961). See also Miller & Potthoff, *Volksbeauftragten,* 2, pp. 174ff.

58. See the hair-raising report on the problems of dealing with the Berlin unemployed by trade unionist Johann Sassenbach of Feb. 1–2, 1919, in Schönhoven, *Gewerkschaften,* pp. 630ff.

59. Meeting of Jan. 6, 1919, BayHStA, Abt. IV, Mkr., Nr. 14413.

60. Wermuth to Ebert, Dec. 12, 1918, BAP, DMA, Nr. 20, Bl. 192–95.

61. Fischbeck to DMA, Dec. 20, 1918, and meeting of Jan. 10, 1919, ibid., Nr. 19, Bl. 94f., and Nr. 20, Bl. 2f.; and Bauer to DMA, Dec. 21, 1918, Nr. 20, Bl. 16.

62. Letter to DMA, Jan. 16, 1919, ibid., Nr. 19, Bl. 98f.

63. Meeting of Jan. 8, 1919, ibid., Nr. 19, Bl. 152–54.

64. Meeting of Jan. 9, 1919, ibid., Bl. 155f. See above, p. 102.

65. Königsberger in *Zeitschrift des Bayerischen Statistischen Landesamtes* (1920), pp. 216–21.

66. Miller & Potthoff, *Volksbeauftragten,* 2, p. 286.

67. Sassenbach at a meeting on Feb. 1–2, 1919, in Schönhoven, *Gewerkschaften,* p. 636.

68. Verordnung betreffend Abänderung der Verordnung über Erwerbslosenfürsorge vom 13. November 1918 vom 15. January 1919, *RGBl* (1919), p. 82ff., and BAP, DMA, Nr. 20, Bl. 6–9, 94.

69. Meeting of Jan. 16, 1919, BayHStA, Abt. IV, MKr., Nr. 14413, and meetings of Jan. 22 and 29, 1919, ibid., Nr. 14414.

70. Meeting of Jan. 14, 1919, in Kolb and Rürup, *Zentralrat,* p. 366.

71. Müller at a Cabinet meeting of Jan. 21, 1919, in Miller & Potthoff, *Volksbeauftragten,* 2, p. 287, 300.

72. Report by Rohmer, Jan. 31, 1919, BayHStA, Abt. II, Gesandtschaft Berlin, Nr. 1096, and meeting of Jan. 29, 1919, ibid. Abt. IV, MKr., Nr. 14414.

73. Mayor of Mannheim to RWA, Jan. 3, 1919, BAP, RAM, Nr. 1760, Bl. 174–76.

74. Meeting of Jan. 29, 1919, BayHStA, Abt. IV, MKr., Nr. 14414.

75. Report of Jan. 29, 1919, BAP, DMA, Nr. 20, Bl. 255–58. For a detailed account, see Gerald D. Feldman, "Saxony, the Reich, and the Problem of Unemployment in the German Inflation," *AfS* 27 (1987), pp. 102–44, esp. p. 111.

76. See the illuminating article by Richard Bessel, "The Great War in German Memory: The Soldiers of the First World War, Demobilization, and Weimar Political Culture," *German History. The Journal of the German History Society* 6 (1988), pp. 20–34.

77. The discussion and quotations below are taken from a series of letters to the Reich Labor Office of late December 1918 in BAP, RAM, Nr. 1760, Bl. 166–76.

78. For an excellent discussion of the underemployment of women during the war as well as the plans to replace them in the demobilization, see Ute Daniel, "Fiktionen, Friktionen und Fakten—Frauenlohnarbeit im Ersten Weltkrieg," in Mai, *Arbeiterschaft 1914–1918,* pp. 277–323; on the demobilization, see especially Richard Bessel, "Eine nicht allzu große Beunruhigung des Arbeitsmarktes. Frauenarbeit und Demobilmachung nach dem Ersten Weltkrieg," *GuG* 9 (1983), pp. 211–29.

79. For this quote and the discussion and quotations which follow, see meeting of Jan. 22, 1919, RWWK, 5/23/37. There is an excellent discussion of the situation of female workers in Berlin by Susanne Rouette, "'Gleichberechtigung' ohne 'Recht auf Arbeit,'" in Christiane Eifert and Susanne Rouette, eds., *Unter allen Umständen. Frauengeschichte(n) in Berlin* (Berlin, 1986), pp. 159–81.

80. This illustrates rather well Jürgen Kocka's point about the low regard for manual labor in Germany as one of the major differences between American and German society. See Jürgen Kocka, *White Collar Workers in Germany and America, 1890–1940. A Social-Political History in International Perspective* (London & Beverly Hills, 1980), pp. 26ff.

81. Bavarian ambassadorial report from Berlin of Jan. 31, 1919, BayHStA, Abt. II, Gesandtschaft Berlin, Nr. 1096.

82. Ibid.

83. See Feldman, Kolb, and Rürup in *PVS,* 13, pp. 95ff., and Oertzen, *Betriebsräte,* for the fullest discussion of this movement.

84. This is attempted in my "Socio-Economic Structures in the Industrial Sector and Revolutionary Potentialities, 1917–1922," in Charles Bertrand, ed., *Revolutionary Situations in Europe 1917–1922: Germany, Italy, and Austria-Hungary* (Montreal, 1976), pp. 159–69.

85. Report of Feb. 8, 1919, BAP, Informationsstelle der Reichsregierung, Nr. 34, Bl. 103.

86. Ibid., Nr. 29b, Bl. 182f.

87. On the importance of the new plants and uprooted workers, see Feldman in Bertrand, *Revolutionary Situations,* p. 160ff. On Merseburg, see the report of the Magistrate, Feb. 13, 1915, BAP, Informationsstelle der Reichsregierung, Nr. 34, Bl. 94. On the miners, see Gerald D. Feldman, "Arbeitskonflikte im Ruhrbergbau 1919–1922. Zur Politik von Zechenverband und Gewerkschaften in der Überschichtenfrage," *VfZ* 28 (April 1980), pp. 168–223, esp. p. 187.

88. On the demographics and their implications as well as on the special problems of postwar youth, see Klaus Tenfelde, "Großstadtjugend in Deutschland vor 1914. Eine historische-demographische Annäherung," *VSWG* 69 (1962), pp. 182–218; and Detlev J.K. Peukert, *Jugend zwischen Krieg und Krise. Lebenswelten von Arbeiterjungen in der Weimarer Republik* (Cologne, 1987), esp. Chap. 1.

89. Meeting of Jan. 15, 1918, BAK, NL Luders, Nr. 159.

90. Report of Jan. 29, 1919, BAP, Informationsstelle der Reichsregierung, Nr. 30, Bl. 126.

91. Report of Captain Dreyfus, March 31–April 8, 1919, PRO, FO 371/3776/555f.

92. For the concepts of societal and state corporatism, see the important article by Ulrich Nocken, "Corporatism and Pluralism in Modern German History," in Dirk Stegmann et al., eds., *Industrielle Gesellschaft und politisches System. Beiträge zur politischen Sozialgeschichte. Festschrift für Fritz Fischer* (Bonn, 1978), pp. 37–56. On the retreat from the ZAG concepts discussed here, see Feldman & Steinisch, *Industrie und Gewerkschaften,* pp. 42ff.

93. Heinrich Potthoff, *Gewerkschaften und Politik zwischen Revolution und Inflation* (Düsseldorf, 1979), pp. 32ff.

94. Ibid., p. 58.

95. Holtzendorff report of May 22, 1919, HAPAG Archiv.

96. Ehlert, *Wirtschaftliche Zentralbehörde*, pp. 213–37.

97. Ibid., pp. 261–92.

98. Report in VdESI meeting of March 1, 1919, BAK, R 131/156.

99. Ibid.

100. Feldman & Steinisch, *Industrie und Gewerkschaften*, pp. 39ff.

101. I am grateful to Susanne Rouette for some of her critical suggestions here. For a good discussion of the situation, see Richard Bessel, "Unemployment and Demobilisation in Germany After the First World War," in Richard J. Evans and Dick Geary, eds., *The German Unemployed. Experiences and Consequences of Mass Unemployment from the Weimar Republic to the Third Reich* (New York, 1987), pp. 23–43.

102. For the statistics, see *JHS, Volkswirtschaftliche Chronik 1919* (Jena, 1919/1920), pp. 51ff., 97f., 154, 218f.; *RABl* 17 (1919), p. 12. On the Düsseldorf experience, see DMA meeting, April 26, 1919, BayHStA, Abt. IV, MKr., Nr. 14412.

103. Meeting of Feb. 28, 1919, ibid.

104. Königsberger, *Zeitschrift des Bayerischen Statistischen Landesamtes* (1920), pp. 211f.

105. BAP, RAM, Nr. 1740, Bl. 227, and DMA, Nr. 19, Bl. 114f.

106. Königsberger, *Zeitschrift des Bayerischen Statistischen Landesamtes* (1920), p. 212.

107. Report of Feb. 1, 1919, BAP, Informationsstelle der Reichsregierung, Nr. 296, Bl. 176.

108. VdESI meeting, March 1, 1919, BAK, R 131/156.

109. RWWK, 20/46/5. See also Lothar Burchardt, "Zwischen Kriegsgewinnen und Kriegskosten: Krupp im Ersten Weltkrieg," *Zeitschrift für Unternehmensgeschichte* 32 (1987), pp. 71–123.

110. Königsberger in *Zeitschrift des Bayerischen Statistischen Landesamtes* (1920), p. 222.

111. BayHStA, Abt. IV, MKr., Nr. 14412.

112. For the quotations and discussion which follows, see BAP, RWM, Nr. 4252, Bl. 112ff.

113. Meeting of the state Finance Ministers in Weimar, Jan. 29–30, 1919, GStAKM, Rep. 151, HB, Nr. 1444, Bl. 457–529, quote on Bl. 465.

114. Ibid., Bl. 526.

115. Ibid., Bl. 527.

116. See the important analysis of this problem by Peter-Christian Witt, "Bemerkungen zur Wirtschaftspolitik in der 'Übergangswirtschaft' 1918/19. Zur Entwicklung von Konjunkturbeobachtung und Konjunktursteuerung in Deutschland," in Dirk Stegmann et al., *Industrielle Gesellschaft und politisches System*, pp. 79–96.

117. Ehlert, *Wirtschaftliche Zentralbehörde*, pp.

311f., 525; and Eugen Schiffer, *Ein Leben für den Liberalismus* (Berlin, 1951).

118. Eugen Schiffer, *Deutschlands Finanzlage und Steuerpolitik* (Berlin, 1919); Denkschrift über die Finanzen des deutschen Reichs in den Rechnungsjahren 1914 bis 1918, in *VN*, Vol. 338, Drucksache Nr. 158; National Assembly speech of Feb. 15, 1919, *VN*, Vol. 336, pp. 93ff.

119. GStAKM, Rep. 151, HB, Nr. 1444, Bl. 469.

120. Meeting with state Finance Ministers, Jan. 29–30, 1919, ibid., Bl. 470.

121. *VN*, Vol. 326, Feb. 15, 1919, pp. 93ff.

122. Miller & Potthoff, *Volksbeauftragten*, 1, pp. 344ff.

123. Ibid., pp. 344–67. See also Peter-Christian Witt, in Witt, *Wealth and Taxation*, pp. 145–47.

124. See Krüger, *Nationalökonomen*, pp. 152ff.

125. This discussion is based on the lengthy protocol of the meeting of Jan. 29–30, 1919, GStAKM, Rep. 151, HB, Nr. 1444, Bl. 457–529R.

126. Ibid., Bl. 513.

127. Ibid., Bl. 520.

128. Ibid., Bl. 498.

129. Ibid., Bl. 500.

130. Miller & Potthoff, *Volksbeauftragten*, 1, pp. 356f.

131. Jan. 29–30, 1919, meeting, GStAKM, Rep. 151, HB, Nr. 1444, Bl. 481.

132. Ibid., Bl. 482.

133. Ibid.

134. Report by Holtzendorff, March 25, 1919, HAPAG Archiv.

135. Hagen Schulze in *Kabinett Scheidemann*, p. xlvii.

136. Meeting of March 21, 1919, *Kabinett Scheidemann*, p. 79.

137. Report by Holtzendorff on Meeting of May 24, 1919, HAPAG Archiv.

138. Cabinet meeting of April 26, 1919, *Kabinett Scheidemann*, p. 243.

139. Miller & Potthoff, *Volksbeauftragten*, pp. 206n11, 242, 246, 278.

140. Peter Krüger, *Deutschland und die Reparationen 1918/19. Die Genesis des Reparationsproblems in Deutschland zwischen Waffenstillstand und Versailler Friedensschluß* (Stuttgart, 1973), pp. 9–11, and his "Die Rolle der Banken und der Industrie in den deutschen reparationspolitischen Entscheidungen nach dem Ersten Weltkrieg," in Mommsen et al., *Industrielles System*, pp. 568–82.

141. See the excellent analysis of the stalemated character of the Scheidemann government by Hagen Schulze, *Kabinett Scheidemann*, p. xlivff. The conflict over economic policy has been studied in the excellent work of Hans Schieck, *Der Kampf um die deutsche Wirtschaftspolitik nach dem Novemberumsturz 1918* (Heidelberg, 1958). For a fine biography of Wissell, see David E. Barclay, *Rudolf Wissell als Sozialpolitiker 1890–1933* [*Einzelveröffentlichungen der Historischen Kommission zu Berlin, Bd. 44*] (Berlin, 1984), Chap. 3. See also his articles, "A Prus-

sian Socialism? Wichard von Moellendorff and the Dilemmas of Economic Planning in Germany 1918–1919," *CEH* 11 (1978), pp. 50–82, and "The Insider as Outsider: Rudolf Wissell's Critique of Social Democratic Economic Policies 1919 to 1920," in Feldman et al., eds., *The Adaptation to Inflation* [*Beiträge zu Inflation und Wiederaufbau in Deutschland und Europa 1914–1924*] (Berlin & New York, 1986), pp. 451–71. In general, Barclay is more sympathetic to Wissell and Moellendorff than I am.

142. See Feldman, *Iron and Steel*, pp. 82ff.

143. Ibid. See also Warburg to Havenstein, March 7, 1919, Warburg Papers.

144. Meeting of March 23, 1919, BAK, R 13I/190, Bl. 7.

145. Ehlert, *Wirtschaftliche Zentralbehörde*, pp. 293ff.

146. Feldman, *Industrie und Gewerkschaften*, pp. 45ff.

147. Meeting of May 15, 1919, BAK, R 13I/191, Bl. 30–47.

148. Vögler to Gerwin, June 24, 1919, WA/ATH, Allgemeiner Schriftwechsel Fritz Thyssen; and Feldman, *Iron and Steel*, pp. 105ff.

149. Ehlert, *Wirtschaftliche Zentralbehörde*, p. 305ff.; and Böhm, *Anwalt*, pp. 187ff.

150. Hamburg Association of Exporters to the RWM, May 1919, BAK, R 43I/1078, Bl. 4–12, quote on Bl. 7.

151. Böhm, *Anwalt*, p. 191.

152. Warburg to Havenstein, March 7, 1919, Warburg Papers, Hamburg.

153. For the discussion and quotations which follow, see his "Bemerkungen zu den vom Reichswirtschaftsministerium aufgestellten Grundlinien für die künftige Gestaltung des Wirtschaftslebens," ibid.

154. Hagen Schulze in *Kabinett Scheidemann*, pp. xlivff.

155. Meeting of May 5, 1919, ibid., pp. 260f.

156. Meeting of May 6, 1919, ibid., pp. 264f.

157. Ibid., p. 268n2.

158. Ehlert, *Wirtschaftliche Zentralbehörde*, pp. 320ff.

159. The memorandum and program are reprinted in *Kabinett Scheidemann*, respectively, on pp. 272–83, 284–89, quote on p. 275.

160. Ibid., p. 276.

161. Ibid., p. 280.

162. Ibid.

163. I am grateful to Adolf Löwe for this characterization made in the course of our 1982 conversation.

164. Gothein's memorandum is reprinted in *Kabinett Scheidemann*, pp. 297–303. The quotation is on p. 301.

165. Schmidt's memorandum is reprinted in ibid., pp. 289–97. For the quote, see p. 291.

166. Ibid., p. 294.

167. Ibid., p. 293.

168. Ibid.

169. For the "Guidelines for the German Peace Negotiators" of April 21, 1919, see ibid., pp. 193–204.

170. For Dernburg's lengthy Cabinet presentation of April 26, 1919, on Germany's economic capabilities, see ibid., pp. 233–43. Quotation on p. 234.

171. Ibid., p. 235.

172. Ibid., p. 241.

173. Report by Holtzendorff, May 22, 1919, HAPAG Archiv.

174. For a good, brief discussion and analysis of the peace terms as well as their reception and survey of the immense literature as it pertains to Germany, see Kolb, *Weimar Republic*, pp. 23–33, 166–78. See also Peter Krüger, *Die Außenpolitik der Republik von Weimar* (Darmstadt, 1989), pp. 65–76. On the formation of the reparations terms, see Kent, *Spoils*, pp. 66–82.

175. For this position, see the important but exaggerated arguments of Gerhard Weinberg, "The Defeat of Germany in 1918 and the European Balance of Power," *CEH* 2 (Sept. 1969), pp. 248–60.

176. Hajo Holborn, *Kriegsschuld und Reparationen auf der Pariser Friedenskonferenz 1919* (Berlin, 1932), and "Diplomats and Diplomacy in the early Weimar Republic," in Gordon Craig and Felix Gilbert, eds., *The Diplomats 1919–1939* (Princeton, 1953), pp. 132–48.

177. For a useful summary of the treaty terms and their economic implications, see Holtfrerich, *German Inflation*, pp. 137ff.

178. The discussion and quotations which follow are based on the Holtzendorff report of May 24, 1919, HAPAG Archiv. See also Gerald D. Feldman, "Foreign Penetration of German Enterprises after the First World War: The Problem of Überfremdung," in Alice Teichova, Maurice Lévy-Leboyer, Helga Nussbaum, eds., *Historical Studies in International Corporate Business* (Cambridge, 1989), pp. 87–110.

179. Krüger, *Deutschland und die Reparationen*, pp. 174–81. The idea of French participation was propagated with considerable enthusiasm by the potash industrialist Arnold Rechberg and strongly opposed by Stinnes. See Peter Wulf, *Hugo Stinnes. Wirtschaft und Politik 1918–1924* (Stuttgart, 1979), pp. 177f.

180. Krüger, *Deutschland und die Reparationen*, pp. 181ff.

181. Quoted in ibid., p. 190.

182. Haupts, *Deutsche Friedenspolitik*, p. 372f.n163.

183. Max Warburg, *Memoiren* (privately printed), 1919, p. 6, Warburg Archiv.

184. Quoted in Haupts, *Deutsche Friedenspolitik*, p. 372.

185. *Kabinett Scheidemann*, pp. 376f., 432f.

186. Richard Hauser, "Zur Währungsfrage," *Bank=Archiv* 19 (July 1, 1919), pp. 197–99.

187. Willi Prion, *Inflation und Geldentwertung. Finanzielle Maßnahmen zum Abbau der Preise. Gut-*

achten erstattet dem Reichsfinanzministerium (Berlin, 1919).

188. Ibid., p. 93.

189. Ibid., p. 105.

190. Ibid., pp. 99f.

191. Friedrich Bendixen, *Kriegsanleihen und Finanznot. Zwei finanzpolitische Vorschläge* (Jena, 1919), p. 32.

192. Prion, *Inflation und Geldentwertung*, p. 101.

193. See above, Chap. 1, p. 25.

194. Meeting of June 23, 1919, GStAKM, Rep. 151, HB, Nr. 1017, Bl. 234–35. For a summary account of this debate, see Holtfrerich, *German Inflation*, pp. 130ff.

195. Report on meeting with Colonel Conger, June 6, 1919, *Kabinett Scheidemann*, p. 429.

196. ZAG directors meeting, May 20, 1919, BAP, ZAG, Bd. 6, Bl. 7. On the ZAG reaction to the treaty terms, also see Feldman and Steinisch, *Industrie und Gewerkschaften*, pp. 74ff.

197. Holtzendorff report, May 25, 1919, HAPAG Archiv.

198. Holtzendorff report, June 16, 1919, ibid. The struggle in the Cabinet over the acceptance of the treaty terms may be followed in the concluding meetings in *Kabinett Scheidemann*.

199. Hans Staudinger, *Wirtschaftspolitik im Weimarer Staat. Lebenserinnerungen eines politischen Beamten im Reich und in Preußen 1899 bis 1934*, edited by Hagen Schulze (Berlin, 1982), p. 27; Wissell to Schlicke, July 7, 1919, in *Kabinett Bauer*, pp. 78–81; Ehlert, *Wirtschaftliche Zentralbehörde*, pp. 351ff.

200. Meetings of May 28 and June 23, 1919, GStAKM, Rep. 151, HB, Nr. 1017, Bl. 49–61, 227–29.

201. For the memorandum, see *Kabinett Bauer*, pp. 61–71, quotes on pp. 62–63.

202. Memorandum of July 7, 1919, ibid., pp. 82–85, quote on p. 83.

203. Ibid., p. 86.

204. For the meeting, ibid., pp. 93–97, quote on p. 93n12.

205. Ibid., p. 94.

206. Ibid., pp. 94–95.

207. Wissell to the Reich President, July 12, 1919, ibid., pp. 102–5. On the integration of the Reich Food Ministry, which was *de facto* on Aug. 7 and *de jure* on Sept. 15, ibid., pp. 170, 809.

4. The Chaotic Path to Relative Stabilization, July 1919–March 1920

1. Felix Pinner, "Wichtige Entscheidungen," *Berliner Tageblatt*, June 21, 1919, for this discussion and the quotations which follow.

2. See the complaint of the unemployed to the RAM of July 10, 1919, and the reply of the RB of July 29 in BAP, RAM, Nr. 1767, Bl. 339–41.

3. RB to RFM, July 3, 1919, *Kabinett Bauer*, pp. 40–47, quote on p. 42.

4. Ibid., pp. 42f.

5. Ibid., p. 43.

6. For an important analysis that corrects the old view that the Reichsbank was oblivious to the quantity theory of money, see Holtfrerich, *German Inflation*, pp. 163ff.

7. RB memorandum of July 1, 1919, *Kabinett Bauer*, pp. 46f.

8. The classic biography of Erzberger is Klaus Epstein, *Matthias Erzberger and the Dilemma of German Democracy* (Princeton, 1959). For the derivative nature of Erzberger's reforms, see p. 381 and Erzberger's own maiden speech as Minister in the Reichstag, *VN*, Vol. 327, July 8, 1919, p. 1381.

9. For Erzberger's speech of July 8, 1919, see *VN*, Vol. 327, pp. 1376–83, quote on p. 1377.

10. Ibid., p. 1377.

11. Ibid., p. 1383.

12. Ibid.

13. Finance Minister to the Minister Presidents of the States, July 6, 1919, *Kabinett Bauer*, pp. 71–78, especially pp. 74f.

14. Meeting between the Finance Minister and the state Finance Ministers in Weimar, July 13, 1919, ibid., pp. 105–16, quote on p. 108.

15. Ibid., p. 109.

16. Speech of Aug. 12, 1919, *VN*, Vol. 327, p. 2377f.

17. For the debates of August 12–14, 1919, see *VN*, Vol. 329, p. 2363ff. See also *Kabinett Bauer*, pp. 199n16, 231; Epstein, Erzberger, pp. 340ff.; Williamson, *Helfferich*, pp. 291ff.

18. Speech of Aug. 12, 1919, *VN*, Vol. 329, p. 2368.

19. Ibid., p. 2369.

20. Ibid., p. 2374.

21. Ibid., Aug. 14, 1919, pp. 2432ff.

22. Speech of Aug. 13, 1919, ibid., p. 2413.

23. Speech of Aug. 12, 1919, ibid., pp. 2363ff.

24. Ibid., pp. 2507ff., and *Kabinett Bauer*, pp. 41n19, 101n11.

25. RB note of Aug. 3, 1919, and meeting of Aug. 8, 1919, *Kabinett Bauer*, pp. 173–74n6, 191–94. See also notes of Aug. 9 and Aug. 14, 1919, GStAKM, Rep. 120, AX, Nr. 2, Bl. 113ff., 183ff. On the Czech measures, see Alice Teichova, "A Comparative View of the Inflation of the 1920's in Austria and Czechoslovakia," in Schmukler and Marcus, eds., *Inflation Through the Ages*, pp. 531–67, esp. pp. 537ff.

26. *VN*, Vol. 230, pp. 2512ff.; Erzberger to Prussian Minister of Commerce, Oct. 20, 1919, GStAKM, Rep. 120, AX, Nr. 2, Bl. 194; Holtfrerich, *German Inflation*, p. 127.

27. Report by the Württemburg Reichsrat Delegate, Sept. 19, 1919, HStA Stuttgart, E 130, Bü 1248.

28. SäHStA, Gesandtschaft Berlin, Nr. 249, Bl. 235–37. Prussian Minister of Commerce Fischbeck expressed similar views.

29. Staudinger, *Wirtschaftspolitik*, p. 28. I have also benefited from the personal observations of Professor Adolph Löwe, who knew Hirsch during both

the period discussed here and later as a colleague at the New School for Social Research. During World War II, Hirsch put the skills he had learned in World War I to use as an adviser to the Office of Price Administration in Washington. I have learned much from his papers, which were kindly placed at my disposal by his wife, Mrs. Edith Hirsch, as well as from my conversations with her.

30. Economic policy guidelines of the Reich Economics Ministry, Sept. 19, 1919, *Kabinett Bauer*, pp. 260–68, quote on p. 261.

31. Deputy Mittelmann at the meeting of Aug. 14, 1919, *VN*, Vol. 239, p. 2439.

32. Ibid., p. 2441.

33. *Kabinett Bauer*, p. 23; Reich Food Ministry meeting, July 11, 1919, BAK, R 43I/1255, Bl. 56–68; Correspondence with the Städtetag and various municipalities, GStAKM, Rep. 151, HB, Nr. 1017, Bl. 30ff.

34. Meeting of June 23, 1919, GStAKM, Rep. 151, HB, Nr. 1017, Bl. 232, 237.

35. Diary entry for 1919, Julius Hirsch Papers.

36. *Kabinett Bauer*, p. 264, and Cabinet meeting of Sept. 26, 1919, on p. 274. See also the note of the RWM to the states of Oct. 1, 1919, and the RWM meeting of Sept. 18, 1919, GStAKM, Rep. 87B, Nr. 15870, Bl. 246.

37. Meeting of July 11, 1919, BAK, R 43I/1255, Bl. 56ff., for this and other quotes. See also Hirsch's remarks at the June 6, 1919 meeting, GStAKM, Rep. 151, HB, Nr. 1017, Bl. 69.

38. For the discussion of these problems and detailed references to the sources, see Feldman, *VfZ* (1980), pp. 168ff.

39. *Bergarbeiterzeitung*, Nr. 25, June 21, 1919, quoted in Rudolf Tschirbs, "Der Ruhrbergmann zwischen Priviligierung und Statusverlust; Lohnpolitik von der Inflation bis zur Rationalisierung," in Feldman et al., *The German Inflation*, pp. 308–46, quote on p. 316, and his *Tarifpolitik im Ruhrbergbau 1918–1933* [*Beiträge zu Inflation und Wiederaufbau in Deutschland und Europa,* Bd. 5] (Berlin and New York, 1986), pp. 69ff.

40. On the civil service, see Andreas Kunz in Feldman et al., *The German Inflation*, pp. 347–84, as well as his *Civil Servants and the Politics of Inflation in Germany 1914-1924* [*Beiträge zu Inflation und Wiederaufbau in Deutschland und Europa,* Bd. 7) (Berlin and New York, 1986), Chaps. 1–3. On the problem of corruption, see *Kabinett Bauer*, pp. 188f.

41. For the Most speech and the Reichstag debate, see *VN*, Vol. 329, pp. 2206–33. On the miner hostility to the civil servants, see Feldman, *VfZ* (1980) pp. 168ff.

42. Meeting of June 16, 1919, StA Hamburg, Beamtenrat 17, Bd. 1. For the discussion of a wage office, see the meeting of June 4, 1919, in GStAKM, Rep. 120, BB VII 3, Nr. 4, Bd. 7, Bl. 125ff.

43. Cabinet meeting of Aug. 15, 1919, *Kabinett Bauer*, pp. 188f.

44. Ibid., pp. 260f.

45. Ibid., p. 264.

46. On the conflict between Braun and Schmidt, see the Cabinet meeting of Sept. 10, 1919, ibid., p. 246. See also Hagen Schulze, *Otto Braun oder Preußens demokratische Sendung* (Frankfurt a.M., 1977), pp. 274–77.

47. Guidelines of Sept. 19, 1919, *Kabinett Bauer*, pp. 264f.

48. Ibid., pp. 261, 264.

49. Report of Sept. 5, 1919, StA Hamburg, Senatskommission für die Reichs- und auswärtigen Angelegenheiten, III Alc3, Bd. 1.

50. *Kabinett Bauer*, p. 265.

51. The policy is clearly stated in the guidelines of Sept. 19, 1919, ibid., pp. 265–67. The evaluation of the Schmidt–Hirsch policy presented here is not dissimilar to that of William Carl Matthews, "The Continuity of Social Democratic Policy 1919 to 1920: The Bauer-Schmidt Policy," in Feldman et al., *Adaptation to Inflation*, pp. 485–512.

52. *Kabinett Bauer*, p. 267.

53. ZAG directors meeting of Aug. 7, 1919, BAP, ZAG, Nr. 28, Bl. 162ff. On the conflict between the RWM and the ZAG, see Feldman and Steinisch, *Industrie und Gewerkschaften*, pp. 65ff.

54. This quotation and the discussion and quotations which follow are taken from Thelwall's report of Sept. 18, 1919, PRO, FO 371/3778/53–59.

55. American Mission Berlin to State Department, Nov. 19, 1919, NA, 862.51/1237.

56. A. Fecht to State Secretary Albrecht, Nov. 19, 1919, BAK, R 43I/93, Bl. 69.

57. Note of Aug. 7, 1919, BAK, R 43I/93, Bl. 37.

58. Borgmeister to Albert, BAK, R 43I/90, Bl. 26–29.

59. Report to the Reich Chancellery from New York, Dec. 1919, BAK, R 43I/93, Bl. 110–45.

60. Hardy & Co. to Privy Councilor Beil, Aug. 20, 1919, GStAKM, Rep. 120, AX, Nr. 2, Bl. 188.

61. RB memorandum of Dec. 31, 1919, BAP, RWM, Nr. 7621, Bl. 370–88, quote on Bl. 386.

62. Report of the German General Consulate in Zürich, Sept. 20, 1919, GStAKM, Rep. 120, C XIII 1, Nr. 91, Bd. 4, Bl. 160–69—quote on Bl. 164—and Bl. 148ff. for other reports.

63. Letter to the Commerce Ministry of Sept. 9, 1919, ibid., Bl. 102–4, quote on Bl. 103.

64. Ibid.

65. Possehl to Chancellor Bauer, Nov. 7, 1919, BAP, RWM, Nr. 7621, Bl. 238.

66. RB to Prussian Minister of Commerce, Nov. 27, 1919, GStAKM, Rep. 120, C XIII 1, Nr. 91, Bd. 4, Bl. 252f.

67. Report of Dec. 31, 1919, ibid., Bl. 296f.

68. Merton to Schmitz, Dec. 11, 1919, HA der Metallgesellschaft.

69. Merton to Wiedfeldt, Dec. 16, 1919, ibid.

70. Merton to Wiedfeldt, Dec. 30, 1919, ibid.

71. Wiedfeldt to Merton, Dec. 20, 1919, ibid.

72. Unless otherwise noted, the discussion which follows is based on Feldman, *Iron and Steel*, pp. 55f.

73. Ibid., p. 94.

74. Warburg to Wiedfeldt, Nov. 10, 1919, HA Krupp, WA III 225.

75. Wiedfeldt to Hugenberg, Dec. 7, 1919, ibid., Nr. 224.

76. Feldman, *Iron and Steel*, Chap. 2.

77. Meeting of the VDMA directors, Jan. 23, 1920, Heft 4 (1920), VDMA Archiv.

78. RdI, *Geschäftliche Mitteilungen* (Jan. 8, 1920).

79. Ibid. (Feb. 8, 1920).

80. Meeting of the Standing Foreign Exchange Commission, April 8, 1920, GStAKM, Rep. 120, C, XIII 1, Nr. 91, Bd. 5, Bl. 25–29, quote on Bl. 28.

81. Wiedfeldt to Gustav Krupp von Bohlen und Halbach, Jan. 28, 1920, HA Firma Krupp, WA VIII f. 1412.

82. Quoted in Feldman, *Iron and Steel*, pp. 124f.

83. Ibid., pp. 140ff.

84. Ibid., pp. 187ff.

85. Despite its tendentious quality and special pleading, Jakob Reichert's *Rettung aus der Valutanot* (Berlin, 1919) provides a very plastic and accurate portrait of the dumping problems produced by failure to understand the currency depreciation. See also Feldman, *Iron and Steel*, pp. 132ff.

86. Report of Nov. 4, 1919, GStAKM, Rep. 120, C, XIII 5, Nr. 8, Bd. 27, Bl. 116–27.

87. Ibid., Bl. 127.

88. Rohmer report of Nov. 21, 1919, BayHStA, Abt. I, MH 13637.

89. Feldman and Steinisch, *Industrie und Gewerkschaften*, pp. 67ff., and meeting of the ZAG directors on Nov. 16, 1919, BAP, ZAG, Bd. 28, Bl. 1–7, and the program in Bd. 9, Bl. 62, 477–82.

90. Feldman and Steinisch, *Industrie und Gewerkschaften*, p. 68.

91. *Kabinett Bauer*, pp. 449f., 465f., and *RGBl* (1919), p. 2128.

92. *Niederschrift über die Sitzung des Zentralausschusses der Zentralarbeitsgemeinschaft . . . am 12. Dezember 1919*, p. 34.

93. Telegram from North Schleswig, Dec. 13, 1919, and complaint of the Osnabrück Chamber of Commerce, Feb. 2, 1920, GStAKM, Rep. 120, C XIII 1, Nr. 38B, Bd. 1, Bl. 21, 70f. For Hamburg's views, see its petition of Nov. 17, 1919, and the Reichsrat report of Dec. 1, 1919, StA Hamburg, Senatskommission für die Reichs- und auswärtigen Angelegenheiten, III A1c3, Bd. 1.

94. Report of Dec. 12, 1919, PRO, FO 371/3779/242–44.

95. For documents relating to these measures, see BAP, RWM, Nr. 5875, Bl. 95–99 and Nr. 7623, Bl. 71ff. See also the RB memorandum of Nov. 18, 1919, GStAKM, Rep. 120, C XIII 1, Nr. 91, Bd. 4, Bl. 312f. More generally, see Gerald D. Feldman, "Welcome to Germany? The *Fremdenplage* in the Weimar Inflation," in Wilhelm Treue, ed., *Geschichte als Aufgabe. Festschrift für Otto Büsch zu seinem 60. Geburtstag* (Berlin, 1988), pp. 629–49.

96. Discussion of Jan. 9, 1920, BAP, RWM, Nr. 7622, Bl. 103f. See also Hans Jürgen von Kleist, *Die ausländische Kapitalbeteiligung in Deutschland* (Berlin, 1921).

97. RB to Bauer, Jan. 28, 1920, *Kabinett Bauer*, p. 567.

98. Speech of Oct. 13, 1919, *VN*, Vol. 330, p. 2802.

99. Reichert, *Rettung aus der Valutanot*. For a more detailed discussion of this influential pamphlet and the criticisms of it, see Feldman, *Iron and Steel*, pp. 132ff.

100. Meeting of Dec. 17, 1919, GStAKM, Rep. 151, HB, Nr. 1085, Bl. 108–15.

101. Speech of Oct. 1, 1919, *VN*, Vol. 320, p. 2802.

102. Joseph Schumpeter, "Sozialistische Möglichkeiten von Heute," *AfSS* 48 (1920/21), pp. 306–60, quotes on pp. 352f. and 359f.

103. Supervisory Board meeting of the Reich Wheat Board, Dec. 17, 1919, GStAKM, Rep. 151, HB, Nr. 1086, Bl. 109. See also *Kabinett Bauer*, p. 458n14.

104. Remarks at the Reich Wheat Agency Supervisory Board meeting, Dec. 17, 1919, GStAKM, Rep. 151, HB, Nr. 1086, Bl. 109.

105. Cabinet meeting, Jan. 20, 1920, *Kabinett Bauer*, pp. 549–54.

106. Meeting of Feb. 7, 1920, BayHStA, Abt. II, MA 100 705.

107. Ibid.

108. Meeting of the Reich Wheat Corporation, Jan. 25, 1920, GStAKM, Rep. 151, HB, Nr. 1086, Bl. 125.

109. Report of Oct. 25, 1919, NA, 862.00/766.

110. Report of Dec. 23, 1919, SäHStA, LPP, Nr. 28, Bl. 26–31.

111. Report of Dec. 16, 1919, ibid., Nr. 25, Bl. 147.

112. The documentary history of the agency and the commissions is to be found in Brandenburgisches LHA, Pr. Br., Rep. 1A, Nr. 1. See also the report of May 17, 1919, ibid., Nr. 32, Bl. 1f.

113. Report of Jan. 16, 1920, ibid., Nr. 34, Bl. 72–84.

114. Report of Jan. 19, 1920, ibid., Bl. 20; see also reports of Jan. 12, Bl. 36–37, and of Jan. 20, Bl. 36–39.

115. Report of Oct. 28, 1919, ibid., Nr. 33, Bl. 14.

116. Report of Feb. 20, 1920, ibid., Nr. 34, Bl. 2.

117. Report of Jan. 16, 1920, ibid.

118. "Bedeutung und Inanspruchnahme des Verwaltungs- und des Rechtsweges für die Zwecke der Zwangswirtschaft," ibid., Nr. 33, Bl. 175–85, quotes from Bl. 175–77.

119. Reports of Sept. 16, 1919, from the District President of Schwaben and Neuburg and from the District President of Oberfranken, BayHstA, Abt. II, MA 102 145 and 102 150.

120. Meeting of the Oldenburg retailers, Feb. 17, 1919, NStAO, 265/148. For a typical response to the

consumer cooperatives and the municipalization question, see the Chamber of Commerce meeting of Oct. 20, 1919, NStAO, 265/185.

121. Report on the meeting of the State Committee of the Prussian chambers of commerce, June 28, 1919, RWWK, 20/421/1.

122. For such complaints, see the report of the Retailers Committee of the German Chamber of Commerce and Industry, Feb. 25–26, 1920, ibid., 20/422/13.

123. Ibid.

124. Alsberg in *Handbuch der Politik*, IV, p. 159f. See also *Kabinett Bauer*, p. 346, and LHStA Dresden, LPP, Nr. 27, Bl. 11–16.

125. Reichsverband der Verbände deutschen Lebensmittelhandels e.V. to the RWM, Jan. 23, 1920, and reply of Feb. 23, 1920, BAP, RWM, Nr. 12041, Bl. 75–79.

126. Undated RWM memorandum, ibid., Bl. 90–92.

127. Report of Nov. 26, 1919, SäHStA, LPP, Nr. 27, Bl. 56f.

128. Meeting of the representatives of the price examination agencies in Giessen, May 26–28, 1920, StA Hamburg, DHSG III, Pr IV 49/Iff., pp. 18ff.

129. Retailers Committee of the German Chamber of Commerce and Industry, Feb. 25–26, 1920, RWWK, 20/422/13, p. 7.

130. Ibid., p. 16.

131. Reported by Raumer to Saemisch, Nov. 24, 1919, BAK, NL Saemisch, Nr. 67, Bl. 44. More generally, see Potthoff, *Gewerkschaften*, pp. 40ff.

132. Potthoff, *Gewerkschaften*, pp. 71f., 182f.

133. At a meeting on Feb. 7, 1920, Schmidt considered it a sign of "progress" that the workers were finally recognizing the need to give more money to the farmers. BayHStA, Abt. II, MA 100 705.

134. ZAG directors meeting, Dec. 23–24, 1919, BAP, ZAG, Nr. 29, Bl. 30–47, quote on Bl. 45.

135. Feldman and Steinisch, *Industrie und Gewerkschaften*, pp. 82f.

136. Potthoff, *Gewerkschaften*, pp. 141ff.

137. Giesberts to Brauer, Dec. 20, 1919, BAK, K1. Er., Nr. 451, Bd. 6, Bl. 150f.

138. *Kabinett Bauer*, pp. 511ff., 549n3.; Kunz, *Civil Servants*, pp. 187ff.

139. For the discussion of these events, see Feldman, *VfZ* (1980), pp. 180ff.

140. *Kabinett Bauer*, p. 513.

141. Ernst Troeltsch, *Spektator-Briefe. Aufsätze über die deutsche Revolution und die Weltpolitik 1918/1922* (Tübingen, 1924), p. 88.

142. Erich Eyck, *A History of the Weimar Republic*, 2 vols. (Cambridge, 1962), I, pp. 134ff.; Epstein, *Erzberger*, p. 355ff. See also the discussions in Larry Eugene Jones, *German Liberalism and the Dissolution of the Weimar Party System 1918–1933* (Chapel Hill and London, 1988), Chaps. 3–5, and Werner Stephan, *Aufstieg und Verfall des Linksliberalismus 1918–1933* (Göttingen, 1973), pp. 132–65.

143. Report of the Saxon representative in Berlin, SäHStA, Gesandtschaft Berlin, Nr. 349, Bl. 266f.

144. Report by Holtzendorff, Dec. 12, 1919, HAPAG Archiv, for this and the quotations which follow.

145. Valutakommission meeting, Dec. 19, 1919, BAK, R 43I/2432, Bl. 154.

146. Ibid., Bl. 145 and Warburg to Hugenberg, Oct. 11, 1919, BAK, NL Hugenberg, Nr. 30, Bl. 37.

147. Raumer to Hugenberg, July 14, 1919, ibid., Nr. 25, Bl. 227f.

148. Raumer to Saemisch, Nov. 11, 1919, BAK, NL Saemisch, Bd. 8, Bl. 44.

149. Report of the District President of Schwaben and Neuburg, Sept. 9, 1919, BayHStA, Abt. II, MA 102 145. See also Troeltsch, *Spektator-Briefe*, pp. 85, 90f.

150. Report of April 29, 1920, PRO, FO 371/3784/477–86. On the Defence and Defiance League, which developed a propaganda of remarkable intensity and presaged Nazi work in this area, see Uwe Lohlam, *Völkischer Radikalismus. Die Geschichte des Deutschvölkischen Schutz- und Trutz-Bundes 1919–1923* (Hamburg, 1970).

151. The Chemnitz disturbances of August 1919 were the subject of remarkably detailed reports by the Saxon authorities. See SäHStA, MdI, Nr. 11076/1, Bl. 277ff., quote on Bl. 280.

152. Ibid., Bl. 289. It is interesting to note that Chemnitz had a strong Nazi vote in the early 1930s and there is little doubt that the working class contributed to it. See Richard Geary, "Unemployment and Working-Class Solidarity: The German Experience 1929–33," in Richard J. Evans and Dick Geary, eds., *The German Unemployed. Experiences and Consequences of Mass Unemployment from the Weimar Republic to the Third Reich* (New York, 1987), pp. 261–80, esp. p. 262.

153. Session of Oct. 10, 1919 *VN*, Vol. 330, pp. 3055–59 for this episode.

154. Meeting of the Ministerial Council, March 11, 1920, BayHStA, Abt. II, MA 99 514; see also the Saxon ambassadorial report of March 11, 1920, SäHStA, Außenministerium, Nr. 2980/1, Bl. 45ff. Because of the widespread character of this complaint, it reached the Reich Wheat Agency, where it was discussed on March 10, 1920, GStAKM, Rep. 151, HB, Nr. 1086.

155. RB to MdI, Feb. 1, 1919, BAP, RWM, Nr. 7621, Bl. 31–33. More generally, see Maurer, *Ostjuden*, pp. 128ff.

156. See SäHStA, Wirtschaftsministerium, Nr. 1544, Bl. 21ff. The quote is on Bl. 55.

157. Ibid., Bl. 59.

158. For the correspondence, see Stadtarchiv Frankfurt, IHK 1384.

159. See Maurer, *Ostjuden*, p. 104ff. On the procurement of copper, see the memoirs of Capt. Böhm of the Bavarian Army in the Institut für Zeitgeschichte, Munich, Bl. 221.

160. Report to Lord Curzon, Jan. 21, 1920, PRO, FO 371/3779/481.

161. Siegmund Fraenkel of the Munich Chamber of Commerce to the Valutakommission, Dec. 19, 1919, BAK, R 43I/2432, Bl. 152f.

162. Report by v. Reisnitz, Feb. 7, 1920, GStAKM, Rep 120, C, XIII 9, Nr. 1, Bd. 59, Bl. 404–8; *Kabinett Bauer*, pp. 647f.

163. See the list of July 31, 1922, in LA Berlin, AdSt, Nr. 3780.

164. Nordegg to Hans Tauscher, April 1, 1920, BAK, R 43I/89, Bl. 37–39.

165. Ibid.

166. Carl-Ludwig Holtfrerich, "Amerikanischer Kapitalexport und Wiederaufbau der deutschen Wirtschaft 1919–1923," *VSWG* 64 (1977), pp. 497–529, esp. pp. 518, 524ff.

167. See Bendix's lengthy memorandum of Aug. 30, 1919, in BAK, R 43I/93, Bl. 88–99, and his report to the U.S. authorities of Dec. 1919, in NA 862.51/1240.

168. See the reports on these developments in BAP, RWM, Nr. 7621, Bl. 370–82, esp. Bl. 380f., and RB, Bd. 6435, Bl. 15.

169. German Foreign Office memorandum, March 1920, BAK, R 43I/1129, Bl. 138ff., and Hirsch Diary, 1920.

170. The memorandum, which surveys the situation discussed above, is reprinted in *Kabinett Bauer*, pp. 623–32.

171. Ibid., p. 626.

172. Ibid., pp. 634–36.

173. Discussion on March 11, 1920, BAP, RWM, Nr. 7622, Bl. 164.

174. The best general study is Johannes Erger, *Der Kapp–Lüttwitz Putsch. Ein Beitrag zur deutschen Innenpolitik 1919/20* (Düsseldorf, 1967).

175. Carl Duisberg to H.T. von Böttiger, March 15, 1920, WA Bayer-Leverkusen, NL Duisberg, and Gerald D. Feldman, "Big Business and the Kapp Putsch," *CEH* 4 (1971), pp. 91–130.

176. BAP, RWM, Nr. 7622, Bl. 161.

5. The Trials and Tribulations of Relative Stabilization

1. Derek H. Aldcroft, *From Versailles to Wall Street 1919–1929* (Berkeley & Los Angeles, 1977), pp. 66ff.; Dan P. Silverman, *Reconstructing Europe After the First World War* (Cambridge & London, 1982), pp. 40ff. For the concept of "fiscal regime change," see Sargent, in Hall, ed., *Inflation*, pp. 41–98, esp. pp. 41ff., 90ff.

2. Keith Middlemas, *Politics in Industrial Society. The Experience of the British System since 1911* (London, 1979), p. 131. For a comparative analysis, see Gerald D. Feldman, "Die Demobilmachung und die Sozialordnung der Zwischenkriegszeit in Europa," *GuG* 9 (1983), pp. 156–77.

3. On Italy, see Maier, *Recasting Bourgeois Eu-* rope, pp. 109–34 and Chap. 5. On the comparison with Germany, see Carl-Ludwig Holtfrerich, "Moneta e credito in Italia e Germania dal 1914 al 1923," in Peter Hertner and Giorgio Mori, eds., *La transizione dall'economia die guerra all'economia die pace in Italia e Germania dopo la Prima Guerra Mondiale* (Bologna, 1983), pp. 665–92.

4. Julius Hirsch, *Die deutsche Währungsfrage* (Jena, 1924), p. 13, and Bresciani-Turroni, *Economics of Inflation*, pp. 55f.

5. Meeting of Dec. 19, 1919, BAK, R 43I/2432, Bl. 143.

6. Ibid., Bl. 155. On the eight-hour day question, see Gerald D. Feldman and Irmgard Steinisch, "Die Weimarer Republik zwischen Sozial- und Wirtschaftsstaat. Die Entscheidung gegen den Achtstundentag," *AfS* 18 (1978), pp. 353–439.

7. Stinnes at the confidential RdI directors' meeting of April 13, 1920, reprinted in Feldman and Steinisch, *Industrie und Gewerkschaften*, pp. 172f. For Ebert's proclamation of March 14, 1920, see *Kabinett Bauer*, pp. 683f.

8. *Kabinett Bauer*, pp. 722f. and 761n2, and Potthoff, *Gewerkschaften*, pp. 261ff.

9. Kolb, *Weimar Republic*, pp. 38f., 194.

10. See the introductions to *Kabinett Müller* and *Kabinett Fehrenbach* for the discussion of these Cabinets. On Brauns, see William L. Patch, Jr., *Christian Trade Unions in the Weimar Republic 1918–1933* (New Haven & London, 1985), pp. 15, 20, 39f., 60ff.

11. For these events, see Kunz, *Civil Servants*, pp. 196–206.

12. *Kabinett Müller*, pp. 138f.

13. Kunz, *Civil Servants*, pp. 206ff.

14. Kurt Singer & Alfred Schmidt, "Inflation, ihre Entstehung, ihr Verlauf und ihre Heilung, an geschichtlichen Beispielen dargelegt," *Bank = Archiv* (Oct. 25, 1920), Sonderbeilage for the quotations and discussion.

15. This is based on the undated Reichsbank analysis of this phenomenon, BAP, RB, Nr. 6339, Bl. 173–75.

16. The phrase is that of Alfred Lansburgh, *Die Politik der Reichsbank und die Reichsschatzanweisungen nach dem Kriege* [*SVS*, Bd. 166] (Munich and Leipzig, 1924), p. 17.

17. Holtfrerich, *German Inflation*, pp. 167f.

18. Bresciani-Turroni, *Economics of Inflation*, p. 57.

19. Nurske, *The Course and Control of Inflation*, p. 104.

20. "Im Kampfe um die deutsche Währung," Oct. 26, 1920, Hirsch Papers.

21. *FZ*, April 24, 1920.

22. Hesse, *Die deutsche Wirtschaftslage*, pp. 202ff.

23. Letter of Aug. 10, 1920, BAP, RAM, Nr. 1544, Bl. 55–58.

24. Letter of June 2, 1920, ibid., Bl. 23f.

25. Report of Justus Strandes to the Hamburg government, June 7, 1920, StA Hamburg, Senats-

kommission für die Reichs- und auswärtigen Angelegenheiten, III A1a7.

26. Report of RB Curatorium meeting of Sept. 14,
1920, SäHStA, Gesandtschaft Berlin, Nr. 1630, Bl.
61ff.

27. Hirsch memorandum of Oct. 26, 1920, Hirsch
Papers.

28. Meeting of June 17, 1920, GStKMA, Rep.
151, HB, Nr. 1086, Bl. 323f., and meeting of April 21,
1920, Bl. 241.

29. Meeting of June 17, 1920, ibid., Bl. 323.

30. Meeting of April 21, 1920, ibid., Bl. 241.

31. Ibid., Bl. 243.

32. *Kabinett Fehrenbach*, pp. 58ff., and Schumacher, *Land und Politik*, pp. 144ff.

33. Meeting of the Center Party Reichstag Deputies, June 26, 1920, Rudolf Morsey & Karsten Ruppert, eds., *Die Protokolle der Reichstagsfraktion der
Deutschen Zentrumspartei 1920–1925* (Mainz,
1981), pp. 23–26.

34. Quoted in Feldman, *VfZ* (1980), p. 199. See
also Tschirbs, in Feldman et al., *The German Inflation*, pp. 315–20. On Spa and the coal question, see
Charles S. Maier, "Coal and Economic Power in the
Weimar Republic: The Effects of the Coal Crisis of
1920," in Mommsen et al., *Industrielles System*, pp.
530–52.

35. Report of Aug. 19, 1920, NA 862.00/1005.

36. Report of June 5, 1920, NA 862.00/968.

37. Report of Aug. 19, 1920, NA 862.00/1005.

38. Ibid.

39. *Soziale Praxis* 30 (May 1921), p. 511.

40. Valuable information on the conditions of
these and other groups can be gleaned from the reports of the U.S. Consul in Hamburg, NA, 862.00/
985ff.

41. On the problems of the cost-of-living statistics,
see Holtfrerich, *German Inflation*, pp. 25–44, and
Wirtschaft und Statistik (1921), pp. 125–27, 172–75.
On household budgets in the inflation, see Merith
Niehuss, "Lebensweise und Familie in der Inflationszeit," in Feldman et al., eds., *The Adaptation to Inflation*, pp. 237–77.

42. Report of June 1, 1920, NA, 862.00/965.

43. Memorandum of Sept. 3, 1920, SäHStA, Gesandtschaft Berlin, Nr. 6135.

44. On Max Hoelz, see his autobiography, *Vom
"weißen Kreuz" zur Roten Fahne. Jugend-, Kampf-
und Zuchthauserlebnisse* (Berlin, 1929), and Hermann Weber, "Aktionismus und Kommunismus.
Unbekannte Briefe von Max Hoelz," *AfS* 15 (1975),
pp. 331–53.

45. Report of July 31, 1920, ibid.

46. See the interesting analysis of the rhetoric of
Teuerung, which concentrates on Munich in Martin
H. Geyer, "Teuerungsprotest, Konsumentenpolitik
und soziale Gerechtigkeit während der Inflation:
München 1920–1923," *AfS* 30 (1990), pp. 181–216,
esp. pp. 194–98.

47. Holtfrerich, *German Inflation*, p. 239.

48. Much can be learned about conditions from

the special reports to the Reich President from the
RWM for the spring and summer of 1920, BAK, R
431/1147, Bl. 160ff.

49. Workers' Council of the Bismarckhütte to
Ebert, June 28, 1920, BAP, RAM, Nr. 2362, Bl. 4f.
For comparable protests from other areas in west and
south Germany, see BAK, R 431/2414.

50. Report of Aug. 31, 1920, PRO, FO 371/4810/
2ff. On the situation at the Daimler works, see Bellon,
Mercedes, pp. 184–90. See also *Kabinett Fehrenbach*, pp. 118, 139, 147, 175, 181f.

51. U.S. Consular report of July 1, 1920, NA,
862.00/985.

52. Note of July 23, 1920, LHStA Dresden, Wirtschaftsministerium, Nr. 1327, Bl. 128–30.

53. Protest to Minister-President Tantzen, June
28, 1920, NStAO, 136/2815.

54. Protest to the Stadtmagistrat Delmenhorst,
June 28, 1920, ibid.

55. Reichsverband deutscher Spezialgeschäfte to
RWM, July 17, 1920, BAP, RWM, Nr. 12114, Bl.
229–31, and Hauptgemeinschaft des deutschen Ein-
zelhandels to RWM, July 14, 1920, ibid., Nr. 12115,
Bl. 285f.

56. RWM Vermerk, Aug. 28, 1920, ibid., Nr.
12115, Bl. 294f. See also the official protest of the retailers in Duisberg in July 1920 in RWWK, 20/
420/6.

57. Meeting of May 24, 1920, RWWK, 20/420/6.

58. "Grundsätzliches über die Preisbildung im
Einzelhandel, unter besonderer Berücksichtigung
des Lebensmitteleinzelhandels und der Preissteige-
rungen in den Monaten Juli bis Oktober 1920,"
RWWK, 20/503/13.

59. Landrat of Hanau to District President in
Cassel, Aug. 8, 1920, BAP, RWM, Nr. 12115, Bl.
82–86.

60. Würzburg meeting of the price examination
agencies, April 7–8, 1920, StA Hamburg, DHSG III,
Pr IV 49/1ff., p. 13.

61. Ibid.

62. Ibid.

63. Giessen meeting, May 26–28, 1920, pp. 40ff.,
ibid.

64. Würzburg meeting of April 7–8, 1920, ibid.,
pp. 3ff.

65. For this discussion, see the meeting of June
28, 1920, BayHStA Abt. II, MA, Nr. 100 705, and
GStAPrK, Rep. 84a, Nr. 1817, Bl. 335ff.

66. Ibid.

67. Meeting of July 13, 1920, BAP, RAM, Nr.
1031, Bl. 38f.

68. Retailers Committee of the Münster Chamber
of Commerce, Nov. 5, 1920, RWWK, 5/28/13. See
also the note of the Düsseldorf Chamber of Commerce of Aug. 12, 1920, in ibid., 20/503/5 and the
June 20, 1920 Duisburg Chamber of Commerce protest in 20/420/6.

69. Note of June 25, 1920, BAP, RAM, Nr. 1544,
Bl. 5–11.

70. Note of Aug. 15, ibid., Bl. 67–69.

71. Meeting of July 3, 1920, BAP, RWM, Nr. 12114, Bl. 116–18.

72. Meeting of July 3, 1920, BAP, RWM, Nr. 5876, Bl. 102–4. On Braun's opposition to the minimum price guarantees for agriculture and to the RWM support of higher coal prices, see *Kabinett Fehrenbach*, pp. 61, 89f.

73. Kuczynski, *Postwar Labor*, pp. 154f.

74. *RGBl* (1919), p. 1827, and minute of Feb. 14, 1920, BAP, RAM, Nr. 1122, Bl. 344f.

75. See the complaints of the Frankfurt Magistrate of June 24, 1920, and the exchanges which followed in ibid., Nr. 1124, Bl. 261f. and 329f.

76. Report of April 17, 1920, SäHStA, Gesandtschaft Berlin, Nr. 673, Bl. 300f.

77. Report of May 10, 1920, ibid., Bl. 327–33.

78. Report of June 9, 1920, ibid., Bl. 346–60. For the statistics, see the report of June 9, 1920, ibid., Bl. 344f.

79. Report of Oct. 10, 1920, ibid., Außenministerium, Nr. 6135.

80. Report of Dec. 12, 1920, ibid.; subsequent reports in Gesandtschaft Berlin, Nr. 675, Bl. 2ff., 16f., 22f., 40ff. 100f., 119, 144ff.; *Soziale Praxis* (1921), pp. 514f., 1210.

81. *Kabinett Fehrenbach*, pp. 462f.

82. BAP, RAM, Nr. 1025, Bl. 181f.

83. See report of May 19, 1920, BAP, Nr. 1024, Bl. 317f., and note from Berlin, Oct. 25, 1920, Nr. 1025, Bl. 252–55.

84. See the correspondence of July 21–29, 1920, between the RAM and RFM in ibid., Nr. 1031, Bl. 15ff.

85. Ibid., Nr. 1032, Bl. 7–13, and meeting of July 13, 1920, Nr. 1031, Bl. 22ff.

86. Hauptausschuß, Deutscher Städtetag, Köln, Nov. 10, 1920, GStAKM, Rep. 120, A II 5e, Nr. 18B, Bd. 2, Bl. 130ff.

87. July 1920 memorandum, BAP, RAM, Nr. 1025, Bl. 170f.

88. BAP, RAM, Nr. 1031, Bl. 30, and meeting of Sept. 24, 1920, Nr. 1025, Bl. 221f.

89. Ibid., RAM, Nr. 1031, Bl. 35.

90. Cabinet meeting of Sept. 7, 1920, *Kabinett Fehrenbach*, pp. 166f.

91. Materials on this are to be found scattered through the Prussian, Saxon, Bavarian, and Württemberg archives. A fairly substantial collection is in GStAKM, Rep. 120, C XIII 1, Nr. 119, Bd. 1–2, and C XIII 1, Nr. 160, Bd. 1–2.

92. RAM to the Prussian Commerce Minister, Aug. 26, 1920, GStAKM, Rep. 120, BB VII 1 3y, Bd. 3, Bl. 44f.

93. Report of June 12, 1920, BAP, RAM, Nr. 10414, Bl. 68f.

94. *Kabinett Fehrenbach*, p. 437, also pp. 163, 219ff., 435n, and BAP, RAM, Nr. 1544, Bl. 10.

95. For this and the discussion which follows, see especially Peter-Christian Witt, "Inflation, Wohnungszwangswirtschaft und Hauszinssteuer. Zur Regelung von Wohnungsbau und Wohnungsmarkt in der Weimarer Republik," in Lutz Niethammer, ed., *Wohnen im Wandel. Beiträge zur Geschichte des Alltags in der bürgerlichen Gesellschaft* (Wuppertal, 1979), pp. 385–407, esp. pp. 388f.

96. Ibid., and Preller, *Sozialpolitik*, p. 288. See also the excellent discussion of the Munich situation in Martin H. Geyer, "Wohnungsnot und Wohnungszwangswirtschaft in München 1917 bis 1924," in Feldman et al., *Adaptation to Inflation*, pp. 127–62.

97. The Reich was involved in 100 percent of the 60,861 units built in 1919. See Witt in Niethammer, *Wohnungsbau*, esp. p. 43.

98. RWM report of April 7, 1921, BAP, RWM, Nr. 8160, Bl. 17f.

99. RWM reports, Sept. 1920, ibid., Nr. 5916, Bl. 3.

100. Meeting of Nov. 3, 1920, ibid., Nr. 8163, Bl. 2f.

101. RWM report of Dec. 9, 1920, ibid., Nr. 5917, Bl. 18f., and *Kabinett Fehrenbach*, pp. 601f.

102. *Protokoll über die Verhandlungen des Parteitages der Sozialdemokratischen Partei Deutschlands, abgehalten in Görlitz vom 18. bis 24. September 1921* (Berlin, 1921), pp. 82f.

103. See meeting of April 4, 1921, BAP, RWM, Nr. 8160, Bl. 84ff.

104. Ibid., and *SPD Parteitag Görlitz*, pp. 82ff. See also, Robert Adolph, "Baufinanzierung durch Darlehnskassen," *Plutus* (March 2, 1921), pp. 78–81.

105. For the discussion and quotations, see the RB memorandum of Jan. 12, 1921, in BAP, RB, Nr. 6339, Bl. 162–69.

106. Speech to the Reichstag Committee XI, Dec. 1, 1920, BAP, NL Havenstein, Nr. 3, Bl. 238–40.

107. *Kommentar zu der Verordnung betreffend Maßnahmen gegenüber Betriebsabbrüchen und- stillegungen* (Berlin, 1920), p. 6. See also *Kabinett Fehrenbach*, pp. 163–68.

108. Statement by Hecht at an RWR meeting of July 6, 1920, BAP, RWR, Nr. 1, Bl. 129.

109. For this discussion, see Feldman and Steinisch, *Industrie und Gewerkschaften*, pp. 65ff.

110. On the RWR, see Harry Hauschild, *Der vorläufige Reichswirtschaftsrat 1920–1926* (Berlin, 1926).

111. Meeting of July 6, 1920, BAP, RWR, Nr. 1, Bl. 135f.

112. Ibid., Bl. 220f.

113. Ibid., Bl. 230.

114. Ibid., Bl. 238.

115. Feldman, *Iron and Steel*, pp. 189ff.

116. ZAG directors meeting, May 6, 1920, BAP, ZAG, Nr. 30, Bl. 191–207, quote on Bl. 200.

117. ZAG directors meeting, June 10, 1920, ibid., Bl. 84.

118. Reported at an RAM meeting on July 13, 1920, BAP, RAM, Nr. 1031, Bl. 38.

119. ADGB meeting of Nov. 2–4, 1920, Michael Ruck, ed., *Die Gewerkschaften in den Anfangsjahren der Republik 1919–1923* [*Quellen zur Geschichte der*

deutschen Gewerkschaftsbewegung im 20. Jahrhundert, Bd. 2] (Cologne, 1985), p. 242.

120. Report of Jan. 21, 1921, BAP, HAAA, Nr. 64736, Bl. 241f.

121. For the ADGB reactions, see ibid., pp. 193, 238; for the suspicions of the employers that the unions privately wished to contain wages, see the VdA meeting on Nov. 2, 1920, HA/GHH, Nr. 30019324/4; Brauns made his remarks at a meeting on July 3, 1920, BAP, RWM, Nr. 5680, Bl. 116–18.

122. On the shift in the locus of strikes, a trend which continued in 1921, see the important discussions in *Reichsarbeitsblatt* (Nichtamtlicher Teil), Nr. 12 (1922), pp. 365ff., and Nr. 4 (1923), pp. 78ff.

123. Coburg meeting of Oct. 19–20, 1920, in StA Hamburg, DHSG III, Pr IV 49/7, p. 32.

124. Ibid., pp. 9f., 13. These differences among the states repeat themselves regularly in the records of the meetings of the price examination agencies. See also *Kabinett Fehrenbach,* pp. 259ff., 270f., 278ff., 396f.

125. Coburg meeting of Oct. 19–21, 1920, StA Hamburg, DHSG III, Pr IV 49/7, p. 14f.

126. Report of Oct. 8, 1920, AN, AJ5 802/14/15.

127. *Correspondenzblatt,* Oct. 9, 1920, p. 551f.

128. Ruck, *Gewerkschaften,* p. 245f.

129. ZAG meetings of Jan. 13, 1921, and April 1, 1921, BAP, ZAG, Nr. 30, Bl. 93–120.

130. Arbeno to Paul Reusch, June 9, 1921, HA/GHH, Nr. 30019324/6.

131. Report of Hölling, March 14, 1921, BgA, Bestand 13, Bd. 305. For a general discussion of these negotiations, see Feldman, "Arbeitskonflikte," in *VfZ* (1980), pp. 201ff.

132. Diary notation of March 1921, Julius Hirsch Papers.

133. Ten demands of the ADGB, Feb. 26, 1921, Ruck, *Gewerkschaften,* pp. 285–88.

134. *Correspondenzblatt,* March 19, 1921.

135. See the note of Wirth to Fehrenbach of Sept. 17, 1920, and the Cabinet meeting of Sept. 22, *Kabinett Fehrenbach,* pp. 186f., 189–93. See also the correspondence of the RWM with various organizations in BAP, RWM, Nr. 12116, Bl. 131ff.

136. See the meeting with the state Finance Ministers of Nov. 11, 1920, *Kabinett Fehrenbach,* pp. 274–76.

137. Ibid., p. 275n4.

138. Meeting of Nov. 11, 1920, ibid., p. 277.

139. See the Cabinet meetings of Dec. 2, 18, and 20, 1920, and Jan. 2, 1921, in *Kabinett Fehrenbach,* pp. 319ff., 359f., 361ff., 386ff.

140. Cabinet meetings of Jan. 14, 1921, ibid., pp. 407ff., quote on p. 408.

141. PRO, FO 371/5968

142. Report of Nov. 28, 1920, PRO, FO 371/4742/54.

143. Frey to Gwinner, Jan. 5, 1921, HADB. I wish to thank Dr. Manfred Pohl for bringing this document to my attention.

144. *FZ,* Dec. 11, 1920.

145. *FZ,* Sept. 15, 1920. The Association of German Metal Industrialists circulated a memorandum of the Bavarian branch of Feb. 2, 1921, expressing doubts that Germany could continue to escape the international economic crisis on Feb. 21, 1921. It is to be found in the VPI Archiv.

146. A.G. Villiers to Merton, Jan. 11, 1921, HA der Metallgesellschaft.

147. For the discussion and quotations which follow, see Merton to Villiers, Jan. 21, 1921, ibid.

148. Report of February 25, 1921, AN, AJ5 2019/14/16.

6.   What Kind of Reconstruction? The German Business Community Faces the Future

1. Meeting of Feb. 4, 1921, BAP, RWR, Nr. 46, Bd. 2, Bl. 144.

2. On D'Abernon's career in Berlin, see the excellent study by Angela Kaiser, *Lord D'Abernon und die englische Deutschlandpolitik 1920–1926* (Frankfurt a.M., 1989).

3. Memorandum by v. Glasenapp on his conversation with D'Abernon, Nov. 27, 1920, *Kabinett Fehrenbach,* pp. 314–16, quote on p. 315.

4. Ibid., p. 316. For a convincing defense of the Reichsbank discount policy, see Holtfrerich, *German Inflation,* p. 172ff.

5. Saxon report on the Reichsbank Curatorium meeting, Sept. 14, 1920, SäHStA, Gesandtschaft Berlin, Nr. 1630.

6. Holtfrerich, *German Inflation,* p. 288. The 36 percent estimate was based on the investigations of the post-inflation McKenna Committee. Much higher figures—as much as 66 percent—were mentioned during investigations of 1920–1921 to be discussed below, although these were contested.

7. This material is derived from Holtfrerich, *VSWG* (1977), quote on p. 529.

8. Report of Stieber of the RAM, Nov. 20, 1920, BAP, RAM, Nr. 10414, Bl. 170.

9. "Bemerkungen zur Devisenpolitik," undated but of early 1921, BAP, RWM, Nr. 6036, Bl. 2–5.

10. See Stieber report cited in note 7, and *Plutus* (November 24, 1920), p. 374f.

11. RWR meeting, Oct. 10, 1920, BAP, RWR, Nr. 459, Bd. 1, Bl. 9f.

12. *Plutus* (March 24, 1920).

13. *Kabinett Bauer,* p. 264.

14. *Kabinett Bauer,* p. 569fn4. The memorandum was reprinted in *Plutus* (March 10, 1920).

15. Ibid.

16. *Kabinett Bauer,* p. 569, and notes on the meeting in BAP, RFM, Nr. 2800, Bl. 291.

17. *Plutus* (March 20, 1920).

18. Ibid.

19. Ibid.

20. Memorandum of Feb. 18, 1920, BAP, RFM, Nr. 2800, Bl. 182.

21. BAP, RFM, Nr. 2800, Bl. 191.

22. Report of Aug. 2, 1920, Stadtarchiv Frankfurt a.M., IHK, Nr. 615.

23. *Kabinett Fehrenbach*, p. 164.

24. See also his remarks at a meeting on Oct. 1, 1920, in GStAKM, Rep. 120, AX, Nr. 34, Bl. 43.

25. See the reports of the *Berliner Tageblatt*, Aug. 10 and Sept. 11, 1920, in ibid., Bl. 1–3.

26. See the report of Sept. 3, 1920, Stadtarchiv Frankfurt a.M., IHK, Nr. 615.

27. Hamburg Chamber of Commerce to RFM, Aug. 26, 1920, GStAKM, Rep. 120, AX, Nr. 43, Bl. 5–11.

28. Note of Sept. 1, 1920, ibid., Bl. 31–34.

29. Note of Oct. 25, 1920, ibid., Bl. 66f.

30. For a copy, see ibid., Bl. 15.

31. RB to Prussian Minister of Commerce, Nov. 8, 1920, for its formal objections, ibid., Bl. 78–101. For the Reichsbank's motives and actions, see the report to Mayor Landmann of Frankfurt of Sept. 7, 1920, Stadtarchiv Frankfurt a.M., IHK, Nr. 615.

32. RFM to RWM, Sept. 13, 1920, GStAKM, Rep. 120, AX, Nr. 43, Bl. 19f.

33. Meeting Oct. 1, 1920, ibid., Bl. 38–50, quote on Bl. 45.

34. Ibid., Bl. 40.

35. Ibid., Bl. 48.

36. Ibid., Bl. 50. It is not without irony that the collapse of Goldschmidt's Danat Bank triggered the great banking crisis of 1931.

37. Wirth to Scholz, Oct. 9, 1920, ibid., Bl. 36–38.

38. Meeting of the Economic Policy Committee of the RWR, BAP, RWR, Nr. 364, esp. Bl. 176, 200ff.

39. The complete protocols of the Ausschuß zur Prüfung von Maßnahmen gegen die finanzielle Not der produktiven Stände are to be found in ibid., Nr. 459–60. The discussion which follows is based on these protocols, but only the quotations will be cited.

40. Expert testimony of Heinmann, Oct. 28, 1920, ibid., Nr. 459, Bd. 1, Bl. 82f.

41. Statement by Neustadt, meeting of Jan. 28, 1921, ibid., Bl. 313.

42. Ibid., Bl. 282f.

43. Meeting of Feb. 11, 1921, ibid., Nr. 460, Bd. 2, Bl. 185.

44. Meeting of Jan. 29, 1921, ibid., Bl. 130f.

45. Meeting of Feb. 11, 1921, ibid., Bl. 179.

46. Ibid., Bl. 186–93.

47. For the RB memorandum, see GStAKM, Rep. 120, AX, Nr. 43, Bl. 78–101.

48. Meeting of Nov. 16, 1920, BAP, RWR, Nr. 459, Bd. 1, Bl. 155.

49. Ibid., Bl. 152f.

50. Meeting of Jan. 29, 1921, ibid., Nr. 460, Bd. 2, Bl. 58–60.

51. *Ausschuß zur Untersuchung der Erzeugungs- und Absatzbedingungen der deutschen Wirtschaft. Der Bankkredit* (Berlin, 1930), p. 40. See also Richard H. Tilly, "Gemeindefinanzen und Sparkassen in Westfalen in der Inflation, 1918–1923," in Kurt Düwell and Wolfgang Köllmann, eds., *Rheinland und Westfalen im Industriezeitalter, Bd. 2. Von der Reichsgründung bis zur Weimarer Republik* (Wuppertal, 1984), pp. 398–411; and Carl-Ludwig Holtfrerich, "Auswirkungen der Inflation auf die Struktur des deutschen Kreditgewerbes," in Feldman and Müller-Luckner, eds., *Die Nachwirkungen der Inflation*, pp. 187–209.

52. Meeting of Oct. 11, 1920, BAP, RWR, Nr. 364, Bl. 174.

53. Ibid., Bl. 199.

54. Oscar Schlitter to Siegen Bank for Industry and Commerce, April 27, 1921, and Essener Bank to Bergassessor Schleifenbauer, April 30, 1921, HADB. On the Siegen memorandum, see the report by Consul Maurice Parmelee of May 28, 1921, on "Concentration and Combination in German Industry and Finance," NA, 862.60/38, p. 45ff. See also Manfred Pohl, *Konzentration im deutschen Bankwesen (1848–1980)* (Frankfurt a.M., 1982), pp. 3f. 211. The Siegen Bank for Industry and Commerce finally was taken over by the Deutsche Bank in 1925.

55. Comments of Dr. Bendix, meeting of Jan. 29, 1921, BAP, RWR, Nr. 460, Bd. 2, Bl. 109ff.

56. Meeting of Feb. 11, 1921, ibid., Bl. 175f., 195f., quote on 202.

57. Ibid., Bl. 224.

58. RB memorandum of Nov. 8, 1920, GStAKM, Rep. 120, AX, Nr. 43, Bl. 97.

59. Meetings of Jan. 29 and Feb. 11, 1921, BAP, RWR, Nr. 460, Bd. 2, Bl. 98ff., 272ff.

60. *Bank = Archiv* 20 (Nov. 1, 1920), pp. 33ff.

61. *FZ*, Oct. 11, 1920.

62. Note of Oct. 27, 1920, GStAKM, Rep. 120, AX, Nr. 43, Bl. 74.

63. Report to Frankfurt, Oct. 28, 1920, Stadtarchiv Frankfurt, IHK, Nr. 615.

64. *Kabinett Fehrenbach*, p. 164n15.

65. P. Barrett Whale, *Joint Stock Banking in Germany. A Study of the German Credit Banks before and after the War* (London, 1930), p. 196.

66. Whale, *Joint Stock Banking*, pp. 199ff., 224f. See also, Carl-Ludwig Holtfrerich, "Das Eigenkapital der Kreditinstitute als historisches und aktuelles Problem," *Bankhistorisches Archiv. Zeitschrift für Bankengeschichte*, Beiheft 5 (1981), pp. 14–29; "Zur Entwicklung der deutschen Bankenstruktur," Deutscher Sparkassen- und Giroverband, *Standortbestimmung. Entwicklungslinien der deutschen Kreditwirtschaft* (Stuttgart, 1984), pp. 13–42; and in Feldman, ed., *Nachwirkungen*, pp. 187–209.

67. Note by Michalowsky, Oct. 30, 1919, HADB.

68. *FZ*, Aug. 19, 1919, p. 3.

69. Mankiewitz to Klaproth, Feb. 11, 1920, HADB.

70. Wassermann to Klaproth, May 18, 1920, ibid.

71. Mankiewitz to Klaproth, Jan. 30, 1920, ibid.

72. Whale, *Joint Stock Banking*, p. 227f.

73. Wassermann to Klaproth, May 15, 1920, HADB.

74. Karl Erich Born, " The Deutsche Bank during Germany's Great Inflation after the First World War," *Studies on Economic and Monetary Problems*

and Banking History, No. 17 (Frankfurt, 1979), pp. 22f.; Pohl, *Konzentration*, pp. 308–10.

75. Born, *Studies on Economic and Monetary Problems*, p. 22.

76. Klaproth to Mankiewitz, Oct. 2, 1920, HADB.

77. Willi Strauss, *Die Konzentrationsbewegung im deutschen Bankgewerbe. Ein Beitrag zur Organisationsentwicklung der Wirtschaft unter dem Einfluß der Konzentration des Kapitals. Mit besonderer Berücksichtigung der Nachkriegszeit* (Berlin & Leipzig, 1928), pp. 31f, 85f.

78. This is evident from the Hannoversche Bank correspondence in the HADB, but see also Strauss, *Konzentrationsbewegung*, pp. 65–67, and Bresciani-Turroni, *Economics of Inflation*, p. 256ff.

79. Schlitter to Schleifenbaum, April 30, 1921, HADB.

80. Fritz Reisser, "Bankpolitik von 1920," *Plutus* (July 20, 1921), pp. 238–40, quote on p. 239.

81. Whale, *Joint Stock Banking*, p. 238.

82. *Plutus* (July 20, 1921), p. 240.

83. Klaproth to Wassermann, May 11, 1920, HADB.

84. Pinner, *Wirtschaftsführer* (Berlin, 1924), p. 188.

85. Enquête Ausschuß, *Wandlungen in den wirtschaftlichen Organisationsformen. 1. Teil: Wandlungen in den Rechtsformen der Einzelunternehmungen und Konzerne* (Berlin, 1928), p. 187.

86. See Pinner, *Deutsche Wirtschaftsführer*, pp. 192–94; Paul Uffermann, *Könige der Inflation* (Berlin, 1924), pp. 91–96; Paul Uffermann & Otto Hüglin, *Stinnes und seine Konzerne* (Berlin, 1924), p. 75; Arnold Tross, *Der Aufbau der eisenerzeugenden und eisenverarbeitenden Industrie-Konzerne Deutschlands* (Berlin, 1923), pp. 67, 73. Stinnes seems first to have learned about Herzfeld's activities from Albert Vögler in a letter of Nov. 17, 1917, reporting on the then "small Berlin banker's" activities. See Teilnachlaß Hugo Stinnes, Stinnes AG, Mülheim/Ruhr. For efforts by Goldschmidt to compete with Solomonsohn, see Goldschmidt to Stinnes, May 10, 1921, ACDP, NL Stinnes, Nr. 270/1.

87. Feldman, *Iron and Steel*, p. 237.

88. Oppenheim to Schaewen, April 8, 1920, Mannesmann-Archiv, P/1/25/38.

89. See memorandum of Oct. 13, 1921, and accompanying documents in ibid., P/1/26/20.2

90. Examples from the Enquête Ausschuß, *Wandlungen in den Rechtsformen der Einzelunternehmungen*, pp.159ff., esp. p. 169.

91. Lothar Burchardt in *Zeitschrift für Unternehmensgeschichte* (1987), pp. 106ff.

92. Meeting of Sept. 27, 1920, SWW, K2, Nr. 603.

93. Merton to R. von Hemert, Jan. 19, 1920, HA der Metallgesellschaft.

94. Enquête Ausschuß, *Wandlungen in den Rechtsformen der Einzelunternehmungen*, p. 184.

95. Ibid., p. 188. See also "Ausgabe von Vorzugsaktien in 1920," *Wirtschaft und Statistik* (1921), pp.

483–85. See also Knut Wolfgang Nörr, "Zur Entwicklung des Aktien- und Konzernrechts während der Weimarer Republik," *Zeitschrift für das gesamte Handelsrecht und Wirtschaftsrecht* 150 (1986), pp. 155–81, for a discussion of the important legal developments in this area during the Weimar period.

96. Oppenheim to Beukenberg, July 2, 1920, Mannesmann-Archiv, P/1/25/38.

97. *Plutus* (March 24, 1920), pp. 105f.; Feldman, *Iron and Steel*, pp. 264–66. The Deutsche Bank handled the transactions for Wolff, and its archive contains a useful file of correspondence on the operation. Much can be learned about the politics and economics of the transactions from the Oppenheim correspondence in the Mannesmann-Archiv, P/1/25/8.

98. Hamburg HK meeting of June 11, 1920, Commerzbibliothek Hamburg. On the proposed loan and the collateral problem, see Born, *Studies in Economic and Monetary Problems* 17 (1979), p. 19.

99. *Plutus* (May 5, 1920), pp. 152–55.

100. See Vögler to Kirdorf, March 24, 1921, with letter from Siemens to Vögler of the same date and other related documents in ACDP, NL Stinnes, Nr. 253/2.

101. Stinnes to Vögler, March 27, 1921, ibid., and Vögler to Stinnes, June 7, 1921, Nr. 245/5.

102. *Plutus* (Dec. 21, 1921), p. 439.

103. Wiedfeldt to Bohlen, July 8, 1921, HA Firma Krupp, WA III 226, and Feldman, *Iron and Steel*, pp. 259ff.

104. *Plutus* (May 11, 1921), pp. 165–67. See also RWM report of Jan. 15, 1921, BAP, RWM, Nr. 2267/1, Bl. 22, and Tross, *Aufbau*, p. 22.

105. Tross, *Aufbau*, p. 110; Feldman, *Iron and Steel*, pp. 220, 272.

106. Ibid., pp. 116ff., 273ff.

107. Ibid., p. 38, 70f., 115ff., 259ff. For the Vögler memorandum, see Feldman and Homburg, *Industrie und Inflation*, pp. 219–24.

108. Feldman, *Iron and Steel*, chaps. 1–4.

109. Vögler to Stinnes, June 7, 1921, ACDP, NL Stinnes, Nr. 245/5. On the Reusch takeover of the M.A.N. and the Siemens alliance with Stinnes, see Feldman, *Iron and Steel*, pp. 213ff.

110. Quaatz to Vögler, Dec. 30, 1920, ACDP, NL Stinnes, Nr. 001/5.

111. Calculated by Johannes Houwink ten Cate on the basis of his research in BAP, HAAA, 40289ff., as well as in other archives and kindly supplied to the author. See Johannes Houwink ten Cate, "Amsterdam als Finanzplatz Deutschlands," in Feldman et al., *Consequences of the Inflation* [*Einzelveröffentlichungen der Historischen Kommission zu Berlin*, 67. *Beiträge zu Inflation und Wiederaufbau in Deutschland und Europa 1914–1924*] (Berlin, 1989), pp. 149–80.

112. Hamburg HK directors meeting, Jan. 14, 1921, Commerzbibliothek Hamburg.

113. Feldman, *Iron and Steel*, pp. 119f.

114. See the report by a Phoenix observer on his trip to Amsterdam, Feb. 22, 1921, Mannesmann-Archiv, P1/26/20.3.

115. Meeting of April 23, 1920, HA der Metall-gesellschaft.

116. For another reference to the "hate rebate" which German exporters had to offer their customers, see Feldman, *Iron and Steel*, p. 292.

117. Curt Geyer, *Drei Verderber Deutschlands. Ein Beitrag zur Geschichte Deutschlands und der Reparationsfrage* (Berlin, 1924). Helfferich and Havenstein are the other two "destroyers" of Germany discussed in this book.

118. For an excellent survey of the literature on Stinnes, see the introduction to Peter Wulf, *Hugo Stinnes*.

119. Gerd von Klass, *Hugo Stinnes* (Tübingen, 1958), probably wins the prize in this category.

120. This impression comes from my reading of all his papers in the ACDP in preparation for a biography I am writing as well as on a personal interview with Hugo Stinnes, Jr., in 1976 and interviews with other family members. For an account by Edmund, see his *A Genius in Chaotic Times. Edmund H. Stinnes on His Father, Hugo Stinnes (1870–1924)* (privately printed, Bern, n.d., but around 1981 and based on an interview with *Die Zeit* of 1979).

121. For the characterization of the two industrialists as speakers, see the interesting remarks by Arnold Langen, who experienced them both in the Reich Economic Council, in the unpublished biography by Dr. Goldbeck in the Klöckner-Deutz Archive.

122. Stinnes, *A Genius in Chaotic Times*, p. 31.

123. This sketch is based on Ufermann & Hüglin, *Stinnes und seine Konzerne*, pp. 7ff., and Wulf, *Stinnes*, pp. 20ff.

124. For a fine study of these complex developments, see the unpublished Ph.D. dissertation of Edmund Neville Todd III, "Technology and Interest Group Politics: Electrification of the Ruhr, 1886–1930" (University of Pennsylvania, 1984).

125. Ufermann & Hüglin, *Stinnes und seine Konzerne*, p. 10.

126. Stinnes to Thomas, Jan. 3, 1919, ACDP, NL Stinnes, Nr. 268/4.

127. Karl Fehrmann to Clara Stinnes, Oct. 1952, "Erinnerungen an Hugo Stinnes," Teilnachlaß Hugo Stinnes, Mülheim/Ruhr.

128. Testament of March 1920, ACDP, 300/7.

129. Ibid.

130. Stinnes to the Finanzamt, June 21, 1920, as well as the related correspondence, ACDP, NL Stinnes, Nr. 299/3.

131. Ibid.

132. Maier, *Recasting*, pp. 214ff.; Peter Wulf, "Die Auseinandersetzung um die Sozialisierung der Kohle in Deutschland 1920/1921," *VfZ* 25 (1977), pp. 46–98, esp. p. 52.

133. Meeting of Aug. 20, 1920, Teilnachlaß Hugo Stinnes, Mülheim/Ruhr.

134. For this and the quotes which follow, Stinnes to Küchen, August 8, 1920, NL Stinnes, Nr. 182/1. See also the unpublished RWE history of 1948 in the RWE Archiv, Essen.

135. Vögler to Stinnes, Aug. 2, 1920, ACDP, NL Stinnes, Nr. 057/20.

136. Maier, *Recasting*, pp. 214ff.; Wulf, *Stinnes*, pp. 226ff.

137. Kleine to Silverberg, Jan. 6, 1921, BAK, NL Silverberg, Nr. 137, Bl. 178, 179ff.

138. Wiedfeldt to Hugenberg, Sept. 9, 1920, BAK, NL Hugenberg, Nr. 45, Bl. 13f., for this and the quotations which follow.

139. Stinnes to Küchen, Aug. 8, 1920, ACDP, NL Stinnes, Nr. 187/1.

140. Stinnes to Wiedfeldt, Sept. 14, 1920, BAK, NL Hugenberg, Nr. 45, Bl. 10–12, for these quotations.

141. Meeting of Oct. 26, 1920, ACDP, NL Stinnes, Nr. 264/1.

142. Quoted in Feldman, *Iron and Steel*, p. 219. For a detailed history of the founding of the SRSU, see Chap. 4 of that study.

143. Memorandum by Director Heinrich Jastrow, April 7, 1920, reprinted in Feldman and Homburg, *Industrie und Inflation*, pp. 282–86, quote on p. 284.

144. Meeting of Aug. 8, 1920, Teilnachlaß Stinnes, Mülheim/Ruhr. On these beliefs, see also Edmund Stinnes, *Genius*, p. 58.

145. Vögler to Köttgen, Jan. 18, 1922, SAA, 11/Lf 130.

146. Vögler to Stinnes, and to the Supervisory Board of Deutsch-Lux, Feb. 26, 1920, and June 8, 1920, ACDP, NL Stinnes, Nr. 244/1.

147. Stinnes to Raumer, Jan. 16, 1921, and other relevant correspondence in ibid.

148. Stinnes to Berg, Oct. 20, 1920, ibid.

149. Hopkins to Hugo Stinnes, Jr., Oct. 30, 1920; Hugo Stinnes, Jr., to Hopkins, Nov. 6, 1920; Stinnes to Berg, Jan. 7, 1921, ibid.

150. Berg to Hugo Stinnes, March 2, 1922, and Stinnes to Vögler, May 27, 1922, ibid., Nr. 274/4.

151. Köttgen to Vögler, March 29, 1921, SAA, NL Köttgen, 11/Lf 104.

152. Vögler to Köttgen, April 1, 1921, ibid.

153. Ibid.

154. Testament of March 18, 1920, ACDP, NL Stinnes, Nr. 300/7.

155. Letters to Stinnes of Feb. 25 and 26, 1920, ACDP, NL Stinnes, Nr. O57/3.

156. Letters of April 4 and May 10, 1920, ACDP, NL Stinnes, Nr. 157/13. In March 26, 1920, S. Alfred von Oppenheim advised General Director von Schaewen of Phoenix not to concern himself with the depreciation of that company's dollar and gulden holdings, but rather to use them to purchase Swedish kronor in order to finish paying off ore debts and benefit from the latter's depreciation as well. At the same time he actually advised further engagement in Swedish kronor: "Since my feeling is that the improvement of the mark, which in any case is unintelligible in view of our domestic and economic situation, will not last long, we ought to derive profit from the momentary improvement of the mark and, insofar as you have mark holdings available, to change

them into Swedish kronor." Mannesmann-Archiv, P/1/25/38.

157. Letter of Dec. 26, 1920, ACDP, NL Stinnes, Nr. 057/3.

158. Vögler to Stinnes, Nov. 18, 1920, ibid.

159. Stinnes to Vögler, Nov. 19, 1920, ibid.

160. Stinnes to Vögler, Dec. 23, 1920, ibid.

161. Stimmig to Stinnes, Feb. 26, 1921, ibid., Nr. 259/4.

162. Vögler to Stinnes, Dec. 26, 1920, ibid., Nr. 057/3.

163. Vögler to Stinnes, Dec. 31, 1920, ibid.

164. Stinnes to Vögler, June 2, 1921, ibid., Nr. 271/3.

165. Vögler to Stinnes, June 4, 1921, ibid., and Feldman, *Iron and Steel*, p. 267.

166. Ufermann & Hüglin, *Stinnes und seine Konzerne*, pp. 78ff.; Pinner, *Wirtschaftsführer*, pp. 217–23.

167. Stinnes to Vögler, Aug. 19, 1921, and Vögler to Stinnes, Aug. 20, 1921, ACDP, NL Stinnes, Nr. 057/4.

168. For the meetings, see SAA, 54/Lm 123.

169. Stinnes to Vögler, Sept. 1, 1921, ACDP, NL Stinnes, Nr. 038/1.

170. Stinnes to Hoffmann, Feb. 3, 1921, ibid., Nr. 117/4, and Aktennotiz Sempell, April 5, 1922, ibid., Nr. 265/1.

171. Henrich to Stinnes, Aug. 8, 1921, ibid., Nr. 100/2. More generally on the problem of a merger between Siemens and the AEG, see Heidrun Homburg, "Die Neuordnung des Marktes nach der Inflation. Probleme und Widerstände am Beispiel der Zusammenschlußprojekte von AEG und Siemens 1924–1933 oder 'Wer hat den längeren Atem?'" in Feldman, *Nachwirkungen*, pp. 117–55.

172. Meeting of Feb. 9, 1922, with appended report, ACDP, NL Stinnes, Nr. 092/2.

173. Eugen Schmalenbach, *Dynamische Bilanzlehre*, 3rd ed. (Leipzig, 1925); Fritz Schmidt, *Die Wiederbeschaffungspreise des Umsatztages in Kalkulation und Volkswirtschaft* (Berlin, 1923), and *Bilanzwert, Bilanzgewinn und Bilanzumwertung* (Berlin, 1924); Eugen Schmalenbach and Willi Prion, *Zwei Vorträge über Scheingewinne: Die steuerliche Behandlung der Scheingewinne. Die Finanzpolitik der Unternehmung* (Jena, 1922); Willi Prion, *Die Finanzpolitik der Unternehmung im Zeichen der Scheingewinne*, 2nd ed. (Jena, 1922); Walter Mahlberg, *Bilanztechnik und Bewertung bei schwankender Währung* (Leipzig, 1922).

174. See the unpublished history of the VDMA in the VDMA Archiv, Frankfurt a.M.

175. The discussion and quotations which follow are based on his two articles, "Abschreibungen und Geldentwertung" and "Ersatzanschaffungen und Neuanlagen unter dem Einfluß der Geldentwertung," in *Plutus* (Sept. 15, 1920), pp. 285–88, and (Oct. 27, 1920), pp. 334–37.

176. Feldman, *Iron and Steel*, pp. 170ff.

177. On the problems, see Gerald D. Feldman and Ulrich Nocken, "Trade Associations and Eco-
nomic Power: Interest Group Development in the German Iron and Steel and Machine Building Industries," *Business History Review* 49 (1975), pp. 413–45; Gerald D. Feldman, "The Large Firm in the German Industrial System: The M.A.N. 1900–1925," in D. Stegmann et al., eds., *Industrielle Gesellschaft und politisches System. Beiträge zur politischen Sozialgeschichte* (Düsseldorf, 1978), pp. 241–57; Feldman, *Iron and Steel*, pp. 182f.

178. Feldman & Nocken, *Business History Review* (1975), pp. 422f.

179. Enquête Ausschuß, *Entwicklungslinien der industriellen und gewerblichen Kartellierung. Textilindustrie* (Berlin, 1930), p. 7.

180. Ibid., pp. 344f. See also pp. 334ff.

181. "Freibleibend," *Plutus* (Sept. 15, 1920), pp. 282–84, quote on p. 283.

182. "Wirtschaftsenquête," *Plutus* (Aug. 18, 1920), pp. 255–58.

183. For the records of these efforts, see BAP, RWM, Nr. 2267/1.

184. Ibid., Bl. 16, 28, 40.

185. RdI, *Geschäftliche Mitteilungen* 20 (June 7, 1920), Lfd., Nr. 291.

186. See reports of Jan. 8, April 9, June 8, and June 21, 1921, in StA Hamburg, DHSG III, Pr IV 98, Ad. 1.

187. RWM memorandum, July 14, 1921, BAP, RWM, Nr. 2267/2, Bl. 158, and report of Jan. 13, 1922, ibid., Bl. 348f. See also RdI, *Geschäftliche Mitteilungen* 24 (Aug. 11, 1920), Lfd., Nr. 350, and 28 (Sept. 13, 1920), Lfd., Nr. 45.

188. Meetings of the retailers of the Hamburg HK, Dec. 17, 1920, and March 2, 1921, HK Archiv Hamburg, Nr. 102.1A.6.16 and Nr. 102.1A.6.18.

189. Meeting of Nov. 13, 1920, BAP, RWM, Nr. 2267/2, Bl. 17–25, quote on Bl. 25.

190. Meeting of April 6, 1921, ibid., Bl. 130–55, quote on Bl. 133.

191. Ibid., Bl. 154.

192. Report of June 3, 1921, StA Hamburg, Senatskommission für die Reichs- und auswärtigen Angelegenheiten, III Alc3, Bd. V.

193. RWM note of June 12, 1922, BAP, RWM, Nr. 2267/2, Bl. 393–98, quote on Bl. 397f.

194. Ibid., Bl. 398.

7. The Presentation of the Bill

1. John Maynard Keynes, *The Economic Consequences of the Peace* (London, 1920), and *A Revision of the Treaty* (New York, 1922); Etienne Mantoux, *The Carthaginian Peace, or the Economic Consequences of Mr. Keynes* (Pittsburgh, 1965).

2. Not all the authors involved follow this model, but it holds fairly well for Marc Trachtenberg, Stephen Schuker, and Walter McDougall. The most important contributions to the new historiography are: Marc Trachtenberg, *Reparation in World Politics. France and European Economic Diplomacy, 1916–1923* (New York, 1980); Stephen Schuker, *The End*

of French Predominance in Europe. The Financial Crisis of 1924 and the Adoption of the Dawes Plan (Chapel Hill, 1976), "Finance and Foreign Policy in the Era of the German Inflation: British, French and German Strategies for Economic Reconstruction After the First World War," in Büsch and Feldman, eds., *Historische Prozesse*, pp. 343–61, and "Frankreich und die Weimarer Republik," in Michael Stürmer, ed., *Die Weimarer Republik* (Königstein/Ts., 1980); Walter McDougall, *France's Rhineland Diplomacy* (Princeton, 1978), and "Political Economy versus National Sovereignty: French Structures for German Economic Integration After Versailles," *JMH* 51 (1979), pp. 4–23; Maier, *Recasting Bourgeois Europe*; Georges Soutou, "Die deutschen Reparationen und das Seydoux Projekt 1920/21," *VfZ* 23 (1975), pp. 237–70; Carl Schulkin, "Lost Opportunity: The Reparation Question and the Failure of the European Recovery Effort," Ph.D. diss., University of California at Berkeley, 1973; Jon Jacobson, "Strategies of French Foreign Policy after World War I," *JMH* 55 (1983), pp. 78–95; Denise Artaud, *La Question des dettes interalliées et la reconstruction de l'Europe 1917–1929* (Lille & Paris, 1978). A useful recent contribution that transcends some of the debates and puts them in a broader context is Anne Orde, *British Policy and European Reconstruction after the First World War* (Cambridge, 1990).

3. The most balanced and, in this writer's view, most accurate evaluation of German diplomacy and the reparations debate are provided by Peter Krüger in his masterful *Die Außenpolitik der Republik von Weimar* (Darmstadt, 1985), and in his important essay "Das Reparationsproblem der Weimarer Republik in fragwürdiger Sicht," *VfZ* 29 (1981), pp. 21–47. Bruce Kent, *Spoils of War,* provides an invaluable and judicious study of the entire problem.

4. Peter Krüger, "Struktur, Organisation und Wirkungsmöglichkeiten der leitenden Beamten des auswärtigen Dienstes 1921–1933," in Klaus Schwabe, ed., *Das Diplomatische Korps als Elite, 1871–1945* (Boppard am Rhein, 1985), pp. 101–69.

5. Keynes, *Economic Consequences*, Chap. 7. See also the fine discussion in Robert Skidelsky, *John Maynard Keynes. Hopes Betrayed 1883–1920* (London, 1983), Chap. 16.

6. Skidelsky, *Keynes*, pp. 393f.; Keynes to Bonn, Nov. 31, 1919, Duncker & Humblot to Keynes, June 11, 1920, and Keynes to Duncker & Humblot, June 19, 1920, John Maynard Keynes, Economic Papers, Marshall Library, Cambridge University, EC 1₂. In the United States, the book was published by Harcourt, Brace & Howe. The matter was arranged by Walter Lippmann and Felix Frankfurter. See Harcourt, Brace & Howe to Keynes, Oct. 2, 1919, ibid.

7. Warburg to Bonn, March 1, 1920, BAK, NL Bonn, Nr. 48.

8. Keynes to Norman Davis, April 18, 1920, Keynes Papers, Marshall Library, EC 1₂.

9. George Baker to Lionel Curtis, Feb. 9, 1920, ibid.

10. John T. Day of *The Shoe and Leather Record* to E.M. Tomkin, July 15, 1920, BAP, HAAA, Nr. 44935, Bl. 122f.

11. W. Langdon Brown to Keynes, Dec. 31, 1919, Keynes Papers, Marshall Library, EC 1₁.

12. Memorandum by the British Commercial Attaché, Thelwall, transmitted by Lord Kilmarnock to Lord Curzon, June 28, 1920, PRO, FO 371/4742/177–86, quote on 179.

13. Statement of the Union des Commercants et Industriels Francais des Pays Rhénans, Mainz, May 8, 1920; statement by the Chambers of Commerce of the Occupied Areas, Cologne, June 18, 1920; Letter to the Reich Economics and Reich Food Ministries of June 23, 1920, RWWK, 20/492/2.

14. Reports by Dufour of Aug. 4 and Sept. 6, 1920, BAP, HAAA, Nr. 47343, Bl. 8ff., 38ff.

15. Trachtenberg, *Reparation*, pp. 126–44; Maier, *Recasting*, pp. 234f.; Schulkin, "Lost Opportunity," pp. 152ff.

16. Trachtenberg, *Reparation*, pp. 116ff.; Potthoff, *Gewerkschaften*, pp. 235ff.

17. Stinnes to State Secretary Köster, May 25, 1920, ACDP, NL Stinnes, Nr. 027/5. See also Wulf, *Stinnes*, p. 189.

18. Wulf, *Stinnes*, pp. 190–93.

19. Stinnes's opposition to the Versailles military provisions were not without cogency. He favored the militia system because "with every other system we will go from one Putsch to the other and, beside this, cannot afford the cost of a mercenary army." Stinnes to Undersecretary Müller, April 29, 1920, ACDP, NL Stinnes, Nr. 028/3, and *Kabinett Müller*, pp. 158ff.

20. Quoted in Trachtenberg, *Reparation*, p. 148. See also Maier, *Recasting*, pp. 194ff., and Wulf, *Stinnes*, pp. 185ff.

21. Quoted in Trachtenberg, *Reparation*, p. 149.

22. Wulf, *Stinnes*, pp. 214ff.; Hartmut Pogge von Strandmann, ed., *Walther Rathenau. Industrialist, Banker, Intellectual, and Politician. Notes and Diaries 1907–1922* (Oxford, 1985), pp. 243–49; Moritz J. Bonn, *So macht man Geschichte. Bilanz eines Lebens* (Munich, 1953), pp. 244ff.; *Kabinett Fehrenbach*, pp. 41ff.

23. Bonn to Director von Stauss of the Deutsche Bank, July 28, 1920, BAK, NL Bonn, Nr. 48.

24. *Kabinett Fehrenbach*, p. xxxv.

25. D'Abernon to Curzon, July 5, 1920, PRO, FO 371/4738/51–52.

26. A British version of the Memorial dated Jan. 15, 1920 and addressed to Lloyd George, is to be found in the Keynes Economic Papers, Marshall Library, F 1₁, along with other important documents bearing on the Amsterdam meeting and its aftermath. The quotations here are from this version. For an illuminating discussion of the Amsterdam meetings in 1919 and the Brussels Financial Conference, see Silverman, *Reconstructing Europe*, pp. 272ff.

27. Ibid., pp. 276ff.; Carl Bergmann, *The History of Reparations* (New York and Boston, 1927), pp.

44f. The text of the conference reports are to be found in *VR*, Bd. 364, Anlage 922.

28. On Celier, see Trachtenberg, *Reparation*, p. 120. See also Celier to Keynes, June 20, 1920, Keynes Economic Papers, Marshall Library L20/1920.

29. Keynes to Celier, July 8, 1920, ibid.

30. Kent, *Spoils of War*, pp. 110–12.

31. Meeting of Oct. 27, 1920, BAK, NL Le Suire, Nr. 88, p. 70.

32. Ibid., p. 12.

33. Speech by Melchior, ibid., pp. 12ff., and guidelines for the Brussels conference, Dec. 3, 1920, *Kabinett Fehrenbach*, pp. 330ff.

34. RAM to RWM, Sept. 25, 1920, BAK, NL Le Suire, Nr. 105.

35. Bergmann, *Reparations*, p. 37. For Bonn's index schemes, see BAK, NL Bonn, Nr. 7f.

36. März, *Österreichische Bankpolitik*, pp. 367ff.; Orde, *British Policy*, pp. 112ff.

37. Meetings of Oct.–Nov. 1920, BAK, NL Le Suire, Nr. 88, p. 56. See also the remarks of Havenstein at these meetings and at the RB Curatorium's first postwar meeting, Sept. 20, 1920, SäHStA, Gesandtschaft Berlin, Nr. 1630, Bl. 61–80, esp. Bl. 69.

38. *Kabinett Fehrenbach*, p. 5.

39. Bonn to Melchior, Aug. 23, 1920, and reply of Aug. 25, BAK, NL Bonn, Nr. 48.

40. Oct.–Nov. 11, 1920, meetings, BAK, NL Le Suire, Nr. 88, p. 56.

41. Ibid., p. 64.

42. Ibid., p. 62.

43. Ibid., p. 117.

44. Ibid., p. 18.

45. ibid., p. 61.

46. Ibid., pp. 62f. Dietrich pointed out that the similarity of the German proposals to the settlement suggested by Keynes in his famous book was not likely to make them acceptable either.

47. Ibid., p. 63.

48. Ibid., p. 101.

49. Ibid., p. 104.

50. Ibid., p. 66.

51. Ibid., p. 105.

52. Keynes to Smuts, Oct. 22, 1920, Keynes Economics Papers, Marshall Library, L20/1920.

53. Legien at a meeting of the International Federation of Trade unions, Oct. 22–23, 1920, in Ruck, *Gewerkschaften*, pp. 224–27.

54. Wiedfeldt to Brockdorff-Rantzau, Nov. 26, 1920, Ernst Schröder, "Otto Wiedfeldt als Politiker und Botschafter der Weimarer Republik," *Beiträge zur Geschichte von Stadt und Stift Essen* 86 (1971), pp. 168f.

55. Meeting of Nov. 10, 1920, *Kabinett Fehrenbach*, pp. 272–74.

56. Report of Nov. 12, 1920, PRO, FO 371/4742/13.

57. Siemens to Stinnes, Nov. 4, 1920, and Stinnes to Siemens, Nov. 5, 1920, ACDP, NL Stinnes, Nr. 027/5. Wiedfeldt also refused to participate in gov-ernment sponsored negotiations on coal deliveries or reparations, and when the Foreign Office reproached him for this, pointing out that "you will concede that we cannot make foreign policy if everyone in Germany thinks they can run their own show," Wiedfeldt replied that he "had not noticed that the Foreign Office was making foreign policy." Wiedfeldt to Brockdorff-Rantzau, Nov. 26, 1920, in Schröder, *Beiträge* 86, p. 169.

58. *Kabinett Fehrenbach*, pp. 330–32.

59. Undated RWM memorandum from late November or early December 1920, BAK, NL Le Suire, Nr. 81.

60. Meeting of Dec. 16, 1920, BAK, NL Le Suire, Nr. 88, pp. 16ff.

61. Cabinet meeting, Dec. 8, 1920, *Kabinett Fehrenbach*, p. 337f.

62. Cabinet meeting, Dec. 20, 1920, *Kabinett Fehrenbach*, pp. 361–67.

63. Report of Nov. 24, 1920, AN AJ^5 774/14/16.

64. Dec. 16, 1920, meeting, BAK, NL Le Suire, Nr. 88, p. 14.

65. AN, AJ^5 774/14/16.

66. Meeting at Brussels, Dec. 16, 1920, BAK, NL Le Suire, Nr. 88, pp. 12ff.

67. Memorandum on Germany's capacity to pay by R.G. Hawtrey, Sept. 3, 1920, PRO, T/172/1142/18.

68. *VR*, Bd. 364, Drucksache Nr. 876, and *Kabinett Fehrenbach*, pp. 125f., 265f., 336.

69. See Havenstein's remarks to the RB Curatorium on Sept. 20, 1920, LHStA Dresden, Gesandtschaft Berlin, Nr. 1630, Bl. 71ff., and Fritz Naphtali, "Zwangsanleihe," *Plutus* (Dec. 8, 1920), pp. 378ff.

70. Kent, *Spoils of War*, pp. 114f.

71. Bergmann, *Reparations*, pp. 47ff.; Schulkin, "Lost Opportunity," pp. 298ff.; Trachtenberg, *Reparation*, pp. 175ff.

72. The Seydoux plans are discussed in Trachtenberg, *Reparation*, Chap. 4, and Soutou, *VfZ* (1975), pp. 244ff.

73. Le Suire to Scholz, Dec. 21, 1920, BAK, NL Le Suire, Nr. 108.

74. Le Suire to von Buttlar, Dec. 20, 1920, ibid.

75. Bonn to Ministerial Director von Simson, Jan. 10, 1921, BAK, NL Bonn, Nr. 4b. See also his report on Brussels, Dec.–Jan. 1920–1921, *Kabinett Fehrenbach*, pp. 379–86.

76. Ibid.

77. *Kabinett Fehrenbach*, p. 391; Wulf, *Stinnes*, pp. 249ff.

78. Meeting of Jan. 8, 1921, BAK, NL Le Suire, Nr. 120.

79. Report of the Bavarian Ambassador to Berlin, von Rohmer, Jan. 14, 1921, BayHStA, Abt. II, Gesandtschaft Berlin, Nr. 1098. See also Wulf, *Stinnes*, pp. 251ff.

80. Ibid.

81. *Kabinett Fehrenbach*, pp. 416f.

82. Schulkin, "Lost Opportunity," pp. 332ff., for

this quote and the discussion which follows. See also Trachtenberg, *Reparation,* pp. 188ff.

83. Supreme Council meeting, Jan. 27, 1921, DBFP, First Series, Vol. 15, p. 62.

84. Ibid., p. 63.

85. Ibid., p. 66.

86. Ibid., p. 72.

87. Ibid., pp. 102–4.

88. Soutou, *VfZ* (1975), pp. 265ff.

89. *VR,* Feb. 1, 1921, Bd. 347, pp. 2299ff.

90. *Schultheß' europäischer Geschichtskalender* (1921), 1, p. 59.

91. Ruck, *Gewerkschaften,* pp. 289f.

92. *Schultheß* (1921), 1, p. 59, and *Kabinett Fehrenbach,* pp. 476f.

93. Meeting of the experts on Feb. 19, 1921, BAK, NL Le Suire, Nr. 127, p. 31. See also Wulf, *Stinnes,* pp. 224ff.

94. Meeting of Feb. 25, 1921, p. 13, and meeting of Feb. 21, 1921, p. 4, BAK, NL Le Suire, Nr. 127.

95. Meeting of Feb. 22, 1921, ibid., p. 19.

96. Meeting of Feb. 19, 1921, ibid., pp. 22, 31.

97. *Kabinett Fehrenbach,* pp. 489–91, for the draft approved by the Cabinet, and DBFP, Vol. 15, pp. 223–25, for the English version presented to the Allies in London.

98. Meeting of Feb. 25, 1986, *Kabinett Fehrenbach,* pp. 485–89.

99. Report of the Saxon Ambassador to Munich, Feb. 24, 1921, SäHStA, Dresden, Außenministerium, Nr. 2981.

100. Eyck, *Weimar Republic,* Vol. I, p. 175; Kent, *Spoils,* p. 126f.

101. Allied conference, March 1, 1921, DBFP, Vol. 15, p. 227. See also Lloyd George's various remarks at the meetings in early March, ibid., pp. 216ff., and Bergmann, *Reparations,* pp. 63ff.

102. Wiedfeldt to Wirth, March 20, 1921, reprinted in Schröder, *Beiträge* 86, pp. 172f.

103. DBFP, Vol. 15, p. 258.

104. Ibid., pp. 261–65, for the quotations from this speech.

105. Ibid., pp. 246ff., for the Allied discussions of sanctions.

106. Stahmer report, Feb. 17, 1921, BAP, HAAA Handelsabteilung, Nr. 47339, Bl. 31–33. On April 18, 1921, the German Foreign Office passed this advice on to the RdI as well as the German Chamber of Commerce and Industry, warning that such ill-considered bragging increased the "general distaste for us in the world."

107. Stahmer report, Feb. 17, 1921, ibid., Bl. 33.

108. See Christoph Stamm, "Großbritannien und die Sanktionen gegen Deutschland vom März 1921," *Francia* 7 (1979), pp. 339–64, esp. pp. 344f.

109. *Kabinett Fehrenbach,* p. 530n4, and Pogge von Strandmann, *Walther Rathenau,* pp. 251f.

110. Bonn to Albert, March 8, 1921, BAK, NL Bonn, Nr. 2c.

111. *Kabinett Fehrenbach,* p. 544.

112. DBFP, Vol. 15, p. 328. For the negotiations on the new German proposal, see ibid., pp. 301–32. For the reactions in Berlin, see *Kabinett Fehrenbach,* pp. 508ff., 564ff.

113. Krüger, *Außenpolitik,* p. 124.

114. Kraemer to Wiedfeldt, March 12, 1921, ACDP, NL Stinnes, Nr. 019/2. See also Wiedfeldt to Havenstein, March 11, 1921, Schröder, *Beiträge* 86, pp. 175f.

115. Unsigned notes on a conversation with Stinnes on March 11, 1921, ACDP, NL Stinnes, Nr. 039/4, and report of von Rohmer, March 14, 1921, BayHStA, Abt. II, Gesandtschaft Berlin, Nr. 1098.

116. See the analysis by Le Suire made on London on March 3, 1921, BAK, NL Le Suire, Nr. 115.

117. See the remarks of General Director Deutsch of the AEG at the meeting of the Cabinet's Economic Committee on March 12, 1921, *Kabinett Fehrenbach,* pp. 558–62.

118. Meeting of the Economic Committee, March 17, 1921, BAK, NL Le Suire, Nr. 115. See also the remarks by the trade union RWR member, Schweitzer, at the meeting of the Economic Policy Committee of the RWR, March 23, 1921, BAP, RWR, Bd. 5, Bl. 234f.

119. RWR meeting of March 23, 1921, ibid., Bl. 239.

120. Wiedfeldt to State Secretary Albert, March 10, 1921, BAK, R 43I/18, Bl. 377–78; meetings of the directors of the Hamburg HK, Jan. 21, March 11 and 17, 1921, Commerzbibliothek Hamburg.

121. Undated and unsigned report of March 1921, "Two Weeks After London. Effect of Sanctions on the German Financial Market," possibly by Bresciani-Turroni, AN, AJ^5 2250/14.

122. Only New Zealand, Rumania, and Yugoslavia actually imposed the levy. See Stamm, *Francia* 7, pp. 345–52, 362; Report, "Two Weeks After London," AN, AJ^5 2250/14.

123. Ibid. and report of Henry T. Allen, British High Commissioner in the Rhineland, March 24, 1921, NA, 862T.01/268. The British enthusiasm for the occupation and the setting up the customs borders was very limited for both fiscal and political reasons. London was reluctant to supply the personnel necessary for financial reasons, wished to contain French ambitions in the Ruhr, feared that using troops for customs work would corrupt them, and preferred that the French receive the odium for the measures that were taken. See Stamm, *Francia* 7, pp. 352–59.

124. "Two Weeks After London," AN, AJ^5 2250/14.

125. Ibid., 2304/14/16; *Kabinett Fehrenbach,* pp. 595ff.; *Schultheß* (1921), pp. 260–62; Bergmann, *Reparations,* pp. 70f.

126. *Kabinett Fehrenbach,* pp. 561f., 599ff.; Albert to Wiedfeldt, March 18, 1921, BAK, R 43I/18, Bl. 380.

127. Reparations Commission report of April 16,

1921, AN, AJ⁵ 2304/14/16, and *Kabinett Fehrenbach*, p. 586.

128. Havenstein to Fehrenbach, March 4, 1921, BAK, R 43I/18, Bl. 76–79. Significantly, a copy is also to be found in the Stinnes Papers, ACDP, NL Stinnes, Nr. 019/2.

129. Material for the Curatorium meeting, March 21, 1921, BAP, RB, Nr. 6406, Bl. 12–14. For reports on the September 20, 1920, and the March 21, 1921, meetings, see SäHStA, Gesandtschaft Berlin, Nr. 1630, Bl. 61–80, 88–92.

130. Report of Dr. Keck, April 7, 1921, ibid., Bl. 92.

131. Havenstein to Fehrenbach, Feb. 1, 1921, *Kabinett Fehrenbach*, pp. 446–50.

132. Report of April 7, 1921, SäHStA, Gesandtschaft Berlin, Nr. 1622, Bl. 11–12.

133. Ibid.

134. Note of March 22, 1921, to the Saxon Foreign Minister, ibid., Bl. 3.

135. "Notendeckung," *Plutus* (April 13, 1921), pp. 122–27, quote on p. 127.

136. *Plutus* (March 16, 1921), p. 101.

137. Morsey and Ruppert, *Zentrumsparteiprotokolle*, pp. 157ff.; *Schultheß* (1921), pp. 294ff.; *Kabinett Fehrenbach*, pp. 612–14, 661–64.

138. *Zentrumsprotokolle*, pp. 174f.

139. DBFP, Vol. 15, p. 454.

140. Ibid., p. 463.

141. Schulkin, "Lost Opportunity," pp. 429ff.

142. Ibid., pp. 440ff., and Trachtenberg, *Reparation*, pp. 208ff.

143. Becker-Arnsberg at the Center Party *Fraktion* meeting, May 6, 1921, *Zentrumsprotokolle*, p. 185.

144. It is misleading to argue, as does Sally Marks, that "one wonders in what fashion they [the German government] celebrated, behind locked doors no doubt, when they received the Ultimatum of May 5." See Sally Marks, "Reparations Reconsidered: A Reminder," *CEH* 2 (1969), pp. 356–65, quote on p. 364. See David Felix's cogent reply, "Reparations Reconsidered with a Vengeance," ibid. 4 (1971), pp. 171–79, and Marks's response, "Reparations Reconsidered: A Rejoinder," ibid. 5 (1972), pp. 358–61. The most sensible evaluation is by Krüger, *VfZ* 29, pp. 2147. See also the useful analysis of Schulkin, "Lost Opportunity,", pp. 450–52. The Germans never denied that the London terms were an improvement over those of Paris. See Bergmann, *Reparations*, p. 77. For the text of the London Ultimatum, and Lloyd George's delivery of the demands to Ambassador Stahmer, See DBFP, Vol. 15, pp. 568ff.

145. VDESI executive directors meeting, May 6, 1921, BAK R 13/I, Nr. 159, Bl. 35f.

146. Ibid., Bl. 29f.

147. Report of April 28, 1921, SäHStA, Außenministerium, Nr. 2981.

148. Meeting of the Reichsrat Committee on Foreign Affairs, May 7, 1921 (report of May 8), BayHStA, Abt. II, Gesandtschaft Berlin, Nr. 1098.

149. Ibid.

150. Wulf, *Stinnes*, pp. 260ff.; Schröder, *Beiträge* 86, p. 177.

151. Ibid., p. 178f.

152. Henry A. Turner, Jr., *Stresemann and the Politics of the Weimar Republic* (Princeton, 1963), pp. 84ff.; Wulf, *Stinnes*, pp. 262ff.; *Kabinette Wirth*, I, xix–xxiii.

153. See Rudolf Morsey, *Die Deutsche Zentrumspartei 1917–1923* (Düsseldorf, 1966), pp. 379–85; *Zentrumsprotokolle*, pp. 191ff.; Hugo Stehkämper, "Konrad Adenauer und das Reichskanzleramt während der Weimarer Zeit," and Friedrich-Wilhelm Henning, "Finanzpolitische Vorstellungen und Maßnahmen Konrad Adenauers während seiner Kölner Zeit (1906–1933)," in Hugo Stehkämper, ed., *Konrad Adenauer. Oberbürgermeister von Köln. Festgabe der Stadt Köln zum 100. Geburtstag ihres Ehrenbürgers am 5. Januar 1976* (Köln, 1976), pp. 123–53, esp. pp. 140f., and pp. 405–31, esp. pp. 405ff. There does not appear to be any evidence for Henning Köhler's claim that Adenauer was not serious about his candidacy and that his conditions were a tactical maneuver to help Wirth into the candidacy. See Henning Köhler, *Adenauer und die Rheinische Republik. Der erste Anlauf 1918–1924* (Opladen, 1986), p. 128n10.

8. The Domestic Politics of Fulfillment, May 1921–January 1922

1. The Socialist Schweitzer at the Financial Policy Committee of the RWR, June 3, 1921, BAP, RWR, Bd. 547/2, Bl. 189.

2. Meeting of April 4, 1921, ibid., Bl. 279.

3. For the discussion which follows, see Finance Minister to Bergmann, May 14, 1921, Finance Ministry to Wirth, May 17, 1921, BAK, R 43I/19, Bl. 292–95; RB to Wirth, Sept. 5, 1921, BAK, R 43I/21, Bl. 145–53; Havenstein's reports at the RB Curatorium meetings of June 22 and Dec. 20, 1921, SäHStA, Gesandtschaft Berlin, Nr. 1630; RB Zentralausschuß meeting of Dec. 30, 1921, BAP, RB, Nr. 6435, Bl. 68–76; Cabinet meeting of May 17, 1921, and Wirth to D'Abernon, Aug. 16, 1921, *Kabinette Wirth*, I, pp. 2f., 199–201.

4. See Bradbury to Blacket, July 13, 1921, PRO, FO 371/5972/236f.

5. See the record of the discussions with the Guarantees Commission on Sept. 28, 1921, BAK, R 43I/21, Bl. 373. On the industrial contributions, see Vögler to Salomonsohn, July 26, 1921, ACDP, NL Stinnes, Nr. 057/4, and Cuno to Huldermann, July 16, 1920, HAPAG Archiv.

6. Report of the German General Consul in Amsterdam, Aug. 26, 1921, BAP, HAAA, Nr. 40289. Mannheimer had first turned to Rothschild, who had

already refused a similar request from Warburg. He then turned to a group of French banks led by Lazard Frères which, with the initial support of the French Finance Ministry, seemed to show a great interest in providing the loan as a means of preventing excessive fluctuations of the franc harmful to French exports. Although the Reichsbank and Reich government approved the arrangement, the French government suddenly changed its mind. Whether it did so because the last portion of the payment was going to go to Belgium and was thus of lesser interest to the French or for domestic political reasons was unknown. See RB to Wirth, Sept. 5, 1921, BAK, R 43I/21, Bl. 149–52. See also ten Cate in Feldman et al., *Consequences of Inflation*, p. 162f.

7. Vögler to Salomonsohn, July 26, 1921, ACDP, NL Stinnes, Nr. 057/4.

8. RB Curatorium meeting of June 22, 1921, SäHStA, Gesandtschaft Berlin, Nr. 1630, Bl. 97.

9. RB to the Chancellor, Sept. 5, 1921, BAK R 43I/21, Bl. 154.

10. For this and the quotes which follow, see RB Curatorium meeting, Dec. 20, 1921, ibid.

11. Quoted in *Kabinette Wirth*, I, p. 216n3. See also Williamson, *Helfferich*, pp. 296ff., 328f., and Epstein, *Erzberger*, pp. 352ff., 384ff.

12. See Witt in Mommsen et al., eds., *Industrielles System*, pp. 415ff., and in *Wealth and Taxation*, pp. 147ff.

13. See the extraordinary analysis in Peter-Christian Witt, "Reichsfinanzminister und Reichsfinanzverwaltung. Zum Problem des Verhältnisses von politischer Führung und bürokratischer Herrschaft in den Anfangsjahren der Weimarer Republik (1918/1924)," *VfZ* 23 (1975), pp. 1–61. An important and revealing discussion of these organizational questions took place at the Reich Economic Council meetings of Oct. 20–21, 1921, BAP, RWR, Bd. 548/3 and informs the discussion which follows.

14. RWR meeting of Oct. 21, 1921, ibid., Bl. 84.

15. Ibid., Bl. 77.

16. Finance Committee meeting, April 22, 1921, BAP, RWR, Nr. 547/2, Bl. 37.

17. RWR Finance Committee meeting of May 19, 1921, ibid., Bd. 547/2, Bl. 79–98.

18. RWR Finance Committee meeting of June 3, 1921, ibid., Bl. 155.

19. Comment by former Undersecretary Heinrich Göppert at the meeting of Oct. 14, 1921, ibid., Bl. 393f.

20. *Kabinette Wirth*, I, pp. 7–13, and BAK, R 43I/20, Bl. 331–41. The second version, reprinted in Hirsch, *Währungsfrage*, pp. 58–69, is used as the basis of the discussion here.

21. Memorandum of June 27, 1921, BAK, R 43I/20, Bl. 340. As the economic editor of the *FZ*, Anton Feiler, noted: "The idea of seizing so-called gold values apparently also came about because of the realization that the previous Emergency Capital Levy also had a very unjust effect in that it taxed owners of paper obligations according to the same rates as owners of real values, although the development of their respective value had taken an absolutely opposite turn in that the owners of paper values have actually been expropriated through the monetary depreciation, while the owners of real values have been affected by this development to a much lesser degree." See *Verhandlungen der Sozialisierungskommission über die Reparationsfragen*, 3 vols. (Berlin, 1921/22), I, p. 247.

22. See Anton Feiler's remarks, ibid.

23. Wirth at a meeting on Sept. 27, 1921, *Zentrumsprotokolle*, p. 240. This suggests that Ernst Laubach, *Die Politik der Kabinette Wirth 1921/22* (Lübeck, 1968), p. 62, is incorrect in arguing that Wirth initially favored the basic idea of the plan and only changed his mind in June because of the political constellation.

24. *VR*, June 1, 1921, Bd. 349, p. 3711f.

25. Statement by Edler von Braun, June 2, 1921, ibid., p. 3738.

26. *Kabinette Wirth*, I, p. 116. There is an excellent analysis of the political situation by the Bavarian representative in Berlin in a report of June 7, 1921, BayHStA, Gesandtschaft Berlin, Nr. 1098, who could not forebear noting, however, that the Cabinet once again contained "4 Jews or Jewish types [*Judentümliche*]"—Gradenauer, Schiffer, Rosen, and Rathenau. Hirsch's complaints about being left in the lurch by Schmidt and Wirth are to be found in his diary entries for 1921, Julius Hirsch Papers.

27. On Zapf, see Witt, *VfZ* (1975), p. 23, and for his views see his memorandum of May 24, 1921, in BAK, NL Le Suire, Nr. 131, and *Kabinette Wirth*, p. 6f.

28. Zapf memorandum of May 24, 1921, BAK, NL Le Suire, Nr. 131.

29. Undated memorandum, but certainly of May 1921, by Zapf and Privy Councilor Schröder, ibid.

30. Laubach, *Kabinette Wirth*, p. 61n226.

31. See the Reich Finance Ministry memorandum of June 27, 1921, in which a Reichstag speech by Labor Minister Brauns is cited to the effect that a "sick economic body such as the German Reich is today, cannot make experiments." *Kabinette Wirth*, I, p. 97.

32. Cabinet meeting of June 29, 1921, ibid., p. 118.

33. For Hirsch's criticism, see ibid., I, p. 119n1. The RFM proposals were presented in a countermemorandum to the Schmidt program of June 27, 1921, ibid., pp. 91–97. See also the meeting of June 29, 1921, ibid., pp. 155–57. For the relative lack of alarm on the part of those who were to pay the taxes, see Maier, *Recasting*, p. 255. Wirth presented the entire program to the Reichstag on July 6, 1921; that is, nearly two months after taking office. See *VR*, Bd. 350, pp. 4469–73.

34. *Kabinette Wirth*, pp. 2ff., 218f.

35. See the report by Lord D'Abernon of April 2, 1921, and the comments pertaining to it in PRO, FO 371/6047/233–35. The concern was well taken be-

cause the trends noted were to persist through the next two decades. See Petzina et al., *Sozialgeschichtliches Arbeitsbuch III*, p. 74.

36. The memorandum is dated May 24, 1921, BAK, NL Le Suire, Nr. 131. On Beusch, see Witt, *VfZ* 23, p.10n39.

37. Unsigned memorandum, May 24, 1921, BAK, NL Le Suire, Nr. 131.

38. Rathenau diary, June 12, 1921, in Strandmann, *Rathenau*, p. 256.

39. Meeting of Sept. 5, 1921, *Kabinette Wirth*, I, pp. 218f. Previously, the Reich Economic Council had been asked to devise a new index scheme. A report was written by Hilferding, which did a splendid job of showing the inadequacies of the use of exports as a measure of prosperity and which effectively listed all the factors that should be taken into account. The report was published in *Plutus* (July 20, 1921), pp. 240–42.

40. See the Beusch memorandum of May 24, 1921, BAK, NL Le Suire, Nr. 131, and *Kabinette Wirth*, I, pp. 44f.

41. See the meetings of Sept. 28–29, 1921, BAK, R 43I/21, Bl. 368–79.

42. Hirsch had apparently also played a role in these efforts to bring Rathenau into the government, which are described in a discussion of Rathenau in the Julius Hirsch Papers.

43. See David Felix, *Walther Rathenau and the Weimar Republic. The Politics of Reparations* (Baltimore & London, 1971), pp. 67f.; Trachtenberg, *Reparations* pp. 216ff.; Laubach, *Politik*, pp. 73ff.; Strandmann, *Rathenau*, pp. 252ff.; Wulf, *Stinnes*, pp. 317ff. On Rathenau's consultations with industry before and after taking office, see Rathenau to Stinnes, Oct. 20, 1921, and Sorge to Stinnes, Oct. 26, 1921, ACDP, NL Stinnes, Nr. 041/2.

44. For the text, see *VR*, Bd. 369, Drucksache Nr. 2792. See also Kent, *Spoils of War*, pp. 149ff.

45. Strandmann, *Rathenau*, p. 257.

46. Walther Rathenau, *Gesammelte Reden* (Berlin, 1924), p. 257. See also "Der Rathenau = Pakt," *Plutus* (Oct. 12, 1921), pp. 335–37. As one British official wryly commented on the margins of a report of October 13 by the Commercial Secretary Thewall, "An absurd phrase of Rathenau's remote from the facts. It would be equally applicable to Bill Sykes" (the professional thief in Dickens's *Oliver Twist*), PRO, FO 371/5976/205.

47. Stinnes to Rathenau, Oct. 19, 1921, ACDP, NL Stinnes, Nr. 091/2. Copies of the correspondence under discussion here can also be found in the NL Stresemann, 6992/H140573ff. My discussion and argument here run parallel to that of Wulf, *Stinnes*, pp. 317–24.

48. Rathenau to Stinnes, Oct. 20 and 24, 1921; Sorge to Stinnes, Oct. 26, 1921, ACDP, NL Stinnes, Nr. 041/2.

49. Stinnes to Rathenau, Oct. 19, 1920, ibid.

50. For an excellent analysis of these various complexities, see Lothar Albertin, "Die Verantwortung der liberalen Parteien für das Scheitern der Großen Koalition im Herbst 1921," *HZ* 205 (1967), pp. 566–627. See also, *Kabinette Wirth*, I, pp. xxx, xlviiff., and Cabinet meeting of Aug. 4, 1921, pp. 186–89; Laubach, *Politik*, pp. 34ff.; Wulf, *Stinnes*, pp. 269ff.; Ernst Schröder, *Otto Wiedfeldt. Eine Biographie* [*Beiträge zur Geschichte von Stadt und Stift Essen*, 80] (Essen, 1964), pp. 125ff.

51. Rathenau to Gustav Müller, Aug. 18, 1921, Walther Rathenau, *Politische Briefe* (Dresden, 1929), p. 303, and Vögler to Stinnes, Aug. 15, 1929, ACDP, NL Stinnes, Nr. 057/14. For Wiedfeldt's views, see the report of Guggenheimer on the Sept. 3, 1921, meeting of the RdI directors, WA/M.A.N.-A., K75.

52. Vögler to Stinnes, Aug. 29, 1921, ibid., Nr. 043/6, which makes reference to Rathenau's visit. Apparently, the Wiesbaden negotiations were not discussed.

53. Stinnes to Vögler, Aug. 23, 1921, ibid.

54. Ibid.

55. Meeting of RdI directors, Sept. 3, 1921, WA/M.A.N.-A., K75.

56. Meeting of Sept. 7, 1921, *Kabinette Wirth*, I, pp. 237–41, quotation on p. 240.

57. Kraemer to Stinnes, Sept. 9, 1921, and Bücher to Stinnes, Sept. 8, 1921, ACDP, NL Stinnes, Nr. 038/3. Copies of these documents as well as certain others to be discussed below are also to be found in BAK, NL Hugenberg, Nr. 27, Bl. 392–404. It would appear that Hugenberg was kept fully informed by Stinnes.

58. The discussion and quotations which follow are taken from an undated letter to Bücher, ACDP, NL Stinnes, NL O38/3. For some odd reason, this important letter is identified as having been written in "October or November 1921." It is clearly a response to the Bücher–Kraemer letters to Stinnes of Sept. 8–9, while internal evidence clearly demonstrates that another document to be discussed below that is dated Sept. 13 was written between Sept. 10 and 12, 1921.

59. Report on discussion between Bücher and Thomas and Osius, Sept. 13, 1921, ACDP, NL Stinnes, Nr. 038/3.

60. See their remarks at the meeting with Wirth on Sept. 7 as well as Wirth's remarks to the Inter-Party Committee of the Reichstag on Sept. 13, *Kabinette Wirth*, I, pp. 237–41, 254–56.

61. Ibid., and marginal comment on letter from Bücher to Stinnes of Sept. 8, 1921, BAK, NL Hugenberg, Nr. 27, Bl. 395.

62. On the tensions between the "Berliners" in the various industrial organizations and their colleagues and constituents in the provinces, see the illustrations scattered throughout Feldman and Steinisch, *Industrie und Gewerkschaften*. A most revealing account of the entire history of the industrial credit action is to be found in the report given by Director Mann to the Association of Palatine Industrialists on Nov. 25, 1921, VPI Archiv.

63. *Kabinette Wirth*, I, pp. 265–69, 271, for the meetings of September 14 and 17. The bankers at the first meeting were Warburg, Salomonsohn, Gutmann, Bernhard, and Wassermann. Fifty representatives of the banks attended the second meeting. Osius reported on the Sept. 13–14 meetings in a report erroneously dated Sept. 13. Thomas and Osius apparently hoped that the meeting would collapse over the tensions between industry and the banks. Report on discussion between Bücher and Thomas and Osius, Sept. 13 (14), 1921, ACDP, NL Stinnes, Nr. 038/3.

64. Wirth had already discussed the matter, "confidentially," with the Inter-Party Committee on Sept. 13, and the official statement was issued the next day following a report in a Berlin newspaper. See *Kabinette Wirth*, I, p. 255, and BAK, R 43I/2449, Bl. 41f.

65. The sporting metaphor is that of Wirth himself. See Wirth's remarks at the Sept. 27, 1921, meeting of the Center Party Reichstag delegation, *Zentrumsprotokolle*, pp. 238ff. On the Görlitz meeting, see Richard Breitman, *German Socialism and Weimar Democracy* (Chapel Hill, 1981), pp. 83ff.; Winkler, *Revolution zur Stabilisierung*, pp. 434ff.; *Protokoll über die Verhandlungen des Parteitages der Sozialdemokratischen Partei Deutschlands, abgehalten in Görlitz vom 18. bis 24. September 1921* (Berlin, 1921).

66. Meeting of Sept. 26, 1921, *Kabinette Wirth*, I, pp. 286–90.

67. Guggenheimer report on the RdI meeting of Sept. 27, 1921, WA/M.A.N.-A., K75, and report by Director Mann, VPI Archiv.

68. See the excellent report of Oct. 1, 1921, by the Saxon HK representative, SäHStA, Gesandtschaft Berlin, Nr. 471, Bl. 183–89. Important details are also to be found in the report by Director Mann, VPI Archiv.

69. *Kabinette Wirth*, I, p. 325n1.

70. Max Hachenburg, *Lebenserinnerungen eines Rechtsanwalts und Briefe aus der Emigration* [*Veröffentlichungen des Stadtarchivs Mannheim*, Bd. 5] (Mannheim, 1978), p. 199. For the text, see also Hauschild, *Reichswirtschaftsrat*, pp. 614–17.

71. Hachenburg, *Lebenserinnerungen*, p. 200; Maier, *Recasting*, p. 258; *Kabinette Wirth*, I, p. 326n3; Wulf, *Stinnes*, pp. 278ff.

72. Bernhard's idea, which sought to deal with the apparent inability of the Reich tax authorities to handle the assessment problems they faced, was discussed in the Finance Committee of the RWR on November 24–25 (BAP, RWR, Nr. 549, Bd. 4) and was then sent to a special committee which eventually came to the conclusion that no means could be found for such tax communities to organize the distribution of the burden because of the immense individual differences among and within the various industries. See also Hauschild, *Reichswirtschaftsrat*, p. 371. For Bernhard's support of the Hachenburg proposal, see *Plutus* (Nov. 9, 1921), pp. 370–80. For an illustration of how industrialists connected the Bern-

hard and Hachenburg schemes, see Reichert's speech to the VDESI in May 1922, BAK, R 131/160, Bl. 10.

73. Meeting of Oct. 18, 1921, *Kabinette Wirth*, I, pp. 325f. On the unauthorized character of these negotiations, see the report by Director Mann, Nov. 25, 1921, VPI Archiv. On the anticipation that industry could never get its loan, see Bernhard in *Plutus* (Nov. 9, 1921), pp. 370f.

74. NL Stresemann, Nr. 3093/H140554-61.

75. Meeting of the Inter-Party Committee, Oct. 20, 1921, *Kabinette Wirth*, I, p. 331. In this discussion, I follow very closely the analysis of Albertin, *Historische Zeitschrift* 45, pp. 587–601.

76. Laubach, *Politik*, p. 97ff., and the excellent if very antiparliamentary report of the Bavarian representative in Berlin of Oct. 27, 1921, BayHstA, Gesandtschaft Berlin, Nr. 1098.

77. Sorge to Stinnes, Oct. 26, 1921, ACDP, NL Stinnes, Nr. 026/2. Neither Pogge von Strandmann, *Rathenau*, p. 271, nor David Felix, *Rathenau*, pp. 103f., had access to this evidence on Rathenau's actions and motives.

78. Stinnes telegram to Sorge, Oct. 27, 1920, ACDP, NL Stinnes, Nr. 041/2.

79. The invitations to the meeting were sent on October 25, SAA, 11/Lg 748.

80. See his article "Nicht Wirtschaft, Politik ist Schicksal!" from the *Deutsche Zeitung*. Blohm recommended Bang's analyses in a letter to Reichert of Oct. 28, 1921, StA Hamburg, Blohm & Voss, Nr. 64.

81. In early October, Hugenberg seemed very resigned and apathetic about what could be accomplished in the RdI. See his letter to Stinnes of Oct. 7, 1921, ACDP, NL Stinnes, Nr. 025/1.

82. Stinnes to Hugenberg, Oct. 9, 1921, ACDP, NL Stinnes, Nr. 025/1.

83. Report by Osius on discussions with a Mr. Robbins on Oct. 12, 1921, ibid., Nr. 273/1.

84. Ibid.

85. Stinnes to Siemens, Oct. 22, 1921, ibid., Nr. 026/2.

86. Telegram of Nov. 4, 1921, StA Hamburg, Blohm & Voss, Nr. 64. Blohm read the message to the meeting. See also the correspondence between Reichert and Blohm, Oct. 28–29, 1921, as well as his correspondence with Director Stahl of the Vulcan-Werke of Oct. 31–Nov. 4, ibid., and the notes of the Lignite Association and the Mining Branch to the RdI of Nov. 1 and 3, 1921, in BAK, NL Silverberg, Nr. 297, Bl. 1–7.

87. Some of the "atmospheric" details presented here are based on the account in the *Bergisch-Märkische Zeitung* of Nov. 7, 1921, in StA Hamburg, Blohm & Voss, Nr. 64. The same collection also contains an unsigned report on the meeting. The account here and in the discussion which follows is also based on the report given by Director Mann on Nov. 25 in VPI Archiv, and the report given by the representative of the Saxon chambers of commerce of Nov. 7, 1921, SäHStA, Gesandtschaft Berlin, Nr. 471, Bl.

196–210. Citations will be given only for the more significant quotations.

88. Report on meeting in StA Hamburg, Blohm & Voss, Nr. 64.

89. Ibid.

90. Ibid.

91. See the Saxon Representative's report, Sä-HstA, Dresden, Gesandtschaft Berlin, Nr. 471, Bl. 203f.

92. As reported in the notes to be found in StA Hamburg, Blohm & Voss, Nr. 64.

93. See the transcript of his speech in Schröder, *Wiedfeldt*, pp. 181–86, quote on p. 183.

94. Ibid.

95. While the version in Schröder, *Wiedfeldt*, contains an attack on Hasslacher for accusing Wiedfeldt of failing to inform his colleagues in the Ruhr about the credit offer, it does not contain this phraseology. The quotation is taken from the report in the StA Hamburg, Blohm & Voss, Nr. 64. This report was prepared from notes made at the meeting, and it is reasonable to assume that the version in the Krupp archive drawn upon by Schröder may have been "cleaned up" by Wiedfeldt. For Wiedfeldt's reactions to the meeting, see Wiedfeldt to Sorge, Nov. 7, 1921, Schröder, *Wiedfeldt*, pp. 187–90.

96. Schröder, *Wiedfeldt*, p. 188.

97. Report on meeting, StA Hamburg, Blohm & Voss, Nr. 64.

98. Report of Director Mann, VPI Archiv.

99. *Kabinette Wirth*, I, p. 368n1, for the text of the resolution. The passage of the Bücher resolution dealing with the establishment of a legal basis for the action involving compulsion was in fact used as an interpretive gloss on the resolution in subsequent negotiations with the trade unions and the government, ibid., p. 372n9. For the details of the negotiation in the committee, see Wiedfeldt to Sorge, Nov. 7, 1921, Schröder, *Wiedfeldt*, pp. 187–90.

100. Ibid., and report on the meeting in StA Hamburg, Blohm & Voss, Nr. 64.

101. Stinnes to Bücher, Aug. 9, 1921, ACDP, NL Stinnes, Nr. 038/3.

102. For the discussion and quotations in this paragraph, see the meeting of Nov. 10, 1921, *Kabinette Wirth*, I, pp. 368–73. On Stinnes' exploitation of tensions between the various groups of workers, see ibid., p. 386.

103. Meeting of Nov. 10, 1921, *Kabinette Wirth*, I, pp. 375–78.

104. Blohm to Hugenberg, Nov. 7, 1921, StA Hamburg, Blohm & Voss, Nr. 64.

105. Duisberg to Frank, Dec. 28, 1921, WA Bayer-Leverkusen Autographensammlung Duisberg. On the negative attitudes of other industries and industrialists, see Osius to Stinnes, Nov. 24, 1921, ACDP, NL Stinnes, Nr. 022/3.

106. ADGB Bundesausschuß meeting, Dec. 13–17, 1921, in Ruck, *Gewerkschaften*, p. 420. For the Ten Demands, see ibid., pp. 397–99.

107. Duisberg to Frank, Nov. 17, 1921, WA Bayer-Leverkusen, Autographensammlung Duisberg.

108. Reusch to Bücher, Jan. 25, 1922, and Bücher to Reusch, Jan. 26, 1922, HA/GHH, Nr. 30019320/7.

109. Meetings of Nov. 11, 1921, *Kabinette Wirth*, I, p. 385.

110. For a good synopsis of these problems, see *Kabinette Wirth*, I, xxxvi–xxxviii.

111. Discussions of Nov. 14 and 19, 1921, *Kabinette Wirth*, I, pp. 394–96, 411–12.

112. Meeting of Dec. 3, 1921, ibid., pp. 450–52.

113. Blohm to Bang, Nov. 22, 1921, and for similar sentiments on the Wirth committee, Blohm to Sorge, Dec. 10, 1921, StA Hamburg, Blohm & Voss, Nr. 64.

114. Meeting of Dec. 13, 1921, *Kabinette Wirth*, I, pp. 463–65.

115. *Sozialisierungskommission*, II, p. 86.

116. Bonn to Wirth, Nov. 18, 1921, BAK, NL Bonn, Nr. 4b.

117. For a good brief summary, see Carol Fink, *The Genoa Conference. European Diplomacy, 1921–1922* (Chapel Hill, 1984), pp. 14ff. Also, see Trachtenberg, *Reparation*, pp. 216ff. The best discussion of British motives at this time is Orde, *British Policy*, pp. 160ff.

118. Speech by Wirth to the Foreign Policy Committee of the Reichsrat, Jan. 16, 1922, report by von Praeger, BayHStA, Gesandtschaft Berlin, Nr. 1099.

119. Report of Sept. 20, 1921, BAP, RWM, Nr. 7624, Bl. 110f.

120. General Consulate Naples to the RB, Nov. 28, 1921, BAP, RB, Nr. 6435, Bl. 60–62. The General Consulate estimated that there were some six billion marks in Italy, a substantial portion of which were in Naples, which had become a major financial center and center of speculation during and after the war.

121. Report of Bendix, March 6, 1922 (erroneously dated 1921), BAP, HAAA, Nr. 43817, Bl. 125.

122. Austin Hanison, editor of the *English Review*, to Bonn, Nov. 9, 1921, BAK, NL Bonn, Nr. 49.

123. Maier, *Recasting Bourgeois Europe*, p. 267.

124. Report of March 6, 1922, BAP, HAAA, Nr. 43817, Bl. 126–28.

125. Meeting of Nov. 14, 1921, *Kabinette Wirth*, I, pp. 394f. Bendix learned that Kindersley was pushing hard for a moratorium while visiting London in December. See his report of March 6, 1922, BAP, HAAA, Nr. 43817.

126. See his remarks to the Reichsbank Curatorium at its Dec. 20, 1921, meeting, report of Dec. 27, 1921, SäHStA, Gesandtschaft Berlin, Nr. 1630.

127. For this discussion and the quotations, see Norman to Havenstein, Dec. 10, 1921, BAP, RB, Nr. 6394, Bl. 106–10.

128. Ibid.

129. Reprinted in *Kabinette Wirth*, I, p. 465n7. See also the report of the Bavarian Reichsrat Delegate von Praeger on the meeting of the Reichstag Com-

mittee for Foreign Affairs of Dec. 16, 1921, dated Dec. 22, BayHStA, Gesandtschaft Berlin, Nr. 1098.

130. Reported to Rathenau on Dec. 2, 1921, Strandmann, *Rathenau*, p. 277. More generally on the Stinnes trip, see Wulf, *Stinnes*, pp. 289ff., and Fink, *Genoa*, p. 20.

131. See his notes in Strandmann, *Rathenau*, pp. 273–83, and his report to the Cabinet on Dec. 12, 1921, *Kabinette Wirth*, I, pp. 463–66. Rathenau also took advantage of his first visit to London to talk with American Ambassador Harvey in the presence of the American commander in the Rhineland, General Henry T. Allen, on December 1. Rathenau expressed the fear, already stated to Ambassador D'Abernon in early November, that the French would invade the Ruhr if the Germans failed to make their payments and warned that the British would need American backing in trying to prevent this. The Americans appear to have been much impressed with Rathenau's seriousness. See Ernst Schulin, ed., *Walther Rathenau. Hauptwerke und Gespräche* (Heidelberg, 1977), pp. 844f.

132. "Notizen über eine Reise nach London in den Tagen vom 1. bis 8. Dezember 1921," by an unsigned confident of Stinnes, ACDP, NL Stinnes, Nr. 048/4.

133. Ibid., and Pogge von Strandmann, *Rathenau*, pp. 281f.

134. Bendix report of March 6, 1922, on a talk with Rathenau in December 1921. Dunn did not seem to have a very good reputation in some British banking circles, since one banker told Bendix that "it is very regrettable that greater caution is not exercised on the German side in selecting such people to deal with." BAP, HAAA, Nr. 43817, Bl. 129f.

135. Norman to Havenstein, Dec. 10, 1921, BAP, RB, Nr. 6394, Bl. 108f.

136. This discussion is based on the report of von Praeger of Dec. 22, 1921, BayHStA, Abt. II, Gesandtschaft Berlin, Nr. 1098.

137. Ibid.

138. Coded Cable from D'Abernon, Jan. 6, 1922, PRO, FO 371/7473/311/35–37. Ebert took a line similar to that of Wirth in his talk with the British Ambassador.

139. For this discussion, see Trachtenberg, *Reparation*, pp. 225ff.; Felix, *Rathenau*, pp. 115ff.; Fink, *Genoa*, pp. 37ff.; Bergmann, *Reparations*, pp. 113ff. The thirty-one million marks to be paid every ten days represented the amount of foreign currency that the Committee of Guarantees required to be deposited as security for reparation payments from German customs receipts.

140. Report of von Praeger, Jan. 19, 1922, BayHStA, Abt. II, Gesandtschaft Berlin, Nr. 1099.

141. Ibid. In private conversation with Lord D'Abernon on December 1, Rathenau also spoke of the "opium dream of the inflation" coming to an end and foresaw a period of depression both in England and in Germany. Schulin, *Rathenau. Hauptwerke und Gespräche*, pp. 841f.

142. Report of von Praeger, Jan. 19, 1922, BayHStA, Abt. II, Gesandtschaft Berlin, Nr. 1099.

143. "Walther Rathenau," Julius Hirsch Papers.

144. Retold by Hans von Raumer and quoted in Schulin, *Rathenau. Hauptwerke und Gespräche*, p. 847.

9. The Transition to Galloping Inflation

1. For an important discussion of the instrumental character of economic theories and the choices made among them, see Holtfrerich, *German Inflation*, pp. 155–63.

2. Meeting of the RWR Finance Committee, Nov. 11, 1921, BAP, RWR, Nr. 548, Bd. 3, Bl. 363.

3. Ibid., Bl. 364.

4. Maier, *Recasting*, p. 262.

5. BAP, RWR, Nr. 548, Bd. 3, Bl. 369.

6. Ibid., Bl. 376f.

7. Ibid., Bl. 379.

8. Laubach, *Politik*, pp. 69–71.

9. Reports of the employer associations, July 8, 1921, and report of the Chamber of Commerce of Koblenz, June 2, 1921, RWWK, 3/21/10. The exports of the electrotechnical industry dropped from 315 million tons in January 1921 to 169 million in May. See the report of the RWM for May 1921, BAK R 43I/1147, Bl. 466

10. Report of Aug. 4, 1921, NA, 8627.01/309.

11. Ibid.

12. State Secretary Hirsch sought to convince the French that the sanctions and French policies endangered reparations payments. See *Kabinette Wirth*, I, p. 206n12.

13. Meeting of the Retailers Committee of the German Chamber of Commerce and Industry, Nov. 9–10, 1921, WAAK, 20/420/7.

14. British Embassy report, Nov. 27, 1921, PRO, FO 371/5979/49.

15. Report of Nov. 5, 1921, BayHStA, Abt. II, MA 102 147.

16. Report of Nov. 23, 1921, PRO, FO 371/5979/30–31.

17. *Sozialisierungskommission*, I, pp. 173–78.

18. See the letters of the Association of German Piano Dealers, April 19, 1921, the Leather Industry Association of Rhineland–Westphalia of June 27, 1921, the Schauburg Film Theatre of Nov. 5, 1921 in WAAK, 20/48/5.

19. "Börsenterminhandel" in *Plutus* (Nov. 23, 1921), p. 389.

20. In 1920, the index had increased much more modestly; that is, from 100 in January to 165 in December. Bresciani-Turroni, *Economics of Inflation*, p. 260.

21. *Plutus* (Oct. 12, 1921), pp. 350f.

22. Ibid. (Nov. 23, 1921), p. 389.

23. "Sturmtage," *Plutus* (Dec. 7, 1921), p. 408.

24. "Devisenhändler," *Plutus* (Dec. 7, 1921), pp. 416f.

25. "Bankbruch," *Plutus* (Dec. 21, 1921), pp. 424-27.

26. *Plutus* (Nov. 9, 1921), p. 387.

27. "Sturmtage," *Plutus* (Dec. 7, 1921), p. 408.

28. Steinthal to Bierwes, Nov. 7, 1921, Mannesmann-Archiv, M 11.089, Bl. 398.

29. Steinthal to Bierwes, Dec. 7, 1921, ibid., M 11.089, Bl. 35f.

30. Steinthal to Bierwes, Jan. 13, 1921, ibid., Bl. 11.

31. Steinthal to Bierwes, Jan. 26 and Jan. 30, 1922, ibid., Bl. 137f., 152.

32. Steinthal to Bierwes, Jan. 26, 1922, ibid., Bl. 138f.

33. "Spekulation und Wirtschaft," *Plutus* (Dec. 21, 1921), pp. 428-34.

34. Retrospective report by Director Klemme to Director Woltmann, Dec. 27, 1923, HA/GHH, Nr. 300000/5.

35. Lindenlaub, *Maschinenbauunternehmen*, pp. 91f., 100f.

36. Ibid., pp. 114f. See the list of the policies of the export control boards dated Jan. 16, 1922, BAK, R 43I/24, Bl. 318-21.

37. Report of the German consulate in Naples, Nov. 28, 1921, BAP, RB, Nr. 6435, Bl. 60-62.

38. See the reports of Nadolny from the German embassy in Stockholm, Dec. 30, 1921, and Feb. 25, 1922, GStAKM, Rep. 120, C XIII 7, Nr. 1, Bd. 22, Bl. 336-39, 351-54. See also his report of Aug. 16, 1921, and the copy of a letter of the Swedish Deputy Erik Rörig to Ministerial Councillor Sjöberg, Dec. 15, 1921, BAP, HAAA, Nr. 64075, Bl. 337, 353f., and the reports by Nadolny and Wied of Sept. 27 and Oct. 28, in ibid., Nr. 65437, Bl. 71-75.

39. For the formulation of government policy and its economic rationale, see the meeting in the RWM of Oct. 28, 1921, on the reintroduction of export bans and the strengthening of controls, BAP, RWM, Nr. 2434/1, Bl. 626-30.

40. See the lengthy debates in Economic Policy Committee of the RWR in October and November 1921, BAP, RWR, Bd. 6.

41. Report by Justus Strandes, Sept. 21, 1921, StA Hamburg, Staatskommission für die Reichs- und auswärtigen Angelegenheiten, III A1c3, Bd. II. Sept. 21, 1921.

42. Strandes report of Oct. 20, 1921, ibid.

43. BAP, RWR, Nr. 548, Bd. 3, Bl. 382.

44. Ibid., Bl. 389f.

45. For a complete list of the decisions taken by the thirty-six major industrial groups organized in export control boards, see BAK R 43I/24, Bl. 318-21. It should also be noted that some of the subgroups were allowed to make their own arrangements within the general lines laid down by the industrial branch. The reporting of foreign exchange receipts, which was required on a monthly basis, was to be made to a new Reichsbank agency, the "Foreign Exchange Delivery Control Bureau of the Reichsbank" (Devisen-Ablieferungskontrolle der Reichsbank). See the

analysis by Parmelee in his report of Dec. 6, 1921, NA, 620.51/1417.

46. RWR Finance Policy Committee meeting, Nov. 12, 1921, BAP, Nr. 549, Bd. 4, Bl. 14f.

47. Ibid., Bl. 32ff., quote on Bl. 40.

48. Statement by the DVP Deputy Hugo at the RWR Economic Policy Committee, Oct. 17, 1921, ibid., Nr. 6, Bl. 355.

49. Report of Ambassador von Neurath, Nov. 3, 1921, GStAKM, Rep. 120, C XIII l, Nr. 38B, Bd. 7, Bl. 55-57.

50. Report by Adolf Müller, Dec. 31, 1921, ibid., Rep. 120, C XIII 5, Nr. 3, Bd. 28, Bl. 64-72, quote on Bl. 72. See also the meeting of the south German chambers of commerce with the German Chamber of Commerce in Zürich, Nov. 7, 1921, ibid., Bl. 76-94.

51. See "Vorbereitungen zur Arbeitsbeschaffung in der bevorstehenden rückläufigen Konjunktur," drawn up by Dr. Löwe and the "Leitsätze zu dem Programm der Wirtschaftsminister-Konferenz vom 12. Dezember 1921," BAP, RWM, Nr. 2434/2, Bl. 177-79, 193f.

52. Report of Dec. 30, 1921, GStAKM, Rep. 120, C XIII 7, Nr. 1, Bd. 22, Bl. 336-39. On March 3, 1921, the German Ambassador in London, Stahmer, had relayed an interesting report from a well-known English banker on the situation in the United States which is revealing of the prevailing deflationary ideology. The report attributed the signs of recovery to "the cheapness of the raw material . . . the decrease in wages . . . a revival of the demand of the public at reasonable prices." He rapturously went on: "Here showed itself the influence of national deflation. In Europe everyone is begging for goods on credit, everyone is begging for credit in order to get goods. Here—during the time when the tidal wave of crisis swept the country the producer went abegging to find purchasers for his goods and ultimately he found home industry willing to stem the tide. . . . many here have long since realized that under the healthy influence of deflation they will fare better, selling at lower prices, living on a lower priced standard, able to save more than they could during the period of extravagance and inflation." BAP, HAAA, Nr. 47177, Bl. 22f.

53. Report by Heinrich Charles, Oct. 13, 1921, BAP, HAAA, Nr. 4789/1, Bl. 105-13.

54. Report of Jan. 10, 1922, ibid., Nr. 47189/2, Bl. 91-94; the reports in Nr. 47189/1 of October and November 1921, as well as those in this volume for December and January 1922, are filled with such information.

55. Bresciani-Turroni, *Economics of Inflation*, p. 30.

56. The most detailed discussion is Howard Ellis, *German Monetary Theory*, esp. pp. 237-57. See also, Holtfrerich, *German Inflation*, pp. 156ff.; Karl Hardach, "Zur zeitgenössischen Debatte der Nationalökonomen über die Ursachen der deutschen Nachkriegsinflation," in Hans Mommsen et al.,

Industrielle System, pp. 368–75; Czada, in Winkel, ed., *Finanz- und wirtschaftspolitische Fragen*, pp. 9–43, all of which contain extensive references to the various writings in the debate between the quantity and balance-of-payment positions.

57. Holtfrerich, *German Inflation*, pp. 160f.

58. Bonn, *So macht man Geschichte*, pp. 257ff. In his account of his role as a theorist and adviser on pp. 268–71, Bonn accentuates his support of measures of domestic stabilization and struggle with Havenstein at the end of 1922. By the time he wrote his memoirs, he appears to have distanced himself somewhat from the balance-of-payments position, and tends to skirt the position he had taken at the turn of 1921–1922, which was not at all that different from Havenstein's. See John M. Williams, "German Foreign Trade and the Reparations Payments," *Quarterly Journal of Economics* 36 (1922), pp. 482–503. See also Bernard Malamud, "John H. Williams on the German Inflation: The International Amplification of Monetary Disturbances," in Nathan Schmukler and Edward Marcus, eds., *Inflation through the Ages: Economic, Social, Psychological and Historical Aspects* (New York, 1983), pp. 417–34. On Bresciani-Turroni's views, see above, pp. 253f.

59. *Sozialisierungskommission*, III, p. 11.

60. Ibid., p. 10.

61. This phenomenon will be discussed in greater detail later. See Holtfrerich, *German Inflation*, pp. 281ff.

62. *Sozialisierungskommission*, III, p. 18.

63. Ibid., p. 4. For the translation, see Holtfrerich, *Inflation*, p. 297.

64. *Sozialisierungskommission*, III, p. 15.

65. Ibid. On the relations with England, see the report of Havenstein to the Reichsbank Curatorium, Dec. 20, 1921, SäHStA, Gesandtschaft Berlin, Nr. 1630. See also the report by Lang to the German Foreign Office on a conversation with Herbert Hoover of Feb. 3, 1922, in which Hoover pointed out that "A mass of people in England, Germany and other European countries are of the view that the United States has a strong material interest in the restoration of normal economic conditions in Europe. This view is based on the proposition that America is dependent upon Europe as a market for its exports. . . . but this is mistaken. It is true that there is at present unemployment in certain districts and in certain branches of industry . . . but this only has in the smallest amount to do with reduced exports and is to the largest extent an internal American matter, for the portion of America's total production which Europe absorbs in normal times is only about four percent." BAP, HAAA, Nr. 47177, Bl. 93f.

66. *Sozialisierungskommission*, III, pp. 12f.

67. Memorandum by Bonn for Wirth of Jan. 23, 1922, BAK, R 43I/24, Bl. 384–90, quote on Bl. 389.

68. See Rathenau's speech to the Reichstag of March 29, 1922, reprinted in Rathenau, *Gesammelte Reden*, p. 380. More generally, see the speeches on

foreign affairs between January and June 1922 reprinted in this volume beginning with his address to the Allied Supreme Council at Cannes on Jan. 12, 1922, ibid., pp. 361ff.

69. Ellis, *German Monetary Theory*, pp. 207ff., and the literature cited in note 56.

70. Translated in a report of Maurice Parmelee of Feb. 28, 1922, on "The Problem of the Re-establishment of a Gold Currency in Germany," NA, 862.515/31.

71. This criticism was most fully developed in Lansburgh's, *Politik der Reichsbank*.

72. Report of Feb. 28, 1922, NA, 862.515/31.

73. Meeting of Dec. 20, 1921, SäHStA, Gesandtschaft Berlin, Nr. 1630.

74. See the Cabinet meetings of Dec. 26–27, 1921, *Kabinette Wirth*, I, pp. 481–89.

75. RB memorandum of Dec. 28, 1921, BAK, R 43I/23, Bl. 240–48, quote on Bl. 243.

76. Ibid., Bl. 240.

77. Ibid., Bl. 246.

78. Notes by the Centrist Deputy and industrialist Rudolf ten Hompel on a discussion with Havenstein on Jan. 10, 1922, BAK, NL ten Hompel, Nr. 25. It is interesting to note that ten Hompel was much less disturbed by the amount of money in circulation than Havenstein, arguing that the standard of living of those engaged in productive work—workers and employers—was not as low as Havenstein suggested and that the excess circulation was only some tens of millions. On the inflationary character of payments in kind, see Lindenlaub, *Maschinenbauunternehmen*, pp. 144f.

79. Trachtenberg, *Reparations*, pp. 237ff.

80. See his reports of April 7, 1922, and May 15, 1922, which are very typical, NA, 862.515/1462, 1492.

81. *Sozialisierungskommission*, III, p. 358.

82. Ibid.

83. Haller in *Währung und Wirtschaft*, pp. 139ff., and Holtfrerich, *German Inflation*, pp. 146ff.; Webb, *Hyperinflation*, p. 109.

84. See Chapter 8, p. 111.

85. Addison to Lord Curzon, Dec. 2, 1921, PRO, FO 371/5979/73.

86. Ibid.

87. See Chapter 5 and Feldman and Steinisch, *Zentralarbeitsgemeinschaft*, pp. 77f.

88. See the discussions in Schumacher, *Land und Politik*, pp. 164ff.; Moeller, *German Peasants*, pp. 104ff.; *Kabinette Wirth*, I, pp. 40, 42f., 47, 58f.

89. Meeting of the ZAG directors, April 1, 1921, BAP, ZAG, Nr. 30, Bl. 93–103.

90. Meeting of Aug. 11, 1921, ibid., Bl. 30–32.

91. Statement by Grassmann of the ADGB, Aug. 19, 1921, meeting, ibid., Bl. 23f.

92. Memorandum of the Gesamtverband deutscher Metallindustriellen, and guidelines, Aug. 18, 1921, VPI Archiv.

93. Negotiations concerning a cost-of-living in-

crease before the mediation board in Stuttgart, Aug. 24, 1921, HStA Stuttgart, E 392, Fasz. 3, Bd. 18, Anl. 1 zu 2.

94. See Leipart's reports at the ADGB Council meeting of Aug. 16–18, 1921, Ruck, *Gewerkschaften*, p. 353, and the illuminating series of articles of Waldemar Zimmermann, "Der Kampf um die Lohnhöhe und die Lohnpolitik," *Soziale Praxis* 30 (Oct. 1921), pp. 1089–93, 1116–18, 1143–46, esp. pp. 1189–91 for the discussion which follows.

95. Diary entry of June 12, 1921, Friedrich C.A. Lange, *Groß= Berliner Tagebuch 1920–1933* (Berlin, 1951), p. 18.

96. See the insightful discussion in Kunz, *Civil Servants*, pp. 237–59 and *Kabinette Wirth*, I, pp. 195, 198, 215.

97. For the quotation and this discussion, see Tschirbs, *Tarifpolitik im Bergbau*, pp. 147ff., quote on p. 149.

98. *Kabinett Fehrenbach*, p. 599, and *Zahlen zur Geldentwertung*, p. 26.

99. Zimmermann in *Soziale Praxis* 30 (Oct. 1921), p. 1090.

100. Georg Schmidt, "Weltmarktpreis—Weltmarktlohn," *Correspondenzblatt*, Aug. 13, 1921, pp. 458–59.

101. See the report of the RWM on economic conditions in September 1921, BAK, R 43I/1147, Bl. 626.

102. *Correspondenzblatt*, Aug. 13, 1921, p. 459.

103. Meeting of the ADGB Central Committee, Aug. 16–18, 1921, Rück, *Gewerkschaften*, pp. 356, 360.

104. Zimmermann in *Soziale Praxis* 30 (Oct. 1921), p. 1091.

105. ADGB Executive Committee meeting, Aug. 16–18, 1921, in Ruck, *Gewerkschaften*, p. 352.

106. See the Außerordentliche Hauptversammlung des Deutschen Städtetages und des Reichsstädtebundes am 11. November 1921 in Berlin, BAP, RAM, Nr. 10414, Bl. 118.

107. Kunz, *Civil Servants*, pp. 259–69, and his "Variants of Social Protest in the German Inflation: The Mobilization of Civil Servants in City and Countryside, 1920–1924," in Gerald D. Feldman et al., eds., *The Adaptation to Inflation*, pp. 323–53.

108. Diary entry of Dec. 22, 1921, Lange, *Groß= Berliner Tagebuch*, p. 23.

109. Diary entry of Feb. 11, 1922, ibid., p. 25.

110. VDA circular of Oct. 11, 1921, StA Hamburg, Blohm & Voss, Nr. 1329.

111. See the discussion of the social wage in the VDA meeting on Aug. 18, 1921, where Ernst von Borsig strongly supported it, VPI Archiv, and the illuminating discussion of the debate by Zimmermann in *Soziale Praxis* 30, pp. 1116–18, 1143–46. It is interesting to note that the Berlin Chamber of Commerce saw fit to reissue on September 1, 1921, a survey by General Director Felix Deutsch of the AEG of April 1919 on the relationship of wages to capital in

some sixty-six firms and concerns for the period 1908–1917 demonstrating that the portion paid to capital was an average of 13 percent of that paid to labor and in taxes and that the balance had shifted dramatically to the disfavor of capital during the war. See Felix Deutsch, *Das Verhältnis des Anteils von Arbeit und Kapital am Ertrage* (Berlin, 1919).

112. For the Ten Demands, see Ruck, *Gewerkschaften*, pp. 397–99.

113. The discussion which follows is based on the very revealing protocol of the ADGB Federation Executive Committee meetings of Dec. 13–17, 1921, ibid., pp. 400–50.

114. Meeting of Jan. 12, 1922, *Kabinette Wirth*, I, pp. 513f., and meeting of Jan. 17, ibid., pp. 520–22.

115. ZAG meeting of Dec. 2, 1921, BAP, ZAG, Nr. 31, Bl. 170–72.

116. ZAG meeting of Jan. 27, 1922, BAP, ZAG, Nr. 31, Bl. 143–53, quote on Bl. 147.

117. Ibid., Bl. 149.

118. Meeting of the Reparations Committee of the ZAG, Feb. 24, 1922, ibid., Bd. 70, Bl. 269–77, quote on Bl. 276.

119. ZAG meeting of Jan. 27, 1922, ibid., Nr. 31, Bl. 152.

120. Ibid., Bl. 152. For an interesting discussion of such "corporatist" tendencies in the Christian unions, see Patch, *Christian Trade Unions*.

121. Raumer to Stresemann, Dec. 14, 1921, NL Stresemann, 3093/H141136f.

122. Diary entries of Oct. 13 and Nov. 26, 1921, Lange, *Groß= Berliner Tagebuch*, pp. 21f.

10. The Vicious Circles: From Galloping Inflation to Hyperinflation, January–July 1922

1. It seems to me that these considerations and the entire context of German decision making are neglected in Stephen Schuker, *American "Reparations" to Germany, 1919–33: Implications for the Third World Debt Crisis* (Princeton, 1988). See esp. pp. 22f., where I think he misreads the evidence.

2. Wirth to the Reparations Commission, Jan. 28, 1922, *Reparations Commission. III. Official Documents Relative to the Amount of Payments to Be Effected by Germany under Reparations Account*, Vol. I, May 1, 1921–July 1, 1922 (London, 1922), pp. 56–113. See also the useful summary by Wigram of Jan. 28, 1922, in DBFP, Vol. 20, pp. 8–10.

3. Bradbury to Blackett, Jan. 27, 1922, PRO, FO 371/7474/311/19–21.

4. Bradbury to Blackett, Jan. 31, 1922, ibid., 23.

5. Bradbury to Blackett, Jan. 27, 1922, ibid., 19–21.

6. Melchior to Warburg, reporting a conversation of Feb. 18, 1922, Warburg Papers, 1922, pp. 13–16, quote on p. 13.

7. Annex IV of Wirth's letter to the Reparations

Commission of Jan. 28, 1922, *Reparations Commission. III. Official Documents,* Vol. I, pp. 112–13; *Kabinette Wirth,* I, p. 515; Ruck, *Gewerkschaften,* p. 454n10.

8. Meeting of the Foreign Exchange Procurement Board, Feb. 13, 1922, BAP, RB, Nr. 6435, Bl. 77–97, quote on Bl. 83.

9. Ibid., Bl. 82.

10. Cabinet meeting of April 17, 1922, *Kabinette Wirth,* II, pp. 707f.

11. *Kabinette Wirth,* II, pp. 825f.; Schumacher, *Land und Politik,* pp. 169–71.

12. See the Cabinet meetings of Nov. 15, 1921, and Jan. 23, 1922, *Kabinette Wirth,* I, pp. 407f., 527.

13. The discussion here is based on Kunz, *Civil Servants,* Chap. 6.

14. *Kabinette Wirth,* I, p. 566.

15. Report to Stinnes of Feb. 22, 1922, on a conversation between Groener and Dock Director Buschmeyer, and report from Osius to Stinnes of Feb. 24, 1922, ACDP, NL Stinnes, Nr. 005/1.

16. Meeting of March 15, 1922, *Kabinette Wirth,* I, p. 615.

17. Cabinet meeting of May 3, 1922, *Kabinette Wirth,* II, pp. 745–47.

18. Ibid., p. 746.

19. Bresciani-Turroni, *Economics of Inflation,* p. 71, and *Zahlen zur Geldentwertung,* pp. 36f.

20. A point missed by Bresciani-Turroni, *Economics of Inflation,* p. 71, but noted by Robert Kuczynski, *Postwar Labor Conditions,* p. 54.

21. See Carl-Ludwig Holtfrerich, "Deutscher Außenhandel und Goldzölle 1919–1923," in Feldman et al., eds., *The Adaptation to Inflation,* pp. 472–84.

22. See, for example, the report made of remarks at the Committee of Guarantees of Oct. 8, 1921, BAK, R 43I/21, Bl. 315–18.

23. Holtfrerich in *Adaptation,* pp. 481ff.

24. Hesse, *Wirtschaftslage,* pp. 221ff., 488f.; RWM reports to the Reich President of 1921–1922, BAK, R 43I/1147–48.

25. Report on discussion with Kemball-Cook of the Committee of Guarantees, Oct. 8, 1921, BAK, R 43I/21, Bl. 314–17, and Reconstruction Ministry calculations of Dec. 8, 1921, R 43I/23, Bl. 28.

26. This is based on the very useful confidential table and chart of the Reich Coal Association in BAK, NL Silverberg, Nr. 148, Bl. 38f.

27. *Kabinette Wirth,* I, pp. 103f., 150, 237, 330, 341, 360, 410, 415, 563.

28. Meeting of Jan. 24, 1922, BAK, NL Silverberg, Nr. 148, Bl. 20–27, quotes on Bl. 22 and 25.

29. Statement by Emil Girbig, head of the Glass Makers Union, ibid., Bl. 27.

30. Ibid.

31. Vögler to Stinnes, Jan. 20, 1922, ACDP, NL Stinnes, Nr. 052/4.

32. Woltmann report to Reusch of Feb. 16, 1922, HA/GHH, Nr. 3000035/3.

33. Meeting of Feb. 22, 1922, HA/GHH, Nr.

30019320, for this and the quotations and discussion from the meeting which follow.

34. Ibid. See also the similar remarks of Bennhold, the Executive Secretary of the Reich Coal Council in a memorandum of Feb. 28, 1922, BAK, NL Silverberg, Nr. 148, Bl. 68. Among other things, Bennhold pointed out that after all the increases involved in the coal price increase worked themselves out, not the anticipated fifty marks but rather eighteen marks remained for write-offs.

35. Tschirbs, *Tarifpolitik,* pp. 158ff, and *Zahlen zur Geldentwertung,* p. 29.

36. Vögler to Stinnes, March 2, 1922, ACDP, NL Stinnes, Nr. 057/4.

37. These formulations with respect to industrialist behavior, which certainly may be applied to whole interest groups as well, are developed by Lindenlaub in *Maschinenbauunternehmen,* pp. 134ff., 182ff., 205ff.

38. Reports by Director Klemme to Reusch, HA/GHH, Nr. 3000035/3.

39. In general, see Feldman, *Iron and Steel,* pp. 284ff.

40. See the illuminating article of J. Jastrow, "The New Tax System of Germany," *Quarterly Journal of Economics* 37 (1923), pp. 302–41, esp. pp. 307–9.

41. Ruck, *Gewerkschaften,* p. 456.

42. Raumer to Stresemann, Feb. 2, 1922, NL Stresemann, Nr. 3095/H143140f.

43. German Note of Jan. 28, 1922, *Reparations Commission. III. Official Documents,* I, pp. 69ff.; Wirth speech to the Reichstag, Jan. 27, 1922, *VR,* Bd. 352, p. 5561; Holtfrerich, *Inflation,* pp. 134f.

44. *VR,* Bd. 352, p. 5561.

45. *Kabinette Wirth,* I, pp. 562ff., 581f.

46. Report by Fischer, Feb. 8, 1922, BAK, R 43I/25, Bl. 8–24, quote on Bl. 15.

47. Melchior to Warburg concerning his meeting with Horne on Feb. 18, 1922, Warburg Papers, 1922, p. 15.

48. See Justus Strandes's report of Rathenau's appearance before the Reichstag Foreign Affairs Committee, Feb. 25, 1922, StA Hamburg, Hamburgische Gesandtschaft, 1A1d1, Bd. 5a. On the C Bonds, see Fischer's report of Feb. 9, 1922, BAK, R 43I/25, Bl. 24–28. Rathenau undoubtedly found it easy to adopt this view of Genoa because, as D'Abernon reported, he had developed a "passion" for international conferences, viewing them as a path to bringing the world to reason on the reparations issue. See Schulin, *Rathenau. Hauptwerke und Gespräche,* pp. 849f.

49. Strandes report, Feb. 28, 1922, StA Hamburg, Hamburgische Gesandtschaft, 1A1d1, Bd. 5a.

50. On France's inflationary problems at this time, see Maier, *Recasting,* p. 274.

51. Note from the Finance Ministry to the Chancellery, March 21, 1922, BAK, R 43I/25, Bl. 284–86.

52. See his reports of March 9, 24, and 31, 1922, Hoover Institution, Logan Papers, Vol VI, pp. 65f., 76–79.

53. *Reparations Commission. III. Official Documents*, I, pp. 113–21. The language with respect to financial control was very vague, and Bradbury viewed it as limited to a right of "examination, criticism and censure" that was quite a bit less onerous than the kind of machinery of control the French had in mind. See Trachtenberg, *Reparation*, p. 242.

54. Meeting of March 27, 1922, *Kabinette Wirth*, I, p. 643.

55. See the report of von Praeger on the meeting of the Reichstag Foreign Affairs Committee, March 22, 1922, BayHStA, Abt. II, Gesandtschaft Berlin, Nr. 1099.

56. Cabinet meeting of March 24, 1922, *Kabinette Wirth*, I, p. 638.

57. See the meetings of March 23, 24, and 27, 1922, ibid., pp. 623–49. For the RWM position, see the important memorandum written by Hans Staudinger on Hirsch's instructions showing the powerful influence of the reparations news on the exchange rate, March 25, 1922, BAK, R 43I/26, Bl. 40–49, and the RWM position paper on the Allied note, ibid., Bl. 53–57, which pointed out that "Insofar as the demand for new taxes, one can immediately point out that the income from many taxes will increase well over the proposal by the diminution of the value of the money."

58. See his remarks at the March 24 Cabinet meeting, *Kabinette Wirth*, I, p. 630.

59. For a splendid discussion of the pre-Genoa mood of Wirth and Rathenau as a result of the Reparations Commission note, see Krüger, *Außenpolitik*, pp. 166ff. See also Orde, *British Policy*, pp. 160ff.

60. Meeting of March 28, 1922, *VR*, Bd. 353, pp. 6613–22.

61. March 29, 1922, *VR*, Bd. 353, pp. 6643–51, for Stresemann's speech and pp. 6651–57 for Rathenau's address. Quote is on p. 6652.

62. Report of March 31, 1922, PRO, FO 371/7647/311/5. In a report of March 29, D'Abernon deplored the German failure to realize the danger of its currency policies: "The ordinary politician is impressed by the danger of social unrest, which would, in his opinion, arise if there was any scarcity of currency. He either fails to see, or intentionally ignores, the obvious danger which proceeds from continuous inflation, and from the enormous issues of currency paper which pour from the Reichsbank practically every week. It is regrettable that the note of the Reparation Commission, which was much too categorical on some questions, was not more categorical on this," PRO, FO 371/7516/37093/116.

63. Meeting of April 1, 1922, *Kabinette Wirth*, II, pp. 659–62.

64. Meeting of April 4, 1922, ibid., pp. 670–74.

65. Cabinet meeting of April 6, 1922, *Kabinette Wirth*, II, pp. 694–96; Logan to Hoover, March 24, 1922, Hoover Institution, Logan Papers, Vol. VI., pp. 76f.

66. Logan to Hoover, April 14, 1922, ibid., pp. 84–86; *Reparations Commission. III. Official Documents*, I, pp. 121–26.

67. Praeger report of the meeting of the Reichstag Foreign Affairs Committee, April 8, 1922, BayHStA, Abt. II, Gesandtschaft Berlin, Nr. 1099.

68. Meeting between Stinnes and Hermes, March 27, 1922, ACDP, NL Stinnes, Nr. 022/2.

69. Meeting of the Reparations Commission of the ZAG, Feb. 24, 1922, BAP, ZAG, Nr. 70, Bl. 269–77, quote on Bl. 276.

70. RdI directors meeting, March 29, 1922, BAK, NL Silverberg, Nr. 257, Bl. 25f.

71. Meeting of April 7, 1922, HK Hamburg, Plenarsitzungen, Commerzbibliothek.

72. Ibid.

73. Ibid.

74. Here, and in the discussion of Genoa, I follow the convincing interpretation of Krüger, *Außenpolitik*, pp. 171ff.

75. On Russo-German economic relations, see Hartmut Pogge von Strandmann, "Großindustrie und Rapallopolitik: Deutschsowjetische Handelsbeziehungen in der Weimarer Republik," *HZ* 222 (April 1976), pp. 265–341. The discussion of Genoa here relies heavily on Carole Fink's masterful *Genoa Conference*.

76. Krüger, *Außenpolitik*, p. 189; Bonn, *So macht man Geschichte*, pp. 264ff.; Julius Hirsch diary entries for April–May 1922, Hirsch Papers.

77. Bücher to Stinnes, April 17, 1922, ACDP, NL Stinnes, Nr. 019/3.

78. Bücher to Stinnes, April 17, 1922, and Ambassador Lucius to Stinnes, June 17, 1922, and response of June 20, 1922, ibid. Lucius actually suggested that Vlissingen be barred from serving on German supervisory boards, a notion which Stinnes strongly rejected. The Phoenix directors seem to have played some role in fomenting newspaper attacks on Vlissingen, which led to an unpleasant altercation between the Dutch and German groups at the Supervisory Board meeting on June 9, 1922, Mannesmann-Archiv, P/1/25/39.

79. Bücher to Stinnes, April 27, 1922, ACDP, NL Stinnes, Nr. 019/3, and von Raumer to Stresemann, April 21, 1922, NL Stresemann, 7009/H14330.

80. Notes of conversation of May 18, 1922, DBFP, Vol. 19, pp. 990–1001.

81. Maier, *Recasting*, pp. 285f.; Trachtenberg, *Reparation*, pp. 242ff. For the exchanges of notes relating to these arrangements, see *Reparations Commission. III. Official Documents*, I, pp. 129–42.

82. See the relevant Cabinet meetings and documents in *Kabinette Wirth*, II, pp. 782–88, 791–822, 828–36, 839–41; the meetings of the Center Party Reichstag delegation of May 27 and 29, 1922, *Zentrumsprotokolle*, pp. 342–51, 353f.

83. Report of von Praeger, May 31, 1922, BayHStA, Abt. II, Gesandtschaft Berlin, Nr. 1099.

84. Report of May 27, 1922, ibid.

85. Ibid.

86. Extract from the protocol of the Reichstag Foreign Affairs Committee, May 27, 1922, ACDP, NL Stinnes, Nr. 038/3. An abbreviated version of Stinnes's remarks may also be found in the report by von Praeger of May 27, BayHStA, Abt. II, Gesandtschaft Berlin, Nr. 1099.

87. Ibid.

88. Stinnes made a formal complaint to Wirth about Schmidt's behavior on May 28 and threatened to go public unless there was an apology. Although two letters of explanation were drafted, Wirth decided against taking action, especially after Becker of the DVP got into the act by calling Schmidt an "incompetent twit" (*Depp*). It was in this context that Bücher of the RdI paid a call on Wirth about the matter, where Wirth seems to have been very open about his differences with Hermes and Bergmann and to have left Bücher with the impression, as he told Stinnes in a letter of June 17, 1922, that "our suspicion that he is much closer to our viewpoint than that of Hermes–Bergmann with regard to the loan, was confirmed." On this occasion, Wirth also made his bitter complaint about the DVP: "He [Wirth] still is striving seriously to work with the German People's Party, but every time he takes a step in this direction, he receives a kick. He does not know what it is that the German People's Party wants." ACDP Archiv, NL Stinnes, Nr 038/3. On Wirth's displeasure with Schmidt, see also Hugo Stehkämper, ed., *Der Nachlaß des Reichskanzlers Wilhelm Marx* [*Mitteilungen aus dem Stadtarchiv von Köln*, Hefte 52–55], (Cologne, 1968), Teil I, p. 269.

89. Praeger report of May 27, 1922, BayHStA, Abt. II, Gesandtschaft Berlin, No. 1009. The expression Wirth used was "Mitgefangen, mitgehangen."

90. John M. Carroll, "The Paris Bankers' Conference of 1922 and America's Design for a Peaceful Europe," *International Review of History and Political Science* 10 (Aug. 1973), pp. 39–47. See also Werner Link, *Die amerikanische Stabilisierungspolitik in Deutschland 1921–32* (Düsseldorf, 1970), pp. 122ff.

91. Ibid., and Logan report to Hoover of May 12, 1922, Hoover Institution, Logan Papers, Vol. VI, pp. 95–97.

92. Bendix report No. 3 of May 1, 1922, BAP, HAAA, Nr. 43817, Bl. 196–205.

93. See Woltmann to Reusch, Feb. 16, 1922, HA/GHH, Nr. 30019323/8, and Schröder, *Wiedfeldt*, pp. 131ff.

94. Schulin, *Rathenau. Hauptwerke und Gespräche*, p. 851.

95. Wiedfeldt to AA, June 3, 1922, BAP, HAAA, Nr. 43814, Bl. 5456; Link, *Stabilisierungspolitik*, pp. 130f.

96. For the text of the Committee report, see *VR*, Bd. 374, Drucksache Nr. 4484. There are good discussions in Laubach, *Wirth*, pp. 238ff. and Trachtenberg, *Reparation*, pp. 247f. Most useful is the account given to the Cabinet by Bergmann on June 13, 1922, *Kabinette Wirth*, pp. 855ff. Logan shared the German enthusiasm for the report: "The conference of the bankers, notwithstanding the 'impasse' apparently reached, unquestionably will have been of great benefit to the general situation. Their findings constitute an expression of the world's financial opinion that the figure of the present indemnity so far exceeds German capacity as to be fantastic and that the maintenance of this figure can only lead to German bankruptcy. The world's general opinion will undoubtedly follow the majority views of the Commission, backed by the Bankers, on this subject and this must have its ultimate effect on French Government opinion." Report of June 9, 1922, Hoover Institution, Logan Papers, Vol. VI, pp. 105–6.

97. Meeting of June 13, 1922, *Kabinette Wirth*, II, p. 867.

98. Ibid., p. 862.

99. See Hirsch's important memorandum concerning the policy options of July 4, 1922, "Zur Valutakatastrophe," BAK, R 43I/2433, Bl. 351–58.

100. *Zahlen zur Geldentwertung*, p. 9.

101. *Kabinette Wirth*, II, pp. 868f.

102. Ibid., p. 871.

103. Ibid., p. 872.

104. Ibid., p. 874.

105. Ibid., pp. 874ff.

106. Cabinet meeting, June 13, 1922, *Kabinette Wirth*, II, pp. 877–80; Foreign Exchange Advisory Council meeting, July 4, 1922, BAK, R 43I/505, and Hirsch, "Valutakatastrophe," ibid., Bd. 2443, Bl. 351–53.

107. Cabinet meeting of May 9, 1922, *Kabinette Wirth*, II, p. 766. See also Holtfrerich *German Inflation*, pp. 302ff., and Witt in *Wealth and Taxation*, pp. 153ff.

108. See the report on the Reichsbank Curatorium meeting of March 28, 1922, SäHStA, Dresden, Gesandtschaft Berlin, Nr. 1630. See also Karl Helfferich, "Die Autonomie der Reichsbank," *Bank=Archiv* 21 (April 1, 1922), pp. 215–17. For the discussion in the Reich Economic Council in March 1922, see BAP, RWR, Nr. 551, and the excellent summaries of the hearings in GStAKM, Rep. 120A, AX, Nr. 40, Bd. 7, Bl. 265–78. See Holtfrerich, *Inflation*, p. 168. The Autonomy Law is to be found in *RGBl* (1922), II, p. 683.

109. Report by Addison, June 14, 1922, PRO, FO 371/7478/311/188.

110. Here I concur completely with the arguments of Krüger, *Außenpolitik*, p. 187.

111. PRO, FO 371/7479/311/11–31, quote on 13.

112. Ibid., 15–16.

113. Report by Capt. Georgi on conditions in Germany, June 20, 1922, ibid., pp. 12–26.

114. For an illuminating analysis, see Kent, *Spoils of War*, pp. 171f., 398–401.

115. Ibid., and the account drawn up by Stinnes of the events of June 23, 1922, dated July 4, 1922, Stinnes Papers, Stinnes AG. A slightly edited version is to be found in Klass, *Hugo Stinnes*, pp. 282–91, re-

printed in Schulin, *Rathenau. Hauptwerke und Gespräche*, pp. 904–8.

116. Ibid.

117. Ibid. In addition to Stinnes's account, there are two others, one by Logan to Hoover of June 26, 1922, Logan Papers, Box 4, Folder 2, Hoover Institution, and the other by Houghton in a report to the State Department, Dec. 27, 1922, NA, 862.00/1199. Additionally, there is a report by Houghton of June 23/24, 1922, in the D'Abernon memoirs, reprinted in Schulin, *Rathenau. Hauptwerke und Gespräche*, pp. 903f. These reports supplement and support one another, although that of Stinnes tends to gloss over the continuing differences with Rathenau. Since Houghton and Logan were "neutral" observers, and Logan in particular wrote a very detailed and convincing reports, and since his report was written closest to the event, it is reasonable to assume his is the most reliable. The account which follows should show that it is an error to characterize this meeting as a "confrontation," as is done by Kent in *Spoils of War*, p. 185.

118. Stinnes account of July 4, Stinnes AG.

119. Houghton account, NA, 862.00/1199.

120. Logan account, Logan Papers, Box 4, Folder 2, Hoover Institution.

121. Stinnes report of July 4, Stinnes AG.

122. Logan account, Logan Papers, Hoover Institution.

123. Houghton report in D'Abernon, Schulin, *Rathenau. Hauptwerke und Gespräche*, pp. 903f. This was not the first time that Stinnes had tried to persuade Rathenau to keep out of the government. At a breakfast at Ambassador D'Abernon's earlier in the year, Stinnes had offered never to take a position in the government if Rathenau would do the same, an offer Rathenau, shortly to become Foreign Minister, refused, ibid., p. 849.

124. *VR*, June 23, 1922, Bd. 355, p. 7992.

125. Houghton account, NA, 862.00/1190.

126. Stinnes account of July 4, 1922, Stinnes AG.

127. Logan account, Logan Papers, Hoover Institution.

128. For the various warnings received by Rathenau, see Schulin, *Rathenau. Hauptwerke und Gespräche*, pp. 851ff.

129. Hirsch, "Valutakatastrophe," BAK, R 43I/2433, Bl. 354. The reference is to Organisation Consul, a right-wing murder group responsible for numerous political assassinations.

130. Raumer to Stresemann, June 20, 1922, NL Stresemann, 7013H/H143773–79. For his earlier views, see p. 416. Raumer still was wary about entering into the coalition, arguing now, however, that negotiations with the Allies might be easier for the government without the DVP.

131. Gosling to Balfour, July 25, 1922, PRO, FO 371/7517/37093/95–98, quote on 96f.

132. Bendix report of July 3, 1922, BAP, AA, Nr. 43818, Bl. 4853, quote on Bl. 53.

133. Meeting of July 14, 1922, BAP, RWR, Bd. 460, Bl. 287f.

134. Ibid., Bl. 308.

135. Ibid., Bl. 315f.

136. RB Central Committee meeting of July 28, 1922, BAK, R 43I/ 640, Bl. 130–32.

137. *Kabinette Wirth*, II, pp. 924f.

138. "Valutakatastrophe," July 4–5, 1922, BAK, R 43I/2433, Bl. 354–56. This was confirmed at the July 4, 1922, meeting of the Foreign Exchange Advisory Council, where it was reported that the Foreign Exchange Procurement Board was having an easier time because of the dismantling of subsidies and the diminished need for foreign exchange by the Reich agencies.

11. Stabilization Debates and Political Crises, August 1922–January 1923

1. Wirth to the Pope, Aug. 4, 1922, BAK, NL Wirth, Nr. 19.

2. Bergen to the Foreign Office, Aug. 8, 1922, ibid. More generally, see Stewart A. Stehlin, *Weimar and the Vatican, 1919–1933. German–Vatican Diplomatic Relations in the Interwar Years* (Princeton, 1983), pp. 85ff.

3. Coded message to the German embassy in London which Wirth asked be given to Lloyd George's secretary, Grigg, for immediate transmittal to the Prime Minister, Aug. 4, 1922, BAK, NL Wirth, Nr. 14. For a discussion on this note and a similar appeal sent by banker Franz von Mendelssohn to Kindersley on Aug. 10 (ibid., Nr. 2) from the English perspective, see Konrad von Zwehl, *Die Deutschlandpolitik Englands von 1922 bis 1924 unter besonderer Berücksichtigung der Reparationen und Sanktionen*, 2 vols. (Munich, 1974), I, pp. 111ff.

4. Wirth to Archbishop Fritz of Freiburg, Sept. 11, 1922, with a copy of an article on "Foreign Policy" from the *Ingolstädter Zeitung* of Aug. 13, 1922. Fritz responded on Sept. 16, informing Wirth that he had launched a complaint with the Bishop of Eichstätt, BAK, NL Wirth, Nr. 21.

5. Laubach, *Die Politik der Kabinette Wirth*, pp. 263–69, and *Kabinette Wirth*, II, pp. 981–87, 991–1010, 1012f., 1016–19, 1021–37. The best account of these problems is Gerhard Schulz, *Zwischen Demokratie und Diktatur*, 3 vols. (Berlin & New York, 1987ff.), I, Chaps. 8–10.

6. Meeting of Aug. 25, 1922, *Kabinette Wirth*, II, p. 1053.

7. A good account of the clearing operations is to be found in Harold G. Moulton and C.E. McGuire, *Germany's Capacity to Pay. A Study of the Reparation Problem* (New York, 1923), pp. 312–19.

8. Meeting of July 15, 1922, *Kabinette Wirth*, II, pp. 954–56, quote on p. 955. Laubach, *Politik der Kabinette Wirth*, pp. 250ff.

9. Report of July 28, 1922, Logan Papers, Hoover Institution, Vol. VII, p. 116.

10. Bergmann to Wirth, July 29, 1922, *Kabinette Wirth*, II, pp. 974–80.

11. Laubach, *Politik der Kabinette Wirth*, p. 261.

12. McDougall, *Rhineland Diplomacy*, pp. 218ff.; Trachtenberg, *Reparation*, pp. 252, 271. On the rumors concerning political changes in France, see Lucius to Wirth, Aug. 19, 1922, BAK, NL Wirth, Nr. 21.

13. Meeting with the Bavarian representatives, Aug. 19, 1922, *Kabinette Wirth*, II, p. 1023.

14. See the report of the Bavarian Ambassador in Berlin on his conversation with the Austrian Ambassador Riedl, Aug. 26, 1922, BayHStA, Abt. II, Gesandtschaft Berlin, Nr. 1099, and, more generally, März, *Österreichische Bankpolitik*, pp. 483ff.

15. These themes are well-developed in Zwehl, *Deutschlandpolitik Englands*, I, pp. 39ff., 101ff., 204ff.

16. Ibid., pp. 145ff.

17. Cabinet meeting, Aug. 23, 1922, *Kabinette Wirth*, II, p. 1043. For a good illustration of the Foreign Office hostility to Bradbury, see Wigram's "Note on a discussion between the Prime Minister and Sir John Bradbury, held on November 22, 1922," PRO, FO 371/7487/311/214–15 in which Wigram argued that if military officials should be subordinate to the Foreign Office in foreign policy matters, then so should former Treasury officials. For the internal German government discussions of the coal mine and forest question, see BAK, R 43I/30, Bl. 145ff.

18. See Laubach, *Politik der Kabinette Wirth*, p. 263.

19. Von Zwehl, *Deutschlandpolitik Englands*, pp. 175ff.; Link, *Amerikanische Stabilisierungspolitik*, p. 146. See also Logan report from Paris, Sept. 15, 1922, Hoover Institution, Logan Papers, Vol. VII, pp. 128ff.

20. Cabinet meeting of Aug. 23, 1922, *Kabinette Wirth*, II, pp. 1042–45.

21. Cabinet meeting of Aug. 30, 1922, ibid., pp. 1069–71.

22. Report of Aug. 29, 1922, StA Hamburg, Senatskommission für die Reichs- und auswärtigen Angelegenheiten, II A4, Fasz. 29.

23. Memorandum of Sept. 2, 1922, BAP, RB, Bd. 6339, Bl. 75–78, quote on 76f.

24. Ibid., Bl. 78.

25. Meeting of Aug. 28, 1922, ibid., p. 1061.

26. See the discussions of Sept. 6–7, 1922, in the Chancellery, BAK, R 43I/30, Bl. 400–404.

27. Meeting of Sept. 14, 1922, BAK, R 43I/31, Bl. 7–9.

28. Von Zwehl, *Deutschlandpolitik Englands*, pp. 178ff; Laubach, *Politik der Kabinette Wirth*, pp. 276ff.; Logan report of Sept. 15 and 21, 1922, Hoover Institution, Logan Papers, Vol. VII, pp. 128–35. On the clearing arrangements, see the report of Comptroller E.S. Grey of Nov. 7, 1922, PRO, FO 371/7461/273/127–29. The interested Allied parties were able to press the Germans particularly hard on this issue because the Germans had violated the Treaty of Versailles by assuming responsibility for the valorized debts of their nationals. The "provisional" figure of 24.2 millions was substantially more than the German calculation, although somewhat less than the Allies originally claimed.

29. Cabinet meetings of Aug. 24–25, 1922, *Kabinette Wirth*, II, pp. 1049–53.

30. This account is based on an illuminating memorandum on payments in kind by the Ministry for Reconstruction of July 8, 1922, in BAK, R 43I/29, Bl. 291–98.

31. Cabinet meeting of Aug. 25, 1922, *Kabinette Wirth*, II, pp. 1051f.

32. Feldman in *VfZ* (1980), pp. 218ff., and meeting with the trade union leaders, Aug. 29, 1922, BAK, R 43I/30, Bl. 302–4.

33. Meeting with industrialists on Aug. 29, 1922, *Kabinette Wirth*, II, pp. 1066–69, quote on p. 1068.

34. Meeting of Sept. 7, 1922, BAK, R 43I/30, Bl. 400f.

35. Humann's "Aktennotiz zum Thema: Verhandlungen mit Franzosen auf der Heimburg," Aug. 24, 1922, ACDP, NL Stinnes, Nr. 039/2. More generally, see Wulf, *Stinnes*, pp. 234ff.

36. Notes by Humann on discussion with Fehrmann, Aug. 19, 1922, ACDP, NL Stinnes, Nr. 039/2.

37. Wulf, *Stinnes*, p. 326. A copy of the agreement is to be found in the copy sent to the Reich government on Sept. 5, 1922, BAK, R 43I/343, Bl. 142.

38. Notes by Humann on the Heimburg negotiations of Aug. 24, 1922, ACDP, NL Stinnes, Nr. 039/2.

39. Humann conversation with Fehrmann, Aug. 19, 1922, ibid.

40. Ibid.

41. Ibid. It is interesting to note that in later privately written memoirs, Wirth complained that "Stinnes had access everywhere. After May 1921, he saw Ebert every month. The latter then summoned me all the time to tell me the proposals of Stinnes." "Ereignisse und Gestalten von 1918–1933, Pt. III, Nr. 5," BAK, NL Wirth, Nr. 23.

42. Wulf, *Stinnes*, p. 328.

43. Humann report, Sept. 21, 1922, ACDP, NL Stinnes, Nr. 019/4.

44. Report by the Saxon Representative in Munich, Sept. 20, 1922, SäHStA, Außenministerium, Nr. 2984, Bl. 256.

45. Memorandum by Schacht transmitted by Dr. Otto Sprenger of the "Weser" company in Bremen, Sept. 5, 1922, BAK, R 43I/31, Bl. 35–50, quote on Bl. 38.

46. Ibid., p. 42.

47. On Schacht's contacts, see his "Taktische Bemerkungen," ibid., Bl. 43–50.

48. Bavarian report on the meeting of the Reichstag Foreign Affairs Committee, Sept. 9, 1922, BayHStA, Abt. II, Gesandtschaft Berlin, Nr. 1099.

49. For an illustration of government disappointment over the failure of the Belgian accord to im-

prove the exchange rate of the mark, see Schmidt's comments at the Cabinet meeting of Oct. 7, 1922, *Kabinette Wirth*, II, p. 1116. For the reaction to the change in England, see the Cabinet meeting of Oct. 23, ibid., p. 1136.

50. For the Bradbury plan and the German criticism, see the memorandum of the German Finance Ministry of Oct. 25, 1922, BAK, R 43I/31, Bl. 296–327; for the discussions in the Reparations Commission, see the Logan reports of Oct. 13, 17, and 27 in Hoover Institution, Logan Papers, Vol. VII, pp. 138–46. Also, see Trachtenberg, *Reparation*, pp. 276ff.

51. Laubach, *Politik der Kabinette Wirth*, pp. 287f.; *Kabinette Wirth*, II, pp. 1144f.

52. Klöckner to the directors of the Lothringer Hütten- und Bergwerks-Vereine, Oct. 25, 1922, BgA, 25/9.

53. It is to be found not only in Maier, *Recasting*, pp. 296ff, but also in Feldman, *Iron and Steel*, pp. 320ff.

54. Meeting of the directors of the RdI on Sept. 6, 1922, StA Hamburg, Blohm & Voss, Nr. 1299/1. A more general discussion of Bücher's views and the conflicts in the RdI will follow later.

55. Raumer to Wirth, May 13, 1922, BAK, NL Wirth, Nr. 20.

56. Hirsch diary, June 25, 1922, Hirsch papers. His father actually came to Berlin for this purpose, and the episode suggests something of the way prominent Jews felt at this time. In September, Max Warburg, out of concern for the safety of himself and his family, decided to go on a trip to America, Warburg Papers, 1922, p. 26.

57. The memo is to be found in BAK, R 43I/2433, Bl. 351. For the Aug. 17 meeting, see BAP, RWR, Nr. 7, Bl. 1ff.

58. For the discussion of Hirsch's speech of Nov. 11, 1921, see pp. 386–88.

59. Julius Hirsch diary, Aug. 23, 1922, Hirsch Papers.

60. Meeting of Aug. 17, 1922, BAP, RWR, Nr. 7, Bl. 11f.

61. Ibid., Bl. 18.

62. Memorandum of July 4–5, 1922, BAK, R 43I/2433, Bl. 351–58, quote on Bl. 357.

63. Ibid.; Paul Beusch, *Währungszerfall und Währungsstabilisierung* (Berlin, 1928), pp. 12–15; Hirsch, *Deutsche Währungsfrage*, pp. 19–21, 69–75. Beusch, on p. 12, also gives Ministerial Director Dalberg credit along with Hirsch for developing these plans. The gold mark was the mean between a quarter of a dollar and a twentieth of an English pound.

64. Meetings of Aug. 14, 21, and Oct. 7, 1922, *Kabinette Wirth*, II, pp. 1014f., 1039, 1113.

65. Report of the Hamburg representatives to the Reichsrat, Aug. 12, 1922, StA Hamburg, Senatskommission für die Reichs- und auswärtigen Angelegenheiten, III Alc3, Bd. IV.

66. Reusch to Hirsch, Aug. 9, 1920, HA/GHH, Nr. 30019320/2. For the attitude of the Foreign Office, see the remarks of Ritter at the meeting of the Export Levy Committee of the RWR on Aug. 5,

1922, as reported by the Hamburg Representative, Senatskommission für die Reichs- und auswärtigen Angelegenheiten, III Alc3, Bd. IV. The English Parliament and the English colonies had already given the government powers to respond to German dumping, while measures had narrowly been defeated in Sweden and had been introduced by Spain in the midst of trade treaty negotiations with Germany. On the business mobilization, see the report of the Württemberg Representative to the Reichsrat, Aug. 14, 1922, HStA Stuttgart, E 130IV, Nr. 1251. On the use made of the state government Representatives, see Blank to Reusch, Aug. 12 and 14, 1922, HA/GHH, Nr. 30093024.

67. Reports of the Hamburg Representative to the Reichsrat, Aug. 12–13, 1922, StA Hamburg, Senatskommission für die Reichs- und auswärtigen Angelegenheiten, III Alc3, Bd. IV.

68. See the reports in ibid. for August and September.

69. Discussion in RWM of Aug. 11, 1922, GStAKM, Rep. 120, C XIII 1 Nr. 171, Bd. 2, Bl. 14–16, 21–23.

70. Ibid., Bl. 16.

71. Ibid.

72. Secret joint meeting of the Economic Policy and Reparations Committees, Aug. 29, 1922, as reported by the Hamburg Representative to the Reichsrat, StA Hamburg, Senatskommission für die Reichs- und auswärtigen Angelegenheiten, II A4, Fasz. 29.

73. For the text of the memorandum, see Hirsch, *Deutsche Währungsfrage*, pp. 69–75.

74. The Lerchenfeld memorandum will be discussed in more detail in the next chapter. See also Gerald D. Feldman, "Bayern und Sachsen in der Hyperinflation 1922/23," *HZ* 238 (1984), pp. 569–609, esp. pp. 587–92. Hirsch's difficulties with Schmidt are recorded in his diary entries of Aug.–Oct. 1922, Hirsch diary, Hirsch Papers.

75. Cabinet meeting of Oct. 7, 1922, *Kabinette Wirth*, II, p. 1118.

76. Letter to the Chancellor of Oct. 12, 1922, BAK, R 43I/2444, Bl. 313.

77. Meeting of Oct. 7, 1922, *Kabinette Wirth*, pp. 1117–20.

78. Wirth to Hemmer, Oct. 2, 1922, BAK, R 43I/2444, Bl. 295.

79. Telegram Hemmer to Wirth, Oct. 7, 1922, ibid., Bl. 302f., and *Kabinette Wirth*, II, pp. 1117–20.

80. Ibid., pp. 1123f., and *RGBl* (1922), I, pp. 795f.

81. Hirsch diary, 1922, Hirsch Papers. (Newspaper names originally abbreviated.)

82. D'Abernon to Lord Curzon with attached note by Thelwall, Oct. 14, 1922, PRO, FO 371/7518/37093/108f. For samples of the endless petitions, meetings, and protests, see the materials in the Hamburg Chamber of Commerce Papers, HK Hamburg 29 K 12a1, the Münster Chamber of Commerce Papers, RWWK, 5/21/15, the Papers of the Prussian Ministry of Commerce and Industry, which contain

complaints from the stock exchange authorities and the Ministry itself as well as complaints from various chambers of commerce and firms, GStAKM, Rep 120, C XIII 1, Nr. 171, Bd. 2, and the devastating commentary by Otto Bernstein in *Bank = Archiv* (Oct. 15, 1922), pp. 15–20.

83. The Reichsbank letter of Oct. 20, 1922, is reprinted in Hirsch, *Die deutsche Währungsfrage*, pp. 75–77. Havenstein indicated a hundred million goldmark limit at the Cabinet meeting of Oct. 16, 1922, *Kabinette Wirth*, II, p. 1126.

84. The stenographic reports of these lengthy meetings used here is to be found in SäHStA, Gesandtschaft Berlin, Nr. 658, 1. Teil, Bl. 126ff. (meeting of Oct. 2), Bl. 183 (meeting of Oct. 17), and Bl. 200ff. (meeting of Oct. 18). The Hilferding speech is to be found in Bl. 126–30.

85. Ibid., Bl. 130.

86. Ibid.

87. Ibid., Bl. 140.

88. Cabinet meeting of Oct. 24, 1922, *Kabinette Wirth*, II, p. 1142.

89. Meeting of Oct. 2, 1922, SäHStA, Gesandtschaft Berlin, Nr. 658, Teil I, Bl. 150f.

90. Hauschild, *Reichswirtschaftsrat*, pp. 61–66, for the resolution. On the policy of confidentiality, see the speech of Bernhard in the RWR Economic Policy Committee on Nov. 9, 1922, BAP, RWR, Nr. 10, Bl. 316ff.

91. Hermann Müller to Wirth, Oct. 28, 1922, BAK, R 43I/31, Bl. 388f.

92. Bernhard later complained about this rather insulting treatment of Hilferding, ibid., Bl. 322. Bonn was irritated that he was asked to appear at the behest of the Socialists rather than as an independent expert. Bonn to Wirth, Nov. 14, 1922, BAK, NL Bonn, Nr. 8d. For the positions of Urbig and Schumacher, see Havenstein to Bonn, Nov. 19, 1922, ibid. On the attitudes of Cuno and Melchior, see the meeting of German experts with the Chancellor of Oct. 30, 1922, BAK, R 43I/32, Bl. 28–34.

93. *VR*, Bd. 375, Drucksache Nr. 5198. The version here used is that found in the Keynes Papers, Marshall Library, F I/3₁.

94. Ibid. On the motives of Dubois, see Laubach, *Politik der Kabinette Wirth*, p. 304.

95. *VR*, Bd. 375, Drucksache Nr. 5198, pp. 48ff.

96. "Aufzeichnung betreffend eine endgültige Lösung der Reparationsfrage," Nov. 6, 1922, BAK, NL Bonn, Nr. 4c.

97. Bonn to Hermes, Nov. 6, 1922, ibid.

98. On the RdI program, see Feldman, *Iron and Steel*, pp. 319ff., and Hermann J. Rupieper, *The Cuno Government and Reparations 1922–1923. Politics and Economics* (The Hague, Boston, London, 1979), pp. 36ff. Many of the relevant documents are printed in Feldman and Homburg, *Industrie und Inflation*, pp. 313–44, and are to be found in the original in BAK, NL Silverberg, Nr. 132.

99. RdI meeting of Sept. 6, 1922 in Feldman and Homburg, *Industrie und Inflation*, p. 322.

100. Ibid.

101. Ibid., p. 323, and Reusch to RdI, Aug. 30, 1922, HA/GHH, Nr. 30019320/2.

102. Stinnes to Severing, July 3, 1922, ACDP, NL Stinnes, Nr. 046/2. On Severing's role in 1920, see Feldman, *VfZ* (1980), pp. 177ff.

103. Stinnes to Stresemann, Aug. 7, 1922, and Stinnes to Humann, Aug. 7, 1922, ACDP, NL Stinnes, Nr. 002/2.

104. *Protokoll der Verhandlungen des 11. Kongresses der Gewerkschaften Deutschlands, abgehalten zu Leipzig am 17. und 18. Juni 1922* (Berlin, 1922), pp. 498f.

105. The discussion and quotations which follow are from Bücher to Stinnes, Aug. 16, 1922, ACDP, NL Stinnes, Nr. 038/3.

106. See Humann's notes on his discussion with Stinnes on Aug. 24, 1922, ibid., Nr. 039/2.

107. On the non-attendance of VdA representatives at the ZAG, see Bücher to Stinnes, Aug. 16, 1922, ibid., Nr. 038/3. On the wage question in the ZAG, see Feldman and Steinisch, *Industrie und Gewerkschaften*, pp. 97f.

108. Houghton to the Secretary of State, Oct. 30, 1922, NA, 862.00/1192, for the discussion which follows.

109. The copy for Wiedfeldt was sent privately by Houghton to avoid the German Foreign Office channels, ibid.

110. He emphasized the importance of not "putting off" (*verprellen*) England while conducting his negotiations with de Lubersac. See Humann's report of his discussion with Fehrmann, Aug. 19, 1922, ACDP, NL Stinnes, Nr. 039/2.

111. Piggot to Lord Kilmarnock, Nov. 1, 1922, PRO, FO 371/7518/ 37093/209–11 for this report and discussion, quote on 210.

112. Ibid., 211.

113. Humann notes on talk with Stinnes, Aug. 30, 1922, ACDP, NL Stinnes, Nr. 039/2.

114. Ibid. When Wirth complained that the Stinnes-owned *DAZ*, which also functioned as the official newspaper for the government, was attacking him for not appointing a new Foreign Minister, Stinnes ordered an eight-day hiatus before the attack was to be resumed!

115. Humann report of Aug. 31, 1922, ibid., Nr. 046/2.

116. Warburg Papers, 1922, p. 26.

117. Ibid., pp. 30f.

118. Report by the Saxon Representative to Berlin, Gradnauer, Oct. 28, 1922, SäHStA, Gesandtschaft Berlin, Nr. 350, Bl. 95.

119. Gradnauer, who had good contacts in Socialist circles and contacts with Centrists as well, was quite definite on the subject, remarking that "It also would not be very easy to understand how anyone today could have such inclinations," ibid. For Wirth's attacks on Hermes and the Ebert "shadow government," see the Center Party Deputies meeting of Oct. 24, 1922, in *Zentrumsprotokolle*, pp. 394–403. The same group exonerated Hermes of such charges at its meetings between Nov. 13 and 17, ibid.,

pp. 403–12. Wirth continued to believe them, however, and in his 1941 correspondence with the former Prussian Minister-President Otto Braun, the latter confessed that Stresemann and Raumer, at a breakfast with Socialists Hermann Müller and Otto Wels, indicated they were prepared to enter a government provided it was not headed by Wirth. Müller and Wels, in contrast to Braun, showed some inclination to take up this proposition. This in no way proves that Hermes wished to be a party to such an arrangement, which certainly would have been favored by some of the more conservative Centrists. Hermes, after all, was more flexible on the reparations issue than Wirth. See Braun to Wirth, Aug. 25, 1941, and Wirth to Braun, Aug. 29, 1941, BAK, NL Wirth, Nr. 25. It is a measure of Wirth's agitation at the time and his fears of assassination, that he wrote to Hermes on November 4, made mention of the danger to his person, and went on to declare that "he considers it therefore as his obligation as a Christian, to ask forgiveness of those whom he has unintentionally injured [and] therefore takes back all reproaches . . . and sincerely asks for forgiveness." See Stehkämper, *NL Marx*, Teil I, pp. 269f.

120. *Kabinette Wirth*, II, p. 1136.

121. See the revealing analysis of the last days of the Wirth Chancellorship by ten Hompel in BAK, NL ten Hompel, Nr. 15. Wirth emphasized Stegerwald's role in his fall in his correspondence with Otto Braun, BAK, NL Wirth, Nr. 25.

122. "*Hirsch*" is the German word for stag. Center Party Deputies' meeting, Oct. 24, 1922, *Zentrumsprotokolle*, p. 398.

123. Wirth to Schmidt, Oct. 24, 1922, BAK, R 43I/31, Bl. 228f.

124. In the meetings held at this time in the War Burdens Commission and with the Reich Statistical Office, there was a complete consensus that the balance-of-trade deficit was being significantly underestimated. See BAP, RB, Bd. 6594, Bl. 157–83. Germany's actual foreign-trade situation will be discussed in Chapter 13.

125. For the note of Nov. 4, 1922, and the meeting with the party leaders on Nov. 7, see *Kabinette Wirth*, pp. 1148f., 1154–57.

126. Report by Hamburg representative Baumann of Nov. 9, 1922, StA Hamburg, Senatskommission für die Reichs- und auswärtigen Angelegenheiten, Hamburgische Gesandtschaft, Nr. 6. On the Saxon elections, see J. Falter, Th. Lindenberger, and S. Schumann, *Wahlen und Abstimmungen in der Weimarer Republik* (Munich, 1986), p. 108.

127. Winkler, *Revolution zur Stabilisierung*, p. 499.

128. Stinnes to Vögler, Oct. 22, 1922, ACDP, NL Stinnes, Nr. 041/3.

129. See above, p. 462.

130. Thyssen to Wirth, Oct. 14, 1922, BAK, R 13I/1132, Bl. 359–62, and *Schultheß* (1922), p. 130.

131. RWR Economic Committee meeting, Nov. 9, 1922, BAP, RWR, Nr. 10, Bl. 330.

132. Ibid., Bl. 353–68.

133. Ibid., Bl. 368–80.

134. Ibid., Bl. 373.

135. Ibid., Bl. 382.

136. Ibid., Bl. 389.

137. Feldman and Steinisch, *Industrie und Gewerkschaften*, pp. 98ff., 174–85.

138. Winkler, *Revolution zur Stabilisierung*, p. 499.

139. Laubach, *Politik der Kabinette Wirth*, pp. 306f.

140. Klügmann to Hasselmann, Nov. 27, 1922, BAK, R 43I/227–34, quote on Bl. 239.

141. For a strong criticism of the SPD, see Winkler, *Revolution zur Stabilisierung*, pp. 498ff. The importance of the Stinnes speech is also noted in ten Hompel's account of the end of the Wirth regime, BAK, NL ten Hompel, Nr. 15. In a report to the DDP Party Committee, Senator Petersen of Hamburg also emphasized the harmful nature of the speech and suggested that Stinnes had let his rhetoric run away from him. Meeting of Nov. 26, 1922, BAK, R 45III/11, Bl. 196ff. See also Laubach, *Politik der Kabinette Wirth*, pp. 307ff., Jones, *German Liberalism*, pp. 186f., and *Kabinette Wirth*, pp. 1163ff.

142. See his correspondence with Brauns and his own remarks on Stegerwald in BAK, NL Wirth, Nr. 23 and Nr. 25.

143. Wirth's "ultimatum" to the SPD was noted both by Socialist leader Breitscheid, who thought that another tactic might have produced different results, and by the DDP leader Petersen in their subsequent reviews of the crisis. See the report of Klügmann to Hasselmann, Nov. 27, 1922, BAK, R 43I/2662, Bl. 227–34, esp. Bl. 231 and the DDP Party Committee meeting of Nov. 26, 1922, BAK R 45III/11, Bl. 196f.

144. RdI meeting of Sept. 6, 1922, Feldman and Homburg, *Industrie und Inflation*, p. 332. The best discussions of the creation of the Cuno government are by Karl-Heinz Harbeck in his introduction to *Kabinett Cuno*, pp. xixff., and Rupieper, *Cuno Government*, pp. 13–30, and they form the basis of the discussion which follows.

145. See the attack of Rudolf Breitscheid in the Reichstag on Nov. 24, 1922, *VR*, Bd. 357, p. 9112, and Klugmann's report on his conversation with Breitscheid, Nov. 27, 1922, BAK, R 43I/2662, Bl. 230f.

146. On the Stinnes–Cuno conflict, see Peter Wulf, "Schwerindustrie und Seeschiffahrt nach dem 1. Weltkrieg: Hugo Stinnes und die HAPAG," *VSWG* 67 (1980), pp. 1–21. More generally, see Rupieper, *Cuno Government*, pp. 23ff.

147. See Cuno's presentation to the Reichstag on Nov. 24, 1922, *VR*, Bd. 357, pp. 9099–10,005.

148. DDP Party Committee meeting, Nov. 26, 1922, BAK, R 45III/11, Bl. 261f.

149. Ibid., Bl. 203f.

150. Aktennotiz Osius, Nov. 27, 1922, ACDP, NL Stinnes, Nr. 046/3.

151. Rupieper is particularly sensitive to these differences and nuances in his *Cuno Government*, pp. 50ff., and his "Industrie und Reparationen: Einige

Aspekte des Reparationsproblems 1922–1924," in Hans Mommsen et al., eds., *Industrielles System*, pp. 582–92.

152. Logan report of Nov. 24, 1922, Hoover Institution, Logan Papers, Vol. VII, pp. 157–60. See also the anxious November 24, 1922, report of Bergmann, who regretted that Morgan had let his irritation get the best of him in presenting Poincaré with an ultimatum, *Kabinett Cuno*, pp. 8–15, especially, pp. 10–12. On British policy, see Konrad von Zwehl, *Deutschlandpolitik Englands*, I, pp. 264ff., and McDougall, *Rhineland Diplomacy*, pp. 235ff.

153. Bergmann report of Nov. 24, 1922, *Kabinett Cuno*, pp. 12–15, and Warburg to Cuno, Nov. 24, 1922, BAK, R 43I/32, Bl. 276–78.

154. The quotations and discussion are from Wassermann to Cuno, Nov. 30, 1922, BAK R 43I/33, Bl. 3–10.

155. Report by Osius dated Dec. 9, 1922, ACDP, NL Stinnes, Nr. 026/3. On the events leading up to these meetings, see *Kabinett Cuno*, p. 15n10.

156. Stinnes to Reusch, Dec. 7, 1922, ACDP, NL Stinnes, Nr. 026/3.

157. Aktennotiz Osius, Dec. 9, 1922, ibid.

158. *Kabinett Cuno*, p. 51n8.

159. Dec. 12, 1922, meeting, ibid., pp. 63–66, p. 64n4 for quote.

160. Stinnes to Vögler, Dec. 13, 1922, ACDP, NL Stinnes, Nr. 046/2.

161. For this discussion of the negotiations in London, see von Zwehl, *Deutschlandpolitik Englands*, I, pp. 317ff.; Rupieper, *Cuno Government*, pp. 45ff.; Trachtenberg, *Reparations*, pp. 280ff.

162. Von Zwehl, *Deutschlandpolitik Englands*, pp. 332ff., and Bergmann to Cuno, Dec. 11, 1922, *Kabinett Cuno*, pp. 60–63.

163. Ibid., p. 63.

164. The economic and social situation in the Rhineland and the political economy of Germany will be discussed in Chapter 13. For illustrations of the calls for action and reports on the Rhineland reaching the highest levels of government in Berlin in December 1922, see the discussion between State Secretaries Hamm and Brügger of Dec. 4, 1922, and the letter of the Prussian Minister-President Braun to Cuno of Dec. 15, 1922, in *Kabinett Cuno*, pp. 21–25, 68–70.

165. Notes dated Dec. 12, 1922, ACDP, NL Stinnes, Nr. O46/3, and Stinnes to Vögler, Dec. 13, 1922, ibid., Nr. 046/2.

166. Ibid.

167. Quoted from the Hughes papers in Link, *Stabilisierungspolitik*, p. 161. It is interesting to note that this is virtually a literal translation of the proposal discussed in the Stinnes notes on his meeting of Dec. 12 mentioned in note 165.

168. Ibid., pp. 161f. Here I follow Link's interpretation of Cuno's motives. Link does not seem to be aware of Stinnes's role in the Wiedfeldt assignment, and the interpretation of Stinnes's intentions is my own. For other illustrations of Stinnes's unrealistic

expectations at this time, see the discussion which follows.

169. Rupieper, *Cuno Government*, pp. 71f,; Krüger, *Außenpolitik*, pp. 195ff.; Link, *Stabilisierungspolitik*, pp. 163ff.

170. There are reasonably full records of the meetings of Dec. 13 and 16 in BAK, R 43I/33, Bl. 345ff., and 43I/34, Bl. 308ff. but very little information on the meeting of Dec. 21 and 28, although the situation is improved by correspondence, used here for the first time, from the ACDP, NL Stinnes, Nr. 022/2. Some material is reproduced in *Kabinett Cuno*, pp. 73f., 91ff.

171. Meeting of Dec. 16, 1922, BAK, R 43I/308, Bl. 330f.

172. Ibid., Bl. 321.

173. Ibid., Bl. 312.

174. Ibid., Bl. 319.

175. See the useful discussion in Rupieper, *Cuno Government*, pp. 63ff.

176. Ibid., and summary in *Kabinett Cuno*, pp. 73f.

177. *Kabinett Cuno*, p. 91n4.

178. Melchior to Stinnes, dec. 23, 1922, ACDP, NL Stinnes, Nr. 022/2.

179. Stinnes to Melchior, Dec. 26, 1922, ibid.

180. Melchior to Stinnes, Dec. 28, 1922, ibid. See also Stinnes to de Lubersac, Dec. 25, 1922, and de Lubersac to Stinnes, Jan. 1, 1923, ibid, Nr. 020/3. On the Schacht and Cuno talks with Bergeon, see *Kabinett Cuno*, p. 136n3, and for Reusch's remark, see the meeting of Dec. 16, 1922, BAK, R 43I/34, Bl. 321.

181. The formal offer sent for transmittal in Paris is dated, Jan. 4, 1923, *Kabinett Cuno*, pp. 113–16, quote on p. 115.

182. Bücher to Stinnes, Dec. 30, 1922, ACDP, NL Stinnes, Nr. 022/2.

183. Ibid. (Bücher's italics.) For a similar attitude, see Reusch's letter to Cuno of Dec. 31, 1922, *Kabinett Cuno*, pp. 100–103.

184. Stinnes to Bücher, Jan. 1, 1923, ACDP, NL Stinnes, Nr. 046/2.

185. Trachtenberg, *Reparation*, pp. 281ff; von Zwehl, *Deutschlandpolitik Englands*, pp. 359ff.; Rupieper, *Cuno Government*, pp. 72ff.

186. Steven B. Webb, "Fiscal News and Inflationary Expectations in Germany," *Journal of Economic History* 46 (1986), pp. 769–94, quote on p. 94. See also Carl-Ludwig Holtfrerich, "Political Factors in the German Inflation," in Schmuckler and Marcus, eds., *Inflation through the Ages*, pp. 400–416, esp. pp. 410ff. The problem with the adaptive-expectations model, as Holtfrerich shows, is that expectations varied in accordance with events which were in no way predictable by past events.

187. Steinthal to Bierwes, Oct. 12 and 14, 1922, Mannesmann-Archiv, M 11.090, Bl. 255, 269.

188. NA, 862.5151/1048.

189. Houghton report to the Secretary of State of Dec. 27, 1922, NA, 862.00/1199.

190. Memorandum by Hermes of Sept. 21, 1923, in Stehkämper, *NL Marx*, Teil III, p. 99.

12. The Year of Dr. Mabuse: The Hyperinflation and German Society in 1922

1. See the report of Ambassador Stahmer, Nov. 29, 1922, BAP, HAAA, Nr. 47343, Bl. 92–3.

2. From the English-language text accompanying *Dr. Mabuse: The Gambler* (*Dr. Mabuse: Der Spieler*), University of California at Berkeley film collection. On the film of the Weimar Republic, see Siegfried Kracauer, *From Caligari to Hitler* (Princeton, 1947), and Ulrich Gregor and Enno Patalas, *Geschichte des Films 1895–1939* (Hamburg, 1976), pp. 47–63. See also, Norbert Jacques, *Dr. Mabuse: Der Spieler* (reprint, Berchtesgaden, 1961). A useful compendium of events for 1922 is Dieter Struss, ed., *Das war 1922. Fakten. Daten. Zahlen. Schicksale* (Munich, 1982).

3. Report on a conversation of Feb. 18, 1922, Melchior to Warburg, Warburg Papers, 1922, p. 15.

4. Fritz Stern, "The Scientist in Power and Exile," in *Dreams and Delusions. The Drama of German History* (New York, 1987), pp. 51–76.

5. For the Marxist interpretation, see Franz Neumann, *The Rule of Law. Political Theory and the Legal System in Modern Society* (Leamington Spa, 1986), pp. 273ff. See also, Feldman, *AfS* 26 (1986), pp. 8–10.

6. Morus, "System Klante," *Die Weltbühne* 18 (Dec. 21, 1921), pp. 651–52. On Richard Lewinsohn, who later wrote books on the German redistributive effects of the inflation and on money in politics, see Istvan Deak, *Weimar's Left-Wing Intellectuals. Die Weltbühne. A Political History of the Weltbühne and its Circle* (Berkeley & Los Angeles, 1968), p. 256.

7. Rechtsanwalt Dr. Stiel, "Die Beraubung der Mündel," *Deutsche Juristen-Zeitung* (1921), p. 757.

8. Amtsgerichtsrat Dr. Erlanger, ibid. (1922), pp. 55f.

9. See the letter of Oberregierungsrat Dr. Stock, Lübeck, in ibid., p. 248.

10. Oberlandesgerichtspräsident Königsberg an den Jusitzminister, Feb. 25, 1922, GStAPrK, Rep. 84a, Nr. 5535, Bl. 121f.

11. HK Düsseldorf to Oberlandesgerichtspräsidenten, March 22, 1922, ibid., Bl. 98–101, quote on Bl. 98.

12. Report of the Oberlandesgerichtspräsident Köln, March 13, 1922, ibid., Bl. 113–18, quote on Bl. 113, and the report from Kiel of Feb. 14, 1922, Bl. 109–12.

13. Report of April 6, 1922, ibid., Bl. 91–93.

14. Report to the Justice Minister of Feb. 11, 1922, ibid., Bl. 123–25.

15. Although Mügel had begun writing on the subject in August 1921, the writings that drew serious public attention were those that came later in the year: "Gesetzliche Maßnahmen aus Anlaß der Geldentwertung. Die Goldmark als Rechnungswert," *Juristische Wochenschrift* (Oct. 15, 1921), pp. 1267–11, and "Kreditgewährung und wechselnder Geldwert," *Deutsche Juristen-Zeitung* (Feb. 1, 1922), pp. 72–82. He ventured a comprehensive presentation of his views, which was published early in 1923. See Mügel, *Geldentwertung und Gesetzgebung* [*Wirtschaftsrecht und Wirtschaftspflege*, Heft VII] (Berlin, 1923). The presentation of his views which follows is based on these writings.

16. Alois Zeiler, *Meine Mitarbeit* [*Rechts= und Wirtschaftsfragen*] (Braunschweig, n.d.), esp. pp. 141ff. These memoirs were written and published sometime in the 1930s and are an important source on the revaluation question.

17. Mügel, *Juristische Wochenschrift* (Oct. 15, 1921), p. 1270.

18. Ibid., p. 1273.

19. Finance Committee meeting of the RWR, November 12, 1921, BAP, RWR, Nr. 549, Bd. 4, Bl. 14f.

20. For Springer's printed version of his comments at the November meeting in Berlin where Mügel's views were discussed, see Geh. Oberfinanzrat Springer, "Vorkriegshypotheken und Geldentwertung, *Bank=Archiv* 22 (Dec. 20, 1922), pp. 71–73. Mügel sought to answer these attacks in his February 1922 article in the *Deutsche Juristen-Zeitung*, pp. 73–81.

21. Ibid. pp. 72f.

22. Mügel, *Geldentwertung*, p. 102 and report to the Prussian Justice Minister of Nov. 7, 1922, GStAPrK, Rep. 84a, Nr. 5885, Bl. 13. The matter was taken up in a confidential discussion among the Prussian authorities, apparently in response to a proposal that Prussia present a proposal in support of Mügel's ideas in the Reichsrat. The predominant sentiment was negative, however, and the matter was dropped. Report to the HK Frankfurt, Dec. 29, 1922, Stadtarchiv Frankfurt, IHK, Nr. 608.

23. Zeiler, *Meine Mitarbeit*, pp. 146ff.

24. Mügel, *Geldentwertung*, p. 102.

25. "Franklin D. Roosevelt Head of Big German Mark Trust," *New York American*, Sept. 9, 1922, BAP, HAAA, Nr. 43814, Bl. 91.

26. Carl Fincke to the Dresdener Bank, Sept. 9, 1922, and copy of the newspaper report appearing in the American press, ibid., Bl. 66f.

27. Wiedfeldt to Foreign Office, Nov. 16, 1922, ibid., Bl. 91.

28. See the reports of Ludwig Bendix of Oct. 4 and Oct. 10, 1922, ibid., Nr. 43818, Bl. 222–26, and Nr. 43819, Bl. 1–5. For the estimates of U.S. investor losses, see Holtfrerich in *VSWG* 64 (1977), pp. 23–25. For present day support for the argument that German imports played a major role in relieving the depression in the United States, see Carl-Ludwig Holtfrerich, "Die konjunkturanregenden Wirkungen der deutschen Inflation auf die US-Wirtschaft in der Weltwirtschaftskrise 1920/21," in Feldman et al.,

The German Inflation. A Preliminary Balance, pp. 207–34.

29. See above, Chapter 1, p. 45.

30. Mayor of Wittenberge to the Zentralstelle des Deutschen Städtetages, Feb. 3, 1921, and related correspondence in LA Berlin, AdSt, Nr. 3780.

31. Flensburg to the Zentralstelle des Deutschen Städtetages, Dec. 24, 1921, ibid.

32. Charbonnier to Böss, Jan. 24, 1922, and Böss to Charbonnier, Jan. 27, 1922, LA Berlin, AdSt, Nr. 3780. On loans offered by a Danish–Norwegian group, see the letter of the government of Rüstringen to the Magistracy of Wilhelmshaven, May 28, 1922, and on Danish offers of a fifty-year loan to the city of Stralsund, see the letter from the Stralsund authorities to the Städtetag of Aug. 18, 1922. On the problem of taking long-term loans in any currency, see the note of the Städtetag to the government of Kolberg, Sept. 22, 1922, ibid.

33. Descriptions of these various categories of *Valutaschuldner* are to be found in the meeting of the RWR Finance Committee of December 21, 1921, BAP, RWR, Nr. 550, Bd. 5, Bl. 51ff., and an informative report to the HK of Frankfurt a.M. & Hanau of Jan. 26, 1922, Stadtarchiv Frankfurt a.M., IHK, Nr. 609. On the insurance companies, see the report of July 20, 1922, in ibid., as well as the report of U.S. Vice Consul N. P. Davis of January 20, 1923, NA, 862.106/1. For estimates of the amount of the Swiss mortgage debts, see the report of the RWM of April 8, 1922, SäHStA, Gesandtschaft Berlin, Nr. 659, Bl. 46–50.

34. For the German–Swiss Agreement of December 6, 1920, see *RGBl*, (1920), p. 2021. See also *Kabinette Wirth*, II, pp. 789f.

35. *Juristische Wochenschrift* (1922), pp. 1316–18; *Deutsche Juristen-Zeitung* (1922), pp. 511f., 591–94.

36. RWR meeting, Dec. 21, 1921, BAP, RWR, Nr. 550, Bd. 5, Bl. 73.

37. Statement by Beckmann in the RWR as reported to the Frankfurt a.M. & Hanau Chambers of Commerce, Jan. 28, 1922, Stadtarchiv Frankfurt, IHK, Nr. 609.

38. See the letter by the Mayor of Vienna of Sept. 5, 1922, and accompanying materials surveying international practices for the June 14, 1923, meeting of the Financial Committee of the Congress of German Municipalities, LA Berlin, AdSt, Nr. 2527 and Nr. 3780, as well as the meeting of the *Valuta* Committee of the south German chambers of commerce, March 3–4, 1922, Stadtarchiv Frankfurt, IHK, Nr. 609.

39. *Plutus* (Dec. 20, 1922), p. 498; *Kabinette Wirth*, II, pp. 789–91. On the inconclusive negotiations with the Congress of German Municipalities on Dec. 7, 1922, see LA Berlin, AdSt, Nr. 3780.

40. *Volkswirtschaftliche Chronik* (1921), pp. 821f.; (1922), pp. 561, 758; (1923), pp. 256, 608; (1924), pp. 311f. See also the letter from one of the "Valuta-free" companies to the Chambers of Com-

merce of Frankfurt & Hanau, July 20, 1922, Stadtarchiv Frankfurt, IHK, Nr. 609.

41. Congress of German Cities to the Magistracy of Wittenberge, April 13, 1921, LA Berlin, AdSt, Nr. 3780.

42. For a useful survey, see John P. Dawson, "Effects of Inflation on Private Law Contracts: Germany, 1914–1924," *Michigan Law Review* 33 (Dec. 1934), pp. 171–238. See also Dr. Lahusen, "Zur clausula rebus sic stantibus," *Juristische Wochenschrift* (Aug. 1, 1922), pp. 1180–82, and for the influence of Oertmann, see the interesting discussion in Reichsgericht decisions in ibid., (May 15, 1922), pp. 702–6.

43. The legal bureaus of the Rheinischen Stahlwerke and the Wirtschaftsausschuß der Deutschen Werfte were especially diligent in citing court decisions to back up their demands for revision of old contracts. See Rheinstahl's letter to its customers of Feb. 22, 1922, and the shipbuilders circulars of Jan. 30 and March 13, 1922, in StA Hamburg, Blohm & Voss, Nr. 679. See also the widely circulated note of the General Consul in Amsterdam to the German Foreign Office of July 1, 1922, BayHStA, Abt. II, Gesandtschaft Berlin, Nr. 1840.

44. See the circulars sent to the Duisberg Chamber of Commerce of Aug. 1 and Nov. 30, 1922, RWWK, 20/523/3.

45. Letter of A. Stickman, Nov. 7, 1922, BAP, HAAA, Nr. 44935, Bl. 167f., and circular of the Board of Trade of July 13, 1922, ibid., Bl. 169–72.

46. Circular of the Duisberg Chamber of Commerce, Aug. 7, 1922, RWWK, 20/418/12.

47. General Consul Hatzfeld to the Foreign Office, July 1, 1922, BayHStA, Abt. II. Gesandtschaft Berlin, Nr. 1840.

48. For a useful compilation as of May 1922, see Plum, "Schwebende Lieferverträge unter dem Einfluß der staatlichen und wirtschaftlichen Umwälzung seit Krieg und Revolution im Lichte der Rechtsprechung," *Juristische Wochenschrift* (May 1, 1922), pp. 633–56.

49. Nipperdey, "Vertragstreue und Geldentwertung," *Deutsche Juristen-Zeitung* (Nov. 1, 1922), pp. 659–63.

50. Justizrat Kurlbaum at the Fifteenth Representative Assembly of the German Association of Lawyers, Oct. 15, 1922, reprinted in *Juristische Wochenschrift* (Dec. 1, 1922), p. 1. See also the letter to the Reich Minister of Justice of Sept. 1, 1922 reprinted in ibid. (Sept. 1, 1921).

51. Ibid., p. 659.

52. Helpful contributions to this problem have been made by Konrad Jarausch. See his "The Crisis of the German Professions 1918–1933," *Journal of Contemporary History* 29 (1985), pp. 379–98; "Die Not der geistigen Arbeiter: Akademiker in der Berufskrise," in Werner Abelshauser, ed., *Die Weimarer Republik als Wohlfahrtsstaat. Zum Verhältnis von Wirtschafts- und Sozialpolitik in der Industriegesellschaft* [*Vierteljahrsschrift für Sozial- und Wirtschaftsgeschichte*, Beiheft 81] (Stuttgart, 1987),

pp. 280–89; and "Die unfreien Professionen. Überlegungen zu den Wandlungsprozessen im deutschen Bildungsbürgertum 1900–1955," in Kocka, ed., *Bürgertum*, Vol. 2, pp. 124–48.

53. Consul Gosling report of Aug. 30, 1922, PRO, FO 371/7518/37093/13–15.

54. Meeting of the Fifteenth Representative Assembly of the Association of German Lawyers, Oct. 15, 1922, *Juristische Wochenschrift* (Dec. 1, 1922), pp. 22–23.

55. Unless otherwise noted, this discussion is based on Julius Magnus, *Die Rechtsanwaltschaft* (Leipzig, 1929), pp. 1–34; Hans Heiler, *Die Verelendung des Mittelstandes.* [*Heft 106 der Beiträge zur Statistik Bayerns*] (Munich, 1925), pp. 38–42, Schultze, *Not und Verschwendung*, pp. 305–9, and the material to be found in the Verhandlungen der 15. Vertreterversammlung des Deutschen Anwaltvereins am 15. Oktober 1922 (Berlin), printed as the appendix to the Dec. 1, 1922 issue of the *Juristische Wochenschrift*.

56. Ibid., p. 14.

57. Ibid., p. 23.

58. For this quotation, and those which follow, see the meeting of the Unterausschuß zur wirtschaftlichen Förderung der geistigen Arbeit, Dec. 20, 1922, BAP, RWR, Nr. 476, Bl. 131–33.

59. RWR subcommittee meeting, Feb. 12, 1923, ibid., Bl. 178. Hachenburg, it will be remembered, had provided the draft legislation for the abortive credit offer of German industry.

60. For the pre-1914 development of the profession, see Claudia Huerkamp, *Der Aufstieg der Ärzte im 19. Jahrhundert. Vom gelehrten Stand zum professionellen Experten: Das Beispiel Preußens* [*Kritische Studien zur Geschichtswissenschaft*, Bd. 68] (Göttingen, 1985), pp.198f., for the statistics.

61. Ibid., Chap. 7.

62. Ibid., pp. 224–40. See also Michael H. Kater, "Ärzte und Politik in Deutschland, 1848 bis 1945," *Jahrbuch des Instituts für Geschichte der Medizin der Robert Bosch Stiftung*, Band 5, für das Jahr 1986 (Stuttgart, 1987), pp. 34–48, esp. p. 35.

63. Hermann Scholl, "Die Lage der deutschen Ärzte," *Süddeutsche Monatshefte* (1923), pp. 68–74, quote on p. 71.

64. For statistics on the plight of the doctors which are used in this discussion, see Heiler, *Verelendung*, pp. 32–38, and for information on their condition, see Schultze, *Not und Verschwendung*, pp. 296–305. For the polemics, see the speech of the Socialist Deputy Julius Moses, himself a doctor, in *VR*, Nov. 16, 1922, Bd. 357, pp. 9003–10, and the exchange between Hans Oppenheim, "Die Zukunft des Aerztestandes," *Die Weltbühne* 18 (March 22, 1922), pp. 210–11 and Richard Lewinsohn, "Der Aerztestand der Zukunft," ibid. (Aug. 10, 1922), pp. 131–35. The attitude of the profession and its organization is rigorously presented in Georg Kuhns, *Fünfundzwanzig Jahre Verband der Ärzte Deutschlands (Hartmannbund)* (Leipzig, 1925). For more critical perspectives,

see I. Winter, "Ärzte und Arbeiterklasse in der Weimarer Republik," in Kurt Kühn, ed., *Ärzte an der Seite der Arbeiterklasse. Beiträge zur Geschichte des Bündnisses der deutschen Arbeiterklasse mit der medizinischen Intelligenz* (Berlin, 1973), pp. 25–38, and Michael H. Kater, "Professionalization and Socialization of Physicians in Wilhelmine and Weimar Germany," *Journal of Contemporary History* 20 (1985), pp. 677–701.

65. Kuhns, *Fünfundzwanzig Jahre*, p. 352.

66. Preller, *Sozialpolitik*, pp. 234, 284.

67. Speech by Moses, *VR*, Nov. 16, 1922, Bd. 357, p. 9007. For the strike threats and discussion of medical profession demands in the RWR subcommittee, see the meetings of Dec. 20, 1922, and Feb. 23, 1923, BAP, RWR, Nr. 476, Bl. 130ff., 175ff.

68. Georg Bernhard and Prof. Heyde, for example, felt that the entry of the doctors into the ranks of the civil service was inevitable, although the former supported a law granting "free choice of doctor" and the latter opposed it, ibid., Bl. 175–77. For a shrewd analysis of the contradictions in the position taken by the doctors and support for the socialization of the medical profession, see Richard Lewinsohn, "Der Aerztestand der Zukunft," *Die Weltbühne* 18 (Aug. 10, 1922), pp. 131–35. See Käte Frankenthal, *Der dreifache Fluch: Jüdin, Intellektuelle, Sozialistin. Lebenserinnerungen einer Ärztin in Deutschland und im Exil* (Frankfurt a.M. & New York, 1981), p. 105.

69. Arnold Czempin, "Schauspielersorgen," *Die Weltbühne* 17 (April 21, 1921), pp. 438–42.

70. Martin Zickel, "Theaterdirektorenfreuden," ibid. (May 5, 1921), pp. 500–502, and Emil Lind, "Schauspielerkämpfe," ibid. (May 19, 1921), pp. 553–57.

71. Report of July 10, 1919, Hoover Institution Archives, Karl von Wiegand Papers, Box 24. Apparently, the Kaiser continued to subsidize the opera from exile until April 1919. See also Wolfgang Ribbe, ed., *Geschichte Berlins*, 2 vols. (Munich, 1987), Vol. 2, pp. 883ff.

72. Gisella Selden-Goth, "Große Volksoper," *Die Weltbühne* 17 (Oct. 13, 1921), pp. 380–82.

73. Schultze, *Not und Verschwendung*, p. 349.

74. Report of July 8, 1919, Karl von Wiegand Papers, Hoover Institution, Box 24. In this context, it is amusing to read von Wiegand's correspondence with his mistress which was filled with baby talk.

75. *Die Chronik Berlins* (Berlin, 1986), p. 343.

76. Lange, *Groß = Berliner Tagebuch* (Berlin, 1951), p. 22.

77. Schultze, *Not und Verschwendung*, pp. 352ff., and Hans Knudsen, "Theater" in Hans Herzfeld, ed., *Berlin und die Provinz Brandenburg im 19. und 20. Jahrhundert* (Berlin, 1968), pp. 827ff.

78. "Misera, Totentanz, Hypnose," Aug. 30, 1922, Alfred Döblin, *Ein Kerl muß eine Meinung haben* (Freiburg i.B., 1976), pp. 101f. On the *Angestelltenkultur* of the Weimar Republic, see Siegfried Kracauer, *Die Angestellten. Aus dem neuesten Deutschland* (Frankfurt, 1971).

79. Lange, *Tagebuch*, pp. 34f.

80. Siegfried Jacobsohn, "Saisonbeginn," *Die Weltbühne* 18 (Sept. 21, 1922), pp. 315–18. For a more sympathetic view of the strike, during which the actors put on special performances in breweries and wherever they could find room, see Döblin's "Zwischen den Waffen singen die Musen," of Dec. 7, 1922, in *Ein Mann*, pp. 131–34.

81. Siegfried Jacobsohn, "Der Schauspieler-streik," *Die Weltbühne* 18 (Dec. 7, 1922), pp. 601–5, quote on p. 603.

82. Berthold Viertel, "Theater-Not," ibid., Dec. 28, 1922, pp. 673–78, quote on p. 675.

83. Klaus Pringsheim, "Nach dem Schauspieler-putsch," ibid., 19 (Jan. 11, 1923), pp. 45–49, and Siegfried Jacobsohn, "Die Theaterkrise," ibid., (March 15, 1923), pp. 308–9.

84. See the fine discussion by Martin Schumacher, "Autoren und Verleger in der deutschen Inflationszeit," *VSWG* 58 (1971), pp. 88–94.

85. Bruno Rauecker, "Die Fachvereine der deutschen Schriftsteller," in Ludwig Sinzheimer, ed., *Die geistigen Arbeiter. Erster Teil. Freies Schriftstellertum und Literaturverlag* [*Schriften des Vereins für Sozialpolitik*, Bd. 152], (München & Leipzig, 1922), pp. 157–98, quote on p. 195.

86. Karl Bücher, "Gutachten über das Gesamtgebiet der Schriftstellerfrage," ibid., pp. 465–79, quote on p. 475.

87. Ludwig Feuchtwanger, "Die Bezahlung des wissenschaftlichen Schriftstellers," ibid., pp. 273–307, esp. pp. 297f. Feuchtwanger was the business manager of the publishing firm of Duncker & Humblot.

88. Dr. Leon Zeitlin, "Finanzpolitik und Schriftstellerfragen," ibid., pp. 367–84, esp. pp. 379ff.

89. Described in a memorandum of the Börsenverein der Deutschen Buchhändler zu Leipzig of July 12, 1921, BAP, RWR, 463, Bl. 177–84, esp. Bl. 177.

90. Ibid., Bl. 179.

91. Subcommittee meeting of May 30, 1921, ibid., Nr. 467, Bl. 232–70. That it was possible to provide some calculations on how honoraria and royalties were calculated was amply demonstrated by de Gruyter's colleague from Duncker & Humblot, Ludwig Feuchtwanger in Sinzheimer, *Die geistigen Arbeiter*, pp. 273ff.

92. Gustav Kiepenheuer, "Unsre Schriftsteller. Antwort an Herbert Eulenberg," *Die Weltbühne* 20 (Jan. 24, 1924), pp. 105–8, quote on p. 106.

93. Wolff to Schickele, March 29, 1921, Bernhard Zeiler and Ellen Otten, *Kurt Wolff. Briefwechsel eines Verlegers 1911–1963* (Frankfurt a.M., 1967), p. 208.

94. Wolff to Schickele, Nov. 17, 1921, ibid., p. 211.

95. See Wolff to Schickele, June 6, 1923, p. 215, and their published correspondence for 1923 in ibid., pp. 212ff.

96. Erich Mühsam, "Autor und Verleger," *Die Weltbühne* 20 (March 20, 1924), pp. 384–86.

Mühsam supported an authors' publishing cooperative.

97. Alfred Henschke, *Klabund Chansons. Streit- und Leidgedichte* (Vienna, 1930), pp. 36–37. The last stanza of "Der geistige Arbeiter in der Inflation" read:

Ein eigener Sarg, das ist mein Stolz
Aus Eschen- oder Eichenholz
Aus deutscher Eiche.—Das Vaterland
Reichte mir hilfreich stets die Vaterhand
Begrabt mich in deutschem Holz, in deutscher
   Erde, im deutschen Wald
Aber bald!
Wie schläft sich's sanft, wie ruht sich's gut,
Erlöst von Schwindsucht und Skorbut.
Herrgott im Himmel, erwache ich zu neuem
   Leben noch einmal auf Erde:
Laß mich Devisenhändler, Diamantenschleifer
oder Kanalreiniger werden!

98. Klabund, "Unser Verleger," *Die Weltbühne* 20 (Feb. 14, 1924), pp. 213f.

99. See, for example, Bruno Renecker, "Die Not der Schriftsteller," *Soziale Praxis* (1920), pp. 618f.

100. See the various articles supporting continuation of the system in 1921 in BAK, R 431/2488, Bl. 19–25.

101. See Kurt Wolff, "Brief an Eulenberg," *Die Weltbühne* 20 (Jan. 31, 1924), pp. 133–37. The publisher Fritz Cohn, defended the export control system for books in "Unsre Eulenbergs," ibid. (Jan. 17, 1924), pp. 78–80.

102. Herbert Eulenberg, "Unsre Verleger," ibid. (Jan. 10, 1924), pp. 48–49.

103. Wolff, "Brief an Eulenberg," ibid. (Jan. 31, 1924), p. 136.

104. Schickele to Wolff, Nov. 15, 1921, *Wolff. Briefwechsel*, p. 209, and Schumacher, *VSWG* (1971), p. 94. On Schickele, see also Deak, *Weltbühne*, p. 267.

105. "Ausverkauf," *Kunst und Künstler* 18 (Feb. 1, 1920), p. 191.

106. From the catalogue of Hans Goltz, *10 Jahre Neue Kunst in München* (Munich, 1923). I am grateful to Laszlo Glozer for bringing this source to my attention.

107. In addition to the article in note 102 above, see L. Fritzsching, "Die wirtschaftliche Lage der bildenden Künstler seit Kriegsende," in *Annalen des Deutschen Reichs für Gesetzgebung, Verwaltung und Volkswirtschaft. Jahrgang 1921 und 1922* 54/55 (Munich, Berlin & Leipzig, 1923), pp. 133–208, esp. pp. 170ff.

108. Ibid., pp. 147ff.; see also the retrospective comments in "Auktionsnachrichten," *Kunst und Künstler* 22 (1924), p. 154. More generally, see Fritz Hellwag, "Die derzeitige wirtschaftliche Lage der bildenden Künstler," in Ernst Francke and Walther Lotz, *Die geistigen Arbeiter. Zweiter Teil. Journalisten und bildende Künstler* [*Schriften des Vereins*

für Sozialpolitik, Bd. 152] (Munich and Leipzig, 1922), pp. 143–75.

109. Friedrich Dross, ed., *Ernst Barlach. Die Briefe I, 1888–1924* (Munich, 1968), p. 555. On Liebermann, see Lange, *Tagebuch,* p. 30.

110. The first issue of *Kunst und Wirtschaft* appeared in October 1920, and the issues discussed here were mentioned with such regularity and frequency that there is no point in citing individual articles here. They were, so to speak, the subject matter of the journal.

111. Hellwag in *Die geistigen Arbeiter, Zweiter Teil,* p. 172.

112. Carl Zuckmayer, "Katharina Knie," *Komödie und Volksstück* (Frankfurt a.M., 1950), p. 86.

113. RWR subcommittee meeting of Jan. 28, 1921, BAP, RWR, Nr. 467, Bl. 2ff., quote on Bl. 35.

114. Ibid., Bl. 101.

115. Ibid., Bl. 69.

116. *Kunst und Wirtschaft* 2 (April 1922), p. 1.

117. See Hauschild, *Reichswirtschaftsrat,* pp. 92ff., 241ff.

118. Hellwag in *Die geistigen Arbeiter. Zweiter Teil,* p. 174. In a letter to Reinhard Piper of Sept. 17, 1922, Barlach complained mightily about the freight costs of moving his works, which obviously had to be well and carefully packed. See Dross, ed., *Barlach. Briefe I,* p. 682.

119. See the interesting discussion in Fritzsching, *Annalen* 54/55, pp. 152ff.

120. See especially, "Zur Frage des Kunsthandels," *Kunst und Wirtschaft* 4 (Feb. 1923), p. 3; "Mindest-Gebührensätze für bildenden Künstler," ibid. 3 (Aug. 1922), pp. 2ff.; "Zur vergleichende Anatomie," ibid. 3 (Nov. 1922), pp. 3f.; "Bericht des Reichswirtschaftsverbandes," ibid. 4 (Jan. 1923), pp. 1f.

121. For the discussion which follows, see Gerald D. Feldman, "The Politics of *Wissenschaftspolitik* in Weimar Germany: A Prelude to the Dilemmas of Twentieth-Century Science Policy," in Charles S. Maier, ed., *Changing Boundaries of the Political. Essays on the Evolving Balance Between the State and Society, Public and Private in Europe* (Cambridge, 1987), pp. 255–85, esp. pp. 263ff.; "Industrie und Wissenschaft in Deutschland," in Rudolf Vierhaus and Bernhard vom Brocke, eds., *Forschung im Spannungsfeld von Politik und Gesellschaft. Geschichte und Struktur der Kaiser-Wilhelm/Max-Planck-Gesellschaft* (Stuttgart, 1990), pp. 657–72; and "The Private Support of Science in Germany, 1914–1933," in Rüdiger vom Bruch and Rainer A. Müller, *Formen außerstaatlicher Wissenschaftsförderung im 19. und 20. Jahrhundert. Deutschland im europäischen Vergleich* [*VSWG,* Beiheft 88] (Stuttgart, 1990), pp. 87–111, and the literature cited in these articles. On the NGW, see Kurt Zierold, *Forschungsförderung in Drei Epochen. Deutsche Forschungsgemeinschaft. Geschichte. Arbeitsweise. Kommentar* (Wiesbaden, 1968), pp. 5ff., 29ff., and Thomas Nipperdey and Ludwig Schmugge, *50 Jahre Forschungs-*

förderung in Deutschland, 1920–1970: Ein Abriß der Geschichte der deutschen Forschungsgemeinschaft (Berlin, 1970). Schreiber's views are well presented and his role well represented in his *Die Not der deutschen Wissenschaft und der geistigen Arbeiter. Geschehnisse und Gedanken zur Kulturpolitik des deutschen Reiches* (Leipzig, 1923).

122. Nipperdey and Schmugge, *50 Jahre,* p. 14.

123. Zierold, *Forschungsförderung,* pp. 5ff., 29ff.

124. Haber to Schmidt-Ott, Aug. 2, 1920, BAK, R 73, Nr. 37.

125. Harnack to Schmidt-Ott, Dec. 8, 1920, ibid.

126. Haber to Schmidt-Ott, Aug. 2, 1920, BAK, R 73, Nr. 37.

127. Harnack to the Prussian Cultural Minister, May 20, 1920, MPG Archiv, A 1, Nr. 337.

128. See Peter-Christian Witt, "Wissenschaftsfinanzierung zwischen Inflation und Deflation: Die Kaiser-Wilhelm-Gesellschaft 1918/19 bis 1934/35," in Rudolf Vierhaus and Bernhard vom Brocke, eds., *Forschung im Spannungsfeld von Politik und Gesellschaft. Geschichte und Struktur der Kaiser-Wilhelm-/Max-Planck–Gesellschaft* (Stuttgart, 1990), pp. 579–656; Zierold, *Forschungsförderung,* p. 33; KWG meeting of March 24, 1922, MPG Archiv, Nr. 63, and "Denkschrift über Ersparnisse in den von der Kaiser-Wilhelm-Gesellschaft unterhaltenen Instituten und sonstigen Unternehmungen," May 16, 1923, which provides important retrospective material and presents a more differentiated view of KWG growth than that provided by Witt, ibid., Nr. 342.

129. *VR,* Nov. 16, 1922, Bd. 357, p. 9004. The debate began on Nov. 15 with Schreiber's speech, ibid., pp. 8985ff.

130. Report of May 23, 1921, PRO, FO 371/5970/67–63.

131. Quoted in Weindling, *Health, Race and German Politics,* p. 325.

132. The latter decision was taken in March 1922, and Fritz Haber seems to have been instrumental in the matter. See the KWG meeting of March 24, 1922, MPG Archiv, Nr. 63. A memorandum of May 16, 1923, speaks of a decision by the institutes to hire foreigners for half the scientific personnel employed by the institutes for personnel reasons. The same memorandum discusses in detail the problems of keeping up with foreign research and the slowing down of research in various institutes, ibid., Nr. 342.

133. This was a point which Geheimrat Trendelenburg had sought much earlier, apparently with not much effect, to impress upon the representatives of the artistic organizations in a discussion of the distressed situation of German art on Jan. 4, 1921, BayHStA, Abt. II, MK 40850, esp. pp. 1–3, 11.

134. "Das Einkommen der Hochschullehrer," *Mitteilungen des Verbandes der Deutschen Hochschulen* 2 (Oct. 1, 1920), pp. 247–66, quote on p. 247. Unless otherwise noted, this discussion of the conditions of the professorate is based on this valuable report. See also Fritz Ringer, *The Decline of the German Mandarins. The German Academic Commu-*

nity, 1890–1933 (Cambridge, Mass., 1969), pp. 53ff. for a discussion of the social background and character of the German academic community.

135. "Das Einkommen der Hochschullehrer," *Mitteilungen des Verbandes der Deutschen Hochschulen* 2 (Oct. 1, 1922).

136. Ibid., p. 256.

137. "Die Notlage der nichtbeamteten preußischen Privatdozenten," ibid. (Oct. 15, 1922), p. 268.

138. "Amerikanische Einschätzung der finanziellen Lage der deutschen Gelehrten," ibid. (Dec. 15, 1922), pp. 292f.

139. For an excellent discussion of the condition of Germany's students, see the opening chapters of Michael Kater, *Studentenschaft und Rechtsradikalismus in Deutschland 1918–1923* (Hamburg, 1975), with further references to the large contemporary literature. As usual when it came to the support of education, Carl Duisberg was a notable exception, ibid., pp. 79f.

140. Hartmut Titze, ed., *Das Hochschulstudium in Preußen und Deutschland 1820–1944* (Göttingen, 1987), pp. 29f.

141. Report by Mrs. Kathleen Jones, sent by Lord D'Abernon, May 16, 1922, PRO, FO 371/7514/37093/131–32.

142. See Michael Kater, "The Work Student: A Socio-Economic Phenomenon of Early Weimar Germany," *Journal of Contemporary History* 10 (1975), pp. 71–94.

143. Quoted in Hans Gehrig, *Wirtschaftsnot und Selbsthilfe der deutschen Studentenschaft* (Berlin & Leipzig, 1924), p. 22. This is an invaluable source on the condition of students during this period.

144. Verband Hannoverscher landwirtschaftlicher Hausfrauen an den landwirtschaftlichen Hausfrauenverein Hannover, Dec. 6, 1922. See also the letter of Sept. 14, 1922. StA Hannover 320I, Nr. 62.

145. Schreiber, *Not der deutschen Wissenschaft*, pp. 50ff.; for the changing interests of students, see the telling statistics in Titze, *Hochschulstudium*, pp. 86ff. On Verschuer, the later *Doktorvater* of Josef Mengele, and these activities, see Weindling, *Health, Race and German Politics*, p. 322.

146. Holtfrerich, *German Inflation*, pp. 257ff.; Adolf Günther, "Die Folgen des Krieges für Einkommen und Lebenshaltung der mittleren Volksschichten Deutschlands," in Meerwarth et al., *Die Einwirkung des Krieges*, pp. 99–279, esp. pp. 210ff.

147. Hans Guradze and Karl Freudenberg, "Das Existenzminimum des geistigen Arbeiters," *JNS* 120 (1923), Folge III, Bd. 65, pp. 326–33, quote on p. 333.

148. Erich Simon, "Der Haushalt eines höheren Beamten," ibid. 119, (1922), Bd. 64, pp. 425–32, quote on p. 431.

149. Guradze and Freudenberg, ibid. 120 (1923), Bd. 65, p. 333.

150. Verein für Sozialpolitik, *Die Zukunft der So-zialpolitik. Die Not der geistigen Arbeiter. Jubiläumstagung des Vereins für Sozialpolitik in Eisenach 1922* [*SVS*, Bd. 163] (Munich & Leipzig, 1923), pp. 118f, 131f.

151. Ibid., p. 178.

152. Ibid., p. 184.

153. Ibid., p. 221.

154. Ibid., pp. 248–50.

155. Ibid., p. 212.

156. "Geistige Arbeit!" *Plutus* (Sept. 27, 1922), pp. 384–88, quote on pp. 384f.

157. Ibid., p. 387.

158. Meridonalis, "Die Not des Geistes," *Die Weltbühne* 19 (June 21, 1923), pp. 709–12, quote on p. 711.

159. Deputy Strathmann at the Reichstag meeting of Nov. 16, 1922, *VR*, Bd. 357, p. 9012.

160. See Kater, *Studentenschaft und Rechtsradikalismus*, esp. pp. 20ff., and Franz Hamburger, *Lehrer zwischen Kaiser und Führer. Der deutsche Philologenverband in der Weimarer Republik. Eine Untersuchung zur Sozialgeschichte der Lehrerorganisation*, (Phil. diss., Heidelberg, 1974), esp. pp. 111ff.

161. Speech of Nov. 16, 1922, *VR*, Bd. 357, pp. 9016–21, quote on p. 9017.

162. For the application of the concept of "political culture" to the history of the Weimar Republic, see the important article by Detlev Lehnert and Klaus Megerle, "Identitäts- und Konsensprobleme in einer fragmentierten Gesellschaft. Zur politischen Kultur in der Weimarer Republik," in Dirk Berg-Schlosser and Jakob Schissler, eds., *Politische Kultur in Deutschland. Bilanz und Perspektiven der Forschung* (Oplanden, 1987), pp. 80–95.

163. M. M. Gehrke, "Proletarianisierung oder Entproletarianisierung?" *Die Weltbühne*, 18 (Oct. 12, 1922), pp. 398f.

164. Morus, "Bergab!" *Die Weltbühne* 18 (Oct. 26, 1922), pp.448–50.

165. On Raffke, see Hans Ostwald, *Sittengeschichte der Inflation. Ein Kulturdokument aus den Jahren des Marksturzes* (Berlin, 1931), pp. 79ff., and Struss, *Das war 1922* (Munich, 1982), pp. 9f. 31, 53, 64f., 147ff., 152, 174.

166. "Raffke," text by Theobald Tiger, music by Rudolph Nelson (Drei Masken Verlag, Berlin, 1922). I am grateful to Professor Peter Jelavich for providing me with the music and text.

167. Roland Schacht, "Verteidigung des Schiebers," *Die Weltbühne* 18, (Dec. 14, 1922), pp. 618–20, for this and the quotations which follow. On Schacht, see Deak, *Weltbühne*, p. 267.

168. "Selbsthilfe des Mittelstandes," *Niederdeutsche Zeitung*, Oct. 26, 1922, BA, ZSg103, Nr. 1811. The plight of such persons is brilliantly captured in Stefan Zweig's story, "Die unsichtbare Sammlung," the story of a blind old veteran who lovingly "shows" and describes his "unsalable" collection of prints to a dealer when they had actually already been sold by his wife and daughter. See Stefan Zweig, *Novellen* (Frankfurt a.M., 1960), pp. 334–48.

169. Deutscher Rentnerbund to RWM, Aug. 4, 1921, BAP, RWM, Nr. 62052, Bl. 25. It is difficult to ascertain the actual numbers of *Kleinrentner* during the inflation, and the numbers are based on surveys taken after the inflation. The best data are in Bayerisches Statistisches Landesamt, *Sozialer Auf- und Abstieg*, pp. 118–23. For an excellent new discussion, see Karl Christian Führer, "Für das Wirtschaftsleben 'mehr oder weniger wertloser Personen.' Zur Lage von Invaliden- und Kleinrentnern in den Inflationsjahren 1918–1924," *AfS* 30 (1990), pp. 144–80, esp. 168–80.

170. Landesverband der Rentnervereinigungen Bayerns to RWM, Sept. 19, 1921, BAP, RWM, Nr. 62052, Bl. 43–52.

171. See the lengthy pamphlet by Amtsrichter Schneider-Nürnberg, *Die rechtliche Verantwortlichkeit von Reich und Reichsbank für die deutsche Geldpolitik* (Munich, 1922) in ibid., Bl. 140f.

172. See, for example, the request of the Württemberg Finance Ministry for such support, June 21, 1921, and the response of the RAM of Oct. 17, 1921, BAK, R 43I/2104, Bl. 4–6, 19–20.

173. Meeting in RAM of Sept. 26, 1921, SäHStA, Gesandtschaft Berlin, Nr. 2296, Bl. 7–14, quote on Bl. 10.

174. See the memorandum of the RAM, Dec. 16, 1921, ibid., Bl. 3639. See also Führer, *AfS* 30 (1990), p. 174.

175. See the correspondence on this for the period between March and December 1922, in SäHStA, Gesandtschaft Berlin, Nr. 2296, Bl. 59–144. Important detail is also to be found in the papers of the Congress of Municipalities, LA Berlin, AdSt, Bd. 2037/II.

176. This discussion is based on Gerald D. Feldman, "The Fate of the Social Insurance System in the German Inflation, 1914–1923," in Gerald D. Feldman et al., eds., *The Adaptation to Inflation*, pp. 432–47, which also contains reference to the major literature. See also, however, the extraordinarily fine discussion of social insurance in the inflation by Martin H. Geyer, *Die Reichsknappschaft. Versicherungsformen und Sozialpolitik im Bergbau 1900–1945* (Munich, 1987), pp. 83–108.

177. Report of the Staatliche Bayerische Wirtschaftsstelle in Berlin, July 8, 1922 and subsequent reports, BayHStA, Abt. II, MA 104 017.

178. DHV to Reich Insurance Board for white-collar workers, Dec. 6, 1922, BAK, R 112, Nr. 61, Bl. 18ff.

179. Geyer, *Reichsknappschaft*, p. 99.

180. Landesverband bayer. Stadt- und Marktgemeinden an das bayer. Ministerium für Soziale Fürsorge, Oct. 27, 1921, BayHStA, Abt. I, M Arb. Nr. 1190. On the various steps taken, see Geyer, *Reichsknappschaft*, pp. 91ff.

181. Halle Magistracy to the Städtetag, April 22, 1922, LA Berlin, AdSt, Nr. 358/II.

182. Petition of the Plauen social pensioners to the Saxon Labor Ministry, Sept. 18, 1922, SäHStA,

Gesandtschaft Berlin, Nr. 2289, Bl. 30f. The possibility that the new measures were simply disregarded is suggested by a survey taken by the Saxon government among its municipalities in March 1922, which was not only filled with complaints about the financial and administrative difficulties created by the new system but also with explicit refusals to implement the new law on financial grounds. See the report of March 7, 1922, ibid, Nr. 2288, Bl. 96–115. On Braun's calculations, see Geyer, *Reichsknappschaft*, pp. 106, 430n83.

183. Quoted in ibid., p. 107. Similarly, at a meeting of the social pensioners in Plauen on September 18, 1922, they listed among their demands that the pensions "be paid in gold currency because the contributions were so paid." SäHStA, Gesandtschaft Berlin, Nr. 2289, Bl. 30f.

184. See, for example, the meeting of the state and municipality representatives with the Labor Ministry in Nürnberg on Sept. 15–16, 1922, in ibid., Bl. 40–46.

185. Robert Weldon Whalen, *Bitter Wounds. German Victims of the Great War, 1914–1939* (Ithaca and London, 1984), pp. 131ff., and Michael Geyer, "Ein Vorbote des Wohlfahrtsstaates. Die Kriegsopferversorgung in Frankreich, Deutschland und Großbritannien nach dem Ersten Weltkrieg," *GuG* 9 (1983), pp. 230–77.

186. See the discussion of these matters at a meeting of the Reich Committee for the Care of War Disabled and Survivors, July 10, 1922, BAP, RAM, Nr. 10376, Bl. 298–308.

187. Whalen, *Bitter Wounds*, pp. 141–53, esp. pp. 147f.

188. See the meeting of Aug. 15, 1922, and the visit of the head of the association to the Reich Chancellery on Aug. 23, BAK, R 43I/2096. For the ZAG response, see the ZAG meeting of Oct. 14, 1922, BAP, ZAG, Nr. 31, Bl. 101f. See also Führer, *AfS* (1990), p. 172.

189. ZAG meeting of Dec. 21, 1922, BAP, ZAG, Nr. 31, Bl. 53f.

190. Memorandum of the Conference of Westphalian Cities, Nov. 14, 1922, LA Berlin, AdSt, Nr. 4160/II. The latter volume is filled with important information on the 1922 crisis in municipal finances. For a useful brief account, see Karl-Heinrich Hansmeyer, ed., *Kommunale Finanzpolitik in der Weimarer Republik* (Stuttgart, 1973), chap. 3. Much can be learned about municipal finances from Otto Büsch's important *Geschichte der Berliner Kommunalwirtschaft in der Weimarer Epoche* (Berlin, 1960).

191. Popitz of the Finance Ministry to the Städtetag, Dec. 6, 1922, LA Berlin, AdSt, Nr. 4160.

192. RB to the Städtetag, Nov. 5, 1922, ibid. See also the letter of the city of Leipzig to the administration of the loan bureaus, Nov. 4, 1922, ibid.

193. See the report by Mitzlaff of the Städtetag, Nov. 5, 1922, SäHStA, Nr. 2289, Bl. 83–86.

194. Report to Mayor Böss of Berlin, Dec. 27,

1922, and report on the discussion of Dec. 18, 1922, in the Prussian Ministry of the Interior, LA Berlin, AdSt, Nr. 4160/II. See also Holtfrerich, *German Inflation*, p. 303, and *Deutsches Geld- und Bankwesen in Zahlen*, p. 38.

195. See Feldman, *AfS* 27 (1987), pp. 131–37.

196. Denkschrift der sächsischen Staatsregierung über die zunehmende Teuerung, end of May 1922, BAP, RWM, Nr. 12225, Bl. 206–14.

197. The Saxon government still was waiting for a reply and asking for one in mid-February 1923, when its Representative was told by an RWM official that he doubted that one could be sent since the Ministry was too preoccupied with other problems and the memorandum "had been completely overtaken by events." See notation of Reg. Rat Wodtke, Feb. 14, 1923, ibid., Bl. 250.

198. The control inspections were undertaken in Pomerania, Silesia, East and West Prussia, the Rhineland, Schleswig-Holstein, Hannover, Westphalia, and Hessen-Nassau. The last two provinces were visited in early September, the others in the spring. See GStAKM, Rep. 77, Tit. 1059$_b$ Abt. 1m, Nr. 28a. The findings were summarized in a memorandum of Dec. 7, 1922, Bl. 3–5. This discussion is based on the latter, as well as a reading of the reports, and only quotations will be cited.

199. Report of June 30, 1922, ibid., Bl. 126f.

200. Memorandum of March 29, 1922, BAP, RWM, Nr. 12089, Bl. 96f. and BayHStA, Abt. II, MA 100 977.

201. Letter of Gebrüder Kayser, a sewing machine and bicycle producer in Kaiserslautern to the Verband Pfälzischer Industrieller, May 3, 1922, VPI Archiv, "Industriegewinne." This volume contains a good collection of responses to Hamm. See also BayHStA, Abt. II, MA 100 977 for others.

202. See memoranda by Ministerialrat Susat and Dr. Stern, May 1922 and June 29, 1922, BAP, RWM, Nr. 12089, Bl. 100–103.

203. Niederschrift über die 13. Tagung der Landes-, Provinz- und Bezirkspreisprüfungsstellen am 23. und 24. Mai in Dresden, StA Hamburg, DHSG III, Pr IV 49/9. The discussion which follows is based on this protocol.

204. Remarks of Munich Landesgerichtsrat Bretzfeld, ibid, p. 46.

205. Ibid., p. 47.

206. Ibid., p. 23.

207. Ibid.

208. Ibid., pp. 26f.

209. Ibid., pp. 32f.

210. Ibid., p. 33.

211. Witt in *Wealth and Taxation*, pp. 152ff.

212. Felix Pinner, "Anekdoten und Wahrheiten," from the commercial section of the *Berliner Tageblatt*, Sept. 2, 1922, RWWK, Nr. 5/28/15.

213. Report on the meeting of the Advisory Council on Cartels in the RWM, June 30, 1922, StA Hamburg, DHSG III, Pr IV 98, Bd. 1.

214. Report of Director Klemme of the GHH,

Sept. 11, 1922, HA/GHH, Nr. 3000035/3, which contains a record of the steel industry pricing discussions during this period. For a general discussion, see Feldman, *Iron and Steel*, pp. 284–319.

215. For the theoretical discussion, see Gerald Merkin, "Towards a Theory of the German Inflation: Some Preliminary Observations," in Feldman et al., *The German Inflation. A Preliminary Balance* [*Beiträge zu Inflation und Wiederaufbau in Deutschland und Europa 1914–1924*, Bd. 1] (Berlin & New York, 1982), pp. 25–47.

216. Meeting of the Advisory Council on Cartels of the RWM, June 30, 1922, StA Hamburg, DHSG III, Pr IV 98, Bd. 1. See also remarks of Dr. Stern at the meeting of the representatives of the price examination agencies in Hannover on Nov. 16–18, 1922, ibid., Pr IV 49/10, pp. 5ff.

217. Ibid., pp. 23ff.

218. Letter from a Recklinghausen retailer to Deputy Allekotte, June 6, 1922, RWWK, 20/501/16.

219. Report of the Dresden City Council, Nov. 3, 1922, SäHStA, MdI, Nr. 11342, Bl. 18f.

220. Ibid.

221. Report of the Kreishauptmannschaft Dresden of Nov. 13, 1922, ibid., Bl. 20f.

222. Kreishauptmannschaft Leipzig to the Saxon Interior Ministry, Nov. 15, 1922, ibid., Bl. 22f.

223. *Deutscher Nahrungsmittel = Großhandel* (Dec. 1916), RWWK 20/503/9; *Volkswirtschaftliche Chronik 1922*, pp. 707ff.; RWM to Länderregierungen, Dec. 16, 1923, BAK, R 43I/1246, Bl. 243–49; "Das Reichsgericht gegen den Wiederbeschaffungspreis," *Vossische-Zeitung*, Dec. 20, 1922, ibid., Bl. 255.

224. Meeting in Hannover, Nov. 16–18, 1922, StA Hamburg, DHSG III, Pr IV 49/10.

225. Report by Consul William Seeds, Jan. 6, 1921, PRO, FO 371/5986. On Kahr, see above, Chap. 5, pp. 245f., and Chap. 9, pp. 389f.

226. Report of von Dziembowski, April 28, 1922, SäHStA, Außenministerium, Nr. 2983, Bl. 179–81.

227. The memorandum was sent by the Chancellor to the RWM for a reply, and the discussion and quotations which follow are from the memorandum and the commentaries by various RWM officials, see BAP, RWM, Nr. 253/1, Bl. 54ff. For more detail on the origins and fate of the memorandum, see Gerald D. Feldman, "Bayern und Sachsen in der Hyperinflation 1922/23," *HZ* 238 (1984), pp. 569–609, esp. pp. 580ff.

228. Report of the Regierungspräsident of Schwaben and Neuburg, May 19, 1922, BayHStA, Abt. II, MA 192 147, and subsequent reports in 102 136; 102 140; and 102 150.

229. For a full discussion of this problem in Bavaria and elsewhere, see Feldman in Treue, ed., *Geschichte als Aufgabe*, pp. 629–49.

230. Report on conditions in Saxony by the Regierungspräsident of lower Bavaria, Nov. 18, 1922, BayHStA, Abt. II, MA 102 140.

231. Ibid.

232. Ibid.

233. Report of the Reich Representative in Munich, Jan. 3, 1922, BAK, R 43I/2230, Bl. 7f.

234. Jacques, *Dr. Mabuse. Der Spieler*, pp. 16f.

235. Report of Nov. 9, 1922, BAK, R 43I/2230, Bl. 147–49.

236. Report of Nov. 22, 1922, ibid., R 43I/2231, Bl. 267–69.

237. Eberhard Jäckel and Axel Kuhn, eds., *Hitler. Sämtliche Aufzeichungen 1905–1924* (Stuttgart, 1980), pp. 682f.

238. Speech of Sept. 28, 1922, ibid., p. 697.

239. Conversation with Truman Smith, Nov. 20, 1922, ibid., p. 733.

13. Facing Disaster: The State and the 'Productive Estates' on the Eve of the Ruhr Occupation

1. "1923," *Plutus* (Dec. 20, 1922), pp. 493f.

2. See Beusch, *Währungszerfall und Währungsstabilisierung*, p. 1. It is important to remember that the figures in Table 23 are deflated. For the monthly changes, see Steven B. Webb, "Government Revenue and Spending in Germany, 1919–1923," in Feldman et al., *The Adaptation to Inflation* [*Beiträge zu Inflation und Wiederaufbau in Deutschland und Europa 1914–1924*, Bd. 8] (Berlin & New York, 1986), pp. 46–82, Tables 1 and 3. At the Reichsbank Curatorium meeting of Sept. 26, 1922, Havenstein reported: "It is noteworthy that through the severe increases in taxes, the expenditures of the Reich (without reparations) have been more than covered. In the period from April 1921 [*sic*] to June 1922, the expenditures for reparations and related costs were 151 billion marks; the floating debt rose to 135 billion in this period. Accordingly, 16 billion could have remained to be paid out for reparations obligations. This favorable development has been put once again in question by the last drop in the exchange rate." Report in SäHStA, Gesandtschaft Berlin, Nr. 1630.

3. See Witt in *Wealth and Taxation*, pp. 137–60.

4. See the Reichstag debates of Dec. 15–16, 1922, *VR*, Bd. 357, pp. 9360ff., 9398ff.

5. RWR Finance Committee, Dec. 7, 1922, BAP, RWR, Nr. 552, Bd. 7, Bl. 215ff., quote on Bl. 241. On the RWR positions on the forced loan, see Hauschild, *Reichswirtschaftsrat*, p. 376, 395.

6. Cabinet meeting of Dec. 22, 1922, *Kabinett Cuno*, pp. 94f.

7. RWR Finance Committee meeting, Dec. 7, 1922, BAP, Nr. 552, Bd. 7, Bl. 245f.

8. For the Schmalenbach proposals to mandate a reform of balance sheets, see his presentations to the RWR in March 1922, BAP, RWM, Nr. 5581, Bl. 2ff. The gold-mark-balance question was discussed in the RdI on Aug. 15, 1922. For the protocol and statements supporting the RdI decision not to come out in favor of a reform of balancing procedures under existing conditions, see RWWK, 20/471/1. The RdI's position was stated in a circular of Aug. 29, 1922, BAP, RB, Nr. 6542, Bl. 7f. For the RdI's evolving views on tax reform, see the sketch of a tax reform program developed by Dr. Jordan for the projected RdI Economic Program, dated Nov. 22, 1922, NL Funcke, Vergangene Zeiten, Buch 4, Deutsches Industrie-Institut. For complaints from chambers of commerce and wholesaler organizations about the "threatening destruction of capital" through the income and business taxes, see StA Hamburg, Blohm & Voss, Nr. 1405/4. On the general problem, see the report from the U.S. General Consul in Hamburg of Oct. 4, 1922, NA, 862.5151/1017. The right-wing attitude toward the tax question was strongly represented during a meeting between Hermes and the DNVP Deputies Helfferich and Reichert on Nov. 30, 1922, confidentially reported in GHH, Nr. 300193000/6.

9. See the reprinted version of Arthur Salomonsohn's speech to the RWR in *Bank = Archiv* 22 (Nov. 1, 1922), pp. 29–32, and the statement of the various banking organizations and editorial comments in ibid. (Jan. 15, 1923), pp. 111f.

10. See Hermes to the Prussian Ministry of Commerce, Feb. 7, 1922, with attached reports from various finance offices, GStAKM, Rep. 120, AXI 1, Nr. 35, Bd. 2, Bl. 1–10.

11. RB to RFM, Oct. 9, 1922, ibid., Bl. 103–15, with appended reports, Bl. 118–60, quote on Bl. 108.

12. Ibid., Bl. 104ff.

13. Ibid., Bl. 121f., 123f., 127f.

14. Ibid., Bl. 121, 135ff.

15. See the reports of the Bavarian *Regierungspräsidenten* in BayHStA, Abt. II, MA 102 136; 102 140; and 102 150.

16. Whale, *Joint Stock Banking*, pp. 216–18. The gold-mark value of deposits is not entirely reliable because of the varying internal and external value of the mark. What is unquestionable is the fall in real value.

17. Reichsbank to RFM, Oct. 9, 1922, GStAKM, Rep. 120, AXI 1, Nr. 35, Bd. 2, Bl. 103–15. Holtfrerich, *German Inflation*, p. 66.

18. *Plutus* (Jan. 17, 1923), pp. 30f.

19. Meeting of Nov. 30, 1922, HA/GHH, Nr. 30019300/6. Another good example of the exaggerated importance attached to the question was provided by Cuno, who in September had declared that the absence of confidentiality of bank accounts was "a major source of the shortage of money." Whether he still believed this when he became Chancellor at the end of November is difficult to say. See the meeting of the RdI directors of Sept. 6, 1922, reprinted in Feldman and Homburg, *Industrie und Inflation*, p. 318.

20. See Holtfrerich, *German Inflation*, p. 303, the material prepared for the Reichsbank Central Committee meetings of Oct. 28 and Nov. 23, 1922, BAP, Reichsbank, Nr. 6668, Bl. 13–29; the Reichsbank Curatorium meeting of Sept. 26, 1922, *Kabinette*

Wirth, II, pp. 1104–8; the Reichsbank Curatorium meeting of Dec. 19, 1922, SäHStA, Gesandtschaft Berlin, Nr. 1630.

21. See the remarks of RB Director Bernhard at a meeting of June 22, 1922, BAP, RB, Nr. 6460, Bl. 92f.

22. Ibid., Bl. 81–96, for the protocol of the meeting.

23. Ibid., Bl. 84.

24. "Zur Frage der Wiedereinbürgerung des Wechselverkehrs," June 6, 1922, ibid., Bl. 77–80, quote on 78f.

25. Ibid., Bl. 87.

26. Ibid., Bl. 95.

27. Ibid.

28. "Kreditnot und ihre Bekämpfung," *Bank = Archiv*, 21 (July 15, 1922), pp. 319–23. This was a lead article and more than usual length.

29. On the influence of Friedrich's article, see Willy Prion, "Deutsche Kreditpolitik 1919–1922," *Schmollers Jahrbuch* 42 (1924), pp. 163–205, quote on p. 194.

30. *Bank = Archiv* 21 (July 15, 1922), p. 320.

31. Ibid., p. 321.

32. Ibid.

33. Holtfrerich, *German Inflation*, pp. 78f.

34. RdI directors meeting, Sept. 6, 1922, reprinted in Feldman and Homburg, *Industrie und Inflation*, p. 315.

35. Ibid., p. 114.

36. Ibid., p. 319.

37. Holtfrerich, *German Inflation*, pp. 71ff., 290ff.; Prion, "Deutsche Kreditpolitik," pp. 179ff.

38. Report by U.S. Consul Emil Sauer, Sept. 29, 1922, NA, 862.00/1149.

39. Meeting of Sept. 6, 1922, Feldman and Homburg, *Industrie und Inflation*, p. 318.

40. Ibid., p. 320.

41. RB Curatorium meeting of Sept. 25, 1922, SäHStA, Gesandtschaft Berlin, Nr. 1630. For the amount of emergency money issued, see *Zahlen zur Geldentwertung*, p. 47. On the Cologne situation, see the report of the U.S. Consul Emil Sauer, Sept. 29, 1922, NA, 662.00/1149. On the negotiations in Duisburg and Düsseldorf and the arrangements between the various major industrial firms and the local authorities between July and December 1922, see RWWK, 20/525/19.

42. *Kabinette Wirth*, II, p. 1108.

43. Meeting of Oct. 28, 1922, BAK, R 43I/640, Bl. 141.

44. Meeting of Dec. 19, 1922, SäHStA, Gesandtschaft Berlin, Nr. 1630.

45. Meeting of Dec. 23, 1922, BAK, R 43I/640, Bl. 158–63.

46. Stinnes to Vögler, Oct. 22, 1922, ACDP, NL Stinnes, Nr. 035/1. Important details on these credits are to be found in an unpublished study by W. Freund, "Die Siemens–Rheinelbe–Schuckert–Union (1920–1926)," SAA 54/Lm 123.

47. Vögler to Stinnes, Oct. 25, 1922, ACDP Archiv, NL Stinnes, Nr. 097/4.

48. Vögler to K. H. Brunner, Aug. 14, 1922, ibid., Nr. 096/2.

49. Note by Stinnes, ibid., Nr. 047/1. On the negotiations of Aug. 29, 1922 with the banks, see ibid., Nr. 019/4. On the extent of credits taken by the various SRSU members, see the Freund study, SAA 54/Lm 123.

50. Freund study, SAA 54/Lm 123, and Feldman, *Iron and Steel*, pp. 312f.

51. Thus, the machine-building firms investigated by Dieter Lindenlaub do not seem to have made much use of Reichsbank credits, in part also perhaps because some of them, like the M.A.N. and the Maschinenfabrik Esslingen could get credits from their parent company, the Gutehoffnungshütte. See Lindenlaub, *Maschinenbauunternehmen*, pp. 77ff.

52. Steel Federation meeting of Oct. 24, 1922, HA/GHH, Nr. 3000035/3. Some documentation on the negotiations with the Reichsbank as well as mention of the other syndicate arrangements is to be found in negotiations of Dec. 1, 1922, in the Mannesmann-Archiv, P/1/26/31. See also Wirtz to Vögler, Nov. 25, 1922, WA/ATH, FWH, Nr. 120 and the Freund study of the SRSU in SAA 54/Lm 123.

53. Report of Sept. 21, 1922, BAP, HAAA, Nr. 4739, Bl. 222.

54. RdI meeting of Sept. 6, 1922, Feldman and Homburg, *Industrie und Inflation*, p. 316.

55. Ibid., p. 317.

56. Ibid., p. 318.

57. Hamburg-Südamerikanische-Dampfschiffahrts-Gesellschaft to the RFM, Oct. 16, 1922, HK Hamburg Archiv, Nr. 29k12a1. This volume is filled with material on the protests received by the Hamburg Chamber of Commerce as well as its own lobbying efforts against the decree. Excellent descriptions of the workings of the antispeculation decree are to be found in the reports of the U.S. Vice-Consul in Hamburg, Maurice Walk of Nov. 2 and 8, 1922, NA, 862.5151/1025, 1029.

58. See J. Kleynmans of the Coal Dealers Association to Würst of the Münster Chamber of Commerce, Oct. 13, 1922, along with his memorandum of early September and other related correspondence in RWWK, 5/18/28.

59. See the report of the Verband der Kolonialwaren-Großhändler to its members of July 31, 1922, reporting on a meeting with Grützner and various Mayors, the payment conditions imposed on retailers by the Verband der Kolonialwaren-Großhändler in the Rhineland and Westphalia in mid-August 1922, the various complaints about inability to get credit from the banks, and the letter of the Duisburg wholesalers to the Food and Finance Ministries of Aug. 20, 1922, RWWK, 20/475/25.

60. Gebrüder Rath to the Chamber of Commerce in Münster i.W., Nov. 28, 1922, RWWK, 5/21/15.

61. Verein deutscher Wollkämmer und Kammgarnspinner to the Duisburg Chamber of Commerce with appended brochure on "Goldmarkbilanz," Feb. 5, 1923, and circular of the Koblenz

Chamber of Commerce, Nov. 17, 1922, RWWK, 20/47l/1.

62. Alfred Lansburgh, "Banco-Mark," *Die Bank* (1923/I), pp. 215–23. See also, Holtfrerich, *German Inflation*, p. 304, and Georg Bernhard, "Wertbeständigkeit," *Plutus* (Feb. 15, 1923), pp. 55f.

63. Alfred Lansburgh, "Banco-Mark," *Die Bank* (1923/I), p. 222. On the situation of the wholesalers and the proposal for gold accounts, see Centralverband des Deutschen Großhandels to the RWM, GStAKM, Rep. 120, C XIII l, Nr. 171, Bd. 2, Bl. 199–214, and the memoranda by Dalberg, the RdI, and the interministerial discussions in SäHStA, Gesandtschaft Berlin, Nr. 658, 1. Teil, bl. 231–48. See also, Dalberg, "Entwicklung zur Mark-Banco," *Bank = Archiv* (March 1, 1923), pp. 141–43.

64. Reprinted in Elizabeth Johnson, ed., *The Collected Writings of John Maynard Keynes.* XVIII. *Activities 1922-1923: The End of Reparations* (Cambridge, 1978), pp. 47–58.

65. Ibid., p. 50.

66. Holtfrerich, *German Inflation*, pp. 281–96 for a discussion of the various estimates. It is interesting to note that Holtfrerich's research seems to confirm the 1930 estimate of F. D. Graham, *Exchange, Prices and Production*, p. 259. A good illustration of the problems involved in estimating the amounts lost by mark holders is a private letter from the banker de Meulen of Hope & Co. in Amsterdam to Keynes pointing out that in his concentration on foreign bank accounts in Germany and cash mark holdings abroad, he had neglected current account holdings in marks in banks outside of Germany: ". . . an almost incredibly large number of persons and firms have opened an account in marks with their bank in Holland. Even a good many provincial banks do not keep a banking account in Germany, but keep an account in marks with their bank in Amsterdam or Rotterdam. One could compare it to little rivulets of mark accounts disgorging into small rivers at the provincial town banks and all these little rivers flowing into the big river of the bank in Amsterdam or Rotterdam, which carries the whole flood to one of the large banking institutions in Berlin or Hamburg. These rivulets and little rivers tend to swell the account of the Amsterdam or Rotterdam bank with its German correspondent in many cases to a very large figure—1,000,000,000 marks or more. In my opinion the estimated amount of marks in German banknotes in Holland is usually exaggerated, whereas the amount of marks kept in current account is apt to be underestimated." Letter of Sept. 11, 1922, Marshall Library, Keynes Papers, F I/4₁.

67. Johnson, ed., *Collected Writings,* pp. 50f.

68. Maurice Frère, "Report by the Intelligence Service on the Balance of German Accounts," Paris, Oct. 19, 1922, PRO, FO 371/7486/311/166–93.

69. Ibid.

70. Johnson, ed., *Collected Writings,* XVIII, pp. 57f.

71. The various estimates are conveniently summarized in the Report of the Reparations Commission, Delegation of the Committee of Guarantees, Library of Congress, Manuscript Division, Ayres Papers. I am grateful to Prof. Carl-Ludwig Holtfrerich for placing these documents at my disposal.

72. Van Meulen to Keynes, Aug. 2, 1922, and Vissering to Keynes, Aug. 10, 1922, Wallenberg to Keynes, July 31 and Sept. 11, 1922. See also Warburg to Keynes, Sept. 11, 1922, and Havenstein to Keynes, Sept. 13, 1922, Marshall Library, Keynes Papers, F I/4₁.

73. See above, pp. 484f.

74. Holtfrerich, *German Inflation*, p. 283. For a criticism of the German trade statistics and the estimates developed in 1924, see the report of R. Pilotti and the McKenna Report in Library of Congress, Manuscript Division, Ayres papers. The German statistics were defended by Rudolf Meerwarth, "Über die deutsche Zahlungsbilanz," in *SVS*, 167 (Munich & Leipzig, 1924), pp. 1–32. For a positive appraisal of the potential of the commercial balance, see the report by Frère, PRO, FO 371/7486/311/167–68.

75. Thus, in April 1923 the Statistical Office estimated the value of German exports to be 1,747.3 million gold marks in the second half of 1922 as over against 2,062.5 million in the first half. The amount paid for in foreign currency increased from 31 percent in January to 67 percent in December as opposed to a range of 19 to 37 percent in the last half of 1921. See report of April 11, 1923, BAP, RB, Nr. 6594, Bl. 184–88.

76. Graham used values obtained by multiplying values of exports based on 1913 average prices by an index of potential prices calculated on the basis of values in the years 1924–1926, Graham, *Exchange, Prices and Production*, pp. 266–72.

77. Report of the General Consul in Amsterdam, Hatzfeld, May 31, 1922, SäHStA, Außenministerium, Nr. 6921, Bl. 2.

78. Report of Oct. 6, 1922, ibid., Bl. 52.

79. Report of Aug. 4, 1922, ibid., Nr. 7036.

80. Report of Dec. 6, 1922, GStAKM, Rep. 120, C XIII 5, Nr. 3, Bd. 88, Bl. 154f.

81. See the reports of August–November 1922 of the Hamburg representative in Berlin on discussions in the Export Control Committee of the RWR, StA Hamburg, Senatskommission für die Reichs- und auswärtigen Angelegenheiten, III A1c3, Bd. IV.

82. Meeting of the RWR subcommittee, Nov. 15, 1922, report of Nov. 24, 1922, ibid.

83. Report on meeting of Nov. 25, 1922, sent Nov. 27, ibid.

84. Meeting of Nov. 30, 1922, sent on Dec. 1, ibid.

85. M. van Delden & Co. to the Münster Chamber of Commerce, Oct. 26, 1922, RWWK, 5/20/24.

86. Report of Vice-Consul William E. Lane, Cologne, Jan. 3, 1923, NA, 862.655/11, and Chamber of Commerce report to the Prussian Minister of Commerce and Industry, December 30, 1922, RWWK, 5/20/24. See also the report of Consul E. Verne Richardson from Berlin, Nov. 11, 1922, which suggests that similar conditions existed in the textile

industry as a whole, NA, 862.515/47, as does Hesse, *Deutsche Wirtschaftslage*, p. 294.

87. Report of Emil Sauer, Cologne, Oct. 13, 1922, NA, 862.00/1153.

88. Reports by Consul Louis G. Dreyfus, Jr., Aug. 1, 1922, and Dec. 15, 1922, NA, 862.60/42.

89. Lindenlaub, *Maschinenbauunternehmen*, pp. 24ff.

90. Mannesmann Supervisory Board meeting, Oct. 26, 1922, Mannesmann-Archiv, MM.023.

91. Phoenix board meetings of April 24 and Dec. 12, 1922, ibid., P/1/25/39, and Krupp directors meeting of Dec. 20, 1922, HA Firma Krupp, WA IV 2560.

92. Klöckner to Paster Hillebrand of Ickern bei Rauxel, Sept. 20, 1922, BgA, Nr. 25/8.

93. Meeting of Sept. 29, 1922, HA/GHH, Nr. 300193010/17.

94. Fritz Naphtali, "Kapitalmarktpolitik," *Plutus* (Aug. 16, 1922), pp. 337–40, quote on p. 337.

95. Stinnes to the RWE directors, May 27, 1922, ACDP, NL Stinnes, Nr. 230/4.

96. Stinnes to the directors of the RWE, Aug. 19, 1922, and other relevant correspondence in this volume, ACDP, NL Stinnes, Nr. 230/3; see also his letter to Kraiger of June 18, 1922, ibid., Nr. 133/5. See also the Deutsch-Luxemburg directors meeting of June 17, 1922, SAA 11/Lf 129–31.

97. See Stinnes to Kraiger, June 18, 1922, ACDP, NL Stinnes, Nr. 133/5, and to Hoffmann, June 18, 1922, ibid., Nr. 117/3.

98. Vögler to Stinnes, Dec. 23, 1922, and Stinnes marginal comments, ACDP, NL Stinnes, Nr. 057/4.

99. See the excellent discussion in Bresciani-Turroni, *Economics of Inflation*, pp. 263ff. There is also an interesting report by the American Vice Consul in Breslau, John E. Kehl, of Nov. 24, 1922, NA, 862.51/1583.

100. Walther de Gruyter to Reusch, Jan. 3, 1923, HA/GHH, Nr. 300193000/8.

101. Stinnes to Bruhn, Aug. 10, 1922, ACDP, NL Stinnes, Nr. 286/2. The role of the hyperinflation in bringing the credit plans for Russia to a standstill is also emphasized by Pogge von Strandmann, *HZ* (1976), pp. 308ff.

102. Quoted in Lindenlaub, *Maschinenbauunternehmen*, p. 159n98; in general, see his excellent discussion of this problem on pp. 153–61. For Stinnes's promotional activities in the Rhineland, see RWWK, 3/5/62; his linking of the reparations in kind to the reduction of construction work is to be found in his conversation with bankers on Aug. 29, 1922, ACDP, NL Stinnes, Nr. 019/4; for reports on the railroad car industry, see the reports in RWWK, 20/441/1.

103. On the problems of the Alpine, see Chapter 6, p. 297; Feldman, *Iron and Steel*, p. 319; and the correspondence in ACDP, NL Stinnes, Nr. 093/2.

104. Stinnes to Castiglioni, Nov. 4, 1922, ibid.

105. Draft of response, ACDP, NL Stinnes, Nr. 093/2, which also contains a covering letter to Stin-

nes of Dec. 6, 1922, and the memorandum of the worker representative.

106. Report by Consul E. Verne Richardson, Dec. 5, 1922, NA, 862.60/47.

107. Mann, *Neue Rundschau* (1925), p. 237.

108. Report of Oct. 4, 1922, PRO, FO 371/7578/37093/89–91.

109. The conflict in South Germany is described in Feldman and Steinisch, *AfS* (1978), pp. 364–81.

110. Ibid., and the remarks of Leipart at the June 1922 ADGB Congress, *Protokoll der Verhandlungen*, pp. 329f.

111. Reports of Dr. Leopold, the business manager of the Arbeitgeberverband der deutschen Papier-, Pappen-, Zellstoff- und Holzstoff-Industrie, Aug. 5 and 25, 1922, VPI Archiv.

112. See the excellent short discussion and references to the literature in Irmgard Steinisch, *Arbeitszeitverkürzung und sozialer Wandel. Der Kampf um die Achtstundenschicht in der deutschen und amerikanischen Eisen- und Stahlindustrie 1880–1929* [*Beiträge zu Inflation und Wiederaufbau in Deutschland und Europa 1914–1924*, Bd. 6] (Berlin & New York, 1986), pp. 438ff.

113. *Protokoll der Verhandlungen des 12. Kongresses der Gewerkschaften Deutschlands in Breslau* (Berlin, 1925), p. 122.

114. Meeting of Oct. 5, 1922, BAP, RWR, Nr. 522, Bl. 424f.

115. Steinisch, *Arbeitszeitverkürzung*, pp. 451f.

116. Report by Dr. Leopold of the Arbeitgeberverband der deutschen Papier-, Pappen-, Zellstoff- und Holzstoff-Industrie, Aug. 15, 1922, VPI Archiv.

117. Report of the delegate of the RWM for the Anthracite Mining Industry West, Oct. 19, 1922, StA Münster, Nr. 1162, and Feldman, *VfZ* (1980), pp. 205ff.

118. Quoted in Feldman and Steinisch, *AfS*, (1978), p. 377.

119. U.S. Consular report on living and economic conditions in Württemberg, Oct. 25, 1922, NA, 862.50/470.

120. Report of Aug. 15, 1922, PRO, FO 371/7156/123.

121. Report of Nov. 15, 1922, ibid., No. 371. See also Gerald D. Feldman and Merith Niehuss, "Haushaltsrechnungen aus der Inflationszeit. Materialien und Interpretationen," in Feldman et al., *The Adaptation to Inflation*, pp. 265–77, esp. pp. 274–76.

122. See Holtfrerich, *The German Inflation*, pp. 227ff.; Rudolf Meerwarth, "Zur neuesten Entwicklung der Löhne," *Zeitschrift des preußischen statistischen Landesamts 1922/23* 62 (Berlin, 1923), pp. 327–40; Costantino Bresciani-Turroni, "The Movement of Wages in Germany During the Depreciation of the Mark and After Stabilization," *Journal of the Royal Statistical Society* 92, New Series (1929), pp. 374–427, esp. pp. 389ff. Even Werner Abelshauser in "Verelendung der Handarbeiter? Zur sozialen Lage der deutschen Arbeiter in der großen Inflation der frühen zwanziger Jahre," Hans Mommsen and Winfried Schulze, eds., *Vom Elend der Handarbeit. Prob-*

leme historischer Unterschichtenforschung (Stuttgart, 1981), pp. 445–76, cannot present very impressive data for his optimistic thesis on the improved condition of the working classes in the inflation for the second half of 1922. His reliance on hourly rather than weekly real wages for Hamburg (p. 454) is also somewhat dubious, and the weekly real wages for Hamburg supplied by the American Consul in a report of Jan. 18, 1923, suggests a bleaker picture, NA, 862.5041/23.

123. For the alarm in trade-union leadership circles over the high construction-worker wages, see Ruck, *Gewerkschaften*, pp. 608–11. More generally, see Tschirbs, *Tarifpolitik*, pp. 183ff.

124. See the report of Dr. Leopold of the German paper and wood products industry, Aug. 25, 1922, VPI Archive. Paul Silverberg made a strong plea for the restoration of differentials in the extraordinary meeting of the VdA held in Berlin on Oct. 12, 1922, BAK, NL Silverberg, Nr. 2, Bl. 7.

125. Circular of Aug. 25, 1922, VPI Archiv.

126. Ibid.

127. Discussion in the ADGB Bundesausschuß, Nov. 27–28, 1922, Ruck, *Gewerkschaften*, pp. 717–22, quote on p. 717.

128. Ibid., p. 720, and Meerwarth in *Zeitschrift des preußischen statistischen Landesamts 1922/23* (1923), p. 336.

129. A good summation of the employer side is to be found in the meeting of the peak employer association for the metal industry (Gesamtverband deutscher Metallindustrieller) at the June 16–17, 1922, meeting in Berlin, VPI Archiv. For the trade-union position, see the discussions of the Bundesausschuß on Sept. 29 and Nov. 28, 1922, Ruck, *Gewerkschaften*, pp. 644ff., 717ff.

130. On the varying interpretations of Flensburg, see the materials cited in ibid. On the Austrian system, see Max Lederer, "Indexziffer und Löhne in der deutschösterreichischen Industrie," *Soziale Praxis* 31 (Sept. 6, 1922), pp. 953–56, and the report of the German embassy in Vienna on Sept. 29, 1922, and the lengthy report of July 26, 1923, AA Bonn, Nr. 11ᵇ, Sozialpolitik 3, Österreich.

131. Wagner-Roemmich, "Goldlöhne und Goldpreise?" *Soziale Praxis* 31 (Oct. 5, 1922), pp. 1081.

132. Ibid., pp. 901f.

133. *Correspondenzblatt*, Oct. 21, 1922, pp. 548ff., and Tarnow's remarks at the Bundesausschuß meeting on Oct. 1, 1922, Ruck, *Gewerkschaften*, p. 655.

134. *Soziale Praxis* 31 (1922), p. 1296. See also, ibid., pp. 1136ff., 1293ff.

135. See the VdA circular of June 1, 1922, VPI Archiv.

136. Circular of the Wage Policy Committee of the VdA, Sept. 27, 1922, BAK, NL Silverberg, Nr. 2, Bl. 51–54.

137. Report on the meeting of the Wage Contract Committee of Sept. 18, 1922, sent to the members on Sept. 29, 1922, ibid., Bl. 55–58.

138. Gok to Blohm, Sept. 19, 1922, StA Hamburg, Blohm & Voss, Nr. 1329.

139. Zechen-Verband to the RAM, Oct. 12, 1922, BgA, 13/307.

140. Meeting of the Zechen-Verband Managerial Committee, Sept. 30, 1922, ibid.

141. VdA circular of Oct. 6, 1922, on meeting with Wirth of Oct. 5, ibid.

142. Discussion between Brauns and the mine owners, Nov. 8, 1922, ibid.

143. For Reusch's attitude and the price reduction effort, see Feldman, *Iron and Steel*, pp. 337ff.

144. Reusch to Cuno, Dec. 22, 1922, BAK, R 43I/2172, Bl. 188f.

145. Circular of the Fachgruppe Bergbau, Dec. 20, 1922; Labor Association of the Northwest Group of the German Iron and Steel Industry to the Mine Owners Association, Dec. 21, 1922; Hölling to Loewenstein and Wiskott, Dec. 21, 1922, BgA, 13/307.

146. Tschirbs, *Tarifpolitik*, p. 165, and report by Director Klemme of Jan. 9, 1923, HA/GHH, Nr. 3000035/3.

147. Report of Bergrat Hasse, Dec. 29, 1922, StA Münster, Nr. 1864.

148. Report of Jan. 13, 1922, ibid.

149. Statement by Senator Stubbe of Hamburg, meeting of the Food Ministers in Oldenburg, Oct. 27–28, 1921, StA Dresden, Gesandtschaft Berlin, Nr. 487, Bl. 151.

150. See Moeller, *German Peasants*, pp. 110ff.

151. Präsident der preußischen Central-Genossenschafts-Kasse an den preußischen Finanzminister, Sept. 8, 1922, GStAKM, Rep. 151, HB, Nr. 1020, Bl. 342f.

152. Hans Guradze, "Die Brotpreise und Kosten des Lebensbedarfes in Berlin im Jahre 1922," *JNS* 65 (1923), pp. 254–57.

153. Report on discussion with trade union leaders in the RWM, Sept. 12, 1922, BAP, RWM, Nr. 2434/3, Bl. 549–51.

154. Meeting of the ADGB Bundesausschuß, Sept. 28–Oct. 1, 1922, Ruck, *Gewerkschaften*, p. 639.

155. Ibid., pp. 655f.

156. Ibid., pp. 656f.

157. Mayor Külb to the Reich Food Ministry, Sept. 13, 1922, BAP, RAM, Nr. 10554, Bl. 134–38.

158. See the debate on Oct. 23, 1922, *VR*, Bd. 357, pp. 8900ff.

159. Meeting of the Food Ministers of the various states, Sept. 4–5, 1922, SäHStA, Gesandtschaft Berlin, Nr. 488, p. 14. On the experience with delivery strikes by the peasants in Bavaria, see Jonathan Osmond, "German Peasant Farmers in War and Inflation," Gerald D. Feldman et al., *The German Inflation. A Preliminary Balance*, pp. 288–307, esp. pp. 301ff.

160. Meeting of the Food Ministers, Sept. 4–5, 1922, StA Hamburg, Gesandtschaft Berlin, Nr. 488, pp. 5–7. On the Tanzten plan, see Schumacher, *Land und Politik*, pp. 286ff.

161. *Kabinette Wirth*, II, pp. 1110–13; for the draft of the law sent to the Reichsrat, see StA Merseburg, Rep. 151, HB, Nr. 1020, Bl. 351–56.

162. Meeting of the Food Ministers in Berlin,

Dec. 18, 1922, SäHStA, Gesandtschaft Berlin, Nr. 488, p. 12, and, for this discussion in general, see the Cabinet meetings of Dec. 8, 16, and 19, 1922, *Kabinett Cuno*, pp. 54f., 70f., 79f.

163. Ibid., and internal RAM memorandum on "bread stretching," Dec. 12, 1922, BAP, RAM, Nr. 10554, Bl. 169f.

164. Finance Policy Committee meeting of the RWR, Nov. 10, 1922, BAP, RWR, Nr. 552, Bd. 7, Bl. 79.

165. Ibid., Bl. 96.

166. Ibid., Bl. 117, 120.

167. Ibid., Bl. 128f.

168. See the discussion in Kunz, *Civil Servants*, pp. 350ff.

169. See his memorandum on the economic situation of Dec. 21, 1922, *Kabinett Cuno*, pp. 84–89. See also *Zahlen zur Geldentwertung*, p. 43.

170. Kunz, *Civil Servants*, p. 358; *Kabinett Cuno*, pp. 95–100.

171. "Stillegung der österreichischen Notenpresse," *Germania*, Nov. 21, 1922; "Schieberwanderung Wien-Berlin," *Deutsche Tageszeitung*, Nov. 24, 1921, and numerous similar newspaper articles in BAK, R 43I/1246, Bl. 228ff.

172. Report of Dec. 4, 1922, BAK, R 43I/185, Bl. 295–98, quote on Bl. 296.

173. Reports of Dec. 4 and 18, 1922, ibid., Bl. 305–10, 412–16.

174. Piggot to Lampson, Dec. 7, 1922, PRO, FO 371/7489/311/233–35.

14. A Disordered Fortress: Passive Resistance, the Cuno Government, and the Destruction of the Mark

1. Willy Prion, "Kreditpolitik und Ruhrkampf (1923), *Schmollers Jahrbuch* 49 (1925), pp. 109–33, esp. p. 109.

2. For the failure to prepare for the Ruhr occupation, see the telling criticisms of Prion in ibid., pp. 115f. On the productive capacity of the printing presses, see the report on a meeting in the RFM on Jan. 6, 1923, *Kabinett Cuno*, p. 122n1.

3. Rupieper, *Cuno Government*, p. 97, and Ministerial Council meeting of January 9, 1923, *Kabinett Cuno*, pp. 126f.

4. For the Socialist trade union problems, see Michael Ruck, *Die Freien Gewerkschaften im Ruhrkampf 1923* (Cologne, 1986), Chaps. III.

5. Cabinet Council meeting of Jan. 9, 1923, *Kabinett Cuno*, pp. 124f. and report of ADGB Secretary Knoll on his discussions of Jan. 8–10, 1923, Ruck, *Gewerkschaften*, pp. 733ff.

6. Ibid., p. 106.

7. Stinnes to Kirdorf, Jan. 17, 1923, ACDP, NL Stinnes, Nr. 120/1.

8. Report by Knoll of the ADGB, Jan. 8–10, 1923, Ruck, *Gewerkschaften*, p. 740. See also Ruck, *Gewerkschaften im Ruhrkampf*, pp. 52ff.; Wulf, *Stinnes*, pp. 350ff. Ruck, in this writer's opinion, too eas-

ily accepts the charges of Limbertz of the Socialist mining union that Stinnes was pursuing a "catastrophe policy" in his own interpretation. Stinnes was given to extreme language, but his goal remained negotiation, although he certainly was naive about what the French would accept. At the same time, if the Germans were not going to simply give in to the French goals in occupying the Ruhr, it is difficult to see how the decision to move to Coal Syndicate to Hamburg can be faulted.

9. Report by Director Woltmann, Jan. 19, 1923, HA/GHH, Nr. 300193008/7.

10. Stinnes to Kirdorf, Jan. 17, 1923, ACDP, NL Stinnes, Nr. 020/1.

11. Memorandum by Stinnes written in Oberhof, Thuringia, Jan. 23, 1923, ACDP, NL Stinnes, Nr. 020/1.

12. *VR*, Jan. 13, 1923, Bd. 357, pp. 9417–39 and Winkler, *Von der Revolution*, pp. 556ff.

13. Telephone call from Vögler, Jan. 16, 1923, *Kabinett Cuno*, p. 146n3, and meeting of Jan. 10, ibid., pp. 129f. See also, Huber, *Verfassungsgeschichte* 7, pp. 281ff., and Jean-Claude Favez, *Le Reich devant l'occupation franco-belge de la Ruhr en 1923* (Geneva, 1969), pp. 101ff.

14. Ministerial Discussion of Jan. 19, 1923, *Kabinett Cuno*, pp. 176ff., and Reusch to Woltmann, Jan. 21, 1923, HA/GHH, Nr. 300193008/7.

15. Melchior to Warburg, Jan. 12, 1923, Warburg Papers, 1923, p. 7. See also, *Kabinett Cuno*, p. 129, and memorandum of the Essen Chamber of Commerce, Jan. 13, 1923, BAK, R 43I/203, Bl. 222–26.

16. Ernst Leug to Reusch, Jan. 30, 1923, HA/GHH, Nr. 300193008/7.

17. Sogemeier report of Jan. 20, 1923, HA/GHH, Nr. 300193008/7. On the wage-price trade-off in the coal mining industry, see *Kabinett Cuno*, p. 180n2.

18. For a useful summary, see Ruck, *Gewerkschaften im Ruhrkampf*, pp. 175ff., 244ff.

19. Cabinet meeting of Jan. 17, 1923, *Kabinett Cuno*, p. 156n6; Frölich to Cuno, Jan. 19, 1923, ibid, pp. 178f.; Sogemeier report of Jan. 20, 1923, HA/GHH, Nr. 300193008/7.

20. See Geithe, *Lebensmittelzwangswirtschaft*, pp. 144ff., the comments by Hamm of Dec. 21, 1922, and Jan. 17, 1923, *Kabinett Cuno*, p. 89; the memorandum of the Ministries of Justice and Economics sent to the state governments on Dec. 16, 1922 is to be found in BAP, RWM, Nr. 2434/4, Bl. 229–35.

21. *Kabinett Cuno*, pp. 159–73.

22. Note by Hamm, Jan. 17, 1923, BAK, R 43I/2445, partially reprinted in *Kabinett Cuno*, p. 206n3.

23. Report of Consul General Coffin from Berlin, Jan. 30, 1923, NA, 862.60/484.

24. Economic Policy Committee of the RWR, Feb. 7, 1923, BAP, RWR, Nr. 396, Bd. 12, Bl. 34. The information on the coal supply was provided the committee by Coal Commissar Stutz, Bl. 17ff.

25. Ibid., Bl. 58.

26. Prion, "Kreditpolitik und Ruhrkampf," pp. 116f. and Reichsbank Central Committee meeting of Jan. 18, 1923, BAK, R 43I/640, Bl. 167–69.

27. "Vermerk über den Marksturz," Jan. 30, 1923, *Kabinett Cuno*, pp. 206f.

28. Cabinet meeting of Feb. 6, 1923, *Kabinett Cuno*, p. 218.

29. Delbrück, Schickler & Co. to the Reichskanzlei, Jan. 30, 1923, BAK, R 43I/222, Bl. 454–57.

30. Report by Trendelenburg on a conversation with Dr. Max Schlencker of the Saarbrücken Chamber of Commerce, Jan. 23, 1923, and meeting of Reich, Prussian, and Reichsbank officials on Jan. 29, 1923, BAK, R 43I/205, Bl. 246 and R 43I/206, Bl. 361–63. For the ADGB warning, see *Correspondenzblatt*, Jan. 20, 1923, pp. 27f.

31. Aktenvermerk by a Reichsbank official, Jan. 30, 1923, BAP, RB, Nr. 6435, Bl. 161–63.

32. Saxon report on the Reichsbank Curatorium meeting of March 21, 1923, dated April 1, SäHStA, Gesandtschaft Berlin, Nr. 1631. This version of the meeting is important because it records facts about the intervention not to be found in the version in BAP, RB, Nr. 6406, Bl. 207–27. The latter contains very revealing statistical information on the intervention.

33. This is based on a report by Melchior on talks he had with Bergmann, Hermes, and Schroeder on February 13–14, 1923, Warburg Papers, 1923, pp. 12ff. The transcription of the letters here is filled with dating errors arising from the fact that events that took place in January are often ascribed to the corresponding date in February. See also, Bergmann, *History of Reparations*, pp. 185ff.

34. Saxon report on the Reichsbank Curatorium meeting of March 21, 1923, SäHStA, Gesandtschaft Berlin, Nr. 1631.

35. This was reported by Reusch, who had spoken to Hermes and bankers on February 15, see Reusch to Haniel, Feb. 25, 1923, HA/GHH, Nr. 300193000/6.

36. Initially, the banking house of Hallgarten handled the New York end of the operation, but Mendelssohn then insisted and received exclusive control of the operation because of the superior telegraphic connection between Amsterdam and New York. See Warburg Papers, 1923, p. 13.

37. Saxon report on the meeting of March 21, SäHStA, Gesandtschaft Berlin, Nr. 1631.

38. Ibid., and report in BAP, RB, Nr. 6406, Bl. 207ff.

39. Meeting of the Economic Policy and Finance Policy Committees of the RWR, Feb. 8, 1923, BAP, RWR, Nr. 396, Bd. 12, Bl. 120.

40. Ibid., Bl. 79, and Bl. 79ff. for the quotations which follow.

41. Ibid., Bl. 93.

42. Ibid., Bl. 97.

43. Ibid.; U.S. Consular report on the financial situation in Württemberg and Baden, March 27, 1923, NA 862.51/1659; meeting of the Foreign Exchange Procurement Board, March 6, 1923, BAK, R ll/505; conversation between Stinnes and Stresemann, March 19, 1923, NL Stresemann, Nr. 3098/7114H/H145243–45; Ministerial discussion, April 19, 1923, *Kabinett Cuno*, p. 399–402. For Hagen's opposition, which he claimed was shared by all of industry, see Warburg Papers, 1923, p. 15. On Havenstein's feelings about the mark rate, see Woltmann to Reusch, Feb. 26, 1923, HA/GHH, Nr. 300193003/8.

44. On the role of Hermes and Bergmann, see Bergmann, *History of Reparations*, pp. 184ff., and Bernhard's article, "Die Goldanleihe," *Plutus* (March 1, 1923), pp. 69–73, which also compares the Hirsch gold loan plan with the one being implemented. For Melchior's role, which may have been crucial, see Warburg Papers, 1923, p. 14.

45. For the quotes from Havenstein which follow, see Saxon report on Reichsbank Curatorium meeting, March 21, 1923, SäHStA, Gesandtschaft Berlin, Nr. 1631.

46. *Kabinett Cuno*, pp. 276f., and Bernhard, "Devisen = Anleihe," *Plutus* (April 1, 1923), pp. 101–3.

47. Reported in the RWR joint committee meeting of Feb. 21, 1923, BAP, Nr. 396, Bd. 12, Bl. 135. For Havenstein's views on the need to tighten credit, see his report to the Curatorium of March 21, 1923, BAP, RB, Nr. 6406, Bl. 220ff.

48. RWR meeting of Feb. 21, 1923, BAP, RWR, Nr. 396, Bd. 12, Bl. 132–204.

49. Ibid., Bl. 160.

50. Ibid., Bl. 154–55.

51. Warburg Papers, 1923, p. 13.

52. Reusch to Haniel, Feb. 25, 1923, HA/GHH, Nr. 300193000/6, for the RdI complaint to the Reichsbank, see the RdI circular of Feb. 21, 1923, ibid., Nr. 30019320/2.

53. This discussion is based on a report of Peter Klöckner to the directors of his branch in Rauxel, Feb. 25, 1923, BgA, Nr. 25/9.

54. Ibid. Another indication of Klöckner's sensitivity on these matters was his chiding of his directors for the way in which they handled the billion marks they had received as a credit through the Coal Syndicate. He insisted that they cease discounting drafts provided by the Syndicate and, instead, provide their own drafts for the Syndicate to discount, for in the latter method, "there is a world of difference insofar as you are expressly obligated on June 30 to put the credits you have accepted in the balances whereas the drafts you provide which are accepted by others appear as accounts payable."

55. Woltmann to Reusch, Feb. 26, 1923, HA/GHH, Nr. 300193003/8. A report of the American Consul in Stuttgart on the financial condition of firms in Baden and Württemberg of March 27, 1923, suggests that businesses in the unoccupied areas were, in fact, much harder hit, NA, 862.51/1659.

56. Klöckner to Rauxel directors, Feb. 25, 1923, BgA, Nr. 25/9, and Woltmann to Reusch, Feb. 26, 1923, HA/GHH, Nr. 300193003/8.

57. Reusch to Woltmann, Feb. 28, 1923, in response to Woltmann's report of Feb. 26, ibid. More generally, see Feldman, *Iron and Steel*, pp. 359ff.

58. Feldman, *Iron and Steel*, pp. 363ff.

59. Reported by Director Lattau of Phoenix, April 18, 1923, Mannesmann-Archiv, P/1/25/63.

60. Here I follow the excellent discussion of Ruck, *Gewerkschaften im Ruhrhampf,* p. 216ff.

61. For Havenstein's remarks and Cuno's threat to the bankers, see the meetings of April 19, 1923, *Kabinett Cuno,* pp. 399–404. See also Warburg to Cuno, March 30, 1923, Warburg Papers, 1923, pp. 20–22, and a report by Arndt von Holtzendorff on a conversation with Cuno on April 7, 1923. Hermes, in blaming the failure of the dollar loan on German business circles, put the matter quite bluntly a few months later: "One must openly state, that the Cuno Cabinet, which was so publicly greeted by German business when it was formed, was very weakly supported by the same business community." Hermes Memorandum of Sept. 21, 1923, Stehkämper, *NL Marx,* Teil III, p. 103. For Stinnes's remarks to Hermes, see Hermes to Ersing, Oct. 19, 1923, ibid., p. 111.

62. Ibid.

63. Handelskammer Hamburg to the Reichsbank, April 30, 1923, StA Hamburg, Staatskommission für die Reichs- und auswärtigen Angelegenheiten, II A4, Fasz. 29, and Max Warburg, "Das Ergebnis der Dollarschatzanweisungsanleihe des Deutschen Reiches," *Bank = Archiv* (April 15, 1923), pp. 175–77.

64. Ibid., and the penetrating analysis by Morus, "Das Fiasko der Goldanleihe," *Die Weltbühne* (April 12, 1923), p. 428f. See also the U.S. Consular report of Corelius Ferris, March 13, 1923, on the rye and coal loans as well as the more general report by Orsen S. Nielsen on the failure of the dollar loan, NA, 862.61/5 and 862.51/1660.

65. Warburg to Cuno, March 30, 1923, Warburg Papers, 1923, p. 22.

66. Morus, "Das Fiasko der Goldanleihe," *Die Weltbühne* (April 12, 1923), pp. 428f.

67. RB Central Committee meeting, April 23, 1923, BAK, R 43I/640, Bl. 178f.

68. See Hamm to Kempner, April 27, 1923, and an article by Felix Pinner in the *Berliner Tageblatt* of April 28, "Wer sind die großen Devisenkaäufer," BAK, R 43I/2445, Bl. 111f.; summaries of the Reichstag hearings are to be found in ibid., Bl. 148–54. The report of the Reichstag investigation is to be found in *VR,* Bd. 380, Drucksache Nr. 6591. The transcript of twelve of seventeen of the open and closed meetings of the investigation committee held between May 29 and July 9, 1923, are to be found in BAK, R 2/2419 and further transcripts are to be found in the NL of the Socialist committee member Paul Hertz, SPD Archiv, along with very important analyses made in 1957 by Dr. Anspach, and much of the discussion which follows is strongly influenced by his memorandum of March 19, 1957, and the accompanying materials. See also, *Kabinett Cuno,* pp. 421–25, 459–61. The investigation was briefly discussed in the Reichstag debate on May 9, 1923, where the Communist Deputy Frölich, who was also

a member of the committee, made a particularly vicious attack on Stinnes, *VR,* Bd. 359, Sitzung vom 9. Mai 1923, pp. 10930ff., esp. pp. 10951–53.

69. Siemens to Havenstein, April 26 and Stinnes to Havenstein, April 27, 1923, ACDP, NL Stinnes, Nr. 039/1.

70. *Kabinett Cuno,* p. 425f.n5.

71. File memorandum by Groener, Jan. 28, 1923, BAK, R 43I/2445, Bl. 157.

72. This account and analysis is based largely on the materials in the NL Paul Hertz, SPD Archiv.

73. Report of April 7, 1923, HAPAG Archiv.

74. Unsigned letter to Wirth, April 23, 1923, BAK, NL Wirth, Nr. 2. The content of the letter demonstrates that the author had regular contact with the highest levels of the government.

75. Ritter to his mother, March 8, 1923, in Klaus Schwabe and Rolf Richardt, eds., *Gerhard Ritter. Ein politischer Historiker in seinen Briefen* (Boppard am Rhein, 1984), pp. 224–25.

76. See the excellent discussion in Ruck, *Gewerkschaften im Ruhrkampf,* pp. 253–77.

77. Feldman and Steinisch, *Industrie und Gewerkschaften,* pp. 105ff.

78. On Stinnes, see Henry Bernhard, ed., *Gustav Stresemann. Vermächtnis,* 3 vols. (Berlin, 1932), I, pp. 42–44, and Stinnes to Wiedfeldt, March 15, 1923, ACDP, NL Stinnes, Nr. 022/3; on Wolff and Carp, see Rupieper, *Cuno,* p. 144; on Rinkel, see the report by Consul Sauer in Cologne, April 28, 1923, NA, 862t.00.

79. Stinnes to Wiedfeldt, March 15, 1923, ACDP, NL Stinnes, Nr. 022/3.

80. For this and the quotations which follow, see the report by Stinnes on his trip to Rome, dated April 5, 1923, ACDP, NL Stinnes, Nr. 046/1.

81. Report by the Saxon Representative Gradnauer, Feb. 13, 1923, SäHStA, Gesandtschaft Berlin, Nr. 321.

82. Williamson, *Helfferich,* pp. 373ff.

83. Stinnes to Wiedfeldt, March 15, 1923, ACDP, NL Stinnes, Nr. 0221/3, and Stinnes notes on a discussion with the chairman of the committee of Guarantees, Haguenin, April 5, 1923, ibid., Nr. 265/1. Rupieper, *Cuno,* pp. 144f.

84. Rupieper, *Cuno,* pp. 135ff., and Hermann J. Rupieper, "Alanson B. Houghton: An American Ambassador in Germany, 1922–1925," *The International History Review* 1 (Oct. 1979), pp. 490–508.

85. Report by Hamm, April 20, 1923, *Kabinett Cuno,* pp. 412–15, and Rupieper, *Cuno,* pp. 146f.

86. See the correspondence and documents at the end of April and first days of May in *Kabinett Cuno,* pp. 415–19, 430–38, 440–52.

87. The German note is reprinted in *Ursachen und Folgen,* Vol. 5, pp. 121–24. See the analysis in Rupieper, *Cuno,* p. 149.

88. Hamm to Haniel, April 26, 1922, *Kabinett Cuno,* pp. 431f. Hermes defined his criticisms very precisely in a memorandum of Sept. 21 and a letter to Ersing of Oct. 19, 1923, Stehkämper, *NL Marx,*

Teil III, pp. 106f., 113f. Hermes was ill prior to the sending of the note and returned from leave to find it already formulated.

89. Unsigned letter to Wirth, April 25, 1923, BAK, NL Wirth, Nr. 2. The content of this lengthy letter bears great similarity to the views of Albert, but Albert's relations with Wirth were not very good. Another possibility would be Schröder of the Finance Ministry. It was clearly written by someone with very close connections to both the Foreign Office and the Reich Chancellery.

90. Melchior to Warburg, May 10, 1923, Warburg Papers, 1923, p. 36.

91. Here, my assessment is in complete agreement with Rupieper, *Cuno*, pp. 152ff. There are excellent reports on the divisions within the government and the critical comments on Cuno by the Saxon Representatives in Berlin, see especially the reports of May 15 and May 26, 1923, SäHStA, Gesandtschaft Berlin, Nr. 350, Bl. 107–9.

92. Report, probably by Humann, on a conversation with Stinnes of May 17, 1923, ACDP, NL Stinnes, Nr. 039/1. The report is unsigned, but internal evidence points to the authorship of Humann. It was Humann who spoke to "Dr. H.," but this leaves little doubt as to who "H" was. The discussion of Stinnes's views and quotations which follow are based on this report.

93. Geheimer Justizrat Dr. Erger to the Legal Division of Deutsch-Lux, Feb. 14, 1923, and reply of March 5, 1923, ibid., Nr. 057/1.

94. Meeting of the Presidium, May 15–16, 1923, HA/GHH, Nr. 30019320/7.

95. Ibid.

96. Report by Guggenheimer on discussion with Dr. Krekenberg, May 17, 1923, M.A.N Augsburg, Nr. K71.

97. Meeting of May 16, 1923, HA/GHH, Nr. 30019320/7.

98. Eighteen industrial leaders signed the letter of May 25, 1923 which was addressed to the Chancellor and is reprinted in *Kabinett Cuno*, pp. 508–13.

99. *Kabinett Cuno*, p. 539n3, and Solmssen to Bürgers, June 13, 1923, RWWK, NL Solmssen.

100. Bürgers to Fonk, ibid.

101. Socialist trade unions to the Chancellor, June 1, 1923, *Kabinett Cuno*, pp. 537–39.

102. Report of the Commissar for the Surveillance of Public Order, June 15, 1923. For Socialist responses, see, for example, the report of the ADGB trade-union leader in the Rhineland, Meyer, of June 7, 1923, Hiko, NB 158b/153. The themes are repeated over and over again in the reports from the Ruhr and elsewhere. A summary of trade-union criticisms is to be found in *Soziale Praxis* 32 (1923), pp. 554–56.

103. Bücher to Cuno, May 31, 1923, *Kabinett Cuno*, pp.530–32, also, pp. 532n3 and 538n2.

104. See meeting of May 29, 1923 and memorandum of the Reich Agricultural League of June 12, 1923, ibid., pp. 517–19, 554–56.

105. *Ursachen und Folgen*, V, pp. 145f.

106. Stresemann to Litwin, June 26, 1923, NL Stresemann, 3098/7116/H145655–57.

107. In this analysis, I follow the argument of Rupieper, *Cuno*, pp. 163ff., who also provides details on an interesting but unsuccessful effort by John Foster Dulles to mediate.

108. Raumer to Stresemann, July 23, 1923, NL Stresemann, 3098/7117/H145749–53.

109. See the extremely useful detailed accounting of these expenditures made in early July 1923 in BAK, R 43I/214, Bl. 58–68. See also Hermes remarks in his memorandum of Sept. 21, 1923, Stehkämper, *NL Marx,* Teil III, p. 88.

110. For these figures and this discussion, see the report of the Statistisches Reichsamt of the summer of 1923 cited in Table 44 as well as the discussions of May 9, 1923, and August 10, 1923, in GStAPrK, Rep. 84a, Nr. 1410.

111. Unsigned letter to the RWM, BAP, RWM, Nr. 4531, Bl. 110–13. These problems are generally discussed in Feldman, *Iron and Steel*, pp. 365ff.

112. Ibid., pp. 367f.

113. Memorandum of Sept. 21, 1923, Stehkämper, *NL Marx,* Teil III, p. 88. See also the report of the U.S. Consul in Cologne, May 4, 1923, NA, 862.00/1243; Ruck, *Gewerkschaften*, pp. 177ff., and, more generally, Norbert Ranft, "Erwerbslosenfürsorge, Ruhrkampf und Kommunen. Die Trendwende in der Sozialpolitik im Jahre 1923," in Feldman et al., eds., *Adaptation to Inflation*, pp. 163–201.

114. See, for example, the meeting in Darmstadt of May 5, 1923, BAP, RAM, Nr. 2987, Bl. 143–47. As the WAST in Hamm reported in a very revealing account of July 2, 1923, it was very difficult to distinguish between the wage guarantee and what might be called "productive unemployment support for private enterprises." See GStAKM, Rep. 120, BB, VII 1 3^y, Bd. 5/6 Bl. 302–05.

115. Feldman, *Iron and Steel*, pp. 369ff., and report of Section X of the RAM, July 25, 1923, BAP, RAM, Nr. 1724, Bl. 182.

116. Note by Hamm of May 1, 1923, *Kabinett Cuno*, p. 147n3; RWM circular of Feb. 17, 1923, SäHStA, MdI, Nr. 11352, Bl. 89f.

117. Meeting of the State Secretaries on price and wage questions, Feb. 26, 1923, BAK, R 43I/1152, Bl. 48–53, quote on Bl. 50f. See also German Chamber of Commerce and Industry to the RWM, March 3, 1923, BAP, RAM, Nr. 10555, Bl. 2–4; Finance Committee meeting of the RWR, March 10, 1923, BAP, RWR, Nr. 396, Bd. 12, Bl. 304ff.; RWM to the Saxon Landespreisprüfungsstelle, Feb. 27, 1923, SäHStA, Landespreisprüfungsstelle, Nr. 86, Bl. 45f., and the relevant correspondence on cartels in ibid., Nr. 87. On the price reductions, see the remarks of State Secretary Trendelenburg, Cabinet meeting of May 2, 1923, *Kabinett Cuno*, p. 456.

118. *Zahlen zur Geldentwertung*, pp. 26f., 33.

119. Reports of May 4, June 15, and August 16, 1923, NA, 862t. 00/0, 6, and 14.

120. Chancellery report of March 9, 1923, BAK, R 43I/1152, Bl. 109. See the meeting of the ADGB

leaders of April 17–18, 1923, in Ruck, *Gewerkschaften*, pp. 828ff.

121. VdA circular of April 7, and see also the circular of March 31, 1923, StA Hamburg, Blohm & Voss, Nr. 1329. See also VdA to Hamm, Feb. 28, 1923, BAK, R 43I/1152, Bl. 79f.

122. RAM to VdA, March 12, 1923, BAK, R 43I/1152, Bl. 124.

123. ADGB meeting of April 17–18, 1923, Ruck, *Gewerkschaften*, pp. 831, 834.

124. For the meeting of April 16, see BAP, ZAG, Nr. 31, Bl. 814, for that of April 23, ibid., Bl. 15–25.

125. Hauschild, *Reichswirtschaftsrat*, pp. 177ff. and reports of the Hamburg representative of March 1923 in StA Hamburg, Senatskommission für die Reichs- und auswärtigen Angelegenheiten, III Alc 3, Bd. 5.

126. RWR Economic Policy Committee meeting, May 2, 1923, BAP, RWR, Nr. 397, Bd. 13, Bl. 277ff., quote on Bl. 291.

127. Ibid., Bl. 295.

128. Ibid., Bl. 311.

129. Ibid., ZAG, Nr. 31, Bl. 23.

130. See Tänzler's remarks, ibid., Bl. 20.

131. Ibid., Bl. 21, 23.

132. Statement by Dr. Oppenheimer of the Berlin Metal Industrialists Association, ibid., Bl. 24.

133. Report by Knoll, May 8, 1923, Hiko, NB 166/28.

134. VdA circular of May 3, 1923, StA Hamburg, Blohm & Voss, Nr. 1329. See also VdA to Cuno, April 24, 1923, BAK, R 43I/1152, Bl. 171f., and notes between the Chancellery and RAM, ibid., Bl. 175f.

135. Dißmann to Brauns, May 3, 1923 and Grützner to Oeser, May 12, 1923, BAP, RAM, Nr. 2372, Bl. 201, 296; Favez, *Le Reich devant l'occupation*, pp. 238ff.

136. Husemann to the ADGB, May 31, 1923, Hiko, NB 158a/148.

137. Meeting of Ruhr union leaders, May 30, 1923, Hiko, NB 167/137.

138. Schreiber to Leipart, May 30, 1923, Hiko, NB 158a/0143.

139. Schreiber to the Factory Workers Union headquarters, May 28, 1923, Hiko, NB 158a/145a.

140. Meeting with trade-union leaders on May 29, 1923, Ruck, *Gewerkschaften*, p. 861, and Brauns to the VdA, May 25, 1923, BAK, R 43I/1262, Bl. 213.

141. VdA to Brauns, June 1, 1923, ibid., Bl. 214–16, and VdA circular of June 7, 1923, StA Hamburg, Blohm & Voss, Nr. 1329.

142. Hamm memorandum of June 16, 1923, *Kabinett Cuno*, p. 576, and letter of Brauns to Hamm, June 20, 1923, ibid., n.5.

143. ZAG directors meeting, June 23, 1923, BAP, ZAG, Nr. 31, Bl. 1–7, quote on Bl. 6.

144. Ibid., Bl. 7.

145. Meeting of July 4–5, 1923, in Ruck, *Gewerkschaften*, p. 877. For the Reichstag debate of June 7, 1923, see *VR*, Bd. 360, pp. 11205ff.

146. Cabinet meeting of July 7, 1923, *Kabinett Cuno*, pp. 628ff.

147. Quoted in Kunz, *Civil Servants*, pp. 88f., 358ff.

148. *Soziale Praxis* 23 (1923), pp. 819f.

149. Report of the American Consul in Leipzig, July 26, 1923, NA, 862.5045.

150. Meeting of June 19–21, 1923, StA Hamburg, DHSG III, Pr IV 49/11.

151. RAM Report of Oct. 20, 1923, on policies of July–September 1923, BAP, RAM, Nr. 1724, Bl. 234f.

152. RWR Economic and Finance Policy Committee meeting of July 11, 1923, ibid., RWR, Nr. 398, Bd. 14, Bl. 159.

153. See the accounts in Ulrich Rönitz, ed., *Chronik des Zentralverbandes deutscher Haus- und Grundbesitzvereine e.V. 1879–1927* (Berlin, 1929), pp. 99ff., and the excellent discussions in Lyth, *Inflation and the Merchant Economy*, pp. 156–61, 173–78.

154. Joint meeting of the RWR Economic and Finance Policy Committees, May 2, 1923, ibid., Bl. 231f.; on Düringer and his bill, see Michael L. Hughes, *Paying for the German Inflation* (Chapel Hill and London, 1988), pp. 26ff. Düringer was something of a maverick, having departed the DNVP for the DVP in 1920 in opposition to DNVP political radicalism. He was also an experienced judge who had served on the Reich Supreme Court between 1902 and 1915 and had specialized in financial matters.

155. Hughes, *Paying*, pp. 32f. There is an excellent summary of the decisions and judicial reasoning in a report by U.S. Consul Orsen N. Nielsen of June 21, 1923, NA, 862.5156/1066.

156. Joint meeting of the Economic and Finance Policy Committees and the Committee for Housing and Settlement, May 2, 1923, BAP, RWR, Nr. 397, Bd. 13, Bl. 257–62.

157. Ibid., Bl. 238f.

158. RWR Meeting of June 13, 1923, ibid., Bl. 417ff., and Cabinet meeting of June 6, 1923, *Kabinett Cuno*, p. 548n1.

159. RWR meeting of June 13, BAP, RWR, Nr. 397, Bd. 13, Bl. 427.

160. The examples are provided from a report by the American Consul E. Verne Richardson of June 26, 1923, NA, 862.506/12.

161. For the discussion of this aspect at the June 13 meeting, see BAP, RWR, Nr. 397, Bd. 13, Bl. 427, 431, 442ff., 448f.

162. Ibid., Bl. 424.

163. Ibid., Bl. 446.

164. Report of April 23, 1923, BAK R 43I/2445, Bl. 96f., and Frowein to Cuno, April 23, and petition of the Hamburg and Bremen merchants, April 24, Bl. 100ff. See also the government meeting with the bankers of April 19, *Kabinett Cuno*, pp. 403f., and Kühne, *Devisenzwangswirtschaft*, p. 24.

165. The American Consul in Hamburg, Maurice Walk, provided a huge catalogue of the abuses which

American importers could expect in dealing with German forwarders in a report of July 21, 1923, and concluded that there were "no assured methods . . . to protect the principal from the agent's speculation." NA, unnumbered.

166. *Kabinett Cuno*, pp. 575–81.

167. *RGBl* (1923), I, pp. 401f., 509, 511.

168. Meeting of June 22, 1922, *Kabinett Cuno*, pp. 598f.

169. Report by H.C.F. Finlayson on a discussion with Oberregierungsrat Husslein of the Exchange Section of the Finance Ministry, June 27, 1923, PRO, FO 371/8664/37114/277–81, quote on 277.

170. Notes by Kempner of the Chancellery of a discussion on June 19, 1923, BAK, R 43I/2445, Bl. 161f. See also the record of other discussions on 16 and 21 in ibid., Bl. 162ff.

171. Ibid., pp. 598f.n1, 710n1.

172. Report of the Saxon Representative at the Reichsbank Curatorium meeting of July 14, 1923, SäHStA, Gesandtschaft Berlin, Nr. 1631.

173. Meeting of June 22, 1922, ibid., p. 601.

174. Minute by Kempner of June 25, 1923, BAK, R 43I/2445, Bl. 218–20.

175. Minute of June 27, 1923, ibid., Bl. 222.

176. See the reports by the American Consuls Orsen N. Nielsen from Berlin and George D. Hopper from Hamburg, both of July 27, 1923, NA, 862.5151/1072–73; Ritscher to Hamm, July 10, 1923, BAK, R 43I/2446, Bl. 15f., and the discussion in the Chancellery on July 14, 1923, BAK, R 43I/2445, Bl. 281f., and the memorandum by Economics Minister Becker of July 23, 1923, *Kabinett Cuno*, pp. 652–58.

177. Reichsbank-Direktorium to Cuno, July 28, 1923, *Kabinett Cuno,* pp. 688–90.

178. Finlayson report of July 3, 1923, PRO, FO 371/8665/147/20–22 and Addison to Curzon, June 20, 1923, ibid., 371/8664/37114/188.

179. Report on the Reichsbank Curatorium meeting of July 14, 1923, SäHStA, Gesandtschaft Berlin, Nr. 1630.

180. Ibid., and *Kabinett Cuno*, pp. 688–90.

181. The discussion and quotations which follow are taken from the meeting of June 11, BAK, R 43I/640, Bl. 195.

182. Ibid.

183. Ibid., Bl. 207–13.

184. RB Curatorium meeting of July 14, 1923, SäHStA, Gesandtschaft Berlin, Nr. 1631.

185. There is an excellent discussion of this question based on extensive use of the sources in Rupieper, *Cuno*, pp. 187ff. For Becker's views, see *Kabinett Cuno*, p. 656f.n12.

186. See above, Chapter 13, pp. 596f.

187. *Kabinett Cuno*, p. 599fn6.

188. "Goldmarkkonten und Goldmarkkredite im Bankverkehr," *Bank=Archiv* 18, (June 15, 1923), pp. 217–25, quote on p. 224.

189. *Kabinett Cuno*, p. 656fn12, and Rupieper, *Cuno*, pp. 191f.

190. Report on the presentation of Hermes concerning the government's tax plans before the Reichsrat, July 28, 1923, SäHStA, Außenministerium, Nr. 5317.

191. Hauschild, *Reichswirtschaftsrat*, pp. 91f.

192. RWR Economic and Finance Policy Committees Meeting, July 11, 1922, BAP, RWR, Nr. 398, Bd. 14, Bl. 115ff, quote on Bl. 116. The discussion and quotations which follow are taken from this document and especially the Hilferding speech on Bl. 115–36.

193. Bernhard, in his remarks, drew some blood in revenge for Hirsch: "There is a certain irony in the fact that, after one had practically brought the former State Secretary in the Reich Economics Ministry down over this Foreign Exchange Control Decree, today a Foreign Exchange Control Decree and an entire complex of foreign-exchange decrees are carried out in isolation by an opposing government, which, if the measures taken at that time were senseless, leaves the senselessness of those measures very far behind. (Very True!)," ibid., Bl. 157.

194. Ibid., Bl. 131f.

195. See, for example, the meeting of July 24, 1923, BAK, R II/505.

196. Leidig to Stresemann, July 18, 1923, NL Stresemann, 3098/7117/H1451698–700.

197. Besprechung über die Goldrechnung auf dem Gebiete der Steuern, Aug. 2, 1923, BAK, NL Bonn, Nr. 25c. This seems a truer presentation of his attitudes than his retrospective self-defence of Sept. 21, 1923 in Stehkämper, *NL Marx*, Teil III, pp. 90ff. Hermes clearly was more realistic than many of his colleagues, but his fundamental view was that taxation was virtually pointless without a foreign-policy success in the reparations area and that otherwise more taxes would lead to increased inflation. At the same time, his criticism of the Reichstag's unwillingness to support real reforms is well-taken, and he certainly is correct in arguing that the Reichstag would not have voted the August reforms without the panic over the mark collapse of July.

198. Ibid., Teil I, p. 286., and Teil III, pp. 115ff. Hermes gave a rundown of his tax plans to the Reichsrat on July 28, arguing, somewhat sheepishly, that most of the taxes had already been valorized and that the basis for sound fiscal conditions were in place and awaited only a satisfactory resolution of the Ruhr struggle but admitting that the ten trillion paper marks already given out for the Ruhr struggle required the special measures he was now taking. See the report of the Baden Representative to the Reichsrat, Kempff, GLA Karlsruhe, 237/13319.

199. Position paper for the meeting, July 31–Aug. 1, 1923, *Kabinett Cuno*, pp. 697–702. For the Ministerial Council of July 27, ibid., pp. 672–79.

200. Meeting of Aug. 3, ibid., pp. 710f.

201. RdI to the various branches of industry, Aug. 8, 1923, StA Hamburg, Blohm & Voss, Nr. 511.

202. Confidential letter from Siemens, Aug. 6, 1923, ibid. Bücher, in his letter to Rudolf Blohm of Blohm & Voss, Aug. 3, 1923, asked Blohm to pay up

in full since it was a "decision over the existence or non-existence of the Reich." Blohm's exclamation point in the margins suggests that he was not taken with all the drama, a point he made clear in a letter of Aug. 9, in which he told Bücher that neither he nor his industry were prepared to be called upon again to supply monies that should be raised by the public and to do so on such a basis.

203. F. Schichau to the Verein Deutscher Schiffswerften, Aug. 10, 1923, and his letter of Aug. 8, ibid.

204. Atlas-Werke A.G. Bremen to the Verein Deutscher Schiffswerften, Aug. 10, 1923, ibid.

205. On these plans, see the revealing memorandum by Hamm of August 13, 1923, on the undertaken and projected government measures at the moment of transfer of government by Cuno to Stresemann, *Kabinett Cuno*, pp. 748–52.

206. *Kabinett Cuno*, pp. 724f., 750f. This second intervention of the Reichsbank began on August 9 and lasted until November 2, costing some 144 million gold marks and yielding some 8.9 quadrillions of paper marks. The details are to be found in the report of the Foreign Exchange Procurement Board to the RB of Feb. 2, 1924, BAP, RB, Bd. 6406, Bl. 299–301.

207. For the Hamm program, ibid., pp. 662–66; for the Albert-Henrich program, pp. 682–88.

208. For the concept of "regime change," see Sargent in Hall, ed., *Inflation*, pp. 40–97. One could argue that Cuno was heading in a reverse direction with respect to an important component of such regime changes mentioned by Sargent; namely, the autonomy of the central bank. Under the bizarre German circumstances, however, the autonomy of the Reichsbank, at least until the solutions found under Stresemann were put in place, was more likely to inhibit rather than promote a "regime change."

209. Warburg Papers, 1923, pp. 56f.

210. Meeting of the DDP directors, July 28, 1923, in Lothar Albertin and Konstanze Wegner, eds., *Linksliberalismus in der Weimarer Republik. Die Führungsgremien der deutschen demokratischen Partei und der deutschen Staatspartei 1918–1933* [*Quellen zur Geschichte des Parlamentarismus und der Politischen Parteien*, Bd. 5] (Düsseldorf, 1980), pp. 297f.

211. See the Hamm memorandum of Aug. 13, 1923, *Kabinett Cuno*, p. 751.

212. Hugenberg to Stinnes, Aug. 11, 1923, ACDP, NL Stinnes, Nr. 022/2. On the fall of Cuno, see Rupieper, *Cuno*, pp. 211ff.; Jones, *German Liberalism*, pp. 195ff.; Winkler, *Revolution zur Stabilisierung*, pp. 593ff.; Max von Stockhausen, *Sechs Jahre Reichskanzlei. Erinnerungen und Tagebuchnotizen 1922–1927*, edited by Walter Görlitz, (Bonn, 1954), pp. 72ff.

15.   The Politics of Currency Reform, August–October 1923

1. Meeting of the party leaders on Aug. 22, 1923, *Kabinette Stresemann*, I, pp. 58f. On the Decree of August 10, see Huber, *Deutsche Verfassungsgeschichte*, Vol. 7, p. 306.

2. Meeting of Aug. 20, 1923, *Kabinette Stresemann*, I, p. 45.

3. Report of Aug. 6, 1923, ibid., p. 45n14.

4. Schultheß, *Geschichtskalender*, pp. 150f.

5. Ibid., p. 9f.n1–2. The report on the bank notes was provided by August Müller to the RWR on Aug. 31, 1923, BAP, RWR, Nr. 398, Bd. 14, Bl. 322.

6. Walter Fabian, *Ein Stück Geschichte* (Löbau, 1930), pp. 40ff.; for a broader discussion on the fateful conflicts in Saxony, see Benjamin Lapp, "Political Polarization in Weimar Germany: The Saxon Bürgertum and the Left, 1918–1930" (Ph.D. diss., University of California, Berkeley, 1991), esp. chap. 3. For the debates over the amnesty bill and the attachment of the Centuries to the state police, see *Verhandlungen der Sächsischen Volkskammer*, 1923, Vol. 2, meetings of June 21, (pp. 1159ff.), July 9, (pp. 1364ff., 1395ff.), and July 12, 1923 (pp. 1558ff.).

7. Amtshauptmannschaft Kamenz to the Saxon Interior Ministry, Sept. 1, 1923, SäHStA, MdI, Nr. 11108, Bl. 2f.

8. Report from Dresden, Sept. 14, 1923, ibid., Nr. 11110, Bl. 212ff.

9. Report of Aug. 2, 1923, ibid., Nr. 11108, Bl. 6f. On these and other forms of what Benjamin Lapp analyzes as "degradation rituals," see Lapp, "Political Polarization," chap. 3.

10. Report by the City Council of Stollberg, Sept. 4, 1923, SäHStA, MdI, Nr. 11108. Bl. 15f.

11. Report of the Polizeipräsidium Leipzig, Aug. 23, 1923, ibid., Bl. 125–27.

12. Report of the Chemnitz Polizeipräsidium, Aug. 10, 1923, ibid., Nr. 11110, Bl. 36f. More generally, see the report on strikes and unrest in Saxony by the Ministry of the Interior, of October 3, 1923, ibid., Nr. 11111, Bl. 211–13.

13. Report of the Government Commissar on the events in Penig from Aug. 11 to Aug. 17, 1923, ibid., Bl. 169ff.

14. Report of the police in Eibenstock, Aug. 27, 1923, ibid., Bl. 198–200.

15. Report by Syndic Illgen to the Saxon Ministry of the Interior, Aug. 20, 1923, ibid., Nr. 11112, Bl. 168–72.

16. Police Report from Freiberg, Aug. 25, 1923, ibid., Nr. 11108, Bl. 76–79.

17. Report on the unrest in Leipzig, June 4–6, 1923, dated Aug. 10, 1923, ibid., Nr. 11109, Bl. 169–77, esp. Bl. 172.

18. Report of the Leipzig Polizeipräsidium, Aug. 16, 1923, ibid., Nr. 11110, Bl. 291.

19. Report of a criminal inspector, Dresden, Sept. 17, 1923, and of an official of the Railroad Workers Union, Sept. 18–19, 1923, ibid., Nr. 1112, Bl. 77–83, 91f. Both Saxon and Bavarian observers noted the fascist appeal to common people in the Vogtland. See the report of the Bayreuth police, Sept. 26, 1923, BayHStA, Abt. II, Generalstaatskommissar 43.

20. Report of von Henle to the Bavarian Ministry of the Interior, Sept. 19, 1923, ibid., MA 102 150.

21. Ibid.

22. Report of the Regierungspräsident in Niederbayern, Oct. 3, 1923, ibid., MA 102 140. The powerful Bavarian peasant leader Georg Heim openly attacked the new taxes as "brutal, unjust and fateful in their consequences for the German people." See the report of the Reich Representative in Bavaria of Aug. 31, 1923, BAK, R 43I/2233.

23. Report of the Regierungspräsident in Oberbayern, Sept. 6, 1923, BayHStA, Abt. II, MA 102 136.

24. Report of the Regierungspräsidium von Unterfranken u. Aschaffenburg, July 9, 1920, BayHStA, Abt. II, MA 102 150.

25. Report by the Regierungspräsident in Oberbayern, Aug. 24, 1923, ibid., Nr. 102 136.

26. Report of Sept. 28, 1923, ibid., Generalstaatskommissar 43.

27. Unsigned report of Aug. 8, 1923, BAP, RAM, Nr. 812, Bl. 147f., for this quotation and the discussion which follows.

28. Meeting of Aug. 29, 1923, HA/GHH, Nr. 300193020/1.

29. Report of Aug. 11, 1923, Ruhrhauptreferat, BAP, RAM, Nr. 812, Bl. 128f.

30. Report by the Minister for the Occupied Areas, Sept. 11, 1923, BAP, Reichskanzlei, Zentralstelle Rhein-Ruhr, Lageberichte, Nr. 13, Bl. 18.

31. Reports of Aug. 13 and 15, 1923, ibid., Bl. 54, 57f., and the report of Morrison Taylor, U.S. Vice Consul in Cologne, Aug. 16, 1923, NA, 862t.00/14. Taylor's weekly reports reinforce their German counterparts.

32. See the U.S. Consular report of Sept. 15, 1923, NA, 862t.00/20.

33. Report of the State Commission for the Surveillance of the Public Order, Sept. 5, 1923, BAK, R 43I/215, Bl. 11–13.

34. Report from Gelsenkirchen of Sept. 15, 1923, ibid., Bl. 84ff.

35. Telegram from Houghton to Secretary of State, July 30, 1923, NA, 862.00/1265.

36. See RAM to RB, Aug. 15, 1923, BAK, R 43I/666, Bl. 16.

37. Food Ministers' conference of Aug. 17, 1923, SäHStA, Gesandtschaft Berlin, Nr. 488.

38. Petition of the Mecklenburg-Schwerin Landbund, *Kabinette Stresemann*, I, p. 97n11, and petition of the Pomeranian Landbund, Aug. 24, 1923, ibid., pp. 93–98. See also, Schumacher, *Land und Politik*, pp. 180ff., and Moeller, *German Peasants*, pp. 112ff.

39. *Kabinette Stresemann*, I, pp. 60–63, quote on p. 63.

40. See Helfferich's account to the Reichstag on Oct. 9, 1923, *VR*, Bd. 361, p. 12072.

41. Quoted in Williamson, *Helfferich*, p. 386.

42. See the discussions and drafts in Beusch, *Währungsverfall*, pp. 27–37, 116–27; Friedrich Ramhorst, *Die Entstehung der Deutschen Renten-*

bank [*Veröffentlichungen des Reichsverbandes der Deutschen Industrie,* Heft 20] (Berlin, March 1924), pp. 3–7; Karl-Bernhard Netzband and Hans-Peter Widmaier, *Währungs- und Finanzpolitik der Ära Luther 1923–1925* (Basel & Tübingen, 1964), pp. 12–26, Holtfrerich, *German Inflation*, pp. 315f.

43. Helfferich before the Reichstag, Oct. 9, 1923, *VR*, Bd. 361, p. 12072.

44. Cuno to Gildemeister, Jan. 22, 1924, HAPAG Archiv.

45. *VR*, Aug. 15, 1923, Bd. 361, p. 11897.

46. Ibid., p. 11881, and Williamson, *Helfferich*, p. 388.

47. *VR*, Aug. 15, 1923, Bd. 361, p. 11881.

48. This was recounted by Helfferich at the Reichstag on Oct. 9, 1923, *VR*, Bd. 361, pp. 12072f.

49. See his remarks to the DNVP industrialist working committee prior to the Aug. 18 meeting, *Kabinette Stresemann*, I, pp. 24n5, 25n12.

50. For the discussion and quotations from and about the meeting of August 18 which follows, see *Kabinette Stresemann* I, pp. 23–29.

51. *VR*, Aug. 14, 1923, Bd. 361, p. 11840.

52. Report by the Saxon Representative, Aug. 23, 1922, SäHStA, Außenministerium, Nr. 5317.

53. Report of Aug. 22, 1923, ibid., and *Kabinette Stresemann*, I, pp. 56–60.

54. Meeting of Aug. 20, 1923, *Kabinette Stresemann*, I, p. 47.

55. Report of the Saxon Representative to the Reichsrat, Aug. 23, 1923, SäHStA, Außenministerium, Nr. 5317.

56. Report of Aug. 23, 1923, ibid., Gesandtschaft Berlin, Nr. 350, Bl. 119.

57. *Kabinette Stresemann*, I, p. 156n3 and n4.

58. Ibid., p. 155n1, and pp. 155–69, for this important meeting.

59. Ibid., p. 164.

60. See the report on his remarks to the Budget Committee of the Reichstag, Aug. 22, 1923, SäHStA, Außenministerium, Nr. 5317. For a useful but perhaps overly sympathetic appreciation of Hilferding's performance as Finance Minister, see Martin Vogt, "Rudolf Hilferding als Finanzminister im ersten Kabinett Stresemann," in Büsch and Feldman, *Historische Prozesse*, pp. 126–58.

61. *Kabinette Stresemann*, I, p. 156fn6. For petitions protesting the deadlines and requesting delays, see BAK, R 43I/2357, Bl. 188f., 200, 213f.

62. See Karl Ziegler, "Die verlorene Steuerschlacht," *Plutus*, (Sept. 1, 1923), pp. 282f.

63. Kühne, *Devisenbewirtschaftung*, p. 25f.; *Kabinette Stresemann*, I, pp. 173ff.,180f., 185f., 201, 203

64. *Plutus* (Sept. 1, 1923), p. 284.

65. Confidential British Intelligence report of Aug. 28, 1923, PRO, FO 371/8666/127.

66. *Vossische Zeitung* of Sept. 8, 1923, quoted in *Plutus* (Sept. 15, 1923), p. 303.

67. Report of Finlayson, Sept. 17, 1923, PRO, FO 371/8667/44–46. On the razzias and their questionable effectiveness, see the scattered observations in

the RWR Finance Policy Committee discussion of Sept. 28, 1923, BAP, RWR, Nr. 555, Bd. 10.

68. Reusch to August Haniel, Sept. 5, 1923, HA/GHH 30019300/5.

69. RWR meeting, Aug. 31, 1923, BAP, RWR, Nr. 398, Bd. 14, Bl. 311.

70. Cabinet meeting of Aug. 20, 1923, *Kabinette Stresemann*, I, pp. 52–55, especially, p. 53n50.

71. Despatch by D'Abernon, Aug. 18, 1923, PRO, FO 371/8666/48–49.

72. Report on a conversation with Stresemann on Aug. 18, dated Aug. 23, 1923, ibid., 51. Stresemann pointed out that the SPD had demanded Havenstein's dismissal, but that it would be impossible to yield simply to a partisan demand.

73. Ministerial discussion of Aug. 23 and Cabinet meeting of Aug. 30, 1923, ibid., pp. 84, 160.

74. RB to Reich Finance Minister, Aug. 18, 1923, *Kabinette Stresemann*, I, pp. 37–42.

75. For this memorandum of Aug. 22, see *Kabinette Stresemann*, I, pp. 64–68.

76. The protocol of the meeting is to be found in ibid., pp. 101–25, quotes on p. 103.

77. Memorandum for Director Nordhoff, Aug. 31, 1923, BAP, RB, Nr. 6339, Bl. 244f.

78. Georg Bernhard, "Reichsbankreform," *Plutus* (Sept. 1, 1923), p. 278.

79. Meeting of Aug. 25, 1923, *Kabinette Stresemann*, I, p. 114; see also the presentation of the program to the RWR Currency Committee on Sept. 4, 1923, StA Hamburg, Senatskommission für die Reichs- und auswärtigen Angelegenheiten, II A4, Fasz. 29.

80. Ibid., p. 116. For the manner in which the remarks of Havenstein and Salomonsohn were leaked to the press, see BAP, RB, Bd. 6339, Bl. 251–55. For a useful commentary, see Bernhard's article, "Reichsbankreform," *Plutus* (Sept. 1, 1923), pp. 277–81.

81. Cabinet meeting of Aug. 30, 1923, *Kabinette Stresemann*, I, pp. 158–60. Havenstein even received a relatively friendly hearing when he presented his program to the RWR Currency Committee on September 4, although the remarks by the chair, Georg Bernhard, and Undersecretary Dalberg were very much in the tone of "it's about time" in their reception to Havenstein's stable-mark account plan. It was here that Havenstein indicated that the necessary legislation would be available in two weeks time. See the report in StA Hamburg, Senatskommission für die Reichs- und auswärtigen Angelegenheiten, II A4, Faz. 29.

82. *Kabinette Stresemann*, I, p. 164.

83. Meeting of the RWR Economic Policy and Foreign Trade Committee, Aug. 31, 1923, BAP, Nr. 398, Bd. 14, Bl. 293, and Cabinet meeting, Aug. 30, 1923, *Kabinette Stresemann*, I, pp. 157f.

84. Ibid., p. 167.

85. See the minute of ten Hompel of Oct. 31, 1923, BAK, NL ten Hompel, Nr. 28., and the relevant Reich Coal Council meetings in BAK, NL Silverberg, Nr. 148.

86. Reusch to August Haniel, Sept. 5, 1923, HA/GHH, Nr. 30019300/5.

87. Reichert at meeting of Sept. 12, 1923, in the RAM, HA/GHH, Nr. 3001100/18. More generally, see Feldman, *Iron and Steel*, pp. 374ff.

88. *Kabinette Stresemann*, I, p. 166.

89. See his report of Aug. 29, 1923, ibid., pp. 142–44.

90. Quoted in *Kabinette Stresemann*, I, p. 138n1.

91. Discussion in RFM, Aug. 29, 1923, ibid., pp. 138–42.

92. Ibid. For the RB plan, see also the memorandum for Director Nordhoff of Aug. 31, 1923, BAP, RB, Nr. 6339, Bl. 242–50. For the Hilferding plan, see Beusch, *Währungszerfall*, pp. 140ff.

93. Blohm to Helfferich, Aug. 20, 1923, StA Hamburg, Blohm & Voss, Nr. 1382. For the views of Hillger of the Reich Agrarian League, Urbig, and Wassermann, see the meeting of Aug. 29, 1923, *Kabinette Stresemann*, I, pp. 140f.

94. See his remarks to the RWR on Aug. 31, 1923, BAP, RWR, Nr. 398, Bd. 14, Bl. 292.

95. *Kabinette Stresemann*, I, pp. 139–41.

96. Ibid., p. 138n4. Funk's program was summarized in a retrospective article of Jan. 4, 1924, to be found in GStAKM, Rep. 120, AX, Bl. 238. This was the same Walter Funk who later became Hitler's economic adviser and then Economics Minister.

97. Ramhorst, *Entstehung*, pp. 7f.

98. *Kabinette Stresemann*, I, p. 177; for the meeting of Sept. 1, and the Luther memorandum of Sept. 3, ibid., pp. 173–79.

99. Ramhorst, *Entstehung*, pp. 7ff. The RdI committee was composed of Bücher, Frowein, Oskar Funcke, Hugenberg, Kraemer, Lammers, Friedrich Minoux, Müller-Oerlinghausen, Schweizer, and Warmbold. The experts at the Sept. 5 meeting seem to have been the same as those attending the Aug. 29 meeting along with some additional industrialist representatives: Luther, Havenstein, Helfferich, Urbig, Wassermann, Frowein, Kraemer, Lammers, Professor Warmbold, Professor Wagemann, and Hillger.

100. A copy of the article by Friedrich Pilot, "Die Beseitigung der Geldinflation," *DAZ*, Aug. 23, 1923, is to be found in BAK, NL ten Hompel, Nr. 10. It is reprinted in Beusch, *Währungszerfall*, pp. 133–38. The description which follows is based on this source. See also, Wulf, *Stinnes*, pp. 458ff. For the RWR committee meeting of Sept. 4, see the report in StA Hamburg, Senatskommission für die Reichs- und auswärtigen Angelegenheiten, II A4, Fasz. 29.

101. The protocol of the hearings of Sept. 6–7, 1923, is to be found in BAK, R 2/2436. See also *Kabinette Stresemann*, I, p. 174n10.

102. Baumann report, Sept. 7, 1923, StA Hamburg, Senatskommission für die Reichs- und auswärtigen Angelegenheiten, II A4 Fasz. 29.

103. BAK, R 2/2438, and *Kabinette Stresemann*, I, p.176f.n5.

104. Ramhorst, *Entstehung*, p. 15.

105. Hauschild, *Reichswirtschaftsrat*, pp. 97f.; Hirsch, *Währungsfrage*, pp. 23ff.; Georg Bernhard,

"Die Goldnote," *Plutus*, (Sept. 15, 1923), pp. 293–96.

106. *Kabinette Stresemann*, I, pp. 208–13. Important information on the sequence of events is to be found in Bernhard's presentation to the Joint Finance and Economic Policy Committee of the RWR on Sept. 10, BAP, RWR, Nr. 398, Bd. 14, Bl. 417ff.

107. For the meeting of Sept. 10, 1923, see *Kabinette Stresemann*, I, pp. 224–28; on the influence of Bonn, see ibid., p. 209n20, and Bonn's memoranda of Sept. 2, 1923, "Der Plan einer Währungsbank" and undated "Der Beginn der Währungsreform," BA, NL Bonn, Nr. 8d. In my interpretation of Hilferding's theoretical position, I follow Harold James, "Rudolf Hilferding and the Application of the Political Economy of the Second International," *The Historical Journal*, 24 (1981), pp. 847–69, esp. pp 858–60, rather than Klaus-Dieter Krohn's rather laudatory portrayal of Hilferding as an unorthodox innovator of Keynesian persuasion in "Helfferich contra Hilferding. Konservative Geldpolitik und die sozialen Folgen der deutschen Inflation 1918–1923," *VSWG* 62 (1975), pp. 62–92. For the Hilferding plan itself, see Beusch, *Währungszerfall*, pp. 140f.

108. *Kabinette Stresemann*, I, pp. 224–28.

109. RWR meeting of Sept. 11, 1923, BAP, Nr. 398, Bd. 14, Bl. 427.

110. Ibid., Bl. 435.

111. Ibid., Bl. 433.

112. Ibid., Bl. 435.

113. Meeting of Sept. 12, 1923, ibid., Bd. 15, Bl. 9.

114. Ibid., Bl. 5.

115. Ibid.

116. Ibid., Bl. 13.

117. Ibid., Bl. 39.

118. Ibid., Bl. 35.

119. Ibid., Bl. 44.

120. Ibid., Bl. 60ff.

121. Ibid., Bl. 71f., and Hauschild, *Reichswirtschaftsrat*, pp. 98f.

122. See the account and other relevant documents in ten Hompel's memoirs, BAK, NL ten Hompel, Nr. 1; Rupert and Morsey, *Zentrumsfraktion*, Sept. 13, 1923, p. 476f. See also the account of Otto von Glasenapp, "Helfferich, der Schöpfer der Rentenmark," written in 1928, BAP, RB, Nr. 6677, Bl. 175–97, esp. Bl. 183.

123. Cabinet meeting of Sept. 13, 1923, *Kabinette Stresemann*, I, pp. 256–62.

124. Memorandum of Jan. 2, 1928, BAK, NL ten Hompel, Nr. 1.

125. Beusch, *Währungszerfall*, pp. 141–47.

126. For the RB response to the Helfferich plan, ibid., pp. 127–30.

127. Helfferich was in ill-health and left for Italy, from whence he sent this letter of Sept. 18, reprinted in Ramhorst, *Entstehung*, p. 22.

128. Here I follow the account in Beusch, *Währungszerfall*, pp. 50ff., and the text of the Luther proposal and Reichsbank commentary, ibid., pp. 147–52. I do not find Martin Vogt's argument that the

plan developed really was Hilferding's nor his general attribution of initiative to Hilferding on the currency reform question entirely convincing, see Büsch and Feldman, *Historische Prozesse*, esp. pp. 146ff.

129. Ramhorst, *Entstehung*, pp. 25ff.; for the relevant documents and meetings dealing with the period September 19–26, see *Kabinette Stresemann*, I, pp. 308–12, 371f., 375f.

130. Von Richter to Hilferding, Sept. 26, 1923, GStAKM, Rep. 120, AX, Nr. 27a, Bd. 15, Bl. 84–88, for quotations and this discussion.

131. HK Hamburg, Plenarsitzung, Sept. 14, 1923, Commerzbibliothek.

132. Foreign Office report of Sept. 20, 1923, GStAMK, Rep 120, AX, Nr. 27a, Bd. 15, Bl. 90–98.

133. See Hauschild, *Reichswirtschaftsrat*, pp. 414–16, and BAP, RWR, Nr. 555, Bd. 10.

134. Ibid., Bl. 211.

135. Ibid., Bl. 272.

136. Ibid., Bl. 284.

137. Ibid., Bl. 221.

138. Ibid., Bl. 223.

139. Ramhorst, *Entstehung*, pp. 31f.

140. Meeting of Sept. 28, 1923, BAP, RWR, Nr. 550, Bd. 10, Bl. 277f.

141. Ibid., Bl. 295.

142. Ibid., Bl. 293.

143. Ibid., Bl. 242f.

144. Meeting with the Minister-Presidents, Sept. 25, 1923, *Kabinette Stresemann*, I, p. 349.

145. RWR Joint Economic and Finance Policy Committees meeting, Sept. 12, 1923, BAP, RWR, Nr. 399, Bd. 15, Bl. 40f.

146. See Stresemann's meeting with the organizations of the occupied areas, Sept. 24, 1923, ibid., pp. 339–45, quote on p. 344. For Jarres's views, see his memorandum on his participation in the Ruhr conflict and its liquidation, BAK, NL Jarres, Nr. 49, and his memorandum of Sept. 21, 1923.

147. For this meeting, see NL Stresemann, 3159/7394/H171304–311.

148. Ibid.

149. Meeting of Sept. 25, 1923, ibid., H171326–31, quote on 171330. See also Jones, *German Liberalism*, pp. 198ff.

150. Meeting of Sept. 25, 1923, NL Stresemann, 3159/7394/H171326–331

151. Warburg Papers, 1923, p. 61.

152. VdA circular of Aug. 9, 1923, BgA. The discussion here follows the account in Feldman and Steinisch, *Industrie und Gewerkschaften*, pp. 112ff.

153. Meeting of Aug. 20, 1923, BAP, ZAG, Nr. 74/1, Bl. 282–309.

154. Meeting of Sept. 1, 1923, ibid., Bl. 222–27.

155. Köttgen to Siemens, Aug. 24, 1923, SAA 4/Lf 669.

156. Meeting of Sept. 6, 1923, BAP, ZAG, Nr. 74/1, Bl. 218f.

157. Ibid., Bl. 20.

158. Ibid., Bl. 321. Thus, at the meeting of the

DVP Party delegation on Sept. 12, von Raumer pointed out that "we have 17 mines in unoccupied Westphalia; their productivity decreases day by day; it is a scandal. That is why we need a partial elimination of the demobilization decrees. Without an increase of hours there will be no increase of the profitability of the railroads and post office." Stresemann was fully in accord with this point. NL Stresemann, 3159/7394/H171304f.

159. Meeting of Sept. 10, 1923, ibid., Bl. 128–41, quote on Bl. 129f.

160. Ibid., Bl. 386.

161. Ibid., Bl. 383.

162. Meeting of Sept. 19, 1923, ibid., Bl. 96–103, and VdA circular of Sept. 20, 1923, ibid., Bl. 382.

163. Meeting of Oct. 1, 1923, ibid., Bl. 66–73.

164. Meeting of Oct. 15, 1923, ibid., Bl. 82.

165. For the Cabinet meeting of Sept. 30, 1923, see *Kabinette Stresemann*, I, pp. 410–15.

166. For the discussion of Sept. 22, 1923, see the chronology of Seeckt's political activities by Lt.-Gen. von Lieber in *Kabinette Stresemann*, II, Appendix l, pp. 1176–203, esp. p. 1178. More generally, see the grand-breaking article of Günter Arns, "Die Krise des Weimarer Parlamentarismus im Frühherbst 1923," *Der Staat. Zeitschrift für Staatslehre, Öffentliches Recht und Verfassungsgeschichte* 8 (1969/2), pp. 181–216, Hans Meier-Welcker, *Seeckt* (Frankfurt a.M., 1967), pp. 370ff., and Winkler, *Von der Revolution zur Stabilisierung*, pp. 618f.

167. The agrarian leaders who visited Seeckt were Gustav Roesicke, Count Schwerin-Löwitz, Hans von Goldacker, Arno Kriegsheim, and Friedrich von Berg. See the Lieber chronology, *Kabinette Stresemann*, II, pp. 1177–79. Seeckt's chief advisers were Lt.-Gen. Paul Hasse, Major Kurt von Schleicher, and Lt.-Col. Joachim von Stülpnagel. Schleicher's role here is interesting for the comparison it suggests with his role in the crisis of 1932–33.

168. Meier-Welcker, *Seeckt*, pp. 373f.

169. Wulf, *Stinnes*, pp. 454ff.

170. George W. F. Hallgarten, *Hitler, Reichswehr und Industrie. Zur Geschichte der Jahre 1918–1933* (Frankfurt a.M., 1955), pp. 63f.

171. For the situation in Bavaria, see Wolfgang Benz, ed., *Politik in Bayern 1919–1933. Berichte des württembergischen Gesandten Carl Moser von Filseck* (Stuttgart, 1971), pp. 128ff., and the reports of the Saxon Ambassador in Munich of August–September 1923, SäHStA, Außenministerium, Nr. 2989. For the interpretation, see the useful remarks of Wulf, *Stinnes*, pp. 456ff. Stinnes's meeting with Hitler is discussed in the private memoirs of his daughter, Claerenore Stinnes, ACDP, NL Stinnes, Nr. 313.

172. Stinnes to Dauch, Sept. 29, 1923, ACDP, NL Stinnes, Nr. 046/3.

173. *Kabinette Stresemann*, II, p. 1179.

174. For these plans, see *Kabinette Stresemann*, II, pp. 1203–10, and Wulf, *Stinnes*, pp. 461f. See also report by Charles Marling to Lord Curzon from The Hague, Oct. 12, 1923. PRO, FO 371/8745/285.

175. For the letter of Oct. 7, 1923, see NL Stinnes,

Private possession, and Wulf, *Stinnes*, pp. 461f. In a private letter to Hugo Stinnes, Jr., of Nov. 16, 1923, Stinnes also criticized Minoux for talking too much about his intentions to the wrong people and suggested that Minoux had become inattentive to business because of his political ambitions. ACDP, NL Stinnes, Nr. 200/7.

176. Feldman and Steinisch, *AfS* 18 (1978), pp. 388ff. For the telegram of September 30, 1923, see *Kabinette Stresemann*, I, pp. 415f.

177. On these developments, see Huber, *Verfassungsgeschichte*, 7, pp. 347–51; Cabinet meeting Reichsbank to Stresemann, Sept. 30, 1923, *Kabinette Stresemann*, I, pp. 410–17.

178. Ibid., p. 414 for these quotes.

179. Ibid., pp. 429f.

180. The account here follows Winkler, *Von der Revolution zur Stabilisierung*, pp. 625ff.

181. Report on the meeting of the Main Committee of the RdI, Oct. 12, 1923, SäHStA, Gesandtschaft Berlin, Nr. 471, Bl. 288–95, quote on Bl. 292.

182. Meeting of Oct. 9, 1923, *VR*, Bd. 361, pp. 12037–47 for the speeches of Frölich and Müller. The measure required at least 307 of the 459 votes in the Reichstag. In a vote on the reading on October 11, it received only 253 votes, while on the third reading on October 13, it received 316 votes, ibid., pp. 12142–46 and 12152–54. On Stresemann's tactics, see the meeting of Oct. 11, 1923, in *Kabinette Stresemann*, I, pp. 543f.

183. Report of a Saxon Representative on the meeting of the Main Committee of the RdI, Oct. 12, 1923, SäHStA, Gesandtschaft Berlin, Nr. 471, Bl. 292.

184. See the Reichstag meeting of Oct. 9, 1923, *VR*, Bd. 361, pp. 12040f., 12045f., 12060f.

185. For the staggered schedule of reductions, see *Kabinette Stresemann*, I, p. 467n11.

186. Ibid., II, p. 520n6.

187. See discussion between Wolff and the Cabinet on Oct. 10, 1923, ibid., pp. 520–22. On the Role of Dutch interests, see Feldman, *Iron and Steel*, pp. 417ff.

188. Ibid., and Cabinet discussion of Oct. 10, 1923, ibid., pp. 529f.

189. For these events, see ibid., pp. 411ff.

190. *Kabinette Stresemann*, II, p. 509f.n2, and discussion with Cabinet members on Oct. 9, 1923, ibid., pp. 509–18.

191. Reusch to Haniel, Sept. 5, 1923, HA/GHH, Nr. 300193000/5.

192. British report on a conversation between van Vlissingen and the Dutch Chargé d'Affaires in Berlin, Oct. 13, 1923, PRO, FO 371/8748/215–16.

193. Bierweis to Steinthal, Nov. 14, 1923, Mannesmann-Archiv, M11 091.

194. Trachtenberg, *Reparation*, p. 326.

195. Meeting of Oct. 9, 1923, *Kabinette Stresemann*, II, p. 517.

196. Meeting of Oct. 10, 1923, ibid., p. 532.

197. Ibid., p. 550. The letter to Stinnes is reprinted in ibid., pp. 560–63.

198. Koeth to Stresemann, undated, ibid., pp. 566f. On Koeth's relationship to Schacht, see *Plutus* (Nov. 15, 1923), p. 357. On the charges, see Bernhard, ed., *Vermächtnis*, I, pp. 146–48.

199. Schacht to Stresemann, Oct. 6, 1923, ibid., pp. 500–502, and Beusch, *Währungszerfall*, pp. 170–72.

200. *Kabinette Stresemann*, II, p. 501n3.

201. Beusch, *Währungszerfall*, pp. 163–66, 172–76, for the DDP memorandum and the Hirsch plan.

202. The best account from which the discussion and quotations which follow are largely taken is Ramhorst, *Entstehung*, pp. 37–39. See also Beusch, *Währungszerfall*, pp. 54f., 166–70.

203. Holtfrerich, *German Inflation*, p. 317. For this discussion in general, see the Cabinet meeting of Oct. 15, 1923, *Kabinette Stresemann*, II, pp. 573–75, 578–80.

204. Report by Lord D'Abernon of remarks by Dr. Ludwig Kastl, Nov. 25, 1923, PRO, FO 371/8668/147/214. It is interesting to note that Kastl later became the Managing Director of the RdI.

205. Ibid., and Ramhorst, *Entstehung*, pp. 40–43.

206. Undated memorandum of mid-October, PRO, FO 371/8668/35.

16. The Politics of Stabilization, October–November 1923

1. For the details, see Feldman and Steinisch, *Industrie und Gewerkschaften*, pp. 117ff.

2. Meeting of the ZAG Wage Commission, Oct. 15, 1923, BAP, ZAG, Nr. 74/1, Bl. 82.

3. Bundesausschuß meeting of Oct. 16, 1923, in Ruck, *Gewerkschaften*, p. 956.

4. Dißmann at the joint meeting of the ADGB, AfA, and ADB, Oct. 17, 1923, ibid., p. 977.

5. Meeting of Oct. 16, 1923, ibid., p. 966. See also Leipart's remarks on p. 956.

6. Meeting of Oct. 17, 1923, ibid., p. 977.

7. Ibid., p. 970.

8. Meeting of Oct. 16, 1923, ibid., p. 964.

9. Ibid., pp. 967–78.

10. See März, *Österreichische Bankpolitik*, pp. 476ff.

11. See the report of the British Ambassador Keeling to Curzon, Oct. 25, 1923, PRO, FO 371/8817/144. On the meetings between Hornick and the German officials, see BayHStA, Abt. II, MA 104 430.

12. Report by Keeling to Curzon, Oct. 4, 1923, PRO, FO 371/8817/50f.

13. Netzband and Widmaier, *Währungs- und Finanzpolitik*, pp. 101–7.

14. Saemisch to Stresemann, Aug. 31, 1923, *Kabinette Stresemann*, I, pp. 170–172.

15. Ibid., pp. 186f., and Kunz, *Civil Servants*, pp. 368–70.

16. *Kabinette Stresemann*, I, p. 297n8.

17. Ibid., p. 298n11.

18. See the meeting with the civil servants' peak organizations on Sept. 18, 1923, ibid., pp. 296–98.

19. Cabinet meeting of Sept. 10, 1923, ibid., pp. 230f. For the social conflicts among the various categories of government workers and their organizations over this issue, see Kunz, *Civil Servants*, pp. 370–77, and "Stand versus Klasse. Beamtenschaft und Gewerkschaften im Konflikt um den Personalabbau 1923/24," *GuG* 8 (1982), pp. 55–86.

20. Höltzendorff report to the HAPAG, Oct. 9, 1923, HAPAG Archiv.

21. Ebert to Luther, Oct. 10, 1923, *Kabinette Stresemann*, II, pp. 536–40.

22. Cabinet meeting of Oct. 17, 1923, ibid., pp. 608–10; Kunz, *Civil Servants*, p. 55.

23. Ibid., and for only slightly varying figures, Klaus Sühl, *SPD und öffentlicher Dienst in der Weimarer Republik. Die öffentlichen Bediensteten in der SPD und ihre Bedeutung für die sozial-demokratische Politik 1918–1933* (Opladen, 1988), p. 100. Carl Goerdeler was later to become Lord High Mayor of Leipzig, Price Commissioner under the Nazis, and to die a leader of the Resistance. His proposals and the record of the meetings with the state and municipal representatives of Oct. 19–20 are to be found in the files of the LA Berlin, AdSt, Nr. 2440/I.

24. Memorandum by Mitzlaff of Oct. 16, 1923, ibid.

25. Meeting of Oct. 17, 1923, Ruck, *Gewerkschaften*, p. 976.

26. For a report on these meetings, see ibid.

27. For the petition of Nov. 6, 1923, see La Berlin, AdSt, Nr. 2400/II. See also Kunz, *Civil Servants*, p. 53 and the meeting between the government and the civil-service organizations on Nov. 14, 1923, in *Kabinette Stresemann*, II, pp. 1067–70.

28. See the discussion at the meeting between the state and municipal representatives and the Reich Finance Ministry of Oct. 19, 1923, LA Berlin, AdSt, Nr. 2440/I.

29. Finance reform discussions, undated outline, LA Berlin, AdSt, Nr. 2440/I.

30. Order signed by Luther, Oct. 27, 1923, BAK, R 43I/2358, Bl. 36–39.

31. For the Labor Ministry's retrospective on the condition of the system in 1922–1923, see its report for 1924–1925, BAK, R 43I/2088, Bl. 233.

32. Brauns to Luther, Oct. 21, 1923, BAK, R 43I/2096, Bl. 205.

33. Ibid., Bl. 234, and report of Brauns to Ebert, Nov. 17, 1923, BAK, R 43I/2091, Bl. 211f.

34. Dean Göppert of the Göttingen Medical Faculty to the Chancellor, Nov. 17, 1923, ibid., Bl. 213. See also Preller, *Sozialpolitik*, p. 327.

35. Report of the American Vice Consul in Stuttgart, Erik W. Magnuson, Dec. 27, 1923, NA, 862.5042/6.

36. Verband der deutschen Berufsgenossenschaften an den Herrn Reichsarbeitsminister, Oct. 24, 1923, BAK, R 43I/2093, Bl. 250f., 257f.

37. See the letters of the Labor Minister to the Finance Minister of Oct. 21 and Dec. 10, 1923, BAK, R 43I/2096, Bl. 204–6 and 210f. More generally, see Dobbernack, "Entwicklung und Stand der Sozialver-

sicherungsfinanzen unter besonderer Berücksichtigung der Rentenversicherungen, in *RABl* (1933), IV, pp. 254–66. The assets of the old-age and invalid insurance system decreased from 2150.5 million gold marks in 1913 to 329.6 million gold marks in 1924. See Feldman in *Adaptation to Inflation*, p. 445.

38. Labor Minister to Finance Minister, Oct. 21, 1923, BAK, R 43I/2096, Bl. 204–6.

39. Ernst Günther, "Die Anpassung der Sozialversicherung an die Geldentwertung und Lohnsteigerung," *JNS* 121 (1923), pp. 1–54, quote on p. 4.

40. Luppe, "Abbau der Invalidenversicherung," *Soziale Praxis*, 32 (Sept. 20, 1923), pp. 843–45. For reference to the article in the *DAZ*, see BAK, R 42I/2088, Bl. 67.

41. Report of the Saxon Representative to the Reichsrat, Nov. 22, 1923, SäHStA, Gesandtschaft Berlin, Nr. 2289, Bl. 307. On the *de facto* transition to the cost coverage system and abandonment of the capital coverage system, see the RAM to RFM, Oct. 23 and Dec. 10, 1923, BAK, R 43I/2096, Bl. 204–6, 210f.

42. See the article by the head of the Berlin insurance offices, Dr. R. Freundt, "Die Zukunft der Sozialversicherung," Oct. 23, 1923, BAK, R 43I/2088, Bl. 67.

43. Ibid., and see the articles by Ministerialdirektor Griesser of the RAM in the *RABl* (Nichtamtlicher Teil) (1924), pp. 182–84 and 412f.

44. Preller, *Sozialpolitik*, p. 363; Kuczynski, *Postwar Labor Conditions*, pp. 150ff.; Ranft in Feldman et al., *Adaptation to Inflation*, pp. 196ff.; Syrup, *Hundert Jahre*, pp. 330f.

45. See Ranft in Feldman et al., *Adaption to Inflation*, pp. 162–201, figures on pp. 193f. The report of Section X of the RAM for October 1923–March 1924 confirms these figures, see BAP, RAM, Nr. 1724, Bl. 359.

46. See the report on the meeting in the RAM by the Saxon Representative, Dec. 19, 1923, SäHStA, Gesandtschaft Berlin, Nr. 2289.

47. See Böss to the Prussian Commerce Minister, Sept. 17, 1923, GStAKM, Rep. 120, BB, VII 1 3y, Bd. 5, Bl. 577f. For unemployment supports and cost of living in Berlin during the inflation and in 1924, see Kuczynski, *Postwar Labor conditions*, pp. 155f.

48. See report of Sept. 21, 1923, SäHStA, Außenministerium, Nr. 6139, and the reports of the police authorities in Leipzig of Oct. 13 and 16, 1923, MdI, Nr. 11112/I, Bl. 397f., 404–6.

49. Unsigned and undated report on the Hamburg uprising sent to Abteilung N. of the KPD Oberleitung, ibid., Nr. 11107, Bl. 16–18. The excellent and detailed accounts of Oct. 23 and 25, 1923, of the events in Hamburg by the American Consul Theodore Jaeckel support the interpretation provided here, NA, 862.00/1362. For the events in and literature on Saxony, Thuringia, and Hamburg and for Communist policy, see Winkler, *Von der Revolution zur Stabilisierung*, pp. 648ff. On Communist tactics, see Werner Angress, *Stillborn Revolution: The Com-*

munist Bid for Power in Germany, 1921–1923 (Princeton, 1963). On the role of the military in this period, see Heinz Hürten, ed., *Das Krisenjahr 1923. Militär und Innenpolitik 1922–1924* [*Quellen zur Geschichte des Parlamentarismus und der politischen Parteien. Zweite Reihe. Militär und Politik, Bd. 4*] (Düsseldorf, 1980).

50. Report of the British Consulate General in Cologne, Oct. 29, 1923, PRO, FO 371/8748/273/24–26, and report of the High Commissioner in Koblenz, Oct. 19, 1923, ibid., 371/8746/273/13f. On the concessions to the unions with respect to supplementing the unemployment supports, see Ruck, *Gewerkschaften*, p. 962n14. In a memorandum by Luther of Oct. 24, he agreed to pay a supplement of 15 percent on both civil service salaries and unemployment support in the occupied areas. *Kabinette Stresemann*, II, pp. 749f.

51. *Kabinette Stresemann*, II, pp. 807f. for this quotation and the discussion below.

52. See Schultheß, *Geschichtskalender 1923*, pp. 201ff,. and *Kabinette Stresemann*, II, pp. 693–95, 704–6.

53. Report by Ministerialrat Kiep of Oct. 17, 1923, *Kabinette Stresemann*, II, pp. 616f. For Tirard's efforts to create a separate Rhenish state and this currency problem, see also the report of Oct. 29, 1923, ibid., pp. 889–93.

54. Karl-Dietrich Erdmann, *Adenauer in der Rheinlandpolitik nach dem Ersten Weltkrieg* (Stuttgart, 1966), pp. 82ff. Paul Wentzcke, *Ruhrkampf. Einbruch und Abwehr im rheinisch-westfälischen Industriegebiet*, 2 vols. (Berlin, 1930–1932), II, p. 218; Morsey, *Zentrumspartei*, pp. 531ff., Kohler, *Adenauer*, pp. 184ff.; Ruck, *Gewerkschaften im Ruhrkampf*, pp. 510ff.

55. Reported by Jarres at the meeting in Hagen of Oct. 25, 1923, *Kabinette Stresemann*, II, p. 764.

56. Ibid., pp. 766f.

57. The first interpretation is that of Erdmann in *Adenauer*, pp. 187ff., and Kohler, *Adenauer*, pp. 188, 274ff.

58. Meeting of Oct. 20, 1923, *Kabinette Stresemann*, II, p. 668.

59. Ibid., p. 671.

60. Meeting of Oct. 24, 1923, ibid., p. 711.

61. Ministerial discussion of Oct. 24, 1923, ibid., p. 712.

62. For the memorandum of Oct. 24, 1923, see ibid., pp. 749–52, and for his motives, see Hans Luther, *Politiker ohne Partei. Erinnerungen* (Stuttgart, 1960), p. 178.

63. The full text of the Hagen meeting is to be found in *Kabinette Stresemann*, II, pp. 761–836. For Stresemann's attacks on the Jarres and Adenauer proposals, see especially pp. 769–82.

64. For Stresemann's hopes, see Erdmann, *Adenauer*, pp. 103f.; see also Kent, *Spoils of War*, pp. 227ff.

65. Hagen meeting of Oct. 25, 1923, *Kabinette Stresemann*, II, p. 770.

66. Ibid., p. 793.

67. Ibid., pp. 794f.

68. Cabinet meeting and letter from Stresemann to the Committee of Six, Nov. 1, 1923, ibid., pp. 933–35, 941–44.

69. Report by Melchior of Nov. 2, 1923, on a discussion with Smuts of Oct. 27, Marshall Library, Keynes Papers, F I/2.

70. Wiegand to Mason, Oct. 25, 1923, Hoover Institution, Karl von Wiegand Papers, Box 16.

71. Huber, *Verfassungsgeschichte* 7, pp.364–73.

72. Meeting in Hagen, Oct. 25, 1923, *Kabinette Stresemann*, II, p. 781. On the Reichsbank precious-metal reserves in Bavaria and their political complications, see Martin Vogt, "Zum bayerischen Versuch finanzieller Eigenständigkeit im Spätsommer und Herbst 1923," in Büsch and Feldman, eds., *Historische Prozesse,* pp. 224–36.

73. See especially the Cabinet meeting of Nov. 1, 1923, and the discussion among the bourgeois Cabinet meetings on Nov. 2 in *Kabinette Stresemann*, II, pp. 935–38, 944–47. For a balanced discussion, see Winkler, *Von der Revolution zur Stabilisierung*, pp. 665–69.

74. Report of Nov. 2, 1923, by the U.S. Consul in Dresden, Louis G. Dreyfus, Jr., NA, 862.00/1361. See also the report of Melchior of Nov. 2, 1923, on his discussions with Smuts, Marshall Library, Keynes Papers, F I/2.

75. Sollmann to Kempkes, Oct. 22, 1923, *Kabinette Stresemann*, II, pp. 696f.

76. See James M. Diehl, *Paramilitary Politics in Weimar Germany* (Bloomington, 1977), pp. 139ff., and the materials of General von Lieber, *Kabinette Stresemann*, II, pp. 1191ff.

77. Seisser's account of his journey is reprinted in Ernst Deuerlein, ed., *Der Hitler-Putsch. Bayerische Dokumente zum 8./9. November 1923* (Stuttgart, 1962), pp. 301–4. For developments in Bavaria and this interpretation, see Harold J. Gordon, Jr., *Hitler and the Beer Hall Putsch* (Princeton, 1972), pp. 246ff.

78. Meier-Welcker, *Seeckt*, pp. 397f.

79. Report by Kroeger, Nov. 4, 1923, ACDP, NL Stinnes, Nr. 029/1. See also Deuerlein, *Hitler-Putsch*, p. 302.

80. Seeckt's letter to Wiedfeldt of Nov. 4, 1923, is reprinted in *Kabinette Stresemann*, II, pp. 1215f.

81. Meier-Welcker, *Seeckt*, pp. 402–4.

82. Meeting of Nov. 5, 1923, NL Stresemann, 3159/7394/H17435f.

83. Ibid., H171436.

84. See telegraphic report by Ambassador Houghton on a conversation with Stinnes, Nov. 6, 1923, NA, 862.00/1330.

85. Ibid.

86. Melchior report of Nov. 2 on his conversations with Smuts, Marshall Library, Keynes Papers, F I/2. See the Holtzendorff report of Nov. 7, 1923, HAPAG Archiv for this and the discussion which follows.

87. Report of the Regierungspräsident of Oberbayern, Oct. 19, 1923, BayHStA, Abt. II, MA, Nr. 102 136. Reprinted in Deuerlein, *Hitler-Putsch*, pp. 238f.

88. For the reactions in Bavaria, see the report of Nov. 6, 1923, ibid., and the eyewitness reports sent to Berlin on Oct. 31, 1923, in *Kabinette Stresemann*, II, pp. 926–33. See also Monika Richarz, ed., *Jüdisches Leben in Deutschland. Selbstzeugnisse zur Sozialgeschichte 1918–1945* (Stuttgart, 1982), pp. 82–85. For an excellent discussion of the entire affair in its short- and long-term context, see Reiner Pommerin, "Die Ausweisung von 'Ostjuden' aus Bayern 1923. Ein Beitrag zum Krisenjahr der Weimarer Republik," *VfZ* 34 (1986), pp. 311–40.

89. *Münchener Zeitung*, Nov. 11, 1923.

90. Report of Consul-General Clive, Nov. 7, 1923, PRO, FO 371/8756/311/60.

91. Reports of Nov. 18 and Dec. 4, 1923, BayHStA, Abt. II, MA 102 140.

92. Report from upper Bavaria, Dec. 5, 1923, ibid., Generalstaatskommissar 44. Reprinted in Deuerlein, *Hitler-Putsch*, pp. 467f.

93. Report of Dec. 23, 1923, ibid., pp. 548–50.

94. The use of the HAPAG's code and telegraphical facilities shows that Seeckt was serious about the Directory project and clears up Charles Maier's puzzlement over Seeckt's alleged use of the sea mails in contacting Wiedfeldt. See Maier, *Recasting*, p. 383n76. For the details, see Ernst Schröder, "Wiedfeldt und die Seeckt-Ebertschen Direktoriumspläne des Jahres 1923," *Das Münster am Hellweg. Mitteilungsblatt des Vereins für die Erhaltung des Essener Münsters* 19, Beiheft 11 (November 1966), pp. 129–42, esp. pp. 134ff., and Ernst Schröder, *Wiedfeldt*, pp. 158ff., 191f.; Houghton report of Nov. 7, 1923, NA, 862.00/1331.

95. For the behavior of the mob and this interpretation, see Robert Scholz, "Ein unruhiges Jahrzehnt: Lebensmittelunruhen, Massenstreiks und Arbeitslosenkrawalle in Berlin 1914–1923," in Manfred Gallus, ed., *Pöbelexzesse und Volkstumulte in Berlin. Zur Sozialgeschichte der Straße (1830–1980)* (Berlin, 1984), pp. 79–124, esp. pp. 114–17. Scholz appropriates Döblin's contradictory interpretation in Döblin, *Ein Kerl muß eine Meinung haben*, pp. 217–18. The most convincing discussion of these and similar events in Germany at this time is to be found in Maurer, *Ostjuden* (Hamburg, 1986), pp. 329ff.

96. Warburg Papers, 1923, p. 68.

97. Report of Oct. 21, 1923, PRO, FO 371/8686/21. On the measure, see Kühne, *Devisenzwangswirtschaft*, pp. 28f.

98. Melchior to Keynes, Dec. 13, 1923, Marshall Library, Keynes Papers F I/2.

99. See undated report on the Oct. 22, 1923, decree, PRO, FO 327/8668/75–78; Handelskammer Hamburg, Plenarsitzungen, Oct. 26 and Nov. 9, 1923, Commerzbibliothek, Hamburg. For Koeth's hostility and a defense of the effort, see Beusch, *Währungszerfall*, p. 72.

100. Reports of American Consul Emil Sauer from Cologne, Oct. 26, Nov. 2 and 9, 1923, NA, 862t.00/28, 30, 33.

101. Report of Nov. 9, 1923, by Consul Emil Sauer, NA, 862t.00/34. See also his reports of October 26 and Nov. 2, 1923, NA, 862t.00/28, 33.

102. Webb, *Hyperinflation*, pp. 80–82.

103. Report of Consul Dyer, Koblenz, Nov. 2, 1923, NA, 862t.00/30.

104. Scholz in *Pöbelexzesse*, p. 114.

105. Report of Consul M. K. Moorhead, Nov. 2, 1923, NA, 862.5041/36.

106. Ibid.

107. "Nervenbelastung," *FZ*, Oct. 20, 1923, Abendblatt.

108. Ernst to Hans Barlach, Oct. 28, 1923, Ernst Barlach, *Briefe 1888–1938*, 2 vols. (Munich, 1968–1969), Vol. l, p. 709.

109. For the amount of money in circulation, see *Deutsches Geld- und Bankwesen in Zahlen*, p. 15; for the proclamation of the new bank notes, see BAK, R 28, Nr. 23, Bl. 404, 469–71, and *Währung und Wirtschaft in Deutschland*, pp. 171, 175; on the productive capacities available to the Reichsbank, see Prion in *Schmollers Jahrbuch* 49 (1925), p. 132.

110. Hjalmar Schacht, *The Stabilization of the Mark* (London, 1927), pp. 105ff.; *Deutsches Geld- und Bankwesen in Zahlen*, p. 15; Webb, *Hyperinflation*, pp. 69f.; Holtfrerich, *German Inflation*, pp. 312f.

111. Meeting of Oct. 25, 1923, HA Firma Krupp, WA IV 2560.

112. Kriegsdenkschrift, ibid., WA VII f 1081; Webb, *Hyperinflation*, pp. 14f.; Lindenlaub, *Maschinenbauunternehmen*, pp. 194f.

113. The town was able to cover up its operations because they were part of a district-wide arrangement whereby the cities in the M. Gladbach and Neuss regions could issue such money. All such money was supposed to bear the name of the printer who had made it, and Ödenkirchen's "extra" money was finally discovered when the Reichsbank branch noted that some of the money did not have a printing-house name on it. Reichsbankstelle M. Gladbach to the Reichsbank, Dec. 8, 1923, GStAKM, Rep. 120, AX, Nr. 27d, Bd. 3, Bl. 67f.

114. See Harold Winkel, "Das württembergische Notgeld (1914–1924), in Hansjoachim Henning, Dieter Lindenlaub, Eckhard Wandel, *Wirtschafts- und sozialgeschichtliche Forschungen und Probleme. Festschrift für Karl Erich Born* (St. Katharinen, 1987), pp. 310–34, esp. pp. 324ff.

115. Ibid., p. 328.

116. *Vossische Zeitung*, Nov. 4, 1923, quoted by Scholz, in Gallus, ed., *Pöbelexzesse*, p. 114.

117. *FZ*, Oct. 30, 1923, zweites Morgenblatt.

118. See Chap. 15, p. 733.

119. There is a good brief discussion of the bank in Ursula Büttner, *Politische Gerechtigkeit und Sozialer Geist. Hamburg zur Zeit der Weimarer Republik* (Hamburg, 1985), pp. 171ff. The bank is studied in detail in Manfred Försterling, "Die Hamburgische Bank von 1923 Aktiengesellschaft," *Hamburger Wirtschaftschronik* 3 (1965), pp. 1–124. Important details are found in the Warburg Papers, 1923, pp. 72f., Warburg Archiv.

120. Blohm to the Hamburg Bank of 1923, Oct. 31, 1923, StA Hamburg, Blohm & Voss, Nr. 530.

121. Report of the American Consul Jaeckel, Nov. 8, 1923, NA, 862.00/1365. See also the angry letter of the Association of Hamburg Shippers to the Senate of Nov. 13, 1923, about the practices of the retailers, StA Hamburg, Blohm & Voss, Nr. 530.

122. "Der Währungskommissar," *Plutus* (Nov. 15, 1923), p. 358.

123. Ibid., p. 359; Cabinet meeting of Oct. 2, 1923, *Kabinette Stresemann*, II, p. 953. See also Koeth to State Secretary Kempner, Nov. 6, 1923, Nov. 6, 1923, BAK, R 43I/2446, Bl 195, and the analysis in the article "Schuld und Schicksal," *FZ*, Nov. 3, 1923, Abendblatt.

124. See the note of Kempkes to Hagen of Nov. 3, 1923, and the reports of Solmssen's conversations in Berlin, *Kabinette Stresemann*, II, pp. 960–62.

125. See Heidegret Klöter, *Der Anteil der Länder an der Wirtschaftspolitik der Weimarer Republik 1919–1933* (Bonn, 1967), pp. 140ff., and Beusch, *Währungszerfall*, p. 69.

126. On the Bavarian discussions, see the meeting of the Bavarian State Ministry of Nov. 3, 1923, in Deuerlein, *Hitler-Putsch*, pp. 296–301, and, more generally, the revealing article, "Das Geldwesen im Sturme," *FZ*, Oct. 27, 1923, zweites Morgenblatt. See also Vogt in Büsch and Feldman, *Historische Prozesse*, pp. 232f. On Saxony's monetary hanky-panky, see the report on the meeting of the Finance Ministers of Nov. 10, 1923, StA Hamburg, Senatskommission für die Reichs- und auswärtigen Angelegenheiten, II A1, Fasz 3, Bd. I.

127. Hirtseifer to the Prussian ministers, Nov. 10, 1923, GStAKM, Rep. 120, AX, Nr. 27a, Bd. 16, Bl. 159.

128. Report of the Hamburg State Finance Councillor Lippmann, dated Nov. 14, 1923, StA Hamburg, Senatskommission für die Reichs- und auswärtigen Angelegenheiten, II A1, Fasz. 3, Bd. I, Nr. 44, for the discussion and quotations which follow.

129. On Seeckt's measures, see *Kabinette Stresemann*, II, pp. 1197f.

130. Ibid., pp. 1038f., 1199f. For Seeckt's orders, see Hürten, *Das Krisenjahr 1923*, pp. 132f.

131. *Kabinette Stresemann*, II, pp. 1064–66.

132. Ibid., p. 973f.n12.

133. Cabinet meeting of Nov. 5, 1923, ibid., pp. 973f. and 973n14.

134. Cabinet meeting of Nov. 3 and 5 and report of Oberregierungsrat Grävells of Nov. 3, 1923, *Kabinette Stresemann*, II, pp. 956f., 962–64, 968f.; Beusch, *Währungszerfall*, p. 73; Centralverband des Deutschen Bank- und Bankiergewerbes to Luther, Nov. 7, 1923, GStAKM, Rep. 120, AX, Nr 17a, Bd. 17, Bl. 191–96.

135. Beusch, *Währungszerfall*, pp. 73f., and *Kabinette Stresemann*, II, pp. 962, 972; Holtfrerich, *German Inflation*, pp. 317f.

136. Schacht, *Stabilization of the Mark*, pp. 90ff.; Stresemann, *Vermächtnis*, I, pp. 147f.; *Kabinette Stresemann*, II, pp. 990–92, 1037f.; "Der Währungskommissar," *Plutus* (Nov. 15, 1923), pp. 357–61; Fürstenberg, *Erinnerungen*, p. 163.

137. Much can be learned about the early days of the Rentenbank from the report of Rentenbank President Lentze, Dec. 5, 1923, StA Hamburg, Blohm & Voss, Nr. 532. See also Ramhorst, *Entstehung*, pp. 44ff., and Pfleiderer in *Währung und Wirtschaft*, pp. 189ff.

138. Report of Rentenbank President Lentze, Dec. 5, 1923, StA Hamburg, Blohm & Voss, Nr. 532.

139. Since Kastl dealt with reparations questions, this may have been a shrewd way of suggesting that Germany did not need the kind of external controls imposed on the Austrians. His other unflattering comments on the Rentenbank leaders, however, suggest that his remarks were sincere. D'Abernon report, Nov. 25, 1923, PRO, FO 371/8668/147/213. On the events of Nov. 14, see Ramhorst, *Entstehung*, p. 46.

140. Cabinet meeting of Dec. 3, 1923, *Kabinette Marx*, I, p. 19. Ramhorst, *Entstehung*, pp. 45f.; Beusch, *Währungszerfall*, pp. 73f., 178f.; Schacht, *Stabilization*, pp. 102–4, but see the Reichsbank claim that Schacht wanted to abandon the November 20 level in their letter to the Chancellor of Dec. 17, 1923, *Kabinette Marx*, I, pp. 130ff.; report by Robinson on Schacht's testimony, Jan. 19, 1924, Robinson Papers, Hoover Institution, Box 8. On the significance of the depreciation and rigid pegging of the exchange rate, see Dornbusch, in *Macroeconomics and Finance*, esp. pp. 353–57.

141. Warburg Papers, unpublished memoirs, 1923, p. 69.

142. For the speech, see BAP, RB, Nr. 6668, Bl. 141–46. On its significance, see Ramhorst, *Entstehung*, p. 47. See also von Glasenapp, "Rentenbank und Rentenmark," *Bank = Archiv* (Nov. 17, 1923), pp. 29–32.

143. See Reichsbank circular of Dec. 1, 1923, BAK, R 28, Bl. 343f. and Schacht's remarks at the Cabinet meeting of Dec. 3, *Kabinette Marx*, I, p. 19.

144. " . . . daß Notgeld nicht mit Geldnot verwechselt werden dürfe," ibid., p. 21.

145. Central Committee meeting, Nov. 29, 1923, BAP, RB, Bd. 6668, Bl. 143; Schacht, *Stabilization*, pp. 27ff.; *Kabinette Marx*, I, pp. 6f., 14, 21, 26, 65ff., 71, 82f.

146. See the report of Lentze of Dec. 5, 1923, and the agreement of Dec. 1 in StA Hamburg, Blohm & Voss, Nr. 532.

147. See Stresemann's remarks at a meeting of Nov. 17, 1923, *Kabinette Stresemann*, II, p. 1115.

148. *FZ*, Nov. 17, 1923, and *VR*, Nov. 20, 1923, Bd. 361, p. 12164.

149. Lentze report of Dec. 5, 1923, StA Hamburg, Blohm & Voss, Nr. 532.

150. D'Abernon report, Nov. 25, 1923, PRO, FO 371/8668/147/211.

151. RWR Finance Policy Committee meeting, Nov. 13, 1923, BAP, RWR, Nr. 556, Bd. 11, Bl. 4, p. 44.

152. Ibid., p. 38.

153. Ibid., p. 40. This historian can confirm that Feiler was absolutely correct. The files of the RWM dealing with cartels in the BAP are nothing but a collection of newspaper clippings.

154. Paul to Hermann Reusch, Oct. 31, 1923, HA/GHH, Nr. 400101298/37.

155. *Kabinette Stresemann*, pp. 1923f. More generally for this discussion, see Feldman, *Iron and Steel*, pp. 429ff., and Feldman and Steinisch, *AfS* 18 (1978), pp. 397ff.

156. Stinnes to Luther, Nov. 14, 1923, *Kabinette Stresemann*, II, pp. 1072–76.

157. Hugo to Edmund Stinnes, Nov. 16, 1923, ACDP, NL Stinnes, Nr. 300/7. The letter was accompanied by a copy of the above mentioned letter to Luther of Nov. 14.

158. Johannes Bähr, *Staatliche Schlichtung in der Weimarer Republik. Tarifpolitik, Korporatismus und industrieller Konflikt zwischen Inflation und Deflation 1919–1932* (Berlin, 1989), pp. 72ff.; Preller, *Sozialpolitik*, p. 258ff.; Uwe Oltmann, *Reichsarbeitsminister Heinrich Brauns in der Staats- und Währungskrise 1923/24. Die Bedeutung der Sozialpolitik für die Inflation, den Ruhrkampf und die Stabilisierung* (Kiel, 1969), pp. 276ff.; Steinisch, *Arbeitszeitverkürzung*, pp. 464ff. Reichert sent a confidential report on Brauns's plans to the VDESI on Nov. 14, 1923, BAK, R 13I/202, Bl. 166.

159. For the dicussion, see *Kabinette Stresemann*, II, pp. 1083–85.

160. Seeckt to Stresemann, Nov. 20, 1923, *Kabinette Stresemann*, II, pp. 1151f.

161. Meier-Welcker, *Seeckt*, p. 411.

162. Hugo to Edmund Stinnes, Nov. 16, 1923, ACDP, NL Stinnes, Nr. 300/7.

163. Cabinet meeting of Nov. 19, 1923, *Kabinette Stresemann*, II, pp. 1130–36, quote on p. 1131.

164. Stehkämper, *NL Marx.* Teil I, pp. 296, 303f., 323.

165. Luther to Seeckt, Nov. 23, 1923, *Kabinette Stresemann*, II, pp. 1163–65.

166. See the report of the Saxon Representative to the Reichsrat, Nov. 29, 1923, SäHStA, Außenministerium, Nr. 5318.

167. Luther to Ebert, Nov. 30, 1923, in Beusch, *Währungszerfall*, p. 181.

168. Report of the Saxon Representative to the Reichsrat, Dec. 5, 1923, SäHStA, Außenministerium, Nr. 1061.

169. Stehkämper *NL Marx.* Teil I, p. 303. On the crisis, see Winkler, *Von der Revolution zur Stabilisierung*, pp. 678ff. Very well informed reports on the various efforts to form a government were written by the Saxon Representative in Berlin, Gradnauer, SäHStA, Gesandtschaft Berlin, Nr. 350, Bl. 175–79.

On the new government, see *Kabinette Marx*, I, pp. vii–xi. Stresemann's views were expressed to Lord D'Abernon and relayed in a report of Dec. 3, 1923, PRO, FO 371/8818/372/217.

17. Saving the Stabilization, December 1923–April 1924

1. I am grateful to the late Prof. Harold J. Gordon for providing me with his note from Lowenstein's memoirs.
2. Der Verband der Fleischkonservenfabriken von Groß-Hamburg u. Umgebung an die Handelskammer, Nov. 28, 1923, HK Hamburg, 29.H.l.14.
3. Lt. General von Müller to the Saxon authorities, Nov. 17, 1923, SäHStA, Polizeipräsidium Zwickau, Nr. 102, Bl. 36.
4. On upper Bavaria, see the report of Dec. 5, 1923, BayHStA, Abt. II, Generalstaatskommissar 44, and the report from lower Bavaria of Dec. 4, 1923, BayHStA, Abt. II, MA 102 140.
5. Report of Consul Jaeckel, Jan. 4, 1924, NA, 862.515/79.
6. See Webb, *Hyperinflation and Stabilization*, pp. 65–74, who, in my view, correctly emphasizes this point.
7. Report by Höltzendorff for the HAPAG, Oct. 9, 1923, and Pelzer to Höltzendorff, Oct. 14, 1923, Hapag Archiv. It is interesting to note that Oeser's model for the loan was one taken out by the city of Hamburg from English bankers in August 1923 which was secured by the collection of port duties. On this 6 percent sterling loan, see the report of the American Consul George D. Hepper, Aug. 24, 1923, NA, 862.51/1697. On the Reichsbahn loan from the English, see also Warburg's unpublished memoirs for 1923, p. 73, and the discussions on the Foreign Exchange Procurement Board of Nov. 20, 1923, and Jan. 3, 1924, BAK, R 11/505.
8. See the Cabinet meetings of Jan. 31 and Feb. 11, 1924, *Kabinette Marx*, I, pp. 303–7, 347. A similar arrangement was made for the Post Office.
9. Report of the American Consul in Koblenz, Jan. 8, 1924, NA, 562t0/884.
10. See the internal report of Section X of the RAM on conditions between October 1923 and March 1924, BAP, RAM, Nr. 1724, Bl. 359f.
11. Report of Dec. 19, 1923, SäHStA, Gesandtschaft Berlin, Nr. 2289. Also, see Cabinet meeting of Dec. 6, 1923, *Kabinette Marx*, I, p. 48.
12. *Verhandlungen der Sächsischen Volkskammer*, Dec. 18, 1923, Vol. 2, pp. 2144f.
13. Meeting of the Food Ministers, Dec. 18, 1923, SäHStA, Gesandtschaft Berlin, Nr. 488.
14. Report by Theodore Jaeckel, Jan. 19, 1923, NA, 862.00/1359, and report of Consul Magnuson from Stuttgart, Feb. 13, 1924, 862.00/1421. For the report from Koblenz by Consul Francis Dyer of Jan. 28, 1924, see NA, 862t.00/60.

15. Diary entry, Feb. 3, 1924, Ayres Papers, Hoover Institution.
16. Young to Mrs. Young, Feb. 14, 1924, Arthur Young Papers, ibid.
17. Cabinet meeting of Dec. 10, 1923, *Kabinette Marx*, I, p. 76.
18. Ibid., pp. 72–74, and Cabinet meeting of Dec. 13, 1923, ibid. p. 100. For the quotation, see the report of the Regierungspräsident of the Upper Palatinate and Regensburg, Fcb. 16, 1924, BayHStA, Abt. II, MA 102 143.
19. For a discussion, see Feldman and Steinisch, *AfS* (1978), pp. 411f.; Feldman, *Iron and Steel*, pp. 436ff.; Steinisch, *Arbeitszeitverkürzung*, pp. 464–89.
20. See Feldman and Steinisch, *Industrie und Gewerkschaften*, pp. 121–27, 198ff. The Christian unions remained interested in the ZAG and took a different stand on the extension of working hours at this time. For employer efforts to get rid of collective bargaining and frustration with Brauns's pro-union policies, see the VdA circulars of Nov. 7, and Dec. 19, 1923, StA Hamburg, Blohm & Voss, Nr. 1329.
21. Meeting with workers at the GHH, Dec. 27, 1923, HA/GHH, Nr. 300141/16.
22. *Verhandlungen der Sächsischen Volkskammer*, Dec. 18, 1923, Vol. 2, p. 2145.
23. See the report of the Regierungspräsident of lower Bavaria, Feb. 4, 1924, BayHStA, Abt. II, Generalstaatskommissar, 44.
24. See Gerald D. Feldman, "Streiks in Deutschland 1914–1933: Probleme und Forschungsaufgaben," in K. Tenfelde and H. Volkmann, eds., *Streik. Zur Geschichte des Arbeitskampfes in Deutschland während der Industrialisierung* (Munich, 1981), pp. 271–86, and the statistics on pp. 296–305.
25. See the VdA circulars on wage policy of Nov. 30 and Dec. 31, 1923, and the meeting of the Association of Metal Industrialists of Nov. 6, 1923, where a 40 to 50 percent real-wage reduction was advocated, StA Hamburg, Blohm & Voss, Nr. 1329.
26. For the RAM policy with respect to the arbitration boards, see the reports on the meetings of Nov. 14 and Dec. 13, 1923, GStAKM, Rep. 120, BB, VI, Nr. 1, Bd. 1, Bl. 24–27, 70–72. For the correspondence, which came to public attention and led to strong representations by the ADGB, see Kukuck and Schiffmann, *Gewerkschaften*, pp. 136–41. See also Bähr, *Staatliche Schlichtung*, pp. 132–34. The comparative gold wage calculations are based on an extremely informative report by Assistant Trade Commissioner Margaret L. Goldsmith in the Arthur Young Papers, Hoover Institution, Box 2.
27. Ibid., for the wage statistics. For employer complaints about farm and retailer prices, see the petition of the firm of Kronprinz in Ohlig, Nov. 15, 1923, and an analysis of retailer pricing in BAP, RAM, Nr. 10556, Bl. 15ff., and the VdA circulars of Nov. 30 and Dec. 31, 1923, StA Hamburg, Blohm & Voss, Nr. 1329.
28. See the revealing report of Hamburg Repre-

sentative to the Reichsrat Julius Strandes, Nov. 2, 1923, StA Hamburg, Senatskommission für die Reichs- und auswärtigen Angelegenheiten, III A1c3, Bd. 5. See also Knut Wolfgang Nörr, *Zwischen den Mühlsteinen. Eine Privatrechtsgeschichte der Weimarer Republik* (Tübingen, 1988), pp. 143ff.

29. For various versions of the circular of the RWM of Dec. 17, 1923, drafts of the widely distributed price analysis and lists and other pertinent material, see BAP, RAM, Nr. 10556, Bl. 33–35; RWM, Nr. 12089, Bl. 403–14; SäHStA, MdI, Nr. 11352, Bl. 234–44.

30. See the report of the Surveillance Section of the Anti-Profiteering Bureau for the month of December, BayHStA, Abt. II, Generalstaatskommissar 53.

31. For the situation in the Ruhr, see the firm of Albert Wöhrmann to the Chamber of Commerce in Duisburg, Feb. 5, 1924, and the charges against the banks in the area in January and February 1924, RWWK, 20/501/17. For Hamm's report of Jan. 11, 1924, see *Kabinette Marx*, I, p. 226.

32. Report of the Regierungspräsident of Schwaben and Neuburg, Dec. 28, 1923, BayHStA, Abt. II, Generalstaatskommissar 44. This was typical of reports throughout Bavaria.

33. Petition of Dec. 31, 1923, BAP, RWM, Nr. 62055, Bl. 174–80. This volume is filled with such petitions from retailer and craft organizations.

34. Report of the Regierungspräsident in upper Bavaria, Dec. 20, 1923, BayHStA, Abt. II, Generalstaatskommissar 44.

35. Director Hermann Dahl at the meeting of Jan. 18, 1924, BAP, RWR, Bd. 525, Bl. 211.

36. Meeting of Jan. 18, 1924, ibid., Bl. 234.

37. Ibid., Bl. 196.

38. Ibid., Bl. 213.

39. The business journalist Habersbrunner, ibid., Bl. 224.

40. Hughes, *Paying for the German Inflation*, pp. 34ff.; David B. Southern, "The Impact of the Inflation: Inflation, the Courts and Revaluation," in Richard Bessel and E. J. Feuchtwanger, eds., *Social Change and Political Development in Weimar Germany* (Totowa, New Jersey, 1981), pp. 55–76; Dawson in *Michigan Law Review* (Dec. 1934), pp. 171–238; Zeiler, *Meine Mitarbeit*, pp. 153ff.

41. Quoted in Dawson, *Michigan Law Review* (1934), p. 208. For a good legal discussion, see Nörr, *Zwischen den Mühlsteinen*, pp. 55–71. On the role of the Darmstadt court and its decisions, see above, Chap. 14, p. 683.

42. Nörr, *Zwischen den Mühlsteinen*, pp. 65f., 71; Hughes, *Paying for the German Inflation*, pp. 35f.; for an important criticism of the Weimar judiciary, see Ernst Fraenkel, *Zur Soziologie der Klassenjustiz* (Berlin, 1927), pp. 15, 26f.

43. Hughes, *Paying for the German Inflation*, p. 37; for other examples, see Southern in Bessel and Feuchtwanger, *Social Change*, p. 65.

44. Report of the American Vice Consul in Munich, Oct. 23, 1923, NA, 862.51/1727; Hughes, *Paying for the German Inflation*, p. 29.

45. Am Zenhoff to the Prussian State Ministry, Nov. 15, 1923, GStAPrK, Rep. 84a, Nr. 5885, Bl. 583–42, quote on Bl. 534, and Hughes, *Paying for the German Inflation*, pp. 25, 37–41.

46. GStAPrK, Rep. 84a, Nr. 5885, Bl. 540.

47. Wernek to the Prussian Justice Minister, Jan. 7, 1924, ibid., Bl. 725–35, quote on Bl. 726.

48. Ibid., Bl. 734.

49. *Kabinette Marx*, I, pp. 46–48; Luther, *Politiker ohne Partei*, p. 230; Netzband and Widmaier, *Ära Luther*, pp. 138–42. The two new taxes accounted for 56.2 percent of the government's revenues in December, revenues which rose from 15.1 to 88.9 million gold marks between between the last ten days of November and the last ten days of December. See Beusch, *Währungszerfall*, pp. 80.

50. Luther, *Politiker*, pp. 221ff.; for a detailed account of this decree, see Netzband and Widmaier, *Ära Luther*, pp. 142–68.

51. Ibid., pp. 168ff., for the most comprehensive discussion of the Third Emergency Tax Decree.

52. Saxon report on the Reichsrat meeting of Dec. 21, 1923, SäHStA, Außenministerium, Nr. 5318 and Cabinet meetings of Dec. 15 and 17, 1923, *Kabinette Marx*, I, pp. 108–13, 127–29.

53. Ibid., p. 110.

54. Reichsrat meeting of Dec. 21, 1923, StA Dresden, Außenministerium, Dec. 21, 1923.

55. Report of Consul Leslie Reed, Jan. 24, 1924, NA 862.51/1752.

56. Report of the Regierungs-Präsident of Oberfranken, Dec. 18, 1923, BayHStA, Abt. II, MA 102 155/2.

57. Report of Jan. 17, 1923, ibid., Generalstaatskommissar 44.

58. Cabinet meeting of Dec. 17, 1923, *Kabinette Marx*, I, p. 128.

59. Hughes, *Paying for the German Inflation*, pp. 54ff.; Cabinet meeting of Dec. 15 and 17, 1923, and State Secretary Bracht to the Justice Minister, Jan. 24, 1924, *Kabinette Marx*, I, pp. 110, 127, 264f.

60. Quoted in Stehkämper, *NL Marx*. Teil III, pp. 121f., and Marx's response to Cardinal Bertram, ibid., p. 120. More generally, see Hughes, *Paying for the German Inflation*, p. 58.

61. *Kabinette Marx*, I, pp. 343–45, for the negotiations with the party leaders on Feb. 9, 1924, and pp. 360f., for the Cabinet meeting of Feb. 13, 1924. For a good analysis of the politics, see Hughes, *Paying for the German Inflation*, pp. 65f.

62. Hughes, *Paying for the German Inflation*, p. 67.

63. For the text, see *RGBl* (1924), I, pp. 74–90; Netzband and Widmaier, *Ära Luther*, pp. 189f.; Holtfrerich, *German Inflation*, pp. 321ff.

64. Hughes, *Paying for the German Inflation*, pp. 67f.

65. Speech of Luther to Reichsrat, Feb. 2, 1922, SäHStA, Außenministerium, Nr. 5318.

66. Netzband and Widmaier, *Ära Luther*, pp. 203ff.

67. Cabinet meeting of Jan. 25, 1924, *Kabinette Marx*, I, pp. 267f.

68. See Luther's speech to the Reichstag of Feb. 29, 1924, *VR*, Bd. 361, p. 12570f. Here I take issue with the rather uncritical treatment of SPD attitudes toward the Third Emergency Tax Decree in Rosemarie Leuschen-Seppel, *Zwischen Staatsverantwortung und Klasseninteresse. Die Wirtschafts- und Finanzpolitik der SPD zur Zeit der Weimarer Republik unter besonderer Berücksichtigung der Mittelphase 1924-1928/29* (Bonn, 1981), pp. 146ff., and Claus-Dieter Krohn, *Stabilisierung und ökonomische Interessen. Die Finanzpolitik des deutschen Reiches 1923-1927* (Düsseldorf, 1974), pp. 43-53. Leuschen-Seppel shows that the posture of the SPD toward revaluation had already changed in March 1924. For a criticism of both these authors similar to the one presented here, see Gerhard Schulz, *Deutschland am Vorabend der großen Krise. Zwischen Demokratie und Diktatur* (Berlin and New York, 1987), pp. 74ff. For the ADGB–AfA stand on the rent tax and revaluation, see their petition to Marx of Feb. 26, 1923, in Horst-A. Kukuck and Dieter Schiffmann, *Die Gewerkschaften von der Stabilisierung bis zur Weltwirtschaftskrise 1924-1930*, 2 vols. (Cologne, 1986), I, pp. 142-46. More generally, see Peter-Christian Witt, "Die Auswirkungen der Inflation auf die Finanzpolitik des deutschen Reiches 1924-1935," Feldman and Müller-Luckner, eds., *Die Nachwirkungen der Inflation*, pp. 43-95., esp. pp. 69-71.

69. Moritz Bonn, "Die Kapitalflucht aus Deutschland," *Plutus* (Feb. 1, 1924), pp. 36-45, quote on p. 45.

70. Huber, *Verfassungsgeschichte* 7, pp. 484-87.

71. See RB directors to State Secretary Bracht, Dec. 17, 1923, and the latter's acid marginal comments in *Kabinette Marx*, I, pp. 130-33.

72. Warburg Papers, 1923, p. 70. The fact that Schacht was not a Jew did not, of course, prevent his enemies from calling him one! See Fürstenberg, *Erinnerungen*, p. 164. Fürstenberg seems to have voted for Helfferich. For the Central Committee protocol, see SäHStA, Gesandtschaft Berlin, Nr. 1631.

73. Ibid.

74. Reichsrat meeting of Dec. 18, 1923, ibid. On Norman's opposition to Helfferich, see Harold James, *The Reichsbank and Public Finance in Germany 1924-1933: A Study of the Politics of Economics during the Great Depression* (Frankfurt a.M., 1985), p. 20.

75. Bonn to Hamm, Dec. 15, 1923, BAK, NL Bonn, Nr. 8d, Bl. 21, for the quotations and this discussion.

76. Schacht so viewed it himself in his *Stabilization of the Mark*, pp. 124-27. See *Kabinette Marx*, I, p. 146.

77. See Maier, *Recasting*, pp. 396ff.; McDougall,

Rhineland Diplomacy, pp. 323ff.; Hans Otto Schötz, *Der Kampf um die Mark 1923/24. Die deutsche Währungsstabilisierung unter dem Einfluß der nationalen Interessen Frankreichs, Großbritanniens und der USA [Beiträge zu Inflation und Wiederaufbau in Deutschland und Europa 1914-1924, Bd. 9]* (Berlin & New York, 1987), pp. 60ff.

78. Hirtseifer to Brauns, Nov. 13, 1923, GStAKM, Rep. 120, AX, Nr. 27a, Bd. 16, Bl. 160. On the condition of French finances, see Schuker, *The End of French Predominance*, Chap. 2.

79. Schötz, *Kampf um die Mark*, pp. 79-81; *Kabinette Marx*, I, pp. 15f., 29f., 33f., 54.

80. This discussion is based on the report of Bavarian Representative in Berlin von Praeger of Dec. 7, 1923, BayHStA, Abt. II, Gesandtschaft Berlin, Nr. 1100, rather than the report in *Kabinette Marx*, I, pp. 50-52, which is quite a bit less explicit.

81. Meeting of Dec. 13, 1923, *Kabinette Marx*, I, pp. 101-3.

82. See Marx to Hagen, Dec. 22, 1923, Hagen to Marx, Dec. 31, 1923, *Kabinette Marx*, I, pp. 151-54, 183-85, and Schötz, *Kampf um die Mark*, pp. 74-76.

83. Meeting of Dec. 17, 1923, *Kabinette Marx*, I, p. 124.

84. Meeting of Jan. 9, 1924, ibid., p. 211.

85. Wiedfeldt to the Foreign Office, Jan. 7, 1924, BAP, HAAA, Nr. 43814, Bl. 163-68, quote on Bl. 164f.

86. Ibid., Bl. 167.

87. Diary entries of Arthur Young, for Feb. 6, 9-10, 1924, Hoover Institution, Arthur Young Papers, Box 1.

88. Diary entry of Feb. 5, ibid.

89. Diary entry of Feb. 4, 1924, Leonard P. Ayres Collection, Hoover Institution.

90. Warburg Papers, 1923, p. 73. This analysis of the American policy is based on the excellent discussion in Schötz, *Kampf um die Mark*, pp. 121-27.

91. Schacht, *Stabilization of the Mark*, pp. 129f., and *My First Seventy-six Years. The Autobiography of Hjalmar Schacht* (London, 1955), pp. 190ff., for a colorful account of his first days as president of the Reichsbank and his relations with Montagu Norman.

92. Schacht reports from London, BAK, NL Schacht, Nr. 3. See also Schötz, *Kampf um die Mark*, pp. 92-94, and the Cabinet meeting of Jan. 8, 1924, *Kabinette Marx*, I, pp. 206-8.

93. Schacht report on his London visit, BAK, NL Schacht, Nr. 3.

94. For this quote and the discussion which follows, see ibid.

95. Ibid., and *Kabinette Marx*, I, pp. 206-8.

96. Schacht to Stresemann, Jan. 22, 1924, BAK, NL Schacht, Nr. 3.

97. See the report by Henry Robinson of the committee, Jan. 19, 1924, Hoover Institution, Robinson Papers, Box 8.

98. Schacht to Stresemann, Jan. 22, 1924, BAK, NL Schacht, Nr. 3.

99. Diary entry of Feb. 20, 1924, Hoover Institution, Leonard P. Ayres Collection, p. 57.

100. A. N. Young to W. R. Castle of the Dept. of State, Feb. 22, 1924, Hoover Institution, A. N. Young Papers, Box 1.

101. Schacht to Stresemann, Jan. 22, 1924, BAK, NL Schacht, Nr. 3.

102. Ibid., and *Kabinette Marx*, I, pp. 275–83.

103. Schötz, *Kampf um die Mark*, pp. 129–33, and Schacht, *Stabilization of the Mark*, pp. 144–47.

104. Schötz, *Kampf um die Mark*, pp. 135–48. See also *Kabinette Marx*, I, pp. 142f.

105. RB Curatorium meeting of April 29, 1924, SäHStA, Gesandtschaft Berlin, Nr. 1631. In general, I follow Schötz's excellent discussion in *Kampf um die Mark*, pp. 148–57, but Schötz does not seem to be aware of how much the Americans offered in April.

106. A. N. Young to Castle, Feb. 22, 1924, Hoover Institution, Arthur Young Papers, Box 1.

107. See Harold James, "Die Währungs- und Wirtschaftsstabilisierung 1923/24 in internationaler Perspektive," Abelshauser, ed., *Die Weimarer Republik als Wohlfahrtsstaat* , pp. 63–79, esp. pp. 71–73. See also Schötz, *Kampf um die Mark*, pp. 145–48.

108. Schacht, *Stabilization of the Mark*, pp. 164f.

109. See the British report on the credit crisis in Germany of May 30, 1924, PRO, FO 371/9793/372/133–35.

110. Felix Pinner, "Schutz der Rentenmark," Feb. 23, 1924, *Berliner Tageblatt*, Feb. 23, 1924, in GStAKM, Rep. 120, AX, Nr. 27a, Bd. 16, Bl. 164.

111. See the internal RB report, "Angriffe der Presse gegen die Diskontpolitik der Reichsbank," of late February 1924, in BAP, RB, Nr. 6460, Bl. 126–33, for the discussion and quotations in this paragraph.

112. Meeting of April 29, 1924, SäHStA, Gesandtschaft Berlin, Nr. 1631. See also the reports of discussions with Schacht in the spring of 1924 in PRO, FO 371/9793/372. See also the correspondence in the Hamburg Chamber of Commerce, HK Hamburg, 29.H.1.14. More generally, see Webb, *Hyperinflation and Stabilization*, pp. 70–73, 98f. On business conditions and the mentality of both producers and consumers during the first months of 1924, see the report of Consul Louis Dreyfus from Dresden, June 9, 1924, NA, 862.50/552.

113. *Kabinette Marx*, I, p. 558.

114. Report by Karl Fehrmann for Frau Stinnes on his last conversation with Hugo Stinnes on March 18, 1924, Oct. 16–18, 1924, Stinnes Papers, private possession.

115. Quoted in Williamson, *Helfferich*, p. 400.

Epilogue: A Mortgaged Republic

1. A copy of this letter was sent by Consul William Coffin to the Secretary of State, March 21, 1924, as an illustration of the "tendency of German commercial and financial circles to mix political propaganda with business," NA, 862.516/145.

2. From the report of the German embassy in Stockholm of an article in the *Sozialdemokraten*, Feb. 26, 1924, BAP, RWM, Nr. 7625, Bl. 156–61.

3. Ibid.

4. Ruck, *Gewerkschaften*, p. 974. For the industrial production figures, see Holtfrerich, *German Inflation*, p. 204. The costs of the Ruhr occupation between January and the end of June 1923 alone were estimated to be between .75 and 1 billion gold marks in government expenses and between 1.5 and 1.75 billion gold marks in economic losses. See the undated memorandum of the Statistisches Reichsamt, GStAPrK, Rep. 84a, Nr. 1410, Bl. 82–110.

5. It seems to me that Carl-Ludwig Holtfrerich's argument in *German Inflation*, pp. 292–300, and in his "Internationale Verteilungsfolgen der deutschen Inflation 1918–1923," *Kyklos* 30 (1971), pp. 271–92, tends to understate the trauma of 1923 in his effort to prove the value of the hyperinflation in eliminating Germany's foreign private debt and reducing Germany's foreign public debt. While his argument that a stabilization in the spring of 1922 would have undermined this advantage is persuasive, his "cost-benefit evaluation" studiously avoids any consideration of the costs of 1923. It is interesting that even so positive an analyst as Corrado Gini argued that the time for stabilization had come in late 1922, *Weltwirtschaftliches Archiv* (1934), esp. pp. 403, 431. On the bond market and interest rates, more about which will be said below, see T. Balderston, "The Origins of Economic Instability in Germany 1924–1930. Market Forces versus Economic Policy," *VSWG* 69 (1982), pp. 488–514, and "Links between Inflation and Depression: German Capital and Labour Markets, 1924–1931," in Feldman and Müller-Luckner, eds., *Die Nachwirkungen der Inflation*, pp. 156–85.

6. Holtfrerich, *German Inflation*, p. 334. For his convincing demonstration of this point, see his discussion on pp. 271ff.

7. Schulz, *Deutschland am Vorabend der Großen Krise*, pp. 70f.

8. Robert Moeller, "Winners as Losers in the German Inflation: Peasant Protest over the Controlled Economy 1920–1923," in Feldman et al., *The German Inflation. A Preliminary Balance*, pp. 255–88.

9. The best summary discussion on the condition of agriculture is in Schumacher, *Land und Politik*, Chap. 5, but see also Schulz, *Deutschland am Vorabend der Großen Krise*, Chaps. 4–5, and Fritz Beckmann, "Die Kapitalbildung der deutschen Landwirtschaft während der Inflation," *Schmollers Jahrbuch* 48 (1924), pp. 113–33.

10. James, *The German Slump*, p. 246 and Chap. 7, more generally for this discussion and the data.

11. Schulz, *Deutschland am Vorabend der Großen Krise*, p. 164.

12. *Wirtschaft und Statistik* (1925), p. 769. The figures are reprinted as an illustration of industry's

strengthened position in Krohn, *Stabilisierung*, p. 21. For a good criticism of Krohn's approach, see Lindenlaub, *Maschinenbauunternehmen*, pp. 24ff.

13. Ausschuß zur Untersuchung der Erzeugungs- und Absatzbedingungen der deutschen Wirtschaft, *Verhandlungen und Berichte des Unterausschusses für allgemeine Wirtschaftsstruktur. 3. Arbeitsgruppe. Wandlungen in den wirtschaftliche Organisationsformen. Vierter Teil. Kartellpolitik. Erster Abschnitt* (Berlin, 1930), p. 330.

14. Diary Entry of A. N. Young, Feb. 7, 1924, Hoover Institution, Arthur Young Papers, Box 1.

15. A. N. Young to W. R. Castle, Jr., Feb. 22, 1924, ibid.

16. See Julius Hirsch, "Wandlungen im Aufbau der deutschen Industrie," in Bernhard Harms, ed., *Strukturwandlungen der deutschen Volkswirtschaft*, 2 vols. (Berlin, 1928), I, pp. 187–221, esp. p. 197. In fact, the actual increase in the number of locomotives and railroad cars available in 1924 was not substantially in excess of 1913, but a substantial portion of the rolling stock had been replaced and there certainly had been excess production between 1920 and 1923 for "political reasaons." See Peter-Christian Witt, "Anpassung an die Inflation. Das Investitionsverhalten der deutschen Staatsbahnen/Reichsbahn in den Jahren 1914 bis 1923/24," Gerald D. Feldman, et al., ed., *The Adaptation to Inflation*, pp. 392–432.

17. Bresciani-Turroni, *Economics of Inflation*, pp. 359–97, 405–9.

18. Undated and unsigned memorandum "Ueber die Zukunftsaussichten der deutschen Industriekonzerne," which was obviously written in 1924, BAP, RB, Bd. 6406, Bl. 400–405, quote on Bl. 400.

19. Siemens to Vögler, Dec. 27, 1925, SAA 4/Lf 635.

20. The unreliability of the gold mark balances to record the actual condition of firms after a period of such disorder was emphasized by the investigatory commission set up to explore the situation of the German economy in the late Weimar Republic, see *Ausschuß zur Untersuchung der Erzeugungs- und Absatzbedingungen der deutschen Wirtschaft. 1. Arbeitsgruppe. Bd. l. Gesamtbericht* (Berlin, 1931), p. 177.

21. Kronenbrauerei Dortmund to Chamber of Commerce, May 19, 1924, SWW Dortmund, Kl, Nr. 354.

22. See Deutsch-Lux's response of May 21, 1924, ibid. For the quote, see Amberg & Klestadt to the Duisburg Chamber of Commerce, May 14, 1924, RWWK, 20/471/1.

23. See their respective letters to the Duisburg Chamber of Commerce of May 16 and 19, 1924, ibid.

24. Steinthal to Bierwes, Feb. 13, 1924, Mannesmann-Archiv, MM.091.

25. Bernd Weisbrod, *Schwerindustrie in der Weimarer Republik. Interessenpolitik zwischen Stabilisierung und Krise* (Wuppertal, 1978), pp. 85f. See also the article "Goldbilanzen," *Plutus* (June 15, 1924), pp. 181f.

26. Here I follow the arguments of Lindenlaub, *Maschinenbauunternehmen*, pp. 24–30.

27. "Die Umsätze der IG im Jahre 1924," by Dr. W. Thiele, April 22, 1925, WA Bayer-Leverkusen, 15.D1.1. I am grateful to Prof. Peter Hayes for placing this document at my disposal.

28. On the Barmat affair, see the discussion in Eyck, *History of the Weimar Republic*, I, pp. 326ff. For a good illustration of the anti-Semitic as well as anti-Socialist tone of the right-wing attack, see the anonymously authored pamphlet, *Barmat und seine Freunde* (Berlin, 1925) in BAK, Zeitgeschichtliche Sammlung 2, Nr. 173-1.

29. There is a good summary of the phases of the crisis in Bresciani-Turroni, ˙*Economics of Inflation*, pp. 404–9. Two valuable studies of the crisis are Fritz Blaich, *Die Wirtschaftskrise 1925/26 und die Reichsregierung. Von der Erwerbslosenfürsorge zur Konjunkturpolitik* (Kallmünz Opf., 1977), and Dieter Hertz-Eichenrode, *Wirtschaftskrise und Arbeitsbeschaffung. Konjunkturpolitik 1925/26 und die Grundlagen der Krisenpolitik Brünings* (Frankfurt a.M. & New York, 1982).

30. See Krohn, *Stabilisierung und ökonomische Interessen*, pp. 105–12 and Fritz Blaich, "Der '30-Millionen-Fonds—Die Auseinandersetzung um eine soziale Ruhrentschädigung 1925–1927," *Blätter für deutsche Landesgeschichte* 113 (1977), pp. 450–76. The compensation was very important for relieving the liquidity problems of IG Farben, whose members received fifty million marks. See the Thiele report, WA Bayer-Leverkusen, 15.D1.1.

31. Duisberg to Schlubach, June 19, 1925, WA Bayer-Leverkusen, Autographensammlung Carl Duisberg. More generally, see Feldman, *Iron and Steel*, pp. 450ff. Also, Schulz, *Deutschland am Vorabend*, pp. 91ff.

32. Weisbrod, *Schwerindustrie*, pp. 86–92. On the stabilization crisis, see Bresciani-Turroni, *Economics of Inflation*, Chap. 10. More generally, see Harold James, *German Slump*, Chap. 4.

33. Holtfrerich, *German Inflation*, p. 206.

34. The theoretical foundation for this argument is provided by the seminal article of Werner Abelshauser and Dietmar Petzina, "Krise und Rekonstruktion, Zur Interpretation der gesamtwirtschaftlichen Entwicklung Deutschlands im 20. Jahrhundert," reprinted in Werner Abelshauser and Dietmar Petzina, *Deutsche Wirtschaftsgeschichte im Industriezeitalter. Konjunktur, Krise, Wachstum* (Königstein/Ts, 1981), pp. 47–93.

35. *Wirtschaftliche Chronik* (1925), p. 364.

36. Ibid., pp. 366ff.

37. Undated Reichsbank report, BAP, RB, Bd. 6406, Bl. 295–399. More generally, see Carl-Ludwig Holtfrerich, in Feldman and Müller-Luckner, *Nachwirkungen*, pp. 187–209; Manfred Pohl and the comments of Karl Erich Born in Büsch and Feldman,

Historische Prozesse, pp. 83–95, 122f.; Born, *International Banking*, pp. 222f.

38. See Carl-Ludwig Holtfrerich in *Bankhistorisches Archiv*, Beiheft 5 (April 1981), pp. 14–29 and in Deutschen Sparkassen- und Giroverband, *Standortbestimmung. Entwicklungslinien der deutschen Kreditwirtschaft*, pp. 13–42; Knut Borchardt, "'Das hat historische Gründe.' Zu den Determinanten der Struktur des deutschen Kreditwesens unter besonderer Berücksichtigung der Rolle der Sparkassen," Hansjoachim Henning, Dieter Lindenlaub, Eckhard Wandel, eds., *Wirtschafts- und sozialgeschichtliche Forschungen und Probleme* (St. Katharinen, 1987), pp. 270–87.

39. For an excellent discussion of the effort to subordinate economic to financial considerations and its breakdown, see Fred Hirsch and Peter Oppenheimer, "The Trial of Managed Money: Currency, Credit and Prices 1920–1970," in Carlo M. Cipolla, ed., *The Fontana Economic History of Europe*. Vol. 2, *The Twentieth Century* (Glasgow, 1976), pp. 603–97, esp. pp. 608ff. On Germany specifically, see Harold James, "Did the Reichsbank Draw the Right Conclusions from the German Inflation?" in Feldman and Müller-Luckner, *Nachwirkungen*, pp. 211–31.

40. Danat report for 1925 in BAK, NL Silverberg, Bd. 552, Bl. 148f. On these aspects of the 1925–1926 depression, see Blaich, *Wirtschaftskrise*, pp. 28–34, 58–77, 141ff.

41. Here I follow the arguments of Harold James in Feldman, *Nachwirkungen* (statistics on p. 227n14).

42. See the memorandum by State Secretary Hans Schäffer of August 3, 1931, on the banking crisis in Ilse Maurer and Udo Wengst, *Politik und Wirtschaft in der Krise 1930–1932. Quellen zur Ära Brüning. Quellen zur Geschichte des Parlamentarismus und der politischen Parteien. Dritte Reihe. Die Weimarer Republik*, 2 vols. (Düsseldorf, 1980), I, pp. 817–19 for these quotes.

43. See Witt in Feldman and Müller-Luckner, *Nachwirkungen*, pp. 43–116, for the general course of German finances in this period. See also the discussion of reparations and financial policy of Dec. 4, 1929 in *Kabinette Müller*, II, pp. 1211–14.

44. Witt in Feldman and Müller-Luckner, *Nachwirkungen*, p. 93, and Peter Flora and Arnold J. Heidenheimer, eds., *The Development of Welfare States in Europe and America* (New Brunswick & London, 1981), pp. 37–80, esp. 49, 59.

45. See Feldman in Feldman et al., eds., *Adaptation to Inflation*, pp. 433–41 and Witt in Feldman and Müller-Luckner, *Nachwirkungen*, p. 66f.n70.

46. Report on "The Social Charges borne by German Economy," by L. Gaillet-Billotteau of Oct. 15, 1925, Transfer Committee, Economic Service, Note No. 16, Hoover Institution.

47. Ibid., and Blaich, *Wirtschaftskrise*, p. 82.

48. On the Ruhr lockout, see Gerald D. Feldman and Irmgard Steinisch, "Notwendigkeit und Gren-

zen sozialstaatlicher Intervention: Eine vergleichende Fallstudie des Ruhreisenstreits in Deutschland und des Generalstreiks in England," *AfS* 20 (1980), 57–118. The best study of the compulsory arbitration system is Bähr, *Staatliche Schlichtung*.

49. This is not the place to enter into the complicated "Borchardt Controversy." For convenient collections of articles on the subject, see Knut Borchardt, *Wachstum, Krisen, Handlungsspielräume der Wirtschaftspolitik. Studien zur Wirtschaftsgeschichte des 19. und 20. Jahrhunderts* (Göttingen, 1982), Part III; "Kontroversen über die Wirtschaftspolitik in der Weimarer Republik," *GuG*, Vol. 11, No. 3 (1985); Ian Kershaw, ed., *Weimar: Why did German Democracy Fail?* (London, 1990); Jürgen Baron von Kruedener, ed., *Economic Crisis and Political Collapse* (Oxford, 1990). For real wage levels and production, see Bry, *Wages in Germany*, p. 362.

50. On strikes and lockouts, see Feldman in Tenfelde & Volkmann, *Streik*, pp. 271ff. For labor's inflationary expectations, see Balderston in Feldman and Müller-Luckner, *Nachwirkungen*, pp. 168ff. For the argument that savings could have come from wages and salaries, see Carl-Ludwig Holtfrerich, "Arbeitslosigkeit, Sozialabbau, Demokratieverlust. Ergebnis zu hoher Löhne in der Weimarer Republik?" *Gewerkschaftliche Monatshefte* 11 (1983), pp. 714–22. I find the argument more theoretically than historically convincing. On the "growth pact," see Heinrich Volkmann, "Modernisierung des Arbeitskampfes? Zum Formwandel von Streik und Aussperrung in Deutschland 1864–1875," in Hartmut Kaelble, ed., *Probleme der Modernisierung in Deutschland. Sozialhistorische Studien zum 19. und 20. Jahrhundert* (Opladen, 1978), pp. 110–70, esp. p. 168.

51. Ausschuß zur Untersuchung der Erzeugungs- und Absatzbedingungen der deutschen Wirtschaft, *Massenfilialunternehmen im Einzelhandel mit Lebensmitteln und Kolonialwaren. Verhandlungen und Berichte des Unterausschusses für Gewerbe: Industrie, Handel und Handwerk (III. Unterausschuß)* (Berlin, 1929), Bd. 2, p. 269.

52. Ibid., *Konsumvereine, 9. Arbeitsgruppe (Handel)* (Berlin, 1931), Bd. 8, p. 292.

53. Ibid., *Das Deutsche Handwerk (Sonderuntersuchungen über das Bäcker-, Konditor-, Fleischer-Schumacher-, Schneider- und Buchbinderhandwerk), 8. Arbeitsgruppe (Handwerk)* (Berlin, 1930), Bd. 3, pp. 173f.

54. Ibid., *Einzelhandel mit Bekleidung. Teil II. Versandgeschäfte, Etagengeschäfte, Einzelhandel mit Schuhen, Kreditgebender Einzelhandel. 9 Arbeitsgruppe (Handel)* (Berlin, 1930), Bd. 10, pp. 294f.

55. See the excellent article of Sandra J. Coyner, "Class Consciousness and Consumption: The New Middle Class in the Weimar Republic," *Journal of Social History* 10 (1977), pp. 310–31.

56. William L. Patch, Jr., "Class Prejudice and the Failure of the Weimar Republic," *German Studies*

Review 12 (Feb. 1989), pp. 35–54, quotes on pp. 40, 44. More generally, see James, *German Slump*, pp. 218f.

57. Knut Borchardt, "Das Gewicht der Inflationsangst in den wirtschaftspolitischen Entscheidungsprozessen während der Weltwirtschaftskrise," in Feldman and Müller-Luckner, *Nachwirkungen*, pp. 233–60, esp. p. 239.

58. Report of July 20, 1927, by L. Gaillet-Billotteau on "The Status and Salaries of Officials of the Reich from 1924 to July 1, 1927. A Comparison with 1913." Transfer Committee, Economic Service, Note No. 46, Hoover Institution.

59. On the struggle over the employment of American loans and the significance of the depression of 1925–1926, see William C. McNeil, *American Money and the Weimar Republic. Economics and Politics on the Eve of the Great Depression* (New York, 1986), and the essays by McNeil, "Could Germany Pay? Another Look at the Reparations Problem in the 1920's," and Jon Jacobson, "The Reparations Settlement of 1924," in Feldman et al., *The Consequences of Inflation* (Berlin, 1989), pp. 79–124. On public finances, see James, *German Slump*, Chap. 3, and on the problem of Reich reform, see Gerhard Schulz, *Zwischen Demokratie und Diktatur. Die Periode der Konsolidierung und der Revision des Bismarckschen Reichsaufbaus 1919–1930* (Berlin and New York, 1987). For a good discussion of the problems of municipal financing, see Jürgen Reulecke, "Auswirkungen der Inflation auf die städtischen Finanzen," in Feldman and Müller-Luckner, *Nachwirkungen*, pp. 97–116.

60. See the splendid discussion of this strategy in Weisbrod, *Schwerindustrie*, Chap. 5, esp. pp. 457ff. See also Gerald D. Feldman, "Aspekte Deutscher Industriepolitik am Ende der Weimarer Republik 1930–1932," in Karl Holl, ed., *Wirtschaftskrise und liberale Demokratie* (Göttingen, 1978), pp. 103–21.

61. Hans Luther, "1923 und 1930," *Bank = Archiv* (Jan. 1, 1930), pp. 131–34.

62. Harold James, *Reichsbank*, p. 160.

63. See especially Gerhard Schulz, "Inflationstrauma, Finanzpolitik und Krisenbekämpfung in den Jahren der Wirtschaftskrise, 1930–1933," in Feldman and Müller-Luckner, eds. *Nachwirkungen*, pp. 261–96.

64. See David Marquand, *Ramsay MacDonald* (London, 1977), pp. 668ff., and Roger Middleton, "The Treasury in the 1930s: Political and Administrative Constraints to the Acceptance of the 'New' Economics," *Oxford Economic Papers* 34(1982), pp. 48–77, esp. p. 65.

65. I am grateful to Prof. Knut Borchardt for these references. For this discussion more generally, see Borchardt in Feldman and Müller-Luckner, *Nachwirkungen*, pp. 233–60, as well as the essays of Witt and Schulz in the same volume which place more emphasis on the manipulation of inflation anxiety.

65. Quoted in ibid., p. 244.

66. On the turn to reflationary policies and von Papen, see Turner, *German Big Business and the Rise of Hitler* (New York & Oxford, 1985), pp. 227ff. On the connection between rule by decree under presidential government and reflationary measures, see Schulz in Feldman and Müller-Luckner, *Nachwirkungen*, pp. 292–94. On the problem of silencing inflation anxiety, see Witt in ibid., pp. 46f.

67. Holtfrerich, *German Inflation*, pp. 277f. I find this an oddly ecstatic moment in an otherwise very sober and compelling book.

68. See Thomas C. Childers, "Inflation and Political Realignment in Germany," in Gerald D. Feldman et al., eds., *The German Inflation. A Preliminary Balance*, pp. 409–31, esp. p. 420, and *The Nazi Voter. The Social Foundations of Fascism in Germany, 1919–1933*, (Chapel Hill, 1983), Chap. 2.

69. Autobiography of Heinrich Dinse, Theodore Abel Collection, Hoover Institution, Box 1, No. 101. For other illustrations of the influence of the inflation, see Box 1, No. 79; Box 2, Nos. 181, 212, 214, 215, 233, 264; Box 3, Nos. 343, 363, 454, 468, 495, 533.

70. Autobiography of Maria von Belli, ibid., Box 2, No. 212.

71. Quoted in Turner, *Big Business*, p. 81.

72. For an illustration of ADGB rhetoric, see its memorandum of Feb. 22, 1926, in Kukuck and Schiffmann, *Gewerkschaften*, I, pp. 615f. For the quote, see Childers, *Nazi Voter*, p. 96, and more generally, Kunz, *Civil Servants*, pp. 370ff.

73. See Thomas Childers, "Anti-System Politics in the Era of Stabilization," and Larry Eugene Jones, "In the Shadow of Stabilization: German Liberalism and the Legitimacy Crisis of the Weimar Party System," in Feldman and Müller-Luckner, *Nachwirkungen*, pp. 1–41.

74. On the revaluation parties, See Jones, *German Liberalism*, pp. 260ff. For an admirably clear presentation of the complex legislation, see Hughes, *Paying for the German Inflation*, pp. 189–94.

75. Ibid., p. 180. See also his excellent discussions of the comparative question and the present value of the revaluation on pp. 96ff., 176ff.

76. Jones, *German Liberalism*, pp. 262ff., and Childers in Feldman et al., *German Inflation*, pp. 424f.

77. See Konrad J. Jarausch, "Die Not der geistigen Arbeiter. Akademiker in der Berufskrise 1918–1933," in Werner Abelshauser, ed., *Die Weimarer Republik als Wohlfahrtsstaat*, pp. 280–300. Michael Kater, *Doctors Under Hitler* (Chapel Hill and London, 1989).

78. On the language of German politics, see Childers, *AHR* (April 1990), pp. 331–58; on the relevance of modernization theory, see Feldman, *AfS* 26 (1986), pp. 1–26. On the increasing connection between the economic situation and mobility in Weimar, see Bayerisches Statistisches Landesamt, *Sozialer Auf- und Abstieg*.

79. For an important discussion of the tendency to grow weary of interest organization and seek more integrative forms of political identification as well as for a convincing rejection of the notion of bourgeois passivity in the Weimar Republic, see Peter Fritzsche, *Rehearsals for Fascism. Populism and Political Mobilization in Weimar Germany* (New York & Oxford, 1990), esp. Chaps. 7–9.

80. Stefan Zweig, *The World of Yesterday. An Autobiography by Stefan Zweig* (New York, 1943), p. 313.

Bibliography

Unpublished Sources

Archiv der sozialen Demokratie (SPD Archiv), Bonn-Bad Godesberg
   NL Paul Hertz
   NL Carl Severing
Archiv des Bundes deutscher Frauenvereine, Berlin
   Abt. 6 Bundesarbeit in der Kriegs- und Übergangszeit
   Abt. 15 Schriften des Bundes
Archiv des deutschen Gewerkschaftsbundes (DGB Archiv), Düsseldorf
   ADGB Vorstandskorrespondenz
   NL Heinrich Imbusch
Archiv für Christlich-Demokratische Politik (ACDP) der Konrad Adenauer-Stiftung, St. Augustin bei Bonn
   Bestand I-220 NL Hugo Stinnes
Archiv des Vereins deutscher Maschinenbauanstalten (VDMA Archiv), Frankfurt am Main
Archives Nationales (AN), Paris
   Archives of the French Delegation to the Reparation Commission, fonds AJ⁵.
Bayerisches Hauptstaatsarchiv (BayHStA), München
   Abt I, MH Handelsministerium
   Abt. II, Gesandtschaft Berlin
   Abt. IV, MKr. Kriegsministerium
Bergbau-Archiv (BgA), Bochum
   Bestand 13 Zechenverband
   Bestand 15 Fachgruppe Bergbau
   Bestand 25 Klöckner-Bergbau-Victor-Ickern AG
   Bestand 32 Berggewerkschaft Hibernia
   Bestand 42 Gelsenkirchener Bergwerks AG (GBAG)
Brandenburgisches Landeshauptarchiv (LHA) (Potsdam)
   Rep. 1A Verteilungsstelle Berlin
Bundesarchiv Koblenz (BAK)
   Kleine Erwerbungen (Kl. Er.), Nr. 451
   NL Max Bauer
   NL Moritz Bonn
   NL Lujo Brentano
   NL Anton Erkelenz
   NL Georg Gothein
   NL Alfred Hugenberg
   NL Erich Koch-Weser

   NL Karl Jarres
   NL Gunter Le Suire
   NL Marie-Elisabeth Luders
   NL Wichard von Moellendorff
   NL Reinhold Quaatz
   NL Jakob Riesser
   NL Hjalmar Schacht
   NL Eugen Schiffer
   NL Friedrich Saemisch
   NL Paul Silverberg
   NL Rudolf ten Hompel
   NL Joseph Wirth
   R 2 Reichsfinanzministerium (RFM)
   R 13I Verein deutscher Eisen- und Stahlindustrieller
   R 28 Dienststellen der Deutschen Reichsbank
   R 43I Reichskanzlei
   R 45II Deutsche Volkspartei (DVP)
   R 45III Deutsche Demokratische Partei (DDP)
   R 73 Notgemeinschaft der deutschen Wissenschaft
   R 85 Auswärtiges Amt. Handelspolitische Abteilung
   R 112 Reichsversicherungsanstalt für Angestellte
   Zeitgenössische Sammlungen 172–73, 103
Bundesarchiv Potsdam (BAP)
   Demobilmachungsamt (DMA)
   Deutsche Bank
   Deutsche Reichsbank (RB)
   Handelspolitische Abteilung des Auswärtigen Amtes (HAAA)
   NL Rudolf von Havenstein
   Präsidialkanzlei
   Reichs- und Staatskommissar für die besetzten Gebiete
   Reichsarbeitsministerium (RAM)
   Reichskommissar für die Überwachung der öffentlichen Ordnung
   Reichsministerium (Reichsamt) des Innern (RMI)
   Reichswirtschaftsministerium (RWM)
   Reichswirtschaftsrat (RWR)
   Sozialisierungskommission
   Zentralarbeitsgemeinschaft (ZAG)
Commerzbibliothek Hamburg
   Handelskammer (HK) Hamburg, Plenarsitzungen
   Handelskammerakten

Deutsches Industrie-Institut (Cologne)
  NL Oskar Funcke
Doe Library, University of California at Berkeley
  NL Gustav Stresemann (Microfilm)
Geheimes Staatsarchiv Kulturbesitz Merseburg
  (GStAKM)
  Rep. 87B   Ministerium für Landwirtschaft, Do-
    mänen und Forsten
  Rep. 120   Preußisches Ministerium für Handel
    und Gewerbe
  Rep. 151   Preußisches Finanzministerium
Geheimes Staatsarchiv Preußischer Kulturbesitz
  (GStAPrK), Berlin-Dahlem
  NL Friedrich Schmidt-Ott
  Rep 77   Statistisches Landesamt
  Rep 84a   Justizministerium
Generallandesarchiv (GLA) Karlsruhe
  Abt. 233   Staatsministerium
  Abt. 237   Finanzministerium
  Hamburg-Amerika-Linie (HAPAG) Archiv,
    Hamburg
  Arndt von Holtzendorff Correspondence
Handelskammer (HK) Archiv, Hamburg
Haniel Archiv Gutehoffnungshütte (HA/GHH),
  Duisburg
  Hauptverwaltung
  NL Paul Reusch
Hauptstaatsarchiv Düsseldorf
  Regierung Düsseldorf
Hauptstaatsarchiv (HStA) Stuttgart
  E 130   Staatsministerium
Hessisches Staatsarchiv (StA) Marburg
  Bestand 150 Oberpräsidium der Provinz Hessen-
    Nassau
Historische Kommission zu Berlin (Hiko)
  Gewerkschaftliche Restakten (NB)
  NL Rudolf Wissell
Historisches Archiv der Deutschen Bank (HADB),
  Frankfurt a.M.
Historisches Archiv der Fried. Krupp GmbH (HA
  Firma Krupp), Essen
  NL Otto Wiedfeldt
  Werksakten
Historisches Archiv der Höchst AG
Historisches Archiv (HA) der Metallgesellschaft,
  Frankfurt a.M.
  Korrespondenz Richard Merton
Hoover Institution, Stanford
  Theodore Abel Collection
  Leonard P. Ayres Collection
  James A. Logan Papers
  Henry M. Robinson Papers
  Karl von Wiegand Papers
Institut für Zeitgeschichte, Munich
  NL Böhm
Julius Hirsch Papers (private possession, now in the
  BAK)
Klöckner-Humboldt-Deutz AG, Cologne
Landesarchiv (LA) Berlin
  Akten des deutschen Städtetages (AdSt)
Leo Baeck Institute, New York City

Memoirs of Felix Deutsch, Max Merkreich, Georg
  Witkowski, Adolf Riesenfeld, Max Aronsohn,
  Emil Schorch, Philip S. White, Carl Schwabe,
  Arnold Bernstein, Ernst Herzfeld
Library of Congress, Washington, D.C.
  Leonard P. Ayres Papers
Mannesmann-Archiv (Düsseldorf)
  Mannesmannröhren-Werke
  Phoenix AG für Bergbau und Hüttenbetrieb
  Rheinische Stahlwerke (Rheinstahl)
Marshall Library, Cambridge University, England
  John Maynard Keynes, Economic Papers
Max-Planck-Gesellschaft (MPG) Archiv, Berlin-
  Dahlem
National Archives (NA), Washington, D.C.
  Department of State, Decimal File
Niedersächsisches Hauptstaatsarchiv in Hannover
  (NHStAH)
  Bestand 80 II   Regierungspräsidien in Hannover,
    Hildesheim und Lüneburg
  Bestand 320 I   Hausfrauenverein Hannover
Niedersächsisches Staatsarchiv in Oldenburg
  (NStAO)
  Bestand 265   Oldenburgische Industrie- und
    Handelskammer
Politisches Archiv des Auswärtigen Amtes, Bonn
  (AA Bonn)
  11^b Österreich
Private Possession
  Eduard Hamm
Public Records Office, London
  FO 371   General Correspondence, Political
Rheinisch-Westfälisches Wirtschaftsarchiv zu Köln
  (RWWK)
  Abt. 3   Handelskammer Koblenz
  Abt. 5   Handelskammer Münster i.W.
  Abt. 10   Handelskammer Duisburg
  NL Jakob van Norden
  NL Georg Solmssen
Sächsisches Hauptstaatsarchiv (SäHStA)
  Dresden
  Außenministerium
  Gesandtschaft Berlin
  Ministerium des Innern (MdI)
  Wirtschaftsministerium
  Landespreisprüfungsstelle (LPP)
SPD Archiv, Bonn-Bad Godesberg
  NL Emil Barth
Staatsarchiv (StA) Hamburg
  Arbeiterrat Groß-Hamburg
  Beamtenrat Hamburg
  Blohm & Voss
  Demobilmachungskommissar
  Deputation für Handel, Schiffahrt und Gewerbe
    (DHSG)
  Hamburgische Gesandtschaft Berlin
  Reichstagsausschuß für auswärtige Angelegenhei-
    ten
  Senatskommission für Angelegenheiten der
    Staatsarbeiter
  Senatskommission für die Justizverwaltung

Senatskommission für die Reichs- und auswärtigen Angelegenheiten
Staatsarchiv (StA) Münster in Westfalen
Oberbergamt Dortmund
Stadtarchiv Frankfurt am Main
  Industrie- und Handelskammer (IHK), Frankfurt am Main
Stiftung Westfälisches Wirtschaftsarchiv (SWW) Dortmund
  K1 Handelskammer Dortmund
  K2 Industrie- und Handelskammer Bochum
  K3 Handelskammer Bielefeld
  K4 Handelskammer Minden
  F26 Concordia Bergbau AG, Oberhausen
Stinnes AG, Mülheim a.d. Ruhr
  Privatnachlaß Hugo Stinnes (Else Stinnes Collection)
Verband der Pfälzischen Industrie e.V. (VPI Archiv), Neustadt an der Weinstraße
Warburg Family Archive, Warburg, Brinckmann, Wirtz & Co., Hamburg
  Max Warburg Papers
Werksarchiv (WA) Bayer-Leverkusen
  NL Carl Duisberg
Werksarchiv der August-Thyssen-Hütte (WA/ATH), Duisburg
  Friedrich-Wilhelms-Hütte (FWH)
  Fritz Thyssen Correspondence
Werksarchiv Maschinenfabrik Augsburg-Nürnberg, Augsburg (WA/M.A.N.-A.)
  NL Emil Guggenheimer
  Werksakten
Werksarchiv Maschinenfabrik Augsburg-Nürnberg, Nürnberg (WA/M.A.N.-N.)
Werner-von-Siemens-Institut für Geschichte des Hauses Siemens, Munich
  NL Arnold Köttgen
  NL Max Haller
  NL Carl Friedrich von Siemens
  Siemens-Archiv Akten (SAA)

Published Documents

Abelshauser, Werner, A. Faust, D. Petzina, eds. *Deutsche Sozialgeschichte 1914–1945. Ein historisches Lesebuch.* Munich, 1985.
Akten der Reichskanzlei. Weimarer Republik. Herausgegeben für die historische Kommission bei der Bayerischen Akademie der Wissenschaften von Karl Dietrich Erdmann:
Das Kabinett Scheidemann 13. Februar bis 20. Juni 1919. Ed. by Hagen Schulze. Boppard am Rhein, 1971.
Das Kabinett Bauer. 21. Juni 1919 bis 27. März 1920. Ed. by Anton Golecki. Boppard am Rhein, 1980.
Das Kabinett Müller I. 27. März bis 21. Juni 1920. Ed. by Martin Vogt. Boppard am Rhein, 1971.
Das Kabinett Fehrenbach. 25 Juni 1920 bis 4. Mai 1921. Ed. by Peter Wulf. Boppard am Rhein, 1972.
Die Kabinette Wirth I und II. 10. Mai 1921 bis 26. Oktober 1921. 26. Oktober 1921 bis 22. November 1922. Ed. by Ingrid Schulze-Bidlingmaier. 2 vols. Boppard am Rhein, 1973.
Das Kabinett Cuno. 22. November 1922 bis 12. August 1923. Ed. by Karl-Heinz Harbeck. Boppard am Rhein, 1968.
Die Kabinette Stresemann I u. II. 13. August bis 6. Oktober 1923. 6. Oktober bis 30. November 1923. Ed. by Karl Dietrich Erdmann and Martin Vogt. 2 vols. Boppard am Rhein, 1978.
Die Kabinette Marx I und II. 30 November 1923 bis 3. Juni 1924. 3 Juni 1924 bis 15. Januar 1925. Ed. by Günter Abramowski. Boppard am Rhein, 1973.
Das Kabinett Müller II. 28 Juni 1928 bis März 1930. Ed. by Martin Vogt. Boppard am Rhein, 1970.
Albertin, Lothar, and Konstanze Wegner, eds. *Linksliberalismus in der Weimarer Republik. Die Führungsgremien der Deutschen Demokratischen Partei und der Deutschen Staatspartei 1918–1933 [Quellen zur Geschichte des Parlamentarismus und der politischen Parteien, Bd. 5].* Düsseldorf, 1980.
Ausschuß zur Untersuchung der Erzeugungs- und Absatzbedingungen der deutschen Wirtschaft (Enquête Ausschuß). *Das deutsche Handwerk (Sonderuntersuchungen über das Bäcker-, Konditor-, Fleischer- Schumacher-, Schneider- und Buchbinderhandwerk), 8. Arbeitsgruppe (Handwerk).* Berlin, 1930.
––––––. *Die deutsche Zahlungsbilanz.* Berlin, 1930.
––––––. *Einzelhandel mit Bekleidung. Teil II. Versandgeschäfte, Etagengeschäfte, Einzelhandel mit Schuhen, Kreditgebender Einzelhandel. 9. Arbeitsgruppe (Handel).* Berlin, 1930.
––––––. *Gesamtbericht.* Berlin, 1931.
––––––. *Konsumvereine. 9. Arbeitsgruppe (Handel).* Berlin, 1931.
––––––. *Massenfilialunternehmen im Einzelhandel mit Lebensmitteln und Kolonialwaren. Verhandlungen und Berichte des Unterausschusses für Gewerbe: Industrie, Handel und Handwerk (III. Unterausschuß).* Berlin, 1929.
––––––. *Die Reichsbank.* Berlin, 1929.
––––––. *Verhandlungen und Berichte des Unterausschusses für allgemeine Wirtschaftsstruktur. 3. Arbeitsgruppe. Wandlungen in den wirtschaftlichen Organisationsformen. Vierter Teil. Kartellpolitik. Erster Abschnitt.* Berlin, 1930.
Benz, Wolfgang, ed. *Politik in Bayern 1919–1933. Berichte des Württembergischen Gesandten Carl Moser von Filseck.* Stuttgart, 1971.
Deutsche Bundesbank. *Deutsches Geld- und Bankwesen in Zahlen 1876–1975.* Frankfurt a.M., 1976.
Deutschlands Wirtschaft, Währung und Finanzen.

Im Auftrage der Reichsregierung den von der Reparationskommission eingesetzten Sachverständigenausschüssen übergeben. Berlin, 1924.

Documents on British Foreign Policy 1919–1939. First Series. London, 1947ff.

Flemming, Jens, Claus-Dieter Krohn, Dirk Stegmann, and Peter-Christian Witt, eds. *Die Republik von Weimar.* 2 vols. Königstein/Ts., 1979.

Hürten, Heinz, ed. *Das Krisenjahr 1923. Militär und Innenpolitik 1922–1924 [Quellen zur Geschichte des Parlamentarismus und der politischen Parteien. Zweite Reihe. Militär und Politik,* Bd. 4]. Düsseldorf, 1980.

Jäckel, Eberhard and Axel Kuhn, eds. *Hitler. Sämtliche Aufzeichnungen 1905–1924.* Stuttgart, 1980.

Kolb, Eberhard, and Reinhard Rürup, eds. *Der Zentralrat der Deutschen Sozialistischen Republik.* Leiden, 1968.

Kukuck, Horst-A., and Dieter Schiffmann, *Die Gewerkschaften von der Stabilisierung bis zur Weltwirtschaftskrise 1924–1930.* 2 vols. Cologne, 1986.

Lutz, Ralph Haswell. *The Fall of the German Empire.* 2 vols. Stanford, 1932.

Matthias, Erich, and Rudolf Morsey. *Die Regierung des Prinzen Max von Baden.* Düsseldorf, 1962.

Maurer, Ilse, and Udo Wengst. *Politik und Wirtschaft in der Krise 1930–1932. Quellen zur Ära Brüning. [Quellen zur Geschichte des Parlamentarismus und der politischen Parteien. Dritte Reihe. Die Weimarer Republik],* 2 vols. Düsseldorf, 1980.

Miller, Susanne, and Heinrich Potthoff, eds. *Die Regierung der Volksbeauftragten, 1918/19.* 2 vols. Düsseldorf, 1969.

Morsey, Rudolf, and Karsten Ruppert, eds. *Die Protokolle der Reichstagsfraktion der deutschen Zentrumspartei 1920–1925.* Mainz, 1981.

Niederschrift der konstituierenden Sitzung des Zentralausschusses der Zentralarbeitsgemeinschaft der industriellen und gewerblichen Arbeitgeber und Arbeitnehmer Deutschlands am 12. Dezember 1919. Berlin, 1920.

Protokoll der Verhandlungen des 11. Kongresses der Gewerkschaften Deutschlands, abgehalten zu Leipzig am 17. und 18. Juni 1922. Berlin, 1922.

Protokoll der Verhandlungen des 12. Kongresses der Gewerkschaften Deutschlands in Breslau. Berlin, 1925.

Protokoll über die Verhandlungen des Parteitages der Sozialdemokratischen Partei Deutschlands, abgehalten in Chemnitz vom 15. bis 21. September 1912. Berlin, 1912.

Protokoll über die Verhandlungen des Parteitages der sozialdemokratischen Partei Deutschlands, abgehalten in Görlitz vom 18. bis 24. September 1921. Berlin, 1921.

Reparation Commission. III. Official Documents Relative to the Amount of Payments to Be Effected by Germany under Reparations Account.

Vol. I (May 1, 1921–July 1, 1922). London, 1922.

Ruck, Michael, ed., *Die Gewerkschaften in den Anfangsjahren der Republik 1919–1923 [Quellen zur Geschichte der deutschen Gewerkschaftsbewegung im 20. Jahrhundert,* Bd. 2]. Cologne, 1985.

Schönhoven, Klaus, ed. *Die Gewerkschaften im Weltkrieg und Revolution 1914–1919 [Quellen zur Geschichte der deutschen Gewerkschaftsbewegung im 20. Jahrhundert,* Bd. 1]. Cologne, 1985.

Schultheß' europäischer Geschichtskalender. Munich, 1921ff.

Stehkämper, Hugo, ed., *Der Nachlaß des Reichskanzlers Wilhelm Marx [Mitteilungen aus dem Stadtarchiv von Köln,* Hefte 52–55]. Cologne, 1968.

Ursachen und Folgen vom deutschen Zusammenbruch 1918 und 1945 bis zur staatlichen Neuordnung Deutschlands in der Gegenwart. Eine Urkunden- und Dokumentensammlung zur Zeitgeschichte. Ed. by Herbert Michaelis, Ernst Schraepler, and Günter Scheel. Berlin, n.d.

Verhandlungen des Reichstags. Stenographische Berichte und Drucksachen. Berlin, 1920–1924.

Verhandlungen der Sächsischen Volkskammer. Dresden, 1919ff.

Verhandlungen der Sozialisierungskommission über die Reparationsfragen. 3 vols. Berlin, 1921/1922.

Verhandlungen der verfassungsgebenden Nationalversammlung. Stenographische Berichte und Drucksachen. Berlin, 1919.

Zahlen zur Geldentwertung in Deutschland 1914 bis 1923. [Sonderheft 1 zu Wirtschaft und Statistik, Bd. 5]. Berlin, 1925.

Contemporary Newspaper, Journals, and Periodicals

Archiv für Sozialwissenschaft und Sozialpolitik. 1914ff.

Die Bank. Wochenheft für Finanz-, Kredit- und Versicherungswesen. 1919ff.

Bank=Archiv. Zeitschrift für Bank- und Börsenwesen. 1914ff.

Correspondenzblatt der Generalkommission der Gewerkschaften Deutschlands. 1914–1923.

Deutsche Allgemeine Zeitung. 1920ff.

Deutsche Juristen-Zeitung. Berlin, 1919–1924.

Frankfurter Zeitung. 1918ff.

Jahrbücher für Nationalökonomie und Statistik. 1918ff.

Juristische Wochenschrift. Berlin, 1919–1924.

Kölnische Zeitung. 1919ff.

Kunst und Künstler. 1920–1923.

Kunst und Wirtschaft. 1920–1923.

Mitteilungen des Verbandes der Deutschen Hochschulen. 1920ff.

Plutus. Kritische Zeitschrift für Volkswirtschaft und Finanzwesen. 1920ff.

Reichsarbeitsblatt. Berlin, 1914ff.

Reichsgesetzblatt. 1914ff.

Reichsverband der deutschen Industrie. *Geschäftliche Mitteilungen für die Mitglieder des Reichsverbandes der deutschen Industrie.* 1920ff.

Reichsverband der deutschen Industrie. *Veröffentlichungen des Reichsverbandes der deutschen Industrie.* 1920ff.

Schmollers Jahrbuch für Gesetzgebung, Wirtschaft und Verwaltung.

Schriften des Vereins für Sozialpolitik. 1918ff.

Soziale Praxis und Archiv für Volkswohlfahrt. 1919ff.

Statistisches Reichsamt. *Wirtschaft und Statistik.* 1920ff.

Volkswirtschaftliche Chronik der Jahrbücher für Nationalökonomie und Statistik. Jena, 1919ff.

Die Weltbühne. Berlin, 1920–1924.

Die Wirtschaftskurve mit Indexzahlen der Frankfurter Zeitung. 1921ff.

Zeitschrift des Preußischen Statistischen Landesamts. 1920ff.

Contemporary Publications and Writings (to 1930)

ADGB. *Kommentar zu der Verordnung betreffend Maßnahmen gegenüber Betriebsabbrüchen und -stillegungen.* Berlin, 1920.

Aerobee, Friedrich. *Der Einfluß des Krieges auf die landwirtschaftliche Produktion in Deutschland.* Stuttgart, 1927.

Alsberg, Max. "Wirtschaftsstrafrecht. Besonders die strafrechtliche Bekämpfung des Sozialwuchers," in Gerhard Anschütz. et. al., eds. *Handbuch der Politik.* Vol IV. Berlin and Leipzig, 1921. Pp. 143–159.

Bayerisches Statistisches Landesamt. *Die Verelendung des Mittelstandes. Heft 106 der Beiträge zur Statistik Bayerns.* Munich, 1925.

————. *Sozialer Auf- und Abstieg im Deutschen Volk. Statistische Methoden und Ergebnisse. Heft 117 der Beiträge zur Statistik Bayerns.* Munich, 1930.

Beckmann, Fritz. "Die Kapitalbildung der deutschen Landwirtschaft während der Inflation," in *Schmollers Jahrbuch* 48 (1924): pp. 113–33.

Bendixen, Friedrich. *Kriegsanleihen und Finanznot. Zwei finanzpolitische Vorschläge.* Jena, 1919.

————. *Währungspolitik und Geldtheorie im Lichte des Weltkrieges.* Munich, 1919.

Bente, Hermann, "Die deutsche Währungspolitik von 1914–1924," in *Weltwirtschaftliches Archiv* 23 (1926): pp. 117–91.

Bergmann, Carl. *The History of Reparations.* New York and Boston, 1927.

Beusch, Paul. *Währungszerfall und Währungsstabilisierung.* Berlin, 1928.

Briefs, Götz. "Kriegswirtschaftslehre und Kriegswirtschaftspolitik," in *Handwörterbuch der Staatswissenschaften* 5 (1923): pp. 374–414.

Bücher, Karl. "Gutachten über das Gesamtgebiet der Schriftstellerfrage," in Ludwig Sinzheimer, ed. *Die geisten Arbeiter. Erster Teil. Freies Schriftstellertum und Literaturverlag [Schriften des Vereins für Sozialpolitik, Bd. 152].* München & Leipzig, 1922. Pp. 465–479.

Bumm, Franz, ed. *Deutschlands Gesundheitsverhältnisse unter dem Einfluß des Weltkrieges.* Stuttgart, 1928.

Bunzel, Julius, ed. *Geldentwerung und Stabilisierung in ihren Einflüssen auf die soziale Entwicklung in Österreich [Schriften des Vereins für Sozialpolitik, Bd. 169].* Munich & Leipzig, 1925.

Calwer, Richard. *Monatliche Übersichten über Lebensmittelpreise.* Berlin, 1914ff.

Dalberg, Rudolf. *Deutsche Währungs- und Kreditpolitik 1923–1926.* Berlin, 1926.

————. *Die neue deutsche Währung nach dem Dawes Plan.* Berlin, 1924.

Deutsch, Felix. *Das Verhältnis des Anteils von Arbeit und Kapital am Ertrage.* Berlin, 1919.

Elster, Karl. *Von der Mark zur Reichsmark. Die Geschichte der deutschen Währung in den Jahren 1914 bis 1924.* Jena, 1928.

Eucken, Walter. *Kritische Betrachtungen zum deutschen Geldproblem.* Jena, 1923.

Eulenburg, Franz. "Inflation. Zur Theorie der Kriegswirtschaft," in *Archiv für Sozialwissenschaft und Sozialpolitik* 45 (1919): pp. 477–526.

————. "Die sozialen Wirkungen der Währungsverhältnisse," in *Jahrbücher für Nationalökonomie und Statistik* 67 (1924).

————. "Zur Theorie der Kriegswirtschaft. Ein Versuch," in *Archiv für Sozialwissenschaft und Sozialpolitik* 43 (1916): pp. 349–96.

Feuchtwanger, Ludwig. "Die Bezahlung des wissenschaftlichen Schriftstellers," in Ludwig Sinzheimer, ed. *Die geisten Arbeiter. Erster Teil. Freies Schriftstellertum und Literaturverlag [Schriften des Vereins für Sozialpolitik, Bd. 152].* München & Leipzig, 1922. Pp. 273–307.

Francke, Ernst, and Walther Lotz. *Die geistigen Arbeiter. Zweiter Teil. Journalisten und bildende Künstler [Schriften des Vereins für Sozialpolitik. Bd. 152].* Munich and Leipzig, 1922.

Fritzsching, L. "Die wirtschaftliche Lage der bildenden Künstler seit Kriegsende," in *Annalen des Deutschen Reichs für Gesetzgebung, Verwaltung und Volkswirtschaft. Jahrgang 1921 und 1922* 54/55 Munich, Berlin, and Leipzig, 1923. Pp. 133–208.

Gehrig, Hans. *Wirtschaftsnot und Selbsthilfe der deutschen Studentenschaft.* Berlin & Leipzig, 1924.

Geithe, Hans. *Wirkungen der Lebensmittelzwangswirtschaft der Kriegs- und Nachkriegszeit auf den Lebensmitteleinzelhandel.* Halle, 1925.

Geyer, Curt. *Drei Verderber Deutschlands. Ein Beitrag zur Geschichte Deutschlands und der Reparationsfrage.* Berlin, 1924.

Goltz, Hans. *10 Jahre Neue Kunst in München.* Munich, 1923.

Günther, Ernst. "Die Anpassung der Sozialversicherung an die Geldentwertung und Lohnsteigerung," in *Jahrbücher für Nationalökonomie und Statistik* 121 (1923): pp. 1–54.

Guradze, Hans. "Die Brotpreise und Kosten des Lebensbedarfes in Berlin im Jahre 1922," in *Jahrbücher für Nationalökonomie und Statistik* 65 (1923): pp. 254–57.

Guradze, Hans, and Karl Freudenberg. "Das Existenzminimum des geistigen Arbeiters," *Jahrbücher für Nationalökonomie und Statistik* 120 (1923): pp. 326–33.

Hahn, L. Albert. "Die Frage des sogenannten Vertrauens in die Währung," in *Archiv für Sozialwissenschaft und Sozialpolitik* 52 (1924): pp. 119–46.

Harms, Bernhard, ed. *Strukturwandlungen der deutschen Volkswirtschaft.* 2 vols. Berlin, 1928.

Hauschild, Harry *Der vorläufige Reichswirtschaftsrat 1920–1926.* Berlin, 1926.

Heiler, Hans. *Die Verelendung des Mittelstandes. Heft 106 der Beiträge zur Statistik Bayerns.* Munich, 1925.

Helfferich, Karl, *Deutschlands Volkswohlstand 1888–1913,* 3rd ed. Berlin, 1914.

———. *Das Geld,* 6th ed. Leipzig, 1923.

Hellwag, Fritz. "Die derzeitige wirtschaftliche Lage der bildenden Künstler," in Ernst Francke and Walther Lotz. *Die geistigen Arbeiter. Zweiter Teil. Journalisten und bildende Künstler* [*Schriften des Vereins für Sozialpolitik.* Bd. 152]. Munich and Leipzig, 1922. Pp. 143–175.

Hirsch, Julius. *Die deutsche Währungsfrage.* Jena, 1924.

———. "Wandlungen im Aufbau der deutschen Industrie," in Harms, ed. *Strukturwandlungen der deutschen Volkswirtschaft* Vol. I. Berlin, 1928. Pp. 187–221.

Hoche, Alfred and Rudolf Binding. *Die Freigabe der Vernichtung lebensunwerten Lebens.* Leipzig, 1920.

Jacques, Norbert. *Dr. Mabuse: Der Spieler.* Reprint. Berchtesgaden, 1961.

Jaffé, Edgar. "Kriegskostendeckung und Steuerreform," in *Schriften des Vereins für Sozialpolitik.* Bd. 156. Munich, 1917. Pp. 83–118.

Jastrow, J. "The New Tax System of Germany," in *Quarterly Journal of Economics.* 37 (1923): pp. 302–41.

Johnson, Elizabeth, ed. *The Collected Writings of John Maynard Keynes. XVIII. Activities 1922–1923: The End of Reparations.* Cambridge, 1978.

Keynes, John Maynard. *The Economic Consequences of the Peace.* London, 1920.

———. *A Revision of the Treaty.* New York, 1922.

Knauss, R. *Die deutsche, englische und französische Kriegsfinanzierung. Sozialwissensschaftliche Forschungen, hrsg. v. der sozialwissenschaftlichen Arbeitsgemeinschaft.* Abteilung V, Heft 1. Berlin & Leipzig, 1923.

Koeth, Joseph. "Die wirtschaftliche Demobilmachung. Ihre Aufgabe und ihre Organe," in Gerhard Anschütz, ed. *Handbuch der Politik.* Vol. 4. Berlin and Leipzig, 1921. Pp. 163ff.

Königsberger, Kurt, "Die wirtschaftliche Demobilmachung in Bayern während der Zeit vom November 1918 bis Mai 1919," in *Zeitschrift des Bayerischen Statistischen Landesamtes* 52 (1920): pp. 193–226.

Koppenstätter, Eduard. *Die Markentwertung. Astrologische Begründung der Kursentwicklung in den Jahren 1914–1922 mit prognoszierter Währungskurve für die Jahre 1923–1926.* Ried, 1923.

Kuczynski, Robert. "German Taxation Policy in the World War," in *Journal of Political Economy* 31 (Dec. 1923): pp. 763–89.

———. *Postwar Labor Conditions in Germany.* Washington, 1925.

Kuhns, Georg. *Fünfundzwanzig Jahre Verband der Ärzte Deutschlands (Hartmannbund).* Leipzig, 1925.

Labor and Adolf Löwe. *Wirtschaftliche Demobilisation.* Berlin, 1916.

Langgässer, Elisabeth. "Merkur," in *Erzählungen.* Düsseldorf, 1964.

Lansburgh, Alfred. *Die Politik der Reichsbank und die Reichsschatzanweisungen nach dem Kriege.* [*Schriften des Vereins für Sozialpolitik,* Bd. 166]. Munich and Leipzig, 1924.

Lewinsohn, Richard (Morus). *Das Geld in der Politik.* Berlin, 1930.

———. *Die Umschichtung der europäischen Vermögen.* Berlin, 1925.

Löwe, Adolf. *Soziale Förderungen für die Übergangswirtschaft.* Berlin, 1918.

Lotz, Walter. "Darlehenskassen," in *Handwörterbuch der Staatswissenschaften* 3 (1926): pp. 209–15.

———. *Die deutsche Staatsfinanzwirtschaft im Kriege.* Stuttgart, 1927.

Luther, Hans. *Fest Mark—solide Wirtschaft.* Berlin, 1924.

———. Die Stabilisierung der deutschen Währung. Aus persönlichen Erinnerungen erzählt," in *Zehn Jahre deutsche Geschichte 1918–1928.* Berlin, 1928. Pp. 159–78.

Magnus, Julius. *Die Rechtsanwaltschaft.* Leipzig, 1929.

Mahlberg, Walter. *Bilanztechnik und Bewertung bei schwankender Währung.* Leipzig, 1922.

Mann, Heinrich. "Kobes," in *Neue Rundschau* I (1925): pp. 235–66.

Mann, Thomas, "Disorder and Early Sorrow," in Thomas Mann. *Death in Venice and Seven Other Stories.* New York, 1954. Pp. 182–216.

———. *Gesammelte Werke in 13 Bänden.* Bd. 13. *Nachträge.* Frankfurt a.M., 1974.

Meerwarth, Rudolf. "Über die deutsche Zahlungsbilanz," in *Schriften des Vereins für Sozialpolitik*. Bd. 167. Munich and Leipzig, 1924. Pp. 1–32.

————. "Zur neuesten Entwicklung der Löhne," in *Zeitschrift des Preußischen Statistischen Landesamts 1922/23* 62 (1923): pp. 327–40.

Meerwarth, Rudolf, Adolf Günther, and Waldemar Zimmermann. *Die Einwirkung des Krieges auf Bevölkerungsbewegung, Einkommen u. Lebenshaltung in Deutschland*. Stuttgart, 1932.

Mises, Ludwig von. "Die geldtheoretische Seite des Stabilisierungsproblems," in *Schriften des Vereins für Sozialpolitik*. Bd. 164. Munich and Leipzig, 1923.

Moulton, Harold G., and C. E. McGuire. *Germany's Capacity to Pay. A Study of the Reparation Problem*. New York, 1923.

Mügel, Oskar. *Die Aufwertung. Überblick über die Entwicklung*. Berlin, 1926.

————. *Geldentwertung und Gesetzgebung [Wirtschaftsrecht und Wirtschaftspflege, Heft VII]*. Berlin, 1923.

Oertmann, Paul. *Die Aufwertungsfrage bei Geldforderungen, Hypotheken und Anleihen*. Berlin, 1924.

Pinner, Felix. *Deutsche Wirtschaftsführer*. Charlottenburg, 1924.

Plenge, Johann. *Von der Diskontpolitik zur Herrschaft über den Geldmarkt*. Berlin, 1913.

Popitz, Johannes. "Die deutschen Finanzen 1918–1928," in *Zehn Jahre deutsche Geschichte 1918–1928*. Berlin, 1928. Pp. 179–202.

Prion, Willi. "Deutsche Kreditpolitik 1919–1922," in *Schmollers Jahrbuch* 42 (1924): pp. 163–205.

————. *Die Finanzpolitik der Unternehmung im Zeichen der Scheingewinne*. 2nd ed. Jena, 1922.

————. *Inflation und Geldentwertung. Finanzielle Maßnahmen zum Abbau der Preise. Gutachten erstattet dem Reichsfinanzministerium*. Berlin, 1919.

————. "Kreditpolitik und Ruhrkampf (1923)," *Schmollers Jahrbuch* 49 (1925) pp. 109–33.

Quante, Peter. "Lohnpolitik und Lohnentwicklung im Kriege," in *Zeitschrift des Preußischen Statistischen Landesamts* 59 (1919): pp. 323–84.

Ramhorst, Friedrich. *Die Entstehung der Deutschen Rentenbank [Veröffentlichungen des Reichsverbandes der Deutschen Industrie, Heft 20]*. Berlin, March 1924.

Rauecker, Bruno. "Die Fachvereine der deutschen Schriftsteller," in Ludwig Sinzheimer, ed. *Die geistigen Arbeiter. Erster Teil. Freies Schriftstellertum und Literaturverlag [Schriften des Vereins für Sozialpolitik, Bd. 152]*. München & Leipzig, 1922. Pp. 157–98.

Reichert, Jakob. *Rettung aus der Valutanot*. Berlin, 1919.

Reichsarchiv. *Der Weltkrieg 1914–1918. Kriegsrüstung und Kriegswirtschaft. Bd. 1: Die militärische, wirtschaftliche und finanzielle Rüstung*

Deutschlands von der Reichsgründung bis zum Ausbruch des Weltkrieges. Berlin, 1930.

Rönitz, Ulrich, ed. *Chronik des Zentralverbandes Deutscher Haus- und Grundbesitzvereine e.V. 1879–1927*. Berlin, 1929.

Schmalenbach, Eugen. *Dynamische Bilanzlehre*. 3rd. ed. Leipzig, 1925.

Schmalenbach, Eugen, and Willi Prion. *Zwei Vorträge über Scheingewinne: Die steuerliche Behandlung der Scheingewinne. Die Finanzpolitik der Unternehmung*. Jena, 1922.

Schmidt, Fritz. *Bilanzwert, Bilanzgewinn und Bilanzumwertung*. Berlin, 1924.

————. *Die Wiederbeschaffungspreise des Umsatztages in Kalkulation und Volkswirtschaft*. Berlin, 1923.

Schoenthal, Justus. *Papiermark, Rentenmark, Reichsmark. Ein Beitrag zur jüngsten Entwicklungsgeschichte der deutschen Währung*. Leipzig, 1925.

————. *Rentenbank und Rentenmark*. Berlin, 1924.

Scholl, Hermann. "Die Lage der deutschen Ärzte," in *Süddeutsche Monatshefte* (1923): pp. 68–74.

Schreiber, Georg. *Die Not der deutschen Wissenschaft und der geistigen Arbeiter. Geschehnisse und Gedanken zur Kulturpolitik des deutschen Reiches*. Leipzig, 1923.

Schulze, Ernst. *Not und Verschwendung. Untersuchungen über das deutsche Wirtschaftsschicksal*. Leipzig, 1923.

Schumpeter, Joseph. "Sozialistische Möglichkeiten von Heute," in *Archiv für Sozialwissenschaft und Sozialpolitik* 48 (1920/21): pp. 306–60.

————. "Das Sozialprodukt und die Rechenpfennige," in *Archiv für Sozialwissenschaft und Sozialpolitik* 44 (1917/ 1918): pp. 627–715.

Simon, Erich. "Der Haushalt eines höheren Beamten," in *Jahrbücher für Nationalökonomie und Statistik* 119, Bd. 64 (1922): pp. 425–32.

Sinzheimer, Ludwig, ed.. *Die geistigen Arbeiter. Erster Teil. Freies Schriftstellertum und Literaturverlag [Schriften des Vereins für Sozialpolitik, Bd. 152]*. München & Leipzig, 1922.

Skalweit, August. *Die deutsche Kriegsernährungswirtschaft*. Stuttgart, 1927.

Sontag, Ernst. *Hypothekengläubiger und Anleihebesitzer im Kampf um ihr Recht. Eine Kritik des Entwurfs eines Gesetzes über die Aufwertung von Hypotheken und anderen privatrechtlichen Ansprüchen sowie des Entwurfs eines Gesetzes über die Ablösung öffentlicher Anleihen*. Berlin, 1925.

Statistisches Reichsamt. *Deutschlands Wirtschaftslage unter den Nachwirkungen des Weltkrieges*. Berlin, 1923.

Strauss, Willi. *Die Konzentrationsbewegung im deutschen Bankgewerbe. Ein Beitrag zur Organisationsentwicklung der Wirtschaft unter dem Einfluß der Konzentration des Kapitals. Mit be-*

sonerer Berücksichtigung der Nachkriegszeit. Berlin & Leipzig, 1928.

Süskind, W. E. "Raymund." *Neue Rundschau* I (1927): pp. 369–88.

Troeltsch, Ernst. *Spektator-Briefe. Aufsätze über die deutsche Revolution und die Weltpolitik 1918/1922.* Tübingen, 1924.

Tross, Arnold. *Der Aufbau der eisenerzeugenden und eisenverarbeitenden Industrie-Konzerne Deutschlands.* Berlin, 1923.

Tyszka, Karl von. "Die Veränderungen in der Lebenshaltung städtischer Familien im Kriege," in *Archiv für Sozialwissenschaft und Sozialpolitik* 43 (1917): pp. 841–76.

Ufermann, Paul. *Könige der Inflation.* Berlin, 1924.

Ufermann, Paul, and Otto Hüglin. *Stinnes und seine Konzerne.* Berlin, 1924.

Verein für Sozialpolitik. *Die Zukunft der Sozialpolitik. Die Not der geistigen Arbeiter. Jubiläumstagung des Vereins für Sozialpolitik in Eisenach 1922* [*Schriften des Vereins für Sozialpolitik, Bd. 163*]. *Munich & Leipzig, 1923.*

Williams, John M. "German Foreign Trade and the Reparations Payments," in *Quarterly Journal of Economics* 36 (1922): pp. 482–503.

Zeitlin, Leon. "Finanzpolitik und Schriftstellerfragen," in Ludwig Sinzheimer, ed. *Die geistigen Arbeiter. Erster Teil. Freies Schriftstellertum und Literaturverlag* [*Schriften des Vereins für Sozialpolitik, Bd. 152*]. Munich & Leipzig, 1922. Pp. 367–84.

Zehn Jahre deutsche Geschichte 1918–1928. Berlin, 1928.

Memoirs, Biographies, Diaries, Collections of Letters

Barlach, Ernst. *Briefe 1888–1938.* 2 vols. Munich, 1968–1969.

Bernhard, Henry, ed. *Gustav Stresemann. Vermächtnis.* 3 vols. Berlin, 1932.

Bonn, Moritz J. *So Macht Man Geschichte. Bilanz Eines Lebens.* Munich, 1953.

Brüning, Heinrich. *Briefe und Gespräche 1934–1945.* Stuttgart, 1974.

D'Abernon, Viscount. *Ambassador of Peace: Pages from the Diary of Viscount D'Abernon, Berlin 1920–1926.* 3 vols. London, 1929–1930.

Döblin, Alfred. *Ein Kerl muß eine Meinung haben.* Freiburg i.B., 1976.

Fürstenberg, Hans. *Erinnerungen. Mein Weg als Bankier und Carl Fürstenbergs Altersjahre.* Wiesbaden, 1965.

Groener, Wilhelm. *Lebenserinnerungen. Jugend, Generalstab, Weltkrieg.* edited by Friedrich Freiherr Hiller von Gaetringen. Göttingen, 1957.

Hachenburg, Max. *Lebenserinnerung eines Rechtsanwalts und Briefe aus der Emigration* [*Veröf-*

fentlichungen des Stadtarchivs Mannheim, Bd. 5]. Mannheim, 1978.

Hahn, Albert. *Fünfzig Jahre zwischen Inflation und Deflation.* Tübingen, 1963.

Hölz, Max. *Vom 'Weißen Kreuz' zur Roten Fahne. Jugend-, Kampf- und Zuchthauserlebnisse.* Berlin, 1929.

Lange, Friedrich C. A. *Groß=Berliner Tagebuch 1920–1933.* Berlin, 1951.

Luther, Hans. *Politiker ohne Partei. Erinnerungen.* Stuttgart, 1960.

Merton, Richard. *Erinnernswertes aus meinem Leben, das über das Persönliche hinausgeht.* Frankfurt a.M., 1955.

Rathenau, Walther. *Gesammelte Reden.* Berlin, 1924.

———. *Politische Briefe.* Dresden, 1929.

Schacht, Hjalmar. *My First Seventy-six Years. The Autobiography of Hjalmar Schacht.* London, 1955.

———. *The Stabilization of the Mark.* London, 1927.

Scheidemann, Philipp. *Memoiren eines Sozialdemokraten.* 2 vols. Dresden, 1928.

Schiffer, Eugen. *Ein Leben für den Liberalismus.* Berlin, 1951.

Schröder, Ernst. *Otto Wiedfeldt. Eine Biographie* [*Beiträge zur Geschichte von Stadt und Stift Essen, 80*]. Essen, 1964.

Schulze, Hagen. *Otto Braun oder Preußens demokratische Sendung.* Frankfurt a.M., 1977.

Schwabe, Klaus, and Rolf Richardt, eds. *Gerhard Ritter. Ein politischer Historiker in seinen Briefen.* Boppard am Rhein, 1984.

Singer, Kurt, ed. *G. F. Knapp/F. Bendixen, Zur Staatlichen Theorie des Geldes. Ein Briefwechsel (1905–1920).* Tübingen, 1958.

Skidelsky, Robert. *John Maynard Keynes. Hopes Betrayed 1883–1920.* London, 1983.

Staudinger, Hans. *Wirtschaftspolitik im Weimarer Staat. Lebenserinnerungen eines politischen Beamten im Reich und in Preußen 1899 bis 1934.* Ed. by Hagen Schulze. Berlin, 1982.

Stinnes, Edmund. *A Genius in Chaotic Times. Edmund H. Stinnes on his father, Hugo Stinnes (1870–1924).* Bern, n.d.

Stockhausen, Max von. *Sechs Jahre Reichskanzlei. Erinnerungen und Tagebuchnotizen 1922–1927.* Ed. by Walter Görlitz. Bonn, 1954.

Zeiler, Alois. *Meine Mitarbeit (Rechts= und Wirtschaftsfragen).* Braunschweig, n.d.

Zeiler, Bernhard and Ellen Otten. *Kurt Wolff. Briefwechsel eines Verlegers 1911–1963.* Frankfurt a.M., 1967.

Secondary Literature

Abelshauser, Werner. "Inflation und Stabilisierung. Zum Problem ihrer makroökonomischen Auswirkungen auf die Rekonstruktion der deutschen Wirtschaft nach dem Ersten Weltkrieg," in Otto Büsch and Gerald D. Feldman, eds. *Historische Prozesse.* Berlin, 1978. Pp. 161–74.

————. "Verelendung der Handarbeiter? Zur sozialen Lage der deutschen Arbeiter in der grossen Inflation der frühen zwanziger Jahre," in Hans Mommsen and Winfried Schulze, eds. *Vom Elend der Handarbeit. Probleme historischer Unterschichtenforschung.* Stuttgart, 1981. Pp. 445–76.

————. ed. *Die Weimarer Republik als Wohlfahrtsstaat. Zum Verhältnis von Wirtschafts- und Sozialpolitik in der Industriegesellschaft* [*Vierteljahrsschrift für Sozial- und Wirtschaftsgeschichte*, Beiheft 81]. Stuttgart, 1987.

Abelshauser, Werner, and Dietmar Petzina. "Krise und Rekonstruktion. Zur Interpretation der gesamtwirtschaftlichen Entwicklung Deutschlands im 20. Jahrhundert," in W. Abelshauser and Dietmar Petzina, eds. *Deutsche Wirtschaftsgeschichte im Industriezeitalter. Konjunktur, Krise, Wachstum.* Königstein/Ts., 1981). Pp. 47–93.

Albertin, Lothar. "Die Verantwortung der liberalen Parteien für das Scheitern der Großen Koalition im Herbst 1921," in *Historische Zeitschrift*, 205 (1967): pp. 566–627.

Aldcroft, Derek H. *From Versailles to Wall Street 1919–1929.* Berkeley & Los Angeles, 1977.

Ambrosius, Gerold. "Öffentliche Unternehmen in der Inflation 1918 bis 1923. Der Konflikt zwischen der betrieblichen Finanzwirtschaft der städtischen Werke und den fiskalpolitischen Ansprüchen der Kommunen," in Feldman et al., eds. *The Adaptation to Inflation.* Berlin and New York, 1986. Pp. 357–91.

Ambrosius, Gerold, and William H. Hubbard. *A Social and Economic History of Twentieth-Century Europe.* Cambridge, Mass., 1989.

Angress, Werner T. "Das deutsche Militär und die Juden im Ersten Weltkrieg," in *Militärgeschichtliche Mitteilungen* 19 (1976): pp. 77–146.

————. *Stillborn Revolution: The Communist Bid for Power in Germany, 1921–1923.* Princeton, 1963.

Arns, Günter. "Die Krise des Weimarer Parlamentarismus im Frühherbst 1923," in *Der Staat. Zeitschrift für Staatslehre, Öffentliches Recht und Verfassungsgeschichte* 8 (1969/2): pp. 181–216.

Artaud, Denise. *La Question des dettes interalliées et la reconstruction de l'Europe 1917–1929.* Lille & Paris, 1978.

Aubin H. and W. Zorn. *Handbuch der deutschen Wirtschafts- und Sozialgeschichte.* 2 vols. Stuttgart, 1971, 1976.

Bähr, Johannes. *Staatliche Schlichtung in der Weimarer Republik. Tarifpolitik, Korporatismus und industrieller Konflikt zwischen Inflation und Deflation 1919–1932.* Berlin, 1989.

Balderston, Theo. "Links between Inflation and Depression: German Capital and Labour Markets, 1924–1931," in Gerald D. Feldman and Elisabeth Müller-Luckner, eds. *Die Nachwirkungen der Inflation.* Pp. 156–85.

————. "The Origins of Economic Instability in Germany 1924–1930. Market Forces versus Economic Policy," in *Vierteljahrsschrift für Sozial- und Wirtschaftsgeschichte* 69 (1982): pp. 488–514.

————. "War Finance and Inflation in Britain and Germany, 1914–1918," in *Economic History Review* 42 (1989): pp. 222–44.

Barclay, David E. "The Insider as Outsider: Rudolf Wissell's Critique of Social Democratic Economic Policies 1919 to 1920," in Gerald D. Feldman et al., eds. *The Adaptation to Inflation.* Berlin and New York, 1986. Pp. 451–71.

————. "A Prussian Socialism? Wichard von Moellendorff and the Dilemmas of Economic Planning in Germany 1918–1919," in *Central European History* 11 (1978): pp. 50–82.

————. *Rudolf Wissell als Sozialpolitiker 1890–1933* [*Einzelveröffentlichungen der historischen Kommission zu Berlin*, Bd. 44]. Berlin, 1984.

Bariety, Jacques. *Le Relations Franco-Allemands après la Première Guerre Mondiale. l0 Nov. 1918–10. Jan. 1925: De l'Exécution a la négociation.* Paris, 1977.

Bellon, Bernard P. *Mercedes in Peace and War. German Automobile Workers, 1903–1945.* New York, 1990.

Benjamin, Walter. *Einbahnstraße.* Frankfurt a.M., 1969.

Bessel, Richard. "Eine nicht allzu große Benunruhigung des Arbeitsmarktes. Frauenarbeit und Demobilmachung nach dem Ersten Weltkrieg," in *Geschichte und Gesellschaft* 9 (1983): pp. 211–29.

————. "The Great War in German Memory: The Soldiers of the First World War, Demobilization, and Weimar Political Culture," in *German History. The Journal of the German History Society* 6 (1988): pp. 20–34.

————. "Unemployment and Demobilisation in Germany After the First World War," in Richard J. Evans and Dick Geary. *The German Unemployed. Experiences and Consequences of Mass Unemployment from the Weimar Republic to the Third Reich.* New York, 1987. Pp. 23–43.

Bieber, Hans-Joachim. "Die Entwicklung der Arbeitsbeziehungen auf den Hamburger Großwerften zwischen Hilfsdienstgesetz und Betriebsrätegesetz (1916–1920)," in Gunther Mai, ed. *Arbeiterschaft 1914–1918 in Deutschland.* Düsseldorf, 1985. Pp. 77–153.

————. *Gewerkschaften in Krieg und Revolution. Arbeiterbewegung, Industrie, Staat und Militär in Deutschland 1914–1920.* 2 vols. Hamburg, 1981.

Blackbourn, David. "The *Mittelstand* in German Society and Politics 1871–1914," in *Social History* 2 (1977): pp. 409–33.

Blackbourn, David, and Geoff Eley. *The Peculiarities of German History. Bourgeois Society and Politics in Nineteenth Century Germany.* Oxford and New York, 1984.

Blaich, Fritz. "Der '30-Millionen-Fonds—Die Auseinandersetzung um eine soziale Ruhrentschädigung 1925–1927," in *Blätter für deutsche Landesgeschichte* 113 (1977): pp. 450–76.

———. *Der Schwarze Freitag. Inflation und Wirtschaftskrise.* Munich, 1985.

———. *Die Wirtschaftskrise 1925/26 und die Reichsregierung. Von der Erwerbslosenfürsorge zur Konjunkturpolitik.* Kallmünz Opf., 1977.

Böhm, Ekkehard. *Anwalt des Handels- und Gewerbefreiheit. Beiträge zur Geschichte der Handelskammer Hamburg.* Hamburg, 1981.

Boldt, Hans. "Deutscher Konstitutionalismus und Bismarckreich," in Michael Stürmer, ed. *Das kaiserliche Deutschland. Politik und Gesellschaft 1870–1918.* Düsseldorf, 1970. Pp. 119–42.

Boll, Friedhelm. "Spontaneität der Basis und politische Funktion des Streiks 1914 bis 1918. Das Beispiel Braunschweig," in *Archiv für Sozialgeschichte* 17 (1977): pp. 337–66.

Böll, Heinrich. "The Specter That Still Haunts Germany. Inflation." *New York Times Magazine.* May 2, 1976.

Borchardt, Knut. "Das Gewicht der Inflationsangst in den wirtschaftspolitischen Entscheidungsprozessen während der Weltwirtschaftskrise," in Gerald D. Feldman and Elisabeth Müller-Luckner, eds. *Die Nachwirkungen der Inflation.* Munich, 1985. Pp. 233–60.

———. "'Das hat historische Gründe.' Zu den Determinanten der Struktur des deutschen Kreditwesens unter besonderer Berücksichtigung der Rolle der Sparkassen," in Hansjoachim Henning, Dieter Lindenlaub, and Eckhard Wandel, eds. *Wirtschafts- und sozialgeschichtliche Forschungen und Probleme.* St. Katharinen, 1987. Pp. 270–87.

———. "Strukturwirkungen des Inflationsprozesses [Schriftenreihe des Ifo-Instituts für Wirtschaftsforschung, 50]. Berlin & Munich, 1970.

———. *Wachstum, Krisen, Handlungsspielräume der Wirtschaftspolitik. Studien zur Wirtschaftsgeschichte des 19. und 20. Jahrhunderts.* Göttingen, 1982.

———. "Währung und Wirtschaft," in Deutsche Bundesbank. *Währung und Wirtschaft in Deutschland 1876–1975.* Frankfurt a.M., 1976.

Born, Karl Erich. "The Deutsche Bank during Germany's Great Inflation after the First World War," in *Studies on Economic and Monetary Problems and Banking History*, No. 17 (Frankfurt, 1979).

———. *International Banking in the 19th and 20th Centuries.* New York, 1983.

Breitman, Richard. *German Socialism and Weimar Democracy.* Chapel Hill, 1981.

Bresciani-Turroni, Constantino. *The Economics of Inflation. A Study of Currency Depreciation in Post-War Germany, 1914–1923.* London, 1937; reprinted 1968; original Italian 1931.

———. "The Movement of Wages in Germany During the Depreciation of the Mark and After Stabilization," in *Journal of the Royal Statistical Society* New Series, 92 New Series (1929): pp. 374–427.

Bronfenbrenner, M. "Inflation and Deflation," in *International Encyclopedia of the Social Sciences.* Vol. 7. New York, 1968. Pp. 289–301.

Bry, Gerhard. *Wages in Germany, 1871–1945.* Princeton, 1960.

Burchardt, Lothar. "Zwischen Kriegsgewinnen und Kriegskosten: Krupp im Ersten Weltkrieg," in *Zeitschrift für Unternehmensgeschichte.* 1987.

Burghardt, Anton. *Soziologie des Geldes und der Inflation.* Graz, 1977.

Büsch, Otto. *Geschichte der Berliner Kommunalwirtschaft in der Weimarer Epoche.* Berlin, 1960.

Büsch, Otto, and Gerald D. Feldman, eds. *Historische Prozesse der Deutschen Inflation 1914 bis 1924. Ein Tagungsbericht [Einzelveröffentlichungen der historischen Kommission zu Berlin, Bd. 21].* Berlin, 1978.

Büttner, Ursula. *Politische Gerechtigkeit und Sozialer Geist. Hamburg zur Zeit der Weimarer Republik.* Hamburg, 1985.

Cagan, Phillip. "The Monetary Dynamics of Hyperinflation," in Milton Friedman, ed. *Studies in the Quantity Theory of Money.* Chicago, 1956. Pp. 25–117.

Canetti, Elias. *Crowds and Power.* Translated by Carol Stewart. New York, 1963.

Carroll, John M. "The Paris Bankers' Conference of 1922 and America's Design for a Peaceful Europe," in *International Review of History and Political Science* 10 (Aug. 1973): pp. 39–47.

Childers, Thomas C. "Anti-System Politics in the Era of Stabilization," in Gerald D. Feldman and Elisabeth Müller-Luckner, eds. *Die Nachwirkungen der Inflation.* Munich, 1985. Pp. 1–20.

———. "Inflation, Stabilization and Political Realignment in Germany," in Gerald D. Feldman et al. eds. *The German Inflation. A Preliminary Balance,* Berlin and New York, 1982. Pp. 409–31.

———. *The Nazi Voter. The Social Foundations of Fascism in Germany, 1919–1933.* Chapel Hill, 1983.

———. "The Social Language of Politics in Germany: The Sociology of Political Discourse in the Weimar Republic," in *American Historical Review* 95 (April 1990): pp. 331–58.

Costigliola, Frank. *Awkward Dominion. American Political, Economic, and Cultural Relations with Europe, 1919–1933*. Ithaca and London, 1984.

———. "The United States and the Reconstruction of Germany in the 1920s," in *Business History Review* 50 (Winter 1976): pp. 477–502.

Coyner, Sandra J. "Class Consciousness and Consumption: The New Middle Class in the Weimar Republic," in *Journal of Social History* 10 (1977): pp. 310–31.

Craig, Gordon. *Germany 1866–1945*. New York, 1978.

Czada, Peter. *Die Berliner Elektroindustrie in der Weimarer Zeit. Eine regionalstatistisch-wirtschaftshistorische Untersuchung*. Berlin, 1969.

———. "Große Inflation und Wirtschaftswachstum," in Hans Mommsen et al., eds. *Industrielles System und Politische Entwicklung*. Düsseldorf, 1974. Pp. 386–95.

———. "Ursachen und Folgen der großen Inflation," in Harald Winkel, ed. *"Finanz- und Wirtschaftspolitische Fragen der Zwischenkriegszeit* [*Schriften des Vereins für Sozialpolitik*, N.F.. 73]. Berlin, 1973. Pp. 11–43.

Daniel, Ute. *Arbeiterfrauen in der Kriegsgesellschaft: Beruf, Familie und Politik im Ersten Weltkrieg*. Göttingen, 1989.

———. "Fiktionen, Friktionen und Fakten—Frauenlohnarbeit im Ersten Weltkrieg," in Gunther Mai, ed. *Arbeiterschaft 1914–1918 in Deutschland*. Düsseldorf, 1985. Pp. 277–323.

Dawson, John P. "Effects of Inflation on Private Law Contracts: Germany, 1914–1924," *Michigan Law Review* 33 (Dec. 1934): pp. 171–238.

de Cecco, Marcello. "The Vicious/Virtuous Circle Debate in the Twenties and the Seventies." European University Institute Working Paper No. 24. Badia Fiesolana, San Domenico, January 1983.

Deak, Istvan. *Weimar's Left-Wing Intellectuals. Die Weltbühne. A Political History of the Weltbühne and its Circle*. Berkeley & Los Angeles, 1968.

Deuerlein, Ernst, ed. *Der Hitler-Putsch. Bayerische Dokumente zum 8./9. November 1923*. Stuttgart, 1962.

Desai, Ashok V. *Real Wages in Germany 1871–1913*. Oxford, 1968.

Deutsche Bundesbank. *Währung und Wirtschaft in Deutschland 1876–1975*. Frankfurt a.M., 1976.

Diehl, James M. *Paramilitary Politics in Weimar Germany*. Bloomington, 1977.

Dornbusch, Rudiger. "Lessons from the German Inflation Experience of the 1920s," in Rudiger Dornbusch et al., eds. *Macroeconomics and Finance: Essays in Honor of Franco Modigliani*. Cambridge, Mass., 1987. Pp. 337–66.

Ebeling, Richard M. *Money, Method, and the Mar-ket Process. Essays by Ludwig von Mises*. Norwell, Mass., 1990.

Ehlert, Hans Gotthard. *Die wirtschaftliche Zentralbehörde des Deutschen Reiches 1914–1918. Das Problem der "Gemeinwirtschaft" in Krieg und Frieden*. Wiesbaden, 1982.

Eichengreen, Barry. *Golden Fetters: The Gold Standard and the Great Depression, 1919–1939*. Oxford, 1991.

Ellis, Howard, S. *German Monetary Theory 1905–1933*. Cambridge, Mass., 1937.

Epstein, Klaus. *Matthias Erzberger and the Dilemma of German Democracy*. Princeton, 1959.

Erdmann, Karl-Dietrich. *Adenauer in der Rheinlandpolitik nach dem Ersten Weltkrieg*. Stuttgart, 1966.

Erger, Johannes. *Der Kapp-Lüttwitz Putsch. Ein Beitrag zur deutschen Innenpolitik 1919/20*. Düsseldorf, 1967.

Eyck, Erich. *A History of the Weimar Republic*. 2 vols. Cambridge, 1962.

Fabian, Walter. *Ein Stück Geschichte*. Löbau, 1930.

Falter, J., Th. Lindenberger, and S. Schumann. *Wahlen und Abstimmungen in der Weimarer Republik*. Munich, 1986.

Favez, Jean-Claude. *Le Reich devant l'occupation Franco-Belge de la Ruhr en 1923*. Geneva, 1969.

Feldman, Gerald D. "Arbeitskonflikte im Ruhrbergbau 1919–1922. Zur Politik von Zechenverband und Gewerkschaften in der Überschichtenfrage," in *Vierteljahrshefte für Zeitgeschichte* 28 (April 1980): pp. 168–223.

———. *Armee, Industrie und Arbeiterschaft in Deutschland 1914–1918*. Bonn, 1985.

———. *Army, Industry and Labor in Germany, 1914–1918*. Princeton, 1966.

———. "Aspekte deutscher Industriepolitik am Ende der Weimarer Republik 1930–1932," in Karl Holl, ed. *Wirtschaftskrise und liberale Demokratie*. Göttingen, 1978. Pp. 103–21.

———. "Bayern und Sachsen in der Hyperinflation 1922/23" [*Schriften des historischen Kollegs*, Vorträge 6]. Munich, 1984. Also in *Historische Zeitschrift* 238 (1984): pp. 569–609.

———. "Big Business and the Kapp Putsch," in *Central European History* 4 (1971): pp. 91–130.

———. "Die Demobilmachung und die Sozialordnung der Zwischenkriegszeit in Europa," in *Geschichte und Gesellschaft* 9 (1983): pp. 156–177.

———. "Economic and Social Problems of the German Demobilization, 1918–1919," *Journal of Modern History* 47 (1975): pp. 1–47.

———. "The Fate of the Social Insurance System in the German Inflation, 1914–1923," in Gerald D. Feldman et al., eds. *The Adaptation to Inflation*. Berlin and New York, 1986. Pp. 432–47.

———. "Foreign Penetration of German Enterprises after the First World War: The Problem of Überfremdung," in Alice Teichova, Maurice Lévy-Leboyer, and Helga Nussbaum, eds. *Historical Studies in International Corporate Business.* Cambridge, 1989. Pp. 87–110.

———. "Die Freien Gewerkschaften und die Zentralarbeitsgemeinschaft," in Heinz Oskar Vetter, ed. *Vom Sozialistengesetz zur Mitbestimmung. Zum 100. Geburtstag von Hans Böckler.* Cologne, 1975. Pp. 229–52.

———. "Gegenwärtiger Forschungsstand und künftige Forschungsprobleme zur deutschen Inflation," in Otto Büsch and Gerald D. Feldman, eds. *Historische Prozesse. Berlin, 1978. Pp. 3–21.*

———. "German Business between War and Revolution: The Origins of the Stinnes–Legien Agreement," in Gerhard A. Ritter, ed. *Entstehung und Wandel der Modernen Gesellschaft. Festschrift für Hans Rosenberg.* Berlin, 1970. Pp. 312–41.

———. "The Historian and the German Inflation," in Nathan Schmukler & Edward Marcus, eds. *Inflation through the Ages.* New York, 1983. Pp. 386–99.

———. "Industrie und Wissenschaft in Deutschland," in Rudolf Vierhaus and Bernhard vom Brocke, eds. *Forschung im Spannungsfeld von Politik und Gesellschaft. Geschichte und Struktur der Kaiser-Wilhelm/Max-Planck-Gesellschaft.* Stuttgart, 1990. Pp. 657–72.

———. *Iron and Steel in the German Inflation, 1916–1923.* Princeton, 1977.

———. "The Large Firm in the German Industrial System: The M.A.N. 1900–1925," in Dirk Stegmann et al., eds. *Industrielle Gesellschaft und politisches System. Beiträge zur politischen Sozialgeschichte.* Düsseldorf, 1978. pp. 241–57.

———. "The Political and Social Foundations of Germany's Economic Mobilization," in *Armed Forces and Society* 3 (1976): pp. 121–45.

———. "The Political Economy of Germany's Relative Stabilization during the 1920/21 Depression," in Gerald D. Feldman et al., eds. *The German Inflation Reconsidered. A Preliminary Balance.* Berlin and New York, 1982. Pp. 180–206.

———. "The Politics of Stabilization in Weimar Germany," in *Tel-Aviver Jahrbuch für Deutsche Geschichte* 17 (1988): pp. 19–42.

———. "The Politics of *Wissenschaftspolitik* in Weimar Germany: A Prelude to the Dilemmas of Twentieth-Century Science Policy," in Charles S. Maier, ed. *Changing Boundaries of the Political. Essays on the Evolving Balance Between the State and Society, Public and Private in Europe.* Cambridge, 1987. Pp. 255–85.

———. "Politik, Banken und der Goldstandard in der Zwischenkriegszeit," in *Vom Goldstandard zum Multireservewährungsstandard. Neuntes nationales Symposium zur Bankgeschichte am 18. Oktober 1985 im Hause der Deutsche Bank AG, Frankfurt am Main. Bankhistorisches Archiv. Zeitschrift zur Bankgeschichte.* Beiheft 11. Frankfurt a.M., 1987. Pp. 11–20.

———. "The Private Support of Science in Germany, 1914–1933," in Rüdiger vom Bruch and Rainer A. Müller. *Formen außerstaatlicher Wissenschaftsförderung im 19. und 20. Jahrhundert. Deutschland im europäischen Vergleich* [*VSWG*, Beiheft 88]. Stuttgart, 1990. Pp. 87–111.

———. "Saxony, the Reich, and the Problem of Unemployment in the German Inflation," *Archiv für Sozialgeschichte* 27 (1987): pp. 102–44.

———. "Socio-Economic Structures in the Industrial Sector and Revolutionary Potentialities, 1917–1922," in Charles Bertrand, ed. *Revolutionary Situations in Europe 1917–1922: Germany, Italy, and Austria-Hungary.* Montreal, 1976. Pp. 159–69.

———. "Streiks in Deutschland 1914–1933: Probleme und Forschungsaufgaben," in Klaus Tenfelde and Heinrich Volkmann, eds. *Streik. Zur Geschichte des Arbeitskampfes in Deutschland während der Industrialisierung.* Munich, 1981. Pp. 271–286.

———. "Weimar from Inflation to Depression: Experiment or Gamble?," in Gerald D. Feldman and Elisabeth Müller-Luckner, eds. *Die Nachwirkungen der deutschen Inflation.* Munich, 1985. Pp. 385–401.

———. "The Weimar Republic: A Problem in Modernization?," in *Archiv für Sozialgeschichte* 26 (1986): pp. 1–26.

———. "Weimar Writers and the German Inflation," in Gisela Brude-Firnau and Karin J. MacHardy, eds. *Fact and Fiction. German History and Literature 1848–1924.* Tübingen, 1990. Pp. 173–83.

———. "Welcome to Germany? The *Fremdenplage* in the Weimar Inflation," in Wilhelm Treue, ed. *Geschichte als Aufgabe. Festschrift für Otto Büsch zu seinem 60. Geburtstag.* Berlin, 1988. pp. 629–49.

Feldman, Gerald D., Carl-Ludwig Holtfrerich, Gerhard A. Ritter, Peter-Christian Witt, eds. *The Adaptation to Inflation* [*Beiträge zu Inflation und Wiederaufbau in Deutschland und Europa 1914–1924, Bd. 8*]. Berlin and New York, 1986.

———. *The Consequences of Inflation* [*Einzelveröffentlichungen der Historischen Kommission zu Berlin, 67. Beiträge zu Inflation und Wiederaufbau in Deutschland und Europa 1914–1924*]. Berlin, 1989.

———. *The Experience of Inflation. International and Comparative Studies* [*Beiträge zu Inflation und Wiederaufbau in Deutschland und Europa 1914–1924, Bd. 2*]. Berlin and New York, 1984.

———. *The German Inflation. A Preliminary Balance* [*Beiträge zu Inflation und Wiederaufbau in Deutschland und Europe 1914–1924, Bd. 1*]. Berlin and New York, 1982.

Feldman, Gerald D. and Heidrun Homburg. *Industrie und Inflation. Studien und Dokumente zur Politik der deutschen Unternehmer 1916–1923.* Hamburg, 1977.

Feldman, Gerald D., Eberhard Kolb, and Reinhard Rürup. "Die Massenbewegungen der Arbeiterschaft in Deutschland am Ende des Ersten Weltkrieges (1917–1920)," in *Politische Vierteljahrsschrift* 13 (1972): pp. 84–105.

Feldman, Gerald D. and Elisabeth Müller-Luckner, eds. *Die Nachwirkungen der Inflation auf die deutsche Geschichte 1924–1933.* Munich, 1985.

Feldman, Gerald D. and Merith Niehuss. "Haushaltsrechnungen aus der Inflationszeit. Materialien und Interpretationen," in Feldman et al. *The Adaptation to Inflation.* Berlin and New York, 1986. Pp. 265–77.

Feldman, Gerald D., and Ulrich Nocken. "Trade Associations and Economic Power: Interest Group Development in the German Iron and Steel and Machine Building Industries," in *Business History Review* 49 (1975): pp. 413–445.

Feldman, Gerald D., and Irmgard Steinisch. *Industrie und Gewerkschaften 1918–1924. Die überforderte Zentralarbeitsgemeinschaft.* Stuttgart, 1985.

————. "Notwendigkeit und Grenzen sozialstaatlicher Intervention: Eine vergleichende Fallstudie des Ruhreisenstreits in Deutschland und des Generalstreiks in England," in *Archiv für Sozialgeschichte* 20 (1980): 57–118.

————. "The Origins of the Stinnes–Legien Agreement. A Documentation," in *Internationale Wissenschaftliche Korrespondenz zur Geschichte der deutschen Arbeiterbewegung* 19/20 (1973): pp. 45–104.

————. "Die Weimarer Republik zwischen Sozial- und Wirtschaftsstaat. Die Entscheidung gegen den Achtstundentag," in *Archiv für Sozialgeschichte* 18 (1978): pp. 353–439.

Felix, David. "Reparations Reconsidered with a Vengeance," in *Central European History* 4 (1971): pp. 171–79.

Fergusson, Adam. *When Money Dies: The Nightmare of the Weimar Collapse.* London, 1975.

Fink, Carol. *The Genoa Conference. European Diplomacy, 1921–1922.* Chapel Hill, 1984.

Fischer, Wolfram, and Peter Czada. "Wandlungen in der deutschen Industriestruktur im 20. Jahrhundert," in Gerhard A. Ritter, ed. *Entstehung und Wandel der modernen Gesellschaft. Festschrift für Hans Rosenberg zum 65. Geburtstag.* Berlin, 1970. Pp. 116–65.

Flemming, Jens. *Landwirtschaftliche Interessen und Demokratie. Ländliche Gesellschaft, Agrarverbände und Staat 1890–1925.* Bonn, 1978.

Flemming, Jens and Peter-Christian Witt. "Probleme der Sozialstatistik im deutschen Kaiserreich," an introduction to the reprint of the 1909 Reich Statistisches Amt's *Erhebungen von Wirtschaftsrechnungen minderbemittelter Familien im deutschen Reich* and the Deutsche Metallarbeiter-Verbandes's *320 Haushaltsrechnungen von Metallarbeitern.* Berlin & Bonn, 1981.

Flora, Peter, and Arnold J. Heidenheimer, eds. *The Development of Welfare States in Europe and America.* New Brunswick & London, 1981.

Försterling, Manfred. "Die Hamburgische Bank von 1923 Aktiengesellschaft," in *Hamburger Wirtschafts-Chronik* 3 (1965): pp. 1–124.

Fraenkel, Ernst. *Zur Soziologie der Klassenjustiz.* Berlin, 1927.

Frenkel, Jacob A. "The Forward Exchange Rate, Expectations and the Demand for Money: The German Hyperinflation," in *American Economic Review* 67 (1977): pp. 653–70.

————. "Further Evidence on Expectations and the Demand for Money during the German Hyperinflation," in *Journal of Monetary Economics* 5 (1979): pp. 97–104.

Fricke, Dieter, et al., eds. *Lexikon zur Parteiengeschichte. Die bürgerlichen und kleinbürgerlichen Parteien und Verbände in Deutschland (1789–1945).* 4 vols. Leipzig, 1983ff.

Friedrich, Otto. *Before the Deluge. A Portrait of Berlin in the 1920's.* New York & London, 1972.

Fritzsche, Peter. *Rehearsals for Fascism. Populism and Political Mobilization in Weimar Germany.* New York & Oxford, 1990.

Führer, Karl Christian. *Arbeitslosigkeit und die Entstehung der Arbeitslosenversicherung in Deutschland 1902–1927* [*Einzelveröffentlichungen der historischen Kommission zu Berlin, 73. Beiträge zu Inflation und Wiederaufbau in Deutschland und Europa 1914–1924*]. Berlin, 1990.

————. "Für das Wirtschaftsleben 'mehr oder weniger wertloser Personen.' Zur Lage von Invaliden- und Kleinrentnern in den Inflationsjahren 1918–1924," in *Archiv für Sozialgeschichte* 30 (1990): pp. 144–80.

Geary, Richard. "Unemployment and Working-Class Solidarity: The German Experience 1929–33," in Richard J. Evans and Dick Geary, eds. *The German Unemployed. Experiences and Consequences of Mass Unemployment from the Weimar Republic to the Third Reich.* New York, 1987. Pp. 261–80.

Geiger, Theodor. *Die soziale Schichtung des deutschen Volkes. Soziographischer Versuch auf statistischer Grundlage.* Stuttgart, 1987; reprint of the 1932 original.

Gellately, Robert. *The Politics of Economic Despair. Shopkeepers and German Politics 1890–1914.* London & Beverly Hills, 1974.

Geyer, Martin H. *Die Reichsknappschaft. Versicherungsformen und Sozialpolitik im Bergbau 1900–1945.* Munich, 1987.

————. "Teuerungsprotest, Konsumentenpolitik und soziale Gerechtigkeit während der Inflation: München 1920–1923," in *Arichv für Sozialgeschichte* 30 (1990): pp. 181–216.

————. "Wohnungsnot und Wohnungszwangswirtschaft in München 1917 bis 1924," in Feldman et al., eds. *The Adaptation to Inflation.* Berlin and New York, 1986. Pp. 127–62.

Geyer, Michael. "Ein Vorbote des Wohlfahrtsstaates. Die Kriegsopferversorgung in Frankreich, Deutschland und Großbritannien nach dem Ersten Weltkrieg," in *Geschichte und Gesellschaft* 9 (1983): pp. 230–77.

Gilbert, Felix. *A European Past. Memoirs 1905–1945.* New York, 1988.

Gini, Corrado. "Wirkungen der extremen Formen der Inflation auf den Wirtschaftsorganismus," in *Weltwirtschaftliches Archiv*, N.F., 40 (1934): Bd. 2, pp. 399–436.

Gordon, Harold J., Jr. *Hitler and the Beer Hall Putsch.* Princeton, 1972.

Graham, Frank D. *Exchange, Prices, and Production in Hyper-Inflation Germany, 1920–1923.* Princeton, 1930.

Gregor, Ulrich, and Enno Patalas. *Geschichte des Films 1895–1939.* Hamburg, 1976.

Guttmann, William, & Patricia Meehan. *The Great Inflation. Germany 1919–1923.* Westmead, 1975.

Habedank, Heinz. *Die Reichsbank in der Weimarer Republik. Zur Rolle der Zentralbank in der Politik des deutschen Imperialismus.* East Berlin, 1981.

Hall, Robert E., ed. *Inflation. Causes and Effects.* Chicago & London, 1982.

Haller, Heinz. "Die Rolle der Staatsfinanzen für den Inflationsprozess," in Deutsche Bundesbank. *Währung und Wirtschaft in Deutschland.* Frankfurt a.M., 1976. Pp. 115–55.

Hallgarten, George W. F. *Hitler, Reichswehr und Industrie. Zur Geschichte der Jahre 1918–1933.* Frankfurt a.M., 1955.

Hamburger, Franz. *Lehrer zwischen Kaiser und Führer. Der Deutsche Philologenverband in der Weimarer Republik. Eine Untersuchung zur Sozialgeschichte der Lehrerorganisation.* Heidelberg, 1974.

Hansmeyer, Karl-Heinrich, ed. *Kommunale Finanzpolitik in der Weimarer Republik.* Stuttgart, 1973.

Hardach, Gerd. *The First World War 1914–1918.* Berkeley, 1977.

Hardach, Karl. "Zur zeitgenössischen Debatte der Nationalökonomen über die Ursachen der deutschen Nachkriegsinflation," in Hans Mommsen et al. *Industrielles System.* Düsseldorf, 1974. Pp. 368–75.

Haupt, Heinz-Gerhard. "Kleinhändler und Arbeiter in Bremen zwischen 1890 und 1914," in *Archiv für Sozialgeschichte* 22 (1982): pp. 95–132.

Hecker, Gerhard. *Walter Rathenau und sein Verhältnis zu Militär und Krieg.* Boppard am Rhein, 1983.

Heilman, Linda. "Industrial Unemployment in Germany: 1873–1913," in *Archiv für Sozialgeschichte* 27 (1987): pp. 25–50.

Henning, Friedrich-Wilhelm. "Finanzpolitische Vorstellungen und Maßnahmen Konrad Adenauers während seiner Kölner Zeit (1906–1933)," in Hugo Stehkämper, ed. *Konrad Adenauer. Oberbürgermeister von Köln. Festgabe der Stadt Köln zum 100. Geburtstag ihres Ehrenbürgers am 5. Januar 1976.* Köln, 1976. Pp. 405–31.

Hennock, Peter. "Public Provision for Old Age. Britain and Germany, 1880–1914," in *Archiv für Sozialgeschichte* 30 (1990): pp. 81–104.

Henschke, Alfred. *Klabund Chansons. Streit- und Leidgedichte.* Vienna, 1930.

Hertz-Eichenrode, Dieter. *Wirtschaftskrise und Arbeitsbeschaffung. Konjunkturpolitik 1925/26 und die Grundlagen der Krisenpolitik Brünings.* Frankfurt a.M. & New York, 1982.

Hesse, Friedrich. *Die deutsche Wirtschaftslage von 1914 bis 1923, Geldblähe und Wechsellagen.* Jena, 1938.

Heurkampf, Claudia. *Der Aufstieg der Ärtzte im 19. Jahrhundert. Vom gelehrten Stand zum professionellen Experten: Das Beispiel Preussens* [*Kritische Studien zur Geschichtswissenschaft,* Bd. 68]. Göttingen, 1985.

Hirsch, Fred, and John Goldthorpe, eds. *The Political Economy of Inflation.* London & Cambridge Mass., 1978.

Hirsch, Fred, and Peter Oppenheimer. "The Trial of Managed Money: Currency, Credit and Prices 1920–1970," in Carlo M. Cipolla, ed. *The Fontana Economic History of Europe. The Twentieth Century 2.* Glasgow, 1976. Pp. 603–97.

Hoffmann, Walther G. *Das Wachstum der deutschen Wirtschaft seit der Mitte des 19. Jahrhunderts.* Berlin, Heidelberg, New York, 1965.

Holborn, Hajo. "Diplomats and Diplomacy in the early Weimar Republic," in Gordon Craig and Felix Gilbert eds. *The Diplomats 1919–1939.* Princeton, 1953. Pp. 132–48.

————. *Kriegsschuld und Reparationen auf der Pariser Friedenskonferenz 1919.* Berlin, 1932.

Holtfrerich, Carl-Ludwig. "Amerikanischer Kapitalexport und Wiederaufbau der deutschen Wirtschaft 1919–1923," in *Vierteljahrsschrift für Sozial- und Wirtschaftsgeschichte* 64 (1977): pp. 497–529.

————. "Arbeitslosigkeit, Sozialabbau, Demokratieverlust. Ergebnis zu hoher Löhne in der Weimarer Republik?," in *Gewerkschaftliche Monatshefte* 11 (1983): pp. 714–22.

————. "Auswirkungen der Inflation auf die Struktur des deutschen Kreditgewerbes," in Gerald D. Feldman and Elisabeth Müller-Luckner, eds. *Die Nachwirkungen der Inflation.* Munich, 1985. Pp. 187–209.

————. "Deutscher Außenhandel und Goldzölle 1919–1923," in Gerald D. Feldman et al., eds.

The Adaptation to Inflation. Berlin and New York, 1986. Pp. 472–84.

―――. "Das Eigenkapital der Kreditinstitute als historisches und aktuelles Problem," in *Bankhistorisches Archiv. Zeitschrift für Bankengeschichte,* Beiheft 5 (1981): pp. 14–29.

―――. *The German Inflation 1914–1923.* Berlin and New York, 1986; German edition 1980.

―――. "Internationale Verteilungsfolgen der deutschen Inflation 1918–1923," in *Kyklos* 30 (1977): pp. 271–92.

―――. "Die konjunkturanregenden Wirkungen der deutschen Inflation auf die US-Wirtschaft in der Weltwirtschaftskrise 1920/21," in Gerald D. Feldman et al., eds. *The German Inflation. A Preliminary Balance.* Berlin and New York, 1982. Pp. 207–34.

―――. "The Modernisation of the Tax System in the First World War and the Great Inflation, 1914–1923," in Peter-Christian Witt, ed. *Wealth and Taxation in Central Europe. The History and Sociology of Public Finance.* Leamington Spa, 1987. Pp. 125–35.

―――. "Moneta e credito in Italia e Germania dal 1914 al 1923," in Peter Hertner and Giorgio Mori, eds. *La transizione dall'economia die guerra all'economia die pace in Italia e Germania dopo la Prima guerra mondiale.* Bologna, 1983. Pp. 665–692.

―――. "Political Factors in the German Inflation," in Nathan Schmuckler and Edward Marcus, eds. *Inflation through the Ages: Economic, Social, Psychological and Historical Aspects.* New York, 1983. Pp. 400–416.

―――. "Relations between Monetary Authorities and Governmental Institutions: The Case of Germany from the 19th Century to the Present," in Gianni Toniolo, ed. *Central Banks' Independence in Historical Perspective.* Berlin and New York, 1988. Pp. 105–59.

―――. "Zur Entwicklung der deutschen Bankenstruktur," in Deutscher Sparkassen- und Giroverband. *Standortbestimmung. Entwicklungslinien der deutschen Kreditwirtschaft.* Stuttgart, 1984. Pp. 13–42.

Homburg, Heidrun. "Die Neuordnung des Marktes nach der Inflation. Probleme und Widerstände am Beispiel der Zusammenschlußprojekte von AEG und Siemens 1924–1933 oder "Wer hat den längeren Atem?," in Gerald D. Feldman and Elisabeth Müller-Luckner, eds. *Die Nachwirkungen der Inflation.* Munich, 1985. Pp. 117–55.

Hubbard, William H. "The New Inflation History," in *Journal of Modern History* 62 (1990): pp. 552–69.

Huber, Ernst Rudolf. *Deutsche Verfassungsgeschichte seit 1789.* 7 vols. Stuttgart, 1957ff.

Hughes, Michael. "Economic Interest, Social Attitudes, and Creditor Ideology: Popular Responses to Inflation," in Feldman et al., eds. *The*

German Inflation. A Preliminary Balance. Berlin and New York, 1982. Pp. 385–408.

―――. *Paying for the German Inflation.* Chapel Hill and London, 1988.

Jacobson, Jon. "The Reparations Settlement of 1924," in Gerald D. Feldman et al., eds. *The Consequences of Inflation.* Berlin, 1989. Pp. 79–108.

―――. "Strategies of French Foreign Policy after World War I," in *Journal of Modern History* 55 (1983): pp. 78–95.

Jaksch, Hans Jürgen. "Ein einfaches ökonometrisches Modell für die deutschen Hyperinflation von 1923," in Gerald D. Feldman et al., eds. *The German Inflation Reconsidered. A Preliminary Balance.* Berlin and New York, 1982. Pp. 107–31.

―――. "Inflation und Reparationsforderungen in der frühen Weimarer Republik: Eine spieltheoretische Untersuchung," in Gerald D. Feldman et al., eds. *The Adaptation to Inflation.* Berlin and New York, 1986. Pp. 83–123.

James, Harold. "Did the Reichsbank Draw the Right Conclusions from the German Inflation?" in Gerald D. Feldman and Elisabeth Müller-Luckner, eds. *Die Nachwirkungen der Inflation.* Munich, 1985. Pp. 211–31.

―――. "Foreign Crises and Domestic Choices in Weimar Germany," in *Tel Aviver Jahrbuch für Deutsche Geschichte* 17 (1988): pp. 43–58.

―――. *A German Identity. 1770–1990.* New York, 1989.

―――. *The German Slump: Politics and Economics, 1924–1936.* Oxford, 1986.

―――. *The Reichsbank and Public Finance in Germany 1924–1933: A Study of the Politics of Economics during the Great Depression.* Frankfurt a.M., 1985.

―――. "Rudolf Hilferding and the Application of the Political Economy of the Second International," in *The Historical Journal* 24 (1981): pp. 847–69.

―――. "Die Währungs- und Wirtschaftsstabilisierung 1923/24 in internationaler Perspektive," in Werner Abelshauser, ed. *Die Weimarer Republik als Wohlfahrtsstaat.* Stuttgart, 1987. Pp. 63–79.

Jarausch, Konrad. "Die Not der geistigen Arbeiter. Akademiker in der Berufskrise 1918–1933," in Werner Abelshauser, ed. *Die Weimarer Republik als Wohlfahrtsstaat.* Stuttgart, 1987. Pp. 280–300.

―――. "Die Unfreien Professionen. Überlegungen zu den Wandlungsprozessen im deutschen Bildungsbürgertum 1900–1955," in Jürgen Kocka, ed. *Bürgertum im 19. Jahrhundert. Deutschland im europäischen Vergleich.* Vol. 2 München, 1988. Pp. 124–48.

―――. *The Unfree Professions. German Lawyers, Teachers and Engineers 1900–1950.* New York & Oxford, 1990.

Jones, Larry Eugene. "Democracy and Liberalism in the German Inflation: The Crisis of a Political Movement, 1918-1924," in Gerald D. Feldman et al., eds. *Consequences of Inflation*. Berlin, 1989. Pp. 3-44.

————. *German Liberalism and the Dissolution of the Weimar Party System 1918-1933*. Chapel Hill and London, 1988.

————. "In the Shadow of Stabilization: German Liberalism and the Legitimacy Crisis of the Weimar Party System," in Gerald D. Feldman and Elisabeth Müller-Luckner, eds. *Die Nachwirkungen der Inflation*. Munich, 1985. Pp. 21-41.

————. "Inflation, Revaluation, and the Crisis of Middle-Class Politics: A Study in the Dissolution of the German Party System 1923-1928," in *Central European History* 12 (1979): Pp. 143-68.

Jordan, William M. *Great Britain, France and the German Problem*. London, 1943.

Kaelble, Hartmut. *A Social History of Western Europe, 1880-1980*. Dublin, 1989.

Kaes, Anton, ed. *Manifeste und Dokumente zur deutschen Literatur 1918-1933*. Stuttgart, 1983.

————. "Die ökonomische Dimension der Literatur: Zum Strukturwandel der Institution Literatur in der Inflationszeit 1918-1923," in Gerald D. Feldman et al., eds. *Consequences of the Inflation*. Berlin, 1989. Pp. 307-30.

Kaiser, Angela. *Lord D'Abernon und die englische Deutschlandpolitik 1920-1926*. Frankfurt a.M., 1989.

Kater, Michael H. "Ärzte und Politik in Deutschland, 1848 bis 1945," in *Jahrbuch des Instituts für Geschichte der Medizin der Robert Bosch Stiftung*. Stuttgart, 1987. Pp. 34-48.

————. *Doctors Under Hitler*. Chapel Hill and London, 1989.

————. "Professionalization and Socialization of Physicians in Wilhelmine and Weimar Germany," in *Journal of Contemporary History* 20 (1985): pp. 677-701.

————. *Studentenschaft und Rechtsradikalismus in Deutschland 1918-1923*. Hamburg, 1975.

————. "The Work Student: A Socio-Economic Phenomenon of Early Weimar Germany," in *Journal of Contemporary History* 10 (1975): pp. 71-94.

Kent, Bruce. *The Spoils of War. The Politics, Economics, and Diplomacy of Reparations 1918-1932*. Oxford, 1989.

Kershaw, Ian, ed. *Weimar: Why did German Democracy Fail?* London, 1990.

Kindleberger, Charles P. "Collective Memory vs. Rational Expectations: Some Historical Puzzles in Macro-Economic Behavior," in Charles P. Kindleberger, ed. *Keynesianism vs. Monetarism and other Essays in Financial History*. London, 1985. Pp. 129-38.

————. "A Structural View of the German Infla-

tion," in Gerald D. Feldman et al., eds. *The Experience of Inflation*. Berlin and New York, 1984. Pp. 10-33.

Klass, Gerd von. *Hugo Stinnes*. Tübingen, 1958.

Klöter, Heidegret. *Der Anteil der Länder an der Wirtschaftspolitik der Weimarer Republik 1919-1933*. Bonn, 1967.

Kluge, Ulrich. *Soldatenräte und Revolution. Studien zur Militärpolitik in Deutschland 1918/19*. Göttingen, 1975.

Knudsen, Hans. "Theater" in Hans Herzfeld, ed. *Berlin und die Provinz Brandenburg im 19. und 20. Jahrhundert* Berlin, 1968.

Kocka, Jürgen. *Facing Total War. German Society 1914-1918*. Leamington Spa, 1984.

————, ed. *Bürger und Bürgerlichkeit im 19. Jahrhundert*. Göttingen, 1987.

————, ed. *Bürgertum im 19. Jahrhundert. Deutschland im europäischen Vergleich*. 3 vols. München, 1988.

————. *White Collar Workers in Germany and America, 1890-1940. A Social-Political History in International Perspective*. London & Beverly Hills, 1980.

Köhler, Henning. *Adenauer und die rheinische Republik. Der erste Anlauf 1918-1924*. Opladen, 1986.

Kolb, Eberhard. *Die Arbeiterräte in der deutschen Innenpolitik 1918-1919*. Düsseldorf, 1978.

————. *The Weimar Republic*. Winchester, Mass., 1988.

Kracauer, Siegfried. *Die Angestellten. Aus dem neuesten Deutschland*. Frankfurt, 1971.

————. *From Caligari to Hitler*. Princeton, 1947.

Krohn, Klaus-Dieter. "Geldtheorien in Deutschland während der Inflation 1914 bis 1924," in Gerald D. Feldman et al., eds. *The Adaptation to Inflation*. Berlin and New York, 1986. Pp. 3-45.

————. "Helfferich contra Hilferding. Konservative Geldpolitik und die sozialen Folgen der deutschen Inflation 1918-1923," in *Vierteljahrsschrift für Sozial- und Wirtschaftsgeschichte* 62 (1975): pp. 62-92.

————. *Stabilisierung und ökonomische Interessen. Die Finanzpolitik des deutschen Reiches 1923-1927*. Düsseldorf, 1974.

————. *Wirtschaftstheorien als politische Interessen. Die akademische Nationalökonomie in Deutschland 1918-1933*. Frankfurt and New York, 1981.

Kruedener, Baron Jürgen von, ed. *Economic Crisis and Political Collapse*. Oxford, 1990.

————. Die Entstehung des Inflationstraumas. Zur Sozialpsychologie der deutschen Hyperinflation 1922/23," in Feldman et al. *Consequences of Inflation*. Berlin, 1989. Pp. 213-86.

Krüger, Dieter. *Nationalökonomen im wilhelminischen Deutschland*. [Kritische Studien zur Geschichtswissenschaft, 58]. Göttingen, 1983.

Krüger, Peter. *Die Außenpolitik der Republik von Weimar*. Darmstadt, 1989.

————. Die Auswirkungen der Inflation auf die deutsche Außenpolitik," in Gerald D. Feldman and Elisabeth Müller-Luckner, eds. *Die Nachwirkungen der Inflation.* Munich, 1985. Pp. 297–313.

————. *Deutschland und die Reparationen 1918/19. Die Genesis des Reparationsproblems in Deutschland zwischen Waffenstillstand und Versailler Friedensschluß.* Stuttgart, 1973.

————. "Das Reparationsproblem der Weimarer Republik in fragwürdiger Sicht," in *Vierteljahrshefte für Zeitgeschichte* 29 (1981): pp. 21–47.

————. "Die Rolle der Banken und der Industrie in den deutschen reparationspolitischen Entscheidungen nach dem Ersten Weltkrieg," in Hans Mommsen et al., eds. *Industrielles System.* Düsseldorf, 1974. Pp. 568–82.

————. "Struktur, Organisation und Wirkungsmöglichkeiten der leitenden Beamten des auswärtigen Dienstes 1921–1933," in Schwabe, Klaus, ed. *Das Diplomatische Korps als Elite, 1871–1945.* Boppard am Rhein, 1985. Pp. 101–69.

Kühne, Rudolf. *Die Devisenzwangswirtschaft im Deutschen Reich während der Jahre 1916 bis 1926. Eine währungspolitische Reminiszenz.* Frankfurt a.M., 1970.

Kunz, Andreas. *Civil Servants and the Politics of Inflation in Germany 1914–1924 [Beiträge zu Inflation und Wiederaufbau in Deutschland und Europa, Bd. 7].* Berlin and New York, 1986.

————. "Stand versus Klasse. Beamtenschaft und Gewerkschaften im Konflikt um den Personalabbau 1923/24," in *Geschichte und Gesellschaft* 8 (1982): pp. 55–86.

————. "Variants of Social Protest in the German Inflation: The Mobilization of Civil Servants in City and Countryside, 1920–1924," in Gerald D. Feldman et al., eds. *The Adaptation to Inflation.* Berlin and New York, 1986. Pp. 323–53.

————. "Verteilungskampf oder Interessenkonsensus? Einkommensentwicklung und Sozialverhalten von Arbeitnehmergruppen in der Inflationszeit 1914 bis 1924," in Gerald D. Feldman et al., eds. *The German Inflation. A Preliminary Balance.* Berlin and New York, 1982. Pp. 347–84.

Lapp, Benjamin. "Political Polarization in Weimar Germany: The Saxon Bürgertum and the Left, 1918–1930." Ph.D. diss., University of California, Berkeley, 1991.

Laubach, Ernst. *Die Politik der Kabinette Wirth 1921/22.* Lübeck, 1968.

Laursen, Karsten, and Jørgen Pedersen. *The German Inflation 1918–1923.* Amsterdam, 1964.

League of Nations. *International Currency Experience. Lessons of the Inter-War Period.* League of Nations, 1944.

Lehnert, Detlev, and Klaus Megerle. "Identitäts- und Konsensprobleme in einer fragmentierten Ge-

sellschaft. Zur politischen Kultur in der Weimarer Republik," in Dirk Berg-Schlosser and Jakob Schissler, eds. *Politische Kultur in Deutschland. Bilanz und Perspektiven der Forschung.* Opladen, 1987. Pp. 80–95.

Lepsius, M. Rainer. "Parteiensystem und Sozialstruktur. Zum Problem der Demokratisierung der deutschen Gesellschaft," in Wilhelm Abel, et. al. eds. *Wirtschaft, Geschichte und Wirtschaftsgeschichte. Festschrift zum 65. Geburtstag von Friedrich Lütge.* Stuttgart, 1966. Pp. 371–93.

Leuschen-Seppel, Rosemarie. *Zwischen Staatsverantwortung und Klasseninteresse. Die Wirtschafts- und Finanzpolitik der SPD zur Zeit der Weimarer Republik unter besonderer Berücksichtigung der Mittelphase 1924–1928/29.* Bonn, 1981.

Lindberg, Leon N., and Charles S. Maier, eds. *The Politics of Inflation and Economic Stagnation.* Washington, 1985.

Lindenlaub, Dieter. *Maschinenbauunternehmen in der deutschen Inflation 1919–1923 [Beiträge zu Inflation und Wiederaufbau in Deutschland und Europa 1914–1924, Bd. 4].* Berlin and New York, 1985.

————. "Maschinenbauunternehmen in der Inflation 1919 bis 1923: Unternehmenshistorische Überlegungen zu einigen Inflationstheorien," in Gerald D. Feldman et al., eds. *The German Inflation. A Preliminary Balance.* Berlin and New York. Pp. 49–106.

Link, Werner. *Die amerikanische Stabilisierungspolitik in Deutschland 1921–32.* Düsseldorf, 1970.

Linse, Ulrich. *Barfüßige Propheten. Erlöser der zwanziger Jahre.* Berlin, 1983.

Lohlam, Uwe. *Völkischer Radikalismus. Die Geschichte des Deutschvölkischen Schutz- und Trutz-Bundes 1919–1923.* Hamburg, 1970.

Lyth, Peter J. *Inflation and the Merchant Economy. The Hamburg Mittelstand 1914–1924.* New York, 1990.

Mai, Gunther, ed. *Arbeiterschaft 1914–1918 in Deutschland.* Düsseldorf, 1985.

————. "Arbeitsmarktregulierung oder Sozialpolitik? Die personelle Demobilmachung in Deutschland 1918 bis 1920/24," in Gerald D. Feldman et al., eds. *The Adaptation to Inflation.* Berlin and New York, 1985. Pp. 202–36.

————. *Das Ende des Kaiserreichs. Politik und Kriegführung im Ersten Weltkrieg.* Munich, 1987.

————. *Kriegswirtschaft und Arbeiterbewegung in Württemberg 1914–1918.* Stuttgart, 1983.

————. "'Wenn der Mensch Hunger hat, hört Alles auf.' Wirtschaftliche und soziale Ausgangsbedingungen der Weimarer Republik (1914–1924)," Werner Abelshauser, ed. *Die Weimarer Republik als Wohlfahrtsstaat.* Stuttgart, 1987. Pp. 33–62.

Maier, Charles S. "Coal and Economic Power in the Weimar Republic: The Effects of the Coal Crisis of 1920," in Hans Mommsen et al., eds. *Industrielles System*. Düsseldorf, 1979. Pp. 530–52.

———. "Inflation and Stabilization in the Wake of the Two World Wars: Comparative Strategies and Sacrifices," in Gerald D. Feldman et al., eds. *The Experience of Inflation*. Berlin and New York, 1984. Pp. 106–29.

———. "The Politics of Inflation in the Twentieth Century," in Charles S. Maier, ed. *In Search of Stability. Explorations in Historical Political Economy*. Cambridge, 1987. Pp. 187–224.

———. *Recasting Bourgeois Europe: Stabilization in France, Germany, and Italy in the Decade after World War I*. Princeton, 1975; reprinted 1988.

———. "The Two Postwar Eras and the Conditions for Stability in Twentieth-Century Western Europe," in *American Historical Review* 86 (April 1981): pp. 326–67.

Malamud, Bernard. "John H. Williams on the German Inflation: The International Amplification of Monetary Disturbances," in Nathan Schmukler and Edward Marcus, eds. *Inflation through the Ages: Economic, Social, Psychological and Historical Aspects*. New York, 1983. Pp. 417–34.

Mann, Golo. *Deutsche Geschichte des 19. und 20. Jahrhunderts*. Frankfurt a.M., 1958.

Mantoux, Etienne. *The Carthaginian Peace, or the Economic Consequences of Mr. Keynes*. Pittsburgh, 1965.

Marks, Sally. "Reparations Reconsidered: A Reminder," in *Central European History* 2 (1969): pp. 356–65.

———. "Reparations Reconsidered: A Rejoinder," in *Central European History* 5 (1972): pp. 358–61.

Marquand, David. *Ramsay MacDonald*. London, 1977.

März, Eduard. *Österreichische Bankpolitik in der Zeit der großen Wende 1913–1923. Am Beispiel der Creditanstalt für Handel und Gewerbe*. Vienna, 1981.

Mathews, William Carl. "The Continuity of Social Democratic Policy 1919 to 1920: The Bauer–Schmidt Policy," in Gerald D. Feldman et al., eds. *The Adaptation to Inflation*. Berlin and New York, 1986. Pp. 485–512.

Maurer, Trude. *Ostjuden in Deutschland, 1918–1933*. Hamburg, 1986.

McDougall, Walter. *France's Rhineland Diplomacy*. Princeton, 1978.

———. "Political Economy versus National Sovereignty: French Structures for German Economic Integration After Versailles," in *Journal of Modern History* 51 (1979): pp. 4–23.

McNeil, William C. *American Money and the Weimar Republic. Economics and Politics on the Eve of the Great Depression*. New York, 1986.

———. "Could Germany Pay? Another Look at the Reparations Problem in the 1920's," in Gerald D. Feldman et al., eds. *The Consequences of Inflation*. Berlin, 1989. Pp. 109–24.

Meier-Welcker, Hans. *Seeckt*. Frankfurt a.M., 1967.

Mendershausen, Horst. *Two Postwar Recoveries of the German Economy*. Amsterdam, 1955.

Merkin, Gerald. "Towards a Theory of the German Inflation: Some Preliminary Observations," in Gerald D. Feldman et al., eds. *The German Inflation. A Preliminary Balance*. Berlin and New York, 1982. Pp. 25–47.

Middleton, Roger. "The Treasury in the 1930s: Political and Administrative Constraints to the Acceptance of the 'New' Economics," in *Oxford Economic Papers* 34 (1982).

Middlemas, Keith. *Politics in Industrial Society. The Experience of the British System since 1911*. London, 1979.

Miller, Susanne. *Die Bürde der Macht. Die deutsche Sozialdemokratie 1918–1920*. Düsseldorf, 1979.

Mises, Ludwig von. "The Great German Inflation," in Richard M. Ebeling. *Money, Method, and the Market Process. Essays by Ludwig von Mises*. Norwell, Mass., 1990. Pp. 96–103.

Moeller, Robert G. "Dimensions of Social Conflict in the Great War: The View from the German Countryside," in *Central European History* 14 (1981): pp. 142–68.

———. *German Peasants and Agrarian Politics, 1914–1924. The Rhineland and Westphalia*. Chapel Hill, 1986.

———. "Peasants and Tariffs in the *Kaiserreich*: How Backward were the *Bauern*?," in *Agricultural History* 55 (1981): pp. 370–84.

———. "Winners as Losers in the German Inflation: Peasant Protest over the Controlled Economy 1920–1923," in Gerald D. Feldman et al., eds. *The German Inflation. A Preliminary Balance*. Berlin and New York, 1982. Pp. 255–288.

Mommsen, Hans. "Die Auflösung des Bürgertums seit dem späten 19. Jahrhundert," in Jürgen Kocka, ed. *Bürger und Bürgerlichkeit im 19. Jahrhundert*. Göttingen, 1987. Pp. 288–315.

———. *Die Verspielte Freiheit. Der Weg der Republik von Weimar in den Untergang 1918–1933*. Berlin, 1989.

Mommsen, Hans et al., eds. *Industrielles System und politische Entwicklung in der Weimarer Republik*. Düsseldorf, 1974; reprinted in 1977.

Mommsen, Wolfgang J. "The German Revolution 1918–1920: Political Revolution and Social Protest Movement," in Richard Bessel and E. J. Feuchtwanger. *Social Change and Political Development in Weimar Germany*. London, 1981. Pp. 21–54.

Morsey, Rudolf. *Die Deutsche Zentrumspartei 1917–1923*. Düsseldorf, 1966.

Mosse, Werner, and Arnold Paucker, eds. *Deutsches Judentum in Krieg und Revolution 1916–1923*.

[*Schriftenreihe wissenschaftlichen Abhandlungen des Leo Baeck Instituts*, 25]. Tübingen, 1971.

Müller, Klaus-Peter. *Politik und Gesellschaft im Krieg. Der Legitimitätsverlust des badischen Staates 1914–1918*. Stuttgart, 1988.

Neue Deutsche Biographie. Munich, 1953ff.

Neumann, Franz. *The Rule of Law. Political Theory and the Legal System in Modern Society*. Leamington Spa, 1986.

Netzband, Karl-Bernhard and Hans-Peter Widmaier. *Währungs- und Finanzpolitik der Ära Luther 1923–1925*. Basel & Tübingen, 1964.

Niehuss, Merith. *Arbeiterschaft in Krieg und Inflation. Soziale Schichtung und Lage der Arbeiter in Augsburg und Linz 1910 bis 1925*. [*Beiträge zu Inflation und Wiederaufbau in Deutschland und Europa 1914–1924*, Bd. 3]. Berlin and New York, 1985.

———. "Lebensweise und Familie in der Inflationszeit," in Gerald D. Feldman et al., eds. *The Adaptation to Inflation*. Berlin and New York, 1986. pp. 237–77.

Nipperdey, Thomas. *Deutsche Geschichte 1866–1918, Bd. I Arbeitswelt und Bürgergeist*. Munich, 1990.

Nipperdey, Thomas and Ludwig Schmugge. *50 Jahre Forschungsförderung in Deutschland, 1920–1970: Ein Abriß der Geschichte der deutschen Forschungsgemeinschaft*. Berlin, 1970.

———. *Die Organisation der deutschen Parteien vor 1914*. Düsseldorf, 1961.

———. "Wehlers 'Kaiserreich.' Eine kritische Auseinandersetzung," in Thomas Nipperdey. *Gesellschaft, Kultur, Theorie*. Göttingen, 1976. Pp. 360–89.

Nocken, Ulrich. "Corporatism and Pluralism in Modern German History," in Dirk Stegmann et al., eds. *Industrielle Gesellschaft und politisches System. Beiträge zur politischen Sozialgeschichte. Festschrift für Fritz Fischer*. Bonn, 1978. Pp. 37–56.

Nörr, Knut Wolfgang. "Zur Entwicklung des Aktien- und Konzernrechts während der Weimarer Republik," in *Zeitschrift für das gesamte Handelsrecht und Wirtschaftsrecht* 150 (1986): pp. 155–81.

———. *Zwischen den Mühlsteinen. Eine Privatrechtsgeschichte der Weimarer Republik*. Tübingen, 1988.

Nurske, Ragnar. *The Course and Control of Inflation. A Review of Monetary Experiences after World War I*. Geneva, 1946.

Oertzen, Peter von. *Betriebsräte in der Novemberrevolution*. Düsseldorf, 1976.

Offer, Avner. *The First World War: An Agrarian Interpretation*. Oxford, 1989.

Olson, Mancur. *The Rise and Decline of Nations. Economic Growth, Stagflation, and Social Rigidities*. New Haven & London, 1982.

Oltmann, Uwe. *Reichsarbeitsminister Heinrich Brauns in der Staats- und Währungskrise 1923/24. Die Bedeutung der Sozialpolitik für die Inflation, den Ruhrkampf und die Stabilisierung*. Kiel, 1969.

Orde, Anne. *British Policy and European Reconstruction after the First World War*. Cambridge, 1990.

Osmond, Jonathan. "German Peasant Farmers in War and Inflation," Gerald D. Feldman et al., eds. *The German Inflation. A Preliminary Balance*. Berlin and New York, 1982. Pp. 288–307.

Ostwald, Hans. *Sittengeschichte der Inflation. Ein Kulturdokument aus den Jahren des Marksturzes*. Berlin, 1931.

Patch, William L., Jr. "Class Prejudice and the Failure of the Weimar Republic," in *German Studies Review* 12 (Feb. 1989): pp. 35–54.

———. *Christian Trade Unions in the Weimar Republic 1918–1933*. New Haven and London, 1985.

Patton, Craig. "Strikes in the German and British Chemical Industries 1914–1918: The Influence of Inflation and Deflation on Industrial Unrest in Post-War Europe," in Gerald D. Feldman et al., eds. *The Experience of Inflation*. Berlin and New York, 1984. Pp. 303–38.

Petzina, Dietmar et al., eds. *Sozialgeschichtliches Arbeitsbuch. III. Materialien zur Statistik des deutschen Reiches 1914–1915*. Munich, 1978.

Peukert, Detlev J. K. *Jugend zwischen Krieg und Krise. Lebenswelten von Arbeiterjungen in der Weimarer Republik*. Cologne, 1987.

———. *Die Weimarer Republik. Krisenjahre der klassischen Moderne*. Frankfurt a.M., 1987.

Pfleiderer, Otto. "Die Reichsbank in der Zeit der großen Inflation, die Stabilisierung der Mark und die Aufwertung von Kapitalforderungen," in Deutsche Bundesbank. *Währung und Wirtschaft*. Frankfurt a.M., 1976. Pp. 157–201.

Pirlet, Otto. *Der politische Kampf um die Aufwertungsgesetzgebung nach dem Ersten Weltkrieg*. Cologne, 1959.

Plumpe, Gottfried. "Chemische Industrie und Hilfsdienstgesetz am Beispiel der Farbenfabriken vorm. Bayer & Co.," in Gunther Mai, ed. *Arbeiterschaft 1914–1918 in Deutschland*. Düsseldorf, 1985. Pp. 179–210.

Pohl, Manfred. *Konzentration im deutschen Bankwesen (1848–1980)*. Frankfurt a.M., 1982.

Pommerin, Reiner. "Die Ausweisung von 'Ostjuden' aus Bayern 1923. Ein Beitrag zum Krisenjahr der Weimarer Republik," in *Vierteljahrshefte für Zeitgeschichte* 34 (1986): pp. 311–40.

Potthoff, Heinrich. *Gewerkschaften und Politik zwischen Revolution und Inflation*. Düsseldorf, 1979.

Preller, Ludwig. *Sozialpolitik in der Weimarer Republik*. Stuttgart, 1949.

Proctor, Robert N. *Racial Hygiene. Medicine under the Nazis*. Cambridge, Mass., 1988.

Ranft, Norbert. "Erwerbslosenfürsorge, Ruhrkampf und Kommunen. Die Trendwende in der Sozialpolitik im Jahre 1923," in Gerald D. Feldman et al., eds. *Adaptation to Inflation*. Berlin and New York, 1986. Pp. 163–201.

Ratz, Ursula. "Sozialdemokratische Arbeiterbewegung, bürgerliche Sozialreformer und Militärbehörden im Ersten Weltkrieg," in *Militärgeschichtliche Mitteilungen* (1985/1): pp. 9–33.

Reger, Erich. *Union der festen Hand. Roman einer Entwicklung*. Berlin, 1946.

Reulecke, Jürgen. "Auswirkungen der Inflation auf die städtischen Finanzen," in Gerald D. Feldman and Elisabeth Müller-Luckner, eds. *Die Nachwirkungen der Inflation*. Munich, 1985. Pp. 97–116.

———. *Die wirtschaftliche Entwicklung der Stadt Barmen von 1910 bis 1925*. Neustadt an der Aisch, 1973.

Ribbe, Wolfgang, ed. *Geschichte Berlins*. 2 vols. Munich, 1987.

Richarz, Monika, ed. *Jüdisches Leben in Deutschland. Selbstzeugnisse zur Sozialgeschichte 1918–1945*. Stuttgart, 1982.

Richter, Werner. *Gewerkschaften, Monopolkapital und Staat im Ersten Weltkrieg und in der Novemberrevolution*. Berlin, 1959.

Rifkin, Jeremy. *Entropy. A New World View*. New York, 1980.

Ringer, Fritz. *The Decline of the German Mandarins. The German Academic Community, 1890–1933*. Cambridge, Mass., 1969.

———, ed. *The German Inflation of 1923*. New York, 1969.

Ritter, Gerhard A.. *Die deutschen Parteien 1830–1914*. Göttingen, 1985.

———. *Der Sozialstaat. Entstehung und Entwicklung im internationalen Vergleich*. Munich, 1989.

———. *Sozialversicherung in Deutschland und England. Entstehung und Grundzüge im Vergleich*. Munich, 1983.

Ritter, Gerhard A., and Jürgen Kocka, eds. *Deutsche Sozialgeschichte. Dokumente und Skizzen. Band II. 1870–1914*. Munich, 1974.

Roesler, Konrad *Die Finanzpolitik des Deutschen Reiches im Ersten Weltkrieg*. Berlin, 1967.

Rosenberg, Hans. "Die Pseudodemokratisierung der Rittergutsbesitzerklasse," in Hans Rosenberg, ed. *Machteliten und Wirtschaftskonjunkturen*. Göttingen 1978. Pp. 83–101.

Rouette, Susanne. "'Gleichberechtigung' ohne 'Recht auf Arbeit,'" in Christiane Eifert and Susanne Rouette, eds. *Unter allen Umständen. Frauengeschichte(n) in Berlin*. Berlin, 1986. Pp. 159–81.

Ruck, Michael. *Die Freien Gewerkschaften im Ruhrkampf 1923*. Cologne, 1986.

Rupieper, Hermann J. "Alanson B. Houghton: An American Ambassador in Germany, 1922–1925," in *The International History Review* 1 (Oct. 1979): pp. 490–508.

———. *The Cuno Government and Reparations 1922–1923. Politics and Economics*. The Hague, Boston, London, 1979.

———. "Industrie und Reparationen: Einige Aspekte des Reparationsproblems 1922–1924," in Hans Mommsen et al., eds. *Industrielles System*. Düsseldorf, 1974. Pp. 582–92.

Rürup, Reinhard, ed. *Arbeiter und Soldatenräte im rheinisch-westfälischen Industriegebiet. Studien zur Geschichte der Revolution 1918/19*. Wuppertal, 1975.

———. "Demokratische Revolution und 'dritter Weg.' Die deutsche Revolution von 1918/19 in der neueren wissenschaftlichen Diskussion," in *Geschichte und Gesellschaft* 9 (1983): pp. 278–301.

———. *Probleme der Revolution in Deutschland 1918/19*. Wiesbaden, 1968.

Salemi, Michael K. "Adapative Expectations, Rational Expectations and Money Demand in Hyperinflation Germany," in *Journal of Monetary Economics* 5 (1979): pp. 593–604.

Sargent, Thomas J. "The Ends of Four Big Inflations," in Robert Hall, ed. *Inflation: Causes and Effects*. Chicago, 1982.

———. *Rational Expectations and Inflation*. New York, 1986.

Scherf, Harald. "Inflation," in *Handwörterbuch der Wirtschaftswissenschaften*. Vol. 4. Göttingen, 1978. Pp. 159–84.

Schieck, Hans. *Der Kampf um die deutsche Wirtschaftspolitik nach dem Novemberumsturz 1918*. Heidelberg, 1958.

Schmidt, Carl T. *German Business Cycles, 1924–1933*. New York, 1934.

Schmölders, Günter. *Psychologie des Geldes*. Reinbek, 1966.

Schmukler, Nathan, and Edward Marcus, eds. *Inflation through the Ages: Economic, Social, Psychological and Historical Aspects*. New York, 1983.

Schneider, Michael. *Die christlichen Gewerkschaften 1894–1933*. Bonn, 1982.

———. "Deutsche Gesellschaft im Krieg und Währungskrise 1914–1924," in *Archiv für Sozialgeschichte* 16 (1986): pp. 301–20.

Scholz, Robert. "Die Auswirkungen der Inflation auf das Sozial- und Wohlfahrtswesen der neuen Stadtgemeinde Berlin," in Gerald D. Feldman et al., eds. *The Consequences of Inflation*. Berlin, 1989. Pp. 45–75.

———. "Ein unruhiges Jahrzehnt: Lebensmittelunruhen, Massenstreiks und Arbeitslosenkrawalle in Berlin 1914–1923," in Manfred Gallus, ed. *Pöbelexzesse und Volkstumulte in Berlin. Zur Sozialgeschichte der Straße (1830–1980)*. Berlin, 1984. Pp. 79–124.

———. "Lohn und Beschäftigung als Indikatoren für die soziale Lage der Arbeiterschaft in der Inflation," in Gerald D. Feldman et al., eds. *The Adaptation to Inflation*. Berlin and New York, 1986. Pp. 278–322.

Schötz, Hans Otto. "Der britisch-französische Gegensatz in der Deutschlandpolitik—am Beispiel des Versuchs der Gründung einer Notenbank für die besetzten Gebiete am Jahreswechsel 1923/24," in Gerald D. Feldman et al., eds. *Consequences of Inflation*. Berlin, 1989. Pp. 125–48.

———. *Der Kampf um die Mark 1923/24. Die deutsche Währungsstabilisierung unter dem Einfluß der nationalen Interessen Frankreichs, Großbritanniens und der USA. [Beiträge zu Inflation und Wiederaufbau in Deutschland und Europa 1914–1924, Bd. 9]*. Berlin and New York, 1987.

Schröder, Ernst. "Otto Wiedfeldt als Politiker und Botschafter der Weimarer Republik," in *Beiträge zur Geschichte von Stadt und Stift Essen* 86 (1971).

———. "Wiedfeldt und die Seeckt–Ebertschen Direktoriumspläne des Jahres 1923," in *Das Münster am Hellweg. Mitteilungsblatt des Vereins für die Erhaltung des Essener Münsters* 19, Beiheft 11 (November 1966): pp. 129–42.

Schroeder, Hans-Jürgen. "Die politische Bedeutung der deutschen Handelspolitik nach dem Ersten Weltkrieg," in Gerald D. Feldman et al., eds. *The German Inflation Reconsidered. A Preliminary Balance*. Berlin and New York, 1982. Pp. 235–51.

Schröter, Alfred. *Krieg-Staat-Monopol. 1914 bis 1918. Die Zusammenhänge von imperialistischer Kriegswirtschaft, Militarisierung der Volkswirtschaft und staatsmonopolistischer Kapitalismus in Deutschland während des Ersten Weltkrieges*. Berlin, 1965.

Schuker, Stephen A. *American "Reparations" to Germany, 1919–33: Implications for the Third World Debt Crisis*. Princeton, 1988.

———. *The End of French Predominance in Europe. The Financial Crisis of 1924 and the Adoption of the Dawes Plan*. Chapel Hill, 1976.

———. "Finance and Foreign Policy in the Era of the German Inflation: British, French and German Strategies for Economic Reconstruction After the First World War," in Otto Büsch and Gerald D. Feldman, eds. *Historische Prozesse*. Berlin, 1978. Pp. 343–61.

———. "Frankreich und die Weimarer Republik," in Michael Stürmer, ed. *Die Weimarer Republik. Belagerte Civitas*. Königstein/Ts., 1980. Pp. 93–112.

Schulin, Ernst, ed. *Walther Rathenau. Hauptwerke und Gespräche*. Heidelberg, 1977.

Schulkin, Carl. "Lost Opportunity: The Reparation Question and the Failure of the European Recovery Effort." Ph.D. diss., University of California, Berkeley, 1973.

Schulz, Gerhard. "Inflationstrauma, Finanzpolitik

und Krisenbekämpfung in den Jahren der Wirtschaftskrise, 1930–1933," in Gerald D. Feldman and Elisabeth Müller-Luckner, eds. *Die Nachwirkungen der Inflation*. Munich, 1985. Pp. 261–96.

———. *Zwischen Demokratie und Diktatur. Deutschland am Vorabend der Großen Krise*. Berlin & New York, 1987.

———. *Zwischen Demokratie und Diktatur. Die Periode der Konsolidierung und der Revision des Bismarckschen Reichsaufbaus 1919–1930*. Berlin & New York, 1987.

Schumacher, Martin. "Autoren und Verleger in der deutschen Inflationszeit," in *Vierteljahrsschrift für Sozial- und Wirtschaftsgeschichte* 58 (1971): pp. 88–94.

———. *Land und Politik. Eine Untersuchung über politische Parteien und agrarische Interessen*. Düsseldorf, 1978.

———. *Mittelstandsfront und Republik. Die Wirtschaftspartei—Reichspartei des deutschen Mittelstandes 1919–1933*. Düsseldorf, 1972.

Schumann, Horst. *Oberschlesien 1918/19. Vom gemeinsamen Kampf deutscher und polnischer Arbeiter*. Berlin, 1961.

Schwabe, Klaus, ed. *Die Ruhrkrise 1923. Wendepunkt der internationalen Beziehungen nach dem Ersten Weltkrieg*. Paderborn, 1985.

Silverman, Dan P. *Reconstructing Europe After the First World War*. Cambridge & London, 1982.

Simmel, Georg. *The Philosophy of Money*. Translated by Tom Bottomore and David Frisby. London, Henley & Boston, 1978.

Southern, David B.. "The Impact of the Inflation: Inflation, the Courts and Revaluation," in Richard Bessel and E. J. Feuchtwanger, eds. *Social Change and Political Development in Weimar Germany*. Totowa, New Jersey, 1981. Pp. 55–76.

———. "The Revaluation Question," in *Journal of Modern History* 51 (1979).

Soutou, George. "Die deutschen Reparationen und das Seydoux Projekt 1920/21," in *Vierteljahrshefte für Zeitgeschichte* 23 (1975): pp. 237–70.

———. *L'or et le Sang. Les buts de guerre économiques de la Première Guerre Mondiale*. Paris, 1989.

Specht, Agnete von. *Politische und wirtschaftliche Hintergründe der deutschen Inflation 1918–1923*. Frankfurt a.M., 1982.

Stamm, Christoph. "Großbritannien und Die Sanktionen gegen Deutschland vom März 1921," in *Francia* 7 (1979): pp. 339–64.

Stegmann, Dirk. *Die Erben Bismarcks. Parteien und Verbände in der Spätphase des wilhelminischen Deutschlands. Sammlungspolitik 1897–1918*. Cologne, 1970.

Stehkämper, Hugo. "Konrad Adenauer und das Reichskanzleramt während der Weimarer Zeit," in Hugo Stehkämper, ed. *Konrad Adenauer. Oberbürgermeister von Köln. Festgabe*

der Stadt Köln zum 100. Geburtstag ihres Ehrenbürgers am 5. Januar 1976. Köln, 1976. Pp.
123–153.

Stehlin, Stewart A. *Weimar and the Vatican, 1919–
1933. German–Vatican Diplomatic Relations in
the Interwar Years.* Princeton, 1983.

Steinisch, Irmgard. *Arbeitszeitverkürzung und sozialer Wandel. Der Kampf um die Achtstundenschicht in der deutschen und amerikanischen
Eisen- und Stahlindustrie 1880–1929.* [*Beiträge
zu Inflation und Wiederaufbau in Deutschland
und Europa 1914–1924, Bd. 6*]. Berlin & New
York, 1986.

Stephan, Werner. *Aufstieg und Verfall des Linksliberalismus 1918–1933.* Göttingen, 1973.

Stern, Fritz. "The Scientist in Power and Exile," in
*Dreams and Delusions. The Drama of German
History.* New York, 1987.

Strandmann, Hartmut Pogge von. "Großindustrie
und Rapallopolitik: Deutsch-sowjetische Handelsbeziehungen in der Weimarer Republik," in
Historische Zeitschrift 222 (April 1976): pp.
265–341.

————, ed. *Walther Rathenau. Industrialist,
Banker, Intellectual, and Politician. Notes and
Diaries 1907–1922.* Oxford, 1985.

Struss, Dieter, ed. *Das war 1922. Fakten. Daten.
Zahlen. Schicksale.* Munich, 1982.

Stürmer, Michael, ed. *Die Weimarer Republik. Belagerte Civitas.* Königstein/Ts., 1980.

Sühl, Klaus. *SPD und öffentlicher Dienst in der Weimarer Republik. Die öffentlichen Bediensteten
in der SPD und ihre Bedeutung für die sozialdemokratische Politik 1918–1933.* Opladen,
1988.

Svennilson, Ingvar. *Growth and Stagnation in the
European Economy.* Geneva, 1954.

Syrup, Friedrich and Otto Neuloh. *Hundert Jahre
Staatliche Sozialpolitik 1839–1939.* Stuttgart,
1957.

Teichova, Alice. "A Comparative View of the Inflation of the 1920's in Austria and Czechoslovakia," in Nathan Schmukler and Edward Marcus, eds. *Inflation through the Ages.* New York,
1983. Pp. 531–67.

Ten Cate, Johannes Houwink. "Amsterdam als Finanzplatz Deutschlands," in Gerald D. Feldman et al., eds. *Consequences of the Inflation.*
Berlin, 1986. Pp. 149–80.

Tenfelde, Klaus. "Großstadtjugend in Deutschland
vor 1914. Eine historische-demographische Annäherung," in *Vierteljahrsschrift für Sozial-
und Wirtschaftsgeschichte* 69 (1962): pp.
182–218.

Tenfelde, Klaus, and Heinrich Volkmann. *Streik.
Zur Geschichte des Arbeitskampfes in Deutschland während der Industrialisierung.* Munich,
1981.

Terhalle, Fritz. "Geschichte der deutschen öffentlichen Finanzwirtschaft vom Beginn des 19.
Jahrunderts bis zum Schlusse des Zweiten Welt-

krieges," in *Handbuch der Finanzwissenschaft.*
2nd ed., Vol. 1. Tübingen, 1952. Pp. 273–326.

Teuteberg, Hans J. "Der Verzehr von Nahrungsmitteln in Deutschland pro Kopf und Jahr seit Beginn der Industrialisierung (1850–1975)." in *Archiv für Sozialgeschichte* 19 (1979): pp. 331–88.

Tilly, Richard H. "Gemeindefinanzen und Sparkassen in Westfalen in der Inflation, 1918–1923,"
in Kurt Düwell and Wolfgang Kollmann, eds.
*Rheinland und Westfalen im Industriezeitalter.
Bd. 2. Von der Reichsgründung bis zur Weimarer Republik.* Wuppertal, 1984. Pp. 398–
411.

Titze, Hartmut, ed. *Das Hochschulstudium in
Preußen und Deutschland 1820–1944.* Göttingen, 1987.

Tobin, James. "Inflation: Monetary and Structural
Causes and Cures," in Nathan Schmukler and
Edward Marcus, eds. *Inflation Through the
Ages.* New York, 1983. Pp. 3–16.

Todd, Edmund Neville III. "Technology and Interest
Group Politics: Electrification of the Ruhr,
1886–1930." Ph.D. diss., University of Pennsylvania, 1984.

Trachtenberg, Marc. *Reparation in World Politics.
France and European Economic Diplomacy,
1916–1923.* New York, 1980.

Trevithick, J. A. *Inflation. A Guide to the Crisis in
Economics.* New York, 1980.

Triebel, Armin. "Variations in Patterns of Consumption in Germany in the Period of the First
World War," in Richard Wall and Jay Winter,
eds. *The Upheaval of War. Family, Work and
Welfare in Europe 1914–1918.* Cambridge,
1988. Pp. 159–96.

Trumpp, Thomas. "Statistikmaterial zur Wirt-
schafts- und Sozialgeschichte der deutschen Inflation in Archiven der Bundesrepublik
Deutschland," in Gerald D. Feldman et al., eds.
*The German Inflation Reconsidered. A Prelim-
inary Balance.* Berlin and New York, 1982. Pp.
132–48.

Trumpp, Thomas, and Renate Köhne, eds. *Ar-
chivbestände zur Wirtschafts- und Sozialgeschichte der Weimarer Republik. Übersicht über
Quellen in Archiven der Bundesrepublik
Deutschland.* Boppard am Rhein, 1979.

Tschirbs, Rudolf. "Der Ruhrbergmann zwischen
Priviligierung und Statusverlust; Lohnpolitik
von der Inflation bis zur Rationalisierung," in
Gerald D. Feldman et al., eds. *The German In-
flation. A Preliminary Balance.* Berlin and New
York, 1982. Pp. 308–46.

————. *Tarifpolitik im Ruhrbergbau 1918–1933.*
[*Beiträge zu Inflation und Wiederaufbau in
Deutschland und Europa 1914–1924, Bd. 5*].
Berlin and New York, 1986.

Turner, Henry A. *German Big Business and the Rise
of Hitler.* New York and Oxford, 1985.

————. *Stresemann and the Politics of the Weimar
Republic.* Princeton, 1963.

Ullmann, Hans-Peter. *Interessenverbände in Deutschland*. Göttingen, 1988.

Vogt, Martin. "Rudolf Hilferding als Finanzminister im ersten Kabinett Stresemann," in Otto Büsch and Gerald D. Feldman, eds. *Historische Prozesse*. Berlin, 1976. Pp. 126–58.

――――. "Zum bayerischen Versuch finanzieller Eigenständigkeit im Spätsommer und Herbst 1923," in Otto Büsch and Gerald D. Feldman, eds. *Historische Prozesse*. Berlin, 1976. Pp. 224–36.

Volkmann, Heinrich. "Modernisierung des Arbeitskampfes? Zum Formwandel von Streik und Aussperrung in Deutschland 1864–1875," in Hartmut Kaelble, ed. *Probleme der Modernisierung in Deutschland. Sozialhistorische Studien zum 19. und 20. Jahrhundert*. Opladen, 1978. Pp. 110–70.

Wagenführ, Rolf. *Die Industriewirtschaft. Entwicklungstendenzen der deutschen und internationalen Industrieproduktion 1860–1932. Vierteljahreshefte für Konjunkturforschung*, Sonderheft 31. Berlin, 1933.

Webb, Steven B. "Fiscal News and Inflationary Expectations in Germany," in *Journal of Economic History* 46 (1986): pp. 769–94.

――――. "Government Revenue and Spending in Germany, 1919–1923," in Gerald D. Feldman et al., eds. *The Adaptation to Inflation*. Berlin and New York, 1986. Pp. 46–82.

――――. *Hyperinflation and Stabilization in Weimar Germany*. New York and Oxford, 1989.

――――. "Money Demand and Expectations in the German Hyperinflation: A Survey of the Models," in Nathan Schmuckler and Edward Marcus, eds. *Inflation Through the Ages*. New York, 1983. Pp. 435–49.

Weber, Hermann. "Aktionsmus und Kommunismus. Unbekannte Briefe von Max Hoelz," in *Archiv für Sozialgeschichte* 15 (1975): pp. 331–53.

Wehler, Hans-Ulrich. *The German Empire, 1871–1918*. Leamington Spa/Dover, New Hampshire, 1985.

Weill-Reynal, Etienne. *Les Réparations Allemandes et la France* 3 vols. Paris, 1947.

Weinberg, Gerhard. "The Defeat of Germany in 1918 and the European Balance of Power," in *Central European History* 2 (Sept. 1969): pp. 248–60.

Weindling, Paul. *Health, Race and German Politics between National Unification and Nazism 1870–1945*. Cambridge, 1989.

Weisbrod, Bernd. *Schwerindustrie in der Weimarer Republik. Interessenpolitik zwischen Stabilisierung und Krise*. Wuppertal, 1978.

Welskop-Deffaa, Eva Maria. "Die 'Inflationsnovelle' aus dem 'Tryptychon des Teufels'. Ein wirtschaftsgeschichtlicher Essay zur Nachwirkung der Inflation im Frühwerk Elisabeth Langgässers," in Gerald D. Feldman et al., eds. *The Consequences of Inflation*. Berlin, 1989. Pp. 287–330.

Wentzcke, Paul. *Ruhrkampf. Einbruch und Abwehr im rheinisch westfälischen Industriegebiet*. 2 vols. Berlin, 1930–1932.

Whale, P. Barrett. *Joint Stock Banking in Germany. A Study of the German Credit Banks before and after the War*. London, 1930.

Whalen, Robert Weldon. *Bitter Wounds. German Victims of the Great War, 1914–1939*. Ithaca and London, 1984.

Williamson, John G. *Karl Helfferich 1872–1924. Economist, Financier, Politician*. Princeton, 1971.

Winkel, Harald. "Das Württembergische Notgeld (1914–1924)," in Hansjoachim Henning, Dieter Lindenlaub, and Eckhard Wandel, eds. *Wirtschafts- und sozialgeschichtliche Forschungen und Probleme. Festschrift für Karl Erich Born*. St. Katharinen, 1987, Pp. 310–334.

Winkler, Heinrich August. *Mittelstand, Demokratie und Nationalsozialismus. Die politische Entwicklung von Handwerk und Kleinhandel in der Weimarer Republik*. Cologne, 1972.

――――. *Von der Revolution zur Stabilisierung. Arbeiter und Arbeiterbewegung in der Weimarer Republik 1918 bis 1924*. Berlin and Bonn, 1984.

――――. *Zwischen Marx und Monopolen. Der deutsche Mittelstand vom Kaiserreich zur Bundesrepublik Deutschland*. Frankfurt a.M., 1991.

Winter, I. "Ärzte und Arbeiterklasse in der Weimarer Republik," in Kurt Kühn, ed. *Ärzte an der Seite der Arbeiterklasse. Beiträge zur Geschichte des Bündnisses der deutschen Arbeiterklasse mit der medizinischen Intelligenz*. Berlin, 1973. Pp. 25–38.

Witt, Peter-Christian. "Anpassung an die Inflation. Das Investitionsverhalten der deutschen Staatsbahnen/Reichsbahn in den Jahren 1914 bis 1923/24," in Gerald D. Feldman et al., eds. *The Adaptation to Inflation*. Berlin and New York, 1986. Pp. 392–432.

――――. "Die Auswirkungen der Inflation auf die Finanzpolitik des deutschen Reiches 1924–1935," in Gerald D. Feldman and Elisabeth Müller-Luckner, eds. in *Die Nachwirkungen der Inflation*. Munich, 1985. Pp. 43–95.

――――. "Bemerkungen zur Wirtschaftspolitik in der 'Übergangswirtschaft' 1918/19. Zur Entwicklung von Konjunkturbeobachtung und Konjunktursteuerung in Deutschland," in Dirk Stegmann et al., eds. *Industrielle Gesellschaft und politisches System*. Düsseldorf, 1978. Pp. 79–96.

――――. *Die Finanzpolitik des deutschen Reiches von 1903 bis 1913. Eine Studie zur Innenpolitik des wilhelminischen Deutschland*. [*Historische Studien*, Heft 415]. Lübeck & Hamburg, 1970.

――――. "Finanzpolitik und sozialer Wandel in Krieg und Inflation 1918–1924," in Hans

Mommsen et al., eds. *Industrielles System.* Düsseldorf, 1974. Pp. 395–426.

————. "Inflation, Wohnungszwangswirtschaft und Hauszinssteuer. Zur Regelung von Wohnungsbau und Wohnungsmarkt in der Weimarer Republik," in Lutz Niethammer, ed. *Wohnen im Wandel. Beiträge zur Geschichte des Alltags in der bürgerlichen Gesellschaft.* Wuppertal, 1979. Pp. 385–407.

————. "Reichsfinanzminister und Reichsfinanzverwaltung. Zum Problem des Verhältnisses von politischer Führung und bürokratischer Herrschaft in den Anfangsjahren der Weimarer Republik (1918/1924)," in *Vierteljahrshefte für Zeitgeschichte* 23 (1975): pp. 1–61.

————. "Staatliche Wirtschaftspolitik in Deutschland 1918–1923: Entwicklung und Zerstörung einer modernen wirtschaftspolitischen Strategie," in Gerald D. Feldman et al., eds. *The German Inflation Reconsidered. A Preliminary Balance.* Berlin and New York, 1982. Pp. 151–79.

————. "Tax Policies, Tax Assessment and Inflation: Towards a Sociology of Public Finances in the German Inflation, 1914–1923," in Peter-Christian Witt, ed. *Wealth and Taxation in Central Europe. The History and Sociology of Public Finance.* Leamington Spa, 1987. Pp. 137–60.

————. "Wissenschaftsfinanzierung zwischen Inflation und Deflation: Die Kaiser-Wilhelm-Gesellschaft 1918/19 bis 1934/35," in Rudolf Vierhaus and Bernhard vom Brocke, eds. *Forschung im Spannungsfeld von Politik und Gesellschaft. Geschichte und Struktur der Kaiser-Wilhelm/Max-Planck-Gesellschaft.* Stuttgart, 1990. Pp. 579–656.

Wulf, Peter. "Die Auseinandersetzung um die Sozialisierung der Kohle in Deutschland 1920/1921," in *Vierteljahrshefte für Zeitgeschichte* 25 (1977): pp. 46–98.

————. *Hugo Stinnes. Wirtschaft und Politik 1918–1924.* Stuttgart, 1979.

————. "Schwerindustrie und Seeschiffahrt nach dem 1. Weltkrieg: Hugo Stinnes und die HAPAG," in *Vierteljahrsschrift für Sozial- und Wirtschaftsgeschichte* 67 (1980): pp. 1–21.

Wurm, Clemens. "Frankreich, die Reparationen und die interalliierten Schulden in den 20er Jahren," in Gerald D. Feldman and Elisabeth Müller-Luckner, eds. *Die Nachwirkungen der Inflation.* Munich, 1985. Pp. 335–83.

Zierold, Kurt. *Forschungsförderung in drei Epochen. Deutsche Forschungsgemeinschaft. Geschichte. Arbeitsweise. Kommentar.* Wiesbaden, 1968.

Zilch, Reinhold. *Die Reichsbank und die finanzielle Kriegsvorbereitung 1907–1914.* Berlin, 1987.

————. "Zum Plan einer Zwangsregulierung im deutschen Bankwesen vor dem Ersten Weltkrieg und zu seinen Ursachen. Dokumentation," in B. A. Aisin and W. Gutsche, eds. *Forschungsergebnisse zur Geschichte des deutschen Imperialismus vor 1917.* Berlin, 1980. Pp. 228–56.

Zimmermann, Waldemar. *Die Veränderungen der Einkommens- und Lebensverhältnisse der deutschen Arbeiter durch den Krieg.* Stuttgart, Berlin, and Leipzig, 1932.

Zuckmayer, Carl. "Katharina Knie," in *Komödie und Volksstück.* Frankfurt a.M., 1950.

Zunkel, Friedrich. *Industrie und Staatssozialismus. Der Kampf um die Wirtschaftsordnung in Deutschland 1914–18.* Düsseldorf, 1974.

Zwehl, Konrad von. *Die Deutschlandpolitik Englands von 1922 bis 1924 unter besonderer Berücksichtigung der Reparationen und Sanktionen.* 2 vols. Munich, 1974.

Zweig, Arnold. "Alter Mann am Stock," in *Novellen.* Frankfurt a.M., 1987.

Zweig, Stefan. "Die unsichtbare Sammlung," in *Novellen.* Frankfurt a.M., 1960. Pp. 334–48.

————. *The World of Yesterday. An Autobiography by Stefan Zweig.* New York, 1943.

Index